U0897874

2022 世界交通运输大会（WTC2022）论文集

（桥梁工程与隧道工程篇）

世界交通运输大会执委会　编

人民交通出版社股份有限公司

北京

内 容 提 要

本书为2022世界交通运输大会(WTC2022)论文集　桥梁工程与隧道工程篇,是由中国公路学会、世界交通运输大会执委会精选的118篇论文汇编而成。此论文集重点收录了桥梁工程与隧道工程领域的前沿研究及创新成果,可供从事交通运输工程等领域的人员参考,也可供院校相关师生学习。

图书在版编目(CIP)数据

2022世界交通运输大会(WTC2022)论文集：桥梁工程与隧道工程篇／世界交通运输大会执委会编. — 北京：人民交通出版社股份有限公司，2022.8

ISBN 978-7-114-18287-7

Ⅰ.①2…　Ⅱ.①世…　Ⅲ.①桥梁工程—文集②隧道工程—文集　Ⅳ.①U-53

中国版本图书馆CIP数据核字(2022)第194351号

2022 Shijie Jiaotong Yunshu Dahui (WTC2022) Lunwenji　Qiaoliang Gongcheng yu Suidao Gongcheng Pian

书　　名：**2022世界交通运输大会(WTC2022)论文集　桥梁工程与隧道工程篇**
著 作 者：世界交通运输大会执委会
责任编辑：韩亚楠　郭晓旭
责任校对：席少楠　赵媛媛
责任印制：刘高彤
出版发行：人民交通出版社股份有限公司
地　　址：(100011)北京市朝阳区安定门外外馆斜街3号
网　　址：http://www.ccpcl.com.cn
销售电话：(010)59757973
总 经 销：人民交通出版社股份有限公司发行部
经　　销：各地新华书店
印　　刷：北京建宏印刷有限公司
开　　本：889×1194　1/16
印　　张：50.75
字　　数：1536千
版　　次：2022年8月　第1版
印　　次：2022年12月　第2次印刷
书　　号：ISBN 978-7-114-18287-7
定　　价：288.00元
(有印刷、装订质量问题的图书,由本公司负责调换)

编　委　会

主　　席	沙爱民	张占民	刘文杰	
副 主 席	龙奋杰	陈春阳	安　实	顾祥林
	王云鹏	刘　攀	赵　鹏	何　川
	杜修力	严　伟	王小勇	谈传生
	吴超仲	周建庭	巨荣云	王大鹏
委　　员	汪海年	陈艾荣	陈建勋	陈　峻
	姚恩建	葛颖恩	张卫华	曹先彬
	王兴举	等		
执行编辑	游汉波	洪梓璇	冯　娜	陈　琨
	陈　敏	刘晓玲	张雷军	

目　录

桥梁工程篇

隧道工程篇

桥梁工程篇

Analysis and Correction of Temperature Effect of PC Cable-Stayed Bridge during Construction

Siyu Zhu* Yifan Song Hanhao Zhang Huichen Ge Kang Wang Qixiang Hui Fuhua Zhang
(Highway College, Key Laboratory of Bridge Detection Reinforcement Technology
Ministry of Communication, Chang'an University)

Abstract In order to study the influence of temperature effect on main beam alignment and cable force in cable-stayed bridge construction process:, this paper analyses the characteristics of temperature field of main beam and cable, based on the basic theory of heat conduction, a simulation calculation method of structure plane temperature field is proposed. This method can easily and accurately calculate and predict the temperature field distribution of girder and stay cable. Then analyses the influence of structure temperature field on cable force and line shape through temperature field distribution obtained by simulation calculation. The influence of temperature effect on subsequent unmade segments is predicted and a method to correct the influence of temperature effect is proposed according to the actual alignment of the segments. Taking a cable-stayed bridge (Jun'an Waterway Bridge) as an example, the temperature field simulation results obtained in this paper are very similar to the actual measured temperature data. The method of correcting temperature effect in this paper ensures the rationality of main beam alignment and cable force.

Keywords Highway bridge Plane temperature Field simulation Field test Temperature effect Correction method Cable force Elevation error

0 Introduction

Jun'an Waterway Bridge is a large bridge in Foshan section of Fojiang Expressway in Guangdong Province. Its bridge layout is: 119m + 250m + 119m three-span double tower double cable plane PC wide cable-stayed bridge. There are 20 cantilever construction sections in the main span and 14 cantilever construction sections in the side span. The main beam section is 36.8m wide, 3m high, separated single box double chamber section. The construction technology is the cantilever casting construction of the rear fulcrum hanging basket, and the design reference temperature is 21.9℃ (shown in Fig. 1).

Since entering the summer construction, the cable force changes greatly within a day due to the temperature effect of main beam elevation. In addition to the schedule requirements, part of the construction conditions, measurement conditions (such asmolding, marking elevation belt, etc.) can not be completely under the ideal temperature. Therefore, in summer construction, especially after entering the large cantilever stage: ① It is necessary to analyse and predict the distribution of the temperature field of the structure (main beam and stay-cable) and calculate the influence of the temperature field on the elevation of the main beam and cable force of the stay cable; ②put forward the correction method for the influence of temperature effect, so as to ensure the rationality of elevation and cable force in the construction process of main beam.

1. Fund: Science and technology supported by China Postdoctoral Foundation (2015M572511).

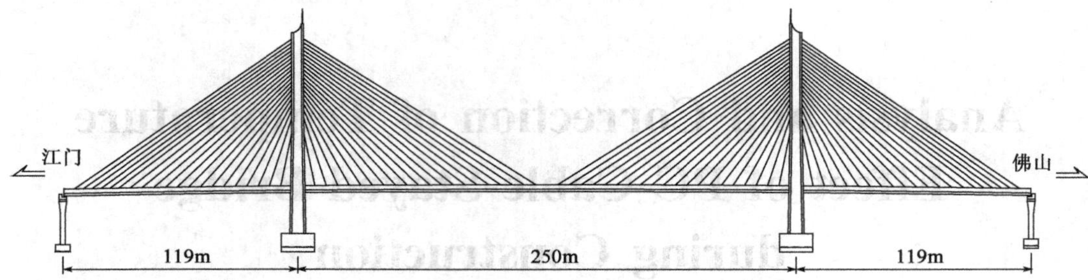

Fig. 1 Bridge layout

1 Temperature field simulation calculation and test

1.1 Structure temperature field characteristics

The influence of ambient temperature field on the structure is divided into overall temperature influence and local temperature influence.

The influence of overall temperature refers to the phenomenon of temperature change of uniformity of the overall structure or a single component over time, such as the overall seasonal temperature change of the bridge (construction stage generally does not occur), the overall temperature change of the stay-cable. The temperature field of the structure is only related to time:

$$T_1 = u_1(t) \tag{1}$$

The influence of local temperature difference refers to the non-uniform and local temperature change generated by the structure in the ambient temperature field. Such as the temperature gradient distribution on the top surface of the main beam. The temperature field of the structure is related to three-dimensional coordinates of the structure:

$$T_2 = u_2(x,y,z,t) \tag{2}$$

A large number of data shows that the temperature distribution of the stay-cable and the main beam axis is consistent:

$$T_2 = u_2(x,y,t) \tag{3}$$

1.2 Theoretical basis of structure temperature field calculation

1.2.1 Derivation of differential equations for heat conduction

All the structural materials are homogeneous and isotropic, and only the plane temperature field is considered. The following deduction can be made.

The relationship between temperature and energy is established through specific heat relation:

$$Q = \int_{t_1}^{t_2}\left(\iiint_V cp\frac{\partial u}{\partial t}dV\right)\mathrm{d}t \tag{4}$$

The energy of the external temperature field entering the structure through the structure boundary:

$$Q_1 = \int_{t_1}^{t_2}\left[\iiint_V\left(\frac{\partial^2 u}{\partial x^2}+\frac{\partial^2 u}{\partial y^2}+\frac{\partial^2 u}{\partial z^2}\right)\cdot k(x,y,z)\,dV\right]\mathrm{d}t \tag{5}$$

Energy provided Internal heat source of structure:

$$Q_2 = \int_{t_1}^{t_2}\left[\iiint_V F(x,y,z,t)\,dV\right]\mathrm{d}t \tag{6}$$

According to the law of conservation of heat energy: $Q = Q_1 + Q_2$, and joint (3), the plane heat conduction equation with internal heat source can be written as follows:

$$\frac{\partial u}{\partial t}-\frac{k}{cp}\left(\frac{\partial^2 u}{\partial x^2}+\frac{\partial^2 u}{\partial y^2}\right)=\frac{F(x,y,t)}{cp} \tag{7}$$

c: Specific heat capacity of materials; p: The density of material; k: Coefficient of thermal conductivity.

1.2.2 Initial and boundary conditions of temperature field

Initial conditions: The initial temperature of the structure is the same as the initial temperature of the external environment.

Boundary conditions: Since the convective heat exchange on the surface of concrete or stay cable is known, the third type of boundary conditions (mixed boundary conditions) are adopted:

$$\lambda\left(\frac{\partial u}{\partial n}\right)_s = \beta(T_s - T_\alpha)$$

$$\beta = 3.06 + 4.11v \quad (8)$$

β: Convective heat transfer coefficient of material exposed to air which can be calculated according to the linear fitting function proposed in literature, within the wind speed range of 1m/s ~ 25m/s.

T_s-T_α: Temperature difference between structure surface and surrounding boundary.

v: wind speed, value based on daily average wind speed.

1.3 Simulation calculation of temperature field

1.3.1 Assumptions and calculation parameters of simulation calculation

(1) The three-dimensional temperature field is simplified to the two-dimensional plane temperature field. The plane temperature distribution of main beam section and stay cable section is calculated by establishing plate elements.

(2) For the structural boundary that receives solar radiation (top surface of main beam, side of stay-cable), the local hourly solar radiation intensity (considering the radiation absorption coefficient of structure surface) is converted into heat source. The change of angle between normal and solar rays caused by sunshine direction within a day is not considered (that is, the change of radiation absorption coefficient is not considered). The radiation absorption function with time is simply defined in the volume element of the radiated surface. The heat source function of the volume element inside the structure and the volume element on the surface that is not affected by radiation is defined as 0.

The plane heat source function is expressed as follows:

$$F(x,y,t) = \rho s \quad (9)$$

ρ: Daily radiation absorption coefficient, top surface of concrete is 0.5 according to literature, and the side of stay-cable is 0.6 according to literature.

S: Hourly radiation energy per day (function of time).

Referring to the actual local meteorological data and relevant specifications, the heat source function can be calculated as the following piecewise function after curve fitting:

$$F_{\text{concrete}}(x,y,t)\begin{cases}0 & t\in[0,7)\\ 0.37t^4-19t^3+346t^2-2593t+6851 & t\in[7,18)\\ 0 & t\in[18,24)\end{cases}$$

$$F_{\text{stay-cable}}(x,y,t)\begin{cases}0 & t\in[0,7)\\ 0.00t^4-22.8t^3+415t^2-3112t+8221 & t\in[7,18)\\ 0 & t\in[18,24)\end{cases}$$

$$R^2 = 0.91 \quad (\text{unit: W/m}) \quad (10)$$

(3) The fitting was carried out according to the atmospheric temperature predicted by the weather (chamber temperature did not change much, so the constant temperature was simulated according to the initial temperature), and the atmospheric temperature was calculated by substituting the following function:

$$T(t) = (4t^4 - 2.5t^3 + 3.75t^2)\times 10^{-4} - 1.76t + 30.1$$

$$R^2 = 0.89, t\in[0.24] \quad (\text{unit: C}) \quad (11)$$

(4) The surface boundary of the structure shall define the convective heat transfer coefficient according to Equation (8), and simulate the heat exchange between the contact surfaces caused by the temperature difference, as shown in Tab. 1 (the interior and exterior of the box shall be defined separately).

Convective heat transfer coefficient Tab. 1

Boundary location	Inside the box	Outside the box
Convective heat transfer coefficient kJ/(m · hr · ℃)	20.1	56.2

(5) The thermal properties of structural materials are calculated according to the actual conditions and satisfy the plane heat conduction equation (Tab. 2).

Thermal properties of structural materials Tab. 2

Material	Concrete	HDPE	High strength steel wire
Coefficient of thermal conductivity[W/(m · ℃)]	2.33	0.4	80
Specific heat[kJ/(kgf · ℃)]	0.96	2.3	0.46

(6) The initial temperature of the structure is the same as that of the external environment:

$$u(x,y,t_0) = T(x,y,t_0) \tag{12}$$

(7) Generally, 15:00 is the time with the highest temperature and strong radiation in summer. Therefore, it is possible to directly calculate the temperature field distribution of the main beam and stay-cable at the most unfavorable time.

1.3.2 The calculation results

According to the above assumptions and calculation parameters, the plane finite element program is used to calculate the following results (Fig. 2 ~ Fig. 5):

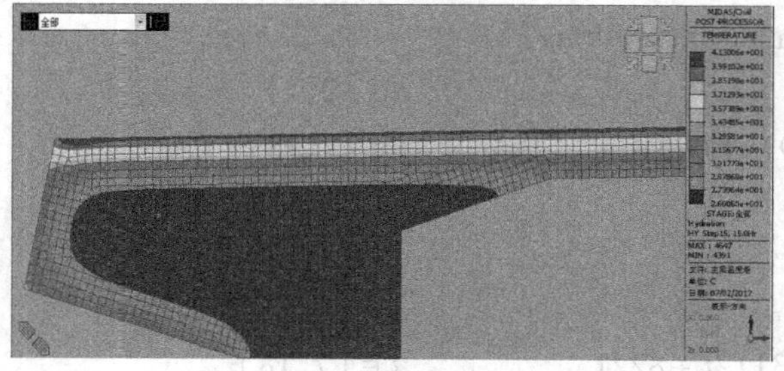

Fig. 2 Temperature field distribution diagram at the side web of box girder

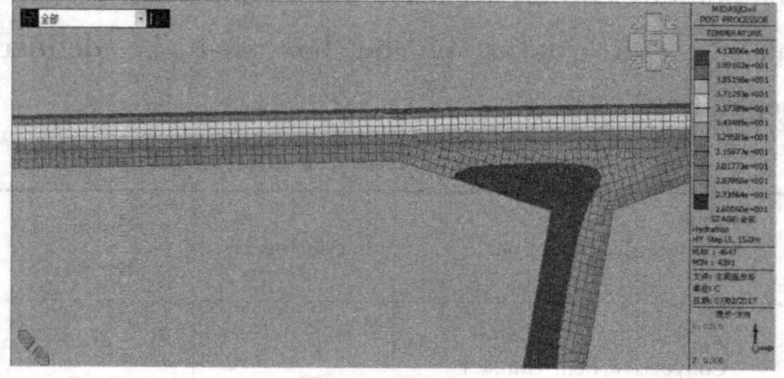

Fig. 3 Distribution of temperature field at middle web of box girder and top plate of box chamber

It can be seen from the temperature field distribution at this time in the figure:

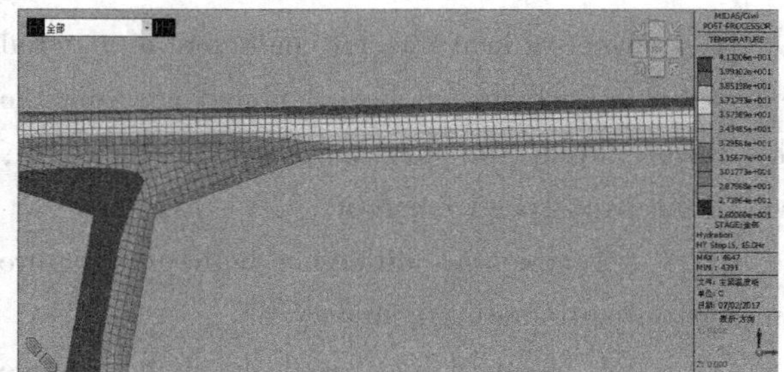

Fig. 4 Distribution of temperature field at hollow top plate of box girder

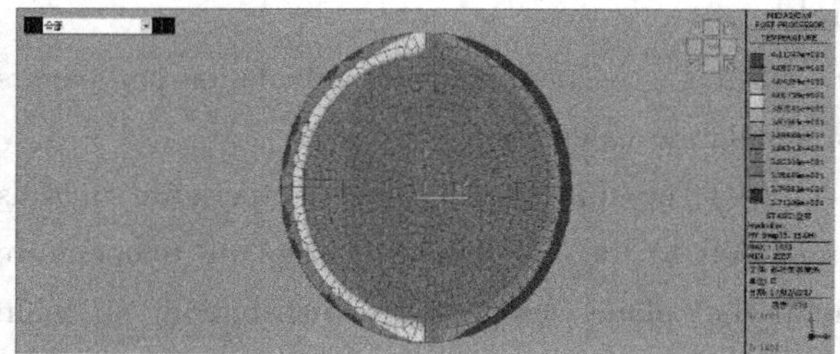

Fig. 5 Distribution of temperature field at stay-cable

(1) The temperature distribution of the roof at box girder is 41℃ ~ 28℃, and the distribution is basically linear; the range affected by temperature at the side web is about 40cm, and the temperature distribution at the side web is basically the same as that at the roof of the box. Due to different ambient temperatures on both sides of the middle web, the linear temperature distribution (from the inner side to the outer side) is 27℃ ~ 30℃; the bottom surface of hollow roof is affected by environmental convection, and its linear temperature distribution is 41℃ ~ 32℃.

(2) The temperature of HDPE sheath on the exposed surface of the cable is about 42℃; uniform temperature distribution of Internal high strength parallel steel wire is 39℃ due to fast thermal conductivity; the HDPE sheath on the back has a temperature of about 37°C.

1.4 Test of temperature field

1.4.1 The test content

The temperature field test was conducted in sunny weather with high temperature. When section 11 is completed, readings will be taken at approximately 7 a. m and 15 p. m.

The embedded situation of temperature sensor is shown in Fig. 6 and Fig. 7.

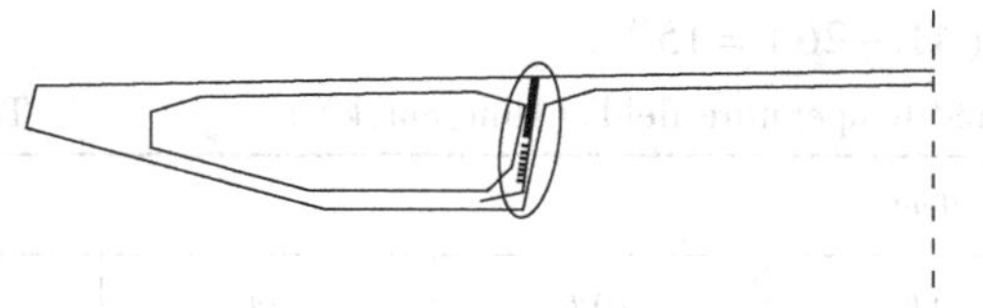

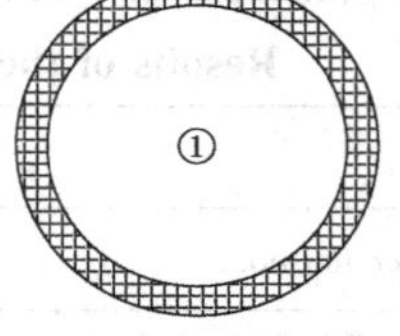

Fig. 6 Layout of temperature measuring points of main beam

Fig. 7 layout of steel wire temperature measuring points

1.4.2 The test results

The temperature field data collected for the completed section of the bridge (main beam block 12#) is shown in Tab. 3.

Measured temperature of temperature field test(Unit:℃) Tab. 3

	Time	The environment temperature	Average temperature of stay-cables	Average temperature of top surface of roof	Average temperature of bottom surface of roof
Simulation calculation	7:00	26	26	26	26
	15:00	36	39	41	30
	Δtemperature	10	13	15	4
Measured data	7:00	24	25	25	26
	15:00	35	36	37	28
	Δtemperature	11	11	12	2
Simulation error	Δ	—	2	3	2

There is about 2℃ ~ 3℃ (about 15%) error between the temperature change value calculated by finite element simulation and the measured data in temperature test. The large numerical value of the simulation is due to: the decrease of the daily radiation absorption coefficient of the structure caused by the change of solar incident angle is not taken into account; the wind speed on the test day is obviously greater than the monthly average wind speed given by meteorological data, resulting in the convective heat transfer coefficient at the structure boundary is greater than the calculated value.

The temperature distribution obtained by the plane temperature field simulation method proposed in this paper is unfavorable, and it is safe to calculate the linear shape, cable force and stress in the process of construction monitoring. It can be used to predict and correct the influence of temperature effect on cable force and line shape.

2 Calculation, analysias and prediction of tempreature effect

2.1 Temperature field data and calculation results used in calculation

Taking the main beam block 12# of the bridge as an example, the temperature field data calculated by simulation (shown in Tab. 3) is substituted into the finite element program for calculation.

In order to facilitate the analysis, the influence of temperature is separately calculated from the following two aspects according to Tab. 3: cable heating and temperature gradient of main beam. The calculation results are shown in Tab. 4.

(1) Temperature rise of stay-cable is calculated according to uniform temperature rise of steel wire (39 - 26) = 13℃.

(2) In the range of roof thickness, the temperature

field of the main beam changes greatly. The linear temperature gradient of roof's top surface is calculated according to temperature rise of (41 − 26) = 15℃. The linear temperature gradient of roof's buttom surface is calculated according to temperature rise of (41 − 26) = 15℃.

Results of theoretical calculation (simulated temperature field) (Unit: cm, kN) Tab. 4

Temperature effect						
Section no.		12#	11#	10#	9#	8#
Cable warming	Δelevation	−2.4	−2.2	−2.0	−1.8	−1.6
	Δcable force	−10	−9	−10	−13	−18
Temperature gradient	Δelevation	−1.9	−1.4	−0.9	−0.5	−0.2
	Δcable force	163	113	66	37	12
Total	Δelevation	−4.3	−3.6	−2.9	−2.3	−1.8
	Δcable force	153	104	56	24	−6

The temperature rise of the cable and the temperature gradient of the main beam have great influence on the line shape. The temperature gradient of main beam has great influence on cable force. The effect of cable temperature rise on line shape is uniform; the influence of temperature gradient of main beam on line shape and cable force is local, generally affecting only four or five adjacent segments.

2.2 Predict the impact of temperature effect on subsequent segments

The measured elevation data of main beam block 12# after completion of construction is shown in Tab. 5.

Measured data results (Unit: cm) Tab. 5

Measured elevation of main beam block 12#											
Section		12#		11#		10#		9#		8#	
		Side span	Mid span	Side span	Mid span	Side span	Mid span	Side span	Mid span	Side span	Mid span
Time	7:00	26.820	28.477	26.875	28.335	26.893	28.247	26.964	28.216	27.028	28.130
	15:00	26.782	28.441	26.844	28.302	26.870	28.220	26.944	28.197	27.012	28.114
Δelevation		−3.8	−3.6	−3.1	−3.3	−2.3	−2.7	−2	−1.9	−1.6	−1.6

The influence of theoretical calculation (simulated temperature field) and measured temperature effect on the alignment of the main beam is shown in Fig. 8.

The agreement between the simulated calculation and the measured data proves that the calculated results are reliable.

The temperature effect in the construction stage has at least 3 ~ 4 cm influence on the elevation of the main beam; the influence of temperature effect on subsequent segments can also be roughly predicted (calculated based on the above temperature field, as shown in Tab. 4): Before the side span is closed, the temperature effect affects the elevation of 5.2cm; before mid-span closure, temperature effect affects elevation of 10.4cm. Therefore, after entering the summer construction, the temperature has a great influence on the main beam alignment and cable force. When the construction process is not at the design reference temperature, relevant measures must be taken to correct the influence of temperature (Tab. 6).

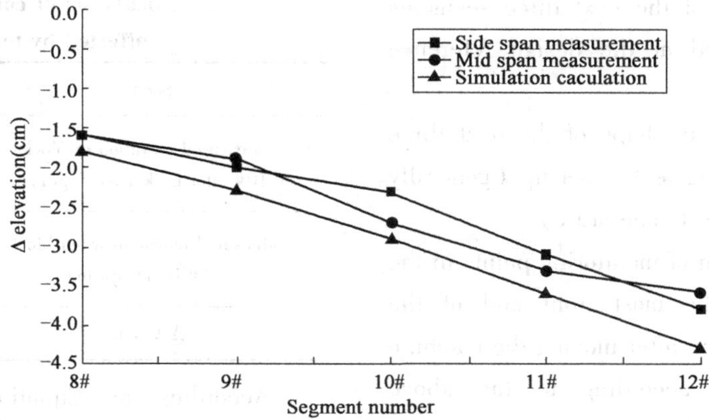

Fig. 8 Comparison between theoretical calculation and measured elevation

Impact of predicted temperature effect on each construction stage(Unit: cm,kN) Tab. 6

Temperature field type		The influence of temperature effect on the front end of cantilever		
		Work to section 12#	Work to section 14#(Before side span is closed)	Work to section20#(Before mid span is closed)
Temperature difference between beam and cable	Δelevation	-2.4	-3.1	-8.0
	Δcable force	-10	-5	-7
Temperature gradient of main beam	Δelevation	-1.9	-2.1	-2.4
	Δcable force	163	151	140
Total	Δelevation	-4.3	-5.2	-10.4
	Δcable force	153	146	133

3 Correction method for temperature effect in construction process

3.1 Correction of cable tension force of stay-cable

The cable force variation is mainly caused by the temperature gradient of the main beam. If the cable is not at the design reference temperature, the tension of the cable should be corrected according to the theoretical calculation. For example, at 15: 00, the tension of the 12# cable should be 3600 + 153 = 3753kN (3600kN is the tension at the design reference temperature). When the temperature returns to the reference temperature, the cable force returns to the design value.

However, due to the complexity and uncertainty of temperature gradient distribution, theoretical analysis is difficult to accurately simulate cable force variation and correction. Therefore, it is generally recommended to stretch the cable late at night or early in the morning. The cable tension of Jun'an Waterway Bridge is generally before 6: 00 in the morning, so there is no need to modify the cable force.

3.2 Correction of mold elevation

3.2.1 Correction of mold elevation

In order to meet the requirements of construction schedule, the time of establishing a mold is close to noon or 3 p. m. Commonly, at this time, the temperature has a great influence and must be adjusted according to the measured alignment before the mode adjustment.

As Fig. 9 below:

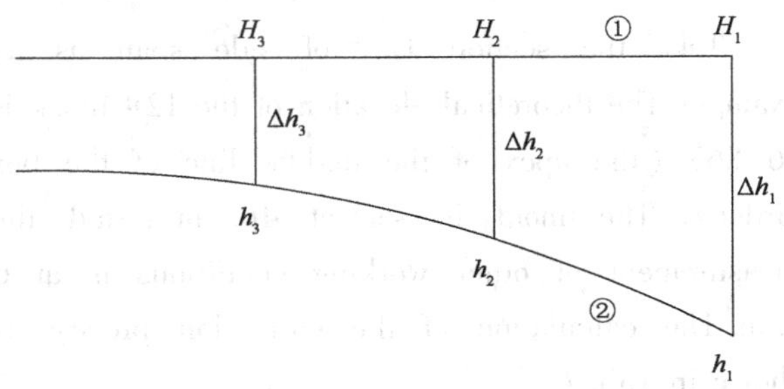

Fig. 9 Diagram of temperature influence

①: The line shape of the next three segments after the basket is moved at the design reference temperature.

②: The measured line shape of the next three segments when the new segment is set up (generally not at the design reference temperature).

H_1, H_2, H_3: Elevation of monitoring points in the next three sections of the most front end of the cantilever of the main beam after moving the machine (it can be calculated according to the above calculation).

h_1, h_2, h_3: Elevation of monitoring points measured relative to the setting up of the model.

$\Delta h_1, \Delta h_2, \Delta h_3$: The temperature effect value of the corresponding monitoring point during modeling.

Δh_0: Influence of real-time temperature effect of mold segments.

H_0: Mold elevation of new section at design reference temperature.

$\tilde{H}_0$: Temperature corrected mold elevation. Namely, $\tilde{H}_0 = H_0 - \Delta h_0$.

As a segment is only 6 meters, the stiffness of individual segments is large. The change value of each two segments is basically linearly increasing[16], so there is $\Delta h_2 - \Delta h_1 = \Delta h_3 - \Delta h_2$. Therefore, it can be predicted that the mold segments are affected by temperature in this temperature environment: $\Delta h_0 = \Delta h_1 + (\Delta h_1 - \Delta h_2) = 2(H_1 - h_1) - (H_2 - h_2)$.

Namely, the elevation of the mold at this temperature:

$$\tilde{H}_0 = H_0 - \Delta h_0 = h_0 - 2(H_1 - h_1) + (H_2 - h_2) \tag{13}$$

3.2.2 An engineering example

Take the section 12 # of side span as an example. The theoretical elevation of the 12# block is 26.863 (the apex of the middle line of the box girder). The mold is set at 4p. m., and the measurement of other working conditions is at 6 a. m. The calculation of the correction process is shown in Tab. 7.

Calculation of correction value affected by temperature Tab. 7

Section	10#	11#
Measured elevation of block 10# after basket moving(m)	26.890	26.866
Measured elevation when block 11# is set up(m)	26.862	26.834
Δ h(cm)	2.8	3.2

According to Equation (13), the setting elevation of block 12# at the current temperature is 26.863-2 × 3.2/100 + 2.8/100 = 26.827m. The actual construction elevation change process of Block 12# is shown in Tab. 8. The construction process of block 12 # is in a reasonable state, and the modification method basically eliminates the influence of temperature effect on the alignment of main beam in the construction process.

Actual construction elevation changes Tab. 8

Working condition	Theoretical value of elevation(m)	Measured value of elevation(m)	Δh(cm)
Formwork erection	26.863	26.827	-3.6
After casting	26.721	26.726	+0.5
After tensioning cable	26.817	26.820	+0.3

4 Conclusions

To sum up, the conclusions are as follows:

(1) The influence of temperature effect on concrete cable-stayed bridge cannot be ignored, especially in summer construction or large cantilever construction stage.

(2) The numerical values calculated by the plane temperature field simulation method proposed in this paper are highly similar to the data obtained by the temperature test method. The influence of temperature effect on cable-stayed bridge can be predicted and corrected in advance by the simulation method proposed in this paper.

(3) The temperature difference between cable

beams and the temperature gradient of the main beam have great influence on the elevation of the main beam, the temperature gradient of main beam has great influence on cable force.

(4) The temperature gradient of the main beam can only affect the elevation and cable force of the four or five adjacent segments of the largest cantilever end, and has little influence on the next segment; the temperature difference between cable beams affects the elevation of the cantilever end, and the closer the cable beam is to the maximum cantilever end, the greater the influence is.

(5) According to the engineering example, the correction method of temperature effect in the construction process proposed in this paper is reasonable. The modification method basically eliminates the interference of temperature factors to the construction process and ensures the alignment of the main beam, which has a certain practical value.

(6) The correction method proposed in this paper can be used not only for the correction of temperature effect, but also for the correction of temporary construction load, so as to reduce the construction error caused by external factors.

References

[1] Lin Yuanpei. Cable-stayed Bridge [M]. Beijing: People's Communications Press, 2004.

[2] Liu Shilin. Design of Cable-stayed Bridge [M]. Beijing: People's Communications Press, 2006.

[3] Veeehio, F. Nonlinear Analysis of Reinforced Concrete Frames Subjectd to Thermal and Mechanical Loads [J]. Journal of ACI Structure, 1987, 84(6): 492-501.

[4] Sivakumaran, KS. Analysis of Concrete Structures Subjected to Sustained Temperature Gradients [J]. Can Journal Civil Eng., 1984, 11 (3): 404-410.

[5] Zhang Yi, Guo Enzhen. Heat Transfer [M]. Nanjing: Southeast University Press, 2004.

[6] Zhang Jianrong, Liu Zhaoqiu. Experimental Study on Convective Heat Transfer Coefficient of Concrete in Wind Tunnel [J]. China Civil Engineering Journal, 2006(9): 39-42 + 61.

[7] Zhang Jianrong, Zhou Yuanqiang, Lin Jianping, et al. Effect of Solar Radiation on Temperature Of Concrete Box Girder [J]. Journal of Tongji University (Natural Science), 2008 (11): 1479-1484.

[8] Dilger W. H, Ghali A, Chan M, et al. Temperature stresses in composite e box girder bridges [J]. Journal of Structural Engineering, ASCE, 1983, 109(6): 1460-1478.

[9] Zhang Jianrong, Xu Xiangdong, Liu Wenyan. Study on Solar Radiation Absorption Coefficient of Concrete Surface [J]. Building Science, 2006 (1): 42-45.

[10] Ge Yaojun, et al. Temperature field test report of main bridge of Yongjiang Bridge during construction period [J]. Shanghai Institute of Urban Construction, 1992.

[11] Ge Yaojun, Zhai Dong, Zhang Guoquan. Experimental Study on Temperature Field of Concrete Cable-stayed Bridge [J]. China Journal of Highway and Transport, 1996(2): 76-83.

[12] Ministry of Construction, PRC. Design Code for Heating, Ventilation and Air Conditioning: GB 50019—2003 [S]. Beijing: China Planning Press, 2003.

[13] Wang Di, Li Yang, Hou Ning. Design code for heating ventilation and air conditioning [S]. Beijing: China Planning Press, 2003.

[14] Shi Saiying, Wang Weifeng. Research on Temperature Effect of Cantilever Construction of Concrete Cable-stayed Bridge [J]. Science Technology and Engineering, 2012 (33): 9110-9113.

[15] Guo Qiwu, Fang Zhi, Pei Bingzhi, et al. Research on Temperature Effect of Cantilever Construction of Concrete Cable-stayed Bridge [J]. Science Technology and Engineering, 2012(33): 9110-9113.

[16] Su Cheng, Xu Yufeng, Deng Jiang. Analysis of Temperature Effect of Concrete Cable-stayed Bridge [J]. China Journal of Highway and Transport, 2002(2): 51-54.

公路下穿既有高铁桥墩基础影响规律分析

张健伟*
(长安大学公路学院)

摘　要　为保证新建公路下穿高铁桥梁时的施工与运营安全,需对既有桥梁墩台基础进行影响性分析。本文以福州市南江滨东大道下穿福厦高铁为工程依托,采用 MIDAS/GTS 建立三维有限元数值模型,分析了道路施工阶段及运营阶段对桥墩基础位移的影响以及公路沉降。结果表明:在公路施工过程中,垫层的开挖对桥墩承台的影响较大,沉降变化速率较快,后期的运营阶段有较大的不均匀沉降,应及时采取措施予以控制。现场监测资料显示,垫层开挖时承台沉降变化量达到 3.6mm,且变化率较大,在施工时应当予以重视。现场实测验证了数值模拟的结果和规律,可为类似工程设计与施工提供一定参考。

关键词　公路工程　数值分析　下穿高架桥　墩台

0　引言

近年来,随着基础建设的快速发展,交通出行愈发便利,隧道下穿桥梁、公路下穿高铁高架桥的情况也越来越普遍[1-3]。利用下穿公路的交叉方式在节省大量的工程投资,取得较好的经济效益的同时也给既有的高铁高架桥带来安全隐患。

目前,很多学者对该问题做了大量研究。彭坤等[4]以地铁盾构隧道下穿既有桥梁桩基工程为依托,利用数值模拟的方法分析了两种不同的桩基加固方案下地表沉降和桩身变形规律。尚艳亮等[5]利用数值模拟与现场监测的方法分析了双线盾构对桥梁桩基础的影响。张俭[6]为保证既有高铁运营安全,提出了"U"形槽和桥梁两种下穿高铁方案。张振[7]以公路下穿沈丹高速边牛大桥工程为依托,分析了桥下道路对既有桥梁桥墩的影响,并提出了减小影响的方法。

本文以福州市南江滨东大道下穿福厦高铁工程为依托,采用 MIDAS/GTS 对下穿高架桥路基进行动态数值模拟,分析了道路施工各个阶段及运营阶段对桥墩基础位移的影响,路面沉降以及桩身水平位移变化规律[8-11],并依托工程实测验证了数值计算的结果,可为类似工程设计与施工提供一定参考。

1　工程概况

福州市南江滨东大道全长约 3330m,沿江而建,作为城市主干道,该线路设计速度为 50km/h,如图 1、图 2 所示位置关系,路线北为闽江,南为规划城市用地,在 K5 + 986 处与福厦高铁相交,该处桥墩的节点为 52#、53#。根据地勘资料,工程区域地层从上到下依次是杂填土、黏土、粉土、粉细砂、砂岩。

图 1　南江滨东大道与福厦高铁位置关系

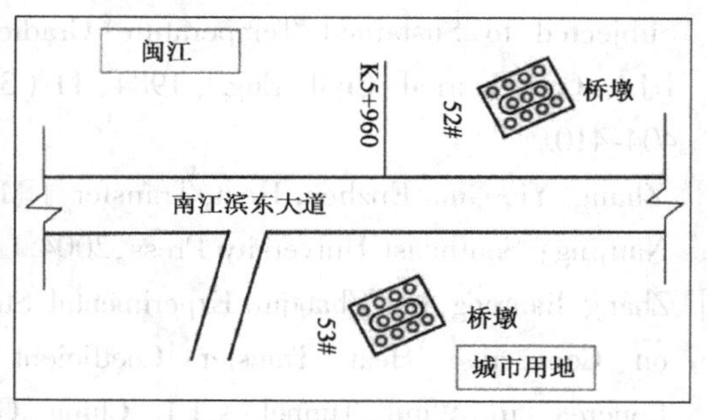

图 2　路线与桥墩位置关系

大幅的路基开挖或过大的填高都会对现有福厦高铁桥墩产生不利的侧向压力。因此，在施工方案确定前可通过数值模拟，分析路基施工过程中对桥墩影响的规律，以验证方案的可行性。

2 有限元模型

2.1 模型建立

本文采用 MIDAS/GTS 对下穿高架桥路基进行动态数值模拟，根据实际工程情况建立三维模型，64.4m×82m×82m（长×宽×高）。其共包含 5 层土，各层深度分别为 5m、13m、14m、10m、23m；道路面层、基层和垫层的厚度分别为 0.2m、0.65m、1m；桥墩、承台以及桩基的厚度分别为 15m、3m、45m。三维有限元模型如图 3 所示。各个土层、道路及桥墩等参数如表 1～表 3 所示。

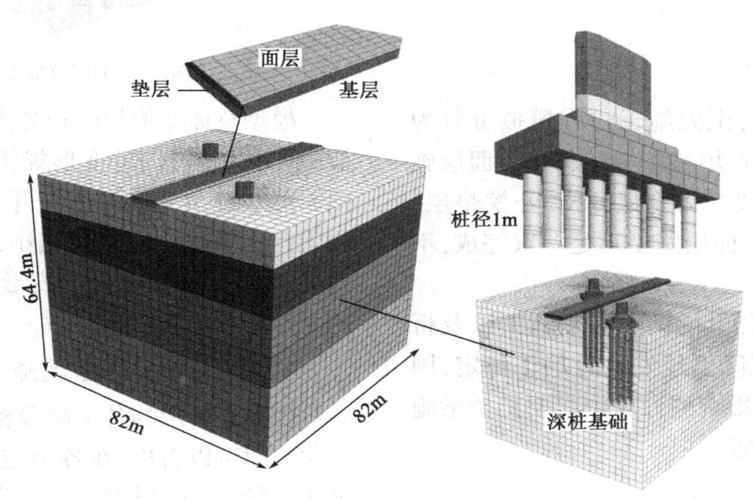

图 3 三维有限元模型

土层物理力学参数 表 1

类别	h/m	γ/kPa	E_{50ref}/MPa	E_{oedref}/MPa	E_{urref}/MPa	μ	e_0	n	ψ/(°)	c/kPa
杂填土	5	17.0	4.5	4.5	13.5	0.35	0.3	0.3	18	8
黏土	13	17.7	8	8	24	0.35	0.4	0.2	12	24
粉土	14	17.7	15	15	45	0.33	0.3	0.2	21	15
粉细砂	10	19.4	8	8	24	0.30	0.25	0.3	33	1
砂岩	23	21.8	75	75	225	0.20	0.5	0.3	35	400

公路的计算参数 表 2

类　别	厚度/m	重度/($kN \cdot m^{-3}$)	泊松比/μ	弹性模量/GPa
面层	0.2	27.0	0.35	3.00
基层	0.65	26.0	0.25	4.50
垫层	1.0	26.0	0.30	0.84

高架桥的计算参数 表 3

类　别	厚度/m	重度/($kN \cdot m^{-3}$)	泊松比/μ	弹性模量/GPa
桥墩	15.0	25.0	0.20	31.5
承台	3.0	25.0	0.20	31.5
桩基	45.0	25.0	0.20	33.5

2.2　基本假定

各土层的应力应变特性服从摩尔—库伦准则,而面层、基层、垫层、桥墩、承台和桩基满足弹性变形特性。所有材料均为均质、连续、各项同性体,其中道路面层、基层、垫层、桥墩和承台以三维实体单元模拟,桩基采用梁单元模拟,桩端设有桩端单元以表示底部砂岩对桩基的支撑作用。初始应力只考虑土体以及桥梁结构的自重应力,在道路施工完毕开始运营后,在面层施加15kPa均布压力。

2.3　施工模拟

根据实际状况,有限元施工过程模拟可分为初始阶段、开挖垫层、换填垫层、基层施工、面层施工、道路运营六个阶段。为简化分析,开挖垫层、换填垫层、基层施工和面层施工均是一次完成,不进行分区分段。

在公路施工之前,由桥梁的桩基施工以及桥梁荷载引起的先期沉降已经发生且趋于稳定,因此在针对公路施工的影响的计算中需要把桥梁施工引起的先期沉降清零。

3　计算结果及分析

3.1　整体位移分布

通过有限元计算结果可知,在最后一个阶段即运营期模型的竖向变形占了总变形的90%以上。因此,对于工程场地内的土体而言,其变形以竖向为主,且由竖向位移云图可知大部分土体均发生沉降,极少部分区域有轻微隆起(小于0.4mm),可忽略不计。图4、图5分别为运营期模型整体变形、运营期模型Z方向变形。

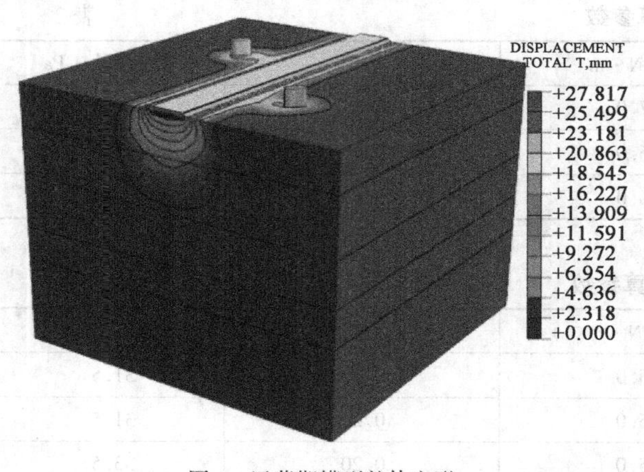

图4　运营期模型整体变形

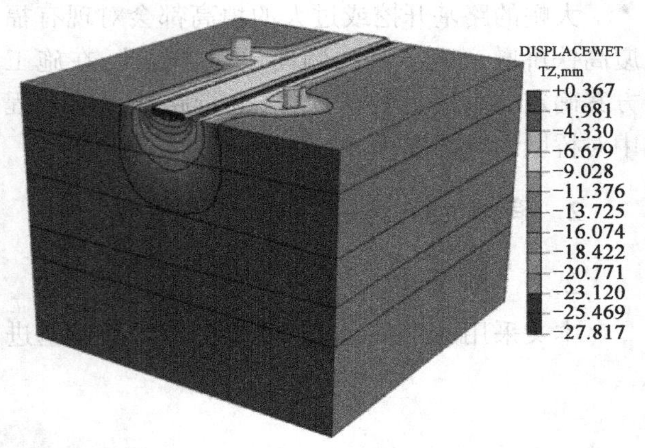

图5　运营期模型Z方向变形

模型整体变形规律和Z方向的变形规律较相似,本文以Z方向的变形规律分析为主。由图4、图5可知最大变形发生在开挖路面处,变形较为均匀且由路面向外逐渐减小;桥墩的存在对变形有一定的影响,桥墩处的变形达到6.679mm,Z向的变形影响深度约为18m。

3.2　桥墩、承台沉降分析

由图6所示的各个阶段桥墩以及承台的沉降变化规律可以看出,在各个施工阶段52号桥墩的整体沉降较53号桥墩大,沉降的峰值都出现在承台的边角处。接下来分析各施工阶段墩台沉降的特点:

(1)开挖垫层阶段,沉降最大值出现在52号桥墩承台左边角,约为3.9mm,右边角的沉降最小,约为3.1mm,故而整个桥墩及承台呈现左倾的趋势。53号桥墩沉降最大值仅为3.5mm,整体呈现右倾的趋势。

(2)换填垫层阶段,沉降最大值仍出现在52号桥墩承台左边角,约为4.1mm,右边角的沉降最小,约为3.9mm,但差异沉降较小,较第一阶段整个承台出现右倾的趋势。53号桥墩沉降最大值在左边角,为3.9mm,最小沉降出现在右边角,为3.6mm,整体呈现左倾的趋势。

(3)基层施工阶段,沉降最大值出现在52号桥墩承台右边角,约为4.5mm,左边角的沉降最小,约为4.1mm,整个承台呈现右倾的趋势。53号桥墩沉降最大值在左边角,为4.4mm,最小沉降出现在右边角,为3.6mm,整体呈现左倾的趋势。此阶段,两桥墩桥台开始向道路中间倾斜。

(4)后期运营阶段,沉降最大值仍出现在52号桥墩承台右边角,约为5.5mm,左边角的沉降最小,约为 4.2mm,差异沉降较上一阶段增大,右倾的趋势较为明显。53 号桥墩沉降最大值在左边角,为 3.9mm,最小沉降出现在右边角,为 3.6mm,差异沉降较小,整体呈现左倾的趋势。

四个施工阶段的沉降逐渐增大,且 52 号桥墩呈现先左倾后右倾的趋势,后期运营阶段的承台不均匀沉降较为明显,应及时采取措施予以控制。相对而言,53 号桥墩整体未产生较大的不均匀沉降。

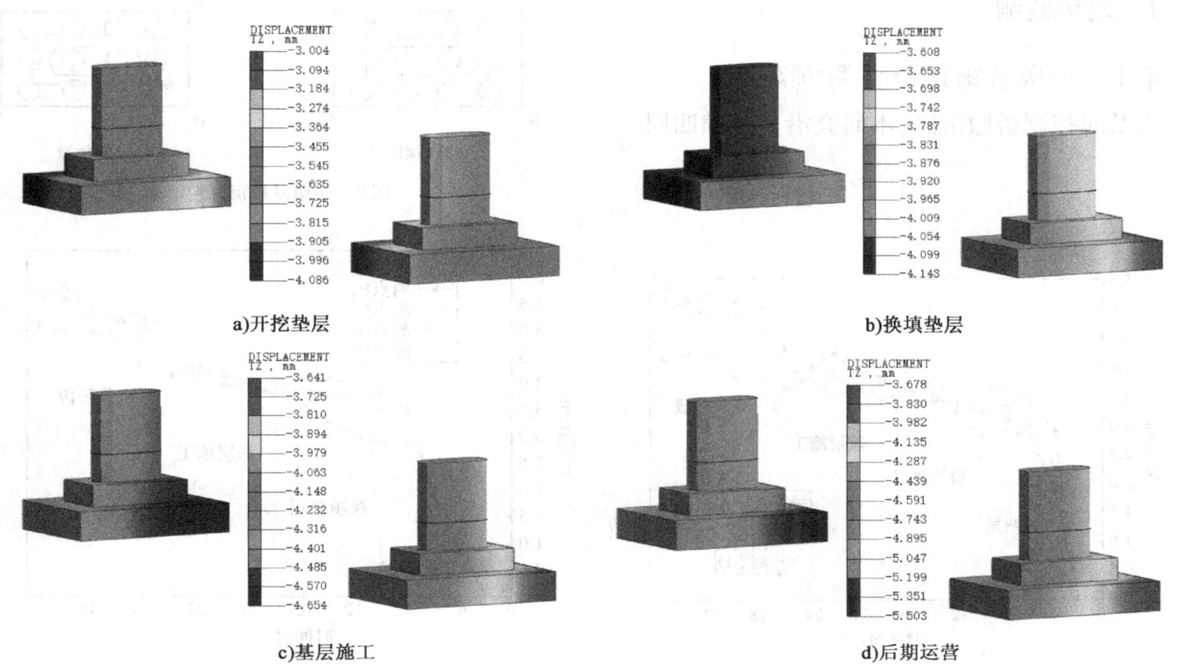

a)开挖垫层　b)换填垫层

c)基层施工　d)后期运营

图 6　各个阶段桥墩、承台沉降规律

3.3　道路施工后沉降分布

如图 7 所示,在道路运营期间,沉降最大位移变形发生在基层与垫层的交界处,高达 27mm,路面的沉降约为 7.9mm,基层和垫层的沉降较为接近,同时因为两层面厚度较大,沉降也较大,约为 16mm。面层、基层和垫层虽然沉降不一,但均未出现不均匀沉降。

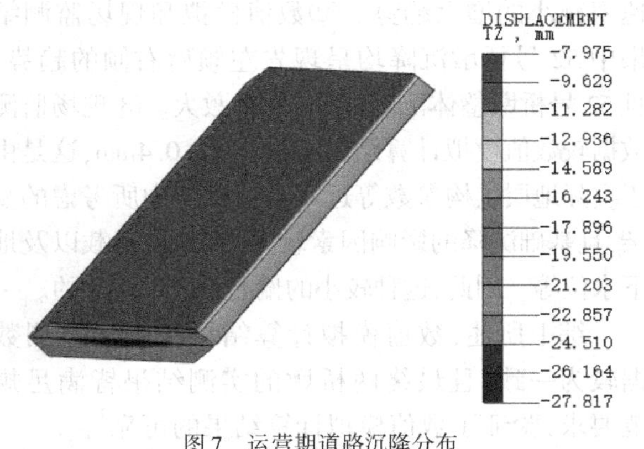

图 7　运营期道路沉降分布

3.4　桩身水平位移分析

图 8 所示为各个施工阶段 53 号桥墩桩身水平位移的变化规律,从中可以看出,初始阶段的水平位移为 0。随着桩身深度的增加,各个施工阶段的水平位移变化规律相似,都随着深度的增加逐渐减小。随着施工的推进,各个阶段的桩身水平位移向着路面偏移,且位移整体逐渐增大。其中开挖垫层时,桩身的水平位移偏离路面,向外侧倾,最大值为 0.45mm。其后的各个阶段桩身的水平位移都是向着路面方向,最大值发生在道路运营阶段,约为1.26mm。在换填垫层阶段,浅层的

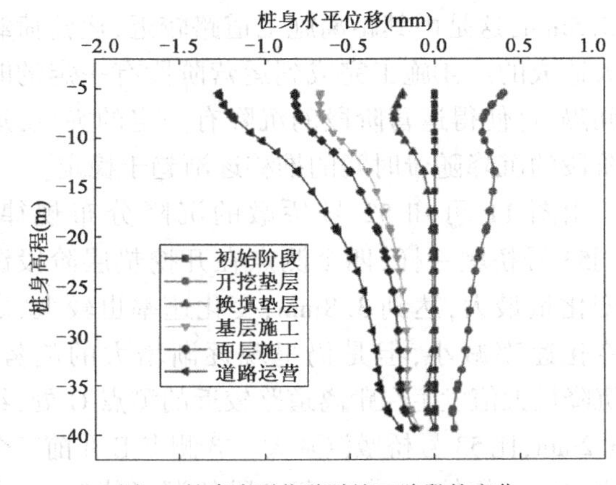

图 8　桩身水平位移随施工阶段的变化

桩体有较小的水平位移,随着深度的继续增大,桩身水平位移皆没有受到影响。在其他各个施工阶段,桩身深度为 40m 时,水平位移都较小,可认为无影响。

4　现场监测

4.1　桥墩基础沉降监测方案

为及时控制桥墩沉降,本研究沿其基础四周埋设监测点,长边布置 4 个监测点,短边布置 3 个监测点(每条边上有 2 个重合点),如图 9 所示,得到施工过程中两桥墩的沉降分布曲线,如图 10、图 11 所示。

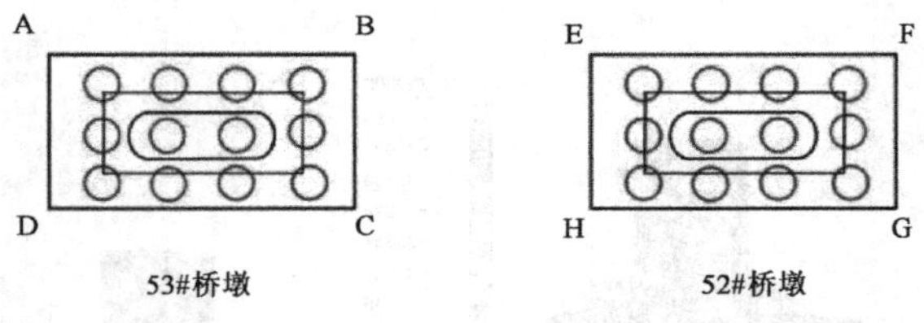

图 9　桥墩基础沉降监测点

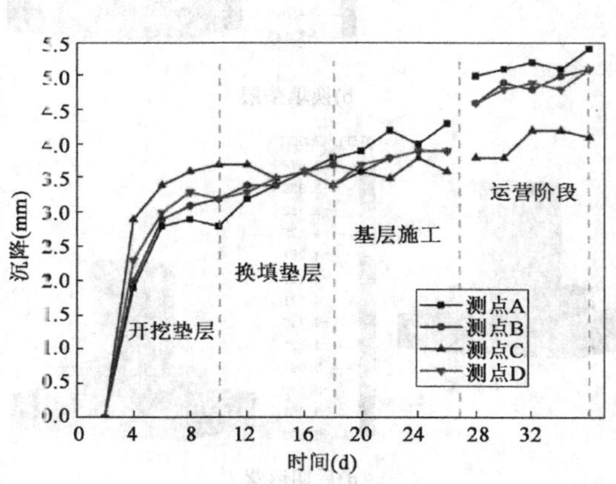

图 10　53#桥墩基础沉降分布规律

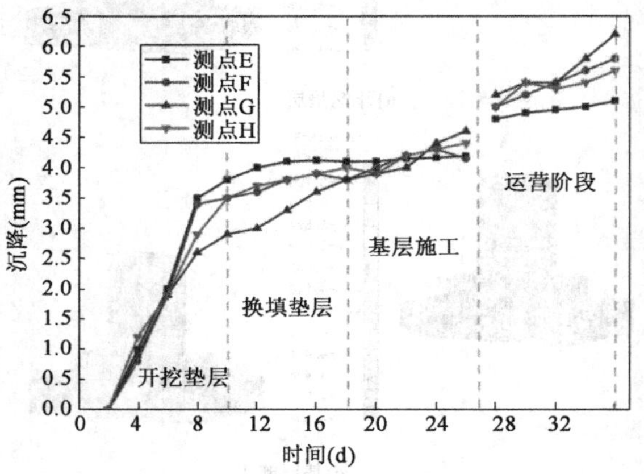

图 11　52#桥墩基础沉降分布规律

4.2　监测结果

由图 10 可知 53#桥墩的沉降分布规律:①四个测点在开挖垫层阶段沉降变化量最大,达到 3.6mm,变化速率也较大,之后变化速率减小,但是仍呈现逐渐增大的趋势。在施工过程中应对此阶段予以重视,积极采取措施,保证施工安全。②测点 C 因为距离施工道路相对较远,在开挖垫层之后的施工过程中沉降变化不大,有较小波动,约为 3.5mm。③沉降最大值发生在测点 A 处,约为 5.5mm,这是由其距离施工道路较近,运营荷载较大造成的。④施工完成到运营阶段有一定的时间间隔,这使得运营阶段的沉降有一定的突变,运营阶段的沉降随着时间的推移逐渐趋于稳定。

由图 11 可知 52 号桥墩的沉降分布规律:①同53 号桥墩一样,四个测点在开挖垫层阶段沉降变化量最大,达到 3.8mm,变化速率也较大,之后变化速率减小,但是仍呈现逐渐增大的趋势。②沉降最大值发生在距离道路较近的测点 G 处,约为6.2mm,比 53 号桥墩沉降大。③测点 E 在前三个阶段的沉降值较大,在运营阶段的沉降值较小,主要是由于其距离施工道路较远,运营荷载较小。

4.3　监测数据与计算结果对比

分析对比数值模拟计算结果和现场监测数据结果可知:①数值模拟和现场监测结果中桥墩沉降随时间的变化规律基本一致,52 号与 53 号桥墩均在开挖垫层阶段迅速产生较大沉降,随后在换填垫层、基础施工和运营阶段沉降逐步呈现变化速率减小的增大趋势。②数值模拟和现场监测结果中 52 号桥墩沉降均呈现先左倾后右倾的趋势,且 52 号桥墩整体沉降比 53 号桥墩大。③现场监测数据较数值模拟计算结果略大,约为 0.4mm,这是由于实际地层结构参数等远比数值模拟中所考虑的复杂,且基础沉降的影响因素较多,如地表荷载以及地下水位等。因此,这种较小的偏差是可以接受的。

综上所述,数值模拟计算结果和现场监测数据较为一致,且最终两桥墩的实测结果皆满足规范要求,验证了数值模拟计算结果的可靠性。

5　结语

(1)随着施工的不断推进,桥墩及承台沉降逐渐增大,道路施工后运营阶段52号桥墩呈现先左倾后右倾的趋势,后期运营阶段的承台不均匀沉降较为明显,应及时采取措施予以控制。相对而言,53号桥墩整体未产生较大的不均匀沉降。

(2)道路开挖完成之后最大位移变形发生在基层与垫层的交界处,高达27mm,路面的沉降约为7.9mm,基层和垫层的沉降较为接近,同时因为两层面厚度较大,沉降也较大,约为16mm。面层、基层和垫层虽然沉降不一,但未出现不均匀沉降,效果较好。

(3)随着桩身深度的增加,各个施工阶段的水平位移变化规律相似,都随着深度的增加逐渐减小。随着施工的推进,各个阶段的桩身水平位移向着路面偏移,且位移整体逐渐增大,最大值发生在道路运营阶段,约为1.26mm。桩身深度为40m时,水平位移都较小,可认为无影响。

(4)数值模拟计算结果与实测结果基本一致,且实测结果表明,在开挖垫层阶段承台沉降变化量最大,达到3.6mm,变化速率也较大,应对此阶段予以重视,保证施工安全。运营阶段的沉降随着时间的推移逐渐趋于稳定。

参考文献

[1] 韦京,王芳,孙明志. PBA工法地铁车站下穿桥梁方案优化研究[J]. 现代隧道技术,2014,51(6):101-107.

[2] 孙宗磊. 石济客专临近既有高速铁路桥梁设计[J]. 铁道工程学报,2016,33(2):37-42.

[3] 郑熹光,何平,张安琪,等. 地铁施工对邻近桥梁桩基础内力影响分析[J]. 现代隧道技术,2015,52(3):110-118.

[4] 彭坤,陶连金,高玉春,等. 盾构隧道下穿桥梁引起桩基变位的数值分析[J]. 地下空间与工程学报,2012(8):485-489.

[5] 尚艳亮,师文君,杜守继,等. 盾构近距离下穿桥梁数值分析与监测[J]. 沈阳建筑大学学报(自然科学版),2018(2):247-256.

[6] 张俭. 新建道路下穿运营高速铁路桥梁的设计方案[J]. 中外公路,2014,34(2):185-188.

[7] 张振. 浅析新建公路下穿高速公路既有桥梁对桥墩的影响[J]. 北方交通,2014(6):24-26.

[8] 杨红春. 新建道路下穿高速铁路桥梁对高铁桥墩和桩基影响的分析[J]. 中国市政工程,2016(2):7-9.

[9] 熊桂开,钟恒. 新建道路路基对既有上跨桥的安全影响分析及保护对策[J]. 内蒙古公路与运输,2015(1):11-13.

[10] 周建明. 桥梁或高架渡槽下相邻墩台间新建铁路路基的处理措施[J]. 铁道建筑技术,2016(2):79-83.

[11] 肖昊,叶长宏,宋文超,等. 高架桥下路面不均匀沉降机理及车辆荷载影响研究[J]. 交通科技,2018(2):8-11.

Experimental Study on the Effect of Wind Yaw Angle on Buffeting Response of Long-span Cable-stayed Bridge under Maximum Single Cantilever State

Jun Wang[1,2] Shuangrui Liu[1,2] Jiawu Li[*1,2]

(1. School of Highway, Chang'an University; 2. Wind Tunnel Laboratory of Chang'an University)

Abstract The buffeting response of wind yaw angle to long-span bridge cannot be ignored. In order to study the wind yaw angle effect on buffeting response of long-span cable-stayed bridge in the state of the cantilever, aeroelastic model test of full bridge was conducted, wind yaw angle was set −45 °~45 °, a total of 7 working condition, buffeting response at key section was measured. Skew wind decomposition and superposition method was used to calculate the corresponding buffeting response, and compared with the test results. The results show that the buffeting response at the cantilever end of the cable-stayed bridge increases with the increase of the absolute wind yaw angle, and the maximum buffeting response values occurred at $-45° \sim -30°$ and $30° \sim 45°$. The buffeting response at the bridge pylon top decreases with the increase of the absolute value of wind yaw angle, and the maximum response approximately appears in the normal wind condition, namely $-15° \sim 15°$. In the range of $-15° \sim 15°$, the error of the skew wind decomposition and superposition is less than 10%, but it will be higher than the experimental value. The error increases with the increase of wind yaw angle, but the influence of wind speed on the error is not obvious.

Keywords Bridge engineering Cable-stayed bridge Cantilever state Buffeting Wind yaw angle Aeroelastic model test of full bridge Skew wind decomposition and superposition

0 Introduction

The development and application of high-strength materials, the updating of calculation methods and technologies, and the increasing progress in design and construction technology have expanded the application space of cable-stayed bridges. Especially in the range of 200m ~ 1000m span, cable-stayed bridges are more effective than arch bridges and suspension bridges. The construction of long-span cable-stayed bridge is often carried out by cantilever pouring method or cantilever assembly method. In the cantilever state, the main girder has not been closed, the natural frequency and damping of the structure are small, and its wind resistance performance is weak, especially in the maximum cantilever state, which belongs to the wind-induced sensitive system. Therefore, the problem of wind-induced vibration in the maximum cantilever state of long-span cable-stayed bridges is one of the key hotspots in the study of wind resistance of such bridges. At the same time, the pulsating component of the air flow in the natural environment may cause the buffeting of the bridge structure. The buffeting start-up wind speed is low, which is easy to occur during the construction stage. Excessive buffeting response will affect the construction progress and construction safety. Therefore, it is necessary to analyse the buffeting of the bridge at the maximum cantilever stage.

The proposed bridge is located in the coastal area of Guangdong Province, China. The bridge site is open and flat, and may encounter strong winds of different directions or even typhoons. The influence of skew wind cannot be ignored, and it may be more dangerous under the action of illegal direction wind. It is necessary to consider the influence of wind yaw angle on bridge buffeting response.

At present, the research methods of buffeting of cable-stayed bridges by scholars include wind tunnel tests, numerical calculations and so on. Kimura et al. analysed the buffeting response of the wind yaw angle to the cantilever slab structure from the perspective of vibration theory based on experimental data, and proposed the skew wind decomposition and superposition method. Scanlan et al. studied the response of cable-stayed bridges under the action of skew wind during the construction phase on the basis of Kimura. Liu et al. studied the buffeting response of a long-span cable-stayed bridge during the construction period using the method of field measurement. Shen et al. used numerical calculation methods to study the effect of MDTMD on buffeting control of long-span cable-stayed bridges. Su et al measured the buffeting response of cable-stayed bridges under mountain wind conditions through wind tunnel tests. Hu et al. studied the buffeting response of the bridge tower in the self-standing state under the action of skew wind based on the wind tunnel test, and found that the maximum buffeting response of the bridge tower under the action of non-orthogonal wind. Che et al. also studied the influence of wind yaw angle on buffeting response of bridge tower in self-supporting state through aeroelastic model test, and found that the displacement response curve changes parabola with wind speed. Tang et al. used aeroelastic test and numerical simulation to analyse the buffeting response of a single-tower cable-stayed bridge during the construction phase.

In summary, the research on buffeting response of cable-stayed bridges is mostly based on wind tunnel tests. Considering the working conditions of different wind yaw angles, the research objects are mainly the cantilever state of the symmetrical cable-stayed bridge or the independent state of the tower. There are few reports on the buffeting of the bridge in the maximum cantilever state. Therefore, taking a long-span cable-stayed bridge in the maximum cantilever state as the research object and the inflow wind direction as the variable, the buffeting response of the long-span cable-stayed bridge in the maximum cantilever state is studied through the aeroelastic model wind tunnel test of full bridge and the skew wind decomposition superposition method.

1 Engineering background

A large-span cable-stayed bridge is a double-tower, double-cable-plane cable-stayed bridge, which is planned to be built in the coastal area of Guangdong Province, China. The bridge site locates open terrain, spans a river and is less than 100km away from the sea to the southeast. The maximum cantilevered bridge layout is shown in Fig. 1. The span layout is 402. 5m + 234. 5m = 637. 0m, the tower height is 259. 0m, the side span ratio of the main span is about 1. 716 : 1, and the tower height ratio of the main span is about 1. 554 : 1, the structure has obvious asymmetric characteristics. At the same time, in summer and autumn, the bridge site is the main area for typhoons landing along the coast of China, which is vulnerable to tropical cyclones from the Pacific. The statistical data shows that there were 129 typhoonsaffecting the bridge site from 1973 to 2008, with an annual average of about 3. 6 times, mainly from July to September.

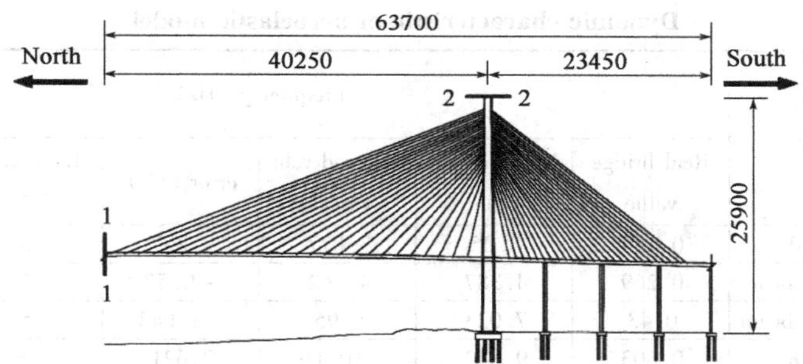

Fig. 1 Cable-stayed bridge at maximum cantilever state (Unit: cm)

2 Aeroelastic model test of full bridge

2.1 Model design

According to the actual bridge size at the maximum cantilever stage of the cable-stayed bridge, the test section size of the CA-1 atmospheric boundary layer wind tunnel of Chang' an University and the blocking rate, the geometric scale ratio of the aeroelastic model is determined to be 1 : 266. 4.

Generally speaking, aeroelastic similarity includes the similar conditions of the length, density, elasticity and internal friction of the structure, as well as the similar conditions of the density and viscosity, velocity and gravitational acceleration of the airflow. Therefore, the similarity conditions that must be met in aeroelastic model wind tunnel test can be expressed by these dimensionless parameters, as shown in Tab. 1. The parameter ρ in the table represents the air mass density, generally $\rho = 1.225\text{kg/m}^3$; U is the average wind speed; B is the characteristic size of the structure, and the bridge deck width is generally taken for aeroelastic model wind tunnel test; μ is the viscosity coefficient of air movement; g is gravitational acceleration; f is the natural frequency of the structure; E is the elastic modulus of structural material; ρ_s is the mass density of structural material; ζ

is the structural damping ratio.

Nondimensional similar parameters of aeroelastic model Tab. 1

Parameters	expression	Physical meaning	Similar requirements
Cauchy	$E/\rho U^2$	Structure elastic force/aerodynamic inertia force	Strictly similar
Froude	gB/U^2	Structure gravity/aerodynamic inertia force	Strictly similar
Strouhal	fB/U	Time Scale	Strictly similar
Damping ratio	δ	Energy consumption per cycle/total vibration energy	Strictly similar
Density ratio	ρ_s/ρ	Structure inertial force/air flow inertial force	Strictly similar
Reynolds	$\rho UB/\mu$	Pneumatic inertia force/air viscous force	Relaxation requirements for bluff bodies

For the conventional low-speed wind tunnel test, the fluid density ratio between the model and the prototype = 1, the fluid viscosity coefficient ratio = 1, and the gravity acceleration ratio. Thus, it can be seen from the definition in Tab. 1 that among the above dimensionless parameters, only when the geometric scale ratio is 1, the gravity parameters and viscosity parameters can be met at the same time. Since the geometric scale ratio of the aeroelastic model is ≪1, it is generally difficult to meet the consistency conditions of the viscosity parameters in the low-speed wind tunnel test of the aeroelastic model. Therefore, in the design of the bridge aeroelastic model, the similar requirements for the viscosity parameter (Reynolds number) are relaxed.

The aeroelastic model is made of aeronautical wooden outerwear with a gap of 2 mm. The outerwear does not provide stiffness and only serves to simulate the aerodynamic shape. It has aluminum alloy core beams and lead block counterweights.

In order to verify the accuracy of the model, the free excitation method is used to measure the dynamic characteristics of the aeroelastic model. The frequency and damping ratio are shown in Tab. 2. The dynamic characteristics of real bridges are shown in Fig. 2.

Dynamic characteristic of aeroelastic model Tab. 2

Vibration model	Vibration characteristics	Frequency (Hz)					Damping ratio (%)	
		Real bridge value	Model actual value	Measured value of model	error (%)	Limit value (%)	Measured value	Limit value
1	Main beam side bend	0.187	3.05	3.077	0.857	5	0.75	0.5 ~ 0.8
2	Vertical bending of main beam	0.269	4.387	4.362	-0.57	5	0.55	0.5 ~ 0.8
3	Vertical bending of main beam	0.43	7.023	6.95	-1.043	5	—	—
4	Torsion of main beam	0.603	9.842	10.1	2.621	5	0.7	0.5 ~ 0.8
5	Vertical bending of main beam	0.639	10.43	10.25	-1.722	5	—	—

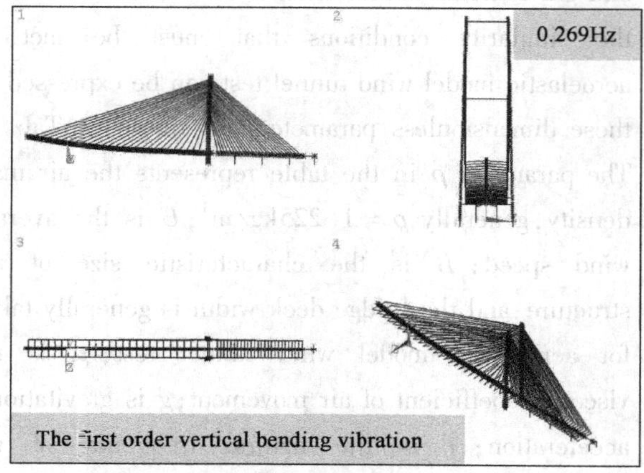

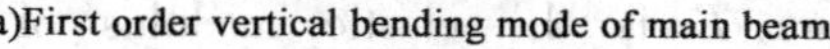

a)First order vertical bending mode of main beam

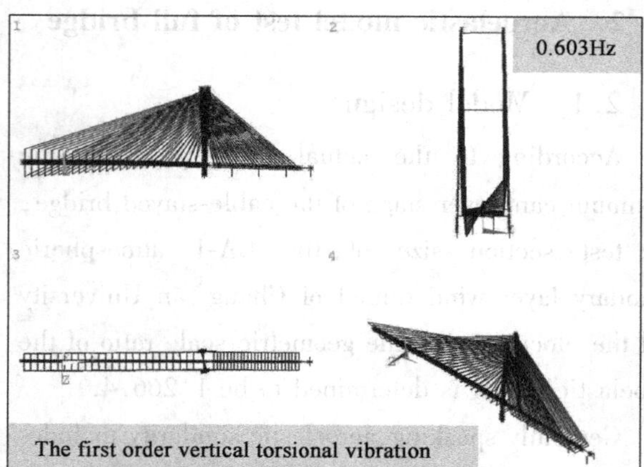

b)First order torsional mode of main beam

Fig. 2 Dynamic characteristics of real bridges

2.2 Wind field simulation

According to the analysis of the wind environment at the bridge site, in the CA-1 atmospheric boundary layer wind tunnel of Chang'an University, the passive simulation technology of wedge and rough element is used to simulate the type B geomorphic turbulent wind field with a scale ratio of 1:266.4, and the target value of wind speed profile index α is 0.16. The aeroelastic model and turbulent wind field of the maximum cantilever state of the long-span cable-stayed bridge are shown in Fig. 3.

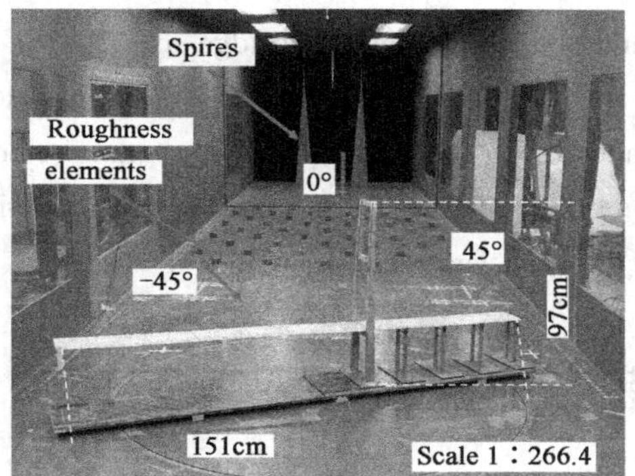

Fig. 3 Atmospheric boundary layer wind field and aeroelastic model

$$\frac{U}{U_{\mathrm{ref}}} = \left(\frac{H}{H_{\mathrm{ref}}}\right)^{\alpha} \tag{1}$$

$$\frac{TI}{\alpha} = \left(\frac{H_{\mathrm{ref}}}{H}\right)^{TI_{\mathrm{ref}}} \tag{2}$$

Where U_{ref} is the reference wind speed, U is the wind speed, H_{ref} is the reference height, H is the height, α is the surface roughness coefficient, TI is the turbulence intensity, and TI_{ref} is the reference turbulence intensity.

There are many forms of pulsating wind power spectrum. In this paper, the widely used Simiu spectrum, Panofsky spectrum, and von Karman spectrum are compared with the measured spectrum, and the measured wind power spectrum is fitted with two spectral functions A and B, the power spectrum functions are shown in equations (3) to (9) respectively.

$$\frac{nS_u(n)}{u_*^2} = \frac{200f}{(1+50f)^{5/3}}\text{---Simiu} \tag{3}$$

$$\frac{nS_w(n)}{u_*^2} = \frac{6f}{(1+4f)^2}\text{---Panofsky} \tag{4}$$

$$\sigma_u^2 = 6u_*^2 \tag{5}$$

$$\frac{nS_u(n)}{\sigma_u^2} = \frac{4F}{(1+70.8F^2)^{5/6}}\text{---von Karman} \tag{6}$$

$$\frac{nS_u(n)}{\sigma_u^2} = \frac{A_u f}{(1+B_u f)^{5/3}}\text{---A} \tag{7}$$

$$\frac{nS_u(n)}{\sigma_u^2} = \frac{A_u f}{(1+B_u f)^2}\text{---B} \tag{8}$$

Where $S_u(n)$ is the downwind fluctuating wind power spectrum, $n$is the fluctuating wind frequency, u_* is the friction velocity, f is the dimensionless Mourning coordinate, which is calculated by equation (9). $F = nL_x^u/\overline{U}$ is the calculation of the von Karman power spectrum dimensionless wind speed, $\overline{U}$ is the average wind speed, $L_x^u = \frac{1}{\sigma_u^2}\int_0^{\infty} R_{u1u2}(x)\,dx$is the turbulence integrating ruler along the x-axis of the wind direction degree, A_u、B_u are the parameters to be fitted, and σ_u is the standard deviation of the fluctuating wind in the downwind direction.

$$f = \frac{nz}{U(z)} \tag{9}$$

Where $U(z)$ is the wind speed at height z.

The downwind fluctuating wind power spectrum at the height of the bridge deck is shown in Fig. 4. It can be seen that the fitting effect of the von Karman power spectrum and the measured power spectrum is better than the Simiu spectrum and the Panofsky spectrum, and the B fitting spectrum is better than the A fitting spectrum

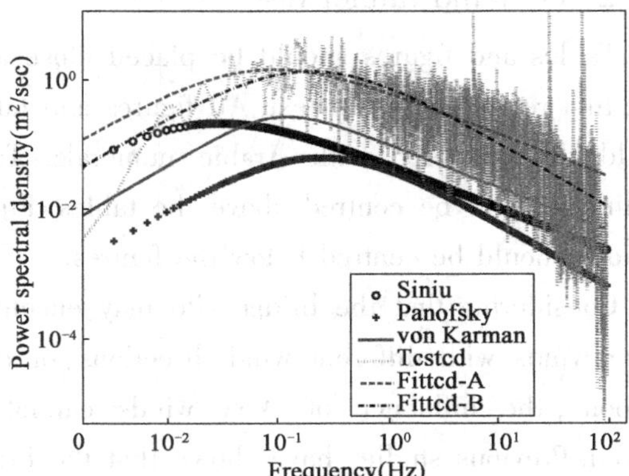

Fig. 4 Downwind fluctuating wind power spectrum at bridge deck height

The downwind speed and turbulence intensity are fitted according to equations (1) and (2). As shown in Fig. 5 ~ Fig. 6, it can be seen that the fitting effect of the wind speed profile and the turbulence intensity profile is better, which is similar to the specification.

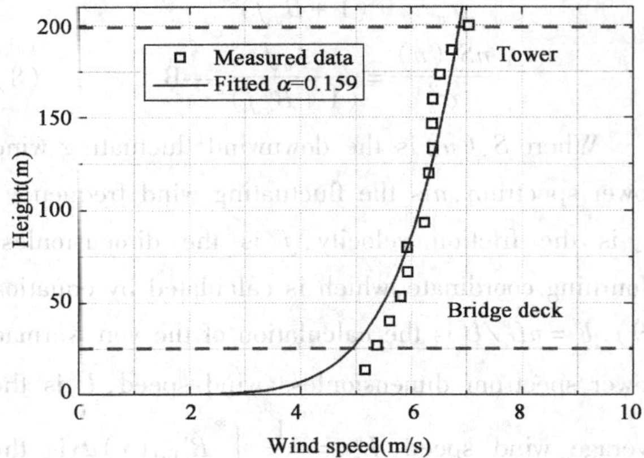

Fig. 5 Perpendicular wind speed profiles

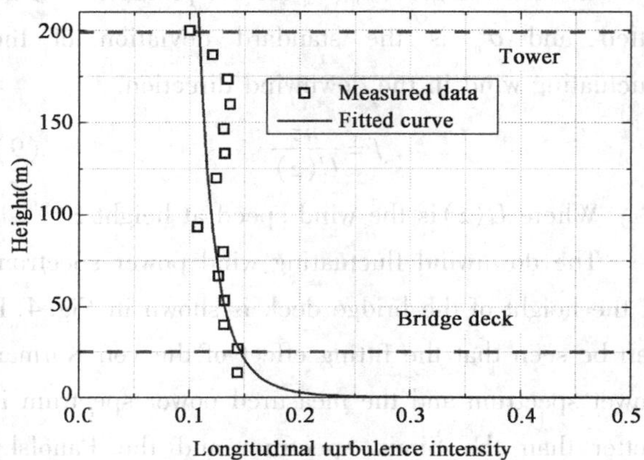

Fig. 6 Downwind turbulence intensity profiles

2.3 Wind tunnel test

Tables and figures should be placed close after their first reference in the text. All figures and tables should be numbered with Arabic numerals. Table headings should be centred above the tables. Figure captions should be centred below the figures.

Considering that the bridge site may encounter strong winds with different wind directions, or even typhoons, the influence of skew winds cannot be ignored. Previous studies have shown that the bridge structure may be in a more dangerous state under the action of illegal winds, especially for long-span cable-stayed bridges in the construction stage. Therefore, it is necessary to study multiple wind yaw angles. According to the structural characteristics, 7 working conditions are designed, and the wind yaw angles are shown in Fig. 7, respectively, $-45°$, $-30°$, $-15°$, $0°$, $15°$, $30°$, $45°$. The geometric midpoint of the aeroelastic model is placed at the center of the beta device turntable in the test section, and the wind yaw angle is controlled by adjusting the turntable angle of the beta device. The main research factor in this paper is the wind yaw angle, so the wind attack angle only considers the 0° wind attack angle.

The definition of wind yaw angle β: the angle between the average wind direction of the incoming flow and the normal of the bridge axis. A wind yaw angle of 0° indicates that the incoming flow is perpendicular to the bridge axis. The counter clockwise rotation when viewed from above is the direction in which the wind yaw angle increases.

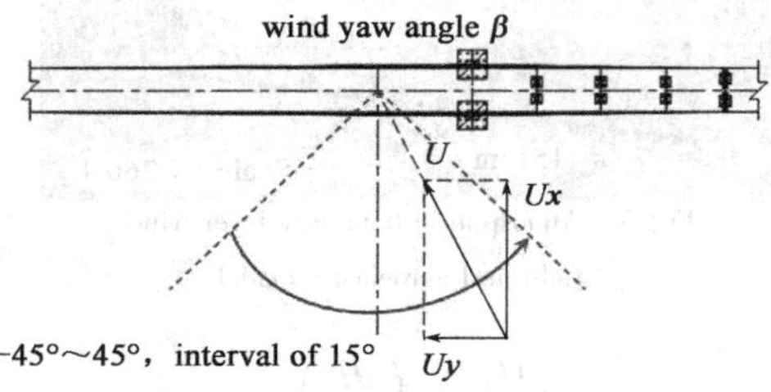

Fig. 7 Diagram of wind yaw angle and skew wind decomposition

Combining the first-order mode of the bridge, as shown in Fig. 2, the deformation of section 1-1 at the cantilever end and section 2-2 at the tower top is the largest. In order to measure the buffeting response of the structure, three measuring points are set at the cantilever end and tower top respectively, and the vibration response is measured by laser displacement sensors, as shown in Fig. 1 and Fig. 8.

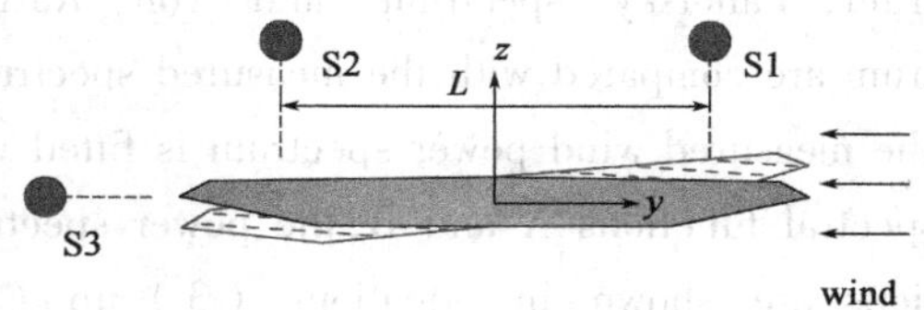

Fig. 8 Diagram of sensors setting

The vertical (forward-bridge) response, transverse-bridge response and torsional response of the control section can be measured through geometric relations, as shown in equation (10) ~ (12).

$$D_{ver} = \frac{1}{2}(d_1 + d_3) \quad (10)$$

$$D_{lat} = d_3 \quad (11)$$

$$D_{rot} = \frac{1}{L}(d_1 - d_2) \quad (12)$$

Where d_1, d_2 and d_3 are the measurement results of the laser displacement sensors S1, S2, and S3 respectively, D_{ver} is the vertical vibration response, D_{lat} is the transverse vibration response, and D_{rot} is the torsion response.

3 Analysis of test results

3.1 Buffeting response at the cantilever end of the main beam

It can be seen from Tab. 2 and Fig. 9 that the vertical bending vibration of the cantilever end is the main vibration mode, and the first-order vibration frequency is close to the design value with a difference of 0.57%, which reflects that the design of the aeroelastic model is reasonable and the follow-up experimental research is reliable. It can be seen from Fig. 10 that when the design wind speed of the main girder is 32.64m/s during the construction stage, the vertical RMS value of buffeting presents a "W" shape with the wind yaw angle, and the orthogonal wind response with the RMS value on both sides greater than 0°. The transverse RMS value is approximately twice that of the vertical response, and the trends are similar, with the maximum values appearing at 0° and −30°; the buffeting torsion RMS value is approximately U-shaped with the yaw angle of the wind. When the wind yaw angle is between-15° and 30°, the torsional RMS value is approximately unchanged, but the torsional response at 45° is about twice that of the orthogonal wind. In addition, the cloud map of the cantilever end buffeting response with wind speed and wind yaw angle in Fig. 11, it can be preliminarily determined that the buffeting response of cantilever end of main beam of the largest cantilever cable-stayed bridge in the turbulent field does not always appear under the orthogonal wind condition, but more often increases with the increase of the absolute value of wind yaw angle, and the maximum value appears −45 ° ~ −30 ° and 30 ° ~45 °.

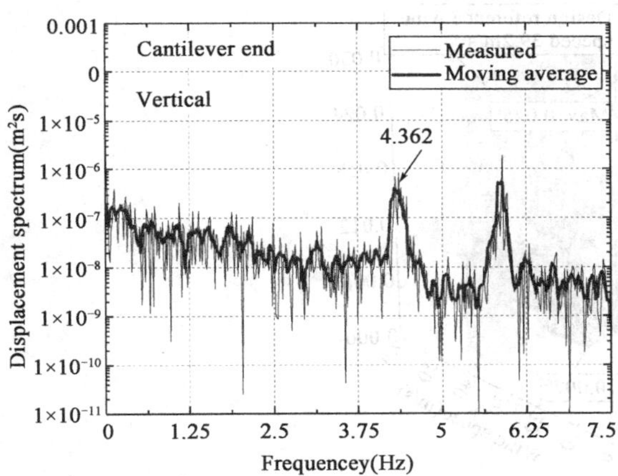

Fig. 9 Amplitude frequency diagram of vertical vibration at cantilever end

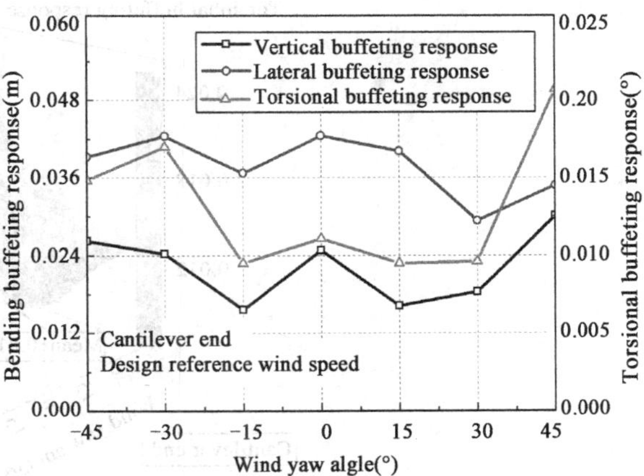

Fig. 10 Buffeting response of cantilever end (design wind speed)

3.2 Buffeting response of bridge tower top

It can be seen from Tab. 2 and Fig. 12 that the vibration frequency along the bridge direction of the tower top is consistent with that of the main beam, which is 4.362 Hz, indicating that the main vibration mode of the bridge in the maximum cantilever state is the first-order vertical bending vibration of the main beam. It can be seen from Fig. 13 that when the design wind speed of the main girder is 32.64m/s during the construction stage, the RMS value of buffeting along the bridge is in an inverted V-shaped with the yaw angle of the wind, and the maximum value of the RMS appears at −15°, which is about 9% greater than the orthogonal wind condition. The buffeting transverse RMS value is less than 1/2 of the vertical response, and the trend is similar. The maximum value appears at the wind yaw angle of 15°, which is obviously different from the situation at the cantilever end of the main beam. The influence of wind yaw angle on the buffeting torsional RMS value of the bridge tower top is also approximately inverted "V", and the maximum RMS value appears at 0 °, which is 0.122 °. In addition, from the cloud diagram of buffeting response of bridge tower top with wind speed and wind yaw angle in Fig. 14. It can be seen that the buffeting response of bridge tower top of the largest cantilever cable-stayed bridge in the turbulent field mostly occurs under approximately orthogonal wind conditions, the wind yaw angle is within the range of − 15 ° ~ 15 °, and the buffeting response decreases with the increase of the absolute value of wind yaw angle.

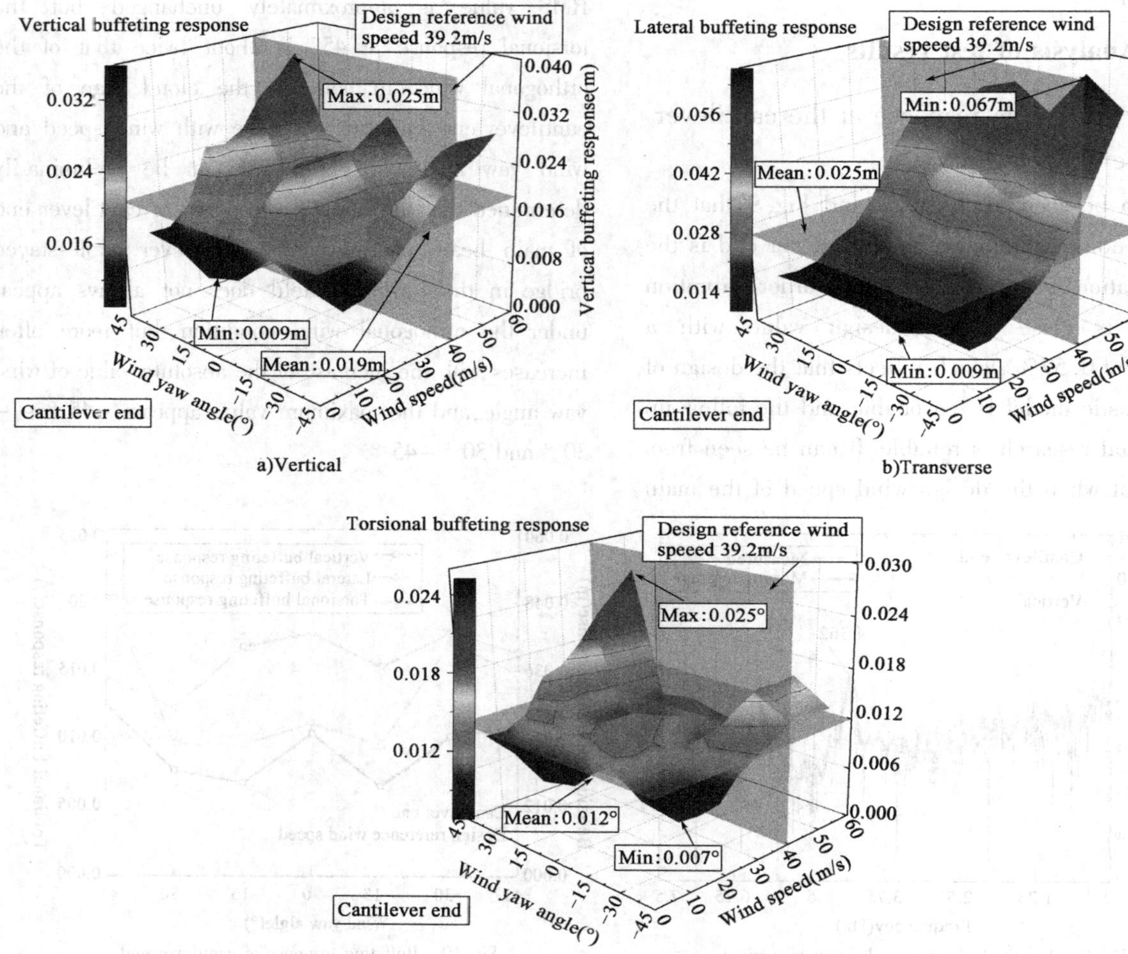

Fig. 11 Buffeting response of cantilever end

4 Skew wind decomposition and superposition method

According to Kimura's paper, the oblique wind load acting on the structure is decomposed into two sets of load components in the forward and transverse directions according to the relationship of the trigonometric function, and then the wind-induced response of the bridge under the two load components is obtained. Then they are linearly superimposed.

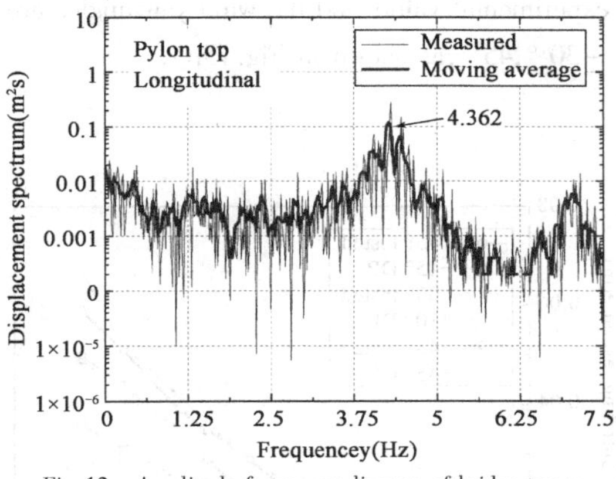

Fig. 12 Amplitude frequency diagram of bridge tower top vibration along the bridge direction

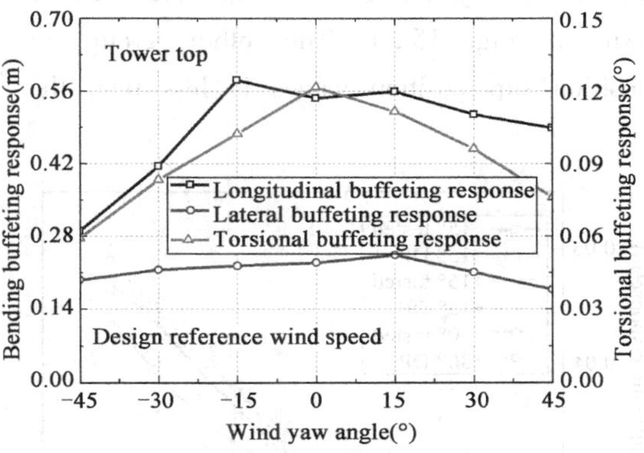

Fig. 13 Buffeting response of bridge tower top (design wind speed)

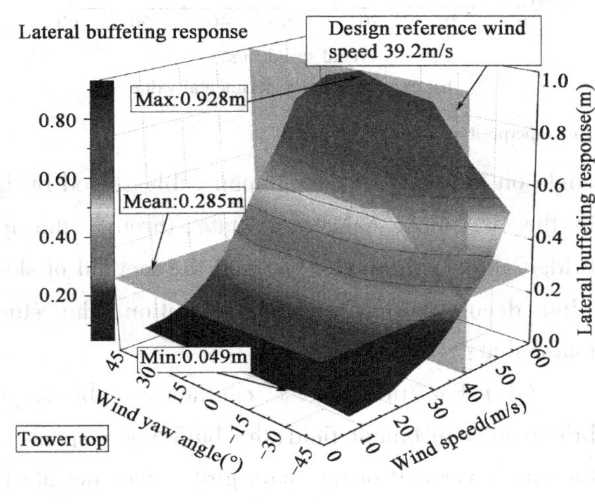

a)Vertical

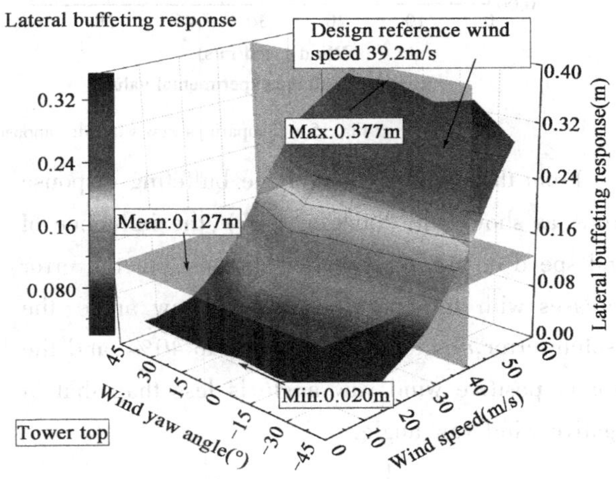

b) Transverse

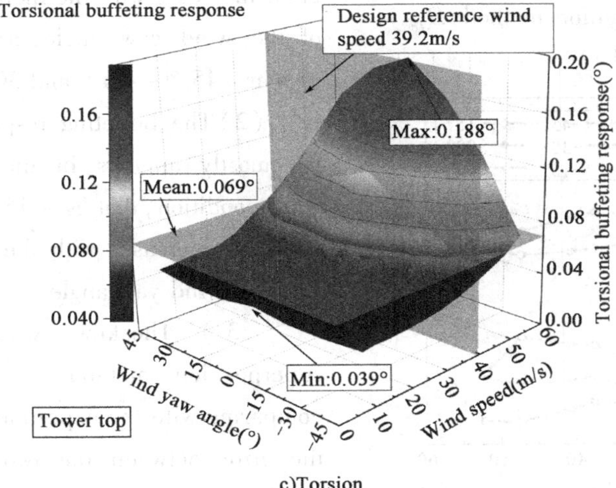

c)Torsion

Fig. 14 Buffeting response of bridge tower top

The results obtained by the skew wind decomposition and superposition method are different from the experimental values. From the point of view of the buffeting response value, it can be divided into two groups. One group is that the decomposition superposition value is greater than the experimental value, and the wind yaw angles are −15 °, 15 °, 30 °, as shown in Fig. 15a). The other group of decomposition superposition values is less than the experimental value, and the wind yaw angles are −45 °, −30 °, 45 °, as shown in Fig. 15b).

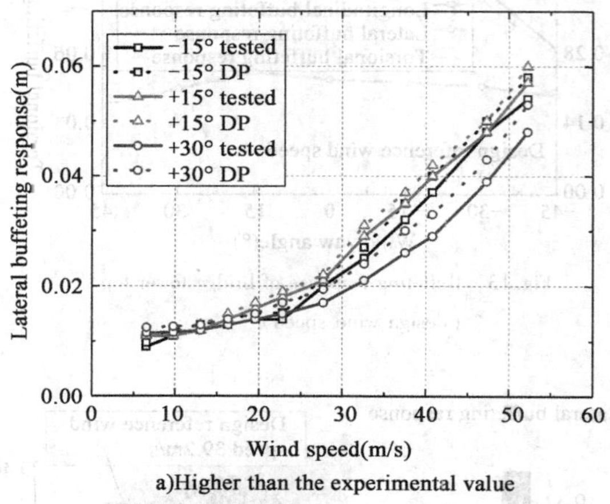

a)Higher than the experimental value

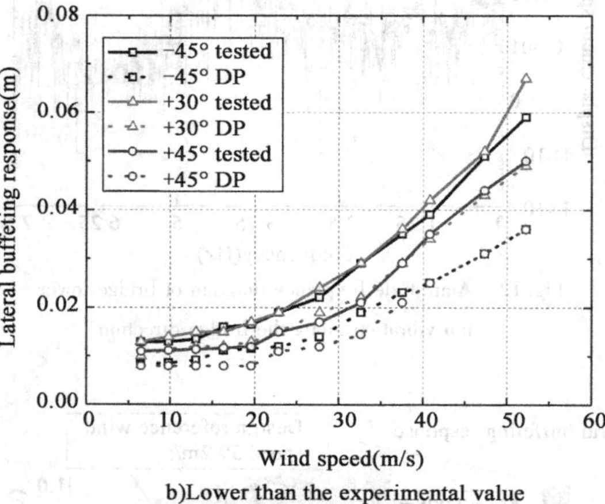

b)Lower than the experimental value

Fig. 15　Comparings kew wind decomposition and superposition method with test data

From the point of view of the buffeting response error ε, as showed in equation (13), the influence of wind speed on the error is not obvious, but the error increases with the increase of wind yaw angle, the absolute error ε increases from 10% to 40%, and the error of positive wind yaw angle is less than that of negative wind yaw angle.

$$\varepsilon = \frac{1}{D_{Test}}(D_{DS} - D_{Test}) \tag{13}$$

Where D_{DS} is the response calculated by skew wind decomposition and superposition method, D_{Test} is the test buffeting response (Fig. 16).

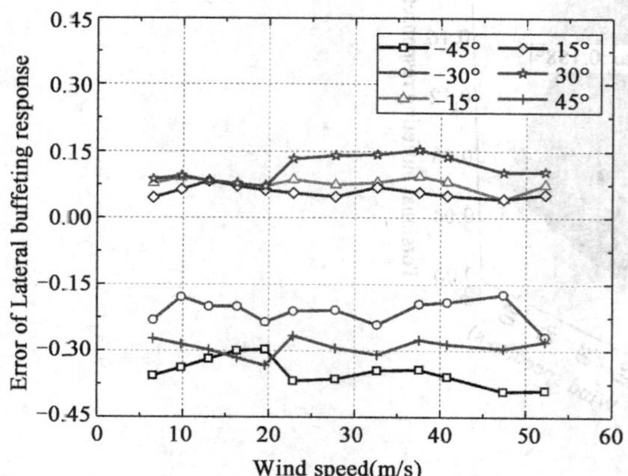

Fig. 16　Skew wind decomposition and superposition method error

5　Conclusions

In order to study the influence of wind yaw angle on buffeting of a long-span cable-stayed bridge in the maximum cantilever state, through the full bridge aeroelastic model test and the method of skew wind decomposition and superposition, the study found that:

(1) For the largest cantilever cable-stayed bridge in a turbulent field, the buffeting response at the cantilever end of the main girder does not always appear under orthogonal wind conditions, and more often increases with the increase of the absolute value of the wind yaw angle, and the maximum values appear −45 ° ~ -30 ° and 30 ° ~ 45 °.

(2) The buffeting response of the bridge tower top mostly appears in the approximate orthogonal wind condition, that is −15 ° ~ 15 °. The buffeting response decreases with the increase of the absolute value of wind yaw angle.

(3) Theskew wind decomposition and superposition method is easy to calculate. By comparing with the experimental data, it is found that the error between the two is within 10% within −15° ~ 15°, but the calculated value is higher than the actual value. This method is suitable for conservative estimation of buffeting response. In addition, the error increases with the increase of wind yaw angle.

6 Acknowledgements

This work was financially supported by the National Natural Science Foundation of China (51978077).

References

[1] Che Xin, Li Jiawu, Gao Fei, et al. Wind tunnel test and analysis of buffeting performance of free-standing pylon of cable-stayed bridge under skew wind [J]. Journal of Highway and Transportation Research and Development, 2012, 29(10):84-87 + 101.

[2] Gimsing N. J, Georgakis C. T. Cable supported bridges: Concept and design [M]. 3 ed. Wiley. 1983.

[3] Gong Cheng, Liu Zhiwen, Xie Gang, et al. Control of wind-induced vibration in large span cable-stayed bridge with high piers during cantilever construction stages [J]. Engineering Mechanics, 2015, 32(S1):122-128.

[4] Guo Jun, Huang Chongfu, Ai Fuli. Study of the typhoon dynamic risk in Guangdong province with respect to months and early warning [J]. Systems Engineering Theory & Practice, 2015, 35(6):1604-1616.

[5] Hu Qingan, Qiao Yunqiang, Liu Jianxin, et al. Buffeting performance of bridge tower under yawed wind during construction [J]. Journal of Traffic and Transportation Engineering, 2008 (2):40-43.

[6] Design code for wind resistance of highway bridges: JTG/T 3360-01—2018 [S]. Beijing: People's Communications Press, 2018.

[7] Kimura K, Tanaka H. Bridge buffeting due to wind with yaw angles [J]. Journal of Wind Engineering and Industrial Aerodynamics, 1992, 42(1):1309-1320.

[8] Liu Zhiwen, Ding Dong, Jia Yaguang, et al. Field measurement of wind-induced vibration responses of a large cable-stayed bridge during construction stages in mountainous terrain [J]. Journal of Hunan University (Natural Sciences), 2017, 44(1):16-22.

[9] Liu K. B, Shen C, Louie K. S. A 1,000-Year history of typhoon landfalls in Guangdong, Southern China, reconstructed from Chinese historical documentary records [J]. Annals of the Association of American Geographers, 2001, 91(3):453-464.

[10] Lu X, Yu H, Ying M, et al. Western north pacific tropical cyclone database created by the china meteorological administration [J]. Advances in Atmospheric Sciences, 2021, 38 (4):690-699.

[11] Ma Tingting, Ge Yaojun, Zhao Lin. Wind-resistant behavior of a long span cable-stayed bridge during construction [J]. Journal of Vibration and Shock, 2013, 32(12):100-104 + 115.

[12] N. J. Gimsing, C. T. Georgakis. Cable supported bridges: Concept and design [J]. Structural Engineer, 2012.

[13] Pang Jiabin. Field investigation and wind tunnel simulation of strong wind characteristics in coastal and mountainous regions [D]. Shanghai: Tongji University, 2006.

[14] Scanlan, H Robert. Bridge buffeting by skew winds in erection stages [J]. Journal of Engineering Mechanics, 119.

[15] Shen Zhengfeng, Hu Zhaotong, Li Jiawu, et al. Controlling the modal coupled buffeting response of the long span dense-frequency cable-stayed bridge by MDTMD [J]. China Journal of Highway and Transport, 2019, 32 (10):135-149.

[16] Su Yi, Li Mingshui, Yang Yang, et al. Buffeting response and equivalent wind load of single cantilever corridor bridge in mountainous areas [J]. Journal of Southwest Jiaotong University, 2019, 54(1):121-128.

[17] Tanaka H, Davenport A. Response of taut strip models to turbulent wind [J]. Journal of Engineering Mechanics-Asce, 1982, 108:33-49.

[18] Tang Yu, Hu Pan, Jia Hongyu, et al. Buffeting responses of single-tower cable-stayed bridge with rigid frame system during construction [J]. Journal of Southwest Jiaotong University, 2021, 56(3):485-492.

[19] Wang P. H, Tang T. Y, Zheng H. N. Analysis of cable-stayed bridges during construction by cantilever methods [J]. Computers & Structures, 2004, 82(4): 329-346.

[20] Wang Yu, Ma Rujin, Tu Xi. Test on transversal wind load effect of long-span arch bridge with influence of skew wind [J]. Journal of Chang'an University (Natural Science Edition), 2011, 31(5): 38-43.

[21] Ying M, Zhang W, Yu, H, et al. An overview of the China meteorological administration tropical cyclone database [J]. Journal of Atmospheric & Oceanic Technology. 2014, 31: 287-301.

[22] Zan S. J. The effect of mass, wind angle, and erection technique of the aeroelastic behaviour of a cable-stayed bridge model. Retrieved from Ottawa, Canada, 1987.

[23] Zhang Y, Wei K, Shen Z, et al. Economic impact of typhoon-induced wind disasters on port operations: A case study of ports in China [J]. International Journal of Disaster Risk Reduction, 2020, 50: 101719.

[24] Zhu Ledong, Wang Miao, Guo Zhenshan, et al. Buffeting performance of double-cantilever state of a long-span cable-stayed bridge under yawed wind [J]. Engineering Mechanics, 2006(4): 86-92.

基于三次样条曲线和APDL的拱轴系数优化调整

周 静*[1] 谭红梅[1,2] 李益达[1] 曾 勇[1,2]

(1. 重庆交通大学山区桥梁与隧道工程省部共建国家重点实验室;
2. 重庆交通大学山区桥梁结构与材料教育部工程研究中心)

摘 要 本文基于对拱轴系数优化计算要领的总结,分析了三种拱轴系数计算方法(最小弯曲能法、压力线与拱轴线偏离最小法、三次样条插值曲线拟合法)的优点以及不足之处。并通过APDL语言编写了三次样条函数计算流程,来进行拱轴系数优化。本文以某上承式混凝土拱桥为基础,开展一系列优化调整过程。分析研究得出,“三次样条插值函数的拟合法”可以控制全桥各个截面的弯矩,得到的拱轴线已不再是常规的抛物线、圆弧形或者悬链线,而是一条样条曲线。同时,拱截面在1/8、3/8、5/8等截面的弯矩都显著降低了。由此可见,此优化方法更加适用于计算大跨径拱桥的拱轴系数。

关键词 桥梁工程 拱轴系数 优化算法 大跨拱桥 三次样条插值曲线 APDL

0 引言

计算拱轴系数作为拱桥设计中的重要内容,其取值的多少极大程度地影响着拱桥主拱截面的高度。拱轴系数代表着拱脚结构重力强度与拱顶结构重力强度的比,反映了拱轴线曲率的大小。

计算拱轴系数的过程,其实就是找出由于压力线与拱轴线不重合弯矩值达到最小时的曲线。于是设计中想得到的拱轴线就为与多种类型荷载压力线重合的曲线,此时主拱断面只存在轴向压力而不存在弯矩以及剪力。在这种理想情况下,不仅截面受力均匀,混凝土材料也会体现出较好的抗压性。但现实中,主拱圈不仅受到不变荷载的作用还受到活载的作用,其中不变荷载占全部荷载的比值较大,而活载因其变化很难控制。所以,常规采用的计算方式是以恒载压力线作为拱轴线,常规计算拱轴系数的方法是“五点重合法”。

侯春辉、宋顺心研究对比了计算拱轴系数的“最小弯曲能法”与“五点重合法”。结果表明,“最小弯曲能法”可得到更优的拱轴系数,还能得

1. 基金项目:重庆交通大学山区桥梁结构与材料教育部工程研究中心开放基金资助(QLGCZX-JJ2017-5);重庆市留学人员回国创新项目(CX2020117)。

到拱结构受力较好的立柱之间的距离以及设计方式。田振生、崔文杰等人剖析了悬链线拱轴系数的计算本质,对比了“最小弯曲能法”与“压力线与拱轴线偏离最小法”,结果表明基于 APDL 语言的“最小弯曲能法”在设计拱轴系数的过程中存在运算的局限。而“压力线与拱轴线偏离最小法”可快速获取拱轴系数,改善拱轴截面受力,但对拱脚来说所受弯矩过大。刘永来、段永宝等人针对传统插值模型存在的问题,分析研究了三次样条插值曲线法,并对其模型本质以及边界条件进行系统的分析研究,得出三次样条插值曲线法线性逼近能力强,线性光滑性好,可以充分表征变形体的变化形式。由此可见,三次样条插值曲线法还未在桥梁领域中有所应用,这些研究也并未将其与拱轴系数计算相结合。

本文总结了三种计算拱轴系数的优化方法,最终得出“三次样条插值函数”的方法最优,并用 APDL 语言编写了三次样条插值函数的命令流,对某上承式混凝土拱桥进行拱轴系数优化。结果表明,此方法可对全桥各截面的弯矩进行控制,非常适合大跨径拱桥拱轴系数的计算。

1 拱轴系数的计算原理

设计中,多见的拱轴曲线形状除了圆弧线、抛物线和悬链线之外,还有许多工程得出的曲线形状,如高次抛物线、悬索线、组合曲线等。但在现实中,大、中跨径的拱桥常以悬链线作为拱轴线的线形,方法为“五点重合法”,即让拱轴线接近其恒载作用下各个断面全部是受压时的轴线,即规定拱轴线在拱五个断面处(两个拱脚、两个 1/4 点、拱顶)与其三铰拱压力线吻合,而达到五点弯矩为 0 的要求来确定拱轴系数,可利用公式:

$$m = \frac{1}{2}\left(\frac{f}{y_{1/4}} - 2\right)^2 - 1 \tag{1}$$

$$\frac{y_{1/4}}{f} = \frac{\sum M_{1/4}}{\sum M_j} \tag{2}$$

式中:m——拱轴系数;

$\sum M_j$——半拱恒载对拱脚截面的力矩;

$\sum M_{1/4}$——自拱顶至拱跨 1/4 点的恒载对 1/4 截面的力矩;

f——矢高;

$y_{1/4}$——拱顶到跨径的 1/4 处。

通过以上公式算出 m 值后,若与假定的 m_0(首次拟定的拱轴系数)不吻合,则以算出的 m 值作为下一次的假定值,再次计算,一直计算到两者相近为止。此计算流程需进行多次的重复迭代,而且某些断面点断面压力线与拱轴线吻合得并不好,可变荷载、降温、材料收缩徐变的影响也都无法解决。针对以上问题,本文总结了三种优化拱轴系数计算的流程,分别是最小弯曲能量法、压力线与拱轴线偏离最小法、三次样条插值曲线拟合法。

2 计算拱轴系数的优化方法

优化设计是找到某个最优设计方式的流程,所以“最优设计”其实是一种方案,在充分符合设计规定的同时,所需花费最小。换句话说,最优设计方法是最有时效的方案。依据拱桥的受压性能好、抗弯性能弱的特点以及拱轴线的选取本质,拱桥设计中应尽量降低由荷载作用出的弯矩值。

2.1 最小弯曲能量法

最小弯曲能量法是用来确立斜拉桥在成桥阶段最优索力的一种方法,当弯曲能量达到最小时,主梁所受到的弯矩不大且分布比较均匀,这是从节约原料、减小成本的角度来优化索力的一种方法。由于拱桥和斜拉桥的主梁受力的本质是相通的,可以假设最小弯曲能量法与拱桥拱轴系数的优化是可以类比的,当拱轴系数为某个值时,拱轴线能尽量地吻合压力线,而权衡吻合的程度就是主拱的弯曲应变能的大小,即

$$U = \int_s \frac{M^2(s)}{2EI} ds \tag{3}$$

式中:U——桥梁任意截面应变能;

$M(s)$——桥梁任意截面弯矩;

E——拉伸弹性模量;

I——惯性矩。

以式(3)弯曲应变能作为目标函数来优化拱轴系数,然后以优化的拱轴系数作为设计变量,以拱圈的应力作为状态变量即可求解。由于 ANSYS 程序的优化技术规定最优拱轴系数的要点是在结果中获得目标函数,需要计算式(3),而且 ANSYS 软件的计算未提供完全的弯曲应变能,因此需要参数化设计语言 APDL 运用数值积分来求解。计算公式为:

$$\int_a^b f(x)dx = \frac{h}{3}[f(a) + f(b) + 2\sum_{k=1}^{m-1} f(x_{2k}) +$$

$$4\sum_{k=1}^{m-1}f(x_{2k-1})] \tag{4}$$

式中:$h=\frac{b-a}{n}$——计算所取得步长;

k、m——表示1,2,3,…,n。

为了使积分具有一定的精度,需要把单元划到充足的精度。

2.2 压力线与拱轴线偏离最小法

压力线是主拱圈各断面合力点的连线,而拱轴线是指拱圈各个截面形心的连线,如图1所示。拱桥中的主拱圈主要以抗压为主,同时断面中受到其他作用,如轴向力、弯矩和剪力等内力。除了拱脚断面以外,其余断面剪力是较小,可以忽略。图1的i-i截面在截面形心处有弯矩M和轴向力N,这两个作用恰好可用偏心合力来联立,此时合力点与截面形心的距离表示为e,如下式:

$$e=\frac{M}{N} \tag{5}$$

式中:e——合力点与截面形心的距离;

M——弯矩;

N——轴向力。

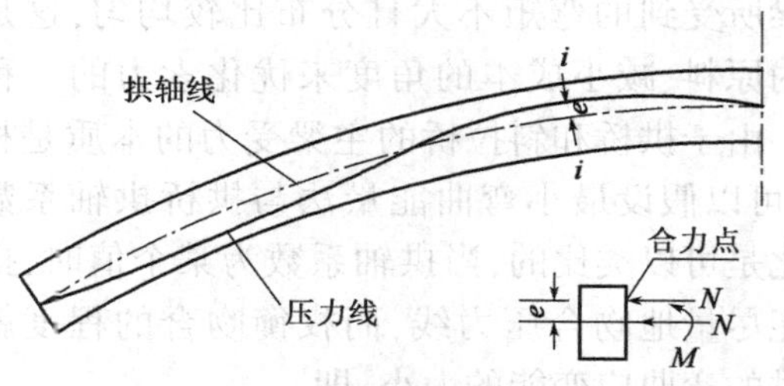

图1 压力线与拱轴线关系图

此方法需要提供拱圈多个断面的弯矩和轴向力,得到各断面的偏心距,相比上节介绍的最小弯曲应变能法,其需要将结果进行数值积分的方式才能获得优化目标值而言。压力线与拱轴线偏离最小法更容易在ANSYS程序中实现,但对于拱脚来说改善的作用并不显著。

2.3 三次样条插值曲线拟合法

按照常规的计算拱轴系数的方法,确定拱轴线时只确定主拱上的五个截面(两个拱脚、两个1/4点、拱顶),去吻合恒载压力线,这就会导致主拱在荷载作用下远离控制断面的某些截面压力线而与拱轴线偏离较大的现象,从而引起主拱过大的弯矩。随着拱桥跨径的不断增大,拱轴线合理性对结构受力来说越来越重要的。确立合理拱轴线,采用样条拟合的方式可解决上述问题,具体方法如下:

设在节点上$a\leqslant x_0<x_1<x_2<\cdots<x_n\leqslant b$,$m_i=S'(x)(i=0,1,2,\cdots n)$由三次样条插值函数的定义,插值函数$S(x)$在每个区间$[x_i,x_{i+1}]$上是一个不超过三次的多项式,若记为$S_i(x)$(因变量$x$的三次样条插值函数),则可设:

$$S_i(x)=a_ix^3+b_ix^2+c_ix+d_i \quad (i=0,1,2,\cdots n) \tag{6}$$

从而有

$$S(x)=\{S_0(x)S_1(x)\cdots S_{n-1}(x)\}^T \tag{7}$$

其中$S_i(x)$由a,b,c,d四个未知数唯一确定,因此要确定[a,b]上的三次样条插值函数$S(x)$,就要确定$4n$个未知系数$\{a_i,b_i,c_i,d_i\}(i=1,2,3,\cdots,n-1)$。得出这$4n$个未知系数的方式有很多,下面介绍三转角法。

由三次分段Hermit插值多项式可知,在区间$[x_i,x_{i+1}]$上,$S_i(x)$可表示为:

$$\begin{aligned}S_i(x)=&\frac{(x-x_{i+1})^2(x-x_i)}{h_i^2}m_i+\\&\frac{(x-x_i)^2(x-x_{i+1})}{h_i^2}m_{i+1}+\\&\frac{(x-x_{i+1})^2[2(x-x_i)+h_i]}{h_i^3}y_i+\\&\frac{(x-x_i)^2[2(x_{i+1}-x)+h_i]}{h_i^3}y_{i+1}\\&(i=0,1,2,\cdots,n-1)\end{aligned} \tag{8}$$

其中,$h_i=x_{i+1}-x_i(i=0,1,2,\cdots,n-1)$,对$S_i(x)$求二阶导数得:

$$\begin{aligned}S''_i(x)=&(6x-2x_i-4x_{i+1})\frac{m_i}{h_i^2}+\\&(6x-4x_i-2x_{i+1})\frac{m_{i+1}}{h_i^2}+\\&6(x_i+x_{i+1}-2x)\frac{y_{i+1}-y_i}{h_i^3}\end{aligned} \tag{9}$$

利用函数$S(x)$在插值区间$[a,b]$上的各内节点$x_i(i=1,2,3,\cdots n-1)$处有二阶连续导数的条件:$S''(x_i-0)=S''(x_i+0)$,经整理可得关于参数m_{i-1},m_i,m_{i+1}的一个方程:

$$\lambda_im_{i-1}+2m_i+\mu_im_{i+1}=d_i \tag{10}$$

其中,$\lambda_i=\frac{h_i}{h_{i+1}+h_i}$,$\mu_i=\frac{h_{i-1}}{h_{i-1}+h_i}$,$d_i=3\left(\lambda_i\frac{y_{i+1}-y_i}{h_i}+\mu_i\frac{y_i-y_{i-1}}{h_{i-1}}\right)$。

(10)式中是关于$n+1$个待定参数$m_0,m_1,\cdots$,

m_n 的 $n-1$ 个方程，所以有无穷多组解，要唯确定 $m_i(i=1,2,3,\cdots n)$ 的值还需要补充两个条件：

$$S'(x_0)=m_0, S'(x_n)=m_n \tag{11}$$

根据上式(10)、(11)，$m_0,m_1,\cdots,m_n$ 有唯一解，将其带入式(8)，区间 $[a,b]$ 上的三次样条插值函数 $S(x)$ 也被唯一确定。

根据桥跨设计方式，可知主拱肋的跨径 L、矢高 f 以及拱肋以上的结构。将半拱分为足够多的节点 $0=x_0<x_1<x_2<\cdots<x_n=L/2$，以悬链线拟合拱顶、拱脚及1/4三个控制点(或以二次抛物线拟合拱顶、拱脚等控制点)，作为第一次的拱轴线，并依次计算各个节点 $x_i(i=1,2,3,\cdots n)$ 的纵坐标 y_i^0 (上标0表示初始值)。此外，根据拱轴线的特点，在两个端节点有下式的几何边界条件：

$$m_0=S'(x_0)=(y_1-y_0)/(x_1-x_0) \tag{12}$$

$$m_n=S'(x_n)=0 \tag{13}$$

m_0、m_n 的物理含义分别是两端点处的斜率。将上式代回到式(11)中，结合式(10)并写成矩阵的形式有：

$$\begin{bmatrix} 1 & 0 & 0 & \cdots & \cdots & \cdots & 0 \\ \lambda_1 & 2 & \mu_1 & & & & \\ & \lambda_2 & 2 & \mu_2 & & & \\ & & \ddots & \ddots & \ddots & & \\ & & & \lambda_{n-1} & 2 & & \mu_{n-1} \\ 0 & & & 0 & 0 & & 1 \end{bmatrix} \begin{bmatrix} m_0 \\ m_1 \\ m_2 \\ \vdots \\ m_{n-1} \\ m_n \end{bmatrix} = \begin{bmatrix} (y_1-y_0)/(x_1-x_0) \\ d_1 \\ d_2 \\ \vdots \\ d_{n-1} \\ 0 \end{bmatrix}$$

求得 $m_0,m_1,\cdots,m_n$ 后，利用有限元软件计算各单元在节点处的弯矩 M_i 以及轴力 $N_i(i=1,2,3,\cdots n)$，同时与式(14)联立对内节点坐标做如下修正：

$$\Delta x_i=\frac{M_i}{N_i}\frac{m_i}{\sqrt{1+m_i^2}}, \Delta y_i=\frac{M_i}{N_i}\frac{1}{\sqrt{1+m_i^2}} \quad (i=1,2,3,\cdots n-1) \tag{14}$$

重新计算控制节点 (x_i^k,y_i^k) (上标k表示第k次重复计算后的数值)并以三次样条插值曲线拟合后，再进行下一轮的有限元分析计算，直到式 $e=\sqrt{\sum_0^n\left(\frac{M_i}{N_i}\right)^2}(i=1,2,3,\cdots,n)$ 达到最小值。整个计算流程如图2所示。

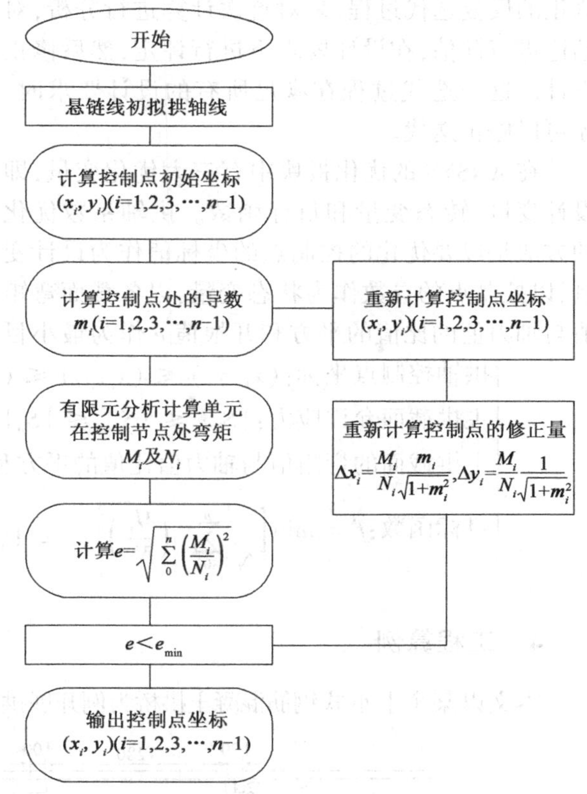

图2　合理拱轴线计算流程图

对于一次落架拱桥，拱圈上的外荷载是较容易确定的。对于无支架施工的拱桥，特别是拱上建筑与拱圈分担外荷载的组合体系拱桥，结构的自身重量并不完全等效于作用在拱圈上的外荷载，拱桥分担的荷载与架设流程有关，应按照架设过程来进行模拟计算，按上述流程进行拱轴线模拟。

3　基于APDL语言的拱轴系数优化

20世纪70年代，ANSYS有限元软件就一马当先在有限元分析中联立了图形技艺以及开放的使用方式，使有限元分析迈出了很大的一步。如今该软件拥有较好的前处理器以及方便的后处理器，同时提供多种语言，如用户界面设计语言、用户编程特性和参数设计语言等。ANSYS在工程上的一个很大的优点就是能进行参数化建模。

ANSYS程序给用户提供了两种优化的方法，这两种方法可以解决大多数优化问题。第一种方法是零阶方法，这是一个较为完备的处理方法，可以高效率地解决许多工程难题。第二种方法是一阶方法，它是在目标函数基础上对设计变量的灵敏程度的表达，因此对精确的优化分析更有利。

对于以上方法,ANSYS 提出了许多分析—评估—修正的反复迭代过程,来对首次计算进行分析,对结论进行评估,在设计要求下进行评定,然后修正设计。这一迭代过程在满足所有的设计要求时,才可以停止迭代。

在 ANSYS 的优化板块中有三大优化变量,即设计变量、转态变量和目标函数。拱轴系数优化的方法是以要优化的控制点的坐标值作为设计变量,以控制点的导数作为状态变量,以各截面弯矩值与轴力值的比值的平方和开根值 e 作为最小目标函数进行求解。具体步骤为:

(1)建立模型分析文件。该文件需要具有整个分析流程,且需满足下列要求:以控制点坐标值为设计变量建立参数化模型(PREP7),求解(SOLUTION),提取并指定状态变量和目标函数(POST1)。

(2)构建优化控制文件。该文件包括进入 OPT 处理器,指定分析文件(OPANL),声明优化变量,选择优化方法,指定优化循环控制方式,优化迭代分析,查看优化设计的序列结果。

$$\begin{cases}\text{拱轴控制点坐标}:(x_1,y_1)\leqslant(x_i,y_i)\leqslant(x_u,y_u)\ (i=1,2,3,\cdots,n)\\ \text{主拱截面允许应力}:\{S_1\}\leqslant\{S_j\}\leqslant\{S_u\}\ (j=1,2,3,\cdots n)\\ \text{主拱截面的弯矩值与轴力值比值的平方和开根}:\{e_1\}\leqslant\{e_k\}\leqslant\{e_u\}\ (u=1,2,3,\cdots n)\\ \text{目标函数}:f=\min\left[\sqrt{\sum_0^n\left(\dfrac{M_i}{N_i}\right)^2}\ (i=1,2,3,\cdots,n)\right]\end{cases}$$

4　工程算例

本文以某个上承式钢筋混凝土拱桥为例开展拱轴系数优化研究。该桥计算跨径为 115m,计算矢跨比为 1/5,立柱间距为 12.8m。桥面板采用空心板,主拱圈采用箱形截面。半桥总体布置如图 3 所示。

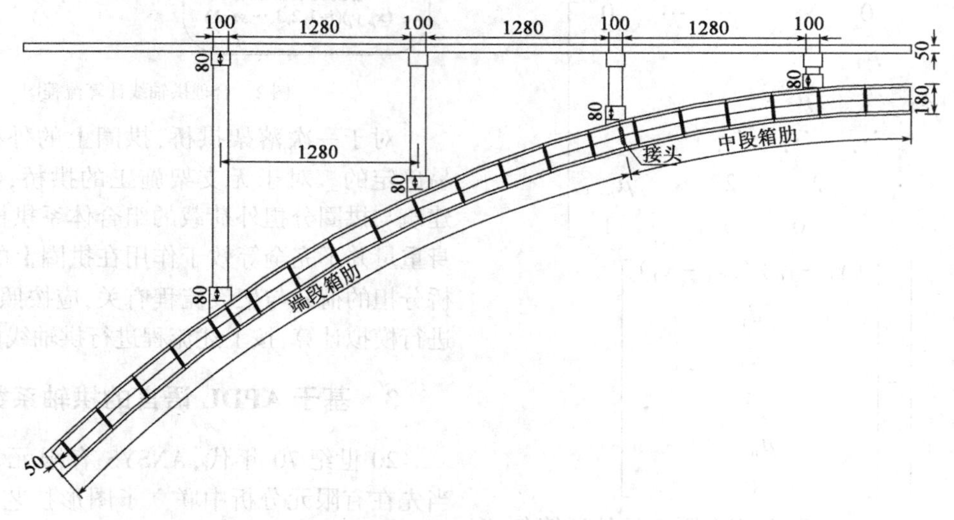

图3　半桥总体布置图

半桥有限元模型如图 4 所示,所用单元类型为 beam188,共 387 个节点。主拱与拱上立柱以及桥面板与拱上立柱采用的约束类型为主从连接,拱脚为固结,拱顶为滑动连接,桥面板两端点采用铰接。

全拱分为 24 个截面,由于主拱左右对称,本文仅取一半的主拱圈数据值进行对比分析研究,如图 5、图 6 所示。提取数据值见表 1。

从图 5、图 6 可见,控制点的各截面弯矩值都得到了一定的控制。优化前主拱最大正弯矩为 4862.183kN/m,最大负弯矩为 −1347.567kN/m;优化后主拱最大正弯矩为 2211.005kN/m,最大负弯矩为 −7.78kN/m。优化后的主拱拱脚正弯矩相比优化前减少 52%,优化后的主拱最大负弯矩相比优化前减少 99%,优化程度显而易见。若截面划分得足够细致,那么全拱的弯矩都将得到有效的控制,对主拱的受力也会更加有利。第一次与第九次拟合后输出的坐标数值见表 2。

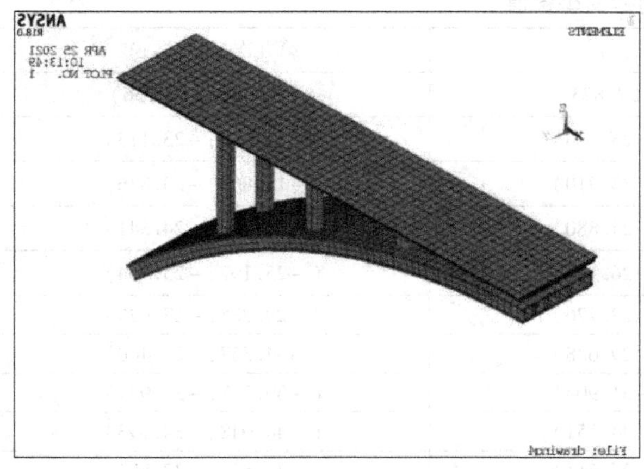

图4 半桥有限元模型

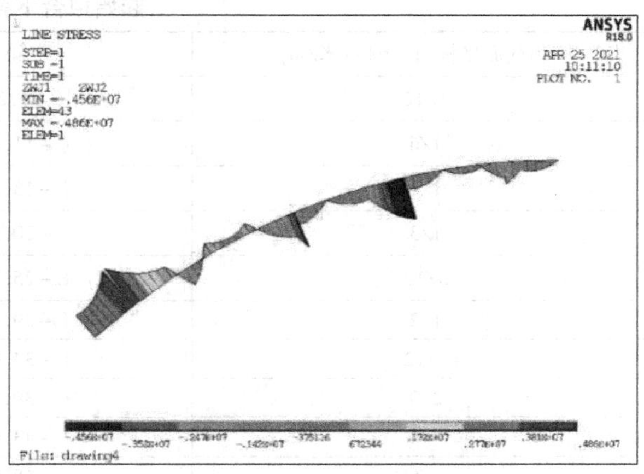

图5 优化前的主拱弯矩图

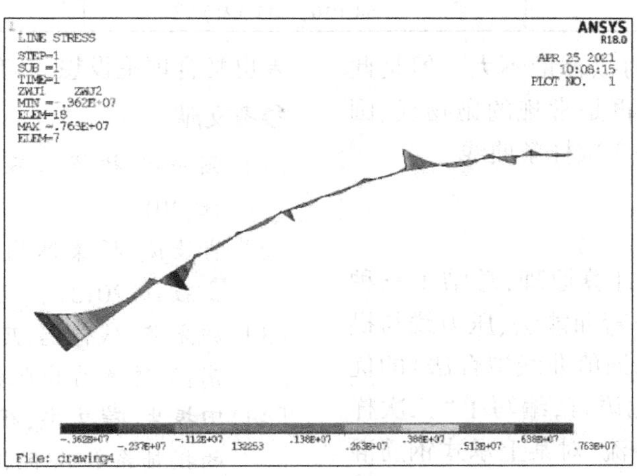

图6 优化后的主拱弯矩图

起始拟合下各控制截面弯矩值 表1

控制截面弯矩值(kN/m)	第一次拟合	第九次拟合
1/12	-1670.806853	41.369596
1/6	-560.100432	-7.778361
1/4	-619.464437	16.204406
1/3	-4263.954930	-1.230128
5/12	-1347.566547	42.646295
1/2	-538.116498	71.142339
7/12	-2285.059927	129.328244
2/3	726.749505	236.129113
3/4	216.064087	420.360811
5/6	1600.236196	759.434246
11/12	4862.182772	1739.950397
拱脚	4242.924130	2211.005403
e	0.322637893	0.095641328

起始拟合下各控制截面坐标值　表2

控制截面坐标值(单位:米/m)	第一次(x,y)	第九次拟合(x,y)
1/12	(-6.546,-22.823)	(-6.506,-22.756)
1/6	(-11.179,-23.226)	(-11.129,-23.113)
1/4	(-15.863,-23.910)	(-15.860,-23.836)
1/3	(-20.548,-24.880)	(-20.485,-24.541)
5/12	(-25.233,-26.147)	(-25.192,-25.964)
1/2	(-29.918,-27.726)	(-29.885,-27.629)
7/12	(-34.603,-29.638)	(-34.537,-29.460)
2/3	(-39.287,-31.904)	(-39.317,-31.971)
3/4	(-43.971,-34.551)	(-44.048,-34.693)
5/6	(-48.653,-37.611)	(-48.821,-37.881)
11/12	(-53.333,-41.121)	(-53.812,-41.848)
拱脚	(-58.010,-45.121)	(-58.632,-45.721)

由表2可知,坐标值的拟合量不大。但是此时得到的拱轴线形状已不再是常规的抛物线、圆弧线或考悬链线,而是一条三次样条曲线。

5　结语

本文通过拱轴系数的计算原理,总结了三种计算拱轴系数的方法(最小弯曲能法、压力线与拱轴线偏离最小法、三次样条插值曲线拟合法)的优缺点,并联立APDL参数化语言,编写了“三次样条插值曲线拟合法”的命令流,对某上承式钢筋混凝土拱桥开展拱轴系数优化研究,得出了优化的拱轴线形状。现总结如下:

(1)根据多次数据值拟合,最终计算得到的拱轴线形状不再是常规的悬链线,而是一条由函数插值得出的三次样条曲线。

(2)常规计算拱轴系数的方式是“五点重合法”,只对五个点的弯矩进行计算,让这五点与压力线重合确定悬链线,忽略了主拱其他断面的受力。三次样条插值曲线拟合法不仅可以使五点的弯矩值达到最小,也可以对其他截面的弯矩进行控制。若断面分得足够细致,那么主拱各截面弯矩数值都可以得到控制。对于大跨径拱桥来说,其主拱跨径的各截面若只保证五点的弯矩值,对拱桥受力来说是不利的,此时采用三次样条插值曲线拟合法可对多个截面的弯矩进行控制。所以,对于大跨径拱桥来说此种方法更加适用。

(3)本文首次将“三次样条函数”的理论与拱桥拱轴系数优化有机结合在一起,得到了更能体现现实问题特点的三次样条插值函数,其算例结果也契合理论设想,具有一定的工程价值。

参考文献

[1]　顾安邦.桥梁工程[M].北京:人民交通出版社,2013.

[2]　肖汝诚.桥梁结构体系[M].北京:人民交通出版社,2013.

[3]　施光燕,钱伟懿,庞丽萍.最优化方法[M].北京:高等教育出版社,2007.

[4]　田振生,崔文杰,杨柄楠,等.基于APDL语言的拱轴系数m优化设计[J].北方交通,2020(3):2-28.

[5]　陈波旭.大跨径钢筋混凝土拱桥拱轴系数优化设计[J].青海交通科技,2017(6):2-28.

[6]　侯春辉,宋顺心.基于APDL语言的拱轴系数优化及立柱布置研究[J].铁道工程学报,2017(10):55-58.

[7]　刘典宏,张冰,张德凯.基于三次样条插值的木料抛光机轨迹优化[J].科技创新导报,2019(31):109-110.

[8]　颜伟,耿路,周雷,等.基于海情和三次样条插值算法的舰船雷达散射截面优化分析方法[J].电子与信息学报,2018(40):579-585.

[9]　刘永来,段永宝,官立祥.三次样条插值方法及其在形变数据预处理中的应用[J].勘察技术科学,2017(6):47-50.

[10]　宁云,颜东煌,涂光亚,等.基于APDL参数化语言实现拱轴系数m的优化设计[J].长沙理工大学学报(自然科学版),2006(3):34-38.

[11]　Yang Wu, Yao Wenjuan, Liu Xiaoyu. Fitting

analysis of catenary arch axis equation in changing section [J]. International Journal of Applied Mathematics and Statistics, 2013(14): 21-27.

[12] Hong Shao-Hua, Wang Lin, Truong Trieu-Kien. An improved approach to the cubic-spline interpolation [J]. Source: Proceedings International Conference on Image Processing, 2018: 1468-1472.

加固后独柱墩曲线梁桥抗倾覆性能分析

徐 康* 钟强铭 张修石 王佳盈

(长安大学公路学院)

摘 要 近年来独柱墩曲线梁桥的倾覆事故屡有发生,对原有独柱墩曲线梁桥的抗倾覆稳定性进行评价并选择经济合理的加固措施成为研究的热点问题。本文以江西省某高速匝道桥加固工程为例,依据设计规范,采用支座失效法分析其抗倾覆稳定性能,建立了 MIDAS 三维有限元模型,研究独柱墩曲线梁桥加固前后的支座受力异同和新增支座的类型和数量对桥梁抗倾覆稳定性能的影响。研究结果表明,新增支座不参与恒载受力;曲线内侧的新增支座对桥梁抗倾覆性能影响较小,加固时可以仅增设曲线外侧的支座;采用可受拉的一般连接模拟新增支座时会放大桥梁的抗倾覆性能,需根据验算目的和支座的实际受力形式进行模拟。本文的研究成果可为独柱墩曲线梁桥加固后的抗倾覆性能评价和同类型的加固工程提供参考和指导。

关键词 独柱墩曲线梁桥 抗倾覆性能评价 支座失效法 独柱墩加固

0 引言

独柱墩桥梁因美观和占地少等优点,在市政桥梁和高速匝道桥上得到了广泛的应用。而近年来,国内各地发生过多起独柱墩连续梁桥整体倾覆事故,造成了较大的财产损失和人员伤亡,引起了社会各界极大的反响[1]。各地相关部门也迅速行动,对独柱墩桥梁进行了相应的加固。

目前业内学者对独柱墩曲线梁桥抗倾覆稳定性的影响因素、验算方法和加固措施研究较多:刘鹏[2]、王紫玉[3]和崔鑫[4]等学者对独柱墩桥梁抗倾覆稳定性分析方法和影响因素进行了研究,结果表明独柱墩曲线梁桥倾覆危险性受横向支座间距、桥梁曲率半径的影响很大,基础变位和温度效应对其也有一定影响;吕毅刚等[5]对已有的独柱墩曲线箱梁桥抗倾覆计算方法进行了总结,并提出了一种基于稳定效应的简化计算方法;贺志勇[6]对比了加固前、后独柱墩曲线梁桥的抗倾覆稳定性,对于其研究对象来说,最佳支座预偏心为11cm;周健民[7]研究了独柱墩桥梁倾覆的力学过程,提出了一种基于拉压杆的抗倾覆加固新型结构。但对于加固后曲线梁桥的受力方式和计算方法的不同,已有研究较少涉及,而加固后独柱墩桥梁的抗倾覆稳定性分析与验算方法、加固方式和支座设置等因素有关,与原桥存在一定差异。因此,本文以某独柱墩连续曲线梁桥加固工程实例为基础,通过 MIDAS 建模,探究用有限元方法分析加固后曲线梁桥抗倾覆性能时合理的模拟方法,同时分析增设的支座类型(可受拉支座和单向受压支座)和支座数量对其抗倾覆性能的影响,为日后其他类似加固工程提供参考。

1 抗倾覆稳定性验算理论

依据《公路钢筋混凝土及预应力混凝土桥涵设计规范》(JTG 3362—2018)(以下简称《规范》),梁桥倾覆失稳过程存在两个特征状态:在特征状态1,箱梁的单向受压支座开始脱离受压;在特征状态2,箱梁的抗扭支承全部失效。梁桥抗倾覆稳定性采用支座失效法进行分析验算。

(1)特征状态1:在作用基本组合下,单向受压支座不出现负反力,即满足:

$$1.0R_{Gki}+1.4R_{Qki}\geqslant 0 \tag{1}$$

式中：R_{GEi}，R_{Qki}——恒载和活载作用下单向受压支座的支反力，支座受压取正值。

(2)特征状态2：上部结构抗倾覆稳定性系数应大于2.5，即满足：

$$\frac{\sum S_{bk,i}}{\sum S_{sk,i}} \geqslant k_{qf} \tag{2}$$

式中：k_{qf}——横向抗倾覆稳定性系数，取$k_{qf}=2.5$；

$\sum S_{bk,i}$——使上部结构稳定的效应设计值；

$\sum S_{sk,i}$——使上部结构失稳的效应设计值。

$\sum S_{bk,i}$和$\sum S_{sk,i}$的值根据各支座的支反力，结合支座间距计算求得。

2　工程概况

本文以江西省某高速匝道桥加固工程为例进行分析计算。该桥位于半径320m的圆曲线内，跨径组合20m+21.366m+23m+22.55m+21.626m+20m+20m，上部结构采用单箱双室整体连续箱梁，下部结构为桩柱式桥墩。主梁横断面布置如图1所示。

2.1　原支座布置

原桥共设12个支座。其中，1、6、7、8号台(墩)为双排支座，支座间距均为6.1m；2、3、4、5号桥墩为独柱墩，设置单支座。原支座布置如图2所示。

2.2　加固后支座布置

该桥加固时，对原2、3、4和5号独柱墩单支座进行改造，先在独柱墩顶部外包1.7m钢套筒，并钻孔植锚杆，使钢套筒与墩柱形成整体，然后在钢盖梁两侧各增加一个支座，两个新加支座与原墩顶支座间距1.75m。独柱墩加固方案如图3所示，加固后支座布置如图4所示。

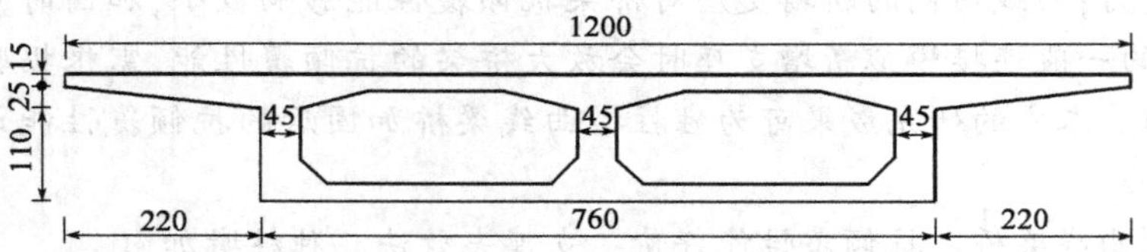

图1　主梁横断面图(尺寸单位：cm)

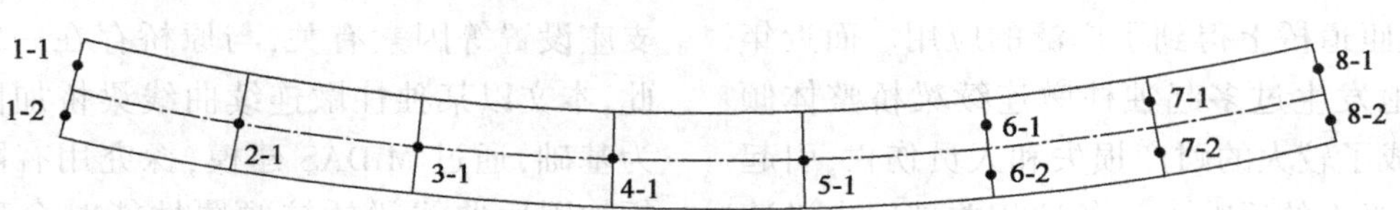

图2　原支座布置图

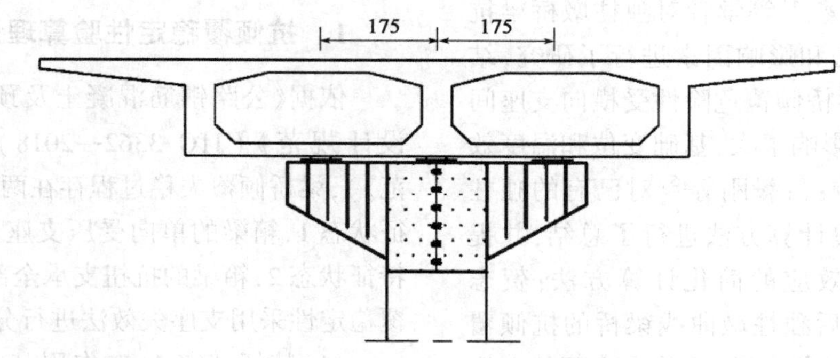

图3　独柱墩加固图(尺寸单位：cm)

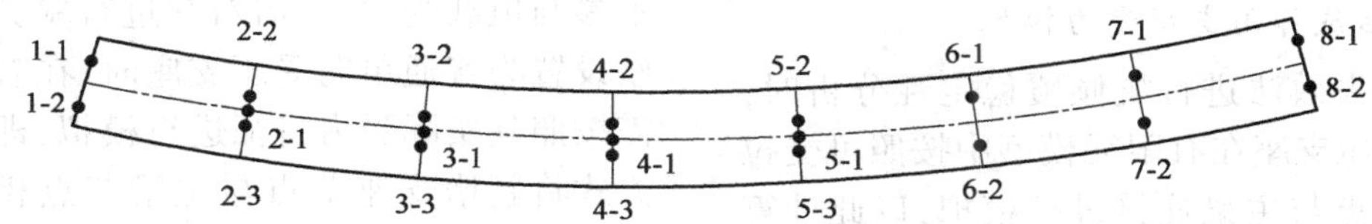

图4　加固后支座布置图

3　加固前后抗倾覆稳定性分析

3.1　桥梁有限元模型

本文采用 MIDAS 进行上部结构的建模计算，主梁共建立 300 个节点、299 个单元，未加固前桥梁模型共 12 个支座节点。其中，4-1 支座节点约束 x、y、z 三个方向自由度（x 方向为顺桥向，y 方向为横桥向，z 方向为竖向，均为局部坐标系）；6-1 和 7-1 支座节点约束 y、z 两个方向自由度；其他支座节点以及加固后模型新增支座节点的边界条件相同，仅约束 z 方向的自由度。有限元三维模型如图 5 所示。本研究在加固前后不同阶段钝化或激活新增支座的边界节点，改变支座节点与主梁的连接方式以实现支座类型的模拟；验算荷载考虑公路Ⅰ级荷载，最大车道数为 3，按最不利情况布载。

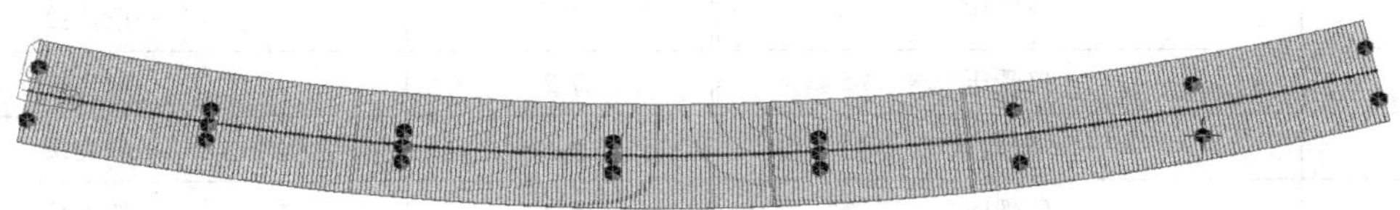

图5　有限元三维模型

3.2　加固前后支座受力分析

3.2.1　恒载作用支座受力差异

加固前桥梁已处于稳定的受力状态，在恒载作用下，主梁与原支座的变形相互协调，加固后增设的新支座几乎不参与受力。将两种体系下恒载作用的支反力分别进行计算，结果如表 1 所示。可以看到，原支座在加固前后的恒载支反力变化不超过 0.02%，可以不考虑新增支座在恒载作用下的受力，即进行抗倾覆稳定性验算时恒载作用下的支反力按照原桥体系进行计算。

恒载支反力对比　　表 1

支座编号	加固前(kN)	加固后(kN)	相对变化量	支座编号	加固前(kN)	加固后(kN)	相对变化量
1-1	691.91	691.82	0.01%	4-3	—	0.00	—
1-2	709.10	709.11	0.00%	5-1	3842.61	3842.42	0.01%
2-1	3923.90	3923.76	0.00%	5-2	—	0.20	—
2-2	—	0.23	—	5-3	—	0.00	—
2-3	—	0.00	—	6-1	1736.92	1737.35	-0.02%
3-1	3769.58	3769.20	0.01%	6-2	1746.66	1746.22	0.02%
3-2	—	0.00	—	7-1	1928.35	1928.03	0.02%
3-3	—	0.35	—	7-2	1906.98	1907.37	-0.02%
4-1	3974.33	3974.22	0.00%	8-1	693.26	693.23	0.00%
4-2	—	0.12	—	8-2	722.92	722.88	0.01%

3.2.2　活载作用支座受力模拟

采用支座失效法进行抗倾覆稳定性分析时，桥梁的单向受压支座在有限元模型中按照可受拉连接将支座节点与主梁连接进行模拟，以此计算出其活载作用下的负反力，验算时将其与恒载作用效应进行组合；对于加固后桥梁，其新增支座不参与恒载受力，无需对其进行验算。当新增支座设置为普通单向受压支座时，在有限元模型中需按照其实际受力特征进行模拟，即以仅受压的方式将新增支座节点与主梁节点相连接。加固后桥梁各支座在有限元模型中的受力类型见表 2。

支座类型模拟　　表 2

支座编号	类型	支座编号	类型
1-1	一般连接	4-3	仅受压
1-2	一般连接	5-1	一般连接
2-1	一般连接	5-2	仅受压
2-2	仅受压	5-3	仅受压
2-3	仅受压	6-1	一般连接
3-1	一般连接	6-2	一般连接
3-2	仅受压	7-1	一般连接
3-3	仅受压	7-2	一般连接
4-1	一般连接	8-1	一般连接
4-2	仅受压	8-2	一般连接

3.3　抗倾覆稳定性分析

本文按照第 1 节中抗倾覆稳定性验算理论对该桥进行分析，采用 MIDAS 有限元模型计算各个支座的恒载支反力以及最不利活载的支反力，再分别计算稳定效应和失稳效应，最后得到抗倾覆稳定系数。双排支座中的曲线内侧支座为不利支座，即 1-1、6-1、7-1 和 8-1 号支座。不利支座特征状态 1 计算结果如表 3 所示，特征状态 2 荷载作用效应和抗倾覆稳定系数如表 4 所示。表 4 中荷载效应数据正值表示稳定效应，负值表示失稳效应，抗倾覆稳定系数为稳定效应与失稳效应的比值，“—”意为无失稳风险。

不利支座特征状态 1(kN)　　表 3

不利支座编号			1-1	6-1	7-1	8-1
不利支座对应的活载支反力	加固前	$1.0R_{GKi}+1.4R_{QKi,11}$	-200.32	1163.97	1967.60	687.17
		$1.0R_{GKi}+1.4R_{QKi,61}$	56.97	760.25	2016.92	-14.17
		$1.0R_{GKi}+1.4R_{QKi,71}$	1010.93	2309.11	1741.29	-5.25
		$1.0R_{GKi}+1.4R_{QKi,81}$	405.80	1519.78	2090.78	-147.24
	加固后	$1.0R_{GKi}+1.4R_{QKi,11}$	541.52	1762.32	1957.32	682.37
		$1.0R_{GKi}+1.4R_{QKi,61}$	676.44	1552.53	2354.06	904.61
		$1.0R_{GKi}+1.4R_{QKi,71}$	699.77	1910.37	1748.82	694.02
		$1.0R_{GKi}+1.4R_{QKi,81}$	674.97	1807.08	2072.62	550.49

荷载作用效应及抗倾覆稳定系数　　表 4

不利支座编号		1-1	6-1	7-1	8-1
加固前	恒载效应(kN·m)	30823	30823	30823	30823
	活载效应(kN·m)	-6251	-6659	3074	-2118
	抗倾覆稳定系数	4.93	4.63	—	14.55

续上表

不利支座编号		1-1	6-1	7-1	8-1
加固后	恒载效应(kN·m)	57948	57948	57948	57948
	活载效应(kN·m)	-2066	-2590	2567	-469
	抗倾覆稳定系数	28.04	22.38	—	123.60
抗倾覆稳定系数相对变化量		468.62%	383.47%	—	749.37%

由计算结果可以看出，加固前独柱墩桥在活载作用下，1-1 和 8-1 支座均出现了负反力，不满足《规范》的要求；而加固后所有不利支座均保持受压状态，且抗倾覆稳定系数大大提高。给该桥独柱墩增设两个支座的加固方式使其抗倾覆性能得到明显提升。

4 增设的支座类型和支座数量对计算结果的影响

4.1 支座类型的影响

前文在有限元模拟时将新增支座设置为仅受压支座，为了探究支座的模拟方法对抗倾覆稳定性能的影响，下面分别建立两种支座类型的有限元模型：

(1)模型 1：与原加固后模型保持一致，新增支座设置为仅受压支座。

(2)模型 2：新增支座设置为可受拉支座，采用一般连接。

计算结果如图 6、图 7 所示。采用一般连接时，对独柱墩相邻桥墩上的支座最小支反力有一定程度的影响：1-1 和 6-1 号支座最小支反力有小幅度减小，而对远离独柱墩的桥墩上的支座影响甚微。另一方面，采用一般连接后，活载对各个支座的作用效应均变为了稳定效应，即不存在倾覆失稳风险。可见，新增支座的类型对原桥抗倾覆性能影响较大，若选择一般连接进行模拟将会放大桥梁的抗倾覆性能。进行有限元模拟时，需根据支座的实际类型选择支座节点和主梁的连接方式。

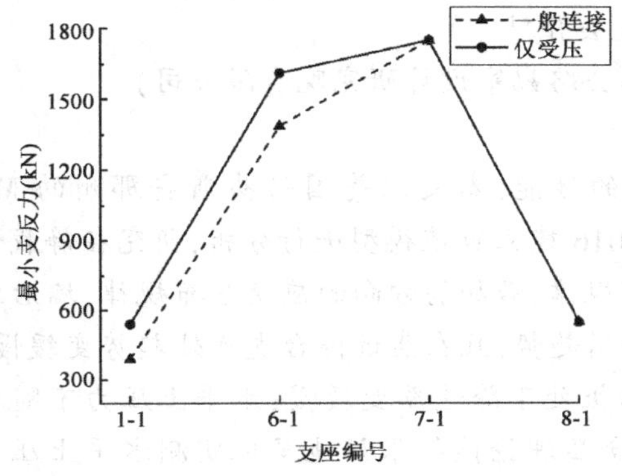

图 6 支座类型对最小支反力的影响

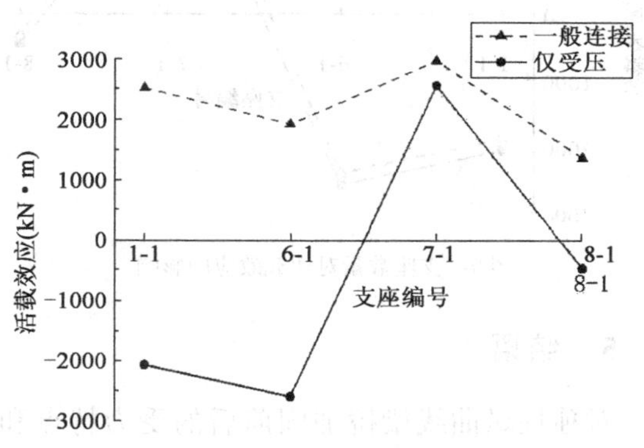

图 7 支座类型对活载效应的影响

4.2 支座数量的影响

有限元模拟时新增的支座均按照仅受压支座进行模拟，而独柱墩曲线梁桥发生倾覆失稳时会绕倾覆轴向曲线外侧翻转[3]。为考虑曲线内侧的新增支座对桥梁抗倾覆稳定性能的影响程度，现将独柱墩加固的新增支座中的内侧支座移除，即将 2-2、3-2、4-2 和 5-2 号支座移除，然后进行抗倾覆稳定性分析，并与原新增双侧支座的结果进行对比，如图 8、图 9 所示。

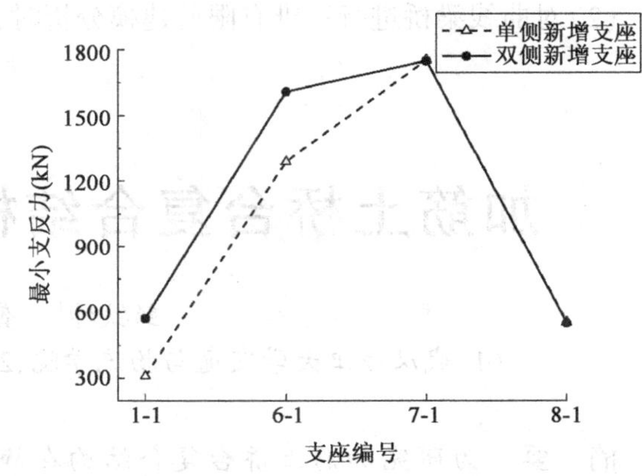

图 8 支座数量对最小支反力的影响

从图中可以看出，将独柱墩新增的内侧支座移除后，各不利支座的最小支反力有所减小，但最小值仍大于 300kN，未出现受拉情况；活载的作用效应，正值为稳定效应，负值为失稳效应，与原新增双侧支座的情况相比差别很小；桥梁的抗倾覆稳定性仍保持在较高水平,可见新增的内侧支座对抗倾覆稳定性的影响较小。

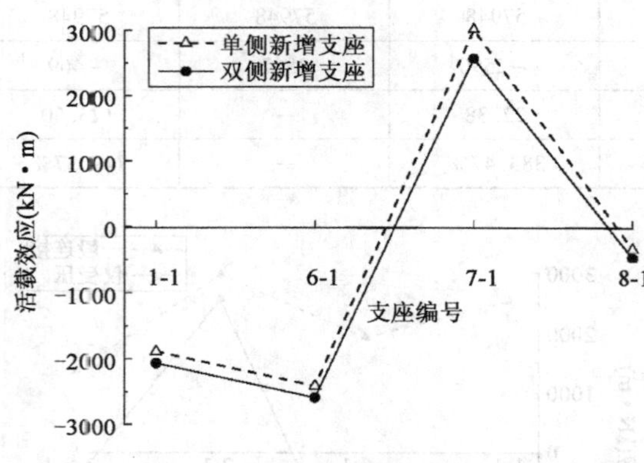

图9　支座数量对活载效应的影响

5　结语

对独柱墩曲线梁桥加固前后的受力特点和抗倾覆稳定性进行分析,有助于选择更加合理、经济的加固措施,对独柱墩加固工程具有很大的指导意义。本文通过对江西省某匝道桥加固工程进行分析,讨论独柱墩曲线梁桥加固前后在恒载、活载作用下的受力异同,以及新增支座的类型和数量对其抗倾覆稳定性的影响,可得出以下结论:

(1)采用新增支座的方式对独柱墩曲线梁桥进行加固时,恒载作用下新增支座几乎不参与受力。分析桥梁抗倾覆稳定性时,恒载作用效应的计算不考虑新增支座的作用,而活载作用效应的计算按照加固后的新体系进行。

(2)对曲线梁桥进行三维有限元建模分析时,不利支座采用可受拉的方式进行模拟,而新增支座与主梁的连接模拟方式对计算结果有很大的影响:新增支座按照可受拉的一般连接进行模拟时会很大程度上放大桥梁的抗倾覆性能。

(3)曲线内侧新增的支座对桥梁最不利支座最小支反力有一定程度的影响,但对抗倾覆稳定系数影响很小。进行加固时可以考虑仅增设曲线外侧的支座,以减少加固成本。

参考文献

[1] 张利鹏. 大件运输车辆荷载下独柱墩曲线梁桥抗倾覆稳定性研究[D]. 西安:长安大学,2020.

[2] 刘鹏. 独柱墩曲线梁桥倾覆参数敏感性分析[J]. 工程建设,2020,52(4):29-32.

[3] 王紫玉. 浅析独柱曲线梁桥稳定性及抗倾覆对策[J]. 城市道桥与防洪,2021,268(8):152-155.

[4] 崔鑫. 基于新规范的独柱墩曲线梁桥抗倾覆稳定性分析[J]. 上海公路,2020,157(2):26-29.

[5] 吕毅刚,饶攀,韩伟威,等. 独柱墩曲线箱梁桥抗倾覆实用计算方法研究[J]. 交通科学与工程,2021,37(3):35-40.

[6] 贺志勇,王野. 某独柱墩曲线梁桥安全性评估与加固设计[J]. 中外公路,2018,38(3):124-130.

[7] 周健民,吴文明,王辰杰. 基于拉压杆的独柱墩抗倾覆加固结构及设计方法研究[J]. 公路交通科技,2021,38(8):110-115.

加筋土桥台复合结构在静载下的性能研究

彭铁坤[1]　龚　硕[2]　朱云升*[1]

(1. 武汉理工大学交通与物流学院;2. 中交第二公路勘察设计研究院有限公司)

摘　要　为研究加筋土桥台复合结构在静载作用下的性能,本文以美国路易斯安那州的 Maree Michel 桥为工程背景,采用二维有限元分析软件 Plaxis 2D 2016 建立数值模型进行分析,研究在静载作用下桥台前墙面板的水平位移分布规律、桥台基础的沉降分布规律、沿加筋方向的应变分布规律、墙后水平土压力分布规律。结果表明,墙后水平位移随墙高大致呈递增趋势,且在靠近桥台支座处趋势变缓慢;沿加筋材料的应变呈现出中间大两端低的趋势,其中在靠近面板处下降速率变缓慢;水平土压力不随墙高增加而呈现线性增大的规律,不符合经典朗肯理论,而利用仓压理论能够很好地呈现实测水平土压力的变化规律。本文提出仓压理论中的系数 k 值应根据面板刚度和回填土重度等因素取值。

关键词 加筋土桥台复合结构 Plaxis 2D 软件 加筋材料 水平土压力 仓压理论

0 引言

加筋土桥台复合结构(Geosynthetic Reinforced Soil Integrated Bridge System,简称 GRS-IBS)是在土工合成材料加筋土(Geosynthetic Reinforced Soils,简称 GRS)的基础上发展起来的一种新型结构。将加筋土的性质与桥梁设计结合而成的加筋土桥台复合结构具有普通桥台难以拥有的优点,包括施工周期短、施工难度低、造价低等。此结构最重要的一个优点是能够减小或消除桥梁承台的水平土压力,甚至可用以代替传统桩基支撑上部桥梁结构自重和交通荷载,从而减小甚至消除桥台与连接路堤之间的差异沉降,很好地解决了中小桥梁的桥头跳车问题[1-3]。基于此,这种结构最近几十年得到国外工程师们的青睐,并对此展开了大量的理论研究和工程实践。而国内尚处于探索阶段,大多停留在理论研究[4]。

GRS-IBS 是由加筋土基础、桥台、综合引道三部分组成[5]。由于 GRS-IBS 是一项新兴技术,大量的研究包括现场实验以及理论研究都从各方面验证了此结构具有优异的性能。FHWA 提出了两种设计桥台承载力的方法:第一种方法是参考 Wu[6]提出的解析方法,把加筋间距、粒料尺寸、加筋材料抗拉强度和回填土摩擦角作为设计参数纳入设计中;第二种方法是基于实验确定的特定材料的应力—应变关系来预估由此材料建造而成的桥台的承载力[7]。根据 FHWA 的设计准则,GRS-IBS 的极限承载能力为竖向应变的 5%,最大允许承载压力为 200kPa[8]。Nicks[9]尝试设计并施工建造了 GRS-IBS 结构,在结构上进行了一系列现场静载实验,结果表明在静载作用下 GRS 具有良好的性能以及较高的承载力。此外,大量的数值模拟也研究了 GRS-IBS 桥台的性能,Wu[10]建立了一个加筋间距较小的有限元模型对加筋间距较小的加筋土进行性能分析,研究了加筋间距、刚度、土体性质等对土体膨胀的影响。结果表明,当加筋间距小于 0.3m 时,土工合成材料的加入降低了土体的膨胀性,并在零体积应变假设下产生了更强的土体复合体。Zheng 和 Fox[11]使用有限差分软件分析了 GRS 桥台在静载下的性能,数值结果表明加筋间距、回填土密实程度和桥梁荷载对 GRS 桥台的侧向变形和桥台沉降有显著影响。

这些研究强调加筋间距、加筋长度、刚度等因素对 GRS-IBS 的影响,但对墙后水平土压力分布规律的研究较少。本文结合工程背景,利用 Plaxis 2D 软件建模,分析了墙后水平位移、沿加筋材料方向应变分布、加筋基础沉降规律,重点研究了墙后水平土压力分布规律,并验证了仓压理论在分析水平土压力分布方面的合理性,为后续设计 GRS-IBS 结构提供理论参考。

1 工程概况

本文以美国路易斯安那州的 Maree Michel 桥为工程背景。该桥采用 GRS-IBS 结构,跨径为 19.8m,挡土墙面板最大高度为 4.8m,桥台宽 13m,如图 1 所示。此桥的主梁直接由 GRS 桥台支撑,避免使用传统的深基础桥台。为了监测结构的使用性能,在施工时安装了四种监测传感器,水平和竖向压力计安装在墙后,用来监测墙后水平和竖向土压力;位移传感器用来监测墙体变形以及差异沉降;沿加筋材料方向放置应变计,用以监测沿加筋材料方向的应变。监测仪器布置情况如图 2[12]所示。

图 1 Maree Michel 大桥

2 数值模型

2.1 模型几何形状及边界条件

本文采用二维有限元软件 Plaxis 2D 2016 建立模型。图 3 显示了模型的几何形状以及边界条件。

模型主梁长 $L_a = 7.3\text{m}$,高 $D_a = 1\text{m}$,由 GRS 桥台结构支撑,支座宽 $d_b = 1.7\text{m}$,高 $d_a = 0.2\text{m}$;采用引道过渡到路面,引道由加筋材料分层填筑压实

而成,长 $L_b = 6.5\text{m}$,厚 $L_c = 1.3\text{m}$。桥台总高 $H = 4\text{m}$,由碎石填料和加筋材料分层填筑而成,加筋材料采用高强度土工布,长 $L_r = 2.6\text{m}$,竖向间距 $S_v = 0.2\text{m}$;天然土开挖面坡度为2∶1,碎石堆砌在挡土墙墙角前形成一个坡面,顶面坡度3∶1,地面坡度1∶1,此结构能减少冲刷腐蚀,同时限制挡墙的水平变形;加筋土基础由土工布填筑而成,宽 $B_r = 2.5\text{m}$,高 $B_a = 0.5\text{m}$。为了减小边界条件对计算的影响,模型地基长15.5m,深8m;底部边界固定,两侧限制水平方向的位移。

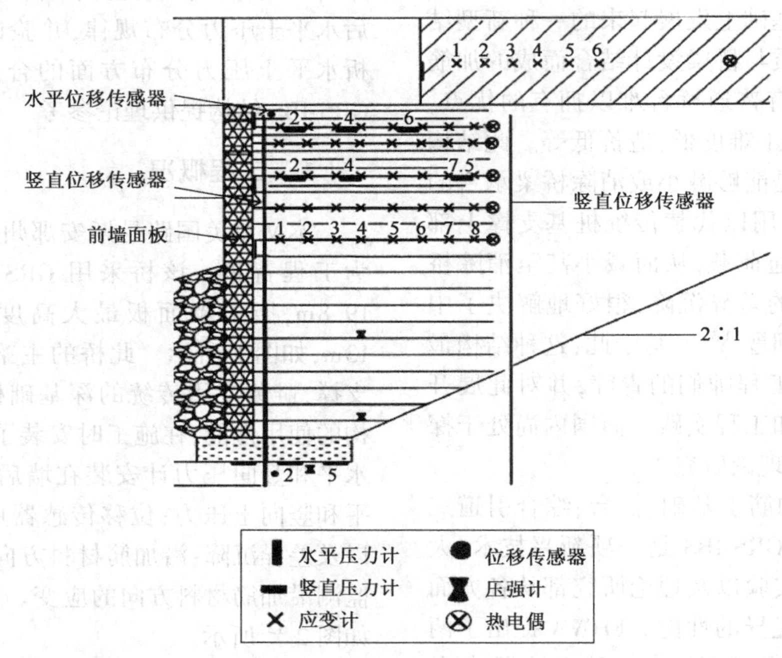

图2　监测仪器布置图

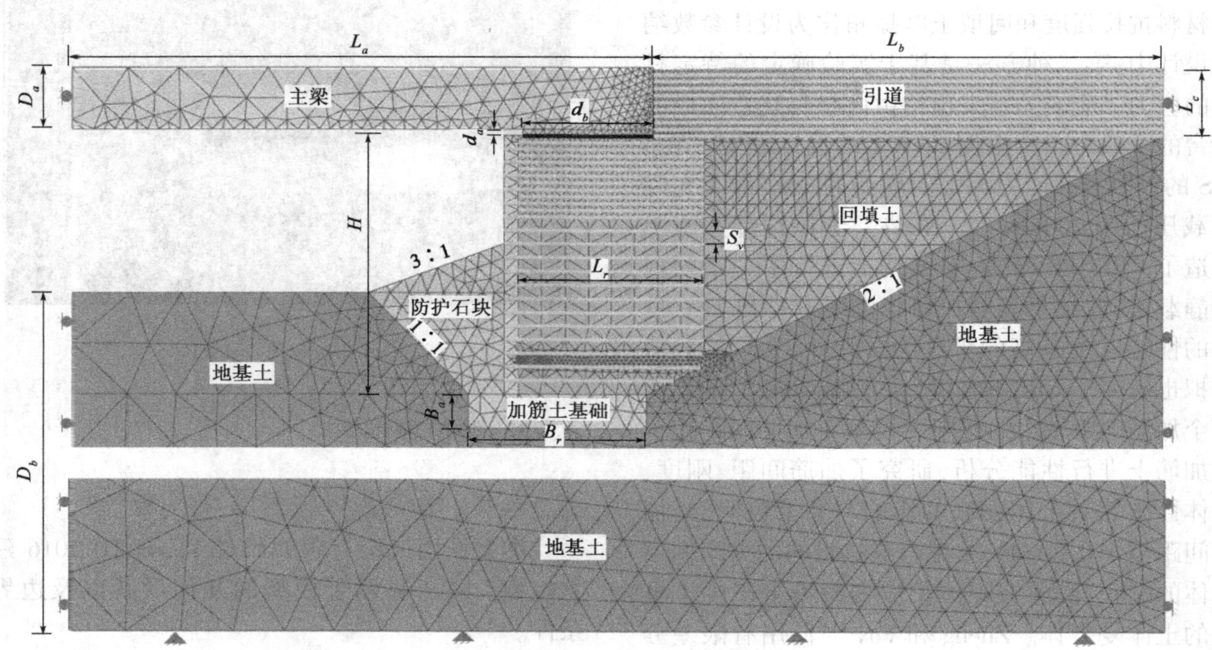

图3　模型几何形状及网格划分

2.2 材料模型

本文采用土体硬化本构模型(the Hardening Soil 简称 HS)模拟回填土材料。该模型为二阶高级本构模型,属于双曲线弹塑性模型,是在塑性剪切硬化理论框架下发展而来的,考虑了剪切硬化,可模拟主偏量加载引起的不可逆变形。HS 模型需输入 9 个主要参数,标准三轴排水试验割线刚度 E_{50}^{ref}、侧限压缩试验切线刚度 E_{oed}^{ref} 可通过三轴试验获得;刚度的应力相关幂指数 m 可从 0.5 ~1 中选取;卸载/重加载刚度 E_{ur}^{ref} 根据假设 $E_{ur}^{ref}=3E_{50}^{ref}$[13] 计算获得;有效粘聚力 c'、有效内摩擦角 φ'、剪胀角 ψ 可通过室外大型直剪实验获得;卸载—重加载泊松比 ν_{ur} 取 0.2,破坏比 R_f 取 0.8;其他高级参数取默认值。表 1 列出了参数的具体值[12]。

本文选用线弹性模型(the Elastic Model,简称 LE)模拟主梁、加筋土基础、挡土墙砌块、加筋材料、支座,地基土采用摩尔库伦模型模拟,具体参数值见表 1;采用 Plaxis 软件自带的界面单元模拟砌块与砌块、回填土与加筋材料之间的接触面。在此软件中,界面单元的属性与周围土体有关,界面参数依赖周围土体选取的本构模型。当周围材料为线弹性模型、摩尔库伦模型、土体硬化模型时,界面的主要参数为强度折减系数 R_{inter},使用弹塑性模型描述界面行为以模拟土-结构相互作用,采用摩尔库伦准则区分界面的弹性行为和塑性行为,即当剪应力 τ 满足下式时界面保持为弹性:

$$|\tau| < -\sigma_n \tan\varphi_i + c_i \tag{1}$$

式中:σ_n——有效正应力;

φ_i——有效内摩擦角;

c_i——有效粘聚力

当剪应力 τ 满足下式时界面将表现出塑性行为:

$$|\tau| = -\sigma_n \tan\varphi_i + c_i \tag{2}$$

界面的强度属性可根据相关材料的土体强度属性和强度折减因子 R_{inter}(在本文模拟中,$R_{inter}=0.8$)按如下规律计算得出:

$$c_i = R_{inter} c_{soil}$$

$$\tan\varphi_i = R_{inter}\tan\varphi_{soil} \leqslant \tan\varphi_{soil}$$

$$R_{inter} < 1 \text{ 时 } \psi_i = 0°;\text{否则 } \psi_i = \psi_{sol}$$

为了模拟现场施工,本研究在模拟桥台施工时采用分段填筑,即桥台被分成 20 层施工,每层厚 0.2m。在每一层施工时,铺筑回填材料以及土工格栅,并在每层的顶部施加均布荷载模拟压实过程。因实际施工中靠近砌块处的填土无法采用大型机械车压实,一般采用人工夯实,故模拟压实过程施加的均布荷载由两部分组成:靠近砌块处荷载为 10kPa,布置长度 $L_s=0.5$m,剩下部分的荷载大小为 63kPa。一层施工完成后,继续按此过程模拟下一层直至整个桥台模拟完成。均布荷载的布置方式以及材料接触面形式如图 4 所示,相关的材料参数值见表 1。

材料参数值 表1

单元类别	参数值
面板	线弹性模型;$E=3\times10^7$kPa;$\gamma=12.5$kN/m^3;泊松比 $\nu=0$
土工格栅	线弹性塑性模型;抗拉强度 $T_u=80$kN/m;轴向刚度 $EA=600$kN/m
回填材料	土体硬化模型;干重度 $\gamma_d=18$kN/m^3;湿重度 $\gamma_t=19$kN/m^3;粘聚力 $c=20$kPa;摩擦角 $\varphi=51°$;剪胀角 $\psi=21°$;$E_{50}^{ref}=34000$kPa,$E_{ur}^{ref}=103200$kPa,$E_{oed}^{ref}=26400$,$\nu=0.2$,$m=0.5$
地基土体	莫尔库伦模型;干重度 $\gamma_d=15.2$kN/m^3;湿重度 $\gamma_t=18.65$kN/m^3;粘聚力 $c=17.7$kPa;摩擦角 $\varphi=27°$;$E=30000$kPa;$\nu=0.2$
填料与格栅间的接触面	具有莫尔库伦破坏准则的线弹性模型;粘聚力 $c=8.6$kPa;摩擦角 $\varphi=40.4°$
面板与格栅间的接触面	具有莫尔库伦破坏准则的线弹性模型;粘聚力 $c=8.6$kPa;摩擦角 $\varphi=40.4°$
防护石块	线弹性模型;$E=50$MPa;$\gamma=22$kN/m^3;$\nu=0.5$

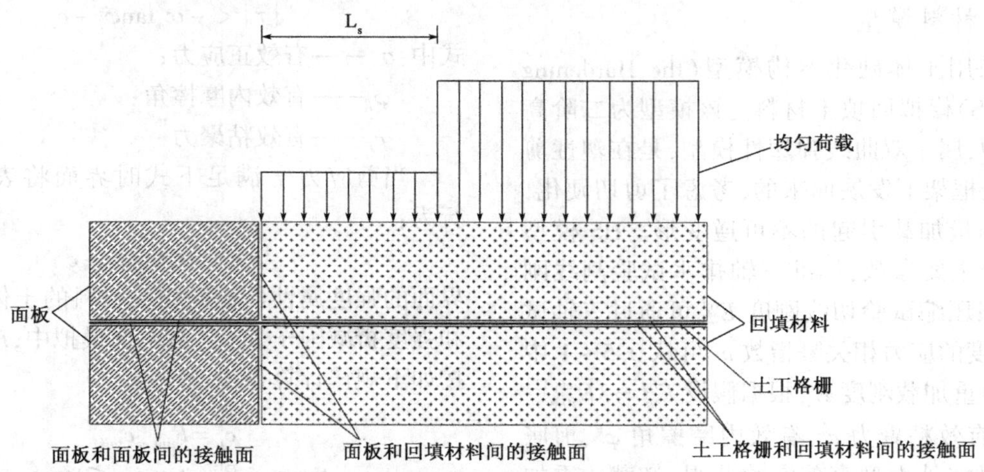

图4　均布荷载布置方式及材料接触面形式

2.3　计算结果

2.3.1　面板水平位移

本文将桥台结构的主梁施工完成时的现场检测数据与数值模型的模拟结果对比,包括桥台挡墙侧向位移、加筋土基础沉降、沿加筋材料方向的应变等参数,进而验证所建模型的合理性。图5为挡土墙面板水平位移实测结果与数值模拟结果。从图中可以看出,挡土墙水平位移沿墙高大致呈递增趋势,越靠近上部桥座处,递增速率越低,这是由于支座下为密筋承载区,且承受较大的由桥梁上部荷载传递的附加压力,加筋材料发挥了较大的加筋作用,有效地约束了土体水平位移,形成的加筋复合体强度和刚度较大,能抵消附加荷载产生的土压力,故而产生的位移较小。由图可知,实测最大水平位移为3mm,模拟最大水平位移为3 5mm,远低于FHWA建议的最大水平位移17mm(不超过支座长度的1%,1% d_b = 0.01 × 1700 = 17mm);实测位移和模拟位移在1/3H处较为吻合,在1/3H至H处略有差别,原因在于实测数据取自主梁施工完成时,挡墙上部分水平位移还未完全形成,但总的来说,模拟结果非常接近实测结果。

2.3.2　加筋土基础沉降

图6为四个阶段的加筋土基础沉降量。其中,阶段一为第七层施工完成时的基础沉降,阶段二为第十二层施工完成时的基础沉降,阶段三为桥台施工完成时的基础沉降,阶段四为主梁施工完成时的基础沉降。模拟结果非常接近实测结果,沉降量总体呈增大趋势,且最大沉降为3.5mm;在阶段一和阶段二处,现场测量值低于数值模拟结果,可能是由旧桥造成的土体超固结所致。

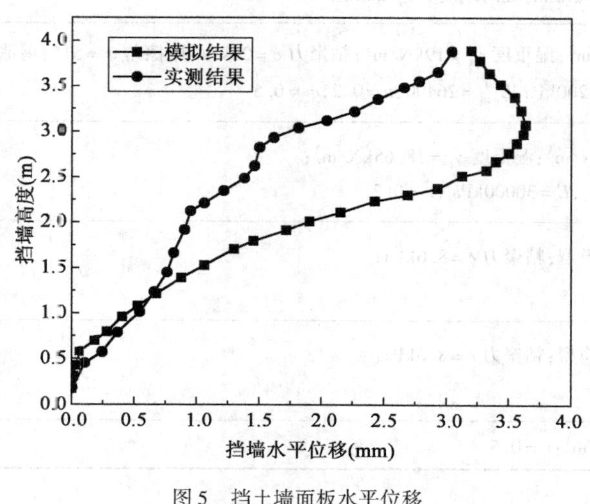

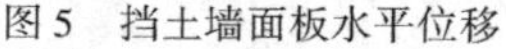
图5　挡土墙面板水平位移

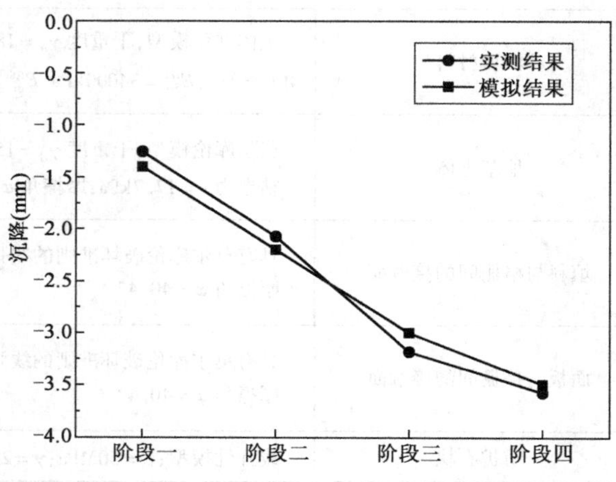

图6　加筋基础沉降

2.3.3 沿加筋材料方向的应变

图7和图8分别为第十二层和第十六层沿加筋材料方向的应变,图9为桥台结构的加筋材料层数分布情况。从图7和图8可知,两层应变最大值为0.7%,均低于FHWA建议的最大应变值2%,由此可知加筋桥台中的筋材所受的轴力远小于抗拉强度,且应变最大值位于其长度的一半处。从面板至应变最大处,实测结果略低于模拟结果,原因可能是前墙处防护石块的存在影响墙后应变的形成。总体来说,模拟结果和计算结果在变化趋势上基本相同,都是沿着面板方向先逐渐增加,到达峰值再缓慢过渡到面板。

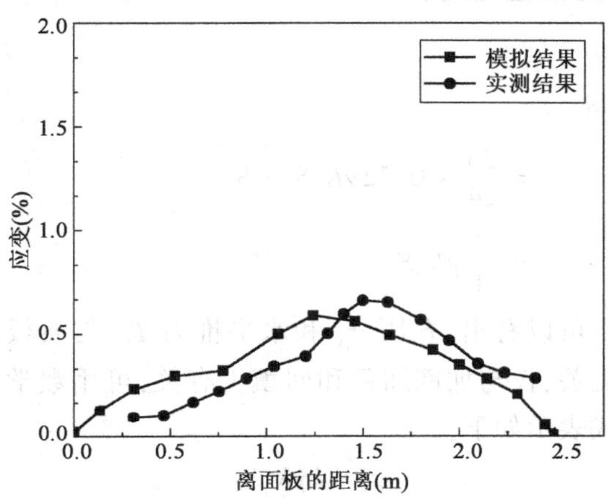

图7 第十二层沿加筋材料方向的应变

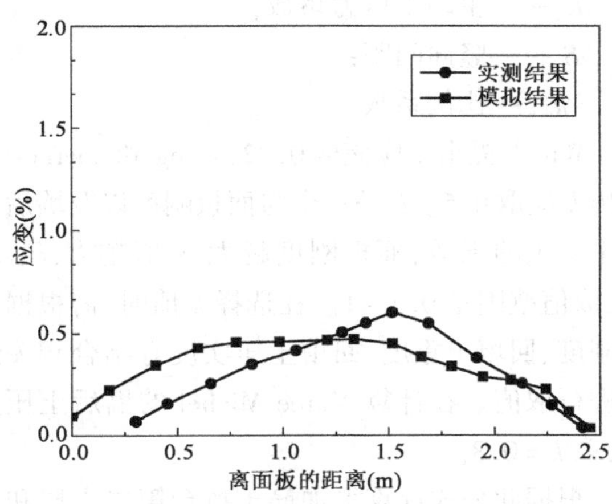

图8 第十六层沿加筋材料方向的应变

2.3.4 墙后水平土压力

图10为墙后水平土压力模拟数据与实测数据的对比。由图可知,第二十层和第十七层水平土压力接近,为290Pa,第十三层的实测水平土压力接近500Pa。根据经典朗肯理论的土压力分布规律,土压力应随深度增加而不断增加,这与实测数据不符,原因在于加筋材料与回填土形成的加筋复合体在水平方向的变形受挡土墙面板影响较小,主要受到筋材的约束作用的影响。

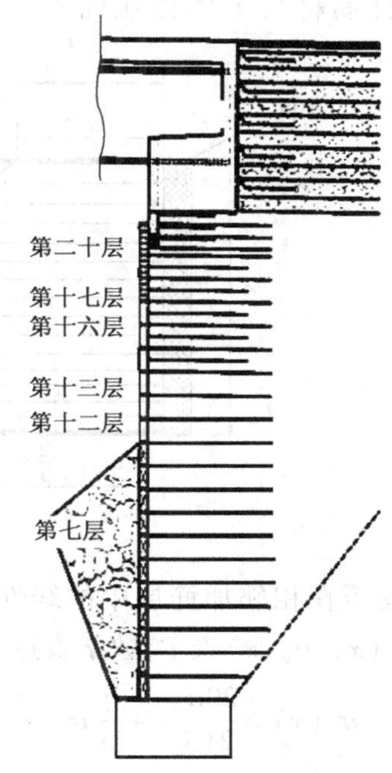

图9 加筋材料层数分布情况

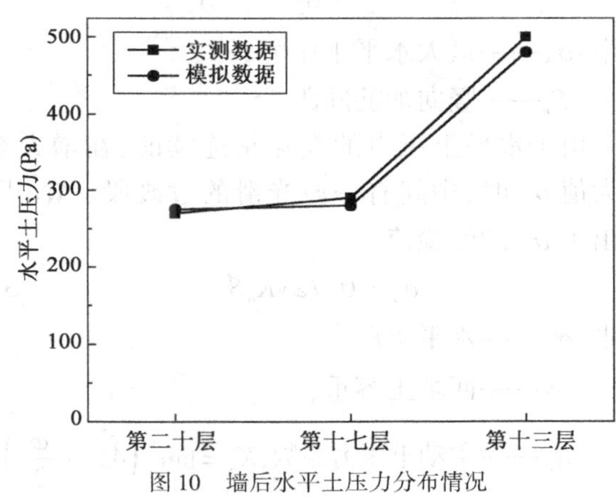

图10 墙后水平土压力分布情况

从实测数据可知,第十三层的水平土压力约是第二十层的两倍;桥台顶部六层为承载区,布置了较密的加筋材料,竖向加筋间距 $S_{vu}=0.2\mathrm{m}$,桥台下部加筋间距 $S_{vd}=0.1\mathrm{cm}$,顶层加筋间距恰为桥台下部加筋间距的一半。由此可以猜想,加筋作用下的水平土压力与加筋间距成正比。对于这一猜想,Wu[14]提出了一种理论,把呈现这种规律的水平土压力命名为仓压(bin pressure)。其理论大致如下:在理想状态下,加筋土中的每一层加筋材料能完全抑制其上下附近处的土体的变形,则在此层处的土压力为零;在重力作用下,土压力随深度增加而约呈线性增大趋势,至最大值 σ_h 后相邻的另一层处减小到零,这两层之间的水平压力就称作仓压。由于实际情况下加筋材料不是完全刚性的,且筋材与土体接触面不是绝对粘附的,在加筋层与面板接触处会产生一定的水平压力。基于此,本文设计了一个仓压理论图,如图11所示。

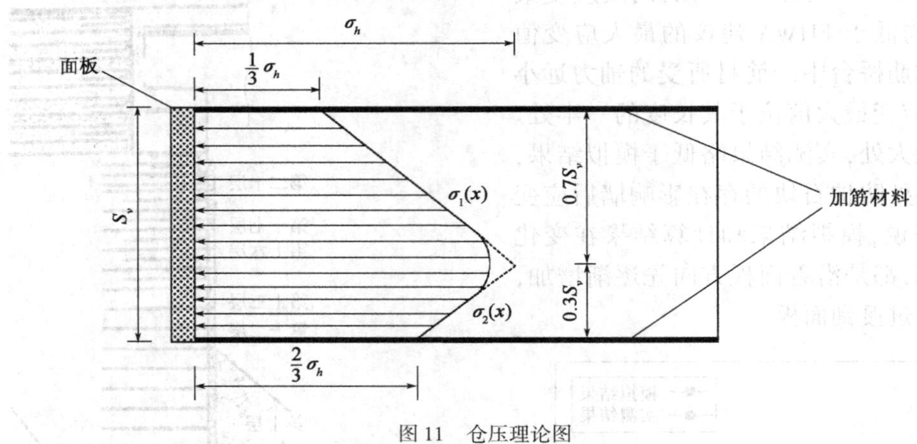

图11　仓压理论图

其中,仓压在相邻加筋层中的线性分布情况可用函数 $\sigma_1(x)$、$\sigma_2(x)$ 表示,数学表达式分别为:

$$\sigma_1(x)=\frac{20\sigma_h}{21S_v}x+\frac{1}{3}\sigma_h \tag{3}$$

$$\sigma_2(x)=-\frac{10\sigma_h}{9S_v}x+\frac{16}{9}\sigma_h \tag{4}$$

式中:σ_h——最大水平土压力,

S_v——竖向加筋间距

由于水平土压力的变化是连续的,在增大至最大值 σ_h 时,中间有一段光滑的过渡段。Wu[14]给出了 σ_h 的经验值:

$$\sigma_h=0.72\gamma K_aS_v \tag{5}$$

式中:σ_F——水平土压力;

γ——回填土容重;

K_c——主动土压力系数,$K_a=\tan^2\left(45°-\dfrac{\varphi}{2}\right)$。

当间距 S_v 足够小时,可用线段代替过渡段中的曲线,此时对 $\sigma_1(x)$、$\sigma_2(x)$ 在间距 S_v 范围内进行积分可得加筋土体对面板的总水平推力 T_{bin}:

$$T_{bin}\approx\int_0^{0.7S_v}\sigma_1(x)\mathrm{d}x+\int_{0.7S_v}^{Sv}\sigma_2(x)\mathrm{d}x$$

$$=\int_0^{0.7S_v}\left(\frac{20\sigma_h}{21S_v}x+\frac{1}{3}\sigma_h\right)\mathrm{d}x+\int_{0.7S_v}^{Sv}\left(-\frac{10\sigma_h}{9S_v}x+\frac{16}{9}\sigma_h\right)\mathrm{d}x$$

$$=\frac{25}{24}\sigma_hS_v$$

$$=\frac{25}{24}\times0.72\gamma K_aS_v\cdot S_v$$

$$=\frac{3}{4}\gamma K_aS_v{}^2$$

可以看出,仓压 σ_h 和水平推力 T_{bin} 与面板高度无关,仅与加筋间距和回填土有关,可用数学表达式表示如下:

$$\sigma_h=k\gamma K_aS_v$$

式中:γ——土体重度;

K_a——主动土压力系数;

S_v——竖向间距;

k——比例系数。

Wu[14]提出 k 应该取0.72,soong 和 koerner[15]提出 k 应取0.5。k 是一个与面板刚度以及墙后回填土有关的系数,面板刚度越大,k 值越大,σ_h 越大,取值范围是0.5~1。在选择 k 值时,需根据面板刚度、回填土重度、回填土压实度等结合相关经验进行取值。在计算 Maree Michel 的墙后土压力时,取 $k=0.8$。

根据此公式计算得加筋土桥台第二十层和第十七层的水平土压力 σ_{hup}:

$$\sigma_{hup}=0.8\gamma K_aS_{vup}$$

$$=0.8\gamma\tan^2\left(45°-\frac{\varphi}{2}\right)S_{vup}$$

$$=0.8\times21.3\times\tan^2\left(45°-\frac{51°}{2}\right)\times0.1$$

$$=0.213\text{kPa}$$

计算得第十三层的水平土压力 σ_{hdown}：

$$
\begin{aligned}
\sigma_{hdown} &= 0.8\gamma K_a S_{vdown} \\
&= 0.8\gamma \tan^2\left(45° - \frac{\varphi}{2}\right) S_{vdown} \\
&= 0.8 \times 21.3 \times \tan^2\left(45° - \frac{51°}{2}\right) \times 0.2 \\
&= 0.42\text{kPa}
\end{aligned}
$$

本文在不考虑桥梁附加荷载作用时利用经典朗肯理论计算土压力，得第二十层、第十七层、第十三层的土压力值分别为 0.523kPa、1.57kPa、3.668kPa。图 12 为实测数据与理论计算所得结果的对比，可以看出实测水平土压力介于两种理论之间，采用仓压理论计算得到的数据更接近真实值，而采用朗肯理论计算得到的土压力在不考虑桥梁附加荷载时比实测值大，若考虑附加荷载则误差更大。由此可以验证在计算加筋挡土墙中的水平土压力时使用仓压理论更精确，计算得到的值略小于真实值，故在计算桥台结构的稳定性时，验算加筋材料的轴力时可采用仓压理论计算。根据仓压理论的推导结果，水平推力 $T_{bin} \propto S_v^2$，当稳定性不满足要求时，相比改换回填材料，减少竖向加筋间距的作用更明显；在设计桥台时需要通过计算加筋材料的轴力来选取筋材，不宜选取仓压理论，而选取经典朗肯理论计算设计轴力则更加安全，但由此计算得到的筋材所需的抗拉强度较高，导致选材时的耗费较大。如何根据具体情况选择合适的理论计算加筋桥台中筋材的轴力还有待研究探讨。

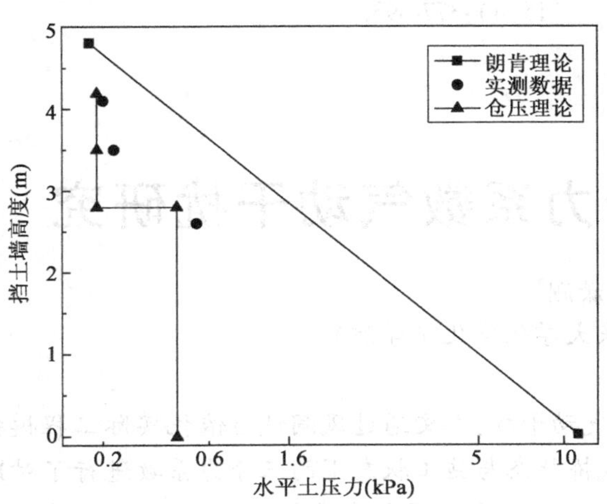

图 12　不同理论下的水平土压力对比

3　结语

本文使用 Plaxis 2D 2016 软件对 Maree Michel 桥进行数值模拟分析，模拟结果与实测结果非常接近，同时验证了仓压理论的合理性，现对上述研究结果总结如下：

(1)墙后水平位移随墙高增加呈逐渐增大趋势，在靠近上部 1/3H 处达到峰值，之后略微减小。这说明加筋密集区的加筋材料能够有效地约束加筋土体的变形，且实测值与模拟值都远低于 FHWA 的极限值，最大水平位移为 3mm，表明此桥台结构在桥梁荷载作用下变形较小，完全能够代替传统深基础桥台，并且能有效地减小差异沉降，拥有极大的发展潜能，是未来我国桥台结构发展的方向。

(2)墙后第十二层和第十六层沿加筋材料方向的应变最大值为 0.7%，低于 FHWA 建议的最大应变值2%，呈现出中间高两端低的趋势，在靠近面板处，减小趋势较缓慢，可能是由于面板前的防护石块的存在影响墙后应变的形成；加筋材料的应变不足 1%，表明加筋材料完全没有达到其极限强度，变形较小，在未来研究中采用线弹性本构模型分析加筋材料的变形性能是完全可行的。

(3)墙后水平土压力不随高度呈线性变化，但与加筋间距密切相关，因此墙后的水平土压力不符合经典朗肯理论，但与仓压理论计算得到的土压力分布非常吻合；仓压理论中的系数 k 需根据面板刚度、回填土重度、回填土压实度等结合相关经验进行取值，除了考虑这几个参数外，关于系数 k 的取值还需进一步的研究；在未来计算桥台稳定性时，可考虑选择仓压理论计算轴力；在设计桥台结构选取加筋材料时，可考虑选择经典朗肯理论。除此之外，仓压理论是否适合分析墙后竖直土压力还有待研究探讨。

参考文献

[1] Adams M. T, Schlatter W, Stabile T. Geosynthetic reinforced soil integrated abutments at the Bowman Road Bridge in Defiance County, Ohio [C]. Geosynthetics in Reinforcement and Hydraulic Applications, American Society of Civil Engineers, 2007:1-10.

[2] Kost A. D, Filz G. M, Cousins T. Full-scale investigation of differential settlements beneath a geosynthetic reinforced soil bridge abutment[J]. Transportation Research Record, 2014, 2462(1): 28-36.

[3] Talebi M., Meehan, C. L., Cacciola, D. V., Design and construction of a geosynthetic reinforced soil integrated bridge system[C]. Geo-Congress, Atlanta, Georgia, Reston, 2014: 4176-4190.

[4] 朱晨,蔡晓光,黄鑫,等.土工合成材料加筋土柔性桥台研究现状[J].防灾科技学院学报,2021,23(2):10-19.

[5] Adams M, Nicks J, Stabile T. Geosynthetic Reinforced Soil Integrated Bridge System, Interim Implementation Guide[R]. 2011, No. FHWA-HRT-11-026.

[6] Wu J. T. H, Pham T. Q. Load-carrying capacity and required reinforcement strength of closely spaced soil-geosynthetic composites[J]. Journal of Geotechnical & Geoenvironmental Engineering Geotech, 2013, 139(9):1468-1476.

[7] Berg R. R, Christopher B. R, Samtani N. C. Design and Construction of Mechanically Stabilized Earth Walls and Reinforced Soil Slopes-Volume I[R]. 2009, No. FHWA-NHI-10-024.

[8] Nicks J. E, Adams M. T, Ooi P. S. K. Geosynthetic reinforced soil performance testing—Axial load deformation relationships[R]. 2013, No. FHWA-HRT-13-066.

[9] Nicks J. E, Esmaili D, Adams M. T. Deformations of geosynthetic reinforced soil under bridge service loads[J]. Geotextiles and Geomembranes, 2016, 44(4):641-653.

[10] Wu J. T. H, Yang K. H, Mohamed, et al. Suppression of soil dilation—a reinforcing mechanism of soil-geosynthetic composites[J]. Transportation Infrastructure Geotechnology, 2014, 1(1):68-82.

[11] Zheng Y, Fox P. J. Numerical investigation of geosynthetic-reinforced soil bridge abutments under static loading[J]. Journal of Geotechnical & Geoenvironmental Engineering, 2016, 142(5): 1090-0241.

[12] Saghebfar M, Abu-Farsakh M, Ardah A, et al. Performance monitoring of Geosynthetic Reinforced Soil Integrated Bridge System (GRS-IBS) in Louisiana[J]. Geotextiles and Geomembranes, 2017, 45(2):34-47.

[13] Schanz T, Vermeer P. A, Bonnier P. G. The Hardening Soil Model: Formulation and Verification[J]. Beyond 2000 in Computational Geotechnics, 1999, :281-296.

[14] Wu J. T. H, Pham T Q. Load-Carrying Capacity and Required Reinforcement Strength of Closely Spaced Soil-Geosynthetic Composites [J]. Journal of Geotechnical & Geoenvironmental Engineering, 2013, 139(9):1468-1476.

[15] Yang Soong, Robert M. Koerner. On the required connection strength of geosynthetically reinforced walls[J]. Geotextiles and Geomembranes, 1997, 15(4):377-393.

并行双幅旧桥对新桥三分力系数气动干扰研究

王 涵*1 辛潇澜2

(1.长安大学公路学院;2.重庆大学化学化工学院)

摘 要 为研究并行的双幅旧桥对新桥三分力系数气动干扰,本文通过风洞试验依托实际工程模拟了拟修建新桥与旧桥的上下游位置关系,对拟修建新桥成桥状态与施工状态下的三分力系数进行了对比分析。结果表明:已有的并行旧桥会对新建桥梁的三分力系数产生不同程度的气动干扰,当旧桥位于上游时,旧桥对新桥有明显的遮挡作用,新桥的阻力系数会减小30%左右;新桥的升力系数和升力矩系数的变化对于风攻角的改变较为敏感,当风攻角为负角度时,各工况升力系数和升力矩系数的偏差非常大,在正攻角时偏差较小;在新建桥梁的成桥状态与施工状态下测得的三分力系数有明显偏差。

关键词 桥梁风工程 三分力系数 风洞试验 并行桥梁 气动干扰 新旧桥梁

0 引言

随着我国政治、经济、文化的飞速发展,我国人口已经突破14亿,全国机动车保有量超过3.78亿,交通量也急剧增长,已有的桥梁等基础设施无法满足目前的交通需求,因此需要在一些旧桥的临近位置建造新桥以满足交通需求,但是由于新修建的桥梁与旧桥的间距宽度较小,风经过上游断面作用到下游断面时会互相干扰。楼小峰[1]利用二阶投影法计算研究了高雷诺数时串列的两个圆柱间的绕流,并利用此方法预测了拱桥两拱肋的三分力系数。陈素琴[2]改进了MAC标志网格方法研究了串列方柱的阻力与方柱间距的关系,结果表明随着两方柱的间距逐渐增大,其阻力系数并不是连续变化,而是在特殊间距时存在"跳跃现象"。郭震山、郭春平等[3-4]学者利用计算流体力学针对变截面的双幅连续刚构桥研究了两跨中箱梁截面的气动干扰效应,发现气流经过上游截面会增加其紊流度,从而导致下游截面的来流不是均匀流,即使当两桥间距大于8倍的桥宽时,气动干扰的影响仍然存在。苟国涛[5]使用FLUENT研究了连续刚构双幅箱梁桥之间的阻力系数干扰,定义了"干扰因子"来表征这种干扰的大小,通过模拟计算得到了各个工况下的风压分布,从而对两桥阻力系数的干扰做出了基于表面压力的机理分析。刘志文等[6-7]学者首先针对串列的三种典型断面,利用CFD分析的结果验证了风洞试验的结果,再通过与已有文献的数据进行对比证实了数值模拟手段的可行性与精度,得到了各种形式断面的气动干扰因子与断面间距的关系。陈政清等[8-11]学者采用风洞试验的方法对双幅扁平钢箱梁桥面间的颤振稳定性、涡振特性和静力特性进行了研究,结果表明两幅桥面间的气动干扰可能会降低主梁的颤振临界风速、增大涡振的振幅及其三分力系数。以上研究主要是针对最初设计时就采用的双幅并行桥梁,且两断面形式相同,对不同断面形式的新旧桥梁气动干扰研究较少。因此,本文以广东省某拟修建的实际工程为背景,对不同形式断面的旧桥对新桥的静力气动干扰进行研究。

1 研究工程背景

拟修建的新桥为328m+153m的独塔斜拉桥,设有2个辅助墩和1个过渡墩,如图1所示。大桥全宽33.9m,由于索塔两边拉索采用不对称布置,为平衡自重,主跨328m采用扁平钢箱梁,如图2所示,边跨153m采用大容重的混凝土梁。旧桥为80m+128m+80m的双幅连续刚构桥,桥位实景如图3所示,主梁为直腹板的预应力混凝土大箱梁,左右幅桥桥面宽度分别为17.5m和15.0m。旧桥箱梁横断面如图4所示。

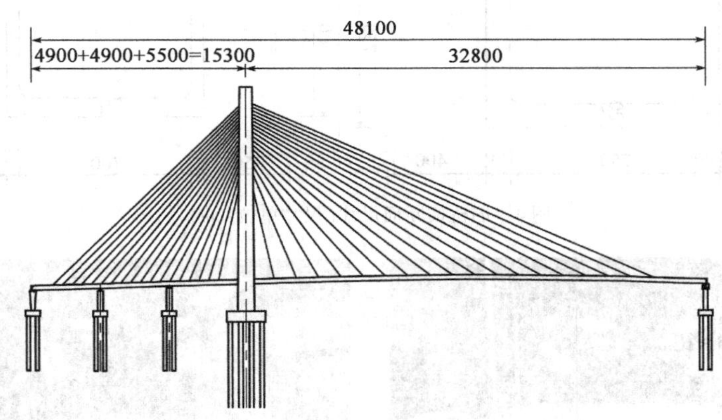

图1 新建桥梁立面布置(尺寸单位:cm)

2 风洞试验

三分力系数是桥梁结构承受风荷载时的重要参数,考虑到在新桥施工阶段时没有二期桥面铺装、路灯、人行道栏杆等影响气动外形的附属设施,整个桥梁气动外形与成桥阶段有较大的差别,而气动外形的变化又会影响其三分力系数,因此试验工况考虑节段模型分为成桥状态(旧桥在上游、无旧桥和旧桥在下游)和施工状态(旧桥在上游、无旧桥和旧桥在下游)。新桥的成桥、施工状态模拟分别如图5、图6所示。试验段宽3m,高2.5m,试验模型由测量段与二元端板构成,试验时将端板与外接铝合金杆固结,由铝合金杆和天平连接,天平连接在α机构和测力内支架上。节段测力模型缩尺比为1:50,长1.5m,长宽比为2.21:1,宽0.678m,高0.0614m;共考虑21个风攻角,从-10°~10°按每1°间隔;试验流场为10m/s的均匀流场,试验用测力天平为中国空气动力研究中心研制的杆式5分量应变天平。试验工况安排如表1所示。原拟修建新桥与旧桥实际间距为9.7m,缩尺后为0.194m。

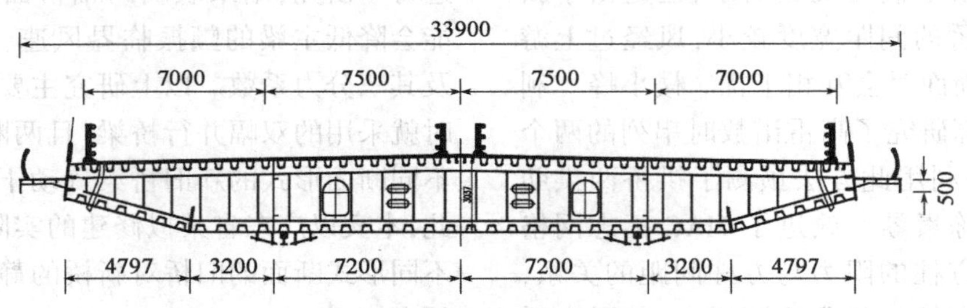

图2　新建桥梁横断面尺寸(尺寸单位:mm)

图3　旧桥实景图

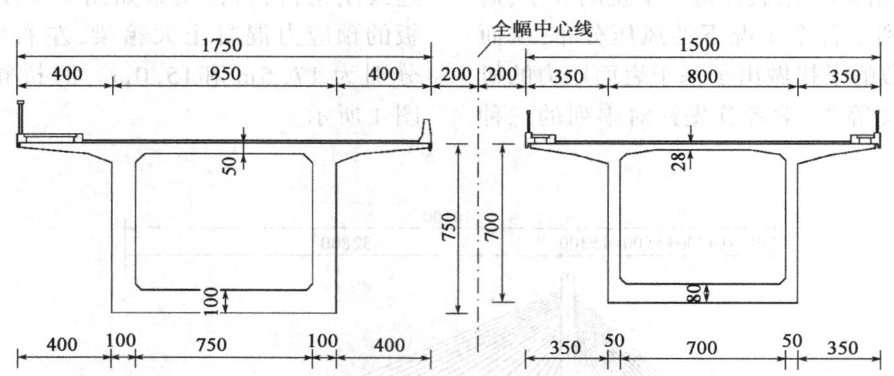

图4　旧桥横断面尺寸(尺寸单位:cm)

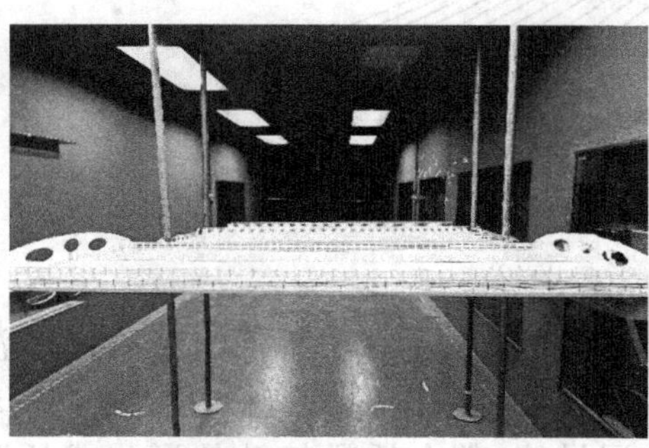

图5　成桥阶段试验模型(旧桥在上游)

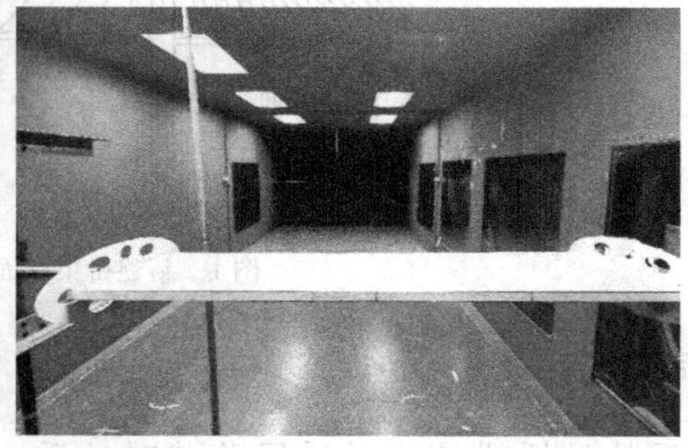

图6　施工阶段试验模型(无旧桥)

试验工况安排　　表1

工况序号	阶　段	相对位置	风　攻　角
1	成桥状态	无旧桥	－10°～10°
2		旧桥在上游	
3		旧桥在下游	
4	施工状态	无旧桥	
5		旧桥在上游	
6		旧桥在下游	

3　试验结果分析

为方便将新旧桥相对位置各工况的试验结果进行对比分析，本文分别将同一气动力系数的三种位置关系工况绘于同一张图上，图中的三分力系数定义如下：

$$C_D = \frac{F_D}{q_w A_H} \qquad C_L = \frac{F_L}{q_w A_V} \qquad C_M = \frac{M_T}{q_w A_V B}$$

式中：C_D、C_M、C_L 分别为无量纲化的风轴坐标系下的阻力系数、升力矩（扭矩）系数和升力系数，F_D、M_T、F_L 分别为对应的风轴坐标下的阻力、升力矩（扭矩）和升力，$q_w = \frac{\rho U^2}{2}$为来流动压；ρ 和 U 分别为空气密度和来流速度；A_H 和 A_V 为相应的参考面积，$A_H = HL$，$A_V = BL$，L、B 和 H 分别为模型的长、宽和高。新桥试验模型尺寸如表2所示。

新桥试验模型细部尺寸　　表2

物　理　量	符　　号	尺　　寸
长（m）	L	1.50
宽（m）	B	0.678
高（m）	H	0.0614
迎风面积（m^2）	A_H	0.0921
侧风面积（m^2）	A_V	1.017

成桥状态的试验结果如图7～图9所示，施工状态的试验结果如图10～图12所示。

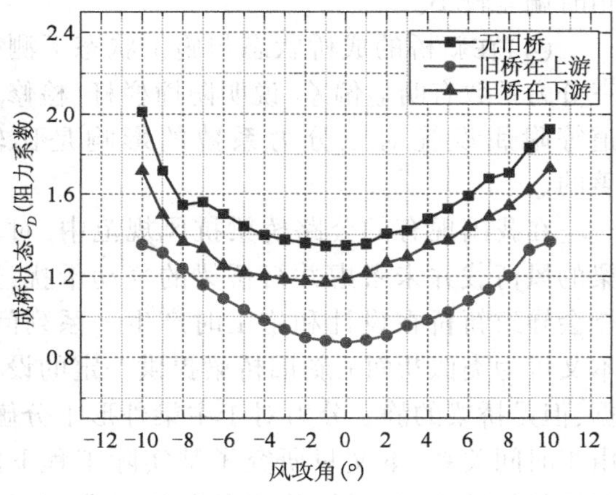

图7　成桥状态阻力系数-风攻角

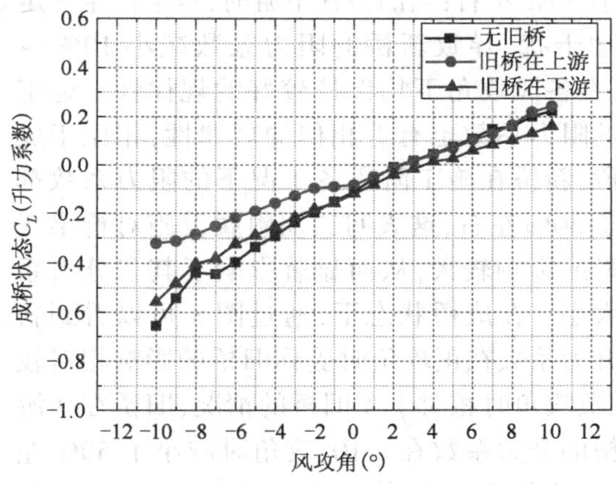

图8　成桥状态升力系数-风攻角

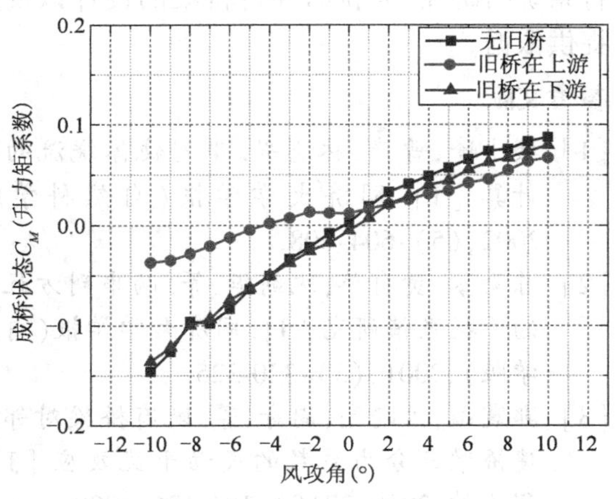

图9　成桥状态升力矩系数-风攻角

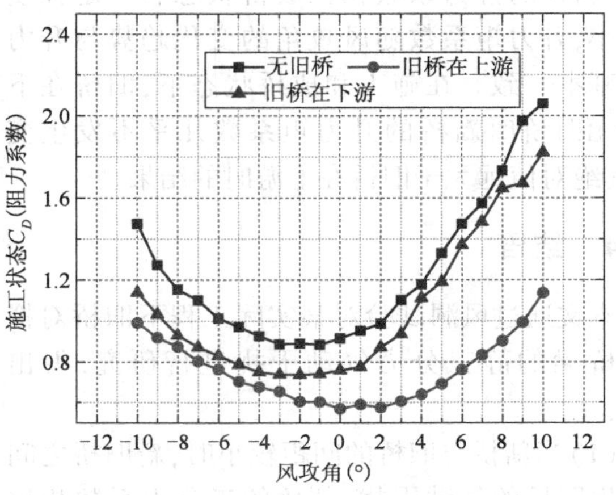

图10　施工状态阻力系数-风攻角

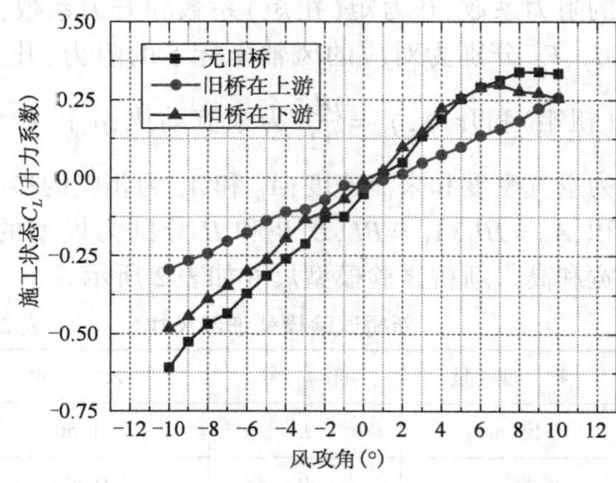

图 11　施工状态升力系数-风攻角

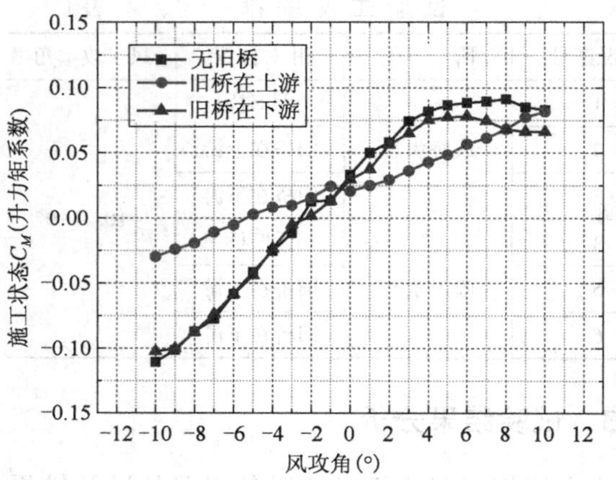

图 12　施工状态升力矩系数-风攻角

由以上试验结果可知,新旧桥梁之间存在明显的三分力系数干扰效应,在成桥状态和施工状态下,新桥的阻力系数都是在无旧桥时最大。成桥状态下,当旧桥在上游时,会对新桥产生明显的遮挡效应,导致新桥的阻力系数在各个风攻角下均减小 30% 左右;当旧桥在下游时,也会产生一定的气动干扰,导致新桥的阻力系数减小 10% ~ 15%,在各风攻角下均保持较好的规律性。施工阶段的阻力系数也有着相似的规律性,相比于成桥阶段,新桥在施工阶段各工况下的阻力系数都减小了 30% 左右,这表明二期附属设施对桥梁气动外形的影响较大,从而显著影响了其三分力系数的大小。在成桥状态下,通过图 8 可以看到新桥的升力系数在正攻角时受到旧桥的影响相对较小,在负攻角时相对于无旧桥的情况,旧桥在上游时新桥的升力系数在 -10°攻角时减小了 50% 左右,随着攻角的变化,其偏差逐渐减小。在施工状态下,新桥的升力系数相比成桥状态有一定程度的减小,升力矩系数随风攻角的变化趋势与升力系数基本一致。在施工和成桥状态下,旧桥在下游和无旧桥时新桥的升力矩系数几乎不发生变化,其绝对值远大于旧桥在上游时的结果。

4　结语

本文通过风洞试验对某实际工程下旧桥对拟新建桥梁的静三分力气动干扰进行研究,得出结论:

(1)当新桥与旧桥的间距较小时,新旧桥之间会产生明显的气动干扰,新桥的三分力系数相比于无旧桥时有明显的变化。

(2)旧桥对新桥存在明显的遮挡效应,当旧桥在上游时,新桥的阻力系数有明显的减小,相对于无旧桥时偏差可达 30% 以上。

(3)新桥的升力系数和升力矩系数的变化对于风攻角的改变较为敏感,当风攻角为负时,各工况升力系数和升力矩系数的偏差非常大,在正攻角时偏差较小。

(4)在新桥的成桥状态与施工状态下测得的三分力系数有明显偏差,说明防撞栏杆、检修车轨道等附属设施对三分力系数的影响是比较显著的。

在我国现有的公路桥梁抗风规范中,对于主梁的风荷载并未考虑并行桥梁的气动干扰,这可能会导致新桥在设计和施工时产生一系列问题。本文可为类似断面的新旧桥梁提供一定的设计依据,但是桥梁的静三分力对于主梁外形十分敏感。由于时间关系,本文只研究了某实际工程下的新旧桥的气动干扰,后续将对各种桥梁典型断面进行系统的研究,为新旧并行桥梁的设计以及规范提供依据。

参考文献

[1] 楼小峰,曹产,林志兴. 串列钝体绕流的数值计算[J]. 同济大学学报(自然科学版),2002,(5):604-608.

[2] 陈素琴,黄自萍,沈剑华,等. 两串列方柱绕流的干扰数值研究[J]. 同济大学学报(自然科学版),2001,(3):320-325.

[3] 郭震山,孟晓亮,周奇,等. 既有桥梁对邻近新建桥梁三分力系数的气动干扰效应[J]. 工程力学,2010,27(9):181-186 +200.

[4] 郭春平,白桦,洪光. 双幅桥静分力系数气动干扰效应研究[J]. 重庆交通大学学报(自然

科学版),2011,30(5):899-902+942.
[5] 苟国涛,叶征伟,项贻强,等.双幅并行连续刚构桥箱梁断面三分力系数气动干扰效应数值模拟[J].公路工程,2013,38(2):196-201.
[6] 刘志文,陈政清.串列双幅典型断面三分力系数气动干扰效应[J].振动与冲击,2015,34(5):6-13.
[7] 刘志文,陈政清,胡建华,等.大跨度双幅桥面桥梁气动干扰效应[J].长安大学学报(自然科学版),2008,28(6):55-59.
[8] 陈政清,刘小兵,刘志文.双幅桥面桥梁三分力系数的气动干扰效应研究[J].工程力学,2008(7):87-93.
[9] 陈政清,牛华伟,李春光.并列双箱梁桥面风致涡激振动试验研究[J].湖南大学学报(自然科学版),2007(9):16-20.
[10] 陈政清,牛华伟,刘志文.平行双箱梁桥面颤振稳定性试验研究[J].振动与冲击,2006(6):54-58+178.
[11] 陈政清,牛华伟,刘志文.双幅桥面桥梁主梁气动干扰效应研究[J].桥梁建设,2007(6):9-12.

Strain-based Identification of Moving Truck Loads of Short-span Steel Bridges

Jun Wu*[1] Ming Yang[1] Kai Dong[1] Fan Yang[2]
(1. Department of Bridge Engineering, Chang'an University;
2. China Communication's Highway Investment and Construction Company-Hainan Division Ltd.)

Abstract As the long-term repetitive dynamic loading, the vehicle load, especially the truck load, is one of the dominant causes of bridge deterioration, and the occasional overloading may lead to bridge collapse. The monitoring and measurement of the truck loads with high accuracy can be very helpful to assess the performance of bridges. The traditional vehicle weighing way, theoretically, cannot achieve high accuracy in measuring dynamic load. Comparatively, identifying the vehicle loads through the bridge response is a new way of great potential. In this paper, the identification of light-truck and heavy-truck loads for a typical short-span steel bridge is studied. The time history of truck load is identified through the generalized orthogonal function of the bridge strain. The Tikhonov regularization technique is applied to solve the unstable problem of the inverse dynamic problem. The influence of critical parameters of bridge model's element number, vehicle speed, road roughness, and signal noise areanalysed. From the results of numerical simulation, the identification accuracy is significantly influenced by signal noise, and the result of light truck is better than that of heavy truck.

Keywords Bridge-vehicle interaction Truck load identification Steel bridge Tikhonov regularization technique

0 Introduction

The vehicle loads, especially truck loads, have significant impact on bridges' serviceability and durability. As one of the most frequent and long-term external forces, the vehicle load causes bridge's dynamic vibration and fatigue problem. Thus, the identification of the moving vehicle load is a critical problem for bridge's health monitoring system.

At present, the widely-used instruments of measuring vehicle load on bridge are static scale and pavement weigh-in-motion (WIM) system. The static scale is time-consuming and disturbs the traffic flow. The pavement WIM, buried under the pavement, the installment and maintenance is inconvenient and costly. In recent years, more researchers have started to develop a more efficient and economic WIM system, i. e. the Bridge WIM (B-WIM). The core technology of the B-WIM is that the vehicle identification is realized through measuring the bridge response. In 1979, Moses firstly proposed the concept of B-WIM: identifying the vehicle load through bridges' influence line. This is an efficient way to identify the static vehicle load for short-span bridge and culvert. Further, researchers proposed the dynamic B-WIM algorithm, which is also called the moving force identification (MFI). MFI can obtain the vehicle load time-history of the whole process crossing the bridge. With the efforts of scholars, MFI has made great progress. The bridge type has developed from simply supported girder bridge to continuous girder bridge, and the vehicle model has developed from simple moving load to moving mass-stiffness-damping system model. More new methods are introduced to MFI. Dowling et al. utilized the first order regularization method in the back-casting algorithm. Chen et al. identified vehicle axle loads from bridge responses using preconditioned least square QR-factorization algorithm. Liu et al. shortened the sample length of bridge response by applying compressed sensing theory. In order to reduce the influence of random effect on vehicle identification, Wu and Law proposed a random identification algorithm, which successfully improved the calculation accuracy of MFI algorithm. Mohammed proposed a moving load identification method that can reduce the calculation time, making real-time load monitoring possible.

Besides, the input parameter of B-WIM has several choices. Researchers tried the bending moment, the mode shape, the displacement and the strain. Among them, strain is the most common used index and has better accuracy. Up to now, the basic framework of MFI is established while further work needs to be conducted to improve each module's efficiency and applicability. We find there are few studies focusing on comparing the accuracy of load identification for different vehicle types.

In this paper, we mainly focus on the sensitivity analysis of key parameters influencing the moving load identification's accuracy under different truck types. The first part is to introduce the inversed dynamic method to identify the vehicle loads through the bridge strain. Subsequently, a 20m steel bridge under two vehicle types (light truck and heavy truck) is studied. The robustness of the method is verified for parameters including element numbers, vehicle speed, measurement noise, and road roughness.

1 Identification method of moving vehicle load

1.1 Forward calculation of vehicle-bridge system

The vehicle-bridge system is presented in Fig. 1. The vehicle model is composed of mass, stiffness, and damping. The load $\mathbf{P}_{\text{int}}$ transmitted from the vehicle to the bridge includes two parts: static and dynamic part. With the assumption of Rayleigh damping, the motions of bridge and vehicle can be expressed by the following equations, respectively.

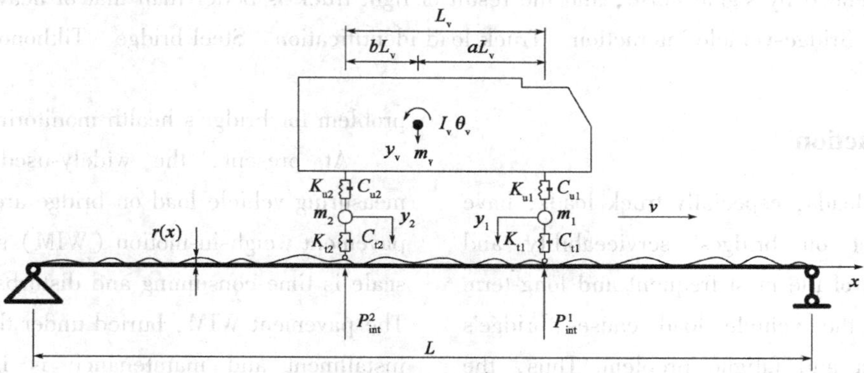

Fig. 1 Vehicle-Bridge Model

$$\mathbf{M}_b\ddot{\mathbf{Y}}_b + \mathbf{C}_b\dot{\mathbf{Y}}_b + \mathbf{K}_b\mathbf{Y}_b = \mathbf{H}_c\mathrm{P}_{int} \quad (1a)$$

$$\mathbf{M}_v\ddot{\mathbf{Y}}_v + \mathbf{C}_v\dot{\mathbf{Y}}_v + \mathbf{K}_v\mathbf{Y}_v = \mathbf{P}_{sta} - \mathbf{P}_{int} \quad (1b)$$

where **M**, **C**, **K** are the mass, damping and stiffness respectively. **Y**, $\dot{\mathbf{Y}}$ and $\ddot{\mathbf{Y}}$ are the vectors of vertical displacement, velocity and acceleration, respectively. Subscripts b and v denote bridge and vehicle, respectively. $\mathbf{H}_c$ is the conversion vector of $\mathbf{P}_{int}$ to the bridge's nodal load, which is composed of 0 and the Hermitian cubic interpolation shape functions (Law et al., 2004). $\mathbf{P}_{sta}$ is the static load of the vehicle.

The interaction force of axle i between the vehicle and the bridge can be calculated through:

$$P_{int}^i = K_{ti}[y_{vi} - y_b(x_i(t)) - r(x_i(t))] + C_{ti}[\dot{y}_{vi} - \dot{y}_b(x_i(t))] + [m_i + (b - a_i)m_v]g \quad (2)$$

where y denotes the vertical displacements; $x(t)$ is the position of the axle i at time t; $r(x_i(t))$ is the road roughness at the position of axle i, K_{ti}, C_{ti} is the tire stiffness and damping of the axle i. The aim of this study is to identify the value of P_{int}^i.

Combining Equation. (1) and (2), the vehicle-bridge's coupling system can be written as:

$$\begin{bmatrix} \mathrm{M}_b & \mathrm{M}_{bv} \\ 0 & \mathrm{M}_v \end{bmatrix}\begin{Bmatrix} \ddot{\mathrm{Y}}_b \\ \ddot{\mathrm{Y}}_v \end{Bmatrix} + \begin{bmatrix} \mathrm{C}_b & \mathrm{C}_{bv} \\ 0 & \mathrm{C}_v \end{bmatrix}\begin{Bmatrix} \dot{\mathrm{Y}}_b \\ \dot{\mathrm{Y}}_v \end{Bmatrix} + \begin{bmatrix} \mathrm{K}_b & \mathrm{K}_{bv} \\ 0 & \mathrm{K}_v \end{bmatrix}\begin{Bmatrix} \mathrm{Y}_b \\ \mathrm{Y}_v \end{Bmatrix} = \begin{Bmatrix} \mathrm{H}_c\mathrm{P}_{sta} \\ 0 \end{Bmatrix} \quad (3)$$

Equation (3) can be solved through the Newmark-Beta method to obtain the bridge's nodaldisplacement $\mathbf{Y}_b$. The bridge's strain ε can be computed through the bridge's displacement:

$$\varepsilon(x,t) = \left(-h\frac{\partial^2 H(x)}{\partial x^2}\right)y_b(t) = uy_b(t) \quad (4)$$

where $H(x)$ is the component of h is the distance between the lower surface and the neutral axis of the bridge's cross section $u = -h\{u_1(x), u_2(x), \cdots, u_N(x)\}$, a vector composed of the second derivatives of H_i. H_i is the component of the Hermitian cubic interpolation shape function.

In matrix form, Equation (4) can be written as:

$$\varepsilon = U\mathbf{Y}_b \quad (5)$$

where: $U = -h\begin{bmatrix} u_1(x_1) & u_2(x_1) & \cdots & u_N(x_1) \\ u_1(x_2) & u_2(x_2) & \cdots & u_N(x_2) \\ \vdots & \vdots & \vdots & \vdots \\ u_1(x_{Ns}) & u_2(x_{Ns}) & \cdots & u_N(x_{Ns}) \end{bmatrix}$;

$\mathbf{Y}_b = \{y_{b1}(t), y_{b2}(t), \cdots, y_{bN_s}(t)\}^T$.

1.2 Backward calculation of vehicle load

The vehicle load can be identified through the bridge response: deflection-related indicators (deflection, strain), internal forces (reactions, bending moment), and dynamic indicators (acceleration, mode shape etc.). In this paper, the strain is taken as the indicators for vehicle load's identification. In the following part, we derived the relationship between the moving vehicle load and the strain of the bridge.

If the number of measuring strain points is N_s, the strains at location $\{x_1, x_2, \cdots, x_{N_s}\}$ can be expressed by the matrix form:

$$\varepsilon = \mathbf{CT} \quad (6)$$

where $\varepsilon = \{\varepsilon(x_1, t), \varepsilon(x_2, t), \cdots, \varepsilon(x_{N_s}, t)\}^T$ and $\mathbf{T} = \{T_0(t), T_1(t), \cdots, T_{N_f}(t)\}^T$. N_f is the number of terms for the generalized orthogonal function. $T_i(t)$ is the generalized orthogonal function, for example, Chebyshev polynomial of the first kind; the element of matrix C needs to be determined. By the least-squares method, we obtain the coefficient matrix C:

$$\mathbf{C} = \varepsilon\mathbf{T}^T(\mathbf{TT}^T)^{-1} \quad (7)$$

Through the least-square method and substituting Equation. (7) into Equation. (5), we obtain:

$$\mathbf{Y}_b = (\mathbf{G}^T\mathbf{G})^{-1}\mathbf{G}^T\varepsilon = (\mathbf{G}^T\mathbf{G})^{-1}\mathbf{G}^T\mathbf{CT} \quad (8a)$$

$$\dot{Y}_b = (\mathbf{G}^T\mathbf{G})^{-1}\mathbf{G}^T\mathbf{C}\dot{\mathbf{T}} \quad (8b)$$

$$\ddot{\mathrm{Y}}_b = (\mathbf{G}^T\mathbf{G})^{-1}\mathbf{G}^T\mathbf{C}\ddot{\mathbf{T}} \quad (8c)$$

Substituting Equation. (8) into Equation (1a), we can calculate theidentified moving vehicle load $\mathbf{P}_{ide}$:

$$\mathbf{\Phi} = \mathbf{H}_c\mathbf{P}_{ide} \quad (9)$$

where $\mathbf{\Phi} = \mathrm{M}_b\ddot{\mathrm{Y}}_b + \mathrm{C}_b\dot{\mathrm{Y}}_b + \mathrm{K}_b\mathrm{Y}_b$. It should be noted that in Equation. (1), it is a general equation to compute the interaction load between vehicle and bridge. Thus, it can also be used to calculate the identified vehicle load P_{ide}.

Inherently, Equation. (9) is an ill-conditioned

problem, which cannot be solved directly by least-square method. In this study, the Tikhonov regularization is applied to avoid the ill-conditioned problem:

$$J(\mathbf{P},\lambda) = \| \mathbf{BP}_{ide} - \mathbf{\Phi} \|^2 + \lambda \| \mathbf{P}_{ide} \| \quad (10)$$

where λ is the optimal regularization value and can be determined by L-curve method, $\| \cdot \|$ is the norm of matrix.

The identified moving vehicle load can then be computed by:

$$\mathbf{P}_{\text{ide}} = (\mathbf{H}_c^T\mathbf{H}_c + \lambda\mathbf{I})\mathbf{H}_c^T\mathbf{\Phi} \quad (11)$$

whereI is the identify matrix.

1.3 Error Quantification

To quantify the result's accuracy from the above-mentioned method, the relative percentage error between real value and identified value is calculated as:

$$E_r = \frac{\| \mathbf{P}_{\text{ide}} - \mathbf{P}_{\text{int}} \|_2}{\| \mathbf{P}_{\text{int}} \|_2} \times 100\% \quad (12)$$

2 Numerical simulations

2.1 Bridge and vehicle model

In this study, a 20m simply-supported steel box girder bridge (Fig. 2) is taken as the prototype bridge. The bridge is designed according to the Chinese bridge design code (JTG D60—2015). The bridge uses Q235 steel and its mechanical parameters are shown in Tab. 1.

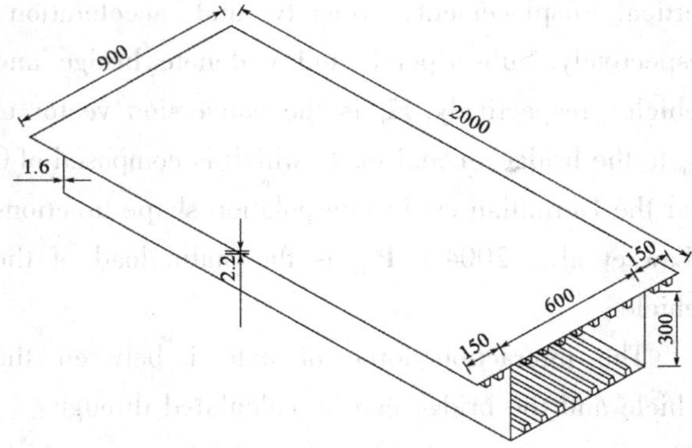

Fig. 2　Finite element model of the bridge (Unit: cm)

The road surface roughness is set according to Equation. (13) (ISO 8608, 1995):

$$r(x) = \sum_{k=1}^{N}\sqrt{2S(\bar{\phi}_k)\Delta\bar{\phi}}\cos(2\pi\bar{\phi}_k x + \theta_k) \quad (13)$$

where $\bar{\phi}$ (cycle/m) is the spatial frequency; $\bar{\phi}_k$ is the wave number and N is the number of frequencies; Δ is the distance interval between successive ordinates of the surface profile; θ_k is the random phase angle uniformly distributed between 0 and 2π; $S(\bar{\phi}_k)$ (cycle/m) is the PSD function for road surface roughness.

Physical and Material Parameters of Bridge　　Tab. 1

Item	Density (kg/m³)	Area (m²)	Moment of inertia (m⁴)	Elastic modulus (N/m²)	Damping ratio
Value	7850	0.526	0.96001	2.1E11	0.3%

The vehicle model adopts half-vehicle model (Fig. 1) with two axles. We use two vehicle types—light truck and heavy truck— to conduct the load identification analysis. The static weight of the light truck is 2970kg, and the heavy truck is 20235kg. The axle distances of them are 2.66m and 4.27m, respectively. The main parameters of two vehicles are shown in Tab. 2.

Physical and material parameters of bridge　　Tab. 2

Parameter	Unit	Light truck	Heavy truck
[a b L_v]	m	[0.35 0.65 2.66]	[0.519 0.481 4.27]
[m_v m_1 m_2]	kg	[1460 800 710]	[17735 1500 1000]
I_v	kg·m²	1.52E3	1.47E5
[K_{u1} K_{u2}]	N/m	[3.99E5 3.99E5]	[2.47E6 4.23E6]
[K_{t1} K_{t2}]	N/m	[3.51E5 3.51E5]	[3.74E6 4.60E6]
[C_{u1} C_{u2}]	N·s/m	[2.32E4 5.18E3]	[3.00E4 4.00E4]
[C_{t1} C_{t2}]	N·s/m	[8.00E2 8.00E2]	[3.90E3 4.30E3]

2.2 Simulation results

The load identification of two trucks is conducted considering the cases under different bridge's element number, vehicle speed, road surface roughness, and noise level. The error quantification is computed based on Equation(12).

The baseline bridge-vehicle coupling model is: the bridge model is discretized uniformly into $N_b = 10$ elements; the vehicle moves with v = 15m/s (54km/h); the road roughness profile is Class B (ISO 8608, 1995); the strain measured with 5% signal noise expressed as:

$$\varepsilon = \varepsilon_o(1 + E_p N_{oi}) \tag{14}$$

where ε and ε_o are the vectors of measured and actual responses, E_p is the noise level (in this part, $E_p = 5\%$), and N_{oi} is a standard normal distribution vector with zero mean and unit standard deviation.

The baseline model's load identification results are shown in Fig. 3. In the figure, N_b means the element number of the bridge. $\mathbf{P}_{ide}$ is the identified vehicle load, $\mathbf{P}_{int}$ is the realistic interaction force between bridge and vehicle, and $\mathbf{P}_{sta}$ is the vehicle's static axle load, which is calculated by $(m_1 + bm_v)g$ and $(m_2 + am_v)g$ for the front and rear axle, respectively. According to the parameters listed in Tab.2, the $\mathbf{P}_{sta}$ is [17.14 11.97] kN of two axles for light truck, and [98.3 100] kN for heavy truck. As shown in Fig. 3, the identification results (blue line) are close to the realistic value (red line), and they fluctuate around vehicle's static axle load (green line).

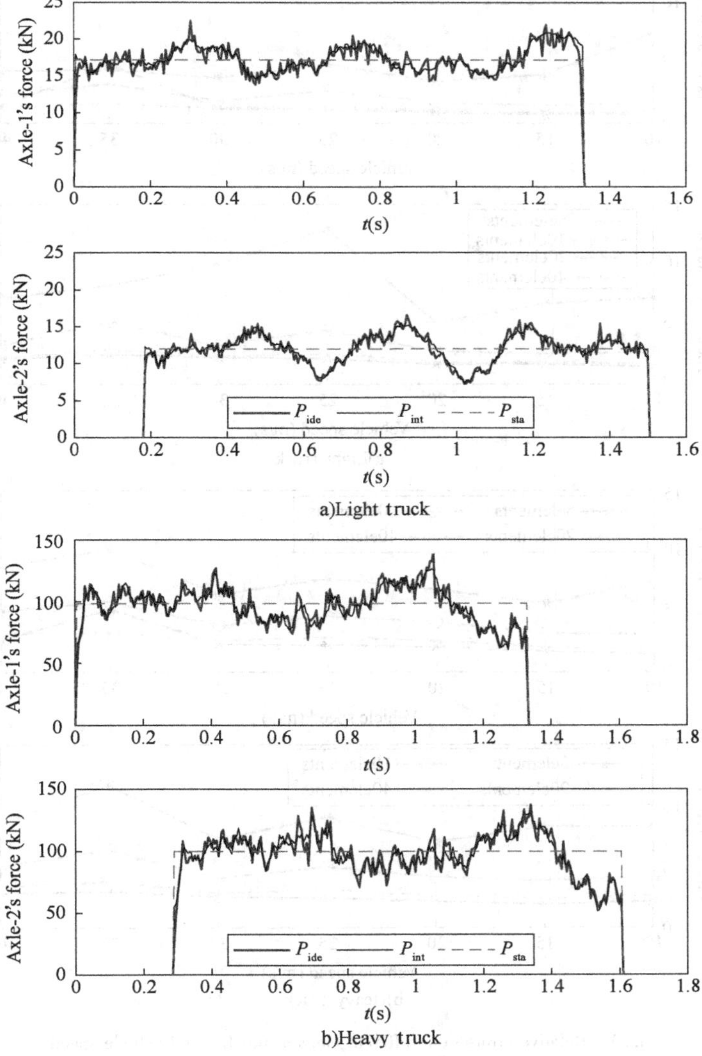

Fig. 3 Load identification (v = 15m/s, $N_b = 10$)

2.2.1 Influence of bridge's element number and vehicle speed

For comparison, we observed the identification results under different bridge's element number Nb (5 to 20) and vehicle speed v (10, 15, 20, 25, 30, 35, 40m/s). Different N_b implies different number of strain's measuring points. In this study, the strain gauges are set at the model's node except the two ends of the beam.

Theidentification error E_r obtained through Equation(12) is shown in Fig. 4 for light truck and heavy truck. For most cases, E_r decreased with the increasing of N_b. When $N_b \geqslant 10$, the identification error's difference is small among different bridge's element numbers, and the identification error does not fluctuate largely under different vehicle speed. For axle-1, the relative error is 0.74% to 4.89% for light truck, and 1.46% to 5.82% for heavy truck. For axle-2, the relative errors of light and heavy truck change from 1.38% to 5.16%, and from 1.89% to 6.41%, respectively. In general, the relative error is slightly affected by the vehicle speed, and the axle-1 has better identification than axle-2. The light truck's identification accuracy is higher than the heavy truck.

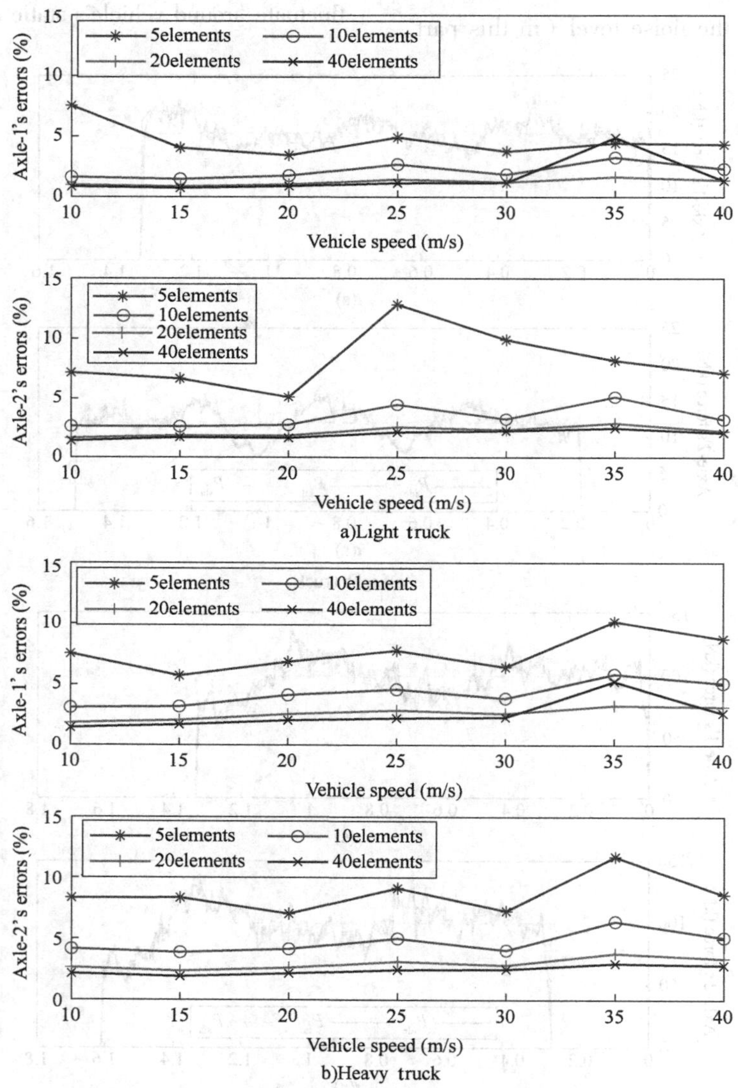

Fig. 4 Relative errors from different element number and vehicle speed

2.2.2 Influence of road roughness and signal noise

In this part, the identification error under different road roughness profiles and noise levels are discussed and the results are shown in Fig. 5. Three road roughness cases are taken into account of "B", "C", and "D" classes. Four noise levels E_p (0, 5%, 10% and 15%) are simulated according to Equation(14).

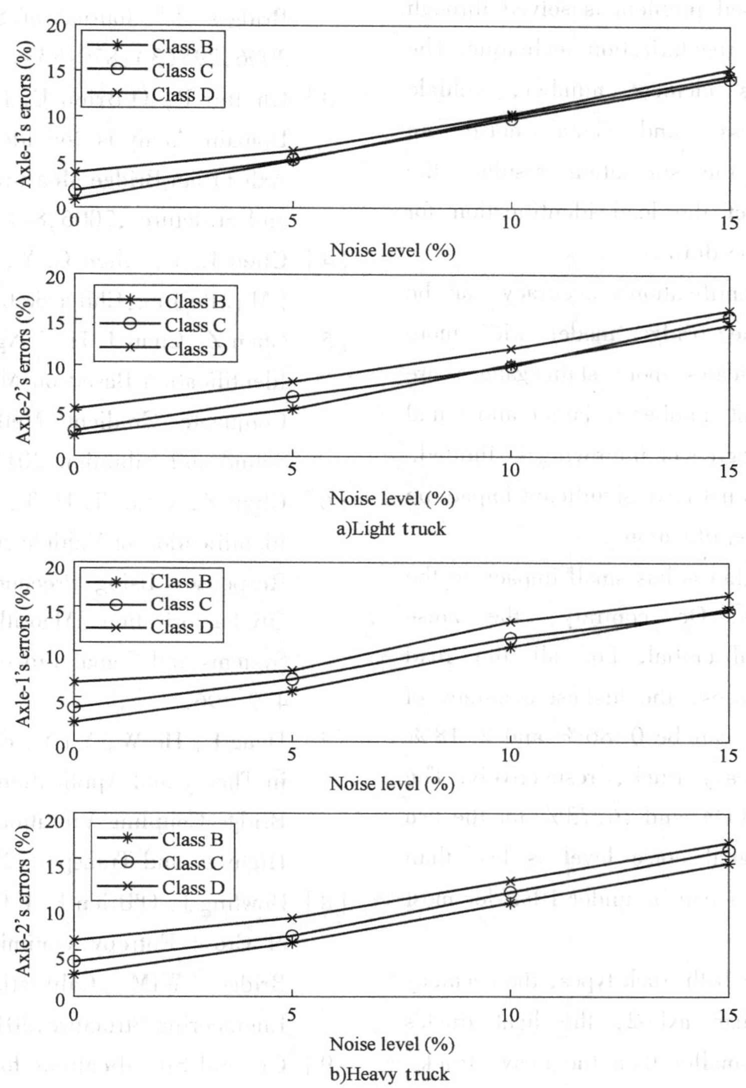

Fig. 5 Relative errors from different road roughness and signal noise

As shown in Fig. 5, the identification errors increased with the noise level and the unevenness degree of road roughness. Obviously, the noise level has significant impact on relative errors, while the road roughness's impact is small. For all levels of noise and roughness, the light truck's errors of axle-1 and axle-2 rang from 0.86% to 15.31%, and 2.29% to 16.11%, respectively. Regarding the heavy truck, the errors range from 2.18% to 16.40% of axle-1, 2.34% to 16.73% of axle-2. In general, the error of axle-1 is less than around 1% of axle-2 for both trucks. The error of light truck is less than around 1% of heavy truck.

3 Conclusions

In this paper, a light truck and a heavy truck with two axles are identified on a 20m simply-supported steel box girder bridge. The bridge's strain is taken as the identification indicator and the time-domain dynamic inversed problem is solved through applying the Tikhonov regularization technique. The influences of bridge's element number, vehicle speed, road roughness, and signal noise are discussed. Based on the simulation results, the following conclusions of the load identification for different vehicles can be drawn:

(1) The load identification's accuracy can be improved if using the bridge model with more elements, which implicates more stain gauges are used. When the element number is larger and equal to 10 elements, the degree of improving is limited. The vehicle speed does not have significant impact on the accuracy of load identifications.

(2) The road roughness has small impact on the identification accuracy. On contrary, the noise signal's impact is substantial. For all the road roughness and noise cases, the highest accuracy of axle load identification can be 0.86% and 2.18% for light truck and heavy truck, respectively. The lowest accuracy is 16.11% and 16.73% for the two truck types. If the signal noise level is less than 10%, the relative errors can be under 10% for most cases.

(3) In general, for both truck types, the accuracy of axle-1 is higher than axle-2, the light truck's identification error is smaller than the heavy truck. The difference of identification accuracy between the two trucks is less than 1%, which means that the truck weight's influence on identification accuracy is trivial.

4 Acknowledgements

This work was supported by Natural Science Foundation of Shaanxi Province (2020JM-230), and the Fundamental Research Funds for the Central Universities (CHD 300102219220).

References

[1] Chan T. H. T, Law S. S, Yung T. H. An Interpretive Method for Movin Force Identification[J]. Journal of Sound and Vibration, 1999, 219(3): 503-524.

[2] Chan T. H. T, Ashebo D. B. Theoretical Study of Moving Force Identification on Continuous Bridges[J]. Journal of Sound and Vibration, 2006, 295(3): 870-833.

[3] Chatter P, O'Brien E. J, Lia Y. Y. Wavelet Domain Analysis for Identification of Vehicle Axles from Bridge Measurements[J]. Computers and Structures, 2006, 84(28): 1792-1801.

[4] Chen L. Y, Chen C. Y, Liu F. X. Statistics [M]. BeiJing: China Statistics Press, 2015.

[5] Chen Z, Chan T. H. T, Nguyen A. Moving Force Identification Based on Modified Preconditioned Conjugate Gradient Method [J]. Journal of Sound and Vibration, 2015, 423(9): 100-117.

[6] Chen Z, Chan T. H. T, Nguyen A, et al. Identification of Vehicle Axle Loads from Bridge Responses Using Preconditioned Least Square QR-Factorization Algorithm [J]. Mechanical Systems and Signal Processing, 2009, 128(1): 479-496.

[7] Deng L, He W, Yu Y, et al. Research Progress in Theory and Applications of Highway Vehicle-Bridge Coupling Vibration[J]. China Journal of Highway and Transport, 2018, 31(7): 38-54.

[8] Dowling J, O'Brien E. J, Gonzǘlez A. Adaptation of Cross Entropy Optimization to A Dynamic Bridge WIM Calibration Problem [J]. Engineering Structure, 2012, 44: 13-22.

[9] General Specifications for Design of Highway Bridges and Culverts: JTG D60—2015 [S]. Beijing: China Communications Press, 2015.

[10] Hansen P. C. Analysis of Discrete Ill-Posed Problems by Means of the L-curve[J]. Siam Review, 1992, 34(4): 561-580.

[11] Henchi K, Fafard M, Talbot M. An Efficient Algorithm for Dynamic Analysis of Bridges Under Moving Vehicles Using A Coupled Modal and Physical Components Approach [J]. Journal of Sound and Vibration, 1998,

212(4):112-175.

[12] ISO 8608,(1995). Mechanical Vibration-Road Surface Profiles-Reporting of Measured Data.

[13] Law S. S, Chan T. H. T, Zeng Q. H. Moving Force Identification: A Time Domain Method [J]. Journal of Sound and Vibration, 1997, 201(1):1-22.

[14] Law S. S, Fang Y. L. Moving Force Identification: Optimal State Estimation Approach[J]. Journal of Sound and Vibration, 2001, 239(2):233-254.

[15] Law S. S, Chan T. H. T, Zhu X. Q, et al. Regularization in Moving Force Identification [J]. Journal of Engineering Mechanics, 2001, 127(2):136-148.

[16] Law S. S, Bu J. Q, Zhu X. Q, et al. Vehicle Axle Loads Identification Using Finite Element Method[J]. Engineering Structures, 2004, 26(8):1143-1153.

[17] Law S. S, Wu S. Q, Shi Z. Y. Moving Load and Prestress Identification Using Wavelet-Based Method[J]. Journal of Applied Mechanics, 2008, 7(2):021014.

[18] Law S. S, Wu S. Q. Vehicle Axle Load Identification on Bridge Deck with Irregular Road Surface Profile [J]. Engineering Structures, 2011, 33(2):591-601.

[19] Law S. S, Wu S. Q. Statistical Moving Load Identification Including Uncertainty [J]. Probabilistic Engineering Mechanics, 2012, 29(2):70-78.

[20] Liu H, Yu L, Luo Z. W, et al. Compressed Sensing for Moving Force Identification Using Redundant Dictionaries [J]. Mechanical Systems and Signal Processing, 2020, 138:106535.

[21] Moses F. Weigh-in-motion System Using Instrumented Bridges [J]. Journal of Transportation Engineering, 1979, 105(3): 233-249.

[22] Mohammed Y. M, Uddin N, O'Brien E. J. Moving Force Identification for Real-time Bridge Weigh-in-motion [J]. Bridge Structures, 2018, 14(4):139-145.

[23] O'Connor C, Chan T. H. T. Dynamic Wheel Loads from Bridge Strains [J]. Journal of Structural Engineering, 1988, 114(8): 1703-1723.

[24] O'Connor C, Chan T. H. T. Wheel Loads from Bridge Strains: Laboratory Studies [J]. Journal of Structural Engineering, 1988, 114(8):1724-1740.

[25] Pei J, Wu Y. C, Li S. C. Chebyshev Polynomial [M]. Harbin: Harbin Institute of Technology Press.

[26] Wu S. Q, Law S. S. Moving Force Identification Based on Stochastic Finite Element Model [J]. Journal of Sound and Vibration, 2010, 20(1):10-32.

[27] Wu S. Q, Law S. S. Vehicle Axle Load Identification on Bridge Deck with Irregular Road Surface Profile[J]. Journal of Sound and Vibration, 2011, 21(3):8-25.

[28] Xiao H. Z, Wen Y. H, Wei X. R. Vehicle Weight Identification for A Bridge with Multi-T-Girders Based on Load Transverse Distribution Coefficient [J]. Advances in Structural Engineering, 2019, 22(16): 3435-3443.

[29] Yuan X. R, Chen E. L, Yang, S. P. Identification of Moving Loads by Response of Orthotropic Plates[J]. Journal of Vibration, Measurement and Diagnosis, 1995(3):30-34.

[30] Zhu X. Q, Law S. S. Identification of Vehicle Axle Loads from Bridge Dynamic Responses [J]. Journal of Sound and Vibration, 2000, 236(4):705-724.

爆炸作用下空心板损伤及铺装层影响分析

曹思源*[1]　徐　岳[1]　董尧一[2]　刘文强[3]
(1.长安大学公路学院;2.中铁西安勘察设计研究院有限责任公司;
3.中交瑞通路桥养护科技有限公司)

摘　要　为研究铺装层的设置方式对爆炸作用下混凝土空心板桥动力响应的影响,本文基于任意拉格朗日-欧拉法(ALE法),采用有限元软件LS-DYNA进行数值模拟以及不同铺装层设置形式的空心板数值分析。研究表明,当爆炸高度为1.5m,炸药TNT当量为12.5kg时,炸点正下方空心板挖空处顶端、桥面铺装层部分单元首先失效,空心板于1/4跨径处产生纵桥向裂缝,并有向失效区贯通的趋势;考虑铺装层与铺装层内钢筋网明显减小了空心板顶的超压及竖向挠度峰值,为提高数值模拟准确性,在进行桥梁结构爆炸作用数值分析时考虑铺装层是有必要的,无铺装层模型与有铺装层空心板模型于超压峰值和竖向位移峰值上的偏差与炸药当量成负相关。

关键词　公路桥梁　抗爆性能　ALE法　空心板　流固耦合

0　引言

随着我国交通网的日益完善,桥梁结构在面临爆炸等偶然荷载时所表现的脆弱性越发受到人们的重视。当桥梁承受爆炸作用时,其安全性能会大幅降低,容易造成严重的经济损失与社会影响。

对于桥梁结构爆炸作用的研究方向主要有材料本构模型的研究与验证、结构动态响应分析和桥梁受损评定。李世民等[1]研究了几种常用的混凝土动态损伤模型,分析了各模型优缺点,对混凝土抗冲击作用数值模拟有参考意义;Xiangzhen Kong等[2]、Wei Wang等[3]进行了爆炸作用下混凝土靶板的响应试验,得到了爆炸作用下混凝土靶板的损伤状况并进行了数值分析,验证了爆炸作用下混凝土本构模型的正确性;王芳等[4]对一组四边约束钢靶板在爆炸冲击波下的塑性大变形情况进行了试验,并采用钢板在塑性大变形时的半经验公式对试验结果进行了对比,结果表明所采用的钢板塑性大变形半经验公式与计算结果匹配,有良好的一致性;Li等[5]和Rong等[6]对梁式构件在爆炸冲击荷载下的动态响应进行了可靠性分析,重点研究了结构的变形与动力响应对各参数不确定性的敏感程度。

以上研究成果大多集中在爆炸作用下桥梁结构的响应与损伤分析,且在进行实桥爆炸模拟时,往往采用忽略铺装层或通过提高混凝土顶板厚度的方式简化模型,减少了数值分析的工作量,而这种简化方式对桥梁构件爆炸响应的影响程度尚不明确。为明确钢筋混凝土空心板的损伤机理,提高数值模拟的计算精度,在验证数值模拟方法正确性的前提下,本文研究铺装层的设置方式对空心板爆炸响应的影响程度,为桥梁结构抗爆性能研究提供参考。

1　爆炸作用的数值分析

1.1　爆炸作用模拟方法

爆炸作用是一种在极短时间内发生包含复杂物理、化学能量释放的作用,其发生过程短暂,往往在几百毫秒内完成,爆炸瞬间伴随着高温高压与碎屑侵彻。在处理多物质流固耦合问题时,根据材料所采用的计算网格坐标系的不同可以分为拉格朗日法、欧拉法与任意拉格朗日-欧拉法。

拉格朗日法认为材料依附空间网格,随着网格的运动而变形。该算法计算精度与计算效率较高,避免了计算物质材料输入所带来的误差,且物质截面与单元面重合,能够准确描述单元所在的位置,但该算法在结构发生大变形的情况下往往容易发生畸变,导致较大的数值计算误差,计算时间进一步延长,使运算无法运行。

欧拉法认为模型采用固定的空间网格进行计算,材料在固定的空间网格中流动。该方法由于空间网格不发生变化,不存在空间网格畸变的问题。

然而,该方法在计算物质间流动问题时会产生物质界面穿过单元,需要时间对运动的界面进行重建。

任意拉格朗日-欧拉法(ALE 法),结合了拉格朗日法与欧拉法的优点,将空间网格节点的速度作为独立的变量进行控制,在让物质界面的节点速度与材料速度相同的同时,使物质界面和单元的边界重合,能够准确刻画物质的边界,同时由于其采用了松弛算法,可以用于求解材料大变形的问题。

本文采用的 ALE 法相比于冲量法与经验公式法精度更高,并结合了欧拉法与拉格朗日法的优势,在爆炸作用的仿真模拟中最为常用。

1.2 材料本构模型与状态方程

材料本构模型与状态方程的选用对数值模拟结果的正确性至关重要[7],本文涉及的材料包括炸药、空气、混凝土及钢筋,不同的材料需要选择与实际情况相匹配的本构模型与状态方程。

采用 ALE 法进行流固耦合显式动力学分析时,TNT 炸药状态方程可采用爆轰产物状态方程(JWL)描述:

$$P=A\left(1-\frac{\omega}{R_1V}e^{-R_1V}\right)+B\left(1-\frac{\omega}{R_2V}\right)e^{-R_2V}+\frac{\omega E_0}{V} \tag{1}$$

式中:P——爆轰压力;

E_0——初始内能密度;

V——相对体积。

其余为 JWL 状态方程常数,具体取值见表 1。

炸药 JWL 状态方程参数 表 1

A(kPa)	B(kPa)	R_1	R_2	ω
3.71×10^8	3.23×10^6	4.15	0.95	0.35

空气状态方程可采用线性多项式描述:

$$P=C_0+C_1\mu+C_2\mu^2+C_3\mu^3+(C_4+C_5\mu+C_6\mu^2)E_0 \tag{2}$$

式中,$C_0=C_1=C_2=C_3=C_6=0$,$C_4=C_5=0.4$,均为多项式系数;$\mu=\rho_{air}/\rho_0-1$,其中 ρ_{air} 为空气当前密度,ρ_0 为空气初始密度;P 为爆轰压力,$E_0=2.5\times10^{-6}J$,为单位体积内能。

本文选择 RHT 模型作为混凝土在爆炸作用下的本构模型,模型涉及的相关参数见表 2。

混凝土 RHT 模型特征参数 表 2

f_t/f_c	f_s/f_c	G	a	N	Q	B_Q	$COMP$	$TENS$	B_r	M
0.1	0.18	16.7	1.6	0.61	0.6805	0.0105	0.53	0.7	1.6	0.61

ρ(g/cm³)	P_{crush}(MPa)	P_{lock}(MPa)	n	A_1	A_2	A_3
2.314	23.3	600	3	35.27	39.58	9.04

D_1	D_2	$E_{f,\min}$	$SHRATD$	T_1	T_2	B_0	B_1
0.1	0.18	16.7	1.6	0.61	0.6805	0.0105	0.53

表 2 中参数符号含义:f_t/f_c 为拉压强度比,f_s/f_c 为剪压强度比,G 为材料剪切模量,a、N 为失效面参数,Q 为拉压子午比参数,B_Q 为脆性韧性转化系数,$COMP$ 为单轴压缩弹性极限与单轴压缩强度比,$TENS$ 为单轴拉伸弹性极限与单轴拉伸强度比,B_r、M 为残余应力强度参数,$SHRATD$ 为残余剪切模量缩减系数,ρ 质量密度,A_1、A_2、A_3、B_0、B_1、T_1、T_2 为$p-alpha$ 状态方程的材料参数,P_{crush} 为孔隙开始压碎时的压力;P_{lock} 为孔隙压实时的压力,P_{lock} 为压缩指数,D_1、D_2 为损伤参数,$E_{f,\min}$ 为失效最小等效塑性应变。

钢筋本构模型可采用塑性随动模型:

$$\sigma_y=[1+(\dot{\varepsilon}/C)^{1/P}]\cdot(\sigma_0+\beta E_p\varepsilon_p^{eff}) \tag{3}$$

式中:σ_y——屈服应力;

$\dot{\varepsilon}$——应变率;

C、P——模型参数;

σ_0——静载屈服应力;

β——硬化参数;

E_p——塑性硬化模量;

ε_p^{eff}——有效塑性应变。

经对比分析,采用本节材料本构模型与状态方程能够有效模拟结构在实际爆炸下的动态响应,且损伤状况与现场试验结果匹配度较高,能够满足数值模拟的需求。

2 研究对象及有限元模型

为给爆炸作用下空心板桥的损伤分析奠定基础,现以空心板局部损伤特性分析为出发点,以 10m 跨径钢筋混凝土空心板桥为研究对象,取其中的两片混凝土空心板为主体结构,其单板构造如图 1 所示:桥面板长 1000cm,板宽 100cm,板厚 50cm,纵向钢筋直径 12mm,空心板其余钢筋 10mm,桥面铺装采用单层钢筋网,钢筋直径

10mm,间距10cm,空心板端面一侧定义为对称面,一侧释放纵桥向位移与全部转动约束;空气域尺寸75cm×50cm×200cm,除对称面外的其他边界面为无反射边界;炸药尺寸25cm×25cm×25cm,与空气域组成流体组;选择初始起爆高度1.5m,炸药当量12.5kg,爆轰中心在空心板水平中心正上方。

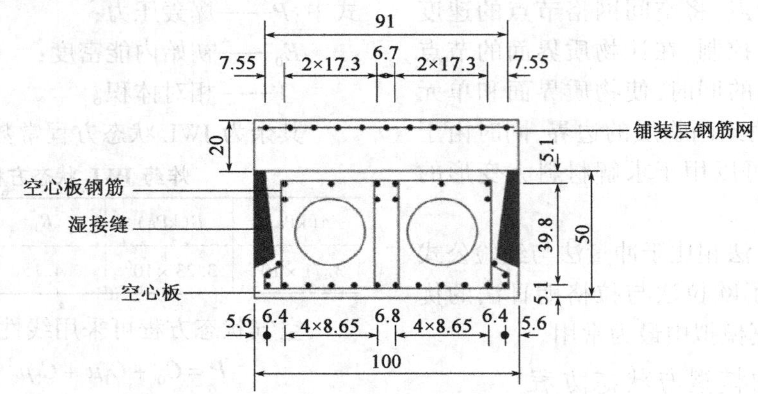

图1　空心板中板横截面构造(尺寸单位:cm)

通过结构的对称性简化模型,建立炸药、空气域、铺装层及空心板的1/4有限元模型,采用同1.2节的材料模型与相关参数,钢筋采用梁单元,其余均采用实体单元;钢筋采用共节点分离式布置,忽略钢筋与混凝土间的滑移,认为两种材料变形协调;混凝土铺装层与空心板间设置绑定接触;1/4有限元模型的梁单元和实体单元共计140.8万个。数值分析1/4有限元模型如图2所示(隐藏空气域与炸药模型)。

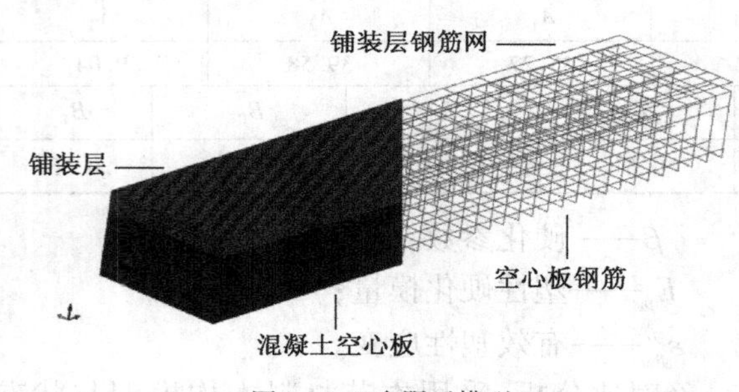

图2　1/4有限元模型

3　空心板动态力学响应与损伤分析

3.1　超压冲击波与结构破坏形式

RHT模型通过损伤度描述结构的损伤状况,损伤度越大,区域的损伤程度越高,当损伤度为1时,单元失效。当$t=0.3$ms时空心板损伤变化趋于稳定,图2镜像后的1/2空心板跨中损伤云图如图3所示,1/4空心板不同平面位置损伤云图如图4所示。

从图3可以看出,当爆炸发生时,炸药正下方空铺装层与空心板挖空处顶部首先发生失效,跨中截面空心板中度以上的损伤面积为0.21m^2。从图4可以看出,爆炸发生后铺装层底与空心板顶损伤较严重,约为2.16m^2;空心板底损伤范围有一定程度的增加,底部产生沿纵向钢筋与箍筋的裂缝,纵向裂缝最大长度达到1/2空心板跨径;空心板于支座处顶出现纵向裂缝;炸药正下方铺装层与空心板顶面发生不同程度的冲剪破坏,钢筋网发生弯曲并部分裸露,空心板产生明显下挠。

3.2　铺装层构造方式影响分析

为探究铺装层混凝土与铺装层钢筋网对空心板结构爆炸响应的影响程度,本文建立了不同铺装层处理形式的空心板有限元模型,统计空心板顶底损伤度大于0.5的损伤范围,如图5所示;空心板顶超压与板底竖向位移时程曲线如图6所示。

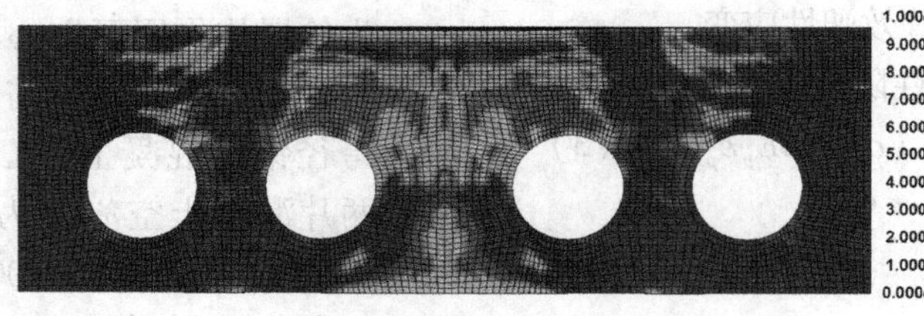

图3　空心板跨中截面损伤示意($t=0.2$ms)

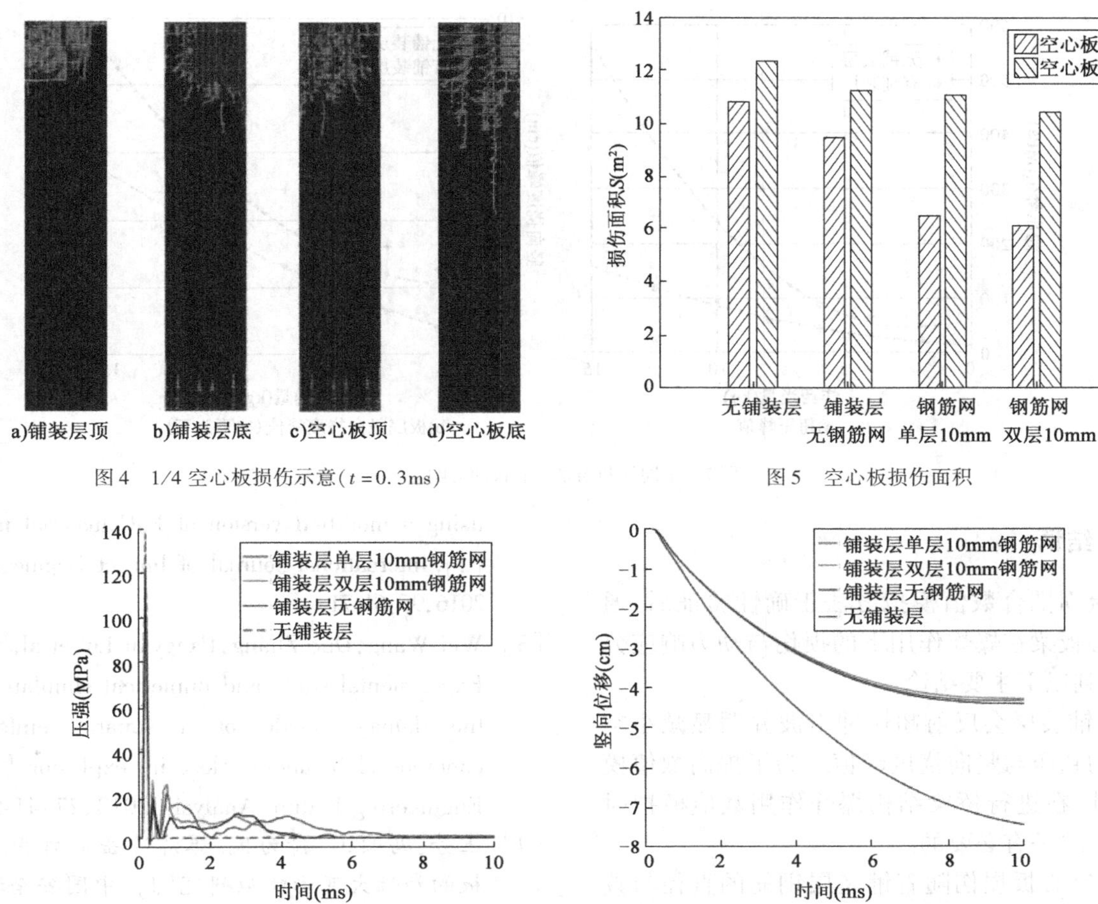

图4 1/4 空心板损伤示意($t=0.3\text{ms}$)

图5 空心板损伤面积

图6 空心板时程曲线

从图5可以看出,不同构造铺装层下空心板底损伤面积明显大于板顶,其中不设置铺装层时板顶与板底损伤最严重,板顶损伤面积为 10.8m^2,板底损伤面积为 12.3m^2,板顶与板底损伤面积较其他铺装处理形式分别扩大了 13% ~44% 与 9% ~16%;随着铺装层钢筋网数量的增加,空心板损伤面积逐渐减小,当采用双层 10mm 钢筋网时,空心板的板顶与板底损伤面积均最小,分别为 6.1m^2 与 10.4m^2。

从图6a)可以看出,不设置铺装层时空心板顶的超压峰值最大,为 137.8MPa,较其他铺装层处理方式增大了 13% ~29%,随着铺装层钢筋网数量的增加,空心板顶超压峰值逐渐减小,当采用双层 10mm 钢筋网时板顶超压峰值最小,为 97.3MPa;从图6b)可以看出,无铺装层的空心板竖向位移最大,为 7.4cm,其他铺装层处理方式板底竖向位移偏差不大,其中采用双层 10mm 钢筋网时板底竖向位移最小,为 4.2cm。

3.3 TNT 当量影响分析

为进一步探寻不同炸药当量对空心板动力响应的影响,计算不同 TNT 当量的炸心正下方空心板顶超压峰值与板底竖向位移峰值并采用二次多项式拟合,计算结果如图7所示。

从图7a)中可以看出,在不同炸药当量下,无铺装层的空心板炸心下方单元的超压峰值与板底竖向挠度均明显高于有铺装层空心板。当炸药当量为 12.5kg 时,无铺装空心板超压峰值为 341.9MPa,较有铺装空心板提高了 132.9MPa;当炸药当量为 1kg 时,无铺装空心板超压峰值为 249.1MPa,较有铺装空心板提高 132.9MPa。两者偏差仅为 30.1MPa,随着炸药当量的减小。两者的偏差也逐渐减小。空心板底的竖向位移峰值的绝对值也有相似的规律,如图7b)所示。有无铺装层的空心板超压峰值与竖向位移峰值的绝对值均与炸药当量成正相关,且随着炸药当量的提升,有无铺装层的动力响应峰值偏差逐渐变大。

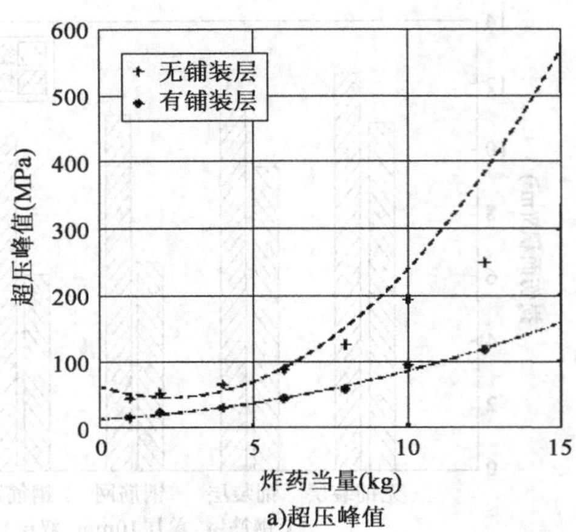

a)超压峰值

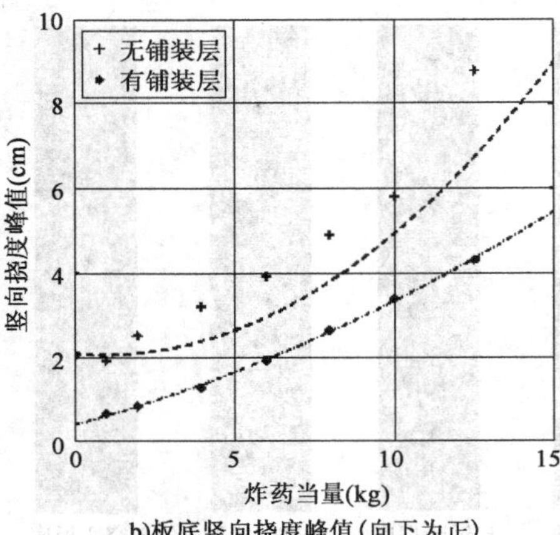

b)板底竖向挠度峰值(向下为正)

图7 不同炸药当量空心板动力响应

4 结语

在流固耦合数值模拟方法正确性验证后,通过对空心板梁在爆炸作用下的损伤与动力响应分析,可得到以下主要结论:

(1)铺装层会反射超压冲击波并明显减小空心板顶的超压与竖向挠度峰值。为了提高数值模拟准确性,在进行桥梁结构爆炸作用数值模拟时考虑铺装层是有必要的。

(2)空心板损伤随着铺装层钢筋的直径与数量的提高而增加,不同炸药当量下有铺装层的空心板动力响应峰值均低于无铺装层的空心板,无铺装层模型与有铺装层模型空心板超压峰值及竖向位移峰值的绝对值与比例距离成负相关,且两者间的偏差与比例距离成负相关。

参考文献

[1] 李世民,李晓军.几种常用混凝土动态损伤本构模型评述[J].混凝土,2011(6):19-22.

[2] Xiangzhen Kong, Qin Fang, Hao Wu, et al. Numerical predictions of cratering and scabbing in concrete slabs subjected to projectile impact using a modified version of HJC material model [J]. International Journal of Impact Engineering, 2016,95:61-71.

[3] Wei Wang, Duo Zhang, Fangyun Lu, et al. Experimental study and numerical simulation of the damage mode of a square reinforced concrete slab under close-in explosion [J]. Engineering Failure Analysis, 2013, 27:41-51.

[4] 王芳,冯顺山,俞为民.爆炸冲击波作用下靶板的塑性大变形响应研究[J].中国安全科学学报,2003(3):61-64+84.

[5] Li Q M, Meng H. Pressure-mpulse diagram for blast loads based on dimensional analysis and single-degree-of-freedom model [J]. Journal of Engineering and Mechanics, 2002, 128(1):87-92.

[6] Rong H C, Li B. Probabilistic response evaluation for RC flexural members subjected to blast loadings [J]. Structural Safety, 2007, 29(2): 146-163.

[7] 辛春亮,薛再青,涂建,等.有限元分析常用参数材料手册[M].北京:机械工业出版社,2020.

大位移弹性控制伸缩装置动力学模型的建立

张修石*[1] 李鹏程[1] 谢 青[1] 李光玲[2]

(1.长安大学公路学院;2.西安石油大学机械工程学院)

摘 要 为实现运营期大跨径桥梁大位移伸缩装置服役性能的仿真与评估,本文基于多弹簧多滑块多杆机构的运动机理,建立了弹簧控制伸缩装置的动力学仿真分析模型。首先,利用机械平衡关系建立力学平衡方程,结合相似关系和函数解析法确定结构动力学关系方程;其次,以某一弹性控制伸缩装置的运动实验为基础,验证弹性控制伸缩装置动力学仿真分析模型的准确性及有效性。本文提出了一种建立精确、高效的伸缩缝动力学仿真模型的方法。

关键词 桥梁工程 动力学仿真模型 理论分析 弹性控制伸缩装置 伸缩缝

0 引言

桥梁伸缩缝是桥梁结构重要的部件之一,其主要作用是适应在移动荷载、温度及混凝土收缩徐变等作用下桥梁上部结构的变形需要。由于悬索结构体系柔度较大,上部结构会产生较大的变形。为了实现桥面的连续以及满足上部结构变形的需要,应在桥梁端部与桥台之间和各桥段之间布置伸缩缝,以用于覆盖结构所预留的缝隙。对于不同结构形式和梁端位移要求的桥梁结构,目前存在多种形式的伸缩缝装置,包括模数式、毛勒式、对接式等。而模数式伸缩缝中的弹性控制伸缩装置由于具有良好的弹性变形能力可以应用于大变形结构中,该装置由多根主梁和支撑梁组成,通过支撑梁上各滑块间的弹性控制带动主梁发生位置变化。由于伸缩装置的间距不是固定的,伸缩装置需要能够在所有子间隙上均匀地分割这种运动,以确保伸缩装置在最终状态下各构件达到平衡状态。

在桥梁运营过程中,弹性控制伸缩装置由于会产生较大的位移往往导致轴承和弹性支承产生过度磨损和破坏,从而使弹性控制伸缩装置出现疲劳开裂的现象,进而导致位移控制弹簧顶部螺帽脱落。国内外学者致力于研究大位移伸缩装置病害的形成原因以及伸缩装置的保养维修,主要集中在伸缩缝状态评估及使用寿命预测等方面,包括伸缩装置动力分析、极端荷载下伸缩缝的响应分析等研究[1]。

目前,伸缩缝的结构设计和理论研究逐渐从基于静态模型和准静态模型向基于动态模型发展,大部分研究者通过伸缩装置实测数据或其精细化有限元模型进行动力分析。Ancich E J 等[2]分别建立了单支撑梁和多支撑梁的伸缩缝动态有限元模型,分析了结构的振动频率,提出伸缩缝的设计应从基于静态模型分析向基于动态模型分析发展。王军[3]运用简化的几何模型关系,建立了模数式装置有限元模型,对其进行静力、动力以及梁体顶升状态下的仿真分析。Michael Tahedl 等[4]通过建立桥梁伸缩缝的多体运动学模型,并考虑不同的摩擦力本构关系,在合理的时间范围内模拟地震荷载作用过程中伸缩缝各部件的运动关系。Emily McCarthy 等[5]建立了一个适用于多种结构的单支撑梁模数式桥梁伸缩缝的有效分析模型,并通过工厂加工进行动力实验,结果表明该模型能够有效预测桥梁在役期间伸缩缝各部件的运动特性。

基于上述研究,本文主要采用理论分析方法建立一种新型弹性控制伸缩装置的动力学模型,通过力学平衡条件和几何关系平衡条件预测了在伸缩装置边梁发生位移的情况下,支撑梁上各滑块的运动特性;通过理论结果与实测数据对比验证该理论模型的可靠性,从而为建立有限元模型奠定理论基础。

1 弹性控制伸缩装置

1.1 结构简介

本文研究的是模数式伸缩缝中的弹性控制伸缩装置,其一般由具有良好缓冲性能的橡胶材料及刚度较大的钢材组成,既能满足大跨径桥梁大位移的要求,也能承受较大的移动荷载;其由于具有良好的使用性能常用于公路桥梁。弹性控制伸缩装置 BIM 模型如图 1 所示。

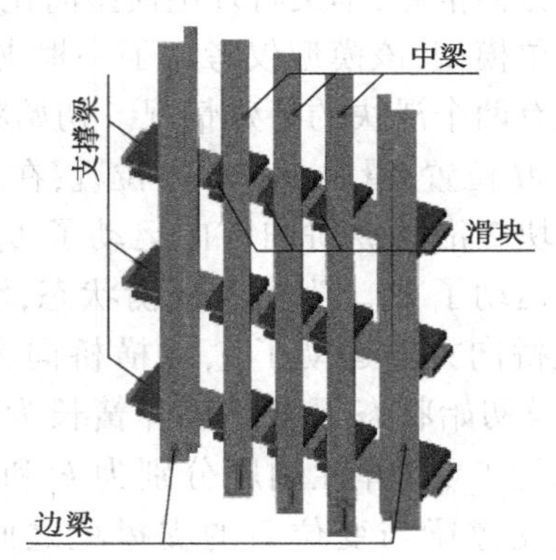

图 1 弹性控制伸缩装置 BIM 模型

模数式伸缩缝中由 V 型橡胶密封条镶嵌于异型钢边梁和工型钢中梁内,主梁和支撑梁之间通过滑块装置和弹性支承连接。荷载通过支撑系统传递给桥梁结构,在荷载作用下伸缩装置开始运动,主梁间的间距变化给滑块上的弹性支承施加控制力,弹性支承可以带动滑块沿着支撑梁顶部滑动,并且这些滑块始终固定在主梁上。滑块通过在支撑梁上滑动带动主梁发生平动,以达到结构的整体平衡,其工作原理如图 2 所示。当梁间隙缝宽开启到最大时,密封橡胶条被拉直,控制弹簧随之拉伸,受到最大拉力,但仍在弹簧的允许变形范围之内。当伸缩缝闭合时,控制弹簧处于完全松弛状态。主梁在运动过程中始终保持平行状态,并且支撑梁与主梁的相交线满足截距定理。伸缩缝外侧的边梁固定在相应的上部结构中。当上部结构产生纵向变形导致钢梁间距改变时,弹簧产生一个微小的位移 ΔS 和附加力 ΔF,此力使支承横梁产生位移,并带动与其刚性连接的中梁移动,最终使弹簧达到一个新的平衡状态。

本文根据实际结构建立了图 3 所示的多弹簧多杆多滑块理论模型,其中垂直于弹簧的杆件代表主梁,圆圈表示支撑梁上的滑块,滑块通过两端连接的弹簧在支撑梁上滑动。

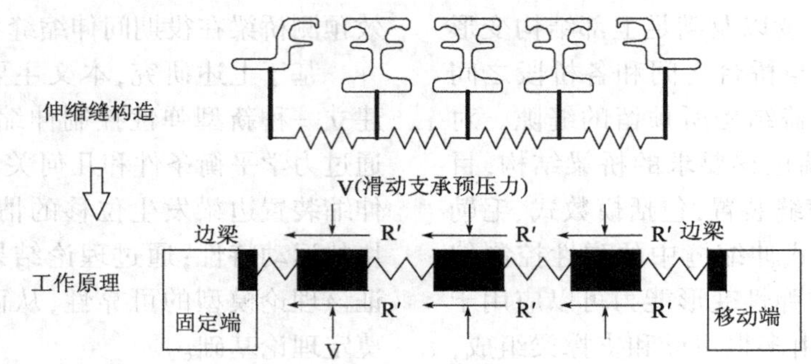

图 2　弹性控制伸缩装置工作原理

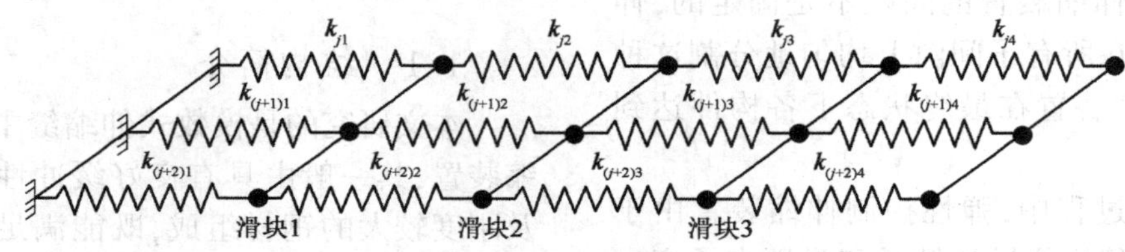

图 3　弹性伸缩控制装置理论模型

1.2　理论推导

为了方便推导,本文将理论模型简化成如图 4 所示的简单模型,该模型仅考虑了一根支撑梁,支撑梁上仅有两个滑块的特殊情况。初始状态下滑块 1 位于 M 位置,滑块 2 位于 A 位置;在移动荷载作用下滑块 2 沿着纵桥向方向运动了 L_A,沿着横桥向方向运动了 L_B。为达到平衡状态,滑块 1 相应地在纵桥向方向运动了 x,在横桥向方向运动了 y。假设初始状态下第一根弹簧长为 L_1,第二根弹簧长为 L_2;其弹性刚度分别为 k_1 和 k_2,初始状态下的支撑梁与变位后的支撑梁之间的夹角为 α。

根据几何关系有:

$$\alpha = \arctan\left(\frac{L_B}{L_1 + L_2 + L_A}\right) \tag{1}$$

由三角形相似关系有:

$$\frac{y}{L_B} = \frac{L_1 + x}{L_1 + L_2 + L_A} \tag{2}$$

解得:

$$x = \frac{y \cdot (L_1 + L_2 + L_A) - L_1 \cdot L_B}{L_B} \tag{3}$$

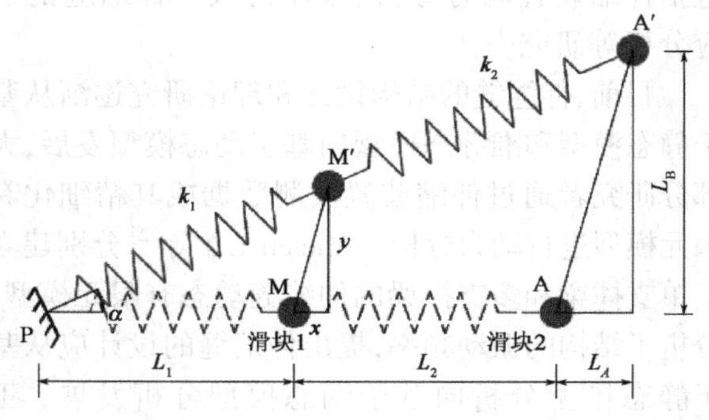

图 4　单支撑梁双滑块理论模型

由于滑块最终达到平衡状态,根据力学平衡条件有:

$$k_1 \cdot [y/\sin\alpha - L_1] = k_2 \cdot [(L_B - y)/\sin\alpha - L_2] \tag{4}$$

将方程(1)、(3)、(4)联立求解方程组可得：

$$y = \frac{(k_1L_1 - k_2L_2)(L_1L_2 + L_1L_A + L_B) + k_2L_1L_B\sqrt{\left(L_2 + L_A + \frac{L_B}{L_1}\right)^2 + 1}}{(k_1L_1 + k_2L_2)\sqrt{\left(L_2 + L_A + \frac{L_B}{L_1}\right)^2 + 1}} \tag{5}$$

$$x = (L_1 + L_2 + L_A)\left[\frac{(k_1L_1 - k_2L_2)(L_1L_2 + L_1L_A + L_B) + k_2L_1L_B\sqrt{\left(L_2 + L_A + \frac{L_B}{L_1}\right)^2 + 1}}{L_B(k_1L_1 + k_2L_2)\sqrt{\left(L_2 + L_A + \frac{L_B}{L_1}\right)^2 + 1}}\right] - L_1 \tag{6}$$

由此求得滑块1的位移-时程关系。根据对简单模型的理论推导，可以扩展到复杂模型的各支撑梁上滑块的位移-时程关系。由于支撑梁在运动过程中始终满足截距定理，只需要确定第一根支撑梁上滑块的位移-时程关系，其与支撑梁上滑块的相对位移与第一根支撑梁上相对应滑块的相对位移保持一致。对任一时刻 t，滑块1在支撑梁上的瞬态位置为 $l(t)$，则 $t+1$ 时刻滑块1的瞬态位置为 $l(t+1)$，则滑块1沿支撑梁滑动的轨迹位移为：

$$S_1 = \Delta l = l(t+1) - l(t) \tag{7}$$

将式(7)对时间 t 求导，可得滑块1滑动的速度方程为：

$$v = d(l(t+1) - l(t))/dt \tag{8}$$

将式(7)对时间 t 求二阶导数，可得滑块1滑动的加速度方程为：

$$a = d^2(l(t+1) - l(t))/dt^2 \tag{9}$$

由以上运动学仿真模型可知，如果已知支撑梁最外侧滑块运动的位移，便可获得其余滑块的运动轨迹状态，这为以单支撑梁双滑块为基本单元的复杂机构运动仿真提供了数学理论模型。

2 弹性控制伸缩装置模型理论结果验证

本文以文献[5]中的弹性控制伸缩装置为例，验证已建立的伸缩装置动力学仿真分析模型。弹性控制伸缩装置中主梁、支撑梁均采用Q345钢材，连接各滑块的弹性元件材料为氯丁橡胶，整个模型中的材料均为线弹性材料，材料特性见表1。主梁梁宽0.09m，梁长6m。支撑梁分别位于距主梁两端0.5m、3m以及5.5m处，伸缩装置立面图如图5所示。初始状态下各主梁处于平行状态；支撑梁垂直于主梁，主梁间间距为0.3m，$k_1 = k_2 = 980$(N/mm)。边梁做如图6所示的正弦往复运动，每个完整周期(−90mm，+242mm)耗时约11s，平均正弦加载速度为56mm/s。根据理论模型推导图3中第一根支撑梁上的各滑块运动轨迹与实测对比结果如图7所示。

伸缩缝装置主要材料特性　　表1

材　　料	弹性模量	泊松比	密　　度
Q345钢材	2.05e+005MPa	0.25	7800kg/m³
氯丁橡胶	980MPa	0.48	0.94kg/m³

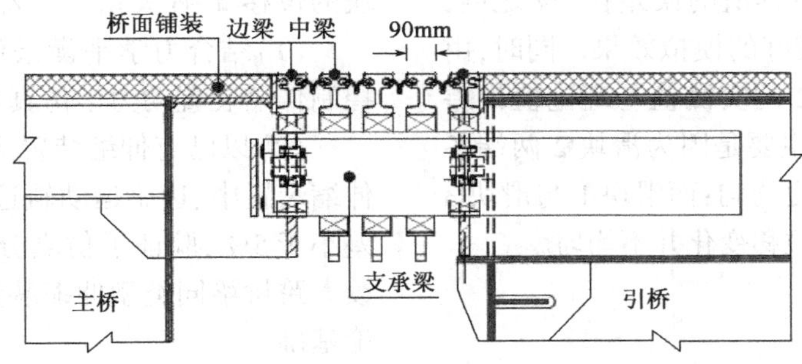

图5　伸缩装置立面图

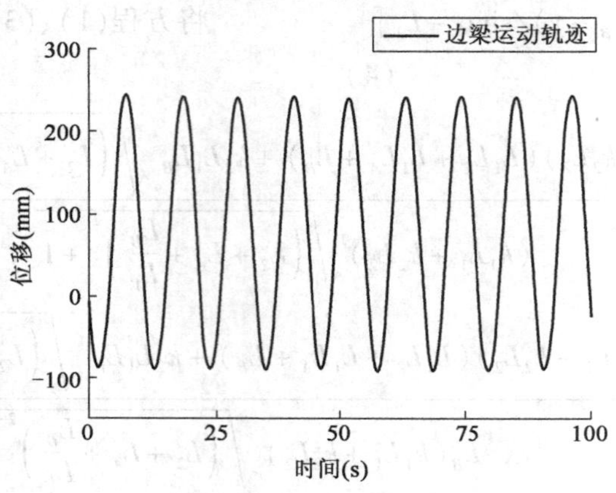

图6　边梁运动轨迹位移-时程曲线

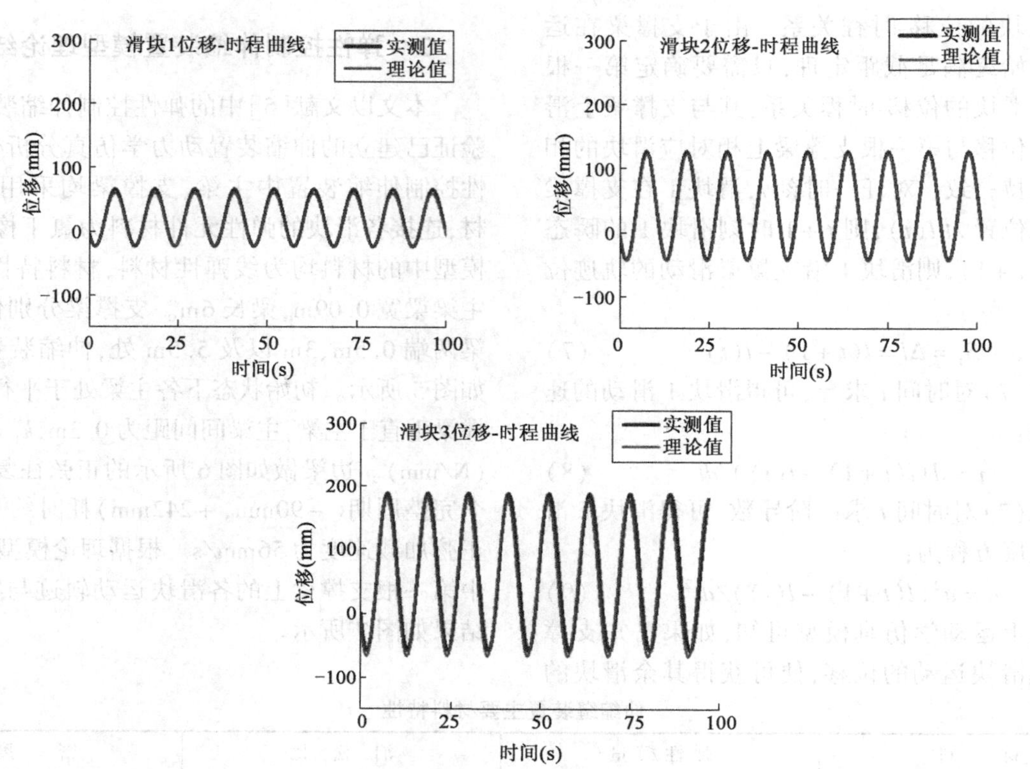

图7　各滑块位移-时程曲线

由图7可知,在100s测试时间内支撑梁上各滑块的实测位移值与理论位移值的误差在5%之内,可以认为该理论模型有较好的模拟效果。同时,由对比结果可以发现滑块2的实测值与理论值误差最小,模拟效果最好。这主要是因为滑块2两端各有两组弹簧,其位移变化更均匀;而滑块1与滑块3两端弹簧组数不同,滑块位移变化并不均匀。

3　结语

本文研究如何建立弹性控制伸缩装置理论模型,并通过理论推导确定了主梁以及支撑梁上滑块的位移-时程关系。主要结论如下:

(1)结合力学平衡条件和相似关系建立弹性控制伸缩装置动力学仿真分析模型。

(2)以已有伸缩装置运动试验结果,对比分析伸缩装置中、边梁运动轨迹时程曲线,时程位移误差小于5%,验证了仿真分析模型的准确性,为后续大跨桥梁同类型伸缩装置的仿真评估提供了理论基础。

但该模型仍有不足之处,实际模型中弹簧支承与支撑梁之间在滑动过程中存在摩阻力,模型中尚未考虑这一因素对滑块位移时程的影响,并且由实测数据与理论数据对比可知,随着时间的积累,两者之间的相对误差逐渐越大,因此应该进一步研究在长时间范围内如何消除这种累计误差。

相关数据参数含义见表2。

参数解释表　　表2

L_i ($i=1,2$)	第 i 根弹簧长度	K_i ($i=1,2$)	第 i 根弹簧弹性刚度
S	位移	v	速度
a	加速度	α	夹角

参考文献

[1] 黄灵宇. 大跨钢桥伸缩缝的性能评估与病害控制研究[D]. 南京:东南大学,2017.

[2] Ancich E J, Chrigwin G J, Brown S C. Dynamic anomalies in a modular bridge expansion joint [J]. Journal of Bridge Engineering, 2006, 11 (5):541-554.

[3] 王军. 公路桥梁模数式伸缩缝受力性能研究[D]. 南昌:南昌大学,2018.

[4] Michael Tahedl, Andreas Taras, Fredrik Borchsenius, et al. Assessment of the Seismic Retrofit Potential of Bridge Expansion Joint by means of Multibody Simulations [C]. XI International Conference on Structural Dynamics,2020.

[5] Emily McCarthy, Timothy Wright, J E. Padgett, et al. Development of an Experimentally Validated Analytical Model for Modular Bridge Expansion Joint Behavior[J]. Journal of Bridge Engineering,2014,19(2):235-244.

基于 POD 和 DMD 的双矩形断面非定常绕流分析

仵广策*

(长安大学公路学院)

摘　要　本文采用数值模拟方法对宽高比为 5:1、宽与间距比为 1:1.2 的双幅矩形进行了非定常绕流计算,结果表明上下游矩形断面间存在明显的气动干扰;采用本征正交分解(POD)和动态模态分解(DMD)方法对断面绕流稳定阶段流场进行了分析,两种方法均准确提取了稳定阶段流场的主要流动特征,且 DMD 方法进一步得出流场脉动部分由涡脱频率及高阶倍频对应的流场模态组成。

关键词　数值模拟　双幅矩形　非定常绕流　本征正交分解　动态模态分解

0　引言

改革开放以来,国民经济不断发展,交通量也日益增加,由于良好的经济效益,双幅桥的数量也与日俱增。但双幅桥断面之间由于距离过近,存在着明显的气动干扰效应,这给主梁的抗风带来了不利影响。已有学者对此开展了研究工作,丁林等对不同间距的串联双方柱流致振动进行了数值模拟,发现在间距为 4D 时流致振动最强[1]。杜晓庆等对间距比为 2 和 4 的串列双方柱进行了涡激振动数值模拟,从能量和涡的角度分析了流场的流态和演变过程[2]。Wang F 等对不同间距比的串联双方柱断面绕流进行了数值模拟,并采用 POD 和 DMD 方法对流场进行了分解,揭示了间距对流场的影响规律[3]。刘小兵等对均匀风场中串联双矩形断面气动力相互干扰进行了研究,发现上下游断面间距对阻力及升力系数根方差值有显著影响[4]。刘志文等对均匀流场下不同阻尼比、不同间距比的双矩形断面涡激振动气动干扰进行了风洞试验分析,发现阻尼比对扭转振幅有显著影响,而间距比对扭转锁定区间有较大影响[5]。马凯等对不同约束情况和不同竖向和水平间距的双矩形断面涡振性能进行了研究,发现不同约束情况不会显著改变相关参数的分布趋势,水平和竖向间距的增大对涡振性能有利[6-7]。本文采用了 POD 和 DMD 方法对双幅矩形断面非定常绕流流场进行了分解,从流场本身层面对双幅矩形的非定常绕流进行了分析,得出了稳定阶段绕流流场的三要特征,对以往学者的研究做了有力补充。

1　POD和DMD方法

1.1　POD方法

如具有 N 个相同时间间距 Δt 的流场快照(如各点的压力、速度信息),则流场可分解为基本流动和脉动流动的叠加,即为:

$$u(x,t_i)=u_0+u'(x,t_i) \tag{1}$$

采用POD方法的目的为将流场脉动部分正交分解为用少量POD基和其模态系数的乘积来表示的形式:

$$u'(x,t_i)=\sum_{j=1}^{N}a_j(t_i)u_j(x) \tag{2}$$

其中:$\{u_j\}_{j=1}^{N}$ 表示POD的基,t_j 时刻,第 j 个POD基模态系数定义为 $a_j(t_i)$。要计算POD基,应先求出相关矩阵 C:

$$C=P^TP \tag{3}$$

其中:$P=[u'(x,t_1)\ u'(x,t_2)\ \cdots\ u'(x,t_N)]$ 是减去均值后的快照序列矩阵。矩阵 C 为对称矩阵,具有非负特征值,故可得:

$$CA^{[j]}=\lambda_jA^{[j]} \tag{4}$$

其中:特征矢量 $A^{[j]}$ 为模态系数矩阵,$A^{[j]}=[a_j(t_1)\ a_j(t_2)\ \cdots\ a_j(t_N)]$。POD基为:

$$u_j(x)=\frac{1}{N\lambda_j}\sum_{i=1}^{N}a_i^{[j]}(u(x,t_i)-u_0(x)) \tag{5}$$

依据特征值 λ 按能量对各模态排序,可得主要流场模态。依据式(2)得到的任意时刻流场脉动量与平均流场相加可得任意时刻流场。

1.2　DMD方法

N 个等时间间距 Δt 的流场快照序列 $u_i=[u_1\ u_2\ u_3\cdots u_N]$,将其分配为 X_{N-1} 和 Y_{N-1}:

$$\begin{cases}X_{N-1}=[u_1\ u_2\cdots u_{N-1}]\\ Y_{N-1}=[u_2\ u_3\cdots u_N]\end{cases} \tag{6}$$

假设 X_{N-1} 通过做如下转换可得到 Y_{N-1}:

$$Y_{N-1}=AX_{N-1} \tag{7}$$

则对 X_{N-1} 做奇异值分解 $X=USV^*$。转换矩阵 A 可通过下式求解:

$$A=U^*YVS^{-1} \tag{8}$$

各阶DMD模态为:

$$\phi_j=U\Lambda_j \tag{9}$$

对矩阵 A 求解其特征值,得到特征值 μ_j 和特征向量 Λ_j。各阶DMD模态频率及衰减率分别为:

$$\begin{cases}f=\mathrm{Im}(\ln(\mu_j))/(2\pi\Delta t)\\ \sigma=\mathrm{Re}(\ln(\mu_j))/(\Delta t)\end{cases} \tag{10}$$

按照下式计算的模态范数对各阶模态进行排序:

$$\|\phi_j\|=\frac{1}{\|V^*S^{-1}\Lambda_j\|} \tag{11}$$

2　数值模拟及计算结果

模型宽度B为300mm,高H为60mm、两矩形净间距为D为360mm,中心距风场上下边界均为600mm、距风场左右边界分别为2000mm和3000mm,全部采用非结构网格进行划分。为保证计算结果的精确,壁面网格的尺寸取0.1mm,同时为了后续处理结果的精确,网格划分数量约为105万,满足网格无关性要求。网格划分如图1所示。风场入口采用速度入口,来流速度 V 取5m/s,出口采用压力出口,上下边界设置为对称边界,壁面设置为无滑移壁面。采用效果较好的 $SST\ k-\omega$ 模型,计算方法为速度-压力耦合的simple方法,采用二阶迎风格式,为保证单周期有足够采样步数,时间步长取0.0001s。升力系数(C_l)计算结果如图2所示。

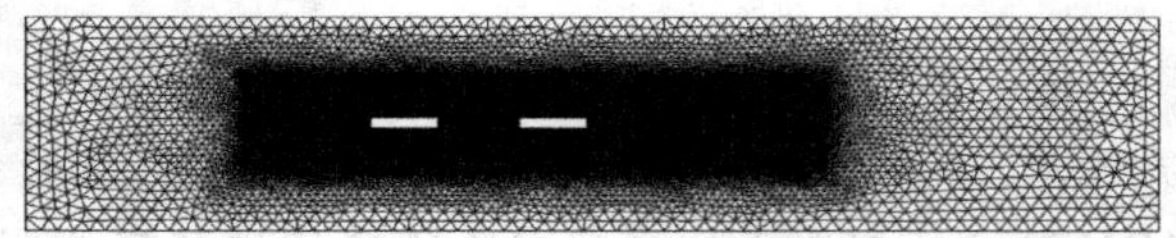

图1　网格划分图

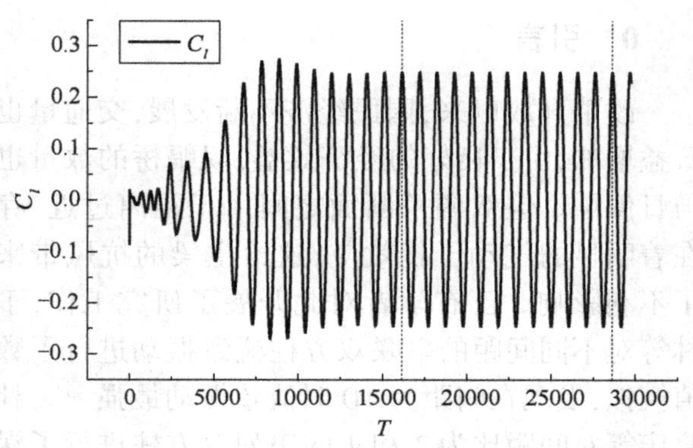

图2　升力系数计算结果

对如图2所示的稳定阶段进行分析后,结果如表1所示,与其他已有文献对比发现升力系数、阻力系数和斯托罗哈数均吻合较好。

CFD 计算结果　表1

不同文献	参数数据计算结果		
	$C_{l,rms}$	$C_{d,mean}$	St
本文	0.176	0.202	0.599
文献[8]	0.144	0.232	0.528
文献[9]	0.177	0.206	0.435
文献[10]	0.24	0.23	0.45

单个周期内的压力云图如图3所示,可以观察到整个周期内上游矩形上下缘均依附有一大涡,并在尾端持续涡产生并分离;下游矩形在T时刻前端部上缘及后端部下缘各有一涡旋,结合周期后三个时刻可知,此刻上缘的涡刚刚产生,随后紧贴矩形上缘运动至下缘并最终发生分离,而下缘的涡旋是上半个周期在前端下缘产生的涡运动至此处,随后同样在尾端发生脱离,形成与上缘分离的反对称的涡旋。

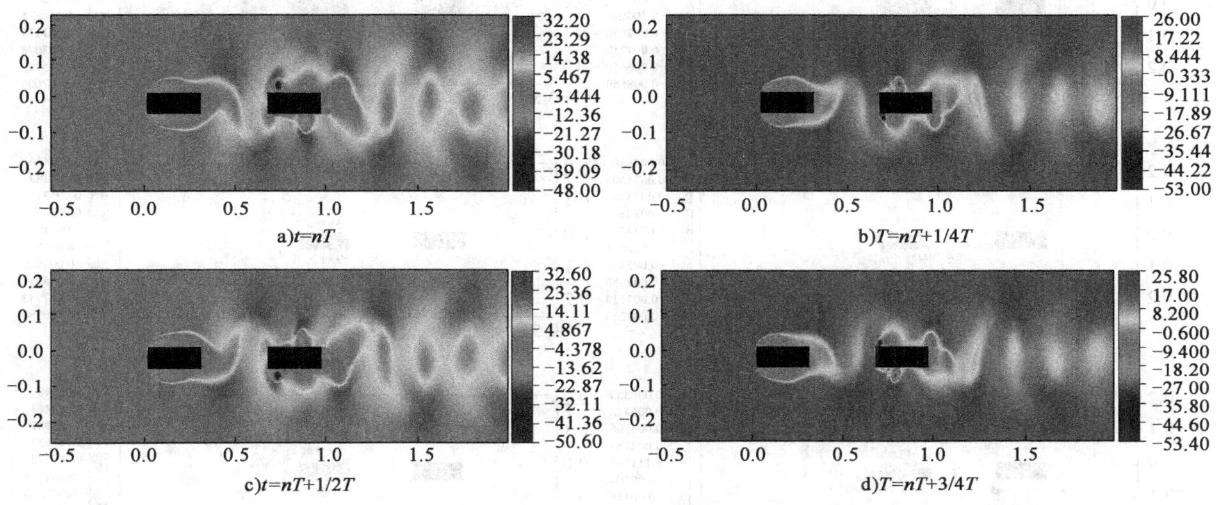

图3　单周期速度云图

3　计算结果分析

本文对稳定阶段升力系数做FFT变换得到的主频为9.99Hz。

3.1　POD计算结果及分析

图4所示为对发展阶段(每间隔10时间间隔输出一个快照,故快照间隔$\Delta t = 0.001\mathrm{s}$)流场的压力快照进行POD分解后得到的各阶模态图。

图5为前20阶模态从大到小排列的各模态的能量分布图。表2为前$i(i=1,5,9,11)$阶模态能量占模态总能量的比例。

前i阶模态能量比例　表2

前 i 阶	能量 E	能量占比
1	1.20E+09	40.5%
5	2.68E+09	90.2%
9	2.92E+09	98.0%
11	2.95E+09	99.0%

从图5中可以看出,前2阶模态能量超过总模态能量的一半,为流场脉动部分的主要模态,且前6阶模态两两成组,流场特征相近。第1阶模态和第2阶模态流场特征大致相同,都是从上游矩形的前端部位上下缘各产生一个大小几乎相同、方向相反的涡,在向下游移动中涡不断发展壮大,直到到达下游矩形的前端受到干扰,模态1中在此处前涡与此处发展的涡汇合,形成更大的涡向后继续发展;而模态2则是互相干扰最后在后方形成一个原处旋转的涡旋,并最终发生分离,前涡向远离矩形的方向运动发展,而后形成的涡旋则紧贴断面向后运动,最后在尾端脱离。模态3和模态4主要流场特征亦大致相同,都为上游矩形尾部产生的涡运动到下游矩形前缘与此处产生的涡碰撞干扰并最终分离,且上下缘的涡在尾端发生融合,最终一起向后运动,不同点在于模态4的涡的运动趋势相较于模态3略明显。模态5和

模态 6 同样大致相同,都为上游矩形尾端分别产生一个大小相同、方向相反的涡旋,发展并运动至下游矩形前端与此处的涡作用并发生分离,与前组流场不同点在于紧贴矩形运动的涡在尾端并未发生融合而是自始至终分离。模态 7 和 8、模态 9 和 10 同样分别为 1 组特征相同的流场模态,不再进行赘述。

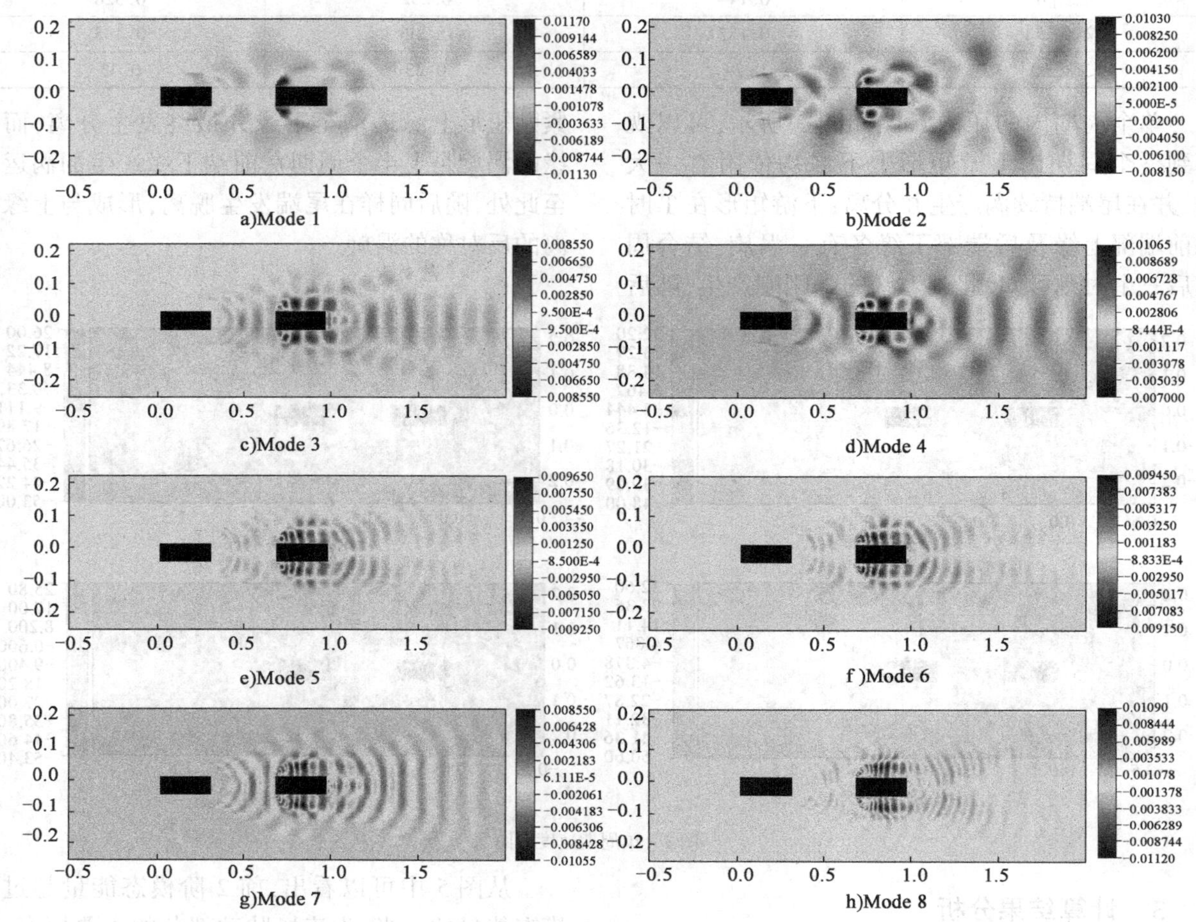

图 4　POD 速度模态云图

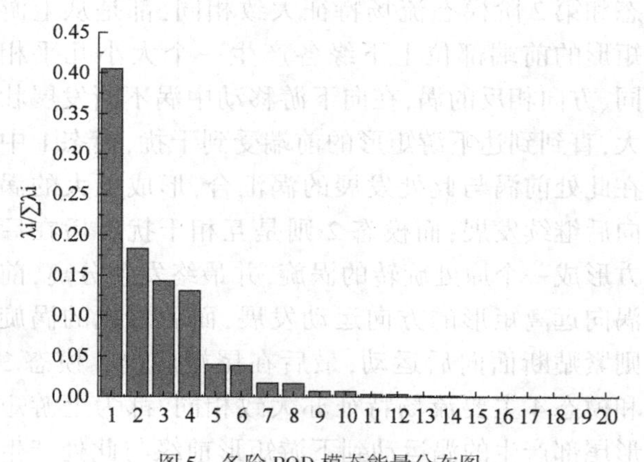

图 5　各阶 POD 模态能量分布图

图 6 所示为前 4 阶流场的时间系数。从图中可以看出,每组的两个模态波动的频率大致相同,但存在一定的相位差;而第二组模态比第一组模态波动的频率明显加快,无固定的相位差,可见同组之间模态表现为"此消彼涨",不同组模态之间相互杂糅,共同组成复杂流场。除此以外,本文还对其进行了 FFT 分析,发现每一阶模态包含多个主要频率。

3.2　DMD 计算结果及分析

图 7 所示为对稳定阶段流场的压力快照进行 DMD 分解,并按模态范数的大小进行排序之后得到的前 11 阶 DMD 模态的压力云图。图 8 为以实部为横轴,虚步为纵轴,DMD 特征值的实部和虚部在单位圆上的分布,绿色菱形表示在单位圆外,红色菱形表示在单位圆上或圆内,紫色菱形为第 1 阶模态在单位圆上。图 9 为前 30 阶各阶 DMD 模态的能量分布图。表 3 为前 11 阶模态对应的模

态频率和模态衰减率。从中可以看出，DMD 分解与 POD 分解不同，它不仅可以将复杂的流场分解成各阶简单流场，且每个流场仅对应单个频率，而 POD 分解的单阶模态流场则包含多种频率信息。在分解得到的 DMD 模态中，第一阶模态为平均流场，频率为 0Hz，占据了流场部分能量，而 POD 则因为分解过程中减去了平均流场部分，故第一阶不是平均流场。之后的 DMD 模态与 POD 模态类似，也是成对出现，其特征值共轭。第 2 ~ 3 阶模态的频率为 9.602Hz，与对升力系数进行 FFT 分解得到的主频 9.99Hz 相近，可见此阶模态对应频率为该风速下的涡脱频率，而 4 ~ 5 阶模态的频率为 19.204Hz，为涡脱频率的 2 倍频，之后的模态均为涡脱频率的高倍频，POD 分解得到的模态与 DMD 分解得到的模态流场特征也相互对应，可见稳定阶段流场的主要部分由其涡脱频率和高倍频模态组成。结合 Ritz 特征值及能量分布图也可以看出此时大部分模态都在环上或环内，代表其处于稳定状态，前几阶涡脱频率及其 2 倍频、低倍频代表的模态占据了除平均流场外大部分能量，且其衰减率为小于 10^{-4} 级，无不印证其反映了此流场的主要特征。

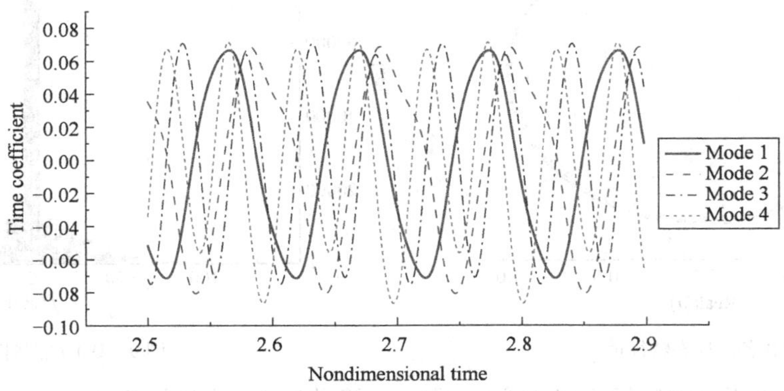

图 6 前 4 阶 POD 模态系数变化图

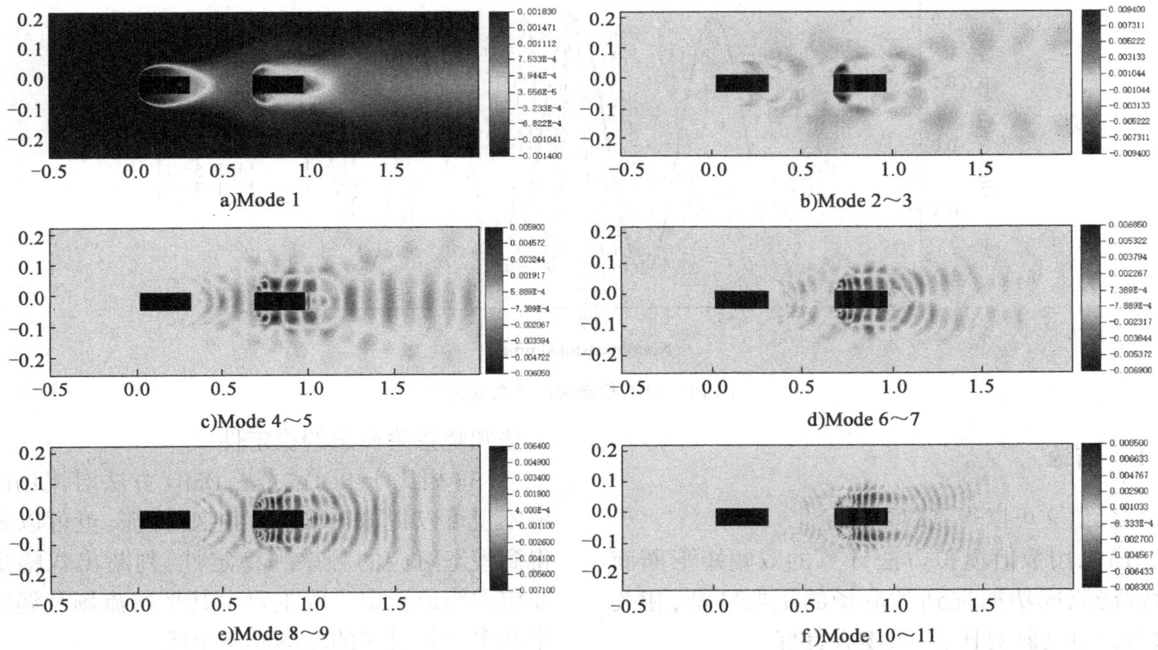

图 7 DMD 速度模态云图

前 11 阶 DMD 模态频率及其对应衰减率　　表 3

模　态	频率(Hz)	衰　减　率
1	0	-1.436E-05
2~3	9.602	1.667E-04
4~5	19.204	1.566E-04
6~7	28.806	4.406E-04
8~9	38.408	2.365E-04
10~11	48.010	-5.588E-05

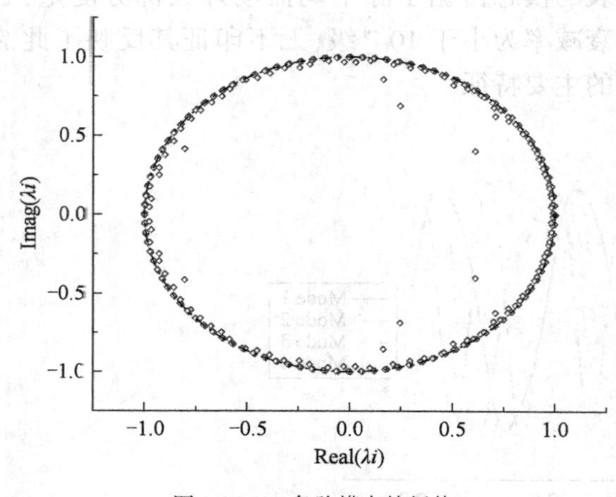

图 8　DMD 各阶模态特征值

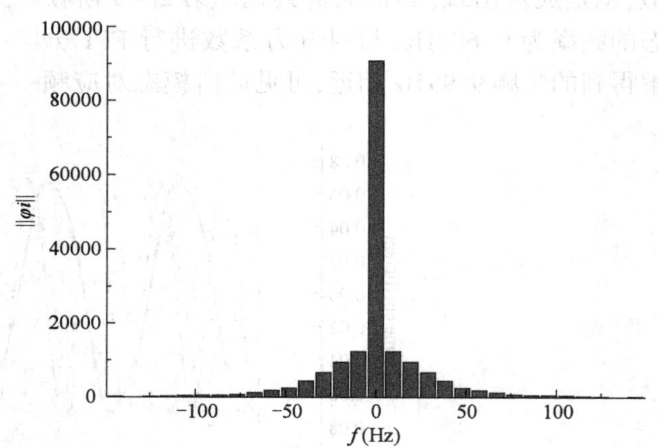

图 9　DMD 能量图

图 10 所示为 2~9 阶 DMD 模态的时间系数变化图,可见这几阶模态均较为稳定地做周期性简谐振动。同时,模态越高,振动频率越高,且频率间为倍数关系,印证了前文观点。

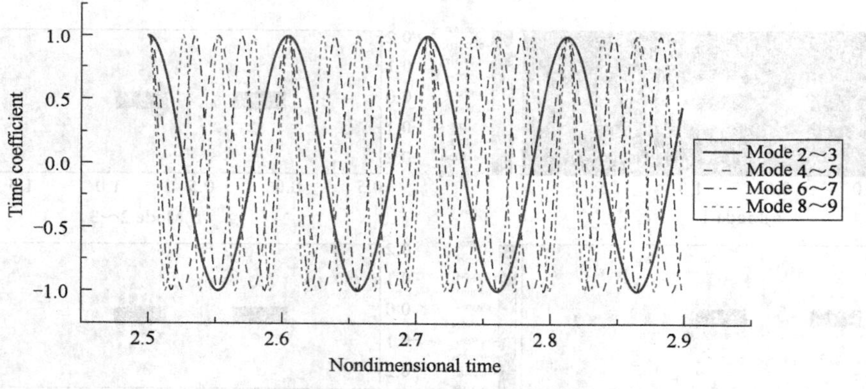

图 10　DMD 模态时间系数变化图

4　结语

综合上文可以得到以下结论:

(1)采用数值模拟方法计算的双幅矩形断面非定常绕流成功捕捉到了流场的主要特征,相关参数与已有文献对比,结果吻合良好。

(2)采用 POD 方法对流场压力快照进行分解,可以有效提取流场的主要流动特征,但对流场的分解不彻底,每阶流场中包含多个频率成分,且无法知晓各阶模态的稳定性。

(3)相比于 POD 方法,DMD 方法对流场的分解不仅可以提取出流场的主要特征,更可以直接得到模态对应的频率和稳定性,判断出双幅矩形非定常绕流稳定阶段主要由其平均流场及涡脱频率和多倍频对应的流场模态组成。

参考文献

[1] 丁林,叶倩云,王海博,等.不同间距串列双方柱流致振动运动特性分析[J].振动工程

学报，2019，32(2)：331-339.

[2] 杜晓庆，邱涛，郑德乾，等.低雷诺数中等间距串列双方柱涡激振动的数值模拟［J］.哈尔滨工业大学学报，2020，52(10)：94-101.

[3] Wang F, Zheng X D, Hao J M, et al. Numerical Analysis of the Flow around Two Square Cylinders in a Tandem Arrangement with Different Spacing Ratios Based on POD and DMD Methods［J］. Processes, 2020, 8(8)：15.

[4] 刘小兵，陈政清，刘志文，等.均匀风场中串列双矩形断面气动力干扰的数值研究［J］.振动与冲击，2008，27(12)：83-87+181.

[5] 刘志文，栗小祜，陈政清.均匀流场串列双矩形断面涡激振动气动干扰试验［J］.中国公路学报，2010，23(5)：44-50.

[6] 马凯，胡传新，周志勇.不同约束情况下双矩形断面的涡振性能分析［J］.振动与冲击，2020，39(10)：141-147+205.

[7] 周志勇，马凯，胡传新，等.水平和竖向间距对双矩形断面涡振性能的影响［J］.哈尔滨工程大学学报，2021，42(4)：505-513.

[8] 刘小兵，杨群.双幅典型断面静力系数气动干扰试验研究［J］.工程力学，2012，29(S2)：107-112.

[9] 马凯，胡传新，袁万城，等.基于风洞试验和数值模拟的双矩形断面涡振气动干扰研究［J］.振动与冲击，2020，39(1)：157-168.

[10] Larsen A. Advances in aeroelastic analyses of suspension and cable-stayed bridges［J］. Journal of Wind Engineering and Industrial Aerodynamics, 1998, 74(2)：73-90.

优化响应面法在简支梁有限元模型修正中的应用

杨雅勋*[1,2] 陆嘉诚[1] 王林柯[1]

（1.长安大学公路学院；2.西安长安大学工程设计研究院有限公司）

摘 要 针对桥梁实际结构与其有限元模型之间的偏差，本文提出以基于响应面法和线性递减权重粒子群算法的优化响应面法来进行有限元模型的修正，并以一简支梁为例，结合静载测试数据对其有缺陷部位的材料参数进行修正。采用中心复合试验设计和F检验法进行参数显著性分析，以不含交叉项的二次函数拟合响应面模型，采用线性递减权重粒子群算法进行优化求解，证明了其算法高效稳定，能迅速收敛到全局最优解的优点，提高了求解效率，且误差显著降低，证明了优化响应面算法的可行性与精确性，可作为桥梁运营期间的模拟与分析的重要方法，对桥梁实际结构的健康监测与损伤识别具有指导意义与实用价值。

关键词 桥梁工程 有限元模型修正 优化响应面法 简支梁桥

0 引言

采用有限元模型模拟桥梁实际结构的过程中，往往由于模型结构、参数、阶次等因素，造成二者之间存在偏差。因此，应采用适当的优化方法对有限元模型进行修正，以降低误差，从而更准确地模拟实际结构。

经过近半个世纪的发展，国内外主要提出了矩阵修正法、设计参数修正法、响应面法等修正方法[1]。矩阵修正法主要针对质量矩阵和刚度矩阵，其主要缺陷是修正后的矩阵不具备原有的物理意义，且改变了初始矩阵的带状和稀疏性，因此逐渐被淘汰。Berman 等以部分模态信息为基准，根据结构动力学方程构造约束条件，采用拉格朗日乘子法推导出质量修正矩阵[2]。设计参数修正法主要针对设计参数的修正，其主要缺陷是选择待修正参数的随机性大,迭代速率慢,修正效率低。陈彦江等采用灵敏度分析法筛选参数,结合健康监测数据对一座连续刚构模型完成了修正,显著降低了误差[3]。而响应面法克服了上述二者的缺陷,因其准确性和高效性而被广泛应用。杨雅勋等通过试验设计构造了代替原有复杂有限元模型的响应面模型,以序列二次规划法完成了求解修正[4]。

本文将以基于响应面法和线性递减权重粒子群算法的优化响应面法来修正一座简支梁桥的有限元模型。选择损伤节段的弹性模量和密度作为修正对象,以中心复合试验进行设计,采用 F 检验法筛选出显著性高的参数,再通过拟合函数建立响应面模型,然后依据测试数据在响应面模型内求解,从而利用最优解对有限元模型进行优化。优化后的误差显著降低,证明了优化响应面法在简支梁桥模型修正方面的正确性。

1　优化响应面法的有限元模型修正理论

1.1　响应面法基本原理

1.1.1　特征值与响应值的选取

特征值的选择要符合实际的力学特性以及参数的物理意义。本文以损伤部位的弹性模量和密度作为输入特征值。测试点的挠度、应力、应变作为静力响应值,结构的频率、模态振型作为动力响应值。

1.1.2　试验设计与响应面模型的建立

本文选择 Design-Expert 设计,其主要优点是精度高且试验次数少[5-7],在进行响应面拟合时,其样本个数为 $n=(k+1)(k+2)/2$(k 为待修正参数的数量)。

响应面模型的建立需考虑函数的简洁与计算的高效,因此以二次多项式响应面函数为例进行推导。

含交叉项的二次项的统一形式为:

$$y=\sum_{i=1}^{k-1}\beta_i x_i \tag{1}$$

将 m 个样本点对响应值 $y^{(i)}$ $(i=0,1,2,\cdots,m-1)$ 代入(2)得到估计值:

$$\begin{cases} y^{(0)}=\sum_{i=0}^{k-1}\beta_i x_i{}^{(0)} \\ y^{(1)}=\sum_{i=0}^{k-1}\beta_i x_i{}^{(1)} \\ \cdots\ \vdots \\ y^{(m-1)}=\sum_{i=0}^{k-1}\beta_i x_i{}^{(m-1)} \end{cases} \tag{2}$$

上述二式通常存在误差,构造误差函数 $\sum_{i=1}^{m-1}(\varepsilon^{(j)})^2$,使其最小化,可以确定系数 β_i 的取值。

$$S(\beta)=\sum_{i=1}^{m-1}(\varepsilon^{(j)})^2=\sum_{j=0}^{m-1}\Big(\sum_{i=0}^{k-1}\beta_i x_i{}^{(j)}-y^{(j)}\Big) \tag{3}$$

其极小值的必要条件为:

$$\frac{\partial S}{\partial \beta_l}=2\sum_{j=0}^{m-1}\Big(\sum_{i=0}^{k-1}\beta_i x_i^{(j)}-y^{(j)}\Big)=0\cdots(l=0,\cdots,k-1) \tag{4}$$

求解上式即为求解 k 个方程和 k 个未知数的方程组,其矩阵形式为:$(\boldsymbol{X\beta}-\boldsymbol{y})^T\boldsymbol{X}=\boldsymbol{0}$

$$\boldsymbol{X}=\begin{bmatrix} 1 & x_1{}^{(0)} & x_2{}^{(0)} & \cdots & x_{k-1}{}^{(0)} \\ 1 & x_1{}^{(1)} & x_2{}^{(1)} & \cdots & x_{k-1}{}^{(k-1)} \\ \cdots & \cdots & \cdots & \cdots & \cdots \\ 1 & x_1{}^{(k-1)} & x_2{}^{(k-1)} & \cdots & x_{k-1}{}^{(k-1)} \end{bmatrix},$$

$$\boldsymbol{y}=\begin{bmatrix} y^{(0)} \\ y^{(1)} \\ \cdots \\ y^{(k-1)} \end{bmatrix},\beta=\begin{bmatrix} \beta_0 \\ \beta_1 \\ \cdots \\ \beta_{k-1} \end{bmatrix} \tag{5}$$

对上述矩阵进行运算得到系数矩阵 $\boldsymbol{\beta}=(\boldsymbol{X}^T\boldsymbol{X})^{-1}\boldsymbol{X}^T\boldsymbol{y}$。

1.1.3　响应面精度检验

确定响应面模型后还需对其精度进行评定[8-10]。通常选择复相关系数 *R-Squard* 和修正的复相关系数 *adjR-Squard*。

(1)复相关系数 *R-Squard*。

$$R\text{-}Squard=\frac{SSR}{SSY}=1-\frac{SSE}{SSY} \tag{6}$$

其中:

$$SSY=\sum_{i=1}^{m}(y_i-\bar{y})^2=\sum_{i=1}^{m}y_i^2-m\,\bar{y}^2=y^Ty-\frac{(I^Ty)^2}{m} \tag{7}$$

$$\begin{aligned} SSE&=\sum_{i=1}^{m}(y_i-y)^2\\ &=(y-X\beta)^T(y-X\beta)\\ &=y^Ty-\beta^TX^Ty \end{aligned} \tag{8}$$

$$SSR = SSY - SSE = \beta^T X^T y - \frac{(I^T y)}{m} \quad (9)$$

计算得到的 *R-Squard* 值可用来描述响应面的拟合程度,其越趋近 1,则误差的影响越小,回归方程越精确。

(2)修正的复相关系数 *adjR-Squard*。

传统意义上的 *R-Squard* 随着 k 值增大在一定程度上有所增大,因此引入了修正的复相关系数 *adjR-Squard*,该表达式为:

$$adjR\text{-}Squard = 1 - \left(\frac{m-1}{m-k}\right)\frac{SSE}{SSY} \quad (10)$$

adjR-Squard 越接近 1,说明响应面的拟合精度越高。

1.2 线性递减权重粒子群算法基本原理

1.2.1 算法原理

通过改变标准群算法中的权重与学习因子来改变粒子对自我认知和对全局认知的能力,可以提高算法的求解效率,更快速地进行全局或局部的求解。速度更新及权重 ω 变化如下式:

$$v_{ij}(t+1) = \omega v_{ij}(t) + c_1 r_1(t)[p_{ij}(t) - x_{ij}(t)] + c_2 r_2(t)[p_{gj}(t) - x_{ij}(t)] \quad (11)$$

$$\omega = \omega_{max} - \frac{\omega_{max} - \omega_{min}}{t_{max}} \times t \quad (12)$$

其中 ω_{max}、ω_{min} 表示 ω 的最值,t 为当前迭代步数,t_{max} 表示最大迭代步数。

1.2.2 收敛能分析

本节将通过对比自适应权重法来说明线性递减权重法的有效性。自适应权重法的权重 ω 是根据适应度函数不断变化的,其 ω 可设置为:

$$\omega = \begin{cases} \omega max - \dfrac{(\omega_{max} - \omega_{min}) \times (f - f_{min})}{(f_{avg} - f_{min})}, & f < f_{avg} \\ w_{max}, & f > f_{avg} \end{cases}$$

其中 ω_{max}、ω_{min} 表示取值限值,f 表示适应度值,f_{avg}、f_{min} 分别表示当前所有粒子的平均适应度值和最小适应度值。

为了对算法性能进行测试,常选用 Sphere 函数和 Rosenbrock 函数作为测试函数。本节将取二维函数对两种粒子群算法进行测试,其中最大迭代步数设置为 200。为了对比其收敛性能,各算法的参数应设为相同,见表 1。

各算法参数设置表 表 1

算法类型	ω	c_1	c_2	粒子数	最大迭代步数
自适应权重 PSO	$\omega_{max}=0.9$、$\omega_{min}=0.4$	2	2	40	200/500
线性递减权重 PSO	$\omega_{max}=0.9$、$\omega_{min}=0.4$	2	2	40	200/500

本节对每种算法各进行 30 次运算,记录其平均、最优适应度等数据,并对其标准差和计算时间等进行汇总,得到对比结果见表 2。

二维函数各算法对比 表 2

测试函数类型	算法类型	适应度平均值	最小适应度值	最差适应度值	标准差	平均计算时间(s)
Sphere	自适应权重 PSO	5.27e-7	1.83e-9	2.14e-6	7.48e-7	0.46670
	线性递减权重 PSO	2.86e-19	3.10e-23	2.72e-18	8.12e-19	0.47165
Rosenbrock	自适应权重 PSO	1.31e-03	1.89e-06	1.14e-02	3.36e-03	0.51144
	线性递减权重 PSO	8.89e-13	5.19e-21	8.87e-12	2.67e-12	0.51575

由表 2 可知,对于二维 Sphere 和 Rosenbrock 的优化求解,线性递减权重 PSO 的精度优于自适应权重 PSO,且其标准差远小于自适应权重 PSO,说明稳定性较好。因此,对于两参数的优化问题,线性递减权重粒子群算法具有精度高、稳定性好等优点。

1.3 优化响应面法有限元模型修正流程

优化响应面法在桥梁结构有限元模型修正中可分为 5 个部分,即有限元模型部分、响应面部分、现场试验部分、优化算法部分、优化求解部分。其流程图如图 1 所示。

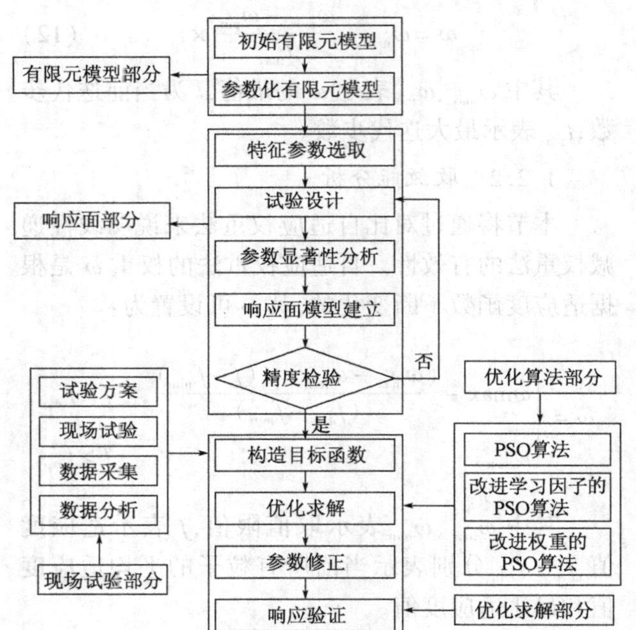

图1　有限元模型修正流程图

2　单梁加载试验

2.1　测点布置

本次试验选择简支箱梁的跨中截面和四分点截面进行挠度测试,每个断面布置两个挠度测点,并在支座处(F-F、G-G)设置挠度测点,消除其变形的影响。在损伤节段1、2(截面D-D、E-E)处各布置四个应变测点。测点断面图与测点布置图如图2、图3所示。

2.2　现场试验测试

对所测试的简支梁分三级加载,每级加载121kN,所得到的挠度值、应变值与其初始值的对比结果见表3、表4。

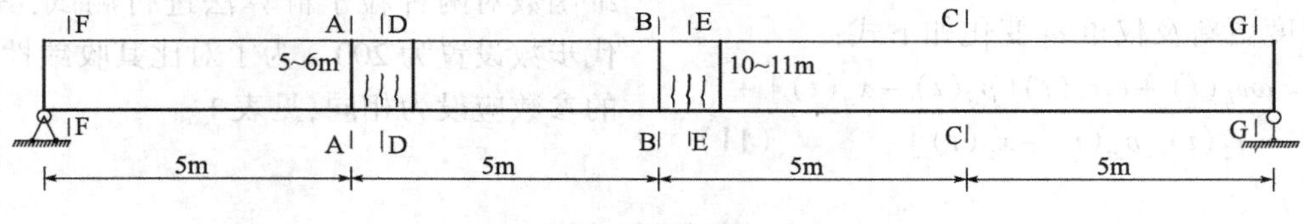

图2　测试断面图

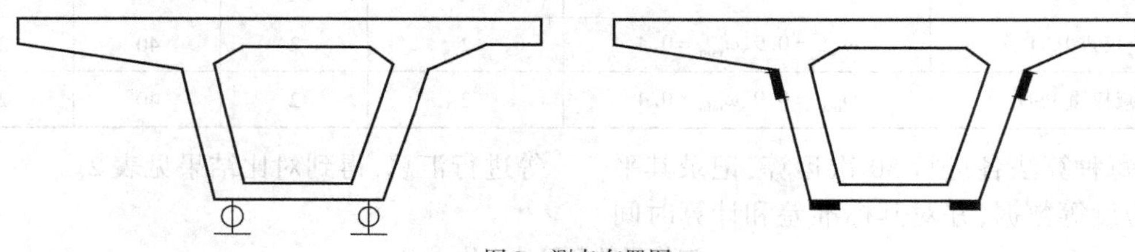

图3　测点布置图

注:⏀为挠度测点,▬为应变测点。

挠度初始计算值与其实测值对比　　表3

测　点	d_A(mm)	d_B(mm)	d_C(mm)
初始计算值	6.345	9.51	6.598
实测值	6.913	10.303	6.802
相对误差	8.22%	7.70%	3.00%

应变对比表　　表4

测　点	初始计算值(10^{-6})	实测值(10^{-6})	相对误差
1	-26	-29	10.34%
2	-26	-30	13.33%
3	98	111	11.71%
4	98	109	10.09%

续上表

测 点	初始计算值(10^{-6})	实测值(10^{-6})	相对误差
5	-48	-53	9.43%
6	-48	-56	14.29%
7	182	205	11.22%
8	182	212	14.15%

3 有限元模型修正

3.1 参数选择与试验设计

本次试验采用中心复合试验设计，选取损伤节段1的弹性模量(E1)和密度(D1)、损伤节段2的弹性模量(E2)和密度(D2)作为试验设计参数。得到中心复合试验设计表，见表5。

中心复合试验设计表 表5

试验点	A-E_1($\times10^4$MPa)	B-E_2($\times10^4$MPa)	C-D_1($\times10^3$kg/m^3)	D-D_2($\times10^3$kg/m^3)	d_A(mm)	d_B(mm)	d_C(mm)
1	4.1400	2.0700	2.9997	2.9997	7.3111	11.0457	7.3974
2	4.1400	2.0700	1.9994	2.9997	7.3111	11.0457	7.3974
3	2.0700	4.1400	1.9994	2.9997	7.1468	10.1864	6.9262
…	…	…	…	…	…	…	…
28	3.1050	3.1050	2.4995	2.4995	6.5912	10.0659	6.8798
29	3.1050	3.1050	2.4995	2.4995	6.5912	10.0659	6.8798
30	4.1400	4.1400	2.9997	2.9997	6.3905	9.6822	6.6741

3.2 参数显著性分析与响应面建立

(1)F检验法参数显著性分析。

根据得到的样本值进行计算统计分析得到参数显著性分析图，如图4所示。

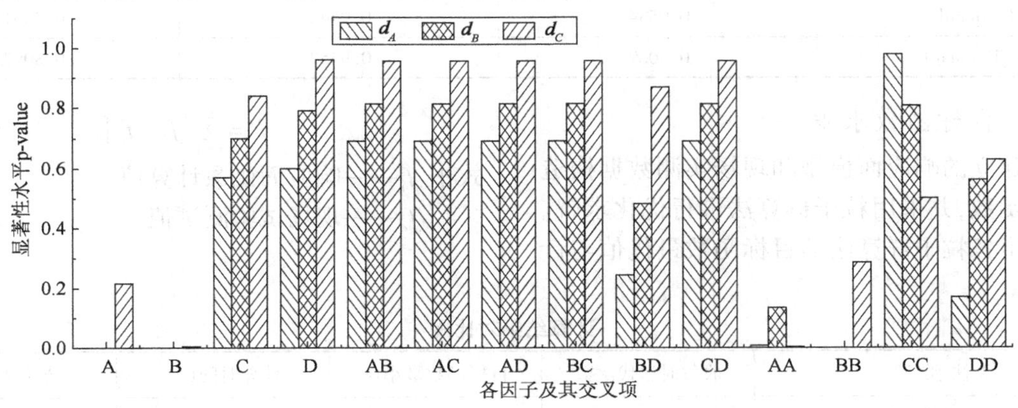

图4 参数显著性分析图

在本次方差分析中设置显著性水平为0.05，当$p\in[0,0.001]$时，该参数影响高度显著；当$P\in(0.001,0.05)$时，该参数影响显著；当$P\in(0.05,1)$时，该参数影响不显著。由图4可知，挠度d_A、d_B、d_C对其弹性模量一次项影响显著，对密度一次项、二次项及其交叉项影响不显著。d_B对弹性模量的E1的二次项影响不显著，d_C对弹性模量的E2的二次项影响不显著。

(2)响应面模型的建立。

合理对参数进行取舍，选取显著性高的参数建立二阶响应面模型，如图5所示。并计算其精度见表6。

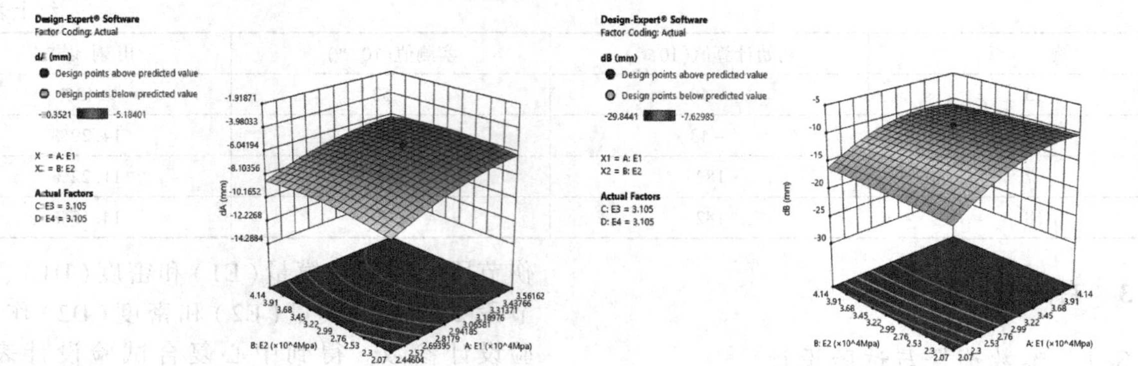

a)d_A关于E1、E2的二阶响应面图像　　b)d_B关于E1、E2的二阶响应面图像

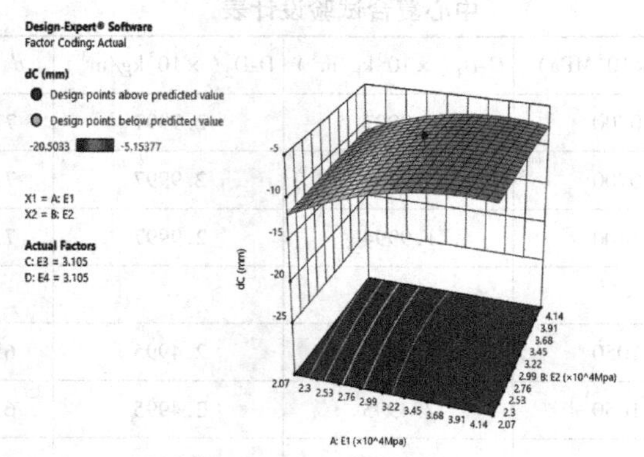

c)d_C关于E1、E2的二阶响应面图像

图5　d_A、d_B、d_C 二阶多项式响应面图像

二次多项式响应面精度检验表　　表6

评价准则	d_A	d_B	d_C
R-squard	0.9534	0.9844	0.9051
AdjR-squard	0.9069	0.9352	0.8067

3.3　目标函数求解

根据建立的响应面模型和现场实测数据构造误差目标函数,并采用粒子群算法进行优化求解。表7给出了各粒子群算法的目标函数最优值与计算时间。

$$F = \sum_{i=1}^{n} |f_i - f_c| \tag{13}$$

式中:f_i——响应面函数计算值;

f_c——现场试验测试值。

计算结果对比图　　表7

算法类型	收敛时迭代次数	目标函数最小值	计算时间(s)	最优解取值
标准PSO算法	115	0.1047	0.536679	(2.8039,3.1289)
同步变化学习因子PSO算法	185	0.1047	0.537390	(2.8039,3.1289)
异步变化学习因子PSO算法	109	0.1047	0.546170	(2.8039,3.1289)
线性权重递减PSO算法	70	0.1047	0.532080	(2.8039,3.1289)

由表7可得,正后损伤节段1的弹性模量为2.8039×104 MPa,下降18.7%;损伤节段2的弹性模量为3.1289×104 MPa,与设计值相比下降9.3%。究其原因,施工质量不高导致混凝土振捣不够密实,造成该部位出现损伤,且裂缝的存在会降低混凝土的刚度,因此节段的整体弹性模量

降低。

3.4 响应验证

将目标函数的计算结果代入初始模型进行参数修正,并计算得到修正后的有限元模型计算结果,如表8、图6、表9、图7所示。

修正后挠度与误差对比图　　表8

测　　点	d_A(mm)	d_B(mm)	d_C(mm)
初始计算值	6.345	9.510	6.598
实测值	6.913	10.303	6.802
修正后计算值	6.620	10.090	6.690
初始误差	8.22%	7.70%	3.00%
相对误差	4.43%	2.11%	1.67%

修正后应变与误差对比表　　表9

测　　点	初始计算值($\mu\varepsilon$)	实测值($\mu\varepsilon$)	修正值后计算值	初始相对误差	修正后相对误差
1	-26	-29	-28	10.34%	3.45%
2	-26	-30	-28	13.33%	6.67%
3	98	111	104	11.71%	6.31%
4	98	109	104	10.09%	4.59%
5	-48	-53	-51	9.43%	3.77%
6	-48	-56	-51	14.29%	8.93%
7	182	205	194	11.22%	5.37%
8	182	212	194	14.15%	8.49%

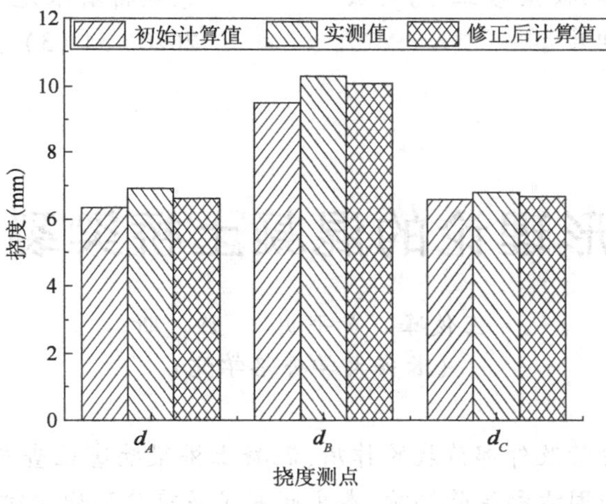

图6　修正前后挠度对比图

由表8、表9及图6、图7可得,修正后的模型挠度计算值与应变计算值均明显降低,其中修正后的挠度结果最小误差降到2%以内,应变误差最小降到4%以内。修正后的有限元模型静力特性与实际结构相吻合,能够反映结构力学性能,实现了对简支单梁的有限元模型修正和损伤识别。

4　结语

本文以简支梁为例,应用优化响应面法并结合静力实测数据对其有限元模型进行修正,得到以下结论:

(1)结合线性递减权重粒子群算法,分别以两种不同的算法对目标函数进行优化求解,结果表明线性递减权重粒子群算法能快速完成对目标函数的求解过程,高效精确。

(2)将优化求解结果代入初始模型进行响应验证,其计算值与实测值趋于一致,验证了基于响应面-线性递减权重粒子群算法的模型修正方法的可行性与准确性。

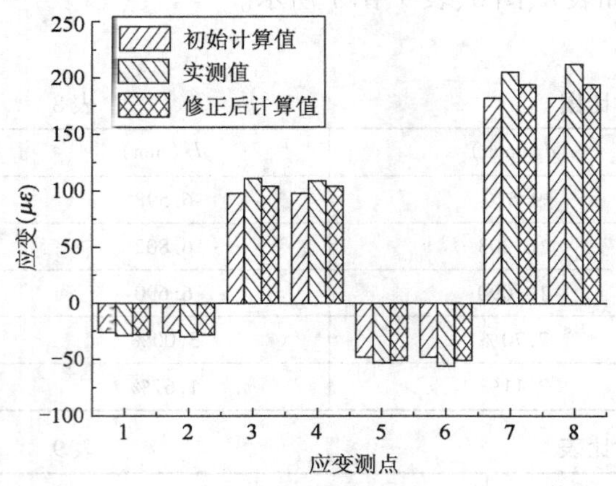

图7 修正前后应变对比图

参考文献

[1] 吴杰. 桥梁结构损伤识别若干问题研究[D]. 广州:华南理工大学, 2020.

[2] Berman A. Comment on Optimal Weighted Orthogonalization of Measured Modes [J]. AIAA Journal, 1979, 17 (8) : 927-928.

[3] 陈彦江, 程永欢, 李勇, 等. 基于参数灵敏度分析的连续刚构桥有限元模型修正 [J]. 公路, 2014, 59(7) : 144-149.

[4] 杨雅勋, 杨福利, 陈东. 改进响应面法在桥梁结构有限元模型修正中的应用 [J]. 公路交通科技, 2020, 37 (10) : 83-91 + 133.

[5] 陈东. 基于响应面法的桥梁结构有限元模型修正与应用 [D]. 西安:长安大学, 2017.

[6] Deshan Shan, Qiao Li, Inamullah Khan, et al. A Novel Finite Element Model Updating Method based on Substructure and Response Surface Model [J]. Engineering Structures, 2015, 103 (15) : 147-156.

[7] 付雷, 马闻达, 高鹏, 等. 基于 RSM-WOA 的桥梁结构有限元模型修正 [J]. 中国科技论文, 2021, 16 (8) : 875-882.

[8] 徐喆, 辛景舟, 唐启智, 等. 基于响应面法和麻雀搜索算法的结构有限元模型修正 [J]. 科学技术与工程, 2021, 21 (21) : 9094-9101.

[9] 宋晓东, 颜永逸, 李佳靖, 等. 基于子结构的大型桥梁有限元模型修正方法 [J]. 桥梁建设, 2021, 51 (2) : 40-46.

[10] 张梓乔, 雷建平. 基于改进响应面的刚构-连续梁桥有限元模型修正 [J]. 工程与建设, 2020, 34 (3) : 386-388.

基于多重分形理论的混凝土桥梁裂缝特征研究

王俊峰 黄平明* 许 昕
(长安大学公路学院)

摘 要 由于长时间的运营及外部荷载的作用,混凝土桥梁病害检查与养护工作面临巨大的挑战。为了消除人工视觉检查的人为因素和经验影响,本文研究了多重分形理论对于混凝土桥梁裂缝特征描述的适用性,为混凝土桥梁裂缝快速特征定量分析及快速检测提供技术支撑。首先,介绍多重分形的理论依据及关键参数求解方法;其次,根据影响混凝土桥梁裂缝特征的四种因素,即粗糙度、方向、宽度及数量,给出9种不同裂缝分布图像;最后,计算得到不同影响因素下裂缝多重分形谱的结果,并进行对比分析。结果表明:不同裂缝分布图像符合多重分形特征,基于线性拟合估计关键参数的方法拟合优度较好。多重分形谱的演变规律与裂缝的发展规律一致,具体表现为:随着裂缝粗糙度、宽度及数量的增大,多重分形谱向更大的值移动,谱最大值(分形维数)不断增大,分形谱的形状也发生明显变化。裂缝方向不同,多重分形谱的最大值不变,但分形谱的谱宽发生改变。由此可以看出,多重分形理论对于定量描述混凝土桥梁裂缝特征及桥梁快速检测具有一定的应用潜力。

1. 基金项目:国家自然科学基金(51878058);国家得点研发计划项目(2019YEB1600702)。

关键词 桥梁工程 裂缝特征 多重分形理论 混凝土桥梁 影响因素

0 引言

钢筋混凝土是我国基础设施建设中常用的建筑材料之一，尤其在桥梁建设方面应用更为广泛。我国桥梁统计数据显示，截至2020年我国公路桥梁总数达到了91.28万座，其中超过90%为混凝土桥梁。随着服役时间的增长及外部荷载（超载、大件运输及地震、撞击等极端荷载）的作用，部分桥梁产生了大量的病害，其中梁体裂缝是混凝土桥梁养护工作中最为突出的挑战[1]。为此，我国颁布了一系列公路桥梁日常养护及技术状况调查规范，如《公路桥涵养护规范》《公路桥梁技术状况评定标准》等，这些规范对桥梁病害的描述及评级做了详细的规定，其中对于混凝土构件的开裂特征及分级描述更加具体，一定程度上规范了桥梁养护工作[2]。但目前我国公路混凝土桥梁病害调查工作多基于人工视觉检查，桥梁技术状况评定结论与检测人员的专业水平和从业经验息息相关，受人为因素影响较大，且无法对其进行准确的定量分析研究，与结构性能间的关系也不明确。为了解决这一问题，近年来，基于图像识别的混凝土桥梁裂缝自动检测及评估成了桥梁病害检测的热门技术[3-5]。

对混凝土桥梁裂缝进行定量描述，以及表征结构的力学性能需要合适的数学工具，为了解决这一问题，分形几何理论被引入混凝土开裂特征分析中。分形几何理论是用来描述复杂形状内在规律的一门学科，它将表现复杂的几何形状用简单的参数和公式表达出来。经过一个多世纪的发展，分形几何理论在材料学科及土木工程学科中的应用日益广泛，为钢筋混凝土材料的裂纹分析提供了新的研究思路[6-8]。不少学者也开展了关于混凝土构件的分形试验研究，殷亚娟等[9]对多组混凝土试件的单轴拉伸力学行为进行损伤数值研究，利用分形维对混凝土开裂全过程中的裂纹分布进行表征，研究了分形维数与混凝土损伤发展之间的联系。于江等[10-11]基于分形理论研究了无腹筋混凝土梁的抗剪性能及再生混凝土梁裂纹演化规律，分析了分形维数与试验梁力学性能间的函数关系。栾海洋等[12]研究了受腐蚀CFRP布增强混凝土梁表面裂缝分布的分形特征，基于分形理论分析了受腐蚀混凝土梁在弯曲荷载作用下的开裂及破坏过程，详细讨论了梁表面裂缝的分形维数与其抗弯性能参数之间的关系。

综上所述，为解决混凝土桥梁最为突出的病害问题，诸多学者对混凝土桥梁裂缝识别及评估技术开展了研究。分形理论作为一种实用的几何形状分析工具，被广泛用于混凝土构件裂缝特征描述中，但在已有的研究中最常采用的特征参数为分形维数，这是单重分形的唯一参数。虽然已有的研究成果验证了分析混凝土裂缝特征的潜力，但众所周知，混凝土桥梁裂缝的产生和发展具有较强的离散性及随机性，裂缝分布形式复杂，单一参数无法表征其更深层次的特征。多重分形理论作为单重分形理论的进一步拓展，弥补了单一特征参数的缺陷，但多重分形对混凝土桥梁裂缝的描述尚未得到有效的研究和验证。

因此，本文首先对分形理论及多重分形理论的分析方法进行介绍，然后设置不同影响因素下的混凝土桥梁裂缝图像，最后基于多重分形理论对其进行分析，验证分析的有效性，分析不同影响因素下多重分形特征的演变规律，为多重分形理论在混凝土桥梁裂缝特征研究及桥梁快速检测方面的应用提供技术支撑。

1 多重分形理论

1.1 分形理论

1965年，Mandelbrot针对“英国的海岸线有多长”这一问题第一次提出分形理论。1975年，他提出了分形维数（Fractal Dimension，FD）的概念[13]。分形维数是表征分形分析结果最核心的参数，它突破了传统欧式几何学对维数的限制，为自然界中复杂形状的构造描述提供了定量分析工具。以一条长为L的线段为例，如果以尺度r测量这条线段，得到$N(r)$个r，则有下述关系式存在：

$$N(r) \times r^1 = L \tag{1}$$

同理，对于面积为S的平面图形及体积为V立体图形，分别以尺度r^2、r^3去测量，则有下述关系式存在：

$$N(r) \times r^2 = S \tag{2}$$

$$N(r) \times r^3 = V \tag{3}$$

上述关系式可以用统一的表达式表示为：

$$N(r) \times r^d = C \tag{4}$$

式中 C 为所测量的几何形状的物理表征，d 为拓扑维数。对于规则几何体而言，拓扑维数在欧氏几何中都是整数，但如果去除整数的限制，则可以将欧式几何维数推广为分形维数，以 FD 表示。

将式(4)中的拓扑维数 d 替换为分形维数 FD，可以得出：

$$FD = \frac{\ln[C/N(r)]}{\ln r} \tag{5}$$

对式(5)进行变换可得：

$$\begin{aligned} FD \cdot \ln r &= \ln C - \ln[N(r)]; \\ -\ln(N(r)) &= FD \cdot \ln r - \ln C; \\ \ln(N(r)) &= -FD \cdot \ln r + \ln C; \\ \ln(N(r)) &= FD \cdot \ln r^{-1} + \ln C \end{aligned} \tag{6}$$

由式(6)可以看出，$N(r)$ 与 $\ln r^{-1}$ 呈线性关系，其斜率即为分形维数的大小。减小 r 的尺寸，$N(r)$ 将随之增大。根据 $N(r)$ 与 $\ln r^{-1}$ 的线性关系，盒形计数法(Box-counting method)被提出用于计算图像的分形维数，这也是目前最常用的一种计算分形维数的方法。其主要思路为以边长为 r 的盒子去覆盖所要分析的图像，然后对非空盒子(所分析的图像穿过该盒子)进行计数，结果记为 $N(r)$。在实际应用中取 n 个不同尺度的 r，将会有 n 个 $N(r)$ 与之对应，将这 n 组数据绘制在双对数坐标上，求得直线的斜率即为分形维数的大小。可以预见，对于平面图形而言，分形维数的取值范围为[1,2]。

1.2 多重分形

对于简单的分形，用一个分形维数就可以描述它的特征。但对于混凝土构件的表面裂纹而言，其分布路径较为复杂，且具有较强的随机性和不均匀性，包含多个不同层次的统计特征。此时，单一参量无法准确描述裂纹分布的特征，需要多个参量才能描述，由此多位学者提出了多重分形理论的概念[14]，用来解决复杂分形图像的描述问题。

下面接着盒形计数法的概念介绍多重分形的主要思想。盒形计数法在计数过程中每个盒子中落入一个或多个像素点均被记数为1，也就是说含有一个点或多个点的盒子具有的权重相等，不能反映图像的不均匀性。因此，我们通过计算每个盒子中像元密度的大小，来表示图像中各点落入各个盒子的概率，本文称之为狭义概率密度值：

$$P_i(r) = \frac{N_i(r)}{\sum_{i=1}^{N(r)} N_i(r)} \tag{7}$$

$P_i(r)$ 的大小与 r 的大小是相关的，因此我们定义 $P_i(r) \sim r^{\alpha_i}$($\sim$ 表示正比于)，其中 α_i 一般称为奇异指数，反映了局部区域内概率子集的分布特征。如果将具有相同 α 值的盒子数记为 $N_\alpha(r)$，则它与盒子尺寸的大小同样存在幂函数关系，可以写为 $N_\alpha(r) \sim r^{-f(\alpha)}$，$f(\alpha)$ 的物理意义表示具有相同 α 值的子集的分形维数。$f(\alpha) \sim \alpha$ 的函数关系称为多重分析谱或奇异谱。

为进一步了解 $f(\alpha)$ 与 α 的分布特征，引入统计物理中的矩表示方法，定义函数 $\chi_q(r)$，对各个盒子的概率进行加权求和，函数表达式为：

$$\chi_q(r) = \sum_{i=1}^{N(r)} P_i^q(r) \sim r^{\tau(q)} \tag{8}$$

由式(8)可以得出 $\tau(q) = \lim\limits_{r\to 0} \frac{\ln \sum_{i=1}^{N(r)} P_i^q(r)}{\ln r}$，同时，定义 $\sum_{i=1}^{N(r)} P_i^q(r) \sim r^{(q-1)D_q}$，式中 $D_q = \frac{1}{q-1} \lim\limits_{r\to 0} \frac{\ln \sum_{i=1}^{N(r)} P_i^q(r)}{\ln r}$。

式中，$\tau(q)$ 称为质量系数，D_q 称为广义分形维数，二者存在 $D_q = (1/q-1)\tau_q$ 的函数关系。q 为每个盒子的权重系数，当 q 大于1时，代表增强概率密度高值的影响；当 q 小于1时，代表增强概率密度低值的影响；当 q 等于0时，$\chi_q(r)$ 退化为 $N(r)$，D_q 退化为 FD，即分形维数。

如果 $\chi_q(r)$ 和 r 在双对数坐标图中呈线性关系或 $\tau(q)$ 为 q 的凸曲线函数，则认为该研究对象具有多重分形特征。因此，$f(\alpha)$ 与 α 均可通过线性拟合的方法求解。Chhabra 等在1989年提出了一种多重分形谱的简化计算方法，主要步骤如下：

(1)首先定义正则化函数：

$$\mu_i(q,r) = \frac{P_i^q(r)}{\sum_{i=1}^{N(r)} P_i^q(r)} \in [0,1] \tag{9}$$

式中 $\mu_i(q,r)$ 为 q 和 r 的函数，本文称之为广义概率密度，当 $q=1$ 时，$\mu_i(q,r)$ 退化为 $P_i(r)$，对于任意尺度的盒子尺寸都存在 $\sum\mu_i(q,r)=1$。

(2)计算 $\alpha(q)$ 与 $f(q)$：

$$\alpha(q)=\lim_{r\to 0}\frac{\sum_{i=1}^{N(r)}\mu_i(q,r)\ln[P_i(r)]}{\ln(r)} \tag{10}$$

$$f(q)=\lim_{r\to 0}\frac{\sum_{i=1}^{N(r)}\mu_i(q,r)\ln[\mu_i(q,r)]}{\ln(r)} \tag{11}$$

在实际应用中，我们需要取不同的 q，然后分别绘制 $\sum_{i=1}^{N(r)}\mu_i(q,r)\ln[P_i(r)]$ 与 $\ln(r)$ 的散点图和 $\sum_{i=1}^{N(r)}\mu_i(q,r)\ln[\mu_i(q,r)]$ 与 $\ln(r)$ 的散点图，通过线性拟合的方法分别求得两组数据的斜率，即为 $f(q)$ 与 $\alpha(q)$。$\tau(q)$、D_q 同样可以采取线性拟合的方法进行计算。多重分形谱的形状为凸曲线，曲线最高点即为分形维数 FD。

2 不同混凝土桥梁裂缝特征影响因素

大量的混凝土构件试验及现场检测结果表明，混凝土桥梁裂缝表面特征的主要影响因素有裂缝表面粗糙度、裂缝发展方向、裂缝宽度、裂缝数量。本节根据四种影响因素，设置 9 种不同发展阶段的裂缝分布图，图幅像素尺寸均为 1276 × 1276，详细构造如图 1 所示；然后应用多重分形理论计算各种影响因素下的多重分形谱，并进行对比分析。

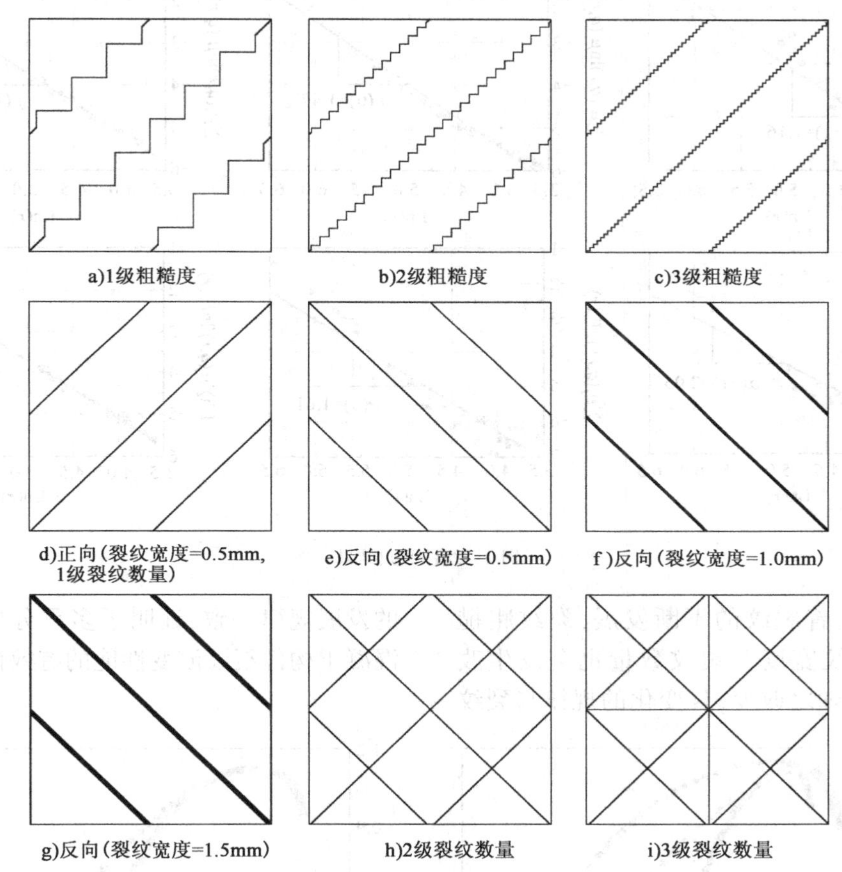

图 1　不同形式的裂纹图像

3 多重分形结果

1.2 节指出，多重分形谱的关键参数 D_q、$f(q)$ 和 $\alpha(q)$ 可以通过在整个盒子尺寸范围内使用回归线计算得到，图 2 列出了图 1i) 的部分回归分析结果，q 的取值分别为 −1,0,1。由图 2 可以看出，当 q 小于 0 时，线性拟合优度小于 $q\geq 0$ 时的拟合优度，但拟合效果总体较好，证明了 1.2 节计算方法的准确性。

基于线性拟合方法对图 1 不同形式的裂纹图像进行多重分形，结果如图 3 所示。由图 3 可以看出：①随着裂纹不断扩展，表面粗糙度不断加深，裂纹方向、裂纹宽度及数量也会发生改变。在裂纹演变的进程中，多重分形谱的形状不断发生改变;②裂纹粗糙度等级、裂纹宽度及裂纹数量的增大导致多重分形谱不断向右上方移动,即分形谱的顶点 FD 向更大的值移动;③裂纹方向不影响分形谱的最大值,但不同裂纹方向分形谱的宽度有所不同。

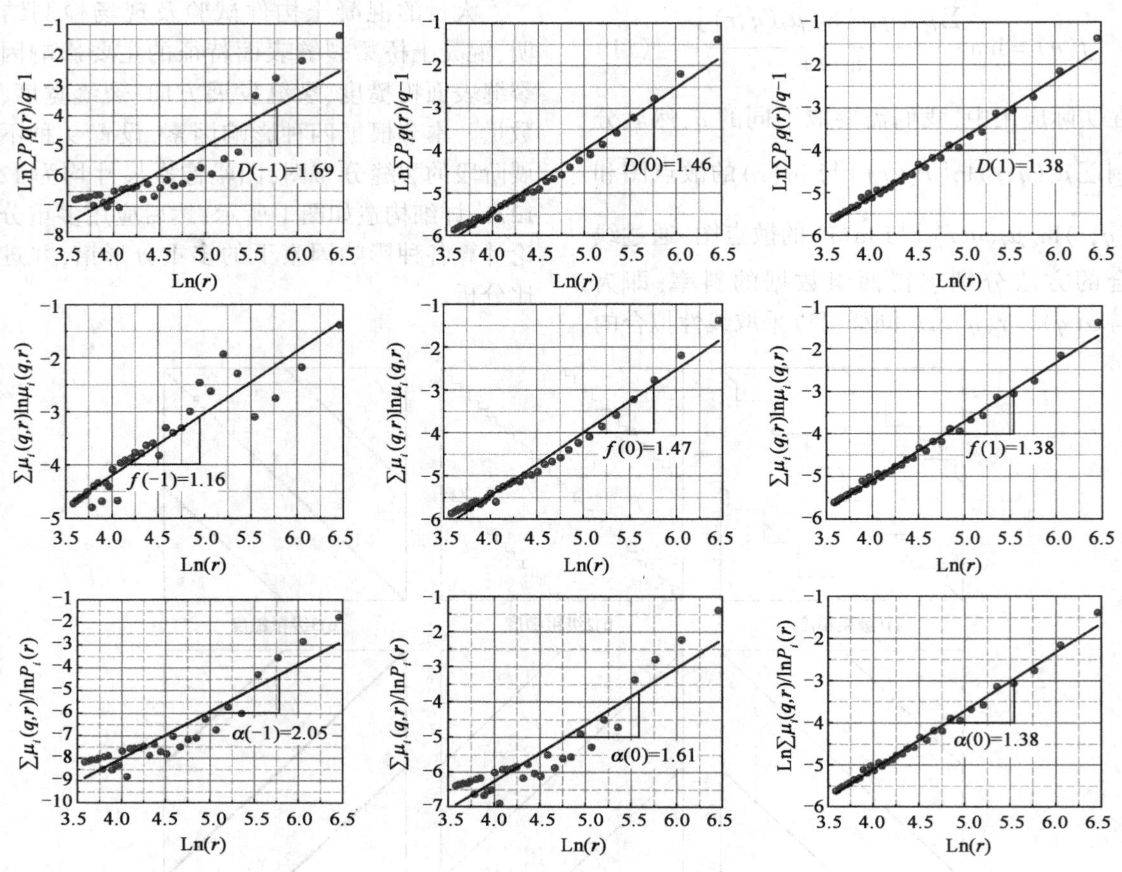

图2　线性回归结果

综上所述,随着裂纹的不断发展,裂纹粗糙度、裂纹方向、裂纹宽度及裂纹数量也会发生改变,多重分形谱也随之改变,且变化的规律与裂纹的发展规律一致,证明了多重分形对于定量表征混凝土构件裂纹演变性能的有效性。

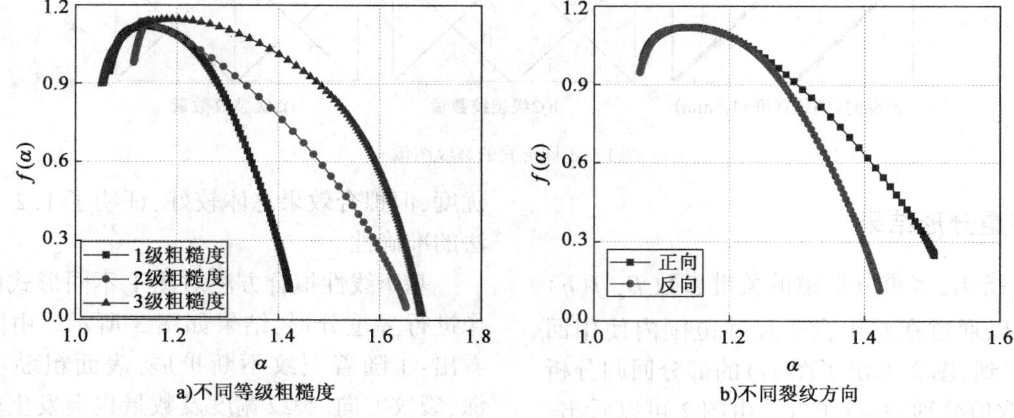

a)不同等级粗糙度　　b)不同裂纹方向

图　3

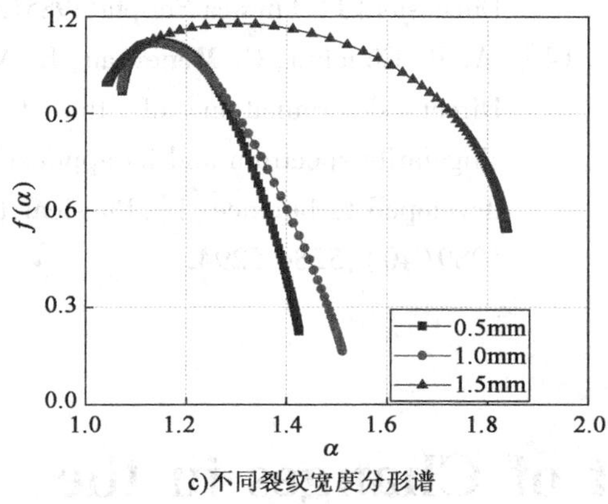

c)不同裂纹宽度分形谱

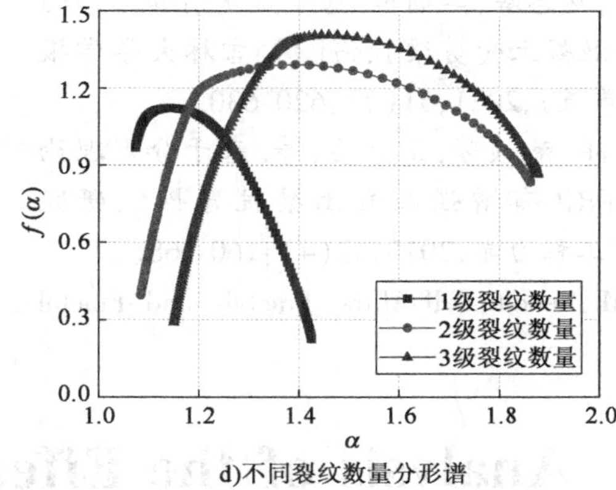

d)不同裂纹数量分形谱

图3　不同裂纹形态的多重分形谱

4　结语

本文给出了多重分形理论的理论基础及求解过程,基于裂纹粗糙度、裂纹方向、裂纹宽度及裂纹数量4种混凝土裂纹的主要影响因素,设置9种不同形式的裂纹图形,利用多重分形理论对其进行分析,展示了多重分形谱中关键参数的部分线性回归结果及最终的多重分形谱图形。得到的主要结论如下:

(1)利用线性回归的方法对多重分形谱的关键参数进行估计的结果较为合理,权重系数 q 越大,回归直线对参数的拟合程度越好。

(2)随着裂纹粗糙度等级、裂纹宽度及裂纹数量不断增加,多重分形谱的形状不断向右上方移动,谱最大值(FD)也不断增加。裂纹方向的改变不影响多重分形谱的最大值,但裂纹方向不同,分形谱的形状有较大差异。

(3)多重分形谱的变化规律与裂纹的演变规律一致,随着裂纹演变进程的深入,多重分形谱上的值向更大的值移动,不同裂纹方向对分形谱的演变也有一定的影响。上述规律证明了多重分形理论对于混凝土裂纹演变规律的响应效果较好,可以作为混凝土裂纹定量描述的工具。

本文初步验证了多重分形理论对于混凝土裂纹演变规律定量描述有一定的应用潜力,基于裂纹图像可以快速对混凝土开裂情况进行勘察,提高了混凝土桥梁日常养护工作的效率。但多重分形在混凝土桥梁中的实际应用还需要进一步的模型试验和现场测试等工作,后续将对此展开进一步研究。

参考文献

[1]《中国公路学报》编辑部. 中国桥梁工程学术研究综述·2021[J]. 中国公路学报,2021,34(2):1-97.

[2] 贺拴海,赵祥模,马建,等. 公路桥梁检测及评价技术综述[J]. 中国公路学报,2017,30(11):63-80.

[3] 阮小丽,王波,荆国强,等. 桥梁混凝土结构表面裂缝自动识别技术研究[J]. 世界桥梁,2017,45(6):55-59.

[4] 高庆飞,王宇,刘晨光,等. 基于卷积神经网络算法的混凝土桥梁裂缝识别与定位技术[J]. 公路,2020,65(9):268-274.

[5] B. Omondi, D. G. Aggelis, H. Sol, et al. Improved crack monitoring in structural concrete by combined acoustic emission and digital image correlation techniques [J]. Structural Health Monitoring,2016(15):359-378.

[6] 郭伟,秦鸿根,陈惠苏,等. 分形理论及其在混凝土材料研究中的应用[J]. 硅酸盐学报,2010,38(7):1362-1368.

[7] 陈万春,师晖军,晁宗棋. 基于分形理论的钢筋混凝土梁式桥裂缝发育特征[J]. 长安大学学报(自然科学版),2003(6):44-46.

[8] 成盛,金南国,田野,等. 混凝土裂缝特征参数的图形化定量分析新方法[J]. 浙江大学学报(工学版),2011,45(6):1062-1066.

[9] 殷亚娟,任青文,沈雷,等. 基于分形维的混凝土裂纹扩展及损伤演化过程研究[J/OL]. 水利学报:1-11.

[10] 于江,吕旭滨,秦拥军. 基于分形理论无腹筋混凝土梁的受剪性能[J]. 工程科学学报,2021,43(10):1385-1396.

[11] 于江,赵志浩,秦拥军.基于声发射和分形的钢筋混凝土受剪梁损伤[J].吉林大学学报(工学版),2021,51(2):620-630.
[12] 栾海洋,范颖芳,王大为,等.基于分形理论的CFRP布增强混凝土梁抗弯性能研究[J].工程力学,2015,32(4):160-168.
[13] B. M. Benoit. Self-Affine Fractals and Fractal Dimension[J],Physica Scripta,1985(32):257.
[14] A. B. Chhabra, C. Meneveau, R. V. Jensen. Direct determination of the f (alpha) singularity spectrum and its application to fully developed turbulence[J],Physical Review A, 1989(40):5284-5294.

Analysis of the Effect of Changes in the Vertical-to-span Ratio of Suspension Bridges on the Structure

Wentao Ma* Pei Tao[2]
(Department of Traffic Engineering,College of Transportation Engineering,Chang'an University)

Abstract Based on a twin-tower single-span suspension bridge,combined with its design information and bridge non-linear analysis, the influence of the suspension bridge's main cable unstressed length, main cable force,main cable hollow cable line shape and saddle pre-deflection is analysed with the suspension bridge vertical-to-span ratio as the variable,to derive the influence on the suspension bridge's main cable and provide effective suggestions for the design and construction of this type of bridge.

Keywords Single span suspension bridges Vertical to span ratio Unstressed length of main cable Hollow cable line shape Pre-deflection

0 Introduction

Suspension bridges are bridges consisting of main cables, stiffening beams, cables, anchors, towers and deck systems, with the cables as the main load-bearing structure, whose load characteristics include: firstly, the load acting on the bridge deck is transferred to the main cables through the stiffening beams via the cables, and then the main cables are divided into the tangential direction and vertical direction of the main cables along the side spans into the pressure on the towers and anchors. The main load-bearing element of a suspension bridge is the main cable strand in tension, the tensile strength of the high-strength steel wire in the strand can be brought into full play, making it the most powerful form of bridge in terms of spanning capacity.

The vertical to span ratio is the ratio f/L between the drape f of the main cable in the main bore and the span L of the main bore. The size of the vertical to span ratio has a great influence on the tension in the main cable and is an important indicator in the overall design. The vertical to span ratio is inversely proportional to the tension in the main cable and the pressure on the tower, and is positively proportional to the height of the tower. The larger the vertical to span ratio, the greater the vertical deflection and lateral deflection of the suspension bridge. The vertical to span ratio is generally between 1/9 and 1/12. The vertical to span ratio of the main cable of a suspension bridge has an effect on the overall stiffness of the structure, but it also has a certain influence on the vibration characteristics of the structure. This paper mainly studies the influence of the vertical span ratio on the stress length, force, hollow cable shape and saddle precession of the main cable of suspension bridges, in order to provide a technical reference for the selection of the vertical span ratio in the future design of such bridges.

1 Project example

The project example is a single span stiffened girder suspension bridge, the span of the main bridge is composed into 255m + 920m + 255m, the mid-span sagittal span ratio is 1/10, the transverse centre distance of the sling is 27.5m, the longitudinal centre distance of the sling is 12.0m, Transverse wind bearing, vertical main bearing and longitudinal limit damping device are set at the cable tower, one expansion joint is set at each end of the stiffened girder, the total unconstrained expansion is 1800mm. The stiffening beam is a streamlined flat steel box girder, 3.0m high and 31.0m wide (including wind spout). The main cables are made of prefabricated parallel steel wire strands (PPWS). In each main cable, there are 154 through-length strands from one side anchorage to the other, with no back ropes in the side spans. The example project bridge layout is shown in Fig. 1.

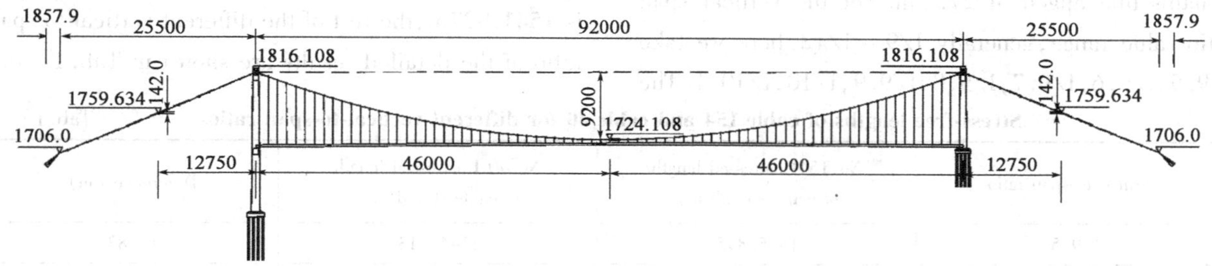

Fig. 1 Bridge arrangement (unit: cm)

The arrangement of the main cable strands is shown in Fig. 2.

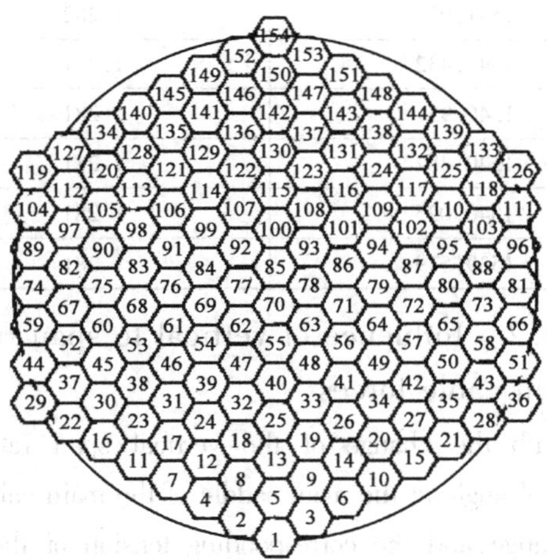

Fig. 2 Main cable strand arrangement

2 Calculation model and key assumptions

For the non-linear analysis of bridges, the following three assumptions are used in the analytical calculation of the main cables:

(1) The main cable material is linearly elastic and conforms to Hooke's Law.

(2) The main cables are ideally flexible and can only withstand tensile forces. The effect of cross-sectional bending stiffness on the cable shape is negligible.

(3) Do not consider the change in crosssectional area of the main cable before and after deformation.

Through the above assumptions, the self-weight constant load of the main cable is constant along the cable, and the curve of the main cable is suspended under self-weight, and satisfies the linear stress-strain relationship.

In the design of suspension bridges, the vector height of the main cable is always given first, and the design of the suspension bridge main cable system is based on the given information to determine the shape of the main cable, the unstressed length, the length of the sling, the offset of the saddle during construction and the installation position of the cable clamp.

In this paper, we study the effects of changing the span-to-span ratio of suspension bridges on various aspects of suspension bridges, and therefore only change the span-to-span ratio, which is set in the range of 1/9 to 1/12, where the main towers and stiffening beams and other parameters are unchanged.

3 Influence of vertical to span ratio on suspension bridge structures

This paper mainly studies all aspects of the suspension bridge's influence on the suspension bridge after the change of the sag-span ratio. When the sag-span ratio changes, the parameters of the main tower and stiffening beam are unchanged, and the distance between the two main cables of the mid-span remains unchanged at 27.5m. For the vertical span ratio value range, generally 1/9 ~ 1/12, here we take 1/9.5, 1/9.6, 1/9.7, 1/9.8, 1/9.9, 1/10, 1/10.1. The eleven sets of sag ratios of 1/10.2, 1/10.3, 1/10.4 and 1/10.5 are compared with each other, and the sag ratio of 1/0 is used as the reference value.

3.1 Effect of vertical-to-span ratio on the stress-free length of the main cable

With the above eleven sets of vertical to span ratios on the twin-tower single-span suspension bridge for the main cable stress-free length analysis, where we selected the longest cable strand 154 and the shortest cable strand 40 to calculate for comparison, the vertical to span ratio of 1/10, 154 cable stress-free length is 1543.209m, 40 cable stress-free length is 1541.927m, the rest of the different vertical to span ratio of the detailed results are shown in Tab. 1.

Stress-free lengths of cable 154 and cable 40 for different vertical-to-span ratios Tab. 1

Vertical-to-span ratio	No. 154Unstressed length of cable strand(m)	No. 40 Unstressed length of cable strand(m)	Difference (m)
1/9.5	1545.895	1544.613	1.282
1/9.6	1545.328	1544.046	1.282
1/9.7	1544.776	1543.494	1.282
1/9.8	1544.239	1542.957	1.282
1/9.9	1543.717	1542.435	1.282
1/10.0	1543.209	1541.927	1.282
1/10.1	1542.714	1541.432	1.281
1/10.2	1542.232	1540.951	1.281
1/10.3	1541.763	1540.482	1.281
1/10.4	1541.306	1540.025	1.281
1/10.5	1540.860	1539.579	1.281

The above results were plotted and are shown in Fig. 3.

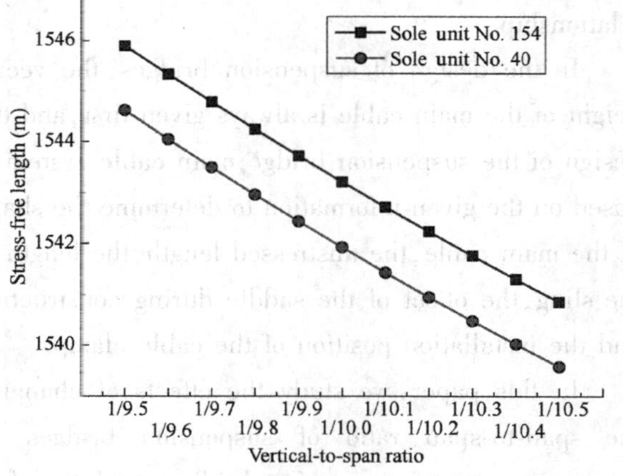

Fig. 3 Stress-free length of two strands at different vertical-to-span ratios

3.2 Influence of vertical to span ratio on main cable forces

With the change of the vertical span ratio, the horizontal angle at the main saddle of the main cable will also change, and the corresponding tension of the main cable will also change as a result, in which the vertical span ratio increases, the horizontal home church of the main cable measured in the middle span gradually becomes smaller, which will lead to its vertical angle constantly becoming larger, thus causing changes in the horizontal tension, the eleven sets of vertical span ratios selected above for the corresponding horizontal force calculation, and the results are obtained as shown in Tab. 2.

Effect of vertical-to-span ratio on horizontal rension Tab. 2

Vertical-to-span ratio	Horizontal tension of cables on both sides of the left saddle (kN)	Horizontal tension of cables on both sides of the right saddle (kN)	Rate of change relative to base value
1/9.5	136078.3	136078.3	-0.0497
1/9.6	137503	137503	-0.0398
1/9.7	138927.8	138927.8	-0.0299
1/9.8	140352.6	140352.6	-0.0199
1/9.9	141777.5	141777.5	-0.0100
1/10.0	143202.4	143202.4	0.0000
1/10.1	144627.4	144627.4	0.0100
1/10.2	146052.5	146052.5	0.0199
1/10.3	147477.5	147477.5	0.0299
1/10.4	148902.6	148902.6	0.0398
1/10.5	150327.8	150327.8	0.0498

The above results were plotted and are shown in Fig. 4.

As can be seen from the graphs and data, the horizontal tension of the main cable on the saddle continues to increase as the vertical to span ratio becomes smaller, with the largest rate of change of 4.98% at 1/10.5 vertical to span ratio compared to the base value.

Next we look at the variation in the total tension on the main cable, details of which are shown in Tab. 3.

The above results were plotted and are shown in Fig. 5.

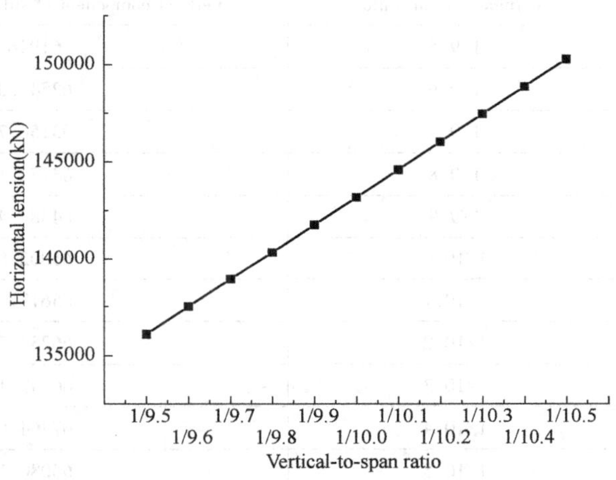

Fig. 4. Effect of vertical-to-span ratio on horizontal rension

Effect of drape-to-span ratio on total tension Tab. 3

Vertical-to-spanratio	Total tension in the mid-span lateral cable of the tower (kN)	Rate of change relative to base value	Total cable tension on the side span of the tower(kN)	Rate of change relative to base value
1/9.5	147524.4	-0.0427	149506.3	-0.0493
1/9.6	148837.4	-0.0342	151057.9	-0.0395
1/9.7	150152.6	-0.0257	152609.6	-0.0296
1/9.8	151469.8	-0.0171	154161.4	-0.0197
1/9.9	152789.1	-0.0086	155713.2	-0.0099
1/10.0	154110.3	0.0000	157265.1	0.0000
1/10.1	155433.5	0.0086	158817	0.0099
1/10.2	156758.6	0.0172	160369	0.0197
1/10.3	158085.5	0.0258	161921.1	0.0296
1/10.4	159414.1	0.0344	163473.1	0.0395
1/10.5	160744.5	0.0430	165025.3	0.0493

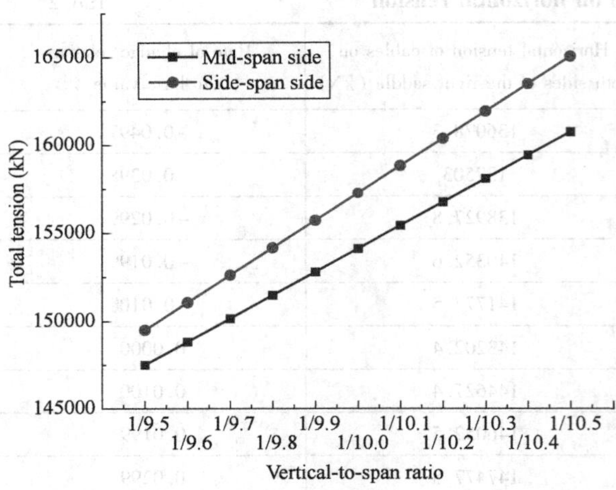

Fig. 5 Effect of vertical-to-span ratio on total tension

As can be seen from the graphs and data, as the vertical span ratio becomes smaller, the total tension in both the middle and side spans continues to increase, with the rate of change being greatest at 1/10.5 vertical span ratio compared to the base value, reaching 4.30% for the middle span and 4.93% for the side spans.

For the vertical forces, the horizontal component of the side span causes a change in the total tension, which in turn causes a change in the vertical component of the main cable in the side span, as shown in Tab. 4.

Effect of vertical span ratio on vertical forces in side spans Tab. 4

Vertical-to-span ratio	Vertical component of side span cable(kN)	Rate of change relative to base value
1/9.5	61926	-0.0473
1/9.6	62541.3	-0.0379
1/9.7	63156.7	-0.0284
1/9.8	63772.1	-0.0189
1/9.9	64387.4	-0.0095
1/10.0	65002.8	0.0000
1/10.1	65618.2	0.0095
1/10.2	66233.7	0.0189
1/10.3	66849.1	0.0284
1/10.4	67464.6	0.0379
1/10.5	68080.1	0.0473

The above results were plotted and are shown in Fig. 6.

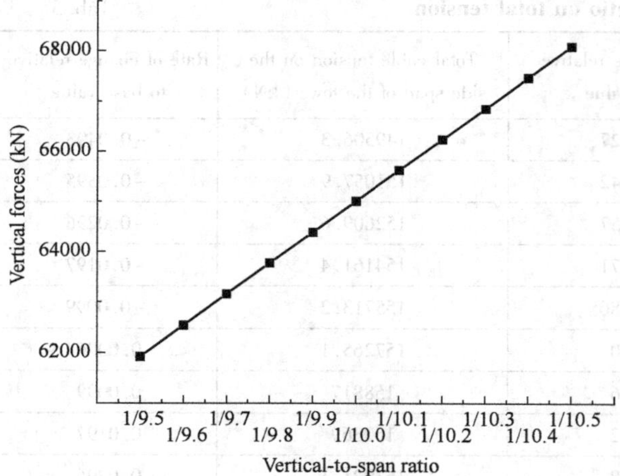

Fig. 6 Effect of vertical span ratio on vertical forces in side spans

According to the above graph and data, the vertical force in the side span increases as the vertical span ratio decreases, with the highest rate of change of 4.73% at 1/10.5 vertical span ratio compared to the base value.

The data above shows that as the vertical span ratio of the main cable becomes smaller, the horizontal tension, total tension and vertical force will increase, but the rate of change is within ± 5% compared to the base value for the range of vertical span ratios set in this paper.

3.3 Influence of vertical-to-span ratio on the shape of aerial cables

For empty cables, the main cable is not subjected to any external load, but only to its own gravity. In this case, the main cable is in the shape of a suspended chain line under its own gravity, and it satisfies the linear stress variation relationship. As the unstressed length of the main cable in the empty condition is the same as the unstressed length of the main cable in the bridge condition, changing the vertical-to-span ratio will also have a greater impact on the alignment of the bridge. Therefore, the same vertical-to-span ratio change as described above was used to calculate the change in line shape of the empty cable. The detailed results are shown in Tab. 5.

Influence of vertical-to-span ratio on the shape of aerial cables Tab. 5

Vertical-to-span ratio	Coordinates of the span centre(m)	Mid-span cable elevation(m)
1/9.5	715	1727.4752
1/9.6	715	1728.5875
1/9.7	715	1729.68104
1/9.8	715	1730.75646
1/9.9	715	1731.81434
1/10.0	715	1732.85527
1/10.1	715	1733.8798
1/10.2	715	1734.88845
1/10.3	715	1735.88175
1/10.4	715	1736.86018
1/10.5	715	1737.82421

The above results were plotted and are shown in Fig. 7.

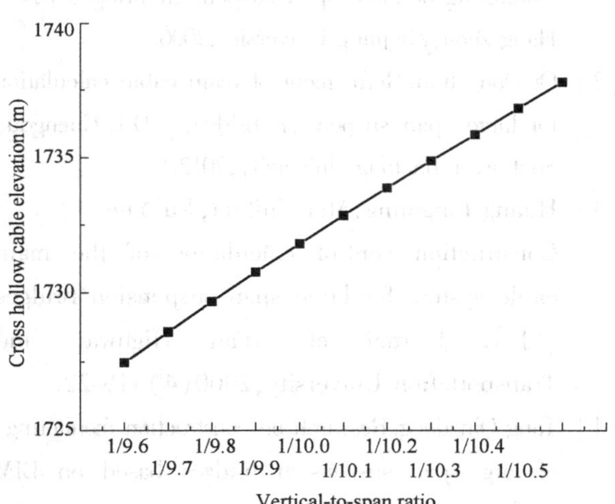

Fig. 7 Effect of vertical-to-span ratio on elevation of empty cables

As can be seen from the above structure, as the vertical to span ratio continues to get smaller, the empty span elevation of the middle span continues to get larger and the change is close to a linear change.

3.4 Influence of vertical to span ratio on saddle precession

As can be seen from the above results, the line shape of the main cable in the bridge state will also change when the vertical to span ratio is changed, and the shape of the main cable will also change when the cable is empty, so the saddle pre-deflection will also change accordingly. The same vertical-to-span ratio change as described above was used to calculate the pre-deflection, the results of which are shown in Tab. 6.

Effect of vertical-to-span ratio on precession Tab. 6

Vertical-to-span ratio	Left main rope saddle pre-deflection(m)	Right main rope saddle pre-deflection(m)	Left scattered saddle precession(°)	Right scattered saddle precession(°)
1/9.5	-1.12738	1.12738	0.66799	-0.66799
1/9.6	-1.12423	1.12423	0.67456	-0.67456
1/9.7	-1.12135	1.12135	0.68111	-0.68111
1/9.8	-1.11872	1.11872	0.68765	-0.68765
1/9.9	-1.11633	1.11633	0.69417	-0.69417

continue

Vertical-to -span ratio	Left main rope saddle pre-deflection(m)	Right main rope saddle pre-deflection(m)	Left scattered saddle precession(°)	Right scattered saddle precession(°)
1/10.0	-1.11416	1.11416	0.70067	-0.70067
1/10.1	-1.11222	1.11222	0.70715	-0.70715
1/10.2	-1.11049	1.11049	0.71362	-0.71362
1/10.3	-1.10895	1.10895	0.72006	-0.72006
1/10.4	-1.10761	1.10761	0.72649	-0.72648
1/10.5	-1.10646	1.10646	0.73289	-0.73289

From the above results, it can be seen that although the change in span ratio has a significant effect on the line of the main cable when it is empty, the change in span ratio has a relatively small effect on the amount of pre-deflection, both for the main saddle pre-deflection and for the loose saddle pre-deflection. Therefore, the effect on the saddle precession is also small when the vertical span ratio is changed by a small amount.

4　Conclusions

This paper is mainly based on a two-tower single-span suspension bridge, selected different vertical-to-span ratios, its main cable unstressed length, main cable stress, main cable's empty cable line shape and saddle's pre-deflection are studied and analyzed, and the corresponding conclusions are drawn:

(1) Changing the span ratio will affect the stress-free length of the main cable, so when the stress-free length is insufficient, the span ratio can be changed accordingly to adjust the stress-free length, and when the span ratio is adjusted within a small range, the change in stress-free length is linearly related to the change in span ratio.

(2) The change of vertical span ratio also has a corresponding effect on the tension of the main cable, as the vertical span ratio increases, the tension of the main cable will also increase accordingly.

(3) The change in span ratio has a greater impact on the shape of the main cable, so the impact of changes in the shape of the main cable needs to be considered when adjusting the span ratio.

(4) The influence of a small change in span ratio on the pre-deflection of the saddle is very limited and is basically within the range of adjustment reserved for the general saddle, therefore, when adjusting the span ratio in a small range, no adjustment of the saddle can be considered for the small amount of adjustment.

References

[1] He Wei. Research on some problems in construction monitoring of large span suspension bridges [D]. Hang zhou:Zhejiang University,2006.

[2] Qi Dongchun. Refinement of main cable calculation for large span suspension bridges [D]. Chengdu: Southwest Jiaotong University,2012.

[3] Huang Pingming, Mei Kuihua, Xu Yue. Construction control calculation of the main cable system for large span suspension bridges [J]. Journal of Xi'an Highway and Transportation University,2000(4):19-22.

[4] Tang Qingdong. Research on construction monitoring of large-span suspension bridges based on BIM [D]. Chengdu:Southwest Jiaotong University,2017.

[5] Peng P, Li Y H, Dai B H. Study on the linear control scheme of main cables of spatial main cable suspension bridges [J]. Construction Technology,2021,50(12):53-56.

[6] Chen Ce, Zhong Jianchi. Influence of variation of vertical-to-span ratio on structural hydrostatic properties of three-tower suspension bridges [J]. Bridge Construction,2008(6):12-14.

[7] Wang Xiulan, Zhang Yunlong, Chai Shengbo, et al. Reasonable value of the vertical-to-span ratio

of the main cable of a two-cable multi-tower suspension bridge[J]. Road Traffic Science and Technology,2021,38(7):51-59.

[8] Tang Maolin,Qiang Shizhong,Shen Ruili. The segmental suspension chain line method for calculating the main cable shape of suspension bridges [J]. Journal of Railways, 2003 (1): 87-91.

[9] Wu Bingjun. Analysis of suspension bridge construction monitoring calculation [J]. Traffic World (Construction and Maintenance. Machinery),2009(11):78-80.

[10] Zhao Yue. Research on the control of main cable of suspension bridge and its Poisson effect[D]. Xi'an:Chang'an University,2016.

[11] Shen Ruili. Research on the design and erection calculation method of suspension bridge main cable system[J]. Journal of Civil Engineering,1996(2):3-9.

无人机在桥梁检测中的应用

刘博恺　刘　佳*　张　阳

(长安大学公路学院)

摘　要　本文从技术进展、方法与案例、标准与规程三个方面进行分析,阐述了无人机在桥梁检测中的发展现状,探讨了无人机在桥梁检测中的挑战。在技术进展方面,介绍了病害图像识别、软硬件发展、航迹规划的研究现状;在方法与案例方面,根据无人机桥梁巡检案例总结出无人机桥检的三种方法;在标准与规程方面,介绍了国内外无人机桥检技术规程的发展现状,并提出了合理的建议。

关键词　无人机　桥梁检测　病害　系统　航迹规划　标准规程

0　引言

桥梁大规模建设时期已经结束,随之而来的桥梁维养工作变得尤为重要。目前国内外常规的桥梁检测普遍采用目视检查或望远镜、桥检车等辅助设备来检查桥梁病害。常规检测手段虽然易于实施,但存在一定的安全隐患,对于全长较长或构件繁杂的桥梁来说,会出现检测耗时长、漏检率高等诸多问题,并且巡检结果存在较大的主观因素。无人机作为一种体积小、灵活、独立性高的新型智能设备,在军事、农业、救灾、测绘、巡检等领域应用广泛。在桥梁巡检中,对于人工不易检查的部位可采用无人机进行辅助巡检。本文从技术进展、方法与案例、标准与规程三个方面对无人机在桥梁检测中的应用进行总结,分析发展现状并为研究人员提供建议。

1　无人机桥梁巡检技术进展

1.1　无人机桥检病害图像识别

在桥梁巡检中,无人机作为一种载具,搭载智能设备采集桥梁各部位图像,并通过一定的手段将图像中可能的桥梁病害信息提取出来,故图像成像、图像拼接、病害定位与识别成为了至关重要的三个方面。

1.1.1　图像成像

桥梁周围复杂的环境会对无人机采集图像造成较大的干扰,严重影响了图像成像的质量,如拍摄角度较偏、环境光线过暗、桥梁构件遮挡等因素的影响会增加识别病害的难度,部分学者尝试采用激光扫描、红外成像、热成像等图像成像技术去解决这个问题;风场作用也会使图像拍摄清晰度下降,许超[1]研究了风场对无人机桥面病害识别稳定成像的具体影响,得出了简支梁桥和拱桥在低风速作用下成像的安全距离在3m左右。

1.1.2 图像拼接

桥梁结构巡检范围广、面积大,在一次拍摄中记录桥梁巡检区域全部的表观特征,以现有的拍摄技术是无法完成的,因此图像拼接技术十分重要。高俊祥[2]提出了一种基于图像拼接算法获取桥梁表面全景图的技术,实现了桥梁箱梁翼板表观图像的拼接;王艳等[3]提出了一种基于遗传算法优化的无人机图像拼接算法,缩短了寻找匹配点的时间。

1.1.3 病害定位与识别

在病害定位方面,张鹏等[4]认为可以通过无人机采集图像时记录的GPS信号来定位病害,这种方法较为简便,但无法确定病害的精准位置;李海东[5]提出了一种基于无人机图像采集和Faster R-CNN的路面病害定位方法,这种方法基本不受路面材料和图像采集环境的影响,可以准确定位路面病害且定位区域的无病害面积较小,有利于后续的病害形态信息提取。

在病害识别方面,基于深度学习的图像识别方法是研究热点。岑静航[6]利用无人机搭载相机进行桥梁图像拍摄,并引入二维信息熵进行裂缝图像评价,结合传统图像处理方法测量已知含有裂缝的图片,得到桥梁裂缝几何信息;Kim等[7]提出了一种基于深度学习的无人机桥梁检测方法,可有效地检测裂缝,并实现了裂缝在点云图上的可视化。

1.2 无人机桥检相关软硬件发展

在软件方面,许多研究人员研发了无人机桥梁巡检系统。陈显龙等[8]开发了一款无人机桥梁病害检测系统,其由无人机避障系统、病害识别系统和桥梁无人机巡检管理系统三部分组成,实现了对桥梁病害的高效检测。许宏元[9]提出了一种全自动的无人机桥检系统,即依据设计图纸,建立桥梁三维模型,桥检系统自动规划无人机巡检航线,无人机依据航线自行飞行,自动实时采集图像并上传云端,桥检系统对图像进行处理,最后使桥检信息在桥梁模型上展示。

在硬件方面,近年来无人机感知能力飞速发展,主要体现在以下两个方面:

(1)无人机搭载各种功能的智能设备,如红外相机、激光扫描仪以及各种智能传感器等,以满足不同巡检需求。交通运输部公路科学研究所等单位使用大疆经纬M210 RTK(搭载光学摄像机X5S、数字红外成像系统)对江海航道桥进行巡检,发现了斜拉索点坑、保温层破裂等表观及内部隐含缺陷[10]。欧盟委员会开展的BridgeScan项目中将激光扫描集成到无人机中,可获取桥梁的三维地形数据点,并自动处理数据[11]。瑞士Flyability公司研制了一种搭载碳纤维保护笼的无人机Elios,可以防止无人机在复杂的桥梁环境中巡检时遭受外界冲击。

(2)以其他检测手段辅助无人机进行桥检作业。国内外研究人员以无人机为主,辅助以智能指挥车、轨道检测车、无人船、爬壁机器人、吸附式机器人等,各类设备之间功能互补,实现了桥梁结构的高效巡检[12]。

1.3 无人机桥检航迹规划

无人机桥检时面临诸多难题。例如,无人机在环境风速高的地区巡检时运行不稳定;无人机巡检复杂桥梁结构时需合理避障;无人机在桥下巡检时GPS信号弱,定位困难;若桥梁存在较多的钢结构、护栏等铁磁性构件,无人机巡检时会受到干扰。所以,无人机桥梁巡检航迹规划是至关重要的。

许多学者对无人机桥梁巡检航迹规划方面做了研究。敬家炽[13]建立了桥梁风场模型以确定不同风速下无人机可达区域,并采用改进后的人工势场算法进行了航迹规划,确定了在风场及其他各种约束条件下无人机桥检路线;徐伟[14]设计了一种针对斜拉桥斜拉索及索塔巡检的无人机航迹规划算法,解决了斜拉桥索塔高度高、斜拉索障碍区域大而难以巡检的问题;名古屋大学研究学者提出了一种利用中继无人机辅助桥下巡检无人机定位的方法[15]。

2 无人机桥梁巡检方法与案例

笔者根据国内外无人机巡检案例,总结出无人机桥梁巡检的三种方法。

第一,检测人员操纵无人机,对桥梁进行目视检查,发现桥梁病害并拍照。这种方法在国外应用较多。例如,美国交通部门认为无人机是执行初始和常规桥梁检查的有效工具,目前其主要按照美国桥梁检查手册《AASHTO Guide Manual for

Bridge Element Inspection》上的要求,使用无人机进行目视检查[16]。俄勒冈州立大学对威拉米特河独立大桥进行无人机巡检,发现了混凝土表观缺陷及钢构件病害[16];南卡罗来纳州交通厅使用无人机对贝茨桥进行巡检,发现了支座缺陷、混凝土裂缝、螺栓松动等病害[17]。然而这种方法依赖人工,自动化程度较低。

第二,检测人员首先使用无人机对全桥进行拍照,将拍摄的照片进行拼接,对病害进行定位,使用计算机视觉算法或人工识别桥梁病害。方留杨等[18]提出了基于无人机倾斜摄影的桥梁检测方法,实现了病害多视角检查。这种方法自动化程度、检测效率较高,但检测结果受图片成像质量和病害定位识别时的算法或人工因素影响较大。

第三,无人机按照巡检系统设定的路线自动飞行巡检,实时自动识别病害,并将采集到的病害信息传输回系统,如图1所示。广州誉宸信息科技有限公司研发了桥梁边坡无人机巡检管理系统,实现了电脑端可视化管理,无人机按照预先设定好的路线自行飞行巡检,并可以多机协同编队飞行巡查[19]。这种方法自动化程度、检测效率最高,但目前的应用较少。

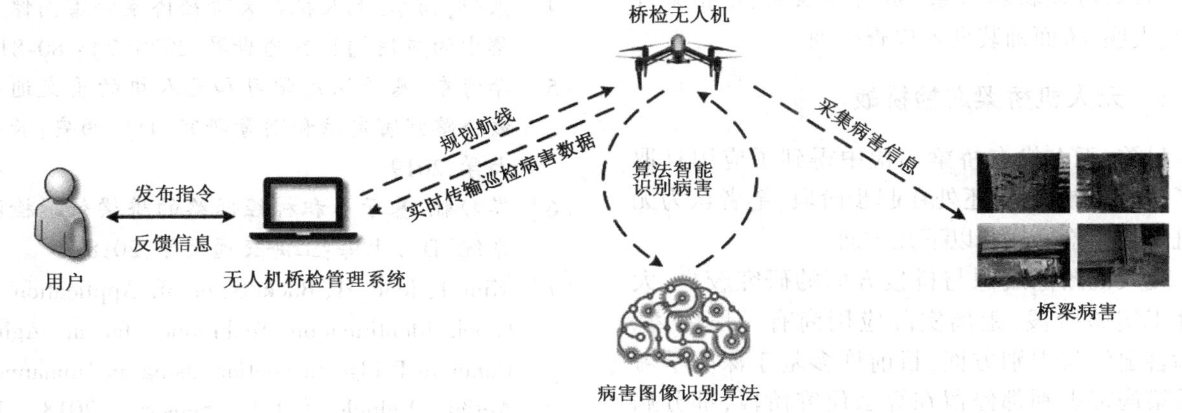

图1 无人机全自动飞行巡检流程

3 无人机桥梁巡检标准与规程

建立一套无人机操作手册和工作规范是极其必要的[20],国外部分地区制定了无人机桥梁巡检技术规程。

美国明尼苏达州交通运输厅于2017年开展了无人机系统桥梁巡检示范二期工程,并制定了一份无人机桥检技术规程,将无人机桥检流程划分为5个阶段:桥梁概况分析、场地安全评估、无人机巡检前准备、巡检实施、病害识别[21]。

日本交通部门制定了桥检无人机性能评价技术规程,将无人机桥检时的机动性能、数据获取性能纳入了评定指标,如图2所示。机动性能分为在桥梁附近巡检时的稳定性能和接触、碰撞时的稳定性能;数据获取性能分为近距离获取图像的性能和获取敲打声音的性能。同时,提出了对桥梁上部结构、下部结构、支座系统的巡检实验方法[22]。

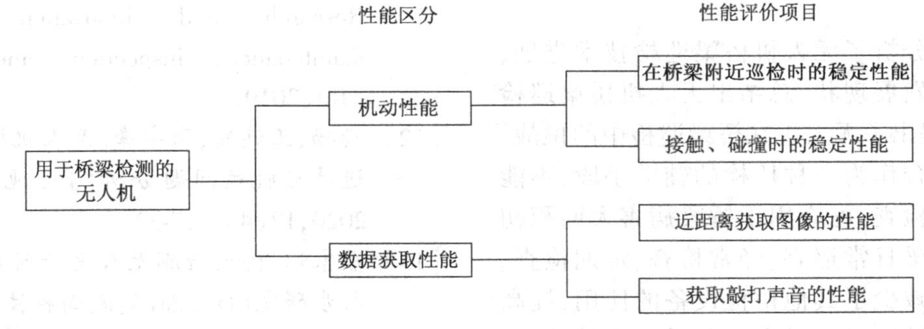

图2 桥检无人机性能分类及评价项目

目前,国内缺乏无人机桥梁巡检标准与规程方面的资料,笔者依据《公路桥涵养护规范》(JTG 5120—2021)中对日常巡查、经常检查、定期检查的规定以及无人机适宜检查的部位及病害,将无人机巡检融入其中。

在日常巡查中,可通过无人机自行巡查实时识别病害的方法,检查桥面铺装是否存在明显破损、开裂、变形等病害;对于索塔和斜拉索,可用人工操纵无人机目视巡查的方法,检查索塔是否存在大面积破损、明显倾斜与变形,斜拉索是否有明显扭曲的病害。在经常检查和定期检查中,以斜拉桥为例,可以将斜拉索、索塔外表面、钢箱梁外表面、支座、桥面铺装列入检查范围。

4 无人机桥梁巡检挑战

目前,无人机在桥梁巡检中得到了应用且取得了较好的效果,但还处在起步阶段,笔者认为无人机桥梁巡检挑战有以下几方面:

无人机图像成像与拼接方面的研究较少,大多处于实验阶段,距离实际应用尚有一段距离。在病害定位与识别方面,目前许多基于深度学习的桥梁病害识别都停留在算法研究阶段,部分病害缺少用于训练的大量图像,不同的病害识别的准确率也不一样,而且没有实现病害信息测量系统化、规范化。

在无人机效能与操纵方面,目前大多数无人机续航时间短、载荷小,满足不了大跨桥梁检测时间长、拍摄照片数量极多的要求,高续航、大载荷的新型桥检无人机是未来的研发重点;在复杂的桥梁检测环境下,对无人机操手要求较高且受主观性影响较大,故应让无人机桥检人员取得无人机执照,使无人机桥检流程更加专业化、规范化。

5 结语

本文系统分析了无人机桥梁巡检技术进展、标准与规程的发展现状,总结出无人机桥梁巡检的三种方法,提出了无人机在桥梁巡检中的挑战。目前无人机适合作为一种桥检的辅助手段,不能完全替代人工检查,可应用于桥梁病害大面积初筛以及辅助桥梁日常巡查、经常检查、定期检查。无人机的应用减少了其他桥检设备的使用,提高了巡检效率,降低了发生事故的风险与巡检费用。随着无人机各方面技术的发展,无人机会越来越多地应用于桥梁巡检,桥梁检测无人机是十分有价值的。

参考文献

[1] 许超.基于无人飞机桥梁病害识别稳定成像安全飞行距离实验研究[D].湘潭:湖南科技大学,2018.

[2] 高俊祥.基于图像处理和机器学习的桥梁检测新技术研究[D].南京:东南大学,2018.

[3] 王艳,祁萌.基于GA-SIFT算法的无人机航拍图像实时拼接[J].测绘通报,2021(8):28-32+47.

[4] 张鹏,杨军.无人机在大跨径桥梁病害图像采集中的应用[J].交通世界,2020(7):80-81.

[5] 李海东.基于深度学习和无人机的重交通荷载公路病害定位和测量研究[D].西安:长安大学,2019.

[6] 岑静航.基于卷积神经网络的桥梁裂缝检测系统[D].上海:上海交通大学,2018.

[7] Kim I, Jeon H, Baek S, et al. Application of Crack Identification Techniques for an Aging Concrete Bridge Inspection Using an Unmanned Aerial Vehicle [J]. Sensors, 2018, 18(6): 1881.

[8] 陈显龙,陈晓龙,赵成,等.无人机在路桥病害检测中的设计与实现[J].测绘通报,2016(4):79-82.

[9] 许宏元.无人机在桥梁检测中的应用[J].中国公路,2017(10):39-40.

[10] 马晔,邹露鹏,张理轻.无人机加载光学摄像及红外成像系统对海上特大桥塔索质量检测的运用技术[J].公路交通科技,2018,35(8):89-93.

[11] Gkoumas K, L M D S F, van Balen M, et al. Research and innovation in bridge maintenance, inspection and monitoring [R]. 2019.

[12] 杨扬,王连发,张宇峰.无人机桥梁检测技术进展与瓶颈问题分析[J].现代交通技术,2020,17(4):27-32.

[13] 敬家炽.桥梁检测无人飞行器系统航迹规划初步研究[D].湘潭:湖南科技大学,2016.

[14] 徐伟.面向斜拉桥索塔巡检的旋翼UAV避障航迹规划与跟踪控制研究[D].西安:长

安大学,2020.

[15] 木村圭佑,前田圭吾,麻晃太朗,等.無人航空機による構造物外観自動計測のための補助用無人航空機群を用いた無人航空機位置推定システム[D].2020.

[16] GILLINS D T, PARRISH C, GILLINS M N. Cost-Effective Bridge Safety Inspections Using Unmanned Aerial Vehicles (UAVS) [R].2016.

[17] BURGETT J M, BAUSMAN D, COMERT G. Unmanned Aircraft Systems (UAS) Impact on Operational Efficiency and Connectivity [R].2019.

[18] 方留杨,陈华斌,吴晓南,等.基于无人机三维建模技术的桥梁检测方法研究[J].中外公路,2019,39(1):109-113.

[19] 兰建雄,苏义坤,谭勇,等.基于无人机的仁新高速养护智能巡检系统设计[J].黑龙江交通科技,2021,44(9):214-215.

[20] Lee J K, Kim J O, Park S J. A study on the UAV image-based efficiency improvement of bridge maintenance and inspection[J]. Journal of Intelligent & Fuzzy Systems,2019,36(2):967-983.

[21] WELLS J, LOVELACE B. Unmanned aircraft system bridge inspection demonstration project phase II final report. [R].2017.

[22] 橋梁点検のための無人航空機性能評価手順書 Ver. 1.0 [R]. 東京:経済産業省,2018.

受载混凝土超声参数特性数值模拟研究

杨雅勋*[1,2] 王林柯[1] 陆嘉诚[1]

(1.长安大学公路学院;2.西安长安大学工程设计研究院有限公司)

摘　要　混凝土的材料随机性使得确定超声参数与其应力状态之间的关系非常困难。本文采用均质弹性材料模拟骨料,损伤塑性材料模拟砂浆,内聚力单元模拟黏结界面,对比以此建立的随机骨料模型和纯水泥砂浆模型在单激励源下超声波传播状态。选定了波速、首波幅值、主频幅值、非线性系数及超声波谱面积五个超声参数,研究了不同超声参数与混凝土应力状态间的关系。结果表明:本文模型数值模拟效果较好,相比纯水泥砂浆模型,随机骨料模型中的骨料会影响超声波的传播形态;这五个参数均可反映混凝土损伤累积程度,其中超声波谱面积对混凝土应力增加比较敏感,并能明显分辨出砂浆单元开始损伤累积和形成贯通裂缝的应力状态。

关键词　超声参数　细观混凝土　数值模拟　无损检测　应力识别

0　引言

混凝土结构在长期受载状态下内部会存在应力累积,导致结构准脆性断裂而影响使用[1],在结构发生破坏之前确定结构状态并采取修复措施可避免重大损伤。许多学者对超声波开展混凝土结构方面的研究。超声波检测是一种常用的方法。Demirboa 对超声波波速和混凝土强度之间的相关性进行了研究[2]。Woodward 等研究了超声波随混凝土损伤水平的变化规律[3]。Park 等研究了循环荷载作用下的混凝土应力相关的超声非线性变化[4]。Vainshtok 等对加筋混凝土的结构强度进行了超声波试验研究[5]。Quiviger 等研究了混凝土中微裂纹对弥散超声的影响[6]。León 等对无侧限压缩荷载下混凝土的材料损伤演化进行了动态超声试验[7]。Moradi Marani 等用超声波对钢筋混凝

1.基金项目:国家重点研发计划项目(2018YFB1600300);国家自然科学基金项目(51878059)。

土板弯曲损伤进行了评价[8]。钟贤毅分析了受载钢筋混凝土工作应力的超声特征[9]。林军志等对改性混凝土的声学参数与应力相关性进行了试验研究[10]。但是以上学者对混凝土模型的细观破坏研究不够,基于此,本文建立了细观混凝土模型,研究了超声波在无应力介质中的传播规律,进行了超声相控阵平行激发与聚焦激发方式对比,并对模型进行加载,研究了声时、波速以及非线性系数等超声特征参数随混凝土应力变化的规律,可以为工程实践提供一定的借鉴。

1　超声波在混凝土中传播数值模拟

1.1　细观混凝土模型建立

本文用 abaqus 建立 150mm×150mm 细观混凝土二维数值模型,将混凝土材料视为由骨料、砂浆和粘结界面三者组成的多相复合材料。

1.1.1　骨料

基于骨料级配理论投放随机骨料,以 Fuller 最大密实度曲线作为最优连续级配曲线[11],表达式为:

$$P = 100\sqrt{\frac{D_0}{D_{\max}}} \tag{1}$$

式中:P——通过筛孔直径 D_0 骨料占所有骨料重量的比值;

$D_{\max}$——骨料的最大粒径。

根据体视学原理[12],由式(1)可得二维截面任意粒径骨料出现的概率 P_c 为:

$$P_c(D<D_0) = P_k\left[1.065\left(\frac{D_0}{D_{\max}}\right)^{0.5} - 0.053\left(\frac{D_0}{D_{\max}}\right)^{4} - 0.012\left(\frac{D_0}{D_{\max}}\right)^{6} - 0.0045\left(\frac{D_0}{D_{\max}}\right)^{8} + 0.0025\left(\frac{D_0}{D_{\max}}\right)^{10}\right] \tag{2}$$

式中:P_k——试件中骨料体积所占的百分比,取 75%。

本文中 $D_{\max}=40$mm,骨料粒径概率分布计算如表 1 所示。

混凝土二级配概率　　表 1

D_0	40mm	20mm	5mm
$\frac{D_0}{D_{\max}}$	1	0.5	0.125
P_C	0.7485	0.5622	0.2824

为计算方便,本文采用圆形骨料。骨料投放规则为:

(1)骨料投放的所有颗粒都保证位于投放区域 Ω 中。

(2)不同骨料颗粒间保证足够距离。

(3)所有投放域中的颗粒不相切且不相割。

(4)骨料外有水泥砂浆层厚度,这一厚度内不存在骨料颗粒[13-15]。

各材料的参数如表 2 所示。

材 料 参 数　　表 2

材料	弹性模量 E(MPa)	泊松比	密度 ρ(t/mm³)	膨胀角(°)	偏移量 ε	不变应力之比 K_c	双、单轴抗压强度之比 α_f	初始刚度 K(MPa/mm)	抗拉强度 T(MPa)	断裂能量 W_f(N·mm)
骨料	75000	0.2	2.5×10^{-9}	—	—	—	—	—	—	—
砂浆	25000	0.167	2.2×10^{-9}	30	0.1	0.6667	1.167	—	—	—
黏结界面	—	—	2.2×10^{-9}	—	—	—	—	6×10^{6}	4	0.06

1.1.2　砂浆

砂浆基体采用 CDP 模型,参考《混凝土结构设计规范》(GB 50010—2010),损伤因子 d 的计算公式为:

$$d = 1 - E_D/E_0 \tag{3}$$

式中:E_D——材料损伤后的折减弹性模量;

E_0——材料处于弹性阶段的弹性模量。

所采用的数据如图 1 ~ 图 4 所示。

1.1.3　黏结界面

本文采用内聚力单元模拟黏结界面。内聚力

单元定义完成后，无需设置初始裂纹，在满足断裂准则时便自发随机产生初始裂纹[16]。其三维空间表示如图5所示。

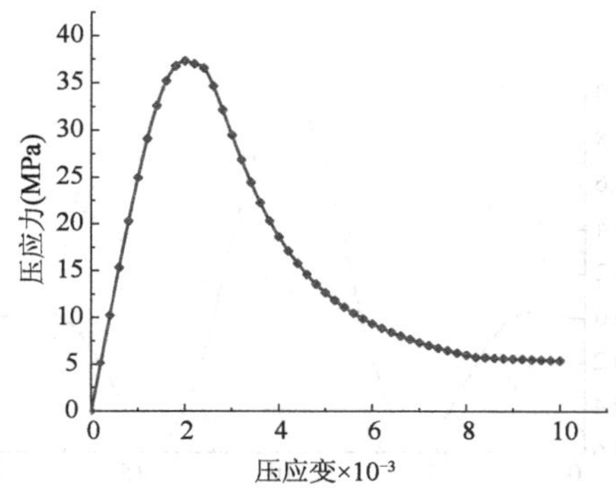

图1 单轴受压应力—应变曲线

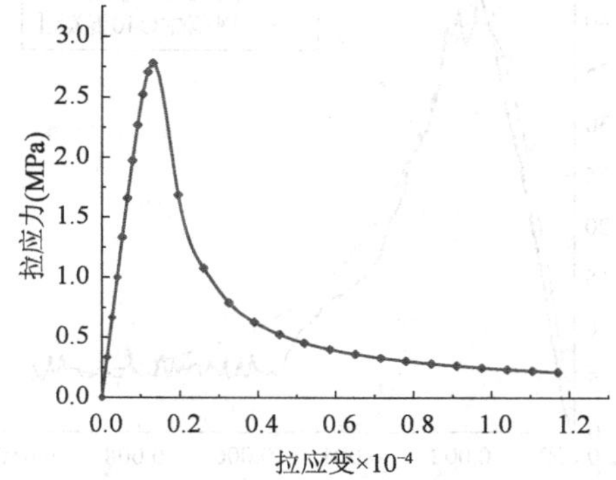

图2 单轴受拉应力—应变曲线

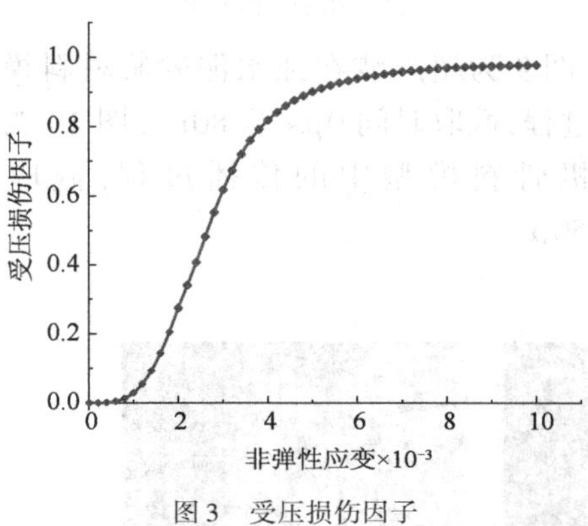

图3 受压损伤因子

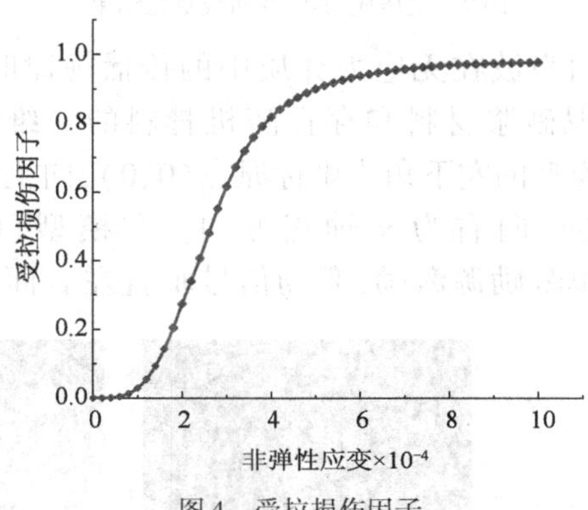

图4 受拉损伤因子

按照表1生成随机骨料，建立模型。单元形状划分采用四边形以减小单元形状对裂缝开展的影响。模型网格大小为1.45mm，共划分为14094个单元。在骨料-砂浆界面中插入内聚力单元模拟界面开裂行为，由此建立的150mm×150mm二维细观混凝土有限元模型如图6所示。

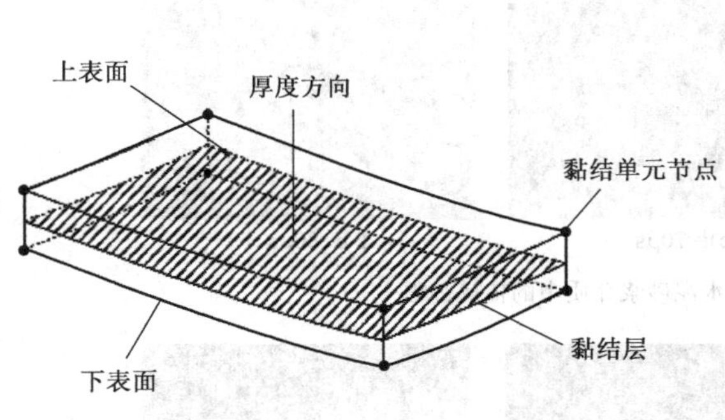

图5 三维内聚力单元的空间表示

图6 有限元模型

将得到的该随机骨料模型的受压应力-应变曲线与规范中C40混凝土单轴受压应力-应变曲线对比，如图7所示，可知按上述方法建立细观混凝土模型可以得到较好的数值模拟结果。

1.2 超声波在无应力介质中传播规律分析

超声波信号采用经过Hanning函数调制的正弦波信号，信号长度为2个周期，发射频率为

100kHz。该激励源信号图如图 8 所示。

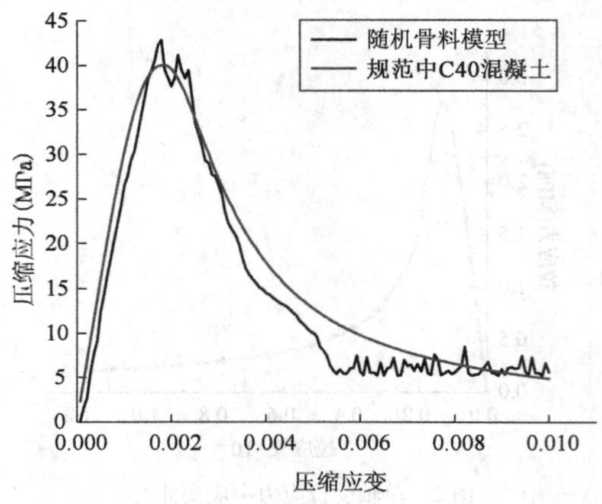

图 7　受压应力-应变曲线对比结果

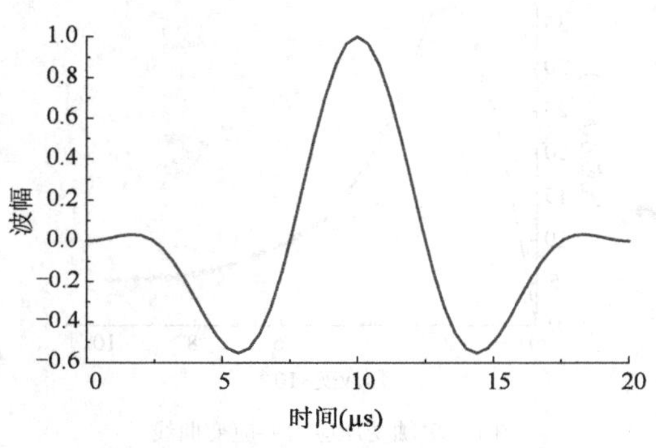

图 8　激励源信号图

研究超声波在无应力介质中的传播规律时，建立纯水泥砂浆材料和存在随机骨料的二维模型。定义模型的左下角为坐标原点(0,0)，向上为 y 轴正方向，向右为 x 轴正方向。在模型(0，75mm)处单激励源激励，激励信号垂直左表面入射，图 9 为超声波在纯水泥砂浆材料模型中的传播过程，截取时间 0μs 至 80μs；图 10 为超声波在随机骨料模型中的传播过程，截取时间 0μs 至 50μs。

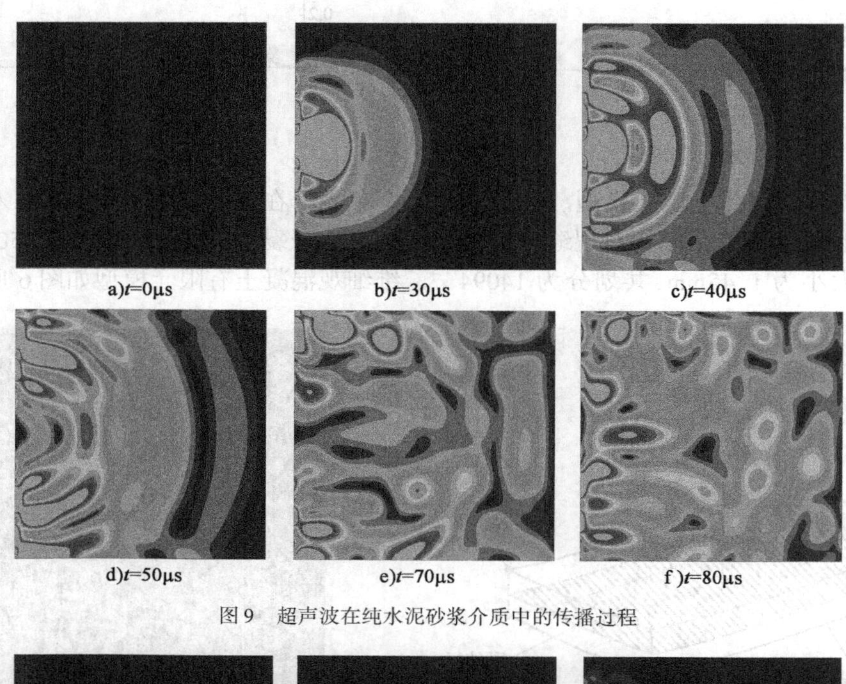

图 9　超声波在纯水泥砂浆介质中的传播过程

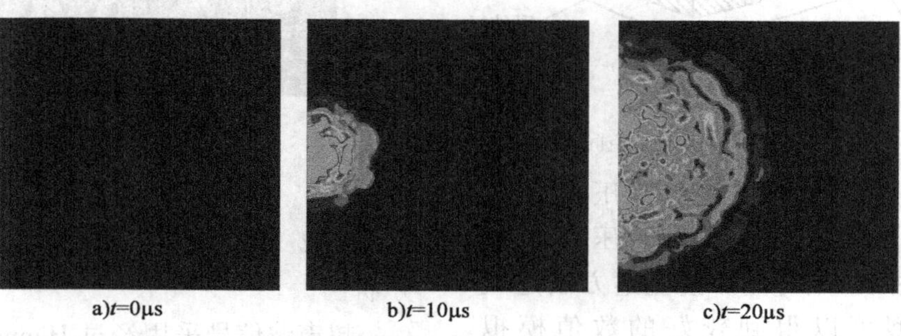

图　10

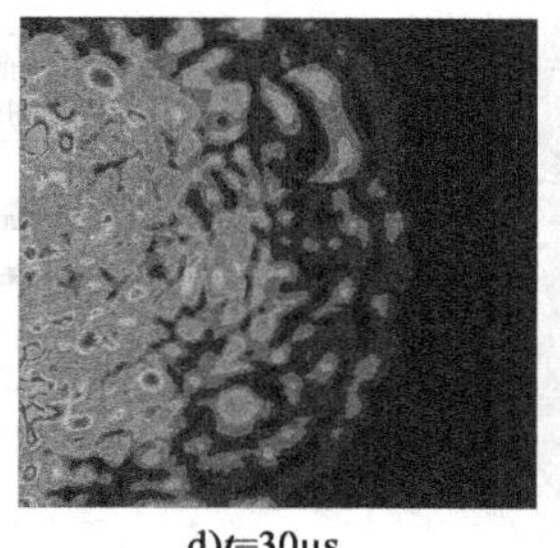
d)t=30μs

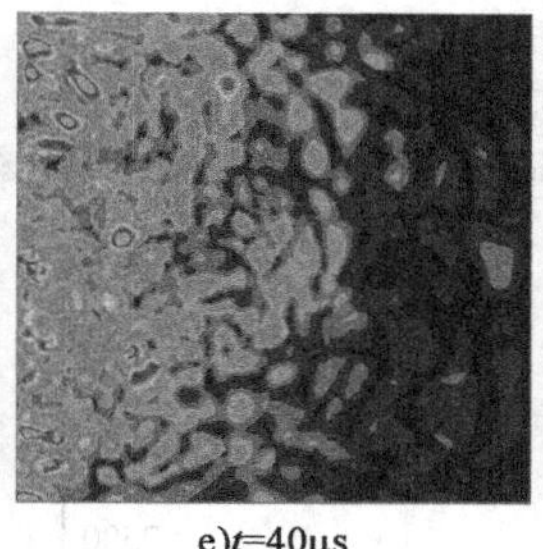
e)t=40μs

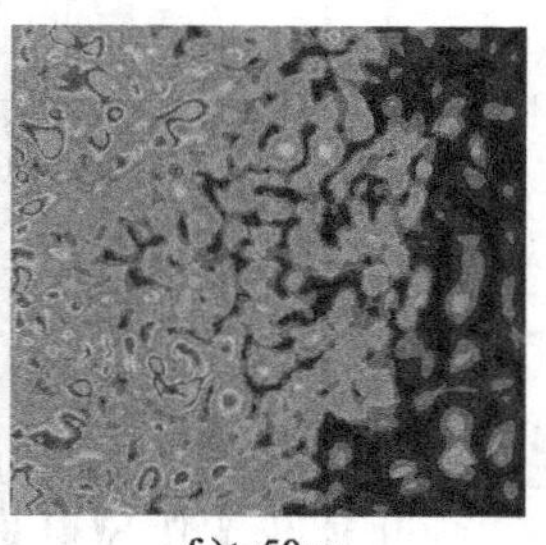
f)t=50μs

图 10 超声波在随机骨料混凝土中的传播过程

对比图 9 和图 10 可知,骨料的存在会使得超声波在传播过程中产生大量无规则的反射波,能够明显观察到混凝土骨料引起的波动,两种模型中超声波传播方式基本一致,水泥砂浆基体在波的传导中占主导地位。

图 11 为两个模型在(150mm,75mm)处的质点位移时程曲线。由图 11 可知,传播距离相同时,随机骨料混凝土模型中质点首波幅值比纯水泥砂浆模型小;随机骨料模型中的波速比纯水泥砂浆模型大;纯水泥砂浆模型质点振动完成后,波在模型内部反射重新回到接收点,引起接收点处质点二次振动,接收点处质点基本静止;随机骨料介质接收处质点在纵波到达后不停振动,因为随机骨料会导致超声波在经过后存在振动残余,引起质点不规则波动。

2 超声波在受载混凝土中传播过程模拟结果分析

2.1 声学参数选择

选用 1.2 节建立的两种模型进行加载,分为 16 级加载,每级加载 60kN 至 900kN。得到接收点的位移时程曲线,对应力做归一化处理,即应力比 $\bar{\sigma}=\sigma_i/\sigma_{\max}$,其中 $\sigma_{\max}=40$MPa。

声学参数选择为:

(1)超声波波速 V。

速度最快的是纵波,纵波波速为:

$$V=\sqrt{\frac{E_d(1-v)}{\rho(1+v)(1-2v)}} \tag{4}$$

式中:E_d——弹性模量;

v——泊松比;

ρ——密度。

(2)首波幅值 A。

首波幅值 A 为接收点位移时程曲线的第一个最值的绝对值。

(3)主频幅值 A_f。

主频幅值 A_f 为接收点位移时程曲线进行傅里叶变换后频域的幅值最大值。

(4)非线性系数 β。

非线性系数正比于二阶谐波幅值 A_{2f}与主频幅值 A_f 的平方,即为:

$$\beta\propto\frac{A_{2f}}{A_f^2} \tag{5}$$

为简化计算,取 $\beta=\frac{A_{2f}}{A_f^2}$。

(5)超声波谱面积 M。

超声波谱面积 M 通常表示为:

$$M=\sum_i^{N/2}A_f(i)\cdot df_i \tag{6}$$

对除波速外的超声参数做归一化处理,即:$\bar{A}=A_i/A_0$,$\bar{A}_f=A_{fi}/A_{f0}$,$\bar{\beta}=\beta_i/\beta_0$,$\bar{M}=M_i/M_0$.

2.2 超声参数特性分析

数值模型的超声参数随应力比变化规律分别如图 12 ~ 图 16 所示。

可将随机骨料模型超声参数随应力比变化规律分为以下几个阶段:

(1)$\sigma_i/\sigma_{\max}<0.2$。

此时模型整体弹性模量基本保持不变,纵波波速、主频幅值及超声波谱面积基本保持稳定;首波幅值和非线性系数则随应力增加呈现略微下降的趋势。

(2)$0.2<\sigma_i/\sigma_{\max}<0.5$。

模型内部开始出现微小裂缝,波速与首波幅值仍基本保持稳定;主频幅值在 $\sigma_i/\sigma_{\max}<0.4$ 时保持稳定,$\sigma_i/\sigma_{\max}>0.4$ 后开始呈现下降趋势;非线性系数继续以略微下降趋势发展;随着裂缝的发展,杂波能量开始显现,超声波谱面积则逐渐增加。

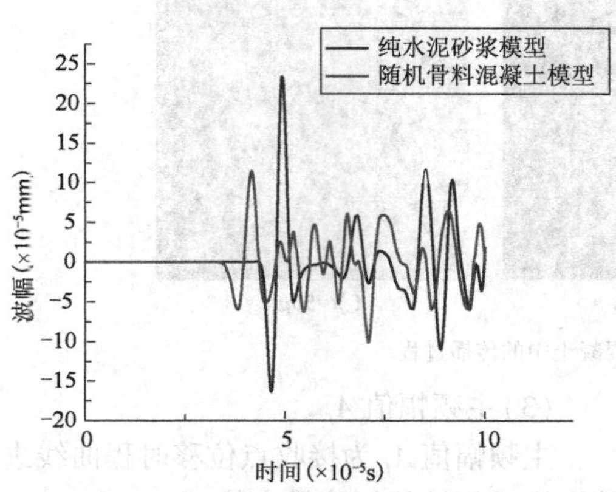

图 11　质点位移时程曲线

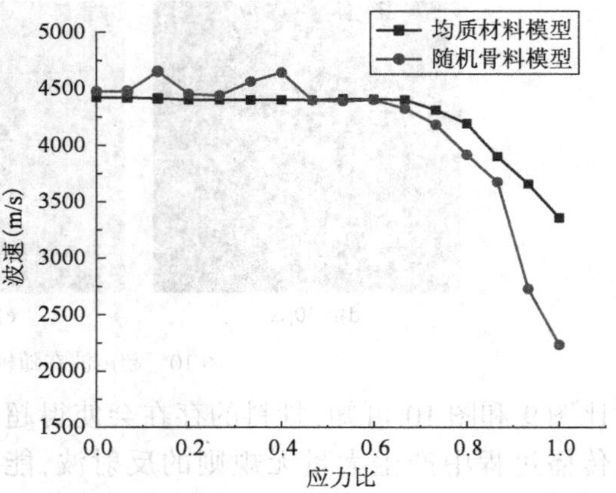

图 12　波速与应力相关性

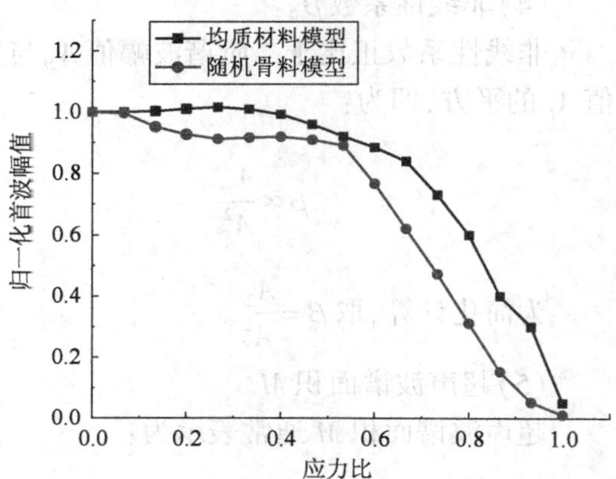

图 13　首波幅值与应力相关性

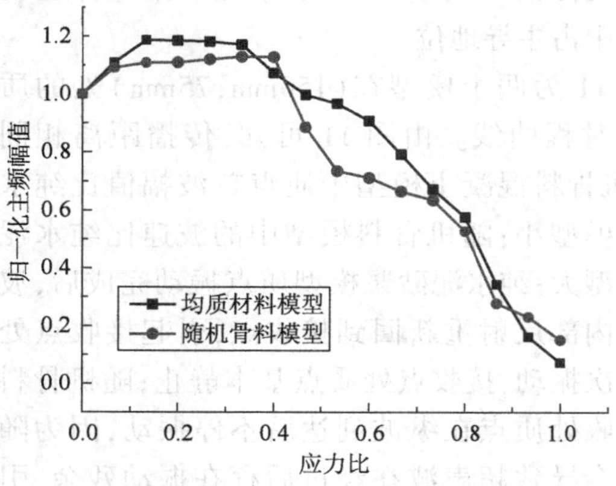

图 14　主频幅值与应力相关性

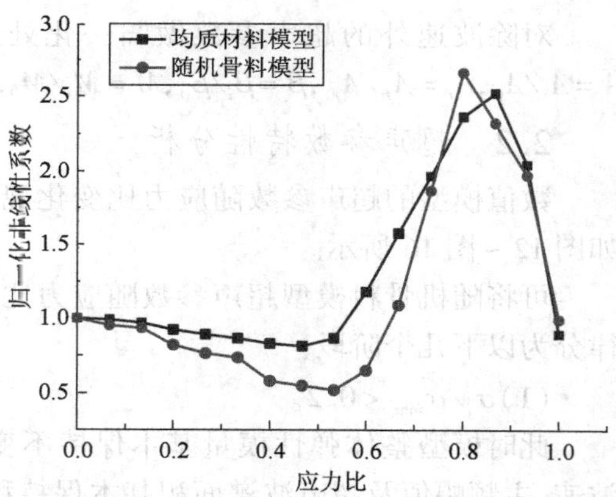

图 15　非线性系数与应力相关性

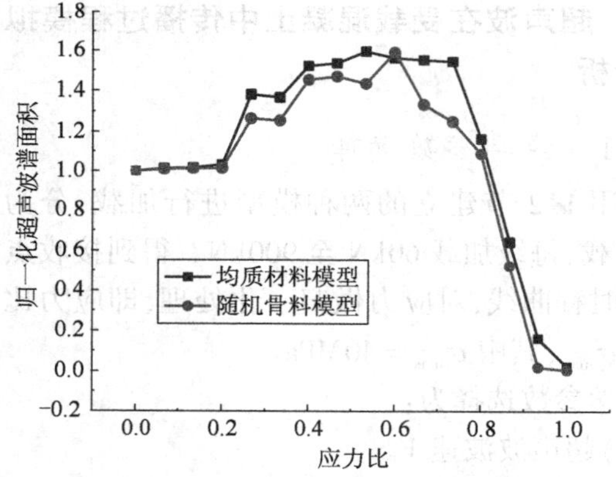

图 16　超声波谱面积与应力相关性

(3)$0.5<\sigma_i/\sigma_{max}<0.7$。

模型内部微小裂缝继续发展，模型整体弹性模量呈现下降趋势。波速呈现较小的下降趋势；首波幅值随着整体弹性模量下降而大幅下降；主频幅值在这个阶段开始呈现下降趋势；非线性系数随着应力比的增大线性增长；杂波能量继续发展，超声波谱面积继续增加。

(4)$\sigma_i/\sigma_{max}>0.7$。

模型内部损伤逐渐扩大，形成贯通裂缝，当$\sigma_i/\sigma_{max}=1$时，已经形成贯通裂缝。波速下降速度不断加快；首波幅值继续以较大趋势下降；主频幅值也继续减少；非线性系数先持续增长，$\sigma_i/\sigma_{max}>0.8$后，高阶频率信号衰减较多，二阶谐波急剧下降，非线性系数骤降；超声波谱面积持续下降，在应力比接近于1时，虽然杂波能量显著，但是由于主频幅值的下降，超声波谱面积下降甚至接近于0。

均质材料模型波速在弹性阶段和损伤起始阶段都是比较稳定的，在损伤大量产生后才快速下降；与波速相比，首波幅值随应力增加下降更快，说明首波幅值对应力变化的敏感度更高；其主频幅值随应力比变化规律与随机骨料模型基本一致，但是随机骨料模型主频幅值随应力增加下降更为剧烈；其非线性系数变化趋势与随机骨料模型基本一致，但是均质材料模型的变化幅度不大；超声波谱面积受混凝土内部应力增加影响较大，并且能够明显分辨出混凝土模型的砂浆单元开始损伤累积和形成贯通裂缝的应力状态。

3 结语

本文通过数值模拟分析了超声波在受载混凝土中的传播过程，得到以下结论：

(1)运用随机骨料投放原理生成了二级配混凝土骨料模型，采用损伤塑性模型模拟砂浆基体，内聚力单元模拟砂浆和骨料的黏结界面，与规范相比可知数值模拟效果较好。

(2)在纯弹性材料模型中，超声波在纯砂浆体中比在随机骨料混凝土模型中传播速度慢；随机骨料会影响超声波在材料中的传播状态，同时导致接收点能量降低，但是水泥砂浆基体在超声波的传播中仍占主导地位。

(3)非线性系数反映了混凝土材料损伤积累程度，超声波谱面积表征了接收点处超声波的全部能量。五个超声参数都能够反映加载过程中的模型内部的应力累积、裂缝开展后的应力释放过程，并且能够明显分辨出混凝土模型的砂浆单元开始损伤累积和形成贯通裂缝的应力状态。

参数解释表如表3所示。

参数解释表　　表3

V	超声波波速
A	首波幅值
A_f	主频幅值
β	非线性系数
M	超声波谱面积
$\bar{\sigma}=\sigma_i/\sigma_{\max}$	应力比

参考文献

[1] Gasser T C, Holzapfel G A. Modeling 3D crack propagation in unreinforced concrete using PUFEM [J]. Computer Methods in Applied Mechanics and Engineering, 2005, 194 (25-26): 2859-2896.

[2] Demirboa, R. Relationship between ultrasonic velocity and compressive strength for high-volume mineral-admixtured concrete [J]. Cement & Concrete Research, 2004, 34 (12): 2329-2336.

[3] Woodward C, Roe S E, Cramer M. Ultrasonic attenuation changes with damage level in concrete [C]//AIP Conference Proceedings. American Institute of Physics, 2007, 894 (1): 1340-1344.

[4] Park S J, Kim G J, Kwak H G. Characterization of stress-dependent ultrasonic nonlinearity variation in concrete under cyclic loading using nonlinear resonant ultrasonic method [J]. Construction and Building Materials, 2017, 145: 272-282.

[5] Vainshtok II, Goikhman A Y, Yamshchikov V S. Ultrasonic testing of strength of loaded concrete and reinforced-concrete structures[J]. Soviet Physics Acoustics-ussr, 1976, 22 (4): 336-338.

[6] Quiviger A, Payan C, Chaix J F, et al. Effect of the presence and size of a real macro-crack on diffuse ultrasound in concrete [J]. NDT & E International, 2012, 45(1): 128-132.

[7] León Ramírez J A, Juan L M, Carrillo J. Material damage evolution for plain and steel-fiber-reinforced concrete under unconfined compression loading by dynamic ultrasonic tests [J]. Arabian Journal for Science and Engineering, 2018, 43(10): 5667-5675.

[8] Moradi-Marani F, P Rivard, C P Lamarche, et al. Evaluating the damage in reinforced concrete slabs under bending test with the energy of ultrasonic waves. [J] Construction and Building Materials, 2014(73): 663-673.

[9] 钟贤毅. 受载钢筋混凝土工作应力超声特征分析[D]. 西安：长安大学，2020.

[10] 林军志，赵明阶，杨洪武. 改性混凝土声学参数与应力相关性试验研究[J]. 岩土力学，2009(S1): 69-74.

[11] 余涛. 超声波在混凝土中传播的数值模拟[D]. 长沙：中南大学，2013.

[12] 刘国权,刘胜新,黄启今,等.金相学和材料显微组织定量分析技术[J].中国体视学与图像分析,2002,7(4):248.

[13] 胡大琳,张立兴,陈定市.二维细观随机混凝土模型的建立和应用[J].长安大学学报(自然科学版),2017,37(3):53-63.

[14] 陈定市.混凝土多因素侵蚀耦合随机细观研究[D].西安:长安大学,2016.

[15] 高政国,刘光廷.二维混凝土随机骨料模型研究[J].清华大学学报(自然科学版),2003(5):710-714.

[16] 徐海滨,杜修力.基于预插黏性界面单元的混凝土细观拉伸断裂过程数值模拟[J].北京工业大学学报,2014,40(11):1666-1672+1686.

定制运输车辆横向偏心作用下桥梁安全性评估

钟强铭 徐 康 韩万水*

(长安大学公路学院)

摘 要 定制运输车辆通常被规定沿桥梁中心线匀速、低速行驶。然而,当桥上出现紧急情况导致车道部分关闭时,定制运输车辆无法按照规定居中行驶。为了研究定制运输车辆能否以横向偏心荷载的方式通过多主梁桥梁,本文通过5个临界车辆荷载、35种不同的荷载工况有限元模拟分析,对横向偏心定制运输车辆荷载作用下的多主梁连续T梁桥进行了结构响应敏感性分析和安全性评估。结果表明:对于本文选择的连续T梁桥,桥梁结构响应的敏感性随着横向偏心距离的增加而增强;定制运输车辆小范围偏载对结构响应产生影响不大,但严重偏载会对结构响应产生较大的影响;C-Ⅰ、C-Ⅱ型定制运输车辆在所有工况下均可安全过桥,C-Ⅲ、C-Ⅳ、C-Ⅴ型定制运输车辆对所有工况均不具备安全通行权。

关键词 桥梁工程 安全性分析 荷载效应比 多主梁桥 横向偏心定制运输车辆荷载

0 引言

为推动国民经济发展,公路运输作为最灵活的运输方式,需要运输不可分割的工业货物,如发电厂、风力涡轮机部件、锅炉、横梁、驳船等,通常需要采用定制的运输车辆,其重量多为正常卡车重量的几倍,对沿线公路桥梁构成了潜在威胁。同时,由于运输货物的特殊性,定制运输车辆的通行是强制性的,因此国内外已有不少学者对桥梁在定制运输车辆荷载作用下的安全性展开了研究[1-5]。

根据相关规定[6],定制运输车辆应以相对较低的速度沿桥梁中心线行驶。然而,桥上的紧急情况,如交通事故或桥面维修等,可能导致交通车道部分关闭[7],定制运输车辆无法严格遵循沿桥梁中心线行驶的原则。桥梁运营管理人员需要知道定制运输车辆能否以横向偏心荷载的方式通过桥梁。闫君媛等[8]从优化结构受力的角度确定了普通超限运输车辆过桥时的最佳横向行驶位置。Zhao等[9]研究了普通卡车的横向偏心载荷及其对结构安全性的影响。然而,人们对横向偏心定制运输车辆荷载对桥梁安全性的影响关注甚少。因此,有必要研究相应的问题。

本文主要研究横向偏心定制运输车辆荷载对桥梁结构安全性的影响。根据文献[5]确定的5种定制运输车辆荷载信息,选取高速中最常见的装配式连续T梁桥建立桥梁模型,对35种不同的横向偏心定制运输车辆荷载工况(7种横向载工况×5种关键定制运输车辆荷载工况)进行分析,并通过与设计车辆荷载效应的对比,研究连续T梁桥在横向偏心定制运输车辆荷载作用下的安全性。

1 模型信息及横向偏心荷载工况

1.1 桥梁模型

本文研究对象为装配式T形截面预应力混凝土连续梁桥,跨径适用范围为30~50m,跨径组合较为多样化。以某高速公路单向两车道的4m×30m跨径连续梁为例,其典型横断面如图1所示,单幅桥宽11.65m,桥面布置为0.5m防撞栏

+10.65m 行车道 +0.5m 防撞栏。全桥设 5 片混凝土 T 形梁,主梁梁高为 2m,横向间距为 2.4m。路面由沥青路面和混凝土路面两部分组成,厚度分别为 10cm 和 9cm。该连续梁桥采用先简支后连续的施工方式。

本文采用有限元软件 Midas/Civil 建立连续 T 梁桥的全桥有限元模型,如图 2 所示,其中主梁与横隔板均按实际布置情况采用梁单元(Beam)模拟。边界条件为每片 T 梁底均施加竖向约束,其中对 3#主梁下的支座增加横向约束,中支点下的支座施加纵向约束。

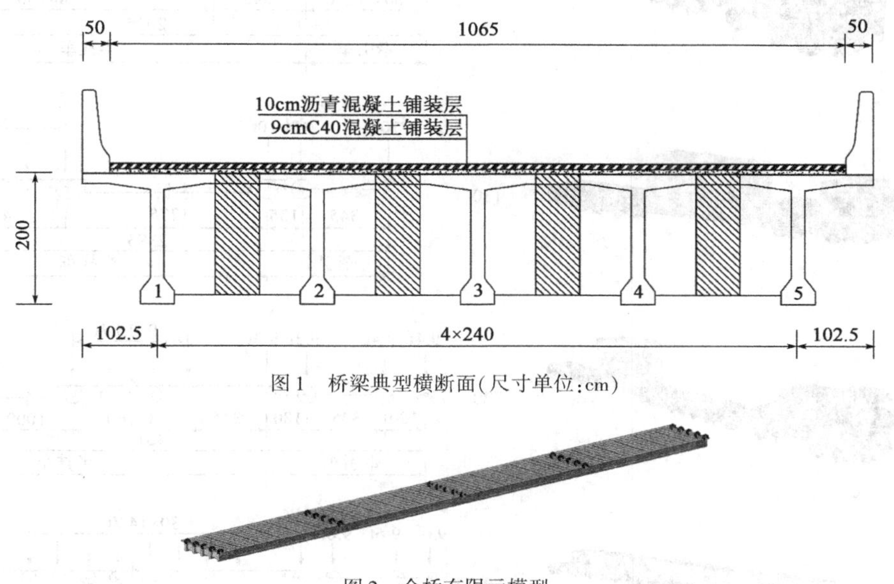

图 1　桥梁典型横断面(尺寸单位:cm)

图 2　全桥有限元模型

1.2　定制运输车辆模型

Han 等[5] 收集了 2012—2015 年河南省高速公路通行的大件运输车辆信息,然后将其中超过 7 轴线的 2011 辆定制运输车辆进行分类,最终提取了 5 类定制运输车辆,并将每一类中总重最大的车辆作为该类别的关键定制运输车辆,如图 3 所示。因此,本文选择这 5 类关键定制运输车辆进行下面的安全评估分析。

1.3　横向偏心荷载工况

当定制运输车辆行驶时,桥梁上可能会出现紧急情况,如交通事故或紧急维修等,导致车道部分关闭。对于具有多车道的桥梁,一条或多条车道关闭的情况均有可能出现。为了进行横向偏心距离对桥梁响应和安全性的敏感性分析,本文为关键定制运输车辆和桥梁确定了 6 种横向偏心荷载工况。图 4 描述了双轴定制运输车辆的横向位置和相应的横向偏心距离。最大横向偏心距离确定为 3m,是因为运输货物的外部尺寸可能超过车辆边缘,且护栏与外轮之间的距离应大于 0.5 m。本文共研究了 35 种不同的荷载工况,即 1 座桥梁原型 ×5 种关键定制运输车辆荷载 ×7 种荷载工况 (1 种工况为中心车辆荷载,6 种工况为横向偏心车辆荷载)。

2　荷载效应分析

分别计算定制运输车辆在上述 7 种荷载工况下各片主梁的响应,取各工况下最不利主梁的荷载效应作为桥梁响应,然后将 6 种偏载工况下的桥梁响应与中载工况下的桥梁响应进行比较,变化率可用式(1)表示:

$$\delta = \frac{E_{e=d} - E_{e=0}}{E_{e=0}} \times 100\% \tag{1}$$

式中,$E_{e=0}$表示横向偏心距离为 0m(中载工况)时的桥梁荷载效应,$E_{e=d}$表示横向偏心距离为 d(d=0.5,1,1.5,2,2.5,3m)时的桥梁荷载效应。

根据式(1)的定义,若变化率为正,说明偏载工况作用下的桥梁响应大于中载工况,偏载工况更不利;反之则说明偏载工况作用下的桥梁响应小于中载工况,中载工况更不利。图 5 显示了以 C-Ⅱ、C-Ⅳ为例的荷载效应变化率,可以看出,随着横向偏心距离的增加,不同临界车辆荷载和荷载效应类型对应的荷载效应百分比变化趋势相似,均为先小幅下降后迅速上升。荷载效应变化率在 d=0.5 和 1m 时为负值,表明这两个偏载工

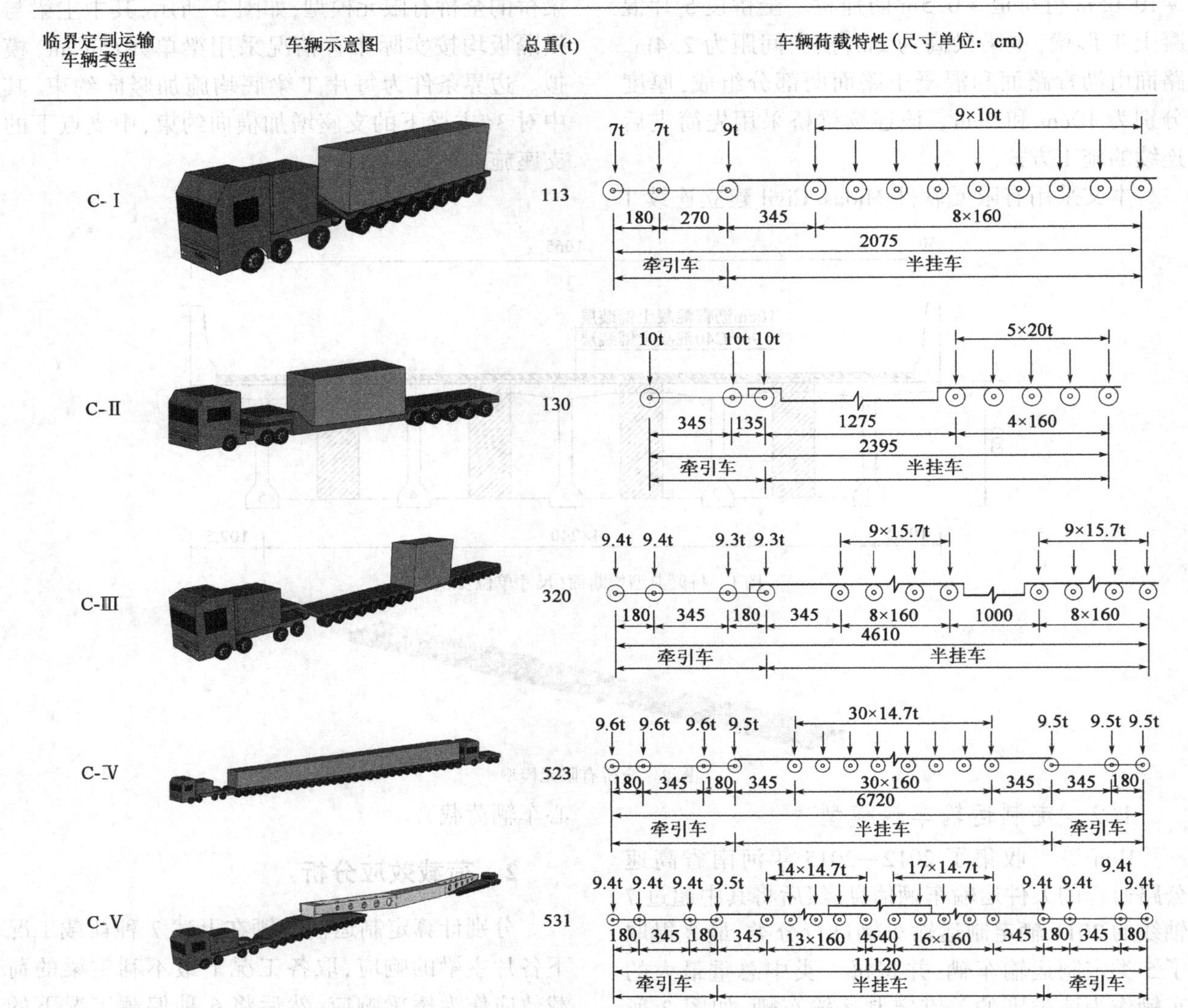

临界定制运输车辆类型	车辆示意图	总重(t)	车辆荷载特性(尺寸单位:cm)
C-Ⅰ		113	7t, 7t, 9t, 9×10t; 180, 270, 345, 8×160; 2075; 牵引车, 半挂车
C-Ⅱ		130	10t, 10t, 10t, 5×20t; 345, 135, 1275, 4×160; 2395; 牵引车, 半挂车
C-Ⅲ		320	9.4t, 9.4t, 9.3t, 9.3t, 9×15.7t, 9×15.7t; 180, 345, 180, 345, 8×160, 1000, 8×160; 4610; 牵引车, 半挂车
C-Ⅳ		523	9.6t, 9.6t, 9.6t, 9.5t, 30×14.7t, 9.5t, 9.5t, 9.5t; 180, 345, 180, 345, 30×160, 345, 345, 180; 6720; 牵引车, 半挂车, 牵引车
C-Ⅴ		531	9.4t, 9.4t, 9.4t, 9.5t, 14×14.7t, 17×14.7t, 9.4t, 9.4t, 9.4t, 9.4t; 180, 345, 180, 345, 13×160, 4540, 16×160, 345, 180, 345, 180; 11120; 牵引车, 半挂车, 牵引车

图3　5种类型的临界定制运输车辆

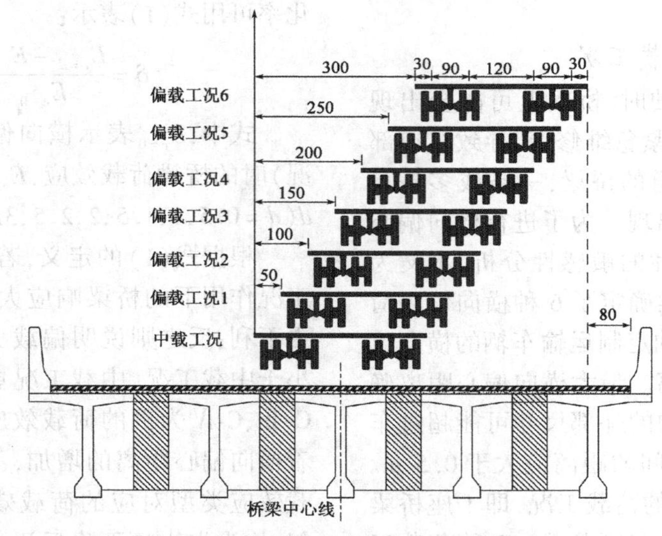

图4　定制运输车辆横向偏心荷载工况(尺寸单位:cm)

况下的桥梁荷载效应小于中载工况下的桥梁荷载效应,定制运输车辆居中行驶对结构受力不是最有利的;其余工况均为正值,且横向偏心距离从2.5m到3m时,荷载效应变化率急剧增大,表明严重偏载会造成结构受力非常不利。主要原因是边梁的荷载效应主要由内力的横向分布引起,随着横向偏心距离的增加,荷载位置逐渐靠近边梁,从而导致边梁的荷载效应增大。对相同定制运输车辆类型,正、负弯矩效应的敏感性相对接近,且与剪力效应相比,对车辆荷载横向偏心行为更为敏感。

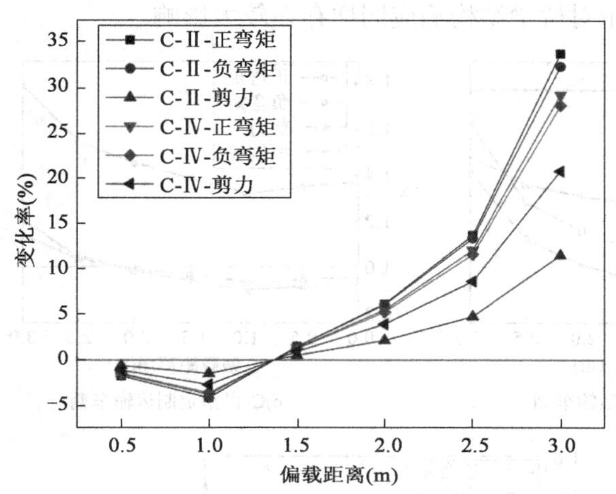

图5 定制运输车辆横向偏心敏感性分析

3 安全性评估

3.1 评估方法

国内外学者在大件运输车辆过桥评估实践中,提出了适用于定制运输车辆安全性快速评估的荷载效应比较法[10]。荷载效应比较法无需进行结构抗力计算便可相对保守地判别车辆过桥的安全性,只需将横向偏心定制运输车辆作用下的荷载效应与设计汽车荷载作用下的荷载效应进行对比,当荷载效应比β大于1时,定制运输车辆无法安全通过桥梁,反之则可安全通过。定制运输车辆过桥安全性判别公式如下:

$$\beta = \frac{\gamma_d S_D}{(1+\mu)\gamma_q S_Q \xi} \leqslant 1 \tag{2}$$

式中,γ_d为横向偏心定制运输车辆荷载分项系数;S_D为横向偏心定制运输车辆荷载效应;μ为冲击系数;γ_q为设计汽车荷载分项系数;S_Q为设计汽车荷载效应;ξ为桥梁承载能力折减系数。

定制运输车辆荷载可视为偶然作用,不属于桥梁设计时的常规车辆荷载,根据《公路桥涵设计通用规范》(JTD 60—2004)规定,偶然作用的荷载组合分项系数取1.0,但当车辆超过《道路车辆外廓尺寸、轴荷及质量限值》(GB 1589—2004)中的限值时,进行桥梁承载能力检算,此类车辆的荷载分项系数取1.1,因此定制运输车辆荷载组合分项系数取1.1。定制运输车辆通过桥梁时,一般有如下规定:低速、匀速行驶,通常要求速度为5km/h以下,严禁变速、制动,尽量减少对桥梁的动力作用。因此,在计算定制运输车辆荷载效应时可不考虑冲击作用的影响。在进行设计汽车荷载效应计算时,根据规范考虑汽车冲击作用和1.4的分项系数。此外,式(2)还通过桥梁技术状况等级增加了桥梁承载能力折减系数,更符合在役桥梁的实际状况。《公路桥梁承载能力检测评定规程》(JTG/TJ 21—2011)规定,一类、二类、三类桥梁的承载能力折减系数分别为1.15,1.1,1.0[11]。定期检查将本文选择的桥梁评定为三类桥梁,因此桥梁承载能力折减系数取1.0。

3.2 设计汽车荷载效应

本文所选择的特例连续T形梁桥设计汽车荷载等级为公路-I级,且该桥于2008年建成,按照《公路桥涵设计通用规范》(JTD 60—2004)中的规定,车道荷载是一个均布荷载与集中力的组合,当计算跨径小于或等于5m时,集中力为180kN,当计算跨径大于或等于50m时,集中力为360kN,中间跨径的集中力大小通过直线内插得到,均布荷载为10.5kN·m^{-1}。装配式T梁桥桥面净宽为10.65m,由此确定设计荷载名义车道数为3,根据横向最不利加载原则布载,最后得到各主梁响应极值并将其作为其汽车荷载效应设计值。

3.3 评估结果分析

根据上述计算参数假定,本文分别计算了35种横向偏心定制运输车辆工况下的荷载效应和设计汽车荷载效应,代入式(2)进行安全性分析。图6给出了5种临界定制运输车辆的荷载效应比值,可以看出,对于C-Ⅰ型定制运输车辆,荷载效应比值均处于控制线下方,且最大值为0.784,有一定的安全储备,因此,C-Ⅰ型定制运输车辆在所有偏载工况下均可安全过桥,此外,正弯矩效应比值均大于负弯矩和剪力效应比值,可将正弯矩作为控制荷载效应类型;对于C-Ⅱ型定制运输车辆,虽然荷载效应比值均处于控制线下方,具有安全通行权,但最大值可达0.936,已经存在安全隐患,为保证车辆顺利过桥,建议对交通进行临时封闭,防止其他车辆与大件车同时在桥,加强对桥梁结构关键部位内力、变形的监控,并做好紧急情况预案;对于C-Ⅲ型定制运输车辆,负弯矩效应比值远高于正弯矩与剪力效应比值,全位于控制线上方区域,表明该车型不能安全通过桥梁,此外,正弯矩与剪力效应比值在偏载未到达2.5m时均位于控制线下方,即可以安全通过桥梁,表明严重偏载可能造成定制运输车辆无法安全通行;对于C-Ⅳ、C-Ⅴ型定制运输车辆,所有荷载效应类型均高于控制线,不具备安全通行权。综合分析5种临界定制运输车辆的荷载效应比值,对于该连续T梁桥,荷载效应比值随着横向偏心距离的增加先减小后增大,最不利正弯矩、负弯矩、剪力效应比值对应C-Ⅴ、C-Ⅳ、C-Ⅳ型定制运输车辆,其值分别为1.521、2.254、1.352。此外,C-Ⅲ型定制运输车辆的总重远小于C-Ⅴ型定制运输车辆,但最不利荷载效应比值却大于C-Ⅴ型定制运输车辆,表明除了定制运输车辆的总重,其轴重、轴距、轮轴分布对桥梁结构响应同样存在较大影响。

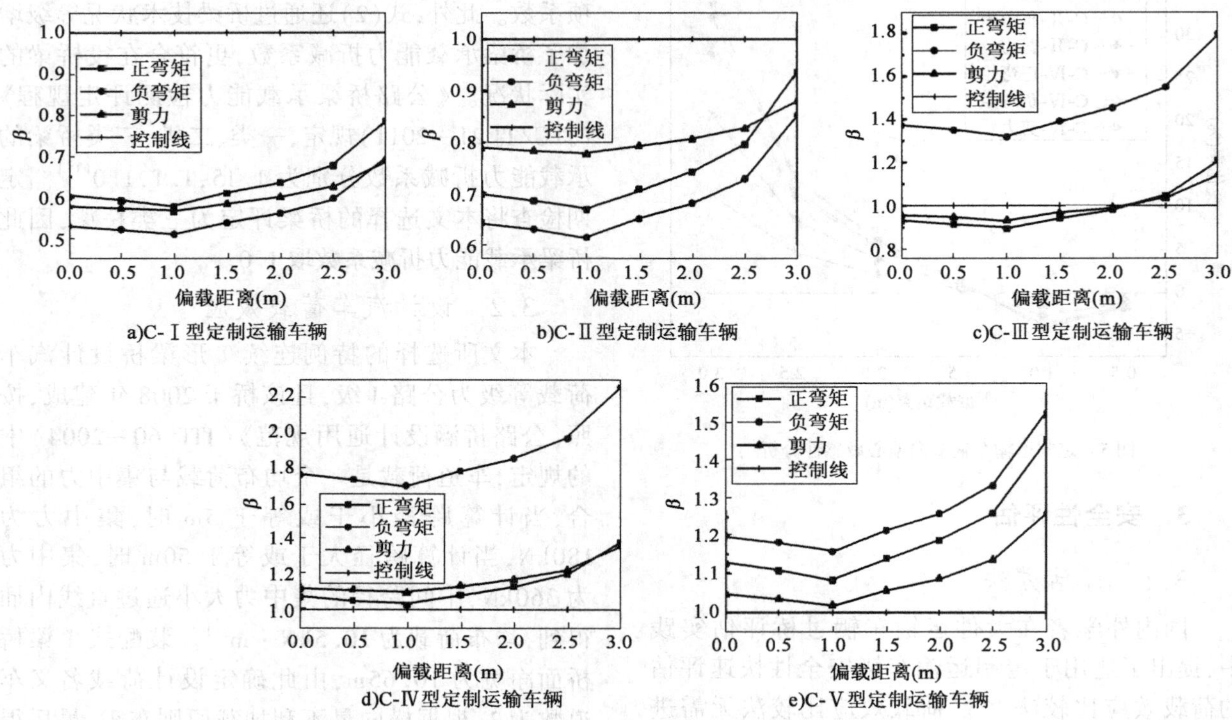

图6　定制运输车辆荷载效应比值

4　结语

本文基于5种临界定制运输车辆荷载,考虑实际车道关闭情况,研究了定制运输车辆能否以横向偏心方式通过连续T梁桥,主要得到以下结论:

(1)桥梁结构响应的敏感性随着横向偏心距离的增加而增强。对相同定制运输车辆类型,与剪力效应相比,正、负弯矩效应的敏感性相对接近,且对车辆荷载横向偏心行为更为敏感。

(2)对于本文选择的连续T梁桥,定制运输车辆居中行驶对结构受力不是最有利的,横向偏心距离在1m范围内时,结构响应相对于中载工况略有减小,但当横向偏心距离超过1m后,结构响应会大幅增加,严重偏载会造成结构受力非常不利。

(3)针对该连续T梁桥,C-Ⅰ、C-Ⅱ型定制运输车辆在所有工况下均可安全过桥,C-Ⅲ、C-Ⅳ、C-Ⅴ型定制运输车辆对所有工况均不具备安全通行权。荷载效应比值随着横向偏心距离的增加先减小后增大,最不利定制运输车辆类型为C-Ⅳ型。

(4)除了定制运输车辆的总重,其轴重、轴距、轮轴分布对桥梁结构响应同样存在影响。本文只针对5类临界定制运输车辆具体的荷载特性进行了分析,并未对其中某一参数进行分析。为制造对桥梁结构最有利的定制运输车辆,之后需进一步研究相关车辆参数对桥梁结构响应的影响。

参考文献

[1] 袁阳光,周广利,高文博,等.考虑安全性与正常使用性能的大件车辆过桥评估方法[J].工程力学,2021,38(7):147-158.

[2] Kim Y J. Safety assessment of steel-plate girder bridges subjected to military load classification [J]. Engineering Structures, 2012, 38 (5): 21-31.

[3] 周广利.定制运输车辆过桥能力的快速评定[J].公路交通技术,2018,34(5):73-77+86.

[4] Deng L, Yan W. Vehicle weight limits and overload permit checking considering the cumulative fatigue damage of bridges [J]. Journal of Bridge Engineering, 2018, 23 (7): 04018045. 1-04018045. 8.

[5] Han W, Yuan Y, Chen X, et al. Safety assessment of continuous beam bridges under overloaded customized transport vehicle load[J]. Journal of Bridge Engineering, 2018, 23 (6): 04018030. 1-04018030. 13.

[6] Bae H U, Oliva M G. Moment and shear load distribution factors for multigirder bridges subjected to overloads [J]. Journal of Bridge Engineering, 2012, 17(3): 519-527.

[7] Zhu B, Frangopol D M. Time-variant risk assessment of bridges with partially and fully closed lanes due to traffic loading and scour [J]. Journal of Bridge Engineering, 2016, 21 (6): 04016021.

[8] 闫君媛,邓露.超限运输车辆通过T梁桥的合理横向位置分析[J].湖南大学学报(自然科学版),2018,45(11):5.

[9] Zhao Y, Zhai X. Reliability assessment of aluminum alloy columns subjected to axial and eccentric loadings [J]. Structural Safety, 2018, 70: 1-13.

[10] Correia J R, Arruda M R T, Branco F A. Structural assessment of reinforced-concrete arch underpasses subjected to vehicular overloads [J]. Journal of Performance of Constructed Facilities, 2014, 28 (2): 321-329.

[11] 李键,钟明全,吴海军,等.桥梁技术状况对公路大件运输承载力的影响[J].公路,2016,61(11):84-89.

基于性能的桥梁系统震后通行能力评估方法

李紫豪* 袁浩允

(长安大学公路学院)

摘 要 桥梁作为公路交通运输线上的关键节点,在地震作用下极易发生破坏。当桥梁震害发生时,往往会中断交通,导致灾区交通网络瘫痪,严重影响震后救援工作的开展,从而进一步加重人员伤亡和财产损失。本文提出了一种基于性能的桥梁系统震后通行能力评估方法,对算例桥梁系统震后运营状态进行了评估。研究结果表明:基于性能的桥梁震后通行能力评估对于评估震后桥梁系统运营状态,进行运营管理决策具有十分重要的应用价值;在桥梁构件易损性分析的基础上,采用I-PCM法可快速建立桥梁系统易损性曲线,同时结合基于性能的震害桥梁通行能力评估模型,可以实现对震后桥梁通行能力的快速评估。

关键词 地震 桥梁 系统易损性 通行能力 评估方法

0 引言

我国环处两大地震带,地震活动频发且强度大,给社会带来巨大的人员伤亡和财产损失。当地震来临时,公路交通运输系统会发生不同形式和程度的破坏,这些破坏状态会导致灾区交通运输线路中断,引发次生灾害,给后续抗震救援工作的开展带来不可估量的影响。例如,1995年日本阪神7.3级大地震,造成城市道路交通线路中断,救援人员无法迅速抵达受灾严重的地区,导致灾区人员错失了最佳的救援时机[1];2008年我国汶川地震,尽管救援速度举世罕见,却依旧因为道路桥梁破坏而导致救援工作延迟,次生灾害频发。

国内外学者对桥梁系统震后通行能力进行了相关研究。美国在20世纪70年代建成了CATS系统,用来对公路系统震后通行能力进行评估[2];日本则从早期评估和现场评估两个方面对桥梁承载能力和通行能力进行评估[3]。兰日清等[2]提出了对单一桥梁结构在地震作用下损伤程度和通行能力的评估方法;段满珍等[4]基于已有的桥梁震害损失数据,对现有的评估震后道路通行能力的模型进行了修正,研究表明新的评估模型预测的结果更加精确;张菊辉等[5]对震后桥梁通行能力理论模型进行了研究,并通过算例进行了验证,证明了该理论模型的有效性;葛胜锦等[12]以桥墩漂移率、支座相对变形作为损伤指标,并将损伤指标予以量化。

目前大多数文献基于桥梁检测技术或理论分析模型对震害桥梁系统通行能力进行评估,基于性能的桥梁系统震后通行能力评估方法往往基于桥梁构件层面,或者仅止于理论模型研究。例如,林庆利首先建立了支座和桥墩两种构件的易损性曲线,随后利用一阶界限法合成了整座连续梁桥的易损性曲线[9];蒋知之等定义了地震对于公路桥梁通行能力的修正系数,进而建立了震后公路桥梁通行能力评估的理论模型[10];周军杰[11]从构件的角度对墩柱的易损性进行了分析研究,通过计算分析了桥墩的剩余承载力及震后桥梁的通行能力。众所周知,桥梁系统比任一单个构件在地震作用下更容易受到破坏,目前相关方面的研究还比较少。

本文提出一种基于性能的桥梁系统震后通行能力评估方法,以一座中小跨径连续梁桥为例,考虑地震动输入的不确定性,利用有限元程序OpenSees建立非线性时程分析模型,对桥墩、支座构件进行易损性分析;然后采用改进的边缘乘积法进行桥梁系统易损性分析;最后结合评估模型,实现对算例桥梁系统震后通行能力的快速评估。

1 桥梁系统震后通行能力评估方法

1.1 桥梁结构易损性分析方法

基于性能的桥梁结构易损性分析方法的实质是将结构性能抗震设计理论运用到易损性分析方法中。易损性分析是指结构在给定的地震强度 IM 的作用下,达到或超出既定极限状态的概率。可用下式表示:

$$P_f = P[EDP \geqslant S_C | IM] \tag{1}$$

式中,EDP 为结构需求;S_C 为结构能力。地震易损性分析作为全概率决策框架的一部分,可为抗震设计、加固以及评估提供依据。目前,工程中常采用理论分析法即数值分析法,本文采用基于非线性动力分析的理论易损性分析法。

1.2 桥梁系统易损性分析方法

目前,国内外学者对于桥梁结构易损性分析展开了大量的研究工作,这些研究成果基本上都停留在桥梁构件层面[5-7],然而,桥梁作为一种大型的结构,是由不计其数的构件根据一定的逻辑关系的组成的系统。有研究表明[8,13],桥梁作为一个系统比任何一个单一构件更容易在地震中受到破坏,不考虑构件之间的相关性,会低估桥梁系统的失效概率。因此,在对震后桥梁通行能力进行评估时,应基于桥梁系统易损性分析结果。

事实上,桥梁系统中各构件失效模式间的逻辑关系十分复杂,想要准确获取其系统失效概率几乎是不可能的,因此在桥梁易损性分析中,常见的做法是将其简化成串联模型,即桥梁系统中有一个构件失效,则认为整个系统失效。这样做的好处是能够保守估计桥梁系统失效概率,使得分析结果偏安全。那么对于串联系统,桥梁系统失效概率 P_{sys} 可由下式表示[11]:

$$P_{sys} = 1 - \Phi(\beta,\rho) = 1 - \int_{-\infty}^{\beta_1}\int_{-\infty}^{\beta_2}\cdots \int_{-\infty}^{\beta_m}\frac{1}{(2\pi)m/2\ |\rho|1/2}\times \exp\left(-\frac{1}{2}X^T\rho^{-1}X\right)dx_1dx_2\cdots dx_m \tag{2}$$

式中，$\Phi(\beta,\rho)$为多元正态累积分布函数；β_i 为第 i 个构件对应的可靠度指标；m 为失效模式数；$\rho=[\rho_{ij}]_{m\times m}$为失效模式相关系数矩阵；$X$ 为 m 维标准正态随机向量。

由式(2)可知，结构系统失效概率求解的核心是对 $\Phi(\beta,\rho)$ 的求解。目前对于 $\Phi(\beta,\rho)$ 的求解，有数值积分法、边界法、近似法。数值积分法计算结果最为精确，但是计算过程较为烦琐，计算效率较为低下；边界法计算原理简单，但是受限于所给出的较宽的失效概率范围[15]。为了克服以上两种计算方法的缺点，Yuan 和 Pandey[14]提出了条件边缘乘积法的改进版本，即 I-PCM 法，其计算原理如下：

$$\begin{aligned}\Phi(\beta,\rho)&=P[(X_m\leqslant\beta_m)\mid\bigcap_{k=1}^{m-1}(X_k\leqslant\beta_k)]\times\\&\quad P[(X_{m-1}\leqslant\beta_{m-1})\mid\bigcap_{k=1}^{m-2}(X_k\leqslant\beta_k)]\times\cdots\times\\&\quad P(X_1\leqslant\beta_1)\approx\Phi[\beta_{m\mid(m-1)}]\times\Phi[\beta_{(m-1)\mid(m-2)}]\times\cdots\times\Phi[\beta_{2\mid1}]\times\Phi(\beta_1)\\&=\prod_{k=1}^{m}\Phi[\beta_{k\mid(k-1)}]\end{aligned}\tag{3}$$

式中，$\beta_{k\mid(k-1)}$为条件正态分位数，可见其计算实质是一个复杂的多维积分过程。Yuan 和 Pandey 提出了一种简化表达式：

$$\beta_{i\mid k}=\Phi^{-1}\left\{1-\frac{\Phi[-\beta_{i\mid(k-1)}]-[-\beta_{i\mid(k-1)},-\beta_{k(k-1)};\rho_{ik\mid(k-1)}]}{\Phi[\beta_{k\mid(k-1)}]}\right\}\tag{4}$$

$$\Phi[-\beta_{i\mid(k-1)},-\beta_{k(k-1)};\rho_{ik\mid(k-1)}]\approx\Phi(c_{i\mid k})\Phi(c_{k\mid(k-1)})\tag{5}$$

$$c_{i\mid k}=[-\beta_{i\mid(k-1)}+\rho_{ik\mid(k-1)}D_{k\mid(k-1)}]/\sqrt{1-\rho_{ik\mid(k-1)}^2D_{k\mid(k-1)}[-\beta_{i\mid(k-1)}+D_{k\mid(k-1)}]}\tag{6}$$

$$D_{k\mid(k-1)}=\phi[c_{k\mid(k-1)}]/\Phi[c_{k\mid(k-1)}]\tag{7}$$

$$c_{k\mid(k-1)}=-\beta_{k\mid(k-1)}\tag{8}$$

式中，$k=1,\cdots,m-1$；$i,j=k+1,\cdots,m$。式(4)～式(8)即改进的条件边缘乘积法(I-PCM 法)的计算流程。由 I-PCM 法的计算原理可知，只需知道结构不同失效模式间的相关系数 $\rho_{(m\times m)}$ 以及不同构件间的可靠度指标 $\beta_{(1\times m)}$，即可使用 I-PCM 法计算出结构系统的失效概率。

1.3 基于性能的桥梁系统震后通行能力评估方法

在基于性能的抗震设计理论中，结构损伤通常被划分为五个等级，即无损伤、轻微损伤、中等损伤、严重损伤、完全破坏。文献[2]根据既往桥梁震害统计结果给出了这五个损伤状态下的通行状况，如表 1 所示。

基于性能的桥梁系统通行能力权重值　　表 1

损伤状态	无损伤	轻微损伤	中等损伤	严重损伤	完全破坏 0 = ≤
通行能力	$0.85<TA\leqslant1.0$	$0.75<TA\leqslant0.85$	$0.5<TA\leqslant0.75$	$0.3<TA\leqslant0.5$	$0<TA\leqslant0.3$
权重值 K_i	1	0.8	0.65	0.3	0

桥梁震后通行能力模型可由下式计算：

$$TA=\sum P_i\times K_i\tag{9}$$

式中，TA 为震后桥梁系统通行能力指标；P_i 为桥梁系统五种损伤状态所占的百分比；K_i 为表 1 中各破坏状态权重值。

对于 P_i，可通过下式进行计算：

$$\begin{cases}P_0=1-P_{f_1}(E_1\mid im)\\P_1=P_{f_1}(E_1\mid im)-P_{f_2}(E_2\mid im)\\P_2=P_{f_2}(E_2\mid im)-P_{f_3}(E_3\mid im)\\P_3=P_{f_3}(E_3\mid im)-P_{f_4}(E_4\mid im)\\P_4=P_{f_4}(E_4\mid im)\end{cases}\tag{10}$$

式中，P_0,P_1,P_2,P_3,P_4 分别代表结构系统五种状态所占的百分比；$E_1,E_2,E_3,E_4,P_{f_1},P_{f_2},P_{f_3},P_{f_4}$分别代表易损性分析中轻微损伤、中等损伤、严重损伤、完全破坏事件和对应的系统失效概率。

最后，根据 TA 值的大小对桥梁系统震后通行能力进行评估，评估结果如表 2 所示。

基于性能的桥梁系统通行能力判定　表 2

TA	$0.75<TA\leqslant1$	$0.5<TA\leqslant0.75$	$0<TA\leqslant0.5$
通行能力	可以通行	限制通行	禁止通行
车流量	100%	50%	0

2 算例桥梁分析模型及地震动输入

2.1 有限元模型建立

本文以一座国内常见的中小跨径连续梁桥为例，跨径布置为 3m×30m。上部结构采用 C50 混凝土 T 梁，由 4 片 T 梁组成，桥面宽 8m。下部结构采用 C40 混凝土。桥墩采用双柱式桥墩，直径为1.5m,钢筋采用HRB335钢筋,纵向配筋率为0.8%,配箍率为0.4%。1#、4#墩处采用聚四氟滑板支座,2#、3#墩处采用板式橡胶支座。算例桥梁所处场地类别为Ⅱ类。

本文基于OpenSees分析平台建立算例桥梁非线性动力分析模型。主梁采用弹性梁单元进行模拟,结构自重及二期铺装等荷载以附加荷载形式均匀施加在梁单元上;桥墩按延性构件设计,因此采用弹塑性纤维单元模拟;混凝土和钢筋本构关系采用Concrete 01和Steel 02材料;支座采用OpenSees中zero length element模拟。由于算例桥梁所处的地址条件较好,为简化计算,不考虑桩土效应。桥型布置图及力学模型如图1所示。

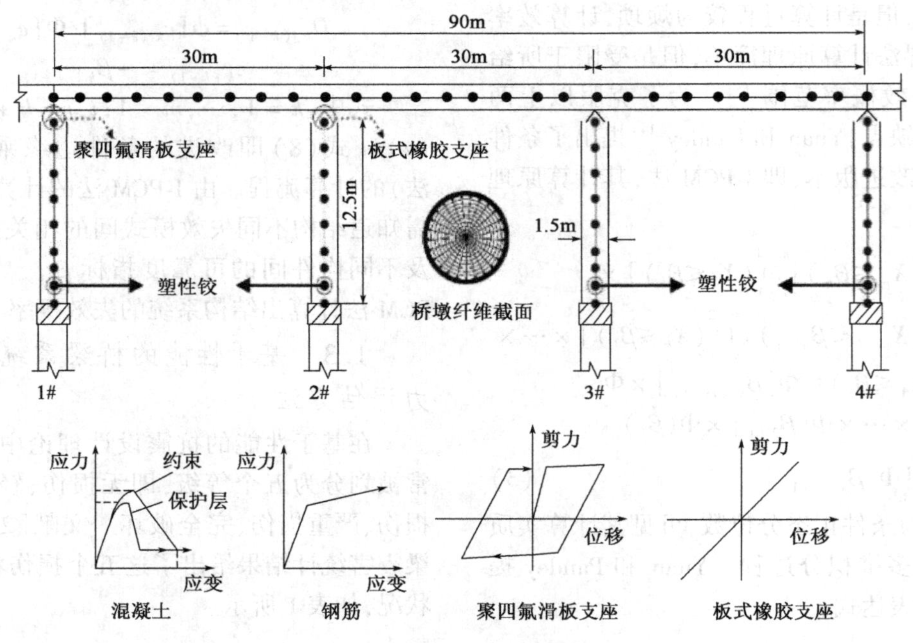

图1　桥型布置图及力学模型

2.2　地震动输入

本文从美国PEER强震数据库中筛选出符合算例桥梁场地类型的50条地震波。这些地震波震中距大于20km,震级为6.0~7.0,所选用的50条地震波在阻尼比$\zeta=5\%$时反应谱均值和均值±标准差如图2所示。根据已有的研究成果,能够表征地震动的参数多种多样,本文基于Padgett等人[17]关于地震动参数进行效率、适用性等方面的研究成果,选择峰值加速度(PGA)作为算例桥梁地震动参数,同时仅研究算例桥梁在纵向地震波作用下的结构响应。

3　桥梁系统易损性分析

3.1　构件损伤指标

大量桥梁震害调查报告指出,支座、桥墩等构件在地震作用中极易受到破坏,从而导致桥梁通行能力下降甚至丧失。因此,本文选取桥墩、板式橡胶支座、聚四氟滑板支座作为构件易损性分析对象。在进行桥梁结构易损性分析时,需基于性能水准来量化不同类型的结构损伤指标。

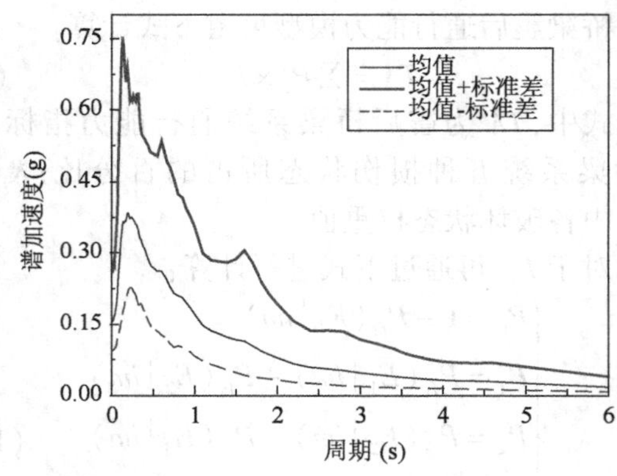

图2　50条地震动反应谱特性($\zeta=5\%$)

已经有大量的研究根据损伤状态或承载力损失制定出结构损伤指标及相应的极限状态。结构损伤指标通常采用曲率延性比、位移延性比或相对位移来量化结构损伤。本文结合相关文献的研究成果[8,18]，从不同方面定义了算例桥梁关键构件损伤指标，如表3所示。

桥梁构件损伤判定准则 表3

构件名称	损伤指标	轻微损伤	中等损伤	严重损伤	完全破坏	参考文献
桥墩	曲率延性比(μ_φ)	$1<\mu_\varphi\leqslant2$	$2<\mu_\varphi\leqslant4$	$4<\mu_\varphi\leqslant7$	$\mu_\varphi>7$	[9,12]
板式橡胶支座	位移延性比(μ_d)	$1<\mu_d\leqslant1.5$	$1.5<\mu_d\leqslant2.0$	$2.0<\mu_d\leqslant2.5$	$\mu_d>2.5$	[8]
聚四氟滑板支座	相对位移(Δ,m)	$0.09<\Delta\leqslant0.15$	$0.15<\Delta\leqslant0.2$	$0.2<\Delta\leqslant0.3$	$\Delta>0.3$	[8]

3.2 系统易损性分析

在桥梁地震易损性分析中，常假定结构承载力与结构需求服从对数正态分布，那么式(1)可以改写成标准正态分布形式：

$$P_f=\Phi\left[\frac{\ln(\overline{EDP})-\ln(\bar{S}_C)}{\sqrt{\beta_{EDP}^2+\beta_C^2}}\right] \tag{11}$$

式中，$\overline{EDP}$，β_{EDP}为结构需求均值和对数标准差；$\bar{S}_C$，β_C为结构承载能力均值和对数标准差。根据HAZU99，当IM采用PGA时，$\sqrt{\beta_{EDP}^2+\beta_C^2}=0.5$。

根据Cornell等人[19]的研究成果，$\overline{EDP}$与IM存在以下关系：

$$\ln(\overline{EDP})=a\ln IM+b \tag{12}$$

式中，a，b为常数，可通过最小二乘法回归得到。

那么根据式(11)、式(12)可计算得到算例桥梁构件易损性曲线，然后运用I-PCM法计算得到算例桥梁系统易损性曲线，如图3所示。

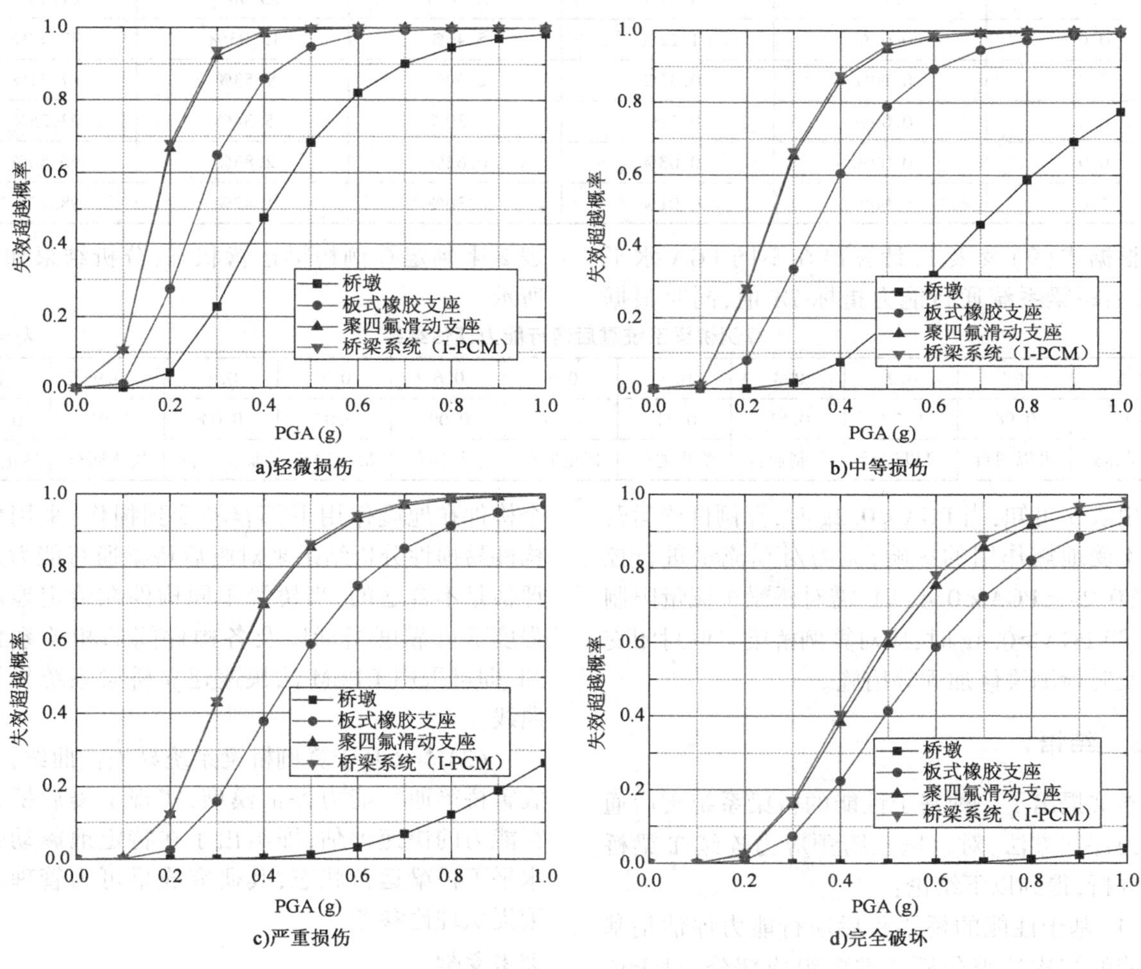

图3 算例桥梁构件及系统易损性曲线

由图3可知，随着PGA的增大，对于桥梁系统中的各类构件来说，在四种损伤状态下其失效超越概率均表现出增大的趋势；在地震作用下，支座结构相对桥墩结构更容易受到破坏，在严重损伤和完全破坏两种状态下表现尤为明显;与此同时,聚四氟滑动支座与其他构件相比在各个损伤状态下失效超越概率最大,成为算例桥梁系统中最易受到地震损伤的构件;与构件易损性曲线相比,在同一PGA水平下,桥梁系统失效概率要大于系统中任一单个构件失效概率,因此,采用单一构件易损性曲线来评估桥梁结构易损性,其结果是高估了结构抗震能力。

4 基于性能的桥梁系统震后通行能力评估

本文基于I-PCM法形成的桥梁系统易损性曲线,对算例桥梁震后通行能力进行评估。根据式(10)计算桥梁系统在给定的PGA下处于五种损伤状态的概率,其结果如表4所示。

桥梁系统在给定的PGA下处于损伤状态的概率 表4

PGA	损伤状态				
	无损伤	轻微损伤	中等损伤	严重损伤	完全破坏
0	100.00%	0.00%	0.00%	0.00%	0.00%
0.1	89.35%	9.48%	0.95%	0.21%	0.01%
0.2	31.97%	39.84%	16.00%	9.76%	2.43%
0.3	6.35%	27.21%	23.68%	26.25%	16.51%
0.4	1.02%	11.37%	17.94%	30.05%	39.62%
0.5	0.15%	3.91%	10.49%	23.96%	61.49%
0.6	0.02%	1.22%	5.46%	15.93%	77.37%
0.7	0.00%	0.37%	2.69%	9.53%	87.41%
0.8	0.00%	0.11%	1.30%	5.34%	93.25%
0.9	0.00%	0.03%	0.62%	2.85%	96.50%
1.0	0.00%	0.01%	0.30%	1.47%	98.22%

根据式(9)及表1,计算出在不同PGA水平下,震后桥梁系统通行能力指标*TA*值,同时根据表2来判定算例桥梁运营状态,分析结果如表5所示。

算例桥梁系统震后通行能力评估结果 表5

PGA	0.1	0.2	0.3	0.4	0.5	0.6	0.7	0.8	0.9	1
TA	0.98	0.77	0.51	0.31	0.17	0.09	0.05	0.03	0.01	0.01
运营状态	可以通行	可以通行	限制通行	禁止通行	禁止通行	禁止通行	禁止通行	禁止通行	禁止通行	禁止通行

由表5可知,当PGA<0.2g时,算例桥梁运营状态不受地震作用的影响,无需对车流量进行控制;当0.2g<PGA<0.4g时,需对桥梁车流量限制50%;当PGA≥0.4g时,应对算例桥梁采取封闭交通和及时检测维修加固等措施。

5 结语

本文提出了一种基于性能的桥梁系统震后通行能力评估方法,对一座三跨预应力连续T梁桥进行分析,得到以下结论:

(1)基于性能的桥梁震后通行能力评估是基于性能的结构抗震分析的重要组成部分,对于评估震后桥梁系统运营状态,进行运营管理决策具有十分重要的应用价值。

(2)桥梁作为一个复杂的结构系统比任何一个构件在地震作用下都容易受到损伤,采用单一构件易损性分析结果来对震后桥梁通行能力进行评估是不合适的;当桥梁不同构件在给定地震动强度下可靠度指标以及各构件间的相关系数已知,即可采用I-PCM法快速建立桥梁系统易损性曲线。

(3)本文基于算例桥梁系统易损性曲线,结合震害桥梁通行能力评估模型,实现了震后桥梁通行能力的快速评估,即给出了在特定地震动强度水平下桥梁运营状态,其研究成果可为管理者决策提供理论参考。

参考文献

[1] 兰日清,李小军,丰彪,等.近场强震作用下城市桥梁结构灾害评价方法研究[J].自然灾害学报,2017,26(4):135-142.

[2] 兰日清,丰彪,王自法. 震后公路桥梁通行能力快速评估技术研究[J]. 世界地震工程,2009,25(2):81-87.

[3] 高洪. 日本的灾难预警与早期评估系统[N]. 中国社会科学院院报,2008-08-07.

[4] 段满珍,轧红颖,李珊珊,等. 震害道路通行能力评估模型[J]. 重庆交通大学学报(自然科学版),2017,36(5):79-85.

[5] 张菊辉. 基于数值模拟的规则梁桥墩柱的地震易损性分析[D]. 上海:同济大学,2006.

[6] 王建民,王国亮,聂建国,等. 基于概率的桥梁结构地震危害性分析[J]. 土木工程学报,2010,43(11):86-93.

[7] 李立峰,吴文朋,黄佳梅,等. 板式橡胶支座地震易损性分析[J]. 湖南大学学报(自然科学版),2011,38(11):1-6.

[8] 李立峰,吴文朋,黄佳梅,等. 地震作用下中等跨径RC连续梁桥系统易损性研究[J]. 土木工程学报,2012,45(10):152-160.

[9] 林庆利. 基于汶川地震震害的公路桥梁易损性研究[D]. 北京:中国地震局工程力学研究所,2017.

[10] 蒋知之,李永义,孙庆峰,等. 震后公路桥梁通行能力理论模型研究[J]. 防灾减灾工程学报,2015,35(2):226-231.

[11] 周军杰. 基于易损性的钢筋混凝土桥墩的剩余承载力评估方法[D]. 北京:北京交通大学,2013.

[12] 葛胜锦,熊治华,翟敏刚,等. 中小跨径混凝土连续梁桥地震易损性研究[J]. 公路交通科技,2013,30(7):60-65.

[13] Nielson B G, Desroches R. Seismic fragility methodology for highway bridges using a component level approach [J]. Earthquake Engineering & Structural Dynamics, 2007, 36(6): 823-839.

[14] Yuan X X, M D Pandey. Analysis of approximations for multinormal integration in system reliability computation[J]. Structural Safety, 2006, 28(4):361-377.

[15] Melchers R E. Structural reliability: analysis and prediction [M]. Chichester, UK: John Wiley & Sons Ltd. ,1999.

[16] M D Pandey. An effective approximation to evaluate multinormal integrals[J]. Structural Safety, 1998, 20(1):51-67.

[17] Padgett J E, Nielson B G, Desroches R. Selection of optimal intensity measures in probabilistic seismic demand models of highway bridge portfolios [J]. Earthquake Engineering & Structural Dynamics, 2008, 37(5):711-725.

[18] Choi E, Desroches R, Nielson B. Seismic fragility of typical bridges in moderate seismic zones[J]. Ksce Journal of Civil Engineering, 2004, 26(2):187-199.

[19] Cornell C A, Jalayer F, Hamburger R O. Probabilistic Basis for 2000 SAC Federal Emergency Management Agency Steel Moment Frame Guidelines [J]. Journal of Structural Engineering, 2002, 128(4):526-532.

基于对流扩散耦合方程求解的沿海混凝土结构耐久性分析

彭文锋[1] 陈 峰*[1] 郝 磊[1] 张亚博[1] 查 斌[2]

(1. 长安大学公路学院;2. 在役长大桥梁安全与健康国家重点实验室)

摘 要 本文对沿海城市深圳市大气环境中氯离子侵蚀作用下的混凝土结构服役寿命进行分析,根据干湿交替下氯离子的传输机理,推导了氯离子在非饱水混凝土内传输的对流扩散方程,给出了温湿度等边界条件对传输机制的影响,建立数值分析模型计算了氯离子中在非饱水混凝土中的对流扩散规律,通过实测数据验证了模型的有效性。在对深圳市温湿度等大气资料进行统计分析的基础上,确定所需的等代干湿交替函数,借助数值求解模型计算混凝土结构的服役寿命。所给出的计算结果可为深圳市大气区混凝土结构的耐久性设计提供定量指标。

关键词　桥梁工程　混凝土耐久性　数值模拟　氯离子传输　大气环境

0　引言

如何准确预测氯离子的传输过程是混凝土耐久性设计的重要环节。传统的Fick第二定律仅能描述氯离子在饱水混凝土中的传输过程,但是在沿海大气环境下,混凝土往往处于非饱水状态,单纯的扩散理论求解必将带来较大的误差。李春秋[1]、金伟良[2]等学者建立了能很好描述干湿交替下氯离子传输的对流扩散耦合方程,该方程可以很好地模拟非饱水状态混凝土内氯离子侵蚀问题。对于位于沿海地区大气环境下的混凝土结构,氯离子侵蚀过程受到温度、湿度和降雨等因素的综合影响。应敬伟等[3]建立了氯离子扩散系数受水灰比、环境温度、时间和环境湿度等因素影响的氯离子扩散模型。现有文献多研究了大气环境对氯离子传输的影响,但对由降雨等干湿交替引起的水分迁移对氯离子传输的影响问题缺乏研究,更未涉及水分迁移造成的对流作用的影响,因而真实描述大气环境下氯离子的传输过程对于沿海混凝土结构耐久性设计具有更为重要的意义。

本文通过建立的氯离子对流扩散耦合求解方程,推导并确定温湿度变化曲线简化求解方法,确立等代干湿交替函数,并以深圳市为例,讨论了大气环境下混凝土结构服役寿命参数的计算方法,为南方沿海城市混凝土结构耐久性设计提供理论参考。

1　模型建立

1.1　氯离子在非饱水混凝土内的传输模型

大气降雨导致的干湿交替作用下以耦合扩散和对流作用来模拟氯离子传输方式。在大气环境下,由于大气湿度的反复变化,混凝土内的氯离子不仅受自身浓度梯度驱动而扩散,更会因孔隙内的毛细负压吸附导致水分迁移而产生对流,只有建立对流和扩散同时耦合的传输方程,才能客观描述和预测氯离子在非饱水混凝土内的传输状态。

由水分传输导致的氯离子对流通量表示为:

$$J_{Cl,conv} = -C_{Cl} \cdot D_c(s) \cdot \frac{\partial s}{\partial x} \tag{1}$$

式中:C_{Cl}——自由氯离子浓度(%);

s——混凝土相对含水量;

x——氯离子传输深度(m);

$D_c(s)$——水分扩散系数(m^2/s);

$J_{Cl,conv}$——氯离子对流通量(m/s)。

由氯离子扩散导致的扩散通量表示为:

$$J_{Cl,diff} = -D_{Cl}(s) \cdot \frac{\partial C_{Cl}}{\partial x} \tag{2}$$

式中:$D_{Cl}(s)$——氯离子扩散系数(m^2/s);

$J_{Cl,diff}$——氯离子扩散通量(m/s)。

联合氯离子对流通量和扩散通量公式,氯离子在干燥阶段和湿润阶段的传输通量可表示为:

$$J_{Cl} = -D_{Cl}(s) \cdot \frac{\partial C_{Cl}}{\partial x} - C_{Cl} \cdot D_c(s) \cdot \frac{\partial s}{\partial x} \tag{3}$$

式中:J_{Cl}——氯离子总通量(m/s)。

最后,根据氯离子的质量守恒方程,在混凝土干燥阶段和湿润阶段氯离子的对流扩散耦合作用方程可表示为:

$$\begin{cases} \dfrac{\partial C_{Cl}}{\partial t} = \dfrac{\partial}{\partial x}\left[D_{Cl}(s) \cdot \dfrac{\partial C_{Cl}}{\partial x} + C_{Cl} \cdot D_d(s) \cdot \dfrac{\partial s}{\partial x}\right], \\ \text{干燥阶段} \\ \dfrac{\partial C_{Cl}}{\partial t} = \dfrac{\partial}{\partial x}\left[D_{Cl}(s) \cdot \dfrac{\partial C_{Cl}}{\partial x} + C_{Cl} \cdot D_w(s) \cdot \dfrac{\partial s}{\partial x}\right], \\ \text{湿润阶段} \end{cases} \tag{4}$$

式中:$D_d(s)$——干燥阶段水分扩散系数(m^2/s);

$D_w(s)$——湿润阶段水分扩散系数(m^2/s)。

1.2　温湿度变化曲线

干燥阶段混凝土表面相对含水量可近似看成大气湿度,故可认为混凝土表面湿度等于环境湿度[4]。

Bastidas Arteaga E[5]假定全年温湿度变化为正弦函数。但实际的温度早晚低而中午高,湿度相反,并且南方沿海城市温度和湿度变化虽然较北方城市而言较为稳定，但仍旧随着月份更替变化，故本文建立以 1 小时为步长的温湿度各自的时变函数，可表示为：

$$\begin{cases} T_i = T_{av,i} - 0.5T_{am,i}\cos\left(\dfrac{\pi}{12}t\right) \\ RH_i = RH_{av,i} + 0.5RH_{am,i}\cos\left(\dfrac{\pi}{12}t\right) \end{cases} \tag{5}$$

式中： t——时间（h）；

T_i，RH_i——第 i 月一天中某时刻的温度、湿度；

$T_{av,i}$，$RH_{av,i}$——第 i 月平均温度、湿度；

$T_{am,i}$，$RH_{am,i}$——第 i 月平均最高温度与平均最低温度差值、平均最高湿度与平均最低湿度差值。

2 模型求解

公式（4）建立的传输模型是高度非线性偏微分方程，可基于 COMSOL 仿真软件建立非饱水混凝土对流扩散传输求解模型，以及混凝土细观求解数值模拟模型，进行氯离子对流扩散传输方程的求解。本文选取 Costa 等[6]的实海暴露试验来验证计算模型的准确性，材料参数的取值与文献[7]一致。

2.1 环境参数取值

该模型温湿度等边界条件取文献[6]给出的气象数据，包括大气温度、大气湿度。

模型的温度变化曲线假定为：

$$T = 16.8 - 5.8\cos(2\pi t_1) \tag{6}$$

式中：t_1———时间（a）。

模型的湿度变化曲线表示为：

$$RH = 78 + 10.5\cos(2\pi t_1) \tag{7}$$

2.2 模型验证

本文取文献[6]中码头－20 区域 C1 对应气候条件为细观混凝土求解模型的边界条件进行数值模拟分析，数值模拟的氯离子分布结果如图 1 所示。不同深度氯离子含量计算值与实测值对比如图 2 所示，图中数据分布显示，实测结果与分析计算结果规律基本一致，二者都呈现了浅层对流为主深层扩散为主的分布特性。由于干湿交替频率和浸泡时间未明确，模拟计算的氯离子分布与实测值存在一些偏差。总体而言，对流扩散传输计算分析能较好地预测氯离子在非饱水混凝土中的传输过程。

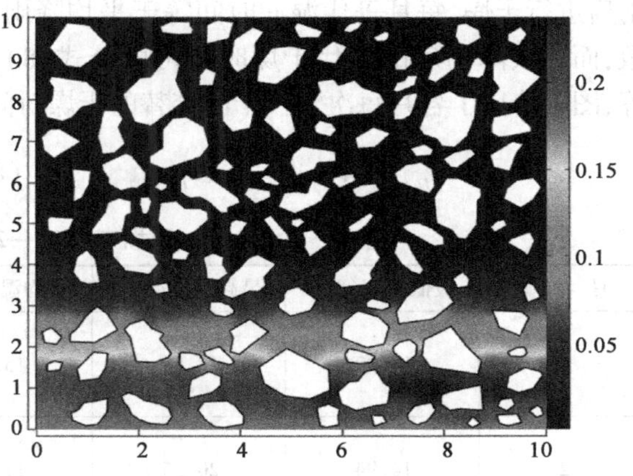

图 1 数值模拟的氯离子浓度分布

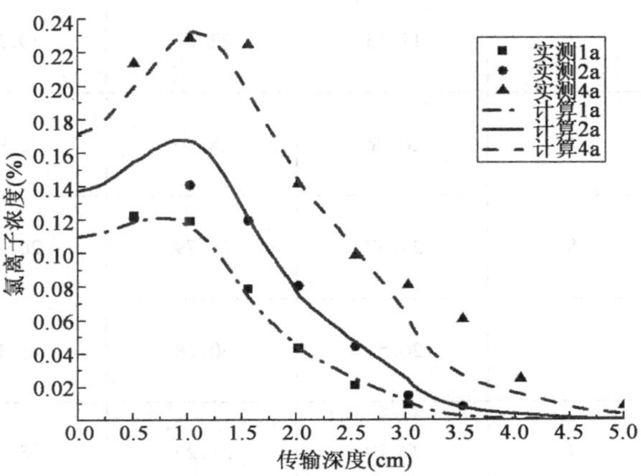

图 2 不同暴露期混凝土内部氯离子浓度计算值和实测值

3 深圳市大气环境下混凝土服役寿命预测

3.1 深圳市温度、湿度和降雨频率统计

环境温度、环境湿度以及干湿交替时间等是影响干湿交替区混凝土内氯离子传输的重要外部因素，本文假定每一次降雨都代表一次干湿交替。以上述三个因素作为氯离子在干湿交替混凝土中传输问题的关键因子，通过对流扩散传输计算模型对深圳市的混凝土结构耐久性进行分析。

根据深圳市 2005—2020 年的气象数据，通过自编 Matlab 程序计算相关温度、湿度变化曲线，平均各月计算结果如表 1 和表 2 所示。图 3 直观表示了一月某天的温湿度变化。由于降雨天数对模型干湿循环参数有决定性影响，本文根据气象资料总结出深圳市各月平均降雨天数，如图 4 所示。为了简化干湿交替模型，假定降雨为湿润混凝土的过程，并不考虑降雨冲刷混凝土导致其表面氯离子浓度变化。假定每次降雨持续时间为 24h，降雨后进行干燥,每月等代湿润时间等于平均降雨天数,而每次降雨后的等代干燥时间可由公式(8)计算,图4给出了各月每次等代干湿交替的干燥时间。

$$t_{D,i}=24\times\left(\frac{D_i}{k_i}-1\right)\tag{8}$$

式中:$t_{D,i}$——第 i 月一次干湿交替的干燥时间(h);

D_i——第 i 月天数;

k_i——第 i 月平均降雨天数。

深圳市2005—2020年各月温度变化曲线　　表1

月　份	最低温度(℃)	最高温度(℃)	平均温度(℃)	温度幅值	温度变化曲线
1	13.32	18.89	15.71	2.78	$T_1=15.71-2.78\cdot\cos\left(\frac{\pi}{12}t\right)$
2	14.94	20.35	17.07	2.71	$T_2=17.07-2.71\cdot\cos\left(\frac{\pi}{12}t\right)$
3	17.53	22.62	19.52	2.55	$T_3=19.52-2.55\cdot\cos\left(\frac{\pi}{12}t\right)$
4	20.96	25.80	22.92	2.42	$T_4=22.92-2.42\cdot\cos\left(\frac{\pi}{12}t\right)$
5	24.37	28.79	26.22	2.21	$T_5=26.22-2.21\cdot\cos\left(\frac{\pi}{12}t\right)$
6	26.53	30.28	28.15	1.88	$T_6=28.15-1.88\cdot\cos\left(\frac{\pi}{12}t\right)$
7	27.19	31.29	28.92	4.10	$T_7=28.92-4.10\cdot\cos\left(\frac{\pi}{12}t\right)$
8	26.91	31.23	28.73	2.16	$T_8=28.73-2.16\cdot\cos\left(\frac{\pi}{12}t\right)$
9	26.24	30.68	28.07	2.22	$T_9=28.07-2.22\cdot\cos\left(\frac{\pi}{12}t\right)$
10	23.59	28.44	25.62	2.43	$T_{10}=25.62-2.43\cdot\cos\left(\frac{\pi}{12}t\right)$
11	19.71	24.75	21.79	2.52	$T_{11}=21.79-2.52\cdot\cos\left(\frac{\pi}{12}t\right)$
12	14.95	20.38	17.23	2.71	$T_{12}=17.23-2.71\cdot\cos\left(\frac{\pi}{12}t\right)$

深圳市2005—2020年各月湿度变化曲线　　表2

月　份	最低湿度(%)	最高湿度(%)	平均湿度(%)	湿度幅值(%)	湿度变化曲线
1	53.89	77.91	66.79	12.01	$RH_1=66.79+12.01\cdot\cos\left(\frac{\pi}{12}t\right)$
2	59.84	83.20	73.11	11.68	$RH_2=73.11+11.68\cdot\cos\left(\frac{\pi}{12}t\right)$
3	62.91	85.01	75.48	8.50	$RH_3=75.48+8.50\cdot\cos\left(\frac{\pi}{12}t\right)$

续上表

月　份	最低湿度(%)	最高湿度(%)	平均湿度(%)	湿度幅值(%)	湿度变化曲线
4	65.54	87.60	78.16	11.03	$RH_4=78.16+11.03\cdot\cos\left(\frac{\pi}{12}t\right)$
5	67.25	88.05	79.23	6.00	$RH_5=79.23+6.00\cdot\cos\left(\frac{\pi}{12}t\right)$
6	70.53	88.43	80.71	8.95	$RH_6=80.71+8.95\cdot\cos\left(\frac{\pi}{12}t\right)$
7	66.80	86.78	78.33	10.00	$RH_7=78.33+10.00\cdot\cos\left(\frac{\pi}{12}t\right)$
8	66.32	87.34	78.47	10.51	$RH_8=78.47+10.51\cdot\cos\left(\frac{\pi}{12}t\right)$
9	61.32	83.14	73.84	10.91	$RH_9=73.84+10.91\cdot\cos\left(\frac{\pi}{12}t\right)$
10	53.97	77.47	67.48	11.75	$RH_{10}=67.48+11.75\cdot\cos\left(\frac{\pi}{12}t\right)$
11	55.10	77.75	67.75	11.33	$RH_{11}=67.75+11.33\cdot\cos\left(\frac{\pi}{12}t\right)$
12	49.50	71.74	61.54	11.12	$RH_{12}=61.54+11.12\cdot\cos\left(\frac{\pi}{12}t\right)$

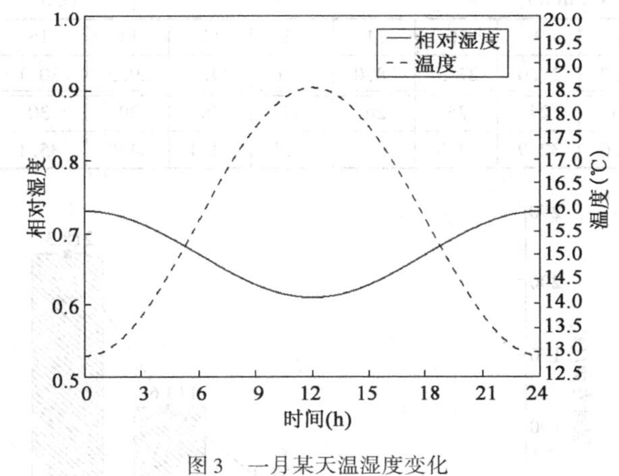

图 3　一月某天温湿度变化

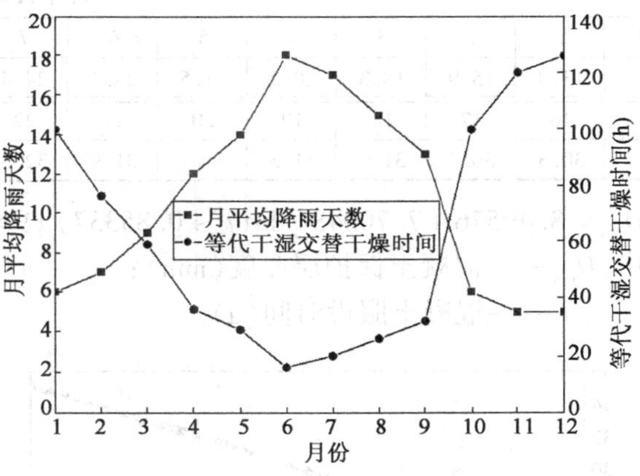

图 4　各月平均降雨天数和等代干湿交替干燥时间

3.2　深圳市大气环境下混凝土服役寿命计算

本文根据温湿度曲线及等代干湿交替函数，进行基于对流扩散传输计算模型的氯离子传输求解，并据此进行沿海环境混凝土结构抗氯离子侵蚀耐久性分析。

假定大气环境下混凝土表面氯离子浓度可以达到稳定状态而不随时间积累，假定 c_s 恒定并取值为 0.2%[8]。按照混凝土结构耐久性设计规范[9]取混凝土保护层厚度 30mm，近海环境临界氯离子浓度 c_{cr} 参考规范取值为 0.1%，混凝土的水灰比取值为 0.4。根据前文中计算的各月温度、湿度和等代干湿交替函数，基于对流扩散传输计算模型以月为单位依次计算处于深圳市大气环境下的氯离子在非饱水混凝土内的浓度参数。当保护层处氯离子浓度达到临界氯离子浓度时，结构处于耐久性失效状态，而不再进行时间演进计算。各年份氯离子沿深度方向的分布计算结果如图 5 所示，结果显示：在第 15 年年末距混凝土表面 30mm 处的氯离子浓度达到临界氯离子浓度，由此可知按照此保护层厚度设置,服役 15 年左右,结构将处于耐久性失效第一状态(钢筋可能脱钝),说明深圳市沿海大气环境下钢筋混凝土结构的诱导期为 15 年。而混凝土结构耐久性设计规范规定的近海大气区桥梁上部结构最低设计使用年限为 30 年,由计算分析可知,设置 30mm 的保护层厚度并不能有效满足沿海环境混凝土结构的耐久性要求。

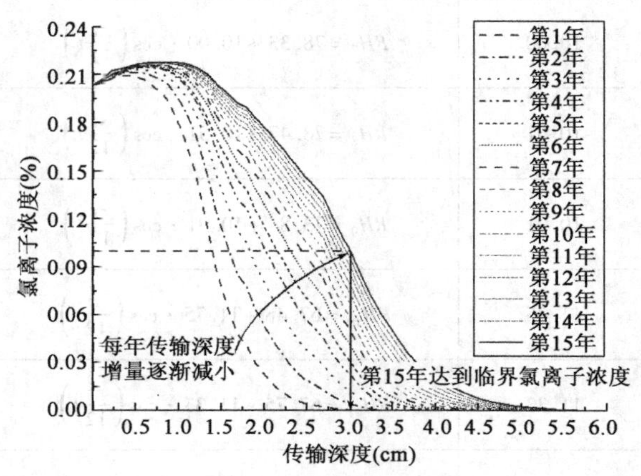

图 5　氯离子逐年传输深度

3.3　深圳市大气环境下钢筋混凝土服役寿命预测模型

现有混凝土结构耐久性规范对近海环境混凝土结构的保护层厚度要求分别为 30mm、35mm、40mm,所要求的服役寿命为 30 年、50 年、100 年,而实际近海环境下的钢筋混凝土结构诱导期往往达不到预计寿命[10]。

考虑深圳市全年各月气候环境的变化,可进一步基于对流扩散传输计算模型计算 30 年的氯离子传输深度,计算所得各年的传输时变深度见表 3,其中 i 表示氯离子侵蚀时间。

根据计算的各年氯离子传输时变深度,可拟合出氯离子达到临界浓度的时间与对应保护层厚度的关系,如公式(9)所示,$R^2=0.995$。对流扩散传输数值模拟计算结果与该拟合公式结果对比如图 6 所示,该公式可以基本精确地给出服役寿命与保护层厚度之间的关系,模型更为精确地计算出了氯离子的侵蚀深度,该方法对保障结构耐久性具有重要意义。

各年传输深度 x_i(mm)　　表 3

i	1	2	3	4	5	6	7	8	9	10	11	12	13	14	15
x_i	13.9	15.9	18.3	20.2	21.5	23.1	24.4	25.7	27.0	27.5	28.0	28.6	29.0	29.5	30.1
i	16	17	18	19	20	21	22	23	24	25	26	27	28	29	30
x_i	30.3	30.7	31.0	31.3	31.7	31.9	32.3	32.6	32.9	33.3	33.7	34.1	34.4	34.8	35.1

$$D_{cov}=8.49576+7.70048\cdot\ln(t_s+0.85337)\quad(9)$$

式中:D_{cov}——混凝土保护层厚度(mm);

t_s——混凝土服役时间(a)。

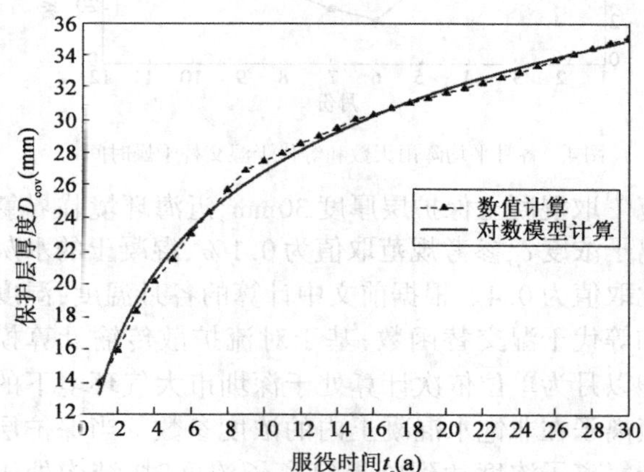

图 6　自然对数模型与数值模型混凝土保护层厚度曲线对比图

可进一步将保护层厚度分别取值为 30、35、40、45、50mm,计算对应的服役寿命为 15.6、30.4、59.0、113.6、218.3a,如图 7 所示。

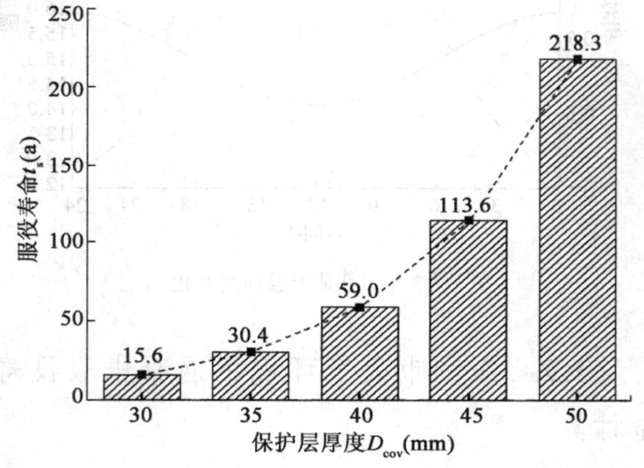

图 7　不同保护层厚度的混凝土服役寿命

混凝土耐久性规范给出了大气区 100 年服役寿命的保护层厚度设计值为 40mm,而针对南方沿海特定的城市(以深圳市为例),其服役寿命 100 年所需的保护层厚度为 44mm。可见,由于我国南方特殊的潮湿高温气候和降雨所致的干湿交替现象,现有混凝土结构耐久性设计规范给出的保护层厚度并不能完全满足我国沿海城市(尤其是深圳市)大气环境下混凝土结构的耐久性要求。

4 结语

本文针对沿海大气环境混凝土非饱水状态下氯离子对流扩散耦合传输特征,建立考虑温度、湿度和降雨等大气环境因素的氯离子对流扩散耦合混凝土细观求解模型,对南方沿海大气环境下混凝土中氯离子侵蚀规律进行计算,并通过现场实测数据验证了模型和计算方法的有效性和计算精度。以该模型为基础,在分析地域温湿度变化规律的基础上,分析了深圳市沿海大气环境下混凝土结构耐久性寿命,并得出如下结论:

(1)建立了考虑大气环境干湿交替因素影响的氯离子对流扩散耦合方程,通过现场实测数据验证了该模型能很好地描述氯离子在干湿交替混凝土内的传输过程。

(2)给出了用深圳市温度、湿度和等代干湿交替函数来表征沿海大气环境参数的方法,并以之为对流扩散耦合方程边界条件,计算分析混凝土的耐久性服役寿命,分析结果表明现有规范给出的保护层厚度不能完全满足南方沿海城市混凝土结构的耐久性要求。

(3)根据前述分析方法,给出了深圳市大气环境下混凝土服役寿命和保护层厚度相关拟合公式和保证其耐久性寿命所需的混凝土保护层厚度建议值,为深圳市大气区混凝土结构的耐久性设计提供了定量指标。

参考文献

[1] 李春秋,李克非.干湿交替下表层混凝土中氯离子传输:原理、试验和模拟[J].硅酸盐学报,2010,38(4):581-589.

[2] 金伟良,张奕,卢振勇.非饱和状态下氯离子在混凝土中的渗透机理及计算模型[J].硅酸盐学报,2008(10):1362-1369.

[3] 应敬伟,赵治超,张喜德.地方气候环境下氯离子扩散系数的研究[J].广西大学学报(自然科学版),2008,33(S1):32-34+37.

[4] 赵娟.海洋环境中考虑温湿传导耦合的氯离子渗透模型[J].上海应用技术学院学报(自然科学版),2011,11(4):294-298.

[5] Bastidas Arteaga E, Chateauneuf A, Sanchez-Silva M, et al. A comprehensive probabilistic model of chloride ingress in unsaturated concrete[J]. Engineering Structures, 2011, 33(3):720-730.

[6] Costa A, J Appleton. Chloride penetration into concrete in marine environment—Part I: Main parameters affecting chloride penetration[J]. Materials and Structures, 1999, 32(4): 252.

[7] Wong S. F, Wee T. H, Swaddiwudhipong S, et al. Study of water movement in concrete[J]. Magazine of Concrete Research, 2001, 53(3): 205-220.

[8] 赵尚传.基于混凝土结构耐久性的海潮影响区环境作用区划研究[J].公路交通科技,2010,27(7):61-64+75.

[9] 公路工程混凝土结构耐久性设计规范.2019,中华人民共和国国家标准. JTG/T 3310-2019, Code for Durability Design of Concrete Structures in Highway Engineering[S].

[10] 罗大明.深圳市混凝土结构耐久性环境区划研究[J].西安:西安建筑科技大学,2011.

Verification and Analysis of Fire Resistance of Constrained Steel Column

Fanglong Zhang*[1] Yining Shen[2]
(1. College of Architecture and Civil Engineering, Wenzhou University;
2. School of highway, Chang'an University)

Abstract Steel structure is widely used in bridge field and building field. In order to promote the comprehensive development of steel structure bridges and steel structure buildings in the field of fire prevention research, it is necessary to study and summarize the fire prevention technology and fire resistance of steel structure. In this paper, the finite element analysis software ABAQUS was used to simulate the confined steel column and beam in a certain test condition. The thermocouple temperature data measured in the test was used as the initial load to conduct the heat conduction analysis, and the temperature field distribution of the whole confined steel column and beam was obtained, which was used as the input temperature field for thermal analysis. In this paper, the deformation and displacement of constrained steel column under fire condition are simulated and verified by comparing the relationship between the displacement and temperature calculated by finite element analysis software and the experimental data, and by introducing the constraint effect of axial force on steel column.

Keywords Steel structure Constraint steel Finite element analysis The fire resistance The thermal analysis

0 Introduction

Steel structure is widely used in the field of large buildings andbridges, but the fire resistance of steel structure has hidden danger in the aspect of safety. Effective fire resistance analysis of steel structure is of vital significance to the healthy development of large steel structure buildings and Bridges.

In the field of bridge, in order to ensure the steel structure bridge can serve safely in the whole life cycle, the study of extreme load such as fire is extremely urgent, and its protection technology is extremely important. Therefore, the Guidance of the Ministry of Transport on promoting the construction of highway steel structure bridges emphasizes once again that " fire prevention measures of steel structure bridges should be improved to improve the ability of steel structure bridges to resist fire" to prevent bridge collapse and other malignant accidents.

The emergence of large steel structure and the development of computer computing power make the fire resistance analysis object of steel structure gradually shift from single or part members to the whole steel structure fire resistance. CECS200 "Technical Code for Fire Prevention of Building Steel Structure" (Submitted for review in September 2010) article 3. 2. 2 clearly requires large space, large span, high-rise, prestressed structures and particularly important buildings must be steel structure overall fire resistance analysis. At the same time, compared with the analysis of a single steel component or steel frame, the analysis of the overall fire resistance of steel structure buildings can more accurately reflect the characteristics of steel structure buildings under different structural forms under fire damage, and the conclusions and measures proposed on this basis are more in line with the actual needs.

The finite element method has been used to analyze the fire resistance of steel structures, including steel beams, steel columns, steel joints and steel frames. However, previous studies using entity unit analysis of steel members, as well as the overall refractory analysis of large steel structure, also can ignore the temperature change of the single steel members, the emergence of large-scale steel structure building and the development of computer computing power prompted analysis of refractory refractory steel members from the individual or the whole steel structure gradually transferred to the object.

The above reasons show that the analysis based on the fire resistance checking calculation of the whole structure represents the development direction of the fire resistance analysis field of steel structure, which is in line with the idea of performance-based fire prevention. The finite element analysis method using line element in finite element analysis software has important practical significance.

1 Test conditions

The fire resistance test of restrained steel column carried out by Li Guoqiang et al., State Key Laboratory of Disaster Prevention in Civil

Engineering, Tongji University, is adopted as the simulation object.

1.1 Test object

The experiment mainly studied the restrained steel column fixed by restrained steel beam under the action of axial load F1 and mid-span concentrated load F2, in which, the restrained steel column is uniformly heated through the test furnace according to ISO834 heating curve. The test model and load distribution are shown in Fig. 1.

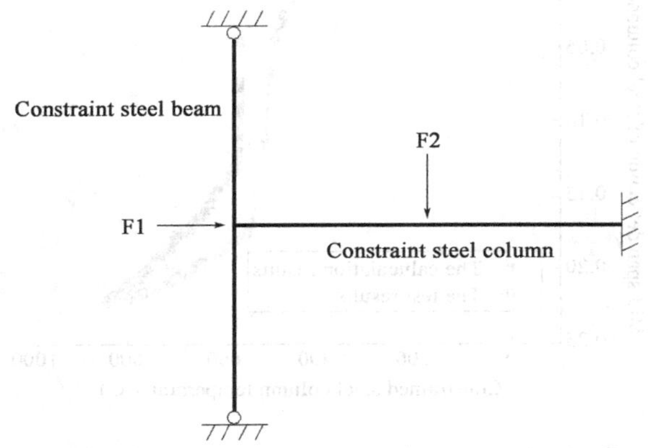

Fig. 1 Test model and load diagram

1.2 Temperature measurement results

The surface temperature of the constrained steel column was measured by the thermocouple prearranged at both ends of the constrained steel column. Due to the systematic error of the test conditions, the temperature changes of the left end and the right end of the restrained steel column measured under the two test results are different. The simulation is carried out under the condition that the temperature distribution is uniform and the temperature at the left and right ends of the constrained steel column changes with time basically the same.

2 The establishment of finite element model

The establishment of finite element modelis divided into two steps. First, the heat transfer model of the steel member is established by using the line element according to the change of temperature of the constrained steel column with time, and then the stress model is established under the condition of the change of temperature field inside the steel member.

2.1 Heat transfer model

The physical property parameters of materials at high temperature are set according to the "Technical Code for Fire Prevention of Building Steel Structure", as shown in Tab. 1.

Input parameters of heat transfer model

Tab. 1

Parameter	Heat conductivity [W/(m · ℃)]	Specific heat capacity [J/(kg · ℃)]	Density (kg/m³)
Numerical value	45	600	7 850

According to the time-varying relationship of average temperature of moderately constrained steel column measured by thermocouple in the reference test, the temperature change curve was extracted as the input of temperature boundary conditions in the heat transfer model, and the extracted curve was shown in Fig. 2.

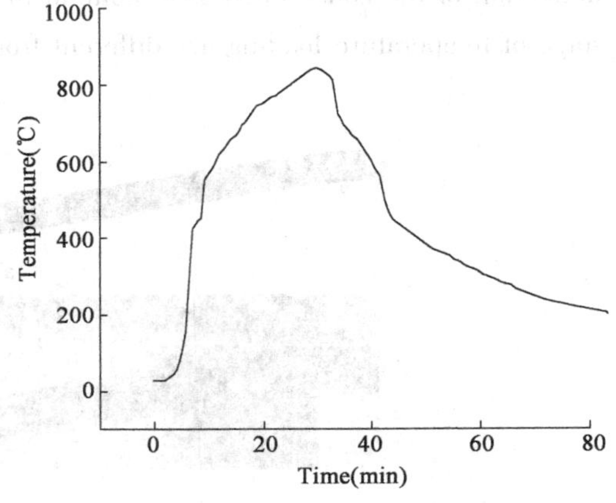

Fig. 2 Temperature curve of heat transfer analysis input

2.2 Mechanical model

Temperature affects the deformation of steel structure under load mainly by changing the deformation parameters and mechanical parameters of steel. Tab2 shows the initial values of each parameter at room temperature. According to the relationship between deformation parameters and mechanical parameters of steel members with temperature given in "Technical Code for Fire Prevention of Steel Structures in Buildings", Poisson's ratio is less affected by temperature, and the initial value is kept unchanged in calculation, thermal expansion coefficient, elastic modulus and yield strength change with temperature, refer to CECS200 for details.

Values of parameters in the force model Tab. 2

Parameter	Coefficient of thermal expansion [m/(m · ℃)]	Modulus of elasticity [N/mm²]	The yield strength [N/mm²]	Poisson's ratio
The initial value	1.4×10^{-5}	2.024×10^{5}	360	0.3

3 The result comparison

Fig. 3 shows the comparison between the test value and the calculated value of the mid-span deflection of the constrained steel column with the change of temperature under the calculated working condition. It can be seen that the variation trend of the calculated mid-span deflection with temperature is basically consistent with the test results, and both the test and simulated constraint columns start to lose stability at about 500℃. As the temperature load continues to increase, when the mid-span deflection increases rapidly (plus and minus sign indicates the deflection change direction) to a certain value, the tensile stress caused by the end constraint increases, and both the calculated results and the test results show the phenomenon of deformation slowing down.

Because the constitutive relation between the test material and the simulated steel member material is difficult to be completely unified, and the boundary constraint conditions are different to some extent, the calculation results of the transition point of the mid-span deflection of the constrained steel column in the later stage of temperature loading are different from the test results, but the error is acceptable for the whole deformation situation.

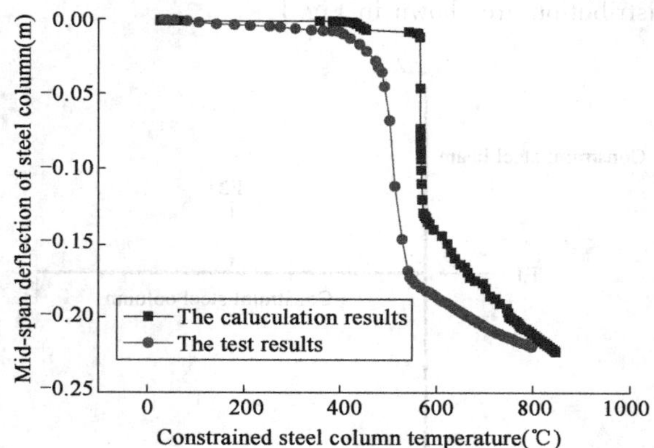

Fig. 3 Comparison of test and calculated values of mid-span deflection of constrained steel column

Fig. 4 shows the comparison of the residual deformation of the constrained steel column between the calculated results and the experimental results, which are basically consistent with the experimental results. In order to compare the results, the deformation of the calculated results is represented by steel columns with cross-section characteristics, and the line element simulation is used in the actual calculation process.

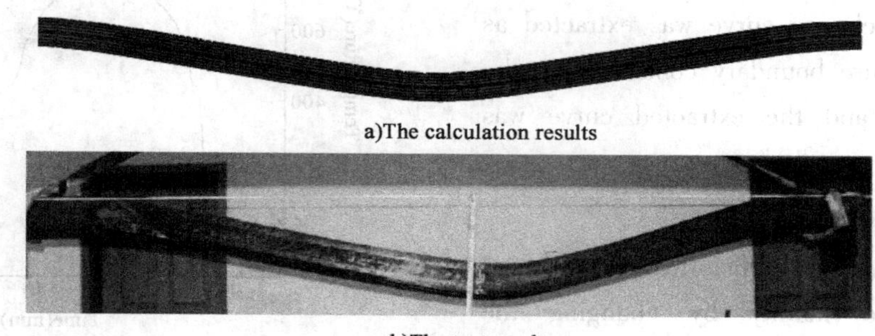

a)The calculation results

b)The test results

Fig. 4 Comparison of test and calculation results

4 Conclusions

Use of finite element simulation software for fire resistant design for steel structure with considerable accuracy, the author adopts the model based on heat transfer and stress distribution of line unit not only can be used for a single fire resistance of steel components analysis, but also can provide the plethora of steel structure bridge and high-rise steel structure building to analyze the overall resistance to fire. It can promote the development of thermal coupling analysis of steel structure from single temperature criterion to whole structure in performance-based fire prevention design. In addition, the internal force and deformation of the structure under the simulated fire situation are designed to ensure that the structure as a whole will not be unstable or damaged in the possible fire accident.

References

[1] Zheng Y. G, Han L. H. Study on mechanical Properties of Beam-column Joints under fire [J]. Steel Structure, 2007, 22 (1) : 89-94.

[2] Ma H. B. Temperature Field and Global Effect Analysis of Steel Frame Structure under Fire [D]. Xi 'an: Xi 'an University of Architecture and Technology, 2009.

[3] Ministry of Transport of the People' s Republic of China. Several Opinions of the Ministry of Transport on Promoting the Construction of Highway Steel Structure Bridges [EB/OL]. (2016-07-13) [2020-11-17]. http://xxgk.mot.gov.cn/jigou/glj/201607/t20160713_2979314.html.

[4] Li G. Q, Xu Y. B, A Usmani. Study on Structures Responses of Steel-concrete Composite Highway Bridge Under Fuel Tanker Fire [J]. Journal of Disaster Prevention Mitigation Engineering, 2016, 36 (3) : 444-452.

[5] Song C. J, Zhang G, Qin Z. Y, et al. Fire Resistance of Steel-concrete Composite Continuous Bridge Grider [J]. Journal of Chang'an University (Natural Science Edition), 2019, 39 (6) : 89-98.

[6] Zhou H. Y, Zhang Z. Y, Hao, C. L, et al. Fire Resistance of Prestressed Continuous Steel concrete Composite Beams [J]. Journal of Changàn University (Natural Science Edition), 2018, 38 (6) : 40-48.

[7] Gao X, Pan W. Application of ABAQUS in finite element analysis [J]. Yunnan Architecture, 2008(1):62-65.

[8] CECS200, Technical Code for Fire Prevention of Steel Structures in Buildings [S].

[9] Li G. Q, Wang P. J, Wang Y. C. Experimental Study on Fire Resistance of Constrained Steel Column [J]. Journal of Building Structures, 2009, 30 (5) : 184-190.

Investigation on Time-varying Ultimate Bearing Capacity of Multi-girder RC Bridge Based on OPENSEES

Jie Zou* Xuan Luo

(Chang' an University)

Abstract Due to vehicle loads and environmental effects, the ultimate bearing capacity of multi-girder RC bridge may deteriorate with the increase of service time, and cause unnecessary loss of life and property. In this paper, an analysis approach is developed for evaluating the time-varying ultimate bearing capacity of multi-girder RC bridge. The approach uses OPENSEES fiber element to establish macro model. The influence of material degradation on the ultimate bearing capacity of multi-girder RC bridge is investigated. In addition, the accuracy of the analysis approach is verified by the failure test of a multi-girder RC bridge, The feasibility and satisfactory performance of the proposed analysis approach are evaluated, then the time-varying ultimate bearing capacity of the bridge is obtained. The results demonstate that the material degradation affects the ultimate bearing capacity of multi-girder RC bridge.

Keywords Multi-girder RC bridge OPENSEES Ultimate bearing capacity Material degradation

0 Introduction

According to statistics, multi-girder RC bridge accounts for a large proportion of many bridges in service. In service multi-girder RC bridge under the coupling action of environment and vehicle load, the degradation of some bridges is accelerated, the reduction of bridge bearing capacity seriously threatens the traffic safety during the service period, and even causes unnecessary loss of life and property. In the past decades, bridge accidents caused by environment and heavy load have occurred frequently, for example, I-35W Mississippi River Bridge and I-5 Skagit River Bridge and Wuxi Single Column Bridge collapsed in 2019. Therefore, it is very important for traffic safety to investigate the time-varying ultimate bearing capacity of multi-girder RC bridge in the whole service cycle.

In recent years, researchers haveinvestigated the ultimate bearing capacity of girder bridges. For example, the Second Highway Survey and Design Institute of the Ministry of Communications conducted failure tests on a single T-shaped simply supported girder to investigate its ultimate bearing capacity. Chen et al. conducted destructive tests on a multi-girder prestressed concrete beam bridge on an highway, and measured the ultimate bearing capacity of the bridge. However, these investigations are based on destructive tests and require expensive test costs. In order to solve these problems, some researchers use the finite element method to analyze the bridge, Zhu et al. investigated the ultimate bearing capacity of a prestressed T-girder bridge by using refined finite element method. Lee et al. made a detailed analysis of post tensioned prestressed concrete girder by using ABAQUS solid element. However, these investigations do not consider the time-varying degradation properties of materials, and they are time-consuming.

To sum up, the time-varying ultimate bearing capacity analysis framework of multi-girder RC bridge is established based on OPENSEES fiber element, The framework is verified by failure test. It provides an analysis method to balance accuracy and efficiency for the time-varying ultimate bearing capacity analysis of multigirder RC bridge.

1 Time-varying material properties

Among many factors that lead to the degradation of the bearing capacity of reinforced concrete structures, the influence of ordinary reinforcement is the most common and the greatest. Corrosion of reinforcement will lead to section loss, reduction of ultimate yield strength and stress concentration of reinforcement. Thus, the structural resistance of a single component and the whole system is reduced. According to the different corrosion mechanism, the corrosion of ordinary reinforcement and prestressed reinforcement can be divided into uniform corrosion and pit corrosion González et al. found that the penetration depth caused by pitting corrosion is much greater than that caused by uniform corrosion. Due to the faster development rate of pit erosion, the consequences are more serious. Therefore, this paper only considers the influence of corrosion caused by chloride ion on the structure. Since chloride ions are mainly transmitted in the form of diffusion in concrete, the existing investigations often use Fick's second diffusion theorem to describe this process, it can be expressed as

$$\frac{\partial C(x,t)}{\partial t}=D_c\frac{\partial^2 C(x,t)}{\partial x^2} \tag{1}$$

Where $C(x,t)$ is defined as the chloride ion concentration at the distance x from the concrete surface at time t; D_c is the diffusion coefficient of chloride ion, and the unit of this coefficient is cm²/year.

Assuming that the chloride concentration of concrete at the initial time is C_0 and the chloride concentration of concrete surface is C_s, the analytical solution can be obtained by substituting the initial condition ($t=0$, $C(x,t)=C_0$) and boundary condition $[x=0, C(x,t)=C_s]$ into Equation (1) respectively:

$$C(x,t)=C_s+(C_s-C_0)\left[1-erf\left(\frac{x}{2\sqrt{D_c t}}\right)\right] \tag{2}$$

When the chloride ion concentration reaches a certain critical value C_{cr} [$C(d,t)=C_{cr}$] and d are the concrete cover thickness of the reinforcement), the reinforcement begins to rust. It may be assumed that the chloride ion concentration of concrete at the initial time is C_0, and the start time of reinforcement corrosion t_i can be obtained by substituting $C(d,t)=C_{cr}$ into Equation (2):

$$t_i=\frac{d}{4D_c[erf^{-1}(1-C_{cr}/C_0)]^2}\frac{1}{} \tag{3}$$

Generally, the development process of reinforcement corrosion is regarded as an electronic chemical process. Once the reinforcement begins to rust, this process can be described by determining the relationship between corrosion current and reinforcement loss weight. The corrosion development rate can be expressed as a function of current density i_{corr} (μA/cm²). Rust pit depth at time t, *i. e.* $p(t)$ can be expressed as

$$p(t)=0.0016(t-t_i)i_{corr}R \tag{4}$$

Where R is the ratio between the depth of local corrosion pit caused by chloride ion and the reduction of reinforcement radius mainly caused by uniform corrosion caused by carbonization under the action of the same current density i_{corr}. Remaining area of reinforcement $A_r(t)$ can be expressed as

$$A_r(t)=\begin{cases}\dfrac{\pi D_0{}^2}{4}-A_1-A_2 & \text{if } p(t)\leqslant\dfrac{\sqrt{2}}{2}D_0\\ A_1-A_2 & \text{if } \dfrac{\sqrt{2}}{2}D_0<p(t)<D_0\\ 0 & \text{if } p(t)\geqslant D_0\end{cases} \tag{5}$$

The calculation diagram of reinforcement residual area $A_r(t)$ is shown in Fig. 1.

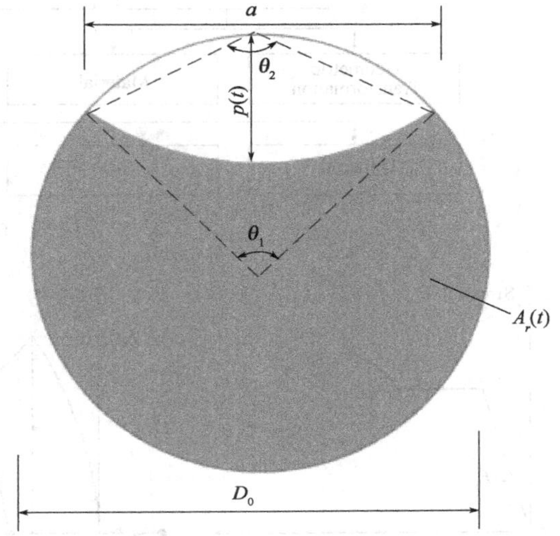

Fig. 1 Calculation diagram of reinforcement residual area $A_r(t)$

2 Time varying ultimate bearing capacity analysis framework of multi-girder bridge based on opensees

2.1 Opensees analysis architecture and constitutive model

OPENSEESmodeling adopts macro fiber element. Firstly, the structure or component needs to be divided longitudinally from large to small, which is divided into element, section and fiber. The fiber constitutes the section, the section constitutes the element, and the element constitutes the structural member. The relationship between load and displacement is reflected from the element level, the relationship between bending moment and curvature is reflected from the section, and the constitutive relationship of material, that is, the relationship between stress and strain, is reflected from the fiber level. The specific structure is illustrated in Fig. 2.

The establishment of the model first needs to divide the member into elements, endow the section on the element with restraint and torsion characteristics, then divide the section into fibers, endow the material constitutive relationship with corresponding fibers according to different material types, and consider the restraint effect of confined concrete. OPENSEES has a rich library of constitutive models. In this paper, the Concrete 01 constitutive model is adopted for confined concrete and unconstrained concrete fibers, and the Reinforcing Steel constitutive model is adopted for reinforcement fibers, as illustrated in Fig. 3.

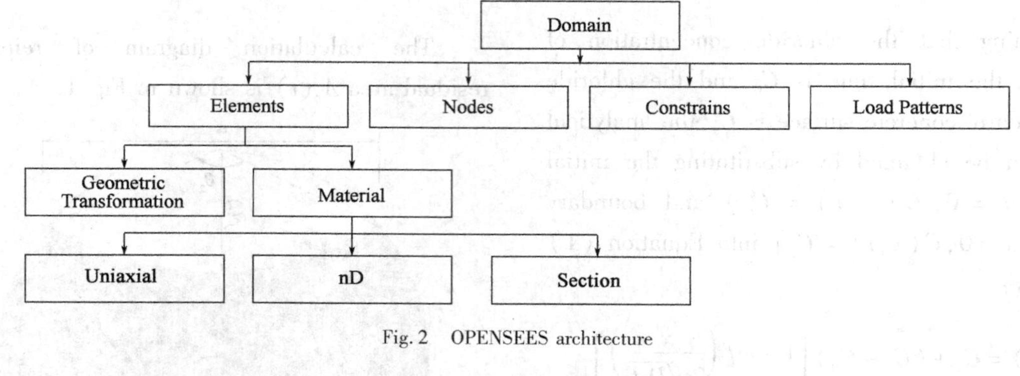

Fig. 2 OPENSEES architecture

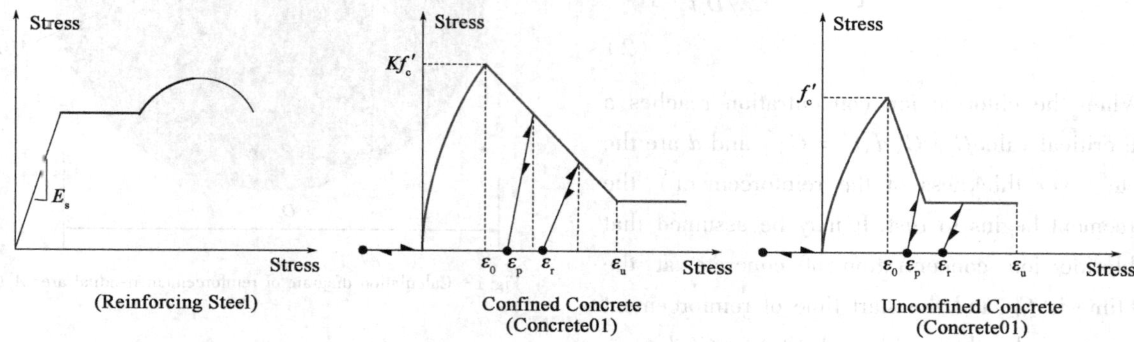

Fig. 3 Constitutive relationship between concrete and reinforcement

2.2 Analysis steps

Step 1: when $t = 0$, the reinforcement is not degraded. Thefiber model of multi-girder RC bridge is established by using OPENSEES analysis framework, and the uniaxial constitutive model of each fiber is given according to the actual material properties. The ultimate bearing capacity at $t = 0$ is calculated by numerical increment algorithm.

Step 2: at time $t = i$, obtain the degradation parameters of reinforcement from Chapter 2, modify the corresponding constitutive parameters of reinforcement fiber and the shape parameters of reinforcement after degradation, and repeat step 1 to obtain the ultimate bearing capacity at time $t = i$.

Step 3: the analysis method of step 2 is adopted in the whole service period. When $t = 100$ years, the analysis is completed to obtain the time-varying ultimate bearing capacity of the whole service period.

3 Case study

3.1 Project overview and analysis results

In order to verify the accuracy of multi beam time-varying ultimate bearing capacity analysis framework based on OPENSEES applied to the system level of multi-girder RC bridge, a simply supported multi beam RC-T-girder bridge is selected for research in this paper. The span of the bridge is 9.2m. Four T-beams are arranged horizontally in a single span, and the bridge width is 6.5m. Transverse diaphragms are set at the midspan and support, including 2 end transverse diaphragms and 1 middle transverse diaphragms. The detailed dimensions and bridge layout are shown in Fig. 4. Through core drilling sampling, the measured elastic modulus E_c of concrete is 23.53GPa, the tensile strength f_t is 2.21MPa, the compressive strength f_c is 23.5MPa, and the measured yield strength f_y of reinforcement is 254.8MPa. Song et al. conducted a full-scale destructive test on the bridge. In the field full-scale destructive test arrangement, in order to simulate the action of actual vehicles, the method of applying concentrated load on four loading points and loading step by step until the main beam is damaged is adopted to obtain the ultimate bearing capacity of the bridge. Fig. 4 a) and c) show the specific loading mode. The rock anchor, main pad beam and lower cross beam in the figure are the equipped devices during loading.

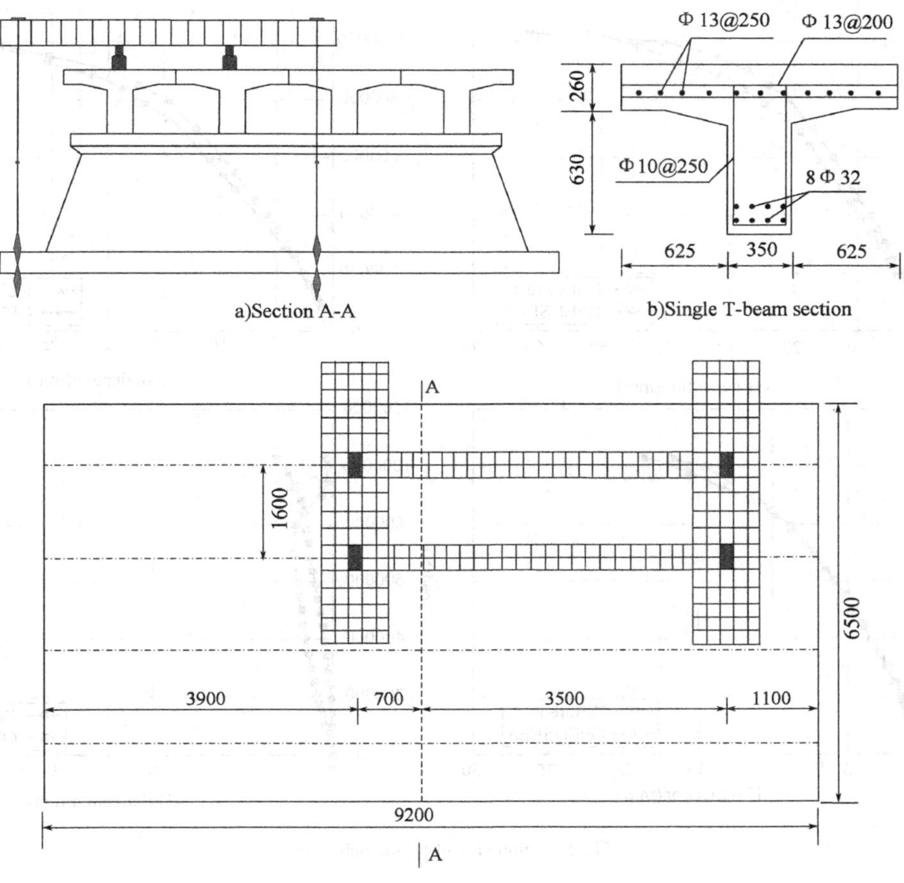

Fig. 4 Geometric dimensions and loading of multi-girder Bridge(Unit: mm)

The whole failure process of this simply supported multibeam RC-T beam bridge is simulated by using OPENSEES fiber macro element analysis technology, and compared with the test data. The test results and model analysis results are shown in Fig. 5. The structure shows that the simulation technology based on OPENSEES fiber macro element obtains satisfactory accuracy in the analysis of multibeam RC bridge system.

The development of main beam deflection and reinforcement stress is shown in Fig. 6.

3.2 Time varying ultimate bearing capacity

Using the analysis framework in Section 3.2, the time-varying ultimate bearing capacity of multi beam RC bridge is obtained at an interval of 10 years. Asillustrated in the Fig. 7, it can be concluded that in the whole service cycle, the ultimate bearing capacity is reduced from 408ton to 312ton, and the ultimate bearing capacity is degraded by 23.5%.

4 Conclusions

This paper aims at the traffic safety of typical multi-girder bridges in China, by dividing the beam section into several fibers, according to the service life, Fick's second diffusion theorem is used to calculate the time-varying material characteristics, and the corresponding uniaxial constitutive material is given by the fiber to realize the accurate simulation of the time-varying behavior of the material. In addition, for the common vehicle loading mode of multibeam bridge, monotonic loading is carried out to the ultimate bearing capacity. The approach was verified by full-scale destructive test, and then formed the time-varying ultimate bearing capacity analysis technology based on OPENSEES. The main conclusions are as follows:

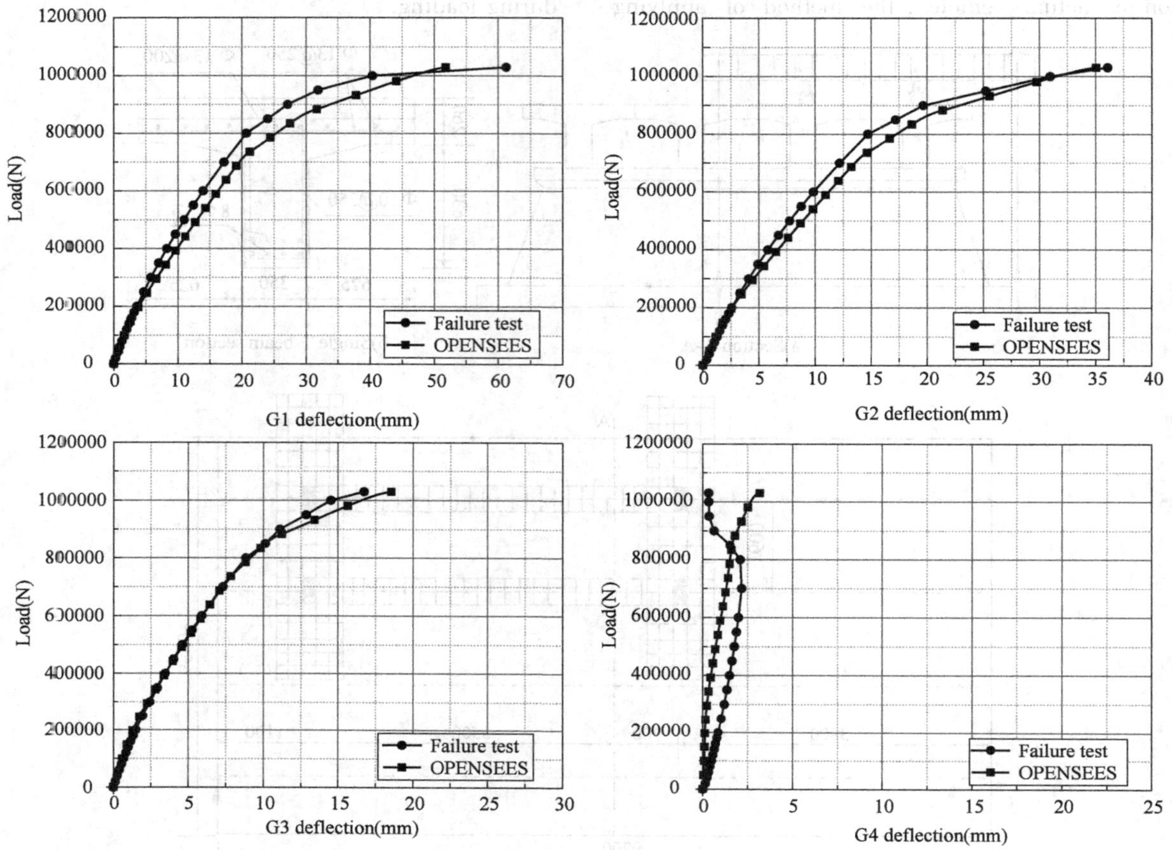

Fig. 5　Applied load versus deflection

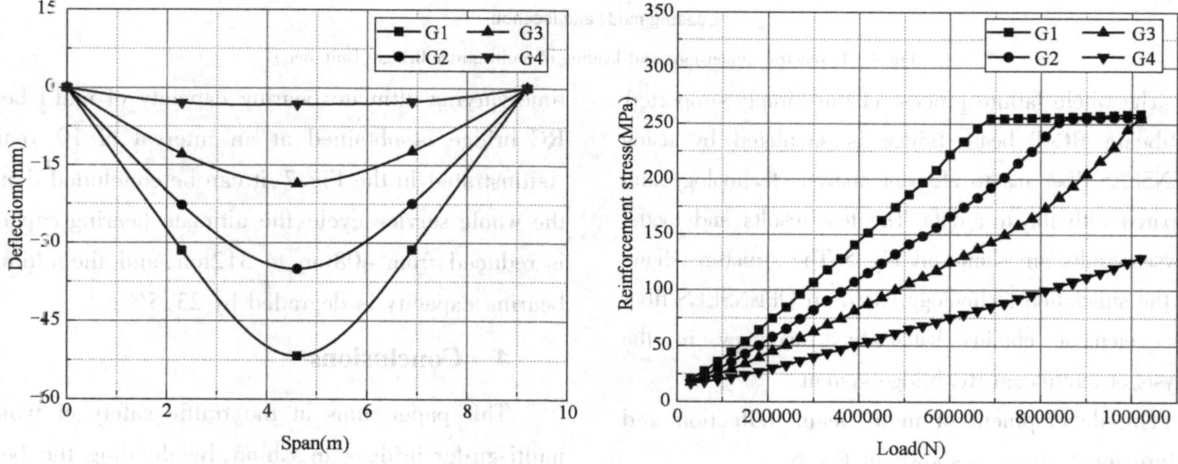

Fig. 6　Main beam deflection and reinforcement stress

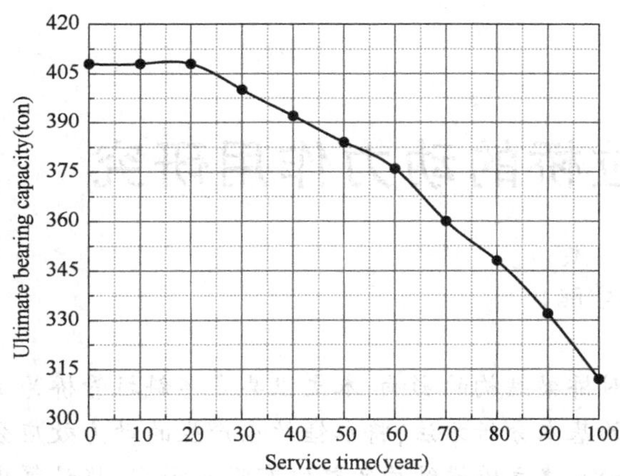

Fig. 7 Time-varying ultimate bearing capacity

(1) The time-varying ultimate bearing capacity analysis framework of multi-girder RC bridge based on OPENSEES can weigh accuracy and efficiency, and provide a new approach for the analysis of ultimate bearing capacity of multi-girder RC bridge.

(2) The corrosion of reinforcement leads to the reduction of reinforcement cross-sectional area and the degradation of material properties, which leads to the significant reduction of the ultimate bearing capacity of multi-girder RC bridge.

References

[1] Chen X, Xu W, Lin C, et al. A comparative study on wave-deck interactions of T-type and box girder decks under regular waves [J]. Ocean Engineering, 2021, 231(1): 109067.

[2] Collepardi M, Marcialis A, Turriziani R. Penetration of Chloride Ions into Cement Pastes and Concretes [J]. Journal of the American Ceramic Society, 1972: 55(10): 534-535.

[3] Dong Y, Frangopol D. M, Saydam D. Sustainability of highway bridge networks under seismic hazard [J]. Journal of Earthquake Engineering, 2014, 18: 41-66.

[4] Enright M. P, Frangopol D. M. Probabilistic analysis of resistance degradation of reinforced concrete bridge beams under corrosion [J]. Engineering Structures, 1998, 20(11): 960-971.

[5] Gonzálex J. A, Andrade C, Alonso C, et al. Comparison of rates of general corrosion and maximum pitting penetration on concrete embedded steel reinforcement [J]. Cement and Concrete Research, 1995, 25(2): 257-264.

[6] Kulprapha N, Warnitchai P. Structural health monitoring of continuous prestressed concrete bridges using ambient thermal responses [J]. Engineering Structures, 2012(40): 20-38.

[7] Lee S H, Abolmaali A, Shin K J. et al. ABAQUS Modeling for Post-tensioned Concrete Beams [J]. Journal of Building Engineering, 2020 (30): 101273.

[8] Shekhar S, Ghosh J, Padgett J. E. Seismic life-cycle cost analysis of ageing highway bridges under chloride exposure conditions: modelling and recommendations [J]. Structure and Infrastructure Engineering, 2018, 14 (7): 941-966.

[9] Songa H W, You D W, Byuna K J, et al. Finite element failure analysis of reinforced concrete T-girder bridges [J]. Engineering Structures, 2002(24): 151-162.

[10] Stark T. D, Benekohal R, Fahnestock L. A, et al. I-5 Skagit River Bridge Collapse Review [J]. Journal of Performance of Constructed Facilities, 2016, 30(6): 04016061.

[11] Vall D. V, Melchers R. E. Reliability of deteriorating RC slab bridges [J]. Journal of Structural Engineering, 1997, 123(12): 1638-1644.

[12] Wang Z, Jin W, Dong Y, et al. Hierarchical life-cycle design of reinforced concrete structures incorporating durability, economic efficiency and green objectives [J]. Engineering Structures, 2018, 157 (15): 119-131.

[13] Zhang J, Xu Y, Mai Z, et al. Flexural performance of RC T-beams strengthened with external double steel channel [J]. Journal of Building Engineering, 2021, 42(3): 102453.

[14] Zhu D, Yuan P, Dong Y. Probabilistic performance of coastal bridges under hurricane waves using experimental and 3D numerical investigations [J]. Engineering Structures, 2021, 242: 112493.

水锤效应对大型输水斜拉桥的动力作用研究

罗 轩* 邹 杰
(长安大学公路学院)

摘 要 为研究大型输水管桥上管道发生水锤效应对桥梁结构的影响,本文以某多塔斜拉管桥为工程背景,通过研究水锤效应的基本理论,并结合桥梁结构的基本分析方法,将水锤效应产生的动力效应分为竖向冲击和纵向冲击两部分;使用通用有限元软件ANSYS建立桥梁结构的整体有限元模型,将计算出的水锤效应的作用力施加于桥梁结构上,研究水锤效应发生时桥梁主要构件的动力响应。计算结果表明:斜拉管桥与输水管道的固有频率相差较大,二者不会产生共振现象;在水锤冲击力作用下,半漂浮体系斜拉桥将产生一定程度的动力响应,主要以顺桥纵向为主,纵向位移衰减很缓慢,竖向位移幅值与纵向相近,但衰减迅速。

关键词 桥梁工程 动力响应 数值模拟 斜拉管桥 水锤效应 冲击作用

0 引言

我国水资源和人口分布不均匀,人口聚居区经常出现缺水现象,而水资源丰富的地区通常位于人口稀少的山区。因此,国家大力发展南水北调等输水工程,这将促进我国水资源的合理配置与使用。在水资源运输过程中,输水管道经常需要跨越山谷和河流。目前传统的方法是倒虹吸管及隧道穿越,还有一种方法是将管道铺设在桥面上,作为桥梁的一种附属设施,从而不需要建设额外的输水工程,可以充分利用现有桥梁,具有经济性与可行性。但是,该方法对于水流量较小的输水管道尚可适用,若是管道中水流较大,管径较粗,可能会对桥梁本身产生不良影响。因此,产生了一些专门用来输送水资源的桥梁,这类桥梁上仅设置输水用的水管以用于运输水流。但是随着直径的增大,输水管道对桥梁结构的影响显著增大,除了考虑输水管道较大的自重,还应考虑管道中水流的水锤效应,这些由水产生的荷载可能远远大于常规桥梁上的车辆荷载。在由于突发情况而关闭阀门的瞬间,管道内会产生水锤效应,水锤效应会对桥梁产生显著的动力作用。

国内外大量学者对水锤效应进行了深入的研究:在流体力学方面,杨超[1]以Timoshenko梁为基础,推导了管道发生水锤效应时在X、Y、Z三个方向上的振动方程;张建伟等[2]使用直接耦合法模型求解了结构的振动特性;张挺等[3]引入指数衰减函数模拟水锤效应发生时流速呈现的衰减特性;郭强等[4]研究了厚壁输水管道在水锤作用下的振动特性,得到了管道的运动方程并做了数值求解;杨志强等[5]使用分离系数矩阵差分法对管道的振动特性进行了研究,并研究了水锤作用下的流固耦合效应。流体力学界对水锤效应已经有了较为深入的研究,但是对于输水管桥这类结构,关于如何将水锤效应与桥梁结构相结合的研究仍然不足。孙建渊等[6]以一独塔斜拉桥为背景,研究了输水管道的水锤效应对桥梁结构的影响,但是该输水管道的直径很小,仅作为桥梁结构的附属设施。

本文以某四塔斜拉输水管桥工程为背景,根据水锤效应的基本理论,计算水锤效应发生时管道对桥梁结构的冲击作用,然后将荷载施加到桥梁的有限元模型上,分析在冲击作用下桥梁结构的动力响应。

1 工程概况

某桥梁工程主桥长490m,为四塔多跨斜拉桥,跨径布置为(65+3×120+65)m,桥梁全长1.346km,桥梁总宽18.5m;主塔采用水滴形混凝土结构,桥塔总高约72m,桥面以上44.2m,桥面以下27.8m,截面为3.5m×4.0m;主梁采用钢桁梁,桁内净宽16.5m,考虑管道检修吊装,净空暂按6.5m控制;双索面布置,斜拉索间距8.0m,单塔布置12对,全桥共布置48对;基础为承台接桩基础;标准断面宽16.5m。桥上敷设双根输水压力钢管道,管道设计流量$27m^3/s$。输水管桥的布置如图1和图2所示。

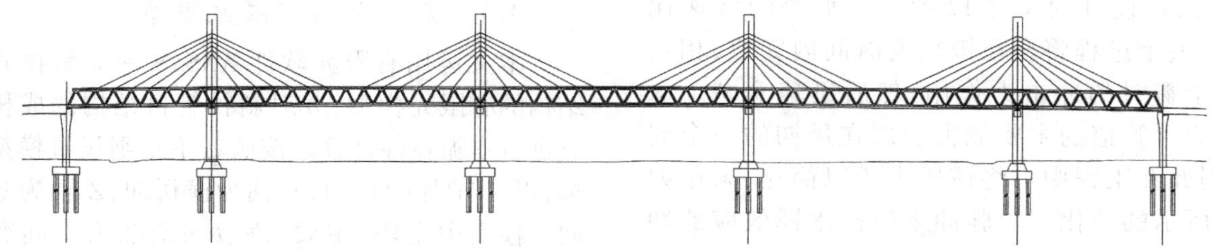

图1 输水管桥立面图

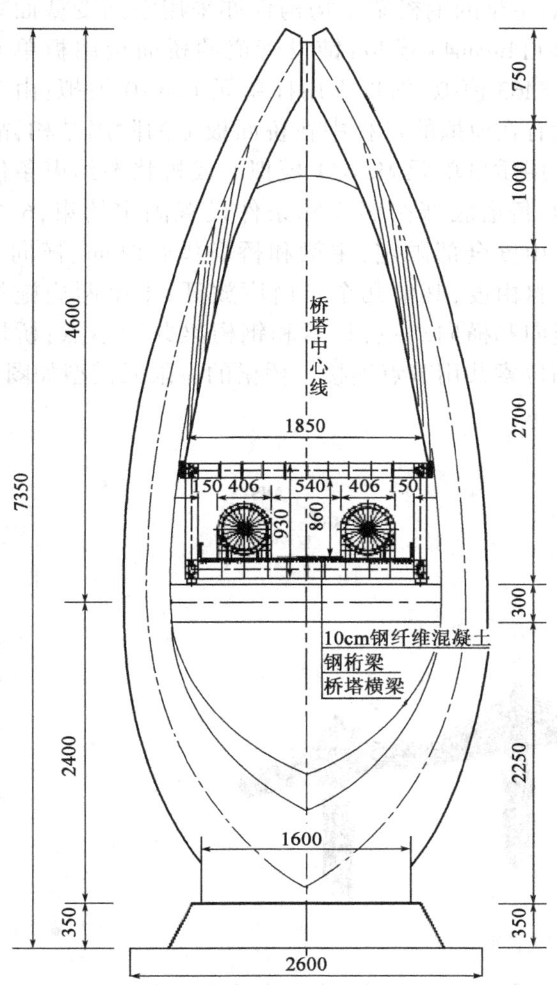

图2 输水管桥管道布置图(尺寸单位:cm)

2 水锤效应的计算与分析

2.1 水锤效应的计算理论

输水管道系统遍布市政、水利、农业等很多工业领域,给人们的日常生活和城市工业发展带来了便利。但是,在有压管道中,输水阀门的关闭等会使得管道中水流的流态发生变化,从而引起管道的剧烈振动,这种现象称为水锤效应。水锤产生时,管道内部的水压会剧烈变化,压强能达到正常工作时的数百倍,这种压强波动会导致管道发生剧烈振动和噪声,会引起结构的破坏甚至爆管等严重工程事故。

当管道系统的流态发生变化时,就会产生动量转换,引起管内压力脉动,进而导致管道振动。管道的振动根据其振动方向分为纵向振动、横向振动、竖向振动三种。

能量会以波的形式进行传递,从而引起管道压强的变化。对于主要的纵向振动,本文采用经典的水锤模型。图3为管道发生水锤效应时,阀门上的压强变化。其中,ΔP为作用在管道阀门上的压强,水锤压强可用以下公式计算:

$$\Delta P = \rho c \Delta v \tag{1}$$

$$c = \frac{\sqrt{Kg/\gamma}}{\sqrt{1 + \dfrac{DK}{\delta E}}} \tag{2}$$

其中,ρ为水的密度;Δv为水流速的变化量;c为水锤波速;K为水的体积弹性模量,一般取2×10^3 MPa;g为重力加速度;γ为水的容重;D为管道内径;δ为管壁厚度;E为管壁材料的纵向弹性模量。

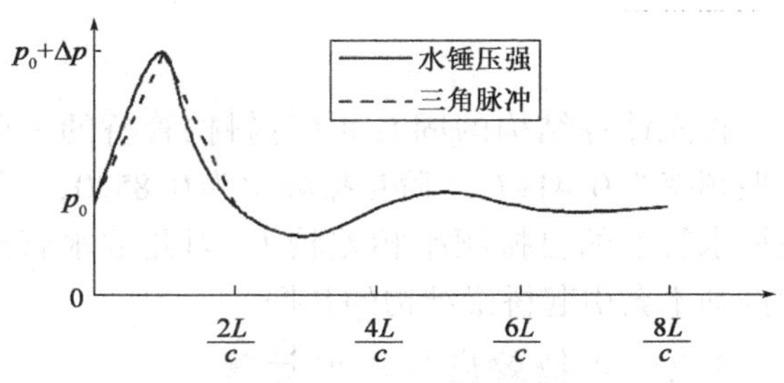

图3 输水管道压强波动过程图

2.2 水锤效应的考虑方法

对于纵桥向振动,水锤效应对管道阀门的压力是一种正弦波的形式,保持周期性的振荡,并且很快衰减直至消失。另一方面,若管道的振动周期与斜拉管桥的自振频率接近,可能会引起结构的共振,在设计时应予以考虑。水锤的波速比较大,整个过程将会在极短的时间内完成,相当于一个瞬时的冲击力作用,然后迅速衰减。水锤效应对管道的主要危害表现在最初的一个周期,因此在工程中可将该压力予以简化,采用如图3所示的简化三角脉冲来模拟水锤效应的冲击作用。

对于横桥向振动,首先其振动的幅度比较小,其次管道的横向振动对桥梁的影响也比较小。只需在设计时对其横向予以加固,即可很好地避免横桥向振动对桥梁的影响。因此,横桥向振动在本文中不予考虑。

对于竖向振动,在发生水锤效应时,管道对桥梁会施加一个瞬间的竖向力,并且该力会周期性地减小,为简化计算,可将其看作常规桥梁中车辆对桥梁的冲击力,并进行如下计算:首先计算出装满水时管道的重量,再将该重量产生的力乘以一个冲击系数并施加于桥梁结构的相应位置上。冲击系数根据管道的计算模型偏安全地取1.4。

3 计算模型的建立

3.1 斜拉管桥有限元模型

本文运用有限元软件ANSYS建立斜拉管桥结构的有限元模型,并对斜拉管桥结构的成桥状态进行自振特性计算。按照右手定则设置模型坐标,以X轴为顺桥向,Y轴为横桥向,Z轴为竖桥向。模型中主塔、主梁、桥墩均离散为空间梁单元:桥塔和桥墩采用空间变截面梁单元Beam44模拟;主梁的钢桁架结构构件亦采用空间变截面梁单元Beam44模拟;铺设管道的桥面板用板单元Shell63模拟;斜拉索用杆单元Link10模拟;由于没有在模拟的过程中在桥面板上的附属结构,故采用质量单元Mass21模拟。成桥状态约束条件为:桥塔底部按照实际条件设置固定约束,6个自由度全部限定;主梁和桥塔耦合纵向、横向2个自由度,其他几个自由度放开;主梁两边施加竖向和横向约束;拉索和钢桁梁共用节点;桥塔和拉索共用节点连接。桥梁的有限元模型如图4所示。

图4 输水管桥有限元模型

首先计算结构的固有频率:斜拉管桥的一阶自振频率为0.4197,二阶自振频率为0.8520,与常规输水管道的自振频率相差较大,因此输水管道的振动不会引起桥梁结构的共振。

3.2 水锤效应作用力计算

综合考虑水量工况,可以认为两个管道都满载时为该桥梁的最不利工况,本文以最不利工况进行计算,得到的结果是保守且安全的。对于水锤的冲击作用,水流的设计流速为2m/s,假设管道的阀门关闭时间为4s,则水体流速在4s内由2m/s减少为0,在2s时管道对阀门的冲击力达到最大。首先计算水锤的冲击力,将水锤力分为水平的冲击作用和竖向的冲击作用,并分别施加于桥梁模型上。竖向冲击力通过公式(1)计算,管道材料为球墨铸铁,弹性模量 $E = 1.0 \times 10^5$ MPa,密度 $\rho = 7300 \mathrm{kg/m^3}$,泊松比 $\upsilon = 0.3$,$K = 2.0 \times 10^3$ MPa,$g = 9.8$ m/s,$\gamma = 1 \mathrm{g/cm^3}$,$D = 3850$ mm,$\delta = 100$ mm,$E = 1.0 \times 10^5$ MPa,$\rho = 7800 \mathrm{kg/m^3}$,$\Delta\upsilon = 2$ m/s,计算可

得 $c = 1228.2\text{m/s}$,压强变化量 $\Delta P = 2456476\text{Pa}$。

管道的直径为3850mm,则水锤产生的竖向总压力 $N_1 = 28597223\text{N}$。管道的刚性很大,因此假设水锤冲击力平均分配给每个支座,管桥上共设61排共122个支座,每个支座所受的竖向冲击力 $n_1 = 234403\text{N}$。

竖向冲击力(图5)按水量满载情况计算,水管和管道的总重量 $M = 6194000\text{Kg}$,产生的总压力 $N_2 = 60701200\text{N}$。未受水锤冲击时,每个支座所受竖向荷载为 $n_2 = 497549\text{N}$;受到水锤冲击时,每个支座所受的水锤竖向冲击力 $n_3 = 199020\text{N}$。

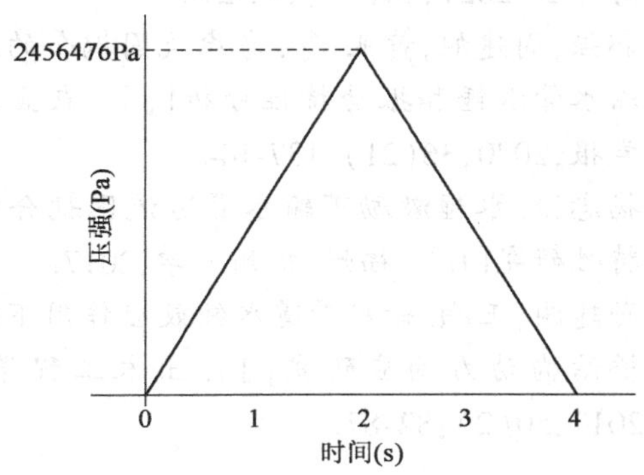

图5 竖向冲击力示意图

4 结果分析

4.1 加载分析

本文主要研究水锤效应对斜拉桥的影响,因此为排除其他因素的干扰,仅考虑水锤效应作用前后斜拉桥的位移情况,应在桥梁因受重力和二期荷载的影响产生的变形完成后再施加水锤效应的作用力。待桥梁变形完成后,对斜拉管桥进行完全法瞬态动力分析,分别施加大小为 n_1 的纵向冲击力和大小为 n_3 的竖向冲击力。

4.2 桥梁的动力响应分析

将水锤冲击力施加到桥梁的有限元模型上,对桥梁进行动力分析,得到斜拉管桥结构在水锤效应作用下主要节点的动力响应。

图6a)为主梁的纵向位移时程曲线。该斜拉桥为半漂浮体系,结构在纵向方向具有一定的柔度,因此结构在纵向的水锤冲击力作用下发生纵向位移,在第一个周期内,位移的幅度和时间与水锤冲击力的规律一致,在以后的周期内位移不断衰减直至消失。水锤的冲击能量主要沿纵向传递,因此纵向的位移衰减较慢且变化平缓。

图6b)为斜拉管桥中间跨和边跨的跨中竖向位移,两者的竖向位移相反,但变化规律相同。与纵向位移相比,竖向位移在水锤冲击发生时更明显,但是在水锤冲击结束后位移衰减得也更快。

图7为斜拉管桥中塔和边塔塔顶的纵向位移时程曲线。塔顶位移在水锤冲击力逐渐增加的过程中出现振荡,并且边塔和中塔的位移相反,但很快两者的变形趋于一致,并与主梁的纵向位移情况一致,大小相近,且都呈现周期性衰减的情况。

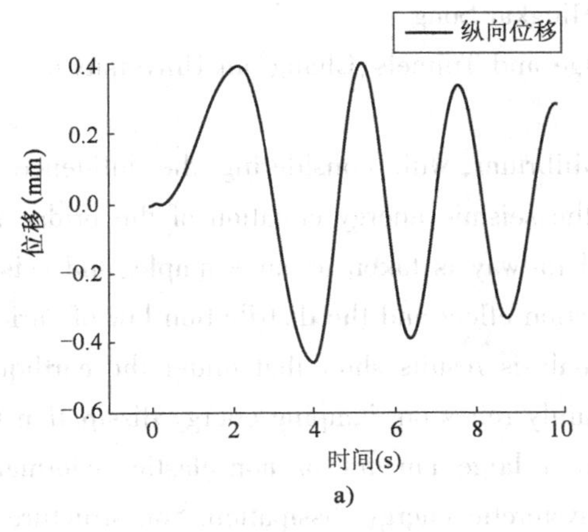

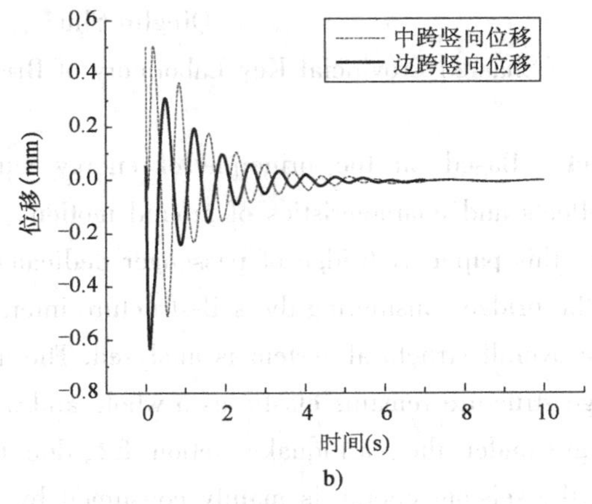

图6 主梁节点位移时程曲线

5 结语

本文以专用的输水四塔斜拉管桥为工程背景,分析了管道发生水锤效应时的动力作用,并研究了此动力作用对桥梁的影响。结论如下:

(1)正常使用情况下管道荷载约为同宽度车道荷载的7倍,发生水锤效应时,荷载增加到同宽度车道荷载的9倍。

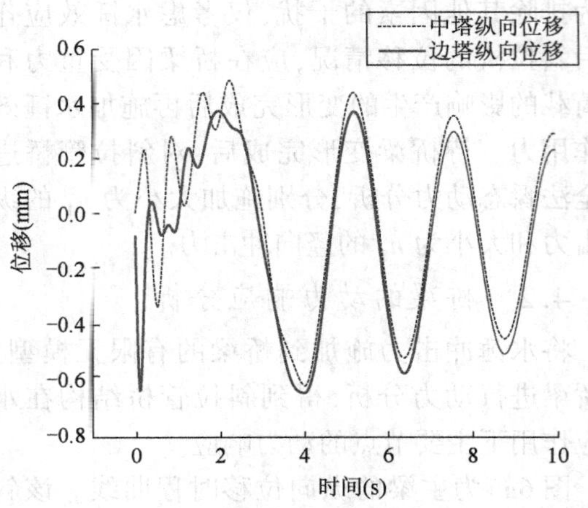

图7　桥塔塔顶位移时程曲线

(2)半漂浮体系斜拉管桥在水锤冲击作用下,桥梁构件的位移主要以纵向为主,位移时程曲线与水锤冲击力的波动一致,呈正弦曲线变化并缓慢衰减。

(3)水锤效应会引起结构竖向的动力响应,但衰减很快。

(4)本文所使用的水锤效应模型为简化模型,实际情况更为复杂,今后可对水锤效应模拟进行进一步的研究。

参考文献

[1] 杨超.非恒定流充液管系统耦合振动特性及振动抑制[D].武汉:华中科技大学,2007.

[2] 张建伟,王涛,曹克磊,等.基于流固耦合效应的梯级泵站输水管道振动特性分析[J].农业机械学报,2017,48(3):134-140.

[3] 张挺,林震寰,林通,等.内激励型振荡衰减流作用下输流管道动力不稳定分析[J].振动与冲击,2021,40(3):284-290.

[4] 郭强,周建旭,黄亚,等.考虑流固耦合的厚壁输水管水锤和振动特性分析[J].农业工程学报,2020,36(21):137-144.

[5] 杨志强.水锤激励下输水管道流固耦合响应特性研究[D].福州:福州大学,2017.

[6] 孙建渊,王灏.输水管道水锤效应作用下斜拉桥结构动力响应研究[J].土木工程学报,2017,50(2):82-87.

Analysis of Seismic Energy Response of Railway Girder Bridge under Different Levels of Earthquake

Qinglin Shu*　Mingkai Song

(Shaanxi Provincial Key Laboratory of Bridge and Tunnels, Chang'an University)

Abstract　Based on the principle of energy equilibrium, with considering the influence of flexible foundation effects and characteristics of ground motions, the seismic energy equation of the bridge structure is established in this paper. A bridge of passenger dedicated railway is taken as an example, and seismic energy response of the bridge considering the soil-structure interaction effect and the distribution law of various types of energy in the overall structural system is analyzed. The analysis results show that under the earthquake action E1, the bridge structure remains elastic as a whole and mainly relies on damping energy dissipation to consume seismic energy; under the earthquake action E2, due to a large amount of non-elastic deformation of the substructure, the seismic energy is mainly consumed by hysteretic energy dissipation. Soil-structure interaction and seismic peak acceleration have significant effects on the seismic total input energy, hysteretic energy dissipation, and damping energy dissipation of the bridge structure.

Keywords　Bridges of passenger dedicated railway　Seismic energy response　Flexible foundation effects　Hysteretic energy dissipation　Damping energy dissipation

0 Intrduction

China is focusing on the large-scale building of passenger dedicated railway lines. The objective of "Eight Longitudinal and Eight Cross" for example, is supported by Layout of Railway Network in the Medium-tern. China had constructed a 38, 000-kilometres passenger dedicated railway by 2020. Following that, China will construct the passenger dedicated railway covering cities with populations of more than 200000, based on 200000 kilometers of rails and using the "Eight Longitudinal and Eight Cross" framework. Although China has conducted many years of preliminary research on the design of passenger dedicated railway and has successfully built the Qin-Shen passenger dedicated railway, systematic research on key issues such as seismic design methods and seismic analysis methods are lacking for passenger dedicated railway bridges. As a result, this paper is devoted to the investigation of the seismic energy response of passenger dedicated railway bridges to give a reference for the energy-based seismic design of such bridges.

The idea of evaluating the seismic response and damage level of structures from an energy perspective has gotten a lot of interest from earthquake engineers bothdomestic and abroad in recent years. Housner[1] was the first to propose the energy-based earthquake design theory and apply it to traditional structures in 1956. In 1988, Akiyama [2] proposed that a two-fold line can be used to represent the total input energy spectrum of a single-degree-of-freedom system and that the total input energy of a multi-degree-of-freedom system can be approximated by the total input energy of a single-degree-of-freedom system with the same basic period. Michel Bruneau and Wang [3] investigated the energy approach for determining the nonelasticity response of a single-degree-of-freedom system in 1996 and discovered that energy is a good indication of the structure's nonelasticity seismic behavior. Luis D. Decanini et al. [4] examined the energy-based approach for assessing seismic demand in 2001 and produced elastic and nonelastic input seismic energy spectra. Xiong et al. [5] established a two-stage seismic design technique based on energy indicators after doing theoretical research on energy-based seismic response analysis of frame structures in 2003. Scholars from home and abroad have begun to apply energy strategies to bridge structures. Anindya Dutta[6] researched energy-based seismic analysis of highway bridges and their design in 1999. Jiang and Zhu[7] suggested an energy technique of seismic design based on bridge structure performance during near-field earthquakes in 2006. Yang[8] estimated the seismic total input energy spectrum appropriate for bridge isolation design and utilized it to construct the bridge structure for seismic isolation design in 2007.

Although the above-mentioned scholars have done a lot of research on the seismic resistance of bridges[1-14], the majority of their efforts have been focused on highways and ordinary railway bridges, with only a few studies focusing on the seismic energy response analysis of bridges of passenger dedicated railway and their energy-based seismic design methods. So, a double-column pier of passenger dedicated railway bridge is taken as an example, considering the influence of flexible foundation effects and characteristics of ground motions, using the two-stage seismic design method (the pier remains elastic under frequent-occurred earthquake E1; the bottom of the pier enters plasticity under rare-occurred earthquake E2; plastic hinges at the bottom of the pier are simulated by bilinear rotation springs), and the FEA model for the bridge is established in this paper. And it studied the seismic energy response and the distribution rules for the bridges of passenger dedicated railway after entering the nonelastic state.

1 Seismic energy equation for bridges of passenger dedicated railway

The ground motions' influence on the bridge structure is fundamentally a process of energy input, transformation and dissipation. The ability of the bridge structure to dissipate seismic energy determines whether it can resist major earthquakes.

The seismic energy equation for passenger dedicated railway bridges will be presented in the next section. The motion equation[9] for the bridge structure of passenger dedicated railway is:

$$[M]\{\ddot{x}(t)\}+[C]\{\dot{x}(t)\}+[K]\{x(t)\} = -[M]\{r\}\{\ddot{x}_g(t)\} \quad (1)$$

In the formula, $\{\ddot{x}(t)\}$、$\{\dot{x}(t)\}$、$\{x(t)\}$ are the vector of acceleration, velocity and displacement of the particle relative to the ground respectively; $[M]$ is the structural mass matrix; $[C]$ is the structural damping matrix; $[K]$ is the structural stiffness matrix; $\{\ddot{x}_g(t)\}$ is the seismic acceleration. Then integrate the relative displacement of the structure[10-11] at both ends of formula (1):

$$\int_0^t \{dx(t)\}^{\mathrm{T}}[M]\{\ddot{x}(t)\} + \int_0^t \{dx(t)\}^{\mathrm{T}}[C]\{\dot{x}(t)\} + \int_0^t \{dx(t)\}^{\mathrm{T}}[K]\{x(t)\} = -\int_0^t \{dx(t)\}^{\mathrm{T}}[M]\{\ddot{x}_g(t)\} \quad (2)$$

In the formula: the left terms are respectively kinetic energy $E_K(t)$ of the bridge structure based on relative displacement, damping energy dissipation $E_D(t)$, the sum $E_H(t)+E_S(t)$ of hysteretic energy dissipation and elastic deformation energy; the right term is the total input energy $E_I(t)$ of the ground motions to the bridge structure. The total input energy of the system is balanced with the sum of other energies, namely:

$$E_I(t)=E_K(t)+E_D(t)+E_H(t)+E_S(t) \quad (3)$$

2 Establishment of the fea model for bridges of passenger dedicated railway

2.1 Basic parameters of double-column piers

The subject of this study is the simply supported girder bridges of passenger dedicated railway located in the 7-degree seismic zone (the first zone in earthquake groups) and the Ⅲ-type site. The basic design parameters are shown in Fig. 1 and Fig. 2: ①The upper structure is a (24 + 24) m ballastless track double-track simply supported box girder (each beam weighs 503.6t per hole), which is connected to the piers through the JHPZ high-speed railway basin-type rubber fixed hinge support; ②The height of the piers is 15m, the distance between piers and columns is 2.4m, and its body has a rectangular cross-section, and its vertical and horizontal dimensions are 3.3m and 2.2m respectively; ③The pier body is made of C35 concrete, 82 HRB335 longitudinal bars (16mm in diameter) and Q235 stirrups (10mm in diameter, 100mm in spacing); ④The foundation is made of C20 concrete, which is the integral open-cut spread foundation, divided into two layers, each layer thickness is 1m, the size of the bottom layer is 9.6m × 6.1m, and the buried depth of the foundation is $e=4$m.

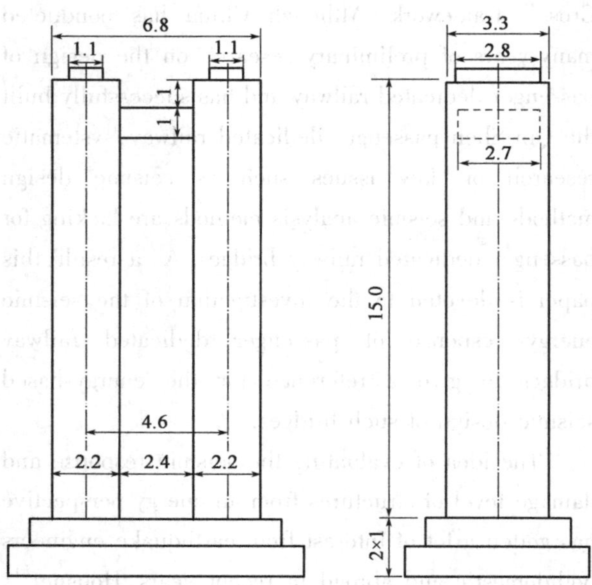

Fig. 1 Double-column pier(Unit:m)

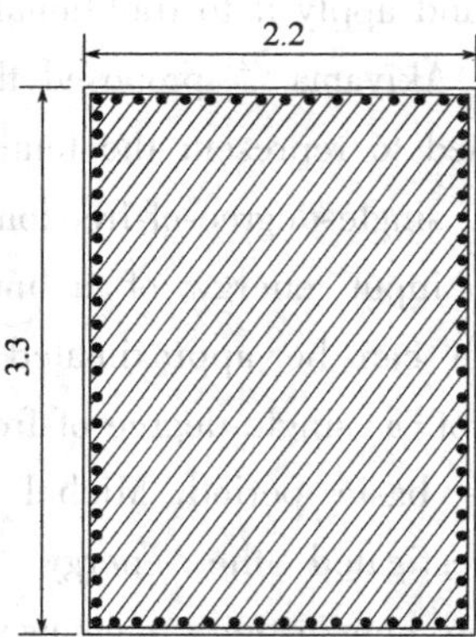

Fig. 2 Rebar arrangement(Unit:m)

2.2 Establishment of the FEA model

An FEA model of the passenger dedicated railway's double-column piers was created in the paper (longitudinal direction) (Fig. 3), in which: ①The pier body and foundation is simulated by beam elements, the pier is divided into 10 units, and the mass of each pier element is distributed on the nodes at both ends; ②The basin-type rubber fixed hinge support is simulated by the connection element, and the support element and the beam mass center node are connected by a rigid arm; ③In this research a spring element is used to model the flexible foundation and determine its translational, rotational, and linked stiffness following Article 7.2.6 of the "Ministry-Promulgated Code" [16].

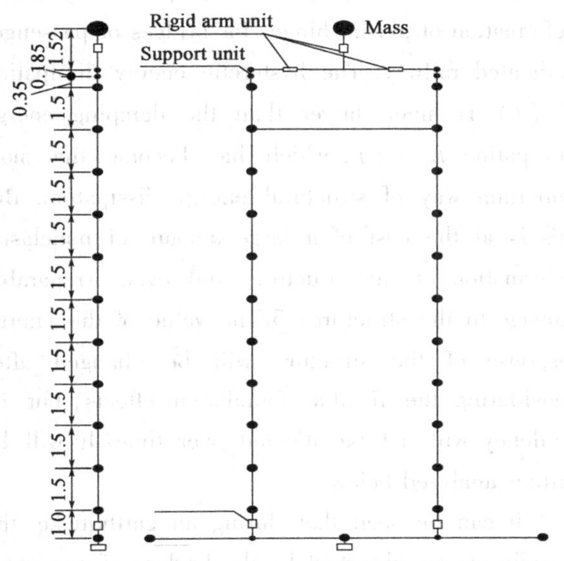

Fig. 3 FEA model (Unit: m)

The bridge construction will have an elastoplastic seismic response when subjected to strong earthquakes, and its plastic deformation is mostly dictated by the deformability of the pier column's plastic hinge. The bottom section of the pier column for the simply supported beam bridge is the plastic hinge area, according to Article 6.2.2 of the "Ministry-Promulgated Code"[17]. The formula for calculating the length of a plastic hinge is given in clause 7.4.3.

$$L_P = 0.08H + 0.022f_y d_s \geqslant 0.044 f_y d_s \quad (4)$$

In the formula: L_p is the equivalent plastic hinge length (cm); H is the height of the cantilever pier or the distance from the plastic hinge to the reverse bending point (cm); f_y is the standard value of the tensile strength of the longitudinal bars (MPa); d_s is the diameter of the longitudinal bars (cm). In addition, Ucfyber software can be used to obtain the bending moment-curvature relationship of the plastic hinge section of the pier bottom, as well as the yield point and limit point of the section, and finally, the skeleton curve of the Takeda bilinear stiffness degeneration restoring force model is shown in Fig. 4.

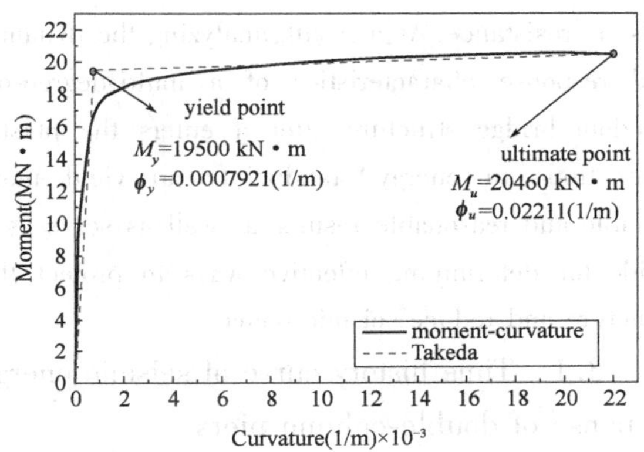

Fig. 4 M-φ relation and skeletal curves

2.3 Selection of seismic records

Since the bridge pier in the calculation example is located in a Ⅲ-type site, according to the principle of wave selection in paragraph 5.3.2 of the "Ministry-Promulgated Code". The 8 strong earthquake records of the fault distance of 6.2 ~ 45.1km and the magnitude of 6.5 ~ 7.6 from the PEER strongly seismic record database in the United States are taken as ground motion input, the specific parameters are shown in Tab. 1.

Earthquake events used in the analysis of seismic energy response of double-pillar piers Tab. 1

No.	Earthquake events	Record number	Mw	R(km)	Site	PGA(g)	PGV(cm)	PGD(cm)
1	1968 Borrego Mtn	A-ELC270	6.8	45	Ⅲ	0.057	13.2	10.03
2	1979 Imperial Valley	H-BCR140	6.5	6.2	Ⅲ	0.59	45.2	16.76
3	1979 Imperial Valley	H-BCR230	6.5	6.2	Ⅲ	0.77	45.9	15.01

continue

No.	Earthquake events	Record number	Mw	R(km)	Site	PGA(g)	PGV(cm)	PGD(cm)
4	1979 Imperial Valley	H-BRA315	6.5	43.2	Ⅲ	0.22	38.9	13.49
5	1989 Loma Prieta	HDA165	6.9	45.1	Ⅲ	0.27	43.8	18.42
6	1989 Loma Prieta	HDA255	6.9	45.1	Ⅲ	0.28	35.6	13.06
7	1999 Chi-Chi	CHY036-N	7.6	20.4	Ⅲ	0.207	41.4	34.17
8	1999 Chi-Chi	CHY036-W	7.6	20.4	Ⅲ	0.294	38.9	21.19

3　Analysis on seismic energy response for double-column piers of passenger dedicated railway

Energy can fundamentally provide a better explanation of the mechanism of the structure's seismic resistance. As a result, analyzing the dynamic and response characteristics of a multi-degree-of-freedom bridge structure after it enters the plastic state from an energy standpoint can yield more reliable and reasonable results, as well as serve as a guide for determining effective ways to protect the structure and reduce seismic damage.

3.1　Time history curve of seismic energy response of double-column piers

Under the impact of seismic waves, the seismic energy response time history curve of the double-column pier rigid foundation and flexible foundation model of the passenger dedicated railway are depicted in Fig.5 (the scale factor of the foundation coefficient $m = 20000\text{kN/m}^4$) (1989 Loma Prieta-HDA165-III-5). It can be seen as follows: ①The kinetic energy $E_K(t)$ and elastic strain energy $E_S(t)$ of the two types of models both increase in the initial stage, and then rapidly attenuate with the increase of time t. When the earthquake ends, $E_K(t)$ and $E_S(t)$ are almost reduced to zero; ②The seismic total input energy $E_I(t)$, structural hysteretic energy consumption $E_H(t)$ and damping energy consumption $E_D(t)$ of the two are gradually accumulated with the increase of time t, and reach the maximum value at the end of the earthquake; ③At each instant, the seismic total input energy $E_I(t)$ of the two is always equal to the sum of other energies in the system, which satisfies the seismic energy balance equation (Equation 3) of the above-mentioned bridges of passenger dedicated railway; ④The seismic energy is mainly consumed by their damping and hysteretic deformation of plastic hinges for bridges of passenger dedicated railway. The hysteretic energy dissipation $E_H(t)$ is much larger than the damping energy dissipation $E_D(t)$, which has become the most important way of structural energy dissipation. But this is at the cost of a large amount of nonelastic deformation of the structure, and even irreparable damage to the structure; ⑤The value of the energy response of the structure will be changed after considering the flexible foundation effects, but its tendency will not be affected over time. It will be further analyzed below.

It can be seen that during an earthquake, the seismic energy absorbed by the bridges of passenger dedicated railway is mainly dissipated by damping energy dissipation $E_D(t)$ and hysteretic energy dissipation $E_H(t)$, with only a small portion of the energy being converted into kinetic energy $E_K(t)$ and elastic strain energy $E_S(t)$. The hysteretic energy consumption $E_H(t)$ is the most engineering-significant energy response index, as it can better reflect the impact of the duration of strong earthquakes on the structural response and is one of the important parameters to measure the cumulative damage of the structure.

3.2　Influence of flexible foundation effects

To calculate the seismic energy response value of the rigid foundation model and the flexible foundation model ($m = 20000\text{kN/m}^4$) under different earthquakes, the peak acceleration PGA amplitude of the 8 strong earthquake records of III-type site in Tab. 1 was adjusted to 0.4g and used as the strongly seismic input for the rigid foundation model and the flexible foundation model ($m = 20000\text{kN/m}^4$).

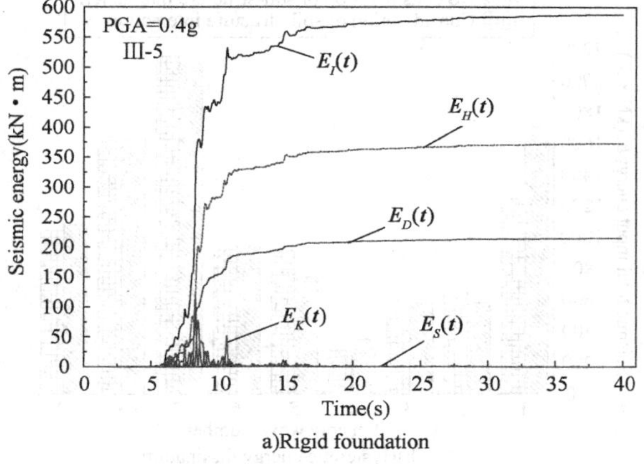

a)Rigid foundation

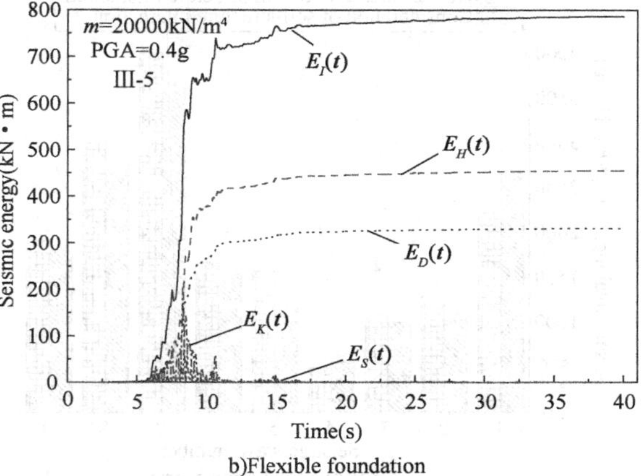

b)Flexible foundation

Fig. 5 Time history curve of seismic energy response of double-column piers

It isillustrated in Fig. 6 that after accounting for flexible foundation effects, the seismic total input energy E_I and damping energy dissipation E_D for passenger dedicated railway bridges would grow, however, the hysteretic energy dissipation E_H will exhibit a trend of attenuation. The influence of flexible foundation effects on the seismic energy response distribution rules of the bridge construction is shown in Fig. 7. The flexible foundation effects will result in a decrease in the proportion (λ_H) of E_H in E_I and an increase in the proportion (λ_D) of E_D in E_I, as can be shown.

In summary, when the foundation soil is included in the FEA model of the structure, the damping for the bridges of passenger dedicated railway increases, increasing the structural damping energy dissipation ratio λ_D; however, the foundation soil deformation shares part of the nonelastic deformation of the dedicated line bridge, lowering the structure hysteretic energy dissipation ratio λ_H.

3.3 The influence of the scale coefficient of the foundation coefficient

The m method[12] is used to calculate the spring stiffness of the foundation soil corresponding to the different values m of the Ⅲ-type site and establish the corresponding double-column pier finite element model of the passenger dedicated railway in this paper, and then the 8 ground motion PGA in Tab. 1 with amplitude modulation of 0.4g are taken as ground motion input, the average value of the seismic energy response of the double-column pier corresponding to the proportional coefficient values m of the different foundation coefficients under the category Ⅲ-type site was calculated.

It isreflected in Tab. 2 that the influence of the change of the scale coefficient value m of the foundation coefficient on the seismic energy response and distribution law of bridges of passenger dedicated railway. It can be seen from it: When the value of the scale coefficient m of the foundation coefficient decreases (that is, as the soil condition of the site softens), the seismic total input energy E_I, damping energy dissipation E_D, and damping energy dissipation ratio λ_D of the structure all increase, whereas the hysteretic energy dissipation E_H and the hysteresis energy consumption ratio λ_H both decrease. This is due to the following reasons: ①With the softening of the site soil, the seismic energy consumed by the foundation soil has increased, while the hysteretic deformation of the plastic hinge of the structure has decreased, resulting in a reduction of E_H and λ_H; ②After including the foundation soil in the FEA model for the bridges of passenger dedicated railway to participate in the dynamic response of the structure, the structural system's damping will increase, which causes the increase of E_D and λ_D.

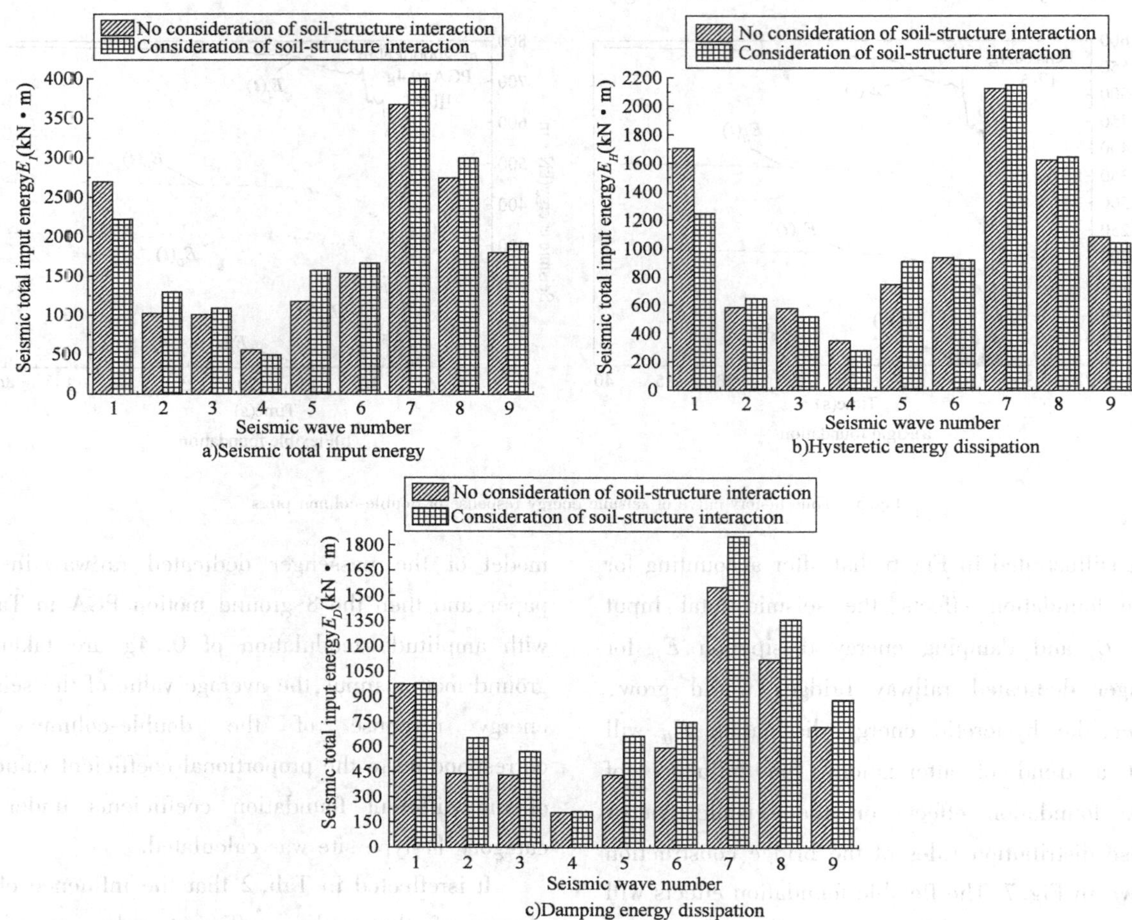

Fig. 6 The influence of flexible foundation effects on the seismic energy response of double-column piers

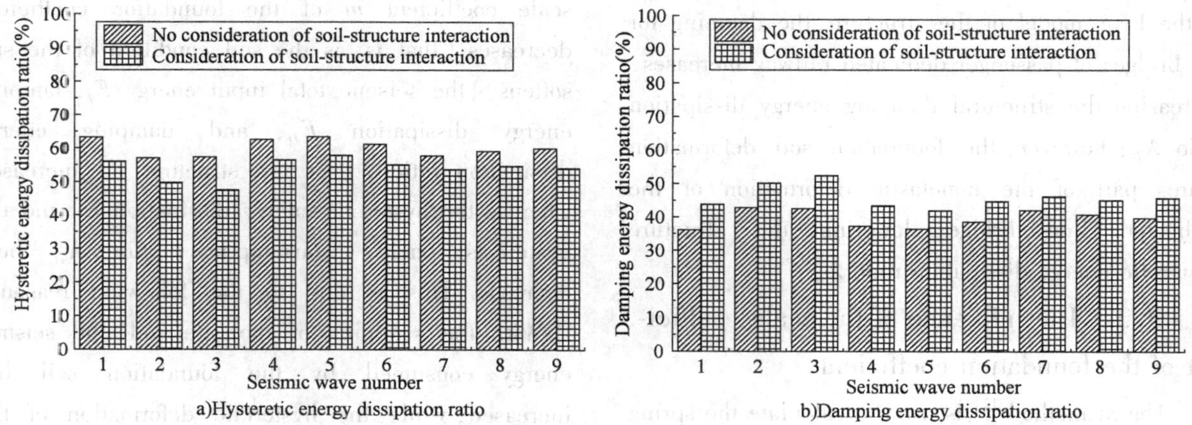

Fig. 7 The influence of flexible foundation effect on the distribution law of structural seismic energy response

The influence of the proportional coefficient value of the foundation coefficient on the seismic energy response of double-column piers and its distribution law Tab. 2

Foundation coefficient	Fundamental period	Seismic total input energy	Hysteretic energy dissipation	Damping energy dissipation	Hysteretic energy dissipation ratio	Damping energy dissipation ratio
m/KN · m4	T/s	EI /kN · m	EH/kN · m	ED/kN · m	λH /%	λD /%
10000	0.63679	1972.35	1041.93	930.43	52.83	47.17
15000	0.61979	1939.23	1041.35	897.88	53.70	46.30
20000	0.61108	1916.73	1038.33	878.40	54.17	45.83
25000	0.60574	1900.45	1034.35	866.10	54.43	45.57
30000	0.60201	1890.08	1032.53	857.55	54.63	45.37

3.4 The influence of seismic peak acceleration

Theseismic peak acceleration PGA is an important factor affecting the intensity of ground motions. To study the influence of PGA on the seismic energy response and its distribution rules of the multi-degree-of-freedom bridge structure, the PGA of the 8 strong earthquake records selected in Tab. 1 are adjusted to 0.1g, 0.2g, 0.4g and 0.6g respectively as the seismic input of the double-column pier flexible foundation model ($m = 20000 kN/m^4$) of the passenger dedicated railway. The seismic energy response of the passenger dedicated railway bridge under the action of different seismic acceleration peaks PGA is calculated.

It isdepicted in Fig. 8 that the impact of PGA on the seismic energy response of the passenger dedicated railway's double-column piers. As can be shown, the seismic total input energy E_I, structural hysteretic energy consumption E_H, and damping energy consumption E_D corresponding to various ground motions all show an increasing tendency as PGA grows, and their increasing amplitude also increases. This is because PGA is a crucial metric for determining the strength of ground motions. The larger the PGA, the more intense the ground motions are, and the more energy is input to the bridge structure from ground motion, resulting in amplification of the structure's dynamic response, which leads to nonelastic deformation of the structure, resulting in an increase in hysteresis energy consumption E_H. Furthermore, because each instantaneous seismic energy response of the structure must fulfill the seismic energy balancing equation, the structural damping energy consumption E_D will increase in lockstep with E_I and E_H.

Furthermore, the hysteretic energy dissipation ratioλ_H and the damping energy dissipation ratio λ_D of the structure reflect the seismic energy consumption capacity of the multi-degree-of-freedom bridge structure's damping and plastic hinges. The seismic energy consumption capacity of double-column piers is affected by changes in PGA, as shown in Fig. 9. It can be seen as follows:

(1) When PGA is equal to 0.1g, the average values of λ_H and λ_D corresponding to 8 strong earthquake records are respectively 11.32% and 88.7%. It is revealed that under the action of a 7-degree design earthquake, the bridge structure is in a linear elastic state, relying mostly on damping to consume seismic energy, and the structure has very little nonelastic deformation, and even plastic hinges have not yet developed.

(2) When PGA is equal to 0.2g, the average value of λ_H rapidly increased to 39.6%, whereas the average value of λ_D dropped to 60.4%. It is demonstrated that under the action of an 8-degree design earthquake, although damping energy dissipation still is used by the bridge structure as the main way, plastic hinges begin to appear in the bridge structure, and its nonelastic deformation increases

sharply and participates in the seismic energy consumption process. However, at this time, the damage induced by nonelastic deformation can be survived by the bridge construction.

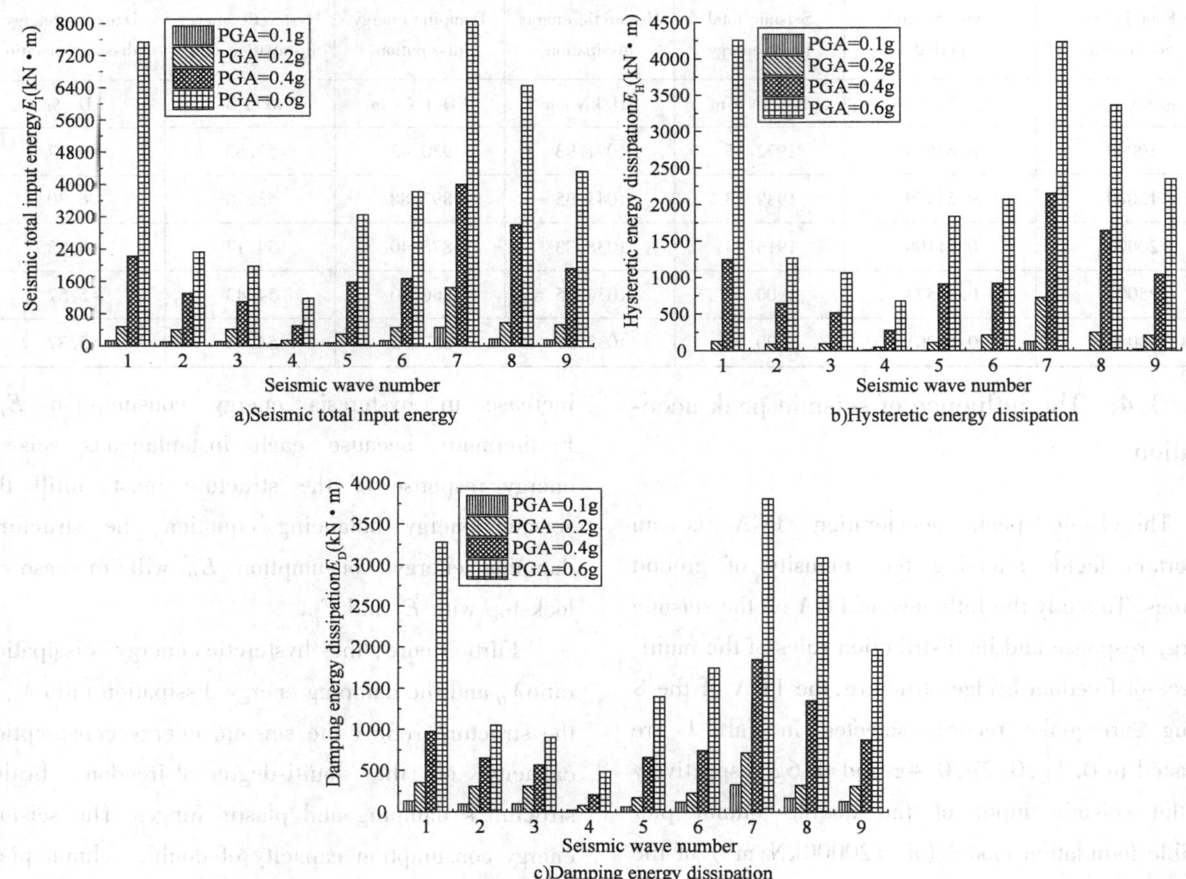

Fig. 8 The influence of PGA on the seismic energy response of double-column piers

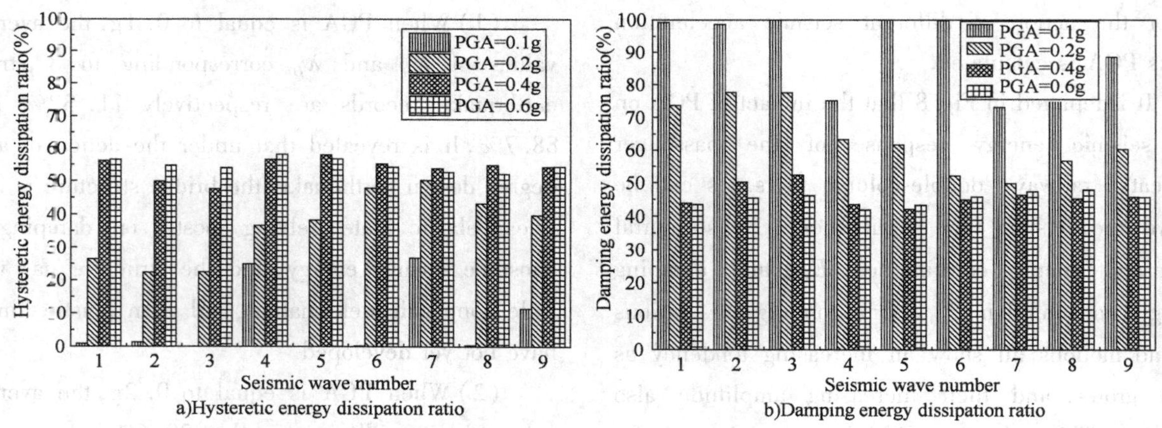

Fig. 9 The influence of PGA on the distribution law of seismic energy response of double-column piers

(3) When PGA is equal to 0.4g, the average value of λ_H exceeds the average value of λ_D, increasing to 54.17%, while the average value of λ_D is only 45.8%. It can be seen that under the action of a 9-degree design earthquake, the damping energy dissipation capacity of the structure has reached the maximum, and the hysteretic energy dissipation E_H accounts for a larger proportion of the seismic total input energy E_I consumed by the structure, thereby replacing the damping energy dissipation E_D has

become the main way of structural energy consumption. However, this is at the cost of a large amount of irreparable deformation of the structure, causing great damage to the structure.

(4) When PGA is equal to 0. 6g, the average values of λ_H and λ_D are respectively 54. 23% and 45.67%, which are not much different from λ_H and λ_D when PGA is equal to 0.4g. It is shown that under the action of a 9-degree rare-occurred earthquake action, the hysteretic energy dissipation capacity of the structure has no more room to rise, and the permissible nonelastic deformation of the structure has been saturated. At this time, the structure has reached the edge of collapse and destruction.

4 Conclusions

The seismic energy response and distribution laws of railway girder bridges under different levels of earthquakes are studied in this paper. The conclusions are obtained as follows:

(1) The seismic energy absorbed by the example bridge in the earthquake is dissipated by damping energy dissipation and hysteretic energy dissipation. The hysteretic energy dissipation can better reflect the influence of the duration of strong earthquakes on the structure response, which is one of the important parameters to measure the cumulative damage of the structure.

(2) With the consideration of the foundation soil, the system damping will increase, which will lead to an increase in structural damping energy consumption and a decrease in hysteretic energy consumption. The trend will also be more significant as the soil quality of the site becomes softer.

(3) Under the earthquake action E1, the example bridge is in a linear elastic state, with very little nonelastic deformation of the structure, and mainly relies on damping to consume seismic energy.

(4) Under the earthquake action E2, the example bridge will have an elastoplastic seismic response, which will produce a large amount of nonelastic deformation, and consume seismic energy through hysteretic energy dissipation. Hysteretic energy consumption accounts for about 55% of the seismic total input energy consumed by the structure, replacing the damping energy consumption as the main way of energy consumption for the structure.

References

[1] Housner G. W. Limit Design of Structures to Resist Earthquake[C]. Proceedings of 1st Conference on Earthquake Engineering, Berkeley, 1956.

[2] Akiyama H. Earthquake Resistant Design Based on the Energy Concept[C]. Proceedings of 9th WCEE, 1988, 905-910.

[3] Michel Bruneau, Niandi Wang. Some aspects of energy methods for the inelastic seismic response of ductile SDOF structures [J]. Engineering Structures, 1996, 18(1): 1-12.

[4] LuisD. Decanini, Fabrizio Mollaioli. An energy-based methodology for the assessment of seismic demand [J]. Soil Dynamics and Earthquake Engineering, 2001, 21: (2) 113-137.

[5] Xiong Zhongming, Shi Qingxuan. Theoretical study on seismic response and design method of frame structures with energy method[J]. World Information On Earthquake Engineering, 2005, 21 (2): 141-146.

[6] Anindya Dutta. Bridge on Energy-Based Seismic Analysis and Design of Highway[D]. Faculty of the Graduate School of the State University of New York at Buffalo, 1999.

[7] Akiyama H. Earthquake Resistant Design Based on the Energy Concept [C]. Proceedings of 9th WCEE, 905-910, 1988.

[8] Uang CM, Bertero V. V. Evaluation of seismic energy in structures[J]. Earthquake Engineering and Structural Dynamics, 1990, 19: 77-90.

[9] Gaetano Manfredi. Evaluation of seismic energy demand [J]. Earthquake Engineering and Structural Dynamics, 2001, 30(4): 485-499.

[10] Mario Ordaz, Benjamin Huerta. Exact computation of input-energy spectra from fourier amplitude spectra[J]. Earthquake Engineering and Structural Dynamics, 2003, 32(16): 597-605.

[11] Jiang Hui. Performance-based seismic design of bridge structure excited by near-fault

earthquake using energy concept[D]. Beijing: Beijing Jiaotong University, 2007.

[12] Fengli Yang. Study on Design Method and Parameters for Seismically Isolated Railway Bridges [D]. Beijing: Beijing Jiaotong University, 2007.

[13] Lichu Fan. Seismic Design of Bridge[M]. Shanghai: Tongji University Press, 1997.

[14] Jufang Li. Energy Based Seismic Response and Design Method of Building Structures[D]. Xi'an: Xi'an University of Architecture and Technology, 2004.

[15] Mingkui Xiao. Analysis Method of Displacement and Energy Responses for Evaluating the Performance of Seismic Structures [D]. Chongqing: Chongqing University, 2004.

[16] Ministry of Railways of the People's Republic of China. Code for seismic design of railway engineering: GB 50111—2017[S], Beijing: China Planning Press, 2020.

[17] Ministry of Transport of the People's Republic of China. Guidelines for Seismic Design of Highway Bridges: JTG/TB 02-01—2008[S]. Beijing, China Communications Press, 2008.

不对称箱梁断面气动性能研究

刘博祥*

(长安大学公路学院)

摘 要 为研究不对称箱梁断面涡振性能,本文采用节段模型风洞试验方法分析了不对称箱梁断面在不同迎风侧下的三风力系数和涡振响应,并采用数值模拟的方法,通过断面流场分析了其涡振产生的机理。试验结果表明:对于不对称箱梁断面,迎风侧的不同对断面三风力系数影响较小;不同来流风向下主梁在+3°和+5°攻角都出现了明显涡振现象;通过对迎风侧宽工况下断面附近流场的数值模拟发现涡振的发生主要是由一个周期内两次旋涡规律脱落造成的。不同来流风向发生涡振的工况相似,窄迎风侧下的涡振振幅相比较大。

关键词 桥梁工程 不对称箱梁断面 三分力系数 涡振 数值模拟

0 引言

随着桥梁设计和施工技术的不断发展和改进,绝大多数桥梁断面采用对称断面,无论是设计、施工、管理都达到了成熟的阶段,关于对称桥梁断面的相关研究也十分完善。在桥梁设计中,对称断面的理论研究和技术创新十分完备,是首选的一种常规结构。箱梁作为最常见的一种桥梁断面,因其具备良好的结构性能在各种桥梁结构中得到广泛应用。

在满足安全和使用功能的前提下,对桥梁的美观设计要求也越来越高,特别是桥梁作为景观桥或城市地标性建筑物出现的时候,桥梁的设计往往不遵常规。不对称桥梁断面可以与周边建筑物融合,又能有效地利用空间资源。但不对称断面也存在问题,主要表现在受力性能和抗风性能方面。相关学者也进行过相似的研究。姜晓彬通过对比对称箱梁断面和不对称箱梁断面的受力特性,指出不对称箱梁断面在荷载作用下受力不均匀、恒载作用下产生扭矩等差异,并对其进行优化[1]。桥梁抗风性能是近年来关注的热点,不对称桥梁断面的抗风性能研究也不可忽略。李明利用节段模型风洞试验研究了非对称Π型梁和流线型箱梁在不同来流风向下的三分力系数、涡振以及颤振特性,研究结果表明:断面的非对称性会严重影响不同来流风向下主梁的涡振及颤振性能,包括出现涡振的风攻角、涡振响应振幅、起振风速以及锁定区间、颤振临界风速等[2]。

目前关于桥梁主梁断面的气动性能研究内容多为对称形式的主梁断面,不对称形式的主梁断面气动性能研究较少。为了研究不对称主梁断面的气动性能，本文利用节段模型风洞试验研究了不对称箱梁断面的气动性能，包括主梁的三分力系数、涡振，并通过数值模拟的方法分析了涡振产生的机理。

1 节段模型风洞试验

主梁断面如图1所示，为不对称箱梁断面。由于断面的不对称性，根据来流风向的不同分为迎风侧窄和迎风侧宽。根据主桥典型断面尺寸、风洞试验段尺寸等要求，选取节段模型的缩尺比为1∶12，模型长1.200m，宽0.417m，高0.083m。

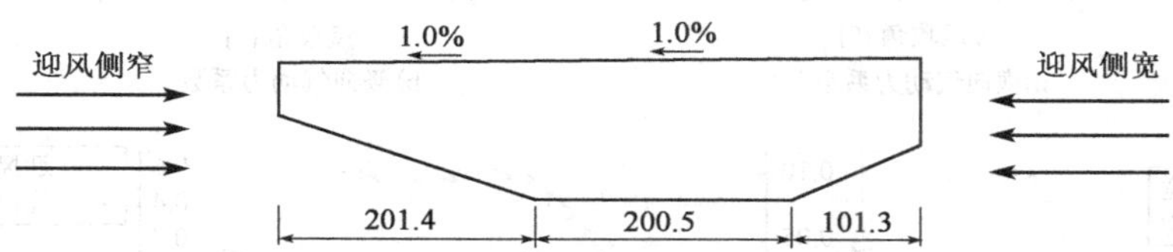

图1 断面及工况示意图（单位：cm）

2 三分力系数

静三分力系数是描述静风荷载的无量纲参数，可通过其计算出任意风速下主梁所受的静力风荷载，得到风荷载后就可对相应的静力变形和静风失稳等进行分析。

如图2所示，沿横桥向的均匀风场中，试验攻角为α，体轴坐标系下桥梁节段模型受到横向气动力和竖向气动力以及扭转力矩F_H、F_V和M_T。风轴坐标系下的阻力和升力由式(1)换算得到，扭转力矩与体轴坐标系下的M_T相同。由式(2)～式(4)计算出体轴的三分力系数C_H、C_V和C_M，风轴坐标系下的阻力系数C_D和升力系数C_L可由式(5)～式(6)算出。

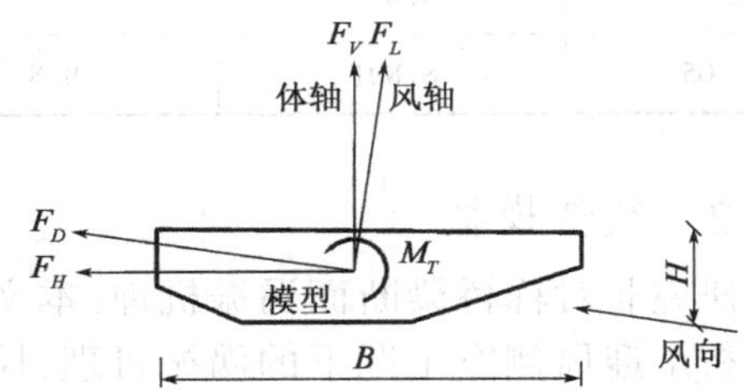

图2 风轴与体轴的相互关系及气动力方向

风轴坐标下的阻力和升力为：

$$\begin{cases} F_D = F_V\sin\alpha + F_H\cos\alpha \\ F_L = F_V\cos\alpha - F_H\sin\alpha \end{cases} \tag{1}$$

式中，α为水平方向与风向的夹角。横向气动力系数C_H、竖向气动力系数C_V和气动扭矩系数C_M以及风轴阻力系数C_D、升力系数C_L定义如下：

横向气动力系数

$$C_H: C_H(\alpha) = F_H(\alpha)/(0.5\rho U^2 HL) \tag{2}$$

竖向气动力系数

$$C_V: C_V(\alpha) = F_V(\alpha)/(0.5\rho U^2 BL) \tag{3}$$

阻力系数

$$C_D: C_D(\alpha) = F_D(\alpha)/(0.5\rho U^2 HL) \tag{4}$$

升力系数

$$C_L: C_L(\alpha) = F_L(\alpha)/(0.5\rho U^2 BL) \tag{5}$$

力矩系数

$$C_M: C_M(\alpha) = M_T(\alpha)/(0.5\rho U^2 B^2 L) \tag{6}$$

式中，$0.5\rho U^2$为气流动压；H、B、L分别为节段模型的高度、宽度和长度。

为研究非对称主梁的静力三分力系数（图3），在均匀流场中分别进行了不同迎风侧下的静力三分力试验。试验攻角$\alpha = -10° \sim +10°$。

对于三分力系数，迎风侧的改变不会影响其变化趋势。

对于升力系数，风攻角小于$-5°$时，迎风侧宽工况下的升力系数大于迎风侧窄工况；风攻角大于$-5°$时，迎风侧宽工况下的升力系数小于迎风侧窄工况。

对于力矩系数，迎风侧窄工况下的力矩系数都大于迎风侧宽工况。由于迎风侧宽和迎风侧窄工况下的腹板倾角不同，对来流的分流作用效果也不同。迎风侧宽工况下，腹板倾角较大，对来流的分流效果较差，造成升力和升力矩小于迎风侧窄工况。

对于阻力系数，迎风侧宽工况下的阻力系数小于迎风侧窄工况，这是由于主梁断面几何不对称，几何中心便倾向于迎风侧宽一侧，且腹板角度不同,造成在相同风攻角下迎风侧窄工况下的迎风面积大于迎风侧宽工况,造成阻力系数偏大。

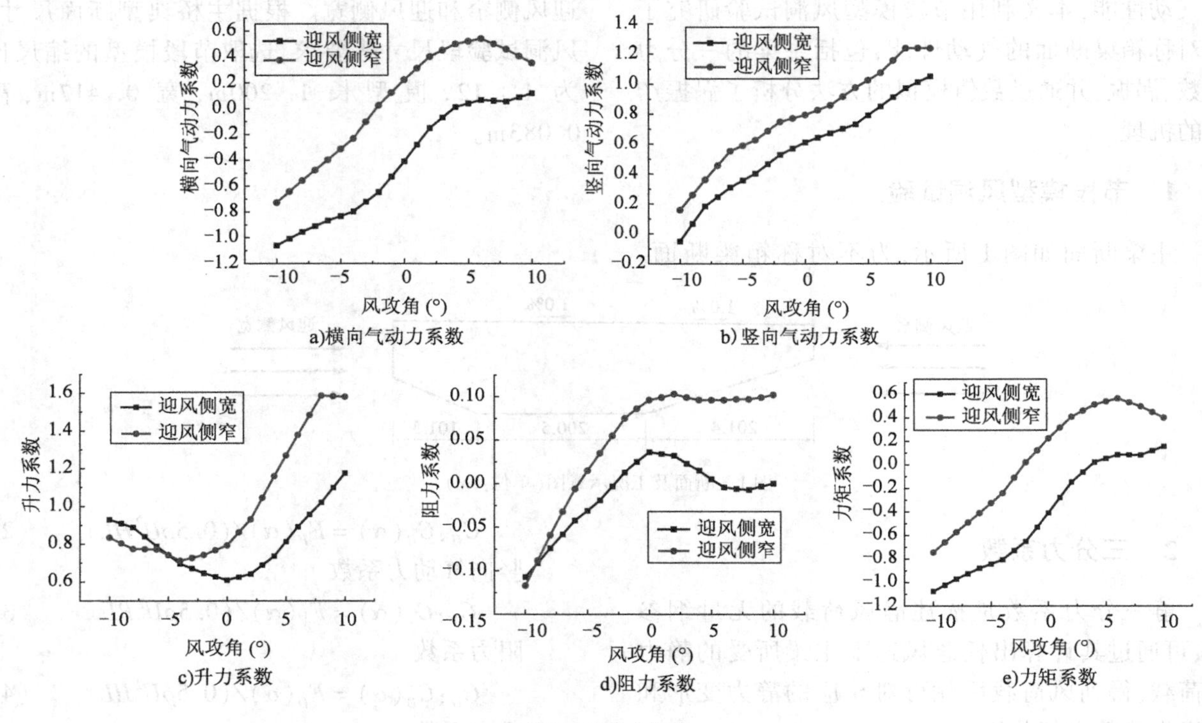

图3　三分力系数

3　涡振响应

3.1　风洞试验

为研究不同类迎风侧在各个攻角下的涡振响应,本文设置了试验断面在迎风侧窄和迎风侧宽这两种工况下在 −5°、−3°、0°、+3°、+5°风攻角下的竖弯涡振试验。节段模型相关参数如表1所示。

节段模型试验参数　　表1

参　　数	实 桥 值	缩 尺 比	模型设计值	实 测 值
等效质量(kg/m)	2094	$1/12^2$	14.542	15.129
等效质量惯矩(kg·m²/m)	14490	$1/12^4$	0.699	—
竖弯基频(Hz)	2.237	12/3.05	8.801	8.8

由图4可知,迎风侧窄工况下,+5°和+3°攻角出现了明显竖弯涡振现象,竖向振幅峰值分别为28.72mm和17.96mm;迎风侧宽工况下,+5°和+3°攻角同样出现了竖弯涡振现象,其中+5°攻角时竖向振幅峰值最大,为20.64mm,+3°攻角涡振峰值为9.03mm。不同来流风向下+3°和+5°攻角都出现了两个较明显的涡锁区间。其他攻角并没有出现明显涡振,且+5°攻角下的竖向振幅最大,该攻角为最不利工况。主梁迎风侧窄比迎风侧宽更容易出现竖弯涡振现象,相同条件下,迎风侧窄的振幅也更大。

3.2　数值模拟

为研究非对称桥梁断面涡振机理,本文通过流场分析了迎风侧宽工况下的涡振机理,风攻角为+5°。计算区域尺寸为10B×40B,如图5所示。入口距主梁断面形心距离为10B,出口距主梁断面形心距离为30B。边界条件:来流方向设置为速度入口,出口设置为压力出口,主梁断面边界设置为无滑移固体壁面边界,计算域上下两侧边界设置为对称边界。数值模拟采用SST k-ω 湍流模型,湍流强度设置为0.5%,湍流粘性比设置为10%。采用SIMPLE算法求解压力-速度耦合问题,压力场和动量场均采用二阶格式离散,收敛残差控制在1e-6。

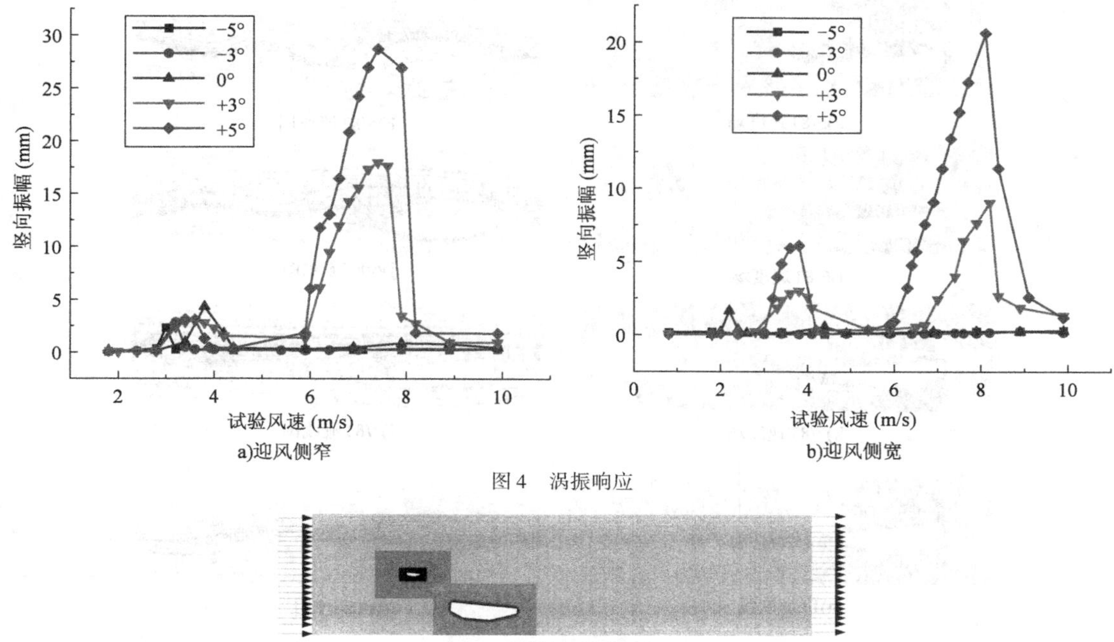

a)迎风侧窄

b)迎风侧宽

图4　涡振响应

图5　计算域及网格设置

相比于风洞试验,数值模拟可以将断面绕流场展现出来,以便更好地分析断面产生涡振的机理。图6给出了桥梁断面迎风侧宽工况下在一个周期T内的流场演变,2/8T时刻,断面附近形成1个主要涡结构,位于断面正上方;2个次要涡结构,分别位于断面右侧翼缘和腹板下方。3/8T时刻,2个次要涡结构向断面右上方脱落并合并,同时主要涡结构发展至最大尺度并开始脱落。4/8T时刻,主要涡结构脱落与合并的次要涡结构伴随脱落。5/8T时刻,涡结构脱落完成,伴有生成涡结构的趋势。6/8T时刻,上个时刻的涡结构脱落造成在断面右上方和翼缘右侧生成两个较小的涡结构。7/8T时刻,涡结构脱落。1T时刻,涡结构脱落完成,至此一个周期结束。由此可见,涡振的发生主要是由风荷载作用下两次涡脱造成的,在主梁断面上方形成一个大的涡结构,涡结构的规律脱落使主梁发生涡振。

图7给出了桥梁断面迎风侧宽工况下在一个周期T内的压力分布变化。与流场图相对应,两次涡脱的发生是由断面上方和下方负压区的形成造成的。可以明显看出在第一次涡脱发生的时候,在断面上方存在一个较大的负压区,同理在第二次涡脱发生的时候,在桥梁断面下方也存在一个较大的负压区,由于压力差的存在,桥梁断面受到向上和向下的升力,发生涡振。

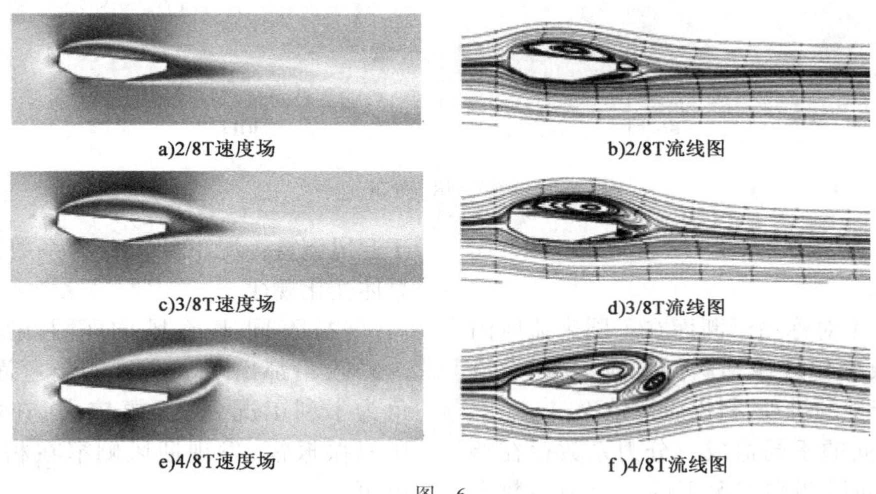
a)2/8T速度场　b)2/8T流线图

c)3/8T速度场　d)3/8T流线图

e)4/8T速度场　f)4/8T流线图

图　6

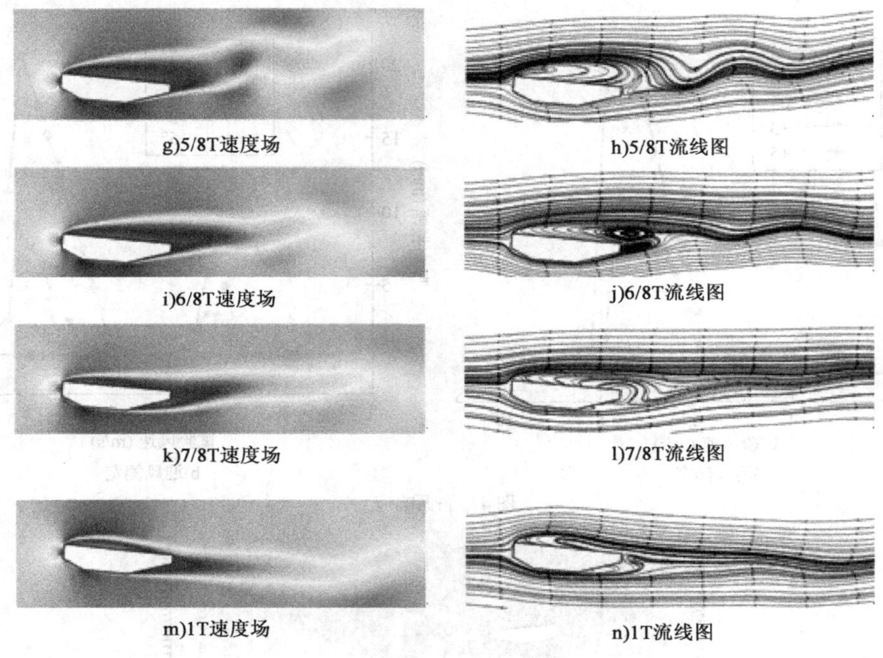

图6　瞬态绕流

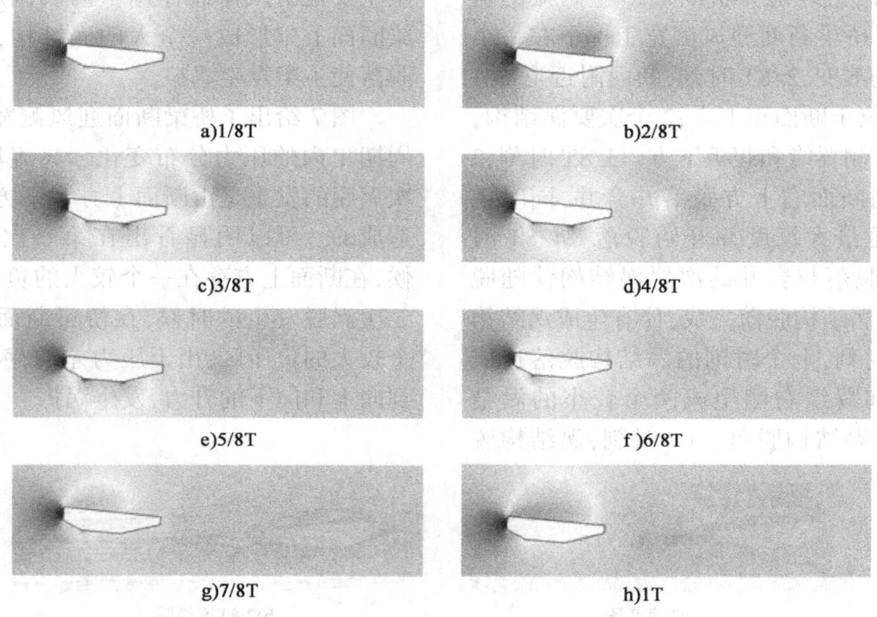

图7　压力分布

4　结语

本文研究了不对称箱梁断面在不同来流风向下的三分力系数变化规律和涡振响应,并通过流场分析了涡振产生的机理,得出以下结论:

(1)来流风向的不同造成三分力系数存在差异,总体表现为迎风侧窄工况下的三分力系数大于迎风侧宽工况下的三分力系数,但不会影响其总体变化规律。

(2)不同来流风向下主梁断面在 +3°、+5°攻角都出现了明显的竖弯涡振现象,正攻角为不利工况,且振幅较大,在相同工况下对比涡振振幅,发现迎风侧窄在相同攻角下的振幅更大。

(3)涡振的发生主要是由一个周期内两次旋涡规律脱落造成的。

参考文献

[1] 姜晓彬. 兰溪金角大桥不对称箱梁断面受力特性研究[D]. 杭州:浙江大学,2014.

[2] 李明,孙延国,李明水,等. 非对称Π型梁和流线型箱梁气动性能风洞试验研究[J]. 振动与冲击,2019,38(8):54-60.

[3] 王骑,廖海黎,李明水,等. 流线型箱梁气动外形对桥梁颤振和涡振的影响[J]. 公路交通科技,2012,29(8):8.

[4] 汪家继,樊健生,聂建国,等. 大跨度桥梁箱梁的三分力系数识别研究[J]. 工程力学,2016,33(1):95-104.

[5] 马凯. 典型桥梁断面静力三分力系数研究[C]//第二十一届全国桥梁学术会议论文集(下册),2014:104-113.

[6] 刘钥,陈政清,张志田. 箱梁断面静风力系数的CFD数值模拟[J]. 振动与冲击,2010(1):5.

可拓展的公路涵洞技术状况模糊综合分层评定

刘 佳 刘博恺* 张 阳 刘裕泓

(长安大学公路学院)

摘 要 鉴于目前不完善的公路桥涵技术状况评定现状,本文提出了一种可拓展的、基于模糊可拓理论及层次分析法(AHP)的公路涵洞技术状况综合评定方法。首先根据公路涵洞构造形式和病害特点,自定义部件、病害指标及其分级评定标准来构造公路涵洞技术状况评定层次分析模型并确定相应指标权重;其次构造AHP-模糊可拓评价模型,基于模糊可拓理论确定各部件技术状况等级及公路涵洞总体技术状况等级。本文量化了公路涵洞技术状况评定过程,使得评定结果不但能反映涵洞总体技术状况,也能反映涵洞各部件技术状况;且充分考虑了涵洞构造形式和病害的多样性,采用自定义部件和自定义病害的方式拓展了可拓层次分析模型,使得本方法的适用性更高。

关键词 桥梁工程 技术状况评定 模糊可拓层次分析法 公路涵洞 自定义病害

0 引言

公路涵洞虽然是公路交通基础设施的重要组成部分,但其技术状况评定等相关研究并未得到如桥梁一般足够的重视。但若由于涵洞技术状况不明发生垮塌事故,公路交通运输也必然会受到影响,因此对公路涵洞技术状况评定方法的研究应进一步深入。在公路涵洞技术状况评定领域,目前的评定方法主要有两种:基于规范的评定方法和基于层次分析法(Analytic Hierarchy Process,AHP)的评定方法。

基于规范的评定方法主要是指根据《公路桥涵养护规范》(JTG 5120—2021)对涵洞总体技术状况进行评定。该方法具有较好的适用性,但是由于没能量化和细化涵洞病害指标,严重依赖专业技术人员的经验知识,是一种主观定性的总体评定方法,也不能反映涵洞各部件的技术状况。基于AHP的评定方法是一种定量分析方法,也是学者研究的热点。徐建武等采用缺陷扣分法和分层综合评定法评定公路混凝土箱涵的技术状况,但其评定结果难以反映涵洞各部件技术状况。覃乐勤等提出了基于层次分析法的涵洞技术状况评定模型,该模型难以满足不同构造形式的涵洞部件划分需求。贺国峰研究了涵洞部件权重和病害权重的求解方法并以盖板涵为例对其进行综合评价,但未考虑涵洞构造及病害的多样性。综上所述,目前公路涵洞技术状况评定方法大多存在的缺陷有:①现行公路涵洞总体技术状况评定方法偏主观定性,缺乏定量分析过程;②即使采用了定量分析方法,由于其适用性不足,也没能充分考虑病害及构造的多样性。

在涵洞技术状况评定中,无论是选取指标还

是确定权重,过程中都存在着不同程度的矛盾,而可拓学研究解决的中心问题也是矛盾,因此可以考虑将可拓学理论应用于公路涵洞的评价。近几年,关于可拓学的评价方法在其他领域应用的研究有所发展。例如,杨卓等基于熵权物元可拓理论评估隧道塌方风险。高炜等采用改进的可拓层次分析法和动态加权相结合的方法对航天军用高技术指标体系进行评价。Xu 等基于物元理论将地震风险评估方法应用于中国西南某山区隧道。Ma 等运用物元可拓理论建立了分布式能源系统的项目后评价指标和评价模型。Zhou 等提出了一种基于层次分析法-可拓物元的公交服务质量评价方法。韩亚坤等利用层次分析法和可拓学理论,建立了绿色建筑节能技术经济评价模型。Du 等基于可拓理论,建立了确定重型机床再制造最优方案的决策模型,利用 AHP 熵权法确定了各评价指标的权重。

本文针对现有技术的缺陷或改进需求,研究了一种可拓展的公路涵洞技术状况模糊综合分层评定方法。首先采用层次分析法(AHP)确定评价指标的权重,实现量化评定过程;其次通过引入自定义部件以及自定义病害,提高评定方法的适用性;而后建立 AHP-模糊可拓评价模型,确定评价指标的经典域、节域和待评价物元,构建关联函数,对指标进行可拓评价,并利用模糊理论客观全面地得出了公路桥涵技术状况等级;最后在案例中验证了该模型的可行性和实用性。

1 AHP 确定评价指标权重

1.1 构建 AHP 评价模型

本文建立了包含目标层、准则层和指标层的公路涵洞技术状况评定层次分析模型,如图1所示。其中的 i 表示某个部件,j 表示某个指标。

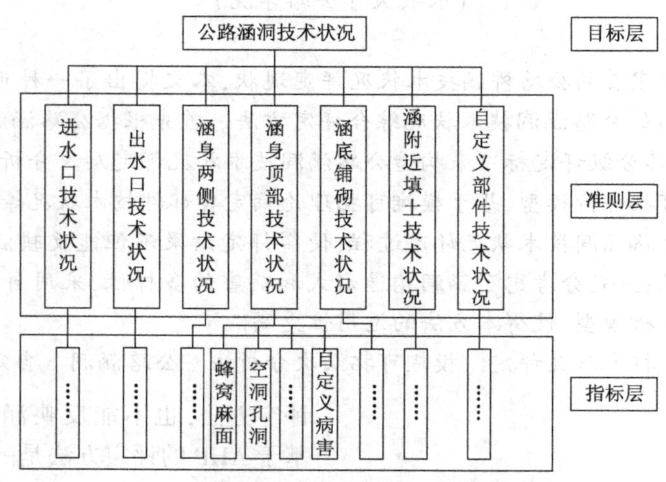

图1 公路涵洞技术状况评定层次分析模型

1.2 构建判断矩阵

按照层次结构模型,每一层元素都以相邻上一层次各元素为基准构造判断矩阵,选用一致矩阵法来确定不同指标之间的权重,即将指标两两对比,采用相对比较值来衡量结果。判断矩阵是表示某一目标的所有指标之间相对重要性的比较,采用 1~9 的标度方式给出,如表1所示。

比较标准意义 表1

标度	定义	标度	定义
1	同样重要	7	强烈重要
3	稍微重要	9	绝对重要
5	明显重要		

注:标准值2,4,6,8分别表示上述两相邻标准值判断的中值。

1.3 一致性检验

为确定所建立的矩阵是否成功、计算的权重结果是否合理,需对判断矩阵的一致性进行检验,首先计算检验指标

$$CI = \frac{\eta_{\max} - n}{n - 1} \tag{1}$$

式中,n 表示判断矩阵的阶数,$\eta_{\max}$ 为判断矩

阵的最大特征根。

其次采用随机一致性指标来检验矩阵 B 的一致性

$$CR = CI/RI \tag{2}$$

式中 RI 表示矩阵的平均随机一致性指标，其取值如表 2 所示；当 $CR < 0.1$ 时，一致性可行。

平均随机一致性指标值 表 2

n	1	2	3	4	5	6	7	8	9
RI	0	0	0.58	0.90	1.12	1.24	1.32	1.41	1.45

1.4 计算权重

在判断矩阵满足一致性检验的条件下，即可求得各层评价指标的权重 α_i。若由于某涵洞构造形式特殊或其他原因需要新增部件时，可在所述准则层自定义部件，该自定义部件的权重 α_m 可采用专家调查法等方法确定，同时其他部件权重修改为

$$\alpha'_i = \alpha_i \times (1 - \alpha_m) \tag{3}$$

如果需要删减某个权重为 α_m 的部件，则剩余部件的权重为

$$\alpha'_i = \alpha_i \times (1 + \alpha_m) \tag{4}$$

2 建立 AHP-模糊可拓评价模型

2.1 待评物元

在可拓学中，常用物元将事物的质和量有机地集成在一起。它是由事物、特征及量值三 个要素组成，通常用一个有序三元组来表示，简称物元，待评物元表示为

$$\boldsymbol{R}_T = (T, u_i, x_i) = \begin{pmatrix} & u_1 & x_1 \\ & \vdots & \vdots \\ T & u_i & x_i \\ & \vdots & \vdots \\ & u_n & x_n \end{pmatrix} \tag{5}$$

式中，x_i 为 T 关于 u_i 的量值，即待评涵洞的所有数据。

2.2 经典域及节域

经典域是指当评价等级 V 的特征 U 发生时，特征 U 所对应的量值的范围，物元的经典域表示为

$$\boldsymbol{R}_j = (V_j, u_i, x_{ij}) = \begin{pmatrix} & u_1 & x_{1j} \\ & \vdots & \vdots \\ V_j & u_i & x_{ij} \\ & \vdots & \vdots \\ & u_n & x_{nj} \end{pmatrix} = \begin{pmatrix} & u_1 & \langle a_{1j}, b_{1j} \rangle \\ & \vdots & \vdots \\ V_j & u_i & \langle a_{ij}, b_{ij} \rangle \\ & \vdots & \vdots \\ & u_n & \langle a_{nj}, b_{nj} \rangle \end{pmatrix} \tag{6}$$

式中，V_j 为评价对象的第 $j(j = 1,2,\cdots,m)$ 个等级；u_i 为第 $i(i = 1,2,\cdots,n)$ 个评价指标；x_{ij} 为评价对象属于第 j 个等级时，对应 u_i 指标的量值；$\langle a_{ij}, b_{ij} \rangle$ 为评价对象 i 属于第 j 个等级时的取值范围，即经典域。

物元的节域表示为

$$\boldsymbol{R}_P = (P, u_i, x_{ip}) = \begin{pmatrix} & u_1 & x_{1p} \\ & \vdots & \vdots \\ P & u_i & x_{ip} \\ & \vdots & \vdots \\ & u_n & x_{np} \end{pmatrix} = \begin{pmatrix} & u_1 & \langle a_{1p}, b_{1p} \rangle \\ & \vdots & \vdots \\ V_j & u_i & \langle a_{ip}, b_{ip} \rangle \\ & \vdots & \vdots \\ & u_n & \langle a_{np}, b_{np} \rangle \end{pmatrix} \tag{7}$$

式中，P 为评价等级的全体，$\langle a_{ip}, b_{ip} \rangle$ 为评价指标 u_i 的所有取值范围，即节域。

2.3 关联函数

各单项评价指标关于各等级的关联度为

$$K_j(x_i) = \frac{\rho(x_i, x_{0ij})}{[\rho(x_i, x_{ip}) - \rho(x_i, x_{0ij})]} \tag{8}$$

式中，$\rho(x_i, x_{0ij}) = \left| x_i - \frac{a_{0ij} + b_{0ij}}{2} \right| - \frac{b_{0ij} - a_{0ij}}{2}$，$\rho(x_i, x_{ip}) = \left| x_i - \frac{a_{ip} + b_{ip}}{2} \right| - \frac{b_{ip} - a_{ip}}{2}$。

2.4 模糊综合评价

$$E_k = \sum W_{ki} K_j(x_{ki}) \tag{9}$$

式中，E_k 为涵洞准则层中第 k 个部件的关联度模糊综合评价结果向量；W_{ki} 为指标层中第 i 个指标的权重。

$$C = WE, \sum_{k=1}^{s} W_k = 1 \tag{10}$$

式中，C 为涵洞目标层的模糊综合评价结果向量；W 为涵洞准则层各部件的权重组成的矩阵；E 为涵洞准则层各部件关于各等级的关联度组成的矩阵。

最后，根据最大隶属度原则确定涵洞的技术状况等级。

3　案例分析

某箱涵在某年检测中被发现存在以下病害：涵身两侧存在累计约55%部件面积的蜂窝麻面，涵身顶部局部存在3%部件面积的混凝土空洞孔洞，涵身顶部局部出现小面积的渗漏水现象，涵顶沥青混凝土路面铺装出现8%铺装面积的波浪拥包，其他部件没有病害。

3.1　指标权重的计算

由于在该涵洞技术状况评定时，需要考虑涵顶路面的病害，因此需要自定义部件。另外，《公路桥涵养护规范》(JTG 5120—2021)中没有渗漏水的评定指标的相关规定，也需要自行定义。该箱涵的准则层包括进水口、出水口、涵身两侧、涵身顶部、涵底铺砌、涵附近填土以及涵顶路面等部件技术状况。自定义病害渗漏水的分级评定标准见表3。

涵洞渗漏水分级评定标准　表3

标度值	定性描述
0	完好
(0,1]	局部有轻微渗水现象
(1,2]	局部有明显渗水现象
(2,3]	多处有明显渗水现象
(3,4]	多处有严重渗水现象，渗水处伴有晶体的析出现象

本文通过专家调查法及AHP确定的进水口、出水口、涵身两侧、涵身顶部、涵底铺砌、涵附近填土各部件的权重 α_i 依次为0.14、0.14、0.3、0.3、0.07、0.05。同时，采用专家调查法所确定的新增的自定义部件——涵顶路面的权重为0.08，则箱涵进水口、出水口、涵身两侧、涵身顶部、涵底铺砌、涵附近填土等部件的权重按式(3)计算，结果分别为0.1288、0.1288、0.276、0.276、0.0644、0.046，空洞孔洞及渗漏水对于涵身顶部的权重分别为0.323、0.677。

3.2　物元模型的确定

对于定量指标，该涵洞的经典域和节域参照《公路桥梁技术状况评定标准》(JTG/TH 21—2011)来确定；对于定性指标，则根据病害严重程度来考核，如表3对于渗漏水的规定。参照《公路桥涵养护规范》(JTG 5120—2021)将涵洞技术状况划分为5类：$V = \{V_1, V_2, V_3, V_4, V_5\}$ = {一类，二类，三类，四类，五类}，该公路涵洞的技术状况评定中经典域、节域、各评价指标的实测值见表4，其中无病害的部件指标为技术状况得分。

3.3　评价指标的关联度计算

根据公式计算公路涵洞技术状况评价指标的关联度，计算结果及最终所得的部件等级见表5。

指标经典域、节域和实测值　表4

箱涵部件	指标	经典域					节域	指标实测值
		V_1	V_2	V_3	V_4	V_5		
进水口	—	[95,100]	[80,95)	[60,80)	[40,60)	[0,40)	[0,100]	100
出水口	—	[95,100]	[80,95)	[60,80)	[40,60)	[0,40)	[0,100]	100
涵身两侧	蜂窝麻面(%)	0	(0,20]	(20,50]	(50,60]	(60,100]	[0,100]	55
涵身顶部	空洞孔洞(%)	0	(0,5]	(5,10]	(10,20]	(20,100]	[0,100]	3
	渗漏水	0	(0,1]	(1,2]	(2,3]	(3,4]	[0,4]	1.8
涵底铺砌	—	[95,100]	[80,95)	[60,80)	[40,60)	[0,40)	[0,100]	100
涵顶路面	变形(%)	0	(0,10]	(10,20]	(20,50]	(50,100]	[0,100]	8

评价指标关联度　表5

准则	指标	V_1	V_2	V_3	V_4	V_5	等级
进水口	—	1	−1	−1	−1	−1	V_1
出水口	—	1	−1	−1	−1	−1	V_1
涵身两侧	蜂窝麻面(%)	−0.55	0.4375	−0.1	0.125	−0.1	V_4

续上表

准　则	指　标	V_1	V_2	V_3	V_4	V_5	等　级
涵身顶部	空洞孔洞(%)	-0.5	2	-0.4	-0.7	-0.85	V_2
	渗漏水现象	-0.5	0.3077	0.125	-0.1	-0.4	V_2
涵底铺砌	—	1	-1	-1	-1	-1	V_1
涵顶路面	变形(%)	-0.5	0.3333	-0.2	-0.6	-0.84	V_2

3.4 模糊综合评价

用 $E_k(k=1,2,\cdots,6)$ 代表箱涵进水口、出水口、涵身两侧、涵身顶部、涵底铺砌、涵附近填土等部件。将箱涵部件对应指标关联度及权重带入式(9)和(10)可得出对应的涵洞技术状况等级。

$$E_4=\sum_{i=1}^{2}W_{4i}\cdot K_j(x_{4i})=(0.323\quad 0.677)\cdot\begin{pmatrix}-0.5 & 2 & -0.4 & -0.7 & -0.85\\ -0.5 & 0.3077 & 0.125 & -0.1 & -0.4\end{pmatrix}=(-0.5\ 0.8543\ -0.0446\ -0.2938\ -0.5454)$$

同理可得其余 E_k。

$$C=WE=(0.1288\ 0.1288\ 0.276\ 0.276\ 0.0644\ 0.046)\cdot\begin{pmatrix}1.0000 & -1.0000 & -1.0000 & -1.0000 & -1.0000\\ 1.0000 & -1.0000 & -1.0000 & -1.0000 & -1.0000\\ -0.5500 & 0.4375 & -0.1000 & 0.1250 & -0.1000\\ -0.5000 & 0.8543 & -0.0446 & -0.2938 & -0.5454\\ 1.0000 & -1.0000 & -1.0000 & -1.0000 & -1.0000\\ -0.5000 & 0.3333 & -0.2000 & -0.6000 & -0.8400\end{pmatrix}=(0.0092\quad 0.0499\quad -0.3711\quad -0.3962\quad -0.5388)$$

基于最大隶属度原则,可知该涵洞综合技术状况等级为二类。

以上案例证实了模糊可拓层次分析法和自定义部件、病害在涵洞技术状况评定的应用是可行的,相关机构可根据该技术状况评定结果采取对应措施对该涵洞进行维修养护。

4 结语

总体而言,本文采用层次分析法将涵洞技术状况拆分成目标层、准则层以及指标层三个层次,并且应用可拓理论量化了技术状况评定过程,基于模糊理论对涵洞总体技术状况进行了综合评价。该方法不但降低了现有技术的主观性,而且能反映涵洞各部件技术状况,有利于突出公路涵洞养护的重点部件。本方法与目前涵洞的技术状况评定方法相比,其方法体系是可拓展的,适用性较高。技术人员能够根据涵洞构造形式和病害多样性的特点,通过自定义部件和自定义病害指标来拓展涵洞技术状况评定层次分析模型。这种可拓展的涵洞技术状况评定方法能够适用于不同构造形式和发生特殊病害的涵洞的技术状况评定工作。

参考文献

[1] Liu Y, Eckert C M, Earl C. A review of fuzzy AHP methods for decision-making with subjective judgements[J]. Expert Systems with Applications,2020,161(15): 113738.

[2] Darko A,Chan A P C,Ameyaw E E,et al. Review of application of analytic hierarchy process (AHP) in construction[J]. International Journal of Construction Management,2019,19(5): 436-452:43.

[3] Piratla K R, Jin H, Yazdekhasti S. A Failure Risk-Based Culvert Renewal Prioritization Framework [J]. Infrastructures, 2019, 4 (3):43.

[4] Lyu H M,Zhou W H,Shen S L,et al. Inundation risk assessment of metro system using AHP and TFN-AHP in Shenzhen[J]. Sustainable Cities, 2020,56(3): 102103.

[5] Kumar P,Singh S K. A comprehensive evaluation of aspect-oriented software quality (AOSQ) model using analytic hierarchy process (AHP) technique[C]. 2nd International Conference on Advances in Computing, Communication, & Automation (ICACCA),2016: 1-7.

[6] 徐建武,李照奇. 公路混凝土箱涵技术状况评定方法探讨[J]. 交通运输研究,2015,1(2): 76-80.

[7] 覃乐勤,毛建平,蒋凌杰.基于层次分析法的涵洞技术状况评定[J].西部交通科技,2018(4):94-98.

[8] 贺国峰.基于层次分析法(AHP)的公路涵洞综合评价[J].中国公路,2018,5:100-101.

[9] 杨卓,戎晓力,卢浩等.基于熵权物元可拓理论的隧道塌方风险评估[J].安全与环境学报,2016,16(2):15-19.

[10] 高炜,张庆普,敦晓彪,等.基于改进的可拓层次分析法和动态加权的航天高技术综合评价研究[J].系统工程与电子技术,2016,38(1):102-109.

[11] Xu J S, Xu H, Sun R F, et al. Seismic risk evaluation for a planning mountain tunnel using improved analytical hierarchy process based on extension theory [J]. Journal of Mountain Science,2020,17(1):244-260.

[12] Ma L, Chen H, Yan H, et al. Post evaluation of distributed energy generation combining the attribute hierarchical model and matter-element extension theory [J]. Journal of Cleaner Production, 2018, 184 (20): 503-510.

[13] Zhou D, Qin P, Li W, et al. Quality Evaluation of Public Transport Service Based on AHP-Extensible Matter Element [J]. Open Journal of Transportation Technologies, 2020, 9 (3): 182-191.

[14] 韩亚坤,陈汉利.基于层次分析—可拓学的绿色建筑节能技术经济评价[J].工程管理学报,2018,32(5):18-23.

[15] Du Y, Zheng Y, Wu G, et al. Decision-making method of heavy-duty machine tool remanufacturing based on AHP-entropy weight and extension theory [J]. Journal of Cleaner Production,2020,252(10):119607.

[16] 赵德金,李冬阳,朴成道,等.基于AHP-熵权可拓学理论的加工中心可靠性评价研究[J].制造技术与机床,2021,11:114-119+126.

基于能量原理悬吊双层桥气动性能研究

洪　光*[1,2]　李加武[1]　王佳盈[1]

(1.长安大学公路学院;2.兰州理工大学土木工程学院)

摘　要　本文通过风洞试验对悬吊双层桥进行了节段模型测振试验,对悬吊双层断面振动加速度进行监控和采集,通过带通滤波器对加速度信号进行滤波处理,采用变分模态分解(VMD)法对振动信号进行模态分解,基于能量法对悬吊双层桥的气动性能进行分析。能量分析结果表明:下层断面输入能量来源于自激气动力与结构耦合阻尼力所做正功,输入能量与下层断面阻尼耗散能量平衡,导致下层断面颤振模态保持等幅振动形态;上层断面输入能量来源于结构耦合力所做正功,其在振动过程中不断向气流输出能量,上层断面的能量增量与其阻尼耗散能量平衡,导致上层断面保持等幅振动形态。

关键词　双层桥梁　气动性能　风洞试验　能量法　软颤振

0　引言

随着我国交通量的增长,双层桥面桥跨结构不仅能够实现不同交通流的渠化,而且能够减小下部结构工程量、缓解交通压力、提高车辆通行效率。因此,在大跨度桥梁桥跨结构设计中,双层桥面布置已成为重要发展趋势。

大跨度桥梁对风荷载动力作用异常敏感,极易诱发风致振动。在各种风致振动中,自激发散性颤振会导致桥梁结构整体风毁,因此大跨度桥梁颤振性能在桥梁抗风领域始终备受关注。国内外学者通过风洞试验,针对桥面开槽、中央稳定板、导流板等各种气动措施对单层桥面桁架梁颤振性能的影响进行了研究，侧重分析了各种气动措施的颤振抑制效果，但是针对气动措施颤振抑制机理及双层桥面桁架梁气动性能的研究较少。其中，徐昕宇等[1]分析了栏杆透风率与高度、桥面板中央开槽及中央稳定板等多种气动措施对双层桥面桁架梁颤振临界风速的影响，研究结果表明：上层桥面内侧不透风栏杆可以发挥上中央稳定板的效果，增大下层桥面外侧栏杆透风率能够提高颤振临界风速。李永乐等[2]对双层桥面铁路桥梁的静风特性进行了研究，分析了“车桥气动干扰”对车辆和桥梁静风气动力的影响。伍波等[3]通过风洞试验对双层桥面桁架梁的软颤振性能进行了研究，分析了风攻角和扭弯频率比对双层桥面桁架梁软颤振的影响，研究表明双层桥面桁架梁的软颤振振幅与发振风速具有唯一对应关系和稳定性，而与初始激励状态无关。截至目前，关于混凝土梁或钢箱梁双层桥气动性能的研究还很少。国内仅有李永乐等[4]对分离式公铁双层箱形梁桥的气动干扰进行了研究，采用“风—车—桥耦合振动”分析方法，分析了气动干扰对车辆行驶的影响。本文在大跨度悬索桥钢箱梁下部，通过吊杆悬吊钢箱梁，构造“悬吊双层桥面”，目前尚未见到类似“悬吊双层桥面”气动性能研究的相关文献资料。悬吊双层桥断面与分离双层断面相似，双层桥面之间也存在着气动干扰现象。气动干扰是近年桥梁抗风领域的研究热点，其中国内外学者刘小兵[5]、Jin 等[6]通过风洞试验对相邻上、下游桥梁或双幅桥的气动干扰问题进行了研究。

悬吊双层桥不仅存在气动干扰，而且双层断面之间存在结构静力耦合，所以与双层桥面桁架梁相比，其气动性能显得更加复杂。基于悬吊双层桥气动性能的研究现状，本文以扁平箱梁断面所构成的悬吊双层桥为研究对象，在风洞实验室通过节段模型测振试验，对其气动性能进行了研究。对试验获取的悬吊双层断面加速度信号，通过积分获取速度与位移信号，采用变分模态分解（VMD）法对振动信号进行模态分解，在此基础上通过能量原理对悬吊双层桥的气动性能进行分析。

1 悬吊双层桥风洞试验

1.1 试验概况

本文以悬吊双层桥为研究对象，在长安大学 CA-1 风洞实验室开展节段模型测振试验。悬吊双层断面（简称双层断面）上、下层断面共同构成了两质点四自由度的“弹簧-质量-阻尼”振动系统，如图 1 所示。

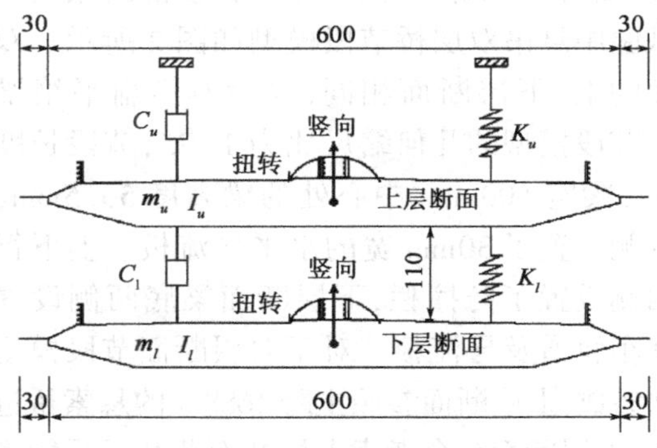

图 1 动力学振动模型简图（mm）

根据结构动力学，双层断面动力学方程组为：

$$m_l\ddot{h}_l(t)+C_{hl}\dot{h}_l(t)-C_{hl}\dot{h}_u(t)+K_{hl}h_l(t)-K_{hl}h_u(t)=F_l(t) \tag{1}$$

$$m_u\ddot{h}_u(t)-C_{hl}\dot{h}_l(t)+(C_{hl}+C_{hu})\dot{h}_u(t)-K_{hl}h_u(t)+(K_{hl}+K_{hu})h_u(t)=F_u(t) \tag{2}$$

$$I_l\ddot{\alpha}_l(t)+C_{\alpha l}\dot{\alpha}_l(t)-C_{\alpha l}\dot{\alpha}_u(t)+K_{\alpha l}\alpha_l(t)-K_{\alpha l}\alpha_u(t)=M_l(t) \tag{3}$$

$$I_u\ddot{\alpha}_u(t)-C_{\alpha l}\dot{\alpha}_l(t)+(C_{\alpha l}+C_{\alpha u})\dot{\alpha}_u(t)-K_{\alpha l}\alpha_l(t)+(K_{\alpha l}+K_{\alpha u})\alpha_u(t)=M_u(t) \tag{4}$$

其中，m_l、C_{hl}、K_{hl} 分别为下层断面竖向振动的单位长度等效质量、固有阻尼、固有刚度；I_l、$C_{\alpha l}$、$K_{\alpha l}$ 分别为下层断面扭转振动的单位长度等效质量惯性矩、固有阻尼、固有刚度；m_u、C_{hu}、K_{hu} 分别为上层断面竖向振动的单位长度等效质量、固有阻尼、固有刚度；I_u、$C_{\alpha u}$、$K_{\alpha u}$ 分别为上层断面扭转振动的单位长度等效质量惯性矩、固有阻尼、固有刚度；$\ddot{h}_l(t)$、$\dot{h}_l(t)$、$h_l(t)$ 分别为下层断面 t 时刻竖向振动加速度、速度、位移；$\ddot{h}_u(t)$、$\dot{h}$、$h_u(t)$ 分别为上层断面 t 时刻竖向振动加速度、速度、位移；$\ddot{\alpha}_l(t)$、$\dot{\alpha}_l(t)$、$\alpha_l(t)$ 分别为下层断面 t 时刻扭转振动加速度、速度与位移；$\ddot{\alpha}_u(t)$、$\dot{\alpha}_u(t)$、$\alpha_u(t)$ 分别为上层断面 t 时刻扭转振动加速度、速度、位移；$F_l(t)$、$M_l(t)$ 分别为下层断面 t 时刻升力、升力矩；$F_u(t)$、

$M_u(t)$分别为上层断面t时刻升力、升力矩。各变量下标含义分别为:下标l表示下层断面,下标u表示下层断面,下标h表示竖向振动,下标α表示扭转振动。为了反映双层桥断面振动特性,节段模型上层断面通过 8 根弹簧悬挂在支架上,下层断面通过 4 根弹簧悬挂在上层断面上。梁端设置了椭圆形二元端板,二元端板固定于上层断面并与下层断面分离,不仅可以消除双层断面的梁端效应,而且可以保证下层断面能够自由振动。风洞试验中悬吊双层桥节段模型如图 2 所示。双层断面的上、下层断面相同,均为典型扁平箱梁断面。节段模型的几何缩尺比为 1∶75,节段长度为 1.5m,梁宽 600mm,中心处的梁高度 56.5mm,梁端两侧设置了 30mm 宽的水平导流板。上下行车道两侧设置了防撞栏,下层断面梁底两侧设置了检修车轨道及导流板。对于双层断面节段模型的振动参数,上层断面参照主跨 1688m 的悬索桥进行设计,下层断面综合考虑上层断面荷载承受能力及弹簧拉伸等因素人为选取振动参数进行设计。

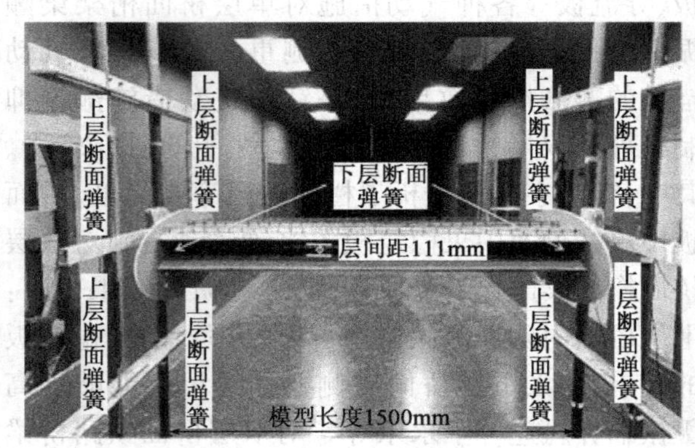

图 2　风洞试验悬吊双层扁平箱梁节段模型照片

试验过程中,通过加速度传感器与数据采集仪分别对上、下层断面的加速度信号进行监控和采集,作为能量法分析双层断面气动性能的基础数据。在施加风速前,通过人工激励获取双层断面节段模型的加速度信号,采用"对数衰减法"对上、下层断面固有振动特性进行识别,其振动特性如表 1 所示。

双层断面振动特性表　　表 1

位　置	单位长度等效质量(kg·m⁻¹)	单位长度等效扭转质量惯性矩(kg·m²/m)	竖向振动频率(Hz)	扭转振动频率(Hz)	竖向振动阻尼比	扭转振动阻尼比
上层断面	11.756	0.43	4.45	9.58	0.36%	0.40%
下层断面	6.26	0.15	2.01	2.19	0.97%	0.50%

1.2　风洞试验结果

1.2.1　双层断面的气动响应

在试验过程中,风速由 1m/s 逐级增大至 6.2m/s:在 1m/s 至 4m/s 风速区间,风速间距为 0.5m/s;在 4m/s 至 5.8m/s 风速区间,风速间距为 0.3m/s;在 5.8m/s 至 6.2m/s 风速区间,风速间距为 0.2m/s。

对于双层断面而言,上层断面固有竖向、扭转振动频率分别为 4.45Hz、9.58Hz,下层断面固有竖向、扭转振动频率分别为 2.01Hz、2.19Hz。因此,选取中心频率 2.5Hz 带宽 1Hz 和中心频率 6.5Hz 带宽 7Hz 的矩形滤波器,分别对上、下层断面加速度信号进行频域滤波处理,根据加速度滤波信号进行频域积分获取速度与位移信号。在 6.2m/s 风速下,上、下层断面加速度滤波时程曲线如图 3、图 4 所示。从图中可以看出:在 6.2m/s 风速下,上层断面竖向振动频率为 2Hz ~ 3Hz,而扭转振动频率为 3Hz ~ 10Hz;下层断面的竖向与扭转振动频率均为 2Hz ~ 3Hz。

双层断面卓越振动频率随风速变化规律如图 5 所示,其加速度 RMS 值随风速变化曲线如图 6 所示。上、下层断面振动频率与 RMS 值随风速变化趋势表明:在风速高于 5.5m/s 时,下层断面竖向与扭转振幅均突变增大,竖向与扭转振动的频率均为 2.258Hz,可以判明下层断面发生弯扭耦合颤振,其颤振临界风速介于 5.5m/s 与 5.8m/s 之间。根据《公路桥梁抗风设计规范》(JTG/T 3360-01—2018)中扁平箱梁颤振临界风速估算公式(5),下层断面颤振临界风速为 6.15m/s。由此可见,下层断面在上层断面气动干扰下颤振临界风速有所降低。

$$U_f = 2.5\eta_s\eta_\alpha\sqrt{\mu\frac{r}{b}}f_t B \tag{5}$$

其中,U_f为颤振临界风速;η_s为形状系数,带分流板的扁平箱梁为 0.80;η_α为攻角效应系数,带分流板的扁平箱梁为 0.80;$\mu = m/2\pi\rho b^2$,m为竖向振动等效质量,ρ为空气密度 1.225kg/m³,b为半桥宽;r

为截面回转半径，$r=\sqrt{\frac{I}{m}}$，I 为扭转振动等效质量惯性矩；f_t 为扭转振动频率，B 为截面宽度，$B=2b$。

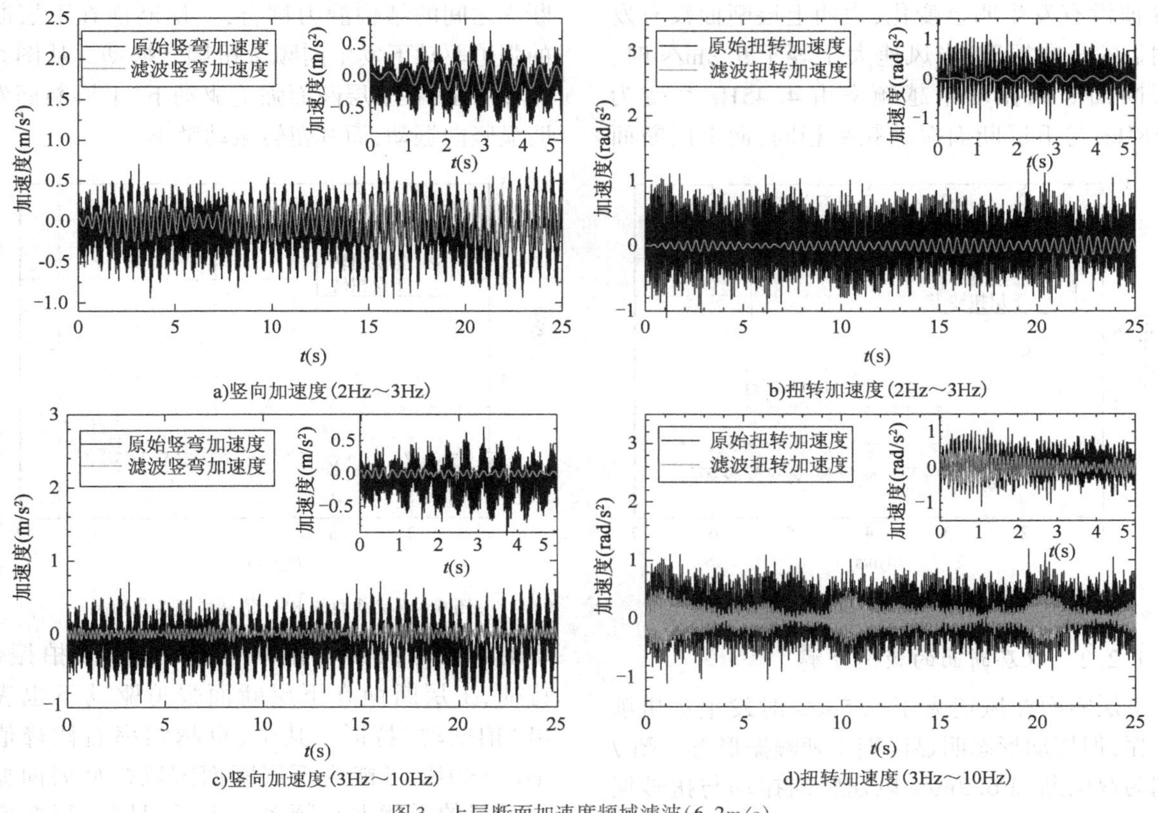

图3 上层断面加速度频域滤波(6.2m/s)

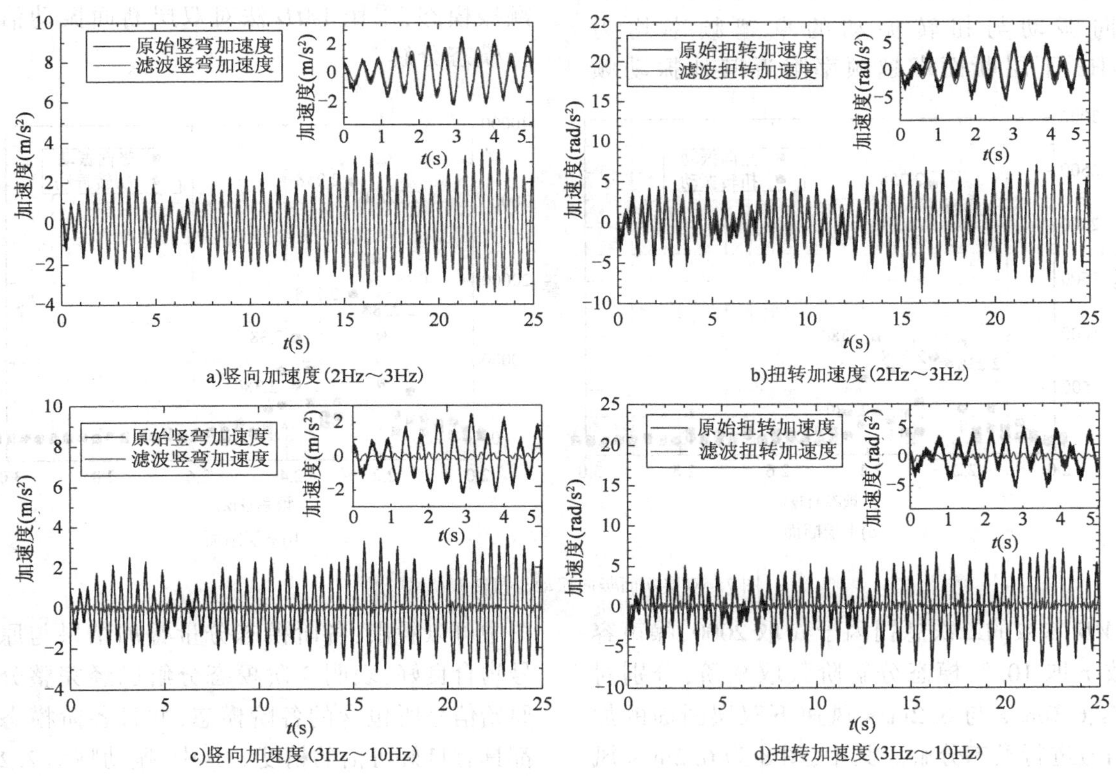

图4 下层断面加速度频域滤波(6.2m/s)

当风速小于5.8m/s时,上层断面竖向振动频率基本保持在竖向振动固有频率4.45Hz附近,*RMS*值没有发生明显变化,表明上层断面没有发生明显的竖向振动;当风速大于等于5.8m/s时,上层断面竖向振动卓越频率由4.45Hz突变为2.258Hz,与下层断面振动频率相同,而上层断面扭转振动卓越频率始终保持在其扭转振动固有频率9.58Hz附近。根据结构动力学可知,由于双层断面之间的结构静力耦合,上层断面在下层断面的强迫驱动下发生同频弯扭耦合振动。从图6中可以看出,在下层断面强迫驱动下,上层断面发生明显竖向振动,而其扭转振动微小。

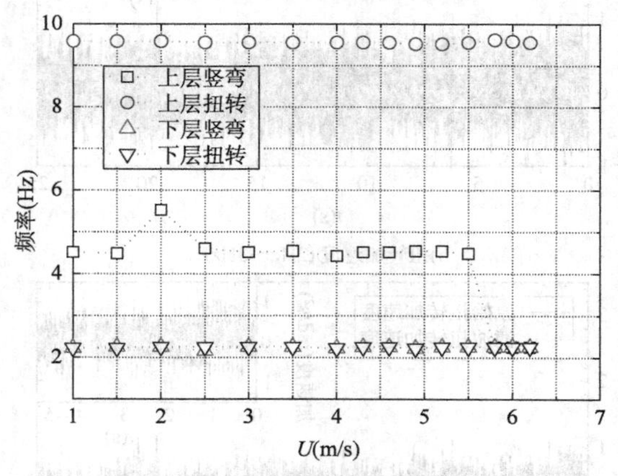

图5　双层断面卓越频率随风速变化情况

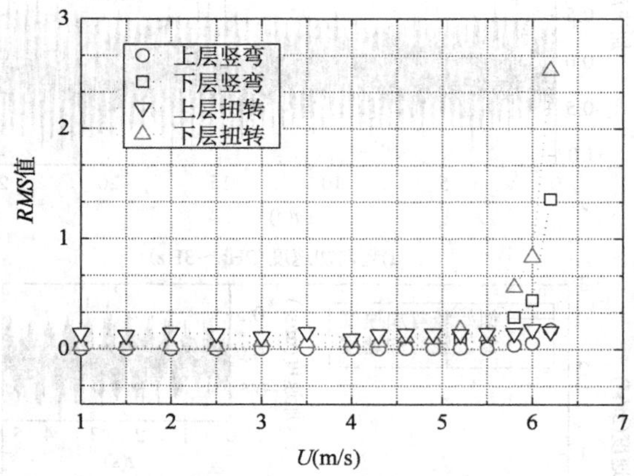

图6　双层断面的RMS值随风速变化情况

1.2.2　双层断面的模态分解

下层断面在风速大于5.5m/s时发生弯扭耦合颤振,但振动形态明显区别于硬颤振形态。图7分别为双层断面6.2m/s风速竖向振动与扭转振动加速度幅频谱。从图中可以看出,上、下层断面竖向振动与扭转振动的卓越频率均为2.258Hz,下层断面卓越频率附近其他振动频率的干扰导致其弯扭耦合振动呈现"拍振动"特征,上层断面在下层断面强迫驱动下也表现出"拍振动"特征。其中,卓越频率右侧峰值频率2.380Hz可能为下层断面节段模型展向振动所引起的干扰振动频率。为了识别双层断面的颤振模态,采用*VMD*法对双层断面振动信号进行模态分解。

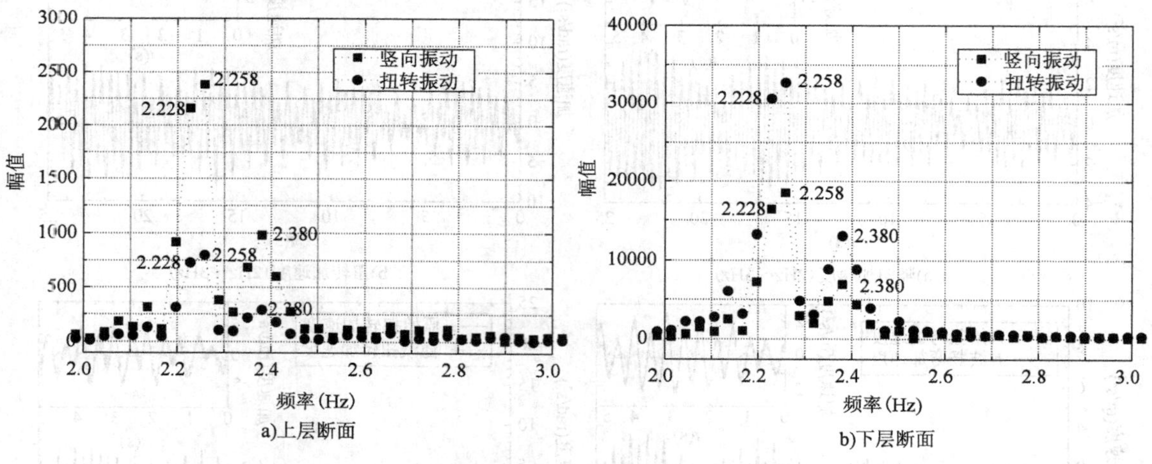

图7　双层断面竖向振动与扭转振动幅频谱

*VMD*参数的二次惩罚因子α取2000,噪声容限参数τ取10^{-6},模态分解阶数取9阶,分别对5.8m/s、6.0m/s与6.2m/s风速下双层断面的加速度信号进行模态分解。其中,图8为6.2m/s风速时,下层断面*VMD*所识别的各阶模态分量。从图中可以看出,各阶模态分量叠加结果与原始信号吻合良好,表明9阶模态分解已经完整分解出原始信号所包含的各阶模态,并且各阶模态分量都具有良好可信的精度。其中,振动频率2.258Hz模态分量即为下层断面在6.2m/s风速下的颤振

模态。在5.8m/s、6.0m/s 风速下,*VMD* 所识别的颤振模态也表现为等幅振动。

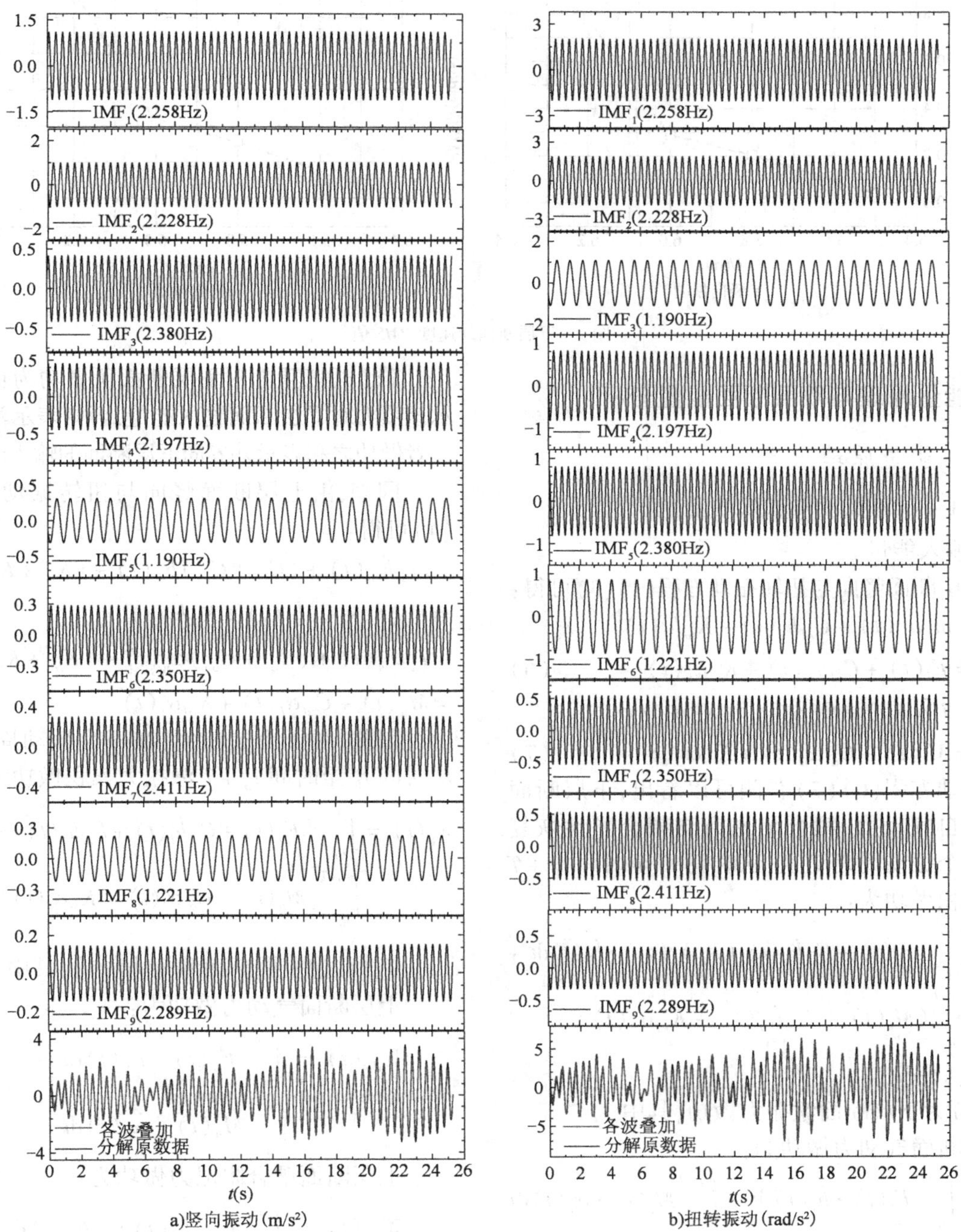

图8 下层断面加速度各阶模态($U=6.2\text{m/s}$)

下层断面弯扭耦合颤振加速度 *RMS* 值随风速变化状况如图9所示。从图中可以看出,当风速大于5.5m/s时,下层断面竖向、扭转振幅均随风速增加缓慢增大,并且在各级风速下下层断面弯扭耦合颤振形态均为等幅振动,其振幅并没有随风速增加呈现发散性。近年有关颤振的研究成果表明,颤振可以分为"硬颤振"与"软颤振"。其中,"硬颤振"具有明显的颤振临界风速,当风速超过颤振临界风速后发生明显的发散性振动;而"软颤振"在风速超过颤振临界风速后并不出现发散性振动,而是随风速增加表现出多个稳定振幅状态。由此可以判明下层断面的弯扭耦合颤振属于"软颤振"范畴。

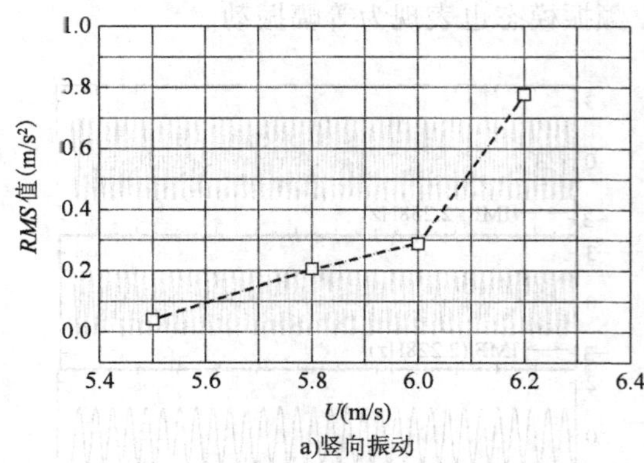

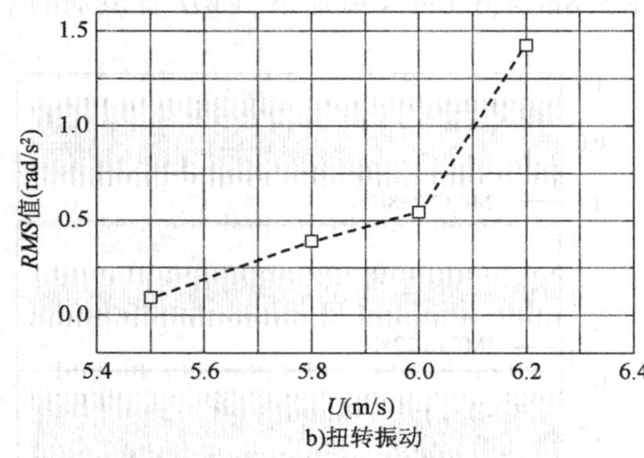

图9　下层断面加速度 *RMS* 值

2　能量原理与双层断面能量分析

2.1　能量原理

2.1.1　输入能量与耗散能量

(1)输入能量。

由下层断面竖向与扭转振动方程(1)(3)可得：

$$m_l\ddot{h}_l(t)+C_{hl}\dot{h}_l(t)+K_{hl}h_l(t)=F_l(t)+C_{hl}\dot{h}_u(t)+K_{hl}h_u(t) \tag{6}$$

$$I_l\ddot{\alpha}_l(t)+C_{\alpha l}\dot{\alpha}_l(t)+K_{\alpha l}\alpha_l(t)=M_l(t)+C_{\alpha l}\dot{\alpha}_u(t)+K_{\alpha l}\alpha_u(t) \tag{7}$$

从振动方程(6)(7)右侧可以看出,下层断面激振力来自气动力、耦合阻尼力与耦合弹性恢复力。在一个振动周期 T 上,从时间 t_0 至时间 t_0+T 激振力累积做功为：

$$W_l(t)=\int_{t_0}^{t_0+T}(F_l(t)+C_{hl}\dot{h}_u(t)+K_{hl}h_u(t))\cdot\dot{h}_l(t)\mathrm{d}t+\int_{t_0}^{t_0+T}(M_l(t)+C_{\alpha l}\dot{\alpha}_u(t)+K_{\alpha l}\alpha_u(t))\cdot\dot{\alpha}_l(t)\mathrm{d}t$$

$W_l(t)$为下层断面激振力做功,其中,

下层断面气动力做功为：

$$W_{Fl}(t)=\int_{t_0}^{t_0+T}F_l(t)\cdot\dot{h}_l(t)\mathrm{d}t+\int_{t_0}^{t_0+T}M_l(t)\cdot\dot{\alpha}_l(t)\mathrm{d}t$$

下层断面耦合阻尼力做功为：

$$W_{Cl}(t)=\int_{t_0}^{t_0+T}(C_{hl}\dot{h}_u(t))\cdot\dot{h}_l(t)\mathrm{d}t+\int_{t_0}^{t_0+T}(C_{\alpha l}\dot{\alpha}_u(t))\cdot\dot{\alpha}_l(t)\mathrm{d}t$$

下层断面耦合弹性恢复力做功为：

$$W_{Kl}(t)=\int_{t_0}^{t_0+T}(K_{hl}h_u(t))\cdot\dot{h}_l(t)\mathrm{d}t+\int_{t_0}^{t_0+T}(K_{\alpha l}\alpha_u(t))\cdot\dot{\alpha}_l(t)\mathrm{d}t$$

若上述三项力对下层断面所做功为正功,则表示该项力对下层断面输入能量,否则表示消耗能量。三者做功之和表示外界向下层断面的输入能量。

同理,由上层断面竖向与扭转振动方程(2)(4)可得：

$$m_u\ddot{h}_u(t)+(C_{hl}+C_{hu})\dot{h}_u(t)+(K_{hl}+K_{hu})h_u(t)=F_u(t)+C_{hl}\dot{h}_l(t)+K_{hl}h_l(t) \tag{8}$$

$$I_u\ddot{\alpha}_u(t)+(C_{\alpha l}+C_{\alpha u})\dot{\alpha}_u(t)+(K_{\alpha l}+K_{\alpha u})\alpha_u(t)=M_u(t)+C_{\alpha l}\dot{\alpha}_l(t)+K_{\alpha l}\alpha_l(t) \tag{9}$$

因此,对于上层断面,在一个振动周期 T 上,从时间 t_0 至时间 t_0+T 激振力累积做功为：

$$W_u(t)=\int_{t_0}^{t_0+T}[F_u(t)+C_{hl}\dot{h}_l(t)+K_{hl}h_l(t)]\cdot\dot{h}_u(t)\mathrm{d}t+\int_{t_0}^{t_0+T}[M_u(t)+C_{\alpha l}\dot{\alpha}_l(t)+K_{\alpha l}\alpha_l(t)]\cdot\dot{\alpha}_u(t)\mathrm{d}t$$

$W_u(t)$为上层断面激振力做功,其中,

上层断面气动力做功为：

$$W_{Fu}(t)=\int_{t_0}^{t_0+T}F_u(t)\cdot\dot{h}_u(t)\mathrm{d}t+\int_{t_0}^{t_0+T}M_u(t)\cdot\dot{\alpha}_u(t)\mathrm{d}t$$

上层断面耦合阻尼力做功为：

$$W_{Cu}(t)=\int_{t_0}^{t_0+T}(C_{hl}\dot{h}_l(t))\cdot\dot{h}_u(t)\mathrm{d}t+\int_{t_0}^{t_0+T}(C_{\alpha l}\dot{\alpha}_l(t))\cdot\dot{\alpha}_u(t)\mathrm{d}t$$

上层断面耦合弹性恢复力做功为：

$$W_{Ku}(t)=\int_{t_0}^{t_0+T}(K_{hl}h_l(t))\cdot\dot{h}_u(t)\mathrm{d}t+\int_{t_0}^{t_0+T}(K_{\alpha l}\alpha_l(t))\cdot\dot{\alpha}_u(t)\mathrm{d}t$$

若上述三项力对上层断面所做功为正功,则表示该项力对上层断面输入能量,否则表示消耗能量。

三者做功之和表示外界向上层断面的输入能量。

(2)耗散能量。

上层断面与下层断面结构阻尼耗散能量分别为:

$$W_{Du}(t)=\int_{t_0}^{t_0+T}[(C_{hu}+C_{hl})\dot{h}_u(t)]\cdot\dot{h}_u(t)\mathrm{d}t+\int_{t_0}^{t_0+T}[(C_{\alpha u}+C_{\alpha l})\dot{\alpha}_u(t)]\cdot\dot{\alpha}_u(t)\mathrm{d}t \quad (10)$$

$$W_{Dl}(t)=\int_{t_0}^{t_0+T}(C_{hl}\dot{h}_l(t))\cdot\dot{h}_l(t)\mathrm{d}t+\int_{t_0}^{t_0+T}(C_{\alpha l}\dot{\alpha}_l(t))\cdot\dot{\alpha}_l(t)\mathrm{d}t \quad (11)$$

2.1.2 稳定性判断准则

当输入断面能量大于结构阻尼耗散能量,即 $W_l(T)>W_{Dl}(T)$ 或 $W_u(T)>W_{Du}(T)$ 时,随着时间的增加振动系统能量不断增加,振动趋向发散;当输入断面能量等于机构阻尼耗散能量,即 $W_l(T)=W_{Dl}(T)$ 或 $W_u(T)=W_{Du}(T)$ 时,断面输入能量被阻尼消耗掉,振动处于等幅振动状态;当输入断面能量小于阻尼耗散能量,即 $W_l(T)<W_{Dl}(T)$ 或 $W_u(T)<W_{Du}(T)$ 时,随着时间的增加振动系统的能量不断减小,振动不断衰减。因此,可将能量增量作为振动稳定性判断准则:

$$\Delta E_l(\mathrm{t})=W_l(T)-W_{Dl}(T)=0 \quad (12)$$

$$\Delta E_u(\mathrm{t})=W_u(T)-W_{Du}(T)=0 \quad (13)$$

2.2 双层断面能量分析

基于双层断面 *RMS* 值随风速的变化趋势可以看出,下层断面在风速超过5.5m/s时发生软颤振。因此,在试验风速5.8m/s、6.0m/s、6.2m/s下,对双层断面展开能量分析。采用"梯形"数值积分方法,在一个完整振动周期上分别计算出气动力、耦合阻尼力与耦合弹性恢复力做功和结构阻尼耗散能量。

2.2.1 上层断面能量分析

在一个完整振动周期上,上层断面在5.8m/s至6.2m/s风速范围内,能量随时间变化规律相似。其中,图10分别为6.2m/s风速上层断面竖向振动能量随时间累积变化曲线图及单位周期累积能量柱状图。从图中可以看出,在竖向振动模态上,上层断面单位周期气动力累积做功为负值,表明上层断面向气流输出能量。竖向振动耦合阻尼力 $C_{hl}\dot{h}_l(t)$ 对上层断面做正功,并随时间呈线性增加,表明下层断面通过耦合阻尼力不断向上层断面竖向振动输入能量。

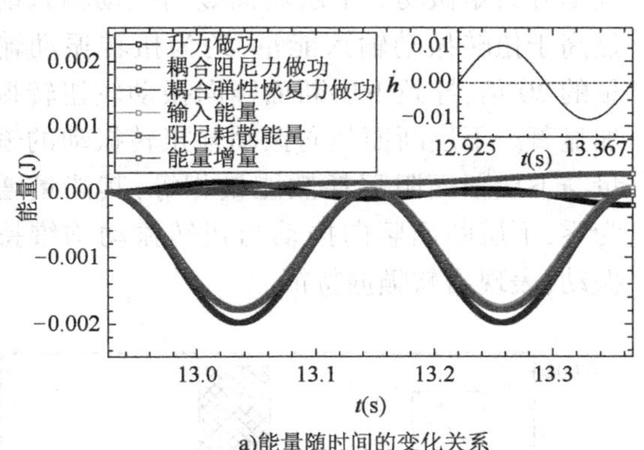

a)能量随时间的变化关系

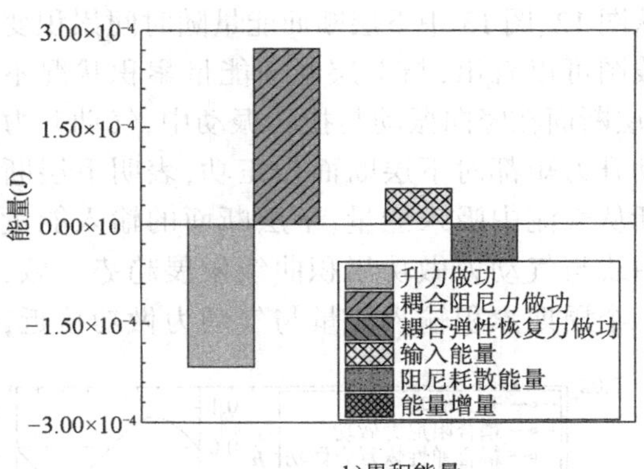

b)累积能量

图10 上层断面竖向振动能量

设下层断面软颤振竖向振动位移为 $h_l(t)=A_{hl}\sin(\omega_h t)$,上层断面与下层断面竖向振动基本同频同相,设上层断面竖向振动位移为 $h_u(t)=A_{hu}\sin(\omega_h t)$,则上层断面竖向振动速度 $\dot{h}_u(t)=\omega_h A_{hu}\cos(\omega_h t)$。根据能量计算公式,耦合弹性恢复力在 t_0 至时间单位振动周期上做功为:

$$W_{Ku}(t)=\int_{t_0}^{t_0+T}(K_{hl}h_l(t))\cdot\dot{h}_u(t)\mathrm{d}t=\int_{t_0}^{t_0+T}(K_{hl}A_{hl}\sin(\omega_h t))\cdot\omega_h A_{hu}\cos(\omega_h t)dt=0$$

其中,振动周期 $T=2\pi/\omega_h$,表明竖向振动耦合弹性恢复力 $K_{hl}h_l(t)$ 对上层断面做功为零,没有向上层断面输入能量。综合以上分析可以判明,上层断面竖向振动的输入能量来源于下层断面通过耦合阻尼力所做正功。图11分别为6.2m/s风速上层断面扭转振动能量随时间累积变化曲线图及单位周期累积能量柱状图。从图中可以看出,上层断面气动升力矩对上层断面做负功,上层断面向气流输出能量；扭转振动耦合阻尼力 $C_{\alpha l}\dot{\alpha}_l(t)$ 对上层断面做正功，并随时间呈线性增加，表明下层断面通过耦合阻尼力不断向上层断面扭转振动输入能量；扭转振动耦合弹性恢复力 $K_{\alpha l}\alpha_l(t)$ 对上层断面做功为零。上层断面竖向、扭转振动的输入能量与其阻尼耗散能量相等，能量增量为零。因此，上层断面竖向与扭转振动均表现为等幅振动。同时，上层断面竖向振动输入能量显著高于扭转振动输入能量，导致上层断面竖向振动显著。

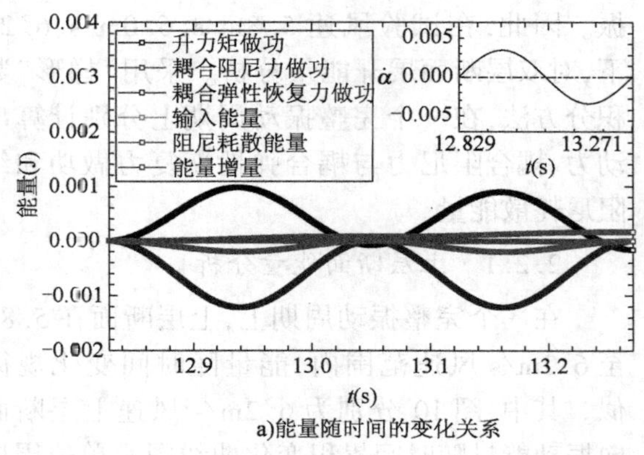

a)能量随时间的变化关系

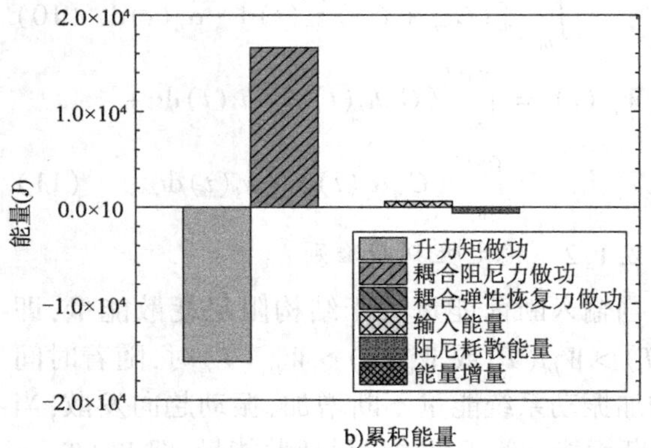

b)累积能量

图 11　上层断面扭转振动能量

2.2.2　下层断面能量分析

下层断面在 5.8m/s 至 6.2m/s 风速范围内，能量随时间变化规律相似。其中，图 12、图 13 分别为 6.2m/s 风速下层断面竖向、扭转振动能量随时间累积变化曲线图及单位周期累积能量柱状图。从图 12、图 13 中下层断面能量随时间累积变化曲线图可以看出，与上层断面能量累积状况不同，下层断面在竖向振动与扭转振动中，气动升力与气动升力矩都对下层断面做正功，表明下层断面不断从气流中吸入能量；下层断面的输入能量累积曲线与气动力做功累积曲线发展趋势一致，并且一个周期累积输入能量与气动力做功接近，表明下层断面的输入能量主要来源于气动力做功。从图 12、图 13 下层断面单位周期累积能量柱状图中可以看出，下层断面竖向振动输入能量近 90% 来自气动升力做功，其余来自耦合阻尼力做功，而下层断面扭转振动输入能量几乎全部来自气动升力矩做功。下层断面竖向振动输入能量明显高于扭转振动输入能量，约为扭转振动输入能量的 20 倍，导致下层断面竖向振动较扭转振动更加显著。下层断面竖向振动与扭转振动的输入能量与下层断面阻尼耗散能量相等，其能量增量均为零，下层断面竖向振动与扭转振动均维持等幅振动，表现出软颤振特征。

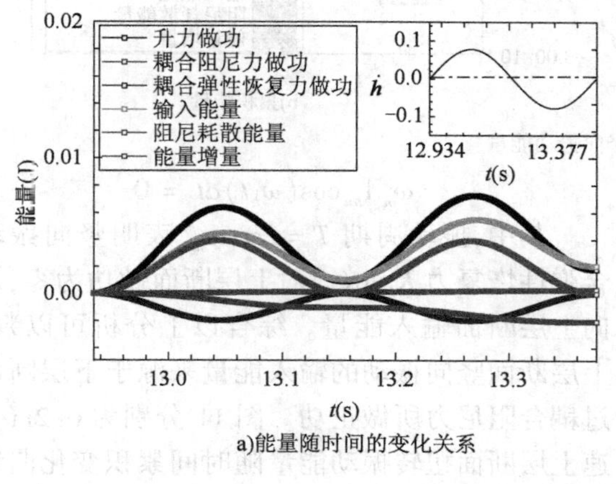

a)能量随时间的变化关系

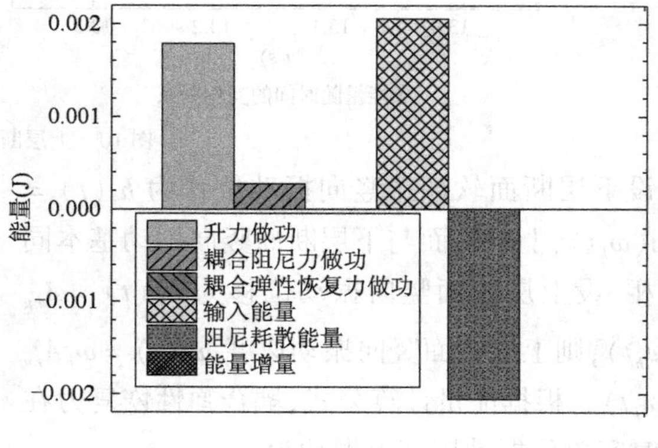

b)累积能量

图 12　下层断面竖向振动能量

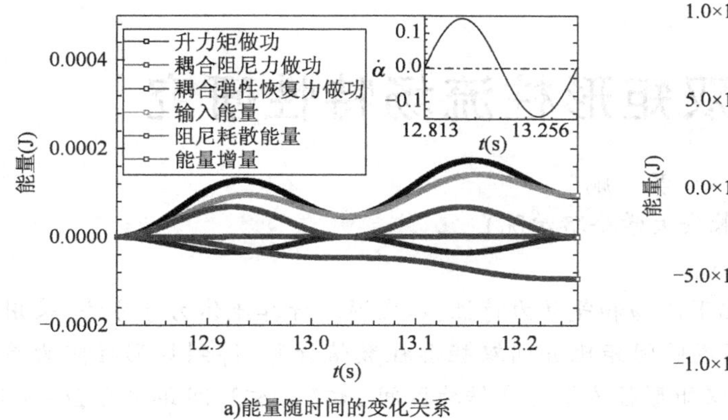

a)能量随时间的变化关系

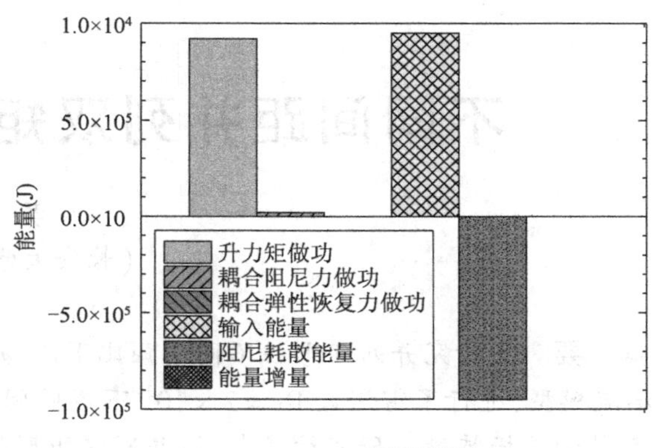

b)累积能量

图 13 下层断面扭转振动能量

3 结语

本文通过风洞节段模型测振试验，采用能量方法对悬吊双层桥气动性能进行了分析，综合分析结果得出以下结论：

（1）在上层断面气动干扰下，当风速达到颤振临界风速时下层断面发生弯扭耦合软颤振，并且其颤振模态倾向于竖向振动；由于双层断面之间的结构静力耦合，上层断面在结构耦合力强迫驱动下发生相同频率弯扭耦合振动；对于双层断面振动系统，下层断面软颤振导致整个振动系统发生软颤振。

（2）上层断面竖向振动与扭转振动的输入能量均来自耦合阻尼力所做正功，上层断面气动升力与升力矩均做负功，表明上层断面在振动过程中主动拍击周边气流，不断向周边气流输出能量。下层断面输入能量主要来源于下层断面气动力所做正功，结构静力耦合力对其输入能量贡献不大，尤其是下层断面扭转振动输入能量几乎全部来自气动升力矩所做正功；下层断面竖向振动输入能量显著高于扭转振动输入能量，导致下层断面软颤振模态倾向于竖向振动；随着风速的增加下层断面输入能量增加，虽然下层断面竖向与扭转振幅不断增大，但输入能量与阻尼耗散能量始终保持平衡，导致下层断面弯扭耦合颤振始终保持等幅软颤振形态。

本文在下层断面的振动参数设计过程中，人为选取了扭弯频率比接近于 1 的极端情况，这与悬吊双层桥梁实际情况存在着一定差异，但对悬吊双层桥梁颤振性能的认识具有一定的借鉴意义。后续研究将会进一步完善，深入研究悬吊双层断面的颤振性能。

参考文献

[1] 徐昕宇，李永乐，廖海黎，等. 双层桥面桁架梁三塔悬索桥颤振性能优化风洞试验[J]. 工程力学，2017，34(5)：142-147.

[2] 李永乐，徐昕宇，郭建明，等. 六线双层铁路钢桁桥车桥系统气动特性风洞试验研究[J]. 工程力学，2016，33(4)：130-135.

[3] 伍波，王骑，廖海黎. 双层桥面桁架梁软颤振特性风洞试验研究[J]. 振动与冲击，2020，39(1)：191-198.

[4] 李永乐，姜孝伟，苏洋，等. 分离式公铁双层桥面相互气动干扰及对列车走行性的影响[J]. 振动与冲击，2016，35(9)：74-78+93.

[5] 刘小兵，李少杰，杨群，等. 并列双箱梁的气动干扰效应对阻力系数的影响[J]. 中国公路学报，2017，30(11)：108-113.

[6] Jin P, Kim S, Kim H K. Effect of gap distance on vortex-induced vibration in two parallel cable-stayed bridges [J]. Journal of Wind Engineering and Industrial Aerodynamics, 2017, 162: 35-44.

不同间距并列双矩形柱流场特性研究

吴　鹏*
(长安大学公路学院)

摘　要　为研究并列矩形柱不同间距比下流场和气动力特性,本文通过计算流体力学方法,采用κ-ω SST湍流模型,进行了雷诺数 $Re = 2 \times 10^3$ 下不同间距比并列双矩形柱数值计算,得到矩形柱阻力系数、升力系数和流场特性。研究结果表明:并列双矩形柱流场存在转换区间 $2 \leqslant L/D \leqslant 3$,间距比 $L/D \geqslant 3$ 时每一个矩形柱流场逐渐接近单矩形柱流场,$L/D \leqslant 2$ 时整个流场类似于单矩形柱;$L/D \geqslant 3$ 时两个矩形柱阻力系数相等,升力系数绝对值相等;$L/D < 3$ 时两矩形柱气动力系数不再相同。

关键词　桥梁工程　流场特性　数值模拟　并列双矩形柱

0　引言

并列双矩形柱结构广泛应用在桥梁结构等实际工程中。流体流过双矩形柱时,两矩形柱间距将会影响流场,进而导致气动力系数发生变化,可能对结构产生不利影响,并且这一影响不能忽视[1]。

许多学者研究了矩形柱气动力、流场特性与结构截面宽厚比(B/D)的关系(B 为顺风向宽度、D 为横风向厚度)。研究表明,矩形柱平均阻力系数在 $B/D = 2$ 左右达到最小值[2]。杜晓庆等[3]研究单矩形柱流场特性,结果表明 $B/D = 1$、2 时矩形柱分离剪切层不会产生再附现象,并且 $B/D = 2$ 时矩形柱在尾流附近存在二次旋涡。王新荣等[4]研究了低紊流度下 B/D 为 2、2.5、3 等工况下的风压特性,发现 $B/D = 2$ 时,矩形柱侧面处于分离剪切层旋涡中。

(1)串列双柱情况下。杨青等[5]基于浸入式边界方法研究不同雷诺数以及间距下柱间流场以及气动力系数,表明 $Re = 200$ 时前柱屏蔽效应随间距比增大而减弱,流场失去稳态特征的临界距离为 $5D$;$Re = 300$ 时流场失去稳定特征的临界距离减少为 $3D$。邵林媛等[6]采用CFD方法,开展不同串列矩形柱数值模拟,发现气动力系数存在临界间距,该临界间距的范围是 $3D \sim 3.2D$。丁林等[7]研究不同间距串列双方柱发现,当双方柱间距大于 $4D$ 时,上游方柱振动响应同单柱相似;当双方柱间距为 $4D$ 时,上、下游方柱达到最大振幅,分别为 $1.06D$ 和 $1.1D$。

(2)并列双柱情况下。吴倩云等[8]通过实验研究发现,当间距在 $1.2D \sim 2.5D$ 时,并列双方柱内侧面平均风压系数干扰明显,平均阻力系数和脉动升力系数干扰效应为减小效应;当间距大于 $2.5D$ 时,气动力系数干扰效应均不明显。赵小军等[9]采用大涡模拟的方法对并排双方柱绕流流场进行数值模拟,计算得到方柱绕流速度场和涡量场。郑宇华等[10]对并列矩形柱进行PIV试验,结果表明矩形柱间距在 $1.3D \sim 1.4D$ 时存在临界值,在临界值以外两矩形柱开缝下方形成的旋涡数量、形态及紊流强度有较大差异。

综上所述,当前有关并列双柱情况的研究针对双方柱进行较多,但是对双矩形柱研究较少。对此,本文采用数值模拟方法,针对雷诺数 $Re = 2 \times 10^3$,宽高比为1:2的并列双矩形柱,研究不同间距下矩形柱气动特性和流场。

1　数值模拟模型

图1所示为本文数值计算的计算域。图1a)代表数值计算采用的流场尺寸,计算域入口到矩形柱几何形心的距离为 $10D$,计算域出口到矩形柱几何中心的距离为 $30D$,上下边界与矩形柱几何中心的距离为 $10D$;图1b)表示并列两矩形柱的几何关系,L 代表两矩形柱几何中心竖向距离,本文计算 L/D 分别为1.5、2、3、4、5总共5个工况。

计算边界采用速度入口,来流为均匀流,风速为 U_0(根据矩形柱横风向厚度 D、雷诺数 $Re = 2 \times 10^2$ 确定);计算域上下边界设置为无滑移对称边界;出口边界设置为压力出口。计算采用 κ-ω SST

湍流模型,求解方法采用 SIMPLEC 二阶隐式算法,时间步设置为 0.025s。

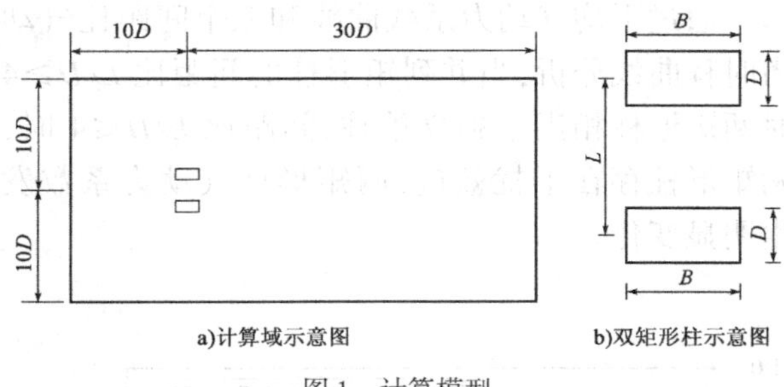

图1 计算模型

计算使用结构化网格,整体网格如图2所示。计算模型局部网格如图3所示,第一层网格的高度设置为0.001D,近壁面网格高度增长率设置为1.08。

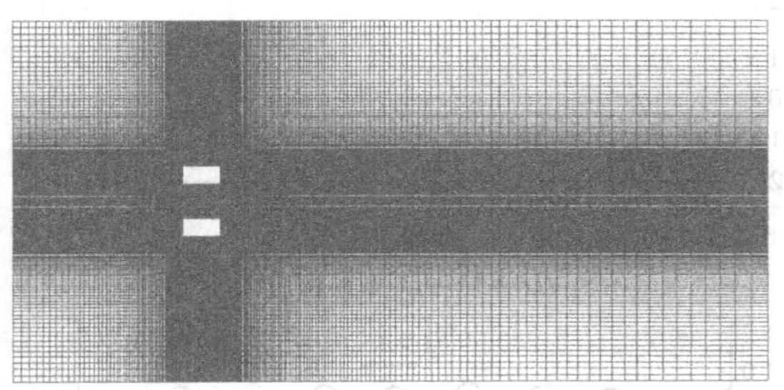

图2 整体网格

图3 局部网格

2 数值模拟结果分析

2.1 气动力分析

定义矩形柱的升力系数和阻力系数为:

$$C_L = \frac{1}{2}\frac{F_L}{\rho U_0^2 B};C_D = \frac{1}{2}\frac{F_D}{\rho U_0^2 D} \tag{1}$$

式中,F_L 和 F_D 分别为单位长度矩形柱气动升力和气动阻力;ρ 为空气密度。

图4表明,矩形柱间距 $L/D=4$、5 时,上下两个矩形柱阻力系数基本相等,为1.66;$L/D=3$ 时,上下两个矩形柱阻力系数基本相等,为1.78;$L/D=2$ 时上下矩形柱阻力系数相差较小,上部为1.79、下部为1.84;$L/D=1.5$ 时上下矩形柱阻力系数相差最大,上部为1.96、下部为1.73。图5表明,矩形柱间距 $L/D=3$、4、5 时,上下两个矩形柱升力系数绝对值基本相等,分别为0.57、0.36、0.85;$L/D=2$ 时上下矩形柱升力系数绝对值不相同,上部为0.8、下部为0.91;$L/D=1.5$ 时上下矩形柱升力系数绝对值相差最大,上部为0.15、下部为0.73。通过对比分析不同间距比的升力系数和阻力系数,可以认为,当 $L/D \geqslant 3$ 时,上部和下部矩形柱的流场的相互影响较小;当间距比 $L/D<3$ 时,上下两个矩形柱的气动力系数变化显著,存在两个矩形柱流场的相互影响。

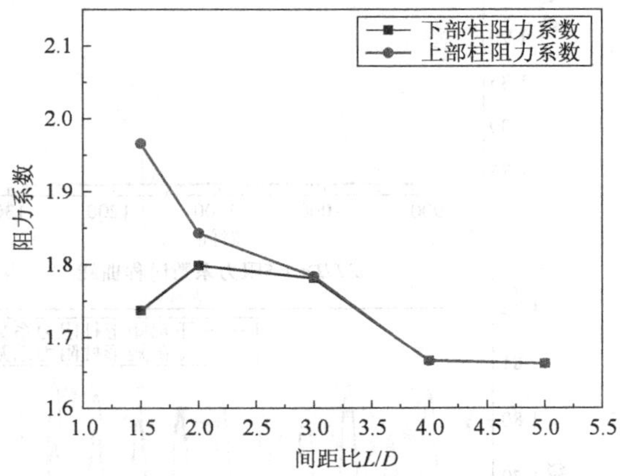

图4 上下部矩形柱平均阻力系数

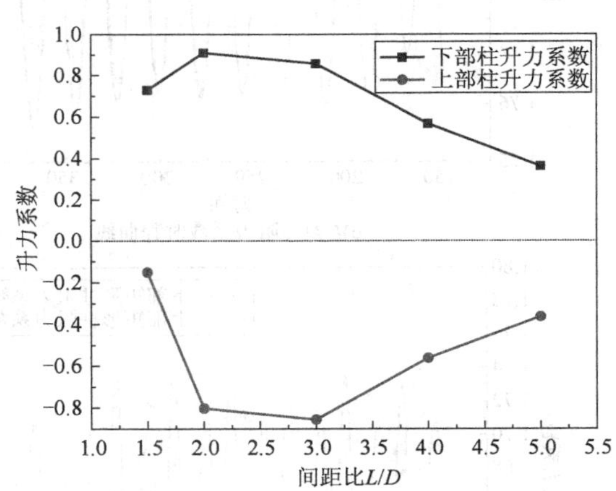

图5 上下部矩形柱平均升力系数

图6展示了 $L/D=1.5$、3、5 三个间距比下并列双矩形柱阻力系数和升力系数的时程曲线。其中a)、b)表明当 $L/D=1.5$ 时,上下部矩形柱的阻力和升力系数为定值,表明两矩形柱之间的干扰效应保持稳定;c)、d)表明当 $L/D=3$ 时,上下部矩形柱的气动力系数都呈现周期性变化,但气动力

系数变化范围比$L/D=1.5$大;(e)(f)表明当$L/D=5$时,上下部矩形柱的气动力系数都呈现周期性变化,以及气动力系数峰值保持稳定,可以认为上下两矩形柱为相对独立单矩形柱,即两矩形柱间没有干扰效应。分析图6可知,上下两矩形柱的阻力系数在同一时刻到达波峰值和波谷值;但是两矩形柱的升力系数的波峰和波谷值存在180°的相位差,即上部矩形柱处于波峰值,下部矩形柱则处于波谷值,上部矩形柱处于波谷,值下部矩形柱则处于波峰值。

通过平均气动力系数曲线和三个间距比气动力时程曲线分析,当并列矩形柱的间距比$L/D\geqslant4$时两矩形柱相当于独立单柱;间距比$L/D\leqslant4$时,两矩形柱存在干扰效应,两矩形柱气动力系数发生明显变化。

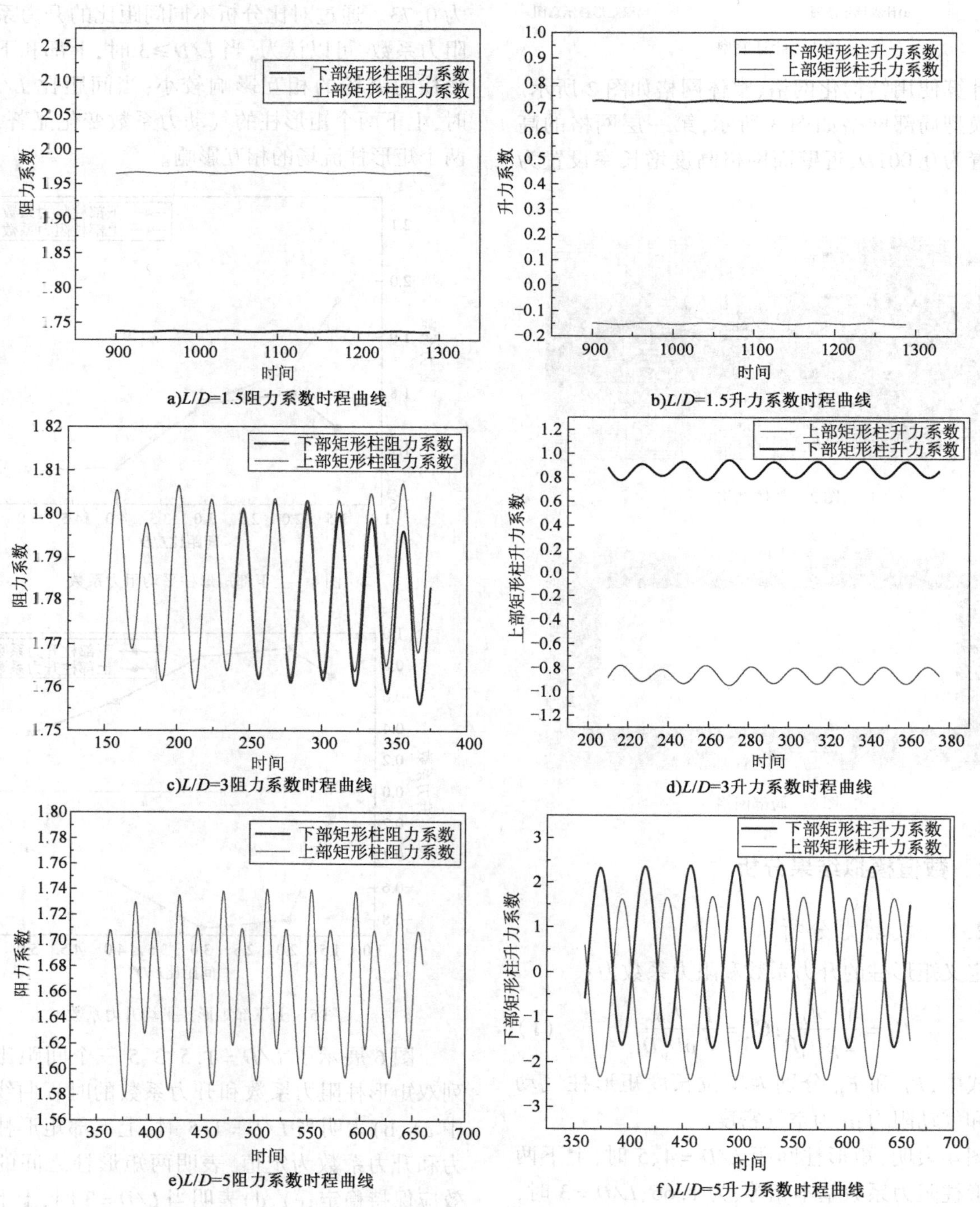

图6　不同间距比下的阻力和升力系数时程曲线

2.2 流场分析

图7给出了不同间距比下并列矩形柱流场的流线和涡量。从图7a)可知,当 $L/D=1.5$ 时两个矩形柱的尾流都没有出现旋涡脱落,并且中间间隙在尾流中产生的旋涡在上矩形柱尾部发展,造成两个矩形柱气动力系数不同;从图7b)可知,当 $L/D=2$ 时其流场结构类似于单矩形柱流场,上部矩形柱上缘旋涡与下部矩形柱上缘旋涡由于在尾流中相互干扰最终形成卡门涡街的上部,两矩形柱下部同理,最终在两矩形柱尾流中形成卡门涡街;从图7c)可知,当 $L/D=3$ 时在每一个矩形柱的尾部都有卡门涡街的形成,但是流线表明两个矩形柱间隙处卡门涡街的旋涡产生相互影响;从图7d)、e)可知,当 $L/D=4$、5时每一个矩形柱尾部都存在卡门涡街,并且流线表明两个矩形柱的尾流没有相互影响。

通过分析 $L/D\geqslant3$ 时的涡量图可知,当两个矩形柱尾流都存在卡门涡街时,上部矩形柱涡量为正的旋涡脱落时,下部矩形柱涡量为负的旋涡相应地也产生脱落,这就表明上矩形柱升力系数达到最大值时下矩形柱升力系数达到最小值;通过分析 $L/D=1.5$ 时的涡量图可知,矩形柱尾部没有旋涡产生,因此升力系数为定值。

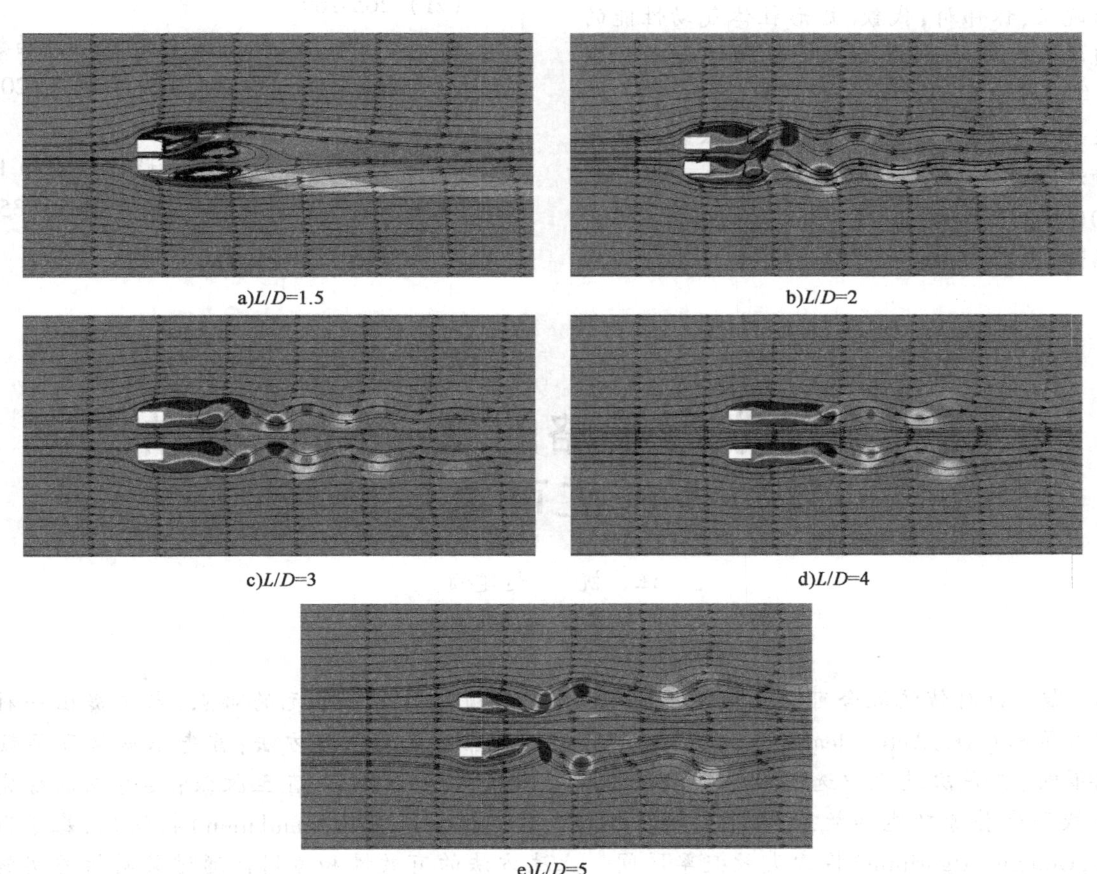

图7 不同间距比下的流场图

3 结语

本文通过数值模拟方法,计算雷诺数 $Re=2\times10^3$ 时并列双矩形柱流场,研究分析了不同间距比情况下并列矩形柱的气动特性和流场特性。主要结论如下:

(1)间距比 $L/D\geqslant3$ 时,两个矩形柱的阻力系数相同;升力系数绝对值相同,且上部矩形柱平均升力系数小于0,下部矩形柱平均升力系数大于0。间距比 $L/D<3$ 时,两矩形柱气动力系数在数值上不再相等。

(2)并列双矩形柱在间距 $L/D\leqslant2$ 时流场整体类似单矩形柱,在间距 $L/D\geqslant3$ 时每一个矩形柱流场逐渐接近单矩形柱。

(3)间距比2≤L/D≤3时存在一个临界值,使得两矩形栏间隙处尾流中的旋涡消失,使得流场从每一个矩形柱接近单矩形柱的流场转换为两个并列矩形柱的整体类似单矩形柱的流场。

参考文献

[1] 徐枫,欧进萍,肖仪清.不同截面形状柱体流致振动的CFD数值模拟[J].工程力学,2009,26(4):7-15.

[2] Yu D, Butler K, Kareem A, et a1. Simulation of the Influence of aspect ratio on the aerodynamics of rectangular prisms[J]. Journal of Engineering Mechanics. 2013,139(4): 429-438

[3] 杜晓庆,林伟群,代钦.矩形柱体气动性能的流场机理研究[J].西安建筑科技大学学报(自然科学版),2019,51(1):51-58.

[4] 王新荣,顾明,全涌.二维矩形柱体表面风压频域特性的雷诺数效应研究[J].工程力学,2016,33(7):100-107.

[5] 杨青,曹曙阳,刘十一.基于浸入式边界方法的串联双矩形柱绕流数值模拟[J].物理学报,2014(21):229-238.

[6] 邵林媛,靖洪淼,张卓杰,等.不同间距串列双矩形柱气动特性的数值模拟研究[C].中国力学学会结构工程专业委员会.第30届全国结构工程学术会议论文集(第Ⅰ册).广州:《工程力学》杂志社,2021:5.

[7] 丁林,叶倩云,王海博,等.不同间距串列双方柱流致振动运动特性分析[J].振动工程学报,2019,32(2):331-339.

[8] 吴倩云,孙亚松,刘小兵.并列双方柱气动特性的干扰效应研究[J].工程力学,2020,37(z1):265-269.

[9] 赵小军,魏文礼.并排方柱绕流的大涡数值模拟及显示[J].西安理工大学学报,2012,28(4):469-473.

[10] 郑宇华,顾杰.两并列矩形柱绕流的PIV试验研究[J].应用力学学报,2018,35(3):465-471.

基于主动学习策略的Kriging模型的斜拉桥施工可靠度分析

汪 帆* 赵建领

(长安大学公路学院)

摘 要 针对传统混合可靠性分析计算量大、需要频繁调用有限元的难点,本文提出一种基于主动学习策略(AK, Active-learning)的Kriging模型的可靠度区间求解方法:首先根据学习函数U建立查询策略,在每次迭代中选取对模型精度提升贡献最大的样本点,直至收敛;接着以训练完成的Kriging模型代替原功能函数,并与蒙特卡罗模拟(MCS, Monte Carlo Simulation)相结合,基于遗传算法(GA, Genetic Algorithm)搜索失效概率区间。上述方法的有效性和适用性通过某斜拉桥实例得到了验证。

关键词 桥梁工程 区间可靠度 基于主动学习的Kriging模型 斜拉桥施工

0 引言

实际工程结构的功能函数表现出高度非线性特征且难以显式化表达,往往只能通过耗时的有限元分析(FEM, Finite Element Method)计算结构响应,这导致传统基于蒙特卡罗模拟(MCS)的可靠度求解方法效率很低。解决上述问题的一种有效思路是建立准确的代理模型来代替真实功能函

1. 基金项目:国家自然科学基金项目(52178104)。

数,如针对钢管混凝土拱桥主梁竖向位移失效模式。崔凤坤等[1]利用BP神经网络拟合极限状态函数,基于粒子群算法全局搜索验算点并求解可靠度指标;贾布裕等[2]提出Kriging响应面法,进行钢筋混凝土框架结构整体抗震可靠度计算与灵敏度分析。然而,由于响应面方法多采用二阶多项式在最可能失效点逼近极限状态平面,对于高维非线性问题的拟合精度较低。此外,人工神经网络虽然具有很强的非线性映射能力,能以任意精度拟合非线性函数,但泛化性能较差,往往需要大量的样本点支持。因此,为了提升采样效率,与上述被动学习策略相对,近年来发展了基于主动学习策略的Kriging模型来预测可靠度[3-4]。其主要思路是:建立初始代理模型,并根据合适的查询策略有偏好地选择最佳样本点,并在下次迭代中添加至实验设计(DoE,Design of Experiment)中,从而逐步提高模型精度。由于新训练点并非任意选取,而是位于感兴趣的区域,从而避免了训练样本选择的盲目性。

然而,上述研究均局限于概率可靠性模型,因而对不确定变量的统计特征非常敏感,不准确的概率分布假设可能会对失效概率预测产生重大影响,从而导致可靠性分析的巨大偏差。事实上,由于不确定信息相对有限和模糊,部分参量难以用精确的概率分布来描述,只能通过其波动区间上下界来度量[5]。因此,工程问题往往表现出概率-区间的混合不确定特征。与概率可靠性分析相比,当引入区间变量以后,失效概率并不是一个确定的值,而是一个区间数,混合可靠性分析成为一个区间分析和概率分析的双环嵌套过程[6],即内环定位功能函数关于区间变量的极值,外环执行概率可靠性分析计算失效概率上下界,其计算负担无疑是非常大的。

为突破概率-区间混合可靠度的计算精度与效率瓶颈,本文将适用性强的MCS方法与AK模型结合,形成AK-MCS求解框架,以代理模型取代实际功能函数,最后通过基于遗传算法的寻优过程准确定位失效概率上下界。所述方法的准确性和适用性在某斜拉桥静力可靠度计算中得到了验证。

1 基于主动学习策略的Kriging模型

1.1 基本框架

AK模型可以实现仅在感兴趣的区域对目标函数进行近似,从而最大程度提高了采样效率[7]。结构失效概率本质上是符号预测问题,即根据功能函数的正负对样本点进行"可靠"与"失效"的分类。因此,在功能函数 $G(x)=0$ 附近获得训练样本能在最大程度上提升采样效率和预测精度。图1展示了建立AK模型的基本流程。

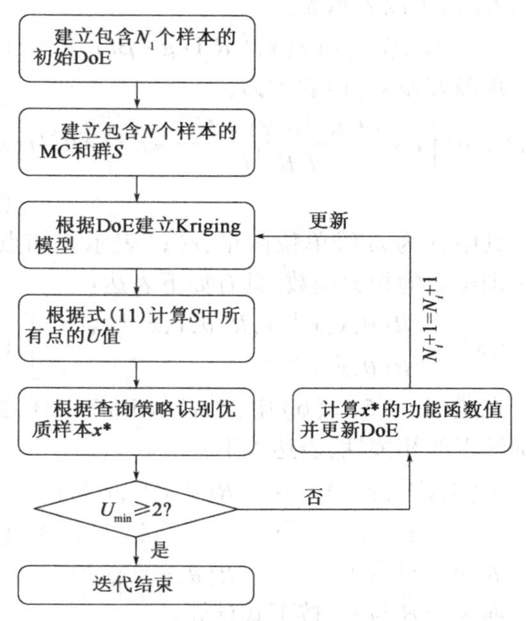

图1 AK模型流程图

1.2 Kriging模型

与其他代理模型不同,Kriging模型在预测未知点函数值的同时,还可以得到预测方差,这反映了模型在不同位置的预测精度,体现了预测信息的趋势和动态,也是主动学习的基本依据。与不同的学习函数相结合赋予了Kriging模型强大的局部逼近能力,因此被广泛应用于工程可靠度分析,其表达如下:

$$\hat{G}(x)=\hat{\beta}+z(x) \tag{1}$$

其中,$\hat{G}(x)$是Kriging模型预测的功能函数取值,$\hat{\beta}$为预测均值,$z(x)$是一均值为0的高斯过程,其方差为:

$$E(z(x_i)z(x_j))=\sigma^2 R(\theta,x_i,x_j) \tag{2}$$

其中,$E(\cdot)$表示期望算子,σ^2表示克里金方差,x_i,x_j是实空间内任意两点,$R(\theta,x_i,x_j)$是由参数θ确定的相关函数。本文采用应用最广的高斯相关模型:

$$R(\theta,x_i,x_j)=\exp(-\sum_{k=1}^{n}\theta_k\ |xi_k\text{-}xj_k|2) \tag{3}$$

其中,θ_k,x_k^i,x_k^j 分别为 n 维向量的第 k 个

元素。

Kriging 模型的建立需要进行实验设计(DoE, Design of Experiment)。考虑一个具有 m 个点的 DoE,样本向量为 $[x^{(1)},x^{(2)},\cdots,x^{(m)}]^T$,对应的输出值 $g=[G(x^{(1)}),G(x^{(2)}),\cdots,G(x^{(m)})]^T$。以此为训练点建立的 Kriging 模型在某个未知点 x 的预测值 $\widehat{G}(x)$可以表示为:

$$\widehat{G}(x)=\widehat{\beta}+r(x)^T R\text{-}1(g-\widehat{\beta}I) \tag{4}$$

预测方差 $s^2(x)$表示为:

$$s^2(x)=\sigma^2\left[1+\frac{(I^TR^{-1}r(x)-1)^2}{I^TR^{-1}I}-r^T(x)R^{-1}r(x)\right] \tag{5}$$

其中,I 为 m 维单位向量,$r(x)$表示未知点与任一训练点的相关函数,具有如下表达:

$$r(x)=\begin{bmatrix}R(\theta,x,x^{(1)}),R(\theta,x,x^{(2)}),\cdots,\\R(\theta,x,x^{(m)})\end{bmatrix}^T \tag{6}$$

在式(4)、(5)、(6)中,R 表示 DoE 中任意两个训练点的相关性,表达如下:

$$R=\begin{pmatrix}R(\theta,x^{(1)},x^{(1)}) & \cdots & R(\theta,x^{(1)},x^{(m)})\\ \vdots & \ddots & \vdots\\ R(\theta,x^{(m)},x^{(1)}) & \cdots & R(\theta,x^{(m)},x^{(m)})\end{pmatrix} \tag{7}$$

而参数 $\widehat{\beta}$ 与 $\widehat{\sigma^2}$ 按下式计算:

$$\widehat{\beta}=(I^TR^{-1}I)^{-1}I^TR^{-1}g \tag{8}$$

$$\widehat{\sigma^2}=\frac{1}{m}(g-\widehat{\beta}I)^TR^{-1}(g-\widehat{\beta}I) \tag{9}$$

注意到式(8)与(9)中 $\widehat{\beta}$ 与 $\widehat{\sigma^2}$ 的值由参数 θ 决定,可以通过下式描述的优化问题来求解:

$$\theta*=\arg\min_{\theta}(|R|\frac{1}{m}\sigma^2) \tag{10}$$

本文在 Matlab Dace 工具箱中执行上述过程,通过一个内置的梯度算法确定最优建模参数 θ^*。

1.3　学习函数

构建 AK 模型的关键在于选择高效的查询策略。针对不同工程应用场景,可以选择相应的学习函数来有偏好地选择最有价值的优质样本,如应用于复杂函数全局优化的 EGO 算法(Efficient Global Optimization),通过 EI 指标来评价待选样本对模型精度的改善程度;以 EFF 函数(Expected Feasible Function)来指示响应真实值在多大程度上满足等式约束 $G(x)=z$。为了提高 AK 模型预测功能函数符号的准确程度,文献[8]首次引入 U 函数来定位对模型精度提升最有价值的样本点,其具有类似于可靠度指标 β 的表达式,定义如下:

$$U(x)=\frac{|\mu_{\widehat{G}}(x)|}{\sigma_{\widehat{G}}(x)} \tag{11}$$

其中,x 为样本点输入侧,$\mu_{\widehat{G}}(x)$与 $\sigma_{\widehat{G}}(x)$为 AK 模型在该点处的预测值与预测方差。

对应的选择样本点为:

$$x^*=\arg\min_{x}U(x) \tag{12}$$

显而易见,U 函数对样本点的选择偏好与可靠性分析的需求是完全一致的。U 值较小,即 $\mu_{\widehat{G}}(x)$接近于零或 $\sigma_{\widehat{G}}(x)$值较大,表明该样本点靠近极限状态,具有较大的预测误差或同时表现这两个特征,其对模型精度提高有显著效果,应当被添加至 DoE 中。

基于学习函数 U 的 AK 模型一般采用的收敛判据为 $U_{min}\geqslant 2$,即对于 MC 种群内所有个体,均能保证 $\Phi[U(x)]\geqslant 0.977$,从而确保了功能函数符号预测正确率高于 97.7%。

1.4　算例讨论

本文采用文献[9]中的一维高次非线性方程,对比三种不同学习函数的性能表现。极限状态方程如式(13)所示,其中,随机变量 x 服从正态分布 $N(2.5,0.5^2)$。

$$G(x)=1.0417x^5-13.25x^4+59.792x^3-112.75x^2+75.167x \tag{13}$$

在该算例中,由 MCS 生成的备选样本数目为 10^5。为了对比四种学习函数对样本点的选择差异,采用了完全相同的初始 DoE,在区间[0,5]内均匀取 6 个点,即 $x=[0,1,2,3,4,5]$,在此基础上构建初始模型,再根据由学习函数决定的选择策略逐步增加优质样本点,直至达到收敛条件。最后,以 20 次样本数为 10^6 的 MCS 抽样计算的失效概率均值为标准,评价四种 AK 模型精度与效率,结果如表 1 所示。其中,N_{call} 表示功能函数的调用次数,P_f 为求得的失效概率,ε_{Pf}为与标准值的相对误差,拟合效果对比如图 2 所示。

不同学习函数的性能表现　　表 1

Methods	N_{call}	P_f	ε_{Pf}(%)
MCS	20×10^6	0.2765	—
AK-EGO	14	0.2707	2.098
AK-EFF	15	0.2764	0.036
AK-U	13	0.2786	0.759

在该一维算例中,三种方法的实际功能函数调用次数差异不明显,AK-U 调用次数相对较少;

在计算精度方面，EGO模型预测的失效概率为0.2707，与MCS方法的相对误差达到了2.098%；而其他三种算法均实现了较高的预测精度，相对误差小于1%。显而易见，三种方法对最佳样本点的选择存在差异：面向全局优化的EGO算法倾向于选择功能函数极小值附近(区间[4,5]内)的点作为优质样本，在此处拟合效果明显优于其他方法；EFF算法强调极限状态附近和设计空间整体的均衡搜索特性，因此一般需要更多的样本点来保证全局拟合精度；基于U函数的AK模型不关心目标区域外的拟合效果，只在$G(x)=0$附近高度逼近原函数，这保证了较高的功能函数符号预测正确率和采样效率。基于U函数的AK模型在规模为13的DoE条件下，预测失效概率为0.2786，相对误差仅为0.759%，表现出了较高的计算精度与效率。

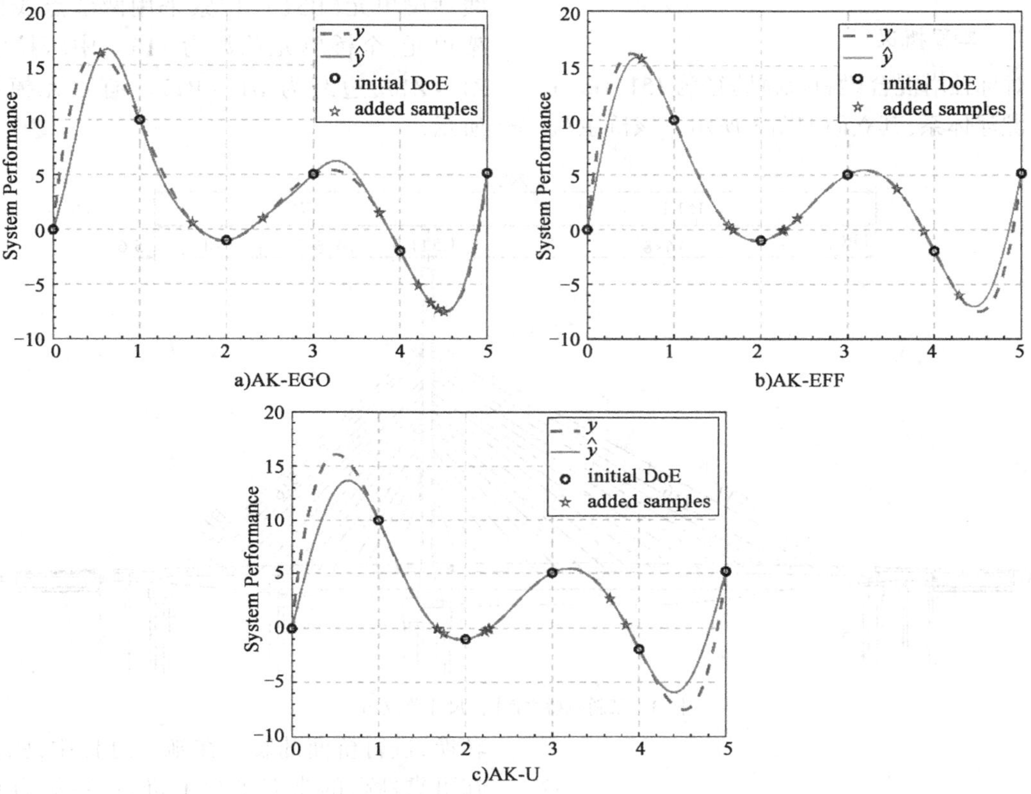

图2　不同学习函数的拟合情况

2　基于AK模型的混合可靠性分析

2.1　AK-MCS

如前所述，包含区间变量的混合可靠度分析是一个双层嵌套寻优的过程，结构失效概率成为一区间值，表达如下：

$$P_f^U = P\{\min_{Y^I}\widehat{G}(X,Y^I)<0\} \tag{14}$$

$$P_f^L = P\{\max_{Y^I}\widehat{G}(X,Y^I)<0\} \tag{15}$$

其中，$\widehat{G}(\cdot)$为Kriging模型代理的功能函数；X为随机变量，Y^I为区间变量。

式(14)、式(15)可改写为：

$$P_f^U = \iint\cdots\int I_F^U(X)f(X)dX \tag{16}$$

$$P_f^L = \iint\cdots\int I_F^L(X)f(X)dX \tag{17}$$

其中，$I_F(\cdot)$为失效指示函数，其表达式如下：

$$I_F^U(X) = \begin{cases} 1, \min\limits_{Y^I} G(X,Y^I)<0 \\ 0, \min\limits_{Y^I} G(X,Y^I)\geqslant 0 \end{cases} \tag{18}$$

$$I_F^L(X) = \begin{cases} 1, \max\limits_{Y^I} G(X,Y^I)<0 \\ 0, \max\limits_{Y^I} G(X,Y^I)\geqslant 0 \end{cases} \tag{19}$$

根据随机变量概率密度函数产生N个样本，按下式计算失效概率上下界：

$$P_f^U = \frac{1}{N}\sum_{j=1}^{N} I_F^U(X^j) \tag{20}$$

$$P_f^L = \frac{1}{N}\sum_{j=1}^{N} I_F^L(X^j) \tag{21}$$

其中,X^j 为第 j 个样本。

最后,将失效概率转化为可靠度指标:

$$\beta^L = -\Phi^{-1}(P_f^U) \tag{22}$$

$$\beta^U = -\Phi^{-1}(P_f^L) \tag{23}$$

式(18)、(19)通过全局收敛性能良好的遗传算法求解,通过选择、交叉、变异等操作定位极值点,上述操作均在 Matlab 遗传算法工具箱内进行。

2.2　工程算例

2.2.1　工程概况

某非对称独塔混合梁斜拉桥跨径为 151.1m + 91.1m,半漂浮体系,其立面如图 3 所示。该桥主跨采用钢-UHPC 组合梁,边跨为混凝土箱梁,边中跨比 0.6,在边跨设有一辅助墩;桥塔为钢箱结构,左塔高 105.12m,右塔高 120.12m;拉索采用平行钢丝镀锌成品索,按扇形空间索面布置。桥宽 46m,双向八车道布置,车辆荷载按城-A 级设计。

本文在通用有限元软件 ABAQUS 中建立该桥的整体模型,以等效弹性模量考虑拉索的几何非线性特征。其中,主梁和桥塔均采用两节点空间线性梁单元(B31),拉索采用两节点线性三位桁架单元,全桥单元总数为 715。中跨拉索编号为 Z1 ~ Z17,边跨为 B1 ~ B17。有限元模型如图 4 所示。

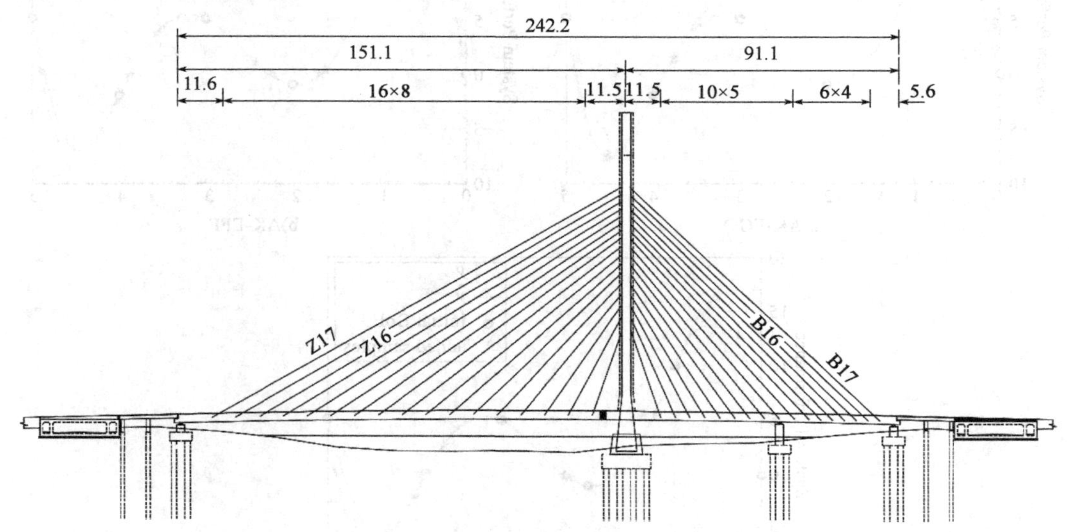

图 3　某斜拉桥立面图(尺寸单位:m)

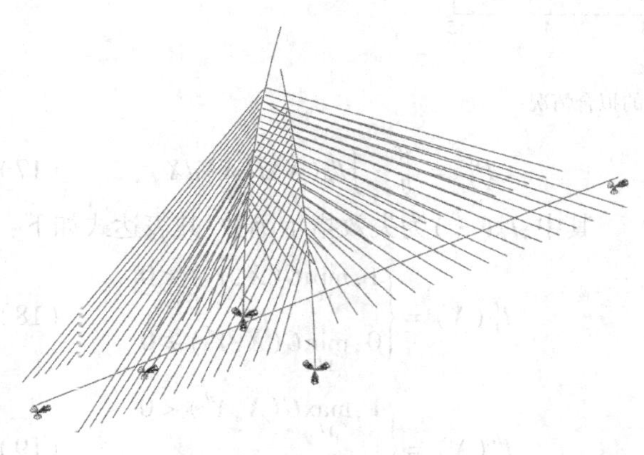

图 4　ABAQUS 有限元模型

2.2.2　施工过程桥塔可靠度分析

该桥采用传统的支架法施工。钢主塔与钢主梁在工厂分段预制完成后,在现场吊装;混凝土主梁则采用支架法现浇,待形成强度后,由塔侧向两端对称张拉 17 对拉索;最后拆除支架,完成体系转换,进行桥面铺装。在施工过程中,张拉操作均在可靠性高的支架平台上进行,主梁自重主要由支架体系承担,大大缓解了桥塔的受力情况,因而安全风险较低。本文以风险最大的二期铺装后桥梁结构体系为研究对象,针对塔顶纵桥向偏位 Δ 建立极限状态方程如下:

$$G(X, Y^I) = \Delta^T - \Delta(X, Y^I) \tag{24}$$

式中,X 为随机变量,Y^I 为区间变量,在本算例中为外侧两对拉索张拉索力,其统计特性如表 2 所示;Δ^T 为允许最大偏位值,按《公路斜拉桥设计规范》(JTG/T 3365-01—2020)取 30mm。

首先经过 60 次迭代建立 AK 模型,收敛过程如图 5 所示。显然,靠近极限状态的样本点更容易被选中,将其加入 DoE 可以显著提高模型精度。再根据遗传算法搜索最大与最小失效概率,结果如表 3 所示。结果表明,该桥在施工过程中最大失效概率为 0.4%,施工风险较小。

变量统计参数　表2

变　量	单　位	参　数　1	参　数　2	分布类型
桥塔弹模 E_1	MPa	2.06×10^5	2.06×10^4	正态
钢主梁弹模 E_2	MPa	2.06×10^5	2.06×10^4	正态
砼主梁弹模 E_3	MPa	3.45×10^4	3.45×10^3	正态
斜拉索弹模 E_4	MPa	1.95×10^5	1.95×10^4	正态
单根拉索钢绞线面积 a	m^2	4.9×10^{-5}	2.5×10^{-7}	对数正态
主梁二期恒载 q	kN/m	98	9.8	极值I型
Z16 索力	kN	2324.1	2569.3	区间变量
Z17 索力	kN	2339.5	2586.2	区间变量
B16 索力	kN	2825.4	3122.7	区间变量
B17 索力	kN	2834.8	3133.2	区间变量

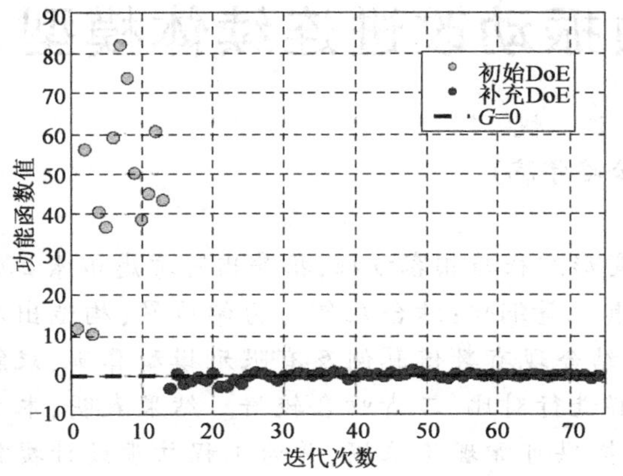

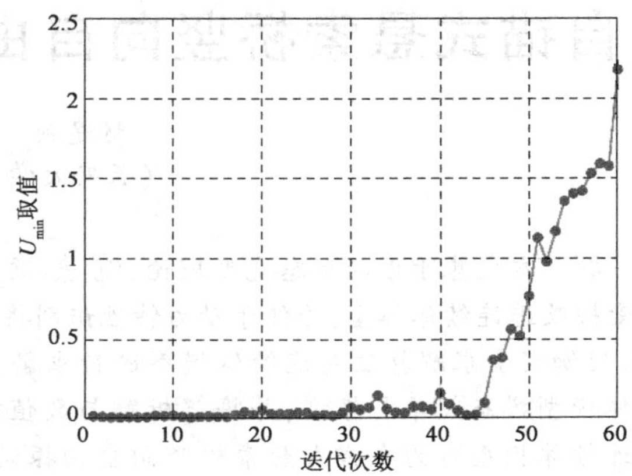

图5　AK模型训练情况

可靠度计算结果　表3

方法	P_f^L	P_f^U	β^L	β^R	模型训练耗时 t(s)	可靠度计算耗时 t(s)
AK-MCS	0.000191	0.00432	2.6260	3.5222	619.1	67.2

3　结语

(1)基于学习函数U的AK模型能够在每次迭代中选择极限状态附近的样本,从而大大改善了采样效率与模型精度,大幅减少实际功能函数调用次数。

(2)以某混合梁斜拉桥为例,分析结果表明了基于AK-MCS的混合可靠性分析方法的有效性和适用性。

(3)该桥在施工阶段的塔偏失效概率范围为0.01%~0.4%,具有较高的可靠指标。

(4)该桥可靠度指标区间为[2.62,3.52],但仍有较大提升空间,后续研究可聚焦于基于区间反演的可靠度优化设计领域,通过对可控参量的调整,实现各项目标最优。

参考文献

[1]　崔凤坤,王虎军,徐岳,等.基于BP神经网络和粒子群算法的钢管混凝土拱桥可靠度分析[J].合肥工业大学学报(自然科学版),2016(8):1103-1109.

[2]　贾布裕,余晓琳,颜全胜,等.基于ISC-Kriging响应面法的桥梁抗震动力可靠度分析[J].华南理工大学学报(自然科学版),2015(10):10.

[3]　吴海波,刘海龙,魏丽君.基于粒子群优化Kriging模型的边坡可靠度分析[J].数学的实践与认识,2021,51(2):120-128.

[4]　李天正,Dias Daniel.主动学习型克里金模型在掌子面可靠度分析中的应用——以双层土隧道为例(英文)[J].Journal of Central South

University,2019,26(7):53-64.

[5] 郑宇宁. 多源不确定性条件下气动弹性系统颤振可靠性分析方法[J]. 振动与冲击,2021,40(3):9.

[6] Du X. Interval reliability analysis[C]. International Design Engineering Technical Conferences and Computers and Information in Engineering Conference,2007:1103-1109.

[7] Yang X. An active learning kriging model for hybrid reliability analysis with both random and interval variables [J]. Structural & Multidisciplinary Optimization,2015,51(5):1003-1016.

[8] Echard B, Gayton N, Lemaire M. AK-MCS: An active learning reliability method combining Kriging and Monte Carlo Simulation [J]. Structural Safety,2011,33(2):145-154.

[9] Wang Z, Wang P. A new approach for reliability analysis with time-variant performance characteristics [J]. Reliability Engineering & System Safety,2013,115(7):70-81.

自锚式悬索桥竖向自由振动改进连续体模型

赵建领* 汪 帆

(长安大学公路学院)

摘 要 本文基于振动形态挠度理论、缆-索-梁变形方程与相容方程,推导出可考虑吊索拉伸的自锚式悬索桥改进连续体模型,为便于动力特性识别将其无量纲化;结合几何与力学边界,构造出对应形函数,采用伽辽金求解算法对连续体模型进行求解;结合现有数值算例及有限元模型算例,求解出改进连续体模型模态频率与振型,并将解析解与数值解进行对比,二者吻合较好。结果表明,本文提出的改进连续体模型可为自锚式悬索桥竖向自由振动提供可靠理论依据,并为工程初步设计提供有效参考。

关键词 自锚式悬索桥 竖向自由振动 改进连续体模型 无量纲化 伽辽金求解算法

0 引言

自锚式悬索桥静动力分析模型通常分为两类:离散模型和连续体模型。基于有限元方法的离散模型多被用于计算结构力学响应的精确数值解[1-2],但有限元模型建模过程中需要进行复杂的初始平衡状态分析[3],找形分析过程中将消耗大量时间;基于解析方法的连续体模型则无需进行初始平衡状态分析,通过求解微分方程便能识别结构力学行为[4-5]。

作为桥梁抗风抗震及车桥耦合等动力问题的基础,自由振动特性的连续体模型研究受到广泛关注。自锚式悬索桥振动系统包含缆-索-梁与塔-墩两类子体系,其解析方法可分为两类:近似方法和经典解析法。近似方法多基于能量守恒原理,采用 Rayleigh-Ritz 法对振动系统进行求解,通过引入形函数而避免对复杂方程直接求解,且可同时考虑两类子体系对振动系统的贡献,得到较为简洁的近似解析解[6-7],但近似方法求解精度过度依赖于振动形函数的合适与否,无法拓展至高阶振动特性研究。经典解析法多基于挠度理论和 Hamilton 原理,推导缆-索-梁子体系微分方程并对其直接求解。国外学者 Bleich 等[8]率先建立了竖向自由振动连续体模型,Abdel-Ghaffar 等[9]研究发现微幅振动可将竖弯与扭转模态解耦,Hayashikawa[10]和 Kim[11]等的研究表明主梁剪切变形与转动惯量对振动特性影响有限,Luco 等[12]系统回顾了 Bleich 等的经典理论,并研究了缆、梁相对刚度对振动特性的影响。然而上述研究均针对地锚式悬索桥,罕见自锚式悬索桥振动特性的连续体模型研究。国内学者刘春城等[13]建立大位移不完全广义势能泛函推导出自锚式悬索桥竖向弯曲振动微分方程及解析解,结果表明忽略主梁剪切,竖弯可与纵飘、横弯及扭转三种模态解耦。

为降低振动微分方程求解难度,上述经典解析法均忽略缆-索-梁子体系中吊索弹性刚度的贡献,即认为缆-梁位移一致,Turmo 等[14]考虑吊索拉伸重新推导了缆-索-梁振动方程并进行无量纲处理,研究证明地锚式悬索桥主梁相对弹性抗弯刚度更大时,吊索弹性刚度对较高阶次模态频率有较大影响。在此基础上,Gwon 和 Choi 等[15-16]研究了平行索面和空间索面地锚式悬索桥连续体模型在静动力和温度荷载下的结构响应,并与有限元模型对比,表明结果准确可靠。与地锚式悬索桥相比,自锚式悬索桥因"自平衡"特性非线性问题更为显著、动力特性更为复杂,直接影响结构适用性与安全性。缆索大变形、主梁压弯等特点使其非线性振动方程求解更为复杂。

在此背景下,为探明自锚式悬索桥的竖向自由振动特性,本文在挠度理论基础上推导出考虑吊索拉伸的缆-索-梁自由振动微分方程组,对其进行无量纲处理得到包含 6 个无量纲特征参数在内的连续体模型;采用伽辽金算法将控制方程组转化为矩阵形式,求解无量纲连续体模型的模态频率及振型;利用现有平行索面自锚式悬索桥数值算例验证连续体模型的普适性与准确性。

1 基本假设与微分方程

1.1 基本假设

自锚式悬索桥改进连续体模型遵循以下假定:①恒载沿全桥均匀分布,且由主缆承担,恒载作用下处于初始平衡态构形;②主缆线形为抛物线;③吊索无质量,沿全桥竖直均匀分布,振动中仍保持竖直且可拉伸;④振动引起的主缆附加水平力远小于初始恒载水平力,且各跨附加水平力相等;⑤振动过程中由于吊索可拉伸,缆-梁位移不等,但都遵循小位移假定。

图 1 所示为自锚式悬索桥示意图,其中,m_c、m_g分别为单位长度主缆、主梁质量;E_c、I_c 和 A_c 分别为主缆弹性模量、惯性矩和面积;E_g、I_g和 A_g分别为主梁弹性模量、惯性矩和面积;E_h、A_h分别为吊索弹性模量、面积;L_h为主缆 IP 点至桥面的长度分量;d_h为吊杆间距;L_j 为各跨跨长;f_j 分别为各跨主缆垂度;z_{cj} 为初始平衡状态下各跨主缆的坐标。

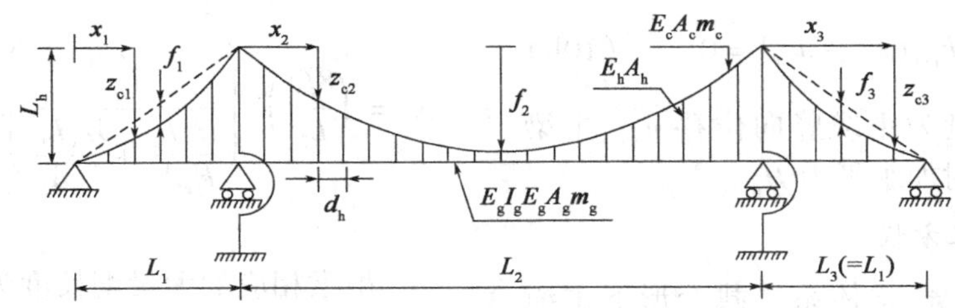

图 1 自锚式悬索桥结构参数示意图

主缆抛物线线形坐标可依次表示为:

$$z_{c1}(x_1)=L_{hz}-\frac{L_{hz}}{L_1}x_1-\frac{4f_{z1}}{L_1^2}x_1(x_1-L_1),$$

$$z_{c2}(x_2)=\frac{4f_{z2}}{L_2^2}x_2(L_2-x_2),$$

$$z_{c3}(x_3)=\frac{L_{hz}}{L_3}x_3-\frac{4f_{z3}}{L_3^2}x_3(x_3-L_3) \tag{1}$$

1.1.1 缆-索-梁变形方程

H_w为初始平衡态下主缆初始水平力,H_p为振动引起的主缆附加水平力。由假设①②可得主缆初始平衡态下平衡方程为:

$$H_w\frac{d^2z_c}{dx^2}+(m_cg+h_z)=0 \tag{2}$$

其中,h_z 为吊索力。在初始平衡态下,$h_z=m_g g/2$,则主缆初始水平力:

$$H_w=(m_c+\frac{m_g}{2})gL^2/(8f) \tag{3}$$

振动过程中索平衡方程为:

$$h_z=\frac{m_g g}{2}+h_p \tag{4}$$

式中,h_p是由振动引起的吊索附加索力,可表示为:

$$h_p=k_{ho}\delta_{ho} \tag{5}$$

其中,由假设③可得吊索沿主梁方向的分布轴向弹性刚度 k_h为:

$$k_h=\frac{E_hA_h}{l_hd_h} \tag{6}$$

式中,l_h为吊索长度,$l_h=L_h-z_c$。

其中,振动引起的吊索伸长量 δ_{ho}可表示为:

$$\delta_{ho} = w_g - w_c \tag{7}$$

式中,w_g为振动引起的主梁竖向位移,w_c为振动引起的主缆竖向位移。

1.1.2 振动方程

主缆振动中平衡方程可表示为[17]

$$m_c \frac{\partial^2 w_c}{\partial t^2} - (H_w + H_p)\frac{\partial^2 (z_c + w_c)}{\partial x^2} - (m_c g + h_z) = 0 \tag{8}$$

主梁振动中平衡方程可表示为[17]

$$\frac{m_g}{2}\frac{\partial^2 w_g}{\partial t^2} + \frac{E_g I_g}{2}\frac{\partial^4 w_g}{\partial x^4} + (H_w + H_p)\frac{\partial^2 w_g}{\partial x^2} - \left(\frac{m_g g}{2} - h_z\right) = 0 \tag{9}$$

由假设④引得,$H_w + H_p \approx H_w$;将式(4)~式(7)依次代入式(8)~式(9),化简、重排并拓展至多跨,得到微分方程组:

$$D_{cj}(x_j,t) = m_c \frac{\partial^2 w_{cj}}{\partial t^2} - H_w \frac{\partial^2 w_{cj}}{\partial x_j^2} - H_p \frac{d^2 z_{cj}}{dx_j^2} - k_{hj}(w_{gj} - w_{cj}) = 0 \tag{10a}$$

$$D_{gj}(x_j,t) = \frac{m_g}{2}\frac{\partial^2 w_{gj}}{\partial t^2} + \frac{E_g I_g}{2}\frac{\partial^4 w_{gj}}{\partial x_j^4} + H_w \frac{\partial^2 w_{gj}}{\partial x_j^2} + k_{hoj}(w_{gj} - w_{cj}) = 0 \tag{10b}$$

其中,方程未知量为主缆竖向位移 w_{cj}、主梁竖向位移 w_{gj} 和主缆附加水平力 H_p。

1.1.3 变形相容方程

自锚式悬索桥缆-索-梁体系受载变形下主缆伸长水平分量与主梁压缩量一致,变形相容方程可表示为:

$$\sum_{j=1}^{3}\left\{\frac{H_p}{E_c A_c}\int_0^{L_j}\left[1 + \left(\frac{dz_{cj}}{dx_j}\right)^2\right]^{\frac{3}{2}} dx_j + \frac{H_p L_j}{E_g A_g}\right\} = \sum_{j=1}^{3}\left(8\frac{f_2}{L_2^2}\int_0^{L_j} w_{cj} dx_j\right) \tag{11}$$

将式(12)化简,振动引起的主缆附加水平力可表示为:

$$H_p = \sum_{j=1}^{3}\left(8\frac{f_2}{L_2^2}\int_0^{L_j} w_{cj} dx_j\right) \bigg/ \left(\frac{L_E}{E_c A_c} + \frac{L_b}{E_g A_g}\right) \tag{12}$$

式中,$L_E = \sum_{j=1}^{3}\left\{\int_0^{L_j}\left[1 + \left(\frac{dz_{cj}}{dx_j}\right)^2\right]^{\frac{3}{2}} dx_j\right\}$,$L_b = \sum_{j=1}^{3} L_j$。

1.2 方程无量纲化

对式(11)进行无量纲处理,基本变量无量纲变换可表示为[14]:

$$x_j = L_2 \bar{x}_j, t = \sqrt{\frac{8f_2}{g}}\bar{t}, w_{cj}(x_j,t) = 8f_2 \bar{w}_{cj}(\bar{x}_j,\bar{t}),$$

$$w_{gj}(x_j,t) = 8f_2 \bar{w}_{gj}(\bar{x}_j,\bar{t}) \tag{13}$$

式中,$\bar{x}_j$、$\bar{t}$ 分别为无量纲横坐标、无量纲时间;$\bar{w}_{cj}(\bar{x}_j,\bar{t})$、$\bar{w}_{gj}(\bar{x}_j,\bar{t})$ 分别是主缆无量纲竖向位移、主梁无量纲竖向位移。

将式(13)代入式(10),得到无量纲振动微分方程组:

$$D_{cj}(\bar{x}_j,\bar{t}) = (1-\bar{m})\frac{\partial^2 \bar{w}_{cj}}{\partial \bar{t}^2} - \frac{\partial^2 \bar{w}_{cj}}{\partial \bar{x}_j^2} - \lambda^2 \sum_{j=1}^{3}\int_0^{\bar{L}_j} \bar{w}_{cj} d\bar{x}_j - \chi^2 \frac{8\bar{f}}{\bar{l}_{hj}}(\bar{w}_{gj} - \bar{w}_{cj}) = 0 \tag{14a}$$

$$D_{gj}(\bar{x}_j,\bar{t}) = \bar{m}\frac{\partial^2 \bar{w}_{gj}}{\partial \bar{t}^2} + \alpha^2 \frac{\partial^4 \bar{w}_{gj}}{\partial \bar{x}_j^4} + \frac{\partial^2 \bar{w}_{gj}}{\partial \bar{x}_j^2} + \chi^2 \frac{8\bar{f}}{\bar{l}_{hj}}(\bar{w}_{gj} - \bar{w}_{cj}) = 0 \tag{14b}$$

式中的无量纲参数分别为:

$$\bar{m} = \frac{\frac{m_g}{2}}{m_c + \frac{m_g}{2}}, \bar{L}_j = \frac{L_j}{L_2}, \bar{f} = \frac{f_2}{L_h}, \alpha^2 = \frac{E_g I_g}{2H_w L_2^2},$$

$$\lambda^2 = \left(\frac{8f_2}{L_2}\right)^2 \left(\frac{L_2}{\frac{H_w L_E}{E_c A_c} + \frac{H_w L_b}{E_g A_g}}\right), \chi^2 = \frac{E_h A_h}{\left(m_c + \frac{m_g}{2}\right) g d_h} \tag{15}$$

吊索相应的无量纲长度为:

$$\bar{l}_{h1} = \bar{x}_1\left[\frac{1}{\bar{L}_1} + 4\bar{f}\cdot(\bar{x}_1 - \bar{L}_1)\right], \bar{l}_{h2} = 1 + 4\bar{f}\cdot \bar{x}_2(\bar{x}_2 - \bar{L}_2), \bar{l}_{h3} = 1 - \frac{\bar{x}_3}{\bar{L}_3} + 4\bar{f}\cdot \bar{x}_3(\bar{x}_3 - \bar{L}_3) \tag{16}$$

其中,$\bar{m}$是主梁相对质量;$\bar{L}_j$是边跨相对长度;$\bar{f}$是主缆相对垂度。λ^2为 Irvine 刚度系数,即主缆相对弹性轴向刚度;α^2为 Steinman 刚度系数,即主梁相对弹性抗弯刚度;χ^2是吊索相对弹性轴向刚度。

2 伽辽金求解算法

2.1 边界与形函数

式(13)未知量分别为主缆无量纲竖向位移 $\bar{w}_{cj}(\bar{x}_j,\bar{t})$和主梁无量纲竖向位移$\bar{w}_{gj}(\bar{x}_j,\bar{t})$,采用

伽辽金算法计算其近似解。主缆有 6 个边界条件,即每跨两端竖向为 0:

$$\bar{w}_{cj}(0,\bar{t})=0,\bar{w}_{cj}(\bar{L}_j,\bar{t})=0 \tag{17}$$

主梁为三跨连续梁,有 12 个边界条件,即各支点处竖向位移为 0、跨内支点两端转角及弯矩相等以及边支点弯矩为 0:

$$\begin{aligned}&\bar{w}_{gj}(0,\bar{t})=0,\bar{w}_{gj}(L_j,\bar{t})=0,\\&\bar{w}''_{g1}(0,\bar{t})=0,\bar{w}_{g3}''(L_3,\bar{t})=0\\&\bar{w}'_{g1}(\bar{L}_1,\bar{t})=w'_{g2}(0,\bar{t}),\bar{w}'_{g2}(\bar{L}_2,\bar{t})=w'_{g3}(0,\bar{t}),\\&\bar{w}''_{g1}(\bar{L}_1,\bar{t})=w''_{g2}(0,\bar{t}),\bar{w}''_{g2}(\bar{L}_2,\bar{t})=w''_{g3}(0,\bar{t})\end{aligned} \tag{18}$$

主缆和主梁的无量纲位移设定为:

$$\bar{w}_{cj}(\bar{x}_j,\bar{t})=\sum_{n=1}^{N}c_{jn}(\bar{t})\times C_{jn}(\bar{x}_j) \tag{19a}$$

$$\bar{w}_{gj}(\bar{x}_j,\bar{t})=\sum_{n=1}^{N}g_n(\bar{t})\times G_{jn}(\bar{x}_j) \tag{19b}$$

式中,N 为形函数阶次;$c_{jn}(\bar{t})$、$g_n(\bar{t})$ 为待定系数;$C_{jn}(\bar{x}_j)$ 是满足式(16)几何和力学边界的主缆振动形函数,可表示为:

$$C_{jn}(\bar{x}_j)=\sin\left(\frac{n\pi\bar{x}_j}{\bar{L}_j}\right)\quad(0\leqslant\bar{x}_j\leqslant\bar{L}_j) \tag{20}$$

$G_{jn}(\bar{x}_j)$ 是满足式(17)几何和力学边界的主梁振动形函数,具体形式参见文献[18]。

2.2 矩阵求解形式

将式(18)代入式(13)后乘主缆、主梁相应形函数并积分,可得到 $4N$ 个方程和 $4N$ 个未知数 $(c_{j1},\cdots,c_{jN}、g_{j1},\cdots,g_{jN})$,格式如下:

$$\int_0^{\bar{L}_j}C_{jm}D_{cj}\mathrm{d}\bar{x}_j=0,\sum_{j=1}^{3}\int_0^{\bar{L}_j}G_{jm}D_{gj}\mathrm{d}\bar{x}_j=0 \tag{21}$$

将式(20)化简并重排成矩阵形式,可表示为:

$$[M]_{4N\times4N}\{\ddot{U}(\bar{t})\}+[K]_{4N\times4N}\{U(\bar{t})\}=\{0\}_{4N\times1} \tag{22}$$

式中,$\{U(\bar{t})\}_{4N\times1}=\{\{c(\bar{t})\}^{\mathrm{T}}_{3N\times1},\{g(\bar{t})\}^{\mathrm{T}}_{N\times1}\}$ (23)

$$\begin{aligned}\{c(\bar{t})\}^{\mathrm{T}}_{3N\times1}=\{&c_{11}(\bar{t}),\cdots,c_{1N}(\bar{t}),c_{21}(\bar{t}),\cdots,\\&c_{2N}(\bar{t}),c_{31}(\bar{t}),\cdots,c_{3N}(\bar{t})\}\end{aligned} \tag{24a}$$

$$\{g(\bar{t})\}^{\mathrm{T}}_{N\times1}=\{g_1(\bar{t}),\cdots,g_N(\bar{t})\} \tag{24b}$$

式(22)中无量纲质量矩阵 $[M]_{4N\times4N}$ 为对角矩阵,可表示为:

$$[M]_{4N\times4N}=\mathrm{diag}\{[M_j^{\mathrm{c}}]_{N\times N},[M^{\mathrm{g}}]_{N\times N}\}\quad(j=1,2,3) \tag{25}$$

式中,

$$[M_j^{\mathrm{c}}]_{N\times N}=\begin{bmatrix}M_{j1}^{\mathrm{c}}&0&0\\0&\ddots&0\\0&0&M_{jN}^{\mathrm{c}}\end{bmatrix}\qquad[M^{\mathrm{g}}]_{N\times N}=\begin{bmatrix}M_1^{\mathrm{g}}&0&0\\0&\ddots&0\\0&0&M_N^{\mathrm{g}}\end{bmatrix} \tag{26}$$

其中:

$$M_{jn}^{\mathrm{c}}=(1-\bar{m})\int\bar{L}_{j0}C_{jn}^2\mathrm{d}\bar{x}_j\quad M_n^{\mathrm{g}}=\bar{m}\sum_{j=1}^{3}\int\bar{L}_{j0}G_{jn}^2\mathrm{d}\bar{x}_j \tag{27}$$

式(22)中无量纲刚度矩阵 $[K]_{4N\times4N}$ 可表示为:

$$\begin{aligned}[K]_{4N\times4N}=&[K^{\mathrm{cg}}]_{4N\times4N}+[K^{\mathrm{ce}}]_{4N\times4N}+\\&[K^{\mathrm{ge}}]_{4N\times4N}+[K^{\mathrm{he}}]_{4N\times4N}\end{aligned} \tag{28}$$

其中,$[K^{\mathrm{cg}}]_{4N\times4N}$ 为主缆无量纲几何刚度矩阵;$[K^{\mathrm{ce}}]_{4N\times4N}$ 为主缆无量纲弹性轴向刚度矩阵;$[K^{\mathrm{ge}}]_{4N\times4N}$ 为主梁无量纲压弯刚度矩阵;$[K^{\mathrm{he}}]_{4N\times4N}$ 为吊索无量纲弹性轴向刚度矩阵。

主缆无量纲几何刚度矩阵 $[K^{\mathrm{cg}}]_{4N\times4N}$ 为对角矩阵,可表示为:

$$[K^{\mathrm{cg}}]_{4N\times4N}=\mathrm{diag}\{[K_j^{\mathrm{cg}}]_{N\times N},[0]_{N\times N}\}\quad(j=1,2,3) \tag{29}$$

式中,

$$[K_j^{\mathrm{cg}}]_{N\times N}=\begin{bmatrix}K_{j1}^{\mathrm{cg}}&0&0\\0&\ddots&0\\0&0&K_{jN}^{\mathrm{cg}}\end{bmatrix}\quad K_{jn}^{\mathrm{cg}}=-\int\bar{L}_{j0}C_{jn}C''_{jn}\mathrm{d}\bar{x}_j \tag{30}$$

主缆无量纲弹性轴向刚度矩阵 $[K^{\mathrm{ce}}]_{4N\times4N}$ 可表示为:

$$[K^{\mathrm{ce}}]_{4N\times4N}=\begin{bmatrix}[K^{\mathrm{cen}}]&[0]_{N\times N}\\[0]_{3N\times N}&[0]_{N\times N}\end{bmatrix} \tag{31}$$

式中,

$$[K^{\mathrm{cen}}]_{3N\times3N}=\begin{bmatrix}[K_{11}^{\mathrm{ce}}]&[K_{12}^{\mathrm{ce}}]&[K_{13}^{\mathrm{ce}}]\\ [K_{21}^{\mathrm{ce}}]^{\mathrm{T}}&[K_{22}^{\mathrm{ce}}]&[K_{23}^{\mathrm{ce}}]\\ [K_{31}^{\mathrm{ce}}]^{\mathrm{T}}&[K_{32}^{\mathrm{ce}}]^{\mathrm{T}}&[K_{33}^{\mathrm{ce}}]\end{bmatrix}$$

$$[K_{ji}^{\mathrm{ce}}]_{N\times N}=\begin{bmatrix}K_{ji11}^{\mathrm{ce}}&\cdots&K_{ji1N}^{\mathrm{ce}}\\ \vdots&\ddots&\vdots\\K_{jiN1}^{\mathrm{ce}}&\cdots&K_{jiNN}^{\mathrm{ce}}\end{bmatrix} \tag{32}$$

其中：

$$K_{jimn}^{ce}=\lambda^2\int_0^{L_j}C_{jn}\mathrm{d}\bar{x}_j\int_0^{L_i}C_{in}\mathrm{d}\bar{x}_i \tag{33}$$

主梁无量纲压弯刚度矩阵$[K^{ge}]_{4N\times4N}$为对角矩阵，可表示为：

$$[K^{ge}]_{4N\times4N}=\mathrm{diag}\{[0]_{3N\times3N},[K^{ge}]_{N\times N}\} \tag{34}$$

式中，

$$[K^{ge}]_{N\times N}=\begin{bmatrix}K_1^{ge} & 0 & 0\\ 0 & \ddots & 0\\ 0 & 0 & K_N^{ge}\end{bmatrix}$$

$$K_n^{ge}=\alpha^2\sum_{j=1}^{3}\int_0^{L_j}G_{jn}G_{jn}'''\mathrm{d}\bar{x}_j+\sum_{j=1}^{3}\int_0^{L_j}G_{jn}G_{jn}''\mathrm{d}\bar{x}_j \tag{35}$$

吊索无量纲弹性轴向刚度矩阵$[K^{he}]_{4N\times4N}$可表示为：

$$[K^{he}]_{4N\times4N}=\begin{bmatrix}\mathrm{diag}\{[K_j^{hecc}]_{N\times N}\} & \{[K_j^{hecg}]_{N\times N}\}^{\mathrm{T}}\\ sym. & [K^{hegg}]_{N\times N}\end{bmatrix}$$

$$(j=1,2,3) \tag{36}$$

式中，

$$[K_j^{hecc}]_{N\times N}=\begin{bmatrix}K_{j11}^{hecc} & \cdots & K_{j1N}^{hecc}\\ \vdots & \ddots & \vdots\\ K_{jN1}^{hecc} & \cdots & K_{jNN}^{hecc}\end{bmatrix}$$

$$[K_j^{hecg}]_{N\times N}=\begin{bmatrix}K_{j11}^{hecg} & \cdots & K_{j1N}^{hecg}\\ \vdots & \ddots & \vdots\\ K_{jN1}^{hecg} & \cdots & K_{jNN}^{hecg}\end{bmatrix} \tag{37}$$

$$[K^{hegg}]_{N\times N}=\begin{bmatrix}K_{11}^{hegg} & \cdots & K_{1N}^{hegg}\\ \vdots & \ddots & \vdots\\ K_{N1}^{hegg} & \cdots & K_{NN}^{hegg}\end{bmatrix}$$

其中：

$$K_{jmn}^{hecc}=\chi^2\cdot 8\bar{f}\int_0^{L_j}\frac{C_{jm}C_{jn}}{\bar{l}_{hj}}\mathrm{d}\bar{x}_j$$

$$K_{jmn}^{hecg}=\chi^2\cdot 8\bar{f}\int_0^{L_j}\frac{C_{jm}G_{jn}}{\bar{l}_{hj}}\mathrm{d}\bar{x}_j$$

$$K_{jmn}^{hegg}=\chi^2\cdot 8\bar{f}\sum_{j=1}^{3}\int_0^{L_j}\frac{G_{jm}G_{jn}}{\bar{l}_{hj}}\mathrm{d}\bar{x}_j \tag{38}$$

最终，无量纲连续体模型固有频率$\bar{\omega}_n$、待定特征向量$U_{(\bar{t})}$可通过下式求得：

$$([K]-\bar{\omega}_n{}^2[M])\{U(\bar{t})\}=\{0\} \tag{39}$$

连续体模型对应的振型可通过式(19)获得，连续体模型固有频率为$\omega_n=\bar{\omega}_n\sqrt{g/8f_{c2}}$。

3 算例

将本文提出的连续体模型编制成程序，计算现有数值算例，验证连续体模型的可靠性与准确性。程序运行环境为：MATLAB R2016a，处理器Intel(R) Core(TM) i7-6700HQ CPU @ 2.60GHz、内存8GB。

3.1 文献算例

3.1.1 结构参数描述

本文采用文献[13]中平行索面混凝土自锚式悬索桥作为算例，主要结构参数见表1。连续体模型中将形函数阶次设定为$N=10$，求解本算例的固有频率及振型，程序运行共耗时25.24sec。

文献算例结构参数 表1

桥跨布置							
L_1(m)	L_2(m)	L_3(m)	d_h(m)	f_1(m)	f_2(m)	f_3(m)	L_h(m)
90	240	90	6	4.56	34.88	4.56	36.88

主梁				主缆			吊索	
m_g(t/m)	E_g(GPa)	A_g(m²)	I_g(m⁴)	m_c(t/m)	E_c(GPa)	A_c(m²)	E_h(GPa)	A_h(m²)
47.5031	35	18.6	19.633	1.3235	195	0.1653	195	0.0059

3.1.2 模态参数计算结果

固有频率结果对比见表2，其中数值解1为大连理工大学专用程序DDJ-W计算结果，数值解2为ANSYS计算结果；解析解1为文献[13]经典解析结果，解析解2为文献[7]近似解析结果，解析解3为本文连续体模型给出的经典解析结果。以数值解均值为参考对比三类解析解准确性,连续体模型固有频率误差与文献结果基本吻合,保证了连续体模型的可靠性与准确性。连续体模型计算的1阶对称、反对称振型如图2所示。

文献[7,13]与连续体模型固有频率结果对比　表2

模态	固有频率(Hz)					结果比较(%)		
	文献[13]		文献[7]		连续体模型	文献[13]	文献[7]	连续体模型
	解析解1	数值解1	数值解2	解析解2	解析解3			
1S	0.3419	0.3713	0.3926	0.4038	0.4263	-2.62	1.43	2.90
1AS	0.4194	0.4642	0.4756	0.5181	0.4775	-2.69	2.56	0.40

注:1S代表1阶对称模态。1AS,代表1阶反对称模态。

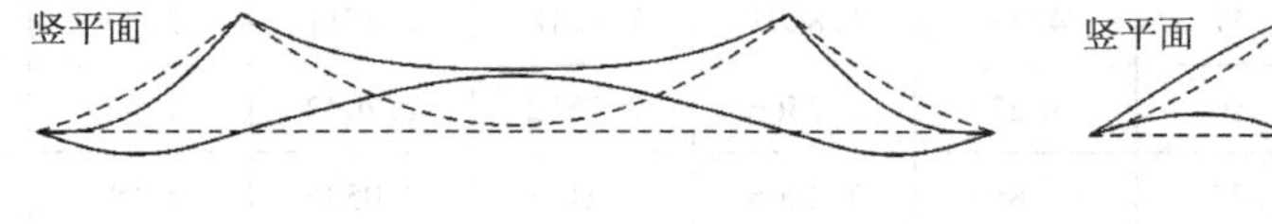

a)1S(连续体模型) ω=0.4263Hz

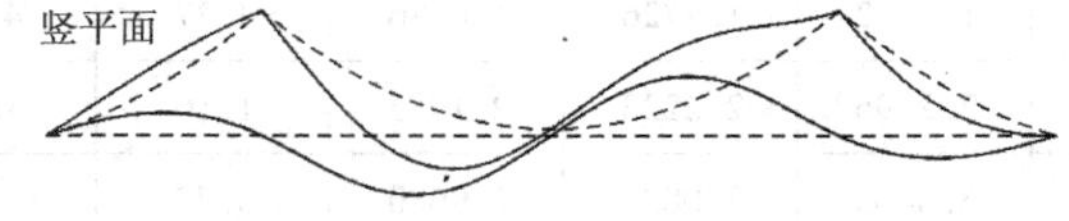

b)1AS (连续体模型) ω=0.4775Hz

图2　平行索面自锚式悬索桥算例振型

3.2 有限元模型算例

3.2.1 结构参数描述

本文采用MIDAS CIVIL建立有限元模型进行特征值分析,如图3所示,桥塔、主梁均采用梁单元模拟,主缆、吊索均采用索单元模拟;吊索-主梁刚性连接,主缆-梁端刚性连接且主梁全桥连续,桥塔塔底固结,结构参数见表3。

3.2.2 模态参数计算结果

按照是否考虑吊索拉伸效应可将连续体模型分为两类:CM-Ext为考虑吊索拉伸效应的连续体模型,χ^2为实际参数计算值。反之,CM-InExt则不考虑吊索拉伸效应,认为吊索刚度足够大而无法变形,设定$\chi^2=1\times10^6$。

图3　自锚式悬索桥有限元模型

有限元模型结构参数　表3

桥跨布置							
L_1(m)	L_2(m)	L_3(m)	d_h(m)	f_1(m)	f_2(m)	f_3(m)	L_h(m)
190	400	190	10	18.05	80	18.05	85

主梁				主缆			吊索	
m_g(t/m)	E_g(Gpa)	A_g(m²)	I_g(m⁴)	m_c(t/m)	E_c(Gpa)	A_c(m²)	E_h(Gpa)	A_h(m²)
14.858	206	1.2784	1.3309	0.2251	200	0.0256	200	0.0013

连续体模型形函数阶次设定为$N=24$,求解固有频率及振型,程序运行共耗时90.49sec。前8阶对称与反对称模态的固有频率与有限元模型固有频率结果对比见表4,1阶反对称模态固有频率误差为-6.10%,2阶反对称模态固有频率误差为-7.74%,其余各阶次模态固有频率误差均在±6%以下,连续体模型与有限元模型结果基本吻合。

连续体模型与有限元模型固有频率结果对比 表4

模态阶次	对称模态(S)固有频率(Hz)					反对称模态(AS)固有频率(Hz)				
	连续体模型		有限元模型(FEM)	结果比较(%)		连续体模型		有限元模型(FEM)	结果比较(%)	
	CM-Ext	CM-InExt		CM-Ext	CM-InExt	CM-Ext	CM-InExt		CM-Ext	CM-InExt
1	0.1406	0.1413	0.1441	-2.43	-1.94	0.1739	0.1741	0.1852	-6.10	-5.99
2	0.3560	0.3597	0.3551	0.25	1.30	0.2740	0.2746	0.2970	-7.74	-7.54
3	0.5012	0.5068	0.5013	-0.02	1.10	0.6932	0.6938	0.6872	0.87	0.96
4	0.8182	0.8193	0.8050	1.64	1.78	0.8924	0.8941	0.8757	1.91	2.10
5	1.1639	1.1658	1.1293	3.06	3.23	1.5549	1.5556	1.5022	3.51	3.55
6	1.7712	1.7726	1.6986	4.27	4.36	1.8691	1.8718	1.7711	5.53	5.69
7	2.2196	2.2223	2.1955	1.10	1.22	2.7566	2.7572	2.7042	1.94	1.96
8	3.0806	3.0820	2.9680	3.79	3.84	3.2065	3.2105	3.0536	5.01	5.14

CM-InExt计算得出的频率均大于CM-Ext得出的频率,这表明不考虑吊索拉伸将提升结构部分刚度,导致频率有所增大,尤其对高阶反对称模态频率影响较大,8阶反对称模态频率二者相差0.004Hz,相比于CM-InExt,CM-Ext更符合工程实际,计算结果也更为精确、可靠。

4 结语

本文基于挠度理论,推导了考虑吊索拉伸的自锚式悬索桥连续体模型,为识别其动力特性,通过无量纲处理得到包含6个无量纲特征参数在内的连续体模型,结合数值及有限元算例验证其准确性,得出以下结论:

(1)根据振动形态挠度理论并结合缆-索-梁变形方程可直接建立起自锚式悬索桥竖向自由振动连续体模型,主梁压弯耦合项抵消了主缆恒载初始水平力的影响,使得方程进一步简化,其竖向自由振动特性可由6个无量纲特征参数共同决定。

(2)未考虑吊索拉伸效应使得结构刚度得到部分提升,以致模态频率增大,对高阶反对称模态影响明显。

(3)与有限元模型相比,本文提出的改进连续体模型能高效准确地计算自锚式悬索桥竖向自由振动固有频率及振型,可为工程初步设计阶段的动力特性提供参考。

(4)自锚式悬索桥主缆真实线形并非二次抛物线,振动过程中还需要考虑非线性与垂度效应。连续本模型可从上述两方面进行改进。

参考文献

[1] 康俊涛,袁敏,王同民.大跨径自锚式悬索桥成桥状态动力特性参数分析[J].桥梁建设,2013,43(6):64-70.

[2] 贺耀北,邵旭东,张欣,等.钢-UHPC组合梁自锚式悬索桥力学性能与经济性分析[J].桥梁建设,2021,51(1):51-57.

[3] 李传习,柯红军,刘海波,等.空间主缆自锚式悬索桥成桥状态的确定方法[J].工程力学,2010,27(5):137-146.

[4] Fei Han, Zichen Deng, Danhui Dan. Vertical Vibrations of Suspension Bridges: A Review and a New Method [J]. Archives of Computational Methods in Engineering, 2021, 28:1591-1610.

[5] Tao Li, Zhao Liu. An Improved Continuum Model for Determining the Behavior of Suspension Bridges during Construction [J]. Automation in Construction, 2021, 127:103715.

[6] 郭俊,刘胜红,高嵩,等.自锚式独塔悬索桥竖向弯曲振动基频估算公式[J].重庆交通大学学报(自然科学版),2019,38(5):27-32.

[7] 张筱雨,刘来君,宋涛,等.计入主塔刚度的双塔自锚式悬索桥竖向弯曲频率估算公式[J].江苏大学学报(自然科学版),2017,38(3):355-360.

[8] Bleich F, McCullough C B, Rosecrans R, et al. The Mathematical Theory of Vibration in Suspension Bridges [M]. Washington: US

Government Printing Office,1950.

[9] Abdel-Ghaffar A M. Suspension Bridge Vibration: Continuum Formulation [J]. Journal of the Engineering Mechanics Division, 1982, 108 (6): 1215-1232.

[10] Hayashikawa T, Watanabe N. Vertical Vibration in Timoshenko Beam Suspension Bridges [J]. Journal of Engineering Mechanics, 1984, 110 (3):341-356.

[11] Kim M Y, Kwon S D, Kim N I. Analytical and Numerical Study on Free Vertical Vibration of Shear-Flexible Suspension Bridges[J]. Journal of Sound and Vibration, 2000, 238 (1): 65-84.

[12] J. Enrique Luco, José Turmo. Linear Vertical Vibrations of Suspension Bridges: A Review of Continuum Models and Some New Results [J]. Soil Dynamics & Earthquake Engineering, 2010, 30 (9):769-781.

[13] 刘春城,张哲,石磊,等. 混凝土自锚式悬索桥竖向自由振动的理论研究[J]. 工程力学,2005,22(4):126-130.

[14] Jose Turmo, J. Enrique Luco. Effect of Hanger Flexibility on Dynamic Response of Suspension Bridges [J]. Journal of Engineering Mechanics, 2010, 136 (12):1444-1459.

[15] Sun-Gil Gwon, Dong-Ho Choi. Static and Dynamic Analyses of a Suspension Bridge with Three-Dimensionally Curved Main Cables Using a Continuum Model [J]. Engineering Structures, 2018, 161(15):250-264.

[16] Sun-Gil Gwon, Dong-Ho Choi. Continuum Model for Static and Dynamic Analysis of Suspension Bridges with a Floating Girder [J]. Journal of Bridge Engineering, 2018, 23 (10):04018079. 1-04018079. 13.

[17] Myung-Rag Jung, Sang-Uk Shin, Mario M. Attard, et al. Deflection Theory for Self-Anchored Suspension Bridges under Live Load[J]. Journal of Bridge Engineering, 2015, 20 (7):04014093.

[18] T. G. Konstantakopoulos, G. T. Michaltsos. A Mathematical Model for a Combined Cable System of Bridges[J]. Engineering Structures, 2010, 32 (9):2717-2728.

训练形式对 NARX-ANN 桥上列车轮轨力预测代理模型精度的影响

韩 艳[1] 张 迅[1] 王力东*[1] 朱志辉[2] 刘汉云[1]

(1. 长沙理工大学土木工程学院;2. 中南大学土木工程学院)

摘 要 本文基于带外生输入的非线性自回归人工神经网络(NARX-ANN),建立了桥上列车轮轨力预测代理模型。在此基础上,研究了训练形式对 NARX-ANN 模型预测精度的影响。该研究以 CRH2 型列车通过 3 跨 32 m 简支梁桥为例,首先,建立车-桥耦合振动模型,并计算列车通过桥梁时的竖向和横向轮轨力时程;其次,建立 NARX-ANN 模型,分别采用闭环和先开后闭的训练形式对代理模型进行训练;最后,对比分析利用两种训练形式的 NARX-ANN 模型对轮轨力的预测精度。结果表明:NARX-ANN 模型能有效地预测竖向和横向轮轨力,并且对竖向轮轨力时程的预测精度高于横向力。相对于先开后闭的训练形式,闭环训练的神经网络对轮轨力时程的预测精度更高。

关键词 车-桥耦合系统 NARX-ANN 模型 训练形式 轮轨力 可靠度

1. 基金项目:国家自然科学基金资助项目(51822803, 51778073);国家重点研发计划项目(2017YFB1201204);湖南省研究生科研创新资助项目(CX20200840)。

0 引言

为保证高速列车运行的安全性和舒适性，同时为解决铁路线路占用耕地较多、难以穿越复杂地形等问题，我国常采用以桥代路的建设方式。据统计，我国高速铁路网中桥梁平均占比大于50%[1]。车-桥系统可靠度成为各国学者的重要研究内容。然而，车-桥耦合振动响应的计算效率是制约可靠度分析的瓶颈。

为解决传统时域求解法计算耗时巨大的问题，Gualano等[2]运用带外生输入的非线性自回归人工神经网络(NARX-ANN)模型，直接利用轨道不平顺预测了竖向轮轨力时程，大幅度提高了计算速度，但预测精度有待提高。庞学苗[3]等和潘丽莎等[4]对比了多种神经网络结构对轮轨力时程的预测精度，并提出NARX神经网络更适合列车轮轨力时程预测。Han等[5]提出了基于重要样本的NARX-ANN车-桥耦合代理模型，分析了轨道高低不平顺作用下列车通过简支梁桥时车体的竖向加速度。

NARX-ANN模型属于黑箱模型，其超参数的选择、训练算法和训练形式等多个方面都会影响NARX神经网络代理模型精度和训练效率[6]。文献[4,7]利用交叉验证，研究了NARX-ANN模型结构的层数、各层神经元个数以及延迟阶数对代理模型精度的影响；文献[3,8]对不同的训练算法进行了对比研究，得到了有意义的结论。目前，虽然已有部分学者开始对NARX-ANN模型代理模型进行研究，但对训练形式的研究为数甚少。

因此，本文以CRH2型列车通过3跨32m简支梁桥为例，建立NARX-ANN车-桥耦合振动代理模型，并以分离迭代法计算的竖向和横向轮轨力作为训练样本，对比闭环和先开后闭两种训练形式下轮轨力时程和最大值的预测精度，并探讨响应初始值和正则化系数对代理模型预测精度的影响，从而为NARX-ANN车-桥耦合振动代理模型选择合理的训练形式和超参数设置提供参考。

1 NARX-ANN车-桥耦合振动代理模型

1.1 NARX-ANN模型

NARX模型是统计学上常用的时间序列模型，适用于非线性动力系统拟合[9,10]。该模型利用历史时刻的输入和输出信息，以及当前时刻的输入信息，预测当前时刻的输出，其表达式为[11]：

$$y_t = f(\mathrm{O}_t) = f(x_t, x_{t-1}, \cdots, x_{t-n_x}, y_{t-1}, y_{t-2} \cdots y_{t-n_y}) \tag{1}$$

式中：x_t 和 x_{t-n_x} 分别表示当前时刻和 $t-n_x$ 时刻的输入向量，y_t 和 y_{t-n_y} 分别表示当前时刻和 $t-n_y$ 时刻的输出向量，其中 n_x 和 n_y 分别表示输入和输出的延迟阶数；$\mathrm{O}(t)=[x_t, x_{t-1}, \cdots, x_{t-n_x}, y_{t-1}, y_{t-2} \cdots y_{t-n_y}]^T$ 表示整合后的当前值和历史值向量；$f(\cdot)$ 表示非线性映射函数，当利用神经网络拟合 $f(\cdot)$ 时，称该模型为NARX-ANN模型。NARX-ANN模型结构如图1所示。

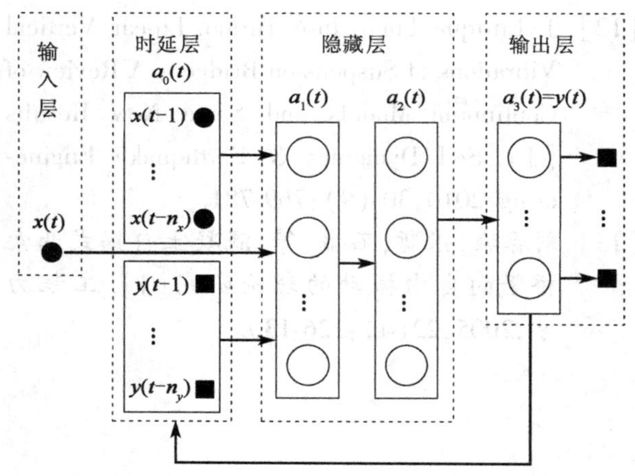

图1 NARX-ANN模型结构

NARX-ANN模型由多个神经元组成，分别包含输入层、时延层、隐藏层和输出层。当前时刻第 l 层神经元的输出 $a_l(t)$ 可以表示为：

$$\begin{aligned} z_l(t) &= W_l\, a_{l-1}(t) + b_l \\ a_l(t) &= f_l(z_l(t)) \end{aligned} \tag{2}$$

式中：W_l 和 b_l 分别表示第 $l-1$ 到第 l 层的权重矩阵和偏置向量；$z_l(t)$ 表示第 l 层神经元的净输入向量；$a_l(t)$ 表示第 l 层神经元的输出向量，当 $l=0$ 时，$a_0(t)$ 为当前值和历史值向量 $\mathrm{O}(t)$；$f_l(\cdot)$ 表示第 l 层神经元的激活函数，对于隐藏层 $f_l(z)=\tanh(z)=(e^z-e^{-z})/(e^z+e^{-z})$，对于输出层 $f_l(z)=z$。

1.2 训练形式

训练神经网络的过程是通过优化算法，利用已有的样本数据，调整式(2)中的权重 W_l 和偏执 b_l，从而提高神经网络的预测精度。NARX-ANN

模型与一般的循环神经网络模型不同,它直接将输出层的输出值作为隐藏层的活性值输入延迟层。由于在训练的过程中真实输出是已知的,因此,可将 NARX-ANN 模型配置成开环或闭环的形式(图 2)进行训练。当采用开环形式训练时,该模型为传统的静态神经网络,可利用真实的输出采用标准 BP 算法进行训练。采用开环形式训练的模型结构简单,训练速度较快,但对噪声有偏。当采用闭环形式训练时,该模型为循环神经网络,必须利用模型反馈的输出采用随时间的 BP 算法(BPTT)或实时递归学习算法(RTRL)等循环神经网络的训练方法进行训练。采用闭环形式训练的模型对噪声无偏,但训练过程复杂,训练速度较慢。因此,部分学者提出先利用开环形式快速训练神经网络,当权重W_l 和偏执b_l 收敛后,再利用闭环形式进行训练,以消除噪声的影响,从而提高神经网络预测精度。

本文采用均方差(MSE)函数作为损失函数:

$$L(\theta)=\frac{1}{TSN}\sum_{s=1}^{S}\sum_{n=1}^{N}\sum_{t=\max(n_x,n_y)+1}^{T}[y_{s,n,t}-\hat{y}_{s,n,t}(\theta)]^2+\lambda\ell_p(\theta) \tag{3}$$

式中,S 表示训练样本的个数;N 表示 NARX-ANN 模型输出特征的个数;T 表示训练样本序列的长度;$\theta=[W_l,b_l]$表示 NARX-ANN 模型的参数;λ 表示正则化系数,是神经网络的超参数;ℓ_p 表示范数函数;y 表示训练样本的真实输出;$\hat{y}(\theta)$表示模型反馈的输出,当采用开环形式训练时 $\hat{y}_{s,n,t}=f(x_{s,t},x_{s,t-1},\cdots,x_{s,t-n_x},y_{s,t-1},y_{s,t-2}\cdots y_{s,t-n_y})$,当采用闭环形式训练时 $\hat{y}_{s,n,t}=f(x_{s,t},x_{s,t-1},\cdots,x_{s,t-n_x},\hat{y}_{s,n,t-1},\hat{y}_{s,n,t-2}\cdots\hat{y}_{s,n,t-n_y})$。

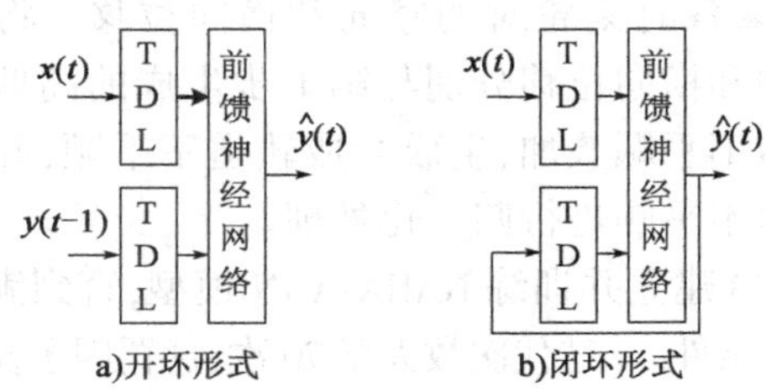

图 2 训练形式

1.3 预测流程

轨道不平顺和桥梁各位置刚度不同是车-桥系统耦合振动的重要激励源。因此,本文将轨道不平顺、无轨道不平顺作用下的轮对位移以及初始轮轨力作为 NARX-ANN 模型的输入,竖向和横向轮轨力作为 NARX-ANN 模型的输出。具体分析流程如图 3 所示。

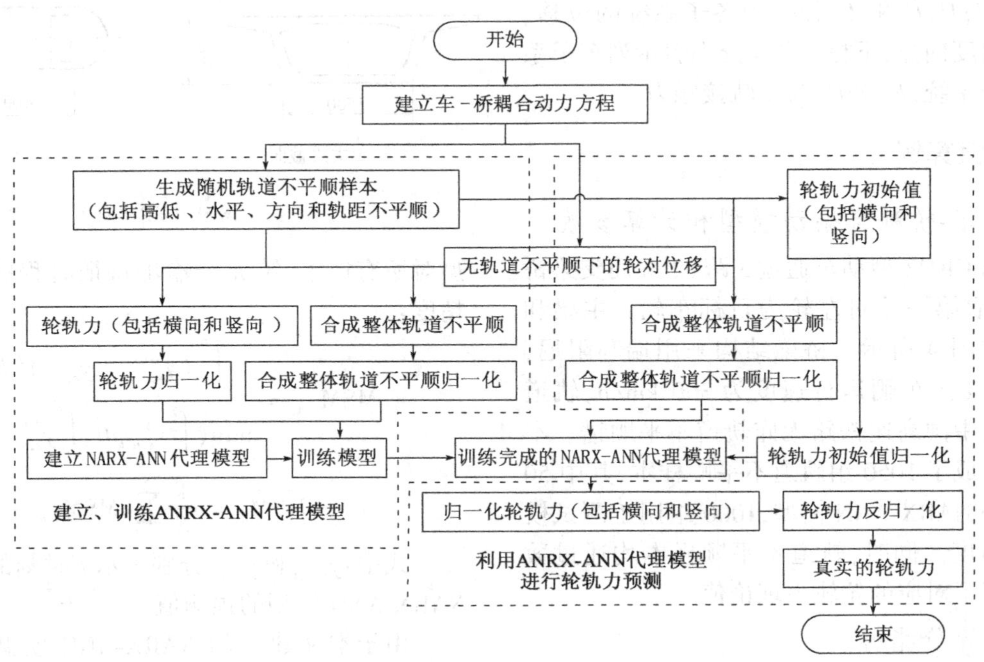

图 3 神经网络预测轮轨力流程图

(1)随机生成多组轨道不平顺样本(包含高低、水平、方向和轨距不平顺),并利用分离迭代法计算各组轨道不平顺作用下的车-桥耦合振动响应。确定需要预测的目标车轮,提取该车轮的轮轨力(包含竖向和横向轮轨力)时程,并对轮轨力进行归一化处理。

(2)计算无轨道不平顺下的车-桥耦合振动响应,提取各时刻轮对的竖向和横向位移。将轮对的竖向和横向位移分别与第 1 步生成的高低和方向轨道不平顺叠加,生成合成轨道不平顺,并对合成轨道不平顺进行归一化处理。

(3)建立并训练 NARX-ANN 模型,直到满足迭代终止条件。[迭代次数大于 70 次,惩罚因子μ大于10^{10},验证失败次数(validation checks)大于 6 次]。

(4)再次生成多组轨道不平顺样本,利用分离迭代法计算前$n_{\max}=\max(n_x,n_y)$步的初始轮轨力向量或将初始轮轨力向量设置为 0。在此基础上,利用第 2 步的方法生成合成轨道不平顺,并对合成轨道不平顺和初始轮轨力向量进行归一化处理。

(5)将归一化处理后的合成轨道不平顺和初始轮轨力输入训练完成的 NARX-ANN 模型,预测初始轮轨力向量之后的归一化轮轨力,对预测的归一化轮轨力进行反归一化处理,得到最终的轮轨力时程。

2　车-桥耦合系统分析模型

车-桥耦合振动模型由列车模型和轨道-桥梁模型组成并通过轮轨接触关系相互联系。列车采用多体动力学建模,其中车体和转向架考虑横移、浮沉、侧滚、摇头和点头运动,轮对则考虑横移、浮沉、侧滚和摇头运动,共计 31 个自由度;轨道-桥梁采用有限元方法建模,并通过直接刚度法形成模型的动力矩阵;在考虑轨道不平顺的基础上,采用迹线法确定列车和轨道-桥梁子系统的轮轨接触关系,并分别利用赫兹非线性接触理论和 Johnson-Vermeulen 理论计算轮轨法向力和蠕滑力。最终,车-桥耦合振动模型的动力方程可以写成如下形式:

$$\begin{bmatrix} M_v & 0 \\ 0 & M_b \end{bmatrix}\begin{bmatrix} \ddot{U}_v(t) \\ \ddot{U}_b(t) \end{bmatrix}+\begin{bmatrix} C_v & 0 \\ 0 & C_b \end{bmatrix}\begin{bmatrix} \dot{U}_v(t) \\ \dot{U}_b(t) \end{bmatrix}+\begin{bmatrix} K_v & 0 \\ 0 & K_b \end{bmatrix}\begin{bmatrix} U_v(t) \\ U_b(t) \end{bmatrix}=\begin{bmatrix} F_{vb}(t) \\ F_{bv}(t) \end{bmatrix} \tag{4}$$

式中:M、C 和 K 分别为各子系统的质量、刚度和阻尼矩阵;U、$\dot{U}$ 和 $\ddot{U}$ 分别为各子系统的位移、速度和加速度向量;下标 v 和 b 分别表示列车子系统和桥梁子系统;F_{vb}和F_{bv}为轮轨接触力。

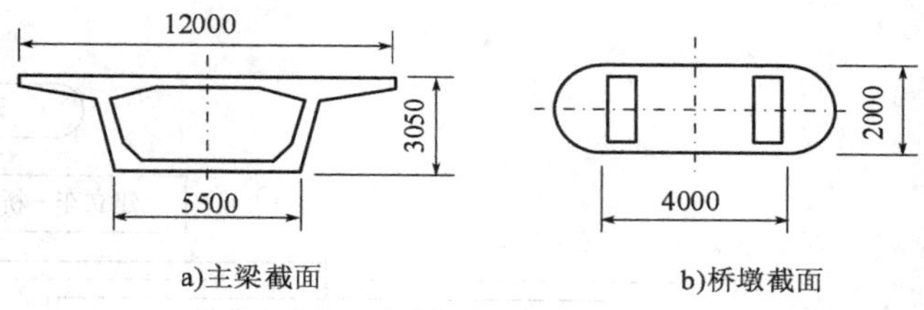

图4　桥梁截面

3　数值算例

3.1　车-桥耦合振动模型和计算参数

本文以 CRH2 型动车通过 3 跨 32 m 简支梁桥为例,并选取第一轮对左轮为目标车轮。主梁和桥墩截面如图 4 所示。桥梁结构采用瑞利阻尼,阻尼比取 5%。车辆运行速度为 300 km/h,轨道不平顺采用中国高速铁路无砟轨道不平顺谱。本研究随机生成了 1050 组轨道不平顺样本,其中 50 组用于训练 NARX-ANN 模型,1000 组用于测试模型的预测精度。同时,轨道不平顺样本均通过数值积分计算了对应的轮轨力理论值。

3.2　评价指标

本文采用均方误差(MSM)[7]来衡量 NARX-ANN 模型对第 s 个样本、第 n 个输出特征时程的预测精度,并采用平均均方误差($\overline{\text{MSM}}$)来衡量模型对所有样本、第 n 个输出特征时程的平均预测精度:

$$\text{MSM}_{s,n}=\frac{\int_0^T (y_{s,n,t}-\hat{y}_{s,n,t})^2 dt}{\min\left(\int_0^T y_{s,n,t}^2 dt,\int_0^T \hat{y}_{s,n,t}^2 dt\right)} \tag{5}$$

$$\overline{\text{MSM}}_n=\frac{1}{S}\sum_{s=1}^{S}\text{MSM}_{s,n} \tag{6}$$

式中:$y_{s,n,t}$和$\hat{y}_{s,n,t}$分别表示 t 时刻的理论值和 NARX-ANN 模型的预测值。

由于本文建立的 NARX-ANN 模型包含竖向和横向轮轨力两个输出特征,在对比多个代理模型的预测精度时会发现,有可能对竖向和横向轮轨力预测精度最高的代理模型并不是同一个模型。另外，根据以往研究可知，神经网络对竖向轮轨力的预测精度高于对横向轮轨力的预测精度[7]，若简单采用竖向和横向轮轨力的$\overline{\mathrm{MSM}}$之和去对比不同神经网络的精度，会导致横向轮轨力的$\overline{\mathrm{MSM}}$对模型精度的评价起决定性作用。为了更合理地评价不同模型的精度，本文提出了整体误差系数(WEC)来比较多输出特征模型的整体精度。其具体表达式为：

$$\mathrm{WEC}_j=\frac{1}{N}\cdot\sum_{n=1}^{N}\frac{\overline{\mathrm{MSM}}_{j,n}}{\min(\overline{\mathrm{MSM}}_{1,n},\overline{\mathrm{MSM}}_{2,n},\cdots,\overline{\mathrm{MSM}}_{J,n})}-1 \tag{7}$$

式中：J表示需要对比的模型总个数；$\overline{\mathrm{MSM}}_{j,n}$表示第$j$个模型预测的第$n$个输出特征的$\overline{\mathrm{MSM}}$。该式以最优输出特征的$\overline{\mathrm{MSM}}$的倒数作为权重，在提高竖向力预测精度权重的同时，降低了横向力预测精度的权重，从而消除竖向力和横向力预测精度相差较大的影响。WEC为大于等于0的实数，同时WEC越小，表明模型的整体预测精度越高，若某个模型对竖向力和横向力的预测精度都最高，则该模型的WEC = 0，表明该模型在所有代理模型中整体预测精度最高。

3.3 超参数分析

本文通过试算和查阅相关文献，确定了包含两个隐藏层的NARX-ANN模型结构，第一个和第二个隐藏层的神经元个数分别为15和10。为了全面分析闭环和先开后闭两种训练形式对NARX-ANN模型对轮轨力时程预测精度的影响，确定两种训练形式对应的最优延迟阶数，本文分别对表1所示模型进行对比研究。图5为输出延迟$n_y=5$时，代理模型对时程的预测精度随输入延迟阶数n_x的变化曲线。可以看出，采用闭环形式训练的模型精度明显高于采用先开后闭形式训练的模型精度。当$\lambda=0$时，采用先开后闭形式训练的模型误差较大，横向力和竖向力的$\overline{\mathrm{MSM}}$在$n_x=55$时最小，分别为0.76%和154.4%，表明该配置下采用先开后闭形式训练的模型不适用于横向轮轨力预测。当$\lambda=0.02$时，采用先开后闭形式训练的模型预测精度明显提高，但仍不及采用闭环形式训练的模型。除B_1和B_2模型外，其余模型的预测精度随输入延迟阶数n_x的增加显著提高，以A_2神经网络为例，n_x由5增加至55时，竖向力和横向力的$\overline{\mathrm{MSM}}$分别降低了86.0%和92.0%，这表明增加输入延迟阶数能有效提高NARX-ANN模型的预测精度。

NARX-ANN模型配置 表1

名　称	A_1	A_2	B_1	B_2	C_1	C_2
训练形式	闭环	闭环	先开后闭	先开后闭	先开后闭	先开后闭
正则化系数λ	0	0	0	0	0.02	0.02
初始输出值	理论值	0	理论值	0	理论值	0

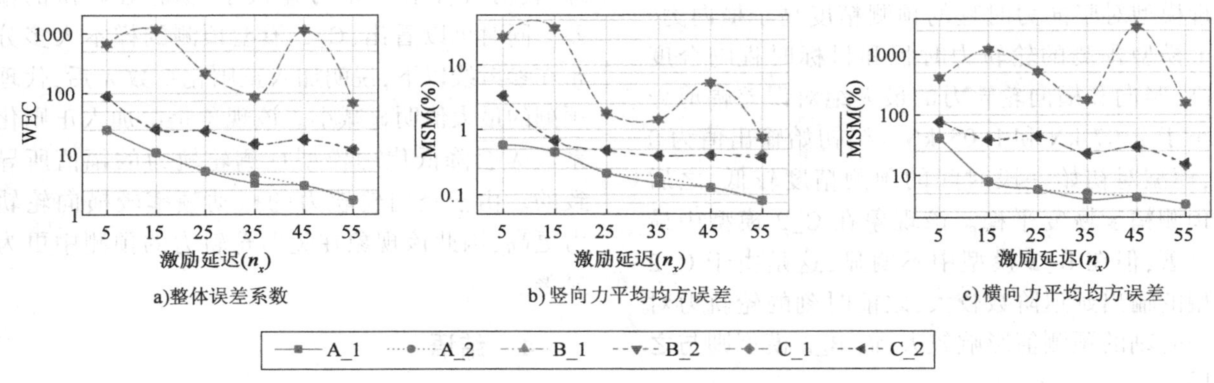

图5 神经网络精度随激励延迟变化曲线

图6为输入延迟阶数 n_x 为55时,NARX-ANN模型对时程的预测精度随输出延迟阶数 n_y 的变化曲线。可以看出,随着响应延迟阶数 n_y 的增加,A_1模型的整体误差系数呈下降趋势,并在 n_y = 35时达到最小值,此时竖向力和横向力的 $\overline{\text{MSM}}$ 分别为0.026%和1.78%。C_1和C_2模型对输出延迟阶数 n_y 不敏感,WEC基本维持在8.08左右,但在 n_y > 35时,利用真实初始输出会提高该模型的预测精度。当 n_y ≤ 2时,A_1、A_2和B_1、B_2模型的整体预测精度基本一致,说明该配置下训练形式对模型影响不大,但当 n_y > 2时,B_1和B_2神经网络的精度急剧降低。当 n_y > 5时,A_1和A_2神经网络的变化趋势不再一致,说明此时初始输出是影响神经网络精度的重要因素。根据上述分析,本文确定各配置下神经网络的最优延迟阶数如表2所示。

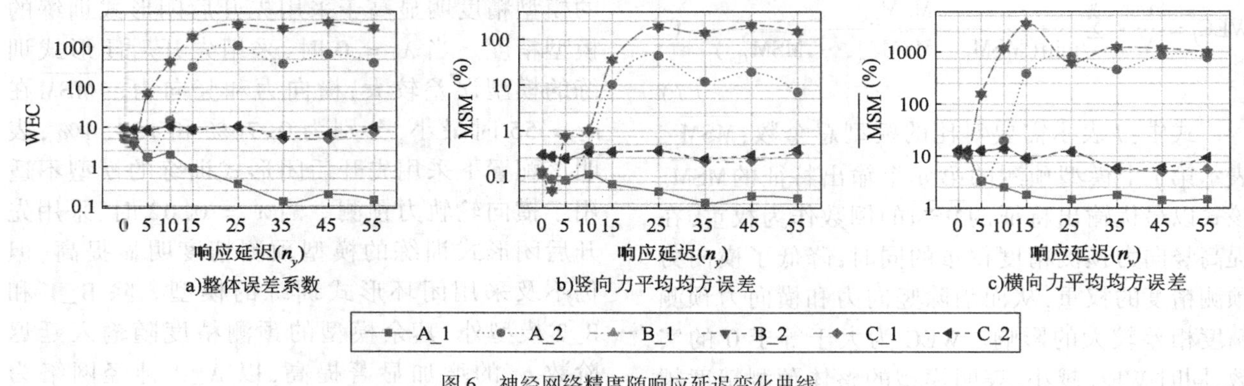

图6　神经网络精度随响应延迟变化曲线

神经网络配置　　表2

名　称	A_1	A_2	B_1	B_2	C_1	C_2
最优延迟阶数[n_x,n_y]	[55,35]	[55,5]	[55,2]	[55,2]	[55,35]	[55,35]
WEC	0.13	1.71	3.56	3.56	8.62	8.62

3.4　时域分析

为进一步研究NARX-ANN模型对时程的预测精度,本文对所有测试样本中与模型 $\overline{\text{MSM}}$ 值最接近的样本进行分析。图7给出了轮轨力预测时程和目标时程的对比曲线。由于B和C模型受初始输出值的影响较小,因此对于B、C模型,仅展示初始输出值为0条件下的对比曲线。可以看出,代理模型对竖向力时程的预测精度高于横向力。A_1模型预测的轮轨力时程和目标时程吻合度最高,竖向和横向轮轨力的最大绝对误差幅值分别小于1.07 kN和1.05 kN。当初始输出值为0时,模型对初始一段时间的预测精度较低,之后的预测精度恢复平稳。该现象在C_2模型中最为显著,但在B_2模型中不明显,这是由于C_2模型的输出延迟阶数较大,之前时刻的轮轨力对下一时刻的预测值影响较大,而B_2模型则与之相反。

3.5　最大值分析

轮轨力最大值是影响列车行车安全的重要指标,本节对NARX-ANN模型时程预测的最大值进行分析。图8给出了列车通过第二跨桥梁时,轮轨力目标时程最大值和预测时程最大值对比图,图中每一个点表示一个测试样本,其横坐标表示通过数值积分计算的目标时程最大值,纵坐标表示代理模型预测的时程最大值。由图8a)可以看出,A_1模型最接近参考线,但较参考线略有下降,表明A_1模型的方差最小,但存在轻微的偏差。同时可以看出,C_2模型预测的样本大多分布在参考线以下,说明加入正则化系数 λ 后,代理预测的最大值明显减小。该现象是由加入正则化系数 λ 会降低代理模型预测轮轨力的幅值所导致的。由于竖向轮轨力的振动频率较横向轮轨力更高,因此该现象在竖向轮轨力的预测中更为显著。

4　结语

本文建立了NARX-ANN桥上列车轮轨力代理模型,并以CRH2型动车通过3跨32 m简支梁桥为例,对比分析了训练形式、初始输出值和正则化系数对轮轨力时程和最大值预测精度的影响，得到以下结论：

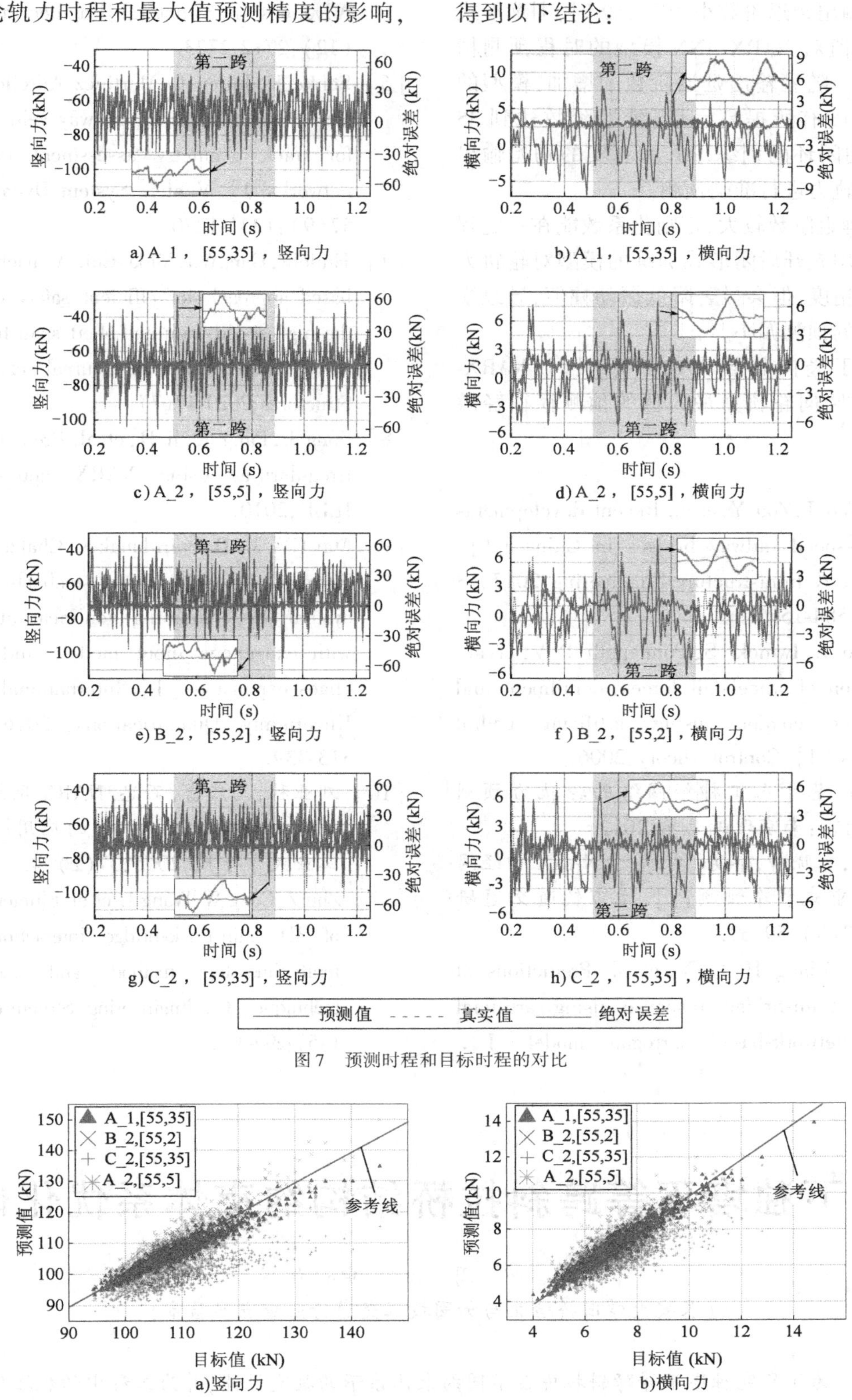

图7 预测时程和目标时程的对比

图8 轮轨力最大值对比

(1) NARX-ANN 模型能通过轨道不平顺有效地预测轮轨力时程曲线，并且对竖向轮轨力时程的预测精度高于横向轮轨力。同时，采用闭环形式训练的模型对轮轨力时程的预测精度较高。

(2)当输出延迟阶数小于等于2时,训练形式和初始输出值对NARX-ANN模型的时程预测精度影响不大。随着输出延迟阶数的增加,模型的时程预测精度有所提高,但当延迟阶数达到35时,必须采用闭环的训练形式和真实的初始输出值才能对轮轨力进行准确预测。

(3)若延迟阶数较大,正则化系数能在一定程度上提高采用先开后闭形式训练的模型对轮轨力时程的预测精度,但会显著降低振动幅值,导致模型对最大值的预测偏小。

(4)由于竖向轮轨力的频率很高,NARX-ANN模型对竖向轮轨力最大值的预测存在轻微偏差。

参考文献

[1] He X, Wu T, Zou Y, et al. Recent developments of high-speed railway bridges in China [J]. Structure & Infrastructure Engineering, 2017, 13(12):1584-1595.

[2] Gualano L, Iwnicki S, Ponnapalli P V, et al. Prediction of wheel-rail forces, derailment and passenger comfort using artificial neural networks [J]. Control Theory, 2006.

[3] 庞学苗. 基于人工神经网络的轮轨力预测[D]. 南京:南京理工大学, 2012.

[4] 潘丽莎, 程晓卿, 秦勇, 等. 基于NARX神经网络的轮重减载率预测[J]. 城市轨道交通研究, 2012(9):59-62.

[5] Han X, Xiang H, Li Y, et al. Predictions of vertical train-bridge response using artificial neural network-based surrogate model [J]. Advances in Structural Engineering, 2019, 22(12):2712-2723.

[6] Sönke K, Julien C, Martinez Aurélie. Black-box modelling of nonlinear railway vehicle dynamics for track geometry assessment using neural networks[J]. Vehicle System Dynamics, 2019, 57(9):1241-1270.

[7] HuileLi, GangWu, Mida Cui. A machine learning based approach for efficient safety evaluation of the high speed train and short span bridge system [J]. Latin American Journal of Solids and Structures, 2020, 17(7).

[8] Song L, Pang X, Ji H, et al. Prediction of track irregularities using NARX neural network. IEEE, 2010.

[9] Mai CV, M. D. Spiridonakos, Chatzi E N, et al. Surrogate modeling for stochastic dynamical systems by combining nonlinear autoregressive with exogenous input models and polynomial chaos expansions[J]. International Journal for Uncertainty Quantifications, 2016, 6(4):313-339.

[10] 刘亚秋, 马广富, 石忠. NARX网络在自适应逆控制动态系统辨识中的应用[J]. 哈尔滨工业大学学报, 2005, 37(2):4.

[11] Zhu Z, Gong W, Wang L, et al. Efficient assessment of 3D train-track-bridge interaction combining multi-time-step method and moving track technique[J]. Engineering Structures, 2019, 183(15):290-302.

地震下独塔不等跨斜拉桥结构约束体系优化研究

冯 昭 周 敉* 申心力

(长安大学旧桥检测与加固技术交通行业重点实验室)

摘 要 为了研究独塔不等跨斜拉桥在不同约束体系下的抗震性能,并为工程中的独塔斜拉桥选取

1. 基金项目:陕西省重点研发计划项目(2019KW-051);陕西省创新人才推进计划-科技创新团队项目(2018TD-040);国家自然科学基金资助项目(51978062);陕西省自然科学基础计划项目-联合基金项目(2021JLM-47);项目大跨度、大流量、多塔斜拉压力输水管桥关键技术研究(Program No. 2021JLM-47)资助。

最合适的约束体系，本文以某 160m + 120m 的独塔不等跨斜拉桥为研究对象，使用有限元分析软件 CSI Bridge 建立全桥模型，并采用时程分析的方法对多种不同约束体系的斜拉桥进行地震反应分析，通过对比塔底、墩顶、墩底等关键截面的弯矩值和位移值来确定独塔斜拉桥的最佳约束体系方案。结果表明，对于本文所研究的斜拉桥而言，在主塔处布置仅纵向滑动的摩擦摆支座，在主跨过渡墩上布置双向摩擦摆支座的体系是整体抗震性能较好的一种约束体系，可以使主塔和各墩的地震响应合理分配，从而提升桥梁整体抗震性能。

关键词 桥梁抗震 约束体系 摩擦摆支座 独塔不等跨斜拉桥

0 引言

斜拉桥是一种塔、梁、索共同受力的结构体系，由于拉索的存在主梁在其跨内多了很多弹性支承点，主梁受力更加均匀，因此斜拉桥有着较为良好的跨越能力。斜拉桥的结构体系随着塔、梁、墩之间结合方式的改变而改变，通过改变塔、梁、墩的结合方式，可以使整体结构受力更加合理均匀[1-2]。

斜拉桥常用体系有飘浮体系、刚构体系和支承体系等[3]。一般而言，对于独塔斜拉桥，在仅考虑正常使用荷载作用的情况下选用刚构体系是较为适宜的，但刚构体系桥在地震高烈度地区响应强烈，往往在主塔底部产生较大的地震力[4]，因此有必要对独塔斜拉桥的约束体系进行更深入的研究。黄鸣柳等[5]以珠海洪鹤大桥为例，研究了双座串联大跨度斜拉桥的合理横向约束体系；王照伟等[6]则以某大跨度三塔斜拉桥为例对其纵向约束体系展开研究；周敉等[7]结合多种减隔震装置对大跨连续刚构桥合理约束体系进行了研究；国内外其他学者也针对斜拉桥的约束体系展开了许多研究[8-9]。还有一些学者将减隔震装置与斜拉桥结合在一起，对其进行参数优化和约束体系分析[10-12]。

本文以某 160m + 120m 的独塔斜拉桥为研究对象，结合桥梁自身情况拟定不同的约束体系，通过对比各体系下关键截面的地震响应展开研究分析，从而确定该独塔斜拉桥的最优约束体系。

1 工程概况

本文研究对象为独塔不等跨斜拉桥，跨径布置为 160m + 120m。较短跨的一边在距主塔 85m 处设置辅助墩，桥型布置如图 1 所示。根据《建筑抗震设计规范》(GB 50011—2001)中附录 A 的界定，拟建工程区抗震设防烈度为 7 度，设计基本地震加速度值为 0.10g。主桥上部结构采用扁平箱形预应力混凝土主梁。桥塔为 C50 的异型倒 Y 形桥塔，塔柱均采用空心箱形截面。辅助墩横桥向为门式结构，边墩为带盖梁的桩柱式形式，基础均采用钻孔灌注桩群桩基础。

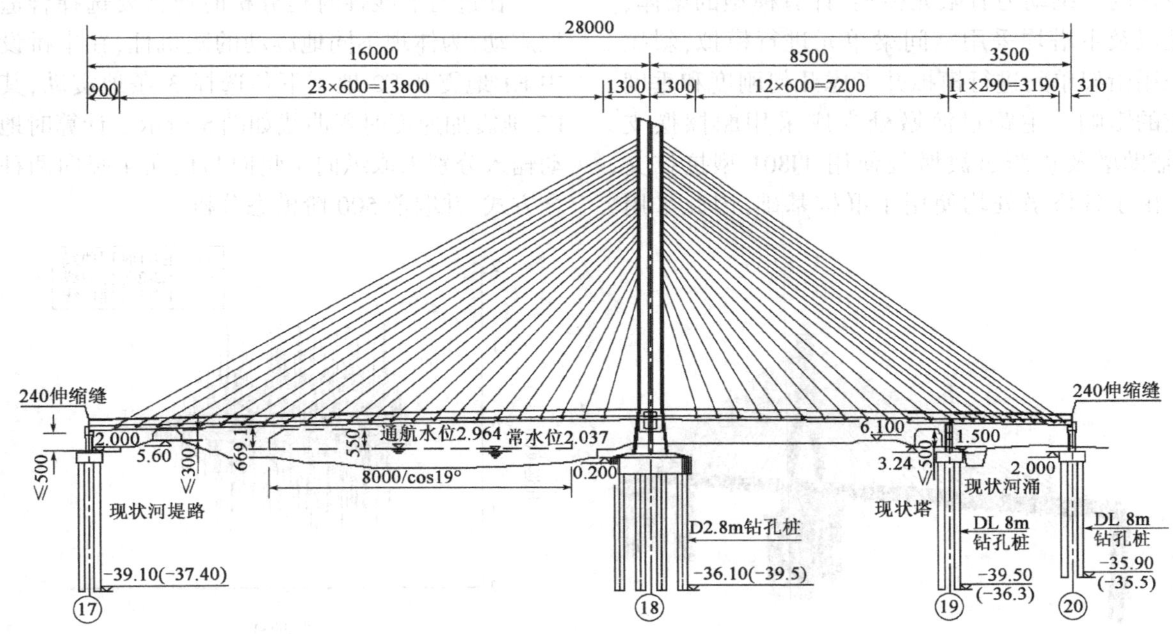

图 1 桥梁总体布置(尺寸单位：cm)

2 装置简介和参数设置

2.1 摩擦摆支座和抗拉支座

辅助墩和边跨交接墩由于拉索有可能出现拉力,采用TJ801-12500和TJ801-10000级别的抗拉支座,主跨交接墩采用摩擦摆支座,如图2和图3所示。

2.2 支座技术参数

表1为摩擦摆支座和TJ801抗拉支座的技术参数表。

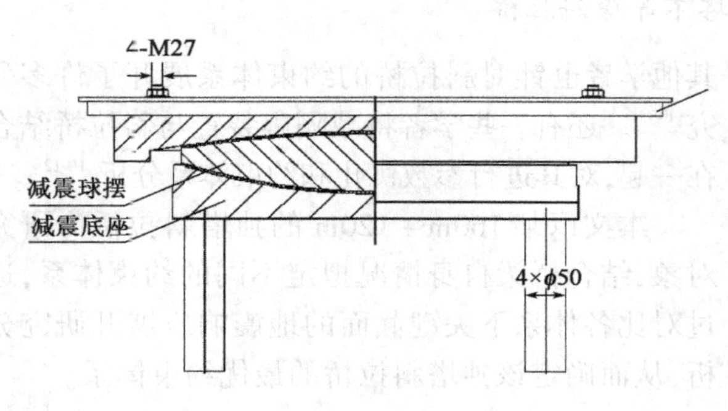

图2 摩擦摆支座示意图

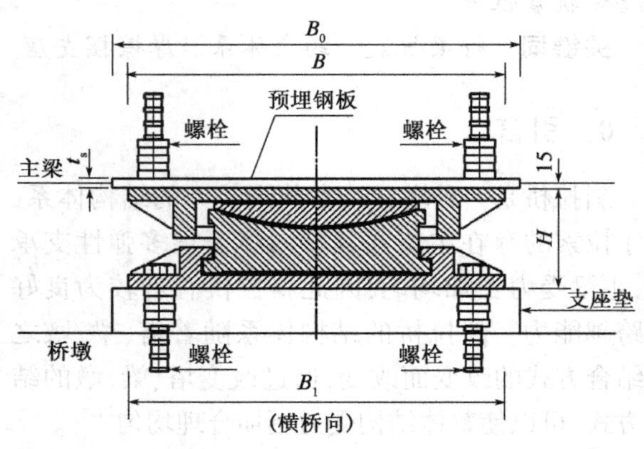

图3 TJ801抗拉支座示意图

支座技术参数表 表1

支座类型	竖向受压承载力(kN)	竖向受拉承载力(kN)	纵桥向位移(mm)	横桥向位移(mm)	转角(rad)
摩擦摆支座	10000	—	±200	±200	0.02
TJ801-10000-SX	10000	3400	±150	±50	0.02
TJ801-12500-SX	12500	4750	±150	±50	0.02

3 空间动力分析模型

3.1 空间动力模型

本文采用有限元分析软件CSI Bridge建立该斜拉桥的三维动力有限元模型,计算模型的梁体、墩柱以及主塔均采用空间梁单元进行模拟,斜拉索采用桁架单元进行模拟并考虑几何刚度和垂度效应的影响。主跨过渡墩处支座采用摩擦摆支座,辅助墩及边跨过渡墩处使用TJ801型抗拉支座。由于各桥墩处均使用了群桩基础,因此采用分层土弹簧模型对桩基进行模拟,竖向每隔1m施加一个土弹簧,土层m值按照建议值表取值。全桥有限元模型如图4所示。

3.2 地震动输入

在进行非线性时程分析时通常要选择合适的地震动,为体现不同地震动的随机性,在本桥设计中E1地震和E2地震下各选择3条地震动,其中E2地震加速度时程曲线如图5所示。计算时地震动输入分别采取纵向+竖向与横向+竖向两种组合方式,并取前500阶模态分析。

图4 全桥有限元模型

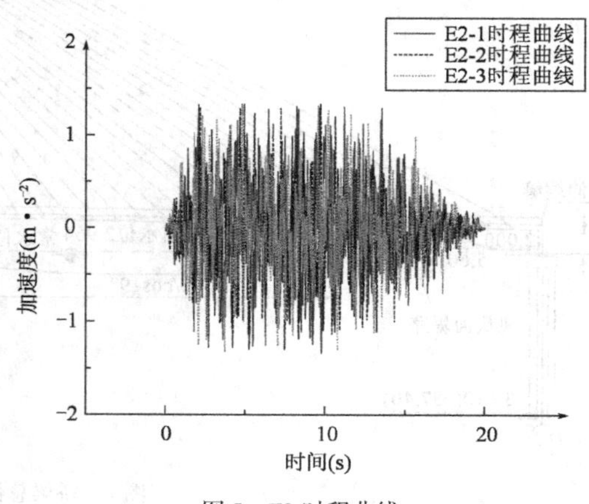

图5 E2时程曲线

4 约束体系方案与结果分析

4.1 约束体系方案

为了减小地震作用下桥梁关键截面的地震响应,结合该桥梁自身实际情况,本文提出以下三种约束体系方案,如图6～图8所示。在辅助墩及边跨过渡墩布置抗拉支座的前提下,体系1是主塔刚构体系+主跨过渡墩上布置双向摩擦摆支座;体系2和体系3在主塔处解除塔梁墩固结,体系2在主塔处布置双向摩擦摆支座,主跨过渡墩上则沿横向布置一个单向摩擦摆支座和一个双向摩擦摆支座;体系3在主塔处布置单向摩擦摆支座,主跨过渡墩上布置双向摩擦摆支座。

体系1:刚构体系+双向摩擦摆支座

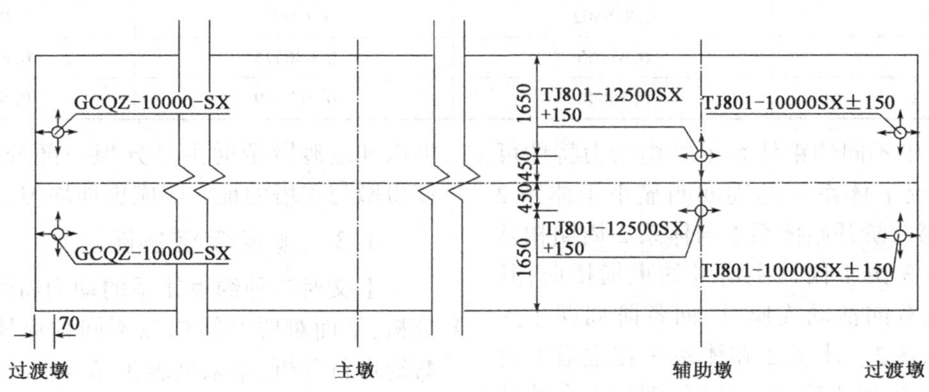

图6 约束体系1

体系2:支承体系(双向)+单双向摩擦摆支座

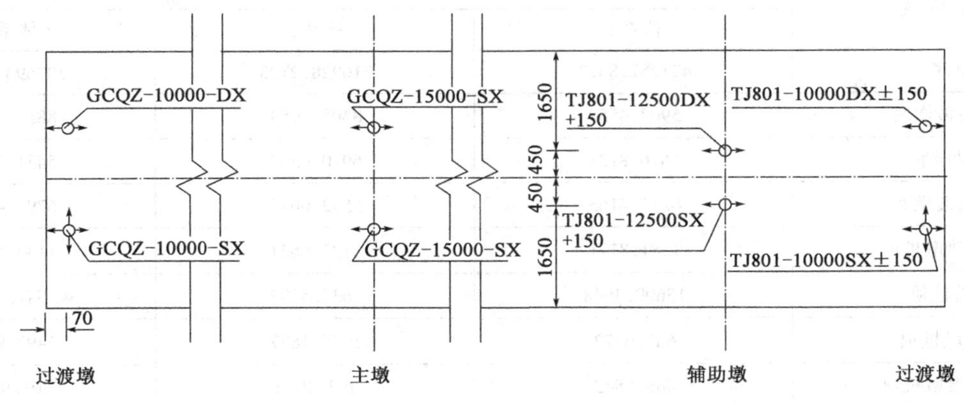

图7 约束体系2

体系3:支承体系(单向)+双向摩擦摆支座

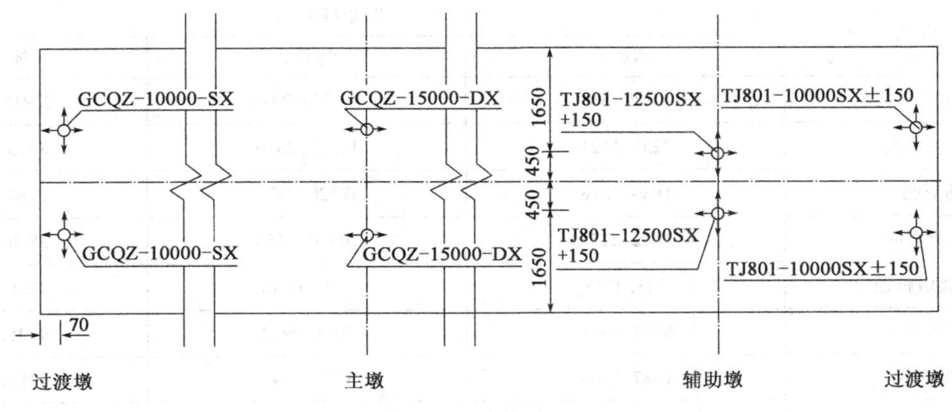

图8 约束体系3

4.2 结构动力特性和阻尼分析

对以上三种体系进行分析,得到不同约束体系下桥梁的动力特性,在此仅列出体系1、体系2和体系3的前五阶周期以做比较,具体内容见表2。

动力特性 表2

阶数	周期(s)		
	体系1	体系2	体系3
1	1.513805	3.98804	4.547053
2	1.014837	1.116793	4.037299
3	0.815502	1.01471	1.014482
4	0.67165	0.636575	0.858627
5	0.48048	0.587339	0.636576

对比表2中不同约束体系下结构动力特性可知,第一阶情况下体系1的周期明显小于体系2和体系3,从第二阶开始体系1与体系2周期相差较小。而体系3由于仅在主塔处约束横桥向,其他墩顶均布置双向活动支座,因而各阶周期稍大于体系1和体系2。体系2和体系3在主塔处解除塔梁墩固结,布置支座支承体系,理论上会使辅助墩和过渡墩帮助主塔分担一部分地震力,从而使得墩与主塔的地震响应更加均匀。

4.3 地震弯矩分析

上文对三种约束体系的动力特性进行了对比分析,下面对桥梁结构在不同约束体系下产生的弯矩进行分析,结果见表3、表4。

体系1、2、3地震弯矩(纵向+竖向输入) 表3

截面位置	弯矩(kN·m)		
	体系1	体系2	体系3
塔底	421252.8322	310928.2193	303693.2366
1号过渡墩底	5907.4554	8408.3654	8851.5111
辅助墩底	1616.8128	6970.0269	5431.5915
2号过渡墩底	4211.4163	5592.6649	6792.4858
1号过渡墩桩顶	1181.8171	1122.6621	1144.5501
主塔桩顶	13699.3648	7633.5392	7542.1415
辅助墩桩顶	667.6272	1975.1837	1492.9959
2号过渡墩桩顶	468.9542	703.4972	708.9109

体系1、2、3地震弯矩(横向+竖向输入) 表4

截面位置	弯矩(kN·m)		
	体系1	体系2	体系3
塔底	210411.6896	132270.2947	229182.663
1号过渡墩底	7255.1121	11311.2876	8313.5043
辅助墩底	1839.9218	12720.8878	2784.6829
2号过渡墩底	3442.2173	10570.7458	3808.4564
1号过渡墩桩顶	745.0485	1357.6643	820.7849
主塔桩顶	8794.7001	7085.0972	9195.0313
辅助墩桩顶	1387.2863	3810.2446	1310.9159
2号过渡墩桩顶	719.2557	1109.8566	653.4227

如图9所示，在纵向地震动输入下，体系2和体系3的塔底绕横轴弯矩均明显小于体系1；在横向地震动输入下，体系2的塔底绕纵轴弯矩小于体系1和体系3。这是因为体系2和体系3在主塔处墩塔梁并非固结，但由于在主塔处限制了横向的位移，因此横向地震动输入下塔底弯矩同体系1相比并未减小。

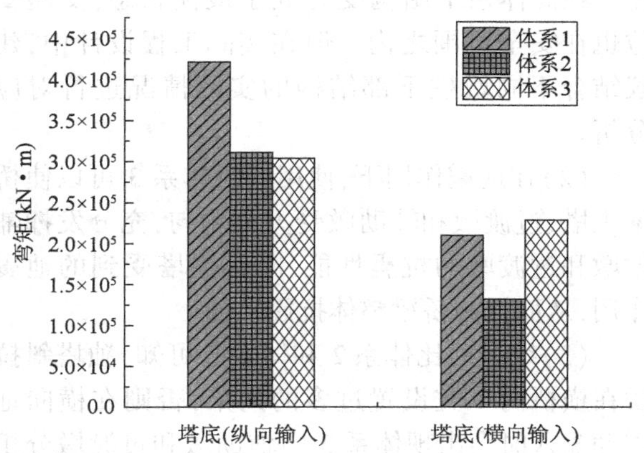

图9 体系1、2、3主塔底部地震弯矩响应

结合表3和图10来分析，在纵向地震动输入下，体系2和体系3在主塔桩顶处地震弯矩远小于体系1，最大减少了44.95%，而其他墩底及桩顶截面的地震弯矩则普遍大于体系1的弯矩响应值，可以看出体系2、3的过渡墩及辅助墩帮助主塔底部及主塔桩顶分担了一部分地震响应。从这一角度来讲，体系2、3均优于体系1。

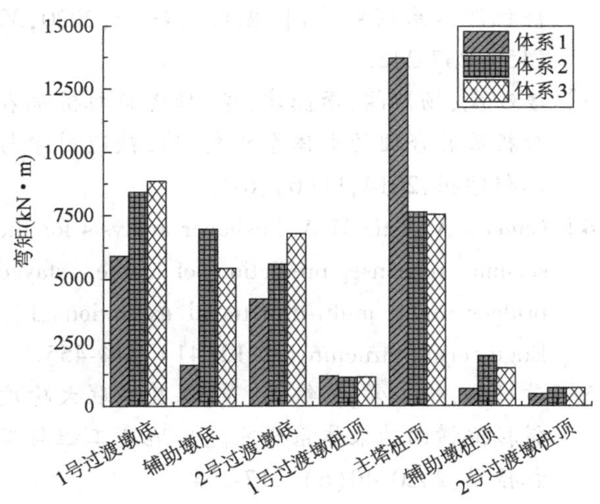

图10 体系1、2、3地震弯矩响应(纵向+竖向输入)

由表4和图11可知，在横向地震动输入下，体系3和体系1的各个关键截面地震响应相差不大，体系3略高于体系1；而体系2由于在主塔处解除了塔梁墩固结，主塔桩顶处地震弯矩小于体系1和体系3，最大减少了22.95%；但在过渡墩及辅助墩处体系2的墩底和桩顶弯矩均明显大于体系1和体系3，这是因为体系2在辅助墩及过渡墩顶布置了单向摩擦摆支座，限制了横桥向的位移，导致横向地震动输入时，这些墩底截面绕纵轴的地震弯矩增大。综合纵向和横向地震动输入来看，体系3优于体系2优于体系1。

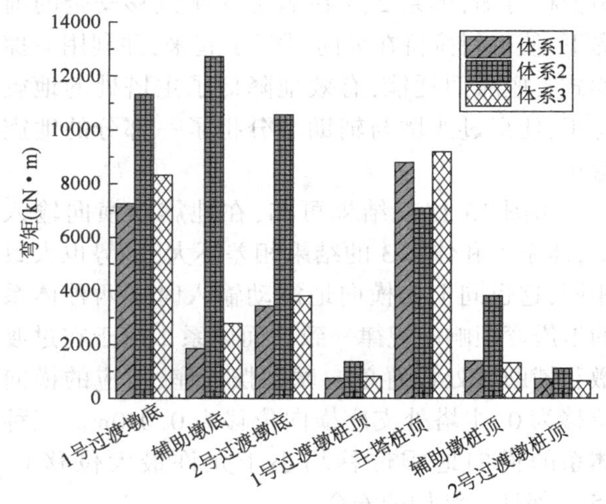

图11 体系1、2、3地震弯矩响应(横向+竖向输入)

4.4 地震位移分析

在对斜拉桥的不同约束体系进行分析时，除了需要进行地震作用下的弯矩对比分析之外，还需要进行结构变形能力的对比分析，主要体现在墩顶的支座位移方面。不同约束体系在地震作用下的墩顶支座位移值如图12、图13所示。

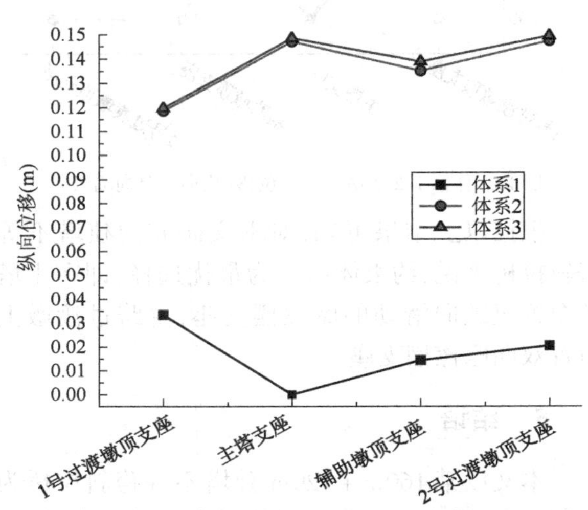

图12 体系1、2、3墩顶支座位移(纵向+竖向输入)

图12描绘的是纵向地震动输入下各墩顶及主塔处支座的纵向位移,可以看出在体系2、3下,各支座纵向位移明显大于体系1,这是因为体系1为塔梁墩固结的刚构体系,而体系2、3在主塔处纵向允许位移。体系1的最大纵向位移为0.0335m,体系2各支座纵向位移在0.1186m到0.1476m之间,体系3最大纵向位移为0.149m,均小于支座纵向最大允许位移0.15m。结合地震弯矩分析可知,体系2、3在满足支座位移安全的前提下,使得斜拉桥在纵向"摆"了起来,并利用摩擦摆式支座带回耗能,有效地降低了主塔处的地震弯矩,使得过渡墩与辅助墩分担了一部分的地震弯矩。

由图13比较结果可知,在地震动横向输入下,体系1和体系3的结果相差不大,趋势也大致相同,这也同上文横向地震动输入时这两种体系的地震弯矩响应规律一致。而体系2由于在过渡墩和辅助墩处设置单向摩擦摆支座,对应的横向位移为0,主塔处支座横向位移为0.040m。三种体系的横向地震位移均小于允许最大位移0.05m,保证了结构的安全。

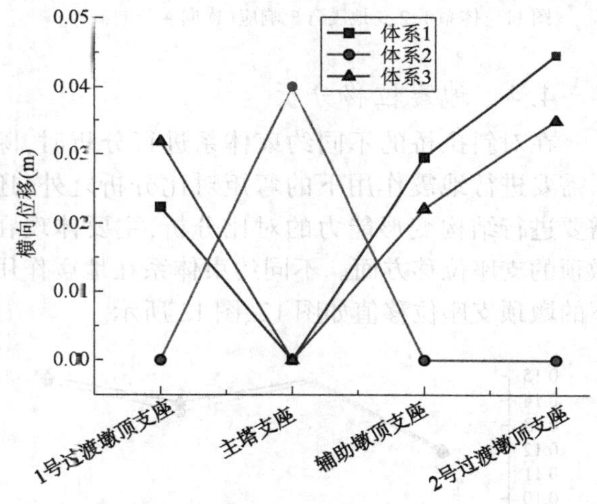

图13 体系1、2、3墩顶支座位移(横向+竖向输入)

根据以上结果可知,对本文研究的独塔不等跨斜拉桥来说,约束体系3为最优选择,即在主塔处布置仅纵向滑动的摩擦摆支座,主跨过渡墩上布置双向摩擦摆支座。

5 结语

本文以某160m+120m独塔不等跨斜拉桥为分析对象,提出了3种不同的约束体系方案,并通过计算主塔、过渡墩和辅助墩的弯矩以及各墩顶支座变位,分析对比了3种体系的抗震性能。根据分析结果得到如下结论:

(1)通过桥梁结构在地震动输入下的受力和变形结果分析可以得出,该独塔不等跨斜拉桥的最优约束体系是体系3:在主塔处布置仅纵向滑动的摩擦摆支座,主跨过渡墩上布置双向摩擦摆支座。在此体系下结构受力处于最优状态,支座变位也在安全范围之内。但在实际工程设计中,建议结合不同墩柱下部结构的实际情况进行对应分析。

(2)在地震作用下,使用约束体系3可以使桥梁主塔、过渡墩和辅助墩受力更均匀,充分发挥辅助墩和过渡墩的抗震性能,减小主塔受到的地震作用,从而提高桥梁整体抗震性能。

(3)综合对比体系2和体系3可知,独塔斜拉桥在横桥向不宜设置过多的约束,否则在横向地震动输入时会出现体系2中辅助墩和过渡墩分担过多地震弯矩的情况。在设计时应根据地震弯矩和地震位移适当调整约束体系,推荐在主塔处设置横向约束。

参考文献

[1] 陈宝魁,王东升,李宏男,等.塔梁间设置BRB跨海斜拉桥减震约束体系及其地震反应[J].振动工程学报,2021,34(3):452-461.

[2] 黄永福,马健,夏支贤.强震区中等跨度斜拉桥抗震体系研究[J].振动与冲击,2020,39(15):237-242.

[3] 姜冲虎,杨博闻,李德建,等.独塔斜拉桥抗震分析及其合理约束体系研究[J].铁道科学与工程学报,2014,11(6):6-12.

[4] Camara A, Astiz M A. Pushover analysis for the seismic response prediction of cable- stayed bridges under multi-directional excitation[J]. Engineering Structures,2012(41):444-455.

[5] 黄鸣柳,沈文爱,何铁明,等.双座串联大跨度斜拉桥横向约束体系研究[J].地震工程与工程振动,2020,40(6):217-224.

[6] 王照伟,陈占力,刘得运,等.大跨度三塔斜拉桥纵向约束体系设计研究[J].世界桥梁,2021,49(4):42-48.

[7] 周敉,朱国强,吴江,等.地震下大跨径连续刚构桥合理约束体系研究[J].振动与冲击,

2019,38(10):98-104.

[8] 邓鹏.超大跨度斜拉桥塔梁纵向约束体系研究[D].成都:西南交通大学,2020.

[9] 徐源庆,吴玲正,徐军,等.斜拉桥合理横向抗震约束体系研究[J].铁路工程技术与经济,2019,34(4):1-5.

[10] 周敉,刘阳,赵威.地震作用下采用UHPC铺装钢箱梁斜拉桥阻尼器参数优化[J].长安大学学报(自然科学版),2021,41(2):89-101.

[11] 王龙.独塔宽幅斜拉桥基于阻尼器的非对称横向抗震约束体系研究[D].重庆:重庆交通大学,2019.

[12] 马长飞,汪正兴,王胜斌,等.大跨度斜拉桥斜置阻尼约束体系参数设计[J].桥梁建设,2018,48(5):33-37.

Study on Mechanical Properties of Self-anchored Suspension Bridge during Hanger Tensioning Process

Pei Tao* Zezhong Qi Pengfei Li

(Department of Bridge Engineering, School of Highway, Chang'an University)

Abstract During the construction of self-anchored suspension bridge, frequent loading and structural boundary changes will cause complex stress and configuration changes. This process is a complex dynamic process with nonlinearity. In different stages of construction, the cable saddle displacement, main tower stress, main beam mechanical characteristics, hanger force, etc. can be used as control factors for construction monitoring to ensure the safety of the structure during construction. Based on the general finite element software, considering the nonlinear effect, combined with the formal installation method and the unstressed state method, this paper determines the reasonable construction scheme of a self-anchored suspension bridge, simulates the whole process of system transformation construction, analyses the mechanical properties of each component in different construction stages, and summarizes the variation rule of internal force and displacement of main cable and stiffening beam. It is verified that as long as the installation process adopts the unstressed state quantity of the reasonable completed bridge state, the internal force of the completed bridge state calculated by installing the tower and beam, main cable and hanger in stages must meet the requirements of the reasonable completed bridge state.

Keywords Construction stage Self-anchored suspension bridge Hanger tensioning procedure Unstressed length

0 Introduction

Self-anchored suspension bridge has gradually developed into a mature bridge type because of its unique shape, flexible adaptability and economy. In particular, the self-anchored suspension bridge anchors the main cable on its own stiffening beam. Compared with the ground anchored suspension bridge, it not only does not need a huge anchorage structure, but also has the advantages of beautiful appearance of the traditional suspension bridge, so it has been widely used in urban bridges.

Long span suspension bridges generally go through multiple construction stages. In these stages, frequent loading and structural system transformation will inevitably lead to complex stress and configuration changes. Therefore, the process is a complex dynamic process with nonlinear time-delay characteristics. Especially for the self-anchored suspension bridge, during construction, it is necessary to first build the stiffening beam on the temporary support, then install the main cable, and then install and tension the hanger between the main cable and the beam according to the predetermined sequence[1], so as to realize the stiffening beam from temporary support to hanger support through hanger tension. This process is also called the system transformation of self-anchored suspension bridge. In the process of system transformation, we should first determine the reasonable completion state. On this basis, we should seek the construction control objectives of each stage according to various constraints, adopt a reasonable hanger tensioning scheme, and comprehensively determine the main technical indicators of construction control. The nonlinear mechanical behavior of self-anchored suspension bridge is mainly concentrated in the system transformation process. In this process, not only the main cable deformation and hanger cable force show significant nonlinear characteristics due to the large geometric deformation of the main cable, but also the contact nonlinearity between the beam and the temporary support with the increase of the main cable axial force and hanger cable force. These nonlinear mechanical behaviors lead to the complex transformation process of self-anchored suspension bridge system, which is much more complex than that of ground-anchored suspension bridge or cable-stayed bridge.

Based on the above analysis of various factors in thehanger tensioning construction, the cable saddle deflection, the force on the main tower, the mechanical characteristics of the main beam and the hanger cable force can be used as the control factors for construction monitoring in different construction stages, so as to ensure the safety of the structure in the construction process. During the hanger tensioning construction, the deformation, internal force change law and other mechanical properties of each component can be studied. It is helpful for engineers to understand the mechanical mechanism evolution law of each part of the structure in the construction process, so as to further improve the grasp of each construction monitoring content in the hanger tensioning process of self-anchored suspension bridge.

1 System transformation of self-anchored suspension bridge

1.1 Methods of system transformation

The main methods of system transformation ofself-anchored suspension bridge are beam dropping method ang hanger tensioning method.

The beam dropping method is to lift the completed bridge line of the stiffening beam to a certain height as the installation configuration of the stiffening beam, install the main cable and hanger according to the completed bridge state, and realize the system transformation by gradually loosening the top and unloading the frame. The key of this method is to reasonably determine the sequence of roof loosening and frame unloading. Generally, the hanger force needs to be adjusted after the system conversion, because the temporary support and jack are arranged at each lifting point, the calculation of the construction process is complex, and the construction operation and construction control are difficult[2]. The hanger tensioning method takes the multi-span continuous stiffening beam as its initial state, and transfers the stiffening beam from the temporary support to the elastic support of the hanger by tensioning the hanger. The key of this method is to determine the tensioning sequence and tensioning force of the hanger. This method has relatively simple construction operation and fast construction speed, and is suitable for self-anchored suspension bridges of various structural forms[3].

Self-anchored suspension bridges generally adopt the method of "beam before cable" and tensioning hangers to convert the stiffening beam supported on the temporary support into hanger elastic support[4], therefore, different states have different structural features[5], as shown in Fig. 1. The process of hanger tensioning is a process of gradually loading the main cable. In the process of system transformation, not only the reasonable tensioning sequence and tensioning force of the hanger should be determined, but also the elastic deformation of the stiffening beam, the shrinkage and creep of the concrete, the tensioning force and tensioning times of the hanger, as well as the jacking times and timing of the tower top saddle should be considered.

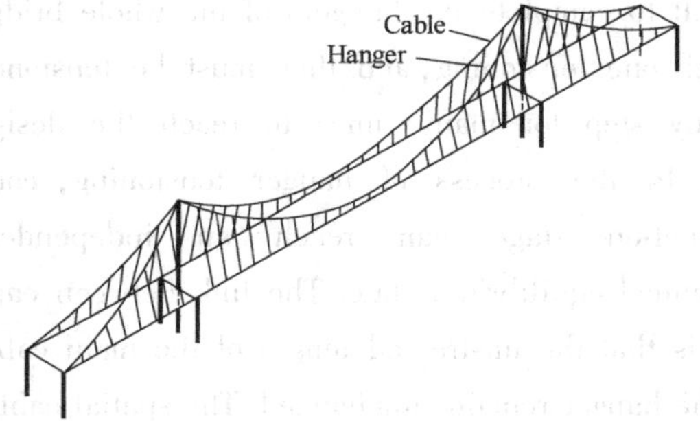

a) Completed stage

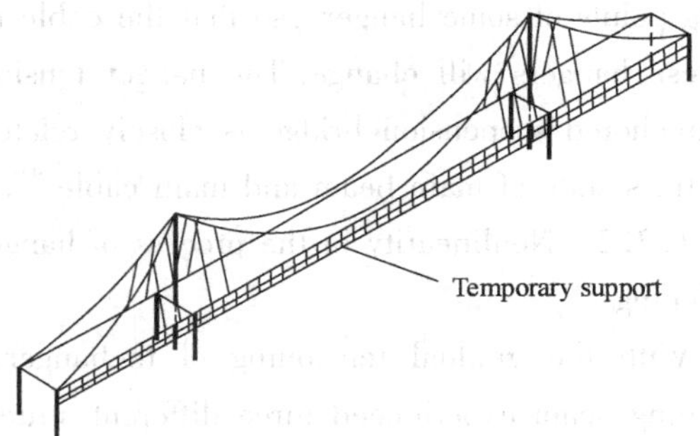

b)Construction stage

Fig. 1 State of self-anchored suspension bridge

The cable will also elongate axially when the line shape changes. It is necessary to constantly adjust the offset of the saddle of the main tower to adapt to the displacement caused by the deformation of the main cable during construction, otherwise the tower may be damaged under the action of bending moment[6]. At the same time, for the convenience of construction, the pushing times of the saddle shall be minimized. In the process of hanger tensioning, the beam will produce certain vertical displacement, and the displacement and deformation of stiffening beam in different tensioning areas will produce positive and negative bending moments in the joint. In the process of hanger tensioning, the bending moment and displacement of main beam will continue to change, and the range of change depends on the hanger tensioning force and hanger tensioning method. Therefore, in order to prevent excessive displacement of the beam body during the construction of self-anchored suspension bridge, it is necessary to select a reasonable hanger tensioning method.

1.2 Analysis method of hanger tensioning process

1.2.1 Reasonable completion state and construction state

The ultimatetarget of hanger tensioning of self-anchored suspension bridge is to make the alignment and stress of the completed bridge meet the design requirements, and ensure the safety of the structure in the process of hanger tensioning. According to the theory of unstressed state method: for the structure composed of certain external load, structural system, support boundary conditions and unstressed state quantity of element, the corresponding structural internal force and displacement are unique and independent of the formation process of the structure, when determining the reasonable completion state of self-anchored suspension bridge, we can determine the reasonable completion state by one-time completion without considering the construction process and drawing up the size of each component. As long as the installation process adopts the unstressed state quantity of reasonable completed bridge state, in this paper, the unstressed length of hanger and main cable is taken as the unstressed state quantity, and the internal force of completed bridge state calculated by installing tower beam, main cable and hanger in stages must meet the requirements of reasonable completed bridge state under dead load, the dead load includes the weights of the stiffening girder, the floor system, and the other parts of the bridge itself[7].

During thehanger tensioning construction, the unstressed cable length of the hanger in the two adjacent construction stages remains unchanged[8]. When a hanger is tensioned in a construction stage, some nodes of the main beam and the main cable will produce corresponding displacement, which will change the distance between the upper and lower lifting points of some hangers, so that the cable force of these hangers will change. The hanger tension of self-anchored suspension bridge is closely related to the stress state of main beam and main cable[9].

1.2.2 Nonlinearity in the process of hanger tensioning

With the gradual tensioning of thehanger, the stiffening beam experienced three different structural systems: support, partial off frame and full off frame, and finally realized the system transformation and reached the pre-bridge state[10]. The determination of the reasonable state of hanger tensioning construction is to determine several states between the empty cable and the completed bridge based on the empty cable state, so as to realize the gradual transformation from the empty cable state to the completed bridge state.

The linear superposition method cannot be used in the calculation ofhanger tension, but the nonlinear iterative method must be used. Hanger force is the function of main cable shape and stiffening beam. The change of hanger force directly affects the main cable shape. The simulation of construction process shows that the self-anchored suspension bridge shows strong geometric nonlinearity and contact nonlinearity in the following aspects: ①In the construction process, the large geometric deformation of the main cable in the transverse and vertical directions produces significant geometric nonlinear response; ②Under the action of hanger tension, the evolution of hanger tension is phased. The change law from tension to target force is complex. Stretching a hanger will have a great impact on all hangers installed before, especially the tension of adjacent hangers; ③ The process of hanger tensioning can raise the main beam, resulting in the redistribution of reaction force of temporary support, resulting in considerable contact nonlinearity.

1.2.3 Hanger tensioning analysis

It is ideal to directly tension thehanger of self-anchored suspension bridge to the unstressed length. However, in actual construction, due to various restrictions such as the bearing capacity of hangers, the number and capacity of tensioning equipment, the bearing capacity of main beams and main towers, it is difficult to complete the hangers of the whole bridge through one tensioning, and they must be tensioned step by step for many times to reach the design value. In the process of hanger tensioning, each construction stage can reach an independent mechanical equilibrium state. The link between each stage is that the unstressed length of the main cable and the hanger remains unchanged. The spatial cable-shaped hanger is inclined along the transverse bridge, so the sag effect needs to be considered. The accurate method is to regard the hanger as an elastic catenary. The calculation diagram is shown in Fig. 2. The force required for hanger tensioning is determined by the following formula[11].

$$\sqrt{(z_{di}-z_i)^2+(x_{di}-x_i)^2}=\frac{S_{di}P_{zi}}{E_dA_d}+\frac{P_{zi}}{q_d}\left[\operatorname{arcsinh}\left(\frac{P_{vi}}{P_{zi}}\right)-\operatorname{arcsinh}\left(\frac{P_{vi}-q_dS_{di}}{P_{zi}}\right)\right]$$
$$y_{di}-y_i=\frac{S_{di}}{E_dA_d}\left(P_{vi}-\frac{q_dS_{di}}{2}\right)+\frac{1}{q_d}\left[\sqrt{P_{zi}^2+P_{vi}^2}-\sqrt{P_{zi}^2+(P_{vi}-q_dS_{di})^2}\right] \tag{1}$$

As shown in Fig. 2, in above equation: is coordinates of lifting points of hanger on main cable, (x_{di}, y_{di}, z_{di}) is coordinates of anchor points of hanger on beam section. S_{di} is unstressed length of hanger, P_{vi} is vertical load of hanger, P_{zi} is transverse horizontal force of hanger, E_d, A_d, q_d are respectively the elastic modulus, cross-sectional area and weight per linear meter of hanger.

2 Determination of design parameters and construction scheme

2.1 Design parameter

Taking a double tower three spanself-anchored suspension bridge (Fig. 3) as an example, the span arrangement is 99m + 200m + 99m, and the rise span ratio of the cable is 1∶6 5. Steel stiffening beams are used for the middle span and side span, and the whole bridge has 2 × 37 hangers, the spacing of hangers near the two bridge towers is 10m, and the spacing of other hangers is 9m. See Tab.1 for material characteristics of main components. The hanger adopts high-strength steel wire, and the hanger is tensioned from the bridge tower to the main span and side span in turn.

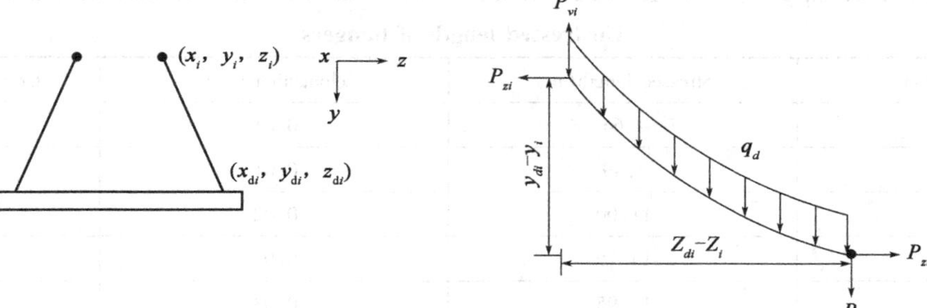

Fig. 2 Calculation of hanger force during tensioning

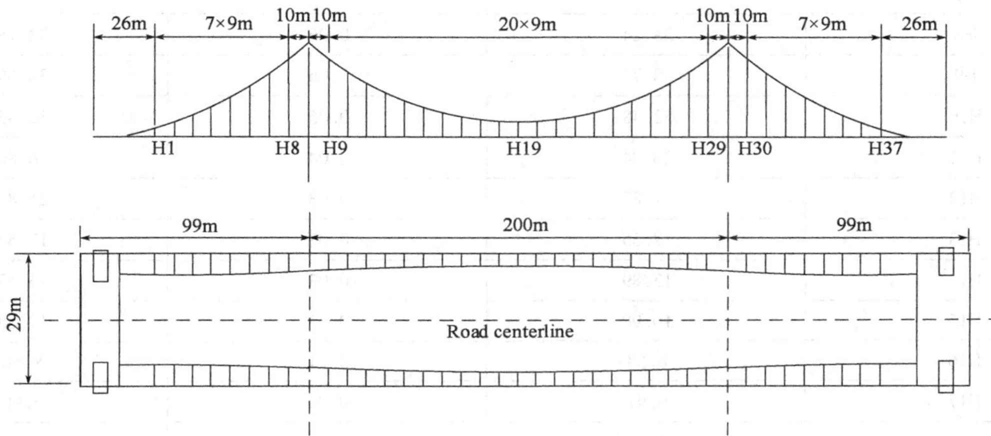

Fig. 3 Bridge layout diagram

Material characteristics Tab. 1

Parameter	Unstressed intensity of cable(kN/m) or Unit weight of main girder(kN/m³)	Area (m²)	Elastic modulus (×10⁸kN/m²)
Main Cable	2.976	3.815×10^{-2}	2.02
Hanger	0.252	2.965×10^{-3}	2.02
Girder	171.1	1.087	2.06

2.2 Unstressed length of hangers

Midas civil is used to establish the calculation model of the whole bridge to solve the internal force, alignment and geometric dimension of the structure in the completed state. According to the hanger length and cable force in the completed state, the unstressed length of the hanger is calculated. The bridge adopts the sequence of symmetrical tensioning from the bridge tower to the side span and the middle of the main span. Therefore, in this paper, the hanger tensioning of the left half of the bridge is taken as an example, as shown in Tab. 2.

2.3 Determination of construction scheme

The hanger tensioning process aims at tensioning the hanger to the unstressed length, that is, by knowing the unstressed length of the hanger and the main cable, the hanger is tensioned to the specified length during the tensioning process. In the process of hanger tensioning, when the bridge tower is offset and the stress exceeds the limit, in order to ensure the stress safety of the bridge tower, it is necessary to push the cable saddle at an appropriate time to balance the horizontal components on both sides of the bridge tower. After the hanger tensioning is completed, remove the temporary support of the stiffening beam, and then apply phase Ⅱ loads such as bridge deck pavement. Finally, concrete the tower top cable saddle to fix the position of the cable saddle, fine tune the cable force and finally achieve a reasonable bridge completion state.

Unstressed length of hangers Tab. 2

Hanger number	Stressed length(m)	elongation (m)	Unstressed length(m)
H1	4.64	0.01	4.63
H2	7.49	0.01	7.48
H3	11.00	0.02	10.99
H4	15.16	0.02	15.13
H5	19.95	0.03	19.92
H6	25.40	0.04	25.36
H7	31.50	0.05	31.45
H8	38.24	0.06	38.18
H9	38.75	0.06	38.69
H10	32.48	0.05	32.43
H11	26.84	0.04	26.80
H12	21.87	0.03	21.83
H13	17.55	0.03	17.52
H14	13.89	0.02	13.87
H15	10.90	0.02	10.88
H16	8.58	0.01	8.56
H17	6.91	0.01	6.90
H18	5.92	0.01	5.91
H19	5.58	0.01	5.58

Based on the unstressed state method and the forward installation method ofself-anchored suspension bridge, the hanger tensioning construction scheme of the bridge is formulated by comprehensively considering the hanger tensioning force and tensioning sequence, the number of cable saddle pushing, the removal of temporary buttresses and the transformation of boundary conditions. The specific construction stages are shown in Tab. 3.

Construction stage Tab. 3

Construction stage	Procedure
Stage 1	Cable saddle pushing
Stage 2 to stage 10	Tensioning H8 to H1(H30 to H37),H9 to H15(H29 to H23)
Stage 11	Cable saddle pushing
Stage 12	Tensioning H16,H17(H21,H22)
Stage 13 to stage 14	Cable saddle pushing
Stage 15	Tensioning H18,H19,H20
Stage 16	Remove the temporary support
Stage 17 to stage18	Pavement and other facilities
Stage 19	Fixed boundary
Stage 20	Adjustment of structure

3 Mechanical properties of components during hanger tensioning

In different system transformation construction stages, the changes ofhanger cable force, main cable displacement, stiffening beam bending moment and vertical displacement show different laws[12].

3.1 Hanger force in construction state

The cable force of thehanger mainly depends on the unstressed cable length of the hanger and the distance between the upper and lower lifting points of the hanger. After the reasonable completion state of self-anchored suspension bridge is obtained, the construction stage is established, the cumulative model in Midas civil construction stage analysis is adopted, and the nonlinear analysis is included to obtain the hanger force in each construction stage, as shown in Fig. 4.

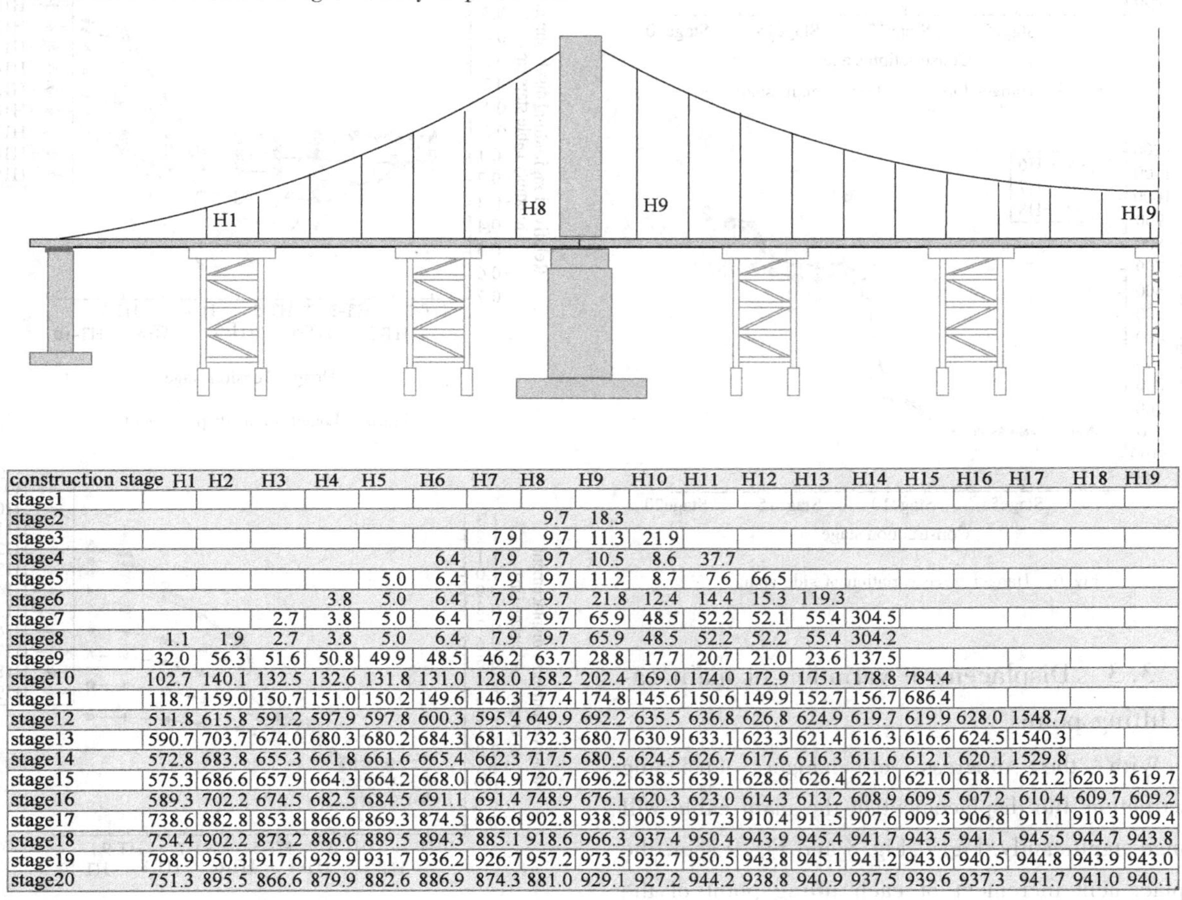

construction stage	H1	H2	H3	H4	H5	H6	H7	H8	H9	H10	H11	H12	H13	H14	H15	H16	H17	H18	H19
stage1																			
stage2								9.7	18.3										
stage3							7.9	9.7	11.3	21.9									
stage4						6.4	7.9	9.7	10.5	8.6	37.7								
stage5					5.0	6.4	7.9	9.7	11.2	8.7	7.6	66.5							
stage6				3.8	5.0	6.4	7.9	9.7	21.8	12.4	14.4	15.3	119.3						
stage7			2.7	3.8	5.0	6.4	7.9	9.7	65.9	48.5	52.2	52.1	55.4	304.5					
stage8	1.1	1.9	2.7	3.8	5.0	6.4	7.9	9.7	65.9	48.5	52.2	52.2	55.4	304.2					
stage9	32.0	56.3	51.6	50.8	49.9	48.5	46.2	63.7	28.8	17.7	20.7	21.0	23.6	137.5					
stage10	102.7	140.1	132.5	132.6	131.8	131.0	128.0	158.2	202.4	169.0	174.0	172.9	175.1	178.8	784.4				
stage11	118.7	159.0	150.7	151.0	150.2	149.6	146.3	177.4	174.8	145.6	150.6	149.9	152.7	156.7	686.4				
stage12	511.8	615.8	591.2	597.9	597.8	600.3	595.4	649.9	692.2	635.5	636.8	626.8	624.9	619.7	619.9	628.0	1548.7		
stage13	590.7	703.7	674.0	680.3	680.2	684.3	681.1	732.3	680.7	630.9	633.1	623.3	621.4	616.3	616.6	624.5	1540.3		
stage14	572.8	683.8	655.3	661.8	661.6	665.4	662.3	717.5	680.5	624.5	626.7	617.6	616.3	611.6	612.1	620.1	1529.8		
stage15	575.3	686.6	657.9	664.3	664.2	668.0	664.9	720.7	696.2	638.5	639.1	628.6	626.4	621.0	621.0	618.1	621.2	620.3	619.7
stage16	589.3	702.2	674.5	682.5	684.5	691.1	691.4	748.9	676.1	620.3	623.0	614.3	613.2	608.9	609.5	607.2	610.4	609.7	609.2
stage17	738.6	882.8	853.8	866.6	869.3	874.5	866.6	902.8	938.5	905.9	917.3	910.4	911.5	907.6	909.3	906.8	911.1	910.3	909.4
stage18	754.4	902.2	873.2	886.6	889.5	894.3	885.1	918.6	966.3	937.4	950.4	943.9	945.4	941.7	943.5	941.1	945.5	944.7	943.8
stage19	798.9	950.3	917.6	929.9	931.7	936.2	926.7	957.2	973.5	932.7	950.5	943.8	945.1	941.2	943.0	940.5	944.8	943.9	943.0
stage20	751.3	895.5	866.6	879.9	882.6	886.9	874.3	881.0	929.1	927.2	944.2	938.8	940.9	937.5	939.6	937.3	941.7	941.0	940.1

Fig. 4 Hanger force in construction state

3.2 Variation of hanger force during construction

In the process ofhanger tensioning, the changes of hanger force on both sides of the bridge tower, main span and side span are shown in Fig. 5 and Fig. 6. It can be seen that the cable force of H6 ~ H11 hanger tensioned early is very small. The cable force under the first 10 construction stages is consistent and small. The cable force gradually increases under the influence of subsequent hanger tensioning, which indicates that the stiffness of the main cable in the early stage is very low. As shown in Fig. 4, when H17 is tensioned to the unstressed length, the cable force is large, but when adjacent hangers are tensioned, the cable force suddenly decreases to a lower level. Under the action of subsequent hanger tensioning, the cable force gradually increases to the bridge completion target, which indicates that the main cable stiffness has been large[13].

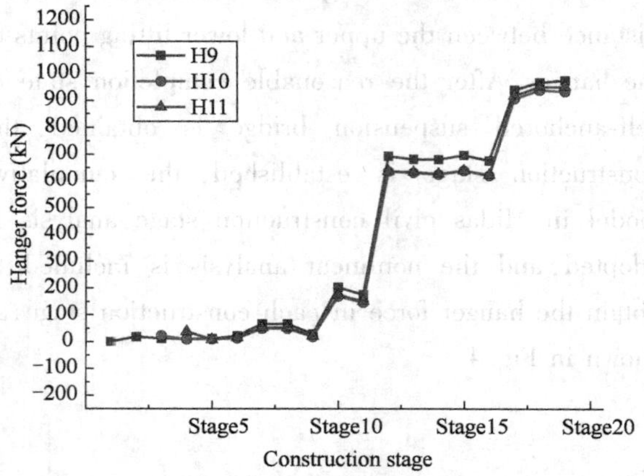

Fig. 5 Hanger force variation of main span

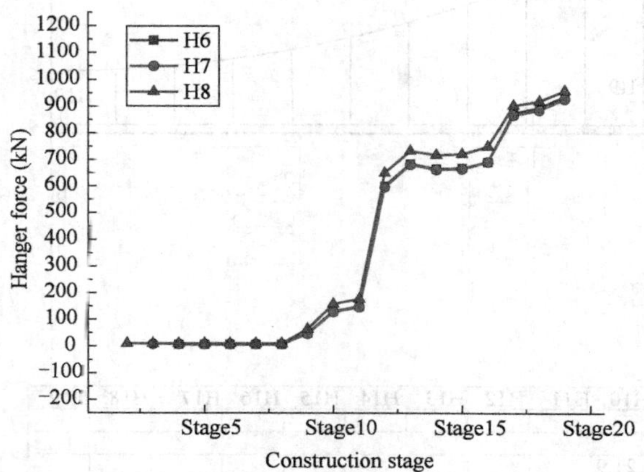

Fig. 6 Hanger force variation of side span

3.3 Displacement variation of main cable lifting point

With the progress of hanger tensioning construction, the displacement of the main cable will change significantly. Fig. 7, Fig. 8 and Fig. 9 show the displacement increment of each lifting point of the main cable of the main span relative to the empty cable state in the longitudinal, transverse, and vertical directions in 10 hanger tensioning construction stages. After the hanger tensioning is completed, except that the longitudinal bridge displacement of the vertical point (H19) in the middle of the main cable span remains unchanged, the other lifting points move to the middle of the span from the empty cable state, and the longitudinal displacement of the lifting point (H9) at the bridge tower is the largest. The transverse bridge displacement of each lifting point gradually increases to the outside with the progress of hanger tensioning. After tensioning, the main cable reaches the spatial cable shape of the bridge state. During hanger tensioning, the middle point of the main cablespan The vertical displacement change of (H19) is the largest, and the vertical displacement change of the main cable near the main tower is small.

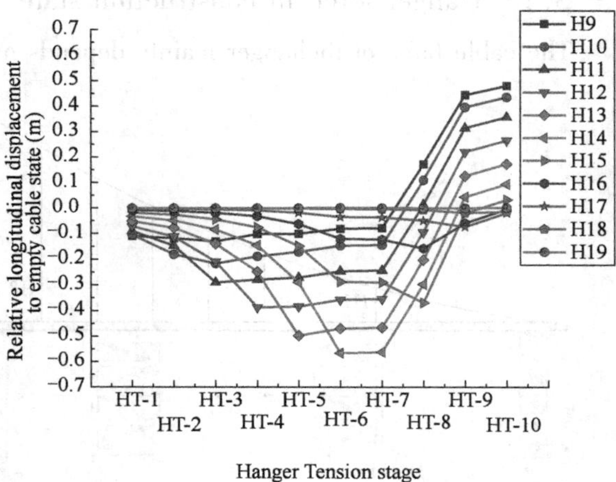

Fig. 7 Longitudinal displacement

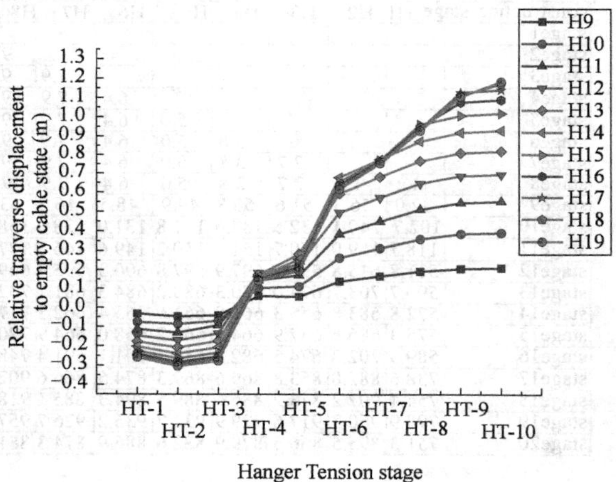

Fig. 8 Transverse displacement

3.4 Variation of bending moment and displacement of stiffening girder

In the process ofhanger tensioning and system transformation, the main cable completes large spatial displacement, and the main beam changes from the support state of temporary pier to the stress of hanger support, resulting in large vertical displacement changes[14]. In order to ensure the safety of the main beam structure, the bending moment and vertical displacement of the stiffening beam are also important factors to control the hanger tensioning construction.

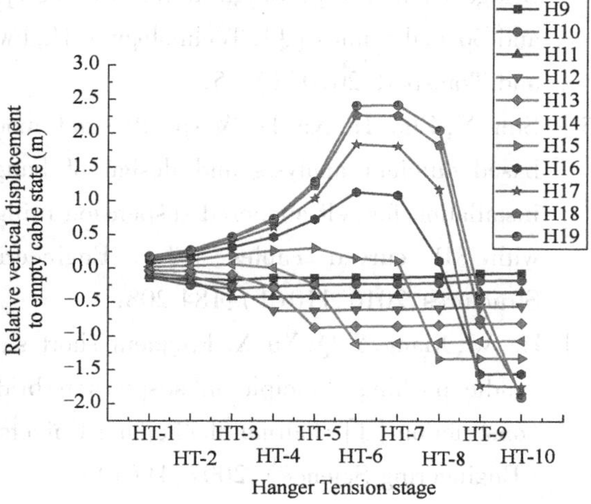

Fig. 9 Vertical displacement

The bending moment change of stiffening beam is shown in Fig. 10. In the early stage of hanger tensioning construction, because the cable force of tensioning the hanger to the unstressed length is small, the stiffening beam is mainly supported by temporary supports. In the middle stage of construction, due to the obvious change of main cable shape, the stiffness of main cable gradually increases, the cable force increases, the stiffening beam gradually demoulds, the main span The bending moment of the stiffening beam at the side span and bridge tower changes greatly. After the construction of cable saddle jacking, bridge deck pavement and cable force adjustment in the later stage, the suddenly increased bending moment of the stiffening beam decreases to reach the main beam state before hanger tensioning, that is, the stress state designed and constructed according to the initial equilibrium state.

The displacement change of stiffening beam is shown in Fig. 11. At the initial stage of tensioning construction, the displacement of stiffening beam basically remains unchanged. In the middle and later stage of tensioning construction, as the main beam is gradually pulled away from the temporary support by the lifting cable, the vertical main beam at each lifting point changes greatly. The closer it is to the middle of the span, the greater the vertical displacement of the main beam. After the completion of bridge deck construction in the later stage, the main girder is restored to designed and constructed alignment of initial equilibrium state.

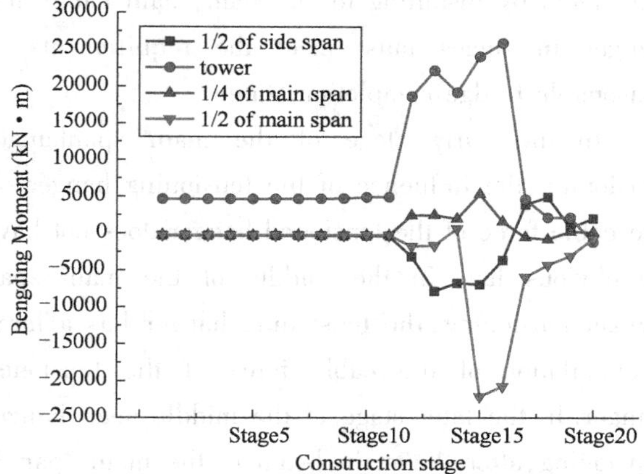

Fig. 10 Bending moment of main stiffening girder

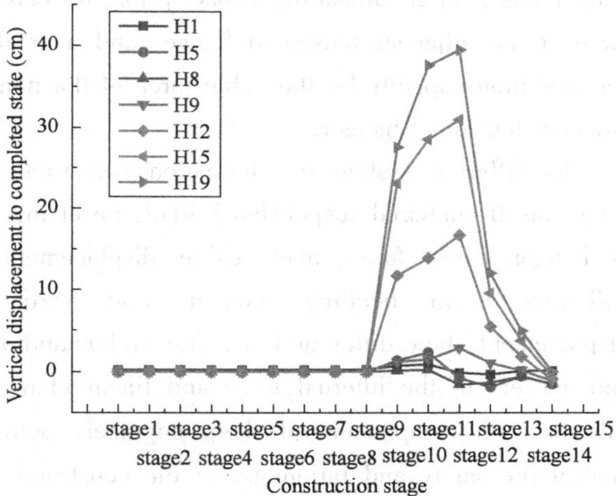

Fig. 11 Vertical displacement of main stiffening gider

4 Conclusions

Based on the finite element method, combined with the positive installation method and the stress-free state method, this paper simulates the whole process of system transformation construction of aself-anchored suspension bridge, and further studies the mechanical properties such as internal force and displacement of different components in each construction stage of the self-anchored suspension bridge:

In the process ofhanger tensioning, due to the changes of boundary conditions and main cable displacement, the hanger cable force will change greatly in different construction stages. However, as long as the unstressed state quantity of reasonable bridge completion state is adopted in the installation process, the internal force of bridge completion state calculated by installing tower beam, main cable and hanger in stages must meet the requirements of reasonable bridge completion state.

In the early stage of the main spanhanger tensioning, the influence of the tensioning hanger on the cable force of the tensioned hanger does not have an obvious law. In the middle of the main span hanger tensioning, the tensioning hanger has a large accumulation of the cable force of the tensioned hanger. In the later stage of the middle span hanger tensioning, after the main beam of the main span is separated from the temporary pier, the tensioning hanger has a large unloading capacity for the cable force of the adjacent tensioned hanger and a small accumulation capacity for the cable force of the non-adjacent tensioned hanger.

In different system transformation construction stages ofself-anchored suspension bridge, the changes of hanger cable force, main cable displacement, stiffening beam bending moment and vertical displacement show different laws. The understanding and mastery of the internal force and linear change rule of each component will help engineers better control the safety and rationality in the construction process of self-anchored suspension bridge.

References

[1] Yang M, Chen Z. An Analysis of Construction Stages Simulation for Self-Anchored Suspension Bridges [J]. Journal of Hunan University (Natural Sciences), 2006, 33(2): 5.

[2] Li C, Ke H, Liu J, et al. Key technologies of construction control in system transformation for Pingsheng Bridge [J]. China Civil Engineering Journal, 2008, 41(4): 6.

[3] Li C, Ke H, Yang W, et al. Comparative study on the optimal system transformation schemes for Taohuayu self-anchored suspension bridge [J]. China Civil Engineering Journal, 2014, 47 (9): 120-127.

[4] Tang Q, Li C, Ke H. Determination of Conversion Plan for Self-Anchored Suspension Bridge System with Single-tower, Double-span and Spacial Cables [J]. Technology of Highway and Transport, 2010(1): 5.

[5] Sun Y, Zhu H, Xu D. A specific rod model based efficient analysis and design of hanger installation for self-anchored suspension bridges with 3D curved cables [J]. Engineering Structures, 2016, 110(1): 184-208.

[6] He W, Xiang Y Q, Xu X. Frequent short steps saddle pushing principle in suspension bridge construction [J]. Journal of Zhejiang University (Engineering Science), 2007, 41(1): 5.

[7] Zhang W, Shi L, Li L, et al. Methods to correct unstrained hanger lengths and cable clamps' installation positions in suspension bridges [J]. Engineering Structures, 2018, 171(15): 202-213.

[8] Li C, Ke H, Liu H, et al. Determination of Finished Bridge State of Self-anchored Suspension Brdige with Spatial Cables [J]. Engineering Mechanics, 2010(5): 10.

[9] Liu H, Liu Z. Design of hanger tension and cable configuration for self-anchored suspension bridges [J]. China Civil Engineering Journal, 2008, 41(3): 5.

[10] Zhang J, Huang H, Liu A, et al. An overall bridge model test study on the mechanical behaviors in the process of system transformation of self-anchored suspension bridge with spatial cable system [J]. China Civil Engineering Journal, 2011, 44 (2): 108-115.

[11] Wang X, He S, Duan R. Hanger tensiong process analysis of self-anchored suspension bridge with spatial cables [J]. Engineering Mechanics, 2016, 33(10): 9.

[12] Wu H, He L, Guo H, et al. Analysis on the Displacement Characteristics of the Main Cable in the Transformation Process of Cable-suspension System of Self-anchored Suspension Bridge [J]. Highway Engineering, 2021, 46

(3):6.

[13] Wang S,Zhou Z,Wu H. Experimental study on the mechanical performance of super long-span self-anchored suspension bridge in construction process [J]. China Civil Engineering Journal,2014,47(6):70-77.

[14] Yuan M,Wang T,Huang X. Study of Hanger Tensioning and System Transformation Techniques for Long-Span Self-Anchored Suspension Bridge [J]. World Bridges,2015,43(3):5.

不同波流方向下双墩动力响应影响分析

郑晨辉[1] 孙 昊*[1] 高 源[2]

(1. 长安大学公路学院;2. 山东高速股份有限公司)

摘 要 深水区桥梁在复杂水动力环境下的流固耦合效应会显著影响桥梁结构的动力响应,而目前研究多集中在单一方向波、流作用,因此开展不同方向波、流作用下深水区桥墩动力响应的研究具有重要的工程应用价值。为了研究水流、波浪方向与流速对双墩动力响应的影响,本文运用ADINA软件建立双圆形空心墩的流固耦合有限元模型,考虑传播方向与双墩中心连线呈30°、45°、60°三种情况,分析了桥墩在波、流作用下的动力响应,主要分析不同工况下墩顶位移、墩底弯矩和墩底剪力的变化规律。分析结果表明:流场中的双墩受遮蔽效应影响,沿水流方向前墩(上游墩)动力响应大于后墩(下游墩),两墩的动力响应差值随流速的增加而增大;随着波浪传播角度的增大,遮蔽效应对波峰作用下后墩动力响应正向最值的削弱作用始终大于波浪绕射效应对应的增强作用,但遮蔽效应对波谷作用下后墩动力响应负向最值的削弱作用逐渐小于波浪绕射效应对应的增强作用。

关键词 深水区桥梁 动力响应 数值模拟 波流传播方向 流固耦合

0 引言

随着世界各国经济的飞速发展,各大经济体已经规划或建设了许多跨海大桥,如我国的“一带一路”、战略规划、粤港澳大湾区发展规划,美国近年修建的奥克兰-旧金山海湾大桥,连接德国费马恩岛与丹麦洛兰岛的费马恩大桥计划等。深水区桥梁处于江海、水库等地区,除了承受常规荷载外,还会承受波浪和水流(波、流)荷载的作用。在这种复杂水动力环境下,对跨海大桥动力响应的研究显得尤为重要。

自20世纪初便有诸多学者开展了关于深水结构物动力响应的研究。Westergaard于1933年提出大坝在地震情况下的动水压力计算公式[1]。Morison基于绕射流理论提出了一种适用于小直径圆柱体的规则波浪力解析方法[2]。随着计算机技术的发展,数值模拟的方法开始成为主要的手段。Wu等运用ANSYS有限元分析软件,建立了波流及地震荷载联合作用下的桩基数值模型,研究了桩基布置方式对桩基动力响应的影响[3]。Burke等发现,当塔式结构所处水深超120m,自振周期达到2.4s时,结构因波浪作用产生较大的动力响应,因此必须重视波浪荷载对深水桥墩的影响[4]。Kascachek G D和Wanzakov O M等基于圆柱结构提出了一种波峰作用下的波浪压强计算公式[5]。Baarholm和Faltinsen以二阶Stokes波作为入射波,对水平板进行冲击试验,验证了非线性边界元法解决波浪冲击问题的有效性[6]。居艮国分析了规则波和随即波作用下钢管桩施工平台的动力响应[7]。康啊真采用浸没边界法,对波浪场中不同型式的围堰进行了动力响应研究[8]。江辉和白晓宇等运用ADINA有限元分析软件,建立了考虑波、流及地震共同作用的双向流固耦合计算模型,讨论了不同参数下圆形桥墩的地震响应特性及参数影响规律[9-10]。张超根据势流体的有限单元法建立了单墩的流场数值分析模型,研究了有无内域水对圆形空心桥墩在地震、波流作用下动力响应的影响[11]。

综上,现阶段的双墩结构流固耦合研究多集中在以双墩串联或并列布置为前提,考虑单一方向来流,对其他来流方向的桥墩动力响应差异研究较少。因此,本文以某跨海大桥为背景,选取流体单元法作为流固耦合分析的计算方法,运用ADINA流固耦合分析软件,建立波流传播方向与双墩中心连线呈30°、45°、60°三种工况的有限元模型,研究各工况下双墩的动力响应差异,获得波、流方向与流速对双墩动力响应的影响规律。

1　双墩流固耦合分析模型的建立

1.1　实体桥墩的建立

本文以某跨海大桥下部结构尺寸为原型,建立双圆形空心桥墩ADINA有限元模型。桥墩与水域接触的外表面为流固耦合特殊边界,假定桥墩底部固结,通过在墩顶截面质心高度建立集中质量节点考虑桥梁上部结构质量,并使该节点与墩顶平面节点集建立刚性连接来模拟上部结构对桥墩的约束作用。墩高40m,桥墩直径5m,壁厚0.7m,C50混凝土,弹性模量3.45×10^{10}Pa,泊松比0.2,钢筋混凝土等效密度2500kg/m^3,墩顶质量3061000kg。上部结构等效模型如图1所示。

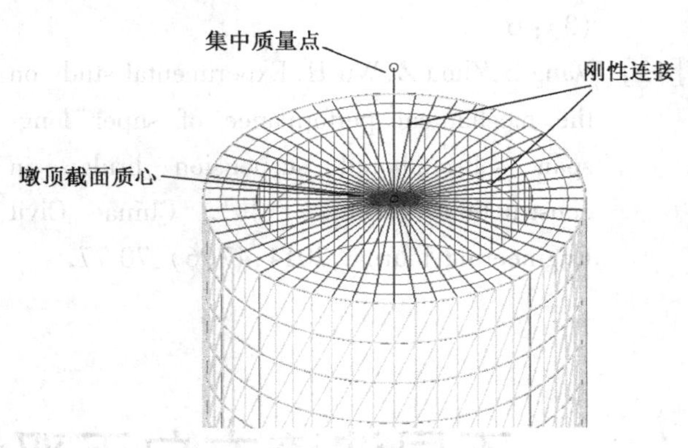

图1　上部结构等效示意图

1.2　水流水槽的建立

在ADINA-CFD模块中建立流体模型,改变入口处流体流入速度,在入口处设置定常流模拟水流。选用基于FCBI-C算法的八节点Fluid流体单元。水槽上表面定义为自由液面边界,水流方向两侧及水槽下边界定义为固壁边界,顺水流方向两侧分别施加速度荷载及一致流出口,流场与桥墩交互边界定义为流固耦合边界。水槽尺寸100m×40m×30m,流速1m/s和4m/s,流体密度1025kg/m^3,体积模量1.0×10^{20}Pa,动力黏度1.05×10^{-3}Pa·s。水流水槽模型如图2所示。

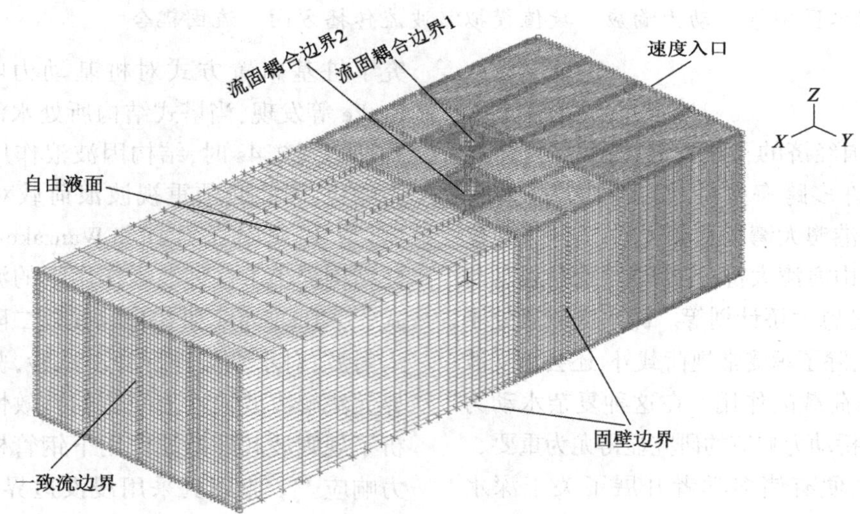

图2　水流水槽示意图

1.3　波浪水槽的建立

本文从规则波理论中选取二阶近似Stokes波作为数值波浪的模拟波浪。

目前,二阶Stokes波势函数近似公式为:

$$\Phi=\frac{HL\cosh kz}{2T\sinh kd}\sin(kx-\omega t)+\frac{3\pi H^2}{16T}\frac{\cosh 2kz}{\sinh^4 kd}\sin 2(kx-\omega t) \tag{1}$$

式中:H为波高;T为波周期;d为静水面水深;z为水质点所在位置的深度;k为波数,$k=2\pi/L$;ω为波浪圆频率,$\omega=2\pi/T$。

波剖面：

$$\eta = \frac{H}{2}\cos(kx - \omega t) + \frac{\pi H^2}{4L}\left(1 + \frac{3}{2sh^2 kd}\right)\coth kd \cdot \cos 2(kx - \omega t) \quad (2)$$

采用边界条件造波法，在 ADINA 中，边界造波法的具体实现方法是将数值波浪水槽入口处设置为扰动源，通过定义入口速度来生成波浪。根据 Dean 和 Dalrymplede 的线性造波理论，入口处的速度函数可由下式计算：

$$U = \eta \frac{\omega}{T(\omega)} = \frac{\partial X}{\partial t} \quad (3)$$

式中，X 为造波板冲程；ω 为造波板角频率；η 为波面方程。$T(\omega)$ 为造波板运动和所模拟波浪间的传播函数，表达式为：

$$T(\omega) = \frac{4\sinh^2 kd}{2kd + \sinh(2kd)} \quad (4)$$

建立三维波浪水槽模型，测试生成波浪。选取试验波浪参数为：波高 5m，周期 6s。由 Stokes 二阶波浪理论计算可得：波频 $\omega = 1.047197551$，波长 $L = 56.0721398797$，波数 $k = 0.1120553865$，入口处造波板运动函数如图 3 所示。墩前流体域沿传播方向网格划分密度为 $L/400$，墩后采用渐变网格划分，垂直于传播方向网格尺寸 $\Delta y = 0.714$m，沿水深方向网格尺寸 $\Delta z = 1$m，分别对两墩 2 倍墩距范围内流体域进行加密。流体域与双墩模型如图 4 所示。

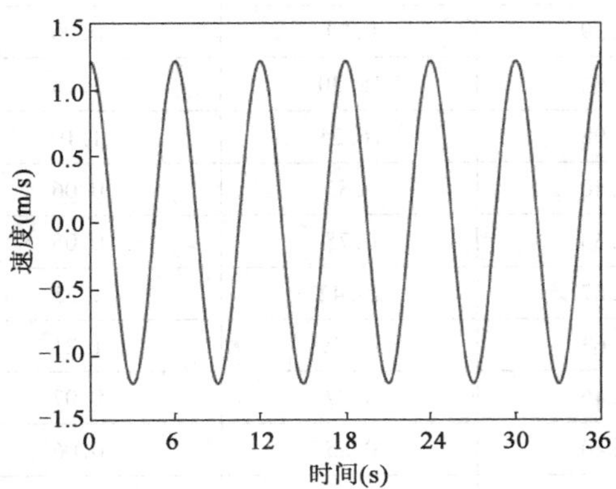

图 3　造波板运动函数

由于动边界造波法生成的波浪与随距速度入口距离的增加而衰减，导致达不到理想波高[9-10]。提取距速度入口一倍波长处波面高程进行分析，通过测试发现，当速度放大系数设置为 7.215 时，波面高程与 Stokes 二阶波浪理论波高达到较高拟合度。距速度入口一倍波长处的波浪高程与理论值对比如图 5 所示，即通过放大系数的调整，可以实现在既定位置处使波高达到理论波高，满足对波高的要求。

图 4　流体域与双墩模型

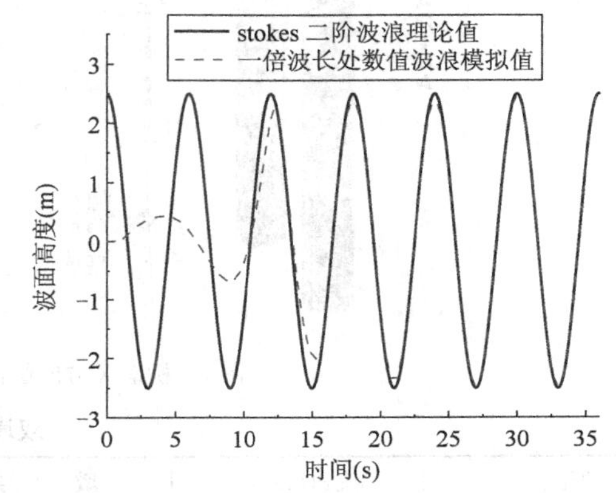

图 5　波浪高程与理论值对比

1.4　双墩桥位布置形式

本文选取在两墩中心距与墩径比值 S/D 为 3，即墩距 s 为 15m 的工况下，分析双墩的动力响应特性。双墩模型桥位布置图及流体域尺寸如图 6 所示。

2　双墩动力响应差异分析

2.1　水流作用下双墩动力响应分析

在速度入口处施加 $u = 1$m/s、4m/s 的水平流速，考虑水流入射角为 30°、45°、60°三种工况。以水流入射角与桥墩中心连线呈 30°及流速为 1m/s 工况为例，$t = 40$s 时双墩 X 方向位移云图及墩顶位移响应如图 7 所示，其中沿水流方向上游墩为 1 号墩，下游墩为 2 号墩。不同工况下双墩动力响应稳定值具体见表 1。

由图 7 可知，1 号墩动力响应最值偏大，这是因为桥墩受遮蔽效应[12]影响，水流绕过前墩发生分离,在其尾流区形成一系列旋涡,尾流区流速明显减小,后墩受前墩尾流区影响所受的正向水流力减小,从而导致动力响应小于前墩。

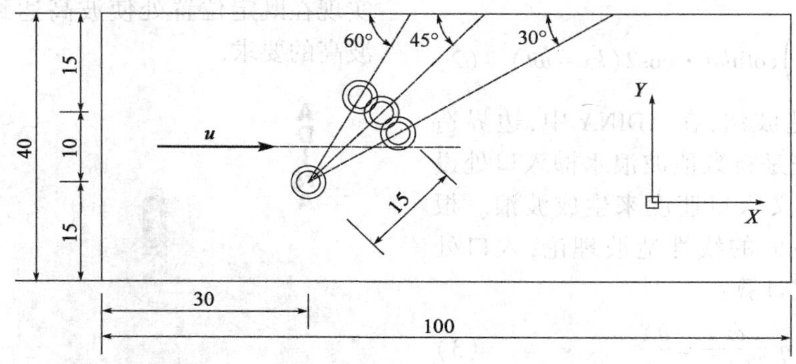

图6　双墩桥位布置图

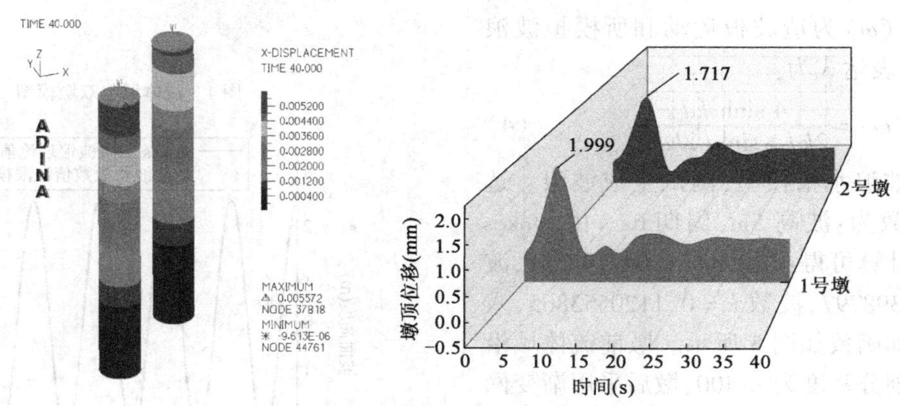

图7　桥墩X方向位移分布云图及墩顶位移响应(单位:m)

双墩动力响应稳定值　　表1

角度(°)	流速(m/s)	墩　号	位移(mm)	弯矩(MN·m)	剪力(MN)
30	1	1	0.44	0.93	0.06
		2	0.39	0.84	0.06
	4	1	9.64	18.30	1.28
		2	7.98	16.25	1.10
45	1	1	0.40	0.85	0.06
		2	0.35	0.75	0.05
	4	1	9.67	20.42	1.35
		2	8.63	18.39	1.21
60	1	1	0.46	0.97	0.07
		2	0.40	0.85	0.06
	4	1	11.85	23.25	1.51
		2	9.37	18.70	1.26

定义差异系数C,分析不同入射角度对双墩结构动力响应产生的影响:

$$C = \frac{F_1 - F_2}{F_1} \times 100\% \tag{5}$$

式中,F_1为1号墩动力响应数值;F_2为2号墩动力响应数值;C为1号墩动力响应与2号墩动力响应差值的比例系数。

由表1可知,墩顶位移稳定值差异在高流速入射角为60°时达到最大,为20.96%;墩底弯矩稳定值差异在高流速入射角为60°时达到最大,为

19.58%；墩底剪力稳定值差异在高流速入射角为60°时达到最大，为16.53%。不同入射角及水流流速下的双墩动力响应差异系数如图8所示。

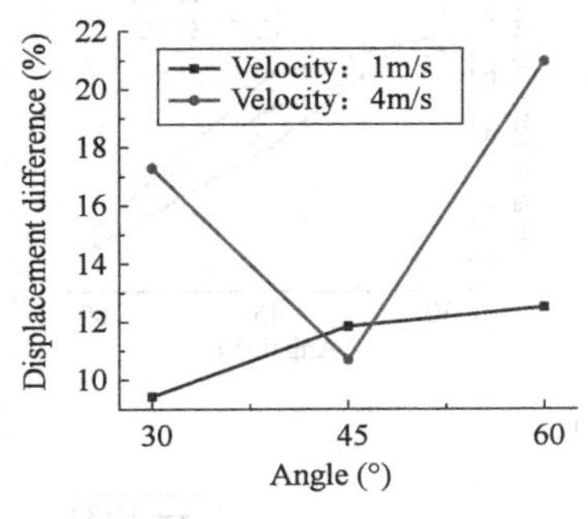

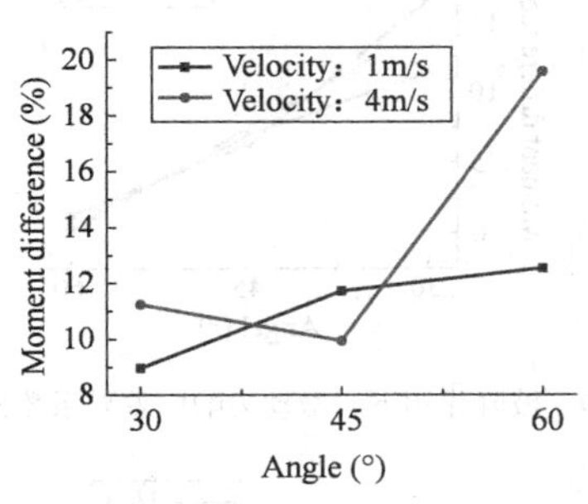

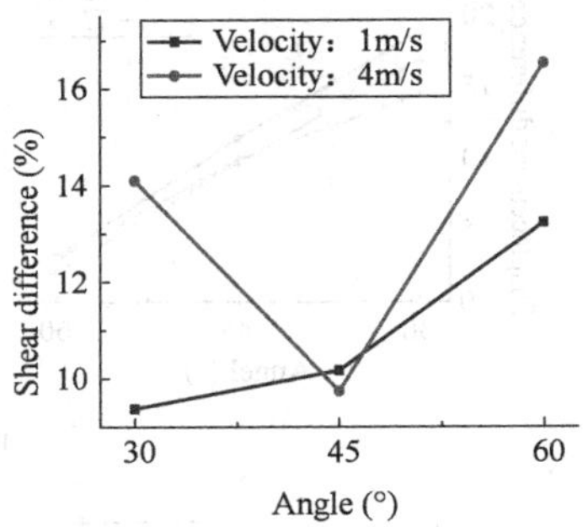

图8 双墩动力响应差异系数分布

2.2 波浪作用下双墩动力响应分析

结合某跨海大桥海域资料，三百年一遇的有效波高在5m左右，故选取波高3m、4m、5m，周期6s的波浪进行分析。不同波浪作用下双墩动力响应具体结果见表2。

波浪作用下双墩动力响应 表2

角度(°)	波高(m)	墩号	位移(mm)		弯矩(MN·m)		剪力(MN)	
			波峰	波谷	波峰	波谷	波峰	波谷
30	3	1	5.31	-5.41	9.57	-10.00	0.41	-0.45
		2	4.31	-4.76	8.00	-8.92	0.38	-0.44
	4	1	6.95	-6.73	12.47	-12.53	0.54	-0.58
		2	5.79	-5.89	10.66	-11.09	0.51	-0.55
	5	1	8.63	-7.46	15.28	-14.04	0.67	-0.66
		2	7.38	-6.88	13.55	-12.97	0.62	-0.64
45	3	1	5.21	-5.16	9.17	-9.46	0.42	-0.45
		2	4.62	-4.99	8.59	-9.42	0.39	-0.44
	4	1	6.79	-6.47	12.28	-12.17	0.53	-0.58
		2	6.13	-6.25	11.36	-11.84	0.50	-0.56
	5	1	8.55	-7.20	15.24	-13.66	0.66	-0.67
		2	7.71	-7.08	14.18	-13.52	0.63	-0.65
60	3	1	5.13	-4.95	9.22	-9.18	0.41	-0.42
		2	4.97	-4.95	9.10	-9.25	0.40	-0.44
	4	1	6.70	-6.16	11.97	-11.48	0.53	-0.53
		2	6.56	-6.23	11.97	-11.71	0.52	-0.56
	5	1	8.39	-6.67	14.88	-12.73	0.63	-0.60
		2	8.13	-6.97	14.81	-13.21	0.63	-0.64

由表2可知，在波浪场中，波浪传播方向为30°和45°时，在波峰与波谷作用下1号墩动力响应均大于2号墩；传播方向为60°时，在波峰作用下，上游墩动力响应大于下游墩，而在波在谷作用下，上游墩动力响应负向最值小于下游墩，且双墩动力响应差异系数均在波峰作用下达到最大。

波峰作用下的双墩动力响应差异系数如图9所示。在同一波高的波浪作用下，随着波浪传播方向与桥墩中心线夹角的增大，前后墩的波峰动力响应差异不断减小，且在角度为60°时接近0。

波谷作用下的双墩动力响应差异系数如图10所示。在同一波高的波浪作用下，随着波浪传播方向与桥墩中心线夹角的增大,前后墩的波谷动力响应差异先减小后增大。

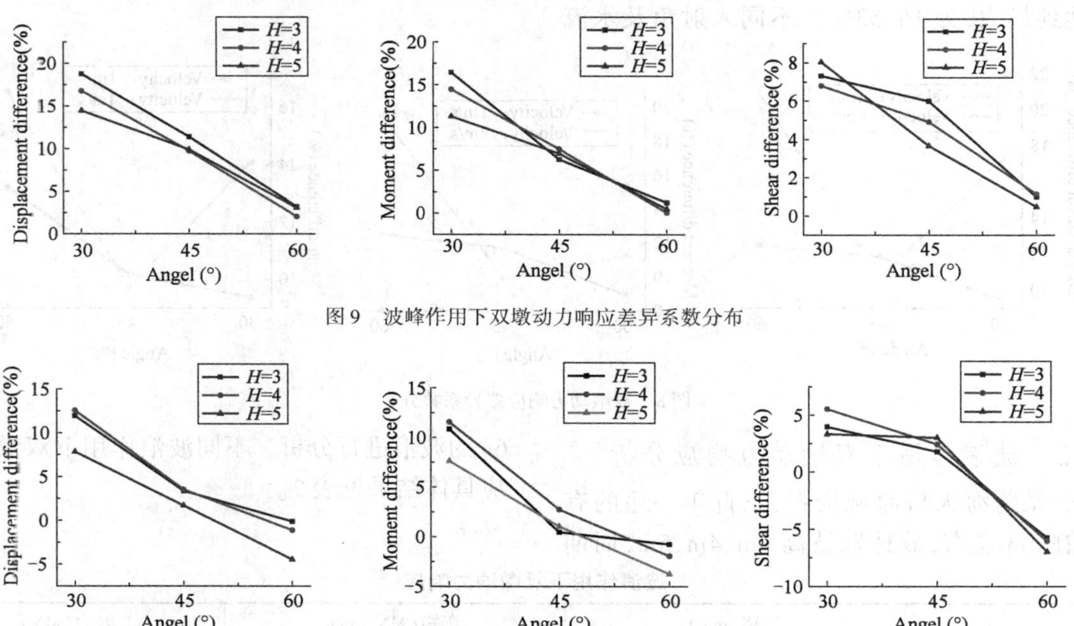

图 9　波峰作用下双墩动力响应差异系数分布

图 10　波谷作用下双墩动力响应差异系数分布

3　结语

本文对不同方向波、流作用下的双墩结构进行详细的数值模拟研究,得出的主要结论有:

(1)水流入射角为 30°、45°、60°下布置的双墩,受遮蔽效应影响,在水流场中上游墩动力响应稳定值不同程度地大于下游墩。在低流速时,双墩动力响应稳定值的差异随着入射角的增加而增大;在高流速时,双墩动力响应稳定值的差异表现为 45° < 30° < 60°,即高流速情况下,在水流入射角度为 45°时,下游墩动力响应与上游墩最接近。

(2)波浪传播方向为 30°、45°、60°下布置的双墩,仅在夹角为 60°的波谷作用下,出现下游墩动力响应大于上游墩的情况。波峰作用于双墩结构时,上游墩动力响应偏大,下游墩动力响应随着夹角的增大而增大,但不会超过上游墩,即遮蔽效应的削弱作用始终大于绕射效应的增强作用;波谷作用于双墩结构时,随着夹角的增大,遮蔽效应的影响逐渐减弱,使得下游墩动力响应逐渐增大,又由于相互靠近的两个墩之间的流体在收缩段流速增大,形成了射流,波浪绕射效应引起了压力和流速的增加,最终绕射效应对下游墩动力响应负向最值的增强作用逐渐大于遮蔽效应的削弱作用,出现下游墩动力响应大于上游墩的情况。

参考文献

[1] Westergaard H M. Water Pressures on Dams during Earthquakes [J]. Transactions of the American Society of Civil Engineers, 1933, 98(2):418-432.

[2] Morison J R, O&Brien M P, Johnson J W, et al. The Force Exerted by Surface Wave on Piles[J]. Journal of Petroleum Technology, 1950, 2(5): 149-154.

[3] Wu Anjie, Yang Wanli. Numerical Study of Pile Group Effect on the Hydrodynamic Force on a Pile of Sea-crossing Bridges during Earthquakes [J]. Ocean Engineering, 2020, 199(1):106999.

[4] Burke B G, Tighe J T. A Time Series Model for Dynamic Behavior of Offshore Structures[J]. Society of Petroleum Engineers Journal, 1972, 12(2): 156-170.

[5] Kascachek G D, Wanzakov O M. Interaction between Regular Wave and Circular Breakwaters[C]. ASCE, 1971:97-105.

[6] Baarholm R, Faltinsen O M. A Boundary-element Method for Solving Water Impact on a Platform Duct[C]. ASME, 2001, 18(3):16-18.

[7] 居艮国. 波浪荷载作用下深水墩钢管桩施工平台动力性能研究[D]. 上海:同济大学,2007.

[8] 康啊真. 三维波浪作用下跨海深水桥梁围堰的动力响应研究[D]. 成都:西南交通大学,2014.

[9] 江辉,白晓宇,黄磊,等. 波浪、海流环境中跨海桥梁深水桥墩的地震响应特性[J]. 铁道学报,2019,41(3):117-127.

[10] 白晓宇. 波、流环境中深水桥墩地震响应特性研究[D]. 北京:北京交通大学,2017.

[11] 张超. 深水桥墩流固耦合动力响应分析[D]. 西安:长安大学,2019.

[12] 廖瑾. 不同深水桥梁基础型式的波浪响应分析[D]. 北京:北京工业大学,2011.

钢结构桥梁点蚀的元胞自动机模拟方法

祁泽中* 李鹏飞 陶 沛
(长安大学公路学院)

摘 要 为了模拟钢结构桥梁在腐蚀环境中的点蚀坑演化过程,本文基于电化学腐蚀原理建立了模拟钢结构点蚀坑电化学腐蚀演化过程的元胞自动机模型,将参与腐蚀的六种主要物质抽象成六种元胞类型,并将整个腐蚀系统离散成100×500的网格,通过定义演化规则模拟点蚀在介观尺度上的腐蚀演化进程,分析了金属氧化概率、金属阳离子水化概率和金属水化物扩散沉降因子对点蚀进程的影响。研究表明:当采用合理的演化参数和演化规则时,蚀坑形貌和金属腐蚀量随时间的变化趋势与实际状况基本一致。在腐蚀模拟过程中,金属氧化概率和金属水化物扩散沉降因子对蚀坑的演化起主导作用,金属氧化概率在腐蚀的前期对金属腐蚀速率起到促进作用,金属水化物扩散沉降因子在后期会对金属腐蚀速率起到抑制作用。因此,采用元胞自动机模拟钢结构点蚀是可行的,控制影响腐蚀速率的影响因素和腐蚀介质与铁基质的接触概率是减缓点蚀坑发展的有效途径。

关键词 钢结构桥梁 点蚀模拟 元胞自动机 蚀坑

0 引言

沿海地区潮湿多盐分的气候环境使得钢结构桥梁面临着严重的腐蚀问题。钢结构的腐蚀不仅会引起材料性能的下降,还会引发钢结构的疲劳,导致桥梁结构的关键部件过早失效,继而引发桥梁结构的破坏和过早的退役[1]。因此,为了保证桥梁结构的使用安全性和抗腐蚀性能,对钢结构的腐蚀机理、腐蚀演化过程和长期性能预测的研究至关重要。

研究桥梁结构钢构件的腐蚀问题主要有试验和数值模拟两种方法。试验方法主要有四种:天然暴露试验法、人工环境加速腐蚀法和电化学加速腐蚀法[2]。数值模拟方法主要有有限元法、元胞自动机理论、相场理论等。相较于数值模拟方法,试验方法虽然具备贴近真实环境、试件材料性能与实际结构基本一致、微观的腐蚀特征更细致等优势,但是存在试验周期长、成本高、可调节性差等缺点。因此,数值模拟在钢材的腐蚀研究中同样发挥着举足轻重的作用。目前,通过数值模拟研究钢材腐蚀虽然取得了较为丰富的研究成果,但是数值模拟仍存在着许多不确定性需要进行深入研究。因此,本文将针对元胞自动机理论在钢材腐蚀模拟方面的应用进行研究。

元胞自动机是一种允许使用者通过定义简单的演化规则来模拟和理解实际生活中存在的复杂物理机制和数理方程的工具。近年来,元胞自动机已广泛地应用于生命科学、交通运输和火灾等领域。除此之外,已有研究表明元胞自动机在金属腐蚀模拟研究方面也相当出色。Cui Chuanjie 等[3]采用三维 Von Neumann 元胞自动机模型模拟了钢材点蚀的初始过程和发展过程,并通过调正参数观察了不同参数下点蚀坑的形貌。Fatoba O. O 等[4]采用二维元胞自动机结合有限元分析模拟了应力作用下钢材的点蚀过程。Chen Mengcheng 等[5]采用二维元胞自动机模型模拟了钢管混凝土外钢管的均匀腐蚀过程。

上述元胞自动机模型主要集中在钢材的腐蚀、钝化、金属阳离子和腐蚀介质的扩散模拟。事实上,金属在腐蚀过程中还存在着金属阳离子的水化以及金属水化物的沉积。因此,本文将考虑金属的氧化、金属阳离子的水化和金属水化物的沉积探索钢材的点蚀过程。

1　钢材点蚀模型

1.1　元胞自动机模型概述

元胞自动机(Cellular Automata. CA),是一种复杂的动力系统。元胞自动机模拟是将一个连续的动态响应过程通过差分方程的形式离散为若干个离散时间节点的演化过程[6]。如图 1 所示,一个完整的元胞自动机模拟过程主要由四项基本元素组成:元胞、元胞空间、元胞邻居与演化规则。元胞是元胞自动机组成结构中的最基本元素。元胞空间是各类元胞分布和演化的空间,实际模拟中主要采用的元胞空间有一维、二维和三维元胞空间。元胞邻居是目标元胞附近的元胞,其中 Von Neumann 元胞邻居和 Moore 元胞邻居常被用于二维元胞自动机模拟[7],其具体特征如图 2 所示。演化规则是元胞自动机模拟最核心的部分,它是根据当前时刻中心元胞及其邻居元胞的状态演化成下一时刻中心元胞状态的规则。

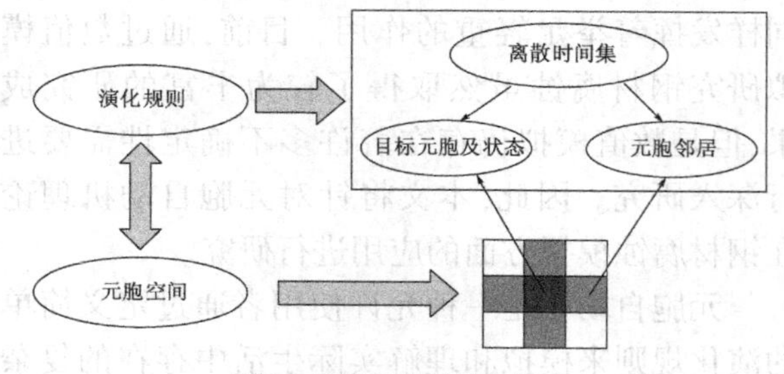

图 1　元胞自动机基本组成

钢材的点蚀是复杂的电化学腐蚀过程,但是元胞自动机可以通过设定演化规则的方式来简化这个过程,因此已有众多研究者将元胞自动机用于金属腐蚀的模拟。为了保证模拟的高效性和准确性,本文采用二维元胞自动机模型模拟钢材点蚀,模型通过 Matlab 编程的方式实现。

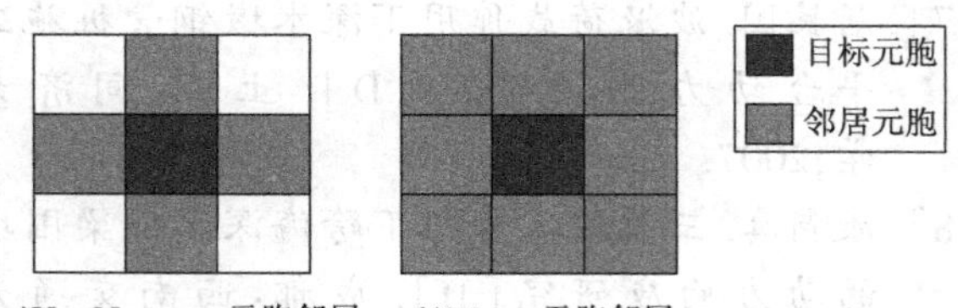

图 2　Von Neumann 元胞邻居和 Moore 元胞邻居

1.2　电化学腐蚀机理

本文的元胞自动机模型基于中性环境建立。为了提高模型的运行效率和简化编程的难度,除腐蚀性介质和水分子之外,模型考虑将 Fe、Fe^{3+}、$Fe(OH)_3$ 这三种主要物质用于元胞状态的选取,三种物质参与的电化学反应过程如电化学方程式(1)~式(3)所示。根据上述电化学反应过程,整个模拟系统有六种物质用于元胞状态的定义。为了表述的方便,六类物种分别采用特定的代码表述,其相应关系如表 1 所示。

$$Fe \rightarrow Fe^{3+} + 3e^- \quad (1)$$

$$4Fe^{3+} + 6H_2O + 3O_2 \longleftrightarrow 4Fe(OH)_3 + 12e^- \quad (2)$$

$$Fe(OH)_3 + 3Cl^- \longleftrightarrow Fe^{3+} + 3OH^- + 3Cl^- \quad (3)$$

元胞自动机中元胞的状态　　表 1

元胞的状态	对应物质	标志
中性溶液元胞	水	*W*
腐蚀溶液元胞	氯离子溶液	*C*
金属 Fe 元胞	非活性金属	*Z*
金属 Fe^{3+} 元胞	活性金属	*N*
金属水化物 $Fe(OH)_3$ 元胞	腐蚀产物	*H*
钝化元胞	钢材保护层	*A*

1.3　元胞自动机模型定义

元胞自动机模型实施过程可由函数关系式 $g = g(c, s, r, \Phi)$ 表述,其中 c 代表元胞,s 代表元胞空间,r 代表元胞邻居,Φ 代表演化规则。由 1.2 节可知,整个模拟过程有六种元胞状态,因此元胞的状态 c 可表述为 $c = c(W, C, Z, F, H, A)$。根据排他原则,同一时间步,同一元胞的状态只能是上述六种状态的一种[8]。为了提高分析效率,本文采用 Von Neumann 元胞邻居。因此,目标元胞在某一时间步的状态将取决于目标元胞自身和相接触的上下左右四个邻居元胞。

如图 3 所示,本文采用 100 × 500 的二维元胞空间进行钢材点蚀过程的模拟。其中,第 1 ~ 40

行代表腐蚀溶液范围，内部包括水溶液元胞 W 和腐蚀溶液元胞 C，腐蚀溶液元胞 C 以一定数量随机分布于水溶液元胞内；第 41 行中间 150～250 列位置用溶液元胞代替代表钢材的局部缺陷，其余位置被抗腐蚀性的钝化元胞 A 占据；剩余位置将被非活性金属元胞 Z 占据。在模拟过程中，元胞尺寸和每一分析步的时间采用单位尺寸和单位时间。

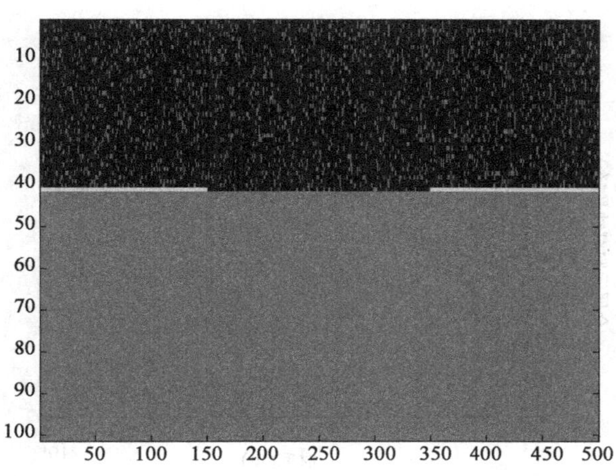

图 3　钢材点蚀元胞自动机模型

材料的腐蚀过程是物质的扩散过程和电化学腐蚀过程的耦合。为了模拟上述过程，元胞自动机模型通过定义扩散规则和腐蚀规则来实现。在每一分析时步，所有元胞被随机抽取并按照设定的规则进化。根据上述电化学反应过程，扩散元胞包括腐蚀元胞 C、铁离子元胞 N 和金属水化物元胞 H。基于随机行走理论、质量守恒定律和各项同性原则，腐蚀元胞 C 和铁离子元胞 N 在每一扩散时步以相同的概率分别向其任意一个邻居元胞移动；金属水化物受重力作用有向下运动的趋势，因此金属水化物元胞向下扩散概率在 0.25 的基础上加重力沉降因子 F 来考虑重力作用。当腐蚀元胞与金属相关的三类元胞相互接触时，三种电化学反应将会发生。当金属元胞与腐蚀元胞相互接触并满足腐蚀概率 $P\text{-}corr$ 时，金属元胞被金属离子元胞代替；当金属离子元胞与腐蚀元胞相互接触并满足水化概率 $P\text{-}hyd$ 时，金属离子元胞被金属水化物元胞代替；当金属水化物元胞与腐蚀性元胞相互接触并满足溶解概率 $P\text{-}diss$ 时，金属水化物元胞被金属离子元胞代替。上述初始参数如表 2 所示。

元胞自动机模拟初始参数　　表 2

P-corr	0.05	*P-diss*	0.002
P-hyd	0.001	F	0.03

2　模拟结果及参数分析

2.1　模拟结果

如图 4 所示，金属元胞腐蚀量随时间呈非线性增加，腐蚀速率随时间逐渐减小，该变化趋势与文献[9]试验结果相一致。当模拟分析进行至 10000 步时，金属元胞腐蚀量达到 2600 个，点蚀形貌呈现凹坑形，点蚀坑内分布着溶液元胞与腐蚀产物元胞，且腐蚀产物向点蚀坑外部扩散，该模拟结果与实际钢材点蚀状况相一致。当模拟分析分别进行至 20000 步和 30000 步时，点蚀坑继续加深，蚀坑内部和外部腐蚀产物不断增加，蚀坑深度变化逐渐减小。从模拟结果可知，采用该模型模拟钢材点蚀过程是可行的。

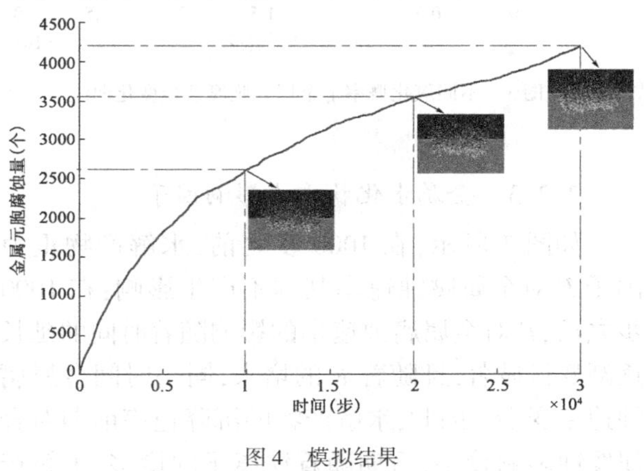

图 4　模拟结果

2.2　参数分析

钢材的点蚀是一个复杂的过程，它受到材料的腐蚀、腐蚀介质和腐蚀产物的扩散、金属离子的水化等因素的影响。基于材料的电化学腐蚀特性，拟对如下几个主要影响参数进行分析：①金属转化为金属离子 Fe^{3+} 速率，②金属离子 Fe^{3+} 转化为金属水化物 $Fe(OH)_3$ 速率，③金属水化物 $Fe(OH)_3$ 受重力作用向下堆积。为了明确单一因素的影响，分析时仅改变单一因素，其他因素保持不变，其初值设定如图 3、表 2 所示。

2.2.1　铁基质氧化速率

作为金属腐蚀的关键因素，铁基质氧化对铁

离子对钢材的点蚀速率有重要影响。元胞自动机模型通过引入腐蚀概率参数 *P-corr* 来反映铁基质的氧化速率。如图5所示,随着 *P-corr* 的增大,金属腐蚀速率也增大。然而,当反应进行至10000步后,不同 *P-corr* 的情况下,金属腐蚀曲线变化趋势逐渐趋于一致,这表明金属腐蚀速率逐渐受到抑制。因此,铁基质氧化速率前期对金属的腐蚀速率有着较大的影响,后期由于其他因素的作用被制约。

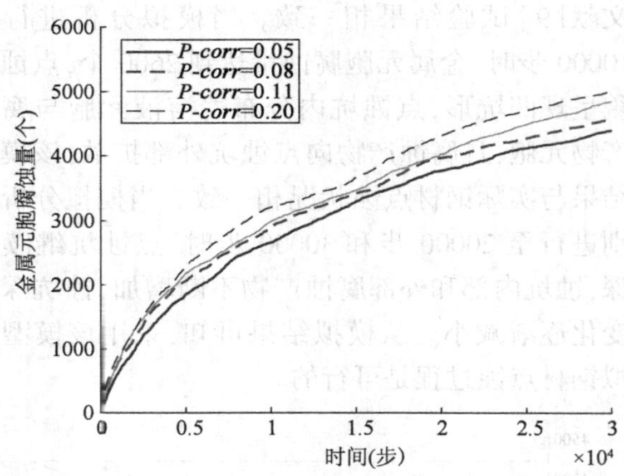

图5　不同氧化概率下金属元胞腐蚀量变化曲线

2.2.2　铁离子水解速率

如图6所示,在1000步之前,*P-hyd* 对金属腐蚀速率基本不产生影响;在1000步之后,*P-hyd* 对金属腐蚀速率的影响随着时间的延长逐渐变得显著,且随着 *P-hyd* 的增大,同一时间金属腐蚀速率变小。因此,铁离子水解速率前期对金属的腐蚀速率影响较小,后期随着铁离子的增多对金属腐蚀速率的影响逐渐变大。

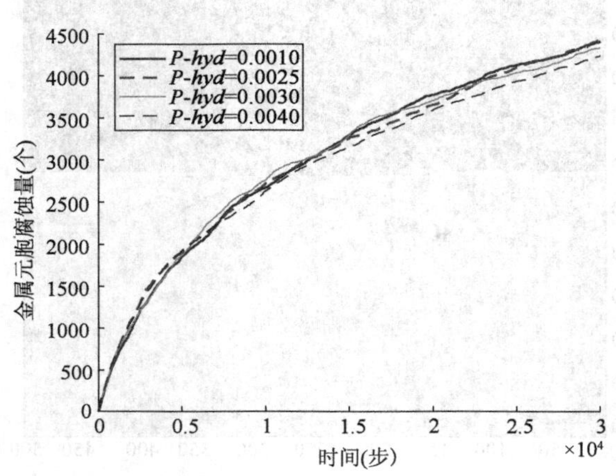

图6　不同水解概率下金属元胞腐蚀量变化曲线

2.2.3　金属水化物重力影响因子

如图7所示,在1000步之前,水解产物重力因子 *F* 对金属腐蚀速率基本不产生影响;在1000步之后,*F* 对金属腐蚀速率的影响随着时间的延长逐渐变得显著,且随着 *F* 的增大,同一时间金属腐蚀速率变小。因此,水解产物的沉降速率前期对金属腐蚀影响较小,后期随着铁离子的增多,水解产物的沉降速率对金属腐蚀速率的影响逐渐变大。

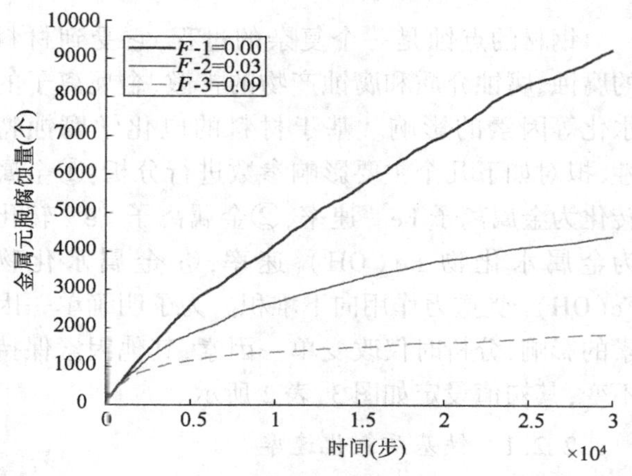

图7　不同金属水化物扩散沉降因子下金属元胞腐蚀量变化曲线

3　结语

采用元胞自动机模拟钢结构点蚀坑的电化学腐蚀过程,将参与电化学腐蚀的关键物质抽象为六种类型的元胞,并通过定义的演化规则在介观尺度上对钢材的点蚀过程进行模拟,分析了铁氧化概率 *P-corr*、铁离子水化概率 *P-hyd* 和金属水化物扩散沉降因子 *F* 三个钢材点蚀进程的影响因素。

(1)当采用合理的演化参数时,元胞自动机模拟产生的蚀坑形貌和金属腐蚀量变化趋势与实际状况基本一致。

(2)金属的腐蚀速率前期随金属氧化概率的增大而增大,后期这种影响会受到限制,因此前期采取合理的防护措施可有效抑制金属的腐蚀。

(3)金属水化物扩散沉降因子的大小对金属腐蚀速率会产生重要影响,这种影响会随着时间的延长不断放大。

(4)本文仅考虑了电化学腐蚀过程中的关键物质,略了其他次要物质,后续的研究可以将其他物质考虑进去。

参考文献

[1] 刘新华,张建仁. 锈蚀对Q550E高性能钢梁抗弯承载力影响的试验研究[J]. 中国公路学报,2019,32(11):184-191+201.

[2] Bierwagen Gordon P, He L, Li J, et al. Studies of a new accelerated evaluation method for coating corrosion resistance-thermal cycling testing[J]. Progress in Organic Coatings, 2000, 39 (1): 67-78.

[3] Cui Chuanjie, Ma Rujin, Chen Airong, et al. Experimental study and 3D cellular automata simulation of corrosion pits on Q345 steel surface under salt-spray environment [J]. Corrosion Science, 2019, 154(1): 80-89.

[4] Fatoba O. O, Leiva-Garcia R, Lishchuk S. V, et al. Simulation of stress-assisted localised corrosion using a cellular automaton finite element approach[J]. Corrosion Science, 2018, 137(6): 83-97.

[5] Chen Mengcheng, Wen Qingqing, Zhu Qi, et al. Simulation of corrosion process for concrete filled steel tubular columns with the cellular automata method [J]. Engineering Failure Analysis, 2017, 82: 298-307.

[6] 郭增伟,陈汉林,黎小刚,等. 拉索钢丝电化学腐蚀进程的元胞自动机模拟方法[J]. 重庆大学学报,2019,42(9):18-26.

[7] 马俊军,蔺鹏臻. 混凝土箱梁氯离子扩散效应分析与寿命预测的CA模型[J]. 长江科学院院报,2019,36(6):121-126.

[8] Wang Haitao, Han En-Hou. Computational simulation of corrosion pit interactions under mechanochemical effects using a cellular automaton/finite element model [J]. Corrosion Science, 2016, 103: 305-311.

[9] Lishchuk S. V, Akid R, Worden K, et al. A cellular automaton model for predicting intergranular corrosion[J]. Corrosion Science, 2011, 53 (8): 2518-2526.

Reliability Prediction Method of Self-anchored Suspension Bridge Based on Artificial Neural Network

Pengfei Li* Pei Tao Zezhong Qi
(Department of Bridge Engineering, School of Highway, Chang'an University)

Abstract Self-anchoredsuspension bridge has gradually become one of the preferred bridge types of urban landscape bridge because of its excellent aesthetic functions. However, because the main cable is a flexible structure, the change of the hanger tension will inevitably affect the line shape of the main girder and the force of the bridge tower. At the same time, due to various factors such as construction errors, the hanger tension is difficult to accurately tension to the design value, but fluctuates in a certain range. In order to ensure the safety of the finished state of the self-anchored suspension bridge, it is necessary to calculate its reliability. This paper takes a two-tower three-span self-anchored suspension bridge as the engineering background, a reliability prediction method of self-anchored suspension bridge is proposed. Finite element model is established in ANSYS to get the response of the structure, and then the BP neural network (BPNN) model is established in MATLAB to simulate the response of the structure. Finally, Monte Carlo simulation is used to predict the reliability of the bridge. The results show that the safety of the self-anchored suspension bridge with uncertainty of hanger tension meets the requirements. And the proposed method can also be applied to the reliability prediction of other cable-supported bridges, prestressed structures and so on.

Keywords Bridge engineering Self-anchored suspension bridge Reliability Artificial neural network Finite element simulation Monte Carlo simulation

0 Introduction

In recent years, as the bridge landscape and aesthetics are becoming more and more important in bridge design, self-anchored suspension bridge presents a blowout development. Self-anchored suspension bridge has the advantages of no large-volume anchorage structure, small topographic constraints, flexible span layout, high material utilization and beautiful appearance, therefore, it has gradually become one of the most competitive bridge types in urban landscape bridges. A beautifully shaped self-anchored suspension bridge can usually be used as a landmark building in a city.

However, the self-anchored suspension bridge is a flexible structure, and the shape of the main cable will continuously reach a self-balanced state as the load changes. Therefore, the structural response of self-anchored suspension bridge is highly sensitive to construction errors, and the hanger tension error is the main sensitive factor. The tension error of the hanger will inevitably affect the line shape of the main girder and the force of the bridge tower, and in serious cases, it will threaten the safety of the self-anchored suspension bridge. Moreover, during the hanger tensioning stage, due to the influence of many factors such as error of construction machinery and operation error of construction personnel, it is inevitable that the hanger tension is under-tensioned or over-tensioned. And it is difficult to accurately tension the hanger tension to the design value. Therefore, it is necessary to calculate the reliability of the self-anchored suspension bridge under the uncertainty of suspender tension to ensure the safety of the whole bridge.

Many achievements have been made in reliability research of self-anchored suspension bridges. Li proposed an improved response surface method to solve the problem that the limit state function of the large, complex bridge structures can not be expressed explicitly, and established the program for any complex structural reliability analysis under service limit state based on MATLAB and ANSYS; Yu proposed a uniform design method and support vector machine based approach to analyze the reliability of self-anchored suspension bridge under serviceability limit state. In recent years, machine learning technology represented by artificial neural networks (ANN), due to its strong nonlinear fitting capabilities, feature extraction capabilities, and highly flexible structural forms, has penetrated into various research directions in civil engineering, and has been used to solve the difficulties of traditional methods. The problems dealt with show great potential for engineering applications. It has been used to solve the problems that are difficult to be solved by traditional methods, showing a good engineering application potential. For example, Zhu proposed an efficient bridge flutter failure probability analysis method based on radial basis function (RBF) neural network; Niu established a GA-BP neural network model based on BP neural network (BPNN) and genetic optimization algorithm to fit the limit state function of the prestressed concrete continuous beam bridge.

In this paper, a reliability prediction method of self-anchored suspension bridge based on BPNN is proposed to improve the calculation efficiency of Monte Carlo method and realize the rapid prediction of reliability. The multi-story frame structure problem is used to verify the accuracy and efficiency of the proposed method. After that the proposed method is used to predict the reliability of self-anchored suspension bridge. Finite element model is established and analyzed in ANSYS to calculate the response of the bridge and generate training samples. And the generated samples were then used for BPNN model training in MATLAB. Finally, the Monte Carlo method based on BPNN is used to predict the reliability of self-anchored suspension bridge in MATLAB.

1 Review of reliability analysis

1.1 Performance function of structure

In structural reliability analysis, in order to correctly describe the working state of the structure, the performance function of the structure is usually introduced. If $X = (X_1, X_2, \cdots, X_n)$ is used to represent the basic random variable of the structure, then $Z = g(X_1, X_2, \cdots, X_n)$ is called the performance function of the structure. There are three types of working states of structures:

$$Z = g(X)\begin{cases} <0 & \text{Failure state} \\ =0 & \text{Limit state} \\ >0 & \text{Reliable state} \end{cases} \quad (1)$$

1.2 Structural reliability index

Structural reliability is defined as the probability that the structure completes the predetermined function within the specified time and under the specified conditions, expressed as P_S. On the contrary, if the structure cannot complete the predetermined function within the specified time and under the specified conditions, the corresponding probability is the failure probability P_f of the structure. Obviously:

$$P_s + P_f = 1 \quad (2)$$

It can be seen that the core problem of structural reliability analysis is the calculation of structural failure probability. If the joint probability density function of $X = (X_1, X_2, \cdots, X_n)$ is $f_X(x) = f_X(x_1, x_2, \cdots, x_n)$, then the failure probability of the structure can be calculated by the following formula:

$$\begin{aligned} P_f &= P(Z<0) = \int_{Z<0} f_X(x)d(x) \\ &= \iint\cdots\int_{Z<0} f_X(x_1, x_2, \cdots, x_n)dx_1 dx_2 \cdots dx_n \end{aligned} \quad (3)$$

Usually, the joint probability density function of basic random variables is difficult to know, and it is also very difficult to calculate multiple integrals. Therefore, the introduction of reliability index β corresponding to failure probability P_f is a simple method to obtain sufficient accuracy. The corresponding relationship between P_f and β is:

$$P_f = \Phi(-\beta) \quad (4)$$

Due to the one-to-one correspondence between P_f and β, β is often used to express the structural reliability in practical engineering.

1.3 Monte Carlo simulation

Monte Carlo method is based on mathematical statistics and uses random numbers to solve computational problems. If the performance function and random variable distribution of the structure are known, the reliability can be solved by Monte Carlo method. Because this method is suitable for any random variable distribution and performance function type, the reliability result calculated by Monte Carlo method is the closest to the exact solution.

Assuming that $X = (X_1, X_2, \cdots, X_n)$ is randomly sampled N times, the sample value x is brought into the performance function $Z = g(X)$, the value of Z is calculated, and the number of times $Z < 0$ is calculated, the estimated value of failure probability is:

$$\hat{P}_f = \frac{n_f}{N} \quad (5)$$

The coefficient of variation of $\hat{P}_f$ is defined as:

$$\delta_{Pf} = \sqrt{\frac{1-P_f}{NP_f}} \quad \text{or} \quad N = \frac{1-P_f}{\delta_{Pf}^2 P_f} \quad (6)$$

In order to obtain higher calculation accuracy, a smaller coefficient of variation is required. It can be seen from the above formula that for structures with low failure probability, the number of samples taken needs to be very large. It can be seen that the disadvantage of Monte Carlo method is low computational efficiency. Therefore, artificial neural network is considered to improve the computational efficiency of Monte Carlo method.

2 Efficient reliability analysis with artificial neural network

2.1 Back-propagation neural network (BPNN)

BPNN is a kind of multilayer feed-forward neural network, which is characterized by signal forward propagation and error back propagation. In forward transmission, the input signal is processed layer by layer from the input layer through the hidden layer to the output layer. Neurons in each layer only affect the state of neurons in the next layer. If the output layer can not get the expected output, it turns to back propagation, and adjusts the weights and thresholds of the network according to the prediction error, so that the predicted output of the neural network is constantly approaching the expected output. The topological structure of BPNN with single hidden layer is shown in Fig. 1.

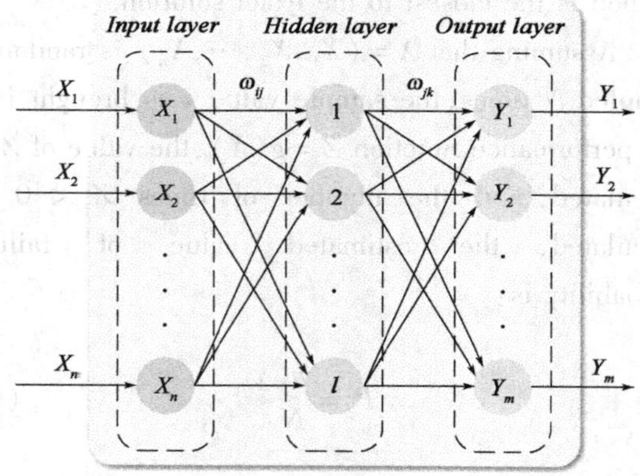

Fig. 1 Topological structure of BPNN with single hidden layer

In Fig. 1, $X_1, X_2, \cdots, X_n$ are the input value of BPNN, $Y_1, Y_2, \cdots, Y_m$ are the output value of BPNN, ω_{ij} and ω_{jk} are the weight of BPNN. As can be seen from Fig. 1, BPNN can be understood as a nonlinear function, expressing the functional mapping relationship from n independent variables to m dependent variables.

The training of BPNN includes the following steps:

Step 1: Initialization. Determine the number of network input layer nodes n, hidden layer nodes l and output layer nodes m, initialize the connection weights between the neurons of the input layer and the hidden layer ω_{ij}, the connection weights between the neurons of the hidden layer and the output layer ω_{jk}, the hidden layer threshold a and the output layer threshold b. Give the learning rate and neuron excitation function.

Step 2: Hidden layer output calculation. Calculate the hidden layer output H according to the input vector X, the connection weight between the input layer and the hidden layer ω_{ij} and the hidden layer threshold a:

$$H_j = f\left(\sum_{i=1}^{n} \omega_{ij} x_i - a_j\right) \quad (j = 1, 2, \cdots, l) \tag{7}$$

Where f is the hidden layer excitation function, which is expressed in many forms. In this paper, the function is selected:

$$f(x) = \frac{1}{1 + e^{x}} \tag{8}$$

Step 3: Output layer output calculation. According to the hidden layer output H, the connection weight ω_{jk} and threshold b, the prediction output O of BPNN is calculated:

$$O_k = \sum_{j=1}^{l} H_j \omega_{jk} - b_k \quad (k = 1, 2, \cdots, m) \tag{9}$$

Step 4: Error calculation. According to the predicted output O and expected output Y, the network prediction error e is calculated:

$$e_k = Y_k - O_k \quad (k = 1, 2, \cdots, m) \tag{10}$$

Step 5: Update the weights. Network connection weights are updated according to network prediction error e.

$$\omega_{ij} = \omega_{ij} + \eta H_j (1 - H_j) x(i) \sum_{k=1}^{m} \omega_{jk} e_k$$
$$(i = 1, 2, \cdots, n; j = 1, 2, \cdots, l)$$
$$\omega_{jk} = \omega_{jk} + \eta H_j e_k \quad (j = 1, 2, \cdots, l; k = 1, 2, \cdots, m) \tag{11}$$

Step 6: Update the thresholds. Update network node thresholds a and b according to network prediction error e.

$$a_j = a_j + \eta H_j(1-H_j)\sum_{k=1}^{m}\omega_{jk}e_k \quad (j=1,2,\cdots,l) \tag{12}$$

$$b_k = b_k + e_k \quad (k=1,2,\cdots,m)$$

Step 7: Check whether the algorithm iteration is complete. If not, return to Step 2.

2.2 Reliability prediction process based on BPNN

The reliability analysis process based on BPNN is shown in Fig. 2.

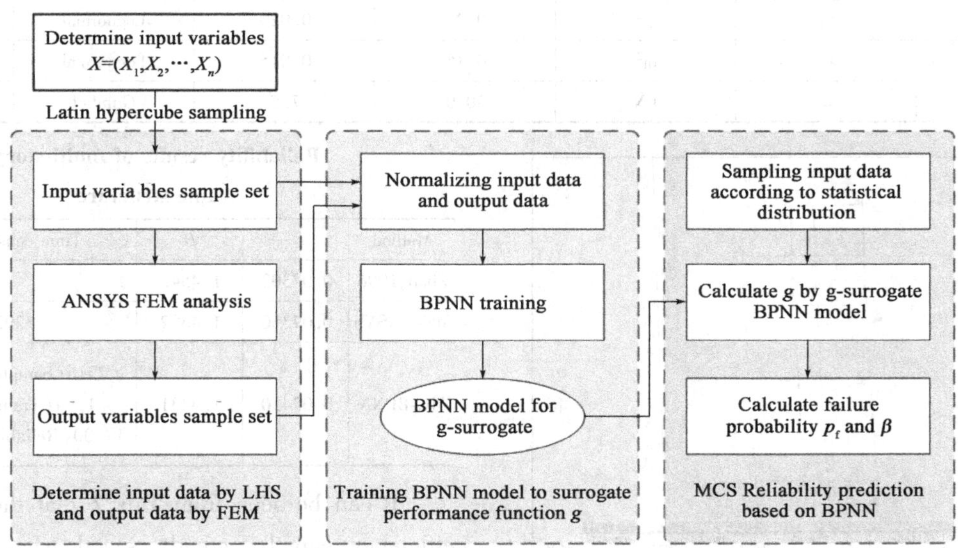

Fig. 2 Reliability analysis process based on BPNN

2.3 Example to verify accuracy and efficiency

In order to verify the accuracy and efficiency of the proposed framework, this paper selects the multi-story frame structureas an example. The multi-story frame structure is shown in Fig. 3.

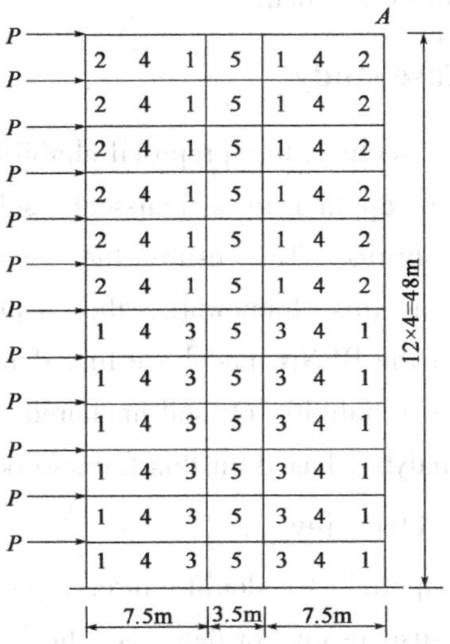

Fig. 3 Structure sketch of multi-story frame structure

The elastic modulus E of each element is $2.0\times10^7\,\mathrm{kN/m^2}$. The relationship between the moment of inertia of the element section and the section area is $I_i = a_i A_i^2\,(i=1,2,\cdots,5)$. The statistic parameters of random variables A_i and P are shown in Tab. 1. Takes the maximum horizontal displacement of node A as u_A, and when $u_A > 0.096\mathrm{m}$, the structure is failure. The limit state equation of theframe structure can be expressed as:

$$Z = 0.096 - u_A(x_1,x_2,x_3,x_4,x_5,x_6) \tag{13}$$

It can be seen from equation (13) that the relationship between the horizontal displacement of node A and random variables cannot be expressed explicitly. Therefore, it is necessary to call finite element software to solve the horizontal displacement of node A. ANSYS finite element software is used in this paper. The finite element model is established and analyzed as shown in Fig. 4.

550 groups of samples are generated by calling ANSYS software for 550 times. Among them, 500 groups of samples are randomly selected to train BPNN, and the remaining 50 groups are used to test the accuracy of BPNN. The regression coefficient of BPNN is shown in Fig. 5.

Random variable statistic parameters of multi-story frame structure Tab. 1

Random variable	Symbol	Unit	Mean value	Standard deviation	Distribution	a_i
A_1	x_1	m^2	0.25	0.025	Lognormal	0.08333
A_2	x_2	m^2	0.16	0.016	Lognormal	0.08333
A_3	x_3	m^2	0.36	0.036	Lognormal	0.08333
A_4	x_4	m^2	0.20	0.020	Lognormal	0.26667
A_5	x_5	m^2	0.15	0.015	Lognormal	0.20000
P	x_6	kN	30.0	7.5	Gumbel	

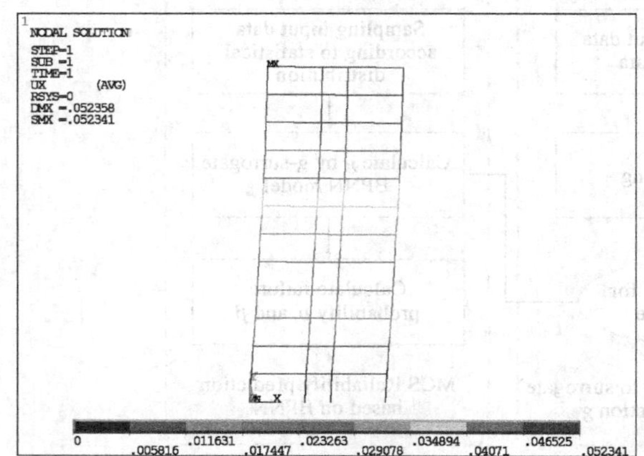

Fig. 4 ANSYS finite element model

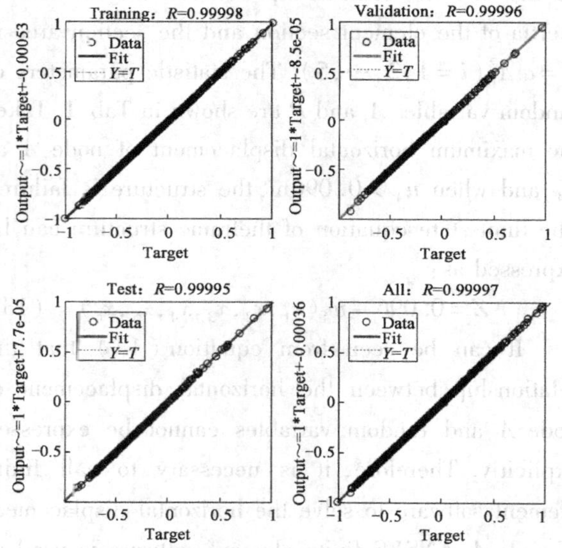

Fig. 5 Regression coefficient of BPNN

Fig. 5 shows that the regression coefficient of BPNN is very close to 1, indicating that its accuracy is high enough. Therefore, BPNN can be used to predict the reliability of frame structures.

The Monte Carlo method based on BPNN is used to calculate the reliability of frame structure, and the calculation results are shown in Tab. 2.

Reliability results of multi-story frame structure Tab. 2

Method	P_f	β	Time consuming(s)
Zhao, 1996	0.07303	1.4542	
MC-ANSYS	0.07350	1.4502	3292.78
MC-BPNN	0.07450	1.4431	2316(Sample generation) 1.94(Training BPNN) 17.00(Reliability prediction)

It can be seen from Tab. 2 that the calculation efficiency can be greatly saved when the neural network is used to fit the limit state function of the structure. Although the sample generation stage in the early also needs to call ANSYS finite element analysis, which takes a long time, a trained BPNN with high accuracy is ready for reliability prediction. When predicting the structural reliability in the final stage, the prediction results can be given quickly by using BPNN, and the time-consuming ANSYS software can be avoided.

3 Case study

In this section, the proposedreliability analysis framework is applied in a real-scale self-anchored suspension bridge. To ensure the accuracy and efficiency of this framework, the accuracy and efficiency of the BPNN model are first demonstrated. Finally, the reliability of self-anchored suspension bridge is analyzed based on this framework.

3.1 Overview

This papertakes a double-tower three-span self-anchored suspension bridge as the engineering background, and the elevation of the whole bridge is shown in the Fig. 6. The bridge is 490m long with a span layout of 50m + 95m + 200m + 95m + 50m. Among them, the main span is 200m, the side span is 95m, the anchor span is 50m. The main span and side span adopt the section of steel girder, the anchor span adopts concrete box girder section form. The total width of the bridge deck is 29m. The main cable is arranged in a quadratic parabolic line and the sag-to-span satio is 1 : 5, 37 pairs of hangers are arranged throughout the entire span. The bridge towers are the most commonly used portal frame structure, concrete material and box section, and are 70m above the deck.

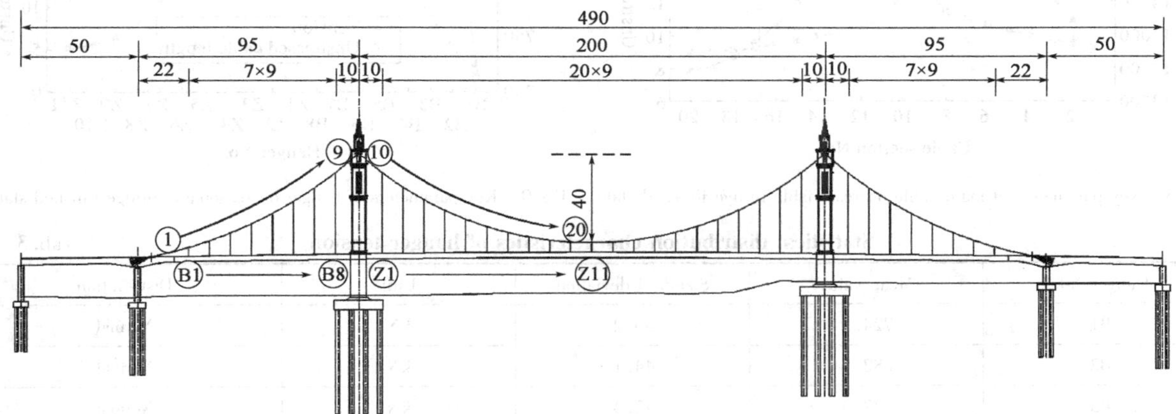

Fig. 6 Elevation of the bridge (unit: m)

3.2 Reasonable bridge finished state simulation

The main cable number increases from the most side span to the middle of the span, and the numbers are 1, 2, 3, ⋯ 19 and 20. The number of side span hangers starts from the anchorage to the tower and increases from B1 to B8. The number of mid span hangers starts from the tower to the mid span and increases from Z1 to Z11. As shown in Fig. 6. For the number on the other side, add "#" after the previous number.

The finite element model of the whole bridge is established in MIDAS/civil, as shown in the Fig. 7.

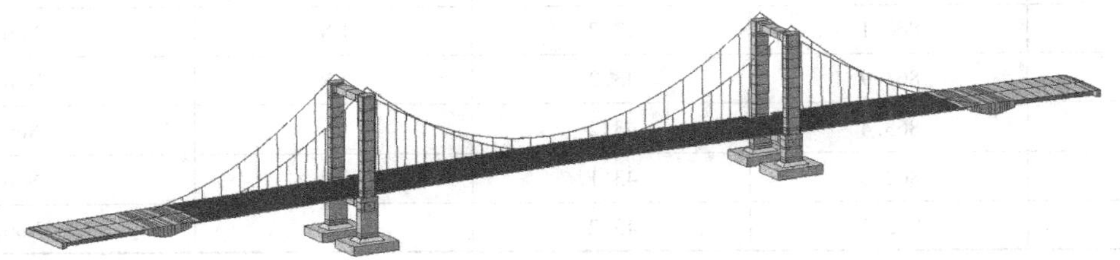

Fig. 7 Elevation of the bridge

The key parameters of main cable and hanger obtained through reasonable bridge finished state analysis are shown in Fig. 8 and Fig. 9.

3.3 Uncertainty of hanger tension

Due to construction errors and various uncertain factors, the tension of thehanger is difficult to accurately tension to the design tension, but fluctuates within a certain range. In this paper, it is assumed that the hanger tension obeys normal distribution, and the statistical distribution characteristics of hanger tension is shown in Tab. 3.

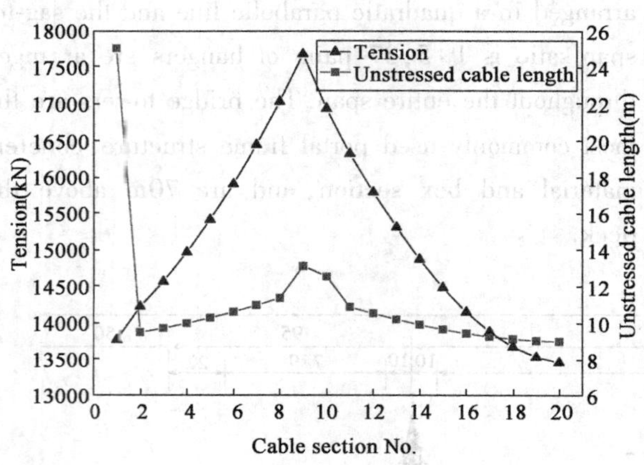

Fig. 8 Key parameters of main cable on reasonable bridge finished state

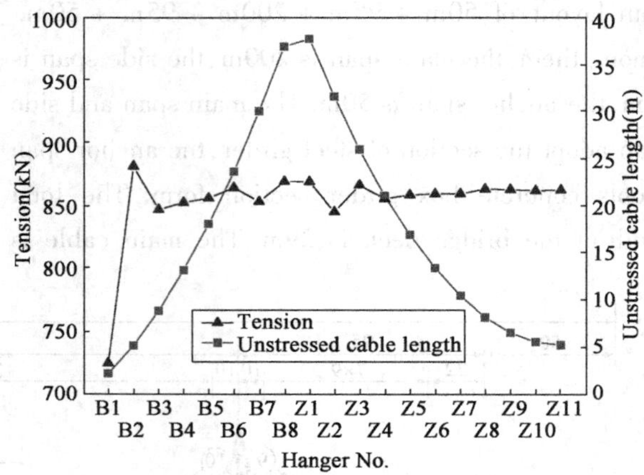

Fig. 9 Key parameters of hanger on reasonable bridge finished state

Statistical distribution characteristics of hanger tension Tab. 3

Hanger No.	Mean value	Standard deviation	Unit	Distribution
B1	724.5	36.2	kN	Normal
B2	882.1	44.1	kN	Normal
B3	847.3	42.4	kN	Normal
B4	852.9	42.6	kN	Normal
B5	856.5	17.1	kN	Normal
B6	864.9	17.3	kN	Normal
B7	853.7	17.1	kN	Normal
B8	869.9	17.4	kN	Normal
Z1	869.7	17.4	kN	Normal
Z2	845.4	16.9	kN	Normal
Z3	867.0	17.3	kN	Normal
Z4	856.1	17.1	kN	Normal
Z5	859.2	17.2	kN	Normal
Z6	860.0	17.2	kN	Normal
Z7	860.1	17.2	kN	Normal
Z8	863.9	43.2	kN	Normal
Z9	863.4	43.2	kN	Normal
Z10	862.6	43.1	kN	Normal
Z11	863.1	43.2	kN	Normal

3.4 Sample generation and BPNN training

The training samples were generated by calling ANSYS finite element software. The finite element model of self-anchored suspension bridge is established in ANSYS as shown in Fig. 10. And in ANSYS finite element model, the tension of the hanger is applied by the way of initial strain. Therefore, the tension in section 3. 3 needs to be converted to the initial strain.

The Latin hypercube sampling of random variables is realized by using the program written by Matlab. In this paper, a total of 550 groups of hanger tension are randomly generated. Among them, 500 groups were used to train BPNN and the other 50 groups were used to test the accuracy of BPNN. The hanger tension is converted into initial strain, which is used as the input variable of BPNN. Then the MATLAB program is used to call ANSYS for finite element analysis and solution. The horizontal displacement of the tower-top and the vertical deformation of the main girder at midspan are obtained as the output variables of BPNN.

In this paper, two BPNNs are trained. BPNN-1 is used to predict the relationship between the hanger tension and the horizontal displacement of the tower-top, and BPNN-2 is used to predict the relationship between the hanger tension and the vertical deformation of the main girder at midspan. The training results are shown in Fig. 11 and Fig. 12.

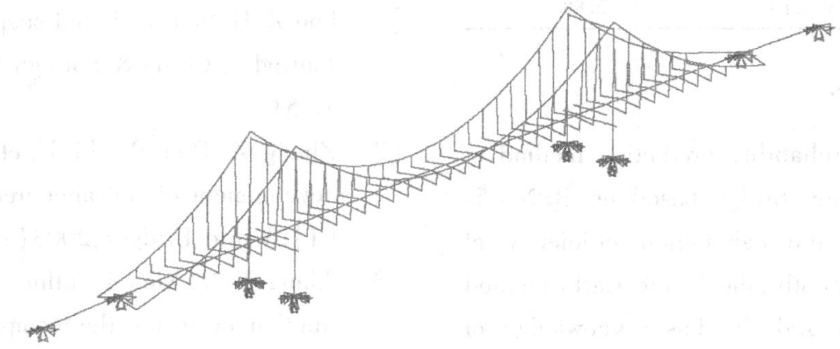

Fig. 10 ANSYS finite element model of the whole bridge

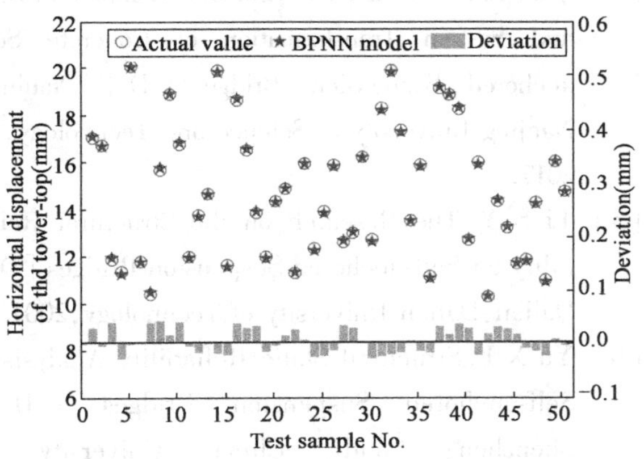

Fig. 11 Training result of BPNN-1

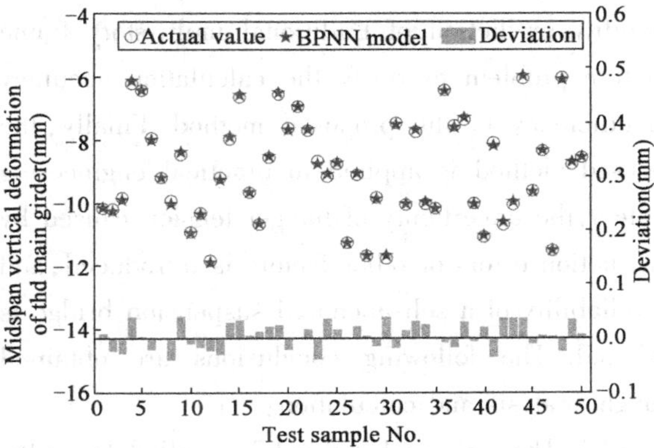

Fig. 12 Training result of BPNN-2

As shown in Fig. 11, the deviation between the artificial neural network predicted value and the actual value of the horizontal displacement of the tower-top fluctuates between − 0.0302mm and 0.0397mm, and the maximum error is 0.35%. As shown in Fig. 12, the deviation between the artificial neural network predicted value and the actual value of the vertical deformation of the main girder at midspan fluctuates between −00368mm and 0.0382 mm, and the maximum error is −0.62%. It can be concluded that the accuracy of the two BPNNs meets the requirements. And then, these two BPNNs will be used to predict the reliability of self-anchored suspension bridge.

3.5 Reliability prediction of selfanchored suspension bridge

In this paper, two failure modes of self-anchored suspension bridge are selected for reliability analysis. Failure mode 1: The horizontal displacement of the tower-top exceeds the allowed maximal value. Failure mode 2: The vertical deformation of the main girder at midspan exceeds the allowed maximal value. Therefore, the corresponding limit state equation is as follows:

$$g_1 = a_{allow} - a(X) \text{ and } g_2 = \Delta_{allow} - \Delta(X)$$

The coefficient of variationis set as 0.05, and taking 10^6 samples, the Monte Carlo method based on BPNN is used to calculate the reliability of the self-anchored suspension bridge. The results are shown in Tab. 4.

Results of the Monte Carlo method based on BPNN Tab. 4

Failure mode	P_f	β
1	5.06×10^{-4}	3.287
2	1.959×10^{-3}	2.885

4 Conclusions

In this paper, a reliability prediction method of self-anchored suspension bridge based on BPNN is proposed to improve the calculation efficiency of Monte Carlo method. Firstly, the Monte Carlo method for reliability solution and the basic knowledge of BPNN are introduced. Then, a reliability prediction framework of Monte Carlo method based on BPNN is proposed. Next, the method is applied to the reliability prediction of traditional multi-story frame structure problem to verify the calculation accuracy and efficiency of the proposed method. Finally, the proposed method is applied to practical engineering problem, the uncertainty of hanger tension caused by construction errors or other factors is introduced, and the reliability of a self-anchored suspension bridge is predicted. The following conclusions are obtained through analysis and calculation:

(1) The proposed method is applied to multi-story frame structure problems and compared with the results of original literature. The results show that the proposed method has high accuracy and efficiency in reliability prediction.

(2) The reliability of the self-anchored suspension bridge is predicted. The results show that the reliability of the main girder and the tower on bridge finished state meet the requirements.

(3) The reliability of the main girder is less than that of the tower, which indicates that the line shape of the main girder is more sensitive to the variation of the hanger tension than that of the tower, so more attention should be paid to the line shape monitoring of the main girder in practical engineering problems.

The results show that the proposed method has good applicability and can also be applied to the reliability prediction of other cable-supported bridges, prestressed structures and so on.

References

[1] Lou Z. H. Self-anchored suspension bridge [J]. Journal of China & Foreign Highway, 2002(3): 49-51.

[2] Zhang Z, Dou P, Shi L, et al. Review on the development of self-anchored suspension bridge [J]. World Bridges, 2003(1): 5-9.

[3] Liang Y X, Xiao J, Influence analysis of construction error for the completed line shape of concrete self-anchored suspension bridge [J]. Construction Technology, 2021, 50(11): 41-45.

[4] Qian L. Research on Reasonable Completion State and System Transformation of Concrete Self-anchored Suspension Bridge [D]. Nanjing: Nanjing University of Science and Technology, 2017.

[5] Li S Y. The Research on the Structural Reliability for Self-anchored Suspension Bridges [D]. Dalian: Dalian University of Technology, 2007.

[6] Yu X L. Structural Static Reliability Analysis of Self-anchored Suspension Bridges [D]. Shenzhen: South China University of Technology, 2011.

[7] Zhu G S. Application of Machine Learning Approaches to Structural Reliability Analysis and Damage Identification [D]. Hefei: Hefei University of Technology, 2021.

[8] Niu H F. Research on Reliability of Prestressed Concrete Continuous Beam Bridge based on neural network algorithm [D]. Changsha: Central South University of Forestry and Technology, 2021.

[9] Zhao G F. Reliability Theory and Its Applications for Engineering Structures [M]. Dalian: Dalian University of Technology Press, 1996.

考虑波浪相位差影响的深水桥墩动力响应研究

向宇恒[1] 路晨雨[2] 肖莉丽*[1] 王佳佳[1] 许 昕[1]
(1. 长安大学公路学院;2. 哈尔滨工业大学土木工程学院)

摘 要 深水桥墩会在海洋环境中受到不同形式的波浪荷载作用,研究波浪相位差引起的桥梁动力响应具有重要的意义。本文以平潭海峡大桥群桩基础为工程背景,对波浪荷载作用下的深水桥墩进行数值模拟分析。首先,采用线性波理论和 Morison 方程计算桥墩所受的波浪荷载;其次,采用 ANSYS 建立考虑桩土作用的群桩模型;最后,分析在考虑相位差和群桩效应的情况下波浪对结构位移、速度、加速度、内力动力响应的影响。计算结果表明考虑波浪相位差和群桩效应都会使深水桥墩的动力响应增大,最大的动力响应幅值达到了 83.95%。由此得出结论:深水桥墩动力响应分析应合理考虑波浪相位差和群桩效应。

关键词 桥梁工程 波浪相位差 数值模拟 桩—土作用 动力响应 群桩效应

0 引言

跨海大桥作为陆地和岛屿之间的连接纽带,处于复杂多变的海洋环境中,会受到巨浪、风暴、急流、地震等多种极端荷载的影响[1]。其中,波浪作用是造成桥梁破坏的常见因素,其对跨海大桥的破坏不仅会造成巨大的经济损失,也会对后续的救援工作带来一定的挑战。Padgett 等[2]分析了 2005 年 Katrina 飓风对美国墨西哥湾沿岸桥梁的破坏,亚拉巴马州等州有超过 44 座桥梁受到不同程度的影响,损失超过十亿美元,其中桥梁基础绝大多数遭到了波浪破坏。因此,在深水桥墩的设计过程中,需考虑波浪荷载等复杂海洋环境对桥墩动力响应的影响。

关于桩基础在波浪荷载作用下的动力响应问题,国内外有许多学者都展开了相关研究。郭俊杰等[3]建立了海浪—海床—桩基数值模型模拟桩基和海床的作用,分析了水深对桩身弯矩、水平位移的影响。胡俊杰[4]通过有限元软件 SAP2000 对简支梁桥进行波浪动力响应分析,评价了波浪作用下不同类型支座设置的减隔震效果。董伟良等[5]针对桥梁大尺寸承台,基于 Fluent 建立三维数值波浪水槽,分析波高、周期及淹没系数等对承台波浪力的影响,得出承台波浪力与波高基本呈线性变化的结论。李忠献等[6]针对波浪的入射方向展开研究,纵桥向入射采用绕射波浪理论,横桥向采用 Morison 方程计算波浪力,基于 ABAQUS 建立连续梁桥计算模型,分析波浪荷载作用下的深水桥梁桩基的应力和相对位移响应。潘良等[7]采用 Morison 公式计算波流荷载,建立三维有限元跨海桥梁桩基模型,分析不同荷载工况下多土层跨海桥梁桩基在波流荷载作用下的动力响应。Tong 等[8]结合数值模拟分析群桩的桩土效应,对桩径、桩间距和埋深等进行了参数化研究,得出桩径和桩间距对桩土效应影响最大的结论。

大多数学者研究波浪荷载作用下的桥墩动力响应时,未考虑桩土之间的相互作用和波浪相位差产生的附加效应。首先,在大多数研究中一般都将桩底固结处理,但实际复杂的海洋环境会对土体的孔隙水压力、粘结强度等产生影响,导致桩土之间产生相互作用;其次,往往不考虑波浪荷载峰值作用在不同桩上的时间差,但波浪荷载作为一种周期性荷载,到达每个桩的时间并不相同。因此,为同时考虑桩—土作用和波浪周期性荷载对桥梁基础的影响,本文采用 m 法模拟桩—土作用,以平潭海峡大桥元洪航道桥 N04 号墩为例建立深水桥墩群桩基础有限元模型,基于线性波理论和 Morison 方程计算波浪对群桩基础的荷载,利用 ANSYS 进行瞬态动力分析,研究深水桥墩在波浪荷载作用下的动力响应问题,讨论波浪荷载峰

1. 基金项目:高烈度地震带峡谷河道型水库对库区公路影响评测与工程对策研究(云交科教〔2008〕12 号)。

值到达桩前的时间(相位差)和群桩效应对结构动力响应的影响。

1　工程概况

平潭海峡大桥元洪航道桥为钢桁梁斜拉桥，桥跨布置为 132m + 196m + 532m + 196m + 132m，全长 1188m，桥型布置形式如图 1 所示。该群桩基础采用 22 根桩直径为 4.0m 的钻孔灌注桩，采用 C50 混凝土，平均桩长 68.0m，桩的入土深度 42m，自由高度 26m，横纵向桩间距 l 为 8.2m。承台为 C50 混凝土哑铃式承台。群桩基础的平面布置和立面布置如图 2、图 3 所示。

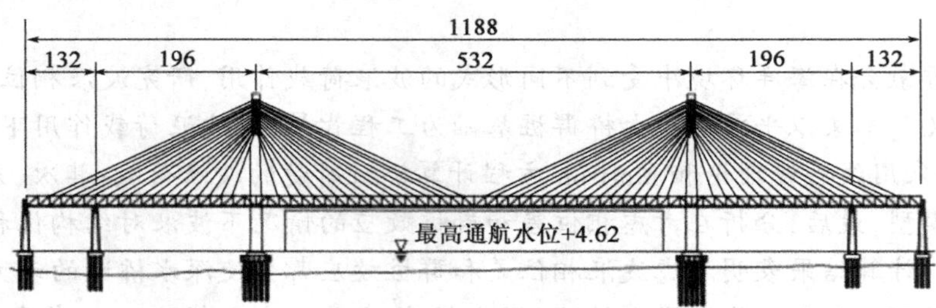

图 1　平潭海峡大桥元洪航道桥桥型布置图(尺寸单位:m)

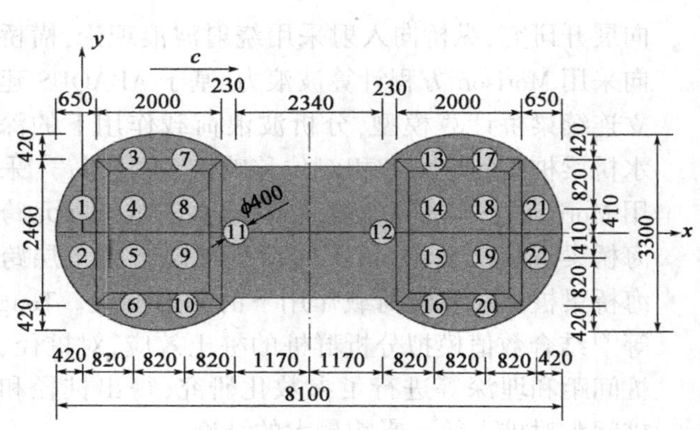

图 2　墩承台群桩基础平面布置图(尺寸单位:cm)

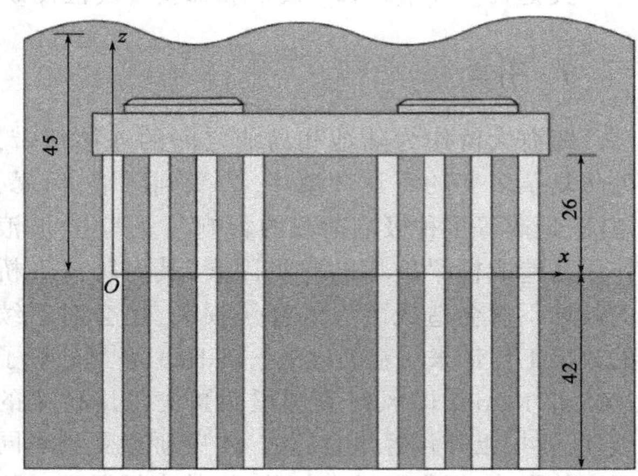

图 3　墩承台群桩基础立面布置图(单位:m)

经查阅桥址处海域的水文资料，桥位 97% 区段位于海况复杂区域，各墩位平均水深 21m，最大水深达到 46m。其中，100 年一遇的波高 $H_{5\%}$ 为 7.29m($H_{5\%}$ 指累计频率为 5% 的波高)，周期 T 为 10.2 s，水深 d 取 45m，此时桩位于水面以下，海水密度 ρ 取 1000kg/m³。本文主要关注波浪力与桩柱之间的作用，承台与桩柱之间采用固结处理，故承台在计算中作为一个集中质量加载，不作为主要分析对象关注其受力情况。

2　计算方法及分析模型

2.1　桩基波浪荷载

本文的桩基所受波浪荷载根据各波浪理论的适用范围判断，$T\sqrt{g/d} = 10.2\sqrt{9.8/45} = 4.76 < 6.0$，且 $H/d = 7.29/45 = 0.162 < 0.2$，所以采用线性波理论计算。经计算，波长 $L = 154.20$m，波数 $k = 2\pi/L = 0.041$，圆频率 $\omega = 2\pi/T = 0.616$rad/s。

已知桩径 $D = 4.0$m，计算 $D/L = 0.026 < 0.2$，属于小尺度结构物，采用 Morison 方程计算作用其上的波浪力。Morison 方程中单位段圆柱体所受的水平波浪力：

$$f_H = f_D + f_I = \frac{1}{2}C_D\rho A u_x|u_x| + C_M\rho V_0\frac{du_x}{dt} \quad (1)$$

其中 ρ 为海水密度，C_D 为拖曳力系数，C_M 为惯性力系数，A 为垂直于波速方向单位柱高的投影面积，V_0 为单位柱高排出水的体积。根据《港口与航道水文规范》(JTS 145—2015)，本文计算桩基所受波浪荷载时取 $C_D = 1.2$，$C_M = 2.0$。

圆柱体任意高度 z 处 dz 微段上的水平波浪力表达式如下：

$$dF_H = f_H dz = \frac{1}{2}C_D\rho D\left(\frac{\pi H\cosh kz}{T\ \sinh kd}\right)^2\cos\theta\left|\cos\theta\right|dz + C_M\rho\frac{\pi D^2}{4}\frac{2\pi^2 H\cosh kz}{T^2\ \sinh kz}\sin\theta dz \tag{2}$$

其中，θ 为考虑波浪到达桩前时间的相位差，$\theta = kx - \omega t$。

基于两种理论计算所得水平波浪力 f_H 沿圆柱体高度和相位的分布规律如图4所示。

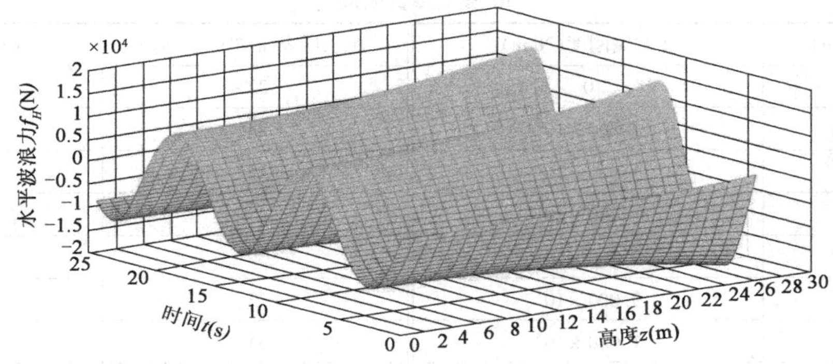

图4　水平波浪力 f_H 沿高度 z 和时间 t 的分布

由于群桩基础中桩柱分布位置带来的波浪力相位差以及群桩效应的影响，每个桩柱上的波浪力分布存在差异，本文讨论一致性波浪力（不考虑相位差 $\Delta\theta_i$ 和各桩的群桩系数 K_i）和非一致性波浪力（分为只考虑相位差 $\Delta\theta_i$ 而不考虑各桩的群桩系数 K_i，考虑相位差 $\Delta\theta_i$ 及各桩的群桩系数 K_i 两种情况）作用在群桩上时的动力响应。图5为考虑相位差 $\Delta\theta_i$ 时，$t = 2.5$s 和 $t = 7.5$s 各桩的水平波浪力沿桩身高度分布图。

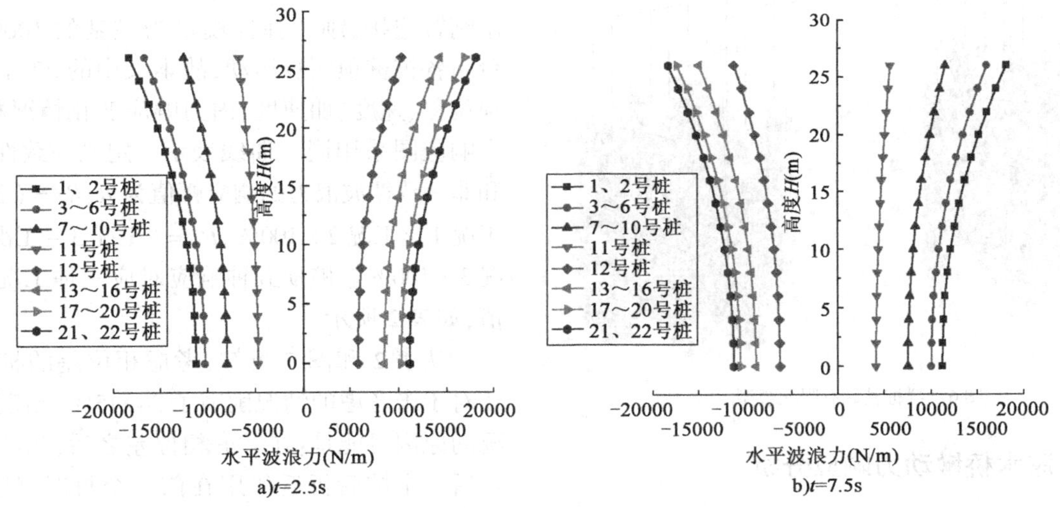

图5　$t = 2.5$s 和 $t = 7.5$s 时22个桩的水平波浪力沿桩基高度的分布

2.2　深水桥墩有限元模型

本文采用ANSYS（APDL）建立深水桥梁的群桩基础有限元模型，由于m法现在工程上使用较多且解法比较成熟，故本文采用m法模拟桩土之间的相互作用。

桩基础采用Beam188两节点三维梁单元模拟，桩身材料为C50混凝土，弹性模量为 3.4×10^{10}Pa，泊松比为0.3，密度为2500kg/m³。由于承台面积大，整体性强，将其简化为集中质量，采用Mass21点单元，集中质量单元与桩身单元采用Beam44单元做刚臂连接，刚臂的弹性模量取桩的1000倍。承台采用C50混凝土，密度为2500kg/m³，高9m，承台集中质量单元三个方向的质量均为 4.71785×10^7kg，转动惯量分别为 3.60212×10^9kg·m²、2.40059×10^{10}kg·m²、2.10407×10^{10}kg·m²。

群桩桩长68m(入土长度42m,置于水中的自由桩长26m),沿桩长方向每2m划分一个单元,采用m法模拟桩—土作用,选取Combin14弹簧单元模拟土体,不同高度土弹簧刚度计算结果如表1所示。边界采用约束桩底节点和弹簧单元一侧节点的所有自由度的方法进行模拟。深水桥墩有限元模型及约束情况如图6所示。

m法土弹簧刚度　　表1

距土层表面的距离(m)	土弹簧刚度(N/m)	距土层表面的距离(m)	土弹簧刚度(N/m)
0	0	22	2.376×10^{8}
2	1.800×10^{7}	24	2.592×10^{8}
4	3.600×10^{7}	26	2.808×10^{8}
6	5.400×10^{7}	28	3.024×10^{8}
8	7.200×10^{7}	30	5.400×10^{8}
10	9.000×10^{7}	32	5.760×10^{8}
12	1.080×10^{8}	34	6.120×10^{8}
14	1.260×10^{8}	36	6.480×10^{8}
16	1.440×10^{8}	38	6.840×10^{8}
18	1.944×10^{8}	40	7.200×10^{8}
20	2.160×10^{8}	42	7.560×10^{8}

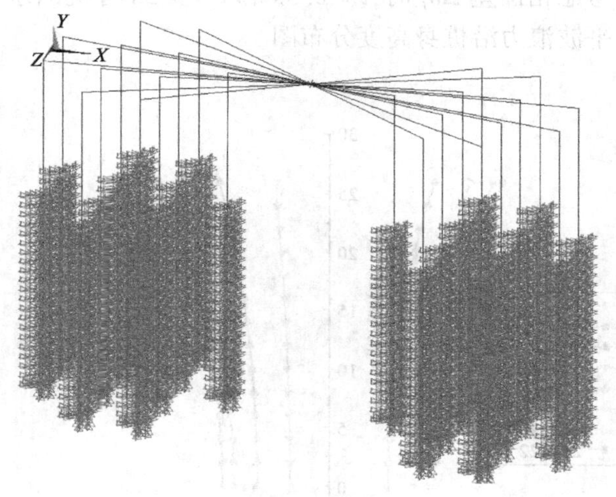

图6　群桩基础有限元模型

3　深水桥墩动力响应分析

本文采用完全法瞬态分析对群桩基础进行位移、速度、加速度和内力时程响应分析。根据瞬态动力分析参数选取原则,时程分析时间取50s,共五个周期,积分时间步长取0.2s。

为了研究相位差和群桩系数对深水桥墩动力响应的影响,本文将波浪力加载分为三种情况:

(1)工况1:一致性波浪力,即不考虑相位差$\Delta\theta_i$和各桩的群桩系数K_i。

(2)工况2:非一致性波浪力,即考虑相位差$\Delta\theta_i$但不考虑群桩系数K_i。

(3)工况3:非一致性波浪力,即同时考虑相位差$\Delta\theta_i$和群桩系数K_i。

由于承台刚度大、整体性强,且承台与各桩采用刚臂连接,刚臂弹性模量为桩基的1000倍,承台与各桩桩顶同步运动,故本文中的22个桩的桩顶位移、速度、加速度、内力响应变化情况相同,动力响应图采用同一曲线表示。定义一致性波浪力和非一致性波浪力的响应幅值为R,R_1=(工况2－工况1)/工况2×100%、R_2=(工况3－工况2)/工况3×100%。桩顶五种响应对应三种工况的最大值,如表2所示。

从表2和图7可知,考虑相位差的桩顶位移相对于未考虑的情况削减了24.45%,出现这一情况的原因可能是:在考虑相位差之后,当波浪作用在后一个桩后折返作用在前一个桩时,波浪力会有抵消作用,但是本文将所有桩简化为一个位移,所以位移会有减小的情况出现。当考虑相位差和群桩效应之后,桩顶位移动力响应增加20.00%。结果表明,按照一致性波浪力计算的桩顶位移相对保守。

由图8、图9和表2可知,考虑相位差后,桩顶最大速度增加45.78%,最大加速度增加69.10%;考虑群桩效应后,桩顶最大速度增加16.33%,最大加速度增加16.18%。结果表明,相位差和群桩系数对桩基础动力响应的影响较大,尤其是相位差的影响,其使结构的加速度和速度都有较大增幅,分析时不可忽略。

不同工况下的桩顶动力响应计算结果 表2

响　　应	位移(mm)	速度(m/s)	加速度(m/s²)	弯矩(kN·m)	剪力(kN)
工况1	2.34×10^{0}	2.25×10^{-3}	4.48×10^{-3}	2.08×10^{3}	2.44×10^{1}
工况2	1.88×10^{0}	4.15×10^{-3}	1.45×10^{-2}	2.32×10^{3}	1.52×10^{2}
工况3	2.25×10^{0}	4.96×10^{-3}	1.73×10^{-2}	2.80×10^{3}	1.96×10^{2}
R_1(%)	-24.45	45.78	69.10	10.34	83.95
R_2(%)	20.00	16.33	16.18	17.14	22.39

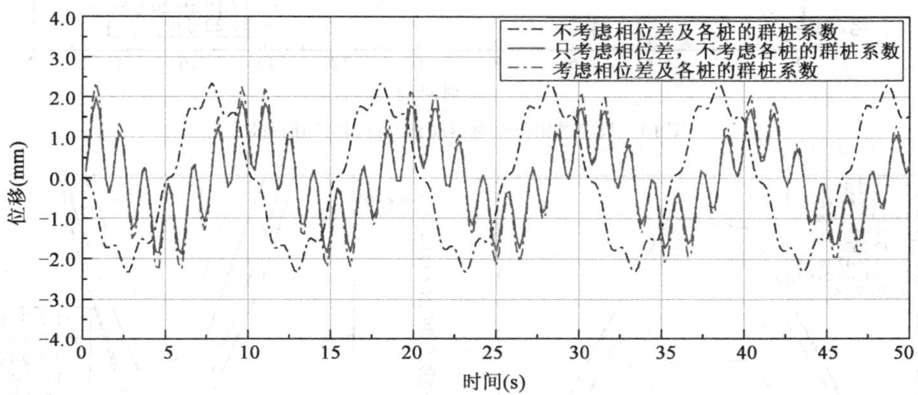

图7　三种工况下各桩顶位移时程图

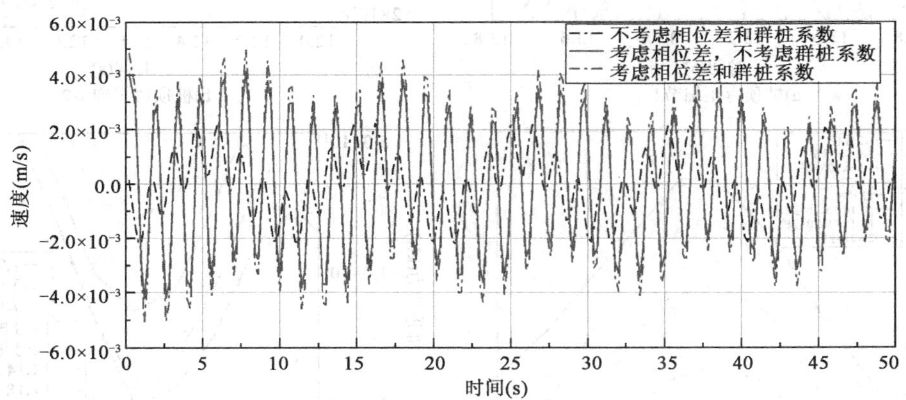

图8　三种工况下各桩顶速度时程图

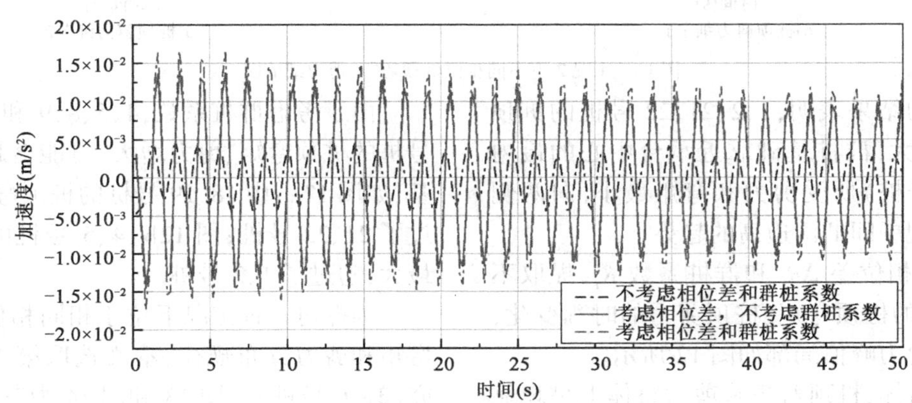

图9　三种工况下各桩顶加速度时程图

只考虑相位差 $\Delta\theta_i$，不考虑各桩的群桩系数 K_i 时，提取不同相位的桩基桩顶弯矩、桩顶剪力时程变化如图 10 所示，并放大其弯矩、剪力峰值局部如图 11 所示。

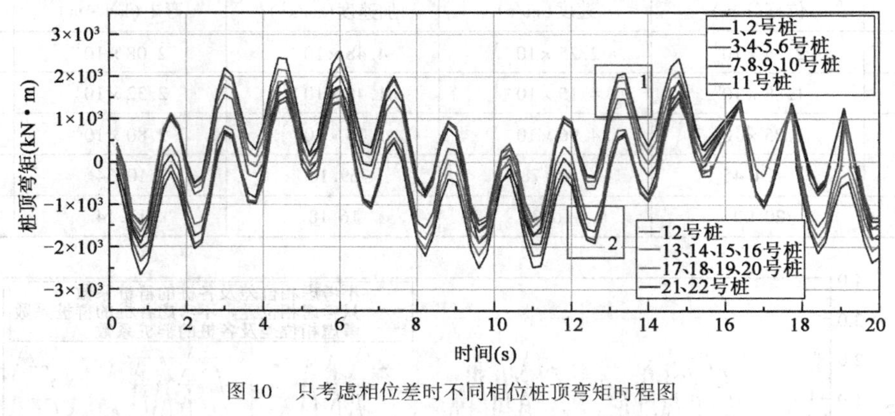

图 10　只考虑相位差时不同相位桩顶弯矩时程图

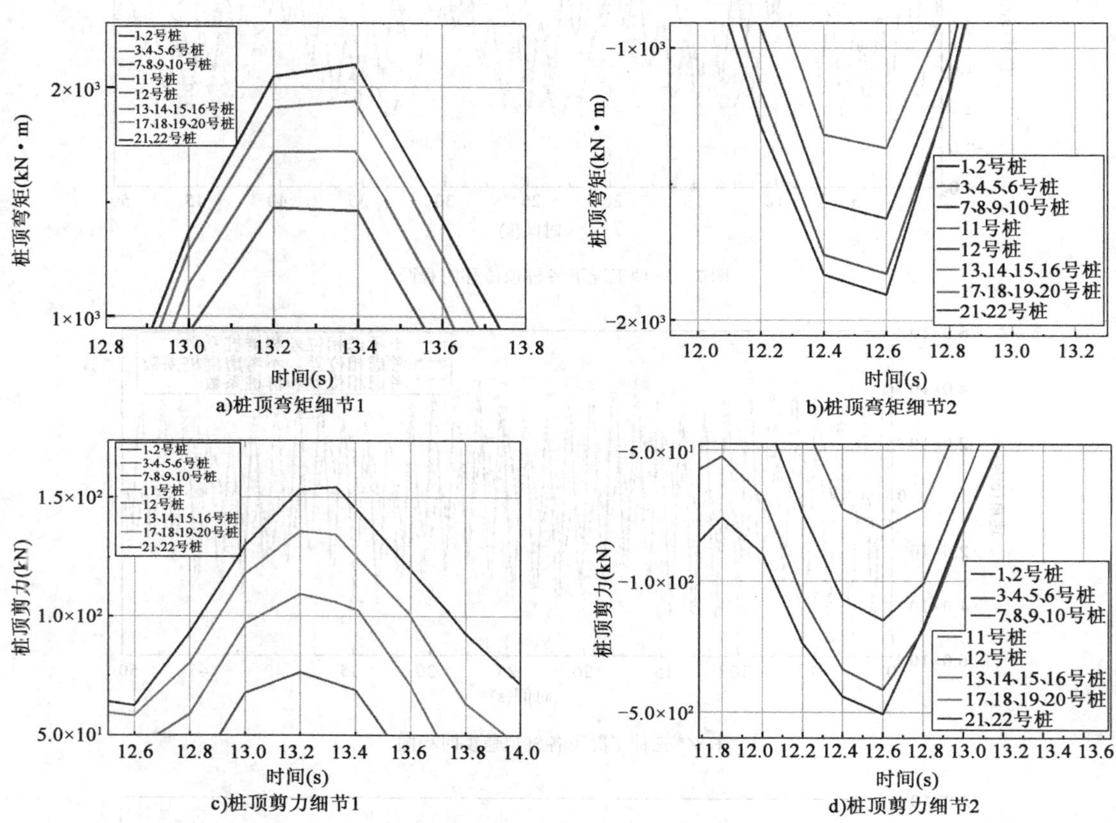

图 11　工况 2 下不同相位桩顶弯矩、剪力细节图

图 11 中的结果表明，1、2、21、22 号桩的桩顶弯矩和剪力最大，群桩基础靠近承台中心的最内侧桩(11、12 号桩)所受剪力和弯矩最小，向两侧逐渐增大，呈现中间低两边高的趋势。

同时考虑相位差 $\Delta\theta_i$ 和群桩系数 K_i，提取不同相位的桩基的桩顶弯矩、桩顶剪力的时程变化，并放大弯矩、剪力峰值局部如图 12 所示。

由图 12 可知，桩顶弯矩和剪力整体上呈现靠近承台中心处小，向两侧逐渐增大的趋势。

由于考虑群桩系数，4、5、8、9 和 14、15、18、19 号桩的桩顶弯矩、剪力增大，可能会超过其外侧桩基，如图 12a) 中 18、19 号桩的桩顶弯矩值最大，超过了 21、22 号桩；图 12b) 4、5 号桩的桩顶弯矩值最大，超过了 1、2 号桩。

为探讨三种工况下位于相同相位的桩的桩顶弯矩和剪力分布规律，本文选取第二列桩进行研究(3 ~ 6 号桩)。图 13 和图 14 为三种情况下 3 ~ 6 号桩的桩顶弯矩和剪力时程图。

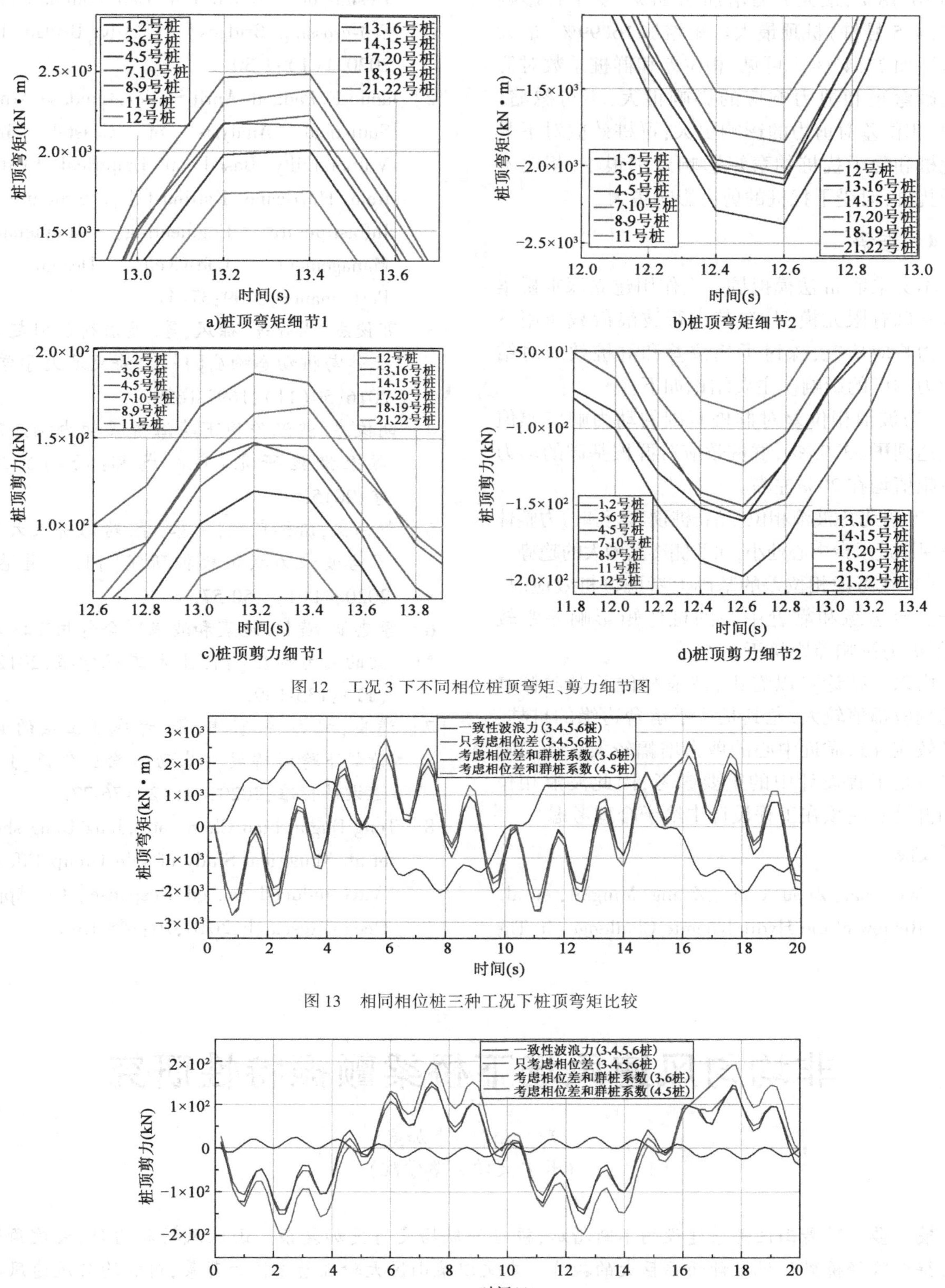

a)桩顶弯矩细节1

b)桩顶弯矩细节2

c)桩顶剪力细节1

d)桩顶剪力细节2

图12　工况3下不同相位桩顶弯矩、剪力细节图

图13　相同相位桩三种工况下桩顶弯矩比较

图14　相同相位桩三种工况下桩顶剪力比较

由图13和图14可知,对于相同相位的桩(3、4、5、6号桩),考虑相位差后,桩顶最大弯矩增加10.34%,最大剪力增加83.95%。考虑群桩效应后,不受干扰影响的桩(3、6号桩)桩顶最大弯矩

增加16.18%,最大剪力增加6.54%;受干扰影响的桩(4、5号桩)桩顶最大弯矩增加16.99%,最大剪力增加27.47%。可见,相位差和群桩系数对群桩基础弯矩和剪力响应的影响很大,不可忽略。其中,相位差对剪力的影响更大;群桩效应对不受干扰桩和受干扰桩的弯矩影响差别很小,相比不受干扰桩,对受干扰桩的剪力影响更大。

4 结语

本文采取m法模拟桩—土作用建立深水桥梁群桩基础有限元模型,对其进行波浪荷载作用下的动力响应研究,探讨了相位差和群桩效应对结构动力响应的影响。主要结论如下:

(1)波浪相位差对群桩基础的动力响应幅值最大达到了83.95%,群桩效应对群桩基础的动力响应幅值均在20%左右。

(2)在考虑波浪相位差后,桩顶弯矩和剪力整体上呈现靠近承台中心处小,向两侧逐渐增大的趋势。

(3)在考虑相位差的基础上考虑群桩效应时,位于承台边缘和靠近中心的桩弯矩影响差距较小,但剪力影响差距接近20%。

由以上结论可以看出,波浪相位差对群桩基础的响应幅值较大,尤其是位于承台边缘的桩柱,群桩效应导致靠近中心的剪力增幅较大。动力响应参数是工程设计中的重要参考,因此波浪相位差和群班效应该在工程设计中给予合理考虑。

参考文献

[1] Wei Kai, Zhou Cong, Zhang Mingjin, et al. Review of the Hydrodynamic Challenges in The Design of Elevated Pile Cap Foundations for Sea-crossing Bridges [J]. Adv. Bridge. Eng, 2020,1(1):1-30.

[2] Jamie E. Padgett, April Spiller, Candase Arnold. Statistical Analysis of Coastal Bridge Vulnerability Based on Empirical Evidence from Hurricane Katrina [J]. Structure and Infrastructure Engineering: Maintenance, Management, Life-Cycle Design and Performance,2009:37-41.

[3] 郭俊杰,周香莲,徐风,等.波浪荷载引起海床土体与桩动态响应[J].上海交通大学学报,2016,50(11):1697-1699.

[4] 胡俊杰.波浪作用下跨海桥梁动力响应及减隔振措施研究[D].成都:西南交通大学,2015.

[5] 董伟良,诸裕良,胡金春,等.跨海桥梁大尺寸承台波浪力数值模拟研究[J].水道港口,2020,41(1):50-57.

[6] 李忠献,黄信.地震和波浪联合作用下深水桥梁的动力响应[J].土木工程学报,2012,45(11):135-139.

[7] 潘良,祝兵,张家玮,等.考虑多土层的波-流荷载下跨海桥梁桩基动力响应分析[J].铁道设计标准,2020,64(12):76-77.

[8] Tong Dagui, Liao Chen cong, Jeng Deng-sheng, et al. Numerical Study of Pile Group Effect on Wave-induced Seabed Response [J]. Applied Ocean Research,2018,76:148-158.

非均匀风速风场下桥梁颤振特性研究

邢 松* 李加武

(长安大学公路学院)

摘 要 随着山区桥梁建设的不断增加,桥址处风场变得更加复杂。山区风场非均匀,大攻角等特点使得大跨径桥梁抗风设计面临巨大的挑战。本文以某山区大跨径悬索桥为背景,对非均匀风速风场下的桥梁颤振特性进行研究。首先,对现有山区风场进行梳理,归纳风速横向分布模型,并以此为基础设计

1.基金项目:国家自然科学基金项目(51978077)。

非均匀风场研究工况；其次，由风洞实验得到大跨径悬索桥的气动参数，并通过有限元分析方法对其进行设定工况的颤振研究。结果表明，山区风场风速横向分布可以用指数函数来表示。非均匀风场颤振分析结果明显有别于同攻角下均匀风场结果，风速两个特征参数（均值和最大值）随着风场非均匀性的变化而发生显著变化，且两参数变化趋势是相反的。

关键词 桥梁工程 颤振 有限元分析 非均匀风场

0 引言

随着交通建设的不断发展，桥梁跨径不断增加，桥址环境也更加复杂。大跨径桥梁结构轻柔，在风荷载的作用下容易产生大幅振动。桥梁风致振动不仅会影响行车安全，甚至会对桥梁结构造成致命破坏，对其结构本身和来往行人安全造成巨大威胁。桥梁风致振动主要包括颤振、涡振、抖振和驰振，其中颤振因其发散性和破坏性而备受关注。抗风设计逐渐成为大跨径桥梁设计的决定性环节，而在桥梁抗风设计中颤振问题是必须解决的。尽管此前学者们已经对桥梁颤振进行了大量研究，但基本都是针对均匀流场的。而随着山区桥梁建设的不断增加，桥址风环境更加复杂。现有研究表明山区风场有明显的非均匀、大攻角以及紊流度高等特点，这对山区大跨径桥梁抗风设计带来挑战[1]。山区风场与均匀风场的显著差异使得我们需要对该情况下的桥梁颤振特性展开进一步的研究。

山区风场的研究方法主要包括现场实测、风洞地形模型实验以及数值模拟三种。相比于现场实测和风洞地形模型实验，数值模拟因其成本低、采样点密集等优势而被广泛使用。靖洪淼[2]对山区风场特性的数值模拟方法进行探索，并对某大跨径悬索桥桥址处山区风场进行研究。数值模拟结果显示，主梁位置处风速沿桥跨变化较大，且主梁风攻角远高于$\pm 5°$。张子剑[3]以西部某斜拉桥桥址处山区峡谷作为研究对象，结合前期风洞地形模型实验的结果通过CFD（计算流体力学）方法进行桥位处风场特性研究。结果表明实际山区风场更加复杂，地形参数和来流风向角会对风场特征参数产生明显影响，现有规范已不能完全适用。洪凡[4]使用数值模拟方法对山区U形和V形峡谷桥址区风场特性进行研究，发现峡谷两侧山体越高，坡度越大，峡谷越窄，峡谷对风场的加速效应越明显。胡朋[5]通过CFD模拟得到某大跨斜拉桥桥址处风场特性，并通过有限元软件进行非均匀风场下的桥梁静风稳定性分析。研究表明非均匀风攻角风场较均匀风攻角风场对桥梁静风稳定性影响更大，非均匀风攻角风场下桥梁的静风失稳风速要远低于均匀风攻角风场，且主要受最大风攻角控制。洪新民[6]拟定理想峡谷模型，并对其风场特性进行数值模拟研究。结果表明峡谷内风速沿水平方向自两侧山体向峡谷中心先迅速增大再缓慢减小，大致呈抛物线形状。峡谷中心处风剖面最大风速高度与峡谷高宽比呈线性关系，且随峡谷高宽比增大而减小。李永乐[7]对深切峡谷桥址处地形进行数值模拟研究，发现主梁处风速、风向角及风攻角顺桥向均有较大变化，且不同来流风向工况下风速变化差异明显。沈炼[8]对澧水大桥所在峡谷风场进行现场实测与数值模拟，发现入口风向与峡谷走向之间夹角是影响峡谷加速效应以及风速变化规律的主要因素。张忠义[9]研究了V形和矩形峡谷风场特性，并与丁海平风洞实验结果对比证明其可靠性。研究结果表明在水平方向上风速会随着摩擦力的减弱而迅速增大，并在最大值之后渐渐趋于平稳。晏聪[10]通过数值模拟得到某大跨悬索桥桥址处风场特性分布规律，并以此为基础进行桥梁颤振分析。研究发现山区风场具有明显的时空不均匀分布特性，在桥梁颤振分析中考虑风速及风攻角的非均匀性是非常必要的。宋佳玲[11]对理想V形峡谷进行风环境数值模拟分析，研究了高度及坡度等参数对风速及风攻角分布的影响，并提出数学模型。

通过上述研究可知，此前对山区桥梁风致振动特性的研究主要针对某一特定地形，且主要专注风场参数与地形之间的关系，而风场与桥梁振动响应之间的关系需要我们进一步研究。本文对现有山区风场研究中风速的横向分布规律进行总结，得到其分布模型并以此为基础设置非均匀风速风场研究工况；进一步通过有限元分析方法对拟定工况进行桥梁颤振特性分析，探究风场特征参数对桥梁颤振稳定性的影响。

1 山区非均匀风场分布

为了对山区非均匀风场下桥梁风致振动进行

研究,首先要先确定山区风场风速沿顺桥向的分布情况。李晋琴[12]在对U形断面流体特性的研究中,将实验数据与不同数学模型进行比对,最终认为指数形分布最能反映实际情况。严军[13]对矩形断面流速分布的研究也表明平均流速的横向分布是满足指数律的。宋佳玲[11]对V形峡谷的数值模拟结果表明山区风场风速分布也可以近似通过指数函数来拟合。因此,我们通过公式(1)所示指数函数模型对以往山区风场研究进行拟合,得到各,自的模型参数。

$$y = 1 + ae^{bx} \tag{1}$$

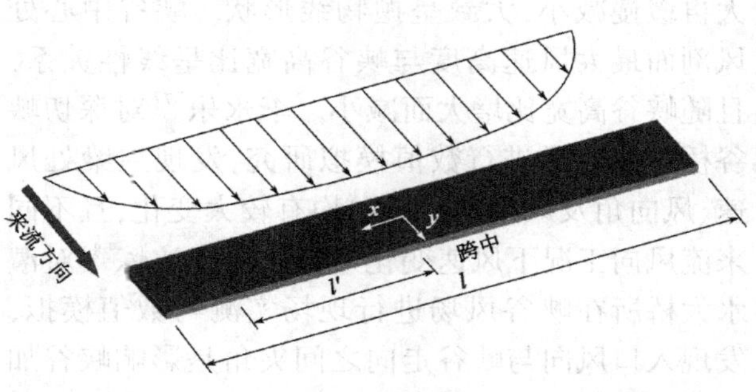

图1　非均匀风速分布示意图

其中x为桥梁某位置到跨中距离l'与桥梁跨径l的比值,跨中为0,两端为±0.5。y代表来流的风速系数(各位置风速与跨中风速的比值),a和b分别为拟合公式系数。非均匀风速分布如图1所示。

图2a)和图2b)分别为张忠义[9]60°V形峡谷数值模拟以及非均匀风场工况2的拟合结果,拟合系数分别为$a = -3.54\times10^{-4}$,$b = 14.69$以及$a = 0.01$,$b = 9.21$。图2c)为丁海平[14]60°V形峡谷实验结果及其拟合曲线,拟合系数为$a = -8.77\times10^{-4}$,$b = 13.97$。图2d)为晏聪[10]山区风场数值模拟结果及其拟合曲线,拟合系数为$a = -0.0039$,$b = 8.04$。

本文将上述拟合曲线以及宋佳玲研究结果汇总于图3,并绘制其两侧的包络线,确定外包络线拟合系数为$a = -0.001$,$b = 10.5$,内包络线拟合系数为$a = -0.01$,$b = 9.2$;根据内外包络线的拟合系数线性内插确定实验工况,得到的工况及曲线如图4所示。其中工况1($a = -0.015$,$b = 8.48$)风速沿横向变化最大,随后变化依次减小,直至工况7($a = -0.01$,$b = 10.5$)。

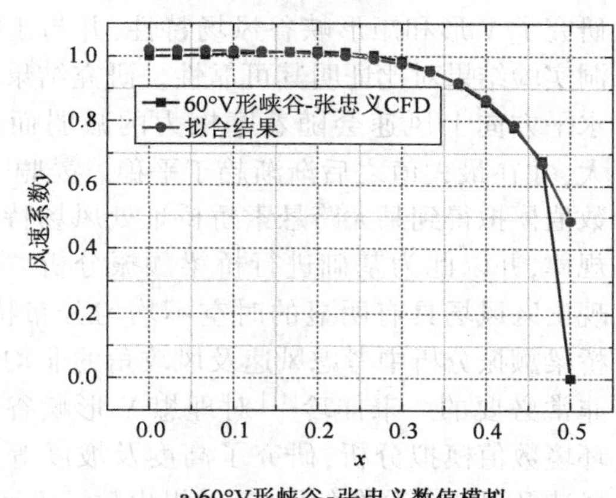

a)60°V形峡谷-张忠义数值模拟

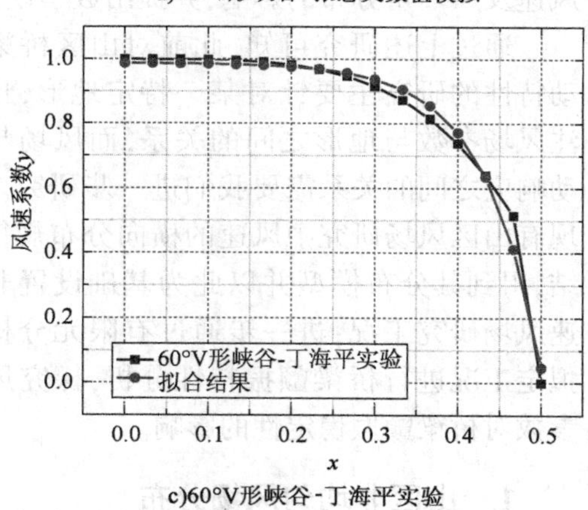

c)60°V形峡谷-丁海平实验

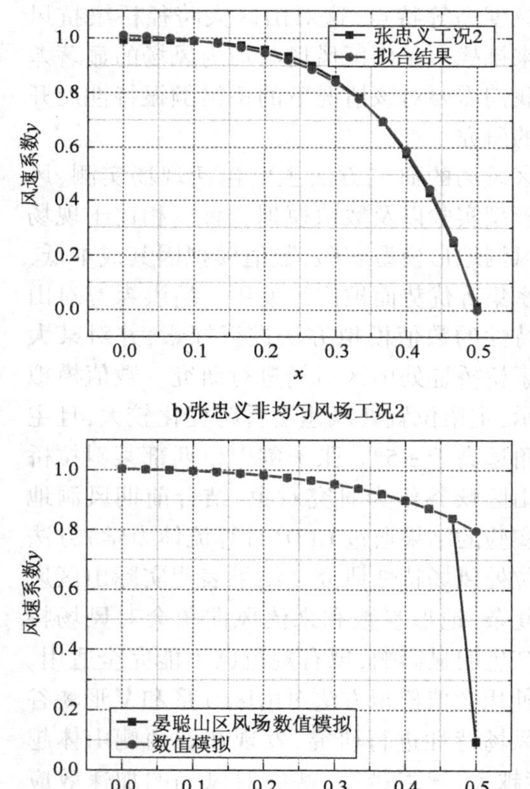

b)张忠义非均匀风场工况2

d)晏聪山区风场数值模拟

图2　非均匀风速分布及其拟合曲线

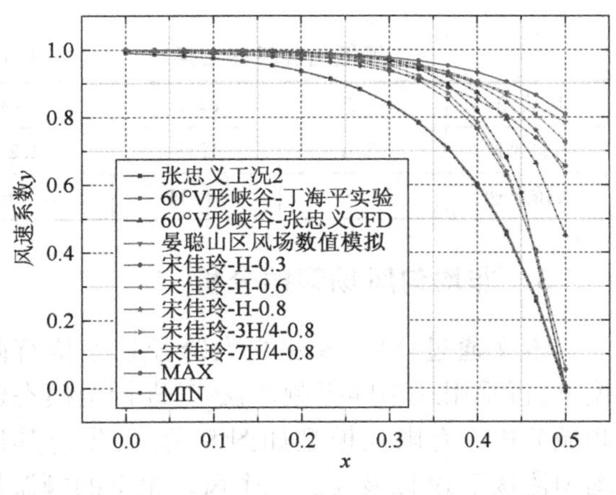

图3 非均匀风速分布汇总

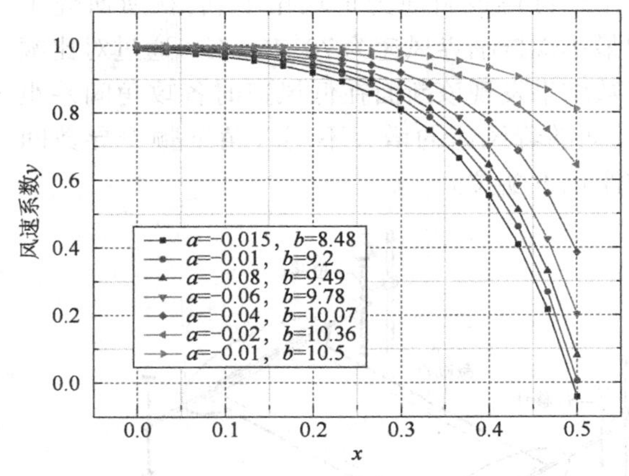

图4 非均匀工况设置

2 大跨径悬索桥风洞实验

本文以一座大跨径悬索桥作为研究对象，先通过节段模型风洞测振实验得到该桥梁的颤振导数，再以此为基础进行后续的桥梁颤振分析。节段模型风洞测振实验在长安大学CA-01号风洞内进行，该风洞为回流式大气边界层风洞。试验段长15m，横截面宽3.0 m×高2.5 m，最高风速可达53m/s。

桥梁主梁为扁平钢箱梁，实验断面为该桥成桥状态，带有防撞护栏以及检修道护栏，且在两侧安装水平导流板以及上中央稳定板来改善断面的气动稳定性能，其在风洞中整体状态以及附属设施细节分别如图5a)和5b)所示。按照缩尺比1:80来设计节段模型，模型长度为1.8m，宽0.8725m，长宽比为2.06:1，具体模型参数如图5c)所示。模型质量 m = 9.1127kg/m，质量惯距 Im = 0.7567kg×m2/2，竖弯频率 fh = 2.5657Hz，扭转频率 fa = 5.3347Hz，实测竖向阻尼比为0.31%，扭转阻尼比为0.21%。

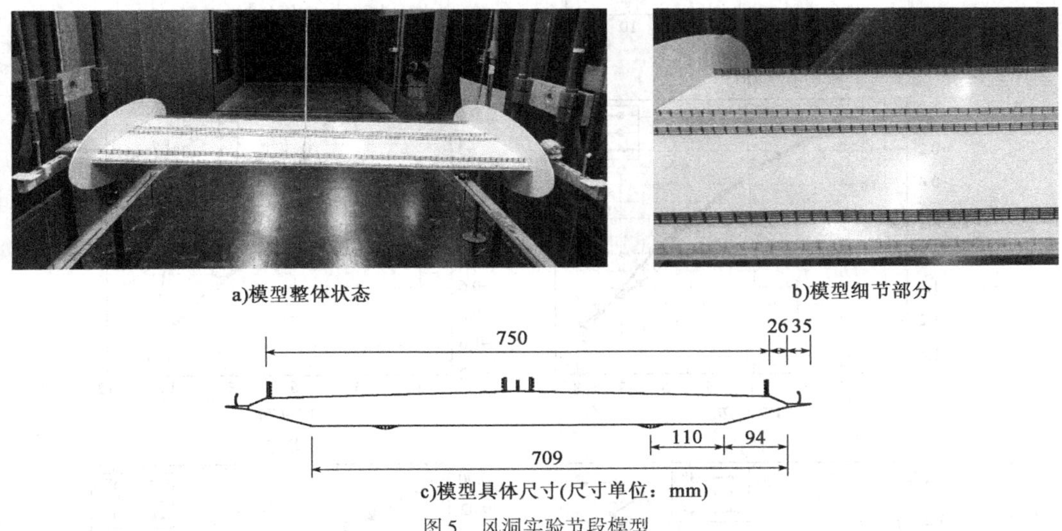

图5 风洞实验节段模型

模型有8根弹簧固定，实验中采用三个激光位移计来采集模型振动过程中的位移数据。模型布置及位移计布置如图6所示。其中，两个对角位置位移计用来计算模型的竖向位移，两个同侧位移计用来计算模型的扭转位移，两个同侧位移计间距为1.36m。模型前后各拉两道长细铁丝以限制模型振动过程中的侧向位移。实验过程中逐级加风并对模型进行激励，通过自由振动法来采集识别颤振导数。实验均在均匀流场中进行，风度比为1:5.8。

实验工况包括-3°，0°以及3°三个风攻角，表1为三个风攻角工况下的颤振临界风速结果。通过修正的最小二乘法[15]得到颤振导数随折减风速的变化情况如图7所示。通过颤振临界风速实验结果可得该断面为负攻角不利,在所研究工况内最小颤振临界风速为70.76m/s。通过对比颤振导数结果发现该断面在低风速时各攻角间差距不大,而随着风速的增大不同攻角下颤振导数间的差距也不断拉大。

颤振临界风速结果　　表1

风攻角	α=3°	α=0°	α=-3°
实验风速	12.6	12.3	12.2
实桥风速	73.08	71.34	70.76

3　非均匀风场颤振分析

本文通过ANSYS建立大跨径悬索桥有限元模型,再采用最小颤振频率法[16]进行全模态颤振频域分析。有限元模型如图8所示,先对其进行均匀流场下0°以及±3°三个风攻角下的颤振临界风速计算。表2为计算结果及其与实验结果的对比。通过结果对比可知有限元分析方法的结果和风洞实验结果非常接近,这验证了本文所用计算方法的可靠性。

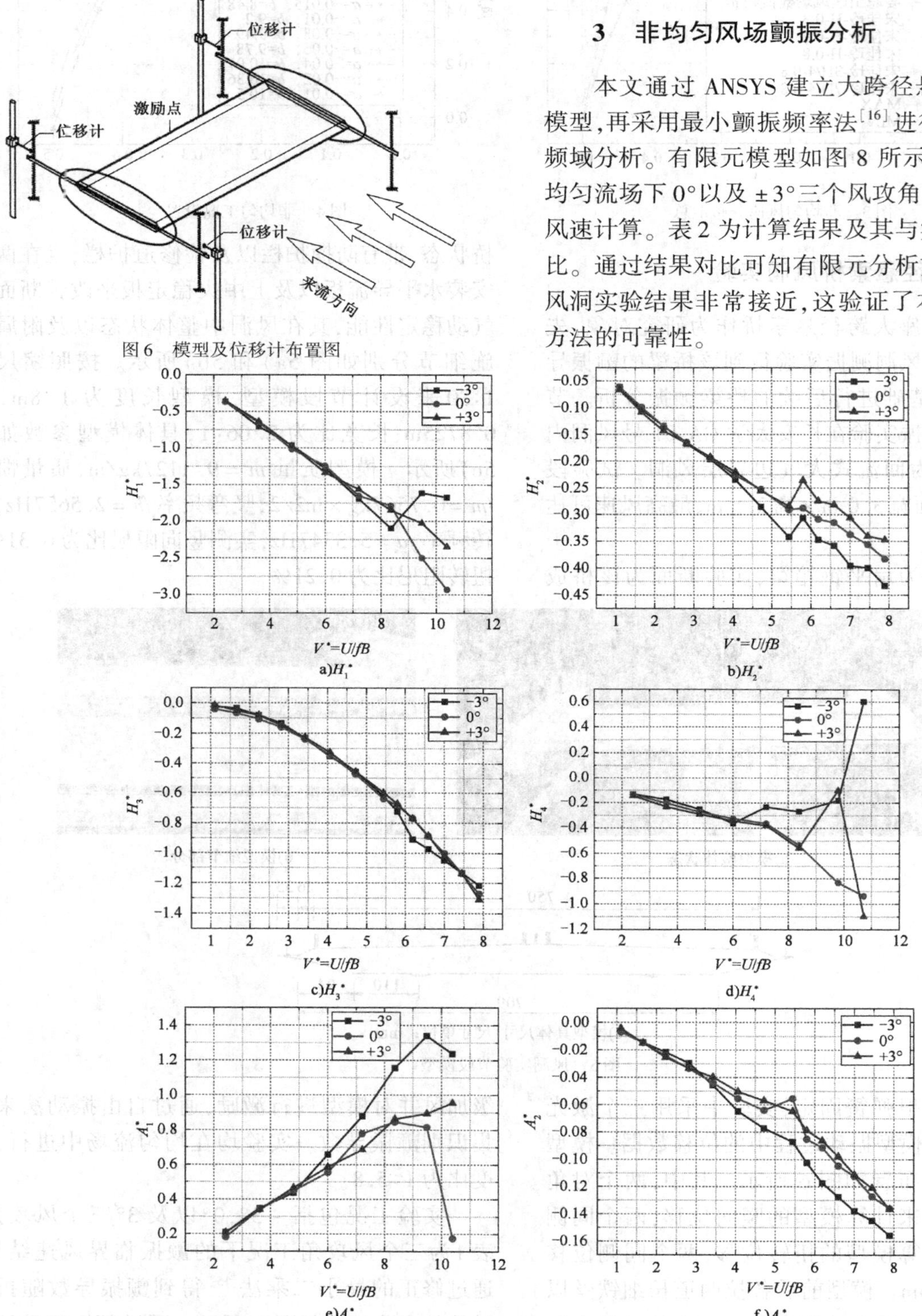

图6　模型及位移计布置图

图　7

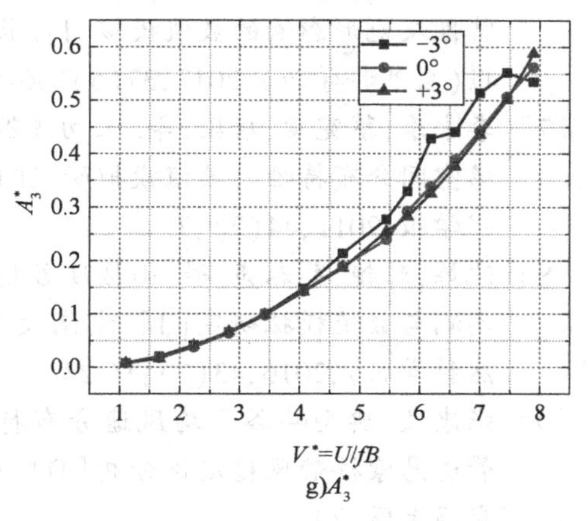

g)A_3^*

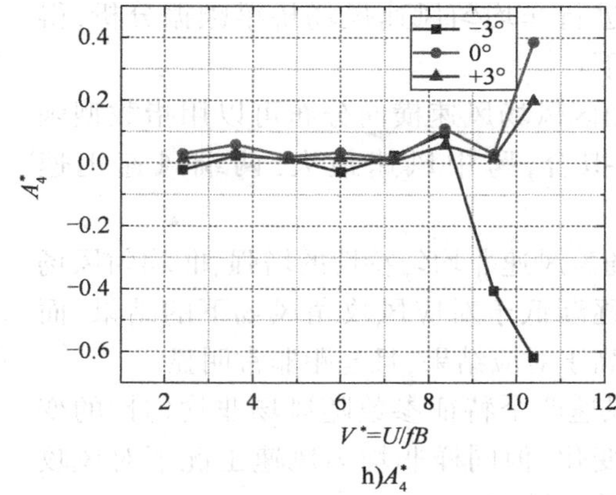

h)A_4^*

图7　颤振导数识别结果

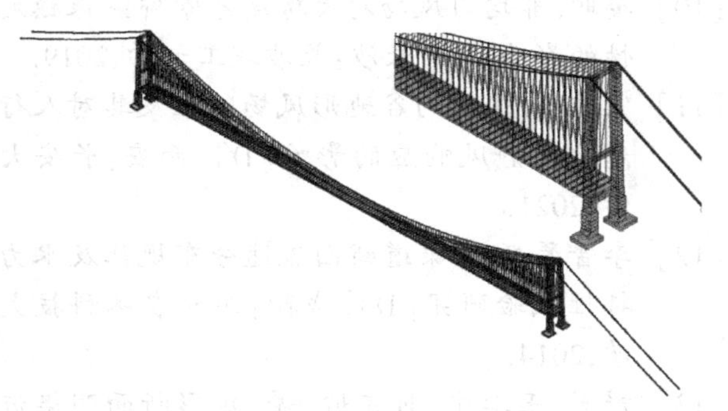
图8　大跨径悬索桥有限元模型

计算结果汇总　　表2

风攻角	风洞实验结果	有限元分析结果	误　差
3°	73.08	73.63	0.75%
0°	71.34	73.47	2.98%
-3°	70.76	73.17	3.41%

下面按照前文所设置的非均匀风场工况对该大跨径悬索桥进行非均匀风场颤振分析。由于风速沿桥梁主跨是非均匀变化的，因此此处将风速的平均值及最大值作为衡量桥梁颤振稳定性的特征参数，分别得到3个风攻角各自7个非均匀工况下的两个特征参数，并将其与对应风攻角均匀风场下的结果进行对比，两者的相对误差汇总于图9。图中横坐标为设定的7个非均匀风速工况，竖坐标为风速结果相对误差，即$(U_{nun}-U_{un})/U_{un}$。其中U_{nun}代表非均匀风场下风速特征参数，U_{un}代表U_{nun}所对应风攻角下均匀风场颤振临界风速。

总的来看，两个特征参数随非均匀风速工况的变化趋势是相反的，且非均匀风场的风速均值均小于所对应风攻角下的均匀风场风速。因此，如果将非均匀风场风速均值作为桥梁颤振的评价标准，则该结果表明山区风场风速的非均匀性会降低桥梁的颤振稳定性。由前文工况设定可知，工况从7到1横向风速分布的非均匀特性逐渐增强。通过图9结果可知随着风速非均匀性的加强，风速均值不断减小，与对应均匀风场下结果的差距不断拉大，甚至超过10%。而风速最大值的变化幅度则更加明显，随着风场风速非均匀特性的增强，风速最大值与对应均匀风场下结果的差距拉大至接近20%。尽管随着风场非均匀特性的变化两个特征参数变化明显，但对于某一工况，三个风攻角间的差距并不显著。相比之下0°和+3°风攻角结果更加接近，而颤振稳定性最差的-3°风攻角下平均风速相比另外两个风攻角与均匀风场下的结果更加接近。

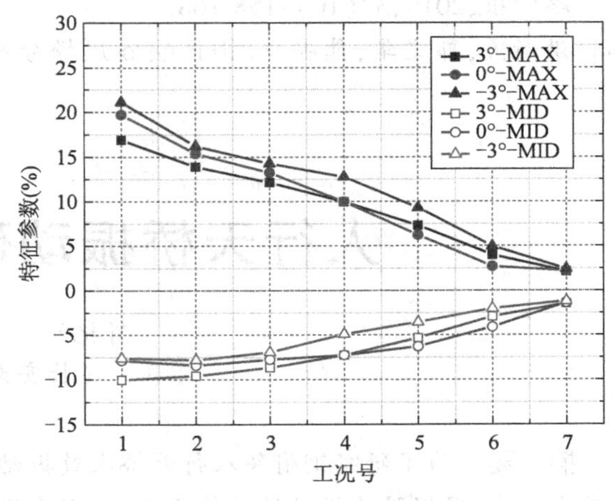

图9　非均匀风速颤振分析结果

4　结语

本文梳理归纳了山区非均匀风场风速分布模型，以此为基础设定非均匀风速颤振研究工况；通过节段模型风洞实验得到大跨径桥梁的颤振临界风速以及颤振导数，并进一步通过有限元模型对

设定工况进行非均匀风速风场桥梁颤振分析,得到结论如下:

(1)山区风场风速横向分布可以用指数型函数来近似拟合,跨中风速最大,两端风速迅速减小。

(2)随着风速非均匀特性的增强,非均匀风场风速均值逐渐低于对应风攻角风场下的结果,而最大值则高于对应结果,且差距非常明显。

(3)风速两个特征参数随风场非均匀性的变化而明显变化,但同样非均匀风速工况下对风攻角的变化并不敏感。

参考文献

[1] 李永乐,喻济昇,张明金,等.山区桥梁桥址区风特性及抗风关键技术[J].中国科学:技术科学,2021,51(5):530-542.

[2] 靖洪淼,廖海黎,周强,等.一种山区峡谷桥址区风场特性数值模拟方法[J].振动与冲击,2019,38(16):8.

[3] 张子剑.基于峡谷地形参数的桥位风特性研究[D].西安:西安科技大学,2021.

[4] 洪凡.山区U型和V型峡谷桥址区风特性研究[D].西安:西安科技大学,2020.

[5] 胡朋,颜鸿仁,韩艳,等.山区峡谷非均匀风场下大跨度斜拉桥静风稳定性分析[J].中国公路学报,2019,32(10):158-168.

[6] 洪新民,郭文华,熊安平.山区峡谷风场分布特性及地形影响的数值模拟[J].长安大学学报(自然科学版),2017,37(5):56-64.

[7] 李永乐,蔡宪棠,唐康,等.深切峡谷桥址区风场空间分布特性的数值模拟研究[J].土木工程学报,2011,44(2):7.

[8] 沈炼,韩艳,蔡春声,等.山区峡谷桥址处风场实测与数值模拟研究[J].湖南大学学报(自然科学版),2016,43(7):16-24.

[9] 张忠义.典型峡谷平均风速分布特性及跨谷管道悬索桥静风稳定性分析[D].成都:西南交通大学,2017.

[10] 晏聪.非均匀风场对大跨度悬索桥颤振稳定性的影响[D].长沙:长沙理工大学,2019.

[11] 宋佳玲.山区沟谷地形风场特性及其对人行悬索桥静风响应的影响[D].西安:长安大学,2021.

[12] 李晋琴.U形渠道断面流速分布规律及水力特性试验研究[D].咸阳:西北农林科技大学,2014.

[13] 严军,王二平,孙东坡,等.矩形断面明渠流速分布特性的试验研究[J].武汉大学学报(工学版),2005(5):59-64.

[14] 丁海平.峡谷平均风空间分布特性研究[D].成都:西南交通大学,2015.

[15] 胡峰强.山区风特性参数及钢桁架悬索桥颤振稳定性研究[D].上海:同济大学,2006.

人行天桥振动研究和舒适度评价

肖艳婷* 　周勇超　赵　亮

(长安大学公路学院)

摘　要　为了研究钢桁架人行天桥人致振动和舒适度评价问题,本文采用傅里叶三角级数模拟行人脚步力荷载,根据强迫振动的计算原理,应用有限元软件进行动力时程分析;采用同步行走人群代替随机行走人群的方法,计算人行天桥在不同工况下的结构峰值加速度响应;参考德国规范EN03(2007)进行不同行人密度下的动力响应研究,并且对钢桁架人行天桥进行了舒适度评价,针对不满足舒适度的工况进行了减振控制。结果表明:桥梁结构在无控状态下动力响应显著,舒适度难以达到要求,而安装TMD减振装置后,减振效率超过73%,人行天桥满足舒适度控制要求。

关键词　桥梁工程　舒适度评价　有限元分析　人行天桥　动力响应

0 引言

现代人行天桥随着使用年限的增加,结构的刚度会逐渐变小,所以在行人荷载的作用下,极易发生人—桥共振问题。国内外桥梁如武汉长江大桥、伦敦千禧桥、日本户田T桥等都出现过行人密度过大引起高频振动的问题。目前,人行天桥振动研究主要集中在行人模型的建立、人群舒适度评价及相关减振措施的制定方面。早期的研究学者对振动进行了分级并以加速度为控制指标给出了限制值。陈政清等[1]总结前人经验,研究了行人步频、步幅等参数对结构振动响应的影响;高世桥[2],BrownJohn[3]采用连续体模型和单自由度模型研究了行人的不同姿态对结构动力响应的影响;操礼林等[4]也研究了人体质量、人体刚度、人体阻尼对结构的自振频率和阻尼比的影响。另外,还有许多科研人员针对不同类型的人行桥梁进行了振动分析和舒适度评价[5-7]。研究表明:人行天桥振动问题关乎结构稳定性,桥梁的行人动力响应和舒适度评价是不可忽视的重要研究领域。

本文针对钢桁架人行天桥的受力特点,在杆件内力和挠度变形良好的基础上,采取符合中国行人参数的行人步行模型,分析钢桁架人行天桥在不同人群密度下的结构动力响应,并且对结构的舒适度进行了评价。

1 人行桥人致振动求解分析原理

1.1 单人竖向力模型的建立

在单人竖向力模型中,影响结构竖向力荷载的因素主要是步频、荷载影响因子、结构自重、初始相位。而在结构竖向力荷载的研究中,行人步行参数对结构步频的影响极其重要。目前,关于行人步频参数的研究已经十分成熟,学者们也提出了不同参数的竖向动载因子,具体如表1所示。

不同竖向单人动载因子及步频 表1

学　者	动载因子	步频(Hz)
Blanchard	$\alpha_1=0.257$	<4
Bachmann	$\alpha_1=0.37,\alpha_2=0.1,\alpha_3=0.12$	2
Allen	$\alpha_1=0.5,\alpha_2=0.2,\alpha_3=0.1,\alpha_4=0.05$	2
孙立民	$\alpha_1=0.36,\alpha_2=0.13$	1.6~2.4
Yao 等	$\alpha_1=0.7,\alpha_2=0.25$	2
Young	$\alpha_1=0.41(f-0.95),\alpha_2=0.069+0.056f$ $\alpha_3=0.033+0.0064f,\alpha_4=0.013+0.0065f$	1~2.8

为了适应我国行人行走的步频特点,本文采用孙利民等[8]提出的竖向行人荷载$F(t)$:

$$F(t)=\begin{cases}0.36\times0.7\sin(2\pi f_s t)\cdots(1.6\text{Hz}\leqslant f_s\leqslant2.4\text{Hz})\\0.13\times0.7\sin(2\pi f_s t)\cdots(3.2\text{Hz}\leqslant f_s\leqslant4.8\text{Hz})\end{cases}\tag{1}$$

图1是采用孙利民等建议的单人荷载按2.0Hz连续行走10s的人行荷载曲线。

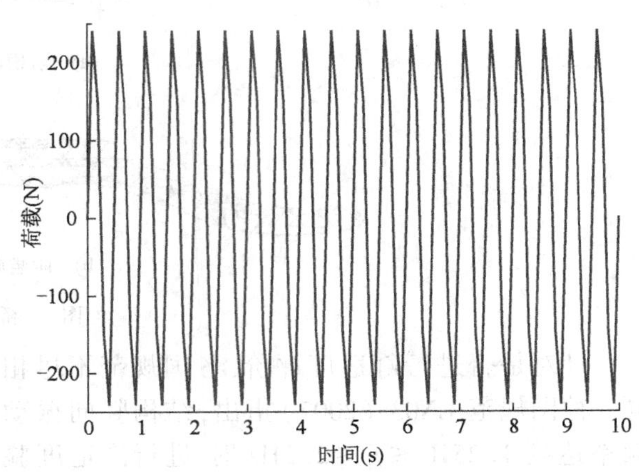

图1 单人行走步频图

1.2 多人荷载模型的建立

(1)小组结伴而行模型。

小组结伴而行时,考虑到每个人状态一致,即相位角、步频、步长均一致,可以认为小组行人动荷载$F_p(t)$用单人脚步动荷载乘以小组人数n来估计。

$$F_p(t)=F(t)\times n\tag{2}$$

(2)低密度人群行走模型。

低密度人群行走将具有不同人行特征参数的随机人群简化成相同步频的人群状态。行走过程中,行人互不干扰,其人群密度上限界定为 0.5 人/m²。根据 Matsumto 等的研究,假设行人上桥服从 Passion 分布,则人行桥等效人数计算公式为:

$$N_p = \sqrt{n} \tag{3}$$

(3)高密度人群行走模型。

当人群密度超过 1 人/m² 时,行人行走相互掣肘,行人前后间距变小。按照随机概率分布模拟方法,其等效人群荷载计算公式为:

$$N_p = 1.85\sqrt{n} \tag{4}$$

n 是不同人群密度人数,考虑不同人群密度的计算是将竖向人群荷载转化为单人作用荷载乘以等效人数 N_p。

人致振动分析,是在结构自振基频的基础上施加简谐荷载引起振动,进行结构动力响应分析。在单人荷载模型的基础上,本文根据振动响应分析理论,运用有限元软件进行数值分析。现有的振动响应理论主要有强迫振动理论、自激励振动理论和随机振动理论。本文主要研究结构的竖向振动,采用强迫振动理论研究结构的动力响应。

2　人行桥动力特性

2.1　人行桥概况

本文研究的人行桥主桥为钢桁架连续梁桥,桁架总高 4.2m,桁架横向间距约为 6m(桥面净宽 5m),主桥全长约为 120m。桥梁的主弦杆、腹杆均采用箱型截面,桥面由下横梁、下弦杆、纵肋构成纵横梁体系,桥面铺装转化为二期荷载进行模拟。桥梁主桁架材料均采用 Q345,主桁节点采用整体式焊接节点。全桥模型及边界约束条件如图 2 所示。

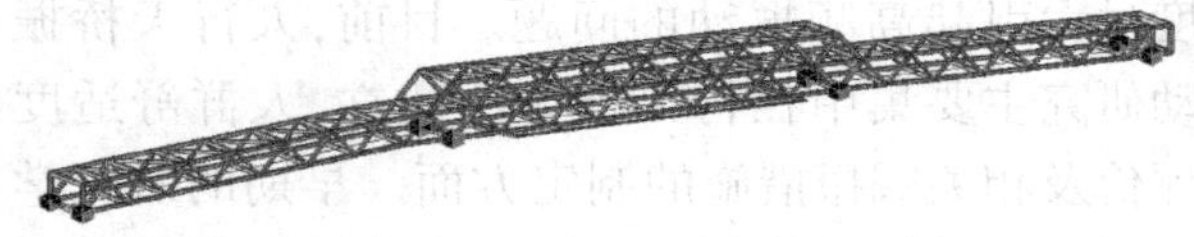

图 2　成桥效果图

2.2　人行桥动力特性

人行桥的动力特性为结构的固有属性,只与结构的刚度、质量和阻尼比有关。本文在考虑结构自重和模态分析的基础上求解结构自振特征值。结构前 5 阶自振频率见表 2,一阶横向弯曲和一阶竖向弯曲如图 3 所示。

频率计算表格　　表 2

序号	自振频率	振型描述
1	1.815	边跨侧弯
2	2.156	边跨侧弯
3	2.378	边跨侧弯
4	2.659	一阶竖弯
5	3.325	二阶竖弯

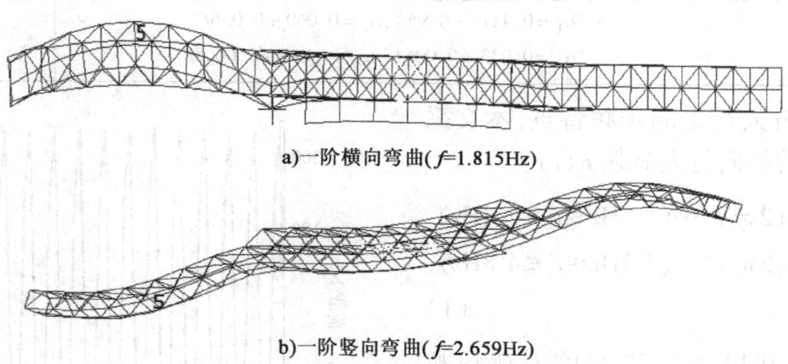

a)一阶横向弯曲(f=1.815Hz)

b)一阶竖向弯曲(f=2.659Hz)

图 3　桥梁的一阶振型

针对是否进行舒适度评价,各国规范不尽相同。德国规范 EN03 (2007)指出,结构竖向振动频率达到 $1.25\text{Hz} \leqslant f_i \leqslant 2.3\text{Hz}$ 时 进行舒适度验算,而中国的《城市人行天桥与人行地道技术规范(征求意见稿)》验算竖向舒适度的频率则为 $1.25\text{Hz} \leqslant f_i \leqslant 3\text{Hz}$。本桥处在人口密集路段,人流量大,可以进行舒适度评价。

3　人致振动竖向力振动分析和舒适度评价

3.1　行人组队不同速度过桥

根据结构动力响应分析以及步频与速度的公式 $v = 0.71f$,本文分别验算了行人在 2.11Hz、2.67Hz、3.52Hz、4.22Hz、4.92Hz、5.63Hz、6.33Hz、7.04Hz步频下结构的加速度响应和位移响应。将行人荷载按照节点动力荷载加载在一阶竖向基频变形最大的节点(5号节点,边跨跨中位置),读取结构的加速度响应见表3,变化趋势如图4所示。

不同步频下结构动力响应表 表3

行人速度(m/s)	步频(Hz)	加速度(mm/s²)	结构振动速度(mm/s)	位移(mm)
1.5	2.11	17.3	1.090	0.075
2	2.67	173	10.29	0.612
2.5	3.52	37.8	0.182	0.008
3	4.22	6.249	0.233	0.023
3.5	4.92	11.5	0.308	0.009
4	5.63	14.2	0.011	0.011
4.5	6.33	35.5	0.888	0.023
5	7.04	15.8	0.381	0.009

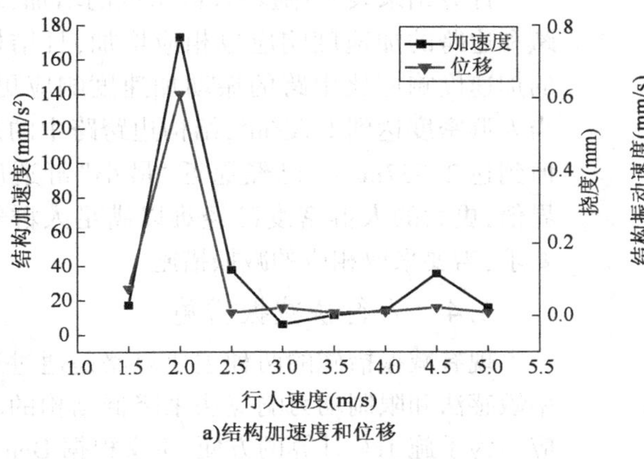

a)结构加速度和位移

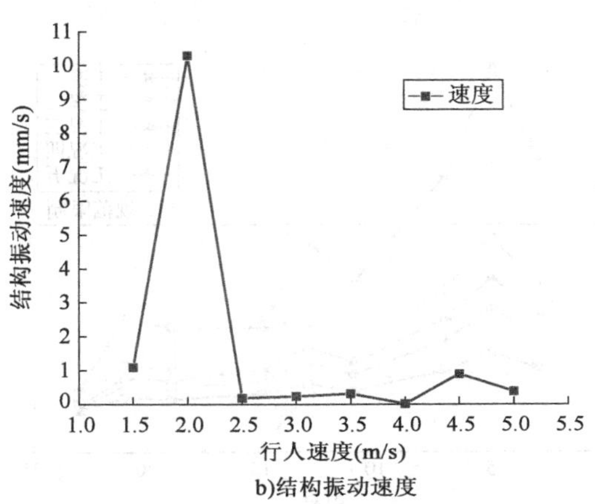

b)结构振动速度

图4 不同步频下结构动力响应图

从速度梯度下的结构动力响应可知,当以2m/s速度行走时,冲击效应最大。这是因为此速度产生的步频为2.67Hz,与结构一阶竖向自振基频相吻合。通过比对分析发现,当行人步频达到结构的基本频率时,结构会产生强烈的动力响应,超过这个限值后,结构的动力响应会相应下降。

3.2 人行荷载工况的确定

为了研究结构在行人结伴行走时以及不同人群密度下的结构荷载响应,本文采用孙利民等的行人脚步力模型研究结构的动力响应,主要分为以下五个工况考虑:

(1)8人组队过桥。

(2)在行人自由行走的状态下,取人群密度为0.3人/m²,人群较疏松,以2m/s速度过桥,通过时间为60s,桥宽5m,计算得到每秒上桥人数为3。此时桥上大约有180人。

(3)取人群密度为0.5人/m²,桥上行人处于稍密状态,计算得到每秒上桥人数为5。此时桥上大约有300人。

(4)取人群密度为1人/m²,桥上人群处于拥挤状态,计算得到每秒上桥人数为10。此时桥上大约有600人。

(5)取人群密度为15人/m²,桥上人群处于严重拥挤状态,计算得到每秒上桥人数为15。此时桥上大约有900人。

本文主要采用以上五种工况进行结构验算。

3.3 不同人群密度下行人舒适度评价及减振措施

本文参考德国规范进行舒适度评价,主要根据竖向加速度和横向加速度划分了四个级别评价标准,如表4所示。

加速度评价舒适级别 表4

舒适级别	舒适度	竖向 a_{limit}(m/s²)	侧向 a_{limit}(m/s²)
CL1	最好	<0.5	<0.1
CL2	中等	0.5~1.00	0.10~0.30
CL3	最小	1.0~2.5	0.3~0.8
CL4	不能接受	>2.5	>0.8

本文采用时程分析法,确定桥梁在脚步力荷载作用下结构的振动速度、位移、加速度响应。选取每跨的四分点,二分点,四分三点的节点动力时程数据,分别对比不同工况荷载激励作用下的竖向加速度响应值。其关键节点加速度响应值见表5和图5,工况四下的时程分析如图6所示。

关键节点加速度响应　　表5

工况	第一跨最大加速度响应(m/s²)			第二跨最大加速度响应(m/s²)			第三跨最大加速度响应(m/s²)		
	1/4L(3)	1/2L(5)	3/4L(7)	1/4L(11)	1/2L(13)	3/4L(15)	1/4L(19)	1/2L(21)	3/4L(23)
工况一	0.614	0.831	0.589	0.317	0.414	0.279	0.208	0.229	0.059
工况二	1.03	1.393	0.988	0.531	0.69	0.468	0.349	0.384	0.101
工况三	1.33	1.798	1.275	0.686	0.89	0.605	0.451	0.496	0.129
工况四	1.728	2.337	1.651	0.8999	1.170	1.259	0.595	0.661	0.164
工况五	3.375	4.564	3.137	1.742	2.27	1.146	1.146	1.259	0.328

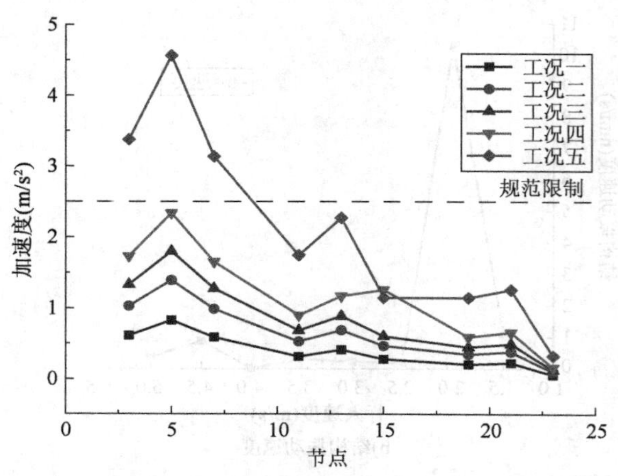

图5　不同工况下不同节点竖向加速度响应值

计算结果表明:随着人群密度的增加,结构中跨和边跨的加速度响应也相应增加,且结构边跨的加速度响应比中跨的振动加速度响应更敏感。当人群密度达到1人/m²,结构边跨跨中的加速度值到达2.337m/s²,已经逼近"最小"舒适度的临界值,更大的人群密度已经难以满足人群舒适度要求,需要采取相应的减振措施。

3.4　人行桥减振措施

现有减振措施的两种主要思路是通过避开频率敏感法和限制动力响应法来降低结构的动力响应。为了施工和计算的方便,本文根据Den Hartog提出的减振计算原理确定减振阻尼器TMD的阻尼器质量、最佳刚度 κ_{opt} 和最佳阻尼 c_{opt}。

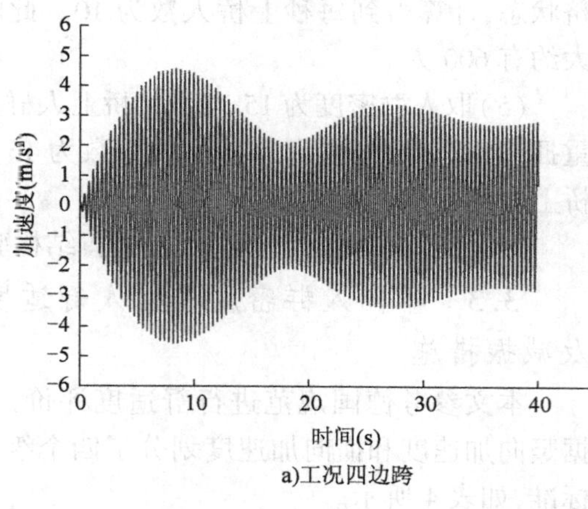

a)工况四边跨

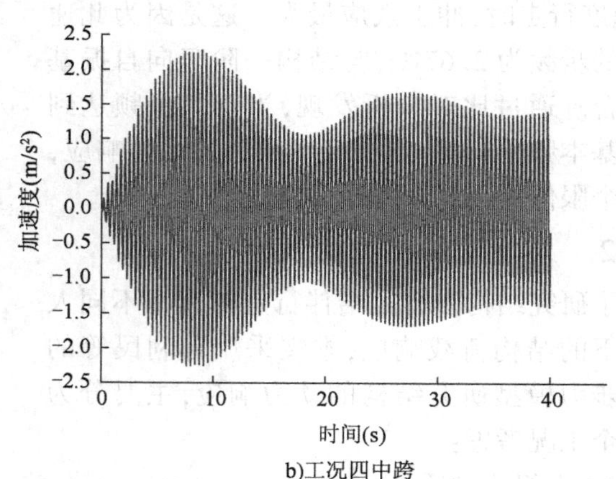

b)工况四中跨

图6　关键节点动力时程响应频谱图

$$\lambda_{opt}=\frac{1}{1+\mu}=,\kappa_{opt}=\lambda_{opt}{}^2 g\omega_0^2 m_d \tag{5}$$

$$c_{opt}=\sqrt{\frac{3u}{8\ (1+\mu)^3}},c_{opt}=2\xi_{dopt}\lambda_{opt}g\omega_0 g m_d \tag{6}$$

式中 μ 为TMD质量与主体结构质量之比;ω_0 为一阶竖向自振频率;m_d 为一阶竖向振型参与质量。

根据有限元计算结果,一阶竖向振型参与质量为145893.57kg,μ 取1%阻尼质量为振型参与质量的1%,ω_0 取20rad/s。TMD设计参数见表6。

TMD 设计参数 表6

TMD 个数	单个阻尼器质量 m_0(Kg)	刚度 κ_{opt}(N/m)	阻尼 c_{opt}(N·s/m)
2	1459	571986	3466

将2个阻尼器对称布置在两侧边跨的二分点处，然后再次对工况三、工况四进行动力时程分析。计算结果表明，添加TMD后结构跨中的振动加速度峰值显著降低。其减振效率见表7，其单个控制节点的减振时程分析如图7所示。

目标工况减振效率 表7

工况		未安装TMD的加速度响应(m/s^2)	安装TMD的加速度响应(m/s^2)	减振效率
工况四	边跨跨中(5)	2.337	0.575	75%
	中跨跨中(13)	1.170	0.318	73%
工况五	边跨跨中(5)	4.564	0.697	84%
	中跨跨中(13)	2.27	0.372	83%

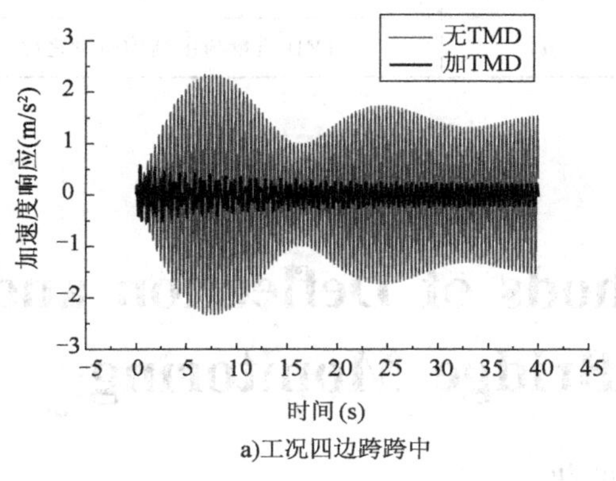

a)工况四边跨跨中

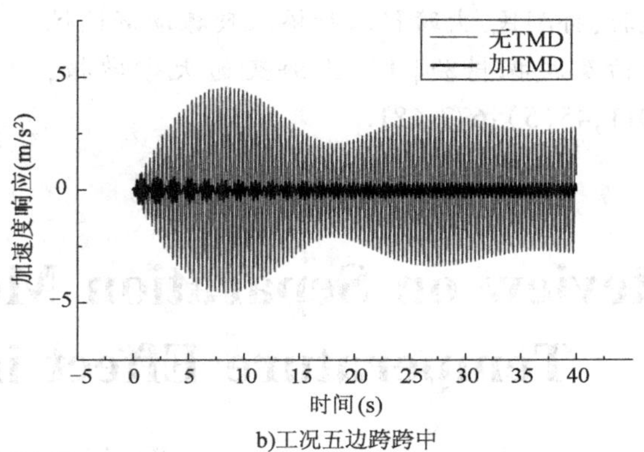

b)工况五边跨跨中

图7 目标工况减振时程示意图

采取减振措施后，工况四和工况五的最大竖向加速度响应分别降到$0.575m/s^2$和$0.697m/s^2$，减振效果良好；舒适度评价指标达到“中等”，符合计算要求，降低了行人在桥上行走时的晃动感和不舒适感。

4 结语

对比各国规范对人行桥人致振动舒适度评价的规定后，本文选取了德国规范EN03(2007)的舒适度评价标准对本桥进行了研究分析，人群荷载采取了符合中国人体行走参数的脚步力模型，结合有限元软件对人行天桥进行了人致振动响应的数值分析，结果如下：

(1)本桥基频依据中国规范，其一阶竖向频率小于3Hz，其横向加速度满足基本规范要求。可以不进行横向舒适度评价，而进行结构的竖向舒适度验算。

(2)在考虑不同人群密度的人群激励下，当人群密度达到1人/m^2，其桥梁的竖向加速度响应值已经逼近“最小”指标的临界值，舒适度较差，对结构采取减振措施后，结构的最不利工况舒适度评价达到“中等”。

(3)本文仅仅研究了结构的竖向加速度响应，得到了一定的规律结果，而结构的横向加速度响应有待进一步研究。另外，本文采用了确定性人群荷载模型，针对随机行人行走模型的动力响应分析还有待深入研究。

参考文献

[1] 陈政清，华旭刚. 人行桥的振动与动力设计[M]. 北京：人民交通出版社，2009.

[2] 高世桥，王栋，牛少华. 人-结构耦合系统动态特性分析[J] 北京理工大学学报，2013，33(3)：235-238.

[3] Brownjohn James W M. Energy dissipation from vibrating floor slabs due to human-structure interaction [J]. Shock and Vibration，2001，8(6)：315-323.

[4] 操礼林,吕亚兵,曹栋,等.行人动力学参数对大跨简支人行桥人致振动的影响分析[J].东南大学学报(自然科学版),2020,50(2):260-266.

[5] 王智丰,李贤军,易锦,等.大跨胶合木拱桥人致振动及其优化控制[J].土木工程学报,2021,54(4):79-94.

[6] 张雪松,陈永辉,王继祥.某异形景观桥人致振动荷载取值及舒适度分析[J].重庆交通大学学报(自然科学版),2018,37(4):1-6.

[7] 许竞,李泽玉,李静.某轻钢人行桥的力学特性研究及舒适度评价[J].建筑结构,2021,51(4):131-135.

[8] 钱骥,孙利民.大跨径人行桥人致振动舒适性评估及减振措施[J].上海交通大学学报,2011,45(5):677-681.

参数解释表:

参 数	名词解释
$F_p(t)$	竖向行人荷载
n	不同人群密度人数
N_p	人行桥等效人数
f_i	结构自振基频
f_s	行人步频
m_0	单个阻尼器质量
C_{opt}	阻尼器最佳阻尼
κ_{opt}	阻尼器最佳刚度
ω_0	一阶竖向自振频率
μ	TMD质量与主结构质量之比

Review on Separation Methods of Deflection and Temperature Effect in Bridge Monitoring

Wu Xiaoyang Liu Jie*

(School of Highway, Chang'an University)

Abstract To more comprehensively summarize the existing bridge deflection temperature effect separation methods and provide systematic and effective information for the further development of bridge deflection temperature effect separation, the existing deflection temperature effect separation methods are summarized, mainly including separation based on the corresponding relationship between temperature and deflection and layer by layer separation based on the period of each component in deflection; The application status, advantages and disadvantages of the existing bridge deflection temperature effect separation methods are analyzed.

Keywords bridge engineering signal separation deflection temperature effect separation

0 Introduction

The deflection change of bridge structure is an important parameter to evaluate the safety state of bridge structure during the safe operation of the bridge, and the deflection component is complex, which is often composed of complex components such as environmental noise, vehicle, and pedestrian live load, temperature effect, the change of structure material and working state. For long-span cable-stayed bridges, the temperature effect in the deflection components during the actual operation has exceeded the theoretical design temperature effect by a lot. At the same time, this type of bridge has a large span, strong flexibility and great impact on the deflection by vehicles. Therefore, it is particularly important to evaluate the real-time performance of deflection monitoring and the components of deflection monitoring data respectively. According to the principal component division, the bridge deflection data collected by the long-term monitoring system can be regarded as the superposition of long-term deflection, daily temperature difference effect, annual temperature difference effect, and live load effect[1]. The quantitative contribution of every single factor to bridge deflection must be separated to provide a reliable basis for bridge performance and safety evaluation.

1 Temperature effect separation based on the corresponding relationship between temperature and deflection

There are many ways to establish the corresponding relationship between temperature and deflection, such as auto associative neural network, artificial neural network, regression statistics, particle swarm optimization algorithm, least squares and multi least squares support vector machine models, etc.

1.1 Regression Statistics

According to the characteristics of different time scales of bridge deflection monitoring information, Liang Zongbao[2] used wavelet analysis theory to peel off the live load effect, established the empirical regression equation of temperature effect according to the correlation analysis of temperature effect and temperature, and eliminated the temperature effect in the structural response information. The regression statistical method is simple and easy, but the accuracy is low, and the environmental factors are complex and changeable. It is not reliable to separate the action effect of a single factor by this method. The schematic diagram of wavelet decomposition is shown in Fig. 1: (CA1 and CD1 are the low-frequency coefficients and high-frequency coefficients after wavelet decomposition, Ca2 and CD2 are the low-frequency and high-frequency coefficient junctions obtained after CA1 wavelet decomposition, and so on).

1.2 Least squares and multi least squares support vector machine models

Liu Xiaping et al.[3] used support vector machine based on the least squares (LS-SVM) model is used to separate the temperature effect, and the separated results are more accurate. By establishing the equation between temperature and temperature effect, taking temperature as a variable and temperature effect as a function, the functional relationship between temperature and temperature effect is established by using the approximation ability of the least squares support vector machine. When the temperature change is known, the variation of the corresponding temperature effect can be calculated So as to achieve the purpose of temperature deflection separation. The schematic diagram of the least squares vector machine model is shown in Fig. 2.

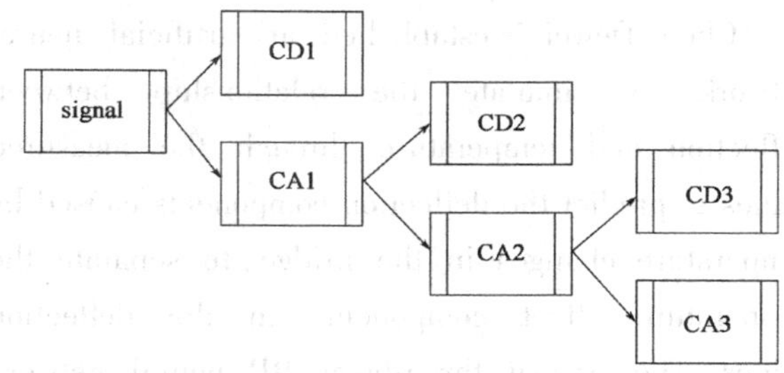

Fig. 1 Schematic Diagram of Wavelet Decomposition

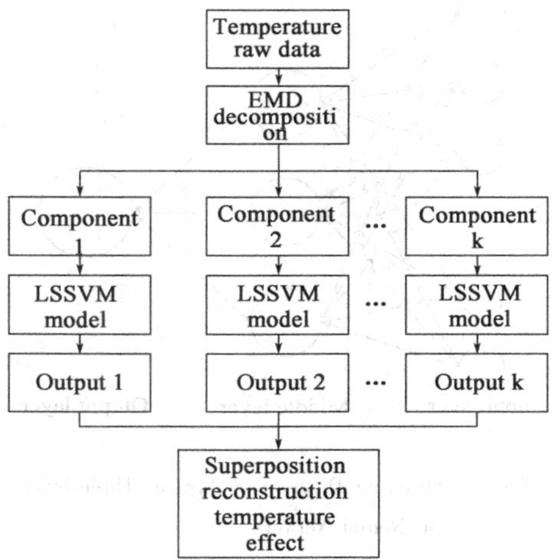

Fig. 2 Schematic Diagram of Least Squares Vector Machine Model

However, the model is a single model structure. With the increase of training data, the complexity of the system will increase sharply. Moreover, due to the existence of data outliers, the single regression model is often unsatisfactory.

Yang Hong et al.[4] Based on the LS-SVM model studied by Liu Xiaping, A method based on multi least squares support vector machine is proposed (M-

IS-SVM) modeling method. In this method, the input data are classified by clustering algorithm, the corresponding LS-SVM sub model is established according to the classification results, and then the LS-SVM sub model is recursively connected through the principal component to form the M-IS-SVM model. Compared with the LS-SVM model, the M-IS-SVM model is more accurate in fitting the mapping relationship between temperature and deflection, so it is separated by the M-IS-SVM model The results are also more accurate.

1.3 Neural network

Chen Dewei[5] established an artificial neural network to simulate the relationship between deflection and temperature through the measured values to predict the deflection components caused by temperature changes in the bridge, to separate the temperature effect components in the deflection values. The typical three-layer BP neural network structure is shown in Fig. 3.

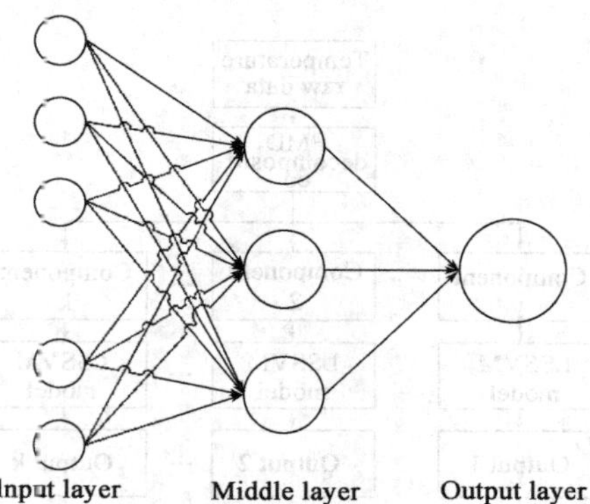

Fig. 3 Structure Diagram of Typical Three-layer BP Neural Network

Different from the finite element calculation method, the artificial neural network method is a special numerical analysis method, which has the characteristics of strong nonlinear mapping ability, fault tolerance, and robustness. It can be used to fit the deflection change relationship of the main beam generated by the temperature distribution at different times. The specific calculation flow is shown in Fig. 4.

It can be seen from the above induction that the neural network method finds the fitting change law through network training, and finds the characteristics of the structural temperature response of the bridge at the same time.

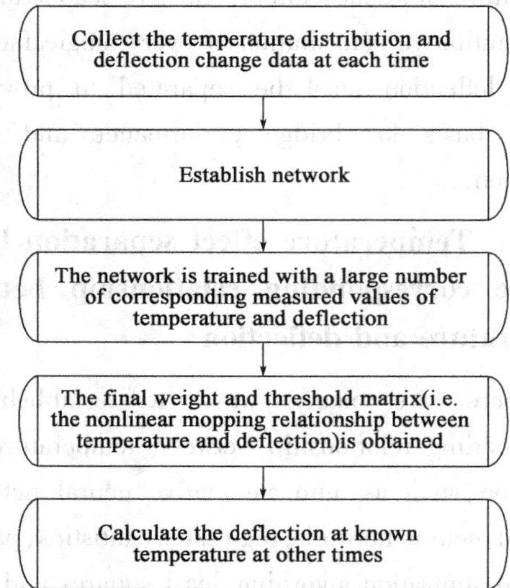

Fig. 4 Specific Calculation Diagram of Neural Network

However, the effectiveness of the neural network method depends on the integrity of the original database and network structure, and the convergence of its training processcan not be guaranteed.

1.4 Particle swarm optimization algorithm

Liu Gang[6] proposed an adaptive bandwidth filtering method to accurately separate temperature effects by using the multi-scale characteristics of structural long-term monitoring signals. According to the idea of multi-scale analysis, the temperature and temperature effect are expanded on different time scales such as daily temperature difference, annual temperature difference, and natural cooling. Using the characteristic that only the daily temperature difference effect is not coupled with other structural effects in time scale, it is obtained that the temperature and temperature effect have linear correlation characteristics through theoretical demonstration, Combining particle swarm optimization algorithm and filtering algorithm, the frequency bandwidth of the time scale of daily temperature difference effect is adaptively changed, to accurately separate the temperature effect in the monitoring signal by regression statistics of daily temperature difference and daily temperature difference effect. The principle of separating temperature effect by particle swarm adaptive filter is shown in Fig. 5.

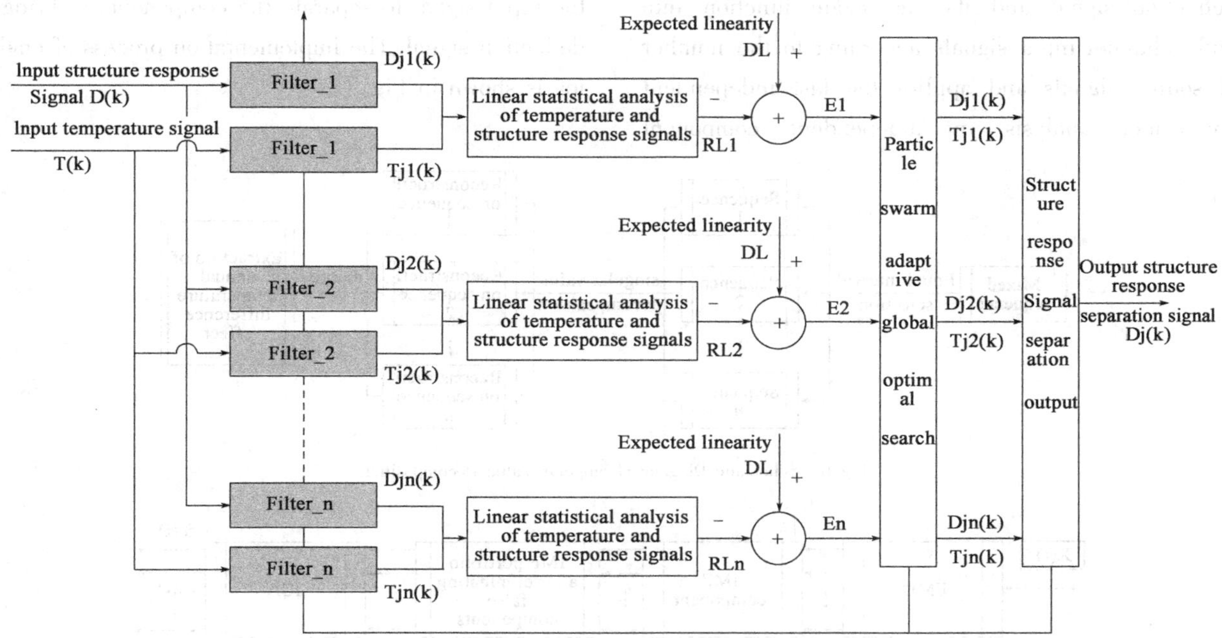

Fig. 5 Schematic Diagram of Separating Temperature Effect by Particle Swarm Adaptive Filter

However, for the signal components with similar center frequency and overlapping bandwidth, such as daily temperature difference deflection, annual temperature difference deflection, and long-term deflection, the separation effect is poor.

2 Separate layer by layer based on the temperature effect of each component period in the deflection

The difference between these methods is mainly that the separation methods after determining the period of each component are different, mainly including singular value decomposition, eigenvalue analysis, fast independent component analysis, center moving average method, and so on.

2.1 Singular value decomposition

A. Deraemaeker et al. [7] used singular value degradation method to eliminate the influence of temperature effect; Liu Xiaping[8] realized the accurate separation of each periodic component of temperature effect in deflection signal by using the periodic characteristics of temperature effect and singular value decomposition; Yang Jian et al. [9] filtered out high-frequency signals such as live load effect through FIR low-pass filter to obtain a group of low-frequency signals, applied singular value decomposition to them, and eliminated singular values close to zero, to realize the extraction of temperature effect in a structural deformation. The flow of the singular value decomposition algorithm is shown in Fig. 6.

However, this method requires that the effects of various environmental factors are not coupled with the damage effects, and all combinations of different effects need to be obtained in the healthy state, which is difficult to meet in the actual bridge.

2.2 Fast independent component analysis

Yang Hong and Liu Xiaping[10] used empirical mode decomposition (EMD) to decompose nonlinear and non-stationary signals into a series of linear and stationary eigenmode functions For the deflection signal separation of single-channel long-span bridge, combined with the advantages of blind source separation and empirical mode decomposition, a blind source separation method based on empirical mode decomposition is proposed (singular value decom position, referred to as SVD) estimates the number of signal sources, recombines the single channel deflection signal and its eigenmode function into multi-channel input signals according to the number of source signals and applies the fast independent component analysis in independent component analysis (ICA) theory Fast independent COM component analysis (FastICA) algorithm decomposes the input signal to separate the components of bridge deflection signal. The implementation process of emd-ica is shown in Fig. 7.

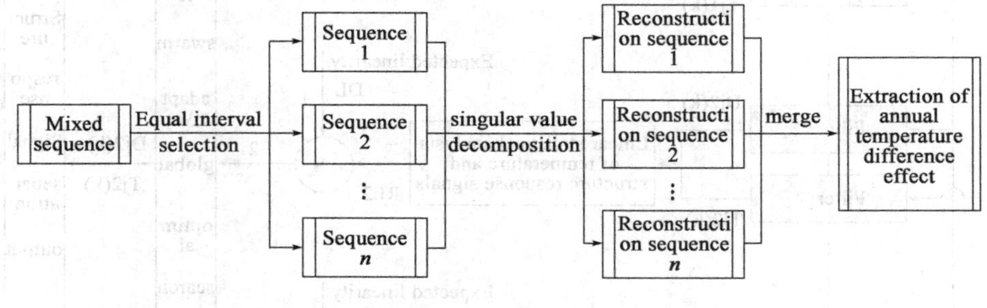

Fig. 6 Schematic Diagram of Singular Value Decomposition

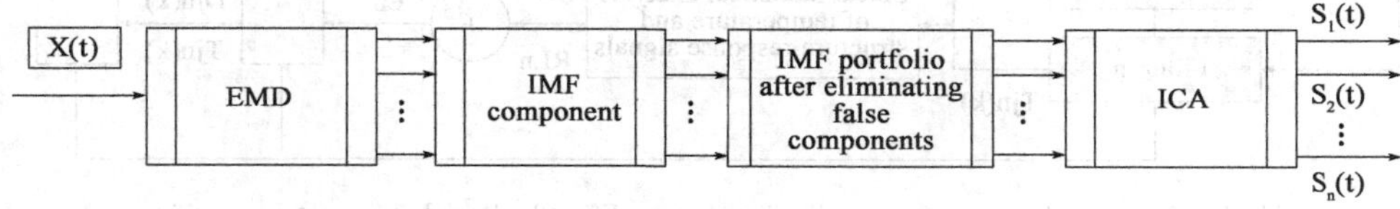

Fig. 7 Schematic Diagram of EMD-ICA Implementation Process

2.3 Center moving average method

According to the multi-scale characteristics of long-term monitoring signal of deflection and the characteristics of periodic variation of deflection under temperature load, ChenGuoliang and Lin Xungen[11] obtained the period length of a signal component by using the modified average periodic diagram method, combined with the deflection temperature effect separation strategy based on the center moving average method, extracted the structural deformation characteristics, and established the prediction model of structural deformation trend by using ARIMA model. The flow diagram of the modified average periodic chart method is shown in Fig. 8.

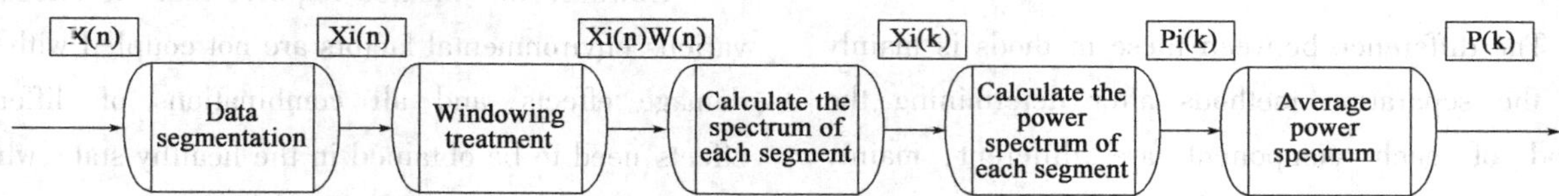

Fig. 8 Flow Chart of Modified Average Periodic Chart Method

3 Conelntions

At present, the deflection temperature effect separation method is mainly divided into two directions: one is to establish the corresponding relationship between temperature and deflection, to realize the separation of temperature effect; Second, after the accurate period of each periodic component in the deflection can be determined, the temperature effects of different periods are separated layer by layer.

However, the process of most methods is too complex, and it seems a little weak when dealing with the long-term massive data of health monitoring, especially it is very difficult to achieve real-time monitoring. Therefore, the subsequent research should focus on optimizing and simplifying the algorithm as much as possible under the condition of ensuring a certain separation accuracy to realize the rapid separation of the temperature effect.

References

[1] Liu Gang. Research on safety state assessment method of large bridges based on long-term static monitoring data [D]. Chongqing: Chongqing University, 2010.

[2] Liang Zongbao. Research on bridge structure safety evaluation based on statistical analysis of monitoring information [D]. Chongqing: Chongqing University, 2006.

[3] Liu Xiaping, Yang Hong, Sun Zhuo, he Qingping, Wang Yanping. Temperature effect separation in bridge deflection monitoring based on LS-SVM [J]. Journal of railways, 2012, 34 (10): 91-96.

[4] Yang Hong, Sun Zhuo, Liu Xiaping, Zhu Weian, Wang Yanping. Separation of bridge temperature deflection effect based on multi least squares support vector machine [J]. Vibration and shock, 2014, 33 (01): 71-76 + 88.

[5] Chen Dewei, Jing Guoqiang, Huang Zheng. The deflection behavior of bridge under temperature is estimated by artificial neural network method [J]. Structural engineer, 2006, (04): 24-28.

[6] Liu Gang, Shao Yimin, Huang Zongming, et al. A new method for separating structure temperature effect in long-term monitoring [J]. Engineering mechanics, 2010, 27 (03): 55-61 + 100.

[7] A. Deraemaeker, E. Reynders, G. De Roeck, et al. Vibration-based structural health monitoring using output-only measurements under changing environment [J]. Mechanical Systems and Signal Processing, 2007, 22(1):

[8] Liu Xiaping, Yang Hong, Sun Zhuo, et al. Airong Research on bridge deflection separation based on singular value decomposition [J]. Journal of Sun Yat sen University (NATURAL SCIENCE EDITION), 2013, 52 (03): 11-16.

[9] Yang Jian, Liu Xiaping, Yang Hong, et al. A new method for extracting temperature effect in bridge structure deformation [J]. Journal of Guangzhou University (NATURAL SCIENCE EDITION), 2013, 12 (03): 38-44.

[10] Yang Hong, Liu Xiaping, Cui Haixia, et al. Separation of real-time dynamic deflection signals of long-span bridges [J]. Vibration. Testing and diagnosis, 2015, (01): 42-49 + 186.

[11] Chen Guoliang, Lin XunGen, Yue Qing, et al. Long term deflection separation and prediction of Bridges Based on time series analysis [J]. Journal of Tongji University (NATURAL SCIENCE EDITION), 2016, 44 (06): 962-968.

Mechanical Performance of Steel Frame Retrofitted with CFRP

Zhao Xiaonan* Li Yujie Wang Peng He Peiwen He Runxiang Niu Jiawei

(School of Highway, Chang'an University)

Abstract Carbon fibre reinforced polymer (CFRP) is regarded as an excellent choice in retrofitting of civil engineering. CFRP retrofitting method for structures has been developed for bridges and an other civil engineering vulnerable to deterioration. In this paper, geometric and material properties are discussed based on the assumption of an equivalent cross-section consisting of steel and CFRP. Pushover analysis of two configurations of steel frames including 40m K-shaped and 80m X-shaped frames is studied to carry out the members which need rehabilitation. Then, the performance of the frame after being retrofitted with CFRP is analysed and compared to the original frame. According to numerical analysis, it is found that the ultimate strength capacity could increase by 7% to 16% for steel frames retrofitted with CFRP.

Keywords CFRP Steel frame Retrofitting Pushover

0 Introduction

Carbonfibre reinforced polymer (CFRP), among other fibre reinforced materials, has been increasingly replacing conventional materials as a result of their excellent strength and low specific weight properties. Their manufacturability in varying combinations with customized strength properties, also their high fatigue, toughness and high temperature wear and oxidation resistance capabilities render these materials an excellent choice in engineering applications. Retrofitting with CFRP materials has been significantly accepted by the civil engineering community around the world in recent years for its technically sound and cost-effective repair technology (Sarker 2011).

Considerable studies have been researched for engineering structures retrofitted with CFRP. For reinforced concrete structure, externally bonded CFRP sheets help in enhanced performance of deficient reinforced concrete (RC) beams in carrying an additional load (Raja 2018), RC columns retrofitted with CFRP composites exhibited a ductile behaviour under cyclic lateral loading (Saljoughian 2019), RC storey building strengthened by CFRP reached larger lateral load-carrying capacity (H. R. Ronagh 2013). For steel structure, CFRP retrofitting could increase the strength of the deteriorated steel girder, behave in a ductile manner and eliminate the early peel off of the CFRP sheet (K. Galal 2011), and significantly increase the compression force and flexural capacity in steel beam-columns retrofitted with CFRP strips (Movaghari 2010).

However, the research work onstrengthening tubular steel frame structures is very limited. In this study, an equivalent CFRP beam element is presented to check the mechanical performance of CFRP retrofitted steel frames.

1 Moldeling of CFRP element

In order to model the composite action between the steel brace and CFRP during pushover analysis, the equivalent CFRP beam element with new geometric and material properties are discussed in this unit.

1.1 Geometric properties of the equivalent CFRP beam element

The cross-sectional area of the equivalent CFRP beam element is calculated as:

$$A_e = A_s + \frac{E_c}{E_s}A_c \qquad (1)$$

And the moment of inertia of the equivalent CFRP beam element is obtained by

$$I_e = I_s + \frac{E_c}{E_s}I_c \qquad (2)$$

Where,

A_s, A_c: cross-section area of steel section and CFRP section

I_s, I_c: the moment of inertia of steel section and CFRP section

E_s, E_c: Young's modulus of steel and CFRP

Using the area and moment of inertiaas the equivalent CFRP beam element, the outer diameter D and thickness of wall t of the equivalent CFRP beam element are obtained.

1.2 Material properties of the equivalent CFRP beam element

According to the previous study of the research group, the greatest contribution on the elastic axial stiffness comes from four layers of CFRP. Thus, four layers of CFRP retrofitting are adopted in this study. The elastic axial stiffness of the equivalent CFRP beam element, viz. E_e = 221GPa and yield stress σ_s = 365MPa.

2 Pushover analysis of steel frame before retrofitted with CFRP

Two steel schemes of steel frames: 40m K-brace and 80m X-brace shown in Figures 1 and 2 are adopted to this study. Pushover analysis is subjected to the two frames in order to obtain the ultimate strength capacity of the original steel frames. During pushover analysis, bulking members are determined, which provides abasis for retrofitting.

2.1 40 K-brace steel frame

The scheme of the original 40 K-brace steel frame is shown in Fig. 1.

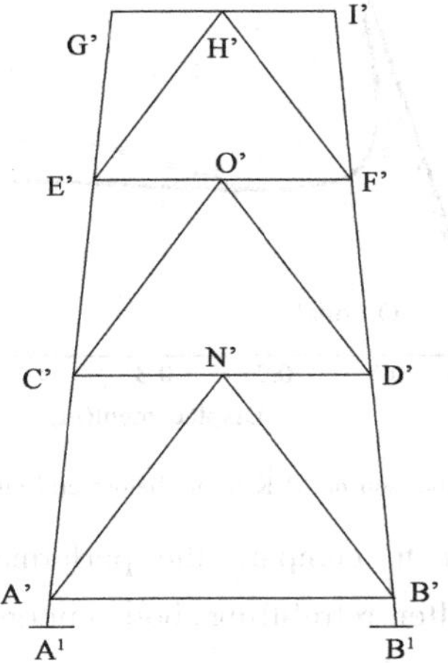

Fig. 1 Original 40 K-brace steel frame

Pushover indicates thatthe first buckling occurs in the intermediate compressive brace O' D' before the ultimate load is reached. A rapid fall-off in load once the compressive brace in the intermediate brace buckles. A second fall-off in load takes place after the compressive brace in the upper frame buckles. The legs acquire additional load shed by the compressive braces and enable the overall residual strength to pick up as the deflection proceeds until collapse occurs.

The forces in the compressive and tension braces in the bottom continue to increase even when the two compressive braces O' D' and H' F' have buckled during the loading procedure, which means that the braces in the bottom do not fail during the pushover analysis. A sudden drop in the load corresponds to adrop in the overall resistance of the structure due to buckling elsewhere. The axial forces in the compressive brace H' F' and tension brace H' E' increase when the intermediate brace O' D' starts unloading due to buckling and the axial forces in member H' F' increase until it buckles.

2.2 80 X-brace steel frame

The scheme of the original 80 X-brace steel frame is shown in Fig. 2.

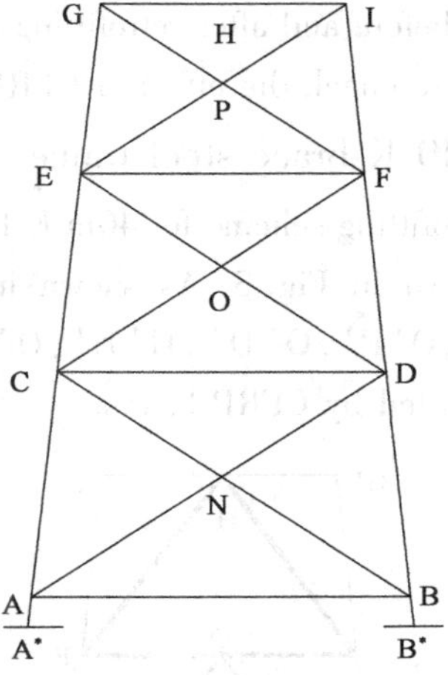

Fig. 2 Original 80 X-brace steel frame

Pushover indicates that after the member BN buckles, the structure still carries additional load because the braces in the intermediate frame and horizontal member CD acquire the load shed by the compressive braces BN and CN in the bottom frame. When the compressive braces OD and OE in the second frame buckle, the braces in the upper frame and the horizontal member EF acquires the load shed by these compressive braces. When the tension failure occurs in the brace AN at the bottom frame, the structure attains the ultimate load. The braces acquire the additional load and enable the overall residual strength to remain substantial as the deflection proceeds until collapse occurs.

When the compressive braces buckle, the horizontal members and tension braces begin to carry the additional load. When the compressive brace BN buckles, the horizontal member CD in the same level and the braces OD and OE in the intermediate frame acquire the load shed by the compressive braces. When the compressive braces BN, OD and OE buckle, the forces in the horizontal members change from tensile to compressive.

3　Pushover analysis of steel frame retrofitted with CFRP and comparison

CFRP rehabilitation iscompleted considering the failure of the members. The performance of the steel frame retrofitted with CFRP will be presented in this section. Then, a comparison of mechanical performance before and after retrofitting of frames will be discussed to check the effect of CFRP retrofitting.

3.1　40 K-brace steel frame

The retrofitting scheme for 40m K-braceframe by CFRP is shown in Fig. 3. As shown in the figure, brace H'F', O'F', O'D', H'E', O'E', and O'C' are retrofitted by CFRP layers.

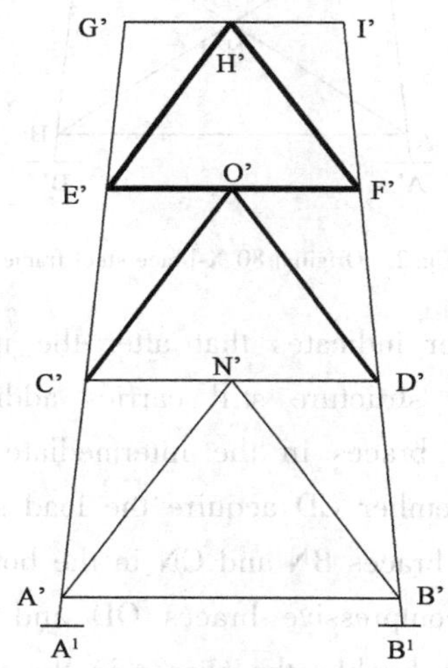

Fig. 3　Strengthen scheme of 40 K frame

According to Fig. 4, it can be seen that the maximum horizontal displacement is 0.12m and the maximum base shear is 8.32 × 103 kN. The member forces and stresses in the structural elements were investigated and it was found that there was no buckling or yielding in any structural element.

The results from the pushover analysis of the frames before and after retrofitting are compared in Fig. 4. The maximum base shear of the steel frame retrofitted with CFRP is 8.32 × 103 kN and the percentage increase of the ultimate capacity is 16% (from the 7.17 × 103 kN to 8.32 × 103 kN).

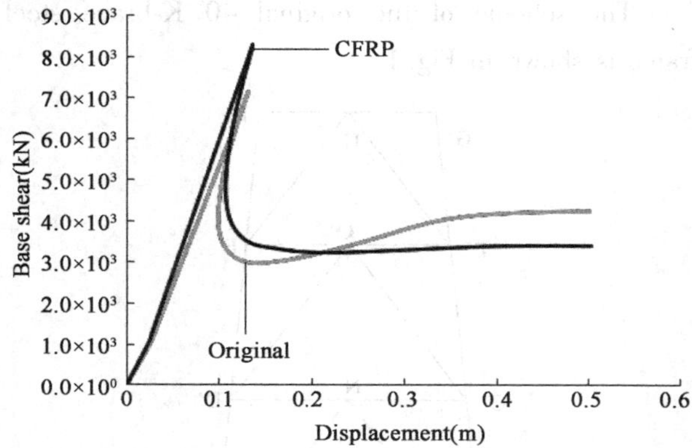

Fig. 4　Comparison of 40 K frame before and after retrofitting

In order to compare the performance offrames before and after retrofitting, both energies-based and load-based performance measures mentioned in Offshore Technology Report -OTO 1999 081 (2000) are adopted in this study. The following parameters are selected.

$$R_1 = \frac{\textit{environmental load at untimate strength capacity}(Q_m)}{\textit{environmental load at first plastic hinge}(Q_p)}$$

$$R_2 = \frac{\textit{environmental load at deflection equal to twice the deflection at ultimate strength capicity}(Q_n)}{\textit{environmental load at ultimate strength capacity}(Q_m)}$$

$$R_3 = \frac{\textit{energy at deflection equal to twice the deflection at ultimate strength capacity(area of ABCD)}}{\textit{energy at ultimate strength capacity(area of ABE)}}$$

The first performance measure R_1 is an indication of the available reserve strength up to the point where the ultimate load of the frames has been reached. Hereafter referred to as pre-ultimate performance measure. The second performance measure R_2 indicates the residual strength expressed as a ratio of ultimate strength, whereas the third performance measure R_3 indicates post-ultimate energy dissipation capacity. R_2 and R_3 are hereafter referred to as post-ultimate performance measures.

The retrofitted frame shows an improved reserved strength R_1 due to an increase in the strength of compressive braces by CFRP. The residual strength R_2 of the frame retrofitted with CFRP is smaller than the original structure due to the buckling of member B'N' at the bottom. However, the retrofitted frame shows a better post-ultimate energy dissipation capacity R_3 (Tab. 1).

Performance measures for 40-meter K-brace frame Tab. 1

Type	Base shear at first plastic hinge (kN)	Ultimate base shear (kN)	Base shear at twice the deflection at ultimate load (kN)	Energy at ultimate capacity (kJ)	Energy at twice the deflection at ultimate load (kJ)	R_1	R_2	R_3
Original	7.11E+03	7.17E+03	4.15E+03	3.54E+02	6.30E+02	1.01	0.58	1.77
CFRP	7.63E+03	8.32E+03	3.91E+03	4.33E+02	8.58E+02	1.09	0.47	1.98

3.2 80 X-brace steel frame

The retrofitting scheme for 80m X-brace frame by CFRP is shown in Fig. 5. As shown in the figure, brace DN, CN, AN and BN are retrofitted by CFRP layers.

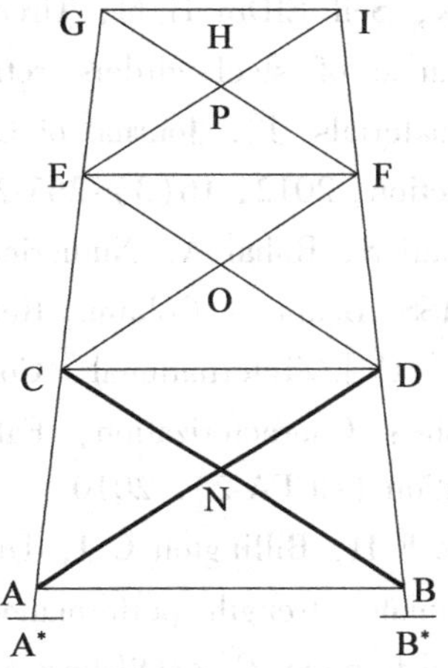

Fig. 5 Strengthen scheme of 80 X frame

The results from the pushover analysis of the frames before and after retrofitting are compared in Fig. 6. The maximum base shear of steel frame retrofitted with CFRP is 1. 23 × 104 kN and the percentage increase of the ultimate capacity is 7% (from 1. 13 × 104 kN to 1. 23 × 104 kN).

Tab. 2 shows the performance measures for the 80m X-brace frame before and after retrofitting. CFRP retrofitted frame shows decreased reserved strength R_1, residual strength R_2, and post-ultimate energy dissipation capacity R_3.

4 Conclusions

(1) CFRP retrofitting could increase the ultimate strength capacity of steel frames. The percentage increase of the ultimate strength capacity of the 40m K-shaped and 80m X-shaped frames are 16% and 7% respectively.

(2) The 40 K-shaped frame shows a better reserve strength R_1 than the original frames. Due to the change of buckling members, the retrofitted have a lower residual strength R_2 but higher post-ultimate energy dissipation capacity R_3 while for 80 X-shaped frame, all of the parameters decrease (Tab. 2).

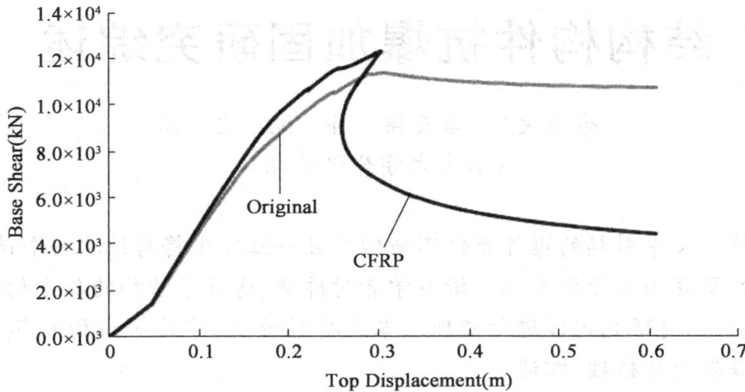

Fig. 6 Comparison of 80 X frame before and after retrofitting

Performance measures for 80-meter X-brace frame Tab. 2

Type	Base shear at first plastic hinge (kN)	Ultimate base shear (kN)	Base shear at twice the deflection at ultimate load (kN)	Energy at ultimate capacity (kJ)	Energy at twice the deflection at ultimate load (kJ)	R_1	R_2	R_3
Original	8.46E+03	1.13E+04	1.07E+04	3.80E+03	8.21E+03	1.34	0.94	2.16
CFRP	1.01E+04	1.23E+04	4.47E+03	4.44E+03	5.66E+03	1.21	0.36	1.28

(3) The performance of the retrofitted frame is related to the scheme. It can be seen that CFRP retrofitting has a greater impact on 40 K-shaped frame compared to 80 X-shaped frame.

It can be found that the CFRP could be useful for application in tubular steel frame structures. Further research is needed to investigate the feasibility of implementing the proposed CFRP retrofitting technique in practice.

References

[1] Sarker P, Begum M, Nasrin S. Fiber reinforced polymers for structural retrofitting: A review [J]. J Civil Eng, 2011, 39(1): 49-57.

[2] Raju A, Mathew L A. Retrofitting of RC beams using FRP [J]. International Journal of Engineering Research and Technology, 2013, 2(1): 1-6.

[3] Saljoughian A, Mostofinejad D, Hosseini S M. CFRP confinement in retrofitted RC columns via CSB technique under reversed lateral cyclic loading[J]. Materials and Structures, 2019, 52(4):1-14.

[4] Ronagh H R, Eslami A. Flexural retrofitting of RC buildings using GFRP/CFRP-A comparative study[J]. Composites Part B: Engineering, 2013, 46: 188-196.

[5] Galal K, Seif ElDin H M, Tirca L. Flexural performance of steel girders retrofitted using CFRP materials[J]. Journal of Composites for Construction, 2012, 16(3):265-276.

[6] Movaghati S, Rahai A. Numerical analysis of steel HSS Beam – Column Retrofitted with CFRP [C]//International Conference on Composite: Characterization, Fabrication and Application (CCFA-2). 2010.

[7] Hamdan F H, Billington C J, Turner R C, et al. Ultimate strength performance of offshore structural framing[C]//Offshore Mechanics and Arctic Engineering Conference, New Orleans. 2000.

结构构件抗爆加固研究综述

余金火* 李天伟 孙 悦 宋 建
(长安大学公路学院)

摘 要 由于恐怖主义等引起的爆炸事件不断增多且一旦发生将对结构安全造成巨大的威胁,所以近年来针对结构抗爆的研究逐渐受到关注。诸多学者对桥梁、建筑等结构的各个构件的抗爆加固进行了研究,但是鲜有人对这些已有研究内容进行梳理。本文将对桥梁、建筑等结构的各个构件抗爆的常用加固措施近几年的研究成果进行梳理、综述。

关键词 桥梁工程 抗爆加固 研究综述 局部构件

0 引言

随着科技的不断进步,土木行业也得到了高速的发展。各种完善的交通网为人们出行提供了极大的便利,各式各样的建筑物也为人类的工作以及娱乐等活动提供了场所。然而,因恐怖袭击、现代战争、偶然因素等引起的爆炸事故频繁发生,这些爆炸事故一旦发生将会造成桥梁、建筑等结构的局部破坏甚至连续倒塌,而对于存在较大爆炸风险的桥梁、建筑等结构,进行事前的防爆加固能有效降低结构在爆炸后的毁伤程度。所以结构抗爆加固的研究一直是国内外学者关注的热点。目前,国内外学者针对桥梁、建筑等结构的各个构件的抗爆加固进行了许多研究。但是鲜有学者对这些已有研究内容进行的梳理、概述。本文将对桥梁、建筑等结构的各个构件的常用加固措施近几年的研究内容进行梳理、概述,为后续的研究提供一定的参考。

1 FRP 材料加固

纤维增强复合物(FRP)具有轻质高强、耐腐蚀、耐疲劳和低导热系数等优点,已经广泛用于土木工程各领域。2007 年,Buchan 等[1]总结了 FRP 约束混凝土及砌体结构抗爆性能的相关研究。2019 年,赵均海等[2]总结了 FRP 约束钢筋混凝土结构的抗爆性能的相关研究。本节将在此基础上对近几年 FRP 约束桥梁、建筑等结构的构件的抗爆性能进行补充。

Ye 等[3]设计制作了一根无 CFRP 加固的钢筋混凝土柱和三根采用不同 CFRP 加固方法(A. 两层横向 CFRP 全包裹缠绕;B. 一层横向一层纵向 CFRP 全包裹缠绕;C. 两层 CFRP 布横向分段包裹缠绕)的钢筋混凝土柱,并进行了近距离、双端起爆的现场试验。研究结果表明:①与无 CFRP 加固的墩柱相比,A、B、C 型加固柱的位移峰值分别减少 12.8%、16.4%、0.01%。②CFRP 加固可以有效地防止钢筋混凝土柱遭受非弹性变形,并使钢筋混凝土柱的破坏行为从典型的压剪破坏转变为不同程度的弯曲变形。陈锐林等[4]基于 LS-dyna 软件建立了分离式钢筋混凝土板及 CFRP 材料的数值模型,研究了 CFRP 材料在爆炸荷载下对于钢筋混凝土板的动力响应和防护机理,对比分析了 CFRP 外贴厚度、外贴形式对钢筋混凝土板的动态响应的影响,并通过现有的试验成果验证了数值模型的可靠性。研究结果表明:外贴 CFRP 条带可以明显延缓混凝土裂缝的发展趋势,延缓结构的破坏时间;CFRP 材料真正发挥其作用是在混凝土裂缝扩展的后期,并且 CFRP 外贴材料越厚,在爆炸荷载作用下,这种抵抗混凝土区域裂缝扩展的效果越明显;不同外贴形式的 CFRP 材料对钢筋混凝土板的影响具有差异性,中间加密型的防护效果最好、均匀分布型防护效果次之、边缘加密型的防护效果相对较差。Reifarth 等[5]对不同比例距离的爆炸荷载下 CFRP 和 GFRP 材料加固的两块钢筋混凝土板进行了试验,对比分析了两种材料的加固性能,并建立数值模型进行了近一步分析。结果表明:CFRP 材料加固钢筋混凝土板可以显著减小 RC 板的损伤区域,而 GFRP 并不总是能改善 RC 板的抗爆性能。Vapper 等[6]为研究 GFRP 加固钢纤维混凝土墩柱和普通钢筋混凝土墩柱的性能进行了爆炸试验和残余承载力试验。试验结果表明:采用 GFRP 材料对钢纤维混凝土柱加固后,混凝土剥落范围减小,残余强度也有明显提高;而对普通钢筋混凝土柱采用 GFRP 加固后,残余强度并未有显著提高。孔祥清等[7]基于 LS-dyna 软件,建立了钢筋混凝土(RC)梁以及芳纶纤维增强复合材料(AFRP)加固后的 RC 梁的数值模型,对比分析了爆炸荷载下 RC 梁在 AFRP 加固前后的破坏形态及跨中位移峰值。结果表明:AFRP 不仅可以改变 RC 梁在爆炸荷载下的破坏形态,还可以明显改善梁的变形程度,加固后相较于未加固梁跨中位移峰值约减小 50.7%。彭培等[8]为研究燃气爆炸下蒸压加气混凝土砌体墙的加固性能,基于 LS-dyna 软件,建立了砌体墙的数值模型,并结合试验和数值模拟对比了玄武岩纤维(BFRP)布对蒸压加气混凝土单向砌体墙的加固效果。研究表明:未加固砌体墙以弯曲破坏为主,随着墙体高度增加,破坏模式由弯曲破坏向剪切破坏转变;BFRP 布条加固可以有效提高墙体抗弯刚度和压拱效应,能显著提高墙体抗爆性能。

总的来说,有许多研究已经表明 FRP 材料加固对于提高混凝土构件的抗爆性能有着显著的效果,但是目前对于 FRP 加固的试验研究主要对单一的材料进行研究(CFRP、GFRP 研究较多),对于不同 FRP 材料加固效果的比较相对较少;对于

FRP加固的数值模拟,大部分文献对于FRP材料与混凝土的界面滑移均未被考虑,而是采用理想化的共节点加以研究;且对于FRP材料如何建立合理的与应变率相关的动态本构方程也需要进一步研究。

2　聚脲材料加固

另外,聚脲材料在防护领域也具有广阔的应用前景。聚脲材料具有强度高、韧性好、耐磨耐老化等优异性能,而且施工快捷、环保无污染。近年来,随着喷涂聚脲弹性体技术的不断发展以及桥梁、建筑等结构对新型材料的急切需求,聚脲材料用于增强桥梁、建筑等结构的抗爆能力逐渐成为国内外研究者们的关注热点。

Shi[9]对普通钢筋混凝土(RC)板、纯聚脲(PU)加固RC板、PU-WGF(纯聚脲中加入编织玻璃纤维网)加固RC板进行了现场试验,比较研究了PU涂层和PU-WGF涂层的加固性能。利用试验结果对PU-WGF钢筋混凝土板的数值模型进行了校核,并利用数值模型研究了涂层破坏模式、爆破破片分布及钢筋混凝土板的损伤程度。结果表明:WGF能提高PU涂层的承载能力、完整性和抗断裂能力,使PU涂层的破坏模式由冲切破坏变为拉伸破坏。许林峰等[10]为了研究聚脲喷涂加固砖填充墙的抗爆特性,进行了聚脲加固砖填充墙的足尺爆炸试验,分析了爆炸荷载下加固砖墙的动力响应特性和破坏模式,揭示了其失效破坏机理。结果表明:聚脲加固可大幅提升砖填充墙构件的抗爆性能,显著增加了砖填充墙构件的变形延性;根据比例爆距不同确定了聚脲加固砖墙的弯曲破坏、剪切破坏和震塌破坏三种模式。赵启明等[11]进行了纯聚脲涂覆钢筋混凝土板爆炸试验,并借助LS-dyna软件对试验结果进行分析。为了提高聚脲涂层的刚度,通过数值模拟对相同条件下聚脲钢板复合加固钢筋混凝土板抗爆性能进行了研究。最后对比分析了聚脲钢板复合加固层和纯聚脲加固层抗爆效果。结果表明:单纯增大聚脲涂覆层数或厚度对于减小跨中动态响应峰值位移作用有限;在相同加固层厚度条件下聚脲钢板复合层的抗爆减振效果优于纯聚脲加固层。Liu等[12]为了研究聚脲涂层对钢筋混凝土拱抗爆性能的影响,进行了内弧面聚脲涂层、全封闭聚脲涂层和内弧面聚脲-纤维网(FRP)复合涂层3种加固方案、8个试件的爆炸试验。并通过准静态中跨集中荷载试验,定量评价了爆炸后拱的损伤程度。结果表明:①全封闭涂层加固取得了最好的防护效果,全封闭聚脲涂层加固残余承载了比内弧面聚脲涂层加固高了39.74%。②内弧面聚脲-纤维网(FRP)复合涂层加固抗爆性能略低于内弧面聚脲涂层加固,这说明聚脲涂层抗爆防护效果可能优于FRP加固。陈潇硕等[13]为了研究聚脲及CFRP布加固地下管廊结构的抗爆性能,进行了9次爆炸试验并测量了结构表面的反射超压、结构位移和应变。结果表明:采用聚脲与CFRP布加固顶板均可提高结构的整体抗爆性能;在比例爆深较小时聚脲的加固抗爆效果优于CFRP布;比例爆深较大时,CFRP布的防护效果强于聚脲,但优势并不明显。

总的来说,许多研究表明聚脲弹性体不仅能通过其高延展性有效地抵消爆炸冲击波,也能提高结构的整体稳定性并能防止碎片飞溅造成的二次伤害。但是,目前聚脲抗爆加固多用于军用领域,而对于交通、建筑领域的研究缺乏体系性,不能准确指导桥梁、建筑等结构的抗爆加固设计。另外,建立聚脲材料在不同应变率下的本构模型及准确考虑聚脲材料与结构的粘结,对进行近一步数值分析也是至关重要的。

3　其他加固方法

Qu[14]采用数值模拟的方法,对炸药当量和位置、钢板的加固长度以及加固方法(如在T梁底部粘贴钢板、在腹板两侧粘贴钢板、在T梁顶部和底部粘贴钢板和全厚钢板)等不同参数或条件对爆破荷载下钢筋混凝土T梁动力特性的影响进行了研究。研究表明:①随着炸药当量的增加,梁的变形模式由弹塑性变形转变为拉弯变形,最终发生弯剪破坏。②随着爆炸垂直方向高度的增加,梁的破坏形式由弯曲剪切变为拉伸弯曲。③与普通钢筋混凝土T梁相比,钢板加固的钢筋混凝土T梁的裂纹萌生时间有所延迟、裂纹扩展速度也显著降低、裂纹的数量也有所减少。④在研究的各种加固方法中,提高梁抗爆性能的最佳加固方法是梁顶部和底部采用钢板加固。⑤通过比较相同爆炸情况下钢板的不同加固长度,得出钢板加固长度的最佳尺寸为80cm左右。

Yang[15]对4块(含有不同体积分数的橡胶颗

粒)钢筋橡胶混凝土板进行了不同炸药量的爆炸试验。此外建立了数值模型,并通过试验数据验证了模型的可靠性。然后利用数值模型进一步研究现场试验中的变形过程。试验结果表明:当炸药当量不高时(2.3kg 或 3.4kg),普通钢筋混凝土板仍处于弹性阶段,损伤较轻;橡胶钢筋混凝土处于塑性阶段,跨中变形较大,受拉区出现细小裂缝。而当炸药当量为 5.6kg 时,普通钢筋混凝土板与橡胶钢筋混凝土板跨中残余位移差减小,橡胶钢筋混凝土板受拉区损伤小于普通钢筋混凝土板。故在大当量爆炸荷载作用下,橡胶颗粒可以有效提高混凝土板的抗爆性能且橡胶颗粒体积替代率低于 30% 时混凝土具有较好的抗爆性能。

Wu[16]对两种类型(不同密度)的泡沫铝保护钢筋混凝土(RC)板进行了一系列的现场爆炸试验,以研究泡沫铝保护 RC 板的性能。试验共设计了 5 个试件,4 块泡沫铝保护(不同密度、不同厚度)的 RC 板和 1 块普通 RC 板。试验表明:采用泡沫铝保护 RC 板能有效减轻爆炸对混凝土板的影响。

4 结语

综上所述,从研究对象来看,目前对于桥梁、建筑等结构的各个构件的抗爆加固研究较多,而对于桥梁、建筑等整体结构,特别是桥梁整体结构的抗爆加固研究较少。另外,由于各个局部构件在爆炸荷载下的动力响应并不能真实地反应桥梁、建筑等整体结构的动力响应,所以今后对桥梁、建筑等整体结构抗爆加固的研究应该会日益增多。从研究手段来看,现阶段主要是通过试验和数值模拟的方法进行研究;对于理论研究,等效单自由度体系应用的较为广泛,但是由于其自身的局限性,目前仅适用于简单的结构体系。对于更深层、适用性更广的理论分析还有待进一步研究。从加固方法来看,目前 FRP 材料在桥梁、建筑等结构的加固和修复中已经得到了广泛应用。但是,FRP 材料制造工艺复杂、施工周期长、应用成本高,不利于大面积使用。与 FRP 材料相比,聚脲弹性体作为一种新型材料具有喷涂工艺简单、黏结能力强、施工便捷、绿色环保等优点且在桥梁、建筑等结构的局部构件抗爆加固中也取得了显著的效果,具有良好的应用前景。然而,目前聚脲弹性体较多用于军用领域,对于桥梁、建筑等结构领域的应用较少。相信以后在桥梁、建筑等结构领域,对聚脲的抗爆加固会进行更系统的研究,更广泛地应用到工程实践中。其他加固方法(钢板、橡胶、泡沫铝等)虽然也取得了比较好的效果,但与 FRP 材料和聚脲材料相比,当前所做的研究较少。

参考文献

[1] Buchan P A, Chen J F. Blast resistance of FRP composites and polymer strengthened concrete and masonry structures-A state-of-the-art review [J]. Composites, Part B. Engineering, 2007, 38 (5/6).

[2] 赵均海,董婧,张冬芳. 爆炸荷载下 FRP 约束钢筋混凝土结构动力响应研究现状[J]. 世界地震工程,2019,35(01):97-109.

[3] Hu Y, Chen L, Fang Q, et al. Study of CFRP retrofitted RC column under close-in explosion [J]. Engineering Structures, 2021, 227:111431.

[4] 陈锐林,李康,董琪,等. CFRP 加固钢筋混凝土板爆炸冲击作用下动力响应分析的数值模拟[J]. 铁道科学与工程学报,2020,17(06):1517-1527.

[5] Reifarth C, Castedo R, Santos A P, et al. Numerical and experimental study of externally reinforced RC slabs using FRPs subjected to close-in blast loads. [J]. International Journal of Impact Engineering. 2021, 156:103939.

[6] Vapper M, Lasn K. Blast protection of concrete columns with thin strips of GFRP overlay[J]. Structures, 2020, 25:491-499.

[7] 孔祥清,戚雪剑,刚建明,等. AFRP 加固钢筋混凝土梁抗爆性能数值模拟研究[J]. 玻璃钢/复合材料,2018(06):54-61.

[8] 彭培,李展,张亚栋,等. 燃气爆炸作用下蒸压加气混凝土砌体墙的加固性能[J]. 爆炸与冲击,2020,40(03):110-123.

[9] Shi S, Liao Y, Peng X, et al. Behavior of polyurea-woven glass fiber mesh composite reinforced RC slabs under contact explosion[J]. International Journal of Impact Engineering, 2019, 132:103335.

[10] 许林峰,陈力,李展,等. 聚脲加固砖填充墙抗爆性能的试验和分析方法研究[J]. 爆炸

与冲击,2021:1-13.
[11] 赵启明,石少卿,李季,等.聚脲钢板复合层加固钢筋混凝土板抗爆性能研究[J].兵器装备工程学报,2020,41(08):214-221.
[12] Liu Y,Wang P,Jin F,et al. Blast responses of polyurea-coated concrete arches[J]. Archives of Civil and Mechanical Engineering,2021,21(1).
[13] 陈潇硕,周健南,周寅智,等.聚脲和CFRP布加固地下管廊结构抗爆对比试验[J].建筑技术,2020,51(12):1511-1513.
[14] Qu Y,Liu W,Gwarzo M,et al. Parametric study of anti-explosion performance of reinforced concrete T-shaped beam strengthened with steel plates[J]. Construction and Building Materials,2017,156:692-707.
[15] Yang F,Feng W,Liu F,et al. Experimental and numerical study of rubber concrete slabs with steel reinforcement under close-in blast loading[J]. Construction and Building Materials,2019,198:423-436.
[16] Wu C,Huang L,Oehlers D J. Blast Testing of Aluminum Foam-Protected Reinforced Concrete Slabs[J]. Journal of performance of constructed facilities,2011,25(5):464-474.

型钢高强混凝土柱破坏模式及判别方法研究

孙　悦*　余金火　李天伟　王计运
(长安大学公路学院)

摘　要　型钢高强混凝土(SRHC)柱具有承载能力高、刚度大、抗震性能好等优点,但在强震作用下会发生设计预期之外的低延性(弯剪或剪切)破坏,从而导致桥梁发生局部或整体倒塌,从而带来不可估量的经济损失。为推广SRHC柱在地震区的应用,收集整理了75根SRHC试件的拟静力试验结果,总结梳理了SRHC柱主要的地震破坏模式以及受力特点,并提出了基于设计参数以及基于抗剪承载力和抗剪需求的SRHC柱破坏模式判别方法。本文提出的SRHC柱破坏模式判别方法准确度高、可靠性强。

关键词　桥梁工程　破坏模式　判别方法　型钢高强混凝土柱　抗震性能

0　引言

随着国家基础建设的迅猛发展,大跨、重载等已成为桥梁结构发展的迫切需求和趋势,桥墩、桥塔等也承受着越来越大的轴力[1]。高强混凝土也被越来越广泛应用在桥梁结构中,而随着混凝土强度的提高,呈现出越来越明显的脆性。因此为了解决高强混凝土桥墩和桥塔在地震区的高脆性以及抗震性能等问题,型钢高强混凝土柱(SRHC)由于承载能力高、刚度大、抗震性能好等优点应运而生。

近年来,地震灾害频发,如汶川(2008年)、海地(2010年)、智利(2010年)、玉树(2010年)及日本(2011年)[2]等强震,具有极强的破坏性。强震使大量桥梁的桥墩、桥塔等破坏甚至倒塌,给震区人们的生命和财产等都带来了巨大的损失。桥墩、桥塔等柱构件是桥梁主要的承重构件,也是承受地震作用的主要构件,在地震作用下,会发生超出设计预期的剪切、弯剪等低延性破坏。对于这些低延性破坏的柱,其耗能能力和延性较差,且承载力会迅速退化,因此容易使桥梁结构发生局部或者是整体倒塌,从而其使用受到限制(尤其在地震区)。为推广SRHC柱在地震区桥梁中的应用,需对其破坏模式以及破坏模式判别方法进行相关

1.基金项目:陕西省自然科学基金(2019JM-172)。

研究。

为了研究地震作用下SRHC柱的地震破坏模式、破坏模式判别方法等，本文对近年来有关SRHC柱的拟静力试验进行详细梳理，归纳出SRHC柱的破坏模式并提出对SRHC柱破坏模式的判别方法，最后对该方法目前存在的问题进行分析，以期推动SRHC柱在地震区大跨、重载桥梁中的应用。

1 地震作用下SRHC柱破坏模式

关于SRHC柱地震的破坏模式、受力影响以及其受力特性等，国内外学者[1,3-6]进行了大量的科学研究工作，从实验研究与理论分析两个方面对其有关特点展开深入研究。李俊华[4]、姜睿[3]、朱伟庆[1]等根据不同的设计参数对SRHC柱进行拟静力试验。如表1所示，他们对柱的地震破坏模式、延性和抗震特性等方面开展了细致的探究；通过实验，并比较SRHC柱的滞回曲线与受剪承载力包络线之间的关系等，将SRHC柱的地震破坏模式可归结为弯曲破坏、剪切(剪切粘结、剪切斜压)破坏、弯剪破坏三类。丧失竖向承载力是在发生剪切破坏后一瞬间出现的，是柱子发生倒塌并且破坏的主要标志。又因为柱子的倒塌破坏中的构件所承受的轴压力和循环荷载作用的历史有关联，因此若想要结构的抗倒塌能力增加，应该规避剪切破坏的现象发生在SRHC柱中。因此对SRHC柱破坏模式的判别方法研究极为重要。

SRHC柱试件设计参数设计及破坏模式 表1

实验者	试件数量	破坏方式	λ	n	箍筋			型钢	
					形式	间距	ρ_{sv}(%)	形式	ρ_{ss}(%)
朱伟庆	16	弯曲破坏	2~3	0.25~0.45	八边形复合	50~100	1.0~2.0	I10	3.58
	3	弯曲破坏	3	0.25~0.38	八边形复合	50~85	1.18~2.0	HW10	5.48
	4	弯曲破坏	3	0.25~0.45	八边形复合	50~80	1.18~2.0	+10	7.15
	1	弯曲破坏	3	0.25	矩形	40	1.70	I10	3.58
	3	弯剪破坏	3	0.25~0.38	矩形	40~85	0.8~1.7	I10	3.58
李俊华	7	弯曲破坏	2~2.5	0~0.36	矩形	90~120	0.8~1.6	I14	6.11
	8	剪切斜压破坏	1~1.5	0.36	矩形	90~120	0.8~1.6	I14	6.11
	7	剪切黏结破坏	2	0.3~0.36	矩形	90~120	0.8~1.6	I14	6.11
姜睿	3	弯曲破坏	2~2.75	0.23~0.35	矩形	44~76	2.2~3	I12	3.7
	8	弯剪破坏	2.75	0.26~0.44	矩形	76~123	0.8~2.2	I12	3.7
	7	剪切斜压破坏	1.5~2	0.29~0.57	矩形	60~123	0.8~2.2	I12	3.7
	7	剪切黏结破坏	2~2.75	0.29~0.57	矩形	83~123	0.8~1.2	I12	3.7

注：λ为柱的剪跨比，n为柱的轴压比，ρ_{sv}为箍筋体积配箍率，ρ_{ss}为型钢的含钢率。

弯曲型破坏一般出现在轴压比较小，但剪跨比相对大且配箍率较大的柱子中，荷载变形关系及主要阶段的受力状态如图1a)所示。在横向水平荷载影响下，首先许多微小的细裂缝出现在柱侧面根部；其次这些微小裂缝会逐渐向柱子的正面延伸，随着荷载增大，发展出更多的水平裂缝，柱子逐渐屈服；接着在柱根部的裂缝变多，外表面混凝土开始剥落，由于柱截面中有型钢使得水平荷载缓慢的下降；最后，位于柱子根部的大面积混凝土块剥落，纵向钢筋屈服，型钢也发生局部屈曲，此时柱子的承载能力快速下降，柱子失效。综上所述，发生弯曲破坏的柱子破坏过程较慢，并且具有较好的延性。

剪切黏结破坏主要在轴压比以及剪跨比均适中的柱中，荷载变形关系及主要阶段的受力状态如图1b)所示。先是弯曲裂缝发生于柱的根部；然后其又会发展成柱中的斜裂缝；其次，在型钢的受压翼缘外侧，产生黏结裂缝，并且其发展的过程速度很快，柱子随后屈服；最后，位于型钢翼缘外侧的混凝土保护层剥落，水平承载力迅速下降，柱子破坏。综上可知，整个破坏的过程从柱子屈服到整个破坏的过程非常快，破坏时柱子具有较低的延性且有较强的脆性。

剪切斜压破坏主要在剪跨比较小、轴压比较大的柱中发生。荷载变形关系及主要阶段的受力状态如图1b)所示。首先弯曲裂缝会发生在柱的根部,斜裂缝则出现在柱的腹部,黏结裂缝在型钢受压翼缘边缘发生;弯曲裂缝和黏结裂缝的发展进程很慢,斜裂缝发展进程很快,同时裂缝的数量也在持续地上升,裂缝宽度也持续地扩大;最后,荷载的作用将位于柱子根部与加载点之间的混凝土劈裂成很多小柱体,这一阶段中水平荷载下降快速,柱子发生破坏。整个破坏过程也是十分的迅速并且柱具有较差的延性。

弯剪破坏的柱子一般是配箍率适中或较大,同时具有较为明显的弯曲和剪切变形特征,且破坏形态介于剪切破坏与弯曲破坏之间,荷载变形关系及主要阶段的受力状态如图 1c)所示。整个破坏的过程变形能力较大,荷载下降速度相对缓慢,抗震的延性相对于剪切破坏来说较好。

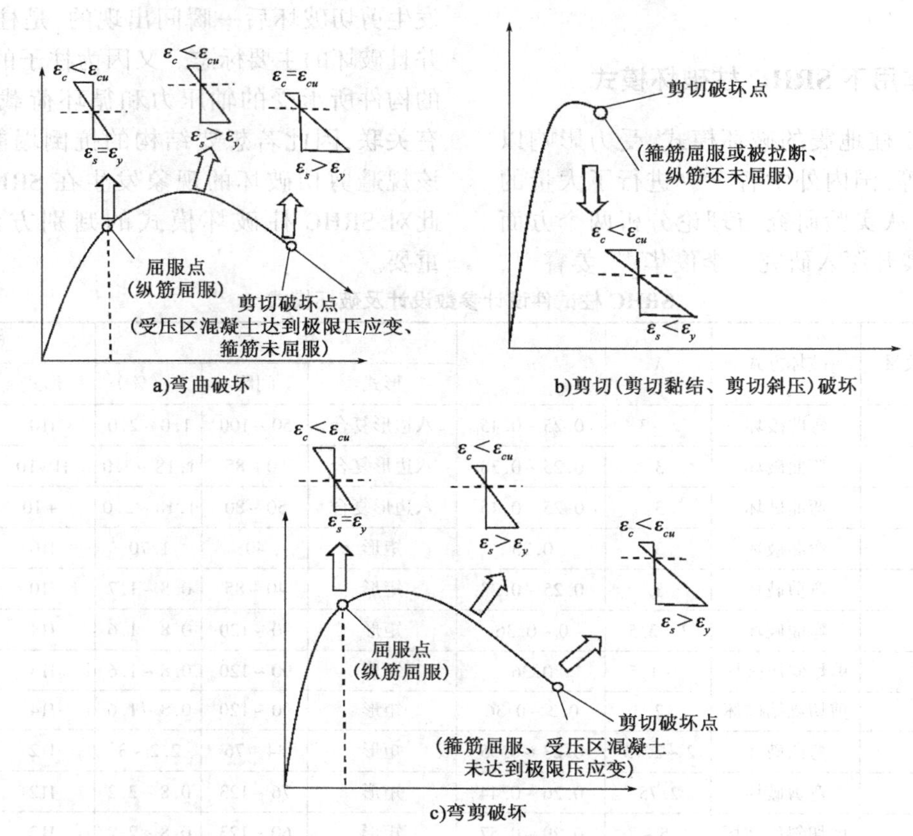

图 1　破坏模式柱受力特点

2　破坏模式判别方法

由于破坏模式不同,SRHC 柱的抗震性能也有明显的差别。为此,设计中应该保证 SRHC 柱具有足够的变形能力和承载能力。若对其可能发生的破坏模式进行判别和控制,可以避免发生弯剪和剪切等不利的破坏模式发生。

2.1　基于设计参数的判别方法

由于 SRHC 柱的破坏形态与剪跨比、轴压比、体积配箍率和含钢率等均有关系,因此,根据表 1 所示的试验数据可以得到破坏形态与但设计参数之间的关系,如图 2 和表 2 所示。

从图 2 可知,通过剪跨比 λ 和轴压比 n 两个指标能够较好的区分 SRHC 柱的破坏形态。由表 2 可知,按剪跨比 λ 与轴压比 n、体积配箍率 ρ_{sv}、配箍形式、含钢率 ρ_{ss} 对破坏形态进行划分,重叠的区段较大,分界线较模糊,使用这些参数无法较好的区分 SRHC 柱的破坏形态。因此需要结合多个参数对 SRHC 柱的破坏模式进行判别:

(1)当剪跨比较大,轴压比适中且箍筋的约束效果较好(八边形复合箍筋)、剪跨比适中,轴压比较小且配箍率较大的试件会发生弯曲破坏。

(2)当剪跨比适中,箍筋的配箍率较小且约束效果一般(矩形箍筋)时,试件会发生弯剪破坏。

(3)当剪跨比较小,轴压比较大时,试件会发生剪切(剪切黏结、剪切斜压)破坏。

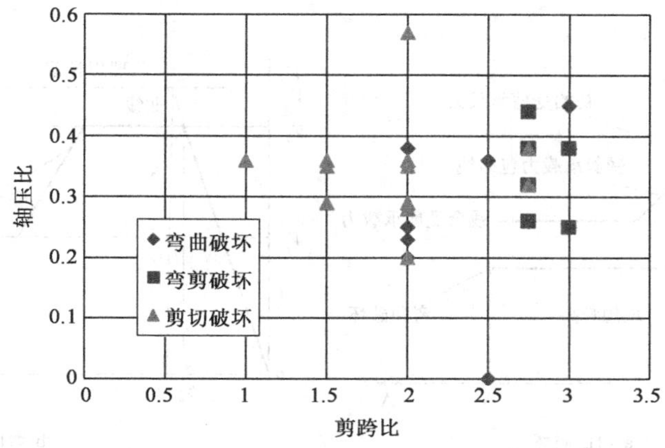

图2 破坏形态与剪跨比和轴压比的关系

破坏模式与剪跨比和轴压比、体积配箍率、含钢率之间的关系 表2

破坏状态	剪跨比 λ	轴压比 n	体积配箍率 ρ_{sv}	含钢率 ρ_{ss}
弯曲破坏	$2.5 \leqslant \lambda \leqslant 3.0$	$0 \leqslant n < 0.45$	$0.8 \leqslant \rho_{sv} \leqslant 3.0$	$3.58 \leqslant \rho_{ss} \leqslant 7.15$
弯剪破坏	$2.0 \leqslant \lambda < 2.5$	$0.25 \leqslant n < 0.45$	$0.8 \leqslant \rho_{sv} \leqslant 2.2$	$3.58 \leqslant \rho_{ss} \leqslant 3.7$
剪切破坏	$1 \leqslant \lambda < 2.0$	$0.2 \leqslant n < 0.36$	$0.8 \leqslant \rho_{sv} \leqslant 2.2$	$3.7 \leqslant \rho_{ss} \leqslant 6.11$

综上分析过程可知，采用基于参数的判别方法可以在构件设计初期，初步预测 SRHC 柱破坏模式。但此方法是基于多个参数共同作用下的判别模式，当其中某个参数发生微小改变时，无法准确的预测出相应的破坏模式的改变。

2.2 基于抗剪承载力和抗剪需求的判别方法

基于受剪承载力的指标进行柱地震破坏模式的判别是目前 RC 柱常用的方法之一[7-8]，现将此法引入 SRHC 柱破坏模式的判别方法之中，该方法是通过比较抗剪需求 V_n（按正截面抗弯承载力计算）和抗剪承载力 V_c 的大小来判断柱的破坏模式。

$$V_n = \frac{M}{a} \tag{1}$$

$$V_c = V_{c1} + V_s + V_a \tag{2}$$

式中：V_n——抗剪需求；

M——正截面抗弯承载力；

a——柱长；

V_c——抗剪承载力；

V_{c1}——混凝土抗剪承载力；

V_s——型钢抗剪承载力；

V_a——箍筋抗剪承载力。

柱发生破坏的整个进程中，当 $V_n/V_c < 1.0$ 时，柱出现弯曲破坏；若当纵筋屈服前有 $V_n/V_c \geqslant 1.0$ 时则会发生剪切（剪切黏结、剪切斜压）破坏；当纵筋屈服后有 $V_n/V_c \geqslant 1.0$ 时，柱将出现弯剪破坏。如图3所示。

图3所示的判别方法，计算简单，概念清晰，可以清楚地预测出 SRHC 柱的破坏模式。但是进行破坏模式判别时由于不同规范所采用的抗剪承载力公式的计算方法不同，所以 SRHC 柱破坏模式的判别的结果会受到影响。这是因为 SRHC 柱的抗剪承载力计算公式目前还没有形成相对统一的计算方法。此处在众多抗剪承载力模型中选取《钢筋混凝土组合机构技术规程》（JGJ—138—2001）提出的抗剪承载力计算公式。

$$V_c = \frac{0.20}{\lambda + 1.5} f_c b h_0 + f_{sv} \frac{A_{sv}}{s} h_0 + \frac{0.58}{\lambda} f_a t_w h_w + 0.07N \tag{3}$$

式中：f_c——混凝土抗压强度设计值；

b——SRHC 截面宽度；

h_0——型钢受拉翼缘和纵向受拉钢筋合力点至混凝土截面受压边缘的距离；

λ——型钢高强混凝土柱的计算剪跨比；

A_{sv}——配置在同一截面内箍筋各肢的全部截面面积；

f_{sv}——箍筋的屈服强度；

s——箍筋间距；

f_a——型钢的屈服强度；

t_w——腹板宽度；

h_w——腹板高度；

N——竖向轴力。

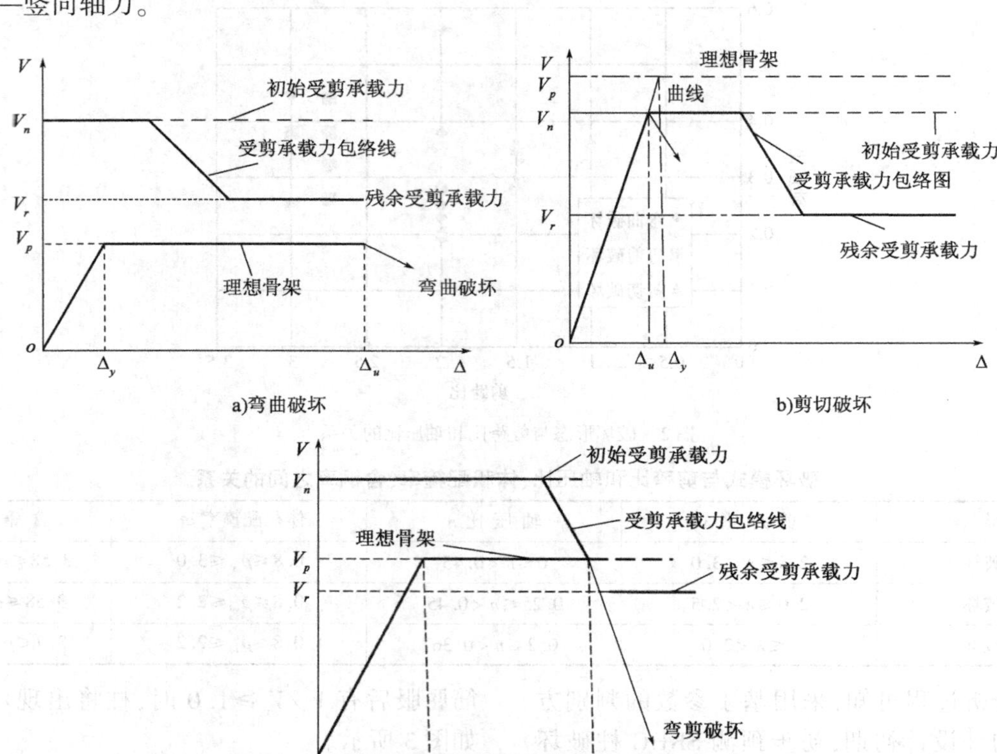

图 3　基于受剪承载力的 SRHC 柱地震破坏模式判别

使用受剪承载力的判别方法，主要是通过预测柱的抗剪承载力 V_c 与抗剪需求 V_n 之间的关系来进行破坏模式的判别。可以准确地掌握柱在地震作用下的破坏模式，提高工程人员对柱的抗震性能和破坏模式的重新认识，使得设计更加合理而不至于发生剪切破坏或弯剪破坏。

3　结语

(1)本文利用收集到的 75 根 SRHC 柱抗震性能试验数据，对现有的 SRHC 柱的破坏形态进行了总结。SRHC 柱在地震作用的影响下，主要会出现三种破坏形式，可以分为：弯曲破坏、剪切破坏和弯剪破坏，后两种破坏模式下的柱具有较差的抗震性能，在设计中应该予以控制。

(2)提出基于设计参数以及基于抗剪承载力和抗剪需求的两种判别方法。其中基于设计参数的判别方法可以较为简单的预测柱的破坏模式，但此方法是基于多个参数共同作用下的判别方法，判断结果误差较大。而基于抗剪承载力和抗剪需求的判别方法则是通过整个受荷过程中抗剪承载力与抗剪需求的变化情况而提出的，此预测方法可靠度高，准确性强。

(3)在型钢混凝土柱承受循环荷载全过程中的抗剪承载力的计算公式有待研究，需要在今后研究中予以重点关注，建立更合理的抗剪承载力退化全过程的计算公式。

参考文献

[1] 朱伟庆.型钢超高强混凝土柱受力性能的研究[D].大连：大连理工大学，2014.

[2] 贡金鑫，张勤，王雪婷.从汶川地震桥梁震害看现行国内外桥梁的抗震设计方法(一)——抗震设防标准与地震计算[J].公路交通科技，2010，27(9)：44-54.

[3] 姜睿.超高强混凝土组合柱抗震性能的试验研究[D].大连：大连理工大学，2007.

[4] 李俊华.低周反复荷载下型钢高强混凝土柱受力性能研究[D].西安：西安建筑科技大学，2005.

[5] 彭胜，许成祥，邓杰，等.基于强度退化的震损加固型钢混凝土柱抗剪承载力分析[J].防灾减灾工程学报，2019，39(1)：158-163.

[6] 白力更,刘维亚,姜维山. 反复荷载作用下型钢混凝土柱受剪承载力模型解析[J]. 建筑结构,2020,50(10):59-66.

[7] 张勤,王娜,贡金鑫. 钢筋混凝土柱地震破坏模式及考虑剪切变形的抗震性能研究进展[J]. 建筑结构学报,2017,38(8):1-13.

[8] Park HG,Choi KK,Wight JK. Strain-based shear strength model for slender beams without web reinforcement[J]. ACI Struct J 2006;103(6):783-93.

双塔自锚式悬索桥施工控制研究

曾科洋 武芳文* 何岚清 左 剑 陈中村

(长安大学公路学院)

摘 要 依托某双塔单跨自锚式悬索桥项目,在施工过程对主缆、主塔、主梁和吊索进行位移和应力监测,使用 MIDAS/CIVIL 建立有限元分析模型;模型计算结果表明吊索的变形与应力均在合理范围内。根据现场实测结果,空缆线形在高程方向和里程方向实测值与理论值之间的偏差较小;在吊杆张拉阶段,主塔根部应力最大偏差值为 6.59%;主梁关键控制截面实测应力值与理论计算值基本相等,应力最大值为 -58.69Mpa,应力最大偏差值为 5.3%。结果表明,各工况下实测值与理论值基本趋势一致,均处于安全状态,且能够满足正常运营阶段要求。

关键词 自锚式悬索桥 施工控制 空缆线形 主塔应力 主梁应力

0 引言

自锚式悬索桥具有结构造型美观、经济性好、对地形条件适应性强等优点[1],逐渐成为城市景观桥梁的有力竞争者。该桥是一种将主缆固定在加劲梁末端的自平衡系统,比之地锚式悬索桥,受力更为复杂[2-4],主缆锚固在加劲梁两端,使加劲梁承受较大的轴向力。当按照特定张拉顺序张拉时,吊索力缺失是随机的[5],吊索在体系转换过程中需要多次张拉[6],吊索受力对最终成桥状态有极其重要影响,施工阶段需要严格控制。桥塔作为传力系统的关键部分,其结构和传力路径复杂[7],因此桥塔施工中的应力需要重点关注。因而有必要对自锚式悬索桥主缆、主梁、吊索和桥塔的应力和位移变化规律进行数值模拟和现场测量等研究。

本文以某座主跨 150m 的自锚式悬索桥为工程背景,对施工过程的关键部位进行监控,研究了主缆线形、主塔应力、主梁控制截面应力的理论值与实测值的变化规律,为此类大桥的施工控制提供参考。

1 工程概况

本文研究的自锚式悬索桥全长 294m,桥跨布置为(32 + 40 + 150 + 40 + 32)m 双塔自锚式悬索桥,主跨 150m,矢跨比为 1/5.3,全桥共设两根主缆,横桥向的中心间距为 28.5m。吊索索距为 5 米。主塔墩上设有竖向支座、约束梁体横向位移的支座及纵向阻尼器。主桥主跨 150m 采用钢混叠合梁,桥宽 29.5m,梁高 3.0m,双向 4 车道,桥面布置为 2m 拉索区 +4.5m 人行非机动车道 +0.5m 分隔带 +15m 车行道 +0.5m 分隔带 +4.5m 人行非机动车道 +2m 拉索区;主桥边跨 32m、40m 采用预应力混凝土连续箱梁,桥宽 25.5m ~ 32.2m(主缆锚固区),梁高 3.0m,双向 4 车道,桥面布置为 4.5m 人行非机动车道 +0.5m 分隔带 +15m 车行道 +0.5m 分隔带 +4.5m 人行非机动车道。桥梁基础采用承台配钻孔灌注桩。大桥总体布置图见图 1。

2 有限元模型分析

2.1 有限元模型

采用 MIDAS CIVIL 2020 桥梁结构专用分析软件进行该桥的施工过程分析。建模时,主梁和桥塔采用梁单元模拟,主梁叠合梁共分为 56 个单元,边跨混凝土梁共分为 82 个单元,主塔共分为

50个单元。缆索系统采用索单元模拟,主缆共分为92个单元,吊杆共分为56个单元。主缆锚固段和加劲梁之间的锚固使用刚性连接来模拟,吊杆下节点和加劲梁预埋钢套管处使用共节点来模拟,桥塔和大地固结。桥梁整体模型见图2。

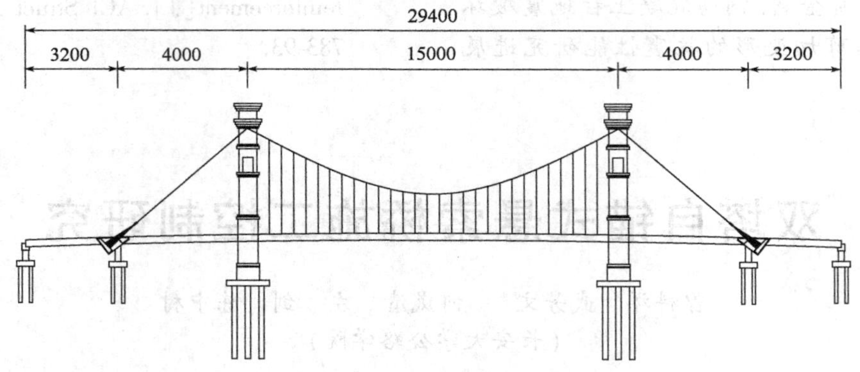

图1　大桥总体布置图(尺寸单位:cm)

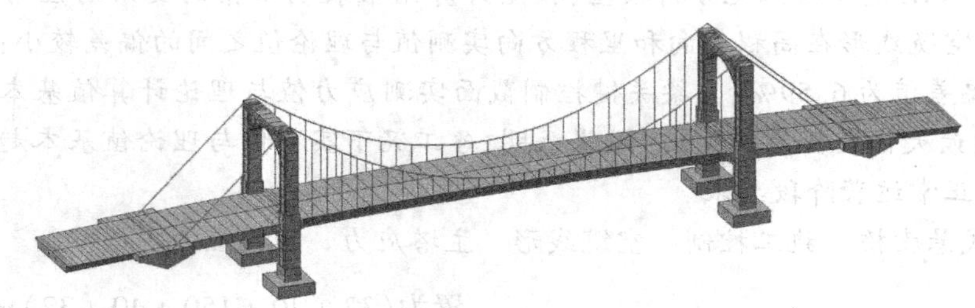

图2　全桥有限元模型

2.2　模型分析结果

吊索为柔性构件,一旦发生破坏,不仅更换困难,而且将会对桥梁结构受力产生巨大的不利影响,甚至导致桥梁垮塌,因而在有限元模型分析阶段需要重点关注其受力情况及其安全性。

由于该桥梁的吊索为对称结构,则选取左幅吊索的一半进行分析,吊索布置见图3。经有限元模型计算得到,吊索在成桥状态和运营阶段的吊索力及安全系数如下表1所示(轴力以受拉为正),安全系数值等于承载能力除以运营阶段最大轴力。根据该表得出,吊索在运营阶段安全系数最小为3.71,满足规范不小于2.5的要求。

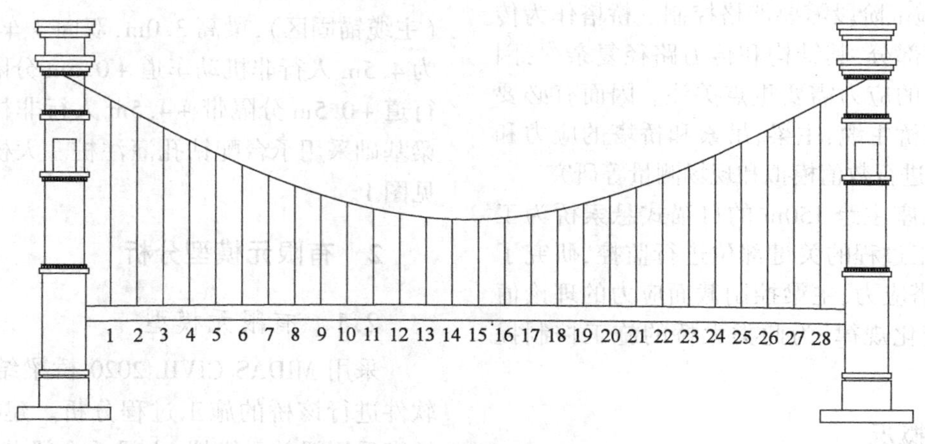

图3　吊索编号图

吊索内力计算结果

表1

吊索编号	成桥轴力(kN)	运营阶段最大轴力(kN)	承载能力(kN)	安全系数
D01	824.0	923.4	4164	4.51
D01	831.9	945.4	3574	3.78
D03	832.2	948.5	3574	3.77
D04	830.3	949.8	3574	3.76
D05	829.2	951.6	3574	3.76
D06	829.9	953.4	3574	3.75
D07	829.3	955.0	3574	3.74
D08	828.7	956.2	3574	3.74
D09	829.8	957.3	3574	3.73
D10	829.4	958.1	3574	3.73
D11	829.1	958.6	3574	3.73
D12	828.9	959.0	3574	3.73
D13	825.5	955.5	3574	3.74
D14	832.2	963.3	3574	3.71

3 施工监测方案

3.1 主缆线形监测

采用高精度莱卡全站仪对主缆线形进行观测。在实际施工过程中,主缆会产生较大的变形,为使棱镜与观测点不产生偏移,使用索箍来固定棱镜。左幅为40个测点,由于左、右幅对称设计,则主缆测点共布置80个点,具体布置见图4。

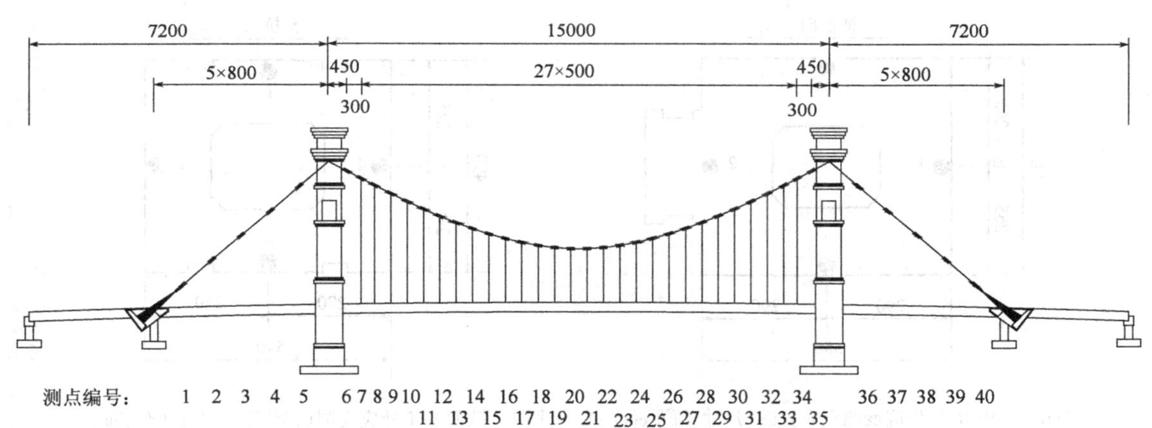

图4 主缆线形测点布置图(尺寸单位:cm)

3.2 主塔应力监测

吊索张拉之后,会使主缆中的拉力增大,致使主塔受到横向的力,使主塔产生附加应力,其最大应力往往分布在主塔的根部位置,所以主塔应力截面主要选择在主塔的根部,尤其是一些变截面位置,具体布置见图5。在不同的控制截面,截面的形式和应力的分布规律也是不相同的,所以在不同的截面,应变计的测点位置布置方式也不相同。在不同截面应变测点布置见图6、图7。

3.3 主梁应变监测

为了保证整个桥梁施工过程的安全并考察主梁内力状态的变化,在主梁的控制段嵌入测试元件,各测点的应力数据随主梁的施工分阶段采集。本文对采集的各施工阶段的应力数据进行分析计算,对施工阶段的异常应力提出应力预警。主梁应变测试断面、测点布置见图8和图9。为了减少温度引起的误差,主梁应变监测应在清晨或深夜开展。

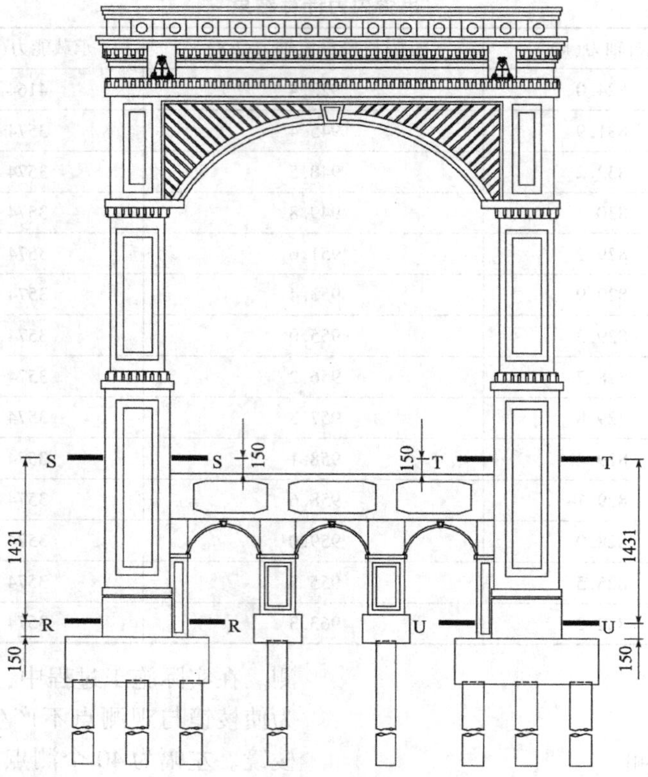

图5　主塔应力截面选取示意图(尺寸单位:cm)

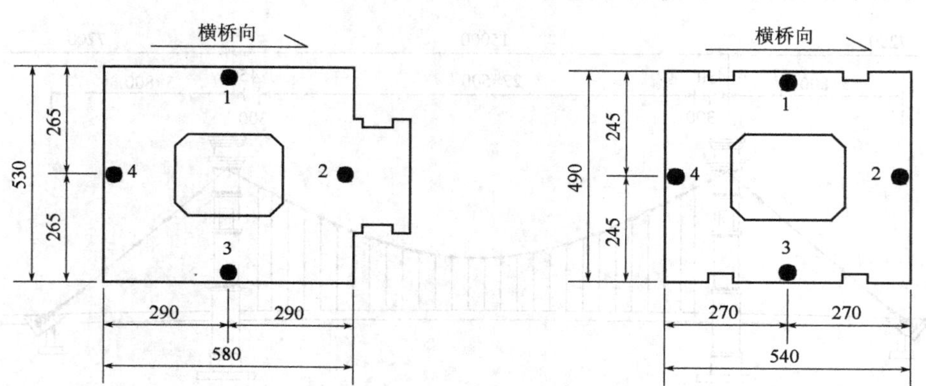

图6　截面R、U处应变测点布置图(尺寸单位:cm)　图7　截面S、T处应变测点布置图(尺寸单位:cm)

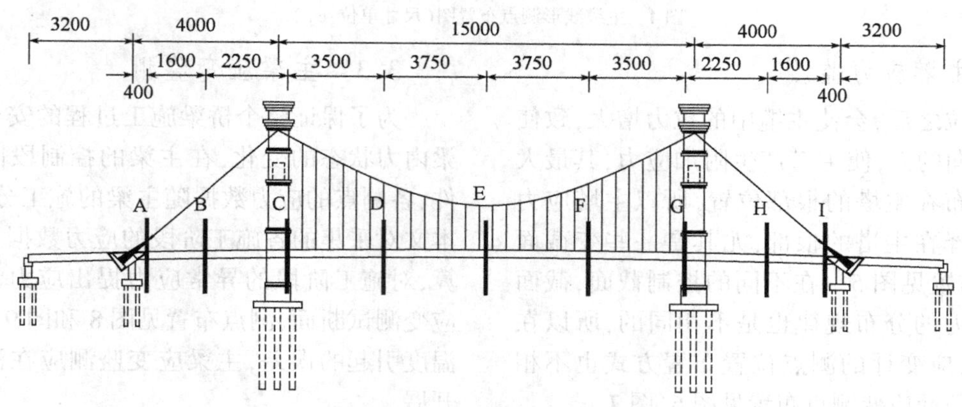

图8　主梁应力控制截面选取图(尺寸单位:cm)

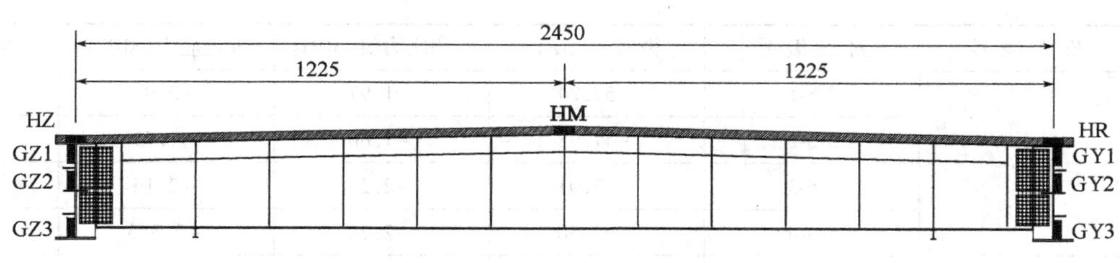

图9 主梁控制断面应变测点布置图(尺寸单位:cm)

注:应变传感器沿纵桥向布置。

4 监测结果及分析

4.1 主缆线形监测结果

本文取空缆状态高程和里程进行主缆线形分析,将实测值与理论值进行相减,得到两者的差值,结果见图10、图11。从图中可以得到:左幅空缆线形的实测数据与理论空缆线形数据在高程方向最大偏差为0.0048m,出现在36号索夹位置,里程方向最大偏差为0.006m,出现在6号索夹位置;右幅空缆线形与理论空缆线形数据在高程方向最大偏差为0.00475m,出现在36号索夹位置,在里程方向最大偏差为0.0056m,出现在6号索夹位置。因此在主缆施工期间,空缆线形符合施工控制的要求。

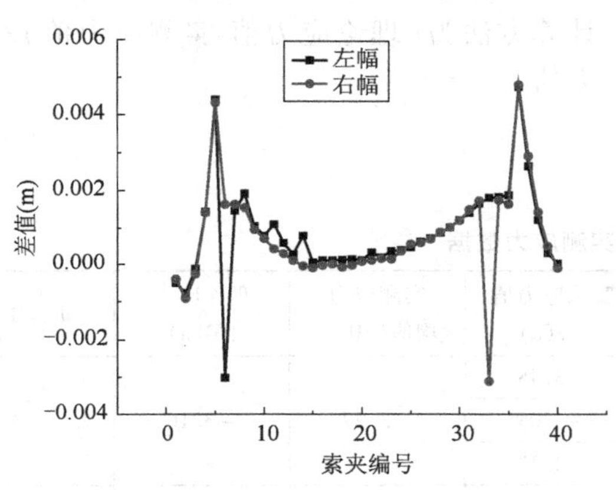

图10 空缆状态高程误差分布图

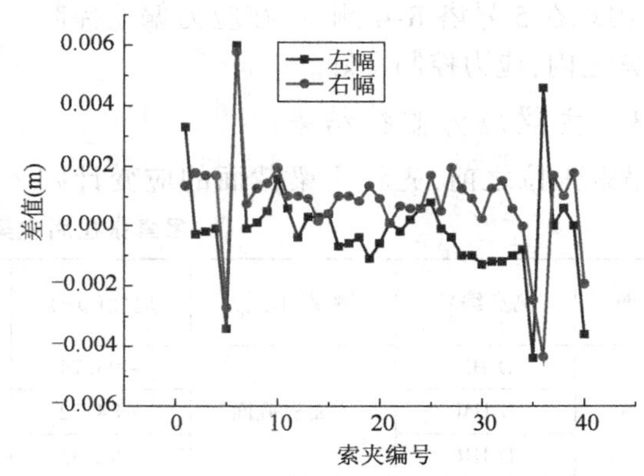

图11 空缆状态里程误差分布图

4.2 主塔应力监测结果

体系转换之前,先将各应变计的读数归零,然后在体系转换完成后,可以读出个应变测点在体系转换过程中产生的应变值,再根据混凝土的本构关系,计算得出混凝土各测点在体系转换过程中产生的应力值。由于5号塔和6号塔对称,选取5号塔进行分析,各控制截面测点的应力值如下表2所示。

五号塔应力数据表 表2

塔号	截面编号	测点编号	微应变(με)	实测应力值(MPa)	理论应力(MPa)	应力偏差
5号塔	5-R	5-R-1	-54.18	-1.87	-1.94	3.61%
		5-R-2	-47.15	-1.63	-1.645	0.91%
		5-R-3	-48.26	-1.67	-1.76	5.11%
		5-R-4	-57.65	-1.99	-2.165	8.08%
	5-U	5-U-1	-53.37	-1.84	-1.91	3.66%
		5-U-2	-57.17	-1.97	-1.85	-6.49%
		5-U-3	-60.93	-2.10	-2.205	4.76%
		5-U-4	-55.92	-1.93	-1.92	-0.52%

续上表

塔　号	截面编号	测点编号	微应变(με)	实测应力值(MPa)	理论应力(MPa)	应力偏差
5 号塔	5-S	5-S-1	-57.24	-1.97	-2.07	4.83%
		5-S-2	-47.98	-1.66	-1.72	3.49%
		5-S-3	-63.91	-2.20	-2.16	-1.85%
		5-S-4	-64.30	-2.22	-2.385	6.92%
	5-T	5-T-1	-62.27	-2.15	-2.16	0.46%
		5-T-2	-48.50	-1.67	-1.725	3.19%
		5-T-3	-84.26	-2.91	-2.73	-6.59%
		5-T-4	-68.82	-2.37	-2.245	-5.57%

由以上的数据表可以看出,最大实测应力出现在 5 号塔的 T-3 测点,应力达到了 -2.91MPa,与理论应力 -2.73MPa 相差了 6.59%,在应力误差控制范围 10% 之内。最小应力出现在 5 号塔 R-2 截面,只有 -1.63MPa,应力偏差只有 0.91%;最大的应力实测值与理论值偏差为 8.08%,出现在 5 号塔 R-4 测点,在应力偏差控制范围 10% 之内,应力控制良好。

4.3　主梁应力监控结果

在吊索张拉之前,先将主梁截面的应变计归零,在吊索张拉之后即可测出在张拉过后主梁截面各测点位置处应力的大小,根据应变计所测得的应变的大小和混凝土钢材的本构关系可以计算出主梁各测点位置出的应力大小,应力如表 3 所示。由于篇幅有限,选取截面 D、截面 E 和截面 F 处的应力情况进行分析,应力偏差值计算方法为(理论应力值-实测应力值)/理论应力值。

吊索张拉后主梁实测应力数据　　表 3

截　面	测点编号	测点位置	应变(με)	实测应力值(MPa)	实测应力均值(MPa)	理论应力(MPa)	应力偏差
D	D-HZ	桥面板截面	-95.74	-3.45	-3.27	-3.16	-3.5%
	D-HM		-84.72	-3.05			
	D-HR		-92.35	-3.32			
	D-GZ1	钢梁截面上缘	-74.25	-15.30	-14.73	-15.42	4.4%
	D-GY1		-68.78	-14.17			
	D-GZ3	钢梁截面下缘	-122.86	-25.31	-26.03	-27.40	5.0%
	D-GY3		-129.84	-26.75			
E	E-HZ	桥面板截面	-68.49	-2.47	-2.47	-2.58	4.1%
	E-HM		-65.51	-2.36			
	E-HR		-71.47	-2.57			
	E-GZ1	钢梁截面上缘	-81.84	-16.86	-15.54	-15.10	-2.9%
	E-GY1		-69.03	-14.22			
	E-GZ3	钢梁截面下缘	-269.06	-55.43	-58.69	-56.52	-3.8%
	E-GY3		-300.72	-61.95			
F	F-HZ	桥面板截面	-81.33	-2.93	-2.86	-2.96	3.2%
	F-HM		-78.79	-2.84			
	F-HR		-77.94	-2.81			
	F-GZ1	钢梁截面上缘	-68.00	-14.01	-14.49	-15.30	5.3%
	F-GY1		-72.68	-14.97			
	F-GZ3	钢梁截面下缘	-134.03	-27.61	-28.33	-28.55	0.8%
	F-GY3		-141.01	-29.05			

根据上表实测应力数据,可知最大应力出现在E截面的钢梁下边缘,应力达到了-58.69MPa,与理论值-56.52MPa相差了3.8%,在应力控制范围10%之内,最大应力偏差在控制截面F的截面上缘,实测应力与理论应力分别为-14.49MPa和-15.30MPa,相差5.3%,在应力偏差控制范围10%之内,应力控制良好。

5 结语

本文以某双塔单跨自锚式悬索桥为工程背景,采用MIDAS CIVIL有限元模型和施工过程实测数据相结合的方法,对主缆、主塔、吊索、主梁的位移和应力的变化规律进行分析,得出结论如下:

(1)空缆阶段,左幅和右幅在高程方向的最大偏差均出现在36号索夹位置,分别为0.048m和0.0475m,左幅和右幅在里程方向的最大偏差均出现在6号索夹位置,分别为0.06m和0.056m,故实测线形与设计线形符合良好。成桥阶段及运营阶段,主缆轴力的安全系数最小为3.02,满足规范不小于2.5的要求,处于安全状态。

(2)主塔在吊索张拉阶段结束状态,其腰部及根部截面的实测应力值与理论应力值的趋势基本一致,应力差值较小,最大偏差值为6.59%,满足规范≤10%的要求。

(3)张拉结束状态,主梁关键控制截面实测应力的最大值出现在E截面的钢梁下边缘,应力为-58.69MPa,在合理的应力控制范围内。最大应力偏差出现在控制截面F的下缘,相差5.3%,在规范的偏差控制范围≤10%内,结构始终处于安全可控状态。

(4)本桥的施工控制合理、结构安全、线形比较顺畅,满足实际运营阶段的要求。

(5)建议对结构应力和线形进行长期监测,及时发现病害,并采取相应维修措施,降低运营阶段综合维护成本,确保该桥结构和行驶安全。

参考文献

[1] 张晨.多塔自锚式悬索桥体系转换分析研究[D].西安:长安大学,2021.

[2] 王春江,戴建国,臧瑜,等.自锚式钢箱梁悬索桥静力稳定性分析[J].桥梁建设,2019,49(2):47-51.

[3] 武芳文,罗建飞,郑伟,等.基于稳健回归法的自锚式悬索桥荷载效率系数优化[J].长安大学学报(自然科学版),2020,40(02):74-82.

[4] 王通.基于稳健回归分析法的自锚式悬索桥荷载试验研究[D].西安:长安大学,2018.

[5] 蒋俊秋,刘祥宇,陈桂成.自锚式悬索桥吊索力缺失分析[J].中外公路,2020,40(1):136-143.

[6] 端茂军,李建慧,索小灿,等.混凝土自锚式悬索桥鞍座的精细化模拟方法[J].南京工业大学学报:自然科学版,2016,38(6):112-115+123.

[7] 刘亚明,伍星,杨鹏.斜塔自锚式悬索桥施工监控[J].公路,2021,66(08):220-225.

[8] 中华人民共和国交通运输部.公路桥涵施工技术规范:JTG/T 3650—2020[S].北京:人民交通出版社股份有限公司,2020.

自锚式悬索桥施工控制多因素敏感性分析

曾科洋 武芳文* 何岚清 樊 州 买少轩

(长安大学公路学院)

摘 要 研究自锚式悬索桥施工控制各参数敏感性,便于在施工过程中对关键参数进行重点控制。以某双塔三跨自锚式悬索桥为例,运用桥梁结构专用软件MIDA CIVIL建立有限元模型,详述吊杆张拉过程,分析了主缆弹性模量、吊杆弹性模量和加劲梁容重对成桥状态下主梁线形和主缆线形的敏感性。通过正交试验设计对该三个参数进行了极差分析,确定各参数敏感度大小。结果表明:主缆弹性模量和加劲梁容重的变化对主缆线形和主梁线形有较大的影响,需重点控制。

关键词　桥梁工程　施工控制　敏感性分析　自锚式悬索桥　正交设计　极差分析

0　引言

自锚式悬索桥凭借造型优美、经济性能好等优点已经成为城市景观桥梁极具竞争力的桥型之一[1]。但在施工过程中,各种材料特性往往无法进行精准控制[2],不可避免地出现细微偏差,使得模型的理论值与现场的实际值存在误差。材料特性的偏差会对结构状态产生影响,敏感性分析能够对各参数进行分析,得出各参数的影响程度,从而确定关键参数[3]。国内外学者在进行各参数敏感性分析时,大多数学者采用单因素试验法[4-6],此类方法操作简便,但是须进行大量的试验。因此,本文推荐使用正交试验设计法[7],当试验因素类别较多时,不仅可以大幅度减少试验次数,而且能够较好的得到试验因素与控制指标之间的敏感性。

本文以某座双塔三跨自锚式悬索桥为工程背景,进行施工阶段多因素敏感性分析。首先确定影响因素及试验水平,运用正交设计试验法进行方案设计;其次采取极差分析,明确各因素对成桥状态桥面线形和主缆线形的影响程度,以便在施工过程中对关键参数进行重点控制。

1　工程概况

本文研究的自锚式悬索桥全长 330m,跨径组合为 30m + 60m + 150m + 60m + 30m,主跨 150m,中跨矢跨比 1/5.5,全桥共两根主缆,横桥向间距 28.5m。全桥共 92 根吊杆,桥梁立面线型为以主桥主跨中心为竖曲线交点,东、西两侧均设置 1.15% 的纵坡,竖曲线半径为 5500m,平面线型为直线。悬索桥主梁采用混合梁,其中 30m 边跨采用预应力混凝土箱梁结构,钢混结合段位于 60m 跨范围内,主梁悬吊部分钢梁全长 270m,钢混结合梁主梁长 248.5m,结合段长 2 × 2.75m,其余部分为锚跨结构。悬索桥两主缆中心距为 28.5m,吊索索距为 5m。主塔墩上设有竖向支座、约束梁体横向位移的支座及纵向阻尼器。桥梁总体布置图如图 1 所示。

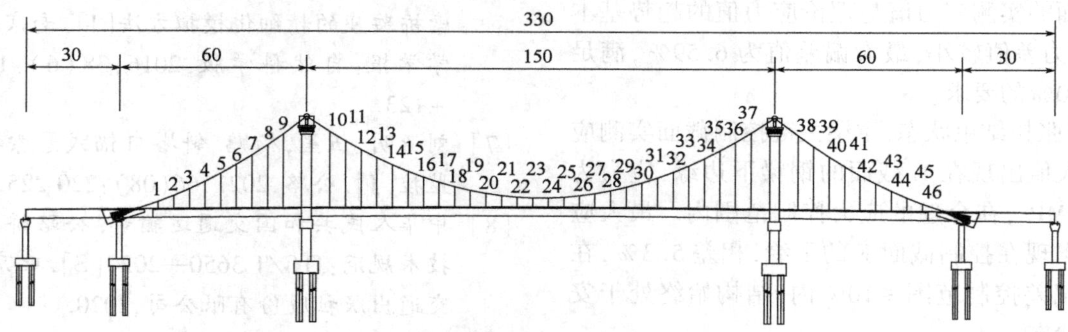

图 1　桥梁总体布置图(尺寸单位:m)

2　有限元模型

2.1　模型建立

本桥采用桥梁结构专用有限元软件 MIDAS CIVIL 进行该桥的施工过程分析。主梁叠合梁、边跨混凝土梁和主塔均采用空间梁单元模拟,缆索系统采用索单元模拟,主缆锚固段和加劲梁之间的锚固使用刚性连接来模拟,吊杆下节点和加劲梁预埋钢套管处使用共节点来模拟,桥塔和大地固结。桥梁有限元模型如图 2 所示。

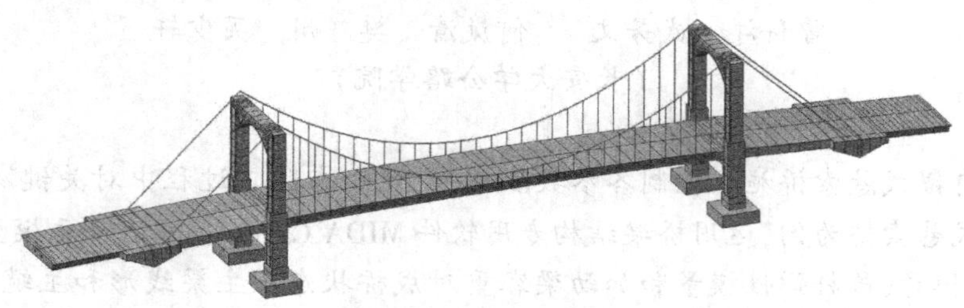

图 2　桥梁有限元模型图

2.2 吊杆张拉阶段划分

该桥左右对称，选取左边一半为分析对象。先从主塔开始向两侧进行张拉，以初步固定主缆形状形成全桥的稳定受力状态，然后将鞍座向跨中方向顶推一定距离，然后从中跨跨中开始，向主塔方向张拉安装、张拉吊索，直至全部吊索张拉完备，张拉过程如表1所示。其间各作业面最多有2对吊索需要临时锚固，每对吊索最多张拉2次。

吊杆张拉阶段划分 表1

步骤	施工内容
1	主缆施工，索鞍向边跨侧预偏27cm
2	张拉安装9、10号吊索至设计位置
3	张拉安装8、11号吊索至设计位置
4	张拉安装7、12号吊索至设计位置
5	鞍座顶推12cm
6	张拉安装6、13号吊索至设计位置
7	张拉安装23号吊索至设计位置
8	鞍座顶推8cm
9	张拉安装22号吊索至设计位置
10	张拉安装21号吊索至设计位置
11	鞍座顶推7cm
12	张拉20号吊索至1100kN
13	张拉19号吊索至1300kN、张拉安装20号吊索至设计位置
14	张拉1、18号吊索至1600kN、张拉安装19号吊索至设计位置
15	张拉2、17号吊索至1600kN、张拉安装1、18号吊索至设计位置
16	张拉3、16号吊索至1300kN、张拉安装2、17号吊索至设计位置
17	张拉4、15号吊索至1000kN、张拉安装3、16号吊索至设计位置
18	张拉安装5、14号吊索至设计位置、张拉安装4、15号吊索至设计位置
19	拆除临时猫道、临时支墩后，进行主缆缠丝、桥面铺装
20	完成体系转换

3 正交设计法

正交试验设计法[8]是指研究多因素多水平的一种试验设计方法。根据其正交性从全面试验中选取一部分有代表性的数据来进行试验，该数据拥有“均匀分散、齐整可比”的特点。例如做一个三因素三水平的实验，按照全面实验的要求，须进行实验有$3^3=27$种。如果按照$L_9(3^3)$正交表安排实验，只需做9次实验，显然大幅度减少了工作量，是一种高效率、快速、经济的实验设计方法。

对正交试验设计结果进行分析，经常采用极差分析。它是考虑某个因素时，认为其他因素对结果的影响是均衡的，从而认为，该因素各水平的差异是由于该因素本身引起的。其包含计算与判断两个部分，计算公式如下所示：

$$K_{jm}=\sum_{l=1}^{n}Y_{jml} \tag{1}$$

$$R_j=\max(K_{j1},K_{j2},\cdots,K_{jm})-\min(K_{j1},K_{j2},\cdots,K_{jm}) \tag{2}$$

式中：K_{jm}——第j列因素在第m水平下对应的控制指标值；

Y_{jml}——第j列因素在第m水平下第l所对应的控制指标值；

n——第j列因素在第m水平下的总次数；

R_j——极差。

R_j反映的是第j列因素水平发生变动时，控制指标产生的变动幅度。R_j越大，说明该因素对控制指标的影响越大，则该因素也就越重要。因此，依据R_j的大小，可判断出各因素敏感性的主次。

3.1　参数选取

对桥梁材料特性进行敏感性分析，首先应明确参数类别。通过查阅文献，选择主缆弹性模量、吊杆弹性模量和加劲梁容重三个因素作为敏感性分析的对象。

在自锚式悬索桥施工控制中，成桥状态主缆线形对全桥受力性能有较大的影响，桥面线形对行车的舒适度有重要的影响，两个均需严格控制。因此本文选择成桥状态主梁跨中点的竖向变形值和主缆跨中点的竖向变形值作为控制指标进行敏感性分析。

根据工程实际情况，将设计参数值作为基准值，在施工过程中各参数特性值出现的偏差程度很小，因而范围取基准值的98%～102%，如表2所示。本次试验因素为3个参数，水平数一般为因素数的1倍，选取为3，则共需进行9次试验。

各因素取值范围　　表2

主缆弹性模量(GPa)	吊杆弹性模量(GPa)	叠合梁容重(kN/m⁻³)
198.00～202.00	198.00～202.00	103.58～107.81

3.2　正交表

正交表的构成是正交实验设计的核心，该表通用符号一般为$L_n(q^s)$，其中，L为正交表；n为试验总次数；q为水平数；s为最多选取的因素数。通过查阅正交表能够得到三因素三水平对应的设计表为$L_9(3^3)$，具体组合方案如表3所示。

试验方案设计　　表3

试验编号	主缆弹性模量E_1(GPa)	吊杆弹性模量E_2(GPa)	加劲梁容重S_1(kN/m⁻³)
1	196.00	196.00	103.58
2	196.00	200.00	105.70
3	196.00	204.00	107.81
4	200.00	196.00	105.70
5	200.00	200.00	107.81
6	200.00	204.00	103.58
7	204.00	196.00	107.81
8	204.00	200.00	103.58
9	204.00	204.00	105.70

4　敏感性分析

4.1　变形值计算

根据正交试验法设计的方案，计算不同水平下成桥状态桥面跨中点和主缆跨中点的竖向变形值。其中成桥状态以完成二期铺装为准，变形值以初始标高为基准。采用桥梁结构专用软件MIDAS CIVIL进行计算，结果如表4所示。

变形值计算结果　　表4

试验编号	桥面变形值h_1(mm)	主缆变形值h_2(mm)
1	65.42	64.98
2	77.90	77.50
3	90.29	89.92
4	63.63	63.06
5	75.82	75.28
6	47.61	47.53
7	61.91	61.20

续上表

试验编号	桥面变形值 h_1(mm)	主缆变形值 h_2(mm)
8	33.21	32.98
9	46.07	45.86

4.2 极差分析

对正交试验结果进行极差分析，以桥面竖向变形值和主缆竖向变形值为控制指标的各参数极差分析结果如表5和表6所示。

h_1 极差分析结果　表5

差数 D(mm)	E_1	E_2	S_1
K_{j1}	233.61	190.96	146.24
K_{j2}	187.06	186.93	187.60
K_{j3}	141.19	183.97	228.02
R_j	92.42	6.98	81.78

h_2 极差分析结果　表6

差数 D(mm)	E_1	E_2	S_1
K_{j1}	232.41	189.25	145.49
K_{j2}	185.87	185.77	186.42
K_{j3}	140.04	183.30	226.41
R_j	92.37	5.94	80.92

对极差分析结果进行分析，可以得到：

(1)以成桥状态下主梁线形为控制指标进行极差分析，显然有各参数极差值的大小为：$E_1 > S_1 > E_2$，且 E_1 和 S_1 的极差值均超过80，远大于 E_2 的极差值。因而主缆弹性模量与主梁容重的变化对主梁线形影响较大，吊杆弹性模量对其敏感性较小。

(2)以成桥状态下主缆线形为控制指标进行极差分析，显然有各参数极差值的大小为：$E_1 > S_1 > E_2$，且 E_1 和 S_1 的极差值均超过80，远大于 E_2 的极差值。因而主缆弹性模量和主梁容重的变化对主缆线形影响较大，吊杆弹性模量对其敏感性较小。

5 结语

本文对某座双塔三跨自锚式悬索桥的三个材料特性参数：主缆弹性模量、吊杆弹性模量和加劲梁容重，进行了多因素敏感性分析，研究各参数变化对主梁线形和主缆线形的影响，得到结论如下：

(1)采用正交试验设计法对桥梁静力特性进行多因素敏感性分析，超越了常规单因素敏感性分析的局限。

(2)在成桥状态主梁线形分析中，主缆弹性模量和加劲梁容重的敏感性较强；在成桥状态主缆线形分析中，主缆弹性模量和加劲梁容重的敏感性较强。因此，在成桥状态下无论对主梁线形还是主缆线形，主缆弹性模量和加劲梁容重的敏感性均较强，故在施工过程中需要密切关注主缆弹性模量和加劲梁容重的参数变化。

(3)在施工监控中，需要重视对主缆弹性模量和加劲梁容重的监测，并根据实测数据及时对有限元模型进行调整。

参考文献

[1] 段向虎. 自锚式悬索桥发展现状与施工技术创新[J]. 铁道建筑,2018,58(11):32-37.

[2] 路韡. 自锚式悬索桥体系转换过程的精细控制研究与参数敏感性分析[D]. 兰州:兰州交通大学,2021.

[3] 王雨威,殷永高,任伟新. 变截面梁与自锚式悬索组合体系桥梁参数分析[J]. 中外公路,2020,(05):54-57.

[4] 朱德华,王立彬,李建慧. 自锚式悬索桥结构设计参数敏感性分析[J]. 林业工程学报,2018,3(01):128-134.

[5] 武芳文,罗建飞,郑伟,等. 基于稳健回归法的自锚式悬索桥荷载效率系数优化[J]. 长安大学学报(自然科学版),2020,40(02):74-82.

[6] 王通. 基于稳健回归分析法的自锚式悬索桥荷载试验研究[D]. 西安:长安大学,2018.

[7] 钟凯琪,肖旸,芦星,等. 煤火热能TPCT提取正交试验设计与极差分析[J]. 中国安全科学学报,2021,31(09):135-141.

[8] 王廷剑,张静静,王黎钦,等. 基于正交试验法的三点接触球轴承结构参数优化设计[J]. 轴承,2020(12):12-15.

多因素影响下简支梁桥冲击系数研究

王志伟* 赵 洋

(长安大学公路学院)

摘 要 为模拟实际状况下车-桥耦合振动响应,得到准确的冲击系数计算结果。采用5轴15自由度空间车辆模型,以3种跨径简支T梁桥与简支箱梁桥为研究对象,建立车-桥耦合振动方程,基于模态叠加原理,使用MIDAS软件建立空间梁格模型获得桥梁模态信息,使用Matlab软件模拟桥梁不平整度信息并计算弯矩冲击系数与挠度冲击系数。针对所得结果进行多参数分析,首先在不同路面不平整度下考虑模态阶数对计算结果的贡献度,其次分析了路面不平整度、车辆速度、桥梁跨径等多参数对冲击系数计算结果的影响,最后对比得到了路面不平整度、车辆速度对于弯矩冲击系数与挠度冲击系数比值的影响规律。分析结果表明:相比于挠度冲击系数,弯矩冲击系数更易受高阶模态影响;路面不平整度对冲击系数计算结果影响显著,车速与桥梁跨径会对结果形成综合影响;在特殊工况下,存在弯矩冲击系数大于挠度冲击系数的情况,此时应用规范进行计算偏不安全,车辆速度对二者比值没有显著影响。研究结果可为简支梁桥动力分析提供参考。

关键词 桥梁工程 冲击系数 数值仿真 简支梁桥

0 引言

随着中国公路交通飞快发展,道路载重日渐增加,移动荷载尤其重载汽车过桥将会引起桥梁振动,同时桥梁的振动将反馈给过桥汽车,产生车-桥耦合振动。为了方便描述上述动力效应对桥梁结构的影响,引入冲击系数概念将动力问题转化为静力问题;冲击系数一般指车辆激励桥梁所产生的动力效应与原有静力效应的比值。

现行《公路桥涵设计通用规范》(2015)中冲击系数计算公式是关于桥梁基频的函数,是1996年吉林省交通科学研究所[1]对7座简支梁桥进行12h不间断数据采集,通过概率回归建立而确立的。近年来,众多学者意识到冲击系数并不是单一变量的函数,其影响因素众多,除桥梁基频外,路面不平整度、车辆类型、车辆速度、截面形式等因素均会对其造成影响[2,3]。对于路面不平整度通常基于三角级数叠加法表达模型,采用功率谱密度函数对其进行描述[4]。用于数值模拟的公路汽车荷载模型较多,经历了从一维到三维的发展,目前由Wang[5]等人提出的3轴车模型被广泛采用,2018年,考虑到中国汽车荷载的现状,邓露[6]等人提出了一种更为精确的5轴车辆模型。早期的冲击系数公式未考虑截面形式对其影响,邓露[7]等研究认为截面形式对桥梁冲击系数有较大影响,相同基频条件下,不同截面桥梁冲击系数相对差值可达30%。

此外,常见的冲击系数包括挠度冲击系数与弯矩冲击系数,15规范中简单只考虑了挠度冲击系数对结构影响,未给出弯矩冲击系数计算公式。目前关于两种冲击系数的关系还不明确,有研究认为弯矩冲击系数小于挠度冲击系数[8],也有学者认为挠度冲击系数大于弯矩冲击系数[9,10],还有研究认为两者的关系受多种因素影响,需要综合考虑[11],因此在桥梁设计的过程中应当同时考虑两种冲击系数的影响,选择较为保守的结果作为设计依据[12]。

基于此,本文将基于模态叠加法使用MATLAB程序编写的车桥耦合分析程序对简支梁桥冲击系数进行分析,将《公路桥涵设计通用规范》(2015)中规定的车道荷载还原为5轴车模型,采用空间加载形式,考虑路面不平整度、桥梁跨径以及截面形式等影响因素计算得到冲击系数,进行参数分析并比较选取不同阶模态对计算精度影

1. 基金项目:国家自然科学基金项目(51978063);

响,所得成果可为后续数值模拟分析冲击系数提供支持。

1 基于模态叠加法的冲击系数分析理论

1.1 车辆模型与振动方程推导

为了更好地模拟车辆过桥的实际过程,本文选取邓露[6]等提出的空间15自由度5轴车车辆模型,其车辆模型如图1所示,车辆模型参数见表1。

采用拉格朗日方程推导其动力学方程,可得到十五自由度五轴车的动力学方程为:

$$[M_V]\{\ddot{Z}\}+[C_V]\{\dot{Z}\}+[K_V]\{Z\}=\{F_{vb}\} \quad (1)$$

式中: $[M_V]$——车辆质量矩阵;

$\{\ddot{Z}\}$、$\{\dot{Z}\}$、$\{Z\}$——各个自由度的加速度向量、速度向量、位移向量;

$[C_V]$——车辆阻尼矩阵;

$[K_V]$——车辆刚度矩阵;

$\{F_{vb}\}$——车辆与桥梁各个接触点处的相互作用力向量。

采用模态叠加法构建桥梁的动力学方程,可以表示为如下形式:

$$[M_b][\ddot{Q}]+[C_b][\dot{Q}]+[K_b][Q]=[F_b] \quad (2)$$

式中:$[M_b]$——桥梁质量矩阵;

$[Q]$——各个模态自由度向量;

$[C_b]$——桥梁阻尼矩阵;

$[K_b]$——桥梁刚度矩阵;

$[F_b]$——桥梁所受外力矩阵。

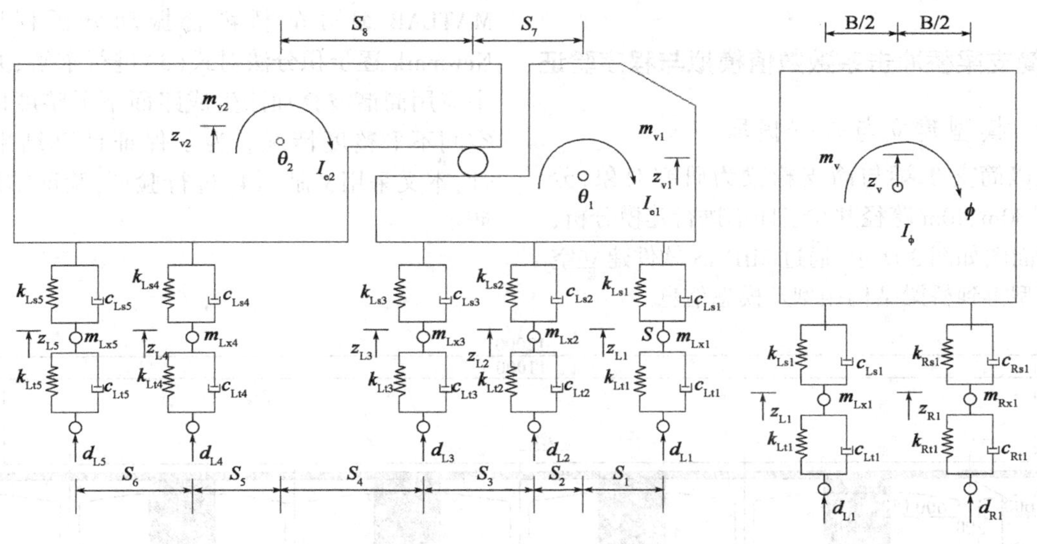

图1 十五自由度五轴空间车辆模型

车辆模型参数 表1

参数	数值	参数	数值
车体质量 M_1(kg)	2276.5	悬架刚度 K_{s1},K_{s2}(kN·m^{-1})	300.0
车体质量 M_2(kg)	45246.0	悬架刚度 K_{s3}~K_{s6}(kN·m^{-1})	500.0
车轴悬挂质量 m_1(kg)	700.0	悬架刚度 K_{s7}~K_{s10}(kN·m^{-1})	1250.0
车轴悬挂质量 m_3(kg)	1000.0	轮胎刚度 K_{t1},K_{t2}(kN·m^{-1})	1500.0
车轴悬挂质量 m_5(kg)	1000.0	轮胎刚度 K_{t3}~K_{t10}(kN·m^{-1})	3000.0
车轴悬挂质量 m_7(kg)	800.0	悬架阻尼 D_{S1},D_{s2}(kN·s·m^{-1})	10.0
车轴悬挂质量 m_9(kg)	800.0	悬架阻尼 D_{S3}~D_{s10}(kN·s·m^{-1})	53.0
		轮胎阻尼 D_{t1}~D_{t10}(kN·s·m^{-1})	3.0

将式(1)车辆动力学方程与式(2)桥梁动力学方程组合,重新排列,便得车-桥耦合振动方程式(3)。

$$\begin{bmatrix} M_V & 0 \\ 0 & M_b \end{bmatrix}\begin{bmatrix} \ddot{Y} \\ \ddot{Q} \end{bmatrix}+\begin{bmatrix} C_v & C_{vb} \\ C_{bv} & C_b \end{bmatrix}\begin{bmatrix} \dot{Y} \\ \dot{Q} \end{bmatrix}+\begin{bmatrix} K_v & K_{vb} \\ K_{bv} & K_b \end{bmatrix}\begin{bmatrix} Y \\ Q \end{bmatrix}=\begin{bmatrix} F_v \\ F_b \end{bmatrix} \quad (3)$$

式中：$[C_{vb}]$——车桥阻尼耦合矩阵；

$[C_{bv}]$——桥车阻尼耦合矩阵；

$[K_{vb}]$——车桥刚度耦合矩阵；

$[K_{bv}]$——桥车刚度耦合矩阵。

1.2　路面不平整度模拟

路面不平整度一般指路面表面偏离理想基准面的程度,研究指出路面不平整度对桥梁冲击系数结果影响较大[13],不可忽略。目前多采用三角级数叠加法和傅里叶变换法生成路面不平整度样本[4]。因三角级数叠加法适应范围更为广泛,故本文采用该方法模拟常见等级路面不平整度样本,并生成10个不平整度样本取平均值以降低平整度随机性影响。图2为生成的一组路面不平整度样本。

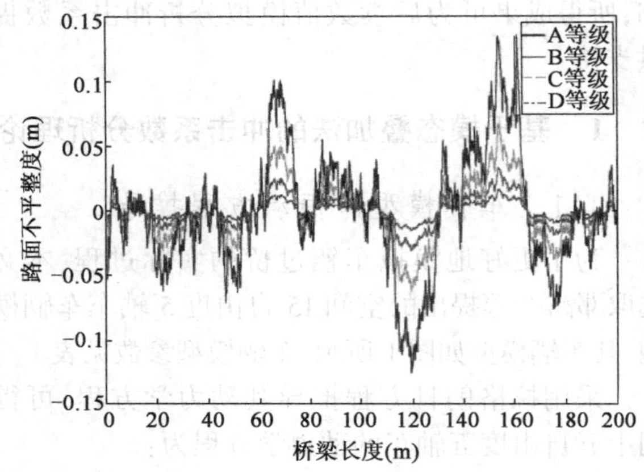

图2　路面不平整度样本

2　简支梁桥冲击系数数值模拟与程序验证

2.1　模型建立与数据提取

本文以简支T梁与简支箱梁为研究对象,分别取20m、30m、40m跨径共6组样本进行建模分析,桥梁横断面图如图3所示,通过MIDAS软件建立空间梁格模型得到桥梁结构振型及模态信息。

2.2　程序编写与验证

为了进一步计算简支梁桥冲击系数,使用MATLAB编写车-桥耦合振动分析程序,应用Newmark逐步积分法对式(3)进行求解,并在分析中应用简谐波叠加法生成路面不平整度信息模拟空间不平整度情况。为了保证计算结果的准确性,本文采用文献[14]进行验证,验证结果如图4所示。

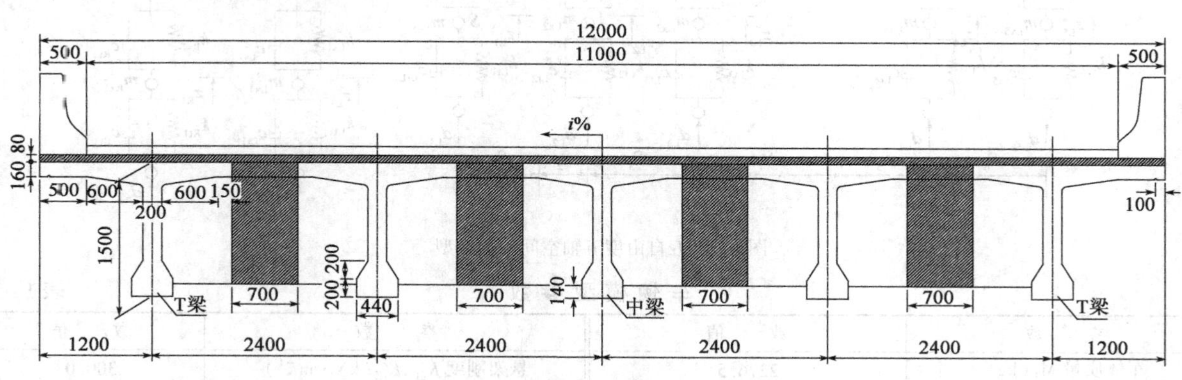

a)典型T梁横断面图

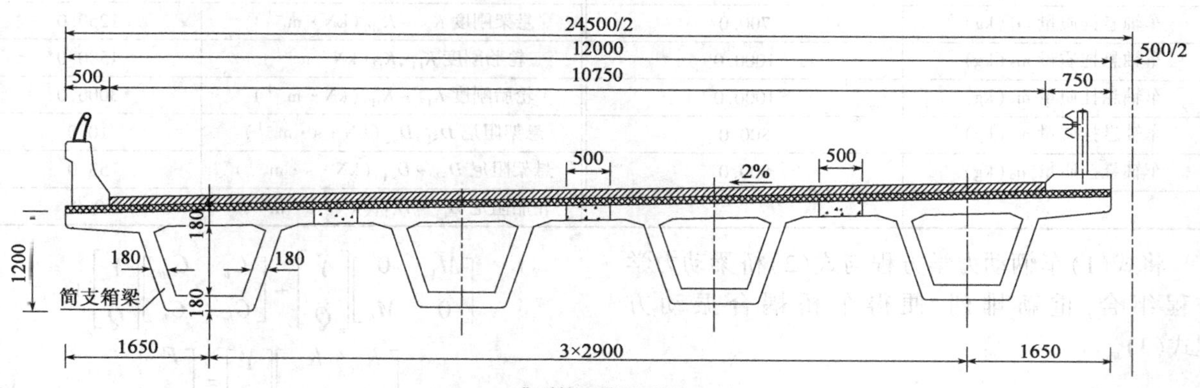

b)典型箱梁横断面图

图3　简支梁桥横断面图(尺寸单位:mm)

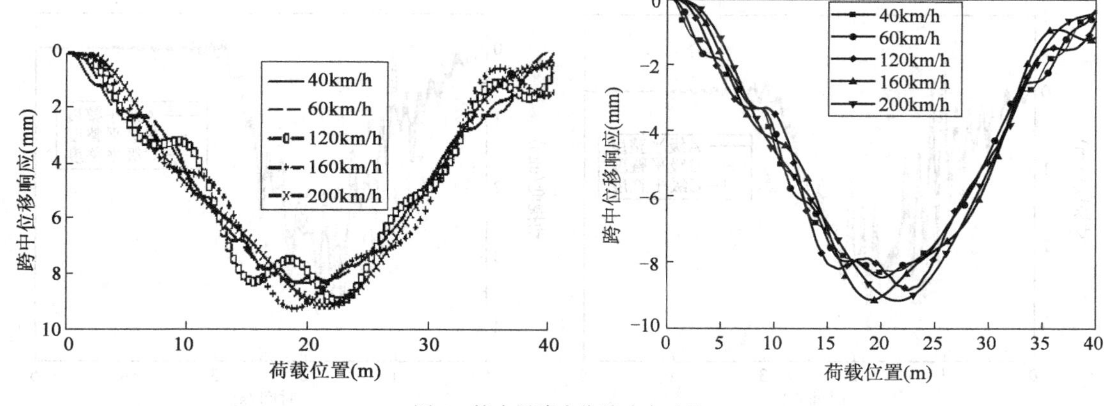

图 4 简支梁跨中位移响应对比

2.3 计算结果

选取前 25 阶模态进行简支梁桥冲击系数,冲击系数计算结果如表 2 与表 3 所示。

简支 T 梁桥冲击系数计算结果 表 2

工况		挠度冲击系数			弯矩冲击系数		
跨径(m)	车速(km/h)	不平整度等级			不平整度等级		
		A 级	B 级	C 级	A 级	B 级	C 级
20	40	1.099	1.210	1.433	1.041	1.143	1.348
	80	1.135	1.276	1.559	1.105	1.221	1.481
	120	1.112	1.226	1.527	1.112	1.213	1.421
30	40	1.102	1.223	1.466	1.026	1.057	1.206
	80	1.075	1.194	1.462	1.063	1.082	1.211
	120	1.066	1.111	1.205	1.099	1.115	1.212
40	40	1.089	1.185	1.376	1.069	1.145	1.326
	80	1.075	1.138	1.446	1.088	1.138	1.371
	120	1.082	1.136	1.245	1.073	1.128	1.244

简支箱梁桥冲击系数计算结果 表 3

工况		挠度冲击系数			弯矩冲击系数		
跨径(m)	车速(km/h)	不平整度等级			不平整度等级		
		A 级	B 级	C 级	A 级	B 级	C 级
20	40	1.073	1.160	1.333	1.031	1.112	1.273
	80	1.160	1.344	1.707	1.129	1.288	1.627
	120	1.053	1.163	1.384	1.034	1.041	1.220
30	40	1.126	1.257	1.517	1.061	1.180	1.418
	80	1.120	1.251	1.514	1.011	1.139	1.398
	120	1.071	1.115	1.205	1.084	1.126	1.212
40	40	1.059	1.127	1.264	1.017	1.080	1.207
	80	1.069	1.195	1.533	1.072	1.119	1.411
	120	1.016	1.038	1.113	1.012	1.036	1.085

跨中截面动挠度时程曲线可以直观表示车桥耦合振动过程,图 5 展示了低速状态(40km/h)下 20m 跨径两种不同截面桥梁的动挠度时程曲线。

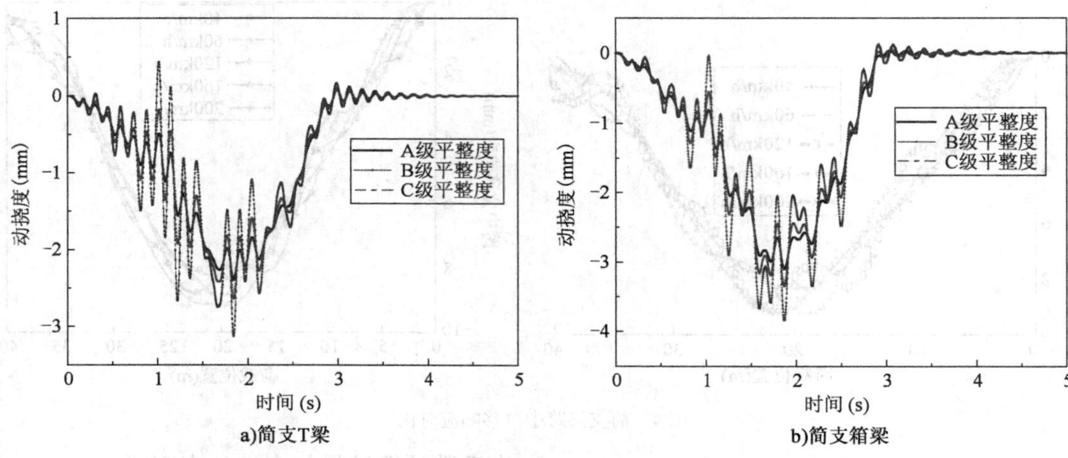

图5　动挠度时程曲线

3　简支梁桥冲击系数结果分析

3.1　多参数对冲击系数影响

影响弯矩冲击系数与挠度冲击系数计算结果的因素十分复杂,模态阶数、截面形式、桥梁跨径以及桥面不平整度等均会对其造成较大影响,本文基于模态叠加法计算结果对影响冲击系数计算结果的因素作简要分析(图6)。

首先以20m简支T梁为例,在行车速度40km/h的工况下分析模态阶数选取对结果影响。

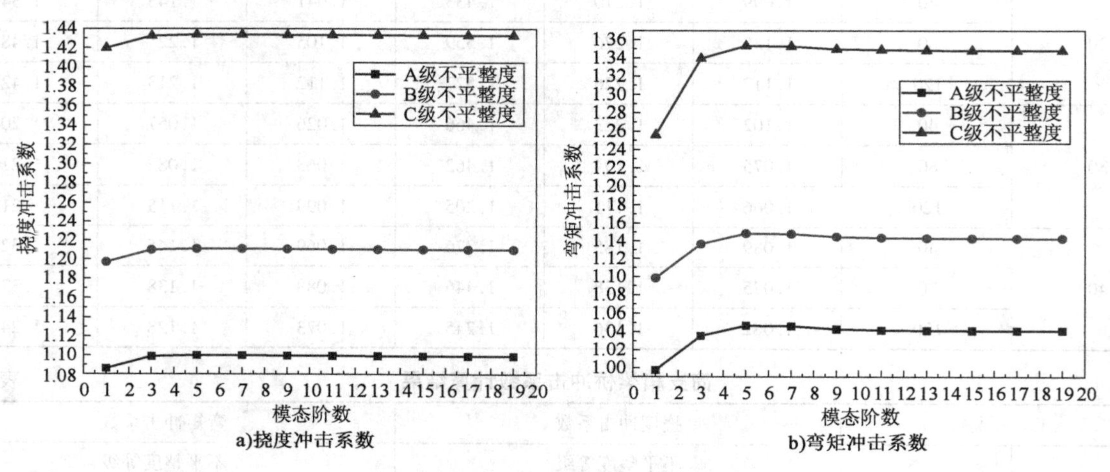

图6　前10阶模态冲击系数

计算发现,对于挠度冲击系数高阶模态影响较小,选取5阶模态即可达到99.9%以上准确度,而对于弯矩冲击系数高阶模态影响较大,一般7阶模态达到稳定,建议选取10阶模态进行计算,此时误差小于0.01%。

此外,由上图还可以明确看到,路面不平整度对冲击系数计算结果产生极大影响,无论是挠度冲击系数或是弯矩冲击系数,C级路面冲击系数值均值高出A级路面的30%以上,由此可见随着桥梁结构服役年限增长,十分有必要对其路面不平整度进行测试,重新评估其动力性能。

为研究桥梁跨径及车辆速度对冲击系数影响,建立20m跨径A级不平整度箱梁模型进行分析,计算结果如图7所示。

由上图可以看出在桥梁跨径较低时,车辆速度对冲击系数影响较为明显,此时冲击系数随车速先增加后减小,随着桥梁跨径增大车辆速度对冲击系数影响减小,但可以观察到车辆在低速行驶与高速行驶时冲击系数均较小,弯矩冲击系数与挠度冲击系数有着类似的规律。

3.2　弯矩与挠度冲击系数关系

弯矩与挠度冲击系数的关系与模态阶数有关(图8、图9),可以用弯矩与挠度冲击系比值ε_{My}表示，根据文献[8]可知：

$$\varepsilon_{My}=\frac{1+\mu_M}{1+\mu_y}=\frac{\pi^2}{12}\times\frac{\sum_{n=1}^{N}n^2\times q_n(t_M)\sin\frac{n\pi}{2}}{\sum_{n=1}^{N}q_n(t_y)\sin\frac{n\pi}{2}} \tag{4}$$

仅考虑一阶模态时，其比值为定值0.822。本文在此基础上以10阶模态冲击系数计算结果，分析桥梁截面形式、跨径、车速等因素对比值影响。

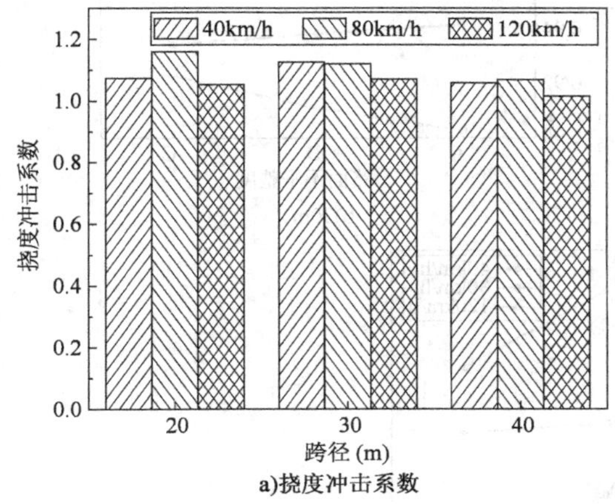

a)挠度冲击系数

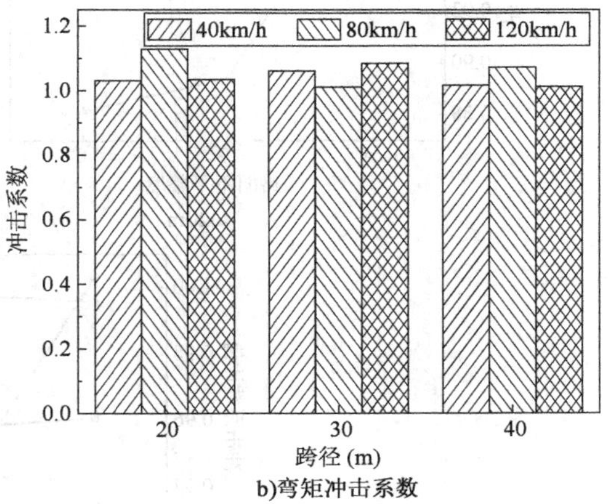

b)弯矩冲击系数

图7　20m箱梁冲击系数

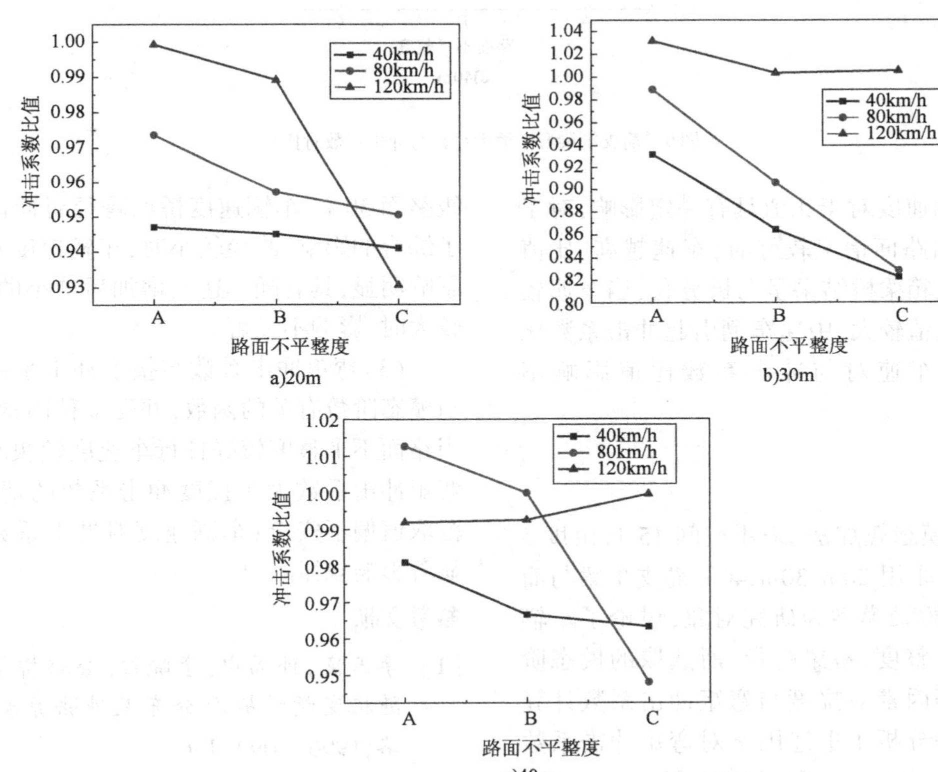

图8　简支T梁弯矩放大系数与冲击系数对比

从图8与图9中可以看出桥面不平整度对弯矩放大系数与挠度放大系数比值具有明显影响，具体表现为比值随着路面等级下降而减小，具体取值范围为0.823～1.032大于一阶模态下0.822结果，可见考虑多阶模态后比值均大于只考虑一阶模态结果，当路面不平整度为A级时部分数据比值大于1，表明此时弯矩冲击系数大于挠度冲击系数，此时按照规范中公式计算冲击系数偏不安全，需同时计算弯矩冲击系数，考虑最不利情况进行设计计算。

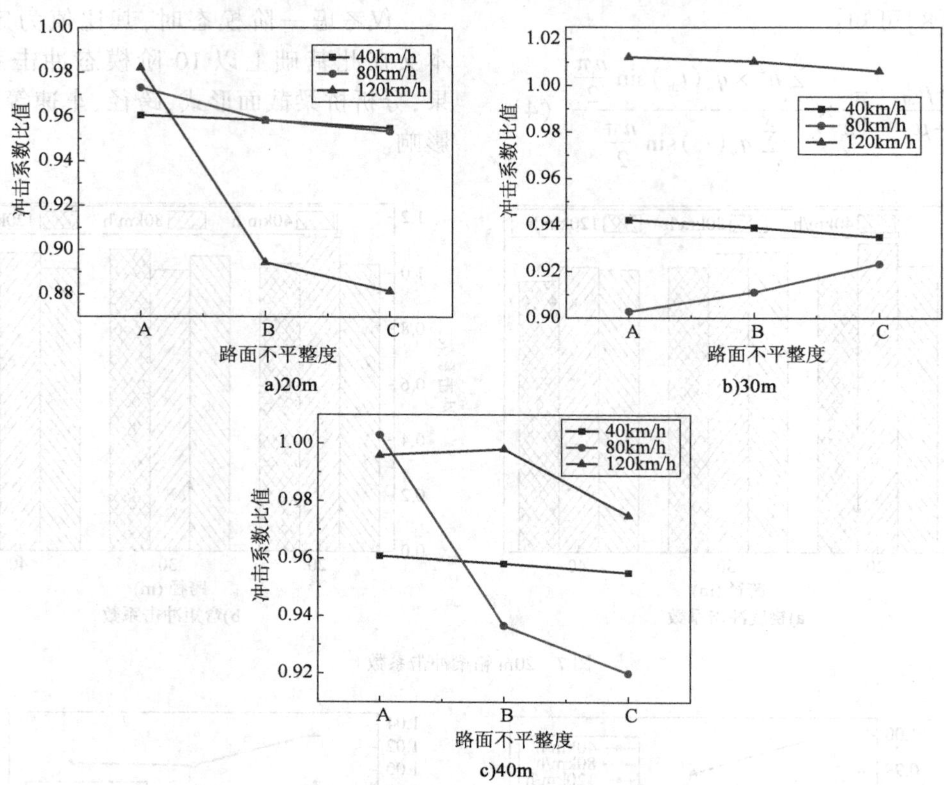

图 9　简支箱梁弯矩放大系数与冲击系数对比

此外,车辆速度对于比值具有一定影响,对于简支 T 梁桥,当路面情况较好时,车速越高,比值越大;对于简支箱梁桥结果呈两极分化,当车速较低或较高时,比值较大,中速车辆引起冲击系数比值较小。因此车速对与冲击系数比值影响不明显。

4　结语

本文基于模态叠加法,采用空间 15 自由度 5 轴车车辆模型,采用 20m、30m、40m 简支 T 梁与简支箱梁各三座桥梁模型为研究对象,讨论了车辆速度、路面不平整度、桥梁跨径、所选取的模态阶数、截面形式等因素对挠度与弯矩冲击系数计算结果的影响,并分析了上述因素对弯矩冲击系数与挠度冲击系数的影响,得出以下结论:

(1)高阶模态对挠度冲击系数影响较小,对弯矩冲击系数影响较大,为获取准去的计算结果,建议取前五阶模态计算挠度冲击系数,取前十阶模态计算弯矩冲击系数。

(2)路面不平整度是影响冲击系数结果最显著的因素,C 级路面下冲击系数计算结果高出 A 级路面 30%,车辆速度桥梁跨径对冲击速度带来了综合的影响,跨径较小时,车辆速度对冲击速度影响明显,具有随车速先增加后减小的趋势,跨径较大时,影响不显著。

(3)弯矩冲击系数与挠度冲击系数的比值是与模态阶数有关的函数,并受多种因素综合影响,当路面不平整度较好且行车速度较快时可能出现弯矩冲击系数大于挠度冲击系数的情况,此时规范取值偏不安全;车辆速度对冲击系数比值没有显著影响规律。

参考文献

[1] 李玉良,孙福申,李晓红. 公路桥梁冲击系数随机变量的概率分布及冲击系数谱[J]. 公路,1996,(09):1-6.

[2] Tso-Chien Pan,Jing Li. Dynamic Vehicle Element Method for Transient Response of Coupled Vehicle-Structure Systems [J]. Journal of Structural Engineering,2002,128(2).

[3] 周勇军,薛宇欣,李冉冉,等. 桥梁冲击系数理论研究和应用进展[J]. 中国公路学报,2021,34(04):31-50.

[4] 沈锐利,官快,房凯.车桥耦合数值模拟桥梁冲击系数随机变量的概率分布[J].振动与冲击,2015,34(18):123-128.

[5] Ton&hyphen, Lo Wang, Dongzhou Huang, Mohsen Shahawy. Dynamic Response of Multigirder Bridges [J]. Journal of Structural Engineering, 1992,118(8).

[6] 邓露,段林利,何维,等.中国公路车-桥耦合振动车辆模型研究[J].中国公路学报,2018,31(07):92-100.

[7] 邓露,何维,王芳.不同截面类型简支梁桥动力冲击系数研究[J].振动与冲击,2015,34(14):70-75.

[8] 邓露,段林利,邹启令.桥梁应变与挠度动力放大系数的大小关系研究[J].工程力学,2018,35(01):126-135.

[9] Aluri S, Jinka C, Gangarao H V S. Dynamic Response of Three Fiber Reinforced Polymer Composite Bridges [J]. Journal of Bridge Engineering,2005,10(6):722-730.

[10] 陈雅仙.适用于我国中小跨径简支梁桥的动力冲击系数研究[D].长沙:湖南大学,2019.

[11] 周勇军,蔡军哲,石雄伟,等.基于加权法的桥梁冲击系数计算方法[J].交通运输工程学报,2013,13(04):29-36.

[12] 高庆飞,张坤,刘晨光,等.移动车辆荷载作用下桥梁冲击系数的若干讨论[J].哈尔滨工业大学学报,2020,52(03):44-50.

[13] 薛宇欣,周勇军,赵煜,王刚强.基于空间桥面不平顺的简支梁桥冲击系数研究[J].合肥工业大学学报(自然科学版),2021,44(03):389-395.

[14] 沈火明,肖新标.求解车桥耦合振动问题的一种数值方法[J].西南交通大学学报,2003(06):658-662.

Two-phase Stiffness Identification Strategy Based on Static Deflection

Zhang Jiading* Li Pengfei
(Key Laboratory for Bridge and Tunnel of Shannxi Province, Chang'an University)

Abstract In this paper, an efficient calculation framework is proposed to solve the problem of static stiffness identification of bridge structures. The problems in the first stage include the overall judgment of structural performance, determining the upper and lower limits of the identification parameters in the second stage, and improving the accuracy and efficiency of the identification in the second stage of the evaluation task. Aiming at the problem in the first stage, a stiffness identification method based on LM algorithm is adopted. The second stage is to divide the beam segments and determine the stiffness value of each divided beam segment to minimize the identification error. Therefore, PSO algorithm is used to optimize the initial value of Kriging model, and a recognition method based on PSO-Kriging model is proposed. Numerical examples show the applicability and effectiveness of the method. The results show that the framework can deal with the timely stiffness evaluation task.

Keywords Structural health monitoring Static stiffness identification FEMU Static defelection PSO-Kriging

0 Introduction

Many bridges have unexpected structural damage during service, which poses a threat to the structure. In order to ensure safety, timely evaluation is necessary, measurements obtained from sensors provide indications of structural service state [1], and interpretation of measurements for obtaining metrics that directly indicate structural health or damage is important.

Stiffness degradation is a widely used indicator to discern whether or not there is damage in a structure2. Many scholars use the measured data to retrieve the structural stiffness, and then evaluate its structural health conditions, Finite-element-model updating (FEMU) is an widely used method, FEMU based on dynamic measurements has been widely studied, Sanayei and Saletnik [2,3] utilized a subset of elemental strain measurements to identify the element stiffness parameters of all or a portion of a finite-element (FE) model of a structure and Sanayei et al. [4] successfully identified the unknown stiffness parameters of the structural components of a tested small-scale steel frame by FEMU strategy using both the static displacements and strains.

The basic idea of FEMU is to make the numerical simulation consistent with the measured results by adjusting the parameters in the finite element model, in the early FEMU method, sensitivity analysis should be carried out to screen design variables and construct complex sensitivity matrices, which greatly affects the performance of the optimization process. At the same time, the FEM needs to be adjusted and recalculated during the optimization iteration.

In recent years, agent model technology has attracted more and more attention in the engineering field. It uses the simulation data of high fidelity FEM to obtain a high-precision approximation to the structural simulation model and realizes the rapid mapping from input data to output data to support real-time decision-making. the response surface method (RSM) and Kriging model are such methods. Xu and Low uses RSM combined with FEM to calculate the reliability index of slope[5], the feasibility of using alternative model in slope reliability analysis is demonstrated. However, the research of Kaymaz and McMahon [6] shows that the traditional RSM requires a lot of calculation work, and its simulation accuracy is not ideal when dealing with strong nonlinear problems. Kriging model, for its integration capability and flexibility or local adaptability, is favored by researchers and tried to be applied to many places. When building Kriging model, the relevant θ should be determined firstly, their values have a great impact on the performance of Kriging model. In DACE (design and analysis of computer experiments)——a Kriging MATLAB toolbox developed by Lophaven [7], the pattern search method is used to find the optimal value of θ. However, this method is easy to fall into a local minimum, and the solution is greatly affected by the given initial value. Therefore, Luo [8] et al. used an artificial bee colony algorithm for optimization θ, You et al. [9] adopts a genetic algorithm, and PSO algorithm is adopted in this paper.

This paper mainly studies the stiffness identification of prestressed concrete continuous beam bridge, and puts forward an efficient FEMU strategy based on LM assisted PSO Kriging model, the method is implemented in two phases. In phase Ⅰ, the identification strategy based on LM algorithm can assist engineers to make a rough judgment on the overall mechanical properties of the structure with only a small amount of calculation, and give the sampling interval in the second stage of identification, so as to improve the identification accuracy and efficiency. In phase Ⅱ, PSO algorithm is used to optimize the initial value of Kriging model to ensure the global optimality of the model under any initial conditions, the accuracy and efficiency of nonlinear fitting are verified through an example. A numerical example is given to illustrate the applicability and accuracy of the method.

1 Two-phase bridge stiffness identification

1.1 Theory of static displacement-based stiffness identification

With the basic assumption of a linear elastic structure, the objective of system identification is defined to be the recovery of element stiffness properties, contained in a finite element model, from static test data. According to the mechanics principle, the mechanical equilibrium equation of the structure under the static response is

$$[K]\{\mu_0\} = \{P\} \tag{1}$$

where $[K]$ is structural stiffness matrix, μ_0 is displacement vector, $\{P\}$ is load vector.

For static parameter identification, two independent stiffness matrices are established[10]: K^a is the analytical stiffness matrix derived from the finite element model, K^m is the measurement stiffness matrix derived from force and displacement measurements. Both are square matrices of the same size. It is assumed that there are no forces applied to the unmeasured degrees of freedom, Eq. (1) can be simplified to

$$f^m = K^a u^m \tag{2}$$

The measured static forces f^m and defelection u^m are obtained on a finite subset of the total degrees of freedom which is used to define the finite element model. The measured force-defelection relationship can be written as

$$f^m = K^m u^m \tag{3}$$

For the same substructurewhich K^m is derived, the corresponding analytical stiffness matrix $K^a(p)$ is obtained by using the finite element method. $K^a(p)$ is adjusted element by element to match K^m, by adjusting the stiffness parameters p, so that the analytical response of the structure is equal to the measured response.

For elastic homogeneous beam, the flexural stiffness$K$ is expressed as the product of E (Yang's Young's modulus) and I (section second moment of inertia)

$$K = EI \tag{4}$$

The contribution of both deflection and alignment is consistent, in this paper, $K^a(p)$ is adjusted by changing the coefficient of young's modulus. But $K^a(p)$ is a nonlinear function that is hard to solve, note that the objective of adjusting $K^a(p)$ is to make the analytical response equal to the measured value, so it can be transformed into an optimization problem with the objective to minimize the error between the theoretically calculated displacement and the measured displacement. The following optimization model is established

$$\begin{aligned} &\mathit{find} \quad p \\ &\min \quad f(p) = \sum_{i=1}^{n}(\Delta_i^m - \Delta_i^\eta) \\ &s.t. \quad ai \leqslant \eta_i \leqslant \beta, i = 1,2,3\cdots n \end{aligned} \tag{5}$$

where Δ_i^m is measured displacement, Δ_i^η is the displacement from FEM, p_i is stiffness coefficient, α_i, β_i are the upper and lower limits of the stiffness coefficient, i is the number of beam segments.

1.2 Two-phase framework for bridge stiffness identification

The general scheme for the two-phase bridge stiffness identification framework is illustrated in Fig. 1, where in the functionality of each phase is described in the following, the calculation method will be described in sections 1.3 and 1.4.

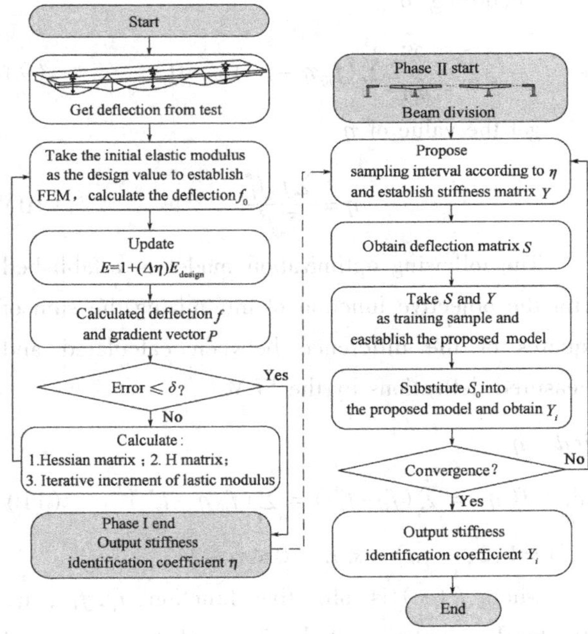

Fig. 1 Frame of two-phase identification

1.2.1 Phase Ⅰ: predicating monolithic bridge stiffness

In many stiffness identification studies, the determination of the range of stiffness coefficient is generally based on the engineer ' s subjective judgment. The rationality of the sampling range affects the accuracy and efficiency of the final identification result directly. The objective of this phase is to assess the overall state of the structure, and provide a basis for determining the upper and lower limits of the recognition coefficient in phase Ⅱ. The first step in stiffness identification by static displacement is assuming the initial elastic modulus E_0 as the design initial value, the long-term deflection under load F_{i0} is calculated by FEM.

Assume that the actual elastic modulus of the structure is

$$E=\frac{E_0}{\eta} \tag{6}$$

The displacement of the measuring point is

$$f_i=f_{i0}\eta \tag{7}$$

Assume all of the measured displacement of each point is f_i^*, the residual sum of squares S is

$$S=\sum_{i=1}^{n}(f_i=f_i^*)=\sum_{i=1}^{n}(f_{i0}\eta-f_i^*)^2 \tag{8}$$

Determine the value of η to minimize the value of S.

According to

$$\frac{\partial S}{\partial\eta}2\sum_{i=1}^{n}(f_{i0}\eta-f_i^*)c_i=0 \tag{9}$$

get the value of η

$$\eta=\frac{\Sigma f_{i0}f_i^*}{\Sigma f_{i0}^2} \tag{10}$$

The following optimization model is established with the objective function of minimizing the sum of squares of the difference between calculated and measured deflections by the FEM

$$\begin{gathered} find\quad \eta \\ \min_{x\in R^n}\ f(\eta)=\sum_{i=1}^{n}(f_i-f_i^*)=\sum_{i=1}^{n}(f_{i0}\eta-f_i^*)^2 \qquad (11) \\ (i=1,2,\cdots,n)\quad s.t.\quad 0\leqslant\eta\leqslant 2 \end{gathered}$$

where $f(s)$ is objective function, f_i, f_i^*, are structural calculation deflection and test measured deflection, f_{i0} is initial deflection calculated with initial elastic modulus E_0, η is stiffness coefficient.

1.2.2 Phase Ⅱ: Identification stiffness by segmented executions

For the same bridge with long service time, due to the different stress conditions of each beam section, the real performance is also quite different, and the global identification results can not reflect the real mechanical state of different positions of the structure. Considering the purpose of stiffness identification is to obtain quantitative indicators for evaluating the real performance and mechanical state of the structure, divide the identified bridge into m segments appropriately and evaluate the performance of the corresponding beam segment with a nominal stiffness in this phase.

Each beam segment of the identified bridge is divided according to the structural characteristics, the initial elastic modulus of each beam segment is taken as the design value E_{design}^i ($i=1,2,\cdots,m$), the deflection of each measuring point under load f_{FEA}^n is calculated by FEM.

Assume that the identification coefficient of each beam segment is η_i ($i=1,2,\cdots,m$), then the actual elastic modulus of each beam section is

$$E_{real}^i=\frac{E_{design}^i}{\eta_i} \tag{12}$$

The measured displacement of each measuring point is $f_{measure}^n$, the residual sum of squares is

$$S=\sum_{i=1}^{n}(f_{FEA}^n-f_{measure}^n)^2 \tag{13}$$

The following optimization model is established

$$\begin{gathered} find\quad \eta_i \\ \min_{x\in R^n}\ f(\eta_i)=\sum_{i=1}^{n}(f_{FEA}^n-f_{measure}^n)^2 \quad (i=1,2,\cdots,n) \\ s.t.\quad a\leqslant\eta_i\leqslant b \qquad (14) \end{gathered}$$

where a, b are the upper and lower limits of the stiffness coefficient determined by the result of phase I.

1.3 L-M algorithm for Stiffness prediction of monolithic bridge

Levenberg-Marquardt (L-M) algorithm is a combination of gradient descent method and Gauss-Newton method. It overcomes the difficulty of dealing with singular matrix and non-positive definite matrix and the requirement of initial value by improving the Hessian matrix of Gauss-Newton (G-N) method

$$G = H + \mu I \tag{15}$$

Suppose $F(x)$ is the sum of the square functions

$$F(x) \sum_{i=1}^{N} v_i^2(x) = v^T v \tag{16}$$

The iteration mode is

$$x_{k+1} = x_k = [J^T(x) J(x) + \mu_k I]^{-1}]^T(x) v(x) \tag{17}$$

where $J(x)$ is Jacobian matrix.

The outstanding feature of this algorithm is that when μ_k increases, the algorithm is close to the steepest descent method.

$$x_{k+1} = x_k - \frac{1}{\mu_K} J^T(x) v(x) = x_k - \frac{1}{2\mu_k} \nabla F(x) \tag{18}$$

When μ_k decreases to 0, the algorithm becomes Gauss-Newton algorithm.

The optimization condition of Levenberg-Marquardt algorithm is to minimize the value of objective function. In this paper, the minimum sum of the square of the difference value between calculated deflection and measured deflection is used to solve the problem. The specific stiffness identification steps are as follows:

(1) Determine deflection f^* from static load testing.

(2) Calculate the structural deflection f_0 of the structure under different working condition with the design initial elastic modulus E_0.

(3) Keep other parameters of the structure unchanged, give a certain increment of elastic modulus ΔE, then analyze the structure again to calculate deflection f_1. The sensitivity parameter which is also called gradient vector of deflection to elastic modulus P is obtained by dividing the long-term deflection difference value calculated twice by the increment of elastic modulus.

(4) Compare the calculated displacement to the measured displacement to judge whether meet the objective function. If it meets the objective function, the structural stiffness coefficient is output, otherwise ΔE should be modified based on P and repeat step (3) until meeting the requirement.

1.4 PSO-Kriging model for bridge stiffness recognition by segmented executions

To find the optimal stiffness coefficient for solving the optimization model of phase Ⅱ, the value of need to change frequently and calculate the FEM. In order to determine the modification value of the identification coefficient of each operation, the sensitivity matrix of the stiffness coefficient of each beam segment to the deflection calculation result needs to be recalculated which is different in each cycle. Meanwhile, the solution of the optimized model requires repeated running the FEM. These steps can be inefficient and costly. In order to overcome the computational limitations previously, a surrogate model is used in this section to fit the constitutive relationship.

1.4.1 Kriging theory

Kriging is a semi-parametric interpolation model, which assumes that the implicit function relationship of the system can be reconstructed with weighting the response value of the known sample function linearly

$$F(x) = \sum^{n} f(x_i) \beta_i \tag{19}$$

Therefore, the performance discreet value of any design scheme in the design space can be obtained as long as the expression of the weighting coefficient β be given. To calculate the weighting coefficients, the Kriging model introduces statistical assumptions that treat the unknown function as a concrete realization of a static random process defined by the following formula

$$F(x) = \beta_0 + Z(x) \tag{20}$$

where β_0 is the mathematical expectation of $F(x)$ which describes the "trend surface" of regionalized variable, it is generally divided into three models: 0th order (constant), linear and quadratic polynomial. $Z(x)$ is a static random process whose mean value is zero and variance is σ^2. A certain correlation of random variables at different positions in the design space can be described as covariance, which can be expressed as

$$Cov[Z(x_i),Z(X_j)] = \sigma_z^2[R_{ij}(\theta,x_i,x_j)] \quad (21)$$

where σ is the standard deviation of pattern response, $R(\theta, x_i, x_j)$ is the correlation function between two sample points x_i and x_j, where θ is the unknown correlation parameter to be determined. The choice of the correlation function is decisive to the simulation accuracy, common functions are as shown in Tab. 1.

Correlation model of Kriging Tab. 1

Correlation model	Function expression
Cubic	$R(\theta,w_i,w_j) = \exp(-\theta_s \mid d_s \mid)$
Exp	$R(\theta,w_i,w_j) = \exp(-\theta_s \mid d_s \mid^{\theta_n+1})$
Gauss	$R(\theta,w_i,w_j) = \exp(-\theta_s \mid d_s \mid^2)$
Lin	$R(\theta,w_i,w_j) = \max\{0,1-\theta_s \mid d_s \mid\}$
Spherical	$R(\theta,w_i,w_j) = 1-1.5\xi_s+0.5\xi_s^3$
Spline	$R(\theta,w_i,w_j) = \zeta(\xi_s)$

Based on the assumption previously, the Kriging model finds the optimal weighting coefficient β to minimize the mean square error

$$MSE[F(x)] = E[(\beta^T Y_s - Y(x))^2] \quad (22)$$

and satisfy the following interpolation condition (or unbiased conditions)

$$E[\sum_{i=1}^{n} F(x_i)\beta_i] = E[F(x)] \quad (23)$$

By applying Lagrange multiplier method, it can be proved that the optimal weighting coefficient β is given by the following linear equations (also called the Kriging model equations)

$$\begin{cases} \sum_{j=1}^{n}\beta_j R(x_i,x_j) + \dfrac{\mu}{2\sigma^2} = R(x_i,x) \\ \sum_{i=1}^{n}\beta_i = 1 \end{cases} \quad (24)$$

where $i = 1,2,\cdots,n$; μ is Lagrange multiplier. It can be written into matrix form as follows

$$\begin{bmatrix} R & F \\ F^T & 0 \end{bmatrix}\begin{bmatrix} \beta \\ \tilde{\mu} \end{bmatrix} = \begin{bmatrix} r \\ 1 \end{bmatrix} \quad (25)$$

where R is "correlation matrix", which is composed of correlation function values of all known sample points. r is "correlation vector", which is composed of correlation function values of all known and unknown sample points. By solving the linear equations (9) and substituting (3), the discreet value of the Kriging model can be obtained

$$\hat{y}(x) = \begin{bmatrix} r(x) \\ 1 \end{bmatrix}^T \begin{bmatrix} R & F \\ F & 0 \end{bmatrix}^{-1} \begin{bmatrix} y_s \\ 0 \end{bmatrix} \quad (26)$$

The model can finally be written as follows by inversion of a partitioned matrix

$$\hat{y}(x) = \beta_0 + r^T(x)\underbrace{R^{-1}(y_s - \beta_0 F)}_{=V_{krig}} \quad (27)$$

where $\beta_0 = (F^T R^{-1} F)^{-1} F^T R^{-1} y_s$, the column vector V_{krig} is only related to the known sample points.

It has been proved that if the optimal correlation parameters θ in the maximum likelihood sense can be guaranteed under any initial conditions, the optimal unbiased characteristic for the Kriging prediction can also be assured. In DACE, the pattern search method was used to find θ. However, this method could not guarantee to find the optimal values of θ under any initial conditions, which will affect the performance of the Kriging model. Therefore, Luo et al. used the artificial bee colony algorithm to optimize θ and You and Jia utilized the genetic algorithm. In this study, PSO, an efficient global optimization algorithm, was used to search θ.

1.4.2 PSO algorithm

In PSO, the behaviour of animals is imitated by moving particles with certain positions and velocities in a searching space, wherein the population is called a swarm, and each member of the swarm is called a particle. Every particle is treated as a point in a d-dimensional design space which adjusts its 'flying' according to its own and other particles' flying experience. Meantime, each particle keeps track of its position in the solution space that is associated with the fitness value that has achieved so far by that particle, and this fitness value is called personal best (pbest). Another best fitness value that is tracked by PSO is the best value obtained by whole swarm, and it is called global best (gbest). The operation of PSO is to gradually change the velocity of each particle toward its pbest and the gbest positions at each time step. The update of velocity and position can follow the following equations, respectively:

$$\begin{cases} V_{i,up} = wV_i + c_1rand1(Best_i - x_i) + c_2rand2(gBest - x_i) \\ x_{i+up} = x_i + V_{i,up} \end{cases} \tag{28}$$

where V_i、$V_{i,up}$ represent the speed of particle i before and after the update, x_i、$x_{i,up}$ represent the position of particle i before and after the update, c_1、c_2 are constants called learning factors, $rand1$、$rand2$ are random numbers uniformly distributed on the interval $[0,1]$, w is inertia weight.

Each particle searches for a better position in the search space and eventually the swarm as a whole, like a flock of birds collectively foraging for food, is likely to move close to the optimum of the fitness function. PSO's multi-point search ability assures itself an efficient global optimization algorithm.

1.4.3 PSO-Kriging model

The multi-point searching ability of PSO algorithm overcomes the limitation of the single-point search and the heavily dependence on the initial imaginative solution. Therefore, the optimal correlation parameters in the sense of maximum likelihood can be guaranteed under any initial conditions, and the optimal unbiased characteristics of the Kriging prediction can also be guaranteed.

To illustrate the advantage of PSO-Kriging, curve $y = (6x-2)^2\sin(12x-4), x \in [0,1]$ is simulated with sample points $S[0 \quad 0.125 \quad 0.25 \quad 0.375 \quad 0.5 \quad 0.615 \quad 0.75 \quad 0.875 \quad 1]^T$. The fitting results of Kriging and PSO-Kriging based on the same sample points are shown in Fig. 2, which shows that both Kriging and PSO-Kriging have a high degree of fitting near the sample points, but the RMSE value of PSO-Kriging is smaller and the fitting effect is much better at non-sample points. It can be seen that the PSO-Kriging model avoids the non-ideal fitting effect of Kriging due to inappropriate selection of initial values, and improves the efficiency and accuracy of model building.

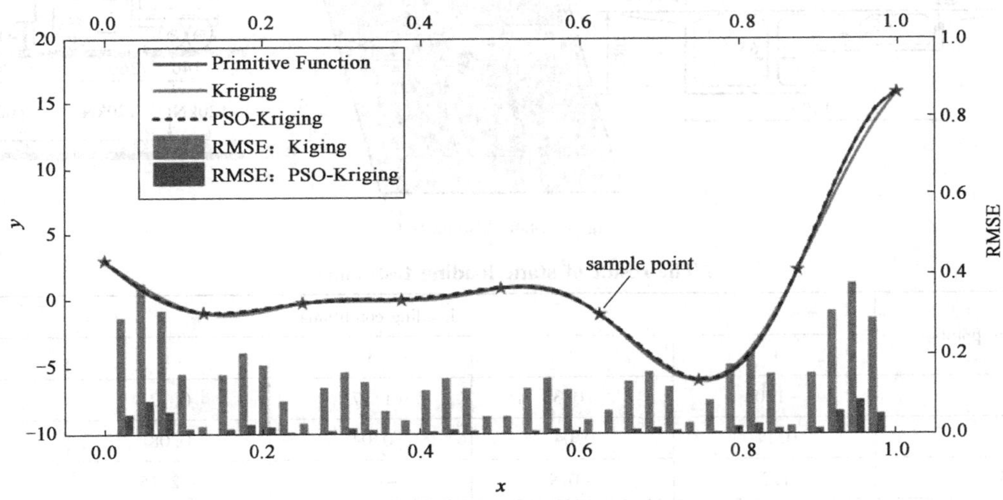

Fig. 2 Fitting effects comparison between PSO-Kriging and Kriging

1.4.4 PSO-Kriging-assisted stiffness identification

The process of applying PSO-Kriging to solve the optimization model established in phase Ⅱ can be described as follows

(1) Divide the identified bridge into several beam segments and draw up the sample interval based on the global stiffness coefficient identified by the L-M method.

(2) The Latin hypercube sampling method is used to get $N = 2n + 1$ sample points recorded as Y, where n is the number of beam segments to be identified. Establish the finite element model, calculate the sampling points, then the defection matrix S is obtained.

(3) Establish the Kriging model with the deflection matrix S and stiffness matrix Y based on MATLAB optimization toolbox, which combined with the PSO algorithm to obtain the PSO-Kriging model.

(4) Substitute the deflection matrix S_0 measured under the static load into the PSO-Kriging model to obtain the stiffness identification coefficient Y_i.

(5) Judge the convergence condition, if it meets the requirement then output the stiffness identification coefficient Y_i and terminate the calculation. Otherwise, select m values agian that meet the constraint conditions according to the MSE value, extract new $2n+1$ sample values by LHS, and a new $2n+1+m$ sample value is used to establish PSO-Kriging model.

(6) Repeat steps (2) to (5) until meeting the requirements.

2 Casestudy

2.1 Structural statement

The calculation example is a variable cross-section prestressed continuous beam bridge with a span of 145m (40 + 65 + 40), as shown in Fig. 3. Load vehicles with a standard axle load of 300kN (front axle load 60kN, rear axle load 120kN) are used, and the arrangement is both 3 vehicles in two rows. Load each measuring point in the figure separately, and the results are shown in Tab. 2.

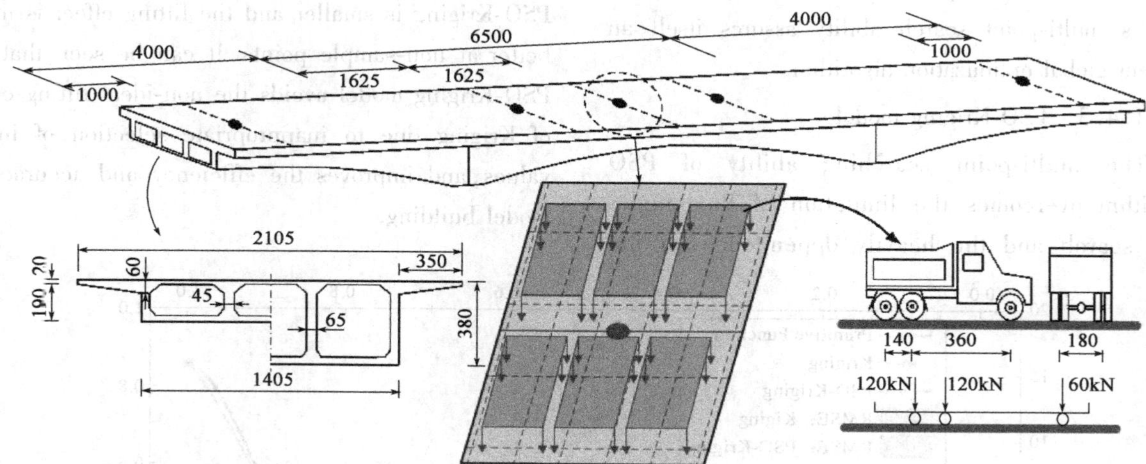

Fig. 3　Static loading test

The result of static loading test (mm)　　Tab. 2

Measuring points	Loading conditions				
	1	2	3	4	5
1	-1.03	-0.35	1.37	0.72	-0.23
2	0.11	0.04	0.04	0.08	1.02
3	1.2	-0.9	-4.25	-2.15	1.25
4	1.02	-0.3	-3.73	-2.38	1.77
5	-0.18	0.21	1.02	1.07	-0.88

2.2 Stiffness identification results and selection of correlation model and regression model

① Phase Ⅰ: Establish a finite element model with the initial elastic modulus whose value is 3.45 × 10^4 MPa. Take the data in each working condition of the mid-section of the mid-span (measuring point 3) as the research basis, the overall stiffness coefficient of the example bridge is identified according to the loading data in each working condition in Tab. 2. The objective function is iteratively optimized through the above process. The calculated deflection from FEM is in good agreement with the measured value after four iterations, and the accuracy of the identification result is evaluated by the sum of squared errors between the theoretically calculated deflection value and the measured deflection. The specific identification results are shown in the Fig. 4.

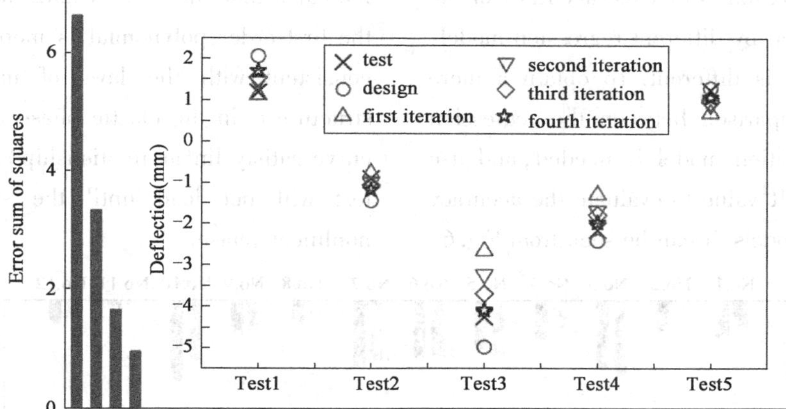

Fig. 4 The identification result of Phase Ⅰ

It can be seen from Fig. 4 that the calculated deflection value through 4 iterations of the FEM calculation for the stiffness identification based on the mid-section of the mid-span is in good agreement with the measured value of the static loading test, and the error is small. The overall stiffness identification coefficient calculated in the iteration method is 1.32. So the structural stiffness identification based on the LM method can effectively reflect the change of the actual global structural stiffness and provide a basis for the preliminary judgment of the structure.

②Phase Ⅱ: In order to verify the feasibility of the identification effect of this model, first assume that each beam segment of the example bridge has stiffness damage. Identify stiffness by the PSO-Kriging model described in this article, and compare the identification results with results under the assumed damage to analyze the accuracy and feasibility of the algorithm. For the same bridge that has been in service for a long time, due to the different stress conditions of each beam section, its real performance is also quite different, therefore, assume the stiffness of the side span beam segment 1 and segment 10 increases by 20%. The stiffness of segment 3, segment 6 and segment 12 increases by 10%. The stiffness of segment 3, segment 6 and segment 12 increases by 10%. The stiffness of segment 3, segment 6, and segment 12 increase by 10%. The stiffness of segment 5, segment 7, and segment 8 decrease by 15%. And the stiffness of the remaining beam segments 2, 4, 9, and 11 decrease by 10%, as shown in Fig. 5. Apply vehicle load at measuring point 6 (the standard vehicle wheelbase is 1.3m + 3.2m, the vehicle weight is 30t, and the arrangement is both 3 vehicles in two rows).

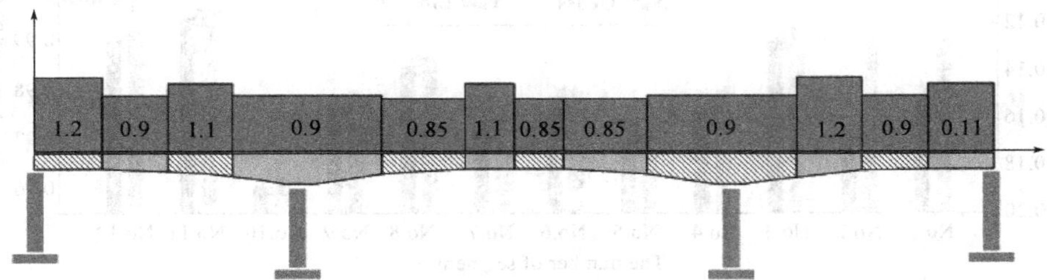

Fig. 5 Beam segment division and stiffness coefficient assumption

Take the variation stiffness coefficient between [0.5, 1.5], the Latin hypercube sampling method is adopted for experimental design, and the response value of the sample points is calculated to establish the initial Kriging model. In the process of establishing the Kriging model, the selection of regression models and correlation models has varying degrees of impact on the accuracy and fitting precision. The main reason is that the accuracy of the Kriging model obtained by different regression models or correlation models is different. To obtain a more accurate model, acomparison between the regression model and the correlation model is needed, and use the RMSE value and R^2 value to evaluate the accuracy of different Kriging models. It can be seen from Fig. 6, that the first order polynomial value of R^2 is closer to 1, and the value of RMSE is closer to 1. That indicates that the PSO-Kriging model established by the first-order polynomial is more accurate, which is more consistent with the laws of mechanics when the structure is in the elastic phase (load and deflection curve satisfy linear relationship). Generally, the load test will not load until the structure enters the nonlinear phase.

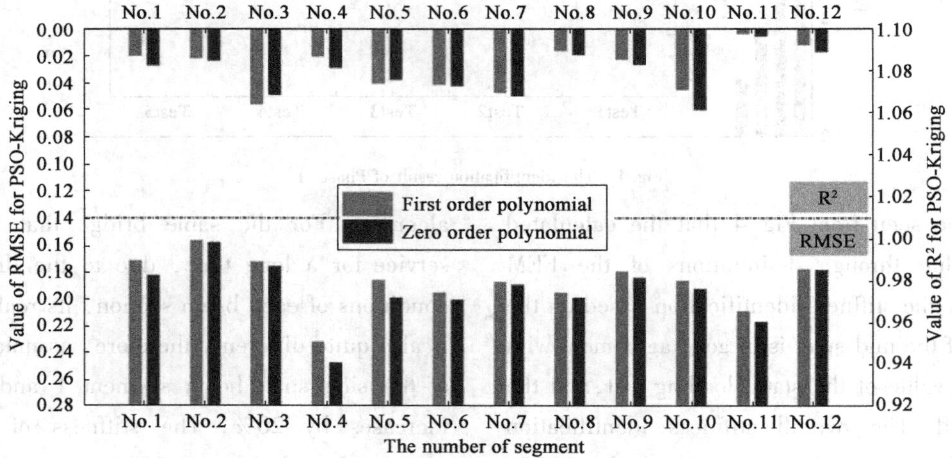

Fig. 6　Accuracy of different regression models

It can be seen from Fig. 7, the Gauss correlation models' value of R^2 is closer to 0, the value of RMSE is closer to 1. It shows that when a first-order polynomial is used as the regression model, the PSO-Kriging model established by Gauss distribution has higher accuracy, and the accuracy of the PSO-Kriging model established by other correlation models is consistent.

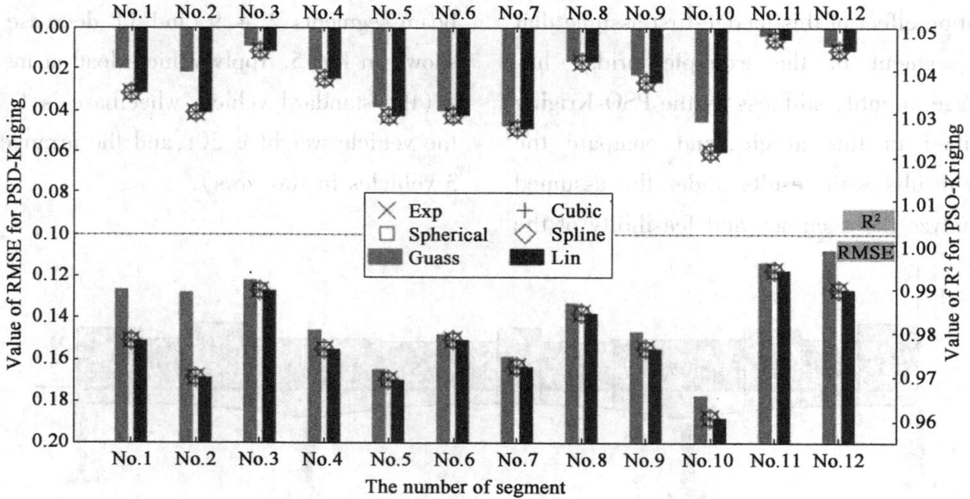

Fig. 7　Accuracy of different correlation models

Therefore, this paper uses the first-order polynomial as the regression model and Gauss distribution as the correlation model to establish the Kriging model, optimize its initial value, establish the PSO-Kriging model, and identify the stiffness. The identification results are shown in the figure below

It can be seen from the above Fig. 8, the stiffness identification based on the PSO-Kriging model achieved a better effect, the revised stiffness coefficient is very close to the proposed stiffness coefficient value, which verifies the feasibility and accuracy of this method.

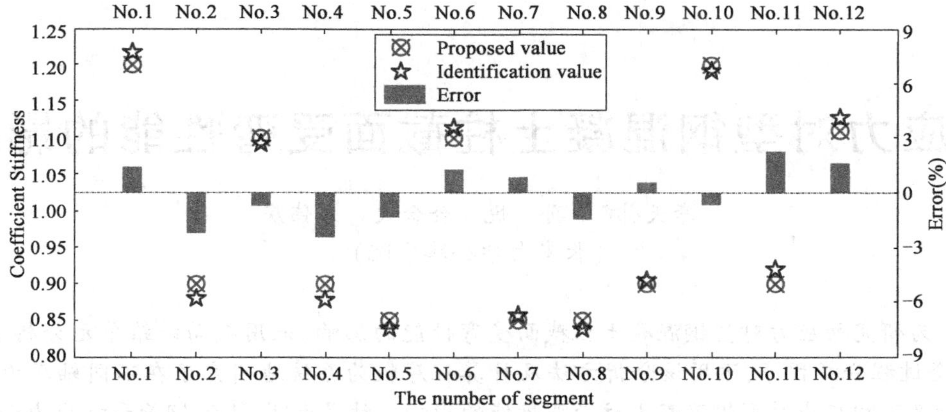

Fig. 8 The identification results in phase Ⅱ

3 Conclusions

In order to improve the accuracy and efficiency of structural parameter identification, a two-stage stiffness identification framework is proposed. Firstly, the overall evaluation method based on LM algorithm is used to evaluate the overall state of the structure and provides a basis for the evaluation of phase II. Then, PSO algorithm is used to optimize the initial value of Kriging model to ensure the accuracy of the model. Finally, the quantitative identification of structural stiffness is realized based on the established PSO Kriging model. The following conclusion can be drawn:

(1) It can be seen that the two-stage identification strategy is suitable for rapid and accurate identification of structural stiffness.

(2) The first stage identification based on L-M method can quickly obtain the overall stiffness parameters of the structure, which provides a strong basis for the preliminary judgment of the operation state of the structure; The piecewise identification method based on PSO Kriging can quickly obtain the stiffness parameters of different parts of the structure.

References

[1] Robert-Nicoud Y, Raphael B, Burdet O, et al. Model Identification of Bridges Using Measurement Data [J]. 2010,20(2):118-31.

[2] Sanayei, Masoud, Saletnik, et al. Parameter Estimation of Structures from Static Strain Measurements. I: Formulation [J]. 1996,

[3] Sanayei M S, M J. Parameter Estimation of Structures from Samtic Strain Mmeasurements. II: Error Sensitivity Aanlysis [J]. Journal of Structural Engineering, 1996, 122(5):563-72.

[4] Masoud Sanayei G R I, Jennifer A. S. Mcclain, Linfield C. brown. Structural Model Updating Using Experimental Static Measurements [J]. Journal of Structural Engineering, 1997, 123 (6).

[5] Xu B, Low B K J J O G, Engineering G. Probabilistic Stability Analyses of Embankments Based on Finite-Element Method [J]. 2006, 132 (11):1444-54.

[6] Kaymaz i, Mcmahon c A jpem. A response surface method based on weighted regression for structural reliability analysis [J]. 2005, 20 (1):11-7.

[7] S N Lophavenh h B N, J Søndergaard. Dace, a Matlab Kriging toolbox [J]. 2002,

[8] Luo X, Xin L, Jing Z, et al. A Kriging-based hybrid optimization algorithm for slope reliability analysis [J]. 2012, 34(1):401-6.

[9] H L You, J X Z. The Construction and Optimization of Kriging Metamodel Based on Genetic

Algorihms [J]. J Comput-Aided Des Comput Graph,2007,019(001):64-8(in Chinese).
[10] Sanayei M, Sampoli S. Structural Element Stiffness Identification from Static Test Data [J]. Journal of Engineering Mechanics, 1991,117.

初应力对型钢混凝土柱截面受弯性能的影响

李天伟* 孙 悦 余金火 朱伟庆
(长安大学公路学院)

摘　要　为研究初应力对型钢混凝土柱截面受弯性能的影响,采用截面纤维单元分析法,编制了截面弯矩-曲率全过程分析程序,运用该分析方法及计算程序较为系统地研究了在不同轴压力水平以及不同含钢率的情况下初应力对型钢混凝土柱受弯性能的影响。结果表明:①型钢承受初应力会降低截面最大抵抗弯矩,随着初应力比例增加,弯矩下降率增加。②轴压力系数越大,初应力比例的影响程度越大。③初应力增加会降低截面曲率延性。由于现行设计规范中尚未考虑初应力的影响,而初应力会引起截面最大抵抗弯矩和延性的降低,在实际工程中应予以关注。

关键词　型钢混凝土柱　初应力　纤维单元分析法

0　引言

随着国家交通强国战略的进一步实施,大跨、重载等已成为桥梁结构发展的迫切需求和趋势。柱构件作为整个桥梁结构抵抗地震作用的关键构件和重要的承重构件将承受着越来越大的轴力,桥墩承载力需要提高,而且还需满足抗震设防的标准,因而对桥梁建设提出了更高的要求。在此背景下,型钢混凝土柱(SRC柱)应运而生,它能够充分发挥型钢和混凝土各自的优势、可利用型钢改善混凝土柱的抗震延性,承载力能力高、刚度大与耐久性较好等优点,表现出很大的优越性。

由于SRC柱的施工特点,在混凝土达到设计强度与型钢组成组合截面共同工作之前,型钢已经预先分担了一部分荷载并在内部产生了一部分初应力,这对组合截面正截面受弯性能有一定的影响,而规范在设计计算时未能考虑,所以研究初应力对型钢混凝土柱截面的受弯影响是很有必要的。

为了更系统地研究初应力对型钢混凝土柱截面的受弯影响,本文采用截面纤维单元法,编制了型钢混凝土柱截面非线性弯矩-曲率全过程分析程序。通过数值分析研究不同轴压力系数、初应力大小及含钢率对型钢混凝土柱受弯性能的影响。

1　截面纤维单元分析法

截面非线性弯矩-曲率全过程分析采用纤维单元分析法。柱截面中不同位置的混凝土受到不同程度的约束,其中箍筋以外的混凝土为未约束混凝土,仅受箍筋约束的混凝土为部分约束混凝土,受到箍筋和型钢约束的混凝土为约束混凝土,如图1a)所示。将柱截面划分成很多较小的单元,赋予每个单元相应的单轴应力-应变关系后,每个单元就可以代表钢筋、型钢或者不同横向约束水平的混凝土,如图1b)所示。为了方便数值分析,曲线边界简化成直线边界。

运用截面纤维单元分析法对型钢混凝土柱组合截面进行弯矩-曲率全过程分析,并可研究不同参数对型钢混凝土柱正截面受弯性能的影响。

1.1　单元应力、应变计算

型钢单元的应变由初应变 ε_0 和组合截面共同工作时的应变组成,其中初应变由型钢单元初应力 σ_0 代入型钢的应力-应变关系求得,组合截面共同工作时的应变可以根据截面曲率 ϕ、中和轴高度 h 和方向角 θ,由平截面假定得出,如图2。对于柱截面中任意一单元A,假设其在 xy 坐标系

中的坐标为(x,y),在$x'y'$坐标系中的坐标为(x',y'),则:

$$\varepsilon_t = \phi h \tag{1}$$

$$\varepsilon_A = \phi(y' + (h - h'_c/2)) \tag{2}$$

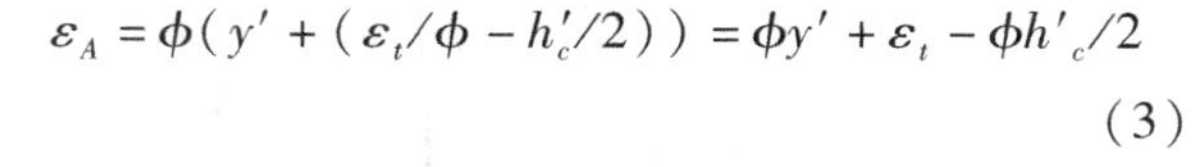

$$\varepsilon_A = \phi(y' + (\varepsilon_t/\phi - h'_c/2)) = \phi y' + \varepsilon_t - \phi h'_c/2 \tag{3}$$

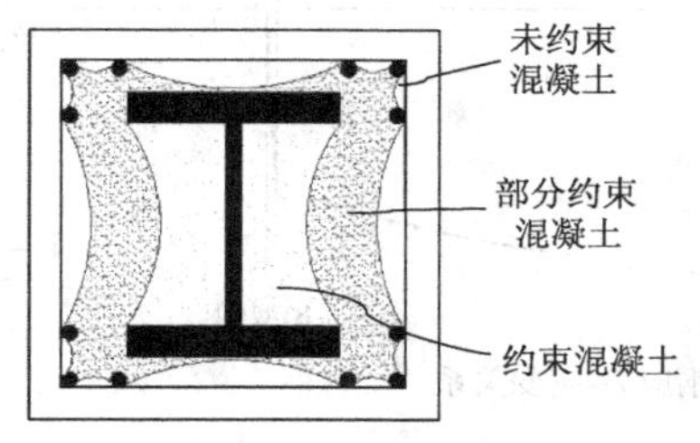

a)不同约束水平的混凝土

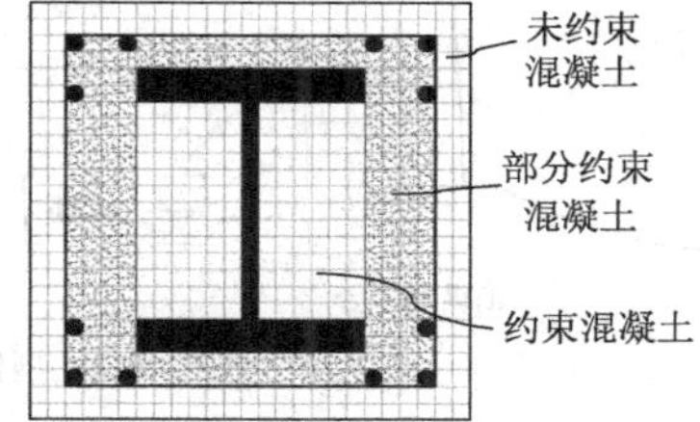

b)型钢混凝土柱截面单元划分

图1 截面纤维单元分析法

坐标(x',y')和(x,y)的关系可由两个坐标系的旋转关系得出:

$$\begin{pmatrix} x' \\ y' \end{pmatrix} = \begin{pmatrix} \cos(-\theta) & -\sin(-\theta) \\ \sin(-\theta) & \cos(-\theta) \end{pmatrix}^{-1} \begin{pmatrix} x \\ y \end{pmatrix} = \begin{pmatrix} \cos\theta & -\sin\theta \\ \sin\theta & \cos\theta \end{pmatrix} \begin{pmatrix} x \\ y \end{pmatrix} \tag{4}$$

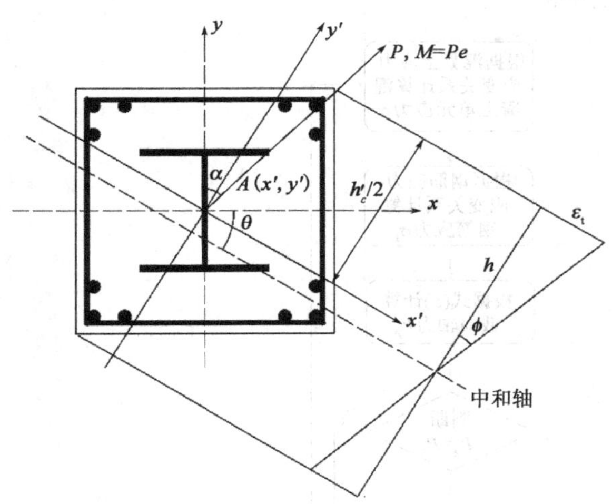

图2 截面应变分布

运用式(4)将A在xy坐标系中坐标转换成$x'y'$坐标系中的坐标后,便可运用式(3)求出A的应变。

混凝土和钢筋的应变只有组合截面共同工作时产生的应变,根据式(1)~式(4)求出。

型钢和钢筋的应力-应变关系采用朱伟庆[2],Chen和Lin[3]推荐的模型,如图3所示。

混凝土的应力-应变关系采用朱伟庆[2],Sherif M. El-Tawil[1]建议的模型。混凝土应力-应变关系曲线如图4所示。

1.2 平衡条件

假设柱端截面作用有轴力P和弯矩M,根据截面的受力平衡有:

$$P = \sum_{i=1}^{nc} \sigma_i A_i + \sum_{j=1}^{ns} \sigma_{ei} A_j + \sum_{k=1}^{nb} \sigma_{ek} A_{bk} \tag{5}$$

$$M_x = Pe\cos(\alpha) = \sum_{i=1}^{nc} \sigma_i A_i y_i + \sum_{j=1}^{ns} \sigma_{ej} A_j y_j + \sum_{k=1}^{nb} \sigma_{ek} A_{bk} y_k \tag{6}$$

$$M_y = Pe\sin(\alpha) = \sum_{i=1}^{nc} \sigma_i A_i x_i + \sum_{j=1}^{ns} \sigma_{ej} A_j x_j + \sum_{k=1}^{nb} \sigma_{ek} A_{bk} x_k \tag{7}$$

式中,P为轴向荷载,由作用在截面上的总轴向荷载N减去型钢预先分担的荷载P_0求得;M_x和M_y分别为对x轴和对y轴的弯矩;e为轴向荷载对柱几何中心的偏心矩;σ_i为第i个混凝土单元的正应力;σ_{ej}为第j个型钢单元的等效应力,通过将型钢单元的应变代入型钢应力-应变关系中求得实际应力再减去型钢单元的初应力σ_0求得;σ_{ek}为第k个钢筋的等效应力;A_i、A_j和A_{bk}分别为第i个混凝土单元、第j个型钢单元和第k个钢筋的面积;x、y为单元质心的坐标;nc、ns、nb分别是混凝土、型钢单元和钢筋的数目;α是荷载的水平倾角。根据“平截面假定”,将单元的应变代入其应力-应变关系中得到单元的应力,应力、应变以受压为正,受拉为负。根据截面平衡条件可以求出中和轴高度和方向角。

1.3 求解过程

采用纤维分析法可编制出一种能够考虑型钢初应力影响规律的分析程序,程序具体分析过程如图5所示。

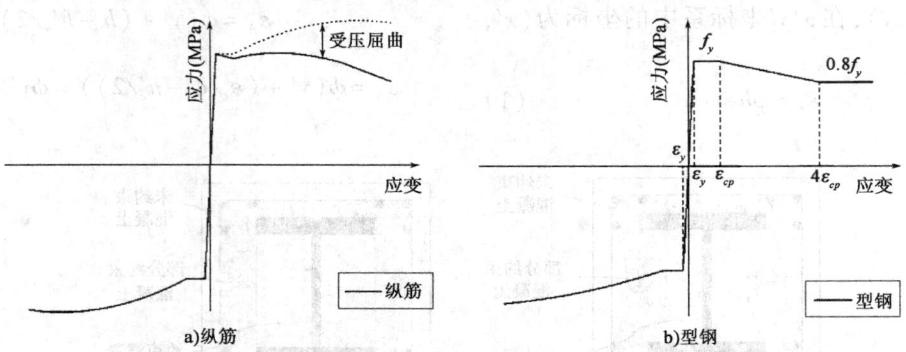

图3　钢筋、型钢应力-应变关系

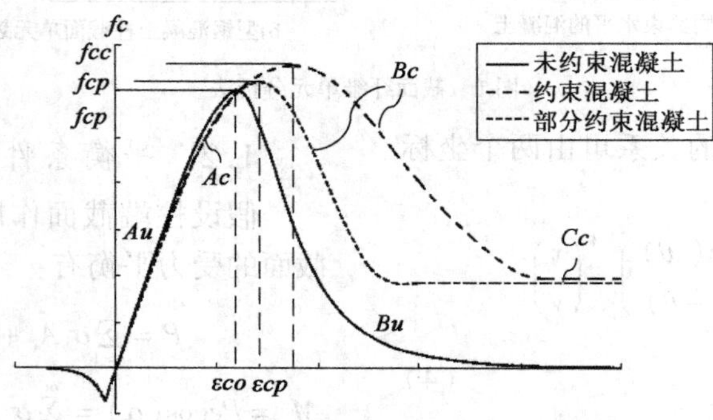

图4　混凝土材料模型

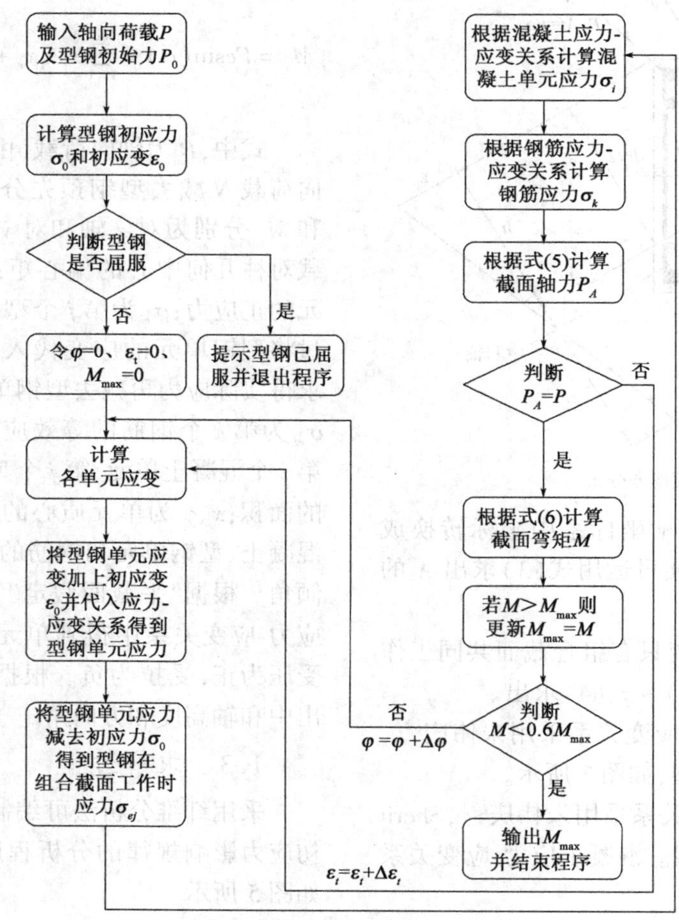

图5　程序流程图

2 截面受弯性能分析

2.1 研究参数及参数水平

设计截面为200mm×200mm的型钢混凝土模型柱，截面形式如图6所示，选取轴压力水平（本章中按照型钢规程[4]和钢骨规程[5]采用轴压力系数n_t来衡量）、型钢先分担的轴力占总轴力的比例，以下用初应力比例表示，及含钢率ρ_{ss}为研究参数，研究各参数对型钢混凝土柱受弯性能的影响。各参数水平如表1所示；纵筋屈服强度f_{yl} = 310MPa；型钢屈服强度f_{ys} = 310MPa。

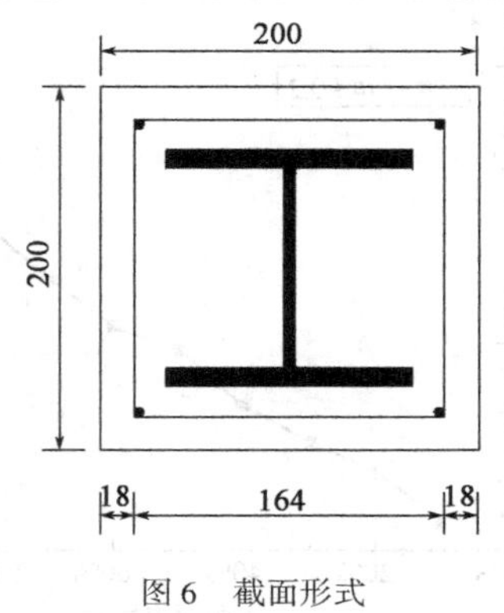

图6 截面形式

参数及各参数水平 表1

参数		参数水平			
轴压力系数	No.	n_1	n_2	n_3	n_4
	nt	0.2	0.3	0.4	0.5
型钢	No.	S1		S2	
	截面形式	130×130×6×13		130×130×11×15	
	含钢率(ρ_{ss})	10%		12.5%	
	No.	S4		S5	
	截面形式	130×130×14×18		130×130×20×20	
	含钢率(ρ_{ss})	15%		17.5%	
初应力比例	No.	P1		P2	
	初应力比例	10%		20%	
	No.	P3		P4	
	初应力比例	30%		40%	
	No.	P5		P6	
	初应力比例	50%		60%	
	No.	P7		P8	
	初应力比例	70%		80%	
	No.	P9		P10	
	初应力比例	90%		100%	

2.2 初应力对截面抵抗弯矩的影响

2.2.1 初应力比例对弯矩的影响标

图7所示为含钢率为0.15，轴压力系数nt = 0.4时弯矩下降率随初应力比例的变化情况。其中，弯矩下降率的计算方法为：（不考虑初应力的弯矩-考虑初应力的弯矩）/（不考虑初应力的弯矩）。由图可以看出，随着初应力比例的增大，弯矩下降率不断增大，且初应力比例较低时，增加速率较快，当初应力比例超过50%后，增加速率减缓，当初应力比例超过60%后，增加速率继续加快。

2.2.2 轴压力系数不同时初应力对弯矩的影响

图8所示为0.15的含钢率时不同轴压力系数下弯矩下降率随初应力比例的变化曲线。由图可知，随着轴压力系数的增大，曲线上各点的数值也随之增加；并且曲线的斜率也随着轴压力系数的增加而增加。由于轴压力系数增加，型钢分担的轴力也越来越大，故当轴压力系数较高时，初应力比例还未达到100%时型钢就已经屈服，表现在图像上就是曲线的水平投影长度的缩短。

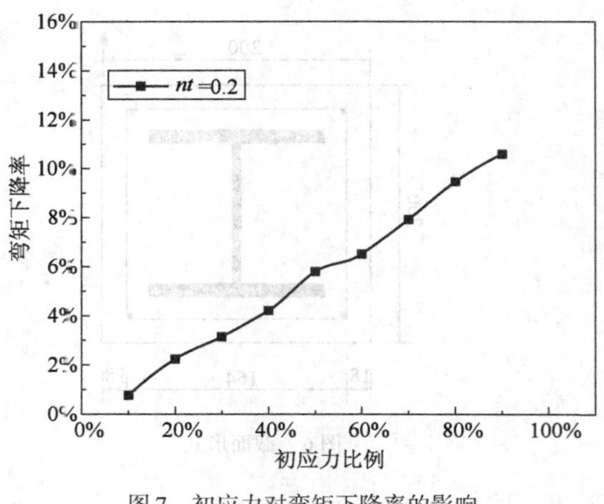

图7　初应力对弯矩下降率的影响

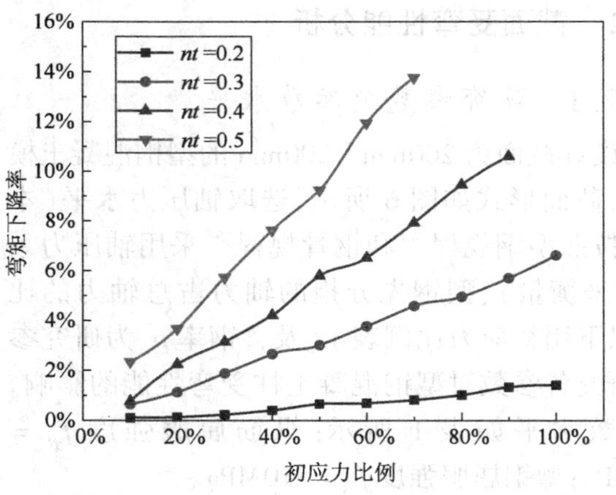

图8　不同轴压力系数下初应力对弯矩下降率的影响

2.2.3　含钢率不同时初应力对弯矩的影响

图9所示为含钢率不同时,初应力对弯矩下降率的影响。由图可以看出,不同含钢率下弯矩下降率随初应力的变化趋势大致相同,只是在数值上有所差别,轴压力系数 n_t 为0.2左右时,不同含钢率下弯矩下降率随初应力变化的曲线在变化趋势和数值上都基本相同,当轴压力系数 n_t 为0.3~0.5时随着含钢率的增加,曲线的峰值降低。此外,由于增加含钢率可使型钢承受更大的轴力,曲线的水平投影长度也随含钢率的增加而增加。

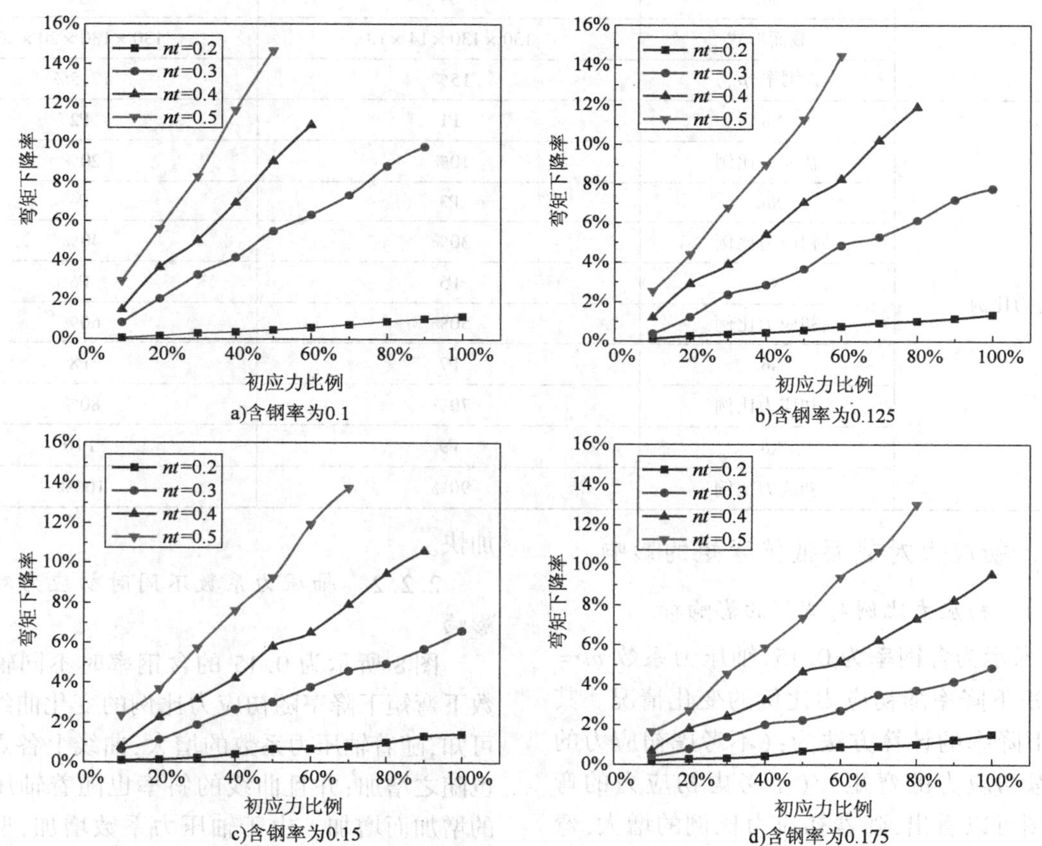

图9　不同含钢率下初应力对弯矩下降率的影响

2.3 初应力对截面曲率延性的影响

描述截面弯曲性能的截面曲率延性采用曲率延性系数μ_φ来描述：

$$\mu_\varphi=\frac{\phi_u}{\phi_y} \tag{8}$$

式中：ϕ_u——截面的极限曲率，取截面弯矩达到峰值M_u后，弯矩下降至0.80M_u时对应的曲率；

ϕ_y——屈服曲率。

图10所示为初应力对截面曲率延性的影响。图10a)所示为含钢率为15%，轴压力系数为0.3时，不同初应力下的截面的弯矩-曲率曲线；由图可知，初应力增大会降低截面的正截面抗弯强度和峰后残余强度，并使弯矩-曲率曲线右移，但是并不改变弯矩-曲率曲线的形状。图10b)为初应力对截面曲率延性系数的影响；由图可知，初应力增大时，截面曲率延性系数降低，当初应力比例超过30%时，延性系数降低速率减慢。

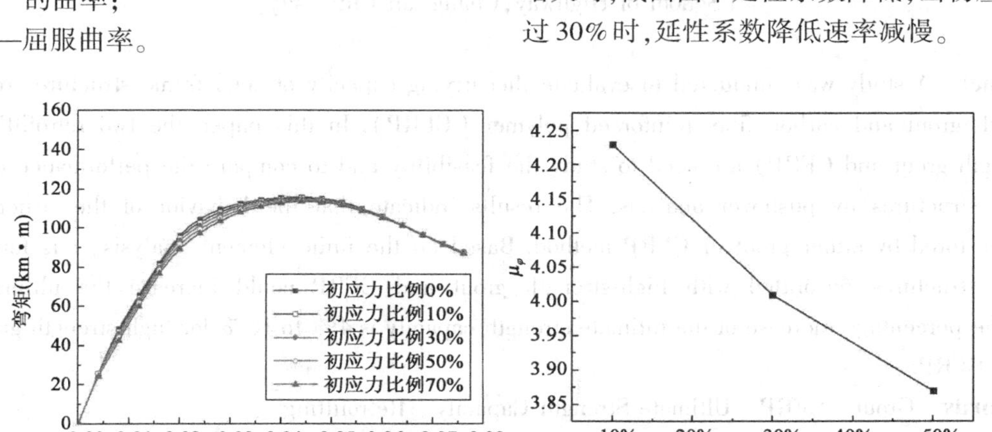

图10 初应力对截面曲率延性的影响

3 结语

(1)型钢承受初应力会降低截面最大抵抗弯矩，随着初应力比例增加，弯矩下降率增加；轴压力系数越大，初应力比例的影响程度越大。

(2)轴压力系数nt = 0.2左右时，初应力的影响基本不随含钢率的变化而变化；轴压力系数nt = 0.3 ~ 0.5时，初应力引起的弯矩下降率的峰值有所不同，含钢率越大，峰值越低。

(3)初应力增加会使截面弯矩-曲率曲线右移，但并不改变其形状；随着初应力比例增加，截面曲率延性系数降低，当初应力比例超过30%后，延性系数降低速率减缓。

(4)本文的研究成果不能考虑斜截面受剪的情况。

(5)型钢混凝土柱在使用过程中，由于混凝土徐变造成轴力在型钢和混凝土上分配不均的情况与本文研究内容类似，本文成果可作为相关研究参考。

参考文献

[1] Sherif M, El-Tawil, Gregory G. Deierlein. Fiber Element Analysis of Composite Beam-column Cross-sections [R]. New York: Structure Engineering, School of civil and environmental engineering, Cornell University, 1996:5-38.

[2] 贾金青，朱伟庆，余芳，等. 型钢超高强混凝土柱截面曲率延性研究[J]. 土木工程学报，2013,46(1):42-51.

[3] Chen C C, Lin N J. Analytical Model for Predicting Axial Capacity and Behavior of Concrete Encased Steel Composite Stub Columns [J]. Journal of Constructional Steel Research, 2006, 62(5):424-433.

[4] 中华人民共和国行业标准. 型钢混凝土组合结构技术规程：JGJ 138—2001[S]. 北京：中国建筑工业出版社，2002.

[5] 中华人民共和国行业标准. 钢骨混凝土结构设计规程：YB 9082—97[S]. 北京：冶金工业出版社，1998.

Carrying Capacity of Steel Structures Retrofitting with Grout and CFRP

Yujie Li* Xiaonan Zhao Wang Peng He Runxiang Niu Jiawei He Peiwen
(School of Highway, Chang' an University)

Abstract A study was conducted to evaluate thecarrying capacity of steel frame structures retrofitted by high-strength grout and carbon fiber-reinforced polymer (CFRP). In this paper, the two retrofitting methods (high strength grout and CFRP) are used to study the feasibility and to compare the performance of retrofitted steel frame structures by pushover analysis. The results indicate that the behavior of the structure can be effectively restored by either grout or CFRP method. Based on the finite element analysis, it is found that the steel frame structures retrofitted with high-strength grout and CFRP could increase the ultimate strength capacity. The percentage increase of the ultimate strength capacity is 4% to 16% for high strength grout and 9% to 19% for CFRP.

Keywords Grout CFRP Ultimate Strength Capacity Retrofitting

0 Introduction

Some steel frame structures which have a long design life may be damaged by accident, such as sudden large earthquake load in low-magnitude areas, while rebuilding is not an economical method. Therefore, the demand for steel structure improvement and reinforcement has been increasing over the years. The most common reinforcement methods for increasing carrying capacity include the enlarged section method and the fiber composite reinforcement method. The enlarged section method as the traditional methods of retrofitting steel structures typically utilizes the steel plates that are bolted or welded to the member. However, constructability and durability are the drawbacks of this method. The steel plates method requires heavy lifting equipment and adds more dead load to the structure. The added steel plates are also susceptible to corrosion, and this may lead to increasing costs in future maintenance. Besides the external steel plate method, the enlarged section method by high-strength grout is also highly used in practical. In other cases, the anti-seepage system in front of the dam of a power station was reinforced by grout under water during the operation period of the power station[1]. Based on the characteristics of the offshore platform, the grouting method was also used for reinforcement[2]. The potential advantages of grouted repair techniques have been recognized for some years. In summary these are: normal fabrication imperfections are easily accommodated by the grout; geometrical damage is easily accommodated; full strength of damaged sections can be restored; where increased strength is required this can readily be provided; repairs can be carried out at any depth within the range of current structures. For fiber composite reinforcement method which has been used to study burning hot these years, the previous study used finite element method to systematically analyze the load transfer coefficient of fiber-reinforced composite materials to strengthen steel structures and proposed several improvements[3-5]. In this paper, the application of high strength grout method for improving the ultimate strength capacity of a steel structure damaged by load and the performamce comparisons of grout and CFRP retrofitted are discussed. In order to investigate the performance of the steel frame structures at external load, the high strength grout, Ducorit® grout produced by Densit ApS company, is chosen for reinforcement due to its high compressive strength and durability which result in extremely high fatigue strength.

1 Modelling of grout members

1.1 Elastic properties

The effective bending stiffness is taken as the sum of the steel and grout bending stiffness:

$$EI = (EI)_s + I_{red} \times (EI)_g \tag{1}$$

where:

EI represents effective bending stiffness of composite material;

$(EI)_s$, $(EI)_g$ represents effective bending stiffness of steel and grout;

I_{red} represents a factor that accounts for a reduced contribution from the grout. According to Eurocode 4, I_{red} = 0.8, while Haukaas, M and Yang, Q, (2000) recommend I_{red} = 1.0. In this study, the value of 1.0 is adopted.

The elastic axial stiffness is taken as the sum of the steel and grout axial stiffness:

$$EA = (EA)_s + (EA)_g \tag{2}$$

where, EA represents elastic axial stiffness of composite material;

$(EA)_s$, $(EA)_g$ represents elastic axial stiffness of steel and grout.

It is beneficial to modify the elastic bending stiffness such that the steel properties can be used, i.e. equivalent moment of inertia and equivalent area are defined as:

$$I_{eq} = I_s + I_{red} \times \frac{E_g}{E_s} I_g \tag{3}$$

$$A_{eq} = A_s + \frac{E_g}{E_s} A_g \tag{4}$$

where, I_{eq}, A_{eq} represents equivalent moment of inertia and equivalent area of composite material;

I_s, I_g represents moment of inertia of steel section and grout section;

A_s, A_g represents area of steel and grout;

E_s, E_g represents elastic modulus of steel and grout.

The equivalent density may be defined such that the total mass of the grouted pipe is correct:

$$\rho_{eq} = \rho_s + \frac{A_g}{A_s} \rho_g \tag{5}$$

where, ρ_{eq} represents equivalent density of composite material;

ρ_s, ρ_g represents density of steel and grout.

1.2 Plastic capacity

The following principles are used when the plastic section properties are calculated, refer to Fig. 1:

(1) the steel tube behaves as an ordinary pipe section;

(2) the grout can only take compressive stresses, the yield stress is assumed to be constant over the compressive section. On the tension side, the stress is zero.

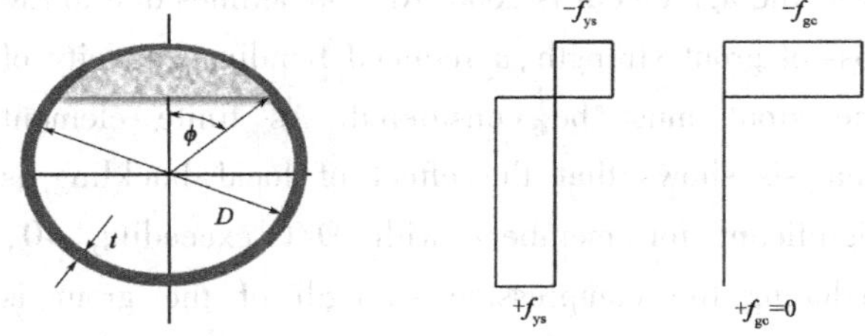

Fig. 1 Plastic stress distribution for grouted section

On this basis the following interaction equation can be calculated for the pipe section:

$$\frac{M}{M_{ps}} = \sin\phi \tag{6}$$

$$\frac{N}{N_{ps}} = \frac{\phi}{\frac{\pi}{2}} - 1 \tag{7}$$

where the plastic capacities in bending and axial tension/compression are

$$M_{ps} = f_{ys} \frac{D^3 - (D - 2t)^3}{6} \tag{8}$$

$$N_{ps} = f_{ys} \frac{\pi (D - 2t)2}{4} \tag{9}$$

where, f_{ys} represents the yield stress for steel;

D and t represents the diameter and thickness of

the tube respectively.

For the grouted section, there is obtained:

$$\frac{M}{M_{pg}} = \sin^3 \phi \tag{10}$$

$$\frac{N}{N_{pg}} = \frac{1}{\pi}\left(\phi - \frac{1}{2}\sin 2\phi\right) \tag{11}$$

where the plastic capacities in bending and axial compression are

$$M_{pg} = f_{yg}\frac{(D-2t)^3}{12} \tag{12}$$

$$N_{pg} = f_{yg}\frac{\pi\,(D-2t)^2}{4} \tag{13}$$

where f_{yg} represents the yield stress for grout, the grouted section contributes only on the compression side of the interaction.

For the composite section, the two interaction equation can be added. The angle to the neutral axial, ϕ, constitutes the interrelation. Haukaas, M. and Yang, Q. (2000)[6] proposed to use $\cos^{1/\beta}$-type function and it adopts $\cos^{1/\beta}$-type function in the study as an approximation to the interaction curve. And the agreement is good. Also sometimes due to the loss of grout strength, a reduced bending capacity of the grout must be considered. As finite element analysis shows that the effect of local buckling is significant for members with D/t exceeding 40, reducing the compressive strength of the grout is necessary.

2 Pushover analysis of platforms and the retrofitted schemes

Pushover analysis is a static, nonlinear procedure in which the magnitude of thelateral loading is incrementally increased in accordance with a certain predefined pattern. The loading is monotonic with the effects of the cyclic behavior and load reversals being estimated by using modified monotonic force-deformation criteria and with damping approximations. In this study, the method of load control is adopted for pushover analysis. The structure is pushed until it becomes unstable and reaches its collapse state. Pushover analysis is based on the assumption that the response of the structure can be related to the response of an equivalent single-degree-of-freedom (SDOF) system. Once the equivalent SDOF system is constructed, its response to any loading can be obtained. One important product of the pushover analysis is the base shear versus top displacement relationship, commonly referred to as the capacity curve of the building. This curve gives an overall summary of the capacity of the structure. Information such as the initial elastic stiffness, the initiation of first yielding, the stage of rapid stiffness deterioration, and the ultimate strength can all be inferred from the capacity curve. In addition, the damage pattern of the building at any post-yield level can be found by examining other response parameters. The weak links and undesirable characteristics in the structure such as carrying capacity can readily be detected from the damage pattern. The process of pushover analysis is shown in the following: first, apply an inverted triangular lateral load from the top to the bottom of the structure, and then gradually increase the load until the structure overturns. And with the increase in the magnitude of the loading, weak links and failure modes of the steel structure are appeared. In this study, pushover analysis is used to measure the reserve and residual strength, the redundancy and the mode of failure of the steel structures.

In pushover analysis, the main failure modes are member buckling of the compressive braces at the bottom and intermediate bays. The strengthening schemes for four-legged X-brace structure with retrofitted braces (80m X-brace and 80m X-brace without horizontal member) are shown in Fig. 2 by the bold solid line. The maximum base shear and maximum topside horizontal displacement from the pushover analysis and failure members are listed in Tab.1. Obviously, the 80m X-brace structure and 80m X-brace structure without horizontal members cannot meet the ductility requirement and requires retrofitting.

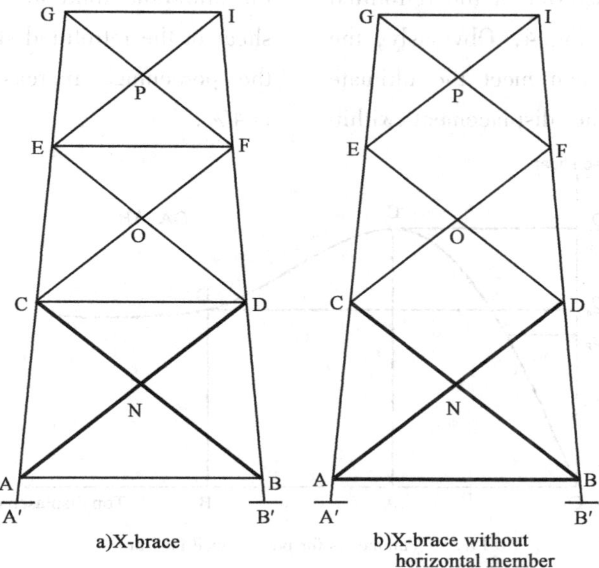

Fig. 2 Strengthening scheme of structures

Max. base shear and Max. horizontal displacement forplatforms Tab. 1

Items	80m (a)		80m (b) structure	
	Max. Base Shear (kN)	Max. Horizontal Displacement (m)	Max. Base Shear (kN)	Max. Horizontal Displacement (m)
Pushover	1.13E+04	0.61	9.60E+03	0.36
Failure members	BN		BC, AB	

3 Pushover analysis of groutstructures compared with cfrp

3.1 Structures retrofitting with grout

In order tocompare the performance of structure before and after strengthening, it adopts energy-based and load-based performance measures in this study. The following parameters in Fig. 3 are selected.

$$R_1 = \frac{\text{environmental load at ultimate strength capacity } (Q_m)}{\text{environmental load at first plastic hinge } (Q_p)}$$

$$R_2 = \frac{\text{environmental load at deflection equal to twice the deflection at ultimate strength capacity } (Q_n)}{\text{environmental load at ultimate strength capacity } (Q_m)}$$

$$R_3 = \frac{\text{energy at deflection equal to twice the deflection at ultimate strength capacity (area of OBDC)}}{\text{energy at ultimate strength capacity (area of OAC)}}$$

The first performance measure R_1 is an indication of the available reserve strength up to the point where the ultimate load of the structures has been reached. Hereafter referred to as pre-ultimate performance measure. The second performance measure R_2 indicates the residual strength expressed as a ratio of ultimate strength, whereas the third performance measure R_3 indicates post-ultimate energy dissipation capacity. R_2 and R_3 hereafter referred to as post-ultimate performance measures.

3.1.1 80m X-brace structures

The retrofitting scheme for 80 meters four-legged X-brace platform is shown in Fig. 2. The braces OD, OE buckled in the pushover analysis, bold solid lines in Fig. 2, were filled with the high strength grout.

The results from the pushover of the retrofitted structure are compared in Fig. 4. Obviously, the structure after strengthening can meet the ultimate strength requirement, with the displacement within the allowable limit for stability. The maximum base shear of the retrofitted structure is 1.18×10^4 kN and the percentage increase of the ultimate capacity is 4%.

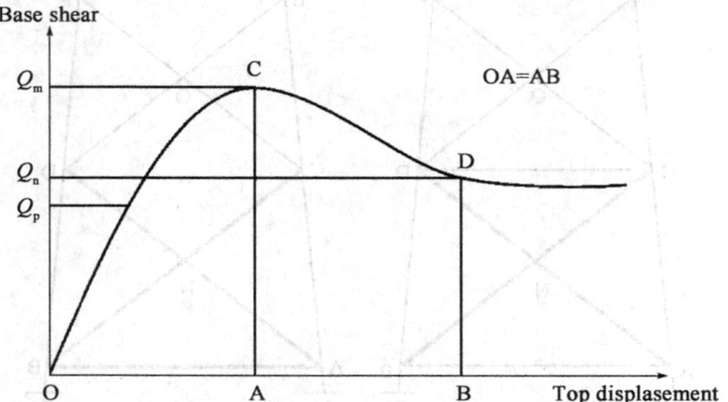

Fig. 3 Parameters for performance measures

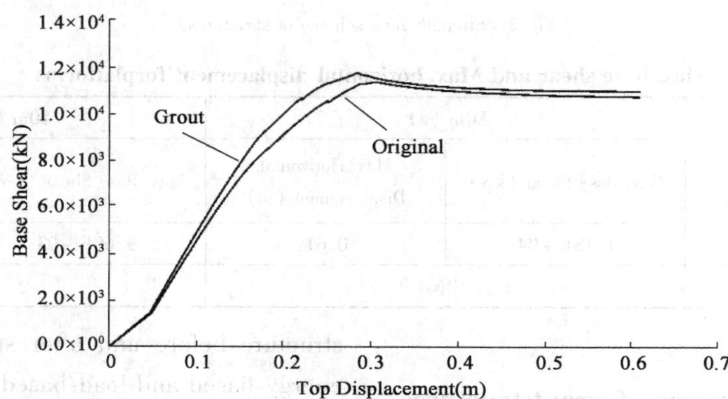

Fig. 4 Comparisons of 80m X-brace structure before and after strengthening by grout

Tab. 2 shows the performance measures for the 80m X-brace structure before and after strengthening. It can be seen that the percentage increase of base shear at the first plastic hinge (23%) is greater than the percentage increase of ultimate base shear (4%) after retrofitted. This Phenomenon results in better pre-ultimate performance for the original structure compared with the retrofitted structure. The residual strength R_2 is similar before and after retrofitting. However, the retrofitted structure shows a better post-ultimate energy dissipation capacity.

Performance measures for 80-meter X-brace structures Tab. 2

Type	Base shear at first plastic hinge (kN)	Ultimate base shear (kN)	Base shear at twice the deflection at ultimate load (kN)	Energy at ultimate capacity (kJ)	Energy at twice the deflection at ultimate load (kJ)	R_1	R_2	R_3
Original	8.46×10^3	1.13×10^4	1.07×10^4	3.80×10^3	8.20×10^3	1.34	0.95	2.16
Grout	1.04×10^4	1.18×10^4	1.10×10^4	3.66×10^3	8.22×10^3	1.13	0.93	2.25

3.1.2 80m X-brace structures without horizontal members

The strengthening scheme for 80 meters four-legged structure without horizontal members is shown in Fig. 2. The buckling braces, bold solid lines in Fig. 2, in pushover analysis were filled with the high-strength grout.

Thepushover results between before and after retrofitting structure are compared in Fig. 5. The member forces and stresses in all structural elements during analysis were investigated and it was found that there was no buckling or yielding in any element. Obviously, the structure after strengthening can meet the ultimate strength requirement, with the displacement within the allowable limit for stability. The maximum base shear of the retrofitted structure is 1.09×10^4 kN and the percentage increase of the ultimate capacity is 13%. Tab. 3 shows the performance measures for the 80m X-brace structure without horizontal members before and after strengthening. The retrofitted structure shows an improved reserved strength R_1 of 5% due to an increase in the strength of compressive braces by the high strength grout. From Fig. 5, it can be seen that the fall-off in load in a retrofitted structure is faster than the fall off in load in the original structure after the ultimate capacity. This phenomenon leads to the decrease in residual strength R_2 and post-ultimate energy dissipation capacity R_3.

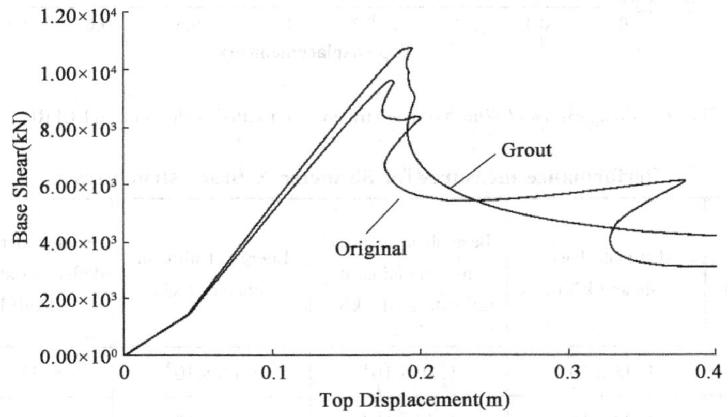

Fig. 5 Comparisons of 80m X-brace structure without horizontal members before and after strengthening

Performance measures for 80m X-brace structures without horizontal members Table 3

Type	Base shear at first plastic hinge (kN)	Ultimate base shear (kN)	Base shear at twice the deflection at ultimate load (kN)	Energy at ultimate capacity (kJ)	Energy at twice the deflection at ultimate load (kJ)	R_1	R_2	R_3
Original	9.54×10^3	9.63×10^3	6.05×10^3	1.33×10^3	2.41×10^3	1.01	0.63	1.81
Grout	1.05×10^4	1.09×10^4	4.13×10^3	1.69×10^3	2.52×10^3	1.04	0.38	1.49

3.2 Comparison of performance retro fitting with grout and CFRP

It can be seen that the externally bonded longitudinal CFRP sheets are effective in increasing the axial strength and stiffness of slender braces. For comparing the performance of grout, this paper quotes the data of the same research group on CFRP. In order to model the composite action between the steel brace and CFRP during pushover analyzing, the equivalent CFRP beam element with special geometric and material properties are used in this study.

3.2.1 80m X-brace structures

Fig. 6 shows the base shear-deflection curves of the structure retrofitted with grout and CFRP. From the results, it can be found that the ultimate strength of the structure retrofitted with CFRP is greater than that value when the structure is retrofitted with grout. The main difference in the post-ultimate behaviors is due to the buckling of members in different bays.

Tab. 4 shows the performance measures for 80m X-brace structure after retrofitting (Grout and CFRP). The structure retrofitted with CFRP shows an improved reserved strength R_1 of about 7% over the structure retrofitted with grout. However, in the structure retrofitted with CFRP the resistance falls off quickly after the ultimate strength capacity. This leads to the decrease in residual strength R_2 and post-ultimate energy dissipation capacity R_3.

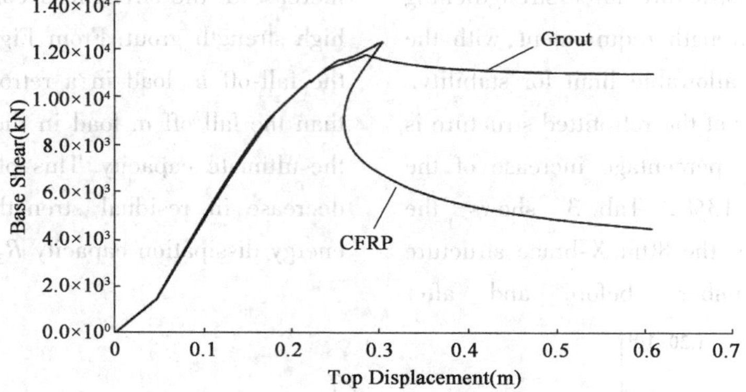

Fig. 6　Comparisons of 80m X-brace structure retrofitted with grout and CFRP

Performance measures for 80-meter X-brace structures　　Tab. 4

Type	Base shearat first plastic hinge (kN)	Ultimate base shear (kN)	Base shear at twice the deflection at ultimate load (kN)	Energy at ultimate capacity (kJ)	Energy at twice the deflection at ultimate load(kJ)	R_1	R_2	R_3
Grout	1.04×10^4	1.18×10^4	1.10×10^4	3.66×10^3	8.22×10^3	1.13	0.93	2.25
CFRP	1.02×10^4	1.23×10^4	4.47×10^3	4.44×10^3	5.66×10^3	1.21	0.36	1.27

3.2.2　80m X-brace structures without horizontal members

Fig. 7 shows the base shear-deflection curves of retrofitted structure with grout and CFRP. The ultimate strength capacity of structure retrofitted with CFRP is greater than the ultimate strength capacity of structure retrofitted with grout. Tab. 5 shows the performance measures for 80m X-brace structure without horizontal members after strengthening. The structure retrofitted with CFRP shows an improved reserved strength R_1 of about 7% over the structure retrofitted with grout. The residual strength R_2 and post-ultimate energy dissipation capacity R_3 of the structure retrofitted with CFRP are almost same as the platform retrofitted with grout. From Fig. 8, it can be seen that the post-ultimate strength for the structure retrofitted with CFRP is marginally higher than the value when retrofitted with grout.

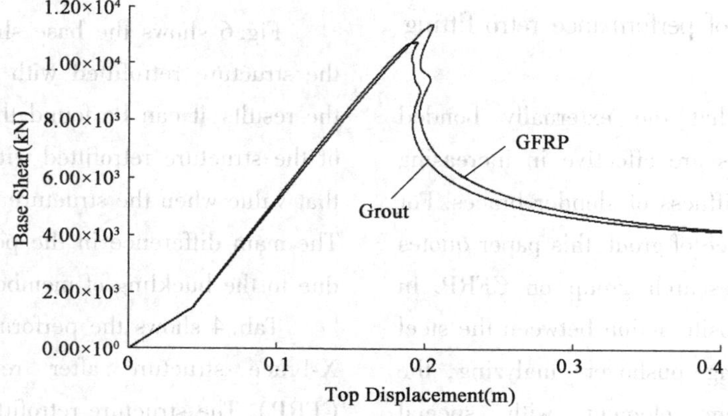

Fig. 7　Comparisons of 80m X-brace structure without horizontal members retrofitted with grout and CFRP

Performance measures for 80m X-brace structures without horizontal members Tab. 5

Type	Base shear at first plastic hinge (kN)	Ultimate base shear (kN)	Base shear at twice the deflection at ultimate load (kN)	Energy at ultimate capacity (kJ)	Energy at twice the deflection at ultimate load (kJ)	R_1	R_2	R_3
Grout	1.05×10^4	1.09×10^4	4.59×10^3	1.88×10^3	2.80×10^3	1.03	0.38	1.49
CFRP	1.04×10^4	1.14×10^4	4.69×10^3	2.10×10^3	3.11×10^3	1.10	0.37	1.48

4 Conclusions

In this study, twostrengthening methods, one with high-strength grout and the other with CFRP are used and compared to check the ultimate strength capacity of the steel frame structures. Based on the finite element analysis, the following results can be obtained:

(1) Thestructures retrofitted with high-strength grout could meet the ultimate strength requirement. The percentage increase of the ultimate strength capacity is 4 to 16%. After retrofitting, the structures show a better reserve strength R_1 than the original structures. The structures after strengthening have exhibited similar residual strength R_2 but show a higher post-ultimate energy dissipation capacity R_3, except for 80m X-brace structure without horizontal members.

(2) Compared with thestructures retrofitted with grout, the structures retrofitted with CFRP show an improved reserved strength R_1 of 4 to 7%. The two strengthening methods show similar values for residual strength R_2 and post-ultimate energy dissipation capacity R_3, except for the 80m X-brace structure.

(3) By comparison, it can be found that the CFRP could be useful forapplication in tubular structures. Further research is needed to investigate the feasibility of implementing the proposed CFRP retrofitting technique in practice.

References

[1] Lin Sen. Application of steel structure platform in reinforcement construction of anti-seepage system of hydropower station[J]. Sichuan water conservancy(in Chinese), 2016, 02.

[2] Etterdal B. Askheim D. Strengthening of Offshore Steel, Components Using High-Strength Grout: Component Testing and Analytical Methods[J]. OTC 2001, 13192:191-208.

[3] Cheng Huang, Tao Chen, Xian Wang. Compressive characteristics of damaged circular hollow section (CHS) steel columns repaired by CFRP or grout jacketing[J]. Thin-Walled Structures, 2017, 119:635-645.

[4] J A Beavers, N G Thompson C. Technologies, External corrosion of oil and natural gas pipelines Corros[J]. Environ. Ind., 2006, 13C (13):1015-1026.

[5] Xiang Zehui, Zhou Jie, Niu Jiangang, et al. Mechanical properties of square concrete short columns strengthened by concrete canvas and CFRP strips under axial compression[J]. Acta Materiae Compositae Sinica (in Chinese), 2022, 39.

[6] Haukaasm M, Yang Q. Development of a Grouted Beam Element for Pushover Analysis[J]. Offshore Design, 2000.

多塔斜拉输水管桥力学特性分析

汪峻松* 　刘双瑞
(长安大学公路学院)

摘　要　目前关于大型输水管桥的研究较少,为分析输水管桥的受力特性,运用 Midas Civil 桥梁分析软件,建立了多塔斜拉输水管桥有限元模型,根据斜拉桥计算理论对成桥状态进行了静力和动力特性分析。研究表明,大型输水管桥的水荷载约为等桥宽汽车荷载的4倍,应着重考虑水荷载对桥梁产生影响;在不同水荷载工况下,满水工况较为安全,偏载工况会产生较大的应力与位移,设计时需要重点关注桥梁的横向刚度。

关键词　桥梁工程　输水管桥　静力分析　动力特性分析

0　引言

近年来,我国各地区的水资源分布不均匀,因此修建了许多战略性的调水基础设施工程。输水桥梁作为跨越河流、山谷的重要手段之一,在调水工程中起着举足轻重的作用。

斜拉桥是常用的输水桥型之一,其结构安全性是整个输水路线中的关键。在管桥力学分析方面,高行行[1]开展了较为全面的大跨度输水斜拉桥力学性能研究。马芹纲等[2]、庄小将等[3]研究了水荷载对斜拉桥产生的影响,分析了输水管道的振动频率,判断其与桥梁的固有频率是否会发生共振,结果表明桥梁结构与输水管道的固有频率相差较大,二者不会产生共振现象,水管不会影响既有桥梁结构的安全运营及行车舒适度。庄小将等[4]通过拟静力分析,将水荷载的影响与使用荷载效应进行对比,发现其对桥梁结构成桥状态的安全运营影响不大。赵静等[5]提出对管道静力分析时可以简化模型,用二维的简单模型来进行简单计算。许萍等[6-7]给出了数值模拟中大跨度斜拉管桥的几何非线性分析方法,指出几何非线性因素存在耦合作用,在结构计算时需要综合考虑其影响。

上述学者所做的研究大多基于小流量、轻型的输水管桥,目前关于大流量、重型的管桥研究还十分缺乏。本文以大流量的多塔斜拉输水管桥为研究对象,通过有限元模拟的手段对多塔斜拉输水管桥的静力特性和动力特性进行分析,分析结果可为后续水管桥的研究提供工程参考。

1　工程概况

该输水管桥主桥长 490m,为四塔五跨斜拉桥,跨径布置为(65 + 3 × 120 + 65)m,桥梁总宽 18.5m;主塔采用水滴形混凝土结构,桥塔总高约 72m,桥面以上 44.2m,桥面以下 27.8m;主梁采用钢桁梁,桁内净宽 16.5m,考虑管道检修吊装,净空按 6.5m 控制;双索面布置,斜拉索间距 8.0m,单塔布置 12 对,全桥共布置 48 对;标准断面宽 16.5m。桥上敷设双根直径为 3400mm 的输水压力钢管道。图1为桥梁立面图。

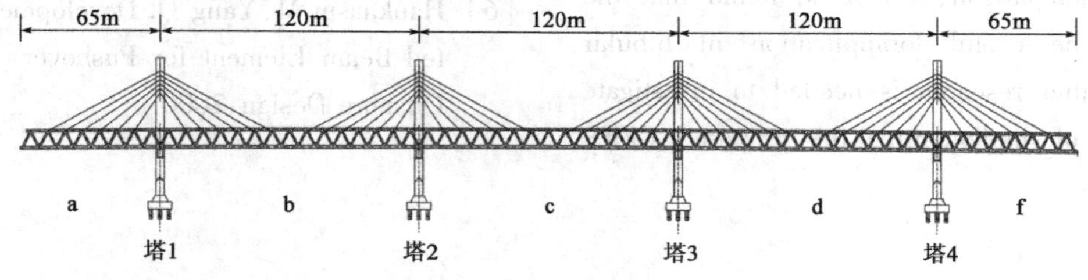

图1　桥梁立面图

2 计算模型

2.1 模型简介

本文采用 Midas Civil 2020 对该桥进行有限元分析。该桥结构较为复杂,全桥模型有 2430 单元、1270 个节点。其中,拉索采用 96 个桁架单元进行模拟,其余均为梁单元。钢桁梁部分包括纵梁、横梁、上下弦杆、腹杆、横撑,主要通过拉索和支座进行支撑,管道以压力的形式作用于桥面板,其刚度不计。图 2 为有限元模型。

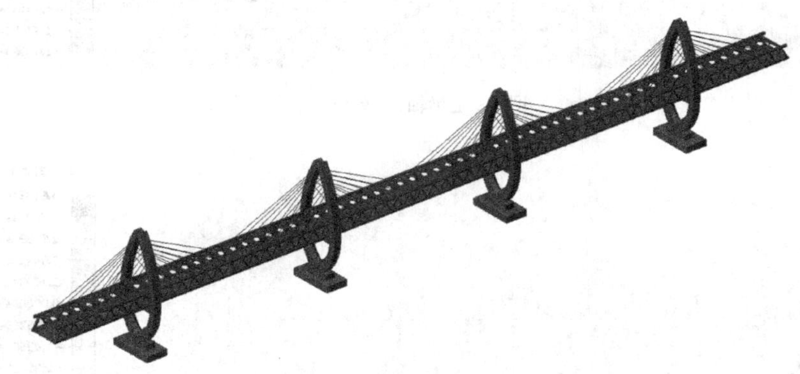

图 2 桥梁有限元模型

2.2 荷载工况

本文在进行成桥阶段静力分析时考虑了以下设计荷载:

(1)结构自重:包括桥梁结构自重、桥面铺装、护栏、管道。其中,桥面铺装荷载为 39.5kN/m,护栏荷载为 10kN/m,管道荷载为 37.0kN/m。

(2)水荷载:荷载为 180kN/m,假定管道阀门设置在桥塔处或端部位置,根据管道中流水可能所处的位置,分为以下 5 种工况:

水荷载 1:水荷载作用于 a 跨;

水荷载 2:水荷载作用于 a、b 跨;

水荷载 3:水荷载作用于 a、b、c 跨;

水荷载 4:水荷载作用于 a、b、c、d 跨;

满水工况:水荷载作用于全桥 5 跨;

将满水工况与汽车荷载工况进行对比,根据《公路桥涵设计通用规范规范》(JTG D60—2015),汽车荷载设为公路 I 级荷载,集中荷载取 360kN/m,均布荷载取 10.5kN/m,按桥面宽度取四车道进行计算,均布作用于全桥约为 45kN/m。由此可得,水荷载约为汽车荷载的 4 倍,应着重考虑水荷载对桥梁的影响。

(3)温度荷载:依据当地温度数据,设置整体升温为 28.4℃,整体降温为 20℃。

(4)预拉力:设置在桥塔横梁处。

3 静力分析

依据不同的荷载工况与效应组合,本文开展了输水管桥成桥状态下的静力分析。

3.1 满水工况

由于输水管桥大多处于满水工况下,此处选取了承载能力极限状态设计时的内力控制组合,具体为"结构自重 + 满水工况 + 整体升温 + 预拉力"。受篇幅所限,以下仅列出了主梁内力、位移和应力。内力组合下的主梁弯矩、剪力、轴力、应力、位移如图 3 ~ 图 7 所示。

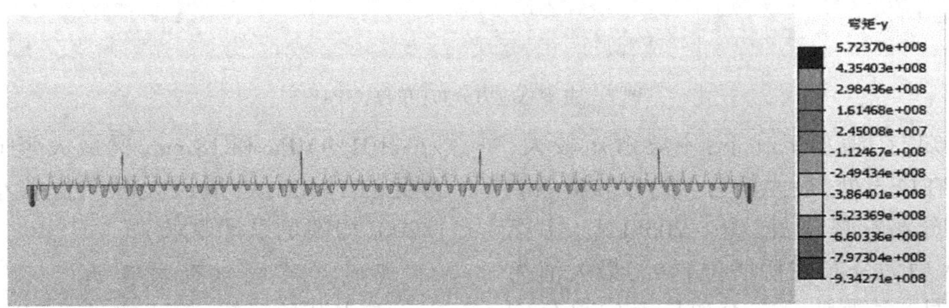

图 3 主梁弯矩(单位:N · mm)

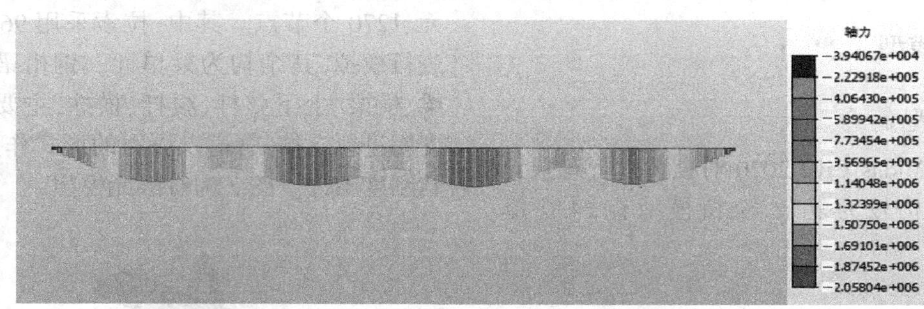

图 4　主梁轴力(单位:N)

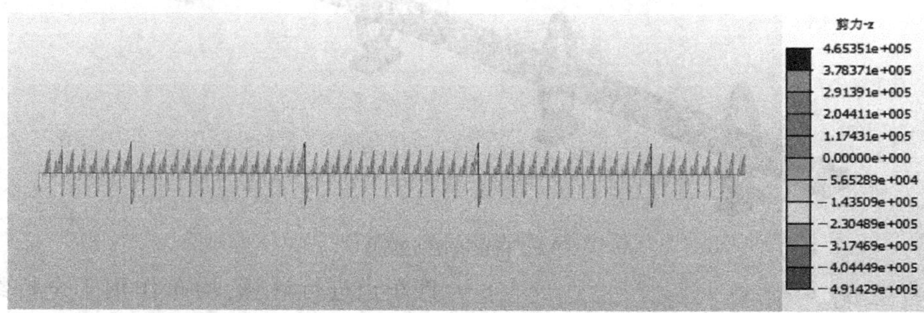

图 5　主梁剪力(单位:N)

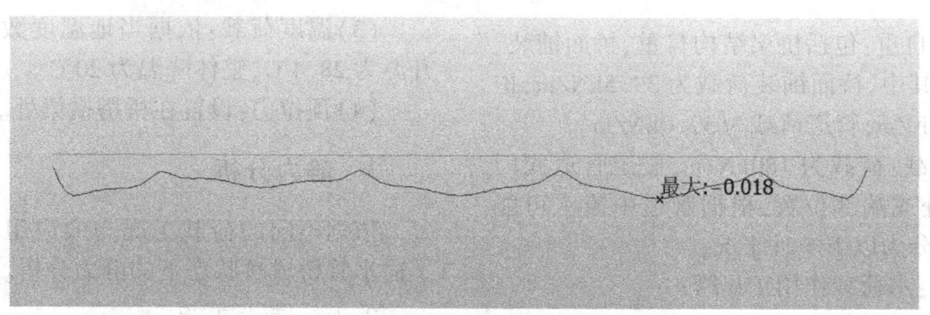

图 6　主梁竖向位移(单位:m)

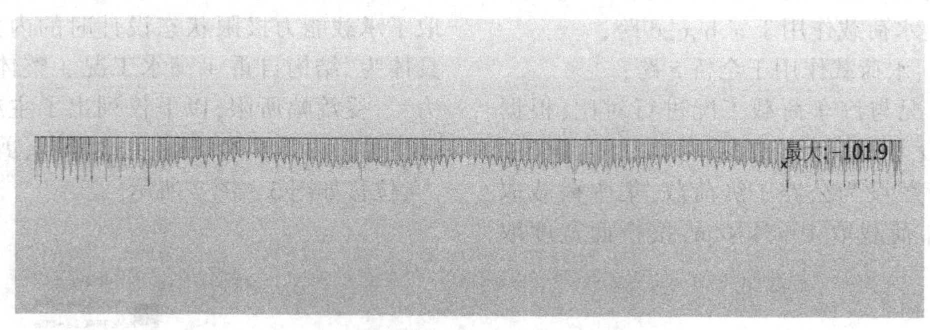

图 7　主梁总应力分布(单位:MPa)

由上图可知,在满水工况下,主梁弯矩较大,最大弯矩分布在塔 3 处,最大值为 −934.3kN · m。主梁最大轴力分布在塔 3 处,为 −2058kN。主梁剪力较小,最大剪力分布在桥塔位置处,最大值为 491.43kN。另外,主梁最大应力和最大位移分别为 −101.9MPa 和 18mm,梁最大竖向位移小于其跨度的 1/400,塔顶最大纵向位移小于其高度的 1/200,均满足设计要求。

3.2　不同水荷载工况

在水开始运输、停止或是受到阀门阻挡时,通常不是充满全桥的,为分析水荷载作用在不同位置对桥梁关键部位的影响,控制荷载组合中其他荷载项不变,仅分析水荷载发生变化时的计算结果。表1和表2列出了桥梁各关键部位的最大应力和最大位移值。水荷载1~4的工况如前面所述。

不同水荷载工况下关键部位的最大应力(MPa) 表1

部件	水荷载1	水荷载2	水荷载3	水荷载4	满水全桥
主梁	-113.8	-155.4	-99.5	-129.7	-101.9
横梁	215.6	231.5	202.5	207.3	188.0
弦杆	113.0	134.2	106.6	81.4	84.4
桥塔	-11.7	-11.3	-11.4	-11.2	-11.1
拉索	456.2	549.0	578.6	567.2	568.3

由表1可知,当水荷载作用于a、b两跨时,主梁、横梁、弦杆应力均达到最大值。主梁应力最大为-155.4MPa,位于塔1处;横梁应力最大为231.5MPa,位于塔1处;弦杆应力最大为134.2MPa,位于桥头支座附近。桥塔应力处于较低水平,最大为-11.7MPa,位于塔梁交接处;拉索应力最大为578.6MPa,位于塔2处。

不同水荷载工况下关键部位的最大位移(mm) 表2

位移	水荷载1	水荷载2	水荷载3	水荷载4	满水全桥
纵主梁竖向位移	81.0	78.4	93.5	23.3	18.0
桥梁竖向位移	83.2	81.3	96.0	25.9	17.2
桥塔纵向位移	80.6	67.2	74.6	53.6	51.4

由表2可知,当水荷载作用于a、b、c三跨时,纵主梁、横梁的竖向位移达到最大值,主梁最大为93.5mm,横梁最大为96.0mm,位置均处于d跨跨中。当水荷载仅作用于a跨,塔1塔顶处的纵向位移最大,为80.6mm。

由上述数据可知,在不同荷载组合下,各构件的应力均满足设计要求,主梁最大竖向位移小于其跨度的1/400,塔顶最大纵向位移小于其高度的1/200,所有变形也满足设计要求。其中,需要注意横梁的刚度,针对偶然荷载要有所预防。

4 动力特性分析

桥梁动力特性分析是桥梁结构分析不可缺少的部分,尤其对于大型输水管桥这种特殊桥型,分析其动力特性具有重要工程意义。本文在Midas中将结构自重和水荷载转化为质量,并通过特征值分析中的子空间迭代法进行计算,表3列出了前10阶的自振频率,图8示出前5阶的振型结果。

桥梁动力特性计算结果 表3

阶数	频率(Hz)	周期(s)	振型描述
1	0.633	1.581	主梁对称横弯
2	0.643	1.556	主梁纵漂
3	0.687	1.457	主梁反对称扭转
4	0.775	1.290	主梁对称横弯
5	0.806	1.241	主梁对称竖弯
6	0.935	1.070	主梁反对称横弯
7	0.947	1.056	主梁对称横弯
8	1.050	0.952	主梁反对称竖弯
9	1.087	0.920	主梁反对称横弯
10	1.104	0.906	主梁对称扭转

通过上述数据分析可知,主梁的横向振型主要为1、4、6、7、9,其相应的频率为在0.63~1.1Hz范围内。其中,第1阶振型的参与质量占多数,4、7、9的振型参与质量在5%~10%之间。

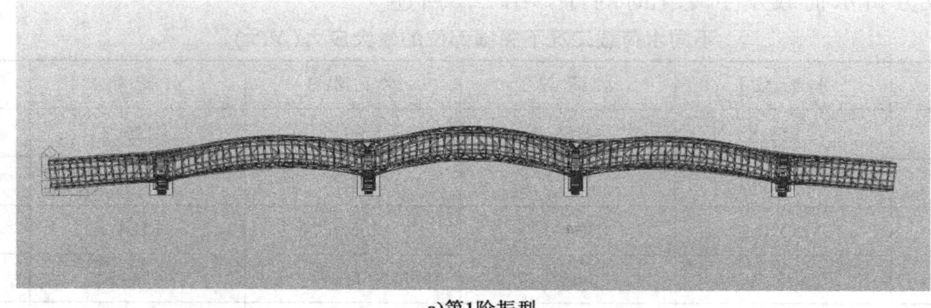

a)第1阶振型

b)第2阶振型

c)第3阶振型

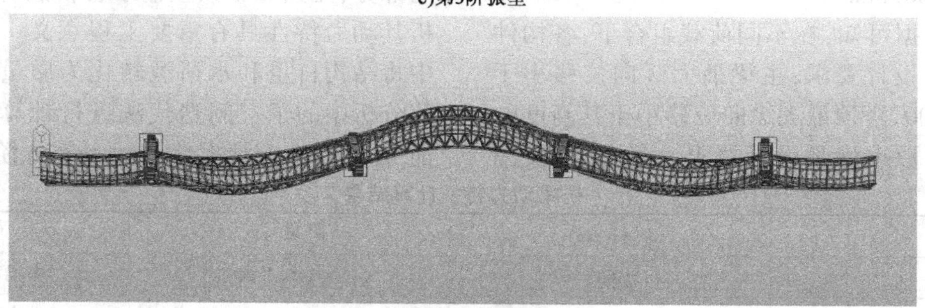

d)第4阶振型

图8　桥梁1~5阶振型

5　结语

通过对大型斜拉输水管桥成桥状态进行力学性能分析,主要得出以下结论:

(1)大型输水管桥的水荷载约为等桥面宽度汽车荷载的4倍,应着重考虑水荷载对桥梁产生影响,需对不同水荷载工况展开分析。

(2)通过对不同水荷载工况进行静力分析,可知满水工况较为安全,偏载工况会产生较大的应力与位移,运营时应尽量避免此种工况。

(3)相比于纵梁、弦杆等关键构件,横梁处的位移与应力较大,其中,横梁位移与应力最大值分别为96.0mm和231.5MPa。由此可见,设计时需要重点关注并加强桥梁的横向刚度部分。

(4)在动力特性方面,由于输水管桥横向刚度较弱,首次出现的振型是主梁横向弯曲,频率为0.633Hz,同时横向弯曲振型大多伴有微小扭转。

参考文献

[1] 高行行. 大跨度管道斜拉桥受力特性分析[D]. 成都:西南交通大学,2016.

[2] 马芹纲,陈方东,庄小将,等. 大跨度斜拉桥过桥水管振动关键问题研究[J]. 世界桥梁,2009,37(04):50-53.

[3] 庄小将,马芹刚,王丰平,等. 大门大桥引桥过桥管线作用效应研究[J]. 桥梁建设,2011,41(06):50-53.

[4] 庄小将,孙建渊,同济大学桥梁工程系. 跨海斜拉桥大型过桥水管振动作用研究[C]. 中国公路学会桥梁和结构工程分会 2009 年全国桥梁学术会议,2009.

[5] 赵静. 汉江管桥的静力分析[J]. 工程与试验,2011,51(01):6-7,38.

[6] 许萍,李著信,高松竹. 斜拉索管桥几何非线性分析的三维有限元模型[J]. 石油工程建设,2008,34(06):14-17,88.

[7] 许萍,李著信,高松竹. 大跨度斜拉索管桥几何非线性分析与数值模拟[J]. 后勤工程学院学报,2008,24(03):31-34,43.

Dynamic Response Analysis of Long-span and Continuous Rigid Frame Bridge under Debris Flow

Qin Xiao *1 Li Da2

(1. Highway College of Chang'an University;

2. Design and Research Institute of CCCC Second Navigation Engineering Bureau Co. ,Ltd.)

Abstract By using the Fluent module and the Transient Structural module in the Ansys Workbench platform, we select appropriate mud-rock flow slurry parameters to carry out the coupling analysis about debris flow impact rigid-frame bridge pier with two different cross-section forms: double thin-walled hollow piers and double thin-walled solid piers. The necessary pictures of the movement of debris flow liquid slurry are obtained, and then the movement and distribution of the slurry in the basin are summarized. Based on the form of the pier and the debris flow slurry parameters such as the change of the factor of continuous rigid frame bridge, the parametric analysis was made on the influences of the dynamic response of bridge pier and then sums up the characteristics of bridge damage.

Keywords Debris flow Continuous rigid frame bridge Impact effect Parameter analysis

0 Introduction

At present, the development of transportation infrastructure is rapid, and the construction of expressways and railways for mountainous areas is also increasing. The mountainous terrain in different regions has its unique hydrogeological conditions, but most of them are characterized by large terrain fluctuations and various adverse geology. Because of such environmental factors, a long-span continuous rigid frame bridge has been widely used in bridge design in the mountainous area due to its advantages of good structural stiffness, strong seismic performance, low construction difficulty and beautiful shape.

As a common geological hazard in mountainous areas, debris flow is relatively serious once it occurs, especially after heavy rains and earthquakes, the probability of secondary geological disasters such as debris flow and landslides caused by this will greatly increase. After encountering a mudslide, if the structure cannot continue to maintain the safety and durability of the design, it will pose a great threat to our public transportation facilities, causing economic losses and other unpredictable consequences.

Because of the frequent occurrence of debris flow accidents in various parts of our country, this will cause many adverse effects on the design and construction of bridges in areas where debris flows are prone. Therefore, based on the actual engineering background of a continuous rigid frame bridge on a certain expressway in Yunnan, this paper conducts research and analysis on the mechanism of debris flow and bridge structure, and discusses the mechanicalbehavior characteristics of the structure under different working conditions. The design and the reinforcement and maintenance of the built bridge provide theoretical support and engineering practice reference.

1 Project overview

In order to study the impact of debris flow on bridges, this paper takes a three-span continuous rigid frame bridge on an expressway in Yunnan province as the engineering background. The main span of the bridge is 118m, and the length of both sides is 64m (Fig. 1). The upper structure of the main beam material is C55, bridge span structure is divided into two left and right, left and right width of the bridge deck is equal, are 11m, the construction of the upper main beam using hanging basket hanging pouring construction and post-tensioned prestressed concrete combination; The substructure is double limb thin-wall hollow pier, the pier body is made of C40 concrete, the pile foundations below the two thin wall pier cap are bored pile foundation and dug pile foundation respectively, and the concrete material of cap and pile foundation is C30.

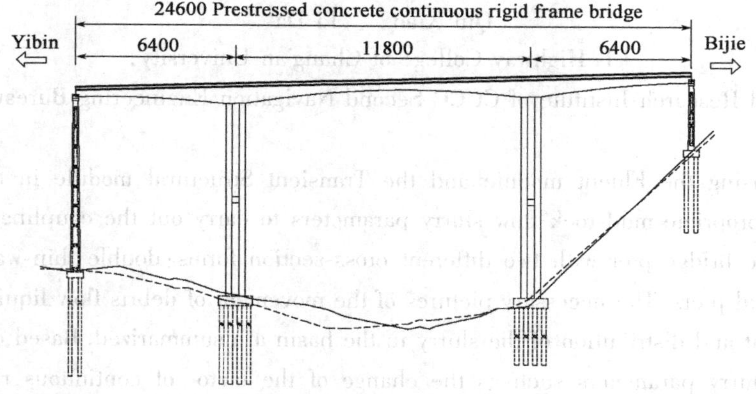

Fig. 1 General layout of the bridge (unit: cm)

2 Model establishment

2.1 Theoretical Basis of Modeling

The geological environment of the research object in this paper belongs to the southwest region. Among the local debris flow cases, most of them are viscous debris flow, and the composition of the viscous debris flow is composed of fine particles, which conforms to the characteristics of the Bingham body model, so its physical model is in accordance with the characteristics of Bingham body are studied.

In actual engineering design, when considering the accidental load of debris flow, it is often simplified as an external effect. Analyzing the impact of debris flow on the bridge impact is simplified to determine the impact force. The impact force of debris flow on the bridge can be divided into two parts: the impact of the mud flow slurry, the impact of the mud composed of water and other small particles on the bridge, also called the overall impact; the impact of large rocks, the impact of the debris flow The impact of coarse-grained solids on the pier. Related studies have shown that both will have a greater impact on the pier structure.

Kang Z conducted a large number of experiments and studies at Dongchuan Station, during which they recorded and saved a large amount of data on important rheological parameters such as flow velocity and bulk density of debris flow. Statistics show that the velocity of debris flow is generally not greater than 10m/s. For the rapid flow caused by the surface of debris flow when the velocity is too high, the maximum velocity can reach 14.5m/s, and the average density of debris flow is generally 2100-2200kg/m^3, the maximum mud depth is about 3m.

In this simulation analysis, we need to set the impact basin of the entire debris flow slurry in advance. Taking into account the actual engineering geology, the slurry basin is set up according to multiphaseflow. The basin is divided into liquid slurry and air. The slurry is a pure fluid with uniform viscosity, and its density is set at 1800-2400kg/m^3, ignoring the heat transfer in the system during the impact of the slurry. At the beginning of the impact, the entire basin was filled with air, and the relative air pressure was zero.

2.2 Selection of model parameters

In order to study the effect of the overall impact of the debris flow slurry on the continuous rigid frame bridge, this section uses the Fluent module to establish the debris flow slurry action model to analyze the distribution of the debris flow slurry within the continuous rigid frame bridge basin under the action of the slurry Fig. 2.

The geometric model of the bridge and the geometric model of the river basin is created in this paper using the 3D modeling software Solidworks. In order to facilitate the division of the mesh, it is imported into the Design Modeler under the Workbench platform to process the model in blocks.

The size of the entire basin is set according to the length, width, and height of 30m, 20m, and 5m respectively. Considering that the geometry of the entire basin is relatively regular, the mesh module that comes with Workbench is used to mesh the basin.

The physical model of the slurry in the impact model adopts the viscous debris flow Bingham model, considering the influence of its gravity, the turbulence model is defined in Fluent according to the k-ε model, the material is set to two-phase flow, the main term is air, and the second term is mud body. According to the fluid parameters, the normal temperature viscosity of the slurry is1.75×10^3 Pa · s, and the volume ratio of sediment is 56.3%. The density of the slurry depends on the specific working conditions, and finally, according to the Bingham body. The model calculates the dynamic viscosity μ of the slurry.

In the fluid analysis, the bridge pier material is C40 concrete, the density is 2800kg/m^3, the modulus of elasticity is 3.25×10^4MPa, and the poisson's ratio is 0.3, The solid grid is divided by a multi-domain grid.

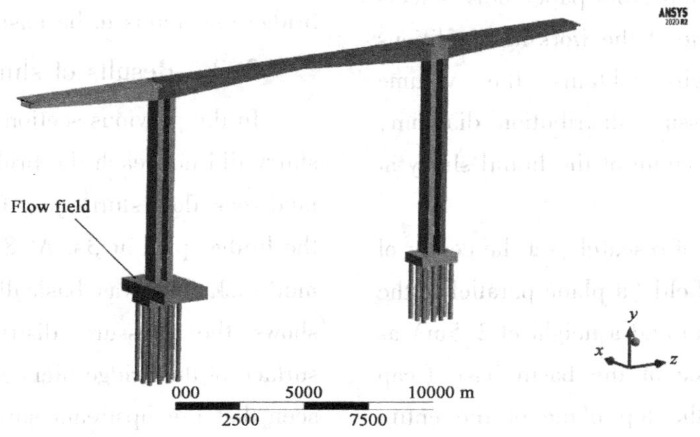

Fig. 2 The coupling model of slurry and bridge

In the boundary conditions of the bridge structure, the bottom of the foundation is set as the fixed end, and the pile side and the cap are set as the elastic support, to simulate the interaction between the pile side soil and the structure. In the transient analysis, an analysis end time is set, calculated according to the total time of 10s, and the time step is 0.02s. Finally, in the pre-processing, output settings for the post-processing results that need to be extracted, such as the structural orientation displacement, the first principal stress, and the equivalent stress.

The analysis type of solid bridge structure is set to transient analysis solution, the end time is set to 8s in the system coupling module, and the time step is consistent with the set value in the solid transient analysis; in addition, the fluid-solid coupling interface defined in the solid needs to be set Create a data exchange with the coupled wall in the fluid (FSI), and finally submit it to the computer to loop iteratively.

3　Analysis of solution results

This paper uses the Ansys CFD-Post post-processing plate as a tool to carry out a complete simulation calculation of the debris flow basin, and then analyze the whole process of the debris flow slurry movement in the basin. Since the basin parameters set in different working conditions have not changed, the analysis results of the same basin are basically the same. Therefore, this paper only selects the debris flow field of one of the working conditions for analysis, and finally obtains the volume distribution diagram, pressure distribution diagram, and flow velocity trace diagram of the liquid slurry at different times.

For the convenience of research, set the center of gravity plane of the flow field (a plane parallel to the bottom surface of the basin and a height of 2.5m) as Plane1, the bottom surface of the basin base (cap plane) as Plane2, and the top plane of the entire basin as Plane3. The flow field analysis takes the typical mud-rock flow slurry (mud depth of 5m and flow velocity of 6m/s) calculated by the actual project at Dongchuan Station in Jiangjiagou, Yunnan Province, as an example.

3.1　Results of slurry volume distribution

Fig. 3 shows the volume distribution at 1s, 3s, 5s and 8s respectively, indicating the change process of volume distribution of debris flow slurry flowing through the free surface of thin-walled hollow piers with double limbs of continuous rigid frame bridge. It can be seen that the debris flow began to contact the front end of the thin-walled pier at 1s, and the liquid slurry appeared in the front end, but the slurry did not reach the back flow surface of the pier. At about 3s, the slurry began to reach the rear of the two thin walls of the bridge pier, but due to the fast speed and high viscosity, the slurry could not immediately immerse in the back flow surface area behind the pier, and its motion mode did not change, in the form of three unconjoined tributaries of the slurry, among which there was a narrow slurry flow between the two thin walls. At 5s, the slurry between the thin wall begins to merge with the slurry outside the wall, and the area on the backflow surface is gradually immersed by the slurry and begins to be impacted by the slurry. Finally, the debris flow slurry is completely distributed in the whole basin at 8s, and the slurry has a complete dynamic response to the bridge pier. After this, the distribution of debris flow slurry will not change much, but the impact height of the whole basin will change slightly, and its impact effect on the bridge pier tends to be basically stable.

3.2　Results of slurry pressure distribution

In the previous section, it was mentioned that the slurry did not reach the bridge pier 1s before, and the mud-rock flow slurry just flowed directly in front of the bridge pier at 3s. At 8s, the entire basin of the mud-rock flow was basically fully developed. Fig. 4 shows the pressure distribution on the coupling surface of the bridge piers at different times. It can be seen that the upstream surface did not interact with the slurry before 1s, so the pressure distribution on the coupling interface was zero before that. After that, the slurry began to contact the pier, and the pressure on the front face of the pier reached 97.1kPa at about 3 seconds and was distributed at the root area of the front face of the thin-walled pier. At this time, the pressure value was the maximum instantaneous impact pressure during the entire process. Subsequently, the debris flow flowed over the back surface of the bridge pier and gradually filled the entire basin, and its instantaneous maximum pressure also decreased. After 5s, the maximum pressure gradually stabilized at about 87.3kPa. At this moment, the pressure value of the oncoming surface is called the stable maximum pressure.

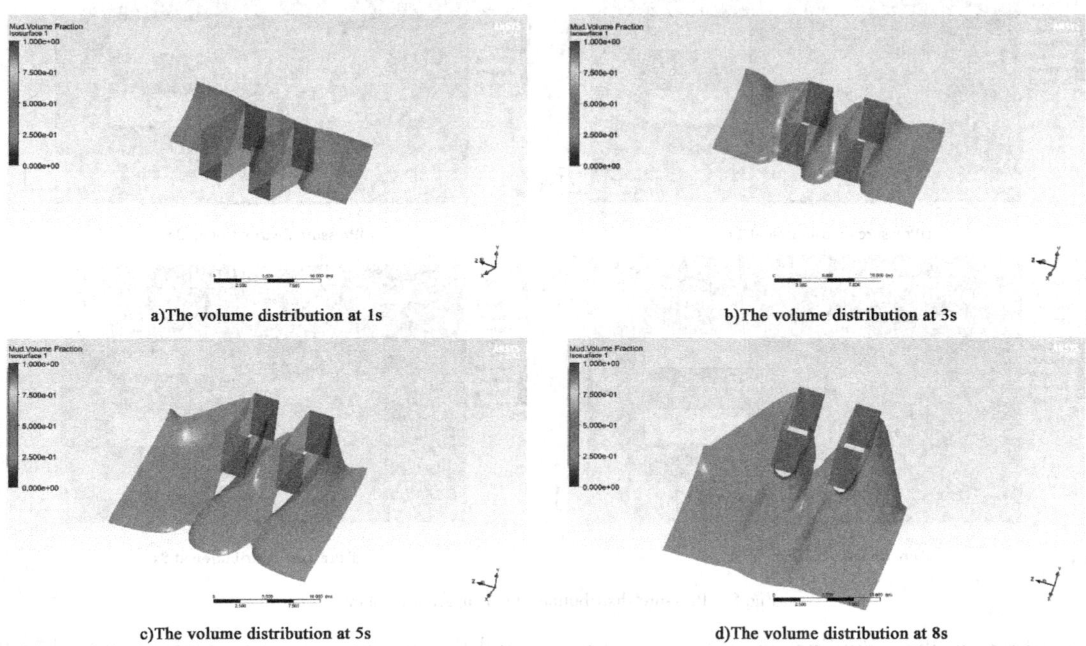

a)The volume distribution at 1s b)The volume distribution at 3s c)The volume distribution at 5s d)The volume distribution at 8s

Fig. 3 Volume distribution diagram of slurry at different moments

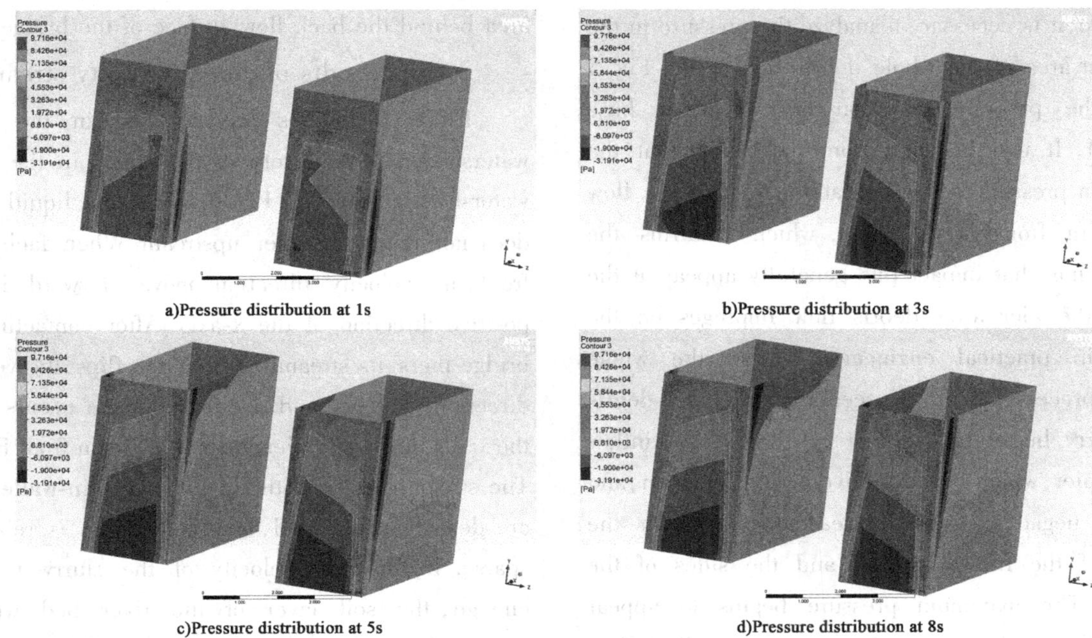

a)Pressure distribution at 1s b)Pressure distribution at 3s c)Pressure distribution at 5s d)Pressure distribution at 8s

Fig. 4 Pressure distribution diagram of fluid-structure coupling interface

It can be seen that the impact pressure generated by the slurry is affected by the hydrostatic pressure. When the depth of the slurry increases, the pressure at the junction of the bottom surface of the structure increases. When the debris flow is fully developed (Fig. 5). The pressure at the highest mud depth is about 48.9kPa, and the calculated value of the theoretical formula is 59.8kPa, so the simulation results are closer to the calculation results.

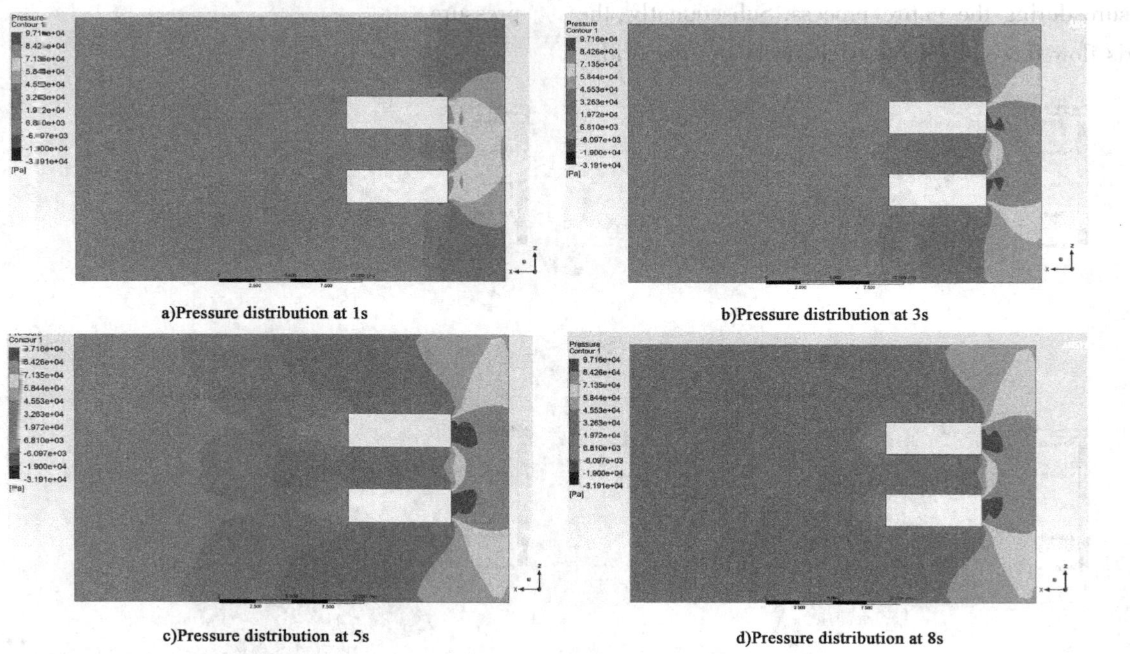

a)Pressure distribution at 1s b)Pressure distribution at 3s c)Pressure distribution at 5s d)Pressure distribution at 8s

Fig. 5 Pressure distribution cloud diagram of planet 2

According to the coupling interface pressure analysis, with the increase of impact mud depth, the pressure at the bottom of the structure will increase. Therefore, it is necessary toanalyze the pressure in the basement area of the whole debris flow basin. Fig. 5 shows the pressure variation of the basin base (Plan2). It can be seen from the figure that the maximum pressure is located at the root of the flow surface in front of the pier, which confirms the phenomenon that impact pits generally appear at the root of the pier after debris flow impinges on the bridge in practical engineering. From the whole impact process, it can be seen that after 1s, debris flow slurry began to overflow in front of the inflow surface pier, which began to diverge phenomenon, and a small negative pressure area appeared near the corner of the inflow surface and the sides of the surface. The maximum pressure begins to appear around 3s, but the distribution range is small. At 8s, the debris flow slurry basically filled the whole basin, and the maximum base pressure appeared in the area directly in front of the flow surface, while the corresponding smaller pressure value appeared in the area behind the back flow surface of the bridge pier.

3.3 Results of slurry velocity streamline

1000 streamlines are selected in the entire watershed. The trajectory of the slurry in the entire watershed is shown in Fig. 6. When the liquid slurry does not reach the pier upstream When facing the front, its velocity direction moves forward in the positive direction of the x-axis. After contacting the bridge piers, its streamline direction flips, the velocity direction changes, and a circumfluence occurs along the walls of the two piers, as can be seen from Fig. 6. The streamlines on both sides of the thin-walled pier are densely distributed, and the middle is relatively sparse. If the flow velocity of the slurry is large enough, the soil layer of the river bed will be destroyed and the bridge foundation will be exposed. When the slurry interacts with the bridge piers, the flow lines behind the piers become sparser, and the flow velocity is reduced a lot compared to before the effect. Moreover, due to the low fluid velocity in the back flow zone, there will be a " vacuum" in a small area, and the movement of the slurry will slow down, which may become a siltation zone for debris flow. In general, the streamline distribution is basically in line with reality.

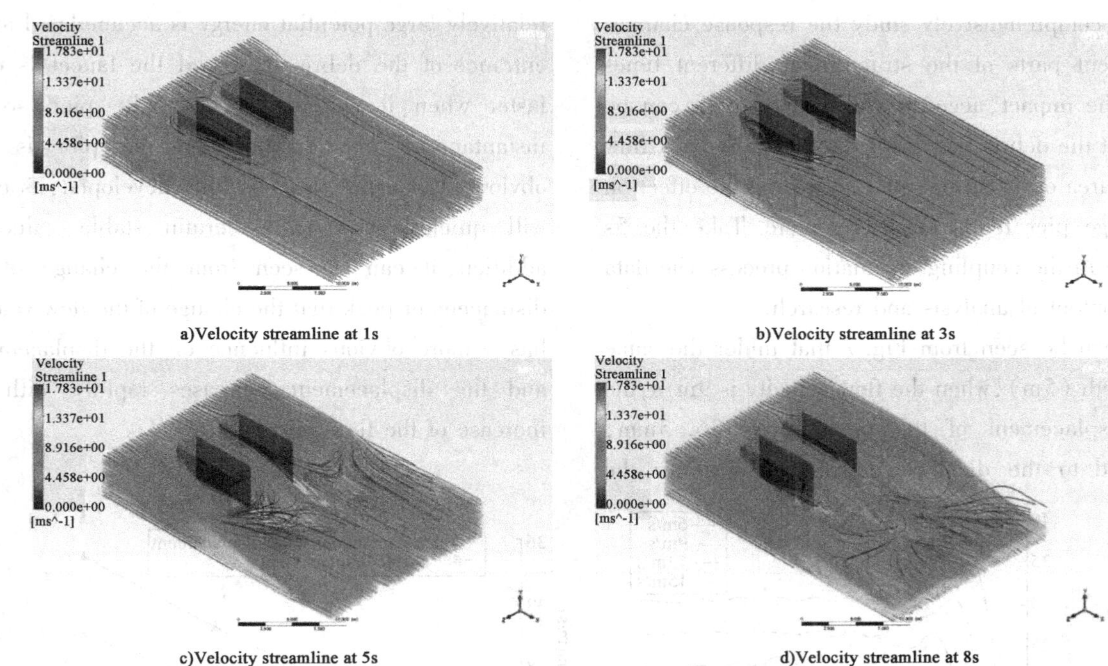

a)Velocity streamline at 1s

b)Velocity streamline at 3s

c)Velocity streamline at 5s

d)Velocity streamline at 8s

Fig. 6 Velocity streamline cloud diagram of slurry flow field

To sum up, the pressure obtained by this simulation is close to the results calculated by the theoretical formula, and the flow line distribution and pressure distribution are in line with the actual engineering. Therefore, it is considered that the flow field simulation is reliable and can be carried out with subsequent parametric analysis.

4 Parameter impact calculation result analysis

Under the action of mud-rock flow slurry load, the dynamic response of the structure is related to the physical properties of the structure and the load. Different structural parameters and load parameters will cause large changes in dynamic response. In order to study the dynamic response of the continuous rigid frame bridge under the action of the mud-rock flow slurry, this section is based on the calculation content of the previous section and continues to use the Fluent module in Ansys Workbench to change the parameterof slurry velocity through the controlled variable method to analyze the displacement of the bridge piers under different parameters, time history changes of stress, impact force, and stability of key parts, to study the influence of different parameters on continuous rigid frame bridge piers.

4.1 Displacement analysis

The dynamic response of the bridge pier under the action of the slurry is related to the amount of energy obtained by the actor, and the energy is affected by the flow velocity and the viscosity and bulk density. In order to study the influence of flow velocity on the dynamic response of continuous rigid frame bridge piers, this section uses flow velocity as a variable to establish an analysis model. The finite element model of the bridge structure is the same as above. In this analysis, four sets of working conditions are set up. Under each set of working conditions, the mud depth, bulk density, and viscosity of the mud-rock flow slurry are the same, and the flow velocity of the slurry is different. The initial impact velocities of the four groups of working conditions are set to 6m/s, 9m/s, 12m/s, and15m/s, respectively.

The impact of liquid slurry on continuous rigid frame bridges is a typical dynamics problem. The mechanical behavior and response changes of bridge piers at different times show different changes. In order to comprehensively study the response changes of different parts of the structure at different times during the impact, according to Chapter 3, it can be seen that the debris flow has submerged the back flow surface area of the bridge pier at 5s, and the effect on the bridge pier tends to be complete. Take the 5s response in the coupling calculation process The data is the content of analysis and research.

It can be seen from Fig. 7 that under the same mud depth (5m), when the flow velocity is 9m/s, the peak displacement of the pier top is 26.5mm, compared to the displacement at 6m/s under the same conditions An increase of 22.7%; when the flow velocity increases to 12m/s and 15m/s, the growth rate of the top displacement of the piers is 15.1% and 14.8%, respectively. This is because a relatively large potential energy is accumulated at the entrance of the debris flow, and the faucet is often faster when it starts to contact the pier, so the instantaneous impact effect on the pier is also obvious. When the slurry is fully developed, its effect will quickly drop to a certain stable value. In addition, it can be seen from the change of the displacement peak that the change of the flow velocity has a more obvious influence on the displacement, and the displacement increases rapidly with the increase of the flow velocity.

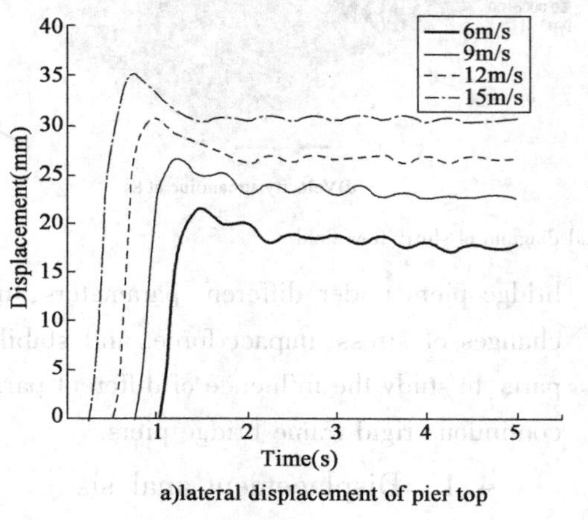

a)lateral displacement of pier top

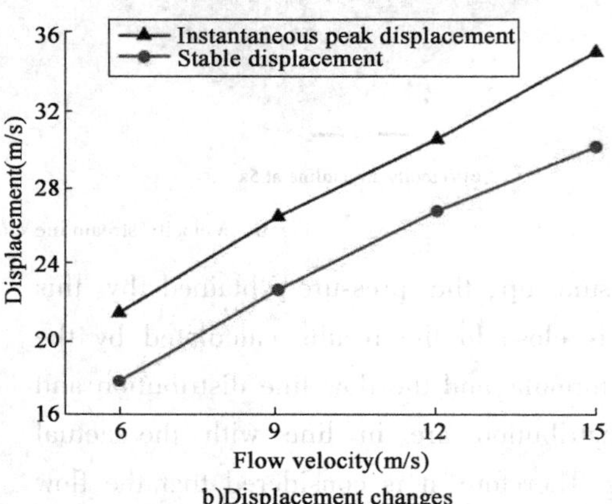

b)Displacement changes

Fig. 7 Time history curve of lateral displacement of pier top and Displacement changes at different flow rates

4.2 Stress analysis

It can be seen from the Fig. 8 that in the four groups of working conditions, the slurry flow velocity gradually increases from 6m/s to 15m/s, and the changing trend of the first principal stress at the upstream surface of the bridge pier substructure is basically the same, all rising first to An instantaneous maximum value, and then stabilizes to a certain stress value after the impact of the slurry stabilizes. In each group of working conditions, it can be found that the stress stability value and peak value are already greater than the ultimate tensile strength required by the pile foundation concrete, and the concrete surface is very likely to appear tensile cracking. In addition, with the gradual increase of the inlet flow rate of the slurry, the possibility of concrete damage to the lower pile foundation further increases. For other parts of the substructure, the stress state is mainly compression, and the increase in flow velocity will increase the compressive stress, but they all meet the limit of the ultimate compressive strength of the pier concrete, which may cause crushing damage.

4.3 Impact analysis

The impact force on the bridge pier is an important part of studying the impact of mud-rock flow slurry. The time history curve comparison of the maximum value of the impact force on the pier under different flow rates is shown in Fig. 9.

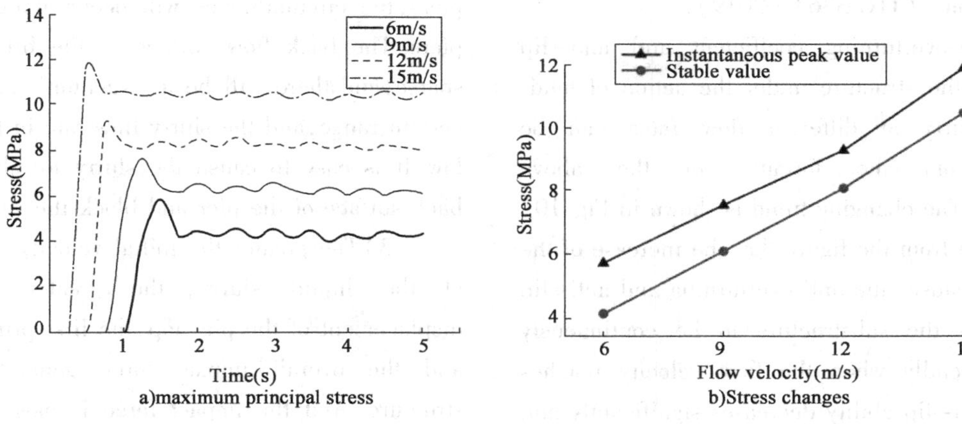

Fig. 8 Time history curve of maximum principal stress and Stress change at different flow rates

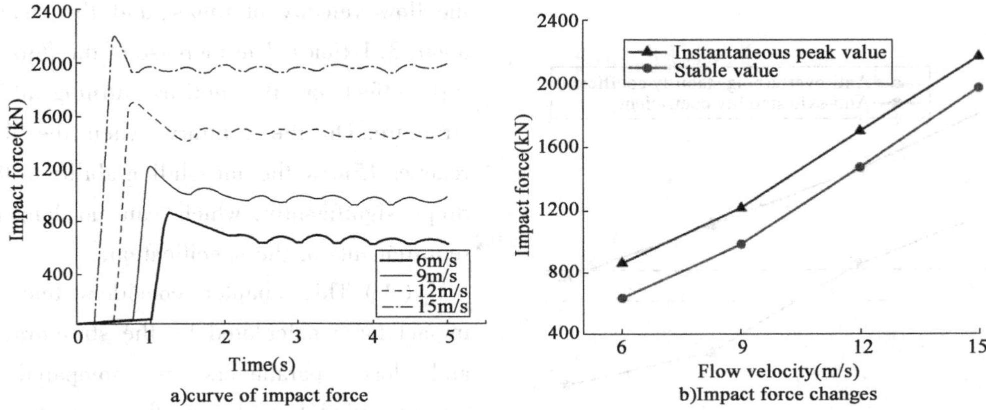

Fig. 9 Time history curve of impact force and Variation of impact force at different flow rates

From the above figure, it is not difficult to see that as the flow rate continues to increase, the peak and stable values of the impact force continue to rise. When the flow velocity reaches 15m/s, the peak impact force is about 2. 5 times that of the flow velocity 6m/s, and the steady value is about 3. 1 times. It can be seen that the influence of the flow velocity on the impact force is more significant.

According to calculations, the ratio of the peak impact force of debris flow slurry to the recommended formula value of the code is about 0. 74, and the ratio of the stable value of the impact force to the recommended value of the code is about 0.62. Compared with the coupled simulation results, the recommended formula method is 30% ~ A margin of about 40%. It can be seen that the calculation method recommended by our country's current codes is relatively safe for the calculation of the impact force of highway bridges and culverts. Because the analysis process considers the viscous and uniform fluid, which mainly consists of fine particles, if the actual project contains larger particlesFor gravel or crushed stone with diameter, it is more reasonable to use the formula method to calculate the value.

4.4 Stability analysis

The stability check generally includes the check of anti-slip and anti-overturning capabilities. When the pier foundation of a bridge culvert cannot meet the stability requirements, the structure will slip or overturn. The related checking calculation method should be carried out according to the " Code for

Design of Highway Bridge and Culvert Foundation and Foundation" (JTG 3363—2019).

The anti-overturning coefficient and anti-slip coefficient of the structure under the action of mud-rock flow slurry at different flow rates can be calculated from the formula in the above specification. The changing trend is shown in Fig. 10. It can be seen from the figure that the increase of the flow velocity causes the anti-overturning and anti-slip coefficients of the substructure to be continuously reduced, especially when the flow velocity reaches 12m/s, its anti-slip ability decreases significantly and will no longer meet the requirements of the specification. (The slip coefficient should not be less than 1.3).

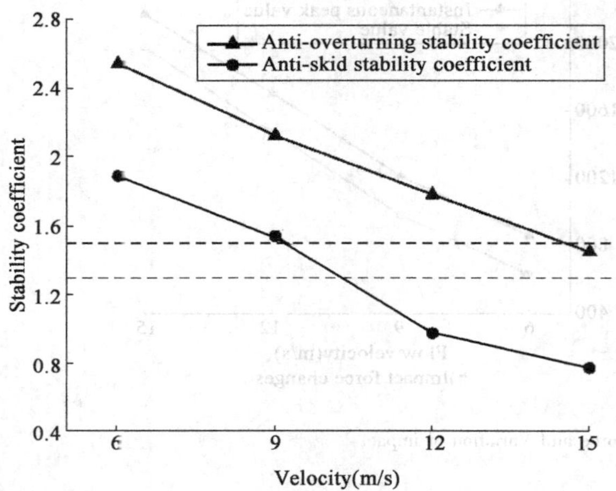

Fig. 10 Stability coefficient of substructure

5 Conclusions

Taking an actual project in the southwest mountainous area as the background, the Ansys software was used to establish a three-dimensional calculation model from the response analysis of the debris flow to the long-span, high-pier, continuous-rigid-frame bridge. And the influence of different mud speeds on the bridge dynamic response was analyzed.

(1) The front face of the double-limbed thin-walled pier is often under greater pressure, especially when the liquid slurry is fully developed and the watershed is filled with slurry, the maximum pressure will appear at the bottom of the front face, and the bottom is prone to impact pits of mudslides.

(2) After the slurry interacts with the bridge piers, the circumfluence will occur along the bridge piers. The back flow surface of the bridge piers is sparse, and there will be a "vacuum" area within a certain range, and the slurry flow rate in this range is low. It is easy to cause the slurry to silt up on the back surface of the pier and block the river.

(3) The greater the initial velocity of the inflow of the liquid slurry, the greater the lateral displacement of the pier top, the first principal stress and the overall impact force generated by the structure. And the impact force is most sensitive to the change of velocity, when the flow velocity reaches 15m/s, the peak impact force is about 2.5 times of the flow velocity of 6m/s, and the steady value is about 3.1 times. The increase of the flow velocity has little effect on the anti-overturning ability of the structure. On the contrary, when the flow velocity reaches 15m/s, the anti-sliding ability of the structure drops significantly, which can no longer meet the requirements of the specification.

(4) This chapter considers that the overall impact force calculated by the structural parameters and load parameters is compared with the recommended formulas in the current codes of our country, and the simulation results are generally 20% to 30% smaller than the value of the code formulas. When considering the debris flow in the actual engineering environment, the medium is not a uniform and pure fluid. If it contains coarse particles, the recommended calculation results are reasonable.

References

[1] Chen M, Chen N. Debris flow prevention mode and engineering value in tourist towns [M]. 2018.

[2] Yao C, Wang Y. State-of-the-art review of debris flow impact forces on bridges in 2019 [J]. Journal of Civil and Environmental Engineering, 2020, 42(5): 28-36.

[3] Ren H, Zhang M. Dynamic Response Analysis of Bridge Pier under the Action of Mudslides [J]. Railway Standard Design, 2016, 60(1): 83-86.

[4] Zhou G. Engineering Geology [M]. 2018.

[5] Qin Y Z. Study of Bridge Pier Impacted by Debris Flow[D]. Chengdu: Southwest Jiaotong University, 2014.

[6] Gou T Y. Dynamic Response Analysis of Continuous Rigid Frame Bridge under Impact Load of Debris Flow[D]. Chengdu: Southwest Jiaotong University, 2017.

[7] Ministry of Land and Resources of the People's Republic of China. Specification for investigation of debris flow disaster prevention and control engineering[S], 2006.

[8] Tamotsu T. Debris Flow on Prismatic Open Channel [J]. Journal of the Hydraulics Division, 1980, 106(3).

[9] Zhou M, Xiong H. Simplified Calculation of Impact Force of Debris Flow Based on the Case Study of Sanyan Valley Debris Flow [J]. Mountain Research, 2017, 35(2): 187-194.

[10] Ministry of Land and Resources of the People's Republic of China. Design code for foundation and foundation of highway bridges and culverts [S]. 2019.

Temperature Field Characteristics Research of Composite Curved Bridge Based on Measured Temperature

Jiachen Liao *

(School of Highway, Chang'an University)

Abstract In order to explore the temperature distribution characteristics of the new type of steel-concrete composite curved bridge in a cold area and make up for the deficiency of the existing standard for the definition of the temperature gradient of the new type of structure, a steel-concrete composite curved bridge in the cold northwest region was taken as the research object. Based on the measured temperature data, the temperature field distribution of the bridge under sunshine is analyzed. The 2D temperature gradient model of the maximum temperature difference is obtained by the least square method. The temperature gradient model is compared with the current code in China. The results show that the sectional function can better describe the daily temperature curve of the box girder compared with the sinusoidal curve; The vertical temperature gradient distribution of the inclined web of steel box girder is cubic polynomial function, the transverse temperature distribution of the bridge deck is an exponential function in the heating stage and the third polynomial function in the cooling stage; The maximum vertical temperature difference of steel box girder web can reach 3℃, which is different from the current specification, and the measured maximum vertical temperature difference can reach 17 ℃, which is quite different from 8.5 ℃ as specified in the code.

Keywords Steel-concrete composite structure Measured data Inclined web Curve fitting

0 Introduction

Steel-concrete composite structure bridges can make full use of the advantages of materials. The connection of a concrete structure and a steel structure making them bear the external forces together has obvious advantages in enhancing the overall structural stiffness, reducing the height of the section and Increasing capacity for carrying loads. Therefore, Steel-concrete composite structure bridges have been rapidly developed in the last 20 years.

In the natural environment, sunlight effects, seasonal changes, and heat conduction affect the temperature distribution of a combined structural bridge, thus causing the temperature of the structure to change continuously over time. Although the coefficients of linear expansion of concrete and steel are similar, their thermal conductivity differs greatly, and the different rates of temperature change of the two materials when subjected to strong direct sunlight heating and drastic changes in day and night temperatures will result in a large temperature difference distribution in the height of the cross-section, so that the different deformations of the two will result in bending stresses between them.

In recent years, it can be seen from the research of previous scholars that many bridge structures generate large tensile stresses under the action of the temperature field, causing serious damage to the structure. According to the experience and findings of Tie-Meng Wang (1997), more than 80% of the cracks generated in actual bridge structures are caused by temperature and settlement. It can be seen that temperature stress has a significant influence on the force and the whole life performance of large span bridges.

For this reason, domestic and foreign scholars have also conducted extensive research on the temperature difference effect of steel-concrete bridges, for example, Chen Xiaoqiang (2009) measured the temperature distribution of a composite structural bridge and analyzed the measured temperature data to determine the distribution of the least favorable temperature gradient; Wu Liuzheng (2011) studied the influencing factors of the temperature field distribution of box girders and carried out transient heat conduction analysis of the structure by finite element to calculate the temperature distribution form the structure at different moments Chen Yanjiang, et al (2014). conducted a two-day observation of the temperature distribution of a composite girder bridge and mathematically fitted the temperature distribution pattern of the structure, and the results showed that there is a significant temperature difference at the intersection of the composite girder, and pointed out the difference between the measured temperature field and the specification. In order to study the temperature difference performance of light-weight composite structures, Liu Yu et al (2015). conducted finite element modeling analysis for two cases, obtained the temperature field distribution of light-weight composite structures, and proposed the deficiencies of the existing codes in China; Wu Qingxiang et al (2016). conducted real-time temperature monitoring of a structural bridge and fitted the measured data to obtain the vertical and lateral temperature distribution patterns of the bridge structure, which showed that the vertical temperature distribution of the steel structure was polynomial and the lateral distribution was exponential. Liu Guanglong et al (2018) measured the temperature field of concrete box girders in the northwest extreme cold region and carried out a finite element modeling analysis, concluding that the same temperature difference model adopted nationwide is a serious underestimation of the temperature effect in the northwest region; Wang Li (2021) used the field temperature observation data to analyze the temperature distribution pattern of this new combination structure under the effect of sunlight, and applied the least-squares fitting to propose its 2-dimensional temperature gradient model; Zhao Guoyun (2020) obtained the temperature distribution pattern of asphalt paving structure by The temperature distribution characteristics of the steel box girder during asphalt paving were obtained by field real measurements and fitted to obtain the least favorable temperature gradient equation, and the prediction equation of the maximum temperature of the top and bottom slabs was also established.

However, most of the existing studies are on steel-concrete straight web bridges, and the research on steel-concrete inclined curved web bridges has not been widely carried out, and the research content is basically on the vertical temperature distribution under the action of solar radiation, and there is little research on the transverse temperature field and its effect. Therefore, it is necessary to study the temperature field distribution characteristics of steel-concrete box girder bridges to provide some theoretical basis for the calculation of the temperature difference stress of steel-concrete structures.

This paper takes a steel-concrete curved girder bridge (Fig. 1) in northwest China as the research object, analyzes the temperature monitoring data obtained from the temperature sensors installed on the bridge, numerically fits the temperature distribution of the bridge measurement points in the transverse and vertical directions with the help of mathematical methods such as function fitting and hypothesis testing, proposes the corresponding temperature gradient distribution formula, and compares it with the current code to find the differences between the measured data and the code, and puts forward the code The shortcomings of the regulations are presented. The results of this paper can be used as a reference for the calculation of the temperature effect of a combined structural girder bridge in the same area.

1 Temperature field measurements

1.1 Study Subjects and Site Arrangement

The background bridge location studied in this paper has annual extreme maximum temperatures between 35℃ and 41.8°C; and extreme minimums between −16℃ and −20℃. The average monthly maximum temperature is the hottest in July, at around 32°C; the average monthly temperature is the coldest in January, at −0.3℃ to −1.3°C. The annual difference reaches 26℃ to 27℃. The temperature difference is large, especially in the short spring and autumn seasons, with drastic temperature changes. In this paper, the test time period was chosen from 2021.3.1 to 2021.3.30, and the temperature test frequency was 1h/time.

a)Appearance of box girder

b)Site construction

Fig. 1 Construction of steel concrete composite beam bridge

The bridge is aligned from northeast to southwest with a span arrangement of 32m + 36m + 28m + 2 × 36m. The width of the bridge deck is 9m and the whole bridge is designed according to a circular curve (R = 114m). The bottom slab is 5m wide and the cantilever slab is 2m wide. vertical top to bottom: 10cm asphalt concrete deck pavement, 8cm C40 concrete deck slab and 140cm steel box girder.

The first two span sections of the second link of the bridge were selected as the measurement point arrangement sections, and 21 measurement points were set in each section, including 10 measurement points for the upper and lower layers of the concrete deck slab, and 11 measurement points for the steel box girder along with the web and the outer layer of the bottom slab, both sections were arranged in the same way, as shown in Fig. 2.

1.2 Test methods and equipment

The internal temperature distribution of the concrete was measured using the buried temperature sensor JM165-C, and the surface temperature of the steel box beam as well as the ambient temperature distribution was measured using the surface-mounted temperature sensor JM165-B. The field test of the temperature field is shown in Fig. 3.

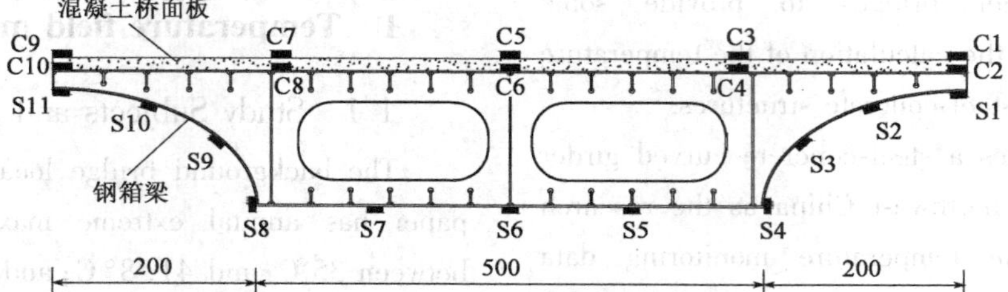

Fig. 2　Layout of temperature measuring points(unit:cm)

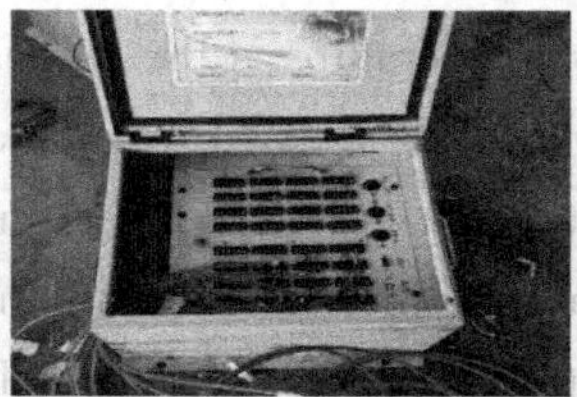

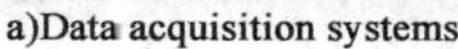

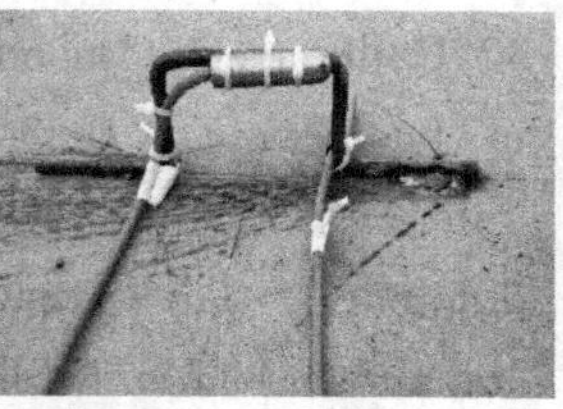

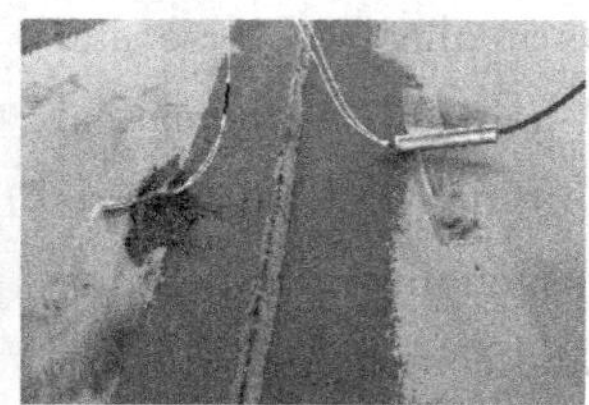

a)Data acquisition systems　b)Concrete temperature measurement points　c)Steel box girder temperature measurement points　d)Solar panels

Fig. 3　Temperature field test

2　Temperature field test results and analysis

The annual temperature variation is more uniform and has less influence on the bridge structure, which is usually considered in the design calculation according to the uniform temperature, which is simpler than the insolation temperature effect. Therefore, the effect of annual temperature difference on the structure is not considered in this study, and only the daily temperature field distribution of the structure caused by insolation is considered. Since the data of the two longitudinal sections are not much different, only one of the sections is analyzed in this paper.

2.1　Daily temperature distribution characteristics

Existing studies concluded that the daily variation of structural temperature can be described by a sinusoidal function, but the actual structural web and the top plate of the bridge deck slab are subject to different solar radiation intensity, so there are certain differences in the daily variation curves. In order to compare the difference of the daily temperature variation curves at different locations, the measurement points: C3, S2, S6, S10 and the ambient temperature data of the concrete bridge deck slab, box girder web, and box girder bottom plate were selected and plot their daily temperature variation curves, as shown in Fig. 4. Where T_{max}, T_{min} are the maximum and minimum values in the daily temperature variation of the bridge deck top plate measurement point C3 to the horizontal line distance from 0:00 to 24:00 of a day, respectively. From the measured data of ambient temperature variation at the bridge site, it can be seen that the ambient temperature variation law with time is basically a sine (cosine) curve variation. The daily maximum temperature occurs at 15:00 and the minimum temperature at 06:00.

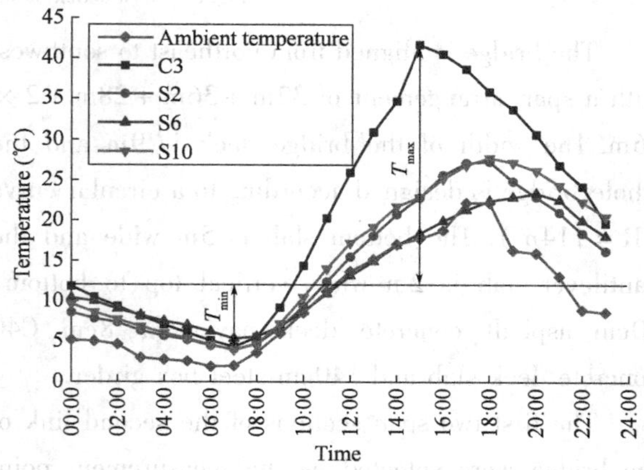

Fig. 4　Daily temperature change curve of section measuring point

The daily temperature variation curves of measurement points S2, S6 and S10 are close to the sinusoidal curve because they are not affected by direct solar radiation. At the same time, because the measurement points S2, S6 and S10 are not subject to direct solar radiation, their daily temperature change curves are close to the sine curve, C3 measurement points are subject to strong solar radiation, its T_{max} (30℃) value is much larger than the T_{min} (7.5℃) value, so the sine curve can not well describe its daily temperature change curve law, this paper uses the segmentation function to describe its change law, the expression is:

$$T_i = \begin{cases} A x^2 + Bx + C & (0 \leqslant x < x_1) \\ A_1 x + B_1 & (x_l \leqslant x < x_2) \\ A_1 x^2 + B_2 x + C_1 & (x_2 \leqslant x \leqslant x_3) \end{cases}$$

Where, *Ti* is the temperature of the measured point in the bridge deck plate, x is the time, ranging from 0h to 24h, vector$A = (A, A_1, A_2)$, $B = (B, B_1, B_2)$, $C = (C, C_1)$ are segmental function coefficients, interval $[0, x_1)$ for the early morning cooling stage, when the bridge structure has not been subjected to solar radiation, $[x_1, x_2)$ for the morning heating stage, when the structure began to be subjected to solar radiation, the temperature significantly increases, and $[x_2, x_3]$ is the afternoon cooling stage, when the intensity of solar radiation gradually decreases and the temperature of the structure gradually decreases.

In this paper, the coefficients corresponding to measurement point C3 are

$A = (0.04, 5.19, -0.17)$

$B = (-1.35, -36.84, 3.54)$

$C = (11.84, 26.14)$, $x_1 = 8$, $x_2 = 15$, $x_3 = 24$

2.2 Characterization of temperature field distribution

In order to distinguish more clearly the distribution characteristics of the temperature at different times of the day, this paper analyzes three periods of the day according to the data characteristics: the early morning cooling stage (00:00 to 07:00), the midday heating stage (08:00 to 14:00), and the evening cooling stage (17:00 to 23:00).

Combined with the characteristics of this bridge as a girder bridge, three temperature gradient distributions will be analyzed in this paper, namely: the vertical temperature gradient distribution of the cross-section (both sides inside and outside the curved bridge), the transverse temperature gradient distribution of the bridge deck slab, and since the temperature difference between the measured points of the steel box girder bottom slab is very small, the transverse temperature of the steel box girder bottom slab is considered to be the same and there is no temperature gradient in this paper. The temperature distribution of the cross-section at different moments is shown in Figure 5 ~ Figure 7. It can be seen from the time course graph of temperature variation at each measurement point:

(1) The maximum temperature occurred at different times, with the highest temperature at the measured point in the concrete of the bridge deck slab occurring at about 14:00, reaching a maximum temperature of 37°C, while the highest temperature in the webs of the steel bridge, both inside and outside, occurred at about 17:00, reaching 27°C. The lowest temperatures both occurred at 07:00 a.m. and both were nearly identical to the ambient temperature, reaching 3.6°C. The bottom slab was not directly exposed to solar radiation, so its temperature changed very slowly and with relatively minimal variation, with a maximum temperature of 27.7°C and a minimum temperature of 3.9°C, which was similar to the ambient temperature.

(2) Comparing the upper and lower measurement points in the concrete deck slab, it can be seen that the top measurement point of the concrete deck slab is more strongly illuminated and closer to the top surface of the deck, which is more sensitive to the change of the ambient temperature, and the temperature change of the lower surface temperature measurement point lags behind that of the upper surface measurement point whether it is cooling or heating. From 00:00 onwards, the temperature

difference between the upper and lower surfaces first becomes smaller and then larger, and then gradually becomes smaller when the upper surface temperature reaches its extreme value.

(3) As can be seen from Fig. 5 to Fig. 7, the temperature distribution patterns for the early morning cooling and evening cooling are roughly the same, while the curve pattern for the midday heating stage is significantly different from, or even diametrically opposed to, the cooling stage.

(4) From the vertical temperature distribution line graph, it can be seen that the vertical temperature distribution of the outer web of the curve shows a trend of increasing from the bottom upward and then decreasing, and the maximum temperature difference is 6℃, which appears at 19:00, while the vertical temperature distribution of the inner web of the curve shows different patterns in the heating and cooling stages, showing a trend of decreasing from the bottom upward and then increasing and then decreasing in the cooling stage, while the heating stage In the cooling stage, the temperature distribution showed a tendency of decreasing from the bottom to the top and then decreasing and then increasing. The maximum temperature difference of 9℃ occurs at 20:00, because the inner side of the curve is exposed to direct sunlight during the heating stage, while there is no interference from sunlight during the cooling stage, and the outer side of the curve is not yet exposed to strong solar radiation during the heating stage, but only in the afternoon, and the intensity of solar radiation is not high.

(5) The transverse temperature distribution in Fig. 7 shows that the transverse temperature distribution of the bridge deck basically becomes a parabolic shape with a downward opening, and in the cooling stage, the temperature distribution is symmetrically distributed along the centerline of the bridge deck, which is more uniform, and in the heating stage, the temperature of the measurement point at the inner end of the curve is more slowly warmed than the measurement point at the outer end of the curve due to the shading effect of the crash barrier and the late direct sunlight.

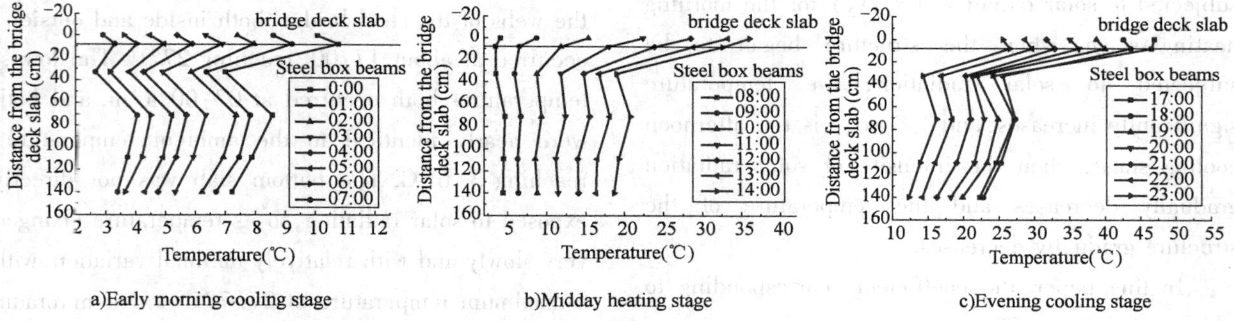

a)Early morning cooling stage b)Midday heating stage c)Evening cooling stage

Fig. 5 Vertical temperature distribution outside the curve

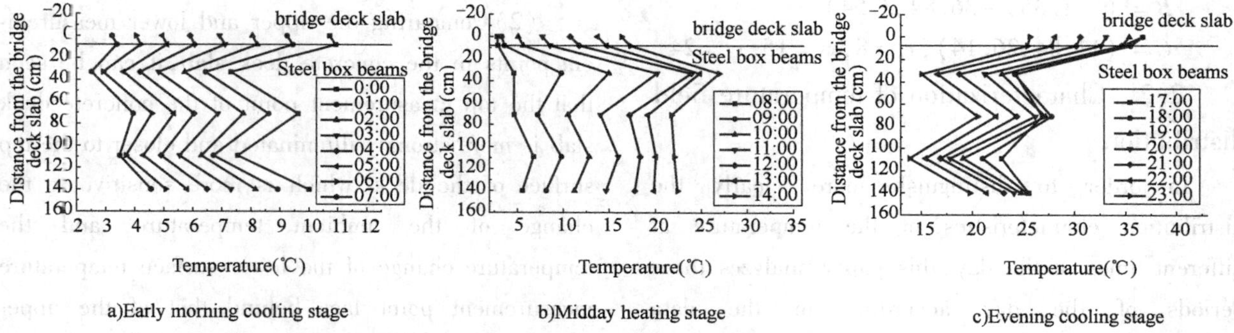

a)Early morning cooling stage b)Midday heating stage c)Evening cooling stage

Fig. 6 Vertical temperature distribution inside the curve

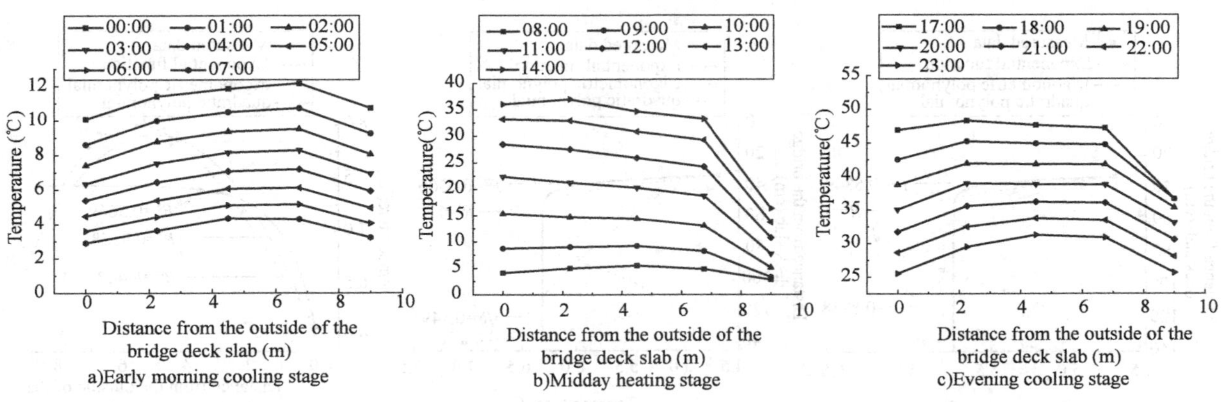

Fig. 7 Transverse temperature distribution of the bridge deck slab

2.3 Selection of the temperature gradient distribution model

In order to select a suitable temperature gradient distribution pattern to describe the temperature distribution of the combined structure, scholars study three commonly used temperature gradient distribution patterns: linear distribution, exponential function distribution, and polynomial.

form distribution, it is clear from the above analysis in this paper that the vertical temperature distribution of the diagonally curved web does not conform to a linear relationship, so the exponential function and the polynomial distribution function (quadratic as well as cubic) are used in this paper to fit the function to the average temperature of the measured points in the cooling stage (as shown in Fig. 8) and the heating stage (as shown in Fig. 9), respectively, and the fitting results are compared and analyzed by the correlation coefficient R^2 (the closer R^2 is to 1, the better the fitting effect). In order to show the curve fitting effect more clearly, the correlation coefficient is divided into three grades A, B, and C, respectively, R^2 is greater than 0.96, R^2 is between 0.8 and 0.96, and R^2 is less than 0.8. The results are shown in Tab. 1.

From the comparison results, it can be seen that the cubic function has good fitting effect for both the inner web and outer web, and also for the transverse side of the bridge deck, especially for the fitting of the vertical temperature gradient pattern of the steel web, the cubic function can go through each point perfectly, so it is considered that the vertical temperature gradient of the steel web meets the cubic polynomial distribution in both the heating and cooling stages, so the following fitting for the least favorable temperature gradient For the deck plate transverse in the cooling stage also conforms to the three polynomial distribution, the temperature distribution in the heating stage, the exponential function of the fitting results more accurate, so the following for the deck plate transverse temperature gradient fitting in the cooling stage using three polynomial functions, in the heating order using the exponential function.

3 Fitting of the least favorable temperature gradient equation

3.1 Principles for fitting the least favorable temperature gradient equation

The temperature distribution is generally considered to be the least favorable temperature gradient when the difference between the highest temperature on the upper surface and the lowest temperature on the girder height reaches its maximum, generally around 14:00 pm. When the bridge is in the heating stage as described above, it is clear from the above analysis that there is a significant difference between the heating stage and the cooling stage, and even an opposite trend in the temperature distribution pattern on the measured section, so it is necessary to adopt a more accurate to determine the moment of the day when the least favorable temperature gradient occurs.

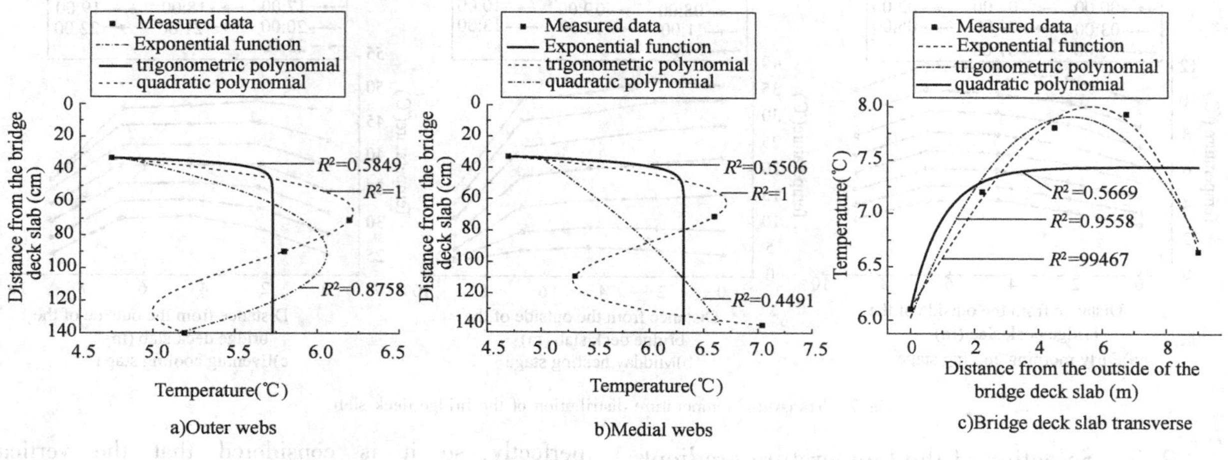

a)Outer webs　　b)Medial webs　　c)Bridge deck slab transverse

Fig. 8　Cooling stage

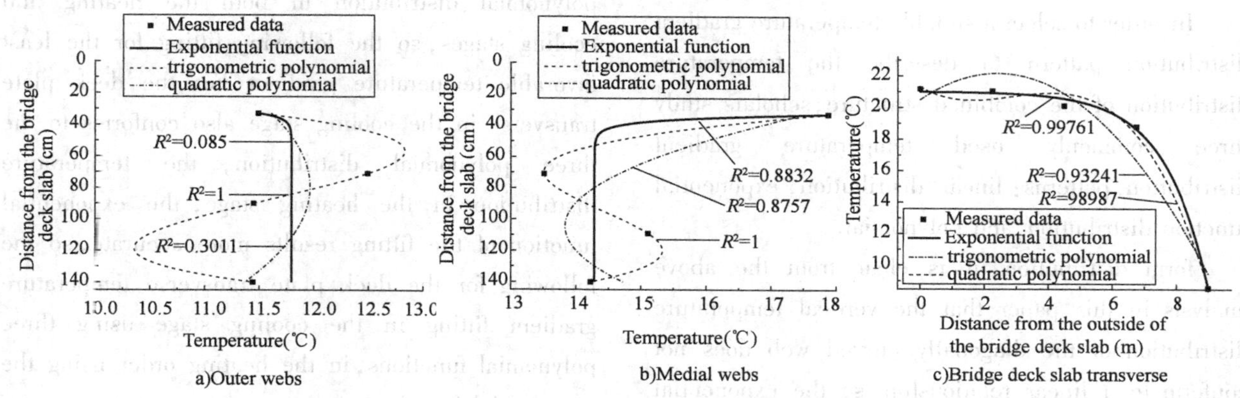

a)Outer webs　　b)Medial webs　　c)Bridge deck slab transverse

Fig. 9　Heating stage

Comparison of temperature gradient fitting results　　Tab. 1

Stage	Outer web vertical			Inner web vertical			Bridge deck plate transverse		
	exponential	2nd polynomial	3rd polynomial	expon ential	2nd polynomial	3rd polynomial	expon ential	2nd polynomial	3rd polynomial
heating stage	C	C	A	B	B	A	A	B	A
cooling stage	C	B	A	C	C	A	C	B	A

In this paper, we adopt the method of selecting the least favorable temperature gradient in the literature (Chen can. 2012): the temperature of one measurement point with the smallest temperature variation in the cross-section is selected as the reference temperature, and the temperature difference distribution of the beam cross-section is obtained according to the temperature of each point, and the temperature gradient with the largest temperature difference is taken as the least favorable temperature gradient.

Considering the different moments of occurrence of the least favorable temperature difference in the vertical direction of the steel web and the least favorable temperature difference in the transverse direction of the bridge deck, the paper considers the least favorable temperature difference in the vertical direction and the least favorable temperature difference in the transverse direction separately, and analyzes the effects of the structure under the action of the least favorable temperature gradient in the vertical direction and the least favorable temperature gradient in the transverse direction respectively.

3.2 Determination of the moment of least favorable temperature difference

From Fig. 10, it can be seen that the sum of the maximum temperature differences in different parts appeared at different moments, the sum of the maximum temperature differences in the vertical direction of the inner web appeared at 16:00. the sum of the maximum temperature differences in the vertical direction of the inner web appeared at 19:00, and the sum of the maximum temperature differences in the horizontal direction of the bridge deck appeared at 14: 00. In the following, the temperature gradient distribution patterns of the whole bridge at each of the three moments will be fitted. Tab. 2 shows the temperature data of all measured points on the inner web, outer web, and deck slab at different moments.

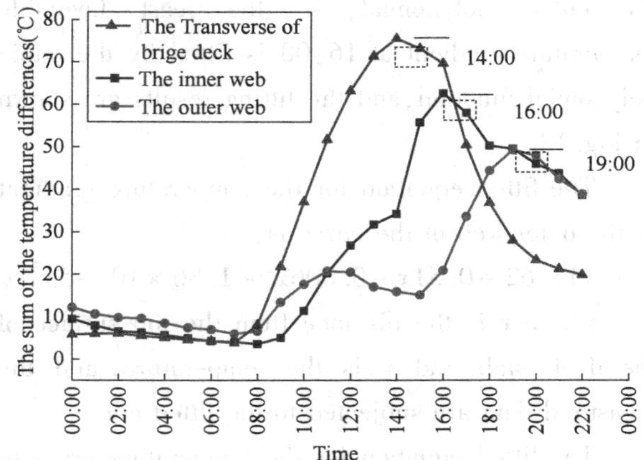

Fig. 10 Sum of temperature difference at different times

Measured data at the moment of the most unfavourable temperature difference Tab. 2

Time	Inner web vertical				Outer web vertical				Bridge deck plate transverse				
	S1	S2	S3	S4	S8	S9	S10	S11	C1	C3	C5	C7	C9
14:00	19.01	20.75	19.28	18.68	26.90	21.74	22.05	22.39	36.03	36.99	34.66	33.26	16.33
16:00	22.95	25.63	23.11	21.46	25.01	25.17	24.14	25.27	50.86	57.77	50.56	51.56	35.26
19:00	21.85	24.85	23.32	19.84	22.88	27.17	19.08	24.78	38.76	44.95	41.85	43.80	35.33

3.3 14:00 most unfavourable temperature gradient fit

Because 14:00 is the heating stage, it is clear from the above analysis that at this stage, the vertical temperature gradient distribution of the steel web is consistent with the cubic polynomial division and, the lateral temperature distribution of the bridge deck slab is close to the exponential form, so both functions were used to fit the least favorable temperature gradient at 14: 00. The fitting results are shown in Fig. 11. The following vertical temperature gradient of the web slab is fitted with the vertical as the x-axis and the lateral as the y-axis, and the following lateral temperature gradient of the bridge deck slab is fitted with the vertical as the y-axis and the lateral as the x-axis.

The fitted equation for the temperature gradient of the outer web of the curve is:

$$y = 11.56 + 0.33x - 0.004x^2 + 1.30 \times 10^{-5}x^3$$

where x is the distance from the top surface of the deck slab and y is the temperature, and the measured data are subjected to the fitted curve.

The fitted equation for the temperature gradient of the inner web of the curve is:

$$y = 32.97 - 0.31x + 0.003x^2 - 9.09 \times 10^{-6}x^3$$

where x is the distance from the top surface of the bridge deck slab, y is the temperature, and the measured data are fitted to the curve.

The fitted equation for the lateral temperature gradient of the deck plate is:

$$y = 36.16958 - 0.01285e - 0.81568x$$

where x is the distance from the outer edge of the deck plate, y is the temperature, and the correlation coefficient is $R^2 = 0.98704$. The fitted results satisfy the requirements.

3.4 16:00 most unfavourable temperature gradient fit

Because 14: 00 is the cooling stage, from the above analysis, it can be seen that at this stage, the vertical temperature gradient distribution of the steel web is consistent with the cubic polynomial distribution. and the transverse temperature distribution of the bridge deck plate is also close to the cubic polynomial, so the least favorable temperature gradient at 16:00 is fitted by the cubic polynomial function, and the fitting results are shown in Fig. 12.

The fitted equation for the temperature gradient of the outer web of the curve is:

$$y = 11.62 + 0.51x - 0.006x^2 + 1.86 \times 10 - 5x^3$$

where x is the distance from the top surface of the deck slab and y is the temperature, and the measured data are subjected to the fitted curve.

The fitted equation for the temperature gradient of the inner web of the curve is:

$$y = 20.71 + 0.22x - 0.003x^2 + 1.25 \times 10 - 5x^3$$

where x is the distance from the top surface of the deck slab and y is the temperature, and the measured data are subjected to the fitted curve.

The fitting equation for the lateral temperature gradient of the deck plate is:

$$y = 51.14 - 0.49x + 0.47x^2 - 0.067x^3$$

where x is the distance from the outer edge of the deck plate, y is the temperature, and $R^2 = 0.9722$, and the fitting results satisfy the requirements.

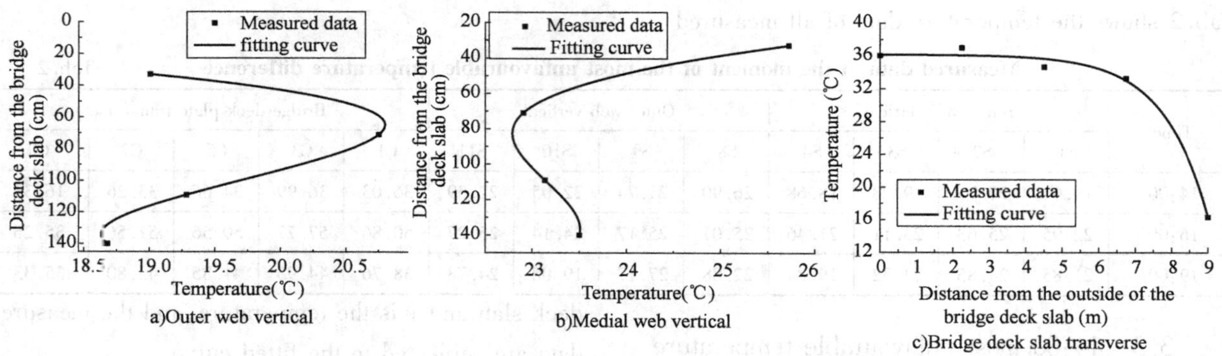

Fig. 11 The least favorable temperature gradient at 14:00

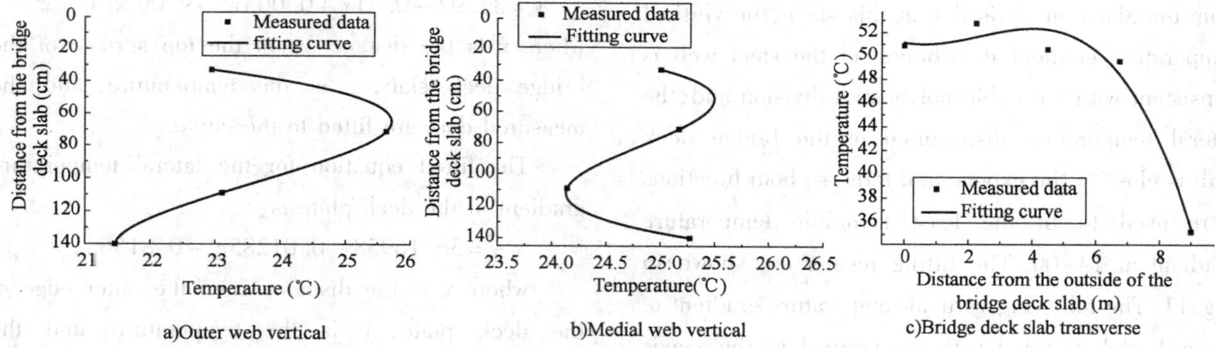

Fig. 12 The least favorable temperature gradient at 16:00

3.5 19:00 most unfavourable temperature gradient fit

Because 19:00 is the cooling stage, it is known from the above analysis that at this stage, the vertical temperature gradient of the steel web and the lateral temperature distribution of the bridge deck slab are in accordance with the cubic polynomial function, so the least favorable temperature gradient at 19:00 is fitted using the cubic polynomial function, and the fitting results are shown in Fig. 13.

The fitted equation for the temperature gradient of the outer web of the curve is:

$$y = 14.32 + 0.31x - 0.002x^2 + 4.9 \times 10 - 6x^3$$

where x is the distance from the top surface of the deck plate, y is the temperature, and the correlation coefficient is $R = 0.9931$, and the curve fitting basically meets the requirements.

The fitted equation for the temperature gradient of the inner web of the curve is:

$$y = -14.82 + 1.84x - 0.02x^2 + 9.37 \times 10^{-5}x^3$$

where x is the distance from the top surface of the deck slab and y is the temperature, and the measured data are subjected to the fitted curve.

The fitted equation for the transverse temperature gradient of the deck plate is:

$$y = 38.90 + 1.13x + 0.03x^2 + 0.02x^3$$

where, x is the distance from the outer edge of the deck plate, y is the temperature, and the correlation coefficient is $R^2 = 0.9591$. The curve fiting basically meets the requirements.

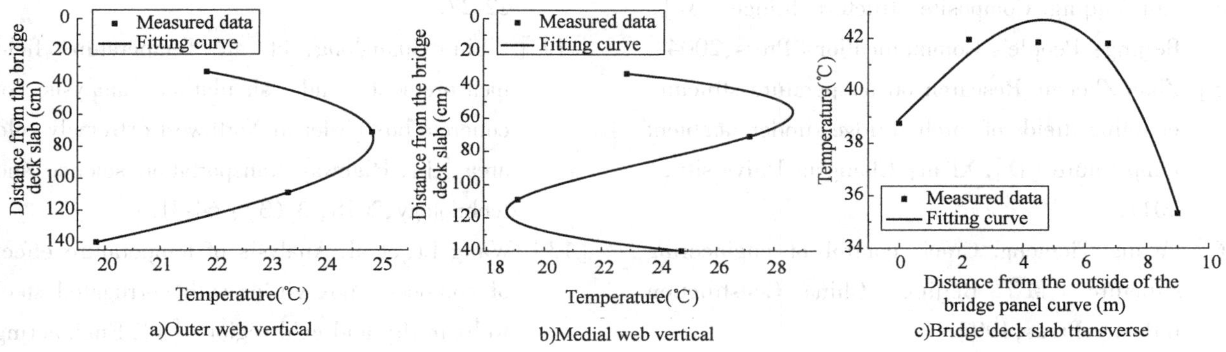

Fig. 13 The least favorable temperature gradient at 19:00

4 Conclusions

Based on the analysis of the measured data of the temperature field of the combined structural girder bridge with diagonal curved web and the determination of the temperature distribution pattern by mathematical means, the following conclusions are drawn in this paper.

(1) In the location of the cross-section not subject to sunlight radiation, or weak sunlight radiation, the daily temperature change curve can be expressed by a sine function, for the bridge deck and other parts of the direct sunlight radiation, the daily temperature change curve is more accurately described by a segmental function.

(2) The pattern of temperature distribution in the beam cross-section is different or even opposite during the heating period by sunlight and the cooling period at night, therefore, when considering the temperature effect, heating and cooling should be considered separately.

(3) The moment of the most unfavourable temperature difference in the web of the bridge and the moment of the most unfavourable temperature difference in the transverse direction of the bridge deck are different, so their effects on the structure should be considered separately in the analysis of temperature effects.

(4) By fitting the measured data, the transverse temperature distribution of the bridge deck slab is in the form of a cubic polynomial and an exponential function, which is recommended to be considered in the specification, while the vertical temperature gradient of the steel web is in the form of a cubic polynomial.

(5) In this paper, only the temperature field and the temperature gradient of the combined structural girder bridge with a diagonal curved web are studied, and the temperature effect calculation of a curved bridge usinga temperature gradient model will be the next stage of the author's research work.

References

[1] Liu Yongjian, Gao Yimin, Zhou Xuhong, et al. Technical and economic analysis of medium and

small span steel-concrete composite girder bridges [J]. Chinese Journal of Highways (in Chinese),2017, 30(3): 1-13.

[2] Priesley M J N. Design of concrete bridges for temperature gradients[J]. ACI Journal, 1978, No. 75-23.

[3] Dilger W H, AmjllGhali ChanMeta1. Temperature stress in composite bridge [J]. Journal of Structural Engineering, ASCE, 1983, 109 (6): 1460-1479.

[4] Liu Yuqing. Composite structure bridge [M]. Beijing: People's Communications Press,2004.

[5] Zhao Zhenyu. Research on temperature structure coupling field of arch bridge under ambient temperature [D]. Xi'an: Chang'an University, 2011.

[6] Wang Tiemeng. Crack control of engineering structure [M]. Beijing: China Construction Industry Press,1997.

[7] Chen Xiaoqiang. Research on temperature field and temperature effect of steel concrete composite continuous box girder bridge [D]. Nanjing: Southeast University,2009.

[8] Wu Liuzheng. Simulation of temperature field of concrete box girder bridge [J]. Highway traffic science and technology, 2011, 28 (10): 65-69.

[9] Chen Yanjiang, et al. Study on temperature field and temperature effect of steel-concrete composite beam bridge [J]. Highway transportation science and technology,2014, 31 (11): 85-91.

[10] Liu Yu, et al. Study on temperature gradient effect of light composite girder bridge deck under sunlight [J]. Highway transportation science and technology, 2015, 32 (6): 54-61.

[11] Wu Qingxiang, et al. Research on sunshine temperature field of a steel-z-concrete composite box girder in Beijing[J]. Journal of Beijing Jianzhu University, 2016, 32 (2): 22-27.

[12] Liu Guanglong, et al. Temperature field measurement and simulation analysis of concrete box girder in Northwest extremely cold area [J]. Highway transportation science and technology,2018, 3 (3): 64-71.

[13] Wang Li, et al. Analysis of temperature effect of composite box girder with corrugated steel webs in dry and cold regions [J]. Engineering Science and technology, 2021, 53 (1): 60-66.

[14] Zhao Guoyun. Temperature distribution of steel box girder during asphalt pavement at high temperature [J]. Science Technology and Engineering, 2020,20 (1): 335-339.

[15] Chen Can. Research on temperature and temperature effect of steel plate composite beam bridge [D]. Changsha: Central South University,2012.

基于 FLAC^{3D} 的土工合成材料加筋土桥台复合结构参数研究

李元昊[1]　彭少龙[2]　朱云升*[1]

(1. 武汉理工大学交通物流学院;2. 中交第二公路勘察设计研究院有限公司)

摘　要　土工合成材料加筋土桥台复合结构(GRS-IBS)是一种可以实现桥梁一体化设计施工的新型技术,但国内针对该种结构的力学性能的研究还不多。本文基于 FLAC^{3D}有限元分析软件以一现有 GRS-IBS 结构为原型建立数值模型,并通过现场监测数据佐证,进行参数研究。研究结果表明:改变土工加筋材料的加筋间距、加筋长度以及回填土内摩擦角均会对 GRS-IBS 结构力学性能产生一定影响。比如增大加筋间距、加筋长度以及减小回填土内摩擦角均会导致面层侧向位移增大,影响 GRS-IBS 结构稳定性;此外,加筋间距与回填土内摩擦角对面层侧向位移的影响比较大,而加筋长度对面层侧向位移的影响较小。

关键词 土工合成材料 加筋土复合体 有限元分析 土工合成材料加筋土桥台复合结构 参数研究 工程应用

0 引言

土工合成材料加筋土(Geosynthetic Reinforced Soil,简称 GRS)技术以其适应性强、节省投资、低碳环保等优势,在公、铁路等土木工程领域得到了广泛应用。在桥梁工程中,采用土工合成材料加筋土桥台复合结构(Geosynthetic Reinforced Soil-Integrated Bridge System,GRS-IBS)能够减小或消除桥梁承台的水平土压力,从而控制桥台与连接路堤的差异沉降,很好地解决了中小桥梁的桥头跳车问题[1]。

自 20 世纪 90 年代后,我国非承重式的加筋土桥台大量涌现。冯焕生[2]总结了京石高速公路北京段三期工程的若干技术措施,通过实践证明外置式加筋土桥台在软土地基上的适用性良好,其密实度和承载力均能满足要求。尹正文等[3]以云南黄登大桥为例,选择外置组合式加筋土桥台作为黄登大桥桥台型式,通过结构设计和稳定性验算,并按设计要求施工完毕,经过 3 年的运行没有出现任何问题,证明黄登大桥加筋土桥台的设计结果是满足规范要求并且满足工程需要。徐超等[4]将 GRS-IBS 结构同之前的加筋土桥台结构进行了对比,认为 GRS-IBS 结构的侧向变形明显小于以往的加筋土桥台,且 GRS-IBS 结构内的筋材应变更小更为均匀。还有一些学者针对 GRS-IBS 结构的抗震性能开展了振动台试验[5,6],认为即便在较大的地震加速度下,GRS-IBS 结构仍能保持整体稳定,仅仅发生微小的变形,并且保持其他条件不变时,减小加筋间距能有效提高该结构的抗震能力。

本文在借鉴国内外对 GRS-IBS 桥台研究的基础上,根据一座现有 GRS-IBS 桥台的现场监测数据,结合 FLAC^{3D}数值模拟进行研究。

1 工程概述

本文以湖北省襄阳市境内 G207 襄阳市襄州至宜城段段改建工程中的一座 GRS-IBS 小桥为原型进行研究。全桥跨径 12m,挡墙高 $H=3$m,且挡墙下部填筑有 2m 高的硬黏土层用以改善土基力学性质,以及防止挡墙内部遭受地下水侵蚀;墙趾处配有加筋土基础(reinforced soil foundation,简称 RSF),使用 C20 混凝土预制件;土工加筋材料的加筋间距 $S_v=0.2$m;墙后填土部分采用碎石砂土进行回填,并分层施工依次碾压至设计压实度。GRS-IBS 左幅结构如图 1 所示。

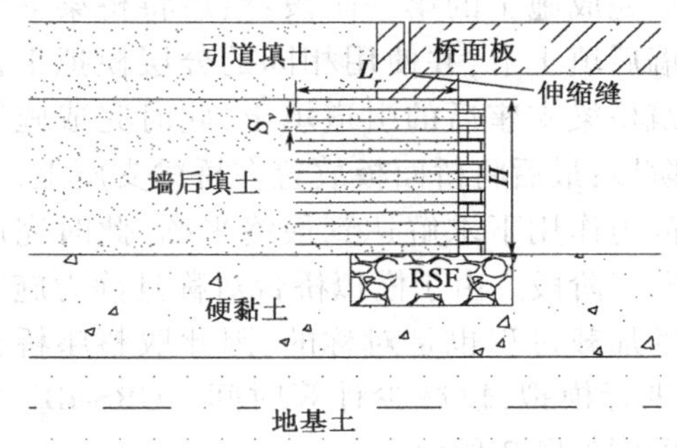

图 1 GRS-IBS 结构图

2 数值模拟验证方案

FLAC^{3D}适用于土与结构相互作用分析,非常适合于本项目研究 GRS-IBS 结构的力学响应分析。通过现场检测,可以得到由桥台自重引起的面层背后侧向土压力以及由桥台自重以及上部荷载引起的桥台面层的侧向位移等数据,进而对数值模拟的结果进行佐证,验证数值模型的可靠性,从而进行更多相关参数的研究。

2.1 数值模拟概述

面层由预制混凝土砌块组成,尺寸为 0.5m(长度)×0.2m(宽度),共 15 层,面层全高 $H=3$m,挡土墙上部包括桥面板、支座、引道填土等高度共 1.5m,桥台总高度 4.5m;桥台位于 7.5m(1.5H)厚的地基土上,且地基土上增加铺设 2m 厚的硬黏土防水层,土基部分共 9.5m;墙角处设有尺寸为 4m(宽度)×1m(高度)的 RSF;面层到侧向土体边界的距离为 15m(5H);面层后填土中的土工加筋材料由土工格栅模拟,从下至上铺设

的土工格栅长度 $L = 3\text{m}(1.0H)$，加筋间距 S_v 为0.2m，且与面层刚性连接。

GRS-IBS桥台数值模型通过分层施工工艺进行模拟，首先铺设地基土并施加边界条件与初始应力状态，然后使用FLAC^{3D}的小应变模式求解，令模型在地基土自重作用下达到平衡；在地基土上建立第一层0.2m高的面层、回填土与土工格栅之后设置面层之间的接触面与面层与回填土之间的接触面，为了模拟实际施工过程中分层施工的摊铺压实过程，对回填土层表面施加8kPa的均布荷载作为压实力[7]，令模型在回填土自重以及均布荷载的作用下达到平衡，且平衡之后将均布荷载移除并进行下一层填土的施工，剩下的14层回填土与面层均使用同样的顺序进行模拟，全部填筑完毕后完成施工的第一阶段；然后将桥梁支座放置在墙后填土上，并使用相同的分层模拟工艺分层填筑桥梁支座后的引道填土，此时完成施工的第二阶段；最后将桥面板放置在桥梁支座上，令模型在静力作用下求解达到最终平衡，此时完成施工的第三阶段。由于模拟桥台对称且静力施工模拟中的加载过程也是对称的，因此取整座桥台的一半进行模拟，以减少计算时间。GRS-IBS结构数值模型如图2所示。

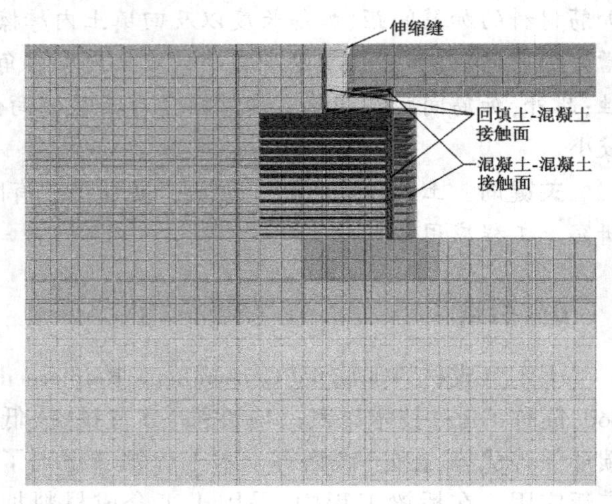

图2 GRS-IBS结构数值模型

2.2 数值模型参数取值

FLAC^{3D}中土体使用摩尔-库伦本构关系进行模拟，其中地基土、硬黏土、回填土的各项主要技术参数已由三轴压缩试验等室内试验得到，如表1所示。

加筋土桥台中的墙板、支座和桥面板均使用C20混凝土预制得到，在FLAC^{3D}数值模型中均使用弹性本构关系模拟，其各项详细参数均由厂商直接提供，如表2所示。

各土体主要技术参数 表1

土体名称	弹性模量 E(MPa)	泊松比 v	密度 ρ(kg/m^3)	内摩擦角 φ(°)	黏聚力 c(kPa)
地基土	28	0.2	1300	25	15
硬黏土	50	0.25	1750	27	20
回填土	33	0.3	1600	35	2

混凝土主要技术参数 表2

混凝土名称	弹性模量 E(GPa)	泊松比 v	密度 ρ(kg/m^3)
C20	25.5	0.17	2400

墙后填土中的土工加筋材料主要与土体发生剪切摩擦作用而无法承受弯矩，因此数值模型中使用土工格栅进行模拟。FLAC^{3D}中土工格栅为各向同性弹性材料，所涉及到的主要参数有弹性模量 E、泊松比 v、厚度 t、耦合弹簧黏结力 c(coupling-cohesion-shear)、耦合弹簧摩擦角 φ(coupling-friction-shear)与耦合弹簧单位面积刚度 k(coupling-stiffness-shear)。其中耦合弹簧黏结力 c、耦合弹簧摩擦角 φ 与耦合弹簧单位面积刚度 k 需要根据经验进行取值[8]。在本次研究中土工格栅界面参数取值如表3所示。

土工格栅界面参数 表3

弹性模量 E (MPa)	泊松比 v	厚度 t (mm)	耦合弹簧黏结力 c(Pa)	耦合弹簧摩擦角 φ (°)	耦合弹簧单位面积刚度 k (kN/m^3)
26000	0.33	5	0	23	2500

数值模型中还需要设置额外的接触面，其中包括回填土与混凝土之间的接触面以及混凝土与混凝土之间的接触面。FLAC^{3D}中接触面涉及到的参数有法向刚度 K_n、剪切刚度 K_s、摩擦角 φ 和黏聚力 c，其中回填土-混凝土接触面摩擦角 φ_{rf} 需要通过强度折减系数($R=2/3$)[9]进行计算，计算公式如式(1)：

$$\varphi_{rf}=\tan^{-1}\left(\frac{2}{3}\times\tan\varphi_p\right) \tag{1}$$

式中：φ_p——回填土峰值摩擦角。

故对于内摩擦角为35°的回填土，此时的回填土-混凝土接触面的摩擦角 φ 约为25°；而对于法向刚度 K_n 和剪切刚度 K_s 均需要根据经验进行取值[9]。接触面的详细参数如表4所示。

接触面参数取值 表4

接触面名称	法向刚度 K_n(MPa/m)	剪切刚度 K_s(MPa/m)	摩擦角 φ(°)	黏聚力 c(kPa)
回填土-混凝土接触面	100	1	25	0
混凝土-混凝土接触面	1000	40	36	58

2.3 数值模型验证

数值模型的验证基于现场监测数据进行，监测结果包括由墙后填土自重与压实力引起的面层后侧向土压力以及由上部结构荷载引起的面层侧向位移。

图3示出了数值模型中得到的侧向土压力分布、根据主动土压力计算公式得到的侧向土压力理论值分布以及安装在4层填土(分别位于高度 $z=0.2H$、$0.4H$、$0.6H$、$0.8H$ 处，H 为面层总高度)中的土压力传感器测量得到的水平土压力分布。由图3可知，现场实测数据与数值分析结果较为吻合，现场数据与模拟结果得到的水平土压力均有随面层高度 z 减小而线性增大的趋势，且对于应力大小而言，现场数据与数值结果的差异在2kPa以内。

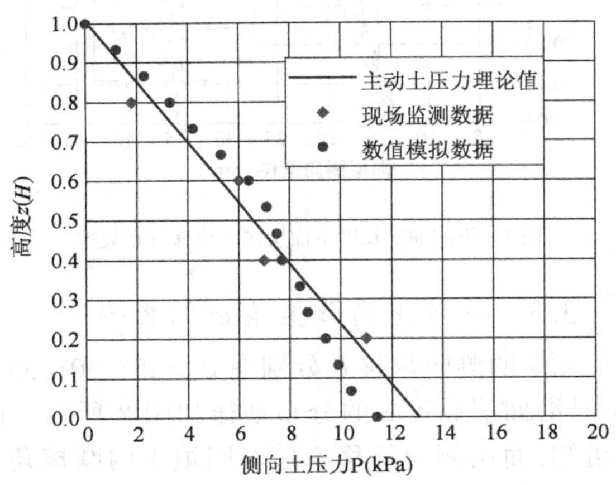

图3 现场实测与数值模拟的侧向土压力分布对比

图4示出了通过位移传感器测量得到的分别位于面层高度 $z=0.2H$、$0.4H$、$0.6H$、$0.8H$ 处的现场实测面层侧向位移与数值模型中得到的面层侧向位移。由图4可知，现场实测数据与数值分析结果同样较为吻合，现场数据呈现出随着面层高度增加而增加的趋势，且同样在高度 $z=0.7H$ 处侧向位移达到最大，偏差在0.2~1.0mm范围内。FLAC^{3D}中侧向位移的计算结果云图如图5所示。

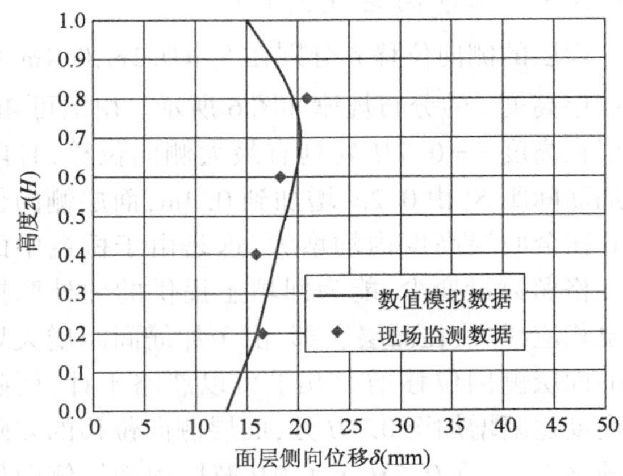

图4 现场实测与数值模拟的面层侧向位移分布对比

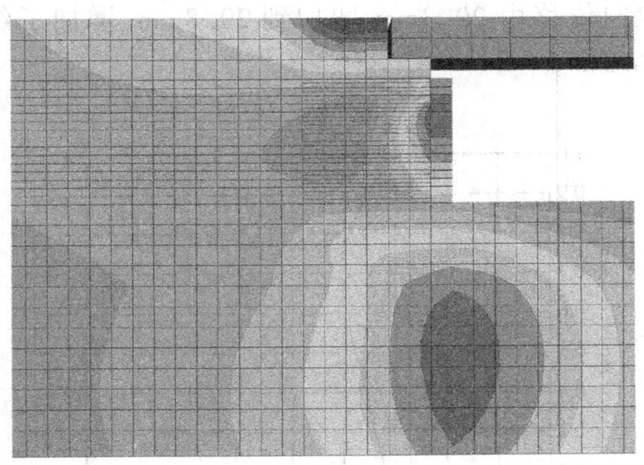

图5 FLAC^{3D}中的侧向位移计算结果

3 数值模拟参数研究

GRS-IBS桥台的力学响应分析参数研究是基于上文中已被现场监测数据验证过的FLAC^{3D}有限

元数值模型进行的。本次研究考虑了3种不同的参数:加筋间距 S_v、加筋长度 L_r 与回填土内摩擦角 φ,并通过沿面层高度 z 的面层侧向位移 δ 来评估这些参数对GRS-IBS的力学性能影响[10],共设计3组工况进行对照研究。

(1)针对加筋间距 S_v 的工况组:加筋间距 S_v = 0.2m,0.4m;加筋长度 L_r = 1.0H(3m);回填土内摩擦角 φ = 35°。

(2)针对加筋长度 L_r 的工况组:加筋间距 S_v = 0.2m;加筋长度 L_r = 0.5H(1.5m),0.7H(2.1m),1.0H(3.0m),1.3H(3.9m);回填土内摩擦角 φ = 35°。

(3)针对回填土摩擦角 φ 的工况组:加筋间距 S_v = 0.2m;加筋长度 L_r = 1.0H(3m);回填土内摩擦角 φ = 25°,30°,35°,40°。

3.1　加筋间距 S_v 的影响

面层的侧向位移 δ 分别在 S_v = 0.2m,0.4m时沿面层高度 z 的分布规律如图6所示。由图可知,面层在高度 z = 0.7H 处具有最大侧向位移,且随着加筋间距 S_v 由0.2m增加到0.4m,面层侧向位移 δ 在全面层高度内均增大,这是由于桥台中的土工格栅数量变少,能为回填土提供的额外摩擦力也相应减少;在面层底部,由于加筋间距增大导致的面层侧向位移增大几乎可以忽略不计,而随着高度逐渐增加至0.7H 处,面层侧向位移的差距逐渐增大,并在0.7H 至1.0H 范围内面层侧向位移的差距逐渐减小;面层在高度 z = 0.7H 处最大侧向位移由20.3mm增加到29.8mm,增加了约46.8%。

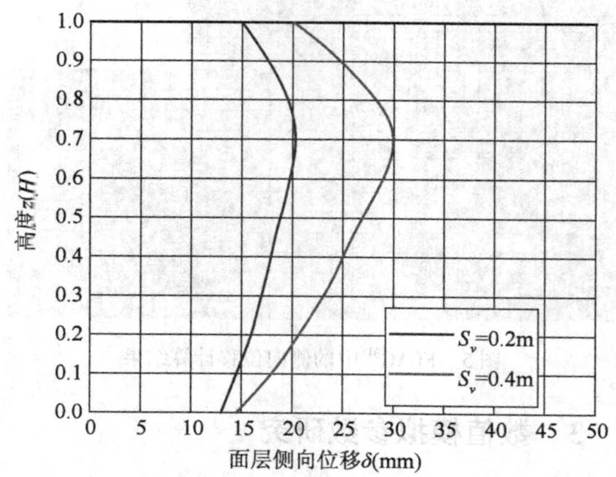

图6　不同加筋间距下面层侧向位移分布规律

3.2　加筋长度 L_r 的影响

面层的侧向位移 δ 分别在 L_r = 0.5H,0.7H,1.0H,1.3H 时沿面层高度 z 的分布规律如图7所示。由图可知,面层同样在高度 z = 0.7H 处具有最大侧向位移,且随着加筋长度 L_r 由1.3H 依次减小到1.0H、0.7H、0.5H,面层侧向位移 δ 在全面层高度内均小幅度增大。这是由于桥台中的土工格栅长度减小时,作用于土工格栅上的总拉力同样减小,从而为回填土内部提供的摩擦力也更少;当加筋长度 L_r 由1.3H 减小到1.0H 时在高度 z=0.7H 处面层侧向位移由19.4mm增加到20.3mm,增加了约4.6%;加筋长度 L_r 由1.0H 减小到0.7H 时在高度 z = 0.7H 处面层侧向位移由20.3mm增加到21.4mm,增加了约5.4%;加筋长度 L_r 由0.7H 减小到0.5H 时在高度 z = 0.7H 处面层侧向位移由21.4mm增加到23.3mm,增加了约8.9%。由此可知随着加筋长度 L_r 逐级减小,面层最大侧向位移的增加幅度也逐渐增大,但是总体而言,改变加筋长度对面层侧向位移的影响较小。

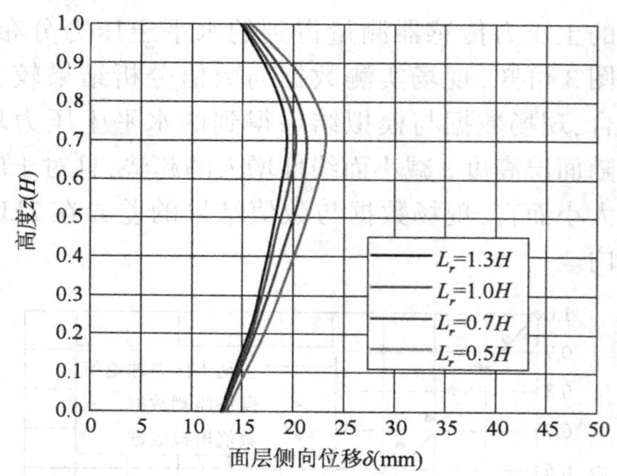

图7　不同加筋长度下面层侧向位移分布规律

3.3　回填土内摩擦角 φ 的影响

面层的侧向位移 δ 分别在 φ = 25°,30°,35°,40°时沿面层高度 z 的分布规律如图8所示。由图可知,面层侧向位移 δ 随着回填土内摩擦角 φ 减小而增大,这是由于内摩擦角减小后回填土的抗剪强度相应减小,且土体与土工格栅之间的摩擦力也减小;面层侧向位移 δ 在内摩擦角 φ = 25°、30°、35°、40°时在高度 z = 0.7H 处分别有最大值28.4mm,23.9mm,20.3mm,17.5mm;内摩擦角 φ 由

40°减小为35°、35°减小为30°、30°减小为25°时，面层侧向位移最大值分别增加了均有一定程度增加，位移最大值分别增加了16%、17.7%、18.8%，增长幅度基本相同，可近似认为呈线性增加。

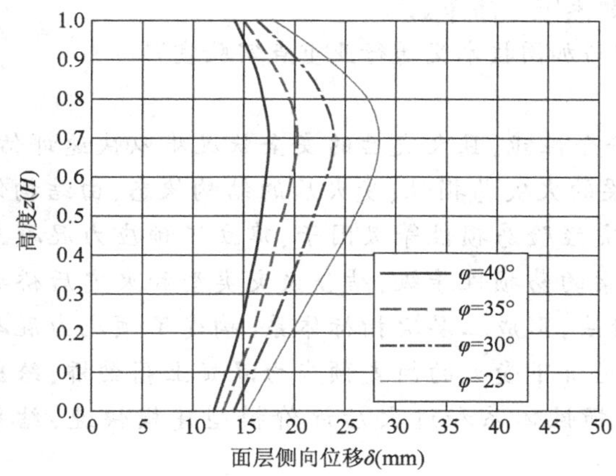

图8 不同回填土内摩擦角下面层侧向位移分布规律

4 结语

本文通过GRS-IBS结构的现场实测数据对$FLAC^{3D}$数值模型验证后，通过进一步数值模拟分析，可总结得出以下相关结论：

(1)通过GRS-IBS结构的现场实测数据，成功验证了$FLAC^{3D}$数值模型，且说明文中所选用的本构模型和接触面等相关参数均可以较好地模拟真实工程中的实际情况。

(2)GRS-IBS结构的面层侧向位移分布曲线呈中间大两头小的分布规律，且在面层高度z=0.7H处具有最大值。

(3)随着加筋间距S_v的增加，面层侧向位移δ也会相应增加；当加筋间距S_v由0.2m增加至0.4m时，面层侧向位移δ最多会增加50%左右，经过对比可知加筋间距S_v对GRS-IBS结构的整体稳定性影响最大，工程中应尽量避免使用较大的加筋间距。

(4)随着加筋长度L_r的减小，面层侧向位移δ呈线性增加，当加筋长度L_r由1.3H减小至1.0H、1.0H减小至0.7H、0.7H减小至0.5H时，面层侧向位移δ的最大值都将分别增加4%～9%，增加幅度较小，因此加筋长度对GRS-IBS结构的整体稳定性影响最小。

(5)随着回填土内摩擦角φ的减小，面层侧向位移δ呈线性增加，当内摩擦角φ由40°减小至35°、35°减小为30°、30°减小为25°时，面层侧向位移δ的最大值分别增加16%～19%，对GRS-IBS结构的整体稳定性影响适中，次于加筋间距的影响，而大于加筋长度的影响，在工程中需要选用具有合适内摩擦角的回填土。

参考文献

[1] Lee K Z Z, Wu J T H. A synthesis of case histories on GRS bridge-supporting structures with flexible facing[J]. Geotextiles and Geomembranes, 2004, 22(4): 181-204.

[2] 冯焕生. 京石公路北京段三期工程及其若干技术措施[J]. 中国公路学报, 1993(04): 33-38.

[3] 尹正文, 杨鹏飞. 黄登大桥加筋土桥台设计及其应用[J]. 云南水力发电, 2014, 30(06): 60-65.

[4] 徐超, 罗敏敏. GRS结构与MSE结构的性能差异及评价方法[J]. 长江科学院院报, 2019, 36(03): 1-7.

[5] 罗敏敏, 徐超, 杨阳, 等. 加筋土柔性桥台复合结构抗震性能试验[J]. 同济大学学报(自然科学版), 2019, 47(11): 1541-1547.

[6] 徐超, 罗敏敏, 任非凡, 等. 加筋土柔性桥台复合结构抗震性能的试验研究[J]. 岩土力学, 2020(S1): 1-9.

[7] Hatami K, Bathurst R J. Development and verification of a numerical model for the analysis of geosynthetic-reinforced soil segmental walls under working stress conditions[J]. Canadian Geotechnical Journal, 2005, 42(4): 1066-1085.

[8] 刘波, 韩艳辉. FLAC原理实例与应用指南[M]. 北京: 人民交通出版社, 2005.

[9] Yu Y, Bathurst R J, Allen T M. Numerical modeling of the SR-18 geogrid reinforced modular block retaining walls[J]. Journal of Geotechnical & Geoenvironmental Engineering, 2016, Vol. 142(5): 1-13.

[10] Rong Wen-yong, Zheng Ye-wei, McCartney, et al. 3D Deformation Behavior of Geosynthetic-Reinforced Soil Bridge Abutments[A]. Geotechnical Frontiers 2017: Walls and Slopes, 2017.

PC桥梁过火后安全评价模型研究

赵晓翠*[1]　张　岗[1,2]　宋超杰[1,2]　陆泽磊[1]
(1. 长安大学公路学院;2. 长安大学旧桥检测与加固技术交通行业重点实验室)

摘　要　火灾严重威胁预应力混凝土(PC)桥梁的安全性能,且火灾后的安全状况难以快速评估。为建立一种简单快捷的评价方法,考虑预应力混凝土桥梁的火灾易损性、受火后的结构状态,由结构体系、跨径、截面类型、车道数和已服役年限,计算了桥梁火灾经验易损性等级因子,建立了预应力混凝土桥梁的火灾后经验易损性体系,确定了预应力混凝土桥梁的易损性等级,结合火灾类型和火灾后桥梁特征推定获得火灾温度。采用基于模糊数学的总体评价法,形成三层次指标体系,构建了预应力混凝土桥梁过火后评价模型。根据工程实例采样,分析了一座桥下受火的简支预应力混凝土箱梁桥,给出了评价结果。研究表明所建立的预应力混凝土桥梁易损性体系和过火后评价模型建模快速,结果可靠。

关键词　预应力混凝土桥梁　经验易损性参数　火灾评价模型　模糊综合评价法　损伤等级

0　引言

预应力混凝土桥梁广泛应用于交通基础设施中,支撑着公路工程、城市道路工程以及铁路工程的建造与运营,对交通运输行业的发展起着非常重要的作用,然而,频发的交通类火灾对预应力混凝土桥梁造成了严重威胁[1]。作为交通支撑的预应力混凝土桥梁,极易发生桥面或桥下火灾,混凝土和钢材遭受火灾后,力学性能退化,导致结构承载能力降低[2]。预应力桥梁因混凝土包裹钢筋而使其耐火性能优于钢结构桥梁,遭遇火灾后变形不大,但过火后桥梁的剩余承载能力不易确定。目前尚未发行与桥梁火灾相关的规范,因此,亟需提出一种快捷可行的预应力混凝土桥梁过火后安全评价模型。

目前,对预应力混凝土桥梁的火灾研究主要集中在桥梁的材料力学性能退化、结构承载能力分析、耐火极限、破坏机理以及桥梁结构发生火灾的可能性等方面[3-5]。Maria 等指出桥梁火灾危险的重要性,建立了为修复桥梁火灾损伤制订方案的实用工具[6]。Kodur 等提出了桥梁抗火设计的重要性因子以及减小桥梁火灾危险性的关键方法,即首先基于火灾的重要性因子评价桥梁的受火重要性,若结果为易于发生火灾破坏则建立相应有限元模型并提出减轻损伤的方法[7-8]。张岗等针对钢-混凝土组合梁遭遇火灾后的安全问题,采用火灾场景反演方法和火灾高温场推定方法,建立了火灾后钢-混凝土组合梁的安全评价方法[9]。宋超杰等以柱式桥墩为研究对象,分析考虑混凝土爆裂的荷载-轴向位移曲线和荷载-横向位移曲线,获得极限承载能力的衰退曲线并建立了火灾后柱式桥墩的“四级损伤指标”[10]。马明雷等采用模糊综合评价的方法建立了车致桥梁火灾发生概率评价模型并进行应用实例分析[11]。孙博等建立了基于火灾分析理论和场景分析的 AHP-FCE 桥梁火灾风险评估体系[12]。然而上述研究主要针对桥梁火灾风险的评估及预防策略或火灾后剩余承载能力的数值分析,未考虑过火后桥梁技术状况评估的实用性。

本文以常见的预应力混凝土桥梁为研究对象,分析实际受火场景,考虑了桥梁对火灾的易损性,受火位置,受火长度,受火温度,持续时间以及火灾类型六个关键因素,通过模糊层次分析法建立数学模型,得到具有一定可信度的预应力混凝土桥梁过火后评价模型;该模型易于理解,使用方便,实用价值较大。

1　火灾后预应力混凝土桥梁易损性体系的建立

预应力混凝土桥梁受火时,桥梁火灾易损性,受火位置,受火长度,受火温度,持续时间以及火灾类型6个因素基本确定了桥梁受火后的结构状态。因此,为评价预应力混凝土桥梁受火后的承载能力,应对过火后的桥梁进行采样。

结合火灾后桥梁数据采样(亦称数据采集),分析既有的桥梁火损特征,并考虑结构的重要性,获得了火灾后经验易损性参数[8],包括结构体系、跨径、截面类型、车道数和已服役年限,如表1所示。通过对以上5个参数的下属参数设置权重因子,即可按照受火桥梁的实际情况确定火灾易损性等级,如表2所示。

PC桥梁火灾后经验易损性参数与权重 表1

桥梁火灾后经验易损性参数	子参数	权重因子	最大权重因子
结构体系	刚构体系	1	3
	连续体系	2	
	简支体系	3	
跨径(m)	>200	1	5
	150~200	2	
	100~150	3	
	50~100	4	
	<50	5	
截面类型	箱型截面	1	5
	实心板截面	2	
	空心板截面	3	
	工字形截面	4	
	T梁截面	5	
车道数	>4	1	3
	4	2	
	2	3	
已服役年限	<10	1	5
	10~25	2	
	26~35	3	
	36~50	4	
	>50	5	

由表1可知,对于不同种类型的桥梁,都有不同的子参数来决定特定桥梁的条件,根据工程经验判断和以前的研究,将权重因子分配给不同的子参数。除桥梁结构体系和车道数按1到3的范围分配外,其余权重因子均按1到5的范围分配。计算火灾易损性等级因子Δ_x。

$$\Delta_x = \frac{\sum \varphi_{i,x}}{\sum \varphi_{i,\max}} \tag{1}$$

式中:$\varphi_{i,x}$——桥梁火灾后经验易损性参数i的子参数权重因子;

$\varphi_{i,\max}$——桥梁火灾后经验易损性参数i的最大权重因子。

PC桥梁火灾易损性等级 表2

易损性等级	等级因子Δ_x	重要性系数
极易受损	>0.95	4
易受损	0.5~0.95	3
中等受损	0.2~0.5	2
不易受损	<0.2	1

受火位置采用观察法,可分为桥面受火、桥下受火、桥面和桥下同时受火三种情况。受火长度采

用测量法，按0～2m、2～5m、5～8m、8～10m、10m以上分级。持续时间及火灾类型均可采用调查法，持续时间按10min以下、10～30min、30～40min、40～60min以上分级。火灾类型可分为垃圾等普通可燃物燃烧、车辆碰撞火灾、油罐车火灾。桥梁受火温度可参照文献[9]采用温度推定方法并结合火灾类型进行推断，如表3所示。通过以上分析，对受火桥梁的采样工作可总结为如图1所示。

火灾后PC桥梁温度推定　　表3

材　料	特　点	标　度	特　征	推定温度(℃)
混凝土	剥落	1	无剥落、掉角	<300
		2	局部混凝土偶掉角	[300,500)
		3	较大范围混凝土剥落或掉角	[500,700)
		4	大范围混凝土剥落或掉角	[700,900)
		5	混凝土酥松、大面积剥落	>900
	颜色	1	灰青色，近视正常	<300
		2	浅灰色，略显粉红	[300,500)
		3	浅灰白色，显浅红	[500,700)
		4	灰白色，显浅黄	[700,900)
		5	显浅黄	>900
	锤击	1	声音响亮、表面不留痕迹	<300
		2	声音较响亮、表面留下较明显痕迹	[300,500)
		3	声音较闷、混凝土粉碎和塌落，留下痕迹	[500,700)
		4	声音发闷、混凝土粉碎和塌落	[700,900)
		5	声音发哑、混凝土严重脱落	>900
钢筋	钢筋外露	1	基本无钢筋外露现象	<300
		2	混凝土保护层稍有脱落，钢筋稍有露出，点状分布	[300,500)
		3	混凝土保护层脱落，钢筋外露不超过3cm	[500,700)
		4	混凝土保护层脱落，钢筋外露部分较明显	[700,900)
		5	混凝土保护层脱落严重，钢筋明显外露	>900
预应力钢束	管道外露	1	无预应力管道外露现象	<300
		2	预应力管道周围混凝土有微裂纹	[300,500)
		3	预应力管道轻微外露，连续长度不超过5cm	[500,700)
		4	预应力管道外露较明显	[700,900)
		5	预应力管道严重外露	>900
梁体	梁体挠度(mm)	1	<5	<300
		2	[5.0,7.5)	[300,500)
		3	[7.5,20.0)	[500,700)
		4	[20.0,40.0)	[700,900)
		5	>40.0	>900

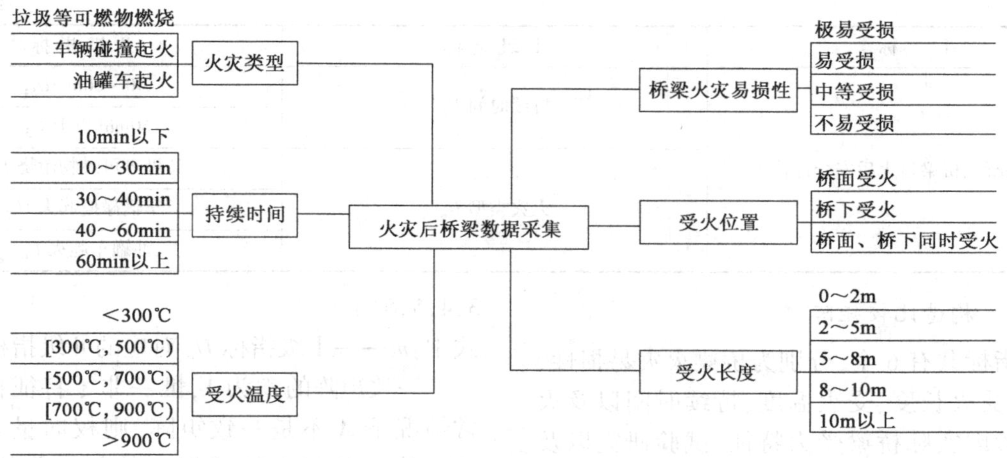

图1　PC桥梁火灾后采样

2　预应力混凝土桥梁过火后安全评价模型的建立

2.1　层次模型的成形

2.1.1　形成评价指标体系

基于火灾后预应力混凝土桥梁的数据采集，将各项指标进行分层，建立层次模型。目标层 U 即为预应力混凝土桥梁过火后的安全评价指标，用于确定桥梁受火后结构状态的6个因素即为 U 的Ⅰ级指标，每一因素对应的子因素又构成了 U 的Ⅱ级指标。根据各级指标之间的关联特点，建立预应力混凝土桥梁过火后的安全评价指标体系[13]，如表4所示。

PC桥梁过火后评价指标体系　　表4

目　标	Ⅰ级指标	Ⅱ级指标
预应力混凝土桥梁过火后安全评价 U	桥梁火灾易损性 U_1	极易受损 U_{11}
		易受损 U_{12}
		中等受损 U_{13}
		不易受损 U_{14}
	受火位置 U_2	桥面受火 U_{21}
		桥下受火 U_{22}
		桥面和桥下同时受火 U_{23}
	受火长度 U_3	0～2mU_{31}
		2～5mU_{32}
		5～8mU_{33}
		8～10mU_{34}
		10m以上 U_{35}
	受火温度 U_4	<300U_{41}
		[300,500)U_{42}
		[500,700)U_{43}
		[700,900)U_{44}
		>900U_{45}
	持续时间 U_5	10min以下 U_{51}
		10～30minU_{52}
		30～40minU_{53}

续上表

目　标	Ⅰ级指标	Ⅱ级指标
预应力混凝土桥梁过火后安全评价 U	持续时间 U_5	40 ~60minU_{54}
		60min 以上 U_{55}
	火灾类型 U_6	垃圾等可燃物燃烧 U_{61}
		车辆碰撞起火 U_{62}
		油罐车起火 U_{63}

2.1.2　构造比较矩阵

Ⅰ级指标共有 6 个，分别为桥梁火灾易损性、受火位置、受火长度、受火温度、持续时间以及火灾类型。考虑实际桥梁受火特征、试验研究以及数值模拟的结果，采用两两互相对比的相对尺度方法，以提高准确度。Ⅰ级指标 U_1,U_2,U_3,U_4,U_5,U_6 对目标层 U 的影响，即可认为对目标 U 的重要性，用 a_{ij} 表示 U_i 与 U_j 对 U 的影响之比，比较尺度采用 1-9 尺度，两两对比的全部结果构成比较矩阵 $\boldsymbol{A}$。

$$\boldsymbol{A}(a_{ij})_{6\times6},a_{ij}>0,a_{ij}=\frac{1}{a_{ij}} \tag{2}$$

同样，可以用 $b_{k,ij}$ 表示 U_{ki} 与 U_{kj} 对 U_k 的影响之比，从而组成比较矩阵 $\boldsymbol{B}_k$。

$$\boldsymbol{B}_k=(b_{k,ij})_{m\times m},b_{k,ij}>0,b_{k,ij}=\frac{1}{b_{k,ij}}(k=\{1,2,3,4,5,6\}) \tag{3}$$

式中：m——Ⅰ级指标 U_k 对应的Ⅱ级指标的数量。

一致矩阵的秩为 1，惟一非零特征根为 n，通常情况下 $\boldsymbol{A}$ 不是一致矩阵，则权向量 ω 取用比较矩阵 $\boldsymbol{A}$ 的最大特征根 λ 的归一化特征向量，在这种情况下应保证比较矩阵 $\boldsymbol{A}$ 的不一致程度满足：

$$CR=\frac{CI}{RI}<0.1,CI=\frac{\lambda-n}{n-1} \tag{4}$$

式中：CR——一致性比率；

CI——一致性指标；

RI——随机一致性指标；RI 的取值如表 5 所示；

n——矩阵 $\boldsymbol{A}$ 的行列数。

***RI* 取值标准**　　表 5

n	1	2	3	4	5	6	7	8	9	10	11
RI	0	0	0.58	0.90	1.12	1.24	1.32	1.41	1.45	1.49	1.51

2.1.3　权重的获取

权重反映了各评价指标在综合评价中的重要程度。将比较矩阵 A 最大特征值对应的特征向量归一化处理，并记为 $\omega=(\omega_1,\omega_2,\omega_3,\omega_4,\omega_5,\omega_6)$，用同样的方法算Ⅱ级指标对Ⅰ级指标的权向量，分别为：

$\omega^{(1)}=(\omega_1^{(1)},\omega_2^{(1)},\omega_3^{(1)},\omega_4^{(1)})$；$\omega^{(2)}=(\omega_1^{(2)},\omega_2^{(2)},\omega_3^{(2)})$；$\omega^{(3)}=(\omega_1^{(3)},\omega_2^{(3)},\omega_3^{(3)},\omega_4^{(3)},\omega_5^{(3)})$；

$\omega^{(4)}=(\omega_1^{(4)},\omega_2^{(4)},\omega_3^{(4)},\omega_4^{(4)},\omega_5^{(4)})$；$\omega^{(5)}=(\omega_1^{(5)},\omega_2^{(5)},\omega_3^{(5)},\omega_4^{(5)},\omega_5^{(5)})$；$\omega^{(6)}=(\omega_1^{(6)},\omega_2^{(6)},\omega_3^{(6)})$

2.2　模糊综合评价模型的建立

2.2.1　火灾后结构安全评价指标的集合

由前述研究过程可知，预应力混凝土桥梁火灾后的安全评价指标集合即为指标体系中所有Ⅱ级指标，共计 25 个子元素，分别为：

$$U=\begin{Bmatrix}U_{11},U_{12},U_{13},U_{14},U_{21},U_{22},U_{23},U_{31},U_{22},U_{33},U_{34},U_{35},\\U_{41},U_{42},U_{43},U_{44},U_{45},U_{51},U_{52},U_{53},U_{54},U_{55},U_{61},U_{62},U_{63}\end{Bmatrix}$$

2.2.2　火灾后结构安全评价等级的集合

假设预应力混凝土桥梁的火灾安全评价等级的集合为 $V=\{V_1,V_2,V_3,V_4,V_5\}$，分别表示无损伤、Ⅰ级损伤、Ⅱ级损伤、Ⅲ级损伤和Ⅳ级损伤。

预应力混凝土桥梁过火后损伤等级的安全评价及剩余承载能力评估如表 6 所示[9]。

各Ⅰ级指标对目标层 U 的权重为 ω，Ⅱ级指标对Ⅰ级指标的权重集合为 $W=\{\omega^{(1)},\omega^{(2)},\omega^{(3)},\omega^{(4)},\omega^{(5)},\omega^{(6)}\}$。

2.2.3　火灾后结构的安全评价矩阵

针对各评价指标，可输入一组专家的火灾安全评价，从而确定评价矩阵 $\boldsymbol{R}$，对不符合此桥梁实际结构状况的指标，则认为这一指标对此桥梁无影响，打分均选择“无损伤”。用评价指标 U_{ij} 的得

分除以专家人数 n_0 作为隶属度 $r_{i,j}$，如表 7 所示。如此，可得 U_i 的单因素模糊评价矩阵 $\boldsymbol{R}_i$。

PC 桥梁过火后评价标准 表 6

损伤等级	安全评价	剩余承载能力
Ⅰ级	主梁刚度基本不变，只需对表面进行处置	>4 倍的作用效应
Ⅱ级	主梁刚度略有下降，经过小修后便可正常使用	3~4 倍的作用效应
Ⅲ级	主梁刚度下降较大，已不能满足正常使用的要求，经过大修可继续承载	2~3 倍的作用效应
Ⅳ级	主梁刚度下降过大，经过维修加固也不能正常使用	<2 倍的作用效应

评价矩阵 $\boldsymbol{R}$ 表 7

指标	无损伤 V_1	Ⅰ级损伤 V_2	Ⅱ级损伤 V_3	Ⅲ级损伤 V_4	Ⅳ级损伤 V_5
U_{11}	$r_{1,1}$	$r_{1,2}$	$r_{1,3}$	$r_{1,4}$	$r_{1,5}$
U_{12}	$r_{2,1}$	$r_{2,2}$	$r_{2,3}$	$r_{2,4}$	$r_{2,5}$
U_{13}	$r_{3,1}$	$r_{3,2}$	$r_{3,3}$	$r_{3,4}$	$r_{3,5}$
…	…	…	…	…	…
U_{62}	$r_{24,1}$	$r_{24,2}$	$r_{24,3}$	$r_{24,4}$	$r_{24,5}$
U_{63}	$r_{25,1}$	$r_{25,2}$	$r_{25,3}$	$r_{25,4}$	$r_{25,5}$

$$\boldsymbol{R}_1=\begin{bmatrix} r_{1,1} & r_{1,2} & r_{1,3} & r_{1,4} \\ r_{2,1} & r_{2,2} & r_{2,3} & r_{2,4} \\ r_{3,1} & r_{3,2} & r_{3,3} & r_{3,4} \\ r_{4,1} & r_{4,2} & r_{4,3} & r_{4,4} \end{bmatrix};\boldsymbol{R}_2=\begin{bmatrix} r_{5,1} & r_{5,2} & r_{5,3} & r_{5,4} \\ r_{6,1} & r_{6,2} & r_{6,3} & r_{6,4} \\ r_{7,1} & r_{7,2} & r_{7,3} & r_{7,4} \end{bmatrix};$$

$$\boldsymbol{R}_3=\begin{bmatrix} r_{8,1} & r_{8,2} & r_{8,3} & r_{8,4} \\ r_{9,1} & r_{9,2} & r_{9,3} & r_{9,4} \\ r_{10,1} & r_{10,2} & r_{10,3} & r_{10,4} \\ r_{11,1} & r_{11,2} & r_{11,3} & r_{11,4} \\ r_{12,1} & r_{12,2} & r_{12,3} & r_{12,4} \end{bmatrix};$$

$$\boldsymbol{R}_4=\begin{bmatrix} r_{13,1} & r_{13,2} & r_{13,3} & r_{13,4} \\ r_{14,1} & r_{14,2} & r_{14,3} & r_{14,4} \\ r_{15,1} & r_{15,2} & r_{15,3} & r_{15,4} \\ r_{16,1} & r_{16,2} & r_{16,3} & r_{16,4} \\ r_{17,1} & r_{17,2} & r_{17,3} & r_{17,4} \end{bmatrix};$$

$$\boldsymbol{R}_5=\begin{bmatrix} r_{18,1} & r_{18,2} & r_{18,3} & r_{18,4} \\ r_{19,1} & r_{19,2} & r_{19,3} & r_{19,4} \\ r_{20,1} & r_{20,2} & r_{20,3} & r_{20,4} \\ r_{21,1} & r_{21,2} & r_{21,3} & r_{21,4} \\ r_{22,1} & r_{22,2} & r_{22,3} & r_{22,4} \end{bmatrix};$$

$$\boldsymbol{R}_6=\begin{bmatrix} r_{23,1} & r_{23,2} & r_{23,3} & r_{23,4} \\ r_{24,1} & r_{24,2} & r_{24,3} & r_{24,4} \\ r_{25,1} & r_{25,2} & r_{25,3} & r_{25,4} \end{bmatrix}$$

2.2.4 火灾后结构的安全综合评价

首先根据单因素模糊评价矩阵 $\boldsymbol{R}_i$ 及其权向量 $\boldsymbol{\omega}^{(i)}$ 对Ⅰ级指标层进行模糊评价，计算Ⅰ级指标的评价函数，得到各Ⅰ级指标的模糊关系子矩阵 Q_i。然后对目标层进行模糊综合评价，由各个模糊关系子矩阵得出模糊关系总矩阵 $\boldsymbol{R}^0$，通过权向量 ω 与评价矩阵 $\boldsymbol{R}^0$ 的模糊变换得可到预应力混凝土桥梁过火后的模糊评判集 S。

$$Q_i=\omega^{(i)}\mathrm{oR}_i \quad i=\{1,2,3,4,5,6\} \tag{5}$$

$$\boldsymbol{R}^0=[Q_1 \quad Q_2 \quad Q_3 \quad Q_4 \quad Q_5 \quad Q_6]^{\mathrm{T}} \tag{6}$$

$$S=\omega\mathrm{oR}^0 \tag{7}$$

式中：o——模糊合成算子。进行模糊变化时要选择适宜的模糊合成算子，本文选择最优的 $\boldsymbol{M}(\cdot,\oplus)$ 算子：

$$S_k=\min\left(1,\sum_{j=1}^{m}\omega_j r_{jk}\right) \quad (k=1,2,3,4) \tag{8}$$

2.3 模型的分析与评定

预应力混凝土桥梁过火后模糊评判集 $S=\{S_1,S_2,S_3,S_4,S_5\}$ 中 S_i 为桥梁损伤等级 V_i 对模糊评判集 S 的隶属度，去除“无损伤 V_1”的评判，按最大隶属度原则得出综合结论，$\boldsymbol{M}$ 所对应的火灾安全评价等级即为综合评价结果。

$$M=\max(S_2,S_3,S_4,S_5) \tag{9}$$

3 工程应用与分析

3.1 工程概况及火灾后数据采集

某简支预应力混凝土箱形截面梁桥，桥梁全长 49m，上部采用预应力混凝土箱梁，全幅总宽 20m，行车道宽 2×6m，人行道宽 2×4m，已服役 9

年。由于桥下堆放垃圾,发生桥下普通可燃物燃烧型火灾,持续时间 25min,受火长度 3m,混凝土有轻微剥落,有烟熏痕迹,未有钢筋外露,也未见预应力钢束管道周围混凝土有裂纹。

采用公式(1),计算桥梁易损性等级因子为:

$$\Delta_x = \frac{\sum \varphi_{i,x}}{\sum \varphi_{i,\max}} = \frac{13}{21} = 0.619048$$

由表 2 可知,此预应力混凝土桥梁的火灾易损性等级为“易受损”;受火位置为桥下受火,受火长度为 2 ~ 5m;火灾类型为垃圾等普通可燃物燃烧;持续时间为 10 ~ 30min;根据温度推定方法并结合火灾类型可推断其受火温度 <300℃。

3.2　计算各级评价指标权重集合

首先构造Ⅰ级指标比较矩阵 A 以及Ⅱ级指标比较矩阵 B_k,使用 MATLAB 软件计算最大特征值(或惟一非零特征值)及相应的归一化特征向量,其一致性检验均通过,从而获得权重集:

$\omega = (\omega_1, \omega_2, \omega_3, \omega_4, \omega_5, \omega_6) = (0.1834, 0.0572, 0.1095, 0.2587, 0.1293, 0.2619)$

$\omega^{(1)} = (\omega_1^{(1)}, \omega_2^{(1)}, \omega_3^{(1)}, \omega_4^{(1)}) = (0.4829, 0.2720, 0.7570, 0.0882)$

$\omega^{(2)} = (\omega_1^{(2)}, \omega_2^{(2)}, \omega_3^{(2)}) = (0.1428, 0.2857, 0.5715)$

$\omega^{(3)} = (\omega_1^{(3)}, \omega_2^{(3)}, \omega_3^{(3)}, \omega_4^{(3)}, \omega_5^{(3)}) = (0.0666, 0.1333, 0.2000, 0.2667, 0.3334)$

$\omega^{(4)} = (\omega_1^{(4)}, \omega_2^{(4)}, \omega_3^{(4)}, \omega_4^{(4)}, \omega_5^{(4)}) = (0.0556, 0.1111, 0.1667, 0.2778, 0.3889)$

$\omega^{(5)} = (\omega_1^{(5)}, \omega_2^{(5)}, \omega_3^{(5)}, \omega_4^{(5)}, \omega_5^{(5)}) = (0.0666, 0.1333, 0.2000, 0.2667, 0.3334)$

$\omega^{(6)} = (\omega_1^{(6)}, \omega_2^{(6)}, \omega_3^{(6)}) = (0.1111, 0.2222, 0.6667)$

3.3　确定火灾安全评价矩阵

邀请 20 位专家对各指标进行打分,单因素模糊评价矩阵如下:

$$R_1 = \begin{bmatrix} 1 & 0 & 0 & 0 & 0 \\ 0 & \frac{1}{5} & \frac{3}{4} & \frac{1}{20} & 0 \\ 1 & 0 & 0 & 0 & 0 \\ 1 & 0 & 0 & 0 & 0 \end{bmatrix}; R_2 = \begin{bmatrix} 1 & 0 & 0 & 0 & 0 \\ 0 & \frac{11}{20} & \frac{9}{20} & 0 & 0 \\ 1 & 0 & 0 & 0 & 0 \end{bmatrix}; R_3 = \begin{bmatrix} 1 & 0 & 0 & 0 & 0 \\ 0 & \frac{9}{10} & \frac{1}{10} & 0 & 0 \\ 1 & 0 & 0 & 0 & 0 \\ 1 & 0 & 0 & 0 & 0 \\ 1 & 0 & 0 & 0 & 0 \end{bmatrix};$$

$$R_4 = \begin{bmatrix} 0 & 1 & 0 & 0 & 0 \\ 1 & 0 & 0 & 0 & 0 \\ 1 & 0 & 0 & 0 & 0 \\ 1 & 0 & 0 & 0 & 0 \\ 1 & 0 & 0 & 0 & 0 \end{bmatrix}; R_5 = \begin{bmatrix} 1 & 0 & 0 & 0 & 0 \\ 0 & \frac{2}{5} & \frac{3}{5} & 0 & 0 \\ 1 & 0 & 0 & 0 & 0 \\ 1 & 0 & 0 & 0 & 0 \\ 1 & 0 & 0 & 0 & 0 \end{bmatrix}; R_6 = \begin{bmatrix} 0 & \frac{3}{4} & \frac{1}{4} & 0 & 0 \\ 1 & 0 & 0 & 0 & 0 \\ 1 & 0 & 0 & 0 & 0 \end{bmatrix}$$

3.4　火灾后安全综合评价

各Ⅰ级指标的模糊关系子矩阵如下:

$$Q_1 = \omega^{(1)} \mathrm{o} R_1 = (0.7280, 0.0544, 0.2040, 0.0136, 0.0000);$$

$$Q_2 = \omega^{(2)} \mathrm{o} R_2 = (0.7143, 0.1571, 0.1286, 0.0000, 0.0000);$$

$$Q_3 = \omega^{(3)} \mathrm{o} R_3 = (0.8667, 0.1200, 0.0133, 0.0000, 0.0000);$$

$$Q_4 = \omega^{(4)} \mathrm{o} R_4 = (0.9444, 0.0556, 0.0000, 0.0000, 0.0000);$$

$$Q_5 = \omega^{(5)} \mathrm{o} R_5 = (0.8667, 0.0533, 0.0800, 0.0000, 0.0000);$$

$$Q_6 = \omega^{(6)} \mathrm{o} R_6 = (0.8889, 0.0833, 0.0278, 0.0000, 0.0000)$$

由各个模糊关系子矩阵得出模糊关系总矩阵为:

$$R^0=\begin{bmatrix}Q_1\\Q_2\\Q_3\\Q_4\\Q_5\\Q_6\end{bmatrix}=\begin{bmatrix}0.7280 & 0.0544 & 0.2040 & 0.0136 & 0.0000\\0.7143 & 0.1571 & 0.1286 & 0.0000 & 0.0000\\0.8667 & 0.1200 & 0.0133 & 0.0000 & 0.0000\\0.9444 & 0.0556 & 0.0000 & 0.0000 & 0.0000\\0.8667 & 0.0533 & 0.0800 & 0.000 & 0.0000\\0.8889 & 0.0833 & 0.0278 & 0.0000 & 0.0000\end{bmatrix}$$

则预应力混凝土桥梁过火后模糊评判集为：$S=\{0.8585,0.0752,0.0639,0.0025,0\}$。

故综合评价结果为：$M=\max(0.0752,0.0639,0.0025,0)=0.0752$，对应的火灾安全评价等级为Ⅰ级损伤，即主梁刚度基本不变，只需对表面进行处置。经过实际桥梁检测，依据《城市桥梁养护技术规范》(CJJ99—2017)，此桥梁为完好级桥梁，与综合评价结果相符。

4 结语

(1)结合火灾后桥梁结构的数据采样，分析既有的桥梁结构火损特征，并考虑结构的重要性，获得了火灾后经验易损性参数，包括结构体系、跨径、截面类型、车道数和已服役年限，建立了结构的火灾后易损性体系。

(2)确定了基于模糊综合评价的预应力混凝土桥梁的火灾后采样过程，主要考虑桥梁火灾易损性、受火位置、受火长度、受火温度、持续时间以及火灾类型6个因素。其中，桥梁火灾易损性需通过火灾后经验易损性参数确定，受火温度需根据桥梁受火后的状态进行推定，其他因素则通过调查直接获得。

(3)基于模糊数学的综合评价方法，结合层次分析指标体系，确定权重集合，可建立预应力混凝土桥梁过火后安全评价模型。

(4)应用本文提出的过火后安全评价模型可对实际工程进行分类评价，其评价过程简单明确，可快速判断PC桥梁过火后的结构状态，为后期检查修复提供理论依据。

参考文献

[1] 张岗，贺拴海. 桥梁结构火灾理论与计算方法[M]. 北京：人民交通出版社股份有限公司，2020.

[2] 张岗，贺拴海，侯炜，等. 预应力混凝土桥梁抗火研究综述[J]. 长安大学学报(自然科学版)，2018，38(06)：1-10.

[3] 宋超杰，张岗，贺拴海，等. 钢-混凝土组合连续弯箱梁抗火设计方法[J]. 交通运输工程学报，2021，21(4)：139-149.

[4] Song CJ, Zhang G, Li XY, et al. Experimental study on failure mechanism of steel-concrete composite bridge girders under fuel fire exposure[J]. Engineering Structure, 2021, 247: 113-230.

[5] Zhang G, Kodur VK, Song CJ, et al. A numerical method for evaluating fire resistance of composite box bridge girders[J]. Journal of Constructional Steel Research, 2020, 165: 105823.

[6] Garlock M, Paya-Zaforteza I, Kodur VK, et al. Fire hazard in bridges: review, assessment and repair strategies[J]. Engineering Structures, 2012, 35: 89-98.

[7] Kodur VK, Aziz EM, Naser MZ. Strategies for enhancing fire performance of steel bridges[J]. Engineering Structures, 2017, 131: 446-458.

[8] Kodur VK, Naser MZ. Importance factor for design of bridges against fire hazard[J]. Engineering Structures, 2013, 54: 207-220.

[9] 张岗，宋超杰，李建章，等. 火灾后钢-混凝土组合梁承载能力评价方法[J]. 长安大学学报(自然科学版)，2021，41(02)：1-11.

[10] 宋超杰，张岗，王富强，等. 火灾后柱式桥墩剩余承载性能安全评价[J]. 长安大学学报(自然科学版)，2021，41(02)：55-65.

[11] 马明雷，马如进，陈艾荣. 车致桥梁火灾发生概率评价模型[J]. 华南理工大学学报(自然科学版)，2015，43(12)：133-140.

[12] 孙博，肖汝诚. 基于层次分析-模糊综合评价法的桥梁火灾风险评估体系[J]. 同济大学学报(自然科学版)，2015，43(11)：1619-1625.

[13] 姜启源，谢金星，叶俊. 数学模型[M]. 4版. 北京：高等教育出版社，2011.

预应力混凝土箱梁桥施工监测研究

陈亚军*　郇晓光
(长安大学公路学院)

摘　要　为研究预应力混凝土箱梁桥施工阶段内力和位移变化规律,以一座 4×25 m 的预应力混凝土箱梁桥为依托工程进行研究。通过 Midas Civil 进行有限元模拟计算,对预应力混凝土箱梁桥的施工过程进行监测,分析各个关键截面的位移和内力的变化规律。研究结果表明:混凝土箱梁桥施工阶段的内力和位移与截面位置和施工阶段有着很大的关系;在混凝土箱梁桥施工过程中,由于相邻节段的影响以及临时支座的安装与拆除,桥梁各个截面的位移和内力会产生较大的变化。

关键词　预应力混凝土箱梁桥　施工监测　内力变化　位移变化

0　引言

根据交通运输部《2020 年交通运输行业发展统计公报》,目前我国中小桥梁数量占到了桥梁总数的 86.15%;中小跨径桥梁占到了我国桥梁的绝大部分,这说明了我国的发展离不开中小跨径桥梁。随着桥梁工程的发展,越来越多的新技术和新理论被应用到桥梁建设过程中,关于桥梁施工过程的研究,许多学者对此展开了研究。崔小芳[1]以重庆某高速公路桥梁为背景,提出了一种基于 BIM 的高速公路桥梁养护综合管理技术,该系统可应用于桥梁建设的全寿命周期中;李悦等[2]通过有限元软件对双塔双索面斜拉桥施工阶段的受力性能进行了分析,归纳了其内力和位移的变化规律,并基于此对依托工程的索力进行了优化;万鹏[3]以杭州德胜路运河二通道桥为工程背景,提出了 3 种不同的施工方法,对比分析桥梁施工过程中的受力状态,优选最合适的施工方法;陈彦恒等[4]依托某单塔双索面折塔斜拉桥,通过 Midas Civil 对其施工阶段斜拉索、主塔和主梁的位移及内力进行了计算分析,并通过现场实测值进行了验证;宋福春等[5]以沈阳四环快速路跨沈西编组站立交桥为背景分析了该桥在施工过程中的受力情况和成桥线形,分别采用正装分析法、倒装分析法和无应力状态分析法 3 种方法进行计算,以此对桥梁的施工进行控制;汪德旺[6]对一座跨度 220 m 的下承式钢管混凝土拱桥进行了分析,通过 Midas Civil 对其最不利受力状态下的施工过程进行了分析,计算了施工过程中不同设计参数对位移、应力和弹性稳定系数的影响,找出了桥梁施工的最不利影响因素;钟文健[7]针对高墩大跨桥梁施工中的墩壁厚度、悬臂等参数对施工稳定性的影响进行了研究,研究结果表明,墩壁厚度对桥梁施工稳定性的影响较大,而横隔板间距的影响很小;周小年[8]以壶口黄河特大桥为依托工程分析了墩身结构对高墩大跨桥梁施工稳定性的影响,通过有限元对比分析不同墩身设计参数的影响,提出了相关建议。

由以上研究现状可知,许多学者通过现场实验和有限元模拟针对大型桥梁施工阶段内力和位移变化展开了深入的研究,相关理论也趋于成熟,但目前相关研究主要集中于大跨径桥梁,从而忽略了中小跨径桥梁。为研究预应力混凝土箱梁桥施工阶段内力和位移变化规律,选取一座跨径 100m 的预应力混凝土箱梁桥为依托工程,对其施工过程进行监测,为同类工程提供参考。

1　工程概况

依托工程为预应力混凝土箱梁桥,设计荷载为汽车 -20 级。桥梁全长为 4×25 m,箱梁采用 C50 混凝土,混凝土弹性模量为 3.45×10^4 MPa,泊松比为 0.2,轴心抗拉强度设计值为 2.65 MPa,轴心抗压强度设计值为 32.4 MPa,线膨胀系数为 1×10^5,混凝土容重为 25 kN/m^3;预应力钢束弹性模量为 1.95×10^5 MPa,泊松比为 0.3,抗拉强度标准值为 1860 MPa,张拉控制应力为 1395 MPa,线膨胀系数为 1.2×10^5,容重为 78.5 kN/m^3。

桥梁截面如图 1 所示。

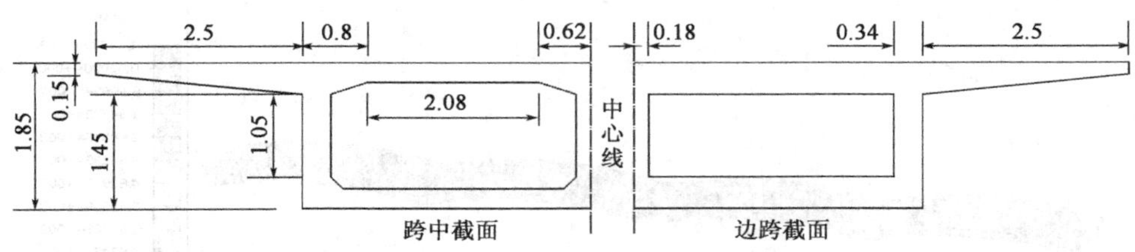

图1　桥梁截面示意图(尺寸单位:m)

2　有限元模型建立

采用 Midas Civil 进行有限元模拟,共计 108 个单元,系统初始温度为 15℃,桥梁施工分为 6 个施工阶段:中边跨浇筑、边跨合龙、中跨合龙、体系转换、桥面铺装、成桥,预应力混凝土箱梁桥模型如图 2 所示,预应力钢束布置如图 3 所示。

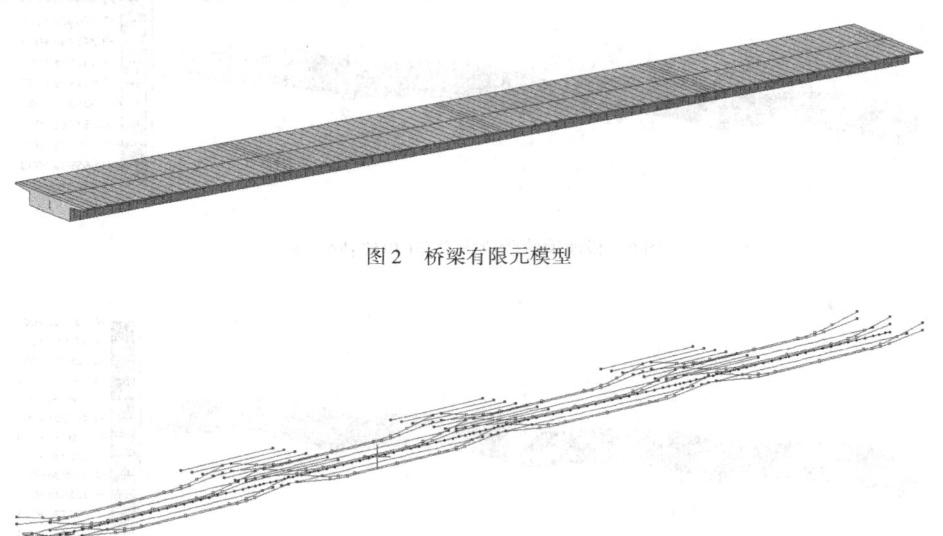

图2　桥梁有限元模型

图3　预应力钢束布置图

3　计算结果及分析

通过 Midas Civil 对预应力混凝土箱梁桥施工阶段内力变化规律进行了研究。由于桥梁左右两侧完全对称,选取边跨左支点截面、1/4 截面、1/2 截面、3/4 截面和中跨左支点截面、1/4 截面、1/2 截面、3/4 截面、中跨右支点截面为关键截面,并依次编号为截面 1 ~ 截面 9;中边跨浇筑、边跨合龙、中跨合龙、体系转换、桥面铺装、成桥 6 个施工阶段分别编号为阶段 1 ~ 阶段 6。

由于篇幅限制,图 4 ~ 图 7 仅给出了阶段 1、阶段 3、阶段 5 和阶段 6 的内力图。

图4　边中跨施工阶段内力图(单位:kN · m)

预应力混凝土箱梁桥施工阶段 1 ~ 阶段 6 的内力及位移变化曲线如图 8 ~ 图 11 所示。

由图 4 ~ 图 11 可知,预应力混凝土箱梁桥施工阶段的内力和位移在不同施工阶段发生了明显

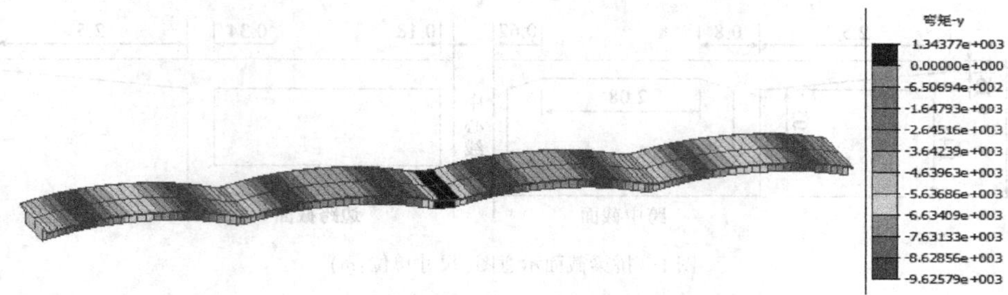

图5　中跨合龙阶段内力图(单位:kN·m)

图6　桥面铺装阶段内力图(单位:kN·m)

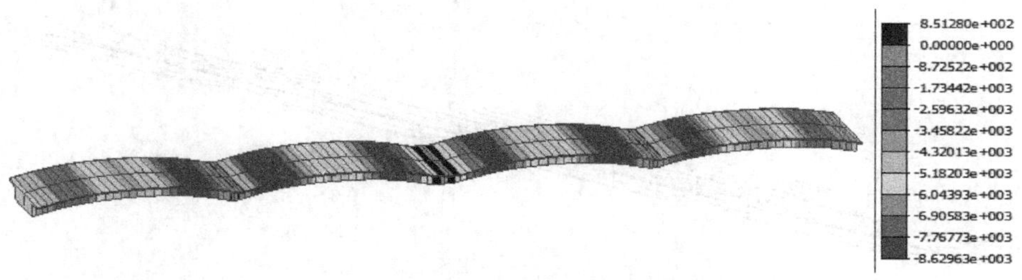

图7　成桥阶段内力图(单位:kN·m)

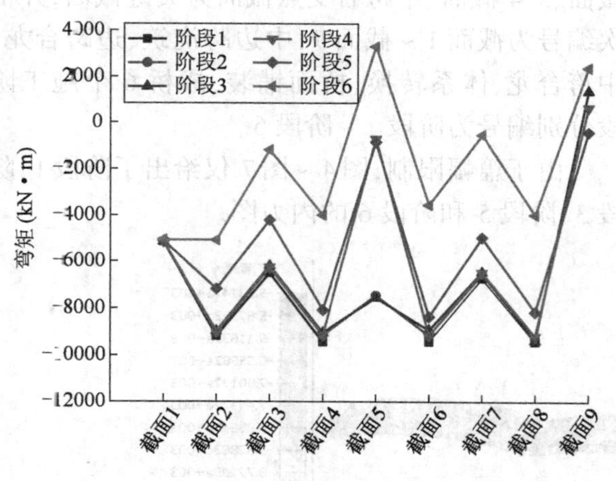

图8　施工阶段弯矩变化图

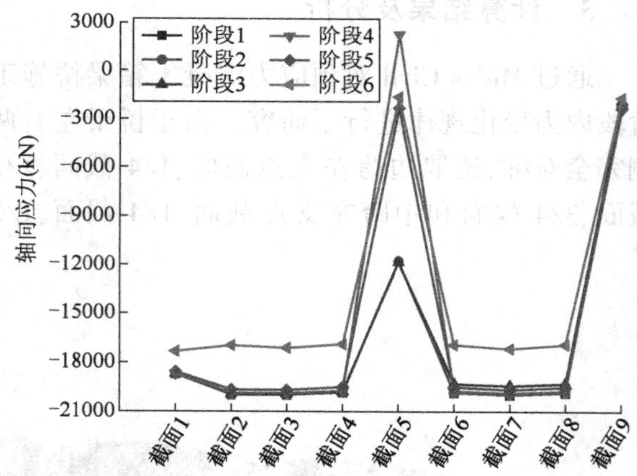

图9　施工阶段轴向应力变化图

的变化,其内力和位移与施工阶段、截面位置有着很大的关系。由图8可知,边跨左支点截面的弯矩在施工过程中几乎没有发生变化,其最大弯矩和最小弯矩出现在中边跨浇筑阶段和成桥阶段,分别为－5156.06 kN·m和－5062.98 kN·m,变化幅度仅为1.81%;其他截面弯矩变化较大,其中中跨左支点截面的弯矩发生了明显的变化,其最大弯矩和最小弯矩出现在中跨合龙阶段和成桥阶段,分别

为 -7476.51 kN·m 和 3287.53 kN·m；截面 2～截面 8 的弯矩在成桥阶段发生了大的变化，这是由于预应力钢束在成桥阶段收缩造成的，由于预应力钢束未达到边跨左支点截面和中跨右支点截面，因此边跨左支点截面和中跨右支点截面的弯矩在成桥阶段未发生较大变化。

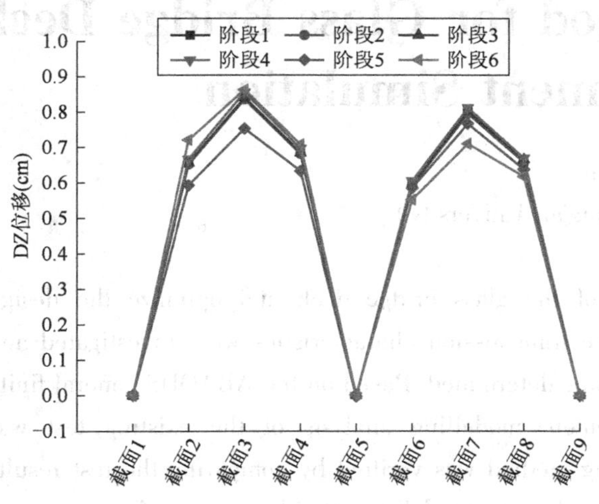

图 10 施工阶段 DZ 方向位移变化图

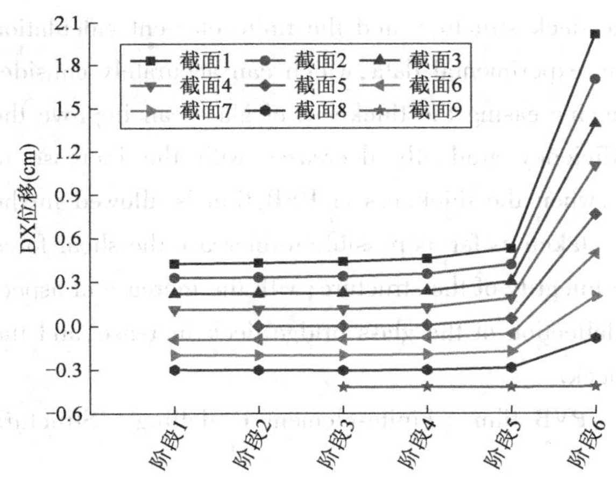

图 11 施工阶段 DX 方向位移变化图

由图 9 可知，中跨左支点截面处的轴向应力在中跨合龙到体系转换阶段的变化最大，由 -11834.14 kN·m 变化到 2265.86 kN·m，这是由于中跨合龙阶段拆除临时支座造成的，其他截面在施工过程中的轴向应力变化很小。由图 10 和图 11 可知，桥梁施工过程中的位移较小，其中最大竖向位移出现在成桥阶段的边跨 1/2 截面处，为 0.86 cm，竖向位移最大变化阶段出现在桥面铺装到成桥阶段的边跨 1/2 截面处；最大轴向位移出现在成桥阶段的边跨左支点截面处，为 2.01cm，轴向位移最大变化阶段出现在桥面铺装到成桥阶段边跨左支点截面处，变化值为 1.49 cm。

4 结语

通过 Midas Civil 对预应力混凝土箱梁桥施工过程进行监测，对其内力的位移的变化进行了研究，主要得到以下结论：

(1)预应力混凝土箱梁桥施工阶段的内力和位移与截面位置和施工阶段有着很大的关系，施工阶段的内力和位移变化线形能够反映桥梁的施工线形。

(2)除边跨左支点截面和中跨右支点截面外，其他截面处的弯矩值在预应力混凝土箱梁桥施工过程中发生了明显的变化，这是由于预应力钢束未达到边跨左支点截面和中跨右支点截面处造成的。

(3)在预应力混凝土箱梁桥施工过程中，中跨左支点截面处的轴向应力在中跨合龙到体系转换阶段的变化较大，其他截面在施工过程中的轴向应力变化很小。预应力混凝土箱梁桥施工过程中的位移较小，最大位移出现在成桥阶段的边跨 1/2 截面处，最大轴向位移出现在成桥阶段的边跨左支点截面处。

参考文献

[1] 崔小芳. 基于 BIM 的高速公路桥梁养护综合管理技术研究[J]. 公路工程，2019，44(03)：253-257.

[2] 李悦，吴国雄，谢远勇. 基于 MIDAS CIVIL 的双塔双索面斜拉桥关键施工阶段受力性能分析[J]. 公路工程，2020，45(04)：141-146.

[3] 万鹏. 大跨双层复合桁架桥施工阶段受力分析[J]. 世界桥梁，2016，44(05)：53-56.

[4] 陈彦恒，占清华. 基于 Midas Civil 的单塔双索面折塔斜拉桥关键施工阶段的有限元分析[J]. 公路工程，2019，44(02)：121-125+200.

[5] 宋福春，张兴，陈冲，等. 大跨预应力混凝土连续梁桥悬臂施工结构控制分析[J]. 沈阳建筑大学学报(自然科学版)，2017，33(02)：226-234.

[6] 汪德旺. 大跨度钢管混凝土拱桥支架法施工仿真分析[J]. 贵州大学学报(自然科学版)，2021，38(06)：104-108.

[7] 钟文健.考虑墩身结构的高墩大跨桥梁施工稳定性研究[J].交通世界,2021(26):160-162.

[8] 周小年.墩身结构对高墩大跨桥梁施工稳定性影响研究[J].中外公路,2018,38(04):181-184.

Optimization of Design Method for Glass Bridge Deck Based on Finite Element Simulation

Bohua Wen*

(School of Highway, Chang'an University)

Abstract To study the mechanical characteristics of the glass bridge deck and optimize the design method, the properties of PVB materials and the shear force transmission characteristics were investigated and studied, and the elastic modulus of PVB used in the design was determined. Based on the ABAQUS general finite element calculation and analysis software, the finite element modelling analysis of the existing test was conducted, and the reliability of the finite element modelling method was verified by comparing the test results with the standard calculation results. Based on the finite element modelling, the bearing performance and parameter analysis of the single-layer reinforced glass thickness, PVB film thickness, and the length-to-length ratio of the glass bridge deck were compared. The results show that: The mechanical properties of PVB interlayer have great influence on the overall stress of the glass bridge deck structure, and the finite element calculation method proposed in this paper is in good agreement with the experimental data, which can accurately consider the shear force transmission characteristics of PVB interlayer; increasing the thickness of glass can improve the bearing capacity of toughened laminated glass, but its efficiency gradually decreases with the increase of thickness, and the thickness of 11 ~ 13mm is recommended; when the thickness of PVB film is allowed in the design of the glass bridge deck, the minimum value should be taken as far as possible to increase the shear force transmission performance of PVB film, thereby increasing the integrity of the structure; with the increase of aspect ratio, i. e. , the increase of short side length, the stress and deflection of the glass bridge deck increase, and the square plate is not suitable as the form of the glass bridge deck.

Keywords Bridge engineering Glass bridge deck PVB film Finite-element modelling Structure design optimization

0 Introduction

With the vigorous development of the tourism industry and the growing needs of the people for a better life, major tourist attractions have successively invested in several glass trestles or corridors to attract tourists to obtain huge economicbenefits[1]. Because of the complicated stress condition of the glass bridge deck, people are also faced with a huge risk of life and safety while they are seeking stimulation. For this type of the glass bridge deck structure, the technical standards for reference are not yet mature, but it has been put into many engineering applications, hidden behind a huge security risk, and there are construction and monitoring units in the market quality problems, engineering quality is difficult to ensure[2]. To ensure the safety of people's lives and property, many local governments have suspended the approval, construction, opening, and operation of glass trestle tourism projects. Therefore, it is necessary to conduct a comprehensive analysis of the bearing capacity of the glass bridge deck and optimize the structural design to avoid such problems. At present, the glass bridge decks in the glass trestle and gallery structures are mostly reinforced plastic sandwich glass plates supported on four sides. Ali S[3-4] designed a new type of composite bridge deck with glass fibre reinforced polymer (GFRP) on the ground floor and laminated glass on the top floor. The safety and service performance of the footbridge are strictly studied, monitoring the stress, deflection, and other important response parameters of pedestrian load, the results show that the suspension bridge can meet the requirements of the bridge design code. Tang Peng[5-7] conducted an experimental study on the load-carrying capacity of three-ply PVB glass panels and single-ply glass bridge decks under different wheel pressures, with emphasis on the continuity of load action, the force acting on the glass plate at different positions is studied, the results show that the load-carrying capacity of the centre, the side and the corner of the laminated glass plate is 2.78, 3.47 and 3.66 times of that of the laminated glass plate in the same position. Tao Zhixiong[8] obtained the material performance parameters of PVB film through tensile test and shear test and conducted the bending bearing capacity test. The test results show that the film has a significant effect on the mechanical performance of laminated glass, and the adhesive effect of the film cannot be ignored, with the increase of temperature, its bearing capacity decreases. Wang Yuanqing[9-12] introduces the classification of the glass load-bearing structure, derives the calculation methods of various structures from the nonlinear large deflection theory, and gives the design examples of the four-side simply supported glass floor and glass rib plate. Centelles X[13] conducted a four-month uniform load test on three layers of laminated glass to study the influence of the creep effect of the laminated glass. It was found that the creep of laminated glass increased with time, the phenomenon that the deflection of glass plate is increasing. It can be seen from the above literature that the current research on the glass bridge deck focuses on the bearing performance test. Many scholars have pointed out that the contribution of PVB to the bearing capacity and the geometric nonlinearity should be considered in the design of the glass bridge deck, and the creep effect of PVB should not be ignored. Compared with the current relevant design codes in China, Europe, and the United States, the Chinese code JGJ 113-2015 and the European code PREN-13474-2 design the laminated glass plate according to the ordinary small deflection laminated plate when dealing with long-term load. The American code ASTME 1300-12a provides the deflection and stress calculation chart considering the influence of PVB for designers through many tests and calculations, but its application range is harsh. Obviously, it is difficult to form a complete set of large deflection theoretical design methods considering creep effect for the glass bridge deck, and finite element simulation becomes a reliable design tool. Therefore, according to the mechanical characteristics of the glass bridge deck, the influence of PVB creep effect is investigated and analyzed in this paper. Based on ABAQUS finite element analysis software, the standard method for finite element simulation of the glass bridge deck is proposed, and the reliability of the method is verified by comparing with the results of previous literature. The structural design of the glass bridge deck is optimized by parameter analysis.

1 Performance analysis of PVB

PVB has an important influence on the bearing capacity of the glass bridge deck. Because of the creep property of PVB atelevated temperature and the influence of temperature and holding time on its shear modulus, it is necessary to calculate the bearing capacity of the glass bridge deck, firstly, the variation of PVB shear modulus with time and temperature should be analysed. This has been studied in detail by the major sandwich glass production companies. In Tab. 1 below, PVB material properties released by some companies.

Shear modulus of PVB Tab. 1

Load Duration	Structural shear relaxation modulus (MPa)						
	Temperature(℃)						
	10	15	20	25	30	35	40
30 sec	571	424	216	69	11	1.9	0.68
1 min	566	389	185	46	6.3	1.3	0.56
5 min	533	308	108	19	2.4	0.68	0.42
30 min	452	213	48	5.0	0.97	0.45	0.4
1 hour	422	182	31	3.5	0.72	0.41	0.9
6 hours	329	99	10	1.2	0.47	0.4	0.37
12 hours	297	76	5.9	0.9	0.42	0.39	0.34

The PVB material is an amorphous polymer which is aviscoelastic material. As can be seen from Tab. 1, the shear modulus of PVB decreases rapidly with the increase of holding time and temperature, which means that the adhesion of PVB decreases and the ability to transmit the interlaminar shear stress of the glass bridge deck decreases, the glass bridge deck is also closer to the common laminate. Since the glass bridge deck generally bears the load of the crowd, the holding time of the load is determined by the open condition of the scenic spot, and the temperature of each scenic spot also varies with the geographical environment and seasons, therefore, the most dangerous situation is considered, the shear modulus of PVB is 0.34MPa, which corresponds to the holding time of 12 hours and temperature of 40℃.

2 Finite element modeling

The modeling method of the glass bridge deck was studied based on ABAQUS general finite element analysissoftware. The basic method of finite element simulation of the glass bridge deck is illustrated by the bearing capacity test of reference [8], and the results are compared with those of reference [8] and JGJ 113-2015, the reliability of the method is verified. The plane size of the glass bridge deck is 1.5m × 1.5m, and the thickness is 6mm + 1.14mmPVB + 6mm, respectively.

The maximum deflection of a supported glass plate in JGJ 113-2015 is as follows:

$$d = \frac{\mu q a^4}{D}$$

where $D = \dfrac{E t_e^3}{12(1-\mu^2)}$ is the rigidity of the glass, E is the elastic modulus of the glass, t_e is the equivalent thickness of the glass plate, and μ is the Poisson's ratio of the glass.

2.1 Material Parameters

The model iscomposed of glass and PVB film. Technical data and drawings of existing glass suspension bridges, and the specific material characteristics of which are shown in Tab.2.

Material parameters Tab. 2

Material	Young's Modulus	Poisson Ratio
glass	72 GPa	0.21
PVB	1.03 MPa	0.5

2.2 Load and Boundary Conditions

From the experimental results in reference [8], it can be found that the two glass plates have not been deboned until destroyed, so the glass plate can be restrained with PVB film tie. The glass bridge deck is a four-sided supporting form, and sliding is not allowed during service. Therefore, the four-sided vertical translational freedom and sliding freedom are restricted on the bottom of the glass bridge deck. Surface load is applied to the top surface, and to simulate the test situation accurately, the dead weight is not considered in the calculation. The concrete load and boundary conditions are shown in Fig. 1.

2.3 Cell Selectionand Mesh Generation

The eight-node linear hexahedral incompatible

mode solid element C3D8I was selected for the glass panel. PVB Poisson's ratio is close to 0.5. To avoid shear self-locking, PVB adopts a hybrid, eight-node linear hexahedron, and non-coordinated mode entity unit C3D8IH. To improve the calculation accuracy and the calculation efficiency, the plane grids of the glass plate and the PVB film are all 10mm × 10mm. Considering the shear force transmission characteristics of the PVB film, and the thickness direction of the PVB film is divided into 3 units, and the thickness direction of the glass plate is divided into 5 units.

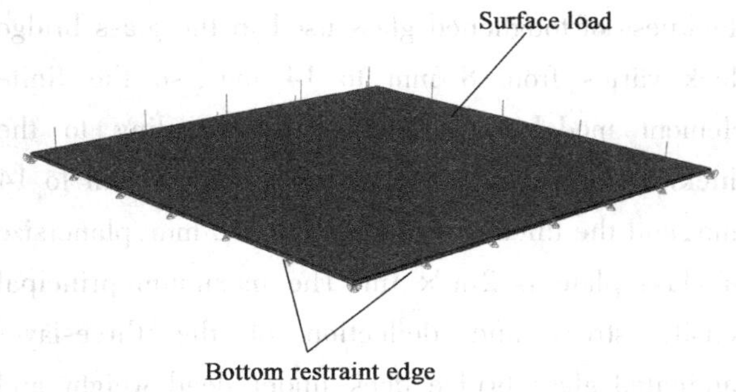

Fig. 1 Load and Boundary Conditions

2.4 Model Validation

Based on the consideration of geometric nonlinearity, the maximum deflection of the glass bridge deck under different load levels is calculated by finite element method. And according to the Chinese code JGJ 113-2015, the maximum deflection is also calculated. The above two results are compared with the results of reference [8]. The results are shown in Fig. 2.

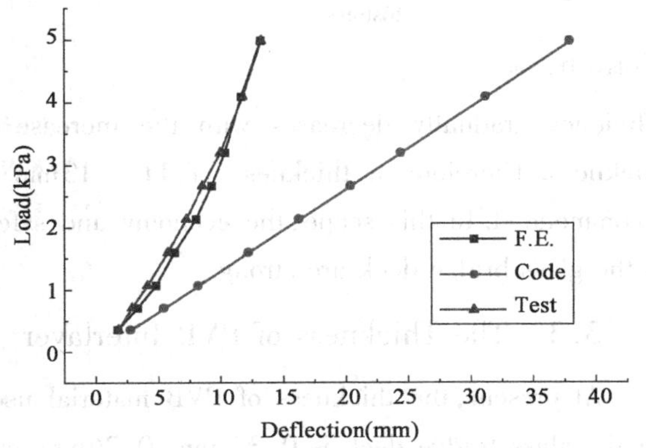

Fig. 2 Results Comparison

As can be seen from Fig. 2, the experimental values are in good agreement with the finite element values, which proves that the finite element simulation method of the glass bridge deck proposed in this paper is dependable, and the load-displacement curves of the test and the finite element show obvious nonlinear characteristics, while the code result is a straight line. It is obvious that the small deflection bending theory adopted in the code seriously underestimates the bearing capacity of the glass bridge deck, the reason is that the standard method does not consider the geometrical nonlinearity and the contribution of PVB material stiffness, which results in a general waste of material properties and poor economy. The finite element simulation value is larger than the test value, because the bearing capacity test of the laminated glass plate in reference[8] does not consider the elevated temperature creep property of PVB material, so the test result is small. By observing the load-displacement curves of finite element simulation and test, it can be found that the deviation between them is large in the initial stage of load increase, and the two have a close trend with the increase of load step by step. It is proved that the creep effect of PVB material begins to appear with the increase of load holding time, which is consistent with the analysis results in section 2 above. It is proved that the contribution of PVB material to the overall stiffness of the structure cannot be completely ignored in the design of the glass bridge deck, and the deflection and stress increment caused by the creep effect of PVB material cannot be ignored. In comparison, the design method recommended by the specification is too safe, and the finite element simulation method is more economical and accurate.

3 Design optimization

It has been proved in theearlier paper that the finite element simulation method of the glass bridge deck is feasible and can replace the normal method in practical design. In order to further optimize the design method of the glass bridge deck, in this section, finite element simulation is used to analyse the parameters of the glass bridge deck, such as the thickness of the glass plate, the thickness of PVB interlayer, and the ratio of length to width of glass plate, the reasonable range of the above parameters is found to provide the basis for the optimal design of the glass bridge deck.

3.1 Pre-phase Analyses

The use of a glass suspension bridge will be subjected to a variety of loads, it includes structure gravity, foundation displacement, soil gravity, soil lateral pressure, crowd load, wind load, snow load, temperature effect, and construction load. The load acting on the glass bridge deck is self-weight, crowd load, snow load, and temperature. According to the Chinese code, the value of the crowd load is 3.5 (kN/m^2) when the bridge deck is designed. The snow load and the crowd load are uniformly distributed loads acting on the top of the glass bridge deck, both usually do not take part in the load combination at the same time and the crowd load is much larger than the snow load, so only the crowd load and the self-weight of the structure are considered in the structural optimization design by finite element simulation. The density of glass is 2.61×10^3 (kg/m^3), temporarily ignoring the weight of PVB. To better evaluate the results, the deflection and stress limit of the glass bridge deck should be determined. According to the local standards issued by Hebei Province, the strength of the end face 30 (MPa) should be taken as the stress limit, and the deflection of the simply supported the glass bridge deck should not exceed 1/200 of the short side length.

3.2 The Thicknessof Glass Plate

After a lot of investigation and research, the thickness of toughened glass used in the glass bridge deck varies from 8 mm to 14 mm, so the finite element models are established according to the thickness of toughened glass plate from 8 mm to 14 mm, and the thickness of PVB is 1.52 mm, plane size of glass plate is 2m × 3m. The maximum principal tensile stress and deflection of the three-layer laminated glass bridge deck under dead weight and crowd load are calculated and the results are shown in Fig. 3.

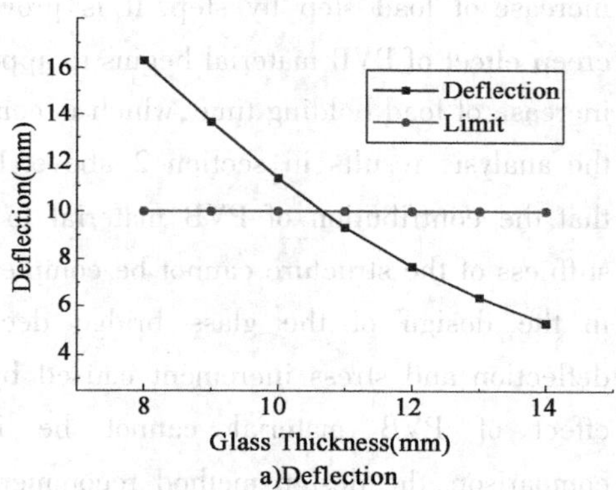

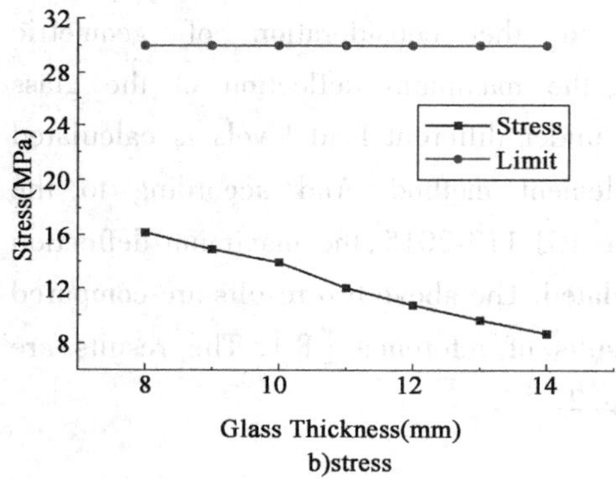

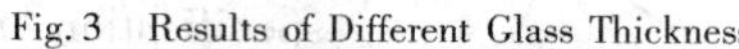
Fig. 3 Results of Different Glass Thickness

It can be seen from the figure that with the increase of glass thickness, the maximum stress and maximum deflection on the glass plate will decrease and are nonlinear changes. For the main tensile stress, all kinds of thicknesses do not exceed the limit, but for the deflection, the glass bridge deck with single layer of toughened glass thickness of less than 11 mm does not meet the requirements. Overall, increasing the thickness of the glass can improve the bearing capacity of toughened laminated glass, but its efficiency gradually decreases with the increase of thickness. Therefore, a thickness of 11 ~ 13mm is recommended. In this scope, the economy and safety of the glass bridge deck are strong.

3.3 The Thickness of PVB Interlayer

At present, the thickness of PVB material used for the glass bridge deck is 0.38 mm, 0.76mm, and 1.52 mm, respectively. The thickness of PVB film has a profound influence on the shear force transmission performance of PVB, which further affects the overall bending performance and stiffness of the glass bridge deck. The thickness of PVB film is 0.38mm, 0.76mm, and 1.52mm, and the thickness of single-layer toughened glass plate is 12mm, plane size of the glass plate is 2m × 3m. The maximum principal tensile stress and deflection of the glass bridge deck are calculated, respectively. The results are shown in Fig. 4.

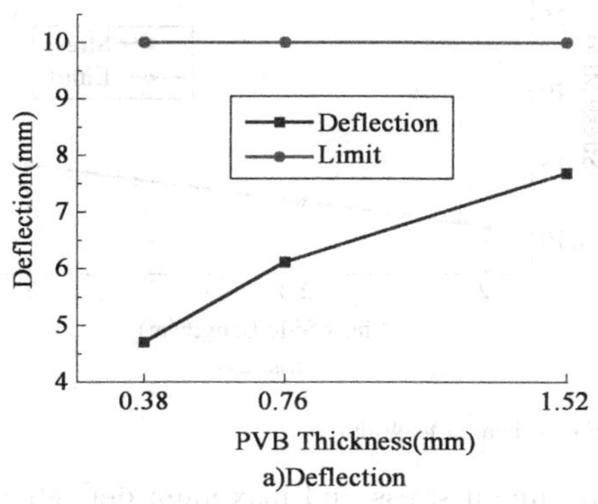

a)Deflection

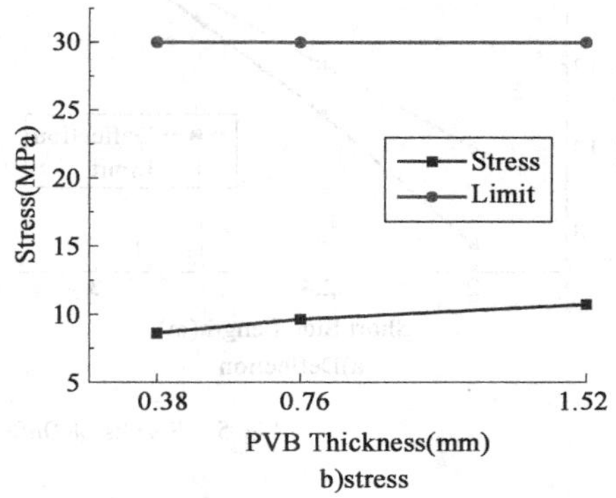

b)stress

Fig. 4 Results of Different PVB Thickness

It can be seen from the above figure that under the same load, the thicker the interlayer film, the greater the deflection of the laminated glass; when the thickness of the interlayer film increases from 0.38 mm to 0.76 mm, the deflection of the laminated glass increases from 4.71 mm to 6.12 mm, an increase of 1.41 mm; when the thickness of the interlayer film increases from 0.76 mm to 1.52 mm, the deflection of the sandwich glass increases from 6.12 mm to 7.69 mm, which increases by 1.57 mm. For the main tensile stress, although there is a similar trend, the increase of PVB film thickness has less influence on the main tensile stress than the deflection. Under different PVB film thicknesses, the deflection and principal tensile stress of the glass bridge deck did not exceed the corresponding limits. In general, the increase of film thickness was not conducive to the improvement of the flexural performance of laminated glass. In summary, when the thickness of PVB film is allowed in the design of the glass bridge deck, the minimum value should be taken as far as possible to increase the shear force transmission performance of PVB film, thereby increasing the integrity of the structure.

3.4 The Ratio of Length to Width of Glass Plate

With the increase of length-width ratio, the force of simply supported plate on four sides transforms from a bidirectional plate to a unidirectional plate, and the deflection limit of the glass bridge deck is related to the short side length, so it is necessary to discuss the reasonable length-width ratio. In the design of a glass suspension bridge, the suspender spacing is fixed, and the longitudinal length of the glass bridge deck is greater than or equal to the transverse length. Therefore, the longitudinal length of the glass bridge deck is fixed to 3 m, and the length-width ratio is 1 : 1, 1 : 1.25, 1 : 1.5, i. e., the short side length is 3 m, 2.4 m, and 2 m The finite element model is established to calculate the maximum principal tensile stress and maximum deflection of the glass bridge deck. The results are shown in Fig. 5.

It can be seen from the above figure that the deflection and main tensile stress of various forms of the glass bridge deck are not exceeding the limit. With the increase of aspect ratio, i. e., the increase of short side length, the stress and deflection of the glass bridge deck increase, and the deflection changes nonlinearly. The main tensile stress changes linearly, and the slope of the deflection curve is large. With the increase of short side length, it quickly approaches the limit value. Therefore, the square plate is not suitable as the form of the glass bridge deck. The short side length of the glass bridge deck is not only related to the stress of the slab itself, but also should be considered comprehensively with the cable system of the glass suspension bridge. The main influencing factors include the main cable spacing and the form of stiffening girder, which should be paid attention to in the design.

Deflection(mm)
Deflection
Limit
Short Side Length(m)
a)Deflection

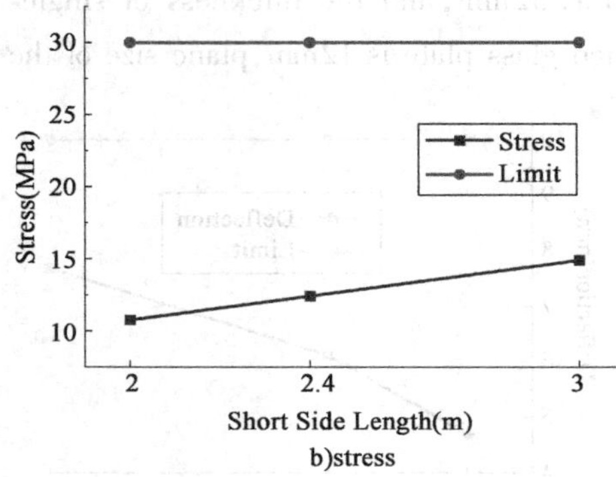

b)stress

Fig. 5 Results of Different Ratios of Length to Width

4 Conclusions

Based on ABAQUS, the high-temperature creep effect of PVB interlayer on the glass bridge deck was investigated and analysed in this paper. The finite element modelling method of the glass bridge deck was studied, and the reliability of the method was verified by comparing it with the experimental data. Based on the finite element modelling, the bearing performance and parameter analysis of the single-layer reinforced glass thickness, PVB film thickness, and the length-to-length ratio of the glass bridge deck were compared. The research conclusions are as follows:

(1) The mechanical properties of PVB interlayer have a profound influence on the overall stress of the glass bridge deck structure, which should be considered in the design and calculation work. The finite element calculation method proposed in this paper is in good agreement with the experimental data, which can accurately consider the shear force transmission characteristics of PVB interlayer. Compared with the traditional theoretical method of thin plate laminated plate with small deflection, the calculation accuracy is improved at the expense of a small amount of efficiency, which can be used as a conventional means for the design of the glass bridge deck.

(2) With the increase of glass thickness, the maximum stress and maximum deflection on the glass plate will decrease and are nonlinear changes. increasing the thickness of glass can improve the bearing capacity of toughened laminated glass, but its efficiency gradually decreases with the increase of thickness. Therefore, a thickness of 11 ~ 13mm is recommended.

(3) The increase of film thickness was not conducive to the improvement of the flexural performance of laminated glass. When the thickness of PVB film is allowed in the design of the glass bridge deck, the minimum value should be taken as far as possible to increase the shear force transmission performance of PVB film, thereby increasing the integrity of the structure.

(4) With the increase of aspect ratio, i. e., the increase of short side length, the stress and deflection of the glass bridge deck increase, and the slope of the deflection curve is large. With the increase of short side length, it quickly approaches the limit value. Therefore, the square plate is not suitable as the form of the glass bridge deck.

References

[1] Huang Xiaokun, Duan Shukun, et al. Advances and engineering practice in glass structures[J]. Journal of Building Structures, 2020, 41 (6): 1-20.

[2] Liu Junjin, Cui Zhongqian, et al. Design method for the glass deck of landscape bridge[J].

Building Science,2020,36(1):1-6.

[3] Ali S, Thambiratnam D, et al. Numerical Study of Pedestrian Suspension Bridge with Innovative Composite Deck[J]. Heliyon,2020,6(7).

[4] Ali S, Thambiratnam D, et al. Performance Evaluation of Innovative Composite Pedestrian Bridge[J]. Structures,2020,26:845-858.

[5] Tang Peng, Gong Sai, et al. Experimental study on bearing capacity of glass bridge deck under different boundary conditions [J]. Journal of Shenzhen University (Science and Engineering), 2020,37(1):84-90.

[6] Tang P, Gong S, et al. Experimental Study on the Bearing Capacity of Glass Deck Under the Condition of Vehicle Traffic [J]. Tehnicki Vjesnik-technical Gazette, 2021, 28 (3): 796-800.

[7] Tang P, Gong S, et al. Experimental Study on Bearing Capacity of Glass Bridge Deck Under Different Wheel Compression Positions [J]. Tehnicki Vjesnik-technical Gazette, 2019, 26 (5):1461-1468.

[8] Tao Zhixiong, Zhang Qilin, et al. Experimental study on flexural capacity and finite element analysis of laminated glass simply supported on four sides[J]. Journal of Building Structures, 2010,31(10):114-119.

[9] Wang Yuanqing, Zhang Hengqiu, et al. The analysis of calculating and design method for load bearing glass structures[J]. Building Science, 2005,21(6):26-30,44.

[10] Wang Yuanqing, Shi Yongjiu, et al. The engineering application and design analysis of load bearing glass structure [J]. Industrial Construction,2005,35(2):6-10.

[11] Wang Yuanqing, Zhang Hengqiu, et al. Finite Element Analysis of Bearing Properties of In-plane Bending Glass Plate [J]. Building Structure,2008,290(2):100,120-122.

[12] Wang Yuanqing, Zhang Hengqiu, et al. Experimental study of the loading capacity and stability of in-plane bending of a glass plate [J]. Journal of Tsinghua University (Science and Technology),2006(6):773-776.

[13] Centelles X, Pelayo F, et al. Long-term Loading and Recovery of a Laminated Glass Slab with Three Different Interlayers [J]. Construction and Building Materials,2021,287.

湿陷性黄土地基闭合型地下连续墙负摩阻力试验及数值模拟研究

李　凡*[1,2]　樊康佳[1,2]　郭红兵[1,2]　王　旭[3]　韩丽丽[1,2]

(1. 陕西交通职业技术学院公路与铁道工程学院;
2. 西安市交通土建结构安全监测工程技术研究中心;
3. 兰州交通大学土木工程学院)

摘　要　湿陷性黄土主要分布于西北地区,其遇水湿陷的特性会严重影响桥梁基础结构的承载能力,为此本文采用石英粉、砂、膨润土、石膏和工业盐制备了人工湿陷性黄土,用于闭合型地下连续墙在湿陷性黄土中遇水湿陷后的负摩阻力模型试验,并采用有限元软件对闭合型地下连续墙遇水湿陷后的负摩阻力发展规律进行了模拟分析。结果表明:闭合型地下连续墙周围土体浸水后,墙体承载力明显降低,轴力沿墙体深度的加深呈现先增大后减小的趋势;墙体外壁侧的摩阻力浸水前为正值,浸水后摩阻力先为负值后为正值,而墙体内壁侧的摩阻力浸水前后均为正值。有限元软件 MIDAS/GTS 模拟得到的墙内、外壁侧摩阻力和墙身轴力的发展规律与室内模型试验结果一致。

关键词　桥梁基础　负摩阻力　模型试验　地下连续墙　湿陷性黄土　数值模拟

0　引言

湿陷性黄土是干旱与半干旱地区一种典型的风成堆积物,由于其特定的生成环境而形成了显著的架空孔隙结构,从而造成了遇水湿陷的独特性质[1]。由于天然黄土在取样过程中不可避免产生的扰动容易使土的结构性释放,其结构性以及力学特性与原状黄土存在显著差异,因此室内模型试验若使用重塑黄土必然达不到天然黄土要求,因此人工制备相似材料此时将能最大限度发挥其作用,满足试验要求。

地下连续墙发展初期仅作为挡土围护结构来使用。随后发展成为集挡土、承重和防水于一身的"三合一"地下结构。在1995年,宝(鸡)—中(卫)铁路中率先在湿陷性黄土地区使用闭合型地下连续墙作为铁路桥梁基础。2006年孟凡超等[2]、程谦恭等[3]、文华等[4-5]对闭合型地下连续墙基础的承载特性、荷载传递机理、负摩阻力等开展了研究并具有重要的参考价值和指导意义。但其现场仍旧采用的是重塑土,与原状黄土仍有差距。

本文通过运用配制而得的湿陷性黄土相似材料,进行室内模型试验,研究湿陷性黄土地区地下闭合墙负摩阻力发展规律。最后采用MIDAS/GTS软件数值模拟了黄土湿陷对地下闭合墙负摩阻力的影响。

1　人工湿陷性黄土制备

黄土中所含的主要矿物成分,可分为无黏结性的粗粒矿物和有胶结性的黏土矿物两大类。本文选取石膏、膨润土、工业盐、石英粉、砂为基本材料制备人工湿陷性黄土[6],如图1所示。通过大量配比试验,采用砂:石英粉:膨润土:石膏:工业盐=0.25:0.3:0.3:0.1:0.05(质量比)的配比。按比例称取各原材料,采用空中自由下落法配制,如图2所示,搅拌均匀,得到湿陷性黄土。湿陷性黄土的物理性质指标如表1所示。

图1　模型试验材料

图2　自由下落法

人工制备湿陷性黄土物理性质指标　　表1

土粒比重	含水率(%)	液限(%)	塑限(%)	最优含水率(%)	最大干密度(g/cm^3)
2.67	10.3	26.02	16.25	14.38	1.96

2　试验研究

依托陕西省境内某一级公路桥梁,其基础为闭合型地下连续墙。现场试验场地选在此桥梁附近,闭合墙地下连续墙平面尺寸为3.4m×3.4m,墙本厚度为0.8m,墙体高度为15.6m,露出地面部分0.6m[13]。通过室内模型试验数据与数值模拟数据进行对比,进而验证模型试验的准确性。

2.1　室内模型试验

室内模型试验依托现场模型墙数据,选取合适相似常数17:1,得到模型墙的边长为3.4/17=0.2m,人土深度为13/17=0.76m,优化取0.57m,墙厚为0.6/17=0.035m,优化取0.025m。弹性模量

$E_p = 1.4 \times 10^3$MPa。本次试验中模型墙材料采用有机玻璃,其弹性模量最为接近相似比计算而得的材料弹性模量,且为更贴近真实墙体测摩擦系数,模型墙表面涂有细砂。

2.1.1 模型墙的制作

本次试验闭合地下连续墙外侧尺寸为200mm×200mm,内侧尺寸为150mm×150mm,厚25mm,墙高570mm,承台高40mm。在裁剪好的有机玻璃板上进行贴应变片、接线以及采用亚克力板专业黏合剂拼接,使其四块板牢固地黏在一起。

2.1.2 应变片布设

为了测量墙身轴力以及墙侧摩阻力,采用24片应变片贴在模型墙表面,具体布置图如图3所示。

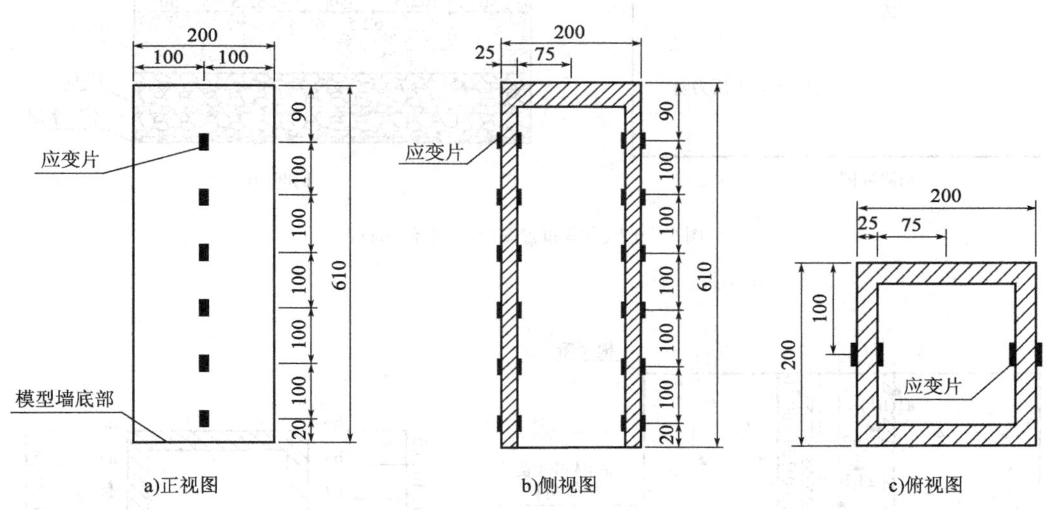

图3 模型墙应变片布置图(尺寸单位:mm)

2.1.3 模型墙布置与模型重塑土铺设

地下连续墙周边土层为湿陷性黄土层,从下往上是不透水层、碎石、中砂、湿陷性黄土。剖面分布如图4所示。

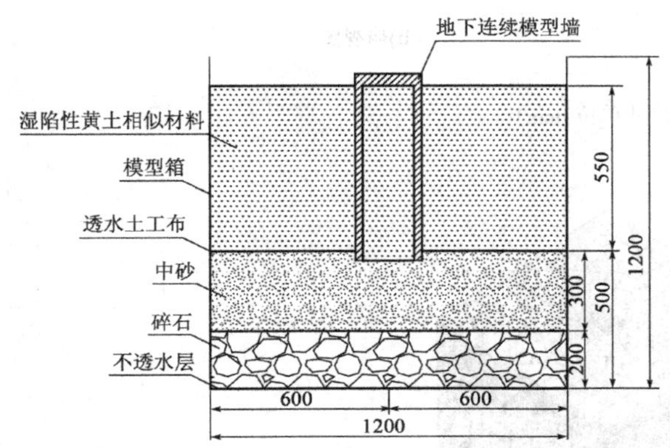

图4 模型墙与土层分布图(尺寸单位:mm)

2.1.4 微型土压力盒布设

试验中共采用8只微型土压力盒测量承台底压力及墙底土压力具体布设如图5所示。

2.1.5 沉降标布设

指定首次采用沉降标测量土体下陷程度,沉降标的布置图如图6所示。

2.1.6 湿陷性黄土地基闭合型地下连续墙土体浸水条件下的负摩阻力试验试验过程

根据要求放置好模型墙及填好湿陷性黄土相似材料,因为地下地连墙加载规范尚不明确,因此按照《桩基检测技术规范》(JGJ 106—2014)相关要求进行加、卸载。室内模型试验对模型墙施加正常工作荷载,正常工作荷载取极限荷载的一半。待加载至正常工作荷载并墙体沉降稳定后,进行土体浸水试验,浸水拟分3次实施。每次对土体加水后,观测土体沉降及墙体应变数据及土压力盒数据。

2.2 数值模拟模型建立

本数值模拟模型尺寸为现场数据尺寸,采用Mohr-Coulomb弹塑性模型对土体进行分析(图7),地下连续墙用MIDAS/GTS中实体单元进行模拟。为更准确模拟分层湿陷,采用土体分层模量折减法模拟湿陷。当闭合墙墙顶施加荷载达到正常使用状态下荷载时,便开始对墙周土体分层进行模量折减,折减系数均取0.5,以达到由上而下分层逐步湿陷的过程。墙内芯土不发生湿陷,因此其属性参数亦不改变。

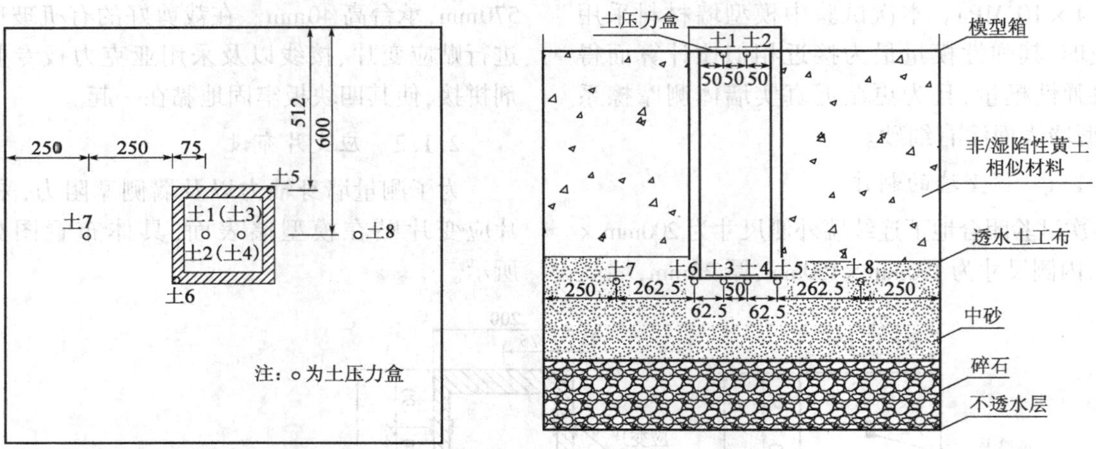

注：o为土压力盒

a)俯视图

b)剖面图

图 5　土压力盒布置图(尺寸单位:mm)

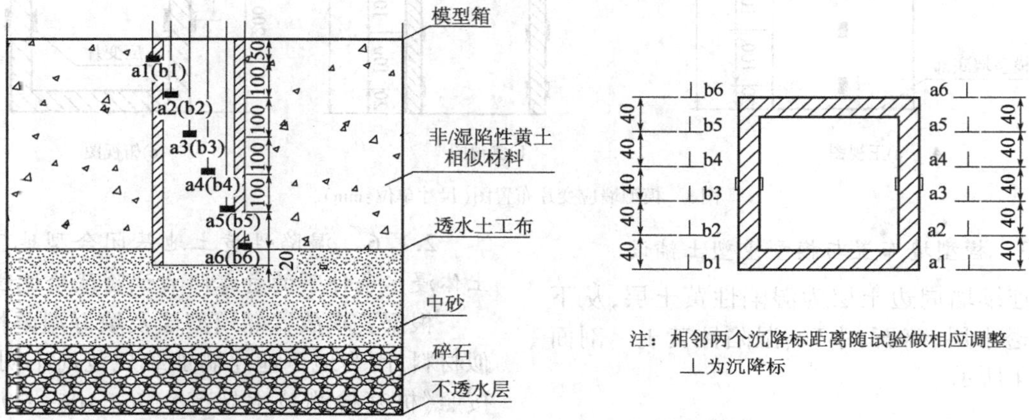

a)侧视图

注：相邻两个沉降标距离随试验做相应调整
⊥为沉降标

b)俯视图

图 6　沉降标布置图(尺寸单位:mm)

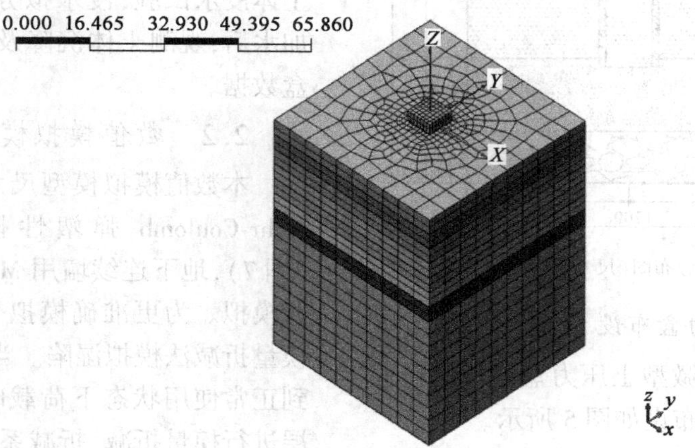

图 7　数值模拟计算模型图

3 土体浸水的负摩阻力模型试验结果与数值模拟结果对比分析

3.1 墙体及湿陷性黄土土层的浸水沉降

从室内模型试验湿陷图中可以看出闭合连续墙周围土体明显下沉，从数值模拟图中同样可以看出土体湿陷呈现环状分布，从外向内土体湿陷程度越大，如图8和图9所示。

图8 室内模型试验湿陷性黄土浸水后湿陷情况

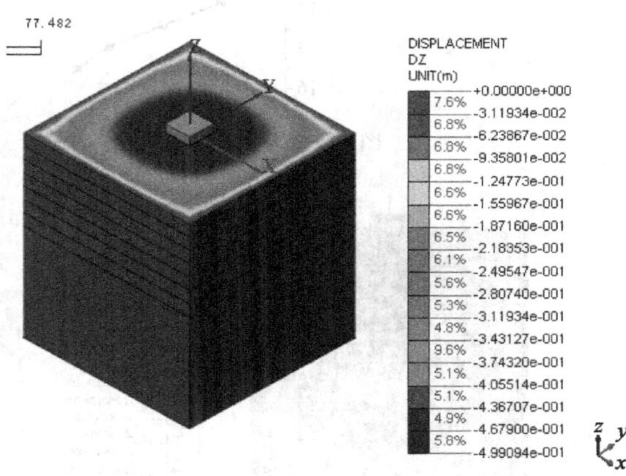

图9 数值模拟湿陷性黄土浸水后湿陷情况

3.2 中性点的确定

中性点是摩阻力、桩土相对位移以及轴向压力沿桩身变化的特征点[4,5]。研究负摩阻力的关键问题在于确定墙侧中性点的位置。下图为室内模型试验和数值模拟对比。

模型墙中性点的位置及变化情况如图10所示，由于有机玻璃材料弹性模量远大于模型土，所以忽略墙身的压缩变形。由图10中可以得出，随着加水次数的增加，中性点位置由浅到深。中性点大致范围在35～45cm左右，且中性点深度与墙体埋深的比例在0.64～0.73之间。

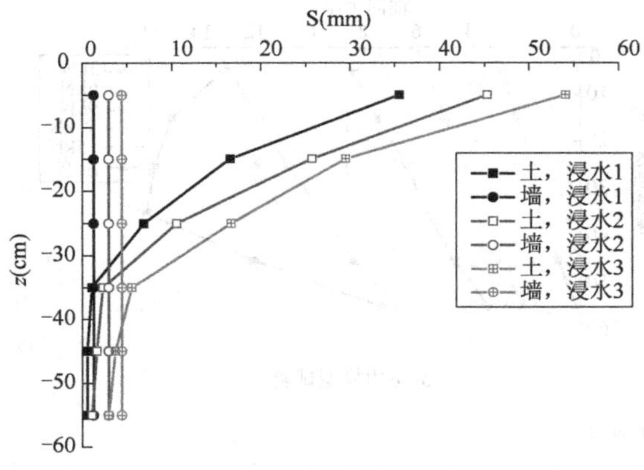

图10 墙土相对位移曲线

墙土位移情况以及相对位移情况如图11和图12所示，墙体下沉位移与土体位移交点在埋深11m附近，且墙土相对位移正负交汇点同样在11m附近。由此推断中性点在10～11m左右，且中性点深度与墙体埋深的比例在0.7左右，与室内模型试验中性点与墙体埋深比例大体一致。

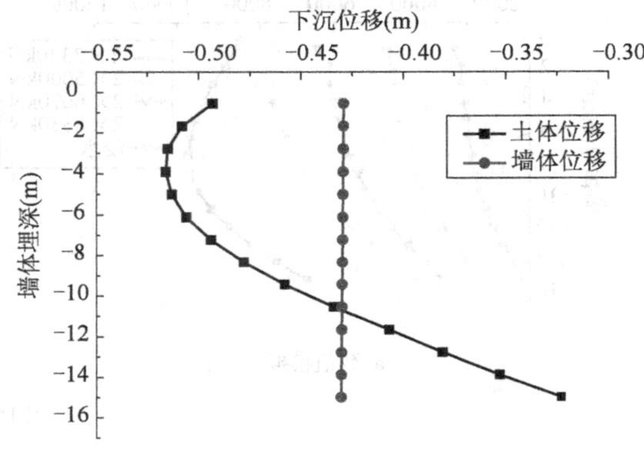

图11 墙/土位移

数值模拟湿陷性黄土浸水后墙体位移如图13所示，从墙土相对位移图中可以看出随着墙体高度向下，相对位移从负到正，说明墙体上部土体下沉大于墙体下沉，下部为正则墙体下沉大于土体，正负交替处则为中性点处。从位移剖面图可明显看出土体湿陷后土体位移大于墙体位移，如图14所示。

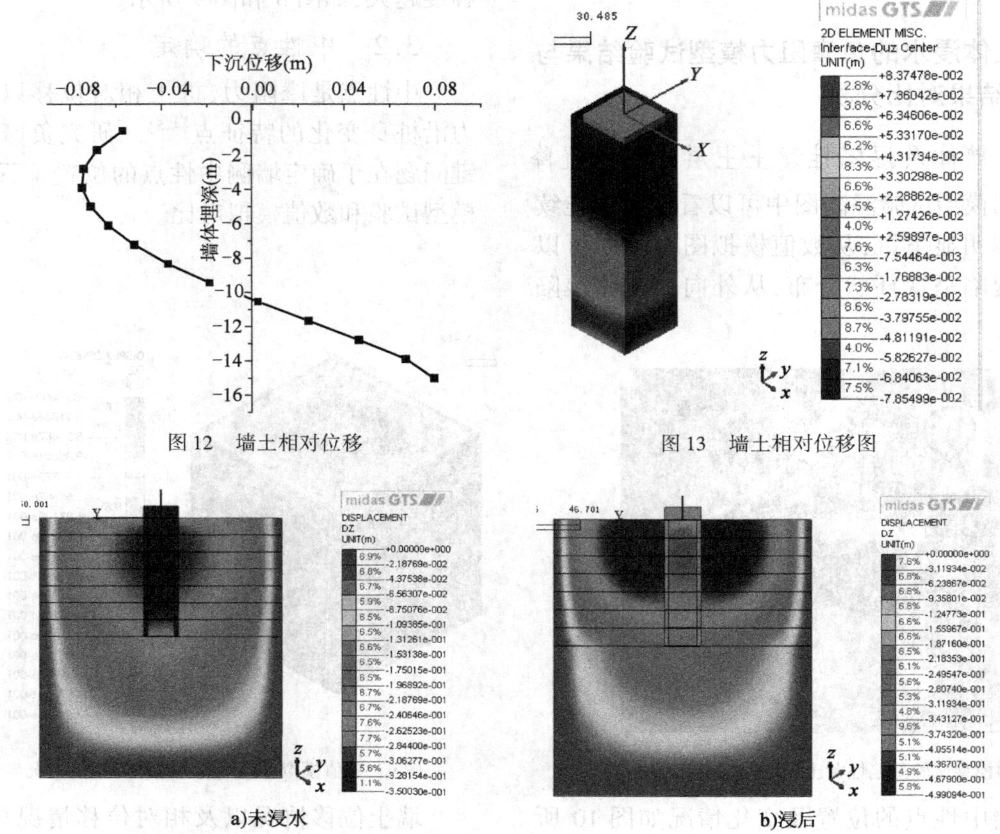

图12　墙土相对位移

图13　墙土相对位移图

图14　位移剖面图

3.3　墙体轴力

墙体轴力分布曲线如图15所示，可以看出无论数值模拟还是室内模型试验加水前轴力均沿墙体埋深不断减小，加水后，轴力沿墙体深度加深呈现先增大后减小趋势，呈“D”型，轴力最大处均为侧摩阻力为0，即中性点处。

a)数值模拟

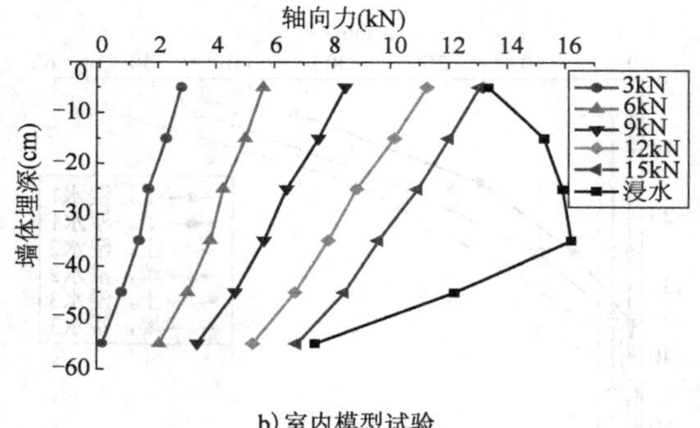

b)室内模型试验

图15　墙身轴力

3.4　墙体负摩阻力的分布

3.4.1　墙外壁侧摩阻力

接触面外墙侧摩阻力如图16所示，墙体从上至下摩阻力呈现先负后正。外墙侧摩阻力浸水前后墙体外壁侧摩阻力数值模拟与模型试验趋势大致相同如图17所示，浸水前均为正摩阻力，浸水后先呈负摩阻力后呈现正摩阻力，正负摩阻力交汇点即中性点且数值模拟得出中性点深度与墙体埋深的比例在0.7左右，数值模拟在0.65附近，大致相同。从图中可以看出土体浸水前墙外侧摩阻力先增加后减小再增加，且多为双峰曲线，随着深度的增加侧摩阻力分布的总趋势是从上小下大到上大下小逐渐变化，但在墙顶和墙端附近均有局部峰值出现,呈“马鞍状”。随着加水量的增大以及湿陷范围的增大,土体的沉降量也在不断加大,当土体沉降大于墙体沉降时,墙侧出现负摩阻力。可以看出负摩阻力分布呈现抛物线型。分析原因是由于模型墙长度较小且嵌入持力层模量较大,所以地下连续墙受力特性类似于短的嵌岩桩性质。墙顶受荷以后,墙身上部首先产生墙-土相对位移,墙周土产生剪切变形,随之上部荷载不断增大,剪切变形到达极限值而导致剪切破坏,墙身上部侧阻开始减小,墙侧阻力向下传递。传递至墙底时受法向应力及相对位移的影响,在墙身下部再次出现极值,随后有减小趋势。然而浸水后由于土体较墙体下沉量大,对墙体有下拽作用,因此呈现先负摩阻后正摩阻力现象。

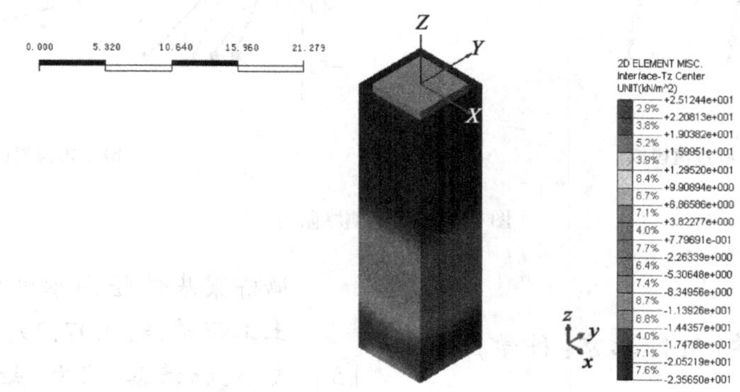

图16 接触面外墙侧摩阻力

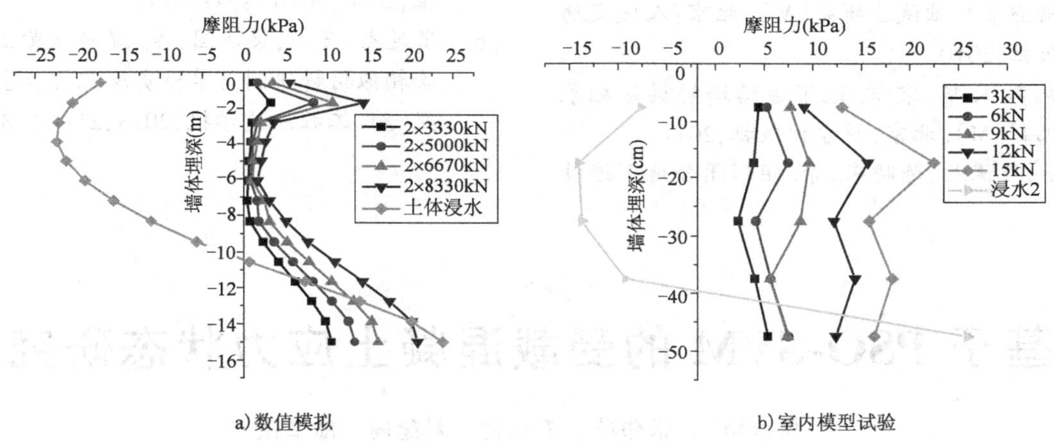

a)数值模拟 b)室内模型试验

图17 墙外壁侧摩阻力

3.4.2 墙内壁侧摩阻力

墙内侧摩阻力浸水前后数值模拟与模型试验趋势大致相同,如图18所示。浸水前后均为正摩阻力,且摩阻力随墙体深度加深摩阻力越大。浸水后摩阻力有加大趋势,这是由于闭合墙土芯被承台与墙身密闭式包起,并且芯土下部进行隔水处理,水无法渗入到芯土内,因此芯土不受外部浸水的影响。然而外侧土体浸水后对墙体有下拉作用加之承台挤压作用,导致内墙摩阻力自然增加。

4 结语

(1)运用湿陷性黄土相似材料于模型试验中,加水后土体发生湿陷,人工湿陷性黄土能很好地模拟原状黄土湿陷过程。

(2)通过室内模型试验和数值模型试验对比发现,室内模型试验中性点在35~45cm左右,且中性点深度与墙体埋深的比例在0.64~0.73之间。数值模拟试验中性点在10~11m左右,且中性点深度与墙体埋深的比例在0.7左右,与室内模型试验中性点与墙体埋深比例大体一致。

(3)闭合型连续墙轴力沿墙体深度加深呈现先增大后减小趋势,呈“D”型。墙体外壁侧摩阻力浸水前均为正摩阻力,浸水后先呈负摩阻力后呈现正摩阻力。而墙体内壁侧摩阻力无论浸水前后均为正摩阻力,且摩阻力随墙体深度加深摩阻力越大,浸水后摩阻力有加大趋势。

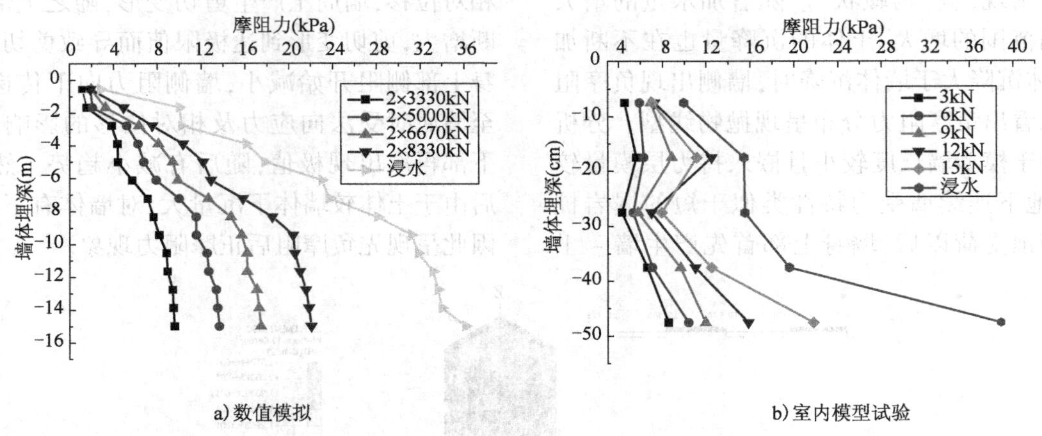

a)数值模拟　　b)室内模型试验

图18　墙内壁侧摩阻力

参考文献

[1] 高国瑞. 近代土质学[M]. 北京:科学出版社,2013.

[2] 孟凡超,陈晓东,程谦恭,等. 黄土地区地下连续墙桥梁基础试验研究[M]. 北京:人民交通出版社,2010.

[3] 程谦恭,文华,宋章. 地下连续墙桥梁基础承载机制[M]. 北京:科学出版社,2011.

[4] 文华,程谦恭,陈晓东,等. 矩形闭合地下连续墙桥梁基础竖向承载特性试验研究[J]. 岩土工程学报,2007,29(12):1823-1830.

[5] 文华,程谦恭,宋章. 矩形闭合地下连续墙基础负摩阻力模型试验研究[J]. 岩土工程学报,2008,30(4):541-548.

[6] 张延杰,王旭,梁庆国,等. 湿陷性黄土模型试验相似材料研制与单桩负摩阻力模型试验研究[J]. 工程地质学报,2013,21(6):857-863.

基于PSO-SVM的受载混凝土应力状态研究

杨雅勋*　张伟德　王林柯　刘德闯　陆嘉诚

(长安大学公路学院)

摘　要　在研究支持向量机(SVM)模拟受压混凝土超声参数与应力的关系时,为提高寻优结果,采用粒子群算法(PSO)对支持向量机参数进行优化,并通过试验验证粒子群优化支持向量机(PSO-SVM)的模拟效果。结果表明:采用粒子群算法优化参数的模型模拟效果明显优于经验参数的简单支持向量机模型。简单支持向量机模拟效果较差,在低应力阶段尤为明显;粒子群算法优化支持向量机模拟效果更好,准确度更高。

关键词　支持向量机　粒子群算法　受载混凝土应力　超声参数

0　引言

支持向量机的应用领域与多层感知器网络和径向基神经网络类似,可以用于解决模式分类问题和非线性回归问题。

支持向量机[1-2]适合于分析小样本和多维数据问题,常被用于分类和预测。文大鹏等将支持向量机与激光诱导击穿光谱相结合,对多种矿石进行分类,大大提高了分类的准确率[3]。杨群等采用支持向量机处理车辆振动信号,用于识别沥青路面横缝[4]。唐诗等运用支持向量机预测水电站机组轴瓦温度[5]。张庆华等采用鲸鱼算法优化支持向量机对铣刀磨损状况进行了监测，提高了识别精度[6]。而超声波检测作为无损检测方法之一，其主要是通过超声波在混凝土结构中传播过程的超声参数特征来判断混凝土结构的状态[7-8]。目前国内外针对该方法的研究也在不断地深入。钟贤毅通过钢筋混凝土试件试验，探究了不同因素对超声参数与工作应力相关性的影响，研究了钢筋位置、空洞大小、试件尺寸等因素对超声参数的影响，建立了钢筋混凝土超声参数与工作应力的[9]。Liu 等人在单轴加载条件下，研究了混凝土波速与应力的关系，并采用最小二乘法拟合了波速与单轴应力的函数关系式[10]。然而，单一的超声参数与应力关系的曲线拟合效果较差，混凝土内部材料力学性能的非线性和结合面的不均匀性限制了超声波技术在识别混凝土应力方面的应用，需要一种更具适用性和精确的方式来拟合超声参数与应力的关系。

在模拟受载混凝土超声参数与应力关系时，采用支持向量机能够处理多维超声参数，可解决样本数量较小的难点。传统的支持向量机预测精度不高，本文采用粒子群算法对支持向量机做了改进，提高了其运算效率与寻优结果。

1 模型的建立和超声参数的选取

大量的研究表明[11-13]，超声波在混凝土材料中传播的特征参数与混凝土结构之间存在着密切的关系。传统的方法通过声时、声速等较少的特征参数来判断混凝土材料的应力状况存在着局限性。通过多种超声参数来拟合参数与应力的关系是非常有必要的，选择合适的参数将直接影响到拟合的效果。因此，通过数值模型的模拟，选择随应力水平变化明显且呈现出规律的超声参数来进行拟合。

考虑到混凝土的非均质性，建立集料、砂浆、集料与砂浆间的相邻界面的三相复合材料二维模型。按集料集配理论，生成粒径小于 40mm 尺寸为 150mm × 150mm 的圆形集料 C40 混凝土模型。在给各相材料赋予材料参数后，约束模型下边界，在上边界上采用位移加载模拟进行 60kN/级的分级加载至 900kN，同时在模型左侧中心处进行超声激励，右侧中心处进行信号接收。发射激励信号：

$$F = \begin{cases} \frac{1}{2}\left[1-\cos\left(\frac{2\pi \cdot f \cdot t}{n}\right)\right] \times \cos(2\pi \cdot f \cdot t) & 0 \leqslant t \leqslant \frac{n}{f} \\ 0 & t > \frac{n}{f} \end{cases} \tag{1}$$

式中：n——周期，$n = 2$；

f——频率，$f = 100\text{kHz}$。

信号图如图 1 所示。加载完成后将采集的超声参数信号进行时域分析和频域分析，得到能够反映混凝土内部结构和应力状态的声学参数，最终选择波速、首波幅值、非线性系数、主频幅值和波谱面积 5 个随应力变化呈规律性且较为敏感的参数以零应力状态为 1 进行归一化处理后，建立与应力的关系，如图 2 所示。

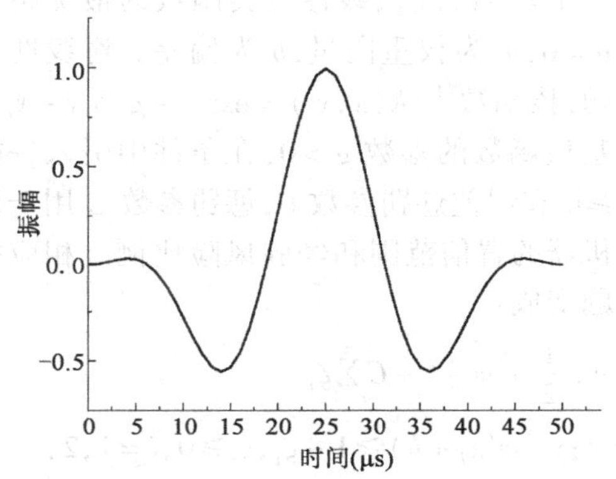

图 1 激励源信号

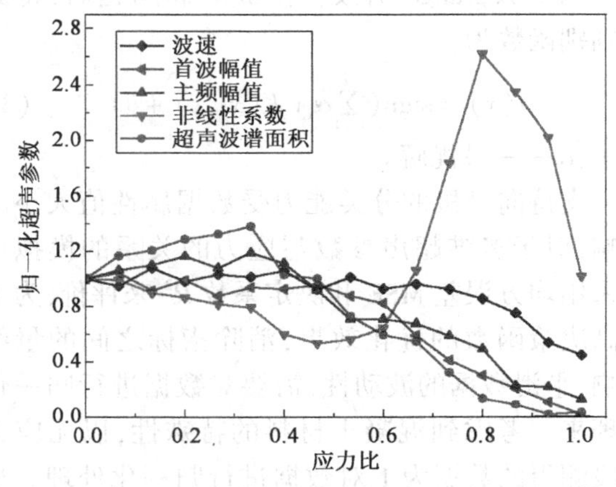

图 2 超声参数与加载应力关系

现有的研究多采用单变量的回归分析来确定超声参数与应力的相互依赖关系，但通过单因素来判断混凝土材料应力是比较单薄的，因此需要结合多参数，以一个整体的数学模型来模拟超声参数与应力的关系是非常有必要的。

2　支持向量机

支持向量机是建立在结构风险最小化原理、统计学习理论的基础上的监督学习算法,将求解过程化为求解一个凸二次规划问题,求解过程具有良好的泛化能力,解具有唯一性和全局最优性[14]。对于非线性问题,基本思想是通过核函数寻找一个非线性的映射将输入空间映射到高维空间来解决原始空间不可分的问题以寻找输入和输出间的关系。

考虑到混凝土材料的复杂性,影响和干扰超声参数的因素众多,超声参数与应力之间存在着明显且复杂的非线性,采用高斯径向基函数为核函数。给定训练集样本 $A=\{(x_i,y_i)|_{i=1}^{n},x_i\in X\subseteq R^n,y_i\in Y=\{-1,1\}\}$,线性分类函数的最优超平面 $wx+b=0$,w 为权重向量,b 为偏差。对线性不可分问题,核函数[15] $K(x,x_i)=\exp(-g\parallel x-x_i\parallel^2)$ 径向基核函数的参数 $g>0$,在条件中引入一松弛项 $\zeta_i\geqslant0$ 和误差惩罚参数 C,惩罚参数 C 用于调节学习机器的置信范围和经验风险比例。相应的优化问题变成:

$$\begin{cases}\min\dfrac{1}{2}\parallel w\parallel^2+C\sum\limits_{i=1}^{n}\zeta_i\\ \text{s. t}:y_i(w^Tx_i+b)\geqslant1-\zeta_i,\zeta_i\geqslant0,i=1,2,\cdots,n\end{cases}\tag{2}$$

利用 Lagrange 函数转换成对偶问题后,得到的判别函数为:

$$f(x)=\text{sign}(\sum_{i=1}^{n}\alpha_iy_iK(x_i,x)+b)\tag{3}$$

式中:α——最优解。

支持向量机的分类能力受数据属性值大小的影响,对于多维超声参数与应力的关系的模拟性能采用均方误差 MSE 和决定系数 R^2 来评价,为了提高决策函数的优化效果,消除指标之间的量纲影响、平滑数据的波动性,需要对数据进行归一化处理来。考虑到混凝土材料的特殊性,以无应力阶段测得的数据为1对数据进行归一化处理。显然,参数 C 和 g 的选取非常明显的影响着支持向量机的性能,选择合适的参数非常重要。采用支持向量机模拟的流程图如图3所示。

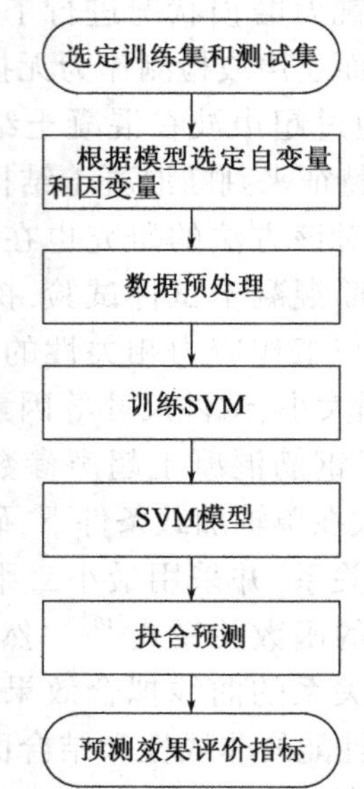

图3　支持向量机算法流程

3　粒子群算法优化支持向量机

粒子群优化算法是一种模拟鸟群的迁徙和群聚行为而提出的基于群体智能的优化算法,借鉴鸟群在飞行过程中个体虽有调整,但个体之间能够保持最适宜的距离的特征。迭代公式及算法过程如下:

$$\begin{cases}\overrightarrow{v_i}(k+1)=w\overrightarrow{v_i}(k)+c_1r_1(\overrightarrow{p_i}(k)-\overrightarrow{x_i}(k))+\\ \qquad c_2r_2(\overrightarrow{p_g}(k)-\overrightarrow{x_i}(k))\\ \overrightarrow{x_i}(k+1)=\overrightarrow{x_i}(k)+\overrightarrow{v_i}(k+1)\end{cases}\tag{4}$$

式中:$\overrightarrow{p_i}$——粒子自身的当前最优位置;

$\overrightarrow{p_g}$——所有粒子的当前最优位置;

w——惯性系数,用于调节搜索范围;

k——当前迭代次数;

c_1,c_2——学习因子,用于调节学习的最大步长,为非负常数;

r_1,r_2——分布于[0,1]之间的随机数,用于增加搜索的随机性。

(1)粒子群算法参数初始化,设定惯性系数、学习因子、最大迭代次数;

(2)确定种群中所有粒子的初始速度$\overrightarrow{v_i}$和位置$\overrightarrow{x_i}$;

(3)计算粒子的适应度;

(4)通过式(4)更新粒子的速度和位置;

(5)判断结束条件。当迭代次数达到设定的最大迭代次数寻优结束,否则返回第(2)步。

采用粒子群算法进行参数优化时，由样本训练集生成的参数 C 和 g 作为初始粒子，计算粒子适应度，以最小适应度的粒子作为全局最优解，以获取最优参数。利用 PSO 优化 SVM 过程如图 4 所示。

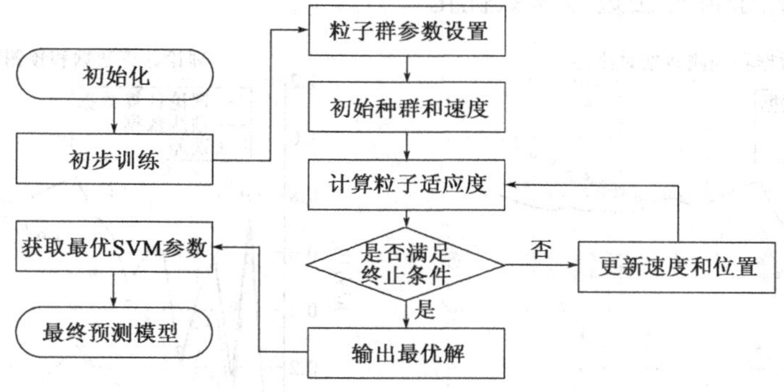

图 4 PSO 优化 SVM 流程

将样本数据作为输入训练后，将模型预测和样本数据之间的均方误差 MSE 和决定系数 R^2 两个指标来评价模型的性能。

4 试验设计验证

4.1 试件设计与测试加载

整个试验共设计 20 个尺寸为 150mm × 150mm × 150mm 的 C40 混凝土试件，水泥选用 42.5 普通硅酸盐水泥，水灰比为 0.49，粒径 5 ~ 20mm 的细集料，20 ~ 40mm 的粗集料，配合比如表 1 所示。

混凝土材料配合比 表 1

组分	水泥	砂	卵石	水
质量比	1	1.5	3.35	0.49

标准养护室内 22 ± 2℃，95% 以上相对湿度养护 28d 之后进行加载试验，过程如下：

（1）试件预处理。在加载前，检查试件几何尺寸误差，擦去试件表面的浮沉和污渍，用由粗至细的砂纸打磨混凝土试件侧面中间部位，直至混凝土表面无灰尘杂。

（2）超声波换能器的连接。将适量的凡士林涂抹在打磨光滑的试件表面和超声波换能器之间，以减少界面上超声波能量损失，提高检测灵敏度。

（3）分级加载。采用压力机对试件按 60kN/级进行分级加载至 720kN 后，按 30kN/级进行加载至试件破坏，记录每级压力数据和接收器采集的信号数据。当压力超过 900kN 时大部分试件还能够继续承压，对超过 1140kN 压力的波形图数据不再进行分析。因此，包括无应力状态共分 27 级进行加载。加载示意图及破坏图如图 5 和图 6 所示。

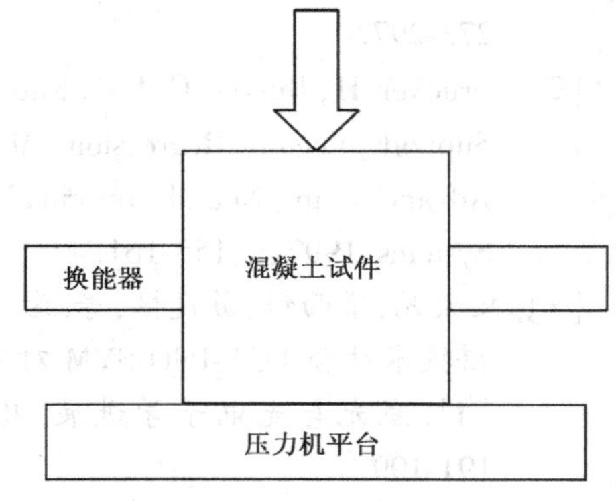

图 5 加载示意图

图 6 试件形成贯通裂缝破坏

4.2 试验结果分析

按照试验方案，完成每个试件加载，随着加载的进行，超声特征参数也不断改变。对 20 个试件的数据归一化后采用支持向量机进行分析。

按经验取惩罚系数 $C = 2$，核函数参数 $g = 1$。

取19个试件513组数据作为训练集,剩余一个试件27组数据作为测试集,得到的支持向量机结果,如图7所示。采用粒子群算法进行参数优化后,得到 $C=0.570466$,$g=0.046285$,以此参数进行支持向量机得到的结果图如图8所示。

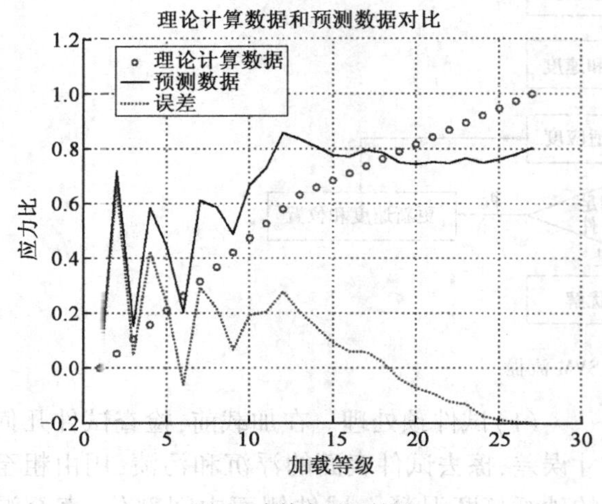

图7　支持向量机结果

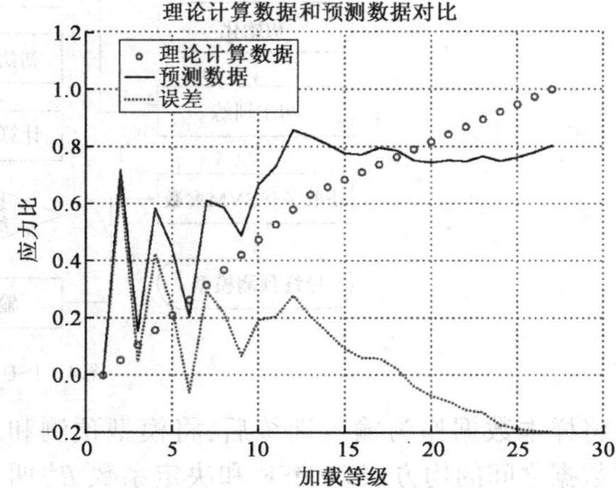

图8　粒子群算法优化后支持向量机结果

参数优化前后支持向量机的均方误差MSE和决定系数 R^2 如表2所示。均方误差越趋于0,决定系数越接近于1,数据模拟的结果越接近于理论计算值。

优化前后结果对比　　表2

	均方误差MSE	决定系数 R^2
参数优化前	0.046217	0.524193
参数优化后	0.024404	0.785318

结果显示,采用粒子群算法优化参数的模型模拟效果明显优于经验参数的支持向量机模型。未进行参数优化的支持向量机与模拟效果不好,特别是在低应力阶段,预测误差很大。参数优化后的模型预测得到的应力结果一般都高于理论计算结果,当加载等级超过20级时($F=930\text{kN}>900\text{kN}$),预测结果偏低,而此时试件的应力已经超过了其抗压强度,混凝土试件已经形成或者将要形成贯通裂缝,此时,试件表面已经能够观察到较为明显的细微裂缝。粒子群算法优化后的模型得到的结果决定系数更高,均方误差更小,模拟的结果效果更好。

5　结语

通过模型仿真和试验验证,对混凝土试件进行分级加载,测试了不同应力状态下的超声参数并采用支持向量机模拟了超声参数与应力的关系。得出以下主要结论:

(1)数值模型模拟结果显示,所选取的波速、首波幅值、主频幅值、非线性系数和超声波谱面积5个超声特征参数与混凝土压应力存在明显的相关性。

(2)试验表明,采用粒子群优化参数的支持向量机模型模拟效果明显优于经验参数的支持向量机模型。在低应力阶段,支持向量机模拟超声参数与应力关系的误差较大,预测结果一般高于真实值模型偏安全。简单支持向量机模拟效果较差,在低应力阶段尤为明显;采用粒子群算法进行参数优化,模拟效果更优,更具有应用价值。

参考文献

[1]　Cortes C, Vapnik V. Support-vector Networks [J]. Machine Learning, 1995, 20(3): 273-297.

[2]　Drucker H, Burges C J C, Kaufman L, et al. Support Vector Regression Machines [J]. Advances in Neural Information Processing Systems, 1997, 9: 155-161.

[3]　文大鹏,梁西银,苏茂根,等.激光诱导击穿光谱技术结合PCA-PSO-SVM对矿石分类识别[J].激光与光电子学进展,2021,58(23):191-199.

[4]　杨群,周师师,王屏,等.信号处理及支持向量机在沥青路面横缝检测中的应用[J]. Journal of Central South University, 2021, 28(08):2451-2462.

[5]　唐诗,李天智,袁永生,等.基于支持向量机的

水电站机组轴瓦温度预测[J]. 人民长江, 2021,52(S2):232-236.

[6] 张庆华,龙伟,李炎炎,等. 基于鲸鱼算法优化LSSVM的铣刀磨损监测[J/OL]. 四川大学学报(自然科学版),2022(01):68-74.

[7] 秦铁男,马化雄,陈韬,等. 混凝土涂层超声波测厚的不确定度评定[J]. 建筑材料学报, 2016,19(01):177-180.

[8] 李俊如,高建光,王耀辉. 超声波检测混凝土裂缝及裂缝成因分析[J]. 岩土力学,2001(03):291-293.

[9] 钟贤毅. 受载钢筋混凝土工作应力超声特征分析[D]. 西安:长安大学,2020.

[10] Liu Z., Ma C, Wei X. P-Wave Velocity and Energy Evolution Process of Concrete in Uniaxial Loading-Unloading Tests[J]. Journal of Materials in Civil Engineering, 2021, 33(6):04021110.

[11] 蒋雨宏. 基于非线性超声特性的混凝土损伤试验研究[D]. 重庆:重庆交通大学,2014.

[12] 聂智超. 混凝土非线性超声传播特性的理论与试验研究[D]. 重庆:重庆交通大学,2021.

[13] 王菲. 低应力条件下混凝土超声传播特性的三维数值模拟研究[D]. 重庆:重庆交通大学,2019.

[14] 奉国和. SVM分类核函数及参数选择比较[J]. 计算机工程与应用,2011,47(03):123-124+128.

[15] 郑小霞,钱锋. 高斯核支持向量机分类和模型参数选择研究[J]. 计算机工程与应用, 2006(01):77-79.

计算机视觉辅助斜拉桥索力测试试验研究

邵 帅[1] 吴 桐[2] 郭劲岑[2] 高燕梅[2] 周志祥[*2]

(1. 重庆航天职业技术学院;

2. 重庆交通大学山区桥梁及隧道工程国家重点实验室)

摘 要 拉索是缆索承重体系桥梁的关键承力或传力构件,在体系构成中的地位至关重要。为进一步提高计算机视觉通用架构下桥梁拉索非接触式测量的精度与效率,拓展其在大型基础设施复杂测试场景下的应用潜力,本文开展了计算机视觉辅助斜拉桥索力测试的试验研究;以全息视觉传感器系统获取拉索数字图像数据,分别计算解析了空间几何构型、全息模态振型、动态位移矢量等全息性态特征参数,在此基础上提出了基于动/静力学形态的拉索索力计算方法。试验结果表明:本文提出的方法可在复杂测试场景下量化分析拉索索力计算参数,相较于常规索力测试方法,最大相对误差为7.31%,均方根误差为1.79%,满足工程实践测试精度及稳定性要求,为斜拉桥索力测试提供了一种新的技术途径。

关键词 桥梁工程 索力测试 计算机视觉 桥梁拉索 空间几何构型

0 引言

我国是桥梁大国,跨江越海大型桥梁工程建设取得了举世瞩目的成就:截至2020年12月,全球在建及拟建主跨400m及以上斜拉桥共计60余座,超70%在中国;主跨300m及以上拱桥共计73座,超50%在中国;主跨500m及以上悬索桥共计107座,超40%在中国。全国300m跨径及以上的大跨径大载荷桥梁中,不低于90%的桥梁都离不开拉/吊/缆索(以下统称"缆索")作为其关键的承力或传力构件:以斜拉索的形式存在于斜拉桥结构体系,以吊杆、主缆的形式存在于悬索桥结构体系,以吊杆、系杆的形式存在于中承式或下承式拱桥结构体系,无支架缆索悬臂拼装中的扣索、猫

1. 基金项目:国家自然科学基金项目(51778094);重庆市自然科学基金面上项目(cstc2020jcyj-msxmX0062)。

道承重主索、体外预应力桥梁的体外索、转体施工中的缆索等。

近 20 年来,缆索结构健康监测与状态识别引起国内外土木工程领域专家学者们的重视。为避免缆索力学性能退化和受力状态变化导致桥梁使用性能和安全性能改变等重大安全事故的发生,结构健康监测(Structure Health Monitoring,SHM)应运而生,被用于在役桥梁拉索、主梁、主塔等关键结构构件长期性能的监测和评估,并在世界范围内实施推广。相较于工作量大、效率低、主观性强、中断交通的传统人工巡检以及常规定期检查,基于自动化监测技术和大规模接触式传感器的结构健康监测系统(Structure Health Monitoring System,SHMS)可全天候、全方位、实时连续、自动化地获取环境荷载效应与结构响应信息。但 SHMS 依赖安装在结构关键测点或关键监测区域的点式传感器,造价高、布设难度大,且仅仅以有限测点进行监测,难以掌握结构或构件的整体性能。要准确掌握结构或构件的技术状态,需要密集的传感器阵列以及严苛的布置方案,技术经济性较差。另一方面,SHMS 经过长期运行监测,采集并积累了相当数量的结构监测数据,这类数据结构形式单一、稳定性差、信息量有限。如何高效运用这类海量监测数据建立结构力学模型,以充分认知结构或构件的技术性能状态并识别可能存在的损伤,仍是限制 SHMS 发展的主要技术瓶颈。

近年来,通信领域与计算机领域的飞速发展为更经济、更便捷、更全息、更可信、更智能、更易维护、更易科学量化的可视化结构健康监测技术奠定了理论基础,使其成为现代结构全寿命周期健康监测技术领域的发展趋势。基于计算机视觉、人工智能与大数据分析的拉索状态识别、检测与长期健康监测成为该领域的研究热点与主攻技术目标,对缆索承重体系桥梁全寿命周期的整体性能进行多方面精准感知与综合健康诊断也成为保证大载荷、大跨径桥梁安全运营的科学前提。本文针对斜拉桥关键构件斜拉索开展基于计算机视觉与全息性态特征的索力状态识别研究,充分发挥计算机视觉与大数据分析在密集全场位移测量与可视化提取全息模态信息方面的优势,为拉索技术状态评估及科学维护提供科学依据与理论支撑,在工程实践中进一步提高 SHMS 的技术经济性,为斜拉桥索力测试提供一种新的技术途径。

1　计算机视觉辅助索力测试试验

1.1　试验概况

为了验证所提出的全息性态特征参数及动力测试理论在大型缆索承重体系桥梁结构位移和振动监测中的性能以及基于动/静力学形态的拉索索力计算方法,在省部共建山区桥梁及隧道工程国家重点实验室分别进行了两类计算机视觉辅助索力测试试验:全息静力形态特征参数索力测试试验与全息动力形态特征参数索力测试试验。

各类传感器布置及测试示意图如图 1 所示。试验现场布置图如图 2 所示。

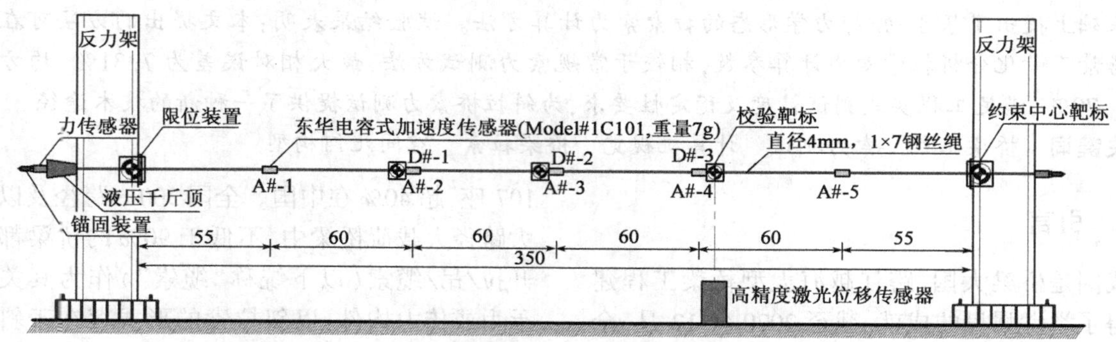

图 1　传感器布置及测试示意图

1.2　测试内容

试验工况设置如表 1 所示。受激励类型和随机数据处理(取样、记录、分析)的影响,拉索全息性态特征参数应采用多次试验结果的平均值,并将单次试验的测量值与平均值的偏差控制在一定范围内。不同测试规范对此范围有不同的取值,在本研究中,该值为 ±3%。

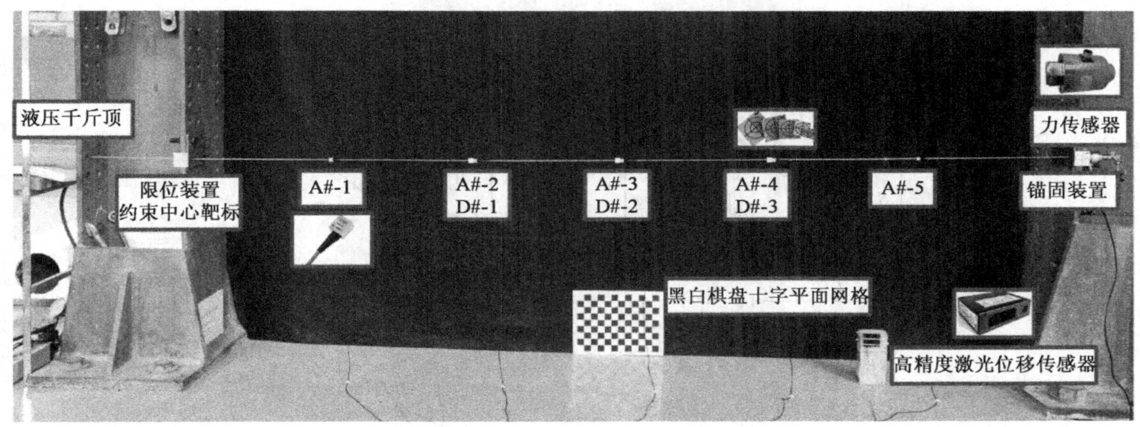

图2 试验现场布置图

试验工况及测试内容 表1

试验工况	试验变量				
	工况序号	倾斜角度	锚固端高差	拉索张力	持荷/测试时间
水平拉索	A1	0°	0cm	~1000N / ~500N	3min/120s
	A2	0°	0cm	~1500N / ~700N	3min/120s
倾斜拉索	B1	21.67°	140.6cm	~1000N / ~500N	3min/120s
	B2	21.67°	140.6cm	~1500N / ~700N	3min/120s

如图3所示,可按课题组已验证方法采用运动信号光谱分量全场光流追踪算法获取多目标特定校验靶标(D#-1、D#-2、D#-3)处拉索位移响应信号及其频谱分析。

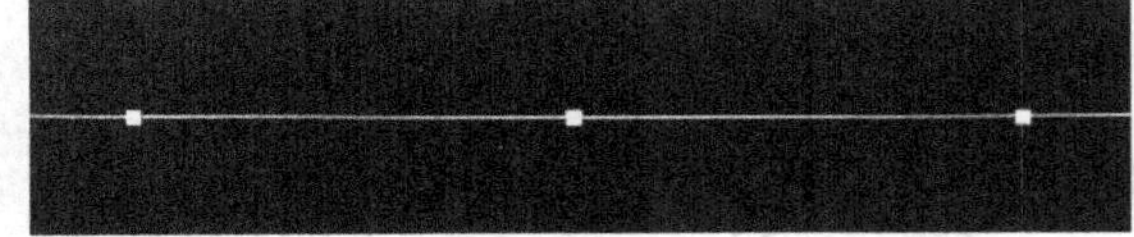

图3 运动信号光谱分量

2 索力计算方法及程序设计

2.1 索力计算原理

2.1.1 全息静力形态特征参数索力计算原理

如图4所示,根据拉索静力力学模型,可建立拉索微元在水平与竖直方向的静力平衡关系,则有考虑节段长度系数 α_1、位置偏移系数 α_2 的全息静力形态法索力计算公式:

$$T(x)=\frac{q(x'_1-x'_0)}{4\left[y(x'_1)-y(x'_0)-2y\left(\frac{x_1}{2}-\alpha_2\Delta d\right)\right]}\sqrt{\alpha_1\,(x'_1-x'_0)^2+(y(x'_1)-y(x'_0))^2} \quad (1)$$

式中,x'_0、x'_1、x_0、x_1 分别为 A、B、A'、B' 在全息视觉传感器的测量坐标系系统水平方向上的坐标。节段长度系数 α_1 表示当前视域拉索节段长度 l' 与整根拉索长度 l 在水平方向投影的比值,即 $\alpha_1=l'/l$。位置偏移系数 α_2 表示当前视域拉索节段中部位置距整根拉索中部位置的差值 Δd 与整根拉索长度 l 在水平方向投影的比值,即 $\alpha_2=\Delta d/l$。拉索节段 $A'B'$ 为整根拉索 AB 在当前视域下的长度范围节段,C 为 AB 中点,C' 为 $A'B'$ 中点,AB 在水平方向的投影长度为 l,$A'B'$ 在水平方向的投影长度为 l',当前视域拉索节段中部位置距整根拉索中部位置的差值为 Δd。

2.1.2 全息动力形态特征参数索力计算原理

如图5所示,根据拉索动力力学模型,可分别建立拉索振动的运动微分方程计算模型、拉索原索计算模型及其等效计算模型,则有带垂度修正项的振动频率法[式(2)]与全息模态振型法[式(3)]索力计算公式。

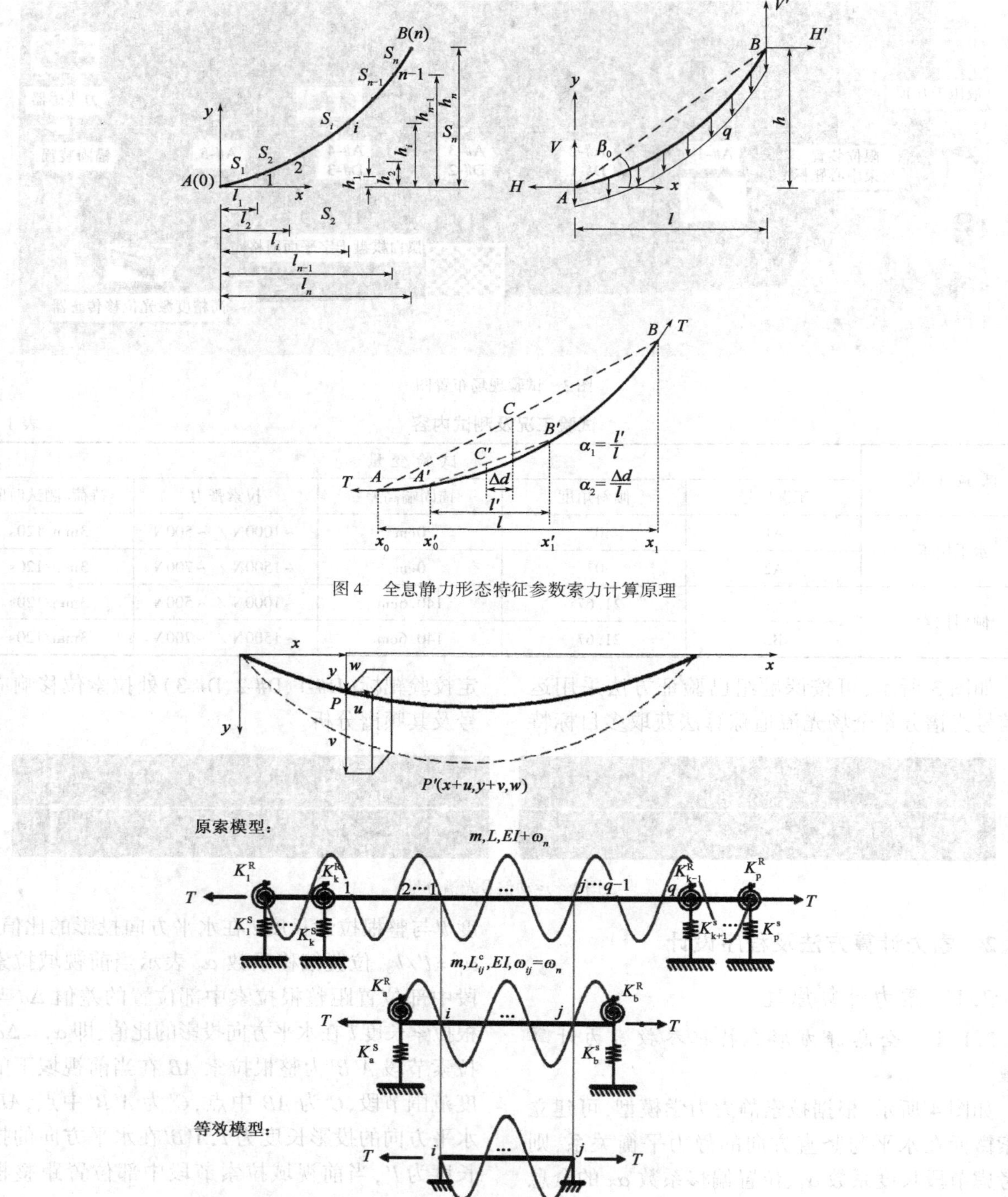

图 4　全息静力形态特征参数索力计算原理

图 5　全息动力形态特征参数索力计算原理

$$T=\frac{4\rho L^2 f_n^{\ 2}}{n^2}-\frac{n^2\pi EI}{L^2}-\frac{mgL\sin\theta}{2}\quad(n=1,2,3,\cdots\cdots)\tag{2}$$

$$T_e=\frac{mf_{ij}^{\ 2}\ (L_{ij}^e)^2}{(j-i)^2\pi^2}-\frac{\pi^2\ (j-i)^2EI}{(L_{ij}^e)^2}\tag{3}$$

式中：f_n 为拉索 n 阶自振频率，L 为拉索弦长计算长度，n 为拉索自振频率阶数，EI 为拉索抗弯刚度，ρ 为拉索线密度（若为非均匀材质，则应以单位长度的质量 m 替代 ρL），f_{ij} 为第 n 阶等效模态频率，$f_{ij}=f_n$ 为第 n 阶原索模态频率，$K_a^R=K_k^R$、$K_b^R=K_{k+1}^R$ 为等效锚固端转动约束，$K_a^S=K_k^S$、$K_b^S=K_{k+1}^S$ 为等效锚固端竖向支撑约束，L_{ij}^e 为 n 阶全息模态振型下驻点 i、j 间的计算长度。

2.2 索力计算程序设计

根据计算机视觉辅助斜拉桥索力测试原理，可得全息静/动力形态特征参数索力计算流程图，如图6、图7所示。

索力计算程序界面如图8所示。

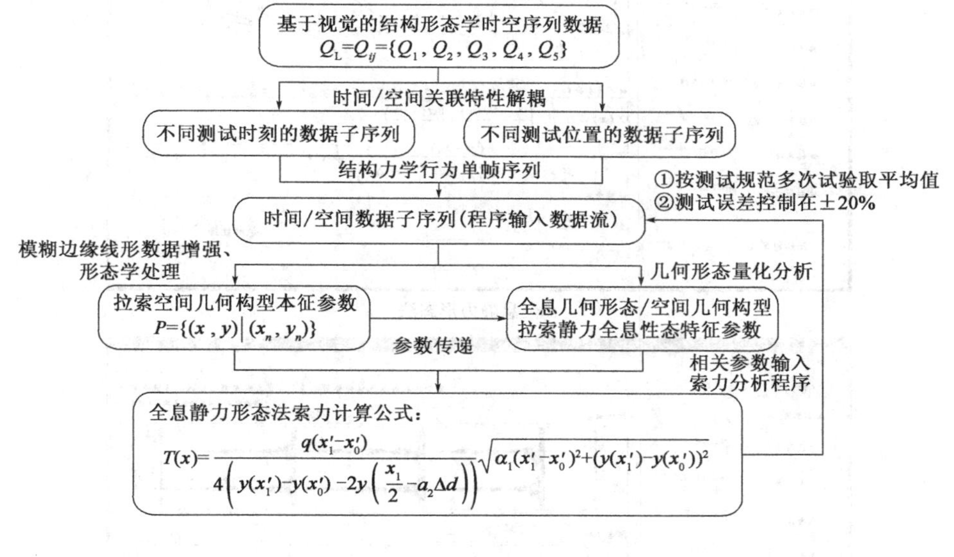

图6 全息静力形态特征参数索力计算流程

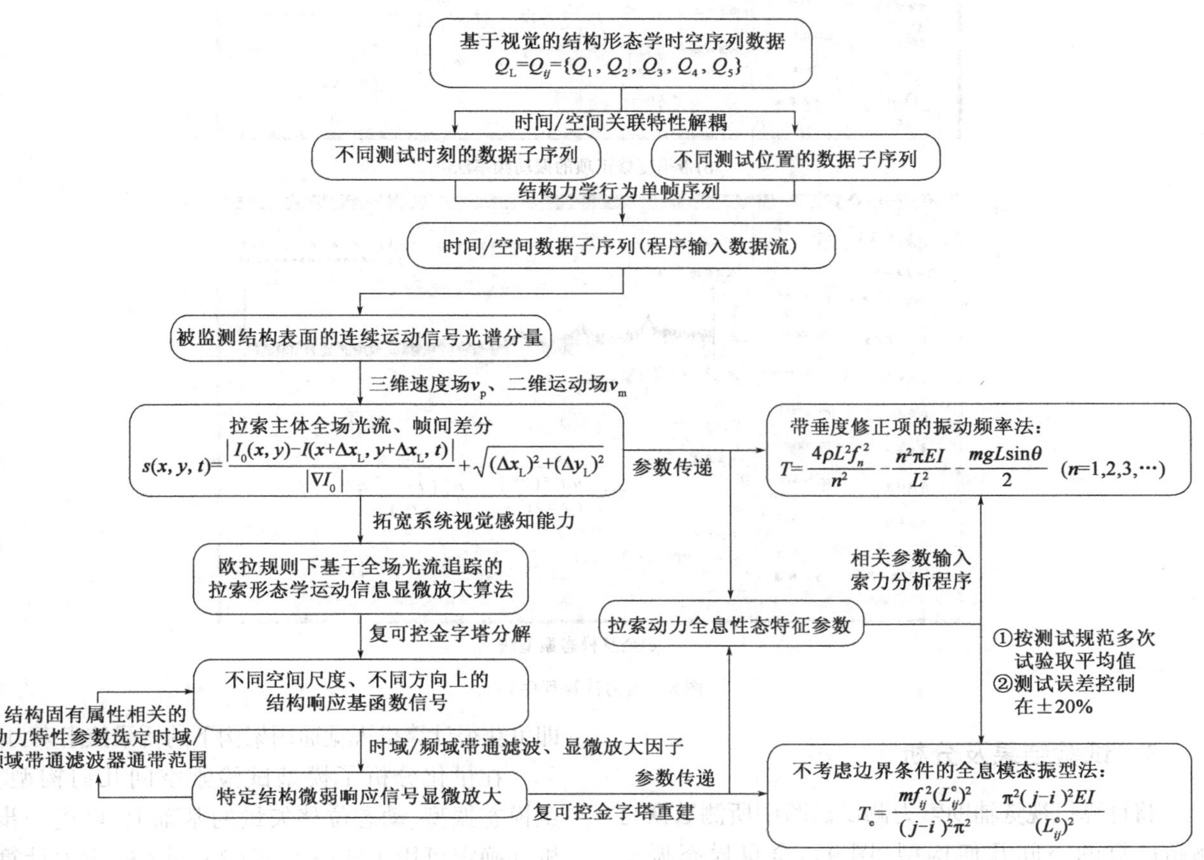

图7 全息动力形态特征参数索力计算流程

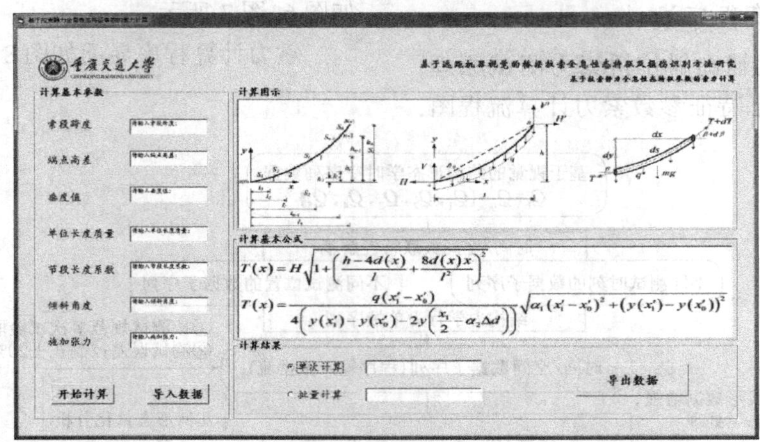

a)全息静力形态法

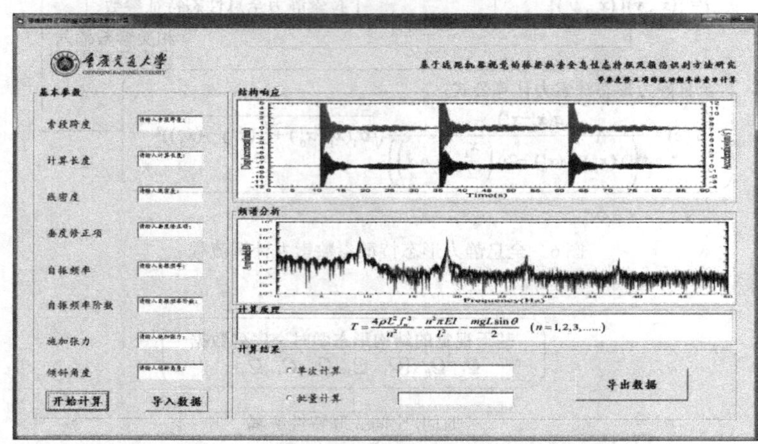

b)带垂度修正项的振动频率法

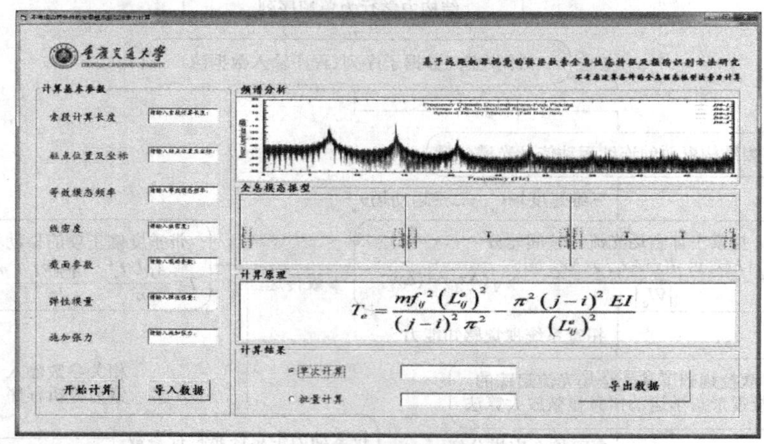

c)全息模态振型法

图 8　索力计算程序界面

3　试验结果及分析

将计算机视觉辅助索力测试试验中所测数据与解析计算的空间几何构型(图 9)、全息模态振型(图 10、图 11)、动态位移矢量(图 12)等全息性态特征参数输入或自动化读入图 8 所示的程序计算界面,即可获得计算机视觉通用架构下的桥梁拉索索力值。

在量化分析了模型试验索空间几何构型、全息模态振型、动态位移矢量的基础上,可进一步解析并确定可用于式(1)、式(2)、式(3)索力计算的测试参数,各试验工况索力计算参数与索力计算结果如表 2、表 3、表 4 所示。

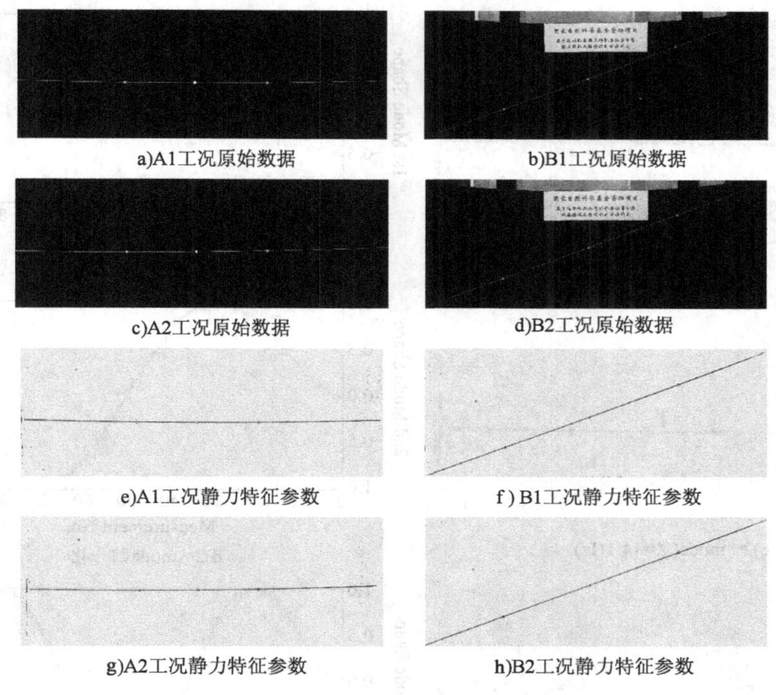

a)A1工况原始数据 b)B1工况原始数据

c)A2工况原始数据 d)B2工况原始数据

e)A1工况静力特征参数 f)B1工况静力特征参数

g)A2工况静力特征参数 h)B2工况静力特征参数

图9 空间几何构型

a)原始序列多帧信号

b)1st mode拉索本征形态数据增强(f_1=6.9Hz)，MAC=99.23

c)2nd mode拉索本征形态数据增强(f_2=14.1Hz)，MAC=98.52

d)3rd mode拉索本征形态数据增强(f_3=20.9Hz)，MAC=97.92

e)1st mode拉索全息模态运动信号光谱分量(f_1=6.9Hz)，MAC=99.23

f)2nd mode拉索本征形态数据增强(f_2=14.1Hz)，MAC=98.52

g)3rd mode拉索本征形态数据增强(f_3=20.9Hz)，MAC=97.92

图10 全息模态振型

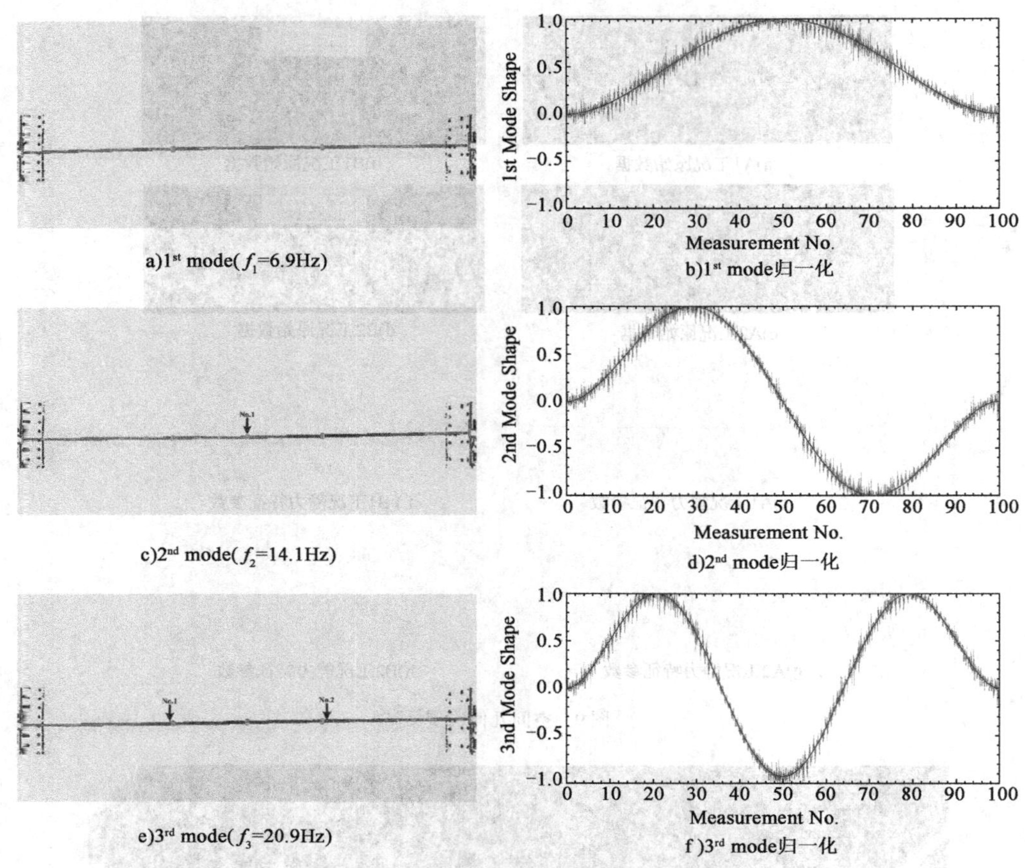

a)1st mode(f_1=6.9Hz) b)1st mode归一化

c)2nd mode(f_2=14.1Hz) d)2nd mode归一化

e)3rd mode(f_3=20.9Hz) f)3rd mode归一化

图11 振型驻点解算及驻点像素坐标

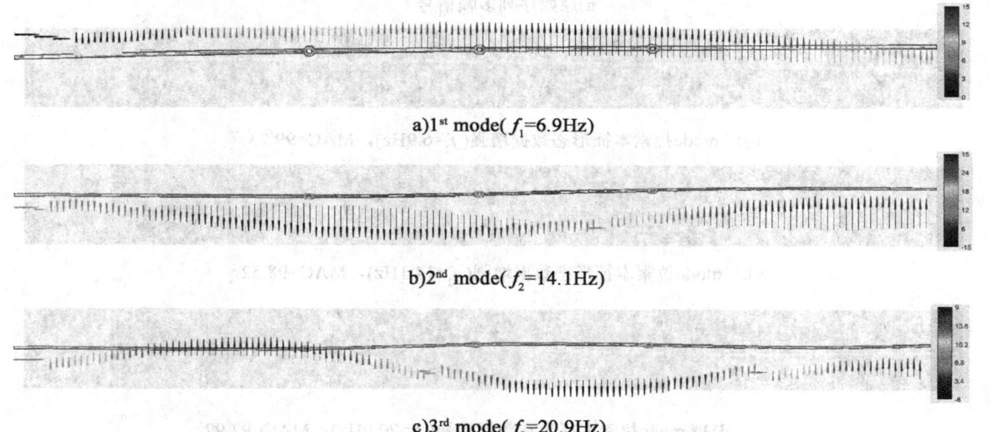

a)1st mode(f_1=6.9Hz)

b)2nd mode(f_2=14.1Hz)

c)3rd mode(f_3=20.9Hz)

图12 动态位移矢量

全息静力形态特征参数索力计算结果 表2

工况序号	像素分辨率(mm/pixel)	计算参数				
		索段跨度 l(mm)	索段高度 h(mm)	垂度值 d(mm)	施加张力/计算索力(N)	相对误差
A1	0.421	3079.2	4.2	22.57	1023.5 / 1001.0	2.20%
A2	0.437	3115.0	3.9	14.72	1523.9 / 1490.8	2.17%
B1	0.321	3085.3	1048.8	19.87	1053.6 / 1130.6	7.31%
B2	0.323	3067.1	1042.8	13.57	1645.5 / 6.93%	6.93%

全息动力形态特征参数索力计算结果　表3

试验工况	工况序号	类别	拉索振动频率索力计算结果					均值
			1st	2nd	3rd	4th	5th	
水平拉索	A1	带垂度修正项	518.3	528.9	505.6	534.6	509.3	516.9
		不带垂度修正项	515.9	526.4	503.2	532.2	506.8	519.3
		相对误差	2.43%	4.53%	0.09%	5.67%	0.64%	2.67%
		传感器索力			503.63			—
	A2	带垂度修正项	708.9	740.0	722.4	745.4	728.2	726.6
		不带垂度修正项	706.5	737.5	720.0	743.0	725.8	729.0
		相对误差	0.67%	5.09%	2.59%	5.87%	3.42%	3.53%
		传感器索力			701.79			—
倾斜拉索	B1	带垂度修正项	517.6	539.1	528.3	558.6	544.5	535.1
		不带垂度修正项	515.1	536.6	525.8	556.0	542.0	537.6
		相对误差	2.28%	6.55%	4.40%	10.41%	7.62%	6.25%
		传感器索力			503.63			—
	B2	带垂度修正项	724.2	758.7	740.4	782.5	—	748.9
		不带垂度修正项	721.7	756.2	737.9	780.0	—	751.5
		相对误差	2.84%	7.75%	5.15%	11.14%	—	6.72%
		传感器索力			701.79			—

全息动力形态特征参数索力计算结果　表4

试验工况	工况序号	类别	等效索力计算结果			索力均值及误差分析	
						视觉/传感器	相对误差
水平拉索	A1	驻点序号	$i=1$	$i=2$	$i=3$	524.0N/503.63N	4.05%
		$j=2$	528.5	—	—		
		$j=3$	524.6	515.3	—		
		$j=4$	521.9	523.4	529.9		
	A2	驻点序号	$i=1$	$i=2$	$i=3$	736.9N/701.79N	5.01%
		$j=2$	746.6	—	—		
		$j=3$	734.4	723.8	—		
		$j=4$	729.3	736.6	750.1		
倾斜拉索	B1	驻点序号	$i=1$	$i=2$	$i=3$	521.8N/504.32N	3.47%
		$j=2$	524.0	—	—		
		$j=3$	524.5	514.4	—		
		$j=4$	521.5	518.9	527.5		
	B2	驻点序号	$i=1$	$i=2$	$i=3$	740.0N/708.49N	4.45%
		$j=2$	752.4	—	—		
		$j=3$	736.1	728.3	—		
		$j=4$	730.5	737.5	755.3		

综上所述，①全息动力形态特征参数索力计算结果间不存在明显差异，趋势相同且稳定，最大相对误差7.31%，验证了基于拉索静力全息性态特征参数的索力估计方法的有效性与稳定性，满足工程实践测试精度及稳定性要求，但不同索段跨度对最终计算出的索力值的精度有较大影响，

较小的索段跨度包含的拉索静力全息性态特征参数信息比较大的索段跨度少,各本征参数点集 P 之间空间几何形态变化接近,偏移较小,容易导致较大测量误差(>20%)。在大型缆索承载体系桥梁现场测试过程中,应根据测试场景及条件应,在满足视域范围及控制要求的前提下尽可能选择较长的索段跨度(如硬件条件允许可针对整个空间几何构型进行全息测试),以反映拉索当前状态信息,保证静力全息测试的精度。②全息动力形态特征参数索力计算结果间不存在明显差异,趋势相同且稳定,最大相对误差6.72%,验证了基于拉索动力全息性态特征参数的索力估计方法的有效性与稳定性,满足工程实践测试精度及稳定性要求,但带垂度修正项的振动频率在本研究的试验中效果不明显。现有索力测试方法受限于传感器数量以及布置方式,较难得到准确的高阶模态信息,易出现较大的误差,且不能简单通过增加传感器数量和减小布置间距来提高精度,因为在实际工程的检测/监测过程中,布置传感器是不便捷甚至是不现实的。

4 结语

针对桥梁拉索(群)的非接触、高效快速测试,本文在计算机视觉通用架构下,开展了计算机视觉辅助斜拉桥索力测试的试验研究,通过解析拉索的静力与动力全息性态参数特征,提出了基于动/静力学形态的拉索索力计算方法,揭示了全息性态特征参数与索力状态特性间的内禀关联机制,可有效解决空间几何构型的测算较为复杂且技术经济性不佳以及动力测试结果易受拉索垂度、刚度、边界条件、温度、梁体振动等因素影响的问题。基于全息动静影像采集装置的索力测试所进行的密集多点以及全息测量,在数据体量与全息测试方面可有效综合多种模态计算分析方法获取拉索精准模态信息,充分发挥了拉索全息性态特征参数在快速、便捷、高效索力测试中的优势,是对现有索力测试理论的扩展与延伸,对索力的精细化计算分析具有积极意义,在工程实践中具有广阔应用前景。

参考文献

[1]《中国公路学报》编辑部.中国桥梁工程学术研究综述·2021[J].中国公路学报,2021,34(2):1-97.

[2] 孙利民,尚志强,夏烨.大数据背景下的桥梁结构健康监测研究现状与展望[J].中国公路学报,2019,32(11):1-20.

[3] 叶肖伟,董传智.基于计算机视觉的结构位移监测综述[J].中国公路学报,2019,32(11):21-39.

[4] D M Feng, M Q Feng. Computer vision for SHM of civil infrastructure: From dynamic response measurement to damage detection-A review[J]. Eng. Struct. 2018,156:105-117.

[5] Billie F Spencer Jr, Vedhus Hoskere, Yasutaka Narazaki. Advances in Computer Vision-Based Civil Infrastructure Inspection and Monitoring [J]. Engineering, 2019, 5:199-222.

[6] 邵帅,周志祥,邓国军,等.基于非接触远程智能感知的桥梁形态监测试验[J].中国公路学报,2019,32(11):91-102.

[7] 鲍跃全,李惠.人工智能时代的土木工程[J].土木工程学报,2019,52(5):5-15.

[8] Xu Y, Brownjohn JMW. Review of machine-vision based methodologies for displacement measurement in civil structures [J]. J. Civ. Struct. Heal. Monit., 2018, 8:91-110.

[9] X. W. Ye, C. Z. Dong, T. Liu. Force monitoring of steel cables using vision-based sensing technology: methodology and experimental verification [J]. Smart Struct. Syst., 2016, 18 (3):585-599.

[10] D. Feng, T. Scarangello, M. Q. Feng, et al. Cable tension force estimate using novel noncontact vision-based sensor [J], Measurement, 2017, 99:44-52.

[11] Dan D H, Ge L F, Yan X F. Identification of moving loads based on the information fusion of weigh-in-motion system and multiple camera machine vision [J]. Measurement, 2019, 144:155-166.

[12] Shuai Shao, Zhixiang Zhou, Guojun Deng, et al. Experiment of Structural Geometric Morphology Monitoring for Bridges Using Holographic Visual Sensor[J]. Sensors, 2020, 20:1187.

[13] Zhixiang Zhou, Shuai Shao, Guojun Deng, et al.

Vision-based modal parameter identification for bridges using a novel holographic visual sensor [J]. Measurement, 2021, 179: 1095.

[14] Guojun Deng, Zhixiang Zhou, Shuai Shao, et al. Novel approach to extract dense full-field dynamic parameters of large-scale bridges using spatial sequence video [J]. Journal of Civil Engineering and Management, 2021, 27 (8): 617-636.

[15] Tong Wu, Liang Tang, Peng Du, et al. Non-contact measurement method of beam vibration with laser stripe tracking based on tilt photography [J]. Measurement, 2022, 18: 110314

[16] Irvine H M. Cable Structures [M]. Ist ed. Cambridge, Mass: MIT Press, 1981.

[17] Banfu Yan, Wenbing Chen, Jiayong Yu, et al. Mode shape-aided tension force estimation of cable with arbitrary boundary conditions [J]. Journal of Sound and Vibration, 2019, 440 (3): 315-331.

曲线连续刚构桥抗震分析

杨元浩 周 敉* 申心力

(长安大学旧桥检测与加固技术交通行业重点实验室)

摘 要 为研究曲线连续刚构桥在地震作用下的性能以及过渡墩支座的受力特点,以白涧河大桥连续刚构为研究对象,使用通用有限元分析软件 CSI Bridge 建立全桥模型,仅考虑 E2 地震作用,采用时程分析法对其桥墩和支座进行验算。结果表明,该曲线连续刚构桥主墩左右两肢内力值相差较大,恒载弯矩的差别最明显。经验算该桥满足 B 类桥梁对应的抗震设防要求。在 E2 地震作用下,过渡墩的固定支座被剪坏,宜将其更换为减隔震支座。

关键词 曲线刚构桥 地震响应 时程分析 支座 有限元模型

0 引言

预应力混凝土连续刚构桥(Prestressed Concrete Continuous Beam Rigid-frame Bridges, PC CBRB),具有较大的纵向和横向刚度,受力性能好,跨越能力大,已成为大跨径梁式桥的主要桥型[1]。近年来,随着我国交通网络的发展,跨越复杂地形、峡谷与河流等的桥梁比重日益增加,连续刚构桥得到广泛应用,其中包括较多的百米高墩大跨情况,且在高地震烈度区占较大比重[2-4]。因此连续刚构桥在震区的表现一直是学者们研究的热点。

杜桃明等[5]研究了高烈度地区不对称刚构-连续梁桥减隔震设计。余孝穷等[6]分析了承台结构形式对分幅连续刚构桥地震响应的影响。周萍[7]研究了桩—土相互作用对高墩连续刚构桥的抗震性能的影响。刘林等[8]对高墩大跨连续刚构的抗震措施进行了一系列研究。郝晓光等[9]对超高墩大跨度刚构—连续梁桥抗震性能进行研究,结果表明设置黏滞阻尼器可有效减小墩弯矩和梁端的纵向地震位移。蒋建军等[10]对大跨连续刚构桥箱梁减震措施进行研究,研究结果表明在辅助墩、交界墩或桥台处设置高阻尼隔震橡胶支座,可以减小箱梁和主墩受力。周敉等[11]对地震下大跨径连续刚构桥合理约束体系进行研究,结果表明,对于所研究的主跨大于 150m 的大跨径连续刚构桥,在过渡墩处设置拉索钢阻尼减震支座和黏滞阻尼器组合体系是最合适的约束体系。近年

1. 基金项目:陕西省重点研发计划项目(2019KW-051);陕西省创新人才推进计划科技创新团队(2018TD-040);国家自然科学基金资助项目(51978062);陕西省自然科学基础研究计划项目联合基金项(2021JLM-47):大跨度、大流量、多塔斜拉压力输水管桥关键技术研究(Program No. 2021JLM-47)资助。

来针对连续刚构抗震表现的研究较多,但针对曲线刚构桥的相关研究较少。

本文以白涧河大桥曲线连续刚构桥为研究对象,采用非线性时程分析的方法,对其桥墩及支座进行了验算。计算结果可为同等跨径的曲线刚构桥抗震设计及支座选用提供参考。

1　工程概况及计算模型

1.1　工程概况

白涧河大桥为济晋高速公路上最长、最高的桥梁,立面布置如图 1 所示。平面位于 $R = 1225\text{m}$ 的圆曲线上,超高横坡度为 2%。主桥上部结构为 75m + 2 × 135m + 75m 连续刚构,下部结构为双薄壁空心墩,最大墩高 104m。

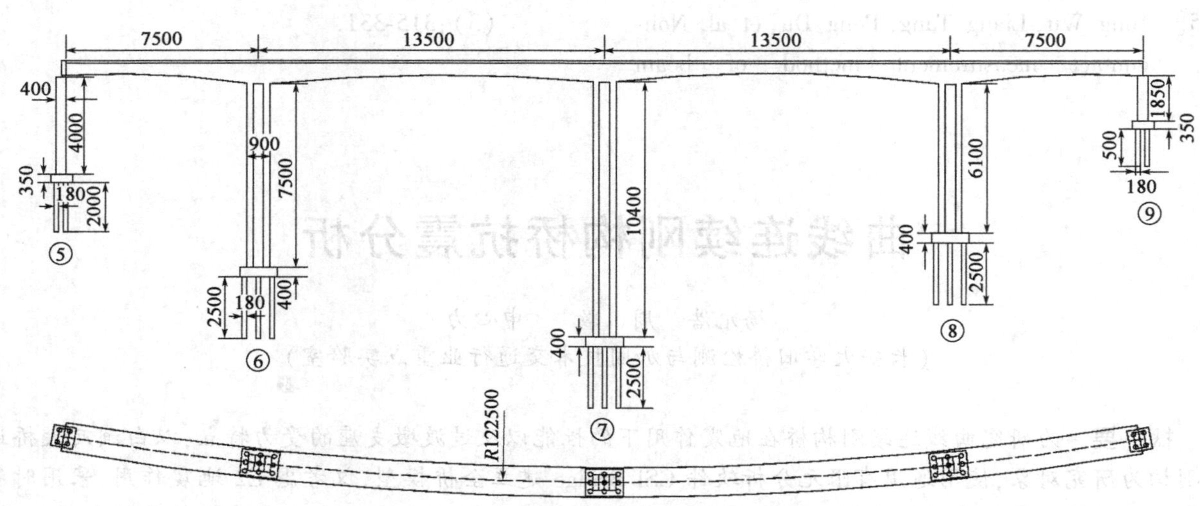

图 1　桥梁总体布置(尺寸单位:cm)

1.2　有限元模型

采用通用有限元分析软件 CSI Bridge 建立全桥模型,计算模型的梁体和墩柱采用空间梁单元模拟,二期铺装采用线荷载和面荷载进行模拟;混凝土结构的阻尼比取 0.05,进行时程分析时,采用瑞利阻尼;桥梁采用桩柱式基础,根据桥址区地质分层情况及砂土液化,采用分层土弹簧模型对桩基进行土层作用力模拟,每隔 1m 施加一个土弹簧,土层 m 值按照地勘报告中的建议值表取值。全桥有限元模型如图 2 所示。

1.3　动力特性

桥梁结构动力计算模型应能正确反映桥梁上部结构、下部结构、支座和地基的刚度、质量分布及阻尼特性,从而保证在 E1 和 E2 地震作用下引起的惯性力和主要振型得到反映。通过 CSI Bridge 模型可知该桥前 5 阶动力特性如表 1 所示。

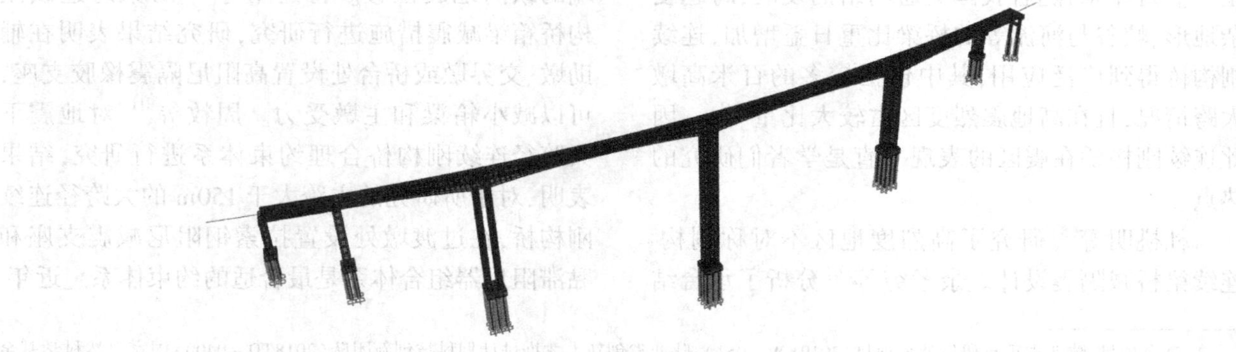

图 2　有限元模型

前 5 阶自振特性列表 表 1

阶　次	周期(s)	频率(Hz)	振 型 特 点
1	4.849335	0.206214	桥墩一阶侧弯
2	4.279039	0.233697	主梁一阶纵漂
3	2.59511	0.38534	桥墩反对称侧弯
4	1.697473	0.589111	引桥桥墩侧弯
5	1.361125	0.734686	引桥主梁纵漂

2　地震动参数

这里仅考虑 E2 地震作用,图 3 为《太澳高速公路济源至晋城段工程场地地震安全性评价报告》提供的反应谱曲线转化而来的 E2 地震动输入情况下的加速度时程曲线,共 3 条,用于本桥非线性时程分析。采用“顺桥向加竖向”和“横桥向加竖向”的加载方式进行计算。其中顺桥向指主桥起终点连线方向,横桥向指垂直主桥起终点连线方向。

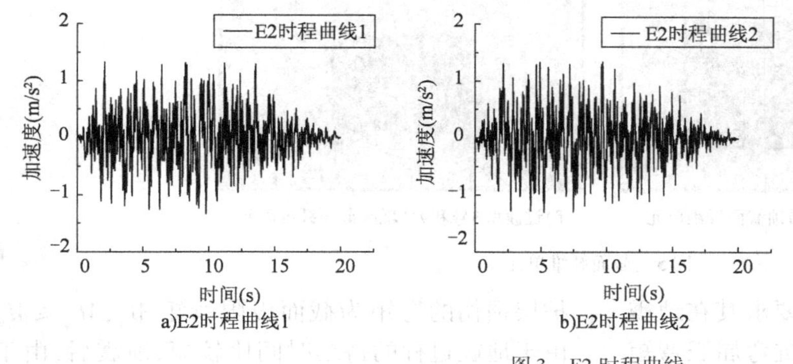

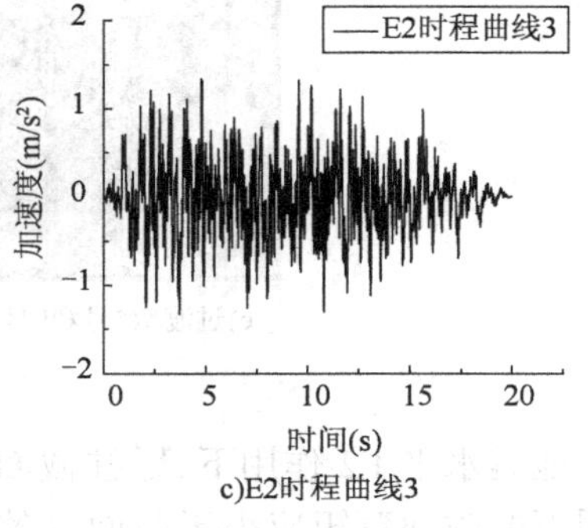

图 3　E2 时程曲线

3　E2 地震作用下墩柱验算

3.1　截面验算原则与方法

3.1.1　验算原则

在设计阶段,根据主墩、过渡墩等重要结构的截面详细配筋图,需要对关键截面、各桥墩墩底墩顶进行验算。钢筋混凝土桥墩的抗弯能力(强度)采用纤维单元进行弯矩-曲率(考虑相应轴力)分析获得,如图 4 所示。

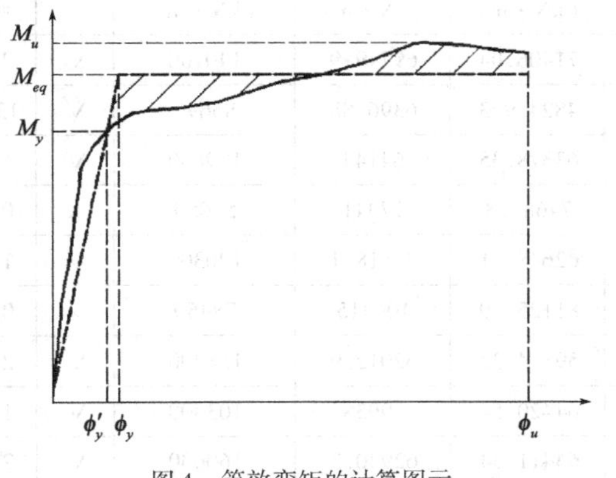

图 4　等效弯矩的计算图示

截面等效抗弯强度实质上是一个理论上的概念值,是将实际的截面弯矩-曲率曲线按能量等效的原则将其等效为一个弹塑性曲线。中间的等效抗弯强度 M_{eq} 计算规则如图 4,由阴影部分面积相等求得。其中 M_y 为截面相应于最不利轴力时最外层钢筋首次屈服时对应的初始屈服弯矩;M_{eq} 为相应于最不利轴力时截面等效抗弯屈服弯矩;M_u 为截面极限弯矩。

对于各验算截面中相应的材料强度均选取实测值。同时,不再考虑材料的安全分项系数。

3.1.2　验算方法

根据前述对桥梁抗震性能的要求,采用如下方法对关键截面进行抗震性能验算,墩柱关键截面的具体验算方法及过程如下:

首先,将桥墩截面划分为纤维单元(图 5),在划分纤维单元时,混凝土和钢筋单元分别划分,钢筋和混凝土单元分别采用实际的钢筋和混凝土应力—应变关系。利用实际的钢筋和混凝土应力—应变关系,采用截面数值积分法进行弯矩-曲率分析(考虑响应轴力),得到图 4 所示弯矩-曲率曲线。

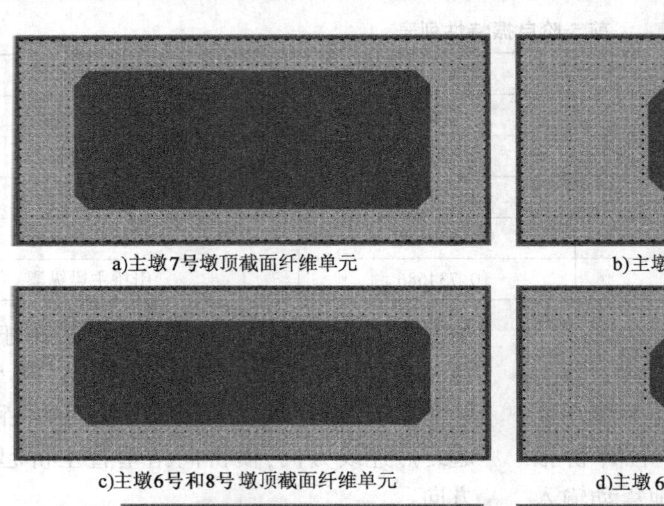

a)主墩7号墩顶截面纤维单元

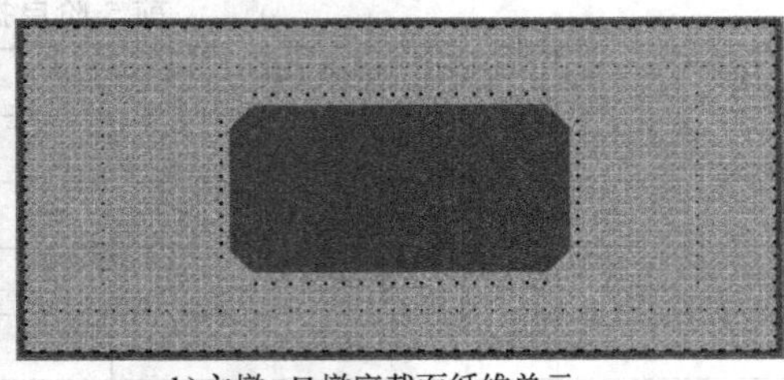

b)主墩7号墩底截面纤维单元

c)主墩6号和8号墩顶截面纤维单元

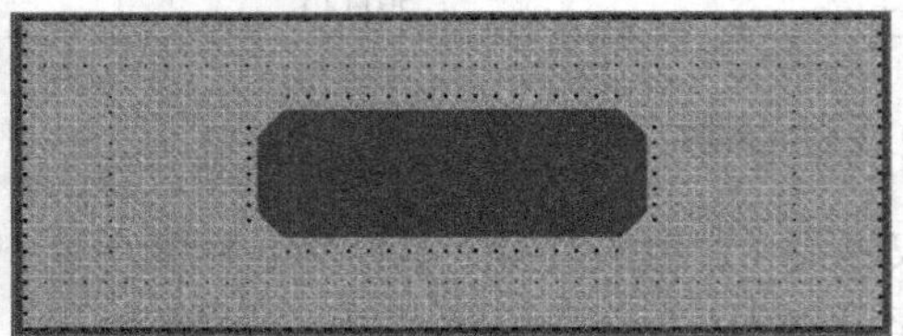

d)主墩6号和8号墩底截面纤维单元

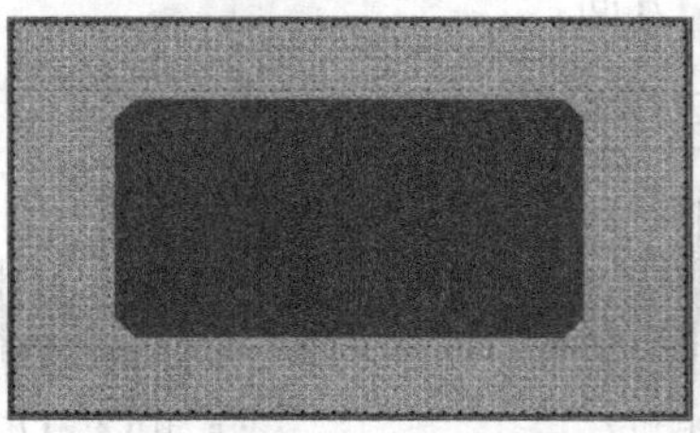

e)过渡墩5号和9号墩顶截面纤维单元

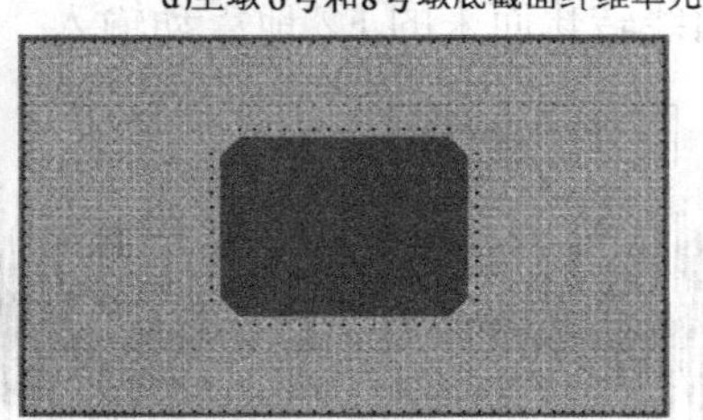

f)过渡墩5号和9号墩底截面纤维单元

图5　截面纤维单元

地震水平E2作用下,墩柱截面要求其在地震作用下的截面弯矩应小于截面等效抗弯屈服弯矩M_{eq}(考虑轴力)。M_{eq}是把实际弯矩-曲率曲线等效为图4中所示理想弹塑性双线性模型时的得到等效抗弯屈服弯矩。从理想弹塑性双线性模型看,当地震反应小于等效抗弯屈服弯矩M_{eq}时,结构整体反应还在弹性范围。实际上,在地震过程中,对应于等效抗弯屈服弯矩M_{eq},截面上还是有部分钢筋进入了屈服。研究表明:截面的裂缝宽度可能会超过容许值,但混凝土保护层还是完好(对应保护层损伤的弯矩为截面极限弯矩M_u,$M_{eq} \leq M_u$)。由于地震过程的持续时间比较短,地震后,由于结构自重,地震过程开展的裂缝一般可以闭合,不影响使用,满足地震水平E2作用下局部可发生可修复的损伤,地震发生后,基本不影响车辆通行的性能要求。

3.2　桥墩验算

对桥墩截面抗弯强度进行了校核,结果如表2和表3所示。

桥墩截面抗弯强度校核(E2顺桥向+竖向)　　表2

桥墩号	位置	恒载轴力(kN)	地震轴力(kN)	组合轴力恒-动(kN)	恒载弯矩(kN·m)	地震弯矩(kN·m)	组合弯矩(kN·m)	等效屈服弯矩(kN·m)	检验	能力/需求
5	墩底	22635.99	-2579.43	25215.417	-1656.17	71406.04	69749.9	140100	√	2.00
	墩顶	7808.19	2110.135	5698.055	1571.91	4824.973	6396.88	85690	√	13.39
6	左墩底	41061.79	7010.155	34051.635	765.61	63378.35	64144	109800	√	1.71
	左墩顶	21106.27	11900.73	9205.541	2656.16	74684.8	77341	58050	×	0.75
	右墩底	53102.16	8561.677	44540.483	14470.02	62648.11	77118.1	120300	√	1.55
	右墩顶	33146.64	5065.928	28080.712	25289.44	81125.59	106415	78450	×	0.73
7	左墩底	58278	9235.63	49042.37	2178.61	59834.33	62012.9	158200	√	2.55
	左墩顶	28570.13	10197.49	18372.638	35517.42	64420.54	99938	103800	√	1.03
	右墩底	55699.54	4700.289	50999.251	-1471.02	64411.34	62940.3	160600	√	2.55
	右墩顶	27452.63	4605.578	22847.052	37736.11	61691.94	99428.1	109800	√	1.10

续上表

桥墩号	位置	恒载轴力(kN)	地震轴力(kN)	组合轴力恒-动(kN)	恒载弯矩(kN·m)	地震弯矩(kN·m)	组合弯矩(kN·m)	等效屈服弯矩(kN·m)	检验	能力/需求
8	左墩底	49782.42	14428.34	35354.082	16125.94	67980.08	84106	111100	√	1.32
	左墩顶	33386.82	4070.85	29315.97	28535.78	68525.82	97061.6	79760	×	0.82
	右墩底	37243.19	21710.65	15532.542	2954.52	75428.67	78383.2	90570	√	1.15
	右墩顶	20847.59	5870.615	14976.975	5966.34	69753.25	75719.6	64380	×	0.85
9	墩底	15135.72	-4934.96	20070.682	1646.31	48739.79	50386.1	131200	√	2.60
	墩顶	7830.76	1716.488	6114.272	1551.77	5384.672	6936.44	86450	√	12.46

桥墩截面抗弯强度校核(E2横桥向+竖向) 表3

桥墩号	位置	恒载轴力(kN)	地震轴力(kN)	组合轴力恒-动(kN)	恒载弯矩(kN·m)	地震弯矩(kN·m)	组合弯矩(kN·m)	等效屈服弯矩(kN·m)	检验	能力/需求
5	墩底	22635.99	-241.486	22877.476	650.74	172323	172974	218200	√	1.26
	墩顶	7808.19	346.482	7461.708	1084.23	32787.79	33872	142700	√	4.21
6	左墩底	41061.79	5896.273	35165.517	8027.63	98984.32	107012	273500	√	2.55
	左墩顶	21106.27	-4198.42	25304.691	10487.06	38037.12	48524.2	175400	√	3.61
	右墩底	53102.16	5455.458	47646.702	-7465.68	121574	114108	304100	√	2.66
	右墩顶	33146.64	3488.132	29658.508	10609.53	30977.56	41587.1	187500	√	4.50
7	左墩底	58278	2202.029	56075.971	11256.66	145854.2	157111	345800	√	2.20
	左墩顶	28570.13	-1465.95	30036.077	11110.52	34549.8	45660.3	248200	√	5.43
	右墩底	55699.54	2352.8	53346.74	11480.74	135920.8	147402	339000	√	2.29
	右墩顶	27452.63	-2687.52	30140.148	10968.85	31179.1	42147.9	248400	√	5.89
8	左墩底	49782.42	-1404.15	51186.565	7470.94	125395	132866	312600	√	2.35
	左墩顶	33386.82	-355.971	33742.791	10612.38	22755.5	33367.9	198700	√	5.95
	右墩底	37243.19	6010.146	31233.044	8258.69	108674.6	116933	263800	√	2.25
	右墩顶	20847.59	7429.03	13418.56	10388.45	34306.33	44694.8	141900	√	3.17
9	墩底	15135.72	159.593	14976.127	-619.85	192373.8	191754	196000	√	1.02
	墩顶	7830.76	1349.375	6481.385	1106.21	29659.05	30765.3	139700	√	4.54

3.3 主桥6号~8号墩顶位移验算

该桥为B类桥梁,E2地震作用下,允许墩柱进入塑性。因此在原有模型基础上,对主墩截面抗弯刚度进行折减,采用有效截面抗弯刚度,然后利用有限元分析模型计算E2地震作用下墩顶位移最大值;并对该桥主桥模型采用Pushover分析,得到其墩柱屈服位移进而计算位移延性系数,经计算,其位移延性系数均满足安全要求。

图6为Pushover分析模型,将引桥结构删除并转化为荷载施加在过渡墩5号和9号,对主墩6号、7号和8号分别进行推导分析,表4为墩位位移验算结果。

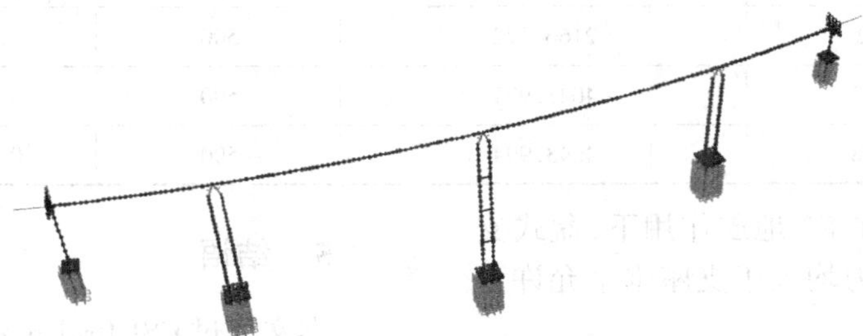

图6 空间动力计算模型图

E2 地震作用下主墩位移验算　表4

墩号	6		7		8	
位置	左肢	右肢	左肢	右肢	左肢	右肢
屈服位移(m)	0.43153	0.50353	0.88324	0.613241	0.290304	0.207504
E2 地震位移(m)	0.200656	0.200667	0.189955	0.189847	0.185722	0.185726
位移延性系数	0.464987	0.39852	0.215066	0.30958	0.63975	0.895048

4　E2 地震下支座验算

4.1　盆式支座活动方向位移验算

按照《公路桥梁抗震设计规范》7.5.2 要求，B 类及 C 类桥在 E2 作用下盆式支座的抗震位移验算应符合下列要求。

$$X_B \leqslant X_{max} \tag{1}$$

$$X_B = X_D + X_H + 0.5X_T \tag{2}$$

式中：X_{max}——活动支座容许滑动水平位移(m)；

X_B——E2 地震作用效应、永久作用效应以及均匀温度作用效应作用组合后的支座滑动水平位移(m)；

X_D——支座水平地震设计力产生的支座水平位移(m)；

X_H——永久作用产生的支座的水平位移(m)；

X_T——均匀温度作用引起的支座的水平位移(m)。

验算结果如表5所示。

盆式支座位移验算(mm)　表5

桥墩号	支座号	E2 地震下 X 向位移	容许位移	能力比	检验
5#	91	195.504	200	1.023	√
	92	194.446	200	1.02856	√
9#	107	159.704	200	1.25232	√
	108	160.657	200	1.24489	√

根据以上计算，不考虑温度作用带来的支座位移，白涧河大桥的盆式支座在 E2 地震作用下位移均小于容许滑动位移。满足规范要求。

4.2　盆式支座固定方向受力验算

按照《公路桥梁抗震设计规范》7.5.2 要求，B 类及 C 类桥在 E2 作用下盆式支座的固定方向上的受力验算应符合下列要求。

$$E_{hzh} \leqslant E_{max} \tag{3}$$

$$E_{hzh} = E_{hze} + E_{hzd} + 0.5E_{hzT} \tag{4}$$

式中：E_{max}——固定支座容许承受的水平力(kN)；

E_{hzh}——E2 地震作用效应、永久作用效应以及均匀温度作用效应作用组合后的固定支座水平力设计值(kN)；

E_{hze}——支座水平地震设计力(kN)；

E_{hzd}——永久作用产生的支座的水平力(kN)；

E_{hzT}——均匀温度作用引起的橡胶支座的水平力(kN)。

验算结果如表6所示。

盆式支座横桥向水平力验算(kN)　表6

桥墩号	支座号	E2 地震下 Y 向剪力	支座剪力能力值	能力比	检验
5#	91	2166.174	500	0.23082	×
	92	2166.172	500	0.23082	×
9#	107	4043.991	500	0.12364	×
	108	4043.994	500	0.12364	×

由以上计算可得，在 E2 地震作用下，盆式支座固定方向所受的地震力均大于支座水平允许水平力，支座被剪坏。

5　结语

本文通过 CSI Bridge 有限元软件，采用非线性

时程法对该曲线刚构桥的桥墩及支座进行了验算,得出了以下结论:

(1)该曲线连续刚构桥,各主墩的左右两肢在恒载作用及地震作用下,内力均有明显差别,其中两肢的恒载弯矩差别最大。

(2)E2 地震作用下,除 6 号和 8 号墩顶截面外所有墩柱最不利截面地震弯矩小于其等效屈服弯矩,截面未进入塑性状态,均满足规范要求。对于 6 号和 8 号墩,E2 地震作用下强度验算虽不满足要求,但经 Pushover 分析可得 E2 地震作用下,其墩顶位移延性系数均小于规范要求,因此 6 号 8 号墩顶虽进入塑性,但结构依然安全。

(3)对于该曲线刚构桥,在 E2 地震作用下,过渡墩上固定支座的水平力超过其容许水平力,盆式支座被剪坏,从而丧失其功能,破坏传力路径。对于同等跨径相似曲率半径的曲线刚构桥宜在过渡墩上设置减隔震支座。

参考文献

[1] 王东升,童磊,王荣霞,孙治国. 大跨 PC 连续刚构桥抗震研究进展综述[J/OL]. 西南交通大学学报:1-16.

[2] Yuancheng Peng, Zixiang Zhang. Development of a Novel Type of Open-Web Continuous Reinforced-Concrete Rigid-Frame Bridge [J]. Journal of Bridge Engineering, 2020, 25 (8): 05020005-05020005.

[3] 石岩,熊利军,李军,等. 考虑内力状态的连续刚构桥典型施工阶段地震易损性分析[J]. 振动与冲击,2021,40(24):136-143 + 179.

[4] Wang H L, Xie C L, Liu D, et al. Continuous reinforced concrete rigid-frame bridges in China [J]. Pract Period Struct Des Constr, 2019, 24 (2):05019002.

[5] 杜桃明,叶仲韬,刘洋,等. 高烈度地区不对称刚构-连续梁桥减隔震设计研究[J]. 世界桥梁,2021,49(03):78-83.

[6] 余孝穷,郭炎峰,等. 承台结构形式对分幅连续刚构桥地震响应的影响研究[J]. 世界桥梁,2021,49(02):57-63.

[7] 周萍. 考虑桩-土相互作用对高墩连续刚构桥的抗震性能分析[J]. 交通世界,2021(28):105-106. DOI:10. 16248/j. cnki. 11-3723/u. 2021. 28. 050.

[8] 刘林,李智宇,袁广学. 高墩大跨连续刚构的抗震措施研究[J]. 公路,2021,66(02):174-177.

[9] 郝晓光,杨未蓬,唐辉. 超高墩大跨度刚构-连续梁桥抗震性能研究[J]. 世界桥梁,2020,48(04):35-39.

[10] 蒋建军,郑万山,唐光武,等. 大跨连续刚构桥箱梁抗震分析与减震措施研究[J]. 公路工程,2020,45(02):28-33. DOI:10. 19782/j. cnki. 1674-0610. 2020. 02. 005.

[11] 周敉,朱国强,吴江,卢伟,刘平均. 地震下大跨径连续刚构桥合理约束体系研究[J]. 振动与冲击,2019,38(10):98-104. DOI:10. 13465/j. cnki. jvs. 2019. 10. 015.

高烈度区中小跨径城市矮墩高架桥梁地震响应分析

刘旭奇　周　敉*　申心力

(长安大学旧桥检测与加固技术交通行业重点实验室)

摘　要　为研究地震作用下高烈度区中小跨径城市矮墩高架桥梁的地震响应,进行延性设计和减隔

1. 基金项目:陕西省重点研发计划项目(2019KW-051);陕西省创新人才推进计划-科技创新团队(2018TD-040);国家自然科学基金资助项目(51978062);陕西省自然科学基础研究计划项目-联合基金项目(2021JLM-47):大跨度、大流量、多塔斜拉压力输水管桥关键技术研究(Program No. 2021JLM-47)资助。

震设计并设置防屈曲支撑进行地震响应分析,结合某 3×30m 矮墩城市高架桥梁,使用有限元软件 CSI Bridge 建立全桥模型,采用非线性时程分析方法,对比分析了不同体系下及设置防屈曲支撑时桥墩和基础的内力响应。结果表明:对于本文所研究的矮墩城市高架桥梁,减隔震设计的内力响应均远小于延性设计,利于抗震,但设置防屈曲支撑减震效果并不明显。该研究可为同类型桥梁的抗震设计提供参考。

关键词　桥梁工程　桥梁抗震　非线性　城市高架　矮墩　抗震体系　防屈曲支撑

0　引言

随着交通建设的发展,越来越多的城市桥梁应运而生。由于城市桥梁承担着城市间交通运输及震后救灾工作,因此对于城市桥梁抗震性能的研究是重中之重。然而相较于大跨径桥梁,一般跨径的城市桥梁抗震设计方法研究比选较少[1]。

尹臻[2]以某机场高速为研究对象,对高烈度区大跨连续梁结构采用延性抗震设计方法,进行地震反应分析与验算。郭良等[3]以某城市高架桥六车道主线模型及匝道桥模型为研究对象,分别采用减隔震设计和延性抗震设计进行分析。闫鹏[4]以一座城市大跨矮墩桥梁为例,采用反应谱法计算结构地震响应,并进行了抗震性能验算。贾奋宗[5]以某全互通立交主线高架桥梁引桥为背景,采用 Midas 软件对双柱墩连续梁桥进行抗震分析。但目前对于下部结构为矮墩,且位于高烈度区的中小跨径城市桥梁的地震响应分析较少。

防屈曲支撑(Buckling-Restrained Braces, BRB)由于耗能优越、造价低、易于安装,在桥梁与结构工程抗震设计颇受青睐[6]。Joel Lanning 等[7]研究探讨了使用防屈曲支撑减轻大跨度桥梁地震响应的可行性。Yuandong Wang 等[8]研究了使用防屈曲支撑对直桥抗震性能的影响。董阳等[8]研究了不同墩高下防屈曲支撑的设置方式及核心段材料屈服强度对桥梁地震反应的影响规律。李晓莉等[9]研究了山区桥梁双柱式桥墩之间设置防屈曲支撑的横向抗震能力。刘子舟等[10]提出了在桥梁双柱墩横桥向设置防屈曲支撑,在纵桥向设置铅芯橡胶支座的双向减隔震体系。目前防屈曲支撑抗震性能相关研究主要集中于桥墩为较高桥墩、体系为延性体系,对应用于矮墩、减隔震体系的地震响应分析较少。

本文以某矮墩城市高架桥梁为研究对象,采用延性设计和减隔震设计进行动力响应分析。通过对比结构的地震响应,得到合理的抗震设计方案,并对比选出的体系设置防屈曲支撑进行优化,为同类型城市桥梁的抗震设计提供参考。

1　工程概况及空间动力分析模型

1.1　工程概况

本文依托的实际工程为矮墩连续梁桥,跨径为3×30m,且在主桥两侧各建一联引桥作为边界条件,桥梁总体布置图如图 1 所示。上部结构为等截面预应力混凝土连续箱梁,梁宽为 12.75m,材料为 C50 混凝土;下部结构为花瓶式双柱墩,墩高均为 4m,材料为 C40 混凝土,桥墩立面布置图如图 2 所示。支座采用 GPZ 系列盆式橡胶支座和 JZQZF 系列三防摩擦摆减隔震支座,支座布置图如图 3 所示。

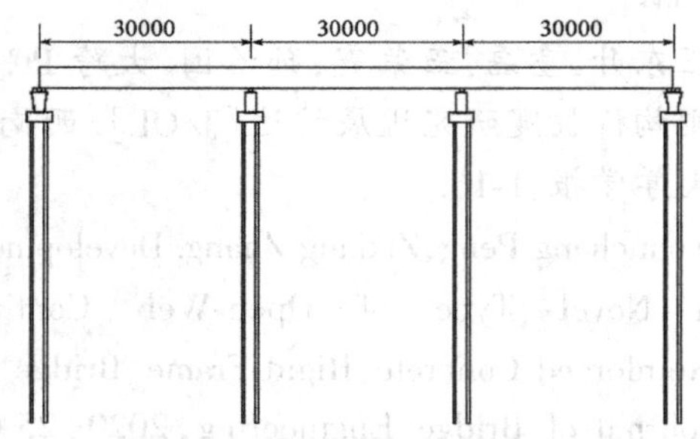

图 1　桥梁总体布置图(尺寸单位:mm)

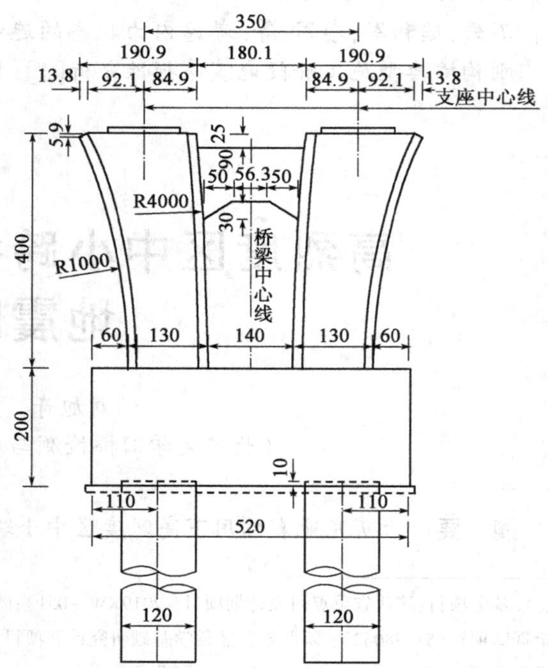

图 2　桥墩立面布置图(尺寸单位:cm)

1.2 空间动力分析模型

使用 CSI Bridge 有限元程序,建立了矮墩连续梁的有限元模型进行抗震性能分析,全桥有限元模型如图 4 所示。模型中主梁、过渡墩、辅助墩及系梁均离散为空间梁单元;承台采用壳单元模拟;基础采用 m 法模拟桩土效应,地震作用下土弹簧的刚度系数按静力作用的 2 倍取值。盆式支座、摩擦摆支座及防屈曲支撑采用 Plastic-Wen 连接单元模拟[11]。

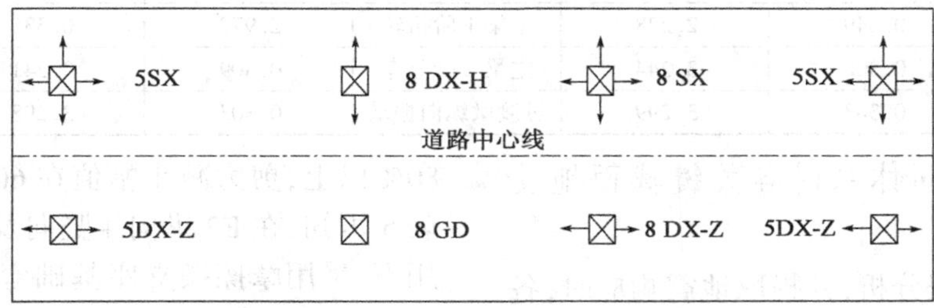

图 3 支座布置图

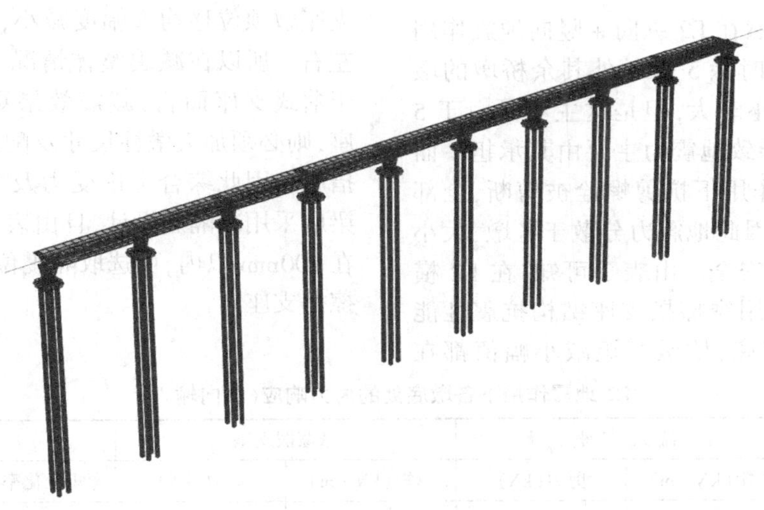
图 4 全桥有限元模型

2 地震动输入

根据项目安评报告及《中国地震动参数区划图》(GB 18306—2015),桥址区地震基本烈度为Ⅷ度,地震动峰值加速度为 0.20g,设防类别为乙类,场地为Ⅱ类场地。本文取 E2 地震波 4 条,作为水平向地震动,竖向地震动取水平向地震动的 2/3 倍。通过非线性时程分析计算,比较不同条件下,矮墩连续梁的地震响应。水平向地震动加速度时程曲线如图 5 所示。

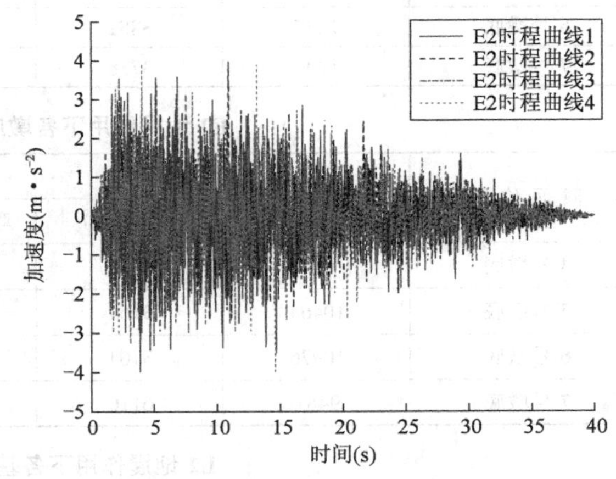

图 5 E2 地震作用时程曲线

3 地震响应分析

3.1 结构动力特性

对延性体系和减隔震体系进行动力分析,得到不同体系下的动力特性,具体内容如表 1 所示。由表 1 可知,桥梁减隔震设计前 3 阶自振周期明显大于延性设计自振周期,更有利于避开结构的卓越周期,提高抗震性能。但是两种体系抗震性能具体如何还需进一步研究。

桥梁动力特性 表1

阶次	延性设计			减隔震设计		
	周期(s)	频率(Hz)	振型特征	周期(s)	频率(Hz)	振型特征
1	0.926	1.080	主梁1阶纵飘	3.049	0.328	主梁竖向振动
2	0.587	1.703	主梁1阶侧弯	3.036	0.329	主梁1阶纵飘
3	0.449	2.228	主梁1阶扭转	2.977	0.336	主梁1阶扭转
4	0.308	3.244	主梁2阶竖弯	0.309	3.241	主梁2阶竖弯
5	0.303	3.299	过渡墩纵向振动	0.303	3.298	过渡墩纵向振动

3.2 采用不同体系时各关键截面地震响应分析

通过非线性时程分析,并提取地震响应时,各关键截面处响应值均取4条地震波作用下的最大值。

由表2可知,虽然在E2纵向+竖向地震作用下,采用摩擦摆支座时除5号墩外其余桥墩的墩底弯矩均较盆式支座时大,但是这主要是由于5号墩盆式支座固定导致地震力主要由其承担。而摩擦摆支座在地震作用下抗剪螺栓被剪断,全部变为双向活动支座,因此地震力分散于各墩,大小基本一致,结构更加安全。由表3可知,在E2横向+竖向地震下,采用摩擦摆支座结构抗震性能更好,相较于盆式支座,桥墩弯矩减小幅值都在80%以上,剪力减小幅值在60%以上。由表4及表5可知,在E2纵向+竖向及横向+竖向地震作用下,采用摩擦摆支座基础弯矩和剪力减小幅值基本达到80%以上。由图6及图7可知,在E2纵向+竖向及横向+竖向地震作用下,采用摩擦摆支座墩顶位移均大幅度减小,减小幅值均在90%左右。所以在减震整体情况上,摩擦摆支座相较于盆式支座而言,减震效果更好,若采用盆式支座,则必须加大墩柱尺寸及配筋率,并增加防落梁措施。因此综合考虑受力及工程造价,此类型桥梁应采用减隔震设计,且由表6可知,支座位移均在200mm以内,可选取隔震位移为±200mm的摩擦摆支座。

E2地震作用下各墩底处的内力响应(纵向输入) 表2

截面位置	盆式支座		摩擦摆支座		地震响应变化	
	弯矩(kN·m)	剪力(kN)	弯矩(kN·m)	剪力(kN)	弯矩变化率(%)	剪力变化率(%)
4号墩底	1343	3738	1939	517	44.375	-86.176
5号墩底	30190	3882	2033	560	-93.266	-85.579
6号墩底	1237	3882	2058	582	66.368	-84.999
7号墩底	1390	3738	1807	514	30.017	-86.238

E2地震作用下各墩底处的内力响应(横向输入) 表3

截面位置	盆式支座		摩擦摆支座		地震响应变化	
	弯矩(kN·m)	剪力(kN)	弯矩(kN·m)	剪力(kN)	弯矩变化率(%)	剪力变化率(%)
4号墩底	10958	6116	1051	791	-90.405	-87.061
5号墩底	10464	3164	1225	1159	-88.298	-63.371
6号墩底	10976	3164	1264	1146	-88.484	-63.771
7号墩底	9481	6116	1008	739	-89.366	-87.912

E2地震作用下各基础的内力响应(纵向输入) 表4

截面位置	盆式支座		摩擦摆支座		地震响应变化	
	弯矩(kN·m)	剪力(kN)	弯矩(kN·m)	剪力(kN)	弯矩变化率(%)	剪力变化率(%)
4号桩	4426	1026	773	219	-82.537	-78.682
5号桩	4596	1065	785	255	-82.932	-76.032

续上表

截面位置	盆式支座		摩擦摆支座		地震响应变化	
	弯矩(kN·m)	剪力(kN)	弯矩(kN·m)	剪力(kN)	弯矩变化率(%)	剪力变化率(%)
6号桩	4755	992	856	181	-82.000	-81.713
7号桩	4846	1089	786	168	-83.769	-84.563

E2地震作用下各基础的内力响应(横向输入) 表5

截面位置	盆式支座		摩擦摆支座		地震响应变化	
	弯矩(kN·m)	剪力(kN)	弯矩(kN·m)	剪力(kN)	弯矩变化率(%)	剪力变化率(%)
4号桩	5013	2934	857	302	-82.916	-89.692
5号桩	5136	2233	827	237	-83.894	-89.370
6号桩	4545	986	849	175	-81.323	-82.254
7号桩	4691	2019	897	192	-80.873	-90.485

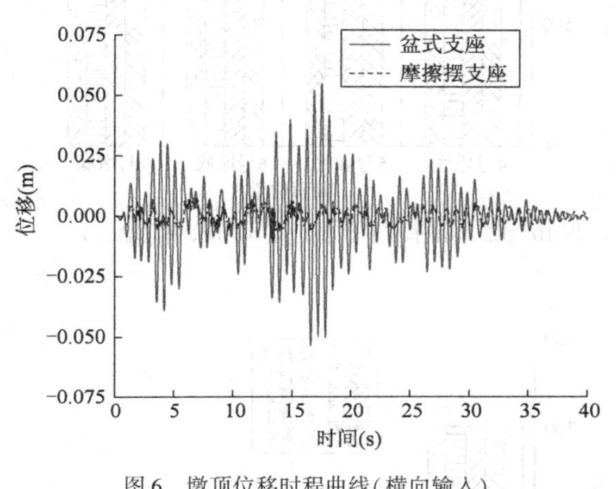

图6 墩顶位移时程曲线(横向输入)

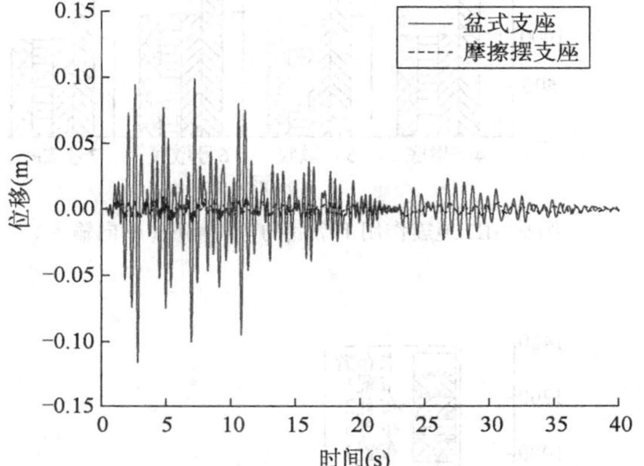

图7 墩顶位移时程曲线(纵向输入)

墩顶支座位移(mm) 表6

纵横向	桥墩号							
	4号左墩	4号右墩	5号左墩	5号右墩	6号左墩	6号右墩	7号左墩	7号右墩
纵向	165.862	165.862	164.283	164.283	164.737	164.737	166.326	166.326
横向	163.907	163.915	160.168	160.222	162.682	162.712	165.971	165.996

3.3 采用防屈曲支撑时各关键截面地震响应分析

目前防屈曲支撑较广泛地应用于双柱墩横向抗震,但主要用于较高桥墩,对于矮墩相关研究较少。因此在上节分析得出结论的基础上,对采用摩擦摆的桥梁结构横向设置防屈曲支撑,分析其对结构横向地震响应的影响,防屈曲支撑布置图如图8所示。

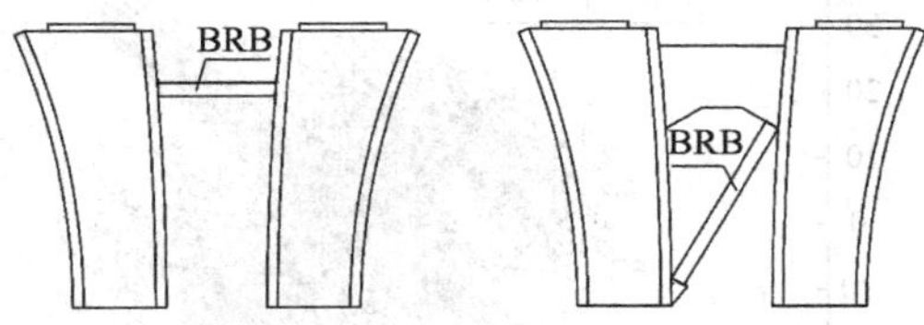

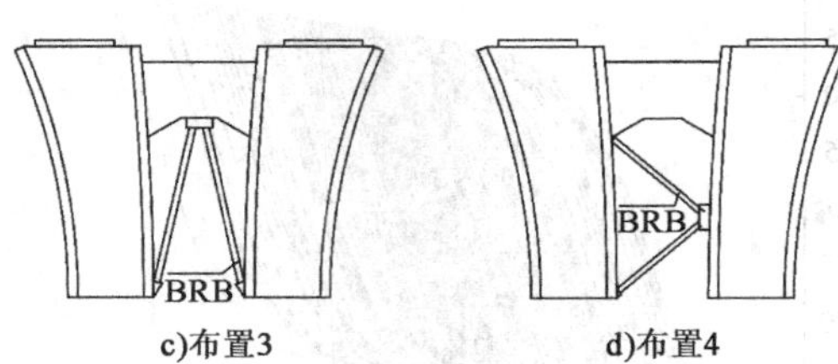

图8 桥墩防屈曲支撑布置图

由图9及图10可知,采用防屈曲支撑替换系梁后,墩底弯矩增加均在140%以上,最高达201.726%;剪力最多减小54.596%。由图11和图12可知,4种防屈曲支撑布置形式对基础的地震响应影响很小。且由图13可知这是由于防屈曲支撑进入屈服状态,其轴向长度发生变化,导致桥墩横向变形增大、弯矩增加。布置2、3、4虽然相较未布置防屈曲支撑的结构地震响应有所减小,但是弯矩最大仅减小3.055%,剪力最大仅减小2.795%。由图14可知防屈曲支撑轴力最大值还未超过50kN,未发生屈服,仅通过改变下部结构中地震力的传力路径,来减小墩身的弯矩和剪力。结合图15可知,防屈曲支撑4种布置形式桥墩墩顶位移相较于未布置防屈曲支撑桥墩的墩顶位移几乎相同,减小幅值接近于0,这样微小的减震效果,综合考虑造价、施工情况,不适用于此类型桥梁。

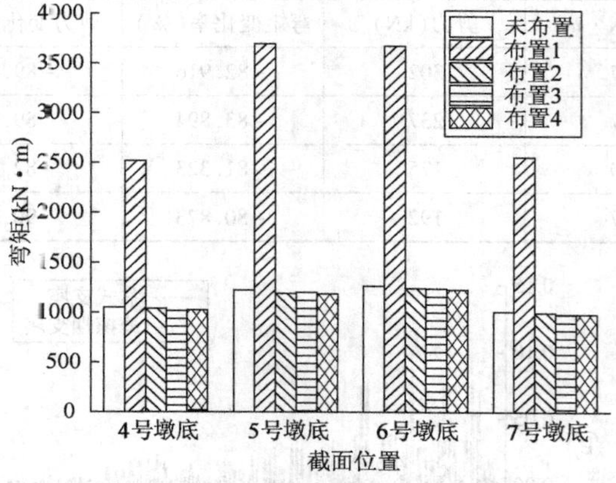

图9 E2地震作用下墩底的弯矩响应(横向输入)

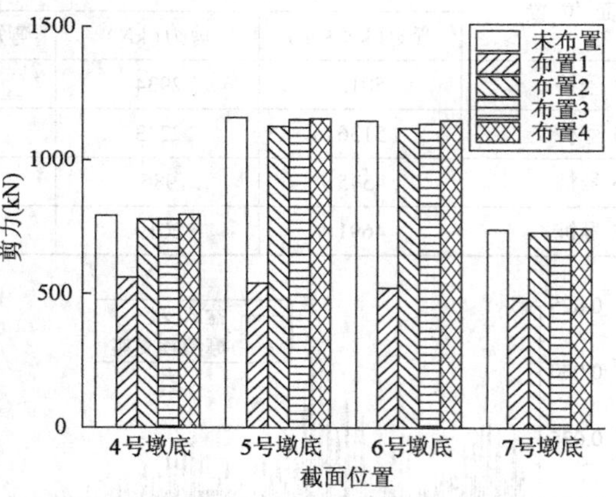

图10 E2地震作用下墩底的剪力响应(横向输入)

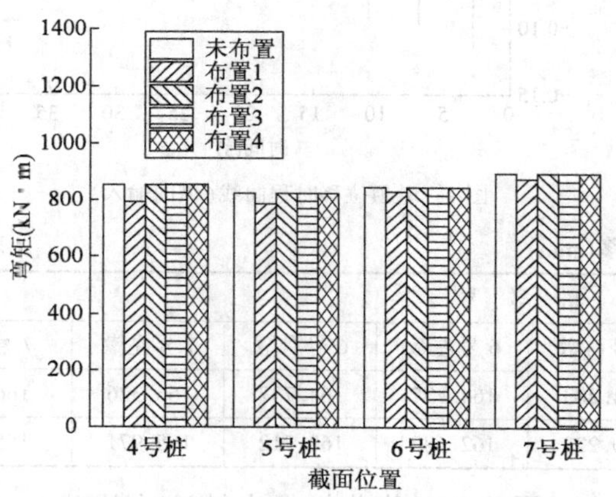

图11 E2地震作用下基础的弯矩响应(横向输入)

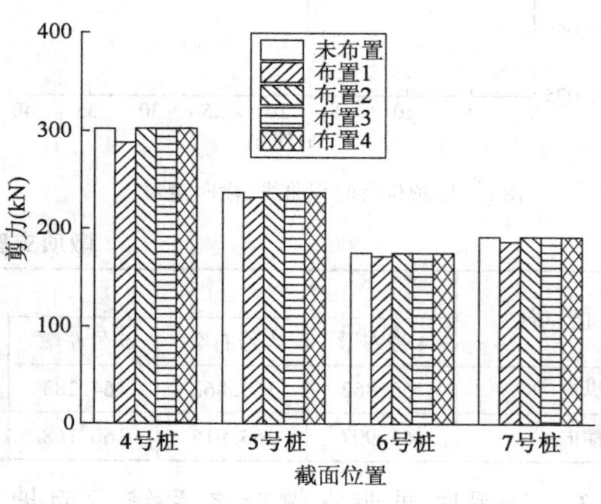

图12 E2地震作用下基础的剪力响应(横向输入)

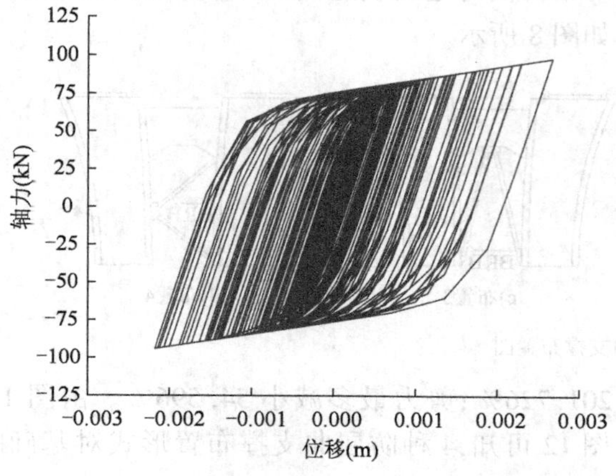

图13 布置1的防屈曲支撑滞回曲线

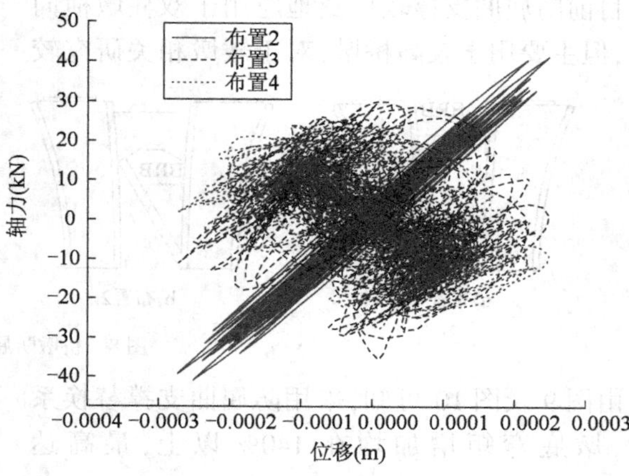

图14 布置2、3、4的防屈曲支撑滞回曲线

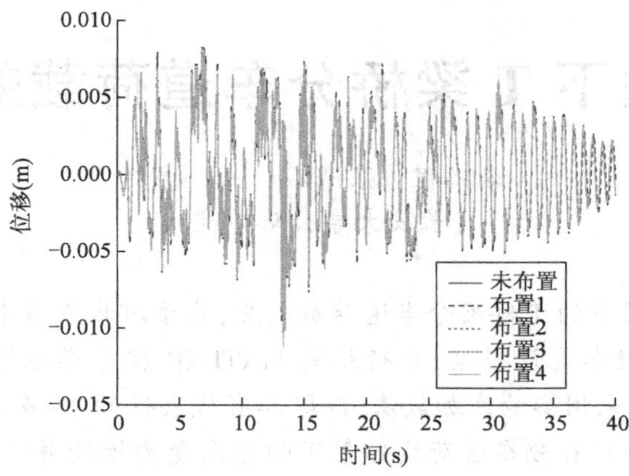

图15 墩顶位移时程曲线(横向输入)

4 结语

本文以某 3×30m 矮墩城市高架桥梁为研究对象,分析了高烈度区中小跨径城市高架桥梁的抗震性能。根据分析结果得出如下结论:

(1)通过对两种体系进行动力特性分析可知,对于本桥型来说,采用减隔震体系相较于延性体系,可以延长自振周期,更利于结构抗震。

(2)通过对两种体系进行地震响应分析可知,减隔震体系抗震性能远超延性体系,桥墩和基础的弯矩及剪力值均减小 60% 以上,并选取隔震位移为 ±200mm 的摩擦摆支座。

(3)对于减隔震体系,桥墩横桥向设置防屈曲支撑,文中几种布置形式均无明显优化效果,该减隔震设计对于本类型桥梁来说已达到最优。

(4)本文仅对Ⅷ度区中小跨径城市高架桥梁的抗震性能进行分析,下一步可以分析不同地震等级、不同墩高及不同桥梁类型,在地震作用下中小跨径城市高架桥梁的抗震性能。

参考文献

[1] 刘鹏,程永欢. 关于城市桥梁在8度强震区的抗震设计讨论[J]. 内蒙古公路与运输,2020(02):11-14+21.

[2] 尹臻. 高烈度区大跨连续梁延性抗震设计[J]. 城市道桥与防洪,2020(12):70-74+13.

[3] 郭良,左路. 城市高架桥梁抗震设计问题探析[J]. 交通世界,2021(26):111-112.

[4] 闫鹏. 城市大跨矮墩桥梁抗震性能分析[J]. 交通世界,2017(29):100-102.

[5] 贾奋宗. 7度地震区双柱墩连续梁桥的抗震设计研究[J]. 城市道桥与防洪,2016(06):132-135+14.

[6] 孙治国,华承俊,石岩,等. 利用防屈曲支撑实现桥梁排架基于保险丝理念的抗震设计[J]. 振动与冲击,2015,34(22):199-205.

[7] Joel Lanning, Gianmario Benzoni, Chia-Ming Uang. Using Buckling-Restrained Braces on Long-Span Bridges. I: Full-Scale Testing and Design Implications[J]. Journal of Bridge Engineering, 2016,21 (5):04016001-04016001.

[8] Yuandong Wang, Luis Ibarra, Chris Pantelides. Seismic Retrofit of a Three-Span RC Bridge with Buckling-Restrained Braces [J]. Journal of Bridge Engineering, 2016, 21 (11): 04016073-04016073.

[9] 李晓莉,孙治国,刘昕,等. 山区桥梁双柱式桥墩设置防屈曲支撑的减震效果研究[J]. 振动与冲击,2018,37(22):173-180.

[10] 刘子舟,王东升,陈磊,等. 近断层地震动下设置防屈曲支撑的双向减隔震桥梁地震反应[J]. 世界地震工程,2020,36(02):155-162.

[11] 周救,朱国强,吴江,等. 地震下大跨径连续刚构桥合理约束体系研究[J]. 振动与冲击,2019,38(10):98-104.

重车作用下T梁桥分车道荷载效应分析

李鹏程 张修石 王 涛*
(长安大学公路学院)

摘 要 为研究重车作用下的T桥梁分车道荷载效应,基于河北某高速289d的动态称重数据,利用行车特性和汽车荷载特性的概率统计模型,自行编写MATLAB程序模拟符合实际交通流的随机车流。以20m简支T梁为验算实例,采用影响线加载法,选取具有代表性的单-多重车工况,分析随机车流下的荷载效应。主要分析多主梁桥型在分车道荷载作用下的横向受力性能并依据临界荷载效应比值法评估其承载能力安全性。结果表明:随着重车行驶车道的不同,T梁不同梁的荷载效应差异较大,当重车加载于行车道2时产生的荷载效应最大;单车工况下的弯矩荷载效应小于公路Ⅰ级荷载效应,但在多车工况下,实际重车荷载效应最大值已超过设计汽车荷载效应,但其临界荷载效应比值仍在合理范围内。

关键词 桥梁工程 T梁桥 影响线加载法 荷载效应 分车道

0 引言

汽车作用是公路桥梁可变荷载的重要组成部分。随着高速公路重型汽车占比不断提高,汽车荷载水平也不断发生变化。对于中小跨径桥梁,现有规范的设计荷载不足以满足实际在役桥梁日益增长的卡车荷载水平[1];同时,为了保证汽车行驶安全和物流效率,现高速公路大多为按车型分车道行驶,这也使得不同行车道的汽车荷载响应产生较大差异[2-3]。因此,分析重车工况下车辆荷载特性以及T梁桥在分车道汽车荷载下的横向分布特性对于汽车荷载研究及T梁桥乃至中小跨径桥梁的运营管养具有实际意义。

关于中小跨径桥梁承载能力与安全性评估,国内外学者已经开展了大量研究。张征文等[4]基于104国道的车辆荷载数据,对简支梁的荷载效应进行了分析;黄平明等[5]基于河北省宣大高速的动态称重数据,研究了重载下空心板桥的承载能力安全性。当然,也有学者对分车道行驶下的桥梁荷载响应研究也做了不少工作,周军勇等[6]对比了分车道交通流量及荷载分布的差异;刘浪等[7]以加州交通厅许可荷载车模型为参照,通过建立的典型超重车辆模型对比了多、单车道超重车荷载效应。而中小跨径桥梁在重车交通流下的分车道荷载效应分析有待进一步完善。

本文将以中小跨径空心板桥为研究对象,首先,基于河北省某高速的汽车概率特性参数[8],将静态的车辆数据与交通流数据合称为模拟车流,方便地利用现有数据建立符合交通流特性的车辆荷载模型。其次,根据影响线加载原理编制影响线加载程序,计算重车或者特定多车工况下的代表性荷载效应值,以重车下荷载效应值与规范所对应设计汽车荷载效应比值评判现有T梁桥的承载能力,研究简支T梁桥在重车荷载作用下的横向分布力学特性。

1 车流荷载模拟

1.1 汽车特性模型

为了更好地反映实际车流特性,需要对实际桥梁运营过程中的汽车荷载参数进行概率统计分析。基于实测的汽车统计数据,建立符合实际运营特性的汽车特性模型。汽车特性模型主要包括车质量、轴距、轴重和车型分布等参数。

1.1.1 交通流量

交通流量作为车流荷载统计的总样本,监测所得的每一个汽车荷载作为其样本之一。基于WIM系统对河北省某高速采集289d、871719组车辆荷载数据。由于称重系统识别精度的局限性,仅选取100708组汽车荷载数据分析其荷载参数特性。车型分类及比例如表1所示。

各轴数卡车数量及百分比　　表1

轴数	2	3	4	5	6
数量	69407	15655	9369	1393	4884
百分比(%)	68.92	15.54	9.3	1.38	4.85

1.1.2　车质量

车质量是最能反映汽车荷载水平的参数,也是最具代表性的车流荷载参数。不难知道,通过桥梁任意一辆汽车的车质量都是随机的,汽车在空载、满载和超载等不同的载重情况下形成不同的样本参数,其往往服从正态混合分布,最低载重是车辆空载时的车辆自重,最高载重为107.48t。其概率密度函数[9]为:

$$W(x)=\sum_{i=1}^{M}\omega_i\frac{1}{\sqrt{2\pi\sigma_i}}\exp\left[\frac{(x-\mu_i)^2}{2\sigma_i}\right] \tag{1}$$

式中:ω_i——第 i 个模型在整体模型中所占的比重;

μ_i、σ_i——第 i 个模型的均值和标准差。

1.1.3　轴重和轴距

汽车的轴重和轴距也会对结构荷载响应产生较大影响,轴重与车质量在各个集中力上的分配比例相关,而车距则影响汽车荷载在桥面上的平面分布。基于概率学理论建立轴重和轴距的概率模型分析,建立考虑轴重和轴距等车辆特性的随机车流模型。根据采集的车辆荷载数据,不同轴数卡车的轴重和轴距均服从双峰-五峰高斯分布。

1.1.4　车型分布

以轴数、轴重和轴距等汽车荷载参数为分类依据,对该高速公路主要车型进行分类。车型分类及其比例如表2所示。

车型分类及比例　　表2

车型编号	车辆参数信息	(平均/最大车质量)(t)
V1 68.93%	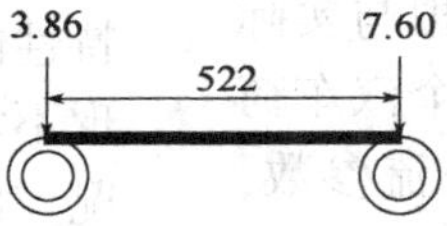 3.86　7.60 522	11.46/48.59
V2 5.68%	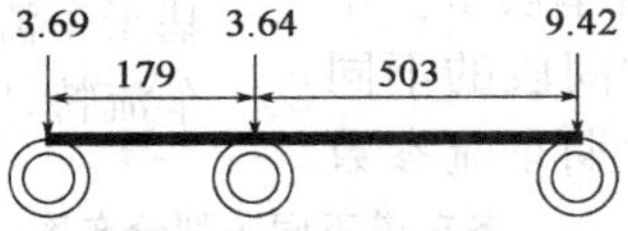 3.69　3.64　9.42 179　503	16.75/54.87
V3 9.87%	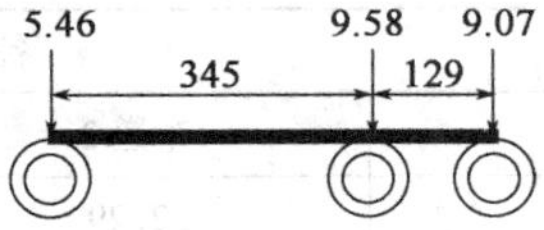 5.46　9.58　9.07 345　129	24.11/63.84
V4 7.68%	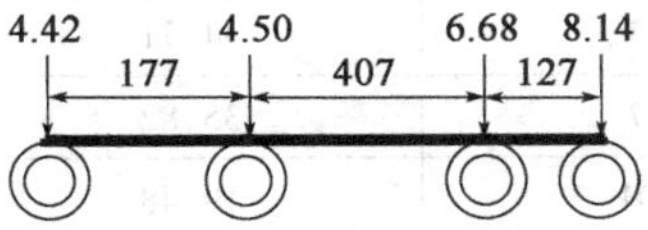 4.42　4.50　6.68　8.14 177　407　127	23.68/93.52
V5 1.63%	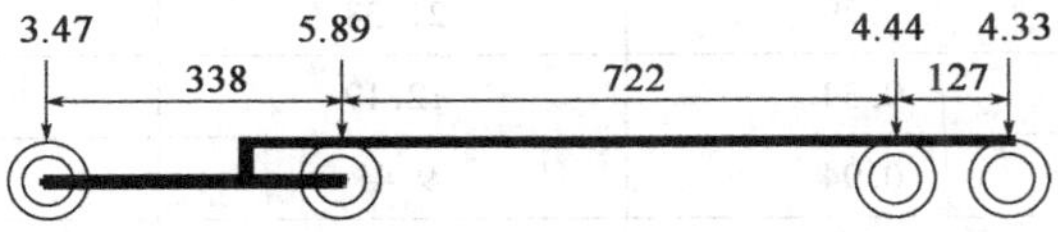 3.47　5.89　4.44　4.33 338　722　127	18.13/77.98
V6 1.26%	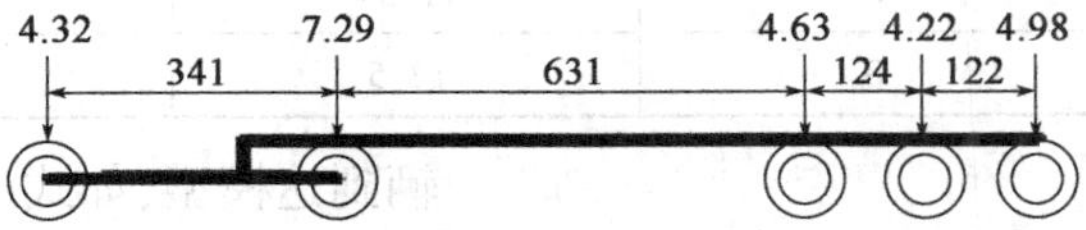 4.32　7.29　4.63　4.22　4.98 341　631　124　122	25.43/104.33
V7 0.13%	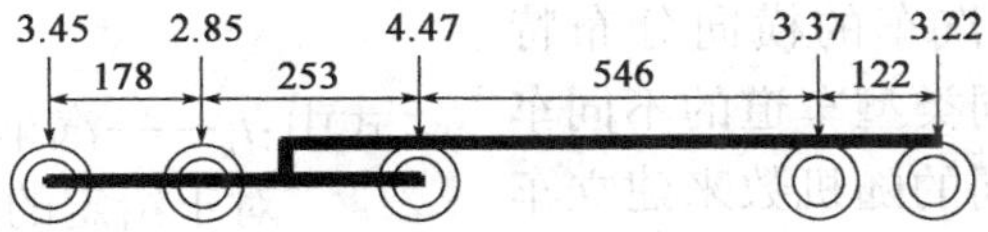 3.45　2.85　4.47　3.37　3.22 178　253　546　122	17.36/54.85

续上表

车型编号	车辆参数信息	(平均/最大车质量)(t)
V8 2.85%	5.14 8.49 8.12 8.20 7.96 8.70 310 129 603 124 124	46.61/143.00
V9 2.00%	3.70 3.50 9.68 6.86 6.32 6.81 166 237 831 124 124	36.86/102.99

由图1可知:该高速公路共包含9种汽车车型,其中两轴车型-V1所占的比例最大,占据所有卡车数量的68.92%,三轴卡车车型-V3和车型-V2分别占到所有车辆的9.87%和5.68%,4轴汽车中,车型-V4占据绝大多数,其占据汽车总量的7.68%,而半挂汽车所占比例相对较小,半挂汽车中,6轴汽车V8所占比例最大,占据汽车总量的2.85%。

1.1.5 汽车特性模拟

Monte Carlo法可以有效地模拟随机性较强的事件[10],故可以采用Monte Carlo法来模拟与实际车流具有相同分布特征的随机车流。单个汽车荷载样本具有车重、轴重和轴距等不同的车流参数,这些车流参数分别服从不同的数学概率模型。车流参数除了具有随机性外,还会随时间段的不同有较大的差异,在实际行车的不同时期车流参数变化较明显。在随机车流建模过程中,基于不同车流参数的数学概率模型,利用产生均匀、相互独立的[0,1]区间上的随机数,然后根据适当的数学转换方法实现随机变量的抽样。

1.2 车流特性模型和车辆到达模型

1.2.1 车流特性模拟

车质量、轴重和轴距反映单个样本的概率特性,交通流量各车型分布及比例更多表现一定时间段内通过桥梁汽车荷载的横向分布特性。通常高速公路包括行车道和超车道,基于分车道交通特性的情况,超车道和行车道车辆类型分布也呈现不均衡。同时剔除掉汽车存在的跨线行驶的情况。两种车道不同类型汽车分布率如表3所示。基于车流特性统计建立符合实际车流交通特性的车流特性模型。

各车道不同车型分布率 表3

车型	各车道分布率			
	车道1	车道2	车道3	车道4
V1	4.71	32.29	39.36	23.64
V2	2.3	34.71	43.39	19.6
V3	3.7	35.82	44.71	15.77
V4	1.01	19.48	38.47	41.04
V5	0.79	21.38	42.75	35.08
V6	0.34	12.19	37.35	50.12
V7	0.94	9.41	42.04	47.61
V8	0	11.59	42.09	46.32
V9	0	12.5	37.48	50.02

1.2.2 车辆到达模型

车流特性模型反映的是汽车的横向分布特征,在指定交通量下,基于不同类型车道的不同车头时距概率统计分布生成不同的随机数来建立车辆到达模型,如式(2)所示。

$$\sum_{k=1}^{i} t_k \geq T \tag{2}$$

式中:t_k——汽车车头时距概率参数。

对于给定的任意时间段T,将基于车头时距概率参数生成的随机数赋予时间段 T 内的 i 个汽车数量。

1.3 车流生成

首先,基于任意给定的时间段,利用车辆到达模型得到指定交通量;其次根据汽车特性模型进行车型、车质量以及轴重轴距的随机抽样。同时,基于车流特性模型进行车速、车型及车道分配的模拟,最后形成符合实际交通流特性的随机车流(图1)。

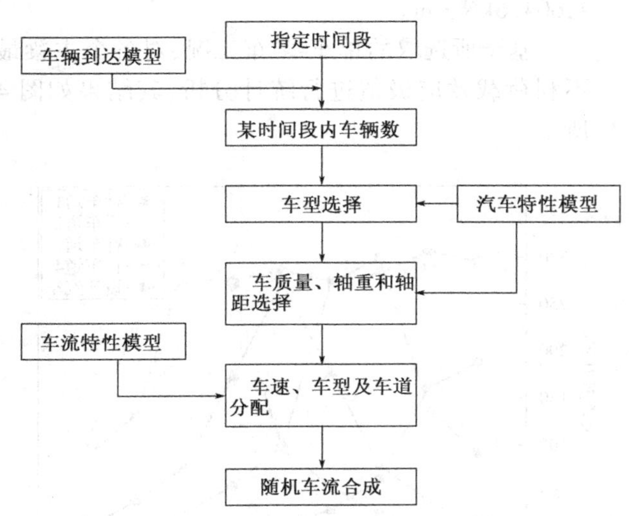

图1 随机车流模拟过程

基于上述随机车流模拟过程,运用 MATLAB 编程建立多车道随即车流模拟程序,生成 180 天的随机车流样本,如图 2 所示。

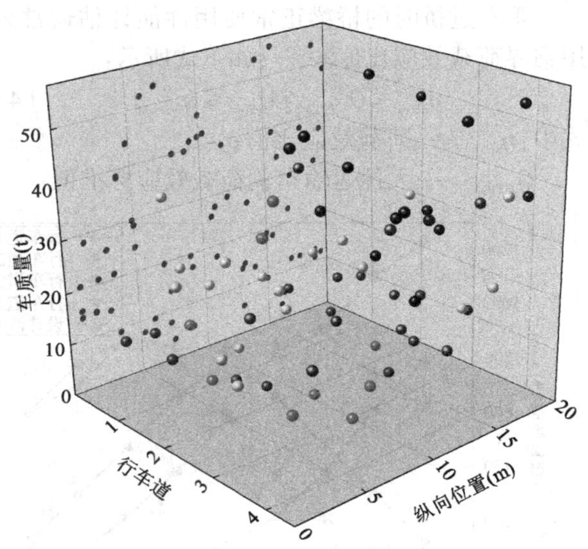

图2 单日随机车流样本

2 车辆荷载效应模拟

选取某单向四车道高速公路上的 20m 简支 T 梁桥为工程背景。桥梁上部结构 9 片 T 梁组成,桥面铺装层采用 8cm 厚沥青混凝土 + 8cm 厚 C40 混凝土桥面铺装层,桥梁设计荷载为公路-I 级。桥梁横断面如图 3 所示,各主梁按顺序编号。

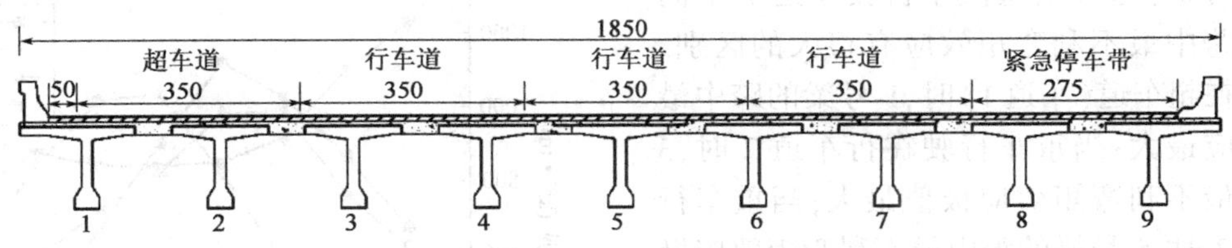

图3 桥梁横断面(尺寸单位:cm)

2.1 荷载工况选取

已有文献研究表明[11-12]:对于中小跨径桥梁,小型汽车对结构影响很小,在进行交通流模拟及汽车加载过程中往往可以略去,而重车过桥的荷载效应与同一时间过桥数量的相关度较高,3 辆或者 3 辆以上重型汽车同时过桥发生的概率很小,而单车过桥或者两辆车同时过桥的概率却很大。因此在选取特定重车荷载工况时,仅考虑单车工况或者 2 辆重型汽车行驶工况。对于后者的累加荷载效应按照下式定义:

$$L_{i\_total}=D_1L_{i1}+D_2L_{i2}+D_3L_{i3}+D_4L_{i4} \tag{3}$$

式中:L_{i_total}——第 i 个荷载工况引起的叠加效应;

L_{i1}、L_{i2}、L_{i3}、L_{i4}——该荷载工况在 1~4 车道引起的荷载效应;

D_1、D_2、D_3、D_4——4 条车道对应的分布系数。

基于前述生成随机车流选取具有代表性的单车道-多车道行驶的车辆行驶工况,对于 2 辆重车行驶工况,由于研究对象为单向 4 车道高速公路上的中小跨径桥梁,故前述式(3)中各车道分项系数可设为[13]:主车道为 1,2 车道为 0.45,3 车道为 0.15,4 车道为 0.05。

2.2　荷载效应分析

按照不同荷载工况加载不同数量的重型汽车. 因为所选取的工况出现的次数较多,若采用有限元软件分别加载不同的重型汽车,会导致计算效率较低的问题,为了提高计算效率,本文用影响面加载的方法计算桥梁的弯矩荷载效应。

重车过桥时的桥梁正常使用性能评估通常采用临界荷载效应比值法[14],如下式所示:

$$\eta_{serve} = Q_{CTV,k}/Q_{design} \leqslant \eta_{critical} \tag{4}$$

式中:η_{serve}——荷载效应比值;

$Q_{CTV,k}$——大件运输车辆荷载效应标准值;

Q_{design}、$\eta_{critical}$——构件的设计汽车荷载效应及临界荷载效应比值。

本文所选用的 20m 简支 T 梁,在计入冲击作用影响的情况下,将规范要求[15]设计荷载水平布置于最不利荷载效应位置。采用 Midas/Civil 软件计算的 1 号 ~ 9 号梁跨中弯矩分别为 1229.4, 1100.4, 916.9, 850.7, 839.7, 843.0, 878.2, 778.4, 604.6kN · m。

基于所选取的单车-多车工况,对各个主梁最不利荷载效应极值进行统计分析,其结果如图 4 所示。

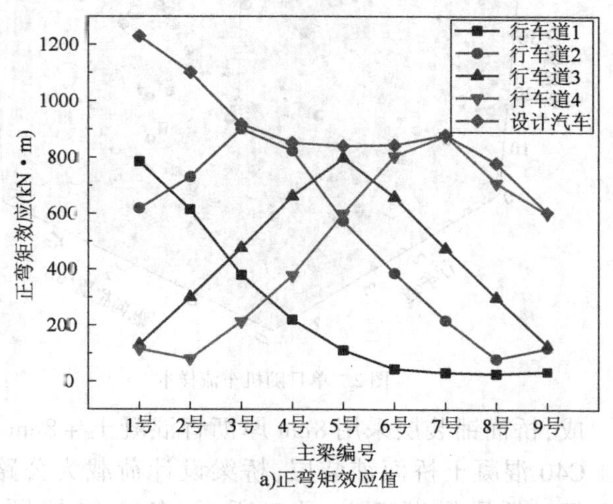

a)正弯矩效应值

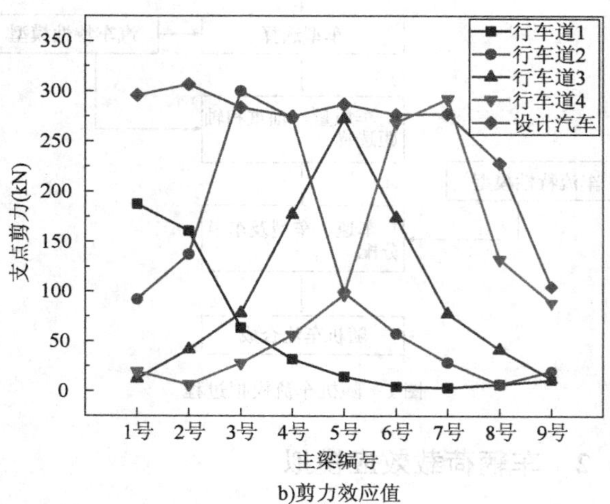

b)剪力效应值

图 4　单车工况下 T 梁桥横向各个梁受力分析

由图 4 可知:随着重型汽车行驶车道的不同各个主梁的跨中最不利弯矩效应有很大的区别。当重车行驶在超车道(车道 1)时,1 号梁的跨中最不利弯矩效应最大;当重车行驶在行车道 2 时,3 号梁的跨中最不利弯矩效应极值最大;当重车行驶在行车道 3 时,5 号梁的跨中最不利弯矩效应极值最大;当重车行驶在行车道 4 时,7 号梁的跨中最不利弯矩效应极值最大。由此可见,汽车在行驶过程中横向分布的不均匀性会对桥梁荷载效应产生较大影响,而在实际运营过程中,交通管制、驾驶员的驾驶习惯等都会产生汽车的横向不均匀分布。

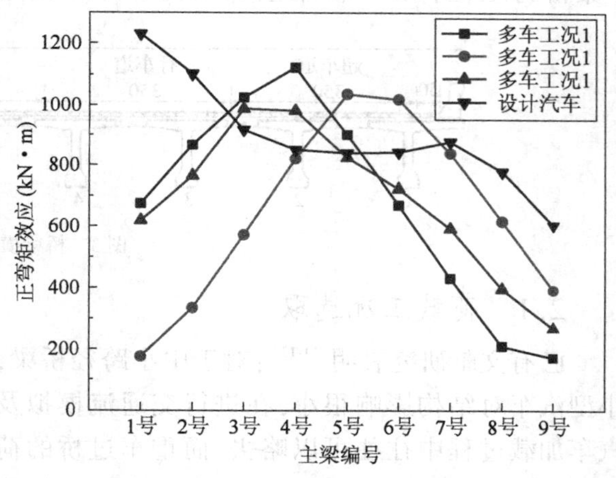

图 5　多车工况下 T 梁桥横向各个梁受力分析

由图 5 可知,3 号、4 号、5 号及 6 号梁多车工况下的汽车荷载最大正弯矩效应均已超过设计汽车荷载效应;当重车在靠近桥梁中心线的车道行驶时,其荷载效应小于车辆偏载时的荷载效应。简支 T 梁边梁的抗弯承载能力还有较大的安全冗余度。

3　结语

(1)根据已有某高速的汽车荷载概率特性建立综合汽车荷载模型和车流特性模型的随机车流,充分表征实际汽车流过桥的横向分布特征,使随机车流能够充分反映实际车辆运营状态。

(2)受重型卡车分车道行驶的影响,各梁随着重型卡车桥上横向分布的不同其荷载效应也有很大区别,往往靠近汽车行驶处T梁其荷载效应值较大,但临界荷载效应比值尚未达到1,表明目前设计水平对应桥梁能满足单辆重型卡车行驶的通行安全性。在重型卡车多车工况下,其实际荷载最大弯矩效应值已经远远超过设计汽车荷载水平。

(3)本文通过单一算例进行重型卡车过桥分车道荷载效应分析,尚不具有代表性,后续还需进行不同跨径、不同桥型下的桥梁分车道荷载效应分析。

参考文献

[1] Kent K Sasaki TerryParet, Juan C. Araiza. Failure of concrete T-beam and box-girder highway bridges subjected to cyclic loading from traffic [J]. Engineering Structures, 2010, 32 (7): 1838-1845.

[2] 刘黎萍,孙立军. 高速公路沥青路面轮迹横向分布研究[J]. 同济大学学报(自然科学版), 2005,33(11):1449.

[3] 阮欣,周可攀,周军勇. 某八车道高速公路车流特性及荷载响应[J]. 同济大学学报(自然科学版),2015,43(4):1449.

[4] 张征文,杨飞,赵建峰. 基于WIM数据的简支梁桥车辆荷载效应分析[J]. 公路交通科技, 2014,31(5):86-92.

[5] 黄平明,袁阳光,赵建峰. 重载交通下空心板桥梁承载能力安全性[J]. 交通运输工程学报,2017,17(3):1-12.

[6] 周军勇,石雪飞,阮欣. 高速公路分车道荷载差异及其响应特性[J]. 同济大学学报(自然科学版),2018,46(4):458-464.

[7] 刘浪,陈东军,任青阳. 超重车模型及多-单车道荷载效应[J]. 西南交通大学学报,2019,54(6):1169-1176.

[8] 袁阳光,郭雷,裴浩楠. G104国道卡车荷载概率特性分析[J]. 北京工业大学学报,2017,43(11):1697-1705.

[9] 刘扬,张海萍,鲁乃唯. 基于WIM的随机车流建模和简支梁桥荷载效应研究[J]. 桥梁建设,2015,45(5):13-18.

[10] 朱本仁. 蒙特卡罗方法引论[M]. 济南:山东大学出版社,1986.

[11] Kin Y J, Tanovic R, Wight R G. Recent advances in performance evaluation and flexural response of existing bridges [J]. J PerformConstr Facil, 2009, 23: 190-200.

[12] 韩万水,赵士良,李彦伟. 特重车荷载下装配式PC板桥荷载效应分析[J]. 科技导报, 2016,34(2):277-281.

[13] Fu Gk, Liu L, Bowman M D. Multiple presence factor for truck load on highway bridges[J]. Journal of Bridge Engineering, 2013, 18(3): 240-249.

[14] 袁阳光,周广利,高文博. 考虑安全性与正常使用性能的大件车辆过桥评估方法[J]. 工程力学,2021,38(7):147-158.

[15] 中华人民共和国行业标准. 公路桥涵设计通用规范:JTG D60—2015[S]. 北京:人民交通出版社股份有限公司,2015.

悬吊支架法施工钢混组合梁的力学行为研究

管 弦*[1] 唐国华[2]

(1. 北京华宏工程咨询有限公司;2. 重庆交通大学)

摘 要 本文通过对钢混组合梁采用悬吊支架法施工的过程进行有限元分析模拟,讨论了风荷载、悬吊点纵向间距、混凝土桥面板厚度、桥面混凝土浇筑过程及悬吊支架拆除等多因素对钢主梁及其组合梁的力学性能的影响,得到了钢混组合梁在悬吊支架法施工过程中的力学行为规律,为类似结构设计、施工提供了理论指导。

关键词 桥梁工程 悬吊支架 钢混组合梁 现浇桥面板 有限元分析

0 引言

工字钢-混组合结构[1-4]是由外露的工字型钢主梁作为三要的承重结构与混凝土桥面板通过剪力键连接形成的一种组合结构。可以直接利用钢-混组合梁中钢结构梁的自承重能力,在钢结构梁下悬挂支架体系来完成这种组合结构中的混凝土构件的现浇施工,这一桥梁施工方法被称为悬吊支架法。这种施工方法的支架不受地形、河流、地基承载力的限制,且占用桥下空间少,是一种经济有效的施工方法。

然而悬吊支架[5-6]这种支架类型在实际工程中却很少使用,主要原因是悬吊支架固定点较少,在风荷载等敏感性因素影响下,支架体系的横向位移难以控制。更为重要的是在混凝土浇筑过程中,随着混凝土重量的增加及浇筑点纵横向位置的变化,悬吊支架系统将发生变形,导致浇筑的混凝土结构也发生变形。针对悬吊支架的这一缺点,为了使采用悬吊支架浇筑的混凝土桥面板成型后其线形能满足设计要求,有必要对这种悬吊支架对钢结构及支架本身在施工过程中的力学行为进行研究。

1 工程背景及悬吊支架计算模型的建立

1.1 工程背景

某大桥的桥位地处低缓丘陵,跨越丘陵间谷地,沿丘陵坡脚展布,地势起伏较大。大桥主梁采用的是双工字钢板组合梁,分左右两幅,桥跨组合为4×40m+4×40m+3×40m+4×40m,共15跨。单幅组合梁桥面宽为12.5m,左右幅中间设置0.5m宽分隔带,双幅全宽25.5m,上部结构梁高均为2.7m(其中钢板梁高2.2m,桥面板高0.4m,铺装层高0.1m)。

1.2 悬吊支架构造

本案例现浇桥面板采用悬吊支架方案,即利用钢梁自承重能力,在钢板梁底板下悬挂横向主承重梁,然后以此为基础安装满堂碗扣支架,铺设方木及竹胶板,实现整联现浇。支架设计如图1所示。

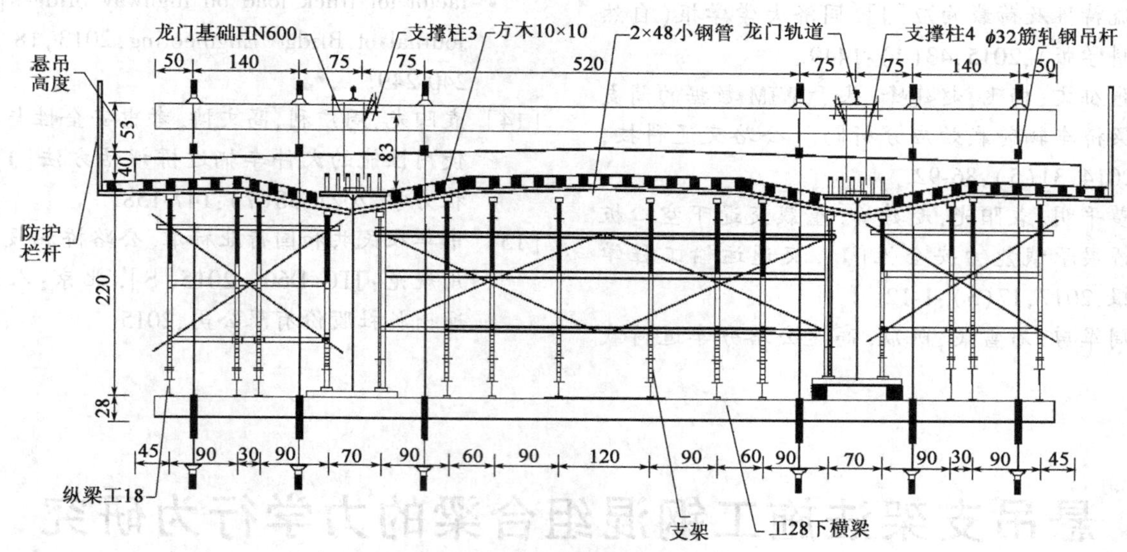

图1 悬吊支架跨中标准断面图(尺寸单位:cm)

悬吊支架系统依托钢板梁双工字钢承受重量,从下至上构件依次的布置情况如下介绍所示:][28下横梁(两端为][22,中间为][28)、工18纵向分配梁、[28钢立柱、][28上横梁、ϕ32精轧螺纹钢吊杆组成。其中,上下横梁均间距400cm布置一道,主纵梁根据受力特性先按30cm、60cm、90cm、120cm间距布置。在横断面上布置6根精轧螺纹钢吊杆,两侧对称布置。碗扣支架立杆横向间距根据不同部位受力情况按30cm、60cm、90cm、120cm间距布置,纵向统一按90cm间距布置。根据碗扣支架的搭设施工规范,设置纵横向的剪刀撑。底模系统由1.5cm厚的竹胶板面板、10cm×10cm截面的纵桥向方木、ϕ48×035cm横桥向小钢管组成。

各材料的参数如表 1 所示。

材料容重及弹性模量表 表 1

材　　料	容重(γ)	弹性模量(E)
桥面板混凝土 C50	$26KN/m^3$	3.45×10^4 Mpa
模板木材	$8KN/m^3$	10×10^3 Mpa
钢管材料及纵横梁 Q235	$76.98KN/m^3$	2.06×10^5 Mpa
精轧螺纹钢吊杆和钢主梁 Q345	$78.5KN/m^3$	2.06×10^5 Mpa

1.3 悬吊支架结构计算模型

本文应用有限元软件建立了该支架系统的计算模型。边界条件设置为:钢主梁的两端下横梁放在盖梁上,两端下横梁中间约束 DZ,两端下横梁按照简支梁添加约束,上横梁与钢主梁之间只考虑只受压弹性连接,上下横梁通过吊杆连接,吊杆采用桁架单元模拟,不传递弯矩。悬吊支架模型建模共计 14500 个节点,18399 个梁单元,72 个桁架单元。悬吊支架有限元计算模型如图 2、图 3 所示。

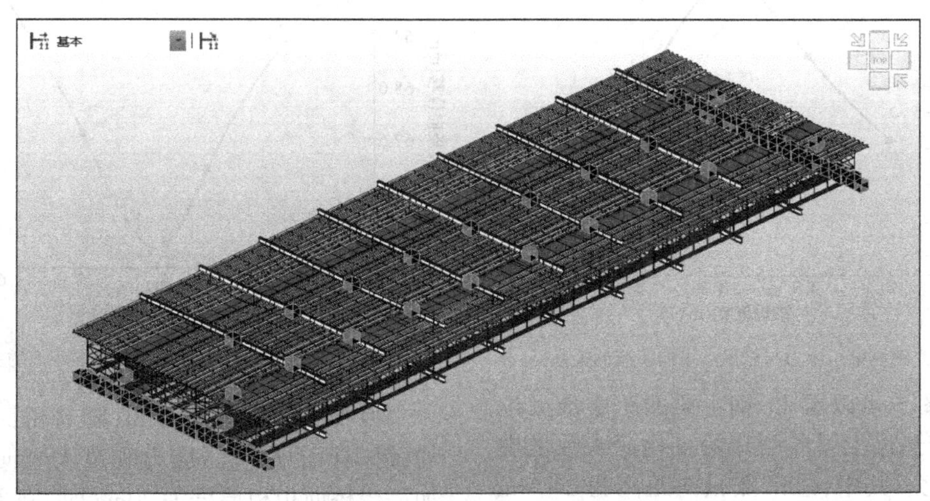

图 2　工字钢主梁作主要承力结构的支架整体计算模型

图 3　工字钢主梁作主要承力结构的支架整体计算模型

2　悬吊支架结构对钢主梁结构力学行为影响研究

2.1　风荷载对钢主梁力学行为的影响

通过查阅相关规范得知桥梁所在地的基本风压为0.35kN/m²。由基本风压公式$\omega_k=\beta_z\mu_s\mu_z\omega_0$计算得出当地的风荷载标准值为$\omega_k=0.75\text{kN/m}^2$，方向考虑为水平；将风荷载标准值转化为节点荷载，再将风荷载以节点荷载的形式施加到悬吊支架和钢主梁的横向迎风面上。

支架的横向位移都发生在钢主梁的$L/2$处。悬吊支架和钢主梁有风荷载作用时的横向位移比没有风荷载作用时大了18.46mm，横向最大位移达到了21.20mm；钢主梁跨中应力值增加了10.05Mpa，增加幅度为26.17%。这说明风荷载对钢主梁的应力与变形影响较大。

2.2　悬吊支架的悬吊点纵向距离对钢主梁力学行为的影响

本文通过调整悬吊支架的悬吊点纵向距离来研究悬吊支架的悬吊点纵向距离对钢主梁力学行为的影响，纵桥分别按照2m、3.5m、4m、5m、6m间距布置。如图4、图5所示。

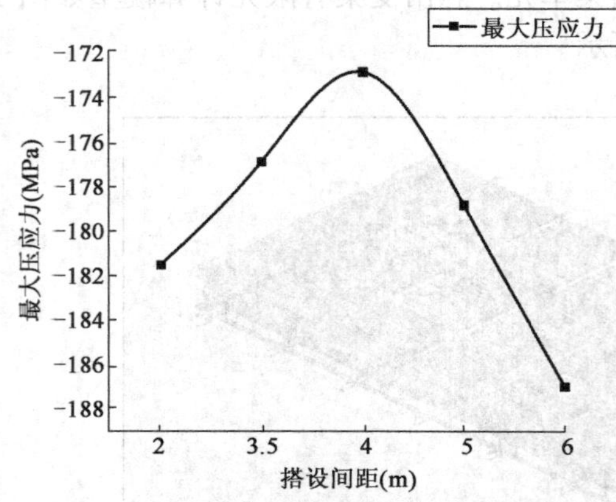

图4　钢主梁压应力与悬吊点纵向距离的关系

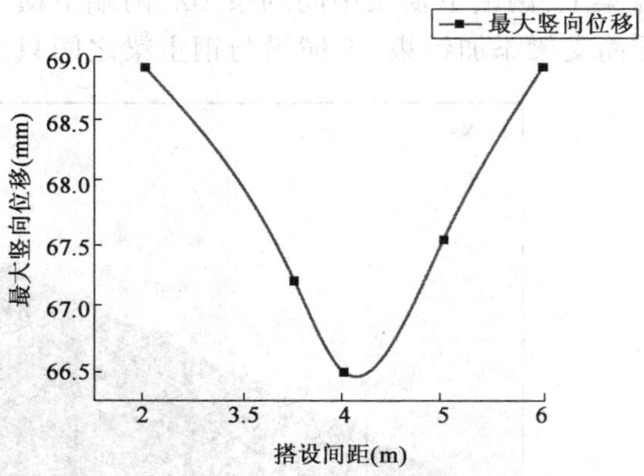

图5　钢主梁跨中位移与悬吊点纵向距离的关系

从图4、图5可以看出，钢主梁的跨中最大位移和应力随着悬吊点纵向距离的变化而大致呈现出抛物线变化。其中，悬吊点纵向距离为2～4m时，最大压应力和最大竖向位移逐渐减小；为4～6m时，最大压应力和最大竖向位移逐渐增大。实际工程悬吊点纵向间距设计合理值为4m，处于抛物线的极值点附近，有利于提高钢主梁的受力。

2.3　混凝土桥面板厚度对钢主梁结构力学行为的影响

本文通过对桥面板厚度进行调整来研究其对钢主梁力学行为的影响，具体研究了桥面板厚度为10cm、20cm、30cm时钢主梁的力学行为，计算结果如表2所示。

混凝土桥面板厚度对钢主梁跨中的影响　　表2

混凝土桥面板厚度(cm)	最大压应力(Mpa)	最大竖面位移(mm)
10	-110.55	48.04
20	-172.90	66.48
30	-232.28	88.90

由表2数据分析可知，随着桥面板厚度的增加，钢主梁的最大压应力和最大竖向位移都在增加。当桥面板板厚度为20cm时，钢主梁的最大压应力为172.90Mpa；当桥面板厚度为30cm时，钢主梁的最大压应力为232.28Mpa，增加了59.38Mpa，增加比例为34.34%。而最大竖向位移为由66.48mm增加到88.90mm，增加了33.72%。由此可以看出，桥面板的重量在整个系统的受力中占据主要地位。

2.4　桥面板混凝土浇筑过程对钢主梁力学行为的影响

混凝土桥面板的浇筑顺序为：横桥向按照先中间再两边的顺序一次浇筑到位，纵桥向由跨中向梁端逐步浇筑到位。依据浇筑顺序，共分4个工况：工况1为悬吊支架安装成功状态(临时施工荷载也施加在了悬吊支架上)；工况2为跨中段混凝土(顺序3)浇筑完成；工况3为三分段混凝土(顺序2)浇筑完成；工况4为梁端段混凝土(顺序1)浇筑完成。

通过图6可以看出由于钢主梁在工况4下所受到的梁部荷载最大，所以应力也最大，最大应力为172.90Mpa。通过图7可以看出由于钢主梁在工况4下所受到的梁部荷载最大，故竖向位移也最大，最大竖向位移为66.48mm。这些数据为钢主梁预拱度的设置提供了依据。

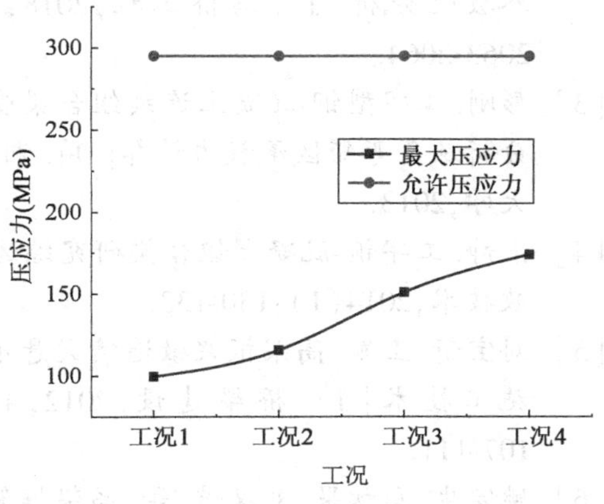

图6 钢主梁跨中应力变化图

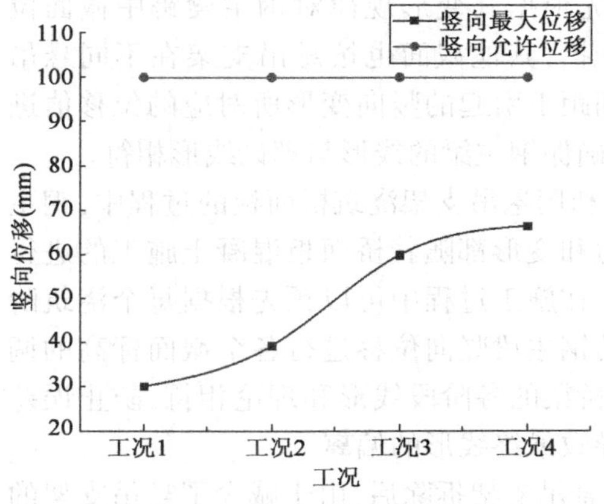

图7 竖向跨中位移变化图

由以上数据分析可知，在支架拆除前后，跨中位置的竖向位移增大了10.13mm；而钢主梁在只承受桥面板混凝土重量和风荷载的情况下跨中的最大竖向位移为45.84mm，相对于支架拆除后的竖向位移减少了10.18mm。由此可见，在桥面板和钢主梁形成一个整体后，桥梁的刚度变大会造成一部分位移不可恢复，而可恢复的位移可以通过一些技术方法来避免。

2.5 悬吊支架结构的拆除对钢主梁结构力学行为的影响

当混凝土桥面板结构强度达到设计要求时即可对悬吊支架进行拆除。当桥面板混凝土达到设计强度后，就可以认为钢主梁和混凝土板已经成为一体，可以作为一个整体共同受力，此时只承受悬吊支架的自重和风荷载作用，不再承受混凝土的振捣荷载和施工荷载。对悬吊支架拆除前后钢主梁的竖向位移变化进行分析，结果如表3、图8所示。

不同工况下时钢主梁的竖向位移(mm)　　表3

工况	梁端	L/4	跨中
拆除前	0	-47.01	-66.15
拆除后	0	-39.81	-56.02

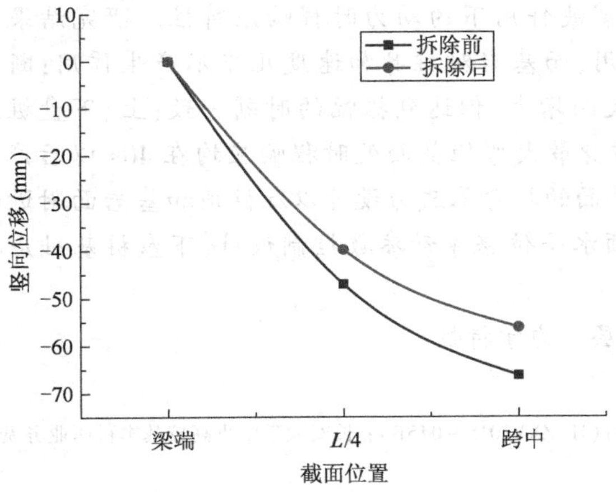

图8 悬吊支架拆除前后钢主梁竖向位移变化图

3 结语

本文通过对悬吊支架的风荷载、悬吊点纵向间距、混凝土桥面板厚度、混凝土浇筑过程和支架拆除对钢主梁力学行为的影响进行研究，得到了悬吊支架与钢主梁的变形规律，以便对悬吊支架施工时钢主梁的力学行为和线形进行控制。通过研究得出以下结论：

(1)悬吊支架的风荷载对钢主梁的位移和应力影响较大，会使其产生较大的横向位移。因此，在钢主梁结构成型前进行线形控制时，为了使计算分析更精确，应在荷载组合分析时将钢主梁和悬吊支架的横风荷载考虑进去，且采取必要措施限制桥面板浇筑过程中钢主梁的横向位移。

(2)钢主梁的位移和应力随着悬吊点纵向距离的变化而呈现出抛物线变化。其中，悬吊点纵向距离为2~4m时，最大压应力和最大竖向位移逐渐减小；为4~6m时，最大压应力和最大竖向位移逐渐增大。因此，悬吊点纵向距离合理取值建议为4m。

(3)钢主梁的跨中最大位移和应力随着桥面板厚度的增加而增大,且桥面板的重量在整个系统受力中占据主要地位。采用不同的桥面板厚度时,可以先根据其变形规律对钢主梁跨中截面位置进行预抬,其他截面也按悬吊支架在不同悬吊点纵向间距下引起的竖向变形所对应的位移值进行预抬,确保钢主梁的线形与理论线形相符。

(4)利用悬吊支架浇筑桥面板的过程中,钢主梁的应力和变形都随着桥面板混凝土施工的进行而增加。在施工过程中可以预先根据每个浇筑阶段引起的钢主梁竖向位移进行各个截面标高的调整,确保桥梁的各阶段线形和理论相符,防止误差的积累导致最终线形的偏离。

(5)悬吊支架拆除后,由于减少了悬吊支架的自重,钢主梁会向上发生回弹,而成桥后由于桥梁的刚度变大会有部分位移不可恢复。因此,预拱度设置时必须充分考虑这些变化,避免成桥时出现下挠或者隆起。

参考文献

[1] 王胜斌,吴肖波,唐国喜,等. 双工字钢-混凝土板组合梁桥车桥耦合振动研究[J]. 世界桥梁,2017,4 (166):38-44.

[2] 马天. 双工字钢混组合梁桥混凝土徐变效应参数化分析[J]. 路桥工程,2018,5(28):2063-2064.

[3] 彭刚. 工字型钢-混凝土连续组合梁受弯性能分析及负弯矩区承载力计算[D]. 湘潭:湘潭大学,2013.

[4] 张静. 工字钢-混凝土组合梁研究综述[J]. 市政技术,2014(1):130-133.

[5] 刘宝新,王军. 高架框架墩连续梁悬吊支架法施工技术[J]. 桥梁建设,2012,42(12):107-111.

[6] 姚宏生,马秋果,刘汉斌,等. 高架框架墩连续梁悬吊支架法的施工技术研究[J]. 石家庄铁道大学学报:自然科学版,2013,11(3):123-128.

地震区跨活动断层桥梁桩基动力时程响应分析

李宇杰[1] 冯忠居*[1] 张 聪[1] 刘 闯[2] 王富春[1] 孙平宽[3]

(1. 长安大学公路学院;2. 海南省交通运输厅;3. 中国公路工程咨询集团有限公司)

摘 要 为了研究强震区桥梁跨活动断层时,桩基在地震中的动力响应,以海文大桥为工程背景,利用 Midas GTS 有限元软件建立其强震-断层-海床岩土体耦合作用的数值模型,研究了桥梁桩基的加速度、位移、弯矩及剪力在不同强度(0.20~0.60g)的5010地震波作用下的动力时程响应特性。研究结果表明:上部大厚度松散土体对桩身加速度有放大及滤波作用,而基岩对桩身加速度几乎不产生作用;断层上、下盘桩基础的桩顶水平位移随输入地震动强度的增大而增大,但达到振幅的时刻一致;上、下盘桩基础桩顶竖向位移时程响应都在50s以后产生永久沉降;桩身最大弯矩截面处时程响应均在40s以后产生永久弯矩;应重点考虑上部覆盖层软硬土体界面和基岩界面的抗弯承载力设计以及桩顶和基岩面附近的抗剪承载力设计;上盘桩基础应按桩身加速度、弯矩、桩顶水平位移等动参数控制设计,下盘桩基础应按动剪应力控制设计。

关键词 地震响应 数值模拟 桥梁桩基 活动断层 力学特性

1. 基金项目:国家自然科学基金项目(51708040);海南省交通科技项目(HNZXY2015-045R);长安大学中央高校基本科研业务费专项资金(No. 300102218115)。

0 引言

地震波会对桥梁桩基础及周围岩土体产生扰动,从而影响桩基础的承载特性和稳定性,甚至造成其破坏失效。现有的桥梁大直径深长桩基础抗震设计理论中,关于活动断层对桥梁抗震性能的影响研究还处于探索阶段,无法满足桥梁桩基工程在跨断层施工时安全和经济上的需求,针对活动断层这一特殊地质条件下的桥梁桩基设计的研究亟待开展。

当前国内外学者分析桥梁桩基在地震作用下动力响应的方法主要是随机振动法、时程分析法与反应谱法。赫永峰等分别运用规范简化算法、弹性、弹塑性时程分析法及反应谱法对比分析了连续梁桥在地震作用下的响应,给出不同计算阶段适合的方法。单德山等基于全国129个汶川主震地震台站记录的反应谱,分析了高墩大跨度连续刚构桥随不同断层距的动力响应特性。刘小璐等利用相对运动法导出了非一致地震激励下的随机振动和随机模拟等结构动力响应分析方法,研究了大跨度桥梁结构在地震中的动力可靠度。在模型试验方面,冯忠居等利用振动台试验较为系统地研究了桩-土-断层耦合作用下,桥梁桩基的抗液化性能及桩身加速度、桩顶水平及竖向位移、弯矩、剪力、桩基损伤情况等动力响应特点。吴琪等进行了3层框架结构群桩基础在不同地震强度下的振动台试验,揭示了地震作用下珊瑚砂场地内地基-桩-上部结构的动力响应。宋波等基于相似准则开展了钢管桩基高桩码头振动台试验,分析了直桩和斜桩结构在不同地震动作用下的动力响应特点以及桩基的震损形式。张恒源等开展了地基-群桩基础-框筒结构在可液化场地中的动力相互作用振动台试验,对比分析了水平和竖向(双向)耦合地震作用下群桩应变、超孔隙水压力、土体加速度等研究结果。Xu等利用大型振动台试验探讨了群桩结构体系在可液化与不可液化砂土中的应变及加速度等动力响应特性。Mohanty等对典型的桩承式桥梁进行了缩尺振动台试验,应用加速度幅值增大的白噪声运动来判断桥梁的逐渐液化和动力特性,研究了可液化沉积物中桩支承桥梁跨中倒塌的机理。在数值模拟方面,Opensees为桥梁的三维有限元模型提供了计算平台。陈旭等通过建立有限元模型研究了土体非线性对高墩桥梁地震响应的影响和土层对基岩地震动的滤波效应。张永亮以铁路简支梁桥为研究对象,建立了考虑桩-承台-土相互作用的Midas/civil有限元单墩抗震计算模型,应用反应谱法分析对桥梁桩基础在承台侧向土埋深和桩侧土m值变化时的地震反应规律。Wu等利用Ansys有限元软件建立了综合考虑波浪、地震、水流作用的流固耦合数值模型,分析了地震振荡流场、地震-流联合流场及地震-波联合流场中的群桩效应。Li等以小型物理砂箱实验模拟受推力断层影响的群桩,并采用粒子流程式(PFC3d)进行数值分析,在剪切带的传播路径、桩帽的位移和桩的变形模式方面,数值分析结果与砂箱试验结果吻合良好。

现有研究成果未能综合考虑活动断层及地震动强度等因素对特大型桥梁大直径深长桩基础动力时程响应产生的影响,本文通过Midas GTS有限元软件建立海文大桥桩基-土-断层相互作用的数值模型,选用非线性动力分析法研究在强震区跨活动断层环境下,桩基础的桩身加速度、桩顶水平及竖向位移、桩身弯矩及剪力的动力时程响应,以期为强震区跨断层桥梁深长桩基础设计提供可靠的技术依据。

1 工程背景

海文大桥项目的路线总长5.597km,其中跨海部分桥长为3.959km。桥梁桩基础位于地震荷载大、风浪频率高、发震活动断层、海相强腐蚀区的环境里,50年超越概率10%和2%的动峰值加速度分别为0.35g和0.59g,为国内最大。抗震设防烈度要求为0.35g(Ⅷ度)。桥址附近22条断层,其中大桥跨越F2、F3、F4三条断层,F3、F4为非活动断层,37号与38号墩之间跨越F2活动断层,大桥桩基础的施工环境在国内外罕见。

海文大桥37号墩位于断层F2的下盘,38号墩位于上盘,承台尺寸为9.2m(横桥向)×9.2m(纵桥向)×3m(厚),承台下接4根群桩。F2活动断层为正断层,宽度约30m,倾向南西,倾角65°,走向345°。37号和38号墩桩基础距离断层大约25m,土层分布从上到下如图1所示。

2 数值模拟

2.1 模型建立与参数选取

土体具有典型的非线性本构关系,为了使分

析结果合理准确,选择有限元软件中的非线性时程计算方法进行地震时程分析。弹性模型适用于承台与桩基础的分析,弹塑性模型适用于岩土体分析,收敛准则采用摩尔-库伦准则,收敛条件采用“位移”及“内力”等非线性计算方式。

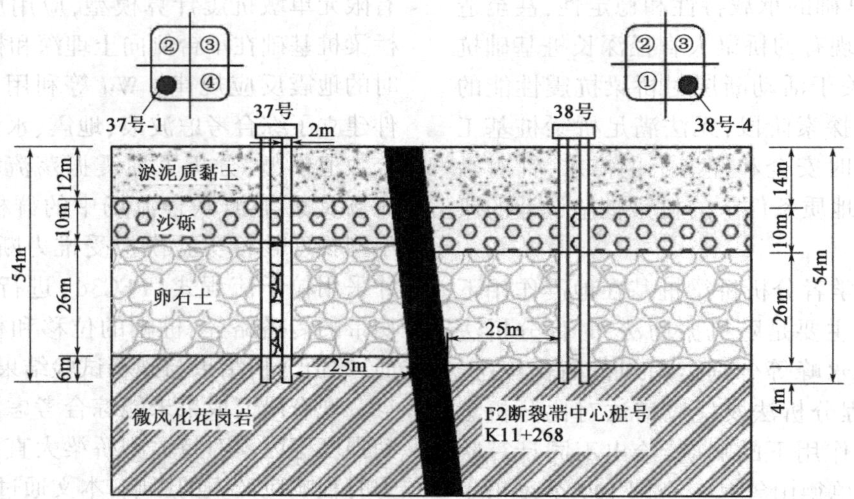

图 1　桩基础与断层相对位置

2.1.1　模型建立

承台尺寸为 9.2m×9.2m×3m,承台下接 4 根桩间距 5.5m、桩径 2m 的群桩;37 号、38 号墩桩长都是 54m,下盘桩端嵌入岩层的深度为 6m,上盘为 4m;承台尺寸均为 9.2m×9.2m×3m;模型的尺寸在 X 方向为 100m,Y 方向 62m,Z 方向 82m。土层分布从上到下依次是淤泥质黏土层(夹砂),上盘厚度为 14m,下盘厚度为 10m;砂砾层,厚度为 10m;卵石土层,厚度为 26m;桩端嵌入的微风化花岗岩层,厚度为 38m。断层破碎带及桩周土体的网格尺寸加密划分为 1m,外侧土体网格尺寸 1 ~ 4m 渐变划分,模型网格划分如图 2 所示。

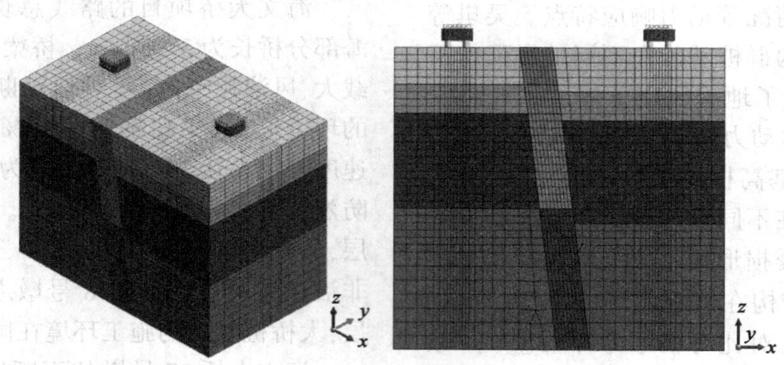

图 2　37 号和 38 号墩模型

2.1.2　参数选取

由海文大桥桥址区域地质勘察报告及有关的规范得到数值分析模型中的材料取值,如表 1 所示。

各材料参数表　　表 1

材　料	弹性模量(MPa)	泊松比	黏聚力(kN/m²)	内摩擦角(°)	重度(kN/m³)
淤泥质黏土(夹砂)	45.68	0.35	48	12	17
粉细砂(含泥)	70.6	0.31	3	14	18.6
砂砾	85.9	0.30	92	21	19

续上表

材料	弹性模量(MPa)	泊松比	黏聚力(kN/m^2)	内摩擦角(°)	重度(kN/m^3)
卵石土	99.8	0.28	180	30	22
中风化花岗岩	40280	0.24	1200	43	24.8
微风化花岗岩	60058	0.20	1760	50	26.5
淤泥质黏土破碎带	24.6	0.36	38	7	15
砂砾破碎带	35.4	0.32	58	18	17
卵石土破碎带	55.8	0.29	150	28	21
中风化岩破碎带	21800	0.26	1000	40	23
微风化岩破碎带	38800	0.22	1500	48	25
钢筋混凝土	40000	0.19	—	—	24

2.1.3 边界条件

(1)振型分析采用弹性边界

在地震时程分析过程中,首先要通过振型分析求得有限元分析体系中的特征值,再利用其来求取阻尼参数。Midas GTS 有限元软件通常利用弹性边界条件分析特征周期,并用曲面弹簧来定义。

(2)时程分析采用黏弹性人工边界

由于波的反射效应,采用一般静力学的方法进行地震时程分析,会有比较大的误差,故采用黏性边界条件,Midas GTS 有限元软件建模时通过在土体外边界添加曲面阻尼弹簧来定义黏性边界。

2.2 计算方案

2.2.1 地震波选取

依照《海南省文昌市海文大桥项目工程场地地震安全性评价报告》(中国地球物理研究所)给出的建议,选择 50 年超越概率为 10% 的 5010 地震波并利用 SeismoSigal 软件对其基线校正及滤波处理,并将其加速度峰值按比例缩放,最终得到如图 3 的波形,选取 0.20 ~ 0.60g 不同峰值的地震动输入。

2.2.2 工况设置

地震动输入选取 5010 地震波的不同峰值 0.20g、0.25g、0.30g、0.35g、0.40g、0.45g、0.50g、0.55g、0.60g,分析跨活动断层桥梁桩基础在不同强度的同种波形地震动作用下的力学特性及地震响应。

由于存在断层的影响,需要考虑地震动水平方向和竖向同时作用的影响,计算工况如表 2 所示。

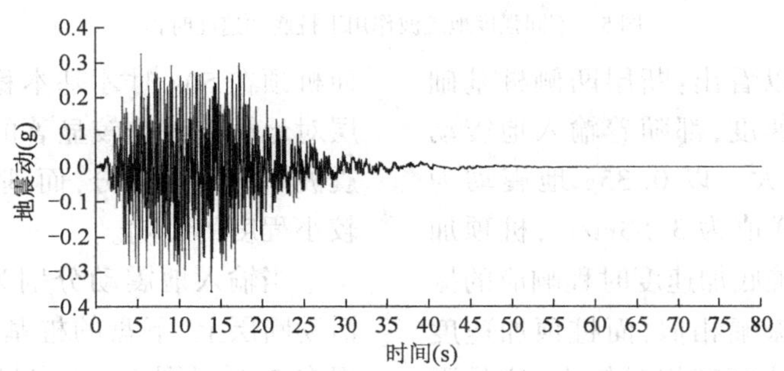

图 3 5010 地震波

计算工况 表 2

桥基础编号	地震波类型	地震波强度	加载方式	备注
37 号-1、38 号-1	5010	0.20g、0.25g、0.30g、0.35g、0.40g、0.45g、0.50g、0.55g、0.60g	水平向 + 竖向	跨活动断层

3　不同强度地震波作用下桩基础力学特性

3.1　桩身加速度时程响应

在不同强度的地震动作用下,位于断层两侧的37号-1和38号-4桩基础桩顶和桩底处的加速度时程响应,如图4~图5所示。

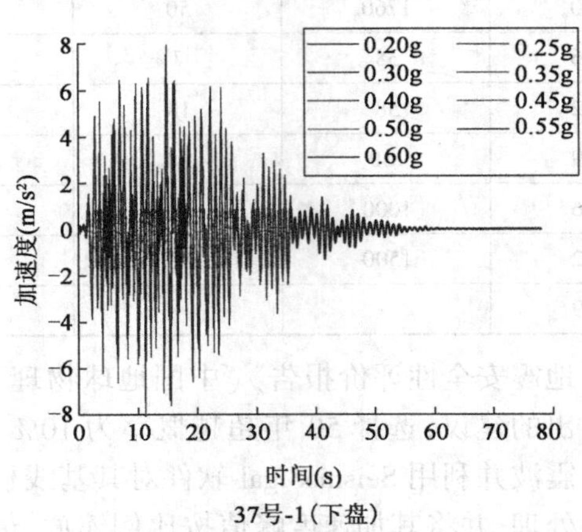

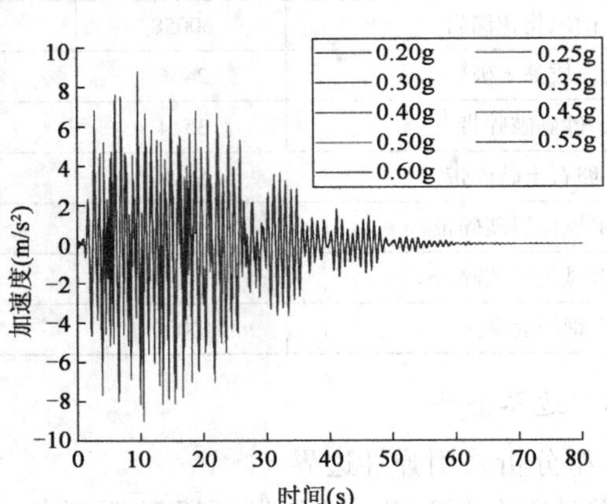

图4　不同强度地震波作用下桩顶加速度时程

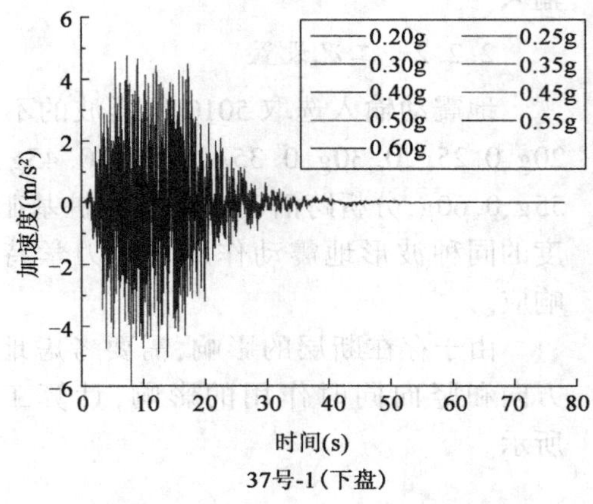

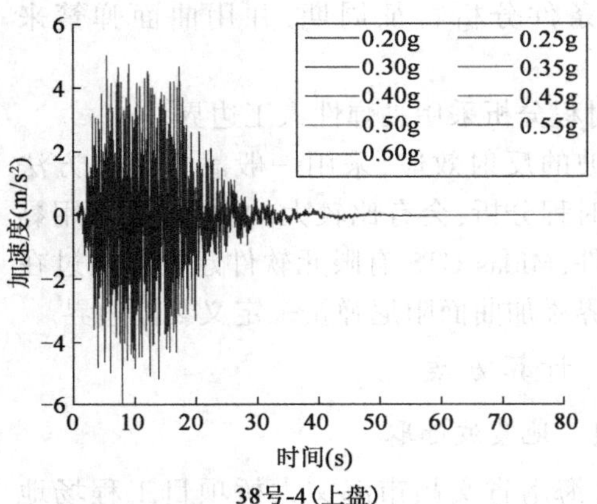

图5　不同强度地震波作用下桩底加速度时程

从图4和图5中可以看出:断层两侧桩基础在桩顶和桩底位置的加速度,都随着输入地震动加速度峰值的增大而增大。以0.35g地震动为例,37号-1桩底加速度峰值为3.53m/s²,桩顶加速度峰值为6.17m/s²。桩底加速度时程响应的振动幅度与输入地震动的振幅相似,而桩顶加速度响应值与输入值相比振动幅度相对较大,这是因为当输入地震动的加速度峰值接近场地的自振周期时,桩土惯性相互作用会增强场地土层对该地震波的放大作用,共振作用使得桩顶对地震波的敏感程度和响应程度增大。

桩底加速度和输入加速度的频率相似,桩顶加速度的频率比桩底的小,分析0.35g地震动作用下的响应,桩底加速度在30s时基本达到稳定,而桩顶在50s时才基本稳定,表明大厚度上覆土层对地震波有比较显著的“过滤”效应,滤掉了地震波中的高频成分,而基岩对地震波的频率产生较小程度的影响。

当输入地震动分别为0.20~0.60g时,位于活动断层上、下盘的桩基础桩底加速度峰值均出现在7.96s(图6);下盘桩基础桩顶加速度峰值出现的时刻在11.28~18.20s之间,上盘桩出现在10.06~15.36s之间,可见与桩底加速度峰值出现的时刻相比,桩顶存在着相对滞后的情况;且桩基础位于下盘,其峰值出现的时刻明显滞后于上盘。由于基岩对输入地震动的响应速度快,而上部覆盖土层因为惯性作用和桩土相互作用,对输入地震动的响应速度与基岩相比存在滞后性,因此出现了“上盘效应”。

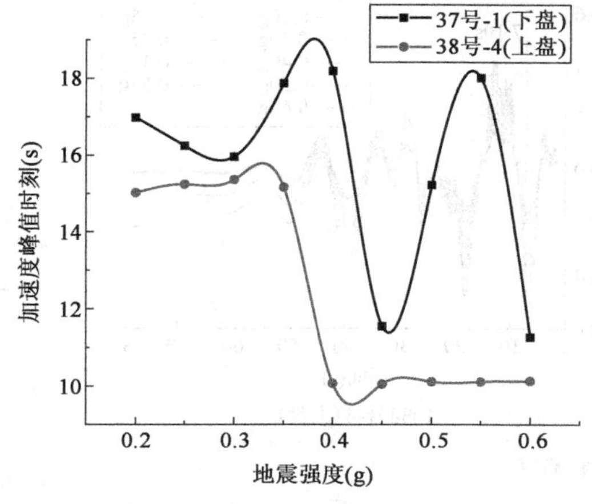

图6　上、下盘桩顶加速度峰值时刻对比

3.2　桩顶水平位移时程响应

在不同强度的地震动作用下，断层两侧桩基础桩顶水平位移时程响应如图7所示。

从图7可以看出：同一强度地震动作用下，位于活动断层上、下盘的桩基础产生的永久位移大小不同，但其桩顶水平位移时程响应的规律类似。当输入的地震动为0.35g时，上、下盘桩基础产生的永久位移分别为0.03m、0.02m，说明在同一强度地震动作用下，位于活动断层上盘的桩基础产生更大的永久位移，存在“上盘效应”。

桩顶水平位移的时程响应幅度在不同强度地震动作用下基本一致，输入0.20～0.60g加速度峰值时，37号-1、38号-4桩基础均分别在6.96s、12.96s达到水平位移的最大值。可知，桩基础达到振幅的时刻是一定的，不随地震动强度增加而变化。

相同强度的地震动下，位于活动断层上盘的38号-4桩顶水平位移最大值明显大于下盘37号-1桩顶水平位移最大值(图8)，由于断层两侧桩周土体存在差别以及桩基嵌岩深度不同，使得地震作用中断层地质显示出显著的“上盘效应”，上盘的桩产生更大的水平位移。

随着输入地震动强度增大，37号-1和38号-4桩基础的桩顶水平位移最大值也增大，呈近似线性增长。在0.20～0.60g地震动作用下，如图8所示，随地震动增大，最大振幅差值逐渐增大，“上盘效应”逐渐显著。

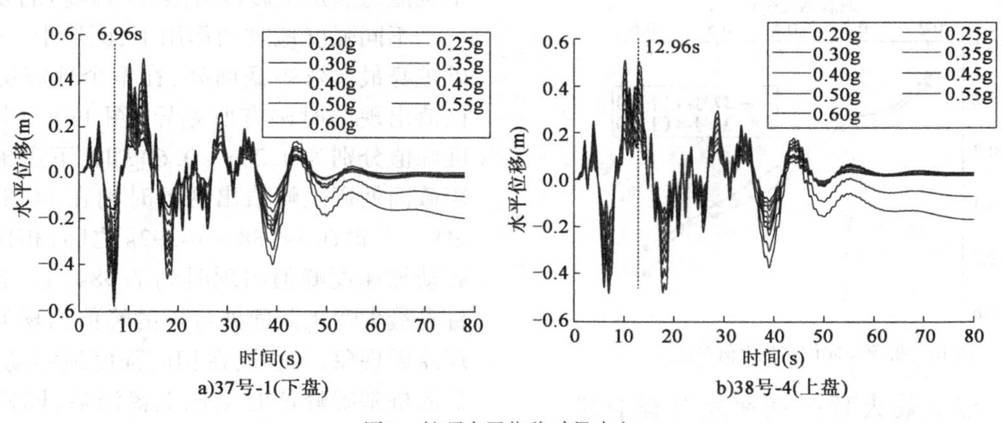

图7　桩顶水平位移时程响应

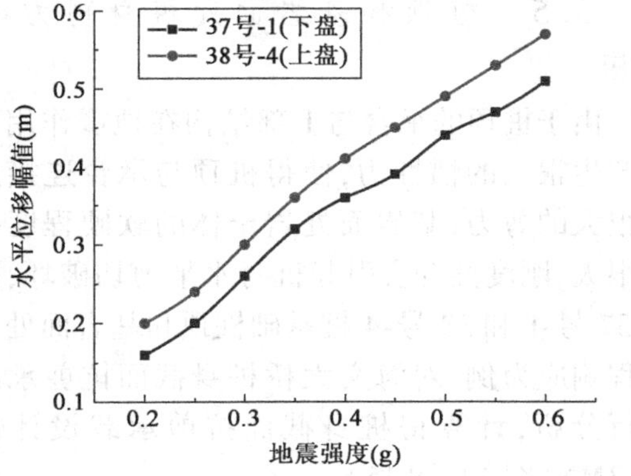

图8　上、下盘桩顶水平位移最大值对比

3.3　桩顶竖向位移时程响应

在不同强度的地震动作用下，37号-1桩基础和38号-4桩基础的桩顶竖向位移时程响应如图9所示。

由图9可看出，相同强度的地震动作用下，位于断层上、下盘的桩基础桩顶竖向位移时程变化规律相似，但桩基础产生的永久竖向位移大小不同。不同强度的地震动作用下，随着地震持时增加，桩顶竖向位移振动规律相同，上、下盘桩基础桩顶竖向位移均在7.10s达到峰值，50s之后基本不再发生振动,且均产生了永久竖向位移。

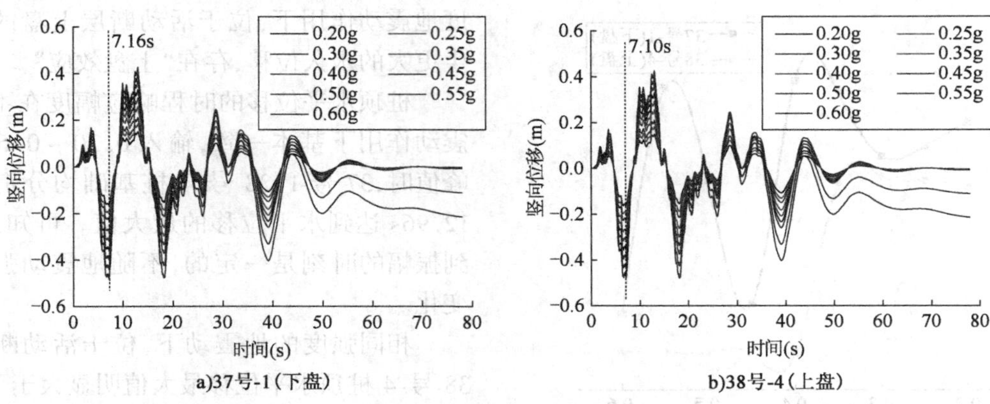

a)37号-1(下盘)　　b)38号-4(上盘)

图 9　桩顶竖向位移时程响应

随着地震强度的增大,上、下盘桩基础的桩顶竖向位移最大值均接近线性增长(图 10)。在 0.20～0.60g 地震动作用下,上、下盘桩基础产生了不均匀沉降,桩顶竖向位移最大值变化趋势如图。位于上盘的 38 号-4 桩基础受地震影响较大而产生较大沉降,有明显的"上盘效应",此外桩周土体及嵌岩深度的差异也会对上、下盘沉降差异产生一定影响。

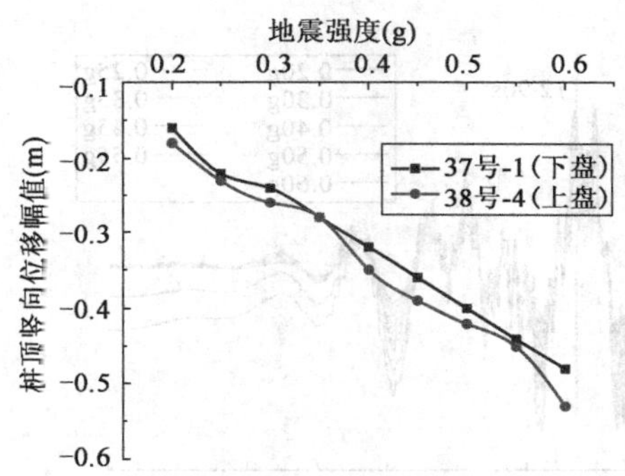

图 10　桩顶竖向位移最大值对比

3.4　桩身最大弯矩截面处时程响应

根据《公路钢筋混凝土及预应力混凝土桥涵设计规范》(JTG 3362—2018),计算海文大桥 37 号、38 号墩桩基础配筋得其抗弯承载力为 37.14MN·m,桩身弯矩在土层界面处达到最大值,分析其最大弯矩截面处时程响应,如图 11 所示。

输入不同强度的地震加速度时,位于断层上、下盘的桩基础在 0～40s 范围内振幅较大(图 12),整个地震历程中桩身产生较大弯矩的持时较长,从 40s 以后弯矩逐渐减小并趋于稳定,最终产生了永久弯矩。当输入加速度峰值分别为 0.20～0.60g时,下盘桩基础产生的永久弯矩为 0.7～1.1MN·m,上盘桩产生的永久弯矩为 1.1～2.6MN·m。相同强度的地震加速度下,上盘桩基础产生的永久弯矩要比下盘桩基础的永久弯矩都大,这是由于上、下盘桩周土体在断层两侧的差异及桩基嵌岩深度不同,导致了地震动作用下明显的"上盘效应"。上、下盘桩基础在 0.35g 强度的地震动作用下,产生的最大弯矩为 26.78MN·m,小于桩基抗弯承载力,说明海文大桥桩基础抗弯承载能力满足抗震设防烈度(Ⅷ度)的要求。

不同强度地震动作用下,断层上、下盘的桩基础桩身最大弯矩截面处,在整个地震历程中弯矩极值出现的时刻有所差异(图 13)。当输入加速度峰值分别为 0.20g～0.60g 时,下盘桩身最大弯矩截面处弯矩峰值出现的时刻在 14.88～21.78s 之间,上盘在 14.88～14.92s 之间;相比于输入地震动加速度峰值出现时刻 7.98s,上、下盘桩基础桩身最大弯矩截面处弯矩的峰值出现的时刻均呈现滞后现象。此外,在相同强度地震动作用下,下盘的桩基础峰值时刻比上盘滞后,同样出现了的"上盘效应"。

3.5　桩顶和基岩面处桩身剪力时程响应

由于桩顶的承台与上部结构在地震作用下摆动产生很大的惯性力,使得桩顶与承台连接处产生很大的剪力;基岩面处岩土体的软硬程度差异性很大,刚度突变会引起桩身水平剪切破坏,因此以 37 号-1 和 38 号-4 桩基础桩顶和基岩面处剪力时程响应为例,对海文大桥桩身截面抗剪承载力进行分析,计算得桩身截面抗剪承载设计值为 11.3MN(图 14、图 15)。

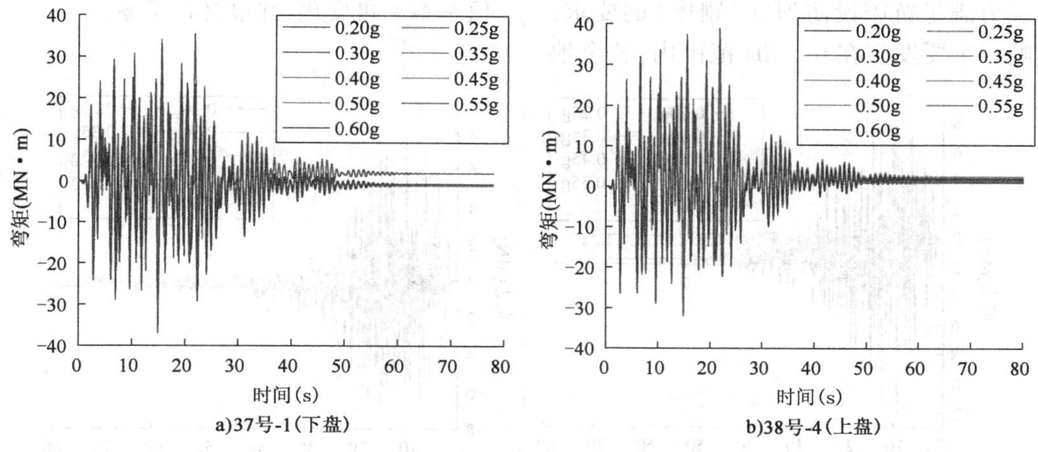

图 11　桩基础桩身最大弯矩截面处时程

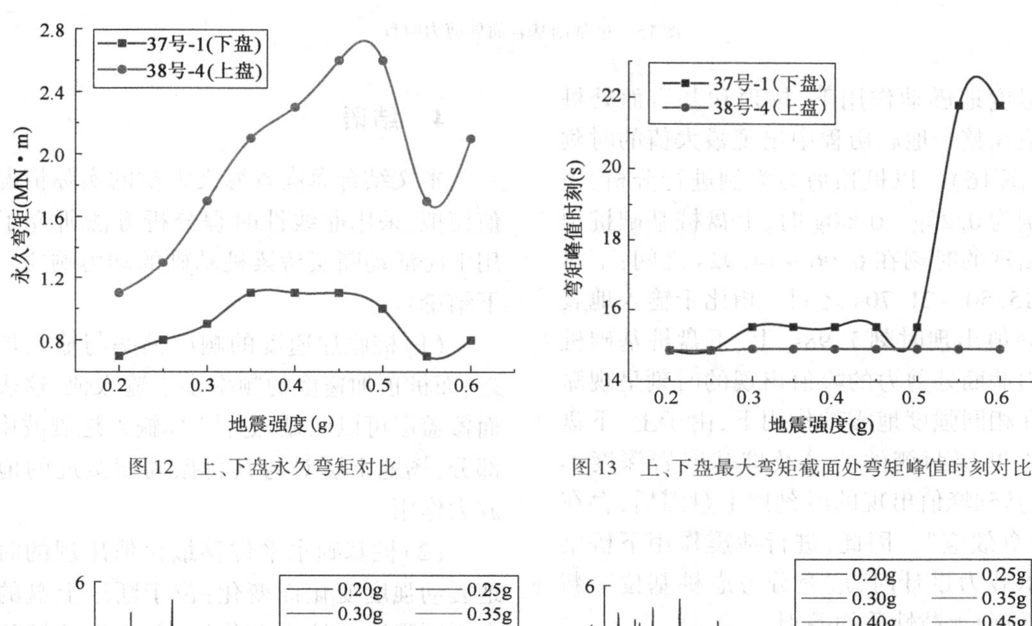

图 12　上、下盘永久弯矩对比

图 13　上、下盘最大弯矩截面处弯矩峰值时刻对比

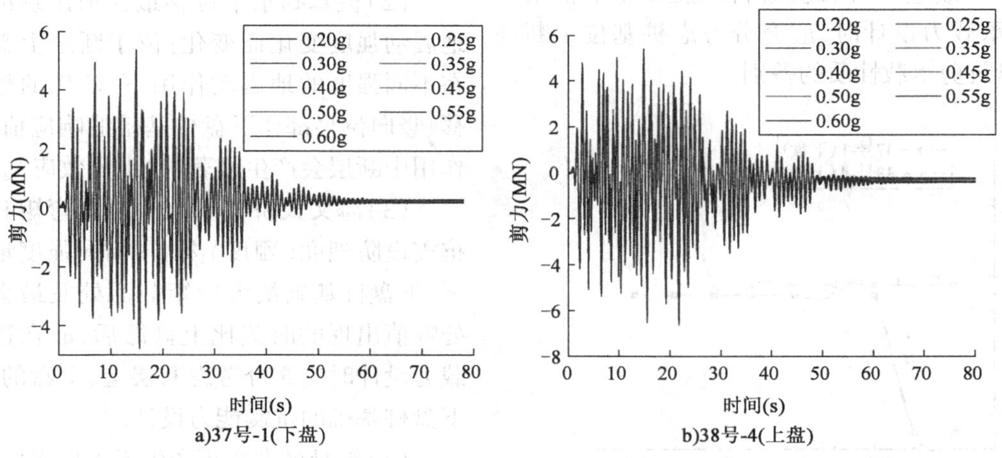

图 14　桩基础桩顶剪力时程

由图 14 和图 15 可知:位于断层上、下盘的桩基础桩顶剪力时程和基岩面处桩身剪力时程变化规律基本相同:桩身同一截面处桩身剪力值随着地震强度的增大逐渐增大,当输入地震动强度为

0.35g时,基岩面处剪力最大值为6.8MN,桩基截面抗剪承载力满足抗震设防烈度(Ⅷ度)的要求;剪力时程响应主要发生在0~40s范围内,整个地震历程中产生较大剪力的持时较长,40s以后剪力值基本不再变化,并最终趋于零。

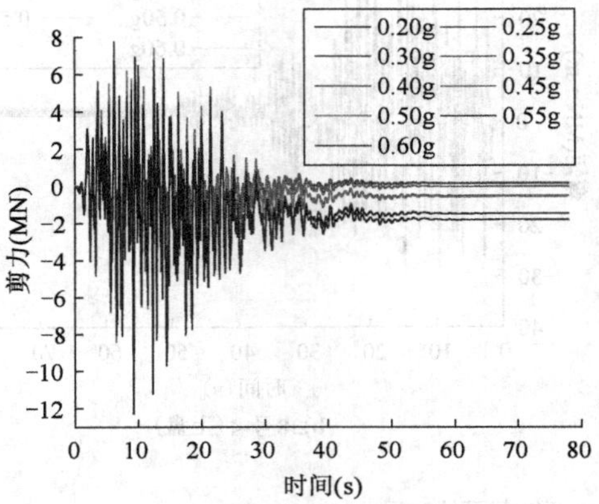

a)37号-1(下盘)

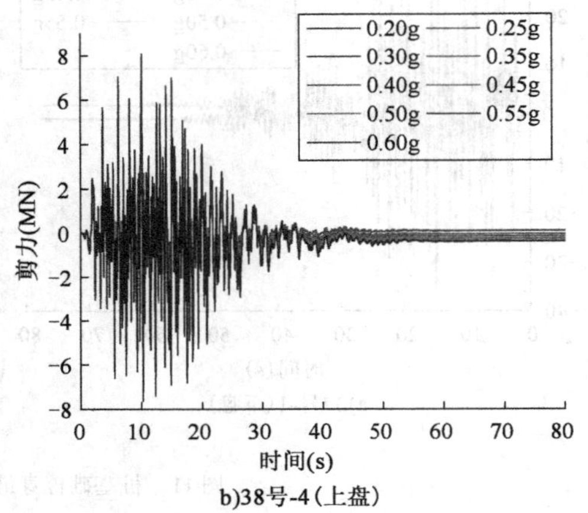

b)38号-4(上盘)

图15　桩基础基岩面处剪力时程

不同强度地震动作用下,桩顶和基岩面处桩身剪力峰值在整个地震历程中出现最大值的时刻有所差异(图16)。以桩顶剪力为例进行分析,当地震波分别为0.20g~0.60g时,上盘桩基础桩顶剪力峰值出现的时刻在6.96~14.92s之间;下盘桩基础在15.50~21.70s之间。相比于输入地震波加速度峰值出现时刻7.98s,上、下盘桩基础桩身最大剪力截面处剪力的峰值出现的时刻呈现滞后现象。在相同强度地震动作用下,由于上、下盘桩周土体在断层两侧的差异及桩基嵌岩深度不同,下盘桩基础峰值出现的时刻比上盘滞后,存在明显的"上盘效应"。因此,进行地震作用下桥梁桩基抗剪承载力设计时,应充分考虑桩基位于断层上、下盘抗剪承载性质的差别。

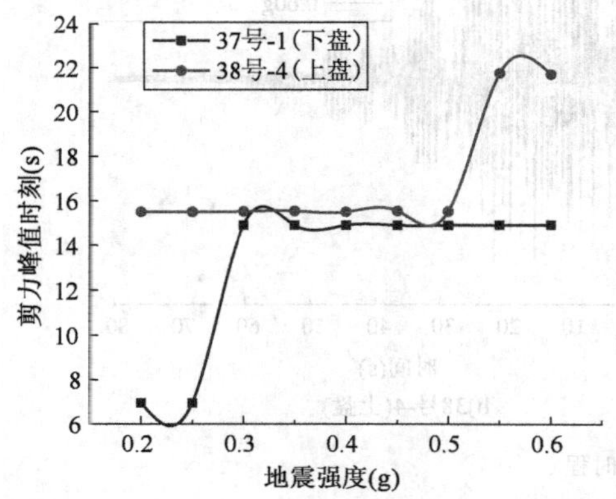

图16　上、下盘桩顶剪力峰值出现时刻对比

4　结语

本文结合海南省海文大桥的实际情况利用数值模拟,采用非线性时程分析方法研究了地震作用下跨活动断层桥梁桩基础的动力响应。得到以下结论:

(1)桩底加速度的响应频率与输入加速度接近,而桩顶加速度的频率小于输入值,这表明海床面覆盖层可以明显"过滤"掉输入地震波中的高频部分;场地土层对与其自振周期接近的地震波有放大作用。

(2)桩基础水平位移最大值出现的时刻不随地震动强度变化而变化;位于断层上盘的桩基础在不同强度的地震动作用下,产生的桩顶水平位移、竖向位移都比下盘桩基础的响应值大,在地震作用中断层会产生显著的"上盘效应"。

(3)海文大桥桩基础的最大弯矩和剪力满足抗震设防烈度(Ⅷ度)要求;相同强度地震动作用下,下盘桩基础最大弯矩截面处及最大剪力截面处峰值出现的时刻比上盘滞后,故在进行桩基承载力设计时应充分考虑断层上、下盘的差异,增强下盘桩基础的抗震能力设计。

(4)桩身最大弯矩产生于土层界面处,最大剪力截面产生于桩顶及软硬岩分界处,应加强重点位置抗弯、抗剪能力的设计。研究成果可为海文大桥桩基工程提供重要的设计与施工技术指导,补充强震-断层-海床岩土体耦合作用下桩基础的设计理论。

参考文献

[1] FengZhongju, Hu Haibo, Dong Yunxiu, et al. Effect of steel casing on vertical bearing characteristics of steel tube-reinforced concrete piles in loess area [J]. Applied Sciences, 2019,9(14):2874.

[2] DongYunxiu, Feng Zhongju, Hu Haibo, et al. The horizontal bearing capacity of composite concrete-filled steel tube piles[J]. Advances in Civil Engineering,2020,1-15.

[3] FengZhongju, Huo Jianwei, Hu Haibo, et al. Research on corrosion damage and bearing characteristics of bridge pile foundation concrete under a dry-wet-freeze-thaw cycle [J]. Advances in Civil Engineering, 2021, 2021(6):1-13.

[4] Jiang Guan, FengZhongju, Zhao Ruixin, et al. Case study on safety assessment of rockfall and splash stone protective structures for secondary excavation of highway slope[J]. Advances in Civil Engineering,2021,2021(2):1-9.

[5] Zhou X,Zhang X. Thoughts on the Development of Bridge Technology in China [J]. Engineering,2019,5(6):1120-1130.

[6] 王启耀,胡志平,王瑞,等.地震作用下地裂缝场地地表加速度响应的振动台试验研究[J].铁道学报,2015,37(12):121-128.

[7] 曾永平,董俊,陈克坚,等.近断层高铁简支梁桥抗震性能分析研究[J].铁道工程学报,2020,37(12):70-76.

[8] 江辉,张鹏,黄磊,等.跨断层简支钢箱梁桥的概率性地震损伤特性研究[J].振动与冲击,2021,(40):253-262.

[9] 管仲国,李建中.大跨度桥梁抗震体系研究[J].中国科学:技术科学,2021,51(05):493-504.

[10] 中国桥梁工程学术研究综述·2021[J].中国公路学报,2021,34(02):1-97.

[11] 贾宏宇,杨健,郑史雄,等.跨断层桥梁抗震研究综述[J/OL].西南交通大学学报:2021,1-16.

[12] 赫永峰,禚一.城际铁路连续梁桥抗震计算方法对比分析[J].铁道工程学报,2017,34(06):43-49.

[13] 单德山,张二华,董俊,等.汶川地震动衰减特性及其大跨高墩连续刚构桥的地震响应规律[J].土木工程学报,2017,50(04):107-115.

[14] 刘小璐,苏成,李保木,等.非一致地震激励下大跨度桥梁随机振动时域显式法[J].土木工程学报,2019,52(03):50-60+99.

[15] 冯忠居,张聪,何静斌,等.强震作用下群桩基础抗液化性能的振动台试验[J].交通运输工程学报,2021,21(04):72-83.

[16] DongYunxiu,Feng Zhongju,He J B,et al. Seismic response of a bridge pile foundation during a shaking table test [J]. Shock and Vibration, 2019:1-16.

[17] 刘闯,冯忠居,张福强,等.地震作用下特大型桥梁嵌岩桩基础动力响应[J].交通运输工程学报,2018,18(04):53-62.

[18] 何静斌,冯忠居,董芸秀,等.强震区桩-土-断层耦合作用下桩基动力响应[J].岩土力学,2020,41(07):2389-2400.

[19] 冯忠居,董芸秀,何静斌,等.强震作用下饱和粉细砂液化振动台试验[J].哈尔滨工业大学学报,2019,51(09):186-192.

[20] 冯忠居,王溪清,李孝雄,等.强震作用下的砂土液化对桩基力学特性影响[J].交通运输工程学报,2019,19(01):71-84.

[21] 吴琪,丁选明,陈志雄,等.不同地震动强度下珊瑚礁砂地基中桩-土-结构地震响应试验研究[J].岩土力学,2020,41(02):571-580.

[22] 宋波,谢明雷,李吉人.不同桩基形式高桩码头地震动力损伤振动台试验研究[J].土木工程学报,2018,51(S2):28-34.

[23] 张恒源,钱德玲,沈超,等.水平和竖向地震作用下液化场地群桩基础动力响应试验研究[J].岩土力学,2020,41(03):905-914.

[24] Xu C S, Dou P F, Du X L, et al. Seismic Performance of Pile Group-structure System in Liquefiable and Non-liquefiable Soil from Large-scale Shake Table Tests [J]. Soil

Dynamics and Earthquake Engineering,2020,138:106299.

[25] Mohanty P, Xu D, Biswal S, et al. A shake table investigation of dynamic behavior of pile supported bridges in liquefiable soil deposits [J]. Earthquake Engineeringand Engineering Vibration,2021,20(1):1-24.

[26] Zhang C, Wu Cw, Wang Pg. Seismic Fragility Analysis of Bridge Group Pile Foundations considering Fluid-Pile-Soil Interaction [J]. Shock and Vibration,2020,2020:8838813.

[27] Feng Zr, Su L, Wan Hp, et al. Three-dimensionalFinite Element Modelling for Seismic Response Analysis of Pile-supported Bridges [J]. Structure and Infrastructure Engineering, 2019,15(12):1583-1596.

[28] 陈旭,李春祥.考虑桩-土相互作用的高墩桥梁抗震性能[J].同济大学学报(自然科学版),2021,49(06):799-806.

[29] 张永亮,徐瑾,刘聪聪,等.承台-桩-土作用下铁路桥梁桩基础地震反应[J].铁道工程学报,2020,37(05):30-35.

[30] Wu Aj, Yang Wl. Numerical study of pile group effect on the hydrodynamic force on a pile of sea-crossing bridges during earthquakes [J]. Ocean Engineering,2020,199:106999.

[31] Li Ch, Lin Ml, Huang Wc. Interaction between pile groups and thrust faults in a physical sandbox and numerical analysis [J]. Engineering Geology,2019,252:65-77.

[32] 中华人民共和国行业标准.公路钢筋混凝土及预应力混凝土桥涵设计规范:JTG 3362-2018[S].北京:人民交通出版社股份有限公司,2018.

连续刚构桥设置防屈曲支撑的减震效果研究

徐梓涛 周 敉*

(长安大学旧桥检测与加固技术交通行业重点实验室)

摘 要 为探究在连续刚构桥设置的防屈曲支撑(Buckling-Restrained Braces,BRB)的减震效果和BRB的合理设置方式,以某110m+210m+110m连续刚构桥为研究对象,使用有限元分析软件CSI Bridge建立全桥模型,并采用非线性时程分析方法对所提出的3种工况下的连续刚构桥进行地震反应分析,通过对比主墩顶部和底部等关键位置的内力值和位移值来确定合理的BRB设置方式。结果表明,对于本文所研究的连续刚构桥而言,在一定程度上BRB的耗能能力越强则减震效果越好,BRB的合理布置形式为主墩双肢间按照单向斜撑式布置。

关键词 桥梁工程 连续刚构桥 减震设计 非线性时程分析 防屈曲支撑

0 引言

连续刚构桥跨越能力强,桥面行车舒顺,同时悬臂施工难度小,经济性好。这些优势使连续刚构桥应用广泛,然而在中高烈度地震区修建大跨径连续刚构桥对桥梁自身抗震性能提出了更高的要求。连续刚构桥梁主墩与主梁固结的结构特点使得抗震设计比较困难,通常做法是在过渡墩与主梁之间考虑不同的减震约束体系来减小桥梁地震响应[1]。本文提出一种新的减震方式,即在连续刚构桥的双肢薄壁墩上设置防屈曲支撑(Buckling-Restrained Braces,简称BRB)来实现减震耗能的作用,从而提高结构抗震性能。

1.基金项目:陕西省用点研发计划项目(2019KW-051);陕西省创新人才推进计划科技创新团队(2018TD-040);国家自然科学基金资助项目(51978062);陕西省自然科学基础研究计划项目-联合基金项目(2021LM47);大跨府、大流量,多塔斜拉压力输水管桥关键技术研究(Program No.2021JLM-47)资助。

BRB是一种金属耗能减震构件，具有耗能能力强、经济性好、安装及更换方便等特点。近年来部分学者将BRB引入桥梁工程领域作为“保险丝”来提高桥梁结构抗震性能。谢文等[2,4]研究了在斜拉桥双柱式辅助墩设置BRB牺牲构件的有效性和可行性，结果表明BRB耗能辅助墩可满足斜拉桥整体损伤控制目标。孙治国等[3]通过拟静力、增量动力分析手段验证了BRB减小桥梁排架地震损伤的效果，发现影响排架屈服顺序的因素是BRB核心段长度。Bazaez R等[5]研究了BRB改造的带缺陷的排架墩的循环行为，大规模拟静力实验的结果表明BRB能有效提高结构的位移延性，同时控制易损构件的损伤。Dong H H等[6]提出了将一种自定心防屈曲支撑(SC-BRB)用于双柱式桥墩抗震改造，非线性动态分析结果表明相比传统BRB，设置SC-BRB能够明显减小结构的残余变形，但会放大桥梁的峰值加速度。石岩等[7]发展了设置BRB的桥梁排架墩基于位移的设计方法并验证了其可行性。李晓莉等[8]研究了山区桥梁双柱式桥墩设置BRB的减震效果，通过数值分析发现小震下BRB可减轻桥墩地震力但会增大基础剪力，大震下BRB能有效减小墩柱最大塑性变形并控制其残余位移角。张永亮等[9]研究了双柱式桥墩BRB设置方式和参数取值对桥梁地震响应的影响规律，揭示了BRB影响结构地震反应的作用机制。石岩等[10]研究了在远场和近断层地震动输入下不同设计参数对设置BRB的排架墩抗震性能的影响，得出了BRB与排架墩水平刚度比和水平屈服位移比的合理取值范围。董阳等[11]研究了不同墩高的双柱式桥墩的BRB合理设置方式和BRB核心段材料屈服强度对桥梁地震响应的规律，得到了不同墩高下BRB合理设置方式和最优参数。Wang Y D等[12,13]研究评估了采用BRB改造桥墩的斜桥的抗倒塌能力和破坏模式，非线性时程分析表明，BRB极大地改善了斜桥抗震性能，但BRB失效后对桥梁抗倒塌能力的影响可以忽略不计，同时BRB的使用大大降低了桥梁的失效概率，降低了斜桥对地震动入射角的敏感性。

综上所述，学者们对双柱式桥墩设置BRB的作用效应已有深入的研究，但对于连续刚构桥的桥墩设置BRB的研究还比较少，所以开展大跨度连续刚构桥设置BRB的减震效果研究能够丰富BRB的应用研究，相关成果也能为中高震区大跨度连续刚构桥的抗震设计提供参考。

1 防屈曲支撑的原理

1.1 防屈曲支撑的构成

防屈曲支撑由可屈服的芯材、约束构件和两者间无黏结材料或间隙组成，如图1所示。可屈服内芯一般由Q235钢材制成，约束构件给内芯提供侧向约束，以防止BRB受压时内芯发生整体或局部屈曲，保证内芯在受拉和受压的工况下都能进入屈服状态，从而实现滞回耗能的作用，无黏结材料的作用是减少内芯与约束构件之间的摩擦力。

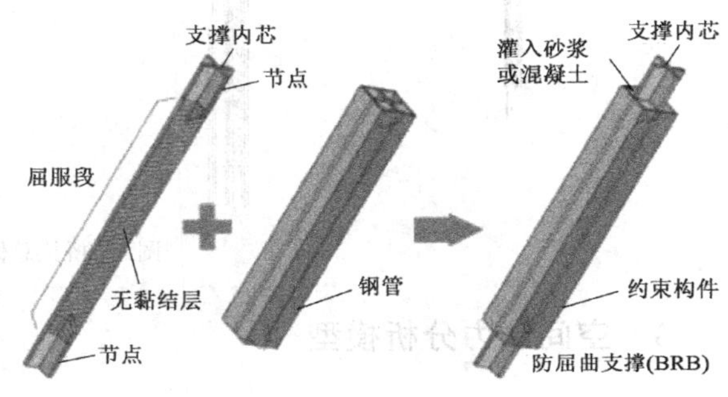

图1 防屈曲支撑组成

1.2 防屈曲支撑的力学模型

防屈曲支承的力学行为可用Bouc-Wen恢复力模型来描述，其非线性力与位移关系可用式(1)和式(2)表示。

$$f = \alpha kd + (1-\alpha)kz \tag{1}$$

$$\dot{z} = \begin{cases} \dot{d}(1-|z|^n), \dot{d}z>0 \\ \dot{d}, else \end{cases} \tag{2}$$

式中：k——弹性刚度；

α——屈服后刚度与弹性刚度的比值；

z——内部滞后变量，此变量范围为$|z|\leqslant 1$，其屈服面由$|z|=1$表示；

n——控制参数，控制着从弹性到非弹性过渡曲线的平滑性，n数值越大曲线越陡，本文取$n=20$。

力-位移关系可用图2表示。

2 工程概况

本文研究桥梁为三跨连续刚构桥，桥跨布置

为110m+210m+110m,上下行分幅布置。主梁为钢筋混凝土箱梁,主墩为双肢薄壁墩,墩高为24.6m,双肢间距6m。桥梁总体布置见图3。根据区域地质勘测资料,桥址区地层结构较复杂,根据规范判定:该桥的桥址区场地类别为Ⅲ类。地震动峰值加速度值为0.2g,场地的地震基本烈度为Ⅷ度,抗震构造措施按Ⅸ度进行抗震设防。

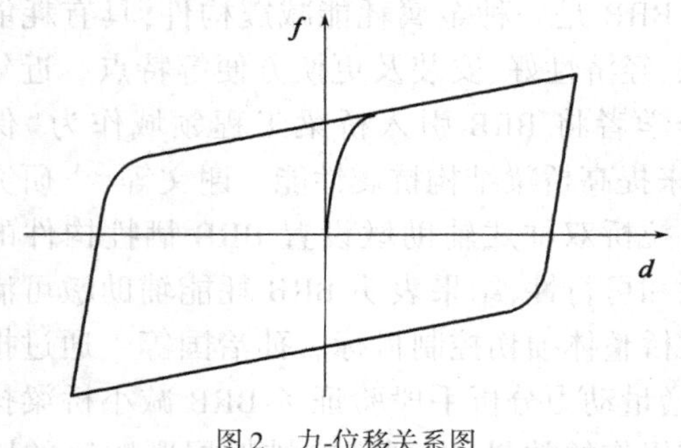

图2　力-位移关系图

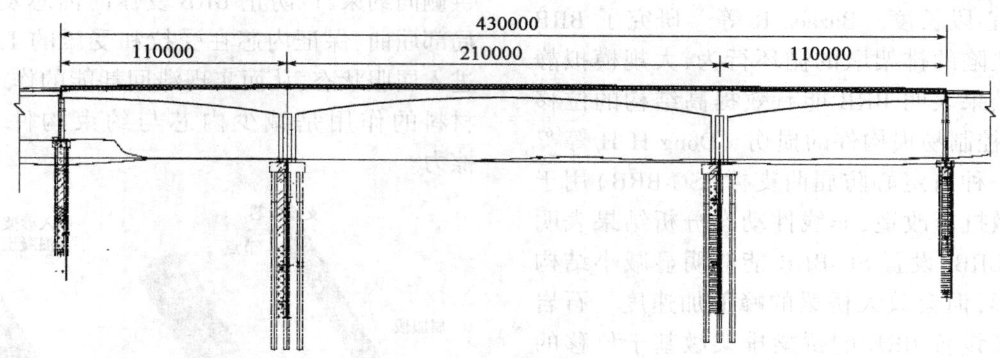

图3　桥梁总体布置(尺寸单位:cm)

3　空间动力分析模型

3.1　空间动力模型

通过有限元分析软件 CSI Bridge 建立全桥动力空间计算模型。有限元模型以顺桥向为 X 轴,横桥向为 Y 轴,竖向为 Z 轴。梁体和桥墩采用空间梁单元模拟,承台采用面单元进行模拟,单元划分反映结构的实际动力特性,二期铺装采用线荷载和面荷载进行模拟。BRB 采用 Plastic (Wen) 单元模拟,只考虑轴向非线性特性。支座单元只考虑理想支承形式。群桩基础采用空间梁单元模拟,竖向每隔 2m 施加一个土弹簧。进行时程分析时,采用瑞利阻尼,有限元模型见图4。

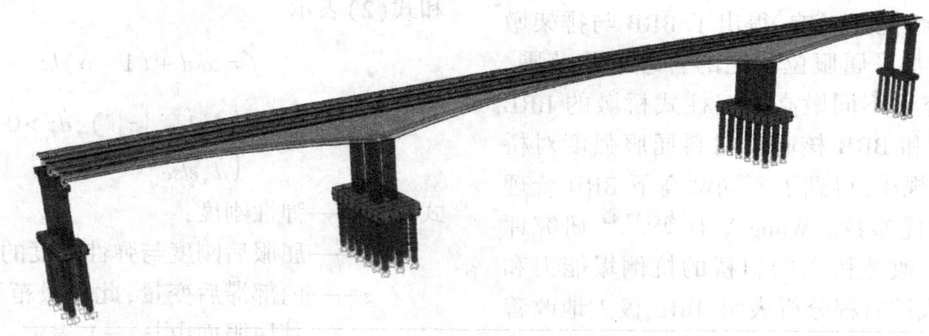

图4　全桥有限元模型

3.2　地震动输入

为体现地震动的随机性,根据该桥"安评报告",在E1地震和E2地震下各选取3条加速度时程曲线用于本桥非线性时程分析,加速度时程曲线如图5所示。地震动输入方向为1倍 X 向 + 0.667倍 Z 向。

4　BRB减震效果分析

4.1　BRB设置工况

结合连续刚构桥主墩构造特点和 BRB 杆件合理布置长度,本文考虑 BRB 技术参数差异和布置方式区别,提出了3种 BRB 布置工况,如图6所示。工况一与工况二的BRB构件布置为单向斜撑式,工况三的BRB构件设置为人字形斜撑式。连续刚构桥两个主墩设置相同的布置工况。

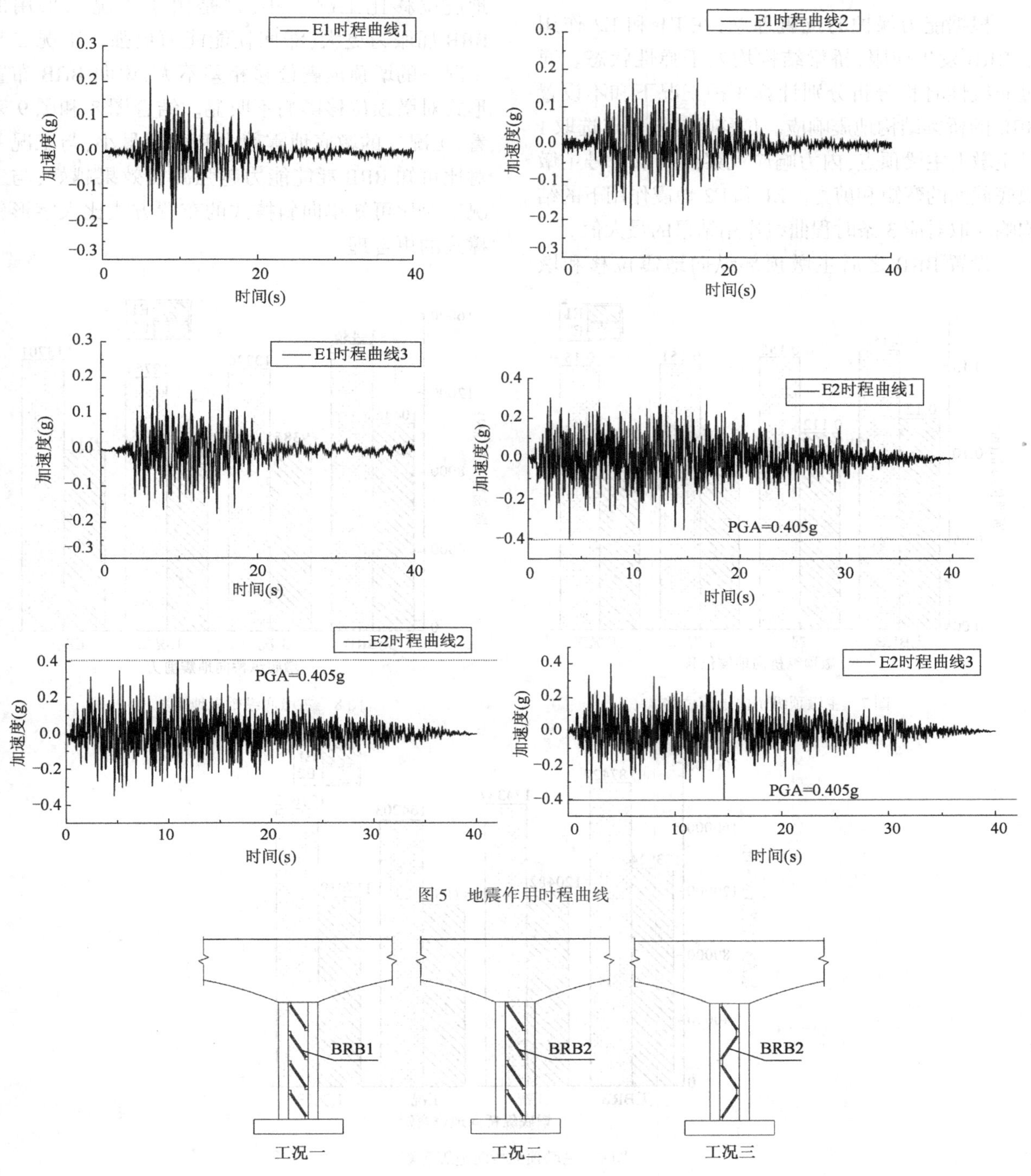

图5 地震作用时程曲线

图6 BRB设置形式

连续刚构桥主墩的构造特点使得桥梁结构纵桥向水平抗推刚度较低,在地震作用下桥墩变形量大,即使在E1地震作用下BRB也难以保持弹性。为使BRB尽早屈服以保护主墩,本文考虑的BRB的屈服力为500kN和1000kN。设计参数见表1。

防屈曲支撑技术参数 表1

BRB类型	屈服力(kN)	初始刚度(kN/m)	屈强比
BRB1	500	650000	0.03
BRB2	1000	650000	0.03

4.2　设置BRB的连续刚构桥减震效果对比

根据能力保护的抗震理念,在E1和E2作用下BRB发生屈服,桥梁结构均处于弹性状态。通过非线性时程分析分别计算3种工况下和不设置BRB的桥梁结构地震响应。位移响应参考点选取1号主墩上主梁顶点,内力响应观察点选取1号主墩底截面的弯矩和剪力。E1和E2地震作用下的结构响应取对应3条时程曲线作用结果的最大值。

设置BRB之后主墩顶部纵向地震位移和墩底剪力及弯矩值均会降低(图7~图9),所以BRB能实现减震的作用。从图7来看,工况二的墩顶地震位移比工况一小,这是由于工况二采用的BRB屈服力更大,滞回耗能能力更强。工况二与工况三的墩顶地震位移相差不大,说明BRB布置形式对墩顶位移影响不明显。结合图8和图9来看,工况二的墩底地震剪力和弯矩最小,与工况一对比可知BRB耗能能力越强减震效果越好,与工况三对比可知单向斜撑式的布置方式比人字形斜撑式的更合理。

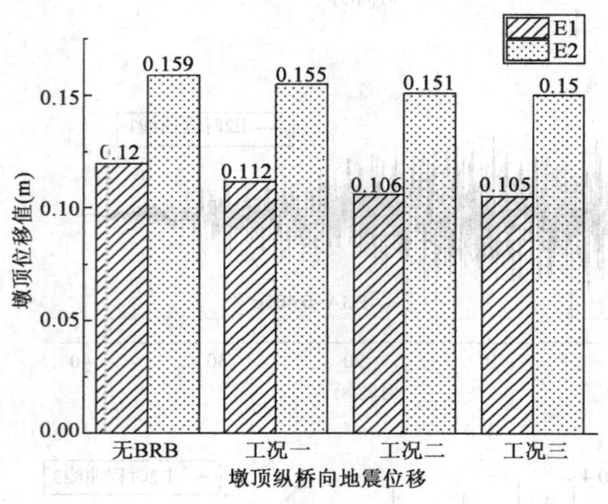

图7　主墩顶纵桥向地震位移

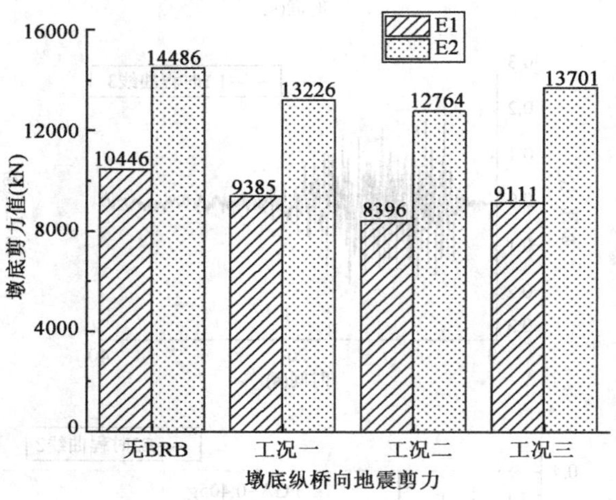

图8　主墩底纵桥向地震剪力

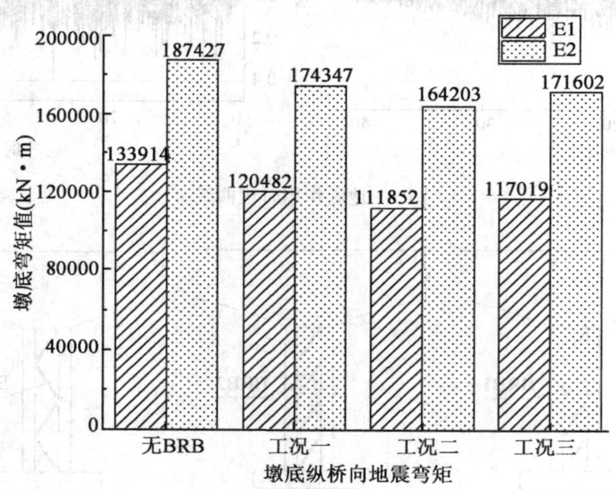

图9　主墩顶纵桥向地震弯矩

4.3　设置BRB的连续刚构桥减震率分析

为进一步量化BRB的减震作用,本文使用减震率定量描述连续刚构桥设置BRB的减震效果。减震率计算公式如下:

$$R=\frac{P_a-P_b}{P_a} \tag{3}$$

式中:R——设置BRB的连续刚构桥的减震率;

P_a——未设置BRB的连续刚构桥的某一地震响应值;

P_b——设置BRB的连续刚构桥的某一地震响应值。

由上述公式分别计算E1和E2作用下墩顶位

移、墩底弯矩和剪力的减震率,如图10和图11所示。

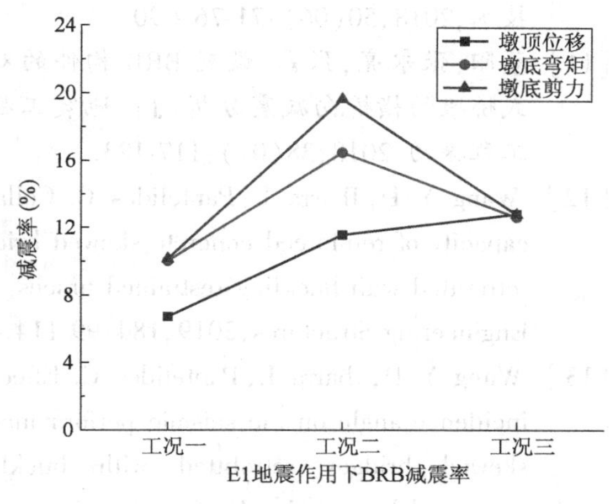

图10 E1地震作用下BRB减震率

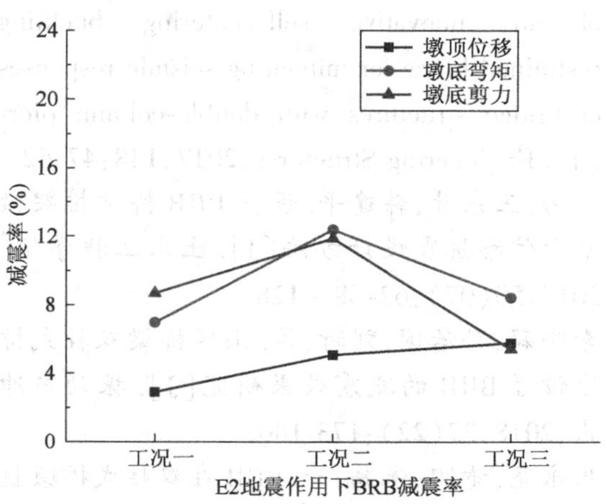

图11 E2地震作用下BRB减震率

结合图10和图11可以看出:3个工况下减震率均较为显著,所以设置BRB能够有效降低结构的地震位移响应和内力响应。E1地震作用下的结构减震率比E2作用下的大,BRB在E1地震作用下减震效果更好。从图10可以看出:E1地震作用下,工况二的墩底剪力和位移的减震率最大,工况三的墩顶位移减震率最大,说明在相同BRB布置形式下,BRB屈服力更大则减震效果更显著。从BRB布置形式来看,单向斜撑式的墩底弯矩和剪力减震效果优于人字形斜撑式,但人字形斜撑式对墩顶位移减震更有效。从图11可以看出,E2地震作用下同样是工况二的墩底弯矩和剪力减震效果最好,工况三的墩顶位移减震率略大于工况二但墩底剪力减震效果较低,这是由于相比于单向斜撑式布置形式,采用人字形斜撑布置形式的主墩纵向刚度更大,减小结构地震位移的同时也增大了墩底剪力。

综合来看,在一定范围内,屈服力更大,滞回耗能能力更强的BRB减震效果更好。本文研究的连续刚构桥主墩的合理BRB设置形式为单向斜撑式。

5 结语

本文以某110m+210m+110m三跨连续刚构桥为分析对象,提出了3种BRB设置工况,通过非线性时程分析方法计算关键位置的地震位移和内力响应,分析比较了3种工况的减震效果。根据分析结果得到以下结论:

(1)通过桥梁结构在E1和E2地震作用下的受力和变形结果分析可以得出,该大跨度连续刚构桥的最优BRB设置方案是工况二。

(2)在地震作用下,主墩上设置的BRB滞回耗能能力越强则减震效果越好。

(3)通过对比可知,连续刚构桥主墩双肢间BRB按单向斜撑的形式布置是合理的。

本文研究结果可为同类型连续刚构桥的减震设计提供参考。本研究存在一些不足,主墩设置BRB提高了主墩纵桥向水平抗推刚度,桥梁静力设计分析时BRB对主墩刚度的影响不能忽略。BRB减震效果的参数敏感性分析和布置形式的影响规律还值得进一步深入研究。

参考文献

[1] 周敉,朱国强,吴江,等.地震下大跨径连续刚构桥合理约束体系研究[J].振动与冲击,2019,38(10):98-104.

[2] 谢文,孙利民.采用耗能辅助墩的超大跨斜拉桥顺桥向地震损伤控制[J].中南大学学报(自然科学版),2013,44(11):4672-4681.

[3] 孙治国,华承俊,石岩,等.利用BRB实现桥梁排架基于保险丝理念的抗震设计[J].振动与冲击,2015,34(22):199-205.

[4] 谢文,孙利民.基于结构"保险丝"概念的双柱式高墩地震损伤控制研究[J].振动工程学报,2016,29(03):420-428.

[5] Bazaez R, Dusicka P. Cyclic behavior of reinforced concrete bridge bent retrofitted with buckling restrained braces [J]. Engineering Structures, 2016, 119:34-48.

[6] Dong H H, Du X L, Han Q, et al. Performance of an innovative self-centering buckling restrained brace for mitigating seismic responses of bridge structures with double-column piers [J]. Engineering Structures, 2017, 148:47-62.

[7] 石岩,王东升,韩建平. 设置 BRB 桥梁排架墩基于位移抗震设计方法[J]. 土木工程学报, 2017,50(07):62-68 +128.

[8] 李晓莉,孙治国,刘昕,等. 山区桥梁双柱式桥墩设置 BRB 的减震效果研究[J]. 振动与冲击,2018,37(22):173-180.

[9] 张永亮,董阳,张磊,等. BRB 在双柱式桥墩抗震体系中的工作机理分析[J]. 地震工程学报,2018,40(05):957-962.

[10] 石岩,张展宏,韩建平,等. 设置 BRB 的桥梁排架墩抗震性能参数分析[J]. 工程科学与技术,2018,50(06):71-76 +90.

[11] 董阳,张永亮,张磊. 设置 BRB 构件的双柱式桥墩的横桥向减震分析[J]. 地震工程与工程振动,2018,38(01):117-123.

[12] Wang Y D, Ibarra L, Pantelides C. Collapse capacity of reinforced concrete skewed bridges retrofitted with buckling-restrained braces[J]. Engineering Structures, 2019, 184:99-114.

[13] Wang Y D, Ibarra L, Pantelides C. Effect of incidence angle on the seismic performance of skewed bridges retrofitted with buckling-restrained braces[J]. Engineering Structures, 2020, 211.

凝冰状态下钢桁梁桥面系温度场研究

周勇超　王丁丁*

(长安大学公路学院)

摘　要　本文基于热力学相关理论,进行了凝冰状态下钢桁梁桥面系温度场的理论推导,建立了相关影响因素之间的联系。首先根据瞬态热传导理论,定义了桥面系温度场的定解条件,将系统初始状态与边界状态进行了解析分析;然后结合现实情况确定如何对边界条件进行取值简化,结合钢桁梁结构特点建立温度场函数微分方程;最后确定了求解温度场分布所需要的相关材料的热力学参数,通过有限元软件对凝冰状态下钢桁梁桥面系进行瞬态温度场分析,提取出了桥梁结构各个节点在 24h 的外界环境作用下的温度变化情况。

关键词　钢桁梁　温度场　热力学　桥面系

0　引言

严寒气候下,在桥面上铺装结构表面的水分或蒸汽会在冷风的影响下迅速凝固成冰,给公路和城市道路的运输造成了巨大安全隐患的同时,也降低了运输效率。桥面结冰大大降低了汽车的附着系数,也降低了汽车轮胎和地面之间的摩擦力,不但会大大降低车速,而且还会增加出现车祸的概率;因桥面会先于路面结冰,在路面尚未结冰的时候,可能会误导驾车司机而诱发交通事故。所以近几十年来,各国学者对于桥面铺装结构除冰的研究从未间断并取得了很多成果。

肖劲松等将弹性材料橡胶和融雪剂掺入了沥青混凝土中,研究了不同掺入比例下的除冰效果,将化学除冰与物理除冰技术相结合为桥面除冰方法提供了一种新思路。吴少鹏等提出了通过在沥青铺装层中埋设管网,用流体捕获光能,以达到融雪除冰的目的;利用清洁能源减少碳排放来除冰无疑会成为未来研究的热点。陈鑫等依托于实际工程进行了能量桩除冰的试验,在桩基础和桥面

1. 基金项目:国家自然科学基金资助项目(52078044)。

板中预埋热力管,利用水泵驱动浅地层的热量来达到除冰效果。陈鑫等人着重研究了桩基础与桥面的换热效率与热力响应,给后续研究方向做了铺垫,并且第一次以实验的方式验证了能量桩的除冰效果。

综合以往的研究成果,不难发现,目前关于桥面融雪除冰的方法与手段日趋成熟,且相关领域的应用也越来越广泛。但是对融雪除冰过程中热力对桥面铺装结构温度场的影响研究较少。受太阳辐射、风力、气温、湿度及太阳光照时间等因子作用,在桥面系温度场的边界条件下具有各种热交换过程,并且温度随时间而不断发生变化。同封闭的钢箱桥比较,钢桁梁桥面系开放式的结构表面边缘情况比较复杂,本文主要根据钢桁梁构造特征,分析并确定某钢桁梁桥面体系在桥面凝冰状态中的温度场状况。

1 桥面凝冰状态下钢桁梁桥面系温度场定解条件

钢桁梁桥面系受太阳辐射、辐射换热和对流换热等各种因素直接影响,温度场的变换可以认为是瞬态热传导问题。它的微分导热方程涉及时间和空间变化,而函数 T 的定解则由初始状态和边界状态构成。

1.1 温度场初始条件

在桥面凝冰期间,桥面结构在自然环境影响下产生了一种初始的瞬时温度场,可由空间位置函数表示。

$$T|_t=0=T_0(x,y,z) \tag{1}$$

式中:x、y、z——桥梁结构的坐标;

t——时间。

1.2 温度场边界条件

边界状态,在传热学中一般包括下列三类[7]:

(1)第一类边界要求,是指结构上任一点在 t 时的温度值。针对钢桁梁,在任一点的环境温度都会随周围环境变化,因此无法利用理论分析方法得到实际温度数值,而且采用现场测定既复杂又会有很大的误差,所以第一类边界条件不适用于有限元计算。

(2)第二类的边界条件要求结构的任意一点在 t 时的热流密度。对于钢桁梁桥面系,理论分析和现场测量的手段,都无法获取任意点的热流密度,所以也不适用于有限元计算。

(3)第三类边界条件,是指确定结构物和外部环境之间的热量交换系数以及外部环境的温度。针对钢桁梁的桥面系,一般采用对流换热和辐射换热,其热量交换系数一般与风力和环境温度有关,而风力和周围环境气温也很易于经过现场检测得到。因此可选择将第三类边态用作有限元计算时的边态,用式(2)表示。

$$k_x\frac{\partial T}{\partial x}n_x+k_y\frac{\partial T}{\partial y}n_y+k_z\frac{\partial T}{\partial z}n_z=\bar{h}_c(T_\infty-T) \tag{2}$$

式中:k_x、k_y、k_z——结构沿 x、y、z 的热量交换系数;

n_x、n_y、n_z——结构边外法线的余弦;

$\bar{h}_c$——辐射换热和对流换热时的整体热量交换系数,单位为:$W/(m^2 \cdot K)$;

T_∞——外部条件的热量;

T——热持续时间。

2 桥面凝冰状态下钢桁梁桥面系温度场理论分析

2.1 太阳辐射

太阳光是钢桁梁桥体系到达最初始温度场的主要加热能量。对于一个区域来说,在日照时间基本相等的情况下,太阳光的距离和太阳高度角都是影响太阳辐射强度的因素。

太阳高度角在同一天里的各个时间会出现周期性变动,导致阳光辐射强度也会出现周期性变动。正午时强度最高,而日出与日落时的强度则最低,其日变过程也可以用式中(3)来描述。

$$q(t)=\begin{cases}q_s\cdot\sin\left(\frac{2\pi}{24}t+\varphi\right), & \left(\frac{2\pi}{24}t+\varphi\right)\in[0,\pi]\\0, & \left(\frac{2\pi}{24}t+\varphi\right)\in[\pi,2\pi]\end{cases} \tag{3}$$

式中:$q(t)$——太阳辐射函数;

q_s——辐射的强度幅值;

φ——初项。

2.2 辐射换热

对于钢桁梁的下铺装层、钢桥面板、纵梁、横隔板等均直接与大气接触,并因此受到大量热辐射。如果把空气看成绝对黑体,桥面系与大气的辐射热流密度就为(4)。

$$q_F = \varepsilon\sigma[(T_1|_{Z=0} - T_Z)^4 - (Ta - T_Z)^4] \quad (4)$$

式中：q_F——有效辐射热流密度系数；

ε——建筑表层的发射比，钢结构取 0.4，桥面系表面取 0.81；

σ——Stefan-Boltzmann 常数，$\sigma = 5.6697e^{-8}$ $W/(m^2 \cdot K^4)$；

TZ——绝对零度值，$T_Z = -273℃$；

T_a——大气环境温度；

$T_1|_{Z=0}$——钢构件及上层表面温度。

若已知温度，经由式中(4)即可得到钢桁梁桥面铺装复合体系地面和空气间的辐射热流密度。

2.3　对流换热

对流换热由于和介质表面面积、流体与物体表面内部的相对温度关系有关所以强度可以用牛顿冷却定律来计量，如式(5)所示。

$$Q = \alpha F(T_W - T_f) \quad (5)$$

式中：Q——换热热量；

α——对流换热系数，单位：$W/(m^2 \cdot K)$；

F——表面面积；

T_W、T_f——流体和结构表面温度。

对于钢桁梁桥面系，由于桥面下和桥上空气接触，通常来说风力并不为零，发生受迫对流现象，而钢桥面板下与表面桥下的空气接触，风力则视作零，故发生了自由对流。查阅有关文献，结构和空气间的对流换热系数 α 可用式(6)来表示。

$$\alpha = 5.768 \times \left[0.775 + 0.35\left(\frac{v}{0.304}\right)^a\right] \quad (6)$$

式中：v——风速大小，单位 m/s；

a——系数，当 $v < 4.88$m/s 时，$a = 1$，当 $v \geq 4.88$m/s 时，$a = 0.78$。可得到钢桁梁表面构造和大气之间的对流换热系数。

2.4　温度场边界条件的确定

针对铺装层、钢桥面板的上表层以及侧表层等，其边界包含太阳辐射、地面与大气环境之间的放射换热以及对流换热等，可表示为：

$$-K\frac{\partial T}{\partial y}\bigg|_{y=0} = \alpha F[T_1(t)|_{y=0} - T_a] + q(t) + \varepsilon\sigma[(T_1(t)|_{y=0} - Ta)^4 - (T_a - T_Z)^4] \quad (7)$$

式中：$T_1(t)|_{y=0}$——钢桁梁桥面系表层温度，有关参数按照 2.2.1 ~ 2.2.3 节选取。

对于钢桥面板下表层、纵梁表层、横隔板表层以及 U 肋外表层，均不受太阳辐射影响，其边界条件则包括空气与大气之间的辐射换热以及自由对流换热等，可描述为：

$$-K\frac{\partial T}{\partial y}\bigg|_{y=y0} = \alpha F[T_1(t)|_{y=y0} - T_a] + \varepsilon\sigma[(T_1(t)|_{y=y}0 - T_a)^4 - (T_a - T_Z)^4] \quad (8)$$

式中：$T_1(t)|y=y0$——桥面板下表层、纵梁表层、横隔板表层以及 U 肋外表层温度，有关参数按照 2.2.1 ~ 2.2.3 节选取。

对于 U 肋内表面，由于不受太阳辐射影响，内部空气处于相对静态状态，可忽视其自由对流影响，边界条件也仅包括太阳辐射换热影响，可表示为：

$$-K\frac{\partial T}{\partial y}\bigg|_{y=y0} = \varepsilon\sigma[(T_1(t)|y=y0 - T_a)^4 - (T_a - T_Z)^4] \quad (9)$$

式中：$T_1(t)|_{y=y0}$——U 肋的表面温度，有关参数按照 2.2.1 ~ 2.2.3 节选取。

2.5　构件内部传热及材料参数

用傅里叶定理可以近似的说明结构内的热传导的现象。

$$Q = -\lambda \cdot gradT \quad (10)$$

式中：Q——热流通量；

λ——导热系数；

$gradT$——温度梯度，根据傅里叶定理得出。

由于热流通量与温度梯度之间具有一定关联，所以根据内部温度场也应定义热流通量。为了获得内部温度场，借助于热力学第一定律，该传热微分方程如下。

$$\rho c\frac{\partial T}{\partial y} = div(\lambda gradT) + q_v \quad (11)$$

式中：q_v——内部热源强度；

ρ、c——密度及比热容。

对于钢桁梁的桥面系，以钢结构建筑为主，铺装材质为沥青混凝土。其热力学参数按表 1 取值。

材料参数 表1

材料	导热系数（W/m·℃）	比热容（J/kg·℃）	密度（kg·m^{-3}）
钢材	58.2	460	7850
混凝土	1.3	930	2450

3 桥面凝冰状态下钢桁梁桥面系温度场数值分析

3.1 工程概况

以某钢桁架连续梁的18m节段桥面为研究对象。桁架的各个杆件、横梁和纵杆为箱型截面，弦杆截面尺寸为0.4m×0.5m，顶板、底板、腹板壁厚16mm；斜腹杆截面尺寸为0.4m×0.3m，顶板、底板、腹板壁厚16mm；主桁节点为整体式节点；横梁和纵杆顶板、底板壁厚16mm，腹板壁厚14mm。桥面系由下横梁、下弦杆、纵肋组成系。纵梁为闭口加劲U肋（上宽300mm×下宽200mm×高度300mm×8mm）。其横截面见图1。

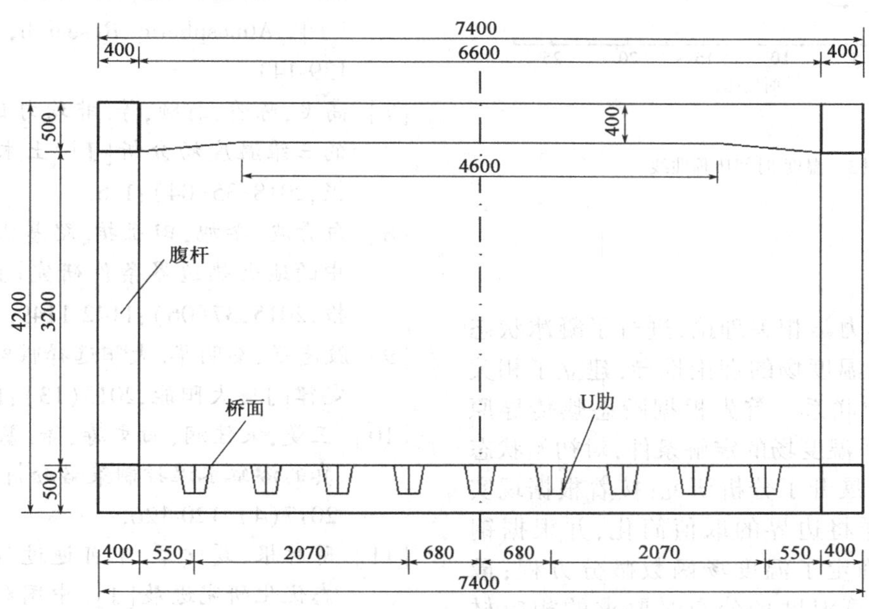

图1 横截面布置图（尺寸单位：mm）

3.2 有限元模型

使用Abaqus建立的瞬态传热钢桁梁温度场分析模型，其中钢桁梁使用四节点壳单体，而路面摊铺则使用八节点六面体的实体单元利用Abaqus建立瞬态传热钢桁梁温度场分析模型，其中钢桁梁单元采用S4R，桥面铺装单元采用C3D8R。模型中所需热力学参数按第2节取。腹杆按0.1m的大小划分网格，其他部分按照0.2m的大小进行网格划分。初始温度采取西安低温季节某一天0时温度，并根据这1d 24h的温度变化，对该桁梁进行温度场分析。温度云图如图2所示。

3.3 温度场分析结果

通过有限元软件对凝冰状态下钢桁梁桥面系进行瞬态温度场分析，提取出了桥梁结构各个节点在24小时的外界环境作用下的温度变化。桥面附近结构影响较大，因此绘制了桥面各构件的温度随时间变化的历程曲线，如图3所示。

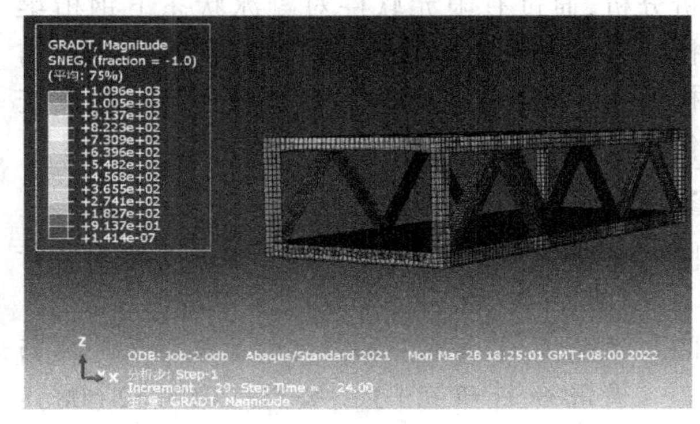

图2 温度云图

由图3可知：U肋温度变化最快，下横梁和下弦杆的变化接近温度值也比较接近，而U肋的温度起伏更大。与横梁和弦杆相比，U肋横截面更小，且离桥面系相对更近。

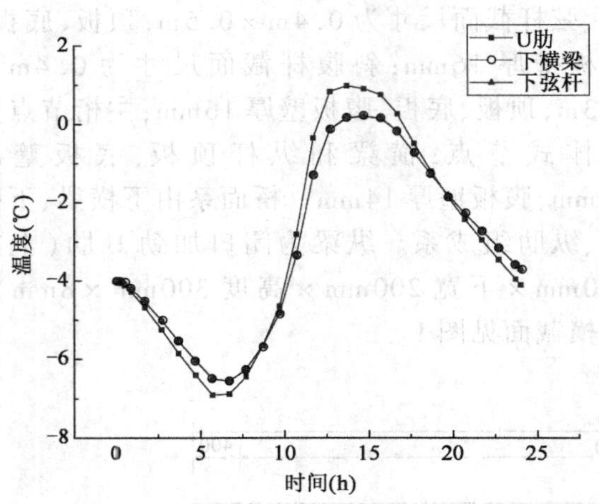

图3 温度-时间历程曲线

4 结语

本文基于热力学相关理论,进行了凝冰状态下钢桁梁桥面系温度场的理论推导,建立了相关影响因素之间的联系。首先根据瞬态热传导原理,定义了桥面系温度场的定解条件,对初始状态与系统边界条件展开了分析研究;接着根据现实情况决定了怎样将边界的取值简化,并根据钢桁梁结构特性确定了温度场函数微分方程;最后,确定了在计算温度场分布时要求的相应材料的热力学稳定性参数并对实际结构进行了有限元分析。将实际状况下的温度场问题进行解析分析,通过有限元软件对凝冰状态下钢桁梁桥面系进行瞬态温度场分析,提取出了桥梁结构各个节点在24h的外界环境作用下的温度变化情况。

参考文献

[1] 曹林涛. 防冰铺装材料的组成与性能分析[J]. 公路,2019,64(12):242-246.

[2] 肖劲松,邹孟秋. 物理-化学综合融雪除冰沥青混合料研究[J]. 公路,2017,62(08):248-252.

[3] Pan Pan, Shaopeng Wu. A review on hydronic asphalt pavement for energy harvesting and snow melting[J]. Renewable and Sustainable Energy Reviews,2015,48:624-634.

[4] 陈鑫,孔纲强,刘汉龙,等. 桥面融雪除冰能量桩热泵系统换热效率现场试验[J/OL]. 中国公路学报:1-12[2021-12-03].

[5] 张楠,夏胜全,侯新宇,等. 土热传导系数及模型的研究现状和展望[J]. 岩土力学,2016,37(06)1550-1562.

[6] Makkonen, Lasse, Ahtikan. Mapping of Ice Loads Basedon Airport Weather Observations [J]. Atmospheric Research, 1995. 36(3): 139-143.

[7] 高飞,陈潘,翁顺,等. 非均匀日照条件下结构的三维温度场分析[J]. 土木工程与管理学报,2018,35(04):1-6.

[8] 白青波,李旭,田亚护. 路基温度场长期模拟中的地表热边界条件研究[J]. 岩土工程学报,2015,37(06):1142-1149.

[9] 殷志强,秦明华. 太阳选择性吸收涂层与物理定律[J]. 太阳能,2013(13):10-14.

[10] 王曼,宋佳润,曲文涛,等. 基于MATLAB仿真的浴缸水温控制策略分析[J]. 大学数学,2017(4):120-126.

[11] 陈林根,夏少军. 不可逆过程广义热力学动态优化研究进展[J]. 中国科学:技术科学,2019,49(09):981-1022.

[12] 刘兴法. 混凝土结构的温度应力分析[M]. 北京:人民交通出版社,1991.

[13] 李兰兰,梁世强,唐大伟,等. 基于电加热融雪系统的道岔结构传热特性[J]. 中国科学院大学学报,2013,30(6):744-756.

[14] 胡汉平. 热传导理论[M]. 合肥:中国科学技术大学出版社,2010.

[15] 刘守花,阳军生,崔高航,等. 季冻区深基坑温度场及冻胀变形研究[J]. 铁道科学与工程学报,2020,17(05):1140-1146.

[16] 张飞. 沥青混合料导热系数测定仪器仿真分析与优化研究[D]. 西安:长安大学,2018.

一种新型空间双曲面混凝土桥塔的模板设计分块方法与实现

高世洪* 郑和晖
(中交第二航务工程局有限公司;长大桥梁建设施工技术交通行业重点实验室;交通运输行业交通基础设施智能制造技术研发中心;中交公路长大桥建设国家工程研究中心有限公司)

摘 要 针对现阶段曲面桥塔模板工程中存在的设计效率低下、工业化程度低、材料消耗量大等问题,提出了一种"标准块+辅助块"模板设计分块方法。该设计方法以建筑工业化思想为基础,采用数字化技术手段,提高了模板设计效率、模板工业化程度。最后,以黄茅海大桥空间双曲面混凝土桥塔模板设计为例,将设计方法实例化,构建了"标准块+辅助块"模板设计数字化实施路线。

关键词 模板设计 方法 分块 混凝土桥塔 双曲面

0 引言

进入21世纪,建筑业得到了高速发展,异型曲面桥塔应用增多。异型曲面混凝土桥塔的建造需要高超的模板设计技术。从工程造价来看,在混凝土结构施工中,工程模板价格约占工程总支出的20%~30%,工程量约为总工程量的30%~40%,工期消耗约为50%左右[1]。模板设计是模板工程的龙头,与后期项目的施工质量、进度、成本存在着紧密的联系。因此,模板设计在整个项目开展过程中起到重要的作用。

目前,桥梁工程上针对异形曲面混凝土桥塔模板的设计主要采用图形设计软件(主要为CAD、Revit、Inventer等)建立桥塔的3D模型;依据桥塔外表皮曲率变化情况对桥塔沿高度方向进行分段;根据拟定模板材料、模板施工工艺设计初始模板的尺寸,依据现场施工反馈情况对模板进行修正[2-4]。该设计方法存在以下缺陷:①需全过程在三维空间进行点、线、面的抓取操作,设计效率较低;②模板设计分块思想落后,模板后期制作工业化程度低,施工时材料消耗量大、沟通成本高。在国家倡导建筑工业化、绿色化、信息化背景下,模板设计也应提质增效,研究高效率、节材、绿色的模板设计技术。

本文针对空间双曲面混凝土桥塔模板设计,提出一种"标准块+辅助块"的模板设计分块方法。该方法以工业化建造思想为基础,辅以数字化研究手段,可将模板设计工作由3维立体空间降至2维平面空间,并实现设计过程的程序化,提高了设计效率;同时,模板设计的标准化,也节省了模板制作周期,减少后期模板材料浪费。

1 "标准块+辅助块"模板设计方法

1.1 设计思想

"标准块+辅助块"模板设计方法脱胎于建筑工业化[5]理念,即以通用标准尺寸块(主模板)分割桥塔各节段外表皮,以辅助块(辅助模板)填补各节段余下空白。在模板安装误差允许范围内,若桥塔多节段共用模板标准块(成组),便可形成桥塔多节段模板设计的1(标准块)+N(辅助块)情况(图1)。再以数字化的技术手段将设计过程程序化,便可产生标准化设计、工业化制造、装配化施工的效果。

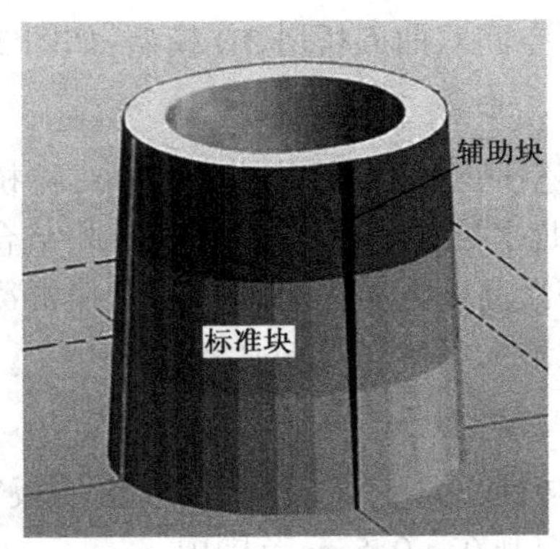

图1 "标准块+辅助块"模板设计

1.2　设计流程

对于空间双曲面混凝土桥塔,“标准块 + 辅助块”模板设计包括三大模块:曲率分析、精度控制、智能分块。“曲率分析”进行桥塔节段划分及节段成组,“精度控制”确定“模板标准块宽度”,“智能分块”输出成组节段模板综合信息并显示分块效果。“标准块 + 辅助块”模板设计流程图,如图 2 所示。

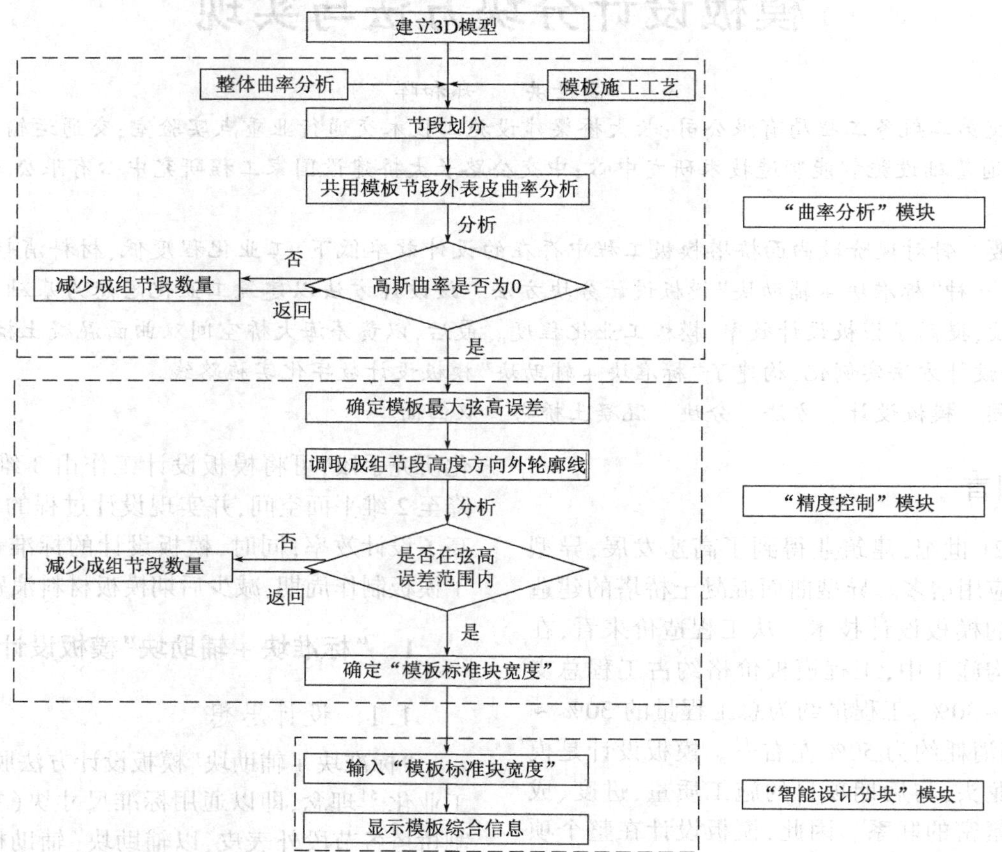

图 2　“标准块 + 辅助块”模板设计流程图

2　技术方案

具体实施包括 9 个步骤。

2.1　步骤 1

建立空间双曲面桥塔 3D 模型,如图 3 所示。

2.2　步骤 2

观察空间双曲面桥塔曲率分布,将桥塔按曲率(高斯曲率接近)分为几个部分,并结合模板工艺将桥塔沿高度方向进行分段。爬模混凝土塔柱分段高度最大不应超过 6m(图 4)。

2.3　步骤 3

限定模板的“弦高误差”。成组模板“弦高误差”通常控制在 ±0.5cm 范围内。

2.4　步骤 4

选取曲率相近若干节段“成组”(共用模板),分析曲率变化,曲率为 0,进行后续操作;曲率非为 0,减少成组节段,以 3 段成组为例(图 5)。

2.5　步骤 5

选取成组最上、最下节段轮廓线 l_a、l_b、l_c、l_d(图 6)。

2.6　步骤 6

将 l_b、l_c、l_d 投影至与 l_a 共点共面分别为 $l_{b'}$、$l_{c'}$、$l_{d'}$。由模板最底下边线 l_a 向模板最高下边线 $l_{c'}$ 引垂线;模板最底上边线 $l_{b'}$ 向模板最高上边线 $l_{d'}$ 引垂线。根据模板最大弦高误差,确定成组节段模板最大标准块宽度(图 7)。

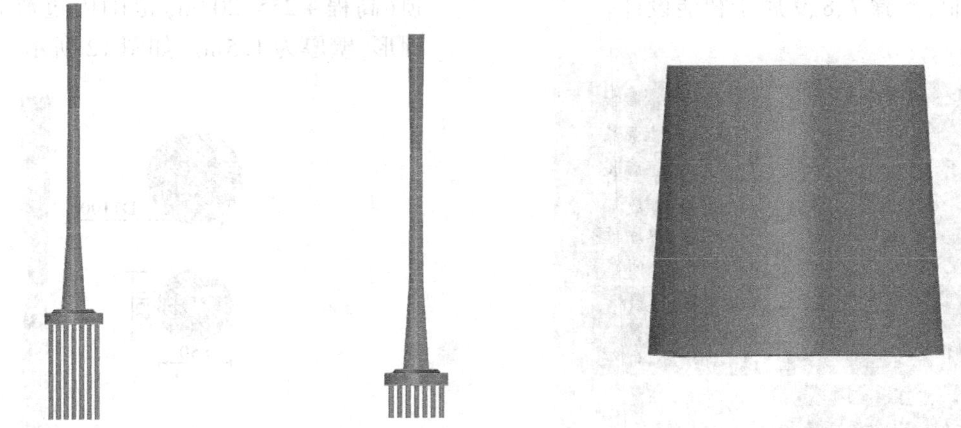

图3　双曲面桥塔3D模型　　图4　桥塔高度方向节段划分　　图5　3节段成组

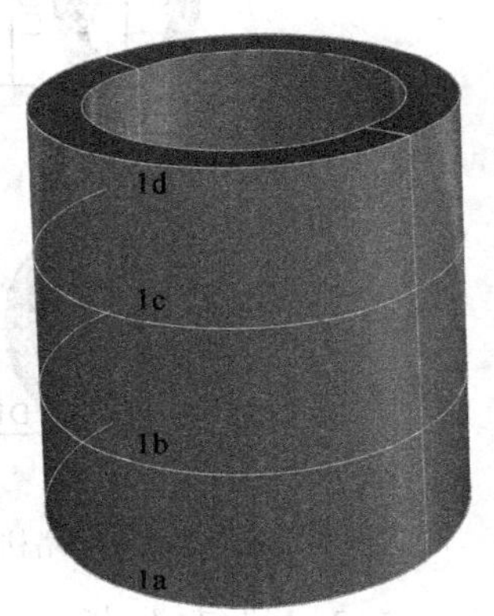

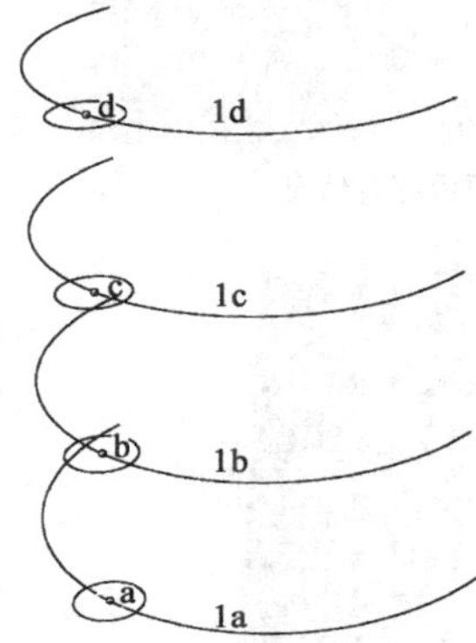

图6　选取成组最上、最下节段轮廓线

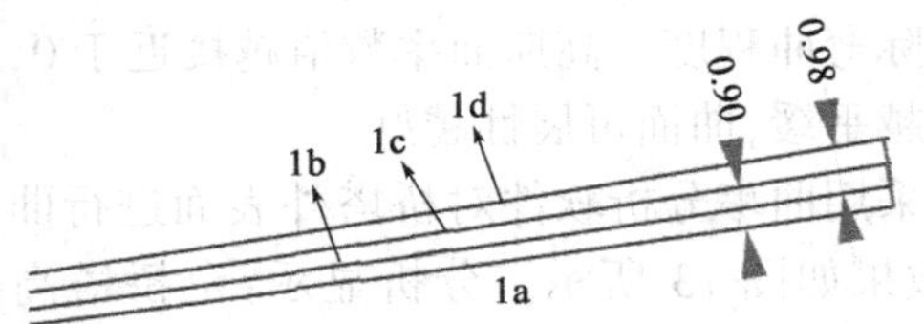

图7　确定成组节段模板最大标准块宽度

2.7　步骤7

对“各组”节段外表皮进行放样并摊平处理(图8)。

图8　成组节段(1/2表皮)摊平

2.8　步骤8

根据“各组模板标准块宽度”等单元分块各组摊平表皮(图9)。

图9　1/2表皮等单元分块

2.9　步骤9

依据项目综合情况调节各组“模板标准块宽度”,程序将可视化输出各组模板“标准块”与“附加块”数量、尺寸及面积(图10);

最终效果如图11所示。

其中步骤2属于曲率分析,步骤3、4、5、6属于精度控制,步骤 7、8、9 属于智能设计。

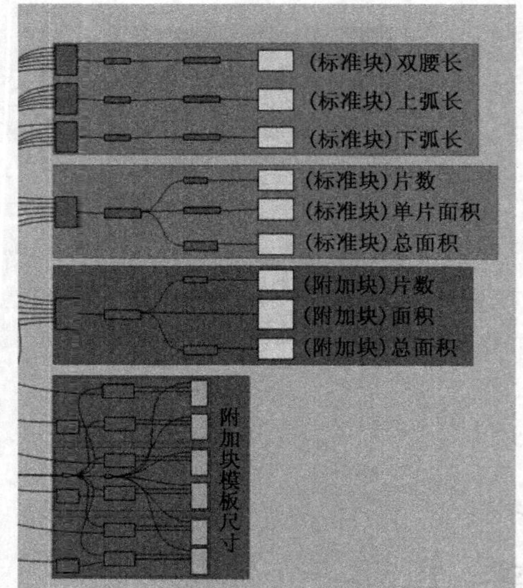

图 10　塔柱模板综合信息

图 11　模板设计分块效果图

其中步骤 2 属于曲率分析,步骤 3、4、5、6 属于精度控制,步骤 7、8、9 属于智能设计。

3　案例

3.1　案例背景

黄茅海大桥(主跨 2×720m)跨越崖门口黄茅海水域,是目前世界最大公路三塔斜拉桥。黄茅海大桥主桥塔采用混凝土独柱型索塔,横断面为圆形和圆端形空心薄壁断面。本文研究以黄茅海西桥塔为背景展开。

黄茅海大桥西塔(以下简称桥塔/索塔)高度 255.203m,塔顶设置 6m 高的塔冠。索塔底截面为圆形截面(高程 +6.500m),直径 18m;在塔底到高程 +69.871m 范围内过渡到圆端形截面,尺寸为 13m×10m(顺桥向×横桥向),壁厚 2m;高程 +69.703m 到 +169.203m 范围内过渡到直径 8.5m 圆形,壁厚在高程 +119.703m 到高程 +125.703m 范围内由 2m 过渡到 1.5m;高程 +169.703m 到塔顶(高程 +255.203m)范围内过渡到直径 11m 的圆形,壁厚为 1.5m。如图 12 所示。

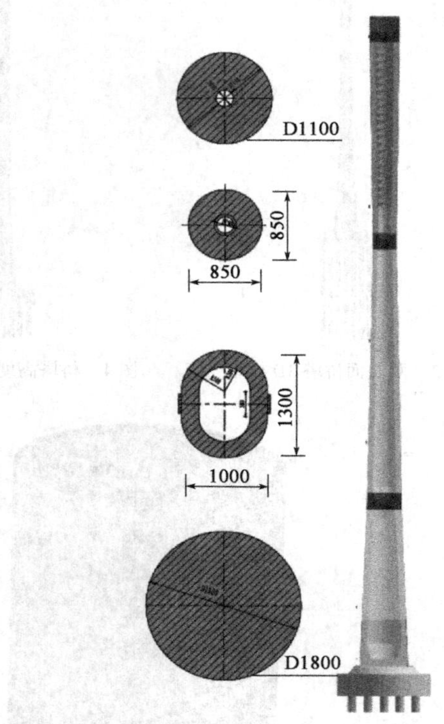

图 12　黄茅海大桥西塔柱效果图(尺寸单位:cm)

3.2　曲率分析

在微分几何中,通常用高斯曲率来反映曲面的实际弯曲程度。高斯曲率数值越接近于 0,表示曲面越平缓,曲面可展性越好。

采用曲率分析软件对桥塔外表面进行曲率分析,效果如图 13 所示。分析显示:全桥塔高斯曲率范围 $-3.4610^{-10}\sim0$ 区间,仅在下塔柱起始段、下塔柱与中塔柱过渡段、中塔柱与上塔柱过渡段,高斯曲率部分小于 0(呈双曲面变化)且接近于 0,整体高斯曲率接近于 0,曲面可展性较好。

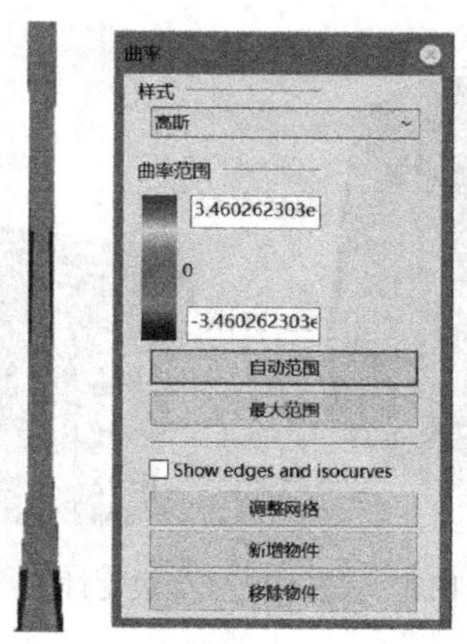

图 13　桥塔外表面曲率分析

爬模施工中,混凝土塔柱标准段模板高度尺寸通常应小于6m。由前文分析可知:本塔柱高斯曲率接近于0,曲面变化平缓,考虑以6m作为塔柱标准节段高;塔柱起始段、下塔柱与中塔柱过渡段、中塔柱与上塔柱过渡段节段高度根据曲面实际情况按小于6m划分。

3.3 节段划分

在以直代曲的基础上,结合桥塔结构与爬模施工的特点,将桥塔塔座以上部分划分为43个节段,标准节段划分高度为6m。整个桥塔划分为4个施工区段:下塔柱、中塔柱、上塔柱、塔冠。如图14所示。

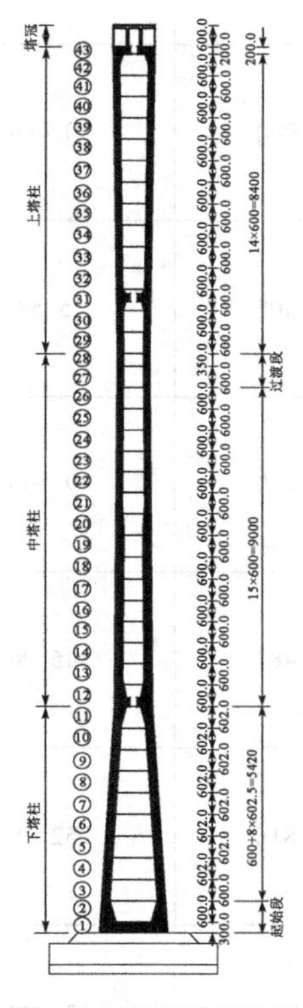

图14 桥塔节段划分图

塔柱起始段(高9m)采用支架施工,其余标准节段采用液压爬模施工。

下塔柱:1~11节段,高63.203m。第1、2节为起始段,第1节高3m,第2节高6m;第3节高6m;第4~11节段高6.025m。

中塔柱:12~28节段,高99.5m。第12~26节为标准节,标准节段高6m;第27~28节为过渡段,第27节段高6m,第28节段高3.5m。

上塔柱:29~43节段,高86m。第29~42节为标准节,标准节段高6m;第43节段为尾段,高2m。

3.4 桥塔模板设计

3.4.1 桥塔节段成组

下塔柱高斯曲率范围:$-3.46\times10^{-10}\sim0$区间,接近于0,曲面表皮可展,如图15所示。

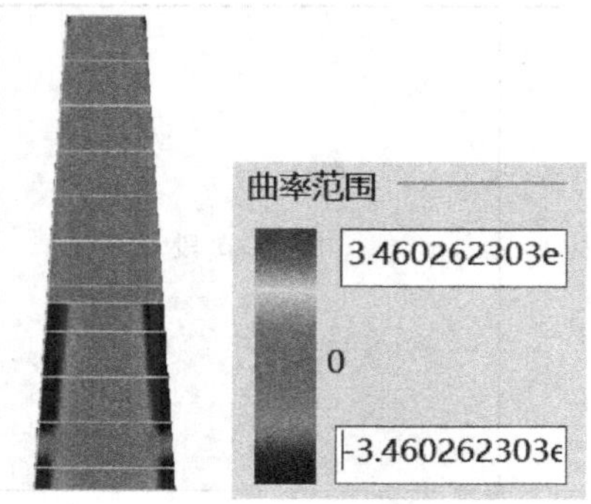

图15 下塔柱曲率分析

下塔柱成组策略:①\②\③\④⑤⑥⑦⑧⑨⑩⑪

中塔柱高斯曲率范围:$-3.46\times10^{-10}\sim0$区间,接近于0,曲面表皮可展,如图16所示。

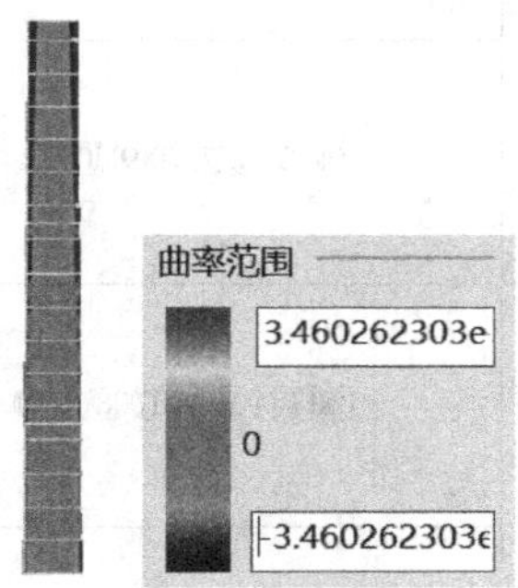

图16 中塔柱曲率分析

中塔柱成组策略:⑫⑬⑭⑮⑯⑰⑱⑲⑳\㉑㉒㉓㉔㉕㉖㉗\㉘

上塔柱高斯曲率为0,曲面表皮可展,如图17所示。

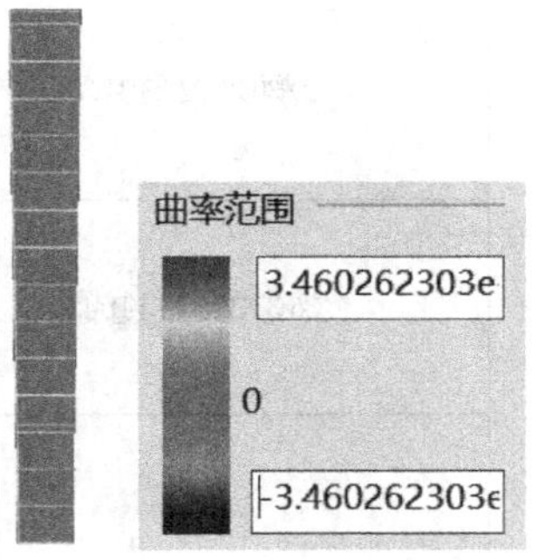

图17 上塔柱曲率分析

上塔柱成组策略:㉙㉚㉛㉜㉝㉞㉟\㊱㊲㊳㊴㊵㊶㊷\㊸

3.4.2　模板成组结果

设定成组模板“弦高误差”为±0.5cm。桥塔全塔段模板信息统计表如表1所示。全塔典型成组节段效果如图18所示。

全塔段模板信息统计表　　表1

目　标	成组节段	模板标准块信息(m) 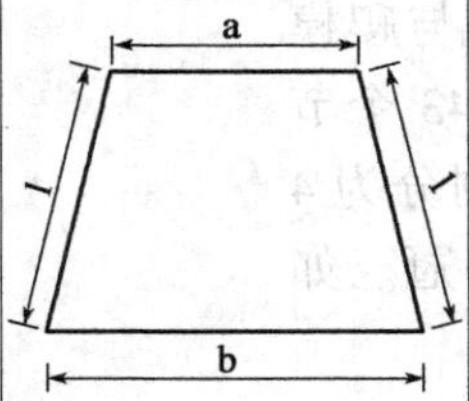	标准块面积(m^2)	辅助块面积(m^2)	总面积(m^2)
下塔柱(11节段)	①	a=2.460 b=2.500 l=3.003	148.980	19.488	168.468
	②③	a=2.415 b=2.500 l=6.007	295.400	55.54	350.940
	④⑤⑥⑦⑧⑨⑩⑪	a=1.080 b=1.136 l=6.035	293.120	59.300	352.420
中塔柱(17节段)	⑫⑬⑭⑮⑯⑰⑱⑲⑳	a=2.200 b=2.228 l=6.000	159.484	345.96	505.444
	㉑㉒㉓㉔㉕㉖㉗	a=2.500 b=2.558 l=6.001	181.816	252.18	433.996
	㉘	a=2.500 b=2.536 l=3.501	70.516	23.520	94.036
上塔柱(15节段)	㉙㉚㉛㉜㉝㉞㉟	a=1.840 b=1.874 l=6.001	175.10	192.886	367.990
	㊱㊲㊳㊴㊵㊶㊷	a=1.867 b=1.900 l=6.001	180.924	94.426	275.350
	㊸	a=2.486 b=2.500 l=2.000	59.844	9.074	68.918

注:模板最大标准块宽度设为2.5m,是参照钢模板施工要求,其他模板材料模板最大标准块宽度可按现场施工要求确定。

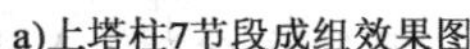
a)上塔柱7节段成组效果图

b)中塔柱9节段成组效果图

c)下塔柱8节段成组效果

图18 塔柱典型成组节段效果

由表1及图18可知:①模板设计分块结果符合全塔曲率变化。曲面曲率变化明显,成组节段模板标准块宽度小;曲面曲率变化小或为0,成组节段模板标准块宽度大。下塔柱曲率变化较中、上塔柱明显,塔柱成组节段模板标准块宽度较中、上塔柱尺寸小;②上、中、下塔柱模板接缝线(由下至上)均有错开,无法形成直线。上塔柱高斯曲率为0,是可展曲面,模板接缝线错开不明显,近乎直线;中、下塔柱高斯曲率接近于0,模板接缝线错开明显。

4 结语

(1)"标准块+辅助块"模板设计方法是以工业化建造思想为基础,目标是实现桥塔模板设计智能化、模板制作工业化、模板施工装配化。

(2)空间双曲面混凝土桥塔模板设计采用"标准块+辅助块法",运用曲率分析将桥塔外表皮分成可展开的各部分,编写对应模板设计程序,可在项目开展前期较迅速得出桥塔模板综合信息,包括:成组标准块、附加块的数量、尺寸、单片面积及总面积。

(3)"标准块+辅助块"模板设计实施路线,对桥塔外表皮成组为高斯曲率为0的可展曲面具有很好的实际操作效果,模板接缝线错开不明显,近乎直线;高斯曲率接近于0的曲面可在模板允许误差范围内参考使用,模板接缝线(由下至上)错开明显;高斯曲率非为0的曲面,成组为可展曲面使用。

(4)本文"标准块+辅助块"模板设计数字化实施路线存在一定局限。对于可展曲面可采用本文所述方法;对于空间不可展开曲面,应考虑在3维空间进行模板设计分块的方式。

参考文献

[1] 王展忠.钢木模板体系与铝合金模板体系对比应用研究[D].绵阳:西南科技大学,2020.

[2] 王明胜,刘海波,陈鸣,等.重庆千厮门嘉陵江大桥索塔爬模设计研究[J].施工技术,2012,41(6):5.

[3] 倪喜雨、郭亮亮、魏鹏等.三维变曲面倾斜混凝土索塔模板体系施工技术[J].施工技术,2020,49(22):3.

[4] 范波,刘小勇,王元鑫.空间多曲面桥梁墩身施工模板设计研究[J].公路交通技术,2018,34(3):5.

[5] 百度百科.建筑工业化[EB/OL].[2021-12-19].https://www.baike.com.

考虑偏轴弹塑性的桥梁用FRP用户材料子程序开发

高卿林[1] 辛灏辉*[1] 刘玉擎[2]

(1.西安交通大学人居环境与建筑工程学院;2.同济大学土木工程学院桥梁工程系)

摘 要 纤维增强复合材料(FRP)呈正交各向异性,当主受力方向与纤维方向呈一定夹角时,FRP

1.基金项目:国家自然科学基金项目资助(51808398.52078362)。中央高校基本科研业务费专项资金资助。

表现出相应的塑性行为。桥梁工程用 FRP 结构通常处于多轴应力状态下,准确评估材料的性能对 FRP 桥梁结构的设计有着重要影响。为此,本文旨在开发可考虑 FRP 材料偏轴弹塑性影响的材料子程序(UMAT),基于返回映射算法在商业软件 ABAQUS 中建立了 FRP 材料三维塑性模型。通过对比 FRP 层合板偏轴拉伸和压缩试验结果和数值模拟结果,验证所开发的用户材料子程序。结果显示了子程序和有限元模型的正确性和合理性,此外网格尺寸和分析步长对模拟结果的影响较为有限。

关键词　桥梁工程　弹塑性本构模型　切平面算法　纤维增强复合材料　有限元分析　UMAT 子程序

0　引言

近年来,纤维增强复合材料(Fiber Reinforced Polymer,FRP)因其重量轻、强度高、可设计性好、抗疲劳性能优异等特点在桥梁结构中得到了广泛的应用[1-4]。随着对 FRP 复合材料在微观和宏观等方面认识的深入,对其本构关系的进一步研究有利于加强对这种新型材料非线性行为的认识,有效保证结构在服役期间的安全性。

已有的试验研究表明,当主受力与纤维方向呈一定夹角时,纤维增强复合材料在外荷载作用下具有明显的非线性行为和拉压性能不对称行为[5-8],学者们认为,非线性行为[6,9]的产生一部分是由于纤维与基体材料本身的非线性,另一部分是加载过程中由于纤维转动或损伤引起的非线性;而拉压性能不对称[9-11]则归因于材料固化时内部的残余热应力和基体材料本身的性能差异。

为了更准确地描述这种材料性能,学者们提出了一系列宏观的力学方法,包括非线性弹性理论、弹塑性理论以及损伤耦合理论。Hahn 和 Tsai[12]提出的余能密度函数方法是最典型的非线性弹性理论方法之一,但由于该方法认为材料的纤维方向为线弹性且不考虑应力高阶项的影响,所以研究[13]表明,Hahn-Tsai 非线性弹性理论相比基于 Sun-Chen 塑性模型的弹塑性理论在预测横向非线性行为明显的材料的应力应变响应时会产生不可忽视的计算误差。基于 Sun-Chen 模型的弹塑性理论中塑性变形的描述依赖于塑性势函数的选取。为了考虑复合材料在单调荷载作用下的拉压性能不对称行为,Wang 和 Xiao[14,15]类比 Drucker-Prager 屈服准则,将考虑各向异性的 Hill 屈服准则修正为考虑静水压效应对材料屈服影响的广义形式,之后利用弹塑性柔度法推导的本构形式对复合材料单向板和斜交板的偏轴拉、压响应与试验结果进行对比,显示了模型的有效性。为避免繁琐迭代过程,在实际计算中忽略了弹性到塑性状态的过渡从而对流程进行了简化[13-15],这种简化在某些复杂的加载过程中可能会导致错误的计算路径并对最终结果造成较大影响。所以应基于屈服面方程在塑性区进行反复迭代计算,使得单元应力状态始终保持在等向扩张的后继屈服面上。

本文在已有的试验及理论研究基础上,利用返回映射算法中的切平面算法对复合材料塑性变形阶段的应力应变进行迭代更新,通过编写描述材料本构关系的 UMAT 子程序,实现单向及斜交层合板偏轴拉伸、压缩的模拟并与试验结果进行比对,验证模型与计算子程序的准确性,并对可能影响模拟结果的因素进行分析。

1　理论模型

1.1　广义 HILL 屈服准则

HILL[16]通过考虑材料的正交各向异性,提出了如式 1 所示的屈服准则:

$$f_{HILL}=H(\sigma_{11}-\sigma_{22})^2+F(\sigma_{22}-\sigma_{33})^2+G(\sigma_{33}-\sigma_{11})^2+2L\sigma_{23}^2+2M\sigma_{31}^2+2N\sigma_{12}^2=1 \tag{1}$$

式中:H、F、G、L、M、N——材料各向异性状态的特征参数;

σ_{11}、σ_{22}、σ_{33}、σ_{12}、σ_{23}、σ_{31}——材料各向应力分量。

将式 1 展开并将 H、F、G、L、M、N 用 a_{ij} 表示,得屈服准则的一般表达式:

$$f_{HILL}(\sigma_{ij})=a_{11}\sigma_{11}^2+a_{22}\sigma_{22}^2+a_{33}\sigma_{33}^2+2a_{12}\sigma_{11}\sigma_{22}+2a_{13}\sigma_{11}\sigma_{33}+2a_{23}\sigma_{22}\sigma_{33}+2a_{44}\sigma_{23}^2+2a_{55}\sigma_{13}^2+2a_{66}\sigma_{12}^2-1=0 \tag{2}$$

该准则可以有效地评估各向异性材料的应力应变响应,但忽略了材料的在拉伸和压缩荷载作用下的差异性,所以不能直接用于构建复合材料的弹塑性模型。

Drucker-Prager(D-P)屈服准则[17]最初是用于反映静水压效应敏感的岩石、岩土材料强度的准

则,该准则考虑的是各向同性材料在单轴拉伸和压缩荷载作用下屈服强度的差异性:

$$f_{DP}(J_1,J_2)=\sqrt{J_2}+rJ_1=k \tag{3}$$

式中:J_1——应力第一不变量;

J_2——应力偏量第二不变量;

r、k——与内摩擦角和黏结力有关的试验常数。

D-P 准则计入了中间主应力的影响,又考虑了静水压力的作用,但没有考虑材料的各向异性,所以同样不能直接用于复合材料的强度计算。

由此,王杰[13-15]等人通过类比 D-P 准则,将静水压效应考虑进原有的 HILL 屈服准则中,提出了准则的广义形式:

$$f^*_{HILL}=\sqrt{f_{HILL}}+I\sigma_{11}+J\sigma_{22}+K\sigma_{33}-1=0 \tag{4}$$

对于纤维增强复合材料,其 2-3 平面内材料属性相同,且一般情况下假定沿纤维方向的性能处于线弹性状态,则可化简部分参数如下:

$$H=G=0\quad M=N\quad F=(Y_2^{\mathrm{T}}\Gamma)^{-2}$$
$$J=K=\frac{\Gamma-1}{Y_2^{\mathrm{T}}\Gamma}\quad a_{44}=\frac{2}{(Y_2^{\mathrm{T}}\Gamma)^2} \tag{5}$$

式中:$\Gamma=\dfrac{2\alpha}{1+\alpha}$,$\alpha=\dfrac{Y_2^{\mathrm{C}}}{Y_2^{\mathrm{T}}}$;

Y_2^{C}、Y_2^{T}——22 方向的压缩和拉伸屈服强度,化简后的广义 Hill 屈服准则为:

$$f^*_{HILL}=\frac{1}{Y_2^{\mathrm{T}}\Gamma}\left[\sqrt{(\sigma_{22}-\sigma_{33})^2+4\sigma_{23}^2+2a_{66}\Gamma^2(\sigma_{31}^2+\sigma_{12}^2)}+(\Gamma-1)(\sigma_{22}+\sigma_{33})\right]-1=0 \tag{6}$$

令

$$\Phi^*=\frac{1}{Y_2^{\mathrm{T}}\Gamma}\left[\sqrt{(\sigma_{22}-\sigma_{33})^2+4\sigma_{23}^2+2a_{66}\Gamma^2(\sigma_{31}^2+\sigma_{12}^2)}+(\Gamma-1)(\sigma_{22}+\sigma_{33})\right]$$

,同时由于 2-3 平面材料横观各向同性,定义平均屈服强度:

$$\frac{1}{(\bar{Y})^2}=\frac{1}{3}\left[\frac{1}{(Y_1)^2}+\frac{1}{(Y_2)^2}+\frac{1}{(Y_3)^2}\right]\Rightarrow\bar{Y}=\sqrt{\frac{3}{2}}Y_2^{\mathrm{T}}\Gamma \tag{7}$$

则定义等效应力为 $\sigma_{\mathrm{eff}}=\bar{Y}\Phi^*$,将式(6)及式(7)带入得

$$\sigma_{\mathrm{eff}}=\sqrt{\frac{3}{2}(\sigma_{22}-\sigma_{33})^2+4\sigma_{23}^2+2a_{66}\Gamma^2(\sigma_{31}^2+\sigma_{12}^2)}+\sqrt{\frac{3}{2}}(\Gamma-1)(\sigma_{22}+\sigma_{33}) \tag{8}$$

这里将等效应力与等效塑性应变关系简化为幂函数形式[13-15]:

$$\varepsilon_{\mathrm{eff}}^{\mathrm{p}}=A\cdot\sigma_{\mathrm{eff}}{}^{n} \tag{9}$$

式中:A,n——表征材料特征的参数。

1.2 返回映射算法

返回映射算法(Return Mapping Algorithms)[18,19]通过将弹性方程与总应变增量进行积分,以获得弹性应力的预测值(试探应力,σ^{trial})。之后通过反复修正塑性应变增量,将试探应力的值回退到后继屈服面。典型的返回映射算法包括最近点投射算法[20](Closest Point Projection Method,CPPM)和切平面算法[21,22](Cutting Plane Algorithm,CPA)。已有研究表明[23-25],CPPM 方法在面向较复杂的模型时可能存在计算量较大且收敛困难的问题,需要额外的线搜索技术保证计算的准确性和稳定性。故本文采用 CPA 方法(图 1),该方法基于最速下降的原理,避免了方程进行隐式处理的需要,从而表现出更好的收敛性。

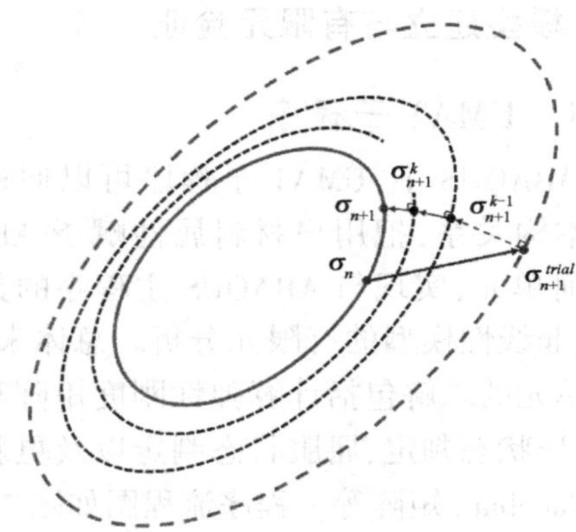

图 1 CPA 方法的应力回退法则

如图 1 所示,在 CPA 方法中,首先通过第 n 步的应力水平σ_n、弹性刚度矩阵D^e及应变增量 $\Delta\varepsilon$ 估算得到第 $n+1$ 步的试探应力σ^{trial}_{n+1}

$$\sigma^{trial}_{n+1}=\sigma_n+D^e\Delta\varepsilon \tag{10}$$

之后通过迭代算法逐步修正塑性应变增量

$$\begin{gathered}\Delta\sigma^1_{n+1}=\sigma^2_{n+1}-\sigma^{trial}_{n+1}=-D^e\Delta\varepsilon^{p,1}\\ \cdots\\ \Delta\sigma^k_{n+1}=\sigma^{k+1}_{n+1}-\sigma^k_{n+1}=-D^e\Delta\varepsilon^{p,k}\end{gathered} \tag{11}$$

式中:k——当前分析步中的迭代次数;

$\Delta\varepsilon^p$——塑性应变增量。

根据关联流动法则得

$$\Delta\varepsilon^p=\Delta\lambda\cdot a\quad a=\frac{\partial F}{\partial\sigma} \tag{12}$$

式中:F——塑性势函数;

$\Delta\lambda$——与塑性加载历史相关的非负标量函数;

a——梯度矢量,其方向为塑性应变增量矢量的方向,即塑性势函数在当前应力点的法线方向。将式(12)带入式(11)得

$$\Delta \sigma_{n+1}^{k} = -\Delta\lambda^{k} D^{e} a^{k} \tag{13}$$

若在每一次迭代中,都将塑性势函数 F 在当前应力值σ_{n+1}^{k}附近线性化,则可以得到

$$F^{k+1} = F^{k} + (a^{k})^{\mathrm{T}}(\sigma_{n+1}^{k+1} - \sigma_{n+1}^{k}) \tag{14}$$

于是当 $F^{k+1}=0$,将式(13)代入式(14)得

$$\Delta\lambda^{k} = \frac{F^{k}}{(a^{k})^{\mathrm{T}} D^{e} a^{k}} \tag{15}$$

通过此方法更新材料在迭代过程中的塑性应变和应力为

$$\varepsilon^{p,k+1} = \varepsilon^{p,k} + \Delta\varepsilon^{p,k} = \varepsilon^{p,k} - (D^{e})^{-1}\Delta\sigma^{k} \tag{16}$$

$$\sigma^{k+1} = \sigma^{k} + \Delta\sigma^{k} \tag{17}$$

2　模型建立与有限元验证

2.1　UMAT子程序

在ABAQUS中,UMAT子程序可以通过定义材料的本构关系,把用户材料属性赋予ABAQUS中的任何单元,实现与ABAQUS主程序的数据交换,完成非线性模型的有限元分析。总体来看,本文中对单元的求解包括计算弹性刚度矩阵和试探应力、拉压状态判定、屈服状态判定以及更新应力应变和Jacobian矩阵等。程序流程图如图2所示,屈服后的应力采用1.2节所介绍的切平面算法(CPA)进行迭代更新,更新算法流程如下:

(1)依照公式10计算初始弹性试探应力($k=1$)

$$k=1 \quad \sigma^{1} = \sigma_{trial} = \sigma + D^{e}\Delta\varepsilon \tag{18}$$

(2)计算屈服面位置与等效塑性应力(式(8)),判定屈服状态

$$\sigma_{HILL}^{k} = \sigma_{\mathrm{eff}}^{k} - \max\{\sigma_{\mathrm{TEMP1}}, \sigma_{\mathrm{TEMP2}}\} \tag{19}$$

$$\sigma_{\mathrm{TEMP1}} = \sqrt{\frac{3}{2}} Y_{2}^{\mathrm{T}} \Gamma \tag{20}$$

其中,$\Gamma = \dfrac{2\alpha}{1+\alpha}$,$\alpha$ 在拉伸与压缩状态下的取值分别为:$\alpha_{\mathrm{C}} = \dfrac{Y_{2}^{\mathrm{C}}}{Y_{2}^{\mathrm{T}}}$,$\alpha_{\mathrm{T}}=1$。

$$\sigma_{\mathrm{TEMP2}} = A^{-\frac{1}{n}} (\varepsilon_{\mathrm{eff}}^{p})^{\frac{1}{n}} \tag{21}$$

若 σ_{HILL}^{k} 的值小于残差 R_{TOL}(一般 $R_{\mathrm{TOL}} \leqslant 10^{-3}$),则认为此分析步的迭代结束,否则:

(3)通过等效塑性应变求解第 k 次迭代的塑性增量[13]

$$\mathrm{d}\varepsilon_{\mathrm{ij}}^{p,k} = \frac{\partial\sigma_{\mathrm{eff}}^{k}}{\partial\sigma_{\mathrm{ij}}^{k}} \mathrm{d}\varepsilon_{\mathrm{eff}}^{p,k} \tag{22}$$

$$\mathrm{d}\varepsilon_{\mathrm{eff}}^{p,k} = \frac{\sigma_{HILL}^{k}}{H_{p} + (\mathrm{d}\varepsilon^{p,k})^{\mathrm{T}} D^{e} \mathrm{d}\varepsilon^{p,k}} \tag{23}$$

$$H_{p} = \frac{1}{A \cdot n \cdot (\sigma_{\mathrm{eff}})^{n-1}} \tag{24}$$

(4)求解应力增量

$$\Delta\sigma^{k} = -\mathrm{d}\varepsilon_{\mathrm{eff}}^{p,k} D^{e} \mathrm{d}\varepsilon^{p,k} \tag{25}$$

(5)由式(16)、式(17)更新应力 $\sigma^{ep,k+1}$ 和塑性应变$\varepsilon^{p,k+1}$,并更新等效塑性应变:

$$\varepsilon_{\mathrm{eff}}^{p,k+1} = \varepsilon_{\mathrm{eff}}^{p,k} + \mathrm{d}\varepsilon_{\mathrm{eff}}^{p,k} \tag{26}$$

(6)更新迭代次数 $k=k+1$,返回②

更新算法的流程图如图2所示。

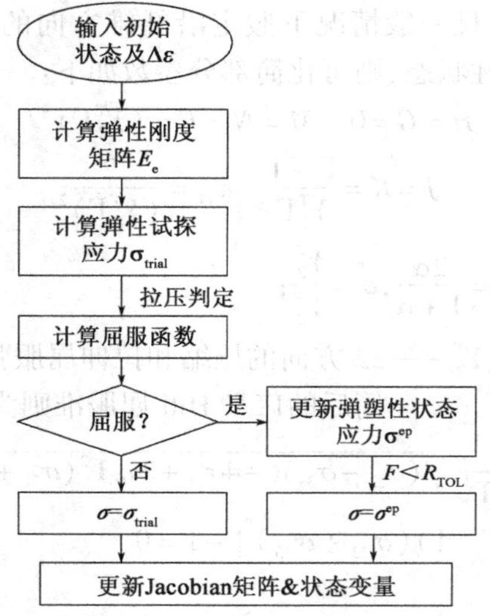

图2　UMAT子程序流程图

2.2　程序验证

文献[13-15]介绍了单调加载下IM600/Q133碳纤/环氧12层层合板的拉伸和压缩试验,为了研究该层合板的力学性能,分别制备了长200mm、宽20mm、厚1.8mm,偏轴角15°、30°、45°、90°、±30°和±45°的长条形试样,试验采用了Xiao等[26]提出的适用于偏轴试验的夹具,试验结果如表1所示。

层合板三维有限元模型采用8节点六面体线性减缩积分单元C3D8R,模型尺寸与试件相同,模型边界条件、加载模式及网格尺寸如图3所示。网格在长宽方向为2mm×2mm,厚度方向划分12层,分析步长为1×10^{-4};参照试验方案,模型左右两侧50mm夹持端分别耦合于参考点RP1、RP2并

释放平行于板的弯矩使其在面内能够自由转动，减少端部约束引发的应力集中。模型加载采用一端固定（$x_1=0$），另一端施加位移（x_2）的方式进行。

IM600/Q133 材料弹性与塑性参数 表 1

应力状态	E_{11} (MPa)	E_{12} (MPa)	G_{12} (MPa)	G_{13} (MPa)	v_{12}	v_{23}	a_{66}	A (MPa^{-n})	n	α
拉伸	137.8×10^3	8.91×10^3	4.41×10^3	3.01×10^3	0.33	0.48	1.2	2.33×10^{-12}	4.6	1.0
压缩	137.8×10^3	8.91×10^3	4.41×10^3	3.01×10^3	0.33	0.48	1.2	2.09×10^{-13}	4.78	1.7

图 3 模型网格及边界条件

图 4 所示为单向层合板的试验及有限元计算结果的对比情况，二者的应力应变关系基本相同，本文编制的子程序与文献[13]计算的结果也基本一致，显示了程序的正确性。

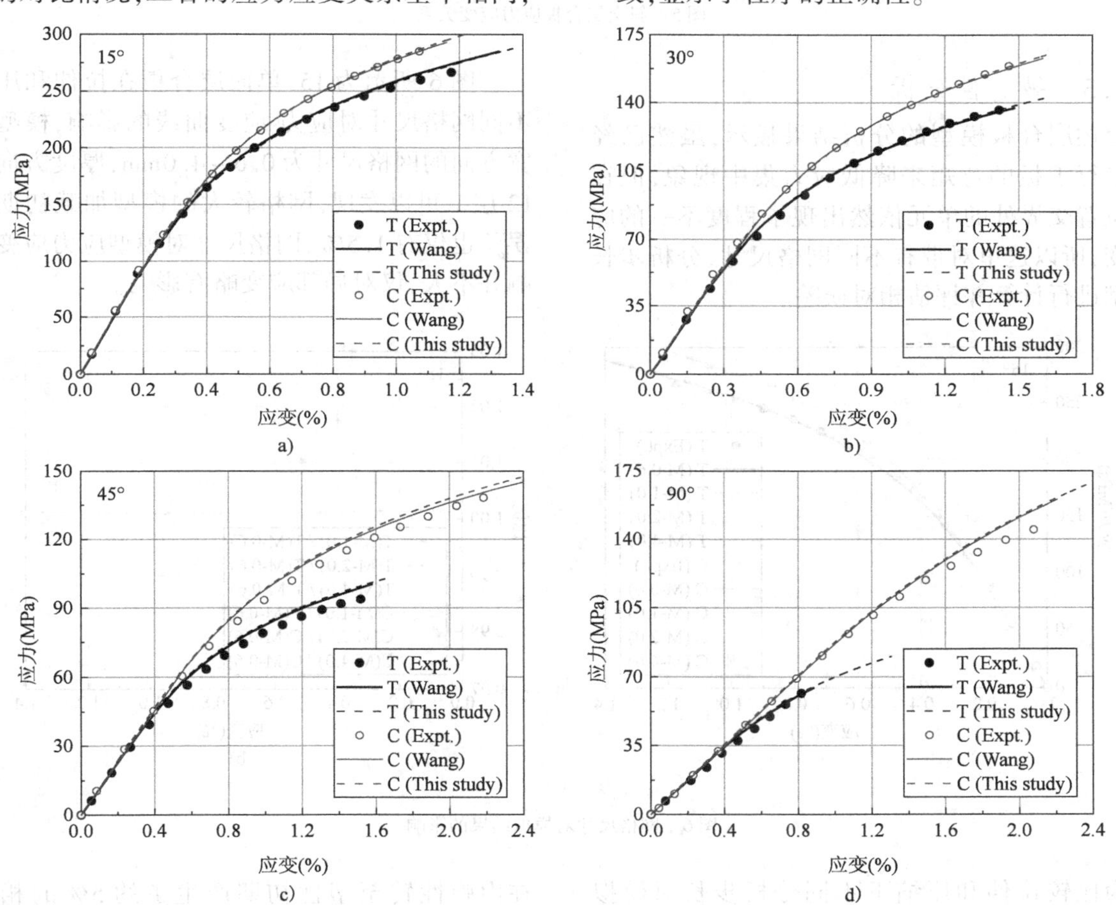

图 4 单向层合板应力应变关系

图 5 所示为 30°和 45°斜交层合板试验和有限元计算结果对比情况，结果显示，本文有限元计算结果相比试验得到的值偏大，与文献[13]的模拟结果在弹塑性阶段也有一定误差，王杰[13]和 Thiruppukuzhi & Sun[27] 认为这是由于应变较大时材料内部可能已经发生损伤，但模型中没有考虑这方面的影响导致的。此外，对于单向层合板的各层应力状态大致相同，但斜交层合板由于各层

纤维方向不同,受力情况的差异不可忽视,有限元模型将层间作用简化为Tie接触,使得层间刚度偏大,得到的模拟结果相比真实值也偏大。

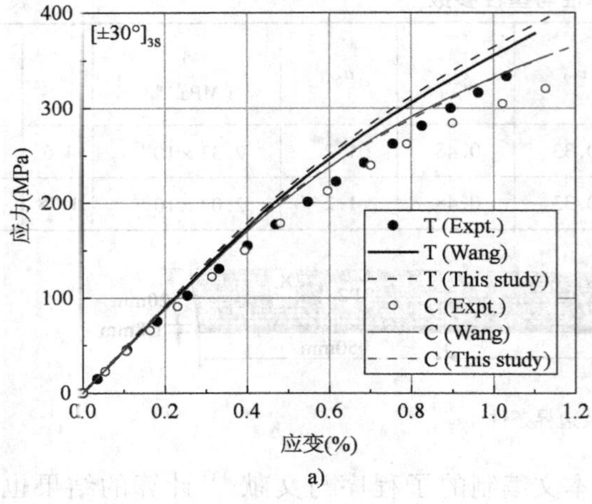

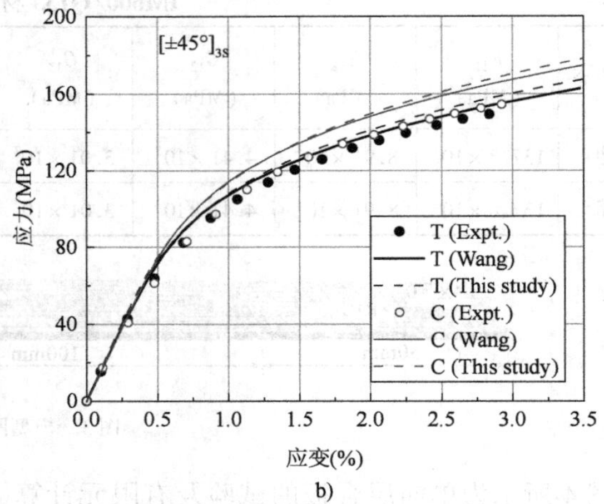

图5 斜交层合板应力应变关系

2.3 敏感性分析

上述层合板模型的分析结果显示,虽然已经释放平行于板的弯矩来降低应力集中现象,但在夹持位置交界处的单元依然出现了程度不一的应力突变,所以这里对带有不同网格尺寸、分析步长的模型进行计算并评估相对误差。

图6所示为15°单向层合板在拉伸和压缩下不同网格尺寸对应力-应变曲线的影响,模型在长宽方向的网格尺寸为0.6~4.0mm,厚度方向划分12层。可以发现,网格较大的模型加载初期相对误差也仅有1.5%,网格尺寸对模型应力应变的影响并不大,仅对局部应变略有影响。

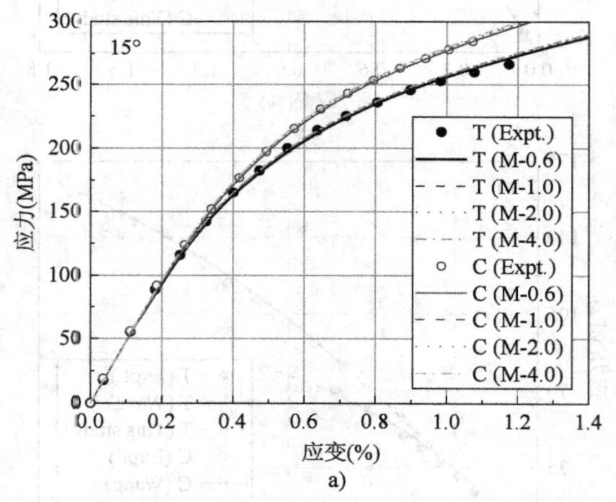

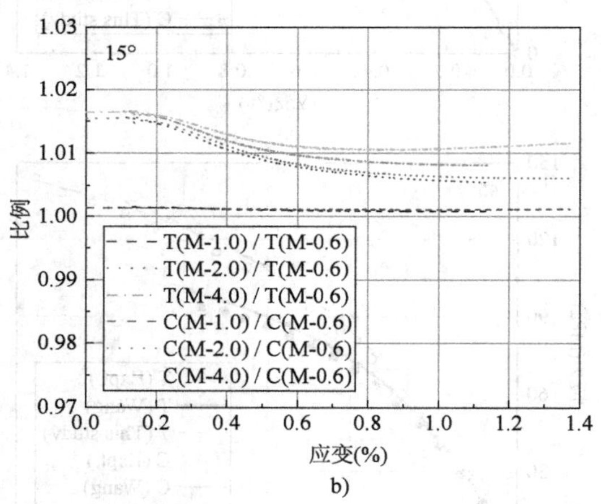

图6 网格尺寸对模拟结果的影响

为比较拉伸和压缩下不同分析步长对模拟结果的影响,分别计算了分析步数量为2×10^2、1×10^3、1×10^4和1×10^5的拉压模拟结果,如图7所示。结果显示,当以分析步数量为1×10^5的工况为衡量基准时,分析步较多的工况保证了较好的稳定性,分析步较少、尤其是2×10^2的工况,在由弹性转至塑性初期产生了约5%的相对误差,这可能是由于文献[13]将等效应力与等效塑性应变关系简化为幂函数关系,所以压缩与拉伸硬化主曲线在加载初期的弹性阶段产生了较小的等效塑性应变导致的。此外,对于分析步较少的工况,模型的收敛性表现也欠佳。

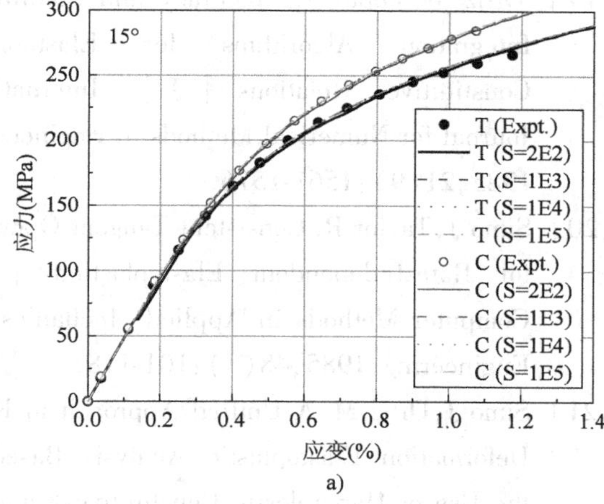

a)

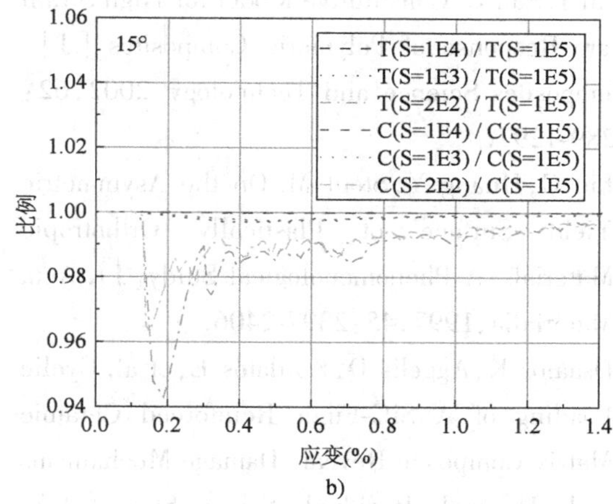

b)

图7 分析步数量对模拟结果的影响

3 结语

纤维增强复合材料(FRP)的应用有利于大跨度桥梁、高层结构体系的发展。对这种材料弹塑性行为的深入研究有利于扩展其在工程结构中的应用。本文通过编写描述桥梁工程用 FRP 材料本构关系的 UMAT 子程序,在 ABAQUS 中实现对 FRP 层合板偏轴拉伸和压缩的模拟,本文结论与展望如下:

(1)在考虑了拉压性能不对称的非线性本构模型基础上,通过切平面算法在 ABAQUS 中实现复合材料弹塑性阶段应力的迭代更新,利用已有试验数据验证了有限元模型和 UMAT 子程序的正确性。

(2)对层合板模型进行敏感性分析的结果显示,网格尺寸和分析步长对模拟结果的影响有限,但分析步数量较少时可能会导致一定的收敛性问题。

(3)大应变下材料往往已经出现损伤,现有分析方法未考虑损伤对模型的影响,故后续应对大应变下塑性变形和损伤效应的耦合作用进一步分析,从而对现有模型进行修正。

参考文献

[1] Bakis C E, Bank L C, Brown V L, et al. Fiber-Reinforced Polymer Composites for Construction-State-of-the-Art Review [J]. Journal of Composites for Construction, 2002, 6(2):73-87.

[2] Xin H, Liu Y, Mosallam A S, et al. Evaluation on Material Behaviors of Pultruded Glass Fiber Reinforced Polymer (GFRP) Laminates [J]. Composite Structures, 2017, 182(12):283-300.

[3] Xin H, Mosallam A S, Liu Y, et al. Analytical and Experimental Evaluation of Flexural Behavior of FRP Pultruded Composite Profiles for Bridge Deck Structural Design [J]. Construction and Building Materials, 2017, 150:123-149.

[4] Xin H, Mosallam A S, Liu Y, et al. Experimental and Numerical Investigation on In-Plane Compression and Shear Performance of a Pultruded GFRP Composite Bridge Deck [J]. Composite Structures, 2017, 180(11):914-932.

[5] 周祝林,姚辉,刘剑,等. 复合材料非线性力学的细观分析[J]. 玻璃钢/复合材料, 2009(01):10-14.

[6] Xiao Y, Hatta H, Kawal M. Observations on Tensile and Compressive Behavior for Off-Axis Fiber Composites[C]// Proceedings of the 10th Japan International SAMPE Symposium. Tokyo: Tokyo Big Sight, 2007: PMC-7-5.

[7] Bert C. Models for Fibrous Composites with Different Properties in Tension and Compression [J]. Journal of Engineering Materials and Technology, 1977, 99(4):344.

[8] Amijima S, Adachi T. Nonlinear Stress-Strain Response of Laminated Composites[J]. Journal of Composite Materials, 1979, 13(3). 206-218.

[9] Tsai J,Sun C. Constitutive Model for High Strain Rate Response of Polymeric Composites [J]. Composites Science and Technology,2002,62:1289-1297.

[10] Liu C,Huang Y,Stout M. On the Asymmetric Yield Surface of Plastically Orthotropic Materials:A Phenomenological Study[J]. Acta Materialia,1997,45:2397-2406.

[11] Dsaaios K,Aggelis D,Kordatos E,et al. Cyclic Loading of A SiC-Fiber Reinforced Ceramic Matrix Composite Reveals Damage Mechanisms and Thermal Residual Stress State [J]. Composites Part A: Applied Science and Manufacturing,2013,44:105-113.

[12] Hahn H,Tsai S,Nonlinear Elastic Behavior of Unidirectional Composite Laminae[J]. Journal of Composite Materials,1973,(7):102 118.

[13] 王杰. 纤维增强复合材料非线性响应的拉压不对称性研究[D] 上海:同济大学,2018.

[14] Wang J,Xiao Y. Some Improvements on Sun-Chen's One-Parameter Plasticity Model for Fibrous Composites-Part I: Constitutive Modelling for Tension-Compression Asymmetry Response[J]. Journal of Composite Materials,2017,51(3):405-418.

[15] Wang J,Xiao Y. Some Improvements on Sun-Chen's One-Parameter Plasticity Model for Fibrous Composites-Part II: Finite Element Method Implementation and Applications[J]. Journal of Composite Materials,2017,51(4):533-545.

[16] Hill R. The Mathematical Theory of Plasticity [M]. Oxford:Oxford University Press,1998.

[17] Drucker D,Prager W. Soil Mechanics and Plastic Analysis or Limit Design[J]. Quarterly of Applied Mathematics,1952,10:157-165.

[18] Huang J, Griffiths D. Return Mapping Algorithms and Stress Predictors for Failure Analysis in Geomechanics [J]. Journal of Engineering Mechanics, 2009, 135 (4): 276-284.

[19] Ortiz M,Popov E. Accuracy and Stability of Integration Algorithms for Elastoplastic Constitutive Relations [J]. International Journal for Numerical Methods in Engineering,1985,21(9):1561-1576.

[20] Simo J,Taylor R. Consistent Tangent Operators for Rate-Independent Elastoplasticity [J]. Computer Methods in Applied Mechanics and Engineering,1985,48(3):101-118.

[21] Simo J,Ortiz M. A Unified Approach to Finite Deformation Elastoplastic Analysis Based on the Use of Hyperelastic Constitutive-Equations [J]. Computer Methods in Applied Mechanics and Engineering,1985,49(2):221-245.

[22] Ortiz M,Simo J. An Analysis of A New Class of Integration Algorithms for Elastoplastic Constitutive Relations [J]. International Journal for Numerical Methods in Engineering,1986,23(3):353-366.

[23] De S,Peri D,Owen D. Model for Elastoplastic Damage at Finite Strains: Algorithmic Issues and Applications [J]. Engineering Computations,1994,11(3):257-281.

[24] Biani N,Pearce C. Computational Aspects of a Softening Plasticity Model for Plain Concrete [J]. Mechanics of Cohesive-Frictional Materials[J],1996,1(1):75-94.

[25] Caddemi S,Martin J. Convergence of the Newton-Raphson algorithm in elastic-plastic incremental analysis[J]. International Journal for Numerical Methods in Engineering,1991,31(1):177-191.

[26] Xiao Y,Kawai M,Hatta H. An Integrated Method for Off-Axis Tension and Compression Testing of Unidirectional Composites [J]. Journal of Composite Materials, 2011, 45: 657-669.

[27] Thiruppukuzhi S,Sun C. Models for the Strain-Rate-Dependent Behavior of Polymer Composites [J]. Composites Science and Technology,2001,61:1-12.

基于健康监测长期数据的伸缩缝性能评估

刘　杰　武晓阳*
(长安大学公路学院)

摘　要　本文基于某大跨度悬索桥健康监测长期数据,提出了伸缩缝性能评估方法。通过线性回归定量分析了主梁梁端位移与结构温度的相关性;并基于高斯混合模型的EM参数估计方法和广义极值分布模型,建立伸缩缝位移的概率密度模型并估计伸缩缝位移在设计基准期内的极值。长期监测结果表明伸缩缝刚度发生退化,伸缩缝伸缩变化总量在设计基准期内小于伸缩缝的设计位移,运营性能满足设计要求。

关键词　桥梁工程　结构健康监测　概率统计　悬索桥　伸缩缝　位移　温度

0　引言

在桥梁结构中,伸缩缝是消减由不均匀沉降所引起的上部结构的二次应力[1]以及调节外部作用下结构产生变形的重要附属结构。伸缩缝的服役状态不仅会影响桥梁的整体功能,更有可能影响到结构本身,导致各种病害与经济损失[2]。实际工程中伸缩缝损坏问题非常普遍,同时,大跨度桥梁的刚度较小,过早失效的情况越来越普遍[3]。因此迫切需要有效的方法对伸缩缝的状态进行监测和评估[4],以便实时准确地发现损伤并及时做出修复策略。

目前,人工检测由于主观性很强同时难以对伸缩缝的状态做出准确、定量的判断,现多采用基于桥梁健康监测数据的性能评估手段。通过布设传感器,在桥梁运营期间采集伸缩缝在各种耦合作用下的位移、主梁温度等数据。基于长期监测数据与相关算法,实时检测到伸缩缝位移的异常情况,从而可以对伸缩缝的运营性能进行评估,为伸缩缝的管养决策提供依据和指导[5]。大量学者通过对伸缩缝位移分析[6-10],对伸缩缝的服役状态评估进行了相关研究。

本文基于某大跨度悬索桥健康监测系统采集的伸缩缝位移与主梁结构温度数据,分析伸缩缝位移与温度的相关性,研究了两者相关性参数长期变化规律,建立位移概率分布模型,并评估了伸缩缝的使用性能。

1　伸缩缝位移长期监测与分析

背景桥梁为576.2m+1418m+481.8m的三跨连续钢箱梁悬索桥,该桥在梁端的南北端上下游各安装了一个伸缩缝位移计,共安装4个,如图1所示。在边跨跨中的位置共安装了6个结构温度测点,如图2所示,从而实时采集梁端伸缩缝处的纵向位移和边跨跨中截面温度监测数据。

分析悬索桥在服役状态下的长期监测结果,分别选取2018年4月10号(春季)、2018年7月10号(夏季)、2018年9月29号(秋季)和2018年1月20号的健康监测数据进行时程与统计分析。本文中所有监测数据均采用10min平均值为计算基本颗粒度,温度的每一个计算值取截面平均值。

大桥伸缩缝位移和主梁温度数据的日时程变化如图3~图6所示,图中,位移时程图包括主桥一侧的上、下游和上下游2个传感器的平均位移时程图,位移均以mm为单位,主梁温度以℃为单位。

从图3~图6可以看出,各个测点的时程变化较一致,并且每天在0:00—8:00之间位移变化量增加,在9:00—17:00之间位移变化量减小,通过比较伸缩缝位移和主梁结构温度时程图,可见两者变化极具一致性;当温度变低时,位移变化量增大,当温度变高时,位移变化量减少,表明了南北两端伸缩缝纵向位移与温度之间存在较强的负相关性。

为进一步分析本悬索桥伸缩缝位移与主梁温度变化之间的关系,表1列出了各个伸缩缝位移和主梁结构温度的统计参数,经过分析,可以得出以下规律和结论:①北侧、南侧各自的上下游的位移变化基本保持一致,表明了各端上下游之间的伸缩缝装置的工作协同一致。②伸缩缝位移与主梁结构温度时程变化均类似于正弦函数。③伸缩缝位移在一年不同季节中变化存在差异。夏季环境温度高,日温差较大,伸缩缝位移日较差大;春秋两季环境温度适中,日温差较小,同时,春季的日温差大于秋季的日温差,春季的伸缩缝位移日较差比秋季的更大;冬季环境温度较低,日温差小,所以冬季的伸缩缝位移日较差最小。综合以上结果,表明了本悬索桥伸缩缝纵向位移与温度之间存在明显的相关关系。

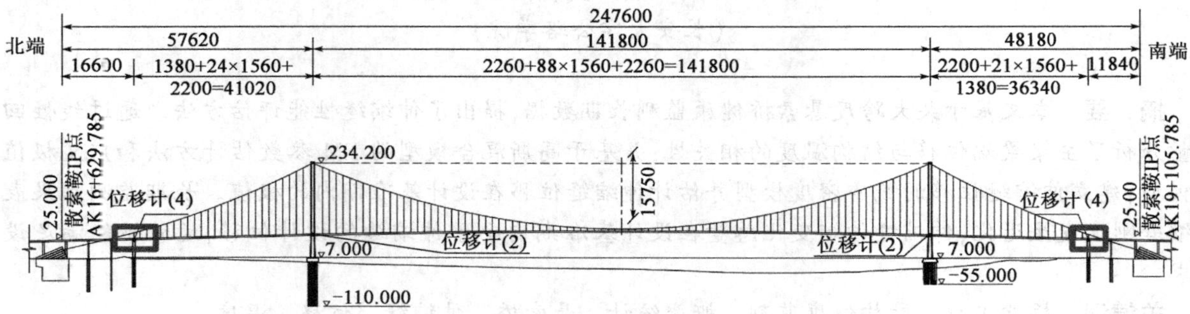

图 1　桥梁位移计测点布设图(尺寸单位:cm)

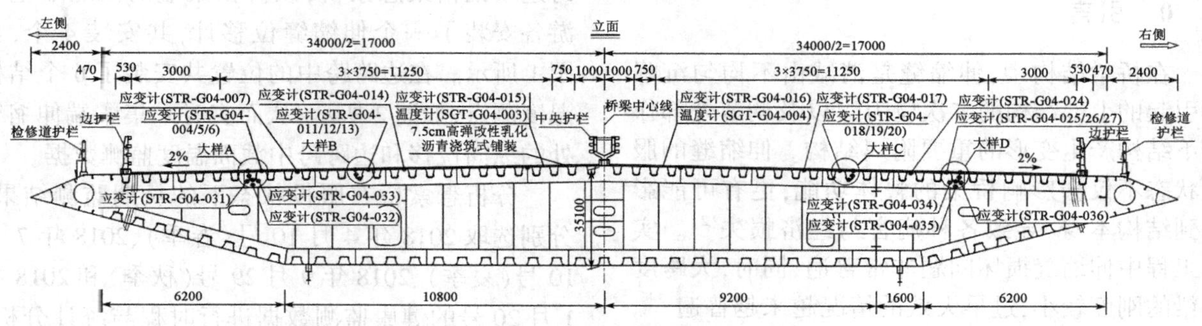

图 2　桥梁结构温度测点布设图(尺寸单位:cm)

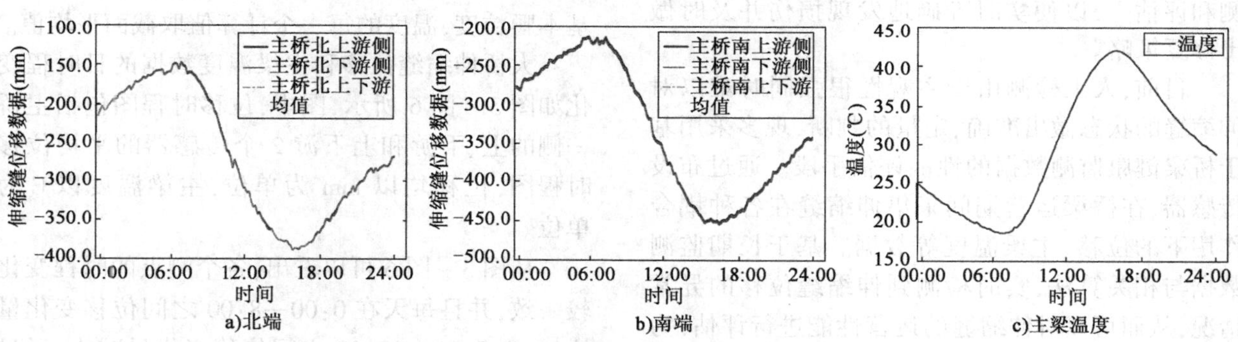

图 3　2018 年 4 月 10 日伸缩缝位移和主梁温度日时程图

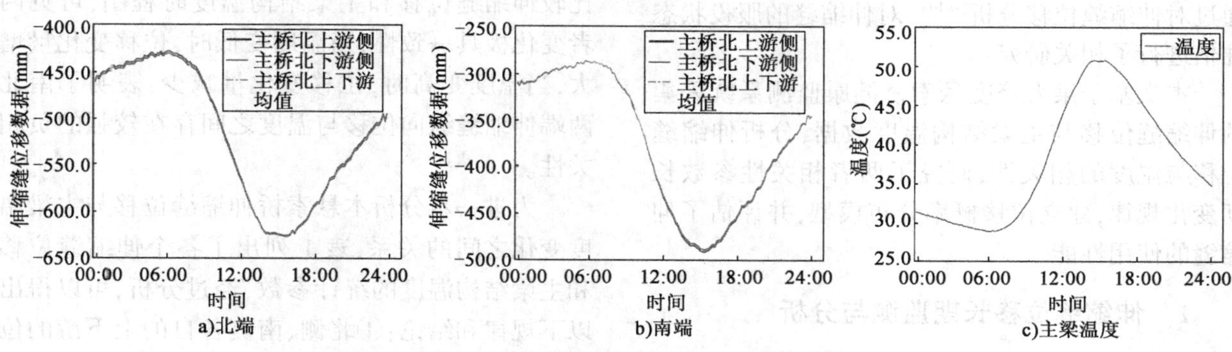

图 4　2018 年 7 月 10 日伸缩缝位移和主梁温度日时程图

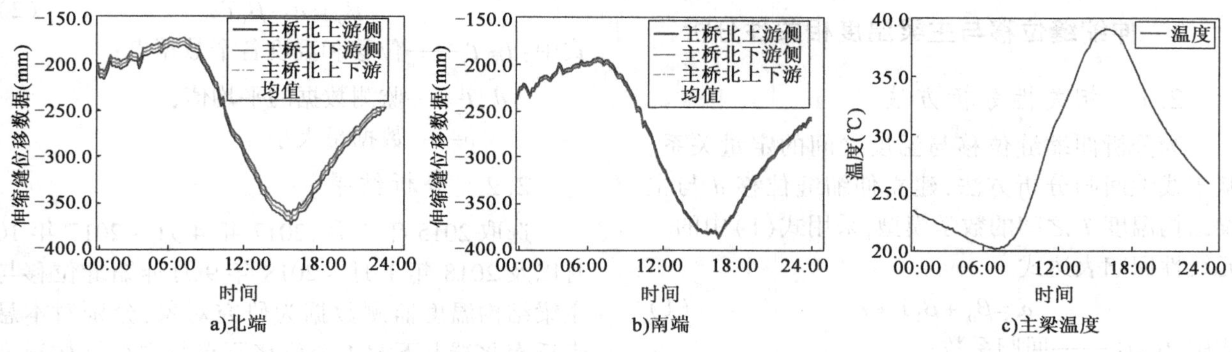

图5 2018年9月29日伸缩缝位移和主梁温度日时程图

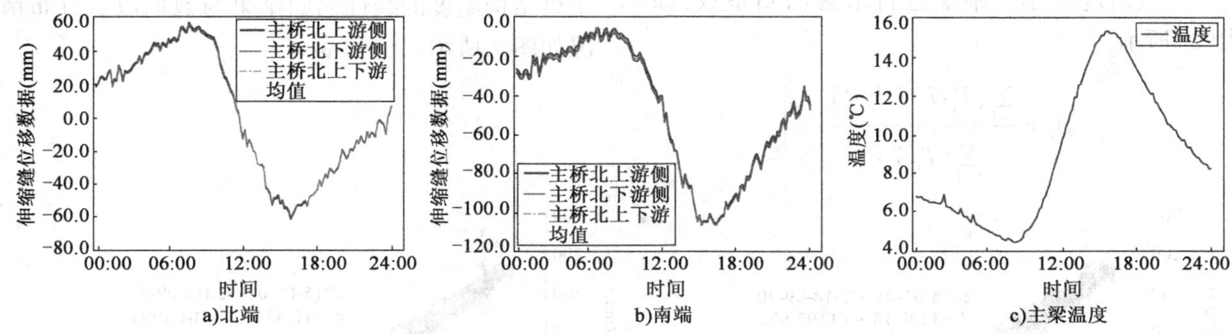

图6 2018年1月20日伸缩缝位移和主梁温度日时程图

本悬索桥南北两端伸缩缝纵向位移与主梁结构温度的统计参数 表1

日期	测点		最大值	最小值	平均值	日较差
2018年4月10号	北端位移(mm)	上游	-146.22	-388.34	-264.94	242.12
		下游	-147.44	-387.88	-265.77	240.44
	南端位移(mm)	上游	-214.02	-453.60	-333.99	239.58
		下游	-211.80	-451.29	-331.35	239.49
	主梁结构温度(℃)		42.11	18.66	29.52	23.45
2018年7月10号	北端位移(mm)	上游	-286.52	-490.77	-376.19	204.25
		下游	-286.25	-488.02	-374.94	201.77
	南端位移(mm)	上游	-430.44	-625.85	-518.33	195.40
		下游	-427.52	-624.57	-515.83	197.05
	主梁结构温度(℃)		50.86	28.91	38.16	21.95
2018年9月29号	北端位移(mm)	上游	-181.03	-373.72	-262.76	192.69
		下游	-173.35	-362.56	-254.26	189.21
	南端位移(mm)	上游	-197.24	-387.56	-279.74	190.32
		下游	-193.40	-385.29	-276.32	191.90
	主梁结构温度(℃)		39.05	20.18	28.20	18.87
2018年1月20号	北端位移(mm)	上游	56.87	-61.27	2.50	118.14
		下游	55.67	-60.35	2.00	116.02
	南端位移(mm)	上游	-7.27	-106.95	-48.68	99.68
		下游	-5.15	-106.41	-46.80	101.26
	主梁结构温度(℃)		15.34	4.42	9.00	10.92

2　伸缩缝位移与主梁温度相关性分析

2.1　相关性分析方法

为分析伸缩缝位移与温度之间的定量关系，基于线性回归分析方法，建立伸缩缝位移 d 与主梁结构温度 T 之间的数学模型，采用式(1)中的一元线性回归表达式。

$$d = \beta_0 + \beta_1 T + \varepsilon \tag{1}$$

式中：β_0、β_1——回归系数；

ε——误差。

一般通过最小二乘法进行求解回归系数，如式(2)所示。

$$\beta_1 = \frac{\sum_{i=1}^{n}(T_i-\bar{T})(d_i-\bar{d})}{\sum_{i=1}^{n}(T_i-\bar{T})^2}$$

$$\beta_0 = \bar{d} - \beta_1 \bar{T} \tag{2}$$

式中：d_i、T_i——位移和温度各个数据点；

$\bar{d}$、$\bar{T}$——监测数据的平均值；

n——数据量大小。

2.2　分析结果

选取2015年1月、2017年4月～2017年10月以及2018年1月～2018年9月伸缩缝位移与主梁结构温度监测数据为研究对象，分别对本悬索桥南北端上下游4个位移测点与主梁结构温度之间进行一元回归分析，各个测点伸缩缝位移和主梁结构温度的线性回归结果与数据散点分布情况如图7所示。

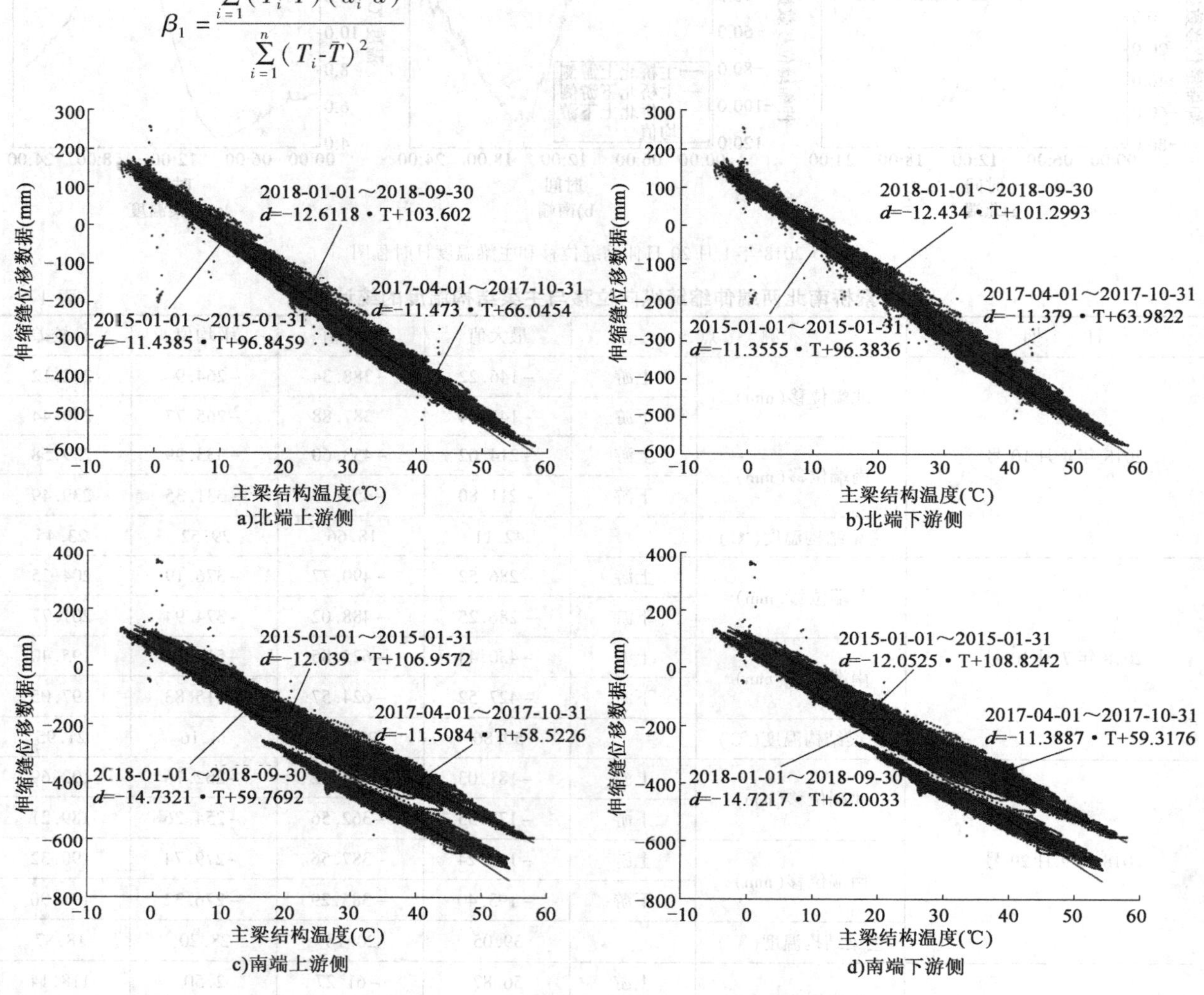

图7　伸缩缝位移与主梁温度相关性分析结果

从图7中可以得出以下结论：①南北端上下游4个伸缩缝的位移数据与主梁结构温度数据存在明显的负线性相关性，各个测点都表现出主梁结构温度高则位移小、主梁结构温度低则位移大的特征。②纵向刚度是表征伸缩缝性能的重要指标，在相关性分析图中，斜率的大小代表了纵向刚度的大小，即斜率越小，纵向刚度越小，在相同的温度变化作用下，伸缩缝的位移更大。从图7中可以看出各个测点的斜率β_1随着时间的推移，均存在着变小的趋势，例如北端上游侧从2015年的-11.4385变化至2018年的-12.6118，南端上游侧从2015年的-12.039变化至2018年的-14.7321，表明了本悬索桥存在着服役性能退化的风险。

3 伸缩缝位移的概率建模分析

3.1 建模方法

基于本大跨度悬索桥健康监测系统所采集的伸缩缝位移数据，根据AIC与BIC准则，选定分量为2的高斯混合和模型来表征各个测点位移数据的概率密度分布，从而准确描述位移数据的统计特性，计算公式如式(3)所示。

$$f(d_i)=\alpha N_1(\mu_1,\sigma_1)+\beta N_2(\mu_2,\sigma_2)$$
$$=\alpha\left[\frac{1}{\sigma_1\sqrt{2\pi}}\mathrm{e}\frac{-(d_i-\mu_1)^2}{2\sigma_1{}^2}\right]+$$
$$\beta\left[\frac{1}{\sigma_2\sqrt{2\pi}}\mathrm{e}\frac{-(d_i-\mu_2)^2}{2\sigma_2{}^2}\right] \quad (3)$$

式中：$f(d_i)$——位移数据d_i的概率密度函数；

$N_1(\mu_1,\sigma_1)$、$N_2(\mu_2,\sigma_2)$——正态分布函数；

μ_1,σ_1、μ_2,σ_2——正态分布函数的均值和方差；

α、β——高斯混合模型中2个正态分布的权重比例，且$\alpha+\beta=1$；

μ_1、σ_1、μ_2、σ_2、α、β——待估计参数，此处采用EM算法对高斯混合模型进行参数估计[11]。

3.2 概率统计分析结果

为保证数据的连续性，选定2018年1月1日至2018年9月30日之间的南北端上下游四个位移测点的数据进行概率建模，计算颗粒度采用10min，公式(4)~(7)为北端上游、北端下游、南端上游和南端下游位移测点的概率密度函数，图8分别展示了不同位移测点的概率密度柱状图以及基于高斯混合模型的拟合概率密度曲线。

$$f(d_i)=0.54N_1(-225.81,98.99)+0.46N_2(27.54,68.05) \quad (4)$$

$$f(d_i)=0.54N_1(-225.16,98.11)+0.46N_2(27.04,67.76) \quad (5)$$

$$f(d_i)=0.54N_1(-321.02,117.96)+0.46N_2(-25.35,74.02) \quad (6)$$

$$f(d_i)=0.54N_1(-323.84,117.63)+0.46N_2(-27.68,74.43) \quad (7)$$

从上述可以得出，北端上下游、南端上下游的概率密度分布相当一致，表明各端的伸缩缝上下游工作协同性较高。

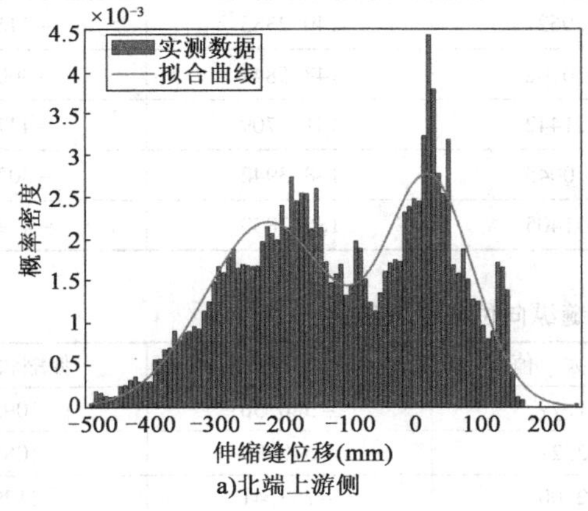

a)北端上游侧

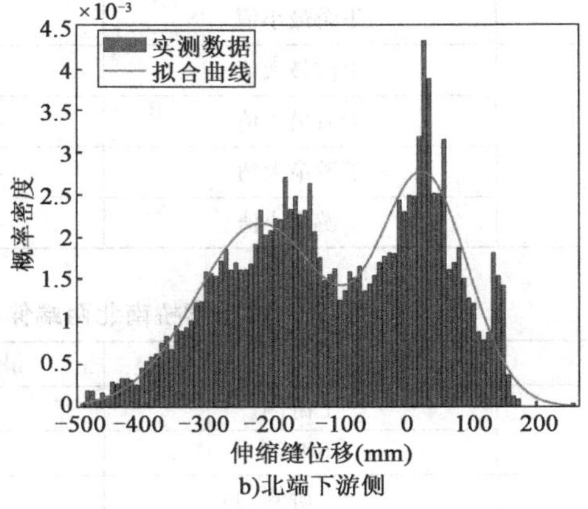

b)北端下游侧

图 8

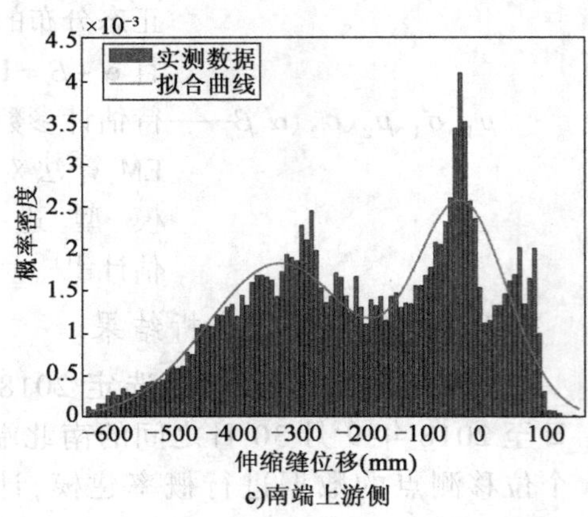

c)南端上游侧

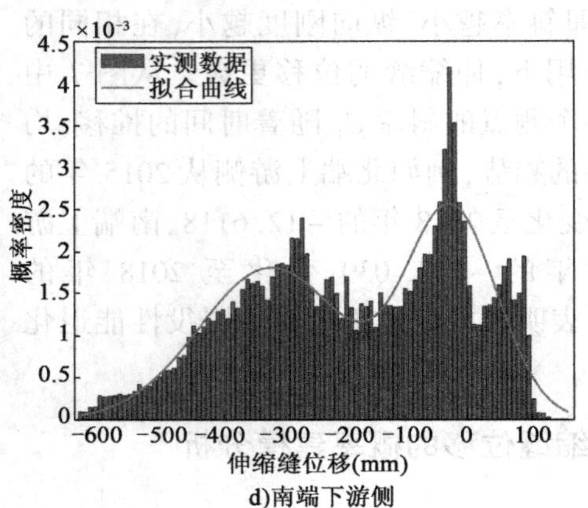

d)南端下游侧

图8　伸缩缝位移概率密度图

4　伸缩缝位移极值估计

4.1　分析方法

为对伸缩缝的位移极值进行估计,选取2018年1月1日至2018年9月30的每天位移监测数据的最值,采用广义极值分布函数[12]建立各个位移测点的概率分布模型,如式(8)所示,从而估计本桥设计基准期内的位移极值,同时可以判断伸缩缝的极值较差能否满足伸缩缝位移的设计性能要求。

$$F(x;k,\sigma,\mu)=\exp\{-[1+k(x-\mu)/\sigma]^{-1/k}\} \tag{8}$$

式中:k、μ、σ——形状参数、位置参数和尺度参数。

4.2　分析结果

本悬索桥南北端上下游测点的极值分布参数如表2所示,概率密度图如图9~图12所示。根据我国桥梁设计规范的设计基准期为100年,可计算得各个伸缩缝位移在基准期内的最值,如表3所示。

从表3可以看出,伸缩缝最大较差总量为南端上游侧的1129.41mm,小于伸缩缝的设计位移量1520mm,说明伸缩缝满足设计要求。

本悬索桥伸缩缝纵向位移最值的广义极值分布参数　表2

测点位置		广义极值分布参数		
		k	σ	μ
北端	上游最大值	0.1614	104.4792	-201.0452
	上游最小值	-0.0675	143.9071	-349.0587
	下游最大值	0.1689	102.1893	-198.6693
	下游最小值	-0.0627	140.2383	-346.2323
南端	上游最大值	-0.0102	148.5841	-300.3341
	上游最小值	-0.1442	181.3709	-447.3642
	下游最大值	-0.0045	148.3942	-303.5506
	下游最小值	-0.1405	180.7839	-449.4750

本悬索桥南北两端伸缩缝纵向位移最值估计　表3

测点位置		最大值	最小值	伸缩较差总量
北端	上游侧	511.77	-580.56	1092.33
	下游侧	512.21	-570.99	1083.20
南端	上游侧	372.00	-757.41	1129.41
	下游侧	367.40	-757.21	1124.61

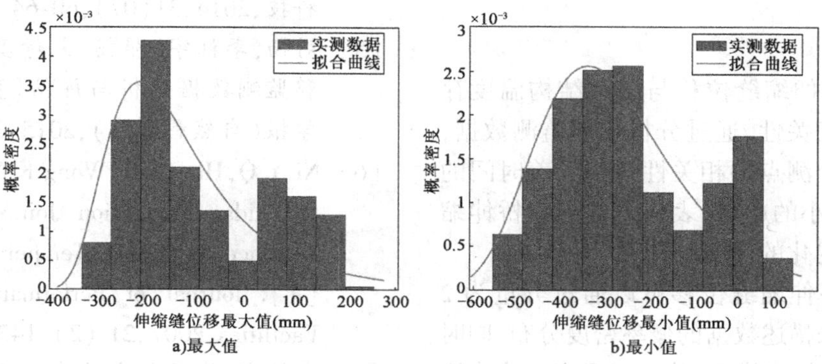

图 9　北端上游伸缩缝位移最值广义极值分布概率密度图

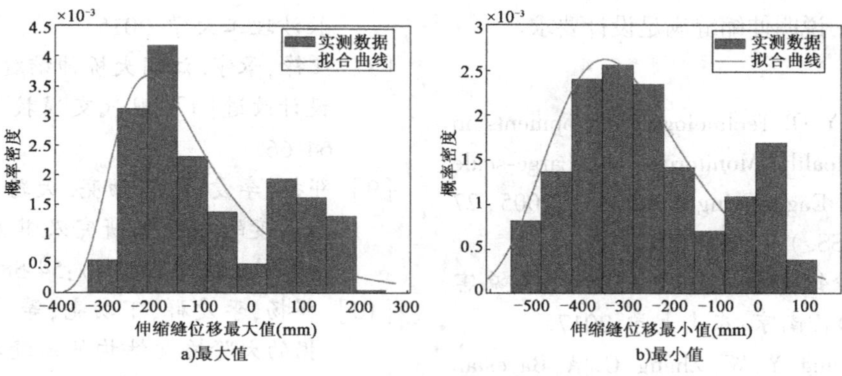

图 10　北端下游伸缩缝位移最值广义极值分布概率密度图

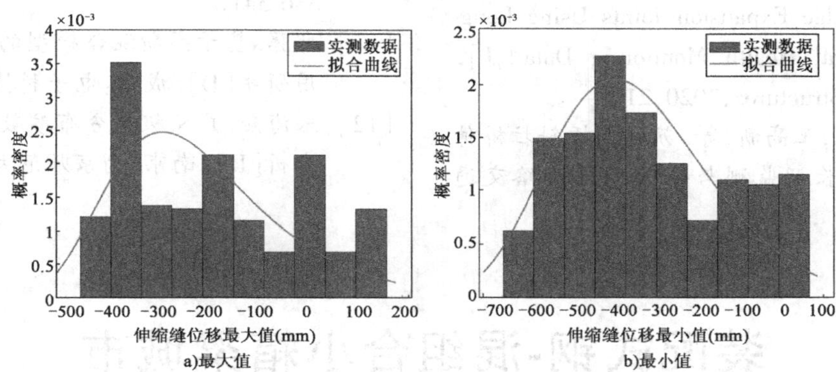

图 11　南端上游伸缩缝位移最值广义极值分布概率密度图

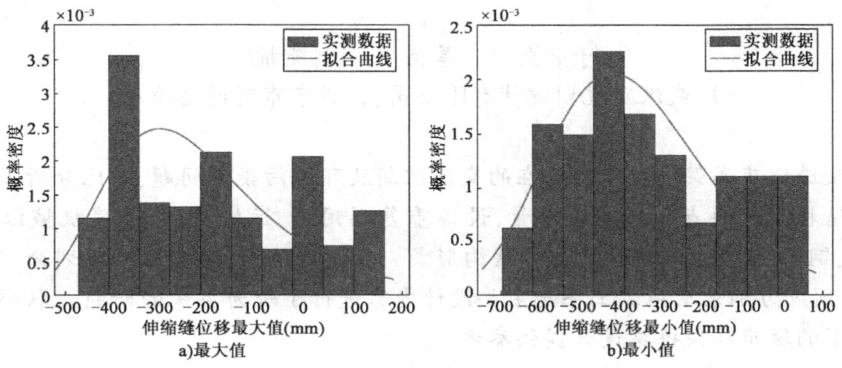

图 12　南端下游伸缩缝位移最值广义极值分布概率密度图

5　结语

(1)本悬索桥伸缩缝位移与主梁结构温度存在良好的线性负相关性,通过分析长期监测数据,南北端上下游4个测点的相关性斜率随着时间的推移,均存在着变小的趋势,表明了本悬索桥伸缩缝存在服务性能退化的风险。

(2)本悬索桥伸缩缝位移可以通过分量为2的高斯混合模型来描述数据的概率密度分布,同时基于广义极值分布概率模型,估计了温度变化作用下位移最大伸缩量为1129.41mm,小于伸缩缝的设计位移量1520mm,说明伸缩缝满足设计要求。

参考文献

[1] Ko J M, Ni Y Q. Technology Developments in Structural Health Monitoring of Large-scale Bridges[J]. Engineering Structures, 2005, 27(12 SPEC. ISS.):1715-1725.

[2] 黄灵宇. 大跨钢桥伸缩缝的性能评估与病害控制研究[D]. 南京:东南大学,2017.

[3] Ni Y Q, Wang Y W, Zhang C. A Bayesian Apprcach for Condition Assessment and Damage Alarm of Bridge Expansion Joints Using Long-term Structural Health Monitoring Data[J]. Engineering Structures,2020,212.

[4] 丁幼亮,周凯,王高新,等. 苏通大桥斜拉桥伸缩缝位移的长期监测与分析[J]. 公路交通科技,2014,31(07):60-64.

[5] 刘扬,李杜宇,邓扬. 大跨度悬索桥伸缩缝位移监测数据分析与评估[J]. 长沙理工大学学报(自然科学版),2015,12(02):21-28.

[6] Ni Y Q, Hua X G, Wong K Y, et al. Assessment of Bridge Expansion Joints Using Long-term Displacement and Temperature Measurement [J]. Journal of Performance of Constructed Facilities,2007,21 (2):143-151.

[7] 李杜宇. 基于长期健康监测数据的南溪长江大桥伸缩缝状态监测与评估研究[D]. 长沙:长沙理工大学,2015.

[8] 汪锋,承宇. 江阴大桥伸缩缝损坏原因分析及设计改进[J]. 现代交通技术,2010,7(02):64-66.

[9] 邓扬,李爱群,丁幼亮. 大跨悬索桥梁端位移与温度的相关性研究及其应用[J]. 公路交通科技,2009,26(05):54-58.

[10] 邓扬,李爱群,丁幼亮,等. 基于长期监测数据的大跨桥梁结构伸缩缝损伤识别[J]. 东南大学学报(自然科学版),2011,41(02):336-341.

[11] 邱藤. 基于高斯混合模型的EM算法及其应用研究[D]. 成都:电子科技大学,2015.

[12] 朱海燕. 广义极值分布参数估计方法的比较分析[D]. 南京:南京师范大学,2014.

装配式钢-混组合小箱梁城市高架桥上部结构方案研究

于长久*[1]　姜兰兰[2]　刘天栋[1]
(1. 武汉市规划设计有限公司;2. 咸宁市交通运输局)

摘　要　为改进城市高架桥梁建设存在的交通阻断及环境污染等问题,对比分析了目前主要应用的装配式桥梁上部结构的优缺点。从吊装重量、设备重复利用率、运输条件、吊装机械以及拼装效率等方面,提出了装配式钢-混组合小箱梁新型上部结构形式。从设计角度,对主梁节段划分、混凝土梁段、钢横梁、钢-混结合段、预应力钢束及施工工序等主要设计内容进行了较为系统的研究。取得的研究成果可以为一定建设条件下的城市高架桥梁设计提供参考。

关键词　钢-混组合小箱梁　上部结构　城市高架桥设计　装配式桥梁　拼装

0 引言

近年来,随着经济的高速发展,城市交通量增长迅猛。国内大中型城市均存在交通量高峰期道路拥堵的问题。为了缓解交通压力,城市建设者常常通过修建高架桥的立体交通方式来疏导交通。目前国内城市高架桥梁多采用宽幅现浇箱梁形式,该方案不需要在城市内占用大片土地来建设预制场。箱梁结构统一,造型较美观,对宽度和跨径变化适应性强。现浇箱梁高架桥的桥墩一般为双柱墩,无帽梁节省桥下净空,为桥下行车创造了条件。但现浇箱梁也有一些缺陷,主梁制造需要搭设满堂支架,长期阻断交通,施工现场会产生粉尘和噪声污染,影响沿线居民的正常生活。为解决现浇箱梁产生的不利影响,近年来预制装配化桥梁得到广泛地重视和应用。目前常用的装配化桥梁上部结构主要有整孔预制混凝土梁(空心板、小箱梁、T 梁)[1,2]、节段预制钢-混组合梁和节段预制混凝土大箱梁。从场地占用面积、设备规模、设备周转利用、构件运输难度等方面分析,上述几种方案均有一定不足。通过对影响预制结构方案优劣的主要因素分析,在整孔预制混凝土小箱梁和节段预制钢-混组合梁的形式基础上,提出了节段预制钢-混组合小箱梁结构。该方案上部结构预制节段体量小,对吊装和运输设备要求低,便于在市区内运输及安装。模板重复利用率高,便于推广。本文主要针对设计及工程应用方面,提出了一种新的桥梁上部结构预制节段形式,完成了结构主要构件的构造设计方案,可供一定建设条件下的城市高架桥梁设计参考。

1 现有主要装配式上部结构方案分析

目前国内城市高架桥采用的装配式上部结构形式主要有整孔预制混凝土梁(空心板、小箱梁、T 梁),节段预制钢-混组合梁和节段预制混凝土大箱梁。三种方案在运输吊装设备要求、模板重复利用率、施工效率以及桥梁景观等方面,都有各自不同的特点。下面针对以上几点主要因素进行分析及综合比较。

1.1 整孔预制混凝土梁

整孔预制混凝土梁结构形式(图 1)主要包括空心板、小箱梁、T 梁。该方案具有设计施工标准化,模板利用率高等优点。早期城市高架桥该类结构形式应用较多,武汉市解放大道高架桥上部结构采用简支空心板,为提高桥梁美观性,桥墩采用隐形帽梁形式。武汉市黄埔大街高架桥上部结构采用简支 T 梁,桥墩同样采用隐形帽梁形式。

该类桥梁上部结构梁高较小,结构轻盈。但整孔预制梁长度一般为 20 ~ 30m,相对于中心城区的建设场地,运输难度大,易造成交通拥堵。

图 1 整孔预制混凝土梁高架桥

1.2 节段预制钢-混组合梁

钢-混组合梁桥(图 2)中比较常见的是简支梁结构[3],一般上翼缘为混凝土板,下翼缘为钢梁。相对于传统的钢筋混凝土结构,钢-混组合梁自重更轻,有利于预制节段的吊装和运输;此外,钢-混组合梁桥还可以更好降低梁高,有助于提升桥下净空利用率。钢-混组合梁的钢梁一般采用螺栓连接,对安装拼装的精度要求较高。预制件的安装需要较高的施工水平,在施工过程中常出现两片梁螺栓孔难以对齐的情况。由于钢-混组合梁相对混凝土梁造价较高,且主梁景观效果一般,故应用有限,导致预制构件模板的利用率较低,造成前期投入的厂房和制造设备处于长期闲置状态。

1.3 节段预制混凝土大箱梁

近年来节段预制拼装大箱梁结构在城市桥梁建设中有所应用,但仍尚未得到量大面广的推广。国内外双向六车道桥梁基本上采用整幅式单箱多室断面或分离式双幅桥梁。城市高架桥常用的断面形式如图 3 ~ 图 5 所示。

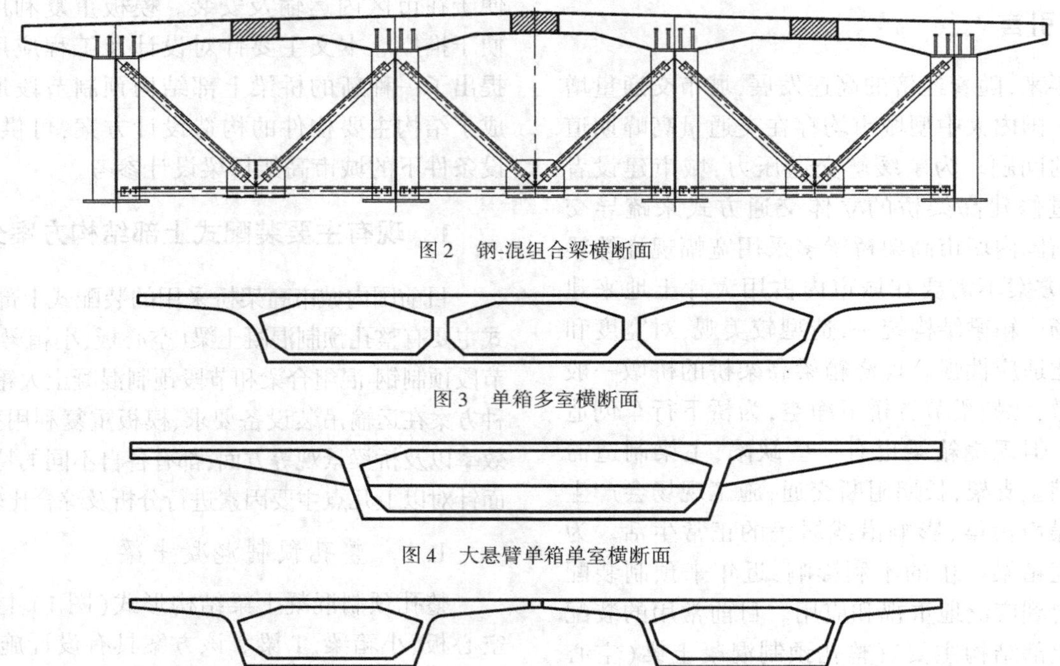

图 2　钢-混组合梁横断面

图 3　单箱多室横断面

图 4　大悬臂单箱单室横断面

图 5　分箱室双主梁横断面

单箱多室和大悬臂单箱单室断面预制效率高,但构件尺寸大,对运输条件、制造及安装设备要求高。横向分幅同步安装的分箱室双主梁结构预制效率相比单箱单室断面略低,单室构件尺寸相对较小,对运输条件、制造及安装设备要求较低。

1.4　主要装配式上部结构方案对比

以跨径 30m、总宽 24m 的双向 6 车道高架桥为例,从节段尺寸、吊装重量、设备重复利用率、运输条件、吊装机械以及拼装效率等方面,对三种城市高架桥的装配化上部结构进行分析对比,具体分析结果如表 1 所示。

装配式上部结构方案对比表　　表 1

断面形式		节段尺寸(长×宽×高)(m)	吊装重量(t)	设备重复利用率	运输条件要求	吊装机械要求	拼装效率
整孔预制小箱梁		30×2.4×1.6	95.7	高	高	较高	低
节段预制钢-混组合梁		10×2.4×1.8	63	较高	低	低	高
节段预制混凝土大箱梁	大悬臂单箱单室	24×4×1.8	132.8	较低	高	高	高
	分箱室双主梁	12×4×1.8	84.6	较低	较高	较高	较高

通过分析比较可以看出,几种主要应用的上部结构形式各有优劣。针对市区内房屋密集、交通拥堵的场地建设条件,三种上部结构均有一定的不足。针对这种情况,本文提出了节段预制钢-混组合小箱梁的新型结构形式,以适应城市一定建设条件的高架桥快速施工需求。

2　节段预制钢-混组合小箱梁

节段预制钢-混组合小箱梁结构形式的提出,主要针对城市内房屋密集、道路交通条件较差的高架桥建设场地情况。从提高制造设备重复利用率,降低预制构件运输难度,减小机械吊装重量降低施工难度角度考虑,对现有的装配化上部结构进行改造,从而适应相对苛刻的建设条件。本文主要从设计角度出发,针对设计过程中需要解决的主要关键技术问题[4],对主梁总体布置及结构体系、节段划分、混凝土梁段、钢横梁、钢-混结合段、预应力钢束及施工工序等进行研究分析[5,6]。

2.1 总体布置及结构体系

以典型的双向6车道24m宽,跨径30m城市高架桥为例进行分析研究。桥梁5跨1联,1联上部结构总长为150m。结构为预应力钢-混组合梁连续体系,主梁整幅布置。横向共布置8片主梁,跨中正弯矩段为预应力混凝土梁,墩顶负弯矩段为钢梁,钢梁与混凝土梁之间通过钢-混结合段连接过渡。

2.2 节段划分

为便于车辆运输预制构件,应尽量减小构件长度。但若要提高拼装效率,则应尽量增大构长度。为达到运输要求与拼装效率的平衡,确定混凝土梁预制节段长度为6m。常规的小箱梁为多支座体系,主梁下方需设置桥墩帽梁。由于帽梁的存在,导致桥墩侵占了桥下净空,并且桥梁也显得不美观。从施工效率角度看,小箱梁墩顶连续段钢筋布置复杂,钢筋现场绑扎及焊接工作量大,使得工期大幅度延长。为提高施工效率并且取消墩柱帽梁,本方案在梁端处用钢横梁代替现浇混凝土横梁,既可以提高施工效率,又可以充分利用钢材的高强度而设置双支座,取消帽梁。钢横梁在连续墩处总宽度取4m,其中横梁部分宽2m,横梁两侧外伸的分体钢箱梁各1m。钢横梁在过渡墩或桥台处总宽度取1.92m,其中横梁部分宽0.92m,横梁一侧外伸的分体钢箱梁长1m。混凝土梁段与钢横梁之间通过钢-混结合段连接,钢-混结合段总长3m,伸入混凝土梁段内2m,外伸1m。图6以中跨一片主梁为例,展示了主梁的节段划分情况。

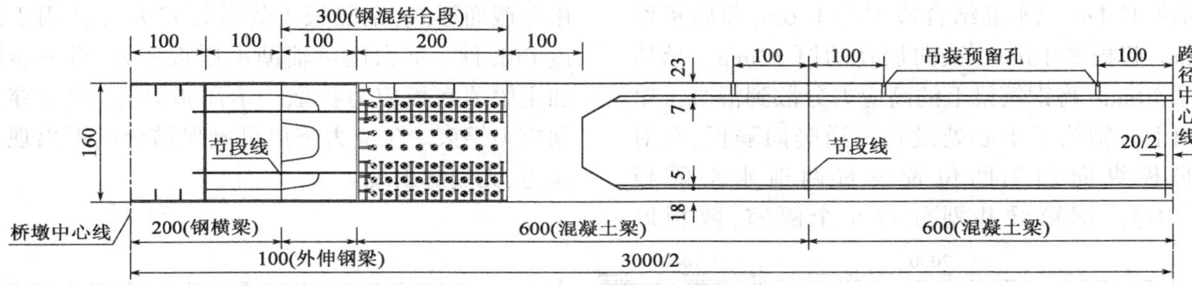

图6 主梁节段划分图(尺寸单位:cm)

2.3 混凝土梁段

混凝土梁段截面形式与常规小箱梁相同,梁高1.6m,中梁顶板宽度2.4m,边梁顶板宽2.85m,顶板厚23cm,底板厚20cm,腹板宽20cm。钢-混结合段侧3m范围为实心段。混凝土节段拼接处设置剪力键,剪力键的布置应避让预应力管道。预制节段剪力键采用多键体系,且均匀布置。腹板内的剪力键横向与腹板等宽,剪力键延腹板全高布置。顶板共设置2处剪力键,剪力键宽46cm,高13cm。底板设置1处剪力键,剪力键宽38cm,高18cm[7]。剪力键截面布置具体见图7。

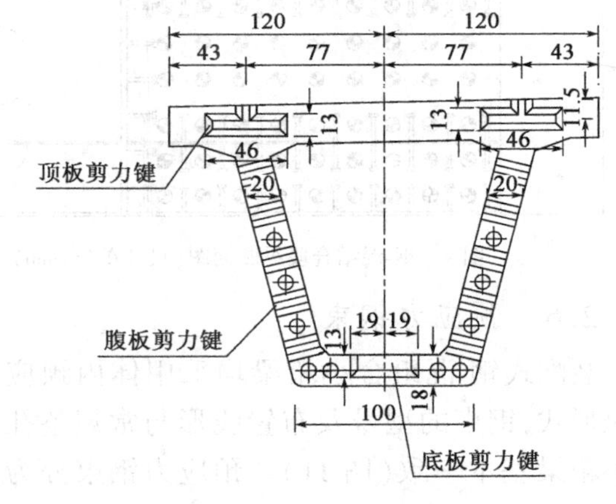

图7 主梁剪力键布置图(尺寸单位:cm)

2.4 钢横梁

钢横梁总长度为24m,总宽度为4m。钢横梁由横梁及外伸分体小箱梁两部分组成(图8)。连续墩顶处横梁宽2m,两侧各1m外伸小箱梁。过渡墩及桥台处横梁宽0.92m,跨中侧1m外伸小箱梁。为便于运输和制作安装,延长度方向每两个箱梁之间翼缘中心处设置拼接缝,节段标准长度约为5.2m。外伸小箱梁外轮廓与混凝土小箱梁对齐,顶底板及斜腹板均设置板式纵向加劲肋。钢横梁梁高与混凝土小箱梁一致,梁高1.6m,顶底板及侧壁均设置板式纵向加劲肋,横梁对应小箱梁腹板位置处设置横隔板。钢横梁顶底板厚24mm,腹板厚16mm,加劲肋板厚12mm。横梁顶板等间距布置剪力钉,加强桥面现浇层与钢顶板之间的连接。帽梁下桥墩考虑为常规的双柱墩，根据墩柱的实际平面布置在支座上方横梁内对应设置支座加劲肋。

2.5　钢-混结合段

钢横梁与混凝土小箱梁在相接位置，由于材料和板件尺寸不同，截面在强度和刚度上存在突变情况。在钢-混结合位置，构件受力复杂，设计上需重点考虑。设计应确保钢-混结合段能可靠传递内力，保证主梁刚度均匀过渡和变形连续。

图8　钢横梁构造图

钢-混结合段主要包括承压板、钢隔室、内置抗剪装置(PBL件及栓钉)、纵向预应力钢束等(图9)。钢-混结合段深入混凝土梁部分长2m，外伸钢梁长1m。钢-混结合段梁高1.6m，顶底板厚24mm，腹板厚16mm，纵向加劲肋厚12mm。承压板厚40mm，将钢箱梁上的高应力分散到混凝土梁截面上。钢箱梁中心处设置一道竖向隔板，在对应腹板纵向加劲肋位置设置两道水平隔板(图10)。钢箱梁共划分为6个隔室，隔板厚16mm，外伸钢箱梁隔板截面延纵向采用变截面形式，主要起到均匀分散钢箱梁应力和刚度渐变过渡的作用。深入混凝土梁段部分钢隔板沿纵向采用等截面形式，钢隔板上焊接栓钉并开孔用于穿过PBL件。剪力键可辅助承压板传力，进一步增加主梁顶底板应力扩散。承压板开孔，用于穿过预应力钢束。预应力钢束可确保结合面不出现拉应力，无裂缝出现。

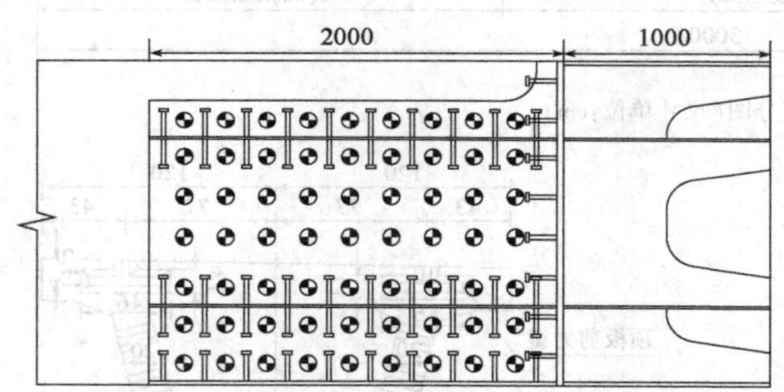

图9　钢-混结合段纵断面图(尺寸单位：mm)

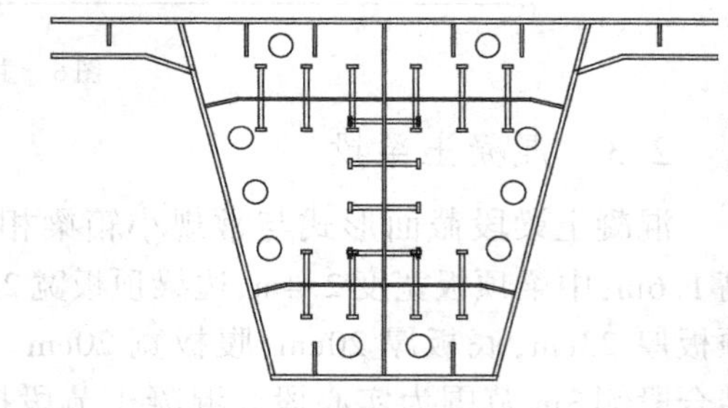

图10　钢-混结合段横断面图

2.6　预应力钢束

装配式钢-混组合小箱梁均采用体内预应力钢束形式，钢束的型号及布置线形与常规整孔预制小箱梁基本一致(图11)。预应力钢束分为底板束和顶板束两部分，正弯矩底板束共有8根，负弯矩顶板束共有4根。预应力钢束采用4-ϕs15.2高强度低松弛钢绞线，其标准强度$f_{pk}=1860\text{MPa}$，$E_p=1.95\times10e^5\text{MPa}$，松弛率小于0.025。钢束张拉端位于钢-混结合段的承压板处，钢束在钢-混结合段范围内竖向线形为水平直线，以使得预应力管道避开PBL键和栓钉。预应力钢束同时起到提高混凝土梁承载力和加强钢-混结合段与混凝土梁连接的作用。

2.7　施工工序

混凝土小箱梁节段及钢构件均在工厂预制，混凝土节段采用短线法预制拼装工艺[8]。在制造钢横梁节段时，应注意外伸钢箱梁纵坡及超高横坡，以保证主梁拼装完成后能够适应道路线形。外伸钢箱梁端部截面应与主梁纵向轴线垂直，便于钢梁节段之间焊接。由于城市高架桥梁大多位于城区内，故考虑预制构件由车辆运载，在桥位处进行吊装。采用下行式架桥机运梁，首先吊装钢横梁节段，并在现场焊接为整体[9,10]。吊装钢-混结合段，就位后将结合段与外伸钢箱梁进行焊接。

依次吊装拼接混凝土梁节段以及桥跨另一端钢-混结合段和钢横梁。一孔桥跨预制主梁节段吊装完成后,在混凝土梁段接缝处灌注环氧树脂胶黏剂。结构胶固化形成强度后,张拉底板正弯矩区钢束。绑扎主梁横向翼缘钢筋并浇筑混凝土,完成主梁横向联系。架桥机移至下一跨,重复上述步骤进行拼装。当整联主梁正弯矩束张拉完毕后,张拉主梁顶板负弯矩束,拆除临时约束,实现体系转换。

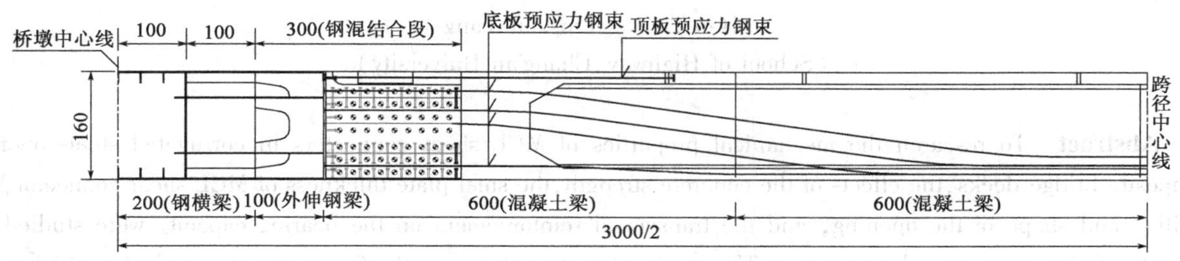

图 11 预应力钢束布置图(尺寸单位:cm)

3 结语

针对市区城市高架桥的建设条件,从节段尺寸、吊装重量、设备重复利用率、运输条件、吊装机械以及拼装效率等方面,分析得出目前主要应用的三种预制装配式上部结构形式的优缺点。基于分析成果,提出了一种新的装配式钢-混组合小箱梁上部结构形式。该方案混凝土梁节段长度为6m,相应吊装重量约16t,对运输条件和吊装机械要求较低。设备重复利用率高,但由于混凝土横向翼缘需现场浇筑,拼装效率相对较低。

本文主要从设计角度,对主梁节段划分、混凝土梁段、钢横梁、钢-混结合段、预应力钢束及施工工序等主要设计内容进行了较为系统的研究。取得的初步设计成果可以为该结构方案的后续深入研究和实践提供一定的研究基础。该方案拼接断面较多,有钢构件焊接和混凝土剪力键拼接两种情况,对构件制造和拼装的精度要求较高。后续研究可就如何保证构件制造和拼装的精度开展工作,提升结构的拼装容错率,为保障实际施工的可操作性提供理论基础。

参考文献

[1] 张子飏,邓开来,徐腾飞. 预制装配式混凝土桥梁结构2019年度研究进展[J]. 土木与环境工程学报(中英文),2020,42(5):184-189.

[2] 杨文武,蔡俊镱,柳欣荣,等. 预制装配化桥梁技术发展及应用[J]. 广东公路交通,2019,(5):67-72.

[3] 邵长宇. 组合结构桥梁的发展与应用前景[J]. 城市道桥与防洪,2016(9):11-15.

[4] 吴东升. 城市节段预制拼装箱梁桥结构设计的技术特点与创新[J]. 中外公路,2021,41(1):70-75.

[5] 中华人民共和国行业标准. 节段预制拼装预应力混凝土桥梁设计标准:DG/T J08-2255—2018[S].

[6] 中华人民共和国行业标准. 城市轨道交通预应力混凝土节段预制桥梁技术标准:CJJ/T 293—2019[S]. 北京:中国建筑出版社,2019.

[7] 沈殷,蔡鹏,陈立生,等. 节段预制拼装混凝土桥梁剪力键接缝的抗剪强度[J]. 同济大学学报(自然科学版),2019,47(10):1414-1420.

[8] 张门哲,涂光亚,王双喜,等. 短线拼装法施工的宽幅多节段混凝土箱梁的预制控制[J]. 中外公路,2018,38(6):148-152.

[9] 杨秀礼,徐杰,夏昊. 中小跨径预制装配化桥梁专用架设方法与智能安装技术研究[J]. 公路,2018,(12):126-129.

[10] 夏昊,范晨阳. 市政装配化桥梁墩梁一体化架设施工关键技术[J]. 公路,2021,(4):85-89.

Analysis of Mechanical Properties of MCL Shear Connectors

Hao Tan* Lingzhu Yang
(School of Highway, Chang'an University)

Abstract To research the mechanical properties of MCL shear connectors in corrugated steel-concrete composite bridge decks, the effects of the concrete strength, the steel plate thickness of MCL shear connector, the position and shape of the opening, and the transversal reinforcement on the bearing capacity were studied by using the finite element analysis method. The results show that the strength of concrete, the steel plate thickness, type of opening, and transversal reinforcement are the main factors affecting the bearing capacity, while the position of the opening does not affed the bearing capacity. During the design, oval openings and reasonable steel plate thickness should be selected to avoid steel failure and steel waste.

Keywords Corrugated steel-concrete Composite bridge decks MCL shear connectors Mechanical properties Finite element analysis

0 Introduction

The profiled steel-concrete composite slab has been widely used in industrial and civil buildings. However, in the building structure, the profiled steel plate is only used as permanent formwork. The bearing and deformation of the structure only consider the role of reinforced concrete slab, While the combined role of The profiled steel plate and reinforced concrete is not considered. If the profiled steel plate and concrete slab can be combined as a whole, the bearing capacity will be greatly improved. In addition, the profiled steel plate can also replace the reinforcement to bear the tensile force, so as to save the amount of reinforcement and reduce the construction costs such as fabrication and installation of reinforcement. Referring to the profiled steel-concrete composite slab in the building, Kim et al proposed the structural form of corrugated steel-concrete composite decks in the bridge, that is, the corrugated steel, concrete, and reinforcement are combined into a whole through shear connectors (Kim et al., 2010). Shear connectors commonly used are mainly stud and PBL shear connectors. And Lorenc et al proposed MCL (Modefied Clothoid) shear connector based on PBL shear connector (Lorenc et al., 2016). MCL shear connector has good static and fatigue performance. It does not need to be manually welded on-site like a stud. It can be processed directly in the factory, and the quality can be guaranteed. At the same time, compared with PBL shear connector, MCL shear key has a larger opening area and the construction of penetrating reinforcement is more convenient. However, there are few studies on the mechanical properties of MCL shear connectors in corrugated steel-concrete composite bridge decks, and there are many studies on PBL shear connectors in steel-concrete composite bridge decks.

Hosain et al. explored the effects of concrete strength, the number andsize of steel plate openings, the distribution of transversal reinforcement, and other influencing factors on the mechanical properties of PBL shear connectors (Hosain et al., 1996). Nishiumi et al. studied the effects of concrete strength, the presence or absence of transversal reinforcement, and the size of steel plate openings on the longitudinal shear ultimate bearing capacity of PBL shear connectors by push-out test (Nishiumi et al. ,1999). Verlllasco et al. analysed the influence of concrete shear area on the longitudinal shear capacity of PBL shear connectors through push-out test (Verlllasco et al. , 2007). Hu et al. studied the effects of reinforcement strength and its diameter, the size of steel plate openings, stirrup strength, steel plate thickness, and other factors on the mechanical properties of PBL shear connectors (Hu et al. , 2007). Li et al. studied the effects of concrete strength, the size of steel plate openings, transverse reinforcement, and the arrangement of shear connectors on the shear capacity of PBL shear connectors(Li et al. , 2008). Wang et al. obtained the failure characteristics and load slip curve of PBL shear connectors through push-out test (Wang et al. ,2011). Xiao[1] et al. analysed the influence of the steel plate thickness on the ultimate bearing capacity and shear stiffness of PBL shear connector through push-out test(Xiao et al. ,2012).

In this paper, the effects of concrete strength, the steel plate thickness of MCL shear connector, opening position and its shape, reinforcement diameter on the mechanical properties of MCL shear connectors in corrugated steel-concrete composite bridge decks are analysed.

1 Push-out Specimen

Push-out specimens are often used to study the mechanical properties of shear connectors. The finite element model established in this paper is also based on the size of push-out specimens.

The size of MCL shear connector and push-out specimen are shown in Fig. 1 and Fig. 2 respectively. In Fig. 1, a and b are the long half axis and short half axis of the ellipse, P is the load, the steel plate thickness is 6mm, the steel plate thickness of the steel plate of MCL shear connector is 14mm, and the diameter of through reinforcement is 16mm. A single layer of reinforcement mesh shall be set at the position 30mm away from the upper surface of the concrete. The longitudinal and transverse reinforcement diameters are 12mm and the spacing is 100mm. The size of the push-out specimen is 460mm × 366mm × 700mm.

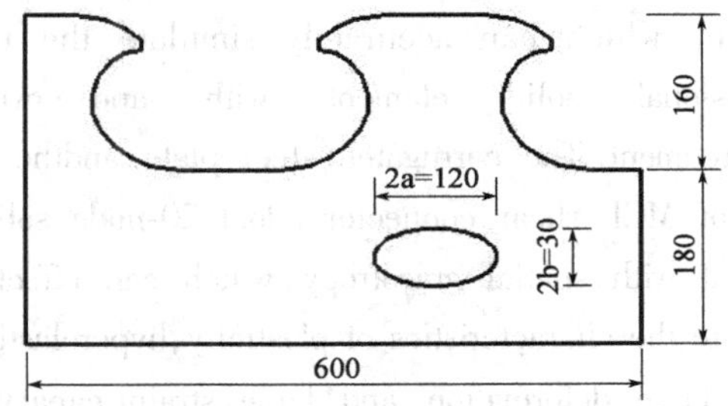

Fig. 1 Size of MCL Shear Connector(Dimensional unit: mm)

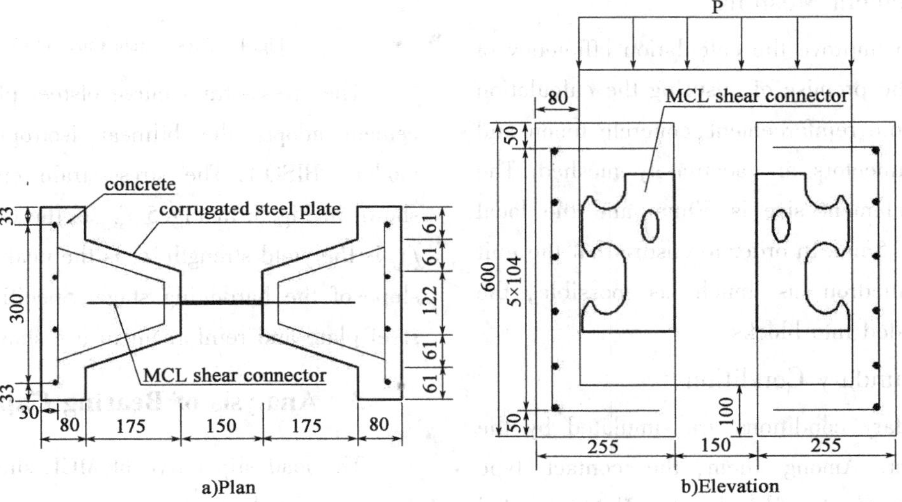

Fig. 2 Size of Push-Out Specimen(Dimensional unit: mm)

2 Finite Element Model

According to the size of the push-out specimen, the finite element model is established by using the finite element software ANSYS. The finite element model is shown in Fig. 3.

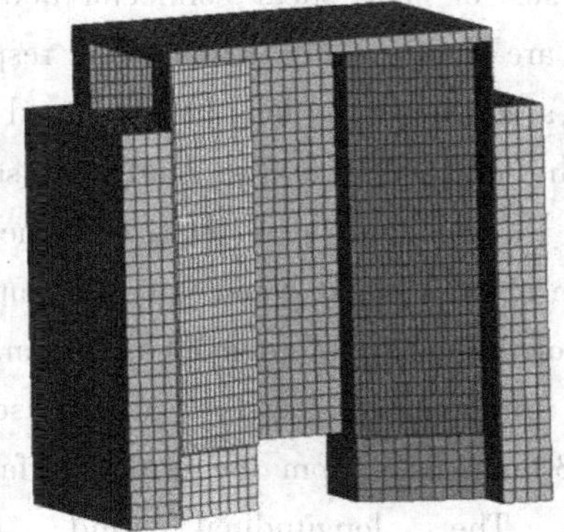

Fig. 3 Finite Element Model

2.1 Unit Type

The concrete structure adopts a 8-node SOLID65 element, which can accurately simulate the three-dimensional solid element with and without reinforcement. The corrugated steel plate andthe steel plate of MCL shear connector adopt 20-node solid186 element with spatial anisotropy, which can effectively simulate the characteristics of plasticity, hyperelasticity, creep, large deformation, and large strain capacity of materials.

2.2 Element Meshing

In order to improve the calculation efficiency of the model, on the premise of ensuring the calculation accuracy, only the reinforcement, concrete tenon and MCL shear connectors are accurately meshed. The overall model element size is 50mm and the local element size is 15mm. In order to ensure that the unit shape is hexahedron as much as possible, the concrete is divided into blocks.

2.3 Boundary Condition

The boundary conditions are simulated by the contact element. Among them, the contact type between reinforcement and concrete adopts bonded contact, and the contact normal stiffness is 10. The contact type between corrugated steel plate and concrete, the side of MCL shear connector and concrete is frictional contact, and the friction coefficient is 0.2. The contact type between the concrete and the sheath of MCL shear connector is frictionless contact, and the normal stiffness is 1.

2.4 Stress-strain Relation and Ruin Rule

The stress-strain curve of concrete adopts multilinear isotropic strengthening model (MISO). The stress-strain curve of concrete is shown in Fig. 4. In Fig. 4, f_c is uni-axial compressive strength, ε_0 is the concrete compressive strain when the concrete compressive stress reaches f_c, ε_{cu} is the concrete ultimate compressive strain. The failure criterion of concrete adopts the W-W five parameter failure criterion suitable for SOLID65 element. The shear retention factor of open crack and closed crack of concrete are 0.50 and 0.95. The compressive strength of concrete is 53MPa and the elastic modulus is 34.5GPa.

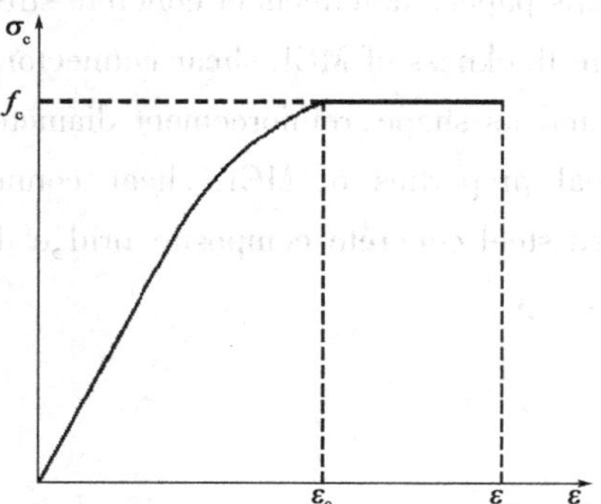

Fig. 4 Stress-Strain Curve of Concrete

The stress-strain curve ofsteel plate and reinforcement adopts the bilinear isotropic strengthening model (BISO). The stress-strain curve of Steel is shown in Fig. 5. In Fig. 5, $f_{st,r}$ is the ultimate strength, $f_{y,t}$ is the yield strength, ε_u is the peak strain, , k is the slope of the hardening stage. Specific parameters of steel plate and reinforcement are shown in Tab. 1.

3 Analysis of Bearing Capacity Factor

The load slip curve of MCL shear connector in the corrugated steel-concrete composite deck can directly reflect its bearing capacity and deformation performance. Based on the finite element model, the load slip curve is drawn by adjusting the influence parameters such as concrete strength, steel plate thickness, opening position, and its shape, and reinforcement diameter, and the influence of parameter changes on the ultimate bearing capacity of MCL shear connector is analysed.

3.1 Concrete Strength

The concrete strength grades are C50, C60, and C70 respectively, and the other parameters are fixed.

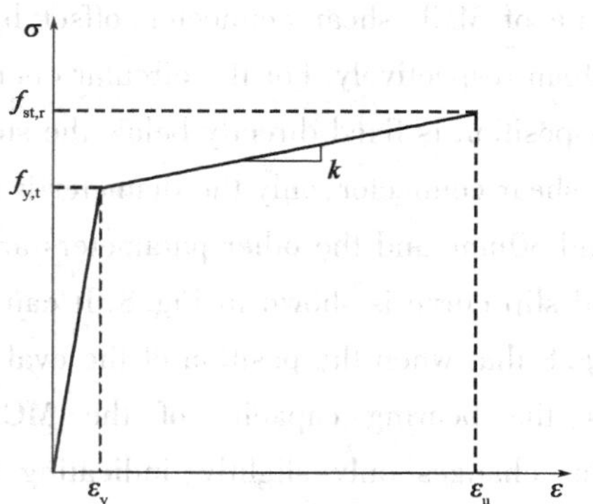

Fig. 5 Stress-Strain Curve of Steel Plate and Reinforcement

Parameters of Steel Plate and Reinforcement Tab. 1

Material	ElasticModulus (GPa)	Yield Strength (GPa)	Ultimate Strength (GPa)
Steel Plate	206	422.6	524.1
Reinforcement	200	446	604.8

The load slip curve is shown in Fig. 6. It can be seen from Fig. 6 that the bearing capacity of MCL shear connector increases obviously with the increase of concrete strength, but its increased speed slows down with the increase of concrete strength. The reason is that under the model state, the structure is damaged due to excessive concrete shear deformation, while the steel plate of MCL shear connector is only slightly deformed. Increasing the concrete strength can effectively increase the bearing capacity of MCL shear connectors. However, when the concrete strength increases to a certain extent, the deformation of the steel plate of MCL shear connector begins to increase, resulting in the speed of increasing load capacity decreases obviously.

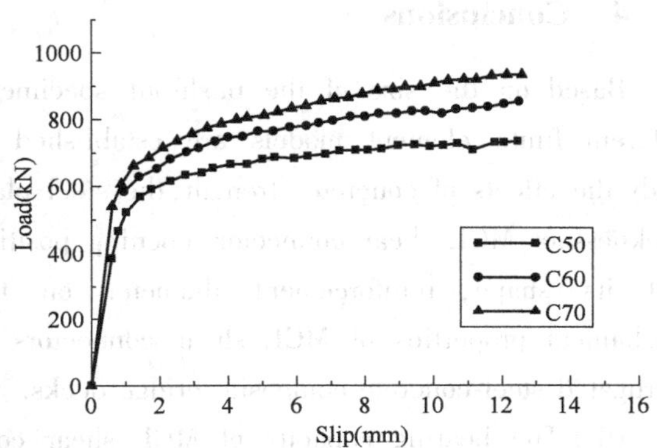

Fig. 6 Influence of Concrete Strength

3.2 MCLShear Connector Steel Plate Thickness

The steel plate thickness of MCL shear connector is taken as 8, 14, and 20mm respectively, and the other parametersare fixed, the load slip curve is shown in Fig. 7. It can be seen from Fig. 7 that when the steel plate thickness of MCL shear connector increases from 14mm to 20mm, the shear bearing capacity increases by about 13.6%, that is, the bearing capacity does not increase significantly. This is because when the steel plate thickness of MCL shear connector is large, the structure is damaged due to excessive shear deformation of concrete, and the influence of concrete strength on bearing capacity is more severe. When the steel plate thickness of MCL shear connector is reduced from 14mm to 8mm, the bearing capacity changes greatly; This is because the steel plate thickness is small, and the failure mode changes from concrete shear failure to steel plate failure. Therefore, when selecting the steel plate of MCL shear connector, it should be considered comprehensively.

3.3 Opening Position and Shape

The opening shapes are oval and circular respectively. For ovalopenings (a = 30mm, b = 15mm), the opening positions are directly below the steel plate of MCL shear connector, offset by 50mm and 100mm respectively. For the circular opening, the opening position is fixed directly below the steel plate of MCL shear connector, only the diameter is changed to 60 and 30mm, and the other parameters are fixed. The load slip curve is shown in Fig. 8. It can be seen from Fig. 8 that when the position of the oval opening changes, the bearing capacity of the MCL shear connector changes only slightly, indicating that the change of the opening position has little effect on the shear bearing capacity of the MCL shear connector.

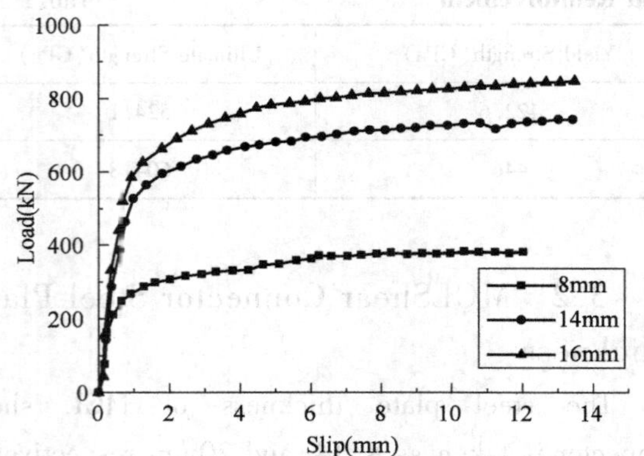

Fig. 7　Influence of Steel Plate Thickness

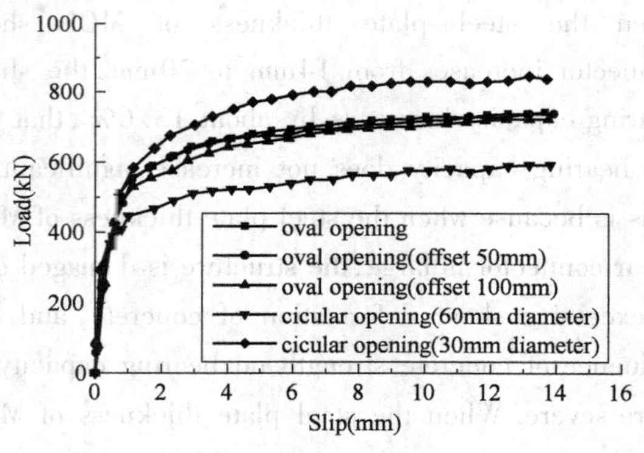

Fig. 8　Influence of Opening Position and Shape

When theopening is circular and its diameter is 30mm and 60mm, the bearing capacity is reduced by 21.9% and increased by 14.7% respectively compared with the oval opening. However, due to the limitation of the height of the steel plate, the selection of the oval opening can increase the shear area of concrete and improve the shear bearing capacity. Therefore, the oval opening should be preferred in the MCL shear connector.

3.4　Reinforcement Diameter

The load slip curve when the reinforcement diameter changes to 14, 16 and 18mm and without reinforcement is shown in Fig. 9. As can be seen from Fig. 9, compared with MCL shear connectors without reinforcement, the bearing capacity of MCL shear connectors is greatly improved after setting reinforcement. However, when the reinforcement diameter is increased from 14mm to 16 or 18mm, the bearing capacity of MCL shear connectors is not significantly improved.

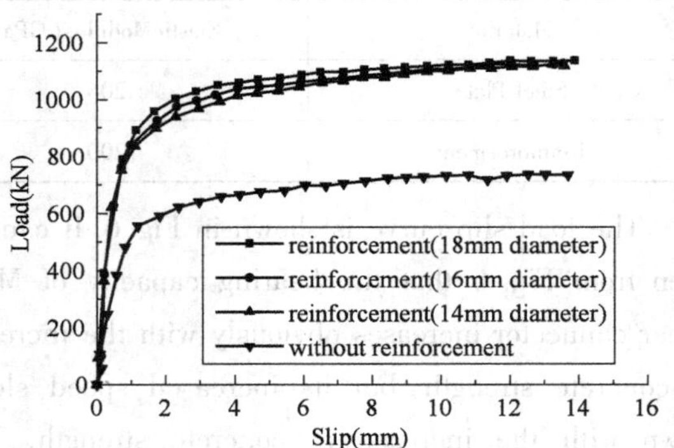

Fig. 9　Influence of Reinforcement Diameter

When there is no reinforcement through, it only depends on the concrete to resist the shear. After setting reinforcement, the joint action of reinforcement, the steel plate, and surrounding concrete makes the concrete in a triaxial compression state, so as to improve the compressive strength of concrete. Therefore, setting through reinforcement can significantly improve the bearing capacity of MCL shear connector

4　Conclusions

Based on the size of the push-out specimen, different finite element models are established to study the effects of concrete strength, the steel plate thickness of MCL shear connector, opening position and its shape, reinforcement diameter on the mechanical properties of MCL shear connectors in corrugated steel-concrete composite bridge decks.

(1) The bearing capacity of MCL shear connector increases obviously with the increase of concrete strength, but its increased speed slows down

with the increase of concrete strength.

(2) When the steel plate of MCL shear connector increases from 14mm to 20mm, the shear bearing capacity increases by about 13.6%, but the shear bearing capacity increases greatly when the steel plate thickness of MCL shear connector increases from 8mm to 14mm. Therefore, when selecting the plate steel of MCL shear connector, it should be considered comprehensively.

(3) The change of the opening position has little effect on the shear bearing capacity of the MCL shear connector.

(4) Setting reinforcement can significantly improve the bearing capacity of MCL shear connector. The reinforcement diameter has little impact on the bearing capacity of MCL shear connectors.

References

[1] Jianhua Hu, Wenqi Hou, Meixin Ye. Study of influence factors and formula for the bearing capacity of PBL shear connectors [J]. Journal of Rail Way Science and Engineering, 2007, 4 (6): 12-18.

[2] Lorenc W J S C. The design concept for the steel part of a composite dowel shear connection [J], 2016, 9 (2): 89-97.

[3] Nishiumi K, Okimoto M J D G R. Shear strength of perfobond rib shear connector under the confinement [J], 1999, (633): 193-203.

[4] Kim H-Y, Jeong Y-J J E S. Ultimate strength of a steel-concrete composite bridge deck slab with profiled sheeting [J], 2010, 32 (2): 534-546.

[5] Oguejiofor E, Hosain M J C. Numerical analysis of push-out specimens with perfobond rib connectors [J]. 1997, 62 (4): 617-624.

[6] Vellasco P C G S, De Andrade S a L, Ferreira L T S, et al. Semi-rigid composite frames with perfobond and T-rib connectors Part 1: Full scale tests [J]. Journal of Constructional Steel Research, 2007, 63 (2): 263-79.

[7] Zhenhai W, Canhui Z, Qiao L I. Experimental Investigation on Load-Slip Relationship of Perfobond Rib Shear Connectors [J]. Journal of Southwest Jiaotong University, 2011, 46 (4): 547-552.

[8] Xiao L, Li X, Wei X. Research on the Static Load Mechanical Properties of PBL Shear Connectors' Push-out Test [J]. China Railway Science, 2010, 31 (3): 15-21.

[9] Xiao L, Qiang S, Li X, et al. Research on Mechanical Performance of PBL SHEAR Connectors Considering the Perforated Plates Thickness [J]. Engineering Mechanics, 2012, 29 (8): 282-288, 296.

An Approach to Solving the Critical Load of Slender Column with Spring Hinges

Peiwen He*

(Department of Bridge Engineering, School of Highway, Chang'an University)

Abstract By analysing the critical buckling load of a slender column with spring hinges, the transcendental equation is obtained and a simple approach for solving it with Taylor series is given in this paper. According to this approach, the critical buckling loads with different boundary conditions of dimensionless flexure rigidity are obtained. Based on the results of the approach presented in this paper, the contour of dimensionless critical buckling load, related to the dimensionless end flexure rigidity, is derived. The research results can avoid the complexity of estimating the critical buckling load and boundary flexure rigidity without computer assistance at site, help the engineers to judge and make decisions simply through charts, and have a specific value for improving solving efficiency.

Keywords Mechanics of material Stability of slender column Taylor series Numerical method Quartic function

0 Introduction

In the practice of bridge engineering, whether the compression column can function normally as a component often determines the safety and reliability of the structure. As early as 1744, Euler proposed a formula for calculating the critical load for the slender column under compression (Euler, 1759), which laid a foundation for the elastic buckling theory of compression bar (Ban, 2021). In the early 1970s, Lansing assumed that the stress of the compression bar on any section was distributed as a semi-sine according to a straight line and a deflection curve, established the equilibrium equation, and obtained the analytical expression of the critical stress by iterative calculation (Gong, 2010). Later, many scholars have studied the instability equation and critical load of the slender column with different materials (Yang, 2021), sections (Wang, 2019), and other parameters (Dong et al., 2012), and discussed the variation of the compression column's deflection curve with the increase of the axial pressure by the accurate formula of curvature (Ding, 2014).

By studying the critical state ofbuckling of slender column, the Euler formula of Slender Column under boundary elastic support is derived (Sun et al., 2009). Moreover, the formula is dimensionless. However, the existing calculation approaches need to be calculated many times, and the field application efficiency in the project is not higher enough (He et al., 2021). Therefore, an approach that provides simply formulas and relevant graphs to a judge or quickly estimating the critical buckling load of the slender column will be of specific value to the engineering practice. Without computer assistance in the field, engineers can simply estimate the critical buckling load and boundary bending stiffness through charts according to the contents of this study. It has a certain reference significance for the research of improving the overall efficiency of the project.

1 Critical Buckling Load Formula of Slender Column

In the practical application of bridge engineering, the slendercolumn carrying axial force plays an important role in many bridges such as steel truss bridges. The end constraints of slender columns welded at both ends are not ideal hinged or fully consolidated. They are between hinge and consolidation state and have a certain rigidity. The boundary condition, in this case, can be regarded as a spring hinge. Spring hinge not only has the characteristics of restraining the lateral displacement of the slender column ends and allowing the ends to rotate, but also can provide a reverse bending moment at the end to resist the rotation. On this basis, the stress analysis of the slender column is carried out (Fig. 1).

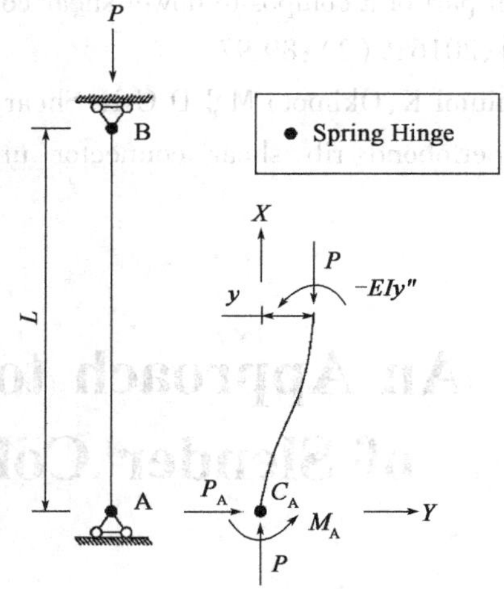

Fig. 1 Force Analysis of Slender Column Restrained by Spring Hinge at both ends

It is assumed that the flexural rigidity of a slender column is determined by the properties of the material itself, which is an invariable constant, and will not change with the variation of column end angle. Taking the spring hinge A as the original point, the coordinate system is shown in Fig. 1.

The Euler formula used in the following derivation has a certain scope of application (Sun et al., 2009). The stress of the compression column under the action of the critical force P_{cr} shall not exceed the proportional limit of the material σ_p. The application scope of Euler formula can be expressed as:

$$\lambda \geqslant \pi \sqrt{\frac{E}{\sigma_p}} = \lambda_p \tag{1}$$

$$\lambda = \frac{\mu l}{i} \tag{2}$$

$$i = \sqrt{\frac{I}{A}} \tag{3}$$

Where: λ_p is the limit value of compression column flexibility that can apply the Euler formula; λ is the flexibility (slenderness ratio); i is the inertia radius of the column section.

The following differential equation can be established according to the theory of material mechanics and stress analysis:

$$EIy'' + Py = P_A x + M_A \tag{4}$$

where: EI is the flexure rigidity of the slender column ($N \cdot m^2$); y is the lateral deflection value of the slender column (m); P is the axial force on the slender column (N); P_i is the horizontal support reaction force (n) at the end i ($i = A, B$) of the slender column (N); x is the length along the length direction of the slender column from point A (m); M_i is the reverse bending moment provided by the support at the end i ($i = A, B$) of the slender column ($N \cdot m$).

Let $k^2 = \frac{P}{EI}$ and substitute it into Equation (4). After simplification and solution, the following equation can be obtained.

$$y = A\sin kx + B\cos kx + \frac{P_A x}{P} + \frac{M_A}{P} \tag{5}$$

where: A and B are constants.

At both ends of theslender column, the balance equation formed by the support reaction P_A and P_B provided by the support and the reverse bending moments M_A and M_B acted by the spring hinge is as follows.

$$P_A = \frac{M_B - M_A}{L} \tag{6}$$

$$P_B = \frac{M_B - M_A}{L} \tag{7}$$

where: L is the length of the slender column.

In order to simplify and calculate Equation (5), the boundary conditions are introduced as follows:

At the hinge A of the slender column, the deflection of the it is 0.

$$x = 0, y = 0: B + \frac{M_A}{P} = 0 \tag{8}$$

At the hinge B of the slender column, the deflection of the it is 0.

$$x = L, y = 0: A\sin kL + B\cos kL + \frac{M_B}{P} = 0 \tag{9}$$

The product of the flexure rigidity of the spring hinge and the rotation angle of the slender column at end A is the reverse bending moment provided by the elastic hinge.

$$M_A = C_A y_A : AkC_A - M_A\left(\frac{C_A}{PL} + 1\right) + \frac{M_B C_A}{PL} = 0 \tag{10}$$

The product of the flexure rigidity of the spring hinge and the rotation angle of the slender column at end A is the reverse bending moment provided by the elastic hinge.

$$M_B = C_B y_B : AkC_B\cos kL + BkC_B\sin kL - \frac{M_A C_B}{PL} + M_B\left(\frac{C_B}{PL} - 1\right) = 0 \tag{11}$$

According to the physical properties of thebuckling of slender columns under pressure, it is necessary to make A, B, M_A, M_B not all zero, that is, the above four Equations (8 ~ 11) are combined as simultaneous equations, and the matrix corresponding to the coefficient of A, B, M_A, M_B is zero. The matrix is as follows.

$$\begin{bmatrix} 0 & 1 & \frac{1}{P} & 0 \\ \sin kL & \cos kL & 0 & \frac{1}{P} \\ kC_A & 0 & -\left(\frac{C_A}{PL}+1\right) & \frac{C_A}{PL} \\ kC_B\cos kL & kC_B\sin kL & -\frac{C_B}{PL} & \frac{C_B}{PL}-1 \end{bmatrix} \times \begin{bmatrix} A \\ B \\ M_A \\ M_B \end{bmatrix} = 0 \quad (12)$$

By simplifying its coefficient determinant, the following equation can be obtained.

$$\left(\frac{\sin kL}{kL}-\cos kL\right)\left(\frac{1}{C_A}+\frac{1}{C_B}\right)+\frac{1}{C_AC_B}\frac{P^2}{kL}\sin kL+\frac{1}{L}(2-2\cos kL-kL\sin kL)=0 \quad (13)$$

In order to avoid the complexity of calculation caused by the inclusion of units, we make the formula dimensionless. Define the critical load level as $\chi=\sqrt{\frac{PL^2}{EI}}$; The dimensionless flexure rigidity of end A is $\overline{C_A}=\frac{C_AL}{EI}$; The dimensionless flexure rigidity of end B is $\overline{C_B}=\frac{C_BL}{EI}$. Thus, the above equation can be simplified shown as follows.

$$\chi^3\frac{\sin\chi}{C_AC_B}-\chi^2\cos\chi\left(\frac{1}{C_A}+\frac{1}{C_B}\right)+\chi\sin\chi\left(\frac{1}{C_A}+\frac{1}{C_B}\right)+(2-2\cos\chi-\chi\sin\chi)=0 \quad (14)$$

In order to solve the value of χ in Equation (11), assume the following function and find the solution of χ in it.

$$f(\chi)=\chi^3\frac{\sin\chi}{C_AC_B}-\chi^2\cos\chi\left(\frac{1}{C_A}+\frac{1}{C_B}\right)+\chi\sin\chi\left(\frac{1}{C_A}+\frac{1}{C_B}\right)+(2-2\cos\chi-\chi\sin\chi) \quad (15)$$

According to the existing research (Sun et al., 2009), for the slender column hinged at both ends, it can be regarded as that the hinge at both ends has no flexure rigidity. In this case, the minimum non-zero solution that χ is π. For a slender column which fixed at one end and hinged at the other, it can be regarded that the flexure rigidity value at the hinged end is 0 and the at the consolidated end is large. In this way, the minimum non-zero solution of χ is 1.43π. For slender columns consolidated at both ends, it can be considered that the flexure rigidity value at both ends is large, and the minimum non-zero solution that χ can obtain is 2π. It can be figure out that when $\overline{C_A}$ and $\overline{C_B}$ are known and the minimum non-zero solution of χ in formula (3-15) is obtained, the results are between π and 2π.

2　Solution for The Transcendental Equation

2.1　Expand the Original Equation According to Taylor Series

Since the original Equation (15) is transcendental, it is difficult to obtain its analytical solution, but its numerical solution under given conditions can be obtained in different ways. This paper aims to provide an approach to figure out numerical solutions with high accuracy. Since the equation is not suitable for Newton iterative method (He et al., 2021), and other iterative methods need repeated calculation, this paper considers expanding the original equation by Taylor Series and combining it with the quartic formula to find the minimum non-zero solution of the original function.

It is known that the solution χ_0 of function $f(\chi)$ is located on the open interval $(\pi, 2\pi)$, and in this interval, the original function has the derivative of order $(n+1)$. Then for any $\chi\in(\pi,2\pi)$, there exists:

$$f(\chi)=\frac{f(\chi_0)}{0!}+\frac{f'(\chi_0)}{1!}(\chi-\chi_0)+\frac{f''(\chi_0)}{2!}(\chi-\chi_0)^2+\cdots+\frac{f^{(n)}(\chi_0)}{n!}(\chi-\chi_0)^n+R_n(\chi) \quad (16)$$

where: $R_n(\chi)$ is the Taylor remainder. And when the value of χ close χ_0, to the equation satisfies $\lim\limits_{\chi\to\chi_0}R_n(\chi)=0$.

The Taylor series at $\chi=\pi, 1.125\pi, 1.25\pi, 1.375\pi, 1.5\pi, 1.625\pi, 1.75\pi, 1.875\pi, 2\pi$ are considered respectively because $\chi\in(\pi,2\pi)$. At these 9 points, the value of each corresponding function of Taylor series is very close to the value of the original function(Tab.1). While the value of each expanded function around its corresponding point has a certain error with the value of the original function. If multiple quartic functions are used to connect to form a multi-segment function when $\chi \in (\pi, 2\pi)$, the values of 9 expanded functions need to be calculated under different $\overline{C_A}$ and $\overline{C_B}$, and they are compared with the original function values, so as to obtain which expanded equation should be used for calculation(Fig. 2).

Let: $Q = 1/A/B$, $P = 1/A + 1/B$, formulas of Taylor series of the original function (15) at $\chi = \pi$, 1.125π, 1.25π, 1.375π, 1.5π, 1.625π, 1.75π, 1.875π, 2π is shown as follows (Taylor remainder is omitted), and the form of formula is $ax^4 + bx^3 + cx^2 + dx + e$

The Taylor series at 9 values of χ Tab. 1

χ	a	b	c	d	e
π	$-0.083-0.333P-Q$	$0.523+1.571P+3.142Q$	0	$-2.026-2.026P$	2.248
1.125π	$-0.077-0.308P-0.924Q$	$0.48+1.441P+2.883Q$	0	$-1.525-1.525P$	1.394
1.25π	$-0.059-0.236P-0.0707Q$	$0.345+1.035P+2.07Q$	0	$0.385+0.385P$	-2.197
1.375π	$-0.059-0.236P-0.707Q$	$0.122+0.365P+0.73Q$	0	$4.208+4.208P$	-10.112
1.5π	0	$-0.167-0.5P-Q$	0	$10.103+10.103P$	-23.457
1.625π	$0.032+0.128P+0.383Q$	$-0.48-1.439P-2.878Q$	0	$17.647+17.647P$	-41.993
1.75π	$0.059+0.236P+0.707Q$	$-0.766-2.297P-4.595Q$	0	$25.676+25.676P$	-63.268
1.875π	$0.077+0.308P+0.924Q$	$-0.971-2.912P-5.825Q$	0	$32.286+32.286P$	-82.046
2π	$0.083+0.333P+Q$	$-1.047-3.142P-6.283Q$	0	$35.059+35.059P$	-90.4

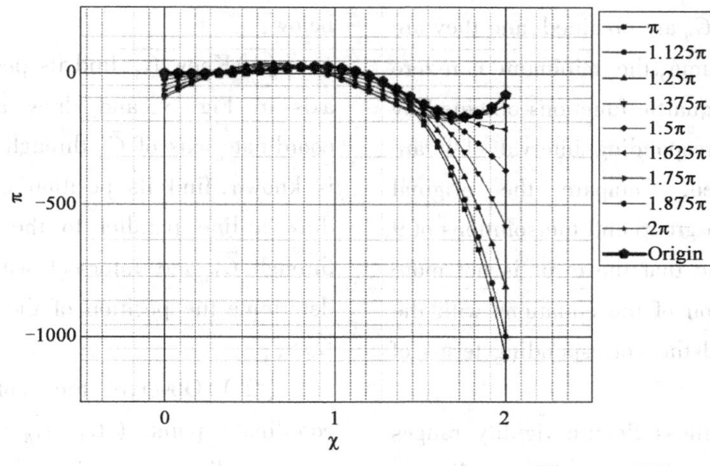

Fig. 2 Curves of Taylor Series and original function when $\overline{C_A} = 1$ and $\overline{C_B} = 1$

2.2 The Approach of Solving Univariate Quartic Function and The Applicable Range of Formulas

2.2.1 The Solution Approach of Univariate Quartic Function

For a univariate quartic function, if it can be written in the following form, it can be solved by using the quartic formula.

$$ax^4 + bx^3 + cx^2 + dx + e = 0 \tag{17}$$

Let:

$$\Delta_1 = c^2 - 3bd + 12ae, \Delta_2 = 2c^3 - 9bcd + 27ad^2 + 27b^2e - 72ace \tag{18}$$

$$\Delta = \frac{\sqrt[3]{2}\Delta_1}{3a\sqrt[3]{\Delta_2 + \sqrt{-4\Delta_1^3 + \Delta_2^2}}} + \frac{\sqrt[3]{\Delta_2 + \sqrt{-4\Delta_1^3 + \Delta_2^2}}}{3\sqrt[3]{2}a} \tag{19}$$

Let:

$$P_1 = -\frac{b}{4a}, P_2 = \frac{1}{2}\sqrt{\frac{b^2}{4a^2} - \frac{2c}{3a} + \Delta},$$

$$P_3 = \frac{b^2}{2a^2} - \frac{4c}{3a} - \Delta, P_4 = \frac{-\frac{b^3}{a^3} + \frac{4bc}{a^2} - \frac{8d}{a}}{4\sqrt{\frac{b^2}{4a^2} - \frac{2c}{3a} + \Delta}} \quad (20)$$

Then, the quartic formulas of quartic function are:

$$x_1 = P_1 - P_2 - \frac{1}{2}\sqrt{P_3 - P_4} \quad (21)$$

$$x_1 = P_1 - P_2 + \frac{1}{2}\sqrt{P_3 - P_4} \quad (22)$$

$$x_3 = P_1 + P_2 - \frac{1}{2}\sqrt{P_3 + P_4} \quad (23)$$

$$x_4 = P_1 + P_2 + \frac{1}{2}\sqrt{P_3 + P_4} \quad (24)$$

2.2.2 The Range of Formulas Applicable to Different $\overline{C_A}$ and $\overline{C_B}$

The original functionis solved iteratively by a computer program, the minimum non-zero solutions of χ under different $\overline{C_A}$ and $\overline{C_B}$ are obtained, and they are recorded. At the same time, the minimum non-zero solutions of 9 univariate quartic functions obtained by Taylor series in the corresponding interval of χ are calculated and recorded. Compare the original function solutions of each group and the solutions of 9 equations. On the premise that the error is not more than 1%, take the solution of the equations with the smallest error, and record the corresponding terms of the quartic formula.

When the dimensionless flexure rigidity ranges from 0 to 1000, thequartic formula corresponding to the following expanded equations is obtained through data comparison. In particularly, when the formula is expanded at 1.5π, the approach of solving cubic equation such as collocation approach and dichotomy can be used, which will not be repeated here, or the expansion formulas at 1.375π and 1.625π can be used for the solution, and the error can also meet the requirements (Tab. 2).

The Taylor series' corresponding terms of quartic formula Tab. 2

χ	Corresponding Term
π	x_4
1.125π	x_4
1.25π	x_4
1.375π	x_4
1.5π	—
1.625π	x_3
1.75π	x_3
1.875π	x_3
2π	x_3

2.3 An Approach of Calculation by Querying Graphs

Through the comparison of data, we can get the following Graph in which the corresponding Taylor series and its quartic formula can be queried when $\overline{C_A}$ and $\overline{C_B}$ are known. The calculation process is given below:

(1) Know $\overline{C_A}$, find its position on the coordinate axis in Fig. 3, and draw a line parallel to the coordinate axis of $\overline{C_B}$ through $\overline{C_A}$; Similarly, when $\overline{C_B}$ is known, find its position on the coordinate axis, draw a line parallel to the coordinate axis of $\overline{C_A}$ through $\overline{C_B}$ and intersect with the previous line to determine the position of the coordinate point ($\overline{C_A}$, $\overline{C_B}$);

(2) Observe the colour area where the coordinate point ($\overline{C_A}$, $\overline{C_B}$) is located, find the corresponding expansion point of Taylor series through the colour diagram on the right side of Fig. 3, and obtain the quartic formula;

(3) Calculate Δ_1 and Δ_2 through Equation (18), and substitute them into Equation (19) to calculate the value of Δ;

(4) The calculation results are obtained by using the quartic formulas of Equations (21 ~ 24).

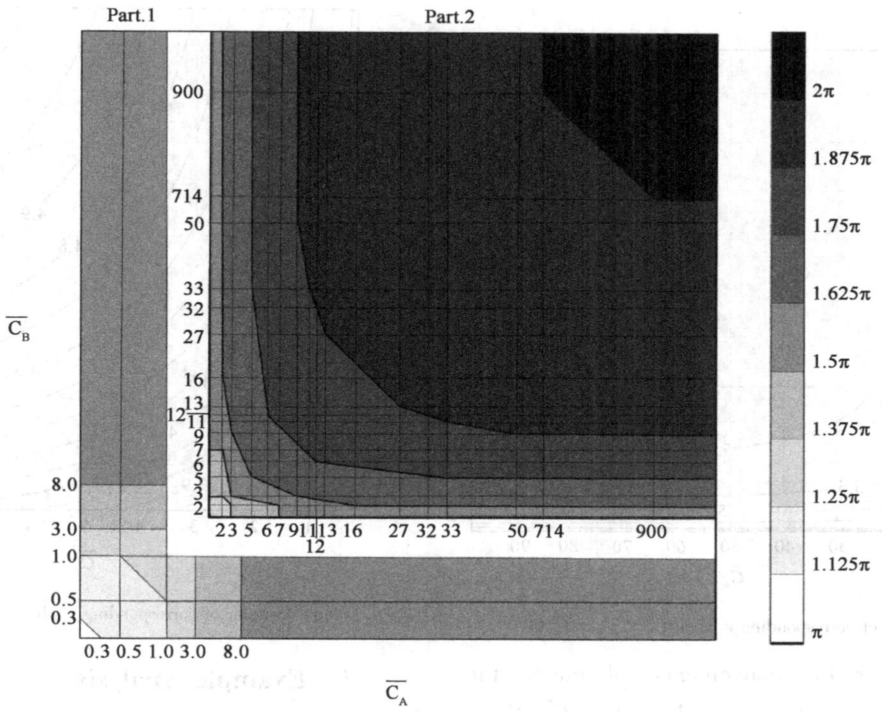

Fig. 3 Graph of Taylor series corresponding to different $\overline{C_A}$ and $\overline{C_B}$

Notes: Part. 1is applicable to the case of $\overline{C_A}$, $\overline{C_B}$ < 1. 0; Part. 2 is applicable to the case of $\overline{C_A}$, $\overline{C_B}$ ∈ (1,1000)

2.4 Query the Contours and Find the Minimum Value of $\overline{C_A}$ And $\overline{C_B}$

Through Section 2.2, the dimensionless critical buckling load χ of slender column can be obtained from different $\overline{C_A}$ and $\overline{C_B}$. If these 3 numbers obtained in the ith calculation are compiled into an array ($\overline{C_{Ai}}$, $\overline{C_{Bi}}$, χ_i), and the results of each calculation in which the dimensionless flexure rigidity of $\overline{C_A}$, $\overline{C_B}$ ∈ (0, 1000) in a fixed step are recorded, a multi-dimensional array **A** can be obtained (n is the total number of calculations):

$$\boldsymbol{A}=\begin{pmatrix}(\overline{C_{A1}} & \overline{C_{B1}} & \chi_1)\\(\overline{C_{A2}} & \overline{C_{B2}} & \chi_2)\\(\overline{C_{A3}} & \overline{C_{B3}} & \chi_3)\\(\overline{C_{A4}} & \overline{C_{B4}} & \chi_4)\\\vdots & \vdots & \vdots\\(\overline{C_{An}} & \overline{C_{Bn}} & \chi_n)\end{pmatrix}$$

When n is large enough, the multi-dimensional array **A** can be used to draw the contour when $\overline{C_A}$, $\overline{C_B}$ ∈ (0, 1000) with $\overline{C_A}$ and $\overline{C_B}$ as the abscissa and ordinate respectively and χ as the corresponding value, as follows Fig. 4.

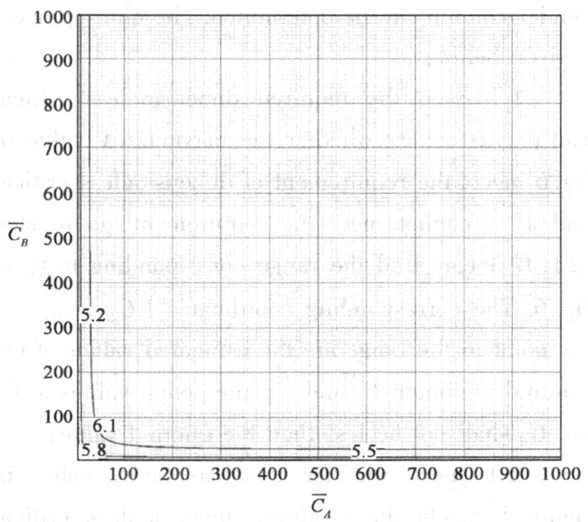

Fig. 4 Contour of corresponding χ when $\overline{C_A}$, $\overline{C_B}$ ∈ (0,1000)

It is not difficult tofigure out that when the value of one of $\overline{C_A}$ and $\overline{C_B}$ exceeds 100, the value of χ exceeds 6.1 and is very close to 2π. In order to get other values easier, the contour corresponding to χ value when $\overline{C_A}$, $\overline{C_B}$ ∈ (0,1000) is drawn as follows

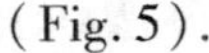
(Fig. 5).

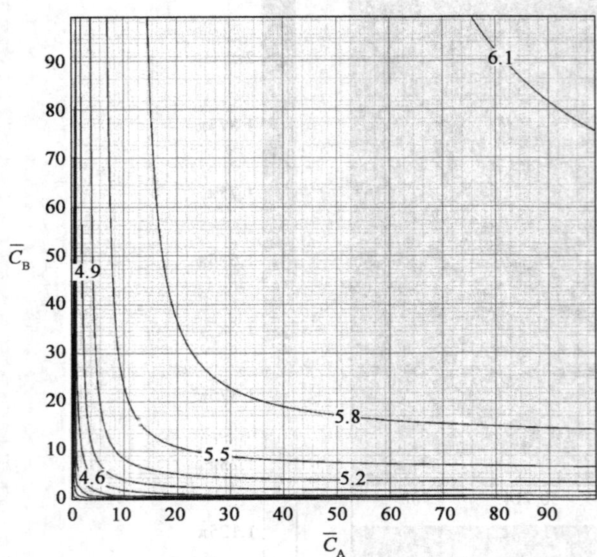

Fig. 5　Contour of corresponding χ when $\overline{C_A}, \overline{C_B} \in (0,100)$

Similarly, for the convenience of query, the contour of the corresponding χ value when $\overline{C_A}, \overline{C_B} \in (0,10)$ is as follows.

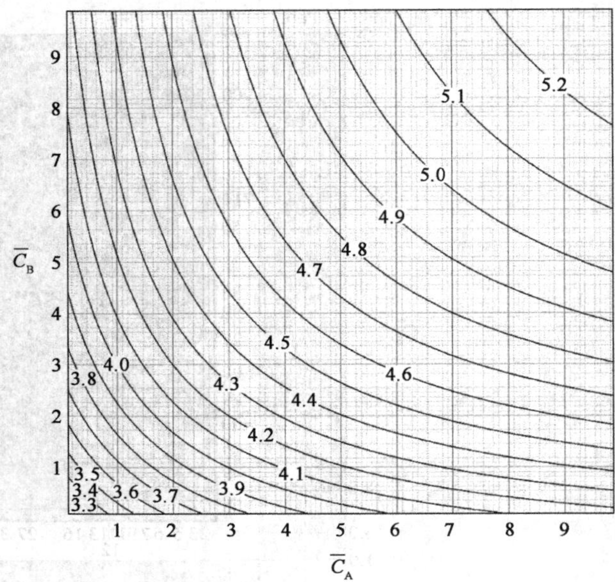

Fig. 6　Contour of corresponding χ when $\overline{C_A}, \overline{C_B} \in (0,10)$

When the dimensionless critical load of the slender column required by the project is χ, the above graphs can be conveniently consulted, and the dimensionless flexure rigidity at both ends of the slender column can be determined. The query process is given below:

(1) Given the required dimensionless critical load χ_0, first query whether the maximum χ value in Fig. 6 meets the requirement of dimensionless critical load. If it cannot meet the requirement, go to step (2). If it can, find the range corresponding to χ_0 in Fig. 6. The corresponding coordinates ($\overline{C_{A0}}, \overline{C_{B0}}$) of any point in the range are the estimated values of the required minimum $\overline{C_A}$ and $\overline{C_B}$, the actual values of $\overline{C_A}$ and $\overline{C_B}$ shall not be less than the queried value;

(2) Query whether the maximum χ value in Figure 5 meets the required dimensionless critical load. If it cannot meet the requirement, go to step (3). If it can, query the minimum estimated values of $\overline{C_A}$ and $\overline{C_B}$ according to Fig. 5 similarly;

(3) Query the required minimum $\overline{C_A}$ and $\overline{C_B}$ estimated values according to the range corresponding to χ_0 in Fig. 4.

3　Example Analysis

3.1　Figure Out The Buckling Load According to The Flexure Rigidity of Ends

3.1.1　Example

The length of a slender column with equal section is $L = 2\text{m}$, which adopts No. 10 Hot-rolled I-beam (GB/T 706—2016), and the section is shown in Fig. 7. The section depth is $h = 120\text{mm}$, the leg width is $b = 74\text{mm}$, the web thickness is $d = 5\text{mm}$, the middle thickness of the legs is $t = 8.4\text{mm}$, the inner arc radius is $r = 7\text{mm}$, the arc radius of the leg end is $r_1 = 4.5\text{mm}$, the section area is 17.80cm^2, the moment of inertia is $I_x = 4.36 \times 10^{-6}\text{m}^4$, the material flexure rigidity is $E = 215 \times 10^9\text{Pa}$, the flexure rigidity of end A and end B is $C_A = C_B = 1450000\text{N} \cdot \text{m}$. Try to figure out the buckling critical load of the slender column.

3.1.2　Result analysis

The flexure rigidity of both ends in the example are known, and they can be transformed into dimensionless flexure rigidity as follow:

$$\overline{C_A} = \frac{C_A L}{EI} = 3.0936$$

$$\overline{C_B} = \frac{C_B L}{EI} = 3.0936$$

Referring to Fig. 3, it can bequeried that the fourth term of the quartic formula should be taken according to the Taylor series expanded by χ at 1.375π.

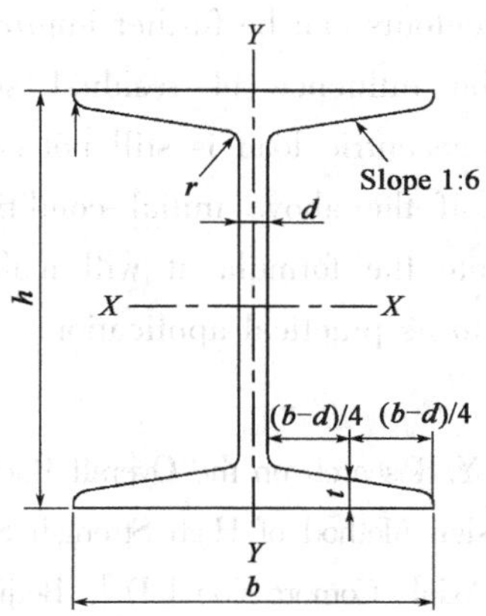

Fig. 7 Schematic diagram of I-beam section

$Q = \frac{1}{C_A C_B} = 0.1045$, $P = \frac{1}{C_A} + \frac{1}{C_B} = 0.6465$ can be obtained, and substitute them into the expanded formula for solution as follows:

$$-0.1543x^4 + 0.4334x^3 + 6.9283x - 10.1128 = 0$$

Substitute the parameters into Equation (18), we can obtain the following equations:

$$\Delta_1 = c^2 - 3bd + 12ae = 0 - 3 \times 0.4334 \times 6.9283 + 12 \times 0.1543 \times 10.1128 = 9.7167$$

$$\Delta_2 = 2c^3 - 9bcd + 27ad^2 + 27b^2e - 72ace = 0 - 0 + 27 \times (-0.1543) \times 6.9283^2 + 27 \times 0.4334^2 \times (-10.1128) = -251.266$$

Substitute Δ_1 and Δ_2 into Equation (19) to obtain the following equation:

$$\Delta = \frac{\sqrt[3]{2}\Delta_1}{3a\sqrt[3]{\Delta_2 + \sqrt{-4\Delta_1^3 + \Delta_2^2}}} + \frac{\sqrt[3]{\Delta_2 + \sqrt{-4\Delta_1^3 + \Delta_2^2}}}{3\sqrt[3]{2}a}$$

$$= \frac{\sqrt[3]{2} \times 9.7167}{3 \times (-0.1543) \times \sqrt[3]{-251.2661 + \sqrt{-4 \times 9.7167^3 + (-251.2661)^2}}} + \frac{\sqrt[3]{-251.2661 + \sqrt{-4 \times 9.7167^3 + (-251.2661)^2}}}{3 \times \sqrt[3]{2} \times (-251.2661)}$$

$$= 16.9076$$

We can figure out:

$$\chi = \frac{0.4334}{4 \times 0.1543} + \frac{1}{2} \times \sqrt{\frac{0.4334^2}{4 \times 0.1543^2} + 16.9076} + \frac{1}{2} \times \sqrt{\frac{0.4334^2}{2 \times 0.1543^2} - 16.9076 + \frac{\frac{0.4334^3}{0.1543^3} - \frac{8 \times 6.9283}{0.1543}}{4 \times \sqrt{\frac{0.4334^2}{4 \times 0.1543^2} + 16.9076}}}$$

$= 4.3731$

Therefore, $\chi = 4.3731$ is the minimum non-zero solution of the transcendental equation when $\chi \in (\pi, 2\pi)$. The difference between this result and the result $\chi' = 4.3730$ calculated by computer is less than 1%. According to $\chi = \sqrt{\frac{PL^2}{EI}}$, the critical buckling load is $P = 4481.7$kN.

3.2 Figure Out The End Flexure Rigidity According to The Required Buckling Load

3.2.1 Example

The length of a slender column with equal section is $L = 2$m, which adopts No. 10 Hot-rolled I-beam (GB/T 706—2016), the column section and material properties are the same as those shown in Section 3.1. In order to make the critical buckling load of the column not less than 4100kN, the flexure rigidity at one end is known to be 1875000N · m, try to conservatively estimate the minimum flexure rigidity required at the other end.

3.2.2 Result analysis

Firstly, the dimensionless critical buckling load is calculated as:

$$\chi = \sqrt{\frac{PL^2}{EI}} = \sqrt{\frac{4100 \times 10^3 \times 2^2}{215 \times 10^9 \times 4.36 \times 10^{-6}}} = 4.1827$$

Then calculate the dimensionlessflexure rigidity of the end of the slender column as:

$$\overline{C_A}=\frac{C_A L}{EI}=\frac{1875000\times 2}{215\times 10^9\times 4.36\times 10^{-6}}=4.0004$$

Referring to Fig. 6, a conservative estimate is made based on the contour line with the dimensionless critical load of 4.2, and the minimum dimensionless flexure rigidity at the other end is approximately $\overline{C_B}=1.6$. Through the verification of the solution shown in Section 2.2 and computer calculation, we can get that under the condition of $\overline{C_A}=4.0004$, $\overline{C_B}=1.6$, the dimensionless critical buckling load of the slender column is 4.2370 and its critical buckling load is 4207.090kN, which meets the given requirement of the critical buckling load of the slender column.

4 Conclusions

In this paper, based on the existing formula for calculating the critical buckling load of slender columns constrained by springs at both ends, an approach is proposed to figure out numerical solutions to transcendental equations in a specific range. Based on the data integration of the paper, the contour of dimensionless critical buckling load, which is related to the dimensionless and flexure rigidity, is derived. The following conclusions can be drawn:

(1) The approach provides a solution for the transcendental equation of the critical buckling load and gives the graphs for querying the applicable Tayler series. It can avoid the complex process of directly solving the transcendental equation and ensure high accuracy.

(2) The quartic formula obtained in this study is proved to be reliable through the examples. For the engineers on site, the graphs provided in this paper are concise and easy to understand. Compared with relying on computer analysis, they can get the solutions more conveniently with the approach.

(3) The curves and contours provided in this study can also be used to estimate whether the current structure meets the requirements of critical buckling load and provide a reference for engineering practice.

(4) The formula calculated and the graph drawn in this paperare suitable for the slender prismatic column with elastic spring support at the end. The fineness of contours can be further improved.

(5) The influence of residual stress, initial bending and eccentric load is still not considered in this formula. If the above initial conditions can be introduced into the formula, it will make a further contribution to its practical application.

References

[1] Ban, H. Y. Research on the Overall BucklingBehavior and Design Method of High Strength Steel Columns under Axial Compression [D]. Beijing: Tsinghua University, 2012.

[2] Ding R. Discussion on the Stability of Compression Bar [J]. Mechanics in Engineering, 2014, 36(05): 636-638.

[3] Dong G W, Li Z Y, Zhao Y J. Unified Deduction of Pressure Lever Stability Critical Force Euler Formula [J]. Journal of Wuhan Institute of Technology, 2012, 34(12): 71-74.

[4] Euler L. Sur la force decolonnes[M]. Memoires de l'Academie de Berlin, 1759.

[5] Gong L L. Internal Force Identification and Stability Analysis of Long Compressed Bar[D]. Guangzhou: South China University of Technology, 2010.

[6] He P W, Yang Z P, Wang P. Numerical Analysis of Bearing Capacity of Elastic Slender Column [C]. World Transportation Convention (WTC2021) Proceedings (I), 2021: 1048-1053.

[7] Sun X F. Mechanics of Materials[M]. 5th ed. Beijing: Higher Education Press, 2009.

[8] Wang L J. Flexural Buckling of Axially Compressed Bars [J]. Building Structure, 2019, 49 (19): 126-135.

[9] Yang Z P. Elasto-Plastic Analysis of Slender Circular Tubular Steel-CFRP Column [D]. Xi'an: Chang'an University.

基于多源信息融合的交通荷载重构方法研究

杨 干* 韩万水 张书颖

（长安大学公路学院）

摘 要 交通荷载是桥梁最重要的外部荷载之一。准确重构桥梁所承受的交通荷载对桥梁结构的状态评估具有重要意义。为了获取车辆的类别、轨迹以及速度等信息，本文提出了基于YOLOx模型结构搭建的车辆检测网络，并采用迁移学习、冻结训练等方法，进而有效、可靠地训练车辆检测网络，其检测的平均准确率均值(mAP)达到了0.975。针对车辆荷载重量信息的获取与匹配，本文提出了实时融合动态称重系统(WIM)数据以及基于统计数据随机抽样两种方法，以适应不同的情况。为了测试这种方法的有效性，选择了国内某一桥梁进行试验。结果表明，车辆得到准确检测，并合理匹配了重量信息，实现了交通荷载的重构。

关键词 桥梁工程 交通荷载重构 信息融合 神经网络

0 引言

作用在公路桥梁上的交通荷载往往呈现出较强的随机性和地域性[1]。它作为主要活荷载对桥梁结构安全有着深远影响。交通荷载信息可以分为时变信息和时不变信息。时变信息主要指车辆行驶在桥梁上的速度、轨迹等；时不变信息指的是车辆的轴数以及重量信息。准确获得交通荷载的时变信息和时不变信息，进而重构真实交通荷载，这对桥梁性能评估，剩余使用寿命预测，耐久性分析和维养工作意义重大。

目前国内外对交通荷载识别进行了大量的研究，很多学者通过间接的方式来获取交通荷载信息，即通过结构响应反演移动荷载。其应用较多的方法主要包括解析法Ⅰ[2]，解析法Ⅱ[3]，时域法[4]及频时域法[5]。陈震等[6]基于时域法，采用预处理共轭梯度法由梁的弯矩响应、加速度响应及其响应组合来识别桥梁移动荷载。随后，又通过引入正则化矩阵，提出采用截断广义奇异值分解法识别桥梁移动荷载[7]。汪新丽[8]使用光纤光栅传感技术，根据传感器的响应拟合应变曲线，通过应变位置系数进行修正，结合应变荷载系数进行荷载识别。陈适之等[9]基于长标距光纤光栅(FBG)传感器序列测得的宏应变时程，提出宏应变曲率的指标，并建立了新型桥梁式动态称重方法，可同时识别车辆车速、轴距及轴重。通过结构响应反演移动荷载，计算规模庞大，干扰因素多，难以同时识别桥梁上的多辆车辆信息。

也有学者依托交通流监控视频，基于计算机视觉技术来直接识别交通荷载的时空信息[10]，进而通过视频识别信息与车重数据的融合实现了交通荷载的重构[11-12]。这些交通荷载重构方法的适用性仍可进一步提高。本文提出了基于多源信息融合，可适用于多种工况的交通荷载重构方法。

1 交通荷载检测

1.1 网络结构

目标检测主要解决了图像中有什么物体以及这个物体在哪里的问题。这有以下难点：首先，物体可以出现在图片中任何位置，并且其大小差异很大；其次，物体的角度和姿态是不确定的；另外，物体的类别有多样性。为了解决上述问题，在传统的目标检测算法中，采用多尺度特征金字塔与遍历滑窗相结合的方式。针对每一个尺度，采用遍历滑窗来判断这个尺度的位置有没有目标物体，这种处理方式十分笨重耗时。后来，出现了锚框(固定参考框)的概念。针对不同的尺度，每个锚框负责检测与其交并比(IOU)大于设定阈值的目标，这就将问题转化成为：在特定的锚框内，有没有认识的目标物体，这个物体偏离锚框有多远。这样就避免了多尺度的遍历，极大地提升了遍历的速度。近年来，出现了一阶段的目标检测算法，只需要对不同尺度的特征图的目标中心点和宽高进行回归,极大地减少了耗时和需要的算力。本文我们采用 YOLOX 模型[13]来进行车辆的检测。

YOLOx 网络模型是在之前一系列 YOLO 模型的改进,其网络结构如图 1 所示。整体过程为特征提取、特征加强以及对特征点的分类和回归。在进行特征提取之前,YOLOx 设置了 Focus 网络结构来进行压缩宽高和拓展通道,具体操是在一张图片中每隔一个像素拿到一个值形成独立的特征层,并将这些特征层进行堆叠。YOLOx 的主干特征提取网络采用了 CSPDarknet 结构,由 Con_BN_SiLU(标准卷积块)、Csplayer(残差结构)以及 SppBottneck(空间金字塔池化结构)组成。其中标准卷积块 Con _ BN _SiLU 由基本卷积层(Convolutional layer)、批量归一(Batch Normalization)以及 SiLU 激活函数组成。SiLU 激活函数是 Sigmoid 激活函数和 ReLU 激活函数的融合改进版,它具备无上界有下界、平滑、非单调的特性,在深层模型的效果更优,表达式为:

$$f(x) = x \cdot sigmoid(x) \tag{1}$$

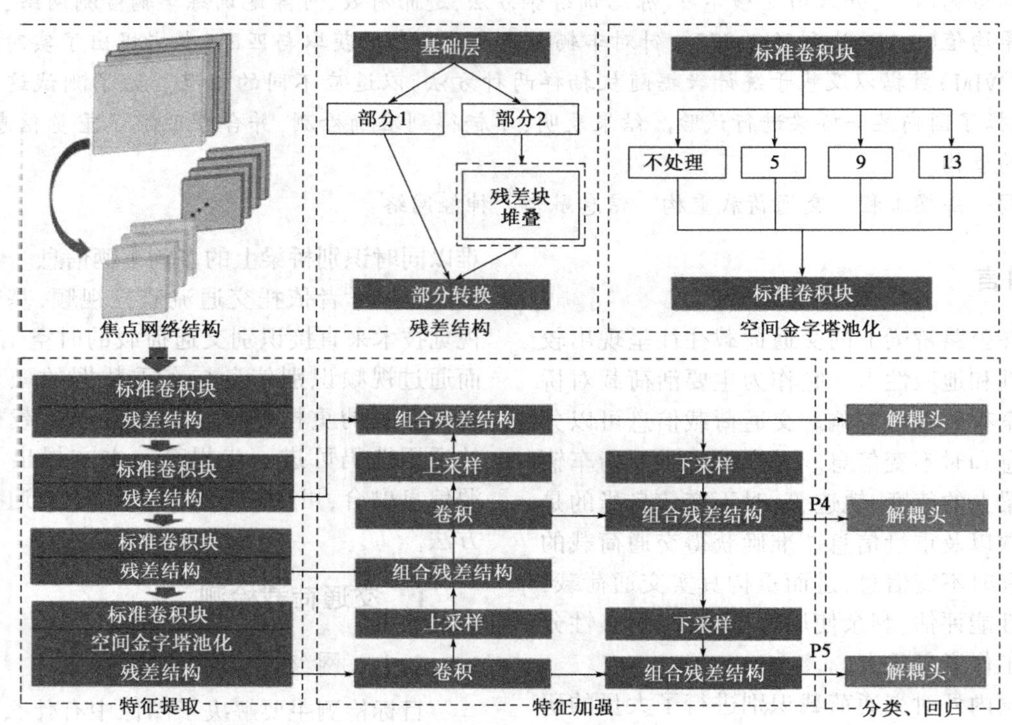

图 1　YOLOx 网络结构图

图形如图 2 所示。

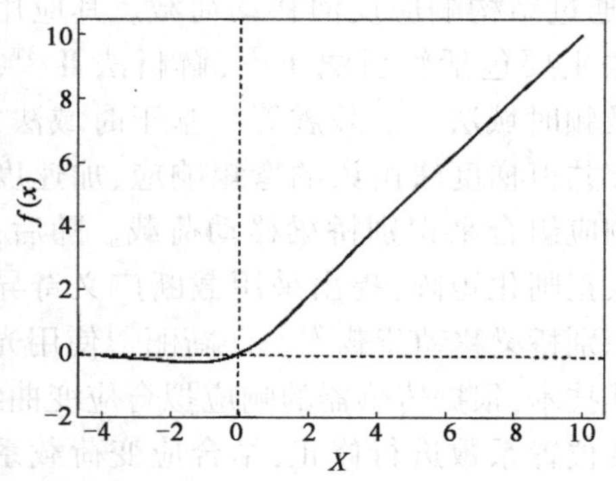

图 2　SiLU 激活函数

使用 Csplayer 可以有效地避免随着神经网络的深度的增加而带来的梯度消失的问题。使用 SppBottneck 结构,通过不同尺度的池化核来进行最大池化完成特征提取,进而提高网络的感受野。通过基础的特征提取,可以得到 3 个有效特征层,其大小分别为(80,80,256)、(40,40,512)以及(20,20,1024)。加强特征提取网络本质上是特征的重复提取,将深层的特征层进行上采样与浅层的特征层融合,然后将浅层特征融合的结果进行下采样与深层特征层融合,结合“从上向下”和“从下向上”来完成特征的加强提取,进而得到 3 个加强后的有效特征层 P3、P4 和 P5。

在特征点的分类和回归部分,YOLOx 与之前所有的版本有很大区别,它将预测分成了两个部分,一部分用来分类、一部分用来回归。首先对加强后的有效特征层(P3/P4/P5)进行特征整合,接下来分两个方向来进行:①用两个标准卷积块进行特征提取,接着用一个卷积实现分类,用于判断这个特征点所属物体的种类(Cls);②用两个标准卷积块进行特征提取,接着分别用两个卷积实现特征点对应的物体边界框的回归结果(Reg)并判别特征点是否有对应的物体(Obj)。其整体过程的流程图如图3所示。

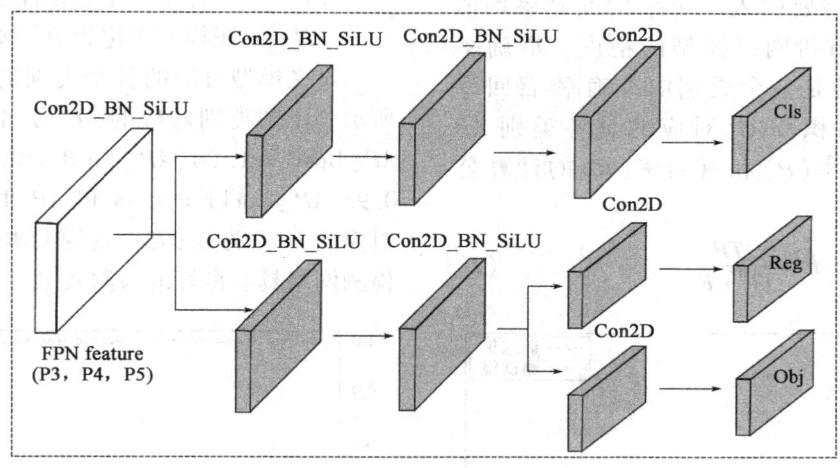

图3　分类、回归过程图

1.2　网络训练和测试

数据集对于一个具有良好检测能力的网络发挥着至关重要的作用,它必须具有足够多的类别,以确保网络的泛化能力。本文收集了不同路段的5000张车辆荷载照片,涵盖了常见的各种车型。这些图片中不同类型的车辆被分别标记。每个标签对应一个标签文件,文件记录车辆的类型和车辆在图片中的位置。在本文中,车辆分为三类:小汽车(car),大巴车(bus)和卡车(truck)。每种类型的车辆的照片都区分为前视图和后视图,例如,小汽车照片分为汽车前视图(carF)和小汽车后视图(carB)。数据集建立完毕后将其划分为训练集和测试集,划分比例为8:2,即4000张照片用来训练,1000张照片用来测试。

准备好数据集之后,接下来进行网络的训练。在训练的过程中,需要将网络的预测结果与真实的结果进行对比计算,进而得到网络的损失函数值。本文网络的损失也包含了三个部分,分别是Reg部分、Obj部分和Cls部分,分别对应着特征点回归参数的判断(利用网络预测框和真实框计算交并比损失)、特征点包含物体的判断(根据正负样本和特征点的是否包含物体的预测结果计算交叉熵损失)、特征点包含物体种类的判断(根据真实框的种类和特征点的种类预测结果计算交叉熵损失)。此外,值得注意的是,YOLOX中采取了SimOTA方法进行动态的正样本数量分配。其整体的流程如下:首先,计算网络在当前特征点的预测框与每个真实框之间的重合程度,其重合程度越高则说明该特征点越近似正确地拟合了真实框,进而其Cost代价就会越小。接着,筛选出与真实框重合度最高的十个预测框,并分别求出其与真实框的交并比(IOU),并求和。然后,计算网络当前预测框与真实框的预测准确度,并判别真实框的中心是否落在了特征点的一定半径内。最后,计算Cost代价矩阵,将Cost代价最低的k个点作为该真实框的正样本。在上述过程中,Cost代价矩阵代表每个真实框和每个特征点之间的代价关系,由三部分构成,分别为特征点预测框与每个真实框的重合程度、特征点预测框与每个真实框的种类预测准确度以及对每个真实框是否落在一定特征点的规定半径内的判断。

整个训练的过程分两个阶段进行,分别是冻结阶段和解冻阶段。在冻结阶段,模型的主干被冻结,特征提取网络不发生改变,此时仅仅对网络进行了微调,所需的计算机的显存较小。在解冻阶段,此时模型的主干被解放,特征提取网络会发生较大的改变,需要的显存较大。在第一阶段赋予初始权重并冻结训练的目的是防止网络并不适应于对应的数据集,进而导致主干网络的参数被无序的破坏。在此,采用两个阶段进行训练主要是借鉴了迁移学习的思想。在冻结训练阶段,参数设置为:回合(*epoch*)为50次,批次数(*batch_size*)为8,学习率(*lr*)为0.001;在解冻阶段,参数设置为：$epoch = 100$，$batch\_size = 4$，$lr = 0.0001$。图4展示了在解冻阶段的损失函数下降图。从损失函数下降图来看，网络未出现过拟合和欠拟合的现象。在这里需要引入一个平均准确率均值（mAP）的概念来评价网络模型的精度。准确率均值（AP）对应的是一个类别的准确率-召回率曲线所包围的面积，mAP 对应的是各类别 AP 的平均值。准确率（P）和召回率（R）的计算公式为：

$$P = \frac{TP}{TP + FP} \tag{2}$$

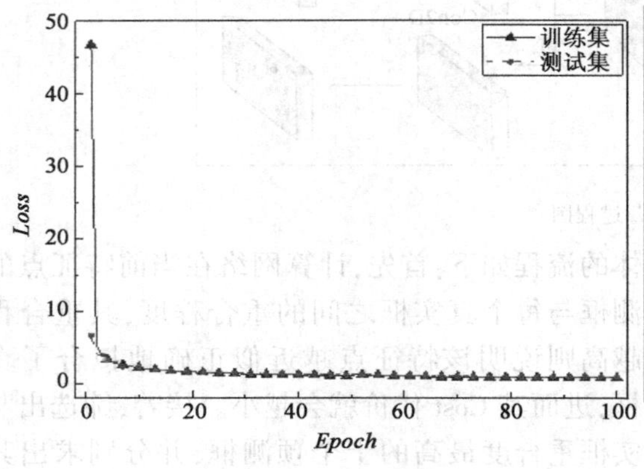

图4 损失函数下降图

$$R = \frac{TP}{TP + FN} \tag{3}$$

式中：TP——正样本判定为正样本；

FP——负样本判定为正样本；

FN——正样本判定为负样本。

本文模型对应的各个类别的 $P-R$ 图如图5所示。不同类别对应的 AP 为：$AP\_BusB = 0.97$、$AP\_BusF = 1.00$、$AP\_CarB = 0.97$、$AP\_CarF = 0.95$、$AP\_TruckF = 0.98$ 和 $AP\_TruckB = 0.98$，故对应的 mAP 为0.975。这说明本文所建立的车辆检测网络具有良好的检测效果。

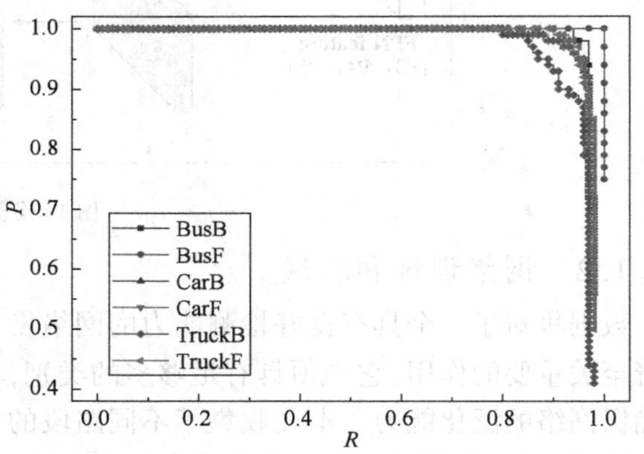

图5 准确率-召回率曲线图

2 车辆荷载的重构

通过上述建立的车辆检测网络获得的车辆坐标是像素坐标，而不是世界坐标。桥面坐标系属于世界坐标系，仅仅获得车辆在图像中的像素坐标是无意义的，因此必须建立起像素坐标系与桥面坐标系之间的转换关系。这通常涉及四种坐标系：世界坐标系，相机坐标系，图像坐标系和像素坐标系。其中：世界坐标系的原点和方向可以人工定义，单位为m；相机坐标系，它的原点是相机中的光心，单位是m；图像坐标系点是图片的中心，单位是mm；像素坐标系的原点是图像的左上角，单位是像素。世界坐标系与像素坐标系之间可以通过坐标转换矩阵进行变换，其具体推导过程可参考文献[10]，在此就不详细介绍。

通过上述过程可以获取车辆荷载的速度、轨迹等时空信息，但是仍无法获取车辆荷载的重量信息。需要融合车辆荷载的重量信息以实现车辆荷载的完备重构。动态称重系统（WIM）作为一种先进的交通调查设备，为研究人员获取真实的车辆重量信息提供了一种有效途径，其可以获取车辆到达时间、车速、轴数、轴重、轴距等信息。本文针对桥头安装有WIM和没有安装WIM两种情况，给出了不同的车辆荷载重构的方式。针对桥头安装有WIM的情况，将WIM记录的车辆重量信息与通过车辆检测网络识别的车辆时空位置信息直接进行匹配，进而实现车辆荷载的重构。WIM系统记录车辆的轴重、轴距信息以及车辆到达时间的同时，车辆检测网络也可以记录车辆的到达时间，并实现对车辆时空信息的识别。车辆到达安装WIM系统桥梁断面处的时间和车道信息，WIM系统和车辆检测网络均可以记录，可以基于此来完成信息的融合，进而完成车辆荷载的完备重构，其过程如图6所示。上述方法，笔者在文献[12]中做了详细阐述，在此不赘述。

针对没有安装WIM系统的情况，可以使用抽样的方法，给不同种类的车辆赋予合理的重量信息。不可否认的是，通过这种方式我们获得的车辆荷载与真实的车辆荷载，在短时间内会有很大的差别。但是，如果我们更为关心的是荷载引起的桥梁结构的累积损伤，对于足够大且无偏的数据集，这种抽样荷载估计的方式是具有价值的。

通过这种方式,我们需要从桥梁所在的路线内收集车辆荷载信息,并从中提取车辆重量分布参数,并拟合其分布的概率密度函数 $f(x)$。图7中给出了某线路中二轴车和三轴车的车质量概率密度分布图,其基础数据来源于安装在线路上的WIM装置。

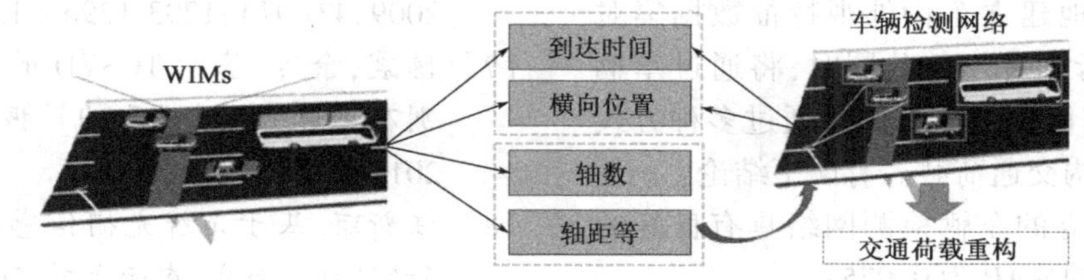

图6 基于WIM数据的交通荷载重构示意图

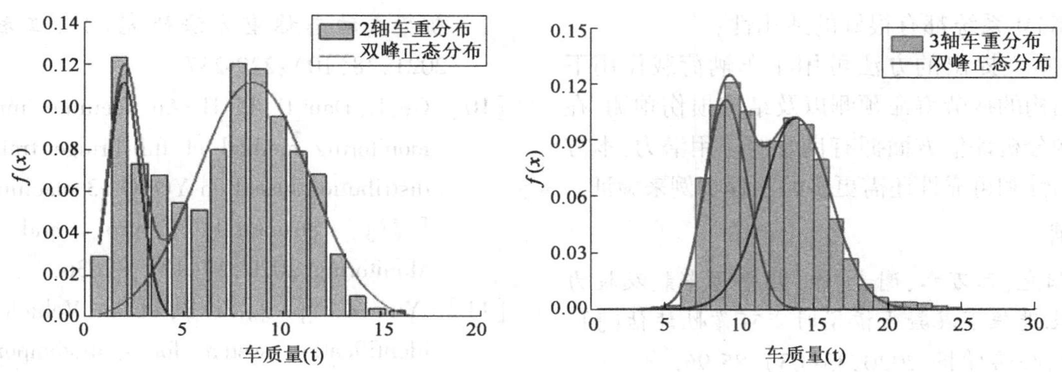

图7 车重概率密度分布示意图

得到了概率密度函数 $f(x)$ 之后,一般可以通过逆分布函数法或者舍选法进行抽样。采用逆分布函数法虽然准确简洁,但是在多数情况下无法直接给出概率累积分布函数的反函数。相对于逆分布函数法,舍选法的应用范围更广。其步骤为:

第一步:产生 $[a,b]$ 区间内均匀分布的随机数 x:

$$x:x=(b-a)r_1+a,r_1\in U[0,1] \tag{4}$$

第二步:产生 $[0,c]$ 区间内均匀分布的随机数 y:

$$y:y=cr_2,r_2\in U[0,1] \tag{5}$$

其中,c 的取值要大于等于概率分布函数 $f(x)$ 在 $[a,b]$ 区间的最大值。

第三步:当 $y\leqslant f(x)$ 时,接受 x 为所需的随机数,否则,返回到第一步重新抽取一对 (x,y)。

根据上述抽样办法进行对车重抽样,进而与车辆位置的进行融合,获取完备的车辆荷载。

为了测试上述方法的有效性,选择了国内某一桥梁进行试验。在此桥梁上并没有安装有WIM系统,故采取抽样的方法进行车重的匹配。如图8所示,车辆被准确地检测、跟踪,并合理匹配了重量信息,成功实现了交通荷载的重构。

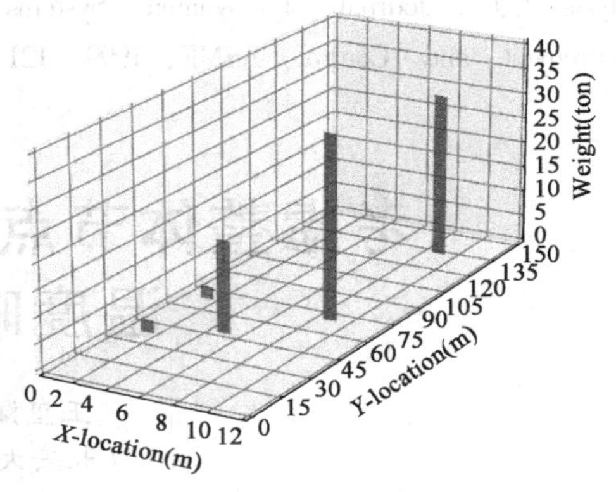

图8 交通荷载重构结果图

3 结语

本文提出了基于YOLOx网络结构的车辆检测网络,并针对性地建立车辆外观特征数据集对车辆检测网络进行训练。与此同时,将通过车辆检测网络得到时空信息与车重信息通过多种方式进行融合,进而重构交通荷载。有以下结论:

(1)本文所建立的车辆检测网络具有良好的检测效果,其对应的 *mAP* 为0.975;

(2)本文提出的多种融合方式对于桥梁是否安装有WIM系统都有很好的适用性;

(3)本文提出的方法可用于车辆荷载作用下的桥梁结构的疲劳寿命预测以及结构损伤预测,在桥梁结构分析评估方面拥有良好的应用潜力,本方法的鲁棒性和可靠性还需更多的工程实例来验证。

参考文献

[1] 袁阳光,韩万水,谢青,等.非平稳车载及抗力劣化进程下混凝土桥梁时变可靠性评估[J].中国公路学报,2020,33(03):85-96.

[2] O'connor C, chan T H T. Dynamic Wheel Loads From Bridge Strains [J]. Journal of Structural Engineering ASCE, 1988, 114(8):1703-1723.

[3] Chan T H T, Law S S, Yung T H. An Interpretive Method for Moving Force Identification [J]. Journal of Sound and Vibration, 1999, 219 (3):503-524.

[4] Law S S, Chan T H T. Moving Force Identification: A Time Domain Method [J]. Journal of Sound and Vibration, 1997, 201(1):1-22.

[5] Law S S, Chan T H T, Zeng Q H. Moving Force Identification: A Frequency and Time Domains Analysis [J]. Journal of Dynamic Systems, Measurement and Control, ASME, 1999, 121: 394-401.

[6] 陈震,余岭.桥梁移动荷载识别及其PCGM预优矩阵选取[J].浙江大学学报(工学版),2009,43(07):1293-1296+1306.

[7] 陈震,余岭.基于TGSVD的桥梁移动荷载识别及正则化矩阵选取[J].振动.测试与诊断,2015(01):24-29+184.

[8] 汪新丽.基于光纤光栅传感的交通荷载识别研究[D].南京:东南大学,2017.

[9] 陈适之,冯德成,杨干,等.基于宏应变曲率的桥梁式动态称重方法研究[J].工程力学,2021,38(10):229-237.

[10] Ge L, Dan D, Li H. An accurate and robust monitoring method of full-bridge traffic load distribution based on YOLO-v3 machine vision [J]. Structural Control and Health Monitoring, 2020, 27(12): e2636.

[11] Yun Z, Yp B, Zl B, et al. Vehicle weight identification system for spatiotemporal load distribution on bridges based on non-contact machine vision technology and deep learning algorithms-ScienceDirect [J]. Measurement, 2020, 159:107801.

[12] Yang G, Wang P, Han W, et al. Automatic generation of fine-grained traffic load spectrum via fusion of weigh-in-motion and vehicle spatial-temporal information [J]. Computer-Aided Civil and Infrastructure Engineering, 2022, 37:485-499.

[13] Ge Z, Liu S, Wang F, et al. YOLOX: Exceeding YOLO Series in 2021 [J]. 2021. arXiv: 2107.08430v2.

考虑整体节点刚度对钢桁梁桥温度响应分析

王玺翔* 刘 佳
(长安大学公路学院)

摘 要 以某钢桁梁桥为工程背景,通过建立铰接桁架模型、常规梁模型和带刚臂梁单元模型,探讨整体节点刚度对温度作用下钢桁梁杆件应力、竖向位移和支座反力响应的影响规律。结果表明,在温度荷载作用下,整体节点刚度对竖向位移和支座反力影响不大;整体节点刚度对钢桁梁桥组合应力温度响应影响较大,其中对腹杆影响较为明显。因此,可通过改变节点刚度,减少钢桁桥梁温度应力。

关键词 钢桁梁桥 整体节点刚度 温度响应 受力性能

0 引言

钢桁梁桥具有刚度大、施工快捷、跨越能力大等特点,在国内得到广泛应用。钢桁梁整体节点,即将节点板与一端的弦杆焊接成为一个整体,其主桁节点板成为箱形弦杆的一部分[1]。20 世纪 90 年代,孙口黄河大桥首次采用焊接整体节点和节点外拼接技术。整体节点因构造简洁,受力合理,工期短等优势,在钢桁结构中得到广泛推广。

目前,国内外学者关于整体节点刚度对钢桁梁力学性能的影响开展了许多研究。Raul Zaharia 等[2]通过试验研究,提出了节点刚度的理论计算公式。陈淮等[3]人通过建立最不利节点精细化模型,得出施工最不利阶段时节点局部受力情况,保证桥梁施工安全。黄永辉等[4]人通过对比挠度、应力、模态等动静特性指标,发现带刚臂梁单元模拟值与现场实测更为吻合。刘海峰等[5]人通过建立变截面梁单元、常截面梁单元、变弹性模量梁单元以及壳单元离散的有限元模型,模拟主材节点刚度对钢管输电塔受力的影响,并与实测值对比。盛兴旺等[6]通过对比所建立的常规梁单元模型、多尺度模型和刚臂梁单元模型,发现直腹杆次应力对节点刚度变化较敏感,应考虑较大的安全富余。综合国内外研究现状,主要集中在节点刚度对桥梁静力特性的影响。温度作为一种桥梁结构的长期作用,它对桥梁结构的影响与结构的刚度有密切的影响。针对整体节点刚度对桥梁结构的温度响应影响的研究工作较少。

本文选取某钢桁梁桥为工程背景,采用 MIDAS CIVIL 有限元分析软件建立三种不同节点刚度的模型,探讨不同节点刚度下桥梁结构的温度受力性能的影响。

1 工程背景

某钢桁梁全长为 679m,主桥的结构形式为 3×80m 上承式钢桁-混凝土组合梁桥,主梁采用双拼桁架组合梁,钢主梁标准间距 6.7m,主桁中心高度 7.2m,节间标准长度 8m,平联、弦杆、腹杆相交处均为整体式节点板连接。钢桁梁桥整体布置如图 1 所示。

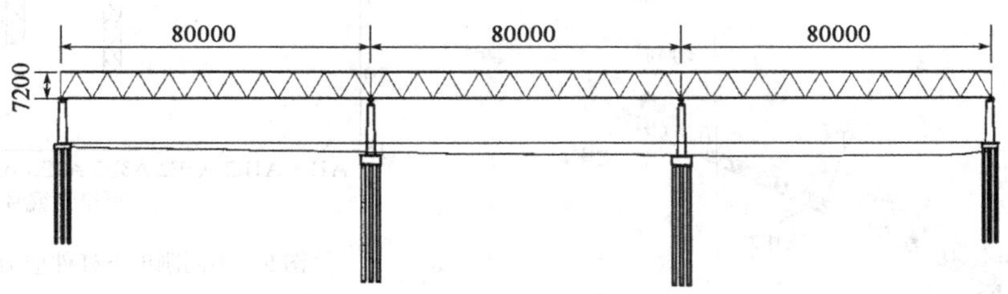

图 1 钢桁梁桥结构整体布置(尺寸单位:mm)

2 建立有限元模型

根据该桥梁结构构造形式和实际尺寸,构建铰接桁架模型、常规梁模型和带刚臂梁单元模型,通过采用三种不同的节点处理方法,以模拟不同节点刚度下桥梁结构的温度效应。本文选取 A2 相邻的两个节间为主要研究对象,各杆件编号及相应位置见图 2。

2.1 铰接桁架模型

铰接桁架模型是最简化的桁架计算模型,将节点板简化为一个“铰”,在结构力学中,认为该节点只能传递轴力,不能传递弯矩。在 MIDAS CIVIL 有限元分析软件中,通过释放一般梁单元的梁端约束模拟节点铰接,如图 3a) 所示。

2.2 节点刚接模型

节点刚接模型是目前桁架计算分析主要的方法,与铰接桁架模型相比,可传递弯矩,考虑抗弯等刚度。节点位置取杆件中心线的交点,且在荷载作用下,节点处各杆件间的夹角保持不变。在 MIDAS CIVIL 有限元分析软件中,可直接通过一般梁单元实现,如图 3b) 所示。

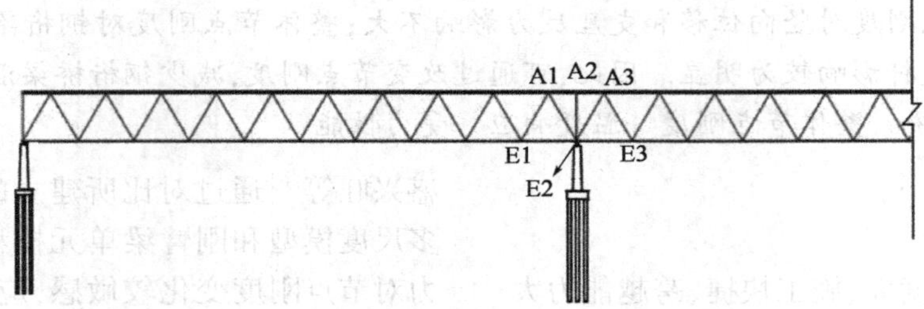

图2　钢桁梁杆件编号及位置

2.3　带刚臂梁单元模型

带刚臂梁单元模型是在节点板区域赋予无穷大刚度。在MIDAS CIVIL有限元分析软件中,可直接通过在一般梁单元施加梁端刚域实现,如图3c)所示。

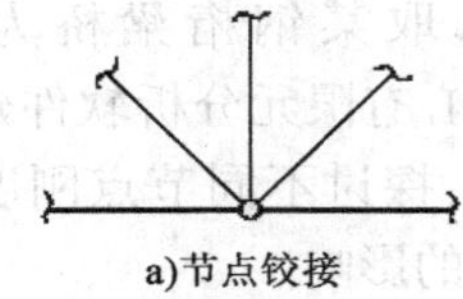

a)节点铰接

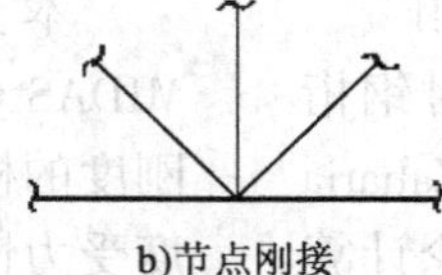

b)节点刚接

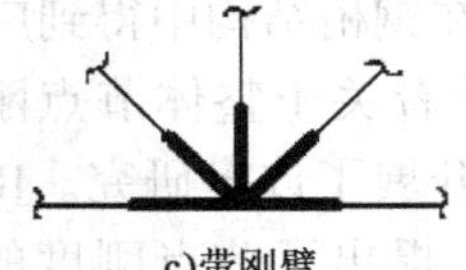

c)带刚臂

图3　整体节点力学图

3　计算结果分析

分析铰接桁架模型、常规梁模型和带刚臂梁单元模型在环境温度升温20℃,钢桁梁桥各杆件的应力以及竖向位移和支座反力。其中各模型中支座的位置及其编号如图4所示,计算结果见图5~图7。

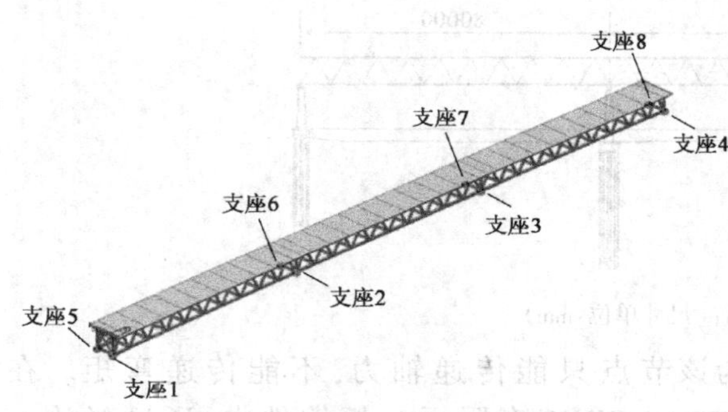

图4　支座位置及编号

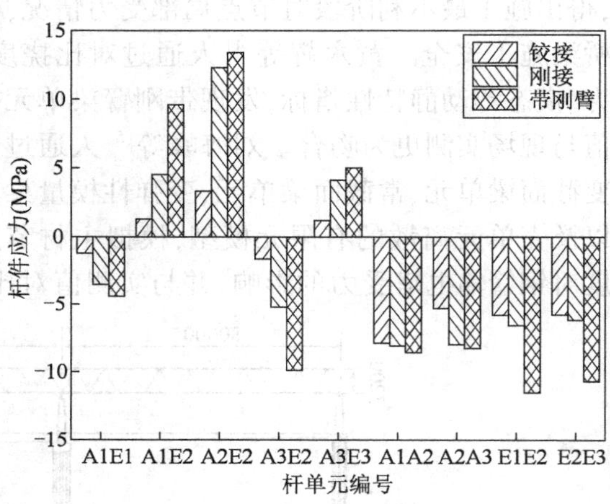

图5　不同刚度下杆件应力温度响应

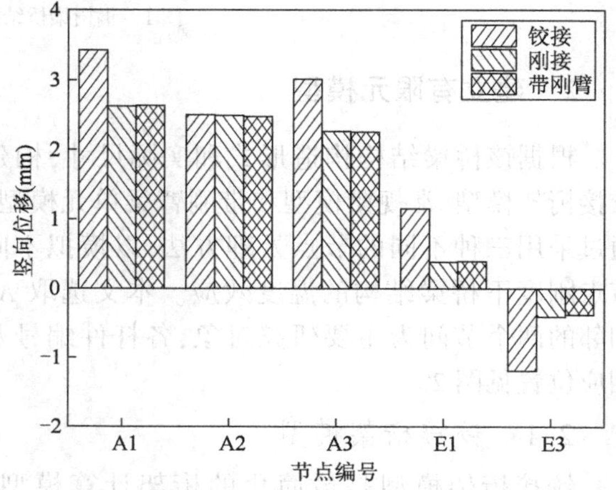

图6　不同刚度下竖向位移温度响应

由图5可以看出,三种模型中各杆件端部组合应力的温度响应分布规律基本一致,应力大小呈现出带刚臂空间梁单元模型>节点刚接模型>节点铰接模型的规律,铰接模型和带刚臂空间梁单元模型的温度应力计算值差异最大,为75%;三个模型的腹杆应力值随刚度增加而增加,弦杆温度应力受刚度影响较小。由此可知,在钢桁梁一类结构的设计中,需要考虑节点刚度对温度次应力的影响,尤其是腹杆,可通过降低腹杆的节点刚度降低桁杆应力对温度的响应。

由图 6 可以看出,A2 节点位于支座上方处,受到约束,整体节点的刚度变化对支座附近的竖向位移影响不大。在结构温度变化下,除 A2 节点外节点铰接模型的竖向位移均比其他两个模型大,铰接模型竖向位移平均相差 23.6%,节点刚接模型和带刚臂空间梁单元模型竖向位移基本一致。

由图 7 可以看出,不同节点刚度下,各支座反力对温度的变化的响应相差不大,节点铰接模型和节点刚接模型的计算结果差异相对较小,最大为 7%,位于支座 2,节点刚接模型和带刚臂空间梁单元模型的计算结果差异相对较大,最大为 17.8%,位于支座 5。说明在温度作用下,节点刚度对支座反力影响不大。

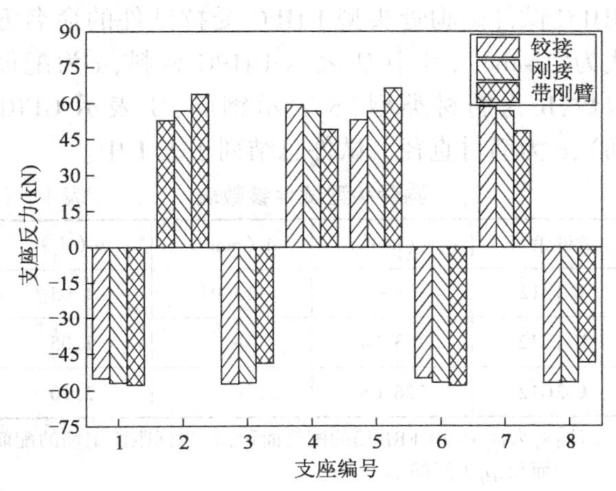

图 7 不同刚度下支座反力温度响应

4 结语

本文以某钢桁梁桥为工程背景,通过建立铰接桁架模型、常规梁模型和带刚臂梁单元模型三种模型模拟不同节点刚度,对比分析三种模型的组合应力、竖向位移以及支座反力对温度变化的响应。通过分析发现,整体节点刚度对钢桁梁竖向位移温度响应和支座反力温度响应影响不大;对钢桁梁应力温度响应影响较大,特别是对腹杆影响较为显著。因此,在钢桁梁桥结构设计中,可考虑减小节点刚度,降低温度荷载对钢桁梁桥的温度应力。

参考文献

[1] 林荫岳,邵克华.我国桥梁钢和整体节点钢桁梁新技术[J].城市道桥与防洪,1994(02):25-29.

[2] ZahariaR, Dubina D. Stiffness of joints in bolted connected cold-formed steel trusses [J]. Journal, 2006, 62: 240-249.

[3] 陈淮,李杰,李谊修.连续钢桁梁施工阶段整体节点局部应力分析[J].桥梁建设,2011(05):21-25+58.

[4] 黄永辉,王荣辉,饶瑞.考虑整体节点刚域影响的钢桁梁桥空间受力计算分析[J].中国铁道科学,2012,33(05):8-14.

[5] 刘海锋,杨靖波,韩军科,等.考虑主材节点刚域影响的钢管输电塔变截面梁单元有限元模型[J].工程力学,2015,32(06):162-170.

[6] 盛兴旺,郑纬奇,戴劲.考虑整体节点刚域模拟影响的钢桁梁力学效应分析[J].桥梁建设,2016,46(06):78-82.

配 GFRP 筋 UHPC 受拉构件力学性能试验

李益达　谭红梅　徐骁青*

(1.重庆交通大学土木工程学院;2.同济大学土木工程学院)

摘　要　配置筋材的超高性能混凝土(UHPC)构件具有良好的工程应用前景。为研究配玻璃纤维复合材料(GFRP)筋 UHPC 受拉构件的力学性能,并与配钢筋 UHPC 构件进行对比,开展了 1 个配钢筋 UHPC 和 2 个配 GFRP 筋 UHPC 狗骨头型试件的轴拉试验。试验结果表明:配筋形式相同时,配 GFRP 筋 UHPC 试件的受拉应变硬化性能要弱于配钢筋 UHPC 试件;在开裂特性方面,配钢筋 UHPC 试件具有多缝开裂特征,而 2 个配 GFRP 筋 UHPC 试件均仅有一条裂缝;U-1S12 试件的可视开裂应变值比 U-1G12 试件大了 4 倍左右,但出现可视裂缝时裂缝宽度更大。此外,GFRP 配筋率增加后,配 GFRP 筋 UHPC 试件的极限抗拉承载力升高,并具有更好的裂缝宽度控制能力。

关键词 GFRP筋 UHPC 受拉性能 应变硬化 裂缝宽度

0 引言

超高性能混凝土(Ultra-high Performance Concrete,简称UHPC)和纤维复合增强材料(Fiber Reinforced Polymer,简称FRP)均是近年来备受关注的高性能材料。将FRP筋与UHPC结合使用,能够充分利用UHPC和FRP筋的高强度特性[1],同时弥补FRP筋普通混凝土构件在正常使用极限状态下挠度大、裂缝宽度大的缺点,得到了越来越多学者的关注[2,3]。

深入研究配筋UHPC构件的受拉应力-应变曲线和开裂特性,对掌握梁、板、柱等工程构件的相关力学性能十分重要。目前已有诸多学者对配钢筋UHPC受拉构件的力学性能进行研究,但配FRP筋UHPC受拉构件的力学性能的研究尚未见报道。Kunieda等[4]的研究指出,配钢筋UHPC受拉构件表现出受拉应变硬化特征,同时构件表面有多条微裂缝。Roy等[5]研究指出,高纤维含量、更好的纤维取向和更高的钢筋强度等级可以使配钢筋UHPC构件获得更高的轴向抗拉强度。Hung等[6]的试验结果表明,钢纤维的加入提高了UHPC与钢筋的黏结强度,使UHPC的受拉破坏模式由多条裂缝转变为单一的局部裂缝,加剧了试件内部钢筋的应变集中。Aghdasi等[7]的研究指出,在配钢筋UHPC受拉构件中,第一个宏观可视裂缝的形成均由钢筋的屈服点(约0.2%~0.4%应变)控制。

综上研究可知,UHPC材料中配置筋材可以改善UHPC的受拉应变硬化性能,获得更高的抗拉强度。FRP筋具有弹性模量低、线弹性等特性,与钢筋不同,对UHPC受拉构件的增强作用可能存在差异。为此,本文通过开展配GFRP筋UHPC试件的轴拉试验,研究配GFRP筋UHPC受拉构件的力学性能,探索GFRP筋与钢筋在UHPC材料中增强作用的区别。

1 试验方案

1.1 试件设置

本次试验共浇筑了3个狗骨头型受拉试件,包括1个配钢筋UHPC试件,2个配GFRP筋UHPC试件。狗骨头型UHPC受拉试件的命名方式为"U-abc",其中U表示UHPC材料,a为配筋根数,b为筋材类型(S表示钢筋、G表示GFRP筋),c为筋材直径。试件总结列于表1中。

狗骨头型试件参数表 表1

试件编号	A_r(mm^2)	A_s(mm^2)	ρ_f(%)
U-1S12	—	113.04	1.05
U-1G12	113.04	—	1.05
U-2G12	226.08	—	2.10

注:A_r为标距段GFRP筋的配筋面积;A_s为标距段钢筋的配筋面积;ρ_f为配筋率。

试件几何形状和配筋详图如图1所示。试件长度900mm,标距段长度为200mm。为了防止构造破坏,所有试件均在端部布置了构造钢筋,如图1中试件内部的粗线条所示。

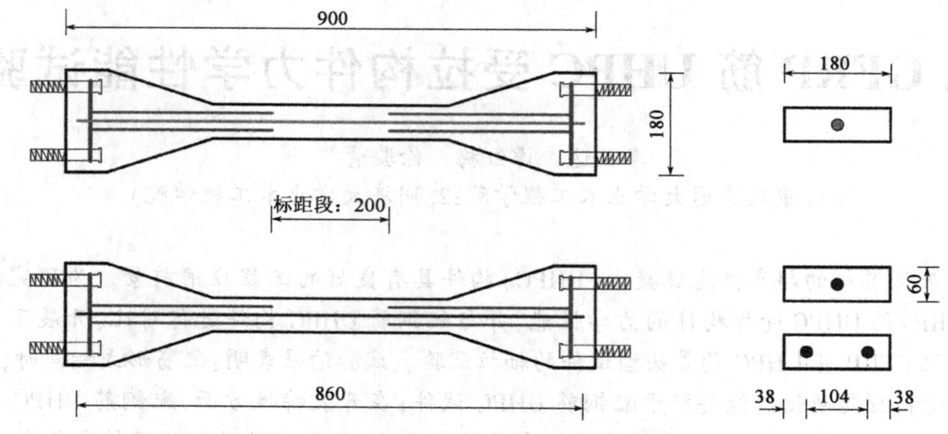

图1 狗骨头型试件几何尺寸与配筋细节(尺寸单位:mm)

1.2 材料

1.2.1 UHPC

UHPC采用湖南固力工程新材料有限责任公司的商用预混料配制。水胶比为0.18，钢纤维的含量为2%（体积占比）。钢纤维的长度为13mm，直径为0.2mm，长径比为65。配合比的其他参数并不清楚。通过单轴拉伸试验，测得UHPC材料的峰值抗拉强度 $f_t = 8.87\text{MPa}$，弹性模量 $E_c = 46800\text{MPa}$。

1.2.2 筋材

钢筋采用HRB335级螺纹钢筋。GFRP筋由海川建材有限公司提供，如图2所示。玻璃纤维材料的固化定型采用了常州天马的不饱和聚酯树脂。GFRP筋的纤维体积含量74%左右。为获得GFRP筋的力学性能参数，开展了其受拉性能实验。根据《拉挤玻璃纤维增强材料塑料杆力学性能实验方法》（GB/T 13096—2008），测得GFRP筋（直径 $d_r = 12\text{mm}$）的弹性模量 $E_r = 41.6\text{GPa}$，极限抗拉强度 $f_u = 901.86\text{MPa}$。

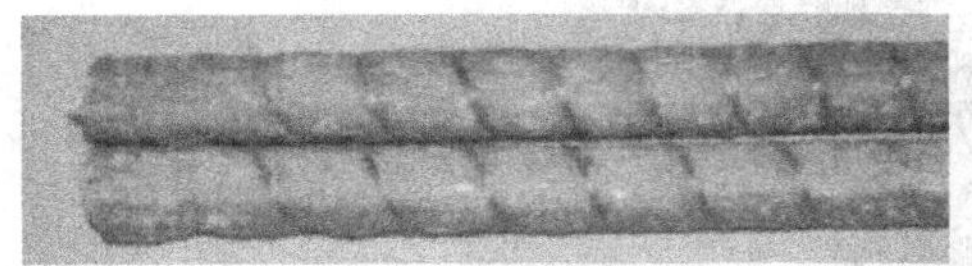

图2 GFRP筋

1.3 加载布置

本次试验由量程为50t的MTS伺服实验机进行加载。为了准确测量标距段的拉应变，在试件的标距段安装4个LVDT位移计。利用江苏东华动态应变采集箱DH5922D同时采集荷载、位移和应变结果。试验加载布置如图3所示。

图3 试验布置

2 试验结果

2.1 配钢筋UHPC试件

图4a）显示了U-1S12试件的荷载-位移曲线。加载至67.0kN时，试件左侧出现多条微裂缝，如图5所示。随后，微裂缝数量有所增加，已有裂缝长度不断增长。加载至70.0kN时，距离上端夹具的一条微裂缝发展成主裂缝（图6），但U-1S12试件承载力高于单根钢筋的受拉荷载，这是因为裂缝截面处钢纤维的桥接作用使得UHPC参与工作。主裂缝形成后测试段内微裂缝的数量不再增加，宽度也没有改变，仅有主裂缝在变宽，并往未开裂的部分扩展。由图4b）可知，U-1S12试件的荷载在达到C点后没有显著下降，这得益于钢筋的屈服强化和钢纤维良好的桥接作用。

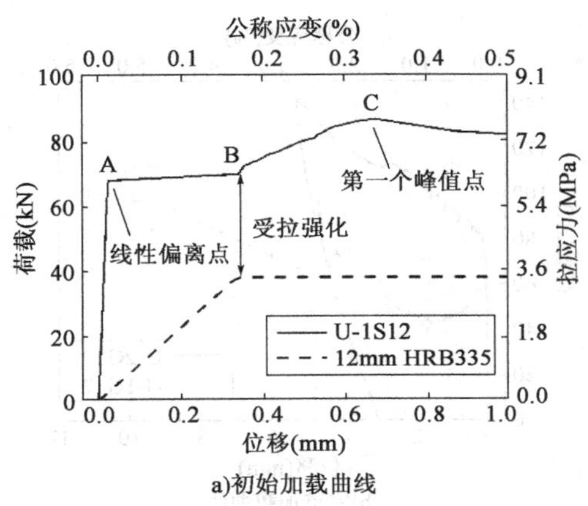

a)初始加载曲线

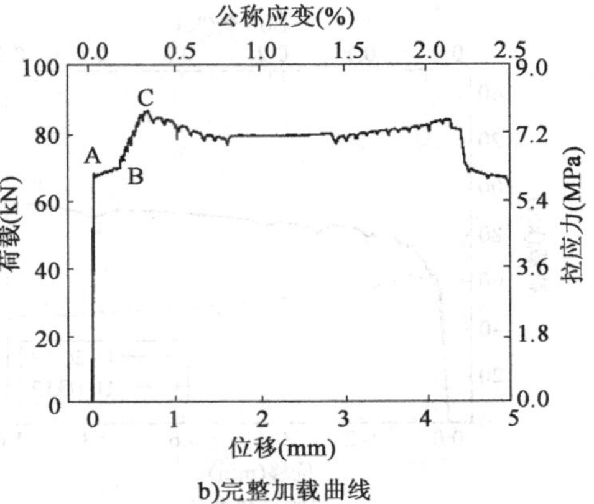

b)完整加载曲线

图4 U-1S12的荷载-位移曲线

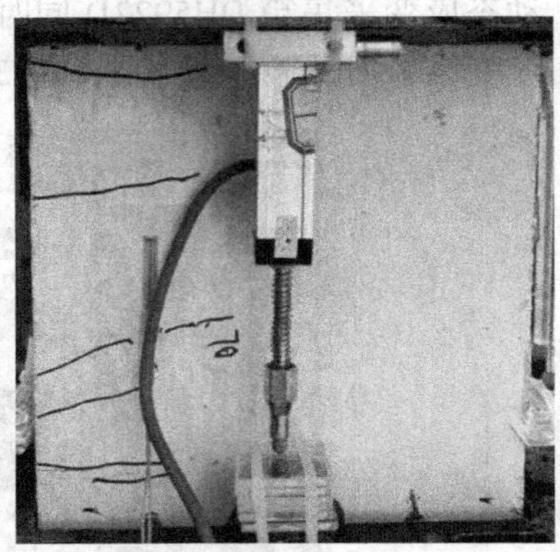

图 5　U-1S12 试件初始开裂

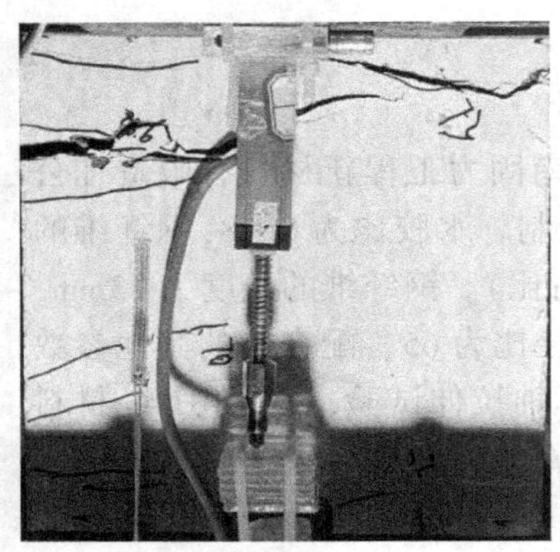

图 6　U-1S12 试件主裂缝形成

A 点之前,U-1S12 试件受拉变形较小,UHPC 和钢筋均处于弹性工作阶段,试件承担的外荷载由两种材料的刚度比例分配。线性偏离之后,进入 AB 段,该阶段为多缝开裂阶段,此时标距段内的微裂缝数量在增加,裂缝间距在减小,但裂缝宽度基本不变。值得注意的是,在多缝开裂阶段 U-1S12 试件的位移显著增加,承担的荷载却几乎不变。B 点过后为主裂缝形成阶段,进入该阶段时某条微裂缝发展成主裂缝,裂缝宽度持续增大,其余微裂缝的宽度、状态基本保持不变。

2.2　配 GFRP 筋 UHPC 试件

图 7、图 8 分别显示了 U-2G12 和 U-1G12 试件的破坏模式,其中 U-2G12 试件以端部破坏失效,U-1G12 试件以 GFRP 筋拉断失效。2 个配 GFRP 筋 UHPC 试件的荷载-位移曲线如图 9 所示。

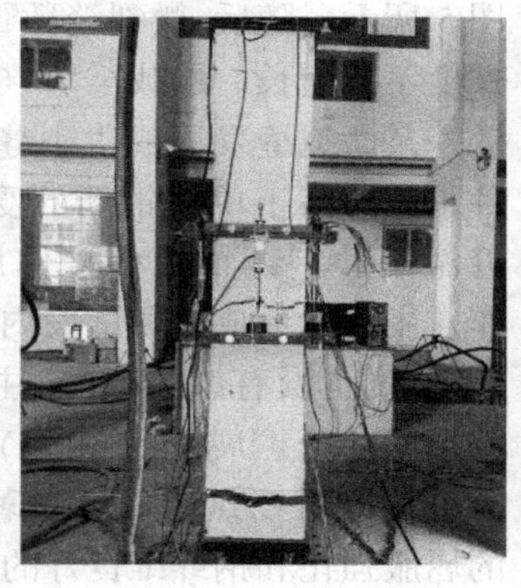

图 7　U-2G12 试件的端部破坏

图 8　U-1G12 试件 GFRP 筋断裂破坏

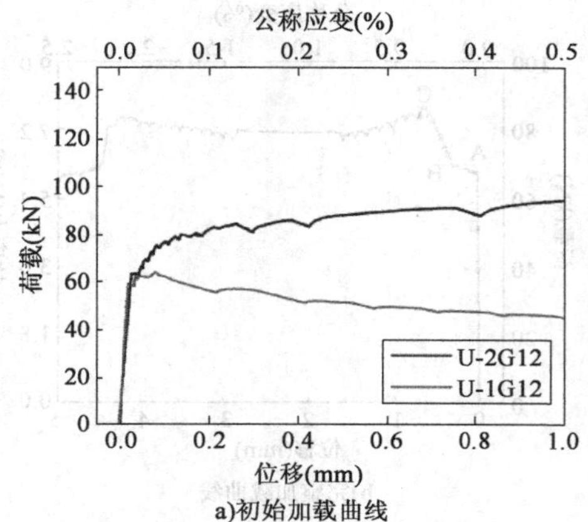

a)初始加载曲线

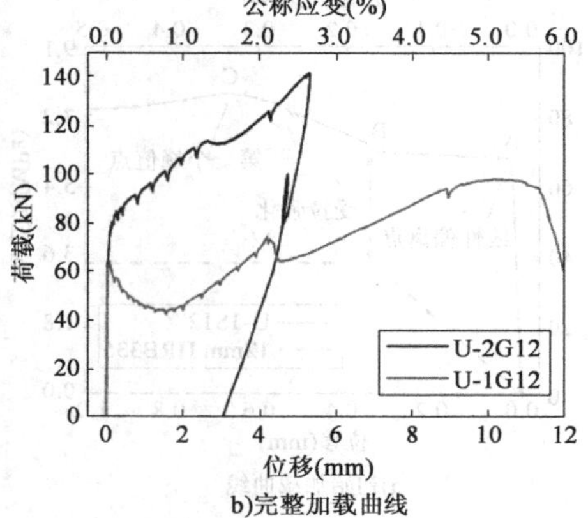

b)完整加载曲线

图 9　配 GFRP 筋试件的荷载-位移曲线

根据图9a),U-1G12的线性偏离点(60.1kN)和U-2G12试件的线性偏离点(60.0kN)很接近,但线性偏离过后U-1G12试件承担的荷载出现下降的现象,而U-2G12试件的刚度明显大于U-1G12试件。加载过程中,U-1G12试件与U-2G12试件在标距段都仅有一条持续扩展的主裂缝,这与U-1S12试件的多缝开裂有所不同。

根据图9b),U-2G12试件的极限承载力高于U-1G12试件,但极限应变却较低,这是因为U-2G12试件以端部破坏失效,破坏荷载不由标距段控制,使得标距段尚未达到峰值承载力。值得注意的是,以GFRP筋断裂失效的U-1G12试件极限承载力(97.8kN)接近单根GFRP筋的承载力(101.9kN),然而U-1G12试件的极限拉应变(0.052)却比GFRP筋单独受拉时的极限应变(0.022)大了一倍以上。另外,在加载过程中通过裂缝所在截面观察到GFRP筋附近有剥离的混凝土碎块,同时GFRP筋表面被磨平,如图10所示。这些试验现象和结果表明,GFRP筋在UHPC中发生了滑移。

图10 磨平的GFRP筋附近有混凝土碎块

3 对比分析

3.1 黏结滑移效应

如图11所示,按名义应变计算U-1G12试件破坏点的GFRP筋应力远大于GFRP筋的断裂应力,这表明,U-1G12试件在线性偏离过后呈现出荷载软化是由GFRP筋滑移引起。在UHPC中钢筋与GFRP筋相比具有更优异的黏结性能,这使得钢筋与UHPC具有良好的变形协调特性,这种黏结作用是UHPC受拉试件具有应变硬化的前提[8]。尽管开裂荷载取决于UHPC材料本身,但开裂后,裂缝截面处应力重分布的前提是需要GFRP筋与UHPC具有良好的黏结作用,才可将UHPC基体的大部分拉应力传递给GFRP筋承担。

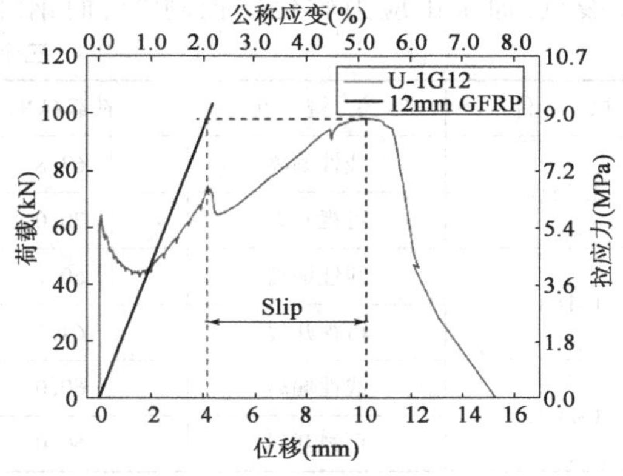

图11 U-1G12试件中GFRP筋滑移

U-1G12试件的荷载-位移曲线在线性偏离点后呈现出波动。这与GFRP筋在UHPC中的嵌入效应(wedging effect)有关。图12解释了嵌入效应。Yoo等[9]研究表明,随着GFRP筋自由端滑移的增加,未黏接部分进入黏接区域,剥离的碎块填充缝隙,使得黏结应力再次增加。本次试验的受拉试件中GFRP筋的埋入长度要远大于其他学者的试验研究,因此,随着黏结应力传递长度范围内GFRP筋滑移的增加,黏结应力为零区域的GFRP筋进入黏结应力工作范围内,使得黏结应力再次增加,重复此过程,使得荷载呈现波动的趋势,表现出与钢筋在UHPC中拔出时不同的特殊效应。与GFRP筋相比,钢筋的肋纹强度较高,埋置在UHPC中并承受拉拔力时几乎不会被损坏,因此嵌入效应不明显。

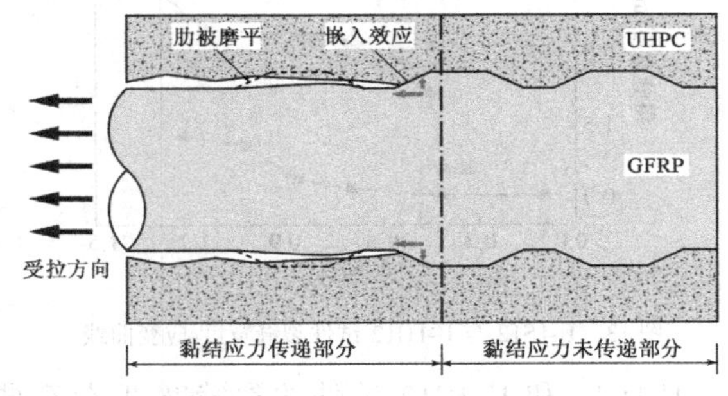

图12 嵌入效应示意

3.2 开裂特性

根据图5和图7可以看出,配钢筋UHPC试件呈现出明显的多缝开裂,而配GFRP筋UHPC试件则以单一裂缝为主。三个试件的开裂特性如

表 2 所示。由表可知,U-1S12 试件的可视开裂应变值分别是 U-1G12 和 U-2G12 试件可视开裂应变值的 4 倍和 7.4 倍。有研究表明 UHPC 材料的可视开裂点,通常由应力软化段控制[10],而钢纤维掺量越低 UHPC 的应变硬化效应越小,越早进入应力软化。这意味着,对于试件的可视开裂时机而言,在 UHPC 中配置钢筋作为增强筋更优于配置 GFRP 筋。

三个试件开裂特性表　　表 2

试　件	关　键　点	荷载(kN)	平均位移(mm)	应变(mm/mm)	裂缝宽度(mm)
U-1S12	线性偏离	67.8	0.025	1.2×10^{-4}	不可视
	可视开裂	70.0	0.341	1.7×10^{-3}	0.60
U-1G12	线性偏离	60.1	0.026	1.3×10^{-4}	不可视
	可视开裂	64.3	0.081	4.1×10^{-4}	0.08
U-2G12	线性偏离	60.0	0.027	1.3×10^{-4}	不可视
	可视开裂	60.0	0.045	2.3×10^{-4}	0.03

图 13 对比了 U-1S12 试件和 U-1G12 试件的裂缝宽度-应变曲线。尽管 U-1S12 试件可视开裂应变达到 0.0017(接近 HRB335 钢筋的屈服应变 0.00167),但可视开裂时裂缝宽度较 U-1G12 试件大,曲线较陡,裂缝宽度发展速率较大。可视开裂后配钢筋 UHPC 试件的裂缝宽度发展较快归因于以下两点:一是螺纹钢筋与 UHPC 之间的强黏结作用,使得这类受拉试件在局部宏观可视裂缝扩展时,钢筋的应变过于集中,若此时钢筋的配筋率较低,便可能导致试件过早的破坏;二是钢筋屈服后,刚度明显下降,不具备 GFRP 筋的线弹性特征。因此,从控制可视裂缝的扩展速度考虑,在 UHPC 中配置 GFRP 筋更优于钢筋。

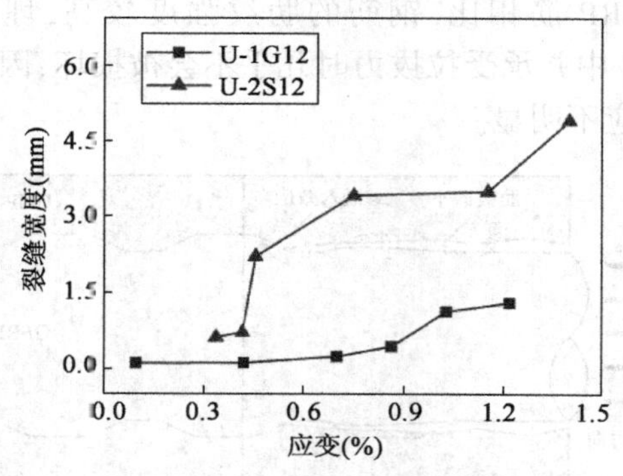

图 13　U-1S12 与 U-1G12 试件裂缝宽度-应变曲线

U-1G12 和 U-2G12 试件的裂缝宽度-荷载曲线,如图 14 所示。可以看出,在相同裂缝宽度下,U-2G12 试件的承载力大于 U-1G12 试件,这说明 GFRP 配筋率的增加提高了试件的裂缝宽度控制能力,但 U-2G12 试件的可视裂缝出现得却比 U-1G12 试件更早。

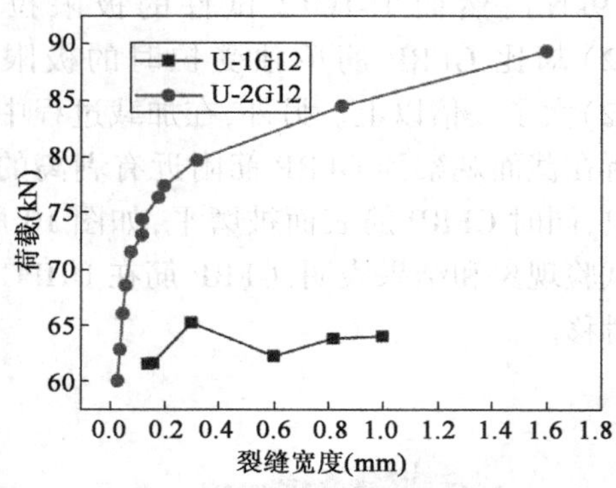

图 14　配 GFRP 筋试件的裂缝宽度-荷载曲线

4　结语

本次研究共浇筑了 3 个狗骨头型受拉试件,其中包括 1 个配钢筋 UHPC 试件,2 个配 GFRP 筋 UHPC 试件。研究内容主要包括不同试件之间的荷载-位移曲线以及开裂特性对比。根据试验结果和已有研究得出以下结论:

(1)相比于钢筋,GFRP 筋在 UHPC 中的黏结性能较差,提高 GFRP 筋与 UHPC 之间的黏结作用,是这类试件开裂后具有应变硬化特性的关键。

(2)配钢筋 UHPC 受拉试件呈现多缝开裂特征,配 GFRP 筋 UHPC 试件则以单一裂缝为主。相比于配钢筋 UHPC 试件,配 GFRP 筋 UHPC 试件的可视开裂得更早。在试件可视开裂后,得益于 GFRP 筋的线弹性特征,配 GFRP 筋 UHPC 试件的裂缝宽度控制能力要优于配钢筋 UHPC 试件。

(3)GFRP 配筋率的增加提高了配 GFRP 筋 UHPC 试件的裂缝宽度控制能力,但降低了可视开裂应变值,使试件更早地出现可视裂缝。

参考文献

[1] Xu X, Hou Z. Experimentalstudy on one-way BFRP bar-reinforced UHPC slabs under concentrated load [J]. Materials (Basel). 2020,13(14).

[2] Yoo D Y, Banthia N, Yoon Y S. Flexural behavior of ultra-high-performance fiber-reinforced concrete beams reinforced with GFRP and steel rebars [J]. Engineering Structures. 2016,111:246-262.

[3] Yoo D Y, Kwon K Y, Park J J, et al. Local bond-slip response of GFRP rebar in ultra-high-performance fiber reinforced concrete [J]. Composite Structures. 2015,120:53-64.

[4] Kunieda M, Hussein M. Enhancement ofcrack distribution of UHP-SHCC under axial tension using steel reinforcement [J]. Japan Concrete Institute. 2010,1:49-57.

[5] Roy M, Hollmann C, Wille K. Influence offiber volume fraction and fiber orientation on the uniaxial tensile behavior of rebar-reinforced Ultra-High Performance Concrete [J]. Fibers. 2019;7:67-87.

[6] Hung C C, Lee H S, Chan SN. Tension-stiffening effect in steel-reinforced UHPC composites: Constitutive model and effects of steel fibers, loading patterns, and rebar sizes [J]. Composites Part B: Engineering, 2019, 158: 269-278.

[7] Aghdasi P, Ostertag CP. Tensile fracture characteristics of Green Ultra-High Performance Fiber-Reinforced Concrete (G-UHP-FRC) with longitudinal steel reinforcement [J]. Cement and Concrete Composites. 2020(114) 103749.

[8] 张哲. 钢-配筋 UHPC 组合桥面结构弯曲受拉性能研究[D]. 长沙:湖南大学,2016.

[9] Yoo D Y, Yoon Y S. Bond behavior of GFRP and steel bars in ultra-high-performance fiber-reinforced concrete [J]. Advanced Composite Materials. 2016,26(6):493-510.

[10] 王俊颜,耿莉萍,郭君渊,刘超,刘国平. UHPC 的轴拉性能与裂缝宽度控制能力研究[J]. 哈尔滨工业大学学报,2017(12):165-169.

基于幅值总和法的系杆拱桥构件重要性系数研究

祁山白*[1] 卢 涛[2] 韩 恒[1] 惠启祥[1] 周子涵[1] 卓鸿杰[1]
(1. 长安大学公路学院;2. 保利长大工程有限公司)

摘 要 在桥梁工程的设计、建造、运维的全寿命周期中,构件重要性系数对保障桥梁的安全起着巨大的作用,但是目前所存在的各类构件安全性的评价方法存在着不全面、复杂、适用性低的问题,基于此现状,本研究梳理了目前存在的几类主流的评价方式,建立了一种通过考虑其他构件效应变化幅值总和的方式计算构件缺损后对局部其他构件的影响的方法,并通过 Midas civil 软件建立有限元模型验证该方法的可靠性。对于一系杆拱桥工程实例而言,发现中间吊杆和 1/4 跨附近的整体影响系数较大,全桥的局部影响系数从两端到和跨中递增,通过局部影响系数的分项系数计算,发现吊杆应力敏感性较大,主梁应力和挠度敏感性较小,拱肋轴力和吊杆应力敏感程度基本在同一数量级,在不同残缺模型中吊杆的断裂次数和构件重要性系数分布规律较为吻合。研究表明,在计算桥梁结构的部件重要性系数时,本文所提出基于幅值总和法的构件重要性系数评价方法是概念清晰的、利于工程应用的、有效的。

关键词 鲁棒性 构件重要性系数 幅值总和法 系杆拱桥

0　引言

对于系杆拱而言吊杆是关键传力构件,在体系中起到的作用是承受和传递荷载,吊杆长期处于加载卸载循环以及受到环境侵蚀的不利作用,使其容易产生锈蚀甚至断裂,从而导致体系整体破坏,造成严重的桥梁倒塌事故。因此探究防止结构因局部破坏而导致结构整体倒塌的设计方法,成为目前相关学科和学者们亟待解决的问题[1]。在意外荷载作用下,结构不产生与其破坏原因不相称的垮塌的能力被称为“鲁棒性”[2]。国内外学者对鲁棒性的定量方法研究较多。基于确定性评价指标有 Starossek 通过结构倒塌过程能量的释放与吸收提出的能量法评价指标等[3]。基于概率性评价指标主要有:Frangopo 基于结构损伤前后的失效概率提出了冗余度指标[4]。Liao 等人在考虑结构倒塌的概率和经济性以及社会影响的角度下提出了基于风险的评价指标[5]。

构件重要性系数是鲁棒性研究的基础,结构构件重要性指的是结构构件的性能退化对整体结构系统所产生的影响作用大小[6]。构件重要性的评价方法分为考虑荷载作用和不考虑荷载作用两大类。不考虑荷载作用的研究成果有胡晓斌[7]把构件依次拆除后的退化率作为评价指标,这种评价方法存在两个问题,一是结构的频率是多阶的,构件的拆除前后频率次序会发生变化,二是对基频影响不大的构件也有较大重要性系数的可能。Agarwal 等[3]基于刚度矩阵行列式提出了整体性指标,该指标有工程含义不明确的缺点。张誉等[9]用层次分析法(AHP 法),该方法有利于经验法进行规范,减小主观性影响,但是对应用者的依赖性还是较大。考虑了荷载作用的研究成果有 Gharaibeh 等[10]提出的利用可靠度计算构件重要性系数的方法计算繁杂适用性不强。胡晓斌等[11]用平均应力比和稳定退化系数,从理想材料的平均应力和结构稳定性的角度考虑。刘西拉[12]以能量为基础建立了反映构件对结构应变能变化大小的重要性系数,这种方法的特点是计算方便但是由于其开放性的特点不利于进行方案对比。

1　构件重要性评价理论

考虑荷载作用的评价方法是目前更加合理和受到认可的构件重要性评定方法。其中针对不同的性能指标提出的方法各有优缺点。但是现有的方法应用于拱桥体系工程实例时计算繁琐,过程复杂,对实际工程建设的应用性不强,因此本文在考虑荷载作用条件下提出一种基于幅值总和法的新构件重要性评价方法,该方法具有以下特点:

(1)考虑外荷载作用,具有确定的评价指标,计算概念清晰。

(2)评价指标具有普遍性,能够进行定性算,可以方便地在实际工程中进行应用。

(3)在考虑荷载作用的基础上综合考虑构件对结构系统的作用和对其他构件的影响。

幅值总和法考虑了当构件缺损时对结构体系整体性和局部影响所提出的一种评价指标,该指标由整体性影响系数 M_i 和局部影响系数 N_i 组成。

1.1　整体性影响系数

本文对整体性影响系数通过承载力 γ 来确定。构件 i 在缺损以后承载能力产生,以变化幅值表征整体影响系数。根据实际工程确定破坏准则,通过放大活载系数 λ 控制结构响应,并根据下式确定结构达到极限承载力时的活载放大系数 λ。

$$S_\lambda \leqslant [S] \tag{1}$$

式中:λ——活载放大系数;

S_λ——放大系数等于 λ 时构件某一效应;

$[S]$——构件某一效应的极限值。

结构在构件缺损前后的极限承载力发生变化,通过下式确定整体性影响系数:

$$M_i = 1 - \frac{\gamma'}{\gamma} \tag{2}$$

$$\gamma = Q_D + \lambda Q_L \tag{3}$$

式中:i——缺损构件号;

M_i——i 号构件的整体性影响系数;

γ——完整模型结构极限承载;

γ'——缺损模型结构极限承载力;

Q_D——恒载;

D_L——活载。

1.2　局部性影响系数

系杆拱桥是一个内部高次超静定结构,在某些部件缺损以后结构已经具有一定冗余度,不一定会发生立即失效,而是产生内力重分布,其他构件会根据所处的位置、连接关系等因素产生不同程度影响。当某一构件缺损以后结构内力变化波及范围广，幅值大则说明该构件在体系体系中具有重要作用，其构件重要性系数相对大。在以往文献中对其他构件的影响评价指标是效应最大值为代表值，表征构件缺损以后其他构件影响大小。但是这种方法的弊端是，当结构设计不合理或者有限元模型计算不合理时，会出现个别构件效应极值，结果的稳定性和可靠性不能保证，会与实际情况不符的状况。因此本位提出采用效应幅值总和法来全面考虑构件缺失对其他构件的影响。

针对不同的桥型，在计算局部影响系数时考虑的效应种类和数量不同，从而产生不同的分项系数，本文定义某一构件缺损后局部影响系数的第 e 种分项系数用下式进行计算：

$$n_e = \frac{\sum_{j=1}^{z} |X_j - X'_j|}{\sum_{j=1}^{z} |X_j|} \tag{4}$$

式中：z——所考虑效应对应的单元或节点号；

e——考虑的效应种类数；

X_j——完整结构第 e 类效应值；

X'_j——缺损结构第 e 类效应。

为了综合考虑各分项系数引入雷达图评价法，雷达图评价方法下结构的局部影响系数 N_i 用下式进行计算：

$$N_i = A_{ne} \tag{5}$$

式中：N_i——构件 i 缺损时的局部影响系数；

A_{ne}——构件 i 缺损时考虑的 e 种类效应 n_e 通过雷达图评价方法得到的面积。

针对不同的构件，对整体承载力和局部构件的影响趋势是一致的，所以考虑构件的重要性评价指标时对整体承载力的贡献度 M_i 和对其他构件的影响程度 N_i 要协调考虑，规定构件重要性系数评价指标：

$$K_i = M_i N_i \tag{6}$$

式中：K_i——第 i 号构件的重要性系数。

2 工程实例计算

2.1 工程背景

2.1.1 总体布置

根据上述原理所提出的重要性系数计算方法，对一座系杆拱桥进行构件重要性计算，以杭甬运河桥为例。

杭绍台高速跨杭甬运河桥（图 1），采用系杆拱桥方案，分左右两幅布置。平面位于半径 1290m 的圆曲线上，两侧拱肋与系杆均采用直线布置。拱肋净跨 102m，矢高 20m，矢跨比为 1:5.1，主拱轴线采用二次抛物线（相对于系杆中心）。左幅桥桥宽 20.5m，横向设两片拱肋，拱肋横向间距 19m。单片拱肋共设 18 根吊杆，吊杆间距 5m。横向两拱肋之间设 1 道一字型横撑和 4 道 K 撑以保证拱肋横向稳定，横撑采用圆管型截面。系杆采用钢箱型断面，两侧系杆间设置普通横梁，在拱脚处设置端横梁。

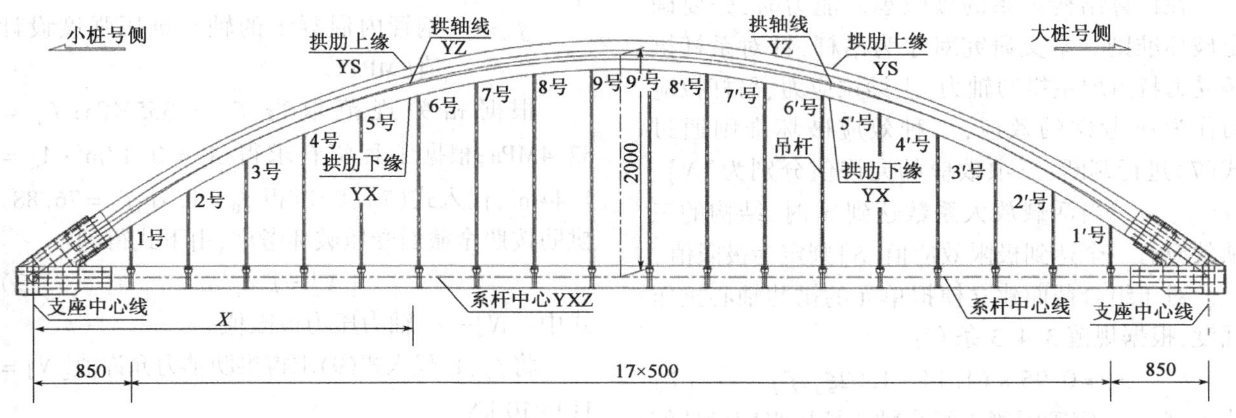

图 1 桥型总体布置

2.1.2 有限元模型

建立有限元模型，采用梁单元和桁架单元进行模拟，根据研究需要，总共建立 1 个全桥模型 18 个缺损模型，全桥模型共建立 680 个节点 789 个单元，如图 2 所示。

拱肋截面和系杆在拱脚段单元是 Q355 钢和 C50 混凝土组合结构，建立组合截面，在进行 SPC 计算时以钢材为基准材料建立。

考虑到桥梁两侧的吊杆具有对称受力规律基本一致,又为了使得计算结果更具有可靠性,故采用朝向大桩号方向的右侧 18 根吊杆进行重要性分析。从小里程到大里程编号依次为 1 号 ~18 号吊杆,如图 3 所示。

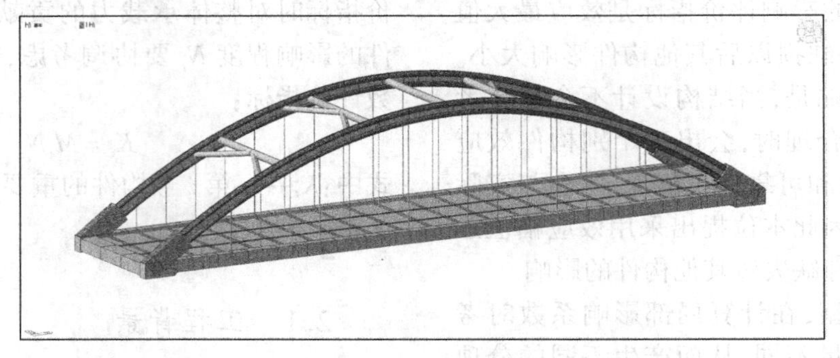

图 2　有限元模型

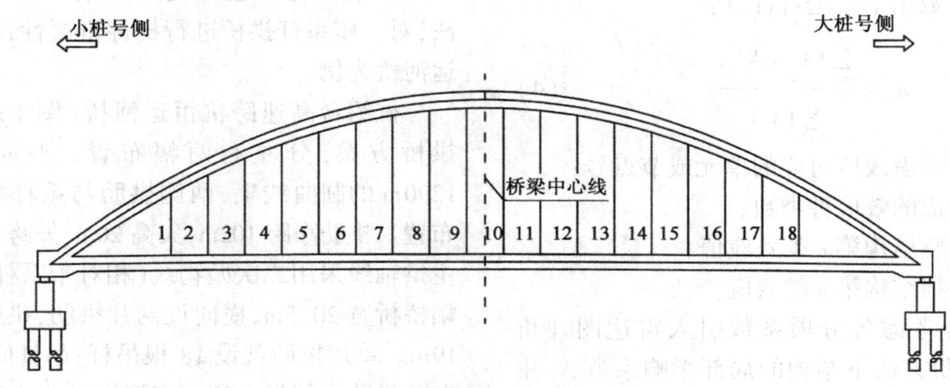

图 3　吊杆编号

2.2　整体性影响系数

2.2.1　破坏准则

在计算结构体系的极限承载能力时,先要确定破坏准则。本文研究对象为吊杆,针对系杆拱桥受力特点取主拱肋轴力、主梁拉应力、吊杆拉应力作为所考虑的效应,三种效应破坏准则通过式(7)进行判断,三项效应的允许值分别为$[N]$、$[\sigma_1]$、$[\sigma_2]$当活载放大系数达到 λ 时,结构的三项效应有一个达到极限效应值$[S]$判定为极限值。

对于组合截面建立模拟单元的拱肋轴心抗压强度,根据规范 3.4.3 条有:

$$f_{sc}=0.96\times(1.14+1.02\xi_0)f_{cd} \tag{7}$$

式中:f_{sc}——钢管混凝土组合轴心抗压强度设计值(MPa);

ξ_0——钢管混凝土约束效应系数设计值,按式(8)计算。

$$\xi_0=\frac{A_s f_{sd}}{A_c f_{cd}} \tag{8}$$

式中:A_s——钢管混凝土钢管的截面面积(m^2);

f_{sd}——钢管的抗拉强度设计值(MPa);

A_c——钢管内混凝土的截面面积(m^2);

f_{cd}——钢管内混凝土的轴心抗压强度设计值(MPa)。

根据相关规范取得 $f_{sd}=355$MPa;$f_{cd}=32.4$MPa;根据工程资料求得 $A_s=0.17m^2$;$A_C=1.44m^2$;代入式(7)(8)求得 $\xi_0=1.31$;$f_{sc}=76.88$,拱肋按照全截面受压破坏考虑,由下式得到:

$$[N]=f_{sc}A_c \tag{9}$$

式中:$[N]$——轴力压力极限值。

将f_{sc}、A_c 代入式(9)求得拱肋轴力允许值$[N]=110\times10^3$kN

根据相关规范主梁和吊杆应力极限值有:

$$[\sigma_1]=355\text{MPa}$$

$$[\sigma_2]=1860\text{MPa}$$

2.2.2　活载放大系数

为了计算方便,求解极限承载力时对自重、二期、汽车荷载按照承载能力极限状态下的基本组合来考虑荷载工况。在全桥模型中通过调整活载系数 λ，使得结构效应逐渐达到2.2.1确定的极限值[S]，将加载过程中的最大效应值和极限值之比作为加载效率，结果如表1和图4所示。

不同活载放大系数下结构响应　表1

活荷载放大系数 λ	主梁最大应力 σ_1(MPa)	拱肋最大轴力 N(10^3kN)	吊杆最大应力 σ_2(MPa)
1	20.00	-27.23	685.00
4	43.40	-30.19	792.90
8	80.90	-34.75	958.90
12	119.00	-39.31	1125.00
16	157.00	-43.86	1291.00
20	194.00	-48.42	1457.00
24	232.00	-52.11	1623.00
28	270.00	-56.47	1789.00
29.694	286.00	-59.46	1860.00

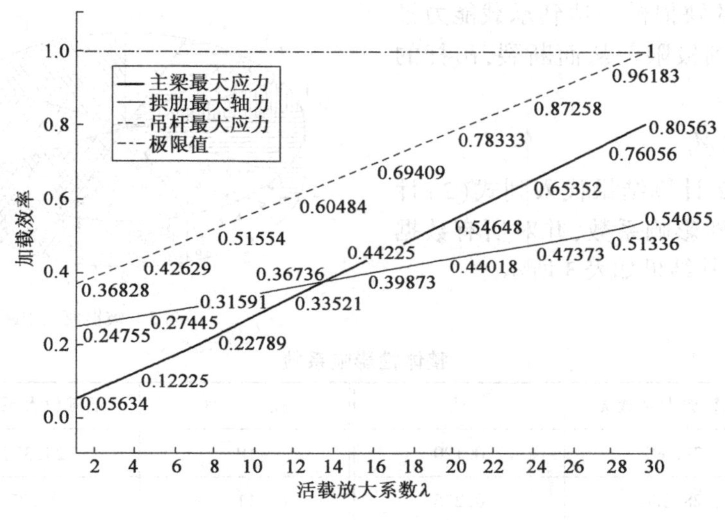

图4　加载效率

随着活载放大系数的增大，拱肋轴力先快速增加然后缓慢增加，未达到极限值[N]，主梁应力增长较快但未达到极限值[σ_1]，单位吊杆应力几乎是线性增长直至达到极限值[σ_2]，此时认为结构体系达到承载能力极限状态无法继续承受荷载，得到对应的活载放大系数 $\lambda=29.694$。

根据研究需要建立在去除1号～18号吊杆后的18个缺损模型，按照1.1所述的方法确定对应模型的活载放大系数 λ_i，并将该加载效率下的三个效应的最大值与极限值之比作为加载效率值，结果如表2所示。

缺损模型活载放大系数　表2

模　型	活荷载放大系数	主梁加载效	拱肋加载效率	吊杆加载效率	破坏构件
1	28.692	0.81	0.54	1	9号吊杆
2	27.384	0.77	0.53	1	3号吊杆
3	25.246	0.69	0.49	1	4号吊杆
4	23.073	0.71	0.50	1	3号吊杆
5	25.327	0.66	0.48	1	4号吊杆
6	25.562	0.70	0.49	1	7号吊杆

续上表

模　型	活荷载放大系数	主梁加载效	拱肋加载效率	吊杆加载效率	破坏构件
7	23.449	0.64	0.47	1	8号吊杆
8	23.358	0.64	0.46	1	9号吊杆
9	21.349	0.62	0.46	1	10号吊杆
10	21.335	0.64	0.46	1	9号吊杆
11	23.37	0.64	0.46	1	10号吊杆
12	23.443	0.64	0.47	1	11号吊杆
13	24.563	0.70	0.49	1	12号吊杆
14	25.375	0.66	0.48	1	15号吊杆
15	23.125	0.71	0.50	1	16号吊杆
16	25.289	0.69	0.49	1	15号吊杆
17	27.418	0.77	0.53	1	16号吊杆
18	28.693	0.81	0.54	1	9号吊杆

可以看出在不同的缺损模型达到承载能力极限状态时都是吊杆达到极限值从而断裂,吊杆的断裂频数如图5所示。

2.2.3　影响系数 M_i

将2.2.1和2.2.2计算结果代入到式(2)计算出各个吊杆的整体性影响系数,并对所有数据在列向上进行归一化,其结果如表3所示。

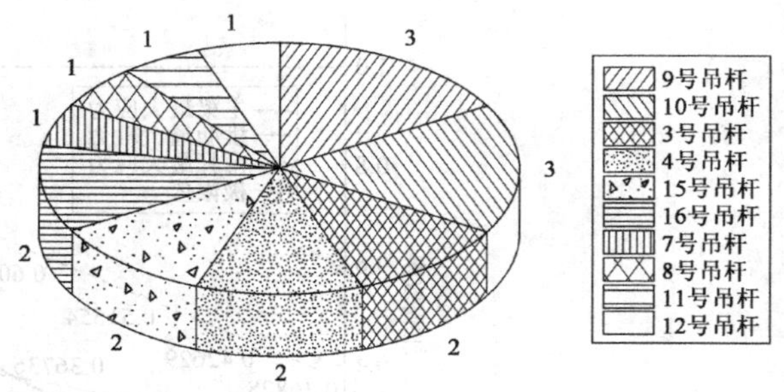

图5　破损模型中断裂吊杆频数

整体性影响系数　　表3

模　型	活载放大系数λ	M_i	模　型	活载放大系数λ	M_i
1	29.692	0.120	10	23.335	1.000
2	28.384	0.276	11	23.37	0.757
3	25.246	0.532	12	23.443	0.748
4	26.073	0.792	13	25.563	0.614
5	24.327	0.522	14	24.375	0.517
6	25.562	0.494	15	26.125	0.786
7	23.449	0.747	16	25.289	0.527
8	23.358	0.758	17	28.418	0.272
9	23.349	0.998	18	29.693	0.120

各吊杆的整体影响性系数分布如图6所示。

从图6可以看出,各吊杆正整体性影响系数 M_i 分布特点是中间吊杆的重要性比两端吊杆大,跨中两根吊杆重要性最大,1/4跨处4号吊杆和15号吊杆重要性也较大,1号和18号吊杆对整体承载能力的贡献度最小。

2.3　局部影响系数

2.3.1　分项系数

根据2.3述所系杆拱桥的受力特点,计算构件的局部影响分项系数时采取的计算效应为:①n_1主梁的应力,②n_2主梁挠度,③n_3拱的轴力,④n_4拱的挠度,⑤n_5吊杆应力。

与计算整体性影响系数 M_i 不同，在计算局部影响系数 N_i 时在对应的缺损模型中以活载系数 $\lambda=1$加载，通过 18 个缺损模型的分析，可以得到不同缺损模型下对五个效应。将数据读取，绘制成折线图如图 7 ~ 图 16 所示。

从图 7 到图 10 可以看出，不同的缺损模型中，主梁应力、挠度幅值分布呈现出中间大两端小的特点，意味着任一构件的缺损对主梁挠度和应力的影响从跨中向两边由大变小；从图 11、图 12 可以看出，不管是哪个构件的确实对各段拱肋轴力的影响幅值相近；从图 13、图 14 可以看出，吊杆的断裂对吊杆附近的拱肋挠度影响远大于其他位置的拱肋；从图 15、图 16 可以看出，吊杆断裂以后相邻的 6 根吊杆影响显著，其影响范围由近及远逐步减小。

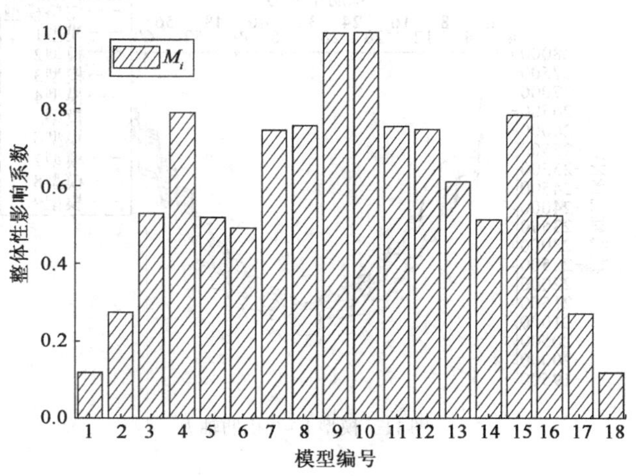

图 6 整体性影响系数 M_i 分布

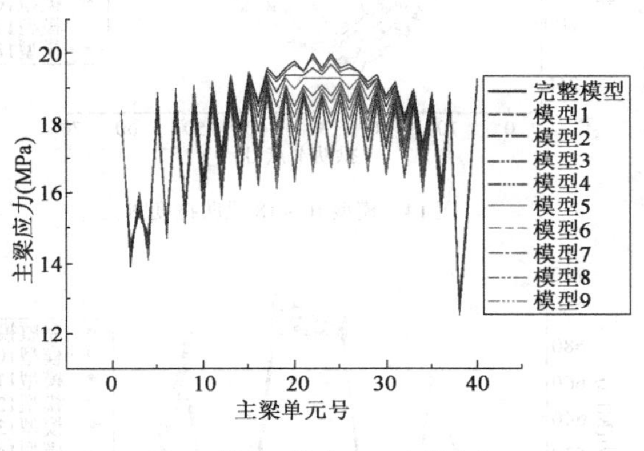

图 7 模型 1 模型 1 ~9 主梁应力

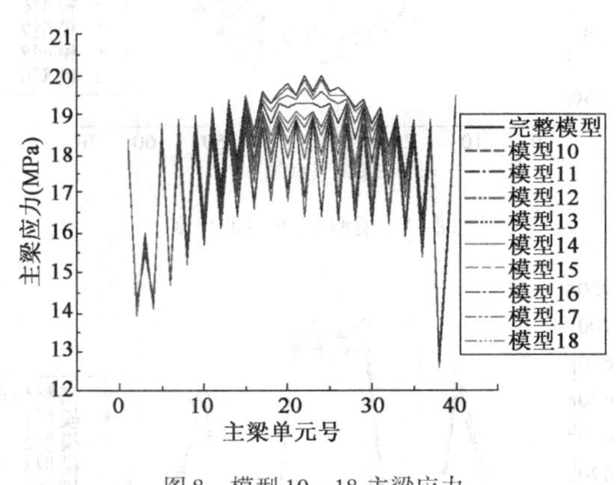

图 8 模型 10 ~ 18 主梁应力

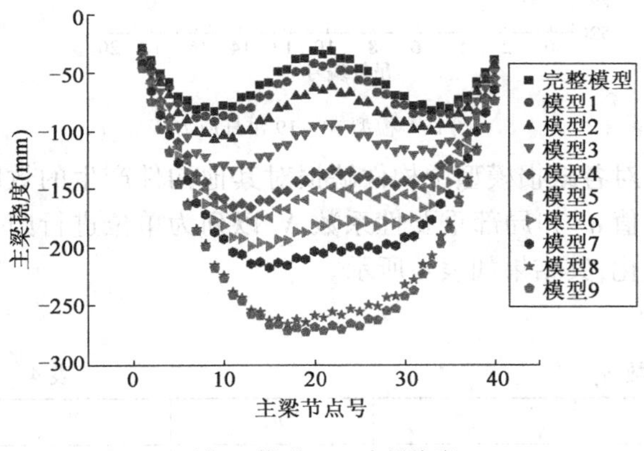

图 9 模型 1 ~9 主梁挠度

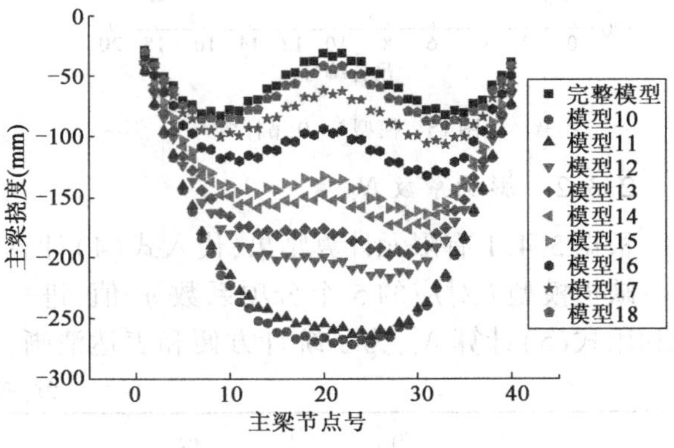

图 10 模型 10 ~ 18 主梁挠度

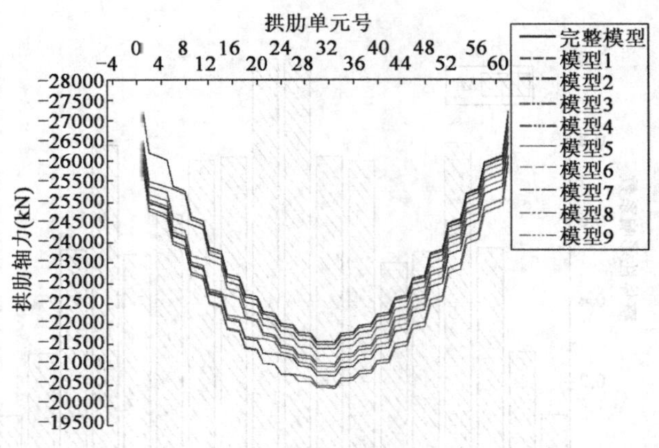

图 11　模型 1~9 拱肋轴力

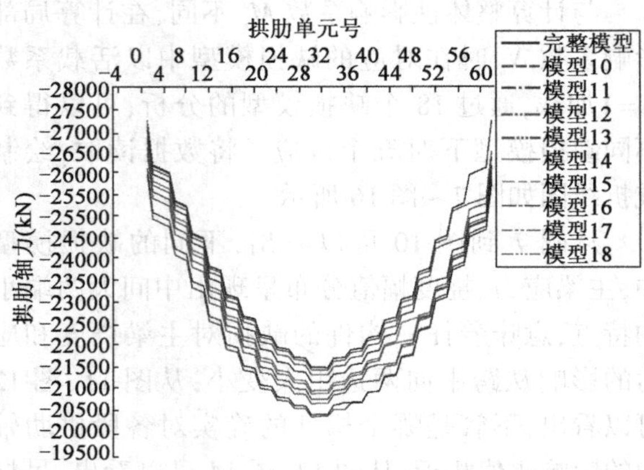

图 12　模型 1~18 拱肋轴力

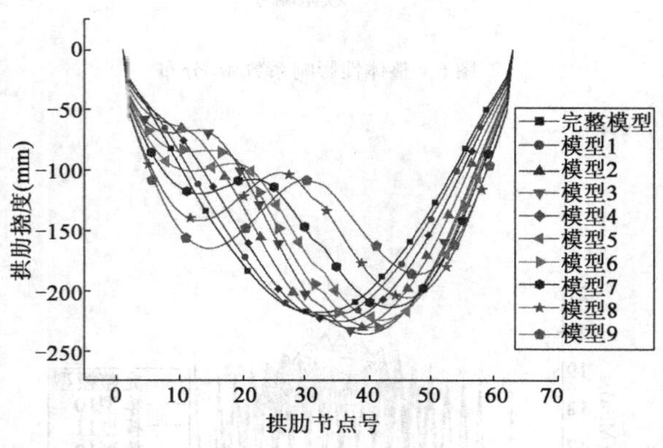

图 13　模型 1~9 拱肋挠度

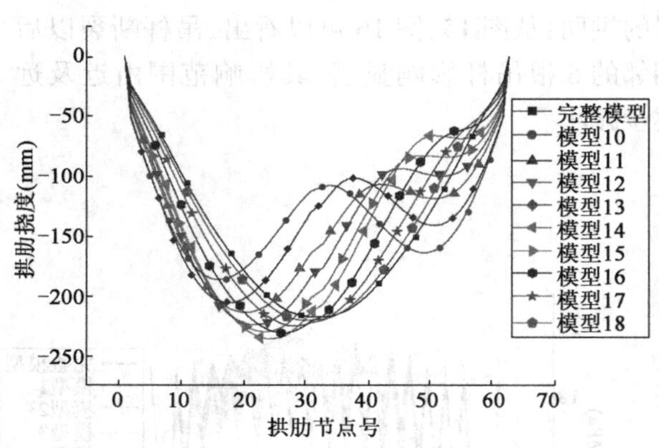

图 14　模型 10~18 拱肋挠度图

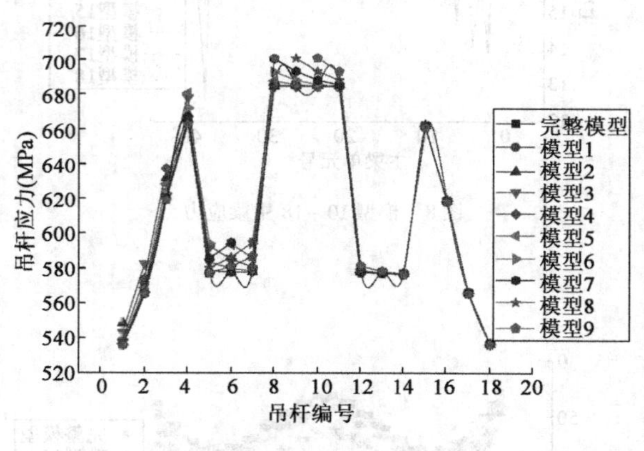

图 15　模型 1~9 吊杆应力

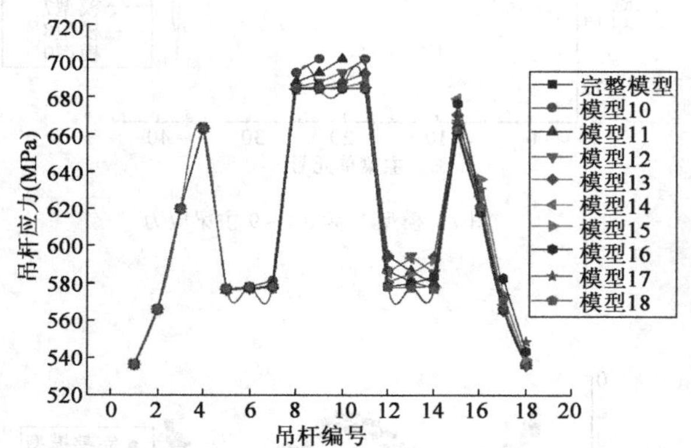

图 16　模型 10~19 吊杆应力

2.3.2　影响系数 N_i

根据 2.4.1 有限元计算结果,代入式(4)计算每一缺损模型 i 对应的 5 个分项系数 n_e 值,进一步利用式(5)计算 N_i,为了统计方便和表达清晰,对各缺损模型中构件缺损对其他构件产生的效应值 n_e 和局部重要性系数 N_i 以列为单位进行归一化,其结果如表 4 所示。

分项系数 n_e　　表 4

i	n_1	n_2	n_3	n_4	n_5	N_i
1	0.053	0.049	0.083	0.190	0.144	0.012
2	0.164	0.144	0.190	0.348	0.527	0.078

续上表

i	n_1	n_2	n_3	n_4	n_5	N_i
3	0.326	0.288	0.339	0.548	0.808	0.167
4	0.499	0.461	0.509	0.747	0.924	0.451
5	0.562	0.524	0.558	0.752	0.952	0.453
6	0.661	0.639	0.662	0.810	0.965	0.502
7	0.751	0.732	0.745	0.831	0.985	0.525
8	0.969	0.960	0.964	0.997	0.997	0.859
9	1.000	1.000	1.000	0.993	0.998	1.000
10	0.989	1.000	1.000	0.995	1.000	0.997
11	0.954	0.960	0.964	1.000	0.997	0.854
12	0.724	0.732	0.744	0.839	0.983	0.549
13	0.637	0.639	0.662	0.822	0.965	0.498
14	0.527	0.524	0.557	0.782	0.950	0.451
15	0.462	0.461	0.509	0.791	0.924	0.433
16	0.291	0.288	0.339	0.589	0.804	0.218
17	0.151	0.144	0.189	0.371	0.526	0.079
18	0.057	0.049	0.083	0.195	0.141	0.012

表中的意义是：每一行代表对应的残缺模型 i 中，缺失该构架时对主梁应力，主梁挠度、拱肋轴力、拱肋挠度、吊杆应力的影响大小；每一列代表对于不同的效应 n_i，不同的残缺模型下影响大小。

为了比较的直观方便，根据表4绘制雷达图如图17～图22所示，由于数据量较大故将3个模型下各个效应值表现在一个雷达图上。

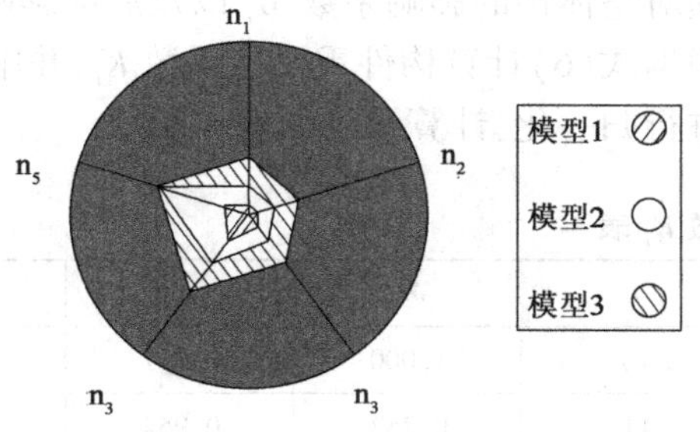

图17　模型1模型2模型3雷达图

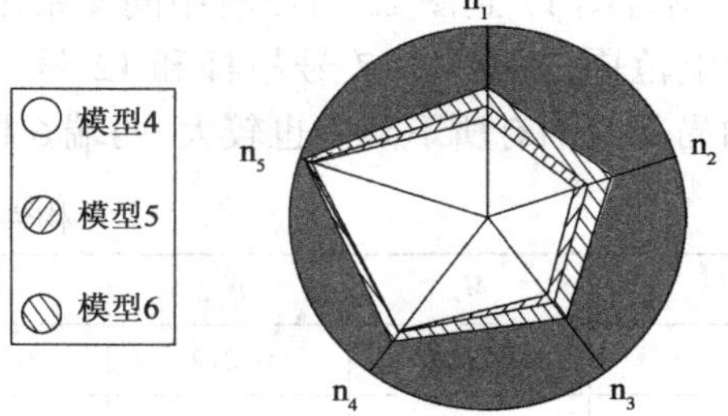

图18　模型1模型2模型3雷达图

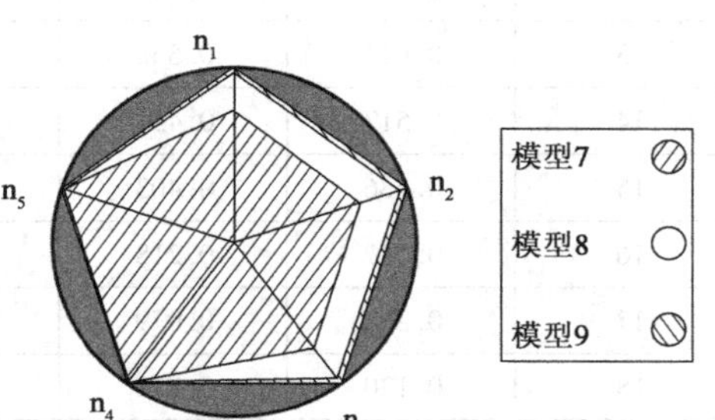

图19　模型1模型2模型3雷达图

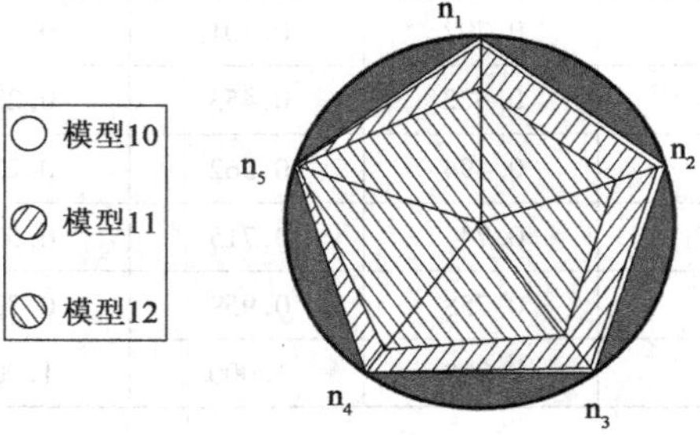

图20　模型1模型2模型3雷达图

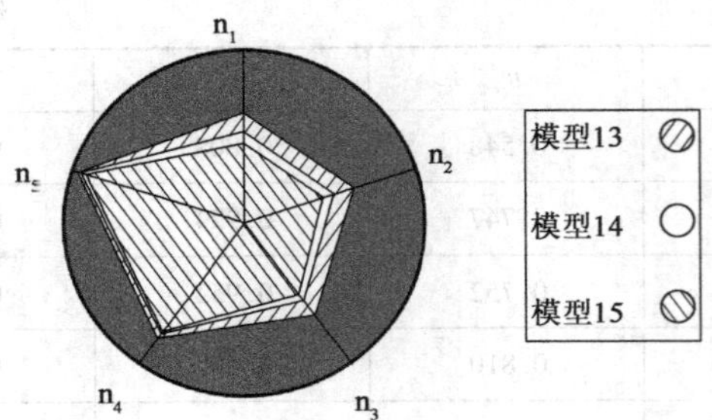

图 21　模型 1 模型 2 模型 3 雷达图

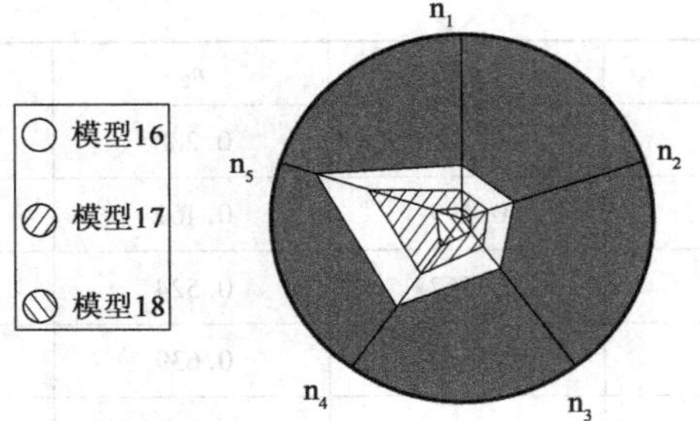

图 22　模型 1 模型 2 模型 3 雷达图

雷达图的半径都是 1,每三个模型数据绘制在同一张图上,用不同的颜色区分,每种颜色的面积表示对应模型下求得的局部影响系数,每个 5 边形的顶点长短反应该模型下对全桥 5 个效应的影响程度大小,通过雷达图可以发现:构件缺损后对 5 个分项系数中 n_4、n_5 较大,基本在在同一量级,即对拱的挠度和吊杆拉应力影响最大;构件缺损后对 n_1、n_2、n_2 影响较小,三者基本在同一量级,即对主梁应力、主梁挠度、拱肋轴力影响相对较小;中部吊杆(7 号 ~ 12 号)缺损后,对 5 种效应的影响都较为显著,两端吊杆除了对吊杆应力重分布影响较大外对其他 4 个效应影响不显著。

根据表 4 的结果可以得到局部影响系数 N_i 的分布规律如图 23 所示。

5 个分项系数综合考虑得出的局部影响系数表明,对于系杆拱桥,总体上看从两端到中跨吊杆影响范围由小变大吊杆的局部影响的大主要分成 3 个梯度,结合图 17 到图 22 可以看中间 4 根吊杆缺损时影响范围广,4 号 ~ 7 号吊杆和 12 号 ~ 15 号吊杆的局部范围有所下降但也较大,两端 6 根吊杆的缺损影响范围和幅度都最小。

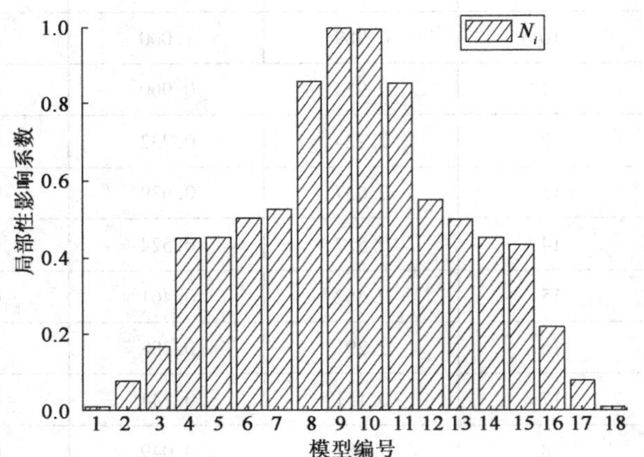

图 23　N_i 分布

2.4　重要性系数 K_i

根据 3.3 和 3.4 部分的研究,得出了构件缺损对整体性的影响系数 M_i 以及局部影响系数 N_i,根据式(6)计算构件重要性系数 K_i,并用在列向上进行归一化,计算结果如表 5 所示。

构件重要性系数 K_i 表　　表 5

i	M_i	N_i	K_i	i	M_i	N_i	K_i
1	0.120	0.012	0.001	10	1.000	0.997	0.998
2	0.276	0.078	0.021	11	0.757	0.954	0.723
3	0.532	0.167	0.089	12	0.748	0.649	0.486
4	0.792	0.401	0.318	13	0.614	0.558	0.343
5	0.522	0.453	0.237	14	0.517	0.451	0.234
6	0.494	0.562	0.278	15	0.786	0.403	0.317
7	0.747	0.715	0.535	16	0.527	0.218	0.115
8	0.758	0.959	0.728	17	0.272	0.079	0.022
9	0.998	1.000	1.000	18	0.120	0.012	0.001

根据上表可以绘制全桥一侧 18 个吊杆的构件重要性系数 K_i 的分布图 2-24。

构件重要性系数是整体性影响系数 M_i 和局部影响系数 N_i 共同影响下产生,可以看出构件整体上是中间吊杆的构件重要性系数大两端小，在1/4跨附近的4号、5号以及15号、16号吊杆也具有较大重要性系数，跨中两根吊杆的重要性系数是平均值的2.8倍是全桥最重要的构件，将本文得到结果和文献[13]对比图5中得到断裂频数分布图，发现构件的重要性系数和断裂频数分布较为吻合，也和其他学者利用已有理论对系杆拱桥吊杆重要性分析计算结果的分布规律基本吻合[13]。

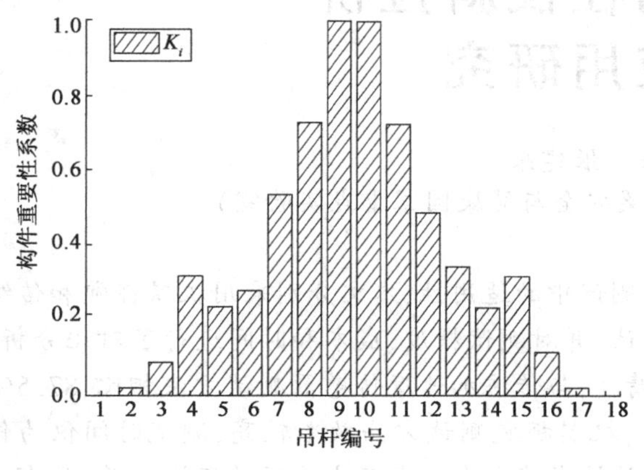

图24 吊杆编号

3 结语

本文总结和回顾了学者们对鲁棒性研究，在其他学者已有的研究的基础上，提出一种新的构件重要性评价方法。该方法重点在于考虑结构不同种类影响效应时，对各个构件的效应幅值进行总和，这样更加全面和稳定地考虑了构件缺损对于其他构件的影响。该方法从整体和局部两个方面着手考虑构件的影响，具有全面性和稳定性的特点。研究结果表明：18根吊杆整体性重要性系数，呈波浪形分布，中间吊杆和1/4处的吊杆位于峰值处，说明在该位置处的吊杆对结构承载能力的贡献度相对较大；计算局部影响系数 N_i 时，发现不同类型的分项系数对构件缺损的敏感程度不同，拱的挠度和吊杆的应力在构件缺失后幅值大；通过对不同缺损模型的分析，发现主梁应力、挠度呈现有两端到中间逐渐变大的特点，拱肋轴力在全范围影响相近，拱肋挠度和吊杆力在构件缺损位置附近影响大，随着距离增大影响幅度很快消失；K_i 的分布特点呈现三个极值点，分别是跨中和两个1/4点附近，与缺损模型中的吊杆断裂频数统计结果较为吻合；利用本文提出的方法进行同一类桥的计算，其结果与该领域学者对类似问题的分析结果相近，表明该方法具有可靠性和适用性。另外，本文存在以下不足：(1)本文只在静力条件下进行了分析，动力荷载下的重要性分析还有待研究；(2)整体影响系数和局部影响系数权重还有待研究；(3)计算 M_i 和 N_i 时选择的构件效应类型、数量可以进行进一步研究；(4)本文是针对系杆拱桥这类桥型进行了吊杆重要性研究，基于本文提出的方法对于其他桥型的、其他部件适用性还有待于进一步研究。

参考文献

[1] 姜健，张其杰，吕大刚，等. 建筑结构鲁棒性定量判定方法的研究进展[J/OL]. 建筑钢结构进展：1-21[2021-11-25].

[2] Giorgio Anitori1, Joan Ramon Casas2, Michel Ghosn, et al. Redundancy and Robustness in the Design and Evaluation of Bridges: European and North American Perspectives[J]. Journal of Bridge Engineering, 2013, 18(12): 1241-1251.

[3] Starossek U. Progressive Collapse of Structures[J]. Collapse Properties, 2009, 16:. 113-117.

[4] Frangopol D M, Curley J P. Effects of Damage and Redundancy on Structural Reliability[J]. Journal of Structural Engineering, 1987, 113(7): 1533-1549.

[5] Liao, K W, Wen Y K, et al. Evaluation of 3Ds-teel moment frames under earthquake excitations II: reliability and redundancy[J] Journal of Structural Engineering, ASCE, 2007, 133(3): 471-480.

[6] Hunley CT, Harik I E. Structural redundancy evaluation of steel tub girder bridges.

[7] 胡晓斌. 新型多面体空间刚架结构抗连续倒塌性能研究[D]. 北京：清华大学，2007.

[8] Agarwal J, Blockley D, Woodman N. Durability of 3-dimensional Trusses[J]. Structural Safety, 2001, 23(3): 203-202.

[9] 张誉，李立树. 旧房可靠性的模糊综合评判[J]. 建筑结构学报，1997, 18(5): 12-20.

[10] Gharaibeh E S, Frangopol D M, Onoufriou T. Reliability-based importance assessment of structural members with applications to complex structures [J]. Computers &

Structures,2002,80(12):1113-1131.

[11] 胡晓斌,钱稼茹.结构连续倒塌分析与设计方法综述[J].建筑结构,2006(S1):573-577.

[12] 张雷明,刘西拉.框架结构能量流网络及其初步应用[J].土木工程学报,2007,40(3):45-49.

[13] 毕来运.吊杆破断对系杆拱桥力学性能的影响研究[D].兰州:兰州交通大学,2019.

基于机器视觉的在役斜拉桥索力测试应用研究

何连海* 刘 朵 张建东

(苏交科集团股份有限公司在役长大桥梁安全与健康国家重点实验室)

摘 要 为研究机器视觉技术在运营期斜拉桥索力测试中的适用性,本文分别采用机器视觉和传统加速度传感器测量方法对一座在役斜拉桥索力进行了测试,并对测试精度、成本和时间进行了对比分析。结果表明,机器视觉技术用于斜拉桥索力测试具有较高精度,与传统加速度传感器测试方法相比,87.5%的测试样本相对偏差小于5%,最大相对偏差仅为5.7%;机器视觉测试方法效率较高,测试时间仅为传统加速度传感器的50%,同时直接成本降低60%以上。该技术将会在未来产生较高的经济效益,具有广泛的应用前景。

关键词 斜拉桥 索力测试 机器视觉 加速度传感器

0 引言

拉索是斜拉桥重要的受力构件,斜拉桥在运营过程中经受车辆循环往复荷载以及不良大气环境的腐蚀作用,容易导致拉索松弛和损伤,使得拉索索力偏离成桥索力,降低结构安全性能,因此需要对在役斜拉桥索力进行检测[1-2]。目前运营期斜拉桥索力测试主要使用基于加速度传感器的振动频率测试方法,加速度传感器测量结果精度高,但是需要人工安装,耗费时间较长,成本较高[3-4]。

基于机器视觉的索力非接触测试技术通过亚像素定位,精确获得目标测点位置,且具有低成本、多点位同步测量等优点,近年来被逐步应用于索力测试中[5]。周子杰[6]为探究计算机视觉方法用于索力测试的适用性,采用伺服静载锚固试验机张拉单根斜拉索钢绞线,并通过相机摄影的非接触测量方法测量拉索动态响应,测试结果表明,计算机视觉方法测试索力与实测值相比最大误差不超过6%,具备开展实际结构索力测试的能力。张宇航等[7]以拱桥吊杆索力测试为背景,讨论了基于相位的欧拉运动放大算法与基于Canny算子的边缘识别算法的适用性,研究表明,与传统基于加速度传感器的索力测试方法相比,基于欧拉运动放大算法的索力测试方法具有易操作、低成本和高效率的优点。晏班夫等[8]制作了斜拉桥拉索室内模型试验,并通过视频图像测振技术和力传感器分别进行了测试,验证了视频图像测振技术检测索振动是可行的。综上所述,机器视觉索力测试方法已在室内实验和实桥测试中得到了一定程度的应用,但该方法应用于在役斜拉桥索力测试的文献报道较少。

鉴于此,本文分别采用机器视觉和传统加速度传感器测量方法对一座在役斜拉桥16根拉索索力进行测试,以传统加速度传感器测试结果为对比基准,从测试精度、时间、成本等维度分析机器视觉测量方法的适用性。

1 技术原理

基于机器视觉的索力测试是指通过二维图像处理技术和图像目标点定位技术,精确测量相机所拍图像上多个目标点在荷载作用下的相对变化像素数,再结合像素与实际位移的转换,输出实际变形结果,得到目标测点振动位移时程曲线,然后经过傅里叶变换得到斜拉桥拉索自振频率,最后将拉索自振频率代入索力-频率对应关系式(1)即可得到索力[9]。主要测量过程包括相机标定、图像预处理、特征点提取等。

$$F = 4ml^2\left(\frac{f_n}{n}\right)^2 \tag{1}$$

式中:m——索的单位长质量(kg/m);

l——拉索计算长度(m);

f_n——拉索的 n 阶频率;

n——拉索的振动阶数。

(1)相机标定是指通过相机内部参数(焦距、光圈等)和外部参数(相机位置、旋转方向等),建立图像二维像素坐标系与世界三维坐标系之间的映射关系。图1为相机标定中像素坐标系 O_1、图像坐标系 O_2、相机坐标系 O_3 和世界坐标系 O_4 相互关系的示意。相机标定是视觉测量的首要任务,标定结果的准确性和可靠性对后续的研究工作起到至关重要的作用。

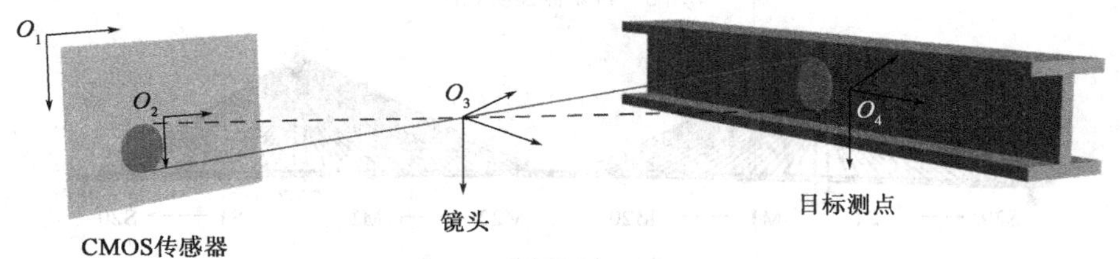

图1 相机标定示意图

(2)图像预处理一般是通过灰度转换、图像增强、阈值分割、二值化、滤波等方法,消除图像噪声、扩大图像中不同特征之间的差别、增强特征点的可检测性、减小运算数据量等。

(3)图像预处理后需要对特征点进行定位,特征点精确定位的关键在于特征点的检测提取,常用的特征点检测算法有基于图像灰度的边缘检测算法。图像的边缘是图像的基本特征(边缘识别就是为了获取这些特征区域),图像的边缘表现为图像的灰度不连续性,根本原因是图像中的元素不止一种,每种元素有自己独有的特征,这些差异反应到图像上就是图像灰度在某些区域发生急剧变化。在斜拉桥索力测量中,可充分利用拉索表面与背景颜色对比明显的斑点,提取到丰富的特征点边缘信息。在基于图像边缘的检测算法中,特征点边缘提取又分为像素级边缘提取和亚像素级边缘提取。对于像素级边缘提取来说,每个像素对应一个整数坐标位置,然而在测量拉索振动位移时,整数坐标位置的精度往往并不能准确反应特征点的位置信息,在整数坐标位置之间还有更加细分的像素存在,称为亚像素,如图2所示。本文测试设备采用亚像素边缘检测算法实现目标特征点的精准定位。

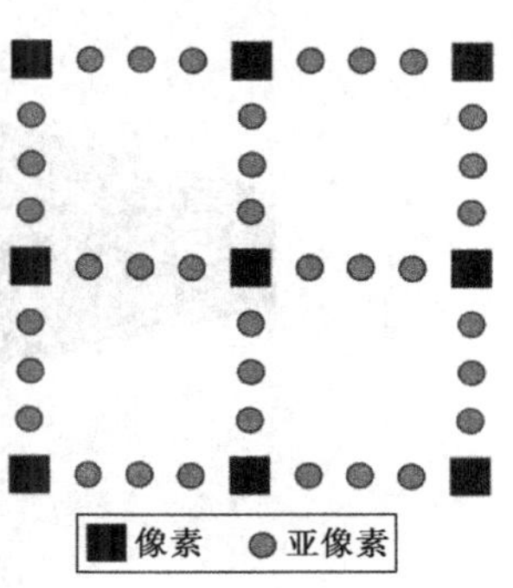

图2 亚像素示意

2 斜拉桥索力测试试验

2.1 试验概况

某双塔双索面三跨式预应力混凝土斜拉桥,全长1080m,全漂浮体系,跨径组合为110m + 270m + 110m,左右幅分离式设计,全桥共有160根拉索,其实景如图3所示。

该桥拉索编号规则如下:北侧为10号塔,南侧为9号塔,边跨侧代号为S,中跨侧代号为M,分别以各个塔为基准,向南北方向由小到大进行编号(从1依次自增1),拉索编号示意如图4、图5所示。

2.2 试验方案

采用如下对比试验方案。

图3　桥梁侧面实景图

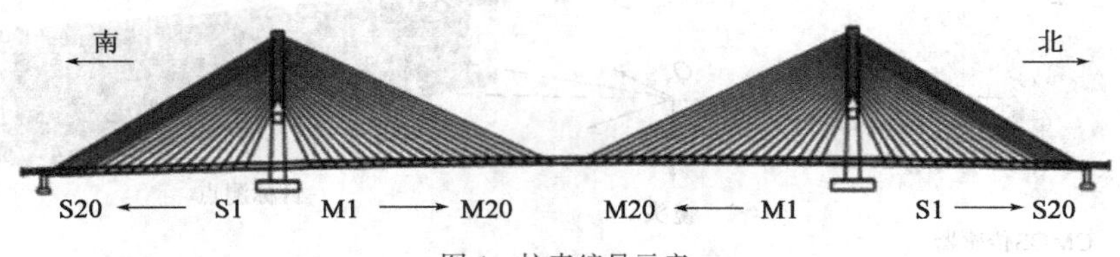

图4　拉索编号示意

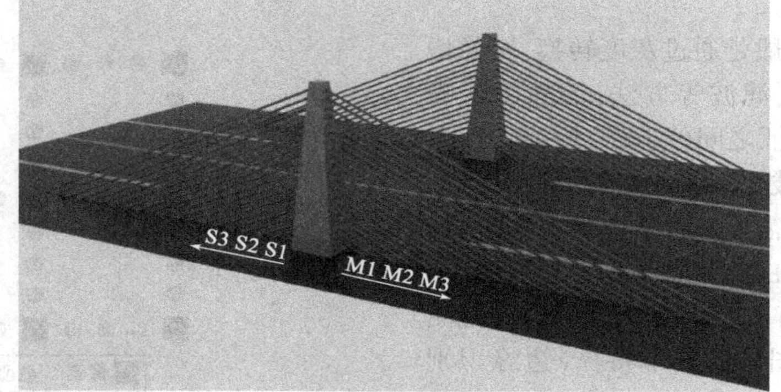

图5　拉索编号局部放大图

(1)硬件设备、测试参数。采用雷图BJQN-V2.0桥梁挠度检测仪搭配Tamron 25mm定焦镜头采集拉索振动的数字图像数据，采用东华DH5901有线加速度传感器采集拉索振动的加速度信号。将桥梁挠度检测仪和加速度传感器的采样频率均设为80Hz。

(2)拍摄地点。本次测试不封闭桥面交通，无法在车行道进行测试；同时由于该桥跨越河流，桥下难以找到合适的观测位置，而桥面两侧有人行通道，拉索也在桥面两侧，因此将拍摄地点选取在该斜拉桥的人行过道上。

(3)测试工况、内容。在自然环境、随机车流工况下分别使用机器视觉和加速度传感器测量方法测量该斜拉桥16根拉索的自振频率。现场测试如图6、图7所示。

图6　加速度传感器测试

2.3　结果分析

2.3.1　测试精度

分别使用机器视觉和传统加速度传感器测量

方法对9号、10号塔最外侧16根拉索自振频率进行测量，选择加速度传感器测量结果作为对比基准，测量结果如表1、图8所示，其中测量相对偏差最大的拉索——9号塔左S20时程曲线、频谱如图9、图10所示。需要注意的是，由于拉索单位长度质量和计算长度均保持一致，这里以基频表征斜拉桥索力，仅对比基频测试精度的差异。

a)视点标记

b)现场测试

图7 机器视觉测试

两种方法测试基频对比 表1

拉索位置	测试结果(Hz)		相对偏差(%)
	机器视觉	加速度传感器	
9号塔左M20	0.978	0.977	0.1
9号塔左M19	0.964	0.968	-0.4
9号塔右M20	1.059	1.062	-0.3
9号塔右M19	1.055	1.069	-1.3
9号塔左S20	1.043	0.987	5.7
9号塔左S19	1.013	0.962	5.3
9号塔右S20	1.059	1.059	0
9号塔右S19	1.046	1.052	-0.6
10号塔左S20	1.031	1.051	1.9
10号塔左S19	1.035	1.040	-0.5
10号塔右S20	1.067	1.042	2.4
10号塔右S19	1.049	1.044	0.5
10号塔左M20	0.971	0.973	-0.2
10号塔左M19	0.958	0.934	2.6
10号塔右M20	0.984	0.975	0.9
10号塔右M19	0.943	0.938	0.5

注：相对偏差=(机器视觉测试基频－加速度传感器测试基频)/加速度传感器测试基频。

从表1和图8可知：

(1)机器视觉与加速度传感器测试结果具有较高的一致性，相较于加速度传感器，机器视觉方法有87.5%的拉索基频测试相对偏差小于5%，9号塔左S20拉索基频测试相对偏差最大，为5.7%。

(2)机器视觉方法测量拉索基频总体上表现出北侧精度高于南侧的特点，这主要是由于北侧光照更加稳定，拍摄图像更加清晰，目标测点的特征提取更加准确。

2.3.2 测试时间和成本

对机器视觉和传统加速度传感器测试方法在时

间、人员和成本方面进行了对比,结果如表2所示。

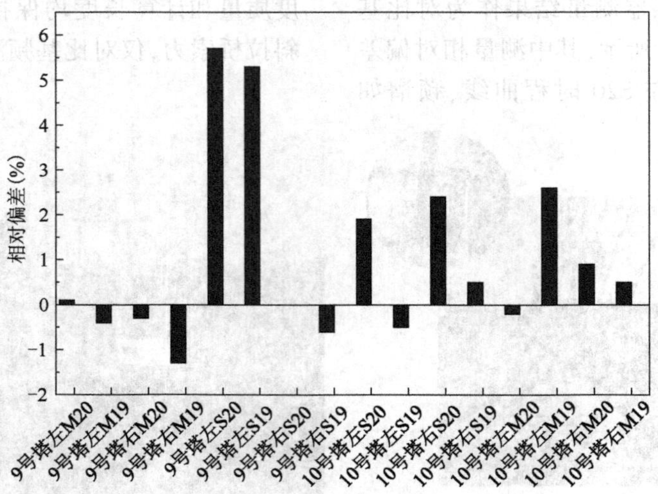

图8　两种方法测试基频相对偏差

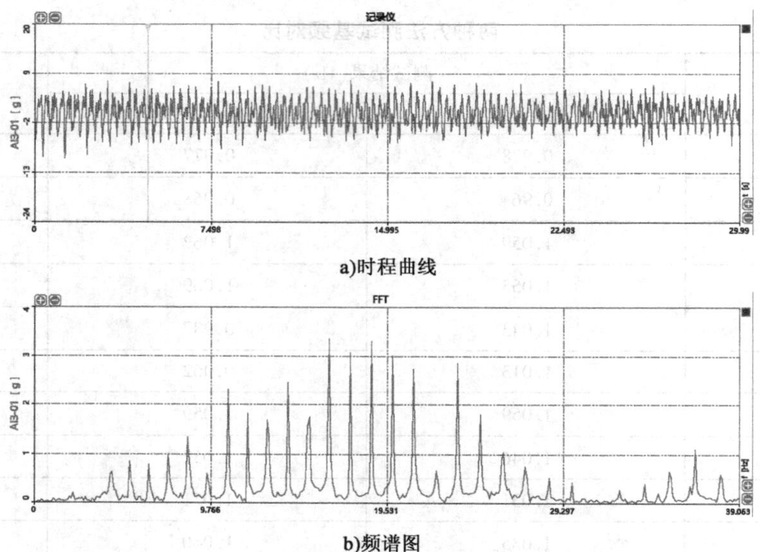

a)时程曲线

b)频谱图

图9　9号塔左S20拉索加速度传感器测试结果

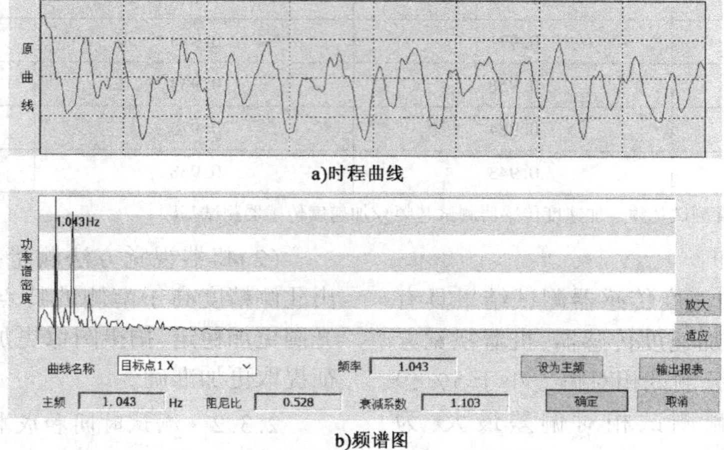

a)时程曲线

b)频谱图

图10　9号塔左S20拉索机器视觉测试结果

测试方法	总试验时间(天)	至少需要人数(个)	测试费(元)
加速度传感器	1	3	30000
机器视觉	0.5	1	10000

测试时间、成本对比 表2

由表2可见,由于机器视觉索力测试方法可以单次测试多根拉索,总测试时间仅需要半天,小于传统加速度传感器测试方法的1天,测试效率高;此外其仅需要1人即可完成现场测试、数据整理;测试费用10000元,远小于传统加速度传感器测试方法的30000元,以上分析进一步表明机器视觉方法在斜拉桥索力测试中具有较好的应用前景。

3 结语

本文开展了机器视觉技术在运营期斜拉桥索力测试方面的应用研究,通过对比机器视觉和加速度传感器两种索力测试方法的测试精度、时间和成本,得到以下结论:

(1)机器视觉索力测试方法可在测试精度达到传统加速度传感器85%以上的前提下,节约部分检测费用、提升测试效率,在斜拉桥索力测试中具有较好的研究前景和应用价值,可作为传统加速度传感器测试方法的补充与拓展。

(2)在光照较差或者不稳定的情况下,机器视觉方法测试噪声会明显增大,影响索力的识别,后续有必要开展相关图像增强算法的研究,以提高机器视觉方法在不同光照环境下测试斜拉桥索力的适用性和可靠性,为在役斜拉桥索力的快速、准确检测提供支撑。

参考文献

[1] Chu C, Ghrib F, Cheng S. Cable tension monitoring through feature-based video image processing[J]. Journal of Civil Structural Health Monitoring, 2021, 11(1): 69-84.

[2] Ya N B, Li D, Chen W, et al. Mode shape-aidedcable force determination using digital image correlation[J]. Structural Health Monitoring, 2020(6): 147592172095216.

[3] 吉伯海,程苗,傅中秋,等.基于振动频率法的斜拉桥索力测试影响因素[J].中南大学学报(自然科学版),2015,46(07):2620-2625.

[4] Du W, Lei D, Bai P, et al. Dynamic measurement of stay-cable force using digital image techniques [J]. Measurement, 2020, 151: 107211.

[5] Tian Y, Zhang C, Jiang S, et al. Noncontactcable force estimation with unmanned aerial vehicle and computer vision[J]. Computer-Aided Civil and Infrastructure Engineering, 2021, 36(1): 73-88.

[6] 周子杰.基于视频亚像素模板匹配算法的索力试验[J].城市道桥与防洪,2021(12):140-143+19.

[7] 张宇航,苏成,邓逸川.基于欧拉运动放大算法的桥梁索力测试方法研究[J].图学学报,2022:1-8.

[8] 晏班夫,陈泽楚,朱子纲.基于非接触摄影测量的拉索索力测试[J].湖南大学学报(自然科学版),2015,42(11):105-110.

[9] 徐昊杰,袁向荣,刘辉等.视频图像测振技术对斜拉索索力的应用[J].实验室研究与探索,2017,36(11):7-10+14.

钢桁-混凝土组合梁二维温度场分布及效应

熊 鑫* 李 洁

(长安大学公路学院)

摘 要 钢桁-混凝土组合梁是大型空间框架式结构,在日照作用下的温度分布空间性很强。为了研究钢桁-混凝土组合梁桥温度梯度分布模式及其力学响应,本文以某三跨钢桁-混凝土组合连续梁桥为背景,通过总结大跨组合结构桥梁的温度监测数据,结合热分析模型得到了混凝土桥面板的竖向温度分布,并提出了钢桁-混凝土组合梁简化的二维温度场分布模式。采用 ANSYS 软件建立了三维空间有限元模型,分析了钢桁-混凝土组合梁在温度梯度作用下的力学响应,得出温度梯度大幅提高了受日照一侧支墩处下弦杆的压应力和边跨跨中的挠度。

关键词　桥梁工程　二维温度场　有限元分析　钢桁-混凝土组合梁　温度梯度效应

0　引言

钢桁-混凝土组合梁桥由钢桁架和混凝土桥面板通过剪力连接装置组合而成,充分利用了钢材良好的抗拉性能和混凝土良好的受压性能,具有自重轻、跨越能力大、承载能力高、维修方便等优点,应用广泛。然而混凝土和钢材的材料特性不同,两者的导热性的差异使其在日照下的温度分布差别很大,许多学者对此类大跨度组合结构桥梁的竖向温度梯度均有研究。耿文宾等[1]指出在无太阳辐射情况下,钢桁梁温度与外界大气温度相差不大,而在有太阳辐射的情况下,钢桁梁温度与外界大气温度相差较大。对某矮塔钢桁梁桥的空间温度场监测结果表明,钢桁梁的斜杆和下弦杆的温度明显高于上弦杆。王达等[2]对某钢桁加劲梁钢-混组合桥面系竖向温度梯度监测数据表明,该类型结构的温度梯度主要集中于混凝土桥面板上、下缘之间;相比组合结构其他位置,混凝土桥面板温度梯度效应尤为突出。刘国飞等[3]对某大跨长联连续钢桁梁桥的部分杆件的温度进行了长期跟踪监测,温度监测结果表明钢桁梁存在明显的竖向温度梯度,且上平联存在明显的横向温度梯度。朱劲松等[4]以某简支钢箱-混凝土组合梁桥为背景,基于三维遮挡算法,考虑太阳辐射、对流换热、结构热传导等因素影响,分析四季典型天气下竖向温度分布变化规律,提出了两种竖向温度梯度模式。

虽然日照作用下组合结构桥梁的竖向温度梯度显著,但横向温度梯度也不容忽视。有研究表明[5],钢桁梁侧桁架上下构件之间存在显著的垂直温度梯度,下桁架构件之间存在显著的横向温度梯度。故日照作用下钢桁-混凝土组合梁的横向温度梯度及其产生的效应亟需研究。目前对于钢桁架的温度效应的研究大多考虑年温差变化(均匀温度作用),而对于日照温差(温度梯度作用)主要集中在竖向温度梯度,对横向温度梯度鲜有考虑。本文通过分析总结已有的温度梯度监测资料,以某钢桁-混凝土组合连续梁为研究对象,考虑了日照引起的钢桁组合梁横向温度梯度,分析了该类结构的二维温度分布,并通过数值模拟研究其力学效应。

1　工程概况

某 3×80m 钢桁-混凝土组合连续梁桥,桥面板翼缘端部厚度为 0.22m,翼缘根部厚度为 0.4m,宽 12.9m,铺设有 8cm 厚的沥青混凝土铺装层;钢桁梁梁高 7.2m,宽 6.7m,标准节间长度为 8m。桥梁全貌如图 1 所示。

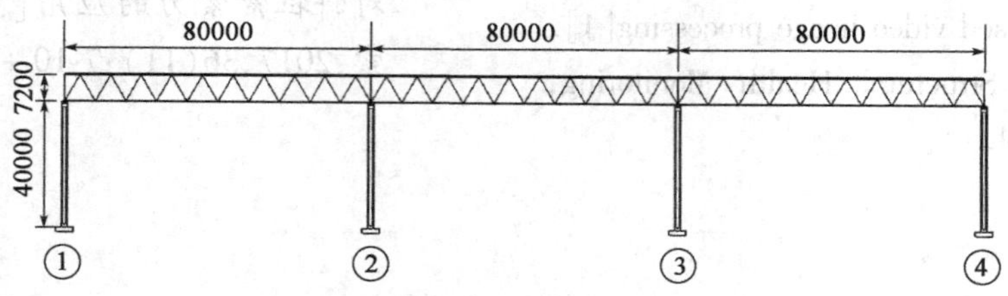

图 1　桥跨布置图(尺寸单位:cm)

2　二维温度场分析

2.1　竖向温度场研究

2.1.1　模型验证

为了验证钢桁-混凝土组合梁竖向温度梯度数值模拟的有效性,本研究对王达等[6]的钢-混凝土组合桥面板的温度加载试验的温度梯度结果进行验证。该试验采用的缩尺梁混凝土桥面板宽 1.582m,厚度为 60mm;工字钢高度为 165mm,试件总长 4.8m。图 2 是缩尺梁加载测点布置图和组合梁竖向温度测点布置图。

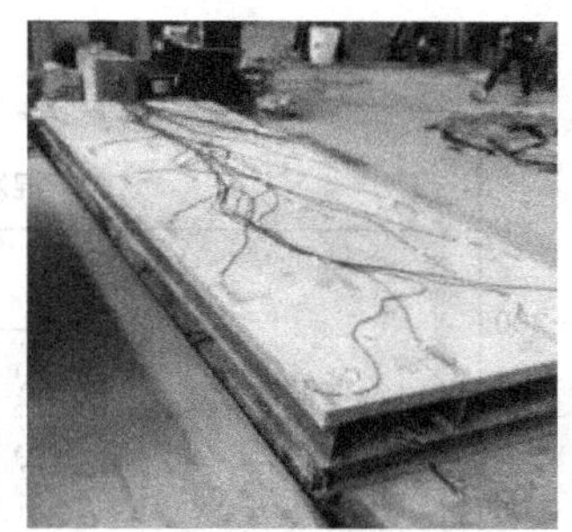

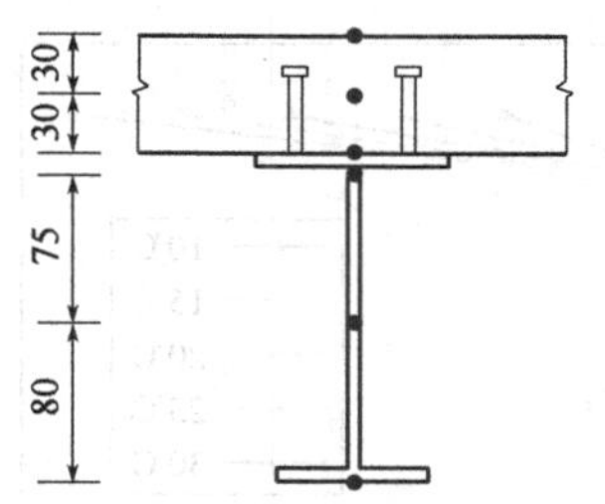

a)桥面板顶端加载测点布置　　b)竖向温度测点布置(尺寸单位：mm)

图2　缩尺梁温度测点布置图

采用有限元分析软件 ANSYS 建立有限元热分析模型对试验梁进行了瞬态热传导分析,有限元模型如图3所示(不考虑温度沿顺桥向变化),混凝土和工字钢均采用 solid 70 单元。组合梁的传热有三种模式,热传导、对流换热和辐射换热,通过对桥面板有限元模型顶端施加10℃到30℃的温度边界条件(第一类边界条件)模拟试验梁的电辅热加热,同时将辐射换热等效为对流换热[7],采用综合对流换热系数考虑对流换热和辐射换热。模型的各项热工参数取值如表1所示。

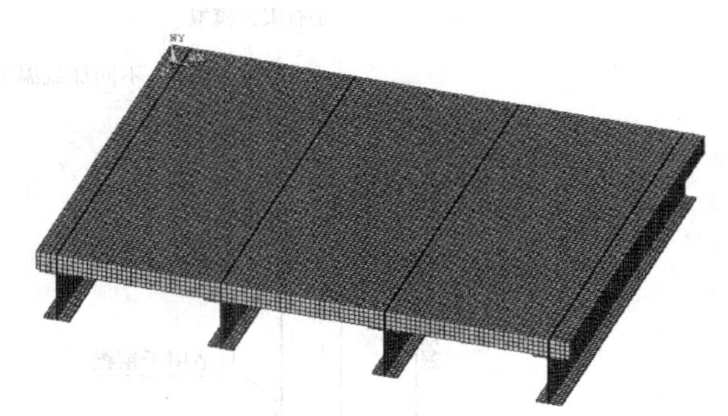

图3　试验梁有限元模型

有限元模型各项热工参数　　表1

材料类型	比热容($J \cdot kg^{-1} \cdot K^{-1}$)	导热系数($W \cdot m^{-1} \cdot K^{-1}$)	密度($kg \cdot m^{-3}$)	综合对流换热系数($W \cdot m^{-2} \cdot K^{-1}$)
混凝土	920	1.54	2500	20
钢	465	54	7850	20

以模型梁顶面加载30℃为例,随着时间的增长,模型梁的热量自上而下传递,当混凝土板底面温度停止加速变化时模型梁横截面的温度分布如图4所示。其他加载温度下组合梁截面温度分布情况汇入图5a),并与图5b)中的试验结果进行比较。

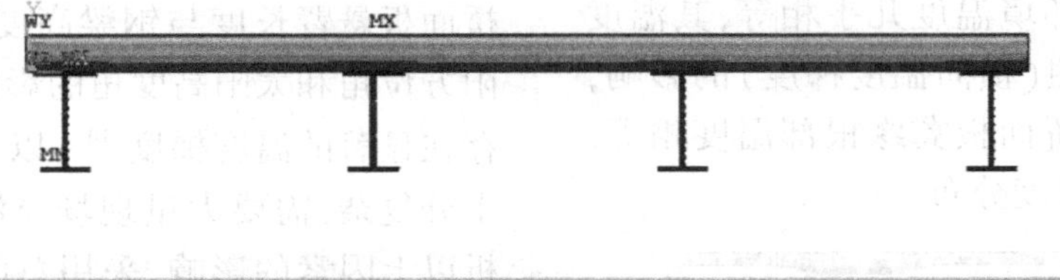

图4　顶部加载30℃时截面温度分布

通过对比,虽然通过数值模拟得到的竖向温度梯度曲线较试验结果变化更平缓(由于试验梁是由缩尺1/4所得,试验数据的截面高度 h 放大了4倍),总体上与试验结果吻合程度较好,故采用数值分析方法进一步研究钢桁-混凝土组合梁的竖向温度梯度。

2.1.2　竖向温度梯度

根据我国 JTG D60—2015《公路桥涵设计通用规范》中的规定,混凝土桥面板表面沥青铺装层为80mm时,由插值可得桥面板竖向日照正温差计算的温度基数 T_1 为16.4℃,T_2 为5.98℃,如图6所示。该桥桥面板厚度为400mm(图7),可知根据规范钢梁的温度基数取值为0℃。

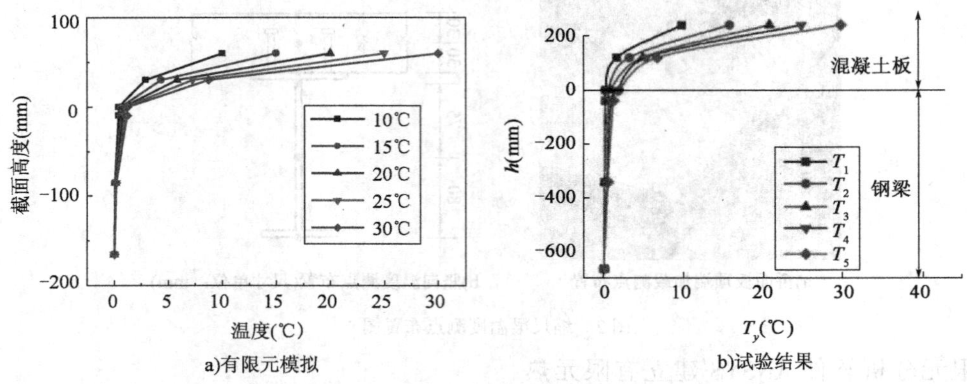

图5　不同加载温度下组合梁截面温度分布

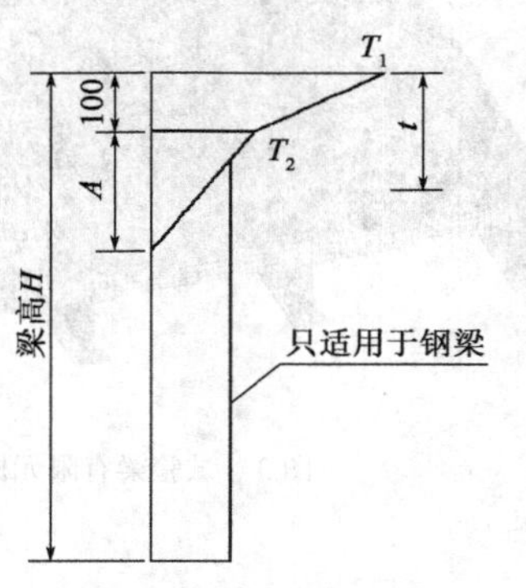

图6　温度梯度规范值

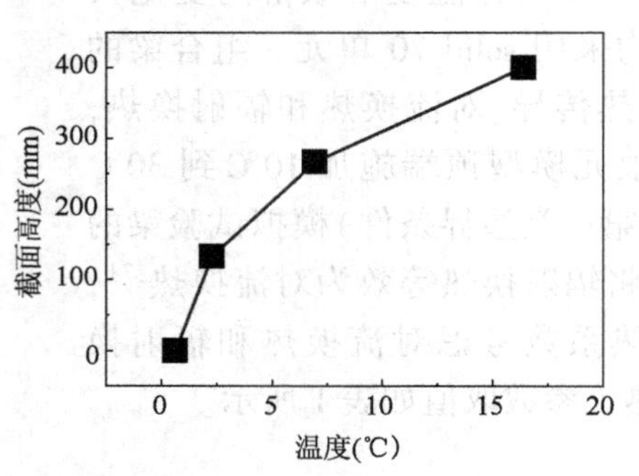

图7　温度梯度模拟值

规范规定的温度梯度服务于通用桥梁设计，可能不适用于个例的研究分析。因此采用上节所述的数值模拟方法，对钢桁-混凝土组合梁的竖向温度梯度进行有限元模拟。由于缺乏气象数据资料，混凝土表面的最高温度仍取规范值16.4℃，混凝土桥面板的温度分布如图8所示。竖向温度梯度下钢桁架的温度与环境温度几乎相等，其温度分布主要受梁侧面日照(横向温度梯度)的影响，可暂时认为与混凝土桥面板翼缘根部温度相等，接下来将分析其横向温度分布。

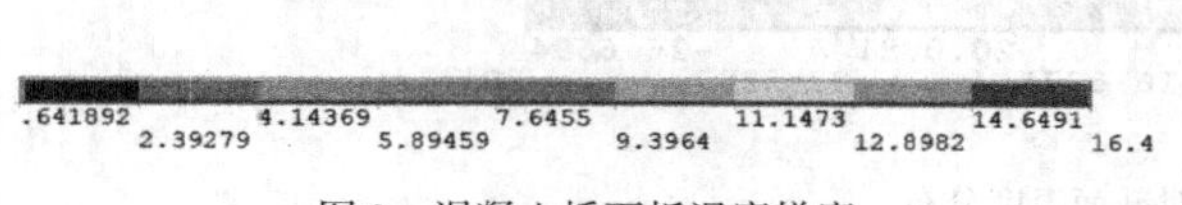

图8　混凝土桥面板温度梯度

2.2　横向温度梯度研究

目前有关钢桁-混凝土组合梁横向温度梯度研究较少，一般认为桥面板悬臂对腹板有遮蔽作用，不考虑结构的横向温度变化，如规范中给出的温度梯度参考。然而肖林等[8]指出，对于钢-混组合桥梁上部结构，钢梁中的温度显著高于规范设计值。钢桁-混凝土组合梁具有很强的空间性，其仅有一侧受日照作用，若仅考虑竖向温度作用，即认为两侧钢桁架的温度一致，可能会低估了温度梯度效应。且该桥混凝土悬臂长度较短，不足以完全遮蔽一侧钢桁架。故一侧钢桁架一部分受日照作用，另一部分处于阴影中。阴影部分不仅受桥面板悬臂长度与钢梁高度之比的影响，还受太阳方位角和太阳高度角的影响[9]。而底部桁架也存在显著的温度梯度[10]，以上因素若要精确考虑十分复杂，需要大量现场监测数据。为了简化分析以上因素的影响，采用总的太阳高度角来考虑由日照引起的温差，与受日照辐射相近的阴影区域及被侧桁架部分遮挡的底部桁架区域温度采用线性变化过渡，其他未受日照辐射区温度仍按竖向温度梯度分布。

2.3　二维温度分布

据检测资料显示，下午2点到5点为为一天中温度最高的时候，假定此时的太阳高度角为30°，受日照辐射一侧桁架直射部分平均温度升高15℃，另一侧桁架不变。考虑钢结果热传导率较大,且杆件横向尺寸相对于纵向较小,故认为钢桁架各杆件的横截面温度分布均匀。则综合以上分析得出钢桁-混凝土组合梁二维温度分布模式如图9所示。

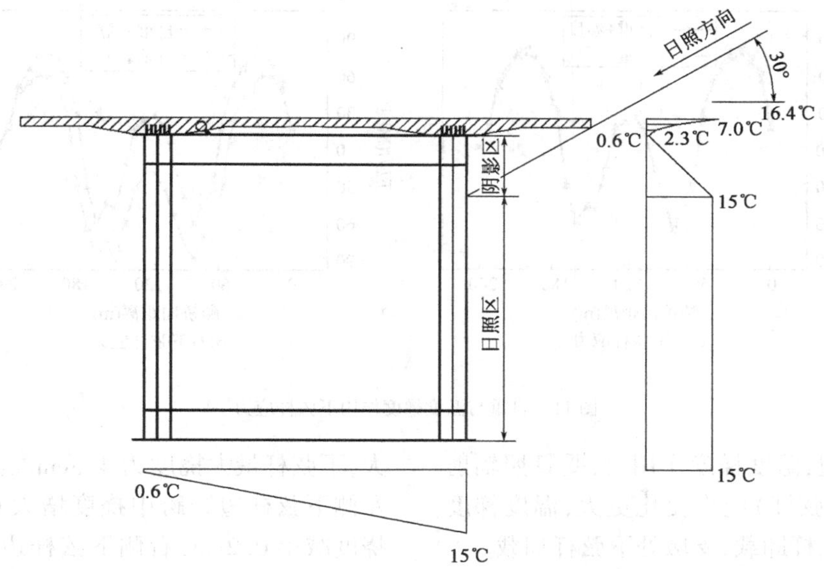

图9 钢桁-混凝土组合梁二维温度分布

3 温度梯度效应

3.1 三维空间有限元模型

为了分析该钢桁-混凝土组合梁温度梯度效应,采用ANSYS软件建立三维有限元分析模型,桥面板采用solid 65实体单元,钢桁架采用beam 188梁单元,全桥共98734个单元,其中实体单元94464个,梁单元4270个,混凝土桥面板和钢桁架采用无滑移连接,有限元模型如图10所示,在2号墩右侧设置固定支座,并在同侧其他支承处设置单向(纵向)活动支座;在2号墩左侧设置单向(横向)活动支座,并在同侧其他支承处设置双向活动支座。温度梯度荷载按图9所示加载,桁架右侧为受日照辐射区,图中给出了桥面板、钢桁架右侧与下侧杆件的温度分布,其他部位杆件的温度均匀,为0.6℃(与桥面板底部相同)。

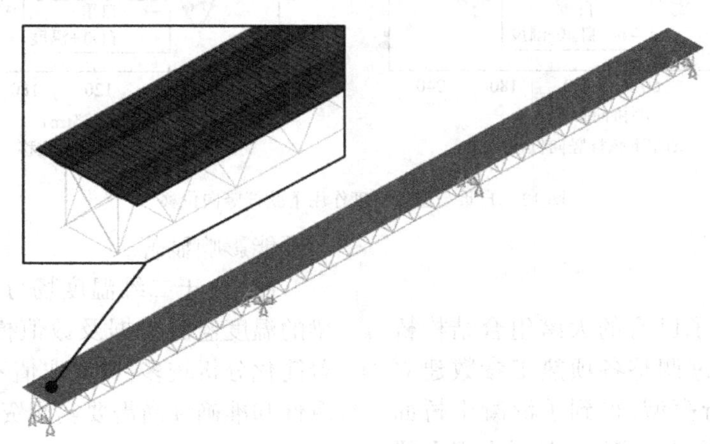

图10 ANSYS有限元模型

3.2 应力分析

在自重与温度梯度共同作用下,钢桁-混凝土组合梁的两侧下弦杆沿顺桥向应力变化如图11所示。

由图11可知,自重作用下,边跨跨中下弦杆拉应力最大,为75.3MPa,支墩处下弦杆压应力最大,为64.4MPa。温度梯度作用下,左侧下弦杆应力相比自重应力变化不大,仅在边跨跨中引起拉应力增大4.5MPa,而右下弦杆应力变化幅度较大,边跨跨中拉应力减小24.0MPa,支墩处压应力增大27.2MPa,达到91.6MPa。

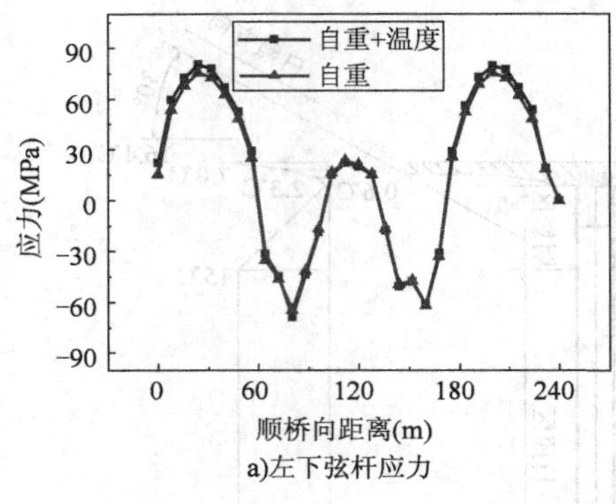

a)左下弦杆应力

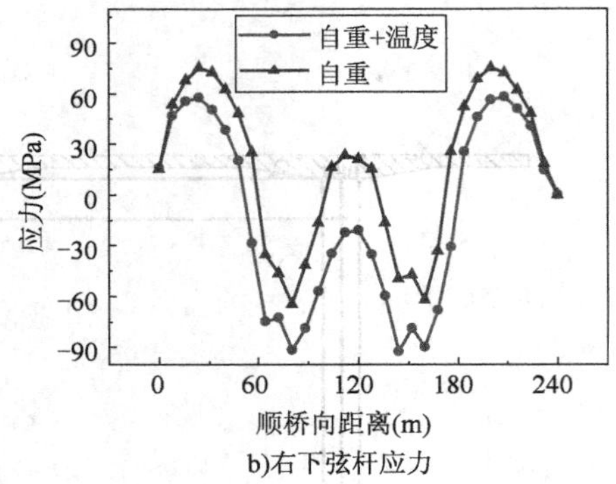

b)右下弦杆应力

图11　自重与温度梯度作用下弦杆应力

经过对比发现,温度梯度作用时,受日照辐射一侧下弦杆(右下弦杆)应力变化更大,温度梯度引起边跨跨中下弦杆卸载,支墩处下弦杆加载。

3.3　位移分析

在自重与温度梯度共同作用下,钢桁-混凝土组合梁的两侧下弦杆沿顺桥向挠度变化如图12所示。

由图12可知,自重作用下,边跨跨中挠度最大,下弦杆最大挠度为4.3cm。温度梯度作用下,左侧下弦杆边跨跨中挠度增大0.2cm,中跨跨中挠度减小0.2cm;右侧下弦杆边跨跨中处挠度增大0.6cm,中跨跨中挠度减小0.3cm。因此可以得出,温度梯度作用时,受日照辐射一侧下弦杆挠度变化更大,温度梯度引起边跨挠度增加,中跨挠度减小。

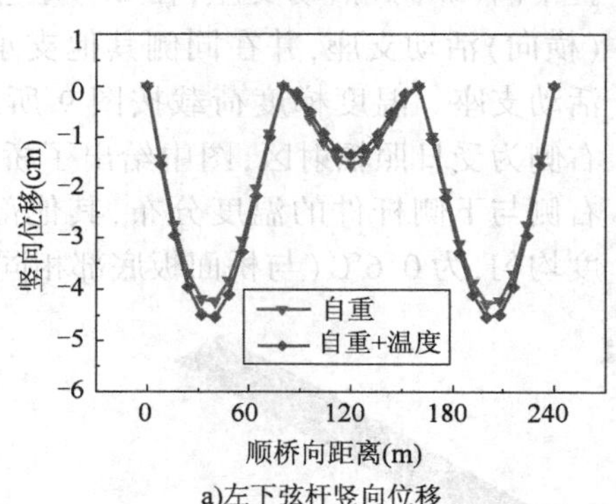

a)左下弦杆竖向位移

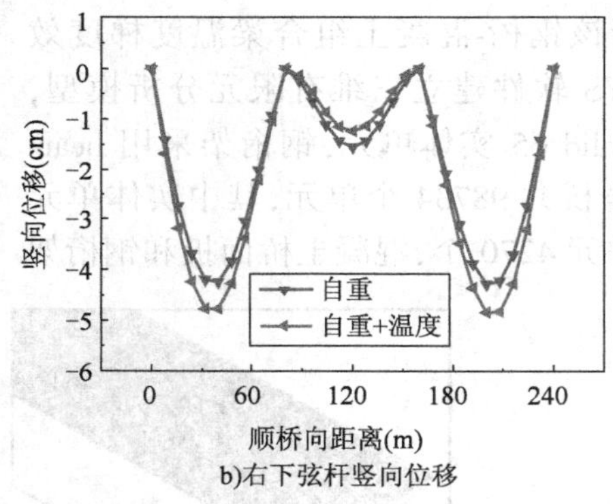

b)右下弦杆竖向位移

图12　自重与温度梯度作用下弦杆竖向位移

4　结语

(1)本文总结分析了已有的大跨组合结构桥梁的温度监测数据,通过调整各项热工参数建立符合实测资料的热分析模型,得到了混凝土桥面板的竖向温度梯度,并提出了钢桁-混凝土组合梁简化的二维温度场分布模式。

(2)建立了三维空间有限元模型,分析了钢桁-混凝土组合梁的温度梯度的力学响应。温度梯度作用使得支墩处下弦杆压应力增大27.2MPa,边跨跨中处挠度增大0.6cm。对结构的力学性能影响显著。

(3)由于二维温度场分析参考了类似结构桥梁的温度监测数据及数值模拟结果,该方法存在着简化分析较多,参数取值不够精确等问题,其可取性和准确性尚需要实测资料进一步验证。

参考文献

[1]　耿文宾,刘康,周俊龙,等.高-矮塔斜拉钢桁梁桥空间温度场监测分析[J].天津建设科技,2021,31(05):20-22.

[2]　王达,张永健,刘扬,等.基于健康监测的钢桁加劲梁钢-混组合桥面系竖向温度梯度效应

分析[J].中国公路学报,2015,28(11):29-36.

[3] 刘国飞.大跨长联连续钢桁梁桥施工阶段温度效应研究[J].铁道建筑技术,2021(10):16-20+39.

[4] 朱劲松,李雨默,顾玉辉,等.钢箱-混凝土组合梁桥竖向温度梯度分析[J].公路工程:1-18.

[5] Wang G-X, Ding Y-L. Long-Term Monitoring of Temperature Effect on Horizontal Rotation Angle at Beam Ends of a Railway Steel Truss Bridge[J]. Journal of Bridge Engineering, 2019,24(10).

[6] 王达,谭本坤,赵鹏鑫.钢-混凝土组合桥面板温度梯度效应的试验研究与数值模拟[J].建筑结构学报,2021,42(S2):74-82.

[7] 段飞.大跨度钢桥日照温度场和温度效应研究[D].西南交通大学,2010.

[8] 肖林,蔡俊宇,杨妍秋,等.桥梁温度作用与效应2020年度研究进展[J].土木与环境工程学报(中英文),2021,43(S1):167-174.

[9] 刘江,刘永健,马志元,等.钢-混凝土组合梁桥的温度梯度作用(Ⅰ)——作用模式与极值分析[J].中国公路学报:1-29.

[10] 刘永健,刘江,张宁.桥梁结构日照温度作用研究综述[J].土木工程学报,2019,52(05):59-78.

钢-混组合梁可靠性及施工误差分析

张柳煜[1] 曾 斌*[1] 史小川[1]
(长安大学)

摘 要 根据钢-混凝土组合梁的弹性理论和塑性理论对其进行了不同条件下的可靠性分析,研究了组合梁在不同混凝土强度、不同钢材强度、不同混凝土板的宽厚比影响下的可靠度变化规律,并研究混凝土板厚度和宽度施工误差的合理控制范围。结果表明:随着混凝土强度以及钢材强度的增大,组合梁的可靠度也会随之增加;随着混凝土翼板宽度的增加,最佳混凝土翼板厚度呈抛物线形式下降;混凝土板厚度和宽度的施工误差应分别控制在(0,+5)和(-3,+3)范围内较安全。

关键词 钢-混凝土组合梁 可靠度 施工误差 弹性理论 塑性理论

0 引言

钢-混凝土组合梁近年来由于其优异的性能得到广泛推广使用,其充分发挥了钢材和混凝土两种不同材料的性能,不但能够满足结构的受力要求,而且达到了充分利用材料特性的目的,具有良好的经济效益。

目前已有相当多的关于钢-混凝土组合梁的可靠性研究,廖汶和陈忠延[1]提出将可靠度理论与组合梁截面设计联系起来,以经济效益为目标进行组合梁的优化设计;龚志刚[2]研究了桥梁整体可靠度和单梁可靠度,发现桥梁整体受力时的可靠度要比某一根梁单独承受作用时的可靠度高很多;张文等[3]提出了组合梁的两种挠度计算方法,并以此为基础进行了正常使用极限状态的可靠度分析;李明达[4]研究了不同参数对正常使用极限状态下的组合梁的可靠度影响规律;王立宪等[5]研究了组合梁的跨度、混凝土标号、钢材牌号、混凝土板厚对基于挠度控制的正常使用极限状态的可靠度影响分析;弥衡[6]研究了截面几何尺寸、材料等对组合梁分别处于承载能力和正常使用两种极限状态下的可靠度影响规律;张俊民等[7]研究了组合梁梁高和钢梁下底板厚度对处于承载能力极限状态时的简支组合梁的可靠度影响;潘明杨[8]研究了混凝土材料分项系数对组合梁的可靠度影响规律。王建超等[9]从组合梁的抗弯、纵向抗剪及竖向抗剪三个方面研究了材料分项系数对组合梁的可靠性影响规律。

本文根据钢-混凝土组合梁的塑性分析理论,研究分析了各项参数对其可靠度的影响规律,以及以弹性理论和可靠度理论为基础，研究施工误差对可靠度的影响以及确定较合理的施工误差。

1 钢-混凝土组合梁抗力

组合梁在生产和施工的过程中，由于各种各样的原因，其材料和截面尺寸等都会产生差异，所以需要对影响抗力的因素进行统计分析。实际工程中影响结构抗力的因素较多，归纳起来有构件的截面尺寸的不定性、材料性能的不确定性以及由于截面尺寸大小等因素引起的计算模式不定性。截面几何统计参数、材料统计参数和计算模式统计参数分别见表1、表2、表3。

构件截面几何统计参数　　表1

随机变量(X_K)		$K_X=\mu_X/X_K$	$\delta_X=\sigma_X/\mu_X$
混凝土	板厚	1.0121	0.0835
	板宽	1.0019	0.0076
钢梁	厚度	0.9790	0.0220
	翼缘宽度	1.0050	0.0110
	腹板高度	1.0030	0.0110

材料强度统计参数　　表2

随机变量(X_K)	$K_X=\mu_X/X_K$	$\delta_X=\sigma_X/\mu_X$	随机变量(X_K)	$K_X=\mu_X/X_K$	$\delta_X=\sigma_X/\mu_X$
C20混凝土	1.7182	0.2363	Q235钢	1.2160	0.1460
C30混凝土	1.5012	0.1773	Q345钢	1.1760	0.1210
C40混凝土	1.4840	0.1578	Q390钢	1.0370	0.0830
C50混凝土	1.3877	0.1374	Q420钢	1.0080	0.0830

计算模式不定性统计参数　　表3

随机变量(X_K)	$K_X=\mu_X/X_K$	$\delta_X=\sigma_X/\mu_X$
组合梁	1.0889	0.1181

上述表中：K_X 是随机变量的标准值，如尺寸、材料强度等的设计值；μ_X 和 σ_X 是随机变量 X_K 的平均值和标准差。

抗力统计参数 X_K 用下式计算，标准差 σ_R 可通过文献[10]中的误差传递公式计算。

$$R=g(X_1,X_2,\cdots,X_n) \tag{1}$$

$$\mu_R=g(\mu_{X_1},\mu_{X_2},\cdots,\mu_{X_n}) \tag{2}$$

$$K_R=\frac{\mu_R}{R} \tag{3}$$

$$\delta_R=\frac{\sigma_R}{\mu_R} \tag{4}$$

式中：$g(\cdot)$——抗力计算方式；

R——按设计参数计算的抗力；

μ_R——按统计参数计算的抗力。

后续研究的算例采用上述截面尺寸等参数。通过上述公式计算所得抗力的统计参数见表4。

抗弯承载力统计参数结果　　表4

混凝土强度等级	Q235		Q345		Q390		Q420	
	K_R	δ_R	K_R	δ_R	K_R	δ_R	K_R	δ_R
C20	1.3812	0.1324	1.3659	0.1211	1.2814	0.1135	1.2594	0.1143
C30	1.3339	0.1358	1.3245	0.1060	1.1968	0.0886	1.1817	0.0905
C40	1.3309	0.1348	1.2912	0.1123	1.1548	0.0805	1.1325	0.0823
C50	1.3210	0.1377	1.2856	0.1131	1.1459	0.0801	1.1157	0.0803

2 荷载效应及可靠度计算方法

2.1 荷载效应

本文按规范对于公路桥涵设计只考虑永久作用，也就是结构恒载以及汽车荷载，文献[9]中给出了结构恒载和汽车活载的统计参数，结果见表5。

荷载统计参数　　表5

荷载分类	分布类型	实测平均值/标准值	变异系数
永久作用	正态分布	1.0148	0.0431
汽车荷载	极值Ⅰ型	0.7995	0.0862

2.2 可靠度计算方法

计算可靠度的方法多种多样，如规范《公路工程结构可靠性设计统一标准》(JTG 2120—2020)

推荐的一次二阶矩法、改进的一次二阶矩法、Monte Carlo 法以及 JC 法等。本文采用 JC 法进行结构可靠指标的计算，其计算流程图见图 1。

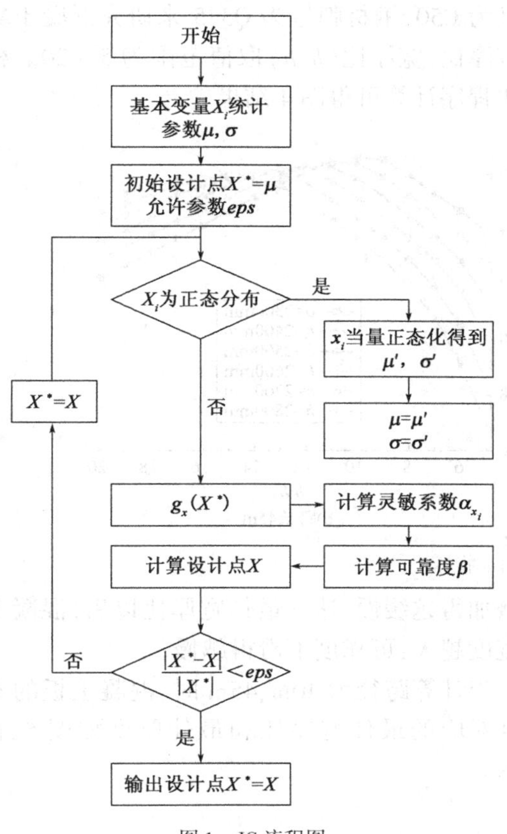

图 1 JC 流程图

3 算例分析

将国内某一高速公路的工字型钢-混组合梁桥作为例子进行可靠度研究，组合梁的横截面尺寸参数见图 2。研究分析了将承载能力极限状态作为目标的工字型钢—混组合梁可靠度变化规律及混凝土板的施工误差控制范围。

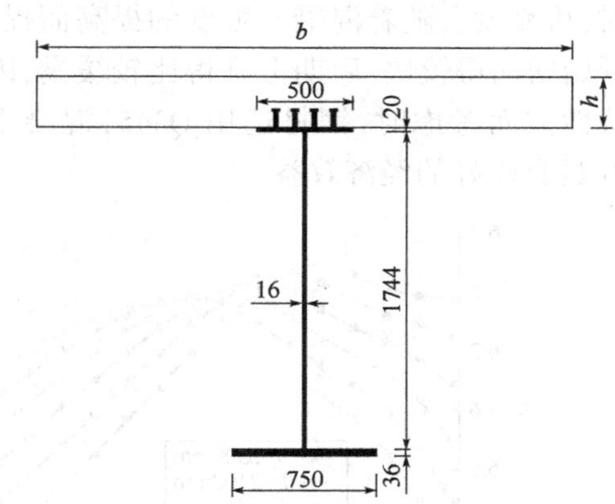

图 2 工字型组合梁横截面尺寸参数图(尺寸单位：mm)

3.1 可靠度指标敏感性分析

取 40m、45m 两种跨径，取强度为 C20、C30、C40、C50 的混凝土，钢材牌号分别取 Q235、Q345、Q390、Q420，混凝土板宽分别取 2300mm、2400mm、2500mm、2600mm、2700mm、2800mm。根据塑性理论进行研究分析，分析时混凝土容重取 25kN/m^3，钢材密度取 78.5kN/m^3。用 MATLAB 编写三个子程序，分别作为组合梁结构抗力、永久作用和汽车作用效应的计算程序以及可靠度的计算程序，将组合截面尺寸等参数和上述计算得到的统计参数代入程序计算可靠度。对比分析组合梁使用不同混凝土等级、不一样的钢材牌号、不同厚度和宽度的混凝土板以及不同跨径的组合梁的可靠度指标的变化规律。由宽为 2800mm、厚为 230mm 的混凝土板计算所得结果见图 3，图中 β 为可靠度指标。

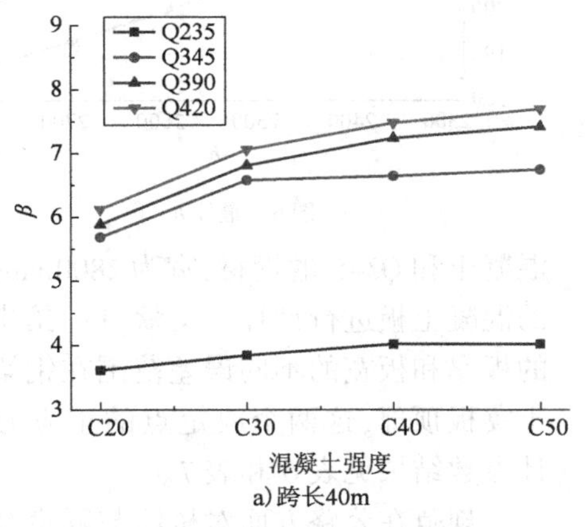

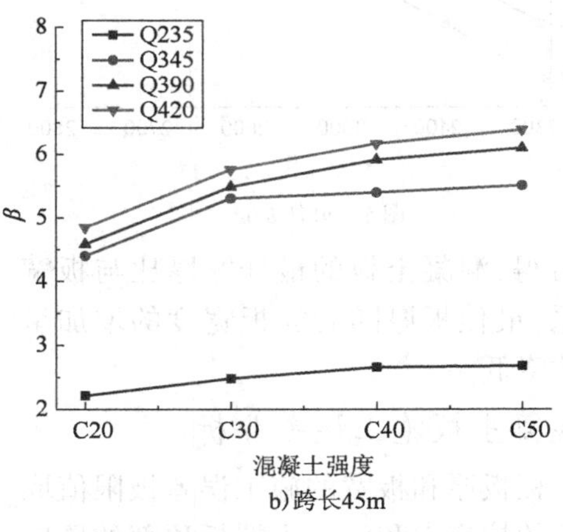

图 3 两种跨径对应不同材料的可靠指标

由图 3 可知，当截面尺寸一定时，只考虑计算跨径的影响，可靠指标随计算跨径的增加而降低；当保持混凝土强度不变时，增加钢材强度会使可靠度也随之增加，并且当钢材牌号从 Q235 上升到

Q345时,可靠指标增加得最快,钢材牌号从Q345到Q420时,可靠指标增加缓慢。当保持钢的强度不变时,可靠度会随着混凝土强度的提高而提高,但刚开始增加得较快,后期上升得比较缓慢,因此从经济性方面考虑时,钢材选用Q345,混凝土采用C40具有较好的经济效益。

影响组合梁可靠指标的因素有很多,在承载能力极限状态下,研究混凝土板的宽度和厚度的比例关系显得非常有必要。下文将取混凝土强度等级为C50,钢材牌号为Q345来研究混凝土翼板的宽厚比,宽厚比(b/h)取值范围为5~20。根据上述程序计算可得图4结果。

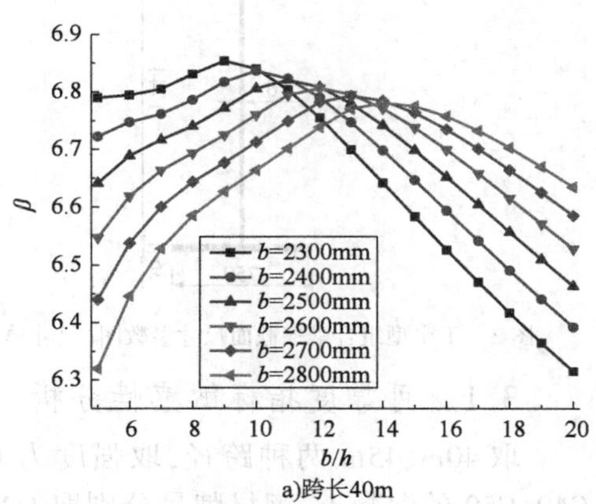

a)跨长40m

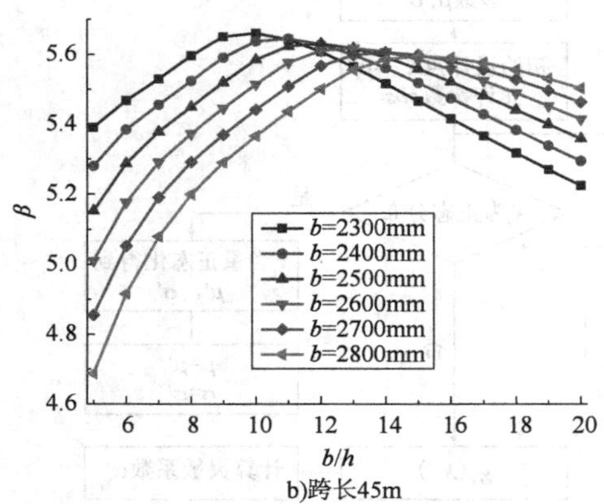

b)跨长45m

图4　两种跨径对应的可靠指标

从图4中可以看出,所有不同板宽可靠度的曲线随着b/h的增大,可靠度呈现出先上升再下降的趋势,即当混凝土板的宽度保持一定时,组合梁的可靠度随着混凝土翼板厚度的降低呈现出先上升再下降的规律。跨径保持相同时,随着b/h的增加,在达到最佳b/h前,混凝土板宽越小可靠度增加得越缓慢,达到最佳宽厚比以后,混凝土板的宽度越大,可靠度下滑得越慢。

当计算跨径为40m、45m时,混凝土板的不同宽度对应的最佳宽厚比和最佳厚度如图5、图6所示。

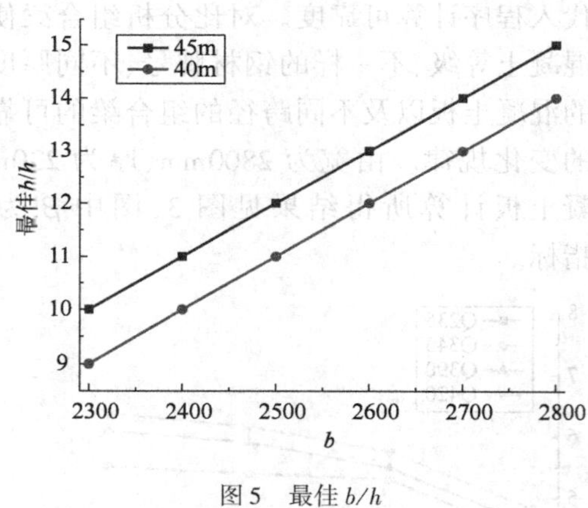

图5　最佳b/h

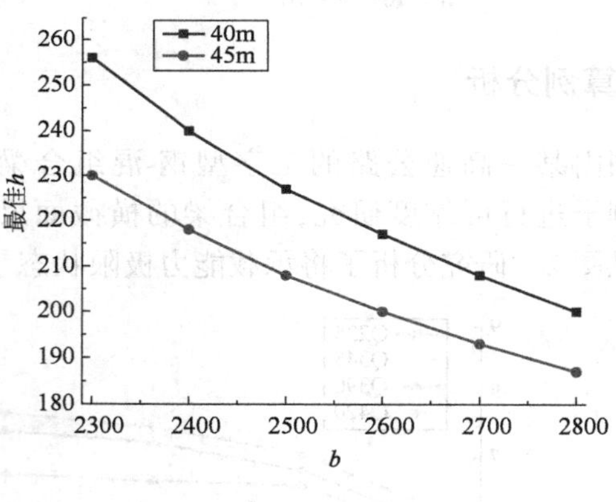

图6　最佳h

由上图可得,混凝土板的最佳宽厚比与板宽呈正比例关系,最佳板厚随着翼板宽度的增加呈抛物线的形式降低。

3.2　混凝土板施工误差分析

混凝土翼板板厚和板宽的施工误差极限值取决于钢梁底部的拉应力和混凝土翼板顶部的压应力,以二者极限允许值为控制目标分析混凝土板厚度与宽度施工误差范围的合理性。采用C50的混凝土和Q345的钢材,宽为2800mm,厚为230mm的混凝土板进行计算。文献[11]给出了混凝土板的板厚和板宽的不同误差范围在钢梁底部和混凝土翼板顶部,这两个决定点的正应力概率特性统计参数结果见表6和表7。

规范在公路方面对桥涵与隧道结构的目标可靠度作了以下规定,当他们的安全等级为一级且破坏为延性破坏时,结构可靠度应不小于4.7。

混凝土板厚度的不同误差范围决定点正应力概率特性统计参数 表6

误差控制范围	应力位置	均值(MPa)	标准差	变异系数
(-5, +5)	混凝土上翼缘	22.5027	0.1204	0.0054
	工字梁下翼缘	275.1509	2.5481	0.0093
(0, +5)	混凝土上翼缘	22.5018	0.0820	0.0036
	工字梁下翼缘	275.1514	2.5473	0.0093
(0, +10)	混凝土上翼缘	22.5027	0.1204	0.0054
	工字梁下翼缘	275.1509	2.5481	0.0093

混凝土板宽度不同误差范围决定点正应力概率特性统计参数 表7

误差控制范围	应力位置	均值(MPa)	标准差	变异系数
(-3, +3)	混凝土上翼缘应力	22.5027	0.1204	0.0054
	工字梁下翼缘应力	275.1509	2.5481	0.0093
(-5, +5)	混凝土上翼缘应力	22.5027	0.1212	0.0054
	工字梁下翼缘应力	275.1512	2.5486	0.0093
(-20, +20)	混凝土上翼缘应力	22.5030	0.1400	0.0062
	工字梁下翼缘应力	275.1511	2.5553	0.0093

该文取可靠度为4.7时，根据弹性理论分析方法编制MATLAB程序计算施工误差在不同范围内对应的混凝土板顶部压应力和工字钢梁底部拉应力，计算结果见表8、表9。

不同混凝土板厚度误差范围决定点的应力 表8

控制点	(-5, +5)	(0, +5)	(0, +10)
混凝土上翼缘压应力(MPa)	23.0686	22.8872	23.0686
工字钢下翼缘拉应力(MPa)	287.1270	287.1237	287.1270

不同混凝土板宽度误差范围决定点的应力 表9

控制点	(-3, +3)	(-5, +5)	(-20, +20)
混凝土上翼缘压应力(MPa)	23.0686	23.0723	23.1610
工字钢下翼缘拉应力(MPa)	287.1270	287.1296	287.1610

由表8知，误差控制范围在(-5, +5)、(0, +10)内不利于结构的安全，在范围(0, +5)内有利于结构的安全。由表9知，误差控制范围在(-5, +5)、(-20, +20)内不利于结构的安全，在范围(-3, +3)内有利于结构的安全。由以上计算结果知，对于混凝土板厚度和宽度的误差控制范围分别在(0, +5)和(-3, +3)范围内较安全。

4 结语

通过考虑不同参数对钢-混凝土组合梁在承载能力极限状态下的可靠度指标进行分析，得到以下结论：

(1)为了提高组合梁的可靠性可以通过增加混凝土的强度或者提高钢材的牌号，为了取得较好的经济效益，采用Q345的钢和C40的混凝土较经济；

(2)不同宽度的混凝土翼板有一个最佳的板厚可以使可靠度指标达到最大；

(3)在同一跨径下，随着混凝土板宽的增加，最佳宽厚比也随之增加，板厚以抛物线的形式随之减小。

(4)在施工时，混凝土板厚度和宽度的误差应分别控制在(0, +5)和(-3, +3)较安全。

参考文献

[1] 廖汶，陈忠延. 钢与混凝土结合梁的可靠度分析[J]. 结构工程师，1999(03):1-6.

[2] 龚志刚. 基于可靠度的结合梁桥评估[J]. 世界桥梁，2007(04):35-39.

[3] 张文,宋永发,李荣庆. 组合梁构件正常使用极限状态可靠度分析[J]. 工业建筑,2006(S1):609-611.

[4] 李明达. 正常使用极限状态下梁式受弯构件的可靠度研究[D]. 兰州:兰州理工大学,2017.

[5] 王立宪,李明达,狄生奎. 基于改进折减刚度法的钢-混凝土组合梁挠度可靠度分析[J]. 建筑科学,2018,34(03):15-21.

[6] 弥恒. 基于蒙特卡洛法的钢-混凝土组合梁桥可靠度参数研究及应用[D]. 长安大学,2009.

[7] 张俊民,朱巍,王付. 基于可靠度的钢-混组合梁抗弯承载力敏感性分析[J]. 公路,2018,63(09):152-155.

[8] 潘明杨. 钢-混凝土连续组合梁抗弯性能及其可靠度分析[D]. 武汉:武汉科技大学,2014.

[9] 王建超,赵君黎,贡金鑫,等. 钢-混凝土组合桥梁承载力可靠度分析[J]. 中国公路学报,2009,22(03):76-82.

[10] 赵国藩,曹居易,张宽权. 工程结构可靠度[M]. 北京:水利电力出版社,1984.

[11] 苏举. 工字型钢-混组合梁焊钉连接件与截面几何参数误差控制范围研究[D]. 西安,长安大学,2019.

热带地区钢-UHPC组合桥面板温度梯度研究

刘吉林*[1] 高庚元[2] 阮 欣[1]

(1. 同济大学土木工程学院;2. 中国水利水电第八工程局有限公司)

摘 要 相较于传统钢-混凝土组合桥面板,钢-UHPC组合桥面板厚度较小,现有文献及规范温度梯度可能不适用,且规范对于热带地区温度预测可能存在偏差。本文以红河特大桥为工程背景,基于桥址处典型热带地区实测气象数据,并设置温带地区气象条件作为对照,采用有限元软件对比分析两个地区年高温日钢-UHPC组合桥面板及钢箱主梁温度场。计算结果表明,桥面板在15:00达到日最高温度,UHPC层温度自上至下线性降低,钢箱梁温度由上至下先逐渐降低,而后基本不变,桥面板底部与钢箱梁间存在较大温差。基于温度场分析结果,采用多折线拟合主梁温度场,与现行公路规范的双折线温度梯度模式有较大差别,且热带地区最大梯度温差35.0℃,大于温带地区的19.8℃与规范的20℃标准。

关键词 热带地区 钢-UHPC组合桥面板 温度场 温度梯度

0 引言

钢-UHPC(Ultra-High Performance Concrete,简称UHPC)组合桥面板是密集配筋超高性能混凝土(UHPC)薄层与传统正交异性钢桥面板通过剪力钉形成的新的组合桥面结构,该种桥面结构可以明显提高桥面板刚度,改善钢板受力,目前已应用在梁桥、拱桥、斜拉桥、悬索桥等各类基本桥型的多座桥梁中[1]。

钢-UHPC组合桥面板为典型的钢-混组合结构,包括热工性能差异的钢材与混凝土,温度效应往往成为控制其设计和应用的关键因素[2]。目前,针对钢-混组合梁桥温度效应开展了很多实桥温度测量[3-4]、温度场数值模拟[5]等研究工作,但这些研究大多针对厚度较大的普通混凝土桥面板,混凝土层一般超过200mm;我国公路规范中[6],规定了带混凝土桥面板的钢结构的温度梯度,也主要针对厚度超过100mm的普通混凝土桥面板。而钢-UHPC组合桥面板厚度较小,一般为35~60mm,其温度效应可能存在差异,应进一步研究。

另一方面,我国公路规范中,对于桥梁温度梯度荷载未考虑区域气候及地理特征影响,而我国不同地区间日照辐射差异很大,由此在不同地区产生不同的温度梯度荷载未在规范中得以体现,在对新疆、西藏等严寒地区以及云南等热带地区的温度模式预测可能有偏差[2]。

红河特大桥为主跨700m的钢箱主梁悬索桥,桥面铺装层采用50mmUHPC层的组合桥面板。

桥址位于云南元阳县(东经 102.835°,北纬 23.255°),地处热带,夏季温度高,太阳辐射强,桥梁温度效应显著。综上所述,本文基于桥址处实测气象数据,并设置江浙某温带气象数据作为对照,采用有限元软件计算钢-UHPC 组合桥面板及主梁日照温度场,确定主梁温度梯度模式,与规范温度梯度模式对比,研究成果可为此类桥面板温度梯度效应计算提供理论依据。

1 自然环境下桥面板温度场计算流程

钢-UHPC 组合桥面板在阳光照射下,存在的热传递现象主要包括:表面接收太阳辐射,主要包括太阳直射、太阳散射和地面太阳反射辐射;表面与空气接触的地方存在对流换热;结构内部存在热传导,如图 1 所示。

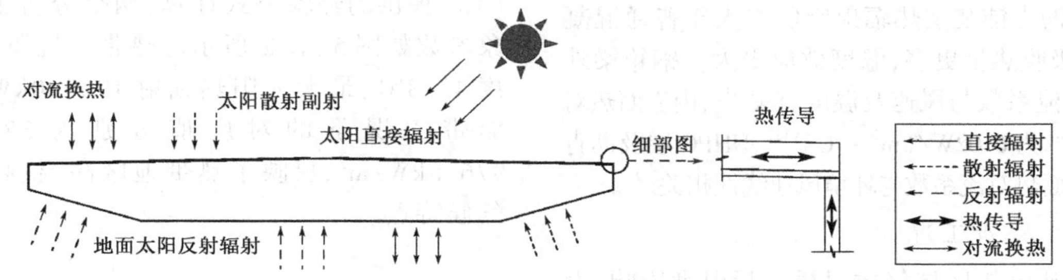

图 1 阳光照射下钢-UHPC 组合桥面板传热示意

根据导热微分方程,桥面板所处热边界条件为第三类边界条件,即周围空气温度和综合换热系数已知,参照文献研究结果,采用综合温度考虑热辐射影响,见式(1)[7]。

$$T = T_\alpha + \frac{\alpha_s I}{h} \tag{1}$$

式中:T——综合温度(℃);

T_α——环境温度(℃);

α_s——结构表面热辐射热量吸收系数;

I——结构表面热辐射强度(kW/m²);

h——对流换热系数(W/(m²·℃))。

采用 ANSYS 有限元软件进行温度时程仿真分析,计算流程如图 2 所示。分析过程首先设定桥面温度场初值,通过循环多天的计算消除初值的误差[8]。各个分析步中,根据太阳入射角,即太阳光方向与外边界法向之间角度,判断外表面是否受到太阳直接照射,然后计算外表面直射辐射值或反辐射值,按照式(1)计算外边界综合温度,将综合温度及热对流系数两类边界条件施加在外边界上,计算桥面板温度场。

基于红河特大桥桥址附近小型气象站 12 月 2 日实测环境温度、风速及太阳热辐射等气象数据,按计算流程得到桥面板 UHPC 层平均温度时程曲线,与当日实测温度对比(图 3)。由图可知,计算温度与实测温度曲线基本吻合,两曲线偏差值在大多数时刻均小于 0.5℃,最大偏差值出现在 12:00,为 1.8℃。计算与实测温度偏差较小,可见采用此计算流程分析桥面板温度场是可行的。

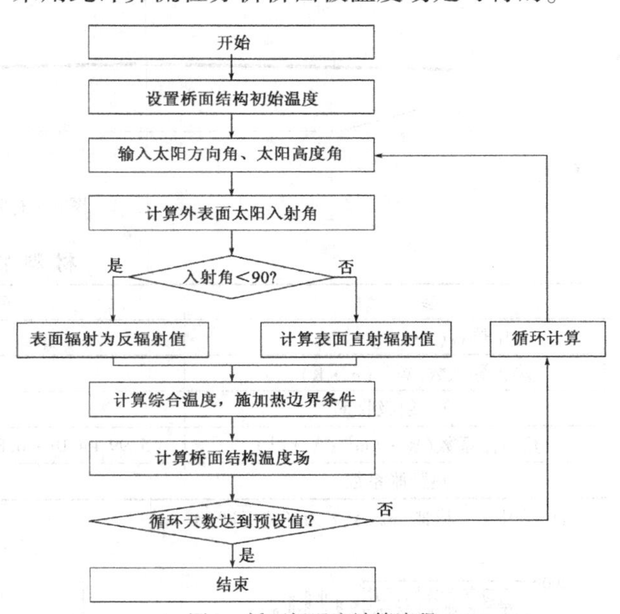

图 2 桥面板温度计算流程

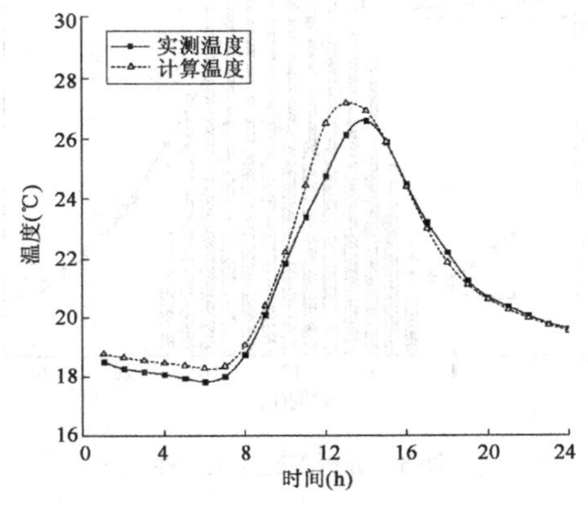

图 3 计算温度与实测温度对比

2 温度场分析

2.1 分析模型

建立红河特大桥钢-UHPC 组合桥面板及钢箱主梁有限元模型，包括沥青铺装层，UHPC 层及下部钢箱梁，如图 4 所示。参照相关文献研究，各材料参数如表 1 所示，其中，沥青铺装层的热辐射吸收率在 0.75～0.90 之间变化[9-10]，本文取值为 0.85[10]，沥青铺装层热辐射吸收率大于普通混凝土，结构吸收热量更多，温度效应更大。钢箱梁外表面热对流系数与风速及温度有关[11]，内表面热对流系数可取为 6.02W/(m²·℃)[12]，UHPC 层及沥青铺装层表面热对流系数与环境风速线性相关[12]。

2.2 分析工况

为对比分析区域气候对桥面板温度影响，设置热带地区及江浙某温带地区两个气象条件分析工况(以下简称热带工况、温带工况)。热带工况下，环境温度、太阳热辐射、太阳反辐射及风速等参数值基于云南省元阳县红河特大桥附近小型气象站长期实测气象数据，选择历史监测温度最高一天的监测数据，经数据平滑处理后用作分析。温带工况下，环境温度及风速参数采用历史天气数据，太阳热辐射及反辐射值按照文献[13]提供的经验公式计算，两个分析工况的气象参数如图 5、表 2 所示。热带工况下，最高温度 43.8℃，最大太阳热辐射 1960.0kW/m²，而温带工况下的对应值分别为 37.1℃及 976.8kW/m²，反映了热带地区高温、高辐射的气候特点。

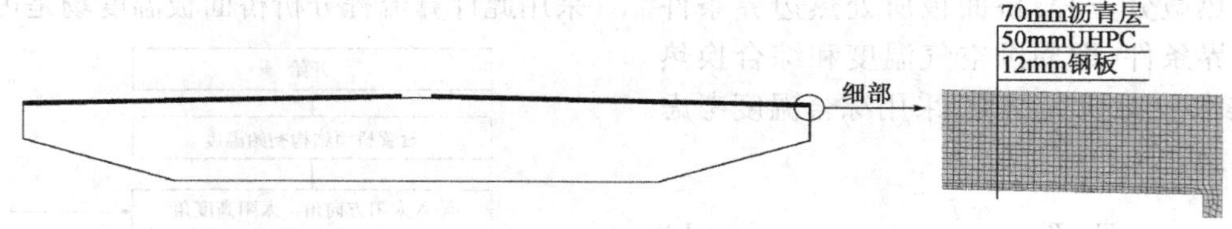

图 4　有限元分析模型

材料物理参数　　表 1

参数	钢材	UHPC 层	沥青铺装层
比热容(J·(kg·℃)⁻¹)	340	960	920
热传导系数(W·(m·K)⁻¹)	45	1.86	1.21
热辐射吸收率	0.7	0.5	0.85
热对流系数(W·(m²·℃)⁻¹)	$5.99+4.0v+0.88[4.8+0.75(T-5)]$	$12.47+3.33v$	$12.47+3.33v$
热膨胀系数	1.2e-5	1.0e-5	1.0e-5

注：表中 v 为风速(m/s)，T 为环境温度(℃)

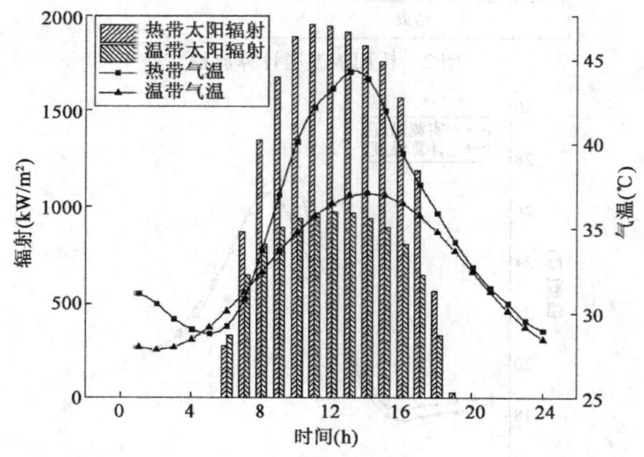

图 5　分析工况气象条件

气象条件汇总　　表 2

分析工况	热带工况	温带工况
气温范围(℃)	29.0～43.8	28.0～37.1
最大太阳热辐射(kW/m²)	1960	976.8
最大太阳反辐射(kW/m²)	210.6	85.4
环境风速(m/s)	3.5	2.3

2.3 桥面板温度场

按分析工况数据，以 1h 为时间间隔，连续计算 5d 至计算结果稳定，取第 5d 的计算结果，两种工况下的桥面板日温度时程曲线如图 6、图 7 所示。白天，受阳光照射影响，沥青铺装层吸收太阳热辐射，通过热传导传递至下部 UHPC 层及钢箱梁,桥面板温度由上至下逐渐降低,并在15:00达到最高温度。夜晚,桥面板通过热对流散热,由于桥面板厚度较薄,散热较快,桥面板各部位温度逐渐趋于一致,与环境温度大致相等,在05:00温度最低。

热带工况下,桥面板顶部日最高温度为80.0℃,底部日最高温度为73.9℃,顶底部温差为6.1℃。温带工况下,桥面板顶部日最高温度为58.9℃,底部日最高温度为55.2℃,顶底部温差3.7℃。桥面板下部钢箱梁竖直腹板接收到上部UHPC层热传导的热量,其平均温度略高于底板。热带工况与温带工况温度场分布特征类似,但热带工况温度更高。

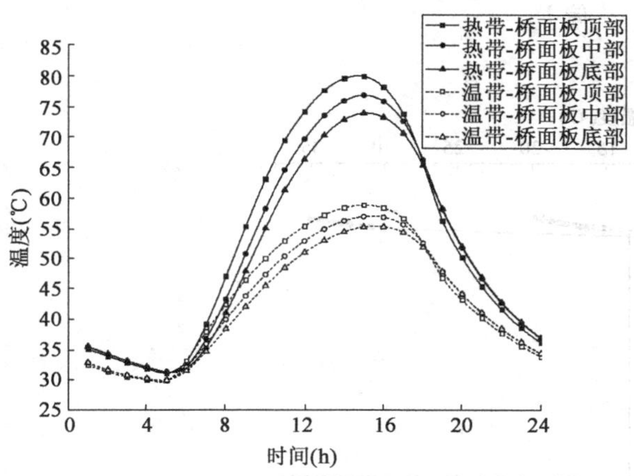

图6 桥面板温度时程曲线

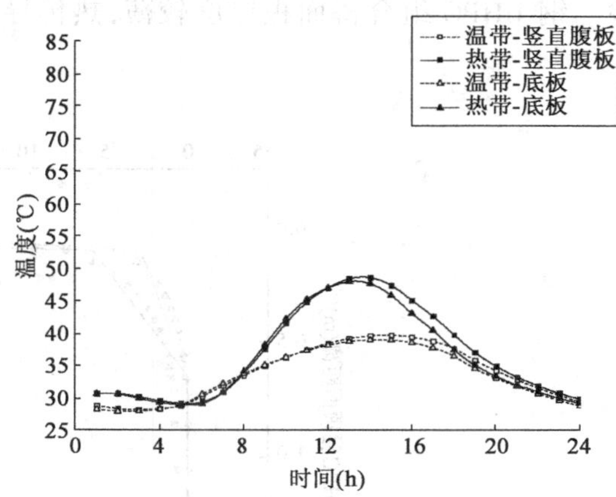

图7 钢主梁各部位温度时程曲线对比

3 温度梯度分析

一般认为,当桥面板上表面最高温度与梁高上最低温度差值最大时,此时温度场为最不利温度场[4],按此方法热带工况与温带工况最不利温度场分别出现在16:00和15:00。提取此时刻有限元模型中各个节点的温度结果,按其至桥面板顶面垂直距离分类统计,得到桥面板温度沿竖向分布,如图8所示。两个计算工况下UHPC层温度由顶面至底面线性下降,在钢梁内温度由上至下先逐渐降低,而后基本不变,钢梁内温差较小,但UHPC层底部与钢主梁间存在较大温差。

我国现行《公路桥涵设计通用规范》中,规定了带混凝土桥面板的钢结构竖向日照温度梯度如图9所示,此种温度梯度模式适用于混凝土桥面板厚度大于100mm的桥梁结构。温度梯度基数T_1、T_2大小考虑铺装层类型及铺装层厚度的影响,沥青铺装层越厚,正温度梯度基数越小,其中,采用50mm沥青铺装层的温度梯度基数T_1、T_2分别为20℃、6.7℃。规范温度梯度未考虑地域影响。

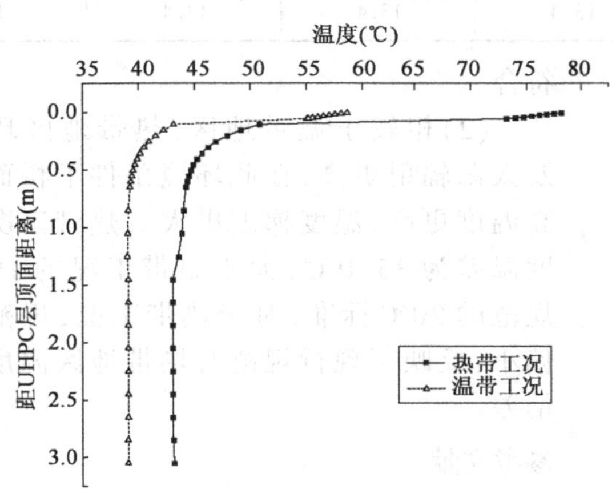

图8 桥面板及钢主梁温度竖向分布

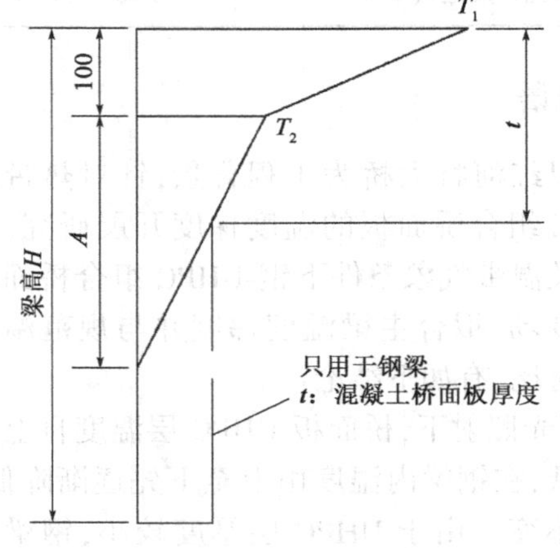

图9 规范温度梯度

根据图8的温度竖向分布图,将温度分解为整体温升及温度梯度,其中整体温升为钢箱梁底板温度,热带工况取为45.9℃,温带工况为39.0℃,两个计算工况温度梯度近似采用多折线拟合,其与规范温度梯度模式对比见图10和表3。

规范温度梯度采用双折线模型,混凝土桥面板底部温度与钢梁温度相等,与本文拟合多折线温度梯度模式,UHPC层与钢箱梁间存在较大温差相比有较大差别。这是由于规范温度梯度主要针对厚度较大的混凝土桥面板,桥面板由上至下的热传导路径较长,由桥面板顶部传递至底部的热量较少。钢-UHPC组合桥面板厚度较薄,热传导路径短,传递至桥面板底部的热量较多,且钢箱梁为薄壁结构,腹板厚度小,桥面板热量难以通过腹板继续向下传递,钢箱梁温度相对桥面板更低。在最大梯度温差方面,热带工况下最大梯度温差为35.0℃,温带工况下为19.8℃,与规范建议值20℃接近。对于热带工况,规范建议值偏小,反映了现行规范对热带地区温度预测的偏差。

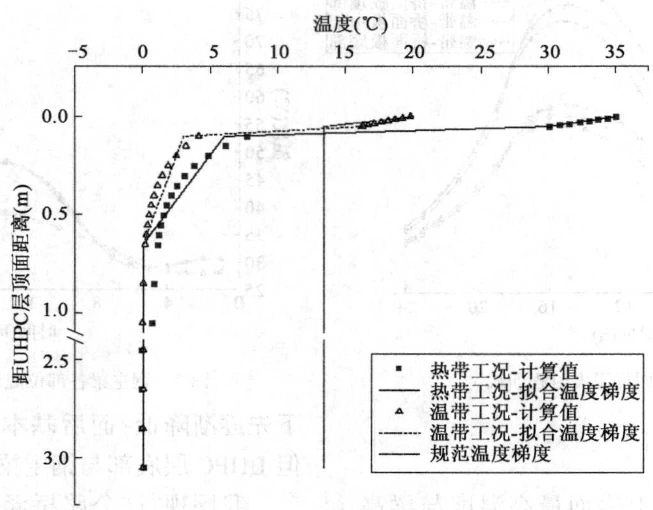

图10　桥面板温度梯度模式

主要参数表格　　表3

普通混凝土桥面板竖向位置(m)	0	0.05	0.10	0.65	3.05
温度值(温带工况)(℃)	19.8	16.2	3.0	0	0
温度值(热带工况)(℃)	35.0	30.0	6.0	0	0
温度值(规范)(℃)	20	13.4	13.4	13.4	13.4

4　结语

本文以红河特大桥为工程背景,针对热带地区钢-UHPC组合桥面板的温度梯度开展研究,对比了热带及温带气象条件下钢-UHPC组合桥面板及主梁温度场,拟合主梁温度梯度并与规范温度梯度进行对比,有如下结论:

(1)阳光照射下,桥面板UHPC层温度自上至下线性降低,在钢梁内温度由上至下先逐渐降低,而后基本不变。由于UHPC层厚度较小,钢梁与UHPC桥面板间存在较大温差,主梁温度梯度近似采用多折线拟合,与现行公路规范混凝土桥面板底部温度与钢梁温度相等的温度梯度假定不相符合。

(2)相较于温带地区,热带地区环境温度及太阳辐射更高,在此环境条件下桥面板日最高温度更高,温度梯度更大。热带工况最大梯度温差为35.0℃,大于温带工况的19.8℃与规范的20℃标准,对于热带工况,规范建议值偏小,反映了现行规范对热带地区温度预测的偏差。

参考文献

[1] 邵旭东,胡建华.钢-超高性能混凝土轻型组合桥梁结构[M].北京:人民交通出版社股份有限公司,2015.

[2] 樊健生,刘诚,刘宇飞. 钢-混凝土组合梁桥温度场与温度效应研究综述[J]. 中国公路学报,2020,33(04):1-13.

[3] 武庆祥,龙佩恒,焦驰宇. 北京地区某钢-混组合箱梁日照温度场研究[J]. 北京建筑大学学报,2016,32(02):22-27.

[4] 陈彦江,王力波,李勇. 钢-混凝土组合梁桥温度场及温度效应研究[J]. 公路交通科技,2014,31(11):85-91.

[5] 陈春苗. 大跨度悬索桥钢-混组合桥面系温度效应分析[D]. 长沙:长沙理工大学,2014.

[6] 中华人民共和国行业标准. 公路桥涵设计通用规范:JTG D60—2015[S]. 北京:人民交通出版社,2015.

[7] 王凯. 混凝土斜拉桥桥塔时变温度场及其温度模式[D]. 上海:同济大学,2016.

[8] Kim S H, Park S J, Wu J, et al. Temperature variation in steel box girders of cable-stayed bridges during construction [J]. Journal of Constructional Steel Research, 2015, 112: 80-92.

[9] 李云龙. 沥青路面热物性参数演化及其对冻土地基温度场影响机理研究[D]. 重庆:重庆交通大学,2018.

[10] 吴赣昌. 层状路面体系温度场分析[J]. 中国公路学报,1992(04):17-25.

[11] 刘丽芳. 钢-混凝土组合梁温度场及温度效应研究[D]. 成都:西南交通大学,2019

[12] 刘照球. 混凝土结构表面对流换热研究[D]. 上海:同济大学,2006.

[13] 陈科旭. 自然环境下大跨度悬索桥空间温度场和温度效应研究[D]. 天津:天津大学,2018.

隧道工程篇

考虑空间约束的隧道塑性区统一强度解析

姚 毅*[1] 高 强[2]
(1. 长安大学公路学院;2. 广州地铁设计研究院股份有限公司)

摘 要 为了探究隧道掘进过程中围岩塑性区的扩展规律及中主应力 σ_2 的影响,本文通过等效模型将空间约束效应简化为沿隧道纵向的虚拟支护力,并基于统一强度准则进行围岩弹塑性分析,对已有深埋圆形隧道的塑性区上限解进行修正。文章讨论了围岩应力释放函数的选取并通过算例与 Kastner 解和文献中的数值解进行对比验证。结果表明:空间约束效应不影响塑性区的上限值,但决定了塑性区的发展路径,考虑该效应能进一步解释围岩塑性区随掌子面掘进的动态扩展过程,相当于给出了"子弹头"形状的三维塑性区范围;中主应力 σ_2 也会影响塑性区的大小,与统一强度准则下的结果相比,经典 Kastner 解给出塑性区范围偏大,但在掌子面附近,σ_2 的影响要弱于空间约束效应。

关键词 隧道工程 塑性区半径 弹塑性分析 空间约束效应 中主应力

0 引言

基于弹塑性理论的收敛约束法对于围岩和支护结构的变形机理给出了较好解释,在隧道工程中应用较广,合理确定围岩塑性区范围至关重要[1]。深埋圆形隧道弹塑性分析中 Kastner 解是一个典型代表,该方法将隧道开挖简化为"厚壁圆筒"平面应变问题,"圆筒"的内径即为隧道开挖内径,外径可视为无限大,通过基于 Mohr-Coulomb 准则的理论解析,给出了围岩塑性区半径公式[2]。后续学者基于该思路,针对应变软化、渗流、蠕变等特性开展了针对性的修正工作[3-6]。

实际上,掘进中的隧道更接近于一个"厚壁深孔"模型,较"厚壁圆筒"多了掌子面处的约束。由于该约束效应的存在,使得在支护结构略滞后于开挖作业的条件下,掌子面附近的围岩仍能暂时维持稳定,随着隧道向前掘进,掌子面与已开挖断面的距离不断增大,对该断面的约束逐渐减小,围岩压力不断释放,围岩塑性区扩展,变形增大。此外,文献[7]中的数值模拟更直观,表明隧道掌子面附近的围岩塑性区是类似于"子弹头"的形状。经典 Kastner 解或"厚壁圆筒"模型可以代表贯通的隧道,给出了塑性区的上限解,却不能解释塑性区随隧道掘进的动态发展过程,有必要考虑掌子面空间约束效应影响进行修正。

Mohr-Coulomb 准则是隧道工程中应用较广的一个二维准则,其形式简单,仅需要黏聚力 c 和内摩擦角 φ 两个参数。但越来越多的文献[8-9]表明,中主应力 σ_2 对围岩强度的影响也不可忽略。Yao 等[7]人在二维广义 Hoek-Brown 准则下研究了塑性区与掌子面约束间的关系,若要进一步探究 σ_2 对塑性区范围的影响则需要依靠三维强度准则。三维准则最大的缺点在于形式复杂,求解难度大,众多三维准则中,俞茂宏[10]提出统一强度准则较为特殊,该准则主要包含 c、φ 两个强度参数,并通过系数 b 来反映中主应力的影响和与其他准则的关系,当 $b=0$ 时可退化为 Mohr-Coulomb 准则;表达式上有较好的连续性,兼顾了简洁性和中主应力 σ_2 影响两个因素。因此,本文进行塑性区解析时拟采用该准则。

综上所述,鉴于掌子面空间约束效应和中主应力 σ_2 均对围岩塑性区范围产生一定影响,而已有的解析解却鲜有同时考虑两类因素作用下的解答。本文基于统一强度准则进行弹塑性分析,通过等效模型将空间约束效应转化为沿隧道纵向分布的虚拟支护力,给出了考虑该效应和中主应力 σ_2 影响下的塑性区半径公式,并和经典 Kastner 解、文献中的数值解行对比,分别探讨了约束效应和 σ_2 的影响,相当于将塑性区半径的上限解拓展为空间范围内的三维解,为动态设计和施工提供了一定的理论支撑。

1 空间约束效应及其等效函数

"新奥法"施工中,支护结构一般略滞后于开挖作业,但无支护断面的围岩却能暂时维持稳定,该效应可视为由掌子面施加了临时约束。隧道向前掘进时,掌子面与某个已开挖断面的距离随时间增大,对该断面的约束逐渐减小,围岩压力不断释放,围岩变形增大。隧道掌子面在时间与空间上体现出这种约束效应,即空间约束效应[11]。

参照Yao等[7]人的相关研究,将掌子面对隧道纵向不同位置的约束可视为一种虚拟支护力,用系数λ表示距掌子面x位置断面的围岩应力或位移的释放程度,即

$$\lambda = \frac{p_x}{p_\infty} = \frac{u_x}{u_\infty} = f(x) \tag{1}$$

式中:p_x、u_x——与掌子面距离x时释放的应力、位移;

p_∞、u_∞——释放的应力、位移最大值。

参照文献[7,11]掌子面空间约束效应等效模型(图1),则对应位置处由掌子面约束等效的虚拟支护力可表示为

$$p_i(x) = p_0(1-\lambda) = p_0 - p_0 f(x) \tag{2}$$

式中:p_0——围岩初始应力,假定$p_i(x)$的方向为沿隧道径向。

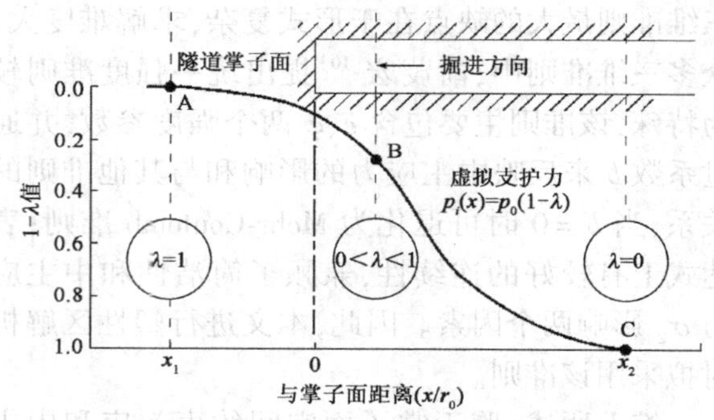

图1 约束效应等效模型

掌子面前方x_1位置的截面A,荷载由围岩本身承担,掌子面后方足够远位置的截面C,围岩所传递的荷载由支护结构承担,那么两截面之间的任意位置B处,由空间约束效应虚拟等效的支护力可由式(2)函数表示。

选取合理的释放函数$f(x)$至关重要。一般情况下硬岩隧道开挖后,围岩应力释放速率快,软岩情况时释放慢,因此不同围岩条件下释放函数应该有所区别。图2列举了文献[12]中关于释放函数的不同取值,A到G代表一组由差到好的围岩应力释放曲线,由图可知,不同围岩条件下曲线并非固定的,Panet,Chern和Unlu and Gercek的曲线基于特定围岩条件下的数据实测或非线性拟合,体现了某种围岩条件下的变形特征,却并不具有普遍适用性。Vlachopoulos[12]的释放函数通过最大塑性区这个过程值代表了一系列围岩曲线,进一步研究可知,在某种特定围岩条件下,Vlachopoulos曲线可与其他四个曲线相重合。因此,本文选取Vlachopoulos的释放函数来进行虚拟支护力等效,即

$$f(x) = \begin{cases} 1 - \left(1 - \dfrac{1}{3}\exp\dfrac{-0.15R_{p\max}}{r_0}\right) \cdot \exp\dfrac{-1.5x}{R_{p\max}}, & x \geqslant 0 \\ \dfrac{1}{3}\exp\dfrac{-0.15R_{p\max}}{r_0} \cdot \exp(x/r_0), & x < 0 \end{cases} \tag{3}$$

式中:$R_{p\max}$——最大塑性区半径;

r_0——隧道开挖半径,后文基于特定围岩参数进行应力释放曲线的计算。

2 约束效应下的塑性区统一强度求解

2.1 统一强度准则

在众多三维强度准则中,俞茂宏[10]提出的统一强度准则应用较广,其定义为当作用于单元体上的两个剪应力以及相应的正应力函数达到某一极值时,材料破坏。通过系数b来反映中主应力σ_2的影响和与其他准则的关系,表达式为:

$$\frac{1-\sin\varphi}{1+\sin\varphi}\sigma_1 - \frac{1}{1+b}(b\sigma_2+\sigma_3) = \frac{2c\cdot\cos\varphi}{1+\sin\varphi} \tag{4}$$

当$\sigma_2 \leqslant \dfrac{\sigma_1+\sigma_3}{2} - \dfrac{\sigma_1-\sigma_3}{2}\sin\varphi$

$$\frac{1-\sin\varphi}{(1+b)(1+\sin\varphi)}(b\sigma_2+\sigma_1) - \sigma_3 = \frac{2c\cdot\cos\varphi}{1+\sin\varphi}, \text{当 } \sigma_2 \geqslant \frac{\sigma_1+\sigma_3}{2} - \frac{\sigma_1-\sigma_3}{2}\sin\varphi \tag{5}$$

式中:b——反应中主应力影响程度的变量,可通过三轴试验获取,若要在π平面上保持包线的全凸性,则b的取值区间为[0,1]。

当$b=0$时,该准则退化为经典Mohr-Coulomb准则,其主应力表达式为:

$$\sigma_1 - \sigma_3 = (\sigma_1+\sigma_3)\sin\varphi + 2c\cos\varphi \tag{6}$$

式中:c——黏聚力;

φ——内摩擦角。

2.2 考虑约束效应影响的塑性区求解

如图3所示,参照经典弹塑性平面应变求解过程[13],提出如下假定:

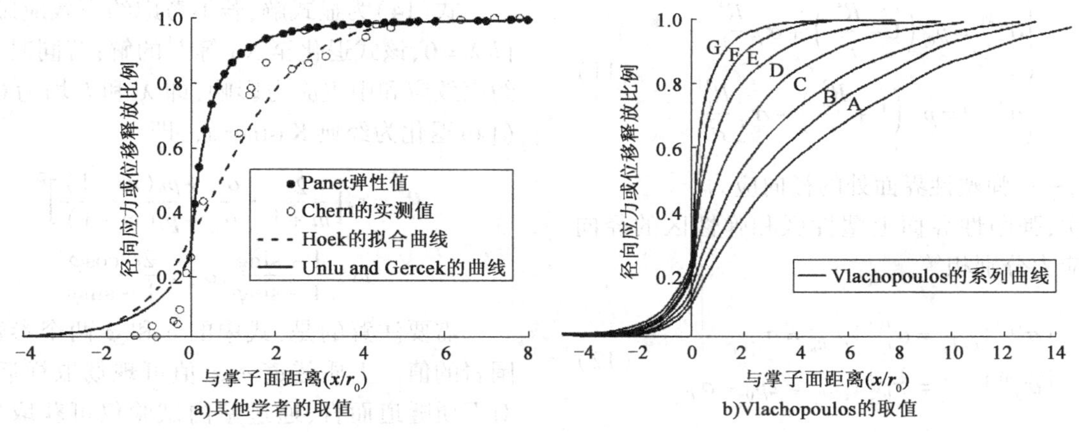

图2 文献中的围岩应力释放曲线[12]

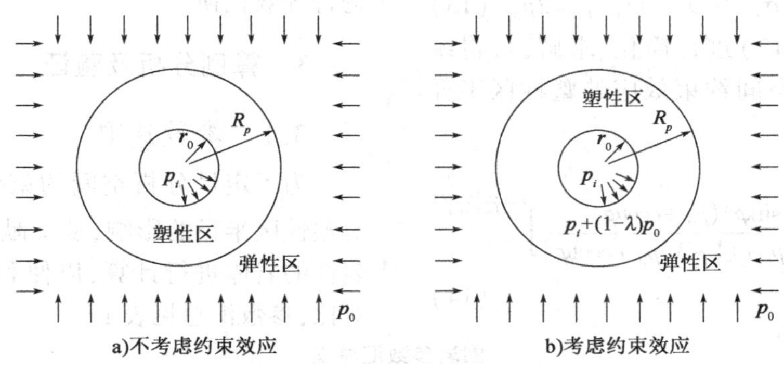

图3 平面应变简化力学模型

(1)围岩均匀、连续、各向同性;

(2)围岩初始应力为静水压力分布;

(3)隧道有足够的深埋,且圆形截面尺寸沿轴线保持不变;

(4)约束效应采用式(2)进行虚拟等效,塑性准则采用2.1节的统一强度准则。

三维平面应变问题求解时一般将垂直于平面的应力 σ_z 当作中主应力,俞茂宏等[8]指出 σ_z 的值会随着平面内塑性应变的增大而迅速接近平面内径向和切向应力的平均值,根据该思路,本文用 $(\sigma_\theta+\sigma_r)/2$ 代替 σ_z 来简化计算过程,即

$$\sigma_2=\sigma_z=\frac{\sigma_1+\sigma_3}{2}=\frac{\sigma_r+\sigma_\theta}{2} \tag{7}$$

首先,通过式(7)对求解过程进行简化,将其代入式(5),得

$$\frac{(1-\sin\varphi)(2+b)}{2+2b}\sigma_\theta-\frac{2+b+(2+3b)\sin\varphi}{2+2b}\sigma_r=2c\cos\varphi \tag{8}$$

平衡方程为

$$\frac{\partial\sigma_r}{\partial r}+\frac{\sigma_r-\sigma_\theta}{r}=0 \tag{9}$$

式中,切向应力 σ_θ 和径向应力 σ_r 分别被视为第一主应力 σ_1 和第三主应力 σ_3。

将式(8)代入式(9),衬砌结构提供的支护力为 p_i,掌子面等效虚拟支护力为 $(1-\lambda)p_0$,总支护力为 $p_i+(1-\lambda)p_0$。因此,考虑空间约束效应影响,隧道内壁处的边界条件由 $\sigma_r=p_i|_{r=r_0}$ 变为 $\sigma_r=[p_i+(1-\lambda)p_0]|_{r=r_0}$,可得考虑约束效应的塑性区范围内应力解。

$$\begin{cases}\sigma_r^{(p)}=[p_i+(1-\lambda)p_0+c\cot\varphi]\left(\dfrac{r}{r_0}\right)^{\frac{4(1+b)\sin\varphi}{(2+b)(1-\sin\varphi)}}-c\cot\varphi\\ \sigma_\theta^{(p)}=\dfrac{2+b+2\sin\varphi+3b\sin\varphi}{(2+b)(1-\sin\varphi)}[p_i+(1-\lambda)p_0+c\cot\varphi]\\ \qquad\left(\dfrac{r}{r_0}\right)^{\frac{4(1+b)\sin\varphi}{(2+b)(1-\sin\varphi)}}-c\cot\varphi\end{cases} \tag{10}$$

式中:p_i——衬砌结构提供的支护力。

其次,弹性区范围应力求解。可直接采用经典的厚壁圆筒问题弹性解[8],即

$$\begin{cases}\sigma_r^{(e)}=p_0\left(1-\dfrac{R_p^2}{r^2}\right)+\sigma_R\dfrac{R_p^2}{r^2}\\ \sigma^{(e)}\theta=p_0\left(1+\dfrac{R_p^2}{r^2}\right)-\sigma_R\dfrac{R_p^2}{r^2}\end{cases}\tag{11}$$

式中:σ_R——弹塑性界面处的径向应力。

再次,弹塑性界面上塑性区和弹性区的径向和切向应力分别相等

$$\begin{cases}\sigma_r^{(p)}|_{r=R_p}=\sigma_r^{(e)}|_{r=R_p}=\sigma_R\\ \sigma_\theta^{(p)}|_{r=R_p}=\sigma_\theta^{(e)}|_{r=R_p}=2p_0-\sigma_R\end{cases}\tag{12}$$

为方便计算,联立式(12)中两个方程消去σ_R

$$(\sigma_r^{(p)}+\sigma_\theta^{(p)})|_{r=R_p}=(\sigma_r^{(e)}+\sigma_\theta^{(e)})|_{r=R_p}=2p_0\tag{13}$$

联立式(10)和(13)进行简化、求解,可得统一强度准则下,考虑空间约束效应的塑性区半径R_p解析解为

$$R_p=r_0\left[\frac{(2+b)(1-\sin\varphi)(p_0+c\cot\varphi)}{(2+b+b\sin\varphi)[p_i+(1-\lambda)p_0+c\cot\varphi]}\right]^{\frac{(2+b)(1-\sin\varphi)}{4(1+b)\sin\varphi}}\tag{14}$$

式(14)为显式解,若不考虑约束效应影响,即仅$\lambda=0$,该式退化至Xu等[8]的解;若同时不考虑约束效应和中主应力影响,即λ和b均为0,则式(14)退化为经典Kastner解,即

$$R_p=r_0\left[\frac{2}{m+1}\cdot\frac{\sigma_{ci}+p_0(m-1)}{\sigma_{ci}+p_i(m-1)}\right]^{\frac{1}{m-1}}\tag{15}$$

$$m=\frac{1+\sin\varphi}{1-\sin\varphi},\sigma_{ci}=\frac{2c\cos\varphi}{1-\sin\varphi}\tag{16}$$

需要注意的是,式中的c和φ两个参数应为围岩的值。土质隧道c、φ值可现场取样后测量,对石质隧道而言,通过室内试验仅可获取岩石的c、φ值,岩体由于结构面的存在,无法直接获取,需进行等效代换。

3 算例分析及验证

3.1 参数选取

为了定量分析空间约束效应及中主应力σ_2对塑性区半径的影响,从文献[12]中选取了某种代表性的岩体进行计算,以便和数值模拟结果进行对比,参数汇总见表1。

围岩参数汇总表 表1

围岩 Hoek-Brown 参数								
σ_{ci}(MPa)	GSI	s	a	m_b	p_0(MPa)	σ_{cm}(MPa)	γ(kN/m³)	r_0(m)
75	60	0.0117	0.503	1.678	28	14	26	2.5

由于文献[12]给出的相关参数为硬质围岩,本文按照Hoek等[14]给出的平均参数法将其换算成岩体对应的c、φ值,即$c=3.26\text{kPa}$,$\varphi=33.4°$。

3.2 不考虑约束效应的塑性区上限解

若不考虑约束效应影响($\lambda=1$),所得结果为塑性区范围的上限解,如经典Kastner解。取支护力$p_i=0$,由于文献未提供中应力σ_2的影响,本文计算了系数b不同取值下的结果,无量纲化计算以消除隧道尺寸效应,汇总见表2。

由表2可知,若不考虑中主应力σ_2的影响,本文解的结果与经典Kastner解一致,在公式形式上也保持了连续性。但随着b值增大,即中主应力影响程度增大,塑性区范围逐渐减小,也印证了Xu等[8]的研究,即不考虑中主应力影响会部分低估围岩强度,进而给出相对保守的塑性区范围。Vlachopoulos[12]给出了表1围岩参数下塑性区上限的数值结果,$b=0$(不考虑中主应力)时理论计算值较模拟值高出约4.7%,与文献中数值计算结果相对应的b值为0.14。

最大无量纲塑性区半径结果汇总表 表2

解的类型		无量纲塑性区半径 $R^*p(R_p/r_0)$
Kastner解		1.57
本文的求解	$b=0$	1.57
	$b=0.2$	1.48
	$b=0.4$	1.42
	$b=0.6$	1.38
	$b=0.8$	1.35
	$b=1$	1.33
Vlachopoulos模拟值		1.50

3.3 空间约束效应和中主应力σ_2的影响

取隧道支护力为$p_i=0.1p_0$,按照与上节数值结果对应的$b=0.14$来计算同时考虑中主应力σ_2

和空间约束效应下的塑性区半径，和不考虑约束效应时的结果进行对比，见图4和图5。

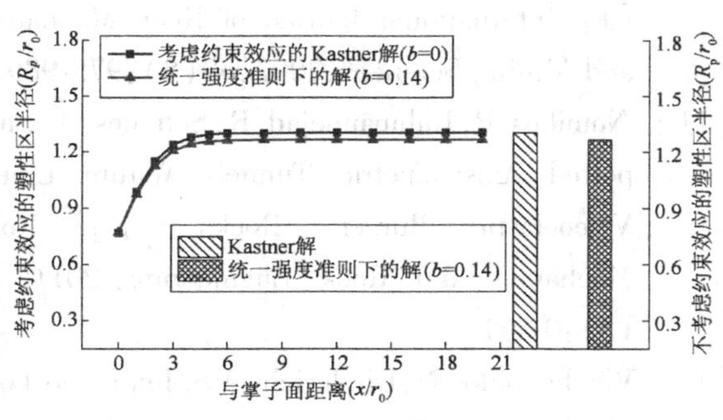

图4 无量纲塑性区范围对比图

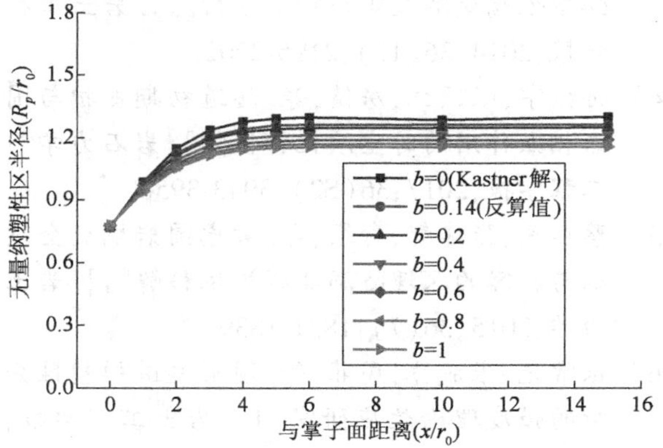

图5 在不同系数 b 条件下的塑性区范围

如图6所示，由于空间约束效应存在，与掌子面间距越大，塑性区越大；当距离足够远时，塑性区不再增长，与不考虑该效应下的结果相同。说明该效应本质上不影响塑性区的上限值，但决定了塑性区的发展路径，形成了三维空间内类似“子弹头”的形状，与Yao等[7]人数值模拟的形状基本吻合，在距掌子面 $2r_0$ 和 $4r_0$ 位置，与文献的误差分别为8.7%和9.5%，误差可能和文献选取的强度准则(Hoek-brown准则)，以及围岩 c、φ 值等效过程相关。不考虑该效应影响，则计算出的掌子面附近初期塑性区范围偏大，不能反映出围岩塑性区随掌子面掘进的发展过程。约束效应的影响范围也仅局限在掌子面附近一段距离，对本文选取的硬岩参数而言，该影响范围约为 $5r_0$，超出该范围则塑性区不再增长。

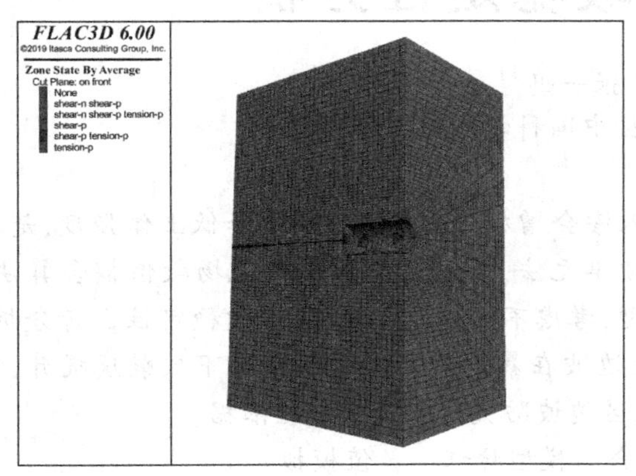

图6 隧道掌子面附近类似“子弹头”形状的塑性区[7]

中主应力 σ_2 同样会影响围岩塑性区大小，在掌子面附近一定范围内，中主应力的影响要弱于空间约束效应，且距离掌子面越近，中主应力的影响越小。在距掌子面 r_0 的断面处，不同中主应力影响程度下(b 的取值区间0~1)，塑性区范围的差异在5%以内，但若不考虑空间约束效应，则与Kastner上限解的误差为25.2%，即中主应力的影响要弱于掌子面约束效应。从动态设计和施工的角度，同时考虑约束效应和 σ_2 影响有助于更好的掌握围岩与支护结构的变形增长过程，以便采用针对性的工程措施。

4 结语

(1)同时考虑空间约束效应和中主应力 σ_2 的影响，基于统一强度准则对隧道塑性区半径公式进行修正，给出了掌子面附近围岩塑性区类似“子弹头”形状的三维分布，反映出塑性区发展与掌子面掘进之间的关系，为动态设计与施工提供了一定的理论支撑。

(2)空间约束效应本质上不影响塑性区范围的上限值，但在一定的约束范围内决定了塑性区的发展路径。

(3)中主应力 σ_2 会影响围岩塑性区的范围，但影响相对较小，就本文中的围岩参数而言，误差在5%以内。

参考文献

[1] 张常光，赵均海，范文. 围岩塑性区变形特性对隧道收敛约束的影响[J]. 中国公路学报，2016，29(3)：106-115.

[2] 夏才初，徐晨，刘宇鹏，等. 基于GZZ强度准则考虑应变软化特性的深埋隧道弹塑性解[J]. 岩石力学与工程学报，2018，37(11)：2468-2477.

[3] 张建智,俞缙,蔡燕燕,等.渗水膨胀岩隧洞黏弹塑性蠕变解及变形特性分析[J].岩土工程学报,2014,36(12):2195-2202.

[4] 孙振宇,张顶立,房倩,等.隧道初期支护与围岩相互作用的时空演化特性[J].岩石力学与工程学报,2017,36(S2):3943-3956.

[5] 蔡燕燕,张建智,俞缙,等.考虑围岩蠕变全过程与扩容的深埋隧洞非线性位移解[J].岩土力学,2015,36(7):1831-1839.

[6] 张常光,张成林,周菲,等.圆形隧道弹塑性分析的强度理论效应研究[J].岩土工程学报,2018,40(8):1449-1456.

[7] Yao Yi,Lai Hong-peng,Zhang Qin,et al. Prediction of Plastic and Fractured Zone Extent Around Deep Circular Tunnel Subjected to Spatial Constraint Effect[J]. Arabian Journal of Geosciences,2021,14(20):2098.

[8] Xu Shuan-qiang,Yu Mao-hong. The Effect of the Intermediate Principal Stress on the Ground Response of Circular Openings in Rock Mass [J]. Rock Mechanics and Rock Engineering, 2006,39(2):169-181.

[9] 张玉,邵生俊,赵敏,等.平面应变条件下土的强度准则在黄土工程问题中的应用研究[J].土木工程学报,2018,51(8):71-80.

[10] Yu Mao-hong,Zan Yue-wen,Zhao Jian,et al. A Unified Strength Criterion for Rock Material [J]. International Journal of Rock Mechanics and Mining Sciences,2002,39(8):975-989.

[11] Nomikos P,Rahmannejad R,Sofianos A. Supported Axisymmetric Tunnels Within Linear Viscoelastic Burgers Rocks [J]. Rock Mechanics and Rock Engineering, 2011, 44 (5):0-564.

[12] Vlachopoulos N,Diederichs MS. Improved Longitudinal Displacement Profiles for Convergence Confinement Analysis of Deep Tunnels [J]. Rock Mechanics and Rock Engineering,2009(2):131-146.

[13] Carranza-torres C. Dimensionless Graphical Representation of the Exact Elasto-plastic Solution of a Circular Tunnel in a Mohr-coulomb Material Subject to Uniform Far-field Stresses [J]. Rock Mechanics and Rock Engineering, 2003(3):237-253.

[14] Hoek E,Carranza-torres C. Hoek-brown Failure Criterion—2002 Edition [C]. Proc. NARMS-TAC Conference,Toronto,2002,1:267-273.

环京道路降雨型边坡稳定性分析

牛 犇[1] 冯 春[2] 张一鸣*[1]

(1. 河北工业大学土木与交通学院;2. 中国科学院力学研究所)

摘 要 降雨是边坡失稳主要诱发因素之一。降雨入渗会增加岩土体容重同时降低土体强度,是典型的连续-非连续水力耦合过程。本研究基于连续-非连续单元法,引入应力场和渗流场数值耦合算法,根据兰营地区边坡地质条件建立高精度三维地质灾害模型,考虑不同降雨工况,对边坡稳定性进行分析,并与监测数据展开对比验证模型可靠性。研究表明,该处边坡在暴雨等恶劣天气情况下破裂度提升,安全系数降低,存在一定失稳危险。本文研究成果可为该地区边坡防灾减灾提供理论依据。

关键词 降雨型滑坡 连续-非连续单元法 水力耦合 模型验证 数值模拟

1. 基金项目:基于裂面优化破裂单元法的岩体边坡水力耦合失稳机理研究(51809069);三维岩体特征-宏观多尺度建模与变形-破坏分析研究(52178324)。

0 引言

近年来,我国地质灾害处于多发态势,滑坡灾害最为突出,滑坡体在脱离母岩后往往产生高速、远程的次生灾害,造成毁灭性破坏和伤亡[1-2]。降雨诱发边坡失稳是一个连续-非连续的过程,降雨入渗则是典型的渗流场和应力场耦合问题[3]。

目前,前人对降雨型滑坡研究主要包括模型试验和数值模拟。模型试验是一种比较直观形象的边坡稳定性分析手段,由于其边界条件容易控制及容易操作等特点,使得模型试验在边坡稳定性分析方面有着广泛的应用。石振明[4]通过模型试验和全自动人工模拟降雨器对不同材料堆积体在降雨作用下的滑坡机理和孔隙水压力变化特征进行分析。周扬[5]开展了人工降雨条件下黄土边坡室内模型试验,对岩土体的变形、含水率和基质吸力进行分析。陈林万[6]结合传感器和人工降雨系统,通过开展室内降雨模型试验,对降雨入渗后边坡内部的变形响应进行研究。朱谭方[7]采用地质分析和降雨离心机模型实验相结合的方法,研究水力作用下的硬土软岩质滑坡的启动机制。但模型实验在成本方面花费较高,在尺度和时间方面不易控制。与模型实验相比,数值模拟具有高效省时和低成本的特点,并且数值模拟方法在分析过程中可以考虑复杂的边界条件,能够模拟复杂工况,不仅可以模拟边坡的破坏和变形,还可以获得边坡在不同位置不同时刻的应力应变状态。田东方[8]提出坡面径流-非饱和渗流分析的渗流场和应力场耦合计算算法,通过有限元对耦合情况和非耦合情况进行对比分析。吕雨桦[9]利用Geo-Studio软件对非饱和土边坡渗流场和应力场进行数值耦合分析,总结非饱和土边坡的稳定性和滑移面的演化规律。李柱[10]利用ABAQUS有限元分析软件,建立渗流-应力耦合控制方程和边坡有限元模型,对渗流应力耦合作用下的露天矿边坡进行稳定性分析。周家文[11]采用二维有限元渗流-应力耦合程序对基于饱和-非饱和渗流有限元计算的渗流场和应力场来计算边坡的危险滑动面和安全系数。目前,连续方法如有限元方法在处理边坡大位移、大变形的破坏问题时容易因为网格畸变而导致计算不收敛;非连续方法如离散单元法在处理水力耦合方面存在一定缺陷。基于连续-非连续单元法引入水力耦合数值算法则会结合两者优势,分析整个系统在大变形大位移状态下的水力耦合问题。王叶[12]基于连续-离散耦合方法FDEM,对两个典型边坡进行稳定性分析,证明了连续-离散耦合方法对于山体滑坡的适用性。司宪志[13]基于连续-非连续耦合分析理论,利用强度折减法简化降雨工况的方法对高填方边坡进行稳定性分析,研究结果表面耦合方法在边坡稳定性分析方面的可行性。

上述研究发现大部分边坡稳定性分析都是将边坡简化为二维模型进行分析计算,很大程度上忽略边坡三维效应。本研究选取兰营地区地质灾害调查点作为研究对象,基于连续-非连续单元法,采用CAD和GID软件进行三维曲面高精度建模,采用模拟数据与实际数据对比方法对模型进行验证,引入应力场和渗流场耦合算法对不同降雨工况下边坡的变形运动和失稳破坏展开数值模拟研究,研究结果可为兰营地区滑坡灾害防灾减灾提供理论依据和科学指导。

1 数值计算方法

1.1 连续-非连续单元法CDEM

本研究依据连续-非连续单元法CDEM,通过数值模拟研究降雨作用下坡体的运动规律和边坡的稳定性[14-15]。CDEM是一种有限元与离散元耦合的显式数值分析方法,不仅可以模拟材料的弹塑性变形及接触碰撞过程,还可以模拟材料从连续到非连续的渐进破坏过程。CDEM包含块体和界面两部分,每个块体单元包括一个或多个有限元单元,用于表征材料的弹性、塑性等连续特征。界面由块体边界组成,块体边界上用弹簧连接,用于表征材料的断裂、碰撞等非连续特征,如图1所示[16-17]。在数值计算过程中,通过块体间及块体内单元间界面的破裂来模拟材料从连续到非连续的渐进破坏过程。

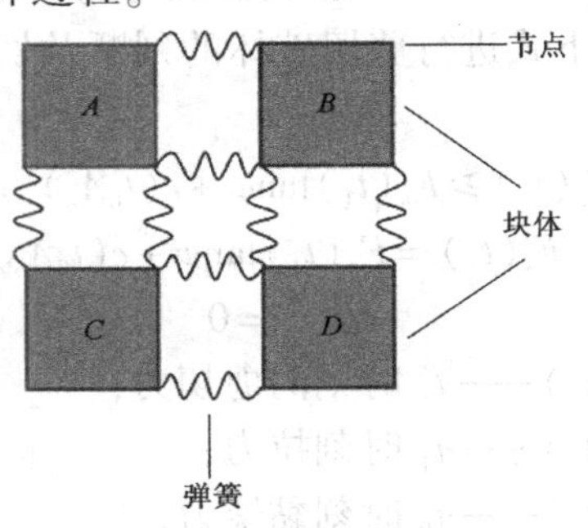

图1 单元界面断裂计算模型

计算过程中,对于块体单元和块体与块体之间的界面选取不同的本构模型,单元的本构模型选择 Mohr-Coulomb 模型,利用下式判断单元的应力是否已经达到或超过 Mohr-Coulomb 准则:

$$\begin{cases} f^s = s_1 - s_3 N_j + 2C\sqrt{N_j} \\ f^t = s_3 - T \\ h = f^t + a^P(s_1 - s^P) \end{cases}$$

式中:C、φ、T——块体的黏聚力、内摩擦角及抗拉强度;

σ_1、σ_2、σ_3——块体的最大、中间和最小主应力;

N_φ、α^P、σ^P——常数,可表述为:

$$\begin{cases} N_\varphi = \dfrac{1+\sin\varphi}{1-\sin\varphi} \\ \alpha^P = \sqrt{1+N_\varphi^2} + N_\varphi \\ \sigma^P = TN_\varphi - 2C\sqrt{N_\varphi} \end{cases}$$

f^s——判断块体是否满足剪切破坏准则的指标;

f^t——判断块体是否满足拉破坏准则的指标;

h——判断块体当前所处应力区域的指标。

如果 $f \geqslant 0$ 且 $h \leqslant 0$,则发生剪切破坏;如果 $f^t \geqslant 0$ 且 $h > 0$ 则发生拉伸破坏。

块体与块体之间的虚拟界面的本构采用 Mohr-Coulomb 脆性断裂模型 brittleMC,并且采用如下公式进行拉伸破坏的判断和法向接触力的修正:

$$\text{if}\quad -F_n(t+\Delta t) \geqslant T_0 A_c$$
$$\text{then}\quad F_n(t_1) = -T(t_0)A_c$$
$$T(t_1) = 0$$

式中:$T(t_0)$——初始时刻的抗拉强度;

A_c——弹簧的特征面积;

$F_n(t_1)$——t_1 时刻弹簧的拉力;

$T(t_1)$——t_1 时刻的抗拉强度。

采用下式进行剪切破坏的判断及切向接触力的修正:

$$\text{if}\quad F_s(t_1) \geqslant F_n(t_1)\tan\varphi + c(t_0 A_c)$$
$$\text{then}\quad F_s(t_1) = F_n(t_1)\tan\varphi + c(t_0 A_c)$$
$$c(t_1) = 0$$

式中:$F_s(t_1)$——t_1 时刻的剪切力;

$F_n(t_1)$——t_1 时刻拉力;

$c(t_0)$——t_0 时刻黏聚力;

$c(t_1)$——t_1 时刻的黏聚力。

1.2 渗流-应力耦合

针对降雨型滑坡,水是最重要的影响因素,水对滑坡的影响主要在于水的入渗作用和渗流-应力耦合效应。岩体内部含有大量的孔隙结构,孔隙介质是水的存在场所和转移通道。当岩土体内部孔隙中产生水头差的作用时,孔隙中的水会产生渗流运动,产生动水压力,动水压力即渗透体积力。动水压力以荷载的形式作用在边坡内的岩土体上,造成岩土体内部应力场的改变,而应力场的改变会使得岩土体的空间位置发生改变。岩土体空间位置的改变是由于岩土体内部孔隙体积变化引起的,而岩土体的渗透系数会随着孔隙率的改变而改变,渗流场与渗透系数息息相关。即降雨作用下渗流场对应力场的作用是通过改变岩土体的动水压力也就是渗透体积力来实现的,而应力场是通过改变岩土体的空隙特征和分布情况来对渗流场造成影响。渗流场与应力场耦合示意图如图2所示。

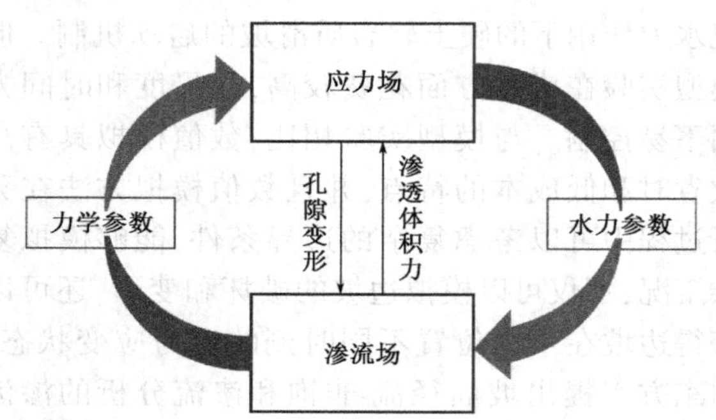

图2 渗流-应力耦合示意图

2 工程分析

2.1 工程背景

调查区位于怀柔北部山区,地貌为典型的低山河谷地貌,白河流域右岸,地势整体西高东低,海拔高度分布在400~1000m之间。地属暖温带型半湿润气候,四季分明,雨热同期,夏季湿润,冬季寒冷少雪。受气候与地形影响,调查区所处位置降水量具有年际变化大,季节分配不均、汛期降水集中等特点。降雨多集中在夏季(6—9月),占全年降雨量的80%以上,年平均降雨量在850mm以上,多年平均最大24h降雨量为80mm。降雨量集中和降雨强度大是引发地质灾害的主要原因。

该调查区为岩质边坡，岩性为砂岩，灾害规模等级为小型，威胁对象为G111国道。隐患点位于G110国道北侧，为人工修路削坡形成陡坡，地表基岩裸露，偶见少量灌木。宏观地质灾害隐患点如图3所示。

图3 地质灾害隐患点

2.2 数值模型

本研究依据勘察报告中地形地貌、地质构造、地层岩性等基本状况，结合CAD和GID软件建立三维数值模型。本模型长约320m、宽约230m、高约205m，其中滑坡隐患区域边坡长约68m、宽约61m、高约21m。模型含有节点48408个，块体259018个，均为四面体单元。边坡模型分为两组，一组为基岩，另一组为基岩上的崩塌体（砂岩）。计算模型及网格如图4所示。

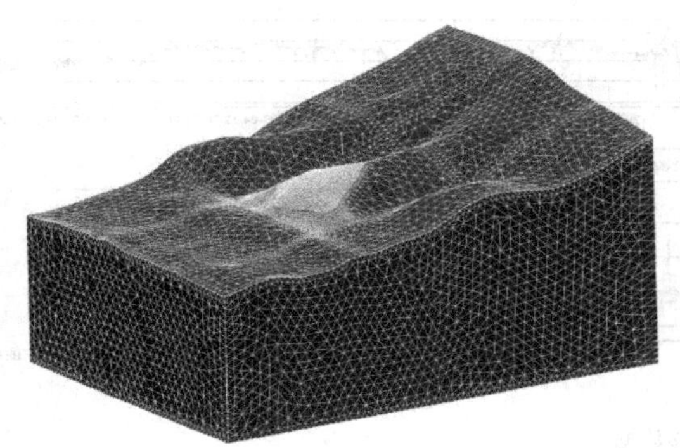

图4 计算模型和网格

CDEM中包含块体和界面两个部分，在界面上引入数值弹簧表述层间作用，界面材料参数包括强度和刚度两部分，强度有黏聚力、抗拉强度和摩擦角，刚度有法向刚度和切向刚度；强度基于弹簧两侧块体的弱值选取，刚度考虑两侧的粗糙度。本研究中界面材料参数基于块体继承获取，刚度基于块体继承，强度基于块体获取，与块体一致。计算过程所用力学参数和渗透参数如表1所示。

计算过程分为两阶段，第一阶段考虑重力作用，计算至平衡状态，获取边坡初始应力、位移等信息；第二阶段基于第一阶段获取的应力场，作为初始计算状态，清除第一阶段位移信息，在边坡上部表面施加流量边界用来模拟降雨过程，分析降雨作用下坡体的运动特性和破坏过程。

针对边界条件，模型的四周及底部采用法向位移约束。边坡顶部表面设置为透水边界，保证雨水自由入渗；假设边坡四周处于无限远处，边坡底部、后部和左右两边设置为不透水边界，边坡前部设置为透水边界，保证雨水自由出渗。降雨流量边界条件施加在边坡表面，计算中不考虑地下水的影响，认为降雨对该滑坡的诱发影响仅为坡面渗流。

2.3 模型验证

在进行数值模拟分析之前，需要对边坡进行初始地应力平衡，还原真实的应力场，保证数值模拟与真实情况相符合。导入模型之后，施加重力和边界条件，计算至平衡状态，清除边坡位移信息，获取边坡初始应力信息。初始应力场如图5所示。

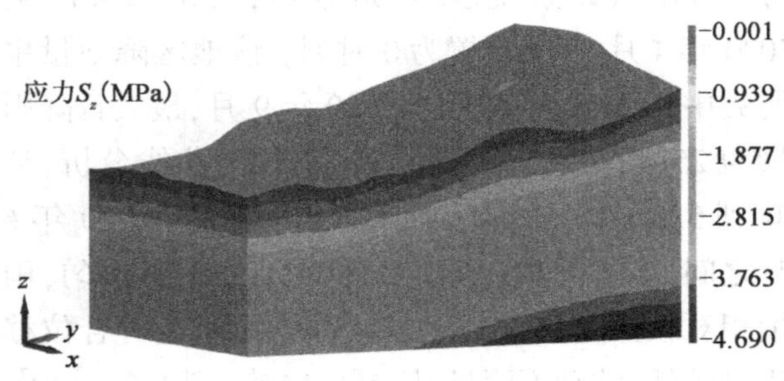

图5 初始应力场云图

计 算 参 数　　表 1

项　　目		弹性模量(GPa)	粘聚力(MPa)	抗拉强度(MPa)	内摩擦角(°)
力学参数	砂岩	0.017	0.086	0.09	20
	基岩	0.032	0.500	0.33	42
性 能 参 数		体积模量(Mpa)	孔隙率	渗透系数($m^2 \cdot Pa^{-1} \cdot s^{-1}$)	比奥系数
渗流参数	砂岩	0.9	0.10	1e-9	1
	基岩	1.0	0.15	2e-10	1

统计兰营地区日降雨量数据以及位移数据，根据勘察资料提供的监测点位置在软件内模型中设置监测点，依据统计的降雨数据在边坡表面施加降雨，将软件内检测的位移数据与兰营地区实际位移数据进行对比，确定模型合理性。现场监测得到的监测点数据如图 6 所示。由于现场采集到的位移数据的特殊性，我们引入合位移记为 Um。

$$Um = \sqrt{(Ux)^2 + (Uy)^2 + (Uz)^2}$$

式中：Ux——监测点 X 方向位移；

Uy——监测点 Y 方向位移；

Uz——监测点 Z 方向位移。

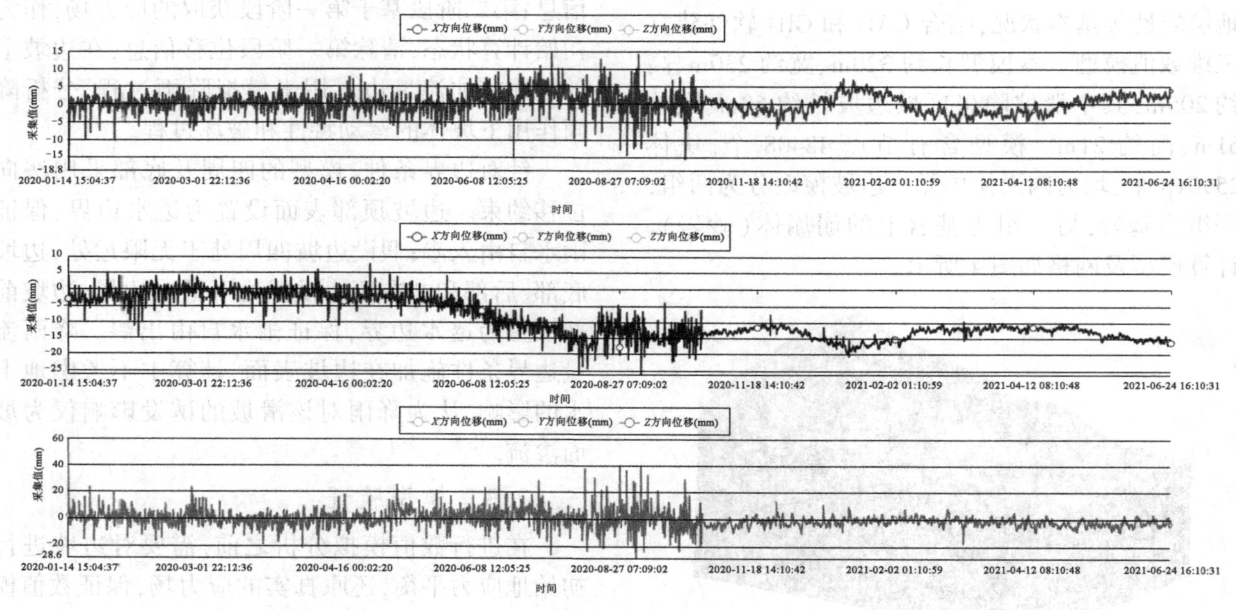

图 6　现场采集位移数据

降雨量统计数据包括 2020 年 4 月至 2021 年 6 月日降雨量数据，总共 430d 左右，约 3.72×10^7s，2020 年 4 月 13 日设置为 0 时刻。该地区降雨量主要集中于 2020 年 6 月至 2020 年 9 月，最大日降雨量为 25mm 左右。根据合位移-时间曲线分析，从 0s 到 5.0×10^6s 大约为 2020 年 4 月到 2020 年 6 月之间，该时间段，降雨量随时间分布不均匀，雨量相对较少，根据位移监测数据可知，此时合位移相对较低，波动不明显；从 5.5×10^6s 到 1.31×10^7s 大约为 2020 年 6 月到 2020 年 9 月之间，该时间段降雨量集中且雨量相对较大，合位移波动明显且位移值较大；从 1.31×10^7s 到 3.72×10^7s 大约为 2020 年 9 月到 2021 年 6 月之间，该时间段降雨量相对较少且仅存在较短时间段的降雨，位移波动不明显。

合位移总体趋势呈现在雨季上升，雨季之后平缓趋势，与兰营地区实际监测点合位移数据相符合。根据位移数据对比分析，认为模型合理，可以用于后续不同降雨工况下的边坡稳定性计算分析。兰营地区降雨量数据以及 GDEM 软件模拟合位移数据如图7所示。

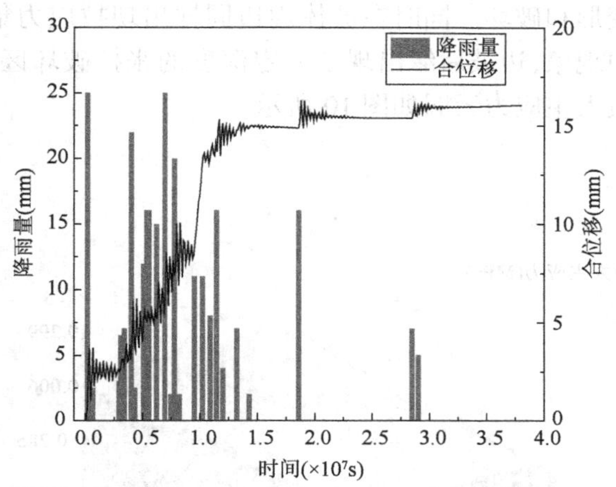

图7　降雨量数据和合位移数据

3　模拟结果及分析

依据上一阶段验证得到的模型在本节开展不同降雨工况下计算，对该边坡的位移场和渗流场等展开分析。通过查阅兰营地区历史降雨量数据，选取日降雨量80mm作为参考数据，进行以下不同降雨工况下的边坡稳定性计算。考虑三种不同的短时强降雨工况，降雨工况1为均匀型降雨，设置降雨强度为80mm/d，保持降雨强度不变，持续时间24h；降雨工况2为递增型降雨，0h降雨强度为0mm/d，之后24h之内降雨强度线性递增至80mm/d；降雨工况3为中强型降雨，0h到12h到降雨强度从0mm/d递增至80mm/d，之后从12h到24h递减至0mm/d。具体降雨工况如图8所示。

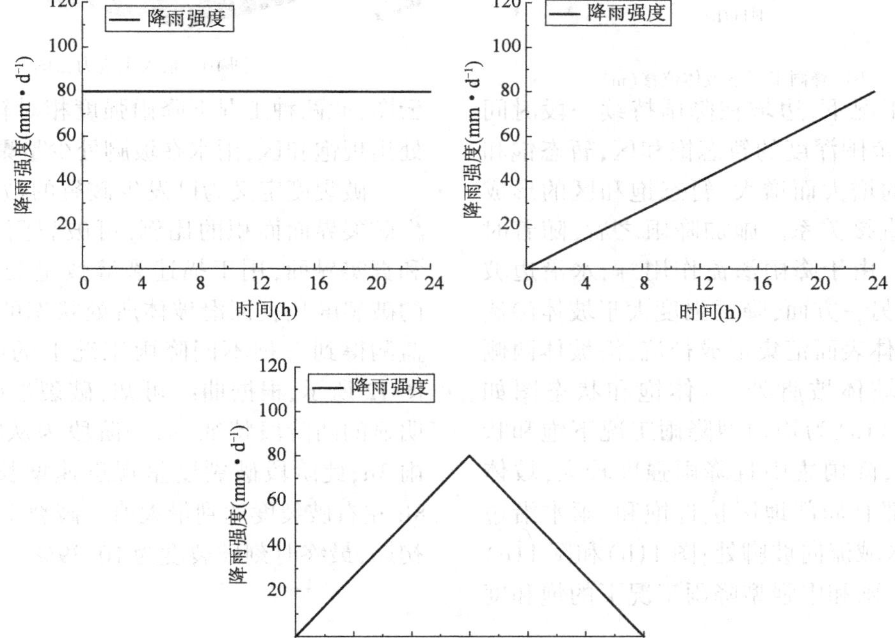
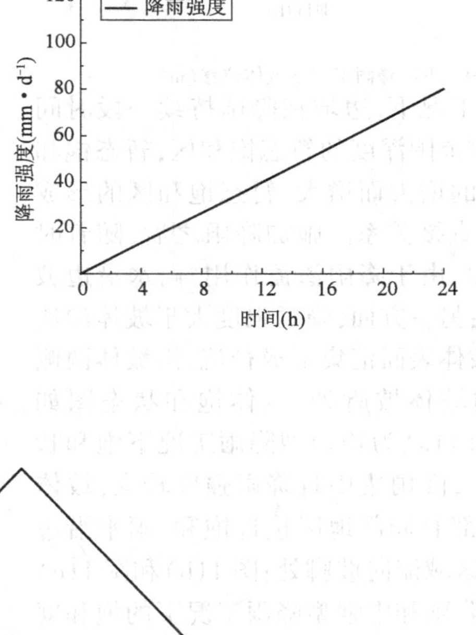

图8　三种不同的降雨工况

考虑三种不同的降雨工况，在滑体坡顶、坡中和坡脚分别设置监测点。降雨作用下，坡体表面土体持续受到雨水冲刷，造成土体强度降低，上部土体下滑压迫坡脚土体，在加上坡脚处土体持续受到雨水的冲刷，造成坡脚处土体位移较大。不同降雨工况下监测点处位移如图8所示。根据合位移-时间曲线分析可知，三种降雨工况下坡顶和坡中处的位移没有明显差别，工况1坡脚处的合位移最大，为24.3cm；工况3坡脚处的合位移最小，为23.2cm。随着降雨持续进行，上部土体由于雨水沿着坡顶和坡面入渗导致坡体自重增大，压迫坡脚处岩土体，再加上坡脚处岩土体持续受到雨水冲刷，产生裂缝，雨水沿裂缝进入土体，造成坡脚处土体强度降低，造成坡脚处土体滑动。

根据图9分析可知，坡顶、坡中和坡脚的位移变化可以分为两个阶段，以降雨渗流10.8h为分界点，位移在降雨10.8h之前迅速上升，在降雨10.8h以后，位移曲线呈缓慢增长趋势。

根据降雨24h边坡最大主应力云图(工况1)可知，在模型四周出现拉应力集中带；在坡顶和坡面表面，出现拉应力；根据滑体部分剖面图可知，在软弱面交汇处，出现拉应力集中现象，容易出现变形和破坏。同时在坡体周边同样出现拉应力集中现象，边坡后缘出现了一定深度的张拉破坏区。最大主应力云图如图10所示。

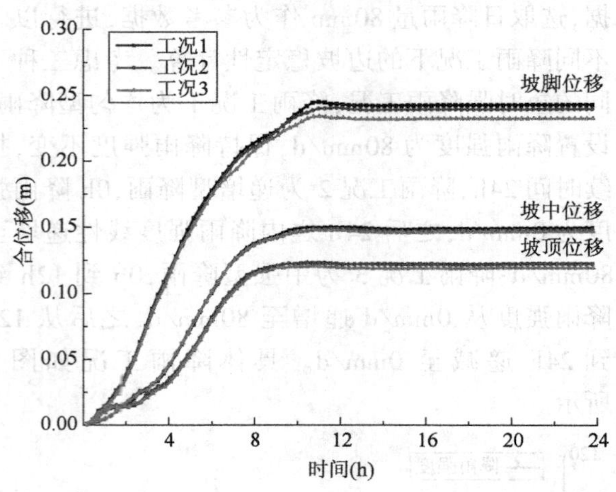

图9　不同降雨工况下坡体位移(m)

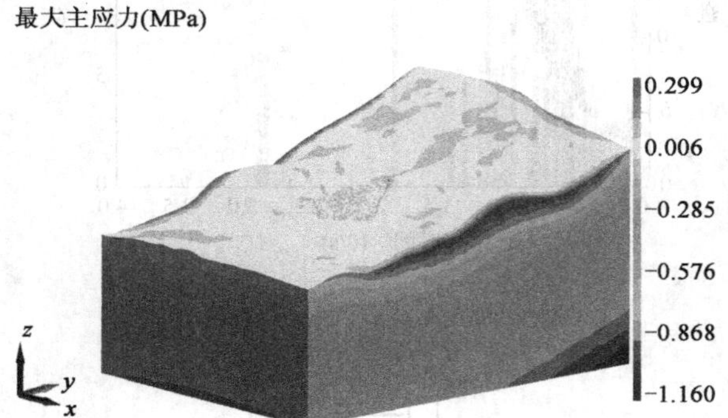

图10　最大主应力云图

三种降雨工况下，边坡在降雨持续一段时间后，表现出一定范围深度的暂态饱和区，暂态饱和区随降雨历时的增大而增大，暂态饱和区的形成与降雨强度有直接关系。施加降雨之后，随着时间推移，一方面，由于降雨渗流作用，雨水沿边坡表面向内入渗；另一方面，降雨强度大于坡体渗透系数，雨水在坡体表面汇集形成径流，沿坡体两侧沟谷区域流向坡体坡脚处，具体饱和状态图如图11所示。图11a)为均匀型降雨工况下饱和状态图，此工况下，降雨集中且降雨强度较大，坡体表面和坡体顶部有局部地区接近饱和，雨水沿边坡两侧的沟谷区域流向坡脚处；图11b)和图11c)分别为递增型降雨和中强型降雨工况下的饱和度云图，此两种工况下降雨强度相对较低，坡体四周处出现饱和区，雨水在坡脚处少量聚集。

破裂度定义为已发生破裂的截面面积占可发生破裂界面面积的比例，可破裂面包括虚拟界面和真实界面，用于描述裂缝数量变化趋势。边坡的破裂度是表征滑坡体所处状态的关键指标[18]。监测得到三种不同降雨工况下的破裂度曲线如图12所示，根据曲线可知，破裂度时程曲线具有明显的两阶段特征，第一阶段为从降雨开始到降雨3h，此阶段破裂度呈现迅速增长阶段，在降雨8h左右破裂度达到最大值。破裂主要发生在降雨初期，最终时刻破裂度为10.39%。

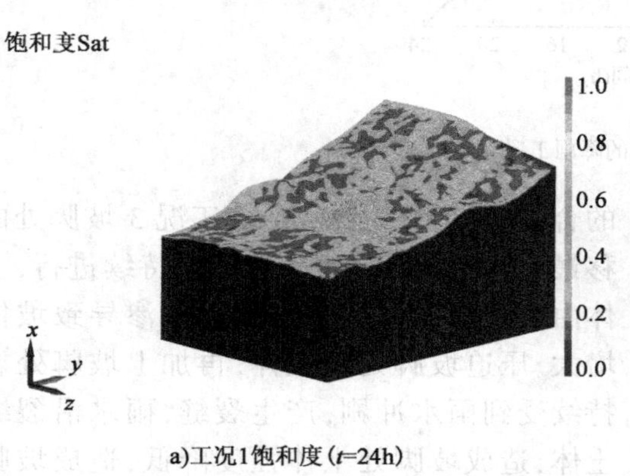

a)工况1饱和度(t=24h)

b)工况2饱和度(t=24h)

图　11

c)工况3饱和度(t=24h)

图 11　三种降雨工况下边坡饱和度

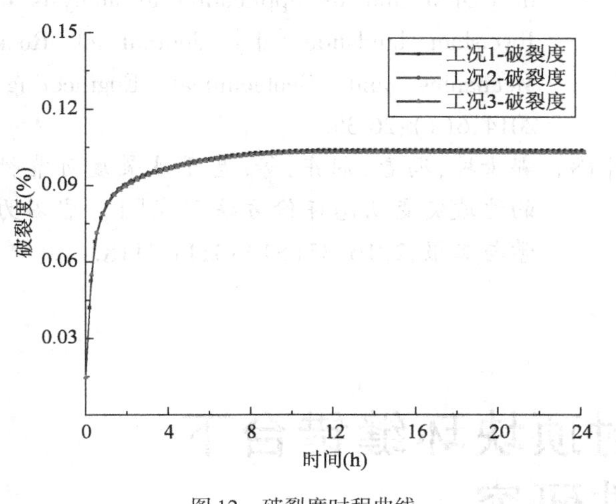

图 12　破裂度时程曲线

根据强度折减法求解边坡安全系数，天然工况下边坡安全系数为 1.79，降雨工况 1 下边坡安全系数为 1.191，降雨工况下 2 边坡安全系数为 1.199，降雨工况 3 下边坡安全系数为 1.199。通过饱和度云图可知，工况 1 情况下大量雨水边坡两侧的沟谷区域流向坡脚处，仅有少量雨水通过渗透进入坡体，造成边坡坡顶和坡脚部分区域饱和，岩土强度降低；工况 2 和工况 3 虽然降雨较少，但同样造成局部区域岩体饱和。故三种降雨工况下，边坡的安全系数和破裂度大致相似。

4　结语

(1)本研究选取京兰营地区地质环境调查点为研究对象，基于连续-非连续单元法，引入渗流-应力耦合计算模型，对降雨-应力-渗流作用下的边坡稳定性进行分析。通过连续方法强度折减法和非连续方法破裂度方法分别对边坡稳定性进行分析，利用连续方法求解边坡安全系数：天然工况下安全系数为 1.79，三种不同短时强降雨工况下边坡安全系数约为 1.20；利用非连续方法求解边坡灾变状态：求得三种不同短时强降雨工况下边坡破裂度为 10.36%。

(2)经稳定性评价该边坡在天然工况下处于基本稳定状态，如遇持续大暴雨等恶劣天气，上覆岩体在重力和雨水冲刷下易沿坡向发生滑塌，在暴雨状态下处于欠稳定状态。

参考文献

[1] 文海家，张岩岩，付红梅. 降雨型滑坡失稳机理及稳定性评价方法研究进展[J]. 中国公路学报，2018，31(2)：15-29.

[2] 黄润秋. 20 世纪以来中国的大型滑坡及其发生机制[J]. 岩石力学与工程学报，2007，26(3)：433-454.

[3] 冯春，李世海，周东. 滑坡研究中的力学方法[M]. 北京：科学出版社，2018.

[4] 石振明，赵思奕，苏越. 降雨作用下堆积层滑坡的模型试验研究[J]. 水文地质工程地质，2016，43(4)：135-140.

[5] 周杨，刘果果，白兰英，等. 降雨诱发黄土边坡失稳室内试验研究[J]. 武汉大学学报(工学版)，2016，49(6)：838-843.

[6] 陈林万，张晓超，裴向军. 降雨诱发直线型黄土填方边坡失稳模型试验[J]. 水文地质工程地质，2021，48(6)：152-161.

[7] 朱谭方，辛鹏，姚磊华，等. 水力作用诱发硬土软岩滑坡启动机制研究[J]. 岩土力学，2021，42(10)：2733-2754.

[8] 田东方，刘德富，王世梅，等. 土质边坡非饱和渗流场与应力场耦合数值分析[J]. 岩土力学，2009，30(3)：810-814.

[9] 吕雨桦，梁德贤，王莹，等. 降雨条件下非饱和土边坡渗流-应力耦合分析[J]. 桂林理工大学学报，2021，41(2)：318-324.

[10] 李柱，谢锋. 渗流-应力耦合作用下露天矿边

坡稳定性研究[J]. 工矿自动化,2018,44(12):83-88.

[11] 周家文,徐卫亚,邓俊晔,等. 降雨入渗条件下边坡的稳定性分析[J]. 水利学报,2008,39(9):1066-1073.

[12] 王叶. 基于连续—离散耦合分析方法的边坡滑动及堰塞体形成过程研究[D]. 武汉:武汉大学,2018.

[13] 司宪志,宁宇,石崇,等. 基于连续-非连续方法的高填方边坡变形稳定性分析[J]. 河北工程大学学报(自然科学版),2021,38(02):53-60.

[14] Li S H, Wang J G, Liu B S, et al. Analysis of critical excavation depth for a jointed rock slope ysing a Face-to-Face discrete element method [J]. Rock Mechanics and Rock Engineering, 2007, 40(4):331-348.

[15] Wang Y, Zhao M, Shihai LI, et al. Stochastic structural model of rock and soil aggregates by continuum-based discrete element method[J]. Science in China, 2005, 48(0z1):95-106.

[16] 冯春,李世海,刘晓宇. 半弹簧接触模型及其在边坡破坏计算中的应用[J]. 力学学报,2011,43(1):184-192.

[17] Chun Feng, Shihai Li, Xiaoyu Liu, et al. A semi-spring and semi-edge combined contact model in CDEM and its application to analysis of Jiweishan landslide [J]. Journal of Rock Mechanics and Geotechnical Engineering, 2014, 6(1):26-35.

[18] 郭汝坤,冯春,周东,等. 基于破裂度可靠性的边坡灾变状态评价方法研究[J]. 岩石力学与工程学报,2016,35(S1):3111-3118.

超大直径盾构隧道封顶块环缝错台下损伤特性研究

张稳军*[1,2]　赵建兵[1,2]　张　弛[1,2]　牛荣健[1,2]　张高乐[1,2]

(1. 天津大学建筑工程学院;2. 天津大学滨海土木工程结构与安全教育部重点实验室)

摘　要　以超大直径盾构隧道施工和运营中封顶块区域环缝错台问题为研究对象,先引用已有试验数据对数值方法进行验证,随后建立超大直径盾构隧道封顶块区域局部精细化模型,对混凝土损伤、螺栓受力与错台量变化的关系规律进行分析;探究了环缝错台引起的封顶块接缝结构损伤特征,建立了错台-封顶块损伤关系表,并通过损伤特性分析给出了超大直径盾构隧道封顶块环缝错台阈值取值建议。研究表明:封顶块接缝处混凝土损伤值与环缝错台量的关系曲线大致呈S状,发生径向逆剪错台的环缝接头处受压损伤最大,发生径向顺剪错台的接头受拉损伤最大;螺栓应力与错台量关系曲线大致呈抛物线状,切向错台下的螺栓应力最大;螺栓等效塑性应变与错台量关系曲线大致呈指数型,径向顺剪错台下产生的等效塑性应变最大;根据各安全指标与错台量的关系建立了错台-封顶块损伤关系表,建议超大直径盾构隧道封顶块错台限值应与其他位置区分,其最大限值应小于13mm。

关键词　超大直径盾构隧道损伤特性　数值模拟　封顶块　环缝错台

0　引言

拼装误差、盾构机姿态调整、隧道沉降差异和管片上浮等因素易导致盾构隧道出现错台,是造成隧道结构损伤、防水性能失效的重要原因。超大直径盾构隧道由于每环衬砌需要拼装的管片数量增多,受外界环境影响更为复杂,尤其是封顶块区域在施工期和运营期面临的错台风险十分严峻。封顶块区域刚度较为薄弱,其错台情况及损伤状态对隧道整体结构的安全性能和防水性能有重要影响。为科学合理地评估封顶块发生环缝错台的超大直径盾构隧道的安全状况和有针对性地对损伤部位进行加固、修补,有必要对其环缝错台量与接缝结构损伤的关系规律进行研究。

众多学者对隧道接缝结构的抗弯特性、抗剪特性等方面进行了大量研究,主要的研究手法有理论分析、数值分析及试验研究等。张冬梅等[1]采用数值方法研究了环缝错台下斜螺栓、凹凸榫对环缝抗剪特性的影响,提出了环缝变形的三级安全评价指标。桑运龙等[2]建立了管片环缝张开与错台模式下的环缝接头计算模型,分析得到了环缝抗拉和抗剪刚度的非线性规律,并运用于地面堆载对管片结构安全的影响评价。张稳军等[3]建立管片-接头三维模型和密封垫-密封槽二维模型,研究了错台对盾构隧道接缝受力和防水性能的影响。除了理论分析和数值计算外,开展足尺试验也是研究盾构隧道接缝受力特征的重要手段。张冬梅等[4]依托上海长江隧道设计并进行了环缝足尺剪切试验,提出了管片环缝剪切刚度计算公式。何源等[5]通过足尺试验研究了盾构隧道环缝的破坏机制,并基于计算力学方法提出了环缝抗剪刚度解析解。闫治国等[6]依托青草沙输水隧道进行足尺试验,研究了环缝的剪切破坏过程。朱瑶宏等[7]依托宁波轨道交通隧道足尺试验得出了不同纵向压力下环缝的抗剪刚度。既有研究大多着眼于接缝弯矩、剪力与错台的关系或单个螺栓孔的破坏过程,研究抗弯、抗剪刚度的变化情况,且研究部位多为标准块段中的纵缝和环缝接头,对封顶块处结构损伤与错台关系鲜有提及,但从工程实践中发现该部位力学性能与其他部位有明显差异,故设计标准和评价准则也应有所区别。

综上所述,本文拟通过建立超大直径盾构隧道封顶块局部三维精细化模型,通过引入混凝土损伤塑性本构和钢材双折线塑性模型充分考虑材料非线性,探究封顶块处环缝错台引起的管片损伤规律及螺栓受力变形特征,为超大直径盾构隧道的安全评估及施工质量控制提供参考。

1 模型验证

1.1 环缝剪切足尺试验

本文引用文献[5]中斜螺栓连接的环缝剪切足尺试验数据来对下文所使用的数值模拟方法进行验证。如图1所示,试验构件由三块管片构成,其中纵向长度剪切块1为350mm,剪切块2为2700mm,剪切块3为350mm,高度均为500mm。试验加载图示如图2所示,水平荷载模拟隧道环缝断面上作用的纵向压力,竖向荷载模拟环缝剪力。加载方案为先施加水平荷载500kN,随后逐级施加竖向荷载,每级10kN,加载直至构件破坏。通过试验获得两条环缝的错台-剪力关系曲线。

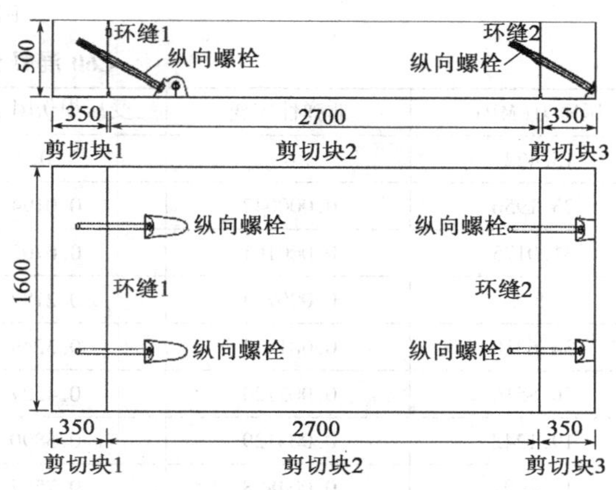

图1 试验构件尺寸图示(尺寸单位:mm)

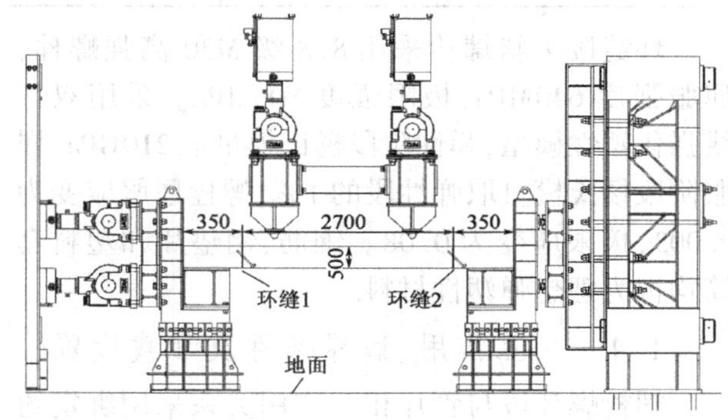

图2 试验加载图示(尺寸单位:mm)

1.2 数值建模

本文依照文献[5]中结构试验所用构件,采用ABAQUS有限元软件进行精细化数值建模,数值模型如图3所示。管片和螺栓采用C3D8R实体单元建模;为防止应力集中,螺栓和管片接触处设有钢垫片和螺栓预埋塑料套筒,采用壳单元模拟;钢筋采用梁单元模拟。

1.3 材料参数

管片混凝土强度等级为C60,本构模型采用ABAQUS材料属性中的混凝土损伤塑性模型。损伤模型参数的计算参考文献[8~9],具体取值如表1所示,通过引入损伤因子 d 来描述混凝土材料拉裂和压碎的破坏程度。

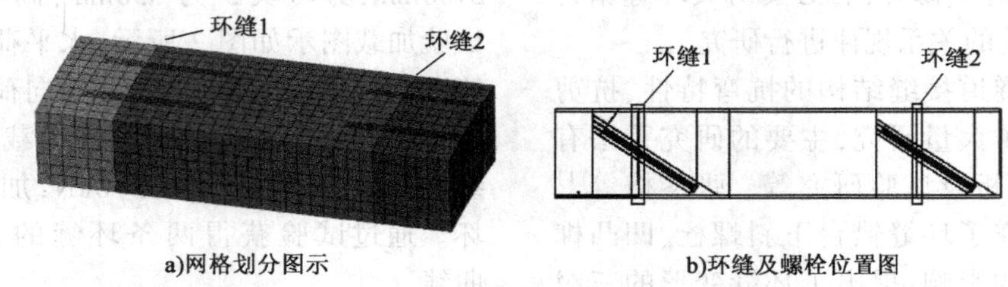

图 3　数值模型

C60 混凝土损伤塑性模型参数　　表 1

压应力(MPa)	非弹性应变	受压损伤因子 d_c	拉应力(MPa)	开裂应变	受拉损伤因子 d_t
15.422	0	0	2.2809	0	0
23.1956	0.000042	0.0194	2.5679	0.0000043	0.0090
31.0175	0.000161	0.0702	2.85	0.0000204	0.0612
38.5	0.000714	0.2182	2.2767	0.0000706	0.2045
34.6218	0.001313	0.3249	1.9906	0.0000942	0.2795
26.8516	0.002124	0.4527	1.4187	0.0001550	0.4633
19.1242	0.003129	0.5890	0.4201	0.0005872	0.8987
11.4091	0.004898	0.7507			
5.6313	0.008606	0.8912			

环缝接头斜螺栓采用 8.8 级 M30 高强螺栓，屈服强度 640MPa，极限强度 800MPa。采用双折线强化塑性模型，弹性阶段杨氏模量取 210GPa，屈服阶段杨氏模量取弹性段的 1%，螺栓屈服应变为 0.003，极限应变为 0.08。钢筋、钢垫片和塑料套筒均视为理想弹塑性材料。

1.4　相互作用、边界条件及加载设置

螺栓螺牙段与管片相互作用关系采用绑定约束，其余部分采用面与面接触，切向采用罚函数摩擦系数取 0.3，法向采用硬接触。管片间采用面与面接触，摩擦系数取 0.4；钢筋采用嵌入接触；钢垫片与螺栓和管片接触摩擦系数取 0.7[1]。

模型在初始分析步约束两端剪切块径向和切向位移，在随后的分析步中先后施加螺栓预紧力、纵向水平力至预定状态，最后逐级施加竖向剪切力。其中螺栓预紧力取 100kN[10]。

1.5　数值结果验证分析

环缝剪切足尺试验结果与数值模拟结果对比如图 4 所示。由图可得，环缝 1 的数值结果在错台达到 3mm 后(即栓杆、栓帽与管片充分接触后)至结构破坏前，与试验结果差值小于 2%，且模拟计算出了环缝 1 后续阶段的剪力-错台关系曲线。环缝 2 的数值结果在错台达到 4mm 后至 16mm (螺栓屈服)前，与试验结果差值小于 2%，后续阶段差值小于 8%。

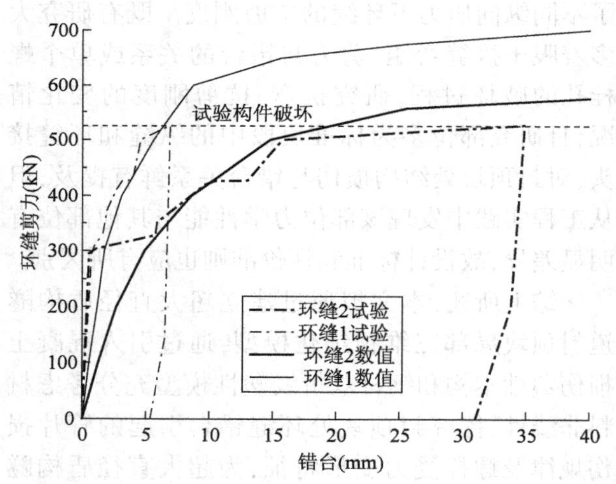

图 4　试验与数值结果对比图

从上述分析可得，初始加载阶段，螺栓杆与孔壁接触前数值模拟模型对于螺栓与管片复杂的接触过程模拟欠佳，但其后数值结果与试验结果吻合较好，能够充分反映结构损伤过程和接头抗剪性能的退化情况。考虑到本文研究重点为错台与结构损伤的关系，且错台 3mm 内不产生结构损伤，故采用上述模型能够满足本文研究需求。

2 环缝错台下封顶块区域损伤规律研究

2.1 工程概况

某超大直径盾构隧道外径 15400mm，内径 14100mm，壁厚 650mm，环宽 2000mm。管片混凝土标号为 C60，每环衬砌管片设计分为 10 块，采用错缝形式拼装；接头螺栓形式采用斜螺栓，强度等级为 8.8 级，设计错台量控制值为 17mm。接缝具体尺寸参数如图 5 所示。

螺帽
56°0'0"
径向线
分块线
325
650
325
220
465
197.7
341.7
238.5
A

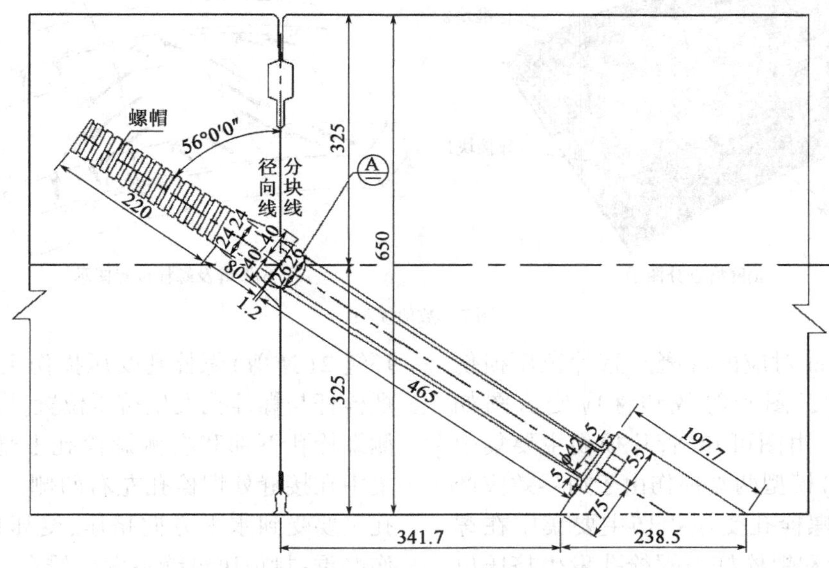

图 5 接缝尺寸图（尺寸单位：mm）

2.2 数值建模及加载设置

下文将对衬砌环中连接强度最为薄弱的封顶块及附近区域进行研究。在管片排版序列中选择图 6 中粗线框部位进行精细化建模分析，模型由两块标准块、两块邻接块及封顶块组成，包含两条环缝及两条封顶块纵缝，建模方法及细部处理与验证模型相同，模型单元总数约 16 万个，如图 7 所示。

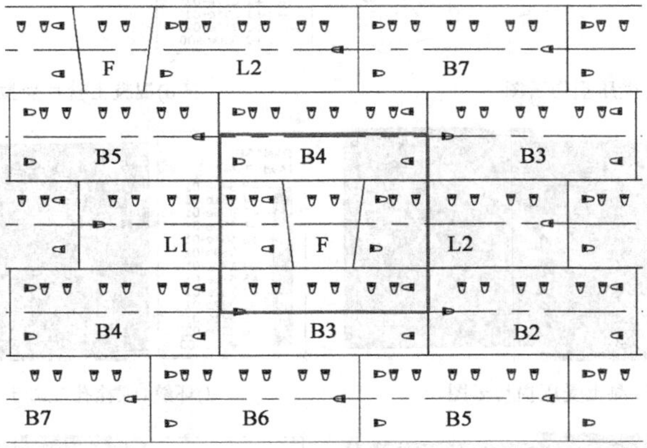

F
L2
B7
B5
B4
B3
L1
F
L2
B4
B3
B2
B7
B6
B5

图 6 建模部位选择

隧道覆土厚度约为 10 ~ 42m，经计算得单位宽度管环内最不利内力组合为正弯矩 1107kN · m 和轴力 5568kN。以此内力组合为初始荷载条件，随后对中间环施加位移荷载模拟环缝错台，位移加载根据位移方向分为两种工况，即径向加载和切向加载，最大加载位移量为 25mm。通过该模型来研究封顶块区域由环缝错台引起的混凝土损伤规律及螺栓特性。

2.3 受力特征分析

在径向加载中，环缝 1 的螺栓处于顺剪状态（手孔端向下错动），环缝 2 的螺栓处于逆剪状态（手孔端向上错动）；封顶块纵缝由于刚度较混凝土段小,在环缝错台发生时会伴随产生纵缝错台,此纵缝处于逆剪状态。在切向加载中,环缝1和环缝2接头受力特征相同,均为切向受剪。由于诸多学者[1,5]已经研究了单根斜螺栓连接的环缝在顺剪、逆剪及切向剪切中的破坏过程,故本文不再对其破坏过程进行分析,而从结构封顶块区域不同位置受力、损伤情况与错台的关系进行深入探究。

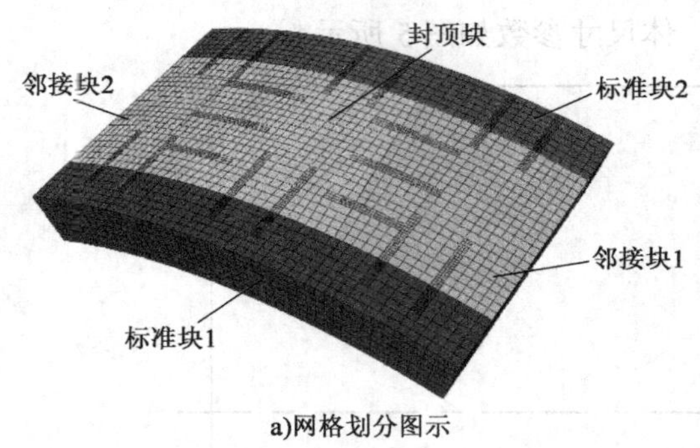

a)网格划分图示

封顶块纵缝

环缝2

环缝1

b)接缝及螺栓位置图示

图7　数值模型

径向错台17mm对应的混凝土管片拉压损伤云图、斜螺栓应力云图和等效塑性应变云图如图8～图10所示。由图可知,管片损伤主要集中在螺栓孔处,图8a)模型两端损伤由于边界效应产生;环缝1(顺剪)螺栓孔受压损伤主要集中在螺母与手孔接触位置和螺栓杆与螺栓孔发生挤压位置,受拉损伤主要集中在螺牙与混凝土接触位置;环缝2(逆剪)螺栓孔受压损伤主要集中在接缝处螺栓杆与螺栓孔发生挤压位置,即图8e)中接缝左侧螺栓孔下部和右侧螺栓孔上部,受拉损伤主要集中在接缝处螺栓孔左右两侧。切向错台下螺栓孔主要受到水平方向挤压,受压侧混凝土受压损伤严重;封顶块纵缝不发生错台,纵缝接头受力远小于径向错台条件下,且不产生混凝土损伤。

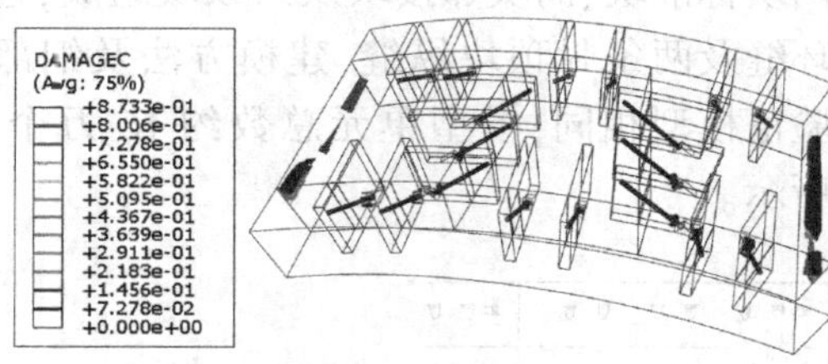

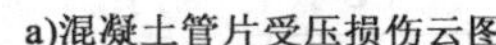

a)混凝土管片受压损伤云图

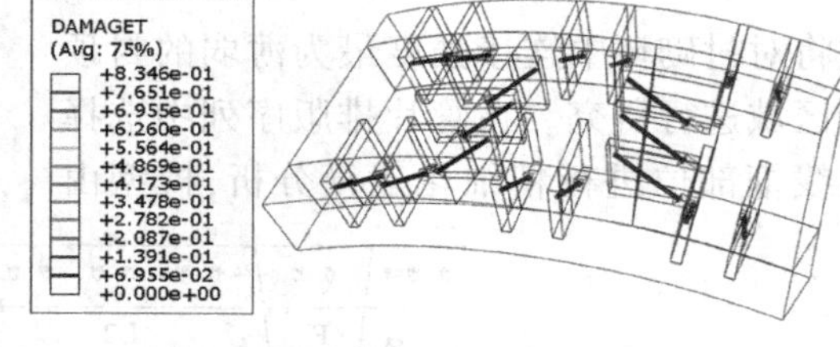

b)混凝土管片受拉损伤云图

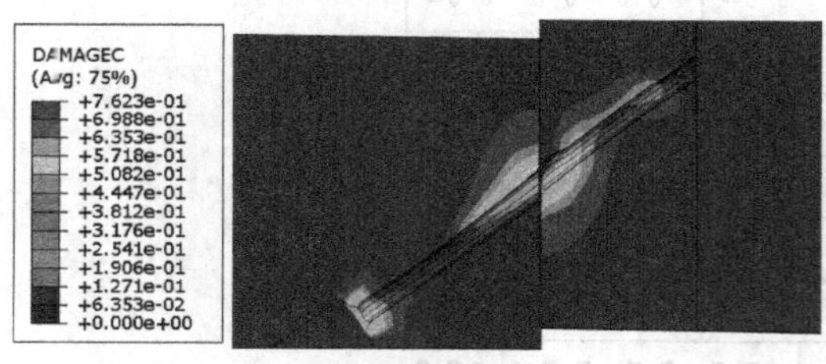

c)环缝1螺栓孔混凝土受压损伤云图

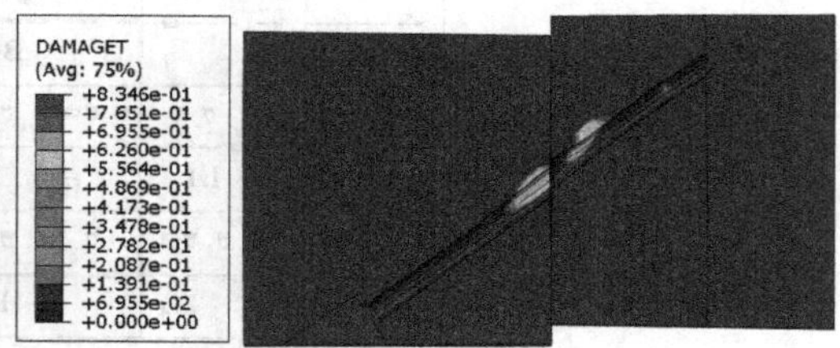

d)环缝1螺栓孔混凝土受拉损伤云图

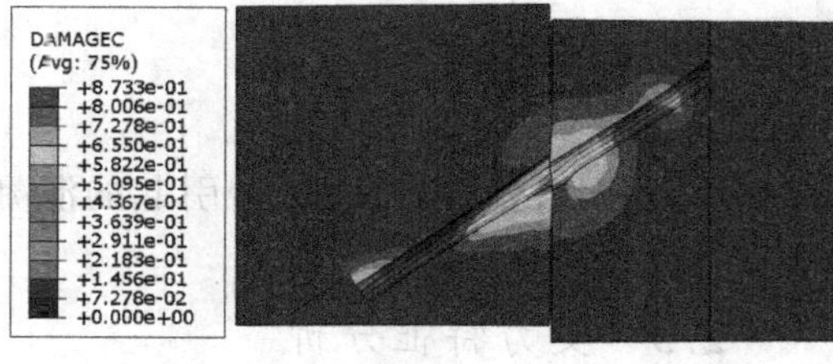

e)环缝2螺栓孔混凝土受压损伤云图

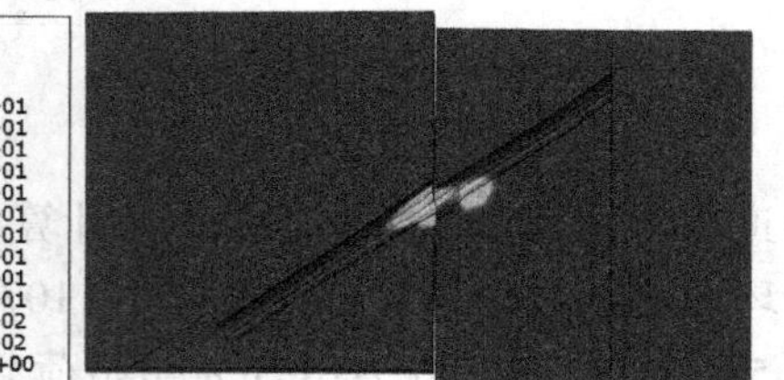

f)环缝2螺栓孔混凝土受拉损伤云图

图8　管片损伤云图

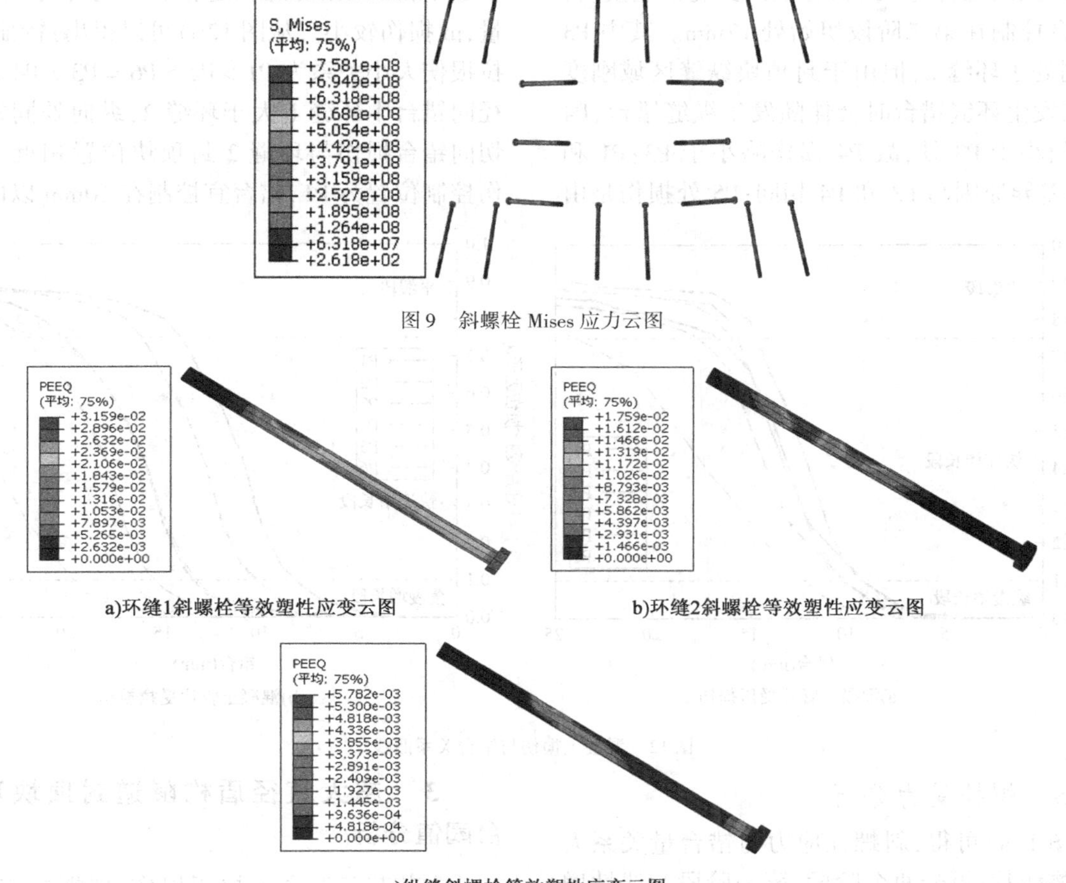

图 9　斜螺栓 Mises 应力云图

a)环缝1斜螺栓等效塑性应变云图

b)环缝2斜螺栓等效塑性应变云图

c)纵缝斜螺栓等效塑性应变云图

图 10　斜螺栓等效塑性应变云图

由图 9 可得，环缝 1 螺栓整体受力均匀，主要承受拉力，螺牙至螺母段应力大小相当，由图 10a)可知螺牙至螺母段同为塑性屈服发生区域，塑性应变在其与螺栓孔接触位置稍大，其余位置分布均匀；环缝 2 斜螺栓应力主要集中在接缝附近，主要承受剪力，受剪屈服区域同样集中分布在接缝错台位置；封顶块纵缝螺栓受力特征与环缝 1 处相似，但应力和塑性发展远小于环缝 1 螺栓。

2.4　管片损伤分析

由于整个结构受力对称，在径向加载中主要选取环缝 1 封顶块螺栓位置 P1、环缝 1 邻接块最大受力螺栓位置 P2、环缝 2 封顶块螺栓位置 P3、环缝 2 邻接块最大受力螺栓位置 P4、纵缝最大受力螺栓位置 P5 共 5 个受力特征有明显差异的位置进行分析，如图 11 所示。切向加载下环缝 1 和环缝 2 螺栓受力特征相同，仅选取环缝受力最大处封顶块螺栓位置 P6 进行分析；该加载条件下未附加产生纵缝错台，纵缝接头受力远小于径向加载条件下，且不产生混凝土损伤，不作分析。从数值模型中提取数据绘制折线图，如图 12 所示。

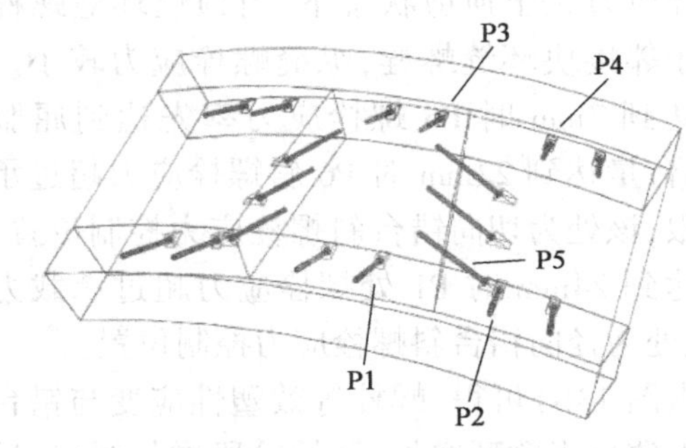

图 11　特征点位图

由图 12 可得，混凝土管片的损伤值与环缝错台量的关系大致呈 S 状，主要可分成三个阶段，第一阶段为缓慢增长段，第二阶段为快速增长段，第三阶段增长趋于平缓。从图 12a) 可以得出，特征位置受压损伤大小关系为 P3 > P4 > P6 > P1 > P2 > P5，径向错台中环缝 2 大于环缝 1，纵缝处最小，切向错台损伤介于径向错台环缝 2 和环缝 1 之间，受压损伤控制位置为P3,为有效减少混凝土损伤,宜将错台控制在第二阶段伊始处12mm。其中P3和P4同处于环缝2,但由于封顶块纵缝区域刚度较小,在发生环缝错台时会伴随发生纵缝错台,P4处错台值小于P3处,故P4损伤略小于P3;P1和P2大小差异原因与P3和P4相同;P5处损伤是由纵缝错台产生的,但纵缝错台量远小于环缝错台量,故损伤较小。从图12b)可以得出,特征位置受拉损伤大小关系为P1 > P2 > P6 = P3 > P4 > P5,即径向错台中环缝1大于环缝2,纵向处同样较小,切向错台损伤与环缝2封顶块位置相近,受拉损伤控制位置为P1,错台宜控制在10mm以内。

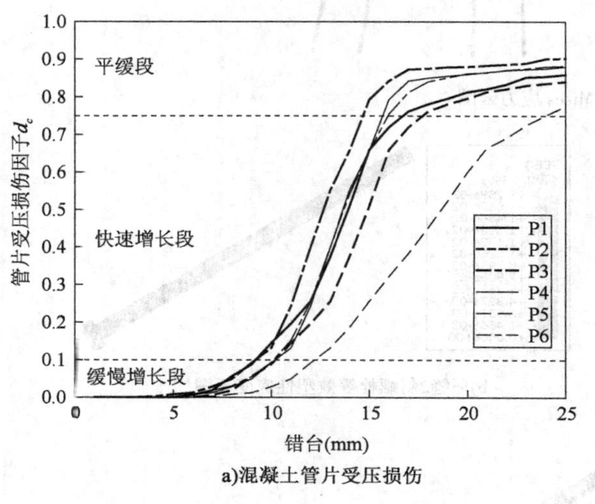

a)混凝土管片受压损伤

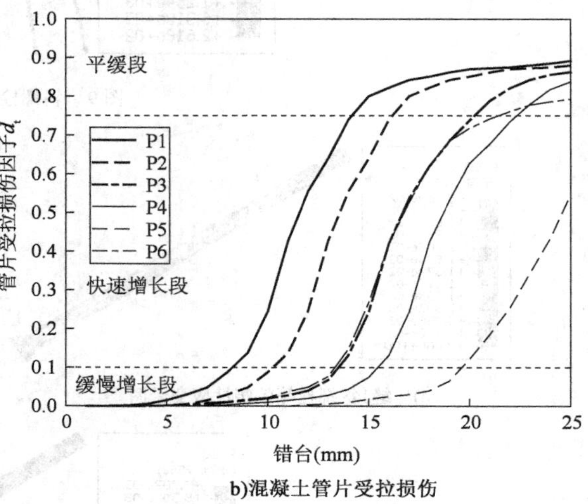

b)混凝土管片受拉损伤

图12　混凝土损伤与错台关系曲线

2.5　螺栓受力分析

由图13a)可得,斜螺栓应力与错台量关系大致呈抛物线状;可分两个阶段,第一阶段为线性增长,第二阶段为斜螺栓屈服后应力缓慢增长。螺栓应力大小依次为P6 > P1 > P2 > P3 > P4 > P5;切向剪切下螺栓应力大于径向剪切下,顺剪状态下斜螺栓应力大于逆剪状态下,封顶块环缝螺栓应力大于邻接块环缝螺栓,纵缝螺栓应力较小。错台量达到7mm时P6螺栓应力率先达到屈服应力;错台量达到22mm时P6斜螺栓应力超过承载力极限,该处为切向错台斜螺栓应力控制位置,错台量达到24mm时P1处螺栓应力超过承载力极限,该处为径向错台斜螺栓应力控制位置。

由图13b)可得,螺栓等效塑性应变与错台量关系大致呈指数型增长,开始阶段增长缓慢,后续阶段随着螺栓屈服塑性应变增长速率加快。各位置螺栓等效塑性应变大小依次为P1 > P2 > P6 > P3 > P4 > P5。由此可知,顺剪错台下螺栓屈服后性能退化较逆剪错台严重,故以P1处为斜螺栓等效塑性应变控制位置。为保证结构的安全性能,螺栓塑性不宜有过大发展,需将螺栓最大塑性应变控制在0.01以内,则错台宜不超过13mm。

3　超大直径盾构隧道封顶块环缝错台阈值分析

本节基于混凝土拉压损伤、斜螺栓应力及等效塑性应变等结构安全指标与环缝错台的关系分析,旨在得出考虑这四项因素时发生错台的结构安全评估数据。下面根据相关研究对每项指标数据进行分级,最后给出封顶块环缝错台阈值建议。

隧道接头处结构的损伤与接缝变形直接相关,拼装误差、施工荷载、隧道上浮沉降等因素引起的接缝错台量达到一定程度后势必会造成混凝土管片局部破损,导致接头力学性能退化和防水失效,对隧道结构产生不可逆的损伤,且后期难于补救,故制定合理的错台控制指标,对控制隧道施工质量具有重要意义。依据混凝土损伤因子在试验中应用的研究[11-12],为便于定量分析将混凝土损伤分为四个等级:损伤因子d为0时定义为无损伤(标记为0),介于0~0.2区间定义为轻度损伤(标记为1),介于0.2~0.7区间定义为中度损伤(标记为2),介于0.7~1区间定义为重度损伤(标记为3)。

螺栓是影响接缝力学性能的主要因素,其受力状态同样对隧道安全和防水其重要作用。本文依据钢材力学特性将螺栓应力情况分为四个等级：螺栓应力 σ 小于 500MPa 时定义为弹性段(标记为0)，介于 500～640MPa 区间定义为弹塑性段(标记为1)，介于 640～800MPa 区间定义为塑性段(标记为2)，大于 800MPa 定义为失效段(标记为3)。将螺栓等效塑性应变划分为四个等级：塑性应变 ε_p 等于 0 定义为无塑性发展(标记为0)，处于 0～0.01 区间定义为塑性轻度发展(标记为1)，处于 0.01～0.03 区间定义为塑性中度发展(标记为2)，大于 0.03 定义为塑性重度发展(标记为3)。将六个特征位置的四项安全指标按照上述分级方法作成错台-封顶块损伤关系表(表2)。

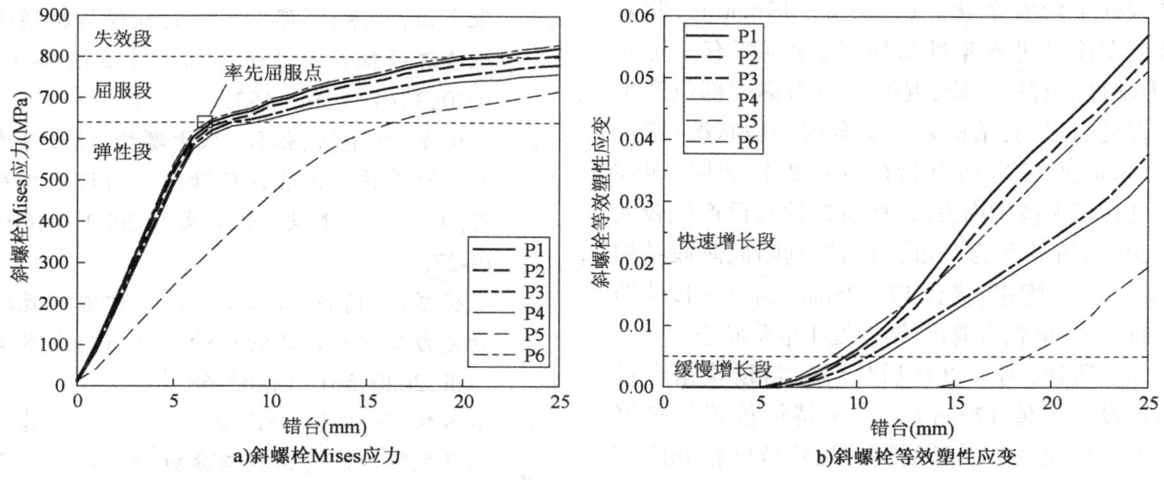

图13　斜螺栓力学特性与错台关系曲线

错台-封顶块损伤关系表　　表2

错台(mm)	P1				P2				P3				P4				P5				P6				损伤状态
	d_c	d_t	σ	ε_p	d_c	d_t	σ	ε_p	d_c	d_t	σ	ε_p	d_c	d_t	σ	ε_p	d_c	d_t	σ	ε_p	d_c	d_t	σ	ε_p	
1～3	0	0	0	0	0	0	0	0	0	0	0	0	0	0	0	0	0	0	0	0	0	0	0	0	未损伤
4	0	0	0	0	0	1	0	0	0	0	0	0	1	0	0	0	0	0	0	0	0	0	0	0	局部轻微损伤
5	0	1	1	0	0	1	1	0	1	0	0	0	1	0	0	0	0	0	0	0	1	1	1	0	
6	0	1	1	0	1	1	1	1	1	0	1	0	1	1	1	0	0	0	0	0	1	1	1	1	
7	1	1	1	1	1	1	1	1	1	1	1	0	1	1	1	1	0	0	0	0	1	1	1	1	
8	1	1	1	1	1	1	2	1	1	1	1	1	1	1	1	1	0	0	0	0	1	1	2	1	局部中度损伤
9	1	1	2	1	1	1	2	1	1	1	1	1	1	1	2	1	0	1	0	0	1	1	2	1	
10	1	1	2	1	1	1	2	1	1	1	2	1	1	1	2	1	1	1	0	0	1	1	2	1	
11	1	1	2	1	1	2	2	1	1	1	2	1	2	1	2	1	1	1	1	0	1	1	2	2	
12	1	2	2	2	2	2	2	2	2	1	2	1	2	1	2	1	1	1	1	0	2	1	2	2	
13	2	2	2	2	2	2	2	2	2	1	2	1	2	1	2	1	1	1	1	0	2	1	2	2	
14	2	2	2	2	2	3	2	2	2	1	2	2	2	1	2	2	1	1	1	0	2	1	2	2	局部重度损伤
15	2	2	2	2	2	3	2	2	2	1	2	2	3	2	2	2	1	1	1	1	2	2	2	2	
16	2	3	2	2	3	3	2	2	3	1	2	2	3	2	2	2	1	1	1	1	3	2	2	2	
17	3	3	2	2	3	3	2	3	3	2	2	2	3	2	2	2	3	1	2	1	3	2	2	2	整体损伤
18	3	3	2	3	3	3	2	3	3	2	2	2	3	2	2	2	3	1	2	1	3	2	2	2	
19	3	3	2	3	3	3	2	3	3	2	2	2	3	2	2	2	3	1	2	1	3	2	2	3	
20	3	3	2	3	3	3	3	3	3	2	2	2	3	3	2	2	3	1	2	1	3	3	3	3	
21	3	3	2	3	3	3	3	3	3	2	2	2	3	3	2	2	3	2	2	1	3	3	3	3	
22～25	3	3	3	3	3	3	3	3	3	3	2	3	3	3	2	3	3	2	2	2	3	3	3	3	

由表2可知,环缝错台1~3mm时,所有特征位置的混凝土均未出现损伤,螺栓均未有塑性发展,结构处于一个非常安全的状态;错台4~7mm时,部分位置出现轻微损伤,在实际工程中出现时,错台量稳定且不继续发展的情况下,一般不进行修补,故根据工程经验和数值研究可判断,此阶段结构处于较安全状态;错台8~13mm时,此阶段部分螺栓已进入塑性阶段,塑性应变有一定发展,力学性能有所下降,混凝土应力集中部位产生中等程度的损伤,结构处于安全度一般状况;错台14~16mm,此阶段所有特征部位螺栓屈服,塑性应变已在较大范围内发展,所有螺栓孔已产生较大损伤,P1位置处尤为严重,由结果判断此阶段结构具有较大安全隐患;错台17~25mm,封顶块接缝结构全面受损,承载力退化,结构处于危险状态。

综上所述,超大直径盾构隧道封顶块错台量在达到设计限值17mm时,六个特征位置处接缝已发生严重损伤。因封顶块的位置特殊性和刚度薄弱性,其错台控制值应较其他位置有所区分,建议封顶块处环缝错台阈值小于13mm(对比原隧道设计限值17mm),必要时应进行加固处理。

4　结语

本文建立了考虑材料非线性的隧道局部三维精细化模型,通过与既有试验结果对比,论证了建模方法的合理性,在此基础上开展了超大直径盾构隧道封顶块环缝错台下的损伤特性研究,主要得出以下结论:

(1)接头混凝土损伤与环缝错台量的关系大致呈S状。相同错台量条件下,径向逆剪下管片受压损伤程度大于径向顺剪,切向错台损伤介于二者之间;受拉损伤则是径向顺剪环缝大于径向逆剪环缝,切向错台损伤大小与径向逆剪相近;封顶块环缝接头损伤大于邻接块。

(2)斜螺栓应力与错台量关系大致呈抛物线状。相同错台量条件下,切向错台下螺栓应力大于径向错台,径向顺剪环缝大于径向逆剪环缝。斜螺栓等效塑性应变与错台量关系大致呈指数型,顺剪状态下产生的等效塑性应变在大小和区域上都明显大于逆剪状态下。

(3)基于错台与封顶块混凝土损伤、接缝螺栓受力等安全指标的关系,提出了错台-封顶块损伤关系表,可借助该关系表实现对环缝错台下超大直径盾构隧道结构安全的量化评估。

(4)基于封顶块错台量与接缝损伤关系分析,建议超大直径盾构隧道封顶块错台限值应与其他位置区分,为避免隧道存在安全隐患其最大限值应小于13mm。

参考文献

[1] 张冬梅,刘杰,李保军,等.大直径盾构隧道斜螺栓环缝抗剪特性研究[J].中国公路学报,2020,33(12):142-153.

[2] 桑运龙,刘学增,张强.基于螺栓-凹凸榫连接的地铁盾构隧道管片环缝接头刚度分析及应用[J].隧道建设(中英文),2020,40(01):19-27.

[3] 张稳军,王博达,张高乐.错台对盾构隧道接缝受力及防水性能的影响分析[J].土木工程学报,2020,53(S1):63-68.

[4] 李冬梅,陈正杰,杨志豪.上海长江隧道管片环缝抗剪性能的试验与分析[J].地下工程与隧道,2011(01):15-17+52.

[5] 何源,杨振华,柳献,等.盾构隧道斜螺栓连接环缝剪切破坏特征理论解析[J].隧道建设(中英文),2021,41(06):933-945.

[6] 闫治国,彭益成,丁文其,等.青草沙水源地原水工程输水隧道单层衬砌管片接头荷载试验研究[J].岩土工程学报,2011,33(09):1385-1390.

[7] 朱瑶宏,张宸,柳献,等.错缝拼装通用环管片环缝抗剪性能试验研究[J].铁道科学与工程学报,2017,14(02):315-324.

[8] 熊进刚,丁利,田钦.混凝土损伤塑性模型参数计算方法及试验验证[J].南昌大学学报(工科版),2019,41(01):21-26.

[9] 张劲,王庆扬,胡守营,等.ABAQUS混凝土损伤塑性模型参数验证[J].建筑结构,2008(08):127-130.

[10] 小泉淳.盾构隧道管片设计[M].北京:中国建筑工业出版社,2012.

[11] 郭嘉伟,徐彬.混凝土损伤塑性模型损伤因子的取值及应用研究[J].甘肃科学学报,2019,31(06):88-92.

[12] 杨飞,董新勇,周沈华,等.ABAQUS混凝土塑性损伤因子计算方法及应用研究[J].四川建筑,2017,37(06):173-177.

基于 FDS 的公路隧道火灾可逆射流风机通风疏散研究

李方舰[1] 李 婧[1] 戎 贤[1,2] 张一鸣[*1]
(1. 河北工业大学土木与交通学院;2. 河北省土木工程技术研究中心)

摘 要 随着我国公路隧道从高速建设期转变为建设与管理并重期,可逆射流风机在隧道通风系统中得到广泛应用。为探究可逆射流风机在隧道火灾下通风运行方式对人员疏散的影响,本文依托广东山隧道,采用5MW、20MW两种火源功率,研究不同射流风机运行方式下隧道中部区域烟气、温度、CO浓度及可见度的变化特性。结果表明,自然风和射流风机的出口气流均会破坏烟气-空气分层结构。在隧道内部1m/s纵向自然风的影响下,面对不同功率火源,射流风机运行模式与人员疏散方向应随之改变。本研究结果可为隧道运营人员及消防部门制定隧道火灾应急通风方案提供理论参考。

关键词 公路隧道 可逆射流风机 火灾通风 人员疏散 FDS

0 引言

随着隧道通风系统的飞速发展,可逆射流风机广泛地应用于我国公路隧道建设中。隧道发生火灾后,可逆射流风机能够通过改变运行方向,控制火灾烟气以最短的路径排出隧道,辅助疏散救援,极大的降低隧道火灾可能造成的损失[1]。

目前,公路隧道机械通风主要有纵向通风、半横向通风、全横向通风以及组合通风4种形式[2]。其中,全射流纵向通风系统施工简单、造价低廉、运维便捷,已成为目前公路隧道使用的主流通风方式。全射流纵向通风系统由安装在隧道顶部或侧壁的若干组射流风机组成。近年来国内众多学者对射流风机的通风效果进行了诸多研究。杨秀军等[3]采用CFD软件进行3车道两风机隧道的数值模拟,得出了不同类型射流风机最小纵向间距的判断依据。方飞龙等[4]通过对隧道现场实测数据处理,发现了隧道纵向射流通风存在延迟效应,提出了隧道纵向射流通风系统流场延迟效应的解析公式。赵黎等[5]通过优化2车道公路隧道射流风机的空间布局,得出了风机最佳安装位置以及横、纵向间距。徐志胜等[6]采用Fluent软件研究风机布置对隧道污染物的分布情况,得出最佳风机横向布置间距为3倍风机直径。赵东平等[7]研究隧道火灾时横通道和平行导洞内射流风机安装位置对防灾通风的影响,提出了射流风机安装位置与不同车道辅助坑道防护门距离的建议值。李小江[8]通过改变射流风机隧道顶部的安装距离,得出安装距离距隧道顶15~20cm时摩阻损失折减系数在75%左右。从前人研究方向来看,大多集中于射流风机安装位置以及横纵向间距对隧道内部通风的影响,射流风机的可逆性在隧道火灾情景下的研究还不够深入。

为提高通风系统的可靠性和效率,射流风机一般分多段布置在隧道两端和中部区域[9]。当火灾发生在隧道两端洞口段时,风机应调整至向较近的隧道出口方向,以减小烟气在隧道内部扩散的距离[10-11];当火灾发生在隧道中部时,由于人员车辆距隧道出口较远,给隧道内部的人员疏散带来巨大困难。因此,研究公路隧道中部区域可逆射流风机不同运行方式对火灾通风疏散的影响具有重要意义。本文依托承秦高速公路广东山隧道,采用FDS软件PyroSim按照隧道实际参数建模,选取5MW和20MW两种火源功率,通过改变射流风机运行方式分析隧道内部烟气、温度、CO浓度和可见度的分布情况及规律,辅助隧道运营

1. 基金项目:河北省自然科学基金(E2019202441);河北省重点研发项目(19275404D);河北省交通运输厅科技资助项目(TH1-202020);天津市交通运输科技发展计划项目(2021-18)

人员优化方案,为公路隧道发生火灾时可逆射流风机的应用提供理论支撑。

1　数值模型建立

1.1　工程概况

广东山隧道位于承秦高速承德段,隧道形式为双洞单向隧道,左线全长2770m,右线全长2772m,是承秦高速公路全线最长的隧道。隧道采用全射流纵向通风方式,车辆设计速度为80km/h。隧道主洞建筑限界宽度为10.25m,限界高度为5m。

1.2　公路隧道模型

依据广东山隧道施工图纸参数建模,隧道模型长度取300m。隧道衬砌材料设置为混凝土,其密度、比热容和导热系数分别设为2280.0kg/m³、1.04kJ/(kg·K)和1.8W/(m·K)。隧道模型内部布置2组射流风机,间距150m,如图1所示。其中每组包含2台可逆射流风机,风机轴线间距2.5m,距隧道建筑限界150mm。风机长度3m,叶轮直径1.12m,射流出口风速30m/s,风机模型两端设置为vent用于正逆向通风,隧道模型两端设置为开放表面。隧道断面尺寸、射流风机模型和数值计算模型如图2所示。

1.3　火源模拟

由于隧道内部行驶车辆车型和车载可燃物的不同,本文选取5MW和20MW作为火源功率的模拟对象[12]。当火灾发生在模型中心处时人员向两侧疏散的距离最远。因此,火源设置在隧道模型地面中心处为最不利位置,火源尺寸设置为5m×3m×2m。

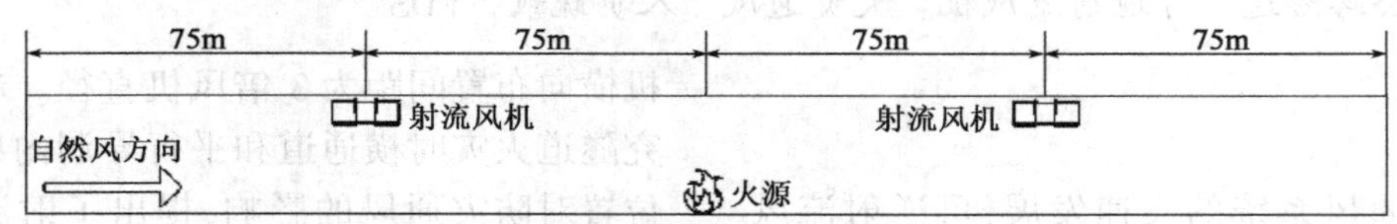

图1　隧道火灾模拟示意图

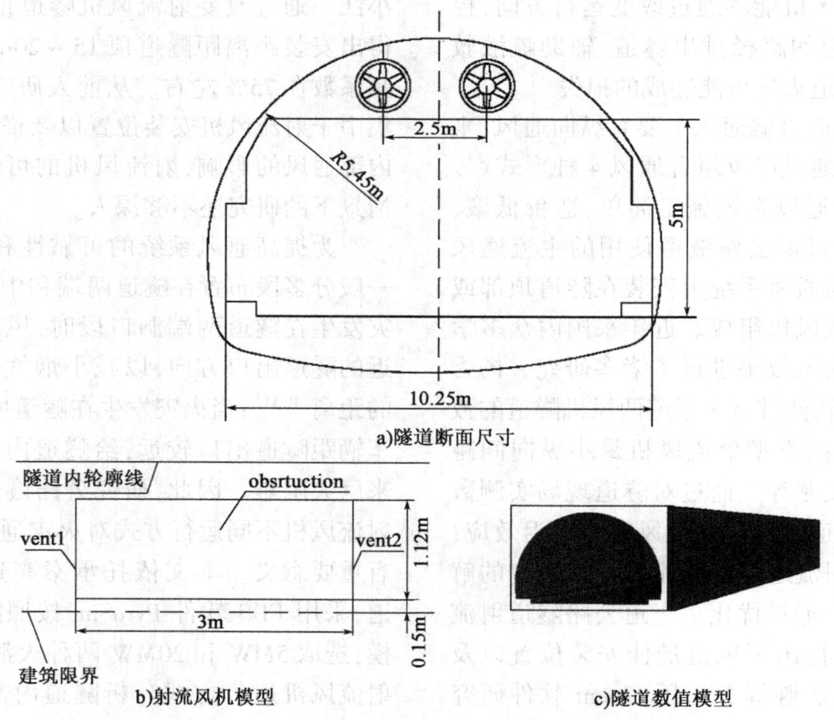

a)隧道断面尺寸

b)射流风机模型

c)隧道数值模型

图2　隧道模型示意图

FDS模拟采用t^2增长模型[13],函数关系式如式(1)所示。

$$Q = \alpha t^2 \tag{1}$$

式中:Q——火灾燃烧时的热释放速率(MW);

α——比例系数;

t——燃烧时间(s)。

考虑到最大火源热释放速率为20MW，故选取最不利情况下比例系数 $\alpha = 0.1876$，即5MW达到最大热释放率的时间为163s，20MW为327s。

1.4 火灾危险临界值

隧道火灾中烟气是影响人员安全的最主要因素，本文分别选取温度、CO体积分数和可见度作为隧道火灾对人员构成危险的条件[14-15]。表1为火灾危险参数临界值，选取高度2m作为人体保护高度。

火灾危险参数临界值　表1

影响参数	临界值
温度	取60℃为温度临界值
CO体积分数	取100ppm为CO浓度临界值
可见度	取10m为可见度临界值

1.5 网格分析

采用FDS模拟时网格大小的选取将直接影响隧道火灾数值模拟的精准度。网格尺寸过大将影响模拟结果，造成较大误差；尺寸过小将影响模拟计算速度，造成资源浪费。因此，选取合适大小的网格尺寸对于隧道火灾数值模拟至关重要。

火源特征直径 D^* 是影响网格质量的关键参数，计算公式如式(2)所示。

$$D^* = \left(\frac{Q}{\rho_0 c_p T_0 \sqrt{g}}\right)^{2/5} \tag{2}$$

式中：D^*——火源特征直径(m)；

Q——火源功率(kW)；

ρ_0——空气密度(kg/m³)；

c_p——空气定压比热容[kJ/(kg·K)]；

T_0——环境温度(K)；

g——重力加速度。

设置隧道内部环境温度为20℃，$\rho_0 = 1.204$ kg/m³，$c_p = 1.004$kJ/(kg·K)，$T_0 = 293$K，g 取9.81m/s²。

参考FDS用户手册[16]可知，可通过火灾特征直径 D^* 和网格实际划分尺寸 d_x 的比值作为网格划分判断的依据。当 D^*/d_x 的值在4～16之间时，能够取得较为准确的数值模拟结果。通过选取较小火源功率5MW进行网格尺寸的计算，能够满足较大火源功率的网格精准度要求，选用的5种工况如表2所示。

网格无关化计算工况　表2

工况	火源功率(MW)	网格尺寸(m)	实际划分尺寸 d_x
1	5	0.125	0.069D*
2	5	0.250	0.137D*
3	5	0.378	0.207D*
4	5	0.500	0.273D*
5	5	0.630	0.345D*

图3为5种工况下火源中心点竖向温度分布情况。从图中可知，随着网格尺寸的减小，距火源中心点较近处的温度逐渐提升，距离火源中心点较远处的温度差异不明显。当网格尺寸减小至0.250m时，温度计算结果与0.125m网格基本一致，因此选取0.250m作为网格基本尺寸。同时考虑到网格尺寸对于距火源较远的位置影响较小，于是将火源前后20m作为网格加密区，非加密区网格尺寸设置为0.500m，以满足隧道火灾模拟精度和速度的要求。

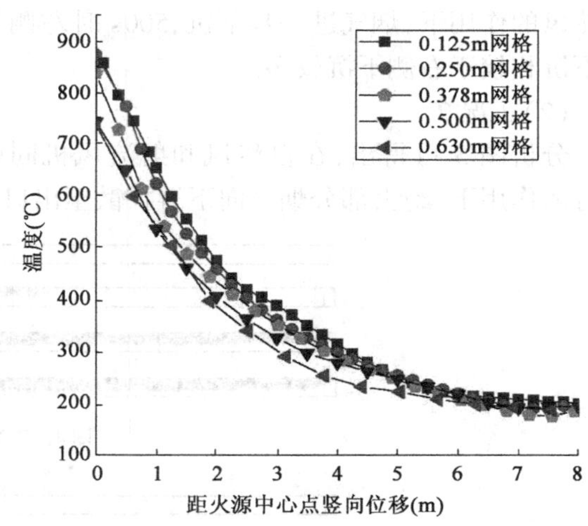

图3　火源中心点竖向温度分布

2 数值模拟及分析

2.1 模拟工况设置

为探究可逆射流风机在隧道火灾下不同通风运行方式对人员疏散的影响，本文采用工况如表3所示。自然风经隧道实地考察后取1m/s，模拟时间取500s。

模拟工况设置　　　　表3

工况	火源功率(MW)	自然风速(m/s)	风机风速(m/s)	风机	送风模式	风机	送风模式
1	5	1	30	左侧风机	停止	右侧风机	停止
2					正向		正向
3					逆向		逆向
4					正向		逆向
5					逆向		逆向
6	20				停止		停止
7					正向		正向
8					逆向		逆向
9					正向		逆向
10					逆向		正向

注:自然风风向为自左向右,取风机正向为向右侧通风,逆向为向左侧通风。

2.2　火源功率 5MW

2.2.1　烟气场

(1)工况 1

由图 4 可知,当隧道内部仅存在自左向右的 1m/s 的纵向自然风时,火灾烟气首先向下游扩散,65s 时开始向上游逆流,140s 时烟气扩散至下游出口,360s 时逆流到达上游出口。此后在纵向自然风的作用下,烟气进一步下沉,500s 时左侧烟气下沉相较于右侧下沉较多。

(2)工况 2

分析图 5 可得出,在自然风和射流风机同向运行的作月下,绝大部分烟气向下游扩散至出口。烟气在 105s 时开始向上游逆流,在 500s 时仅向上游逆流 15m,集中在隧道顶部。

(3)工况 3

由图 6 可知在烟气向下游扩散的过程中,逆向风机的气流破坏了隧道内部烟气-空气分层结构,使得扩散中的烟气快速下沉。220s 时烟气到达上游出口,相较于仅自然风提前了 140s,500s 时烟气已经蔓延至整个隧道模型。

(4)工况 4

由图 7 可知,由于下游风机逆向运行,火灾下游烟气场与工况 3 相似。500s 时相较于工况 2 烟气逆流较多,且在上游风机正向运行下烟气向下扩散较严重。

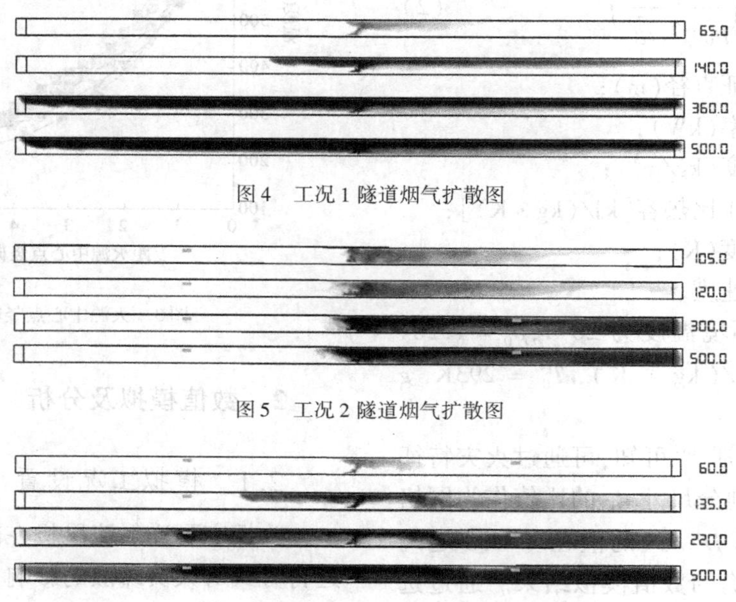

图4　工况 1 隧道烟气扩散图

图5　工况 2 隧道烟气扩散图

图6　工况 3 隧道烟气扩散图

(5)工况5

分析图8可知,当风机向隧道模型两侧运行时,风机中间部分的烟气场与工况1类似,但向两侧射出的气流会影响两侧的烟气场,造成烟气的大面积下沉,500s时隧道模型大部分区域被烟气覆盖。

图7　工况4隧道烟气扩散图

图8　工况5隧道烟气扩散图

2.2.2　2m高度温度、CO浓度及可见度分析

对5MW前5个工况500s时隧道温度、CO浓度和可见度综合分析,取人体高度为2m,见图9。

由图9可知温度和CO浓度分布以火源点为中心近似呈对称分布。火源右侧5m处温度、CO浓度浓度达到最大值,可见度达到最低,主要是由于自然风影响火灾烟气向右侧扩散导致。两侧随纵向距离增加温度和CO浓度下降明显,可见度显著上升,因此火灾发生时应尽快从火源附近撤离。

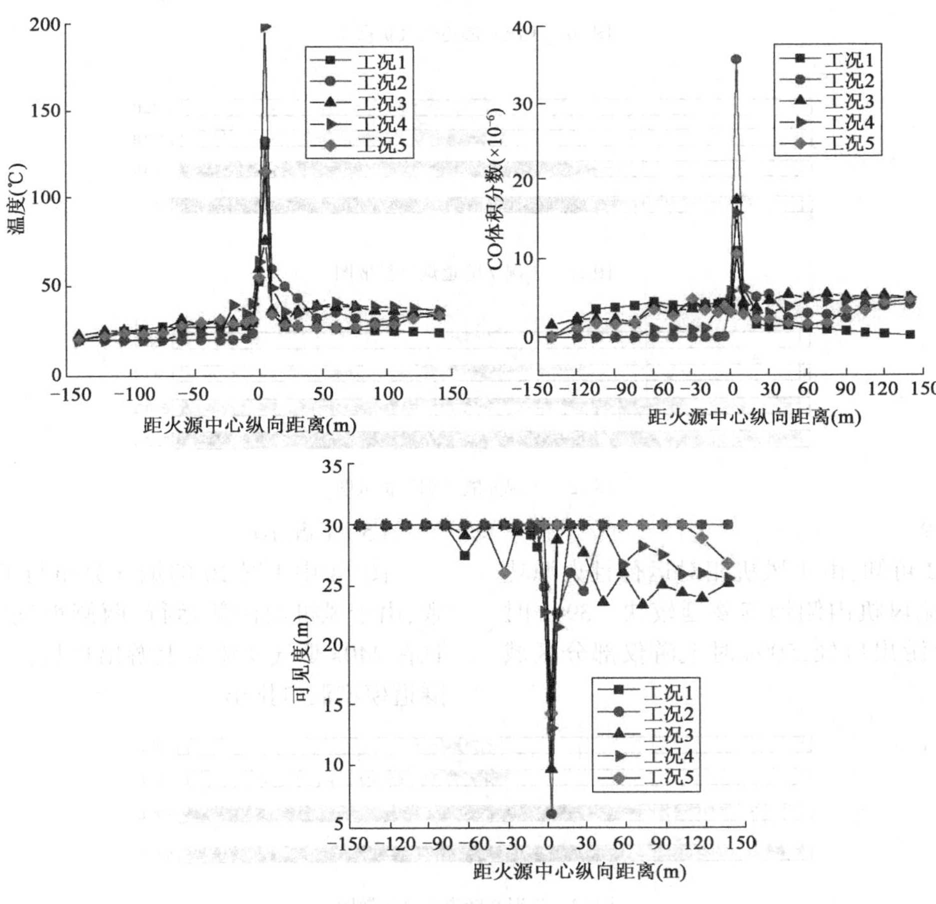

图9　温度、CO浓度、可见度分布图(5MW)

当火源功率为 5MW 时,5 种工况下仅在火源附近温度和可见度超出人体可承受限值。火灾上游距火源 5m 外,温度均低于 40℃,CO 浓度均小于 5ppm,可见度均大于 25m;下游距火源 20m 外,人体高度处温度均小于 50℃,CO 浓度均小于 10ppm,可见度均大于 20m,对人体的影响较小。

工况 2 火灾上游距火源 5m 外,温度测点均小于 25℃,CO 浓度均小于 1ppm,可见度均达到 30m。结合烟气场建议采用工况 2 的通风方案,人员向火灾上游疏散,能够将烟气逆流长度达到最小,最大限度的减小烟气扩散对于疏散人员的心理和行为影响[17]。

2.3 火源功率 20MW

2.3.1 烟气场

(1)工况 6

由图 10 可知,隧道内部烟气扩散与 5MW 一致,但蔓延速度较快,290s 时逆流烟气已到达火灾上游出口,500s 时隧道火灾上游已在纵向自然风的影响下被烟气覆盖。

(2)工况 7

分析图 11 可得,80s 时烟气出现逆流,120s 烟气到达下游出口,320s 时烟气到达左侧风机处,500s 时烟气到达上游 130m 处。与 5MW 不同,烟气逆流较多,且在风机和自然风的作用下下沉,影响了火灾上游烟气的分布。

(3)工况 8

由图 12 可知,烟气扩散规律与 5MW 一致,由于火源功率较大,210s 时烟气已经逆流至火灾上游出口处,500s 时已经充满整个隧道模型。

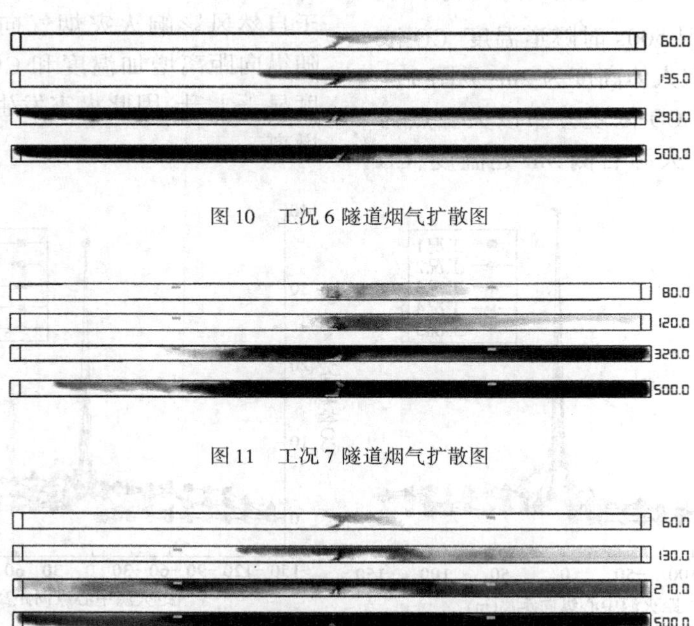

图 10 工况 6 隧道烟气扩散图

图 11 工况 7 隧道烟气扩散图

图 12 工况 8 隧道烟气扩散图

(4)工况 9

分析图 13 可知,由于风机相对运行且火源功率较大,两射流风机内侧烟气蔓延较快。390s 时烟气蔓延至上游出口处,500s 时上游仅部分区域未被烟气覆盖。

(5)工况 10

图 14 中工况 10 的烟气分布与工况 5 基本一致,由于风机向两侧运行,两侧烟气大面积下沉,且在 240s 烟气逆流至上游出口后,大部分烟气自隧道模型洞口排出。

图 13 工况 9 隧道烟气扩散图

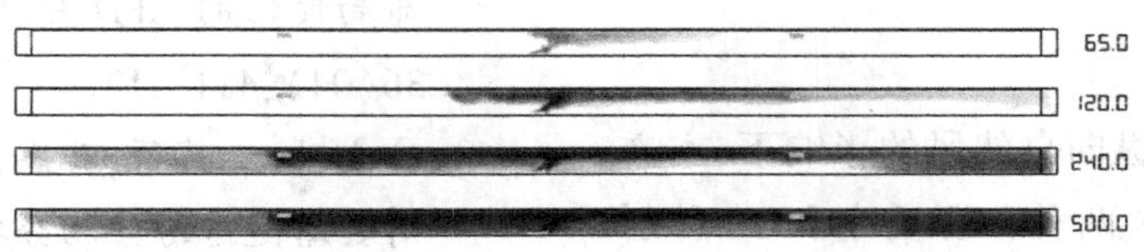

图 14 工况 10 隧道烟气扩散图

2.3.2 2m 高处温度、CO 浓度及可见度分析

对 20MW 火源功率 5 个工况 500s 时人体高度 2m 处隧道温度、CO 浓度和可见度进行综合分析，见图 15。与 5MW 一致，在自然风的作用下火源右侧 5m 处温度、CO 浓度浓度达到最大值，可见度达到最低。但当火源功率增至 20MW 时，在自然风和射流风机共同作用下，火源两侧火灾特性分布差异较大。

工况 6 火灾上游有测点温度超过 50℃，可见度低至 10m，不利于人员安全疏散；下游距火源 20m 外测点温度均小于 45℃，CO 浓度均小于 5ppm，可见度均为 30m，对人体安全影响较小。

工况 7 ~ 10 火源上游大致呈向模型出口递减的趋势，距离火源较近处测点温度超过 55℃，可见度低至 10m；火灾下游大部分测点温度均大于 60℃，可见度低于 10m，不利于人员安全疏散。

综合分析，建议选择工况 6 的通风方案，射流风机停止运行，人员选择火源下游疏散。虽然工况 6 火灾下游存在大量烟气，但存在明显的烟气-空气分层，不会影响人体高度处的温度、CO 浓度和可见度分布，能够保证人员疏散的安全。

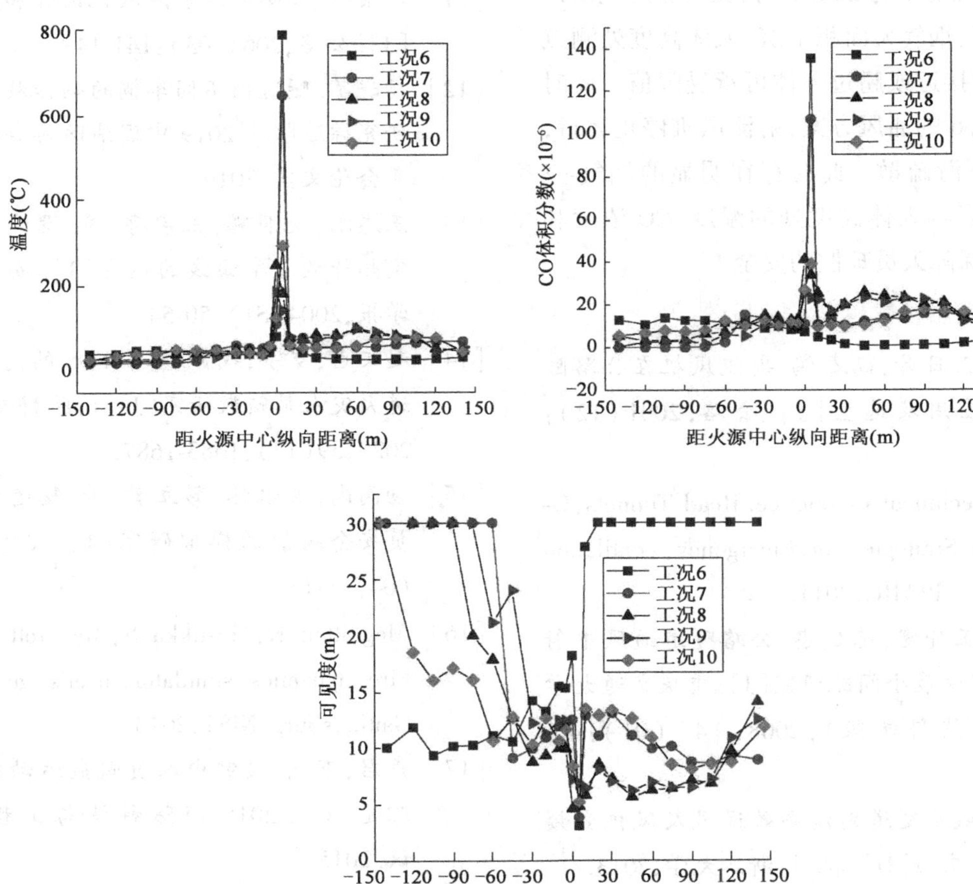

图 15 500s 时温度、CO 浓度、可见度分布图(20MW)

3　结语

在隧道内部1m/s纵向自然风的影响下,本文通过设置5MW和2MW两种火源功率和10种射流风机运行工况,以探究火灾情形下隧道中部区域可逆射流风机不同通风方式对人员疏散的影响,得出如下结论:

(1)当隧道中部发生火灾时,自然风与射流风机都会破坏烟气-空气分层结构,改变隧道内部火灾烟气分布。

(2)当火源功率为5MW时,虽然五种工况下人体高度处温度、CO浓度和可见度均未达到人体承受极限,但工况2能够最大限度的减小烟气逆流长度。此时人员向火灾上游疏散,能够最大限度的减小烟气扩散对于疏散人员的心理和行为影响。

(3)当火源功率为20MW时,在射流风机出口气流的影响下,烟气大面积下沉,人体高度处测点温度和可见度接近或超过人体可承受限值。此时建议选择工况6的通风方案,射流风机停止运行,人员向火灾下游疏散。此时存在明显的烟气-空气分层,不会影响人体高度处的温度、CO浓度和可见度分布,保障人员疏散的安全。

参考文献

[1] 戴国平,王日升,尚春鸽.射流风机在公路隧道中的应用及选型[J].公路,2001(12):66-69.

[2] PIARC Technical Committee. Road Tunnels:Operational Strategies for Emergency Ventilation[R]. Paris:PIARC,2011.

[3] 杨秀军,王晓雯,陈建忠.公路隧道通风中射流风机纵向最小间距研究[J].重庆交通大学学报(自然科学版),2008,{4}(01):40-43,164.

[4] 方飞龙.城市隧道射流高效通风及风机变频节能技术应用[D].杭州:浙江大学,2013.

[5] 赵黎,闫治国.2车道公路隧道射流风机空间布局优化的CFD分析[J].隧道建设,2016,36(04):411-417.

[6] 徐志胜,王蓓蕾,孔杰,等.风机横向布置间距对公路隧道污染物分布的影响研究[J].安全与环境学报,2021,21(01):321-327.

[7] 赵东平,温斯逊,杨柏洪.铁路隧道防灾通风射流风机安装位置对通风效果的影响[J].中国铁道科学,2021,42(01):59-70.

[8] 李小江.城市隧道纵向射流通风技术的应用研究[D].天津:天津大学,2008.

[9] 中华人民共和国行业标准.公路隧道通风设计细则:JTG/T D70/2-02—2014[S].北京:人民交通出版社,2014.

[10] 戴国平.射流风机可逆性在公路隧道中的应用[C].2001年全国公路隧道学术会议论文集.2001:393-395.

[11] 李景银.公路隧道射流风机设计和选型综述[J].公路,2004(03):141-144.

[12] 杨晓菡.隧道内不同车辆的热释放速率试验研究综述[C].2019中国消防协会科学技术年会论文集.2019.

[13] 王志刚,倪照鹏,王宗存,等.设计火灾时火灾热释放速率曲线的确定[J].安全与环境学报,2004(S1):50-54.

[14] 赵文忠,罗宇,戎贤.基于FDS的高速公路隧道火灾人员疏散研究[J].消防科学与技术,2020,39(12):1683-1687.

[15] 杨高尚,安永林,彭立敏,等.隧道火灾时人员安全疏散的模拟研究[J].灾害学,2006(04):8-13.

[16] Mcgrattan K, Hostikka S, Mcderott R, et al. Fire dynamics simulator, user's guide[R]. Gaithersburg:NIST,2013.

[17] 卢君,万竞.火灾中人员疏散运动行为研究综述[C].2015消防科技与工程学术会议.2015.

超大跨度公路隧道施工方法研究

陈文鹏 董方方 王传武* 高本贤 季 瞻 李炎峰 刘龙飞
(长安大学公路学院)

摘 要 为了更好确定超大跨度公路隧道合理施工方法,本文以滨莱高速沿线隧道工程为依托,利用数值模拟手段分别对Ⅳ级围岩采用上台阶CD法、CD法、三台阶七步法开挖,对于Ⅴ级围岩采用上台阶CD法、CD法和CRD法开挖时的施工过程进行探索,获得了不同施工方法下支护结构的变形规律及力学特性,与实测结果吻合度较好。结果表明,超大跨度公路隧道常采用的施工方法是安全可行的,综合考虑支护结构变形受力情况、施工安全、经济性等因素后,建议选择上台阶CD法进行施工。

关键词 隧道工程 施工方法 数值模拟 超大跨度隧道

0 引言

随着机动车保有量急剧增长,原有的单洞两车道、三车道公路隧道逐渐不能满足交通发展的需求,超大跨度公路隧道(单洞四车道公路隧道)应运而生[1]。超大跨度公路隧道结构具有扁平、大跨等特点,支护结构受力更加复杂[2-3],隧道稳定性更差。工程实践中,单洞四车道公路隧道建设难度大,施工不当易发生洞内塌方、洞口滑塌等灾害。

相关学者针对超大跨度施工方法进行了一系列研究,代表性成果有:王春河等[4]以龙鼎隧道工程为依托,对上下台阶法和CRD法开挖方式下围岩控制机制进行数值实验,得出CRD法对隧道拱顶位移、最大塑性应变和支护结构的应力控制效果优于上下台阶法。叶勇[5]以实际工程为依托,通过数值模拟对比分析双侧壁导坑法和三台阶开挖法,指出三台阶法更能有效的控制围岩变形,适用于隧道的快速施工。孙智等[6]和周磊生等[7]分别以实际工程为工程背景,针对CD法和CRD法两种开挖工法的适用性展开了研究,指出CRD法具有更好的围岩控制效果,综合考虑各种因素,现场开挖宜选择CD法。蒋坤等[8]以魁岐2号隧道工程为依托,对比分析了双侧壁导坑法、CRD法和CD法3种施工工法,得出CRD法对围岩有更好的控制效果。欧敏[9]以前鸥隧道工程为背景,研究了双侧壁导坑法的施工力学特性,得到了双侧壁导坑法分部开挖的合理滞后长度和临时支护拆除时机。

上述学者结合实际工程针对超大跨度公路隧道施工工法进行了研究,虽然取得了一定的研究成果,但是对于超大跨度公路隧道施工工法并没有形成统一的认识,同时我国在修建超大跨度公路隧道方面积累的设计和施工经验并不丰富,可供参考的案例有限,给设计和施工造成诸多困扰。因此,亟需对超大跨度公路隧道施工方法进行深入研究。本文以滨莱高速沿线乐疃隧道Ⅳ级围岩YK115+810断面和佛羊岭隧道Ⅴ级围岩ZK105+947断面为依托,针对超大跨度公路隧道Ⅳ级围岩常采用的上台阶CD法、CD法及三台阶七步开挖法和Ⅴ级围岩常采用的上台阶CD法、CD法和CRD法,通过数值模拟方法对不同施工方法建立数值计算模型,分析不同工法下支护结构的变形受力情况,进而提出超大跨度公路隧道合理的施工工法,以供工程设计和施工参考。

1 依托工程概况

滨莱高速沿线隧道隧址区为剥蚀低山丘陵地貌,大部分区域基岩埋深较浅,顶部基岩直接出露,风化现象严重,局部表层覆盖残破积物,谷底堆积有较厚的堆积物、坡积物,隧道场区水文条件简单,受地下水影响较小,隧道地形地貌如图1所示。试验断面地层主要为第四系残破积层(Q_{3dl+el})及太古代(γ_m)混合花岗岩地层,地层风化程度极强烈,结构构造基本破坏,节理裂隙,围岩主要物理力学参数见表1所列。该段隧道为双洞分离式八车道隧道,试验断面采用上台阶CD法进行施工,图2为上台阶CD法施工示意图。

a)乐疃隧道

b)佛羊岭隧道

图1　隧道地形地貌

围岩物理力学参数　　表1

围　岩	弹性模量(GPa)	泊松比μ	重度(kN/m^3)	摩擦角(°)	黏聚力(MPa)
Ⅳ级围岩	4	0.28	23	35	0.5
Ⅴ级围岩	1.3	0.35	22	23	0.1

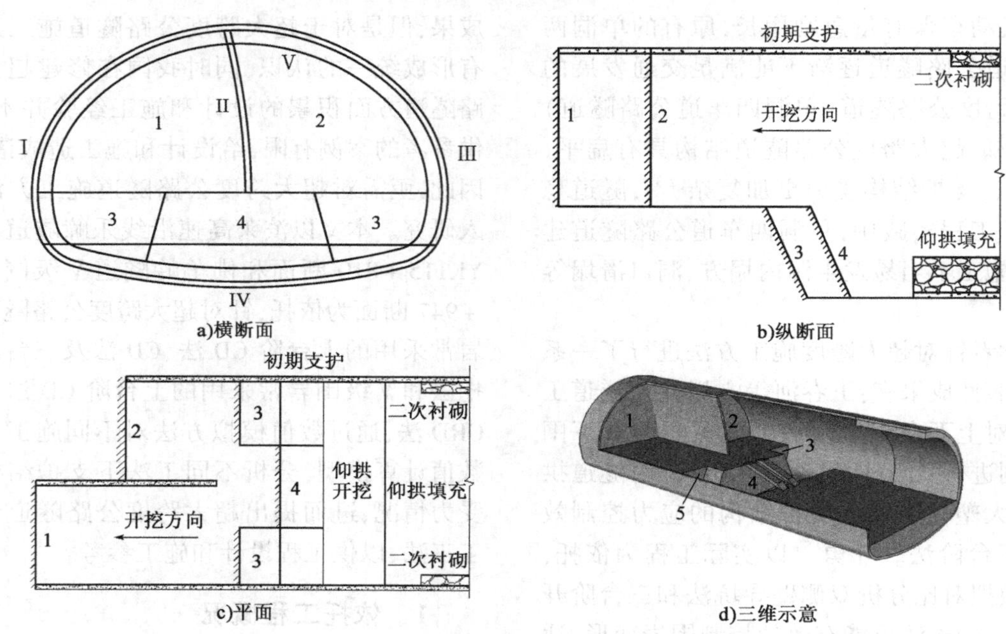

图2　上台阶CD法施工示意

2　数值计算模型及参数选取

针对Ⅳ级围岩采用CD法、上台阶CD法及三台阶七步法和Ⅴ级围岩采用上台阶CD法、CD法及CRD法进行模拟。模型左右边界及下边界均取3.5倍洞径，上边界取至地表。初期支护采用锚喷支护，临时支护采用喷射混凝土、钢架。超前支护采用注浆小导管进行注浆加固，计算模型中将其视为对加固区围岩力学参数的加强，加固区围岩黏聚力和摩擦角均提升20%。模型中支护结构力学参数见表2。

各材料物理力学参数　　表2

材　料	弹性模量(GPa)	泊松比μ	重度(kN/m^3)
钢架	210	0.3	77
喷射混凝土	23	0.22	25
锚杆	210	0.3	77

3　计算结果分析

通过对Ⅳ级围岩、Ⅴ级围岩隧道采用不同施工方法进行模拟计算，得到支护结构的变形及受力在不同施工方法下的分布情况。

3.1 位移分析

隧道开挖后支护结构的变形是判断支护结构稳定性的重要指标,采用不同施工工法开挖隧道时,开挖完成后围岩位移云图如图3~图6所示。

将上图数值计算结果进行整理,得到隧道在不同施工工法下变形结果,见表3。

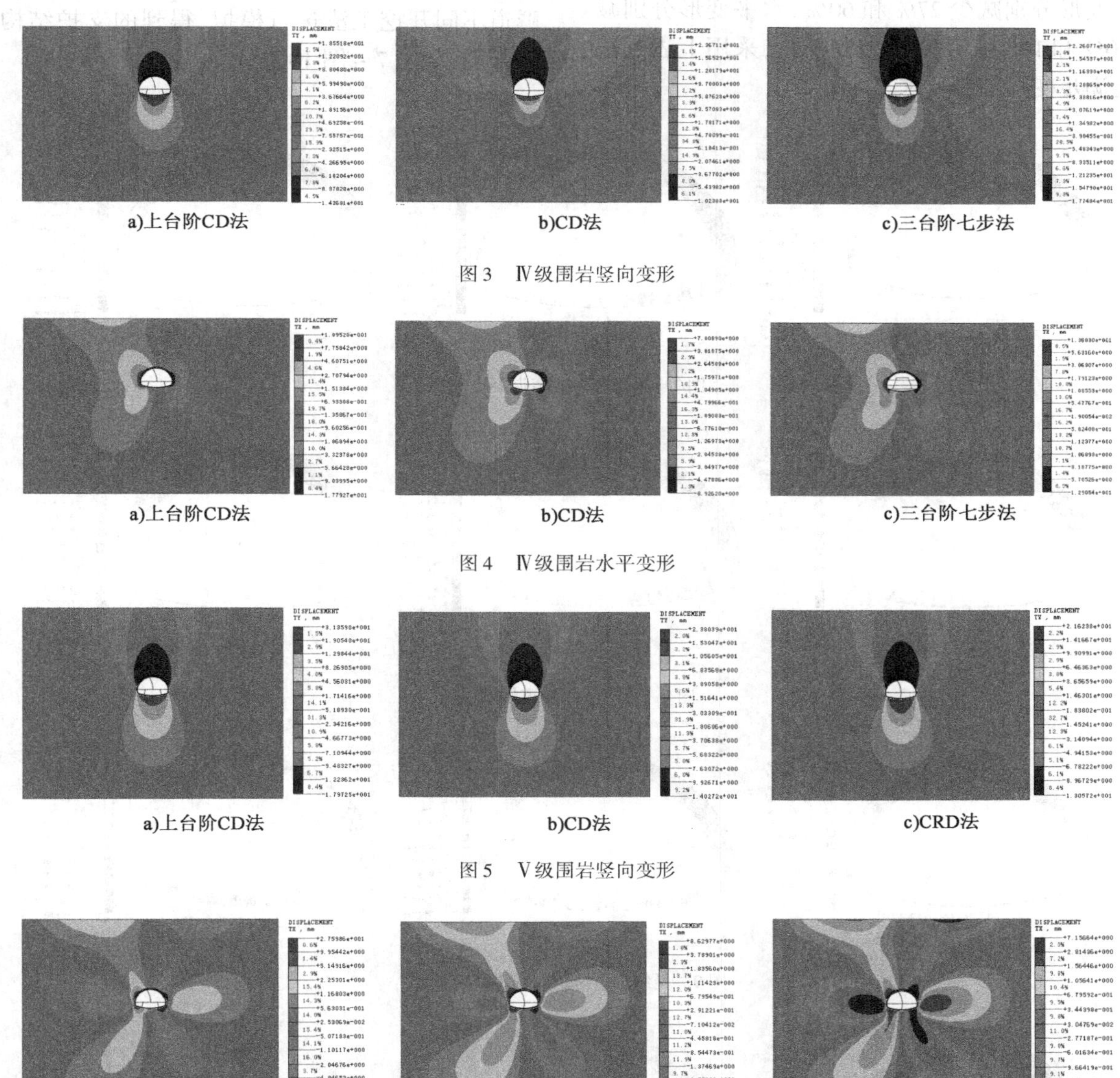

a)上台阶CD法　b)CD法　c)三台阶七步法

图3 Ⅳ级围岩竖向变形

a)上台阶CD法　b)CD法　c)三台阶七步法

图4 Ⅳ级围岩水平变形

a)上台阶CD法　b)CD法　c)CRD法

图5 Ⅴ级围岩竖向变形

a)上台阶CD法　b)CD法　c)CRD法

图6 Ⅴ级围岩水平变形

不同工法下支护结构变形　表3

变形(mm)	Ⅳ级围岩			Ⅴ级围岩		
	上台阶CD法	CD法	三台阶七步法	上台阶CD法	CD法	CRD法
竖向	14.3	10.3	17.7	17.3	13.8	12.7
水平	14.9	10.9	17.1	19.3	15.7	7.7

由表3可知,Ⅳ级围岩隧道三种工法在变形控制上,三台阶七步法变形最大,竖向变形为17.7mm,水平变形为17.1mm。相对于三台阶七步法,上台阶CD法和CD法竖向变形分别减少

19%和42%,水平变形分别减少13%和36%。Ⅴ级围岩隧道三种工法在变形控制上,上台阶CD法变形最大,竖向变形为17.3mm,水平变形为19.3mm。相对于上台阶CD法,CRD法和CD法竖向变形分别减少27%和60%,水平变形分别减少20%和19%。从变形控制上看,采用上述方法都能满足变形控制要求。

3.2　支护结构受力分析

支护结构的的受力情况直接反应隧道开挖后围岩的应力分布情况,因此研究支护结构的受力情况对于选择合理开挖方法是非常重要的。现对隧道不同开挖工法进行模拟,得到的支护结构受力云图,如图7～图10所示。

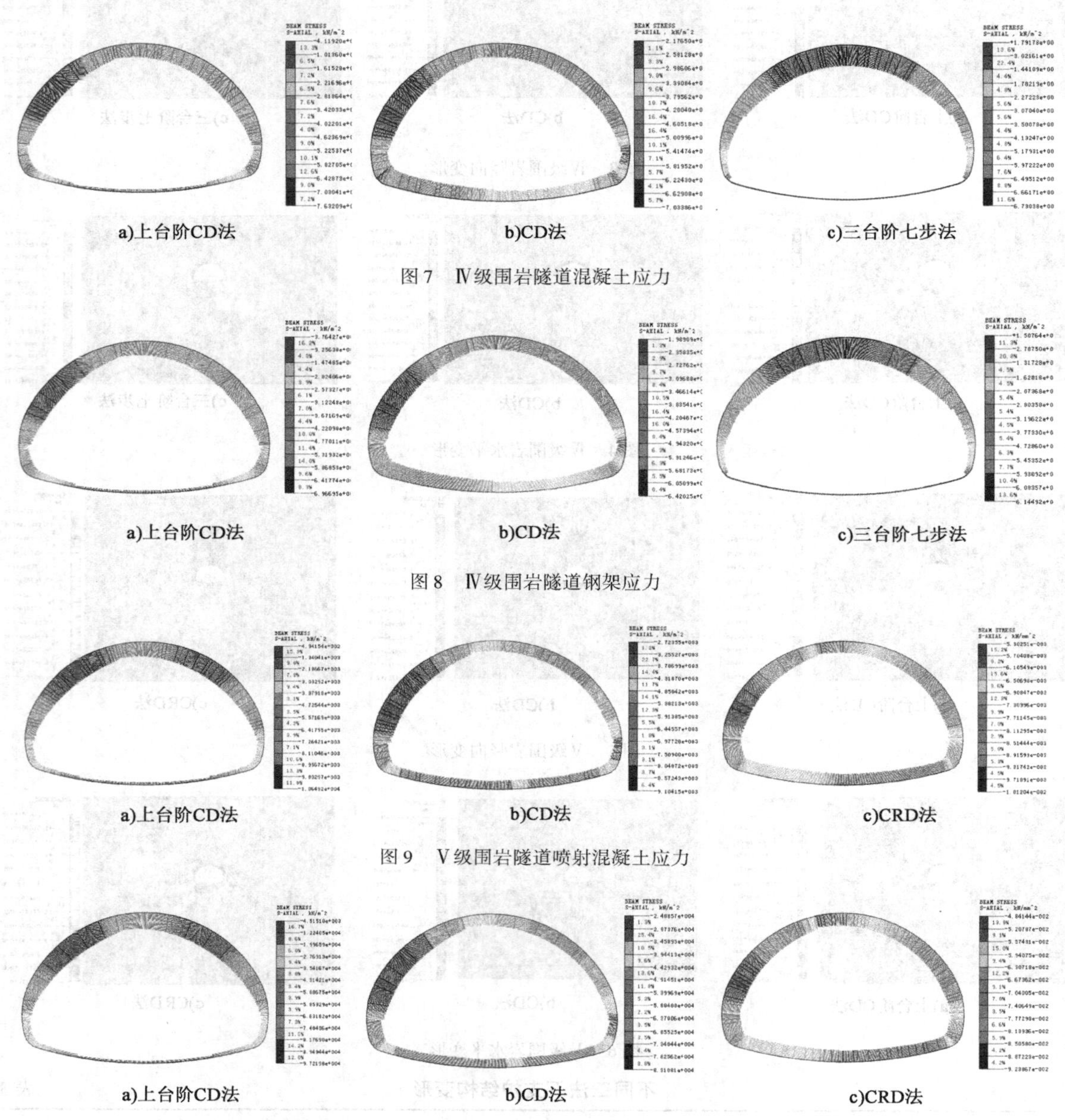

a)上台阶CD法　b)CD法　c)三台阶七步法

图7　Ⅳ级围岩隧道混凝土应力

a)上台阶CD法　b)CD法　c)三台阶七步法

图8　Ⅳ级围岩隧道钢架应力

a)上台阶CD法　b)CD法　c)CRD法

图9　Ⅴ级围岩隧道喷射混凝土应力

a)上台阶CD法　b)CD法　c)CRD法

图10　Ⅴ级围岩隧道钢架应力

从图7、图8可知,Ⅳ级围岩隧道采用上台阶CD法和三台阶七步开挖法时,支护结构受力呈现左右对称的特点,喷射混凝土和钢架受力最大值分别为7.6MPa、6.7MPa和70MPa、61MPa;采用上台阶CD法和CD法时,最大压应力发生在拱腰处,三台阶七步开挖法时最大压应力发生在拱顶处。采用上台阶CD法和CD法时,支护结构全部受压;采用三台阶七步法时,支护结构仰拱受拉,而喷射混凝土抗拉强度较小,因此不利于支护结构的安全稳定。

由图9、图10可知：Ⅴ级围岩隧道采用上台阶CD法和CRD法时，支护结构受力呈现左右对称的特点，喷射混凝土和钢架受力最大值分别为10.6MPa、10.1MPa和97MPa、92MPa；采用CD法施工时，先导所受的压应力要大于后导所受压应力，先导边墙处的受力大于其他部位，喷射混凝土和钢架所受最大的压应力值发生在先导拱腰处为9.1MPa和83MPa，最小压应力值发生在后导拱腰处为1.8MPa和16.0MPa。

4 施工方案选取及监测结果分析

4.1 施工方案选取

通过数值计算分析了支护结构的变形及受力情况，计算结果显示，采用现阶段常采用的工法，支护结构的变形受力都处于安全状态。当考虑施工经济性时，以Ⅳ级围岩采用上台阶CD法和CD法为例，若临时支护采用I20钢架，上台阶CD法每延米临时支护需钢架200kg，喷射混凝土1.7m^2；CD法每延米临时支护需钢架329kg，喷射混凝土2.79m^3；采用上台阶CD法时，每循环可以节省安装、拆除临时支护时间2.5h。

因此从隧道安全性角度考虑，Ⅳ级围岩隧道采用上台阶CD法、CD法、三台阶七步法，Ⅴ级围岩隧道采用上台阶CD法、CD法、CRD法是可行的，均能保证隧道的安全施工。但是施工方法的选择在满足安全性的同时需要兼顾经济性，而采用上台阶CD法施工能够有效地提高施工效率。因此，综合考虑支护结构变形受力情况、施工安全、经济性等因素，建议选择上台阶CD法进行施工。

4.2 监测结果分析

依据隧道现场条件，对现场试验段进行监测，变形监测点布设如图11所示。变形监测结果如图12、图13所示。

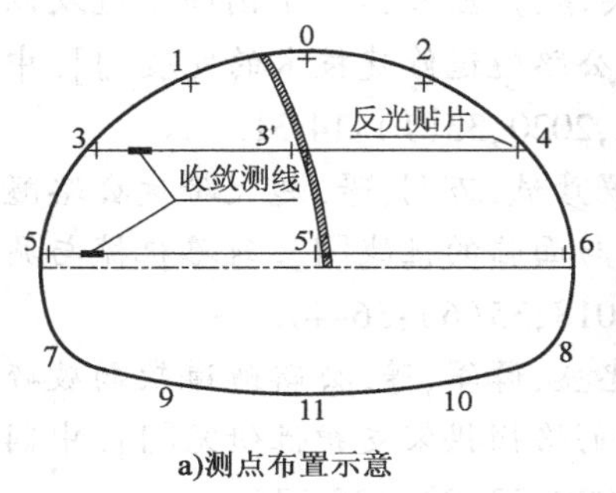

a)测点布置示意

b)现场监测点布设

c)现场监控量测

图11 变形监控量测

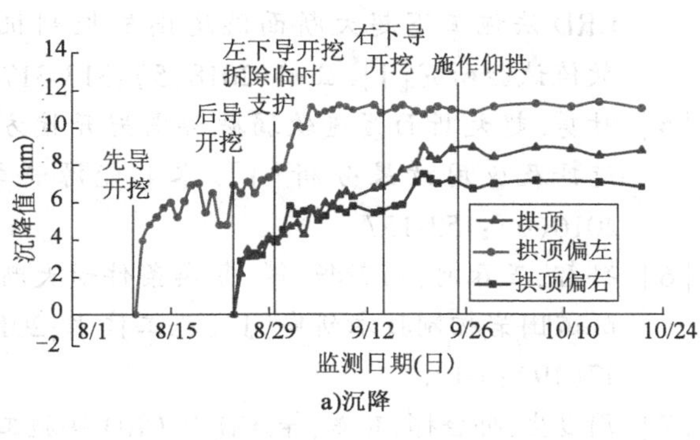

a)沉降

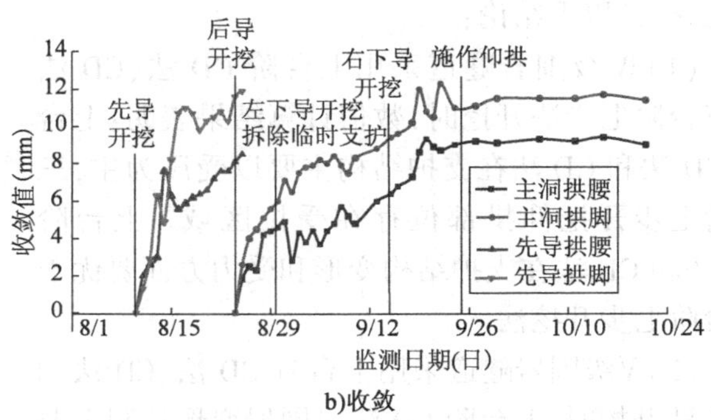

b)收敛

图12 Ⅳ级围岩断面变形时态曲线

从图12、图13可知，Ⅳ级围岩和Ⅴ级围岩监测断面变形量相差不大。隧道开挖后，各监测部位变形规律一致，开挖后相应部位变形量迅速增加，拆除临时支护时各点变形量小幅度增加，初期支护封闭成环后各点变形趋于稳定。其中Ⅳ级围岩监测断面最大沉降值发生在先导拱顶处（拱顶偏左）为12.3mm，最大收敛值发生在主洞拱腰处为12.3mm；Ⅴ级围岩监测断面最大沉降值发生在先导拱顶处（拱顶偏左）为16.8mm，最大收敛值发生在主洞拱腰处为15.2mm。在现场监测中，由于受隧道内复杂的施工环境影响，数据会出现微小波动，但整体保持稳定，且均小于预留变形量，满足安全要求。

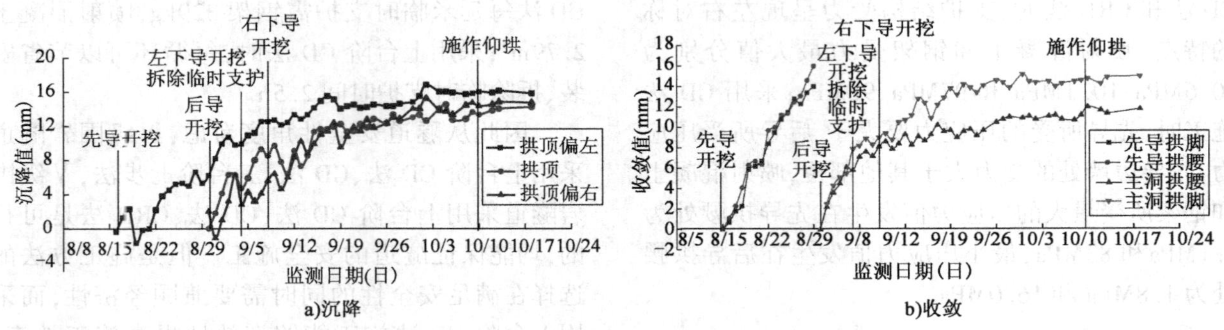

图 13　Ⅴ级围岩断面变形时态曲线

将数值计算中隧道采用上台阶 CD 法开挖得到的位移结果与现场实测结果进行对比分析。数值计算结果Ⅳ级围岩隧道竖向变形和平变形相对实测值分别增大 2mm 和 2.6mm；Ⅴ级围岩隧道竖向变形和水平变形相对实测值分别增大 0.5mm 和 4.1mm。数值计算结果相对实测值略大，这是由于在实际施工过程中，支护结构施作前的变形是无法测得的。综上，说明数值计算结果与现场实测结果吻合性较好，且数值计算结果可靠度较高，选择上台阶 CD 法为施工方法合理。

5　结语

对滨莱高速沿线两座隧道进行的数值模拟，分析了Ⅳ级围岩隧道采用上台阶 CD 法、CD 法和三台阶七步法以及Ⅴ级围岩隧道采用上台阶 CD 法、CRD 法和 CD 法开挖时支护结构的变形受力情况，得到以下结论：

（1）Ⅳ级围岩隧道采用上台阶 CD 法、CD 法和三台阶七步法开挖时，数值计算结果表明：上台阶 CD 法和 CD 法在支护结构主要以受压为主，三台阶七步开挖仰拱部位存在受拉区域。上台阶 CD 法和 CD 法在支护结构变形和受力方面要优于三台阶七步开挖法。

（2）Ⅴ级围岩隧道采用上台阶 CD 法、CD 法和 CRD 法开挖时，上台阶 CD 法对围岩变形控制上要弱于 CD 法和 CRD 法，但均远远小于预留变形量；支护结构的受力三者相差不大，均以受压为主。

（3）从隧道安全性角度考虑，Ⅳ级围岩隧道和Ⅴ级围岩隧道常采用的施工方法都是可行的，均能保证隧道的安全施工。在综合考虑施工安全、经济性、施工效率等因素时，建议选择上台阶 CD 法进行施工。

（4）通过对Ⅳ级围岩和Ⅴ级围岩试验段进行现场试验，并将监测结果与数值计算结果对比分析可知，数值模拟计算结果和现场实测数据吻合度较高，说明数值计算结果可靠，能够为相似工程提供借鉴与参考。

参考文献

［1］张俊儒，吴洁，严丛文，等. 中国四车道及以上超大断面公路隧道修建技术的发展［J］. 中国公路学报，2020，33（1）：14-31.

［2］陈建勋，罗彦斌，万利，等. 超大跨度公路隧道研究现状与面临的挑战［J］. 筑路机械与施工机械化，2018，35（6）：36-44.

［3］杨旸，谭忠盛，薛军，等. 公路隧道软弱破碎围岩高强钢筋格栅拱架支护性研究［J］. 中国公路学报，2020，33（2）：125-134.

［4］王春河，张爱军，樊祥福，等. 上下台阶法和 CRD 法施工下超大断面隧道围岩控制机制数值试验研究［J］. 公路，2018（5）：313-317.

［5］叶勇. 超大断面隧道软弱破碎围岩开挖方案选择及应用效果分析［J］. 水电能源科学，2016（6）：153-157.

［6］孙智，王春河，油新华，等. 复杂条件超大断面隧道围岩控制技术研究［J］. 施工技术，2018，47（19）：9-12.

［7］周磊生，孙会彬，孔军，等. CD 和 CRD 法施工下超大断面隧道围岩变形控制数值计算研究［J］. 公路交通技术，2018，34（S1）：66-69 + 75.

［8］蒋坤，夏才初，卞跃威. 节理岩体中双向八车道小净距隧道施工方案优化分析［J］. 岩土力学，2012，33（3）：841-847.

［9］欧敏. 特大断面浅埋偏压隧道双侧壁工法关键性问题研究［D］. 厦门：华侨大学，2012.

软弱围岩公路隧道预应力锚索支护方案设计

钟道川 陈丽俊 罗彦斌* 张立鑫 田超鹏
(长安大学公路学院)

摘 要 在软弱围岩隧道修建过程中,大变形灾害频发,严重危及施工安全。本文所依托的木寨岭公路隧道,经现场勘查和超前地质预报发现,试验段围岩较破碎,易发生大变形,于是将原设计中的系统锚杆替换为预应力锚索。然后使用 FLAC3D 软件对预应力锚索支护参数进行设计,通过分析单因素下隧道变形情况,最终得到合理的锚索支护参数,即长短锚索组合为 5+10m,锚索环向间距为 0.8~1.0m,锚索预应力为 350~400kN。最后进行现场试验研究,监测结果表明测点最大变形值小于预留变形量,证明预应力锚索支护方案是可行的。本研究成果可以为类似软岩隧道设计和施工提供参考。

关键词 隧道工程 支护方案 数值模拟 预应力锚索

0 引言

随着我国交通事业的迅速发展,在高地应力软弱围岩条件下修建的隧道越来越多。由于高地应力、高压强比等问题,在软岩隧道修建过程中大变形问题频发,严重威胁施工安全,影响施工进度和效益[1]。

目前,国内许多学者对软岩隧道大变形做了大量的研究工作,提出多种软岩大变形控制措施。其中大多数采用的是改变锚杆参数、更换小间距大型号钢架[2-4],采用双层初期支护[5-6],增设锁脚锚管、扩大拱脚[7]等偏向强力被动的支护措施。这些措施控制变形效果是基于初期支护的强度和刚度,即初期支护强度和刚度越高,控制变形效果越好,但工程造价也会随之提高,显然这并不经济。因此,国内学者提出预应力锚固及时主动支护技术,如何满潮院士[8]研发的 NPR(Negative Poisson′s Ratio)锚索支护技术、孙钧院士[9]研发的让压锚杆(索)支护技术以及普通预应力锚索支护技术等。其中普通预应力锚索支护技术,具有锚固深度大,抗拉拔能力强,及时主动支护等特点,在煤矿软岩巷道中广泛使用,已经形成了一套成熟完整的支护体系,但在公路隧道软岩地层中应用较少。因此,有必要对预应力锚索支护技术在公路隧道软岩地层中的应用进行研究。

1 工程概况

1.1 工程简介

渭武高速木寨岭公路隧道是兰海国家高速公路(G75)渭源至武都段的控制性工程,穿越漳河与洮河的分水岭木寨岭,横跨漳县、岷县两县。隧道采用分离式双向四车道设计,其中左线和右线全长分别为 15231m、15173m,洞身最大埋深约 629.1m。隧道进出口分别如图 1 和图 2 所示。

图 1 隧道进口

1.2 试验段地质概况

选取木寨岭公路隧道主洞左线 ZK214+675~ZK214+695 段作为试验段进行支护方案设计,其掌子面揭示围岩主要为灰黑色炭质板岩夹砂质板岩,呈薄～中层状结构,岩层倾角多变,走向近似与隧道轴线方向垂直;围岩裂隙褶皱发育,岩体破碎,自稳能力弱,易产生大变形及大坍塌。又由岩性分析报告可知,岩石饱和单轴抗压强度的平均值为10.1MPa,岩体完整性系数为0.16,岩体基本质量指标修正值为93.3,由相关规范可知,该段围岩属于软岩,围岩级别为Ⅴ级。试验段掌子面围岩如图3所示。

1.3　试验段施工方法

木寨岭公路隧道试验段采用三台阶七步留核心土法开挖,开挖示意图如图4所示,现场开挖如图5所示。

图2　隧道出口

图3　试验段掌子面围岩

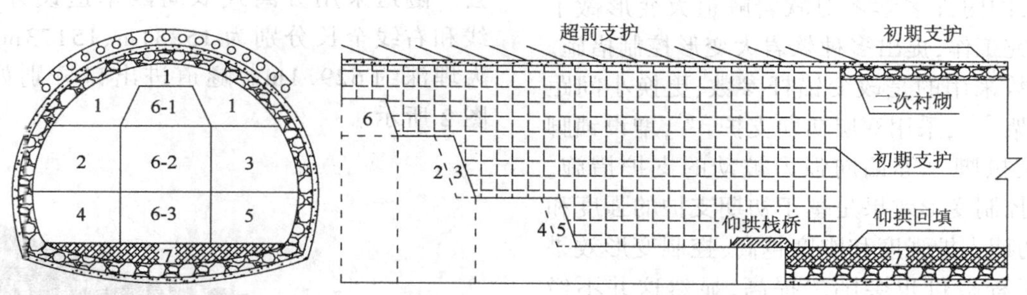

图4　开挖示意图

图5　现场施工图

2 试验段支护方案

2.1 原设计情况

试验段原设计支护参数主要为：Φ42 超前注浆小导管 $L=4.5$m，环向间距 40cm，外插角 $\alpha=10°$；Φ25 自进式中空注浆锚杆 $L=4.0$m，间距 100cm×80cm（环向×纵向）；Φ8 钢筋网，15cm×15cm；HW175 型钢钢架，纵向间距 80cm；喷射早强 C25 混凝土厚 25cm；二次衬砌 C30 钢筋混凝土厚 50cm；预留变形量 20cm。原设计衬砌结构如图 6 所示。

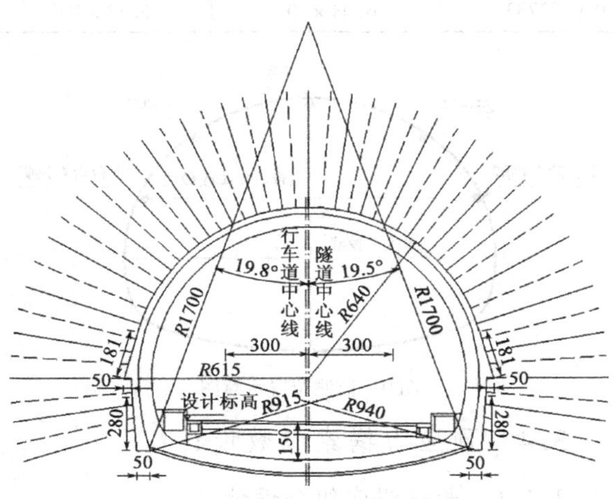

图 6 原设计衬砌结构（尺寸单位：cm）

2.2 试验段支护方案

经现场勘察，试验段掌子面揭示围岩与已施工段落相似，围岩自稳能力较差。又根据超前地质预报分析，雷达波强反射界面明显，振幅较强，波形频率急剧变化，规律性差，同相轴错段不连续，由此推测试验段围岩与已施工段落相似。从已施工段落变形情况来看，其最大沉降值远超预留变形量，平均变形速率高，而且现场存在喷射混凝土剥落、局部掉块、拱架扭曲折断等现象。因此，需对试验段支护方案进行重新设计以控制软岩隧道大变形。

由于原设计中的中空注浆锚杆在软岩地层中锚固效果较差，安装工效低，在软岩大变形隧道中支护效果有限，因此试验段支护方案选择取消原设计中的系统锚杆，替换为长短组合锚索；两种形式的锚索间隔布置，预留变形量调整为 35cm，原设计中其余参数保持不变。锚索施工工序为开挖后进行必要的安全防护→确定锚索位置，固定“W”型钢带→钻机就位，钻孔→清孔→安装锚固剂→插入锚索→搅拌锚固→放置锚垫板→安装锚具→张拉锚固→割掉多余长度锚索。以下将采用数值模拟的方法对锚索支护参数进行设计。

3 数值模拟

3.1 计算模型

依托于木寨岭公路隧道左线试验段 ZK214+675～ZK214+695，使用 FLAC3D 软件对锚索支护进行模拟，模型岩体范围取为 100m×20m×100m（$X\times Y\times Z$），其中 X 方向为水平方向，Z 方向为竖直方向，Y 方向为隧道开挖方向。模型如图 7 所示。

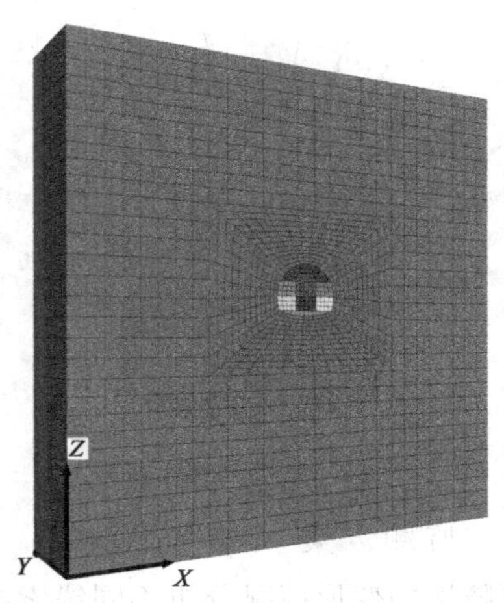

图 7 数值计算模型

3.2 边界条件以及计算参数

模型上表面为自由面，不受任何位移约束，下表面受三个方向的位移约束，沿 X 方向的两个边界和 Y 方向的两个边界分别受该方向的位移约束。根据现有地勘资料以及其他相关资料对模型施加相应的地应力。

岩体选用摩尔-库仑塑性本构模型进行模拟分析，锚索采用 cable 单元进行模拟，钢拱架与喷射混凝土使用等效弹性模量共同构成支护体系，采用 shell 单元进行模拟，等效弹性模量按式（1）考虑。超前支护、锁脚锚管等作为安全储备，不予模拟。以上结构单元所组成的数值模型如图 8 所示。依据现场试验、地质资料、规范等，模型计算采用的参数分别见表 1 和表 2。

$$E_e=\frac{E_cA_c+E_sA_s}{A_c}$$

式中：E_e——等效弹性模量；

E_c——喷射混凝土弹性模量；

A_c——喷射混凝土面积；

E_s——钢架弹性模量；

A_s——钢架面积。

围岩及喷射混凝土参数表　　表1

名　　称	弹性模量 E(GPa)	泊松比 μ	摩擦角 φ(°)	密度 ρ($kg \cdot m^{-3}$)	粘聚力 c(MPa)
围岩	2.0	0.3	26	2560	0.1
喷射混凝土(换算后)	26.53	0.2	—	2200	—

锚索计算参数表　　表2

名　称	弹性模量 E (GPa)	抗拉强度 (kN)	横截面积 (m^2)	单位长度上树脂锚固剂黏结力(N/m)	单位长度上树脂锚固剂刚度(N/m^2)
锚索	200	680	0.0003733	6.08×10^5	5.73×10^7

图8　支护结构模型图

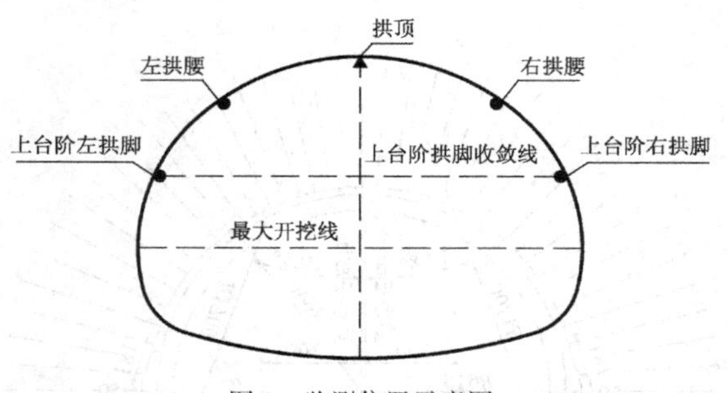

图9　监测位置示意图

3.3　监测方案

根据隧道的变形情况分析不同锚索参数下的支护效果,因此需要对隧道模型变形进行监测,选择变形较大的上台阶进行沉降和收敛变形监测,具体监测位置如图9所示,其中"左"和"右"按照面向掌子面方向进行区分。

3.4　预应力锚索参数设计

3.4.1　长短锚索组合设计

将长短锚索组合分为四种工况即5m+5m、5m+8m、5m+10m和5m+12m进行数值模拟,除长短锚索组合外其余初期支护参数设为不变量,计算结果如表3所示。

不同长短锚索组合下变形统计表　　表3

工况	锚索组合(m)	拱顶沉降(mm)	左拱腰沉降(mm)	右拱腰沉降(mm)	上台阶左拱脚沉降(mm)	上台阶右拱脚沉降(mm)	上台阶拱脚收敛(mm)
1	5+5	290.3	296.4	296.2	327.4	342.9	106.3
2	5+8	268.4	273.6	273.2	300.4	310.7	95.9
3	5+10	254.8	259.5	259.0	281.3	288.6	88.3
4	5+12	252.2	256.6	256.1	278.4	284.5	86.8

由表3可知,锚索长短组合中长锚索越长,沉降变形和收敛变形就越小。锚索长度对沉降变形的影响大于收敛变形,但是当长锚索长度超过10m后,对沉降变形和收敛变形的影响就越来越小,即锚索长度对隧道围岩的变形影响有限。故建议长短锚索组合为(5+10)m。

3.4.2　锚索环向间距设计

基于施工方便和施工安全,预应力锚索只选择在上台阶和中台阶打设。将锚索环向间距分为四种工况:0.6m、0.8m、1.0m、1.2m,其余初期支护参数设为不变量,计算结果如表4所示。

不同锚索环向间距下变形统计表 表4

工况	环向间距(m)	拱顶沉降(mm)	左拱腰沉降(mm)	右拱腰沉降(mm)	上台阶左拱脚沉降(mm)	上台阶右拱脚沉降(mm)	上台阶拱脚收敛(mm)
1	0.6	236.5	238.1	237.4	271.7	278.1	105.4
2	0.8	239.2	242.3	240.1	276.3	282.6	107.7
3	1.0	250.1	253.3	252.2	288.1	298.7	112.6
4	1.2	272.2	274.4	273.3	306.4	331.6	128.6

由表4可知,隧道沉降和收敛变形随着锚索环向间距变小而变小,这主要是由于上台阶和中台阶锚索的密度变大,变形控制效果增强所致,但是锚索环向间距对隧道变形的影响也是逐渐减弱的,尤其锚索环向间距小于1.0m时。因此从经济性和变形控制效果来看,建议锚索环向间距为0.8~1.0m。

3.4.3 锚索预应力设计

锚索预应力分为300kN、350kN、400kN、450kN四种工况进行数值模拟,其余初期支护参数设为不变量,计算结果如表5所示。

不同锚索预应力下变形统计表 表5

工况	预应力(kN)	拱顶沉降(mm)	左拱腰沉降(mm)	右拱腰沉降(mm)	上台阶左拱脚沉降(mm)	上台阶右拱脚沉降(mm)	上台阶拱脚收敛(mm)
1	300	299.8	305.8	306.5	338.4	354.4	124.4
2	350	258.8	263.5	263.0	288.3	296.6	113.0
3	400	234.0	237.3	235.3	256.1	265.0	105.3
4	450	226.1	228.4	224.2	243.9	251.2	100.3

由表5可知,随着锚索施加预应力的增大,沉降和收敛变形在不断减小,但是预应力超过400kN后,隧道沉降和收敛变形控制效果就不太显著。如果施加的预应力过大,锚索很有可能从围岩中拔出,而且工人使用机具张拉锚索也比较困难,故建议锚索预应力为350~400kN。

4 现场试验

为验证预应力锚索支护方案的可行性,在试验段开展现场试验,选择典型断面ZK214+691进行分析,该断面预应力锚索支护参数为长短组合(5+10)m,环向间距1.0m,预应力350kN。选择该断面变形最大的上台阶右拱脚进行沉降变形分析,该测点沉降变形以及变形速率曲线如图10所示。

由图10可知,测点变形初期增长较快,锚索施工后变形速率开始减缓,上台阶右拱脚最终监测累计沉降值为153.4mm,又由于仰拱施作后及时闭合成环,引起的变形较小,所以可以认为测点最终沉降值远小于预留变形量350mm。因此,预应力锚索支护方案是可行的。

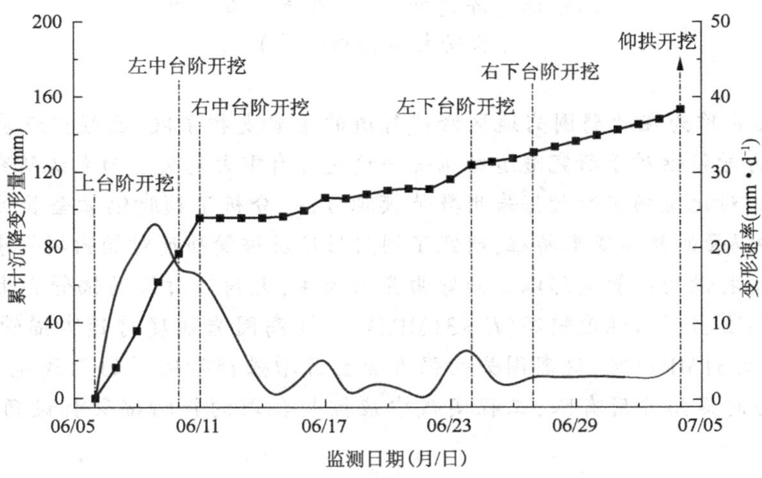

图10 测点沉降变形及变形速率曲线

5　结语

(1)通过对木寨岭公路隧道左线试验段现场勘察及超前地质预报发现,试验段围岩与变形较大的已施工段落围岩相似,围岩破碎,节理裂隙发育,强度低,自稳能力差等。又根据岩性分析报告可知,试验段属于软岩,围岩级别为Ⅴ级,故支护方案中选择取消系统锚杆替换为长短组合锚索。

(2)依托试验段使用FLAC3D软件建立数值模型,通过分析各单因素下的隧道水平收敛和竖向沉降变形,最终得到锚索合理支护参数,即长短锚索组合为5+10m,环向间距为0.8~1.0m,锚索预应力为350~400kN。

(3)通过现场试验来验证锚索支护方案的可行性,选择典型断面ZK214+691进行分析,该断面上台阶右拱脚最终监测累计沉降值为153.4mm,又由于仰拱施作引起的变形较小,故可以认为测点最终沉降值小于预留变形量350mm。因此,预应力锚索支护方案是可行的。

参考文献

[1] 孔超,张俊儒,王海彦,等.深埋软岩大变形隧道支护变形特征及承载机理研究[J].中国铁道科学,2021,42(06):103-111.

[2] 于天赐.软岩隧道大变形控制技术研究[J].土木工程学报,2017,50(S2):112-117.

[3] 资晓鱼,申玉生,朱双燕,等.层状千枚岩隧道形变破坏规律与支护措施研究[J].现代隧道技术,2021,58(03):196-204.

[4] 陈明福.高应力软岩单线铁路隧道大变形控制技术研究[J].公路,2021,66(11):369-374.

[5] 张德华,雷可,谭忠盛,等.软岩大变形隧道双层初期支护承载性能对比试验研究[J].土木工程学报,2017,50(S2):86-92.

[6] 曹小平,魏飞鹏,王波,等.高地应力软岩隧道合理支护方案试验研究[J].铁道工程学报,2018,35(07):65-71+102.

[7] 杨建民,舒东利,张涵,等.软岩隧道初期支护沉降机理及其工程措施研究[J].隧道建设(中英文),2018,38(04):545-550.

[8] 何满潮,李晨,宫伟力,等.NPR锚杆/索支护原理及大变形控制技术[J].岩石力学与工程学报,2016,35(08):1513-1529.

[9] 孙钧,钦亚洲,李宁.软岩隧道挤压型大变形非线性流变属性及其锚固整治技术研究[J].隧道建设(中英文),2019,39(03):337-347.

软弱围岩隧道锁脚锚管力学特性数值模拟分析

周裕锋　陈建勋*　罗彦斌　石　州

(长安大学公路学院)

摘　要　锁脚锚管作为在软弱围岩地区修建隧道的重要支护手段,已经广泛应用于隧道施工建设中,其作用机理以及力学特性对于研究隧道结构安全稳定具有重大意义。为系统研究软弱围岩地区锁脚锚杆的力学特性,本文对比现场实测数据采用数值模拟方法,分析了锁脚锚管全长位移分布变化规律和不同打设角度时锁脚锚管的整体变形特征,研究了围岩强度及锚管强度对锁脚锚管承载能力的影响。研究结果表明:①小角度打设的锚管变形以竖向弯曲变形为主,大角度打设的锚管变形除了竖向弯曲变形外还会发生纵向滑移;②当围岩强度较高($E>31$MPa)时,提高围岩强度对锁脚锚管的承载力影响不明显,围岩强度较低($E\leqslant31$MPa)时,提高围岩的强度会显著增强锁脚锚管的承载能力;③采用高强钢管对锁脚锚管承载能力的提高作用有限,工程实践中应控制合理的锁脚锚管打设角度来提高结构承载能力。

关键词 软弱围岩隧道 锁脚锚管 数值分析 力学特性

0 引言

软弱围岩隧道在修建过程中,由于围岩承载力不足等原因常常出现围岩变形大,沉降难以控制等问题,通常表现为隧道结构整体或局部变形过大、侵限,有时甚至会发生坍塌等安全事故[1-3]。锁脚锚管作为软弱围岩隧道的主要支护手段,以其施工工艺简单、价格低廉、支护效果明显等特点,在软弱围岩隧道中得到了普遍的应用[4-7]并取得了显著的支护效果。

锁脚锚管力学特性的研究方法主要有理论分析、现场检测试验、数值模拟。李健[8]采用数值模拟的方法分析了不同数量(2 根和 4 根)、不同打设角度(10°和 45°)工况下锁脚锚杆的支护效果,指出增加锁脚锚管的数量和角度均对控制隧道变形有利。陈林[9]依托马家庄隧道分析了大跨度黄土隧道中锁脚锚管对围岩变形的控制效果,分析结果表明大跨度黄土隧道支护结构中应取消系统锚管,增设锁脚锚管。王晨昭[10]依托大望山隧道,通过数值模拟的方法研究了锁脚锚杆的合理设计与支护参数。

数值模拟的研究结果显示,锁脚锚管对于控制隧道变形尤其是拱顶下沉有显著作用,且适当增大锚管的管径和延长锁脚锚管的长度可以有效减小隧道的沉降和收敛。但目前学界对于锁脚锚管的合理打设角度研究结果不一[11-12],采用锚索单元或梁单元模拟锁脚锚管作用时不能体现围岩对锁脚锚管的剪切摩擦作用,尤其对于锁脚锚管与围岩接触部分单元的模拟并不合理,并且对于锁脚锚管在围岩荷载作用下的位移分布规律研究不够深入,缺乏对各种因素影响下对锁脚锚管受力变形特性的系统性研究。

为系统研究软弱围岩隧道锁脚锚管的力学特性,本文依托黄延高速公路改扩建工程剪子岔隧道的现场试验结果,利用 Midas GTS NX 建立三维有限元模型对模拟试验进行数值模拟,从而对锚管的全长位移分布以及围岩强度、锚管管材强度对锁脚锚管承载能力的影响进行研究,揭示各种因素影响下的锁脚锚管受力变形特性。

1 模型建立

为全面深入地研究锁脚锚管受力特性与承载特点,本文建立了三维有限元计算模型并选择了合理的支护参数。锚管打设的三维模型如图 1 所示(以 45°打设角为例),各工况下参数选择如表 1、表 2 所示。

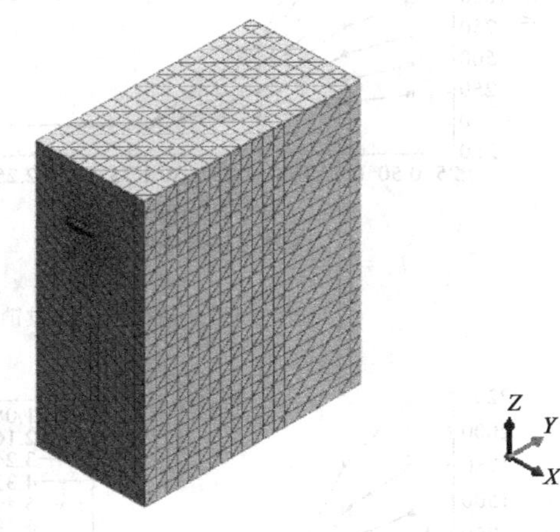

图 1 锚管打设三维限元模型

各打设角度的模型尺寸表 表 1

模型	尺寸类别	打设角度(°)			
		0	30	45	60
锚管	外露部分(cm)	30			
	围岩内部(cm)	220			
	外径(mm)	51			
	壁厚(mm)	4			
围岩	长(cm)	250	230	200	160
	宽(cm)	100	100	100	100
	高(cm)	100	200	250	290

围岩及锚管参数　　　　表2

材　料	弹性模量(MPa)	泊　松　比	重度(kN/m³)	黏聚力(kPa)	内摩擦角(°)
围岩	31	0.3	16.7	35	22
锚管	200000	0.3	75	205000	2.776

2　模型可靠性验证

本文依托黄延高速公路扩建工程剪子岔隧道现场试验结果建立三维有限元模型,对锁脚锚管的管身应变和端部位移进行分析并与实测结果[13]比照,以验证三维模型的准确性和可靠性。

2.1　锁脚锚管管身应变结果对比

锁脚锚管在正常工作状态下主要受竖向力作用,在竖向荷载作用下,锁脚锚管上、下应变明显且对称分布,本文选取锁脚锚管上部应变进行分析研究。结果如图2~图5所示。

(1)0°打设锁脚锚管工况如图2所示。

(2)30°打设锁脚锚管工况如图3所示。

(3)45°打设锁脚锚管工况如图4所示。

(4)60°打设锁脚锚管工况如图5所示。

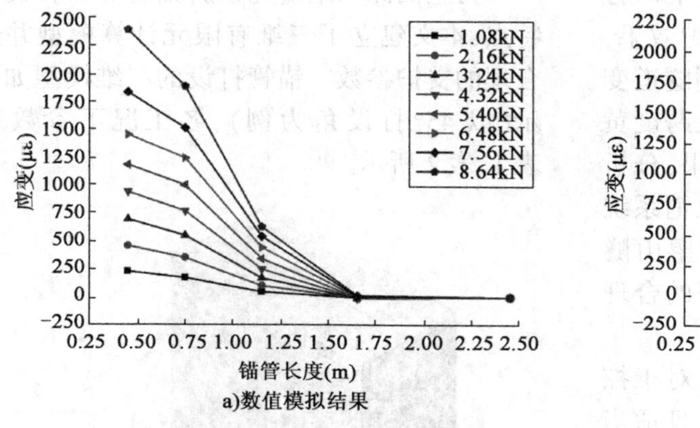

a)数值模拟结果

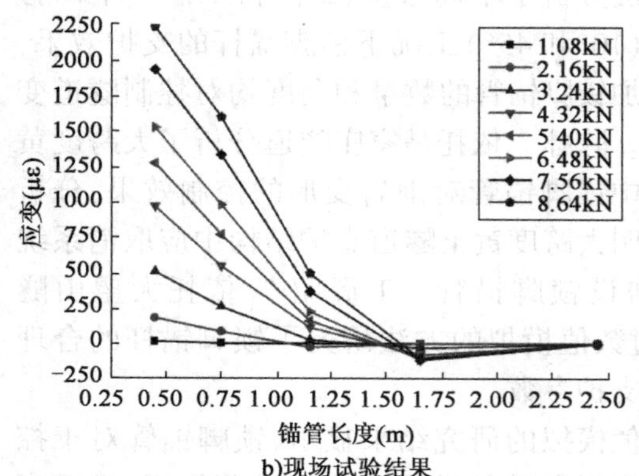

b)现场试验结果

图2　0°打设锁脚锚管上部测点应变结果对比图

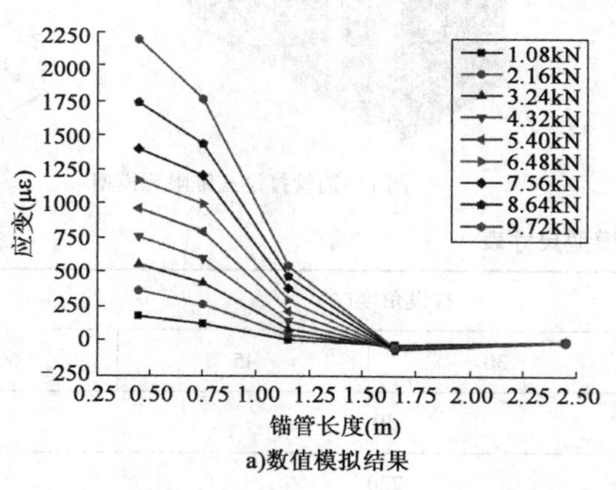

a)数值模拟结果

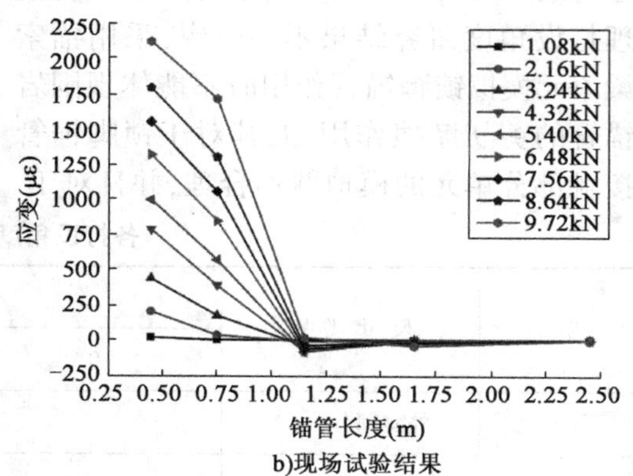

b)现场试验结果

图3　30°打设锁脚锚管上部测点应变结果对比图

由图2~图5的锁脚锚管应变结果可知:①随着锚管深度的不断增加,锁脚锚管应变值不断减小直至为0;②随着锁脚锚管打设角度的增加,同一荷载在同一锚管长度处引起的应变值不断减小;③数值模拟结果和现场实测结果无论在应变值大小还是应变沿着锚管长度的分布变化规律上,均比较接近。由此可知,数值模拟建立的分析模型是合理的,能够较为准确地模拟锁脚锚管的应变变化规律。

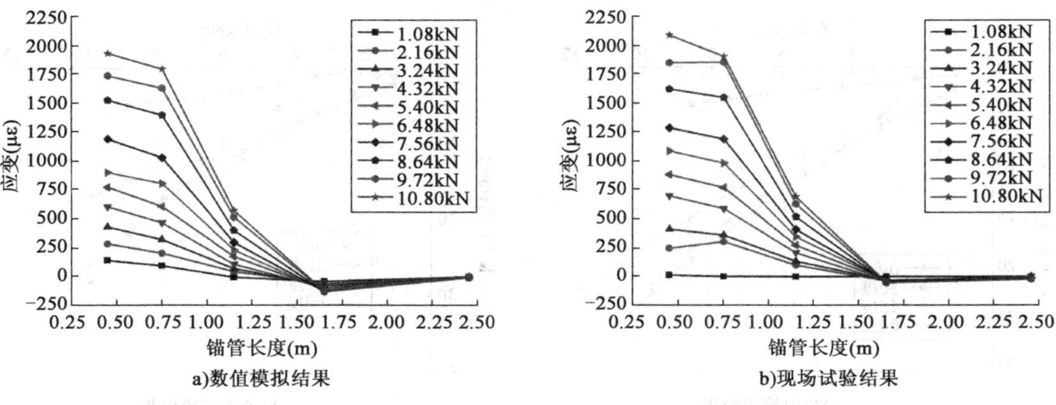

图4 45°打设锁脚锚管上部测点应变结果对比图

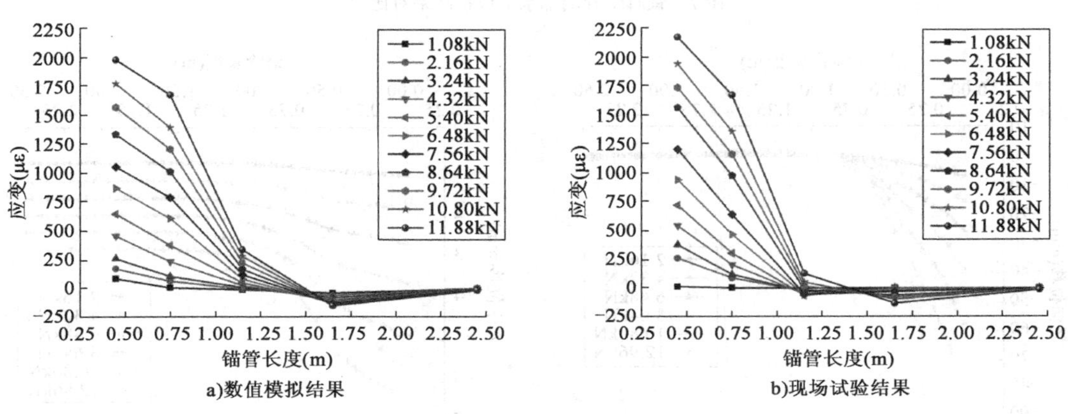

图5 60°打设锁脚锚管上部测点应变结果对比图

2.2 锁脚锚管端部位移结果对比

(1)锁脚锚管端部竖向位移如图6所示。

(2)锁脚锚管端部水平位移如图7所示。

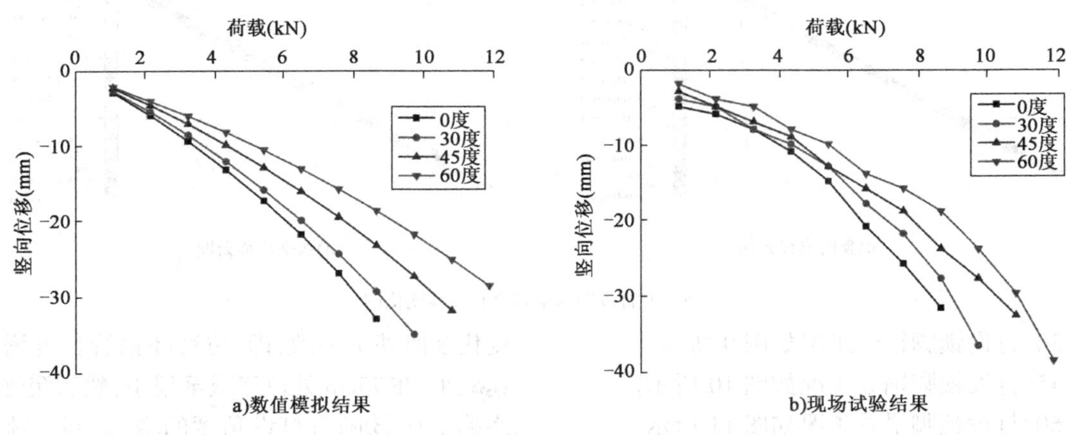

图6 锁脚锚管端部竖向位移结果对比图

由图6、图7可以看出,数值模拟和现场模拟试验的结果不管在曲线变化规律还是数值大小上均非常相近,从而验证了有限元模型的合理性。

3 锁脚锚管全长位移分布变化特征

研究锁脚锚管整体变形规律需要掌握其全长位移分布变化特征,锁脚锚管的位移主要考虑竖向位移和水平位移,并假定竖向位移以向上为正;水平位移以向围岩方向移动为正。选取各断面上侧顶点的位移为代表,不同打设角度下锚管全长位移的分布情况如图8~图11所示。

(1)0°打设锁脚锚管工况如图8所示。

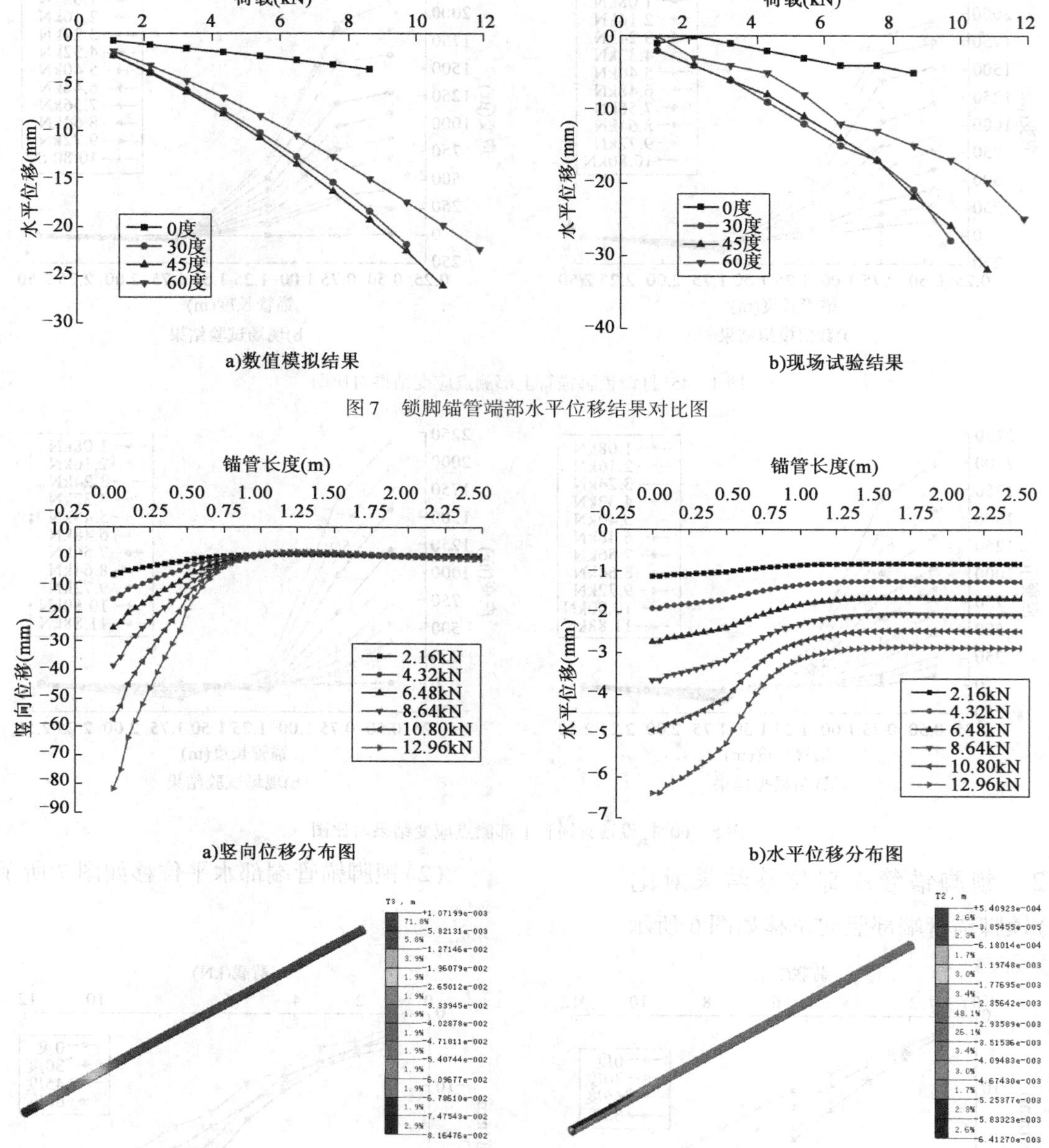

图 7　锁脚锚管端部水平位移结果对比图

图 8　0°打设锁脚锚管全长位移变化图

(2)30°打设锁脚锚管工况如图 9 所示。

(3)45°打设锁脚锚管工况如图 10 所示。

(4)60°打设锁脚锚管工况如图 11 所示。

综合图 8 ~ 图 11,可得到锁脚锚管全长位移变化规律如下:①无论以何种角度打设锚管,锚管的竖向位移和水平位移均为负,说明锁脚锚管工作时向下部、远离围岩方向移动,锚管下侧的围岩受到的压力较大,容易发生较大变形甚至破坏;②竖向位移和水平位移沿着锚管长度方向的分布变化规律基本一致,即:位移随锚管长度增加先迅速减小,在 75cm 处位移减至很小,然后缓慢减小最终趋于 0;③随着打设角度的增大,同一荷载下锚管的端部竖向位移逐渐减小,底部竖向位移逐渐增大;由于钢拱架的沉降主要由锁脚锚管的端部位移控制,所以增大锁脚锚管的打设角度有利于控制隧道的竖向沉降。综合考虑施工条件,锁脚锚管的打设角度应取 45°;④相较于大角度打设的锚管,小角度打设的锚管外端竖向位移更大而底端的竖向位移却很小,说明小角度打设时,锚管以竖向弯曲变形为主,而大角度打设时,锚管除了竖向弯曲变形,还在底端发生了沿锚管纵向的滑移变形;⑤锚管同一长度处的位移增量随着荷载的增加经历了从均匀增加到迅速增加的过程。

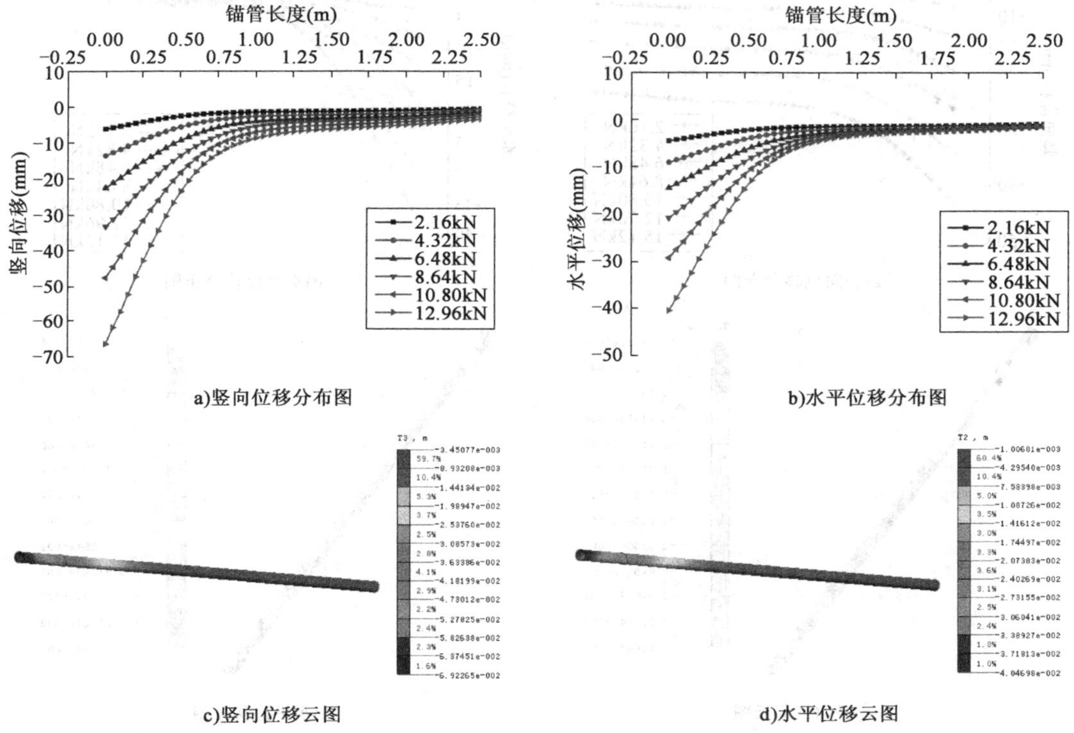

a)竖向位移分布图

b)水平位移分布图

c)竖向位移云图

d)水平位移云图

图9 30°打设锁脚锚管全长位移变化图

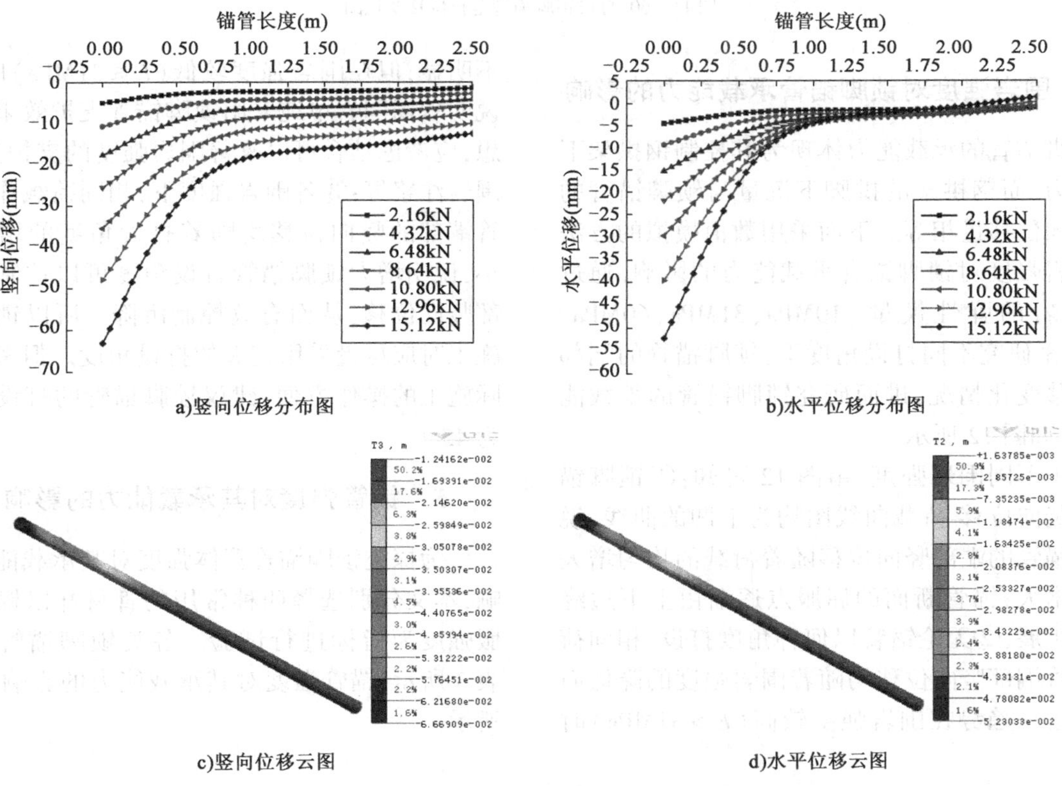

a)竖向位移分布图

b)水平位移分布图

c)竖向位移云图

d)水平位移云图

图10 45°打设锁脚锚管全长位移变化图

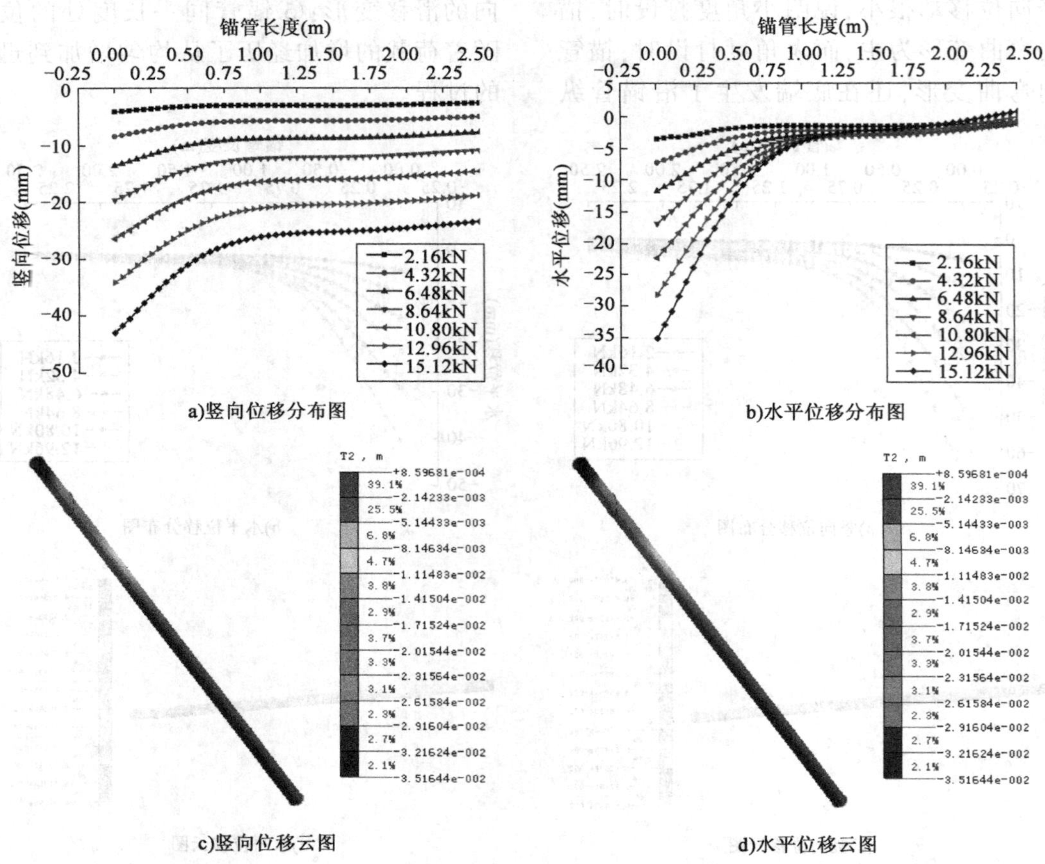

图 11　60°打设锁脚锚管全长位移变化图

4　围岩强度对锁脚锚管承载能力的影响

锁脚锚管的承载能力体现为其控制钢拱架下沉的能力,而钢拱架的拱脚下沉量与锁脚锚管的端部竖向位移量相等。下面采用数值模拟的方法研究围岩强度对锁脚锚管承载能力的影响,通过改变围岩的弹性模量(10MPa、31MPa、60MPa、90MPa)来研究不同打设角度下,锁脚锚管的端部竖向位移变化情况,进而研究锁脚锚管的承载能力,结果如图 12 所示。

对于不同围岩强度,由图 12 可知:①锁脚锚管端部竖向位移-荷载曲线图均为下凹的曲线,说明锁脚锚管的端部竖向位移随着荷载的均匀增大而加速增大,锚管断面的屈服点逐渐由上下边缘向中间扩展;②无论锚管以何种角度打设,相同荷载下锚管端部竖向位移均随着围岩强度的降低而增大。这一趋势在围岩强度较高($E>31$MPa)时不明显,但在围岩强度较低($E\leqslant 31$MPa)时显著。说明软弱围岩单纯采用锁脚锚管支护效果不够理想,应考虑结合可以改善围岩强度的支护措施,如围岩注浆等;③各围岩强度下,相同荷载作用的锚管端部的竖向位移均随着打设角度的增大而减小,说明增大锁脚锚管打设角度可以控制锚管端部竖向位移,从而有效控制沉降。所以锁脚锚管施工时应尽量采用较大的打设角度。但考虑到实际施工的操作方便,建议锁脚锚管的打设角度取为 45°。

5　锚管强度对其承载能力的影响

为探究锁脚锚管管体强度对其承载能力的影响,本文分别选择四种常用的管材并以锚管的屈服强度为指标进行试验。各类锁脚锚管指标如表 3 所示,锚管强度对其承载能力的影响如图 13 所示。

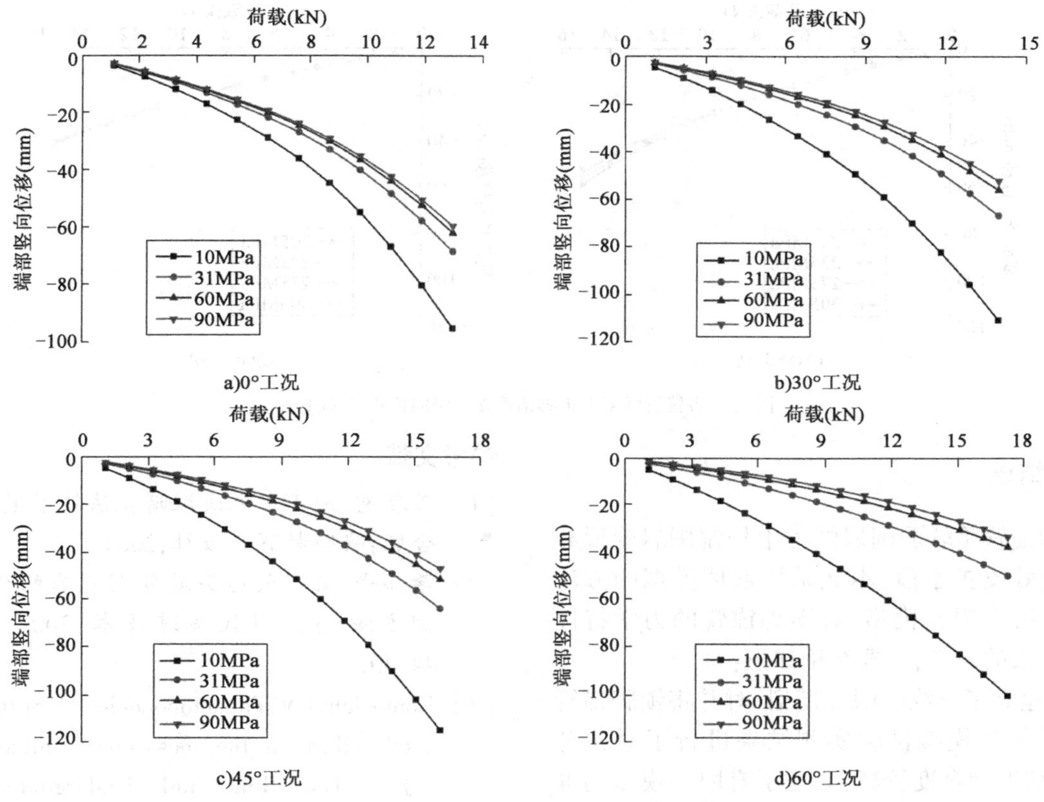

图 12 各围岩强度下锁脚锚管端部竖向位移-荷载曲线

各工况锚管强度指标[14] 表 3

锚管管材型号	10 号	Q235	20 号	35 号
屈服强度(MPa)	205	235	275	305

对于不同锚管强度,由图 13 可知:①各打设角度的锁脚锚管端部竖向位移-荷载曲线走势基本一致,且对于同一打设角度,不同屈服强度的锚管对应的曲线在荷载较小时是重合的,随着荷载地增大,各曲线逐渐分离,分离后的端部竖向位移-荷载曲线表现为端部竖向位移随屈服强度减小而逐渐增大;②若将同一角度不同屈服强度下锚管竖向位移曲线分离的点称为"分离点",打设角度为0°、30°、45°和60°时锚管的分离点对应的荷载值分别为 6.48kN、7.56kN、9.72kN 和 12.96kN,随着锚管打设角度的增大,分离点所对应的荷载值不断增大,大角度打设锁脚锚管时,锚管屈服强度的影响不明显;③无论锚管屈服强度为多少,相同荷载下锚管端部的竖向位移均随着打设角度的增大而显著减小,说明增大打设角度可以有效控制竖向位移,且其效果比提高锚管的屈服强度显著。所以在锁脚锚管设计施工时,应将重点放在采用合理打设角度而非提高锚管强度上。

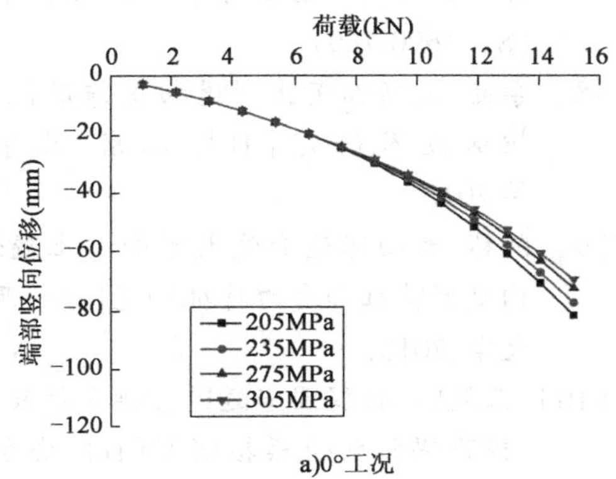

a)0°工况

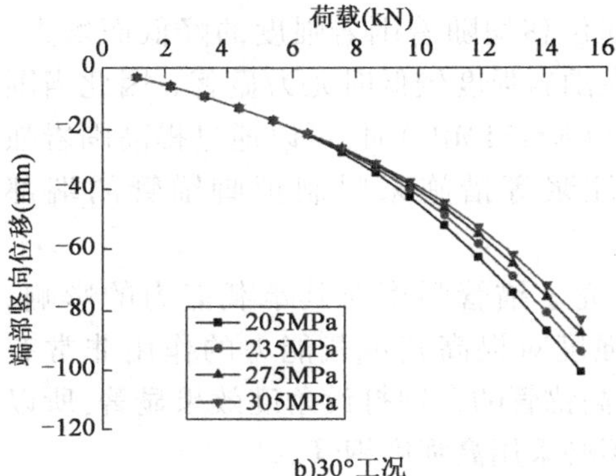

b)30°工况

图 13

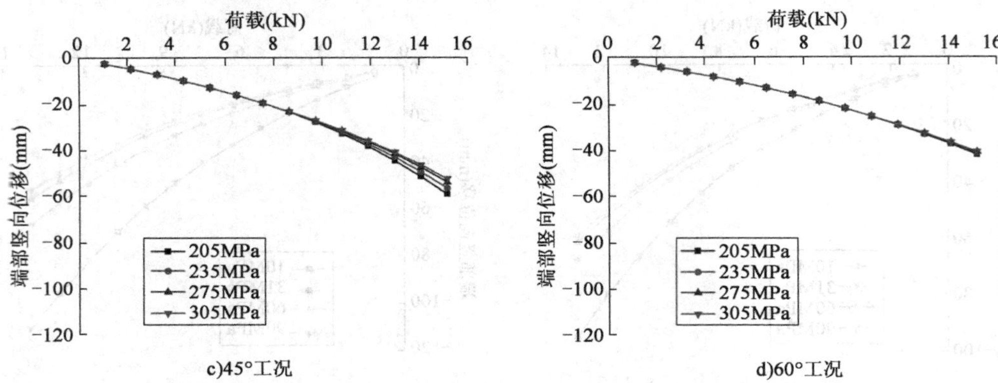

图 13　各锚管强度下锁脚锚管端部竖向位移-荷载曲线

6　结语

锁脚锚管是软弱围岩隧道中控制围岩变形和沉降的有效支护手段,本文采用数值模拟的方法建立了三维有限元模型,对锁脚锚管的力学特性进行了深入的研究,主要结论如下:

(1)建立了三维有限元模型,对并将锁脚锚管的计算结果与模拟试验实测结果进行了对比分析,两者结果吻合度较高,验证了有限元模型的准确性。

(2)研究了锁脚锚管全长位移分布变化特征。在竖向荷载作用下,锁脚锚管竖向位移和水平位移均在锚管长度的前 75cm 左右的范围内较大;随着打设角度的增大,端部竖向位移逐渐减小,而底部竖向位移逐渐增大,从控制隧道竖向沉降角度出发,锚管的打设角度应取较大值,综合考虑施工条件,锁脚锚管打设角度应取 45°;小角度打设的锚管变形以竖向弯曲为主,大角度打设的锚管变形除了竖向弯曲还会发生纵向滑移。

(3)研究了围岩强度对锁脚锚管承载能力的影响。无论锚管以何种角度打设,相同荷载下锚管端部竖向位移均随着围岩强度的降低而增大。这一趋势在围岩强度较低时尤为显著。因此当围岩强度较低(E≤31MPa)时,可以通过提高围岩强度如围岩注浆等措施来限制锁脚锚管的端部位移。

(4)研究了锚管强度对其承载能力的影响。提高锚管强度对提高其承载能力的作用非常有限,没有提高锚管的合理打设角度效果显著,所以锁脚锚管不必采用高强度钢管。

参考文献

[1] 王梦恕. 地下工程浅埋暗挖法技术通论[M]. 合肥:安徽教育出版社,2004.

[2] 李伟平. 公路隧道穿越软弱围岩的变形与控制方法[J]. 现代隧道技术,2009,46(2):44-49.

[3] Kontogianni V, Papantonopoulos C, Stiros S. Delayed failure at the messochora tunnel, greece [J]. Tunnelling and Underground Space Technology, 2008, 23(3):232-240.

[4] 史振宇. 包家山特长隧道富水千枚岩地段快速施工技术[J]. 隧道建设,2009,29(1):72-75.

[5] Bobet A, Einstein H H. Tunnel Reinforcement with Rockbolts [J]. Tunnelling and Underground Space Technology, 2011, 26(1):100-123.

[6] 陈建勋,王超,罗彦斌,等. 高含水量土质隧道不设系统锚杆的试验研究[J]. 岩土工程学报,2010,32(5):815-819.

[7] 陈建勋,乔雄,王梦恕. 黄土隧道锚杆受力与作用机制[J]. 岩石力学与工程学报,2011,30(8):1690-1697.

[8] 李健. 大断面黄土隧道初支作用机理及变形控制技术研究[D]. 北京:北京交通大学 2012.

[9] 陈林. 大西客运专线大断面黄土隧道支护结构变形特征和受力特征研究[D]. 西安:长安大学,2013.

[10] 王晨昭. 软弱围岩隧道管棚支护及其体系下锁脚锚杆数值模拟研究[D]. 哈尔滨:哈尔滨工业大学,2015.

[11] 伍毅敏. 软基隧道支护机理与病害防治技术研究[D]. 西安:长安大学,2008.

[12] 李健. 大断面黄土隧道初支作用机理及变形控制技术研究[D]. 北京:北京交通大学,2012.

[13] 石州,罗彦斌,陈建勋,等. 软弱围岩隧道锁脚锚管力学特性现场模拟试验[J]. 公路交通科技,2021,38(7):96-123.

[14] 中华人民共和国行业标准. 结构用无缝钢管:GB/T 8162—2008[S]. 北京:中国标准出版社,2008.

The Stress-strain State of the Tunnel LINING That Crosses the Fault Zone of Soil Blocks during an Earthquake

Miller Mark *[1] Fang Yong[1] Titov Evgeniy[2] Kharitonov Sergey[2]

[1. Department of Civil Engineering, Southwest Jiaotong University;
2. Department of Bridges and Tunnels, Russian University of Transport (MIIT)]

Abstract The study examines the question of the tunnel behavior under seismic or geophysical load in the zone of changes in the hardness of the surrounding soil mass. In the course of the study, the internal forces and displacements arising in the structure of a tunnel in the zone of intersection of the boundaries of soil layers with different properties, in the case when these layers move relative to each other, were determined. To obtain an analytical solution, the simplest model of a beam on an elastic foundation is used, finite element models in various formulations are presented, with the help of which numerical solutions are obtained, a comparative analysis of the results is carried out.

Keywords Transport tunnels Beam on an elastic foundation Finite elements Tunnel damage Earthquake

0 Introduction

Although tunnels usually have better earthquake resistance properties compared to ground structures, they can be damaged by particularly strong seismic or geophysical impacts or under special conditions, such as soil liquefaction and fault zones. The nature of the occurrence of earthquakes, the propagation of energy in the soil mass, the interaction of seismic waves with structures are very complex processes, for modeling which may require large computing resources, highly qualified engineers, energy-intensive work when creating computational schemes. Despite the fact that computers and software systems are constantly evolving and dynamic calculations are gradually becoming available for solving a wide range of tasks, it is sometimes useful to use quasi-static analysis methods for the initial assessment of the reaction of structures to dynamic impacts. Therefore, the purpose of this article is to obtain an analytical solution and compare it with numerical ones, which are obtained with different approaches to modeling the structure and the environment. Special attention is paid to the issues of three-dimensional modeling.

During an earthquake, soil layers with different properties often move in different ways affecting tunnels that cross such borders. Tunnels located in soft ground can be considered as beams in an elastic medium (or considered as beams on an elastic foundation), as shown in Fig. 1. As a rule, faults are usually the boundaries of soil layers with different engineering and geological characteristics. This study examines the stress-strain state of the tunnel lining that crosses the fault zone of two soil blocks. The initial data are parameters of the lining cross-section, characteristics of the soil and value of the relative displacement of the soil layers.

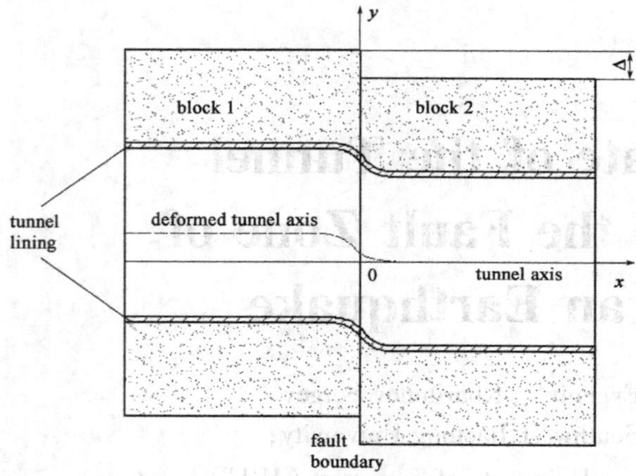

Fig. 1 Scheme of a tunnel throw fault fracture zone

1 The fault is perpendicular to the tunnel axis

1.1 Analytical method

Differential equation of the bending beam (Fig. 2), is:

$$EI_x \frac{d^4 y}{dx^4} + kby = q \tag{1}$$

The well-known solution of equation (1) has the form:

$$y = e^{-\beta x}(C_1\cos\beta x + C_2\sin\beta x) + e^{\beta x}(C_3\cos\beta x + C_4\sin\beta x) + v_0(q) \tag{2}$$

Where $\beta = \sqrt{\frac{kb}{4EI_x}}$, here k is a coefficient of the subgrade reaction, b is the width of a beam, E is Young modulus, I_x is a moment of inertia.

In this case, the deformed view is as in Fig. 3.

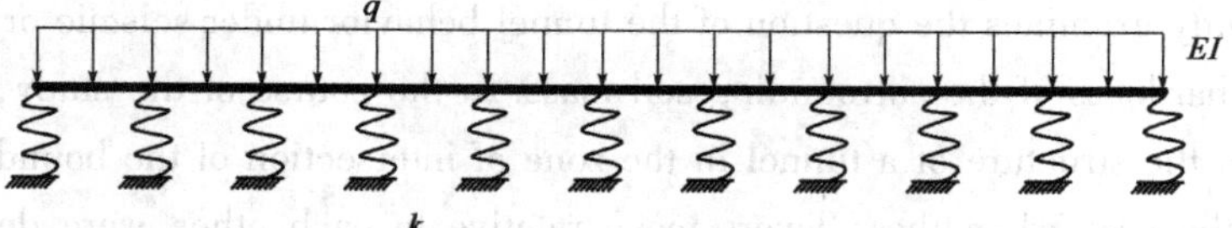

Fig. 2 Classical beam on elastic foundation using the Winkler assumption

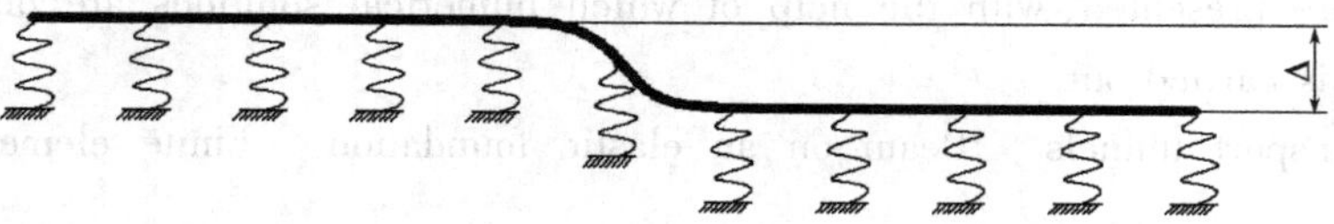

Fig. 3 Deformed view of the calculation scheme

For simplifying the solution, the model of the semi-infinite beam on an elastic foundation is used (Fig. 4), when $0 \leqslant x \leqslant \infty$. In this case, if $x \to \infty$, $e^x \to \infty$, there is no physical meaning, so $C_3 = C_4 = 0$. In addition, from initial data follows that $q = 0$.

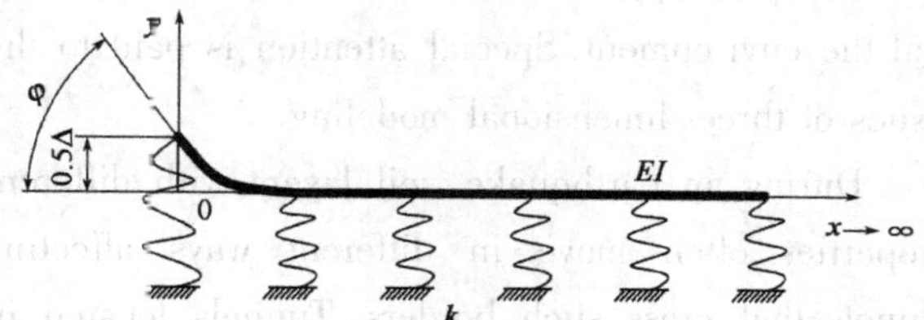

Fig. 4 Accepted calculation scheme

Inview of the above, equation (2) will take a form:

$$y = e^{-\beta x}(C_1\cos\beta x + C_2\sin\beta x) \tag{3}$$

To define the integration constants C_1 and C_2, one has to twice take the derivative of a function in equation (3). Below is the sequence of actions for this operation.

$$y = C_1 e^{-\beta x}\cos\beta x + C_2 e^{-\beta x}\sin\beta x$$

$$y' = C_1(e^{-\beta x}\cos\beta x)' + C_2(e^{-\beta x}\sin\beta x)'$$

$$(e^{-\beta x}\cos\beta x)' = -\beta e^{-\beta x}\cos\beta x + \beta e^{-\beta x}(-\sin\beta x)$$

$$= \beta e^{-\beta x}(-\cos\beta x - \sin\beta x)$$

$$(e^{-\beta x}\sin\beta x)' = -\beta e^{-\beta x}\sin\beta x + \beta e^{-\beta x}\cos\beta x$$

$$= \beta e^{-\beta x}(-\sin\beta x + \cos\beta x)$$

$$y' = C_1[\beta e^{-\beta x}(-\cos\beta x - \sin\beta x)] + C_2[\beta e^{-\beta x}(-\sin\beta x + \cos\beta x)] \tag{4}$$

$$y'' = C_1\beta[-e^{-\beta x}\cos\beta x - e^{-\beta x}\sin\beta x]' + C_2\beta[e^{-\beta x}\cos\beta x - e^{-\beta x}\sin\beta x]'$$

$$y'' = C_1\beta[-\beta e^{-\beta x}(-\cos\beta x - \sin\beta x) - \beta e^{-\beta x}(-\sin\beta x + \cos\beta x)] + C_2\beta[\beta e^{-\beta x}(-\cos\beta x - \sin\beta x) - \beta e^{-\beta x}(-\sin\beta x + \cos\beta x)]$$

$$y'' = C_1\beta^2 e^{-\beta x}[(\cos\beta x + \sin\beta x) - (-\sin\beta x + \cos\beta x)] + C_2\beta^2 e^{-\beta x}[(-\cos\beta x - \sin\beta x) - (-\sin\beta x + \cos\beta x)]$$

$$y'' = C_1\beta^2 e^{-\beta x}[\cos\beta x + \sin\beta x + \sin\beta x - \cos\beta x] + C_2\beta^2 e^{-\beta x}[-\cos\beta x - \sin\beta x + \sin\beta x - \cos\beta x]$$

$$y'' = C_1\beta^2 e^{-\beta x} \times 2\sin\beta x - C_2\beta^2 e^{-\beta x} \times 2\cos\beta x$$

$$y'' = 2\beta^2 e^{-\beta x}(C_1\sin\beta x - C_2\cos\beta x) \tag{5}$$

If the properties ofthe neighboring ground-blocks and bending stiffness of the tunnel lining are constant, for right-hand part of an infinite beam the following boundary conditions can be used:

$$\begin{cases} y(0) = \dfrac{\Delta}{2} \\ \dfrac{d^2y(0)}{dx^2} = 0 => y''(0) = 0 \end{cases} \tag{6}$$

When $x = 0$, the tangent angle takes the extreme value, the second derivative should be equal to zero, whence follows $y''(0) = 0 => M(0) = 0$.

Substituting the boundary conditions in equations (6), (3) and (5) gives:

$$y(0) = \frac{\Delta}{2}: \frac{\Delta}{2} = e^{-\beta * 0}(C_1\cos\beta \times 0 + C_2\sin\beta \times 0) => C_1 = \frac{\Delta}{2}$$

$$y''(0) = 0: 0 = 2\beta^2 e^{-\beta * 0}(C_1\sin\beta \times 0 - C_2\cos\beta \times 0) => C_2 = 0 \tag{7}$$

Taking into the constants found, equation (3) takes the form:

$$y = \frac{\Delta}{2} e^{-\beta x}\cos\beta x \tag{8}$$

Usingthe well-known dependencies between the internal force factors (bending moment M and shear force Q) and a deflection function, one can get equations:

$$\frac{M}{EI} = -y'' = -2\beta^2 e^{-\beta x}\frac{\Delta}{2}\sin\beta x;$$

$$M = -EI\Delta\beta^2 e^{-\beta x}\sin\beta x \tag{9}$$

$$\frac{Q}{EI} = -y''' = -\Delta\beta^2(e^{-\beta x}\sin\beta x)'$$

$$= -\Delta\beta^2[\beta e^{-\beta x}(-\sin\beta x + \cos\beta x)]$$

$$Q = EI\Delta\beta^3 e^{-\beta x}(\cos\beta x - \sin\beta x) \tag{10}$$

The presence of $e^{-\beta x}$ multiplier in equations indicates that all these functions decrease with increasing distance from the block border ($x \to \infty$, $e^{-\beta x} \to 0$). One can assess the zone of influence by function $e^{-\beta x}$. If $x = 0$, $e^{-\beta 0} = 1$.

If $\beta x = \pi$, $e^{-\pi} = 0.043$ and with an accuracy of 5% one can say that it equals to zero. In this case, from $\beta l_{inf} = \pi$ follows:

$$l_{inf} = \frac{\pi}{\beta} \tag{11}$$

1.2 Example

As an example, the stress-strain state of the tunnel lining (Fig. 5) is considered for the beam element. Parameters of concrete are: Young modulus $E = 35500\text{MPa}$, Poisson ratio $v = 0.2$.

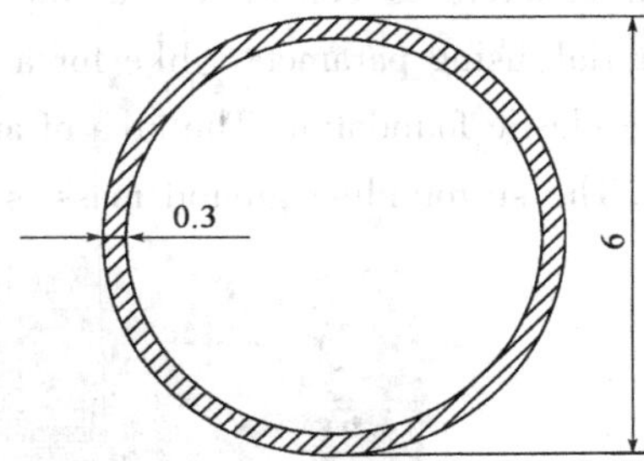

Fig. 5 Cross-section area of the tunnel lining

The vertical deflection of left-hand part is $\Delta = 0.01\text{m}$. The results were obtained by Excel and presented below (comparing the analytical solution to the numerical simulation's one).

1.3 Numerical simulation

1.3.1 Model of a Winkler's beam on elastic foundation

An analytical solution, using a mathematical model of a beam on elastic foundation, allows to quickly and easily assess the inertial forces factors in the tunnel lining from the displacement of blocks along the fault boundary; however that is not a universal solution. Numerical modeling helps to solve this problem. First, the numerical finite element model was created in the MIDAS GTS NX software, based on the calculation scheme of a Winkler beam on an elastic foundation (Fig. 2). The beam nodes are connected to the ground by elastic springs with a step of 1m, the spring stiffness corresponds to the stiffness of the ground foundation. The length of the simulated tunnel section is 200m. The external impact is set as a 0.01m upward shift of the left block. The model is shown in Fig. 6.

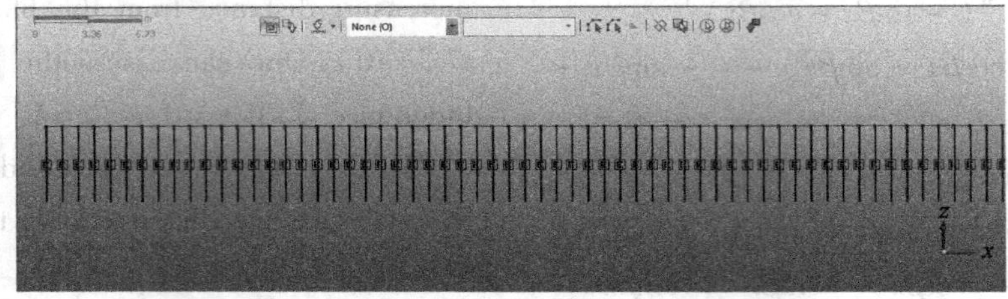

Fig. 6 Part of the finite-element model of a beam on elastic foundation

1.3.2 Model withthe 2D plane strain elements

The next step in verifying the proposed calculation method is to create a 2D model.

The tunnel lining ismodeled by beam finite elements, a concrete is considered as the isotropic elastic material, using parameters like for a model of beam on an elastic foundation. The area of analysis is 200 × 40m. The surrounding ground mass is modeled by the 2D plane stain elements, using Mohr-Coulomb model with parameters: silty clay, Young modulus $E = 37000\text{kPa}$, Poisson ratio $\nu = 0.3$, friction angle $\varphi = 18.4°$, cohesion $c = 33.8\text{kPa}$. A friction was modeled like an interface elements with strength reduction factor $R_c = 0.5$. This model is shown in Fig. 7.

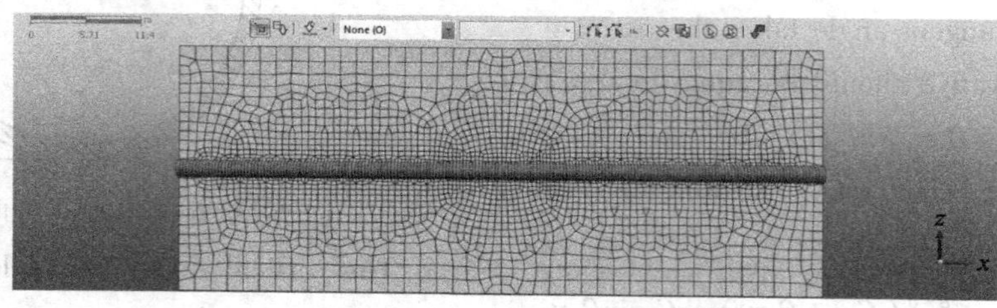

Fig. 7 Model with the 2D plane strain elements

For the integrity of the analysis, the model of a beam on an elastic foundation was used, as well. In this case, one needs to use the coefficient of a subgrade reaction k.

Based on an elastic theory, Scott derived the relation between the coefficient of subgrade reaction and a Young modulus, as follow:

$$k = \frac{E}{d(1-\nu^2)} \tag{12}$$

Where d is a diameter of a pile.

For the presented method, it is acceptable to take d as the tunnel diameter. In this case, for the silty clay the coefficient is $k = 6777\text{kN/m}^2$.

For the convenience of estimating the stress-strain state in each model, the graphs for each case are presented in Fig. 8.

1.4 Practical application

1.4.1 The 1D scheme

Using the numerical simulation model, a study of the changing inertial forces factors was carried with different stiffness of mountain blocks (Fig. 9). Getting analytical results is a difficult procedure in solving such problems, because due to different stiffness of the rock blocks, the deformation and stress plots are not symmetrical.

The stiffness of the first block is characterized by a coefficient of subgrade reaction k_1, the stiffness of the second block by k_3 and the filling space "z" between blocks by k_2.

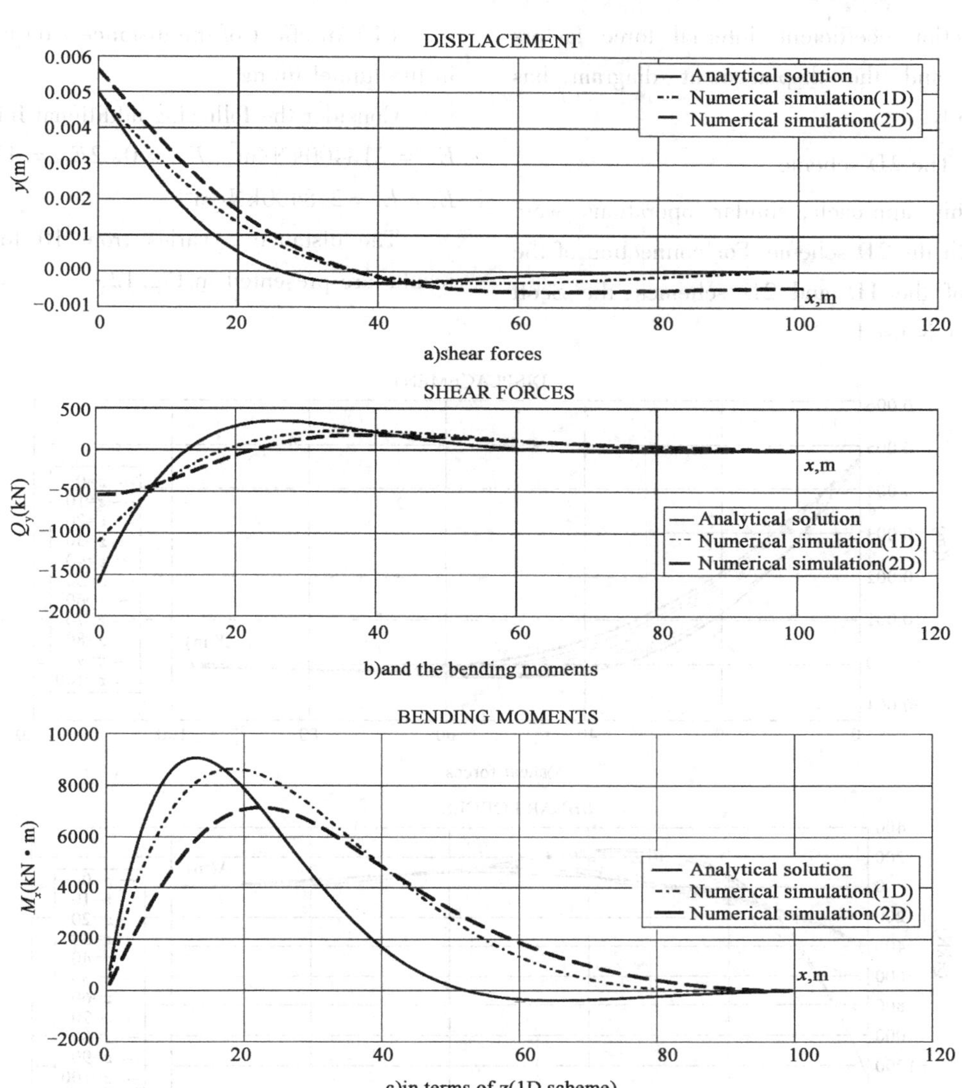

Fig. 8 Results for the silty clay subgrade

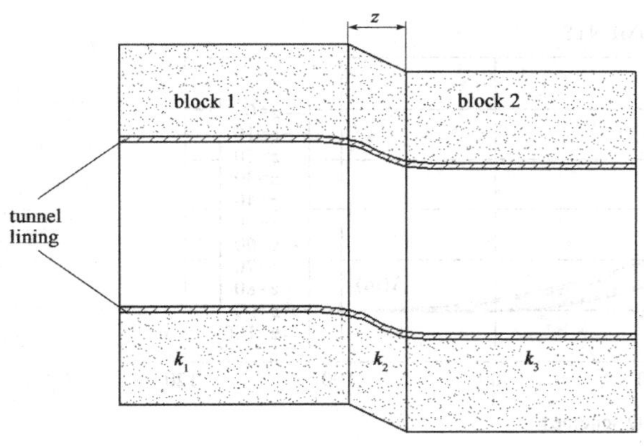

Fig. 9 Using different coefficients subgrade reaction

(1) An effect of the distance z on internal forces in the tunnel lining.

Consider the following additional initial data:

$k_1 = 40000\text{kN/m}^2$, $k_2 = 0.2k_1 = 8000\text{kN/m}^2$, $k_3 = k_1 = 40000\text{kN/m}^2$

The distance z varies from 10 to 100m. The results are presented in Fig. 10.

(2) An effect of the value k_2 on internal forces in the tunnel lining

In this case consider the following additional initial data:

$k_1 = 8000\text{kN/m}^2$, $k_3 = 10k_1 = 80000\text{kN/m}^2$, $z = 40\text{m}$

The coefficient k_2 takes values from 8000 to 80000kN/m^2. The results are presented in Fig. 11. The most interesting is that with increase in the subgrade reaction coefficient, internal force factors increase too and the displacement diagram has changed slightly.

1.4.2　The 2D scheme

Using this approach, similar operations were performed with the 2D scheme. For connection of the soil models of the 1D and 2D schemes, the Scott equation (12) is used.

(1) An effect of the distance z on internal forces in the tunnel lining

Consider the following additional initial data: $E_1 = 218400\text{kN/m}^2$, $E_2 = 0.2E_1 = 43680\text{kN/m}^2$, $E_3 = E_1 = 218400\text{kN/m}^2$

The distance z varies from 10 to 100m. The results are presented in Fig. 12.

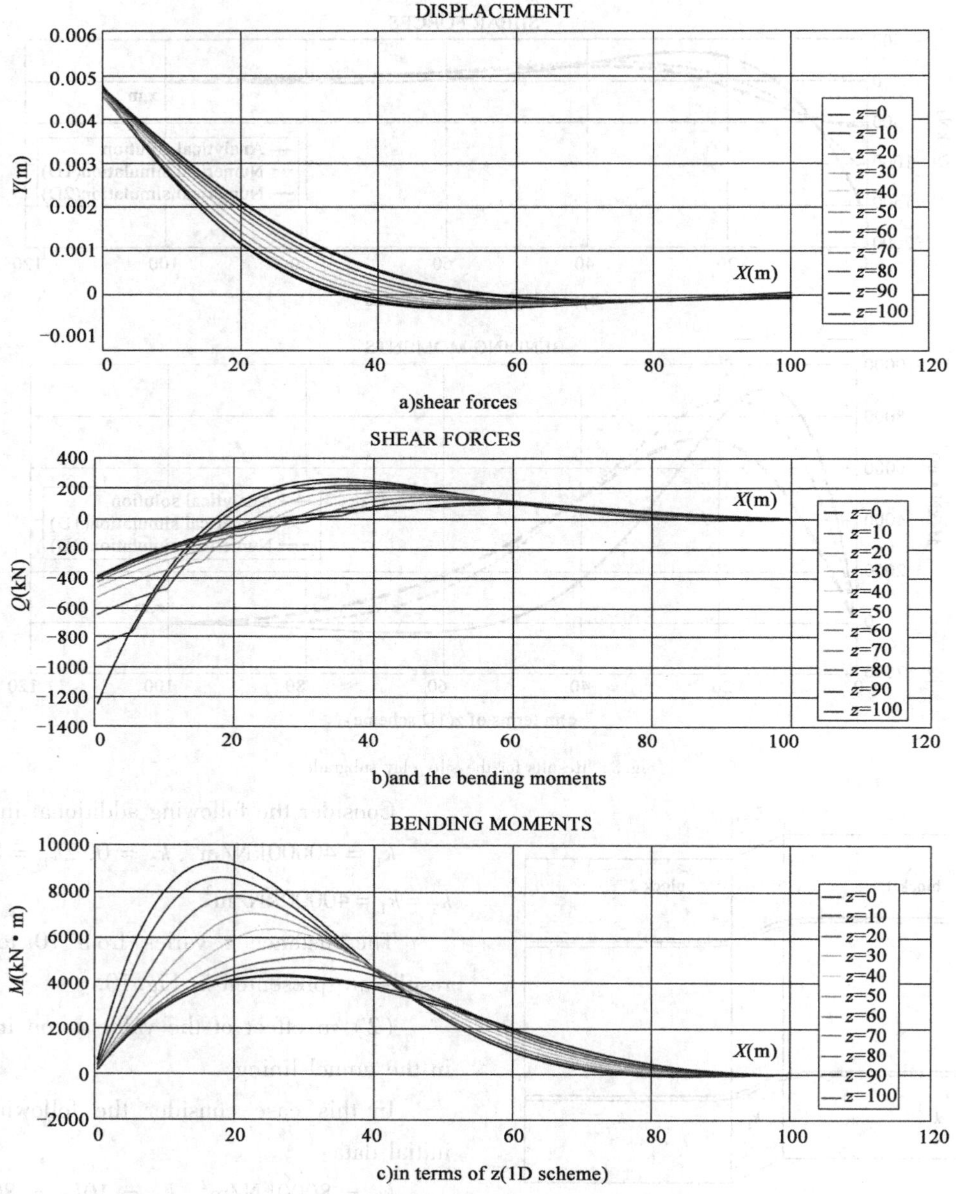

Fig. 10　Diagram of displacement

(2) An effect of the value k_2 on internal forces in the tunnel lining

In this case consider the following additional initial data:

$E_1 = 43680\text{kN/m}^2$, $E_3 = 10E_1 = 43680\text{kN/m}^2$, $z = 40\text{m}$.

E_2 takes values from 43680 to 436800kN/m^2.

The results are presented in Fig. 13.

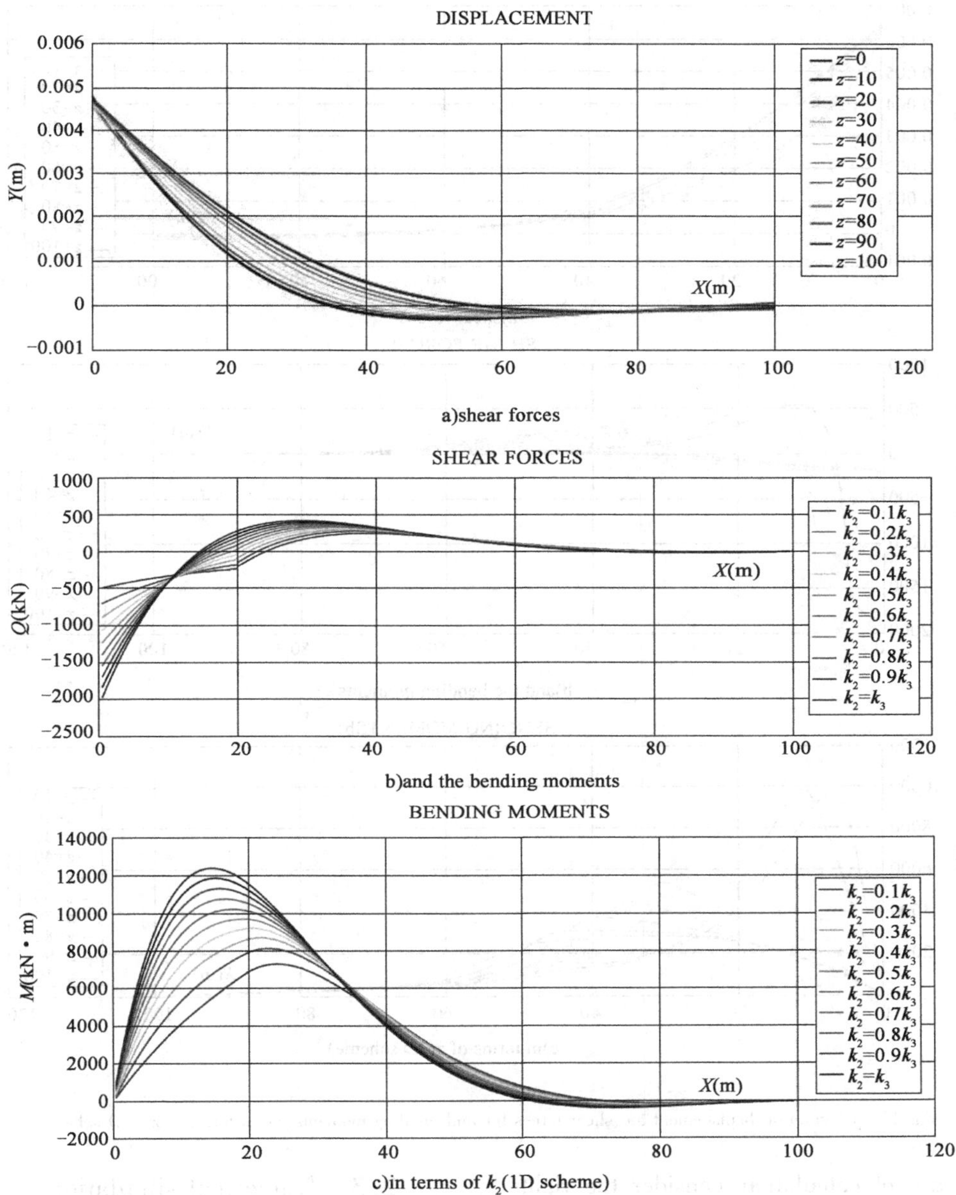

Fig. 11 Diagram of displacement a), shear forces b) and bending moments c) in terms of k_2 (1D scheme)

2 The fault is along to the tunnel axis

2.1 Analytical method

Consider a tunnel with length $2L$, external diameter d, and with compressive (or tensile) stiffness EA. Using the Winkler model to describe the interaction of the surrounding soil mass and the tunnel structure, the coefficient of elastic resistance at the shift k_s is introduced (Fig. 14).

The movement of the tunnel cross-sections w along the x axis is described by the following differential equation:

$$EA\frac{d^2w}{dx^2}-\pi dk_s w=0 \tag{13}$$

2.2 Example

For example, a tunnel lining with the above characteristics was adopted: $d = 6\text{m}$, $t = 0.3\text{m}$. Coefficient k_s is adopted as a quarter of the normal coefficient of subgrade reaction. For silty clay: $k_s = 2000\text{kN/m}^2$.

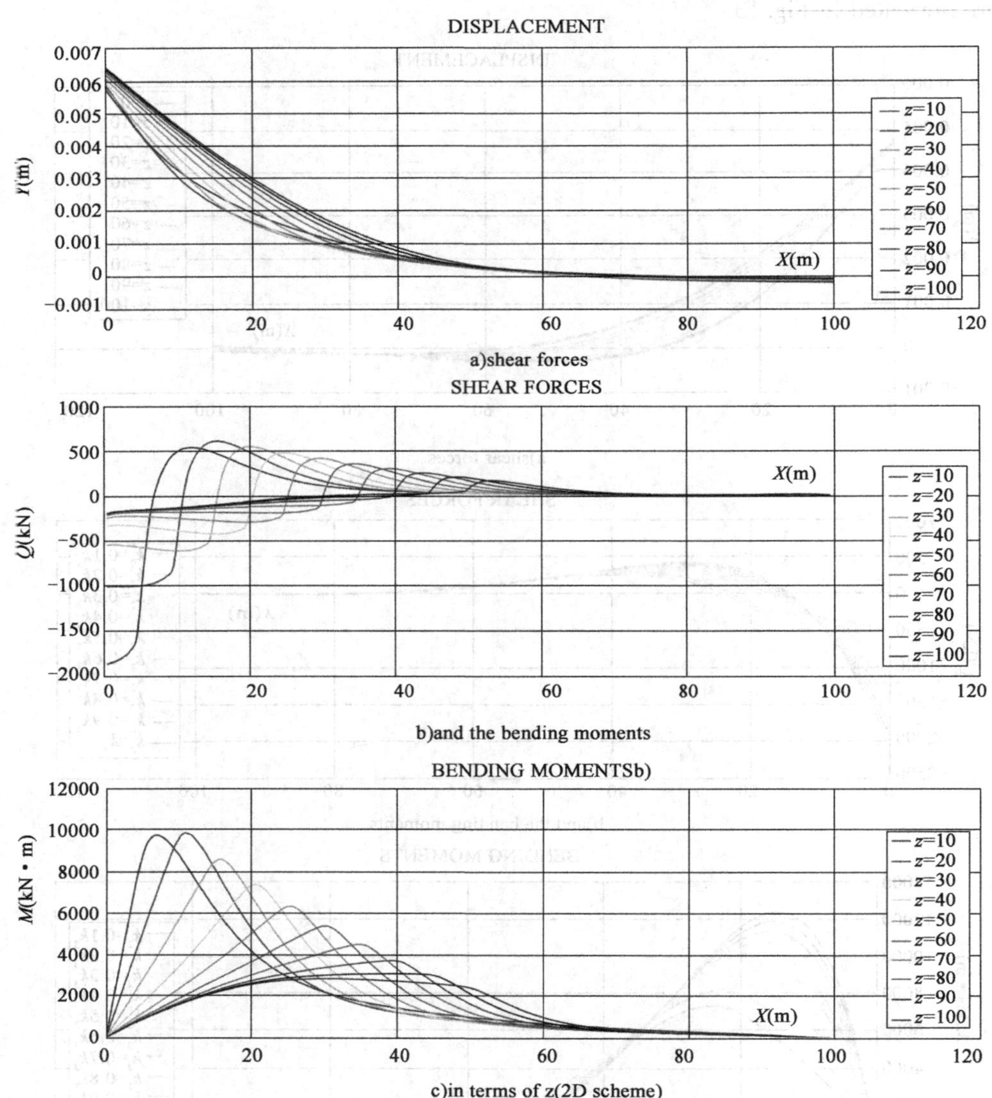

Fig. 12 Diagram of displacement a), shear forces b) and bending moments c) in terms of z (2D scheme)

For the ease of calculation, consider the right-hand cut-off part in accordance with the methods of strength of materials (Fig. 15).

The well-known differential relationship between the force and the deflection is:

$$EA\frac{d^2w}{dx^2} = N_z \tag{14}$$

Given equation (13) and the equilibrium equation for the right-hand cut-off part, one gets:

$$N_z = \pi d k_s w = 1884kN \tag{15}$$

Obviously, the force at the ends of the tunnel is equal to zero. Then, one can plot the diagram internal forces Nz.

2.3 Numerical simulation

For comparing the results, the previously presented models of the tunnel as beams on an elastic foundation with springs (1D) and model with ground given as plane strain elements (2D) are used.

Using these models, with a difference only in the direction of the applied load (the horizontal direction instead of the vertical one). Friction was modeled like an interface element with strength reduction factor R_c = 0.5. The results are presented in Fig. 16.

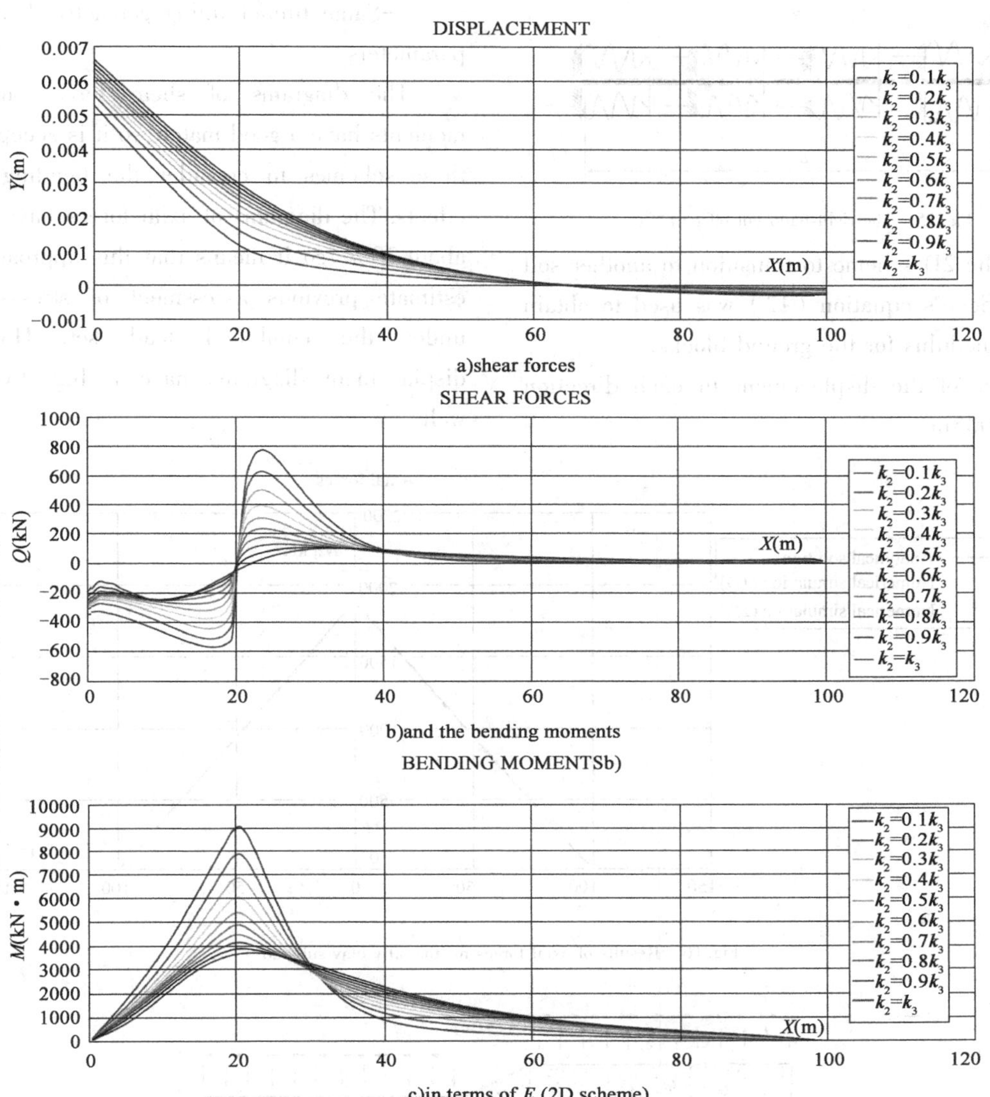

Fig. 13 Diagram of displacement a), shear forces b) and bending moments c) in terms of E_2 (2D scheme)

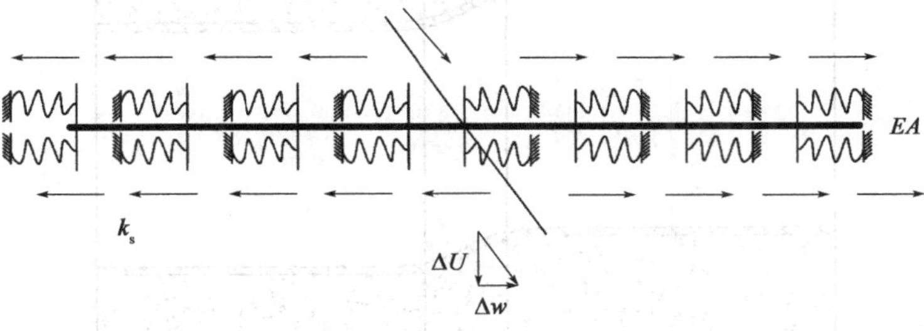

Fig. 14 Calculation scheme for the case when fault is along the tunnel. cross sections axis

3 Simultaneous actions of the fault perpe-ndicular and along the tunnel axis

Usingthe introduced calculation schemes, it is possible to consider the problem combine stress-strain state of the tunnel lining (Fig. 17). For clarity the 1D and 2D schemes were compare, the obtained results are presented in Fig. 18.

Initial data:

—For the 1D scheme:

$k_1 = 40000\text{kN/m}^2$, $k_2 = 0.2k_1 = 8000\text{kN/m}^2$, $k_3 = k_1 = 40000\text{kN/m}^2$

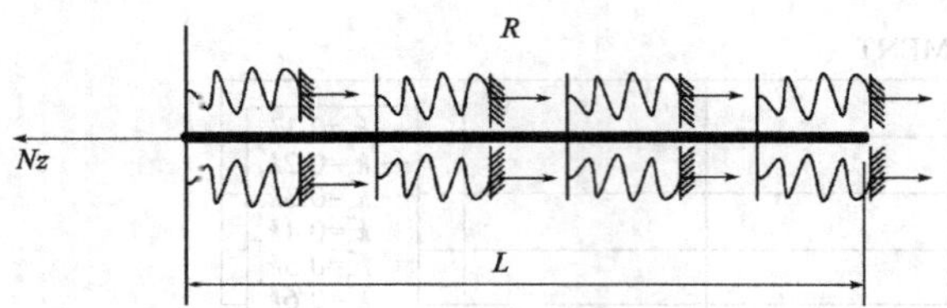

Fig. 15　The right-hand cut-off part

—Forthe 2D scheme to transition to another soil model, the Scott's equation (12) was used to obtain the Young modulus for the ground blocks.

—Valᴌe of the displacement in each direction equalsto 0.005m.

—Same tunnel lining geometrical and physical parameters.

The diagrams of shear forces and bending moments have a good match, so it is acceptable to use these schemes to consider the bending and shear effects. The diagrams of axial forces have error rateof about 20%, so it means that this approach allows to estimate previous assessment of stress-strain state under the combined load set. However, the displacement diagrams have a big divergence, as well.

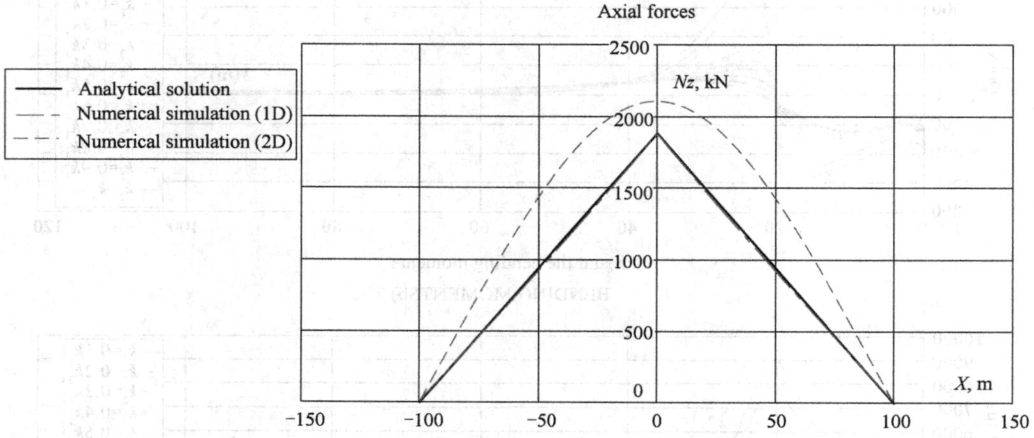

Fig. 16　Results of axial forces for the silty clay subgrade

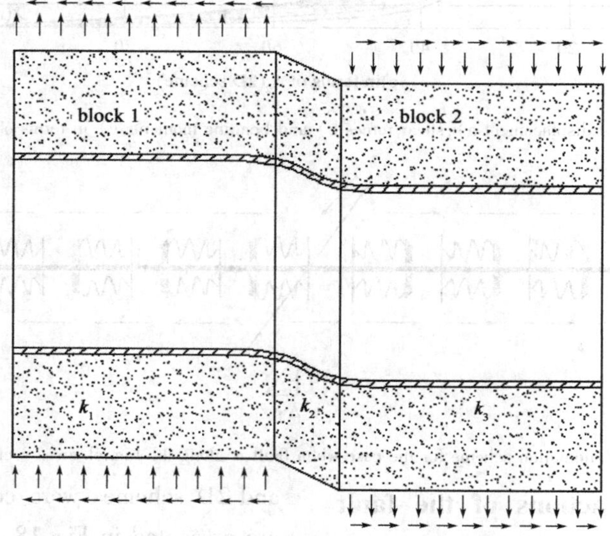

Fig. 17　The combined load set

Inthe 1D scheme it is impossible to consider mass of the ground above the tunnel, moreover, to transit to the 2D scheme, an approach given by Scott (1981) was used. Obviously, these models have

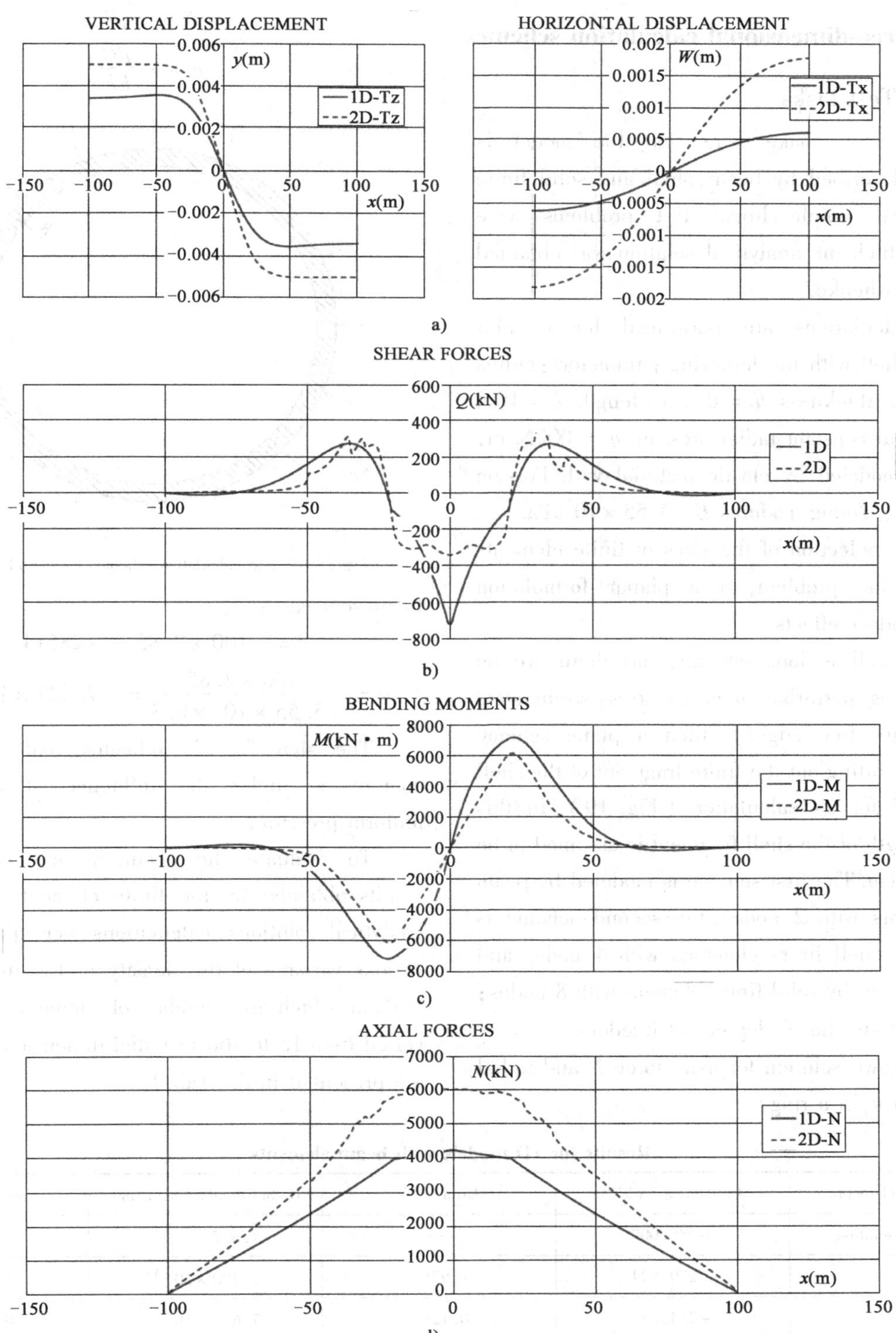

Fig. 18 The combined load set case. Diagrams of displacements a), shear forces b), bending moments c) axial forces d) in terms of distance x

different stiffness of the whole system " ground-structure".

The mainhypothesis is that the coefficient of the subgrade reaction for the tension-compression is a quarter of a normal coefficient of the subgrade reaction for bending and shearing actions $k_s = \frac{1}{4}k$. This investigation was completed for piles and for tunnels it is necessary to continue this research.

4 Three-dimensional calculation schemes

4.1 Test tasks

In order to make sure that the model is adequately described by beam, shell and solid finite elements, two simple linear test problems were solved, for which the analytical solution was obtained by S. P. Timoshenko.

The calculations are performed for circular cylindrical shell with the following parameters: radius $R = 2.85\mathrm{m}$, thickness $h = 0.3\mathrm{m}$, length $l = 10\mathrm{m}$ under external constant radial pressure $q = 100\mathrm{kN/m}$, concrete is modeled by elastic material with Poisson ratio $\mu = 0.2$, Young modulus $E = 3.55\times10^7\mathrm{kPa}$.

4.1.1 Selection of the sizes of finite elements for solving the problem in a planar formulation without boundary effects

If the shell is long enough, and there are no factors causing perturbation of its stress-strain state (a shell with free edges), then a plane scheme obtained by cutting out the finite fragment of the shell can be used for its calculation (Fig. 19). In this case, the length of the shell fragment is assumed to be equal to $l = 1\mathrm{m}$. The first scheme is modeled by beam finite elements with 2 nodes, the second scheme is presented by shell finite elements with 4 nodes and the third one — by solid finite element with 8 nodes; each of the nodes has 6 degrees of freedom.

Well known solution for axial force N and radial dicplasement w in a ring:

$$N = -qR \tag{16}$$

$$w = -\frac{qR^2}{Eh} \tag{17}$$

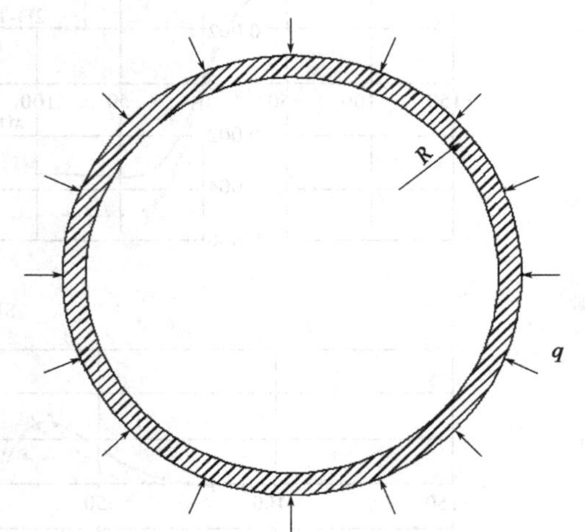

Fig. 19 Planar calculation scheme of a cylindrical shell

In present case:

$$N = -100\times2.85 = -285(\mathrm{kN})$$

$$w = -\frac{100\times2.85^2}{3.55\times10^7\times0.3} = -7.627\times10^{-5}(\mathrm{m})$$

The sign " - " indicates that the ring is compressed under the influence of an external uniform pressure.

To evaluate the accuracy and compare the results obtained by the finite element method with analytical solutions, calculations were performed for various variants of the density of the finite element grid, in which the number of elements in the ring varied from 16 to 160 in radial dimension. The results are presented in the Tab. 1.

Results for 1D models with beam elements Tab. 1

Number of elements	Axial force N(kN)	Error(%)	Radial displacement(m)	Error(%)
Analytical solution	-285.000	—	7.627×10^{-5}	—
16	-279.524	1.92%	7.480×10^{-5}	1.93%
54	-284.657	0.12%	7.618×10^{-5}	0.12%
108	-284.879	0.042%	7.624×10^{-5}	0.039%
160	-284.949	0.019%	7.625×10^{-5}	0.026%

The analysis of Tab. 1 showed that when the sizes of grid is decreased, the axial force and radial displacement approach the exact analytical solutions, which proves the reliability of the work of the beam finite elements using in planar scheme.

Next, the spatial calculation schemes of a cylindrical shell are considered. The shell is modeled by the corresponding four-node shell finite elements, which also have 6 degrees of freedom at each node. For a shell of finite sizes with free edges (the connections made at the ends of the shell do not distort its stress-strain state) the number of finite elements varied from 16 to 160 in the radial direction and from 4 to 40 along the axis of symmetry of the shell. The results are presented in Tab. 2.

Results for 2D models with shell elements Tab. 2

Number of elements	on Mises stress(kN/m^2)	Error(%)	Radial displacement(m)	Error(%)
Analytical solution	950.000	—	7.627×10^{-5}	—
16	903.575	4.89%	7.259×10^{-5}	4.82%
64	914.687	3.72%	7.304×10^{-5}	4.23%
108	916.120	3.57%	7.306×10^{-5}	4.21%
160	918.354	3.33%	7.308×10^{-5}	4.18%

Then, solid elements were used to model a cylindrical shell in the spatial formulation of the problem. The elements have 8 nodes with 6 degrees of freedom at each of them. The number of elements varied from 16 to 600 in the radial direction, from 1 to 8 elements in thickness. The number of elements along the axis of the cylindrical shell varied from 2 to 30 elements, it was selected in such a way that the generated solid finite elements had a shape as close as possible to the cubic one (excluding a grid with obviously unsatisfactorily large dimensions).

It is clearly seen that the presented numerical simulation models perfectly describe the behavior of a cylindrical shell in the considered plane stress-strain state. The error in calculatingthe axial forces, displacements and stresses between the models and the analytical solution is no more than 5% when using shell elements, for beam and solid elements — less than 2%. The results are presented in Tab. 3.

Results for 3D models with solid elements Tab. 3

Number of elements	Axial force N(kN)	Error(%)	Radial displacement(m)	Error(%)
Analytical solution	950.000	—	7.627×10^{-5}	—
16	935.368	1.54%	7.596×10^{-5}	0.41%
64	935.368	1.54%	7.596×10^{-5}	0.41%
108	948.187	0.19%	7.609×10^{-5}	0.24%
160	949.335	0.07%	7.621×10^{-5}	0.079%
360	949.604	0.042%	7.622×10^{-5}	0.066%
600	949.921	0.008%	7.625×10^{-5}	0.066%

4.1.2 Selection of the sizes of finite elements for solving the problem in a spatial formulation with boundary effects

Next, a static calculation of a cylindrical shell with rigidly fixed end faces (Fig. 20), loaded with an internal uniform pressure $q = 100\text{kN/m}^2$ is carried out. Length of the shell is $L = 10\text{m}$, cross-section area and material properties are same like in previous task. In this case, the phenomenon of the edge effect arises.

The well-known differential dependencies between displacementsand internal force factors:

$$w = -\frac{1}{2\beta^3 D}(\beta M_o \Psi(\beta x) + Q_o(\beta x)) - \frac{qR^2}{Eh} \tag{18}$$

$$\frac{dw}{dx} = \frac{1}{2\beta^2 D}(2\beta M_o(\beta x) + Q_o(\beta x)) \tag{19}$$

$$\frac{d^2 w}{dx^2} = -\frac{1}{2\beta D}(2\beta M_o(\beta x) + 2Q_o \xi(\beta x)) \tag{20}$$

$$\frac{d^3 w}{dx^3} = \frac{1}{D}(2\beta M_o \xi(\beta x) + 2Q_o \Psi(\beta x)) \tag{21}$$

$$M = -D\frac{d^2 w}{dx^2} \tag{22}$$

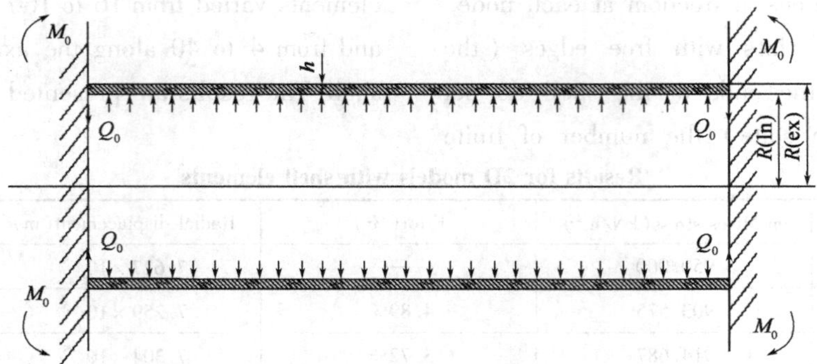

Fig. 20 Calculation scheme of rigidly fixed shell

Where:

$$\beta^4 = \frac{Eh}{4R^2D}; D = \frac{Eh^3}{12(1-\mu^2)}$$

$$M_o = 2\beta^2 D\delta = \frac{q}{2\beta^2}; Q_o = -4\beta^3 D\delta = -\frac{q}{\beta}$$

$$\varphi(\beta x) = e^{-\beta x}(\cos\beta x + \sin\beta x)$$

$$\Psi(\beta x) = e^{-\beta x}(\cos\beta x - \sin\beta x)$$

$$\theta(\beta x) = e^{-\beta x}\cos\beta x$$

$$\xi(\beta x) = e^{-\beta x}\sin\beta x$$

The edgeeffects appears in the vicinity of the fixed boundaries in the form of a bend of the shell in the longitudinal direction and fades as it moves away from the fixed points. It can only be estimated using a spatial calculation model (Fig. 21). In this case, the planar scheme can only be used for sections that are sufficiently far from the end faces, where the edge effect fades.

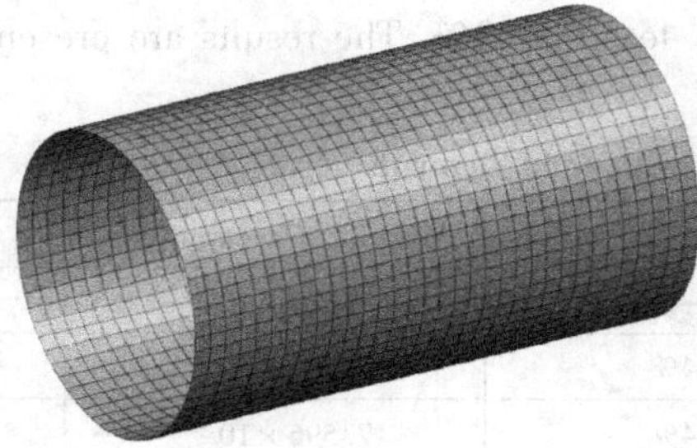

Fig. 21 General and deformed view of shell

In the first case the cylindrical shell is modeled by shell elements. The number of finite elements varied from 16 to 160 in the radial direction and from 10 to 100 along the axis of the shell. The results are presented in Fig. 22.

In the second case solid elements were used. As before, sizes of the grid were selected in such a way that the shape of the finite elements was as close as possible to the cubic one. The number of finite elements varied from 16 to 300 in the radial direction, from 10 to 100 along the axis and from 1 to 5 over the thickness of the cylindrical shell (Fig. 23).

Although this study does not focus on the distribution of stresses over the thickness of the shell in details, it should be noted that one element over thickness does not always correctly describe its stress-strain state, especially in the presence of edge effects. The results are presented in Fig. 24.

Analyzing the graphs shown in Fig. 24 one comes to the conclusion that shell and solid finite elements accurately describe the behavior of closed cylindrical shells, while obtaining quite reliable results, both in terms of displacements and stresses with sufficient density of the model grid.

4.2 Solving the problem in spatial formulation

4.2.1 The fault is perpendicular to the tunnel axis

As in solving test problems, for modeling the tunnel lining, firstly shell finite elements are used, then solid ones.

The surrounding soil array is presented by two blocks consisting of solid finite elements with the properties of the Mohr Coulomb model: silty clay, Young modulus $E = 37000\text{kPa}$, Poisson ratio $\nu = 0.3$, friction angle $\varphi = 18.4°$, cohension $c = 33.8\text{kPa}$. Sizes for each of blocks are 100m × 80m × 40m.

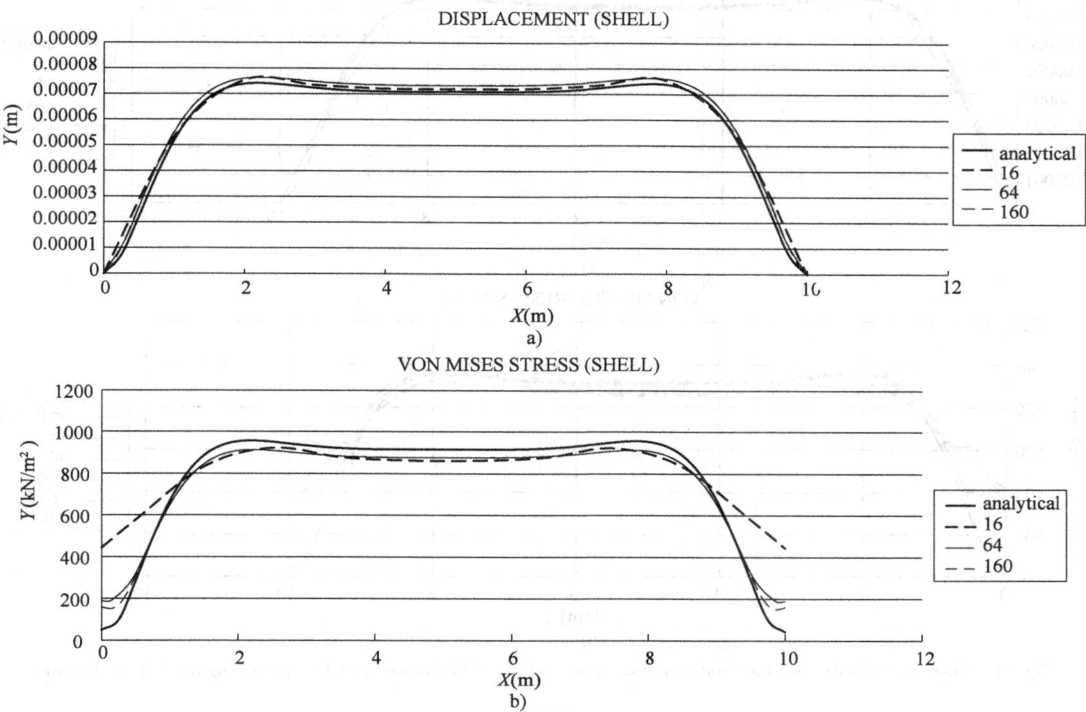

Fig. 22 Diagram of displacement a) and von Mises stress b) shell element models with varying number of elements

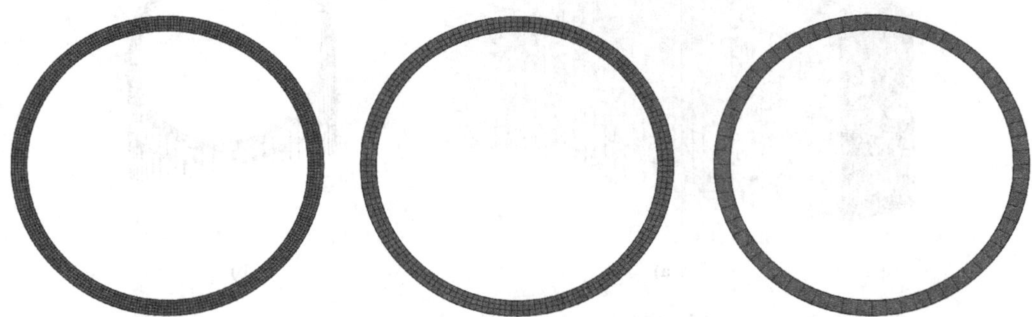

Fig. 23 Variation the number of finite elements in radial direction and over shell thickness

The friction between the tunnel lining and the ground is determined by the strength reduction factor $R_c = 0.5$ and modeled by plane interface elements located between surrounding soil massif and tunnel lining.

To obtain a complete picture of the stress-strain state of the tunnel lining under the described conditions, a model with springs in a three-dimensional formulation with shell and solid finite elements was also considered (Fig. 25).

Fig. 26 below shows the results for all the mentioned models. Dotted lines show the distribution of von Mises stress in models using springs, solid lines correspond to planar and solid finite elements modeling the soil array.

As already noted when solving test tasks, when modeling the lining of a tunnel with three-dimensional finite elements, an important issue is to take into account the stress distribution over the thickness of the shell. It follows from Fig. 27, that in this particular case it is quite acceptable to use one element over shell thickness (the graphs show the maximum values of stress from all obtained ones for each cross-section).

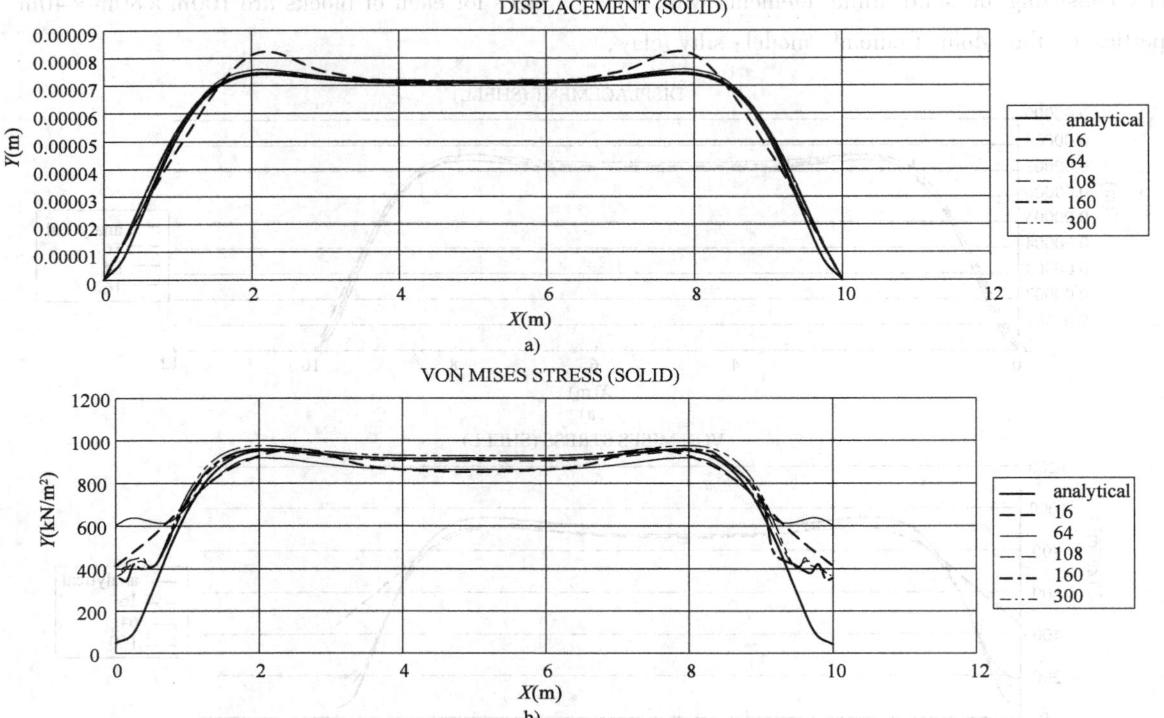

Fig. 24　Diagram of displacement a) and von Mises stress b) for solid element models with varying number of elements

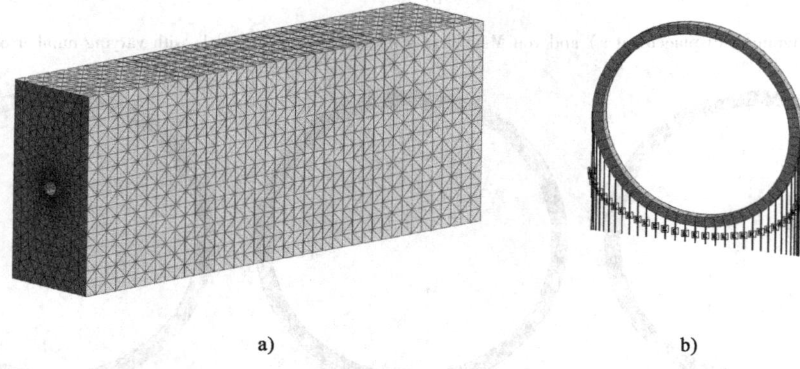

Fig. 25　Spatial calculation schemes with soil massif a) and springs b)

The considered spatial models can be used to analyze the cases mentioned above when two blocks of soil are separated by an intermediate filling space z (Fig. 9). All parameters for the calculation are used similarly for the planar problem. The results are presented in Fig. 28 ~ 31.

4.2.2　The fault is along to the tunnel axis

In the case of movement of the blocks of along the axis of the structure, tension-compression forces arise in the tunnel lining. The soil characteristics and tunnel parameters are taken from the problemabove, the kinematic load is applied as displacement of the left block in the left direction along the tunnel axis by 5mm. The results are shown in Fig. 32.

As can be seen from the graph, the spatial design scheme more accurately describes the behavior of the structure under the action of a given load. Not only the choice of the type of finite elements for the structure and the soil mass has a great influence, but also setting the friction between materials of different stiffness.

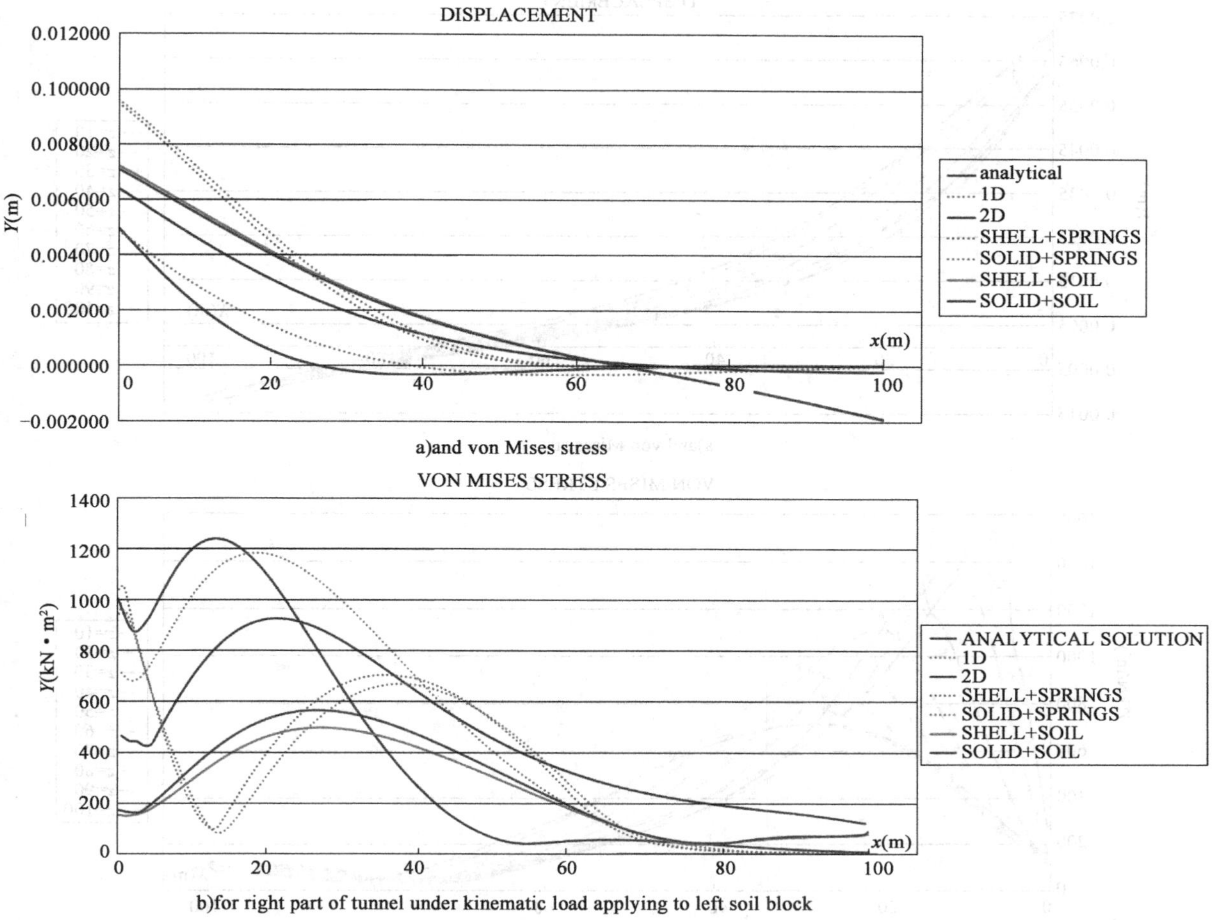

DISPLACEMENT

a)and von Mises stress

VON MISES STRESS

b)for right part of tunnel under kinematic load applying to left soil block

Fig. 26 Diagram of displacement a) and von Mises stress b) for right part of tunnel under kinematic load applying to left soil block

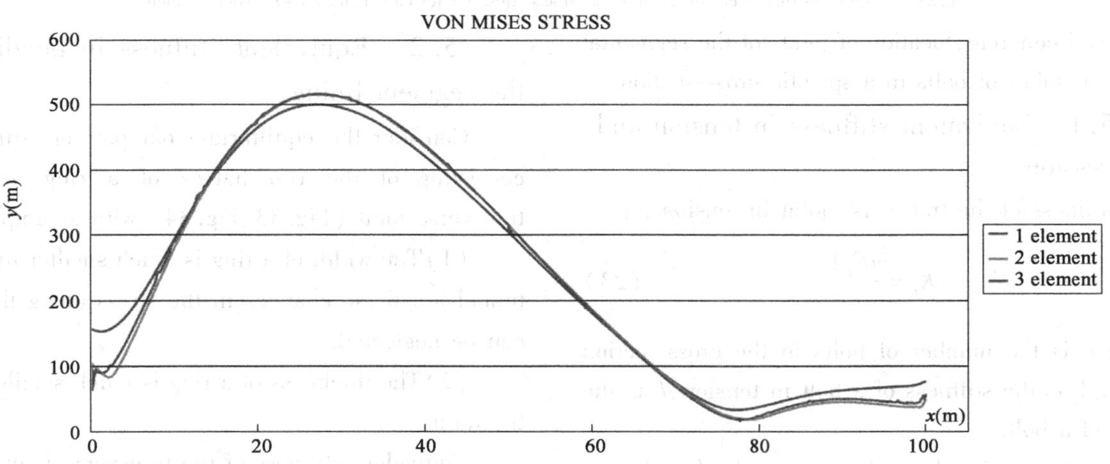

Fig. 27 The results for models with the varies element number over thickness of the shell

5 Equivalent stiffness

In all the tasks discussed above, the tunnel lining is assumed to be made of monolithic concrete with a constant cross-section. However, in engineering practice, the precast structures, made of reinforced concrete or cast iron, are also used. In this case, one needs to take into account the bending stiffness and tensile-compression stiffness, which differ depending on the geometry, type of cast iron, type of bars in the

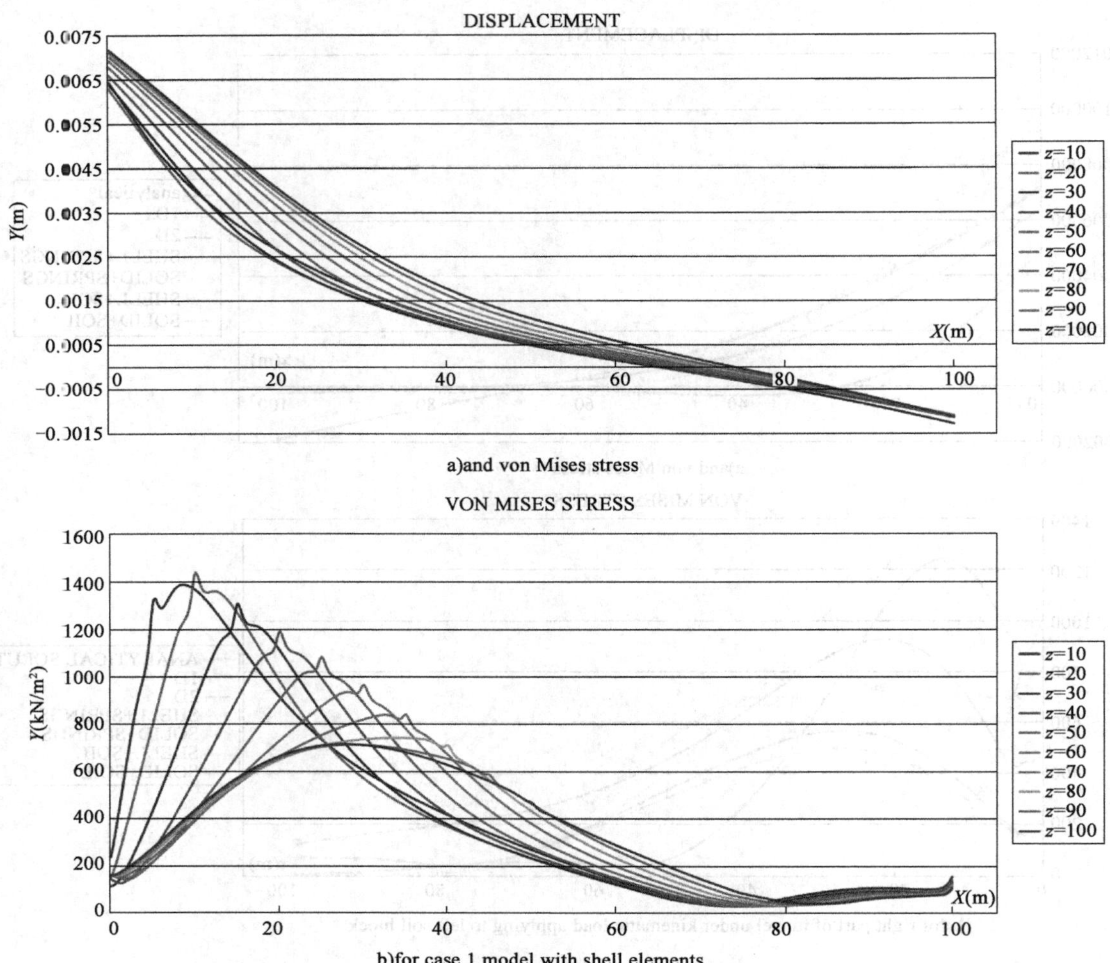

Fig. 28　Diagram of displacement a) and von Mises stress b) for case 1, model with shell elements

reinforced concrete, location of joints of the segmental linings, number of bolts in a specific cross-section.

5.1　Equivalent stiffness in tension and compression

Stiffness of the transverse joint in tension is:

$$K_j = \frac{nE_jA_j}{l_j} \tag{23}$$

Where n is the number of bolts in the cross-section area, E_jA_j is the stiffness of a bolt in tension, l_j is the length of a bolt.

In compression, bolts do not carry load, so in this case equivalent stiffness is determined by the lining stiffness; however in tension the lining ring and the transverse join link work together, so equivalent stiffness can be presented:

$$\frac{l_s}{(EA)_{eq}^{T}} = \frac{1}{K_j} + \frac{l_s}{E_sA_s} \text{ or } (EA)_{eq}^{T} = \frac{K_jE_sA_s/l_s}{K_j + E_sA_s/l_s} \tag{24}$$

5.2　Equivalent stiffness in bending of the segment lining

Consider the equilibrium ofa part of structure, consisting of the two halves of a ring and the transverse joint (Fig. 33、Fig. 34) with assumptions:

(1) The width of a ring is much smaller than the tunnel length, so changes in the stress along the axis can be neglected.

(2) The thickness of a ring is much smaller than the radius.

Equivalent stiffness of the transverse joint is:

$$(EI)_j = \frac{E_sI_Sl_j}{l_s} \frac{\cos^3\theta}{\cos\theta + \left(\frac{\pi}{2} + \theta\right)\sin\theta} \tag{25}$$

Where $I_s = \pi R^3 t$ is an axial moment of inertia of ring's cross-section area.

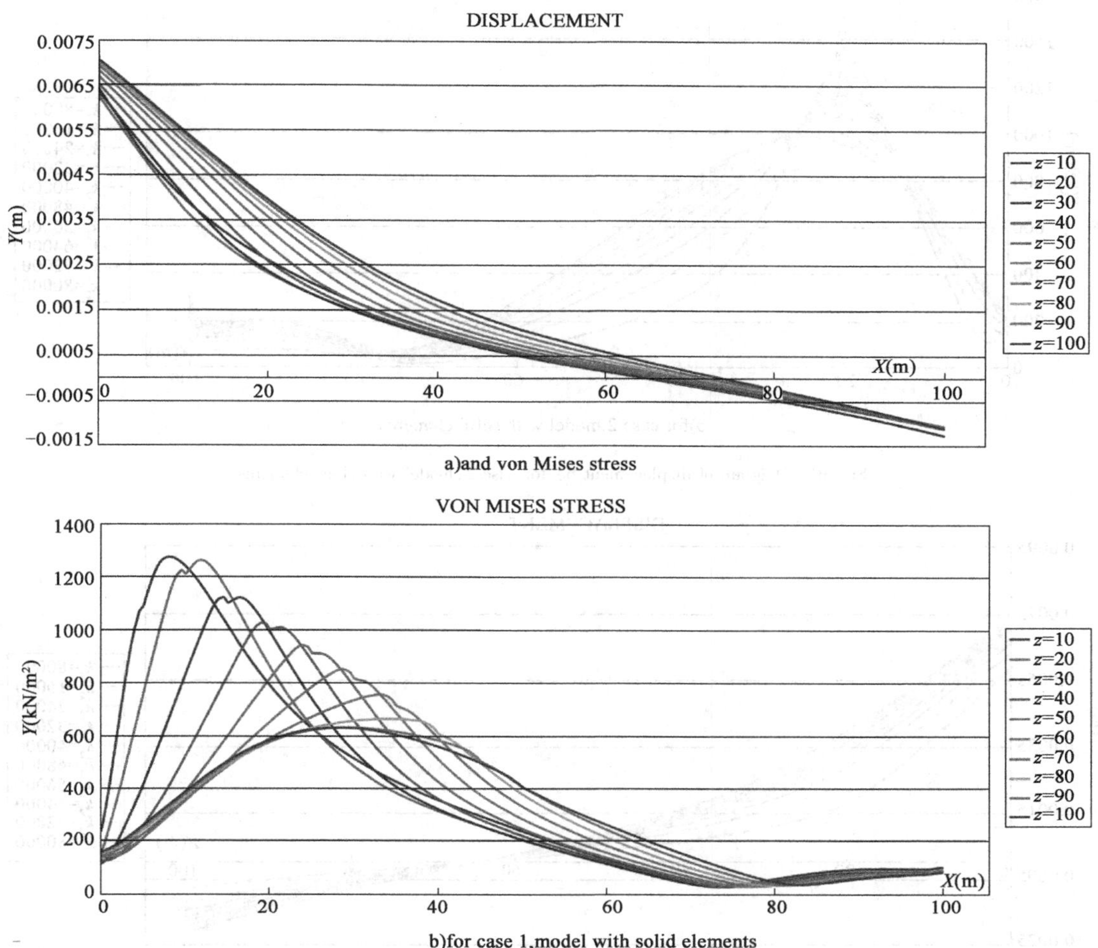

Fig. 29 Diagram of displacement a) and von Mises stress b) for case 1, model with solid elements

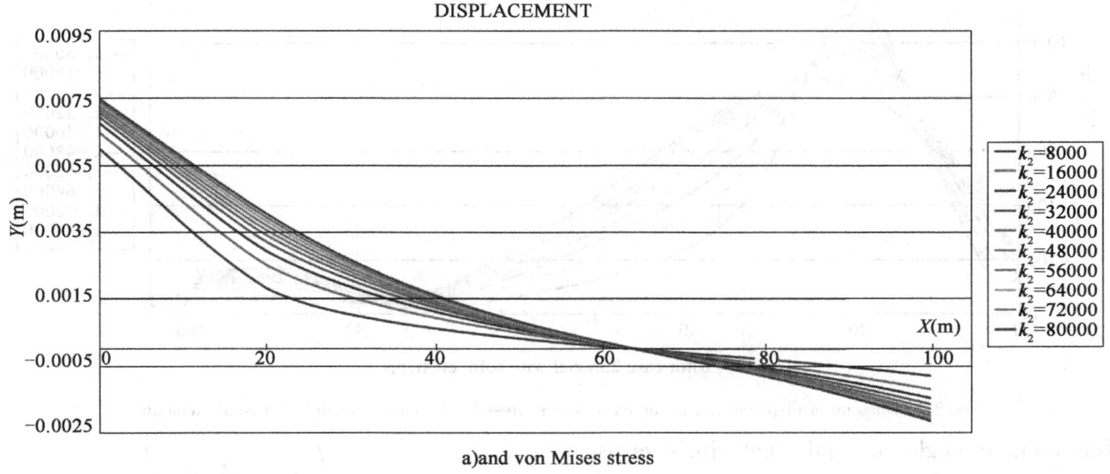

Fig 30

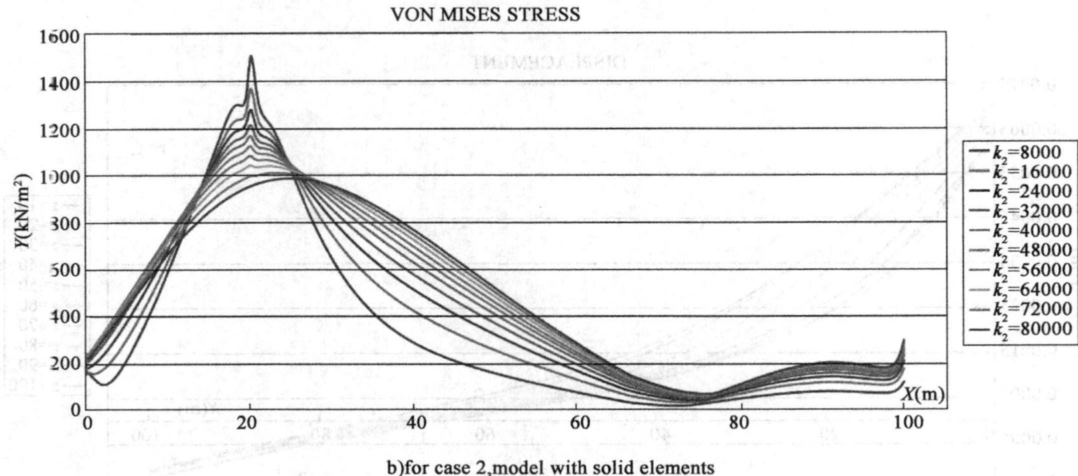

Fig. 30 Diagram of displacement b) for case 2, model with shell elements

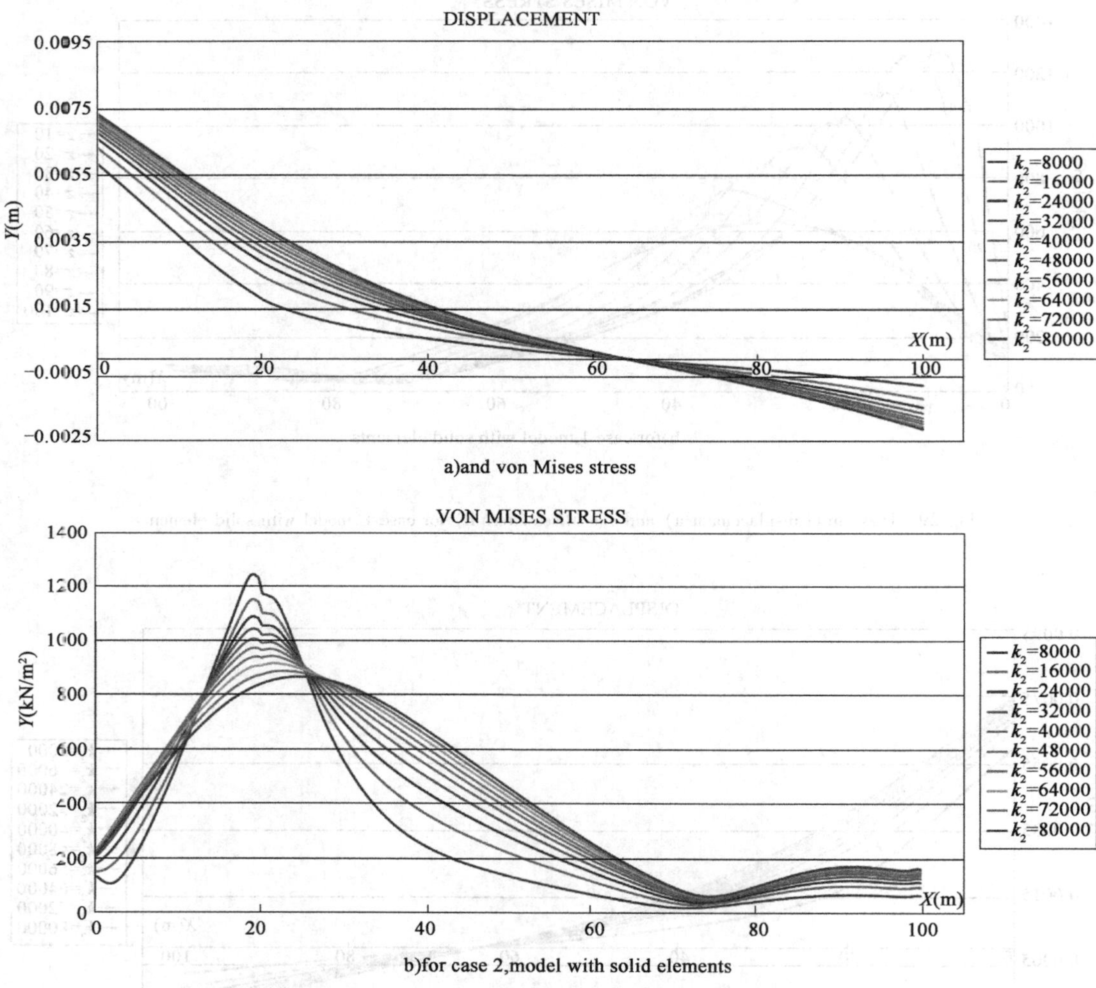

Fig. 31 Diagram of displacement a) and von Mises stress b) for case 2, model with solid elements

The rotation angle of equivalent ring's cross-section area is a sum of rotation angles of the ring and a joint, i. e.

$$\frac{l_s}{(EI)_{eq}} = \frac{l_s}{E_s I_s} + \frac{l_j}{(EI)_j} \tag{26}$$

Combining equations (25) and (26), one obt-

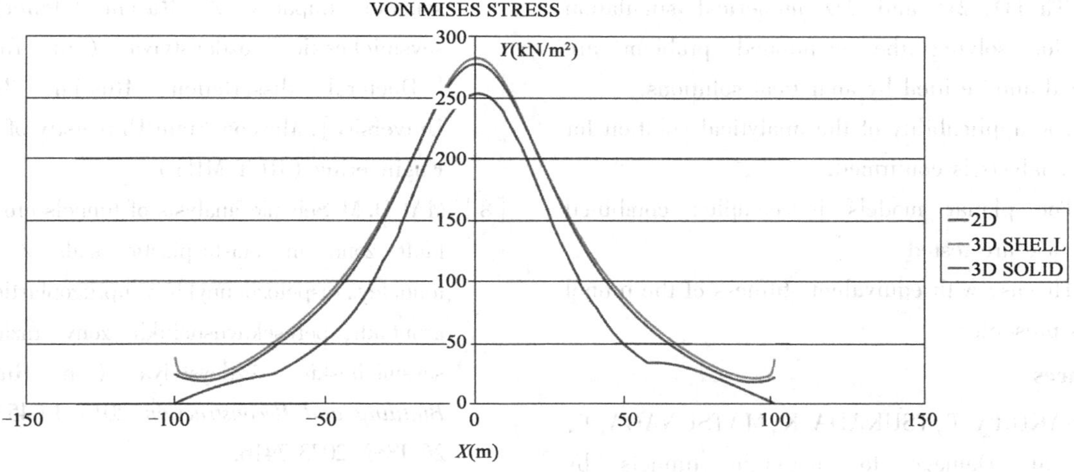

Fig. 32 The results for kinematic load applied along the tunnel axis

ains the equivalent stiffness of the cross-section tunnel lining in bending as:

$$(EI)_{eq} = E_s I_s \frac{\cos^3\theta}{\cos^3\theta + \cos\theta + \left(\frac{\pi}{2} + \theta\right)\sin\theta} \tag{27}$$

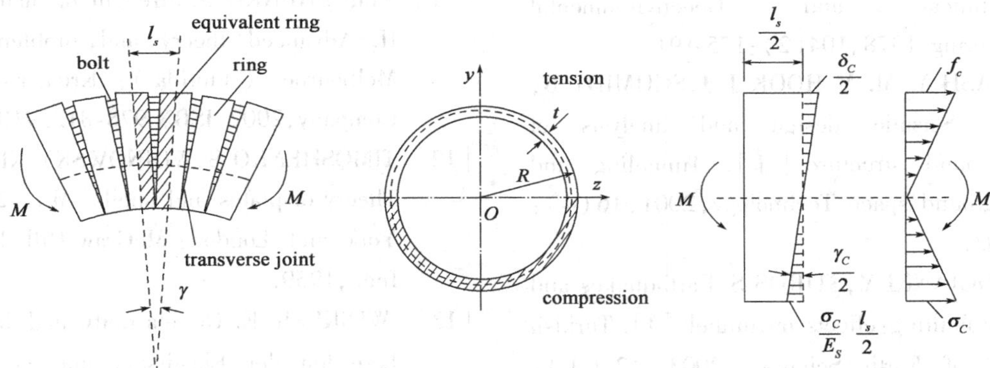

Fig. 33 Stress distribution and angle displacement of the cross-section area in the ring

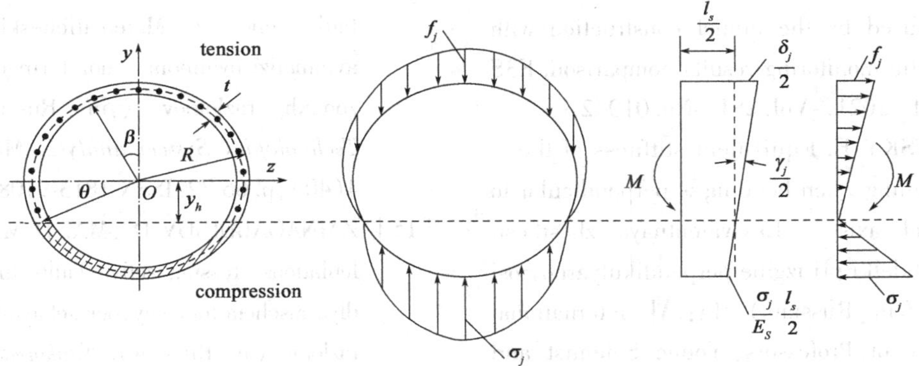

Fig. 34 Stress distribution and angle displacement of the cross-section area in the transverse joint

6 Conclusions

—Classical model of a beam on an elastic foundation is adopted for solving the problem of seismic and geophysics impact on the tunnel in fracture zone.

—The1D, 2D and 3D numerical simulation models for solving the mentioned problem are introduced and verified by analytical solutions.

—The applicability of the analytical solution for primary analysis is confirmed.

—The planar models in complex combined loading case are tested.

—Thecase with equivalent stiffness of the tunnel lining is presented.

References

[1] ASAKURA T, TSUKADA K, MATSUNAGA T, et al. Damage to mountain tunnels by earthquake and its mechanism. *Proceedings of Japan Society of Civil Engineers (JSCE)* [online]. 2000, 2000(659), p. 27-38. eISSN 2187-5103. Available from: https://doi. org/10.2208/jscej.2000.659_27.

[2] DOWDING C. H, ROZEN A. Damage to rock tunnels from earthquake shaking[J]. Journal of Geotechnical and Geoenvironmental Engineering, 1978, 104(2): 175-191.

[3] HASHASH Y. M. A, HOOK J. J, SCHMIDT B, et al. Seismic design and analysis of underground structure [J]. Tunneling and Underground space Technology, 2001, 16(4): 247-293.

[4] KONTOGIANNI V, STIROS S. Earthquakes and seismic faulting: effects on tunnels[J]. Turkish Journal of Earth Sciences, 2003, 12(1): 153-156.

[5] KOSITSYN S, AKULICH V. Numerical methodology for determining the soil mass surface slump, caused by the tunnel construction with the geodetic monitoring results comparison. E3S Web Conf. -2021. -Vol. 281. -No. 01042.

[6] KURBATSKY E. Equivalent stiffness of the segment lining when bending is perpendicular to the tunnel axis / Ekvivalentnaya zhestkostt sbornoy obdelki pri izgibe perpendikulyarnoy osi tonnelya (in Russian). In: Ⅵ international Conference of Professors, Young Scientist and Students: proceedings. 2013. p. 3-6.

[7] MAI D. M. (2014) Calculation of tunnels on seismic impacts / Raschet tonneley na seysmicheskie vozdeystviya (in Russian) [Doctoral dissertation, Russian Transport University]. Moscow State University of Railway Engineering (RUT MIIT).

[8] MAI D. M. Seismic analysis of tunnels crossing the fault zone in elasto-plastic soils / Raschet tonneley, raspolozhennykh v uprugoplasticheskikh gruntakh, peresekayushchikh zony razloma, na seysmicheskie vozdeystviya (in Russian). *Building and Reconstruction*. 2013, 1(45), p. 19-26. ISSN 2073-7416.

[9] REED L. Mosher, William P. Dawkins. Theoretical manual for pile foundations. US Army Corps of Engineers, Engineer Research and Development Cetnter, 2000.

[10] SCOTT R. F. Foundation analysis. New Jersey, Prentice-Hall: Englewood Cliffs, 1981. ISBN 978-0133291698.

[11] TIMOSHENKO S. Strength of materials. Vol. II. Advanced theory and problems. 3. ed. Melbourne (Florida): Krieger Publishing Company, 2002. ISBN 978-8123910772.

[12] TIMOSHENKO S, WOINOWSKY-KRIEGER S. Theory of plates and shells[M]. 2. ed. New York and London: McGraw-Hill Book Co., Inc., 1959.

[13] WINKLER E. On elasticity and fixity / Die Lere fon der Elastitsitet und Festigayt (in German). Prague: Dominicus, 1867.

[14] ZAINAGABDINOV D, MAI D. M. Mathematical models for automated monitoring of tunnels in fault zones / Matematicheskie modeli pri avtomatizirovannom monitoringe tonneley v zonakh razlomov (in Russian). *Modern Technologies. System analysis*. Modelling. 2013, 4(40), p. 66-72. ISSN 1813-9108.

[15] ZAINAGABDINOV D., MAI D. M. Models for calculations crossing active faults tunnels / Modeli dlya rascheta tonneley, peresekayushchikh aktivnye razlomy (in Russian). *Naukovedenie* [online]. 2013, 3, 25TBH313. Available from: https://naukovedenie.ru/PDF/25tvn313.pdf

含水率对第三系半成岩地层公路隧道结构稳定性的影响研究

付文举*
（长安大学公路学院）

摘　要　第三系半成岩地层成岩程度低，遇水软化，隧道围岩极易产生软岩大变形、支护结构开裂侵限、掌子面失稳坍塌甚至涌水涌泥等工程灾害。本文以白鹿原隧道为背景，通过现场取样、室内试验、数值模拟、理论分析等手段，基于含水率对第三系半成岩地层隧道围岩工程特性与结构稳定性进行深入研究。研究结果表明：第三系半成岩的强度与含水率呈负相关，含水率对抗剪强度指标黏聚力影响较大，对内摩擦角影响较小。基于含水率对将第三系半成岩物理力学参数的影响规律，将该地层隧道Ⅴ级围岩分为含水率小于17%、17%～22%、大于22%三个区段。含水率的增加导致隧道围岩变形增大，引起围岩稳定性发生变化，第三系半成岩地层隧道围岩含水率小于22%时可以保证施工的稳定性，当围岩含水率达到饱和后，隧道后导洞开挖极易导致隧道失稳坍塌。第三系半成岩地层隧道围岩含水率处于饱和状态时，初期支护结构可能于后导洞位置局部出现侵限甚至失效。研究结果可为其他第三系半成岩地层隧道设计施工提供指导。

关键词　隧道工程　第三系半成岩　含水率　围岩物理力学特性　结构稳定性　尖点突变

0　引言

随着“一带一路”建设倡议与“十四五”规划的提出，中西部地区的交通事业引来新的发展高潮，隧道由于其独特的优势与建设难点，大多对主线工程起到控制作用。在中西部地区隧道建设中伴随开挖深度的增大，使得隧道频繁穿越第三系地层，由于该地层工程性质和水文地质特征的特殊性，工程界对这一类地层岩土体又称为第三系半成岩，其工程性质介于软岩与硬土之间[1-2]。该地层成岩程度低，遇水易软化，开挖洞室大多位于地下水位以下，使得地下水对岩土体的影响更加明显，隧道开挖极易引起掌子面坍塌、支护结构失效等工程灾害，导致隧道在穿越第三系半成岩地层时地下水成为了极大的挑战[3]。

由于第三系半成岩地层的特殊性，吸引了国内众多学者对其进行研究，并取得了一定成果。马福荣等[4]通过泥岩的室内物理试验发现其抗剪强度随着含水率的减小而增大。张晓宇[5]基于对泥岩夹石膏岩的基本力学特征分析，发现在浸水后极易膨胀、软化，导致其强度降低。张波[6]通过调研与电镜试验，确定含水率为影响砂岩工程性质的主要因素之一，并将砂岩工程地质性质划分为5个等级。谭忠盛[7]等通过室内常规试验，发现随着弱胶结砂岩暴露时间增加，围岩含水率与内摩擦角随之减小，黏聚力增大。翁东郁[8]通过室内试验认为第三系粉质黏土强度随着含水率的增加而减小。王建军[9]通过室内试验与现场物探松动圈测试等方法，发现隧道开挖导致改变了地下水的渗流条件，引起围岩含水率增大，导致砂岩软化与变形。曹峰[10]、王庆林[11]、甄秉国[12]等依托兰渝铁路进行现场监测，得到第三系富水砂岩地层围岩含水率与围岩稳定性的关系以及变化规律。李乐[13]通过数值模拟发现第三系软岩隧道围岩在地下水的影响下，围岩变形破坏形式主要是顶拱塌落。黄明[14]基于物理力学参数建立了考虑含水损伤的泥质粉砂岩蠕变本构模型，通过数值模拟探讨了不同含水率状态下的二衬支护时机与大变形机理。朱举[3]、毛荣吉[15]、陈书玄[16]等依托中条山隧道，通过室内试验、理论分析及数值模拟，展开了地下水渗流对隧道穿越第三系半成岩地层时的稳定性分析研究。

以上研究表明,虽然国内学者对考虑含水率下的第三系半成岩地层物理力学性质及其隧道稳定性做了较多定性研究,但是关于隧道穿越第三系半成岩地层的研究大多集中于兰渝铁路与蒙华铁路等铁路隧道,具有较强的地域性;且考虑含水率对第三系半成岩地层隧道围岩分区的结果几乎没有;加之,公路隧道跨度一般大于铁路隧道,在公路隧道穿越第三系半成岩地层遇水时研究成果较少。

基于此,本文通过原状土现场取样、室内试验、文献调研、理论分析、数值模拟等手段,探索含水率对第三系半成岩的物理力学参数的影响规律,结合白鹿原隧道分析含水率对第三系半成岩地层超大跨度公路隧道稳定性的影响规律,以期为其他第三系半成岩地层公路隧道设计施工提供依据。

1　工程概况

白鹿原隧道是陕西省“2367”外环高速公路南端的控制工程,地处陕西省蓝田县杨木寨村附近。隧道采用分离式双洞六车道设计,设计时速120km/h,隧道净高5.0m,净宽15.25m,毛洞开挖高度12.7m,开挖宽度18.7m,按《公路隧道设计规范》(JTG 3370.1—2018)规定,属超大跨度公路隧道。

隧址区位于白鹿原南侧,以黄土阶地地貌为主,地面起伏不大,被大面积的黄土覆盖,隧道地质纵断面如图1所示。隧道穿越的地层为第三系半成岩地层,具有以下特点:半岩半土,岩、土性质并存,成岩程度低;暴露易崩解,风化程度高;遇水易软化,水稳性极差;自稳性差,围岩等级为Ⅴ级,工程性质差。开挖现场掌子面围岩如图2所示。

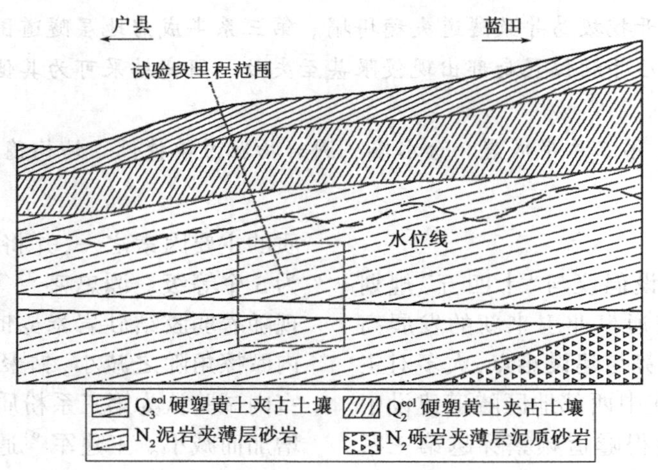

图1　试验段纵剖面图

图2　开挖现场围岩遇水前后对比图

隧址区地形地貌复杂,洞身段位于鲸鱼沟上游下部,沟内常年有水,该区地下水以孔隙裂隙水为主,主要受大气降水、地表水补给。根据钻孔观测,地下水埋深约4.5~6.0m,发现地下水位均高于洞室。隧址区总体位于富水层区段,处于该段的洞室开挖时易坍塌,经沿线地下水的取样分析,地下水对钢筋、混凝土微腐蚀性。

洞内采用单侧壁导坑法进行施工,支护结构按照新奥法原理设计,采用复合式支护结构,支护参数如表1所示。

隧道复合式衬砌支护参数 表1

支护类型		设置部位	设置参数
初期支护	喷射混凝土	全环	强度C25;厚度31cm
	钢筋网	拱墙+边墙	直径$\varphi 8$;间距20cm×20cm;双层
		仰拱	直径$\varphi 8$;间距20cm×20cm;单层
	钢架	全环	I25a工字钢;间距0.5m
	锁脚锚杆	拱脚+墙脚	直径$\varphi 50$;4根
二次衬砌	混凝土	全环	强度C35;厚度65cm
	钢筋	全环	HRB400;直径22mm;间距25cm

2 基于室内试验考虑含水率下的隧道围岩分区研究

隧道施工开挖破坏了地下水走向,隧道周边围岩内地下水易沿上部岩土体孔隙下渗到隧道洞室内,导致围岩遇水崩解为泥塑状,使得围岩软化与变形,从而产生一系列的工程病害:

(1)现场监测发现初期支护拱部存有纵向贯穿裂缝,环向也伴随有4~5条裂缝,且局部出现3~5cm侵限现象,需要对初期支护结构做拆换拱处理;

(2)初期支护结构表面出现渗漏水现象,甚至在洞壁形成点线状水流;

(3)支护结构局部破坏,出现涌水、涌泥现象。

白鹿原隧道工程灾害如图3所示。

白鹿原隧道在穿越第三系半成岩地层遇到水时产生的一系列工程灾害,使得现场施工安全与支护结构的稳定面临巨大挑战。鉴于此,本文从含水率对第三系半成岩物理力学性质影响的室内试验研究入手,建立考虑含水率下的第三系半成岩地层围岩亚分级标准。

a)初期支护侵限

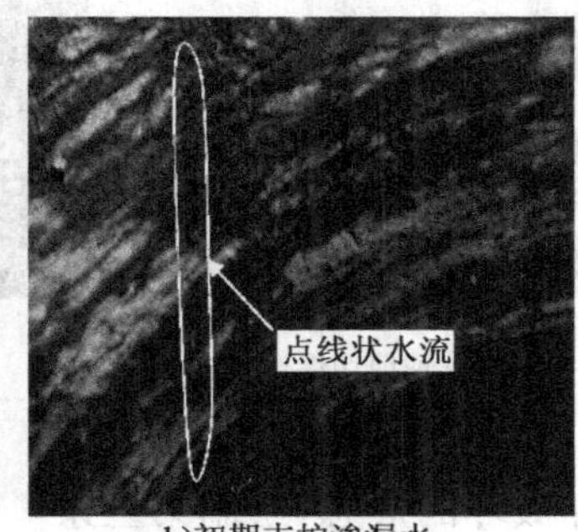

b)初期支护渗漏水

c)涌水

d)涌泥

图3 隧道现场工程灾害

2.1 第三系半成岩物理力学性质试验研究

为准确掌握第三系半成岩的物理力学特性,从白鹿原隧道未扰动掌子面不同部位取不同含水率的岩土试样,依据《公路土工试验规程》对第三系未成岩岩分别展开一系列室内试验研究,包括天然含水率试验、直剪试验、三轴剪切试验等,以获取不同含水率下的第三系半成岩物理力学参数。现场取样与SLB-1A型应力应变控制式三轴剪切渗透仪如图4、图5所示。

对所得原状土试样展开不固结不排水剪(UU)试验,试件破坏状态如图6所示。

图4 现场取样图

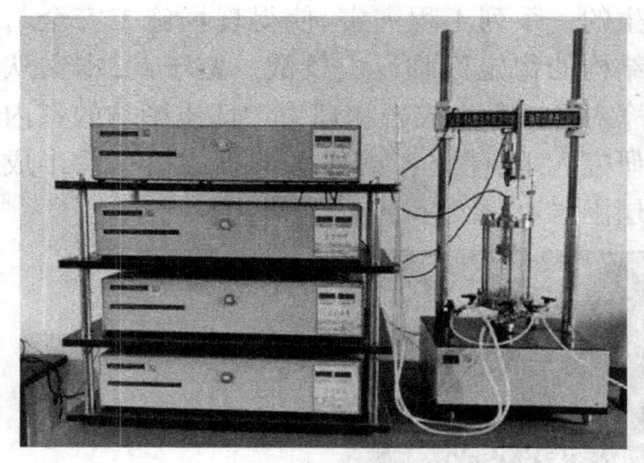

图5 SLB-1A型应力应变控制式三轴剪切渗透仪

图6 土样试件破坏时形态图

基于测得原状土的天然含水率,将试样分为5组,根据试验所得各试样破坏的形态,绘制第三系半成岩在各个含水率条件下的极限摩尔圆和强度包络线,得到第三系半成岩的抗剪强度指标 c、φ 值,结果见表2所示。

为了直观分析含水率对第三系未成岩抗剪强度的影响规律,绘制含水率 ω 与抗剪强度 τ 关系曲线图,如图7所示。

不同含水率下的原状土样的抗剪强度指标 表2

组号	含水率 ω (%)	抗剪强度 τ(kPa)				抗剪强度指标	
		100kPa	200kPa	300kPa	400kPa	c(kPa)	φ(°)
1	15.09	171.93	219.66	270.38	324.45	119.54	26.94
2	17.02	159.43	211.82	265.67	305.55	112.56	26.21
3	19.78	140.96	187.07	233.00	286.81	91.09	25.80
4	21.07	122.54	181.70	214.58	271.35	72.68	25.60
5	23.25	104.72	155.33	199.64	246.49	59.14	25.15

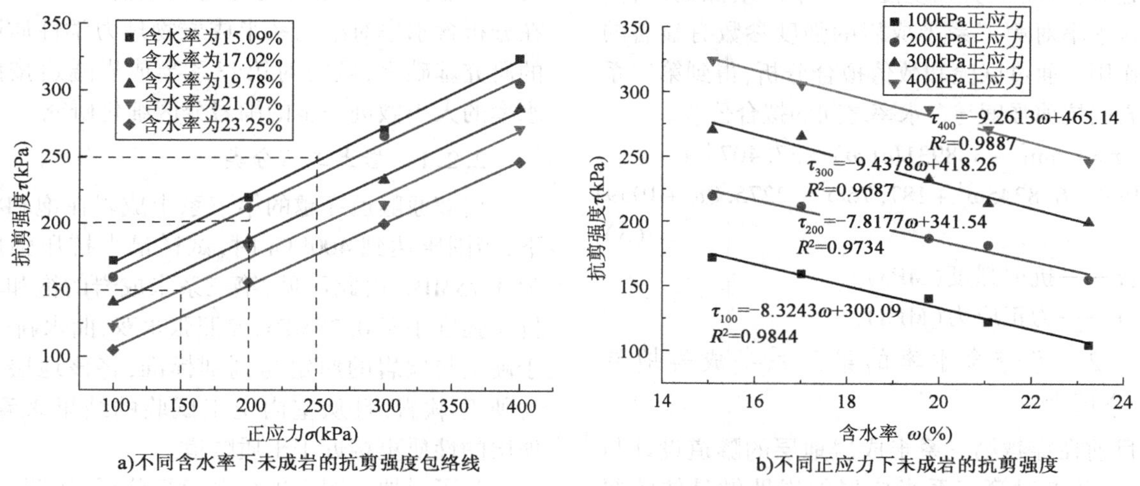

a)不同含水率下未成岩的抗剪强度包络线　　b)不同正应力下未成岩的抗剪强度

图 7　第三系半成岩的抗剪强度包络线

由图 7 和表 2 可知,第三系半成岩的抗剪强度与含水率呈负相关关系,由此得到软弱围岩的天然含水率影响着第三系未成岩地层隧道围岩的强度参数,尤其对第三系半成岩的黏聚力和内摩擦角的影响最为显著。基本上半成岩的抗剪强度和含水率及正应力之间是线性变化的关系:随着含水率的增大抗剪强度降低,且随着正应力增大,相关系数的平方是逐渐减小的。

为了进一步探究第三系半成岩在不同含水率条件下时抗剪强度指标的变化规律,根据表 2 所得试验数据,分别绘制含水率 ω 与黏聚力 c 及内摩擦角 φ 的变化曲线图,如图 8 所示。

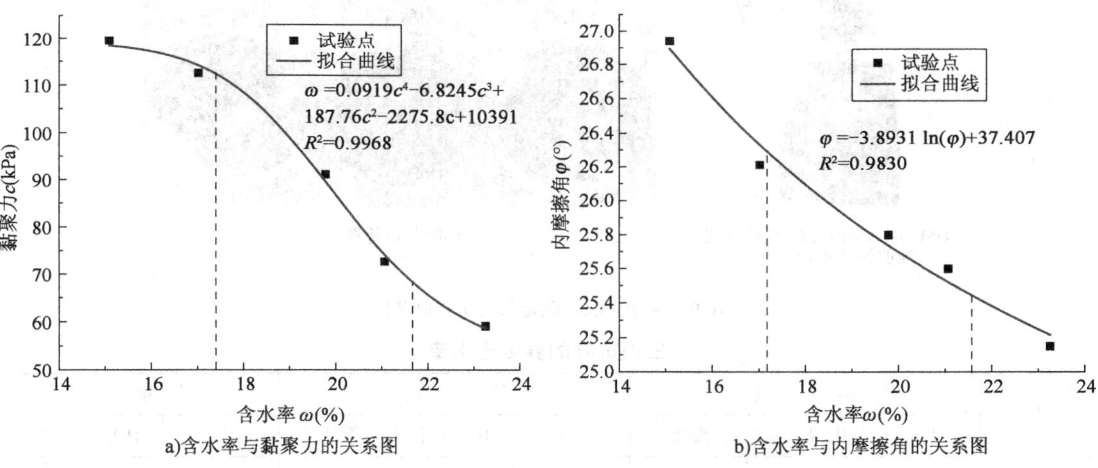

a)含水率与黏聚力的关系图　　b)含水率与内摩擦角的关系图

图 8　含水率与抗剪强度指标拟合曲线图

分析图 5 可以发现,随着含水率的增大第三系半成岩的黏聚力值明显下降,当含水率由 15.09% 增大为 23.25% 时,黏聚力从 119.54kPa 降低到 59.14kPa,下降达到 50.53%。但是随着含水率由 15.09% 增大为 23.25% 时,内摩擦角基本上都在 25°~27°范围内,下降只有 6.64%,并没有明显的变化,所以含水量对内摩擦角影响较小。

含水率与黏聚力的变化用多项式函数拟合,拟合公式见式(1)。

$$c = 0.0919\omega^4 - 6.8245\omega^3 + 187.76\omega^2 - 2275.8\omega + 10391 \tag{1}$$

式中:ω——含水率;

c——黏聚力(MPa)。

含水率与内摩擦角的变化用对数函数拟合,拟合公式见式(2)。

$$\varphi = -3.3981\ln(\omega) + 37.407 \tag{2}$$

式中:φ——内摩擦角(°)。

综上所述,第三系半成岩的黏聚力随含水率的增加而下降,内摩擦角也具有随含水率的增加而下降的趋势,从而抗剪强度随含水率的增加而降低,说明含水率对第三系半成岩的强度参数有显著的弱化作用。通过试验和数值拟合分析,得到第三系半成岩的抗剪强度与含水率之间的拟合公式。

$$\tau = \sigma \tan[-3.8931ln(\omega) + 37.407] + 0.0919\omega^4 - 6.8245\omega^3 + 187.76\omega^2 - 2275.8\omega + 10391 \quad (3)$$

式中:τ——抗剪强度(MPa);

σ——为正应力(MPa)。

2.2　考虑含水率的第三系半成岩地层围岩分区

目前在穿越第三系半成岩地层的隧道设计与施工中,并未对第三系半成岩的岩性做具体的厘定与判别,围岩分级均是笼统的将其归为Ⅴ级围岩,从室内土工试验结果来看,含水率对第三系半成岩的强度有显著的软化作用,加之开挖现场地下水引起的一系列隧道灾害,可以发现这种笼统的分级显然是不能满足现场施工需要的。所以,在分析含水率对第三系半成岩物理力学性质影响的研究基础上,亟需对第三系半成岩隧道按照含水率的大小做进一步的围岩分区细化研究。

2.2.1　岩土工程分类

白鹿原隧道穿越的第三系半成岩在饱和状态下,当围压达到400kPa时,试样最大抗压强度仅为0.75MPa,由此可见,第三系未成岩的饱和单轴抗压强度小于0.75MPa,参照张永双、曲永新[17]关于硬土与软岩的厘定与判别标准,将该地层定义为硬土-软岩,且从室内土工试验的结果来看,该地层的性质更接近于土质隧道。

为了对地层围岩进行自稳行分析,按照《公路土工试验规程》进行液塑性试验,液塑限联合测定仪与试样制备见图9。

通过液塑限联合测定仪测定三组不同试样的界限含水率,见表3。

a)SLB-1A型应力应变控制式三轴剪切渗透仪

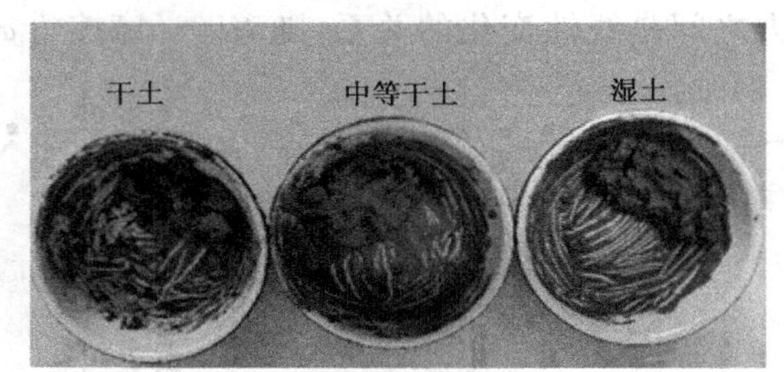

b)制备试样图

图9　液塑限联合测定仪与试样制备图

三组试样的界限含水率　　表3

项目	第一组			第二组			第三组		
	干土	中等干土	湿土	干土	中等干土	湿土	干土	中等干土	湿土
锥入深度(mm)	6.01	10.06	19.99	5.94	9.60	20.07	6.51	11.25	20.05
含水率(%)	31.37	39.72	48.29	35.59	40.77	49.20	36.79	42.16	51.55
塑限(%)	27.69			27.80			24.40		
液限(%)	45.80			48.70			49.50		
塑性指数(%)	18.11			20.90			25.10		
液性指数	-0.21			-0.18			-0.02		

《工程地质手册》中规定塑性指数大于10%且液限小于50%时土为低液限黏土,王明年等[18]认为黏质土液性指数小于0时为坚硬土,由表3可知,该第三系半成岩地层围岩为低液限黏土,且为硬土。

2.2.2　不同围岩含水率分区

土质隧道围岩亚分级已经在我国取得了一定的研究成果,王明年、王玉锁等[19-22]认为土质隧道黏聚力、内摩擦系数与围岩的稳定性有直接的影响,确立了土的抗剪强度指标与内摩擦系数作为围岩亚分级的直接指标；张威[23]、孙长升[24]、周平[25]、杜宇翔[26]等发现随着含水率的增加，昔格达地层围岩抗剪强度降低，并考虑含水率基于围岩物理力学性质建立昔格达地层围岩亚分级标准；吕城等[27]通过黄土的物理力学参数建立了在不同含水率条件下的黄土隧道围岩分区标准。

以上研究表明，围岩在不同含水率条件下，土质隧道的围岩进一步分区的指标有黏聚力 c、内摩擦角 φ、内摩擦系数 $\tan\varphi$。为了得到第三系半成岩地层Ⅴ级围岩基于含水率下的进一步分区标准，由表2得到含水率与抗剪强度指标（黏聚力、内摩擦角）及内摩擦系数之间的变化曲线，如图10所示。

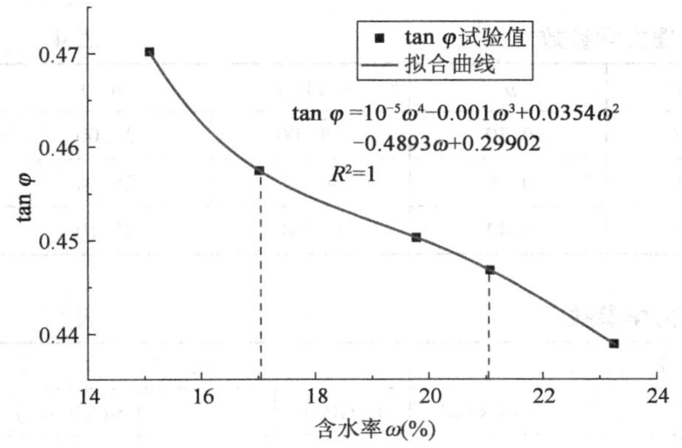

图10　含水率与内摩擦系数关系图

纵观图8a）可以发现含水率在17.3%之前黏聚力随着含水率的增加黏聚力下降不明显，之后迅速降低；含水率在21.8%之后随着含水率的增加，黏聚力下降趋势变缓。从图8b）可以发现含水率在17.1%之前内摩擦角随着含水率的增加黏聚力下降明显，17.1%之后变缓，且含水率在21.7%之后下降速率又有一定程度上的减小。

由图10可得，内摩擦系数随含水率的变化呈座椅状且存在拐点。当含水率低于17%时，随含水率的增大内摩擦系数下降的速度快；当含水率在17%～21.5%之间时，内摩擦系数的变化很小，几乎处于平稳状态；当含水率超过21.5%时，内摩擦系数又恢复下降的趋势。总的来说，含水率低于17%和超过21.5%对第三系半成岩内摩擦系数影响较为明显。

在借助上述含水率对围岩抗剪强度指标和内摩擦系数影响规律的研究基础上，按照含水率的不同，将第三系半成岩地层公路隧道Ⅴ级围岩进一步分为三个区段，分别为含水率小于17%、17%～22%、大于22%。围岩分级包括设计阶段与施工阶段的围岩分级，设计阶段的围岩分级决定隧道开挖方法、辅助施工方法与支护结构参数，施工阶段受开挖扰动后地下水渗流条件发生改变时，根据现场实时监测的隧道围岩含水率对设计阶段的围岩分级做进一步细化，不同围岩含水率采取针对性的施工控制措施，防止含水率过高导致隧道失稳坍塌，达到提前预警与安全控制的目的，保障隧道安全且经济地穿越第三系未成岩地层。为了分析不同围岩含水率条件下的含水率对第三系半成岩地层公路隧道稳定性的影响规律，本文依据《西安外环高速公路南段白鹿原隧道设计附图》进一步对设计方案与现场施工进行有限元模拟。

3　含水率对隧道稳定性影响的数值分析研究

3.1　计算模型建立

本文计算模型依据《西安外环高速公路南段白鹿原隧道设计附图》中的设计方案与现场施工进行建立，隧道跨高分别是18.7m和12.7m。根据圣维南原理，为减小模型的边界效应，计算模型的边界取开挖洞径的3～5倍，故本次模型的左右边界均取距隧道侧面60m，下边界取距隧道底部40m，上边界按隧道断面实际埋深取值，左右侧边界施加水平方向约束，底部施加垂直方向约束。本次模拟视围岩为弹塑性材料，服从摩尔库伦屈服准则，涉及的支护形式包括锁脚锚杆、初期支护喷射混凝土及钢拱架、临时支护喷射混凝土与钢拱架及二次衬砌钢筋混凝土。各支护结构的数值实现方法为：锁脚锚杆为弹性的植入式桁架，钢架等效折算进喷射混凝土，喷射混凝土属性为梁单元，临时支护的钢架和混凝土以及二次衬砌钢筋和混凝土同理进行等效，视为一种均质材料。计算模型如图11所示。

从图11：①先导上台阶开挖并及时支护；②先导中台阶开挖并及时支护；③先导下台阶开挖并及时支护；④先导仰拱开挖并及时支护；⑤后导上台阶开挖并及时支护；⑥后导中台阶开挖并及时支护；⑦后导下台阶开挖并及时支护；⑧后导仰拱开挖并及时支护；⑨拆除临时支护；⑩施作二次衬砌。

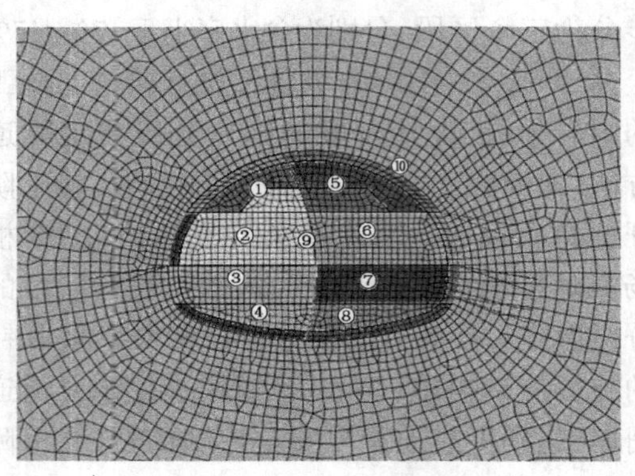

图11 隧道施工阶段模拟图

3.2 计算参数

根据上文中第三系半成岩地层的室内土工试验,本文按照围岩亚分级的结果模拟三种工况,本次模拟选择的围岩物理力学参数见表4,衬砌结构支护参数按照实际依托工程选取,具体物理力学参数见表5。

3.3 含水率对隧道隧道稳定性的影响

3.3.1 尖点突变理论

突变理论首先由 Thom(1972 年)提出,从分叉理论和奇异性理论出发,在岩土工程领域用于分析结构稳定性[28-29]。隧道开挖过程中,围岩变形具有非连续性、非均匀性、非线性的特点,因此用突变过程去分析隧道稳定性[30-33]。

各工况下的围岩物理力学参数 表4

工况	含水率 ω(%)	γ(kN/m³)	E(MPa)	μ	c(kPa)	φ(°)
工况一	小于17	19.00	141.03	0.30	120.00	27.00
工况二	17~22	17.50	97.32	0.36	90.00	25.80
工况三	23(饱和状态)	16.00	63.10	0.42	60.00	25.10

衬砌结构的物理力学参数 表5

支护材料	工况一			工况二			工况三		
	E(GPa)	μ	γ(kN/m³)	E(GPa)	μ	γ(kN/m³)	E(GPa)	μ	γ(kN/m³)
喷射混凝土-钢架	3.44	0.22	23.77	3.44	0.22	23.77	3.44	0.22	23.77
锁脚锚杆	22.00	0.30	78.50	22.00	0.30	78.50	22.00	0.30	78.50
临时支撑	3.54	0.22	24.03	3.54	0.22	24.03	3.54	0.22	24.03
二次衬砌	31.50	0.20	23.50	31.50	0.20	23.50	31.50	0.20	23.50

尖点突变模型是目前7种初等突变模型中应用最广泛的一种[34],势函数 $V(x)$ 标准形式见式(4),突变流形方程见式(5)。

$$V(x)=x^4+\mu x^2+vx \tag{4}$$

$$V'(x)=4x^3+2\mu x+v \tag{5}$$

式中:x——状态变量;

μ、v——控制变量。

定义第 k 步开挖隧道关键点位移向量 $D(k)$ 为:

$$D(k)=\sqrt{\sum_{i=0}^{n}(\Delta k_{ix}^2+\Delta k_{iz}^2)} \tag{6}$$

式中:k——开挖步骤;

Δk_{ix}——i 步开挖下的水平位移;

Δk_{iy}——i 步开挖下的竖向位移。

将计算所得位移向量 $D(k)$ 进行4次多项式拟合,构建变形的四次多项式函数:

$$D=V(k)=a_0+a_1k+a_2k^2+a_3k^3+a_4k^4 \tag{7}$$

根据尖点突变理论的基本原理,对变形函数采用契尔恩豪森变换构建标准势函数,从而得到尖点突变模型标准形式。

$$V(x)=x^4+\mu x^2+vx \tag{8}$$

式中:$\mu=\frac{a_2}{a_4}-\frac{3a_2^2}{8a_4^2}$;$v=\frac{a_1}{a_4}-\frac{a_2a_2}{2a_4^2}+\frac{a_2^2}{8a_4^2}$。

依据尖点突变模型的失稳判据原理,可得到判断岩体演化状态与临界状态的突变特征值 Δ:

$$\Delta=8\mu^3+27v \tag{9}$$

当 $\Delta>0$ 时,围岩系统为稳定状态;当 $\Delta=0$ 时,围岩系统为临界平衡状态;当 $\Delta<0$ 时,围岩系统为失稳状态。由文献[35]可知,Δ 值大于0时,其值越大围岩稳定性越好,反之越差。

3.3.2 基于尖点突变理论的稳定性分析

数值模拟开挖施工完毕后,各工况下的隧道竖向位移见图12所示。

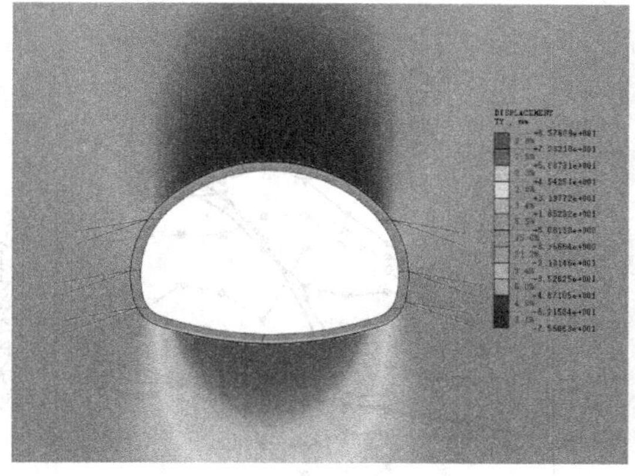

a)工况一

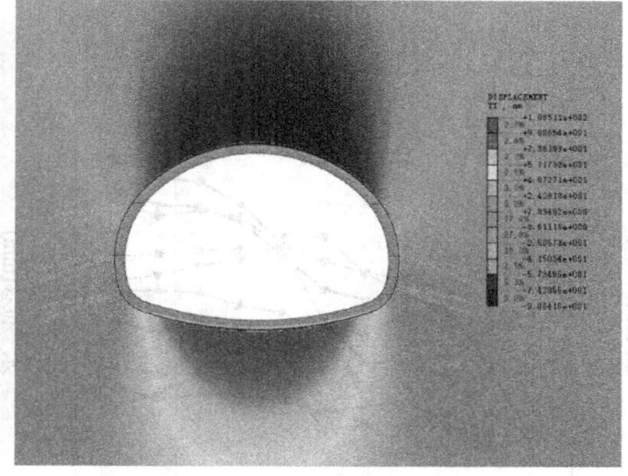

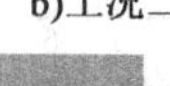

b)工况二

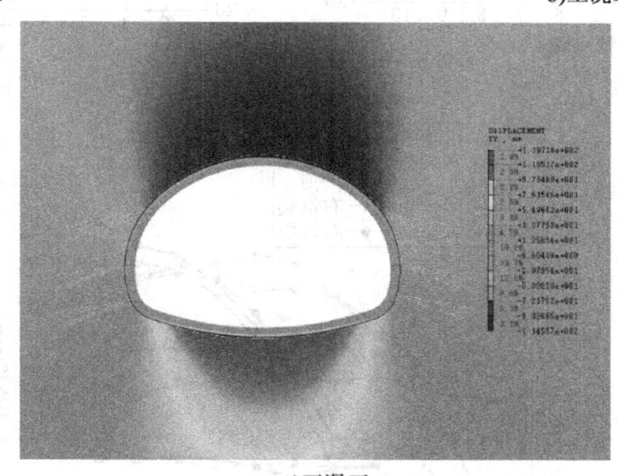

c)工况三

图12　各工况下竖向位移云图

从图12可以看出：各工况下，竖向位移云图均呈现对称分布，除隧道仰拱位置向上隆起，其余位置均产生向下的竖向沉降，最大沉降位置发生在拱顶，工况一拱顶沉降为75.6mm，工况二较工况一增加了20.1%，工况三较工况一增加了51.6%，说明随着含水率的增大最终沉降值也增加。

提取数值计算的各节点位移，得到各工况下的变形特征曲线，见图13，计算得到各开挖步的突变特征值，见表6。

由图13可以看出，各工况下除拱顶外隧道先导洞的竖向沉降始终大于后导洞，后导洞未开挖前隧道水平位移大于竖向沉降，后导洞开挖后隧道竖向沉降变形速率急剧增加，最终沉降值大于水平位移。工况一隧道先导洞的水平位移始终大于后导洞，工况二与工况三隧道后导洞的水平位移大于先导洞，说明第三系半成岩地层隧道围岩随着含水率的增加导致后导洞的水平位移从小于先导洞逐渐过渡为大于先导洞。另外，仰拱施工完成后，隧道收敛基本稳定，竖向沉降仍在增大，应进行反压回填处理，直至隧道变形稳定。

从表6可知，工况一与工况二各开挖步下的突变特征值均大于0，说明当第三系半成岩地层围岩含水率小于22%时，现场设计方案与支护结构可以保证隧道施工的稳定性，工况三在第5步到第6步或第6步到第7步开挖，尖点突变特征值发生突变，表明当第三系半成岩地层围岩含水率大于22%时，后导洞中台阶或下台阶开挖时洞周周围围岩发生突变，围岩失稳，说明含水率的增大引起了塑形区的影响范围，需要超前加固以保证隧道的稳定性。总体而言，工况三的突变特征值大于工况二，工况二大于工况一；即随着含水率的增加各开挖工序的尖点突变特征值整体呈下降趋势，说明第三系半成岩地层围岩随着含水率的增加，施工过程中隧道稳定性逐渐降低，当围岩含水率饱和时，隧道后导洞极易失稳坍塌。因此，在隧道施工过程中，应当加强对尖点特征值发生突变的位置，也就是后导洞变形的监测，及时跟进或者提高支护参数,防止变形过大导致围岩坍塌。

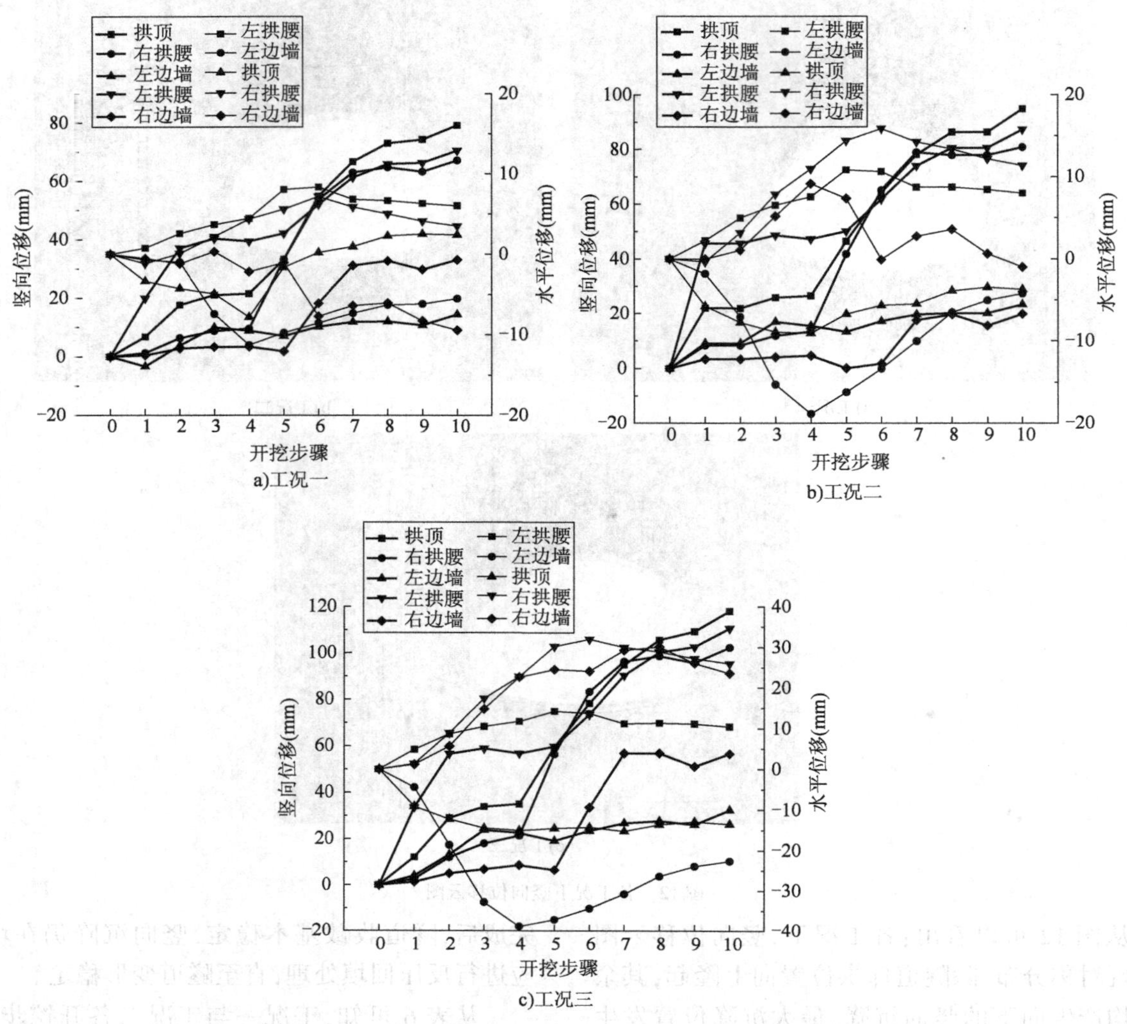

图13　隧道围岩各节点位移曲线图

不同工况下各开挖步的突变特征值计算表　　表6

工　况	类　别	计算值					
工况一	开挖步	5	6	7	8	9	10
	突变特征值	2.2×10^8	1.3×10^{12}	6.7×10^9	2.4×10^8	1.9×10^7	1.3×10^8
工况二	开挖步	5	6	7	8	9	10
	突变特征值	1.2×10^8	8.9×10^{10}	9.7×10^6	3.3×10^6	3.4×10^6	2.6×10^7
工况三	开挖步	5	6	7	8	9	10
	突变特征值	1.1×10^8	8.3×10^6	-8.6×10^{17}	2.1×10^{17}	4.6×10^6	5.7×10^6

3.3.3　含水率对隧道支护结构稳定性的影响

通过上述基于尖点突变理论对隧道施工过程中的稳定性分析,发现第三系半成岩地层围岩含水率对隧道稳定性起到至关重要的作用,所以本文对仰拱隆起与初期支护结构的安全系数进行分析,对上述分析的合理性验证。

数值模拟区段施工完毕后,各工况的轴力、弯矩云图见图14、图15所示。

分析图14、图15发现,各工况下先导洞初期支护结构的轴力明显大于后导洞,且随着含水率的增加支护结构承受的轴力与弯矩也随之增大。根据图14与图15所得初期支护结构内力,采用

《公路隧道设计细则》(JTG/T D70—2010)中的综合安全系数法,计算不同各工况的喷射混凝土抗压系数与钢拱架的抗拉系数,见图16。

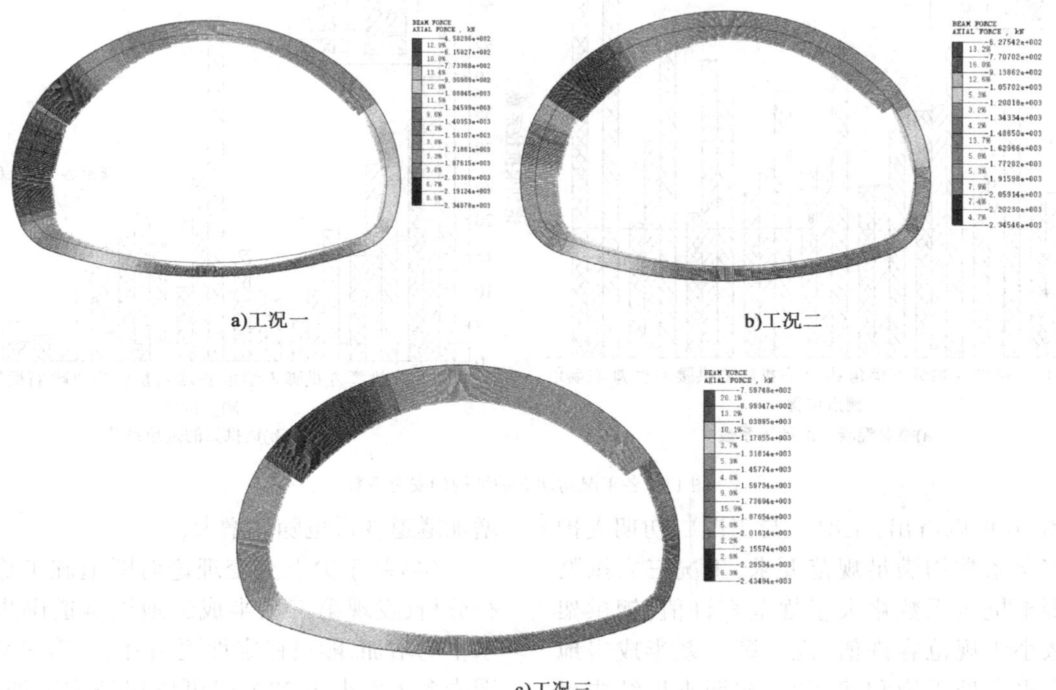

a)工况一

b)工况二

c)工况三

图14 各工况下初期支护轴力云图

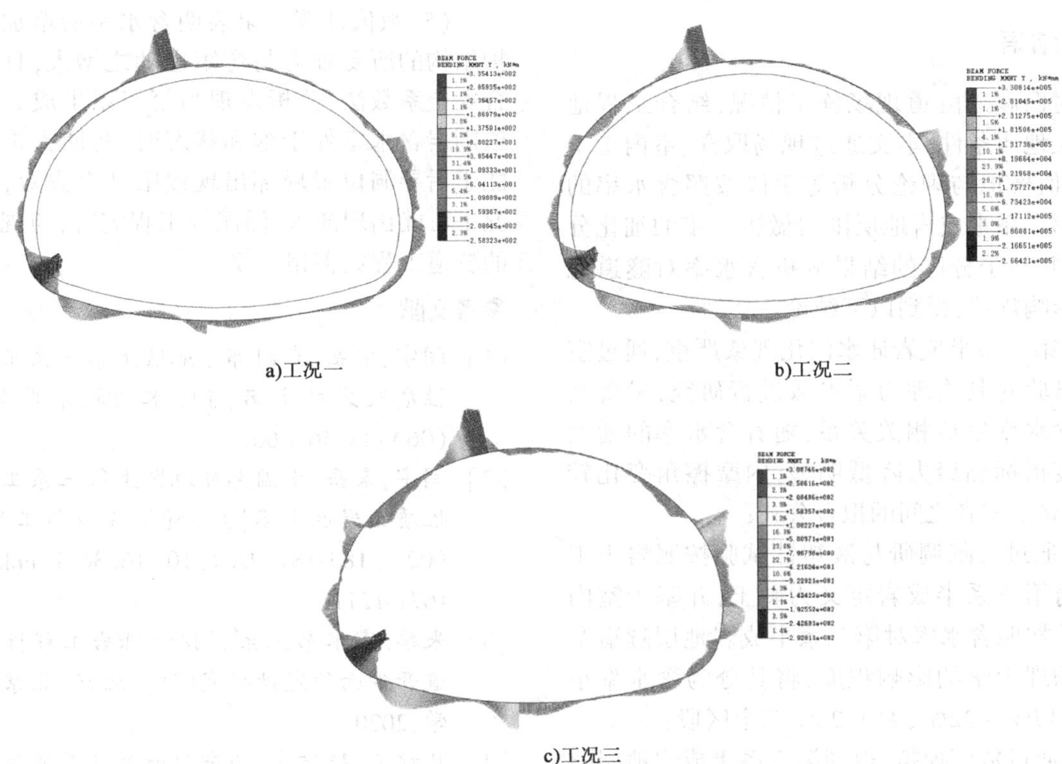

a)工况一

b)工况二

c)工况三

图15 各工况下初期支护弯矩云图

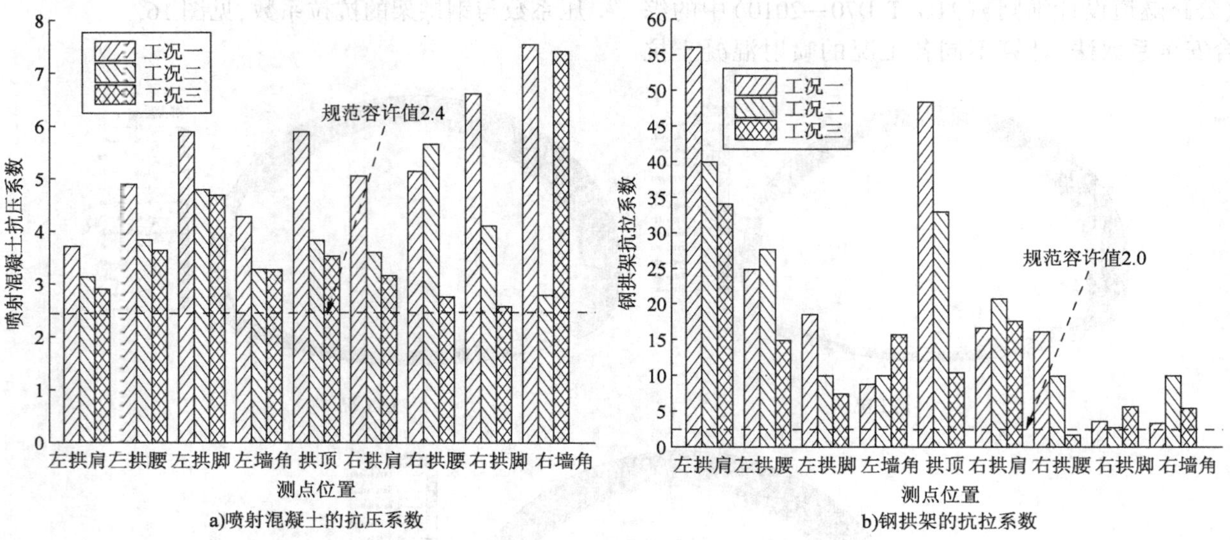

图16 各工况初期支护结构的安全系数

从图16可以看出,工况一与工况二初期支护结构的安全系数均满足规范要求,工况三右拱腰喷射混凝土抗压系数略大于规范容许值,钢拱架抗拉系数小于规范容许值,说明第三系半成岩地层围岩含水率处于饱和状态时,初期支护结构可能于后导洞位置局部出现侵限甚至失效,极端情况下可能出现涌水、涌泥等工程灾害。

4 结语

针对白鹿原隧道现场施工情况,结合工程地质与水文地质条件,本文通过现场取样、室内土工试验、数值模拟与理论分析等手段按照含水率的不同对第三系半成岩地层围岩做进一步的细化分区研究,并基于分区的结果分析含水率对隧道稳定性的影响规律,得到以下结论:

(1)第三系半成岩遇水泥化现象严重,通过室内土工试验对其物理力学参数进行研究,发现其强度与含水率呈负相关关系,随着含水率的增大抗剪强度指标黏聚力降低明显,内摩擦角变化较小,并建立了三者之间的拟合公式;

(2)通过文献调研与液塑性试验按照岩土工程分类将第三系半成岩定义为硬土,并基于室内土工试验按照含水率对第三系半成岩地层隧道V级围岩物理力学的影响程度,将其分为含水率小于17%、17%~22%、大于22%三个区段;

(3)通过数值模拟,得到第三系半成岩地层隧道各围岩含水率分区下的隧道变形曲线,发现后导洞开挖对隧道变形影响较大,且随着含水率的增加隧道变形也随之增大;

(4)基于尖点突变理论对隧道施工稳定性进行分析,发现第三系半成岩地层隧道围岩随着含水率的增加,隧道稳定性逐渐降低,第三系半成岩围岩含水率小于22%时可以保证施工的稳定性,当围岩含水率达到饱和时,隧道后导洞极易失稳坍塌;

(5)数值计算结果表明含水率的增加使得支护结构的所受轴力与弯矩也随之增大,且基于综合安全系数法,分析发现当第三系半成岩地层隧道围岩含水率处于饱和状态时,初期支护结构可能于后导洞位置局部出现侵限甚至失效,极端情况下可能出现涌水、涌泥等工程灾害,与现场实际的隧道工程灾害相一致。

参考文献

[1] 闫宇,宋岳.我国部分地区上第三系工程地质性质及岩性定名[J].水利技术监督,2007(06):43-46+66.

[2] 闫宇,宋岳.中国部分地区上第三系工程地质性质及岩性定名[J].资源环境与工程,2008(02):183-187. DOI:10.16536/j.cnki.issn.1671-1211.

[3] 朱举.富水第三系弱胶结砾岩工程性质及隧道开挖面稳定性研究[D].北京:北京交通大学,2020.

[4] 马福荣,张信贵.南宁盆地第三系泥岩物理性质与强度关系的研究[J].岩土力学,2005,26(S2):123-125.

[5] 张晓宇. 西宁地区第三系地层岩土工程特性及影响[J]. 铁道工程学报,2012,29(08):20-23.

[6] 张波. 兰州盆地第三系砂岩工程地质特性评价研究[J]. 工程地质学报,2014,22(01):166-172.

[7] 王秀英,谭忠盛,王永红,等. 兰渝铁路含水弱胶结砂岩隧道地层特性试验研究[J]. 土木工程学报,2015,48(S1):191-195.

[8] 翁东郁. 隧道穿越第三系粉质黏土工程特性及支护措施研究[J]. 铁道建筑,2014(12):51-54.

[9] 王建军. 兰渝铁路上第三系弱胶结砂岩软化与变形机理探究[J]. 工程地质学报,2013,21(05):716-721.

[10] 曹峰. 兰州第三系砂岩水稳性特征隧道施工研究[J]. 铁道工程学报,2012,29(12):21-25+31.

[11] 王庆林,刘晓翔. 桃树坪隧道、胡麻岭隧道第三系富水粉细砂层围岩含水率与稳定性关系浅析[J]. 现代隧道技术,2012,49(04):1-5+16.

[12] 甄秉国. 兰渝线桃树坪隧道区域上第三系砂岩工程特性分析[J]. 铁道建筑,2013(05):55-57.

[13] 李乐. 滇中第三系软岩工程地质特性及对隧洞工程的影响[D]. 成都:成都理工大学,2014.

[14] 黄明. 含水泥质粉砂岩蠕变特性及其在软岩隧道稳定性分析中的应用研究[D]. 重庆:重庆大学,2010.

[15] 毛荣吉. 流固耦合作用下第三系半成岩地层的隧道稳定性分析[D]. 北京:北京交通大学,2016.

[16] 陈书玄. 第三系泥岩蠕变特性及隧道长期稳定性研究[D]. 北京:北京交通大学,2018.

[17] 张永双,曲永新. 硬土—软岩的厘定及其判别分类[J]. 地质科技情报,2000(01):77-80.

[18] 王明年,魏龙海,李海军,等. 公路隧道围岩亚级物理力学参数研究[J]. 岩石力学与工程学报,2008(11):2252-2259.

[19] 王玉锁,王明年,陈炜韬,等. 砂土质隧道围岩内摩擦系数的试验研究[J]. 岩土力学,2008(03):741-746.

[20] 王玉锁,陈炜韬,王明年. 砂土质隧道围岩黏聚力影响因素的试验研究[J]. 水文地质工程地质,2006(06):48-51.

[21] 王玉锁. 砂质土隧道围岩力学参数及分级方法研究[D]. 成都:西南交通大学,2008.

[22] 王明年,王玉锁,李玉文. 用 SBQ 值作为砂类土质隧道围岩分级基准的构想[J]. 岩土力学,2008,29(12):3235-3240.

[23] 张威,徐则民,刘文连,等. 含水率对西昌昔格达组黏土岩抗剪强度的影响研究[J]. 工程勘察,2011,39(05):1-5.

[24] 孙长升. 含水率对昔格达地层隧道围岩稳定性影响及控制技术研究[D]. 西南交通大学,2015.

[25] 周平,王志杰,徐海岩,等. 考虑含水率的昔格达地层隧道围岩稳定及亚级分级研究[J]. 土木工程学报,2017,50(12):97-110.

[26] 杜宇翔,盛谦,王帅,等. 昔格达组半成岩微观结构与力学性质研究[J]. 岩土力学,2020,41(04):1247-1258+1269.

[27] 吕城. 不同含水率分区的深埋黄土隧道围岩压力与施工关键技术研究[D]. 成都:西南交通大学,2020.

[28] 凌复华. 突变理论及其应用[M]. 上海:上海交通大学出版社,1987.

[29] 付成华,陈胜宏. 基于突变理论的地下工程洞室围岩失稳判据研究[J]. 岩土力学,2008(01):167-172.

[30] 叶继昭. 基于突变理论的顺层偏压隧道围岩稳定性研究[D]. 重庆:重庆交通大学,2019.

[31] 林明才. 基于隧道断面相对变形率判定围岩稳定性研究[D]. 成都:西南交通大学,2019.

[32] 林明才,蒋雅君,杨其新,等. 基于隧道断面相对变形率判定围岩稳定性的研究[J]. 地下空间与工程学报,2021,17(03):872-882+952.

[33] 张艺腾,孙星亮,江勇涛,等. V级围岩隧道不同施工阶段拱顶极限位移研究[J]. 现代隧道技术,2020,57(04):91-97.

[34] 许传华. 岩体破坏的非线性理论研究及应用[D]. 南京:河海大学,2004.
[35] 赵延林,吴启红,王卫军,等. 基于突变理论的采空区重叠顶板稳定性强度折减法及应用[J]. 岩石力学与工程学报, 2010, 29(07):1424-1434.

侧伏充填型溶洞对隧道稳定性的影响研究

欧运起* 　晏长根　魏研博
(长安大学公路学院)

摘　要　岩溶区隧道施工产生的各种工程地质灾害严重制约着我国交通基础设施的发展。针对峨汉高速庙子坪隧道施工可能引发的围岩稳定性问题,本文采用Flac3D软件模拟了侧伏充填型溶洞对隧道围岩变形、应力以及衬砌安全系数的变化情况,并对此进行了分析。结果表明:隧道围岩变形和应力随溶洞与隧道距离的减小而增加,衬砌安全系数则随之减小;间距比 $\lambda_l>1$,即隧道和溶洞的净间距超过隧道跨径时,溶洞对隧道稳定性影响很小,可不予考虑;$\lambda_l<0.33$ 时,对围岩位移和应力影响显著,围岩应力容易超过强度极限值,使得衬砌结构安全性显著降低。施工时应减少围岩扰动,对溶洞进行预处理,并对溶洞区间段的隧道衬砌采取加固措施,增加初支强度,以保障安全施工。

关键词　隧道工程　侧伏充填型溶洞　围岩稳定性　数值模拟

0　引言

我国是世界上岩溶分布最广泛、最发育的国家之一,可溶岩层的分布面积约占国土面积的1/3[1]。岩溶区水岩作用强烈,岩石强度低、极不稳定,容易发生不良地质灾害[2]。工程经验表明,岩溶区隧道修建经常会遇到溶洞、暗河等不良地质条件,极易引发突水、突泥、塌方等工程灾害[3]。岩溶的广泛分布及其孕育的潜在工程地质灾害给隧道建设带来了巨大的挑战,严重制约着我国交通基础设施的建设与发展。因此,如何保证岩溶区隧道的安全施工,已经成为目前岩石力学领域亟待解决的关键问题[4]。

目前,已经有不少专家学者就岩溶对隧道稳定性的影响进行了分析研究。陈禹成等[2]基于COMSOL Mutiphysics多场耦合数值模拟软件分析了多因素条件下充填型隐伏溶洞对隧道围岩稳定性的影响。刘道炎等[5]利用MIDAS GTS软件分析了定间距条件下溶洞填充对隧道稳定性的影响,认为下卧溶洞的填充状态对隧道变形影响很小,填充溶洞无法抑制隧道结构的变形。张良等[6]通过MIDAS GTS数值模拟方法研究了不同洞径和间距条件下顶部溶洞引起的围岩位移、应力以及围岩塑性区的变化情况。宋战平等[7]通过数值模拟和现场原位试验研究了不同位置及尺度的隐伏溶洞对隧道围岩位移变化特征的影响规律。谭代明等[8]通过FLAC^{3D}软件和现场监测手段研究了侧伏溶洞隧道的位移场、应力场以及塑性区的分布情况,塑性区集中于溶洞和隧道之间的围岩,且该处围岩变形大、应力集中,容易发生破坏。

虽然关于溶洞对隧道稳定性影响的研究较多,但到目前为止,关于侧伏充填型溶洞对隧道稳定性的研究还不多,尤其是从围岩位移、围岩应力以及衬砌安全系数角度分析溶洞对隧道稳定性的影响。本文以庙子坪隧道地质预报中揭示的侧伏充填型溶洞为分析对象,采用数值模拟方法研究侧伏充填型溶洞对隧道稳定性的影响规律,研究对指导隧道安全施工、预防工程灾害具有重要意义。

1　工程概况及数值模型

1.1　工程概况

庙子坪隧道是峨眉至汉源高速公路的控制性工程,长度约3.1km,最大埋深约350m。隧址区岩溶发育强烈,形态以漏斗、落水洞、溶洞及溶蚀沟槽为主，复杂的岩溶地质环境成为制约全线工程建设的关键因素。地层岩性主要为中风化泥灰岩，局部夹灰质白云岩，隧道地质纵断面如图1所示。隧址区地表水系主要为徐沟和龙池河的支流及地表冲沟，多呈树枝状分布，补给源为大气降水；地下水类型主要由岩溶水、基岩裂隙水和松散堆积层孔隙水构成。

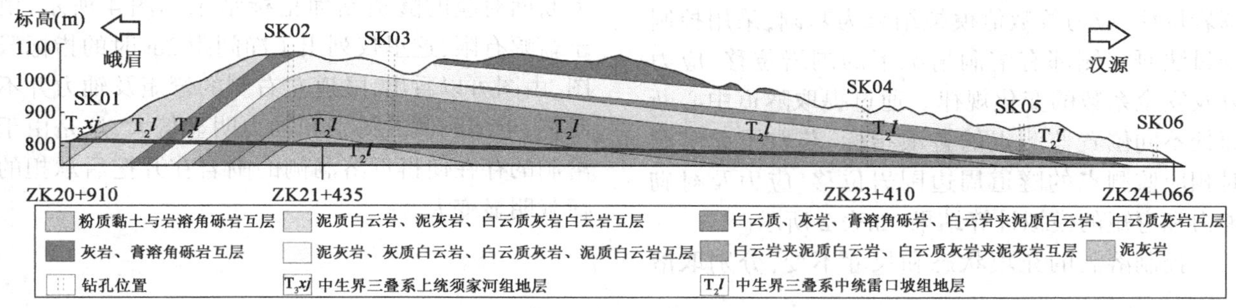

图1 隧道地质纵断面图

1.2 数值模型与参数

由设计资料可知，隧道开挖高度10.4m，宽度11.78m，采用上下台阶法开挖，现场溶洞段隧道埋深约70m左右。为消除边界效应影响，模型边界设定为水平方向 $-30 < x < 30$m，竖直方向 $-30 < z < 70$m，纵向 $0 < y < 8$m。根据现场揭露出溶洞的实际特征，溶洞简化成半径约为3m、高度为14m的圆柱体，走向与隧道纵轴向垂直，计算模型见图2。先在MIDAS软件中建立隧道和溶洞模型，再导入 $FLAC^{3D}$ 软件中采用命令流控制数值模拟全过程。对模型施加如下边界约束条件：顶部为自由表面，只承受围岩自重作用，底部边界施加竖直方向约束，两侧边界施加水平方向约束。

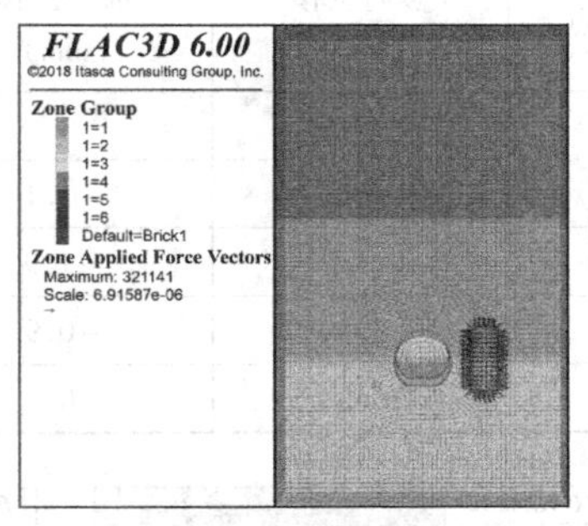

图2 计算模型示意图

围岩采用Mohr-Coulomb理想弹塑性模型，开挖和支护分别采用Null模型和Shell结构单元来模拟。采用适当提高围岩加固区的黏聚力和弹性模量来等效模拟超前支护和注浆加固等措施，模型参数如表1所示。

数值模型参数取值表 表1

材料类型	重度 γ (kN/m³)	泊松比 ν	体积模 K (GPa)	剪切模量 G (GPa)	内摩擦角 φ (°)	黏聚力 c (MPa)
围岩	21	0.32	1.67	0.682	30	0.2
加固区	22	0.32	2.17	0.88	33	0.26
初支	25	0.2	13.9	10.42		

本文仅考虑侧伏溶洞在不同距离时，隧道断面不同位置监测点围岩的位移、应力以及衬砌安全系数的变化规律，隧道断面监测点布置如图3所示。溶腔充填物多为碎石及软塑状软黏土，依据现场溶洞内水压情况及溶腔充填物状态，采用对溶洞内壁施加0.1MPa环向均布压力来模拟充填型溶洞，并在此基础上研究溶腔充填物对隧道稳定性的影响。

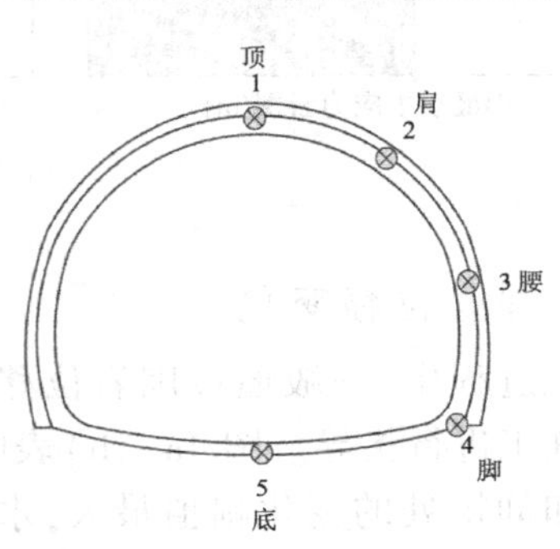

图3 隧道断面监测点布设示意图

2　结果分析

2.1　初步数值模拟

在同等加固支护条件下,以无溶洞情况下的围岩位移、应力等数值模拟结果为基础,采用控制变量法研究侧部有溶洞情况下的围岩位移、应力以及安全系数的变化规律。通过提取隧道中心断面处不同位置监测点的各项指标,获取了无溶洞时相应监测点的隧道周边围岩位移、应力及衬砌轴力和弯矩的模拟计算结果,如表2所示。

控制溶洞的充填状态和尺寸不变,分别取溶洞与隧道的净间距为2m、4m、6m、8m、10m、12m。定义间径比 λ_i 表示为溶洞与隧道之间的净间距与隧道洞径的比值,位移比和应力比为有溶洞与无溶洞时对应指标的比值。有溶洞情况下溶洞最大断面对应的隧道断面指标结果如图4所示,由于篇幅有限,这里仅列出了净间距2m时的指标云图,由图可以看出,隧道左右侧的弯矩及轴力并不对称,近溶洞侧的衬砌和轴力明显偏大,这是由于溶洞的存在使得近溶洞侧的围岩在开挖后承担的荷载明显变大。

无溶洞时各监测点计算结果　　表2

监测点	竖向位移(mm)	水平位移(mm)	最大主应力(kPa)	最小主应力(kPa)	衬砌轴力(kN)	衬砌弯矩(kN. m)
拱顶	-7.9	0	-184	-1006	-749	1.154
右拱肩	-6.7	-1.1	-207	-1465	-1017	0.746
右拱腰	-1.7	-1.9	-306	-1778	-1198	3.067
右拱脚	4.8	-0.9	-234	-1506	-680	-15.52
拱底	6.5	0	-49	-461.63	-560	0.683

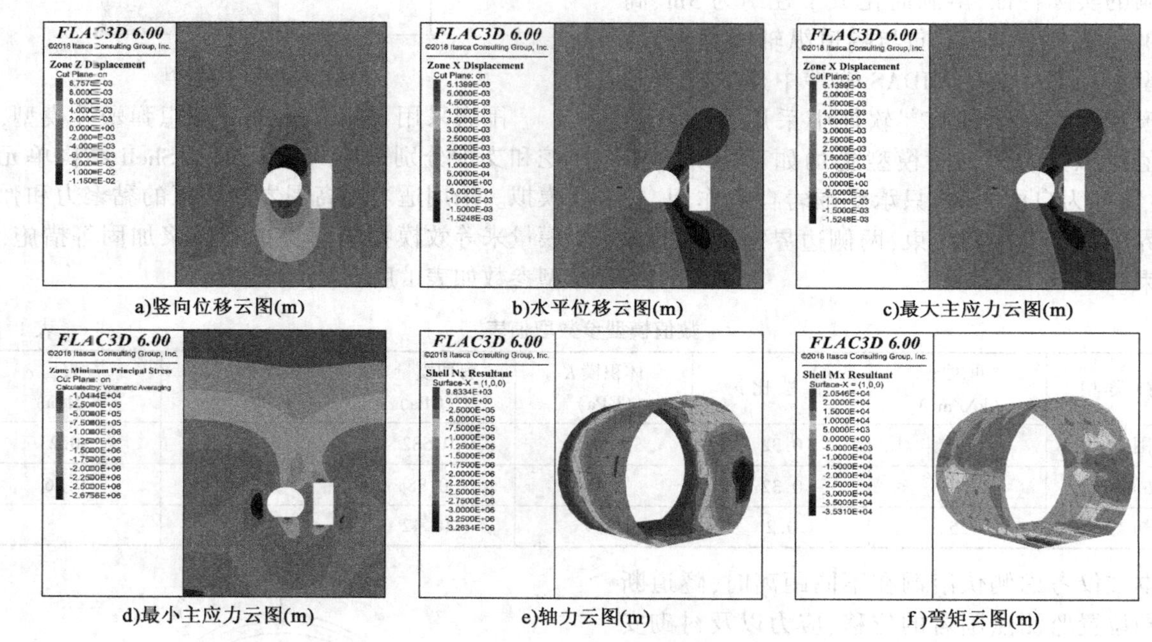

a)竖向位移云图(m)　b)水平位移云图(m)　c)最大主应力云图(m)

d)最小主应力云图(m)　e)轴力云图(m)　f)弯矩云图(m)

图4　净间距为2m时的指标云图

2.2　围岩位移变化

在施工过程中,一般通过围岩位移的动态监测对现场施工进行指导。图4a)、b)表明,竖直位移在拱顶和仰拱处的变化幅值最大,水平位移变化的最大幅值在左右拱腰处,位移的变化不再像无溶洞时呈左右对称分布,整体偏向有溶洞侧。因此,本文主要研究溶洞最大断面处对应的隧道断面的拱顶和仰拱的竖直位移以及拱腰的水平位移。图5表示各个工况下围岩位移变化情况。

当溶洞与隧道净间距为2m时,相比无溶洞时拱顶沉降增加 44.5%；仰拱隆起增加 28%；近溶洞侧拱腰水平位移增加 20%；远溶洞侧拱腰水平位移增加 13%，近溶洞侧拱腰位移增加量明显大于远溶洞侧的位移增加量。这是由于隧道开挖后产生应力重分布，隧道与溶洞之间的岩体产生应力集中现象，所以溶洞侧拱腰的水平位移要更大。随着净间距的增大，左右拱腰水平位移的差值逐渐变小，溶洞对隧道变形的影响越来越小；尤其是净间距超过隧道跨径时，即间径比 $\lambda_l>1$ 时，侧伏充填型溶洞对围岩位移的影响逐渐减小并趋向于无溶洞时的位移状态，此时可忽略溶洞的影响。

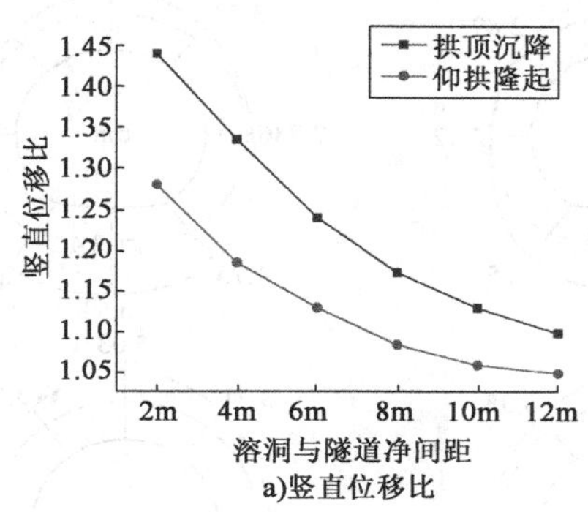

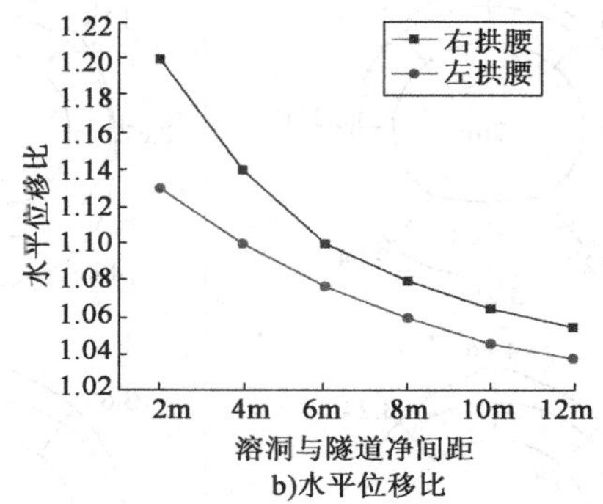

图 5　不同间距时的围岩位移

2.3　围岩应力分析

围岩和初期支护密切接触，围岩的应力变化情况反映了支护结构的受力状态。由于近溶洞侧拱腰属于高应力区也是最危险截面，因此本文分析了侧伏充填型溶洞对拱腰处围岩应力的影响。这里用应力比来表示围岩应力的变化情况，图 6 表示各个工况下拱腰处围岩应力的变化情况。对比各个工况可以发现，应力比随净间距增大而逐渐减小，且近溶洞侧拱腰的围岩应力受溶洞的影响显著，增加值较大。充填型溶洞与隧道净距离为 2m 时，对拱腰处围岩应力的影响最显著，最大主应力提高 75.7%，最小主应力提高 49%；不过随着净间距的增加，溶洞的存在对围岩应力的影响越来越小，当净间距超过隧道跨径，间径比 $\lambda_l>1$ 时，应力的变化量相对较小，趋近于无溶洞时。这是因为溶洞的存在相当于增大隧道在水平方向上的跨度，使得隧道围岩的竖向变形增加，降低了稳定性。此外，由图可知，近溶洞侧拱腰处的围岩应力要大于远溶洞侧拱腰处的围岩应力，侧部溶洞的存在使得溶洞和隧道之间的岩柱产生应力集中现象，削弱了近溶洞侧拱腰处围岩的强度和稳定性，因此近溶洞侧拱腰处的围岩应力较大。

因此，侧伏充填型溶洞与隧道净间距较小时，隧道施工要尽量减少对围岩的扰动，提前对溶洞进行预处理，并提高支护参数对溶洞段隧道进行加固处理，以防岩体失稳产生塌方或突水突泥现象。而随着溶洞与隧道之间的距离增大，隧道围岩应力趋向于无溶洞时。当溶洞与隧道之间的间径比 $\lambda_l>1$ 时，侧部溶洞的存在对隧道位移的影响微乎其微，可不考虑侧伏充填型溶洞对隧道稳定性的影响。

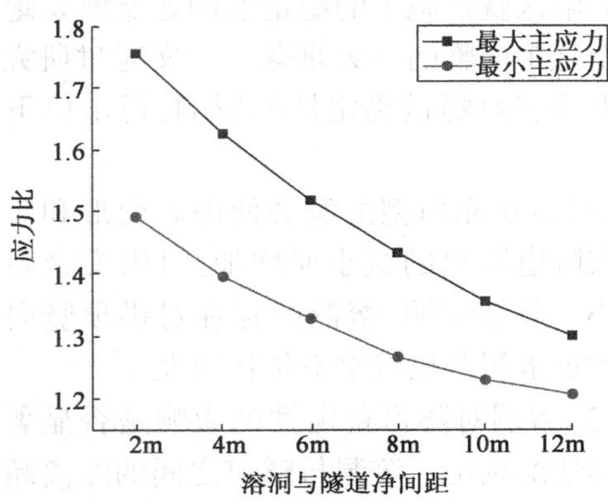

图 6　净间距和应力比关系曲线

2.4　衬砌安全系数分析

衬砌安全系数直接反映隧道结构的稳定性，由衬砌轴力、弯矩推导得出，而溶洞会对衬砌安全系数产生不利影响，通过分析不同工况下衬砌安全系数的变化情况可以评价侧伏充填型溶洞存在对衬砌结构的安全性。图 7 表示不同间距时监测点衬砌安全系数的变化情况。可以看出，隧道衬砌安全系数和溶洞与隧道之间的距离成正比，且近溶洞侧的衬砌安全系数受溶洞的影响较大。间

径比 $\lambda_l<0.33$ 时,近溶洞侧拱腰衬砌安全系数小于规范要求的安全界限值2.4,衬砌结构的安全性低;当间径比 $\lambda_l>1$ 时,隧道各监测点的安全系数就趋近于无溶洞时的状态。因此,应当关注近距离条件下溶洞侧衬砌结构的安全性。对于充填状态的溶洞,溶洞围压的变化会使围岩所承受的应力超过其强度极限值,造成围岩破坏,进一步致使初支开裂,极易发生突水突泥地质灾害,因此需要对近距离溶洞侧衬砌结构需要采取相应的加固措施,以防安全事故发生。

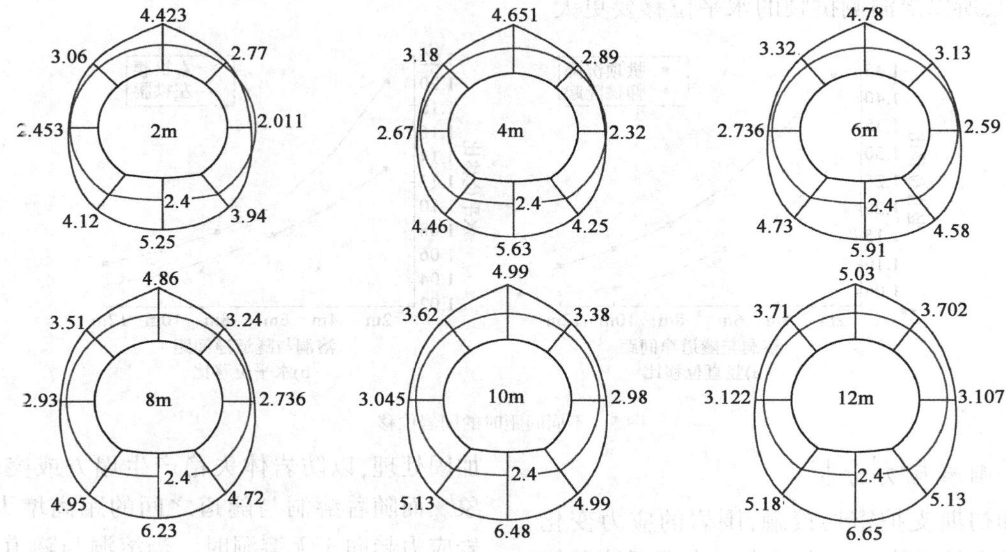

图7　不同间距时的衬砌安全系数

3　结语

岩溶区隧道施工的稳定性问题始终是地下工程安全施工面临的一大难题。本文通过研究侧伏充填型溶洞对隧道稳定性的影响,得出以下几点结论。

(1)侧伏充填型溶洞会使围岩变形和应力随溶洞与隧道距离的减小而增加,衬砌安全系数随之减小。分析表明,溶洞的存在对拱顶竖向位移影响和近溶洞侧拱腰水平位移较大。

(2)溶洞对隧道稳定性的影响是否显著应根据实际情况判定。溶洞与隧道之间的距离超过隧道的洞径($\lambda_l>1$)时,侧部溶洞的存在对隧道围岩位移和应力的影响较小,可不予考虑。而净间距较小,尤其是 $\lambda_l<0.33$ 时,溶洞对隧道围岩位移和应力影响较为显著,隧道施工应尽量减少对围岩的扰动,提前对溶洞进行适当的处理,并做好围岩加固措施,以防岩体失稳产生塌方或突水突泥现象。

(3)间径比 $\lambda_l<0.33$ 时,隧道围岩所承受的应力容易超过其强度极限值,溶洞侧的衬砌结构安全系数显著降低,很容易造成围岩破坏,致使初支开裂,甚至引发突水突泥现象,因此需要对溶洞区间段的隧道衬砌采取加固措施,增加初支强度,预防安全事故发生。

参考文献

[1] 于丽,吕城,汪主洪,等.上伏溶洞下深埋隧道塌落破坏的上限分析[J].中国公路学报,2021,34(4):209-219.

[2] 陈禹成,王朝阳,郭明,等.隐伏溶洞对隧道围岩稳定性影响规律及处治技术[J].山东大学学报(工学版),2020,50(5):33-43.

[3] 张鹏阳.上覆溶洞对隧道施工稳定性的影响及控制研究[D].西安:长安大学,2020.

[4] 李利平.高风险岩溶隧道突水灾变演化机理及其应用研究[D].济南:山东大学,2009.

[5] 刘道炎,谢建斌,黎忠,等.隐覆溶洞对地铁盾构隧道稳定性影响的数值分析[J].隧道建设(中英文),2020,40(S2):151-160.

[6] 张良,王士坤.顶部既有溶洞对隧道稳定性的影响及工程处置[J].公路交通科技(应用技术版),2020,16(7):283-286.

[7] 宋战平.隐伏溶洞对隧道围岩-支护结构稳定性的影响研究[J].岩石力学与工程学报,2006(6):1296.

[8] 谭代明,漆泰岳,莫阳春. 侧部岩溶隧道围岩稳定性数值分析与研究[J]. 岩石力学与工程学报,2009,28(S2):3497-3503.

基于时间效应的深埋隧道围岩-支护体系稳定性分析

毛 伟[1,3] 刘学军*[2,3] 如黑艳·木合买尔[1] 哈月龙[2] 努尔艾合买提江·阿布力孜[1] 姜朝腾[3]

[1. 新疆交通职业技术学院;2. 新疆建筑科学研究院(有限责任公司);
3. 新疆大学建筑工程学院]

摘 要 本文针对公路深埋软岩隧道的围岩变形特点、根据以往研究,在考虑时间效应的围岩力学参数和混凝土时间效应参数的基础上,运用 ANSYS 软件建立有限元模型,按开挖后不施加任何支护和开挖后施加锚杆、钢拱架和喷射混凝土支护两种工况进行数值分析,得到了深埋软岩隧道开挖后围岩-支护稳定性的模拟结果,分析了不同时间效应下的围岩力学性能参数和支护参数对深埋隧道软岩变形以及围岩稳定性的影响,研究结果可为后续深埋软岩隧道安全施工提供理论建议。

关键词 公路隧道 围岩稳定性 数值计算 时间效应 深埋软岩

0 引言

支护与围岩的相互作用关系是深埋隧道工程研究热点之一[1-4]。随着埋深的增加,地应力、温度以及地下水渗透压力逐渐升高,岩体变形的时间效应也将进一步显现,工程稳定性的时效性更加突出。在围岩稳定性较差的情况下,新奥法理论下形成的复合衬砌中初支结构通常采用喷锚+型钢(格栅)拱支护[5],但是何时采用何种支护仍然存在很多困惑。所以,支护形式和支护时机的选择是隧道支护结构设计的重点和难点[6]。

国内外许多学者基于收敛约束法对支护-围岩相互作用进行了系统的研究。Carranza-Torres C[7]对理想弹塑性岩体中不同组合支护形式的作用效果进行了对比分析;侯公羽等[8]结合不同屈服准则,进行理想弹塑性模型下支护与围岩相互作用的全过程分析;张常光等[9]利用应变软化模型分别分析了满足统一强度理论与 Mohr-Coulomb 屈服准则的围岩应力和位移。然而,传统的收敛约束方法在隧道设计中存在明显的局限性,当支护结构投入使用后,隧道围岩与支护特征曲线发生改变后的相交已不具有实际工程意义。具有初支作用的喷射混凝土结构,其力学性能对研究支护与围岩的相互作用具有非常重要的意义。郑颖人等[10]的研究表明,随着围岩断面的不断推进,初支结构承载力在达到极限强度前可能发生临界破坏,这与其时效性密切相关,因此前述理论未能较好地解释初支结构失效行为。目前关于支护结构与围岩相互作用的理论研究尚不完善,这也给隧道支护设计带来一定的困难。

本文基于 Mohr-Coulomb 屈服准则和应变软化本构模型,主要从塑性区面积、塑性区最大深度以及围岩应力状态方面来评价围岩的稳定性,通过模拟不同支护结构在隧道开挖后不同时间区间的稳定特征,得到不同支护结构的安全系数,最后提出相应的支护建议。

1 计算模型与基本参数

本文采用 ANSYS 建立有限元模型,用平面单元、梁单元、杆单元分别模拟围岩、喷射混凝土和钢拱架以及锚杆,锚杆、拱架与围岩共用节点,刚性接触。岩土材料使用理想弹塑性本构模型,按

1. 基金项目:中建新疆建工集团课题(6500022859700X20069);新疆维吾尔自治区重大科技专项(2018A03003-1);中建股份科技研发课题(CSCEC-2020-Z-56)。

照平面应变关联法则下的Druck-Prager屈服准则。进行全断面开挖模拟,不考虑超前小导管、钢筋网和二衬模型。建立的几何模型及有限元单元划分如图1所示。

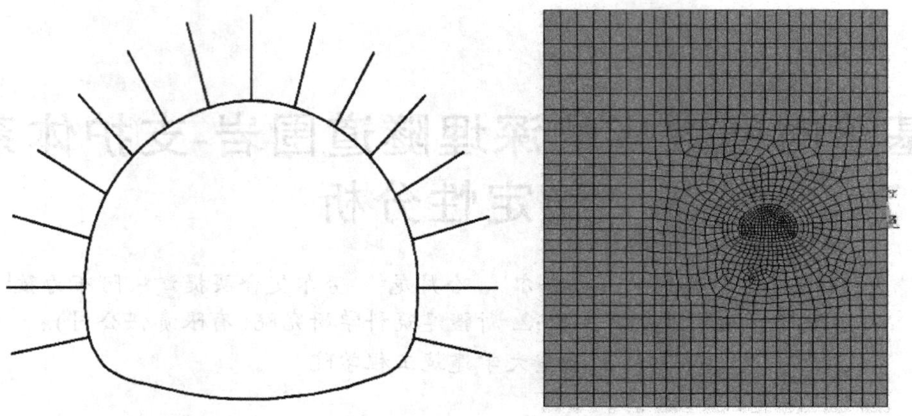

图1　隧洞锚杆及衬砌几何模型与有限元模型

按照平面应变问题考虑隧道纵向和横断面尺寸,数值计算时考虑水平构造应力,计算范围上下部及左右两侧尺寸均大于5倍洞室跨度,左侧施加水平应力场,右侧施加对称边界条件,上下部位施加重力等效的铅直应力场。构造应力的大小根据隧道中心位置的埋深以及实测数据确定,为简化计算,不考虑水平方向的应力梯度,计算施加的应力均使用均布应力。根据隧道地应力测试结果以及现场断面变形的监测数据,试验范围内各测试孔的侧压力系数均大于1,因此在计算分析时需要考虑构造应力。根据现场监测水平和拱顶的累积变形量,两者比值大概为1.1,分别试算侧压系数取1.2、1.15、1.1、1时的隧道水平和拱顶的变形量。计算发现侧压系数$\lambda=1$时,水平和拱顶的变形量比值与实测值最接近。另外,$\lambda=1$时,弹性模量为1160.08MPa,$v=0.3$,计算的水平、拱顶位移与监测数据吻合较好,故本次计算取$\lambda=1$。隧道埋深为115m,根据地应力测试结果垂直方向的应力取$\sigma_v=3.28$MPa。

2　不同时间效应的围岩-支护体系稳定性分析

模拟计算时考虑开挖后不施加任何支护和开挖后施加初支结构两种工况,不考虑围岩的应力释放率以及岩土介质的蠕变影响。

2.1　开挖不支护模拟分析

根据计算条件,隧道开挖不支护的围岩等效塑性应变如图2所示。由图可知,若不施加支护,围岩在开挖时($t=0$d)会发生大范围的塑性屈服,且塑性区的最大半径和面积均随着时间的延长持续增大,拱脚和边墙处的等效塑性应变最大,为最不利位置。

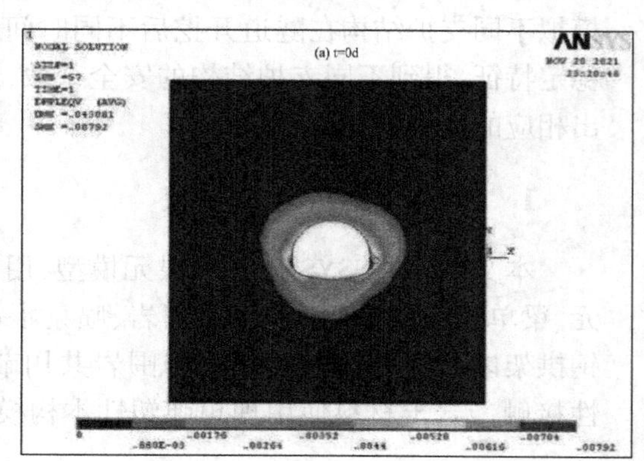

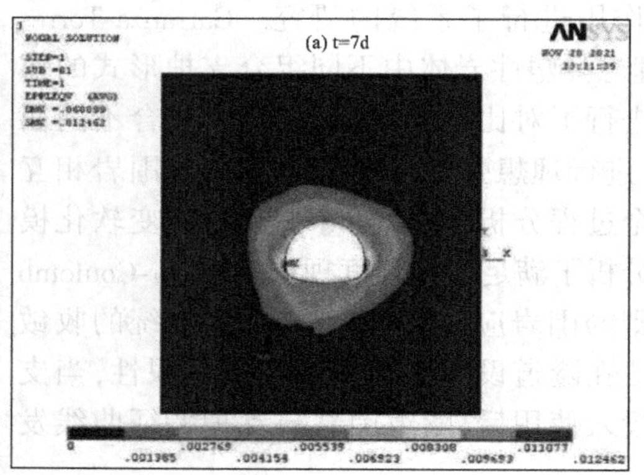

图2　开挖不支护时围岩的等效塑性应变

在构造应力场作用下开挖不支护时的围岩塑性区尺寸，围岩最大、最小主应力如表1和图3所示。根据表1可知，塑性区面积和最大深度均随着时间的延长而持续增大。$t=0$ 即隧洞刚开挖时，不考虑应力释放率，塑性区最大深度达到1.34R。由图3可知，隧洞仰拱处出现最大主应力S1max，右边墙的围岩深部位置出现最大压应力。这也表明右边隧洞的开挖对左边隧洞的围岩应力场有一定的影响。

开挖不支护时围岩的塑性区尺寸以及最大、最小主应力 表1

时刻	塑性区面积(m^2)	Rps 塑性区最大深度(R)	S1max 最大拉应力(MPa)	S3min 最大压应力(MPa)
$t=0$d	538.028	1.34	-0.011	5.53
$t=3$d	681.850	1.59	-0.011	5.57
$t=7$d	904.966	2.02	-0.002	5.92
$t=14$d	1418.117	3.10	-0.003	6.84

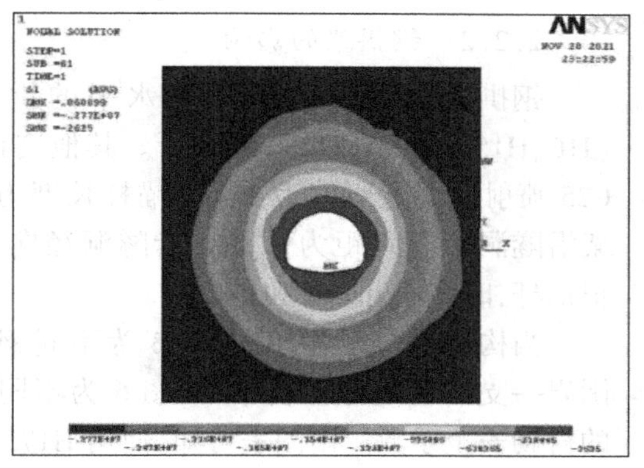
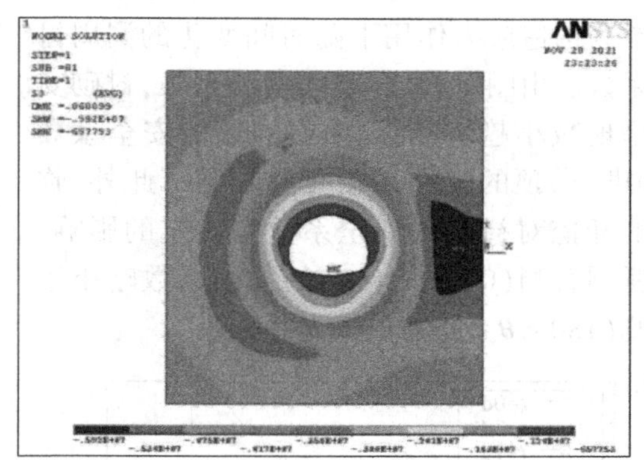

图3 开挖不支护时($t=7$d)围岩的最大、最小主应力

2.2 开挖支护后模拟分析

2.2.1 支护的时间效应

首先讨论在构造应力场作用下，不同时间段的($t=0$、$t=3d$、$t=7d$、$t=14d$、$t=28$d)围岩—支护系统的稳定性。选取的支护条件为：C25喷射混凝土厚度25cm，H150型钢拱架，拱架间距0.6m，锚杆长度3m，沿洞周设15根锚杆。

时间 $t=28$d 时，施加支护后围岩的塑性区范围及应力状态如图4所示。对比图4a)和图3可以明显看出，围岩的塑性区范围、塑性区面积以及塑性区的最大深度均在施加支护后减小，在拱脚处有应力集中现象。

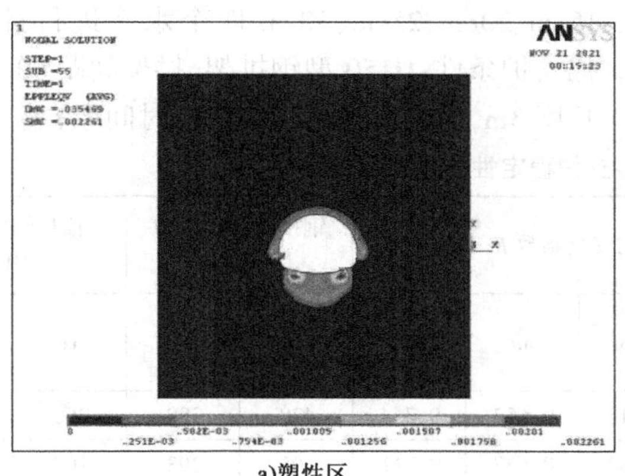

a)塑性区

b)最大主应力

图4 $t=28$d 时隧道支护后围岩的塑性区和最大主应力

表2为不同时间影响下施加支护后的隧道围岩—支护的稳定性结果。由表可知，随着时间的延长，围岩的强度降低，虽然衬砌的强度在增大，但隧洞的塑性区面积以及塑性区的最大深度 R_{ps} 均

持续增大，这表明隧道围岩强度的降低对其稳定性影响较大，隧洞的稳定性、安全性随时间的延长而降低。同时，钢拱架、锚杆的轴向应力随着时间的延长有减小的趋势，初砌安全系数也逐渐减小。

不同时间影响下隧道围岩—支护稳定性结果　　表2

时间 t	围岩					衬砌安全系数 K			钢拱架轴向应力（MPa）		锚杆轴向应力（MPa）	
	$Area_{PS}$	上部 R_{ps}（R）	下部 R_{ps}（R）	S1max（MPa）	S3min（MPa）	max	min	ave	max	ave	max	ave
0d	148.833	0.394	0.858	−0.26	7.02	0.978	0.744	0.868	444	396	266	136
3d	148.959	0.394	0.911	−0.32	7.11	0.878	0.706	0.802	397	360	235	112
7d	131.259	0.394	0.995	−0.40	7.14	0.853	0.706	0.787	356	331	201	92
14d	134.813	0.394	1.008	−0.45	7.40	0.805	0.688	0.758	325	308	179	77
28d	136.995	0.394	1.072	−0.54	7.33	0.773	0.666	0.742	292	281	152	67

图5为构造应力作用下随时间变化的洞周衬砌安全系数。由图可知，随着时间的延长，衬砌安全系数呈现减小趋势，隧洞左右边墙的安全系数最低，仰拱、拱顶的安全系数相对较高。此外，临界隧洞的开挖对衬砌的安全系数有一定的影响。图5中隧洞右侧（$0<\theta<180$）的安全系数略小于隧洞左侧（$180<\theta<360$）的安全系数。

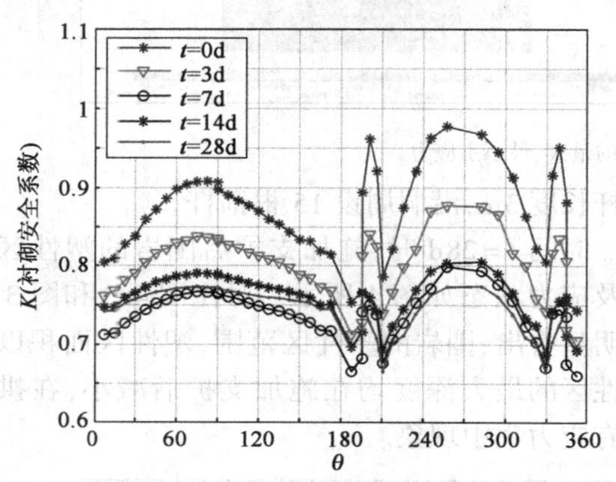

图5　随时间变化的洞周衬砌安全系数

2.2.2　钢拱架的影响

钢拱架的影响选取四个水平的拱架类型（I16、H150、H175、I22a）来分析。其他支护条件：C25喷射混凝土厚度为25cm，锚杆长度为3m，拱架沿隧洞轴向间距为0.6m，沿隧洞径向共设15根锚杆，时间取$t=3$d和$t=28$d。

当构造应力场作用时，表3为不同钢拱架的围岩—支护稳定性分析结果，图6为不同钢拱架的衬砌安全系数。由图表可知，使用H175钢拱架时，围岩的塑性区面积最小、混凝土衬砌的安全系数最高；使用I16钢拱架时，围岩的塑性区面积最大、混凝土衬砌的平均安全系数最低。H175钢架衬砌平均安全系数比I16提高了8%左右，塑性区面积则减小了9.8%。

2.2.3　衬砌厚度的影响

在考虑构造应力场时喷射混凝土厚度选取15cm、20cm、25cm、30cm四个水平进行计算。其他支护条件：H150型钢拱架，拱架间距60cm，锚杆长度3m，沿洞周设15根锚杆，时间取$t=28$d。

不同钢拱架的围岩-支护稳定性结果　　表3

拱架类型	时间 t	围岩				衬砌安全系数 K			钢拱架轴向应力（MPa）		锚杆轴向应力（MPa）	
		$Area_{PS}$（m^2）	R_{ps}（R）	S1max（MPa）	S3min（MPa）	max	min	ave	max	ave	max	ave
I16	3d	160.631	1.008	−0.28	7.04	0.818	0.652	0.744	428	389	260	131
	28d	147.443	1.110	−0.51	7.38	0.742	0.637	0.711	305	293	167	75
H150	3d	148.959	0.911	−0.32	7.11	0.878	0.706	0.802	396	361	235	112
	28d	136.995	1.072	−0.54	7.33	0.773	0.666	0.742	292	281	152	67
I22a	3d	140.313	0.858	−0.30	7.13	0.894	0.722	0.814	391	357	230	109
	28d	136.995	1.072	−0.53	7.32	0.781	0.681	0.749	289	278	150	66

续上表

拱架类型	时间 t	围岩				衬砌安全系数 K			钢拱架轴向应力(MPa)		锚杆轴向应力(MPa)	
		$Area_{PS}$ (m^2)	R_{ps} (R)	S1max (MPa)	S3min (MPa)	max	min	ave	max	ave	max	ave
H175	3d	121.935	0.858	-0.34	7.16	0.932	0.751	0.847	374	342	211	99
	28d	132.961	1.072	-0.54	7.28	0.803	0.700	0.769	282	271	141	61

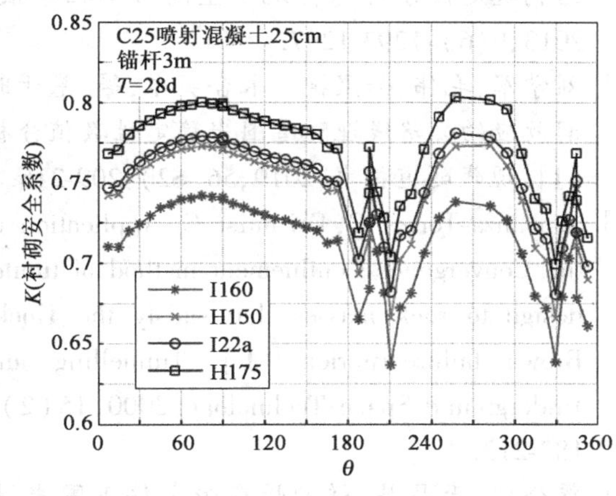

图6 采用不同钢拱架的衬砌安全系数

表4为不同衬砌厚度下的围岩塑性区面积、衬砌安全系数以及钢拱架、锚杆的轴向应力值。由表可知,随着衬砌厚度的增大,围岩的塑性区面积以及最大塑性区深度均减小,衬砌的安全系数增大,钢拱架和锚杆的轴力减小。衬砌厚度取30cm时,塑性区面积较之15cm减小了28.9%,最大塑性区深度由15cm时的1.227R减小到30cm时的1.008R,减小了18%,衬砌的平均安全系数增大了29.9%。这说明增加喷射混凝土厚度对提高围岩稳定性以及衬砌安全性都有较明显的效果,钢拱架轴向应力的最大值及平均值均随着喷射厚度的增大而减小。

构造应力场作用下不同混凝土厚度的围岩-支护稳定性计算结果 表4

混凝土厚度(cm)	围岩				衬砌安全系数 K	钢拱架轴向应力(MPa)		锚杆轴向应力(MPa)	
	$Area_{PS}$(m^2)	R_{ps}(R)	S1max(MPa)	S3min(MPa)	ave	max	ave	max	ave
15	177.871	1.227	-0.45	7.13	0.616	362	340	210	103
20	168.756	1.110	-0.48	7.43	0.681	322	307	181	84
25	136.995	1.072	-0.54	7.33	0.742	292	281	152	67
30	126.478	1.008	-0.57	7.22	0.800	270	260	129	57

2.2.4 锚杆的影响

在考虑构造应力场时,锚杆长度分别取2m、2.5m、3m、3.5m。其他支护条件为:C25喷射混凝土25cm,H150钢拱架,钢拱架间距0.8m,沿隧洞径向共设15根锚杆,时间取 $t=28d$。

在构造应力场作用下,不同锚杆长度的围岩—支护稳定性分析结果见表5。由表可知,锚杆长度主要影响围岩的应力状态,围岩最大拉应力由锚杆2m时的7.63 MPa减小到锚杆3.5m时的7.24MPa,围岩的最大塑性区深度总体呈减小趋势。

构造应力场作用下不同锚杆长度的围岩-支护稳定性分析结果 表5

锚杆长度(m)	围岩				衬砌安全系数 K	钢拱架轴向应力(MPa)		锚杆轴向应力(MPa)	
	$Area_{PS}$(m^2)	R_{ps}(R)	S1max(MPa)	S3min(MPa)	ave	max	ave	max	ave
2	145.497	1.107	-0.48	7.63	0.717	300	290	178	95
2.5	145.761	1.001	-0.51	7.50	0.718	301	290	173	83
3	143.997	1.110	-0.53	7.37	0.719	301	289	163	73
3.5	146.135	1.090	-0.52	7.24	0.721	302	289	152	65

3　结语

(1)在考虑构造应力场作用时,在开挖不支护条件下,拱脚、边墙处出现最大等效塑性应变,而施加支护后,围岩的塑性区面积以及塑性区最大深度均减小。围岩—支护体系的稳定性、安全性(如衬砌的安全系数、钢拱架受力、围岩应力状态等)比自重应力场作用时差。因此,若场区水平构造应力明显,应考虑增加支护条件。

(2)临界隧道的开挖对洞周围岩应力状态、衬砌的安全系数有不利影响。施加支护后,衬砌左右边墙的安全系数最低,且在拱脚处有应力集中现象。围岩的塑性区面积、塑性区最大深度均随着时间的延长而持续增大,但是围岩的稳定性及安全性降低,衬砌的安全系数也逐渐降低。

(3)围岩—支护体系的稳定性随喷射混凝土厚度的增大、拱架以及锚杆长度的增大有所提高,其中混凝土厚度的影响最为明显。所以,在初支时间达到一定的阶段后要及时进行二衬的支护和仰拱的施做,以确保隧道整体稳定。

参考文献

[1]　卢晓颖.考虑时间效应的深埋小净距隧道围岩压力分析[J].公路交通科技,2021,38(10):100-106+143.

[2]　张治国,程志翔,汪嘉程,等.考虑渗流影响的深埋隧道围岩-衬砌相互作用研究[J].隧道建设(中英文),2021,41(S1):108-121.

[3]　夏才初,徐晨,杜时贵.考虑应力路径的深埋隧道黏弹-塑性围岩与支护相互作用[J].岩石力学与工程学报,2021,40(9):1789-1802.

[4]　刘军强,施建仁,王水晶,等.地应力测量在深埋长大隧道岩爆预测中的应用[J].地下空间与工程学报,2011,7 (4):776-788.

[5]　贾剑青,李晶,张宪,等.深埋隧道围岩及支护结构稳定性分析[J].地下空间与工程学报,2013,9(6):1293-1297.

[6]　刘学军,毛伟,如黑艳·木合买尔,等.基于时间效应的公路浅埋隧道围岩稳定性数值分析[J].现代隧道技术,2019,56(S2):209-215.

[7]　Carranza-Torres C, Fairhurst C. Application of the Convergence-Confinement method of tunnel design to rock masses that satisfy the Hoek-Brown failurecriterion [J]. Tunnelling and Underground Space Technology, 2000, 15(2): 187-213.

[8]　侯公羽,李晶晶.弹塑性变形条件下围岩-支护相互作用全过程解析[J].岩土力学,2012,33(4):961-970.

[9]　张常光,张庆贺,赵均海.考虑应变软化及剪胀的井壁稳定统一解[J].煤炭学报,2009,34(5):634-639.

[10]　郑颖人,王永甫,王成,等.节理岩体隧道的稳定分析与破坏规律探讨[J].地下空间与工程学报,2011,7(4):649-656.

暗挖电力管廊隧道施工对桩基及路面影响分析

王豪杰*　程　博　张　亮

(长安大学公路学院)

摘　要　随着地下空间的开发利用,新建地下工程与既有建筑物的相互影响不可忽视。以某综合管廊电力隧道下穿快速路及侧穿高架桥桩基工程为例,对其进行施工阶段响应研究,分析上方路面沉降和侧方桩基位移在隧道开挖过程中的变化规律,并进一步在原工况基础上研究桩基不同分布位置受隧道开挖的影响。结果表明:隧道开挖引起路面纵向沉降变形呈现沿隧道中心线往两侧逐渐减小趋势,路面横向沉降以隧道开挖至其下方前沉降为主;隧道开挖会引起前方较远距离路面表层较早发生沉降,而开挖较近时拱顶上方土体沉降急剧增大;桩基在隧道开挖过程中会产生侧向位移,呈现整体倾斜变形,并且会在隧道薄弱部位对应深度产生较大位移突变;隧道开挖会引起桩基先上移后沉降并逐渐趋于稳定。通过对模拟结果的分析,对隧道、桩基及公路提出合理的加固处理措施,减少相互之间的影响,保证桩基和公路的正常运营和隧道的安全施工。

关键词 电力管廊隧道 路面 桩基 数值模拟 影响分析

0 引言

暗挖综合管廊是随着综合管廊建设的发展而发展起来的。以20世纪90年代上海张杨路综合管廊为起点,我国的现代化综合管廊建设经历了最初的缓慢发展阶段和如今的有序推进阶段。伴随着这个过程,暗挖综合管廊的发展历程分为需求驱动阶段和主动探索阶段[1]。暗挖综合管廊能够有效利用城市地下空间,然而在地下空间的开发利用中,必然存在新建构筑物和既有建筑相互影响的情况。新建地下管廊隧道在开挖过程中存在沉降变形,可能会对已有建筑物的平衡造成扰动进而产生变形和破坏,因此对于上覆重要建筑或管线,合理设计支护显得尤为重要。

针对地下隧道开挖对桩基的影响,已经有诸多学者通过数值分析[2,4]、试验手段[5,8]或简化解析法[9,11]进行了研究。模型试验法具有直观性、真实性,目前多采用离心试验模型较准确的反映出隧道开挖对邻近建筑物的影响。简化分析法目前多基于 Winkler 弹性地基模型,采用两阶段法进行隧道开挖对邻近桩基的作用效应。有限元法以其适用性强,将隧道、桩基和土体作为整体进行计算,因此常被采用[12]。目前,针对隧道对周边建筑物的影响研究,多是以地铁盾构隧道为工程背景,而对于浅埋暗挖法隧道对邻近建筑物的研究则较少。管廊以其独特的优势在市政管网建设中处于不断发展的地位,因此,对于管廊隧道开挖对地下建筑物的影响研究十分必要。

本文以成都某市政管廊为背景,对某电力暗挖隧道下穿三环快速路及穿越既有高架桥桩基进行研究。通过对隧道进行有限元数值模拟,分析出隧道开挖对路面变形和桩基的影响,确定其影响范围和作用大小。由此对已有建筑物的沉降和受力特点进行分析,为后续此类设计提供借鉴参考。

1 工程概况

在建综合管廊为顺接电力规划部门电力接入点,会沿途设置电力隧道,其中一暗挖电力隧道垂直下穿快速路,采用暗挖法施工;全长279.811m,采用2.4m×3.9m的马蹄形结构,起拱线高2.7m,矢高1.2m,隧道初期支护采用喷射混凝土,Φ22砂浆锚杆,初期支护厚度0.2m,隧道断面如图1所示。

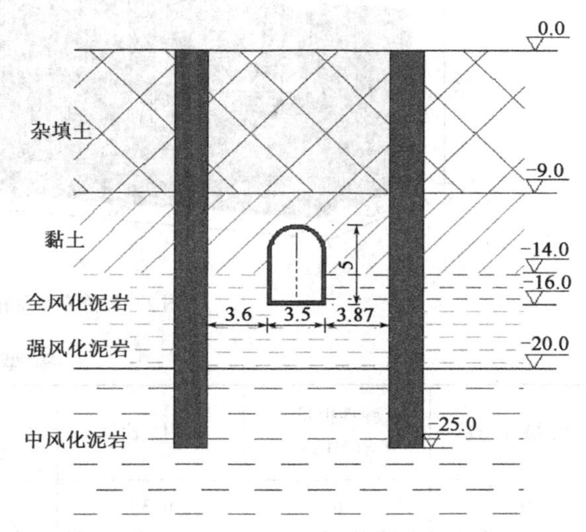

图1 暗挖电力隧道断面图

地层由上而下分别为填土、黏土、全风化泥岩、强分化泥岩和中风化泥岩,隧道开挖断面位于黏土及全风化泥岩层,桩基支承于中风化泥岩层。

电力隧道开挖过程中会侧穿匝道桥三根既有桩基(桥桩为单柱单桩式的端承摩擦桩),距离为3~5m,桩基直径均为2m。

2 有限元模型

采用数值模拟软件 MIDAS GTX 对隧道开挖进行建模,如图2所示。该模型采用三维实体单元模拟,不考虑构造应力影响。隧道埋深11m,横穿快速路,并穿越高架桥桩基,指定沿 x 方向为隧道掘进方向,竖直方向为 z 方向。x、y、z 计算范围分别为76m、35m和35m。模型顶面为自由面,周边约束水平位移,底部施加约束。假设土体为均质、连续、各向同性,采用摩尔库伦本构,土体、喷混、锚杆及桩基分别采用3D实体单元、2D板单元、植入式桁架及1D梁单元模拟,土体、隧道和桩分别采用2m、1m、1m的尺寸控制,均采用自动-实体进行网格划分。模型计算参数如表1所示。

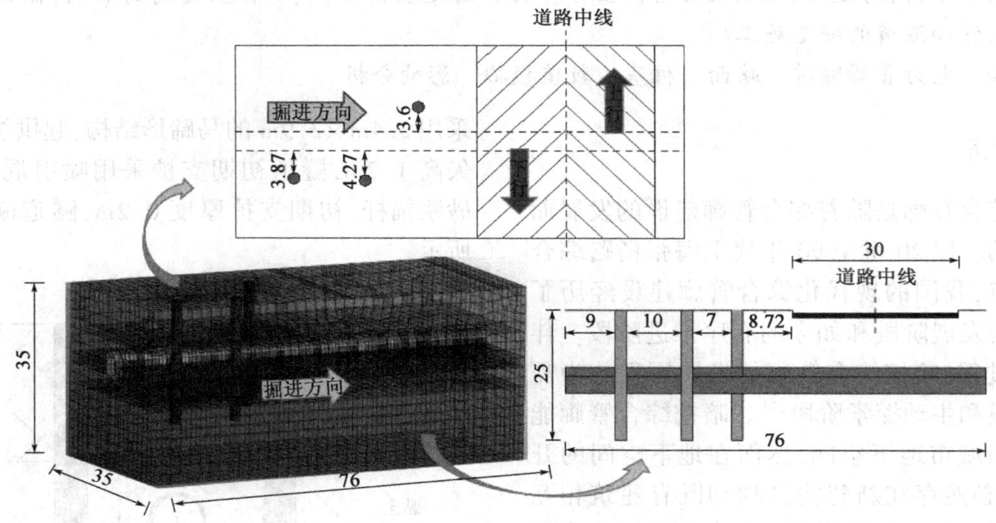

图2　数值模型及相对位置关系(尺寸单位:m)

模型计算参数　　表1

地层名称	弹性模量 E(MPa)	泊松比 ν	重度 γ (kN/m^3)	黏聚力 c(kPa)	内摩擦角 φ(°)	层厚 (m)
填土	6	0.35	19	12	10	5
黏土	7.5	0.33	19.3	30	12	9
全风化泥岩	7.9	0.24	20	40	15.5	2
强风化泥岩	23	0.25	21.2	45	25	4
中风化泥岩	120	0.23	23	200	34	—
锚杆	196×10^3	0.28	78.5	—	—	—
喷混	15×10^3	0.2	24	—	—	—
桩基	30×10^3	0.25	25	—	—	—

隧道采用暗挖法过程施工,每次开挖进尺1.5m,本次共模拟51个开挖步,总计开挖76.5m。每次开挖前进行超前支护,开挖后及时喷混初支,依次进行隧道开挖。其中,桩基1、桩基2和桩基3位置分别对应于隧道开挖步7、开挖步15及开挖步21。

3　数值模拟结果分析

3.1　数值模拟结果分析

为充分考虑隧道施工对上方快速路及侧方桩基影响,数值模型施工阶段分析基于初衬施工,图3为不同开挖步骤下路面中心沉降曲线。由图3可知,随着隧道的开挖,道路各点沉降逐渐增大,隧道中心下沉降变形最大,且隧道中心附近沉降量增大较快,由中心往道路大小里程两侧逐渐减小,呈U型分布。隧道由左幅道路边缘逐步开挖至道路中心时的沉降大于通过道路中心线后隧道开挖引起的沉降。

以西安老城区市政管线改造试验段工程为例,其典型地表沉降监测数据见表2[13],由表中数据可知,数值模拟结果符合工程实际沉降规律,即管廊轴线中心处地表沉降量最大,两边最小。

图4为隧道中心线上方道路范围内沉降变形,道路中心及右幅边缘分别距离左幅边缘15m、30m。由图可知,隧道中心线上方道路路面在开挖

至对应位置下之前的沉降大于通过对应位置后开挖引起的沉降,并且通过沉降曲线可知开挖面后一定范围内为影响区,此区域外土体暂未受开挖影响。因此,应合理确定隧道开挖影响区域,在隧道开挖过程中对影响范围内土体做好沉降监测,变形过大时加强支护。

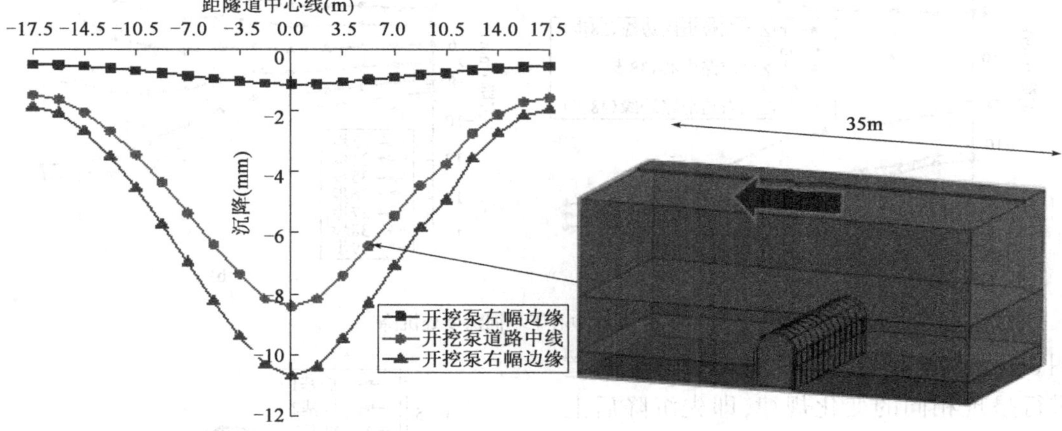

图3　不同开挖步骤下路面中心沉降曲线

断面实测沉降数据　　表2

断面1		断面2		断面3		断面4	
x(m)	S(x)(mm)	x(m)	S(x)(mm)	x(m)	S(x)(mm)	x(m)	S(x)(mm)
-8	-9.27	-9	-6.93	-8	-7.11	-8.5	-14.40
-7	-10.00	-4	-12.10	0	-12.10	-2.5	-26.30
0	-13.40	0	-13.50	5	-10.10	0	-27.70
3	-12.50	6	-10.50	9	-6.79	3	-24.20
9	-7.75	8	-7.10	13	-3.71	7	-18.60
13.3	-4.68	—	—	16	-1.54	—	—
17.7	-2.25	—	—	—	—	—	—
21.3	-0.68	—	—	—	—	—	—

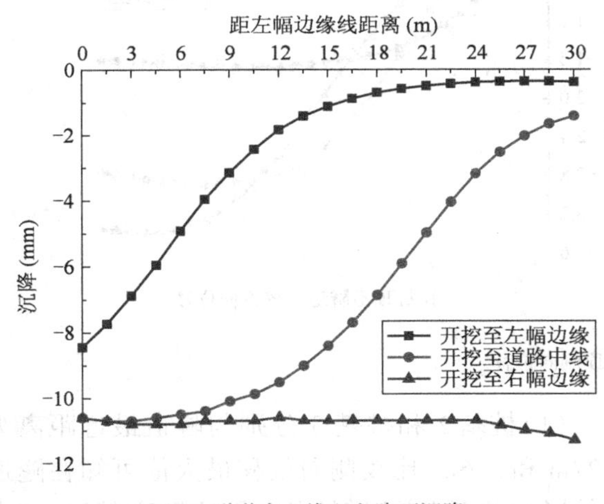

图4　隧道中心线上方路面沉降

图5为道路与隧道两中心线交点处路面至隧道拱顶不同深度的沉降变形量。由图5a)可知,开挖至路面中心之前,拱顶至路面整体沉降较大,而通过中心后开挖引起的沉降整体较小。由图5b)沉降曲线可知:在逐渐开挖至道路中心过程中,0~6m深度范围内土体沉降均匀增大,而6~11m内变化幅度逐渐增大,在拱顶处达到最大值,拱顶沉降逐渐由小于路面沉降增大为大于路面沉降。隧道开挖会先引起后方上部土体产生沉降,随后拱顶上方土体产生较大沉降,拱顶上方影响区域约为隧道开挖半径的3~4倍。

3.2　桩基变形分析

保持桩顶荷载不变,分析隧道开挖引起的桩顶沉降、桩侧沉降及弯矩分布,图6为不同开挖阶段不同位置桩基的桩顶竖向位移。

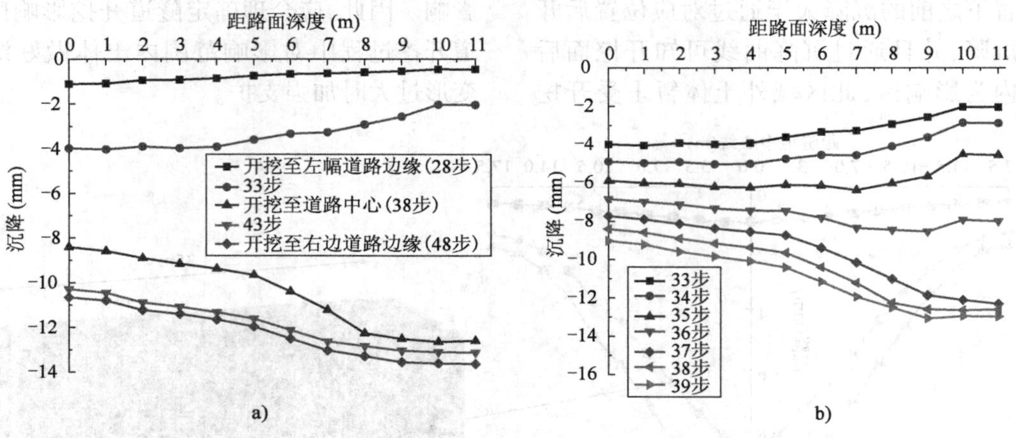

图 5　路面中心下不同深度处沉降

由图 6 可知，各桩基的桩顶竖向位移随隧道开挖的进行呈现相同的变化规律，即先沉降后上移最终趋于稳定。当隧道埋深小于桩底埋深时，隧道开挖最终会导致桩顶上移[3]。距离桩基 1、2、3 最近的开挖步分别为 7 步、15 步、21 步，当开挖步骤为 2 步、9 步、15 步时，各桩基桩顶分别由沉降变为上移，由此可推断当隧道开挖至桩基一定范围内时将引起桩基上移，而在此范围外桩基随土体一起产生向下位移。

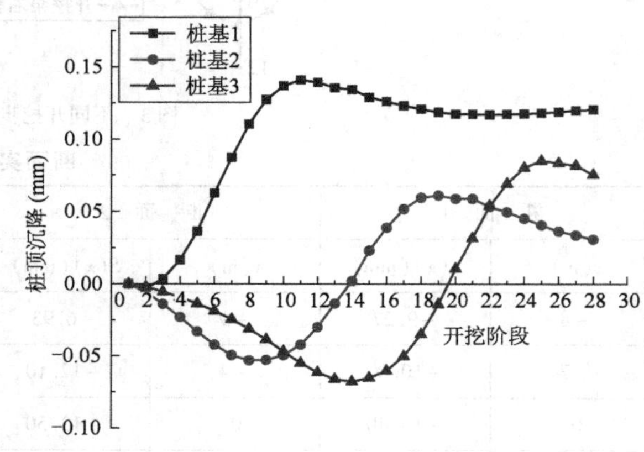

图 6　桩顶沉降曲线

图 7 为隧道开挖引起的桩顶侧向位移，桩基 1 和桩基 2 的桩身沿 Y 轴位移正值表示靠近隧道，桩基 3 负值表示靠近隧道，各桩基沿 X 轴位移正值表示顺开挖方向，负值表示逆开挖方向，下文同。

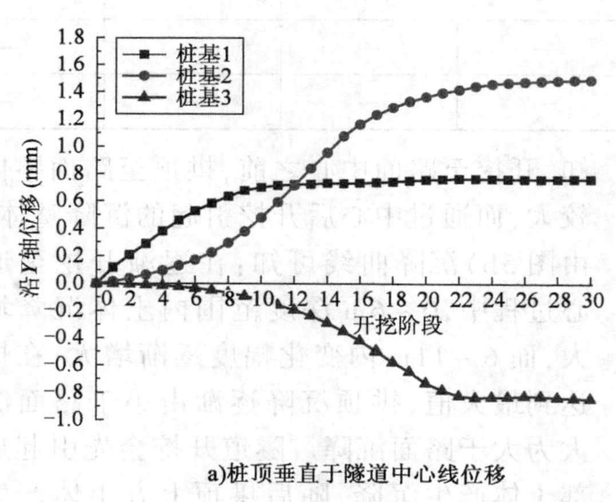

a)桩顶垂直于隧道中心线位移

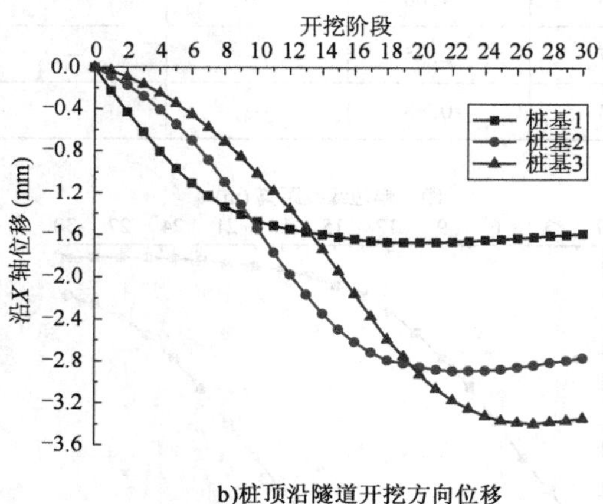

b)桩顶沿隧道开挖方向位移

图 7　不同施工阶段桩顶侧向位移

由图 7a)可知，桩顶将沿隧道开挖中心线一侧产生侧向位移，在桩基一定范围内位移随开挖距离的减小逐渐增大，在对应最近位置位移达到最大，在远离桩基时趋于稳定。各桩基参数均相同，所处位置不同，结合侧向位移曲线可推断：

(1)桩基 2 和桩基 3 分别与隧道最近距离为 4.27m 和 3.6m，比较侧向位移最大值可知在隧道开挖影响范围内，隧道桩基与隧道距离越远，产生的侧向位移越大。

(2)当隧道开挖至桩基 1 和桩基 2 之间时，桩基2侧向位移发展较快,可推断当桩基位于同一侧时,距离开挖起始点较远的桩侧向位移较大。

从图7b)可知:随着隧道开挖的进行,桩基沿开挖方向的位移不断增大,最终趋于稳定;桩基距离隧道开挖起始点越远,最终位移值越大;在通过桩基对应位置后,桩基的侧向位移值仍继续增大,直到开挖至较远位置后才逐渐趋于稳定。桩基沿开挖中心线方向的位移是隧道开挖时掌子面卸荷变形引起的,只有脱离开挖引起的土体挤压范围,桩基的变形才会趋于稳定。

图8为隧道开挖过程中桩身的侧向位移,由于桩基3距离隧道开挖初始位置较远,为更好分析桩身侧向位移发展规律,增设了距离较近的第15开挖步。

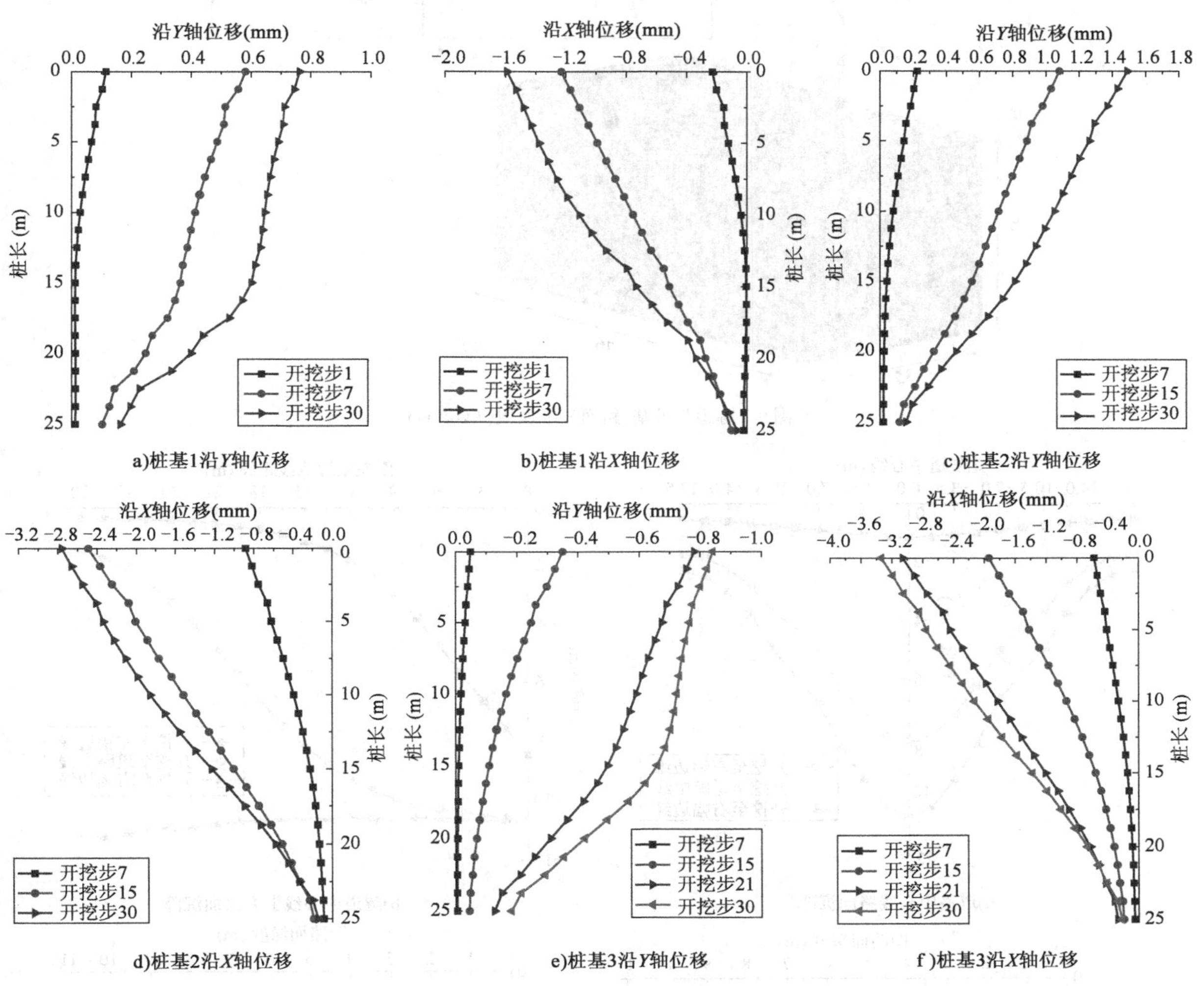

图8 不同开挖阶段下桩身侧向位移

图8a)、图8c)、图8e)表明距离桩基较远的隧道开挖会引起桩身呈现悬臂弯曲变形,当距离逐渐减小时会引起桩身局部受力过大而产生梁弯曲变形,通过桩基深度可以看出,发生突变位置大致在隧道腰部位置。图图8b)、图8d)、图8f)表明桩基在隧道开挖全过程中沿开挖方向均呈现悬臂弯曲变形,没有明显的局部受力集中现象发生。综合图8a)~图8f)可以看出桩身位移在隧道开挖过程中随深度增加而逐渐减小,沿着垂直隧道中心线方向和逆开挖方向呈现整体倾斜变形,当隧道开挖距离桩基较近时会在隧道腰部对应深度产生较大位移突变。

4 对比分析验证

为充分分析隧道开挖对侧方桩基和上方路面的影响并验证上述模拟结果的准确性,依据本工程进一步建立三维模型进行研究。新建隧道与桩基、路面相对位置图及模型如图9所示。

图10为不同开挖阶段对隧道上方路面的变形,由图10可知,隧道的开挖对路面的变形影响

规律与原始工况相一致,仅最终变形值存在差异。

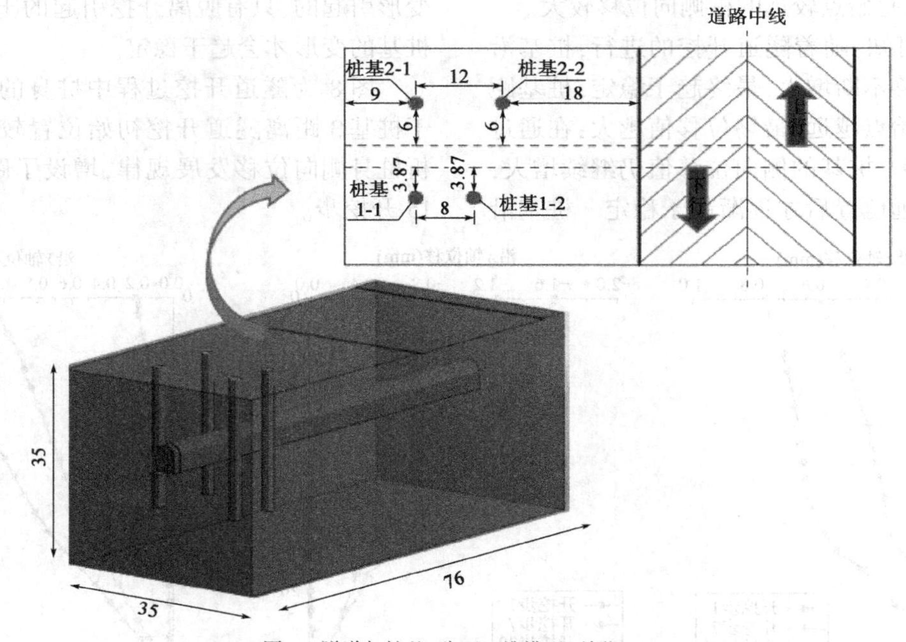

图9 隧道与桩基、路面三维模型(单位:m)

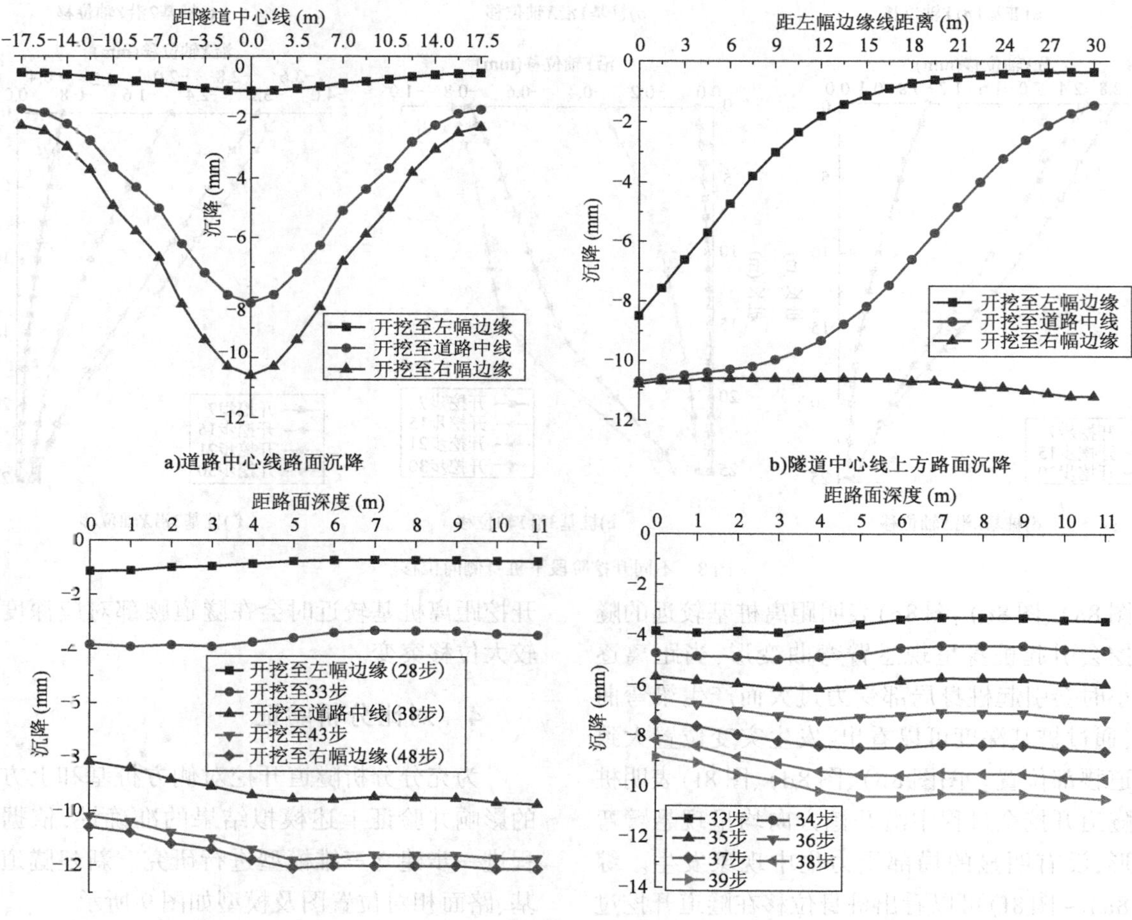

图10 隧道开挖对路面变形影响

图11为不同位置桩基桩顶沉降曲线，桩基的桩顶竖向位移在不同工况、不同位置时随隧道开挖而呈现相同的变化规律，即先沉降后上移最终稍有下降并趋于稳定。由桩基1-1和桩基2-1、桩基1-2和桩基2-2对比可知：桩基距离隧道越远，其变形影响值越小。由桩基1-1和桩基1-2、桩基2-1和桩基2-2对比可知：当桩基位于同一侧时，前方桩基的影响值较后方桩基的影响值较小。

图12为桩基侧向位移曲线，由图12可知，当桩基位于隧道同一开挖面两侧时，桩基与隧道距离越大，产生的侧向位移越大。当桩基位于隧道同一侧时，前方桩基产生的桩顶侧向变形较后方大。

由图12b）可发现随着隧道开挖的进行，桩基沿开挖方向的位移不断增大。随着开挖步远离隧道一定距离后趋于稳定，桩基距离隧道开挖起始点越远，最终位移值越大。但根据桩基1-1和2-1可发现，当桩基位于同一开挖面两侧时，距离隧道越远的桩基桩顶最终沿开挖方向位移稍大。与原工况变化规律一致。

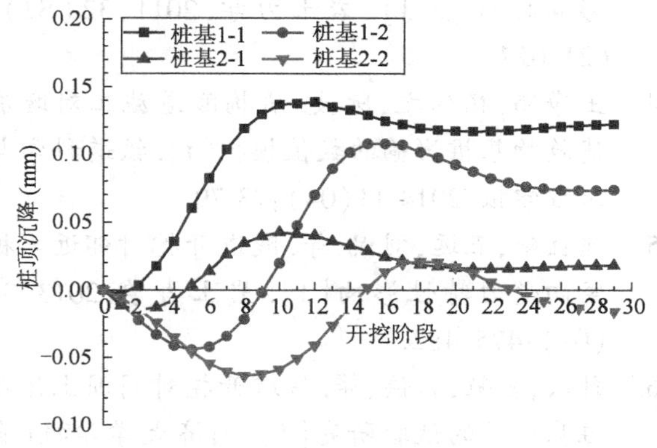

图11 桩基桩顶沉降曲线

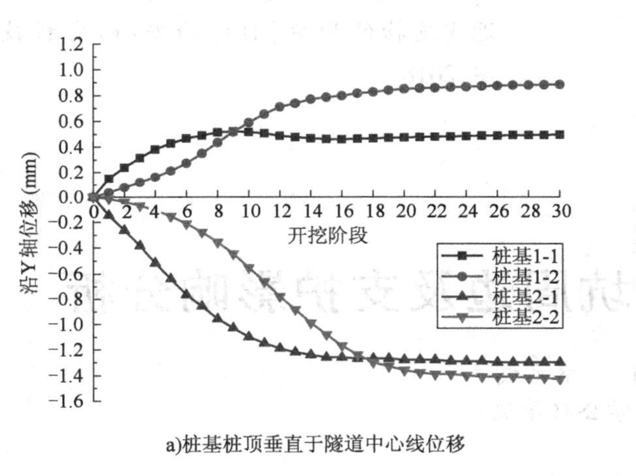

a)桩基桩顶垂直于隧道中心线位移

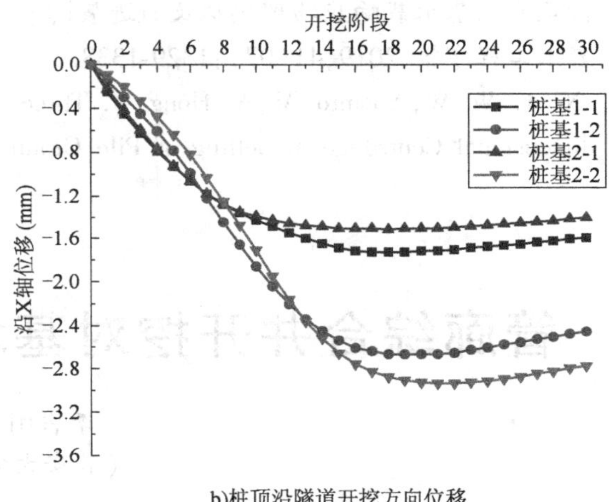

b)桩顶沿隧道开挖方向位移

图12 桩基桩顶侧向位移曲线

5 结语

以某管廊电力隧道下穿快速路及侧穿桩基为背景，研究隧道开挖施工过程对路面及桩基的影响，基于数值模拟，得到如下结论：

（1）隧道开挖对于上方快速路影响显著，沉降变形大致呈现随隧道中心线往两侧逐渐减小趋势，路面在隧道开挖至下方前沉降大于通过下方之后隧道开挖引起的沉降，能达到最终沉降的80%。

（2）路面至隧道拱顶的沉降由逐渐减小变为逐渐增大，当隧道开挖距离较远时，主要引起上部土体沉降；当隧道开挖较近时，会引起隧道拱顶上方一定范围内土体沉降急剧增大。

（3）桩基在隧道开挖过程中会产生侧向位移，沿着垂直隧道中心线方向和逆开挖方向，呈现整体倾斜变形；当隧道开挖距离桩基较近时，会在隧道腰部对应深度产生较大位移突变。

基于上述分析，隧道开挖时对前方一定范围内路面应做好沉降监测工作；桩基施工时一定深度侧向位移较大，应控制此范围内土体的变形，可施加围护桩等措施固定桩基周围受隧道施工扰动的土体。

参考文献

[1] 强健. 暗挖综合管廊的发展和研究方向[J]. 隧道建设(中英文)，2021，41(5)：764-771.

[2] 王丽,郑刚. 盾构法开挖隧道对桩基础影响的有限元分析[J]. 岩土力学,2011,32(S1):704-710.

[3] 王丽,郑刚. 盾构法隧道施工对邻近摩擦单桩影响的研究[J]. 岩土力学,2011,32(S2):621-627.

[4] 王净伟,杨信之,阮波. 盾构隧道施工对既有建筑物基桩影响的数值模拟[J]. 铁道科学与工程学报,2014 11(04):73-79.

[5] 熊巨华,王远,刘侃,等. 隧道开挖对邻近单桩竖向受力特性影响[J]. 岩土力学,2013,34(02):475-482.

[6] 孙庆,杨敏,冉侠,等. 隧道开挖对周围土体及桩基影响的试验研究[J]. 同济大学学报(自然科学版)2011,39(07):989-993+1025.

[7] 刘松玉,李洪江,童立元,等. 地下工程开挖卸荷既有桩基承载响应物理模拟及新进展[J]. 岩土工程学报,2019,41(07):1329-1338.

[8] Ng C W W, Soomro M A, Hong Y. Three-dimensional Centrifuge Modelling of Pile Group Responses to Side-By-Side Twin Tunnelling[J]. Tunnelling and Underground Space Technology, 2014,43(7):350-361.

[9] 章荣军,郑俊杰,蒲诃夫,等. 基于p-y曲线分析隧道开挖对邻近单桩的影响[J]. 岩土工程学报,2010,32(12):1837-1845.

[10] 孙庆,杨敏,汪浩,等. 基于p-y曲线法分析隧道开挖条件下邻近桩基的水平反应[J]. 岩土工程学报,2012,34(11):2100-2107.

[11] 程康,夏唐代,梁荣柱,等. 盾构开挖下邻近既有桩基的竖向响应分析[J]. 岩土工程学报,2018,40(S2):42-46.

[12] 张治国,徐晨,宫剑飞. 考虑桩侧土体三维效应和地基剪切变形的隧道开挖对邻近桩基影响分析[J]. 岩土工程学报,2016,38(05):846-856.

[13] 胡继伟. 地下综合管廊施工对地表沉降和邻近建筑物的影响[D]. 西安:西安科技大学,2018.

管廊综合井开挖对基坑周边及支护影响分析

李吉刚* 蔡元成

(长安大学公路学院)

摘 要 管廊综合井基坑开挖不可避免地会对管廊结构和周边地面产生影响。以成都市某综合管廊项目为基础,对相对位置不同的管廊综合井进行数值模拟,分析在深基坑开挖过程中盾构管廊的变形、基坑周边的沉降及支护体系受力。结果表明:盾构管廊穿越的一侧围护桩最大变形值出现在地面至管廊顶部之间2/3深度位置;中心围护桩在无盾构管廊一侧整体变形值较有管廊一侧大,最大值分别为25.9mm和23.94mm,且不同工况下最大变形值为南北向(25.9mm)>斜向(25.6mm)>东西向(20.78mm);盾构管廊竖向位移沿基坑中心向两侧呈现中间大两边小的趋势,东西向管廊最大隆起量最大,为22.13mm;综合井基坑周边地面变形分为隆起区和沉降区,一定距离内的土体隆起,此距离外的土体发生沉降,临界距离在管廊方向上较大,约为42m。

关键词 管廊综合井 力学响应 数值分析 盾构管廊 支护体系 地面

0 引言

随着城市地上空间的逐步减少,地下空间的开发和利用成为必然趋势,地下综合管廊是城市可持续发展的重要方向,可改善城市空间格局,满足绿色发展需要[1-2]。目前综合管廊随着城市基础设施的建设而不断发展[3],主要采用的施工方法有暗挖法、现浇法、预制装配法[4],其中常见的暗挖工法有顶推法、盾构法、矿山法等[5]。由于城市建设涉及到与周边环境的相互作用,因此需要降低工程对周边环境的影响。盾构技术和预制装配化技术发展讯速,在管廊建设中具有广阔的应用前景。

盾构法可以适用于管廊埋深较大的工程中,利用较深地下空间,避免与浅层地下空间中管线和构筑物的相互影响。目前盾构法在综合管廊建设中已有应用[6-8],由于盾构管廊埋深一般较大,为了将管廊内的管线引出地表,需要在沿线修建综合井。综合井基坑开挖与盾构管廊存在相互作用,目前文献对于基坑和盾构隧道相互作用的研究基本在地铁盾构隧道领域,而缺乏对于管廊盾构隧道与综合井之间相互作用的研究。不少学者研究了盾构隧道对于上覆基坑的影响[9-11]或者基坑开挖对下卧盾构隧道的影响[12-16],但是盾构隧道和基坑位于同一空间的影响研究较少。

以成都市某综合管廊为背景,对综合井深基坑开挖支护过程中支护体系受力、盾构管廊变形及综合井周边地面沉降规律进行分析。并进一步分析管廊与综合井不同相对位置下的变化规律,为类似工程施工提供参考。

1 工程概况

管廊综合井长为29.7m、宽为16.7m、深度为34.6m,采用台阶法分层开挖。台阶高度小于3m,坡度不小于1:1,基坑开挖至支撑中心线下0.5m时停止开挖并及时设置支撑。围护桩采用钻孔灌注桩,直径1.2m,间距2m,深度为41.6m,底部位于基坑底部以下7m。内支撑采用一道混凝土支撑和三道钢支撑,混凝土支撑尺寸为0.6m×0.8m,钢支撑直径为609mm、壁厚16mm,支撑水平间距为4.5m,基坑四角各设置两道斜撑,水平间距为2m。混凝土冠梁尺寸为1.2m×0.8m,钢围檩采用工45C型。盾构管廊外径为9m,管片厚度为0.5m,管片埋深23.1m,底部位于综合井底部以上2.5m。结构如图1所示。地层由上而下分别为人工填土、硬塑黏土、黏土夹卵石、全风化泥岩、强风化泥岩和中风化泥岩。

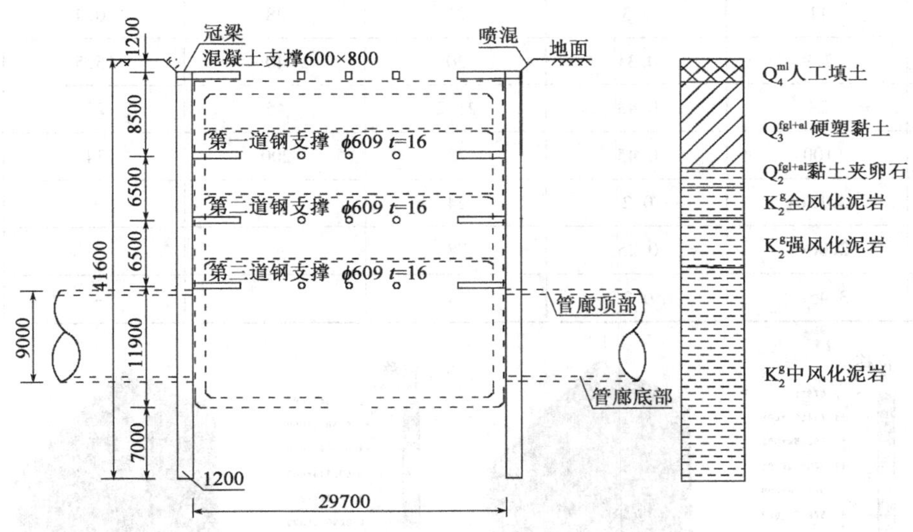

图1 综合井结构图(尺寸单位:mm)

2 建立模型

采用三维有限元软件进行数值模拟分析,模拟范围为183m(长)×177m(宽)×70m(高)。模型顶面为自由面,周边约束水平位移,底部施加约束。基坑围护桩利用等效刚度理论将钻孔灌注桩等效为地下连续墙,采用弹性板单元模拟。支撑、冠梁和围檩均采用梁单元模拟,盾构隧道采用板单元模拟,地层采用3D实体单元模拟,模型如图2所示。岩土体物理参数根据实际勘察获得并采用摩尔-库伦本构模型,而支护结构参数依据类似工程,模型参数如表1所示。

3 结果分析

3.1 基坑支护体系影响分析

在综合井开挖支护过程中,随着基坑的开挖,围护结构将产生一定的应力应变,图3为围护桩模型最终计算结果。南北侧围护桩变形沿深度最大值位于基坑中部深度位置，东西侧围护桩最大值位于盾构管廊以上且靠近管廊顶部，两者最大变形均处于围檩 2 和围檩 3 之间。南北侧整体变形值较大，最大值为 20.78mm，而东西侧最大值为 6.14mm。

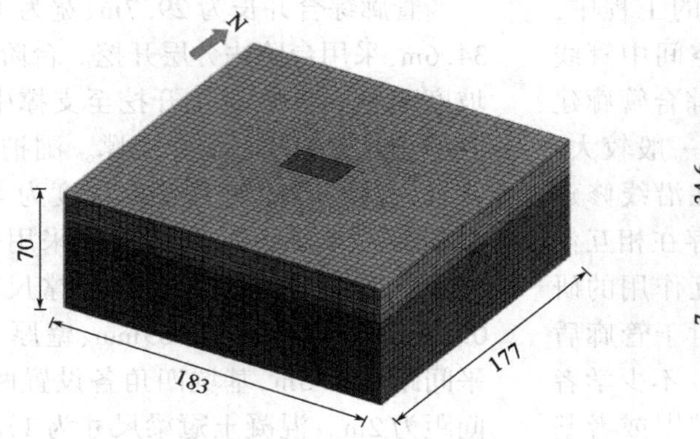

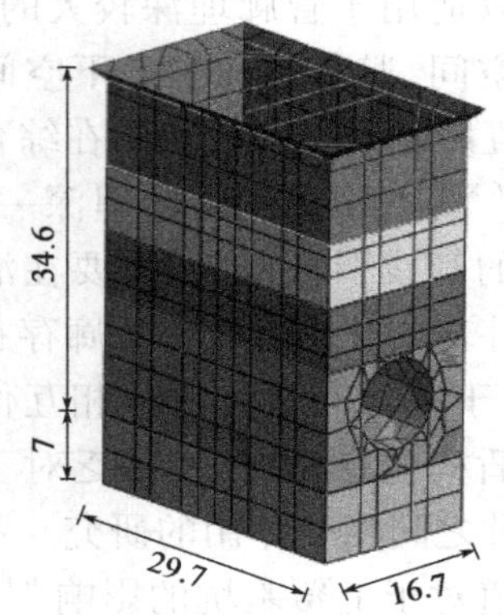

图 2　综合井数值模型(尺寸单位:m)

模 型 计 算 参 数　　表 1

地 层 名 称	弹性模量 E(MPa)	泊 松 比 ν	重度 γ(kN/m^3)	黏聚力 c(kPa)	内摩擦角 φ(°)	层厚(m)
人工填土	4	0.32	19	8	10	2.4
硬塑黏土	7.5	0.32	19.9	55	13.3	8.6
黏土夹卵石	11	0.3	21	38	20.4	2
全风化泥岩	7.9	0.31	20	40	15.5	3.2
强风化泥岩	23	0.43	21.2	45	25	4.8
中风化泥岩	100	0.45	23	200	34	—
C35 混凝土	3.15e4	0.2	24	—	—	—
Q235	2.06e5	0.25	78	—	—	—
盾构管片	3.45e4	0.2	24	—	—	—

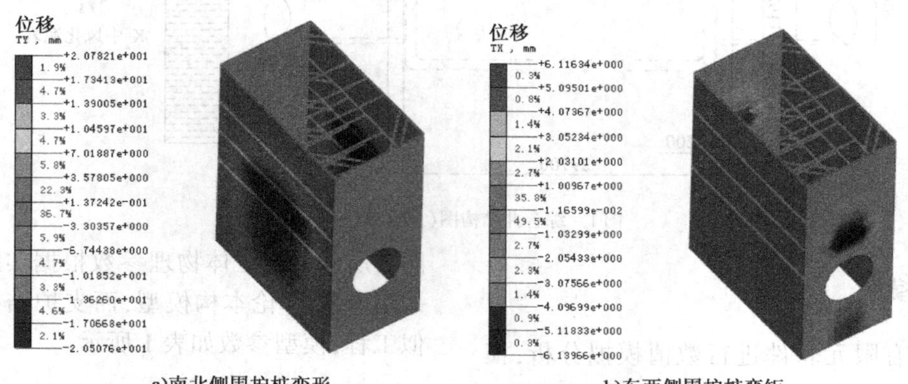

a)南北侧围护桩变形　　b)东西侧围护桩弯矩

图 3　围护桩模型计算结果

图 4 为综合井西侧、南侧中心处围护桩弯矩和变形。由图 4a)、图 4c) 可以看出，从地面至盾构管廊顶部，在支撑处弯矩减小或出现负弯矩，其余位置处弯矩均为正；在盾构管廊底部至综合井底部，在该部分土体未开挖之前(即开挖 1 ~ 开挖 4) 的弯矩为负，在该层土开挖之后的弯矩为正。在盾构管廊以上，围护桩沿基坑内位移呈现先增大后减小的趋势，并且在管廊上部一定位置沿土

体内产生位移,位移随开挖的进行不断增大,最大位移为 6.14mm,在基坑底部土层开挖后略有减小。盾构隧道以下部分同一深度处位移随着隧道的开挖而不断增大,最大位移为 4.21mm。南侧中心围护桩最大位移出现在综合井 1/2 处,为 20.78mm,如图 4b)、图 4d)所示。

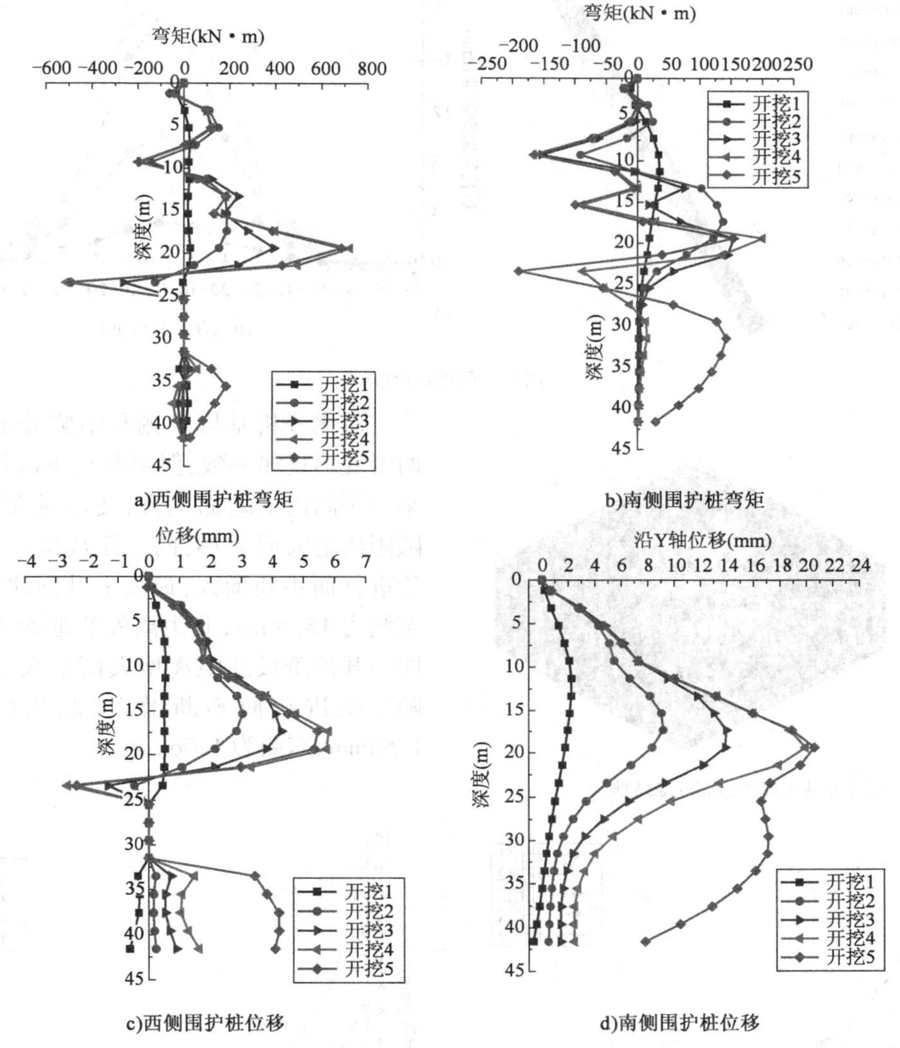

图 4 综合井西侧、南侧中心围护桩位移及弯矩

对比南侧和西侧围护桩弯矩和变形,二者弯矩和变形最大值出现的深度一致。西侧弯矩最大值较南侧大,为 722kN·m,南侧最大弯矩仅为 200.5kN·m;但西侧最大变形值较南侧小,为 6.14mm,而南侧最大变形量为 20.78mm。

3.2 盾构管廊影响分析

综合井在开挖过程中随着土体的卸荷和周围土体的变形,对盾构管廊必然产生影响。对计算模型中盾构管廊布设一系列监测点,图 5 为模型计算结果。

综合井区域内管廊底部变形随着开挖的进行而不断向上隆起,沿管廊方向变形量呈现先增大后减小的趋势,最大位移值出现在综合井中心位置,为 22.13mm。在距综合井一定范围以外,盾构管廊向下产生沉降;距综合井中心 55m,即距综合井边缘约 40m 位置处变形值约为 0mm,该区域为管廊隆起和沉降的过渡位置。

3.3 地面沉降分析

综合井在开挖过程中不可避免引起基坑周边土体变形,图 6 显示了综合井基坑开挖模型周边地面变形。根据数值模拟结果,综合井周边地面沿基坑边缘向外分为隆起区和沉降区,北侧和东侧地面沉降曲线如图 7 所示。

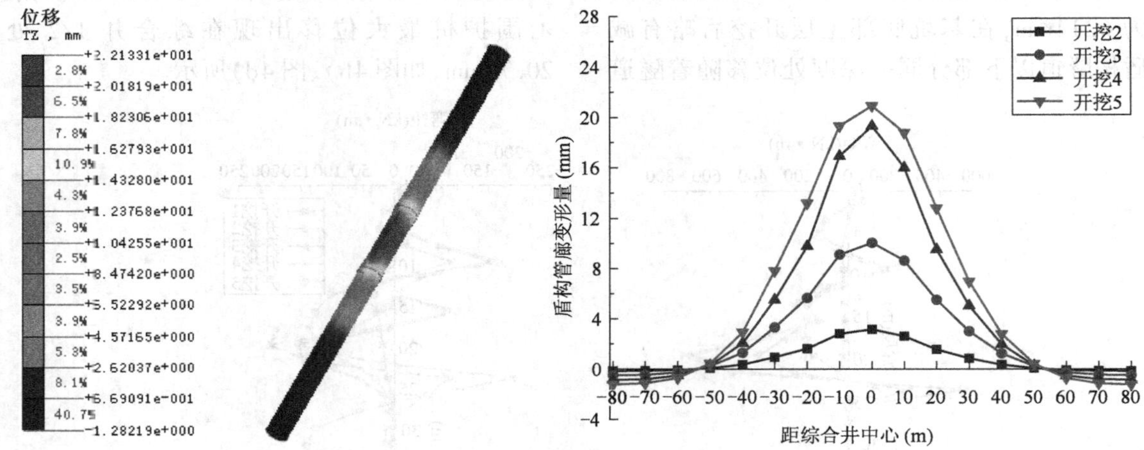

图5　盾构管廊变形

图6　综合井基坑周边地面沉降模型

对比分析基坑东侧和南侧外地面变形曲线：两者变形规律一致，但隆起与下沉过渡距离不同。某一距离内的地面上升，变形量在同一开挖阶段随距离增大而减小，同一距离地面变形量随开挖的进行而不断增大，最大上升值北侧为 15.6mm、东侧为 15.9mm；此距离外的地面下沉，变形量在同一开挖阶段随距离增大而增大，同一距离地面随开挖进行而不断增大，北侧最大沉降量为 1.56mm、东侧为 1.06mm。

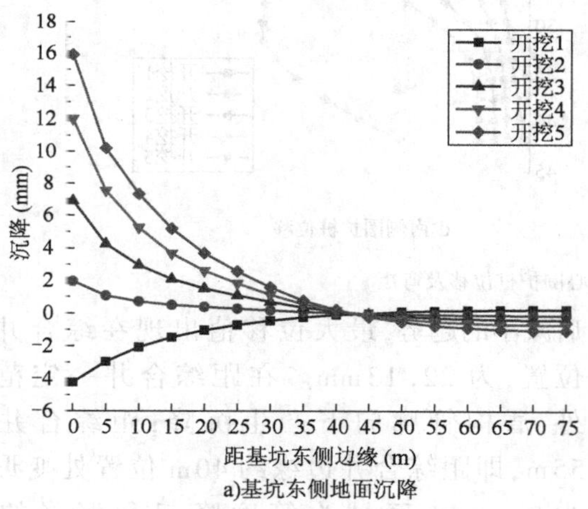

a)基坑东侧地面沉降

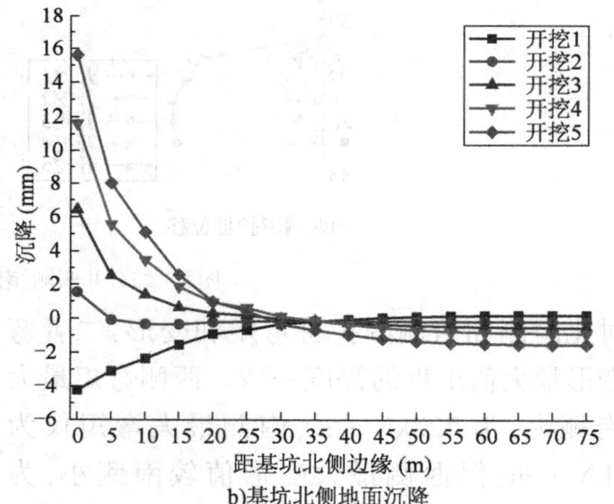

b)基坑北侧地面沉降

图7　不同位置地面随开挖沉降曲线

3.4　实测对比分析

根据数值模拟结果显示，有盾构管廊一侧中心围护桩的位移在管廊顶部以上随深度增加呈现先增大后减小规律，最大变形值出现在地面至管廊顶部之间 2/3 深度位置。通过现场实际观察支护结构变形，在管廊与地面范围之间有裂缝出现，位置与模拟结果接近。

为了进一步验证数值模型的准确性，与已有的研究文献进行对比。吴兰婷[15]通过建立同一深度不同位置的平行隧道研究了明挖基坑与盾构隧道交叉施工相互影响的问题，得出处于基坑中心下隧道变形情况如图 8a)所示，其模拟结果变形规律与本工程一致。罗鑫[16]研究了基坑开挖时下卧盾构隧道的隆起变形,通过数值模拟和现场监测得到图8b),可以发现其数值模拟结果较好地反映了工程实际情况。综合井区域内及距综合井一定范围内盾构管廊随着基坑土体的不断开挖而逐渐向上隆起,且最大变形出现在综合井中心位置处。从中心位置往两端变形值逐渐减小到0mm,在距综合井一定范围以外,盾构管廊向下产生沉降,中心位置两端变形呈现对称分布。上述研究结果佐证了本工程数值模型的准确性,为后续基坑与隧道相对不同位置的研究提供了依据。

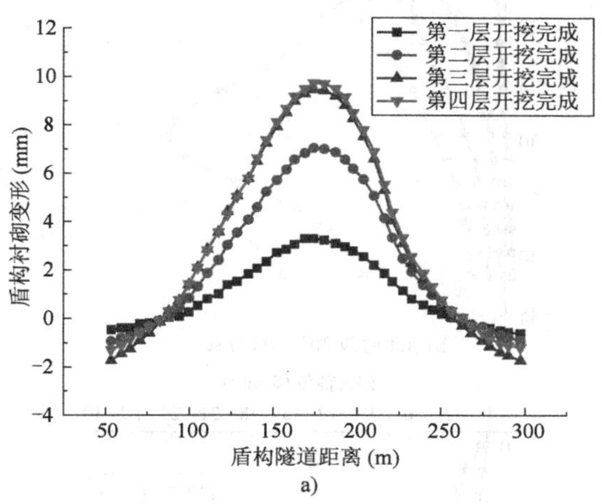

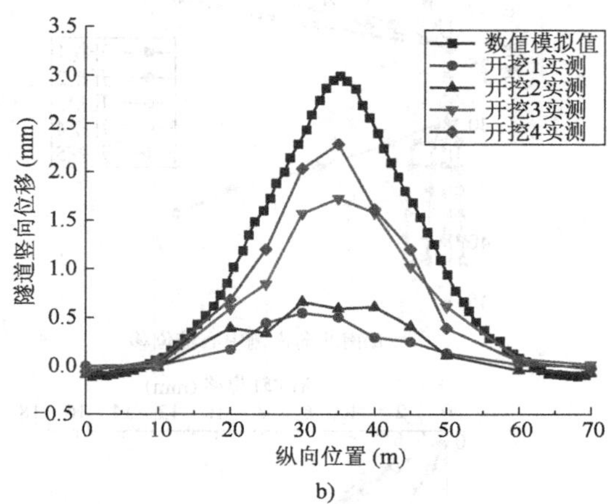

图8 研究结果对比

4 不同管廊位置与综合井相互作用

为研究管廊隧道与综合井不同相对位置产生的相互影响,建立新的数值模型如图9所示。

4.1 基坑围护体系影响对比分析

根据南侧和西侧中心围护桩随深度变形曲线并对比原始工况,综合井中心围护桩变形呈现相似的规律,如图10所示。有盾构管廊穿越的一侧(即综合井南侧)最大变形值较无盾构管廊穿越一侧大;盾构管廊穿越的一侧围护桩最大变形值出现在同一深度,约为15m。南北走向管廊和西南-东北走向管廊工况下无盾构一侧围护桩(即西侧中心围护桩)在同一深度处出现最大变形值,约为30m处;而原始工况出现最大变形值的深度较浅,约为19m处。对比分析不同工况最大变形值,存在南北向(25.9mm) > 斜向(25.6mm) > 东西向(20.78mm)。

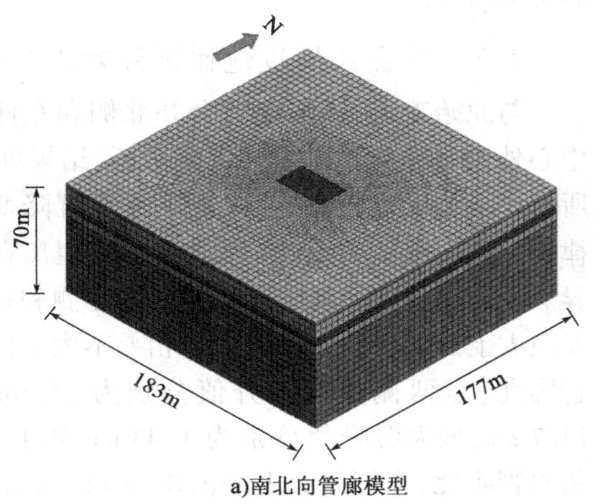

a)南北向管廊模型

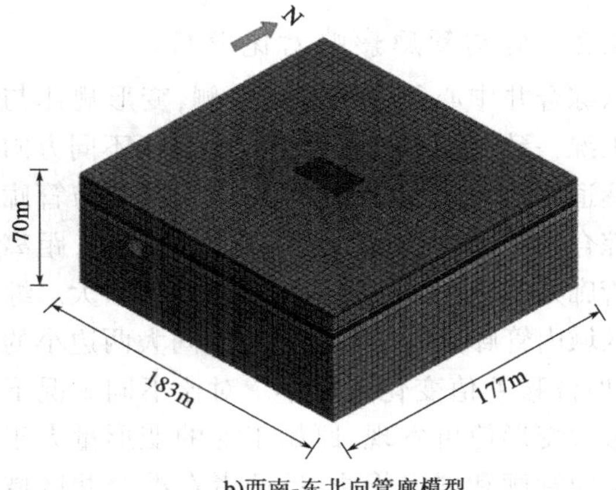

b)西南-东北向管廊模型

图9 不同方向管廊隧道模型

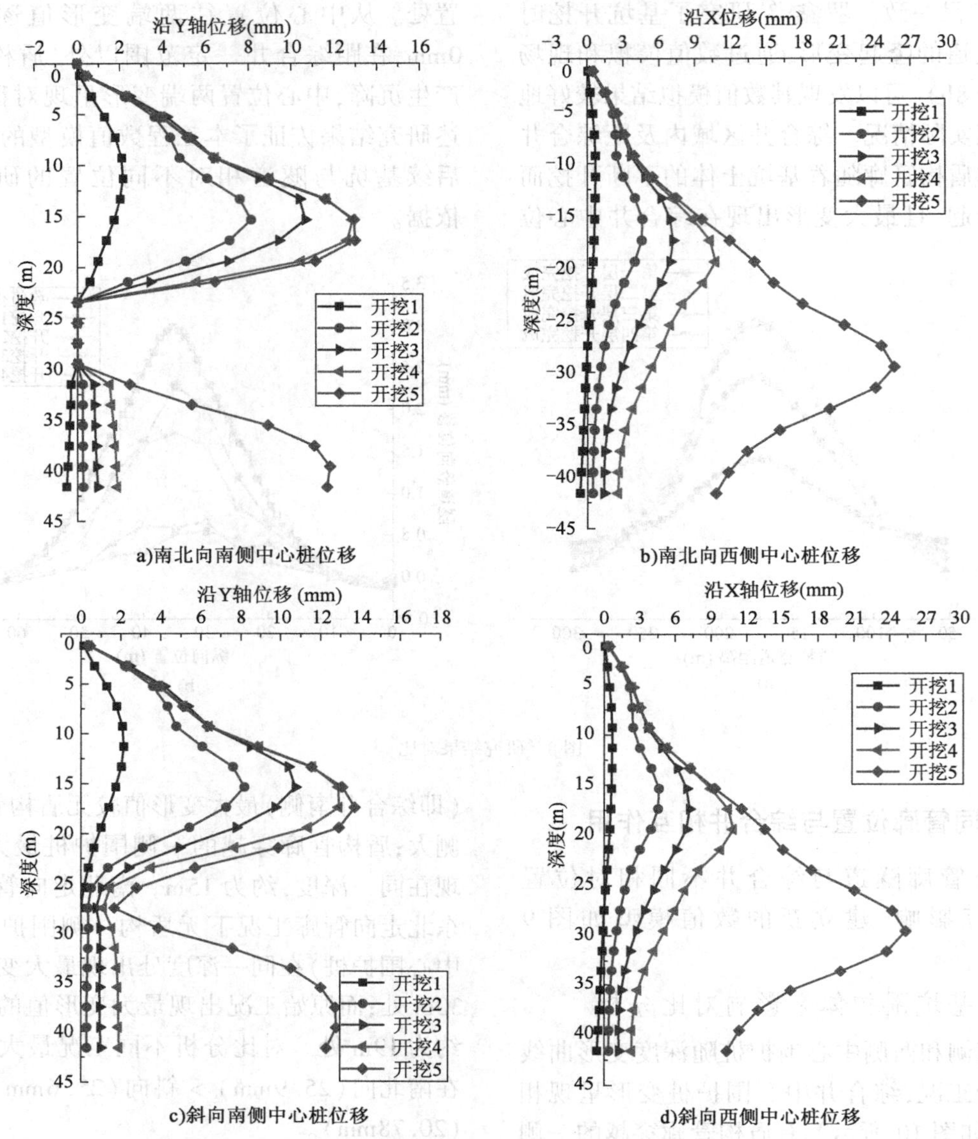

图10　综合井西侧、南侧中心围护桩位移

4.2　盾构管廊影响对比分析

从综合井中心往管廊方向两侧，变形规律与原始工况一致，如图11所示。对比分析不同方向管廊隧道数值模拟结果，可以发现此距离与管廊处于综合井区域内长度可能存在某种联系，距离随着管廊处于综合井区域内长度增大而增大。综合井区域内管廊变形量大致存在中间大两边小的趋势，但位移差值变化量较小。对比不同工况下管廊最大变形值可发现，原始工况的变形量大于南北走向管廊和斜向管廊，后两者在综合井区域内的长度分别为16.7m和19m，相差不大，而原始工况下的长度为29.7m，可见管廊最大变形量随着位于基坑内长度的增大而增大。

4.3　综合井周边地面沉降对比分析

与原始工况一样，取综合井北侧和东侧边缘中心外75m范围地面进行沉降分析，结果如图12所示。从结果发现，两种工况下地面沉降变形规律与原始工况一致，仅变形值和过渡距离存在差异。南北向管廊和斜向管廊工况下北侧和东侧地面最大上升值和最大沉降值均相差不大。南北向管廊北、东两侧最大上升值分别为14.9mm和14.7mm，最大沉降值分别为1.43mm和1.5mm；斜向管廊北、东侧最大上升值均为14.5mm，最大沉降值分别为1.47mm和1.43mm。但二者工况由于管廊方向不同，上升和下沉点至综合井基坑边缘距离不同，南北向管廊北侧距离约为42m，东侧距离约为27m;斜向管廊北侧和东侧距离都约为30m。结合两者计算结果并对比原始工况,在管廊方向上过渡距离较长,而无管廊隧道方向距离较短,在斜向管廊工况下北东侧距离相近。

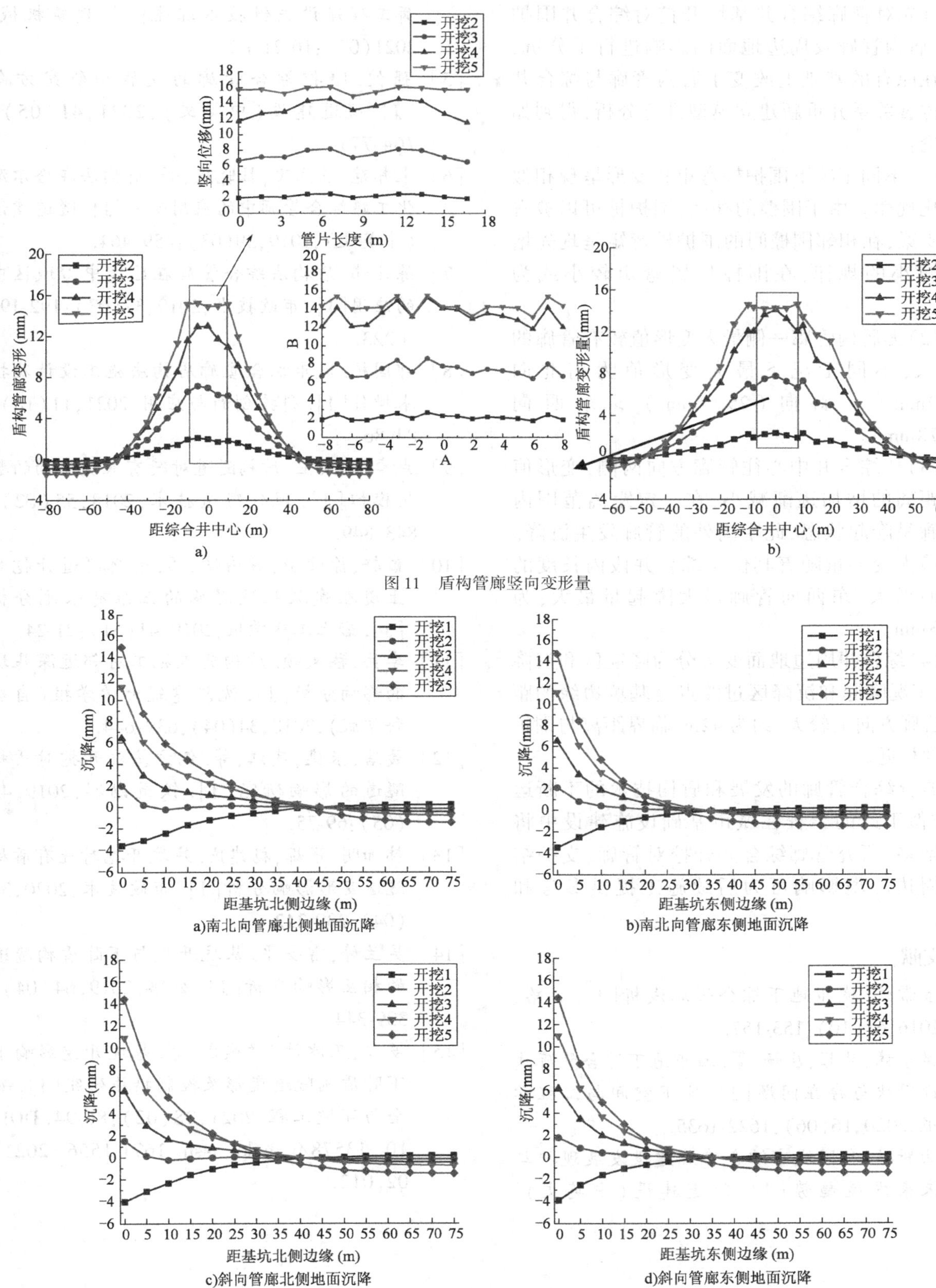

a) b)

图11 盾构管廊竖向变形量

a)南北向管廊北侧地面沉降
b)南北向管廊东侧地面沉降
c)斜向管廊北侧地面沉降
d)斜向管廊东侧地面沉降

图12 综合井基坑周边地面沉降

5 结语

首先对管廊综合井基坑开挖对综合井围护结构、盾构管廊及周边地面的影响进行了分析，然后在原有的基础上改变了盾构管廊与综合井相对位置关系并重新建立模型进行分析，得到如下结论：

(1)不同工况下围护桩弯矩和变形呈现相似的变化规律。由于围檩的存在，围护桩可以被看作简支梁，在相邻围檩间的围护桩弯矩呈现先增大后减小的规律，在围檩位置弯矩较小或为负值。

(2)无盾构管廊一侧最大变形值较有管廊的一侧大，不同工况下最大变形值为南北向(25.9mm)>斜向(25.6mm)>东西向(20.78mm)。

(3)从综合井中心往管廊方向两侧，变形值随着距离的增加逐渐减小，在一定距离范围内的管廊呈隆起状态，此距离外的管廊发生沉降。管廊最大变形量随着其位于综合井段内长度的增大而增大，东西向管廊最大隆起量最大，为22.13mm。

(4)综合井周边地面变形分为隆起区和沉降区，各工况隆起和沉降区过渡点至基坑边缘的距离在管廊方向上较大，约为42m，临界距离与围护桩长度相近。

随着综合管廊的发展和盾构技术的不断运用，类似于此的工程在城市基础设施建设中将逐渐增多，研究管廊综合井开挖对管廊、支护结构及周边环境影响可为后续施工提供参考和借鉴。

参考文献

[1] 余常俊. 城市地下综合管廊浅析[J]. 公路，2016,61(10):153-157.

[2] 梁宁慧，兰菲，庄炀，等. 城市地下综合管廊建设现状与存在问题[J]. 地下空间与工程学报，2020,16(06):1622-1635.

[3] 油新华. 我国城市综合管廊建设发展现状与未来发展趋势[J]. 隧道建设(中英文)，2018,38(10):1603-1611.

[4] 乔高平，刘志军，徐家麟，等. 城市地下综合管廊工程建设关键技术综述[J]. 建筑机械，2021(07):16-21+2.

[5] 强健. 暗挖综合管廊的发展和研究方向[J]. 隧道建设(中英文)，2021,41(05):764-771.

[6] 朱邦范，陈立飞，杜晓庆，等. 盾构法在哈尔滨化工路综合管廊中的应用研究[J]. 隧道建设(中英文)，2019,39(03):459-464.

[7] 陈建伟. 盾构法综合管廊在已建中心城区中的应用[J]. 市政技术，2019,37(03):192-194+223.

[8] 郑国栋. 城市综合管廊盾构法施工设计及技术操作[J]. 科技创新与应用，2021,11(18):84-86.

[9] 卢卓，魏焕卫. 盾构隧道对既有基坑影响的数值模拟[J]. 现代隧道技术，2018,55(S2):843-849.

[10] 戴轩，徐管应，霍海峰，等. 管廊隧道开挖对上覆在建深基坑影响的三维有限元分析[J]. 岩土工程学报，2019,41(S1):21-24.

[11] 李兵，嵇凤颖. 盾构隧道施工对邻近深基坑的影响分析[J]. 沈阳建筑大学学报(自然科学版)，2018,34(04):639-644.

[12] 聂浩，张康，鹿江，等. 侧方基坑开挖对盾构隧道的影响研究[J]. 铁道勘察，2019,45(05):69-75.

[13] 韩加明，张辉，杨建民. 基坑开挖对既有盾构隧道变形影响分析[J]. 市政技术，2020,38(04):239-242.

[14] 吴兰婷，雷安平. 基坑开挖与下卧盾构隧道的相互影响分析[J]. 公路，2019,64(04):339-344.

[15] 罗鑫，王冰洁，尹燕良，等. 基坑开挖影响下下卧盾构隧道变形及控制措施研究[J]. 安全与环境工程，2021,28(02):86-94. DOI:10.13578/j.cnki.issn.1671-1556.2021.02.012.

管棚 + 地表注浆支护的浅埋隧道下穿河道施工分析

张文接* 唐琨杰 窦磊明 徐泽鑫
（长安大学公路学院）

摘 要 随着城际铁路的发展，其穿越河流等水体的情况也越来越普遍。如何在浅覆土的情况下穿越水体，是确保工程安全顺利进行的关键。本文依托某城际铁路下穿河流实际工程，采用有限元数值对比分析了“管棚 + 地表注浆”综合加固与未加固工况下穿施工过程中围岩的位移及管棚的受力。结果表明，围岩变形量：拱顶 > 拱底 > 拱腰。其最大沉降 22.1mm，最大隆起 15.3mm，左右拱腰处的水平位移基本一致，均在 6mm 左右。注浆加固对拱顶的加固效果明显优于拱底，拱顶沉降与拱顶隆起分别减少 47% 与 10.6% 左右。由于高压旋喷桩的弹性模量远大于土体部分，管棚在高压旋喷桩相交部分所受到的应力最大。模拟结果与实测值相差 10% 左右，两者趋势类似。研究结果可为类似工程提供借鉴。

关键词 城际铁路 下穿河流 数值模拟 地表预注浆 管棚注浆 围岩变形

0 引言

随着我国经济的发展，隧道建设日益增多，在隧道的施工建设中遇到下穿水体的情况越来越普遍，如地铁隧道下穿河流湖泊等。对于下穿水体的隧道，如果不能提出安全可靠的施工方案，轻则影响施工进度和质量，重则导致隧道塌方，发生安全事故。因此，如何保证隧道在施工过程中的安全，成为目前隧道施工的关键问题[1-3]。

宋艺[4]以某地铁隧道为例，阐述了盾构隧道覆土较浅时下穿水体的设计方案，并用数值模拟方法进行了验算。黄锋等[5]以旦架哨隧道为例，用数值模拟方法对施工中的围岩位移进行了分析。袁海清等[6]通过 FLAC3D 软件对管棚超前支护作用进行了数值模拟分析。邵迅等[7]以合肥地铁一号线为例，通过数值模拟的方法，研究了盾构隧道开挖时隧道的竖向变形、应力等规律。闫莉等[8]以青岛地铁某隧道下穿河道段为依托，通过数值模拟研究了下穿河流施工时所遇富水软弱地层的结构及其地表变形特性。上述研究分析了下穿水体隧道在施工过程中的变形特征、塑性区分布，并提供了一些加固方法，主要有注浆加固和管棚超前支护。注浆加固是用浆液填充围岩空隙，从而提高围岩强度和刚度；管棚超前支护是通过加固圈起到“承载拱”的作用，而管棚又具有“简支梁”的作用，可承担上部围岩荷载。但目前的研究主要集中在单一加固方法上，而综合考虑管棚支护加地表注浆加固对隧道的加固效果的研究相对较少。

本文以某城际铁路隧道下穿河道实际工程为依托，介绍了下穿河道隧道的施工方法以及支护措施，并通过数值模拟对比分析了“管棚支护 + 地表注浆加固”组合加固措施下隧道围岩位移及管棚受力情况。

1 工程概况

1.1 下穿工程概况

某城际铁路隧道下穿一河流，该河流水深枯水期为 0.8 ~ 1.0m，丰水期为 2.0 ~ 2.5m，河道宽约 26m。隧道采用双洞形式，两洞之间的距离为 15m；开挖方法采用 CD 法，加固方式为超前小导管与管棚复合加固；选用长 4.5m 的超前小导管，环向间距 0.3m，以及长 10m 的管棚，环向间距 0.3m，搭接长度大于 3m。初支采用 C25 混凝土，厚 25cm；二衬采用 C35 混凝土，厚 45cm。河道段采用地表注浆加固，并在施工前施作改河工程。

1.2 下穿隧道与河流基本位置关系

隧道进洞里程为 DK50 + 860，出洞里程为 DK54 + 700，其中在 DK50 + 922 ~ DK50 + 969 段下穿大棉河，城际铁路隧道从河流下方穿过，与河道成 32°角，河底距离隧道顶部约 6.6m，河岸高约 3m。河道与隧道的相对位置如图 1 所示。

图1　河道与隧道平面示意图

河道处主要为粉质黏土和泥质砂岩,从上往下分别为2.2m厚粉质黏土,5.1m厚全风化泥质砂岩,3.7m厚强风化泥质砂岩,其余均为中风化泥质砂岩。隧道基本处于强风化、中风化泥质砂岩层。其地层信息如图2所示。

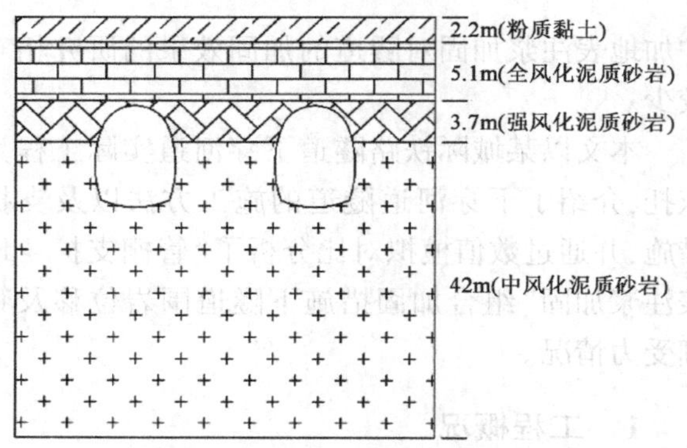

图2　施工现场地质纵断面图

2　区间下穿段施工方案

2.1　地表注浆加固

隧道开挖前施作改河工程并对河道进行注浆加固处理,一般而言,加固范围取隧道开挖半径的3～5倍。本次加固的竖向范围为隧道底部以下2m至地表,横向范围为隧道轮廓线以外1.93m。在加固范围四周设置一圈高压旋喷桩以减少浆液的流失,采用直径800mm、间距600mm、咬合200mm的旋喷桩布置,低于隧道底3m。注浆加固平面如图3所示。

隧道采用水灰比为1:1的纯水泥浆液,扩散半径为1m,其孔位布置设置为横向间距1.7m、纵向间距1.4m。注浆前先进行钻孔,并在孔内放入钢管,通过钢管向围岩内注浆。注浆加固范围如图4所示。

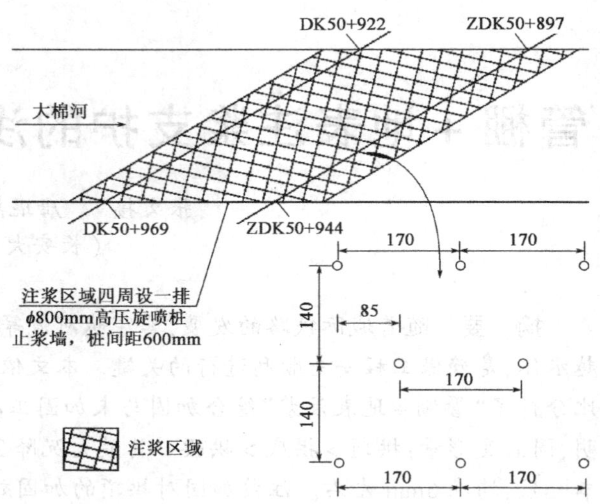

图3　注浆加固平面示意图

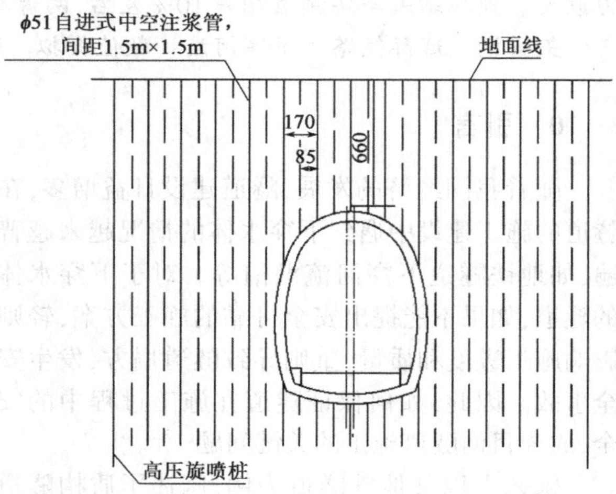

图4　地表注浆加固范围

2.2　超前管棚支护

管棚支护是为了将上部围岩的荷载传递给钢拱架和掌子面前的土体上,以减小掌子面土体所受压力,从而保证掌子面的稳定,提高安全系数。管棚注浆是用浆液填充围岩内存在的裂隙,从而达到提高围岩强度和刚度的目的。常见的管棚注浆形式有单排管和双排管。本工程采用单排管棚,管棚长10m,倾角为11°,布置于洞顶150°范围内,相邻管棚间距为40cm。管棚外径89mm,壁厚5mm,管壁孔位为梅花型布置,孔径10mm,尾部留有150cm止浆段,选用水灰比为1:1的水泥浆液作为注浆材料。

2.3　洞身四步CD法开挖

导坑采用台阶法开挖,每节台阶开挖长度为3m,每节台阶开挖比下一节台阶开挖超前6m,每节台阶开挖完成后立即进行钢拱架的施作并挂钢筋网，喷射混凝土；然后进行初支、横隔板和中隔壁的施作，并尽快将这些结构封闭成环。开挖完一节隧道后喷射8cm厚混凝土封闭掌子面。

3 下穿方案数值模拟

3.1 模型概况

本文采用有限元数值模拟软件对下穿河流隧道施工过程进行数值模拟。考虑边界效应的影响，隧道施工仅对3~5倍洞径范围内的土体产生影响，所以数值模拟隧道的计算范围为：向上取至地表，向下取4倍开挖洞径，左右边界各沿隧道中心取5倍洞径[9-10]，即150m(长)×85m(宽)×53m(高)。模型中各土层以及地表注浆区和管棚加固区采用德鲁克-普拉格本构，高压旋喷桩以及初支部分采用弹性本构。模型共划分了134152个单元，225006个节点。模型及其网格划分如图5所示。

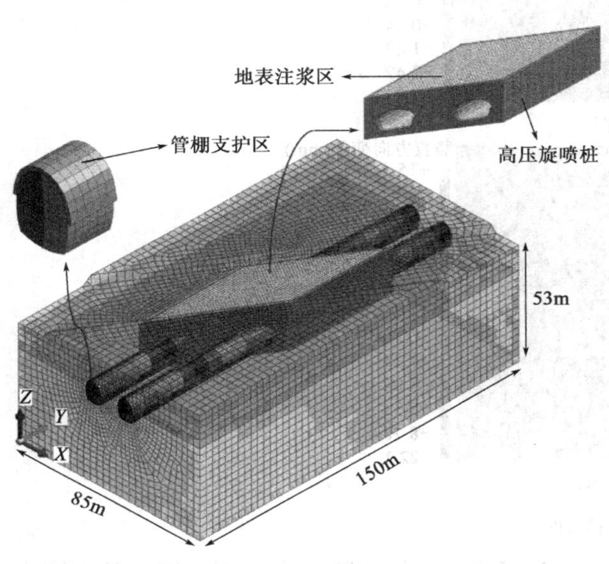

图5 下穿河道计算模型

3.2 参数选取

计算时可按照等效的原则将初支及内支撑中钢拱架的弹性模量折算给混凝土，使之成为一个整体。其计算公式如式(1)所示。

$$E = E_0 + \frac{S_g \times E_g}{S_c} \quad (1)$$

式中：E——混凝土计算后的弹性模量；

E_0——原混凝土的弹性模量；

S_g——钢拱架的截面积；

E_g——钢拱架的弹性模量；

S_c——混凝土截面积。

高压旋喷桩的相互咬合可等效为地下连续墙，如图6所示。等效后地下连续墙的厚度可由等刚度转换原则得到，其计算公式如式(2)所示。

$$E_c \frac{\pi D^4}{64} = E_c \frac{(D-t)h^3}{12} \quad (2)$$

$$h = \sqrt[3]{\frac{3\pi D^4}{16(D-t)}}$$

式中：D——桩的直径；

t——相邻两根桩的咬合距离；

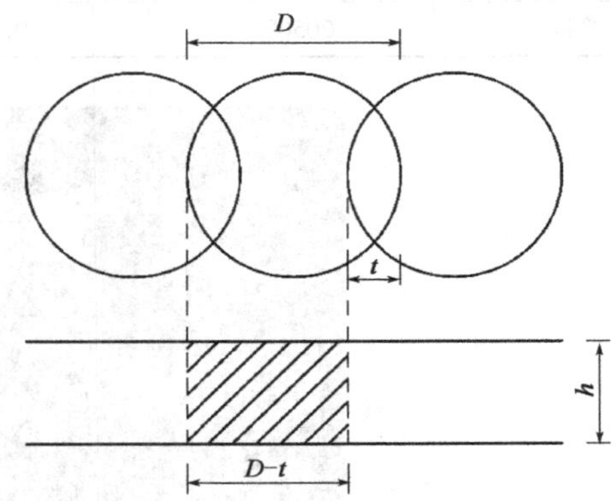

图6 旋喷桩等效地下连续墙

地表注浆加固体与管棚注浆加固体的弹性模量均采用刚度折算法将刚度折算到围岩中，提高围岩刚度。其计算方法类似，在此以管棚注浆加固体的计算为例。

$$E_1 = E_2 + \frac{A_c \times E_c}{A} \quad (3)$$

式中：E_1——管棚加固后围岩弹性模量；

E_2——原始围岩压缩模量；

A_c——注浆体截面面积；

E_c——注浆体硬化后的弹性模量；

A——注浆后钢管混泥土的截面面积。

式(3)中未考虑管棚钢管的弹性模量，因为建立模型时已将管棚钢管以植入式梁的形式添加在管棚实体中。二衬作为长期安全储备，计算时可不予考虑[11]。由于施工前已经施作改河工程，计算时未考虑水的影响。模型中所用材料的参数如表1所示。

4 结果分析

4.1 围岩变形分析

本文取隧道进洞口断面进行拱顶沉降、水平

收敛分析。开挖后围岩的水平收敛及竖向位移如图7所示。

下穿段地层参数　　表1

材料名称	弹性模量(MPa)	容重(KN/m^2)	泊松比	粘聚力(kPa)	内摩擦角(°)
粉质黏土	30	18.5	0.28	38	16
全风化泥质砂岩	37	20	0.23	39	20
强风化泥质砂岩	750	21.2	0.22	120	33
中风化泥质砂岩	1800	22.2	0.21	140	35
地表注浆加固	800	19.6	0.3	122	33
管棚注浆加固	1000	22	0.3	200	35
初期支护	105000	25	0.25	—	—
高压旋喷桩	30000	25	0.2	—	—
管棚	205000	0.3	78	—	—

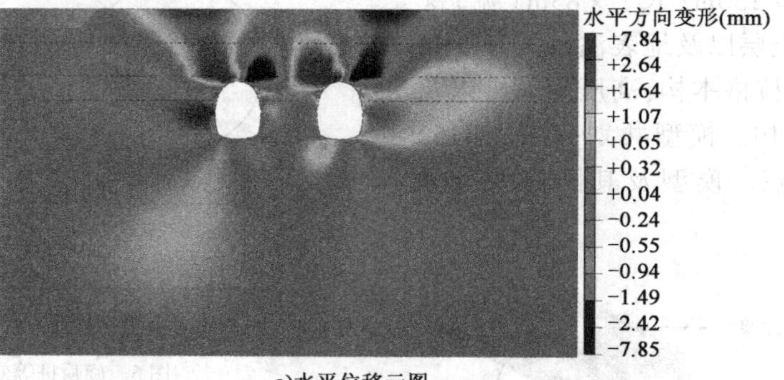

a)水平位移云图

竖直方向变形(mm)
+15.3
+8.86
+6.35
+4.70
+3.35
+2.38
+1.39
+0.20
-1.33
-3.04
-5.33
-8.78
-22.1

b)竖向位移云图

图7　围岩位移云图

隧道开挖后拱顶和拱底围岩向隧道内部移动,但拱顶会把受到的围岩压力转化为左右方向的水平推力,因此隧道会产生左右方向的位移,而且位移基本是对称的,这是因为隧道结构所受到的力基本也是对称的。从图7a)中可以看出向左方向的最大位移发生在左侧隧道的右上方,最大值为7.85mm;向右方向的最大位移发生在右侧隧道的左上方,最大值为7.84mm。隧道拱顶发生沉降,拱底向上隆起,其最大沉降量位于左侧隧道进洞口拱顶处,最大值为22.1mm;最大隆起量位于左侧隧道出洞口拱底处,最大值为15.3mm。

为了进一步探究隧道全长度范围内的沉降和隆起,本文间隔3m提取一次隧道左右洞的拱顶与拱底的沉降数据,绘制成图8所示的曲线图。

从图8a)中可以看出中间部分的沉降明显小于前后部分,且左右洞所对应的隆起曲线变化的位置并不相同,左洞沉降约在距洞口30m时减小,右洞沉降约在距洞口60m时减小,但是左右洞沉降减小段的长度与最小沉降一致。这是由于注浆加固区相对于隧道走向是倾斜的,且左右洞减小的最小值对应的是高压旋喷桩位置。从图8b)中可以看出拱底隆起有四个突变点,这四个点的位置分别对应隧道穿越高压旋喷桩的位置。当穿越旋喷桩后，其隆起量逐渐增大，但是仍小于加固区以外的部分。从图8中可以看出地表注浆对隧道的沉降有明显的控制效果，可减小47%左右的沉降，但是对隧道隆起的控制效果有限，可减小10%左右的隆起。由于高压旋喷桩的弹性模量很大，隧道在高压旋喷桩位置处变形较小，这一变化在拱底隆起曲线中更为明显，其四个尖点对应的就是左右线隧道与高压旋喷桩相交位置。

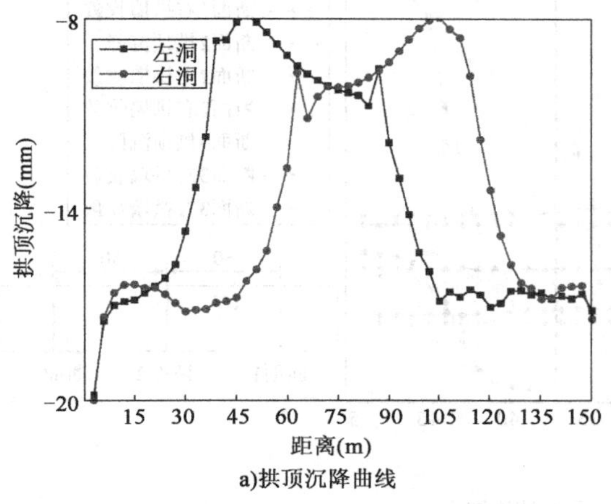

a)拱顶沉降曲线

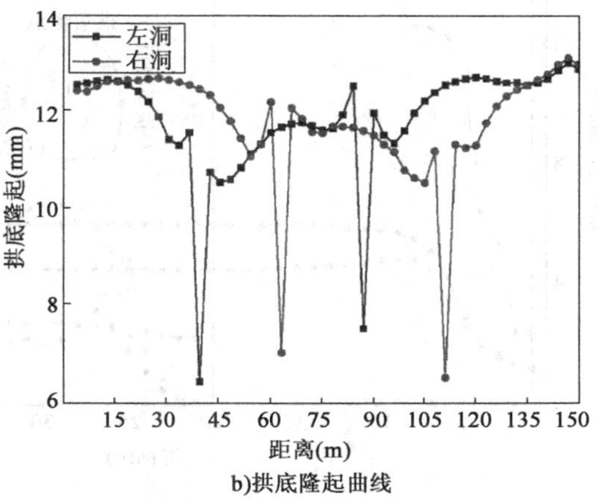

b)拱底隆起曲线

图8 隧道竖向变形曲线

4.2 管棚受力

从管棚所受的应力图(图9)中可以看出其应力主要集中在隧道与高压旋喷桩相交的位置，其他位置应力大致相同，但中间的注浆加固段应力略小于加固段之外的区域。管棚所受的最大拉应力为33280.66KN/m²，最大压应力为-20695.10kN/m²，均位于隧道与高压旋喷桩相交处。在隧道与高压旋喷桩相交处管棚的应力发生突变主要是由于高压旋喷桩的弹性模量与土体以及地表注浆加固区相差太大。而地表注浆区管棚所受的应力小于两端土体，说明注浆加固能在一定程度上减小管棚的弯曲应力，但是改变不大。

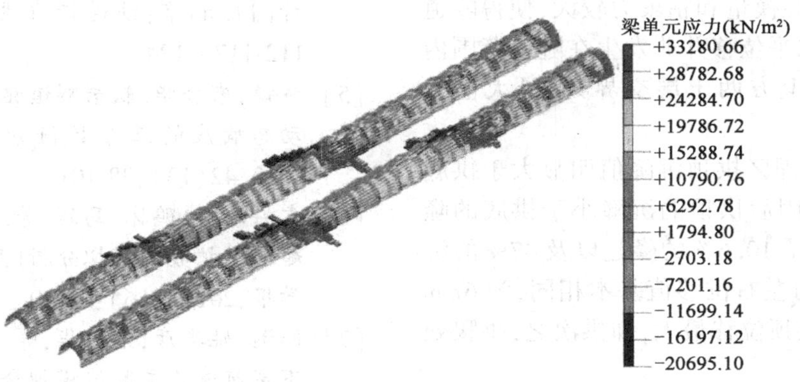

图9 管棚应力图

5 现场实测结果

为了进一步了解隧道在施工过程中注浆加固部分与非注浆加固部分的变形情况，按照10~50m选定断面。本部分共选择三个监测断面，间隔50m，进行了为期48天的现场监测，包括拱顶沉降、周边收敛两项，其中断面2位于注浆加固区内。监测结果如图10所示。

从监测结果可以看出，拱顶沉降与周边收敛具有相似的演变规律，但是在数量级上大约是3:1的关系。这一现象验证了数值模拟的结果，虽然数值模拟结果中两者的关系约为4:1，但也定性说明了在这种复杂地质条件下修建隧道尤其需要控制拱顶的沉降，而左右拱墙的位移基本相同。

从图中可以看出注浆加固区的变形，无论是

拱顶沉降还是左右拱墙的收敛均小于未注浆加固区,约为其1/2,说明地表注浆加固对隧道的变形有很好的控制效果。现场监测结果反映了结构的变形具有一定的阶段性,即在开挖完成后结构会发生较快的变形,完成荷载的释放后变形趋于稳定。

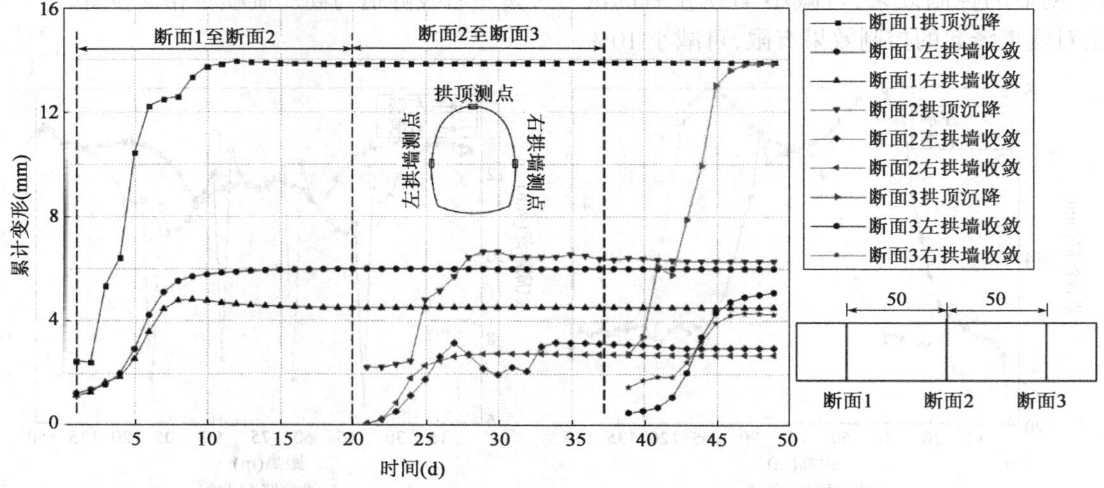

图10 现场监测断面与监测结果

6 结语

本文以某浅埋下穿河流城际铁路隧道工程为依托,采用有限元软件对比分析了未加固与"管棚支护+地表注浆"组合加固工况下围岩的变形及管棚受力情况,得出以下结论:

(1)由于隧道位于中风化泥质砂岩和强风化泥质砂岩中,其弹性模量和粘聚力较大,使得隧道位移较小且最大水平位移并非发生在隧道范围内而是发生在隧道上方两土层交界处,最大值为7.85mm。

(2)未注浆加固区拱顶沉降值明显大于拱底隆起值,但注浆加固后拱顶的沉降小于拱底的隆起,注浆加固减少了10.6%的隆起以及47%的沉降。而两侧拱腰的左右位移值基本相同,为6mm左右。其大小为拱顶位移最大,仰拱次之,拱腰处位移最小。

(3)由于高压旋喷桩的弹性模量远大于土体及地表注浆加固体,管棚在与高压旋喷桩相交部位所受应力最大。因此,在实际施工过程中可通过降低浆液材料配比及材料属性的方法适当降低高压旋喷桩的弹性模量。

参考文献

[1] 房师涛.成都地铁4号线下穿铁路桥三维数值模拟分析[J].重庆交通大学学报(自然科学版),2018,37(7):20-27.

[2] 李自力,潘青,曹志勇,等.盾构长距离下穿越河流数值模拟及施工参数优化设计研究[J].现代隧道技术,2020,57(S1):442-449.

[3] 冉万云.近水库铁路隧道穿越F4断层施工与监测分析[J].重庆交通大学学报(自然科学版),2015,34(6):37-42+47.

[4] 宋艺.地铁区间隧道浅覆土下穿水库方案设计[J].北京:铁道标准设计,2017,61(10):112-117+124.

[5] 黄锋,朱合华.软岩隧道施工过程中围岩位移动态响应的三维数值分析[J].施工技术,2013,42(13):98-101.

[6] 袁海清,傅鹤林,马婷,等.隧道管棚加预注浆超前支护数值模拟分析[J].铁道科学与工程学报,2012,9(6):24-29.

[7] 邵迅,姚华彦,张振华,等.合肥地铁盾构隧道下穿河道施工数值模拟分析[J].合肥工业大学学报(自然科学版),2017,40(1):95-100.

[8] 闫莉,张智慧,朱兴.地铁隧道下穿河流施工遇富水软弱地层的控制技术[J].城市轨道交通研究,2021,24(3):138-141.

[9] 邵保平,陈路海,董赟盛.基于流-固耦合理论的水体下盾构隧道施工渗流规律[J].太原理工大学学报,2020,51(5):634-640.

[10] 赵文财,范飞飞,李子琦,等.基于大管棚支护的大断面黄土隧道穿越冲沟地貌控制效

果分析[J].公路,2020,65(8):380-385.
[11] 陈京贤,曾德荣,王俊召,等.基于应力释放率的大跨径回填土隧道的围岩稳定性研究[J].中外公路,2018,38(6):173-177.

基于BIM二次开发的盾构管片参数化拼装方法

李智昊 贾兴利* 刘 凯 焦泽轩
(长安大学公路学院)

摘 要 盾构隧道建模分析在研究中已经十分成熟,但是盾构隧道管片在建模过程中还面临工作量大、人工操作效率低且模型精度不高等难题,为了解决上述问题,本文提出一种基于BIM二次开发技术的盾构管片参数化建模方法。首先,采用Revit概念体量法创建通用盾构管片模型,并通过12个自适应点位控制管片创建管片自适应族。其次,为减少人为因素误差,基于Civil 3D二次开发读取隧道轴线数据,通过数据运算自动绘制隧道中心线。然后,通过Dynamo可视化程序编辑器选择管片自适应族、调整管片参数、拾取隧道中心线,实现盾构隧道管片自动拼装建模。最后,基于该研究成果,以西安市某工程为例,验证了BIM二次开发技术的实用性和参数化拼装建模的可行性。研究结果表明,盾构管片参数化拼装技术能有效提升工作效率,在保证模型的精度要求下提升建模速度,基于BIM二次开发的盾构管片参数化拼装方法是可行的。

关键词 隧道工程 参数化拼装 BIM 盾构隧道 二次开发

0 引言

BIM技术在国内应用愈加广泛,BIM技术在城市交通工程领域中的应用正处于快速发展阶段[1]。盾构法因其在施工过程中安全性高、掘进速度快、自动化水平高、不受气候影响、无噪声与扰动等优点,广泛应用于城市隧道建设中。将BIM技术运用到隧道工程,实现隧道盾构技术与信息化技术深入结合,可极大地提高隧道工程项目的管理水平[2]。目前,BIM技术在盾构隧道管片的应用还存在一定的局限性。利用BIM技术进行盾构隧道管片建模,虽然可以缩短施工周期,节约施工成本[3],但是预制盾构管片作为异形构件,有着大量独立的信息参数,存在建模重复率高且效率低、工作量大、精细化程度不足和误差较大等问题[4]。因此,利用BIM技术进行隧道管片参数化建模,实现管片快速拼装建模,是BIM技术在盾构隧道应用研究的核心[5]。

国内已有许多学者对隧道参数化建模进行了相关研究。刘兆新等[6]研究了新奥法隧道Revit参数化建模,实现了初期支护模型快速创建与自动布设。朱永学等[7]利用Civil 3D + Revit + Dynamo实现公路隧道参数化建模,有效解决了公路隧道工程BIM参数化程度低、联动性差等问题。赵云辉等[8]通过对地铁区间设计轴线分段拟合处理,基于Revit二次开发技术,提出了管片环坐标、方位角和旋转角等参数的计算方法。唐艳梅等[9]对隧道设计轴线转弯角和转弯环管片的偏转角进行理论计算,建立盾构隧道BIM模型。上述学者主要对基于BIM技术的隧道建模与管片排版方法进行了深入研究,但对于隧道管片模型自动生成技术研究较少。魏章俊等[10]基于Micro Station创建标准双面楔形通用盾构单元环精细模型,并通过二次开发实现了盾构隧道模型的自动化创建。陈曦等[11]基于Revit和Dynamo建立通用管片模型,实现区间管片全过程的自动拼装。以上两位学者基于二次开发技术实现了盾构管片模型自动化生成,但建模流程较为烦琐,建模流程有待进一步优化。

本研究针对上述问题,以盾构隧道为研究对

1.基金项目:陕西省重点研发计划项目(2021SF-514)。

象,通过建立隧道通用管片,基于 Revit + Dynamo 插件,完成盾构隧道管片参数化拼装。并基于 Civil 3D 二次开发,读取 Excel 表格的坐标、高程数据自动生成隧道中心线,通过 Dynamo 插件拾取隧道中心线和管片自适应族后,实现盾构隧道管片快速拼装和自动建模。

1　参数化建模流程

盾构隧道是由环状管片单元连续拼装而成的一段狭长的区间结构,盾构隧道中心线实质是一条空间三维曲线[12]。针对盾构隧道的特点选择合适的建模平台,可以使创建盾构隧道 BIM 模型更加便捷[13]。首先基于 Civil 3D 二次开发实现盾构隧道中心线自动生成,应用 Revit 软件创建盾构隧道管片自适应族,通过 Dynamo 拾取中心线和管片自适应族,以可视化编码程序实现盾构管片自动拼装和 BIM 模型快速生成,具体流程如图 1 所示。

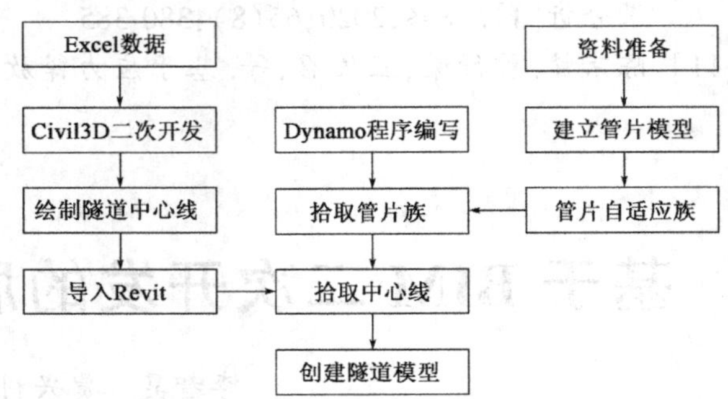

图1　参数化建模流程

1.1　建模平台选择

常见的 BIM 平台有四类,包括以 Revit 和 Civil 3D 为核心软件的 Autodesk 平台,以 MicroStation 为基础平台开发的 Bentley 平台,以 CATIA 为核心软件的 Dassault 平台,还有以 Tekla Structures 为核心软件的 Tekla 平台[14]。几类 BIM 平台的对比如表 1 所示。

BIM 平台对比　　表1

平　台	核心软件	面向专业	优　点	缺　点
Autodesk	Revit、Civil 3D	道路、桥梁、基础设施等	界面与 CAD 相似,使用操作简单,应用范围广	平台之间数据格式不统一,软件对大型数据文件处理不理想
Bentley	Open Roads Designer	公路、桥梁、建筑等	专业性强,数据管理能力出色	学习难度较大,应用成本高
Dassault	CATIA	船舶制造、航空航天等	参数化建模能力强,对复杂的大型结构拥有良好的处理能力	使用和操作上相对比较复杂,不容易掌握
Tekla	Tekla Structures	钢结构	解决大型复杂钢结构工程的难点问题具有独特的优势	主要用于钢结构设计,软件在一般的工程领域应用范围较窄

通过对上述几类 BIM 平台对比分析,结合盾构隧道结构狭长、三维空间变化的特点,最终决定采用 Civil 3D + Revit + Dynamo 创建盾构隧道管片 BIM 模型。

1.2　Dynamo 参数化设计软件

Dynamo 是基于 Revit 的一款参数化设计插件,在 Revit 2018 以上的版本中直接作为内置插件安装在菜单栏中,Dynamo 本身也可作为一款软件独立存在。在 Dynamo 软件中,程序代码以可视化窗口显示,并通过节点图形来访问 Revit API(编程接口),实现 Revit 的扩展功能。在 Dynamo 中,每个节点都能够执行相应的任务。一个窗口节点的输出通过线路连接输入至另一个窗口节点。一系列的窗口通过线路,由一个节点流向另一个节点,最终形成网络,实现 Revit 的参数化设计和自动化建模功能。Dynamo 以其较高的开放性和可塑性,允许用户自定义逻辑算法,满足不同用户的使用需求[15]。

1.3　管片参数化开发思路

1.3.1　通用管片模型创建

(1)通用管片结构

盾构隧道通用管片环由 6 块预制钢筋混凝土管片块环形拼装而成,包括 1 个封顶块(F)、2 个连接块(L_1、L_2)和 3 个标准块(B_1、B_2、B_3),如图 2 所示。

(2)盾构管片自适应族创建

基于 Revit 概念体量法创建盾构管片模型,可以直接拾取平面几何图形生成模型实体,解决管片曲面较为复杂的问题。为了便于后续利用 Dynamo 拾取节点自动生成模型,需要创建管片模型自适应点,以盾构管片标准块为例,在管片每一处圆弧侧的起点、中心点和终点创建自适应点,按照由外到内,由上到下的原则标注序号,如图 3a)所示。创建完成的管片自适应族如图 3b)所示。

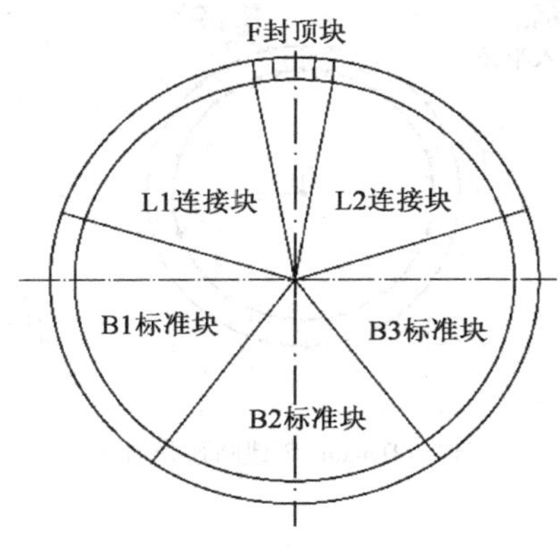

图 2 通用管片环结构

1.3.2 Civil 3D 二次开发

Civil 3D 是基于 AutoCAD 开发的一款具有强大路线设计功能的 BIM 软件,可以根据平面和纵断面线形快速生成对应三维线形[5]。在实际工程中,隧道中心线有时会以表格数据的形式记录,当数据量较大时,手动输入数据建立路线模型工作量大,且操作较为繁琐。为减少上述人为因素引起的误差,提高工作效率,基于 Civil 3D 二次开发实现读取 Excel 数据自动生成路线三维线形,可以减少重复建模工作,节省大量时间。

基于 Civil 3D 的. NET AP,使用 C#编程语言进行 Civil 3D 二次开发。开发工具选择 Visual Studio 2019,. NET API 只提供了程序接口,二次开发命令则需要使用软件自己的程序集,因此在进行二次开发前,应根据开发的需要,向项目中添加必要的引用程序。在项目引用中选择 Civil 3D 安装目录下 acdbmgd. dll、acmgd. dll、accoremgd. dll 等 5 个. dll 文件后,即可编写程序进行二次开发工作,如图 4 所示。

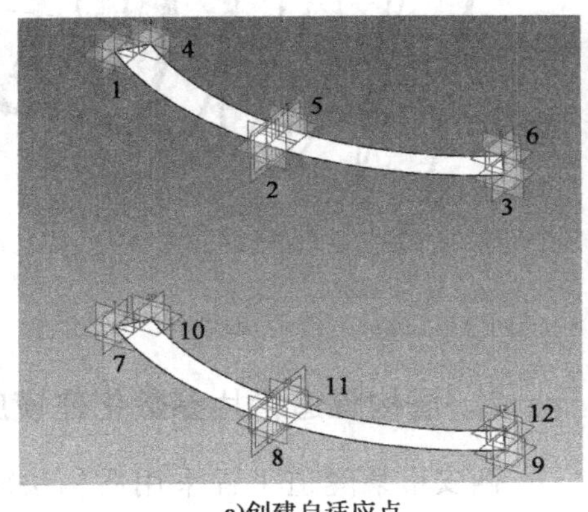

a)创建自适应点

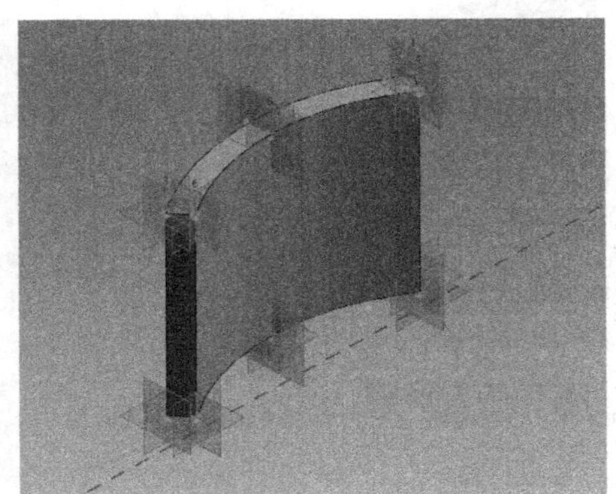

b)管片自适应族

图 3 管片族创建

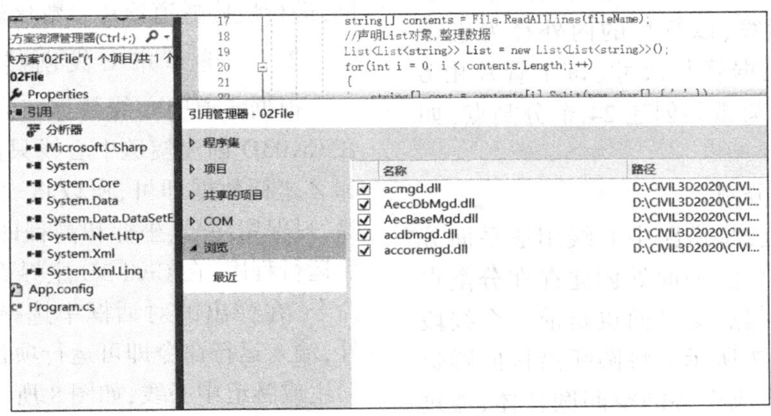

图 4 引用文件

1.3.3　管片参数化建模

隧道管片拼装过程中,传统的方法需要人工处理大量数据,大量重复的建模工作不仅使效率低下,还容易造成误差,降低模型精度。基于Dynamo实现盾构隧道管片自动拼装建模,通过可视化程序编辑器选择管片自适应族、调整管片参数、拾取隧道中心线,运行程序后即可自动生成隧道管片3D模型,并且满足相邻管片、管环间连续紧密贴合的要求,具体思路如下:

(1)隧道基本参数设置

基于Dynamo软件,拾取导入Revit的隧道中心线,选择已经创建完成的管片自适应族,并根据实际需要调整基本参数,如管片外径、管片内径、管片宽度和管片角度,其他可调整参数有环间螺栓个数和参数错缝类型,如图5所示。

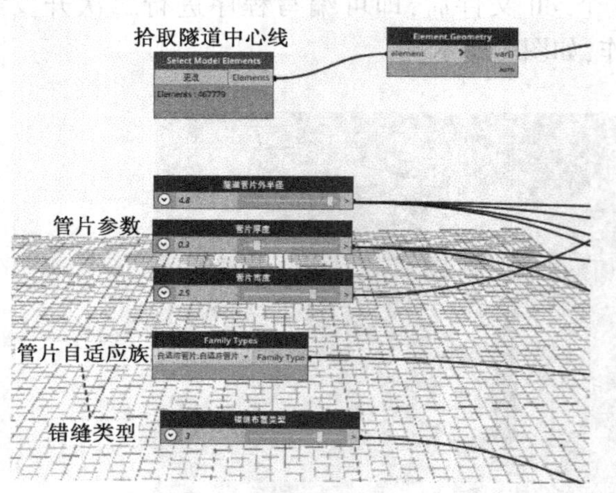

图5　隧道基本参数设置

(2)创建圆弧与圆弧分割点

管片环的平面为圆形,在Dynamo中统一使用圆弧命令。一个管片环由3种类型的6个管片组成,通过程序运算,以管片的内外径为直径分别创建圆弧,并根据管片尺寸,每个管片由6个分割点控制,每个圆弧共创建24个分割点,如图6所示。

(3)隧道中心线分割

根据管片的厚度,将道路中心线用法平面分割成多个线段,在每个法平面处创建存在分割点的圆弧,每个线段的起点法平面也是前一个线段的终点法平面,如图7所示。将圆弧沿按照隧道中心线的线形拉伸形成空心的空间圆柱体,通过数据运算将管片自适应模型填充至分割点包围的区间内,即完成隧道管片模型的创建。

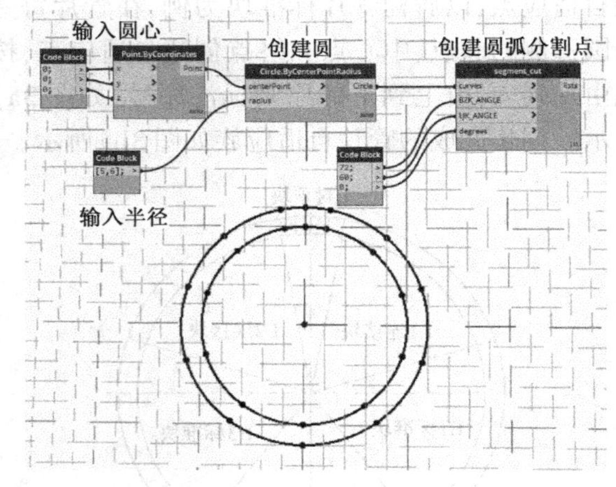

图6　Dynamo创建圆弧分割点

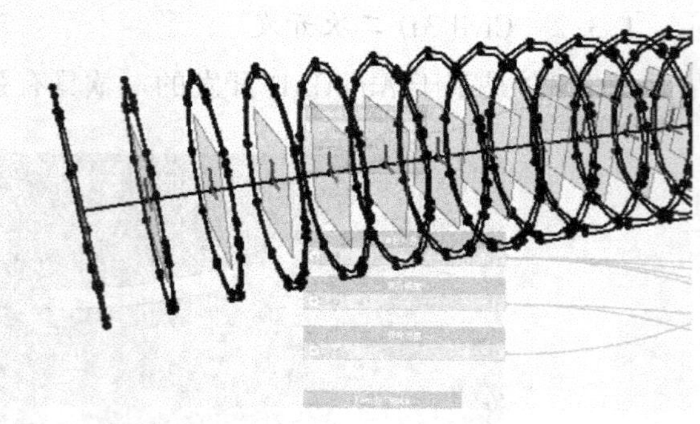

图7　隧道中心线分割

2　盾构隧道管片参数化建模应用

西安市某隧道工程采用盾构法施工,盾构隧道管环基本参数为:管片外径6500mm,管片内径6000mm,管片厚度1600mm,标准块圆心角72°,连接块圆心角62°,封顶块圆心角20°,现以该项目为例,进行盾构隧道管片参数化建模应用。

2.1　隧道中心线创建

根据隧道中心线数据,建立Excel表格,由于在Civil3D创建隧道中心线只需要X坐标、Y坐标和Z坐标数据即可,所以将表格中的其他数据删除,只保留序号、坐标和高程即可。程序编写完成后运行程序,在Civil 3D主界面文字框中输入加载命令,在弹出的对话框中选择加载对应的.dll文件,输入运行命令即可运行项目读取Excel数据自动生成隧道中心线,如图8所示。

2.2　管片模型创建

将创建的隧道中心线保存为dwg文件,Revit

选项栏中选择导入 CAD 文件将隧道中心线导入 Revit 空间,通过导入族文件选项导入管片自适应族,打开管理菜单下的可视化编程软件 Dynamo,拾取隧道中心线和管片模型,根据项目调整参数,点击运行即可自动生成 BIM 模型,如图 9 所示。

隧道点位序号	坐标		高程
	X	Y	
1	390516.567	3412581.272	-19.431
2	390478.898	3412401.208	-18.972
3	390411.752	3412271.642	-18.644
4	390364.2573	3412108.411	-18.423
5	390311.8498	3411953.596	-18.214
6	390259.4423	3411798.781	-17.953
7	390207.0348	3411643.966	-17.642
8	390154.6273	3411489.151	-17.344
9	390102.2198	3411334.336	-17.672
10	390049.8123	3411179.521	-17.947
11	389997.4048	3411024.706	-18.323
12	389944.9973	3410869.891	-18.647
13	389892.5898	3410715.076	-19.012
14	389840.1823	3410560.261	-19.457
15	389787.7748	3410405.446	-19.984
16	389735.3673	3410250.631	-20.215
17	389682.9598	3410095.816	-20.554
18	389630.5523	3409941.001	-21.041
19	389578.1448	3409786.186	-20.499
20	389525.7373	3409631.371	-20.142

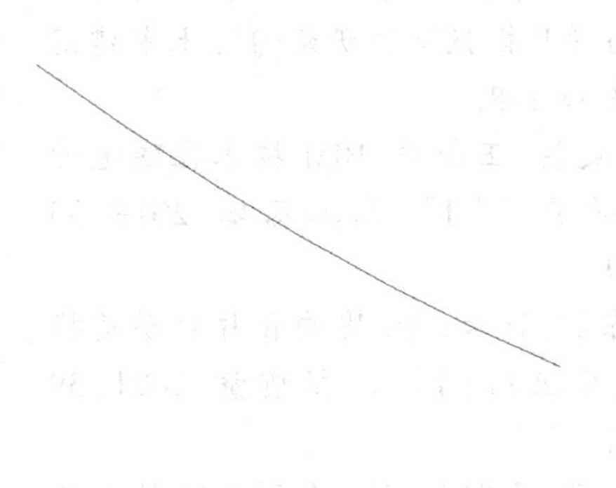

图 8 创建隧道中心线

图 9 盾构隧道管片模型

2.3 应用小结

以西安市某工程为例,基于 Civil 3D 二次开发技术实现自动读取 Excel 表格数据生成道路中心线,并基于 Revit + Dynamo 软件实现盾构隧道管片自动拼装建模,满足了快速与精细化的需求,减少大量重复工作,提高施工便捷性,为盾构隧道施工信息化发展积累了一定经验,也能为其他类似工程项目提供一些参考。

3 结语

本文在现有研究基础上,基于 BIM 二次开发技术实现盾构隧道管片参数化拼装方法,得到如下结论:

(1)本文通过建立通用盾构管片自适应族,利用 Civil3D 二次开发技术创建隧道中心线,基于 Dynamo 软件进行程序编辑,在 Dynamo 程序中拾取管片族和隧道中心线即可自动生成盾构隧道模型。

(2)以西安市某工程为例,结合项目调整盾构管片参数,基于 Dynamo 建立盾构隧道管片自动拼装模型。结果表明,管片参数化拼装技术在满足模型精度的前提下,能够节省人工重复操作,有效提升工作效率。

(3)本研究研究对象为盾构隧道,并未考虑隧道周边的地形影响,后续需要对盾构隧道 BIM + GIS 应用进一步研究。

(4)本文主要针对施工阶段盾构隧道建模进行研究,后续也需针对盾构隧道运营维护阶段的 BIM 应用进行研究。

参考文献

[1] 林懿. BIM 技术在住宅建筑设计中的应用研究[J]. 科技创新与应用,2020(24):172-173.

[2] 欧阳业伟,石开荣,张原. 基于建筑信息模型的地铁工程建模技术研究[J]. 工业建筑,2015,45(10):196-201.

[3] 常建军. BIM 技术在地铁隧道工程施工中的应用[J]. 甘肃科技纵横,2016,45(6):35-42.

[4] 王晓东,喻钢,吴惠明. 基于 Revit 的盾构管片参数化建模应用[J]. 隧道建设(中英文),2018,38(2):249-254.

[5] 陈桂香,徐晨,张文苹,等. 基于 BIM 技术的通用管片精细化建模及应用[J]. 施工技术,2019,48(4):76-80.

[6] 刘兆新,田斌华,陈元培,等. 基于 Revit 的新奥法隧道初期支护构件参数化建模研究[J]. 隧道建设(中英文),2019,39(10):1610-1619.

[7] 朱永学,张向军,张家宝,等. 基于 Civil3D +

Revit + Dynamo的公路隧道参数化建模方法研究[J]. 隧道建设(中英文),2020,40(S2):109-115.

[8] 赵云辉,司典浩,张杨,等. Revit中盾构隧道设计轴线与管片排版算法研究[J]. 土木建筑工程信息技术:1-8.

[9] 唐艳梅,张晨晨,王新龙. BIM技术在隧道管片排版中的应用[J]. 土工基础,2019,33(3):290-294.

[10] 魏章俊,陈前,肖云,等. 盾构管片自动建模方法研究及应用[J]. 工程质量,2021,39(8):63-67.

[11] 陈曦,甘英聪,吴湖英,等. 基于BIM技术盾构隧道管片自动拼装研究[J]. 土木建筑工程信息技术,2021,13(3):75-80.

[12] 张轩. 基于Bentley平台的铁路隧道BIM技术应用研究[J]. 铁道标准设计,2019,63(4):107-112.

[13] 张兆杰,郭鹏,田志宇,等. 公路隧道BIM技术软件平台比选[J]. 北方交通,2019(2):91-94.

[14] 陶建军,王荡,于长海,等. 预制节段梁桥精细化BIM模型构建及平台可视化应用[J]. 公路,2021(12):154-158.

[15] 车冠宇,毛伟栋. Revit + Dynamo参数化隧道模型构建体系探析[J]. 公路交通科技(应用技术版),2018,14(4):246-248.

盾构空推过矿山法隧道管片椭变原因初探

余克鹏[1]　刘庭金*[1,2]　张舒怡[1]

(1. 华南理工大学土木与交通学院;

2. 华南理工大学亚热带建筑科学国家重点实验室)

摘　要　矿山法+盾构法结合工法解决了盾构机在硬岩段掘进速度慢、被困风险高的问题,但也随之带来了矿山法隧道内施作管片的一些问题。为研究盾构空推过矿山法隧道施工过程管片的变形原因和变形机理,本文依托某空推隧道工程中管片衬砌出现的问题,首先初步探究管片的受力模式和椭变原因;然后建立数值模型对管片变形原因进行模拟验证;最后应用数值模型从填充角度范围、填充密实度等影响因素研究该工法施工中填充层对管片变形的控制作用。研究结果表明:管片外壁豆砾石填充不充分和注浆压力不均匀是造成管片椭变的主要原因。建议填充的豆砾石角度范围应大于180°,填充的豆砾石抗力系数应大于20MPa/m。

关键词　盾构隧道　空推　数值模拟　椭变原因　豆砾石填充

0　引言

当在复合地层或孤石地层中进行盾构施工时,盾构机掘进速度缓慢,局部的高强度硬岩或孤石更是可能使盾构机刀具磨损失效。这不仅减缓工程施工进度,还可能导致施工安全问题频发。为解决上述问题,出现了一种新工法:矿山法+盾构法结合工法。该工法是先采用矿山法开挖,施作初支,然后采用盾构机在导台上空推拼装管片,再在管片与初支之间充填豆砾石并进行注浆,最终形成初支+填充层+管片的组合衬砌。

该工法近二十年来在多个大城市地铁隧道中均有应用。该工法既解决了盾构机在硬岩中掘进困难的问题,又大大提高了施工速度。但缺点也是存在的,一是拼装管片时,由于初支承担大部分土压力,管片缺少土体挤压,对外界荷载敏感[1]。二是盾构机顶推力变小,管片纵向压紧不充分,容易发生渗漏水[2]。

1. 基金项目:国家自然科学基金项目(51878296);广东省现代土木工程技术重点实验室资助项目(2021B1212040003)。

针对该工法,已有学者从施工技术、病害原因以及组合衬砌的力学性能等方面开展了研究工作。夏定光[3]认为矿山法隧道底部存在岩粉,易造成底部灌浆不密实,而顶部由于重力原因容易填不满。汪茂祥[4]以广州地铁五号线区杨盾构区间盾构通过40m长的矿山法隧道为例,介绍了盾构通过矿山法隧道的施工关键技术及其成功经验。李锦富[5]对空推工法出现的管片错台、渗漏水、崩角和局部破碎、上浮等问题进行了原因分析,并提出措施。张常光[6]对深圳地铁某区间矿山法+盾构法的管片受力特性进行现场试验,分析了管片环缝接触面应变、土压力和钢筋轴力的变化规律。王明友[7]研究不同回填灌浆密实度对衬砌受力的影响,结果表明密实度过低,会导致管片应力分布不均且产生较大拉应力和屈服区。

可见,对该工法的研究工作主要集中在施工工艺上,工法施工过程管片质量缺陷的规律、成因及发展机理却鲜有研究。为此,本文依托某盾构空推拼装管片过矿山法隧道工程施工过程出现的椭变及病害,提出管片变形原因并进行数值模拟验证,并对施工过程填充层对管片变形的影响展开研究,以更好地为类似工程提供借鉴。

1 工程概况

本文依托某盾构空推过矿山法隧道工程。空推段长708m,区间隧道大多处于强、中和微风化混合花岗岩岩层,局部岩面起伏变化大。设计时针对区间中部地质较好区段采用了矿山法+盾构法结合工法进行施工。图1~图4分别为该工法施工示意图、组合衬砌图、施工现场照片和隧道纵剖面示意图。

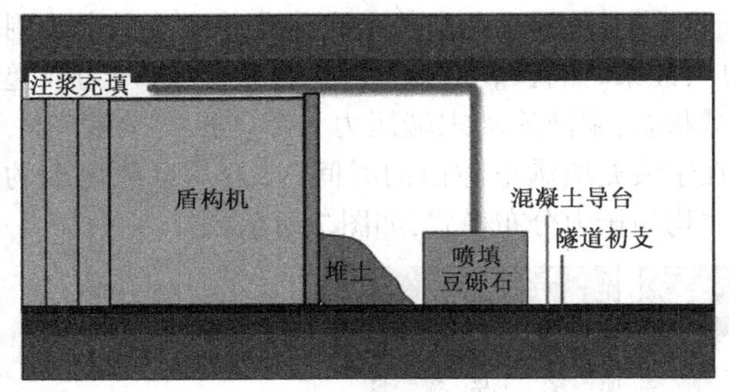

图1 工法施工示意图

空推段矿山法隧道断面近似圆形,净空尺寸6.4m,底部设有混凝土导向平台,用于引导盾构机推进。盾构机空推拼装管片后,需在管片背后填充包括喷射豆砾石、盾尾同步注浆和洞内二次注浆等材料。豆砾石粒径5~15mm,并要求有良好的级配,以形成对管片的有效支撑[8]。

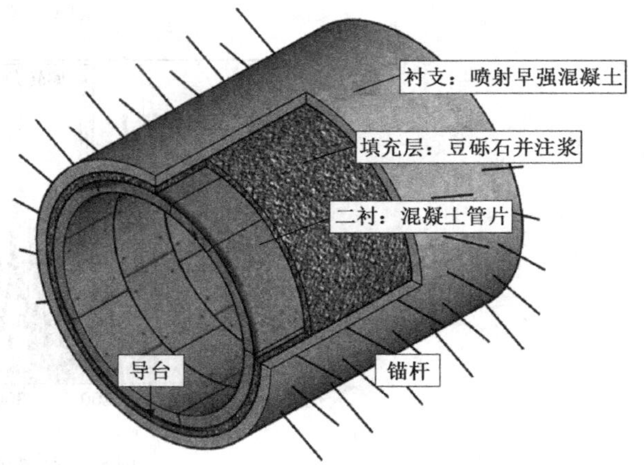

图2 组合衬砌结构示意图

图3 施工现场照片

由于工期紧张,盾构机拼装管片时间急促,且盾构机内部作业运输空间有限,导致豆砾石填充不及时不充分。此外,施工过程中还存在管片背后注浆压力过大的情况。工程质量验收时,发现结构多处存在椭圆度超限,管片错台以及接缝张开等问题,且变形大的地方伴随着崩角破损和裂缝等病害。故本研究以管片椭变为切入点,研究管片椭变原因及变形发展机理,更好地掌握该工法施工过程的力学机理。

2 隧道变形及原因分析

2.1 隧道变形

采用MS100三维激光扫描小车获取管片变形数据。图5为管片椭圆度和偏转角曲线图。

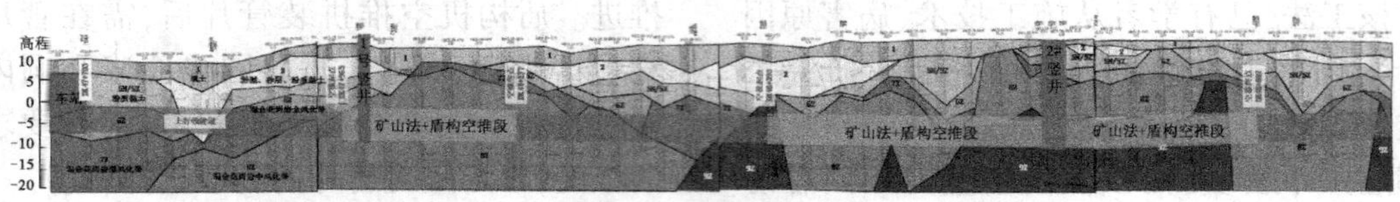

图4　隧道纵剖面示意图

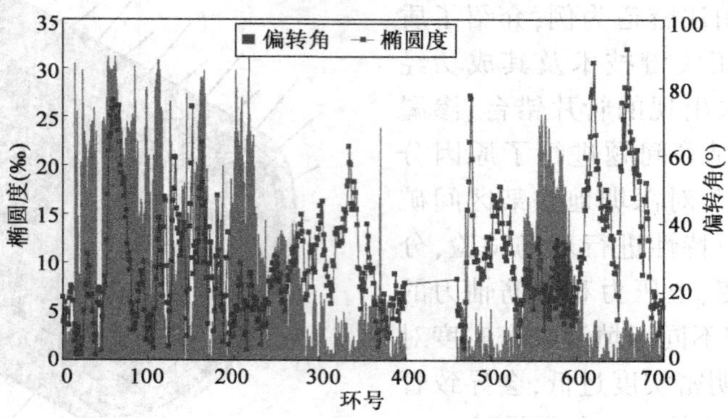

图5　管片椭圆度和偏转角曲线图

根据《盾构法隧道施工及验收规范》(GB 50446—2017),椭圆度是指“圆形隧道管片衬砌拼装成环后隧道最大与最小直径的差值与隧道设计内径的比值”,以‰表示。椭圆度常常被作为评估隧道结构安全的衡量指标。调研结果显示,管片变形超限明显,椭圆度20‰~25‰有31环,25‰以上有19环,最大椭圆度33‰。偏转角0°~90°并存,管片椭变形态多样。

隧道管片间接缝张开显著,拱顶、拱腰和拱脚等多个位置均有出现,封顶块处错台最为显著,最大接缝张开量为10mm。隧道管片间错台情况遍布,环内错台和环间错台均有出现,其中以椭圆度差异大的相邻环错台最为显著,最大错台量为41mm。

2.2　原因分析

矿山法+盾构法结合工法施工过程中,初支和管片之间具有20cm的环形空隙,豆砾石填充前,围岩与管片处于未接触状态,主要通过初支承担外部水土压力,管片并未发挥支护作用。此时管片仅靠螺栓进行固定,外部约束不充分,对外部荷载较为敏感。对空隙回填后,填充层对隧道起到包裹约束作用,隧道整体稳定性增强。因此该空隙的及时回填对管片稳定具有重要的意义。

依托工程的实际施工情况为:盾构机空推拼装管片过程,隧道内运输车忙于运输管片,浆液及豆砾石等运输严重滞后甚至断供;管片拼装完成后,隧道内作业空间及运输车运能恢复,再通过管片注浆孔进行管片壁后注浆工作,因而管片外壁豆砾石充填不充分。因此,认为该区间隧道产生较大变形的原因主要有以下两点:①从结构荷载模式分析,隧道结构外部浆液压力分布不均,且该荷载分布形式存在一定随机性,导致管片处于偏心荷载状态;②从结构约束条件分析,由于管片与初支之间豆砾石充填不充分,导致管片没有收到良好的支撑。常规施工流程与依托工程施工流程对比示意图如图6所示。

由于依托工程中单个注浆孔的注浆需求范围广,注浆时间长。因而浆液为自流灌浆,压力成递减状态,浆液流动末端压力为零。根据文献[9-12],在浆液充填满空隙前的时间内,管片可能出现的非均匀压力分布模式,如图7所示。

矿山法施做初支

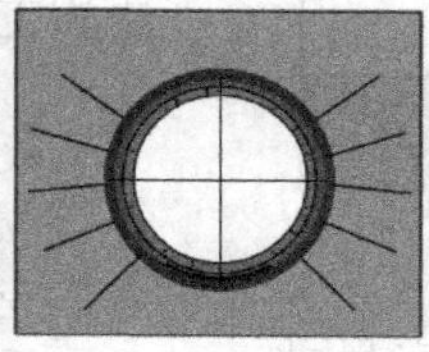

盾构机拼装管片
充填豆砾石

均匀注浆

图　6

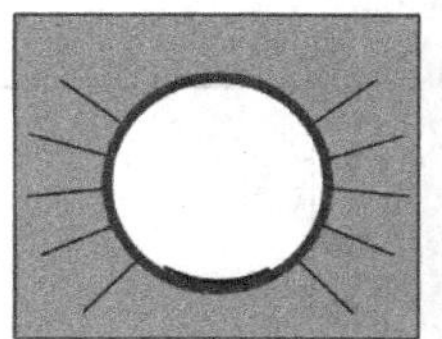

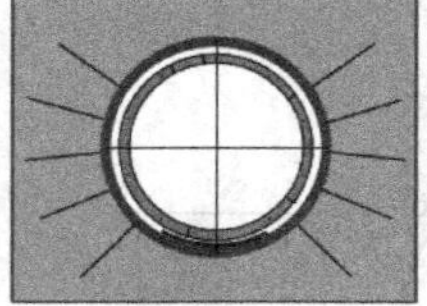

图6 常规与依托工程施工流程对比示意图

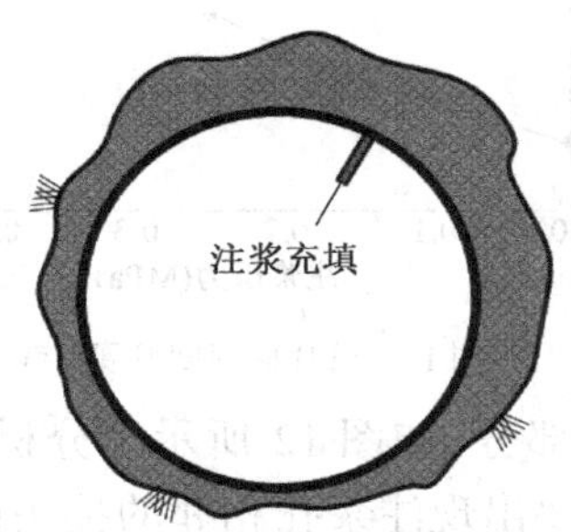

图7 非均匀浆液压力分布

3 有限元分析及验证

3.1 数值模型建立

本文建立的多环管片的三维精细数值模型如图8所示，管片直径为6.0m。模型考虑了管片的环向和纵向手孔、螺栓孔、管片内钢筋和接头螺栓等主要构造。管片螺栓采用实体进行模拟，钢筋采用植入式梁单元模拟。管片混凝土采用混凝土弥散裂缝本构模型，螺栓和钢筋采用范美塞斯弹塑性本构模型。材料参数如表1所示。管片与管片间、管片与螺栓间的界面定义“一般接触”，法向设置为“硬接触”，切向遵从库伦摩擦定律，摩擦系数分别取为0.6、0.3。

3.2 荷载和边界设定

为模拟施工时浆液压力，管片上施加非均匀注浆压力，压力由注浆孔向远处逐渐递减(导台处为0)，以模拟极端情况浆液压力。施加到管片上的注浆压力从0逐步增大到0.5MPa。

实际施工时管片直接落在导台上，因而创建导台实体，并在导台与管片间设置接触模拟导台作用。管片纵向施加沿隧道纵向的位移约束和旋转约束。荷载和边界条件如图9所示。

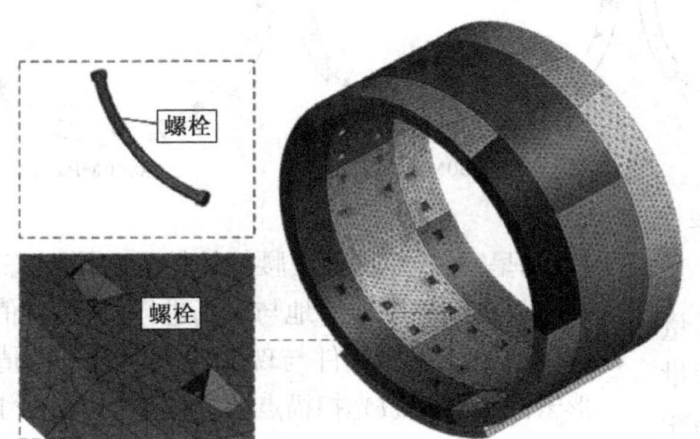

图8 管片三维数值模型

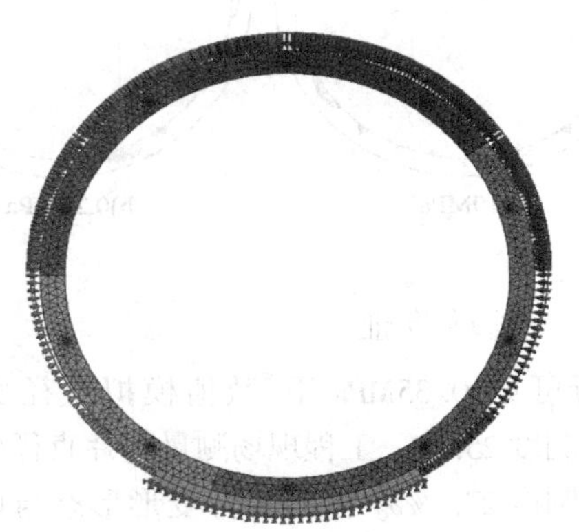

图9 模型荷载和边界模式

材料主要物理力学参数 表1

材　料	重度 (kN/m^3)	弹性模量 (GPa)	泊　松　比	抗压/抗拉强度标准值(MPa)	屈服强度 (MPa)	极限强度 (MPa)
管片混凝土(C50)	25.0	34.5	0.20	32.4/2.64	—	—
钢筋(HRB335)	78.5	200	0.30	—	400	540
弯螺栓(M24,8.8级)	78.5	210	0.30	—	640	800

3.3 结果分析

按照逐步增大注浆压力对模型进行求解后，提取分析中间环管片的计算结果。管片径向位移曲线和椭圆度曲线分别如图10和图11所示。

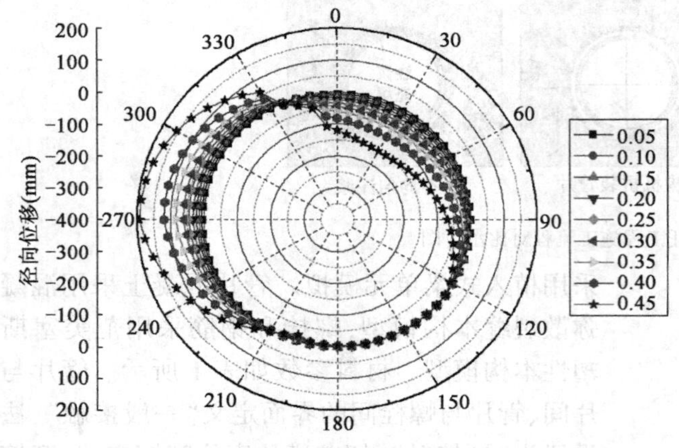

图 10　管片径向位移曲线(注浆压力/MPa)

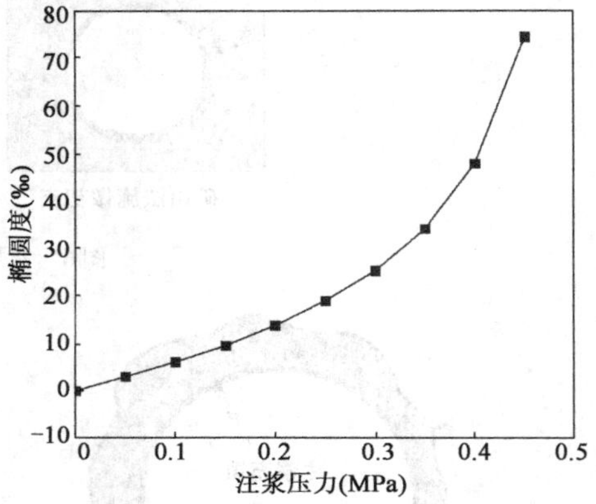

图 11　管片椭圆度发展曲线

分析可见,管片呈现“管片注浆孔处内缩,左拱肩处扩张,封顶块处出现了台阶状错台”的变形形态。管片径向位移、椭圆度变化量增长幅度越来越大,呈现加速增加趋势。0.1、0.2、0.3 和 0.4MPa 压力下管片的最大直径变形量比值为 1.0∶2.3∶4.4∶8.4,管片的椭圆度比值为 1.0∶2.3∶4.1∶7.8。

提取管片应变云图,并仅显示超过两倍极限抗拉应变的部分,如图 12 所示。分析可见,管片的拉应力主要出现注浆孔相邻的接头内弧面以及注浆孔对边的接头内弧面(拱底部位),还有注浆孔左右各 90°的接头外弧面(拱腰部位),因而这些部位容易受拉开裂,出现裂缝病害。0.1、0.2、0.3 和 0.4MPa 下管片拉裂区约占管片的 1.0%、2.9%、8.5% 和 21.3%。

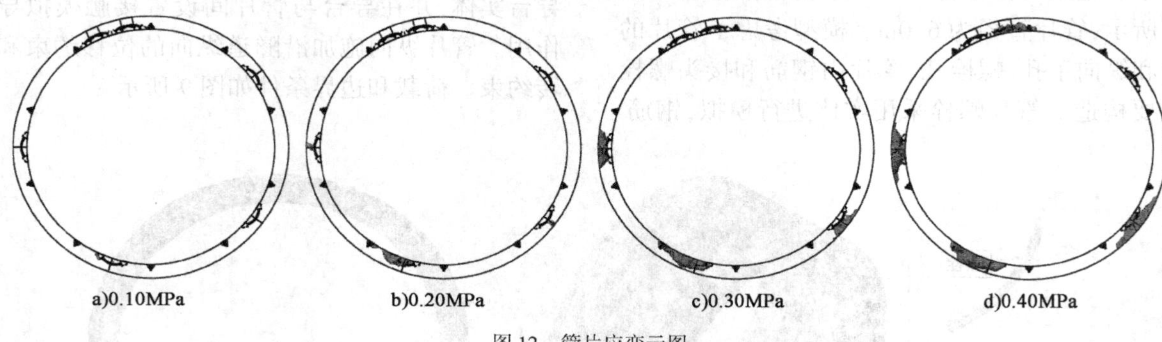

图 12　管片应变云图

3.4　现场验证

分析可见,0.35MPa 下,数值模拟直径变形量 92mm,椭圆度 25.4‰,工程现场测量管片直径变形量 88mm,椭圆度 27.1‰。同时管片变形形态与现场相符,均呈现注浆处回缩,腰部外扩的变形形态。可见,数值模拟结果能较好地与现场进行对应,数值模拟设置的荷载和边界条件与现场较为符合。数值模拟变形云图和三维激光扫描点图分别如图 13、图 14 所示。

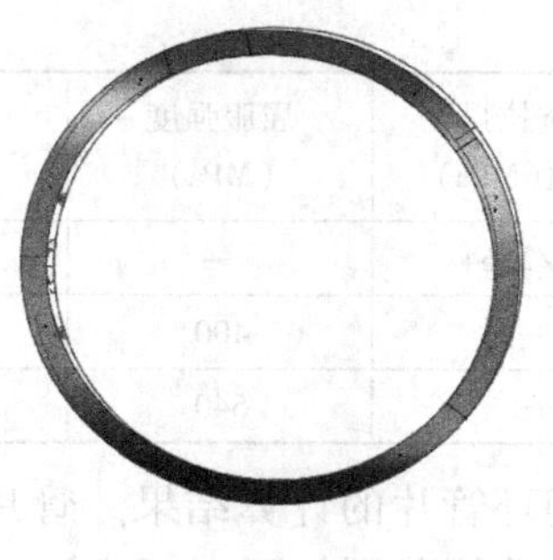

图 13　数值模拟变形云图

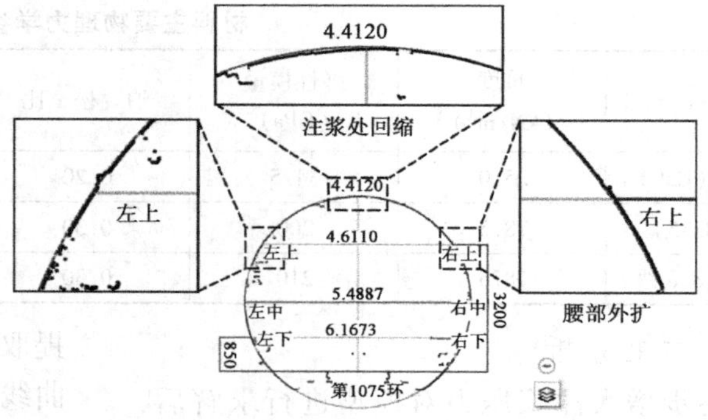

图 14　三维激光扫描点图

4 填充层影响分析

4.1 工况设定

结合施工过程可能出现的豆砾石填充情况，分别设定不同填充范围和填充密实度的多个工况组，并采用仅受压曲面弹簧模拟豆砾石对管片的支持作用。

结合封坤[13]提到的4种抗力计算方法，参考依托工程岩土勘察报告，取填充层抗力系数取为20 MPa/m。并在管片纵向施加沿隧道纵向的位移约束和旋转约束。分析工况组如表2所示。

4.2 填充角度范围对管片影响

0.35MPa压力下管片径向位移如图15所示。填充层填充角度与椭圆度关系曲线如图16所示。

分析工况组 表2

工况组		填充角度范围	抗力系数(MPa/m)
A组	1	下部0°	—
	2	下部60°	20
	3	下部120°	20
	4	半环180°	20
	5	下部240°	20
	6	下部300°	20
	7	全部360°	20
B组	8	全部360°	5
	9	全部360°	10
	10	全部360°	20
	11	全部360°	30
	12	全部360°	40

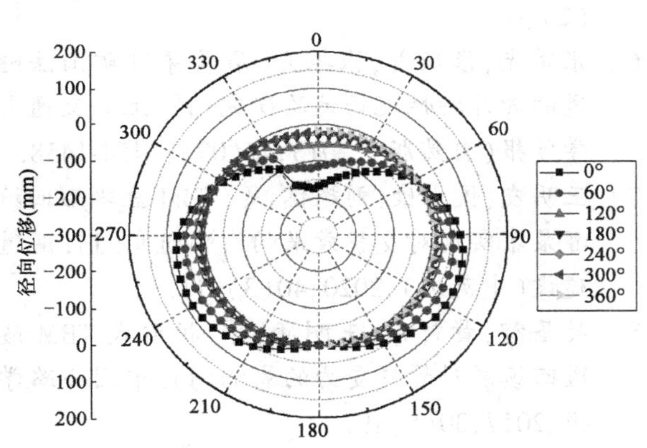

图15 填充角度范围与管片径向位移关系曲线

从径向位移曲线可知，管片顶部内缩，腰部扩张，发生了横鸭蛋状变形，封顶块两侧管片接缝的错台变形最为明显。且填充角度范围越小，管片变形越显著，具体情况是：①当填充0°时，管片整体径向位移非常明显，封顶块处径向位移最大且封顶块接缝发生较大错动。②当填充60°和120°时，管片整体径向位移和接缝处错动仍然明显。③当填充180°及以上时，管片整体径向位移不明显，管片环拱顶略微内陷、拱腰略微外鼓。

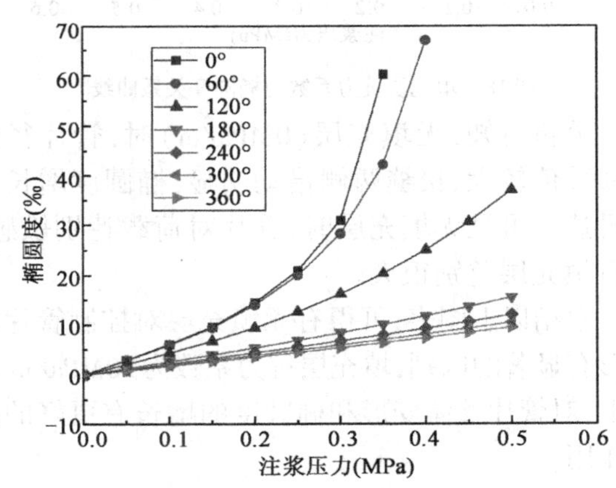

图16 填充角度范围与椭圆度关系曲线

从椭圆度曲线可知，当填充0°~120°时，椭圆度呈加速增加趋势。当填充180°及以上时，椭圆度呈线性增加趋势，且曲线斜率相近。说明填充角度范围为180°及以上，能更好地控制管片椭圆度的增加。

总结以上图表,可得填充 180°及以上,能更好地控制管片整体变形和椭圆度的增长,能对管片环的变形和应力增长起到一定的控制作用。

4.3　填充密实度对管片影响

0.35MPa 压力下管片径向位移如图 17 所示。填充层抗力系数与椭圆度关系曲线如图 18 所示。

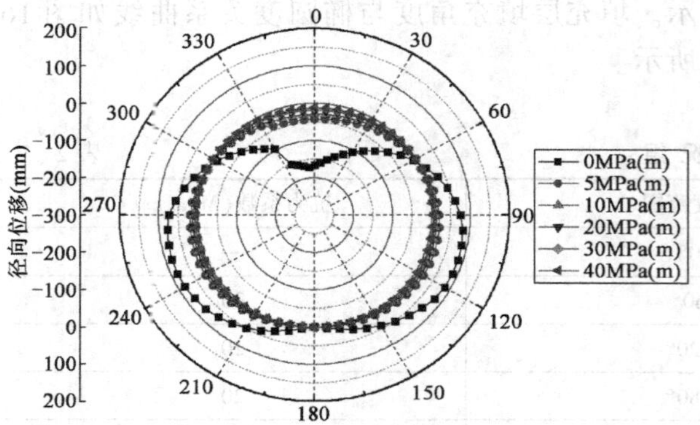

图 17　填充层抗力系数与管片径向位移关系曲线

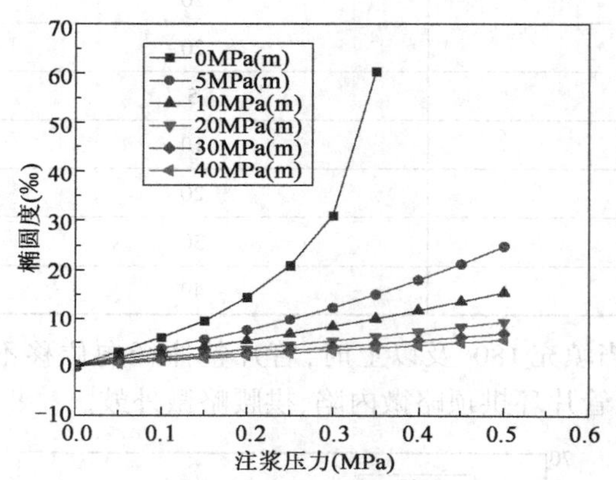

图 18　填充层抗力系数与椭圆度关系曲线

分析可知,无填充层(0MPa/m)时,管片径向位移数值较大,接缝两侧错动明显,椭圆度增长非常迅速。可见无填充层时,管片对荷载特别敏感,与有填充层差别很大。

总结以上图表,可得有无填充层对控制管片的变形有显著的区别,填充层抗力系数为 20MPa/m 及以上,对管片整体变形和椭圆度的增长有更好的控制作用。

5　结语

本文依托某空推隧道工程中管片衬砌出现的问题,初步探究了盾构空推过矿山法隧道管片的椭变原因。认为椭变原因主要有:①从结构荷载模式分析,浆液压力分布不均;②从约束条件分析,豆砾石充填不充分导致管片约束不足。

依据椭变原因设定了管片的受力模式和边界条件,建立数值模型对管片变形原因进行模拟验证。对比数值模拟和工程现场测量结果,管片变形数值大小相近,变形形态相似,一定程度上验证了管片的椭变原因。

本文还研究了填充层角度范围、填充密实度对管片变形的影响。结合数值模拟结果,建议施工中初支和管片间填充豆砾石角度范围应大于 180°及以上、抗力系数应大于 20MPa/m。

参考文献

[1] 王乾屾、陈凡、陈建福,等. 盾构空推过矿山法隧道施工关键技术及数值分析[C]//2020 年工业建筑学术交流会论文集(下册). 北京,2020.

[2] 何锡存. 盾构矿山法联合施工隧道复合衬砌力学性能及质量检测方法研究[D]. 上海:上海交通大学,2020.

[3] 夏定光. 豆砾石回填与灌浆技术探索[J]. 现代隧道技术,2002(01):20-24.

[4] 汪茂祥. 盾构通过矿山法施工隧道段关键技术[J]. 现代隧道技术,2008,45(1):67-70.

[5] 李锦富. 浅议盾构过矿山法隧道空推段施工质量控制[J]. 现代隧道技术,2012,49(2):6.

[6] 张常光,张庆贺,张振光. 盾构穿过矿山法隧道的管片特性现场试验研究[J]. 上海交通大学学报(自然版),2013,47(09):1454-1458.

[7] 王明友,侯少康,刘耀儒,等. TBM 豆砾石回填灌浆密实度对支护效果的影响研究[J]. 隧道建设(中英文),2020,40(3):11.

[8] 吴圣智,黄群伟,王明年,等. 护盾式 TBM 隧道回填层对管片受力的影响[J]. 中国公路学报,2017,30(8):9.

[9] 朱合华,丁文其,李晓军. 盾构隧道施工力学性态模拟及工程应用[J]. 土木工程学报,2000,33(3):6.

[10] 叶飞,朱合华,何川. 盾构隧道壁后注浆扩散模式及对管片的压力分析[J]. 岩土力学,2009(5):6.

[11] Teachavorasinskun S. Evaluation of liner responses due to non-uniform tail void grouting pressure[J]. Geomechanics and geoengineering,

2018,13(3):226-232.

[12] Liang Y,Zhang J,Lai Z S,et al. Temporal and spatial distribution of the grout pressure and its effects on lining segments during synchronous grouting in shield tunnelling [J]. Revue Française De Génie Civil, 2020, 24 (1): 79-96.

[13] 封坤,刘四进,邱月,等.盾构隧道地层抗力系数的修正计算方法研究[J].铁道工程学报,2014,31(6):6.

基于聚类与时间序列的公路隧道围岩变形预测方法研究

刘 智[1] 李欣雨[2] 常建涛*[2] 孔宪光[2]

(1.中交第一公路勘察设计研究院有限公司;2.西安电子科技大学)

摘 要 在公路隧道施工过程中,拱顶沉降与周边收敛的监控量测及其发展趋势的有效预测,对公路隧道安全施工具有重要意义。本文提出一种结合 K-medoids 聚类算法和贝叶斯优化后的长短期记忆网络(Bayes-LSTM)智能算法对拱顶沉降与周边收敛位移进行预测。首先,利用 K-medoids 算法对不同围岩等级的桩号断面量测数据进行聚类分析,针对同一类围岩变形数据利用 LSTM 模型进行训练,并利用贝叶斯优化算法(Bayesian Optimization)对模型参数进行优化,最终动态预测得出未来三天隧道围岩变形数据的预测结果。通过海南某特长公路隧道拱顶沉降与周边收敛的实测数据验证了该方法的有效性。研究结果表明:同一类拱顶沉降与周边收敛位移的时间序列用同一模型预测具有可行性;相比直接用 LSTM 算法建立模型,采用贝叶斯优化方法和 LSTM 结合的算法具有更高的预测精度;以聚类中心断面作为样本预测当前正在监测断面的拱顶沉降与周边收敛位移时,只需要得到当前监测断面的较少数据,从而实现对当前断面的围岩变形的准确预测。

关键词 拱顶沉降 周边收敛 时间序列预测 K-mediods 聚类 LSTM

0 引言

隧道开挖会导致围岩应力重分布,进而产生拱顶沉降与周边收敛的围岩变形。在公路隧道施工过程中,围岩大变形是一种常见的施工灾害,预测隧道内围岩变形一直是岩土工程领域的热点问题,因此针对拱顶沉降与周边收敛的监控量测及其发展趋势的有效预测,将对支护设计提供重要参考,从而确保隧道的稳定性,避免施工中的安全事故。目前针对隧道拱顶沉降与周边收敛的预测一般有以下 3 种,即经验公式法、数值模拟法与人工智能方法[1]。

(1)经验公式法。是根据围岩变形监测数据研究围岩变形的发展规律,并以经验公式表达,拟合出围岩变形的规律。颜杜民[2]基于“S”型函数,建立 Logistic 隧道水平收敛变形预测模型,对马尾山隧道的水平位移进行预测。孙柏林等[3]针对传统的曲线预测模型存在的不足,提出含有 4 个参数的增长曲线模型——Richards 时间函数模型,能较好地拟合出位移-时间曲线,也能拟合速度-时间曲线。

(2)数值模拟法。利用数值仿真的方法根据隧道施工过程中的复杂性与多样性,构建不同模型对隧道围岩变形情况进行分析。俞文生[4]等人针对Ⅲ、Ⅳ级围岩,采用弹-黏塑性有限单元法分析预测不同类别隧道围岩变形。谢宝琎[5]采用有限差分软件建立大断面膨胀土隧道三维数值模型,采用七步开挖方法,分析隧道围岩大变形规律。孙均[6]提出非线性二维黏弹塑性本构模型和

1.基金项目:海南省交通厅科技专项(编号:J-ZX-ZAK-02-2019);中交第一公路勘察设计研究院有限公司科创基金项目(编号:KCJJ2020-19)。

大(小)变形三维弹黏塑性本构模型,针对乌鞘岭铁路隧道软弱围岩施工开挖大变形问题进行研究。

(3)人工智能法。以围岩变形量为因变量,利用人工智能算法构建分析模型,对围岩变形情况展开分析。王文玉等[7]基于生物进化思想,利用遗传算法优化 BP 神经网络的参数,通过马家沟隧道的拱顶沉降数据应用证明模型的精确性。强跃等[8]建立基于集合经验模态分解的多尺度组合核极限学习机模型,对隧道围岩位移进行滚动单步和连续多步预测,验证了模型有较好的精度和实用性。文明等[9]引入动态施工影响因子,建立非线性自回归时间序列预测模型,对史家山隧道的围岩水平收敛和地表变形进行预测。Pan Yue 等[10]建立萤火虫算法和非线性自回归动态神经网络方法结合的 FA-NAR 围岩变形预测模型,通过与最小二乘-支持向量机(LS-SVM)模型对比证明模型有较好的精确度。Guihong Song 等[11]基于累积法对传统的灰色预测模型进行改进,应用证明改进后的灰色预测模型能提高预测精度。Shaoshuai Shi 等[12]基于支持向量机和信息粒化法建立围岩变形预测模型,通过对盘龙山隧道的应用证明模型有较好的准确性。姚凯[13]等人针对隧道围岩变形中的非线性问题,建立了基于果蝇算法改进的广义回归神经网络隧道围岩变形预测模型。

综上所述,国内外学者针对隧道围岩变形预测问题进行了大量的研究,也取得了一些成功的经验。但是与时间相关变形的解析法或先进的时变本构模型数值解需要较强的理论计算能力,这往往超出了许多设计和施工技术人员的能力[14]。随着人工智能技术的发展,回归分析、神经网络、决策树和支持向量机等机器学习方法被广泛应用到隧道围岩变形的预测中。

作为一种典型的人工智能算法,神经网络具有较强的非线性映射能力,而传统神经网络受初值影响较大,同时容易出现梯度爆炸和梯度消失等问题。不同于传统神经网络,长短时记忆网络(Long Short-Term Memory,LSTM)是一种改进的循环神经网络(Recurrent Neural Networks,RNN),可以解决 RNN 无法处理长距离的依赖问题,能够规避 RNN 中梯度爆炸和梯度消失的问题。基于此,本文采用基于 LSTM 的非线性时间序列方法对公路隧道施工期拱顶沉降与周边收敛变形进行预测。目前,针对隧道围岩变形的预测,大部分都是针对单一施工桩号断面的监控量测数据进行分析,在实际施工过程中,一般每隔 10~20m 左右会布置一个监测断面,尤其针对长大公路隧道,可以得到大量不同围岩等级断面的拱顶沉降与周边收敛的监测数据。因此,本文首先利用 K-mediods 算法对不同围岩等级的拱顶沉降与周边收敛的时序数据按时间序列相似度进行聚类,然后对各个聚类中心通过 LSTM 方法建立预测模型,实现了对监测断面的拱顶沉降与周边收敛变形的有效预测。

1　算法

1.1　动态时间弯曲距离(Dynamic Time Warping,DTW)

由于时序数据的特殊性,当比较相似性的两段时间序列长度不等时,传统的欧氏距离有一定的局限性,而动态时间弯曲距离(DTW)具有弹性的度量方式,能够通过时间轴的变化实现“一对多”的比较,有效地解决时间轴不一致的时间序列的相似性度量问题。

DTW 算法按照连续性、单调性等规则构造两时间序列之间的对齐路径,从多条可能的对齐路径中,求得路径距离值最小的对齐路径作为 DTW 对齐路径,将该最小路径距离值作为两条序列的 DTW 距离[15]。

假设有两个时间序列 Q 与 C,长度分别为 n 和 m,基于动态规划构建 Q 和 C 的距离矩阵 $dp[i][j]$,其中 $\mathrm{d}p[i][j]$ 表示时间序列 $Q[0:i]$ 与 $C[0:j]$ 之间相似距离的平方,其中 $dp[i][j]$ 计算公式如下:

$$\mathrm{d}p[i][j] = (Q[i] - C[J])^2 + \min(\mathrm{d}p[i-1][j], \mathrm{d}p[i][j-1], \mathrm{d}p[i-1][j-1]) \tag{1}$$

则 Q、C 的 DTW 距离计算公式如下:

$$DTW(Q,C) = \sqrt{\mathrm{d}p[n-1][m-1]} \tag{2}$$

1.2　K-mediods 算法

K-mediods 算法是基于欧式距离的常用聚类算法,通过均值计算聚类中心点,但当样本中存在异常数据时,可能会使得聚类结果产生偏移。K-mediods 聚类以真实数据对象作为聚类中心,可有效避免数据中的异常值带来的影响。因此本文选用 K-mediods 聚类算法,采用动态时间弯曲距离(DTW)来度量时序数据间的相似距离,K-mediods

算法的流程如下：

(1)确定聚类中心数 K 值，K 值大小的确定，影响 K-mediods 聚类算法离散数据的准确度和合理性。本文采用手肘法确定聚类数 K 值的大小。

手肘法的核心评价指标为簇内误方差(Sum of the Squared Errors，SSE)：

$$\mathrm{SSE} = \sum_{t}^{k} \sum_{p \in C_i} |p - m_i|^2 \tag{3}$$

式中：C_i——样本中的第 i 簇；

p——C_i 中的样本点；

m_i——C_i 中数据的平均值。

手肘法的核心思想如下：随着聚类数 K 的增大，样本会被划分得更加精细，各个簇的聚合程度会逐渐提高，SSE 会逐渐减小。当 K 小于真实聚类数时，K 的增大会大幅增加各个簇的聚合程度，因此 SSE 在此时的下降幅度会很大；当 K 达到真实聚类数后，再不断增加 K 所得到的聚合程度的回报会迅速变小，所以 SSE 的下降幅度会骤减，而后 SSE 随着 K 值的继续增大而逐渐趋于平缓，因此 SSE 与 K 值得变化曲线类似于手肘的形状，而肘部对应的 K 值即为数据的真实聚类数。

(2)随机选择 K 个样本作为聚类中心点 m_1，m_2，$\cdots m_k$。

(3)分别计算样本数据到各个中心点的 DTW 距离，将样本划分到 DTW 距离最小的聚类中心所在簇中：

$$C_k = \{x_i \mid \mathrm{DTW}(x_i, m_k) = \min_{m_j \in m_k} \mathrm{DTW}(x_i, m_j)\} \tag{4}$$

(4)计算各簇内，距离簇内各样本点 DTW 距离最小的点，作为新的中心点。

(5)重复(3)、(4)步，直到样本分类结果不再变化。

1.3 LSTM 算法

RNN 网络模型是一类以序列数据作为输入，在序列演进的方向上进行递归，且所有节点按链式连接的递归神经网络，它具有记忆性，即前一时间步的输出作为下一时间步网络的输入，但是 RNN 在长序列训练过程中存在梯度消失和梯度爆炸问题[16]。

与传统的 RNN 网络相比，LSTM 加入了输入门 i_t，遗忘门 f_t 以及输出门 σ_t 三个门和一个内部记忆单元 c_i，可有效地解决 RNN 存在的问题。输入门控制当前计算的新状态有多大程度更新到记忆单元中；遗忘门控制前一步记忆单元中的信息有多大程度被遗忘；输出门控制当前的输出有多大程度上取决于当前的记忆单元。

LSTM 中第 t 步的更新计算公式为：

$$i_t = \sigma(W_i x_i + U_i h_{t-1} + b_i) \tag{5}$$

$$o_t = \sigma(W_o x_t + U_o h_{t-1} + b_o) \tag{6}$$

$$\tilde{c}_t = \tanh(W_c x_t + U_c h_{t-1}) \tag{7}$$

$$c_t = f_t c_{t-1} + i_t \tilde{c}_t \tag{8}$$

$$h_i = o_t \tanh(c_t) \tag{9}$$

式中，i_t 是通过输入 x_t 和上一步的隐含层输出 h_{t-1} 进行线性变换，再经过激活函数 σ 得到的。输入门 i_t 的结果是向量，其中每隔元素是 0～1 之间的实数，用于控制各维度流过阀门的信息量；W_i、U_i 两个矩阵和向量 b_i 为输入门的参数，是在训练过程中需要学习得到的。遗忘门 f_t 和输出门 o_t 的计算方法与输入门类似，它们有各自的参数 W、U 和 b。与传统的循环神经网络不同的是，从上一个记忆单元的状态 c_t 到当前的状态 c_t 的转移不一定完全取决于激活函数计算得到的状态，还由输入门和遗忘门共同控制。

1.4 贝叶斯优化(Bayesian Optimization)

贝叶斯优化是一种黑盒优化算法，用于求解表达式未知的函数的极值问题。算法根据一组采样点处的函数值预测出任意点处函数值的概率分布，通过高斯过程回归实现。根据高斯过程回归的结果构造采集函数，用于衡量每一个点值得探索的程度，求解采集函数的极值从而确定下一个采样点。最后返回这组采样点的极值作为函数的极值。

算法首先初始化 n_0 个候选解，通常在整个可行域内均匀地选取一些点。然后开始进行循环，每次增加一个点，直至找到 N 个候选解。每次寻找下一个点时，用已经找到的 n 个候选解建立高斯过程回归模型，得到任意点处的函数值的后验概率。然后根据后验概率构造采集函数，寻找函数的极大值点作为下一个搜索点，接下来计算在下一个搜索点处的函数值。算法最后返回 N 个候选解的极大值作为最优解。

1.5 基于 K-mediods 聚类算法与 LSTM 的公路隧道围岩变形预测方法研究

本文针对围岩变形预测方法的研究主要分两个阶段：首先利用 K-mediods 聚类方法对历史变形

趋势数据进行聚类,形成各种不同变化趋势的数据包,并依据聚类结果构建围岩变形的典型轨迹模型;然后利用LSTM算法对围岩变形的典型轨迹构建动态预测模型。算法流程如图1所示,数据处理与重构如图2所示,预测模型构建如图3所示。

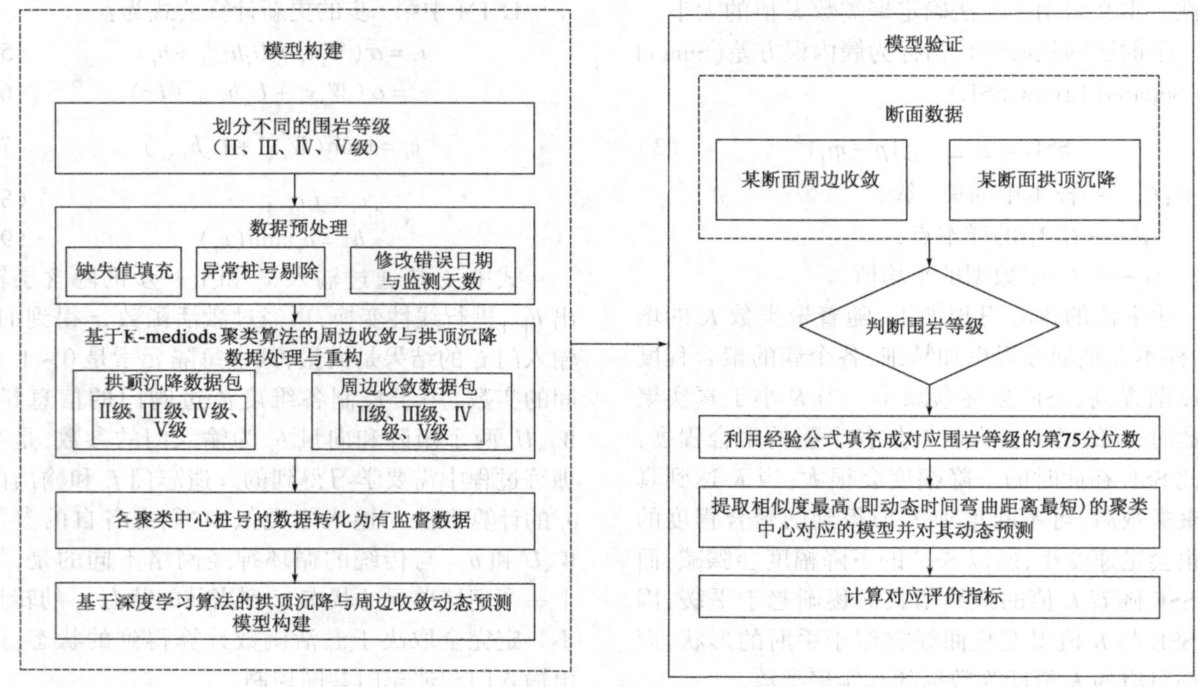

图1　技术方案

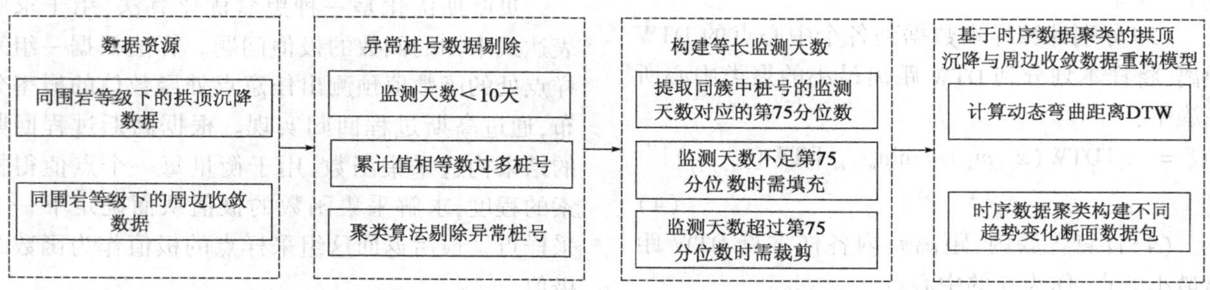

图2　基于K-mediods聚类算法的隧道围岩变形数据的处理与重构

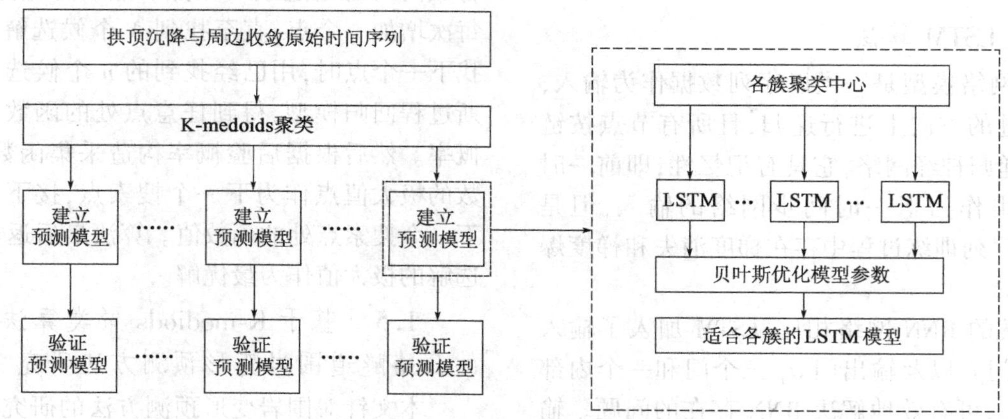

图3　基于LSTM算法的周边收敛与拱顶沉降动态预测模型构建

1.5.1 基于K-mediods聚类算法的隧道围岩变形数据的处理与重构

(1)异常桩号数据剔除

针对存在明显填写错误的桩号、监测天数小于10d的桩号进行剔除,同时利用时序数据聚类分析,剔除各簇中距离聚类中心较大的桩号数据。

(2)构建等长监测天数

由于原始数据中各个桩号的监测天数长度不等,因此需对监测天数进行限制,构建等长监测天数的桩号数据,为后续时序数据聚类做好准备,提取同簇中所有桩号的监测天数对应第75分位数的监测天数,如监测天数不足第75分位数时需进行填充,否则需裁剪。

(3)基于时序数据聚类的拱顶沉降与周边收敛数据重构与处理

按照不同的围岩级别,利用时序数据聚类算法,对多个断面的拱顶沉降与周边收敛数据进行时序数据聚类,将趋势变化相似或相同的量测断面聚为一类,形成不同趋势变化的断面数据包;

1.5.2 基于Bayes-LSTM算法的周边收敛与拱顶沉降动态预测模型构建

针对上述时序数据聚类后形成的各种不同趋势变化的数据包,提取各簇聚类中心,利用LSTM算法对各聚类中心构建预测模型并进行贝叶斯优化(Bayesian Optimization)对所建模型进行优化,形成适用于各种断面数据包的相应模型。最后,任意选取其他断面,对预测模型进行验证。

2 工程实例分析

为了验证该算法的有效性,采用海南省某公路隧道拱顶沉降与周边收敛的变形数据进行分析。该隧道为小净距隧道,最大埋深约380m,围岩主要为Ⅲ、Ⅳ和Ⅴ级围岩。隧道施工过程中的拱顶沉降采用全站仪进行监测,周边收敛位移采用数显收敛计进行监测。Ⅴ级围岩10m一个断面,Ⅳ级围岩20m一个断面,Ⅲ级围岩50m一个断面,实测断面累计共1738个。

2.1 基于K-mediods聚类算法的周边收敛与拱顶沉降的数据处理与重构

选取该隧道左线与右线1738个断面的拱顶沉降与周边收敛数据按照不同的围岩等级进行基于动态时间弯曲距离(DTW)的K-mdeoids聚类分析。在实际监控量测过程中,拱顶沉降与周边收敛的监测天数长度不等,应首先对时间序列进行预处理。本项目中采用不同围岩等级中各个监测桩号中所有监测天数对应的第75分位数对拱顶沉降与周边收敛进行监测天数填充,并利用原有经验公式进行填充,超过的则进行剪切,构建等长监测天数的时间序列。预处理后,按照不同的围岩等级,分别计算时间序列两两之间的DTW距离,衡量时间序列之间的相似程度,如图4所示。

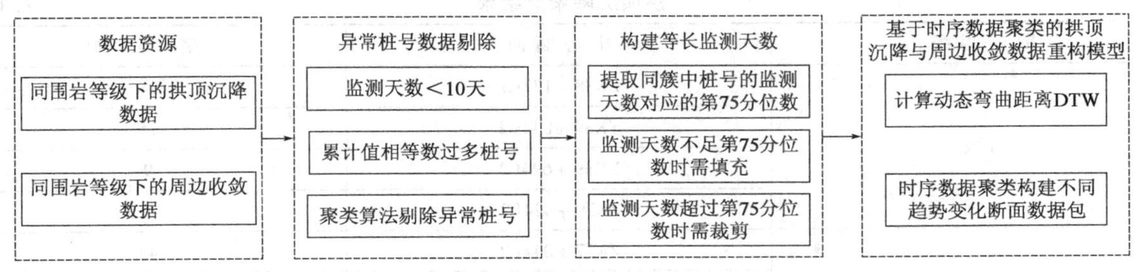

图4 基于K-mediods聚类算法的周边收敛与拱顶沉降的数据处理与重构

2.1.1 异常桩号数据剔除

针对存在明显填写错误的桩号、监测天数小于10d的桩号进行剔除,同时利用时序数据聚类分析,剔除各簇中距离聚类中心较大的桩号数据。

2.1.2 构建等长监测天数

由于原始数据中各个桩号的监测天数长度不等,因此需对监测天数进行限制,构建等长监测天数的桩号数据,为后续时序数据聚类做好准备,提取同簇中所有桩号的监测天数对应第75分位数的监测天数,如监测天数不足第75分位数时需进行填充,否则需裁剪。

2.1.3 基于时序数据聚类的拱顶沉降与周边收敛数据重构与处理

按照不同的围岩级别,利用K-mediods聚类算法,对多个断面的拱顶沉降与周边收敛数据进行时序数据聚类,将趋势变化相似或相同的量测断面聚为一类,形成不同趋势变化的断面数据包。

2.1.4　拱顶沉降聚类结果

根据手肘法对拱顶沉降Ⅱ-Ⅴ等级的桩号进行聚类分析,如图 5～图 8 所示。

拱顶沉降Ⅱ级共有 53 组桩号,有 4 个聚类中心;拱顶沉降Ⅲ级共有 394 个监测桩号,有 6 个聚类中心;拱顶沉降Ⅳ级共有 373 个监测断面,有 5 个聚类中心;拱顶沉降Ⅴ级共有 250 个监测桩号,有 4 个聚类中心。

各等级聚类中心对应的中心断面和聚类数量结果如表 1 所示。

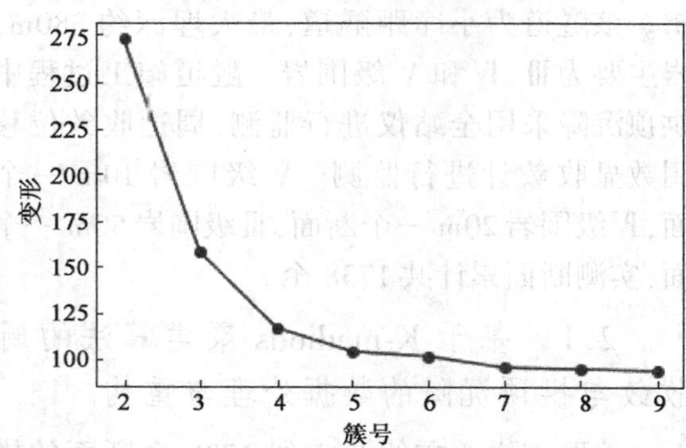

图 5　拱顶沉降Ⅱ级手肘法

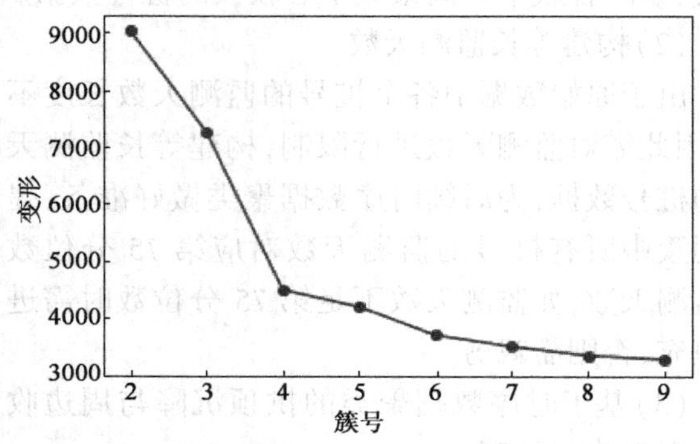

图 6　拱顶沉降Ⅲ级手肘法

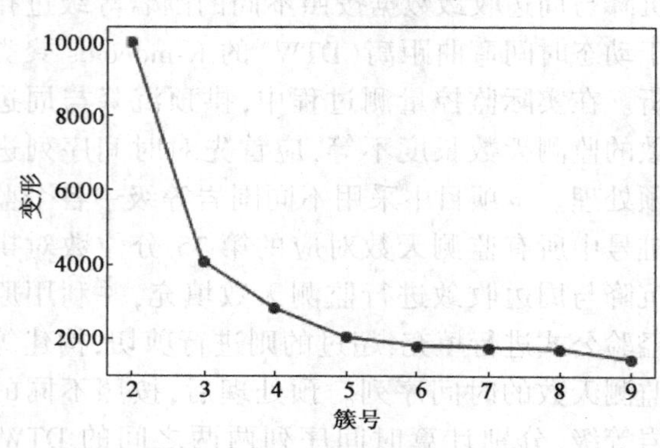

图 7　拱顶沉降Ⅳ级手肘法

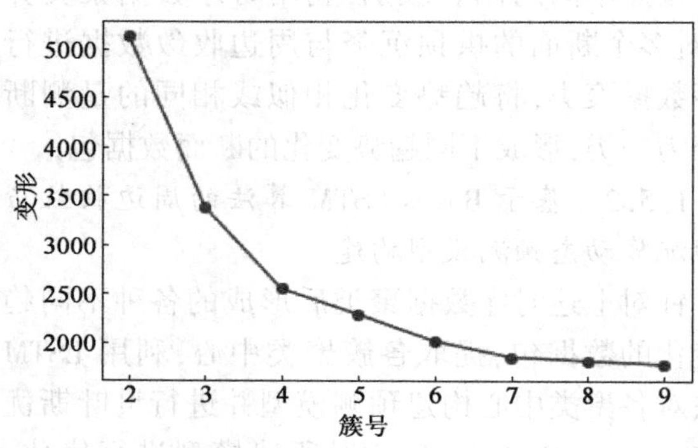

图 8　拱顶沉降Ⅴ级手肘法

拱顶沉降聚类结果　　表 1

围岩等级	中心断面	聚类数
Ⅱ级	ZK38 +177C1	18
	YK39 +844C2	15
	YK39 +694C2	9
	ZK39 +424C2	11
Ⅲ级	ZK37 +047C2	45
	YK36 +187C3	104
	YK38 +090C2	105
	ZK38 +534C3	6
	YK40 +684C3	78
	YK36 +357C3	56
Ⅳ级	ZK36 +617C1	133
	ZK40 +475C3	52
	YK40 +554C3	80
	ZK36 +087C2	79
	ZK36 +837C3	29

续上表

围岩等级	中心断面	聚类数
Ⅴ级	YK37 +177C2	57
	YK40 +804C1	84
	YK36 +537C3	42
	YK36 +067C2	67

利用与拱顶沉降相同的方法，对Ⅱ、Ⅲ、Ⅳ、Ⅴ级的周边收敛提取聚类中心并构建数据包，各等级下对应的聚类中心。周边收敛聚类结果见表2。

周边收敛聚类结果 表2

围岩等级	中心断面	聚类数
Ⅱ级	YK39 +244B1B2	12
	ZK38 +227B1B2	14
	YK39 +544B1B2	15
Ⅲ级	YK38 +940B1B2	25
	ZK40 +555A1A2	29
	YK38 +560B1B2	55
	YK37 +297A1A3	32
	ZK37 +462A1A2	11
Ⅳ级	ZK36 +417B1B2	27
	YK37 +727B1B2	35
	YK40 +494A1A2	29
	ZK37 +487A1A2	14
Ⅴ级	YK40 +804A1A2	24
	YK36 +757A1A3	25
	YK40 +837B1B2	14
	ZK37 +587A1A2	21

2.2 基于Bayes-LSTM算法的动态预测模型构建

提取聚类后各个不同变化趋势数据包对应的拱顶沉降与周边收敛的聚类中心，利用LSTM算法对各聚类中心构建模型并利用贝叶斯优化算法（Bayesian Optimization）对所建模型进行优化，形成适合于各种不同趋势变化的数据包。基于LSTM算法的预测模型构建如图9所示。

2.2.1 基于Bayes-LSTM算法的拱顶沉降动态预测模型构建

以拱顶沉降聚类断面YK36 +187C3为例（图10），此时间序列的时间长度为27，利用Bayes-LSTM算法建立预测模型，输入变量长度为5，输出变量长度为3，则训练样本的个数为27 −5 =22，通过Bayes-LSTM训练并预测，构建适合该种趋势变化的预测模型。然后，将该模型应用于断面YK36 +187C3所在的类的其他所有序列。

为了判断模型的准确性，对实际监测值和模型预测值进行对比，以聚类中心断面YK36 +187C3自身和该类中断面ZK40 +695C1为例，预测数据与真实数据拟合情况如下：均方根误差（RMSE）分别为0.64和0.84，平均绝对误差（MAE）分别为0.50和0.52，决定系数分别为*R*2 =0.95和0.94。监测值和预测值的对比如图11和图12所示。

按照相同的方法得到拱顶沉降其他各类的预测模型，统计每一类中所有断面的RMSE值、MAPE值与R2，此处以拱顶沉降Ⅲ级为例，将结果与未利用贝叶斯优化的LSTM模型的预测结果进行比较（表3）。

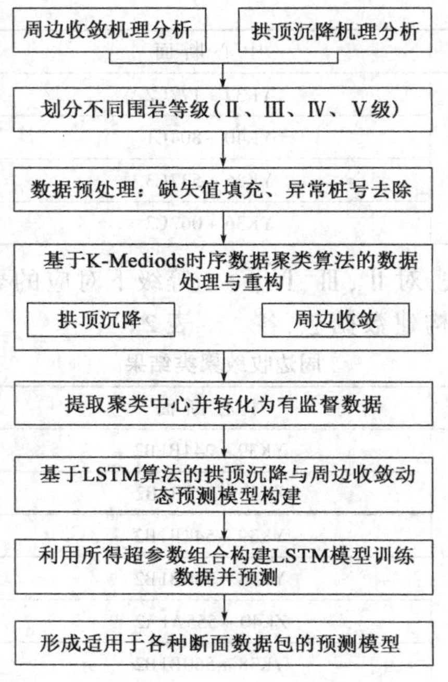

图9　基于LSTM算法的预测模型构建

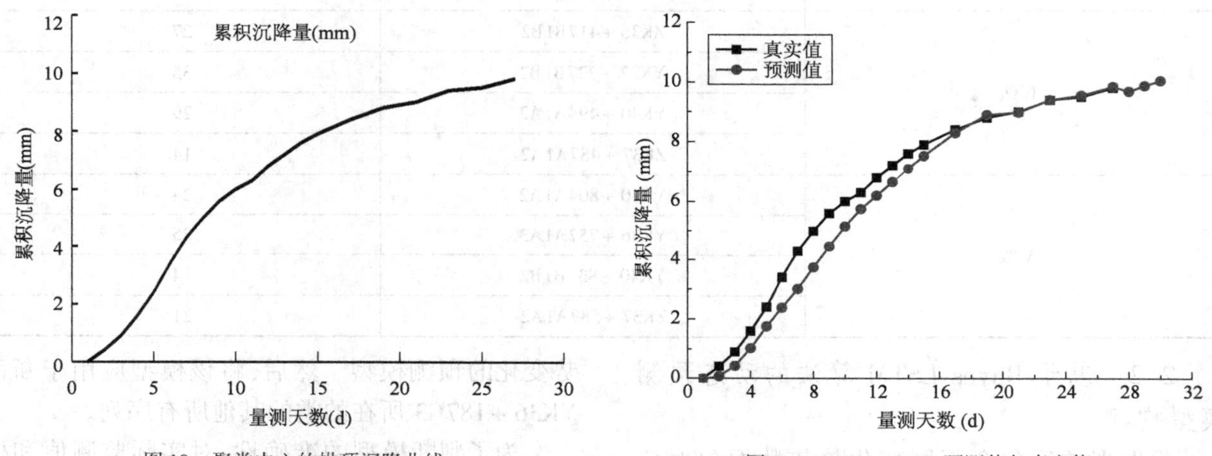

图10　聚类中心的拱顶沉降曲线

图11　YK36 +187C3 预测值与真实值

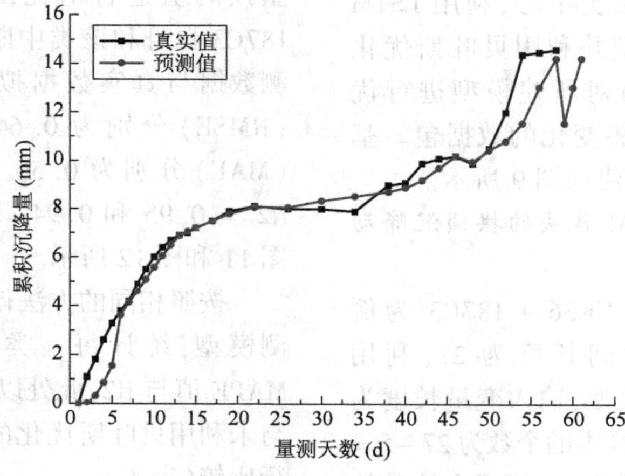

图12　ZK40 +695C1 预测值与真实值

LSTM 和 Bayes-LSTM 模型预测结果对比 表 3

聚类中心	聚类数	RMSE		MAE		R2	
		Bayes-LSTM	LSTM	Bayes-LSTM	LSTM	Bayes-LSTM	LSTM
ZK37 +047C2	45	0.998	2.12	0.96	2.01	0.93	0.69
YK38 +090C2	105	0.55	0.61	0.47	0.59	0.83	0.79
ZK38 +534C3	6	8.6	10.55	5.68	8.21	0.96	0.94
YK40 +684C3	78	0.29	0.3	0.22	0.23	0.98	0.98
YK36 +357C3	56	0.47	0.69	0.34	0.57	0.93	0.85

2.2.2 基于 Bayes-LSTM 算法的周边收敛动态预测模型构建

以周边收敛聚类断面 YK38 +560B1B2 为例,时间序列变化如图 13 所示,此时间序列的时间长度为 25,利用 Bayes-LSTM 算法建立预测模型,输入变量长度为 5,输出变量长度为 3,则训练样本的个数为 25 - 5 = 20,通过 Bayes-LSTM 训练并预测,构建适合该种趋势变化的预测模型。然后,将该模型应用于断面 YK38 +560B1B2 所在的类的其他所有序列。

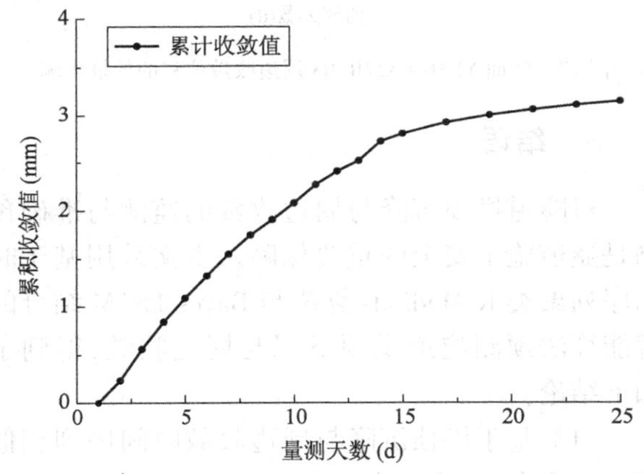

图 13 聚类中心 YK38 +560B1B2 的时间序列

为了判断模型的准确性,对实际监测值和模型预测值进行对比,以聚类中心断面 YK38 +560B1B2 自身和该类中断面 ZK37 +977B1B2 为例,预测数据与真实数据拟合情况如图 14 和图 15 所示,均方根误差(RMSE)分别为 0.07 和 0.086,平均绝对误差(MAE)分别为 0.052 和 0.060,决定系数分别为 R2 = 0.993 和 0.989。

按照相同的方法得到拱顶沉降其他各类的预测模型,统计每一类中所有断面的 RMSE 值、MAPE 值与 R2,此处以周边收敛Ⅲ级为例,将结果与未利用贝叶斯优化的 LSTM 模型的预测结果进行比较(表 4)。

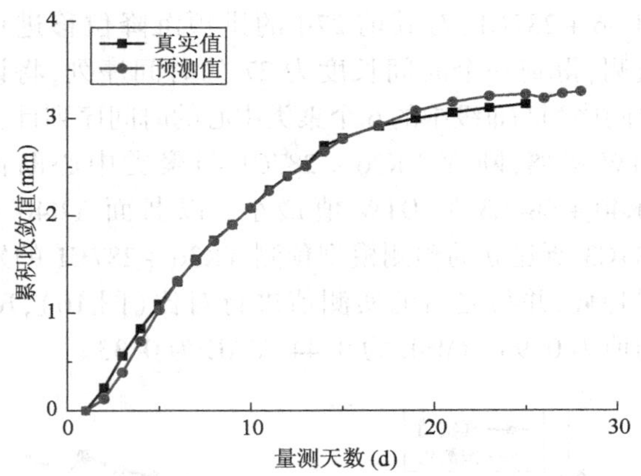

图 14 YK38 +560B1B2 预测值与真实值对比图

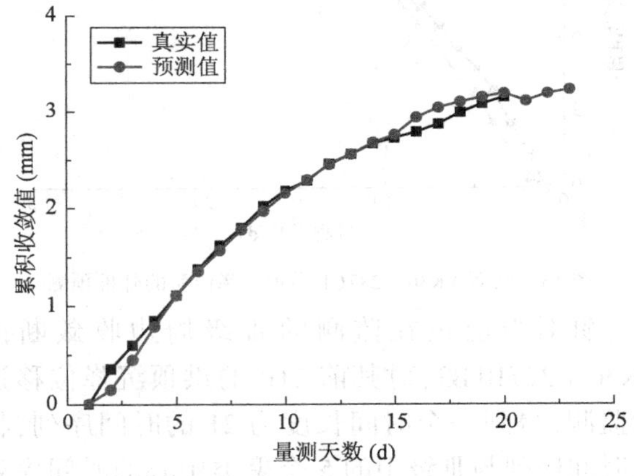

图 15 ZK37 +977B1B2 预测值与真实值对比图

由图 11、图 12、图 14 和图 15 与表 3 和表 4 可知,预测模型在预测同一聚类中其他对象的拱顶沉降与周边收敛位移值上具有较高的预测精度,在实际工程中具有参考意义。同时相比直接采用 LSTM 模型进行建模,贝叶斯优化后的 LSTM 模型在预测隧道拱顶沉降与周边收敛时具有更高的准确性和可靠性。

LSTM和Bayes-LSTM模型预测结果对比　　表4

聚类中心	聚类数	RMSE		MAE		R2	
		Bayes-LSTM	LSTM	Bayes-LSTM	LSTM	Bayes-LSTM	LSTM
YK38+940B1B2	25	0.31	0.32	0.28	0.28	0.93	0.93
ZK40+555A1A2	29	0.069	0.20	0.057	0.19	0.94	0.49
YK37+297A1A3	32	0.18	0.26	0.16	0.24	0.82	0.68
ZK37+462A1A2	11	0.30	0.50	0.25	0.46	0.96	0.88

2.3　拱顶沉降与周边收敛外推预测

针对当前正在监测的Ⅲ级拱顶沉降断面YK36+287C1,对其前27d的拱顶沉降位移进行监测,得到一个时间长度为27的时间序列,将该时间序列与Ⅲ级中的6个聚类中心的时间序列计算DTW距离,断面YK36+287C1与聚类中心断面YK40+684C3的DTW值最小。以断面YK40+684C3所建立的预测模型预测YK36+287C1的发展趋势,并与之后的实测值进行对比(图16),R2的值为0.95,RMSE为0.44,MAE为0.33。

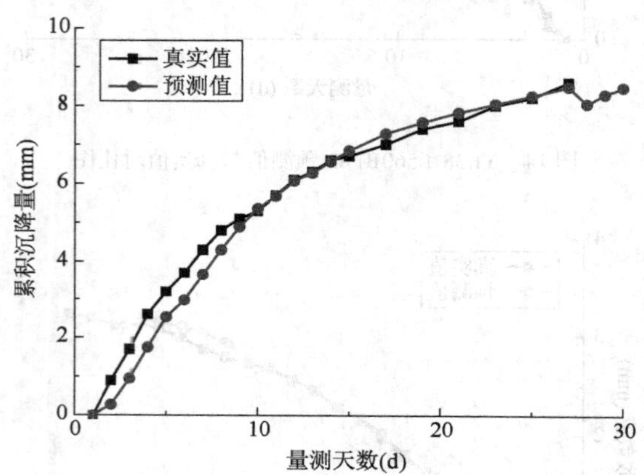

图16　断面YK36+287C1拱顶沉降位移的外推预测

针对当前正在监测的Ⅲ级周边收敛断面YK36+327B1B3,对其前21d的拱顶沉降位移进行监测,得到一个时间长度为21的时间序列,将该时间序列与Ⅲ级中的5个聚类中心的时间序列计算DTW距离,断面YK36+327B1B3与聚类中心断面ZK40+555A1A2的DTW值最小。以断面ZK40+555A1A2所建立的预测模型预测YK36+327B1B3的发展趋势,并与之后的实测值进行对比(图17),R2的值为0.98,RMSE为0.071,MAE为0.053。

由图16和图17可见,对于当前正在监测的断面,基于K-Medoids聚类和Bayes-LSTM结合的算法具有较高的准确性,且该算法仅监测当前断面的部分时间点即可以进行预测,为可能出现较大变形值的断面的处置措施提供更为及时准确的参考。

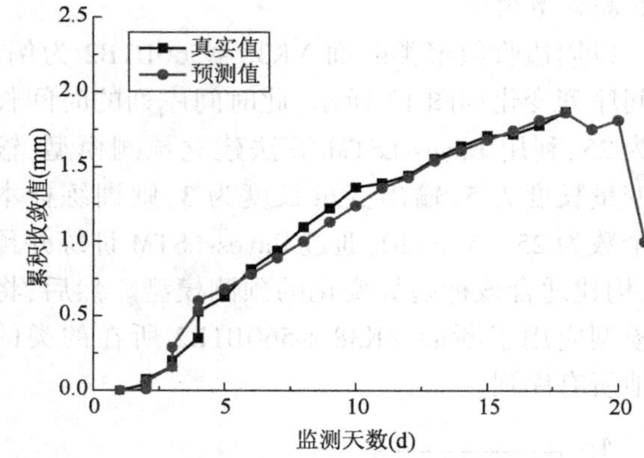

图17　断面YK36+327B1B3周边收敛位移的外推预测

3　结语

对隧道拱顶沉降与周边收敛的监测与准确预测是隧道施工安全的重要保障。本文采用基于时间序列聚类K-Mediods算法与Bayes-LSTM结合的智能算法预测隧道拱顶下沉与周边收敛,得到了如下结论:

(1)基于拱顶沉降与周边收敛时间序列相似度进行聚类,以聚类中心为对象,通过Bayes-LSTM算法建立的预测模型在预测同一聚类中其他对象的发展趋势上具有较高的准确性,验证了同一类时间序列用同一模型预测的可行性。

(2)相比直接利用LSTM建立模型,采用Bayes优化和LSTM结合的算法具有更高的预测精度,能够更真实地反映拱顶沉降与周边收敛的时间曲线。

(3)对于当前正在监测的断面,基于聚类中心的预测可以充分利用已监测断面的数据,在当前断面的监测初期即可以进行及时有效的预测。

参考文献

[1]　杨清浩,胡雄玉,陈子全.基于时间序列聚类和LSSVM的隧道拱顶位移预测[J].公路工

程,2019,44(01):9-15+31.

[2] 颜杜民. 基于"S"型函数的隧道开挖变形预测模型[J]. 地质与勘探,2020,56(02):438-444.

[3] 孙柏林,乔松林,张乾青,等. 隧道拱顶沉降及周边收敛动态过程预测的 Richards 时间函数模型[J]. 公路工程,2015,40(06):114-118.

[4] 俞文生,平洋. 基于黏弹性本构性能的隧道围岩变形预测研究[J]. 岩土力学,2014,35(S1):35-41.

[5] 谢宝琎. 强膨胀土隧道围岩大变形特性及监控预测研究[D]. 阜新:辽宁工程技术大学.

[6] 孙钧,潘晓明. 隧道软弱围岩挤压大变形非线性流变力学特性研究[J]. 岩石力学与工程学报,2012.

[7] 王文玉,王希良,张骞. 基于关联分析和遗传算法优化 BP 的隧道围岩变形预测[J]. 铁道标准设计,2020,64(05):126-132.

[8] 强跃,李绍红,刘超琼. 基于多尺度组合核极限学习机模型的隧道围岩变形预测及应用[J]. 现代隧道技术,2017,54(06):70-76.

[9] 文明,张顶立,房倩,等. 隧道围岩变形的非线性自回归时间序列预测方法研究[J]. 北京交通大学学报,2017,41(04):1-7.

[10] Yue Pan, Liang Chen, Ju Wang, et al. Research on deformation prediction of tunnel surrounding rock using the model combining firefly algorithm and nonlinear auto-regressive dynamic neural network[J]. Engineering with Computers, 2021, 37(2):1443-1453.

[11] Guihong Song, Peng Zhou, Qizhi Hu, et al. Application of Improved Grey Model Based on Cumulative Method to Deformation Prediction of Tunnel Surrounding Rock[J]. Journal of Physics: Conference Series, 2020, 1676(1):012241.

[12] Shaoshuai Shi, Ruijie Zhao, Shucai Li, et al. Intelligent prediction of surrounding rock deformation of shallow buried highway tunnel and its engineering application[J]. Tunnelling and Underground Space Technology incorporating Trenchless Technology Research, 2019, 90:1-11.

[13] 姚凯,朱向阳,张克宏,等. 基于 FOA-GRNN 的软岩隧道围岩变形预测模型[J]. 地下空间与工程学报,2019,15(S2):908-913.

[14] 黄震,廖敏杏,张皓量,等. 基于 SVM-BP 模型非完整数据的隧道围岩挤压变形预测[J]. 现代隧道技术,2020,57(S1):129-138.

[15] 孙茂斌. 基于动态时间规整的时序数据相似度量方法研究[D]. 重庆:重庆邮电大学,2020.

[16] 刘博,王明烁,李永,等. 深度学习在时空序列预测中的应用综述[J]. 北京工业大学学报,2021,47(08):925-941.

基于回归分析的公路隧道拱顶变形预测

苟 超* 龙 欣 刘 智 周春豪

(中交第一公路勘察设计研究院有限公司)

摘 要 隧道施工过程中,拱顶位移是判断围岩稳定性的重要指标。回归分析法作为一种处理测读数据,分析其内在规律的常用方法,被广泛应用于隧道施工过程中围岩变形分析及发展趋势预测,而回归分析中回归函数的选择对数据拟合及预测的精度具有决定性影响。本文基于某公路隧道在不同级别围岩中断面拱顶沉降实测数据,对比分析了现行规范和相关研究中的5种回归函数模型对不同级别围岩下

1. 基金项目:中国交建科技研发项目(编号:2019-ZKJ-08);中交第一公路勘察设计研究院有限公司科技研发项目(编号:KYHT2020-43);中交第一公路勘察设计研究院有限公司科创基金项目(编号:KCJJ2020-19)。

隧道拱顶沉降变形的拟合以及预测精度。研究结果表明:对于该公路隧道各级围岩的实测数据,5种回归函数模型均能对隧道拱顶沉降做出较好的拟合效果,多项式和有理函数的拟合精度均高于规范给出的3种函数,而对数函数的拟合精度相对较差;双曲函数和指数函数可以分别对Ⅴ级和Ⅲ级围岩变形进行有效预测,有理函数适合对Ⅴ级围岩变形进行预测,而多项式函数对实测数据的拟合精度最高,但其不适用于隧道拱顶的变形预测。

关键词　公路隧道　拱顶变形　回归分析　变形预测

0　引言

隧道施工过程中,开挖扰动必然引起隧道围岩发生各种形态的变形。对围岩和支护进行监控量测,可以掌握围岩和支护工作状态,判断围岩稳定性和支护结构的合理性,为施工中调整围岩级别、变更设计方案及参数以及优化施工方案提供依据。隧道拱顶下沉作为隧道监控量测的必测项目之一,对隧道围岩的稳定性判断至关重要。若能通过数据分析对隧道开挖过程中的拱顶下沉进行准确预测,则对隧道施工质量和安全具有重要意义[1-2]。

回归分析是一种处理测读数据,分析数据内在规律的有效方法,常用于数据拟合、趋势预测等问题,具有简洁、准确等特点[3-4]。《公路隧道施工技术规范》(JTG/T3660—2020)(以下简称《规范》[5])中明确规定,公路隧道监控量测应及时进行数据整理和数据分析,对初期的时态曲线应进行回归分析,预测可能出现的最大值和变化速度,掌握位置变化的规律,并建议了3种隧道变形预测回归函数模型。本文基于某公路隧道现场监测数据,对《规范》中3种回归函数以及相关研究中常用的2种函数模型进行适用性分析,分析不同围岩级别下各函数模型对隧道拱顶变形的拟合以及预测精度,为同类工程施工过程中监测数据的分析处理提供指导和依据。

1　工程概况

选取研究的隧道为小净距双洞公路隧道,全长4.8km,洞室净空11.0m×5.0m。隧道穿越地层以Ⅴ级、Ⅳ级和Ⅲ级围岩为主。隧道最大埋深:左线383.18m、右线370.34m,属特长深埋公路隧道。对隧道Ⅴ级围岩地段,采用拱部预留核心土台阶分步开挖法开挖;洞身Ⅳ级围岩地段采用台阶法开挖;隧道洞身Ⅱ、Ⅲ级围岩地段则采用全断面开挖施工。隧道施工按新奥法组织实施,以锚杆、喷射混凝土或钢筋网喷混凝土、钢拱架作为初期支护,模筑混凝土作为二次支护,共同组成永久性承载结构,采用的辅助施工措施主要有超前长管棚、超前小导管加固注浆和超前锚杆支护。

2　工程监测实例

本文分析不同围岩级别下不同函数模型对该隧道拱顶沉降的拟合以及精度预测。由于该隧道施工段没有Ⅰ级围岩,因此选择Ⅱ、Ⅲ、Ⅳ、Ⅴ级围岩段监测断面的拱顶沉降实测数据进行回归分析。选取的断面及拱顶下沉测点的布设如图1所示,本文选择C1测点的监测数据进行分析。不同围岩级别段断面的监测数据如图2所示。

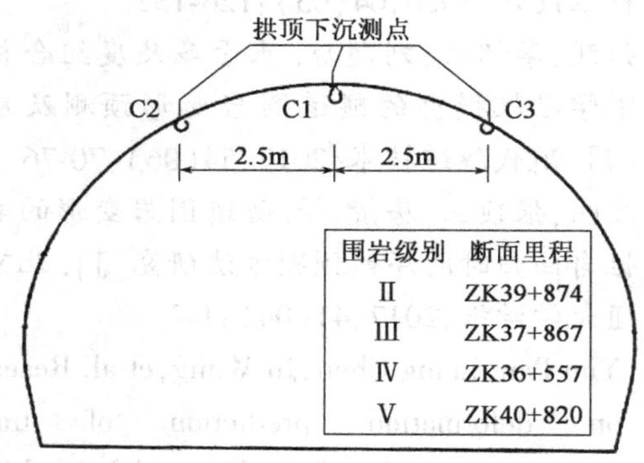

图1　断面及拱顶下沉测点布设示意图

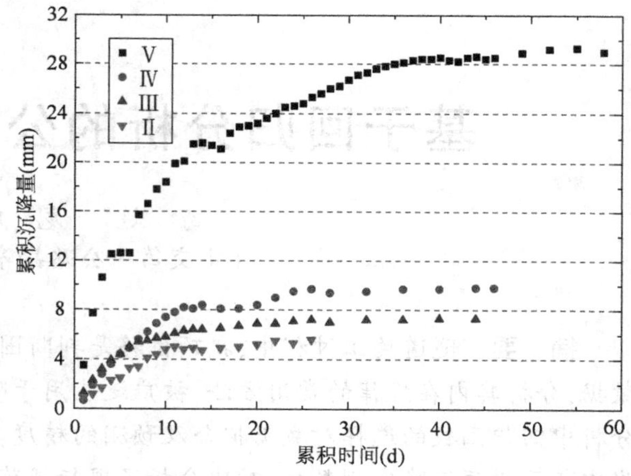

图2　断面拱顶下沉监测数据

由图2可以看出,4个监测断面的拱顶位移均呈现出前期快速增长,中期增长速率降低,后期逐渐平稳的规律。累计时间相同时,拱顶位移随着围岩等级的增大而增大。Ⅴ级围岩段隧道拱顶位移变化最大,最大沉降量达到29.3mm,Ⅱ级围岩段位移变化最小,最大沉降量为5.6mm。

3 监测数据回归分析

3.1 回归模型选取

《规范》中给出了对数、指数、双曲3种建议的隧道围岩变形回归分析函数模型,同时大量研究表明[6-10],多项式函数以及有理函数对于隧道监测数据拟合也具有很好的适用性,因此,本文选取以上5种函数模型进行分析,回归函数模型如表1所示。

3.2 监测数据回归分析

采用选取的5种回归函数对各断面的拱顶沉降数据进行回归分析,回归算法采用Levenberg-Marquardt优化算法,该算法是一种非线性优化方法,具有对过参数化问题不敏感,能有效处理冗余参数问题的特点,对于隧道监测数据拟合具有较好的适用性。5种回归函数模型的拟合结果如图3所示,为更清晰地显示不同函数模型的拟合效果,图3中仅显示后期的监测数据拟合曲线。各回归函数的回归系数以及相关系数平方 R^2 如表2所示。

回归函数模型 表1

序号	函数名称	表达式
1	对数函数	$u = a + b\ln(1 + t)$
2	指数函数	$u = a \cdot e^{-b/t}$
3	双曲函数	$u = at/(b + t)$
4	多项式函数	$u = a + bx + cx^2 + dx^3 + ex^4 + fx^5$
5	有理函数	$u = a + bt/(1 + ct + dt^2)$

注:u 为位移值(mm);a、b、c、d、e、f 为回归常数;t 为初读数后的时间(d)。

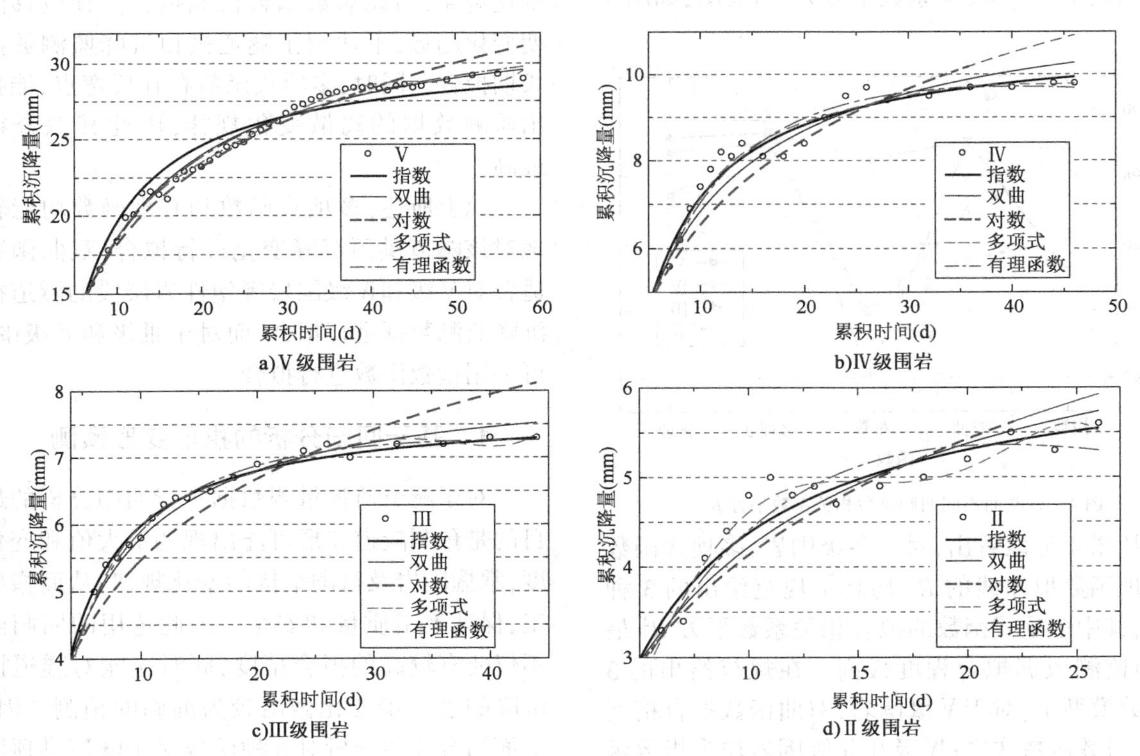

图3 各断面拱顶沉降数据及拟合曲线

不同回归函数拟合结果及相关系数平方 R^2　　表 2

围岩级别	指数拟合	双曲拟合	对数拟合	多项式拟合	有理函数拟合
Ⅴ	$u=30.813e^{-4.528/t}$ $R^2=0.95194$	$u=\frac{33.770t}{8.1991+t}$ $R^2=0.99051$	$u=-0.33226+7.719\ln(1+t)$ $R^2=0.98497$	$u=1.983+2.945t-0.179t^2+0.006t^3-9.583\times10^{-5}t^4+5.839\times10^{-7}t^5$ $R^2=0.99309$	$u=\frac{1.413+3.702t}{1+0.108t-0.1343\times10^{-5}t^2}$ $R^2=0.99154$
Ⅳ	$u=10.895e^{-4.219/t}$ $R^2=0.98452$	$u=\frac{11.948t}{7.484+t}$ $R^2=0.96967$	$u=-0.713+3.022\ln(1+t)$ $R^2=0.93836$	$u=-0.797+1.458t-0.092t^2+0.003t^3-5.033\times10^{-5}t^4+3.237\times10^{-7}t^5$ $R^2=0.99001$	$u=\frac{-1.139+1.717t}{1+0.121t-6.935\times10^{-4}t^2}$ $R^2=0.9874$
Ⅲ	$u=7.731e^{-2.568/t}$ $R^2=0.98798$	$u=\frac{8.243t}{4.223+t}$ $R^2=0.98993$	$u=0.952+1.883\ln(1+t)$ $R^2=0.92138$	$u=0.189+1.266t-0.104t^2+0.004t^3-8.676\times10^{-5}t^4+6.652\times10^{-7}t^5$ $R^2=0.99686$	$u=\frac{-0.588+2.074t}{1+0.236t-5.765\times10^{-4}t^2}$ $R^2=0.99712$
Ⅱ	$u=6.429e^{-3.843/t}$ $R^2=0.96081$	$u=\frac{7.394t}{7.518+t}$ $R^2=0.95574$	$u=-0.656+1.998\ln(1+t)$ $R^2=0.94099$	$u=0.794-0.023t-0.149t^2-0.017t^3+6.989\times10^{-5}t^4-1.005\times10^{-5}t^5$ $R^2=0.99014$	$u=\frac{-0.047+0.726t}{1+0.042t+0.002\times10^{-4}t^2}$ $R^2=0.97456$

由图 3 和表 2 可以看出,5 种回归函数模型的相关系数平方 R^2 均大于 0.9,对于各级围岩段隧道拱顶下沉位移的拟合效果均较好。相比较下,对数函数的拟合效果明显较差,其拟合曲线在后期拟合值有逐渐偏大的趋势。为更直观地比较不同回归函数对不同级别围岩段隧道拱顶下沉位移的回归效果,绘制相关系数平方 R^2 曲线图,如图 4 所示。

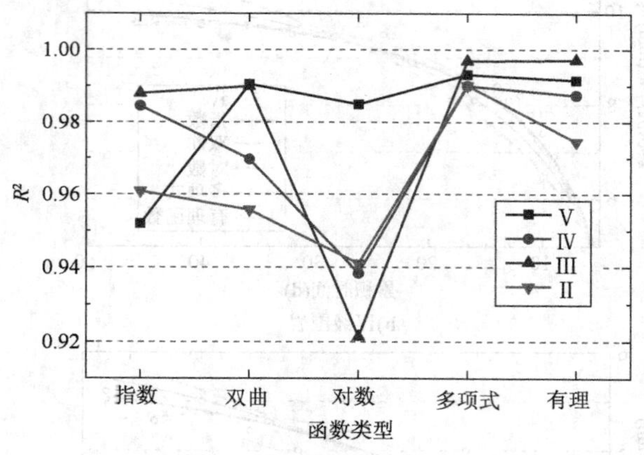

图 4　各断面不同回归函数相关系数平方 R^2

从图 4 可以看出,对于各级围岩,多项式函数和有理函数拟曲线的 R^2 均高于规范给出的 3 种函数,其中多项式函数的拟合相关系数平方 R^2 最大,对监测数据拟合程度最高。在规范给出的 3 种函数模型中,对于Ⅴ级围岩,双曲函数拟合精度最高,对数函数次之;Ⅳ级和Ⅱ级围岩均为指数函数最高,双曲函数次之;Ⅲ级围岩指数和双曲函数 R^2 接近;而对数函数对Ⅳ、Ⅲ、Ⅱ级围岩的拟合效果均较差。分析其原因,双曲函数的曲线变化趋势较为平缓,与塑性岩层的变形情况更为吻合,指数函数曲线具有前期变化较快,后期快速趋于平稳的特点,因此更适合脆性围岩的变形拟合。而由于对数函数不存在极值,其拟合结果会随着时间的延长而持续增大,这不符合隧道拱顶位移的变化规律,因此对数函数仅能拟合拱顶位移的前期变化趋势,不适用于隧道拱顶沉降监测数据的长期拟合。同时,多项式函数存在反弯点,能拟合出监测数据的离散变化规律,因此其拟合精度最高。

综上所述,多项式函数和有理函数均能较好地对该隧道拱顶沉降变化进行拟合,双曲函数更适合对Ⅴ级和Ⅳ级围岩等塑性岩层段的隧道拱顶沉降监测数据进行拟合,而对于Ⅲ级和Ⅱ级围岩,可采用指数函数进行拟合。

4　基于回归分析的拱顶变形预测

对于隧道监控量测数据进行回归分析的最终目的是预测隧道变形可能出现的最大值和变化速度,掌握围岩及衬砌结构的变化规律,从而指导施工,保证施工质量和安全。因此选用的回归函数不仅要有较高的拟合精度,同时应能对隧道拱顶沉降的进一步变化做出较为准确的预测。因此,下面结合前述分析对五种函数对于隧道拱顶沉降的预测能力进行分析。

由前述分析可知,多项式拟合和有理函数对

于隧道拱顶沉降的拟合精度均较高,而双曲函数和指数函数分别适合对塑性岩层段和脆性岩层段进行拟合。因此选择Ⅴ级围岩段和Ⅲ级围岩段的监测数据进行分析。对于Ⅴ级围岩,选择双曲函数、多项式和有理函数进行预测分析。同理,选择指数函数、多项式和有理函数进行Ⅲ级围岩段的隧道拱顶变形预测。

《规范》中规定,当变形速率小于0.2mm/d时,围岩达到基本稳定。因此采用围岩连续3天小于0.2mm/d时对应天数的监测数据进行拟合,采用得到的拟合曲线进行进一步的预测。Ⅴ级围岩和Ⅲ级围岩段分别采用前20天和前14天的数据进行拟合预测。结果如图5、图6所示。

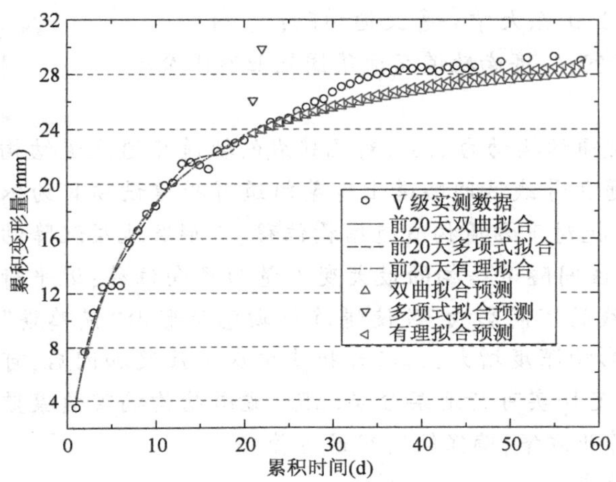

图5　Ⅴ级围岩前20天监测数据预测

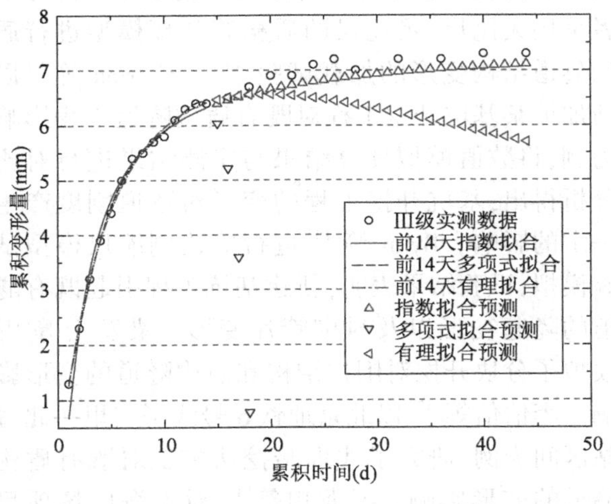

图6　Ⅲ级围岩前14天监测数据预测

由图5和图6可以看出,对于Ⅴ级围岩,通过前20天的监测数据进行拟合,之后用得到的拟合曲线进行长期预测,双曲函数和有理函数的均得到较好的预测效果,在第58天的预测值分别为28.03mm和28.73mm,与实测值的误差分别为-0.97mm和-0.27mm;而对于Ⅲ级围岩,指数函数和有理函数在第44天的预测值分别为7.11mm和5.7mm,指数函数的预测结果较为准确,误差为-0.19mm,而有理函数的预测结果出现了较大的偏差。同时,多项式函数对两类围岩的变形预测偏差均较大,在第二天均出现超过2mm的误差。说明双曲函数和指数函数可以分别对Ⅴ级和Ⅲ级围岩段的隧道拱顶变形进行预测,而有理函数仅适合对Ⅴ级围岩段进行预测,由于多项式函数其本质为一突变模型,存在反弯点,因此不适合对隧道拱顶的变形进行长期预测。

5　结语

本文采用对数、指数、双曲、多项式函数以及有理函数五种回归函数模型,对某公路隧道不同级别围岩段隧道断面拱顶沉降监测数据进行回归分析及预测研究,主要结论有:

(1)对于各级围岩,5种回归函数模型均能对隧道拱顶沉降做出较好的拟合效果。其中,多项式和有理函数的拟合精度均高于《规范》给出的3种函数,而对数函数的拟合精度相对较差;

(2)双曲函数更适合对Ⅴ级和Ⅳ级围岩等塑性岩层段的隧道拱顶沉降监测数据进行拟合,而对于Ⅲ级和Ⅱ级围岩,可采用指数函数进行拟合。

(3)双曲函数和指数函数可以分别对Ⅴ级和Ⅲ级围岩段的隧道拱顶变形进行较为精确的预测,而有理函数适合对Ⅴ级围岩段进行预测。多项式函数对实测数据的拟合精度最高,但其不适用于隧道拱顶的变形预测。

参考文献

[1] 甘洪匀,周建.国内外隧道监控量测技术发展现状综述[J].地下空间与工程学报,2019(S01):16.

[2] 申大为.高速公路隧道的施工监测技术[J].交通世界,2020(33):2.

[3] 汪辉,马淑芝,龙琰.回归分析在隧道围岩稳定性预测中的应用[J].公路,2015(04):296-299.

[4] 吕良,李晓彬,李思宇.公路隧道监测数据处理及回归分析[J].交通科技,2017(2).

[5] 中华人民共和国行业标准.公路隧道施工技术规范:JTG/T 3660—2020[S].北京:人民交

通出版社股份有限公司,2020.
[6] 李梓源,王海亮,张超.隧道洞内监测数据回归分析方法的比较研究[J].市政技术,2016,34(3):4.
[7] 张燕梅,张睿,马进全.基于择优分段回归模型的变形监测数据分析[J].青海大学学报(自然科学版),2017,35(04):36-40+94.
[8] 齐超.回归分析法在隧道监控量测及施工中的应用[J].低碳地产,2016,2(019):73-74.
[9] 徐世强,屈战辉.隧道监控量测相关标准[J].筑路机械与施工机械化,2011,28(1):4.
[10] 包太,言志信,刘新荣.有理函数在隧道监测数据回归分析中的应用[J].地下空间与工程学报,2009,005(005):1029-1032.

顶部卸载对地铁盾构隧道的影响效应分析

黄永亮*[1,2,3]　王　亮[1,4]　曹玉鑫[1,3]　王晓晖[1,3]
(1.济南轨道交通集团有限公司;2.山东大学齐鲁交通学院;
3.山东省智慧轨道交通信息化与装备重点实验室;4.济南轨道交通集团置业有限公司)

摘　要　轨道交通隧道上部开挖会引起下方轨道交通结构动力响应,对已建成的轨道交通隧道结构以及行车安全带来了严重的影响。本文以济南轨道交通3号线区间隧道上部某河道开挖建设项目为依托,采用MIDAS数值计算手段,综合分析河道近平行开挖对下方盾构隧道结构位移、变形及地层沉降的影响。结果表明:上部基坑开挖引起下方近平行的盾构区间隧道结构的最大变形量为竖向位移;近平行河道开挖会引起偏心不平衡卸载对区间隧道左线和右线的不同影响,致使隧道衬砌总变形由“横鸭蛋”形转变为“斜鸭蛋”形;当上部基坑开挖深度增加,有效影响深度增大,但在开挖基坑底部注浆加固后,可有效减小回弹量,并降低影响深度;在实际施工中,应制定切实可行地层分层沉降、隧道结构病害健康监测方案,加强监测预警,并结合监测数据动态调整施工作业方案,确保轨道交通运营安全。

关键词　盾构隧道　开挖卸载　数值模拟　影响效应

0　引言

近年来,我国城市地下空间开发逐渐向更深的地下推进[1]。随着建设规模的扩大,地铁建设规模及其网络覆盖面增大,使得地铁与其他市政工程的相互影响日益凸显,临近地铁保护区建设项目日益增多[2]。

国内外众多学者针对运营地铁保护区近接施工的影响进行了研究。张玉伟[3]等研究了基坑卸载再加载对盾构隧道的影响。Hiroshi等[4]采用有限元数值模拟方法研究了土体开挖时隧道的纵向问题。张鑫海等[5]针对基坑开挖引起下方盾构隧道围压变化的机制进行分析,提出一种能考虑纵向变形影响的盾构隧道横向附加围压变化模型,建立盾构隧道管片环的有限元简化模型。部分学者采用大比尺、足比尺的盾构管片环模型进行盾构隧道结构变形的加载试验[6-8]。Sharma等[9]以新加坡某基坑开挖工程对既有盾构隧道工程影响为例,将数值模拟计算结果与实测结果进行对比分析得出,基坑开挖工程的变形对隧道刚度产生一定的影响。Byun等[10]进行等比例缩尺模型试验模拟,试验结果表明,新建基坑工程引起既有隧道的隆起变形以及衬砌管片变形。梁发云等[11]模拟了分块开挖对围护结构和盾构隧道的变形影响。李倩倩等[12]以北京地铁6号线平安里—北海站区间为例,研究了浅埋暗挖法施工对既有盾构隧道的变形影响。况龙川等[13]对上海广场项目基坑工程进行研究,分析隧道沿线灌注桩和地下

1.基金项目:山东省自然科学基金资助项目(ZR2020QE256);交通运输部2021年交通运输行业重点科技项目清单项目(2021-MS1-006);山东省交通运输科技计划项目(2021B02)。

连续墙施工、盾构隧道上方及侧方基坑开挖引起隧道变形监测数据，得出不同施工情况下盾构隧道的变形特点。Schroeder 等[14-15]采用有限元分析的方法研究了桩基加载对既有隧道的影响。魏纲等[16]以杭州地铁 1 号线为研究对象，分析了不同施工阶段下盾构隧道位移变形的特点。

综上，学者对临近地铁保护区施工领域进行了较多研究，但对运营轨道交通隧道上部河道开挖影响效应研究方面报道较少。鉴于此，本研究依托济南轨道交通 3 号线某区间隧道上部河道长距离、平行基坑开挖卸载项目，采用有限元软件 MIDAS 建立数值计算模型，分析开源中路位置处盾构隧道上方龙脊河河道开挖、电力沟基坑开挖以及过河直埋管线基坑开挖对运营地铁隧道产生的影响，根据计算结果进行区间盾构隧道结构和运营的安全影响综合评价，提出保护改进建议。

1 工程概况

济南市轨道交通 3 号线某区间隧道上部为规划河道，河道在轨道交通工程建设完成后进行施工建设。轨道交通区间为双单洞隧道，采用盾构法施工。盾构区间过区间近接平行下穿规划龙脊河，如图 1 所示。

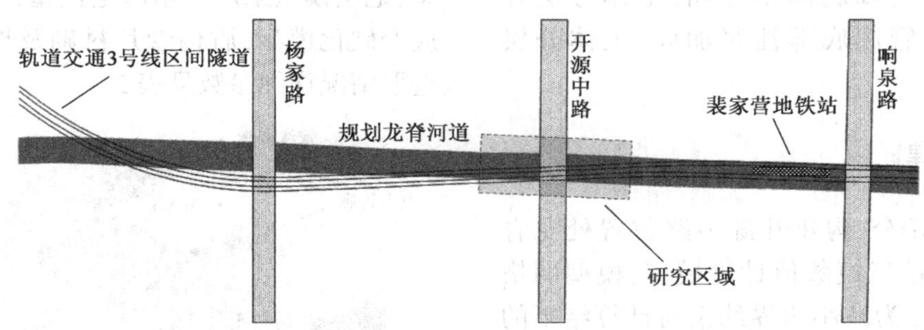

图 1 王裴区间下穿规划龙脊河平面图

研究区域除规划河道外，还涉及电力沟与给水管道施工，管线分布在盾构区间正上方，电力沟由桥涵南侧下穿河道，其最低点高程为 21.98m，距离轨道外顶的净距为 9.3m，其他管线（给水、直饮水、通信、热力、燃气）由桥涵北侧下穿河道，且管道埋深均浅于南侧电力沟，距离轨道外顶的净距为 11.1m，位置关系如图 2 所示。

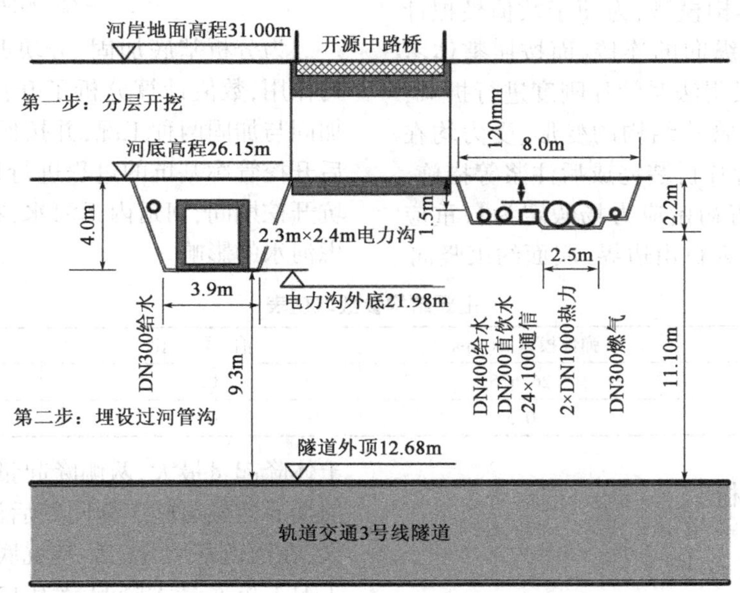

图 2 上部基坑分布与地铁隧道位置关系图

研究区域地质条件较为复杂，表层为 0.3 ~ 3.2m 为素填土，顶部为耕土含植物根系，向下 3.2 ~ 23.8m 为非常规粉质黏土层，具有较强的竖向透水性。向下 27.8 ~ 33.0m 范围内为碎石层，成分以石灰岩碎块为主,多呈棱角状、次棱角状,块径2～6cm,含量55～60%,局部泥质胶结,黏性土充填。底部为含碎石粉质黏土、全风化闪长岩地层。地层参数如表1所示。

地层参数表　表1

地　层	层厚(m)	压缩模量(MPa)	泊松比 ν	密度 γ(kN/m³)	黏聚力 c(kPa)	摩擦角 φ(°)
素填土	3.2	5.85	—	19.4	—	—
粉质黏土	4.8	9.00	0.30	19.8	20.70	10.79
粉质黏土	20	9.83	0.30	19.7	24.3	10.6
碎石	8	20	0.20	18.2	8.0	38.0
全风化闪长岩	10	25	0.30	18.4	28	30

为分析基底加固、分块开挖对减小隧道隆起的作用,数值模型分别进行了以下两个工况的计算:①河道底部、管廊底部不加固,土体分层开挖;②河道底部、管廊底部注浆加固,土体分层开挖。

2　模型构建

文章采用MIDAS构建开源中路位置处龙脊河和管廊基坑开挖三模数值计算模型,模型网格划分如图3所示。为减小边界约束对计算结果的影响,使模拟结果更接近实际情况,模型沿Y方向长度取126m,垂直于线路方向即X方向取100m(河道外缘两侧各约30m),竖直方向为Z方向取49.2m。

模拟假设土层各向同性且沿水平层状分布,采用修正摩尔-库伦本构模型,为便于数值模拟计算,不考虑管片环向、纵向的连接,而按照整体考虑,计算时则按修正惯用法对管片刚度进行折减,折减系数取为0.75。管片结构的变形、受力均在弹性范围内,不考虑管片拼装完成后注浆等措施,同时忽略构造应力,将初始应力场假定为自重应力场。设置模型顶面为自由边界,底面约束竖向位移,四周为法向约束。盾构管片采用C50混凝土。为提高计算的可靠性,计算中采用线弹性模型,地层模型采用摩尔库伦模型,注浆加固层采用应变硬化模型,盾构管片衬砌及地层各力学参数选取情况详细参数见表2。

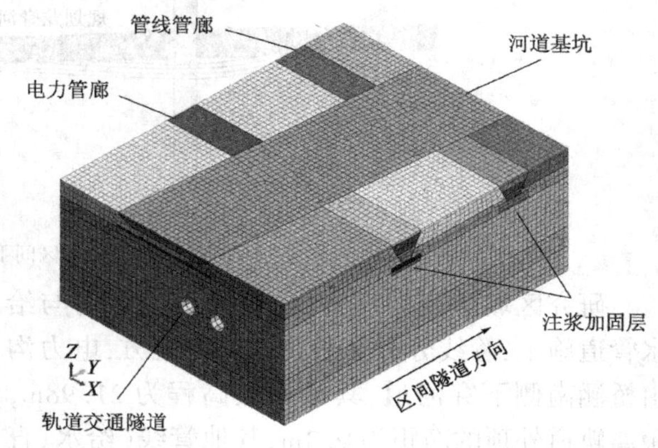

图3　三维模型网格划分

为分析基底加固、分块开挖对减小隧道隆起的作用,数值计算分析了开挖河道及管廊底部不加固与加固两种工况,并按照先开挖河道基坑,然后开挖管廊基坑的过程进行计算分析。因河道基坑开挖期间,河道内无河水,在计算过程中暂不考虑河水的影响。

主要结构参数取值表　表2

材　料	弹性模量 E(Gpa)	泊松比	密度(kN/m³)
管片结构钢筋混凝土	26.625	0.2	26
地层加固区	0.3	0.3	21

3　计算结果分析

3.1　变形特征分析

3.1.1　地层变形

图4为河道开挖完成后地层竖向位移。可以看出,龙脊河的开挖会造成土层的隆起,河底处的土体隆起量最大,两侧隆起量逐渐减小,主要是因前期盾构隧道施工期间壁后注浆造成土体应力增大,在河道基坑开挖后基坑底部卸载导致的隆起。工况1坑底最大隆起量为13.45mm,工况2坑底最大隆起量为12.32mm,与工况1相比较,河道底部和管廊底部加固能够使得坑底最大隆起量减小1.13mm,减少了约8.4%。因此,对基坑底部的注

浆加固,明显可以降低河道底部的卸载和隆起变形,对工程实践具有指导作用。

图5为位管廊开挖完成后地层竖向位移。可以看出,管廊的开挖会继续造成土层的隆起,坑底处隆起量最大,两侧隆起量逐渐减小,不加固时下坑底最大隆起量为15.96mm,比龙脊河开挖后隆起量增加了2.51mm;加固后下坑底最大隆起量为13.93mm,比龙脊河开挖后隆起量增加了1.61mm。相较而言,河道底部和管廊底部加固能够使得管廊开挖完成后河底土体的最大隆起量减小2.03mm,减少了约12.7%。

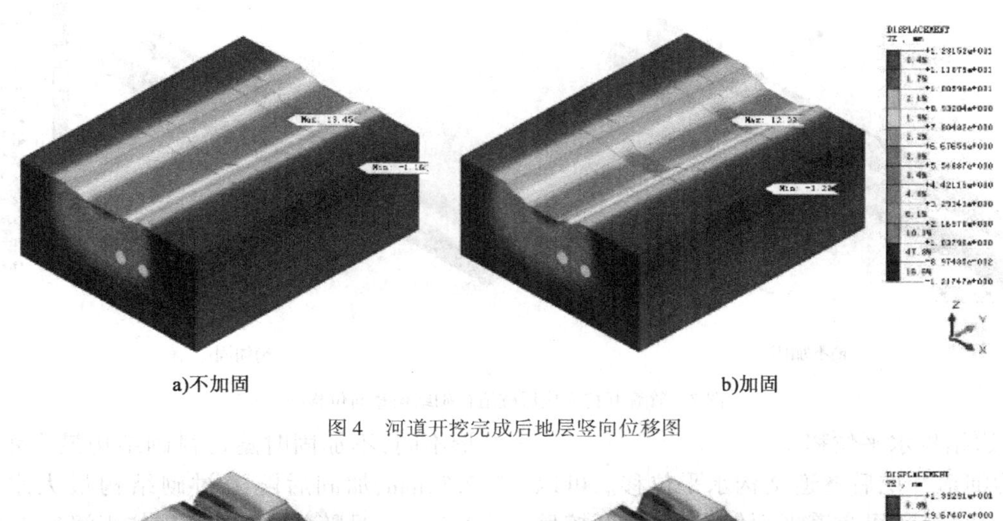
a)不加固 b)加固

图4 河道开挖完成后地层竖向位移图

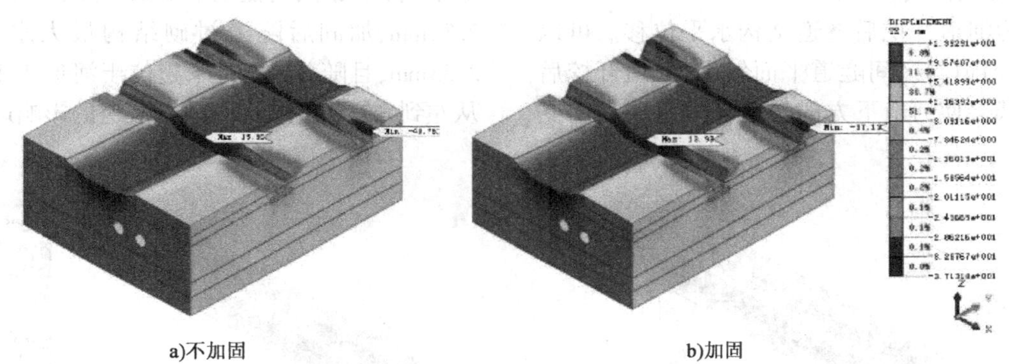
a)不加固 b)加固

图5 管廊开挖完成后地层竖向位移图

3.1.2 隧道衬砌结构位移

(1)隧道结构竖向位移

图6为河道开挖完成后隧道衬砌竖向位移。可以看出,河道开挖后会使河道正下方隧道产生向上的位移,不加固时隧道衬砌结构最大隆起变形量为5.83mm,加固后隧道衬砌结构最大隆起变形量为5.72mm,且随着隧道越来越位于河道正下方(图中从左到右),开挖卸载对下部隧道的影响逐渐增大。

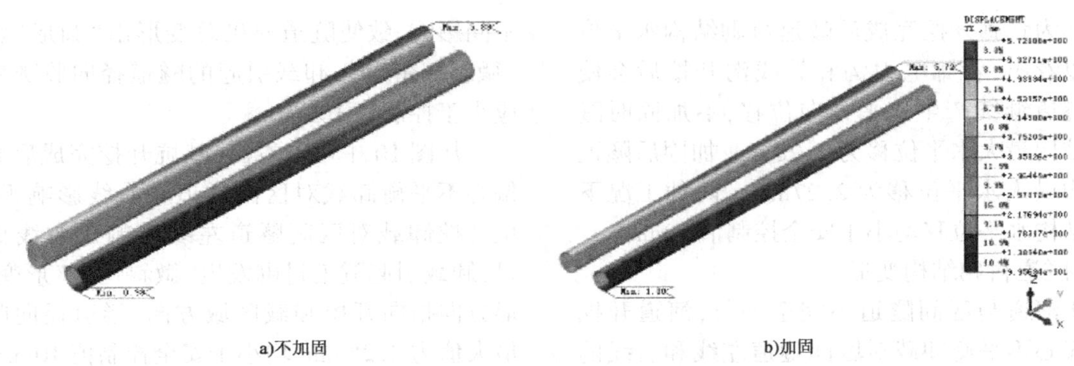
a)不加固 b)加固

图6 河道开挖完成后隧道衬砌竖向位移图

图 7 为管廊开挖完成后隧道衬砌结构竖向位移。可以看出,管廊电力沟和管线沟开挖后会使正下方隧道继续产生向上的位移,不加固时隧道衬砌结构最大隆起变形量为 6.81mm,加固后隧道衬砌结构最大隆起变形量为 6.82mm,且位于管廊电力沟和管线沟开挖正下方处的隧道衬砌结构隆起变形比周围其他衬砌更加明显,反映出管廊电力沟和管线沟开挖卸载对下部隧道结构的有进一步的影响,但加固后影响相对较小。

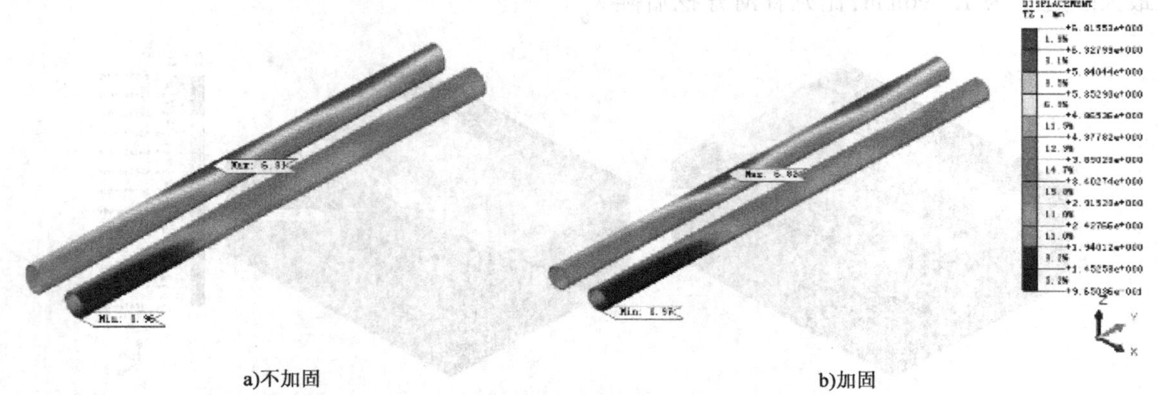

a)不加固　　b)加固

图 7　管廊开挖完成后隧道衬砌结构竖向位移图

(2)隧道结构水平位移

图 8 为河道开挖后隧道结构水平位移。可以看出,由于河道与区间隧道平面斜交,河道开挖后不平衡卸载会使河道下方的隧道结构水平方向变形不同,不加固时隧道衬砌结构最大水平位移为 2.38mm,加固后隧道衬砌结构最大水平位移为 2.33mm,且随着隧道越来越位于河道正下方(图中从左到右),开挖卸载对下部隧道的影响逐渐增大。

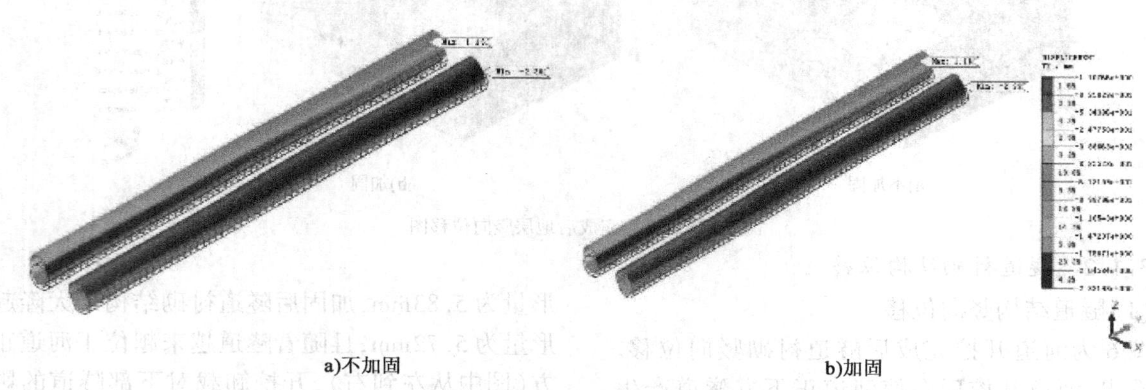

a)不加固　　b)加固

图 8　河道开挖完成后隧道衬砌水平位移图

图 9 为管廊开挖完成后隧道衬砌结构水平位移。可以看出,管廊电力沟和管线沟开挖后会使正下方隧道继续产生水平方向位移,不加固时隧道衬砌结构最大水平位移为 2.28mm,加固后隧道衬砌结构最大水平位移为 2.27mm。两种工况下的隧道结构水平位移均小于安全控制值 10mm。

(3)隧道衬砌结构变形

由于河道与区间隧道不完全平行,河道开挖会引起偏心不平衡卸载对区间隧道左线和右线的不同影响,致使隧道衬砌总变形由“圆形”转变为“微斜鸭蛋”形,卸载引起的隧道径向收敛变形值应小于控制值 10mm。

从图 10 中可以看出,基坑开挖完成后会引起偏心不平衡卸载对区间隧道左右线影响不同,基坑开挖卸载对区间隧道左线影响比右线更加明显,卸载引起隧道衬砌发生“微斜鸭蛋”形变形,变形方向指向开挖卸载区域方向,隧道径向收敛值最大值为 4.26mm,均小于安全控制值 10mm。

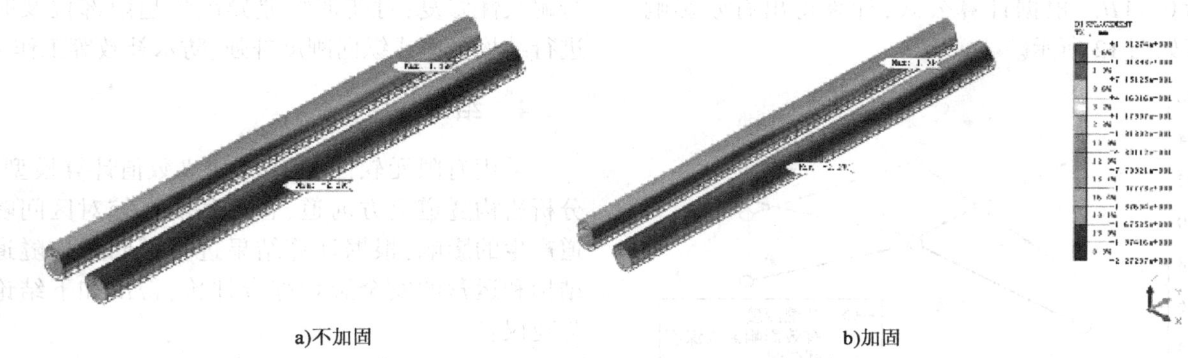
a)不加固　　b)加固

图9　管廊开挖完成后隧道衬砌结构水平位移图

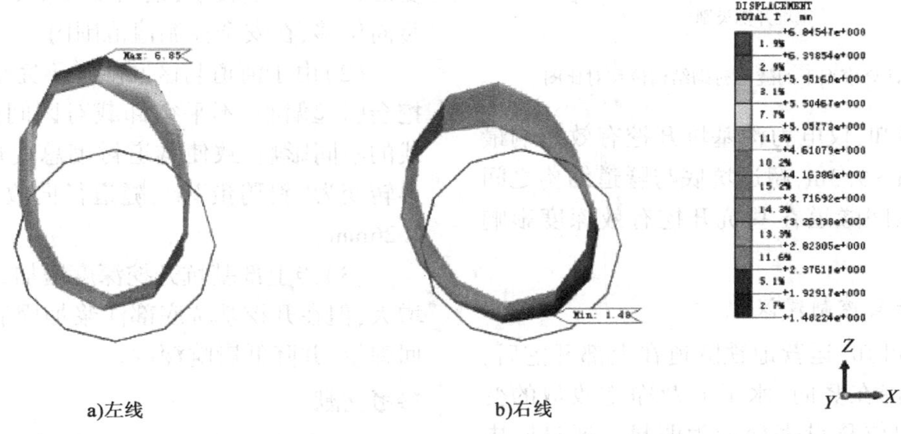
a)左线　　b)右线

图10　基坑开挖完成后隧道衬砌结构总变形位移云图

3.2　结构安全分析

3.2.1　隧道衬砌结构变形分析

图11为河道和管廊基坑开挖引起盾构隧道衬砌结构最大水平位移、竖向位移及径向收敛。相对而言,河道和管廊同步开挖的部位位移量相对仅有河道开挖段较大。在有管廊开挖段,隧道结构在竖向变形量最大,为6.82mm,径向收敛次之为4.26mm,水平径向收敛量最小,为2.27mm,最大变形量小于安全控制标准10mm。

3.2.2　有效影响深度分析

在不考虑基坑边界条件、地下水等因素的影响下,基坑中心点下一定深度处卸荷比可由式(1)进行简化估算。

$$R=\frac{\gamma H}{\gamma(H+D)} \tag{1}$$

式中:R——卸荷比;

γ——土的密度(kN/m^3);

H——基坑开挖深度(m);

D——基底以下卸荷影响深度(m)。

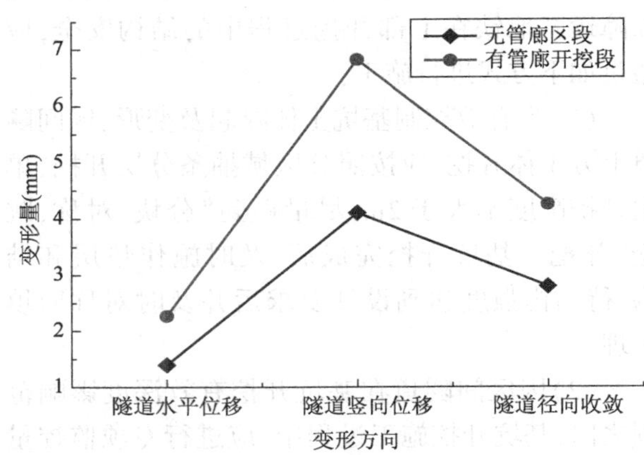

图11　不同计算模型下的隧道衬砌结构位移对比图

在不考虑基坑开挖中时空效应影响的条件下,可计算出基坑开挖所引起的回弹变形有效影响深度和极限卸荷比所对应的回弹量大的土层厚度,取黏性土的有效影响深度参考值为1.44H,其中在有效影响深度内的回弹量大的土层厚度参考值为0.11H。根据计算公式,计算得出有效影响深度如图12所示。

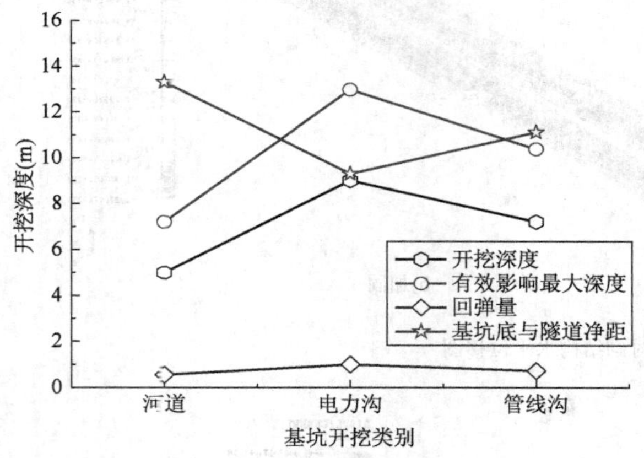

图12　不同计算模型下的隧道衬砌结构位移对比图

由图12可知,仅电力沟基坑开挖有效影响最大深度12.96m>9.3m,超过坑底与隧道结构之间的实际距离,区间隧道在基坑开挖有效深度影响范围之内。

3.2.3　安全控制建议

由上分析可知,运营地铁隧道在上部开挖后,加剧了隧道结构在竖向、水平向及净空收敛的变形量,其中竖向位移量表现最为明显。通过国内外文献资料报道可知,对盾构隧道衬砌结构安全的威胁主要来自隧道拱顶处内侧挤压、隧道竖向椭圆度的增加和接缝两侧管片的不平整接触,为保障运营地铁在上部开挖过程中的结构安全,应通过如下方式进行施工:

(1)为有效控制基坑土体隆起及变形,区间隧道上方土体开挖,应按照分区域抽条分层开挖,单次开挖高度不大于2m,尽量做到"分块、对称、跳仓"开挖。基坑开挖完成后,及时施作垫层和结构,待结构强度达到设计要求后并及时对称回填处理。

(2)因区间隧道在基坑开挖有效深度影响范围之内,基坑开挖施工过程中,应进行专项监控量测,轨道几何形态尺寸应采用自动化监测。监测内容包括结构裂缝、结构变形及轨道几何形态尺寸变化等。结构监测应贯穿于基坑工程作业的全过程,直至外部作业完成且监测数据趋于稳定后方可结束。

(3)基坑工程施工中,应对既有地铁结构局部出现的宽度大于0.2mm的裂缝进行灌缝处理,进行耐久性修复;对变形缝差异沉降超限部位及时进行结构横向或纵向刚度补强、防水补救等工作。

4　结语

采用有限元软件MIDAS建立数值计算模型,分析盾构隧道上方河道、管廊基坑开挖对区间隧道产生的影响,根据计算结果进行区间盾构隧道结构和运营的安全影响综合评价,得出如下结论与建议:

(1)上部河道、管廊基坑开挖会引起近下方近平行的盾构区间隧道结构发生沉降、侧移、倾斜等变形,但变形量较小,最大变形量6.82mm,来自于竖向位移,在安全控制值范围内。

(2)由于河道与区间隧道不完全平行,河道开挖会引起偏心、不平衡卸载对区间隧道左线和右线的不同影响,致使隧道衬砌总变形由"横鸭蛋"形转变为"斜鸭蛋"形,隧道径向收敛值最大值为4.26mm。

(3)当上部基坑开挖深度增加,有效影响深度增大,但在开挖基坑底部注浆加固后,可有效减小回弹量,并降低影响深度。

参考文献

[1] 郑刚,朱合华,刘新荣,等.基坑工程与地下工程安全及环境影响控制[J].土木工程学报,2016,49(06):1-24.

[2] 范建军.软土地层盾构隧道上部开挖卸载扰动位移特性及灾变研究[D].上海:上海交通大学,2015.

[3] 张玉伟,谢永利,翁木生.非对称基坑开挖对下卧地铁隧道影响的离心试验[J].岩土力学,2018,39(7):2555-2562.

[4] Hiroshi, Takeda, Morito, et al. Finite element analysis of general contact problems and Application for excavation of Shield tunnel[J]. Doboku Gakkai Ronbunshu,1998,1998(603):1-10.

[5] 张鑫海,魏纲,林心蓓.考虑纵向变形影响的基坑下方盾构隧道横向受力变化研究[J].岩石力学与工程学报,2020,v.39;No.372(11):196-209.

[6] 封坤,何川,苏宗贤.南京长江隧道管片衬砌结构原型加载试验[J].中国公路学报,2013,026(001):135-143.

[7] 柳献,黄晓冬. 通缝拼装盾构隧道衬砌结构抗倒塌性能的试验研究[J]. 岩石力学与工程学报,2015(S2):3703-3714.

[8] 方勇,汪辉武,郭建宁,等. 下穿黄河盾构隧道管片衬砌结构受力特征模型试验[J]. 湖南大学学报(自然科学版),2017,44(005):132-142.

[9] J. S, Sharma,. Effect of large excavation on deformation of adjacent MRT tunnels [J]. Tunnelling & Underground Space Technology, 2001,(16):93-98.

[10] Byun G W, Kim D G, Lee S D. Behavior of the ground in rectangularly crossed area due to tunnel excavation under the existing tunnel [J]. Tunnelling and Underground Space Technology, 2006, 21(3):361-361.

[11] 梁发云,褚峰,宋著,等. 紧邻地铁枢纽深基坑变形特性离心模型试验研究[J]. 岩土力学,2012(03):22-29.

[12] Liang Fayun, Chu Feng, Song Zhu, et al. Centrifugal model test study on deformation characteristics of deep foundation pit adjacent to Metro Hub [J]. Geotechnical mechanics, 2012(03):22-29.

[13] 李倩倩,张顶立,房倩,等. 浅埋暗挖法下穿既有盾构隧道的变形特性分析[J]. 岩石力学与工程学报,2014,033(z2):3911-3918.

[14] 况龙川,李智敏,殷宗泽. 地下工程施工影响地铁隧道的实测分析[J]. 清华大学学报(自然科学版),2000(S1):79-82.

[15] Schroeder F C. The influence of bored piles on existing tunnels: a case study [J]. Ground Engineering, 2002, 55(7):32-34.

[16] Schroeder F C, Potts D M, Addenbrooke T I. The influence of pile group loading on existing tunnels [J]. Geotechnique, 2004, 54(6):351-362.

[17] 魏纲,李钢,苏勤卫,等. 基坑工程对运营地铁隧道影响的实测分析[J]. 现代隧道技术,2014,51(1) 179-185.

隧道预应力锚杆压力拱理论的数值模拟研究

张 浩*[1] 李博融[2]

(1. 海南省交通工程建设局;2. 中交第一公路勘察设计研究院有限公司)

摘 要 为了明确隧道预应力锚杆的加固机理,本文依托五指山隧道采用数值模拟手段对预应力锚杆的压力拱理论开展了研究。其中,采用有限差分法分析了不同锚杆间距下压力拱的形态及围岩稳定性,采用离散元法分析了预应力锚杆对岩块强度的影响。研究表明:预应力锚杆为主动支护结构,能通过预应力明显提高围岩的强度参数,并在锚杆周围形成压应力集中区域;当锚杆间距偏大时,各锚杆所形成的压应力集中区域无法叠加,不能形成压力拱;当锚杆间距合理时,各锚杆所形成的压应力集中区域发生相互叠加,并形成三维压力拱,有效减小围岩塑性区范围及围岩位移,提高围岩稳定性,充分发挥了预应力锚杆的加固作用。

关键词 围岩稳定性 预应力锚杆 压力拱 数值模拟

0 引言

传统砂浆锚杆在围岩发生变形且砂浆达到一定强度后才能发挥加固作用,而预应力锚杆能通过施加预应力,快速、高效的加固围岩,有效提高围岩的稳定性。随着锚固技术的不断发展,预应

1. 基金项目:海南省交通科技项目(J-ZX-ZAK-02-2019)。

力锚杆在隧道及地下工程中得到了广泛的应用,并取得了良好的加固效果,尤其适用于大跨径及高地应力软岩隧道[1-3]。

刘江等[4]通过对郑万高铁高家坪隧道软弱围岩段涨壳式预应力中空注浆锚杆进行研究,分析了其加固作用机理,并提出了锚杆注浆比例。汪波等[5]依托苍岭特长公路隧道,揭示了预应力中空注浆锚杆控制岩爆的作用机理,并基于此提出了锚杆设计防岩爆原则。朱宏锐[6]报道了涨壳式高强度预应力中空注浆锚杆的快速支护施工方法,同时指出预应力锚杆在高地应力条件下,可保证特大断面隧洞开挖围岩稳定。何思明和李新坡[7]阐述了预应力锚杆荷载传递机制,为预应力锚杆支护设计奠定了基础。李铀等[8]开展了模型试验研究,结果表明预应力锚索的破坏机理及荷载传递方式与锚索结构联系紧密。何宗礼和陈高君[9]根据数值模拟及现场测试结果,提出采用预应力锚杆协同支护技术,能充分发挥锚杆、锚索的加固作用,并产生协同支护的效果。李元[10]采用数值模拟手段对铁路隧道施工新技术开展了研究,指出锚杆、锚索的协同作用能更有效的加固围岩。

综上,国内外学者针对预应力锚杆的加固机理已开展了大量的研究,并取得了丰富的研究成果。研究表明:预应力锚杆的加固机理主要有悬吊理论、组合梁理论、压力拱(承载拱)理论、松动圈理论、销钉理论等[11]。随着人们对预应力锚杆加固机理认识的逐渐深入,压力拱理论受到了广泛的关注。压力拱理论认为预应力锚杆能有效提高围岩参数、改善围岩应力状态,从而提高围岩稳定性。但目前的相关研究主要从预应力锚杆对围岩塑性区、位移场的影响出发,而对于预应力锚杆压力拱理论的研究较少。对此,本文依托五指山隧道工程,采用有限差分法及离散元法,针对预应力锚杆的压力拱理论开展了研究,对完善预应力锚杆的加固机理具有一定的参考价值。

1　预应力锚杆在五指山隧道中的应用

五指山隧道位于五指山市冲山镇,属特长深埋小净距隧道。左线起讫桩号 ZK36 +010 ~ ZK40 +855,长 4845m,隧道最大埋深约 383m;右线隧道起讫桩号 YK36 +000 ~ YK40 +870,长 4870m,隧道最大埋深约 370m。五指山隧道Ⅳ级围岩段拟采用新型涨壳式预应力中空注浆锚杆对围岩进行加固。如图 1 所示,涨壳式预应力锚杆由全螺纹中空锚杆体、半球形钢制垫圈、螺母、拱形垫板、钢制胀壳锚固件等部分组成。钢制涨壳锚固件外径 4.4cm,全螺纹中空杆体直径 25mm,单根长度 4.05m,重量 11.95kg。施工过程中通过旋紧杆体使锚杆前端涨壳头张开,给锚杆施加一定的预应力,促使围岩及早形成压力拱,以达到主动加固围岩,提升围岩稳定性的效果,施工工艺流程如图 2 所示。

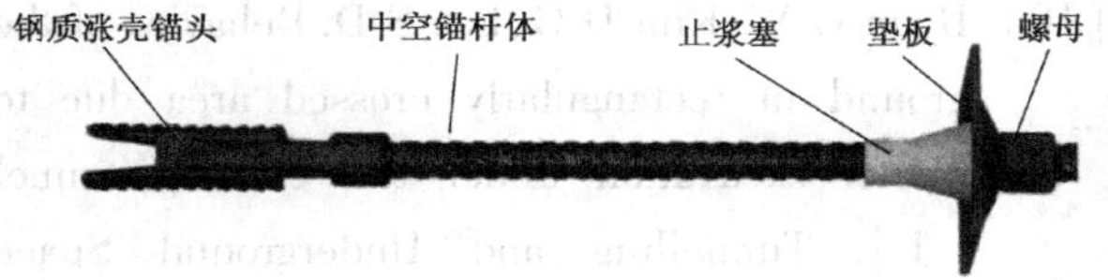

图 1　涨壳式预应力中空注浆锚杆

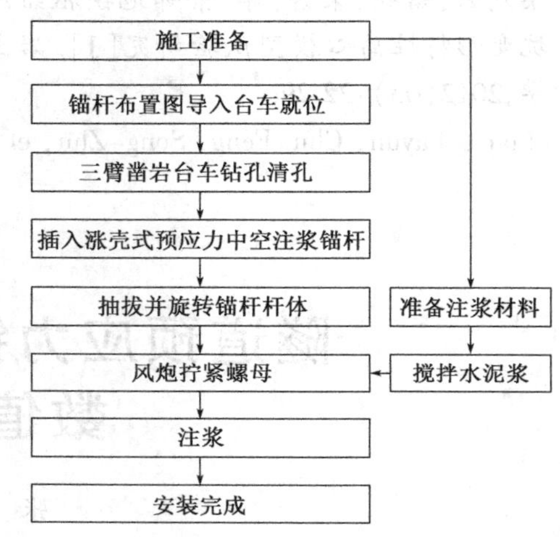

图 2　预应力锚杆施工工艺流程

2　预应力锚杆对隧道围岩稳定性的影响分析

2.1　计算模型

针对五指山Ⅳ级围岩段,建立数值计算模型。如图 3 所示,采用实体单元模拟围岩,采用锚索单元模拟锚杆,围岩及锚杆-围岩界面为理想弹塑性体且满足摩尔-库伦强度准则,锚杆单元为线弹性体。模型的几何范围为 100m × 100m × 1m,隧道开挖高度为 12.5m,开挖跨度为 15 m,埋深为 200m。计算模型采用位移边界条件,四周边界约束法向位移,底部边界约束法向及切向位移,顶部为自由边界,并施加等效于实际埋深的竖向应力。

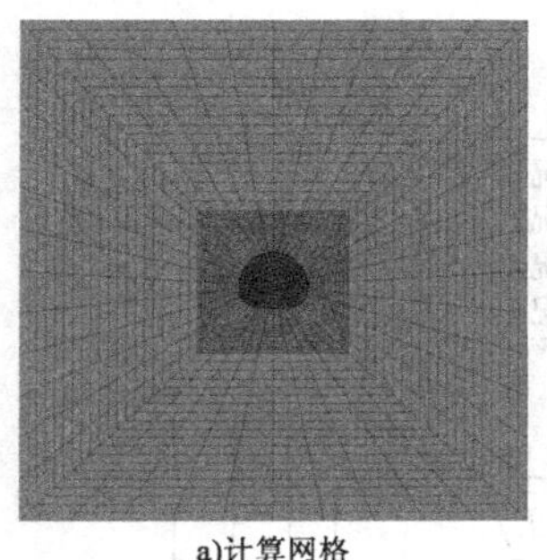
a)计算网格

b)锚索单元

图3 计算模型

模拟预应力锚杆时，需要考虑垫板、黏结段、锚头及预紧力施加等问题，因此在模拟时需要进行一定的处理。如图4所示，本文将锚杆杆体赋予不同的属性来模拟预应力锚杆。其中，锚杆力学参数如表2所示，锚杆两端单元的围岩-锚杆界面强度、刚度分别为1×10^6kN/m、2000MPa，防止两端产生变形、破坏，以模拟锚杆垫板及锚头的作用，并将预应力施加在锚杆的黏结段。

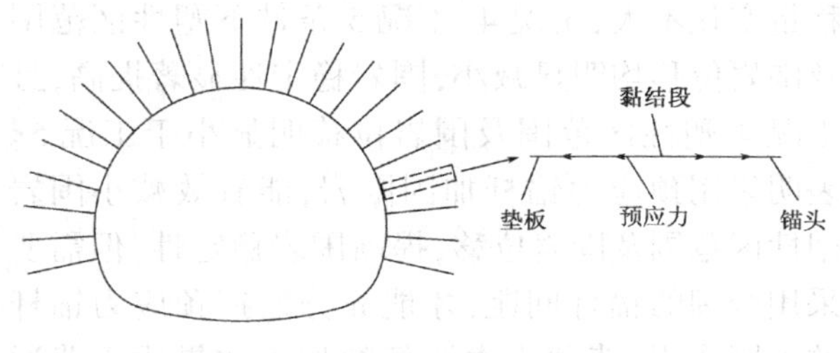

图4 预应力锚杆模拟示意图

2.2 计算参数及工况

根据五指山隧道勘察设计资料及相关规范，选取围岩及锚杆计算参数分别如表1、表2所示。为研究预应力锚杆压力拱理论，本文共计算了5种工况：无加固、单根预应力锚杆加固、间距5m预应力系统锚杆加固、间距1m预应力系统锚杆加固、间距1m普通系统锚杆加固，如表3及图5所示。其中，各种工况下锚杆长度均为4m，预应力均为50kN。

围岩力学参数 表1

围岩级别	γ(kN/m^3)	E(GPa)	c(MPa)	φ(°)	ν
IV	2200	2.6	0.2	27	0.33

锚杆力学参数 表2

弹性模量E(GPa)	横截面积A(mm^2)	单位长度上砂浆的黏结力c_g(kN/m)	砂浆摩擦角φ(°)	单位长度上水砂浆刚度k_g(MPa)	砂浆外圈周长P_g(mm)	抗拉强度F_c(MPa)
200	490.6	10000	55	20	125.6	3100

计算工况 表3

编号	工况描述
1	无加固
2	单根预应力锚杆加固
3	间距5m预应力系统锚杆加固
4	间距1m预应力系统锚杆加固
5	间距1m普通系统锚杆加固

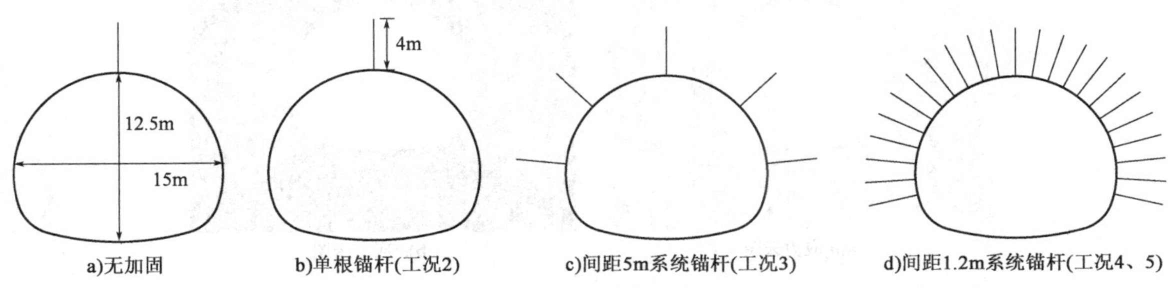

图5 预应力锚杆布置示意图

2.3 围岩塑性区及位移分析

不同工况下围岩塑性区范围及围岩最大位移分别如图6、表4所示。与无加固条件(工况1)相比，工况2及工况3条件下塑性区范围及围岩位移量变化不大,工况 4、工况 5 条件下塑性区范围及围岩位移均明显减小,围岩稳定性显著提高,且工况 4 塑性区范围及围岩位移明显小于工况 5。表明采用预应力锚杆加固围岩,能有效减小围岩塑性区范围及围岩位移,提高围岩稳定性,但需要采用合理的锚杆间距,才能充分发挥预应力锚杆的加固作用,使预应力锚杆的加固效果优于普通锚杆。

2.4　围岩横向压力拱分析

当预应力系统锚杆支护参数合理时,能在隧道周边一定范围内形成压力拱,从而充分发挥预应力系统锚杆的加固作用[4]。因此,本文采用压力拱的范围定量的分析预应力系统锚杆的加固效果。根据文献[12],以隧道围岩径向应力恢复到原岩应力的 90% 处为外边界,并将数值模拟得到的应力场与压力拱边界定义结合起来,则可得到压力拱外边界。

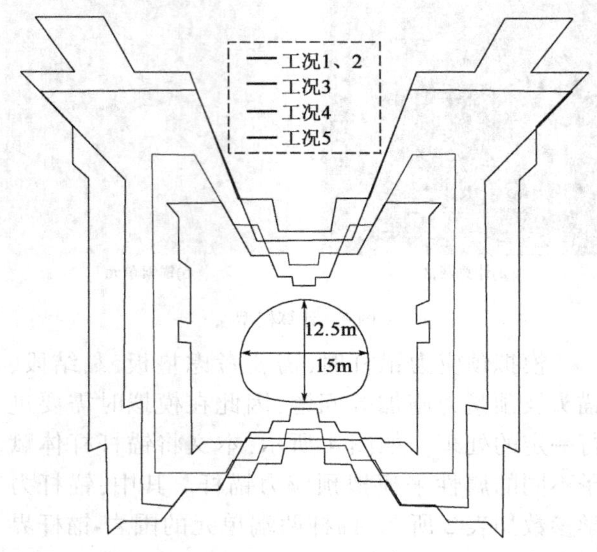

图 6　各工况下围岩塑性区范围

各工况下围岩最大位移　　表 4

编　号	工 况 描 述	最大水平位移(mm)	最大竖向位移(mm)
1	无加固	96.3	94.9
2	单根预应力锚杆	96.1	94.7
3	间距 5m 预应力系统锚杆	85.2	87.3
4	间距 1m 预应力系统锚杆	49.6	47.4
5	间距 1m 普通系统锚杆	64.6	61.9

2.4.1　单根预应力锚杆加固(工况 2)

单根预应力锚杆加固下,围岩应力场如图 7 所示。在锚杆周围的围岩中产生一个类似锥形的压应力集中区域,但影响范围不大。表明预应力锚杆能在围岩中产生压应力集中区域,但单根锚杆的影响范围是有限的,它只能引起围岩中局部的压应力集中,且随着离锚杆距离的增加,应力值迅速衰减,加固效果迅速减小。

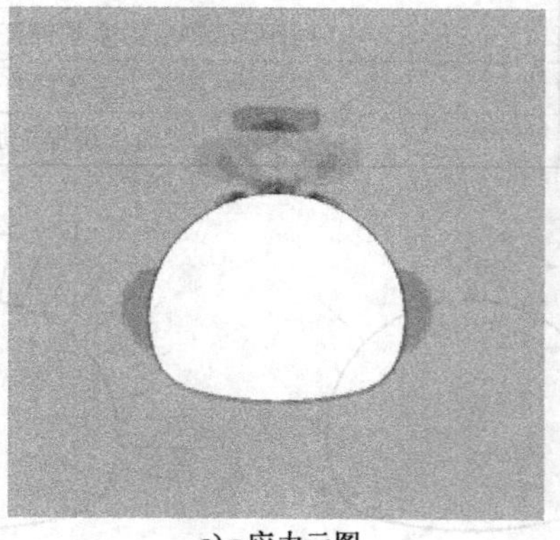

a)σ_x应力云图

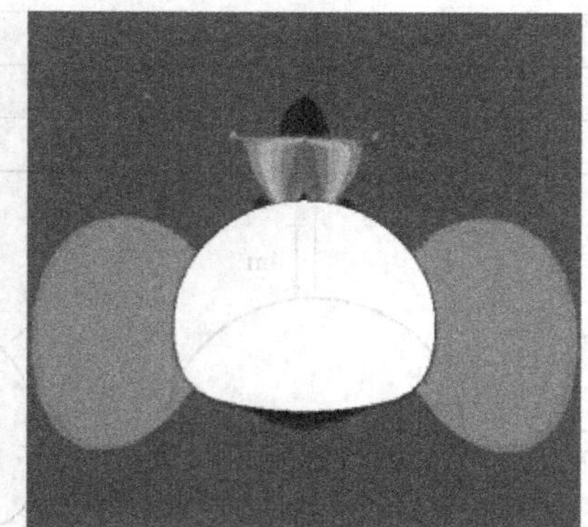

b)σ_z应力云图

图 7　工况 2 围岩应力场

2.4.2　间距 5m 预应力系统锚杆加固(工况 3)

间距 5m 系统预应力锚杆加固下,围岩应力场如图 8 所示。各锚杆的加固范围内均出现了压应力集中的现象,但由于锚杆间距较大,相邻锚杆所形成的加固区域并未相交，因此没有形成整体的压力拱，导致预应力锚杆的加固效果并未充分发挥。

2.4.3 间距 1m 预应力系统锚杆加固(工况 4)

间距 1m 系统预应力锚杆加固下，围岩应力场如图 9 所示。随着锚杆间距由 5m 减小为 1m，各锚杆所形成的压应力集中区域产生了叠加效应，并形成了明显的压力拱区域，充分发挥了预应力系统锚杆的加固效果。

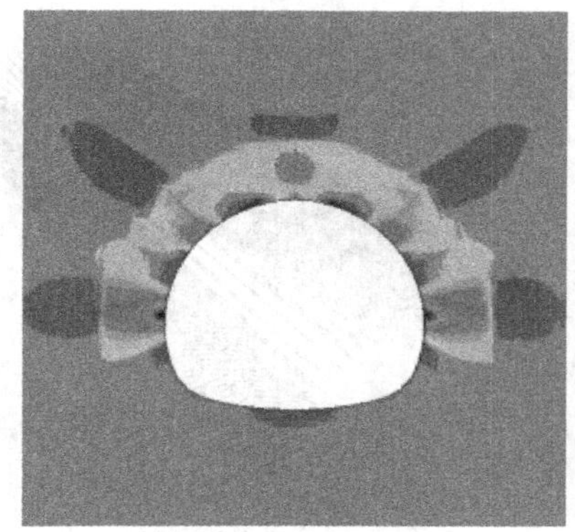

a)σ_x应力云图

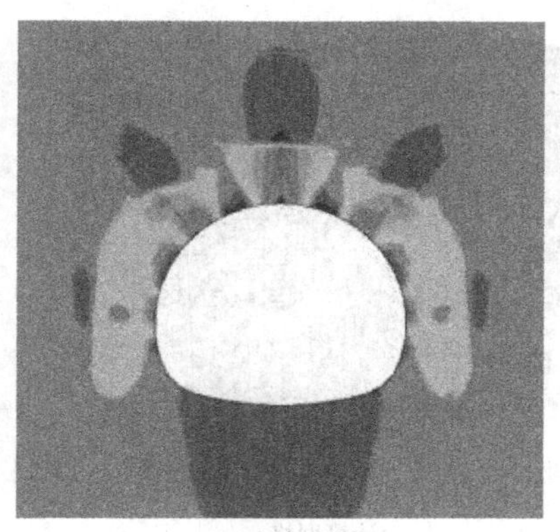

b)σ_z应力云图

图 8 工况 4 围岩应力场

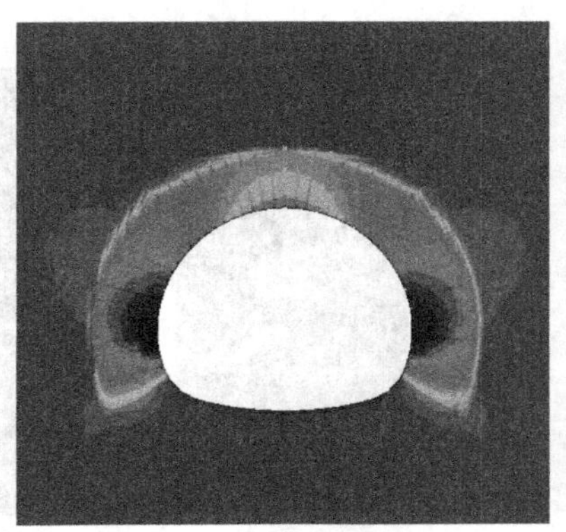

a)σ_x应力云图

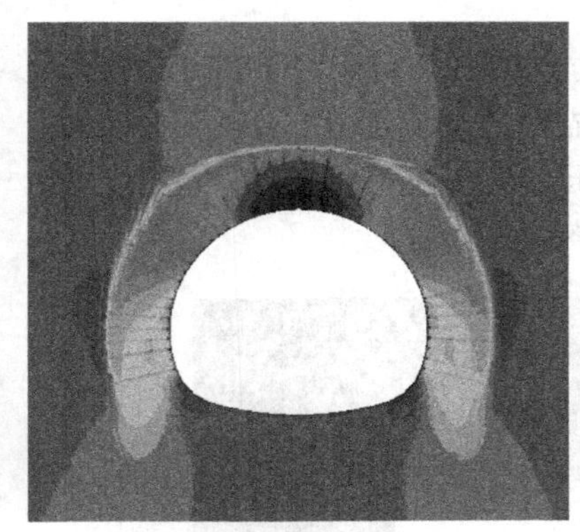

b)σ_z应力云图

图 9 工况 4 围岩应力场

2.4.4 间距 1m 普通系统锚杆加固(工况 5)

间距 1m 普通系统锚杆加固下，围岩应力场如图 10 所示。各锚杆所形成的压应力集中区域产生了叠加效应，并形成了明显的压力拱区域，但压力拱范围明显小于预应力系统锚杆(图 9)，表明预应力系统锚杆得加固效果优于普通系统锚杆。

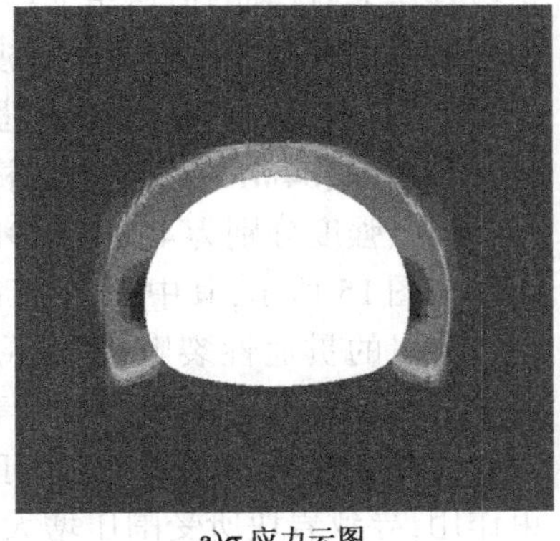

a)σ_x应力云图

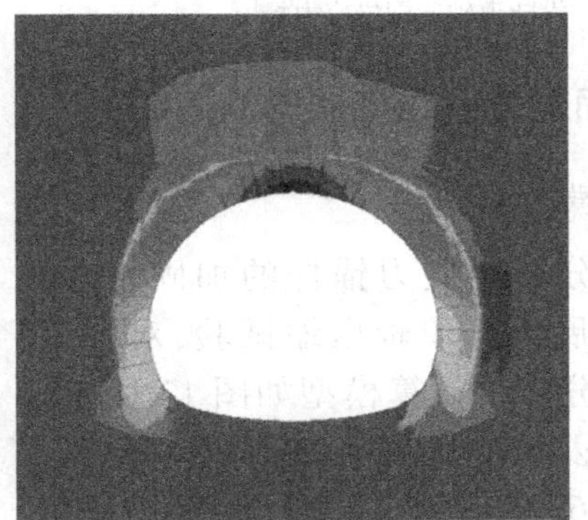

b)σ_z应力云图

图 10 工况 5 围岩应力场

2.5　围岩纵向压力拱分析

为了进一步研究预应力锚杆加固作用下压力拱的分布规律,在平面应变模型的基础上,进一步建立三维计算模型,如图 11 所示。其中,围岩及锚杆计算参数如表 1、表 2 所示,锚杆为梅花形布置,间距为 2m。

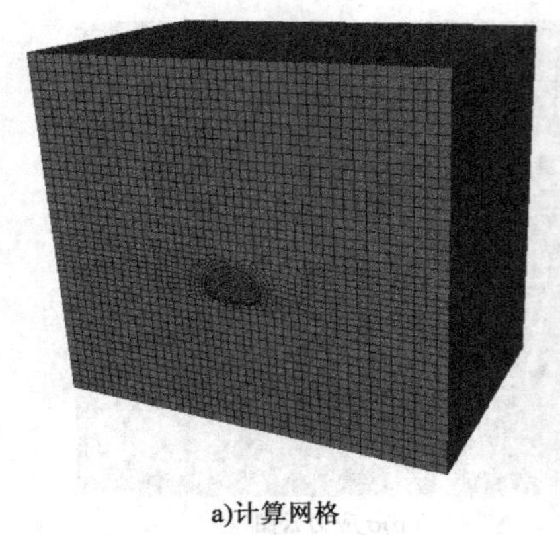

a)计算网格

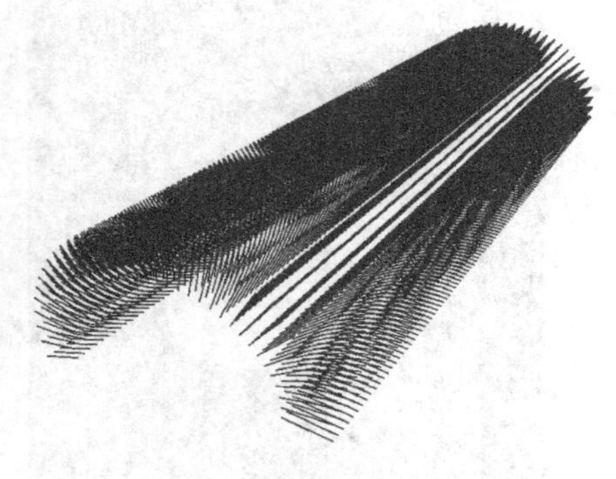

b)锚索单元

图 11　计算模型

沿隧道轴线方向的围岩应力场如图 12 所示。由于预应力系统锚杆的加固作用,沿隧道轴向在隧道洞周形成了压力拱。表明预应力系统锚杆能有效提高围岩的整体稳定性。

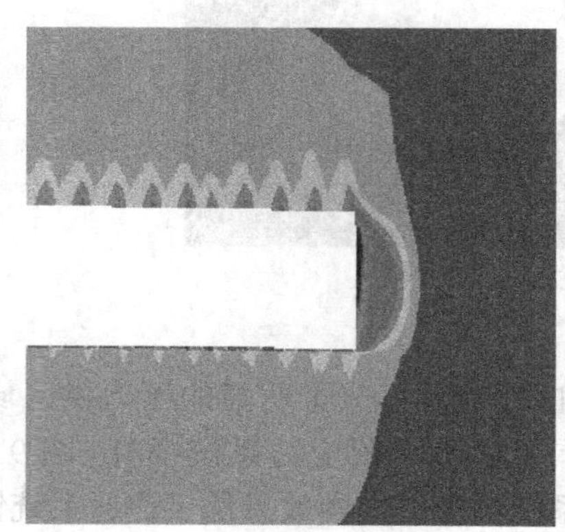

图 12　沿隧道轴向围岩应力场

3　锚杆加固对岩石强度的影响研究

3.1　计算模型

为了进一步分析预应力锚杆的加固机理,采用离散元法开展岩块单轴压缩试验,对锚固岩块的强度进行分析。计算模型如图 13 所示,分别模拟无加固及预应力锚杆加固两种情况,岩块的大小为 0.6m × 0.25m(长 × 宽),锚杆预紧力取 50kN,具体的岩块及锚杆计算参数如表 5 所示。

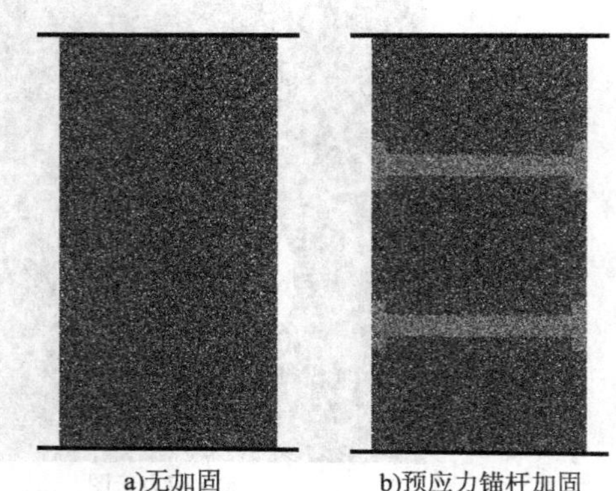

a)无加固　　b)预应力锚杆加固

图 13　岩块单轴压缩试验模型

3.2　岩块强度分析

岩块应力-应变曲线如图 14 所示,两条曲线均呈现出相似的规律,即随着应变的增大,压力首先呈线性增大,达到峰值后呈非线性减小,达到残余值后基本不再变化。但两种工况下的岩石强度区别较大,其中无加固下的峰值强度和残余强度分别为 82MPa、64MPa,预应力锚杆加固下的峰值强度和残余强度分别为 46MPa、19MPa。岩块的破坏模式如图 15 所示,其中无加固工况下的岩块中出现了大量的贯通性裂隙,而预应力锚杆加固下的岩块中的裂隙数量明显较少,且未出现明显的贯通性裂隙。计算结果表明:由于预应力锚杆的约束作用,导致岩块所受围压增大,因此锚固岩块的强度显著提高。

岩块及锚杆计算参数 表5

参数名称	岩块	预应力锚杆
颗粒数量	21079	3579
接触模型	线性平行黏结模型	
孔隙率	0.1	0.05
颗粒平均密度(kg/m^3)	2265	11325
颗粒弹性模量 GPa	24.3	200
颗粒刚度比	6	2000
摩擦系数	0.85	0.90
平行粘结刚度比	1.6	20.2
平行黏结法向强度(MPa)	89.6	1000
平行黏结切向强度(MPa)	115.3	1000

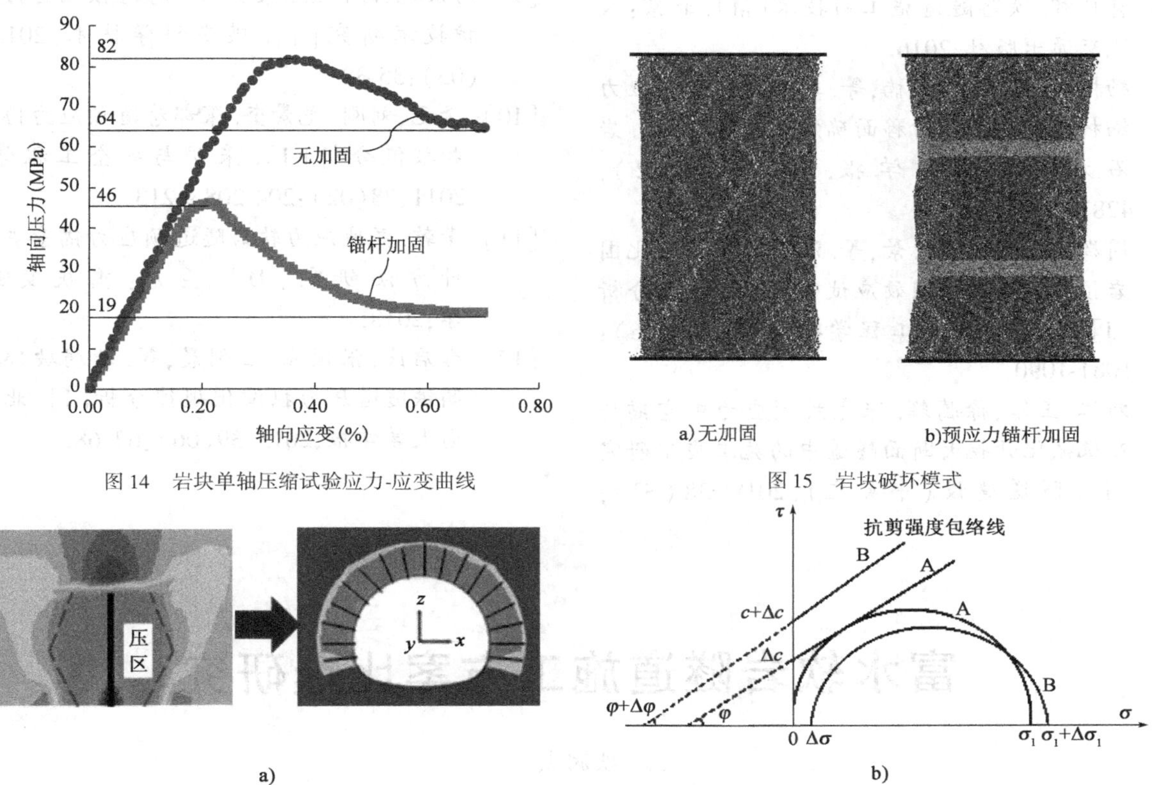

图14 岩块单轴压缩试验应力-应变曲线

图15 岩块破坏模式

图16 预应力锚杆加固机理示意图

4 预应力锚杆加固机理分析

根据以上计算结果可知，预应力锚杆的初始锚固力主要来自于锚杆的初始张拉荷载，属于主动支护形式。围岩在多根预应力锚杆的作用下，单根锚杆形成的压应力集中区相互叠合，可形成一个承受围岩压力的均匀压缩带，即压力拱，如图16a)所示。在压力拱内部，岩石处于三向受压状态，且围岩黏聚力、内摩擦角、弹性模量等均有不同的提高，根据莫尔-库伦强度准则，围岩强度将会增大，提高了其承担荷载的能力，如图16b)所示。

5 结语

本文依托五指山隧道工程背景，采用FLAC3D有限差分软件及PFC2D离散元软件分析了预应力锚杆的压力拱效应，得到以下结论：

(1)预应力锚杆能在其周围形成压应力集中

区域;当锚杆间距较大时,各锚杆所形成的压应力集中区域无法叠加,不能形成压力拱;当锚杆间距合理时,各锚杆所形成的压应力集中区域发生相互叠加,形成三维压力拱。

(2)采用预应力锚杆加固围岩,能有效减小围岩塑性区范围及围岩位移,提高围岩稳定性,但需要采用合理的锚杆间距,才能充分发挥预应力锚杆的加固作用。

(3)预应力锚杆为主动支护结构,能通过预应力明显提高围岩的强度参数,从而提高围岩的自承能力。

参考文献

[1] 肖广智.铁路隧道施工新技术[M].北京:人民交通出版社,2016.

[2] 杨校辉,朱彦鹏,郭楠,等.软岩深基坑预应力锚杆承载特性与滑移面确定试验研究[J].岩石力学与工程学报,2014,33(S2):4287-4298.

[3] 周辉,徐荣超,卢景景,等.深埋隧洞板裂化围岩预应力锚杆锚固效应试验研究及机制分析[J].岩石力学与工程学报,2015,34(06):1081-1090.

[4] 刘江,王军,徐腾辉.涨壳式预应力中空锚杆在机械化开挖大断面隧道中的施工应用研究[J].隧道建设(中英文),2018,38(S2):324-329.

[5] 汪波,何川.预应力中空注浆锚杆在苍岭隧道防岩爆设计中的应用[J].公路,2011(10):206-210.

[6] 朱宏锐.高地应力下高强预应力锚杆快速施工技术研究[J].铁道建筑,2009(06):63-66.

[7] 何思明,李新坡.预应力锚杆作用机制研究[J].岩石力学与工程学报,2006(09):1876-1880.

[8] 李铀,白世伟,方昭茹,等.预应力锚索锚固体破坏与锚固力传递模式研究[J].岩土力学,2003(05):686-690.

[9] 何宗礼,陈高君.煤矿深部巷道预应力协同支护技术研究[J].煤炭科学技术,2013,41(03):35-38.

[10] 李元,刘刚,龙景奎.深部巷道预应力协同支护数值分析[J].采矿与安全工程学报,2011,28(02):204-208+213.

[11] 李乾.高地应力软岩隧道预应力锚索支护设计方法研究[D].重庆:重庆交通大学,2018.

[12] 台启民,张顶立,王剑晨,等.软弱破碎围岩高铁隧道压力拱演化规律分析[J].北京交通大学学报,2015,39(06):62-68.

富水软岩隧道施工方案比选研究

默润杰*
(长安大学公路学院)

摘　要　西安外环高速公路控制性工程白鹿原隧道洞身所处第三系半成岩地层含水率为19.8%,地下水位埋深均高于洞室,施工中易产生涌泥、涌水、沉降变形过大等问题。本文以白鹿原隧道为背景,基于流固耦合理论,采用Midas GTS NX建立模型,对比分析注浆条件下富水大断面第三系半成岩地层隧道采用双侧壁导坑法与中隔壁法两种施工方案,分析考虑流固耦合条件下初期支护的受力特点及孔隙水压力场分布特征。结果表明:在控制围岩变形方面,两种施工方法均能有效控制围岩变形,且区别并不显著;在对初期支护受力验算时,两种施工方法均满足规范要求,安全系数最小值均出现在隧道最大开挖线及拱脚处;孔隙水压力场均在隧道周围形成低水压区,并呈漏斗状分布;在隧道内部上台阶全断面注浆后,隧道拱部上方渗水量较小,隧道内的渗漏水主要集中在边墙及仰拱。从数值模拟结果及工法评价角度综合考虑,中隔壁法优于双侧壁导坑法。

关键词 超大跨度隧道 第三系半成岩地层 富水段落 流固耦合 施工方法

0 引言

随着我国西部大开发力度的不断加大，西部交通事业高速发展。我国地势西高东低，西部地区多以山地、高原等地形为主，地质构造复杂，地层岩性种类繁多，在隧道建设的施工过程中，经常遭遇软弱破碎围岩等地质情况相对较差的地层，尤其是第三系半成岩地层。第三系地层成岩时间短，岩、土性质并存，是介于岩石与土之间的过渡性地层，第三系地层的岩性主要包括泥岩、砂质泥岩，一般成岩作用较差，节理不发育，遇水易软化，暴露易风化。在隧道开挖扰动及地下水的作用下胶结松散的砂层塌落，随着流水涌出，极易发生涌水、涌泥等工程灾害。鉴于这种特性，在隧道施工过程中，当隧道变形过大时或者围岩自稳能力较差时，就需要采取一定的加固措施来保证施工安全。

目前注浆加固是该地层隧道施工的一项重要工法。注浆技术是指通过将适宜的胶凝材料配制成针对性浆液，利用压力设备直接或间接注入岩土体，以改变岩土体的力学分布和结构组成，对加固范围内的裂隙岩体起到有效封闭作用，从而降低围岩的渗透性能，阻隔岩体内部孔隙水对隧道的补给，增强围岩的稳定性。

流固耦合是研究富水地层隧道的一项重要内容，由于地下水的储存和流动对岩石产生渗透水压，从而影响岩石的应力场分布；同时岩石应力场的改变，使裂隙产生变形，影响裂隙的渗透性能和水压的分布。渗流场和应力场相互交叉相互作用的现象即为流固耦合。在隧道建设过程中，不同的施工方法会对围岩变形、支护结构受力等产生不同影响。因此，在流固耦合基础上，众多学者对合理的施工方法进行了研究。

李明等对比分析了大断面黄土隧道双侧壁导坑法和 CRD 法施工的初支受力特点及围岩变形机理；结果表明，在考虑流固耦合作用下 CRD 法控制围岩变形效果要优于双侧壁导坑法。朱苦竹等对深埋隧道进行 CRD 法与双侧壁导坑法开挖模拟，分析开挖过程中的渗流变化、拱顶沉降、地表沉降等；综合表明双侧壁导坑法更有利于围岩稳定性。曹彬等对比环形开挖预留核心土法、CRD 法、三台阶法 3 种开挖方式下的隧道模型的围岩位移，分析不同开挖间距、注浆圈厚度对于地表沉降的影响，得出合理的开挖间距以及注浆圈厚度。朱永全等基于流固耦合理论，考虑降水前后 CD 法和三台阶预留核心土法，分析隧道施工中的地表沉降、洞周位移和支护结构内力；得出降水前后合理的开挖方式；降水前可以采用 CD 法施工，但是施工效率低下，降水后三台阶预留核心土法可以满足施工稳定性要求，且省时省工。

综上分析，在富水地区修建隧道，合理施工方法的选择有利于施工的安全与高效。本文以西安外环高速公路工程白鹿原隧道为依托，采用 Midas GTS NX 建立模型，对隧道富水段的开挖方法进行对比分析。在注浆条件下，研究隧道支护结构的受力特点，采用综合安全系数法对钢架及混凝土的内力进行强度校核，分析围岩变形及孔隙水压力场的分布特征，并对工法的灵活性、适应性等进行评价，综合分析得出适合该地层隧道富水段的施工方案。

1 工程概况

西安外环高速公路南段设有白鹿原长隧道一座，右洞长 2819m，最大埋深 135m；左洞长 2754m。最大埋深 133 米。隧道单洞开挖面积为 192.3m^3，开挖高度为 12.7m，毛洞开挖宽度达 18.7m。《公路隧道施工技术细则》规定隧道开挖宽度 $B \geqslant 18$m 属于超大跨度隧道。

隧址区揭露地层由老至新依次有新近系(N_2)泥岩、砾岩、中更新统黄土(Q_2^{eol})和上更新统黄土 Q_3^{eol}。室内试验表明白鹿原隧道具有成岩度低、胶结性较差、岩石强度低、水敏性强、遇水易软化甚至崩解的特点。加之洞身段整体位于地下水位线之下，严重威胁隧道建设人员安全。隧道在下穿凫峪沟富水段落时，现场发生了涌水、涌泥灾害，如图 1 所示。

为保障隧道顺利穿越富水段地层，现场采用“周壁径向注浆 + 上台阶全断面高压注浆”的方式进行超前加固。掌子面注浆加固后效果如图 2 所示。

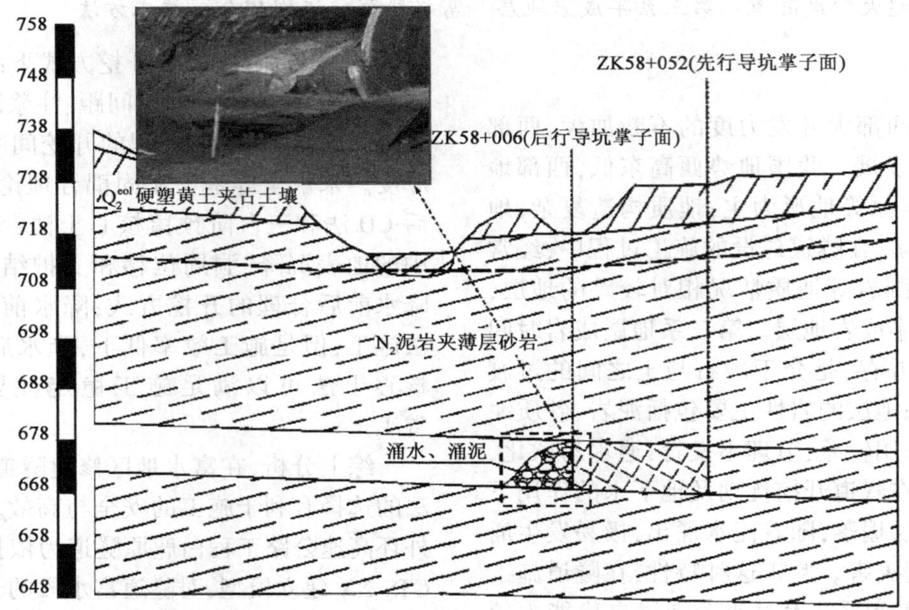

图1　白鹿原隧道涌水、涌泥段纵断面图

图2　现场注浆加固后效果图

2　施工方案比选研究

注浆加固是隧道涌水、涌泥灾害处治的关键技术,通过注浆可以提高围岩的力学参数以及抗渗性,从而达到治理病害或地质灾害,改善工程地质条件的目的。在隧道开挖过程中,围岩应力、应变等在时间和空间上具有不可逆转性。目前,对于隧道发生地质灾害后的施工手段有多种,施工方法的合理性、可靠性直接影响甚至决定工程的施工安全。

2.1　施工方案

水的存在会使第三系半成岩地层工程条件恶化。现场发现,白鹿原隧道涌泥、涌水段进行注浆加固后,围岩仍存在渗水的情况,仍有施工风险。因此,在现场采用“周壁径向注浆＋上台阶全断面高压注浆”的注浆加固条件下,本文对白鹿原隧道涌泥、涌水段的施工方案进行比选研究。工况一为中隔壁法,工况二为双侧壁导坑法如图3、图4所示。

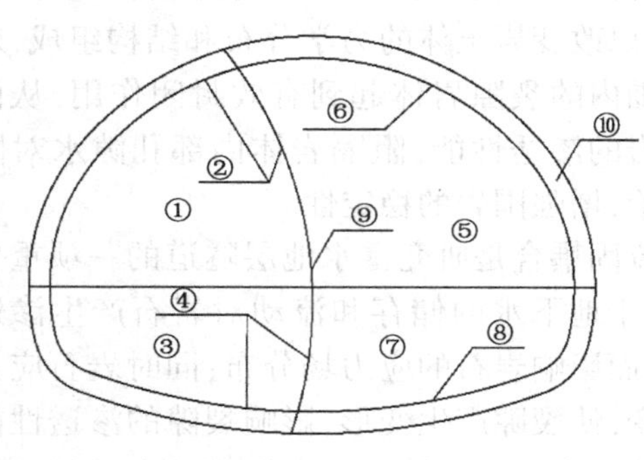

图3　中隔壁法

2.1.1　工况一

中隔壁法的施工方案如下:

①先行导坑上部开挖;②先行导坑上部初期支护(包括施作临时支护);③先行导坑下部开挖;④先行导坑下部初期支护(包括施作临时支护);⑤后行导坑上部开挖;⑥后行导坑上部初期支护;⑦后行导坑下部开挖;⑧后行导坑下部初期支护;⑨拆除中隔壁临时支护;⑩施作二次衬砌。

2.1.2　工况二

双侧壁导坑法的施工方案如下:

①先行导坑上部开挖;②先行导坑上部初期支护(包括施作临时支护);③先行导坑下部开挖;

④先行导坑下部初期支护(包括施作临时支护);⑤后行导坑上部开挖;⑥后行导坑上部初期支护(包括施作临时支护);⑦后行导坑下部开挖;⑧后行导坑下部初期支护(包括施作临时支护);⑨中导洞上部开挖;⑩中导洞上部初期支护;⑪中导洞中部开挖;⑫中导洞下部开挖;⑬中导洞下部初期支护;⑭拆除临时支护;⑮施作二次衬砌。

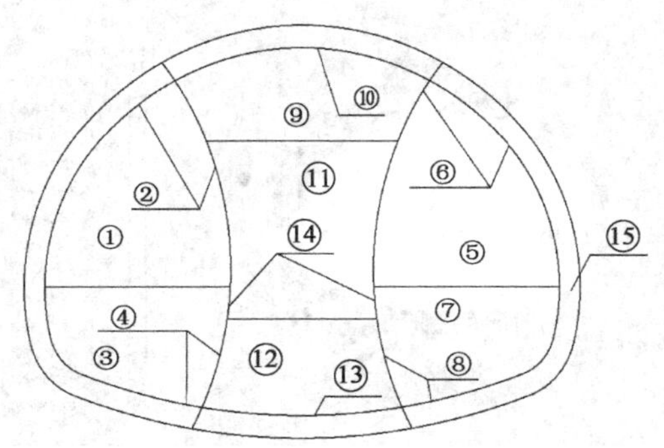

图4 双侧壁导坑法

2.2 建立模型

根据圣维南原理,为减小模型边界效应,计算范围水平方向取3倍洞径,底部纵向取3倍洞高,上部取至地表。建立二维隧道模型,模型尺寸为126.7m×90.8m。建模时各层土及注浆加固区均采用莫尔—库仑本构模型,初期支护、临时支护采用弹性模型,在渗流分析时围岩采用各向同性渗流模型,围岩颗粒假设不可压缩。

对各种支护措施进行简化等效考虑,初期支护由喷射混凝土、钢架和钢筋网等组成,其整个结构可看作为型钢混凝土柱的组合结构构件。材料参数采用将喷射混凝土和钢架进行等效后的喷射混凝土参数。在进行结构内力和变形计算时,型钢混凝土组合结构构件的抗弯刚度可按下式(1)计算:

$$EI = E_a I_a + E_c I_c \tag{1}$$

式中:EI——型钢混凝土构件截面抗弯刚度;

$E_a I_a$——型钢部分的截面抗弯刚度;

$E_c I_c$——喷射混凝土部分的截面抗弯刚度。

模型将土层自上而下划分为2层,地下水的埋深为5.6m。模型左右边界受到水平方向的约束,下部边界受到垂直位移的约束,上部边界不受任何方向的约束,为自由面。在地下水的埋深处设置总水头边界,并在隧道洞周设置零压力水头边界。计算模型参数的选取见表1,两种施工方法的模型整体网格划分如图5所示。

计算模型参数表 表1

模型项目	弹性模量 E(MPa)	泊松比 ν	重度 (kN/m³)	黏聚力 C(kPa)	内摩擦角 φ(°)	渗透系数 (cm/s)
黄土	265	0.30	19.1	28.0	20.0	2.69×10^{-5}
泥质砂岩	306	0.32	19.2	91.1	25.8	2.54×10^{-5}
注浆加固区	1075	0.25	19.8	26.7	19.3	2.69×10^{-6}
初期支护	34.4×10^3	0.22	23.8	—	—	—
临时支护	35.4×10^3	0.22	24.1	—	—	—

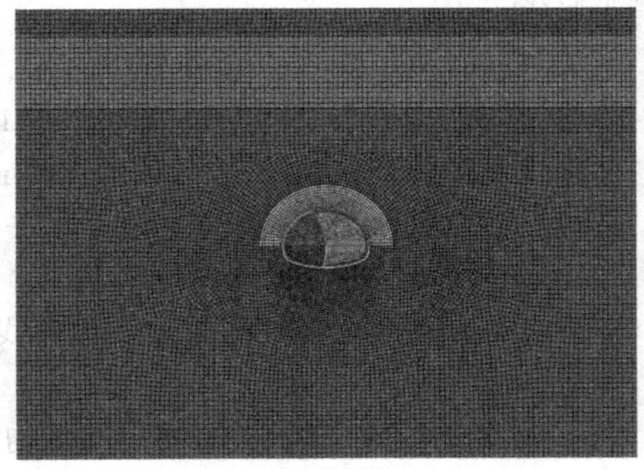

a)中隔壁法

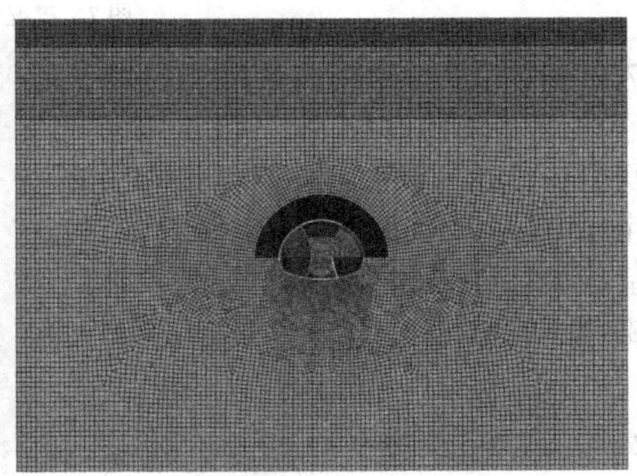

b)双侧壁导坑法

图5 模型整体网格划分

3　数值计算结果分析

3.1　变形分析

3.1.1　工况一变形分析

隧道开挖位移云图如图 6 所示。

由图 6 可知,工况一施工最大沉降值为 -74.7mm,位于隧道拱顶位置处。左右拱腰测点的竖向沉降值分别为 -60.7mm、-55.7mm;收敛值最大位于最大开挖线处,收敛值为 44.7mm。左拱腰及左侧最大开挖线处水平位移均为正值,而右拱腰及右侧最大开挖线处水平位移均为负值。

随开挖工序的隧道变形曲线图如图 7 所示。

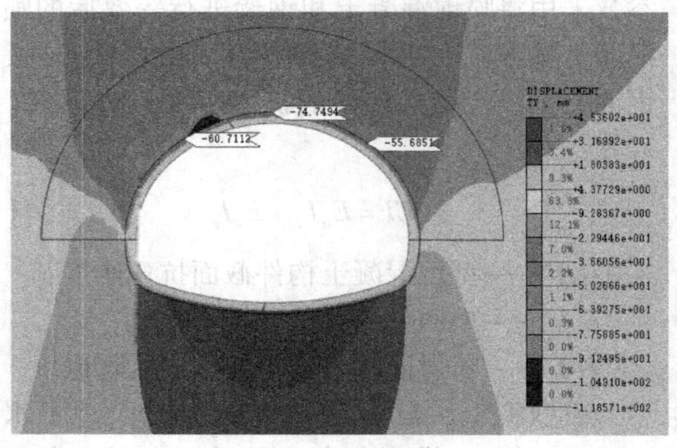

a)垂直位移

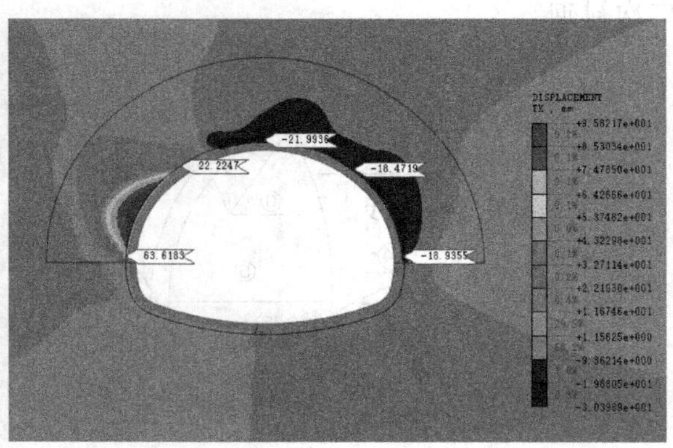

b)水平位移

图 6　隧道开挖位移云图

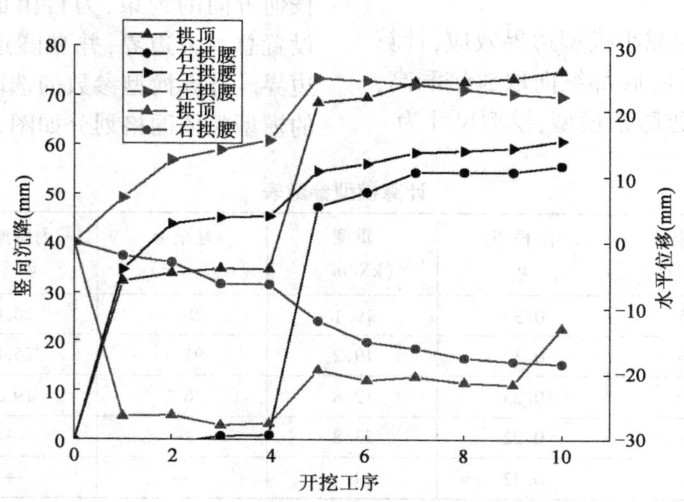

图 7　工况一变形曲线图

由图 7 可知,工况一的竖向沉降均呈增长趋势,当隧道开挖至各测点部位时,各测点竖向沉降变形值急剧增长,当后导上台阶开挖时,右拱腰测点变形值由 1.08mm 增长至 47.46mm;拱顶处的水平位移呈减小趋势,而左、右拱腰处的水平位移均呈增长趋势,但拱腰处水平收敛值先增大后减小。

3.1.2　工况二变形分析

隧道开挖位移云图如图 8 所示。

由图 8 可知,工况二施工最大沉降值为 -62.7mm,位于隧道拱顶位置处。左、右拱腰测点的竖向沉降值分别为 -42.2mm、-41.8mm;收敛值位于最大开挖线处,收敛值为 40.4mm。双侧壁导坑法左拱腰、右拱腰及拱顶处水平位移均小于中隔壁法相应测点的水平位移。

工况二随开挖工序的测点变形曲线图如图 9 所示。

由图 9 可知,工况二的竖向沉降均呈增长趋势,当隧道开挖至各测点部位时,各测点竖向沉降变形值急剧增长,当后导上台阶开挖时,右拱腰测点变形值由 1.16mm 增长至 27.66mm；拱顶、左拱腰处的水平位移呈减小趋势，而右拱腰处的水平位移均呈增长趋势。

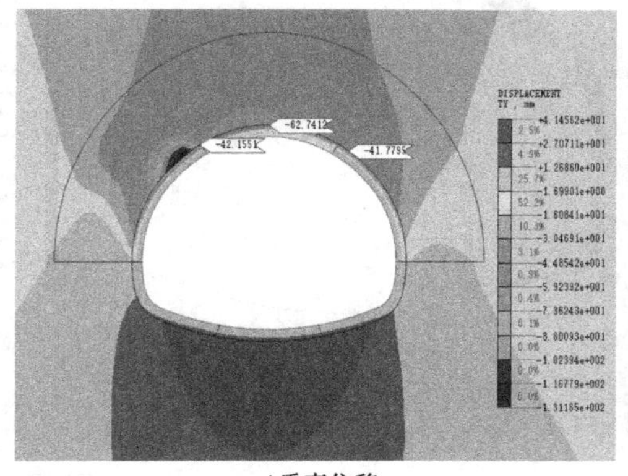

a)垂直位移

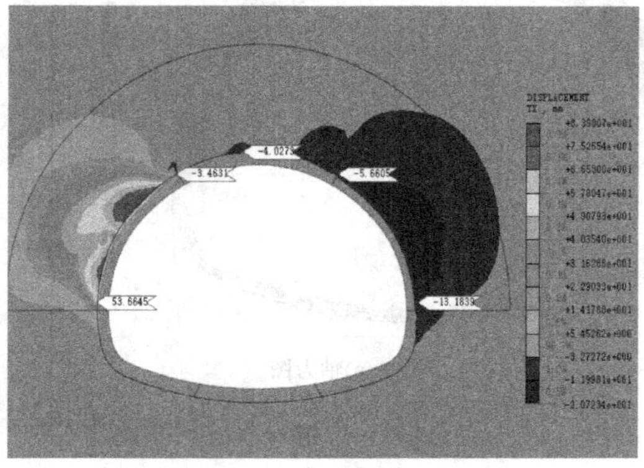

b)水平位移

图 8　隧道开挖位移云图

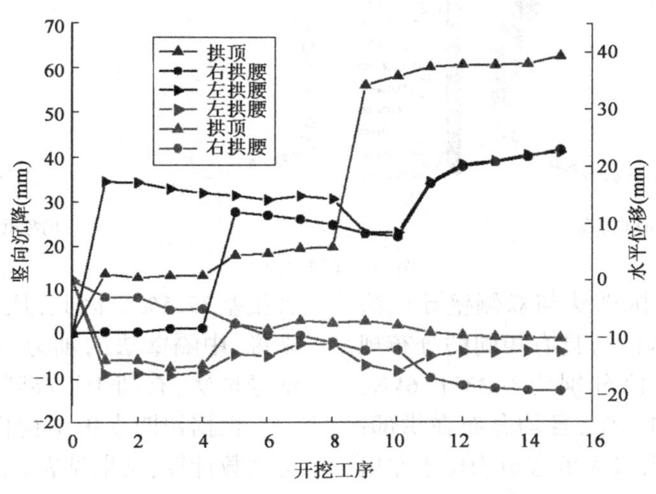

图 9　工况二变形曲线图

综上可知，中隔壁法和双侧壁导坑法均能有效控制隧道变形。其中，中隔壁法最大沉降值为 74.7mm，双侧壁导坑法最大沉降值为 62.7mm，两者相差 12mm，仅占设计预留变形量 250mm 的 4.8%。中隔壁法全断面最大收敛值为 44.7mm，双侧壁导坑法最大收敛值为 40.4mm，两者相差为 4.3mm，仅占设计预留变形量的 1.72%。显然，从变形控制效果来说，无论是采用中隔壁法还是双侧壁导坑法，两者区别并不显著。

3.2　初期支护受力分析

对钢拱架与喷射混凝土进行强度校核时，轴力由钢拱架与喷射混凝土共同承担，弯矩仅由钢拱架承担，可按式(2)~式(5)，计算得到初期支护结构中钢拱架与喷射混凝土分别所承担的内力。进而采用综合安全系数法验算钢拱架受拉强度、钢拱架受压强度以及喷射混凝土截面受压强度。

喷射混凝土承担的轴力：

$$N_h = N\frac{A_h E_h}{A_h E_h + A_g E_g} \tag{2}$$

喷射混凝土承担的弯矩：

$$M_h = 0 \tag{3}$$

钢拱架承担的轴力：

$$N_g = N\frac{A_g E_g}{A_h E_h + A_g E_g} \tag{4}$$

钢拱架承担的弯矩：

$$M_g = M \tag{5}$$

两种工况的初期支护结构内力如图 10、图 11 所示。

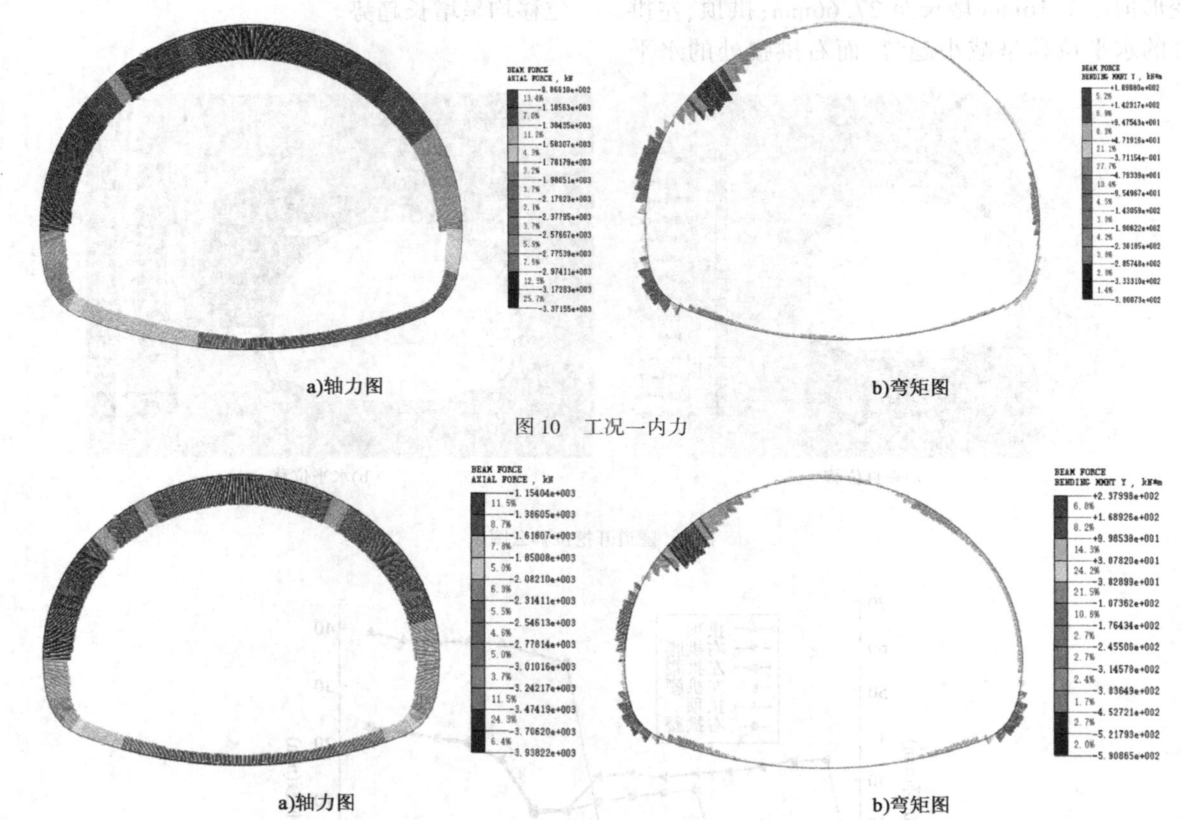

a)轴力图　　b)弯矩图

图10　工况一内力

a)轴力图　　b)弯矩图

图11　工况二内力

由图10、11可知，中隔壁法与双侧壁导坑法两种工况的初期支护结构内力具有相同的分布规律，轴力均为压力，最大值分别为 -3371.6kN、-3938.2kN，两者相差14.4%，且均分布在拱部；最大正弯矩均分布在墙脚，最大负弯矩均位于左拱腰，最大弯矩分别为380.9kN·m、590.8kN·m，两者相差35.5%。因此，从初期支护结构受力角度来说，中隔壁法的轴力、弯矩最大值均小于双侧壁导坑法，有利于提高隧道支护结构的稳定性。

根据初期支护结构内力，对控制截面进行安全系数计算，结果见表2。

初期支护各控制截面内力及安全系数计算　　表2

施工方法	测点	轴力(kN)	弯矩(kN·m)	综合安全系数		
				钢架抗压	钢架抗拉	喷混抗压
工况一	0	2814.3	26.0	4.3	17.9	2.6
	1	2732.8	80.8	2.4	7.5	2.6
	2	2812.4	14.1	5.2	10.4	2.6
	3	2916.8	90.2	2.2	6.5	2.5
	4	2673.7	73.0	2.6	9.1	2.7
	5	1563.2	61.0	3.5	8.0	4.6
	6	1021.3	24.8	7.4	31.9	7.1
	7	1087.1	4.5	14.2	24.9	6.6
工况二	0	2654.9	57.8	3.0	16.9	2.7
	1	2872.3	55.3	3.0	25.2	2.5
	2	1854.3	57.5	3.5	10.1	3.9
	3	2156.7	89.6	2.4	5.2	3.3

续上表

施工方法	测　点	轴力(kN)	弯矩(kN·m)	综合安全系数		
				钢架抗压	钢架抗拉	喷混抗压
工况二	4	2314.6	66.3	2.9	9.5	3.1
	5	1760.7	64.1	3.3	7.9	4.1
	6	1630.5	65.0	3.3	7.4	4.4
	7	1243.9	2.7	13.8	18.4	5.8

由表2可知，采用综合安全系数法对初期支护结构中的喷射混凝土及钢拱架进行强度校核时，中隔壁法和双侧壁导坑法均能满足规范要求。其中，在钢拱架抗压强度及抗拉强度校核方面，中隔壁法与双侧壁导坑法的最小安全系数均出现于隧道左侧最大开挖线处，且两者值差别不大，值分别为2.2、6.5和2.4、5.2，均大于2.0，满足规范要求；在喷射混凝土抗压强度校核方面，两者喷射混凝土抗压安全系数最小值均为2.5，大于2.4，满足规范要求。但两者安全系数最小值出现在不同测点，中隔壁法最小安全系数出现于隧道左侧最大开挖线处，双侧壁导坑法最小安全系数出现于隧道左拱腰处。因此，从安全系数角度来说，无论是采用中隔壁法还是双侧壁导坑法，两者区别并不显著。

3.3　孔隙水压力场分析

考虑流固耦合效应，对数值模型进行分析，不同施工方法的孔隙水压水头以及竖直方向渗流流速如图12、图13所示。

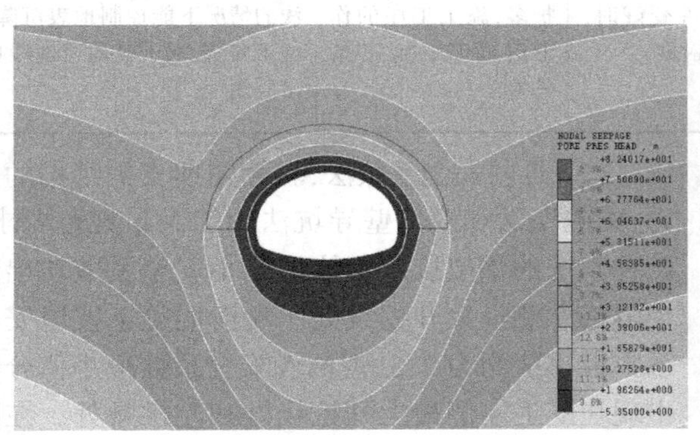
a)孔隙水压水头云图

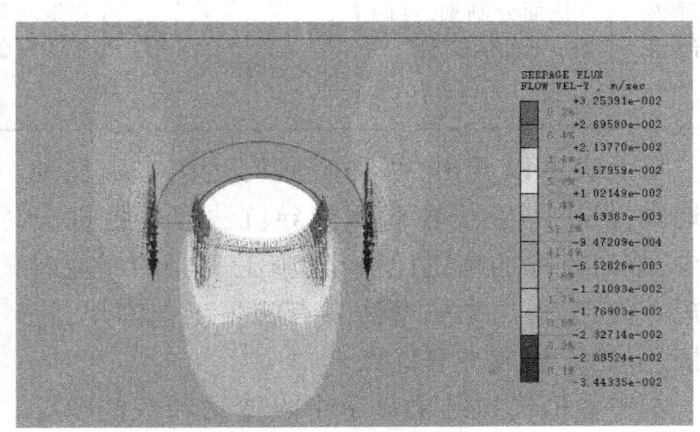
b) 渗流速度图

图12　工况一孔隙水压水头和渗流速度

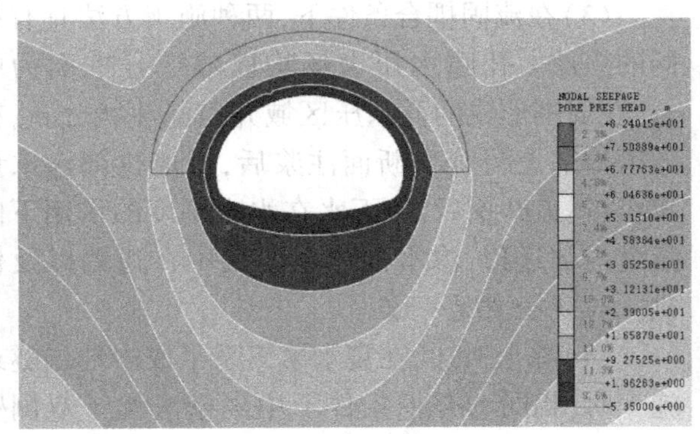
a)孔隙水压水头云图

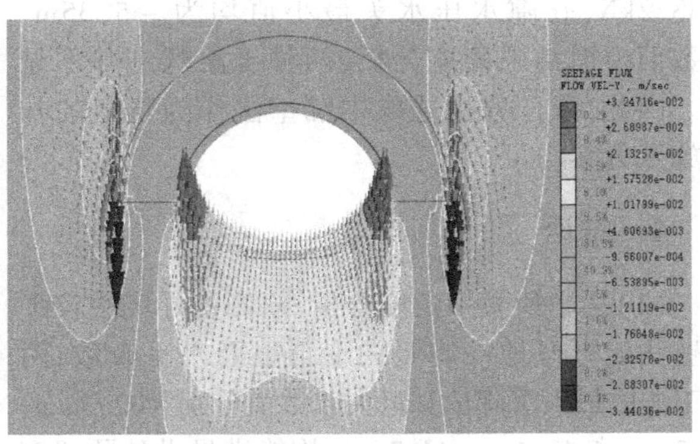
b)渗流速度图

图13　工况二孔隙水压水头和渗流速度

由图12、图13可知，中隔壁法与双侧壁导坑法的孔隙水压力水头云图均在隧道周围形成的低水压区域并呈漏斗状分布，孔隙水压水头最小值均为－5.35m，分布在隧道轮廓线外侧，且在远离隧道时，孔隙水压力水头逐渐增大；在隧道内部上台阶全断面注浆后，隧道拱部渗水量较小。对于中隔壁法及双侧壁导坑法,在隧道开挖后,地下水在水力梯度的作用下向隧道内部迁移,渗水部位主要集中在边墙以及仰拱,在隧道内部渗流流速最大值均分布在边墙处,分别为 325.4m/sec、324.7m/sec,两者仅相差 0.21%,区别并不显著。施工时应注意边墙及仰拱处防排水。综上所述,中隔壁法与双侧壁导坑法两种施工方案具有相同的渗流场分布规律,且两种工况的孔隙水压力水头及渗流流速最大值均比较接近。显然,从渗流角度来说,无论是采用中隔壁法还是双侧壁导坑法,两者区别并不显著。

3.4　综合分析

在选定隧道涌水涌泥段施工方案时,需考虑施工工序的作业时间、施工的支护措施、拆除临时支撑的圬工比例、工程的进度和工程造价等综合因素。中隔壁法和双侧壁导坑法两种工法的综合评价如表 3 所示。

两种工法的综合评价　　表 3

开挖方法	工作面稳定性分析	洞周围岩变形控制效果分析	对地质条件改变的适应性分析	施工灵活性与经济性	综合评价
中隔壁法	开挖跨度减半,开挖面稳定性较好	开挖跨度小,可及时封闭成环,防止洞周围岩变形的急剧扩大	当地质条件变好时可取消临时仰拱,变为台阶法	拆除中隔壁作业复杂,不宜采用大型机械快速施工	属于大断面分割施工,在埋深浅的情况下能控制地表沉降,施工安全,在不良地质地段也可应用
双侧壁导坑法	开挖面分割细,可确保掌子面的稳定	因分割断面细,及时支护,能控制洞周围岩变形的扩大	当地质条件变好时,工法改变困难	开挖断面小,临时支护多,施工工序的作业时间长。施工条件差	属于大断面分割施工,在埋深浅的情况下能控制地表沉降,施工安全,在不良地质地段也可应用

从上表可以看出,两种工法均适用于不良地质地段,但中隔壁法较双侧壁导坑法有开挖面分部少、临时支撑的圬工比例小、施工工序的作业时间短等特点,得出中隔壁法具有施工工艺简单,进度快、节约工程成本等优点。

本文数值模拟结果显示中隔壁法和双侧壁导坑法控制隧道拱顶竖向位移分别是 74.7mm 和 62.7mm,初期支护轴力最大值为 3371.6kN 和 3938.2kN,孔隙水压水头最小值均为 –5.35m。从数值模拟结果角度分析,两种工法区别并不显著。因此,综合分析选取中隔壁法作为隧道的开挖施工方案。

4　结语

(1)从数值模拟角度分析,双侧壁导坑法较中隔壁法能更好地控制竖向变形以及水平收敛,两种工法的最大沉降值和最大收敛值分别为62.7mm、74.7mm 和 40.4mm、44.7mm,均能满足设计预留变形量的要求;从工法特点角度分析,在保证隧道稳定的前提下,中隔壁法施工工艺简单、施工进度快,有利于加快工程的建设以及节约工程成本。综合评价分析,中隔壁法优于双侧壁导坑法。

(2)通过安全系数法,验算初期支护结构的受力,中隔壁法和双侧壁导坑法均能满足规范要求。两种工法的钢架抗压和抗拉最小安全系数均出现于隧道左侧最大开挖线处。喷射混凝土抗压安全系数最小值均为 2.5,但两者安全系数最小值分别出现在隧道左侧最大开挖线处和左拱腰处。在隧道施工中应注意安全系数最小值处钢架连接的完整性,喷射混凝土厚度及均匀性,保证施工质量。

(3)在流固耦合条件下,两种施工方法具有相同的规律。孔隙水压力场均以隧道开挖面为中心,在周围形成的低水压区域并呈漏斗状分布;在隧道内部上台阶全断面注浆后,隧道拱部渗水量较小;隧道开挖后,地下水在水力梯度的作用下向隧道内部迁移,渗水部位主要集中在边墙以及仰拱。与现场情况一致。

(4)综上所述,在富水第三系半成岩地层隧道施工时,相同的开挖条件下中隔壁法优于双侧壁导坑法。

参考文献

[1] 祁卫华. 第三系富水砂岩铁路隧道施工技术[J]. 现代隧道技术,2015,52(01):177-183.

[2] 王建军. 兰渝铁路上第三系弱胶结砂岩软化

与变形机理探究[J]. 工程地质学报,2013,21(05):716-721.

[3] 张民庆,何志军,肖广智,等. 第三系富水砂层隧道工程特性与施工技术研究[J]. 铁道工程学报,2016,33(09):76-81.

[4] 马志富,杨昌贤. 第三系高压富水砂泥岩地层隧道技术研究——以牡绥铁路双丰隧道为例[J]. 隧道建设(中英文),2018,38(03):434-442.

[5] 曹峰. 兰州第三系砂岩水稳性特征隧道施工研究[J]. 铁道工程学报,2012,29(12):21-25+31.

[6] 朱举. 富水第三系弱胶结砾岩工程性质及隧道开挖面稳定性研究[D]. 北京:北京交通大学,2020.

[7] 秦正贵,陈勇. 蒙华铁路中条山隧道第三系地层工程地质特征研究[J]. 隧道建设,2014,34(12):1163-1167.

[8] 刘盼. 第三系砂泥岩隧道涌水涌泥段施工方案研究[D]. 兰州:兰州交通大学,2016.

[9] 高广义. 百店隧道第三系富水砂层快速施工关键技术研究[J]. 隧道建设,2014,34(09):908-912.

[10] 杨昌贤,马志富,张凤武,等. 牡绥铁路双丰隧道富水第三系砂泥岩地层超前注浆加固施工技术[J]. 铁道标准设计,2017,61(07):125-130.

[11] 贾元霞. 超前深孔劈裂注浆技术在高含水率黄土高铁隧道中的应用研究[J/OL]. 铁道标准设计:1-5[2021-12-01]. http://doi-orgs.vpn.chd.edu.cn:8080/10.13238/j.issn.1004-2954.202101080001.

[12] 秦鹏飞. 地下工程注浆技术研究新进展[J]. 现代隧道技术,2020,57(02):55-60.

[13] 杨赛舟,何川,李铮,等. 富水地区隧道注浆圈内部水压分布规律[J]. 中国矿业大学学报,2017,46(03):546-553.

[14] 卓越,李治国,高广义. 隧道注浆技术的发展现状与展望[J/OL]. 隧道建设(中英文):1-11[2021-12-01]. http://kns-cnki-net.vpn.chd.edu.cn:8080/kcms/detail/44.1745.U.20211109.0853.002.html.

[15] 王晓蕾,秦启荣,苏培东,等. 破碎围岩注浆加固技术研究现状及发展趋势[J]. 科学技术与工程,2017,17(23):122-131.

[16] 王刚. 隧道富水地层帷幕注浆加固圈参数及稳定性研究[D]. 济南:山东大学,2014.

[17] 李明,潘春阳,张旭斌. 兰州地铁富水大断面黄土隧道流固耦合作用机理研究[J]. 公路,2018,63(07):323-327.

[18] 朱苦竹,王阳,罗剑航,刘治军. 流固耦合下的软弱围岩隧道施工工法优化研究[J]. 中外公路,2017,37(04):206-210.

[19] 曹彬,刘海明,郭伟,张延杰,杨志华. 基于流固耦合理论下不同开挖方式的位移影响分析——以阿嘎下隧道为例[J]. 工业安全与环保,2021,47(09):27-31+82.

[20] 朱永全,冯宝才. 基于流固耦合的富水软岩地层隧道施工方法研究[J]. 石家庄铁道大学学报(自然科学版),2013,26(S2):85-87.

寒区山岭隧道温度场研究综述

徐浩男* 李 昂

(长安大学公路学院)

摘 要 随着西部地区"一带一路"战略的持续推进,山岭隧道的建设快速发展,寒区山岭隧道遭受冻害现象时有发生,同时在冻害下产生的病害也越来越严重,对隧道的施工和运营均造成了较大危害。而对隧道温度场的研究是冻害研究的突破口,寒区山岭隧道温度场的研究对于隧道冻害的防治是尤为重要的。为了促进寒区山岭隧道温度场体系研究的发展,本文介绍了冻土分布及隧道冻害现状并从现场监测分析、理论解析、模型试验和数值模拟四个方面归纳总结了寒区山岭隧道温度场的学术研究现状,指出现有研究中存在的不足和尚需讨论的方面。建议深入开展温度场、渗流场、应力场等多场耦合作用、离心机模型试验及隧道精细化建模等方面的研究,以期为寒区山岭隧道温度场领域的学术研究提供新的视角和基础资料。

关键词 隧道工程 冻土 温度场 研究综述

0 引言

随着西部地区"一带一路"战略的持续推进,山岭隧道的建设将成交通建设的重点,越来越多的山岭隧道需要穿越寒区。而在寒区修建隧道受到寒冷气候的影响极易发生隧道冻害现象,主要表现为隧道洞门墙体开裂、衬砌开裂挂冰、截排水沟结冰堵塞及路面积水冻胀开裂沉降等[1-2]。这些病害严重影响车辆及行人的正常通行,给隧道安全运行带来了巨大隐患,造成巨大的经济损失和资源浪费。国内外许多学者分析了寒区山岭隧道冻害产生的机理,0℃温度波动被视为形成冻害的三个必要条件之一[3-5]。只有正确了解山岭隧道温度的变化规律与分布特征才能防治隧道冻害,为寒区山岭隧道的设计与修建提供帮助,避免由于冻土可能引起的工程事故及安全隐患[6]。

为了更好地了解寒区山岭隧道温度场的研究现状与进展,本文介绍了冻土分布及隧道冻害现状,将寒区山岭隧道温度场研究分为现场监测分析、理论解析、模型试验和数值模拟四部分进行总结归纳,并展望未来可能研究的方向。

1 冻土分布及隧道冻害

1.1 冻土分布

据统计世界上短时冻土、季节性冻土、多年冻土地区面积占全球陆地面积的50%,主要分布在挪威、加拿大、美国、中国、俄罗斯和日本等地。我国寒区面积为417.4×10^{4}km^2,占我国陆地面积的43.5%[7],主要包括多年冻土区和季节性冻土区。

1.2 隧道冻害

在我国,大量的寒区山岭隧道在施工和运营期间面临着严重的冻害威胁,造成了巨大的经济损失和资源浪费,如新疆"天山第一隧"玉希莫勒盖隧道[8]、秦皇岛梯子岭隧道[9]、内蒙古自治区兴安岭隧道[10]等。国外的寒区山岭隧道也饱经冻害的侵袭[11-12],在日本约有34%的寒区山岭隧道发生冻害[13]。隧道冻害发生模式如图1所示。研究寒区山岭隧道温度场的分布规律及其与渗流场、应力场间的耦合关系以及衬砌冻胀力变化规律等问题变得尤为重要。

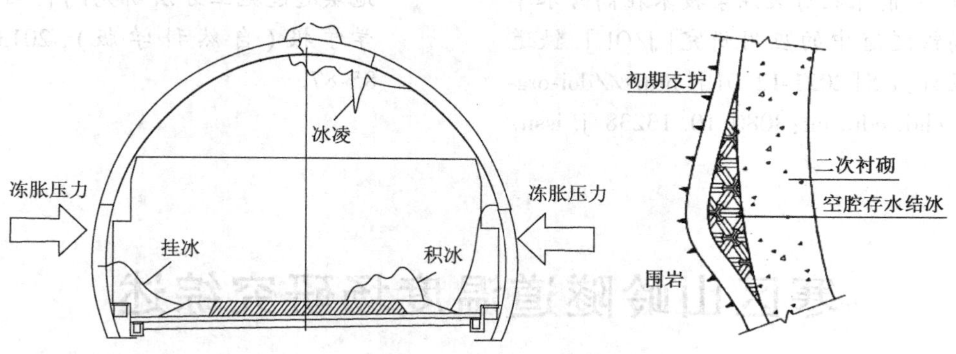

图1 隧道冻害发生模式及局部存水冻胀理论示意图

2 现场监测分析

现场监测数据是各种敏感性因素综合作用的结果,能够即时准确的反映理论研究的实际效果。众多学者对隧道温度场的现场监测数据进行了深入的研究,从隧道内温度分布规律开始逐渐发展到衬砌及围岩温度分布规律。作者列举了国内外寒区山岭隧道温度场现场监测分析案例[14],如表1所示。

寒区隧道温度场分布规律现场监测典型案例 表1

编号	工程名称	工程概况	研究内容	冻土类型
1	西罗奇岭2号隧道[15]	位于东北嫩林线，为直线坡度14‰的上坡越岭隧道，全长1160m	隧道内气温分布规律	季节性冻土
2	正盘台隧道[16]	位于张家口崇礼，为单洞双线隧道，设计长度12.974km	隧道温度场影响因素	季节性冻土
3	梯子岭隧道[18-20]	位于秦皇岛市青龙满族自治州，全长1142.72m，纵坡为4.1%的直线隧道	隧道内外气温变化规律	瞬时冻土
4	Nanaori-Toge隧道[11]	位于日本本州福岛县Aizu-bange，长1045m	隧道内外微观气象	—
5	昆仑山隧道[17]	位于青藏铁路青海境内，地处昆仑山北麓低、中高山区，气温、气压低，全长1686m	隧道内气温分布规律	多年冻土
6	左木台隧道[22]	位于吉林省长白山北部，为单向双车道公路隧道，全长约3000m	隧道内气温分布规律	季节性冻土
7	兴安岭公路隧道[25]	位于内蒙古自治区呼伦贝尔市东北部，全长3960m	隧道温度场的时空演化规律	多年冻土
8	青沙山公路隧道[26]	位于青藏高原东部青沙山区，为分离式单洞双线隧道，左线长3350m，右线长3340m	衬砌及围岩温度分布规律	季节性冻土
9	鹧鸪山隧道[27-28]	位于四川省，海拔3400余m，最低气温达-30℃，全长4448m	衬砌及围岩温度分布规律	季节性冻土
10	风火山隧道[24]	位于可可西里无人区，全长1338m，平均高程4800m以上	冻结围岩体热学响应规律	多年冻土

2.1 隧道内温度分布规律

乜风鸣[15]对西罗奇岭2号隧道温度场进行了测试和分析。王仁远等[16]以京张高铁第一长隧道正盘台隧道为研究对象，分析了影响隧道温度场的因素。张先军[17]在昆仑山隧道进行现场监测，对隧道内气温分布特征进行了分析。分析认为：洞内气温呈抛物线分布，中间高，两边低，在暖季则相反，且洞内与洞外气温年较差的比值随着隧道长度增长而减小。

陈建勋等人对梯子岭隧道进行了温度场的现场测试和分析[18-20]。Islam等[11]对Nanaori-Toge隧道进行现场试验，研究了隧道内外微观气象条件的差异。Du等[21]研究了安装电伴热系统后隧道的温度场分布规律。Zhao等[22]对我国左木台隧道的气温进行了综合测量。研究发现：隧道洞内的年气温变化具有周期性，随时间大致呈正弦曲线变化，并与隧道外空气温度呈近似三角函数周期性变化，沿纵向温度变化呈指数函数曲线变化关系。

2.2 衬砌及围岩温度分布规律

隧道内围岩的初始温度是影响隧道整体温度场的分布的重要因素[16]，对于隧道衬砌及围岩温度分布的规律的研究是必不可少的。陈建勋等[23]依托某寒区隧道，对11处断面的温度进行了为期1.5年的测试，揭示了衬砌及围岩内部温度的变化规律。张德华等[24]结合风火山隧道的修建对冻结围岩体的热学响应规律进行了现场试验研究。赵鑫等[25]基于傅里叶传热定律推导寒区隧道温度简谐波径向传热表达式，探究了寒区隧道温度场的时空演化规律。结果表明：隧道围岩温度在径向一定范围内，随着径向深度的增加，年平均温度上升，年温度振幅衰减，并且呈指数函数曲线变化关系，隧道背后围岩地温随时间及深度呈线性变化趋势。

赖金星等[26]对地处青藏高原东部的青沙山公路隧道地温场进行现场实测与分析，确定了围岩表面温度与围岩最大冻结深度之间的关系，研究了隧道运行初期的温度场演化规律。谢红强[27]、马建新等[28]分别对鹧鸪山隧道的结构和围岩温度场进行了实测研究，前者建立了二维温度场计算模型，探究了保温层施作前后围岩和衬砌温度场的分布情况，后者采用统计分析得到了隧道围岩及支护结构温度场分布规律。分析认为：洞内地温随着围岩深度的加深而增加，隧道围岩及结构体温度沿隧道径向存在某一比较稳定的温度边界条件该范围内的温度随环境温度有一定的升高和降低变化，在此范围外温度趋于稳定。

综上所述隧道洞内气温呈抛物线分布，如图2

所示。暖季则相反,其随隧道外环境空气温度呈近似三角函数周期性变化,年气温变化具有周期性,随时间大致呈正弦曲线变化;隧道围岩温度在径向一定范围呈指数函数曲线变化关系,存在某一比较稳定的温度边界条件。未来应对隧道细部结构的温度变化规律进行更加详细的监测分析,山岭隧道的结构设计优化都应建立在温度场准确预测的基础之上。

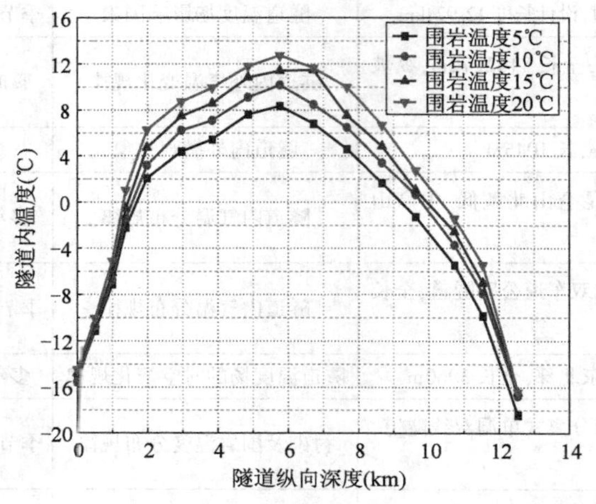

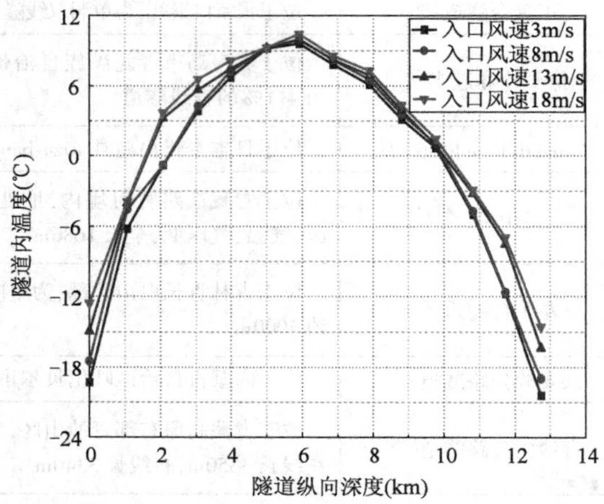

图 2　工程 5[16] 隧道内温度纵向分布图

3　理论解析

现场监测并不适用于未施工的隧道,不能预测其温度场的分布及变化规律。而理论解析则不受隧道施工的影响,其具有明确的物理概念,只需有洞口处气温、风速以及围岩的热物性等参数即可确定洞内气温的分布情况[29]。

3.1　温度场二维理论解析

Shamsundar[30] 提出了沿管道轴向变温边界条件下圆形管道外侧温度的解析解。Bon 等[31] 给出寒区隧道非线性温度场解析解的求解方法。Comini 等[32] 提出一种普遍适用的求解具有非线性物理性质和边界条件的瞬态热传导问题的方法,给出考虑相变的非线性温度场的数值计算方法。Prashantk 等[33-34] 利用叠加原理和分离变量法得到了考虑温度随坐标变化的对流边界条件下圆形截面瞬态温度场的解析解。Lu 等[35] 建立了含时边界条件下多维复合材料圆柱板瞬态热传导问题的解析解。但这些研究成果仅适用于小口径的管道,并不适用于大断面隧道的温度场理论解的研究。

Takumi 等[36] 利用叠加原理和能量守恒原理,得到了寒冷地区隧道内空气温度场的解析解。张国柱等[29] 建立寒区圆形隧道传热模型,利用叠加原理及贝塞尔特征函数的正交及展开定理,得到了寒区隧道围岩径向温度的理论解。郑波等[37-38] 基于现场大量实测数据,分析了高海拔地区特长公路隧道温度沿隧道纵向分布规律、经验公式以及防冻措施。周小涵等[39] 推导寒区隧道围岩-衬砌-气流的非稳态热传导的有限差分方程。Zeng 等[40] 基于有限差分法建立了非稳态传热计算模型,采用正交试验法对隧道温度场的影响因素进行了敏感性研究。

3.2　温度场三维理论解析

上述研究都是二维的,但是国内外各学者研究表明山岭隧道的温度分布并不是均匀而是随空间变化分布的,乜凤鸣[15] 对西罗奇岭 2 号隧道的实测结果也证实了隧道洞口的气温与中间段的气温是不同的,因此要清楚隧道围岩沿轴向的温度变化规律,就必须对隧道温度场进行三维空间分析。

张学富等[41-44] 推导了寒区隧道三维温度场有限元计算公式,并考虑冻土渗流场和温度场的耦合影响,建立冻土渗流场和温度场耦合问题的三维数学模型,推导出考虑围岩与空气热对流交换及围岩自身热传导之间相互耦合作用下的温度场有限元计算模型。张全胜等[45] 基于相变控制微分方程得到了寒区隧道三维温度场的有限元公式。

3.3　多场耦合

渗流场和应力场对寒区山岭隧道的冻害有极大的影响,在工程设计的过程中应充分考虑这两因素对温度场的影响[46]。在多场耦合作用方面的研究早在20世纪中期前苏联学者就提出了水热输运模型,后来学者相继进行了这方面的研究。

黄涛等[47]通过隧道裂隙围岩体渗透性能与热物理性能的等效连续化处理,初步建立了隧道围岩温度场与渗流场耦合作用数学模型。赖远明等[48-49]研究了寒区隧道温度场、渗流场和应力场非线性耦合模型,提出了其控制方程。夏才初等[50]根据能量守恒,建立隧道洞内气体的气-固耦合传热模型,得到了洞内气体年平均温度和温度振幅的显式解析解。但是多场耦合作用的研究仍处于初步发展阶段,不能够满足工程设计的要求,温度场、渗流场、应力场等多场耦合作用是未来研究的重点。

4 相似模型试验及数值模拟

隧道温度场模型试验基于相似理论进行设计,能够重现工程现场实际情况,直观地观察隧道结构,在室内及室外可控环境下获取相应的数据并进行方案改良,模型设计如图3所示。而数值模拟既能较大程度地贴合现场实际工况,充分考虑寒区隧道的不同地质条件,还能通过改变参数来分析不同敏感性因素对寒区隧道温度场的影响效果,分析问题全面,效果直观,相对于现场试验具有其独有的优势。

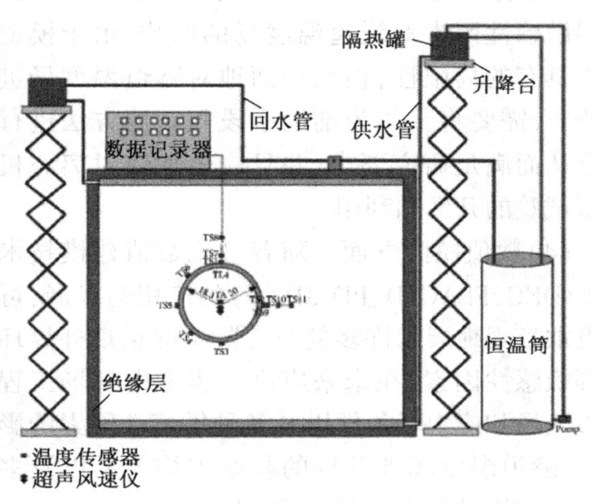

a)横截面

b)剖面

图3 模型设计示意图

4.1 相似模型试验

作者归纳总结了国内外寒区山岭隧道温度场相似模型试验的研究成果,如表2所示。Zhang等[51]使用1:26.83几何缩小尺度的模型试验,研究了施工过程中温度扰动和边界温度对多年冻土隧道围岩温度分布的影响。Feng等[52]开发了一种由制冷系统、循环系统和温度控制系统组成的寒区隧道模型,以研究寒区隧道的温度场、霜升力及保温层的可靠性。Liu等[53]研究了温度场的分布规律以及进气气流温度和风速下霜锋的膨胀规律。Zeng等[40]在通风条件下通过1:30几何减速尺度的模型测试,探究了入口气流温度和机械通风对围岩温度分布的影响。Cao等[54]对寒区隧道温度场进行了系统研究,研究了地下水渗漏与隧道通风耦合的模型试验。郭瑞等[55]研制了一种模拟寒区隧道纵向温度场分布的室内模型试验装置,分析了隧道长度、洞口气温和风速对寒区隧道纵向温度场分布的影响及其规律。

寒区山岭隧道温度场相似模型试验研究 表2

编号	文献来源	试验平台/模型尺寸	试验土壤	隧道模型材料	几何相似比
1	[51]	2.5m×1.6m×0.5m	含水率10%的黏土	钢管	26.83:1
2	[52]	罐体直径1.9m,高度1.75m	细混凝土	土石	25:1
3	[53]	长度3m,内半径12.2cm	细混凝土	组态材料	37:1
4	[40]	8m×3m×1.5m	—	石膏加筋织物	30:1

续上表

编号	文献来源	试验平台/模型尺寸	试验土壤	隧道模型材料	几何相似比
5	[54]	1.4m×1.2m×1.2m	沙子	混凝土管	30:1
6	[55]	隧道直径25cm,长度分别为6、13、27m	—	2 cm厚圆形抽水橡胶管道	50:1
7	[49]	8m×3m×1.5m	—	石膏加单层钢筋网	30:1

4.2　数值模拟

王仁远等[56]分析了外界温度、围岩温度、列车运行速度和列车运行间隔时间对隧道温度场变化规律的影响并利用有限元软件Ansys Fluent验证控制方程的准确性。胡俊等[57]对大直径杯型冻土壁温度场的发展与分布规律进行研究,分析不同因素对该温度场的影响规律。韩跃杰等[6]针对高温多年冻土区隧道传热模型及温度场分布规律开展深入的理论分析、数值模拟和现场监测研究。晏启祥等[58]利用三维瞬态有限元程序抽象出简化的瞬态温度场计算模型,分析在有无保温隔热材料下温度场的应力分布情况。赖金星等[59]基于有限元理论的数值模拟及理论分析等手段对高海拔地区复杂围岩隧道温度场特征和结构性能进行系统研究。

综上所述模型试验很难综合反映不同敏感性因素对隧道温度场的影响,而数值模拟对工程细节进行了简化处理,难以完全模拟工程实际情况。离心机模型试验、精细化建模及对隧道内部特征规律和多场耦合作用进行精确描述将是未来研究的重点。

5　结语

隧道冻害问题随着西部“一带一路”战略推进导致的山岭隧道发展加速而变得愈发复杂,把握寒区山岭隧道洞内外及衬砌围岩温度场的变化规律,是做好隧道防冻设计的前提。如何降低冻害对隧道通行的危害,保证隧道的安全运营是当下学者研究的重点。本文较为系统地总结了国内外学者关于寒区山岭隧道温度场所取得的研究成果。基于此,作者认为以下几个方面有待进一步探讨和深入研究。

(1)现场监测分析方面。国内外学者对于隧道温度场从隧道内部温度分布规律到衬砌及围岩温度分布规律的研究愈发成熟,未来应重点关注隧道细部结构的温度变化预测,为隧道冻害的防治提供依据。

(2)理论解析方面。现有解析方法考虑了不同的侧重因素和简化条件,但公式复杂且工程实用性差,应提出考虑各影响因子修正的简化解析公式,建立更加全面的计算模型并给予验证。目前,对于隧道温度场的三维空间分析较为欠缺,如何考虑温度场、渗流场、应力场等多场耦合作用将是未来研究的重点。

(3)模型试验方面。模型试验很难综合模拟不同敏感性因素对隧道温度场的影响,由于模型试验具有的局限性,很难全面地对隧道温度场进行研究,需要将其作为辅助手段与其他方法进行结合从而满足研究要求,并且应该加快对离心机模型试验的开发和利用。

(4)数值模拟方面。随着三维数值建模技术(如3DEC、FLAC3D、PFC3D等)的应用与发展,可以更加直观地展示许多复杂实际工况重现外界环境等敏感性因素,在未来应进一步考虑现场工程的渗流场和应力场条件以及各种敏感性因素的影响,对隧道温度场涉及到的复杂本构关系以及多场耦合作用进行更加周密的建模。

本文厘清寒区隧道温度场的发展现状及趋势,希望可以给予工程实践者一些启发和帮助,为本领域研究提供一定的参考。

参考文献

[1] 薛翊国,孔凡猛,杨为民,等.川藏铁路沿线主要不良地质条件与工程地质问题[J].岩石力学与工程学报,2020,39(03):445-468.

[2] Ma Q, Luo X, Lai Y, et al. Numerical investigation on thermal insulation layer of a tunnel in seasonally frozen regions[J]. Applied Thermal Engineering, 2018, 138: 280-291.

[3] 周小涵,曾艳华,杨宗贤,等.高纬度寒区浅埋隧道的温度场及防寒抗冻探讨[J].冰川冻土,2016,38(01):121-128.

[4] Chen R, Kang E, Ji X, et al. Cold regions in China[J]. Cold regions science and technology, 2006, 45(2): 95-102.

[5] Lai Y, Wu Z, Zhang S, et al. Study of methods to control frost action in cold regions tunnels[J]. Journal of cold regions engineering, 2003, 17(4):144-152.

[6] 韩跃杰,富志鹏,李博融.多年冻土区隧 道传热模型及温度场分布规律[J].中国公路学报,2019,32(07):136-145.

[7] 陈仁升,康尔泗,吴立宗,等.中国寒区分布探讨[J].冰川冻土,2005(04):469-475.

[8] 王余富.寒区公路隧道温度场特征研究[D].西安:长安大学,2006.

[9] 陈建勋.隧道冻害防治技术的研究[D].西安:长安大学,2004.

[10] 胡国双.兴安岭隧道改建工程施工简介[J].铁道建筑技术,1998(03):37-39.

[11] Islam M S, Fukuhara T, Watanabe H, et al. Horizontal U-tube road heating system using tunnel ground heat [J]. Journal of snow engineering of Japan, 2006, 22(3):229-234.

[12] Luettger H, Poyda F. Brandversuch in waermegedaemmtem tunnel [J]. Tunnel, 1992, 12(3).

[13] 苏林军.寒区隧道冻害预测与对策研究[D].成都:西南交通大学,2007.

[14] 万建国.我国寒区山岭交通隧道防冻技术综述与研究展望[J].隧道建设(中英文),2021,41(07):1115-1131.

[15] 乜风鸣.寒冻地区铁路隧道气温状态[J].冰川冻土,1988(04):450-453.

[16] 王仁远,朱永全,高焱,等.正盘台隧道洞内空气和围岩温度场分析[J].科学技术与工程,2020,20(18):7464-7471.

[17] 张先军.青藏铁路昆仑山隧道洞内气温及地温分布特征现场试验研究[J].岩石力学与工程学报,2005(06):1086-1089.

[18] 陈建勋,昝勇杰.寒冷地区公路隧道防冻隔温层效果现场测试与分析[J].中国公路学报,2001,14(4):75-79.

[19] 陈建勋.公路隧道冻害防治技术[J].长安大学学报:自然科学版,2006,26(4):68-70.

[20] 陈建勋,罗彦斌.寒冷地区隧道防冻隔温层厚度计算方法[J].交通运输工程学报,2007,7(2):76-79.

[21] Yaohui DU, Yang X, Yan C, et al. Numerical analysis of tunnel temperature field in seasonal frozen regions[J]. Journal of Glaciology and Geocryology, 2017.

[22] Pengyu Zhao, Jianxun Chen, Yanbin Luo, et al. Field measurement of air temperature in a cold region tunnel in northeast China[J]. Cold Regions Science and Technology, 2020, 171(C).

[23] 陈建勋,罗彦斌.寒冷地区隧道温度场的变化规律[J].交通运输工程学报,2008(02):44-48.

[24] 张德华,王梦恕,任少强.青藏铁路多年冻土隧道围岩季节活动层温度及响应的试验研究[J].岩石力学与工程学报,2007(03):614-619.

[25] 赵鑫,张洪伟,杨晓华,等.寒区隧道温度简谐波传热特征与影响因素的敏感性[J].交通运输工程学报,2020,20(06):148-160.

[26] 赖金星,谢永利,李群善.青沙山隧道地温场测试与分析[J].中国铁道科学,2007(05):78-82.

[27] 谢红强,何川,李永林.寒区公路隧道保温层厚度的相变温度场研究[J].岩石力学与工程学报,2007(S2):4395-4401.

[28] 马建新.高寒地区特长公路隧道温度场及保温隔热层方案研究[D].成都:西南交通大学,2004.

[29] 张国柱,夏才初,殷卓.寒区隧道轴向及径向温度分布理论解[J].同济大学学报(自然科学版),2010,38(08):1117-1122+1160.

[30] Shamsundar N. Formulae for freezing outside a circular tube with axial variation of coolant temperature[J]. International Journal of Heat & Mass Transfer, 1982, 25(10):1614-1616.

[31] Bonacina C, Comini G, Fasano A, et al. Numerical solution of phase-change problems [J]. International Journal of Heat Mass Transfer, 1973, 16(6):1852-1832.

[32] Comini G, Guidice S D, Lewis R W, et al. Finite element solution of non - linear heat conduction problems with special reference to phase change [J]. International Journal for

Numerical Methods in Engineering, 1974, 8 (3):613-624.

[33] Prashantk J, Suneet S, Rizwan-Uddin. Analytical solution to transient asymmetric heat conduction in a multi layer annulus [J]. Journal of Heat Transfer. 1 (2009) 73-92.

[34] Suneet S, Prashantk J, Rizwan-Uddin. Analytical solution to transient heat conduction in polar coordinates with multiple layers in radial direcrion[J]. International Journal of Thermal Sciences. 47 (2008) 261-273.

[35] Lu X, Tervola P, Viljanen M. Transient analytical solution to heat conduction in multi-dimensional composite cylinder slab [J]. International Journal of Heat & Mass Transfer, 2006, 49(5/6):1107-1114.

[36] Takumi K, Takashi M, Kouichi F. An estimation of inner temperatures at cold region tunnel for heat insulator design [C]. Proceedings of Structural Engineering Symposium. 2008, 32-38.

[37] 郑波,吴剑,郑金龙,等. 高海拔严寒地区特长公路隧道保温层铺设长度研究[J]. 地下空间与工程学报,2017,13(S1):353-359.

[38] 郑波,吴剑,郭瑞,等. 川西高原隧道冻害类型与防冻设计参数研究[J]. 现代隧道技术,2019,56(S1):58-65. DOI:10.13807/j.cnki.mtt.2019.S1.008.

[39] 周小涵,曾艳华,范磊,等. 寒区隧道温度场的时空演化规律及温控措施研究[J]. 中国铁道科学,2016,37(03):46-52.

[40] Zeng Y, Liu K, Zhou X, et al. Tunnel temperature fields analysis under the couple effect of convection-conduction in cold regions [J]. Applied Thermal Engineering, 2017, 120: 378-392.

[41] 张学富,苏新民,赖远明,等. 寒区隧道三维温度场非线性分析[J]. 土木工程学报,2004(02):47-53.

[42] 张学富,赖远明,喻文兵,等. 寒区隧道三维温度场数值分析[J]. 铁道学报,2003(03):84-90.

[43] 张学富,王成,喻文兵,等. 风火山隧道空气与围岩对流换热和围岩热传导耦合问题的三维非线性分析[J]. 岩土工程学报,2005(12):1414-1420.

[44] 张学富,喻文兵,刘志强. 寒区隧道渗流场和温度场耦合问题的三维非线性分析[J]. 岩土工程学报,2006(09):1095-1100.

[45] 张全胜,高广运,杨更社. 寒区隧道温度场的三维有限差分分析[J]. 苏州科技学院学报(工程技术版),2006(03):15-20.

[46] 周小涵. 寒区隧道围岩与风流的对流—导热耦合作用及其应用研究[D]. 成都:西南交通大学,2017.

[47] 黄涛,杨立中. 隧道裂隙岩体温度-渗流耦合数学模型研究[J]. 岩土工程学报,1999(05):554-558.

[48] 赖远明,吴紫汪,朱元林,等. 寒区隧道温度场、渗流场和应力场耦合问题的非线性分析[J]. 岩土工程学报,1999(05):529-533.

[49] 赖远明,喻文兵,吴紫汪,等. 寒区圆形截面隧道温度场的解析解[J]. 冰川冻土,2001(02):126-130.

[50] 夏才初,张国柱,肖素光. 考虑衬砌和隔热层的寒区隧道温度场解析解[J]. 岩石力学与工程学报,2010,29(09):1767-1773.

[51] Zhang X, Zhou Z, Li J, et al. A physical model experiment for investigating into temperature redistribution in surrounding rock of permafrost tunnel [J]. Cold Regions Science and Technology, 2018, 151:47-52.

[52] Feng Q, Jiang B S, Zhang Q, et al. Reliability research on the 5-cm-thick insulation layer used in the Yuximolegai tunnel based on a physical model test[J]. Cold Regions Science and Technology, 2016, 124:54-66.

[53] Liu L, Li Z, Liu X, et al. Frost front research of a cold-region tunnel considering ventilation based on a physical model test[J]. Tunnelling and Underground Space Technology, 2018, 77: 261-279.

[54] Cao S, Lu T, Zheng B, et al. Experimental Study on the Temperature Field of Cold Region Tunnel under Various Groundwater Seepage Velocities[J]. Advances in Civil Engineering,

2020.
[55] 郭瑞,郑波,方林,等.寒区隧道纵向温度场分布特征的模型试验研究[J].现代隧道技术,2021,58(05):129-139. DOI:10.13807/j.cnki.mtt.2021.05.016.
[56] 王仁远,朱永全,高焱,等.寒区隧道温度场模型试验及空气幕保温措施[J].中国铁道科学,2021,42(03):70-82.
[57] 胡俊,杨平.大直径杯型冻土壁温度场数值分析[J].岩土力学,2015,36(02):523-531.
[58] 晏启祥,何川,曾东洋.寒区隧道温度场及保温隔热层研究[J].四川大学学报(工程科学版),2005(03):24-27.
[59] 赖金星.高海拔复杂围岩公路隧道温度场特征与结构性能研究[D].西安:长安大学,2008.

全强风化砂页岩注浆压密特性室内试验研究

樊文胜*[1] 王一达[2] 翁贤杰[3] 张连震[2]
(1.江西省交通投资集团有限责任公司;2.中国石油大学(华东)储运与建筑工程学院;
3.江西交通咨询有限公司)

摘 要 为研究全强风化砂页岩地层在注浆过程中的压密变形特性,基于侧限固结室内试验,得到了不同含水率情况下全强风化砂页岩压密过程的应力-应变曲线,分析了含水率对全强风化砂页岩地层压密过程的影响。建立了可描述不同含水率条件下全强风化砂页岩地层压密过程的二次抛物线数学模型,可用于准确描述劈裂压密注浆过程中全强风化砂页岩的压密过程。研究结果表明:在全强风化砂页岩地层压密过程中,应力-应变关系呈现出明显的非线性特征;全强风化砂页岩地层最终应变与地层的初始含水率有关系,即地层初始含水率越大,土体的最终应变就越大;通过二次抛物线模型拟合得到的曲线与实际试验数据吻合对应情况良好,可为全强风化砂页岩劈裂压密注浆过程的综合分析及其应用提供参考。

关键词 岩土力学 注浆 全强风化砂页岩 压密特性 室内试验

0 引言

公路建设过程中需修建大批隧道工程,复杂的地形地质条件、丰富的地下水资源给隧道工程建设带来了前所未有的挑战,特别是隧道穿越富水全强风化砂页岩等软弱富水围岩时,由于上述地层具有富水性强、自稳能力差等显著特点,隧道工程开挖施工时极易诱发塌方、突水突泥等地质灾害事故,严重影响隧道工程建设安全。劈裂注浆是改善全强风化砂页岩地层力学性能及抗渗性能,提高隧道围岩稳定性的有效措施。在全强风化砂页岩地层劈裂注浆扩散过程中,地层在注浆压力作用下被压密,其压密特性对最终浆脉厚度、注浆扩散半径、注浆压力等关键注浆参数具有显著的影响。

国内外对软弱地层劈裂注浆开展了大量研究,张伟杰等[1,2]认为浆液本构模型为宾汉流体,基于平板窄缝假设建立了初步的劈裂注浆扩散理论模型。张忠苗等[3]建立了幂律型浆液劈裂注浆时各个注浆参数与浆液扩散距离的定量关系。邹金锋等[4,5]假定劈裂注浆在土体中形成的裂缝宽度为均匀裂缝宽度,推导出劈裂注浆的注浆压力沿裂缝长度的衰减规律。然而上述学者的研究仍存在着很大局限性,多是假设劈裂通道开度在劈裂注浆过程中恒定,浆液扩散劈裂通道一次形成,这种假设并不能够动态地描述劈裂注浆过程,并且忽略了浆液与被注介质的耦合,这与实际工程明显不符。在后续研究中,张庆松等人[6]证明了

1.基金项目:国家自然科学基金项目(No.51909270);江西省交通运输厅科技项目(No.2019C0001;No.2020C0005)。

劈裂注浆是一个动态过程,浆液在压力的作用下劈开被注介质,在被注介质中形成浆液劈裂通道;随着注浆的进行,劈裂通道的开度不断增大且浆液扩散距离不断增长,在劈裂注浆扩散过程中伴随着地层的压密。叶飞等[7]基于球形扩张理论,建立注浆压密的力学模型,证明了在压密注浆阶段所注介质所受压力与浆液扩散机理及土体本身压密特性密切相关。但是前人都对特定地层的压密特性未深入开展相关研究。

为研究全强风化砂页岩地层在注浆过程中的压密变形特性,以分析其压密变形特性对注浆扩散过程的影响,本文在充分参考前人[7-9]建立的有关压密特性及土体压缩变形机制模型基础上,基于侧限固结室内试验,考虑不同含水率的影响,研究了全强风化砂页岩压密过程的应力-应变曲线,分析了含水率对全强风化砂页岩地层压密特性的影响规律,建立了可描述不同含水率条件下全强风化砂页岩地层压密应力-应变关系的数学模型。本文的研究不仅证明了劈裂-压密注浆的浆液扩散理论,也在一定程度上进行了全风化砂页岩注浆压密过程的动态分析,同时为劈裂注浆在具有相似压密特性地层中的实际应用提供了理论依据。

1　室内试验

1.1　试验方法

本节依托江西省萍乡至莲花高速公路莲花隧道工程,选取工程典型地层,取得全强风化砂页岩土样,如图1所示。该地层土样的一般含水率为26%,在此土样基础上调整试验土样的地层初始含水率,使得土样的含水率在12%、14%、16%、18%、20%、22%、24%、26%、28%、30%、32%之间,依照《土工试验方法标准》[10]进行试验。

图1　全风化砂页岩现场土样

固结试验采用南京土壤仪器厂生产的WG型单杠杆固结仪(三联高压),在实际注浆工程中,注浆压力区间一般为0～4MPa,为了更好地模拟注浆过程,获得土体压密特性,对土样进行固结试验的荷载确定为0～4MPa,施加荷载的顺序与重量梯度为:0、25kPa、50kPa、100kPa、200kPa、300kPa、400kPa、800kPa、1600kPa、3200kPa、4000kPa。新加一级荷载1h以内,高压固结仪百分表读数变化不超过0.005mm,则可以认定在这一级荷载下,试样稳定不再压缩变形,可以进行下一步加载。

原状土试样的初始地层含水率调整后分为11组,各原状土试样地层初始含水率分别为12%、14%、16%、18%、20%、22%、24%、26%、28%、30%、32%。

1.2　试验结果分析

以土体所受侧限固结应力(kPa)为横坐标,以土体发生的压缩变形应变为纵坐标建立坐标系,绘制全强风化砂页岩的应力-应变曲线。不同地层初始含水率条件下土样的应力-应变曲线如图2所示。分析图2可知:

(1)在土体的压缩过程中,应变随着施加应力的增加而增加,并且增长过程呈现出明显的非线性特征。在较低的应力范围内(0～1600kPa),应变随应力迅速增加,在较高的应力范围内(1600kPa～4000kPa),应变随应力增长而缓慢增加。这就说明全强风化砂页岩发生压缩变形的难度随着压缩过程的推进而不断增加。在地层初始含水率在较小范围(12%～20%)时,当固结应力从0kPa到达1600kPa,地层初始含水率状土样的压缩变形量变化为0.10左右,占整个土层压缩过程总应变(0.14)的70%左右。

(2)土体的最终应变与地层的初始含水率有关系,地层初始含水率越大,土体的最终应变就越大,地层初始含水率为32%的土体在4000kPa压力作用下,最终应变为0.211,而地层初始含水率为12%的土体最终应变为0.123。

(3)不同初始含水率的土体应变随着固结压力的变化趋势基本一致,都是一个上凸的抛物线。初始含水率对土体的压密过程呈现阶段性的影响,当土体所受到的压应力处于较低范围(大致在0～800kPa),土体的压缩应变量随应力增长较快,初始含水率较低的土层应变增长较慢;当压应力处于中间范围(大致在 800 ~ 3200kPa)时,土体的压缩应变量随应力增长速度逐渐变慢,而到了较高压力范围(大致在 3200 ~ 4000kPa),土体的压缩应变量随应力增长并不明显。

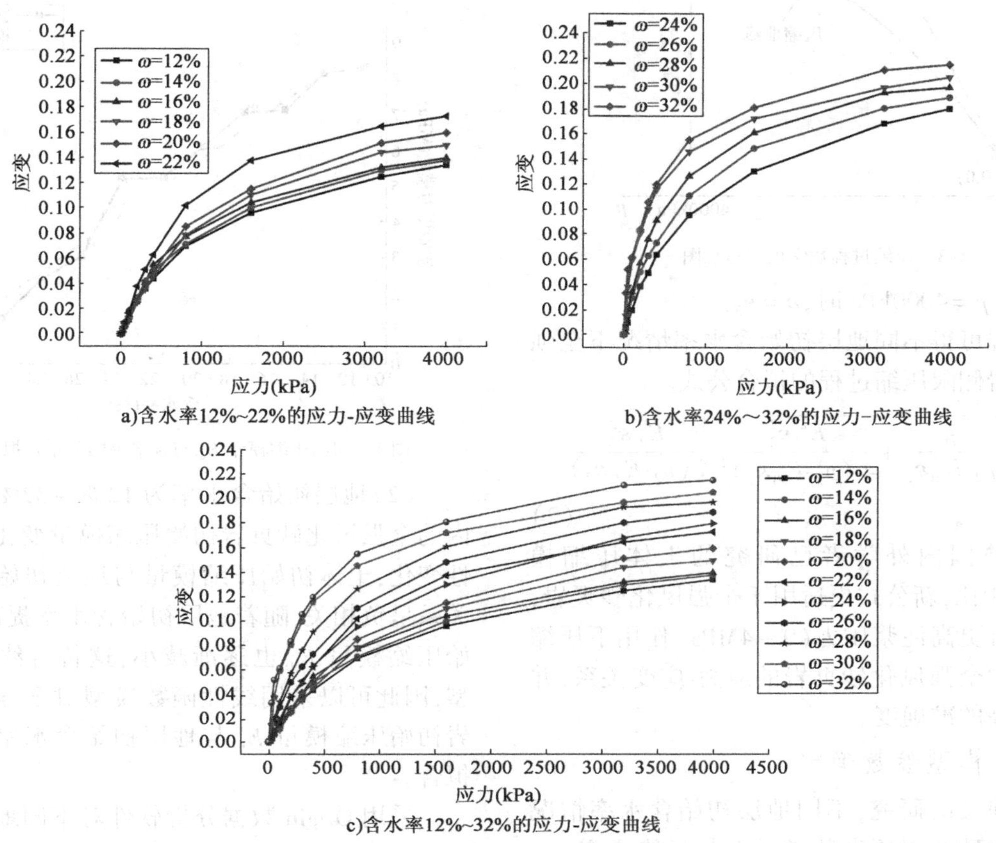

图 2 不同含水率应力与应变关系

2 压密过程数学模型

为了能够更好地研究不同地层初始含水率情况下土体所受浆液压力与土体压缩变形的关系,基于已经得到的不同地层初始含水率情况下室内固结压缩试验数据,建立数学模型方程,拟合试验数据,建立不同地层初始含水率情况下全强风化砂页岩压密过程的数学模型。

2.1 数学模型建立

根据前文室内侧限压缩试验,可以得到全强风化砂页岩的应力-应变曲线如图 3 所示,该应力-应变曲线穿过坐标轴的原点,即当不施加固结压力时,土体的压缩变形量为 0。在施加固结压力的开始阶段,土体压缩变形量增加比较快,在固结应力增长到最大固结压力的一半(2000kPa)时,整体变形量就已经完成了 70% 以上,在压缩的中后期缓慢上升,这具有十分明显的非线性特性。因此拟合模型可以选用二次抛物线模型,经过拟合后的全强风化砂页岩在压缩固结过程中方程式如下:

$$\varepsilon = A\sqrt{p+B}+C \tag{1}$$

式中:ε——全强风化砂页岩的土层应变;

p——土体所受应力大小;

A、B、C——表征初始含水率等土体特性的待定常数项。

初始压缩模量 E_{s0} 和最终应变 ε_2 用于拟合全强风化砂页岩压缩曲线,初始压缩模量 E_{s0} 可以反映地层初始压缩段的压缩速度,而最终应变 ε_2 可以反映地层的最终压密程度。式(2)和 E_{s0},ε_2 中的常数项应满足以下条件:

(1)ε-p 曲线通过原点(0,0),即$0=A\sqrt{B}+C$;

(2)$E_{s0}=\frac{dp}{d\varepsilon}|p=0$;

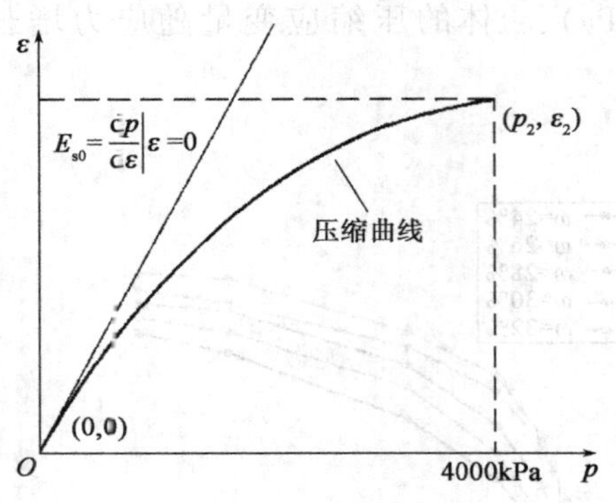

图3　压缩过程数学模型示意图

(3)当 $p=4000\text{kPa}$ 时，$\varepsilon=\varepsilon_2$。

解方程可得不同地层初始含水率情况下全强风化砂页岩侧限压缩过程的拟合公式。

$$\varepsilon=\varepsilon_2\sqrt{\frac{p}{p_2\text{-}E_{s0}\varepsilon_2}+\frac{E_{s0}^2\varepsilon_2^2}{4(p_2\text{-}E_{s0}\varepsilon_2)^2}}\text{-}\frac{E_{s0}\varepsilon_2^2}{2(p_2\text{-}E_{s0}\varepsilon_2)} \tag{2}$$

与之前国内外学者已研究的土体压缩模型[8-9,11-12]相比，新公式更适用于全强风化砂页岩，且能够拟合更高注浆压力(0～4MPa)作用下压缩变形过程中全强风化砂页岩的应力-应变关系，并且具有较高的准确度。

2.2　模型参数确定

根据前文的研究，不同地层初始含水率情况下全强风化砂页岩压密数学模型与最终应变 ε_2、初始压缩模量 E_{s0} 以及最大固结压力有关。

在全强风化砂页岩压密的数学模型中，可以直接从测试数据中获得最终应变 ε_2，而初始压缩模量 E_{s0} 由割线压缩模量0～50kPa确定。只考虑不同地层初始含水率对全强风化砂页岩的初始压缩模量 E_{s0} 和最终应变 ε_2 的影响。通过拟合实验数据得到初始压缩模量 E_{s0}、最终应变 ε_2 与初始含水量之间的定量关系，建立全强风化砂页岩压密数学模型。

以地层初始含水率(%)为横坐标，全强风化砂页岩初始压缩模量(MPa)为纵坐标，建立坐标系，土体初始压缩模量 E_{s0} 在不同地层初始含水率下的变化曲线如图4所示。

(1)在不同初始含水率条件下全强风化砂页岩初始压缩模量均不相同，且随地层初始含水率变换而变化。当地层初始含水率为12%时候，全强风化砂页岩的初始压缩模量最大，达到8.23 MPa，当地层初始含水率为32%时候，全强风化砂页岩的初始压缩模量最小，只有1.1MPa，这说明地层初始含水率越大，土体初始压缩模量 E_{s0} 就小，土体就越疏松，抵抗变形的能力就越弱。

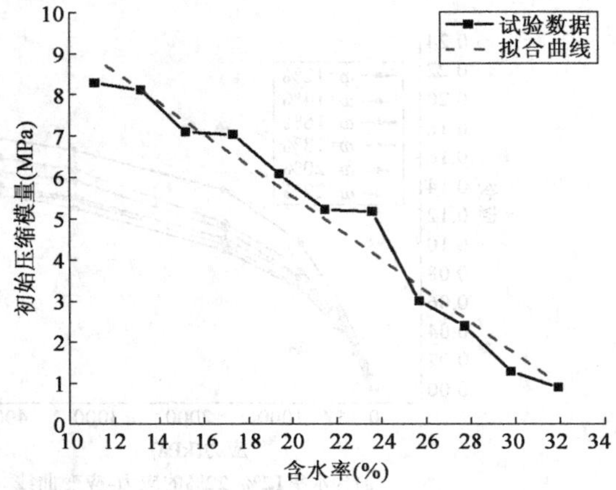

图4　初始压缩模量 E_{s0} 与含水率的关系及拟合曲线

(2)地层初始含水率为12%～32%这一区间内的全强风化砂页岩初始压缩模量变化基本呈线性变化，土体初始压缩模量与地层初始含水率的关系呈负相关，随着地层初始含水率提高，土体初始压缩模量 E_{s0} 也逐渐减小，这符合线性函数模型，因此可以采用线性函数模型对全强风化砂页岩初始压缩模量 E_{s0} 与地层初始含水率关系进行拟合。

采用Origin数据分析软件对不同地层初始含水率 ω_0 下的全强风化砂页岩初始压缩模量 E_{s0} 进行线性数据拟合，土体初始压缩模量 E_{s0} 与地层初始含水率拟合关系如下式：

$$E_{s0}=-0.39415\omega_0+14.03999 \tag{3}$$

式中，E_{s0} 单位为MPa。拟合后拟合优度为0.9964，拟合情况良好。

全强风化砂页岩初始压缩模量 E_{s0} 与地层初始含水率关系的试验数据与拟合数据如图4所示。由图可以看出，全强风化砂页岩初始压缩模量 E_{s0} 与地层初始含水率的拟合关系与实际实验数据基本重合，拟合优度为0.9964，拟合情况良好。

土体在 $p=4000\text{kPa}$ 时的最终应变量 ε_2 与地层初始含水率之间的关系也会影响土体压密数学模型的参数，以地层初始含水率(%)为横坐标，土体最终应变量 ε_2 为纵坐标，建立坐标系，最终应变量 ε_2 与地层初始含水率关系的关系如图5所示。

(1)在不同初始含水率条件下，土体最终压缩变形量均不相同且随地层初始含水率变换而变化。当地层初始含水率为12%时候，全强风化砂页岩的最终压缩变形量最小，只有0.135，当地层初始含水率为32%时候，土体的最终压缩变形量最大，达到0.213，比最小最终压缩变形量高出0.078，这说明地层初始含水率越大，土体的结构就越疏松，受到浆液的压力作用后越容易发生压缩变形，且压缩变形量越大。

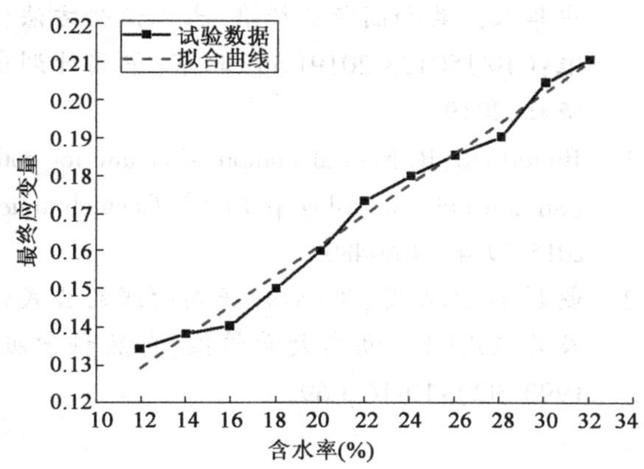

图5 最终应变量 ε_2 与含水率的关系及拟合曲线

(2)地层初始含水率为12%～32%这一区间内的土体最终压缩变形量变化基本呈线性变化，土体初始压缩模量与地层初始含水率的关系呈正相关，随着地层初始含水率提高，土体初始压缩模量 E_{s0} 也逐渐增高，当地层含水率在13%～17%和21%～27%范围内，最终压缩变形量 ε_2 随地层含水率变化比较缓慢，而在其他范围内，最终压缩变形量 ε_2 随地层初始含水率变化相对较大，但从总体趋势上来看，最终应变量 ε_2 随地层初始含水率 ω_0 变化在含水率12%～32%范围内是呈线性正相关关系，即地层初始含水率 ω_0 越高，土体最终压缩应变量 ε_2 越大。

综上所述，土体最终应变量 ε_2 与地层初始含水率变化关系符合一次线性函数模型，因此可以采用一次线性函数模型对土体最终应变量 ε_2 与地层初始含水率关系进行拟合。拟合所用的程序为Origin绘图应用程序，拟合得到的方程如式(4)所示。

$$\varepsilon_2 = 0.00408\omega_0 + 0.07613 \tag{4}$$

式中：ε_2——最终压缩应变量。

土体最终应变量 ε_2 与地层初始含水率关系的试验数据与拟合数据如图5所示。由图可以看出，土体最终应变量 ε_2 与地层初始含水率的拟合关系与实际实验数据基本重合，拟合优度为0.98423，拟合情况良好。

结合前文的研究结果，将已经建立的土体压密过程数学模型与最终应变量 ε_2 公式以及初始压缩模量 E_{s0} 拟合公式相结合，可以得到完整的拟合公式(5)，该公式建立了全强风化砂页岩的压密特性与地层含水量之间的定量关系。此公式可用于准确预测萍莲高速工程全强风化砂页岩劈裂压密注浆过程中土体的压密过程。

$$\begin{cases} \varepsilon = \varepsilon_2\sqrt{\dfrac{p}{p_2 - E_{s0}\varepsilon_2} + \dfrac{E_{s0}^2\varepsilon_2^2}{4(p_2 - E_{s0}\varepsilon_2)^2}} - \dfrac{E_{s0}\varepsilon_2^2}{2(p_2 - E_{s0}\varepsilon_2)} \\ E_{s0} = -0.39415\omega_0 + 14.03999 \\ \varepsilon = 0.00408\omega_0 + 0.07613 \end{cases} \tag{5}$$

式中：ε——土体压缩应变量；

p——土体所受压应力；

E_{s0}——土体初始压缩模量(MPa)；

ε_2——土体在 $P = 4000\text{kPa}$ 对应的最终压缩量；

ω_0——地层初始含水率。

该公式适用范围：(1)地层初始含水率在13%～33%区间内；(2)注浆过程中注浆压力在0～4MPa区间内。

3 结语

(1)在全强风化砂页岩地层压密过程中，应力-应变关系呈现出明显的非线性特征。在较低的应力范围内(0～1600kPa)，应变随应力迅速增加，在较高的应力范围内(1600kPa～4000kPa)，应变随应力增长而缓慢增加。

(2)在注浆压密过程中，全强风化砂页岩地层最终应变与地层的初始含水率有关系，地层初始含水率越大，土体的最终应变就越大，地层初始含水率为32%的土体在4000kPa压力作用下，最终应变为0.211，而地层初始含水率为12%的土体最终应变为0.123。

(3)建立了可描述不同含水率条件下全强风化砂页岩地层压密过程的二次抛物线数学模型，拟合得到的曲线与实际试验数据吻合对应情况良好，可为全强风化砂页岩劈裂压密注浆过程的综合分析及其应用提供参考。

参考文献

[1] 张伟杰. 隧道工程富水断层破碎带注浆加固

机理及应用研究[D]. 济南:山东大学,2014.
[2] 李术才,张伟杰,张庆松,等. 富水断裂带优势劈裂注浆机制及注浆控制方法研究[J]. 岩土力学. 2014(03):744-752.
[3] 张忠苗,邹健. 桩底劈裂注浆扩散半径和注浆压力研究[J]. 岩土工程学报. 2008(02):181-184.
[4] 邹金锋,李亮,杨小礼. 劈裂注浆扩散半径及压力衰减分析[J]. 水利学报. 2006(03):314-319.
[5] 孙锋,陈铁林,张顶立,等. 基于宾汉体浆液的海底隧道劈裂注浆机制研究[J]. 北京交通大学学报(自然科学版),2009,33(4):1-6.
[6] 张庆松,张连震,刘人太,等. 基于"浆-土"界面应力耦合效应的劈裂注浆理论研究[J]. 岩土工程学报. 2016(02):323-330.
[7] 叶飞,陈治,苟长飞,等. 基于球孔扩张的盾构隧道壁后注浆压密模型[J]. 交通运输工程学报,2014,14(1):8.
[8] 曹文贵,李鹏,张超,等. 土的初始和再压缩曲线分析模型[J]. 岩石力学与工程学报,2015(A01):8.
[9] 王志亮,郑明新,李永池. 求前期固结应力的数学模型研究及应用[J]. 岩土力学,2005(10):1587-1590.
[10] 中华人民共和国行业标准. 土工试验方法标准:GB/T50123-2019[S]. 北京:中国计划出版社,2019.
[11] Butterfield, R. Natural compression law for soils (an advance on e-log p′)[J]. Geotechnique, 2015,29(4):469-480.
[12] 赵明华,王贻荪,肖鹤松. 压缩曲线的公式化及其应用[J]. 湖南大学学报:自然科学版,1990(02):10-16+69.

上覆流砂层隧道围岩大变形与衬砌受力特征现场监测研究

李嘉琦*　王志丰　王亚琼　常宏涛
(长安大学陕西省公路桥梁与隧道重点实验室)

摘　要　上覆流砂层结构松散,层间结合力较差,在隧道开挖过程中易出现大变形、钢拱架扭曲破坏、支护混凝土开裂剥落等灾害。以宁夏中香隧道工程为依托,开展对拱顶沉降、围岩压力和钢拱架应力等的现场监测,探讨了上覆流砂层隧道围岩大变形与衬砌受力特征,并针对性地提出相应的变形控制措施与施工建议。研究结果表明:拱顶沉降、围岩压力和钢拱架应力随时间变形规律基本保持一致;拱顶沉降和围岩压力呈现出明显的"左大右小"的非对称性分布特征,最大值均发生在左拱肩位置,分别为492.8mm和0.541MPa;围岩压力和钢拱架应力在横断面空间分布上表现出"上部大,下部小"的离散性分布特征。研究方法和结论可为类似上覆流砂段隧道工程的设计、施工和灾害处置提供一定的参考。

关键词　隧道工程　流砂地层　现场监测　围岩变形　衬砌受力

0　引言

随着我国交通基础设施投资的持续增长,高速铁路的建设也迎来了一个崭新的时期。截止到2019年底,我国高速铁路运营总里程已突破3.5万km,越来越多的特长隧道修建在复杂的地质环境中。在隧道施工过程中,流砂层作为一种复杂地质软岩体,由于其结构松散,胶结程度低、抗拉及抗压强度低、自稳能力差[1-2],隧道在穿越该类地层时极易发生工程灾害,造成较大的经济损失。

目前,国内外学者在软弱围岩隧道大变形现场测试方面开展了丰富的研究,取得了一定的研究成果。晏长根等[3]以成武高速武都西隧道为工程依托开展现场测试,获得了深埋千枚岩偏压隧道3层支护变形及荷载分布规律。戴永浩等[4]依托兰新铁路大梁隧道工程开展围岩大变形现场监测,并针对性的提出了提出了软岩大变形洞段联合支护方案。郭健等[5]对香丽高速海巴洛隧道进行现场测试,探讨了不同施工阶段炭质板岩隧道大变形段衬砌受力特征。韩现民等[6]依托关角隧道开展现场试验,根据现场监测结果确定了炭质板岩隧道的合理支护参数。刘志春等[7]对乌鞘岭隧道F4断层大变形段进行了现场测试,对开挖后的衬砌结构稳定性进行了分析判断。李鹏飞等[8]依托宜万铁路堡镇隧道开展围岩变形及衬砌受力现场监测,得到围岩压力与初期支护体系各子构件的力学特性。而现阶段关于隧道穿越流砂层支护受力方面的研究则相对较少,如:李清川等[9]依托青岛地铁M2号啤苗区间施工段,建立了开挖面失稳破坏力学模型,并通过数值模拟得到了上覆流砂层地质下开挖面的典型破坏参数。刘平等[10]通过建立数值模型,研究了富水砂层影响下隧道围岩的变形破坏机制。综上可知,现阶段缺乏隧道穿越流砂段时断面开挖后隧道围岩变形规律与支护结构受力特征的研究,且针对上覆流砂层隧道施工变形控制措施和灾害处置技术的研究相对较少。

基于此,本文以宁夏中香隧道上覆流砂段为工程背景,选取典型施工断面开展围岩变形、围岩压力、钢拱架应力等的现场监测,探讨上覆流砂层隧道施工过程中围岩变形规律及衬砌结构受力特征,研究成果以期为类似工程提供一定的参考。

1 工程概况及测试方案

1.1 工程概况

依托工程为宁夏省中卫市中香隧道,为双线单洞特长铁路隧道,设计开挖高度为13.09m,跨度为14.98m。隧址区内断裂带极为发育,与线路相交的断裂带主要为北西向,由北向南依次分布有9条大型断裂带。受F5断裂带影响,K44+175~K44+420段围岩条件较差,在施工中多次遭遇流砂、涌水、初期支护开裂等现象。

隧道施工至断面K44+180断面时,掌子面揭露围岩分别为砂质黄土和灰褐色砂岩夹泥,如图1所示,围岩整体稳定性差,拱顶左侧有间歇性流砂涌入,初期支护发生不均匀沉降,喷射混凝土局部开裂、剥落,钢拱架部分发生弯折破坏。

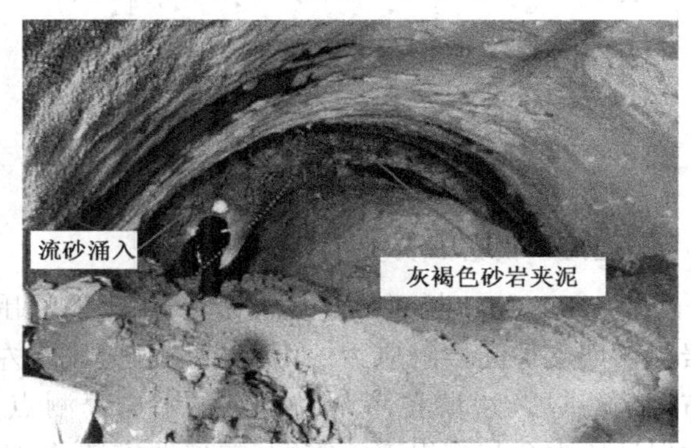

图1 掌子面揭露围岩情况

该区段原设计采用三台阶预留核心土法开挖,原设计参数如表1所示。

隧道支护原设计参数 表1

支护类型	项目	支护参数
初期支护	喷射混凝土	24cm厚C25
	钢筋网	Φ8钢筋网
	边墙锚杆	Φ22砂浆锚杆
	锚杆长度	4m
	钢拱架型号	I22a
	钢拱架间距	70cm
二次衬砌	二衬混凝土型号	C35
	拱墙厚度	50cm
	仰拱厚度	60cm

1.2 测试方案

针对中香隧道在前期施工过程中出现局部间歇性流砂涌出、初期支护变形过大等问题,为进一步探究上覆流砂段隧道初期支护沉降规律和结构受力特征,依据文献指导[11],选取 K44 + 200 断面,除拱顶沉降、水平收敛等必测项目外,增设围岩压力和钢拱架应力监测项目。

1.2.1　围岩变形监测

K44 + 200 断面围岩变形测点布置图如图 2 所示,围岩变形采用非接触坐标法测量,采用测量精度为 0.01mm 的徕卡全站仪进行观测,通过坐标换算得到每一测点的拱顶沉降量和水平收敛量。

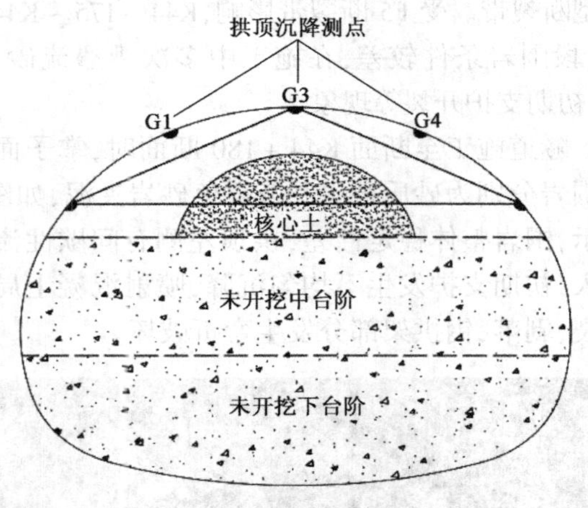

图 2　围岩变形测点布设图

1.2.2　围岩压力监测

在 K44 + 200 断面布设土压力盒,用以监测围岩与初期支护间接触应力。沿开挖轮廓分别在左右拱肩/拱腰/边墙位置对称布设,共 6 个测点。为保证压力盒与围岩表面密贴,在仪器安装前,需锤击整平围岩并用水泥砂浆找平,各测点布设一个土压力盒,共计 6 个压力盒。同时,为避免喷射混凝土施工时破坏仪器导线,将监测导线沿着竖向钢筋固定。布设情况如图 3 所示。

1.2.3　钢拱架应力监测

在 K44 + 200 断面钢拱架上布设钢拱架应力计,用以监测钢拱架应力。沿开挖轮廓分别在左/右拱肩/拱腰/边墙位置对称布设,共 6 个测点,每个测点均在钢拱架上下翼缘内侧布设一个应力计,共计 12 个应力计。布设情况如图 4 所示。

2　监测结果与分析

2.1　拱顶沉降测试分析

K44 + 200 断面拱顶沉降数据如图 5 所示,分析拱顶沉降时程曲线图,可得结论如下:

(1)典型断面拱顶各测点的沉降速率与累积沉降值存在较大差异,但是沉降变形随时间增长的规律基本保持一致,总体上可概括为“急剧变形期、持续变形期、变形稳定期”三个阶段;

(2)隧道上台阶开挖后的 13d 内,拱顶沉降处于急剧变形期,各测点最大沉降速率分别为 39.2mm/d、23.6mm/d 和 21.9mm/d,平均沉降速率为 25.9mm/d、17.3mm/d 和 15.7mm/d,此阶段沉降变形量约占总沉降量的 68% ~77%;

(3)K44 + 200 断面采用三台阶法开挖,受中下台阶施工扰动的影响,拱顶各测点沉降值在断面开挖后第 6d(中台阶开挖)和第 19d(下台阶开挖)均有不同程度“跃迁”,其中左拱肩测点表现最为明显。笔者分析认为中下台阶开挖导致上部拱架短期悬空,断面左侧围岩为第三系松散流砂层,围岩自稳能力差,因此对施工扰动的敏感性较强;

(4)典型断面隧道拱顶沉降存在明显的“非对称性”,呈现出左侧沉降大于右侧沉降的特点。左拱肩测点在断面开挖后 28d 左右逐渐趋于稳定,最终沉降累积值为 492.8mm;拱顶和右拱肩测点稳定时间约为 24d,拱顶中线测点最终沉降值为 302.9mm,右拱肩测点最终沉降值为 264.2mm。

2.2　围岩压力测试分析

图 6 给出了 K44 + 200 断面围岩压力时程曲线图,通过分析得到如下结论:

(1)断面开挖后,各测点的围岩压力随时间而迅速增加,除左拱肩测点外,其他测点在开挖后 7d 内处于急剧增大期,之后增长速率逐渐放缓,围岩压力趋于稳定。

(2)左拱肩测点围岩压力随时间变化的规律与沉降变形的时程曲线类似,开挖后 8d 内围岩压力急剧增长,达到 0.32MPa;中台阶开挖及支护施作后,围岩压力增速减缓,处于持续增长期;下台阶开挖及仰拱闭合后,围岩压力逐渐趋于稳定。

(3)围岩压力在洞周的空间上呈现明显的“上大下小”的离散性分布特征,整体分布规律为:拱肩 > 拱腰 > 边墙,围岩压力最大值位于左拱肩位置,与普氏理论塌落拱的形状基本保持一致。

(4)受上覆流砂层的影响,上台阶围岩与初期支护结构的接触应力呈现明显的“非对称性”,左拱肩围岩压力远大于右拱肩;与拱顶沉降相类似,左拱肩测点处的围岩压力受中下台阶施工扰动的影响,出现小幅度跃迁,之后随着围岩应力的重分布和围岩与初期支护的协调变形而回落。

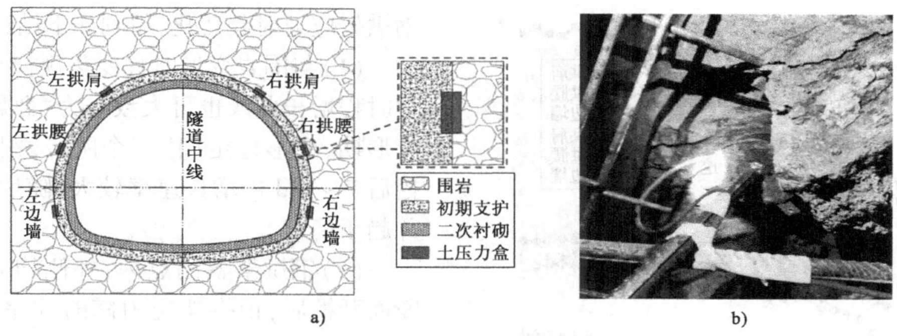

a) b)

图3 围岩压力测点布设图

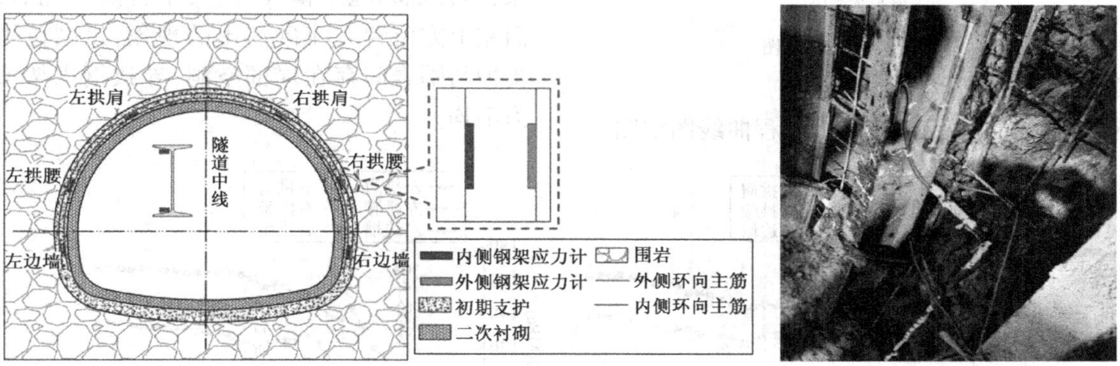

a) b)

图4 钢拱架应力测点布设图

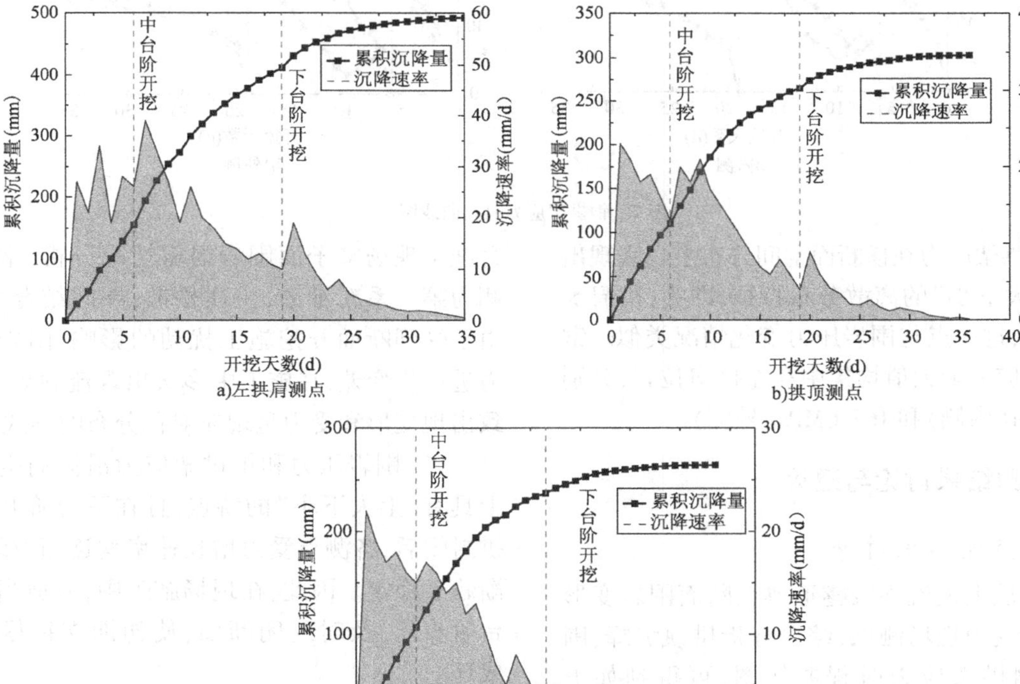

a)左拱肩测点

b)拱顶测点

c)右拱肩测点

图5 拱顶沉降时程曲线图

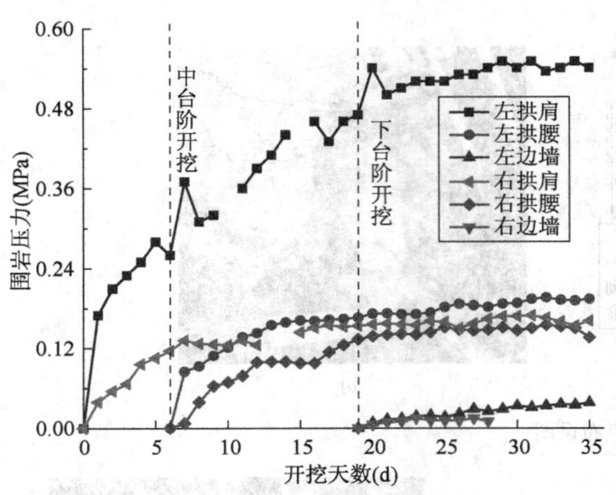

图6　围岩压力时程曲线图

2.3　拱架应力测试分析

K44+200断面钢拱架应力时程曲线图如图7所示(规定压应力为正,拉应力为负)。通过分析钢拱架应力时程变化,得到如下结论:

(1)与围岩变形时程变化规律类似,钢拱架应力时程增长曲线也可大致分为"急剧变形期、持续变形期、变形稳定期"三个阶段,钢拱架应力在开挖后7~10d内增长速率较大,随后增长逐渐放缓并趋于稳定。

(2)钢拱架各测点内、外侧均处于受压状态,断面开挖后,钢拱架应力随时间呈线性增长的趋势。左拱腰测点在开挖初期出现了应力降低的现象,结合现场施工情况分析,中台阶开挖后,掌子面左上方位置有流砂涌出的现象,拱腰位置初期支护与围岩间存在局部空洞,导致钢拱架整体受力不均。

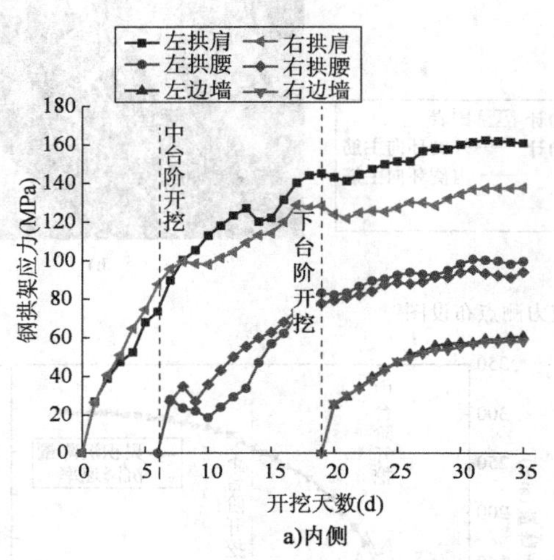

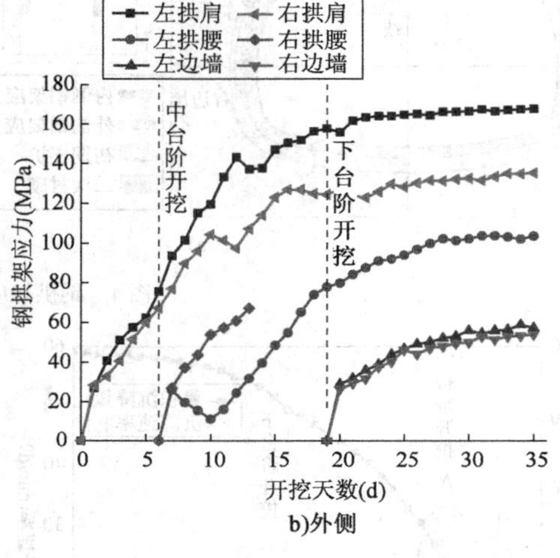

图7　钢拱架应力时程曲线图

(3)钢拱架应力在横断面空间分布上也表现出明显的"上大下小"的离散分布特征,即为:拱肩>拱腰>边墙,这一点与围岩压力变化情况类似。钢拱架内外侧应力最大值均集中在左拱肩位置,分别为160.9MPa(内侧)和167.6MPa(外侧)。

3　监测结果讨论与建议

3.1　监测结果讨论

通过开展上覆流砂段隧道典型断面围岩变形与初期支护受力现场测试,综合分析拱顶沉降、围岩压力和钢拱架应力时程曲线图,可得到如下结论:

(1)拱顶沉降与围岩压力呈现显著的"左大右小"的非对称分布特点,具体表现为:左拱肩测点的沉降值和围岩压力值均大于右拱肩相应值。结合施工现场掌子面围岩揭露情况分析,掌子面左侧为第三系粉细砂,土质松散,层间结合力较差,由于受到断面开挖施工扰动的影响,围岩自稳能力进一步变差,在施工中多次出现流砂等现象,导致出现变形和受力呈现非对称分布的形式。

(2)围岩压力和钢拱架应力沿洞周空间分布上具有"上大下小"的特点,且在下台阶开挖及仰拱封闭后,各测点受力增长速率均逐渐放缓,并逐渐趋于稳定。因此,在现场施工中,应适当缩短各台阶步长,及时封闭断面,使初期支护尽早封闭成环。

(3)拱顶沉降、围岩压力和钢拱架应力随时间增长规律基本保持一致,在断面开挖后7~10d内数值均处于急剧增长期;中下台阶开挖后,各测点监测值均有不同幅度的"跃迁"现象。在上覆流砂段隧道施工中,要严格控制各分部开挖,尽量减少对围岩和已有支护结构的扰动,避免进一步加剧断面变形。

3.2 变形控制措施及建议

针对中香隧道上覆流砂层隧道施工段(K44 + 175 ~ K44 + 420 段),断面开挖后发生围岩变形过大、初期支护混凝土局部剥落、钢架扭曲等灾害,提出如下变形控制措施及建议[12-13]:

(1)调整支护参数。对初期支护结构参数进行调整加强,钢拱架由现阶段的 I22a 调整为 I25b,钢拱架间距由 70cm 调整为 60cm,C25 喷射混凝土厚度由 24cm 调整为 28cm。

(2)拱脚局部加固。中、下台阶开挖后,在断面左侧拱脚位置采用长度为 7.5m 的 Φ108mm × 6mm 钢管进行注浆加固,钢管纵向间距为 60cm,外插角度为 55°。

(3)超前注浆加固。对未开挖部分采用长度为 4.2m 的 Φ40mm × 4.5mm 的小导管进行超前注浆加固,纵向间距为 50cm,外插角度为 30°,注浆材料采用水灰比为 0.8 ~ 1.0 的硅酸盐水泥单浆液。

(4)施工辅助措施。增设超前泄水孔,对后续区段的地下水进行引排,降低围岩含水率;局部断面变形过大时,及时插入临时钢拱架和竖向钢架支撑,控制初期支护变形。

4 结语

(1)拱顶沉降、围岩压力和钢拱架应力在断面开挖后,数值均随时间呈线性增长趋势,时程增长曲线可大致分为“急剧变形期、持续变形期、变形稳定期”三个阶段。

(2)上覆流砂层隧道断面开挖后,拱顶沉降和围岩压力呈现明显的“左大右小”的非对称性分布特点,拱顶沉降和围岩压力最大值有较强的对应关系,均出现在左拱肩位置,最终监测值分别为 492.8mm 和 0.541MPa。

(3)围岩与初期支护的接触应力和钢拱架应力沿洞周在横断面空间分布上表现出“上部大,下部小”的离散性分布特征,即为:拱肩 > 拱腰 > 边墙。

(4)通过对现场监测结果进行分析和讨论,为解决上覆流砂层隧道施工阶段出现的大变形等灾害,应适当提高初期支护强度,减少分部开挖时的施工扰动;同时提出“调整支护参数、拱脚局部加固、超前注浆加固和施工辅助设施”的变形控制措施及建议。

参考文献

[1] 何满潮,景海河,孙晓明. 软岩工程力学[M]. 北京:科学出版社,2002.

[2] 张红军. 上覆富水砂层隧道开挖面稳定性分析与注浆加固对策研究[D]. 山东大学,2017.

[3] 晏长根,罗鑫,王凯,等. 深埋软岩大变形偏压公路隧道 3 层支护结构受力变形特征[J]. 中国公路学报,2016,29(2):98-107.

[4] 戴永浩,陈卫忠,田洪铭,等. 大梁隧道软岩大变形及其支护方案研究[J]. 岩石力学与工程学报,2015,34(增2):4149-4156.

[5] 郭健,阳军生,陈维,等. 基于现场实测的炭质板岩隧道围岩大变形与衬砌受力特征研究[J]. 岩石力学与工程学报,2019,38(04):832-841.

[6] 韩现民,孙明磊,李文江,等. 复杂条件下隧道断面形状和支护参数优化[J]. 岩土力学,2011,32(增1):725-731.

[7] 刘志春,李文江,孙明磊,等. 乌鞘岭隧道 F4 断层区段监控量测综合分析[J]. 岩石力学与工程学报,2006,25(7):1 502-1 511.

[8] 李鹏飞,田四明,赵勇,等. 高地应力软弱围岩隧道初期支护受力特性的现场监测研究[J]. 岩石力学与工程学报, 2013, 32 (S2): 3509-3519.

[9] 李清川,李术才,王汉鹏,等. 上覆流沙层隧道开挖面稳定性分析与数值试验研究[J]. 岩土力学,2018,39(07):2681-2690.

[10] 刘平,刘池,王洪涛,等. 富水砂层影响下隧道围岩变形破坏机制的数值模拟研究[J]. 现代隧道技术,2020,57(04):74-81.

[11] 中华人民共和国行业标准. 公路隧道施工技术规范:JTG/T 3660-2020[S]. 北京:人民交通出版社股份有限公司,2020.

[12] 刘晓杰,梁庆国,刘传新,等. 富水深埋黄土隧道变形规律及控制措施[J]. 隧道与地下工程灾害防治,2021,3(2):23-32.

[13] 宋瑞霞,赵永虎,米维军,等. 帷幕注浆在富水大跨度黄土隧道中的应用[J]. 隧道与地下工程灾害防治,2021,3(2):43-48.

超大断面盾构隧道纠偏引发的管片衬砌损伤研究

张稳军*　周鑫南
(天津大学建筑工程学院)

摘　要　为探明盾构动态纠偏的偏载对管片力学特性的影响,本文采用 ABAQUS 建立模型来模拟千斤顶荷载和盾尾刷反力对盾构隧道的作用,通过损伤面积比来定义管片的损伤程度。最后总结管片损伤的规律,对超大断面盾构隧道纠偏给出合理化建议。研究结果表明:①盾构机直线掘进时最大应力出现在第四环管片,曲线掘进时最大应力出现在作用有施工荷载的管片。②深埋状态下曲线掘进是最不利的工况。③各工况下损伤最严重的是存在千斤顶推力和盾尾刷反力的管片。

关键词　盾构隧道　纠偏　数值模拟　千斤顶荷载　盾尾刷反力　管片损伤

0　引言

盾构纠偏是指当盾构掘进方向与设计方向相比发生了偏移,需要调整千斤顶推力来让盾构机转向回到设计位置,该过程会对后面的管片产生偏载。为减小纠偏导致的损害,研究盾构纠偏之后管片的力学分析尤为重要。

近年来针对盾构隧道管片损伤因素和盾构纠偏问题,业界已积累了一定经验。许鸣蝉、张子新[1]结合虹梅南路金海路通道越江段工程,对管片损伤状况进行了调查,总结出了管片开裂的主要原因。秦建设[2]分析了盾构掘进时管片受到的作用力,对于姿态控制引起的管片错台进行了分析。段红海、方诗诗、赵东华[3]等通过数值模拟发现管环纵向应力最大值出现在管片的水平方向内及外侧。王宏[4]对盾构处于小半径曲线且坡度大的情况进行受力分析,发现造成管片破损的主要原因是撑靴对管片的侧向分力。杨栓民[5]通过对盾构隧道的曲线拟合得出了楔形量、管片长度、拟合误差等参数之间的关系,使盾构的施工更加接近设计曲线。张文萃[6]通过汇总提炼纠偏曲线类型,提出了综合考虑盾尾间隙、千斤顶行程差和管片柔和度的点位计算方法。陈俊生、莫海鸿[7]通过建立块体类盾构机尾实体模型,得到了盾尾刷反力在盾构机姿势调整时对管片的内力和错台量的影响规律。高超[8]结合软土地层盾构掘进施工实例,分析研究了盾构掘进施工中姿态控制要点并相应施工注意事项。

目前国内盾构纠偏已不局限于小半径,开始向隧道断面更大、纠偏更加精准的趋势发展。鉴于此,本文以右纠偏为例,针对纠偏造成管片衬砌损伤力学开展研究分析,利用 ABAQUS 模拟纠偏阶段千斤顶推力和盾尾刷反力对超大断面盾构隧道衬砌管片的作用,得到管片的受力变形情况和破坏损伤过程并总结损伤规律。

1　工程背景

某工程路线全长约 16km,新建隧道长度 9.2km,(其中盾构段 7.4km,明挖段 1.8km)。该工程是目前国内最大直径隧道,属于超大直径盾构隧道。盾构段隧道穿越的地层主要为粉细砂、中砂、粉质黏土、透水性高,另外隧道埋深大、承压水头高:隧道覆土厚度约为 10~42m,近 3~5 年平均水位高程:15.0m(潜水),承受最大的水压约 0.59MPa。

2　数值模型建立

该工程盾构隧道主体结构单环衬砌采用 1 块封顶块、2 块邻接块、7 块标准块的分块方式,其中衬砌环外径为 15.4m,内径为 14.1m,衬砌厚度为 0.65m,衬砌宽度平均为 2m,其管环分块情况如图 1 所示。

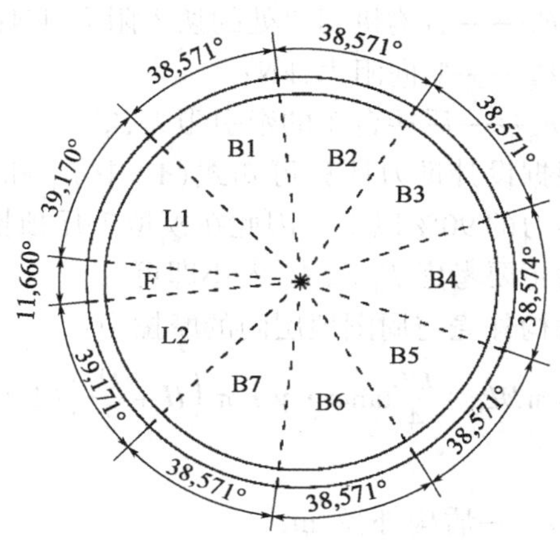

图1 管环分块图

隧道主体结构衬砌管片采用 C60 钢筋混凝土，混凝土抗渗等级为 P12。钢筋采用 HPB300、HRB400 级的钢筋；隧道采用错缝拼装，管片环向接缝采用斜螺栓连接，纵向接缝采用直螺栓连接，连接盾构管片的环、纵向螺栓均为机械性能等级 8.8 级的普通螺栓。

本模型中选取的相互作用类型是表面与表面接触，采取的滑移公式为小滑移公式。定义接触面上的切向行为为“罚”摩擦公式，摩擦系数取 0.3；定义接触面上的法向行为为硬接触，即主接触面和次接触面已经分离不发生接触关系。其余的选择默认。

盾构机直线推进时，加载千斤顶推力的一边不固定，另一边采用绞接固定边界；盾构机曲线推进时将另一边从铰接变为完全固定。数值模型如图2所示。

图2 实体模型图

2.1 材料参数及本构模型

本文在弹性模型试算的基础上引入混凝土塑性损伤模型。管片的塑性损伤参数如表1所示。

混凝土塑性损伤主要参数 表1

E(Pa)	θ	ρ(kg/m^3)	μ	c	φ(°)	fb_0/fc_0	k
3.6×10^{10}	0.2	2600	0.005	0.1	40	1.16	0.67

其中 E 为杨氏模量，θ 为泊松比，ρ(kg/m^3) 为混凝土密度，μ 为黏滞系数，c 为偏心率，φ 为剪胀角，fb_0/fc_0 为混凝土双轴受压与单轴受压极限强度比，k 为屈服常数。除此之外其余材料全部为钢材料，其弹性杨氏模量为 20.6GPa，泊松比为 0.3。

2.2 荷载参数

2.2.1 土荷载

本文采用 Mohr-Coulomb 模型作为土体的本构模型，采用太沙基理论计算土压力，土体主要物理力学参数见表2。

土体主要物理力学参数（根据地质勘察报告） 表2

土层名称	黏聚力 c(kPa)	内摩擦角 φ(°)	侧压力系数 λ	γ(kN/m^3)/γ_{sat}(kN/m^3)	分布深度(m)
粉土素填土	8	10	—	18.5/19.5	20～15
细砂	0	30	0.42	19.5/20.5	15～0
黏土	30	10	0.45	18.5/19.5	0～-2
细砂	0	30	0.42	19.5/20.5	-2～-8
粉质黏土	30	18	0.43	19.0/20.0	-8～-12
细砂	0	30	0.42	19.5/20.5	-12～-16
粉质黏土	30	18	0.43	19.0/20.0	-16～-40

2.2.2　千斤顶推力

本文以压强的形式来代替环缝面上的千斤顶推力,将整个环缝面分为 A、B、C、D 四个区(每个区域被两条蓝色虚线所夹),除封顶块只有一个千斤顶作用外,其余每个管片上都有 2 个千斤顶,千斤顶分区图如图 3 所示,千斤顶推力如表 3 所示。

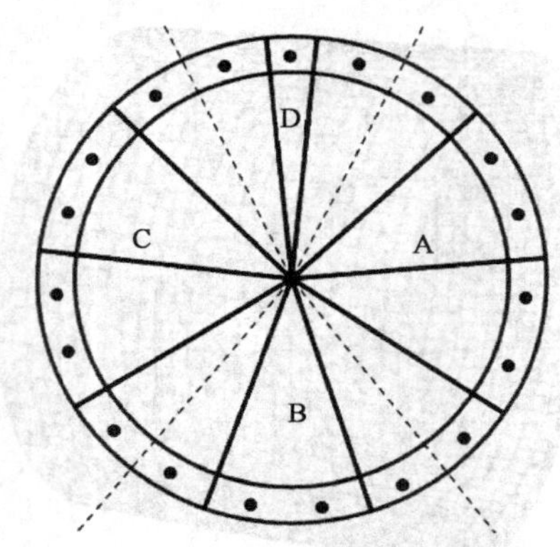

图 3　千斤顶分区图

千斤顶推力设计值 F_d 由五部分组成[9]:

$$F_d = F_1 + F_2 + F_3 + F_4 + F_5 + F_6 \quad (1)$$

式中:F_1——盾构外壳与周围地层间的摩擦力,kN;

F_2——盾构机推进时的正面推进阻力,kN

F_3——管片与盾尾间的摩阻力,kN;

F_4——盾构机切口处的切入阻力,kN;

F_5——变向阻力,kN;

F_6——后接台车的牵引阻力,kN。

根据设计推力计算可知式(1)中 F_1 和 F_2 占整个推力的 90% 以上。因此在模拟千斤顶推力的大小时主要考虑 F_1 和 F_2 大小即可。

盾构外壳与周围地层间的摩擦力:

$$F_1 = \pi DLc + \frac{DL}{4}\tan\varphi \cdot \gamma \cdot \pi \left(H + \frac{D}{2}\right)(1 + K) \quad (2)$$

式中:D——盾构外径,m;

L——盾构长度,m;

c——土体黏聚力;

φ——内摩擦角;

H——覆土厚度,m;

K——静止侧压力系数。

$$F_2 = \frac{\pi D^2}{4}(1-\alpha_0)KH_c\gamma \quad (3)$$

式中:γ——土体重度;

H_c——地面到盾构机轴线的距离,m。

由以上式(2)、式(3)可得深埋、中埋、浅埋工况下的千斤顶设计推力;又因为总推力要大于各项阻力之和,因此需要有一定的余裕量,一般取 2 倍设计推力。其值如表 3 所示。

三种工况下的千斤顶推力　　表 3

埋置深度	千斤顶设计推力(kN)	千斤顶设备推力(kN)	单个千斤顶推力(kN)
浅埋(16m)	65784.1	131568.1	6924.6
中埋(30m)	94360.5	188720.9	9932.7
深埋(40m)	114772.3	229544.6	12081.3

曲线推进时会受到大小不同的千斤顶力。根据某地铁工程隧道施工数据,曲线推进时受偏载作用的千斤顶上的推力应是在直线推进的基础上提高 66%。

2.2.3　盾尾刷反力

管片在纠偏阶段或着转弯时盾尾刷会对管片产生一定的挤压作用,这就是盾尾刷反力。盾构机一般设置 3 ~ 5 道盾尾刷。由于盾尾刷的材质是钢丝,刚度很小,起初不会对管片起到挤压作用;但当盾构机工作一段时间后,浆液会充满盾尾刷的间隙,凝固后使得盾尾刷的刚度增大,在盾构机纠偏或转弯时对管片造成一定的挤压。

本文中用作用在环面上的集中力代替盾尾刷反力,根据某工程的盾尾刷反力取值范围为 115 ~ 189kN[10],本文取盾尾刷反力为 120kN。

3　右纠偏荷载工况下的管片内力影响分析

3.1　右纠偏浅埋工况下的管片应力分析

3.1.1　直线掘进管片应力分析

图 4 为浅埋工况下直线管片的应力图。

由图 4 可知,盾构整体结构受力合理,盾构左右受力对称,应力最大地方在第四环管片内侧一圈。浅埋直线时管片受到的最大应力值为 2×10^6 N,混凝土管片的屈服应力为 3.6×10^7 N,因此管片未超过屈服应力,管片损伤不明显。

3.1.2　曲线掘进(右纠偏)管片应力分析

在千斤顶推力和盾尾刷反力的作用下混凝土

管环受压损伤云图如图 5 所示。

图 4 盾构机直线管片 Mises 应力图

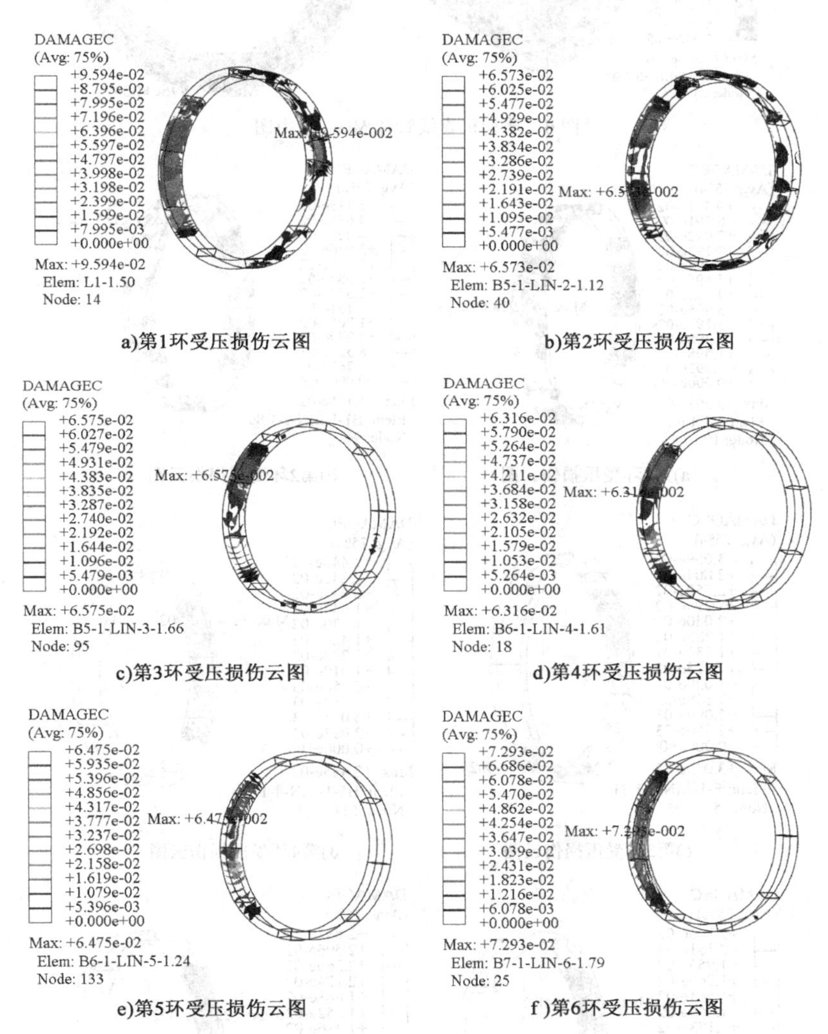

图 5 浅埋下第 1 ~ 6 环管片损伤云图

由图 5 可知,管片 1 ~ 6 环中受压面积主要集中在分区千斤顶推力增大的地方,曲线掘进或者是纠偏过程中管片最先受到破坏的就是这一部分管片。此外,第 1、2 环管片右半部分都有受压面积存在(第 3 环右半部分受压面积很小,可忽略不计),这是由于管片第 1 环、第 2 环右半部分受到了盾尾刷反力的作用,但盾尾刷反力在量级大小上与千斤顶推力有较大差异,因而受压面积有明显不同。

3.2　右纠偏中埋工况下的管片应力分析

3.2.1　直线掘进管片应力分析

图 6 为中埋工况下直线管片的应力图。

由图 6 可知,盾构机管片受到的最大应力出现在第 4 环管壁内侧一圈、第 4 环外侧拱顶及拱腰左右两侧。另外第 5 环、第 3 环靠近第四环的边界处也有较高的应力存在。因此这些地方也是管片最为危险的区域。与浅埋直线工况类似,第 4 环是管片应力最大的地方。

3.2.2　曲线掘进(右纠偏)管片应力分析

图 7 为中埋工况下管片损伤云图。

图 6　盾构机直线管片 Mises 应力图

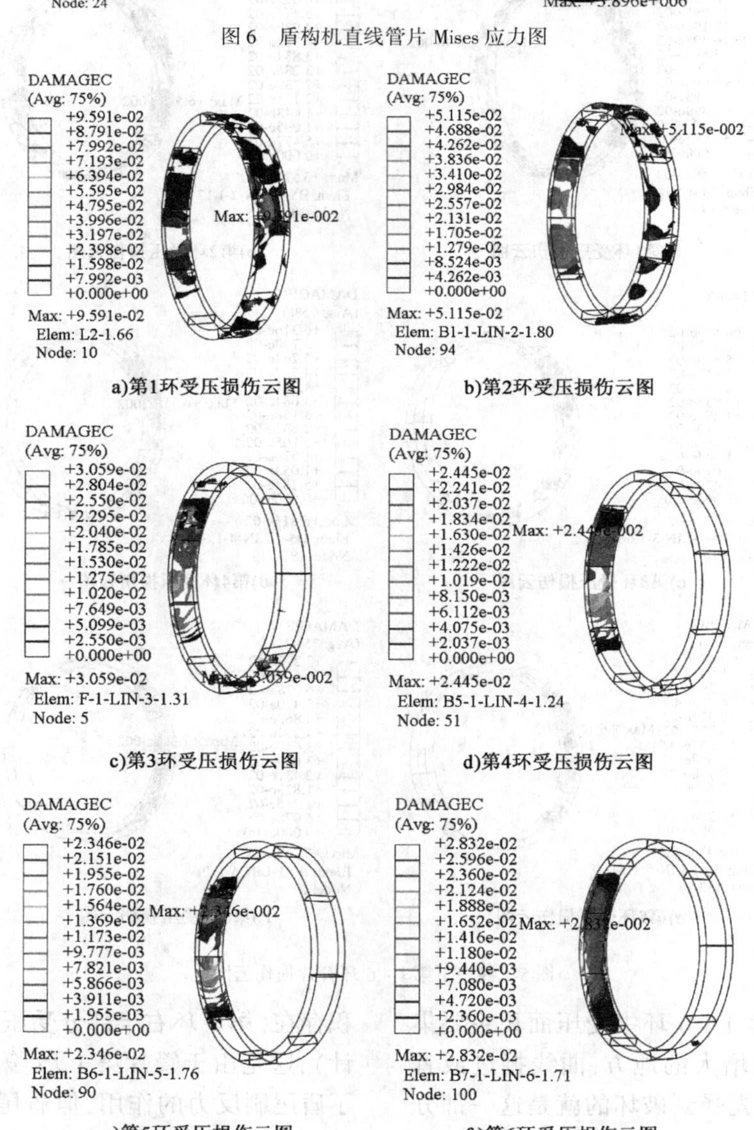

a)第1环受压损伤云图　b)第2环受压损伤云图

c)第3环受压损伤云图　d)第4环受压损伤云图

e)第5环受压损伤云图　f)第6环受压损伤云图

图 7　中埋下第 1 ~6 环管片损伤云图

由图7应力云图可知，第1环管片的损伤面积主要在千斤顶偏载区和受到盾尾刷反力作用的部分区域。在受到盾尾刷反力作用的区域里还存在局部高应力。这是由于封顶块处盾尾刷反力分布较密集才有了局部高应力的产生。因此封顶块此处成为第1环管片最为薄弱的位置，容易发生混凝土管片损伤和混凝土剥落。另外除2环、3环、6环里很小的一部分分布在盾尾刷反力作用区域里，第2~5环管片的受压面积大都集中在千斤顶偏载作用区域，4环、5环管片右部分没有一点受压面积。

3.3 右纠偏深埋工况下的管片应力分析

3.3.1 直线掘进管片应力分析

图8为深埋工况下直线管片的应力图。

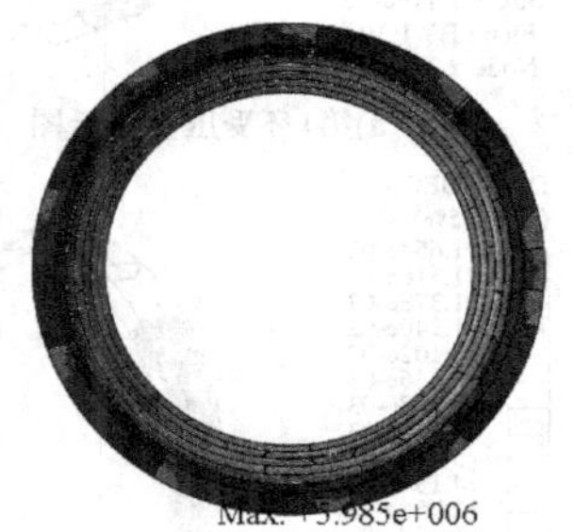

图8 盾构机直线管片 Mises 应力图

由图8应力云图可知，最大Mises应力分布在靠近环边界处的4环、5环的管片内侧，较多较大的应力主要集中在4环。因此4环是管片最为薄弱的位置，结构受力相对合理，在极端情况下4环处极易超过屈服应力最先发生破坏。在引入混凝土塑性损伤后，受压应力云图色彩一致，数值显示为零，说明盾构机在直线掘进时管片一般不会出现损伤。

3.3.2 曲线掘进(右纠偏)管片应力分析

图9为深埋工况下管片损伤云图。

由图9各环受压损伤云图可得，第1环管片损伤面积充满了千斤顶偏载区和拱脚处，受压应力最大的就在千斤顶偏载区，因而这部分管片很容易遭到破坏。第2环管片损伤面积仍主要分布在拱腰和拱脚处，比起第1环的管片损伤面积分布，第2环的损伤面积逐渐向拱脚扩展，但最危险的区域仍然是拱腰处。第3环管片损伤面积则有一半在拱腰处，一半在拱脚处，可见管片受压损伤面积仍在向拱脚处扩展。最危险的区域在拱腰和拱脚交界处及管片附近局部区域。第4环管片损伤面积大部分集中在拱脚处，只有小部分分布在拱腰末端，受压应力最大处位于拱脚。第5、6环管片损伤面积主要分布于拱脚处，但管片受压面积开始变得稀疏且受压应力也有所下降，尤其第5环“片状”十分明显。第6环还有一小部分管片损伤面积已经嵌入了盾构左拱腰末端，最大受压应力云图趋向于平缓，说明千斤顶推力到达第6环时已分散了许多。

3.4 不同工况的数值结果对比分析

3.4.1 Mises应力

图10为直线掘进时三种工况下的应力变化折线图，由图可知，三种工况下直线掘进时管片所受最大应力都在第4环，但由于管片的屈服应力远大于管片在三种工况下的最大应力，因此理论上不会出现破损。

图11是三种工况下曲线掘进的应力变化折线图，由图可知，盾构机曲线掘进时管片的Mises应力大小的关系为深埋 > 中埋 > 浅埋。管片上直接作用的千斤顶推力和盾尾刷反力导致了1号、2号管片的应力最大。

3.4.2 位移分析

图12是各个工况水平位移点线图，由图可知，各个工况下1号管片的水平位移最大，水平位移随着环数的增大而逐级递减。

在分析位移时，为了便于观察，将水平位移和竖向位移云图放大50倍。由图13各工况第1环水平位移云图可知，三种工况下最大水平位移均在拱肩处，此外管片右半部分因为作用有盾尾刷反力，各环管片之间均出现小张角。千斤顶作用区域已有环缝的张开，盾尾刷作用区域的管片表面出现“坑坑洼洼”破损状，变形随着埋深增大而增大。

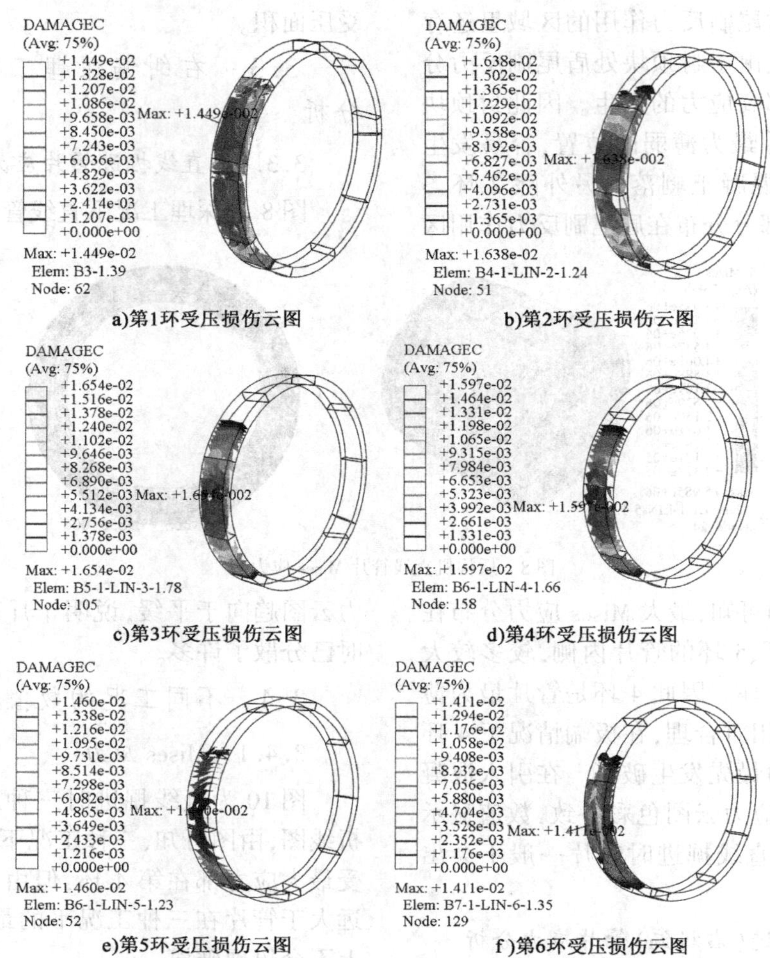

a)第1环受压损伤云图　　b)第2环受压损伤云图

c)第3环受压损伤云图　　d)第4环受压损伤云图

e)第5环受压损伤云图　　f)第6环受压损伤云图

图9　深埋下第1～6环管片损伤云图

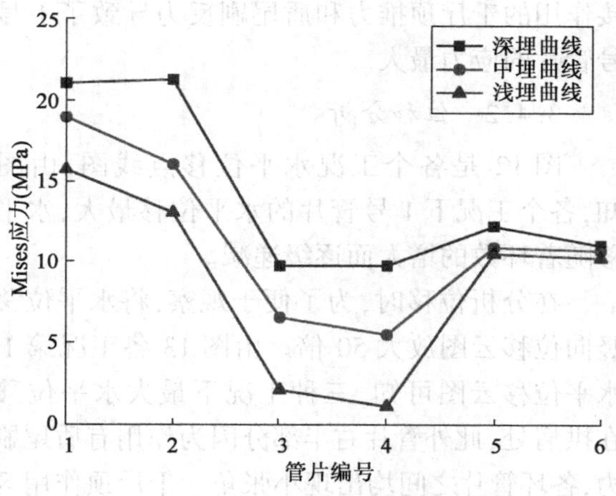

图10　盾构机直线掘进 Mises 应力点线图

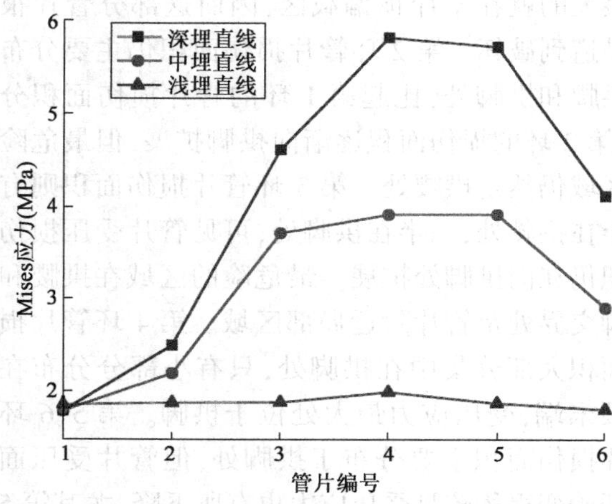

图11　盾构机曲线掘进(右纠偏)Mises 应力点线图

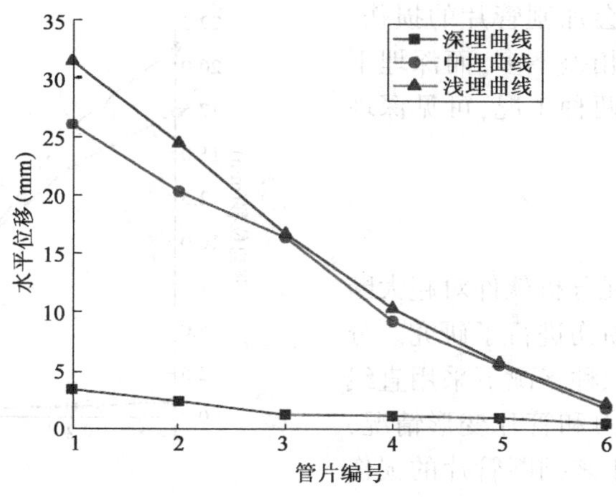

图 12　各个工况水平位移点线图

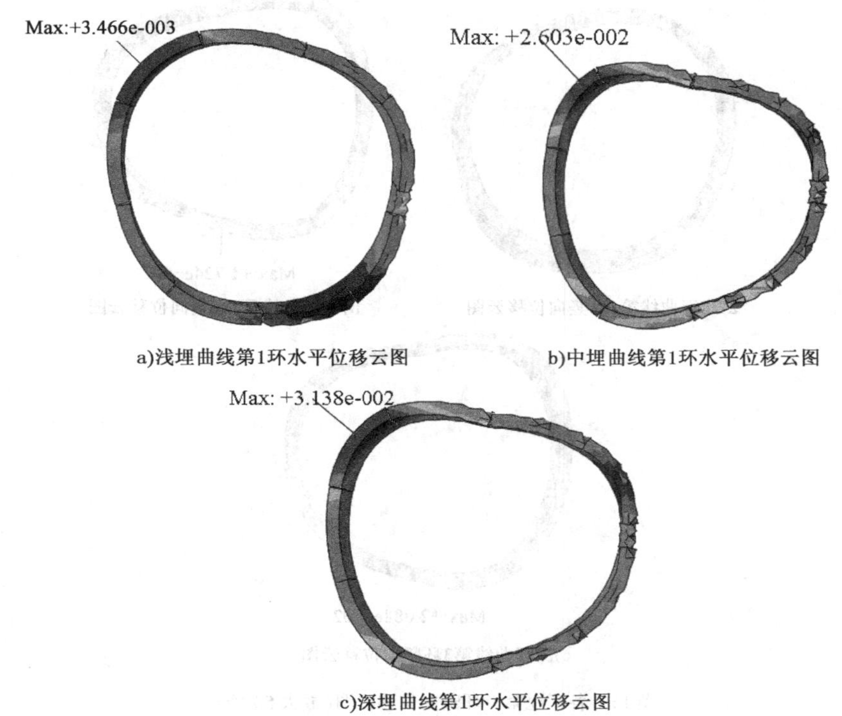

a)浅埋曲线第1环水平位移云图

b)中埋曲线第1环水平位移云图

c)深埋曲线第1环水平位移云图

图 13　各工况第 1 环水平位移云图(放大 50 倍)

图 14 为竖向位移点线图,由图可知,浅埋工况下管片竖向位移变化较小,而中埋和深埋工况下管片竖向位移显著增大,并且第 1、2 环管片的竖向位移明显大于其余管片,说明施工荷载对第 1、2 环管片有较大影响。

图 15 是各工况第 1 环竖向位移云图,由图可知,浅埋工况下最大竖向位移发生在拱肩处,而中埋和深埋工况下的最大竖向位移发生在盾构拱脚处,并且中埋和深埋工况下管片拱脚处变形较严重,很有可能受拉破损,出现小张角。

3.4.3　受损面积分析

本文通过损伤面积比来分析管片的损伤程度,通过像素提取不同区域程度的面积,最后通过损伤面积比公式计算得出管片各环的损伤面积比。三种工况下损伤面积比点线图如图 16 所示。

由图 16 可知,三个工况下的曲线呈递减趋势即管片的损伤程度在慢慢变小,只不过各工况下陡降段各有不同。浅埋下损伤面积比的曲线从第 2 环管片开始陡降,中埋下曲线从第 3 环管片开始陡降。第 1、2 环管片比其余管片损伤更严重,说明千斤顶偏载和盾尾刷反力会加剧管片的损伤。中埋和浅埋管片的损伤程度相差不多,而深埋下管片的损伤程度远大于另外两种工况,可见深埋曲线是管片最不利的工况。

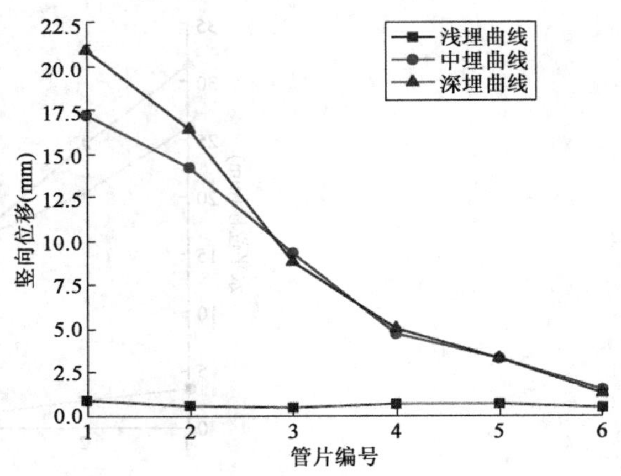

图14　各个工况竖向位移点线图

4　结语

本文通过ABAQUS有限元分析软件对超大断面盾构隧道纠偏引发的管片损伤进行了研究。分析了管片在深埋、中埋、浅埋三种工况下采用直线掘进和曲线掘进时的管片应力和管片变形情况,通过受压应力云图面积的大小来判断管片的损伤程度,得到了以下结论:

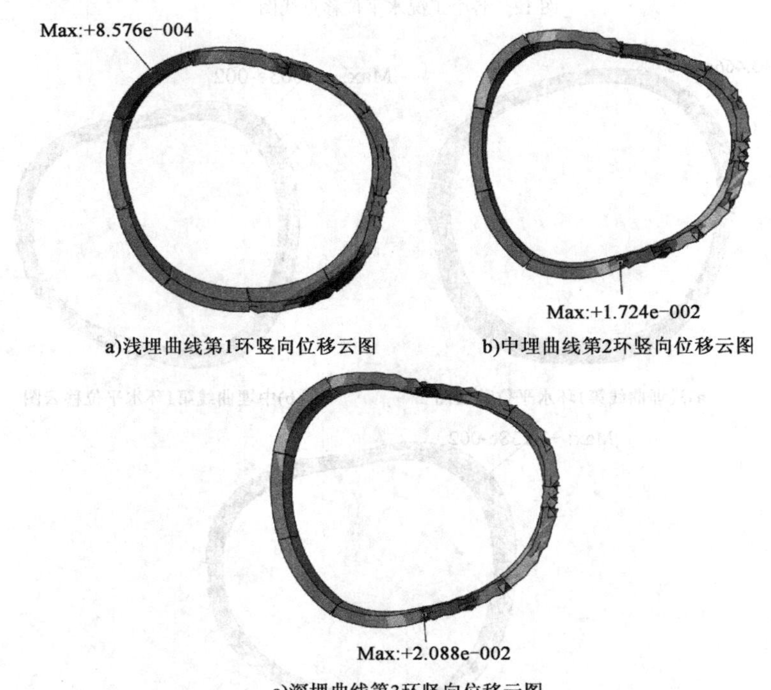

a)浅埋曲线第1环竖向位移云图　b)中埋曲线第2环竖向位移云图

c)深埋曲线第3环竖向位移云图

图15　各工况第1环竖向位移云图(放大50倍)

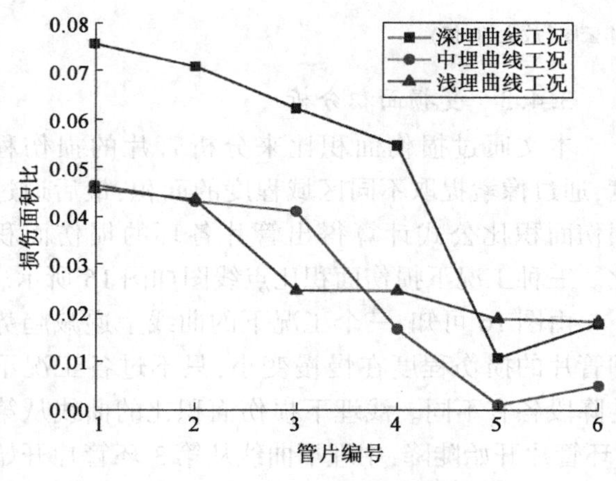

图16　各工况下损伤面积比点线图

(1)直线掘进浅埋时最大压应力值为2.2MPa,中埋时最大压应力值为4.1MPa,深埋时最大压应力值为6.4MPa。曲线掘进浅埋时最大压应力值为14MPa,中埋时最大压应力值为33.2MPa,深埋时最大压应力值为42.9MPa。

(2)三种工况下盾构机直线掘进时第4环管片受损最严重,曲线掘进时离千斤顶越近的第1环管片受损最严重。

(3)三种工况下第1环的水平位移和竖向位移比其他各环要大。右纠偏时最大水平变形发生在拱肩处,最大竖向变形发生在盾构管片拱脚处,实际工程中有必要监测最大变形处。

(4)深埋曲线工况是管片受损最严重的工况,在右纠偏时损伤面积比最大值为0.076。因此在曲线纠偏时要时刻关注离千斤顶近且被盾尾刷反力挤压的管片。

(5)本文仅考虑了千斤顶推力和盾尾刷反力两种施工荷载,没有考虑注浆压力等复杂施工荷载组合,也没有考虑千斤顶撑靴偏心等具体工况下的管片损伤规律。

参考文献

[1] 许鸣蝉,张子新.大直径盾构隧道管片损伤成因分析及处理措施[J].地下空间与工程学报,2013,9(S1):1705-1712.

[2] 秦建设,朱伟,陈建.盾构姿态控制引起管片错台及开裂问题研究[D].南京:河海大学,2004.

[3] 段红海,方诗涛,赵东华,等.地铁盾构管片受力分析及管片破损的控制措施研究[J].工程建设与设计,2016(04):133-136+140.

[4] 王宏.小半径曲线并大坡度盾构施工管片破损及上浮受力分析[J].石家庄铁道大学学报(自然科学版),2012,25(01):74-77.

[5] 杨栓民.盾构隧道曲线拟合研究[J].都市快轨交通,2006,19(5):59~61.

[6] 张文萃.软土地层盾构隧道通用环管片排版纠偏应用技术及施工监控研究[D].西安:西安建筑科技大学,2016.

[7] 陈俊生,莫海鸿.盾构隧道管片施工阶段力学行为的三维有限元分析[A].华南理工大学,2006.

[8] 高超.软土地层盾构掘进施工姿态控制技术研究[J].冶金丛刊,2017,000(003):67-68.

[9] 王明年,于丽,刘大刚,等.隧道与地下工程数值计算及工程应用[M].重庆:西南交通大学出版社,2015.

[10] 高文元.基于盾构隧道整体效应分析的施工荷载确定方法研究[D].天津:天津大学,2019.

超大断面盾构隧道拼装误差引发的管片衬砌损伤研究

张稳军* 李嘉豪
(天津大学建筑工程学院)

摘 要 盾构隧道在施工拼装阶段,衬砌结构力学特性表现出极明显的三维不确定性,使得内部应力集中程度显著提高,进而引发管片损伤行为,破坏结构防水体系。通过建立块体模型,引入混凝土塑性损伤本构与螺栓的双折线强化本构,采用弹塑性模型进行分析,由损伤因子数值来描述衬砌的损伤行为。以错台、张开量为变量分析了管片衬砌的应力分布规律及管片损伤特征,得出了不同错台张开下的内力图和损伤图。通过数值分析得出以下结论:①管片发生错台时产生应力集中,仅影响周围区域,对远处影响不大。②同一错台量下,由于楔形量的存在,混凝土承担一部分剪切力,故封顶块处的错台影响相较于其他管片间错台更大。③同一位置处,随着错台量的增加,管片损伤增大,塑性区域逐渐贯通,全断面产生塑性时,位移将出现不收敛的情况。

关键词 大直径盾构隧道 数值模拟 管片错台 管片张开 管片损伤

0 引言

随着我国城市化进程不断加快,地下空间开发力度持续加大,城市盾构隧道的建设逐渐向大直径和大环宽的方向发展[1-4]。21世纪以前,由于技术方面的局限及经济的落后,隧道在国内还不能普及,但随着技术的提高以及城市需求的不断提升,国内隧道发展进入了新的征程,面对隧道领域的发展也出现一系列急需解决的问题。

在盾构隧道的施工中,防水性能的好坏直接影响着隧道的安全性和耐久性,为了提高隧道的使用寿命,就需要造成防水性能失效的原因入手,即解决拼装误差等造成的管片错台、张开问题,消除错台、张开对防水性能的影响。

衬砌结构由管片及接缝间的螺栓构建而成,衬砌结构的稳定是采用盾构法必须考虑的重要因素。由于隧道所处的高水压环境且管片间存在接缝,所以防水性的研究不可或缺。衬砌管片本身防水性能优越,但在拼装以及运营过程中,容易产生不同程度错台、张开,使得衬砌变形严重,造成防水功能失效,故需要对错台、张开量与防水性能的关系做进一步的研究。

隧道设计的计算理论从一开始的刚性结构设计,到弹性结构设计,再到最后的连续介质设计,一共三个发展阶段[5]。按不同计算方法可划分为荷载位移法和地层位移法,按不同接缝效应可划分为均质圆环模型、接缝等效类模型以及块体类模型三类[6]。

于红梅[7]为了研究用均质圆环法所求得的数据与实际工程中所获得的数据的差别,采用ABAQUS有限元软件进行了实际工程的数值模拟,并在可靠度方面详尽分析了采用均质圆环法对实际工程的指导意义,还构建了相对应的可靠度体系。

常喜军[8]从实际工程的渗漏水分析出发,分析了管片错台的原因以及其机理,并对如何防止或减弱错台影响提出了多项建议。

李翔宇[9]通过分析软土地区渗漏水的分布规律,发现在多种渗漏分布中,接缝处最容易出现渗漏,环缝处的渗漏更大,且主要集中在相邻的标准块之间。

错台形式可分为纵缝错台和环缝错台,前者是同一环中,管片之间发生的错台,后者为环与环之间发生的错台。错台产生的原因有很多,刘永辉、谢玉杰、张广鹏[10-12]等总结如下:

(1)盾构机在推进过程中姿态控制不当,比如纠偏过度等。在出现纠偏过度时,其轨迹与设计轴线出入过大,在盾尾处容易产生较大的径向位移,但是由于螺栓的限制,衬砌的空间形态是确定的,所以径向位移的存在会使得衬砌错台。措施:针对姿态控制问题要严格的遵循“勤纠、缓纠”的原则,使得纠偏的程度严格控制在允许范围内。

(2)拼装作业不规范。在盾构的推进过程中,施工的质量对管片错台影响很大,拼装人员的施工质量直接影响拼装质量的好坏,如砂浆的清理,封顶块拼装的限度,管片的拼装顺序,管片间螺栓的复紧等,这些拼装操作将直接影响到管片的拼装质量,导致产生错台现象。措施:提高拼装人员的责任心,拼装下一环时清理盾尾拼装区的砂浆,严格按照由上到下、左右交叉、最后封顶的原则施工;此外在拼装过程中严格把控衬砌的椭圆度,并在每环拼装完成后对螺栓进行复紧。

(3)管片上浮引起错台。在水含量丰富的地区施工时,衬砌很容易产生上浮进而出现错台现象。为了保证盾构机的姿态控制,需要加快掘进速度,但如果此时注入浆液的初凝时间不足,会使得管片受到的上浮力大于自重,导致管片上浮,进而产生连续的错台现象。措施:提高注入浆液的初凝速度。

(4)注浆参数控制不当。同步注浆中,浆液初凝时间长,管片在浮力作用下有上浮趋势,易引起管片错台;注浆压力过大,对管片造成较大的挤压,易造成管片错台或破损;注浆方量不足,没有充分填充隧道衬砌间隙,管片因为没有被砂浆完全固定而产生错台。措施:根据盾构机掘进情况合理注浆,使注浆量、注浆压力与推进速度等施工参数匹配,同时考虑到上浮的影响,选择合适的浆液配比,满足足够的浆液强度与较短的初凝时间。

赵方[13]通过分析隧道不同地质状况下各种因素的影响,对隧道纵向变形的成因以及如何有效控制纵向变形进行了总结。

高小宁[14]对几种常用的椭圆度计算方法进行了对比分析,总结出了与实际工程最接近的椭圆度拟合形式。

李拼[15]通过ABAQUS对衬砌的错台量、张开量进行了分析,得出了不同错台张开条件下密封垫的应力状态。

王汝宝[16]采用数值模拟纵向沉降进行了研究,得出在纵向沉降中,可以采用高斯曲线进行拟合沉降曲线,最后得出环缝张开量对纵向沉降的影响最大。

卢院[17]为了探究衬砌管片呈现椭化变形的规律,构建三维有限元模型对堆卸载、降水等施工工况下管片变形的规律进行了分析,结果表明封顶块处于拱底时衬砌的横向变形较小，环间产生的错台效应越强，其收敛程度越小。

张劲[18]以混凝土本构关系为基础，引入了损伤因子这一参数，更好地反映出有限元内部的损伤模型与规范中混凝土自身的本构关系。并通过有限元模拟验证了 CDP 模型的可靠性，此外也对 CDP 模型的一些不足进行了改进。

1 盾构隧道数值模型建立

1.1 工程背景

本文依托某工程盾构隧道（隧道覆土厚度约为 10～42m，水位高程为 15m，承受最大水压约 0.59MPa）。隧道主体结构采用“1+2+7”分块方式，如图 1 所示，管片为通用楔形环钢筋混凝土管片。管片衬砌外径 15.4m，内径 14.1m，厚度 0.65m，平均宽度 2.0m。拼装方式为通缝拼装，管片连接采用斜螺栓作为管片接头。管片采用 C60 混凝土，抗渗等级为 P12，钢筋采用 HPB300、HRB400E，环、纵向螺栓为机械性能等级为 8.8 的普通螺栓。

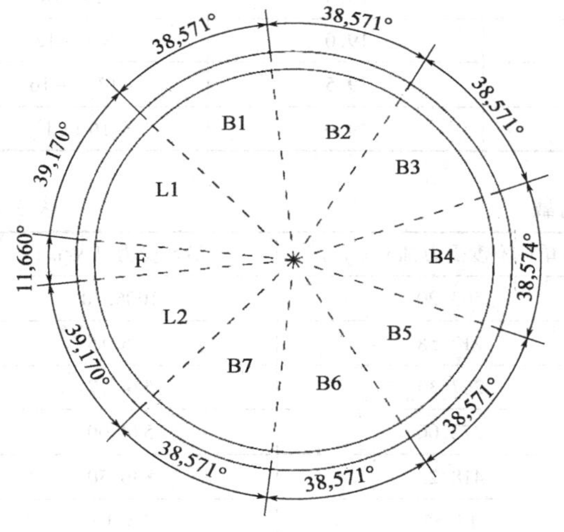

图 1 衬砌分块示意图

1.2 荷载工况

1.2.1 计算理论

本工程隧道埋深在 10～42m，地层条件较差，故采用太沙基理论，假定土体为具有一定黏聚力的松散土体，可以考虑到土体的黏聚力、内摩擦角、隧道埋深以及尺寸的影响，计算示意图如图 2 所示。

竖向土压力计算公式如下：

$$\sigma_V = \frac{B_1(\gamma - c/B_1)}{K_0 \tan\varphi} \cdot (1 - e^{-K_0\tan\varphi H/B_1}) + p_0 \cdot e^{-K\tan\varphi H/B_1} \tag{1}$$

$$B_1 = R_0 \cdot \cot\left(\frac{\pi/4 + \varphi/2}{2}\right) \tag{2}$$

当 $P_0/\gamma < H$ 时，上式可简化为：

$$\sigma_V = \frac{B_1(\gamma - c/B_1)}{K_0 \tan\varphi} \cdot (1 - e^{-K_0\tan\varphi H/B_1}) \tag{3}$$

式中：σ_V——竖向松弛土压力；

B_1——土的一半的松动范围（m）；

K_0——水平与竖向土压之比；

P_0——地面超载（kPa）；

R_0——管片外半径（m）；

c、φ——土层的粘聚力、内摩擦角（°）；

H——覆土厚度（m）；

γ——土的重度（kN/m^3）。

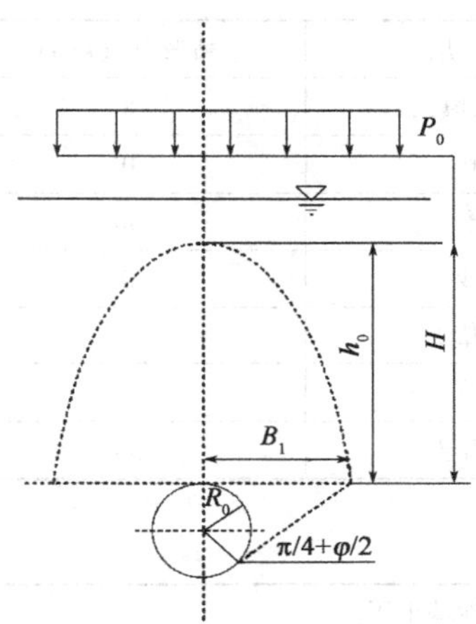

图 2 太沙基土压力示意图

1.2.2 荷载计算

考虑到隧道全程埋深的不同，针对于最不利情况（深埋 42m）进行更为详细的分析。深埋所处地层情况及地层参数如图 3、表 1 所示，考虑地下水位位于地下 15m 处，荷载计算采用水土分算的形式，偏安全考虑设置隧道受到底部水压力数值影响。

埋深土层计算荷载如表 2 所示。

2 纵缝错台对管片力学特性的影响分析

本章根据错台位置的不同以及错台量的不同设立多种工况模型，通过对不同工况下内力、轴力以及弯矩的分析，得到不同错台量以及错台位置对管片衬砌的影响规律。

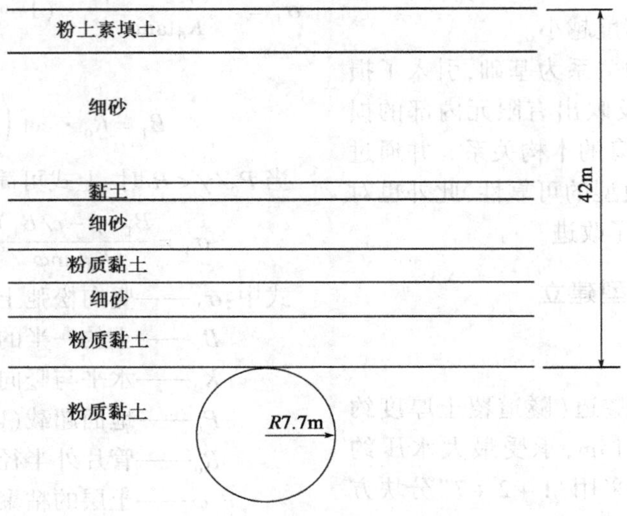

图3　最大深埋土层分布

深埋(42m)隧道土层参数　　表1

土　层	黏聚力 c(kPa)	内摩擦角 φ(°)	重度 γ(N/m^3)	埋深(m)
粉土素填土	8	10	18.5	20～15
细砂	0	30	19.5	15～0
黏土	30	10	18.5	0～-2
细砂	0	30	19.5	-2～-8
粉质黏土	30	18	19.0	-8～-12
细砂	0	30	19.5	-12～-16
粉质黏土	30	18	19.0	-16以下

深埋土层计算荷载　　表2

泰沙基土压		单位宽度受力(kN/m)	沿环受力(kN/m)
竖向土压	$pe1$(kN/m)	503.20	1006.40
顶部水平土压	$qe1$(kN/m)	212.58	425.15
底部水平土压	$qe2$(kN/m)	267.39	534.77
顶部水压	$pw1$(kN/m)	272.00	544.00
底部水压	$pw2$(kN/m)	418.25	836.50
自重	g(kN/m)	17.55	35.10
地面荷载	po(kN/m)	20.00	40.00
隧道正上方荷载	po'(kN/m)	20.00	40.00

2.1　管片计算结果分析

本模型整体采用通缝拼装，各环受力相差不大，但考虑到模型两端约束的影响，故采用6环拼装，最终分析模型时只看中间两环的受力情况，分别记作第3环和第4环。图4为管片混凝土区域应力云图，图5为横向纵向变形位移云图。

从图中可以看出，混凝土管片上应力以压应力为主，且内侧压应力大于外侧压应力，符合管片的变性特征。分析位移云图时，可得横向变形值最大值出现在拱腰附近，竖向变形最大值处于拱顶拱底处，且竖向变形较横向变形数值稍大一些，可以看出隧道整体呈现椭圆化，即拱顶拱底向径向内收敛，拱腰两侧向外侧发展。由此隧道的受力特点，说明模型是合理的。

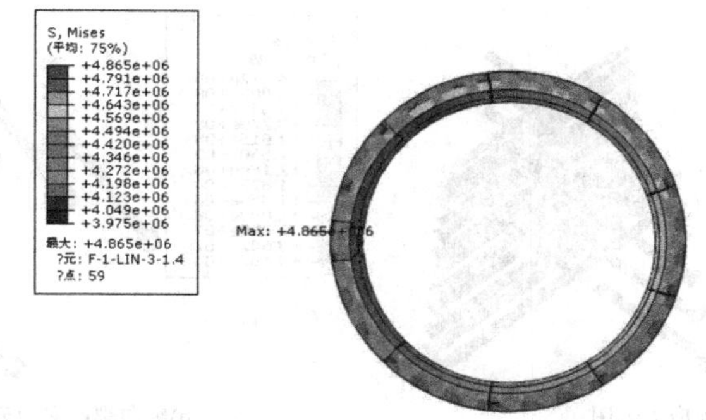

图4　混凝土管片应力云图

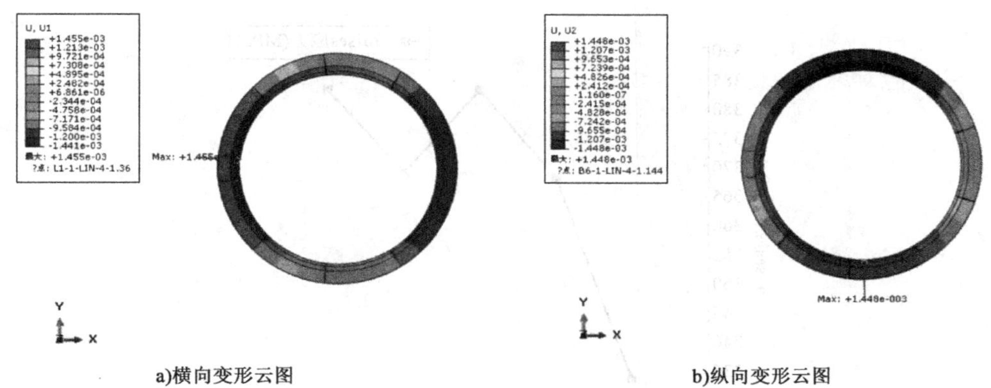

a)横向变形云图　　b)纵向变形云图

图5　管片变形云图

2.2　不同位置同一纵缝错台量影响分析

2.2.1　设置工况

以拼装正常情况下管片的受力及变形情况为标准，再通过强制位移施加位移边界。为探究不同位置对错台的影响，以控制错台为6mm来分析同一错台量影响下不同位置的影响。由于每环管片据横向中心轴对称，故考虑上半环错台量影响共设置5组，设置在封顶块、邻接块与标准管片之间。

内向错台工况设置如表3所示。

不同位置错台工况设置　　表3

工况标号	工 况 设 置	错台量(mm)
1	F 相较 L1 内错	6
2	L1 相较 B1 内错	6
3	B1 相较 B2 内错	6
4	B2 相较 B3 内错	6
5	B3 相较 B4 内错	6

2.2.2　Mises 应力

通过观察螺栓云图（图6）可以看出，不论是环向螺栓还是纵向螺栓，其Mises应力作用于接缝的连接处，螺栓破坏模式为连接处受剪切或拉力，进入塑性状态后失效。

通过不同位置处的Mises应力比较（图7）可得，相较于其他位置错台，封顶块位置处的错台产生的Mises应力最小，这可能由于封顶块处存在楔形量，一部分剪切力由楔形量处的嵌合作用承担，故使得螺栓所受应力相应较小。

2.2.3　最小主应力

由于在衬砌中，螺栓多用于承受拉力，混凝土多用于承受压力，故探讨混凝土的压应力更有意义。混凝土的最小主应力云图如图8所示。通过云图可得在发生部位产生了应力集中现象，且产生的应力影响通过螺栓向周边扩散，使得周边也产生了一定的应力值，但此部位的错台影响仅限于邻近的管片，对相距更远处管片影响很小。

提取最小主应力云图整理数据可以得到应力折线图如图9所示。可以看出相较于工况1，工况2到工况5的应力变化不大，这点刚好与前面分析的螺栓应力相呼应，表明在封顶块处错台时，楔形量的存在会分担一部分错台产生的应力，故导致封顶块部位混凝土受压应力更大，属于不利位置。

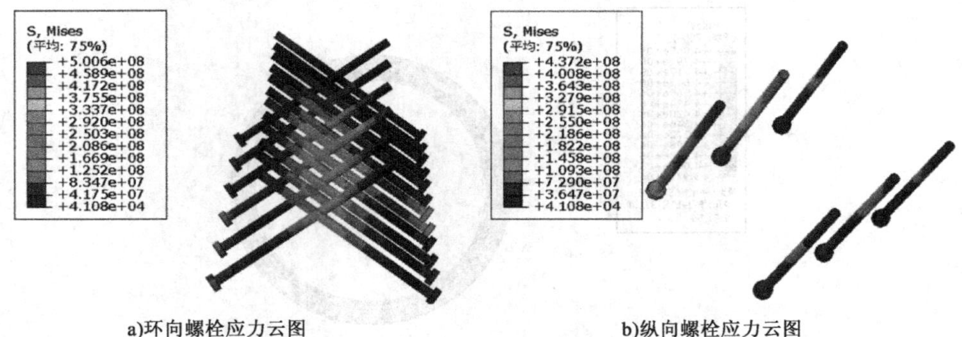

a)环向螺栓应力云图　　b)纵向螺栓应力云图

图6 管片螺栓应力分布云图

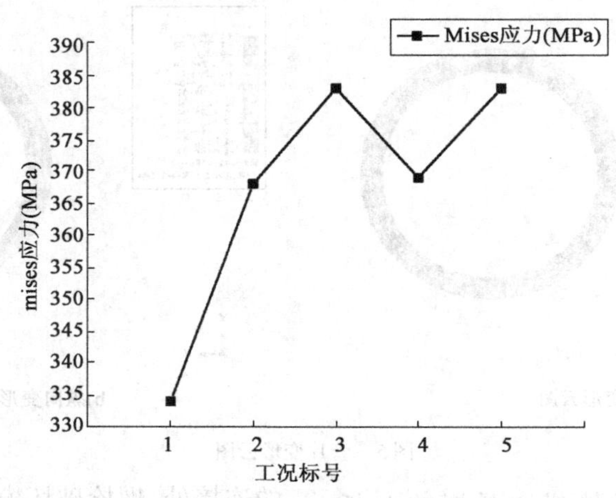

图7 不同位置错台螺栓应力对比图

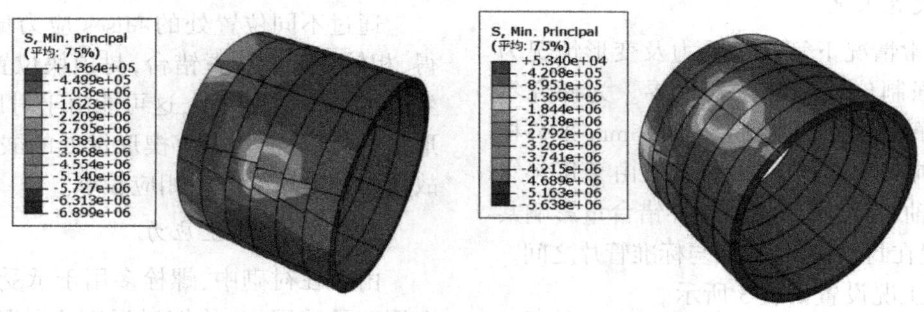

a)封顶块位置错台云图　　b)L1位置错台云图

图8 不同位置错台最小主应力云图

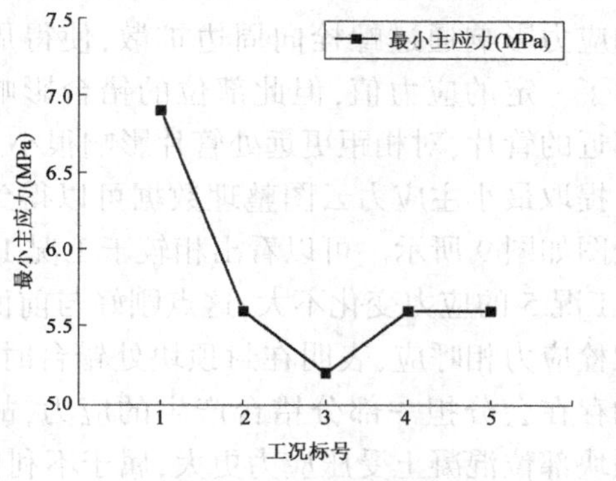

图9 不同置错台最小主应力对比图

2.2.4 损伤分析

提取不同位置损伤因子关系如图10所示，封顶块部位的损伤因子最大，是其他部位损伤因子大小的2到3倍。通过前文叙述可知，损伤因子越大，恢复后的刚度折减越多，故封顶快位置最容易出现损伤。分析原因，楔形量的存在使得管片截面宽度进行了一定的削弱，且在产生内向位移时，嵌合量使得混凝土承担一部分受力。

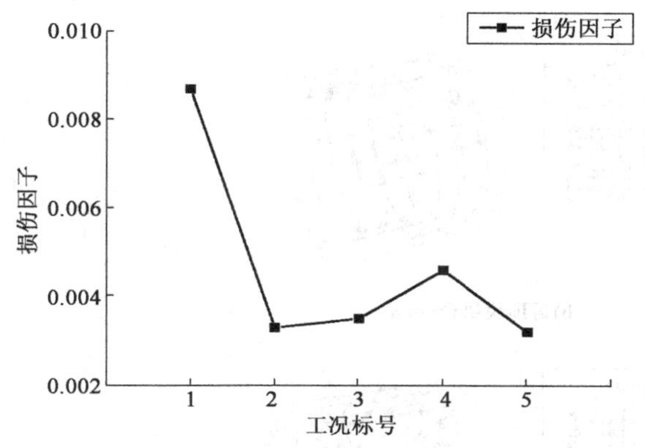

图 10　不同位置错台损伤对比图

2.3　同一位置下不同纵缝错台量影响分析

2.3.1　设置工况

在分析封顶块以及标准块间不同错台量影响时,其工况设置如表 4 和表 5 所示。

封顶块处错台工况设置　表 4

工况标号	工 况 设 置	错台量(mm)
1	F 相较 L1 内错	2
2	F 相较 L1 内错	4
3	F 相较 L1 内错	6
4	F 相较 L1 内错	8
5	F 相较 L1 内错	10

封标准块 B1 处错台工况设置　表 5

工况标号	工 况 设 置	错台量(mm)
1	B1 相较 B2 内错	2
2	B1 相较 B2 内错	4
3	B1 相较 B2 内错	6
4	B1 相较 B2 内错	8
5	B1 相较 B2 内错	10

2.3.2　Mises 应力

设置封顶块不同错台量时提取应力数据如图 11 所示。通过折线图可以看出,Mises 应力随着错台量的增加而增加,且在工况 1 到 4 时,应力随错台量呈线性变化,在错台 8mm 后折线斜率发生了变化。不难得出,在 0 ~ 8mm 错台量变化范围内时,管片呈现弹性特征,在 8 ~ 10mm 变化时,管片呈现塑性特征,在与 B1 错台横向对比时可以发现,封顶块处螺栓应力相较更小。

2.3.3　最小主应力

混凝土最小主应力如图 12 所示。可以看出错台 8mm 之前,应力与错台量呈线性变化,在 8mm 过后斜率发生变化,可以看出混凝土最小主应力与螺栓应力变化趋势相同。通过与 B1 错台横向对比发现,封顶块错台时混凝土所受压应力更大,刚好与分析螺栓应力相对应,表明管片受力为螺栓与混凝土共同作用的结果。

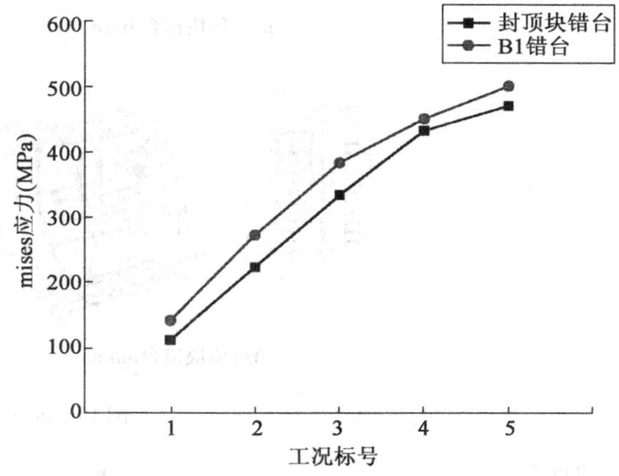

图 11　同一位置错台螺栓应力对比图

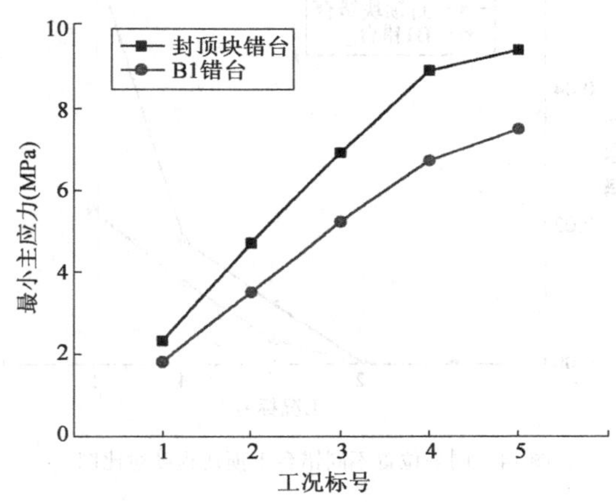

图 12　同一位置不同错台下最小主应力应力对比图

2.3.4　损伤分析

图 13 为工况 1 到 5 的损伤云图,从图可以看出随着错台量的增大,损伤面积开始增多,并逐渐贯通管片,且对比 B1 错台损伤可以看出,由于沿纵向也存在楔形量,故在楔形量朝向的相邻环上也产生了损伤。

分析衬砌损伤时,发现损伤行为从错台 4mm 时开始出现,提取数据如图 14 所示,损伤因子随错台量的增加而增加,错台较小时损伤较小。分析原因,可能只有管片边缘产生了损伤,部分衬砌产生了塑性行为,随着错台继续增加,衬砌损伤开始增大,并在工况四产生了突变。分析原因是由于管片沿宽度塑性贯通,进而使得位移不再收敛。

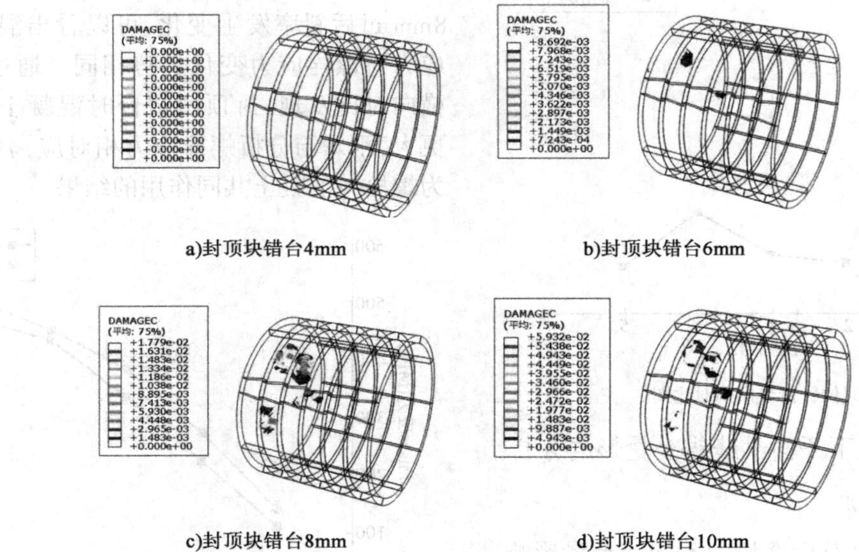

图13 同一位置不同错台损伤云图

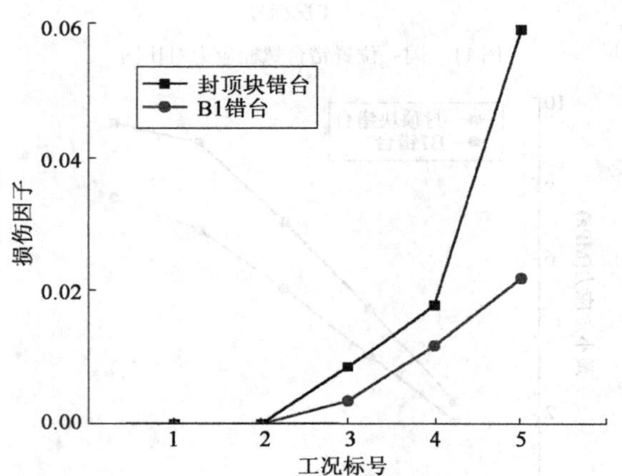

图14 同一位置不同错台下损伤程度对比图

3 结语

(1)管片发生错台时产生应力集中,仅影响周围区域,对远处影响不大。

(2)同一错台量下,由于楔形量的存在,混凝土承担一部分剪切力,故封顶块处的错台影响相较于其他管片间错台更大。

(3)同一位置处,随着错台量的增加,管片损伤增大,塑性区域逐渐贯通,全断面产生塑性时,位移将出现不收敛的情况。

(4)考虑管片间错台位置影响时,封顶块位置由于楔形量的存在,一方面削弱了管片横截面,另一方面相互嵌合阻止了错台。在错台量相同时,封顶块部位相较其他管片间错台更容易发生损伤。故建议在合理范围内,减小楔形量,并对封顶块部位进行严格的监控,以免出现较大的损伤影响衬砌防水性能。

参考文献

[1] 王秀英,王梦恕. 城市的安全发展与地下空间利用[J]. 中国安全科学学报,2003,13(5):76-78.

[2] 朱世友. 国内地铁盾构区间隧道管片结构设计的现状与发展[J]. 现代隧道技术,2002,39(6):23-28.

[3] Hong K R. Typical underwater tunnels in the mainland of china and related tunneling technologies [J]. Engineering, 2017, 3: 871-879.

[4] Tan z s, Li Z L, Tang W, et al. Research on stress characteristics of segment structure during the construction of the large-diameter shield tunnel and cross-passage [J]. Symmetry, 2020, 12(8):1246.

[5] 朱永全,宋玉香. 隧道工程[M]. 北京:中国铁道出版社,2015.

[6] 刘钊. 复杂工况条件下错缝拼装盾构管片变形性能试验与仿真分析研究[D]. 北京:中国铁道科学研究院,2017.

[7] 朱伟译. 隧道标准规范(盾构篇)及解说[M]. 北京:中国建筑工业出版社,2001.

[8] 常喜军. 地铁盾构隧道施工中管片错台控制

技术研究[J].现代城市轨道交通,2020(04):37-40.

[9] 李翔宇,李新源,李明宇,等.地铁盾构隧道渗漏水的产生原因及分布规律[J].建筑科学,2020,36(S1):233-238.

[10] 刘永辉,张亚彬,罗宇勤.盾构隧道管片错台原因分析及措施[J].居舍,2018(31):166.

[11] 谢玉杰,江华.盾构推进中管片错台原因分析[A].北京盾构机专业委员会.2011中国盾构技术学术研讨会论文集[C].北京盾构机专业委员会:市政技术编辑部,2011:3.

[12] 张广鹏,徐海鹏.大直径泥水盾构施工中管片错台原因分析及控制措施[A].中国城市科学研究会轨道交通学组.智慧城市与轨道交通2016[C].中国城市科学研究会轨道交通学组:北京国建信文化发展中心,2016:3.

[13] 赵方.地铁盾构隧道纵向变形影响因素分析[J].土工基础,2018,32(03):326-329.

[14] 高小宁,张航,王哲.盾构隧道椭圆度测量和数据处理[J].测绘技术装备,2020,22(02):73-76.

[15] 李拼,谢宏明,何川,等.基于有效接触应力的大张开量盾构隧道密封垫防水性能分析[J].隧道建设(中英文),2019,39(12):1993-1999.

[16] 王汝宝,徐营,窦顺.隧道管片纵向沉降与环缝张开量的关系研究[J].能源技术与管理,2019,44(05):176-177+189.

[17] 黄大维,周顺华,冯青松,等.软土地区通缝拼装地铁盾构隧道管片纵缝接头的优化[J].中国铁道科学,2017,38(05):62-69.

[18] 张劲,王庆扬,胡守营,等.ABAQUS混凝土损伤塑性模型参数验证[J].建筑结构,2008(08):127-130.

基于水力开度的盾构隧道局部渗漏行为模拟

谢家冲　黄　昕*　张子新

(同济大学地下建筑与工程系)

摘　要　为了模拟盾构隧道衬砌局部渗漏行为及其诱发的衬砌响应与地层变化,引入耦合渗流和变形的CZM(Cohesive Zone Model)方法,基于水力开度概念建立了考虑衬砌局部渗漏的地层-结构模型,并通过与常用的外水内渗模拟方法比对,验证了提出模型的有效性。结果表明:局部渗漏行为对衬砌内力有不利影响,包括衬砌弯矩增加和朝局部渗漏侧的外凸变形;局部渗漏引起邻近地层孔隙压力的大幅降低与渗流速度的提高。与传统的局部水力传导方法相比较,CZM方法用于描述接头水力劣化的开度概念明确,局部渗流区域集中更贴近实际,为隧道外水内渗分析提供了一种优化的模拟方法。

关键词　盾构隧道　局部渗漏　CZM方法　水力劣化　数值模拟

0　引言

衬砌渗漏水是盾构隧道在运营中最常见的病害之一,也经常与开裂、剥落等其他衬砌病害伴随发生。盾构隧道由预制的管片拼装而成并通过螺栓连接,因此衬砌结构并非是连续的防水体系,横向上的收敛变形与纵向上的剪切错台均会引起接缝的力学性能劣化与防水体系失效。

已有研究中一般通过解析方法与数值模拟的手段来研究隧道衬砌的渗漏行为及其所诱发的地层响应和衬砌力学行为的变化。基于解析方法的研究[1-3]通常将衬砌简化为带一定渗透能力的均质圆环,忽略了衬砌在空间上力学和水力特性的非均匀性,但也具备概念清晰、计算简便的特点。相较于解析方法,数值模拟方法[4-8]能够考虑衬砌局部渗漏行为,并能够考虑渗流场与应力场的有

1.基金项目:国家自然科学基金(41877227);上海市科技创新行动计划(21DZ1201104,19DZ1201004)。

效耦合,从而可以更准确地考虑局部渗漏引起的土与结构相互作用变化。然而表征衬砌局部渗漏能力的渗透系数与渗漏区域的确定存在一定主观性,同时渗漏区域的水力与力学行为的耦合也尚未见诸报端。因此,有必要在既有研究建模思路的基础上优化建模手段,反映更真实的局部渗漏区域的水力特性与力学行为。

基于此,本文将常用于模拟岩体裂隙的CZM(Cohesive Zone Model)方法引入盾构隧道的地层-结构模型,描述接头区域的水力劣化行为,能够在一定程度上模拟力学特性与水力开度的耦合特性。文章同时也给出其他两种常用的模拟隧道渗漏的方法并进行了比较,表明了给出的CZM方法的可行性。本文的研究成果可对隧道外水内渗的相关研究提供借鉴,并给出基于水力开度的建模方法指导。

1　基于水力开度的接头渗漏模拟方法

1.1　已有局部渗漏模拟方法概述

图1给出常用的外水内渗模型中衬砌渗透能力的简化方式,区别于等效渗透系数方法[图1a)],部分或局部渗漏模拟方法人为地将特定区域设定较高的渗透性区别于其余的非渗透区域,根据划分的区域范围大小,分别如图1b)和c)所示。

部分水力传导方法(Partial Hydraulic Conductivity Method)[4,5]:即将部分区域(通常是易渗水的区域,例如拱腰范围[4])设定为较高的渗透系数,以模拟现场观测到的较大范围渗水的情况。

局部水力传导方法(Local Hydraulic Conductivity Method)[6-8]考虑到了渗水区域是相对微小的,将防水薄弱的位置(一般考虑为接头区域的水力劣化)设定具有较高的透水能力,相对真实地反映局部渗漏行为。

相比于前一种方法,局部水力传导方法在模拟局部渗漏行为与诱发的地层响应上更为精细与准确,然而这些高渗透区域的渗透系数同样不易确定,一般均需通过给定渗流量来反算得到。另外,不同埋深、不同衬砌形式和设定不同渗水区域大小都会影响渗漏区域渗透系数k_p或k_j的大小。这些通过反算得到的渗透系数同样也是基于渗流量等效的,并非是具有实际物理意义的值,在反映真实的局部渗漏行为上存在缺陷。

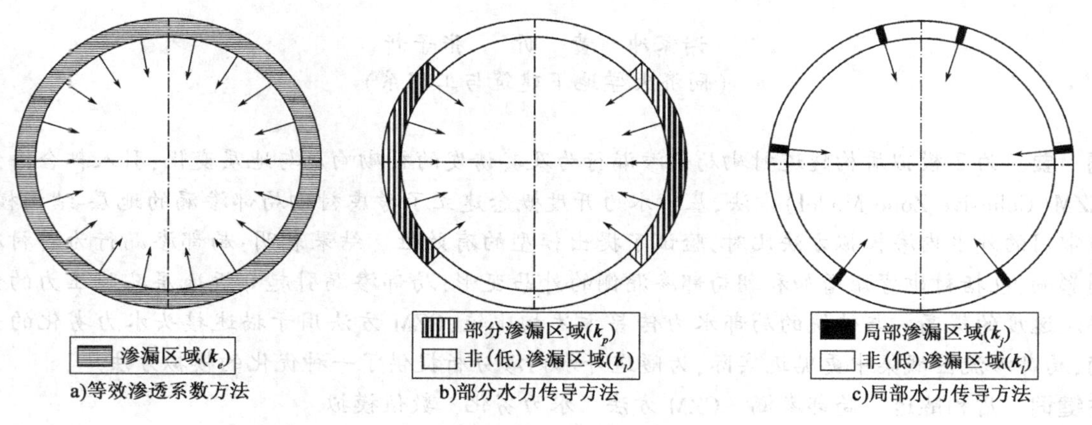

图1　常用衬砌渗漏模拟方法示意图

1.2　考虑渗流的CZM方法

CZM(Cohesive Zone Model)方法被广泛应用于岩石等具有节理面的工程材料裂隙分析[9,10],本文引入该方法用于描述盾构隧道衬砌接缝的局部水力劣化区域,采用ABAQUS[11]中耦合渗流行为的Cohesive单元同时刻画接头区域渗漏与非连续的力学行为。耦合渗流的Cohesive单元中渗流可根据局部方向分为法向滤失(leak off)和切向间隙流(tangential gap flows),分别用以描述Cohesive单元与周围实体单元水力渗透和裂隙中的平板间隙流,如图2所示。在本文中,盾构隧道局部渗漏行为主要表现为切向间隙流,并基于经典的立方定律确定流量,单位时间内单宽开度的渗流量q由式(1)给出。

$$qd = \frac{d^3}{12\mu}\nabla p \tag{1}$$

式中：d——接缝水力开度，m；

∇p——水力梯度，Pa/m；

μ——水的流体黏度，这里取 0.001Pa·s。

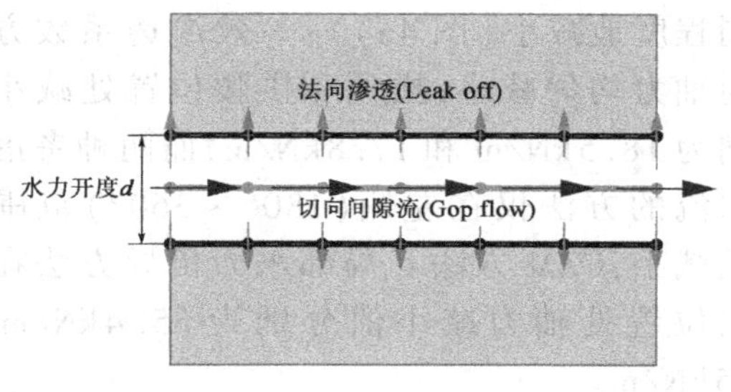

图 2 Cohesive 单元及水力开度示意图

在本文中不考虑内外水压造成的水力劈裂与接头的渐进性力学劣化行为，Cohesive 单元的力学行为简化为线弹性的牵引-分离定律（Traction-Separation law）表达，如式(2)所示。

$$\boldsymbol{t} = \begin{Bmatrix} t_n \\ t_s \\ t_t \end{Bmatrix} = \begin{bmatrix} E_{nn} & E_{ns} & E_{nt} \\ E_{ns} & E_{ss} & E_{st} \\ E_{nt} & E_{st} & E_{tt} \end{bmatrix} \begin{Bmatrix} \varepsilon_n \\ \varepsilon_s \\ \varepsilon_t \end{Bmatrix} = \boldsymbol{E\varepsilon} \tag{2}$$

式中：$\boldsymbol{t}$——法向牵引力张量，包含了 t_n、t_s、t_t 和三个张量分量；

ε——应变张量，包含了 ε_n、ε_s、ε_t 三个张量分量。

本文中的模型为二维模型，则该表达式退化为式(3)。

$$\boldsymbol{t} = \begin{Bmatrix} t_n \\ t_s \end{Bmatrix} = \begin{bmatrix} E_{nn} & E_{ns} \\ E_{ns} & E_{ss} \end{bmatrix} \begin{Bmatrix} \varepsilon_n \\ \varepsilon_s \end{Bmatrix} = \boldsymbol{E\varepsilon} \tag{3}$$

2 不同隧道局部渗漏模型对比分析

为了验证 CZM 模型的有效性，通过相同的其他建模参数建立了低渗透性隧道模型对照组和基于等效渗透系数方法（图 1a））、局部水力传导方法（图 1c））的模型用于比较讨论。根据文献[12]针对上海地铁隧道渗漏情况的现场实测结果，给定计算平衡时的隧道外水内渗速率为 0.5L/m^2/d 以模拟较大渗漏量时的不利情况。通过反复试算确定了三组模型衬砌的渗透能力相关参数，如表 1 所示。

隧道衬砌渗透参数（外水内渗速率为 0.5L/m^2/d） 表 1

模拟方式	渗漏区域渗透参数	非渗透区域渗透参数
全环低渗透性	—	$k_l = 1\times10^{-12}$m/s
等效渗透系数方法	$k_e = 4.14\times10^{-11}$m/s	—
局部水力传导方法	$k_j = 4\times10^{-8}$m/s	$k_l = 1\times10^{-12}$m/s
CZM 方法	$g_0 = 0.026$mm	$k_l = 1\times10^{-12}$m/s

注：g_0 为 CZM 方法中接缝位置 cohesive 单元的初始水力开度。

2.1 模型参数

模型相关参数[13]基于上海地铁隧道区间的外水内渗案例：隧道区间采用土压平衡式盾构隧道施工，隧道内外径分别为 5.5m 和 6.2m。隧道中心距离地表 15m，隧道模型边界设定为 60m×90m，如图 3 所示。地层条件简化为单一的典型粉质黏土层，土体参数：重度 γ 为 18.6kN/m^3，弹性模量 E 为 42.1MPa，泊松比为 0.30，孔隙比为0.85，黏聚力 c 为 12.8kPa，内摩擦角 φ 为 30°，渗透系数 k_s 考虑为各向同性，取 5×10^{-9}m/s。衬砌混凝土采用线弹性材料模拟，弹性模量取 34.5GPa，泊松比取 0.167，渗透系数 k_l 取 1×10^{-12}m/s。

文献[6,13]给出的基于现场监测的上海地铁衬砌渗漏水情况均表明，衬砌接头位置是主要的渗漏点，且多见于拱腰位置。因此在局部水力传导方法和 CZM 方法中，均假设左侧拱腰位置的接头发生水力劣化。为了保证各个模型其他条件一致，除了在 CZM 模型中，其他模型也在接头位置均插入 cohesive 单元，但在计算过程中保持渗流通道关闭。cohesive 单元法向模量 E_{nn} 与切向模量 E_{ss} 分别取 1×10^{10}N/m^2 和 4.17×10^{10}N/m^2，以在渗流状态下考虑接头力学行为对水力开度的耦合影响。

2.2 计算步骤

模型分析步基于 ABAQUS 中 Soils 分析模块展开全过程的应力场与渗流场的耦合分析，设置计算分析步如下：①初始地应力与渗流场平衡；②将开挖区域土体进行模量软化，以模拟隧道开挖过程的土体应力释放；③移除开挖区域土体，进行应力释放；④添加衬砌单元，同时添加用以模拟局部渗流区域的 cohesive 单元等；⑤对隧道内部添加零孔压边界,创造外水内渗条件,计算直至渗流场平衡。

模型的边界条件如下:上部边界为自由边界,且为自由补水的 0 水头面;左右两侧边界约束法向位移,设置不透水边界;模型底部设置法向位移边界,模型底面不透水。外水内渗要求在土体中央开启排水条件,地层四周均会向隧道渗漏区域不同程度地补水,通过试算,在本例的粉质黏土地层较低的渗透系数条件下,给出的边界基本不影响渗流场的计算。

2.3 计算结果对比

通过控制最终达到相同的外水内渗速率一致,从而对各个模型的计算结果进行比较。图 4 和图 5 分别给出最终达到渗流平衡阶段,各个模型的衬砌与墙背土体的计算结果。其中轴力和弯矩以全环低渗透性工况为对照,给出局部渗流作用下内力变化量。相比于全环低渗透的情况,在开启外水内渗阶段后衬砌轴力有不同程度地减小(图 4a)):等效渗透系数方法全周轴力均匀减小,拱顶和拱腰位置处减小值分别为 18.5kN/m 和 17.8kN/m,而两种考虑局部渗流的方法仅在左侧(180° ~360°)范围内大幅减小,CZM 方法和局部水力传导方法在左拱腰位置处轴力减小值分别为 65.4kN/m 和 62.5kN/m。

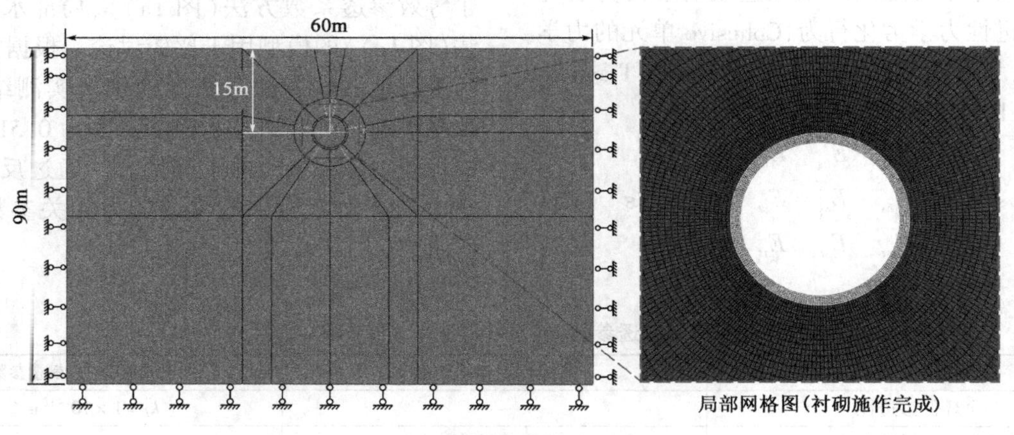

图 3 地层-结构模型示意图

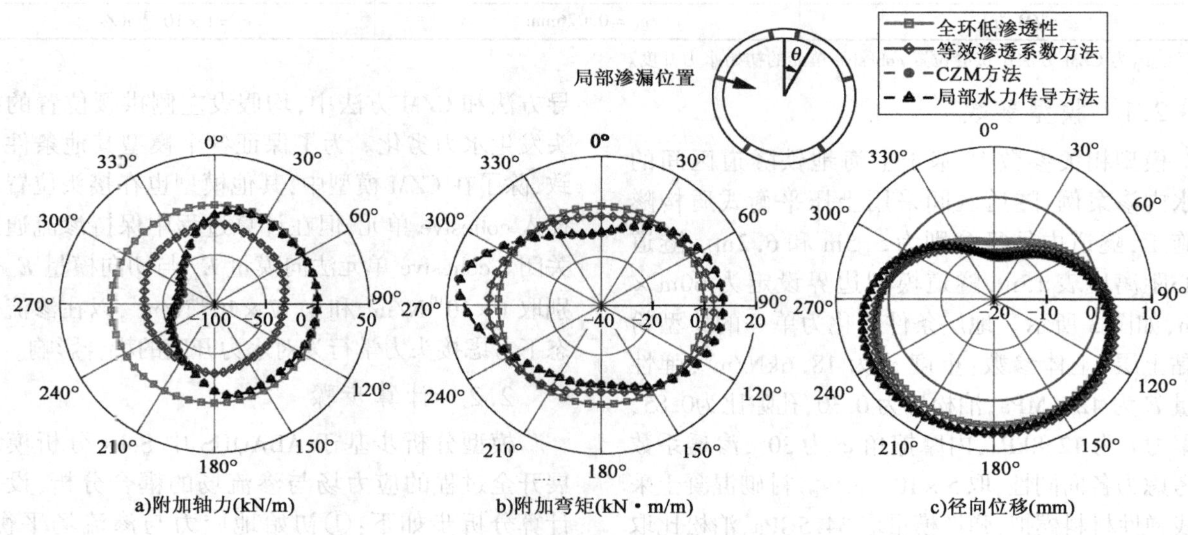

图 4 局部渗漏影响下的衬砌响应

针对衬砌的弯矩的变化情况(图 4b)),等效渗透系数方法的衬砌弯矩在拱腰轻微增加而在拱顶与拱底减小,而两种考虑局部渗流的方法的衬砌弯矩变化幅度更明显,尤其在局部渗流区域,衬砌弯矩增加量达到最大,最大弯矩增加量分别为 16.51kN·m/m 和 15.7kN·m/m,同样是 CZM 方法给出的结果稍大。

由图4c)可见,在考虑外水内渗条件下,隧道有横鸭蛋变形的趋势,且伴随微小的整体沉降。与全环低渗透模型相比,考虑等效渗透系数方法的隧道在拱顶和拱底沉降值分别增加2.26mm和1.62mm,收敛变化量为-0.64mm。两种考虑局部渗流的方法的收敛变化量为-1.65mm和-1.56mm,明显大于全环低渗透性方法的结果。另外,考虑局部渗漏行为后在渗漏区域衬砌有明显外突趋势,CZM方法和局部水力传导方法在渗漏位置处的外凸变化量分别为2.14mm和2mm,是局部渗漏带来的不利影响之一。

局部渗漏在墙背土体的渗流场影响上主要体现为孔隙水压的大幅降低和渗流速度的提高。局部渗流区域对孔隙水压的影响范围约为240°~330°,CZM方法和局部水力传导方法的墙背土体最小孔压值降为24.3kPa和39.9kPa,最大流速则达到了2.70×10^{-7}m/s和1.51×10^{-7}m/s,而同样位置处的全环低渗透性工况和等效渗透系数方法的流速仅为7.87×10^{-11}m/s和1.56×10^{-9}m/s。在局部渗漏条件下,地层对衬砌的径向土压力同样有大幅减小,主要因素是孔隙水压的降低(图5)。

总体来说,基于衬砌与墙背土体响应的变化,本文给出的CZM方法与传统常用的局部水力传导方法具有较高的一致性。局部渗漏条件可能对衬砌带来不利的影响结果,而CZM方法给出的结果变化量稍大于传统常用的局部水力传导方法,分析原因是后者将较大宽度的网格单元视为局部渗流区域,CZM方法中则嵌入0厚度的Cohesive单元,渗流区域相对更集中。

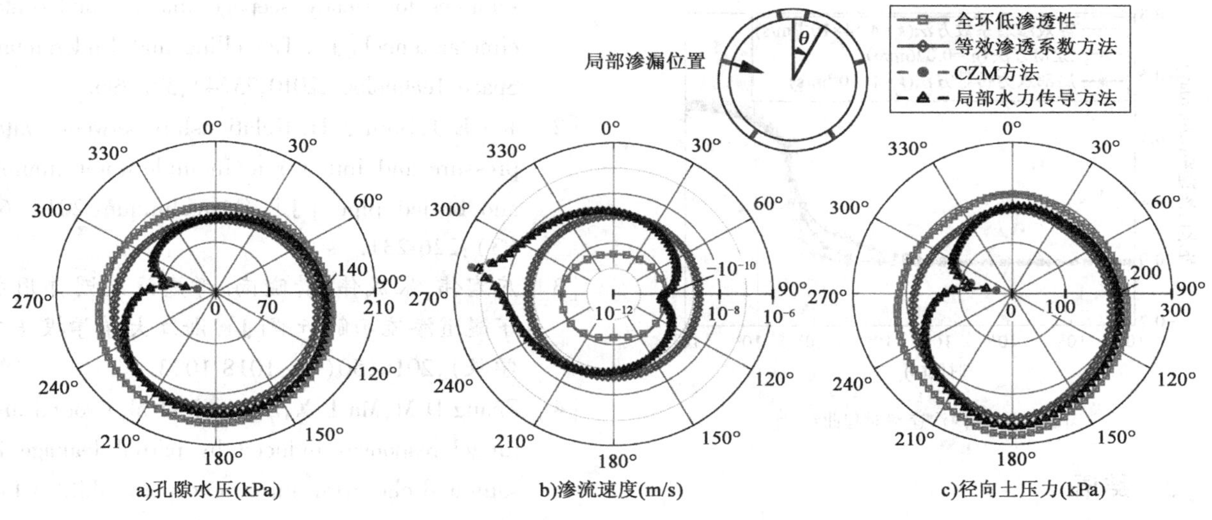

图5 局部渗漏影响下的墙背土体响应

图6给出三组考虑外水内渗的隧道模型地层渗流场结果,结果表明考虑局部渗流的两组模型在局部渗流区域及其上方范围出现明显的地层水力坡降,而且局部渗流区域影响的范围并未遍布衬砌全周,在其直径相反的位置没有明显的渗流场流速,相较于等效渗透系数方法是更加合理的结果。

不同的渗流模式和建模方法也会影响渗流开始至渗流场平衡的时间。由图7可见CZM方法在前期外水内渗速率最快,而等效渗透系数方法最慢。假定到达最终渗流量(0.5L/m²/d)的99%视为已达到渗流平衡,则等效渗透系数法最先达到渗流平衡,耗时1.14×10^{6}s(13.2d),随后是CZM方法,耗时1.70×10^{6}s(19.67d),局部水力传导方法最慢,耗时4.16×10^{6}s(48.1d)。分析原因是局部水力传导方法将渗流区域做了等效,局部渗流范围大但渗透系数小,所需达到渗流平衡的时间更久。

综上所述,通过与其他常用方法的对比,验证了本文给出的CZM方法在模拟衬砌局部渗流上的可行性。相比于常用的局部水力传导方法,其表达局部渗流能力的水力开度含义更明确,渗漏区域更集中,到达最终渗流平衡的时间更快,表明其能够有效模拟接头水力劣化所引发的衬砌与地层响应。

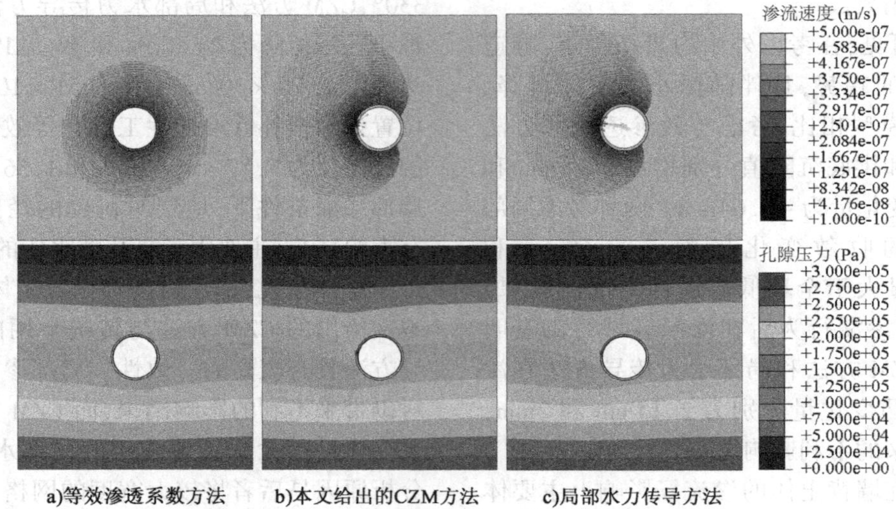

图6　局部渗漏影响下的渗流场分布

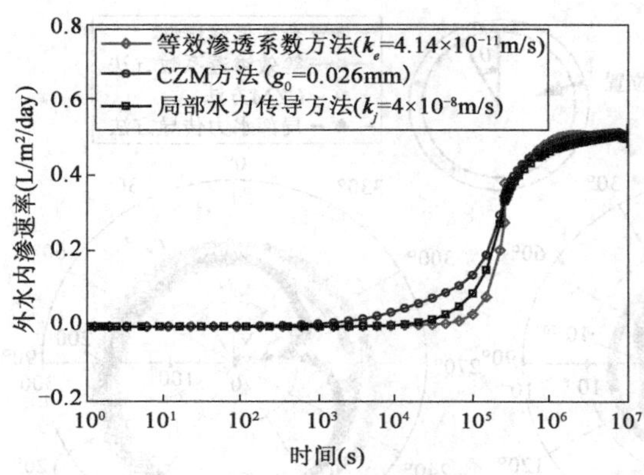

图7　外水内渗速率时程曲线

3　结语

本文引入 CZM 方法用于模拟盾构隧道衬砌的局部渗流行为,通过与常用的渗漏模拟方法对比验证了该方法的有效性。计算结果表明 CZM 方法有以下特点:①通过水力开度概念表达衬砌局部渗流能力,含义更明确,也更接近接缝水力劣化的渗流特性;②相比于局部水力传导方法,CZM 方法的渗流区域更集中,更快到达渗流平衡,同时诱发的衬砌响应变化也更大;③该方法可以有效考虑衬砌局部渗流的水力与力学特性的耦合。更进一步的针对局部渗流的流固耦合分析以及更复杂的局部渗流对衬砌的纵向响应有待后续进一步探讨。

参考文献

[1] Huangfu M, Wang M S, Tan Z S, et al. Analytical solutions for steady seepage into an underwater circular tunnel[J]. Tunnelling and Underground Space Technology, 2010, 25(4): 391-396.

[2] Joo E J, Shin J H. Relationship between water pressure and inflow rate in underwater tunnels and buried pipes[J]. Géotechnique, 2014, 64(3): 226-231.

[3] 应宏伟,朱成伟,龚晓南. 考虑注浆圈作用水下隧道渗流场解析解[J]. 浙江大学学报(工学版), 2016, 50(6): 1018-1023.

[4] Zhang D M, Ma L X, Zhang J, et al. Ground and tunnel responses induced by partial leakage in saturated clay with anisotropic permeability[J]. Engineering Geology, 2015, 189: 104-115.

[5] Wongsaroj J, Soga K, Mair R J. Modelling of long-term ground response to tunnelling under St James's Park, London[J]. Géotechnique, 2011, 63(13), 1103-1115.

[6] Wu H N, Shen S L, Chen R P, et al. Three-dimensional numerical modelling on localised leakage in segmental lining of shield tunnels[J]. Computers and Geotechnics, 2020, 122: 103549.

[7] Shin J H, Kim S H, Shin Y S. Long-term mechanical and hydraulic interaction and leakage evaluation of segmented tunnels[J]. Soils and Foundations, 2012, 52(1): 38-48.

[8] 孙智慧,唐勇,刘涛.盾构隧道局部渗漏水对其力学特性的影响[J].现代隧道技术,2021,58(4):141-149.

[9] Yao Y. Linear elastic and cohesive fracture analysis to model hydraulic fracture in brittle and ductile rocks[J]. Rock mechanics and rock engineering,2012,45(3):375-387.

[10] Zhang G, Zhang Y, Xu A, et al. Microflow effects on the hydraulic aperture of single rough fractures[J]. Advances in Geo-Energy Research,2019,3(1):104-114.

[11] ABAQUS User's Manual[M]. Version 2020. Dassault Systemes Simulia Corp, Rhode Island, USA,2020.

[12] Wu H N, Huang R Q, Sun W J, et al. Leaking behavior of shield tunnels under the Huangpu River of Shanghai with induced hazards[J]. Natural Hazards,2014,70(2):1115-1132.

[13] 刘印,张冬梅,黄宏伟.盾构隧道局部长期渗水对隧道变形及地表沉降的影响分析[J].岩土力学,2013,34(1):290-298.

富水砂层超大直径盾构隧道接缝密封垫防水性能研究

张稳军* 刘 望

(天津大学建筑工程学院)

摘 要 以国内某盾构隧道工程为背景,从盾构管片接缝密封垫防水机理出发,考虑实际工况以及工程需求,借助有限元分析软件 ABAQUS 建立数值模型进行模拟。探究不同接缝错台量、不同接缝张开量对于密封垫防水性能的影响。结果表明:密封垫的防水性能受到张开量和错台量的影响,防水性能随着错台量和张开量的增加而减弱;盾构管片拼装时没有产生错台量时,密封垫的防水性能最好,即使产生一定的张开量,仍能发挥防水效果;当张开量与错台量其中之一超过一定尺寸时,密封垫无法达到要求的防水效果;盾构隧道密封垫设计时,应确保密封垫孔洞被完全压缩,这种情况下的密封垫防水性能最佳。

关键词 盾构隧道 接缝防水 数值模拟 密封垫

0 引言

随着我国经济迅速发展及工程技术水平的不断进步,盾构法施工隧道的数量逐渐增加,同时隧道规模也不断提升,总体上向着大直径、大埋深的方向不断发展。但是在隧道施工及运营过程中,盾构隧道的渗漏水问题也日益突出,渗漏水问题会对隧道的结构稳定性以及安全生产造成较大的影响,因此需要密切关注。盾构隧道的渗漏主要发生在管片的接缝处,主要依靠密封垫进行防水。

国内外研究学者对于盾构隧道管片的接缝防水性能研究一直较为热衷。向科等[1]从弹性密封垫的防水机理出发,考虑实际工况并结合管片拼装的需要,分析并提出盾构隧道管片弹性密封垫断面的主要设计参数。张稳军等[2]用 ABAQUS 网格间求解变换技术,研究不同遇水膨胀橡胶块截面类型和尺寸对复合型密封垫防水性能的影响,得出复合型密封垫的二次防水性能有所提高。赵运臣等[3]模拟了施工极限装配误差,对初步设计进行了防水性能与闭合压缩力试验,并根据试验结果对密封垫进行优化,以确定最优的防水密封垫设计。何太洪等[4]以杭州地铁一号线为背景,设计了适用于该工程的密封垫断面形式。Li 等[5]以南京地铁 10 号线盾构隧道密封垫设计为研究对象,研究了双道密封垫的防水性能。Shi 等[6]建立了管片接缝应力-渗漏耦合模型,并推导出相应的接触面耦合方程,通过试验研究了接缝张开和错台对密封垫防水性能的影响。朱广泉[7]针对某高速铁路盾构隧道,设计了一种新的接缝防水密封性能数值模拟分析方法。孙廉威[8]利用 ANSYS 软件建立了完整的沟槽与弹性密封垫数值模型,模拟水压对弹性密封垫防水的影响。高楠[9]以汕头市苏埃通道工程为背景进行了研究,发现弹性橡胶密封垫的防水能力和装配应力成正比例关系,且随着接缝张开量的增加,比例系数减小。李拼等[10]考虑到弹性密封垫之间、弹性密封垫和沟槽之间的接触应力分配不均,提出了有效应力概念。Zhang 等[11]通过荷载-变形关系测试密封垫的力学性能,通过水压-接缝张开度关系检测防水垫密封性能,得出密封垫偏移量与接缝张开量均对防水性能造成很大影响。

本文基于某富水砂层超大断面盾构隧道工程,分析盾构隧道管片接缝复合型密封垫防水机理,针对纵缝密封垫防水性能开展分析利用有限元软件 ABAQUS 对超大直径隧道中弹性密封垫的防水性能进行了研究,探究富水砂层超大断面隧道中接缝张开量、错台量对于密封垫防水性能的影响。

1　工程概况

本文以某盾构隧道改造工程为背景,管片混凝土强度等级为 C60;混凝土抗渗等级为 P12。衬砌环直径外径为 15400mm,内径为 14100mm,采用“1+2+7”分块结构构成(11.657°×1+39.171°×2+38.571°×7),衬砌厚度为 650mm,平均环宽为 2000mm。拼装方式为错缝拼装,环缝面设置分布式凹凸槽、传力接触面及橡胶垫片,纵缝面设置定位杆。管片接缝型式见图 1,接缝防水为单道密封垫防水形式。

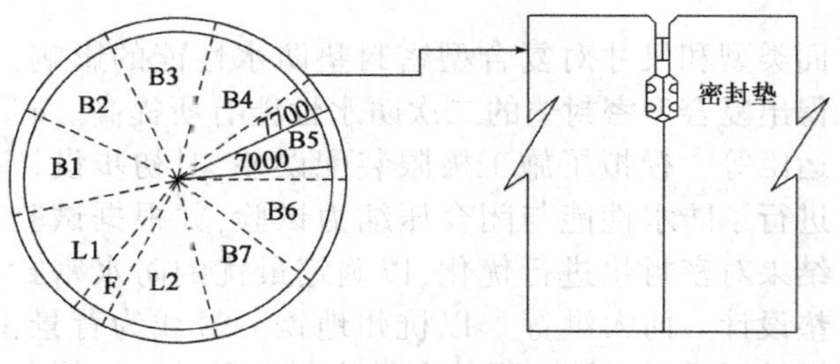

图 1　盾构隧道管片接缝示意图

2　研究情况

运用大型有限元软件 ABAQUS 对橡胶密封垫进行仿真优化,密封垫橡胶材料选用三元乙丙橡胶,其物理特性具有超弹性、非线性以及不可压缩性;本文所研究密封垫主要以压缩为主,因此文章主要研究三元乙丙橡胶的超弹体本构模型。超弹性材料应力-应变的非线性本构关系以应变能函数定义,本次将采用 Mooney-Rivlin 二参数模型,其应变能函数表达式见式(1),材料参数设置见表 1。将混凝土管片看作刚体,并且固定下部刚体,通过对上部刚体施加位移模拟密封垫受压。设置密封垫内部以及密封垫与管片的接触方式,其法向设置为硬接触模式,切向设置为罚模式,摩擦系数取值 0.5。

$$U = C_{10}(I_1 - 3) + C_{01}(I_2 - 3) \tag{1}$$

式中:U——应变势能;

I_1、I_2——应变不变量;

C_{10}、C_{01}——橡胶材料参数。

材料参数　　表 1

硬度(H_A)	C_{10}	C_{01}
A67	0.59238	0.14809

结合工程实际需求与密封垫外形尺寸的限制,确定了最大张开量为 8mm,最大错位量为 12mm。建立密封垫有限元模型如图 2 所示。

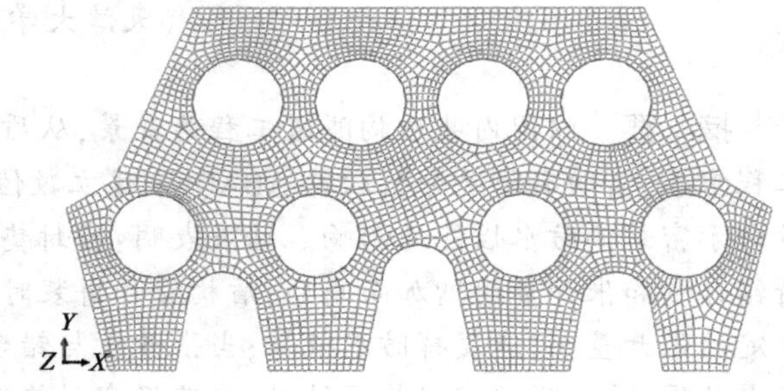

图 2　密封垫有限元模型图

3　计算结果分析

3.1　不同错台量条件下防水性能分析

设置允许最大错台量为 12mm,在 0～12mm 之间设置工况,步长为 2mm。得到张开量为 0mm 时不同错台量下密封垫应力云图(图 3)。根据相关研究[10],采用密封垫接触面平均接触应力表示密封垫防水能力,提取出错台量为 0、4、8mm 时,不同张开量下密封垫-密封垫接触面、密封垫-密封槽接触面两条渗透路径下密封垫防水能力对比如图 4 所示。

根据图 4 可得,在密封垫压缩过程中,渗流路径密封垫-密封槽接触面的接触应力始终大于密封垫-密封垫接触面的接触应力,即防水性能失效由密封垫-密封垫接触面渗流路径控制,因而仅对该路径进行研究。

综合不同张开量的工况下，随着密封垫错台量的变化，密封垫-密封垫接触面平均接触力的数值情况如表2所示，并由此得到密封垫接缝防水能力随着错台量的变化情况如图5所示。通过分析比对不同张开量工况下的数据发现：①在某一定的张开量下，随着密封垫错台量的逐渐增大，接触面上平均接触应力减小，当张开量为0mm时，在错台量为0mm时平均接触应力达到2.626MPa，在错台量为12mm时平均接触应力仅为0.539MPa。②张开量为0mm时，在错台量为8mm的情况下，密封垫依旧满足0.8MPa的工程防水性能要求。③张开量大于4时，错台量变化的全过程中密封垫防水性能始终低于工程防水要求。

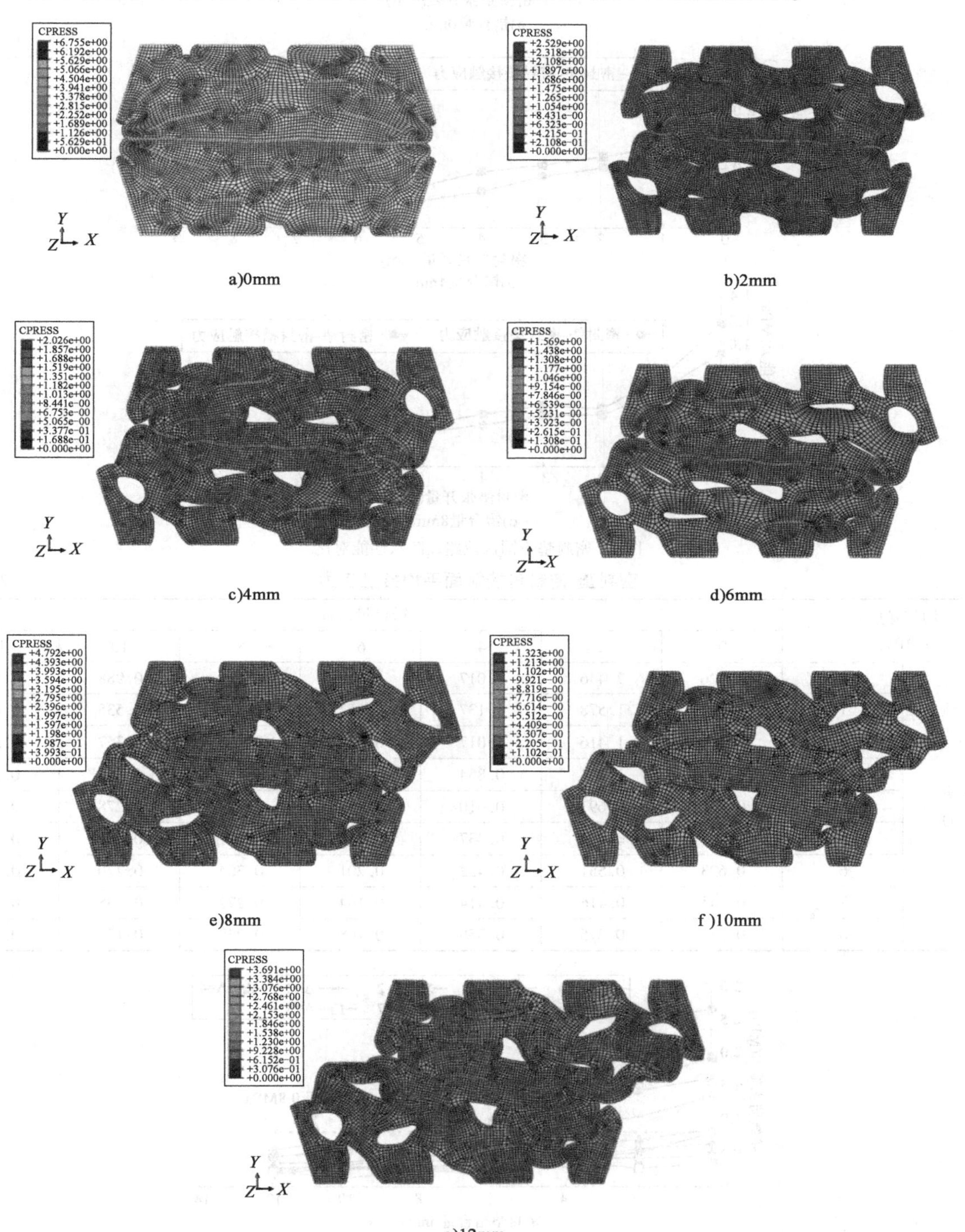

a)0mm b)2mm c)4mm d)6mm e)8mm f)10mm g)12mm

图3 不同错台量密封垫接触应力云图

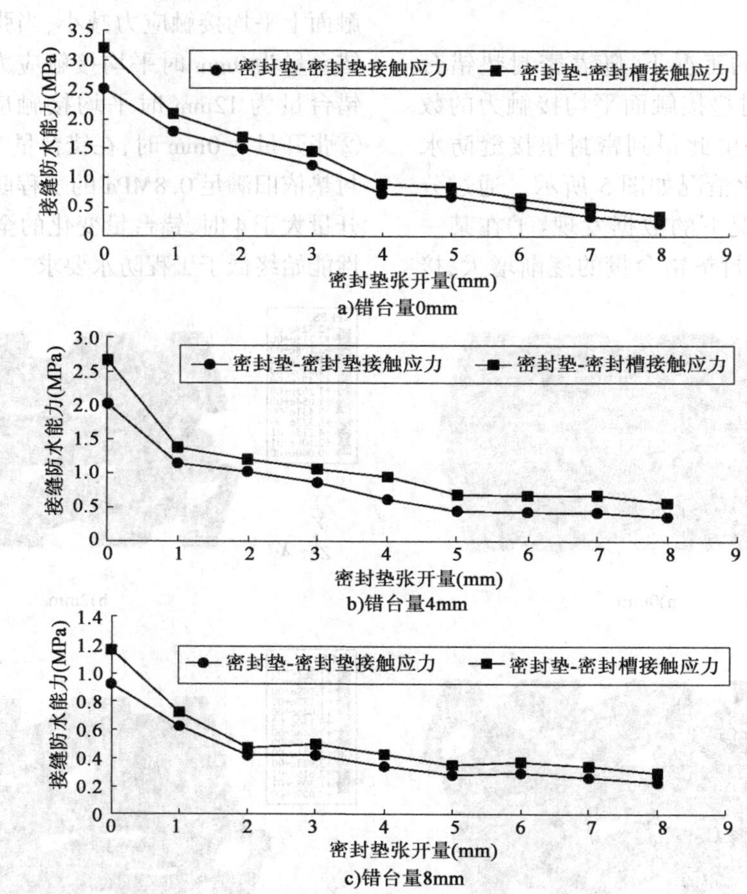

图4　密封垫不同渗流路径防水性能对比

密封垫-密封垫接触面平均接触应力　　表2

平均接触应力(MFa)		错台量(mm)						
		0	2	4	6	8	10	12
张开量(mm)	0	2.626	2.446	2.017	1.686	1.236	0.988	0.539
	1	1.902	1.578	1.137	0.957	0.635	0.535	0.435
	2	1.604	1.416	1.017	0.595	0.430	0.357	0.341
	3	1.320	1.031	0.854	0.557	0.431	0.314	0.262
	4	0.835	0.691	0.610	0.467	0.352	0.278	0.177
	5	0.784	0.497	0.437	0.338	0.291	0.257	0.210
	6	0.623	0.551	0.422	0.201	0.304	0.270	0.262
	7	0.445	0.416	0.414	0.164	0.272	0.255	0.229
	8	0.331	0.275	0.350	0.168	0.239	0.125	0.211

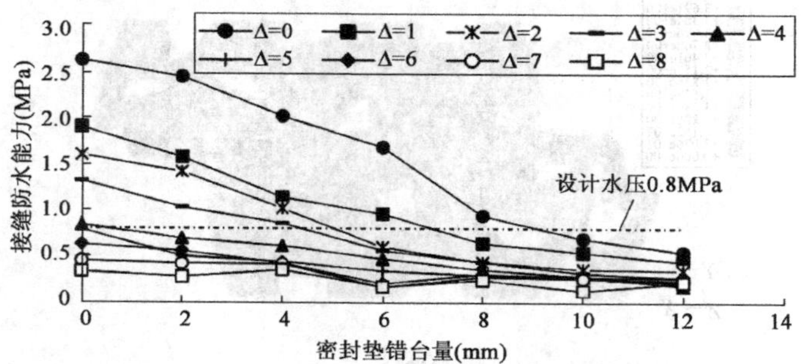

图5　错台量对密封垫防水性能的影响

3.2　不同张开量条件下防水性能分析

参考工程允许最大张开量 8mm，张开量在 0 ~ 8mm 之间设置工况，步长为 1mm。得到错台量为 0mm 时，不同张开量下密封垫的应力云图如图 6 所示。观察分析这几种工况下的云图，可以发现，随着张开量的增加，密封垫间的孔洞逐渐张开，孔洞压紧率降低。如图 6a）所示，在密封垫完全压缩时，张开量为 0mm 情况下，单个密封垫的八个孔洞被完全压紧，此时密封垫的防水效果最佳。随着张开量的增加，单个密封垫的第一排孔洞（靠近密封垫-密封垫接触面一侧）逐渐张开；张开量为 7mm 时，第二排孔洞基本张开。当达到工程允许张开量 8mm 时，单个密封垫两排共 8 个孔洞基本没有受到有效的压缩，此时密封垫的防水性能下降较大。

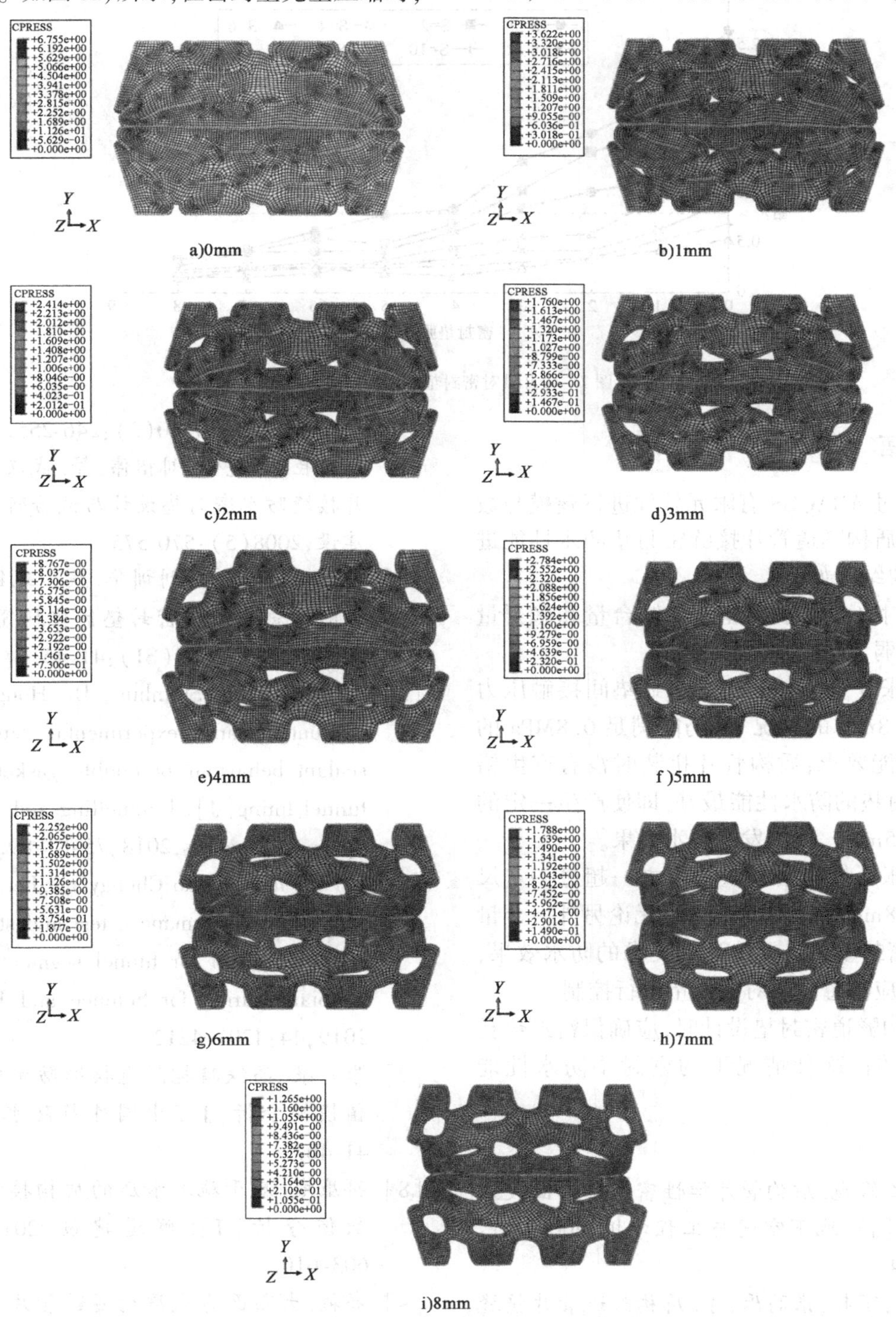

a)0mm　b)1mm　c)2mm　d)3mm　e)4mm　f)5mm　g)6mm　h)7mm　i)8mm

图 6　不同张开量密封垫接触应力云图

根据表2分析总结出张开量对密封垫防水性能的影响,如图7所示。研究不同错台量工况下,密封垫张开量对防水性能影响,可以发现:①密封垫接触应力随密封垫张开量的增大而减少。②在错台量为0mm时,密封垫的防水性能较好,在张开量为5mm时,仍能满足工程防水要求。③当密封垫错台量大于等于8mm时,张开量变化过程中密封垫间平均接触应力基本都不满足工程所需的防水要求0.8MPa。④当密封垫错台量在0~4mm之间,即使张开量达到了3~4mm,该密封垫防水能力也能达到0.8MPa以上,满足工程所需的防水效果。

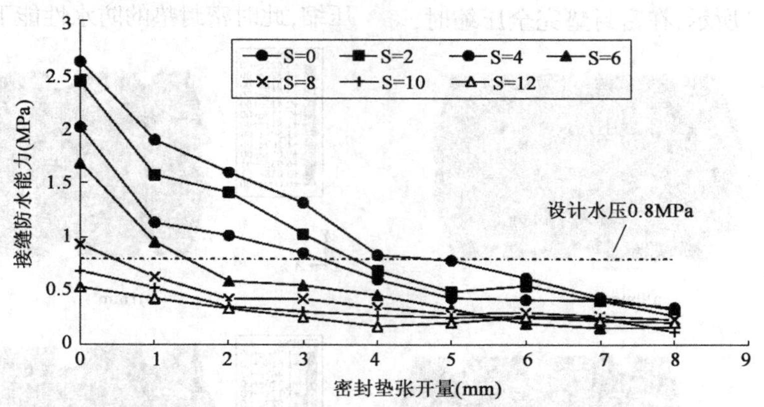

图7　张开量对密封垫防水性能的影响

4　结语

本文通过ABAQUS有限元软件进行建模与数值模拟对某盾构隧道管片接缝密封垫防水性能进行分析,主要结论如下:

(1)密封垫的防水性能随着错台量和张开量的增加而减弱。

(2)在张开量为0mm时,密封垫间接触压力在错台量为8mm的情况下,仍能满足0.8MPa的工程防水性能要求;盾构管片拼装时没有产生错台量时,密封垫的防水性能最好,即使产生一定的张开量(0~5mm),仍能发挥防水效果。

(3)当张开量与错台量其中之一超过一定尺寸时(S>=8mm或者Δ>4mm),无论另外一个量数值如何,密封垫始终无法达到要求的防水效果,因此工程中应注意同时对两个量进行控制;

(4)盾构隧道密封垫设计时,应确保密封垫孔洞被完全压缩,这种情况下的密封垫防水性能最佳。

参考文献

[1] 向科,石修巍.盾构管片弹性密封垫断面设计与优化[J].地下空间与工程学报,2008(2):361-364.

[2] 张稳军,丁超,张高乐,等.盾构隧道管片接缝复合型密封垫选型设计研究[J].隧道建设(中英文),2020,40(2):246-255.

[3] 赵运臣,肖龙鸽,刘招伟,等.武汉长江隧道管片接缝防水密封垫设计与试验研究[J].隧道建设,2008(5):570-575.

[4] 何太洪,周冠南,刘训华.杭州地铁1号线越江隧道管片防水密封垫优化研究[J].地下工程与隧道,2009(S1):41-45.

[5] LI Xue, Zhou Shunhua, Di Honggui, et al. Evaluation and experimental study on the sealant behaviour of double gaskets for shield tunnel lining[J]. T unnelling and Underground Space Technology,2018,75:81-89.

[6] Shi Chenghua,Cao Chengyong,Lei Mingfeng,et al. Sealant performanc e test and stress-seepage coupling model for tunnel segment joints[J]. Arabian Journal for Science and Engineering, 2019,44:4201-4212.

[7] 朱广泉.高铁暗挖隧道接缝防水密封性能数值模拟分析[J].中国建筑防水,2021(3):41-46.

[8] 孙廉威.基于施加水压的盾构接缝防水机制数值分析[J].隧道建设,2018,38(4):603-610.

[9] 高楠.大断面海底盾构隧道管片接缝防水试验研究[D].北京:北京交通大学,2016.

[10] 李拼,谢宏明,何川,等.基于有效接触应力的大张开量盾构隧道密封垫防水性能分析[J].隧道建设,2019,39(12):1993-1999.
[11] Zhang Gao Le, Zhang Wen Jun, Li Hong Liang, et al. Waterproofing behavior of sealing gaskets for circumferential joints in shield tunnels: A full-scale experimental investigation [J]. Tunnelling and Underground Space Technology, 2020(prepublish).

预应力张拉及回淤程度对沉管隧道节段接头变形特性影响分析

牛亚鹏*[1] 岳夏冰[1] 韩瀛光[2]
(1.长安大学公路学院;2.中国石油天然气管道工程有限公司)

摘 要 为了研究预应力张拉控制值、回淤程度对沉管隧道节段接头变形特性的影响。本文采用自平衡柔性加载装置进行了1:100管节缩尺模型试验。分析了预应力张拉程度和回淤荷载变化,对沉管隧道节段沉降、接头张开量的影响。试验结果表明:①施加预应力锚索提高了管节整体的抗弯刚度,减小节段间差异沉降,使沉降在管节内更均匀分布。②管节沉降及接头张开量随着预应力控制值的增加而减小,随着回淤荷载增加而呈线性增加趋势;当预应力控制值从0增大到0.8kN时,管节的沉降和节段接头张开量分别减小了5%~11.94%、73.1%~73.6%,但是当预应力张拉值一定时,随着回淤荷载的增加,管节沉降及节段张开量分别增加了2.63~2.83倍、2.32~2.37倍,表明回淤荷载的增加对节段接头变形特性影响明显,可能会使隧道结构产生漏水甚至破坏。

关键词 沉管隧道 模型试验 节段接头 沉降 张开量 变形特性

0 引言

随着水下隧道的发展,沉管隧道已越来越多地被应用在穿越江河的水下工程领域。节段式沉管隧道由多个节段连接组成管节,管节相互连接形成整个隧道,这种形式更适合地基的不均匀沉降,但由此产生了大量管节接头和节段接头。接头刚度远小于混凝土主体结构,成为整个结构的薄弱部位。在隧道顶部不均匀回淤,沉管碎石垫层处理施工误差,地基不均匀性等的影响下,接头处会产生错动、张开等,有可能使接头部位止水效果降低或失去止水效果,甚至造成节段接头剪力键破坏等。因此针对节段接头变形特性的研究对结构防水和结构设计都有重要意义。

目前,国内外学者对接头力学特性方面开展了一系列研究工作。理论分析方面,刘鹏等[1]通过对接头各部件的力学机理的研究,分别提出了接头轴向、切向与弯曲刚度解析公式。禹海涛等[2]基于变形协调关系和受力平衡方程对接头钢端壳和止水带部件进行了理论分析,推导出了接头刚度解析表达式。模型试验方面,胡指南等[3]通过1:4.69的大比尺沉管隧道节段接头模型试验,研究了沉管隧道节段接头剪力空间分布规律。岳夏冰等[4]通过离心模型试验,揭示了沉管隧道天然地基开挖回弹及回填再压缩应力分布及变形特征。袁勇等[5]通过1:10模型试验,研究了管节接头剪力键在轴力和弯矩作用下变形特性。周舟等[6]通过建立三维有限元模型,分析了预应力锚索对节段接头的力学性能。

综上所述,接头力学特性的研究主要集中在管节接头各部件处,而针对节段接头变形特性的研究很少。特别是考虑预应力张拉程度与回淤程度对节段接头变形特性影响的研究文献较少。

本文在前人研究的基础上,对节段接头变形

1.基金项目:陕西省自然科学基础研究计划(2020JQ-379)。

特性研究进行了1:100管节缩尺模型试验,对比分析了回淤和预应力张拉对沉管隧道沉降、节段接头张开量等方面的影响,相关研究方法与成果可以为沉管隧道节段接头研究及设计提供参考与依据。

1 工程背景

试验以沉管隧道(图1)天然地基段、上部回淤较大的E18管节为原型,其地基土层由上至下分布为淤泥质土10.6m、黏土26.7m、含砾粗砂35m。其中砾石垫层级配好,物料粒径适中,不含杂物,泥浆含量不大于3%,最大粒径不大于31.5mm;沉管隧道节段接头由混凝土剪力键、钢板密封条、OMEGA止水带、预应力锚索组成,如图2所示。地基土参数及沉管结构相关参数见表1、表2。

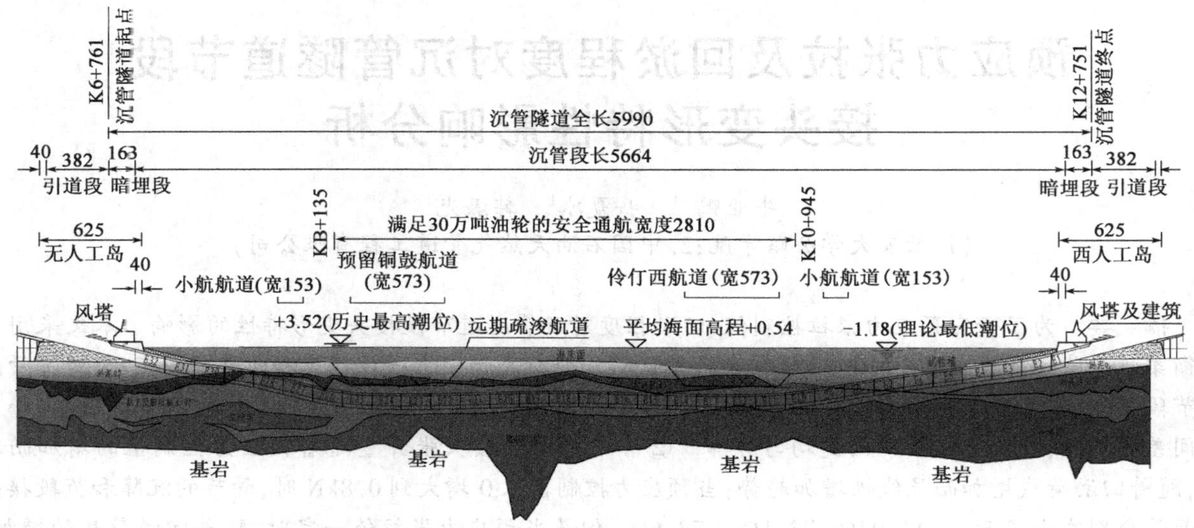

图1 港珠澳海底隧道纵向剖面图(尺寸单位:m)

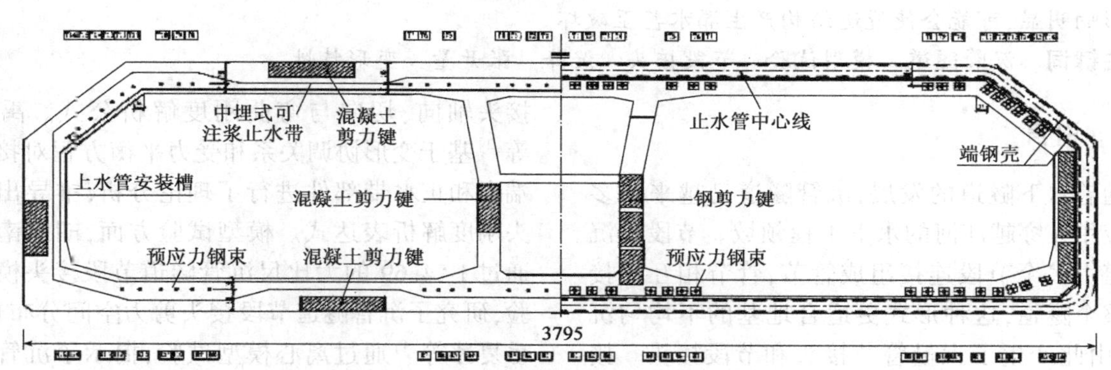

图2 沉管隧道节段横断面图(尺寸单位:cm)

地基土参数[7] 表1

名称	压缩模量E_S(MPa)	重度γ(kN/m³)	黏聚力c(kPa)	内摩擦角φ(°)	泊松比ν	厚度H(m)
淤泥质土	2.68	6.80	9	6	0.43	10.60
黏土	10.78	8.40	26	21	0.40	26.70
含砾粗砂	73.70	11.80	16	33	0.30	35.00

沉管相关参数 表2

材料(混凝土)	弹性模量E(GPa)	密度(t/m³)	泊松比ν	顶底板厚度(m)	边墙厚度(m)	中隔墙厚度(m)	高度(m)
C50	34.5	2.4	0.2	1.5	1.5	0.8	11.4

2 试验设计

2.1 模型相似理论

本次模型试验几何相似比尺为 1:100,沉管隧道原型采用 C50 混凝土、模型材料采用有机玻璃,混凝土的弹性模量 34.5GPa,有机玻璃的弹性模型 5.67GPa,则弹性模量的比值:

$$G_E = \frac{E_p}{E_m} = \frac{34.5}{5.67} \approx 6.08$$

混凝土的密度 2.4t/m^3,有机玻璃的重度为 1.18t/m^3,则重度比尺:

$$c_\gamma = \frac{\rho_p \times g}{\rho_m \times g} = \frac{2.4}{1.18} \approx 2.03$$

已知几何相似常数 $C_l = 100$,弹性模量相似常数 $C_E = 6.08$,重度相似判据

$$c_\gamma = \frac{C_E}{C_L} = \frac{6.08}{100} \approx 0.0608$$

显然,有机玻璃材料的重度不满足相似条件,本文研究回淤荷载和预应力张拉控制值对节段接头变形特性的影响。经过分析,回淤使得相邻节段产生纵向差异沉降,节段接头变形特性主要相邻节段的差异沉降引起,而不是重力作用在沉管上,沉管内部应力积累整体表现出来的,本文忽略重力对回淤荷载和预应力张拉控制值对节段接头变形特性的影响。

2.2 模型制备

2.2.1 模型箱制作

该模型试验所用的模型箱由钢板和有机玻璃组成,模型箱尺寸为 3m(长)×1.2m(宽)×0.6m(高),有机玻璃尺寸为 3m(长)×1.2m(宽)×0.45m(高),如图 3 所示。最大限度保证模型试验的可靠性与真实性,减小边界效应对模型试验的影响。有机玻璃板距离模型箱顶部 0.15m,此部分设计用于观察测量隧道模型,模型箱内壁涂抹凡士林,以减少土箱内壁与模型地基之间的摩擦力。

图 3 模型箱

2.2.2 隧道模型制作

综合考虑沉管隧道在纵向弯曲工况下节段接头的受力特性、试验相似关系及模型箱尺寸,选取有机玻璃作为隧道模型材料,模型试验只保留四组竖向剪力键,水平剪力键及其他防水构造不再进行模拟;通过控制管节两端预应力钢绞线张拉程度,模拟施加于管节中的预应力。节段接头横断面如图 4 所示,管节模型尺寸为 1.8m(长)×0.3795m(宽)×0.114m(高),管节模型如图 5 所示。

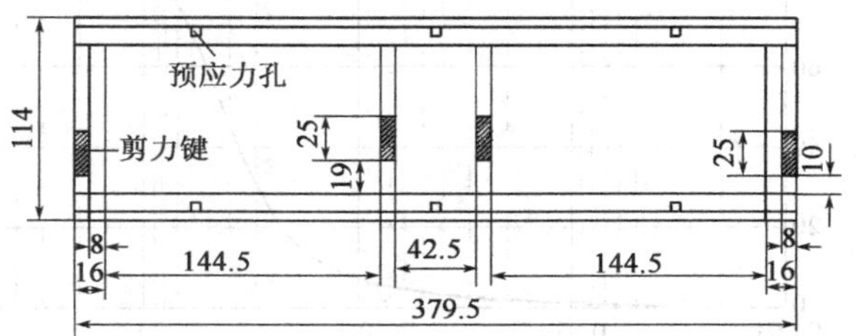

图 4 节段接头横断面(尺寸单位:mm)

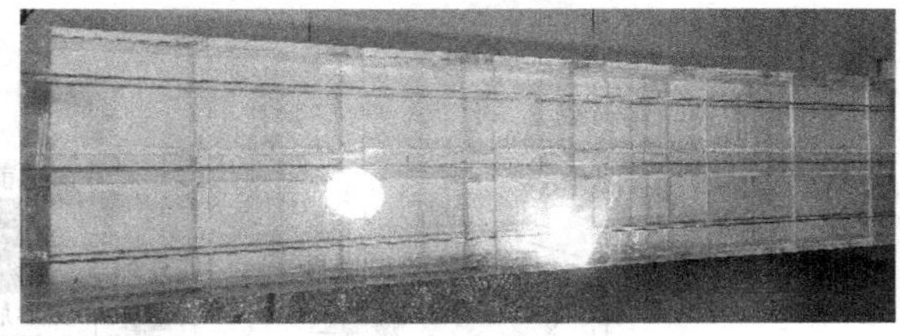

图 5 管节模型

2.2.3 地基土模型的制作

原型地基土层分为三层,分别为淤泥质土、黏土、含砾粗砂。综合考虑场地条件、模型箱尺寸等因素,以压缩模量为控制参数,采用等效替代法,以单层土进行等效代替,等效替代后的地基模型压缩模量为 $E_S = 37.51$MPa。基于相似理论,模型试验地基土压缩模量 $E_S = 6.17$MPa,以压缩模量为控制指标,采用商品砂和 EPS 颗粒混合物模拟地基土。其中细砂的组成:粒径为 1~2mm 占总质量的 6.6%,粒径为 0.5~1mm 占总质量 33.1%、粒径为 0.25~0.5mm 占总质量的 44.9%、粒径为 0.075~0.25mm 占总质量的 13.6%、粒径小于 0.075mm 占总质量的 1.8% 其物理力学指标见表 3,颗粒级配如图 6 所示。

土样参数 表 3

土样	土粒密度 (g·cm^{-3})	最佳含水率 (%)	压缩模量 (MPa)	黏聚力 (kPa)	内摩擦角 (°)
地基土	1.45	4.1	6.17	10.5	28.1

2.3　监测元件布设

测试仪器主要包括土压力传感器(LY-350)、应变片、静态应变仪(TDS-530)与非接触测量仪,监测元件的误差均小于0.5% FS(Full Span,满量程)。本次试验主要针对管节的竖向沉降及节段接头变形特性进行研究,监测元件的布设位置及测量仪如图7、图8所示。

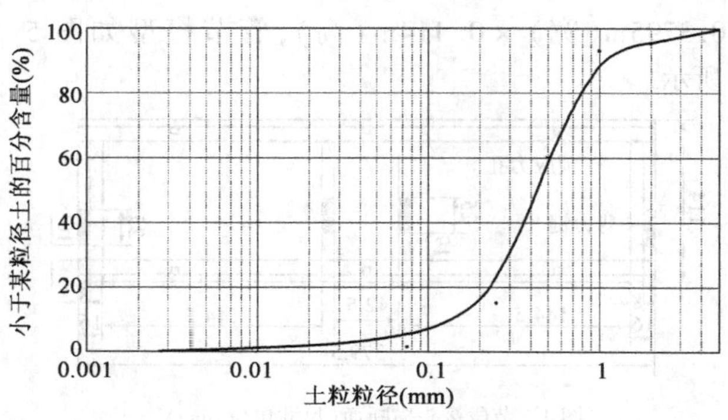

图6　试验用砂颗粒级配曲线

2.4　加载系统

2.4.1　荷载加载方式

本模型试验采用自平衡气压正压加载装置,将气囊放置于已沉放好的沉管模型上方,然后将气囊与气泵连接,最后封闭模型箱顶盖,采用自平衡方式,模拟沉管隧道回淤荷载(图9)。气囊加载模拟柔性荷载,可以尽可能考虑管-土协调变形的能力。

a)管节纵向沉降观测点

b)J4端面应力应变观测点

图7　监测元件布置

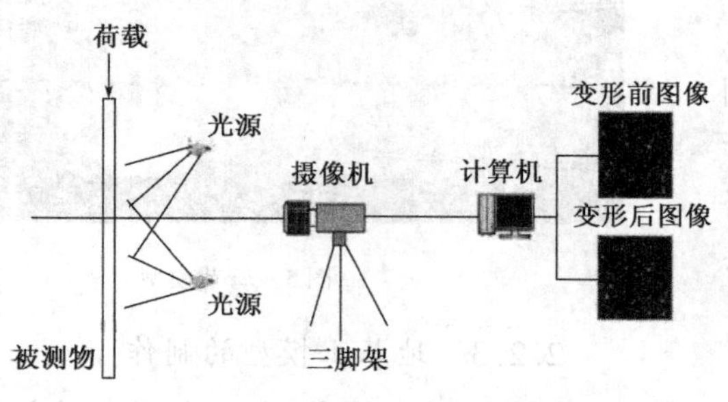

a)非接触测量仪系统

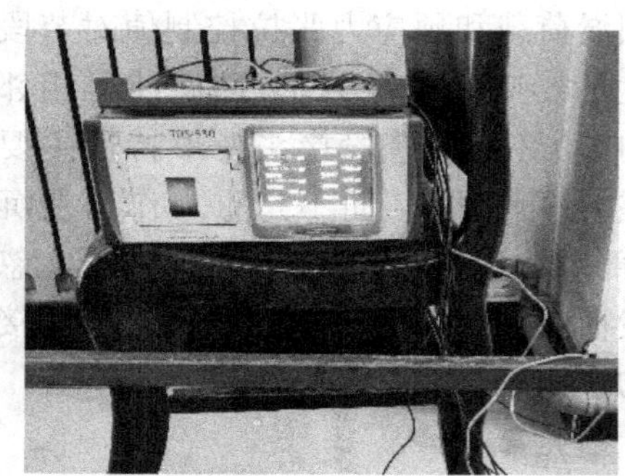

b)静态应变仪

图8　测量仪示意图

a)气囊放置于管节上部

b)封闭模型箱顶盖

图9　自平衡加载装置

2.4.2　预应力加载方式

原型沉管隧道标准管节预应力钢绞线只分布在顶板和底板,共计60孔,每孔预应力张拉程度达到标准强度的100%时,预应力的张拉力为6510kN。采用预应力锚索来增加节段接头处的正压力,提高接头处摩阻力。考虑到试验的目的和实施的难易,本模型试验基于模型相似理论,采用自制预应力加载装置(夹片式锚具、预应力钢绞线、张拉设备)(图10),以轴力为控制变量,模拟结构模型预应力的施加。预应力布置如图11所示。

a)锚具

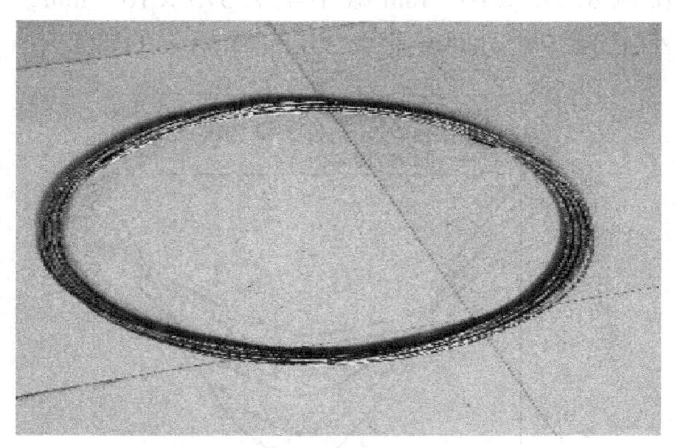

b)预应力钢绞线

c)预应力张拉设备

图10　预应力加载装置

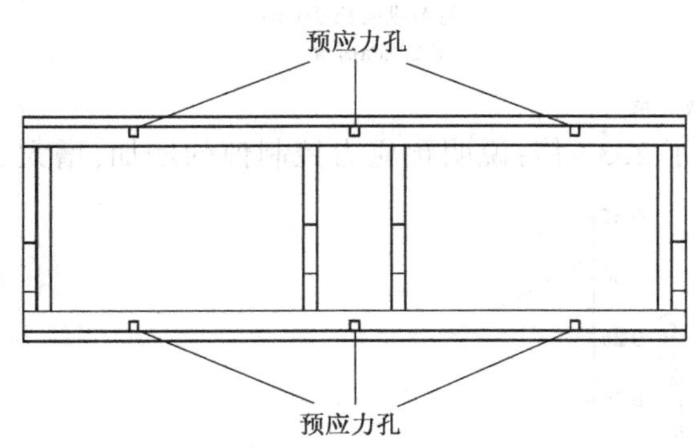

图11　预应力布置示意图

2.5　试验方案

本模型试验共设置了5组试验,进行了预应力张拉值为0kN、0.2kN 、0.4kN、0.6kN和0.8kN 5种工况试验研究,试验工况如表4所示。各试验工况均在最不利回淤荷载下进行。试验所加荷载根据管节所受最不利回淤荷载按1:6.08缩小,取近似20kPa作为最终荷载(本论文最不利回淤荷载换算到工程实际对应的回淤高度为20m)。模拟回淤程度,采用分级加载,分别为5kPa、10kPa、15kPa、20kPa。研究在回淤荷载作用下,预应力控制值对节段接头变形特性的影响。

试验工况　表4

预应力张拉程度	0%	20%	40%	60%	80%
对应荷载(kN)	0	0.2	0.4	0.6	0.8

3　试验结果分析与验证

3.1　沉管隧道沉降影响分析

由图12可知,不同预应力控制值的沉管隧道在回淤荷载作用下,沉管隧道沉降分布沿管节纵向呈向下弯曲姿态,管节的沉降随着回淤荷载的增大而增大,随着预应力控制值的增大而减小,值得注意的是,每条测量线的最大沉降量出现在管节中间节段接头处。当预应力张拉值从0增大到0.8kN时,回淤荷载5kPa作用下的管节中间节段沉降从8.375×10^{-1}mm减小至7.375×10^{-1}mm,减小了11.94%;回淤荷载20kPa作用下的管节中间节段沉降从2.2mm减小至2.09mm,减小了5%。当回淤荷载从5kPa增大到20kPa时,预应力张拉值为0kN的管节中间节段沉降增大了2.63倍;预应力控制值为0.8kN的管节中间节段沉降增大了2.83倍;说明预应力的存在提高了管节整体高度,使管节沉降得到改善,但回淤荷载的增加,会使管节沉降加剧。

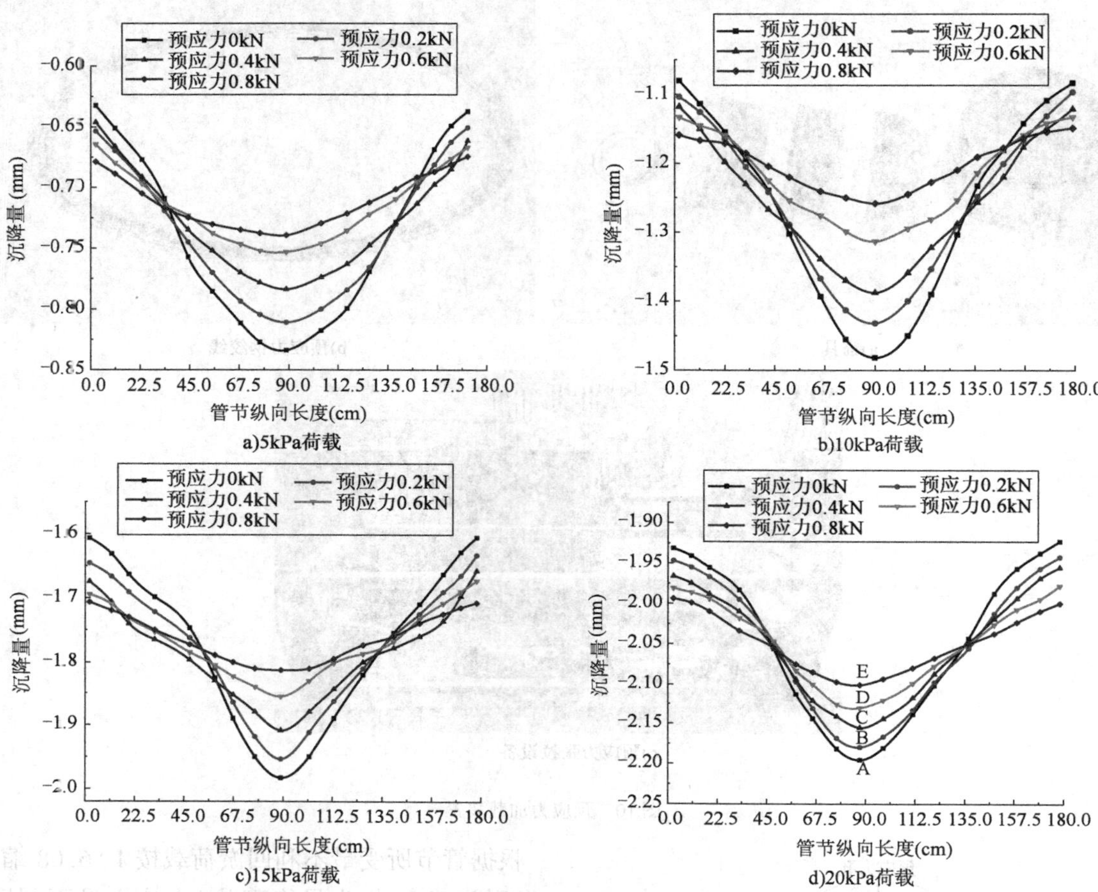

图12 沉降与荷载关系

3.2 节段接头张开量影响分析

由图13可知,管节中间J4端面处,节段接头张开量随着预应力控制值的增加而减小,随着回淤荷载增加而增加。当预应力张拉值从0增大至0.8kN时,在回淤荷载5kPa作用下节段接头张开量从1.37×10^{-1}mm减小至3.622×10^{-2}mm,减小了73.6%;在回淤荷载20kPa作用下节段接头张开量从3.192×10^{-1}mm减小至8.6×10^{-2}mm,减小了73.1%;当回淤荷载从5kPa增大至20kPa时,在回淤荷载5kPa作用下节段接头张开量从1.37×10^{-1}mm增大至3.192×10^{-1}mm,增大了2.32倍;预应力为0.8kN半刚性管节节段接头张开量从3.622×10^{-2}mm增大至8.6×10^{-2}mm,增大了2.37倍;说明预应力控制值的增加,增大了

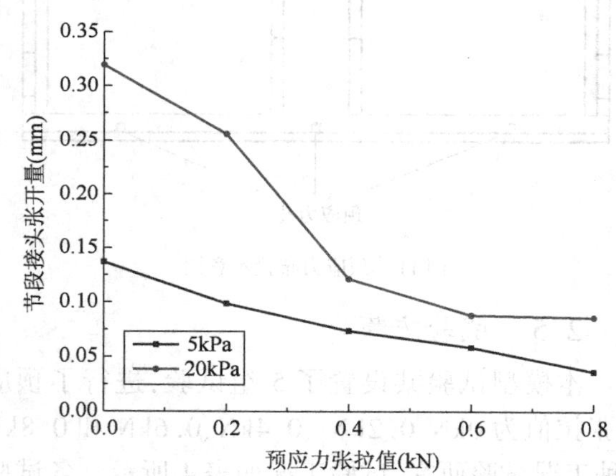

图13 节段接头张开量与预应力控制值关系

节段接头间得摩擦力,提高了节段接头处得剪切刚度,使得节段接头张开量明显减小。

4 结语

(1)在回淤荷载及不同预应力控制值作用下的管节沉降均呈向下弯曲姿态,管节中间沉降大,两端沉降小;沉降及节段接头张开量随着预应力控制值的增加而减小,随着回淤荷载增加而呈线性增加趋势;当预应力控制值从 0 增大到 0.8kN 时,管节中间处的沉降及节段张开量分别减小了 5% ~ 11.94%、73.1% ~73.6%;当回淤荷载从 5kPa 增大到 20kPa 时,管节沉降及节段张开量分别增加了 2.63 ~2.83 倍、2.32 ~2.37 倍;说明回淤荷载的而增大会导致管节沉降及节段接头张开量加剧,但预应力施加提高了管节整体刚度,可以有效改善管节沉降及节段接头张开量,因此,在沉管隧道长期稳定设计中管节结构应考虑保留预应力,以保证其相对稳定性。在运行期,要定期清淤,减小回淤对沉管结构的影响,进一步保证节段接头的安全性。

(2)由于本文主要针对回淤和预应力张拉程度对节段接头变形特性进行研究,在下一阶段的研究中,应综合考虑地基刚度离散型、不均匀回淤及预应力不均匀损失对节段接头的力学特性的影响,使模型试验更加贴合实际,并针对影响因素,提出相应的处治措施。

参考文献

[1] 刘鹏,丁文其,杨波. 沉管隧道接头刚度模型研究[J]. 岩土工程学报,2013,35(增2):133-139.

[2] 禹海涛,萧文浩,袁勇. 沉管隧道接头与管节本体刚度比试验[J]. 中国公路学报,2016,29(12):134-141.

[3] 胡指南,谢永利,张宏光. 超长沉管隧道大型模型试验设计与应用[J]. 现代隧道技术,2014,51 (6):123-128.

[4] 岳夏冰,谢永利,张宏光. 沉管隧道离心模型试验及数值模拟[J]. 工业建筑,2013 年 43 (6):84-89.

[5] 袁勇,禹海涛,萧文浩. 沉管隧道管节接头混凝土剪力键压剪破坏试验研究[J]. 工程力学,2017,34 (3):149-154 +181.

[6] 周舟,丁文其,刘洪洲. 预应力锚索对沉管隧道接头力学特性影响研究[J],地下空间与工程学报. 2015,1:24-29.

[7] 岳夏冰. 外海大回淤沉管隧道软基沉降特征与控制计算[D]. 西安:长安大学,2014.

基于扫视路径速度的隧道入口段安全舒适性分析

梁 波[1,2] 牛佳安[*1] 张红杰[1]

(1. 重庆交通大学土木工程学院;2. 重庆交通大学山区桥梁与隧道工程国家重点试验室)

摘 要 为了更准确地评价公路隧道入口段的安全舒适性,以隧道入口段的驾驶员视觉特性为研究对象,在云南上鹤高速公路的野鸭塘 1 号、2 号和 3 号隧道开展实车试验,采集驾驶员的注视与扫视时间、视点位置、扫视幅度等眼动参数。基于试验数据,提出扫视路径速度指标并验证其合理性。试验结果表明:扫视路径速度能够有效地对隧道入口段的驾驶安全舒适性进行评价。当隧道照明条件相同时,新型蓄能反光发光材料能够使驾驶员的平均扫视路径速度降低 50.6%,峰值扫视路径速度降低 40%。通过对安全舒适指标的关联性分析,进一步表明:扫视路径速度与驾驶员的安全舒适性呈反比关系。随着隧道入口光环境质量的提高,驾驶员的扫视时间占比增加,进而扫视所用时间变长,扫视路径速度减慢。此时驾驶员的安全舒适性较高有利于安全行驶,反之则不利于行车安全。

关键词 交通工程 扫视路径速度 实车试验 隧道入口段 安全舒适性评价

1. 基金项目:国家自然科学基金(51878107);重庆市人才团队项目(2019-9-95)。

0　引言

随着经济建设的全面开展,我国公路建设取得了快速的发展。截至 2020 年末,公路隧道共计 21316 处,总长度达到 2199.93 万延米,同比增长率达到 16%[1]。由于公路隧道特殊的半封闭空间结构导致了隧道内外光环境存在着较大差异,因此当驾驶员驾车经过含有公路隧道的路段时,极易发生交通安全事故。一旦隧道发生交通安全事故,将会使交通通行受阻,进而导致经济效益直线下降[2-3]。交通安全事故由驾驶员、车辆、环境等因素之间的相互不协调性所造成,而隧道环境内的照明质量则是产生交通安全事故不可忽视的重要因素之一。因此,为了更好的预防交通安全事故的发生,有必要对不同隧道光环境下驾驶员在驾驶过程中的安全舒适性进行深入性研究。

驾驶员借助视觉系统获取信息的比例占整体信息的 80%,可见视觉是驾驶员从外界获取信息的最重要途径[4]。目前对驾驶员在隧道中行驶时的视觉特征主要从注视行为、扫视行为以及瞳孔面积变化率三个方面进行研究。如我国学者韩飒[5]和江治东[6]等对驾驶员的视觉注视分布区域进行了划分,并分析其与驾驶员注视行为的关系;王辉[7]、何操[8]和王少博[9]等采用 K-means 聚类分析法分析驾驶员的注视行为变化规律;郭宝义[10]采用了回归拟合法建立了夜间情况下驾驶员注视时间、注视次数、扫视幅度和隧道出入口距离的数学模型,进而为夜间情况下公路隧道的行车条件的改善提供了理论依据。

关于公路隧道内驾驶员的信息感知方面,不少学者已将驾驶员的生物量作为安全舒适性评价指标。例如:陶盼盼[11]选取了驾驶员的瞳孔面积变化率作为舒适性评价指标,并用 MATLAB 构建了速度、反光环色彩(间距)与驾驶员瞳孔面积的拟合模型,进而得到不同行车速度下隧道反光环色彩与间距设置的推荐值;李炳杰[12]以驾驶员的瞳孔面积变化率为评价指标,分析得到了白天不同时段驾驶员驶入隧道洞口过程中时其动态视觉特征的变化规律;尚婷[13]建立了瞳孔面积变化率与减速标线的横向宽度模型;黄发明[14]基于驾驶员的瞳孔面积变化率指标,提出了一种设立在隧道入口接近段 30 ~ 50m 喇叭形结构的遮光设计;洪亮[15]研究了驾驶员瞳孔面积变化率与道路线形指标之间的关系,并提出以瞳孔面积变化率值为 6.0 和 25.0 时作为道路线形指标合理性的判断标准;王春雨[16]采用驾驶员瞳孔面积变化率确定了隧道路段中的驾驶员视觉敏感段。可以看出,目前相关研究所采取的生物量评价指标较为单一,缺乏从驾驶员不同感知角度对隧道的安全舒适性进行评价。

在公路隧道光环境构成物理量信息方面,也有学者研究了其对公路隧道照明安全舒适性的影响。K. Kircher 等[17]借助 VTI 驾驶模拟器,提出适当提高墙面和路面的对比度有利于提高驾驶员驾车经过公路隧道内部时的安全舒适性;杨韬[18]对隧道内不同类型的壁面材料的反射特性进行了研究,得到了具有反射性能的材料能够提高公路隧道内照明的平均亮度;梁波和何世永等[19-21]研究了公路隧道侧壁不同内装材料下的眼动特性,结果表明采用蓄能反光内装涂料的隧道侧壁能显著提高隧道内环境亮度,这种情况驾驶员的瞳孔直径变化较小,变化率较为平稳。然而,目前国内外隧道照明设计和研究大都集中在光环境物理指标的取值和评价方面,未全面考虑人-车-隧道动态光环境这一构成物理信息条件下驾驶员的生物量感知,以及对驾驶行为和交通安全的影响。

综上所述,目前研究偏重于照明环境和信息构成的关系研究,缺乏利用不同生物量评价指标对不同隧道光环境下驾驶员的安全舒适性进行研究。为深入分析公路隧道入口光环境对驾驶安全舒适性的影响,本文以云南上鹤高速公路的野鸭塘 1 号、2 号和 3 号隧道为研究对象,利用眼动仪、照度计等试验设备进行实车试验和现场测量,提出扫视路径速度指标并基于此指标对公路隧道入口段的安全舒适性进行分析,为隧道运营环境安全及品质提升提供理论依据和参考指标。

1　扫视指标的分析研究

1.1　扫视指标

注视和扫视是眼睛固有的生理特征,其中扫视是对连续的两个或多个注视行为进行衔接的眼动过程[22],此过程能够反映人眼对视觉范围的采集广度。其中常用的三种指标为扫视幅度、扫视速度和扫视加速度。扫视幅度为人眼对视觉范围的采集广度;扫视速度是人眼对视觉范围的采集快慢,即扫视幅度与扫视间隔时间的比值,计量单位为°/s;扫视加速度是人眼对视觉范围采集速度的变化快慢。尽管常用的扫视指标已进行相关的研究,但由于人眼扫视过程过于复杂,不可控性因素较多,因此目前对扫视长度指标的研究较少,有必要对扫视参数指标进行优化并使其能反映更多的影响因素。

1.2 扫视路径速度指标的提出

扫视速度是驾驶员眼球扫视幅度 A 与眼动仪记录的扫视过程时间 T 的比值,用公式表示为

$$V_s = \frac{A}{T} \tag{1}$$

式中:V_s——扫视速度(°/ms);

A——扫视幅度(°);

T——眼动仪记录的扫视时间(ms)。

该眼动参数指标的实质为单位时间内眼球的转动角度,但其未考虑眼球的扫视长度对扫视过程的影响。同时,眼动仪记录的扫视时间会遗漏某些扫视幅度较小但实际上进行了扫视的事件时间。因此,本文通过驾驶员的扫视长度来优化扫视速度,提出扫视路径速度指标 S 作为新扫视速度指标,即建立基于扫视路径长度和扫视实际时间的扫视路径速度计算模型

$$S = \frac{L}{t_2 - t_1} \tag{2}$$

式中:S——扫视路径速度指标(px/ms);

L——扫视长度(px);

t_1、t_2——扫视的开始时间和结束时间(ms)。

2 试验设计与数据采集

2.1 试验隧道

试验隧道为云南省上关到鹤庆之间的野鸭塘1号隧道、野鸭塘2号隧道和野鸭塘3号隧道,试验隧道的位置如图1所示。试验隧道的设计速度为80km/h,其他参数如表1所示。

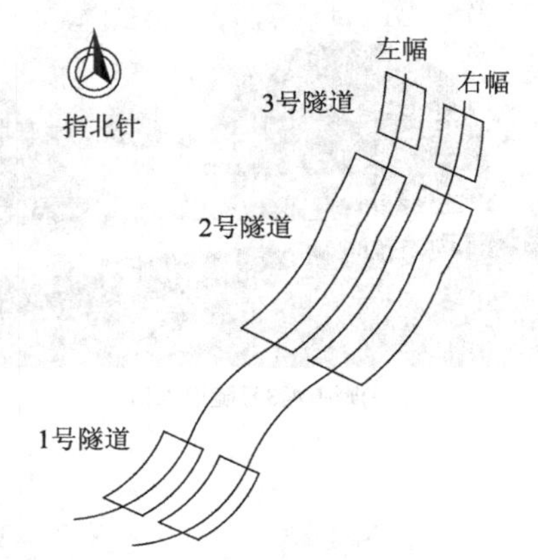

图1 试验隧道位置

隧道的基本参数 表1

试验隧道名称	隧道高度	路面净宽	侧壁材料	隧道长度	入口段布灯方式
1号隧道	7.1m	11m	2.5m高防火涂料	290m	LED加强照明
2号隧道			2.5m高防火涂料	1205m	无加强照明
3号隧道			2.5m高蓄能反光发光涂料	264.93m	LED加强照明

野鸭塘2号隧道入口段的布灯方式与其他隧道存在明显差异,而1号隧道和3号隧道间的最大的区别是采用的侧壁材料不同,分别为防火涂料与新型蓄能反光发光涂料(图2)。防火涂料的反射率为0.64,隧道侧壁布设高度2.5m。蓄能反光发光材料的漫反射率0.82,侧壁布设高度为2.5m,反射光谱 S/P 值(暗视觉光通量与明视觉光通量之比,其值越高,越有利于提升隧道照明质量)整体保持较高水平。同时,比隧道侧壁布设水泥砂浆的路面亮度提升10%以上,而防火涂料的反射光谱 S/P 值则较低。铺设蓄能反光发光材料的隧道侧壁相对于防火涂料侧壁,白天的小目标可见度STV提升12.96%左右[19]。

2.2 试验设备及驾驶员

试验车辆采用长安CX-70,如图3所示。眼动数据采集设备采用德国SMI公司生产的iView ETG 2.1型眼动仪测量驾驶员的动态视觉,见图4。眼动仪采用双眼测试,采样率为30Hz,校准区域为 $1280 \times 960\text{px}^2$,追踪率为99.5%,其结合高分辨率的场景视频,自动视差补偿确保在各种距离的数据精确。使用时与电脑相连,操作者可采集驾驶员的属性、执行校准、观测实时注视轨迹并实时标注被试者的行为。

为了消除不同生理因素段对扫视各参数的影响,选取12名不同年龄段且无色盲色弱的健康驾驶员作为被试者。其中20~35岁青年驾驶员4

名、35~45 中年驾驶员 4 名、45~60 中老年驾驶员 4 名,试验期间无饮酒等特殊情况。

2.3 试验过程

分别对野鸭塘 1 号和 3 号隧道的右幅入口段进行照明参数测定,如图 5 所示。同时,驾驶员戴上眼动仪,以每小时 80km 的速度按照规定的两条驾驶路线行驶,见图 6。第一种驾驶路线:在晚上 19:00~23:00,驾驶员依次驶入野鸭塘 3 号隧道右幅、驶至 2 号隧道右幅中间段,随即掉头,按照原路返回,共完成往返 1 次,此路线共驶入隧道洞门 3 次。第二种驾驶路线:在白天 9:00~17:00,驾驶员依次驶入野鸭塘 3 号隧道右幅、2 号隧道右幅至其车行横通道到 2 号隧道左幅、1 号隧道右幅,驶出野鸭塘 1 号隧道右幅后掉头,按原路返回,直至完成往返 2 次,此路线共驶入隧道洞门 12 次。

a)野鸭塘3号隧道入口

b)隧道入口段蓄能反光发光侧壁

图 2 试验隧道

图 3 试验用车

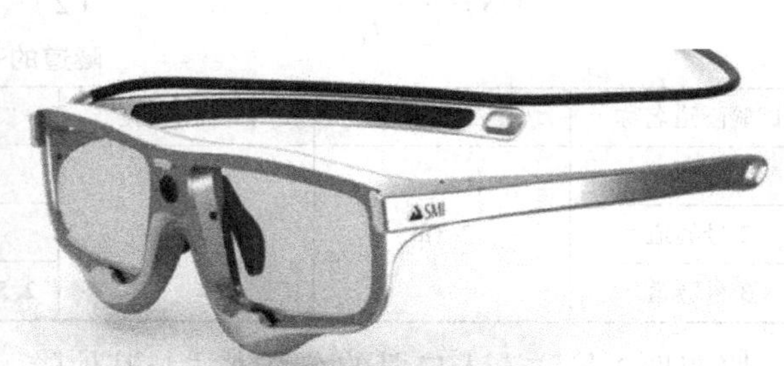

图 4 SMI 眼镜式眼动仪

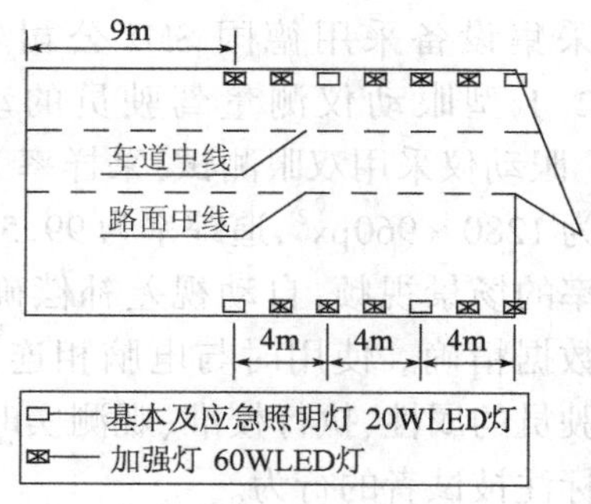

a)入口段灯具布置图

b)照度现场测量情况

图 5 隧道路面与侧壁照度现场测量

a)驾驶员佩戴眼动仪

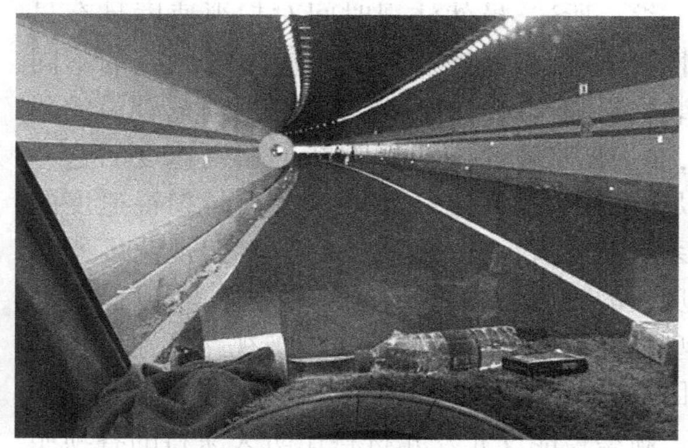
b)隧道入口段眼动情况

图6 眼动参数实车试验过程

3 试验结果与分析

3.1 数据筛选

采用照度计对隧道入口段进行现场照度的测定,然后取其均值,可得到相应的照明参数。其次,运用眼动仪进行数据采集,并使用配套的软件BeGaze3.6.40分析试验数据。根据《公路隧道照明设计细则》(JTG/T D70/2—01—2014)可知入口段长度与隧道净空高度、照明停车视距有关,并结合表1获得野鸭塘1号、2号、3号隧道的入口段长度 D_{th} 均为83.64m,入口段行驶时间为3.76s。因此,利用BeGaze数据处理软件分别筛选出两种路线中的入口段试验数据进行分析研究,即筛选获取到174组试验数据。

3.2 数据处理与分析

3.2.1 安全舒适评价指标分析

野鸭塘1号隧道(防火涂料)与3号隧道(蓄能反光发光涂料)的入口段布灯参数基本一致,但是两个隧道的路面平均照度、路面照度总均匀度和路面照度纵向均匀度、墙面平均照度却存在较大差异,各项数值见表2。

隧道入口段照明参数 表2

照明参数指标	1号隧道防火涂料	3号隧道新型蓄能反光发光材料
路面平均照度	965lx	1080.25lx
路面照度总均匀度	0.72	0.75
路面照度纵向均匀度	0.67	0.68
墙面平均照度	721.51lx	842.04lx
平均扫视路径速度	0.81px/ms	0.4px/ms

如表2所示,新型蓄能反光发光材料涂层侧壁的各项数值均优于防火涂料侧壁的值。同时,蓄能反光发光材料能明显降低扫视路径速度,平均扫视路径速度降低了50.6%。

对试验的174组试验数据进行分析,剔除异常点,得到151组试验样本数据。选取扫视速度、瞳孔面积变化率、不同隧道侧壁材料以及入口段灯具布设情况作为扫视路径速度的影响因素,采用SPSS软件进行单因素方差显著性分析,在显著性水平为0.05的条件下,研究以上各因素对扫视路径速度的影响显著性程度(表3)。

扫视速度差异显著性检验 表3

变　量	显著性水平 P 值.	结　论
注视时间	0.01	影响显著
扫视路径速度	0.03	影响显著
不同隧道侧壁材料	0.10	影响不显著
入口段灯具布设情况	0.25	影响不显著

由表3可知,驾驶员注视时间、扫视路径速度、侧壁材料和灯具布设情况对扫视速度的影响显著性,而对不同隧道侧壁材料与入口段灯具布设情况的影响并不显著。对扫视路径速度而言,扫视速度、不同隧道侧壁材料与入口段灯具布设情况均对其影响显著,而对驾驶员的注视时间影响不显著,见表4。

扫视路径速度差异显著性检验 表4

变　量	显著性水平 P 值..	结　论
扫视速度	0.00	影响显著
注视时间	0.76	影响不显著
不同隧道侧壁材料	0.00	影响显著
入口段灯具布设情况	0.01	影响显著

综上所述,虽然注视时间对扫视速度具有显著性影响,但扫视速度不能反应隧道侧壁的不同内装材料和入口段灯具的布设情况对驾驶员的影响,而扫视路径速度恰好弥补了扫视速度的这一不足。因此,扫视路径速度一方面与扫视速度的关系影响显著,一方面能够反应出扫视速度所不能反应的对驾驶员的影响因素,因此可以作为综合型指标。以上结论为下一步扫视路径速度与其他因素的关系分析提供了基础条件。

新型蓄能反光发光材料比防火涂料的各项照明参数指标更优,同时新型蓄能反光发光材料的扫视路径速度小于防火涂料。因此,随着隧道内环境的照度和均匀度不断增大,扫视路径速度减小,更利于驾驶员的行驶,从而进一步提高驾驶的安全舒适性。

3.2.2　驾驶安全舒适性分析

随着隧道内交通安全事故数量的不断增加,对隧道不同光环境下的驾驶员扫视行为与驾驶安全舒适性的关系研究变得尤为必要。对驾驶员驶入不同隧道入口段的扫视路径速度进行整理分析,如图 7 所示。

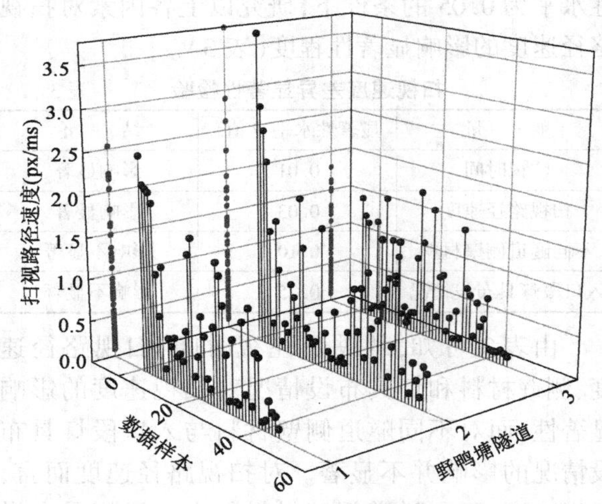

图 7　不同隧道的扫视路径速度

由图 7 中扫视路径速度与野鸭塘 1 号、2 号与 3 号隧道内光环境质量关系图可知,野鸭塘 2 号隧道内未开启加强照明,其侧壁材料为防火涂料,驾驶员的扫视路径速度指标阈值最大达到 3.75px/ms;野鸭塘 3 号隧道内灯具全开,其侧壁材料为新型蓄能反光发光材料,而扫视路径速度指标阈值最大达到 1.5px/ms;野鸭塘 1 号隧道与 3 号隧道采用同样的照明方式,隧道侧壁材料为防火涂料,其扫视路径速度指标的阈值处于野鸭塘 2 号与 3 号隧道阈值之间,阈值大小为 2.5px/ms。这表明,扫视路径速度在与入口段侧壁材料和灯具布设情况存在显著关联性,当侧壁材料和灯具布设情况总体越优时,即环境照明质量越好,扫视路径速度越小。

除此之外,由图 7 分析可知平均扫视路径速度由大到小分别为:野鸭塘 2 号隧道、1 号隧道和 3 号隧道,且三个隧道的峰值扫视路径速度一般出现在隧道洞口附近。这是由于行车环境亮度差异过大时,导致驾驶员视觉难以对周边环境信息进行准确采集,因此紧张程度加剧,为保证行车安全,驾驶员视觉会快速地对周边进行扫视,以获取更多信息。由此说明扫视路径速度与驾驶员的行车安全性具有强相关性,将驾驶员在不同隧道入口段的注视与扫视时间进行分析,各自所占百分比如图 8 所示。

由图 8 可知,野鸭塘隧道 3 号隧道的扫视时间占比最大,其次是 1 号和 2 号隧道,注视时间则与扫视时间占比相反。扫视时间占比越大,注视时间占比越小,表明驾驶员无需在行车过程中对光环境进行专注视认感知就能采集到大量视觉信息,而充足的视觉信息是驾驶员行车舒适性的保障,因此进一步说明各隧道入口段整体行车环境提供给驾驶员的视觉信息由高到低依次为野鸭塘 3 号、1 号和 2 号隧道,即行车舒适性也依此顺序排列。

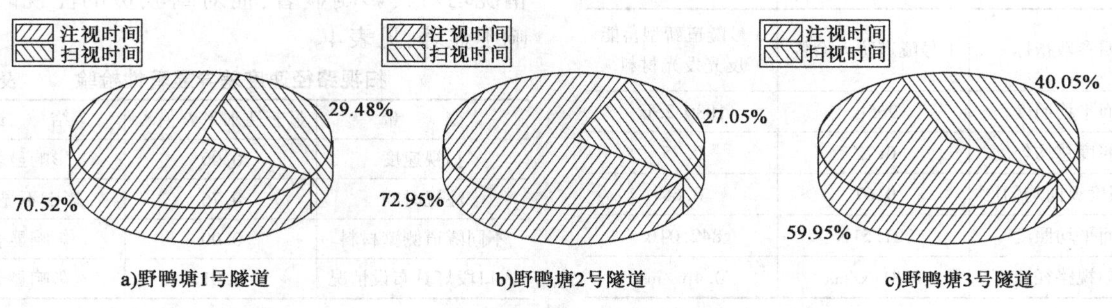

图 8　眼动参数时间占比

综合分析,扫视路径速度指标与驾驶员的驾驶安全舒适性呈反比关系。隧道内环境照明质量越佳,驾驶员在驾驶过程中的安全舒适性越高,此时驾驶员感到安全、舒适与轻松,驾驶员扫视时间占比增大,扫视所用时间变长,扫视路径速度减慢,更利于安全舒适行车;反之,隧道内环境照明质量越差,驾驶员在驾驶过程中的安全舒适性越低,此时驾驶员感到紧张,持续注视时间的比重变大,扫视所用时间变短,扫视路径速度加快,不利于安全舒适行车。

4 结语

眼动行为可反应驾驶员在驾驶过程中生理心理的变化,因此本文通过对不同光环境的隧道进行实车试验,进而分析隧道入口段的驾驶安全舒适性,主要得到以下结论:

(1)扫视路径速度指标能考虑眼球的扫视长度对扫视过程的影响,同时也能反映隧道不同的侧壁材料和入口段灯具的布设方式对驾驶员的影响,该指标与驾驶员的驾驶安全舒适性呈反比关系。

(2)基于蓄能反光发光材料与防火涂料情况下的实车数据,并结合驾驶员感兴趣区域 AOI,确定一般光环境下扫视路径速度指标的安全舒适性阈值在 2.5px/ms 左右,为驾驶员在隧道入口段行驶过程中的安全舒适评价提供了依据。

(3)通过分析三种不同光环境与侧壁材料隧道下的扫视路径速度,可以得出新型蓄能反光发光材料能够明显提高隧道内的行车安全舒适性。当隧道照明条件相同时,该侧壁材料能够使驾驶员的平均扫视路径速度降低 50.6%,扫视路径峰值速度降低 40%。

(4)本文所提出的扫视路径速度指标能更好地评价公路隧道入口段的驾驶安全舒适性,后续有待进一步补充更多光环境隧道和不同车型的试验方案,以增加驾驶员的扫视路径速度样本数量来增强试验的可靠性。

参考文献

[1] 中华人民共和国交通运输部. 2020 年交通运输行业发展统计公报[EB/OL]. (2021-05-19)[2021-06-19]. http://www.gov.cn/xinwen/2021-05/19/content_5608523.htm.

[2] 石雨新. 隧道场景下车辆目标识别中的光照干扰抑制技术研究[D]. 重庆:重庆大学,2016.

[3] 赖金星,张鹏,周慧,等. 高速公路隧道交通事故规律研究[J]. 隧道建设,2017,37(01):37-42.

[4] 梁波,梁加林,何世永,等. 公路隧道光环境信息感知及试验研究[J]. 隧道建设(中英文),2020,40(09):1251-1260.

[5] 韩飒. 山区高速公路隧道路段驾驶员眼动特性研究[D]. 西安:长安大学,2008.

[6] 江治东. 高速公路隧道路段驾驶人视觉注意转移规律研究[D]. 西安:长安大学,2015.

[7] 王辉. 高速公路长隧道路段驾驶人眼动特性研究[D]. 西安:长安大学,2010.

[8] 何操. 山区高速公路隧道路段对驾驶人生理心理影响研究[D]. 西安:长安大学,2009.

[9] 王少博. 高速公路隧道环境下驾驶人注视与负荷特性研究[D]. 西安:长安大学,2017.

[10] 郭宝义. 夜间公路隧道出入口段驾驶员眼动特性研究[D]. 西安:长安大学,2014.

[11] 陶盼盼. 基于驾驶员视觉特性的隧道反光环设置研究[D]. 重庆:重庆交通大学,2016.

[12] 李炳杰. 基于视觉明暗适应变化规律的公路隧道洞口景观优化研究[D]. 重庆:重庆交通大学,2016.

[13] 尚婷,唐伯明,段萌萌. 基于驾驶员瞳孔面积变化率的公路视错觉减速标线横向宽度研究[J]. 重庆交通大学学报(自然科学版),2016,35(01):111-116.

[14] 黄发明. 基于"黑洞效应"的公路驾驶员视错觉改善方法实验研究[D]. 湖北:武汉理工大学,2014.

[15] 洪亮. 驾驶员视觉特性与山区高速公路长大纵坡线形指标关系研究[D]. 湖南:湖南大学,2008.

[16] 王春雨. 隧道路段驾驶员视觉安全技术研究[D]. 重庆:重庆交通大学,2013.

[17] Kircher K, Ahlstrom C. The Impact of Tunnel Design and Lighting on the Performance of Attentive and Visually Distracted Drivers[J]. Accident Analysis and Prevention, 2012, 47:153-161.

[18] 杨韬. 隧道照明反射增量系数研究[D]. 重庆:重庆大学,2008.

[19] 梁波,董越,闫自海,等. 基于眼动特性的隧道中间段光环境参数敏感性分析[J]. 交通

信息与安全,2021,39(06):91-99.

[20] 何世永,梁波,罗红. 不同隧道侧壁涂料对汽车司机视觉反应的研究[J]. 现代隧道技术,2017,54(1):48-54.

[21] He S, Liang B, Pan G, et al. Influence of dynamic highway tunnel lighting environment on driving safety based on eye movement parameters of the driver[J]. Tunneling and Underground Space Technology, 2017, 57:52-60.

[22] Chapman P R, Underwood G. Visual search of driving situations: danger and experience[J]. Perception, 1998, 27 (8):951-964.

山区高速综合管控关键技术与智能场景研究

胡汉桥*[1]　陆　由[1]　周荣贵[2]　刘文智[3]

(1. 湖北交投高速公路运营集团有限公司;2. 交通运输部公路科学研究所;
3. 北京万集科技股份有限公司)

摘　要　根据湖北省山区高速公路安全运营与服务实际,结合智慧高速新政策、新需求和特殊路段安全专项整治要求,以沪渝高速宜恩段最复杂的路段进行试点,分析山区高速公路的运营风险因素,建立长下坡、长大隧道、特大桥风险辨识模型,针对性地采取管理措施、工程措施、交通工程、智能信息化手段,进行智能化综合管控平台研究,探索建立切合实际需求的智慧高速公路建设模型、应用场景、关键技术和运营推广模式。

关键词　山区公路　综合管控　关键技术　智能场景　应用研究

0　引言

在新基建政策刺激下,各省纷纷推出智慧高速公路建设规划与示范工程,各种新概念层出不穷,各建设单位、运营商、集成商、设备商纷纷推出自成体系的智慧高速方案和产品,但由于建设成本、市场规模、顶层设计、系统对接、业务逻辑与应用深度等原因,加上智慧高速概念多、投入大、成效低、公众热度小、复制性差,因此短期内大规模推动智慧高速新建设有较大困难。特别是在湖北高速公路网基本成形的环境下,部分路段传统三大机电系统的应用效率较低,规划新建高速公路的智慧高速工程难度更大。鉴于现状,研究小组思考在现行营运的山区高速公路进行安全管控关键技术研究和智能场景设计,建立智能数字化平台,融入全省交通强国服务体系,探索建立切合实际的智慧高速公路建设、应用与运营推广模式。

1　研究与设计思路

1.1　研究现状

湖北沪渝高速鄂西段(包括宜昌至恩施段、恩施至利川段),2009年12月19日全线建成通车,线型跌宕蜿蜒,高低起伏,纵坡多、桥隧多、弯道多、纵坡长;气候复杂多变,全年暴雨、大雾、冰雪等恶劣天气频繁;辖段通行车辆80%以上为长途过境车,且以13m以上重型货车、半挂车为主,超宽车较多。在以上因素共同作用下,该高速通行和安全管控压力非常大,全线安全管理成为运营管理的首要难题。最复杂区段为椰坪停车区(K1262)至高家堰互通(K1218+475)之间,金龙隧道洞口至高家堰互通段为28km的长下坡路段,海拔落差近900m,平均纵坡为3%,最大纵坡为5%,如图1所示;同时长下坡路段有连续三座特大桥。因此该路段兼具长下坡、隧道群、桥梁段三大治理难点,进行智慧高速场景的研究更具备理论、实践价值和推广价值。

1.2　研究目的

通过现场勘察、历史数据积累、环境调查、事故黑点分析,应用交通安全工程、信息化手段、新基建技术进行综合研究和部分试点,提高道路感知能力、数据融合能力、安全预警监测能力、"一路四方"联动效率,提升道路安全性能、通行能力和服务水平,建立智慧高速公路应用场景模型。

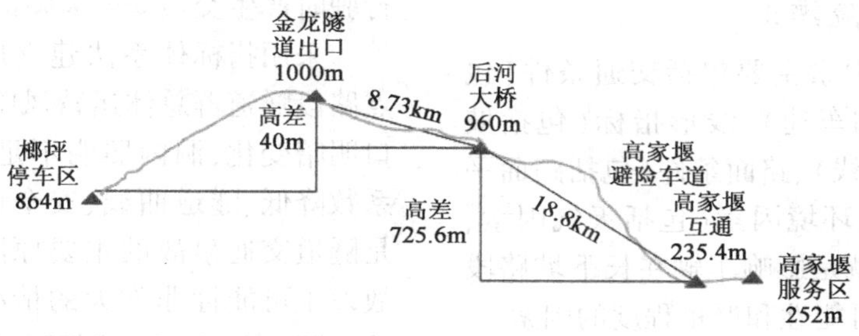

图1　示范路段长下坡坡度示意图

(1)提安全性能:针对该路段长下坡、隧道群、桥梁、急弯路段等复杂路况下危险及事故多发原因分析,通过风险辨识和风险因素分析,有针对性地提出智能化解决方案,在“一路四方”协同联动基础上,研究实施交通智能工程,全面提升示范路段安全性能。

(2)增通行效率:通过实施路段安全提升工程,实现全路段双车道通行,提高通行效率,解决“高速公路不高速”的问题,缓解高峰时段和节假日拥堵程度,实现准全天候通行。

(3)拓智能效能:通过长下坡、隧道群、桥隧连续与综合管控四个智能场景的关键技术与场景应用研究,建立具备推广价值的智慧高速公路示范技术标准、综合平台数据对接指南、公众综合信息服务模型。

1.3　技术路线

基于现场踏勘和原施工设计实际,根据宜恩段交通量、交通组成、路线设计指标、安全设施运行和交通事故等情况,结合目前的安全对策措施,辨识长下坡路段、隧道群、桥梁段存在的交通安全风险,从管理措施、工程措施、交通工程、智能信息化四个方面,研究长下坡路段安全提升与智慧高速应用技术理论,部署智能化管控设备,开发智能综合应用,提升道路交通安全管控水平,为运营单位安全改善工作和智慧高速公路应用场景设计提供支撑。

研究的关键技术路线如下:

(1)根据路段交通量、交通组成、路线设计指标、隧道设施运行和交通事故等情况,分析28km连续长下坡路段和隧道存在的交通安全风险,提出长下坡路段安全管控策略。

(2)基于隧道风险评估结果,面向隧道环境、运营状态全天候监控、运营安全风险预测预警和突发事件抵近处置需求,进行长大隧道设施数字化、图像化、IP化、国产化,完成综合平台智能化升级改进,实现隧道重点路段运行状态预警预测和精准管控。

(3)对山区高速公路应急能力进行评估,结合长下坡路段、隧道、桥梁分布情况,评估隧道各类应急资源、应急预案、周边应急站点设置的合理性,建立数字化与智能化的管控模型,为交通提质专项行动提供优化意见。

(4)进行运营单位养护管理法律责任风险分析与对策,根据交通安全风险评估结果,从管理制度、“一路四方”联动、交通事故相关诉讼等角度开展分析,辨识可能存在的责任风险,建立智能化预警机制与预案体系。

(5)研究示范路段各类信息采集、预警、数据分析、处置和车路协同的关键技术与新设备应用。

2　风险辨识与安全评估

经调查,沪渝高速鄂西段事故95%发生在下坡路段,下坡路段的事故90%涉及大货车,车辆超速超载行驶事故的比例占到六成,因疲劳驾驶、车辆刹车及发动机故障等造成的事故比例较高,涉及大货车的交通事故大都与长下坡刹车失灵有关,占事故总数的39.2%。首发事故黑点距离坡顶为5.5~7.0km,如图2所示。

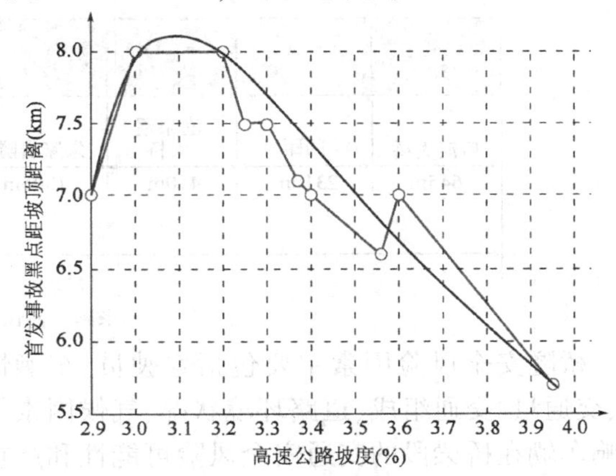

图2　首发事故黑点距离坡顶与坡度关系图

2.1　长下坡风险辨识

长下坡安全风险因素主要包括交通条件(包括交通量、交通组成和车速)、线形指标(包括坡度、坡长、平曲线、竖曲线)、路面条件(包括路面平整度、路面抗滑性能)、环境因素(包括天气因素、时段因素)等,这些也就是影响车辆在长下坡路段行驶时交通安全风险可能性和严重程度的因素。

所研究路段的主要风险的原因是长下坡货车易出现制动过热、爆胎等,应采取预警、管控与交通工程进行处置。

2.2　隧道群风险辨识

长下坡路段包括朱家岩、渔泉溪、扁担娅三座隧道,如图 3 所示。隧道群安全风险因素主要包括隧道群视觉适应、交通条件(包括交通量、交通组成和车速)、线形指标、隧道选址、路面平整度、路面抗滑性能等,这些也就是影响车辆在隧道段行驶时产生交通安全风险的因素。

采用指标体系法建立风险评估模型,评估试点路段隧道群总体运营风险等分为四级。隧道洞口明暗变化、洞内照明不足、能见度低、路面摩擦系数降低、隧道曲线、安全设施不完备、超宽车辆是隧道交通事故的主要原因,针对隧道群道路事故发生可能性非常大的情况,应对隧道群进行处治,消除事故隐患,确保隧道内行车安全。

2.3　桥隧段连续风险辨识

长下坡段包括 3 座大桥,其中渔泉溪大桥、朱家岩隧道、渔泉溪隧道、魏家洲大桥、扁担垭隧道依次相连,具有桥隧连接的特点,如图 4 所示。本路段日均流量 2021 年达 52165pcu,货车占比 43% ~ 50%,而货车中跨省长途货车占货车总流量的 76%,40t 以上的重载货车占比为 35.9 ~ 41.9%。

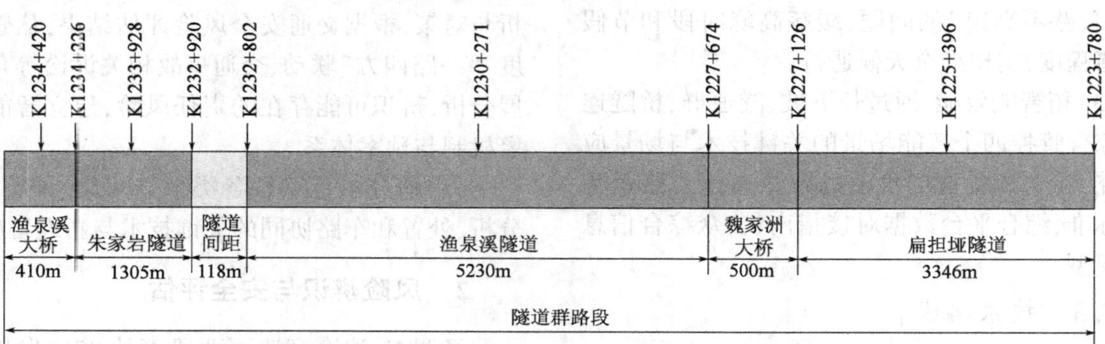

图 3　恩宜向长阳段隧道群布设示意图

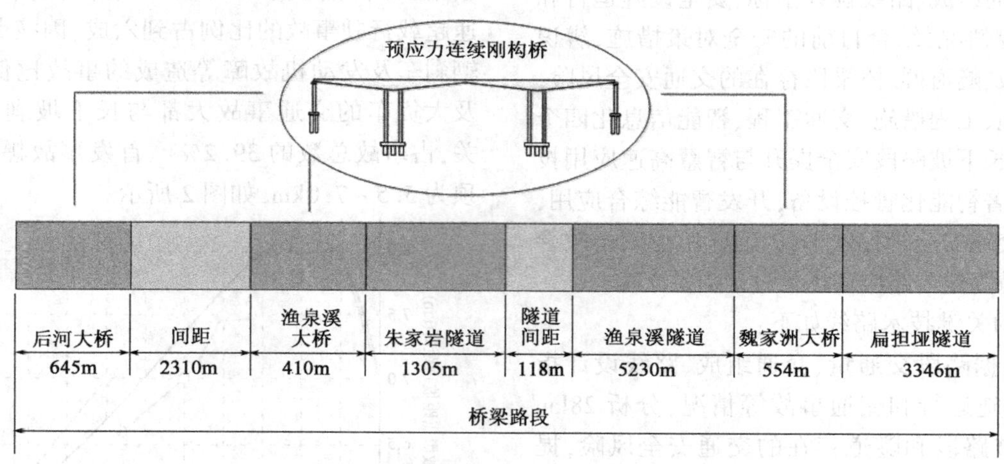

图 4　测试路段桥隧连续示意图

桥隧安全风险因素主要包括驾驶员、车辆性能、交通量、交通组成、道路环境状况、气候因素等影响车辆在桥梁段的交通安全风险可能性和严重程度的因素。其主要风险为所处路段长下坡地段,多与隧道相连,车辆在桥梁段行驶时车速高、车流大、车辆间距小,而下坡因刹车鼓热衰退而刹车失灵,或行驶中车辆出现故障而不能及时停靠,导致车辆追尾或撞击护栏;或因桥隧连接段环境变化剧烈，驾驶员反应不及，引发交通事故。

2.4 综合处置

通过查阅长下坡路段和隧道运营管理单位相关规章制度、应急预案、应急联动协议及突发事件应急处置中反映出的应急组织情况进行评估。构建长下坡路段和隧道段典型突发事件与场景，基于现有应急资源布局和应急响应能力，通过事件仿真与计算模拟等手段以及既有突发事件应急处置，对实际响应救援能力开展评估。

3 关键技术与场景应用设计

3.1 长下坡路段场景设计

连续长下坡路段交通安全事故主要有以下几个特征：①坡度越大，坡长越长，事故数越多；②事故多发生在连续长下坡下半段（坡中、坡底段）；③事故形态多为碰撞和翻车；④事故多发生在1:00—7:00；⑤载重货车比例越高，事故数越多；⑥交通量越大，事故数越多；⑦由天气引发的交通事故比例较高。因此试验路段基于事故与管理需求，对长下坡路段安全提升进行分区，坡前上游路段进行货车车况检查、轮胎温度检查；坡顶起始路段设立速度管理标志、区间测速（开始）和电子警察（限速、车道管理）；坡中路段设立速度管理标志和电子警察（限速、车道管理）；坡底路段设立速度管理标志、区间测速（结束）和电子警察（限速、车道管理），如图5所示。

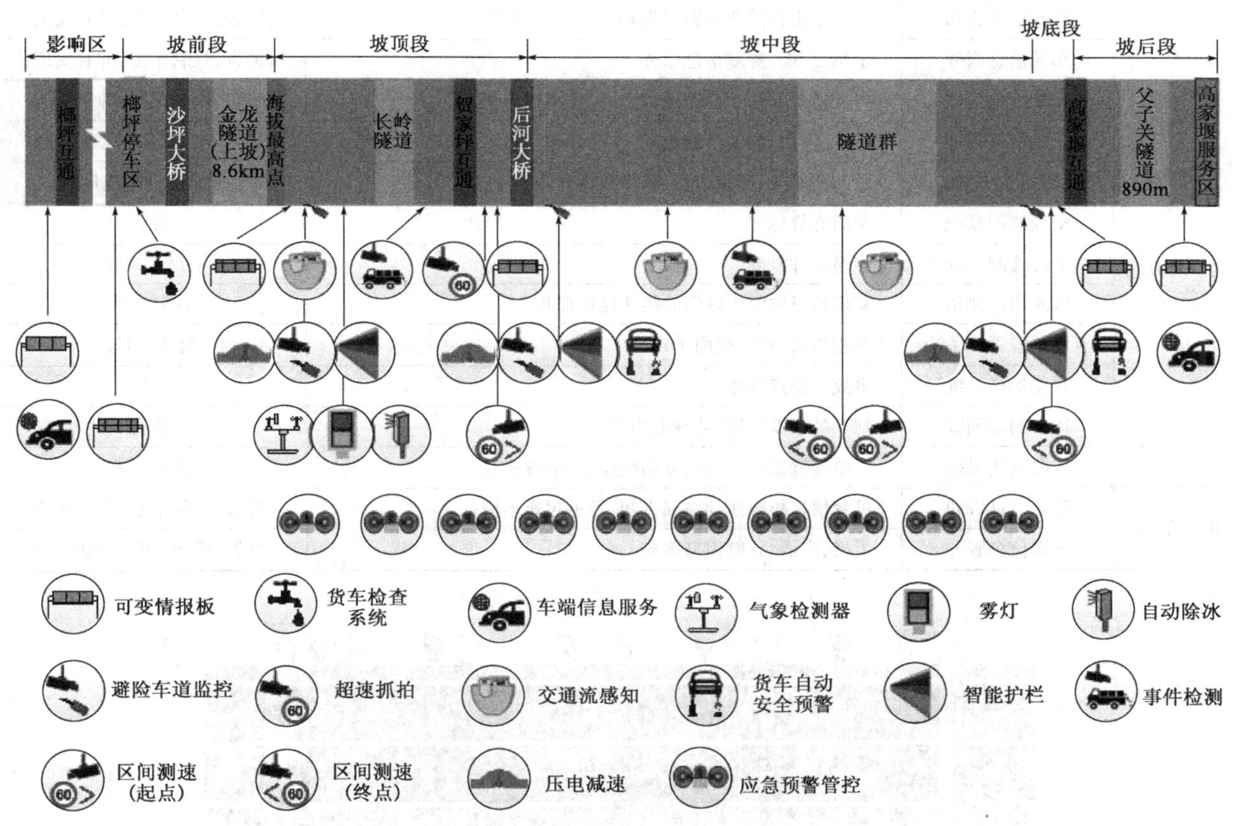

图5 长下坡路段智能信息系统与关键设备布设图

应用的主要关键技术：通过增设各类感知设备，精确检测车辆异常状态，并通过平台算法给予快速信息诱导和"预警"信息，实现"一路四方"联动，加强交通管制与物理措施，减少异常车辆概率。设备主要有：预警可变情报板、货车状态检查管理系统、车端信息服务、气象检测器、雾灯（示廓灯）避险车道监控系统、超速抓拍系统（点速）、交通流感知、货车自动安全预警系统、智能护栏系统、交通事件检测系统、超速抓拍系统（区间测速）、压电减速系统、应急预警管控系统等，如表1所示。

3.2 隧道群场景设计

需对隧道群交通安全运行环境进行综合优化，减少交通事故发生可能性及减轻事故严重程度,从主体结构、交通工程设施、隧道进出口及周边环境、机电系统、应急救援体系等方面,对隧道群进行安全综合场景应用设计。从隧道运营安全能力提升角度分析,进一步完善改进隧道设施设置和机电系统,搭建智能管控平台和设备,实现隧道重点路段运行状态和安全风险的精准管控,如图6所示。

长下坡路段智能综合信息采集与处置系统布设一览表 表1

路段	机电系统	功能	效果
影响区	可变情报板	显示长下坡路况、事故与管控措施	警告,控制车距,抑制变道
坡前上游	可变情报板	显示长下坡路况、事故与管控措施	警告,控制车距,抑制变道
	货车检查管理	根据长下坡路况控制检查、加水进程	消除,控制流量
	车端信息服务	手机、广播、导航信息服务	警告
坡顶路段	恶劣天气预警	气象检测、预警、示廓(雾灯)、自动除冰	警告
	交通流感知	感知交通量、车型比例,支撑控流和限速	警告,控制流量
	单点超速抓拍	单点超速抓拍,控制进入坡中段前的车速	控制车速
	避险车道监控	进行避险车道照明、感知、指示	减轻
	路端信息告知	可变情报板限速和路况告知,警示超速车辆	警告,控制车距,抑制变道
	车端信息服务	手机、广播、导航信息服务	警告,控制车距,抑制变道
坡中及坡底路段	路端信息告知	可变情报板限速和路况告知,警示超速车辆	警告,控制车距,抑制变道
	车端信息服务	手机、广播、导航信息服务	警告,控制车距,抑制变道
	交通流感知	感知交通量、车型比例,支撑控流和限速	警告,控制流量
	全程监控系统	交通态势感知	警告
	事件检测系统	交通事件检测	警告,减轻
	区间限速抓拍	实现长下坡整个区间的超速违法抓拍	控制车速
	应急预警管控系统	全程事故预警,提前干预	警告,减轻
	智能护栏系统	事故多发点预警	减轻
	货车制动预警	刹车鼓温度检测,热衰退预警	警告
	压电减速系统	压电装置振动、变形,被动减速、主动减速	控制车速
坡后下游	路端信息告知	可变情报板限速和路况告知,警示超速车辆	警告,控制车距,抑制变道
	车端信息服务	手机、广播、导航信息服务	警告,控制车距,抑制变道

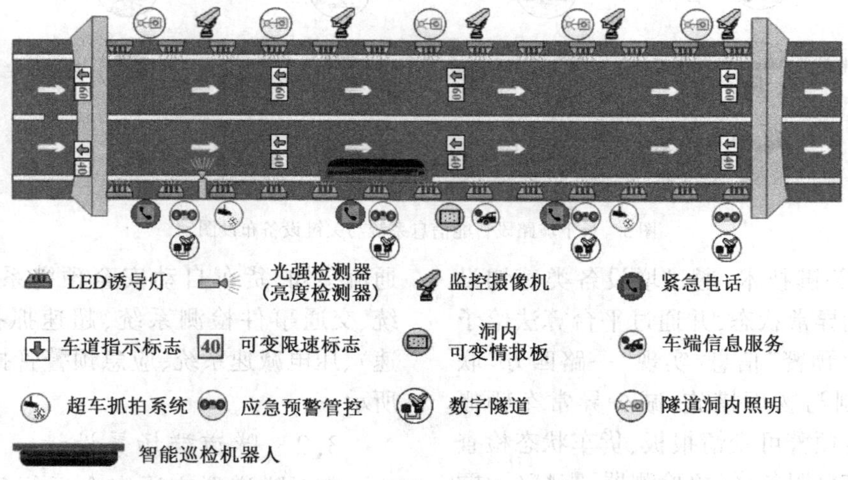

图6 隧道综合智能管控设施布设图

应用的主要关键技术：通过长大隧道设施数字化、图像化、设备的IP化、控制设备国产化，实现安全设施升级，增加人、车、路、环境的检测设施，增强隧道环境、道路感知能力，通过数字化平台建立隧道综合管控平台，对接区域、省级平台和安全管理平台，加强“一路四方”信息联动，提高隧道通行预警能力与处置能力。主要设备包括：超限检测设备、视频分析系统、智能照明管理系统、智能护栏系统、智能巡检机器人、隧道设施数字化图像化、车端信息服务平台、隧道综合管控系统等，如表2所示。

隧道智能综合信息采集与处置系统布设一览表 表2

路段	机电系统	功能	效果
影响区	车辆轮廓检测系统	检测车辆轮廓，提前分流	警告，控制车宽
进口段及进口前路段	传统隧道机电系统	设置、维护、完善可变情报板、交通信号灯、监控摄像机、洞外光强检测器、洞口亮度检测器、紧急电话	警告，积极引导，控制流量，控制车距，抑制变道
	定向音和警报器	向车辆报警，信息交互	警告
	车牌抓拍设备	检测、跟踪车辆	减轻、消除
	LED诱导系统	照明，道路轮廓	视觉适应，积极引导
中间段	分车道限速	车道指示器+车道可变限速标志	控制车速，控制流量
	LED诱导系统	照明，道路轮廓	视觉适应，积极引导
	超车抓拍系统	超车（压实线）抓拍，交警处罚	抑制变道
	数字隧道系统	感知融合、车辆跟踪、事件抓拍	警告、减轻、抑制变道
	应急预警管控	全程事故预警，提前干预	警告、减轻
	路端信息告知	可变情报板限速和路况告知，警示超速车辆	警告，控制车距，抑制变道
	车端信息服务	手机、广播、导航信息服务	警告，控制车距，抑制变道
	隧道机器人	环境、结构健康检测	消除、警告、减轻
	照明系统	隧道照明	视觉适应，积极引导

3.3 桥隧连续应用场景设计

结合交通运输部关于桥梁专项升级的要求，针对长下坡路段桥梁与隧道连续的特点，增设桥梁结构、桥面状态、道路环境、气象情况等监测设备，进一步完善道路运行采集体系，并通过AI算法预警预测道路运行风险，改善桥隧连续段的抗滑能力和自动处置能力，增设道路与预警信息标志，提高与驾驶员信息互动能力与养护人员事件处置能力。

应用的关键技术：通过前端感知监测连续桥隧段道路、环境与车辆实时状态，并通过视频分析、结构数据和气象分析，提高运行预测、预警与预判能力。布设的主要设备有：综合环境检测系统、自动除冰设备、雾灯诱导系统、桥梁健康检测设备等，完成多源数据采集与综合预警平台的建立（图7）。

3.4 综合管控平台升级

在充分利旧前提下，将试点区域（包括影响区、上下游、长下坡、隧道群、桥隧连接段）视为整体，对综合信息系统进行统一规划、建设、管理。加强与相邻路段的互联互通，实现信息实时共享，特别通过影响区实现截流、分流和信息提前预告；实现与上级管理部门互联互通，实时上传交通状态、交通事件、交通事故信息，接收上级部门调度指挥；实现与交通管理部门互联互通，在超速抓拍、超车抓拍、违停抓拍等方面，与公安交管共建共管，通过交警执法提高系统效果；在应急救援方面，通过与公安交管、路政和地方政府协同指挥调度，提高应急救援效率。

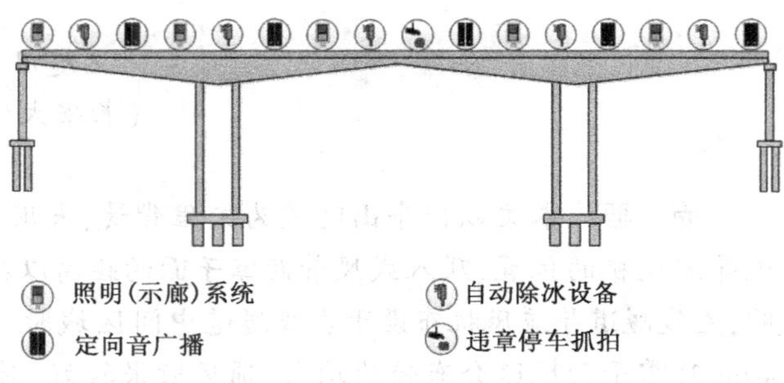

图7 桥隧连续段新增采集与处置单元

3.5　智慧高速试点与技术应用

通过研究沪渝高速鄂西段长下坡、隧道群和桥梁段的风险因素、安全评估等级,根据其影响因素,制定智能场景应用策略,增设信息采集、传感设备、控制设备、显示设备,完善路端、车端信息交互,逐步通过交通工程、信息化工程建立长下坡、隧道群、桥梁段智能化管控模型,实现交通事件发现及处理的全流程管控,重点路段车辆全域跟踪,实现道路安全驾驶,改善交通环境,减少交通事故,形成山区智慧高速公路雏形,通过测试与应用逐步向智慧高速路网进行平滑过渡。

4　结语

智慧高速是系统工程,不仅要从工程、管理、交通和信息化角度思考与推动,更要思考"粗放式"向"数字化"至"智慧化"迭代的关键因素,不是简单设备堆砌,要明确战略定位,加强数字技术与人的相互作用,相互促进;不能单纯以工程角度考虑智慧高速建设,要结合国企改革、国企责任与社会责任宏观要求,通过新基建与数据价值赋予企业"数据智慧"与人的"理性智慧";建立智慧平台,实现企业智能化互联互通;落地智慧流程,推动各方动态互动,实现各种场景应用;培养智慧员工,自我驱动,推动智慧高速、智能交通的智慧进程。

参考文献

[1] 周江华,史玖琦.智慧的企业,还是企业的智慧[J].清华管理评论,2021,7:97-103.

[2] 刘旭,谷岩.浅谈车路协同在高速公路运营服务中的应用[J].中国交通信息化,2021,9:39-40.

[3] 岑晏青,宋向辉,王东柱,等.智慧高速公路技术体系构建[J].公路交通科技,2020,37(7):111-121.

[4] 丁家慧.高速公路长大下坡交通安全风险评估与风险控制技术研究[D].西安:长安大学,2020.

[5] 北京交科公路勘察设计研究院有限公司,云南省交通投资建设集团有限公司,北京中交华安科技有限公司.提升公路连续长陡下坡路段安全通行能力专项行动技术指南[M].北京:人民交通出版社股份有限公司,2019.

[6] 福建省交通运输厅,福建省高速公路集团有限公司,交通运输部公路科学研究院等.公路隧道提质升级行动技术指南[M].北京:人民交通出版社股份有限公司,2019.

[7] 交通运输部公路科学研究院,北京中交华安科技有限公司,贵州省公路局等.提升公路桥梁安全防护能力专项行动技术指南[M].北京:人民交通出版社股份有限公司,2019.

[8] 周颖,陈晨.山区高速公路长下坡与隧道路段安全评价方法研究[J].交通技术,2019,8(3):199-206.

[9] 盛刚.高速公路紧急事件应急救援关键技术研究[D].西安:长安大学,2016.

斜井压入式通风导流风机对通风效果的影响

王庭川*　　任　锐

(长安大学公路学院)

摘　要　本文以伏牛山隧道为工程背景,采用数值模拟的方法并辅以现场实测数据,研究了左线隧道导流风机的位置、压入式风管距掌子面的距离以及压入式风管风速对施工通风效果的影响。研究结果表明,左线隧道导流风机布设于左线隧道中间区域时,对于粉尘颗粒的排出效果较佳。风管距掘进面30~40m时掌子面风速分布较为均匀,通风效果较好,对于粉尘颗粒的排除效果较佳。随风管风速的增大,粉尘颗粒扩散速度更快,扩散范围更广,但除尘效率的增长率却在逐渐降低,因此压入式风管风速22m/s

时，对于斜井压入式通风的通风效果较佳。

关键词　隧道工程　施工通风　风机布置　数值模拟　现场实测

0　引言

随着我国公路隧道建设的迅速发展，越来越多的长大隧道投入建设，截至2020年，全国公路隧道达到21316处、2199.93万延米，其中特长隧道1394处、623.55万延米。目前，长大隧道的施工通风问题尤为重要，逐渐成为隧道快速施工的"瓶颈"。

针对隧道施工通风问题，国内外学者进行了一定的研究。关宝树、杨其新、王明年等人分别开发编制过隧道通风网络计算程序，对二郎山隧道通风、秦岭终南山隧道通风等工程进行过研究[1]。康小兵等[2]对紫坪铺高瓦斯隧道内射流风机不同风速产生不同的通风效果进行了分析。张雪金等[3]建立压入式通风三维数值计算模型，研究了瓦斯涌出量、风量和风管位置等因素对瓦斯扩散的影响。张云龙等[4]利用CFD流体动力学软件得到不同风管出口距掌子面距离下，隧道内风速流场和瓦斯体积分数的分布规律，并与现场测试数据进行对比。王江龙[5]对不同风速条件下，斜井通风管距隧道掌子面不同距离及不同隧道内通风时间条件下道内瓦斯扩散及稀释过程进行了模拟。王阅章等[6]对瓦斯隧道内部流场分布规律进行数值模拟分析。

目前对于长大隧道施工通风的研究通常是对于瓦斯隧道进行的，且大多考虑的是单因素的作用，没有研究对于一般长大隧道的影响，且并无综合考虑压入式通风管与射流风机的共同作用。本文以伏牛山隧道为依托建立三维模型，通过流体力学软件Fluent进行施工通风的数值模拟，对引流风机的位置、风管的布置参数进行优化，为相似的工程提供施工参考。

1　工程概况

伏牛山特长公路隧道位于栾川县庙子镇附近，地属伏牛山系，横跨黄河长江分水岭，隧道左线全长9161m，右线全长9183m，设计行车速度为80km/h。伏牛山隧道共设置车行横通道11处，人行横通道23处，斜井3处，施工时作为施工辅助通道使用，后期用于运营通风。伏牛山隧道1号斜井采用风管压入式通风，由通风机将新风通过风管送向掌子面，污风由斜井排出。

2　数学模型及参数设置

2.1　控制方程

公路隧道在运营期间隧道内空气的流动状态为湍流状态，采用Fluent进行数值计算，选用k-ε模型进行求解，控制方程组如式(1)～式(5)所示[7~8]。

连续方程

$$\frac{\partial u_i}{\partial x_i}=0 \tag{1}$$

动量方程

$$\frac{\partial \rho u_i u_j}{\partial x_j}=\frac{\partial \rho}{\partial x_i}+\frac{\partial}{\partial x_i}\left[\mu\left(\frac{\partial u_i}{\partial x_j}+\frac{\partial u_j}{\partial x_i}\right)\right]+\frac{\partial(-\rho\overline{u_i'u_j'})\rho u_i u_j}{\partial x_j} \tag{2}$$

k方程

$$\rho u_j\frac{\partial k}{\partial x_j}=\frac{\partial}{\partial x_j}\left[\left(\mu+\frac{\mu_t}{\sigma_k}\right)\frac{\partial k}{\partial x_j}\right]+\mu_t\frac{\partial u_i}{\partial x_j}\left(\frac{\partial u_i}{\partial x_j}+\frac{\partial u_j}{\partial x_i}\right)-\rho\varepsilon \tag{3}$$

ε方程

$$\rho u_j\frac{\partial \varepsilon}{\partial x_j}=\frac{\partial}{\partial x_j}\left[\left(\mu+\frac{\mu_t}{\sigma_\varepsilon}\right)\frac{\partial \varepsilon}{\partial x_j}\right]+\frac{c_1\varepsilon}{k}\mu_t\frac{\partial u_i}{\partial x_j}\left(\frac{\partial u_i}{\partial x_j}+\frac{\partial u_j}{\partial x_i}\right)-c_2\rho\frac{\varepsilon^2}{k} \tag{4}$$

黏性系数方程

$$\mu_t=c_\mu\rho k^2/\varepsilon \tag{5}$$

式中：u——平均速度；

u'——脉动速度；

x——位置张量($i,j=1,2,3$)；

μ——动力黏性系数；

μ_t——湍流黏性系数；

k——湍流动能；

ε——耗散率；

$c_1=1.44$，$c_2=1.92$，$c_\mu=0.09$，$\sigma_k=1.0$，$\sigma_\varepsilon=1.92$。

2.2　计算模型

运用计算流体力学软件Fluent建立伏牛山隧道三维数值仿真模型，由于隧道长度较长、规模过大，完全采用1:1的三维模型计算对计算机要求很高，一般计算较难实现，因此如图1所示将模型缩短至350m,压入式风管直径1.6m,风管安装于隧道拱肩处,引流风机置于左线隧道、横通道与右线隧道交界处以及斜井与右线隧道交界处。图2为隧道、横通道及斜井截面示意图。模型统一采用六面体网格进行划分,最终网格划分图如图3所示。

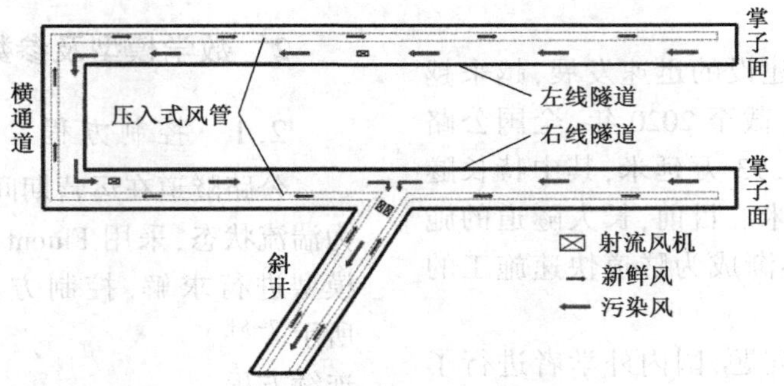

图1　伏牛山隧道数值仿真模型示意图

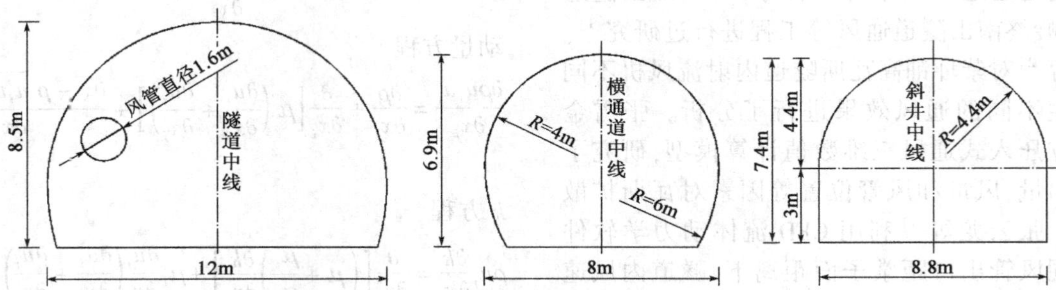

图2　隧道、横通道及斜井截面示意图

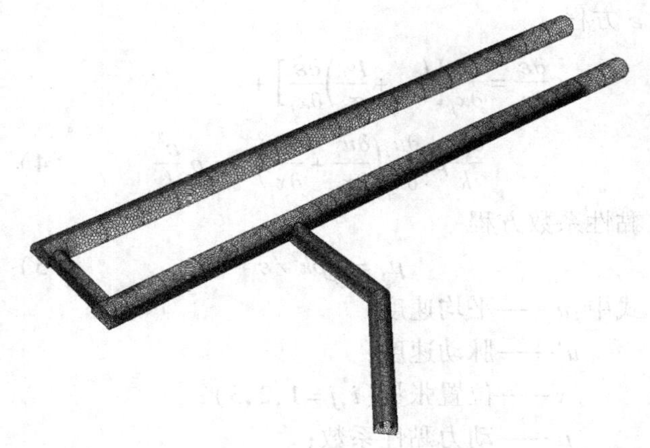

图3　伏牛山隧道模型网格划分示意图

2.3　边界条件

依据施工通风的实际情况设定边界条件如下:

(1)风管出口设置为速度入口边界(Velocity-inlet),直径为1.6m,取值为16~25m/s。

(2)隧道斜井出口设为压力出口边界(pressure-out)。

(3)隧道壁面、地板、掌子面以及风管和射流风机壁面设为固壁边界(wall)。

(4)隧道壁面、顶部边界条件为反弹,隧道底面边界类型为捕获。

(5)射流风机设置为动量源。

(6)实际工程中随着隧道施工的进行,粉尘颗粒绝大部分由掌子面释出,因而假设粉尘颗粒喷射源位于掌子面均匀地释放。

3　研究结果与分析

3.1　左线隧道导流风机位置影响分析

在压入式风管施工通风中,左线隧道掘进面所释放的粉尘颗粒在通风的作用下需要经由最近的横通道至右线隧道中,最后由斜井出口排出,粉尘颗粒所需经过的距离较长,左线隧道内导流风机的位置对于粉尘颗粒能否快速顺利地排出有着很大的影响。为研究左线隧道导流风机位置对施工通风效果的影响,按前述模型进行数值模拟计算,风管距掌子面40m,压入式风管风速22m/s,左线隧道导流风机距掌子面距离按工况要求分别取70m、170m、270m,建立3个模型,分别为工况1-1~1-3。

图4为各工况通风360s之后左线隧道掘进面所产生的粉尘颗粒随位置变化的粉尘浓度变化

图,图中可以看出:

(1)工况1-1至工况1-3的粉尘浓度在隧道内的变化趋势大致相同,随着距掌子面距离的逐渐增大,前期粉尘浓度快速下降,一定距离后趋于平稳。

(2)导流风机附近的粉尘浓度下降速度较快,工况1-1的粉尘浓度在距左线隧道掘进面40~60m位置处大幅度下降77.03%,工况1-2和工况1-3的粉尘浓度分别在距左线隧道掘进面120~160m及230~260m处大幅度下降46.3%与96.1%。同时随着距导流风机位置的距离不断增大,导流风机辅助通风的效果逐渐减弱,粉尘浓度变化减小。

(3)随着导流风机距掌子面距离的增大,导流风机辅助通风的时间位置改变,隧道内粉尘浓度峰值逐渐向隧道外推移,各工况粉尘浓度水平有明显区别。工况1-1的粉尘浓度在至距左线隧道掘进面160m范围内低于其他工况,但趋于稳定后的粉尘浓度较大。工况1-3在近掌子面较大范围内的粉尘浓度过大,230m后粉尘浓度下降速度才增大。而工况1-2虽然在180m后粉尘浓度才低于其他工况,但在较大的范围内粉尘浓度较低,粉尘颗粒的扩散速度与扩散范围更快更大。

综上表明,隧道内导流风机布设于隧道中部对于隧道内粉尘颗粒的排出效果最佳。

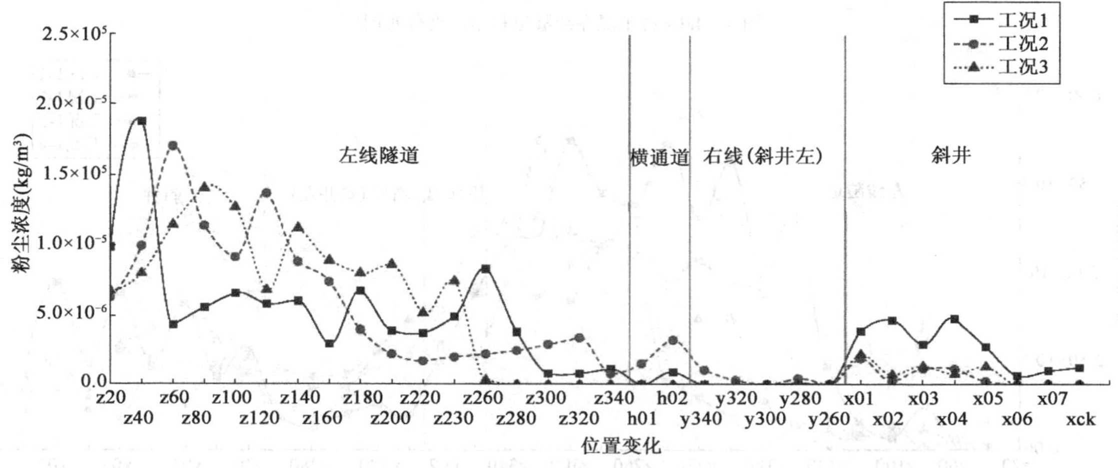

图4 360s各工况左线隧道粉尘浓度分布图

3.2 压入式风管风速影响分析

为了研究压入式风管的风速对斜井压入式通风通风效果的影响,取前述模型进行数值模拟计算,风管距掌子面40m,左线隧道导流风机距掌子面170m,压入式风管风速按工况要求分别取16m/s、19m/s、22m/s、25m/s,建立4个模型,分别为工况2-1~2-4。

图5、图6分别为各工况通风480s及900s后左线隧道粉尘浓度分布图,图中可以看出:

(1)随压入式风管风速的增大,粉尘浓度变化趋势大致相同,但粉尘浓度峰值逐渐减小,且随着风速的增大,隧道内平均粉尘浓度逐渐降低,除尘效率逐渐增大。

(2)工况2-1至工况2-4,随风速的增大,粉尘颗粒扩散范围更广,粉尘颗粒的聚集范围也不断向隧道出口处推移。图5中工况2-1、2-2与2-3分别扩散至260m、300m及340m处,工况2-4粉尘颗粒已扩散至右线隧道内;图6中,随风速的增大,粉尘颗粒的聚集区域不断向隧道出口处推移,工况2-1、2-2粉尘颗粒分别聚集于左线隧道160~300m、180~320m处,工况2-3、2-4粉尘颗粒均聚集于左线隧道260m至横通道范围内。

(3)随着风速的增大,隧道内粉尘浓度有着明显的降低,但粉尘浓度的降低效率也逐渐降低,由16m/s增加至19m/s,除尘效率增加23.49%,由19m/s增加至22m/s;除尘效率增加11.79%,由22m/s增加至25m/s,除尘效率仅增加6.32%。

综上表明,在一定范围内风速越大越有利于隧道内粉尘颗粒的排出,对于施工通风的通风效果也越好;但随着风速的增大,增加相同大小的风速时,增加的除尘效率越来越小,相对于增加风速所需要付出的能耗、经济以及技术相对比,所增长的除尘效率太小,因此工况2-3,即压入式风管风速为22m/s时,在综合考虑除尘效率以及能耗经济下,对于施工通风的通风效果最好。

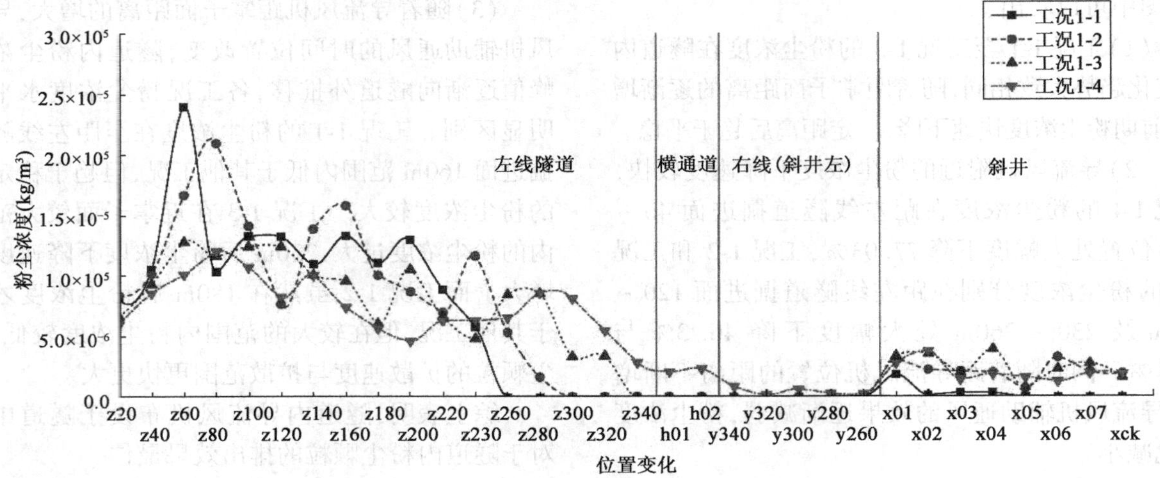

图 5　480s 各工况左线隧道粉尘浓度分布图

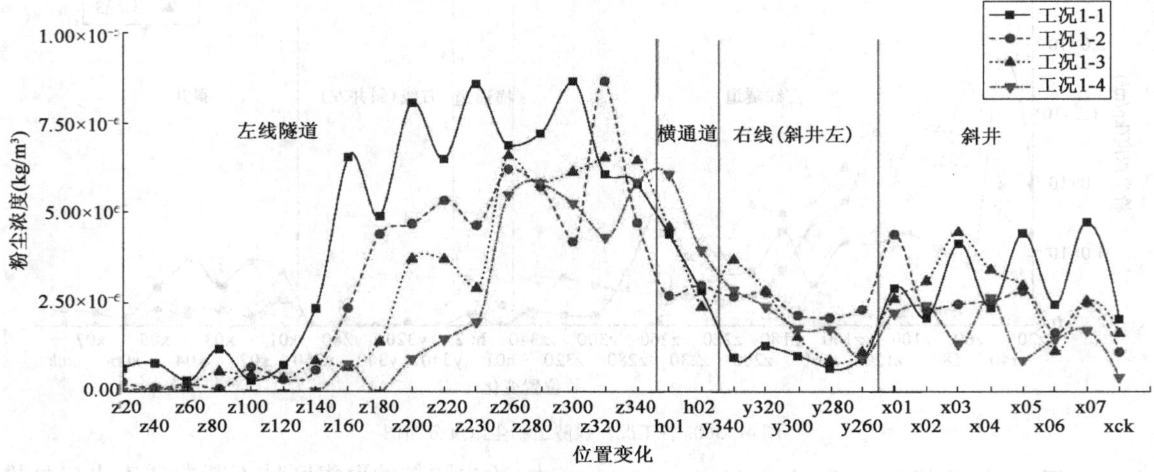

图 6　900s 各工况左线隧道粉尘浓度分布图

3.3　压入式风管距掘进面的距离影响分析

数值计算依然取前述模型进行,压入式风管风速 22m/s,左线隧道导流风机距掌子面 170m,压入式风管距掌子面距离按工况要求分别取 20m、30m、40m、50m,建立 4 个模型,分别为工况 3-1 ~ 3-4。

如图 7 ~ 图 10 所示,随着风管距掌子面距离的增加,工况 3-1 ~ 3-4 的最高风速逐渐降低,分别为 5.5m/s、5m/s、4m/s 及 2.5m/s。且风管距离掌子面过近时,掌子面两侧风速差异较大,工况 3-1 靠近风管放置一侧掌子面风速较高,另一侧区域风速相对较低。工况 3-1 ~ 工况 3-4 随着风管距掌子面距离的逐渐增大,压入式风在吹向掌子面的过程中,风流逐渐偏移并充满隧道,使得在吹向掌子面时风速分布较为均匀,高风速区域逐渐向掌子面中心区域偏移。

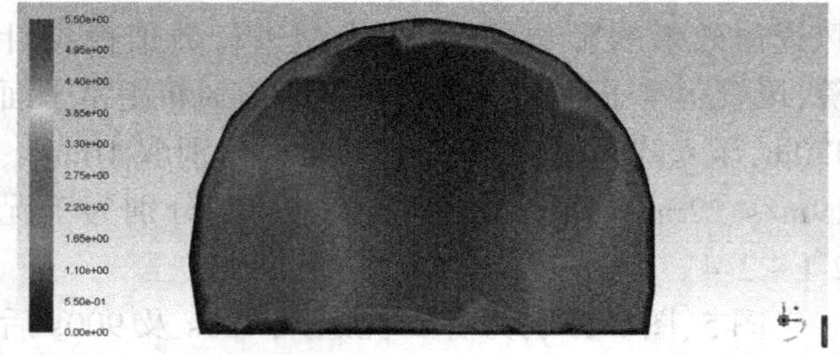
图 7　工况 1 掌子面风速分布

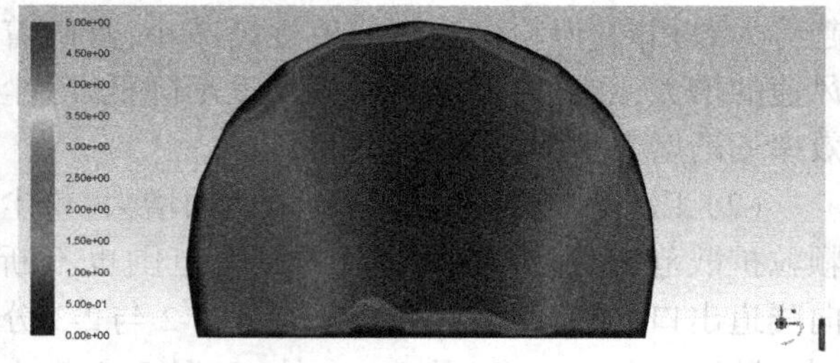
图 8　工况 2 掌子面风速分布

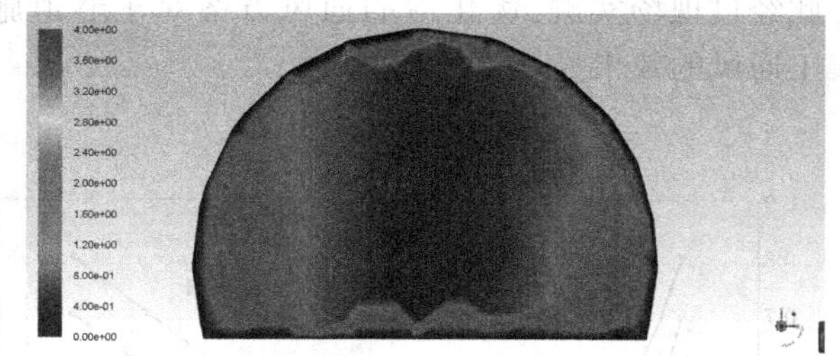

图9 工况3掌子面风速分布

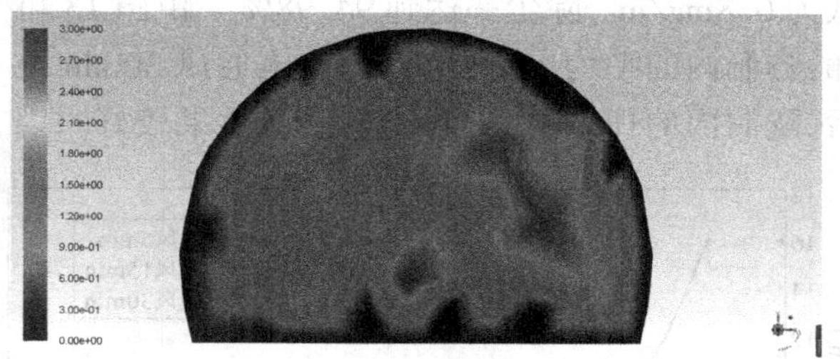

图10 工况4掌子面风速分布

图11为480s时各工况隧道粉尘浓度分布图，由图可知：

(1)随着时间的逐渐增长，工况3-2的隧道内掘进面附近粉尘浓度最高，具有较高的粉尘浓度峰值。

(2)工况3-3平均隧道粉尘浓度最大，工况3-1与工况3-4隧道平均粉尘浓度较低。

(3)工况3-2的粉尘颗粒扩散范围最大，工况3扩散范围最小。

综上，随着压入式风管距掘进面距离的增大，风管距离过近时，掘进面附近的粉尘颗粒扩散效果好，但随距掘进面距离的增大，容易造成粉尘颗粒在距隧道掘进面较远处大面积堆积，通风效果变差。风管距离过大时，在压入式风吹向掘进面的过程中风速不断降低，导致对于掘进面附近粒的通风效果减弱，隧道掘进面附近粉尘颗粒堆积，通风效果变差，综上当压入式风管距掘进面位置适中，即30m左右时对于施工通风的通风效果最佳。

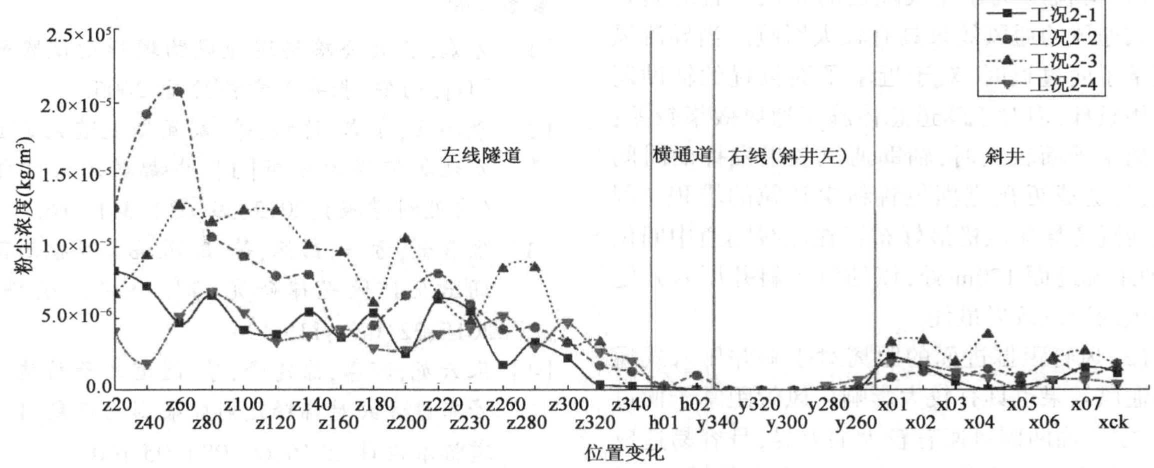

图11 480s各工况隧道粉尘浓度分布图

4 现场实测

为了检测通风方案优化后的现场掌子面的环境情况，在实际左线隧道中部布设导流风机，压入式风管布设于距掌子面30m处，风管风速设为22m/s，在挖掘的过程中进行现场通风测试。为了能够更好地了解掌子面附近的环境随着隧道施工通风的进行的变化情况，对掌子面开挖后，通风5min、通风15min以及通风30min后的测试断面的环境情况进行现场测试评估。

在测试段每隔200m设置一个测试断面，共布设9个测试断面。在隧道中线距离隧底1.7m(隧道内工作人员的平均高度)的高度进行数据检测。对每个测试断面的风速、粉尘浓度进行测量，并根据测量结果进行通风效果的评估。

图12、图13分别为隧道内粉尘浓度以及风速随时间的变化曲线图。由图13可知，在掌子面的开挖初期，通风5min后，粉尘颗粒聚集于掌子面附近，粉尘浓度较高，达到了15.93mg/m³。随着隧道长度的变化，粉尘浓度逐渐降低。随着通风时间的增加，通风15min后，粉尘颗粒逐渐向着斜井迁移，隧道内的粉尘颗粒分布较为均匀。通风30min后，粉尘颗粒大部分已由斜井排出，隧道内的粉尘浓度明显降低，掌子面附近的粉尘浓度降

低为0.8mg/m³,除尘率达到94.98%。由图13可知,隧洞内的平均风速较为稳定,再通风30min之后,隧洞内的环境良好,此时的通风效果较好。因此经过现场实测,优化后的通风方案对于隧道施工通风的效果显著。

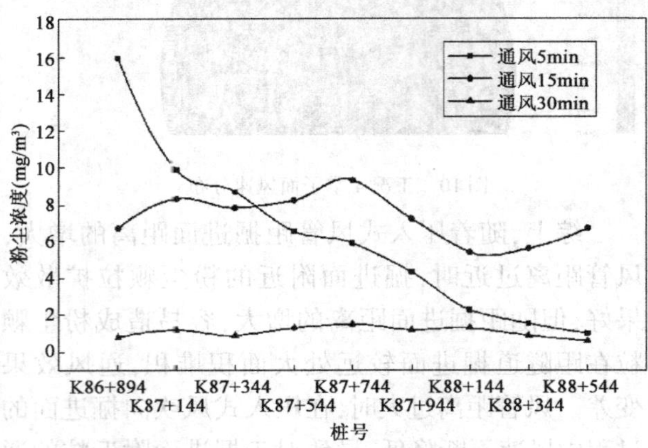

图12 粉尘浓度随通风时间变化图

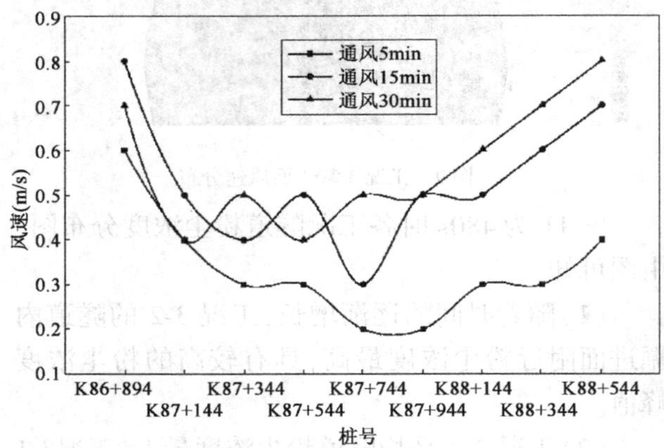

图13 隧道内风速随通风时间变化图

5 结语

(1)导流风机在左线隧道的布设位置对斜井压入式通风的通风效果具有较大影响。当导流风机距掌子面过近时,对于近掌子面位置的辅助通风作用较佳,但对于隧道总体施工通风效果较差;而距离掌子面较远时,辅助通风效果发挥的时间较晚,易造成近掘进面位置粉尘颗粒的堆积。因此左线隧道导流风机最好布置在左线隧道中间位置,即距掘进面170m处,该处对于斜井压入式施工通风的通风效果最佳。

(2)风管距掘进面的距离对于斜井压入式通风的通风效果也具有较大影响。风管距掌子面过近时,掌子面两侧风速有较大的差异,且容易造成粉尘颗粒在距隧道掘进面较远处大面积堆积;风管距掌子面过远,射流不能直接到达掌子面,极大的削弱了对于通风效果的积极影响。风管距掘进面30m左右时,对于斜井压入式通风的通风效果最佳。

(3)压入式风管风速较低时,对于粉尘颗粒的扩散与逸出效果较差;随着风管风速的增大,粉尘颗粒扩散速度更快,扩散的范围更广。但随着风管风速的增大,除尘效率虽然增加但增加比率逐步降低,综合能耗、经济等考虑,压入式风管风速为22m/s时,对于斜井压入式通风的通风效果越好。

参考文献

[1] 方磊. 长大公路隧道通风物理模型试验研究[D]. 西安:长安大学档案馆,2005.

[2] 康小兵,丁睿,许模,等. 高瓦斯隧道施工通风处理数值模拟分析[J]. 成都理工大学学报(自然科学版),2012,39(03):311-316.

[3] 张雪金,方勇,彭佩,等. 隧道施工开挖面瓦斯涌出及扩散规律研究[J]. 公路交通科技,2015,32(02):119-126.

[4] 张云龙,郭春,徐建峰,等. 隧道掌子面施工风管布设方式对稀释瓦斯效果影响研究[J]. 铁道标准设计,2016,60(08):95-100.

[5] 王江龙. 瓦斯隧道通风方案优化[D]. 西安:长安大学,2014.

[6] 王阅章,李鸣,宿成智,等. 公路瓦斯隧道压入式通风数值模拟分析[J]. 中国新技术新产品,2020(19):120-123.

[7] 温玉辉. 特长公路隧道纵向通风系统CFD三维仿真分析[D]. 西安:长安大学,2004.

[8] 马延文,傅德薰. 现代计算流体力学[Z]. 北京:北京航空航天大学档案馆,2002.

德国公路隧道养护和运行管理经验介绍

王璟文*
（交通国际合作事务中心发展部）

摘　要　本文通过对德国隧道运养管理相关政策法律、标准规范，以及欧盟层面的相关法令和指导文件进行梳理，总结分析有效做法和成功经验，为提升我国公路隧道养护和运行水平、完善我国公路隧道运养管理制度及标准规范提供借鉴和参考。本文认为，德国隧道在运行安全管理方面做得非常出色，有高效协作的应急管理体制、完善的危货运输管理体系和全面的安全事件申报和隧道安全宣传机制，对我国具有较大的借鉴意义。

关键词　经验总结　德国隧道运养管理经验　文献研究法　隧道养护和运行管理　隧道危货运输

0　引言

公路运输在我国交通运输中一直占有重要地位，公路建设也取得了举世瞩目的成就。我国公路网不断向大山、西部延伸，跨越了物理阻隔，其中公路隧道建设功不可没。近年来，我国公路隧道数量和里程逐年增长，2020 年中国特长隧道数量 1394 处，较 2019 年增长 219 处；长隧道数量 5541 处，较 2019 年增长 757 处；2020 年中国公路隧道长度 2199.93 万延米，同比增长 15.99%（数据来源：《2020 年交通运输行业发展统计公报》）。与此同时，公路隧道安全管理和应急救援也日益成为社会关注的重点。

德国隧道建设起步较早，多条隧道运行时间长，且安全系数高。但我国对于德国的隧道多关注铁路隧道，且大都聚焦在技术标准以及施工、防火等新技术方面。曾满元、喻渝对德国《铁路标准规范》中隧道标准进行细致的分析并指出，德国《规范》在指导实践方面作用较大；琚国全、陈赤坤、曹彧等对德国铁路隧道设计理念、体系构成、编制内容能方面进行深入分析。此外，相关研究大都围绕新型盾构机和先进施工技术、隧道消防技术等开展，缺少对德国隧道运养管理方面的研究分析。

本文将围绕德国隧道总体概况、管理主体、相关政策法规文件、隧道检查与养护、隧道运行管理等方面展开，重点介绍隧道应急管理、安全管理和危险品运输的经验。

1　德国公路隧道总体概况

德国共有约有 420 公路隧道，总里程约 350km。其中，位于联邦干线公路的隧道由 270 道，总里程约 270km（图 1）（数据来源：德国联邦交通部官网）。巴登符腾堡州拥有超过 80 道联邦干线公路隧道，约占全德国的 30%，是德国拥有最多联邦干线公路隧道的州。全国另有 20 道隧道在建，50 道已取得建筑许可，60 道正在计划中。现今德国最长的公路和高速公路隧道为任斯泰格隧道（Rennsteigtunnel），长 7916m，也是欧洲第四长的双洞公路隧道。

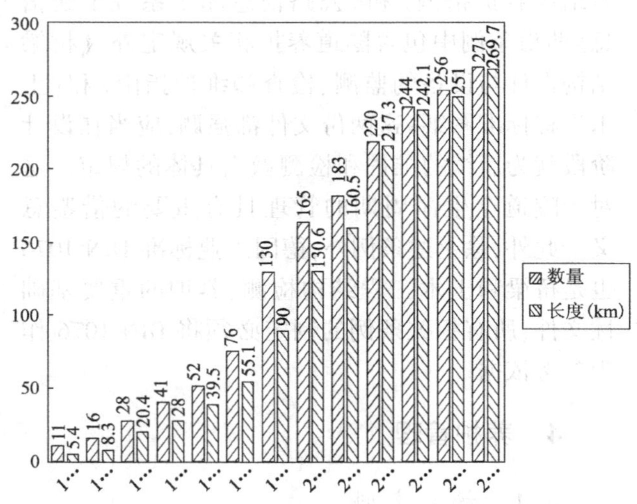

图 1　联邦干线公路数量与长度（截至 2017 年 12 月 31 日）

2　隧道管理主体

德国的隧道由所在公路的管理部门负责。德

国是一个联邦制国家,各州政府在其辖区内拥有较大的自主权,因此,德国公路按照不同业主可分为:联邦干线公路、州级公路、县级公路、市镇公路,分别由联邦交通部、州交通部、县和市镇交通局和其他相关管理机构管理。上述单位既是管理的主体,同时也是联邦有关交通法规、规划和政策的实施主体。在联邦总体的政策框架之下,上述单位根据本地区实际情况,行使诸如交通网络建设、运营管理等职责。

此外,联邦公路研究院(BAsT)也参与制定隧道相关的标准规范,并为政府决策提供咨询。联邦公路研究院(BAsT)是联邦交通部直属的以道路运输为研究重点的科学技术研究机构,该机构以实践为导向,致力于解决人、路、环境之间的关系。同时,它负责为联邦交通部就有关公路交通政策的技术问题做作策咨询,负责起草和协调国家、欧洲和国际的标准规范,其中包括制定隧道相关的指南。

3　相关法律规范文件

在德国,隧道相关的法规文件可分为针对机械设备及隧道运行和针对土木结构的条例两大类。前者主要的法规文件为《关于公路隧道设备和运行的指南》(Richtlinien für die Ausstattung und den Betrieb von Straßentunneln, RABT);后者又细分为为设计、施工和养护三部分,见表 1。

联邦干线上土木结构的条例　　表 1

设　计	施　工	养　护
《土木结构的设计、施工和设备指南》(RE-ING)	《土木结构附加技术合同条件和指南》(ZTV-ING)	《土木结构养护指南》(RI-ERH-ING)
《土木结构设计编制指南》(RAB-ING)	《土木结构的技术交货条件和检验规范》(TL/TP-ING)	《公路信息库子系统土建信息》(ASB-ING)
《土木结构测量与计算规定及指南》(BEM-ING)	《土木工程施工监理规则》(M-BÜ-ING)	—
《公路隧道的建造、设备和运行》(RE-TUNNEL)	—	—
《工程图》(RiZ-ING)	—	—

值得注意的是,除与隧道养护直接相关的《土木结构养护指南》和《公路信息库子系统土建信息》两份条例中包含隧道养护相关规定外,《桥梁结构设计与设备的监测、检查和维护指南》和《土木工程标准图纸》这两份文件都强调,应当在设计阶段就为后续的维护和检测做出具体的规定。这对于隧道全生命周期的管理具有重要的借鉴意义。此外,除上述条例外,德国工业标准 DIN 1076 也是桥梁和土木工程结构检测、养护的重要基础性文件,所有相关条例的制定必须将 DIN 1076 作为参考依据。

4　养护管理

4.1　检查类型

隧道检测分为重点检查、全面检查、年检、半年检查、特殊检查(表 2)6 种。正常情况下,隧道土木结构应每半年一小检(半年检,目测);每年一大检(称年检,目测或用仪器);每 3 年一次全面检查(用仪器),在目测没有问题时照样进行;每 6 年一次重点检查,用各种仪器全面、彻底、详细检查,也可以称为承载能力检测,包括稳定性、排水性能、桥面标志、标线和裂缝,螺丝、锚头松动情况,钢桥锈蚀情况,钢筋是否裸露和各种受力以及密封程度是否正常等都进行彻底的检查。此外,在发生重大特殊情况后,如洪水、地震、车撞等事故,养护部门立即用仪器进行专项检查。该检查不能代替全面检查或重点检查。

4.2　组织形式

大部分联邦州的建设主管部门都会组织对土木结构的检查(图 2)。根据 DIN 1076 标准,监测和检查通常由不同的单位进行。由此形成的“多眼原则”,保证病害评估更加客观。在检查组中,应纳入养护人员,以便其更加了解病害状况,有助于养护工作更加顺利的进行。检查组的规模主要根据现场的工作条件、土木结构数量和平均规模来决定。

土木结构检查类型及频率

表 2

检查类型	工程验收前的检查	保修期内的检查次数					使用寿命结束前的检查次数						
	年份	1	2	3	4	5	6	7	8	9	10	11	后续
半年检查	—	2	2	2	2	2	2	2	2	2	2	2	2
年检	—	1	1	—	1	—	1	1	—	1	1	—	1
全面检查	—	—	—	√	—	—	—	—	√	—	—	—	每6年1次
重点检查	√	—	—	—	—	√	—	—	—	—	—	√	每6年1次
专项检查	—	在发生重大风暴、洪水、交通事故或其他影响隧道土木结构安全的事件后											

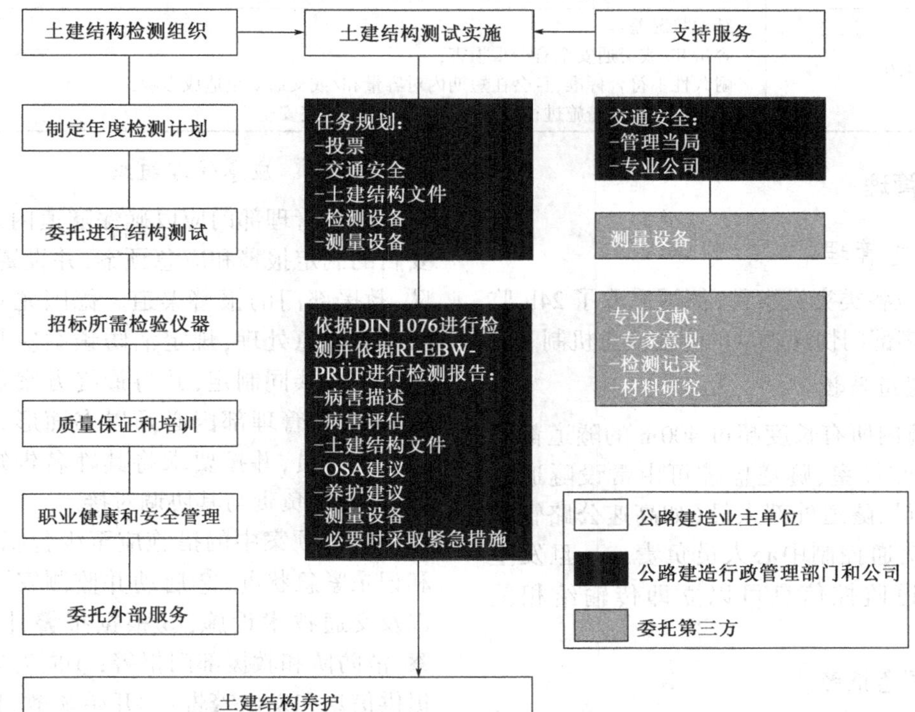

图 2　土木结构检查组织形式

4.3　评分标准

根据 RI-EBW-PRÜF，隧道土木结构所有的组成部分被分为 14 类。根据已定义的目录，可以确定各类对桥梁的容量、交通安全、耐久性造成的影响，并给予相应的评分。评分等级从 1 到 4，其中 1 为最佳评分。在初步评级中，使用矩阵算法获得速率，并同时添加覆盖全部损害蔓延的附加比率，在此基础上，才能确定 14 个类别中每个类别的比率。这些评级是通过 14 个已确定的类别中发生的最大损坏等级来判断的，在此之后，还要根据土木结构被破坏的程度增加权重。最终等级分为 6 种（表 3）。

土木结构状况评分表

表 3

分　　数	土木结构状况和描述
1.0 ~ 1.4	结构状况很好： 容量、交通安全、耐久性均符合标准
1.5 ~ 1.9	结构状况良好： 容量和交通安全符合标准； 至少一个结构部件的耐久性有轻微损害
2.0 ~ 2.4	结构状况满意： 容量和交通安全符合标准； 至少一个结构部件的耐久性有轻微损害，且长期下去会对容量和交通安全造成影响； 短期内需要进行修复或警告，以维护道路安全

续上表

分　数	土木结构状况和描述
2.5~2.9	结构状况及格： 容量符合标准； 交通安全有轻微损害； 至少一个结构部件的耐久性有轻微损害，且中期内会对容量和交通安全造成严重影响； 短期内需要进行修复或警告，以维护道路安全
3.0~3.4	结构状况不及格： 容量和/或交通安全有损害； 耐久性不符合标准，且会在短期内对容量和/或交通安全造成影响； 需要立即采取措施进行修复或警告，以维护道路安全
3.5~4.0	结构状况差： 容量和/或交通安全有严重损害； 耐久性不符合标准，且会在短期内对容量和/或交通安全造成影响； 需要立即采取措施进行修复或警告，以维护道路安全

5　运行管理

5.1　应急管理

为快速响应各类突发事件，德国采取了24h监控、及时报警、多部门快速联动的隧道应急机制。

5.1.1　隧道监控

在德国，境内所有长度超过400m的隧道都设有24h值守的监控室，隧道监控可由常设隧道监控站的工作人员、隧道外部人员(如高速公路管理部门员工)或交通控制中心人员负责。一旦发生紧急情况，隧道监控信息可以立即传输给相关部门。

5.1.2　紧急报警

紧急报警应区分为预警和正式报警两种。在能见度低和交通堵塞时，将发出预警信号；应急电话、火灾警报、开启应急电话亭门、取出灭火器、打开逃生门等情况则会出发正式报警。报警后，监测点的工作人员将会视情况开进紧急预案或消防预案。火灾自动报警还可直接触发消防队报警、隧道封闭、消防通风、应急消防照明和最大日光照明。

5.1.3　应急管理组织

应急管理部门应以确保隧道内人员安全为首要目的制定报警和应急预案，并设置向警方、消防队、救援部门的报警渠道。德国尤其注重隧道火灾事故应急处理，规定消防预案应与负责消防安全的机构共同制定，并将最终方案提供给消防部门。同时，管理部门必须以书面形式指定一名消防安全官员，并按要求将其姓名告知负责防火的部门，专门负责与其协调对接。

应急预案中的措施应至少包括：①快速识别和记录紧急状况；②启动并监测安全设施和装置以及交通技术设施；③根据报警计划，立即向警察、消防队和救援部门报警；④向有安全风险的人提供信息和发出警告；⑤开始疏散，且紧急预案中的各种行动方案每年都要进行审查和演练。

5.2　安全管理

德国非常重视隧道安全，不仅对隧道内的安全设施有全面细致的规定(表4)，还按照欧盟规定建立了安全申报机制，总结安全经验。此外，德国还积极向隧道使用者宣传安全知识，保障交通参与者的安全。

隧道内安全设施要求　　表4

安全设施		隧道长度				
		<400	≥400 <600	≥600 <900	≥900 <1800	≥1800
建筑措施	紧急停靠处	—	—	○	●	●
	掉头口	—	—	○	●	●
	紧急出口	—	●	●	●	●
	紧急人行道	●	●	●	●	●
	排水设施	●	●	●	●	●

续上表

安全设施		隧道长度				
		<400	≥400 <600	≥600 <900	≥900 <1800	≥1800
通信设施	紧急呼叫装置	—	●	●	●	●
	视频监控	—	●	●	●	●
	隧道广播	●	●	●	●	●
	扩音器	—	●	●	●	●
火灾报警设施	手动火灾报警装置	—	●	●	●	●
	自动火灾报警装置	—	●	●	●	●
灭火设施	手提灭火器	—	●	●	●	●
	灭火水源	—	●	●	●	●
引导灯		—	●	●	●	●
逃生通道标志		●	●	●	●	●
控制设施		—	●	●	●	●

●必备
○特殊情况下配备(例如隧道特征受多种风险因素影响)

5.2.1 安全事件申报

按照《欧盟第2004/54/EG号关于全欧路网隧道最低安全要求的指令》的要求,德国需要每两年向欧洲委员会提交一份报告(图3为事故申报流程)。报告包含跨欧公路网隧道发生的严重事故和火灾、其频率及原因以及安全设备和措施有效性等信息。欧委会将欧盟各国事故及处理措施等信息进行汇总,并分享优秀实践和经验,供欧洲各国学习参考。

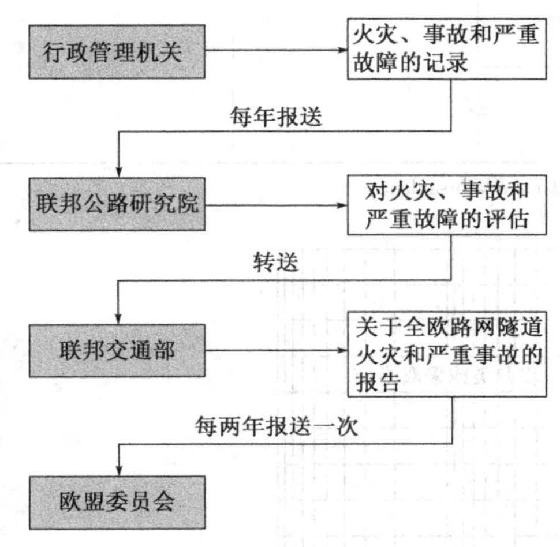

图3 隧道安全事件申报

5.2.2 安全宣传

除了保障隧道的安全设施和运行管理,德国对安全使用隧道也进行了全面的宣传。德国联邦交通部公路局编写了《安全第一——德国的公路隧道》手册,手册向隧道使用者介绍了隧道内重要的安全设施及其在发生故障和火灾时的作用。联邦公路研究院总结小册子的信息,印发"如何正确使用隧道"传单,并制作视频,里面包含了所有隧道安全设施的示意图,以及在不同情况下的行为规范(如入隧道前、正常行驶中、堵车时、发生火灾时等),以保障自身和其他隧道使用者的安全。

5.3 危险品运输

德国针对危险品运输的风险分析将基于《欧洲危险货物国际公路运输协定》(European Agreement Concerning the International Carriage of Dangerous goods by Road, ADR),把隧道分为5个安全等级(表5)。

联邦公路研究院在ADR的基础上,根据《欧盟隧道最低安全条例》和RABT制定了评估危险品等级和确定隧道危险品运输限制的程序,该程序应用于所有公路隧道(无论长短以及业主是谁)。程序分为两个阶段,每个阶段分为两个步骤,共四个环节(图4)。

在粗略评估阶段,首先要对隧道的风险相关特征参数进行检查(表6),若隧道风险参数均达标,则将隧道划入A类。若不达标,将继续按照OECD/PIARC的QRA模型分析隧道运输危险物品的风险。当隧道的指标低于此模型确定的损害预期值,当可以将隧道划入A类,否则,将进行深入分析。

在深入分析阶段,联邦公路研究院将危险品在QRA模型的基础上重新分类(表7),分析危险品的内在风险,并结合各隧道自身的状况,最终以图5所示频率-规模累计曲线形式确定隧道等级。为划入A类的隧道将进行最后的绕路风险核实环节。

隧道安全等级　　表5

等　级	限制运输货物
A	无限制
B	可能引发大型爆炸的危险货物
C	可能引发大范围暴露、大型爆炸或大量有毒物质释放的危险货物,以及B类隧道限制范围内的危险货物
D	可能引发超大型爆炸、大型爆炸或大量有毒物质释放的危险货物,以及C类隧道限制范围内的危险货物
E	除UN2919、UN3291、UN3331、UN3359、UN3373外的所有危险货物

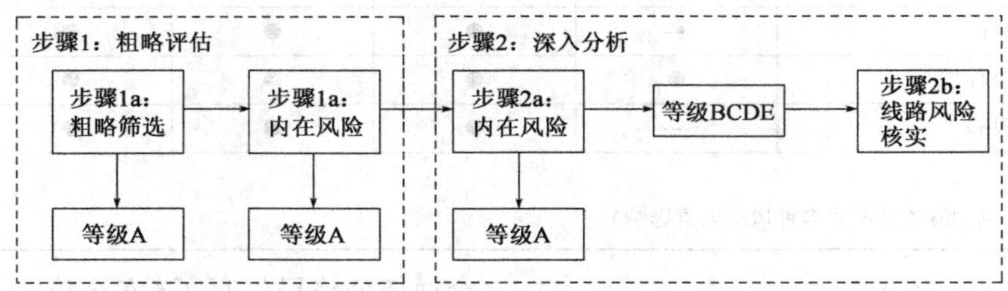

图4　隧道危险品运输分级评定

隧道风险特征参数评价　　表6

参数描述	是	否
隧道<400m	等级A	进入下一阶段
纵坡≤2%		
弧度≤250 gon/km		
出入口没有交叉路口设置		
交通质量优于HBS规定的E级		
卡车占比≤10%		
没有迹象表明危险货物的数量超过平均水平		
无上层建筑和扩建		
符合适用准则的技术或结构安全设备		

注:HBS即《道路交通设施设计手册》(Handbuch für die Bemessung von Straβ enverkehrsanlage)。

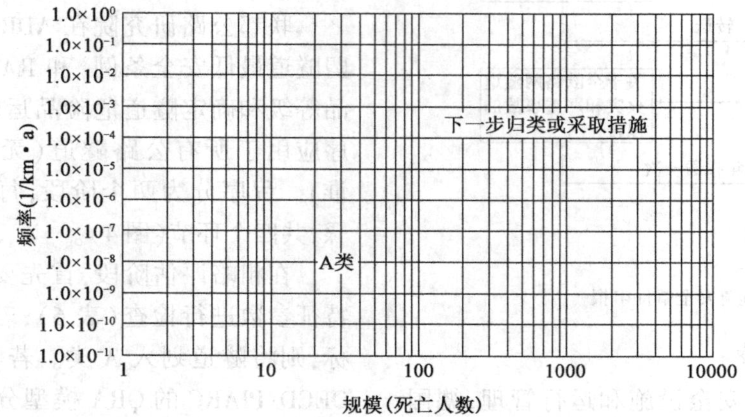

图5　频率-规模模型

危险品分类 表7

代表物品	Nr.	事件	数量	后果
汽油	1	罐式运输;突然或持续释放约 $20m^3$	15t	-立刻点燃和油池火灾 -形成油池,延迟点火 -烟气扩散
	2	小型集装箱运输;突然或持续释放月 $10m^3$	8t	-立刻点燃和油池火灾 -形成油池,延迟点火 -烟气扩散
丙烷	3	罐式运输;以 400kg/s 的速度突然或以 30kg/s 的速度持续释放	12t	-立刻点燃和沸腾液体膨胀蒸汽爆炸(BLEVE) -延迟点火和气云火灾和/或自由流射火灾
	4	小型集装箱运输;以 400kg/s 的速度突然或以 30kg/s 的速度持续释放	1t	-立刻点燃和 BLEVE -延迟点火和气云火灾和/或自由流射火灾
氯	5	罐式运输;突然释放 4t	4t	严重气体泄漏和对人体有毒
	6	小型集装箱运输(总量<50kg);突然释放	50kg	严重气体泄漏和对人体有毒
TNT	7	运输 1000 公斤 TNT 当量,事故发生后,运输车辆着火,引发爆炸。	1t	延迟点火和爆照(可能发生阻尼效应)
	8	运输 1000 公斤 TNT 当量,事故发生后,运输车辆着火,引发爆炸。	100kg	延迟点火和爆照(可能发生阻尼效应)

在绕路风险核实阶段,应为危险品不经过该隧道的运输方案进行分析,评定等级参照风险评定等级。最终,由绕路风险状况结合隧道风险评定状况作出最终评判。

6 结语

德国隧道建设起步较早,多条隧道运行时间长,本文详细介绍了德国隧道养护运行管理经验,在隧道应急处理、安全管理和危险品运输方面德国具有先进的经验,可供我国参考。在应急管理方面,德国为境内超过 400m 的隧道都设置了 24h 值守的监控中心,并制定了多部门联动的、详细的应急预案,以便事故发生时能够迅速做出反应,最大限度保障隧道通行和人员安全。在安全管理方面,德国按照欧盟安全标准配备相应设施,实施安全管理。为每条隧道配备一名隧道管理者,负责编写事故和调查报告;同时设置独立于隧道管理者的检查机构,进行隧道的风险分析,并每 6 个月报告给行政主管部门。此外,德国联邦交通部公路局编写了《安全第一——德国的公路隧道》手册,向大众宣传隧道安全知识,手册向隧道使用者介绍了隧道内重要的安全设施,及其在发生故障和火灾时的作用等。在危货运输方面,德国联邦公路研究院在 QRA 模型的基础上,制定了评估危险品等级和确定隧道危险品运输限制的程序,该程序分为粗略评估和深入分析两个阶段,每个阶段分为两个步骤,共四个环节,应用于所有公路隧道。

参考文献

[1] 曾满元,喻渝. 中德铁路工程隧道技术标准对比分析研究[J]. 现代隧道技术,2008,45(06):34-38.

[2] 琚国全,陈赤坤,曹彧等. 中德高速铁路隧道技术标准对比分析研究[J]. 铁道标准设计,2011,(02),99-103.

短隧道风光互补照明供电多目标设计方法

朱鑫维*　唐　娜
(长安大学公路学院)

摘　要　为降低隧道照明能耗运营管理负担,提出在隧道外建设风光互补发电系统的方法。以隧道照明年总耗电量为控制目标,结合区域风光特性,提出公路短隧道的风光互补发电系统的构建原则,并依据隧道年总照明能耗设计出公路短隧道的多种风光互补发电系统初步建设方案;以各风光互补发电系统建设方案的工程效能、经济效能、生态效能为控制指标,采用层次分析法构建风光互补发电系统建设方案的多目标评价体系,以多目标综合评分定量评价各建设方案的优劣,并以昆明市某隧道为例,实现了风光互补供电系统建设方案的初步设计和优选。

关键词　交通工程　绿色交通　隧道照明　风光互补　层次分析法

0　引言

近年来,我国公路隧道数量在急剧攀升,截至2019年,我国公路隧道里程及数量已增至18966.6km/19067处,随着国家整体能源结构的调整,太阳能、风能等清洁能源的利用率、产品可靠度都在逐步提升,风光清洁能源的应用是降低隧道照明能耗的新发展方向之一。

目前国内针对风、光清洁能源的应用均开展了部分研究。行业内清洁能源的应用范围较广的主要是太阳能及风能,而风电和光伏出力具有随机性、波动性和不可控性等固有属性[1]。风光互补发电系统能够利用风能和太阳能在时间和地域上的天然互补优势,有效平抑风电和光伏出力波动,降低其带来的损失[2]。内蒙古四王子旗居民用电采用"风光互补"系统供电,考虑月日均最低发电量的可靠度与月日均最高发电量弃电率,优化配置风光发电设备[3]。贵州省盘兴高速司家寨隧道照明采用"风光互补+市电"的能源供应方式,其中清洁能源的供应占比在60%以上[4]。赵星虎[5]等考虑区域风光出力相关性,得到风光联合出力场景,以系统的成本、负荷缺电率和弃风弃光浪费率为控制指标建立目标函数优化配置"风光互补"系统。

本文以云南省昆明市某高速公路隧道A为研究对象,基于隧道能耗需求及区域风光特性进行"风光互补离网供电系统"配置方法的研究。

1　区域风光互补特性分析

Kendall秩相关系数(Kendal'τ)是一种基于随机变量秩的相依测度,它反映的是变量间的单调相依性,即变化趋势的一致性[6]。Kendall秩相关系数可以客观反应不同区域内风资源与光资源在不同时间段的出力相关性,用以判断该地区是否适合风光联合发电。Kendall'τ定义的一般形式见式(1)。

$$\tau = P[(x_1 - x_2)(y_1 - y_2) > 0] - P[(x_1 - x_2)(y_1 - y_2) < 0] \tag{1}$$

式中:τ——从样本中随机选取的两组观测值一致的概率与不一致的概率之差;

(x_1, y_1)、$(x_2, y_2)\cdots(x_n, y_n)$——月均风资源和月均光资源组成的样本值。

当$\tau > 0$时,认为区域风光资源不存在互补特性;当$\tau < 0$时,认为区域内风光资源存在互补特性。

1. 研究项目:云南省交通运输厅联合攻关科技项目(云交科教[2019]2号)。

2 风光互补发电系统方案初选

2.1 风光互补发电系统组成

风光互补离网供电系统组成见图1。由于公路隧道外可利用的建筑用地有限,为充分利用隧道建筑用地,提升单位面积内风光发电额能力,推荐采用风光一体化发电设备,风光一体化发电设备的风光发电配件可以依据实际需求进行配置。

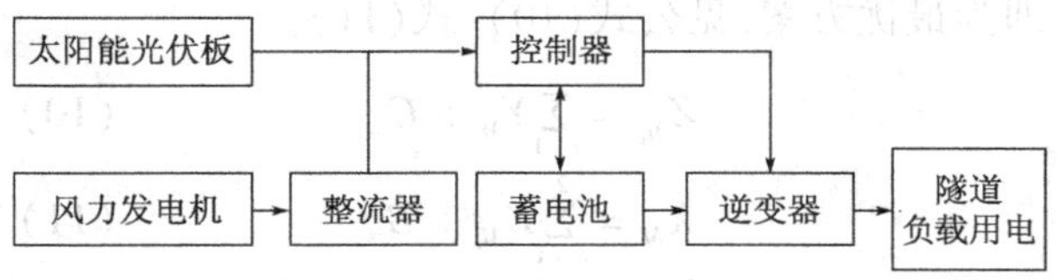

图1 风光一体化发电设备及组成

2.2 风光互补供电方案初选

采用试算法确定风光发电设备布设功率比例:依据隧道照明需求确定隧道年耗电 E_h,计算方法见式(2),再根据风光发电设备的总功率配置计算年均实际发电量 E_f,计算方法见式(3)。为提高风光互补发电系统的供电可靠度,将 E_f 与 $130\% E_h$ 相比较,若 $E_f \geqslant 130\% E_h$,则满足隧道年总耗电量控制目标要求;若 $E_{发} \leqslant 130\% E_{耗}$,则需要反复调整风光发电设备功率比例,直至满足控制目标要求。

$$E_h = \sum_{i=1}^{4} E_i \times N_i \tag{2}$$

式中:E_i——夏季晴天、夏季云天/其他季节晴天、夏季阴天/其他季节云天、其他季节阴天/重阴天四类天气下隧道照明日能耗;

N_i——相应天气分级对应天数。

$$E_f = \sum_{i=1}^{12} (nP_{风} \times T_{风i} + nP_{风} \times T_{风i}) \tag{3}$$

式中:n——风光发电一体化设备数量;

$T_{风i}$、$T_{光i}$——风机、光伏板换算至满功率运行的月均时长,h。

3 风光互补发电照明系统评价体系

3.1 评价方法选取

满足隧道A年总照明需求的风光互补离网供电方案有多种,各建设方案评价属于典型的多目标、多准则、难以量化处理的决策问题,因此可采用层次分析法理念构建目标结构模型(图2),并确定各评价指标权重。

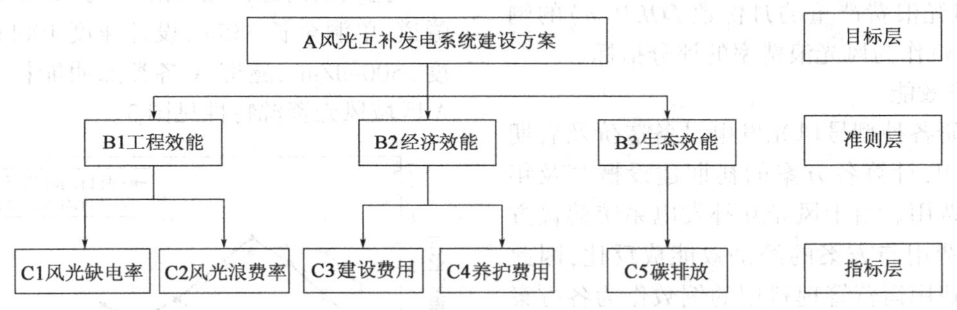

图2 目标层次结构模型

3.2 指标权重确定

3.2.1 构建判别矩阵

对比同一层次的两个指标在上一层次指标中的重要程度,构造判别矩阵,见式(4)。

$$D = (d_{ij})_{n \times n} = \begin{bmatrix} d_{11} & \cdots & d_{1n} \\ \vdots & \cdots & \vdots \\ d_{n1} & \cdots & d_{nn} \end{bmatrix} \tag{4}$$

式中:d_{ij}——指标层中 C_i 相对于 C_j 对准则层 B_m 的重要程度,d_{ij} 的赋值采用1~9标度法,由专家评估赋值结果的平均数确定。

3.2.2 权重值计算及一致性检验

为避免主观判断可能存在的矛盾结论,须对构建的判别矩阵进行一致性检验。

(1)一致性指标 CI 见式(5)。

$$CI = \frac{\lambda_{\max} - n}{n - 1} \tag{5}$$

式中:$\lambda_{\max}$——判别矩阵的最大特征值;

n——评价指标的数量。

(2)计算判别矩阵一致性比率 CR,见式(6)。

$$CR = \frac{CI}{RI} \tag{6}$$

式中:RI——一致性检验指标,可通过查表获取。

若 $CR < 0.1$,则判别矩阵一致性较优;若

$CR>0.1$,则应重新赋值,直至检验结果满足条件。

3.3 评分准则

(1)工程效能

负荷缺电率 LPSP,风光互补发电系统能源供给不能满足负荷端需求的概率即为负荷缺电率,如式(7)所示。

$$LPSP=\frac{\sum_{t=1}^{8760}(P_t-\sum_{i=1}^{3}P_i)}{\sum_{t=1}^{8760}P_t} \tag{7}$$

式中:P_t——负荷端的工作功率;

P_i——各发电设备的输出功率,取 1-LPSP 作为负荷缺电率的评分指标。

风光浪费率 LOEP,风光互补发电系统月总发电量超过负荷端总需求的占比,如式(8)所示。

$$LOEP=\frac{\sum_{i=1}^{30}(P_i\times T_i-W_i)}{\sum_{i=1}^{30}(P_i\times T_i)} \tag{8}$$

式中:LOEP——每月的风光浪费率;

P_i——风光互补发电系统每天输出功率;

T_i——风光互补发电系统每天工作时长。

若 LOFE≥1.3,则可判定该月份风光浪费严重,以全年风光浪费严重的月份数 LOEP(n)的倒数 1/LOEP(n)作为风光浪费率的评分指标。

(2)经济效能

通过调研各种型号风光发电设备造价及后期运营管理费用,计算各方案的初期建设概算及年均运营管理费用。由于风光互补发电系统建设方案需要的总费用与方案的经济效能成反比,因此分别取建设费用运营管理费用的倒数作为各方案的建设成本及运营管理费用指标评分值。

(3)生态效能

计算通过风光互补发电站供给隧道照明用电量,换算为减少的碳排放量,因此可直接采用各建设方案降低的年碳排放量值作为风光互补发电系统建设方案生态效能指标的评分值。

3.4 方案评价方法

本文利用线性归一法对各方案的同一指标评分进行处理,见公式(9)。

$$Y_{Mi}=\frac{X_{Mi}}{\sum_{k=1}^{n}X_{Mi}} \tag{9}$$

式中:Y_{Mi}——方案中指标 i 得分值;

X_{Mi}——第 i 种指标对于方案 M 的评分值;

n——初拟方案数。

根据各指标得分和方案中各指标的权重占比,确定各初定方案的综合得分,分值最高的方案即为最优方案,见公式(10)、式(11)。

$$Z_{Mp}=\sum_{i=1}^{2}Y_{Mi}\times C_{pi} \tag{10}$$

$$\lambda_M=\sum_{u=1}^{2}Z_{Mp}\times B_p \tag{11}$$

式中:Z_{Mp}——方案 M 中准则 p 得分值;

Y_{Mi}——方案 M 中指标 i 得分值;

C_{pi}——指标 i 对准则 p 的权重值;

λ_M——方案 M 的综合得分;

B_p——准则 p 对目标层的权重值。

4 工程案例

4.1 工程概况

昆明某高速公路隧道 A 为双向六车道非光学隧道,单洞全长 355m,设计速度 100km/h,洞外亮度 3500cd/m^2,隧道 A 各类照明能耗见表 1,隧道 A 区域风光资源特性见图 3。

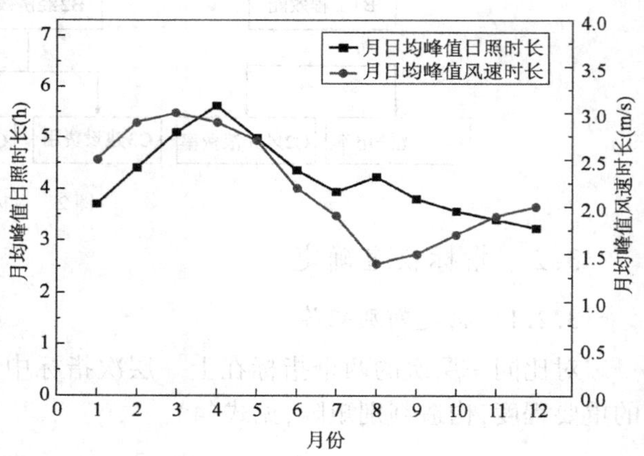

图3　隧道 A 区域风光资源特性

隧道 A 照明能耗　　表 1

月份	1	2	3	4	5	6	7	8	9	10	11	12
月负荷(kW·h)	4927	4068	4842	4152	4189	6403	6645	6743	4420	4311	4998	5106
年耗电(kW·h)	61251											

由 Kendall 秩相关系数（Kendall'τ）法得到隧道 A 区域下半年风光出力具有可靠的互补特性，见表 2，可充分利用太阳能与风能的资源差异特性，实现风光离网供电。

不同时间风光出力相关性 表 2

时段	上半年	下半年
τ	0.47	-0.60

4.2 风光互补系统配置方案初选

基于隧道能耗及区域风光发电特性，提出风光互补系统的 3 种配置方案，风光互补系统的年总发电量均可保证隧道照明的年总功耗，见表 3。

风光互补系统配置方案 表 3

方案	风机功率（W）	光伏板功率（W）	数量（套）	年发电量（kW·h）
1	100	600	96	84936
2	300	450	96	81064
3	250	600	80	82402

4.3 风光互补发电系统方案优选

4.3.1 评价指标权重确定

邀请 12 位从事隧道照明与清洁能源应用方面的专家各评价指标进行评分，以此构建判别矩阵（表 4～表 6），并确定各评价指标的权重值。

经过一致性检验后，上诉矩阵均满足一致性要求，风光互补发电系统建设方案中各指标的权重占比见表 7。

准则层对目标层的判别矩阵 表 4

系统建设方案	工程效能	经济效能	社会效能
工程效能	1.00	4.00	5.00
经济效能	0.25	1.00	2.00
社会效能	0.20	0.50	1.00

各指标对工程效能的判别矩阵 表 5

工程效能	风光缺电率	风光浪费率
风光缺电率	1	5.00
风光浪费率	0.2	1

各指标对经济效能的判别矩阵 表 6

经济效能	建设成本	维护成本
建设成本	1	4
维护成本	0.25	1

风光互补发电系统假设方案指标权重值 表 7

总目标	权重值	控制目标	权重值	控制目标权重值	
系统建设方案	1	工程效能	0.68	风光缺电率	0.83
				风光浪费率	0.17
		经济效能	0.2	建设成本	0.8
				维护成本	0.2
		社会效能	0.12	生态影响	1

4.3.2 风光互补发电系统综合得分计算

各配置方案的在各月的供电能力差异明显，其月发电能力及月负荷见图 4，计算风光互补发电系统建设方案的负荷缺电率 *LPSP* 及风光浪费率

LOEP,并以各方案 1 - *LPSP* 与 1/*LOEP*(*n*)作为方案工程效能评分,经过归一化处理后作为各方案工程效能的得分值,见表8。

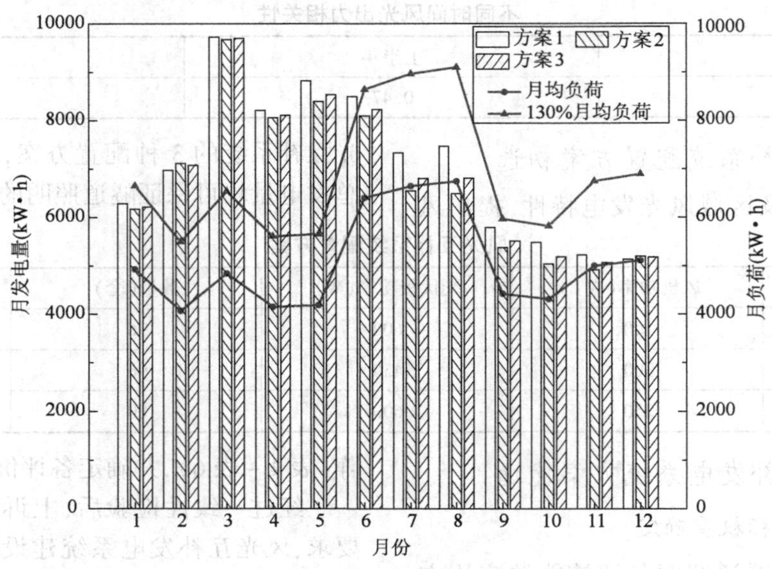

图4　风光互补发电站供电能力

各方案工程效能　　表8

方　案	1 - *LPSP*	归一化处理	1/*LOEP*(*n*)	归一化处理
方案1	1	0.364	1/7	0.222
方案2	0.75	0.273	1/4	0.389
方案3	1	0.364	1/4	0.389

(1)经济效能评价

通过对风光互补发电系统各设备造价及管养费用的调研,以此计算风光互补发电站建设及管养费用,并以建设及管养费用的倒数为各方案经济效能评分,通过归一化处理作为各方案的经济效能评分值,见表9。

(2)生态效能

通过各方案对隧道照明的年供能量,计算各风光互补发电方案降低的碳排放值,经过归一化处理后可直接作为生态效能的评价分值,见表10。

(3)风光互补方案综合得分

风光互补发电系统建设方案综合得分见表11。

各方案经济效能　　表9

方　案	建设成本(万元)	取倒数并归一化处理	年管养成本(万元)	取倒数并归一化处理
方案1	125.58	0.326	7.78	0.338
方案2	122.34	0.334	8.05	0.326
方案3	120.38	0.340	7.83	0.336

各方案生态效能　　表10

方案	年碳排放量(kg)	归一化处理
方案1	36363	0.3341
方案2	36104	0.3318
方案3	36363	0.3341

各方案综合得分　　表11

方案	方案1	方案2	方案3
综合得分	0.337	0.305	0.358

由上表可知，风光互补发电系统建设方案3的综合得分高于方案1、2，因此选择方案3作为该隧道A外风光互补发电系统的建设方案。

5 结语

(1)采用Kendall秩相关系数，可以实现对风电和光伏相关性的定量计算，以定量结果反应区域风光特性更客观、精准，可作为区域风光联合发电可行性的评估手段之一。

(2)本文采用层次分析法理念，对影响风光互补发电系统建设方案的多目标定量化赋权，最后依据各建设方案的综合评分确定风光互补发电系统最优建设方案。

(3)昆明市某高速公路隧道A风光互补离网照明系统选用80套200W风机与600W光伏板的组合实现了工程效能与社会经济效益的统一。

(4)风光互补离网供电系统适用于照明等级不高、风光资源丰富的短隧道，为交通行业实现"碳中和"探索新的发展方向。

参考文献

[1] 乔延辉，韩爽，许彦平，等.基于天气分型的风光出力互补性分析方法[J].电力系统自动化，2021，45(02)：82-88.

[2] 佘梦泽，贾林莉，朱浩骏，等.平抑出力波动的风光储联合发电系统容量优化配置方法[J].电气应用，2014，33(21)：44-48.

[3] 陈松利，闫彩霞，李明，等.中小功率分布式风光互补发电系统的匹配研究[J].现代电子技术，2021，44(15)：94-98.

[4] 雷乃金，卢道勇，戴德江，等.风光互补型公路隧道智能照明系统在高速公路隧道上的应用研究[J].湖南交通科技，2018，44(01)：157-161.

[5] 赵星虎，张会林.计及风光出力相关性的风光互补发电系统优化[J].软件导刊，2021，20(05)：82-85.

[6] 赵继超，袁越，傅质馨，等.基于Copula理论的风光互补发电系统可靠性评估[J].电力自动化设备，2013，33(1)：124-129.

公路隧道入口光伏遮阳棚设计

王 卓*

(长安大学公路学院)

摘 要 选取A隧道为研究对象，基于隧道内轮廓参数及驾驶人视觉舒适，设计遮阳棚断面尺寸及初始长度；依据遮阳棚表面的光伏材料布设形式，以实现光环境均匀渐低为目标，应用Ecotect Analysis仿真模拟，确定光伏遮阳棚透光率参数组合最优方案及遮阳棚合理长度；通过市场调研，比选光伏材料类型；考虑光伏辐射量及光伏材料有效面积计算光伏发电量，并分析其效益。结果表明：碲化镉(CdTe)光伏薄膜材料适宜应用于实际工程，A隧道入口光伏遮阳棚长度48m、透光率组合顶部0.2+侧向0.6－0.4－0.2－0.1时，满足驾驶人视觉过渡舒适，使用年限内发电量为1.64×10^{6} kW·h，可实现隧道入口行车安全和供电功能的合二为一。

关键词 隧道工程 光伏发电 光环境仿真 遮阳棚 透光率组合

0 引言

近年来，随着公路隧道建设的发展，我国已成为目前世界上公路隧道规模最大、数量最多、发展速度最快的国家。截至2020年底，我国公路隧道数量达21236座，总长2199.93万m。研究表明，晴天公路隧道入口内外光照度差异较大形成的"黑洞效应"严重影响驾驶人的视觉感受，易造成生心理紧张、诱发交通事故。为有效解决从明亮的外部进入较暗的隧道内部产生的"黑洞效应"，通常采取两种措施，一是在公路隧道入口设置减光设施；二是隧道内部采用24h全天照明。我国公路隧道每年产生近60亿的电费，隧道里程的增长和品质的提升给隧道照明节能带来了更大压力。

为有效解决隧道入口“黑洞效应”及照明能耗等问题,一些先进的设计理念及技术不断被提出并应用于实际工程中。目前我国关于公路隧道入口设置遮阳棚及隧道内节能设施的研究已取得一定成果。陆远迅等[1]提出了一种结合遮光棚、太阳能LED照明的新型隧道照明方法,并且结合遮光棚的经济性提出了遮光棚的长度计算模型。王兴平等[2]提出一种将不同的隧道照明节能技术进行综合应用的节能化思路,利用太阳能薄膜遮光棚实现隧道入口段照明灯具规模设置及运营能耗的大幅降低。张世平等[3]根据驾驶人视觉适应进行遮阳棚长度设计,研究光伏薄膜在公路上的应用。夏鹏曦等[4]研究季节、行车速度对遮阳棚透光率的影响,结果表明透光率主要受行车速度影响。相关研究及实践中遮阳棚长度设计仅依据行车速度、缺少对驾驶人视觉舒适的考虑,其方法科学性不足,易造成遮阳棚长度过程,导致工程材料浪费。

基于此,本文提出一种将综合性能最优的光伏材料与传统钢拱架+PC板组合的遮阳棚相结合的设计方法。基于运行速度及驾驶人视觉舒适,应用Ecotect Analysis对不同透光参数组合及长度的遮阳棚进行光环境仿真,确定设计方案。依据转换效率、弱光效果等参数比选光伏材料,结合区域太阳光辐射量、光伏材料有效面积分析光伏发电能力及效益。

1 工程概况

A隧道位于云南省,为分离式六车道,断面净宽14.5m,隧道外路基宽度16.75m,设计速度100km/h。隧道所处区域属低度高原季风气候,经纬度为103.26°、25.56°,干旱少雨,年平均日温14.5℃,无霜期230d,地区夏季光照强度高,年平均日照时长2079.3h,属国内典型高光照地区,隧道内外环境的照度水平具有量级差异。隧道右线直线形隧道全长675m,因隧道右幅洞口内外光照差异较大,需设置遮阳棚。

2 光伏遮阳棚遮光效果设计

2.1 光伏遮阳棚尺寸设计

在进行光伏遮阳棚遮光效果设计之前,应先确定遮阳棚尺寸,即遮阳棚的断面尺寸及初始长度。

2.1.1 光伏遮阳棚断面尺寸确定

依据隧道内轮廓,遮阳棚断面采用三圆弧组合式设计,断面尺寸确定时需注意以下两点:①遮阳棚轮廓不得侵入隧道洞口内轮廓范围内,保证道路净空;②遮阳棚净宽不得小于隧道洞外路面的宽度,并与隧道洞外护栏设施保持安全距离[5]。根据项目资料,为保障施工顺利进行,考虑路侧护栏结构宽度及遮阳棚柱脚与护栏立柱间最小距离约为15cm,确定遮阳棚断面尺寸为17.9m,圆弧半径分别为773cm、950cm、773cm,对应圆心角分别为55°、70°、55°,遮阳棚横断面如图1所示。

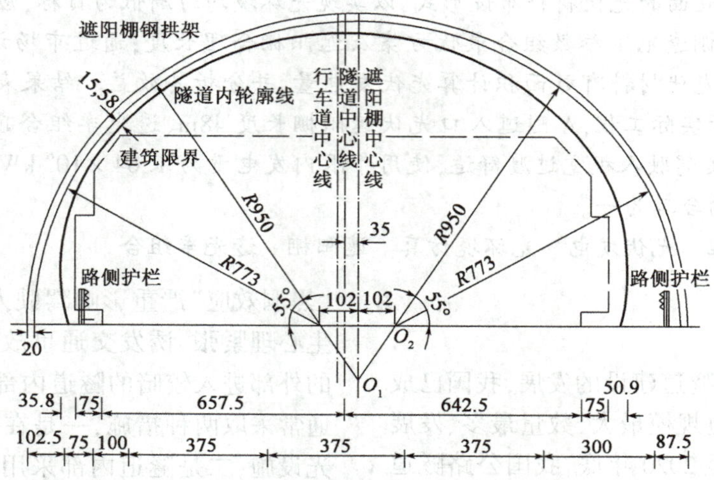

图1 遮阳棚横断面图(尺寸单位:cm)

2.1.2 光伏遮阳棚长度初步确定

为科学实现遮阳棚内光环境均匀渐低及驾驶人视觉舒适,依据车辆运行速度、隧道洞内外视点照度(一般取隧道洞口前50m车内视点照度、隧道入口内10m车内视点照度),以及满足驾驶人视觉舒适要求的指标阈值1.6~1.7[5-7],遮阳棚的理论最小长度计算方法见式(1)、式(2)。

$$l = \frac{V}{3.6} \cdot \frac{\lg \frac{E_w}{E_{in}}}{\lg 1.7} \cdot 0.2 \qquad (1)$$

$$E_{in} = E_{内} \times 1.7^{t/0.2} \qquad (2)$$

式中:V——进入隧道的运行速度,本例取值100km/h;

E_w——隧道外界视点照度,参考项目资料,本例取值3800lux;

E_{in}——遮阳棚末端理论照度值;

$E_{内}$——隧道内10m处视点照度,参考项目资料,本例取值240lux;

t——E_{in}过渡至$E_{内}$的行车时间(s)。

由式(1)、式(2)可得,遮阳棚理论最小长度为18m,为实现光环境均匀渐低,考虑施工条件,依据经验,选择理论最小长度的2倍即36m作为初始长度进行光环境仿真。

2.2 光伏遮阳棚透光率组合及合理长度确定

2.2.1 光伏遮阳棚透光率选择

遮阳棚两侧接收太阳光的射入辐射量只有50%~70%,发电效率低;此外,受太阳入射角的控制,当光伏材料对称布设在遮阳棚中轴线两侧顶部时,可最大化利用太阳能。遮阳棚组合形式应遵循"均匀渐低、追求美观"原则,因此提出"顶部相同,两侧渐变"的透光率组合方案。为实现科学遮光及光伏发电,将遮阳棚长度均分成4~6段(外界光环境较强时取大值,反之取小值);光伏材料采用矩形分布覆盖在各段遮阳棚顶部,每段遮阳棚的最小覆盖角度α_1由光环境而定,约为60°~80°(外界光环境较强时取低值,反之取高值);最大覆盖角度α_2一般由隧道所处位置的太阳入射角β决定,通常为180°-2β,当太阳光以此角度直射在遮阳棚表面时,可最大激发光伏薄膜材料的发电能力。

A隧道入口光伏遮阳棚初始设计长度为36m,因区域光照较强,将遮阳棚长度均分成4段(9m×4)。进行模拟仿真试算后,拟定遮阳棚顶部光伏材料的覆盖角度为60°,透光率0.2,两侧初始段透光率取0.5/0.6,末段透光率取0.1/0.2,中间段视设计情况线性内插。设计4种透光率组合方案,见表1。

遮阳棚透光率参数组合方案 表1

方案	光伏材料布设角度(°)	初始段	中间段1	中间段2	末尾段
方案1	60	0.5	0.3	0.2	0.1
方案2	60	0.6	0.4	0.2	0.1
方案3	80	0.5	0.3	0.2	0.1
方案4	80	0.6	0.4	0.2	0.1

2.2.2 光伏薄膜遮阳棚光环境仿真分析

以遮阳棚初始长度36m进行光环境仿真,受光环境因素影响,结果相差较大,均不满足驾驶人视觉舒适,需要重新设计遮阳棚长度。增加1m分段长度,重新进行光环境仿真,直至实现遮阳棚内光环境均匀渐低。多次调整后,发现分段长度为12m即遮阳棚长度48m时,可较好满足遮光需求。

对以上4种透光率组合方案分别构建遮阳棚及隧道模型,进行遮阳棚前10m至隧道内20m范围的光环境仿真,取所得的0.2s匀速行驶距离(V=100km/h时取5m)的视点照度值绘制照度曲线[5],如图2所示。

分别计算4个方案每0.2s行驶的距离(d=5m)的视点照度数据比值v_{max},见表2。

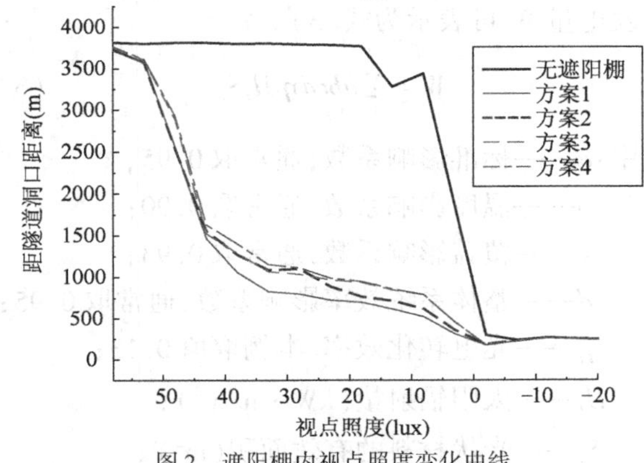

图2 遮阳棚内视点照度变化曲线

3800lux 4 个方案的 v_{max} 值 表2

透光率参数组合方案	无遮阳棚	方案1	方案2	方案3	方案4
v_{max}值	6.29	1.83	1.68	1.92	2.06

由图中曲线和表中结果可知,设置遮阳棚,可有效实现隧道入口前光环境均匀过渡;当遮阳棚长度为48m时,方案2的 v_{max} 符合仿真明暗视觉舒适合理区间(1.6~1.7),满足驾驶人视觉明暗感受舒适的目标。因此,A隧道入口光伏遮阳棚的设计方案为长度48m、透光率组合顶部0.2+侧向0.6-0.4-0.2-0.1,仿真模型如图3所示。

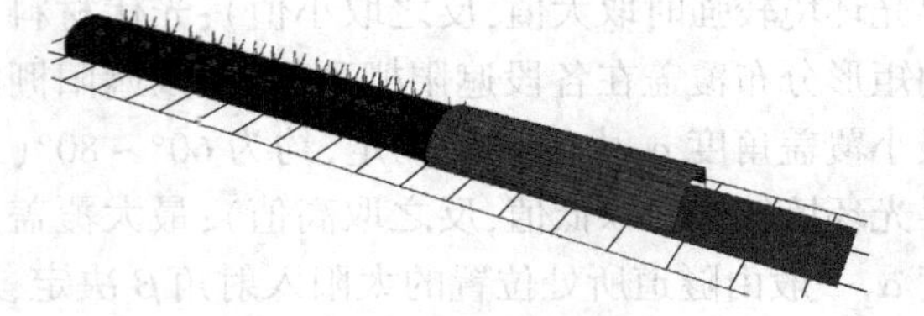

图3 光伏遮阳棚仿真模型

3 光伏发电分析

太阳能转化效率高、无污染气体排放,是一种广为应用的可再生能源,由其衍生出的光伏材料是一种新型高效能源材料。

3.1 光伏材料类型比选

近年来,太阳能材料在公路行业的运用越来越高,对光伏材料进行调研,结果表明在投入生产使用时,与晶硅类光伏电池相比,光伏薄膜电池具有转换效率高、成本较低、弱光性好等特点,更适宜与遮阳棚结合。不同类型光伏电池性能如表3所示。

不同光伏电池性能 表3

光伏电池类别	晶硅太阳能电池	非晶硅薄膜电池	CIGS 薄膜电池	CdTe 薄膜电池
转换效率(%)	13~15	6~7	9~13	9~13
成本	高	较低	高	低
温度系数	高	低	高	低
弱光效果	差	好	好	好
资源	充足	充足	受限	充足
稳定性	高	低	较高	较高

3.2 光伏遮阳棚发电能力

根据选定的光伏材料性能及区域光照条件分析光伏遮阳棚发电能力(光伏发电每年递减约1%,估算年发电量时通常取25年的平均值),光伏发电量W可表示为式(3)。

$$W=\sum_i abcd\eta_i H_t S_i \tag{3}$$

式中:a——标准影响系数,通常取0.95;

b——温度影响系数,通常取0.90;

c——覆盖影响系数,通常取0.93;

d——整体系统效率影响系数,通常取0.95;

η_i——光电转化效率,本例取值0.13;

H_t——太阳辐射量($kW\cdot h/m^2$);

S_i——光伏材料的有效面积(m^2)。

3.2.1 光伏辐射量

光伏遮阳棚发电量的大小由工程所在区域光辐射量决定。为减小误差,采用 Meteonorm7 记录太阳辐射量的平均值。A隧道所处区域寻甸县全年光辐射量为1566$kW\cdot h/m^2$,月最低光辐射量为100$kW\cdot h/m^2$,如图4所示。

3.2.2 光伏材料有效面积

依据遮阳棚断面尺寸及各分段光伏材料覆盖角度计算覆盖宽度(弧长),见式(4)。

$$w_i=\frac{\alpha\pi r}{180} \tag{4}$$

式中:w_i——各分段光伏材料覆盖宽度(弧长)(m);

α——各分段光伏材料覆盖角度(°);

r——遮阳棚半径(m)。

由上式可得 A 隧道入口遮阳棚各分段光伏材料覆盖宽度约为 10m，结合遮阳棚分段长度，计算出光伏材料有效覆盖面积为 $480m^2$。

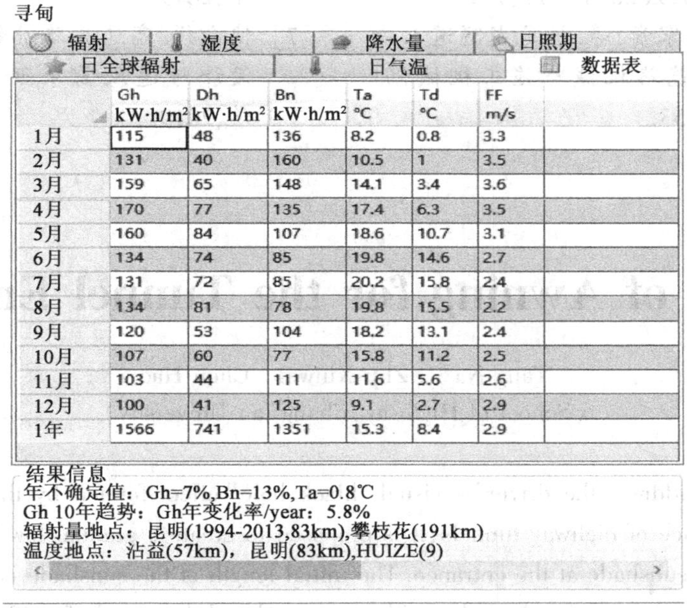

寻甸

辐射 | 湿度 | 降水量 | 日照期

日全球辐射 | 日气温 | 数据表

	Gh kW·h/m²	Dh kW·h/m²	Bn kW·h/m²	Ta ℃	Td ℃	FF m/s
1月	115	48	136	8.2	0.8	3.3
2月	131	40	160	10.5	1	3.5
3月	159	65	148	14.1	3.4	3.6
4月	170	77	135	17.4	6.3	3.5
5月	160	84	107	18.6	10.7	3.1
6月	134	74	85	19.8	14.6	2.7
7月	131	72	85	20.2	15.8	2.4
8月	134	81	78	19.8	15.5	2.2
9月	120	53	104	18.2	13.1	2.4
10月	107	60	77	15.8	11.2	2.5
11月	103	44	111	11.6	5.6	2.6
12月	100	41	125	9.1	2.7	2.9
1年	1566	741	1351	15.3	8.4	2.9

结果信息
年不确定值：Gh=7%,Bn=13%,Ta=0.8℃
Gh 10年趋势：Gh年变化率/year：5.8%
辐射量地点：昆明(1994-2013,83km),攀枝花(191km)
温度地点：沾益(57km)，昆明(83km),HUIZE(9)

图 4　Meteonorm7 计算截面图

3.3　光伏发电效益分析

(1)经济效益

A 隧道入口 48m 光伏遮阳棚在光伏材料使用期限 25 年内(考虑发电能力每年递减 1%)，发电量合计为 1.64×10^6 kW · h，年均发电量为 6.56×10^4kW · h。根据项目相关资料，A 隧道全长为 675m，全段照明年功耗为 2.0×10^5kW · h，光伏遮阳棚可满足约 33% 的用电需求。

(2)生态效益

光伏遮阳棚在使用周期内累计节约煤炭 738.29t，粉尘 502.06t，减排二氧化碳大约 1919.58t，相当于每年种树 4200 棵，具有巨大的生态价值。

4　结语

本文应用 Ecotect Analysis 软件模拟光伏遮阳棚遮光效果，确定透光率组合方案；并依靠市场调研，对比分析光伏材料的类型及特点，基于工程所在区域太阳辐射量及光伏材料布设形式、覆盖面积，分析光伏发电能力，得出如下结论：

(1)光伏遮阳棚宜采取“顶部相同，两侧渐变”的透光率组合，两侧初始段透光率取 0.5/0.6，末段透光率取 0.1/0.2，中间段视设计情况线性内插，一般条件下可满足遮光效果；

(2)碲化镉(CdTe)光伏薄膜材料具有发电能力强、转换效率高、温度系数低、弱光效应好、稳定性高、制作成本低的特点，适宜与公路隧道入口减光构造物相结合，应用于公路设施中；

(3)依托 A 隧道工程，光伏材料覆盖面积 $480m^2$，在碲化镉(CdTe)光伏材料使用期限 25 年内，遮阳棚的发电量合计为 1.64×10^6 kW · h，具有良好的经济效益及生态效益。

目前，光伏技术在低能耗交通安全设施方面已得到广泛应用，且经济效益良好。在太阳能资源丰富地区，研究出可行的公路隧道入口光伏遮阳棚设计方法，对于光伏能源在公路行业的应用具有巨大的推广价值。

参考文献

[1] 陆远迅，刘国贵，王兴平，等. 基于太阳能的公路隧道照明方法[J]. 隧道建设. 2015，35(7)：674.

[2] 王兴平，史玲娜，涂耘，等. 公路隧道照明综合节能技术探讨[C]//2016 中国隧道与地下工程大会(CTUC)暨中国土木工程学会隧道及地下工程分会第十九届年会论文集. 成都：2016：163.

[3] 张世平，王兴平，史玲娜，等. 光伏太阳能薄膜遮阳棚在公路隧道中的应用研究[J]. 公路交通技术. 2018，34(3)：86.

[4] 夏鹏曦,段儒禹,汪主洪,等.公路隧道光伏薄膜遮阳棚的透光率选型及光伏效益估算[J].隧道建设(中英文).2020,40(5):711.

[5] 范新荣,彭余华,高家贵,等.抓地龙隧道入口遮阳棚设计[J].筑路机械与施工机械化.2020,37(12):43,53.

[6] 于亚敏.公路隧道入口"黑洞"效应的数值表征与遮阳棚光环境设计方法[D]:长安大学,2019.

[7] 傅向祥.高速公路毗邻隧道间遮阳棚光环境设计与通风需求研究[D]:西安:长安大学,2019.

Design of Awning for the Tunnel Entrance

Tang Na* Zhu Xinwei Chen Hao
(School of Highway, Chang'an University)

ABSTRACT To address the driver's visual "black hole" effect formed by the drastic change of light environment at the entrance of highway tunnels, it is proposed to create a gradual low transition of driving light environment by setting a sunshade at the entrance. The initial length of the sunshade is determined based on the illumination level of the viewpoints inside and outside the tunnel and the speed of traffic, etc. Based on the initial length, light environment simulation technology is used to analyse the light environment inside the sunshade and determine the "Piecewise single and overall combination". Based on the initial length, the light environment analysis in the sunshade is carried out by using light environment simulation technology to determine the multiple light transmittance parameter scheme and reasonable length of sunshade under the two sunshade material combination methods of "Piecewise single, overall combination" and "same lateral direction, gradual change at the top", and finally the structural arrangement of the sunshade is verified by using structural finite element analysis software, which can provide a reference for the design and application of road tunnel entrance sunshade.

Keywords: Traffic safety Highway tunnel Sunshade Light environment simulation Structural design

0 Introduction

There is a quantitative difference in illumination levels inside and outside the highway tunnel at midday, which can easily cause a transient reduction in the driver's visual function during the process of entering the tunnel, forming a visual "black hole" effect and seriously affecting driving safety. (Du Zhigang et al., 2014). The sunshade is an effective and economical way to reduce the illumination level. Sunshade as an effective and economical facility to reduce light outside the tunnel, in recent years, Its exploration and application of engineering has achieved good social benefits.

Some studies have been conducted in China on key issues such as length selection and light transmission rate of the awning. LiYintao et al consider factors such as illumination inside and outside the cave, driver's vision recovery time, etc., the suggested values of the length of the tunnel entrance light reducing grille under different design speeds are given. (LI Yin-tao et al., 2009). The 3s travel length of the vehicle is used as the length of the shade canopy, and a material with a blue light transmission rate of 40% is selected for the light reduction design. (LI Rong et al., 2012). Zhang Tiangen et al establish the optimal curve of tunnel entrance brightness transition to adjust the length and light transmission rate of the light reducing structure design. (ZHANG Tian-geng et al., 2017). Zhao Xisen et al based on the acceptable threshold of visual brightness change for drivers, the length range of the awning at the entrance of the Arbor Tunnel was studied by combining the travel speed and the stopping sight distance, and the combination of the light transmission rate of the awning was determined by using light environment simulation technology. (ZHAO Xi-seng et al. ,2018). Peng Yuhua et al to solve the visual impact of light and darkness brought by the sudden change of light environment at the entrance of the adjacent tunnel, a model of sunshade with hollowed-out bottom sides and ventilated openings at the top was constructed, and the brightness change law and sunshade light reduction effect of the adjacent tunnel entrance were simulated and analyzed. (PENG Yu-hua et al., 2019). However, the existing research on sunshade still has the following shortcomings: more subjective components for length determination, less reasonable length analysis combined with light reduction transition effect, more light environment design with a single light transmission rate, less research on the combination of multiple light transmission rates and lack of reasonable selection and structural design of sunshade materials, which limit the scientific and reasonable application of sunshade.

Based on the quantitative grading of the visual perception of tunnel entrance drivers, this paper selects the entrance sunshade of the A tunnel as the research object, and analyzes its setting from the aspects of sunshade length, material combination and internal light environment creation, material selection and structural design, which can provide theoretical reference and methodological support for the design of highway tunnel entrance sunshade.

1 Overview of Tunnel

Tunnel A is a separated two-way six-lane tunnel, the average annual sunshine is 2079h, natural light intensity during the midday hours in summer can reach 1.2×10^5 lux, the illumination of the driver's visual position and direction in the car in front of the tunnel (point-of-view illumination) can reach up to 4.3×10^3 lux (illumination under enhanced lighting is generally $10^2 \sim 3 \times 10^2$ lux), the illumination of the environment inside and outside the tunnel cavity The difference is huge; the basic snow pressure of the regional 50-year recurrence period is 0.3kN/m^2, and the basic wind pressure is 0.3kN/m^2.

Tunnel A is 675m long (K54 + 115 ~ 790), with a design speed of 100km/h. The tunnel door is end-wall type. The net width of the tunnel is 14.5m, the roadbed outside the tunnel is 16.75m wide, the route before the entrance is east-west, the safety risk of drivers driving affected by backlight is high.

2 Quantitative Grading of the "Black Hole" effect

The change in illumination of the driver's point of view in the vehicle is closely related to the perception of the visual "black hole" effect . The entrance of 251 road tunnels in the vicinity of Tunnel A was selected for the "black hole" effect experiment. The experimental vehicle was a standard small car (Toyota PRADO), and the illuminance test instrument was a TES1339 illuminance meter (accuracy 0.01lux, test frequency 5 times/s, accorded with the minimum visual stimulation time 0.2s in psychology) (Zwahlen H T et al., 2002). The vehicle was driven into the tunnel at a constant speed during the midday hours of a clear day (11:00 ~ 14:00), and the illuminance meter was placed at the driver's eye position in the same direction as the line of sight, and the point-of-view illuminance readings were measured and recorded in real-time, while the visual perception of the driver's "black hole" effect was recorded. According to the experimental results, the quantitative characterization of viewpoint illuminance parameters and the driver's "black hole" effect on light and dark feelings was established, and the numerical classification of the "black hole" effect feelings was obtained, as shown in Tab. 1.

(1) $E_1/E_2 \leqslant 1.61$ at $E_{ou} = 5000$lux.

(2) $E_1/E_2 \leqslant 1.70$ at $E_{ou} = 4000$lux.

(3) $E_1/E_2 \leqslant 1.84$ at $E_{ou} = 3000$lux.

Numerical classification of"black hole"effect perception Tab. 1

Blackness grading	Blackness Ⅰ	Blackness Ⅱ	Blackness Ⅲ
The "black hole" effect is described by the visual perception K value range	Very dark (extremely uncomfortable)	darker (Uncomfortable)	No darkness (Comfort)
	(28, +∞)	(7.3,28)	(0,7.3)

Notes: $K = \left(\frac{E_{in}}{E_{ou}}\right)0.5 \times \lg\left(\frac{E_1}{E_2}\right)/t$, E_{in}, E_{ou} refers to the illumination level of the viewpoint inside and outside the cave, E_1, E_2 refers to the illumination level of any adjacent viewpoint. Highway tunnel entrance sunshade light environment design needs to meet the requirements of drive- visual comfort, so should ensure that the sunshade within the full length of $K \leqslant 7.3$. cave viewpoint illumination level Ein is generally 50lux ~ 300lux, by mathematical constant transformation to the following conclusions.

3　Analysis of the Light Environment Inside The Tunnel

3.1　Awning and Tunnel Model Construction

Awning section design size should take into account the size of the tunnel profile, the width of the road outside the tunnel and the location of the guardrail, should not encroach on the scope of the original road facilities at the same time pay attention to the pursuit of aesthetic.

The sunshade cross-section adopts the form of a three-section arc combination similar to the inner contour of tunnel A. The supporting arch uses HW200 steel pre-bent into three arc-shaped beams to connect the composition, which is convenient for construction, small self-weight and easy to maintain. In order to avoid the possible influence of the construction error of the sunshade, the inner contour line of the sunshade and the inner contour line of the tunnel are enriched by 10 ~ 15cm, thus the width of the cross-section of the sunshade is 17.9m. The cross section of the sunshade matches the tunnel cross section better and the overall aesthetic appearance is good.

Ecotect Analysis, a widely used light environment simulation software in lighting and architecture, can accurately simulate the building for various natural light (YU Chuan-kun et al., 2017), which can provide a simple and fast way to create a low light environment inside the awning. The simulation base model of the awning and tunnel constructed by using Ecotect Analysis software is shown in Fig. 1.

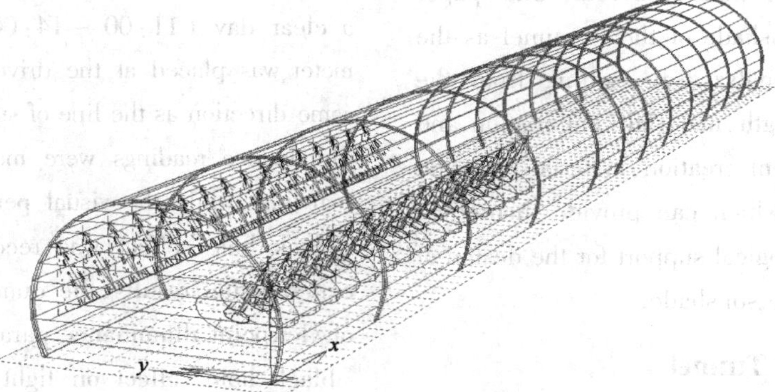

Fig. 1　Awning and tunnel simulation base model

3.2　Design Parameters of the Light Environment Inside the Shade

(1) Tunnel outside viewpoint illumination level

The illumination level of the viewpoint was measured at 50m in front of the entrance of the right line of tunnel A. Before 9:00 a.m. and 18:30 p.m., the illuminance of the viewpoint is weak, after 9:00 a.m., the illuminance of the outside viewpoint is greatly enhanced, reaching the peak value at 11:30 ~ 14:00 p.m., generally fluctuating in the range of 3400 ~ 4100lux, 3800lux is selected as the design parameter of the outside viewpoint illuminance of the tunnel.

(2) The illumination level of the tunnel viewpoint

According to the lighting design level of the tunnel right line, combined with the pre-test tunnel illumination level, selected 240lux as the tunnel viewpoint illumination design parameters.

(3) Control speed

The tunnel speed limit should not exceed the design speed, according to the design documents, 100km/h as the control speed of vehicles entering the tunnel.

(4) The driver's visual comfort criteria

According to the "black hole" effect of numerical grading characteristics, tunnel A "black hole" effect of comfort requirements of the indicator threshold E1/E2 ≈ 1.7. Considering the actual situation of the awning is difficult to achieve the ideal comfort threshold of illumination transition, so the awning viewpoint illumination should be made The gradual low rate should be kept near and slightly below the ideal comfort threshold (too low will lead to too long design length, an unreasonable combination of light transmission parameters, etc.), and 1.6 ~ 1.7 is selected as the driver's comfort criterion.

4 Sunshade Material/Length Combination Design

4.1 Sunshade Material Selection

The selection of sunshade material should take into account the four requirements of light transmission, durability, ease of use and economy, etc. Several common light-reducing materials in engineering are shown in Tab. 2.

Comparison of performance parameters of light reducing materials Tab. 2

Material Type	Maximum light transmittance	Heat resistance	Corrosion resistance	Tensile strength (MPa)	Density ($g \cdot cm^{-3}$)	10mm thick ($yuan \cdot kg^{-1}$)
Plexiglass	92%	Good	Normal	52 ~ 75	1.19	50 ~ 100
PC board	89%	Good	Better	60 ~ 65	1.2	50 ~ 70
ABS plate	84%	Bad	Better	47 ~ 52	1.05	100 ~ 200
Crystal plate	89%	Good	Better	49 ~ 56	1.3 ~ 1.5	67.5
Organic Board	88%	Normal	Normal	44 ~ 50	1.05	87

The comparison found that the PC board has the advantages of high strength, easy processing, light transmission rate variety, etc., more suitable as sunshade material. The PC board is mainly divided into two forms of flat plate and wave board, wave board has better construction performance than flat plate, comprehensive consideration of the selection of 2mm thick PC wave board as awning sunshade material.

4.2 Sunshade Material Transmittance/Length Combination

The realization of the gradual low light environment inside the awning requires that the driver's point-of-view illumination decreases uniformly and continuously from the beginning to the end of the awning, and the decrease is no greater than the comfort threshold to which the driver can adapt. The theoretical minimum length l of the awning is shown in Equation (1), considering parameters such as the level of illumination of the viewpoint inside and outside the cave and the vehicle control speed. (YU Yaming. 2019)

$$l = \frac{V}{3.6} \cdot \frac{\lg \frac{E_{外}}{E_{in}}}{\lg 1.7} \cdot 0.2 \tag{1}$$

Where E_m refers to the theoretical illuminance value at the end of the awning, based on the derivation of Em according to the threshold value of "comfort", the process must meet the formula (2).

$$E_m = E_{in} \times 1.7^{\frac{t}{0.2}} \tag{2}$$

Where t refers to the travel time of E_m transition to E_{in}. It is calculated that the minimum length of the tunnel A entrance sunshade that can realize the ideal transition of illumination is 18 m. Based on experience, 2 times the theoretical minimum length is initially chosen as the initial length of the sunshade for light environment simulation trial calculation.

Based on the principle of "uniformly low and beautiful", the simulation model of "the same lateral direction and gradual change at the top" and "Piecewise single and overall combination" is constructed for the combination of two types of shading materials. Multi-transmittance scheme and length of the sunshade are determined. The net width of evacuation and safety exit of public buildings should not be less than 0.90m, and the net width and net height of firefighters' entry window should not be less than 1.0m, the lower part of both sides of the sunshade will be hollowed out by 1.2m (i.e. no sunshade). The simulation model of the two combined forms of awning is shown in Fig. 2.

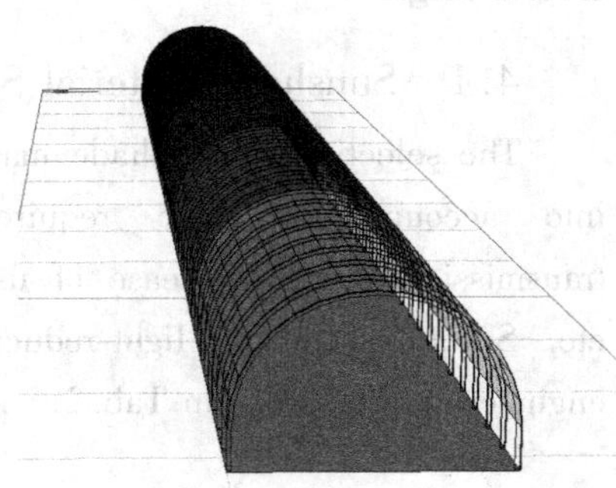

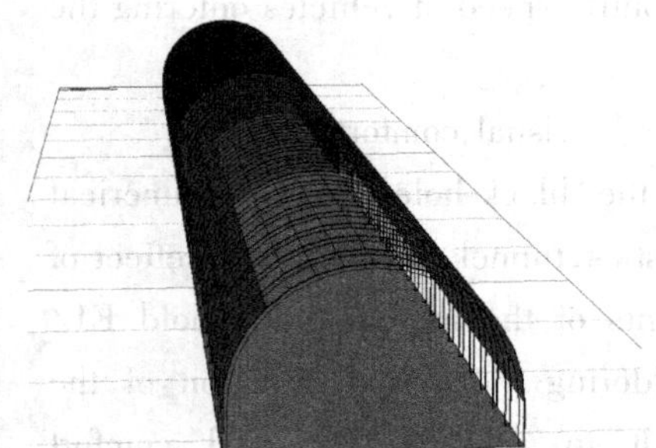

Fig. 2 "Piecewise single, whole combination" type /"Lateral same, top gradient" type model

Firstly, the initial light transmittance combination is designed under the initial length for the light environment simulation of the whole length range, based on the driver's visual comfort judgment standard to evaluate whether the initial sunshade segment combination and length design scheme meet the visual comfort demand, if not, the sunshade length is dynamically adjusted in steps of 1m per segment, and then the light environment simulation is again judged until the visual comfort demand is met, and finally, the sunshade material is determined more The combination of light transmittance and length of shade canopy are finally determined.

(1) Design of "same side-to-side, gradual change at the top" type sunshade combination

Based on the top 60° range of light transmittance gradient design, according to the light environment simulation of the "side-to-side identical, top gradient" type awning model, the light transmittance of the top initial section τ top beginning should be 0.5 ~ 0.6, the light transmittance of the top end section τ top end should be 0 ~ 0.2, the difference of light transmittance parameters of the top adjacent materials should be ≤0.3. 0.3, the lateral light transmission rate τ side is selected considering the matching degree with the initial section and the top material light transmission rate of the end section, and it is appropriate to select 0.2 ~ 0.3.

Light environment simulation analysis for 36m sunshade, found that it is difficult to meet the transition requirements of uniform gradual low light environment. The length of the awning was adjusted to 40m for light environment design, and the length of the top section: 10m + 10m + 10m + 10m, and the following 2 options were designed.

Option 1: Lateral 0.2 + Top 0.5 - 0.3 - 0.2 - 0.1

Option 2: Lateral 0.2 + Top 0.5 - 0.3 - 0.1 - 0

Calculate the maximum value of the ratio w_{max} of the illuminance data of the adjacent 0.2s viewpoints for each scheme, see Tab. 3.

w_{max} **for different parameter options** (40m) Tab. 3

Light transmission parameter combination options	Option 1	Option 2
w_{max}	1.77	1.67

From the above table, the combination of the light transmission rate of option 1 cannot meet the driver' s visual comfort demand, and the combination of the light transmission rate of option 2 meets the driver' s visual comfort threshold. However, considering that the route of tunnel A runs east-west, and the ambient illumination may be high during the daytime in summer, to further guarantee the creation effect of the gradual transition of the light environment in the shed (close to 1.6), the overall length of the shed is appropriately extended to 44m to continue the light environment simulation design, design the length of the top section: 11m + 11m + 11m + 11m, design the combination of light transmission rate scheme: lateral 0.2 + Construct the awning model for viewpoint illuminance simulation analysis, and calculate the ratio of adjacent 0.2s viewpoint illuminance data maximum wmax = 1.61. The change curve of the illuminance of the driver' s viewpoint is shown in Fig. 3.

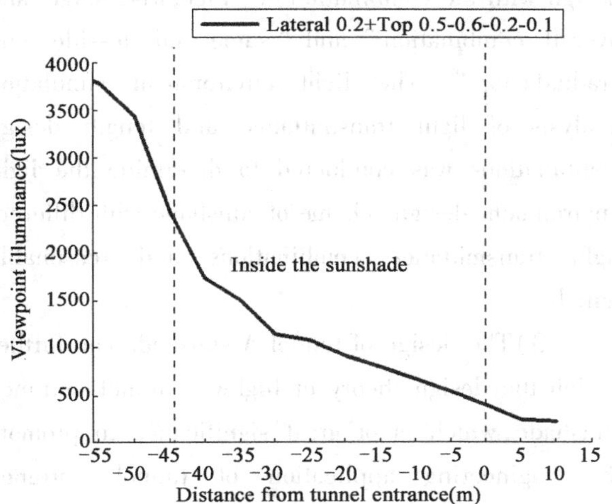

Fig. 3 Illuminance variation curve of viewpoint in 44m awning

It can be seen that the combination of the light transmission parameters of the 44m length sunshade meets the driver' s visual comfort threshold, and the illumination change can better meet the driver' s visual comfort transition needs than 40m, and is more conducive to cope with the light reduction environment under the bright visual environment gradually low transition.

(2) "Piecewise single, overall combination" type sunshade combination design

According to the light environment simulation of "Piecewise single, overall combination" type shade shed model, the segment length should be 9 ~ 12m, the light transmission rate τ of shade shed beginning material should be 0.4 ~ 0.6, and the high value should be taken in the case of high illumination of external viewpoint, the light transmission rate τ of shade shed end material should be ≤0.2, and the light transmission rate of adjacent shade material should be ≤0.3. Should be ≤ 0.3, the first and last difference value ≥ 0.3 of the combination of light transmission parameters can be considered to add the middle section of the transition section, otherwise, illumination is difficult to smooth transition.

The initial length of the sunshade is 36m, considering the economy and reasonable segmentation, it will be divided into 4 segments: 9m + 9m + 9m + 9m. 4 kinds of light transmittance combination programs are designed as follows.

Option 1: 0.5 - 0.4 - 0.2 - 0.1
Option 2: 0.5 - 0.4 - 0.3 - 0.2
Option 3: 0.6 - 0.4 - 0.2 - 0.1
Option 4: 0.6 - 0.4 - 0.3 - 0.1

Calculate the maximum ratioWmax of illuminance data of adjacent 0.2S viewpoints of each scheme, as shown in Tab. 4.

w_{max} for different parameter schemes (36m) Tab. 4

Light transmission parameter rcombination scheme	Option1	Option 2	Option 3	Option 4
w_{max}	1.77	2.33	2.07	1.78

From the above table, it is known that the combination scheme of each light transmission parameter of 36m length awning cannot meet the driver' s visual comfort demand, and the length of the awning needs to be dynamically adjusted. The length of the awning is adjusted to 40m and divided into 4 sections: 10m + 10m + 10m + 10m. The following 4 light transmittance combination schemes are designed.

Option1:0.6 -0.5 -0.3 -0.2

Option 2:0.6 -0.4 -0.3 -0.2

Option3:0.5 -0.4 -0.3 -0.1

Option 4:0.6 -0.4 -0.2 -0.1

Calculate the maximum value of the ratio w_{max} of the illuminance data of the adjacent 0.2s viewpoints for each scheme, see Tab.5.

w_{max} for different parameter options(36m) Tab.5

Light transmission parameter combination options	Option1	Option 2	Option 3	Option 4
w_{max}	2.18	2.17	1.95	1.64

From the above table, it is known that the combination of light transmission rate of 40m length awning scheme 1,2 and 3 cannot meet the driver' s visual comfort demand, while the combination of light transmission rate of scheme 4 meets the driver' s visual comfort threshold and can better realize the light environment gradual low transition. The change curve of illuminance of driver' s viewpoint are shown in Fig.4.

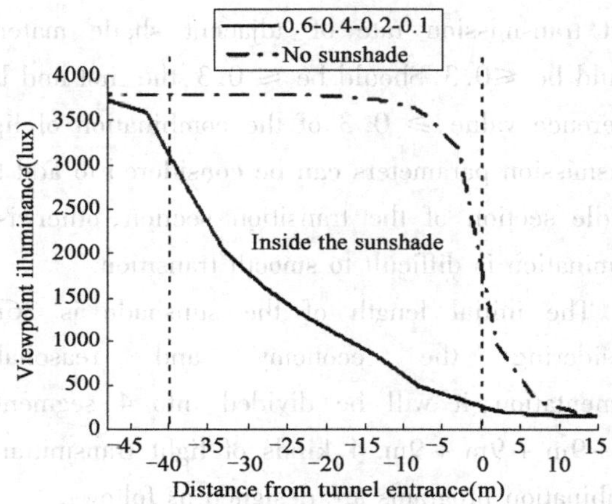

Fig.4 Variation curve of illuminance of viewpoints in Option 4 shade

Comprehensive analysis, " Piecewise single, overall combination "," the same lateral, top gradient" two shading material combination form in certain design conditions can be more economical to create a driver to meet the light and dark visual smooth transition of the driving light environment. In this paper, the design combination of 44m light transmission rate(lateral 0.2 + top 0.5 -0.3 -0.2 -0.1) under the combination of " same lateral, top gradient" shading materials is selected as the design solution for the light environment of tunnel A entrance awning.

5 Conclusions

(1) analyzed the driver' s viewpoint illumination data collected from the multi-tunnel experiment, established a quantitative characterization of the driver' s" black hole" effect of light and darkness, and determined the grading criteria for the driver' s visual perception of light and darkness at different viewpoint illumination levels.

(2) Taking the tunnel A sunshade as the object, the Ecotect Analysis light environment simulation technology was used to carry out a multi-sunshade design with the combination of "Piecewise single and overall combination" and "same side-to-side and gradual top". The light environment simulation analysis of light transmittance and length design combinations was conducted to determine the light environment design scheme of sunshade with different light transmittance combinations and reasonable length.

(3) The design of tunnel A sunshade can further enrich the design theory of highway tunnel entrance sunshade, which is of great significance to promote the engineering application of tunnel entrance sunshade and improve the traffic safety level of tunnel entrance section.

References

[1] Du Zhigang, Zhanji Zheng, Miao Zheng. et al. Drivers' visual comfort at highway tunnel portals: a quantitative analysis based on visual oscillation[J]. Transportation Research Part D: Transport and Environment, 2014, 31, 37-47.

[2] LI Yin-tao. Cheng Guo-zhu. Reasonable Length of Glare proof Grille Section at Exitand Entrance of Highway Tunnel. [J] Highway

Engineering, 2009, 34(05), 13-15 + 20.

[3] LI Rong, Li Qiu, Zhang Li-yun. (2012). The Application of Shade Shed in the Design of Huludan Tunnel. Sichuan Forestry Survey and Design, 02, 76-78.

[4] Peng Yu-hua, Fu Xiang-xiang, Lu Xin. et al. Numerical Simulation on Light Environment and Secondary Pollution of Sunshade Awning of Adjacent Tunnel Portals [J]. Journal of CHONGQINGJIAOTONG University (Natural Science), 2019, 38(01), 23-29.

[5] YU Chuan-kun, Wang Li-xiong, Feng Zi-long. The Study of Office Space under Daylighting in Tianjin Area. Zhaoming Gongcheng Xuebao, 2017, 28(3), 14-19.

[6] YU Ya-ming. Numerical characterization of "black hole" effect at the entrance of highway tunnel and design method of sunshade light environment. Xi'an: Chang'an University, 2019.

[7] Zhang Tian-geng, Zhang Lan-fang, Liu shuo. Study of Natural Light Transition at the Entrance of Highway Tunnels. Journal of Highway and Transportation Research and Development, 2017, 13(01), 137-140.

[8] Zhao Xi-seng, Jing Yi, Tang Peng-fei. Awning Design for the Entrance of the Aruba Tunnel. Journal of Highway and Transportation Research and Development, 2018, 14(10), 256-259.

[9] Zwahlen H T, Badurdeen F F. (2002). Daytime legibility as a function of non-fluorescent and fluorescent traffic sign colors, in "Transportation Research Record 1692" [Z]. Washington DC, America, 2013: 13-17.

考虑人员疏散安全的曲线公路隧道火灾合理风速研究

杨少鹏* 任 锐 李培军 常宏涛
(长安大学公路学院)

摘 要 为了研究纵向通风风速及曲率半径对曲线隧道火灾人员疏散安全的影响，以金家庄螺旋隧道为原型，采用FDS软件建立全尺寸数值模型，分析了纵向风速为0、1、2、3 m/s及隧道半径为890、800、700m条件下，人眼特征高度处(距路面高度1.5m)烟气蔓延及温度分布规律。结果表明：就隧道下部区域而言，温度在距离火源20m外均低于60℃，人体基本都可耐受；考虑烟气，采用不超过1m/s的纵向风速较为适宜，烟气蔓延速率低且火源上游回流长度小于50m；隧道曲率半径越小，烟气蔓延越快，温度越高，但曲率半径对烟气蔓延和温度分布影响程度较低；由于曲线隧道外侧壁面的限制，导致烟气在曲线外侧壁面比内侧更易向下部区域蔓延。

关键词 隧道工程 隧道火灾 数值模拟 曲线隧道 纵向通风 烟气蔓延

0 引言

根据《2020年交通运输行业发展统计公报》，截至2020年底，全国公路总里程519.81万km，公路隧道21316处、2199.93万延m，其中特长隧道1394处、623.55万延m，长隧道5541处、963.32万延m。长大隧道内一旦发生火灾，火灾烟气导致的人员窒息死亡占隧道火灾人员伤亡比重超85%[1]，因此长大隧道内烟气控制显得尤为重要。由于在适应地形方面展现出独到的优越性，同时随着隧道建设技术的不断进步，国内外曲线隧道建设规模日益增长，但同时也给火灾的防灾救灾提出了更大的挑战。长大隧道大多采用纵向通风方式[2]，针对无单独排烟道的纵向通风隧道，阳东等[3]指出过大的风速会破坏烟气热分层稳定性，造成烟气向隧道下部区域蔓延。因此我国《公路隧道通风设计细则》(JTG/T D70/2—02—2014)给出了不会破坏烟气与空气之间的分层结构的纵向排烟风速。李俊梅[4]等对交通拥堵的隧道火灾烟气特性进行了研究,得到了不同功率火源条件下,能够保证烟气分层、有利人员安全疏散的风速。

针对曲线隧道火灾防灾,部分学者对临界风速、烟气蔓延及温度分布特性进行了相关研究。王峰等采用数值计算方法研究了曲线隧道控制烟气的临界风速,结果表明:在半径为600m的曲线隧道内发生规模为10MW火灾时,临界风速为2.5m/s[5];半径为400m的隧道中的临界风速比直线隧道中大7%[6]。伍灿等[7]研究了干海子曲线公路隧道火灾烟气输运特性,并得到了该隧道临界风速为4m/s。芦峰[8]利用FDS建立数值模型,对比了隧道火灾发生在直线段和曲线段的烟气扩散及温度分布,发现火灾发生在曲线段时烟气回流更加严重,温度升高更显著。Zhong等[9]在有坡度曲线隧道中进行现场实验,得到了烟气蔓延的趋势与温度分布特征。

综上所示,当隧道发生火灾时,针对隧道下部人员活动区域的研究较少,但隧道上部空间内的高温及烟气对人员影响较小;针对曲线隧道发生火灾时,考虑人员疏散逃生的合理纵向风速研究还较为缺乏。本文采用数值模拟方法,建立了曲线隧道模型,对纵向通风风速及隧道半径对隧道内人眼特征高度处(本研究取距路面高度1.5m)的能见度及温度分布的影响规律进行了研究,给出了建议的风速值,可以为类似工程的火灾防灾通风和人员疏散策略提供参考。

1 模型建立与工况设置

1.1 模型建立与网格划分

本研究以延庆至崇礼高速公路金家庄特长螺旋隧道为研究对象,该隧道按高速公路双向四车道标准设计,采用分离式隧道方案,设计速度为80km/h,全长4104m,是在建世界最长高速公路螺旋隧道。金家庄螺旋隧道的曲线半径为下行890m,上行860m。采用FDS软件建立曲线隧道模型,模型隧道长度为750m,隧道曲线半径采用890m、800m、700m,隧道净空断面高7.50m,宽13.66m,FDS只能采用立方体网格,要建立曲线隧道模型,只能"以直代曲",采用堆叠的方法建立曲线隧道模型,所建立模型如图1所示。一般来说,当D^*/δ_x在4~16之间时(D^*表示火源特征直径,δ_x表示网格单元的大小),模拟的计算精度能够保证。

根据FDS用户指导手册[10]中给出的火源特征尺寸定义,如式(1)所示。

$$D^*=\left(\frac{Q}{\rho_\infty c_p T_\infty \sqrt{g}}\right)^{\frac{2}{5}} \tag{1}$$

式中:Q——火源热释放速率(kW);

ρ_∞——环境空气密度(kg/m³);

c_p——空气比热容[kj/(kg·K)];

T_∞——环境温度(K);

g——重力加速度(m/s²)。

经计算可知,D^*为2.893。则经计算有δ_x处于0.2m至0.7m之间,综合考虑算机性能和计算结果的精确度,采用火源局部网格加密的方式,取火源附近网格大小为0.3m×0.3m×0.3m;距离火源较远处网格取0.6m×0.6m×0.6m大小,如图1所示。

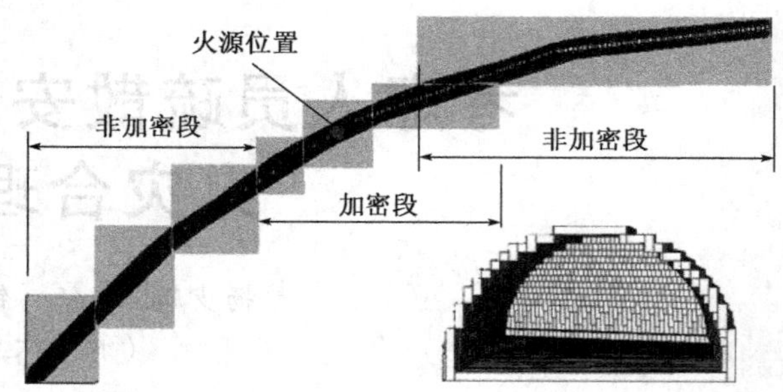

图1 曲线隧道模型图

1.2 火源与环境条件设置

根据《公路隧道通风设计细则》(JTG/T D70/2—02—2014)规定,对于1000m<隧道长度$L\leqslant$5000m的高速和一级公路隧道,隧道火灾最大热释放率为20MW。本文火源位于隧道中心位置,选取非稳态火源,假定火灾热释放速率随时间的平方而增长(式(2)),由于大多数公路隧道火灾是由汽油或柴油燃料的燃烧引发,燃烧速度较快,参考《消防安全工程-火灾场景的选择和火灾设计》[11],选用t^2超快速型火源增长形式,增长系数α取0.1878kW/s²,则火源达到最大火源功率20MW的时间为326.34s。本数值模型设置初始环境压力为一个标准大气压,初始环境温度为298K,隧道洞口设置为自由边界,即烟气可以通过隧道洞口自由地出入计算区域,在其中一个洞口处定义风速,用于向隧道模型内施加纵向风,总模拟时长

为 600s。

$$Q = \alpha t^2 \tag{2}$$

1.3 工况设置与测点布置

根据徐志胜等[7]提出的水平隧道火灾临界风速的理论模型及 Wu 和 Bakar[12]提出的临界风速预计模型可计算得公路隧道 20MW 火灾的临界风速介于2.5~3m/s，且半径为400m 的隧道中的临界速度比直线隧道中大 7%[6]，因此本次数值模拟工况纵向风速最大定为 3m/s，具体工况设置如表 1 所示。

工况设置　　表1

工况编号	曲线半径(m)	风速($m \cdot s^{-1}$)
工况 1	890	0
工况 2	890	1
工况 3	890	2
工况 4	890	3
工况 5	800	0
工况 6	800	1
工况 7	800	2
工况 8	800	3
工况 9	700	0
工况 10	700	1
工况 11	700	2
工况 12	700	3

为了检测环境中温度、能见度的变化，在数值模型中设置了温度、能见度的测试点或测试面，如图 2 所示，在隧道中轴线上设置 6 组共 24 个温度测点，第 1 组位于火源正上方，其余位于火源下游，每组间距 20 米，每组设有 4 个测点，分别距离隧道内地面 1.5m、3.5m、5.5m、7.5m(拱顶)；并设置了三个水平测面，距离隧道内地面 1.5m、3.5m、5.5m。

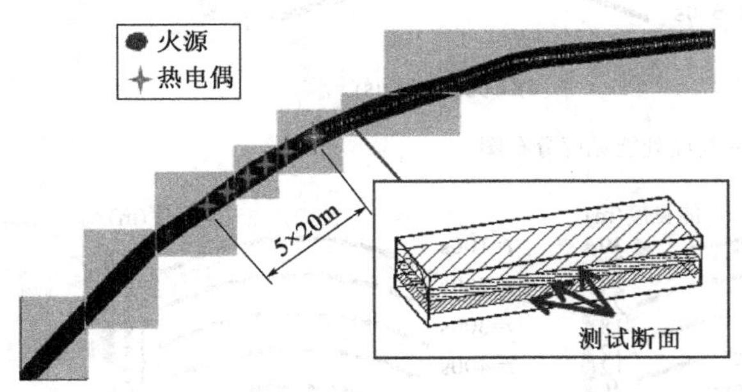

图 2　测点和测面布置图

1.4 模型验证

关于 FDS 数值模拟的可靠性，国内外已有较多学者对其进行验证[13,14]，2009 年，中南大学防灾科学与安全技术研究所在狮子洋水下隧道进行试验研究，试验结果发现，FDS 火灾模拟结果与试验结果吻合较好，如图 3 所示[15]。

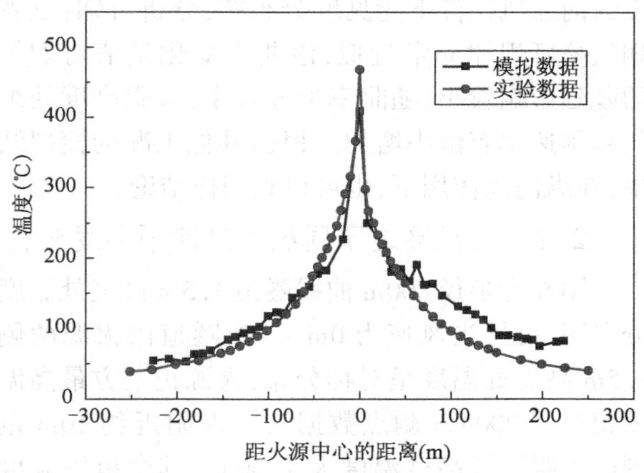

图 3　模拟结果与实验结果对比图

2 模拟结果分析

2.1 曲线隧道不同纵向风速下能见度分析

烟气浓度和能见度存在直接关系，将烟气与能见度对应[16]，认为能见度为 30m 时，认为烟气浓度较低，不影响人员疏散。图 4 为半径 800m 的曲线隧道 1.5m 高度处能见度分布图，可见：当风速为 0m/s 时，隧道内火源两侧 1.5m 高度处能见度呈现对称分布，即烟气蔓延呈对称分布。当隧道内存在纵向风速时，在纵向风速的作用下，火源两侧烟气蔓延出现明显差异，火源下游烟气蔓延速率随风速增加而增大；上游烟气回流长度随风速增加逐渐减小至消失，此种规律与其他学者相关研究内容吻合。纵向风速为 1m/s 时，下部区域烟气回流长度不超过 50m，烟气蔓延速率较慢；纵向风速≥2m/s 时，上游能见度良好，烟气仅向火源下游蔓延，烟气分层被破坏，烟气蔓延速率较快，烟气蔓延速率快于人员逃生速度，且人员需要一定的反应时间，此纵向风速不利于人员疏散。

由图 4-a)、图 4b) 可知隧道两侧边墙能见度下降更快，由图 4c)、图 4d) 可知曲线隧道的外侧边墙能见度下降更快，分析可知：在纵向风速较低情况下，隧道两侧浮升力相对较低，且隧道为马蹄形横断面，两侧更易受到壁面限制，导致了两侧烟气向下蔓延较快;在纵向风速≥2m/s时,烟气分层被破坏,曲线隧道内外侧的差异显著,曲线外侧壁面处烟气受到壁面限制导致更易向下部区域蔓延。

图5为R=890m、800m及700m的曲线隧道无纵向通风条件下能见度分布图,分析可知:三者烟气蔓延规律非常近似,该曲率变化量值对烟气的蔓延影响较小,随曲率半径减小,人眼高度处烟气蔓延速率有微小增加。根据其他工况的模拟结果,在纵向风作用下,也可得到同样结论。

2.2　曲线隧道不同纵向风速下温度分析

图6为半径800m曲线隧道1.5m高度处温度分布图,可见当风速为0m/s时,隧道内火源两侧1.5m高度处温度呈对称分布,火源正上方最高温度超过了900℃(测点数据),火源附近约10m范围内人眼特征高度温度大于40℃,其余范围温度低于40℃。根据已有研究:短时间内人体最高耐受温度为60℃,耐受平均温度为49℃[17],因此对人员的疏散不会造成影响。在纵向风速的作用下,火源温度向下游扩散显著,且风速越高,扩散越快;同时,纵向风速≥1m/s时,火源上游下部区域温度几乎不受火源影响。

图7为各工况下隧道中轴线上1.5m高处各测点温度值,为模拟时间550s至600s的温度平均值,此时火源功率和隧道各测点温度已基本稳定。以曲率半径为800m隧道进行分析,由图7可知,当无纵向通风时,温度很低,距火源20m处仅约33℃,且在距火源80m处降低至接近环境温度20℃;当纵向风速为1m/s时,隧道内温度沿纵向下降迅速,在距火源60m处已下降至49℃以下;当风速为2m/s、3m/s时,结合图6,分析可得:隧道距火源20m至100m处温度降低较小,且趋于稳定,温度值约在55℃至45℃区间。即施加纵向通风,导致隧道除火源附近之外的区域温度增高,但人体可以耐受。

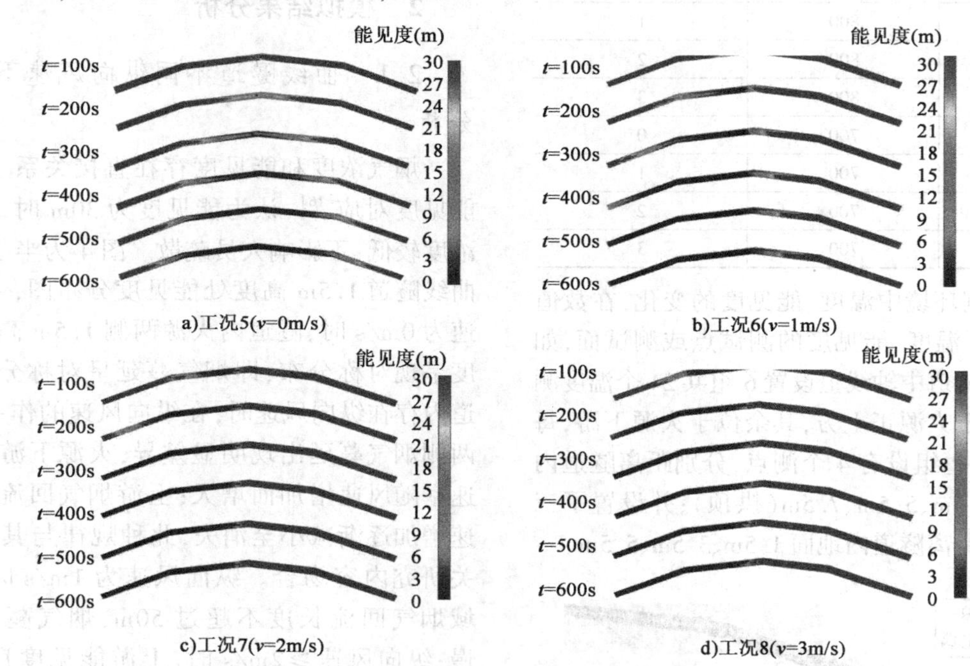

图4　半径800m曲线隧道1.5m高度处能见度分布图

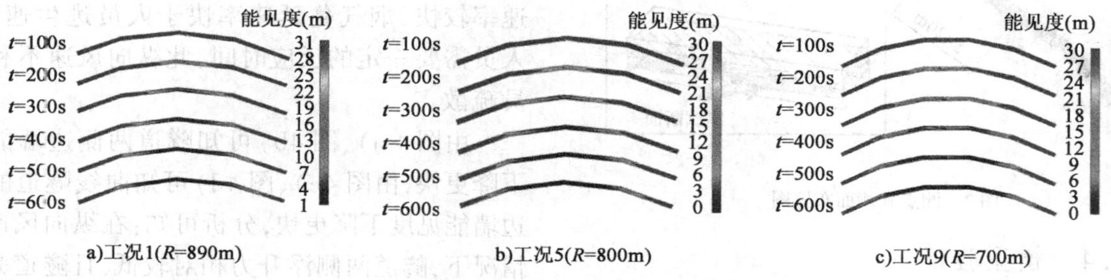

图5　不同半径隧道能见度分布图

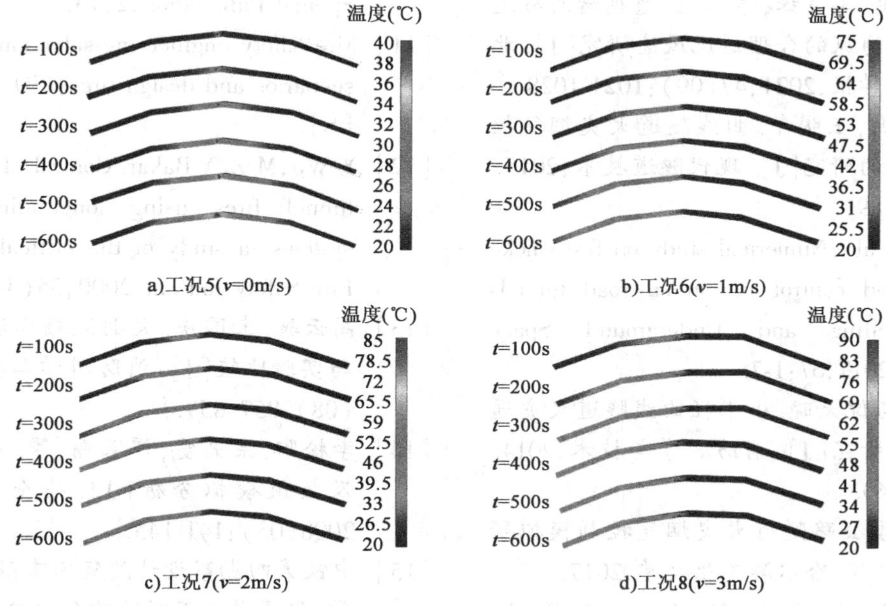

图6　半径800m曲线隧道1.5m高度处温度分布图

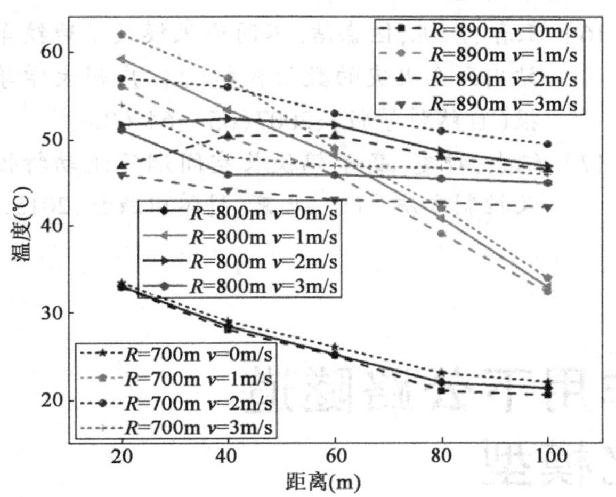

图7　1.5m高度处各测点温度值

对比不同曲率半径隧道温度值可得，曲率半径越小，隧道下部区域的温度越高，但随着至火源距离的增加，差异逐渐减小。同时，曲率半径从890m变化至700m，温度的变化最大值约5℃，平均仅为约2℃～3℃，相对于纵向风速导致的温度分布变化，曲率半径对温度分布的影响很小。

3　结语

本文使用FDS软件建立曲线隧道数值模型，从火灾人员疏散角度出发，研究了隧道内纵向风速及曲率半径对人眼特征高度处(距路面高度1.5m)烟气蔓延与温度分布的影响，研究结果表明：

(1)火灾后人员逃生过程中，隧道内纵向风速值介于0～3m/s，除火源上下游20m范围，隧道下部区域内温度基本都低于60℃，且火源下游60m范围外基本不超过49℃，人体都可以耐受，高温并不是导致隧道火灾人员伤亡的主要因素。

(2)纵向风速越大，火源下游烟气蔓延越快，综合各工况烟气蔓延情况，考虑到人员识别和反应的时间，采用纵向风速为1m/s内较为适宜，上游人眼特征高度烟气回流长度不超过50m，火源下游烟气蔓延速率较慢，能够保证人员安全逃生。

(3)隧道曲率半径对于隧道内能见度和温度存在一定的影响，纵向风速相同条件下，隧道曲率半径越小，下部区域烟气蔓延越快，温度越高，但曲率半径对烟气蔓延和温度分布影响程度较低。曲线隧道内外壁面处烟气蔓延存在差异，尤其当施加纵向通风时差异显著，由于隧道外侧壁面的限制，导致烟气在曲线隧道外侧更易向下部区域蔓延。

参考文献

[1]　钟委，端木维可，李华琳，等．纵向风作用下隧道火灾烟气分岔流动试验研究[J]．中国铁道科学，2016，37(02)：56-63．

[2]《中国公路学报》编辑部．中国隧道工程学术研究综述．2015[J]．中国公路学报，2015，28(05)：1-65．

[3]　阳东，胡隆华，霍然，等．纵向风对通道火灾烟气竖向分层特性的影响[J]．燃烧科学与技术，2010，16(03)：252-256．

[4] 李俊梅,谢飞,李炎锋,等.在交通拥堵的隧道火灾中纵向通风的合理送风风速研究[J].北京工业大学学报,2021,47(09):1021-1028.

[5] 王峰,董国海,王明年.曲线隧道火灾烟气控制临界风速的研究[J].现代隧道技术,2015.52(05):84-89.

[6] Wang,F.,et al.,Numerical study on fire smoke movement and control in curved road tunnels[J]. Tunnelling and Underground Space Technology,2017,67:1-7.

[7] 伍灿,何佳与倪天晓.小半径曲线隧道火灾通风数值模拟研究[J].消防科学与技术,2014.33(01):37-40.

[8] 芦峰.曲线型公路隧道火灾烟气控制模拟研究[D].哈尔滨:哈尔滨工业大学,2017.

[9] Zhong M H, Shi C L, He L, et al. Smoke development in full-scale sloped long and large curvedtunnel fires under natural ventilation[J]. Applied Thermal Engineering, 2016, 108: 857-865.

[10] McGrattan K, Hostikka S, McDermott R. Fire Dynamics Simulator, User's Guide[M]. Nist Special Publication,2013.

[11] Fire safety engineering-selection of design fire scenarios and design fires:ISO/TS16733-2006[S].

[12] Y Wu,M Z A Bakar. Control of smoke flow in tunnel fires using longitudinal ventilation systems -a study of the critical velocity[J]. Fire Safety Journal,2000,35(4):363-390.

[13] 高云骥,朱国庆.火羽流轴向温度大涡模拟与实验比较[J].消防科学与技术,2014,33(08):857-859.

[14] 李松阳,宗若雯,谭家磊,等.室内轰燃试验及数值模拟分析[J].安全与环境学报,2008(05):141-145.

[15] 中铁第四勘察设计院集团有限公司,中南大学.狮子洋水下隧道综合防灾与运营管理技术研究[R].2009.

[16] 王春,江帆,区嘉洁.不同通风模式下地铁车站内列车火灾的数值模拟[J].广州大学学报(自然科学版),2007(05):64-68.

[17] 纪杰,钟委.高子鹤狭长空间烟气流动特性及控制方法[M].北京:科学出版社,2015.

NO_2和弯曲应力作用下公路隧道衬砌碳化模型

王 浩[1] 周志军*[1] 田叶青[1] 张铭驿[2] 张志鹏[1]

(1.长安大学公路学院;2.云南省交通科学研究院有限公司)

摘 要 为研究公路隧道衬砌在酸性气体和弯曲应力作用下碳化耐久性的影响,通过室内快速碳化试验,分析硝酸侵蚀和弯曲应力作用下对混凝土碳化深度的影响规律,建立硝酸和弯曲应力作用下的公路隧道衬砌混凝土碳化深度预测模型。结果表明:酸侵蚀和弯曲应力作用均能提高混凝土碳化深度,且未改变碳化深度增长规律;碳化深度与硝酸浓度和弯曲应力水平成正相关,且符合一定的函数规律;通过与现场实测数据比较,进一步验证了预测模型的可靠性。

关键词 隧道工程 混凝土衬砌 硝酸侵蚀 弯曲应力 碳化 预测模型

0 引言

碳化是导致钢筋混凝土隧道衬砌耐久性劣化的重要原因之一[1-3]。公路隧道衬砌所处环境中除了高浓度的CO_2外,还有汽车尾气所积聚的较高浓度酸性气体(如NO_2)影响混凝土的碳化进程[4-5]。同时,外部应力会影响混凝土气渗透性能和碳化速度[6],围岩荷载的作用使得部分衬砌混凝土处于弯曲受拉状态产生裂缝,加速了衬砌结构的损伤[7]。

混凝土的碳化速度与混凝土材料性质和环境因素密切相关。材料因素对混凝土碳化的影响规律,众多学者进行了大量的试验研究,主要研究内容为水泥种类、水灰比、水泥用量、混凝土强度、外加剂、施工和养护方式等。研究工作还从理论上分析了相应的碳化机理,建立了相关碳化经验模型[8-15]。另一方面,对于环境因素的研究,主要集中于温度因素和湿度因素,部分学者也研究了混凝土应力状态或氯离子侵蚀、冻融等其他因素的影响[16-20]。

综上,本文基于快速碳化试验,研究硝酸侵蚀和弯曲应力作用下混凝土的碳化特性,分析不同硝酸浓度和弯曲应力水平对混凝土碳化的影响,建立公路隧道衬砌碳化深度的预测模型,为公路隧道衬砌结构碳化提供参考。

1 室内快速碳化试验

1.1 原材料及试件制备

水泥采用P·O 42.5 普通硅酸盐水泥;砂为渭河天然砂,细度模数为 3.4;碎石为连续级配 5~15mm的瓜米石;减水剂为聚羧酸系高性能减水剂,减水率 27%。本次试验试件为 100mm × 100mm × 400mm 混凝土棱柱体,强度设计等级为 C30,浇筑成型后静置 24h 后脱模,标号后送入混凝土养护室,在 20℃、95% RH 的环境下养护 28d 后,对试件进行抗折强度测试,对同期浇筑的标准立方体试块进行抗压试验。配合比及 28d 强度如表 1 所示。

混凝土配合比和强度　　表 1

配合比($kg \cdot m^{-3}$)					抗压强度(MPa)	抗折强度(MPa)
水	水泥	砂	碎石	减水剂		
166	360	727	1137	3.6	32.3	5.1

1.2 试验设计

试验参照《普通混凝土长期性能和耐久性能试验方法标准》(GB/T 50082—2009)的规定进行,在试验过程中控制温度为 20℃、相对湿度 70%、CO_2气体浓度 20%;碳化周期为 3d、7d、14d、28d;所有试件均选择一个 100mm × 400mm 的面作为测试面,并将其相邻侧面用石蜡封闭以消除多维碳化对试验结果的影响。

为模拟公路隧道内的酸性气体 NO_2 的侵蚀作用,采用硝酸浸泡的方式进行处理。硝酸溶液浓度分别为 $0.01mol \cdot L^{-1}$、$0.05mol \cdot L^{-1}$、$0.1mol \cdot L^{-1}$。在碳化试验开始前(0d)和碳化进行到 7d、14d、21d 时,将试件的试验面浸泡在对应浓度的硝酸溶液中 1d,如图 1a)所示,待其干燥后,继续进行快速碳化试验。为模拟衬砌受到弯曲荷载的作用,加载方式采用四点弯曲加载法,加载装置如图 1b)所示,弯曲应力水平分别为 $0.3f_f$、$0.5f_f$、$0.7f_f$。为使测区的受力状态一致,选择纯弯段(试件中部 100mm 的范围)为碳化测区,并将其均分为 4 个宽 25mm 的小测区,分别对应 4 个碳化周期。快速碳化试验结束后,将各测区用干锯切片后,采用 1% 酚酞—酒精溶液测试混凝土碳化深度,如图 1c)所示。试验工况见表 2。

a)硝酸浸泡测试面

b)试件加载

c)酚酞测试

图 1　碳化试验

试件编号与对应工况　　表2

应力水平	HNO_3溶液浓度($mol \cdot L^{-1}$)			
	0	0.01	0.05	0.1
0	A-1	B-1	C-1	D-1
$0.3f_f$	A-2	B-2	C-2	D-2
$0.5f_f$	A-3	B-3	C-3	D-3
$0.7f_f$	A-4	B-4	C-4	D-4

1.3　试验结果分析

各试件的在不同碳化时间下的碳化深度 x_c 如表3所示，部分试件的碳化深度-时间曲线如图2所示。显然，各试件的碳化深度发展均呈现出相似的规律，即碳化深度随时间不断增长，增速则呈现减缓趋势。

试件碳化深度　　表3

试件编号	碳化深度(mm)			
	3d	7d	14d	28d
A-1	2.83	4.34	6.06	8.77
A-2	2.77	4.51	6.21	9.16
A-3	2.98	4.65	6.11	9.85
A-4	3.34	5.20	6.83	10.34
B-1	3.14	5.10	6.90	10.52
B-2	3.04	5.33	7.29	10.93
B-3	3.21	5.35	7.36	11.09
B-4	3.38	5.51	8.06	11.42
C-1	3.16	5.56	7.87	11.43
C-2	3.43	5.68	7.90	11.99
C-3	3.59	5.78	8.05	12.41
C-4	3.90	5.81	8.22	12.67
D-1	3.56	5.67	7.89	10.89
D-2	3.86	6.01	7.86	11.96
D-3	4.14	6.36	8.03	12.75
D-4	4.33	6.51	8.40	13.50

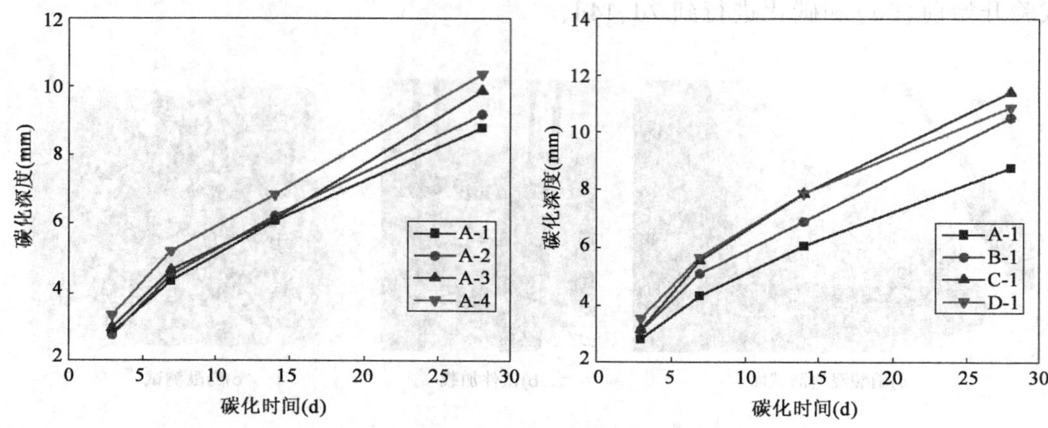

图2　不同工况下的碳化深度曲线

对比图 2a)的 4 条曲线,随着弯曲应力的增大,碳化深度也随之增加。$0.3f_f$、$0.5f_f$、$0.7f_f$ 工况下碳化深度的平均提升幅值分别为 3.65%、7.51%、13.71%,说明相较于较小弯曲应力,较大弯曲应力对碳化深度的提升幅值会有显著提升。由图 2b)可知,碳化深度随着硝酸浓度的增加同样不断提高,且提升效果较弯曲应力更为明显。硝酸浓度 $0.01mol \cdot L^{-1}$、$0.05mol \cdot L^{-1}$、$0.1mol \cdot L^{-1}$ 工况下的碳化深度的平均提升幅值分别为 13.66%、23.88%、30.36%,说明较低的硝酸浓度即可对混凝土的碳化深度造成显著影响。另一方面,随硝酸浓度的增加,碳化深度的提升幅值虽逐渐减小却仍有明显增加,但远小于硝酸浓度的倍数增长幅度,反映了当硝酸浓度较高时,继续增加硝酸浓度对混凝土碳化深度的提升效果较为有限。进一步分析碳化深度与硝酸浓度、弯曲应力水平间的关系,将不同浓度硝酸溶液侵蚀下的试件与无硝酸侵蚀试件的碳化深度比值进行加权平均处理,并将结果根据指数函数拟合,如图 3a)所示;将不同弯曲应力水平作用下的试件与无硝酸侵蚀试件的碳化深度比值进行加权平均处理,并将结果根据 Bradley 函数进行拟合,如图 3b)所示。两者均具有极高的拟合度,如式(1)和式(2)所示。

$$k_A = -0.2406\ln(-0.00193\ln C_{HNO_3}) \quad (C_{HNO_3} \leqslant 0.1mol \cdot L^{-1}) \tag{1}$$

$$k_F = 0.96042 + 0.03983\exp(2.12694f/f_f) \quad (0.3f_f \leqslant f \leqslant 0.7f_f) \tag{2}$$

式中:k_A——酸性气体影响系数;

C_{HNO_3}——硝酸浓度($mol \cdot L^{-1}$);

k_F——弯曲应力影响系数;

f——弯曲应力水平(MPa);

f_f——混凝土的抗折强度(MPa)。

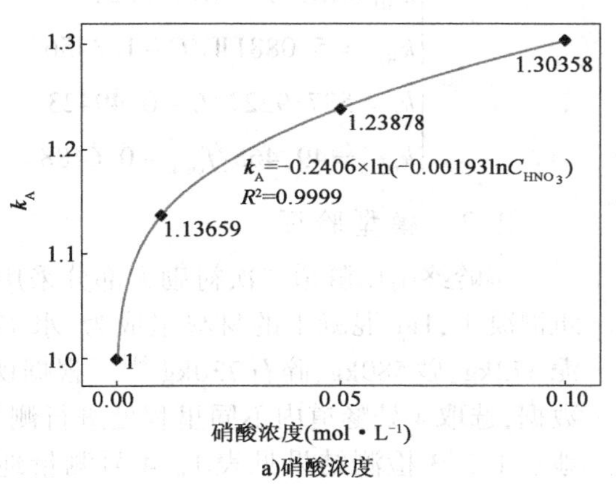

a)硝酸浓度

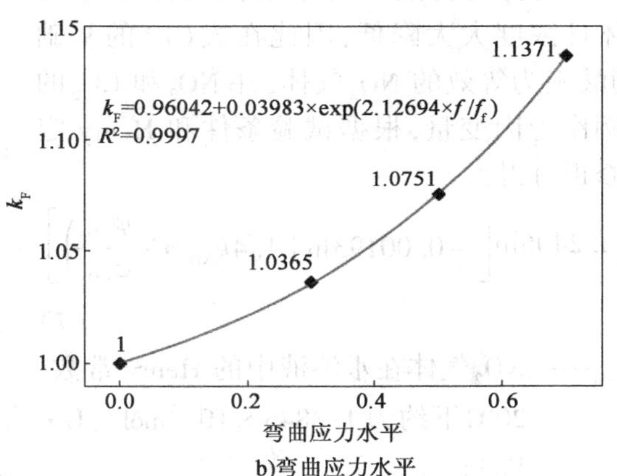

b)弯曲应力水平

图 3 碳化深度影响系数拟合

2 公路隧道衬砌混凝土碳化深度预测模型

2.1 碳化深度预测模型

混凝土碳化模型经过长期的研究和发展,虽然国内外学者使用的手段各不相同,但是碳化深度与碳化时间的平方根成正比的关系已被广泛证实,即经典碳化模型如式 3 所示。

$$x_c = k\sqrt{t} \tag{3}$$

式中:x_c——碳化深度,通常取 mm;

k——综合碳化速度系数,通常取 $mm/a^{0.5}$;

t——时间,通常取 a(年)。

根据 A-1 的碳化深度的拟合结果,可得本文选用混凝土在标准快速碳化环境下的碳化速度系数 $k_0 = 1.644mm/d^{0.5}$,拟合度为 0.9993。此结果基于快速碳化试验,将其运用于实际工程则需要转化为自然条件下的碳化。两者的主要差异在于快速碳化试验中的 CO_2 气体浓度通常为自然环境中的数百倍,因此可引入影响系数 k_{CO_2} 用于反映 CO_2 气体浓度对碳化深度的影响,即

$$x_c = k\sqrt{t} = k_{CO_2}k_0\sqrt{t} \tag{4}$$

Alekseyev 理论碳化模型如式(5)所示。

$$x_c = \sqrt{\frac{2D_c C_0 t}{m_0}} \tag{5}$$

式中:D_c——CO_2 气体在混凝土中的有效扩散系数($m^2 \cdot s^{-1}$);

C_0——环境中 CO_2 气体浓度($mol \cdot m^{-3}$);

m_0——完全碳化时单位体积混凝土吸收的 CO_2 气体的量($mol \cdot m^{-3}$)。

显然,当其他条件相同,则有 $x_c \propto \sqrt{C_0}$。根据定义可得:

$$k_{CO_2} = \sqrt{\frac{\varphi_{CO_2}}{\varphi_0}} = \sqrt{5\varphi_{CO_2}} \tag{6}$$

式中:φ_{CO_2}——环境中 CO_2 气体浓度(%),φ_0 = 20%(标准快速碳化试验的 CO_2 气体浓度)。

根据碳化深度试验数据的分析,在酸性气体侵蚀和弯曲应力作用下的混凝土碳化深度变化规律和仅碳化混凝土基本一致,因此在经典碳化模型的基础上,分别引入酸性气体侵蚀和弯曲应力对碳化深度的影响系数 k_A 和 k_F 对其进行修正。k_F 可根据式(2)计算。由于 k_A 在式(1)中的因变量为硝酸浓度,而自然环境中酸性气体 80% 为 NO_x 气体且浓度大大降低,因此在式(1)的基础上,将硝酸视为等效的 NO_2 气体,并 NO_2 和 CO_2 的浓度比例作为因变量,根据试验条件和 Henry 定律进行修正可得:

$$k_A = -0.2406\ln\left[-0.00193\ln\left(1.4k_{NO_2}p \cdot \frac{\varphi_{NO_2}}{\varphi_{CO_2}}\right)\right] \tag{7}$$

式中:k_{NO_2}——NO_2 气体在水溶液中的 Henry 常数,20℃下约为 1.3845×10^{-5} mol/(L·Pa);

p——标准大气压(101325Pa);

φ_{NO_2}——环境中 NO_2 气体浓度(%)。

在试验基础上,进一步根据公路隧道的环境特点,考虑环境温度 T 和环境相对湿度 RH 对碳化的影响;同时,选取水灰比 W/C = 0.、水泥用量 C、混凝土抗压强度 $f_{cu,k}$ 作为混凝土材料对碳化的影响因素。最终建立如式(8)所示的公路隧道衬砌混凝土碳化深度模型。

$$x_c = k_{CO_2}k_Ak_Fk_Tk_{RH}k_{W/C}k_Ck_{f_{cu,k}}k_0 \cdot \sqrt{t} \tag{8}$$

式中:k_T、k_{RH}、$k_{W/C}$、k_C、$k_{f_{cu,k}}$——环境温度、环境相对湿度、水灰比、水泥用量、抗压强度影响系数。

根据文献[21-23]结合本文的材料参数和环境参数,基于本文选用混凝土在标准快速碳化环境下的碳化速度系数 $k_0 = 1.644 mm/d^{0.5}$ 对以上参数进行修正。设试验选用混凝土的水灰比 W/C = 0.461时的 $k_{W/C} = 1$,试验所用混凝土的水泥用量 $C = 360 kg/m^3$ 的 $k_C = 1$,混凝土抗压强度 $f_{cu,k}$ = 30MPa 的 $k_{f_{cu,k}} = 1$,得到以上影响系数的计算公式:

$$\begin{cases} k_T = \exp(8.748 - 2563/T) \\ k_{RH} = RH(1 - RH)/0.21 \\ k_{W/C} = 5.0881W/C - 1.3456 \\ k_C = 537.9222/C - 0.49423 \\ k_{f_{cu,k}} = 49.465/f_{cu,k} - 0.6488 \end{cases} \tag{9}$$

2.2　模型验证

秦岭终南山隧道二次衬砌大部分采用 C25 模筑混凝土,1m^3 混凝土的材料组成为:水 175kg,水泥 372kg、砂 580kg、碎石 730kg[24]。根据现场检测数据,选取 4 处隧道内不同里程处进行测量,测量地点 1、2、3 检测结果见表 1。4 号测量地点选取距地面 1.5m 位置(4-A)、距离地面 3m 位置(4-B)、距离地面 5m 位置(4-C)进行检测,取平均温度与湿度,测量时间均为 3min。由于围岩压力的不确定性,衬砌受力情况分布较为复杂难以计算,取最大弯曲应力 $0.7f_f$。现场监测数据与计算结果如表 4 所示。

现场监测结果及碳化模型计算值　　　　表 4

测量位置	温度(℃)	湿度(%)	气体浓度(ppm)		实测值(mm)	计算值(mm)	误差(%)
			NO_2	CO_2			
1	15.6	51	0.21	2209	17.15	16.26	5.18
2	19.6	62	1.42	2118	19.05	18.01	5.45
3	24.6	63	3.76	2484	23.50	23.03	2.00
4-A	23.2	63	2.61	2155	21.25	20.42	3.90
4-B			2.35	2210	21.40	20.58	3.83
4-C			3.12	2494	22.30	22.00	1.35

由表4可知,1、2测量点误差较其他测量点误差较大,但误差均能控制在6%以内,测量点3和4-A~C四个点的误差均能控制在4%以内。1、2号点误差原因在于测量点处于隧道前段,测量时的温度、相对湿度、酸性气体等与隧道所处长期环境数据存在一定的人为误差;3和4-A~C的测量点所处隧道中段,空气中除了积聚的NO_2,还存在其他酸性气体(如SO_2)对混凝土衬砌的侵蚀,导致碳化深度实测值与计算值出现误差。图4为碳化深度现场实测值与模型计算值对比结果,两者有较好的吻合度。

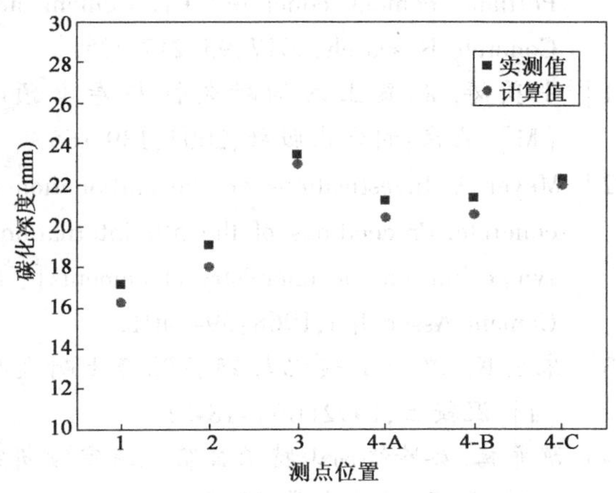

图4 碳化深度实测值与计算值的比较

3 结语

(1)酸性气体和弯曲应力水平影响下的混凝土碳化深度的增长规律仍然符合经典碳化模型;碳化深度和酸性气体(NO_2)浓度及弯曲应力水平均呈正相关关系,分别符合指数函数和Bradley函数规律。

(2)碳化深度随着碳化龄期的增长而不断增加,且增长速率逐渐减小;硝酸浓度和弯曲应力水平的增大均能促进碳化的进行,$0.3f_f$、$0.5f_f$、$0.7f_f$工况下碳化深度的平均提升幅值分别为3.65%、7.51%、13.71%,硝酸浓度0.01mol·L^{-1}、0.05mol·L^{-1}、0.1mol·L^{-1}工况下的碳化深度的平均提升幅值分别为13.66%、23.88%、30.36%。

(3)提出了碳化深度的酸性气体(NO_2)影响系数和弯曲应力影响系数,结合其他学者的碳化深度模型,修正建立了在硝酸侵蚀和弯曲应力作用下的混凝土碳化深度预测模型。预测模型与现场实测数据误差均能控制在6%以内,数据吻合度较好,验证了预测模型的可靠性。

(4)本模型通过室内试验数据修正其他系数,同时在实际隧道环境内还存在其他有害侵蚀气体(如SO_2),影响混凝土衬砌碳化。因此模型修正值及碳化深度的影响系数,还需要在今后研究中进一步完善。

参考文献

[1] 王家滨,牛荻涛.喷射混凝土的硝酸侵蚀:孔溶液H~+与NO_3~-的扩散规律及侵蚀机理[J].材料导报,2019,33(06):991-999.

[2] 王蕾.基于环境因素的公路隧道衬砌结构碳化耐久性研究[D].西安:长安大学,2020. DOI:10.26976/d.cnki.gchau.2020.002107.

[3] 韩兴博,叶飞,梁晓明,等.公路隧道钢筋混凝土衬砌碳化耐久性区划[J].浙江大学学报(工学版),2021,55(08):1436-1443+1463.

[4] 王家滨,牛荻涛.硝酸侵蚀/冻融循环共同作用喷射混凝土耐久性能(I):物理力学性能及孔结构变化[J].材料导报,2019,33(08):1340-1347.

[5] 任光明,赵志祥,聂德新,等.深埋长隧道有害气体发生的地质条件初探[J].山地学报,2002(01):122-125.

[6] 唐官保,姚燕,王玲,等.应力作用下混凝土碳化深度预测模型[J].建筑材料学报,2020,23(02):304-308.

[7] 翁其能,张丽珺,秦伟.公路隧道环境因子对混凝土衬砌耐久性影响综述[J].材料导报,2014,28(15):93-97.

[8] Monteiro I, Branco F A, De Brito J, et al. Statistical analysis of the carbonation coefficient in open air concrete structures[J]. Construction and Building Materials,2012,29:263-269.

[9] 王志杰,王奇,孙长升,等.基于快速碳化试验的纤维喷射混凝土碳化深度预测研究[J].混凝土,2014(02):21-24.

[10] Shi H, Xu B, Zhou X. Influence of mineral admixtures on compressive strength, gas permeability and carbonation of high performance concrete[J]. Construction and Building Materials,2009,23(5):1980-1985.

[11] 赵庆新,齐立剑,潘慧敏.基于混凝土碳化耐

久性的粉煤灰临界掺量[J].建筑材料学报,2015,18(01):118-122.

[12] Song H W,Kwon S J. Permeability characteristics of carbonated concrete considering capillary pore structure[J]. Cement and Concrete Research, 2007,37(6):909-915.

[13] 余波,成荻,杨绿峰.混凝土结构的碳化环境作用量化与耐久性分析[J].土木工程学报,2015,48(09):51-59.

[14] 万朝均,刘晓琴,郭梦君.外加剂对水泥石碳化的影响[J].混凝土,2017(11):87-90.

[15] Lo Y,Lee H M. Curing effects on carbonation of concrete using a phenolphthalein indicator and Fourier-transform infrared spectroscopy [J]. Building and environment,2002,37(5):507-514.

[16] Drouet E, Poyet S, Le Bescop P, et al. Carbonation of hardened cement pastes: Influence of temperature [J]. Cement and Concrete Research,2019,115:445-459.

[17] Leemann A,Moro F. Carbonation of concrete: the role of CO_2 concentration, relative humidity and CO_2 buffer capacity [J]. Materials and Structures,2017,50(1):1-14.

[18] 王家滨,牛荻涛,马蕊,等.弯曲应力作用下喷射混凝土抗碳化性能研究[J].四川大学学报(工程科学版),2015,47(S1):84-90.

[19] Kuosa H,Ferreira R M,Holt E,et al. Effect of coupled deterioration by freeze-thaw, carbonation and chlorides on concrete service life[J]. Cement and Concrete Composites, 2014,47:32-40.

[20] Liu J,Qiu Q,Chen X,et al. Understanding the interacted mechanism between carbonation and chloride aerosol attack in ordinary Portland cement concrete[J]. Cement and Concrete Research,2017,95:217-225.

[21] 牛荻涛.混凝土结构耐久性与寿命预测[M].北京:科学出版社,2003,139-165.

[22] Meyer A. Investigations on the carbonation of concrete. Proceedings of the 5th international symposium on the chemistry of cements[J]. Cement Assoc Jpn,1968:394-401.

[23] 朱安民.混凝土碳化与钢筋混凝土耐久性[J].混凝土,1992(06):18-22.

[24] 陈希梅.秦岭终南山特长公路隧道定额研究[D].西安:长安大学,2009.

挡土墙对土石交界地层浅埋偏压隧道变形的影响

杨晓华[1]　曹杨帆*[1]　肖　靖[2]　尹培杰[1]　陈　锐[1]

(1.长安大学公路学院;2.中交第二航务工程局有限公司)

摘　要　隧道在土岩交界地层施工时由于围岩软硬不均,如果没有相对应的支护措施,可能会导致支护结构开裂甚至发生隧道塌方。本文依托四川省九绵高速大马沟隧道工程,通过模型试验研究土岩交界地层浅埋偏压隧道采用环形开挖预留核心土法以及挡土墙预加固措施对隧道变形的影响。结果表明,地表沉降和拱顶沉降以及围岩压力都在隧道开挖至监测断面时突然增大;地表的最大沉降并没有发生在隧道拱顶正上方处,而是向浅埋侧偏移,这是由于地形偏压以及围岩稳定性低。在有挡土墙预加固措施的情况下,地表沉降明显降低,最大地表沉降从0.527mm减至0.386mm,降低了26.8%。拱顶沉降较左右拱肩大,采用挡土墙的预加固措施后,拱顶沉降值得到显著改善,最大拱顶沉降由0.740mm减小到0.534mm,减小了27.9%。采用挡土墙预加固措施能够减少土岩交界地层浅埋偏压隧道的变形。

关键词　隧道工程　受力与变形　模型试验　土岩交界　环形开挖预留核心土法

0 引言

如今我国山区基础设施建设面临的地质条件更加复杂,许多隧道修建过程中都需要穿越不同地质交界、软硬不均的地层,或者面临浅埋、偏压等不良地质情况。在这种地质条件下修建隧道时围岩稳定性与单一岩层相比存在很大的差异,如果采用的施工方法不合理或者支护措施不当,可能会导致围岩及支护结构变形加剧,支护结构因受力不均出现开裂甚至发生隧道塌方[1-3]。雷明锋等[4]采用20∶1的几何相似比,2∶1的容重相似比施作浅埋偏压隧道衬砌受力和破坏特征模型试验。李林等[5]进行了浅埋偏压洞口段隧道地震响应振动台模型试验研究。江学良等[6]设计并制作了比例1∶10的浅埋偏压小净距隧道物理试验模型。王书刚等[7]使用有限差分软件 FLAC3D 模拟洞口浅埋段的开挖过程。董建华等[8]针对当下洞口段浅埋偏压隧道支护结构容易坍塌、整体位移过大等问题,提出一种新型防护结构。宋战平等[9]基于数值模拟试验确定了大断面偏压隧道洞口段的施工方案。黄维新等[10]分析比较了偏压软弱围岩隧道在不同开挖顺序下各阶段围岩位移变形量。

由于对土石交界地层浅埋偏压隧道开挖的研究较少,本文依托四川省九绵高速大马沟隧道工程,对土石交界地层浅埋偏压隧道开挖过程中围岩和支护结构的变形特征进行研究,并探究挡土墙预加固措施的效果,为工程建设提供指导。

1 工程概况

大马沟隧道介于四川省阿坝藏族羌族自治州九寨沟县郭元乡水沟村和抹地村中间,隧道整体处在白水江左侧,洞口段平均埋深不足20m,岩性主要分为崩坡积碎石土和强-中风化灰岩两种;围岩级别为Ⅴ级,隧道进口段围岩位于土石交界地层,地面横坡的角度约为34°;上部土层为围岩稳定性较差的崩坡积碎石土,岩体也较松散,下部岩层则是中风化灰岩;接触面角度约为45°,土石交界面两侧围岩性质不一,存在严重偏压。在这种地形下进行隧道施工,极易引起隧道支护结构变形不均匀的情况,上部一侧沿土岩交界面进行滑动,容易造成围岩失稳甚至滑塌。围岩物理力学参数见表1。

围岩物理力学参数 表1

围　岩	重度 γ(kN/m^3)	黏聚力 c(kPa)	内摩擦角 φ(°)
崩坡积碎石土	21	14	30
中风化灰岩	26.9	300	38

2 模型试验

2.1 模型箱设计

本次模型试验取几何相似常数 $C_L=50$,容重相似常数 $C_\Gamma=1$,应变、泊松比和内摩擦角相似常数$C_\varepsilon=C_\mu=C_\phi=1$,应力、弹性模量、黏聚力相似常数 $C_E=C_\sigma=C_C=50$。模型试验在特制的模型箱中完成,模型箱的尺寸为1.5m×0.5m×1m(长×宽×高),模型箱示意图如图1所示。为了方便观察,模型箱的正面为1.2cm厚的钢化玻璃,在钢化玻璃中间设置有一个开挖孔,直径为25cm,开挖孔底部距地面25cm,模型箱其余部分皆由钢板焊成。模型箱实物如图2所示。

2.2 试验材料

2.2.1 围岩材料

本模型试验主要研究隧道开挖引起的大变形以及支护结构受力,因此在选用相似材料时主要控制重度、黏聚力、内摩擦角三项指标。参考谈杜勇等人[11-14]的研究成果,确定配比为重晶石粉∶石英砂∶石蜡油=60.5∶30.5∶9的相似材料模拟中风化灰岩,确定配比为重晶石粉∶膨润土∶石蜡油=80.2∶10∶9.8的相似材料模拟崩坡积碎石土。直剪试验测得的围岩材料参数见表2。

围岩相似材料物理力学参数 表2

围　岩	重度 γ(kN/m^3)	黏聚力 c(kPa)	内摩擦角 φ(°)
崩坡积碎石土	21.5	0.27	28
相似比	0.98	51.8	1.07
中风化灰岩	26.1	6.3	37
相似比	1.03	47.6	1.03

2.2.2 衬砌结构材料

参考文献[15]中衬砌结构的相似材料配比,本文采用石膏、石英砂、重晶石粉、水作为原料来模拟原型衬砌,按照 $m_{石膏}:m_{石英砂}:m_{重晶石粉}:m_{水}=$

1.5∶1.7∶1∶1.3的比例进行拌和,并将其制作成3个尺寸为Φ50mm×100mm的圆柱体试件,通过万能压力机测得圆柱体试件的平均弹性模量为540MPa。原型衬砌结构材料与模型衬砌结构材料的物理力学参数见表3。

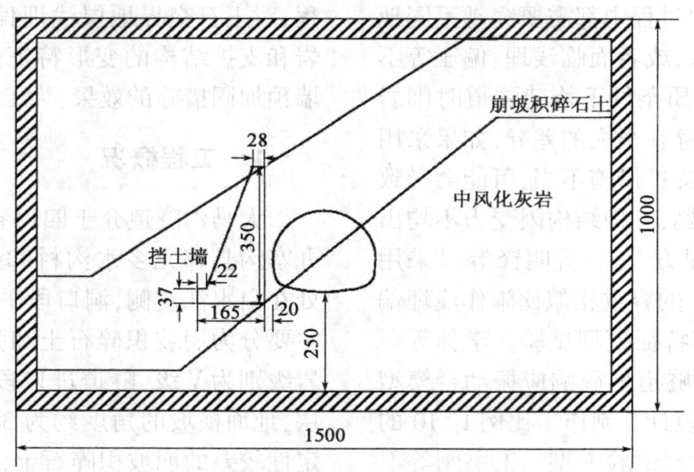

图1　模型箱示意图(单位:mm)

图2　模型箱实物图

衬砌结构相似材料物理力学参数　　表3

材　料	重度 γ(kN/m^3)	弹性模量 E(MPa)
原型材料	25	30000
模型材料	24.50	540
相似比	1.02	55.56

根据 $m_{石膏}:m_{石英砂}:m_{重晶石粉}:m_{水}=1.5:1.7:1:1.3$的比例配制的衬砌结构相似材料,原型与模型的容重相似常数 C_γ 和弹性模量相似常数 C_E 分别为1.02和55.56,基本满足试验条件。

原型初期支护结构的厚度依据几何相似常数换算得到,由于模型初期支护结构的厚度过小,在实际制作过程中不易成型,为了降低浇筑的难度,将初期支护和二次衬砌合为一体。原型初期支护厚度为26cm,二次衬砌厚度为60cm,总厚度为86cm,根据相似比换算得到的模型厚度为1.72cm,预制而成的衬砌结构如图3所示。

图3　衬砌结构实物图

2.2.3　挡土墙材料

挡土墙原型由C20混凝土浇筑而成。综合考虑后,同样采用 $m_{石膏}:m_{石英砂}:m_{重晶石粉}:m_{水}=1.5:$

1.7:1:1.3 的比例配制挡土墙相似材料,挡土墙原型与模型物理力学参数见表4。原型与模型的容重相似常数 C_γ 和弹性模量相似常数 C_E 分别为 0.98 和 47.22,同样满足试验要求。制作成的挡土墙如图4所示。

挡土墙相似材料物理力学参数　　表4

材　料	重度 γ(kN/m³)	弹性模量 E(MPa)
原型材料	25	30000
模型材料	24.50	540
相似比	1.02	55.56

图4　挡土墙实物图

2.3　量测系统

地表沉降总共布置5个测点,中间测点位于拱顶正上方地表处,相邻测点间隔为6cm。拱顶沉降总共布置3个测点,分别布置在隧道拱顶、左右两侧拱肩位置处。地表沉降和隧道拱顶沉降都使用沉降杆量测,在填筑土体时埋设金属沉降杆,并用金属套杆套在金属杆外面进行保护,地表和隧道拱顶沉降测点布置如图5所示。

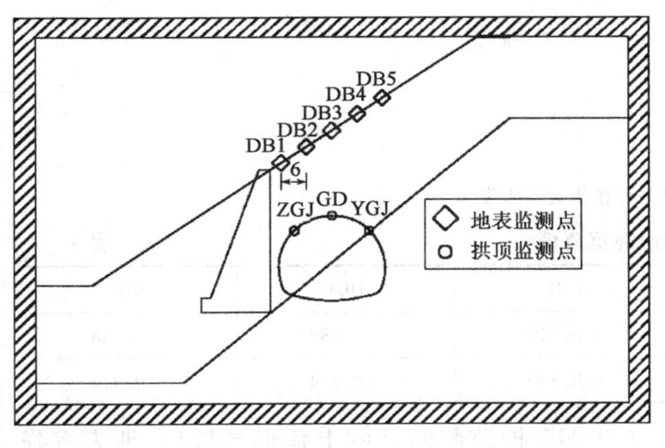

图5　沉降测点布设示意图

2.4　试验过程

(1)围岩相似材料制备。

依据围岩相似材料的配比,将试验所需的材料准备妥当,并进行充分搅拌。

(2)模型填筑。

为了减少围岩与材料箱之间的摩擦对试验结果的影响,在填筑材料之前在模型箱内壁均匀涂抹润滑油。材料搅拌完成后向模型箱内填筑围岩材料,分层填铺,振捣密实。

(3)量测仪器安装。

分别将隧道衬砌、挡土墙、沉降杆埋入预定位置。模型箱填筑完成后将百分表放置在沉降杆上,首先压缩百分表指针,其次将磁性表吸附在模型箱上,模型填筑完成状态如图6所示。

图6　模型填筑完成状态

(4)隧道开挖。

上部弧形导坑开挖和支护;预留核心土开挖;下台阶开挖并进行相应的支护;循环开挖。隧道的开挖进尺为5cm,上部弧形导坑和核心土以及下台阶的开挖各错开5cm。

隧道开挖前将静态应变测试仪清零,每一步开挖后稳定30min再读数,保存数据后进行下一步的开挖,直到隧道开挖完成,总共开挖步数为12步。

3　试验结果分析

3.1　地表沉降分析

在模型箱中间沿地表布置一条测线,测线上布置5个测点,相邻测点间隔为6cm,从左到右分别命名为DB1、DB2、DB3、DB4、DB5,其中DB3位于隧道拱顶正上方地表处,规定地表沉降向上为正,向下为负。地表沉降随开挖步变化曲线如图7~图11所示,地表各监测点的最终沉降值见表5。

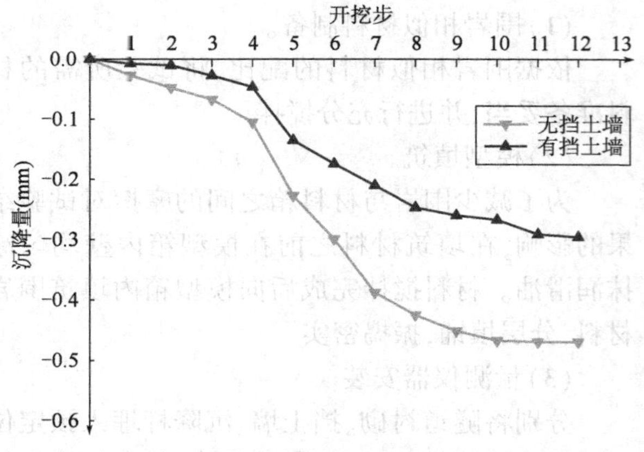

图7 测点DB1沉降与开挖步关系曲线

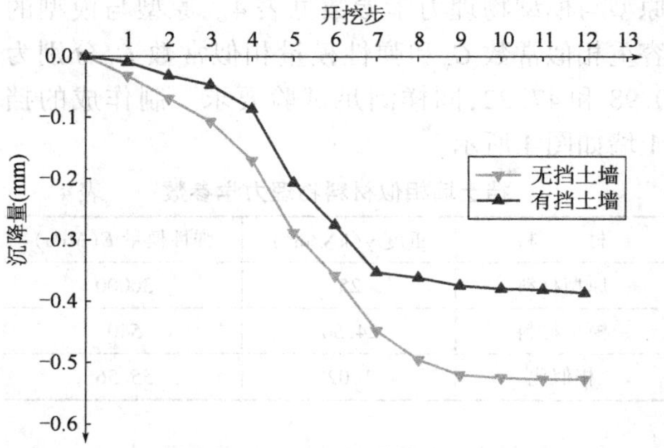

图8 测点DB2沉降与开挖步关系曲线

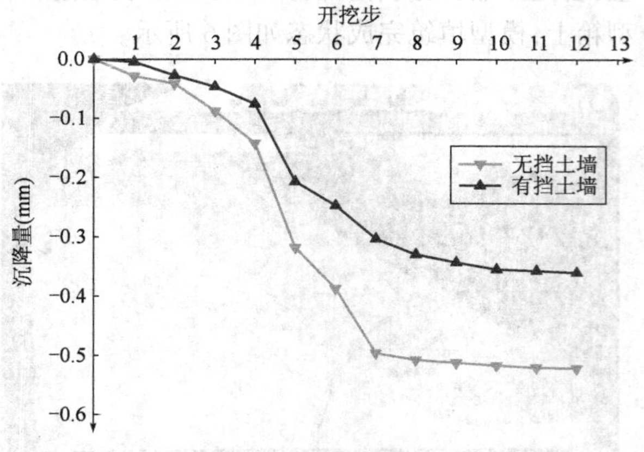

图9 测点DB3沉降与开挖步关系曲线

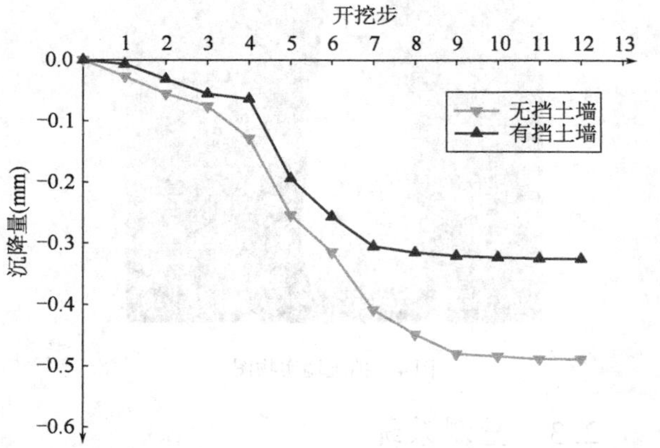

图10 测点DB4沉降与开挖步关系曲线

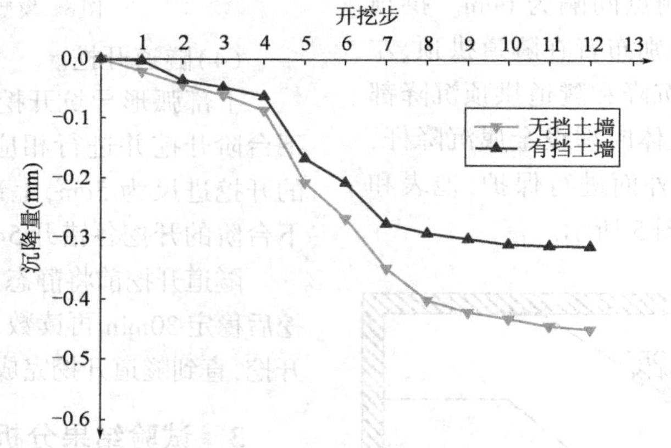

图11 测点DB5沉降与开挖步关系曲线

地表监测点的最终沉降值 表5

地表监测点	DB1	DB2	DB3	DB4	DB5
无挡土墙	-0.469	-0.527	-0.520	-0.488	-0.448
有挡土墙	-0.295	-0.386	-0.359	-0.324	-0.312

(1)地表各监测点的沉降规律相似,地表沉降都是在隧道开挖第五步之前变形较小,在开挖第五步即开挖监测断面的上弧形导坑后,地表沉降突增,在之后开挖第六步和第七步即开挖监测断

面的核心土和下台阶时，地表沉降增量也很大，之后沉降才趋于稳定，表明隧道开挖对上部岩体造成的扰动较大。

(2)地表的最大沉降并不发生在隧道拱顶正上方监测点3位置，而发生在监测点2位置，地表最大沉降向浅埋侧偏移。这是因为地形偏压以及围岩强度低，隧道开挖后岩土体向浅埋侧滑移。

(3)在有挡土墙预加固措施的情况下，地表沉降显著减少。最大地表沉降从0.527mm减至0.386mm，由相似比得到，实际地表沉降从26.350mm减至19.30mm，降低了26.8%。

3.2 围岩位移分析

本次模型试验中，通过沉降杆和百分表监测记录拱顶沉降。在模型箱中间布置三个测点，分别处在隧道左拱肩、拱顶、右拱肩位置，从左到右分别命名为ZGJ、GD、YGJ。拱顶沉降随开挖步变化曲线如图12～图14所示，拱顶监测点的最终沉降值见表6。

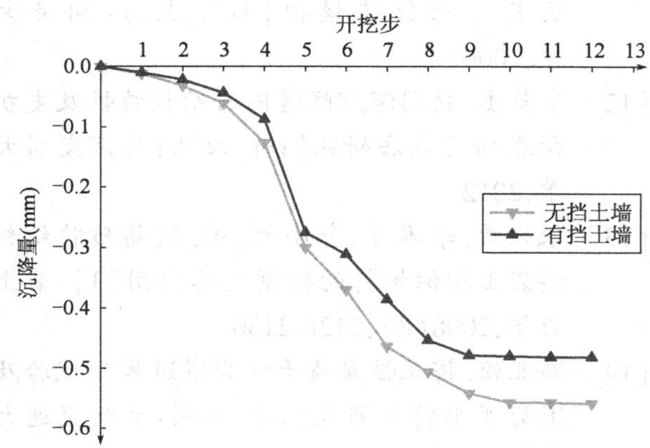

图12 测点ZGJ沉降与开挖步关系曲线

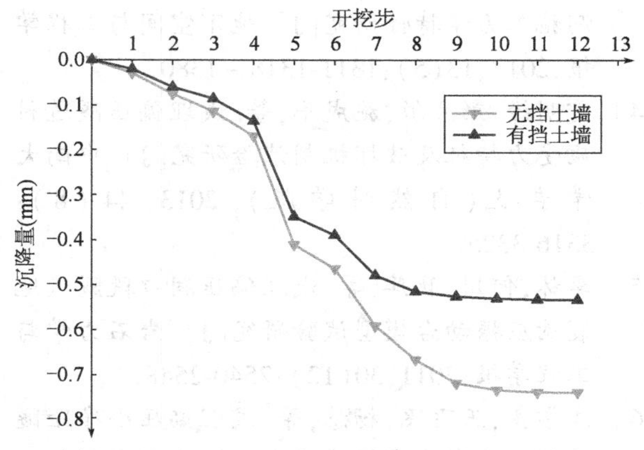

图13 测点GD沉降与开挖步关系曲线

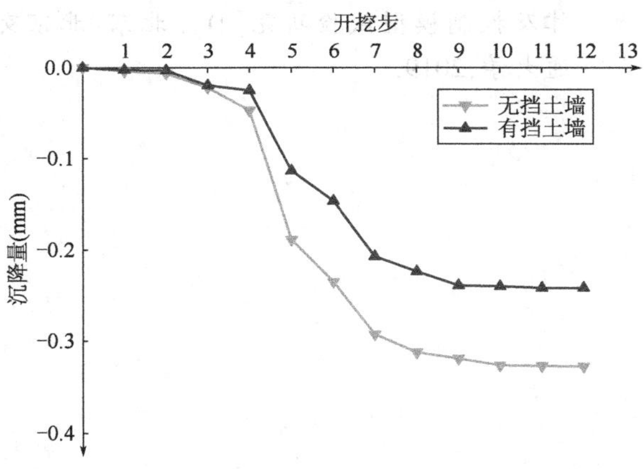

图14 测点YGJ沉降与开挖步关系曲线

拱顶监测点的最终沉降值 表6

拱顶监测点	ZGJ	GD	YGJ
无挡土墙	-0.560	-0.741	-0.328
有挡土墙	-0.482	-0.534	-0.243

(1)拱顶各监测点的沉降规律相似，拱顶沉降都是在隧道开挖第五步之前变形较小，在开挖第五步即开挖监测断面的上弧形导坑后，拱顶沉降突增，而且开挖第五步拱顶沉降的增量大于第六步和第七步，表明上弧形导坑的开挖对围岩稳定造成显著影响，相较而言，预留核心土和下弧形导坑的开挖造成的影响较小。这主要是因为开挖上弧形导坑后拱顶上部围岩发生应力重分布形成拱形受力区，对隧道稳定具有一定的支撑作用。

(2)拱顶沉降大于左右拱肩处，在有挡土墙预加固措施的情况下，拱顶沉降显著降低，最大拱顶沉降从0.740mm减至0.534mm，由相似比得到，实际地表沉降从37.050mm减至26.700mm，降低了27.9%。

4 结语

(1)地表各监测点的沉降规律相似，地表沉降在开挖到监测断面处上弧形导坑时变形突然增大，开挖完监测断面后地表沉降才逐渐趋于稳定。由于偏压的影响，地表的最大沉降向左侧偏移。采用挡土墙预加固措施可以阻止土体的滑移变形。

(2)拱顶各监测点的沉降规律相似，拱顶沉降在开挖到监测断面处上弧形导坑时变形突然增大,开挖完监测断面后拱顶沉降逐渐趋于稳定。隧道拱顶的沉降最大,采用挡土墙预加固措施可以减小围岩变形。

参考文献

[1] 左清军,吴立,陆中功,等.浅埋偏压隧道洞口段软弱围岩失稳突变理论分析[J].岩土力学,2015,36(S2):424-430.

[2] 杨晓华,谢永利.公路隧道坍方综合处治技术[J].长安大学学报(自然科学版),2004(1):61-64.

[3] 徐前卫,程盼盼,苏培森,等.浅埋偏压隧道进洞施工力学特性研究[J].地下空间与工程学报,2017,13(5):1311-1318+1380.

[4] 雷明锋,彭立敏,施成华,等.浅埋偏压隧道衬砌受力特征及破坏机制试验研究[J].中南大学学报(自然科学版),2013,44(8):3316-3325.

[5] 李林,何川,耿萍,等.浅埋偏压洞口段隧道地震响应振动台模型试验研究[J].岩石力学与工程学报,2011,30(12):2540-2548.

[6] 江学良,王飞飞,杨慧,等.浅埋偏压小净距隧道衬砌地震应变规律研究[J].地下空间与工程学报,2017,13(2):506-516.

[7] 王书刚,李术才,王刚,等.浅埋偏压隧道洞口施工技术及稳定性分析研究[J].岩土力学,2006,27(S1):364-368.

[8] 董建华,颉永斌,李建军,等.洞口段浅埋偏压隧道新型防护结构及其简化计算方法[J].中国公路学报,2018,31(10):339-349.

[9] 宋战平,王童,周建军,等.浅埋偏压大断面隧道施工优化及受力特征分析[J].地下空间与工程学报,2017,13(2):459-468.

[10] 黄维新,吴寒,王杰,等.偏压软弱围岩隧道开挖顺序比较研究[J].工程地质学报,2019,27(2):277-285.

[11] 谈杜勇.连拱隧道开挖过程的模型试验研究及其三维数值模拟[D].上海:同济大学,2006.

[12] 李英杰.软弱深埋隧道围岩结构特性及支护荷载确定方法研究[D].北京:北京交通大学,2012.

[13] 张强勇,李术才,郭小红,等.铁晶砂胶结新型岩土相似材料的研制及其应用[J].岩土力学,2008(8):2126-2130.

[14] 冯亚松.挤压性炭质千枚岩隧道模型试验及围岩变形特征研究[D].兰州:兰州交通大学,2015.

[15] 邢宇祺.浅埋软弱围岩暗挖隧道超前变形规律及控制模型试验研究[D].北京:北京交通大学,2019.